CONCORDANCE TO
The Poetry of
WALLACE STEVENS

CONCORDANCE TO
The Poetry of
WALLACE STEVENS

THOMAS F. WALSH

THE PENNSYLVANIA STATE UNIVERSITY PRESS

University Park, Pennsylvania   1963

PREFACE

William Carlos Williams, in *The Trinity Review* of May, 1954, wrote that with *The Auroras of Autumn* Wallace Stevens' "stature as a major poet has reached the full. It is a mark of genius when an accomplished man can go on continually developing, continually improving his techniques." The same issue contained tributes from T. S. Eliot, Marianne Moore, Archibald MacLeish, Conrad Aiken, and many others. His reputation has never been a secret, especially among his fellow poets, but that reputation has grown immeasurably in the last ten years. William Van O'Connor's study (1950) has been followed by three others and a collection of critical essays, with more studies, another collection, and a biography on the way.

All these studies, along with the ever increasing number of articles, have greatly aided the general reader in his appreciation of Stevens' work, but there is still much more to be done, especially in the detailed analyses of individual poems. For Stevens has the reputation of being not only a great poet, but a difficult one. Professor O'Connor describes the nature of the difficulties: "In reading Stevens it is helpful to know in advance that he is employing a complex, ever enlarging symbolism, and a dramatis personae. The abstractness of the later poetry is in part in the mind of the reader who fails to perceive the complexity and to feel the weight of meaning borne by the symbols and characters that live in his mythology. A full examination of this mythology would require a very extensive study of individual images, symbols and figures recurring and growing by accretion from poem to poem over more than forty years." This concordance will make such a full examination possible with the hope that the reader will more easily comprehend each "unfamiliar, difficult fern" which opens out from "the furiously burning father-fire."

THE TEXT

The concordance is based on the following three works by Wallace Stevens:

The Collected Poems of Wallace Stevens. New York, Alfred A. Knopf, 1954.

The Necessary Angel. New York, Alfred A. Knopf, 1951.

Opus Posthumous.   Edited, with an Introduction, by Samuel French Morse.   New York, Alfred A. Knopf, 1957.

The Necessary Angel contains two of Stevens' poems, "Someone Puts a Pineapple Together" and "Of Ideal Time and Choice."   I have included all the original poems of *Opus Posthumous,* but have omitted the translations, "Moment of Light" from the French of Jean LeRoy, and the paraphrases of the prose poems of León-Paul Fargue.

The italicized words in the following lines are misprints in the three works listed above.   The correct word is given following the line:

> Which was, and *if,* chief motive, first delight—Read *is.*
> ("The Comedian as the Letter C," *Collected Poems,* 34.)
>
> The trees *likes* bones and the leaves half sand, half sun—Read *like.*
> ("Farewell to Florida," *Collected Poems,* 118.)
>
> Sour wine to *warn* him, an empty book to read—Read *warm.*
> ("The Good Man Has No Shape," *Collected Poems,* 364.)
>
> Of things were waiting in a *bethrothal* known—Read *betrothal.*
> ("Study of Images II," *Collected Poems,* 464.)
>
> "Concerto for Airplane and *Pinaoforte*"—Read *Pianoforte.*
> ("A Duck for Dinner," *Opus Posthumous,* 62.)
>
> The young *gentlemen* was seen—Read *gentleman.*
> ("Three Travelers Watch a Sunrise," *Opus Posthumous,* 136.)

THE FORMAT

Under each word-entry are included the line in which the word appears, an abbreviation of the title of the poem, and the page and line number.   The lines are numbered according to the page rather than the poem. A *P* at the end of a line designates poems from *Opus Posthumous,* and an *A* poems from *The Necessary Angel.*   If neither *P* nor *A* appears, then the poem is from *The Collected Poems.*   Words from the titles of the poems have been included; for such entries the title of the poem is given, followed by the page number and the word "title."   If the word comes from the title of a *section* of a poem, then the title, the page number, the word "title," and the number of the section are given.

Homographs appear under one word-entry.   A separate word-entry is given to a hyphenated version of a word spelled elsewhere without a hyphen and to proper nouns of more than one word.   Cross references appear for all hyphenated words and for proper names of persons, fictional and nonfictional.   The system of letter alphabetizing has been used.

WORDS OMITTED

I.   Words Entirely Omitted

a	for	more	she	though	wherever
again	from	much	should	through	whether

also	he	my	since	throughout	which
although	her	neither	so	thus	whichever
an	here	nevertheless	such	till	who
and	hers	nor	that	to	whoever
another	him	not	the	toward	whom
any	his	now	their	unless	whose
at	how	of	theirs	until	why
because	however	on	them	upon	with
but	I	onto	then	us	would
by	if	or	there	we	yet
cannot	in	other	therefore	what	you
could	into	others	these	whatever	your
each	it	our	they	when	yours
either	its	ours	this	whenever	
ever	me	shall	those	where	

II. Words Partially Omitted

am [1]	can (aux.)	have (aux.)	no [2]	will (aux.)
are [1]	do (aux.)	having (aux.)	one (pron.)	while (conj.)
as (temporal conj.)	does (aux.)	is [1]	out [3]	
be [1]	did (aux.)	may (aux.)	too (also)	
been [1]	has (aux.)	might (aux.)	was [1]	
being [1]	had (aux.)	mine (pron.)	were [1]	

The concordance also omits foreign equivalents of the above words as well as contractions formed with these words.

---

[1] Forms of the verb "to be" are retained when their meaning stresses existence as such.

[2] "No" is retained when it means the opposite of "yes."

[3] "Out" is retained when in combination with "of."

Most words in the above list will cause readers little surprise. But several have caused editors endless deliberation, eventually forcing them to make arbitrary decisions that cannot entirely satisfy all readers or themselves. I have experienced this same editorial dilemma. A discussion of a few of my decisions may be helpful to the reader.

I have included all reflexive pronouns because Stevens puts a special emphasis on the word "self" that is often carried over to the pronoun. For obvious reasons, forms of the verb "to be" appear in concordances only as random samplings. In Stevens' poetry the verb is often more than a colorless copulative; it can express Stevens' concern with the *fact* of existence. In "The Comedian as the Letter C" he writes, "For realist, what is is what should be." The man in "The Latest Freed Man" is freed because he can exult in the fact of his own unencumbered existence in the center of reality:

> To be without a description of to be,
> For a moment on rising, at the edge of the bed, to be,
>
> .   .   .   .
>
> It was everything being more real, himself
> At the centre of reality, seeing it.

The poet states in "An Ordinary Evening in New Haven" that "as and is are one," thereby using "is" and another seemingly insignificant word, "as," to express the paradoxical relation between seeming and being. I have omitted "as," the temporal conjunction, but have otherwise included it, not only because it is a guide (along with "like" and "than") to Stevens' similes, but also because the poet does not use it automatically—he is always fascinated with the "intricate evasions of as."

The numeral "one" in the statement from "Ordinary Evening" brings attention to a pervasive pattern in Stevens' poetry in which he states that many things are (were) one: for example, "foam and cloud," "a man and a woman," "to be and delight to be," "the blue guitar and I," "the deer and the dachshund," the Whitmanesque "the false and true." The pattern is related to Stevens' concept of the imagination and its power to order and unify reality.

The following words are not included in the concordance, but deserve to be recorded because of their special usage in the lines in which they appear:

AGAIN
   An appearance of Again, the diva-dame. [Adult 353–10

AN
   There was that difference between the and an, [Extracts 255–7
   A few words, an and yet, and yet, and yet—[NH 465–6

I
   The evilly compounded, vital I [Poems Clim 193–19
   Who speaks? But it must be that I, [Peaches 224–7

MORE
   A part of the inhuman more, [Ulysses 105–2 P
   The still inhuman more, and yet [Ulysses 105–3 P

SHALL
   Of was and is and shall or ought to be, [C 40–8
   For him, of shall or ought to be in is. [C 41–9

SHOULD
   Of happens to like, not should. [Table Talk 40–3 P

THAT
   In objects, as white this, white that. [Vari 235–5
   The this and that in the enclosures of hypotheses [Prol 516–14

THE

Where was it one first heard of the truth? The the. [Dump 203–11

There was that difference between the and an, [Extracts 255–7

THIS

In objects, as white this, white that. [Vari 235–5

The this and that in the enclosures of hypotheses [Prol 516–14

WHY

In the weed of summer comes this green sprout why. [Questions 462–4

YET

A few words, an and yet, and yet, and yet—[NH 465–6

The above discussion is intended to demonstrate how some seemingly insignificant words can take on special significance and thus merit at least partial inclusion in this concordance. One must look twice at "the obscurest as, the distant was."

ADDITIONS

The following words should have been included in the concordance, but, through an oversight, were not:

AS. Although I patch it as I can. [MBG 165–12

There's no such thing as life; or if there is, [Parochial 192–4

If the stars that move together as one, disband, [Horn 230–17

But as truth to be accepted, he supposed [Landsc 242–18

Born, as she was, at twenty-one, [Couch 295–6

As he saw it, exist in his own especial eye. [EM 316–19

The most gay and yet not so gay as it was. [Debris 338–13

Its knowledge cold within one as one's own; [Novel 459–3

Not as I, from melons. [Three 129–6 P

Just as the young gentleman [Three 139–9 P

EVERY. Come to us every day. And yet they are [Recit 87–28 P

With something I could touch, touch every way. [Warmth 90–6 P

On every cloud-tip over the heavens, [Letters 107–2 P

HAD. And the world had worlds, ai, this-a-way: [MBG 178–17

What had this star to do with the world it lit, [Martial 238–3

IS. Nothing that is not there and the nothing that is. [Snow Man 10–12

For whom what is was other things. [Oak 272–3

THAN. Than mute bare splendors of the sun and moon. [On Manner 56–8

Than yours, out of our imperfections wrought, [Fictive 87–20

Of it, more than the monstrous player of [MBG 175–8

Than this, in this alone I may believe, [Extracts 257–25

On more than muscular shoulders, arms and chest, [Choc 297–12

WAS. Again, and lived and was again, and breathed again [Martial 238–15

Except what was, [Woman Song 360–9

ACKNOWLEDGMENTS

I am most grateful to the Estate of Wallace Stevens and to Alfred A. Knopf, Inc., the publishers of the poetry of Wallace Stevens, for kindly permitting me to base my concordance on the following editions:

The Collected Poems of Wallace Stevens. New York, Knopf. Copyright 1954 by Wallace Stevens.
The Necessary Angel. New York, Knopf. Copyright 1951 by Wallace Stevens.
Opus Posthumous. Edited, with an Introduction, by Samuel French Morse. New York, Knopf. Copyright 1957 by Elsie Stevens and Wallace Stevens.

Clerical assistance in the project was made available to me through grants from *The Washington Star* and Georgetown University. Professor Franklin B. Williams contributed, whenever possible, the clerical resources of Georgetown's English department.

Miss Joan Krager and Mr. John Solon of the University of Wisconsin were indispensable in their editorial assistance.

To Emilie True, Margaret Mary Dietz, Anne Robertson, Lois Vandeveer, Mary Riggs, José Calvo, Anthony Bruno, James Madjer, and Edward Bednarz, I extend my gratitude and admiration for their assistance in the grueling tasks of typing, filing, and proofreading.

For over a year my colleagues have been made all too aware of my occupation (obsession is a better word) with this concordance. Nevertheless they patiently and sympathetically responded to my many questions. Professor Roland N. Harman deserves special mention in this regard both as friend and counselor.

Thomas F. Walsh

Washington, D. C.
May 27, 1963

ABBREVIATIONS
OF POEM TITLES

CONCORDANCE TO

The Poetry of

WALLACE STEVENS

A. A great disorder is an order. Now, A [Connois 216-9
    The A B C of being, [Motive 288-16
    Suppose we call it Projection A. [Couch 295-3
    It is the infant A standing on infant legs, [NH 469-7
    Its strength and measure, that which is near, point A [Rock
        528-11
ABABBA. Ababba, expecting this king's queen to appear? [Golden
        461-3
ABANDON. With his plough, the peacock may abandon pride [Burnshaw
        48-24 P
ABANDONED. In an abandoned spot. Soft, civil bird, [Cred 377-12
    Like beautiful and abandoned refugees. [Our Stars 455-16
    Beginning of a green Cockaigne to be, disliked, abandoned,
        [Inelegance 25-14 P
    Abandoned because of taxes . . . It was enough: [Greenest 53-2 P
ABASH. Will abash him. [Plot Giant 7-3
ABASHED. Abashed him by carouse to humble yet [C 40-24
ABATE. To abate on the way to church, [Winter B 141-11
ABATES. Prone to distemper he abates in taste, [C 46-3
ABBA. Abba, dark death is the breaking of a glass. [Golden 460-16
ABERRATION. The revealing aberration should appear, [Nigger 153-18
    An impossible aberration with the moon, [Bottle 239-11
    You are familiar yet an aberration. [NSF 406-10
ABHOR. Abhor the plaster of the western horses, [Hartford 226-12
ABHORRENT. A time abhorrent to the nihilist [C 35-29
ABHORRING. Abhorring Turk as Esquimau, the lute [C 38-9
    Abhorring green-blue north and blue-green south. [Archi 18-1 P
ABIDING. Abiding the reverberations in the vaults. [Papini 447-11
ABLAZE. Then, ancientest saint ablaze with ancientest truth, [NH
        467-3
ABLE. Had he been better able to suppose: [Landsc 243-1
    It is only that we are able to die, to escape [Extracts 259-1
    The Got whome we serve is able to deliver [Hero 273-15
    Click, click, the Got whom we serve is able, [Hero 273-20
    But can, that one is sure to be able-- [Crude 305-4
    From lunacy . . . One wants to be able to walk [EM 325-2
    She will think about them not quite able to sing. [Debris 338-9
ABLER. And major man is its exponent, abler [NSF 388-17
ABNORMAL. "Anecdote of the Abnormal" [23-title P
ABOLISHES. "This man abolishes by being himself [NH 485-13
ABOMINABLE. At night, to turn away from the abominable [Sombre
        71-20 P
ABORTION. Abortion, fit for the enchanting of basilisks. [Duck
        63-1 P
ABORTIVE. Should strengthen her abortive dreams and take [NSF
        399-11
    These forms are not abortive figures, rocks, [Owl 432-5
ABOUNDS. The vegetation still abounds with forms. [Lions 125-8
ABOUT. Freemen of death, about and still about [Heaven 56-14
    It comes about that the drifting of these curtains [Curtains 62-1
    Whistle about us their spontaneous cries; [Sunday 70-23
    About the lantern of the beauty [Virgin 71-4
    Of the women about you? [Thirteen 93-23
    The yellow moon of words about the nightingale [Autumn 160-4
    But salvation here? What about the rattle of sticks [Parochial
        191-17
    On tins and boxes? What about horses eaten by wind? [Parochial
        191-18
    About what stands here in the centre, not the glass, [Glass
        197-21
    The women of the time. It has to think about war [Of Mod 240-3
    He felt curious about the winter hills [Extracts 254-26
    And wondered about the water in the lake. [Extracts 254-27
    Whether the water was black and lashed about [Extracts 255-13
    Half desire for indifference about the sky. [Extracts 257-3
    And the most distant, single color, about to change, [Extracts
        258-17
    Amen to the feelings about familiar things, [Montra 260-17
    Living and being about us and being [Hero 276-3
    Unhappy about the sense of happiness. [Pure 331-9
    She will think about them not quite able to sing. [Debris 338-9
    Of propositions about life. The human [Men Made 355-18
    He knows he has nothing more to think about. [Chaos 358-5
    Trace the gold sun about the whitened sky [Cred 373-6
    About the thinker of the first idea, [NSF 387-11
    We reason about them with a later reason. [NSF 399-3
    And scattered them about, no two alike. [NSF 400-24
    He never felt twice the same about the flecked river, [Cata
        424-10
    About the night. They live without our light, [Owl 432-7
    Slowly the room grows dark. It is odd about [Novel 458-19
    Are not precise about the appeasement they need. [NH 467-21
    The truth about themselves, having lost, as things, [NH 470-7
    Part of the res itself and not about it. [NH 473-11
    The statues will have gone back to be things about. [NH 473-24
    Or street or about the corners of a man, [NH 480-1
    Nothing about him ever stayed the same, [NH 483-19
    And spread about them a warmer, rosier odor. [Aug 491-28

"Not Ideas about the Thing but the Thing Itself" [534-title
That blows about in such a hopeless way, [Phases 5-13 P
Why can the horses move about on the ground? [Primordia 8-13 P
The spring about him: [Primordia 9-9 P
Darting envenomed eyes about, like fangs, [Greenest 55-15 P
About the weather and women and the way [Greenest 58-26 P
Of things, why bother about the back of stars? [Greenest 58-27 P
A poem about tradition could easily be [Recit 86-1 P
As a questioner about reality, [Warmth 89-18 P
The right within us and about us, [Ulysses 100-13 P
The right within me and about me, [Presence 105-22 P
One knows at last what to think about [Sol Oaks 111-8 P
And thinks about it without consciousness, [Sol Oaks 111-9 P
That poem about the pineapple, the one [As Leave 117-1 P
About the mind as never satisfied, [As Leave 117-2 P
The one about the credible hero, the one [As Leave 117-3 P
About summer, are not what skeletons think about. [As Leave 117-4P
ABOVE. Already the butterflies flutter above the cabins. [Carolinas
        4-14
    As the flag above the old café-- [Hibiscus 23-2
    In Crispin's mind above a continent. [C 34-1
    Above the forest of the parakeets, [Bird Claws 82-1
    Ashen man on ashen cliff above the salt halloo, [NE Verses 105-7
    I am free. High above the mast the moon [Farewell 117-7
    Last evening the moon rose above this rock [How Live 125-9
    And what's above is in the past [Botanist 2 136-1
    Above the trees? And why the poet as [Eve Angels 136-14
    The sun of Asia creeps above the horizon [Nigger 153-8
    A bridge above the bright and blue of water [Nigger 154-11
    Pushing their buds above the dark green leaves, [Nigger 156-11
    Above the shuttered mansion-house, [Postcard 159-8
    Above the arrowy, still strings, [MBG 169-17
    From crusty stacks above machines [MBG 182-4
    Above her, to the left, [Add 199-5
    Flowing above the rocks, flowing over the sky, [Loaf 200-4
    Occurred above the empty house and the leaves [Sleight 222-4
    She strides above the rabbit and the cat, [Candle 223-3
    That sees above them, that sees rise up above them, [Candle
        223-11
    And above the German camps? It looked apart. [Martial 238-5
    Above the Mediterranean, emerald [Landsc 243-3
    The aureole above the humming house . . . [Beard 247-24
    If just above her head there hung, [Couch 295-10
    Makes him rise above the houses, looking down. [Repet 307-14
    Above him. The moon was always free from him, [EM 314-27
    The flag of the nude above the holiday hotel. [Pure 331-1
    Except that the reader leaned above the page, [House Q 358-12
    Above the table spins its constant spin, [NSF 406-2
    And the pines above and along and beside the sea. [AA 411-9
    Of the pans above the stove, the pots on the table, the tulips
        among them. [Large 423-15
    Are, hanging above you, as you move, [Countryman 428-14
    The crows are flying above the foyer of summer. [Novel 457-1
    Of this present, the venerable mask above [NH 476-17
    Above the real, [Irish 501-14
    Rising out of present time and place, above [Irish 502-1
    On the horizon and lifting himself up above it. [World 520-14
    Both late and alone, above the crickets' chords, [Quiet 523-12
    No longer a battered panache above snow . . . [Not Ideas 534-8
    Wavered in evening air, above the roof, [Phases 5-5 P
    The sky above the plaza widening [Old Woman 43-6 P
    The space above the trees might still be bright [Old Woman 44-29P
    Sing rose-beliefs. Above that urn two lights [Burnshaw 50-1 P
    Because it rose above them all, stippled [Greenest 54-14 P
    And the sun and the sun-reek piled and peaked above [Greenest
        59-3 P
    Above our race, yet of ourselves transformed, [Duck 64-26 P
    Whimpers when the moon above East Hartford [Grotesque 76-18 P
    The chords above your bed to-night. [Child 106-21 P
    Free from everything else, free above all from thought. [Letters
        107-9 P
ABRAHAM. Great mud-ancestor, oozer and Abraham, [Duck 64-29 P
ABREATH. Interior: breathless things broodingly abreath [NH 481-9
ABROAD. Or the phosphored sleep in which he walks abroad [EM 320-16
ABRUTIE. "Poesie Abrutie" [302-title
ABSENCE. Between farewell and the absence of farewell, [Nigger
        152-5
    Whatever it was that he found in their absence, [Nigger 158-8
    An absence in reality, [MBG 176-19
    An absence for the poem, which acquires [MBG 177-2
    Yet the absence of the imagination had [Plain 503-1
    In the absence of fantasia, without meaning more [Course 97-1 P
ABSENT. The shadows that are absent from Euclid, [Common 221-13
    As absent as if we were asleep. [Possum 293-14
    It is not part of what is absent, a halt [NH 487-17
    See how the absent moon waits in a glade [Blanche 10-10 P
ABSENTIA. For neither is it profound absentia, [NH 469-15
ABSOLUTE. Death is absolute and without memorial, [Soldier 97-7
    One string, an absolute, not varying [Montra 263-15
    Is an absolute. Item: The cataracts [Montra 263-21

An innocence of an absolute, [Crude 305-13
It says there is an absolute grotesque. [Feo 334-3
An odor evoking nothing, absolute. [NSF 395-1
The fiction of an absolute--Angel, [NSF 404-10
Yet vested in a foreign absolute, [Owl 434-9
A neuter shedding shapes in an absolute. [NH 479-19
It is the absolute why must it be [Bship 79-8 P
Observed as an absolute, himself. [Ulysses 101-15 P
Like an absolute out of this eloquence." [Presence 106-6 P
As toward an absolute foyer beyond romance. [Local 112-12 P
ABSOLUTES. Of absolutes, bodiless, a head [Men Fall 188-7
ABSOLUTION. Unintelligible absolution and an end-- [Rome 508-5
ABSOLVED. Dismissed, absolved [Mozart 132-16
ABSORB. I absorb them as the Angevine [Peaches 224-3
ABSORBS. Absorbs Anjou. I see them as a lover sees, [Peaches 224-4
Absorbs the ruddy summer and is appeased, [Cred 374-3
ABSTRACT. The true abstract in which he promenades. [Thought 185-12
The abstract, the archaic queen. Green is the night. [Candle
  223-14
An abstract, of which the sun, the dog, the boy [Contra II 270-10
The abstract was suddenly there and gone again. [Contra II 270-13
The abstract that he saw, like the locust-leaves, plainly:
  [Contra II 270-15
As Virgil, abstract. But see him for yourself, [Paisant 335-13
In its abstract motion, [Analysis 348-13
It Must Be Abstract [NSF 380-title 2
In the abstract than in his singular, [NSF 388-18
"The Ultimate Poem Is Abstract" [429-title
Were false. The hidalgo was permanent, abstract, [NH 484-2
The Johnsonian composition, abstract man, [Duck 65-13 P
That bends the particulars to the abstract, [Ulysses 103-23 P
As abstract as porcelain. [Three 131-14 P
ABSTRACTION. To think of man the abstraction, the comic sum.
  [Nigger 156-6
Denies that abstraction is a vice except [Thought 185-7
Escaped its large abstraction, became, [Vase 246-22
Against the edge of the ice, the abstraction would [Extracts
  255-18
Like a white abstraction only, a feeling [Hero 276-26
Who died, the being that was an abstraction, [Gigan 289-6
An abstraction blooded, as a man by thought. [NSF 385-24
The major abstraction is the idea of man [NSF 388-16
The major abstraction is the commonal, [NSF 388-23
Here, then, is an abstraction given head, [Orb 443-7
An expanse and the abstraction of an expanse, [Aug 494-6
A curriculum, a vigor, a local abstraction . . . [R Conn 533-17
The abstraction. He inhabits another man, [Americana 94-10 P
An argentine abstraction approaching form [Real 110-17 P
ABSTRACTIONS. Among Plantagenet abstractions, [Ulysses 103-15 P
As if abstractions were, themselves [Ulysses 103-26 P
ABSURD. That it made the General a bit absurd [NSF 391-18
Were not and are not. Absurd. The words spoken [Rock 525-10
Perhaps, absurd perhaps, but at least a purpose, [Moonlight 532-5
ABULGE. A bullioned blue, a blue abulge, [Two Illus 514-17
ABUNDANCE. And a dissociated abundance of being, [Wom Sun 445-10
ABUNDANT. For his refreshment, an abundant zone, [C 35-17
Like chantering from an abundant [Hero 277-16
The purple odor, the abundant bloom. [NSF 395-3
See flor-abundant.
ABUNDANTLY. Abundantly beautiful, eager, [Homunculus 26-24
ABYSMAL. Foretell each night the one abysmal night, [Heaven 56-18
Abysmal instruments make sounds like pips [NSF 384-5
Plucks on his strings to pluck abysmal glory, [NSF 404-15
Releasing an abysmal melody, [Owl 433-4
An abysmal migration into a possible blue? [Burnshaw 51-9 P
ABYSS. Serenely gazing at the violent abyss, [NSF 404-14
They help us face the dumbfoundering abyss [John 437-14
Singing in the night's abyss; [Phases 4-10 P
ACACIAS. At a town in which acacias grew, he lay [EM 314-17
In spite of the yellow of the acacias, the scent [EM 315-5
ACADEMIC. Hinted autumnal farewells of academic death. [NE Verses
  106-8
"Academic Discourse at Havana [142-title
ACADEMIES. Foolscap for wigs. Academies [Prelude 195-12
Of these academies, the diviner health [Prelude 195-16
The academies like structures in a mist. [NSF 386-21
ACADEMY. And our streams rejected the dim Academy. [Nigger 154-21
"Extracts from Addresses to the Academy of Fine Ideas" [252-title
"Piano Practice at the Academy of the Holy Angels" [21-title P
ACCELERANDO. The breadth of an accelerando moves, [Orb 440-15
ACCELERATIONS. Accelerations that seem inhuman. [Hero 279-4
ACCENT. The tower, the ancient accent, the wintry size. [Antag
  426-6
This is the tragic accent of the scene. [Rome 510-5
The accent of deviation in the living thing [Discov 96-7 P
ACCENTS. In those portentous accents, syllables, [C 45-25
I know noble accents [Thirteen 94-1
Too dark, too far, too much the accents of [EM 314-19
These accents explicate [Inhab 504-2
ACCEPT. For fear the Lord would not accept. [Pourtraicte 21-21

That habit of wishing and to accept the structure [Bed 327-6
The most necessitous sense. Accept them, then, [Man Car 350-17
The direction stops and we accept what is [Cred 374-17
No introspective chaos . . . I accept: [Soldat 11-1 P
ACCEPTANCE. Final for him, the acceptance of such prose, [Armor
  530-7
ACCEPTANCES. Fails to destroy the antique acceptances, [Questions
  462-8
ACCEPTED. But as truth to be accepted, he supposed [Landsc 242-18
Accepted yet which nothing understood, [Choc 297-15
Which she accepted, [Song Fixed 520-4
ACCEPTING. Accepting. He received what he denied. [Landsc 242-17
ACCEPTS. The unpainted shore, accepts the world [Couch 296-4
Demands. It accepts whatever is as true, [EM 323-21
ACCESS. Of final access to its element-- [Pure 333-5
Of access like the page of a wiggy book, [Pure 333-6
The access of perfection to the page. [House Q 358-18
By an access of color, a new and unobserved, slight dithering,
  [Prol 517-2
The only access to true ease, [Ulysses 100-3 P
ACCESSIBLE. The lover sighs as for accessible bliss, [NSF 395-4
The book, hot for another accessible bliss! [NSF 395-13
Or accessible only in the most furtive fiction. [Nuns 93-2 P
ACCIDENT. Which takes a shape by accident. [Stan MBG 73-1 P
The accident is how I play. [Stan MBG 73-3 P
ACCLIMATIZATION. Of Acclimatization, [Analysis 349-5
ACCOMPANIED. You are to be accompanied by more [On Manner 56-7
Accompanied by the exegesis [Thought 185-1
ACCOMPANIMENTS. Become accompaniments of fortune, but [Rome 508-13
ACCOMPANYING. Just rising, accompanying, arranged to cross, [Page
  422-24
ACCOMPLISH. To accomplish the truth in his intelligence. [EM 321-22
ACCOMPLISHED. Accomplished in the immensely flashing East, [Eve
  Angels 137-22
Of sleep, the accomplished, the fulfilling air. [Owl 433-24
The rape of the bourgeoisie accomplished, the men [Bship 77-13 P
ACCOMPLISHING. As the deadly thought of men accomplishing [Monocle
  16-14
This warmth is for lovers at last accomplishing [NSF 391-4
ACCOMPLISHMENT. Is being of the solid of white, the accomplishment
  [AA 412-17
ACCORD. He heard her low accord, [Pourtraicte 22-2
And sounds of music coming to accord [C 45-26
In an accord of repetitions. Yet, [Eve Angels 137-16
"Song of Fixed Accord" [519-title
Of feeling, the things that came of their own accord, [Local
  112-8 P
ACCORDING. And, according to the composer, this butcher, [Thunder
  220-9
If I live according to this law I live [Past Nun 378-15
Is satyr in Saturn, according to his thoughts. [NSF 390-2
As by a custom or according to [AA 412-6
According to his thought, in the Mediterranean [Aug 491-6
ACCORDION. Of the room and on an accordion, half-heard, [AA 419-2
ACCORDS. In transparent accords). [Thunder 220-12
A matching and mating of surprised accords, [NH 468-2
Among the endlessly emerging accords. [Aug 493-2
ACCOSTED. True nothing, yet accosted self to self. [Bouquet 449-18
ACCOUNT. It is like a new account of everything old, [Armor 529-17
ACCOUNTED. For a human that can be accounted for. [Look 519-6
ACCOUTRED. Accoutred in a little of the strength [Repet 307-6
ACCOUTREMENT. A mask, a spirit, an accoutrement. [Gigan 289-20
ACCRETION. An accretion from ourselves, intelligent [Creat 311-2
ACCUMULATES. Now, once, he accumulates himself and time [Papini
  447-12
ACCUMULATION. And flare and Bloom with his vast accumulation
  [Anach 366-14
ACCURATE. To this accurate, exacting eye. Sight [Hero 274-11
My dame, sing for this person accurate songs. [NSF 388-9
Which has no accurate syllables and that [Page 421-8
Be orator but with an accurate tongue [Rome 509-10
ACCUSE. Her words accuse you of adulteries [Red Kit 31-3 P
ACCUSED. And the people suddenly evil, waked, accused, [Sombre 69-2P
ACCUSTOMED. That should be silver, four accustomed seeds [C 45-7
Salt-flicker, amen to our accustomed cell, [Montra 260-20
To sing jubilas at exact, accustomed times, [NSF 398-7
Not yet accustomed, yet, at sight, humane [John 437-8
ACH. Ach, Mutter, [Explan 72-13
ACHE. See sun-ache.
ACHES. The sun aches and ails and then returns halloo [Questions
  462-5
ACHIEVE. That we achieve but balances that happen, [NSF 386-15
ACHIEVED. What meditation never quite achieved. [EM 314-23
Into lands of ruddy-ruby fruits, achieved [Armor 530-3
ACID. An acid sunlight fills the halls. [Contra I 267-2
Of an obvious acid is sure what it intends [NSF 390-8
ACKNOWLEDGE. Away. The night-flies acknowledge these planets,
  [Myrrh 349-16
A-COCK. A-cock at the cross-piece on a pole [MBG 181-21
ACORN. As the acorn broods on former oaks [Oak 272-13

ACQUIRED. The being that yielded so little, acquired [Adieu 127-18
  Acquired transparence and beheld itself [Greenest 54-6 P
ACQUIRES. An absence for the poem. which acquires [MBG 177-2
  And in that mountainous mirror Spain acquires [Descrip 345-13
ACRID. When you were Eve, its acrid juice was sweet, [Monocle 14-14
  From the middens of life, rotten and acrid, [Stan Hero 84-3 P
  And pick the acrid colors out, [MBG 166-6
ACROBAT. An acrobat on the border of the sea [Woman Had 81-12 P
  The acrobat observed [Woman Had 82-7 P
ACROSS. Across the spick torrent, ceaselessly, [Paltry 6-9
  A red bird flies across the golden floor. [Monocle 13-12
  From what he saw across his vessel's prow. [C 35-25
  Across the stale, mysterious seasons. These [On Manner 56-3
  Of the steadfast lanterns creep across the dark? [Heaven 56-20
  Winding across wide water, without sound. [Sunday 67-7
  The yellow rocked across the still façades, [Babies 77-4
  The spittling tissues tight across the bones. [Nigger 155-8
  To nail his thought across the door, [MBG 166-7
  The crack across the pane, [Anything B 211-22
  Across the unscrawled fores the future casts [NSF 383-4
  Across the roofs as sigil and as ward [NSF 384-23
  The wind is blowing the sand across the floor. [AA 412-15
  New stars that were a foot across came out [Page 421-15
  Write pax across the window pane. And then [Puel 456-15
  The shawl across one shoulder and the hat. [NH 483-21
  No turban walks across the lessened floors. [Plain 502-16
  March . . . Someone has walked across the snow, [Vacancy 511-4
  "Looking across the Fields and Watching the Birds Fly" [517-title
  Fly upward thick in numbers, fly across [Red Kit 31-22 P
  Manes matted of marble across the air, the light [Old Woman 45-1P
  Colossal blacks that leaped across the points [Greenest 53-13 P
  Sleekly the serpent would draw himself across. [Greenest 54-27 P
  Hissing, across the silence, puissant sounds. [Greenest 55-16 P
  To be swept across them when they are revealed, [Duck 65-19 P
  A snort across the silverware. [Grotesque 75-16 P
  Of truth. They stride across and are masters of [Role 93-8 P
  Like slits across a space, a place [Dove 98-11 P
ACT. Act I, Scene 1, at a German Staats-Oper. [Niger 153-16
  The poem of the mind in the act of finding [Of Mod 239-17
  Combing. The poem of the act of the mind. [Of Mod 240-22
  A profounder reconciling, an act, [Vase 247-4
  Actor and act but not divided. [Hero 279-12
  In Series X, Act IV, et cetera. [Chaos 357-12
  Or, the persons act one merely by being here. [AA 416-3
  Perception as an act of intelligence [Lytton 39-6 P
  And perception as an act of grace [Lytton 39-7 P
ACTED. Choke every ghost with acted violence, [Nigger 155-6
ACTION. The action of incorrigible tragedy. [Dutch 292-21
  This force of nature in action is the major [EM 324-8
  One feels its action moving in the blood. [EM 324-23
ACTIVE. His active force in an inactive dirge, [C 41-15
  Or else an inherent order active to be [Orb 422-12
  Is active with a power, an inherent life, [Moonlight 531-20
ACTIVITIES. The swarming activities of the formulae [NH 488-17
ACTIVITY. In an immense activity, in which [Past Nun 378-16
  This sense of the activity of fate-- [AA 419-15
  "Reality is an Activity of the Most August Imagination"
    [110-title P
  This invisible activity, this sense. [Clear Day 113-19 P
ACTOR. Of the actor, half his gesture, half [MBG 170-1
  The actor that will at last declaim our end. [Dames 206-20
  And, like an insatiable actor, slowly and [Of Mod 240-6
  Emotions becoming one. The actor is [Of Mod 240-13
  Xenophon, its implement and actor. [Hero 277-1
  Actor and act but not divided. [Hero 279-12
  Destroy all references. This actor [Hero 279-17
  As if nothing had happened. The dim actor spoke. [Repet 306-11
ACTORS. Its actors approaching, on company, in their masks. [AA
  414-21
  These actors still walk in a twilight muttering lines. [NH 479-23
ACTS. Acts in reality, adds nothing [Hero 279-10
ACTUAL. To things within his actual eye, alert [C 40-16
  The actual is a deft beneficence. [Nigger 155-16
  Here is its actual stone. The bread [MBG 184-1
  After that alien, point-blank, green and actual Guatemala.
    [Waldorf 241-9
  That grips the centre, the actual bite, that life [Choc 298-22
  Of the nights, the actual, universal strength, [Repet 309-2
  Within the actual, the warm, the near, [EM 317-7
  Such seemings are the actual ones: the way [Descrip 339-17
  These are the actual seemings that we see, [Descrip 340-17
  Intenser than any actual life could be, [Descrip 344-20
  The actual form bears outwardly this grace, [Pastor 379-17
  Too actual, things that in being real [Roses 430-14
  The infinite of the actual perceived, [Bouquet 451-19
  Behind all actual seeing, in the actual scene, [NH 467-11
  The actual landscape with its actual horns [NH 475-1
  Touch and trouble of the touch of the actual hand. [NH 476-15
  A knowledge that the actual day [Two Illus 513-7
  But his actual candle blazed with artifice. [Quiet 523-15

The need to be actual and as it is. [Armor 530-10
  Its actual appearance, suppose we being [Recit 86-5 P
ACUTE. The real made more acute by an unreal. [Bouquet 451-21
  Of lizards, in its eye, is more acute [Burnshaw 49-17 P
ACUTEST. The sky acutest at its vanishing. [Key W 129-24
  Of the brooder seeking the acutest end [Extracts 259-14
  As acutest virtue and ascetic trove. [Montra 263-12
  Of human things, that is acutest speech. [Choc 300-15
ADAGIO. The dove's adagio may lose its depth [Burnshaw 48-25 P
ADAM. Adam of beau regard, from fat Elysia, [Pure 331-20
  The first idea was not our own. Adam [NSF 383-10
A-DAY. Rumbled a-day and a-day, a-day. [Ord Women 11-18
ADD. Add nothing to the horror of the frost [Nigger 152-13
  "Add This to Rhetoric" [198-title
  Add this. It is to add. [Add 199-13
  Words add to the senses. The words for the dazzle [Vari 234-17
  Casual poet, that to add your own disorder to disaster [Bed 326-15
  Of the sweeping meanings that we add to them. [NSF 384-6
ADDED. Added and added out of a fame-ful heart . . . [NH 484-15
  The smallest lamp, which added its puissant flick, to which he
    gave [Prol 517-3
  A flick which added to what was real and its vocabulary, [Prol
    517-5
ADDICTIONS. Without their fierce addictions, nor that the heat
  [NSF 399-9
ADDICTS. Like their particular characters, addicts [Lots 371-10
ADDING. Creates a fresh universe out of nothingness by adding
    itself, [Prol 517-9
ADDITION. In addition, there were draftings of him, thus: [NH 485-5
ADDRESS. A funny foreigner of meek address. [Lot 371-21
ADDRESSES. "Extracts from Addresses to the Academy of Fine Ideas"
    [252-title
ADDRESSING. "On the Manner of Addressing Clouds" [55-title
ADDS. Acts in reality, adds nothing [Hero 279-10
  Adds to them the whole vocabulary of the South, [Prol 517-7
  Adds very little, [Melancholy 32-10 P
ADDUCE. It is the rock where tranquil must adduce [Rock 528-14
ADEQUACY. "On the Adequacy of Landscape" [243-title
ADEQUATE. Bravura adequate to this great hymn? [Monocle 16-22
ADIEU. "Waving Adieu, Adieu, Adieu" [127-title
  Waved in pale adieu. The rex Impolitor [Aug 495-21
ADIEUX. Select adieux; and he despises this: [EM 322-22
  Adieux, shapes, images-- [Prejudice 369-1
ADIRONDACK. And Adirondack glittering. The cat hawks it [Aug 490-5
ADJECTIVE. The amorist Adjective aflame . . . [MBG 172-8
  It is a choice of the commodious adjective [NH 475-11
  It is difficult even to choose the adjective [Plain 502-13
ADJECTIVES. And peaks outsoaring possible adjectives. [Thought
  185-10
  Leafed out in adjectives as private [Hero 277-25
  Derived from adjectives of deepest mine. [Pastor 379-16
  Except for the adjectives, an alteration [NH 487-5
ADJUST. And barefoot servants round him, who adjust [NSF 390-20
ADMIRAL. O ashen admiral of the hale, hard blue. . . . [NE Verses
  105-8
  The admiral of his race and everyman, [Duck 62-4 P
ADMIRED. Admired by men and all men, therefore, live [Paisant 334-18
  To be admired by all men. Nations live [Paisant 334-19
  To be admired by nations. The race is brave. [Paisant 334-20
ADMIT. Of its propriety. Admit the shaft [Someone 86-2 A
ADMITTED. He first, as realist, admitted that [C 40-26
ADO. Another thought, the paramount ado . . . [What We 460-5
  With holy or sublime ado [Archi 18-15 P
ADOBE. The adobe of the angels? Constantly, [Repet 308-2
ADORN. But these shall not adorn my souvenirs, [Lions 124-17
  In highest night? And do these heavens adorn [AA 417-10
  The father does not come to adorn the chant. [Role 93-6 P
ADORNED. Came like two spirits parleying, adorned [C 31-31
  Adorned with cryptic stones and sliding shines, [Owl 434-10
  Peace stood with our last blood adorned, last mind, [Owl 434-19
  And in bright excellence adorned, crested [Orb 442-17
  Adorned for a multitude, in a gesture spent [Sombre 71-27 P
ADRIATIC. An Adriatic riva rising, [Botanist 1 135-8
ADROITER. And the adroiter harmonies of their fall. [Havana 144-22
A-DUB. A-dub, a-dub, which is made up of this: [AA 416-1
ADULT. "Adult Epigram" [353-title
  Upon the horizon amid adult enfantillages. [Questions 462-6
  Here the adult one is still banded with fulgor, [Aug 495-24
ADULTERIES. Her words accuse you of adulteries [Red Kit 31-3 P
ADVENTURE. This maximum, an adventure to be endured [EM 324-21
  Desire prolongs its adventure to create [NH 482-14
ADVENTURER. The minor of what we feel. The adventurer [EM 325-24
  The interminable adventurer? The trees are mended. [World 520-12
ADVERSARY. "Here am I, my adversary, that [MBG 170-15
AENEAS. The solid shape, Aeneas seen, perhaps, [Recit 87-22 P
AESTHETIC. Of an aesthetic tough, diverse, untamed, [C 31-20
  That helped him round his rude aesthetic out. [C 36-11
  Of his aesthetic, his philosophy, [C 37-14
AETAT. It is the extreme, the expert aetat. 2. [Questions 462-14
AFFABULATION. Romanesque Affabulation [Thought 185-title 3

AFFAIR. Combat, compose their droll affair. [MBG 182-11
  And continue their affair. The shriek [MBG 182-15
  From an old delusion, an old affair with the sun, [Bottle 239-10
  Is the affair of logical lunatics. [EM 324-28
  So little, our affair, which is the affair [Descrip 342-4
  As the fox and snake do. It is a brave affair. [NSF 403-17
  With our affair, our destiny, our hash? [Bship 80-19 P
  Without them it could not exist. That's our affair, [Bship 80-28P
AFFAIRS. Men and the affairs of men seldom concerned [Nigger 156-4
AFFECT. Made to affect a dream they never had, [Burnshaw 47-1 P
  For if we affect sunrise, [Three 134-1 P
  We affect all things. [Three 134-2 P
AFFECTATION. Whose blunt laws make an affectation of mind, [Look 519-9
AFFECTED. Of affected homage foxed so many books, [Havana 142-15
AFFECTING. Like jades affecting the sequestered bride; [C 34-23
  Return, affecting roseate aureoles, [Greenest 56-23 P
AFFECTIONATE. So much for that. The affectionate emigrant found [C 32-11
  That, nameless, it creates an affectionate name, [Pastor 379-15
AFFECTS. That affects the white stones, [Three 135-3 P
  And it affects the green gown. [Three 135-5 P
AFFINED. To blessed syllable affined, and sound [C 43-9
AFFIRM. I affirm and then at midnight the great cat [Montra 264-5
AFFIRMATION. An affirmation free from doubt. [Vase 247-5
AFFIRMED. Out of a thing believed, a thing affirmed: [Beard 247-22
AFFIX. Let the lamp affix its beam. [Emperor 64-15
AFFLATUS. Contained in their afflatus the reproach [C 39-12
  By an afflatus that persists. [Negation 98-2
  Only in misery, the afflatus of ruin, [Rome 509-24
AFFLICTED. Afflicted sleep, too much the syllables [EM 314-20
AFFLUENCE. In a kind of total affluence, all first, [Descrip 342-15
  Some affluence, if only half-perceived, [Planet 533-1
AFIRE. Afire--it might and it might not in that [Page 422-19
AFLAME. The amorist Adjective aflame . . . [MBG 172-8
AFRAID. I felt afraid. [Domination 9-19
  Afraid, the blind man as astronomer, [C 37-18
  The bass lie deep, still afraid of the Indians. [Think 356-8
  Of everything he is. And he feels afraid. [AA 417-3
  They would be afraid of the sun: what it might be, [Page 422-6
  Afraid of the country angels of those skies, [Page 422-7
  Mother was afraid I should freeze in the Parisian hotels. [Novel 457-7
AFRICA. The sun comes up like news from Africa. [Feo 334-12
  By one caterpillar is great Africa devoured [Fuel 456-2
  What god rules over Africa, what shape, [Greenest 52-24 P
  That was never the heaven of Africa, which had [Greenest 54-19 P
  No god rules over Africa, no throne, [Greenest 55-5 P
  And Africa, basking in antiquest sun, [Greenest 55-25 P
  But could the statue stand in Africa? [Greenest 56-27 P
  In endless elegies. But in Africa [Greenest 57-15 P
  In Africa. The serpent's throne is dust [Greenest 58-9 P
  See South Africa.
AFRICAN. Sultan of African sultans, starless crown. [Greenest 60-6P
AFTER. But, after all, I know a tree that bears [Monocle 17-2
  She might, after all, be a wanton, [Homunculus 26-23
  May, after all, stop short before a plum [C 40-28
  After the guitar is asleep, [Venereal 47-21
  And, finger after finger, here, the hand, [Worms 49-21
  After the winter." [Jack-Rabbit 50-13
  Or just after. [Thirteen 93-11
  "Sailing after Lunch" [120-title
  Day after day, throughout the winter, [Medit 124-1
  Still hankers after lions, or, to shift, [Lions 125-4
  Still hankers after sovereign images. [Lions 125-5
  Which led them back to angels, after death. [Eve Angels 137-12
  Of a man gone mad, after all, for time, in spite [Nigger 157-18
  Well, after all, the north wind blows [MBG 174-12
  After long strumming on certain nights [MBG 174-1
  Health follows after health. Salvation there: [Parochial 192-3
  If he will be heaven after death, [Prelude 194-11
  One another washing the mountains bare. [Loaf 200-7
  That's what one wants to get near. Could it after all [Dump 202-28
  Either now or tomorrow or the day after that. [Nightgown 214-20
  After all the pretty contrast of life and death [Connois 215-13
  Is blowing after days of constant rain. [Connois 216-5
  After the sermon, to quiet that mouse in the wall. [Blue Bldg 216-20
  In their hands. The lilacs came long after. [Arcades 225-12
  It is like the season when, after summer, [Cuisine 228-1
  After that alien, point-blank, green and actual Guatemala. [Waldorf 241-9
  Theology after breakfast sticks to the eye. [Les Plus 245-8
  After the final no there comes a yes [Beard 247-9
  In total war we died and after death [Extracts 258-25
  To evil after death, unable to die [Extracts 259-4
  Its evil after death, it dissolves it while [Extracts 259-12
  After the hero, the familiar [Hero 280-23
  After we've drunk the Moselle, to the thickest shade [Phenom 286-16

By water washed away. They follow after. [Somnam 304-8
After all, they knew that to be real each had [Holiday 312-11
After death, the non-physical people, in paradise, [EM 325-21
And after a while, when Ha-ee-me has gone to sleep, [Jouga 337-14
That night, Liadoff, a long time after his death, [Liadoff 346-14
Of the instant to perceive, after the shock, [Liadoff 347-15
Pushing and pushing red after red. [Red Fern 365-4
My Jacomyntje! This first spring after the war, [Extraord 369-16
The bottomless trophy, new hornsman after old? [NSF 390-18
Follow after, O my companion, my fellow, my self, [NSF 392-23
Long after the planter's death. A few limes remained, [NSF 393-3
After a lustre of the moon, we say [NSF 394-19
But your war ends. And after it you return [NSF 407-15
This is form gulping after formlessness, [AA 411-10
And the night, and midnight, and after, where it is. [Bad Time 426-17
After the wind has passed. Sleep realized [Owl 433-19
This was peace after death, the brother of sleep, [Owl 434-7
Twelve and the first gray second after, a kind [What We 459-16
And the bells belong to the sextons, after all, [Luther 462-2
Dark things without a double, after all, [NH 465-13
So, after summer, in the autumn air, [NH 468-5
And more, in branchings after day. One part [NH 468-23
At evening, after dark, is the other half, [NH 482-4
It was after the neurosis of winter. It was [NH 482-17
Before and after one arrives or, say, [NH 485-24
Bergamo on a postcard, Rome after dark, [NH 486-1
After the leaves have fallen, we return [Plain 502-9
To recognize him in after time. [Two Illus 514-5
Night after night because the hemisphere [Spaniard 34-8 P
Long after the worms and the curious carvings of [Burnshaw 47-12P
Angels returning after war with belts [Greenest 56-10 P
Be marble after the drenching reds, the dark [Greenest 57-22 P
Is, after all, draped damask pampaluned, [Greenest 58-4 P
The Bulgar said, "After pineapple with fresh mint [Duck 60-7 P
We went to walk in the park; for, after all [Duck 60-8 P
"Recitation after Dinner" [86-title P
A time existing after much time has passed. [Role 93-11 P
Nothing more, like weather after it has cleared-- [Art Pop 112-14P
AFTER-COLOR. Any azure under-side of after-color. Nabob [Landsc 241-19
AFTER-DEATH. Darkness, nothingness of human after-death, [Flyer 336-12
AFTERNOON. And roamed there all the stupid afternoon. [Hibiscus 23-3
  It was evening all afternoon. [Thirteen 95-1
  In the afternoon, balloons at night. That is [Havana 142-2
  How easily the feelings flow this afternoon [Nigger 151-16
  All afternoon the gramophone [Search 268-1
  All afternoon the gramaphoon, [Search 268-9
  All afternoon the gramaphoon, [Search 268-10
  One chemical afternoon in mid-autumn, [Contra II 270-1
  The afternoon's reading, the night's reflection, [Hero 274-23
  This afternoon the wind and the sea were like that-- [Jouga 337-13
  Morning and afternoon are clasped together [NSF 392-12
  Or before, not the white of an aging afternoon, [AA 412-12
  As on water of an afternoon in the wind [Owl 433-18
  Espoused each morning, each long afternoon, [Orb 441-22
  Of today, of this morning, of this afternoon, [Bouquet 451-13
  At twelve, the disintegration of afternoon [What We 459-7
  So that at the edge of afternoon, not over, [NH 482-22
  Away from them, capes, along the afternoon Sound, [NH 484-7
  In the afternoon. The proud and the strong [Leben 504-17
  The afternoon is visibly a source, [Look 518-17
  With parasols, in the afternoon air. [Parasols 20-14 P
  To search for clearness all an afternoon [Old Woman 44-13 P
  In an autumn afternoon, but two immense [Burnshaw 50-4 P
AFTERNOONS. Inseparable from their afternoons; [Curtains 62-4
  The silken weavings of our afternoons, [Sunday 69-23
  At the end of winter when afternoons return. [Poems Clim 193-11
AFTER-SHINING. Glozing his life with after-shining flicks, [C 46-5
AFTERWARD. That choir among themselves long afterward. [Sunday 70-9
  So afterward, at night, [Weak Mind 212-6
  We chant if we live in evil and afterward [Extracts 259-9
  Waste without puberty; and afterward, [NSF 399-17
AFTERWARDS. See autumn-afterwards.
AGAINST. "Invective against Swans" [4-title
  "The Plot against the Giant" [6-title
  Was it a cry against the twilight [Domination 9-3
  Or against the leaves themselves [Domination 9-4
  Or was it a cry against the hemlocks? [Domination 9-12
  Which had lain folded against the blue [Hibiscus 22-16
  Against his pipping sounds a trumpet cried [C 29-21
  A pungent bloom against your shade. [Venereal 48-17
  Against a tall tree. [Six Sig 74-5
  Against the elders by her side; [Peter 91-15
  Blessed, whose beard is cloak against the snows. [NE Verses 105-6
  Statue against a Clear Sky [NE Verses 105-title 9
  Statue against a Cloudy Sky [NE Verses 105-title 10
  Against your sides, then shoving and slithering, [Farewell 118-15
  The arm of bronze outstretched against all evil! [Mice 123-12

For his rage against chaos [Winter B 141-10
Against the autumn winds [Nigger 152-3
Against the murderous alphabet: [MBG 179-8
Or less, he found a man, or more, against [Horn 230-15
Grows large against space: [Rhythms 245-14
Against the edge of the ice, the abstraction would [Extracts
    255-18
Against enemies, against the prester, [Hero 274-4
High, low, far, wide, against the distance, [Hero 277-22
Against the sight, the penetrating, [Hero 278-28
A parasol, which I had found, against [Phenom 287-9
Steel against intimation--the sharp flash, [Motive 288-19
Against the whole experience of day. [Choc 298-10
Millions of major men against their like [Repet 307-1
I nourish myself. I defend myself against [Repet 308-14
The powdered personals against the giants' rage, [Repet 309-17
Against the gold whipped reddened in big-shadowed black,
    [Repet 309-19
Exquisite in poverty against the suns [EM 317-23
Of the country colors crowding against it, since [EM 318-23
Against the haggardie . . . A loud, large water [EM 321-8
The gross, the fecund, proved him against the touch [EM 322-2
That batters against the mind, silent and proud, [Pure 329-14
Or a barricade against the singular man [Descrip 340-8
The human ocean beats against this rock [Two V 354-19
Of earth, rises against it, tide by tide, [Two V 354-20
"The Prejudice against the Past" [368-title
And this must comfort the heart's core against [Cred 372-15
Against the first idea--to lash the lion, [NSF 385-2
Of an infinite course. The flowers against the wall [AA 412-8
And knock like a rifle-butt against the door. [AA 414-2
In the sense against calamity, it is not [AA 418-2
And against the most coiled thorn, have seized on what was ugly
    [Large 424-3
Against itself. At its mercy, we depend [John 436-12
Against illusion and was, in a great grinding [NH 467-18
In a faithfulness as against the lunar light, [NH 472-15
He preserves himself against the repugnant rain [NH 475-22
Against the trees and then against the sky [Aug 494-12
A light on the candle tearing against the wick [Rome 509-5
He could nor bend against its propelling force. [R Conn 533-12
Oh, bend against the invisible; and lean [Blanche 10-6 P
The constant cry against an old order, [Polo 37-13 P
Contorted, staggering from the thrust against [Old Woman 43-14 P
Crying against a need that pressed like cold, [Old Woman 45-29 P
Hoofs grinding against the stubborn earth, until [Old Woman
    46-10 P
Of the pith of mind, cuirassiers against [Greenest 56-5 P
As against each other, the dead, the phantomesque. [Duck 65-5 P
Against the sleepers to re-create for them, [Sombre 69-7 P
Blew against them or bowed from the hips, when I turned [Bship
    78-17 P
It is the common man against evil, [Stan Hero 84-15 P
It is an arbor against the wind, a pit in the mist, [Discov 95-12P
The gathering of the imbecile against his motes [Discov 95-19 P
A home against one's self, a darkness, [Letters 107-6 P
AGAMEMNON. Like Agamemnon's story. [Phases 3-15 P
Of Agamemnon [Phases 4-18 P
AGATE. The agate in the eye, the tufted ear, [Nigger 153-19
Still bloom in the agate eyes, red blue, [Arcades 225-15
AGE. The old age of a watery realist, [C 28-23
Of blue and green? A wordy, watery age [C 28-25
The song of the great space of your age pierces [God 285-17
An age is a manner collected from a queen. [Descrip 340-5
An age is green or red. An age believes [Descrip 340-6
Or it denies. An age is solitude [Descrip 340-7
By an understanding that fulfils his age, [Cred 374-4
Finally, in the last year of her age, [Past Nun 378-11
Then the stale turtle will grow limp from age. [John 437-22
A great bosom, beard and being, alive with age. [NH 466-3
And yet the wind whimpers oldly of old age [NH 477-2
In an age of concentric mobs would any sphere [Duck 63-25 P
In this he carved himself, he carved his age, [Duck 64-21 P
The solid was an age, a period [Sombre 68-6 P
Did not the age that bore him bear him among [Someone 85-1 A
Its infiltrations? There had been an age [Someone 85-2 A
AGENDA. "Agenda" [41-title P
AGGRANDIZEMENT. His violence was for aggrandizement [C 31-14
AGGRIEVED. And this the spirit sees and is aggrieved. [Anatomy
    108-18
AGING. Or before, not the white of an aging afternoon, [AA 412-12
AGITATIONS. Where luminous agitations come to rest, [Owl 433-12
AGO. A moment ago, light masculine, [Hartford 227-1
Mac Mort she had been, ago, [Oak 272-7
Of thirty years ago. It is looking out [NH 478-8
Regard the freedom of seventy years ago. [Rock 525-4
The vaguest line of smoke (a year ago) [Phases 5-4 P
As they were fifty years ago, [Clear Day 113-9 P
AGONY. And only an agony of dreams can help [Duck 61-24 P
Not the agony of a single dreamer, but [Duck 61-25 P

AGREE. We agree in principle. That's clear. But take [High-Toned
    59-6
Agree: the apple in the orchard, round [Burnshaw 47-30 P
AGREEMENT. Provoking a laughter, an agreement, by surprise. [Gala
    248-15
A good agreement between himself and night, [Extracts 256-5
AGREES. A world agrees, thought's compromise, resolved [Ideal 89-7A
AH. Ah! that ill humors [W Burgher 61-3
And ah! that Scaramouche [W Burgher 61-5
Ah, but the meaningless, natural effigy! [Nigger 153-17
Ah, but to play man number one, [MBG 166-3
Ah! Yes, desire . . . this leaning on his bed, [Men Fall 187-15
Ah! and red; and they have peach fuzz, ah! [Peaches 224-11
Enough. Ah! douce compagna of that thing! [Beard 247-19
Ah! douce campagna, honey in the heart, [Beard 247-20
Felicity, ah! Time is the hooded enemy, [Pure 330-13
Ah, ké! the bloody wren, the felon jay, [NSF 394-1
He is, we are. Ah, bella! He is, we are, [Study I 463-11
Certain and ever more fresh. Ah! Certain, for sure . . .
    [Moonlight 532-6
Ah, good God! That all beasts should have [Parasol 20-7 P
AHEAD. That he sends ahead, out of the goodness of his heart [EM
    320-18
The bass keep looking ahead, upstream, in one [Think 356-11
Upon it, as it flows ahead. [Degen 445-3
AI. And the world had worlds, ai, this-a-way: [MBG 178-17
AI-AI. Lament, willingly forfeit the ai-ai [EM 317-15
AID. In any commonplace the sought-for aid. [C 30-23
The florist asking aid from cabbages, [C 37-16
This cloudy world, by aid of land and sea, [Vari 233-20
The aid of greatness to be and the force. [Ulysses 100-17 P
AILS. The sun aches and ails and then returns halloo [Questions
    462-5
AIMLESS. That a man without passion plays in an aimless way.
    [Sombre 71-12 P
AIR. And giving your bland motions to the air. [Swans 4-8
Untasted, in its heavenly, orchard air. [Monocle 14-15
High up in orange air, were barbarous. [C 30-21
Was like a glacial pink upon the air. [C 34-14
In this hymeneal air, what it is [Lilacs 49-2
From my balcony, I survey the yellow air, [Of Surface 57-3
In the innocent air. [Peacocks 58-26
The grackles crack their throats of bone in the smooth air.
    [Banal 62-13
Wriggling far down the phantom air, [Cuban 65-2
The loneliest air, not less was I myself. [Hoon 65-9
And tall and of a port in air. [Jar 76-12
That the air was heavy with the breath of these swine, [Frogs 78-4
Of flesh and air. [Motion 83-9
Most rare, or ever of more kindred air [Fictive 87-21
And these two never meet in the air so full of summer [Norfolk
    111-20
And then rush brightly through the summer air. [Sailing 121-7
Spread on the sun-bronzed air, [Pascagoula 127-2
However clear, it would have been deep air, [Key W 129-14
The heaving speech of air, a summer sound [Key W 129-15
As the night descended, tilting in the air, [Key W 130-7
That, too, returns from out the winter's air, [Sun March 134-2
Cold is our element and winter's air [Sun March 134-5
Of this ecstatic air. [Botanist 1 135-15
Air is air, [Eve Angels 137-1
Men that repeat antiquest sounds of air [Eve Angels 137-15
Beneath the arches and their spangled air, [Eve Angels 138-2
In the air. [Gray 140-12
Jehovah and the great sea-worm. The air [Havana 142-4
Into this haggard and tenuous air, [Nigger 153-9
Poetry is a finikin thing of air [Nigger 155-17
Made sharp air sharper by their smell [Postcard 159-2
But the name of a bird and the name of a nameless air [Autumn
    160-6
Like a buzzing of flies in autumn air, [MBG 166-20
By gold antagonists in air-- [MBG 169-8
Of the air, in which the blue guitar [MBG 169-14
Good air, good friend, what is there in life? [MBG 175-18
Good air, my only friend, believe [MBG 175-20
Good air. Poor pale, poor pale guitar . . . [MBG 176-2
The sea drifts through the winter air. [MBG 179-14
In the room more like a snowy air, [Poems Clim 193-9
Out of the clouds, pomp of the air, [Idiom 201-5
I stood and sang and filled the air. [Country 207-7
"The Blue Buildings in the Summer Air" [216-title
Stood up straight in the air, struck off [Thunder 220-7
A black line drawn on flat air [Common 221-5
In light blue air over dark blue sea. [Vari 232-6
Until the difference between air [Vari 235-3
The vivid thing in the air that never changes, [Martial 238-12
Though the air change. Only this evening I saw it again,
    [Martial 238-13
The sky was blue. He wanted imperceptible air. [Landsc 241-13
Of air, who looked for the world beneath the blue, [Landsc 241-17

As if the people in the air [Adequacy 243-10
Not the people in the air that hear [Adequacy 244-15
Not as in air, bright-blue-resembling air, [Rhythms 246-7
Flicked into pieces, points of air, [Vase 246-20
An egg-plant of good air. [Extracts 253-15
When he looked, the water ran up the air or grew white
  [Extracts 255-17
One would be drowned in the air of difference, [Extracts 258-12
She held her hand before him in the air, [Hand 271-5
Apparently in air, fall from him [Hero 277-15
Or in a bubble examines the bubble of air. [Phenom 286-8
There are men shuffling on foot in air. [Dutch 290-9
The air attends the brightened guns, [Dutch 290-16
In this bleak air the broken stalks [Possum 293-17
She floats in air at the level of [Couch 295-4
Suspended in air, the slightest crown [Couch 295-11
Of sky, of sea, large earth, large air. It is [Choc 296-10
Or air collected in a deep essay, [Choc 297-10
Political tramp with an heraldic air, [Choc 301-3
He is, the air changes and grows fresh to breathe. [Choc 301-8
The air changes, creates and re-creates, like strength, [Choc
  301-9
Of them in the air still hanging heavily [EM 315-6
As if the air, the mid-day air, was swarming [EM 326-10
Man, that is not born of woman but of air, [Pure 331-16
The forms that are attentive in thin air. [Descrip 344-14
Of air . . . But then that cloud, that piano placed [Liadoff
  347-13
Snow glistens in its instant in the air, [Pieces 351-12
And fire and air and things not discomposed [Two V 355-9
The air is full of children, statues, roofs [Chaos 357-15
In sleeping air. [Woman Song 360-12
In the heavy air. [Attempt 370-14
Sleepless, inhales his proper air, and rests. [Cred 373-24
As placid air becomes. But it is not [Cred 375-15
And Eve made air the mirror of herself, [NSF 383-12
The air is not a mirror but bare board, [NSF 384-2
Say the weather, the mere weather, the mere air: [NSF 385-23
As if--The pigeons clatter in the air. [NSF 390-6
Like a page of music, like an upper air, [NSF 397-13
The golden fingers picking dark-blue air: [NSF 398-15
Are the wings his, the lapis-haunted air? [NSF 404-21
His head is air. Beneath his tip at night [AA 411-2
Of body and air and forms and images, [AA 411-17
The father fetches pageants out of air, [AA 415-13
Of sleep, the accomplished, the fulfilling air. [Owl 433-24
Move lightly through the air again. [Imago 439-20
By such slight genii in such pale air. [Orb 440-8
The blown sheen--or is it air? [Degen 444-18
It is not that there is any image in the air [Wom Sun 445-6
And movement of emotion through the air, [Bouquet 449-17
Fell openly from the air to reappear [Bouquet 450-18
From heaven and float in air, like animals [Study II 464-6
So, after summer, in the autumn air, [NH 468-5
We descend to the street and inhale a health of air [NH 470-17
The pattern of the heavens and high, night air. [NH 472-3
It may be that they mingle, clouds and men, in the air [NH 479-24
There were looks that caught him out of empty air. [NH 483-13
The glass of the air becomes an element-- [NH 488-1
*Have liberty not as the air within a grave [Aug 490-12
The nature of its women in the air, [Aug 491-16
Of that transparent air. [Aug 493-24
And an air of lateness. The moon is a tricorn [Aug 495-20
And sea and air. [Irish 502-8
The tree stood dazzling in the air [Two Illus 514-15
No doubt we live beyond ourselves in air, [Look 518-3
Of air and whirled away. But it has been often so. [Slug 522-4
We make a dwelling in the evening air, [Final 524-1
By our own motions in a freedom of air. [Rock 525-3
It is no longer air. The houses still stand, [Rock 525-5
The rock is the stern particular of the air, [Rock 528-4
In the air of newness of that element, [Armor 530-15
In an air of freshness, clearness, greenness, blueness, [Armor
  530-16
In the great vistas of night air, that takes this form,
  [Moonlight 531-17
It is the third commonness with light and air, [R Conn 533-16
Wavered in the evening air, above the roof, [Phases 5-5 P
This man to take the air. [Soldat 12-16 P
Of mountain pallors ebbing into air; [Soldat 13-10 P
Gesturing grandiose things in the air, [Soldat 16-5 P
Pierce, too, with buttresses of coral air [Archi 18-5 P
With parasols, in the afternoon air. [Parasols 20-14 P
This crust of air? . . (He pauses.) Can breath shake [Infernale
  24-21 P
Fly from the black toward the purple air. [Infernale 25-2 P
Between the matin air and color, goldenest generating,
  [Inelegance 25-16 P
The blueness of the half-night, fill the air [Red Kit 31-23 P
Whipping the air. [Drum-Majors 37-9 P

In thudding air: [Polo 37-21 P
A brilliant air [Polo 38-3 P
In this apologetic air, one well [Lytton 39-16 P
Cooling the sugary air. [Agenda 42-3 P
Manes matted of marble across the air, the light [Old Woman 45-1P
Would flash in air, and the muscular bodies thrust [Old Woman
  46-9 P
Appear to sleep within a sleeping air, [Burnshaw 50-19 P
No longer of air but of the breathing earth, [Burnshaw 52-18 P
Motions of air, robes moving in torrents of air, [Greenest 53-5P
Winding and waving slowly, waving in air, [Greenest 55-14 P
The ecstasy of sense in a sensuous air. [Greenest 56-26 P
Of constellations on the beachy air [Greenest 58-1 P
That rises in the air. The sprawlers on the grass [Duck 64-7 P
Until they changed to eagle in white air, [Sombre 68-4 P
In such an air, poor as one's mule. [Stan MBG 73-11 P
The petals flying through the air. [Grotesque 75-17 P
From constable to god, from earth to air, [Bship 80-22 P
A tall figure upright in a giant's air. [Recit 87-24 P
That move in the air as large as air, [Including 88-10 P
Bands of black men seem to be drifting in the air, [Sick 90-7 P
To be part of a tissue, a clearness of the air, [Nuns 92-16 P
Other men, and not this grass, this valid air. [Americana 94-11P
Than they are in the final finding of the air, in the thing
  [Course 97-2 P
In the central of earth or sky or air or thought, [Conversat
  108-19 P
In the excellences of the air we breathe, [Conversat 109-20 P
And through the air. The smaller ones [Dinner 110-2 P
Night's moonlight lake was neither water nor air. [Real 111-2 P
Neither the cards nor the trees nor the air [Sol Oaks 111-5 P
Young and living in a live air, [Clear Day 113-10 P
Today the air is clear of everything. [Clear Day 113-14 P
A refreshment of cold air, cold breath, [Bus 116-6 P
See mid-air.
AIR-EARTH. Air-earth--Can we live on dry descriptions, [Hero 278-2
AIRPLANE. "Concerto for Airplane and Pianoforte," [Duck 62-29 P
AIRS. All of them, darkened by time, moved by they know not what,
  amending the airs they play to fulfill themselves; [Piano 21-17P
She was all of her airs and, for all of her airs, [Grotesque 74-1P
She was all of her airs and ears and hairs, [Grotesque 74-2 P
In spite of her airs, that's what she was. She was all
  [Grotesque 74-5 P
Of her airs, as surely cologne as that she was bone [Grotesque
  74-6 P
Was what she was and flesh, sure enough, but airs; [Grotesque
  74-7 P
AIRY. That airy dream of the future, [Mozart 132-5
AIX. Less Aix than Stockholm, hardly a yellow at all, [Holiday
  312-4
AI-YI-YI. His robes and symbols, ai-yi-yi-- [MBG 178-11
A fat thumb beats out ai-yi-yi. [MBG 178-22
ALABASTERS. Into the alabasters [Fabliau 23-7
ALARM. Could beat, yet not alarm the populace. [Havana 143-7
ALARMING. Alarming shadows, [Three 138-4 P
ALAS. Alas! Have all the barbers lived in vain [Monocle 14-8
Alas, that they should wear our colors there, [Sunday 69-22
In an excessive corridor, alas! [Antag 426-8
She needs will come consolingly. Alas, [Spaniard 35-3 P
ALBUM. The album of Corot is premature. [Nigger 156-13
ALCHEMICANA. Everything, the spirit's alchemicana [NH 471-22
ALERT. To things within his actual eye, alert [C 40-16
They would march single file, with electric lamps, alert [Page
  423-9
Congenial mannequins, alert to please, [Study II 464-11
Alert us most [Inhab 503-12
In flowery nations, crashing and alert. [Greenest 55-4 P
ALEXANDRINE. The noble, Alexandrine verve. The flies [Contra II
  270-17
ALFRED. See Mrs. Alfred Uruguay.
ALGUAZIL. Of his gold ether, golden alguazil, [Bird Claws 82-8
ALIEN. When he was young), naked and alien, [Anglais 149-2
But the ugly alien, the mask that speaks [Nigger 156-17
After that alien, point-blank, green and actual Guatemala
  [Waldorf 241-9
It is the human that is the alien, [Less 328-3
In the alien freedom that such selves degustate: [Pagoda 92-2 P
ALIENS. Life's foreigners, pale aliens of the mud, [Greenest 59-23P
ALIGHTING. In whose breast, the dove, alighting, would grow still.
  [Think 357-6
ALIGHTS. On which the dove alights. Description is [Descrip 343-21
ALIKE. Puissant speech, alike in each, [Ord Woman 11-26
Are both alike in the routine I know. [Pharynx 96-3
All alike, except for the rules of the rabbis, [Nigger 151-7
The two alike, distinguish blues, [Vari 235-2
This reposes alike in springtime [Yellow 236-11
And the father alike and equally are spent, [EM 324-4
And scattered them about, no two alike. [NSF 400-24
Of the week, queerer than Sunday. We thought alike [AA 419-10
Since both alike appoint themselves the choice [NH 469-16

And alike, a point of the sky or of the earth [NH 483-8
Beyond, the two alike in the make of the mind. [Rome 508-7
And change. If ploughmen, peacocks, doves alike [Burnshaw 48-26P
If platitude and inspirations are alike [Duck 63-3 P
ALIVE. And the earth is alive with creeping men, [MBG 168-14
Wingless and withered, but living alive. [MBG 171-7
Is my thought a memory, not alive? [MBG 173-10
Time swished on the village clocks and dreams were alive,
    [Uruguay 249-26
Shine on the very living of those alive. [Dutch 293-5
Alive, on that people are alive, on that [Wild 328-12
Be alive with its own seemings, seeming to be [Descrip 346-3
In which a real lies hidden and alive. [Novel 458-15
Unreal today, be hidden and alive. [Novel 458-21
A great bosom, beard and being, alive with age. [NH 466-3
Much richer, more fecund, sportive and alive. [NH 469-24
In the warmth of your bed, at the edge of your chair, alive
    [Rome 509-19
It is an illusion that we were ever alive, [Rock 525-1
Were being alive, an incessant being alive, [Rock 526-8
Alive with an enigma's flittering . . . [Ulysses 105-9 P
Alive with an enigma's flittering, [Presence 106-9 P
ALL. Alas! Have all the barbers lived in vain [Monocle 14-8
Found inklings of your bond to all that dust. [Monocle 15-6
I quiz all sounds, all thoughts, all everything [Monocle 16-19
But, after all, I know a tree that bears [Monocle 17-2
To which all birds come sometime in their time. [Monocle 17-5
If sex were all, then every trembling hand [Monocle 17-7
And they were all His thought. [Pourtraicte 22-1
And roamed there all the stupid afternoon. [Hibiscus 23-3
She might, after all, be a wanton, [Homunculus 26-23
Was name for this short-shanks in all that brunt? [C 28-16
In all desires, his destitution's mark. [C 31-11
Decays of sacks, and all the arrant stinks [C 36-10
Of what he saw he never saw at all. [C 36-17
To which all poems were incident, unless [C 36-22
If not, when all is said, to drive away [C 37-7
All dreams are vexing. Let them be expunged. [C 39-31
May, after all, stop short before a plum [C 40-28
Of his own fate an instance of all fate? [C 41-24
For all it takes it gives a humped return [C 43-6
All this with many mulctings of the man, [C 44-3
All din and gobble, blasphemously pink. [C 44-23
Is nothing, what can all this matter since [C 46-11
And sight, and all there was of the storm, [Joost 47-2
The women will be all shanks [Bananas 54-15
Of night, in which all motion [Curtains 62-7
All pleasures and all pains, remembering [Sunday 67-24
Seem all of paradise that we shall know? [Sunday 68-7
Their pleasure that is all bright-edged and cold; [Tallap 72-9
Not all the knives of the lamp-posts, [Six Sig 74-23
And of all vigils musing the obscure, [Fictive 88-4
It was evening all afternoon. [Thirteen 95-1
Beholding all these green sides [Nomad 95-13
Through all its purples to the final slate, [Pharynx 96-11
Incapable master of all force, [Negation 97-17
Widen your sense. All things in the sun are sun. [NE Verses 104-2
That bore us as a part of all the things [Anatomy 107-14
To expunge all people and be a pupil [Sailing 121-3
Who found all form and order in solitude, [Sad Gay 121-17
The arm of bronze outstretched against all evil! [Mice 123-12
All eyes and size, and galled Justitia, [Lions 124-13
Beyond all trees, the ridges thrown [How Live 125-19
It may be that in all her phrases stirred [Key W 129-1
What composition is there in all this: [Botanist 1 135-6
As sure as all the angels are. [Botanist 2 136-2
And then another, one by one, and all [Eve Angels 137-27
When all people are shaken [Fading 139-2
All this is older than its oldest hymn, [Havana 144-28
All night I sat reading a book, [Reader 146-25
All alike, except for the rules of the rabbis, [Nigger 151-7
The cock-hen crows all day. But cockerel shrieks, [Nigger 155-11
For all his purple, the purple bird must have [Nigger 155-20
Of a man gone mad, after all, for time, in spite [Nigger 157-18
Not wisdom. Can all men, together, avenge [Nigger 158-11
And the stillness is in the key, all of it is, [Autumn 160-13
The stillness is all in the key of that desolate sound. [Autumn
    160-14
Melodious skeletons, for all of last night's music [Fish-Scale
    160-15
And all their manner in the thing, [MBG 166-16
And all their manner, right and wrong, [MBG 166-17
And all their manner, weak and strong? [MBG 166-18
Whom all believe that all believe, [MBG 170-11
Is a weed and all the flies are caught, [MBG 171-6
Of a multitude dwindles, all said, [MBG 171-15
Well, after all, the north wind blows [MBG 174-12
Or better not of myself at all, [MBG 175-13
A substitute for all the gods: [MBG 176-3
And the truth, Dichtung und Wahrheit, all [MBG 177-17

One-half of all its installments paid. [MBG 182-2
Like the night before Christmas and all the carols. [Thought
    185-3
With all his attributes no god but man [Thought 186-11
God and all angels sing the world to sleep, [Men Fall 187-9
God and all angels, this was his desire, [Men Fall 188-13
Stripped one of all one's torments, concealed [Poems Clim 193-18
For all your images, [Add 198-19
I am the poorest of all. [Idiom 201-7
(All its images are in the dump) and you see [Dump 202-23
That's what one wants to get near. Could it after all [Dump
    202-28
Could all these be ourselves, sounding ourselves, [Dames 206-11
I know from all the things it touched [Country 207-17
For all the thoughts of summer that go with it [Dwarf 208-5
It is all that you are, the final dwarf of you, [Dwarf 208-9
There was the cat slopping its milk all day, [Rabbit K 209-4
A self that touches all edges, [Rabbit K 209-18
And play concertinas all night. [Jersey 210-19
They think that things are all right, [Jersey 210-20
The bee may have all sweet [Anything B 211-9
Out of all the minds, [Bagatelles 213-23
There has been a booming all the spring, [Nightgown 214-3
If all the green of spring was blue, and it is; [Connois 215-4
And if it all went on in an orderly way, [Connois 215-8
After all the pretty contrast of life and death [Connois 215-13
All this, of course, will come to summer soon. [Connois 216-6
He read, all day, all night and all the nights, [Blue Bldg
    216-16
Searching all day, all night, for the honey-comb. [Blue Bldg
    217-24
The reason can give nothing at all [Dezem 218-19
Bringing the lights of Norway and all that. [Hartford 226-6
But that's all done. It is what used to be, [Cuisine 227-17
Of spray. Let all the salt be gone. [Vari 234-14
So that one lives all the lives that comprise it [Yellow 236-20
He is. The thought that he had found all this [Yellow 237-5
All approaches gone, being completely there, [Waldorf 240-25
A truth beyond all truths. [Landsc 242-19
By thunder, parts, and all these things together, [Landsc 242-26
Was divine then all things were, the world itself, [Landsc 242-29
And that if nothing was the truth, then all [Landsc 242-30
Than a thought to be rehearsed all day, a speech [Beard 247-16
Who was it passed her there on a horse all will, [Uruguay 249-16
That's the old world. In the new, all men are priests. [Extracts
    254-2
Weather of night creatures, whistling all day, too. [Montra
    261-17
All men can speak of it in the voice of gods. [Montra 262-20
All afternoon the gramophone [Search 268-1
And it all spoke together. [Search 268-4
And it spoke all together. [Search 268-6
All afternoon the gramaphoon, [Search 268-9
All afternoon the gramaphoon, [Search 268-10
The premiss from which all things were conclusions, [Contra II
    270-16
And his breast is greatness. All his speeches [Hero 277-12
Destroy all references. This actor [Hero 279-17
A giant's heart in the veins, all courage. [Gigan 289-7
In the will of what is common to all men, [Dutch 291-18
The generations of the bird are all [Somnam 304-7
The spirit and all ensigns of the self? [Repet 308-18
Less Aix than Stockholm, hardly a yellow at all, [Holiday 312-4
After all, they knew that to be real each had [Holiday 312-11
The flowering Judas grows from the belly or not at all. [Holiday
    312-15
All sorts of flowers. That's the sentimentalist. [EM 316-8
All sorts of notes? Or did he play only one [EM 316-12
Softly let all true sympathizers come, [EM 317-4
Indulgence out of all celestial sight. [EM 318-17
The wounds of many soldiers, the wounds of all [EM 318-27
In a world of ideas, who would have all the people [EM 325-13
Of what it sees, for all the ill it sees? [EM 326-1
Speech found the ear, for all the evil sound. [EM 326-5
As those are: as light, for all its motion, is: [Less 327-16
Not span, without any weather at all, except [Wild 329-7
All the Preludes to Felicity [Pure 329-title 1
While all the leaves leaked gold. His mind made morning, [Pure
    331-22
What are the major men? All men are brave. [Paisant 334-13
All men endure. The great captain is the choice [Paisant 334-14
Admired by men and all men, therefore, live [Paisant 334-18
To be admired by all men. Nations live [Paisant 334-19
It is and in such seeming all things are. [Descrip 339-4
In a kind of total affluence, all first, [Descrip 342-15
All final, colors subjected in revery [Descrip 342-16
In which he sat. All chariots were drowned. The swans [Descrip
    343-4
Are shining on all brows of Neversink. [Myrrh 349-14
Out of a storm we must endure all night, [Man Car 351-4

We must endure our thoughts all night, until [Man Car 351-7
In the one ear of the fisherman, who is all [Think 356-9
Of waterish spears. The fisherman is all [Think 356-13
All mind and violence and nothing felt. [Chaos 358-4
And depth, covering all surfaces, [Burghers 362-9
In which the rain is all one thing, [Human 363-8
In the punctual centre of all circles white [Anach 366-8
The spirits of all the impotent dead, seen clear, [Cats 368-8
Now in midsummer come and all fools slaughtered [Cred 372-4
It is the natural tower of all the world, [Cred 373-16
The death of one god is the death of all. [NSF 381-7
Who comes and goes and comes and goes all day. [NSF 381-22
As when the cock crows on the left and all [NSF 386-10
Not to impose, not to have reasoned at all, [NSF 404-2
Do all that angels can. I enjoy like them, [NSF 405-11
Together, all together. Boreal night [AA 413-20
It leaps through us, through all our heavens leaps, [AA 417-16
We were as Danes in Denmark all day long [AA 419-7
As if he lived all lives, that he might know, [AA 420-24
No more that which most of all brings back the known, [Page 422-15
There was so much that was real that was not real at all. [Cata
  425-1
We ask which means most, for us, all the genii [Antag 425-15
Of them. So sense exceeds all metaphor. [Roses 431-6
My memory, is the mother of us all, [Owl 432-15
Nor all one's luck at once in a play of strings. [John 437-13
Blue for all that and white and hard, [Celle 438-13
Itself, a nature to its natives all [Orb 442-13
He wishes that all hard poetry were true. [Papini 447-2
Over all these the mighty imagination triumphs [Puel 456-10
And the bells belong to the sextons, after all, [Luther 462-2
Not faded, if images are all we have. [Study I 464-1
Dark things without a double, after all, [NH 465-13
Behind all actual seeing, in the actual scene, [NH 467-11
No man. The self, the chrysalis of all men [NH 468-21
It took all day to quieten the sky [NH 482-20
In which, for all the breathings [Aug 495-1
And for all the white voices [Aug 495-3
The great pond and its waste of the lilies, all this [Plain 503-6
Which suddenly is all dissolved and gone-- [Hermit 505-19
Now, he brings all that he saw into the earth, to the waiting
  parent. [Madame 507-3
As if the design of all his words takes form [Rome 511-2
As if all his hereditary lights were suddenly increased [Prol
  517-1
Out of all the indifferences, into one thing: [Final 524-6
All over Minnesota, [Primordia 7-10 P
I take all things as stated--so and so [Soldat 11-7 P
All, as Andromache, [Parasol 20-4 P
Ah, good God! That all beasts should have [Parasol 20-7 P
I wish they were all fair [Parasol 20-12 P
All of them, darkened by time, moved by they know not what,
  amending the airs they play to fulfill themselves; [Piano
  21-17 P
All your characters [Demoiselle 23-5 P
And not all birds sing cuck [Lulu M 27-7 P
Take counsel, all hierophants [Sat Night 28-7 P
At all. [Mandolin 29-10 P
The silks they wear in all the cities [Melancholy 32-13 P
Like the mother of all nightingales; be wise [Spaniard 35-10 P
Gray, green, why those of all? [Table Talk 40-8 P
Not those of all. But those. [Table Talk 40-10 P
It cannot matter at all.[Table Talk 40-13 P
To search for clearness all an afternoon [Old Woman 44-13 P
All things destroy themselves or are destroyed. [Burnshaw 46-16P
Come, all celestial paramours, [Burnshaw 47-14 P
And the sound of z in the grass all day, though these [Burnshaw
  51-4 P
It made up for everything, it was all selves [Greenest 53-3 P
Because it rose above them all, stippled [Greenest 54-14 P
As brilliant as mystic, as mystic as single, all [Greenest 55-9P
Is, after all, draped damask, pampaluned, [Greenest 58-4 P
We went to walk in the park; for, after all, [Duck 60-8 P
Will, will, but how and all of them asking how [Duck 61-29 P
Is all the birds he ever heard and that, [Duck 62-3 P
Are all men thinking together as one, thinking [Duck 62-19 P
Confounds all opposites and spins a sphere [Duck 63-20 P
Escape all deformation, much less this, [Duck 63-26 P
All are evasions like a repeated phrase, [Duck 65-14 P
And never will, a subman under all [Sombre 66-14 P
As if it bears all darkness in its bulk. [Sombre 68-18 P
All this is hidden from sight. [Sombre 68-28 P
She was all of her airs and, for all of her airs, [Grotesque
  74-1 P
She was all of her airs and ears and hairs, [Grotesque 74-2 P
In spite of her airs, that's what she was. She was all
  [Grotesque 74-5 P
No thought at all: a gutteral growl, [Grotesque 75-15 P
Like the voice of all our ancestors, [Grotesque 77-10 P
It will be all we have. Our fate is our own: [Bship 81-4 P

To which all other forms, at last, return, [Recit 87-5 P
A countryman of all the bones of the world? [Warmth 90-1 P
In a field, the man on the side of a hill, all men [Americana
  93-16 P
Itself, until, at last, the cry concerns no one at all. [Course
  97-3 P
And if to know one man is to know all [Ulysses 99-20 P
By one, in the right of all. Each man [Ulysses 102-5 P
Whose chiefest embracing of all wealth [Ulysses 104-12 P
And clumped stars dangled all the way. [Ulysses 105-12 P
Through clumped stars dangling all the way. [Presence 106-12 P
On all the rest, in heavy thought. [Child 106-15 P
Free from everything else, free above all from thought. [Letters
  107-9 P
As if we were all seated together again [Letters 107-13 P
And one of us spoke and all of us believed [Letters 107-14 P
From everything would end. It would all meet. [Letters 108-10 P
The one thing common to all life, the human [Conversat 109-1 P
A countryman of all the bones in the world? [As Leave 117-7 P
Unreal, as if nothing had been changed at all. [As Leave 117-14P
All you need, [Three 127-1 P
We affect all things. [Three 134-2 P
Without which it would all be black. [Three 143-9 P
  Its tuft of emerald that is real, for all [Someone 85-16 A
  That steeps the room, quickly, then not at all, [Someone 87-15 A
ALLEGORY. Pure eye. Instead of allegory, [Hero 279-1
ALLEVIATION. Carrying such shapes, of such alleviation, [New Set
  353-1
ALLEY. Through an alley to nowhere, [Grotesque 76-23 P
ALLEYS. To what good, in the alleys of the lilacs, [Lilacs 48-18
ALLIGATOR. Meet for the eye of the young alligator, [Nomad 95-16
ALLIGATORS. Or is it that alligators lie [An Gaiety 33-2 P
ALLITERATIONS. Beautiful alliterations of shadows and of things
  shadowed. [Primordia 8-7 P
ALLONS. But, here, allons. The enigmatical [NH 472-5
ALLOW. Madame, we are where we began. Allow, [High-Toned 59-13
ALLOYS. His infinite repetition and alloys [Havana 144-15
ALL-RELATED. Than green, fidgets of all-related fire. [Pieces
  352-4
ALL-SPEAKING. The end of love in their all-speaking braids.
  [Monocle 14-6
ALMANAC. Repeats the farmer's almanac. [Grotesque 75-11 P
ALMANAGS. Oblivious to the Aztec almanacs, [C 38-22
ALMOND. The almond and deep fruit. This bitter meat [Cuisine 228-13
ALMOST. And reach through him almost to man. [MBG 165-16
  If to serenade almost to man [MBG 165-17
  You could almost see the brass on her gleaming, [Vari 235-19
  Almost a nigger fragment, a mystique [News 265-9
  Or light embodied, or almost, a flash [Choc 297-11
  A sun in an almost colorless, cold heaven. [Holiday 312-6
  It was almost time for lunch. Pain is human. [EM 314-8
  Moving so that the foot-falls are slight and almost nothing.
    [Jouga 337-12
  Almost successfully. Illustration: [Man Car 350-14
  And naked, or almost so, into the grotesque [Lot 371-17
  Of being naked, or almost so, in a world [Lot 371-18
  Almost as predicate. But it exists, [AA 418-17
  Almost as part of innocence, almost, [AA 420-2
  Almost as the tenderest and the truest part. [AA 420-3
  Almost as speed discovers, in the way [Owl 435-10
  The color is almost the color of comedy, [NH 477-10
  Of a mountain, expanded and elevated almost [Moonlight 531-11
  Is almost Byzantine. [Abnormal 24-7 P
  That are almost not our own, but thoughts [Including 88-11 P
  Of almost solid seem show--the way a fly bird [Conversat 108-14P
ALOE. Aloe of ivory, pear of rusty rind.) [Bird Claws 82-5
ALOFT. With lanterns borne aloft to light the way, [Heaven 56-13
  This self, not that gold self aloft, [MBG 176-4
  In an immenser heaven, aloft, [MBG 176-9
ALONE. Or was it that I mocked myself alone? [Monocle 13-6
  It is a theme for Hyacinth alone. [Monocle 15-17
  Shine alone in the sunrise [Nuances 18-6
  Shine alone, shine nakedly, shine like bronze, [Nuances 18-8
  For him, and not for him alone. It seemed [C 34-29
  My candle burned alone in an immense valley. [Valley Candle 51-1
  Alone, shall come fulfilment to our dreams [Sunday 69-1
  The walker in the moonlight walked alone, [Babies 77-7
  The walker in the moonlight walked alone, [Babies 77-16
  And sound alone. But it was more than that, [Key W 129-17
  As we beheld her striding there alone, [Key W 129-30
  Nor night and I, but you and I, alone, [Re-state 146-7
  So much alone, so deeply by ourselves, [Re-state 146-8
  But he remembered the time when he stood alone. [Anglais 149-9
  But he remembered the time when he stood alone. [Anglais 149-11
  But he remembered the time when he stood alone, [Anglais 149-13
  The philosophers alone will be fat [Nigger 152-2
  Alone, but reduce the monster and be, [MBG 175-10
  Alone, one's shadow magnified, [MBG 176-5
  Alone, lord of the land and lord [MBG 176-10
  Alone, a lean Review and said, [MBG 180-20

Sat alone, his great toe like a horn, [Thought 187-7
We said we stood alone. [On Road 203-22
It may be that the ignorant man, alone, [Sleight 222-16
It is she alone that matters. [Scavoir 231-1
And sea exists by grace alone, [Vari 235-4
The philosophers' man alone still walks in dew, [Oboe 250-12
Than this, in this alone I may believe, [Extracts 257-25
Of her, of her alone, at last he knew [Hand 271-20
Alone, the half-arc hanging in mid-air [Repet 309-12
To hear only what one hears, one meaning alone, [EM 320-27
Alone. But in the peopled world, there is, [EM 323-7
Alone is not to know them or himself. [EM 323-18
If they were creatures of the sea alone, [Two V 355-4
They hunt for a form which by its form alone, [Pediment 361-10
By its form alone, by being right, [Pediment 361-13
One seed alone grow wild, the railway-stops [Cats 367-14
Alone and like a vestal long-prepared. [NSF 395-18
Bent over work, anxious, content, alone, [NSF 406-16
Existing in the idea of it, alone, [AA 418-7
The rendezvous, when she came alone, [AA 419-16
Yet Hans lay wide awake. And live alone [Page 422-3
At home; or: In the woods, belle Belle alone [Golden 460-14
That shines with a nocturnal shine alone. [NH 473-2
The oldest-newest day is the newest alone. [NH 476-19
There is an ease of mind that was like being alone in a boat
     at sea, [Prol 515-5
As he traveled alone, like a man lured on by a syllable without
     any meaning, [Prol 516-4
She wanted nothing he could not bring her by coming alone.
     [World 521-7
Both late and alone, above the crickets' chords, [Quiet 523-12
Who knows? The ploughman may not live alone [Burnshaw 48-23 P
Through long cloud-cloister-porches, walked alone, [Greenest 54-3P
And in a bed in one room, alone, a listener [Sick 90-13 P
As if, alone on a mountain, it saw far-off [Pagoda 92-5 P
He was alone without her, [Three 139-8 P
Was alone without her: [Three 139-10 P
ALONG. And which had drowsed along the bony shores, [Hibiscus 22-18
Her old light moves along the branches, [Lunar 107-3
Like Walt Whitman walking along a ruddy shore. [Nigger 150-10
The pines along the river and the dry men blown [Loaf 199-21
As if the sky was a current that bore them along, [Loaf 200-5
The dirt along the sill. [Anything B 211-23
In opal blobs along the walls and floor. [Blue Bldg 217-12
Rumbling along the autumnal horizon, [Dutch 293-7
The wood-doves are singing along the Perkiomen. [Think 356-7
And the pines above and along and beside the sea. [AA 411-9
And along the moving of the water-- [Countryman 429-4
Away from them, capes, along the afternoon Sound, [NH 484-7
Along the walls [Phases 4-13 P
Along the edges of your eye [An Gaiety 33-3 P
Of crisping light along the statue's rim. [Old Woman 43-18 P
In a flapping cloak. She walked along the paths [Old Woman 44-2P
Along the thin horizons, nobly more [Burnshaw 47-10 P
Returns and returns, along the dry, salt shore. [Woman Had 81-24P
Of a ruddier summer, a birth that fetched along [Nuns 92-13 P
ALOUD. Lean from the steeple. Cry aloud, [MBG 170-14
Whistle aloud, too weedy wren. I can [NSF 405-10
As he sat there reading, aloud, the great blue tabulae. [Large
     423-12
ALP. "Botanist on Alp (No. 1)" [134-title
"Botanist on Alp (No. 2)" [135-title
On Europe, to the last Alp, [Inhab 504-4
Up the pineapple, a table Alp and yet [Someone 87-2 A
An Alp, a purple Southern mountain bisqued [Someone 87-3 A
ALPHA. Naked Alpha, not the hierophant Omega, [NH 469-5
Alpha fears men or else Omega's men [NH 469-11
To the end. Alpha continues to begin. [NH 469-20
ALPHABET. Against the murderous alphabet: [MBG 179-8
Teaching a fusky alphabet. [Phosphor 267-16
And the first flowers upon it, an alphabet [Owl 434-16
Or letter of a curious alphabet; [Recit 87-8 P
ALPHABETICAL. Outlined and having alphabetical [Common 221-21
ALPHABETS. From the window-sills at the alphabets, [Ord Women 11-9
Being small, inscribes ferocious alphabets, [Pure 332-23
ALPS. The idea of the Alps grew large, [Thought 184-15
For which the intricate Alps are a single nest. [Connois 216-14
ALREADY. Behold, already on the long parades [Swans 4-9
Already the butterflies flutter above the cabins. [Carolinas
     4-14
Already the new-born children interpret love [Carolinas 4-15
One is already a grandfather and to have put there [Lack 303-18
Even for her, already for her. She will listen [Debris 338-11
Already the green bird of summer has flown [Myrrh 349-15
ALTAR. On the altar, growing toward the lights, inside. [Armor
     529-7
Cover the golden altar deepest black, [Red Kit 31-21 P
The temple of the altar where each man [Greenest 54-17 P
ALTARS. Upon your altars, [Pourtraicte 21-11
Place honey on the altars and die, [MBG 174-3

ALTERATION. Except for the adjectives, an alteration [NH 487-5
ALTERNATE. And of forgetfulness, in alternate strain [C 29-6
Turning in time to Brahms as alternate [Anglais 149-6
In alternate stripes converging at a point [Page 422-22
The things around--the alternate romanza [NH 480-21
ALTITUDE. And that which in an altitude would soar, [Orb 442-9
ALTO. The alto clank of the long recitation, in these [Burnshaw
     52-7 P
ALWAYS. America was always north to him, [C 34-2
Hang always heavy in that perfect sky, [C 69-15
To whom the watermelon is always purple, [Watermelon 88-20
For him the moon was always in Scandinavia [Norfolk 111-10
Encircling us, speaks always with our speech. [Eve Angels 137-18
Of ripest summer, always lingering [Havana 143-14
Always the standard repertoire in line [Nigger 156-19
A mountainous music always seemed [MBG 179-11
One is always seeing and feeling oneself, [Prelude 195-8
Again and again, always there, [Nightgown 214-10
Had got him nowhere. There was always the doubt, [Blue Bldg
     216-17
What will suffice. It has not always had [Of Mod 239-18
We had always been partly one. It was as we came [Oboe 251-17
Was always the other mind. The brightness [Hero 273-11
It was part of a supremacy always [EM 314-26
Above him. The moon was always free from him, [EM 314-27
In one's heart and wished as he had always wished, unable [Bed
     327-2
Weaves always glistening from the heart and mind. [NSF 396-12
For that the poet is always in the sun, [NSF 407-6
He observes how the north is always enlarging the change, [AA
     412-24
There may be always a time of innocence.[AA 418-4
But always of the swarthy water, [Countryman 428-19
Always, in brilliance, fatal, final, formed [Owl 434-23
Oh as, always too heavy for the sense [Orb 441-2
It is a giant, always, that is evolved, [Orb 442-25
Always in emptiness that would be filled, [NH 467-13
He that kneels always on the edge of space [NH 469-9
From a different source. But there was always one: [NH 479-3
The bodiless half. There is always this bodiless half, [NH 481-23
Who watched him, always, for unfaithful thought. [NH 483-15
That which is always beginning because it is part [Armor 530-17
Of that which is always beginning, over and over. [Armor 530-18
Who have always interested me most, [Lytton 38-9 P
That sort of thing was always rather stiff. [Lytton 39-18 P
Triumphant as that always upward wind [Old Woman 44-27 P
Except the future. Always everything [Burnshaw 46-14 P
Leaves are not always falling and the birds [Burnshaw 50-24 P
Of chaos are not always sad nor lost [Burnshaw 50-25 P
In the streets. There will always be cafés and cards [Greenest
     58-15 P
That will always be and will be everywhere.[Greenest 58-18 P
The future for them is always the deepest dome, [Duck 65-21 P
Yet what I mean I always say. [Stan MBG 73-2 P
The scholar is always distant in the space [Recit 86-18 P
And always at this antipodes, of leaden loaves [Discov 95-15 P
Yet always there is another life. [Ulysses 101-21 P
Always, the particular thought [Ulysses 103-14 P
Always and always, the difficult inch, [Ulysses 103-16 P
Repose, always, the credible thought [Ulysses 103-18 P
For which a fresh name always occurred, as if [Local 112-5 P
These were that serene he had always been approaching [Local
     112-11 P
In an always incipient cosmos, [July 115-3 P
What the court saw was always of the same color, [Three 131-22 P
But always of many things. He had not to be told [Someone 85-12A
AM. I am what is around me. [Theory 86-16
Where my spirit is I am, [Sailing 120-23
It is what it is as I am what I am: [Re-state 146-2
And as I am, I speak and move [MBG 180-16
And laid it in the sand. As I am, I am [NSF 395-20
I have not but I am and as I am, I am. [NSF 405-6
Is being and knowing what I am and know. [Angel 496-14
He said, "As I know, I am and have [Ulysses 99-13 P
He said, "As I know, I am and have [Presence 105-16 P
AMASSED. Becomes amassed in a total double-thing. [NH 472-7
AMASSING. The complicate, the amassing harmony. [NSF 403-15
AMBERED. The book and candle in your ambered room, [Rome 510-25
AMBER-EMBER. Dropped out of this amber-ember pod, [MBG 182-6
AMBIANCE. It enfolds the head in a vital ambiance, [Pastor 379-11
A vital, linear ambiance. The flare [Pastor 379-12
AMBIGUOUS. Ambiguous undulations as they sink, [Sunday 70-27
AMBIT. Of an old and disused ambit of the soul [Aug 489-6
A disused ambit of the spirit's way, [Aug 489-8
AMBITIOUS. On the pedestal, an ambitious page dog-eared [What We
     460-1
AMBROSIAL. Who, then, in that ambrosial latitude [Sea Surf 99-5
AME. C'était mon enfant, mon bijou, mon âme. [Sea Surf 99-9
AMEN. Should merely call him dead? Pronounce amen [C 41-17
Lie in the heart's residuum . . . Amen. [Extracts 258-23

But would it be amen, in choirs, if once [Extracts 258-24
But if there be something more to love, amen, [Montra 260-16
Amen to the feelings about familiar things, [Montra 260-17
Amen to thought, our singular skeleton, [Montra 260-19
Salt-flicker, amen to our accustomed cell, [Montra 260-20
Sing for her the seventy-fold Amen, [Grotesque 77-5 P
AMENDING. All of them, darkened by time, moved by they know not what,
    amending the airs they play to fulfill themselves; [Piano 21-17P
AMERICA. America was always north to him, [C 34-2
"United Dames of America" [206-title
Tom McGreevy, in America, Thinks of Himself as a Boy [Our Stars
    454-title 1
See North America.
AMERICAN. "The American Sublime" [130-title
Another American vulgarity. [Celle 438-16
Say that the American moon comes up [Memo 89-11 P
AMERICANA. "Americana" [93-title P
AMETHYST. The spouse beyond emerald or amethyst, [NSF 395-23
AMICAL. By amical tones. [Woman Had 82-6 P
AMID. Suppose these couriers brought amid their train [Monocle
    15-27
A pip of life amid a mort of tails. [Bird Claws 82-3
A promenade amid the grandeurs of the mind, [EM 325-7
Upon the horizon amid adult enfantillages. [Questions 462-6
And died amid uproarious damns. [Lulu M 27-10 P
AMIGAS. Ancient amigas, knowing partisans-- [Souls 95-3 P
AMONG. Among the choirs of wind and wet and wing. [Monocle 13-14
Among the blooms beyond the open sand; [Hibiscus 22-11
And something given to make whole among [C 30-14
Among the purple tufts, the scarlet crowns, [C 32-4
The man in Georgia walking among pines [C 38-15
What is one man among so many men? [C 41-25
Make hue among the dark comedians, [Heaven 56-21
A jovial hullabaloo among the spheres. [High-Toned 59-20
Among the people burning in me still, [W Burgher 61-11
As a calm darkens among water-lights. [Sunday 67-4
He moved among us, as a muttering king, [Sunday 67-30
Magnificent, would move among his hinds, [Sunday 68-1
Naked among them, like a savage source. [Sunday 70-3
That choir among themselves long afterward. [Sunday 70-9
There are no bears among the roses, [Virgin 71-1
You ten-foot poet among inchlings. Fat! [Bantams 76-1
Among the arrant spices of the sun, [Fictive 88-7
She felt, among the leaves, [Peter 90-24
Among twenty snowy mountains, [Thirteen 92-14
Necks among the thousand leaves, [Orangeade 103-5
It is the same jingle of the water among the roots under the
    banks of the palmettoes, [Indian 112-5
Like giant arms among the clouds. [How Live 125-20
More even than her voice, and ours, among [Key W 129-18
Among fireflies. [Gray 140-4
To make him return to people, to find among them [Nigger 158-7
Crying among the clouds, enraged [MBG 169-7
The poet striding among the cigar stores, [Thought 185-5
He sat among beggars wet with dew, [Thought 187-5
It is a state, this spring among the politicians [Glass 198-2
One would have still to discover. Among the dogs and dung,
    [Glass 198-4
On the dump? Is it to sit among mattresses of the dead, [Dump
    203-6
It is she that walks among astronomers. [Candle 223-2
Moving among the sleepers, the men, [Candle 223-5
Among men, in a woman--she caught his breath-- [Yellow 237-6
Among the lascivious poisons, clean of them, [Extracts 252-16
The wind moves like a cripple among the leaves [Motive 288-3
By a lake, with clouds like lights among great tombs, [EM 325-8
Sequences, thought of among spheres in the old peak of night:
    [Bed 326-19
Among fomentations of black bloom and of white bloom. [Attempt
    370-18
Became to-day, among our children and [Lot 371-6
Gulping for shape among the reeds. No doubt, [Lot 371-12
The old seraph, parcel-gilded, among violets [NSF 389-13
Among our more vestigial states of mind. [NSF 392-1
Among the children, like curious ripenesses [AA 415-8
Among these the musicians strike the instinctive poem. [AA 415-16
Of the pans above the stove, the pots on the table, the tulips
    among them. [Large 423-15
Two forms move among the dead, high sleep [Owl 431-13
A man walked living among the forms of thought [Owl 432-20
The mind, among the creatures that it makes, [Owl 436-8
Among the bare and crooked trees, [Celle 438-3
Too exactly labelled, a large among the smalls [Orb 443-11
Twisting among the universal spaces, [Degen 444-15
Among the breathless spices and, sometimes, [Pecul 454-5
And of other holy and learned men, among them [Luther 461-6
Under the birds, among the perilous owls, [NH 474-17
Among time's images, there is not one [NH 476-1
Forms of farewell, furtive among green ferns. [NH 482-15
The statue of Jove among the boomy clouds. [NH 482-19

Among the endlessly emerging accords. [Aug 493-2
The loftiest syllables among loftiest things, [Rome 510-7
The one invulnerable man among [Rome 510-8
Shifted the rocks and picked his way among clouds, [Poem Mt
    512-8
Among the more irritating minor ideas [Look 517-11
Softly she piped among the suns [Song Fixed 519-21
A comic infanta among the tragic drapings, [Slug 522-12
Reverberations leak and lack among holes . . . [Armor 529-8
An ember yes among its cindery noes, [Armor 529-10
As if, among the possible purposes [Moonlight 531-6
It is that Old Man, lost among the trees. [Phases 5-15 P
Among the orchards in the apple-blocks [Good Bad 33-16 P
Painting the saints among palms. [Agenda 41-20 P
Blowing among the trees its meaningless sound. [Old Woman 44-28P
There buzzards pile their sticks among the bones [Burnshaw 49-7P
Become rude robes among white candle lights, [Greenest 53-4 P
Thinly, among the elephantine palms, [Greenest 54-26 P
Intensified and grandiose, but among [Greenest 57-4 P
The medium man among other medium men, [Sombre 71-31 P
As a man among other men, divested [Stan Hero 84-10 P
Among the second selves, sailor, observe [Pagoda 91-19 P
Imagined among the indigenes [Ulysses 101-6 P
Among Plantagenet abstractions, [Ulysses 103-15 P
Among the old man that you know, [Child 106-13 P
That a figure reclining among columns toppled down, [Conversat
    109-7 P
One exists among pure principles. [Sol Oaks 111-4 P
It shines, among the trees, [Three 135-8 P
Among its leaves. [Three 135-11 P
Did not the age that bore him bear him among [Someone 85-1 A
AMORIST. The amorist Adjective aflame . . . [MBG 172-8
AMORISTS. But in our amours amorists discern [Monocle 15-11
When amorists grow bald, then amours shrink [Monocle 15-14
AMOUNTS. This parable, in sense, amounts to this: [Monocle 15-24
AMOUR. Oh! C'etait mon extase et mon amour. [Sea Surf 100-21
But now as in an amour of women [Hartford 227-4
Of the loftiest amour, in a human midnight? [Souls 95-6 P
AMOURS. But in our amours amorists discern [Monocle 15-11
When amorists grow bald, then amours shrink [Monocle 15-14
The suitable amours. Time will write them down. [NSF 398-6
AMPHITHEATRE. Of the Caribbean amphitheatre, [C 30-17
AMPLE. These ample lustres from the new-come moon. [Stan MMO 19-11P
AMPLER. She walks an autumn ampler than the wind [Anatomy 108-3
AMSTERDAM. See New Amsterdam.
ANABASIS. Anabasis or slump, ascent or chute, [C 43-21
ANACHARSIS. "From the Packet of Anacharsis" [365-title
In his packet Anacharsis found the lines: [Anach 365-17
ANALYSIS. "Analysis of a Theme" [348-title
ANALYZED. As in an enchantment, analyzed and fixed [Papini 447-20
ANANKE. The sense of the serpent in you, Ananke, [Nigger 152-11
Fatal Ananke is the common god. [Greenest 59-1 P
Fateful Ananke is the final god. [Greenest 59-20 P
The bold, obedience to Ananke. [Stan Hero 83-24 P
ANARCHIC. Beyond the habit of sense, anarchic shape [Page 422-18
ANATOMY. "Anatomy of Monotony" [107-title
Postpone the anatomy of summer, as [Cred 373-1
ANCESTOR. Ancestor of Narcissus, prince [Jumbo 269-16
To find of sound the bleakest ancestor, [NSF 398-17
The father, the ancestor, the bearded peer, [Aug 494-22
See mud-ancestor.
ANCESTORS. Of parents, lewdest of ancestors. [Prelude 195-20
Like the voice of all our ancestors, [Grotesque 77-10 P
ANCESTRAL. Twelve-legged in her ancestral hells, [Oak 272-8
An ancestral theme or as a consequence [AA 412-7
ANCHOR. The lights in the fishing boats at anchor there, [Key W
    130-6
ANCIENT. An ancient aspect touching a new mind. [Monocle 16-2
you give me, ancient star: [Nuances 18-5
Just so an ancient Crispin was dissolved. [C 29-7
A little juvenile, an ancient whim, [C 35-23
Of its ancient purple, pruned to the fertile main, [C 45-14
The holy hush of ancient sacrifice. [Sunday 67-1
As an autumn ancient underneath the snow, [Nigger 154-2
Are you not le plus pur, you ancient one? [Blue Bldg 217-20
No longer on the ancient cake of seed, [Cuisine 228-12
And in their blood an ancient evil dies-- [Dutch 292-20
Was ancient. He tried to remember the phrases: pain [EM 314-3
The same railway passenger, the ancient tree [Cats 367-16
To have what is not is its ancient cycle. [NSF 382-5
An ancient forehead hung with heavy hair, [NSF 400-7
The tower, the ancient accent, the wintry size. [Antag 426-6
The most ancient light in the most ancient sky, [NH 481-18
A shape within the ancient circles of shapes, [Rome 509-1
In an Ancient, Solemn Manner [Soldat 11-title 2 P
And, while revolving, ancient hyacinths [Sombre 69-17 P
The father. He hides his ancient blue beneath [Recit 87-17 P
Ancient amigas, knowing partisans-- [Souls 95-3 P
The ancient symbols will be nothing then. [Ulysses 102-12 P
ANCIENTEST. Then, ancientest saint ablaze with ancientest truth,

[NH 467-3
ANCIENTNESS. Who reads no book. His ruddy ancientness [Cred 374-2
  With lanterns, like a celestial ancientness. [NH 476-21
AND-A. And-a-rum-tum-tum, and-a [Soldat 15-1 P
  And-a-drum-rum-rum, and-a [Soldat 15-5 P
  And-a-pom-pom-pom, and-a [Soldat 15-9 P
AND-A-DRUM-RUM-RUM. And-a-drum-rum-rum, and-a [Soldat 15-5 P
AND-A-FEE. And-a-fee and-a-fee and-a-fee [Soldat 15-13 P
AND-A-FEE-FO-FUM. And-a-fee-fo-fum-- [Soldat 15-14 P
AND-A-ONE. And his son's son John, and-a-one [Soldat 14-19 P
  And his lean son's John, and-a-one [Soldat 15-3 P
  And his rich son's John, and-a-one [Soldat 15-7 P
  And his wise son's John, and-a-one [Soldat 15-11 P
AND-A-POM-POM-POM. And-a-pom-pom-pom, and-a [Soldat 15-9 P
AND-A-RUMMY-TUMMY-TUM. And-a-rummy-tummy-tum [Soldat 15-16 P
  And-a-rummy-tummy-tum. [Soldat 15-17 P
AND-A-RUM-TUM-TUM. And-a-rum-tum-tum, and-a [Soldat 15-1 P
AND-A-THREE. And-a-two and-a-three [Soldat 14-20 P
  And-a-two and-a-three [Soldat 15-4 P
  And-a-two and-a-three [Soldat 15-8 P
  And-a-two and-a-three [Soldat 15-12 P
AND-A-TWO. And-a-two and-a-three [Soldat 14-20 P
  And-a-two and-a-three [Soldat 15-4 P
  And-a-two and-a-three [Soldat 15-8 P
  And-a-two and-a-three [Soldat 15-12 P
ANDEAN. He felt the Andean breath. His mind was free [C 33-9
ANDERSON. See Mrs. Anderson.
ANDREW. But a ghost for Andrew, not lean, catarrhal [Lack 303-10
ANDREW JACKSON SOMETHING. Andrew Jackson Something. But this book
  [Lack 303-7
ANDROMACHE. All, as Andromache, [Parasol 20-4 P
ANECDOTAL. Yet you persist with anecdotal bliss [Monocle 13-21
  Anecdotal Revery [Soldat 12-title 3
ANECDOTE. "Earthy Anecdote" [3-title
  Without grace or grumble. Score this anecdote [C 45-19
  Or if the music sticks, if the anecdote [C 45-30
  "Anecdote of Men by the Thousand" [51-title
  "Anecdote of Canna" [55-title
  "Anecdote of the Prince of Peacocks" [57-title
  "Anecdote of the Jar" [76-title P
  "Anecdote of the Abnormal" [23-title P
ANEW. Heightened. It is he, anew, in a freshened youth [Myth 118-13P
ANGEL. The garden flew round with the angel, [Circulat 149-16
  The angel flew round with the clouds, [Circulat 149-17
  Angel, convulsive shatterer, gun, [Hero 273-19
  The fiction of an absolute--Angel, [NSF 404-10
  What am I to believe? If the angel in his cloud, [NSF 404-13
  Am I that imagine this angel less satisfied? [NSF 404-20
  "Angel Surrounded by Paysans" [496-title
  I am the angel of reality, [Angel 496-7
  Yet I am the necessary angel of earth, [Angel 496-15
  Of his angel through the skies. They might be mud [Burnshaw
  46-21 P
  He sees the angel in the nigger's mind [Greenest 59-11 P
  The angel at the center of this rind, [Someone 83-6 A
ANGELIC. Its sounds are not angelic syllables [Eve Angels 137-3
  Its animal. The angelic ones [MBG 174-6
  Of that angelic sword? Creature of [Hero 273-17
  At the moment when the angelic eye defines [AA 414-20
  And still angelic and still plenteous, [Orb 443-5
  Mechanisms of angelic thought, [Inhab 503-10
ANGELS. The mules that angels ride come slowly down [Monocle 15-18
  As sure as all the angels are. [Botanist 2 136-2
  "Evening without Angels" [136-title
  Was the sun concoct for angels or for men? [Eve Angels 137-9
  Sad men made angels of the sun, and of [Eve Angels 137-10
  Which led them back to angels, after death. [Eve Angels 137-12
  God and all angels sing the world to sleep, [Men Fall 187-9
  God and all angels, this was his desire, [Men Fall 188-13
  Never angels, nothing of the dead, [Dezem 218-13
  The adobe of the angels? Constantly, [Repet 308-2
  Do all that angels can. I enjoy like them, [NSF 405-11
  Enjoying angels. Whistle, forced bugler, [NSF 405-13
  Than bad angels leap from heaven to hell in flames. [AA 414-12
  Afraid of the country angels of those skies, [Page 422-7
  These illustrations are neither angels, no, [John 437-11
  "Piano Practice at the Academy of the Holy Angels" [21-title P
  The angels come, armed, gloriously to slay [Greenest 55-28 P
  Hé quoi! Angels go pricking elephants? [Greenest 55-30 P
  Angels tiptoe upon the snowy cones [Greenest 56-1 P
  Filleted angels over flapping ears, [Greenest 56-7 P
  Angels returning after war with belts [Greenest 56-10 P
  Forgetting work, not caring for angels, hunting a lift, [Duck
  60-15 P
  Like angels resting on a rustic steeple [Art Pop 113-1 P
ANGER. Which counts for most, the anger borne [Sombre 69-21 P
  In anger; or the fear that from the death [Sombre 69-22 P
ANGERING. And green vine angering for life, [Nomad 95-9
ANGEVINE. I absorb them as the Angevine [Peaches 224-3
ANGLAIS. "Anglais Mort à Florence" [148-title

ANGLED. See right-angled.
ANGRILY. Like humans approaching angrily. [Shifts 83-19
ANGRY. The voice of angry fear, [Mozart 132-11
  Angry men and furious machines [Dutch 290-1
  The angry day-son clanging at its make: [Papini 448-2
ANGUISHING. To the first, foremost law. Anguishing hour! [Monocle
  17-13
ANGULAR. A slash of angular blacks [Public Sq 108-19
  In mornings of angular ice, [Medit 124-5
  To blotches, angular anonymids [Lot 371-11
  And wearing hats of angular flick and fleck, [Bouquet 449-8
  Round summer and angular winter and winds, [Ulysses 102-24 P
ANIMA. Maman. His anima liked its animal [EM 321-16
ANIMAL. And my body, the old animal, [Joost 46-15
  The old animal, [Joost 46-22
  And that white animal, so lean, [Vincentine 53-15
  And that while animal, so lean, [Vincentine 53-18
  That animal eye, [Gubbinal 85-7
  Its animal. The angelic ones [MBG 174-6
  An animal. The blue guitar-- [MBG 174-8
  That animal, that Russian, that exile, for whom [Peaches 224-8
  Maman. His anima liked its animal [EM 321-16
  Of being this unalterable animal. [EM 324-7
  Black beaded on the rock, the flecked animal, [AA 412-2
  That never could be animal, [Two Illus 513-18
  See super-animal.
ANIMALS. Or were to be, animals with men's eyes, [Horn 230-2
  From heaven and float in air, like animals [Study II 464-6
  These are not even Russian animals. [Burnshaw 46-17 P
ANJOU. Absorbs Anjou. I see them as a lover sees, [Peaches 224-4
ANNA. "Anna, Anna, Anna!" [Three 139-7 P
  Is that you, Anna? [Three 140-4 P
  Is that you, Anna? [Three 140-5 P
ANNE. Things are as they seemed to Calvin or to Anne [Descrip
  341-21
ANNEALED. Annealed them in their cabin ribaldries! [C 42-21
ANNIHILATION. In the stale grandeur of annihilation. [Leben 505-9
ANNOTATOR. An annotator has his scruples, too. [C 32-28
ANNOUNCED. The sky. It is the visible announced, [Cred 376-17
ANNUAL. "Annual Gaiety" [32-title P
ANNULLED. The valet in the tempest was annulled. [C 29-8
  When too great rhapsody is left annulled [Havana 144-9
ANOINT. The crows anoint the statues with their dirt. [Swans 4-10
ANON. Anon, their lamps' uplifted flame [Peter 91-18
  This was their ceremonial hymn: Anon [NSF 401-7
  We loved but would no marriage make. Anon [NSF 401-8
ANONYMIDS. To blotches, angular anonymids [Lot 371-11
ANONYMOUS. Thus one is most disclosed when one is most anonymous.
  [Nudity Col 145-13
  Is anonymous and cannot help it. [Hero 279-18
  The eye, completely anonymous, [Couch 295-5
  In the anonymous color of the universe. [NH 470-22
ANSWER. For answer from their icy Elysée. [Heaven 56-23
  The particular answer to the particular question [Ulti 429-13
  As a quick answer modifies a question, [NH 471-6
  A text that is an answer, although obscure. [NH 479-15
  Answer, humming, [Primordia 7-13 P
ANSWERERS. Four questioners and four sure answerers. [C 45-10
ANSWERING. A hatching that stared and demanded an answering look.
  [NH 484-3
  Young catechumen answering the worms? [Sombre 69-24 P
  Response, the completely answering voice, [Ulysses 100-11 P
ANSWERS. This it is that answers when I ask, [Yellow 236-8
  Its attitudes, its answers to attitudes [Aug 489-13
ANT. To have the ant of the self changed to an ox [Freed 205-9
ANTAGONISMS. "In the Element of Antagonisms" [425-title
ANTAGONIST. Over the loftiest antagonist [NSF 390-14
ANTAGONISTS. By gold antagonists in air-- [MBG 169-8
ANTHOLOGY. Should scrawl a vigilant anthology, [C 38-26
ANTIC. Stood, dressed in antic symbols, to display [NH 470-6
ANTICIPATION. Before it comes, the just anticipation [Descrip
  344-12
ANTI-IDEAS. This side of Moscow. There were anti-ideas [Forces
  229-7
ANTI-LOGICIAN. By imagining, anti-logician, quick [Sombre 66-21 P
ANTI-MASTER-MAN. An anti-master-man, floribund ascetic. [Landsc
  241-10
ANTI-PATHOS. An anti-pathos, until we call it [Hero 276-28
ANTIPODAL. But an antipodal, far-fetched creature, worthy of birth,
  [Discov 96-5 P
ANTIPODES. At the antipodes of poetry, dark winter, [Discov 95-7P
  And always at this antipodes, of leaden loaves [Discov 95-15 P
  And the wry antipodes whirled round the world away-- [Discov
  95-20 P
ANTIQUE. Of heaven in an antique reflection rolled [Sea Surf 99-13
  The nocturnal, the antique, the blue-green pines [Parochial
  191-9
  Monsters antique and haggard with past thought? [Dutch 292-11
  Fails to destroy the antique acceptances, [Questions 462-8
ANTIQUEST. Men that repeat antiquest sounds of air [Eve Angels

137-15
And Africa, basking in antiquest sun, [Greenest 55-25 P
To fill, the grindstone of antiquest time, [Bship 80-2 P
And with it, the antiquest wishing [Stan Hero 83-19 P
ANTIQUITY. The warm antiquity of self, [Fading 139-6
ANTITHESIS. The vile antithesis of poor and rich. [NE Verses
 104-6
ANTS. The way ants crawl [Six Sig 74-12
ANXIOUS. Bent over work, anxious, content, alone, [NSF 406-16
ANYONE. To anyone that comes--panic, because [EM 320-19
 Was not his thought, nor anyone's, [Two Illus 513-12
ANYTHING. Rumble anything out of their drums? [Circulat 150-4
 "Anything Is Beautiful if You Say It Is" [211-title
 As anything but sculpture. Good-bye, [Couch 296-5
 The moon is no longer these nor anything [EM 320-20
 To be anything else in the sunlight of the room, [Roses 430-12
 No longer says anything. [Plant 506-9
 In anything that he constructed, so frail, [Quiet 523-2
 If anything would be bliss. [Lytton 38-21 P
 That which is more than anything else [Ulysses 100-12 P
ANYWHERE. There are no shadows anywhere. [MBG 167-8
 Or anywhere beyond, to a different element, [Extracts 258-11
APART. His dark familiar, often walked apart. [Anglais 148-14
 And above the German camps? It looked apart. [Martial 238-5
 Is time, apart from any past, apart [Martial 238-7
 And we feel, in a way apart, for a moment, as if [Gala 248-11
 To that be-misted one and apart from her. [Wild 328-14
 A complex of emotions falls apart, [Cred 377-11
 And polished beast, this complex falls apart. [Cred 377-16
 Of it is not a light apart, up-hill. [Orb 441-27
 The eye's plain version is a thing apart, [NH 465-4
 So much ourselves, we cannot tell apart [NH 466-20
 What path could lead apart from what she was [Old Woman 44-17 P
 Reflections, whirling apart and wide away. [Burnshaw 50-5 P
APARTMENTS. It is the celestial ennui of apartments [NSF 381-16
APENNINES. The strawberries once in the Apennines, [Arcades 225-2
 The strawberries once in the Apennines . . . [Arcades 226-1
APHONIES. Of aphonies, tuned in from zero and [Montra 260-14
APHORISM. And that, then, is my final aphorism. [Soldat 11-3 P
APLOMB. Pure scientist, you look with nice aplomb [Good Bad 33-12P
APOCALYPSE. In an unburgherly apocalypse. [Geneva 24-14
 Resists each past apocalypse, rejects [Extracts 257-27
 Apocalypse was not contrived for parks, [Duck 62-23 P
APOCALYPTIC. One thinking of apocalyptic legions. [Descrip 343-14
APOGEE. The point of survey, green's green apogee, [Cred 373-17
 Axis of everything, green's apogee [Cred 373-20
APOLLO. Uncertain certainty, Apollo [Ulysses 101-5 P
APOLOGETIC. In this apologetic air, one well [Lytton 39-16 P
APOSTROPHE. "The Apostrophe to Vincentine" [52-title
 There seemed to be an apostrophe that was not spoken. [Cata
  424-15
 The volcano Apostrophe, the sea Behold? [Duck 63-29 P
APOSTROPHES. And apostrophes are forbidden on the funicular.
  [Botanist 1 134-11
APOSTROPHIZING. Apostrophizing wreaths, the voice [MBG 177-13
APOTHEOSIS. She said poetry and apotheosis are one. [Past Nun
  378-13
 Are parts of apotheosis, appropriate [NSF 387-20
 Enflashings. But apotheosis is not [NSF 387-23
APOTHICAIRE. Of Phoebus Apothicaire the first beatitude: [NE
  Verses 105-3
APPALACHIAN. Bristles, and points their Appalachian tangs,
  [Bantams 76-3
APPANAGE. Not yesterday, not tomorrow, an appanage [Bouquet 451-14
APPAREL. Performed in verd apparel, and the peach, [C 39-2
APPARELLED. Green is the night, green kindled and apparelled.
  [Candle 223-1
 Of the mind, an apparition apparelled in [Angel 497-8
APPARELS. Apparels of such lightest look that a turn [Angel 497-9
APPARENT. And their blackness became apparent, that one first
  [Nigger 151-2
 Fully made, fully apparent, fully found. [Cred 376-15
APPARENTLY. Apparently in the air, fall from him [Hero 277-15
APPARITION. By apparition, plain and common things, [C 46-7
 This mechanism, this apparition, [Couch 295-2
 Not apparition but appearance, part [Feo 334-10
 What subtlety would apparition have? [Descrip 340-14
 Of the mind, an apparition apparelled in [Angel 497-8
 An apparition, twanging instruments [Duck 63-18 P
 A time, an apparition and nourishing element [How Now 97-11 P
APPARITIONS. Crowded with apparitions suddenly gone [Bouquet
  448-10
APPEAR. The revealing aberration should appear, [Nigger 153-18
 The politics of emotion must appear [EM 324-29
 Will appear like it. But it will be an appearance, [Myrrh 350-1
 Ababba, expecting this king's queen to appear? [Golden 461-3
 The impoverished architects appear to be [NH 469-23
 Appear to sleep within a sleeping air, [Burnshaw 50-19 P
APPEARANCE. Of bliss submerged beneath appearance, [Jasmine 79-10
 Not apparition but appearance, part [Feo 334-10

In flat appearance we should be and be, [Descrip 340-15
Will appear like it. But it will be an appearance [Myrrh 350-1
An appearance of Again, the diva-dame. [Adult 353-10
"The Pediment of Appearance" [361-title
The pediment of appearance. [Pediment 361-9
The whole of appearance is a toy. For this, [Belly 366-16
The intricacies of appearance, when perceived. [Papini 447-17
Cloud's gold, of a whole appearance that stands and is. [Bouquet
 452-18
His own: a chapel of breath, an appearance made [Armor 529-11
Would have a most singular appearance, [Mandolin 29-4 P
Its actual appearance, suppose we begin [Recit 86-5 P
Piercing the spirit by appearance, [Ulysses 104-6 P
APPEARANCES. Its true appearances there, sun's green, [MBG 177-3
 Appearances of what appearances, [NH 465-11
 It is not to be seen beneath the appearances [R Conn 533-13
APPEARED. The sun appeared and reddened great [Country 207-13
 Her hand composed him like a hand appeared, [Hand 271-13
 Mountains appeared with greater eloquence [NH 484-12
APPEARS. Fall, it appears, of its own weight to earth. [Monocle
 14-13
 If one may say so. And yet relation appears, [Connois 215-18
 And say, "The thing I hum appears to be [Landsc 243-7
 On a transmutation which, when seen, appears [EM 318-6
 The barrenness that appears is an exposing. [NH 487-16
 It appears to be what there is of life compressed [Bship 79-1 P
 The rioter that appears when things are changed, [Pagoda 91-20P
APPEASE. Which, being green and blue, appease him, [Aug 491-4
APPEASED. Absorbs the ruddy summer and is appeased, [Cred 374-3
APPEASEMENT. Are not precise about the appeasement they need. [NH
 467-21
APPENDS. The sea appends its tattery hues. [MBG 172-13
APPERCEPTION. A difficult apperception, this gorging good, [Orb
 440-5
APPETITE. For food. The big bird's bony appetite [EM 318-9
 The sun, its grossest appetite becomes less gross, [EM 318-14
 A man of bitter appetite despises [EM 322-20
APPLE. An apple serves as well as any skull [Monocle 14-16
 On bed-clothes, in an apple on a plate. [Blue Bldg 217-16
 The bud of the apple is desire, the down-falling gold, [Holiday
 313-5
 Agree: the apple in the orchard, round [Burnshaw 47-30 P
APPLE-BLOCKS. Among the orchards in the apple-blocks [Good Bad
 33-16 P
APPLES. As apples fall, without astronomy, [Montra 262-7
 The President has apples on the table [NSF 390-19
 To a million, a duck with apples and without wine. [Duck 60-12 P
APPLICATION. Be plain. For application Crispin strove, [C 38-8
APPLIED. They differ from reason's click-clack, its applied [NSF
 387-22
 When applied to the mythical. [Lytton 39-9 P
 Applied on earth to those that were myths [Lytton 39-12 P
 To an untried perception applied [Lytton 39-14 P
APPLIES. As his pure intellect applies its laws, [Bird Claws 82-14
APPOINT. Since both alike appoint themselves the choice [NH 469-16
APPOINTED. The appointed power unwielded from disdain. [C 37-19
 Repeating your appointed paces [Hero 275-16
 Inhaled the appointed odor, while the doves [NSF 389-14
 A syllable of which he felt, with an appointed sureness, [Prol
 516-5
 In an appointed repertoire . . . [Soldat 15-21 P
 Appointed for them and that the pediment [Burnshaw 52-4 P
APPOINTMENTS. Or rising in the appointments of desire, [Greenest
 57-11 P
APPOINTS. Appoints man's place in music, say, today. [NSF 382-2
 Appoints These Marbles Of Itself To Be [Burnshaw 48-6 P
 Appoints its florid messengers with wings [Greenest 57-17 P
APPOSITE. The melon should have apposite ritual, [C 39-1
APPOSITES. Apposites, to the slightest edge, of the whole [Someone
 86-19 A
APPRECIABLE. Of the least appreciable shade of green [Burnshaw
 51-20 P
APPRECIATION. An appreciation of a reality; [Warmth 90-4 P
 An appreciation of a reality [As Leave 117-10 P
APPREHENDED. To be an evasion, a thing not apprehended or [NSF
 396-22
 Not apprehended well. Does the poet [NSF 396-23
 The complexities of the world, when apprehended, [Papini 447-16
 Not that which is but that which is apprehended, [NH 468-13
APPREHENDING. Of the apprehending of the hero. [Hero 279-23
APPREHENDS. That apprehends the most which sees and names,
 [Fictive 88-5
APPREHENSION. His apprehension, made him intricate [C 31-9
 Is like a vivid apprehension [Jasmine 79-7
 Our merest apprehension of their will. [Montra 262-15
 Of greater aptitude and apprehension, [NSF 387-15
 A skillful apprehension and eye proud [Spaniard 35-17 P
APPRENTICE. The apprentice knew these dreamers. If he dreamed [C
 39-29
 Regulae mundi, as apprentice of [Bship 78-21 P

APPRENTICES. Wooden, the model for astral apprentices, [NH 478-19
APPRENTICESHIP. Grotesque apprenticeship to chance event, [C 39-23
APPROACH. The approach of him whom none believes, [MDC 170-10
  A being of sound, whom one does not approach [Creat 311-5
  Is a phase. We approach a society [Bship 79-22 P
  Simplifications approach but do not touch [Bship 80-26 P
  Is an approach to the vigilance [Ulysses 102-6 P
APPROACHED. While she approached the real, upon her mountain,
  [Uruguay 249-8
  Approached this strongly-heightened effigy [NSF 391-14
APPROACHES. All approaches gone, being completely there, [Waldorf
  240-25
  Approaching in the dark approaches [Hero 279-25
  Will look like frost as it approaches them [AA 413-21
  One approaches, simply, the reality [Bouquet 448-14
  Is it Ulysses that approaches from the east, [World 520-11
  A form of fire approaches the cretonnes of Penelope, [World
  520-15
APPROACHING. Approaching like a gasconade of drums. [C 32-18
  Approaching Carolina [C 33-title 3
  Like humans approaching proudly, [Shifts 83-18
  Like humans approaching angrily. [Shifts 83-19
  Approaching the feelings or come down from them, [Montra 260-12
  Approaching in the dark approaches [Hero 279-25
  One foot approaching, one uplifted arm. [Choc 296-16
  Its actors approaching, in company, in their masks. [AA 414-21
  So that the approaching sun and its arrival, [NH 472-17
  Approaching rain [Bowl 7-3 P
  An innocence approaching toward its peak. [Pagoda 92-6 P
  An argentine abstraction approaching form [Real 110-17 P
  These were that serene he had always been approaching [Local
  112-11 P
APPROPRIATE. And peculiar and appropriate glory, [Hero 277-26
  Composed, appropriate to the incomplete, [Repet 309-13
  Of the appropriate creatures, jubilant, [Descrip 344-13
  We were the appropriate conceptions, less [Lot 371-13
  Half pales of green, appropriate habit for [Cred 378-3
  Are parts of apotheosis, appropriate [NSF 387-20
  But still she painted them, appropriate to [NSF 402-4
  For triumphals. These are hymns appropriate to [Papini 447-15
  The appropriate image of himself, [Two Illus 513-13
  With appropriate, largely English, furniture, [Sombre 68-7 P
  To form that weather's appropriate people, [Art Pop 112-18 P
  So, too, of the races of appropriate people [Art Pop 113-4 P
APPROXIMATION. An approximation of an element, [Aug 491-21
APRES. Livre de Toutes Sortes de Fleures d'apres Nature. [EM 316-7
APRICOT. With a single well-tempered apricot, or, say, [Extracts
  253-14
APRICOTS. On porpoises, instead of apricots, [C 27-18
APRIL. Frail as April snow; [Pourtraicte 21-15
  And April hillsides wooded white and pink [C 37-29
  As April's green endures; or will endure [Sunday 68-23
  B. It is April as I write. The wind [Connois 216-4
  On an early Sunday in April, a feeble day, [Extracts 254-25
  At New Year and, from then until April, lay [Extracts 255-2
  For whom the good of April falls tenderly, [NSF 388-7
  Of April here and May to come. Champagne [Greenest 58-24 P
  To April here and May to come. Why think, [Greenest 58-29 P
APRILIAN. Of young identities, Aprilian stubs. [Duck 64-24 P
APT. An eye most apt in gelatines and jupes, [C 27-14
  And apt in versatile motion, touch and sound [Anatomy 108-12
  The clearest woman with apt weed, to mount [Havana 143-17
APTEST. Bottles, pots, shoes and grass and murmur aptest eve:
  [Dump 203-7
APTITUDE. Of greater aptitude and apprehension, [NSF 387-4
APTLY. The muscles of a magnet aptly felt, [Orb 442-15
AQUILINE. Aquiline pedants treat the cart [Prejudice 368-15
  What aquiline pedants take [Prejudice 368-21
  And, therefore, aquiline pedants find [Prejudice 369-4
AQUINAS. The moonlight and Aquinas seemed to. He spoke, [Les Plus
  245-3
ARABESQUES. Arabesques of candle beams, [Phases 4-4 P
ARABIAN. We say: At night an Arabian in my room, [NSF 383-1
ARACHNE. The Arachne integument of dead trees, [Vari 234-19
ARAGONESE. A wide, still Aragonese, [Fare Guit 99-2 P
ARBOR. The four winds blow through the rustic arbor, [Vacancy
  511-12
  It is an arbor against the wind, a pit in the mist, [Discov
  95-12 P
ARBORED. And, arbored and bronzed, in autumn. [Yellow 236-12
ARBORS. In the arbors that are as if of Saturn-star. [Moonlight
  531-18
ARC. The categorical predicate, the arc. [Descrip 344-8
  Like a shelter not in an arc [Celle 438-8
  But in a circle, not in the arc [Celle 438-9
  See half-arc.
ARCADES. "Arcades of Philadelphia the Past" [225-title
ARCADIAN. Straight from the Arcadian imagination, [Novel 459-1
ARCH. Arch in the sea like tree-branches, [Homunculus 26-2
ARCHAIC. Archaic, for the sea. [Paltry 5-7

The abstract, the archaic queen. Green is the night. [Candle
  223-14
  Archaic and future happenings, [Oak 272-19
  This pitter-patter of archaic freedom, [Dutch 292-13
  Voluble but archaic and hard to hear. [Liadoff 347-21
  To be a bronze man breathing under archaic lapis, [Cata 425-10
  Was it as we sat in the park and the archaic form [Aug 494-10
  And the sense of the archaic touched us at once [Aug 494-13
  Was full of these archaic forms, giants [Aug 494-17
  Evoking an archaic space, vanishing [Aug 494-19
  Are chaos and of archaic change. Shall you, [Burnshaw 51-5 P
ARCHANGEL. I am the archangel of evening and praise [Inhab 504-10
ARCHBISHOP. The archbishop is away. The church is gray. [Gray 140-1
ARCHES. That was seen through arches) [Botanist 1 135-3
  The pillars are prostrate, the arches are haggard, [Botanist 1
  135-11
  Beneath the arches and their spangled air, [Eve Angels 138-2
  The grinding in the arches of the church, [Blue Bldg 217-4
  The lean cats of the arches of the churches, [Extracts 254-1
  The lean cats of the arches of the churches [Extracts 254-18
  Under the arches, over the arches, in arcs [Dutch 293-8
  Day's arches are crumbling into the autumn night. [Novel 458-16
  Of bird-nest arches and of rain-stained-vaults. [Rome 510-10
  Its arches in its vivid element, [Armor 530-14
  On which the vast arches of space [Ulysses 103-17 P
ARCHING. Arching cloths besprinkled with colors [Plot Giant 6-18
ARCHITECT. They keep to the paths of the skeleton architect [Duck
  62-10 P
ARCHITECTS. The impoverished architects appear to be [NH 469-23
ARCHITECTURE. And the architecture swoons. [Public Sq 109-8
  Its domes are the architecture of your bed. [Rome 510-14
  "Architecture" [16-title P
ARCS. Under the arches, over the arches, in arcs [Dutch 293-8
  And come to nothing. Let the rainy arcs [Repet 310-3
  The triumph of the arcs of heaven's blue [Duck 60-16 P
ARCTIC. Perhaps the Arctic moonlight really gave [C 34-25
  Artist in Arctic [NE Verses 105-title 8
  An Arctic effulgence flaring on the frame [AA 417-2
ARCTURUS. Or melt Arcturus to ingots dropping drops, [Page 423-3
ARE. You do not play things as they are." [MBG 165-4
  The man replied, "Things as they are [MBG 165-5
  Of things exactly as they are." [MBG 165-10
  Is to miss, by that, things as they are, [MBG 165-18
  So that's life, then: things as they are? [MBG 166-13
  And that's life, then: things as they are, [MBG 167-1
  A tune beyond us as we are, [MBG 167-15
  Of things as they are and only the place [MBG 167-19
  Becomes the place of things as they are, [MBG 168-7
  Detached from us, from things as they are? [MBG 168-19
  The book and bread, things as they are, [MBG 172-20
  Things as they are have been destroyed. [MBG 173-7
  Of things as they are, as the blue guitar [MBG 174-18
  Things as they are. Or so we say. [MBG 176-20
  Concerning the nature of things as they are. [MBG 177-20
  Things as they were, things as they are, [MBG 178-20
  And things are as I think they are [MBG 180-17
  The rhapsody of things as they are. [MBG 183-2
  You as you are? You are yourself. [MBG 183-13
  Invisible, they move and are, [Analysis 348-17
  Took on color, took on shape and the size of things as they are
  [Large 424-8
  Pink yellows, orange whites, too much as they are [Roses 430-11
  Too much as they are to be changed by metaphor, [Roses 430-13
  We are two that use these roses as we are, [Roses 431-10
  Participants of its being. It is, we are. [Study I 463-10
  He is, we are. Ah, bella! He is, we are, [Study I 463-11
  By sight and insight as they are. There is no [NH 473-22
  We hear, what we are, beyond mystic disputation, [Look 518-11
  Were not and are not. Absurd. The words spoken [Rock 525-10
  Were not and are not. It is not to be believed. [Rock 525-11
  And then things are not as they are. [Stan MBG 72-16 P
  I still intend things as they are. [Stan MBG 73-4 P
  But squint and squeak, where no people are: [Stan MBG 73-15 P
  True, things are people as they are. [Stan MBG 73-18 P
AREA. Of property is not an area [Papini 447-14
  In the area between is and was are leaves, [NH 474-2
ARGENT. The red, the blue, the argent queen. If not, [Descrip 340-13
ARGENTINE. Perceived: the white seen smoothly argentine [Bouquet
  449-14
  She had heard of the fate of an Argentine writer. At night,
  [Novel 457-8
  That Argentine. Only the real can be [Novel 458-20
  It is odd, too, how that Argentine is oneself. [Novel 458-22
  An argentine abstraction approaching form [Real 110-17 P
ARGENTINES. These trees and their argentines, their dark-spiced
  branches, [Holiday 313-3
  Did not desire that feathery argentines [NSF 399-5
  For her that she remembered: the argentines [NSF 399-13
  Various argentines, [Archi 18-7 P
ARGUMENT. Victor Serge said, "I followed his argument [EM 324-24

ARIAS. The arias that spiritual fiddlings make, [Orb 440-2
ARID. That the hours of his indolent, arid days, [Frogs 78-10
  Seemed to suckle themselves on his arid being, [Frogs 78-13
ARIEL. Ariel was glad he had written his poems. [Planet 532-7
ARISE. His tattered manikin arise, [Abnormal 24-16 P
ARISTOTLE. Or Aristotle's skeleton. Let him hang out [Less 327-13
  X understands Aristotle [Grotesque 75-4 P
ARITHMETIC. Are we characters in an arithmetic [Recit 87-7 P
ARKANSAW. The jack-rabbit sang to the Arkansaw. [Jack-Rabbit 50-5
ARM. Of a woman's arm: [Six Sig 73-17
  The arm of bronze outstretched against all evil! [Mice 123-12
  Worn out, her arm falls down, [Add 199-3
  His arm would be trembling, he would be weak, [Thunder 220-15
  One foot approaching, one uplifted arm. [Choc 296-16
  Stretched out a shadowy arm to feel the night. [Phases 5-8 P
  Only the surfaces--the bending arm, [Blanche 10-3 P
  Commands the armies; the relentless arm, [Soldat 14-11 P
  The fortifying arm, the profound [Ulysses 100-10 P
ARMED. The angels come, armed, gloriously to slay [Greenest 55-28P
  See hump-armed.
ARMIES. Of the silence before the armies, armies without [Martial
  237-21
  But these are not those rusted armies. [Dutch 292-3
  Grows sharp in blood. The armies kill themselves, [Dutch 292-19
  The armies are forms in number, as cities are. [Choc 296-12
  The armies are cities in movement. But a war [Choc 296-13
  Of the armies, the solid men, make big the fable. [Choc 301-15
  From that strength, whose armies set their own expanses. [Repet
  309-5
  Commands the armies; the relentless arm, [Soldat 14-11 P
ARMORER. See St. Armorer.
ARMORIAL. The binders did it with armorial books. [Greenest 53-16P
ARMS. And would have purple stuff upon her arms, [Paltry 5-12
  That were like arms and shoulders in the waves, [C 29-2
  He for her burning breast and she for his arms. [Norfolk 111-19
  These sudden clouds of faces and arms, [Sad Gay 122-4
  Like giant arms among the clouds. [How Live 125-20
  A running forward, arms stretched out as drilled. [Nigger 153-15
  Either trumpets or drums, the commanders mute, the arms [Martial
  238-1
  Weaving and weaving many arms. [Oak 272-9
  The brightness of arms, said Roma wasted [Hero 273-8
  Of arms, the will opposed to cold, fate [Hero 273-12
  And lither stride. His arms are heavy [Hero 277-11
  Have arms without hands. They have trunks [Possum 293-18
  On more than muscular shoulders, arms and chest, [Choc 297-12
  Integration for integration, the great arms [Choc 301-14
  Of fiery eyes and long thin arms. [Attempt 370-11
  Of a mother with vague severed arms [Celle 438-19
  A giant on the horizon, given arms, [Orb 443-8
  She wanted no fetchings. His arms would be her necklace [World
  521-8
  Entwine your arms and moving to and fro, [Burnshaw 47-17 P
  This is invisible. The supporting arms [Sombre 68-24 P
  Destroyed by a vengeful movement of the arms, [Sombre 69-3 P
  Midmost in its design, the arms grown swift, [Sombre 69-9 P
  A race of dwarfs, the meditative arms [Sombre 70-27 P
  The illustrious arms, the symbolic horns, the red [Bship 79-6 P
  Millions hold millions in their arms. [Memo 89-16 P
  A land would hold her in its arms that day [Letters 108-6 P
AROINTING. Arointing his dreams with fugal requiems? [C 41-11
AROMA. When piled on salvers into aroma steeped [C 35-9
  He must, in the aroma of summer nights, [Montra 261-14
AROSE. A mountain-blue cloud arose [Public Sq 109-3
AROUND. As they flowed around [Infanta 8-5
  On sidelong wing, around and round and round. [Monocle 17-19
  With flowers around, [Pourtraicte 21-5
  That lay elsewhere around him. Severance [C 30-1
  He marked the marshy ground around the dock, [C 36-13
  And sprawled around, no longer wild. [Jar 76-10
  (The rudiments of tropics are around, [Bird Claws 82-4
  Danced around a stump. [Motion 83-4
  I am what is around me. [Theory 86-16
  Walks around the feet [Thirteen 93-22
  Tongues around the fruit. [Orangeade 103-6
  And his nostrils blow out salt around each man. [Grapes 111-3
  The trade-wind jingles the rings in the nets around the racks
    by the docks on Indian River. [Indian 112-4
  And full of yourself. The trees around are for you, [Rabbit K
  209-16
  Threw its contorted strength around the sky. [Sleight 222-8
  Around the sun. The wheel survives the myths. [Sleight 222-11
  Around which silence lies on silence. [Yellow 236-10
  So that the flapping of wind around me here [Choc 299-2
  Words, in a storm, that beat around the shapes . [Sketch 335-22
  Her green mind made the world around her green. [Descrip 339-9
  And throws his stars around the floor. By day [NSF 383-5
  The truth depends on a walk around a lake, [NSF 386-3
  On her trip around the world, Nanzia Nunzio [NSF 395-16
  The vines around the throat, the shapeless lips, [NSF 400-10

  They throw around their shoulders cloaks that flash [AA 419-23
  Birds twitter pandemoniums around [Antag 426-3
  Moving around and behind, a following, [Orb 442-22
  These characters are around us in the scene. [NH 469-13
  Around and away, resembling the presence of thought, [NH 474-5
  The things around--the alternate romanza [NH 480-21
  It wraps the sheet around its body, until the black figure is
    silver. [Plough-Boy 6-6 P
  The child's hair is of the color of the hay in the haystack,
    around which the four black horses stand. [Primordia 8-1 P
  Around it. Thus it has a large expanse, [Red Kit 31-7 P
  The darkest blue of the dome and the wings around [Duck 65-22 P
  Around him and in that distance meditates [Recit 86-19 P
ARPEGGI. Arpeggi of celestial souvenirs, [Spaniard 35-16 P
ARPEGGIOS. While you practice arpeggios, [Mozart 131-19
  At the piano, scales, arpeggios [Hero 274-21
  And its tragical, its haunted arpeggios? [Liadoff 346-19
ARRANGE. You arrange, the thing is posed, [Add 198-16
  Jocunda, who will arrange the roses and rearrange, letting the
    leaves lie on the water-like lacquer; [Piano 22-4 P
ARRANGED. Vermilion smeared over green, arranged for show. [Grapes
  110-14
  Why seraphim like lutanists arranged [Eve Angels 136-13
  Arranged under the stony clouds [Gray 140-6
  Arranged its heroic attitudes. [Hartford 227-3
  The decay that you regard: of the arranged [Cred 377-13
  And of the spirit of the arranged, douceurs, [Cred 377-14
  Just rising, accompanying, arranged to cross, [Page 422-24
  Not as one would have arranged them for oneself, [Novel 458-10
  A knowledge, that which arranged the rendezvous. [Final 524-12
  Lived in the houses of mothers, arranged ourselves [Rock 525-2
  Arranged for phantasy to form an edge [Old Woman 43-17 P
ARRANGEMENT. The arrangement contains the desire of [Couch 296-1
  "Human Arrangement" [363-title
  The arrangement of the chairs is so and so, [Novel 458-9
ARRANGEMENTS. Arrangements; and the violets' exhumo. [EM 322-26
  Without secret arrangements of it in the mind. [Descrip 341-14
ARRANGING. Arranging, deepening, enchanting night. [Key W 130-10
ARRANT. Decays of sacks, and all the arrant stinks [C 36-10
  Among the arrant spices of the sun, [Fictive 88-7
ARRAY. Speak to me that, which spoken, will array me [NSF 396-4
  His utmost statement. It is his own array, [Questions 462-17
ARRAYED. Filled its encrusted fountains, they arrayed [Havana
  142-20
ARRESTED. And fill the foliage with arrested peace, [Cred 373-11
ARRIVAL. This arrival in the wild country of the soul, [Waldorf
  240-24
  So that the approaching sun and its arrival, [NH 472-17
  Await an arrival, [Inhab 503-17
  As at a point of central arrival, an instant moment, much or
    little, [Prol 516-8
ARRIVE. Descensions of their tinkling bells arrive. [Monocle 15-20
  Of bones, he rejected, he denied, to arrive [Landsc 241-20
  And denying what he heard. He would arrive. [Landsc 242-11
ARRIVED. The first word would be of the susceptible being arrived,
  [Discov 96-1 P
ARRIVES. Arrives at the man-man as he wanted. [Hero 280-17
  Before and after one arrives or, say, [NH 485-24
ARROGANCE. An arrogant dagger darting its arrogance, [Aug 491-24
ARROGANT. Dressed poorly, arrogant of his streaming forces,
  [Uruguay 249-22
  The vital, arrogant, fatal, dominant X. [Motive 288-20
  There are potential seemings, arrogant [Descrip 340-19
  An arrogant dagger darting its arrogance, [Aug 491-24
  Of martyrs, to be arrogant in our need, [Bship 81-3 P
ARROGANTLY. Well-booted, rugged, arrogantly male, [Lilacs 49-13
ARRONDISSEMENTS. And in one of the little arrondissements [Winter B
  141-17
  Without his enlargings and pale arrondissements, [Someone 85-5 A
ARROWS. A sheaf of brilliant arrows flying straight, [Tallap 72-7
  Or, if not arrows, then the nimblest motions, [Tallap 72-10
  Intangible arrows quiver and stick in the skin [Holiday 313-9
ARROWY. Above the arrowy, still strings, [MBG 169-17
ART. The thinking of art seems final when [MBG 168-4
  "Thou art not August unless I make thee so." [Bouquet 251-5
ARTICHOKE. Like a word in the mind that sticks at artichoke
  [Burnshaw 47-2 P
ARTICULATE. Articulate its desert days. [MBG 174-10
  Venerable and articulate and complete. [NSF 383-21
ARTIFICE. Or seeing the midsummer artifice [C 33-3
  A little changed by tips of artifice, changed [Myrrh 350-5
  With a sad splendor, beyond artifice, [Owl 435-16
  Of the reality of the eye, an artifice, [Bouquet 448-12
  But his actual candle blazed with artifice. [Quiet 523-15
  Like the artifice of a new reality, [Theatre 91-5 P
  Not the beginning but the end of artifice, [Conversat 109-9 P
  At the bottom of imagined artifice, [Someone 83-9 A
  Here the total artifice reveals itself [Someone 87-12 A
ARTIFICER. She was the single artificer of the world [Key W 129-26
  The artificer of subjects still half night. [Descrip 345-18

ARTIFICIAL. It is an artificial world. The rose [Extracts 252-8
  Man makes the hero artificial. [Hero 280-24
  Beyond intelligence, an artificial man [Creat 311-3
  They are men but artificial men. They are [Paisant 335-7
  It is an artificial thing that exists .[Descrip 344-17
  The lake was full of artificial things, [NSF 397-12
  "Artificial Populations" [112-title P
  This artificial population is like [Art Pop 112-21 P
  A wholly artificial nature, in which [Someone 83-2 A
ARTIST. Artist in Tropic [NE Verses 105-title 7
  Artist in Arctic [NE Verses 105-title 8
  The artist. But one confides in what has no [Couch 296-2
  The monastic man is an artist. The philosopher [NSF 382-1
A-RUB. Preludes a-rub, a-rub-rub, for him that [Hero 278-6
A-RUB-RUB. Preludes a-rub, a-rub-rub, for him that [Hero 278-6
AS. Not as when the goldener nude [Paltry 6-4
  As small as fish-eggs. [Plot Giant 7-1
  Just as they flew from the boughs of the hemlocks [Domination 8-22
  Turning as the flames [Domination 9-6
  Turning as the tails of the peacocks [Domination 9-8
  Loud as the hemlocks [Domination 9-10
  As kildeer do, [Sugar-Cane 12-16
  An apple serves as well as any skull [Monocle 14-16
  And is as excellent, in that it is composed [Monocle 14-18
  But it excels in this, that as the fruit [Monocle 14-20
  As the deadly thought of men accomplishing [Monocle 16-14
  I am a yeoman, as such fellows go. [Monocle 16-26
  Yet is certain as meaning . . . [Magnifico 19-15
  Frail as April snow; [Pourtraicte 21-15
  The mind roamed as a moth roams, [Hibiscus 22-10
  As the flag above the old café-- [Hibiscus 23-2
  It is better that, as scholars, [Homunculus 26-17
  "The Comedian as the Letter C" [27-title
  The sovereign ghost. As such, the Socrates [C 27-8
  As if raspberry tanagers in palms, [C 30-20
  As dissertation of profound delight, [C 31-6
  He was in this as other freemen are, [C 31-12
  And not for stupor, such as music makes [C 31-15
  As sullen as the sky, was swallowed up [C 32-20
  Wrong as a divagation to Peking, [C 34-31
  To him that postulated as his theme [C 35-1
  The vulgar, as his theme and hymn and flight, [C 35-2
  As on this voyage, out of goblinry, [C 35-10
  As being, in a world so falsified, [C 36-19
  Afraid, the blind man as astronomer, [C 37-18
  Abhorring Turk as Esquimau, the lute [C 38-9
  As the marimba, the magnolia as rose. [C 38-10
  With Crispin as the tiptoe cozener? [C 40-2
  Crispin as hermit, pure and capable, [C 40-4
  Little by little, as if the suzerain soil [C 40-23
  He first, as realist, admitted that [C 40-26
  It was as if the solitude concealed [C 42-7
  But the quotidian composed as his, [C 42-25
  His cabin counted as phylactery, [C 43-23
  Lettered herself demurely as became [C 44-31
  As buffo, yet divers, four mirrors blue [C 45-6
  In form though in design, as Crispin willed, [C 45-21
  Concluding fadedly, if as a man [C 46-2
  Lasciviously as the wind, [Venereal 48-1
  Are as natural sounds [Men 1000 51-16
  As the cackle of toucans [Men 1000 52-1
  I figured you as nude between [Vincentine 52-11
  I saw you then, as warm as flesh, [Vincentine 52-16
  As warm, as clean. [Vincentine 52-19
  "Of Heaven Considered as a Tomb" [56-title
  That burial, pillared up each day as porte [Heaven 56-16
  As the sleepless! [Peacocks 58-2
  As if awake [Peacocks 58-7
  As sleep falls [Peacocks 58-25
  Wink as they will. Wink most when widows wince. [High-Toned 59-22
  Should mask as white girls. [W Burgher 61-4
  Permit that if as ghost I come [W Burgher 61-10
  I come as belle design [W Burgher 61-12
  Is full of long motions; as the ponderous [Curtains 62-2
  Deflations of distance; or as clouds [Curtains 62-3
  Is beyond us, as the firmament, [Curtains 62-8
  As the spittle of cows [Depression 63-11
  As they are used to wear, and let the boys [Emperor 64-5
  And spread it so as to cover her face. [Emperor 64-12
  As a calm darkens among water-lights. [Sunday 67-4
  He moved among us, as a muttering king, [Sunday 67-30
  As April's green endures; or will endure [Sunday 68-23
  Not as a god, but as a god might be, [Sunday 70-2
  Who walks there, as a farewell duty, [Virgin 71-5
  As, for example, the ellipse of the half-moon-- [Six Sig 75-12
  Damned universal cock, as if the sun [Bantams 75-16
  As the swine-like rivers suckled themselves [Frogs 78-14
  As to rafters or grass. [Tattoo 81-18
  As his pure intellect applies its laws, [Bird Claws 82-14

I had as lief be embraced by the porter at the hotel [Two Fig 85-14
  Speak, even, as if I did not hear you speaking, [Two Fig 86-4
  As the night conceives the sea-sounds in silence. [Two Fig 86-7
  As in your name, an image that is sure, [Fictive 88-6
  Just as my fingers on these keys [Peter 89-16
  As the immense dew of Florida [Nomad 95-6
  As the immense dew of Florida [Nomad 95-10
  As in a season of autumn. [Soldier 97-2
  As in a season of autumn, [Soldier 97-8
  And moved, as blooms move, in the swimming green [Sea Surf 99-11
  Of ocean, as a prelude holds and holds. [Sea Surf 100-16
  Beheld the sovereign clouds as jugglery [Sea Surf 102-6
  And the sea as turquoise-turbaned Sambo, neat [Sea Surf 102-7
  And heaven rolled as one and from the two [Sea Surf 102-14
  Nature as Pinakothek. Whist! Chanticleer . . . [NE Verses 106-10
  That bore us as a part of all the things [Anatomy 107-14
  Fell slowly as when at night [Public Sq 109-5
  He praised Johann Sebastian, as he should. [Norfolk 111-15
  As if I lived in ashen ground, as if [Farewell 117-12
  The men are moving as the water moves, [Farewell 118-13
  "Ghosts as Cocoons" [119-title
  As of the great wind howling, [Mozart 132-14
  Brings voices as of lions coming down. [Sun March 134-6
  As sure as all the angels are. [Botanist 2 136-2
  As of those crosses, glittering, [Botanist 2 136-10
  Above the trees? And why the poet as [Eve Angels 136-14
  To moodiest nothings, as, desire for day [Eve Angels 137-21
  Within as pillars of the sun, [Fading 139-16
  Lusty as June, more fruitful than the weeks [Havana 143-13
  Imagination as the fateful sin. [Havana 143-22
  As part of nature he is part of us. [Havana 144-18
  It is what it is as I am what I am: [Re-state 146-2
  Sat reading as if in a book [Reader 146-14
  Turning in time to Brahms as alternate [Anglais 149-6
  And sing them in secrecy as lovers do. [Nigger 151-21
  A running forward, arms stretched out as drilled. [Nigger 153-15
  As an autumn ancient underneath the snow, [Nigger 154-2
  Ennobled as in a mirror to sanctity. [Nigger 157-6
  There is no such thing as innocence in autumn, [Nigger 157-12
  As quick as foxes on the hill; [Postcard 158-16
  As if he that lived there left behind [Postcard 159-17
  You do not play things as they are." [MBG 165-4
  The man replied, "Things as they are [MBG 165-5
  Of things exactly as they are." [MBG 165-10
  Although I patch him as I can [MBG 165-15
  Is to miss, by that, things as they are, [MBG 165-18
  So that's life, then: things as they are? [MBG 166-13
  And that's life, then: things as they are, [MBG 167-1
  A tune beyond us as we are, [MBG 167-15
  Ourselves in the tune as if in space, [MBG 167-17
  Of things as they are and only the place [MBG 167-19
  Becomes the place of things as they are, [MBG 168-7
  And shall I then stand in the sun, as now [MBG 168-16
  Detached from us, from things as they are? [MBG 168-19
  High as the hall. The whirling noise [MBG 171-14
  The book and bread, things as they are, [MBG 172-20
  Things as they are have been destroyed. [MBG 173-7
  As it grudges the living that they live. [MBG 173-18
  Of things as they are, as the blue guitar [MBG 174-18
  The wind-gloss. Or as daylight comes, [MBG 175-2
  Two things, the two together as one, [MBG 175-11
  But of that as its intelligence, [MBG 175-14
  Things as they are. Or so we say. [MBG 176-20
  Confusion solved, as in a refrain [MBG 177-18
  Concerning the nature of things as they are. [MBG 177-20
  Sombre as fir-trees, liquid cats [MBG 178-18
  Things as they were, things as they are, [MBG 178-20
  Things as they will be by and by . . . [MBG 178-21
  And think in it as a native thinks, [MBG 180-6
  And yet are fixed as a photograph, [MBG 180-13
  And as I am, I speak and move [MBG 180-16
  And things are as I think they are [MBG 180-17
  As if a blunted player clutched [MBG 182-21
  The rhapsody of things as they are. [MBG 183-2
  You as you are? You are yourself. [MBG 183-13
  As certainly as night is the color [Prelude 194-15
  As of a tragic science should rise. [Prelude 195-13
  As the observer wills. [Pears 197-6
  Brown as the bread, thinking of birds [Loaf 200-1
  As if the sky was a current that bore them along, [Loaf 200-5
  Spreading them as waves spread flat on the shore, [Loaf 200-6
  That it puffs as Cornelius Nepos reads, it puffs [Dump 202-3
  Everything is shed; and the moon comes up as the moon [Dump 202-22
  As a man (not like an image of a man), [Dump 202-24
  Be merely oneself, as superior as the ear [Dump 203-1
  "There is no such thing as the truth," [On Road 203-13
  That they were oak-leaves, as the way they looked. [Freed 205-19
  With faces as with leaves, be gusty with mouths, [Dames 206-9

Neither as mask nor as garment but as a being, [Dwarf 208-11
"A Rabbit as King of the Ghosts" [209-title
You are humped higher and higher, black as stone-- [Rabbit K
    210-1
Of essential unity, is as pleasant as port, [Connois 215-10
As pleasant as the brush-strokes of a bough, [Connois 215-11
As a self that lives on itself. [Thunder 220-20
As if someone lived there. Such floods of white [Sleight 222-6
I absorb them as the Angevine [Peaches 224-3
Absorbs Anjou, I see them as a lover sees, [Peaches 224-4
As a young lover sees the first buds of spring [Peaches 224-5
And as the black Spaniard plays his guitar. [Peaches 224-6
One self from another, as these peaches do. [Peaches 224-20
Of poorness as an earth, to taste [Arcades 225-24
But now as in an amour of women [Hartford 227-4
As they used to lie in the grass, in the heat, [Cuisine 227-18
As if last night's lamps continued to burn, [Cuisine 228-4
As if yesterday's people continued to watch [Cuisine 228-5
Bloomed in sheets, as they bloom, and the girl, [Forces 229-1
Seeming to be liquid as leaves made of cloud, [Forces 229-14
Men fat as feathers, misers counting breaths, [Horn 230-3
False as the mind, instead of the fragrance, warm [Horn 230-12
The figures of speech, as why she chose [Scavoir 231-3
As one improvises, on the piano. [Vari 233-19
As a boat feels when it cuts blue water. [Vari 234-5
In objects, as white this, white that. [Vari 235-5
As one loves visible and responsive peace, [Yellow 236-14
As one loves one's own being, [Yellow 236-15
As one loves that which is the end [Yellow 236-16
And must be loved, as one loves that [Yellow 236-17
Of which one is a part as in a unity, [Yellow 236-18
As the life of the fatal unity of war. [Yellow 236-21
There he touches his being. There as he is [Yellow 237-4
But he came back as one comes back from the sun [Yellow 237-7
Again . . . as if it came back, as if life came back, [Martial
    237-13
But as if evening found us young, still young, [Martial 237-15
Without time: as that which is not has no time, [Martial 237-19
Of destroying, as the mind destroys, [Bottle 239-8
An aversion, as the world is averted [Bottle 239-9
As the mind, to find what will suffice, destroys [Bottle 239-15
In an emotion as of two people, as of two [Of Mod 240-12
It was not as if the truth lay where he thought, [Landsc 242-3
As if the people in the air [Adequacy 243-10
And sun, as if these [Adequacy 244-8
Not as in air, bright-blue-resembling air, [Rhythms 246-7
But as in the powerful mirror of my wish and will." [Rhythms
    246-8
It was as if thunder took form upon [Vase 246-9
And we feel, in a way apart, for a moment, as if [Gala 248-11
Can never stand as god, is ever wrong [Oboe 250-16
As a mirror with a voice, the man of glass, [Oboe 250-21
It was not as if the jasmine ever returned. [Oboe 251-15
To naked men, to women naked as rain. [Extracts 252-14
Beyond the knowledge of nakedness, as part [Extracts 252-18
That evil made magic, as in catastrophe, [Extracts 253-8
If neatly glazed, becomes the same as the fruit [Extracts 253-9
As if designed by X, the per-noble master. [Extracts 254-20
(That being as much belief as we may have,) [Extracts 257-23
Of the weather and in one's self, as part of that [Extracts 258-9
Beyond a second death, as evil's end? [Extracts 258-28
To which we come as into bezeled plain, [Montra 262-3
As apples fall, without astronomy, [Montra 262-7
The naked man, the naked man as last [Montra 262-11
As acutest virtue and ascetic trove. [Montra 263-12
As facts fall like rejuvenating rain, [Montra 263-22
The world as word, [Search 268-11
The world lives as you live, [Search 268-13
Speaks as you speak, a creature that [Search 268-14
Cloud-clown, blue painter, sun as horn, [Jumbo 269-13
"The Hand as a Being" [271-title
As the acorn broods on former oaks [Oak 272-13
Red as a red table-cloth, its windows [Hero 276-1
Into a barbarism as its image. [Hero 277-4
Poet, as if he thought gladly, being [Hero 277-17
Painted by mad-men, seen as magic, [Hero 277-24
Leafed out in adjectives as private [Hero 277-25
Young men as vegetables, hip-hip, [Hero 278-12
There is a feeling as definition. [Hero 278-21
As if the eye was an emotion, [Hero 278-25
As if in seeing we saw our feeling [Hero 278-26
Arrives at the man-man as he wanted. [Hero 280-17
Gold-shined by sun, perceiving as I saw [Phenom 287-13
They could not carry much, as soldiers. [Gigan 289-1
As from an inhuman elevation [Gigan 289-18
As if sounds were forming [Dutch 290-17
Men came as the sun comes, early children [Dutch 291-23
As absent as if we were asleep. [Possum 293-4
The curving of her hip, as motionless gesture, [Couch 295-8
The suspension, as in solid space, [Couch 295-13

Without gestures is to get at it as [Couch 295-17
Between the thing as idea and [Couch 295-19
The idea as thing. She is half who made her. [Couch 295-20
As anything but sculpture. Good-bye, [Couch 296-5
The armies are forms in number, as cities are. [Choc 296-12
He was as tall as a tree in the middle of [Choc 297-19
Experience of night, as if he breathed [Choc 298-7
Grew strong, as if doubt never touched his heart. [Choc 299-5
Now, I, Chocorua, speak of this shadow as [Choc 300-16
How singular he was as man, how large, [Choc 302-1
Which, as a man feeling everything, were his. [Somnam 304-18
Only the eye as faculty, that the mind [Crude 305-15
As if nothing had happened. The dim actor spoke. [Repet 306-11
As if they were desperate with a know-and-know, [Repet 307-24
Nor of time. The departing soldier is as he is, [Repet 308-7
A giant without a body. If, as giant, [Repet 308-10
Sharp as white paint in the January sun; [Holiday 312-2
As each had a particular woman and her touch? [Holiday 312-10
As the body trembles at the end of life. [EM 314-7
The moon rose up as if it had escaped [EM 314-24
As night was free from him. The shadow touched [EM 315-1
As if the health of the world might be enough. [EM 315-25
It seems as if the honey of common summer [EM 316-1
Might be enough, as if the golden combs [EM 316-2
As if hell, so modified, had disappeared, [EM 316-4
As if pain, no longer satanic mimicry, [EM 316-5
Could be borne, as if we were sure to find our way. [EM 316-6
Can we conceive of him as rescuing less, [EM 316-20
As muffing the mistress for her several maids, [EM 316-21
As foregoing the nakedest passion for barefoot [EM 316-22
Is as insatiable as the sun's. The bird [EM 318-10
As the eye closes . . . How cold the vacancy [EM 320-6
As if sight had not its own miraculous thrift, [EM 320-26
As if the paradise of meaning ceased [EM 320-28
Another chant, an incantation, as in [EM 321-5
Because she is as she was, reality, [EM 322-1
Of people, as big bell-billows from its bell [EM 322-13
They press it as epicure, distinguishing [EM 323-2
Demands. It accepts whatever is as true, [EM 323-21
For another, as the son's life for the father's. [EM 323-27
Gives one a blank uneasiness, as if [EM 325-9
As if the air, the mid-day air, was swarming [EM 326-10
Merely in living as and where we live. [EM 326-12
Of ideas and to say as usual that there must be [Bed 326-17
This is the habit of wishing, as if one's grandfather lay [Bed
    327-1
In one's heart and wished as he had always wished, unable [Bed
    327-2
Of things as the structure of ideas. It was the structure [Bed
    327-7
Let him move as the sunlight moves on the floor [Less 327-11
Or moonlight, silently, as Plato's ghost [Less 327-12
As those are: as light, for all its motions, is; [Less 327-16
As color, even the closest to us, is; [Less 328-1
As shapes, though they portend us, are. [Less 328-2
As an element; to the sky, as an element. [Wild 328-17
Yet to speak of the whole world as metaphor [Pure 332-8
As one of the secretaries of the moon, [Feo 533-10
Than Tartuffe as myth, the most Moliere, [Paisant 335-10
The baroque poet may see him as still a man [Paisant 335-12
As Virgil, abstract. But see him for yourself, [Paisant 335-13
Crying as that speech falls as if to fail. [Sketch 336-6
It is as if we were never children. [Debris 338-2
That it is as if we had never been young. [Debris 338-4
As the sun is something seeming and it is. [Descrip 339-2
Her time becomes again, as it became, [Descrip 339-15
To be, as on the youngest poet's page, [Descrip 340-20
That speaks for him such seemings as death gives. [Descrip 341-6
Things are as they seemed to Calvin or to Anne [Descrip 341-21
As if they knew of distant beaches; and were [Descrip 343-8
As, men make themselves their speech: the hard hidalgo [Descrip
    345-11
As if Liadoff no longer remained a ghost [Liadoff 347-8
Plomets, as the Herr Gott [Analysis 349-11
As secondary (parts not quite perceived [Man Car 350-18
The words were spoken as if there was no book, [House Q 358-11
As if, in the presence of the sea, [Silent 359-8
Breathing as if they breathed themselves, [Pediment 361-18
The Good Man Has No Shape, as if they knew. [Good Man 364-14
As a tone defines itself and separates [Anach 366-12
As one of the relics of the heart. [Prejudice 368-16
As one of the relics of the mind . . . [Prejudice 368-19
And brain, as the extraordinary references [Extraord 369-13
Postpone the anatomy of summer, as [Cred 373-1
As good. The utmost must be good and is [Cred 374-18
And is the queen humble as she seems to be, [Cred 374-25
As placid air becomes. But it is not [Cred 375-15
As if twelve princes sat before a king. [Cred 375-25
Must take its place, as what is possible [Cred 376-23
Of its cry as clarion, its diction's way [Cred 377-3

As that of a personage in a multitude: [Cred 377-4
Their parts as in a youthful happiness. [Cred 378-10
As of a general being or human universe. [Past Nun 378-22
Never suppose an inventing mind as source [NSF 381-1
As morning throws off stale moonlight and shabby sleep. [NSF
    382-12
Beating in the heart, as if blood newly came, [NSF 382-21
In heaven as in a glass; a second earth; [NSF 383-14
Across the roofs as sigil and as ward [NSF 384-23
An abstraction blooded, as a man by thought. [NSF 385-24
It feels good as it is without the giant, [NSF 386-1
As when the cock crows on the left and all [NSF 386-10
As a man and woman meet and love forthwith. [NSF 386-16
As on an elevation, and behold [NSF 386-20
As if the waves at last were never broken, [NSF 387-16
As if the language suddenly, with ease, [NSF 387-17
More fecund as principle than particle, [NSF 388-19
The bees came booming as if they had never gone, [NSF 389-19
As if hyacinths had never gone. We say [NSF 389-20
As if--The pigeons clatter in the air. [NSF 390-6
Said that as keen, illustrious ornament, [NSF 391-22
As a setting for geraniums, the General, [NSF 391-23
On one another, as a man depends [NSF 392-5
That walk away as one in the greenest body. [NSF 392-15
A mountain, a pineapple pungent as Cuban summer. [NSF 393-12
The lover sighs as for accessible bliss, [NSF 395-4
As in the top-cloud of a May night-evening, [NSF 395-10
As in the courage of the ignorant man, [NSF 395-11
And laid it in the sand. As I am, I am [NSF 395-20
Evade us, as in a senseless element? [NSF 396-24
And so, as part, to exult with its great throat, [NSF 398-9
As when the sun comes rising, when the sea [NSF 398-23
Yet we are shaken by them as if they were. [NSF 399-2
It might and might have been. But as it was, [NSF 400-20
Each must the other take as sign, short sign [NSF 401-14
And Bawda loved the captain as she loved the sun. [NSF 401-18
She looked at them and saw them as they were [NSF 402-11
Beyond which fact could not progress as fact. [NSF 402-22
Beyond which thought could not progress as thought. [NSF 403-10
He imposes order as he thinks of them, [NSF 403-17
As the fox and snake do. It is a brave affair. [NSF 403-19
Whiter than wax, sonorous, fame as it is, [NSF 403-23
To discover. To discover an order as of [NSF 403-23
I have not but I am and as I am, I am. [NSF 405-6
Even so when I think of you as strong or tired, [NSF 406-15
Made us no less as sure. We saw in his head, [AA 412-1
As by a custom or according to [AA 412-6
An ancestral theme or as a consequence [AA 412-7
As one that is strong in the bushes of his eyes. [AA 414-7
This then is Chatillon or as you please. [AA 415-20
As light changes yellow into gold and gold [AA 416-11
Wild wedges, as of a volcano's smoke, palm-eyed [AA 416-17
As grim as it is benevolent, the just [AA 417-5
Except as needed by way of majesty, [AA 417-14
In the sky, as crown and diamond cabala? [AA 417-15
As pure principle. Its nature is its end, [AA 418-11
Almost as predicate. But it exists, [AA 418-17
As if, awake, we lay in the quiet of sleep, [AA 418-24
As if the innocent mother sang in the dark [AA 419-1
We were as Danes in Denmark all day long [AA 419-7
And fattened as on a decorous honeycomb. [AA 419-13
Bare limbs, bare trees and a wind as sharp as salt? [AA 419-21
Almost as part of innocence, almost, [AA 420-2
Almost as the tenderest and the truest part. [AA 420-3
As if he lived all lives, that he might know, [AA 420-24
As if whatever in water strove to speak [Page 422-9
Took on color, took on shape and the size of things as they are
    [Large 424-8
Through many places, as if it stood still in one, [Cata 424-12
As of a character everywhere, [Countryman 429-6
Is changed. It is not so blue as we thought. To be blue, [Ulti
    429-18
In This Beautiful World Of Ours and not as now, [Ulti 430-6
Pink yellows, orange whites, too much as they are [Roses 430-11
Too much as they are to be changed by metaphor, [Roses 430-13
Of yellow as first color and of white, [Roses 431-1
In which the sense lies still, as a man lies, [Roses 431-2
Not as in metaphor, but in our sense [Roses 431-5
And of as many meanings as of men. [Roses 431-9
We are two that use these roses as we are, [Roses 431-10
Keep you, keep you, I am gone, oh keep you as [Owl 432-14
To see their lustre truly as it is [Owl 432-21
A while, conceiving his passage as into a time [Owl 432-23
Like many robings, as moving masses are, [Owl 433-9
As a moving mountain is, moving through day [Owl 433-10
As on water of an afternoon in the wind [Owl 433-18
Hewn in their middle as the beam of leaves, [Owl 434-2
Underground, a king as candle by our beds [Owl 435-2
Almost as speed discovers, in the way [Owl 435-10
Extremest pinch and, easily, as in [John 437-1

As at the moment of the year when, tick, [John 437-4
Its irrational reaction, as from pain. [John 437-26
Of secluded thunder, an illusion, as it was, [Orb 441-1
Oh as, always too heavy for the sense [Orb 441-2
To seize, the obscurest as, the distant was . . . [Orb 441-3
As if the central poem became the world, [Orb 441-19
Of the other, as if summer was a spouse, [Orb 441-21
Of blue light and of green, as lesser poems, [Orb 442-2
And scintillant sizzlings such as children like, [Orb 442-20
As in a signed photograph on a mantelpiece. [Orb 443-2
As a part, but part, but tenacious particle, [Orb 443-18
"Metaphor as Degeneration" [444-title
If there is a man white as marble [Degen 444-1
As victory. The poet does not speak in ruins [Papini 446-10
As in an enchantment, analyzed and fixed [Papini 447-20
The bouquet stands in a jar, as metaphor, [Bouquet 448-8
As lightning itself is, likewise, metaphor [Bouquet 448-9
The meta-men behold the idea as part [Bouquet 449-22
Toward a consciousness of red and white as one, [Bouquet 450-9
And crawls on them, as if feathers of the duck [Bouquet 450-17
In other shapes, as if duck and tablecloth [Bouquet 450-19
Themselves an issue as at an end, as if [Our Stars 455-21
The fire burns as the novel taught it how. [Novel 458-3
To understand, as if to know became [Novel 459-5
At twelve, as green as ever they would be. [What We 459-11
Twelve meant as much as: the end of normal time, [What We 459-13
The seal is as relaxed as dirt, perdu. [Golden 460-18
Except that the grandson sees it as it is, [Questions 462-9
As far as nothingness permits . . . Hear him. [Questions 463-1
A waking, as in images we awake, [Study I 463-8
As if the centre of images had its [Study II 464-10
Rose--women as half-fishes of salt shine, [Study II 464-15
As if, as if, as if the disparate halves [Study II 464-16
As part of the never-ending meditation, [NH 465-7
As if the crude collops came together as one, [NH 466-1
A porcelain, as yet in the bats thereof. [NH 467-5
As: the last plainness of a man who has fought [NH 467-17
Of dreams, disillusion as the last illusion, [NH 468-11
Reality as a thing seen by the mind, [NH 468-12
Everything as unreal as real can be, [NH 468-18
Searched out such majesty as it could find. [NH 469-3
Out of rigid realists. It is as if [NH 470-4
Men turning into things, as comedy, [NH 470-5
The truth about themselves, having lost, as things, [NH 470-7
That power to conceal they had as men, [NH 470-8
Not merely as to depth but as to height [NH 470-9
But, also, as to their miraculous, [NH 470-11
As that which was incredible becomes, [NH 470-14
To the lover, and blue, as of a secret place [NH 470-21
As a quick answer modifies a question, [NH 471-6
In a faithfulness as against the lunar light, [NH 472-15
The poet speaks the poem as it is, [NH 473-18
Not as it was: part of the reverberation [NH 473-19
Of a windy night as it is, when the marble statues [NH 473-20
By sight and insight as they are. There is no [NH 473-22
Resembling the presences of thoughts, as if, [NH 474-6
Of baker and butcher blowing, as if to hear, [NH 475-2
The gay tournamonde as of a single world [NH 476-3
In which he is and as and is are one. [NH 476-4
As a serious strength rejects pin-idleness. [NH 477-14
In the present state of things as, say, to paint [NH 478-6
As if the eyes were the present or part of it, [NH 478-10
As if the ears heard any shocking sound, [NH 478-11
As if life and death were ever physical. [NH 478-12
Or thinks he does, as he perceives the present, [NH 478-17
For reality is as momentous as [NH 481-5
As of a long, inevitable sound, [NH 482-7
Being part of everything come together as one. [NH 482-11
As rain and booming, gleaming, blowing, swept [NH 484-10
Seen as inamorata, of loving fame [NH 484-14
Touches, as one hand touches another hand, [NH 484-19
Or as a voice that, speaking without form, [NH 484-20
As the fore-meaning in music is." Again, [NH 485-12
As the life of poetry. A more severe, [NH 486-6
As it is, in the intricate evasions of as, [NH 486-10
Have liberty not as the air within a grave [Aug 490-12
Not as the fragrance of Persephone, [Aug 491-10
But as of an exhumation returned to earth, [Aug 491-12
This chorus as of those that wanted to live. [Aug 491-18
The thinker as reader reads what has been written. [Aug 492-4
The world? The inhuman as human? That which thinks not, [Aug
    493-3
In which he exists but never as himself. [Aug 493-8
As if on a taller tower [Aug 493-15
The total of human shadows bright as glass. [Aug 494-23
As in a hermitage, for us to think, [Aug 495-15
It is as he was, [Irish 502-6
To a plain sense of things. It is as if [Plain 502-10
Had to be imagined as an inevitable knowledge, [Plain 503-7
Required, as a necessity requires. [Plain 503-8

With what he is and as he is, [Leben 505-8
It is as if in a human dignity [Rome 508-8
Speak to your pillow as if it was yourself. [Rome 509-9
As in the last drop of the deepest blood, [Rome 509-26
Even as the blood of an empire, it might be, [Rome 510-1
As if the design of all his words takes form [Rome 511-2
The breath of another nature as his own, [Two Illus 513-15
From his project, as finally magnified. [Two Illus 515-4
Gripping their oars, as if they were sure of the way to their
    destination, [Prol 515-7
As at a point of central arrival, an instant moment, much or
    little, [Prol 516-8
As if all his hereditary lights were suddenly increased [Prol
    517-1
We think, then, as the sun shines or does not. [Look 518-23
We think as wind skitters on a pond in a field [Look 518-24
A glass aswarm with things going as far as they can. [Look
    519-12
"The World as Meditation" [520-title
The trees had been mended, as an essential exercise [World 521-4
The trees have a look as if they bore sad names [Slug 522-5
As, for example, a world in which, like snow, [Quiet 523-4
Light the first light of evening, as in a room [Final 524-1
As if nothingness contained a métier, [Rock 526-1
The Poem as Icon [Rock 526-title 2
They bloom as a man loves, as he lives in love. [Rock 527-11
As if its understanding was brown skin, [Rock 527-13
Night's hymn of the rock, as in a vivid sleep. [Rock 528-21
In that which is created as its symbol. [Armor 529-16
The need to be actual and as it is. [Armor 530-1
And there he walks and does as he lives and likes. [Armor 530-22
It is as if being was to be observed, [Moonlight 531-5
As if, among the possible purposes [Moonlight 531-6
In the arbors that are as if of Saturn-star. [Moonlight 531-18
As if some Old Man of the Chimney, sick [Phases 5-6 P
Stiff as stone, [Phases 5-20 P
It seizes a sheet, from the ground, from a bush, as if spread
    there by some wash-woman for the night. [Plough-Boy 6-5 P
I take all things as stated--so and so [Soldat 11-7 P
If I should fall, as soldier, I know well [Soldat 11-10 P
Would taste, precisely, as they said it would. [Soldat 11-12 P
As they enter the place of their western [Soldat 12-8 P
As for a child in an oblivion: [Soldat 13-16 P
Or gaudy as tulips? [Archi 17-8 P
Or melancholy crows as shadowing clouds? [Stan MMO 19-18 P
All, as Andromache, [Parasol 20-4 P
As large ferocious tigers are. [Parasol 20-10 P
As the gum of the gum-tree. [Lulu G 26-22 P
And wronging her, if only as she thinks, [Red Kit 30-15 P
As the moon has in its moonlight, worlds away, [Red Kit 31-8 P
As the sea has in its coastal clamorings. [Red Kit 31-9 P
And equally as scientist you walked [Good Bad 33-15 P
Is at the bottom of her as pique-pain [Spaniard 34-22 P
As a seraglio-parrot; feel disdain [Spaniard 35-11 P
Nobly as autumn moves. [Secret Man 36-12 P
But they are empty as balloons [Drum-Majors 37-1 P
Perception as an act of intelligence [Lytton 39-6 P
And perception as an act of grace [Lytton 39-7 P
As one. [Room Gard 41-3 P
Stood stiffly, as if the black of what she thought [Old Woman
    44-24 P
Triumphant as that always upward wind [Old Woman 44-27 P
Now felt, now known as this. The clouds of bronze [Old Woman
    45-4 P
It was as if transparence touched her mind. [Old Woman 45-9 P
As a place in which each thing was motionless [Old Woman 45-21P
They are horses as they were in the sculptor's mind. [Burnshaw
    46-18 P
Ugly as an idea, not beautiful [Burnshaw 47-7 P
As sequels without thought. In the rudest red [Burnshaw 47-8 P
As if your gowns were woven of the light [Burnshaw 51-24 P
Yet were not bright, came shining as things come [Burnshaw 51-25P
As brilliant as mystic, as mystic as single, all [Greenest 55-9P
As summer would return to weazened days. [Greenest 57-27 P
Each look and each necessitous cry, as a god [Greenest 59-8 P
The workers do not rise, as Venus rose, [Duck 60-9 P
Are the cities to breed as mountains bred, the streets [Duck
    61-3 P
Day came upon the spirit as life comes [Duck 61-5 P
Their destiny is just as much machine [Duck 61-21 P
As death itself, and never can be changed [Duck 61-22 P
Are all men thinking together as one, thinking [Duck 62-19 P
As evils, and if reason, fatuous fire, [Duck 63-4 P
As the man the state, not as the state the man, [Duck 63-9 P
As by a juicier season; and more our own [Duck 65-4 P
As against each other, the dead, the phantomesque. [Duck 65-5 P
Of heaven from heaven to the future, as a god, [Duck 65-27 P
Imagines and it is true, as if he thought [Sombre 66-20 P
He was born within us as a second self, [Sombre 67-3 P
As of insects of cloud-stricken birds, away [Sombre 67-11 P

As a church is a bell and people are an eye, [Sombre 67-19 P
As if it bears all darkness in its bulk. [Sombre 68-18 P
Each one as part of the total wrath, obscure [Sombre 69-5 P
Poised, but poised as the mind through which a storm [Sombre
    69-27 P
Lived as the man lives now, and hated, loved, [Sombre 69-33 P
As the man hates now, loves now, the self-same things. [Sombre
    70-1 P
In marble, but marble massive as the thrust [Sombre 70-24 P
The oranges glitter as part of the sky, [Stan MBG 72-13 P
And then things are not as they are. [Stan MBG 72-16 P
I still intend things as they are. [Stan MBG 73-4 P
In such an air, poor as one's mule. [Stan MBG 73-11 P
True, things are people as they are. [Stan MBG 73-18 P
Of her airs, as surely cologne as that she was bone [Grotesque
    74-6 P
For itself as a world, [Grotesque 76-15 P
As others have, and then, unlike the others, [Bship 77-23 P
My cabin as the center of the ship and I [Bship 78-6 P
As the center of the cabin, the center of [Bship 78-7 P
As man is natural, would be at an end." [Bship 78-19 P
Regulae mundi, as apprentice of [Bship 78-21 P
As the final simplification is meant to be. [Bship 78-30 P
As of a make-believe. [Bship 79-16 P
Gone, as in Calypso's isle or in Citare, [Bship 79-24 P
As a man among other men, divested [Stan Hero 84-10 P
Now. War as a punishment. The hero [Stan Hero 84-16 P
As hangman, a little sick of blood, of [Stan Hero 84-17 P
It was to be as mad as everyone was, [Desire 85-10 P
As if in a golden cloud. The son restores [Recit 87-16 P
"This as Including That" [88-title P
That move in the air as large as air, [Including 88-10 P
Bang cymbals as they used to do. [Memo 89-15 P
As a questioner about reality, [Warmth 89-18 P
And thus an elevation, as if I lived [Warmth 90-5 P
"As at a Theatre" [91-title P
As if, alone on a mountain, it saw far-off [Pagoda 92-5 P
Part of the unpredictable sproutings, as of [Nuns 92-8 P
These things he thinks of, as the buckskin hoop-la, [Americana
    94-13 P
In the much-horned night, as its chief personage. [Souls 94-17 P
Are dissolved as in an infancy of blue snow. [Discov 95-11 P
One feels the life of that which gives life as it is. [Course
    96-18 P
As its autumnal terminal-- [Fare Guit 98-21 P
He said, "As I know, I am and have [Ulysses 99-13 P
As he is, the discipline of his scope [Ulysses 101-14 P
Observed as an absolute, himself. [Ulysses 101-15 P
As a free race. We know it, one [Ulysses 102-4 P
To know established as the right to be. [Ulysses 102-11 P
As if abstractions were, themselves [Ulysses 103-26 P
The self as sibyl. whose diamond, [Ulysses 104-11 P
As these depend, so must they use. [Ulysses 104-23 P
As if another sail went on [Ulysses 105-10 P
He said, "As I know, I am and have [Presence 105-16 P
As if we were all seated together again [Letters 107-13 P
Should be as natural as natural objects, [Conversat 109-4 P
Persist as facts. This is an escape [Sol Oaks 111-6 P
Objects not present as a matter of course [Local 112-1 P
For which a fresh name always occurred, as if [Local 112-5 P
As toward an absolute foyer beyond romance. [Local 112-12 P
As they were fifty years ago, [Clear Day 113-9 P
As if none of us had ever been here before [Clear Day 113-17 P
A churchyard kind of bush as well, [Banjo 114-6 P
A silent sort of bush, as well. [Banjo 114-7 P
As in a page of poetry-- [July 115-1 P
About the mind as never satisfied, [As Leave 117-2 P
As a disbeliever in reality, [As Leave 117-6 P
And thus an elevation, as if I left [As Leave 117-11 P
Unreal, as if nothing had been changed at all. [As Leave 117-14 P
I drink from it, dry as it is, [Three 129-3 P
As you from maxims, [Three 129-4 P
Just as it is true of poets, [Three 129-13 P
As abstract as porcelain, [Three 131-14 P
As the court knew it. [Three 131-16 P
As it gazed [Three 131-20 P
That we are painted as warriors, [Three 132-25 P
That we are painted as three dead men, [Three 133-2 P
At the window, as before. [Three 134-15 P
As there are sides to a round bottle. [Three 136-16 P
As beautiful. [Three 136-18 P
She was as beautiful as a porcelain water bottle. [Three 136-19P
As young. [Three 137-2 P
She was represented as clinging [Three 138-7 P
As you say, [Three 138-23 P
And as the red of the sun [Three 143-4 P
As red is multiplied by the leaves of trees. [Three 143-14 P
The root of a form, as of this fruit, a fund [Someone 83-5 A
It is as if there were three planets: the sun, [Someone 83-11 A
Yet, as it seems, of human residence. [Someone 84-3 A

He seeks as image a second of the self, [Someone 84-7 A
He seeks an image certain as meaning is [Someone 84-12 A
As a part of the nature that he contemplates [Someone 84-17 A
Of Capricorn or as the sign demands, [Someone 86-18 A
As the total reality. Therefore it is [Someone 87-13 A
As of sections collecting toward the greenest cone. [Someone
  87-21 A
ASCENDED. To which the spirit ascended, to increase [Greenest 53-29P
  Like glitter ascended into fire. [Ulysses 102-17 P
ASCENDING. Of the ascending of the dead. [Cortege 80-15
  So that he was the ascending wings he saw [NSF 403-4
  Made by the sun ascending seventy seas. [Burnshaw 47-29 P
  Ascending the humane. This is the form [Recit 87-20 P
ASCENDS. Of clay and wattles made as it ascends [Page 421-11
ASCENT. Anabasis or slump, ascent or chute, [C 43-21
ASCENTS. The wooden ascents [Cortege 80-14
ASCERTAINABLE. On a given plane is ascertainable [Nigger 157-8
ASCETIC. An anti-master-man, floribund ascetic. [Landsc 241-10
  As acutest virtue and ascetic trove. [Montra 263-12
  In an ascetic room, its table [Hero 275-28
ASCETICALLY. Of more or less, ascetically sated [Woman Had 82-5 P
ASH. Burn everything not part of it to ash. [Cred 373-5
  Can I take fire from so benign an ash? [Stan MMO 19-7 P
  Which, from the ash within it, fortifies [Someone 83-17 A
  A green that is the ash of what green is, [Someone 83-18 A
ASHEN. Ashen man on ashen cliff above the salt halloo, [NE Verses
  105-7
  O ashen admiral of the hale, hard blue. . . . [NE Verses 105-8
  As if I lived in ashen ground, as if [Farewell 117-12
  It rose, ashen and red and yellow, each [Page 422-12
  I have neither ashen wing nor wear of ore [Angel 496-9
ASHES. These are the ashes of fiery weather, [Our Stars 455-13
ASHORE. Men would be starting at dawn to walk ashore. [Page 422-5
ASIA. The sun of Asia creeps above the horizon [Nigger 153-8
  Ruled us before, from over Asia, by [Montra 262-14
  There must be mercy in Asia and divine [Montra 262-16
ASIDE. At the finger that brushes this aside [Ulysses 101-1 P
ASIDES. "Asides on the Oboe" [250-title
ASK. Ask us not to sing standing in the sun, [Orangeade 102-17
  That we should ask this often as she sang. [Key W 129-9
  This it is that answers when I ask, [Yellow 236-5
  We ask which means most, for us, all the genii [Antag 425-15
  Poor procurator, why do you ask someone else [Papini 446-1
  Milord, I ask you, though you will to sing, [Red Kit 31-16 P
  Ask of the philosopher why he philosophizes, [Role 93-3 P
ASKED. Consider that I had asked [Desire 85-14 P
  He asked me to walk with him [Three 141-12 P
ASKEW. To be askew. And space is filled with his [EM 318-7
ASKING. The florist asking aid from cabbages, [C 37-16
  One goes on asking questions. That, then, is one [Ulti 429-16
  Will, Will, but how and all of them asking how [Duck 61-29 P
ASLEEP. After the guitar is asleep, [Venereal 47-21
  Drunk and asleep in his boots, [Ten O'C 66-13
  As absent as if we were asleep. [Possum 293-14
  And to the mother as she falls asleep [AA 413-22
  "An Old Man Asleep" [501-title
  The two worlds are asleep, are sleeping, now. [Old Man 501-1
  On which men speculated in summer when they were half asleep.
  [Prol 516-15
  A child asleep in its own life. [Ulysses 104-22 P
  "A Child Asleep in Its Own Life" [106-title P
  See half-asleep.
ASPECT. An ancient aspect touching a new mind. [Monocle 16-2
  Picked up its radial aspect in the night, [NH 478-23
  At another time, the radial aspect came [NH 479-2
  Of that century and of its aspect, a personage, [NH 479-5
  What is the radial aspect of this place, [NH 479-10
  Or of a new aspect, bright in discovery-- [Aug 489-7
  Or else a new aspect, say the spirit's sex, [Aug 489-12
ASPECTS. Increases the aspects of experience, [Papini 447-19
ASPHALT. Below me, on the asphalt, under the trees. [Loaf 200-12
ASPIC. How is it that your aspic nipples [Carolinas 5-2
  Life is a bitter aspic. We are not [EM 322-9
ASPIRIN. See Canon Aspirin.
ASPIRING. A clown, perhaps, but an aspiring clown. [C 39-24
ASSAILED. Lacustrine man had never been assailed [Geneva 24-4
ASSASSIN. Of love and summer. The assassin sings [Extracts 256-8
  Of the assassin that remains and sings [Extracts 256-15
  The assassin flash and rumble . . . He was denied. [EM 320-1
  The assassin's scene. Evil in evil is [EM 324-18
  Comparative. The assassin discloses himself. [EM 324-19
  And daunt that old assassin, heart's desire? [Duck 66-11 P
ASSASSINS. In the end, these philosophic assassins pull [Extracts
  256-1
  A paradise full of assassins. Suppose I seize [Bship 77-20 P
  Once the assassins wore stone masks and did [Bship 78-15 P
ASSAULTED. Summer assaulted, thundering, illumed, [Thought 186-9
ASSEMBLES. That a new glory of new men assembles. [Dutch 292-23
ASSERTING. Asserting itself in an element that is free. [Pagoda
  92-1 P

ASSERTION. In a queer assertion of humanity: [Rock 525-15
ASSERTS. On The Masculine one asserts and fires the guns. [Bship
  80-7 P
ASSIGNS. Untroubled by suffering, which fate assigns [Old Woman
  46-6 P
ASSOCIATES. In an ecstasy of its associates, [EM 316-13
ASSOCIATION. In an association like yours [Including 88-13 P
ASSOCIATIONS. And the associations beyond death, even if only
  [Lack 303-13
ASSUAGED. Who most fecundly assuaged him, the softest [EM 321-14
ASSUAGEMENT. They only know a savage assuagement cries [NH 467-22
ASSUME. Did several spirits assume a single shape? [Les Plus 245-7
  Perhaps, these colors, seen in insight, assume [Bouquet 451-22
ASSUMES. He assumes the great speeds of space and flutters them
  [AA 414-14
  Assumes a pale, Italianate sheen-- [Abnormal 24-6 P
ASSUMPTION. A vital assumption, an impermanence [Rock 526-2
ASTRAL. Wooden, the model for astral apprentices, [NH 478-19
  Astral and Shelleyan, diffuse new day; [Burnshaw 47-26 P
ASTRAY. Led the emperor astray, the torn trumpets [Hero 278-7
ASTRIDE. Man-misty to a race star-humped, astride [Sombre 70-29 P
ASTRINGENT. The chrysanthemums' astringent fragrance comes [Nigger
  157-1
  Disdaining each astringent ripening, [EM 318-20
ASTRONOMER. Afraid, the blind man as astronomer, [C 37-18
ASTRONOMERS. It is she that walks among astronomers. [Candle 223-2
  The self-same madness of the astronomers [Candle 223-8
  And of him that sees, beyond the astronomers, [Candle 223-9
ASTRONOMIES. For that, or a motion not in the astronomies, [Page
  422-17
ASTRONOMY. As apples fall, without astronomy, [Montra 262-7
  Inscribes a primitive astronomy [NSF 383-3
ASTUTE. That tragic prattle of the fates, astute [Spaniard 34-16 P
  Astute in being what they are made to be. [Art Pop 112-20 P
ASWARM. A glass aswarm with things going as far as they can. [Look
  519-12
ASYLUM. Each man in his asylum maundering, [Sombre 68-10 P
ATE. Philadelphia that the spiders ate. [Arcades 225-3
  We drank Meursault, ate lobster Bombay with mango [NSF 401-22
  And if we ate the incipient colorings [Rock 526-16
  Oh! Sal, the butcher's wife ate clams [Lulu M 27-9 P
ATHENS. He had written them near Athens. The farm was white. [Anach
  366-1
  Convinces Athens with its quack. [Grotesque 75-13 P
ATHOS. Remoter than Athos, the effulgent hordes [Greenest 56-22 P
ATLANTIC. In radiance from the Atlantic coign, [C 31-32
  Star over Monhegan, Atlantic star, [Vari 232-15
  And the sheeted Atlantic. [Inhab 504-5
  Say that in the clear Atlantic night [Memo 89-13 P
  See mid-Atlantic.
ATLAS. The bijou of Atlas, the moon, [Public Sq 109-11
ATMOSPHERE. A perfect fruit in perfect atmosphere. [NE Verses 106-9
  Perceived in a final atmosphere; [MBG 168-2
  Is the riches of their atmosphere. [MBG 172-12
  Lashing at images in the atmosphere, [Page 422-29
  Then he breathed deeply the deep atmosphere [Owl 433-23
  Of dulce atmosphere, the fore of lofty scenes [Bouquet 450-3
  At last, in that blond atmosphere, bronzed hard, [NH 487-2
  That, in the shadowless atmosphere, [Aug 493-17
  The stage becomes an atmosphere [Soldat 15-19 P
  This atmosphere in which the horses rose, [Old Woman 44-19 P
  This atmosphere in which her musty mind [Old Woman 44-20 P
  Were the fluid, the cat-eyed atmosphere, in which [Sombre 68-13P
ATMOSPHERES. On high horizons, mountainous atmospheres [Key W
  129-21
  In the crystal atmospheres of the mind, [Ulysses 102-27 P
ATOM. But nakedness, woolen massa, concerns an innermost atom.
  [Nudity Cap 145-10
ATTACH. It seemed haphazard denouement. [C 40-25
ATTAIN. Of the fertile thing that can attain no more. [Cred 373-15
  These lights may finally attain a pole [AA 411-14
  To know what helps and to attain, [Ulysses 104-29 P
ATTAINED. Having attained a present blessedness, [Past Nun 378-12
ATTAINMENT. Not an attainment of the will [Ulysses 101-26 P
ATTAINS. The mind herein attains simplicity. [Tallap 71-14
ATTEMPT. "Attempt to Discover Life" [370-title
ATTEND. Is breathless to attend each quirky turn. [Monocle 15-13
  With rubies then, attend me now. [Country 207-15
  My beards, attend [Extracts 253-16
  At evening, things that attend it until it hears [AA 414-18
  Or stars that follow men, not to attend, [Angel 496-11
ATTENDANT. Came her attendant Byzantines. [Peter 91-13
  The wind attendant on the solstices [Pharynx 96-5
  The moon they made their own attendant ghosts, [Eve Angels 137-11
  Parades of whole races with attendant bands, [Duck 66-2 P
ATTENDED. Attended [Idiom 201-4
ATTENDS. The air attends the brightened guns, [Dutch 290-16
  Now, closely the ear attends the varying [Pure 332-2
  And, now, it attends the difficult difference. [Pure 332-5
  She attends the tintinnabula-- [Hermit 505-15

ATTENTION. Exacted attention with attentive force. [Bouquet 450-21
  The leaves cry. It is not a cry of divine attention, [Course
  96-19 P
ATTENTIONS. Snarling in him for discovery as his attentions
  spread, [Prol 516-17
ATTENTIVE. Attentive to a coronal of things [C 44-14
  The forms that are attentive in thin air. [Descrip 344-14
  Exacted attention with attentive force. [Bouquet 450-21
  With its attentive eyes. And, as he stood, [NH 483-11
ATTIC. But you, ephebe, look from your attic window, [NSF 384-17
  An attic glass, hums of the old Lutheran bells [Golden 460-13
ATTITUDES. Arranged its heroic attitudes. [Hartford 227-3
  Its attitudes, its answers to attitudes [Aug 489-13
  From which they came, make real the attitudes [Burnshaw 52-3 P
ATTRIBUTES. With all his attributes no god but man [Thought 186-11
  Of ex-bar, in-bar retaining attributes [EM 317-24
  Of attributes, naked of myth, true, [Stan Hero 84-11 P
ATTRIBUTIONS. The attributions, the plume and helmet-ho." [NH
  485-15
AUBURN. The total gala of auburn aureoles. [Nigger 154-18
AUDIBLE. Audible at noon, pain torturing itself, [EM 314-4
  It is the visible rock, the audible, [Cred 375-17
  His eye and audible in the mountain of [NSF 403-2
  Or partly his. His voice is audible, [NH 485-11
AUDIENCE. Of which, an invisible audience listens, [Of Mod 240-10
  The audience beholds you, not your gown. [Bad Time 427-9
  A larger poem for a larger audience, [NH 465-18
  And audience to mimics glistening [Sombre 67-24 P
AUDITOR. This auditor of insects! He that saw [C 31-2
AUGUST. And August the most peaceful month. [Rabbit K 209-6
  "Thou art not August unless I make thee so." [Oboe 251-5
  Lie sprawling in majors of the August heat, [EM 325-28
  Tinsel in February, tinsel in August. [Pieces 351-9
  The tinsel of August falling was like a flame [Pieces 352-2
  When the harmonious heat of August pines [NSF 399-18
  "Things of August" [489-title
  The sort of thing that August crooners sing, [Aug 489-9
  "Reality Is an Activity of the Most August Imagination" [110-
  title P
  On an August night, [Three 127-5 P
AUGUSTA. Or: Gawks of hay . . . Augusta Moon, before [Golden
  460-12
AUNT. "Colloquy with a Polish Aunt" [84-title
  ("The Naked Eye of the Aunt") [Stan MMO 19-subtitle P
AUNTS. The aunts in Pasadena, remembering, [Hartford 226-11
AUREOLE. The aureole above the humming house . . . [Beard 247-24
  And live without a tepid aureole, [Angel 496-10
  So she, when in her mystic aureole [Red Kit 31-10 P
AUREOLES. The total gala of auburn aureoles. [Nigger 154-18
  Still weaving budded aureoles, [Postcard 159-14
  Return, affecting roseate aureoles, [Greenest 56-23 P
  In aureoles that are over-dazzling crests . . . [Nuns 92-20 P
AURORAL. So maidens die, to the auroral [Peter 92-6
  To the auroral creature musing in the mind. [Montra 263-24
AURORAS. "The Auroras of Autumn" [411-title
AUSTERITY. In poems of plums, the strict austerity [C 30-8
AUTHOR. Better without an author, without a poet, [Creat 310-18
  Or having a separate author, a different poet, [Creat 311-1
  Of an inhuman author, who meditates [Cred 377-22
  Himself. The author of man's canons is man, [Conversat 109-14 P
AUTOMATON. The automaton, in logic self-contained, [Les Plus 245-5
AUTO-WORKS. Of people, round the auto-works: [News 264-12
AUTUMN. Into the autumn weather, splashed with frost, [Monocle
  16-7
  The stride of vanishing autumn in a park [C 31-3
  Autumn's compendium, strident in itself [C 45-23
  Emotions on wet roads on autumn nights; [Sunday 67-23
  The blackbird whirled in the autumn winds. [Thirteen 93-1
  As in a season of autumn. [Soldier 97-2
  As in a season of autumn, [Soldier 97-8
  The purple dress in autumn and the belfry breath [NE Verses
  106-7
  She walks an autumn ampler than the wind [Anatomy 108-3
  It was autumn and falling stars [Reader 147-1
  In the far South the sun of autumn is passing [Nigger 150-9
  Against the autumn winds [Nigger 152-3
  In an autumn that will be perpetual. [Nigger 152-4
  As an autumn ancient underneath the snow, [Nigger 154-2
  Like these, autumn beguiles the fatalist. [Nigger 155-5
  Noble in autumn, yet nobler than autumn. [Nigger 156-12
  There is no such thing as innocence in autumn, [Nigger 157-12
  One of the leaves that have fallen in autumn? [Nigger 158-12
  And that in autumn, when the grapes [Postcard 159-1
  "Autumn Refrain" [160-title
  Like a buzzing of flies in autumn air, [MBG 166-20
  Of autumn's halloo in its hair. So that closely, then,
  [Parochial 192-2
  The fragrance of the autumn warmest, [On Road 204-11
  It is summer and it is not, it is autumn [Cuisine 228-2
  And, arbored and bronzed, in autumn. [Yellow 236-12

I dreamed, of autumn rivers, silvas green, [Montra 263-2
True autumn stands then in the doorway. [Hero 280-22
How did we come to think that autumn [Hero 280-26
You like it under the trees in autumn, [Motive 288-1
Let Phoebus slumber and die in autumn umber, [NSF 381-9
"The Auroras of Autumn" [411-title
Autumn howls upon half-naked summer. But [John 437-5
Day's arches are crumbling into the autumn night. [Novel 458-16
So, after summer, in the autumn air, [NH 468-5
Becomes the rock of autumn, glittering, [NH 476-10
Wreathed round and round the round wreath of autumn. [NH 486-18
The forgetful color of the autumn day [Aug 494-16
Of autumn days." [Inhab 504-15
The magnum wreath of summer, time's autumn snood, [Rock 526-21
In the rushes of autumn wind [Secret Man 36-2 P
To embrace autumn, without turning [Secret Man 36-3 P
Nobly as autumn moves. [Secret Man 36-12 P
The man of autumn, [Secret Man 36-13 P
So much the sculptor had foreseen: autumn, [Old Woman 43-5 P
A woman walking in the autumn leaves, [Old Woman 45-18 P
Of autumn, these horses should go clattering [Burnshaw 47-9 P
Long autumn sheens and pittering sounds like sounds [Burnshaw
  47-24 P
In an autumn afternoon, but two immense [Burnshaw 50-4 P
Pronouncing its new life and ours, not autumn's prodigal
  returned, [Discov 96-4 P
See mid-autumn.
AUTUMN-AFTERWARDS. And those the leaves of autumn-afterwards,
  [Sombre 69-31 P
AUTUMNAL. Hinted autumnal farewells of academic death. [NE Verses
  106-8
  Much more than that. Autumnal passages [Grapes 111-1
  There is a rumble of autumnal marching, [Dutch 291-3
  Rumbling along the autumnal horizon, [Dutch 293-7
  To the first autumnal inhalations, young broods [Cred 372-6
  Leaves burnished in autumnal burnished trees [NH 474-3
  Of autumnal space becomes [Leben 505-5
  Soother and lustier than this vexed, autumnal exhalation,
  [Inelegance 25-17 P
  Swirled round them in immense autumnal sounds. [Old Woman 43-21P
  As its autumnal terminal-- [Fare Guit 98-21 P
AUTUMNS. Leaves of the autumns in which the man below [Sombre
  69-32 P
AVAILS. You say that spite avails her nothing, that [Good Bad 33-8P
AVANT. The grackles sing avant the spring [Snow Stars 133-1
AVENGE. Not wisdom. Can all men, together, avenge [Nigger 158-11
AVENGES. But the wise man avenges by building his city in snow.
  [Nigger 158-13
AVERSION. An aversion, as the world is averted [Bottle 239-9
AVERT. Of the object. The singers had to avert themselves [Cred
  376-3
  Or else avert the object. Deep in the woods [Cred 376-4
AVERTED. And your averted stride [Nigger 152-12
  An aversion, as the world is averted [Bottle 239-9
AVIGNON. Roma ni Avignon ni Leyden, [Hero 273-2
  In its own dirt, said Avignon was [Hero 273-9
AVILED. That generation's dream, aviled [MBG 183-15
AVOID. But my destroyers avoid the museums. [Nigger 153-13
  To avoid the bright, discursive wings, [Adequacy 243-14
  To avoid the hap-hallow hallow-ho [Adequacy 243-15
  Avoid our stale perfections, seeking out [Dutch 293-1
AVOIRDUPOIS. Romantic with dreams of her avoirdupois, green glade
  [Pure 330-17
AVOWAL. Of recognition, avowal, impassioned cry, [NH 471-3
AVUNCULAR. What avunvular cloud-man beamier than spears? [Greenest
  52-25 P
AWAIT. Await an arrival, [Inhab 503-17
AWAITING. To none, awaiting espousal to the sound [Study II 464-18
AWAKE. Most sisterly to the first, not yet awake [C 44-17
  As if awake [Peacocks 58-7
  To his breath that lies awake at night. [MBG 171-16
  We ought not to be awake. It is from this [Debris 338-5
  As if, awake, we lay in the quiet of sleep, [AA 418-24
  Yet Hans lay wide awake. And live alone [Page 422-3
  A waking, as in images we awake, [Study I 463-8
  See half-awake.
AWAKEN. When people awaken [Fading 139-4
  We more than awaken, sit on the edge of sleep, [NSF 386-19
AWAKENED. Like her remembrance of awakened birds, [Sunday 68-24
AWAKENING. Perhaps there are moments of awakening, [NSF 386-17
AWAKENS. Whose mere savage presence awakens the world in which
  she dwells. [World 520-16
AWARE. Aware of exquisite thought. The storm was one [C 32-31
  With his lunacy. He would not be aware of the lake. [EM 325-11
  In a world of ideas. He would not be aware of the clouds, [EM
  325-15
  A mind exists, aware of division, aware [Cred 377-2
AWASH. Like watery words awash; like meanings said [Angel 497-4
AWAY. Crispin was washed away by magnitude. [C 28-17
  If not, when all is said, to drive away [C 37-7

It made, away from the muck of the land [How Live 126-6
Turned tip and tip away, [Pascagoula 127-3
Run away. [Brave 138-12
Run away. [Brave 138-15
Run away. [Brave 138-18
The archbishop is away, The church is gray. [Gray 140-1
He is away. The church is gray. [Gray 140-9
If thinking could be blown away [Nigger 153-5
Gray grasses rolling windily away [Nigger 155-14
To be falling and to be passing away. [MBG 179-12
Throw away the lights, the definitions, [MBG 183-3
Throw the lights away. Nothing must stand [MBG 183-10
Enough to hide away the face of the man [Dames 206-7
And then nowhere again, away and away? [Dames 206-13
The red cat hides away in the fur-light [Rabbit K 209-20
Now, every muscle slops away. [Hartford 227-9
The thought of her takes her away. [Scavoir 231-14
He brushed away the thunder, then the clouds, [Landsc 241-11
I have wiped away moonlight like mud. Your innocent ear [Uruguay
   249-5
His crust away eats of this meat, drinks [Hero 278-16
Flew close to, flew to without rising away. [God 285-8
Like seeing fallen brightly away. [Possum 294-5
The sounding shallow, until by water washed away. [Somnam 304-6
By water washed away. They follow after. [Somnam 304-8
They follow, follow, follow, in water washed away. [Somnam 304-8
At the railway station, a soldier steps away, [Repet 308-3
Still promises perfections cast away. [EM 318-25
Away. The night-flies acknowledge these planets, [Myrrh 349-16
The wind is like a dog that runs away. [Pieces 352-5
And throws it away like a thing of another time, [NSF 382-11
That walk away as one in the greenest body. [NSF 392-15
And one that chaffers the time away? [NSF 396-19
Away, a little rusty, a little rouged, [NSF 400-14
And normal things had yawned themselves away, [NSF 402-20
Away--and tells and tells the water tells [Bouquet 449-20
That I stay away. These are the words of José . . . [Novel 457-12
Around and away, resembling the presence of thought, [NH 474-5
Away from them, capes, along the afternoon Sound, [NH 484-7
The wind has blown the silence of summer away. [NH 487-13
It was something imagined that has been washed away. [NH 488-2
It is like a boat that has pulled away [Vacancy 511-6
To think away the grass, the trees, the clouds, [Look 517-14
That winter is washed away. Someone is moving [World 520-13
Of air and whirled away. But it has been often so. [Slug 522-4
Still far away. It was like [Not Ideas 534-17
The water runs away from the horses. [Primordia 8-18 P
As the moon has in its moonlight, worlds away, [Red Kit 31-8 P
Why was it that you cast the brass away [Good Bad 33-20 P
What sound could comfort away the sudden sense? [Old Woman 44-16P
Give up dead things and the living turn away. [Burnshaw 49-6 P
Reflections, whirling apart and wide away. [Burnshaw 50-5 P
Yourselves away and at a distance join [Burnshaw 51-15 P
A dewy flashing blanks away from fire, [Burnshaw 51-23 P
O bold, that rode your horses straight away. [Duck 61-31 P
With a tendency to bulge as it floats away. [Duck 63-22 P
And most in what we hear, sound brushed away, [Sombre 67-9 P
As of insects or cloud-stricken birds, away [Sombre 67-11 P
And away, dialogues between incognitos. [Sombre 67-12 P
Cities that would not wash away in the mist, [Sombre 68-9 P
At night, to turn away from the abominable [Sombre 71-20 P
And the wry antipodes whirled round the world away-- [Discov
   95-20 P
Brighter, perfected and distant away, [Ulysses 101-24 P
To that which they symbolized, away [Ulysses 102-14 P
The miles of distance away [Letters 108-9 P
And suddenly denying itself away. [Real 110-18 P
Take away the bushes. [Three 139-15 P
   See far-away.
AWE. The multifarious heavens felt no awe [Geneva 24-8
AWHILE. This field, and tended it awhile, [Frogs 78-8
  Mulberry, shade me, shade me awhile. [Banjo 114-2 P
  Mulberry, shade me, shade me awhile. [Banjo 114-5 P
  Mulberry, shade me, shade me awhile. [Banjo 114-8 P
  Mulberry, shade me, shade me awhile-- [Banjo 114-11 P
  Mulberry, shade me, shade me awhile. [Banjo 114-13 P
AWKWARD. Now like a ballet infantine in awkward steps, [Burnshaw
   47-18 P
AWNINGS. And the awnings are let down. [Mandolin 28-14 P
  And the awnings are too brown, [Mandolin 28-16 P
  If awnings were celeste and gay, [Mandolin 28-18 P
AWRY. Make more awry our faulty human things. [Surprises 98-11
AXIS. Axis of everything, green's apogee. [Cred 373-20
  A man who was the axis of his time, [NH 479-6
AY. Are corrupting pallors . . . ay di mi, [MBG 172-2
AY-MI. With the politest helplessness. Ay-mi! [EM 324-22
AZALEAS. Now, in the time of spring (azaleas, trilliums, [Dump
   202-12
  That are on the dump (azaleas and so on) [Dump 202-15
  And those that will be (azaleas and so on), [Dump 202-16

A-ZAY. Mumbled zay-zay and a-zay, a-zay. [Ord Women 11-2
AZCAN. Chieftain Iffucan of Azcan in caftan [Bantams 75-14
  And fears not portly Azcan nor his hoos. [Bantams 76-4
AZTEC. Oblivious to the Aztec almanacs, [C 38-22
AZURE. Although they paint effulgent, azure lakes, [C 37-28
  Their azure has a cloudy edge, their white [C 37-30
  Any azure under-side of after-color. Nabob [Landsc 241-19
  Of azure round an upper dome, brightest [Greenest 54-13 P
  An azure outre-terre, oranged and rosed, [Theatre 91-14 P
AZURE-DOUBLED. Dressed in its azure-doubled crimsons, [Hero 281-3
AZURY. Breathing his bronzen breath at the azury centre of time.
   [Cata 425-12

B. At beta b and gamma g, [Ord Women 11-10
  And B are not like statuary, posed [Connois 216-10
  The A B C of being, [Motive 288-16
  Projection B. To get at the thing [Couch 295-16
  When B. sat down at the piano and made [EM 316-9
  At B: the origin of the mango's rind. [Rock 528-13
BABBLE. The babble of generations magnifies [Spaniard 34-18 P
BABBLING. There is a monotonous babbling in our dreams [C 39-25
  Babbling, each one, the uniqueness of its sound. [Quiet 523-13
BABIES. "Palace of the Babies" [77-title
  If in a shimmering room the babies came, [Babies 77-10
  "The Woman That Had More Babies Than That" [81-title P
  More babies than that. The merely revolving wheel [Woman Had
    81-23 P
BABOONS. To dream of baboons and periwinkles. [Ten O'C 66-11
  The trombones are like baboons, [Drum-Majors 37-2 P
BABSON. The lin-lan-lone of Babson, [Agenda 41-17 P
BABY. Mrs. Anderson's Swedish baby [Circulat 150-5
  A baby with the tail of a rat? [Horn 230-7
  The sun shone and the dog barked and the baby slept. [Contra II
    270-5
  At least one baby in you. [Primordia 9-23 P
BABYISHNESS. Babyishness of forsythia, a snatch of belief, [Slug
  522-13
BACHELOR. A bachelor of feen masquerie, [Oak 272-5
BACK. And watery back. [Paltry 5-18
  Of what, like skulls, comes rotting back to ground. [Monocle
    14-19
  Knowing that they can bring back thought [Homunculus 26-13
  And then retirement like a turning back. [C 35-11
  Unreal, give back to us what once you gave: [Fictive 88-17
  Brings back an earlier season of quiet [Lunar 107-10
  The floor. Go on through the darkness. The waves fly back.
    [Farewell 117-10
  If the fault is with the lions, send them back [Lions 125-6
  Which led them back to angels, after death. [Eve Angels 137-12
  Falls back to coldness, [Reader 147-6
  So that one would want to escape, come back [Poems Clim 194-5
  Resolved the world. We cannot go back to that. [Connois 215-16
  It is the leaf the bird brings back to the boat. [Blue Bldg
    217-18
  When male light fell on the naked back [Hartford 227-7
  The girl had to hold back and lean back to hold him, [Forces
    229-4
  But he came back as one comes back from the sun [Yellow 237-7
  Again . . . as if it came back, as if life came back, [Martial
    237-13
  Home from Guatemala, back at the Waldorf. [Waldorf 240-23
  It is safe to sleep to a sound that time brings back. [Phenom
    286-12
  Bursts back. What not quite realized transit [Feo 333-20
  That sends us back to the first idea, the quick [NSF 381-17
  The poem, through candor, brings back a power again [NSF 382-23
  The gibberish of the vulgate and back again. [NSF 396-14
  Turn back to where we were when we began: [AA 420-13
  They looked back at Hans' look with savage faces. [Page 421-23
  No more that which most of all brings back the known, [Page
    422-15
  We keep coming back and coming back [NH 471-10
  The statues will have gone back to be things about. [NH 473-24
  They said, "We are back once more in the land of the elm trees,
    [NH 487-3
  Go back to a parent before thought, before speech, [Irish 501-11
  Come back to see a certain house. [Vacancy 511-11
  It dances down a furrow, in the early light, back of a crazy
    plough, the green blades following. [Plough-Boy 6-7 P
  She will leap back from the swift constellations, [Soldat 12-7 P
  Made by a cook that never rode the back [Burnshaw 46-20 P
  Of things, why bother about the back of stars? [Greenest 58-27 P
  That of the son who bears upon his back [Recit 87-12 P
  Makes them a pack on a giant's back, [Ulysses 103-24 P
  A form that is lame, a hand, a back, [Ulysses 104-17 P
  See stallion-back.
BACK-ACHE. "Saint John and the Back-Ache" [436-title
BACKED. See hairy-backed.
BACKGROUND. That night is only the background of our selves,
  [Re-state 146-10
BACKS. A boat carried forward by waves resembling the bright backs
  of rowers, [Prol 515-6
  Your backs upon the vivid statue. Then, [Burnshaw 51-13 P
  From size, backs larger than the eye, not flesh [Sombre 70-23 P
BACKWARD. But let these backward lapses, if they would,[C 35-14
  Related in romance to backward flights, [C 39-10
  Forward of the eye that, in its backward, sees [Descrip 340-3
  And, being straw, turned green, lived backward, shared [Liadoff
    347-9
  She spoke with backward gestures of her hand. [Owl 435-8
  Look backward. Let your swiftly-flying flocks [Red Kit 31-28 P

As I wished, once they fell backward when my breath [Bship 78-16P
BAD. "The Man Whose Pharynx Was Bad" [96-title
  The tea is bad, bread sad. [Fading 139-8
  Is it bad to have come here [Chateau 161-7
  Bad is final in this light. [Possum 293-16
  It is here, in this bad, that we reach [Possum 294-13
  He lived each life because, if it was bad, [Good Man 364-5
  Than bad angels leap from heaven to hell in flames. [AA 414-12
  "In a Bad Time" [426-title
  "Good Man, Bad Woman" [33-title P
BAD-BESPOKEN. The bad-bespoken lacker, [Jumbo 269-15
BADE. And bade the sheep carouse. Or so they said. [NSF 400-22
BADLY. The greenhouse never so badly needed paint. [Plain 502-17
  Oh! it will end badly. [Three 139-2 P
BADROULBADOUR. Out of the tomb, we bring Badroulbadour, [Worms
  49-16
  Out of the tomb we bring Badroulbadour. [Worms 50-3
BAFFLED. Where is it that you think, baffled [Bagatelles 213-10
BAFFLING. Come, baffling discontent. These, too, must be [Sombre
  69-19 P
BAG. In the bag [Soldat 12-20 P
  See paper-bag.
BAGATELLES. "The Bagatelles the Madrigals" [213-title
BAGGED. See big-bagged.
BAKED. Baked through long days, is piled in mows. It is [Cred 374-8
  A green baked greener in the greenest sun. [NSF 393-7
  It is mud and mud long baked in the sun, [Stan MBG 72-6 P
BAKER. The grain is in the baker's shop, [Nigger 154-8
  Of baker and butcher blowing, as if to hear, [NH 475-2
BALANCE. So it is to sit and to balance things [MBG 181-5
  To know that the balance does not quite rest, [MBG 181-9
  Contriving balance to contrive a whole, [AA 420-19
BALANCES. Balances with nuptial song. [MBG 181-4
  Repeats its vital words, yet balances [Search 268-15
  Is well, incalculable balances, [NSF 386-11
  Sets up its Schwärmerei, not balances [NSF 386-14
  That we achieve but balances that happen, [NSF 386-15
BALAYNE. The great ship, Balayne, lay frozen in the sea. [Page
  421-18
BALCONY. From my balcony, I survey the yellow air, [Of Surface 57-3
  But let the poet on his balcony [Havana 144-30
  He might sit on a sofa on a balcony [Landsc 243-2
  On his balcony at night. Warblings became [EM 314-18
  On his balcony, outsensing distances, [NH 483-12
BALD. When amorists grow bald, then amours shrink [Monocle 15-14
  And not a bald and tasselled saint. [Our Stars 455-6
  Bald heads with their mother's voice still in their ears.
    [Woman Had 82-16 P
BALK. To stop the whirlwind, balk the elements. [NSF 401-15
BALKAN. Of the Balkan shoes, the bonnets from Moldau, beards
  [Duck 62-14 P
BALKED. And each blank window of the building balked [Babies 77-8
BALKS. Those feelings that the body balks, [Vari 234-3
BALL. Buffo! A ball, an opera, a bar. [AA 420-12
BALLAD. So far the lady of the present ballad [Three 137-9 P
  It is a doleful ballad, [Three 138-11 P
  The young gentleman of the ballad. [Three 139-13 P
  And the end of the ballad. [Three 139-14 P
BALLAD-EYE. The green, white, blue of the ballad-eye, by night
  [Sombre 71-9 P
BALLADS. But it is a way with ballads [Three 137-15 P
BALLATTA. Ballatta dozed in the cool on a straw divan [NE Verses
  106-5
BALLET. Now like a ballet infantine in awkward steps, [Burnshaw
  47-18 P
BALLETS. And dancers danced ballets on top of their beds-- [Agenda
  42-5 P
BALL-LIKE. The ball-like beads, the bazzling and the bangling
  beads [Grotesque 74-11 P
BALLOON. Someone has left for a ride in a balloon [Phenom 286-7
BALLOONS. In the afternoon, balloons at night. That is [Havana
  142-2
  But they are empty as balloons [Drum-Majors 37-1 P
BALLS. See fire-balls.
BALM. In any balm or beauty of the earth, [Sunday 67-17
  Diffusing balm in that Pacific calm? [Sea Surf 99-8
  He well might find that eager balm [Room Gard 41-10 P
BALMY. I know no magic trees, no balmy boughs, [Monocle 16-27
BALSAM. Those bearing balsam, its field fragrance, [Vari 235-11
BALUSTRADES. The mountainous ridges, purple balustrades, [C 33-14
  A fly crawls on the balustrades. [Including 88-16 P
BANAL. "Banal Sojourn" [62-title
  Through Oxidia, banal suburb, [MBG 182-1
  Of seeping rose--banal machine [Soldat 15-20 P
BANALES. Qui fait fi des joliesses banales, the chairs. [Freed
  205-24
BANANA. Hung heavily on the great banana tree, [NSF 393-14
BANANAS. "Floral Decorations for Bananas" [53-title
  But bananas hacked and hunched . . . [Bananas 54-10
  Pile the bananas on planks. [Bananas 54-14

And deck the bananas in leaves [Bananas 54-17
  And là-bas, là-bas, the cool bananas grew, [NSF 393-13
BAND. A band entwining, set with fatal stones. [Fictive 88-16
  Dismissed the band. [Coroner 30-2 P
BANDEAUX. In the bandeaux of the mothers, would see again. [NSF
  389-18
BANDED. Here the adult one is still banded with fulgor,[Aug 495-24
BANDS. And your braids bear brightening of crimson bands.
  [Burnshaw 51-29 P
  These bands, these swarms, these motions, what of them? [Duck
  62-9 P
  Parades of whole races with attendant bands, [Duck 66-2 P
  Bands of black men seem to be drifting in the air, [Sick 90-7 P
  In the South, bands of thousands of black men, [Sick 90-8 P
  Waits for the unison of the music of the drifting bands [Sick
  90-14 P
BAND-STAND. Then Basilewsky in the band-stand played [Duck 62-28 P
  The man in the band-stand could be orator. [Duck 63-15 P
BANE. Our old bane, green and bloated, serene, who cries, [Banal
  62-16
  I am Solange, euphonious bane, she said. [News 265-4
BANG. To bang it from a savage blue, [MBG 166-11
  Bang cymbals as they used to do. [Memo 89-15 P
BANGLES. And bangles and slatted eyes. [Bananas 54-16
  And beads and bangles of gold and trumpets raised, [Greenest
  56-11 P
BANGLING. The ball-like beads, the bazzling and the bangling beads
  [Grotesque 74-11 P
BANISHMENT. And what descants, he sent to banishment! [C 34-21
BANJO. But on the banjo's categorical gut, [C 38-19
  Sighing that he should leave the banjo's twang. [NSF 393-21
  "Banjo Boomer" [114-title P
BANK. Upon the bank, she stood [Peter 90-21
  And bristling thorn-trees spinning on the bank [Nigger 155-15
  And limbed and lighted out from bank to bank. [Lot 371-3
  Over the top of the Bank of Ireland, [Our Stars 454-14
  Inside our queer chapeaux, we seem, on this bank, [Nuns 92-15 P
BANKS. Tugging at banks, until they seemed [Frogs 78-2
  Grotesque with this nosing in banks, [Frogs 78-11
  It is the same jingle of the water among the roots under the
  banks of the palmettoes, [Indian 112-5
  And savings banks, Fides, the sculptor's prize, [Lions 124-12
  As yet, for the mind, new banks [Mud 147-17
  The shores are banks of muffling mist. [MBG 172-14
  Than creatures, of the sky between the banks, [Lot 371-14
  Here the black violets grow down to its banks [Degen 445-1
  Flashing and flashing in the sun. On its banks, [R Conn 533-9
  Through banks and banks of voices, [Grotesque 77-7 P
  See river-banks.
BANLIEUS. These are not banlieus [Inhab 504-6
BANNERS. And the banners of the nation flutter, burst [NSF 390-22
  How easily the blown banners change to wings . . . [Rome 508-11
  The banners should brighten the sun. [Drum-Majors 37-10 P
BANTAMS. "Bantams in Pine-Woods" [75-title
BAR. From which it sped, a bar in space, [MBG 179-6
  Buffo! A ball, an opera, a bar. [AA 420-12
  See: ex-bar; in-bar.
BARB. And late wanderers creeping under the barb of night, [Dutch
  291-24
BARBARIANS. Lulu sang of barbarians before the eunuchs [Lulu G
  26-9 P
  The manners of the barbarians, [Lulu G 26-15 P
  She described how the barbarians kissed her [Lulu G 26-19 P
BARBARIC. With barbaric glass. [Thirteen 93-13
BARBARISM. Green barbarism turning paradigm. [C 31-22
  Into a barbarism as its image. [Hero 277-4
BARBAROUS. High up in orange air, were barbarous. [C 30-21
  This barbarous chanting of what is strong, this blare.
  [Parochial 191-16
  To its barbed, barbarous rising and has peace. [Extraord 369-11
  Of barbarous tongue, slavered and panting halves [AA 415-18
  Glares, outside of the legend, with the barbarous green [Plant
  506-18
  The barbarous strength within her would never fail. [World 521-15
BARBED. To its barbed, barbarous rising and has peace. [Extraord
  369-11
  See blackly-barbed.
BARBER. Berries of villages, a barber's eye, [C 27-15
BARBERS. Alas! Have all the barbers lived in vain [Monocle 14-8
  Barbers with charts of the only possible modes, [Sombre 68-8 P
BARBICAN. With his men, beyond the barbican. [Vari 234-12
BARE. That is blowing in the same bare place [Snow Man 10-9
  Crispin in one laconic phrase laid bare [C 36-26
  The rich man going bare, the paladin [C 37-17
  Than mute bare splendors of the sun and moon. [On Manner 56-8
  The jar was gray and bare. [Jar 76-14
  And over the bare spaces of our skies [Anatomy 108-6
  Massively rising high and bare [How Live 125-18
  The hotel is boarded and bare. [Botanist 1 135-12
  Bare night is best. Bare earth is best. Bare, bare, [Eve Angels

  137-29
  The earth, for us, is flat and bare. [MBG 167-9
  One after another washing the mountains bare. [Loaf 200-7
  Not father, but bare brother, megalfrere, [Choc 300-21
  The air is not a mirror but bare board, [NSF 384-2
  Bare limbs, bare trees and a wind as sharp as salt? [AA 419-21
  Sordid Melpomene, why strut bare boards, [Bad Time 427-4
  Among the bare and crooked trees, [Celle 438-3
  In primavera, the shadow of bare rock, [NH 476-9
  Bare beggar-tree, hung low for fruited red [NH 483-24
  No memorable muffing, bare and blunt. [Burnshaw 48-8 P
  Like damsels daubed and let your feet be bare [Burnshaw 51-11 P
BARED. And bared yourself, and bared yourself in vain? [Good Bad
  33-21 P
BAREFOOT. Shall a man go barefoot [Am Sub 131-2
  As foregoing the nakedest passion for barefoot [EM 316-22
  And barefoot servants round him, who adjust [NSF 390-20
  They were those that would have wept to step barefoot into
  reality, [Large 423-16
  In the presence of the barefoot ghosts! [Lytton 39-5 P
BARELY. So barely lit, so shadowed over and naught, [Quiet 523-3
BARENESS. When radiance came running down, slim through the bare-
  ness. [Banal 63-2
  The bareness of the house returns. [Contra I 267-1
BARENESSES. And beautiful barenesses as yet unseen, [C 31-26
BARER. Remained, except some starker, barer self [C 29-16
  In a starker, barer world, in which the sun [C 29-17
  She sees a barer sky that does not bend. [Anatomy 108-7
  Falls from that fatal and that barer sky, [Anatomy 108-17
BARES. Up-rising and down-falling, bares [Curtains 62-9
  And bares an earth that has no gods, and bares [Greenest 58-13 P
BAREST. And what she felt fought off the barest phrase. [NSF 402-12
BARGE. To float off in the floweriest barge, [Thought 184-18
BARK. The horses gnaw the bark from the trees. [Primordia 8-8 P
BARKED. The sun shone and the dog barked and the baby slept.
  [Contra II 270-5
BARKING. And bite the hard-bite, barking as it bites. [Novel 458-8
BAR-MEN. And the cooks, the cooks, the bar-men and the maids,
  [Greenest 53-17 P
BARN. See chidder-barn.
BARNS. Than the dew on the barns. [Three 128-2 P
BAROQUE. The baroque poet may see him as still a man [Paisant
  335-12
BAROUCHE. Should have a black barouche. [W Burgher 61-6
BARQUE. Barque of phosphor [Fabliau 23-4
BARRACK. In a book in a barrack, a letter from Malay. [NSF 407-14
BARRED. Ringed round and barred, with eyes held in their hands,
  [Page 422-30
BARREN. Barren, and longing for her; [Sonatina 109-20
  Heard the dogs howl at barren bone, [Thought 187-6
  They are more than leaves that cover the barren rock [Rock 527-6
BARRENNESS. Look at it in its essential barrenness [Cred 373-8
  For what is not. This is the barrenness [Cred 373-14
  The barrenness that appears is an exposing. [NH 487-16
  That its barrenness becomes a thousand things [Rock 527-18
BARRICADE. Or a barricade against the singular man [Descrip 340-8
BARRIER. The solitude, the barrier, the Pole [Thought 186-6
BARRIERS. The spokesman at our bluntest barriers, [NSF 397-2
BARS. The trees were plucked like iron bars [Jumbo 269-1
BASE. At the base of the statue, we go round and round. [Mice 123-2
  Knew the eccentric to be the base of design. [Nigger 151-3
  A space of stone, of inexplicable base [Thought 185-9
  Bulging toward the base. [Pears 196-7
  This is the height emerging and its base [AA 411-13
  At the spirit's base? [Irish 501-8
  The rain falls at its base, [Secret Man 36-7 P
  This base of every future, vibrant spring, [Duck 63-28 P
BASEL. To Nietzsche in Basel, to Lenin by a lake. [Descrip 342-1
  Nietzsche in Basel studied the deep pool [Descrip 342-7
BASIC. The basic slate, the universal hue. [Monocle 15-9
BASILEWSKY. Then Basilewsky in the band-stand played [Duck 62-28 P
  Basilewsky's bulged before it floated, turned [Duck 63-23 P
BASILISKS. Abortion, fit for the enchanting of basilisks. [Duck
  63-1 P
BASIN. Let us erect in the Basin a lofty fountain. [NE Verses 105-1
BASIS. Thus, on the basis of the common drudge, [Polish Aunt 84-8
  How good life is, on the basis of propriety, [Winter B 141-13
BASK. Or bask within his images and words? [C 38-5
  Dark cynic, strip and bathe and bask at will. [NE Verses 106-3
  Bask in the sun in which they feel transparent, [Extracts 254-19
BASKET. Sleeps by his basket. He snores. His bloated breath [Feo
  333-19
BASKETFUL. Grandmother and her basketful of pears [Havana 143-23
BASKETS. In the baskets. [Three 128-15 P
BASKING. The frown like serpents basking on the brow, [NSF 400-11
  Basking in desert Florida? [An Gaiety 33-4 P
  And Africa, basking in antiquest sun, [Greenest 55-25 P
BASS. And mighty Fortitudo, frantic bass. [Lions 124-16
  The bass lie deep, still afraid of the Indians. [Think 356-8
  The bass keep looking ahead, upstream, in one [Think 356-11

There is one dove, one bass, one fisherman. [Think 356-15
BASSES. The basses of their beings throb [Peter 90-10
  May rush to extinguish the theme, the basses thump [Bship 79-27P
BASSO. But a profane parade, the basso [Hero 278-5
BASSOONS. Than the revenge of music on bassoons. [C 32-25
  To the bubbling of bassoons. That's the time [Dump 202-20
BASTARD. Bastard chateaux and smoky demoiselles, [Montra 263-7
BAT. Flies like a bat expanding as it flies, [Pure 332-24
BATARD. C'était mon esprit bâtard, l'ignominie. [Sea Surf 102-9
BATH. You know the mountainous coiffures of Bath. [Monocle 14-7
BATHE. To bathe their hearts in later moonlight, [Homunculus 26-12
  Dark cynic, strip and bathe and bask at will. [NE Verses 106-3
BATHED. She bathed in her still garden, while [Peter 90-8
  Then bathed its body in the leaping lake. [Hand 271-12
  We bathed in yellow green and yellow blue [Lot 371-8
  To study the past, and doctors, having bathed [NSF 391-15
BATHES. And of his works, I am sure. He bathes in the mist [Freed
    204-22
BATHING. "A Lot of People Bathing in a Stream" [371-title
BATHS. One's grand flights, one's Sunday baths, [Sleight 222-1
BATON. Polyphony beyond his baton's thrust. [C 28-21
BATONS. They would throw their batons far up [Drum-Majors 36-20 P
BATS. A porcelain, as yet in the bats thereof. [NH 467-15
BATTER. The winds batter it. The water curls. The leaves [Novel
    457-2
BATTERED. The rusty, battered shapes [Anything B 211-18
  Of ten brilliancies of battered gold [Imago 439-6
  No longer a battered panache above snow . . . [Not Ideas 534-8
BATTERING. It was the battering of drums I heard [Loaf 200-8
  There is a battering of the drums. The bugles [Dutch 291-8
  A retardation of its battering, [Pure 330-5
  A form, then, protected from the battering, may [Pure 330-10
BATTERS. And the river that batters its way over stones, [Loaf
    199-17
  That batters against the mind, silent and proud, [Pure 329-14
BATTLE. For Battle, the purple for victory. But if [Bship 79-7 P
BATTLESHIP. "Life on a Battleship" [77-title P
  It implies a flaw in the battleship, a defeat [Bship 79-15 P
  That's this grandiose battleship of yours and your [Bship 80-29P
BAUBLE. The bauble of the sleepless nor a word [Havana 144-4
BAWDA. Between a great captain and the maiden Bawda. [NSF 401-6
  And therefore married Bawda, whom he found there, [NSF 401-17
  And Bawda loved the captain as she loved the sun. [NSF 401-18
BAWDINESS. Beyond the planets. Thus, our bawdiness, [High-Toned
    59-9
BAWDS. Even the bawds of euphony [Thirteen 94-11
BAWDY. Susanna's music touched the bawdy strings [Peter 92-8
BAY. White dogs at bay. [Cab 21-12 P
  See Mal Bay.
BAYONET. Too long, is like a bayonet that bends. [Soldat 13-7 P
BAYS. Tuck, tuck, while the flamingoes flapped his bays. [C 38-20
  The bays of heaven, brighted, blued? [Botanist 2 136-4
  See window-bays.
BAZZLING. The ball-like beads, the bazzling and the bangling beads
    [Grotesque 74-11 P
BE. Of was and is and shall or ought to be, [C 40-8
  For him, of shall or ought to be in is. [C 41-9
  For realist, what is is what should be. [C 41-31
  The rapey gouts. Good star, how that to be [C 42-20
  Let be be finale of seem. [Emperor 64-7
  So be it. Yet the spaciousness and light [Anatomy 108-15
  The centuries of excellence to be [Havana 143-1
  When to be and delight to be seemed to be one, [Anglais 149-14
  Music is not yet written but is to be. [Nigger 158-3
  Things as they will be by and by . . . [MBG 178-21
  To be without a description of to be, [Freed 205-7
  For a moment on rising, at the edge of the bed, to be, [Freed
    205-8
  To be, in the grass, in the peacefullest time, [Rabbit K 209-7
  But that's all done. It is what used to be, [Cuisine 227-17
  To be again, [Adequacy 244-4
  The will to be and to be total in belief, [Gala 248-14
  To be, regardless of velvet, could never be more [Uruguay 249-13
  Than to be, she could never differently be, [Uruguay 249-14
  To be happy because people were thinking to be. [Extracts 257-5
  They had to think it to be. He wanted that, [Extracts 257-6
  And did not want nor have to be, [Motive 288-12
  To see was to be. He was the figure in [Choc 297-6
  He rose because men wanted him to be. [Choc 299-13
  They wanted him by day to be, image, [Choc 299-14
  That cannot be; to say human things with more [Choc 300-12
  Than human voice, that, also, cannot be; [Choc 300-13
  In day's constellation, and yet remain, yet be, [Choc 300-20
  A civil nakedness in which to be, [Repet 310-6
  What place in which to be is not enough [EM 320-3
  To be? You go, poor phantoms, without place [EM 320-4
  It is possible that to seem--it is to be, [Descrip 339-1
  And seems to be on the saying of her name. [Descrip 339-14
  In flat appearance we should be and be, [Descrip 340-15
  To be, as on the youngest poet's page, [Descrip 340-20

Of the possible: seemings that are to be, [Descrip 342-5
  Seemings that it is possible may be. [Descrip 342-6
  Be alive with its own seemings, seeming to be [Descrip 346-3
  Must bear no name, gold flourisher, but be [NSF 381-14
  In the difficulty of what it is to be. [NSF 381-15
  He is and may be but oh! he is, he is, [NSF 388-10
  When in my coppice you behold me be. [NSF 393-24
  And in harmonious prodigy to be, [Owl 432-22
  In the way what was has ceased to be what is [Owl 435-12
  Are flatly there, unversed except to be, [Bouquet 452-14
  Gone wild, be what he tells you to be: Puella. [Puel 456-14
  To say good-by to the past and to live and to be [NH 478-5
  And it had to be, [Aug 495-12
  The desire to be at the end of distances, [Rock 527-9
  Than the need of each generation to be itself, [Armor 530-9
  And so hydrangeas came to be. [Abnormal 24-3 P
  Beginning of a green Cockaigne to be, disliked, abandoned,
    [Inelegance 25-14 P
  Let this be as it may. It must have tears [Spaniard 35-13 P
  That is is dead except what ought to be. [Burnshaw 46-15 P
  Speak, and in these repeat: To Be Itself, [Burnshaw 52-8 P
  That will always be and will be everywhere. [Greenest 58-18 P
  And must be, when the portent, changed, takes on [Sombre 70-12 P
  Of that which is not seen and cannot be. [Sombre 70-25 P
  That changed in sleep. It is, it is, let be [Sombre 71-15 P
  The way it came, let be what it may become. [Sombre 71-16 P
  In the gesture's whim, a passion merely to be [Sombre 71-28 P
  That I desired. It could be-- [Desire 85-3 P
  Could be, it could be. [Desire 85-6 P
  The right to be." Guiding his boat [Ulysses 99-14 P
  The aid of greatness to be and the force. [Ulysses 100-17 P
  The order of man's right to be [Ulysses 101-13 P
  And the right to be are one. We come [Ulysses 101-19 P
  To know established as the right to be. [Ulysses 102-11 P
  The right to be." He guided his boat [Presence 105-17 P
  Is equal to the right to be. [Presence 106-4 P
  Astute in being what they are made to be. [Art Pop 112-20 P
  On whatever the earth happens to be. [Three 130-23 P
BEACH. On the palmy beach, [Fabliau 23-5
  Deserted, on a beach. It is white, [AA 412-5
  The season changes. A cold wind chills the beach. [AA 412-19
  And the first line spreading up the beach; again [Woman Had
    81-14 P
BEACHES. Or on the beaches, [Solitaires 60-5
  Yet there is no spring in Florida, neither in boskage perdu, nor
    on the nunnery beaches. [Indian 112-7
  As if they knew of distant beaches; and were [Descrip 343-8
  And reaches, beaches, tomorrow's regions became [Descrip 343-13
  These were his beaches, his sea-myrtles in [NSF 393-8
BEACHY. Rose on the beachy floors. [Ord Women 11-20
  Of constellations on the beachy air [Greenest 58-1 P
BEADED. And beaded ceintures. [Ten O'C 66-9
  Black beaded on the rock, the flecked animal, [AA 412-2
BEADS. The beads on her rails seemed to grasp at transparence.
    [Vari 236-2
  Of the image, behold it with exactness through beads [Bouquet
    449-23
  And beads and bangles of gold and trumpets raised, [Greenest
    56-11 P
  And the dewiest beads of insipid fruit [Stan MBG 72-8 P
  Knew her, how could you see the woman that wore the beads,
    [Grotesque 74-10 P
  The ball-like beads, the bazzling and the bangling beads
    [Grotesque 74-11 P
BEAK. In beak and bud and fruity gobbet-skins, [C 32-7
BEAKED. Wildly curvetted, color-scarred, so beaked, [Greenest 57-18P
BEAKS. Poured forth the fine fins, the gawky beaks, the personalia,
    [Somnam 304-17
BEAM. Let the lamp affix its beam. [Emperor 64-15
  First one beam, then another, then [MBG 172-9
  Hewn in their middle as the beam of leaves, [Owl 434-2
BEAMIER. What avuncular cloud-man beamier than spears? [Greenest
    52-25 P
BEAMING. Blooming and beaming and voluming colors out. [NH 484-6
BEAMS. Beams of the huge night converged upon it, [Valley Candle
    51-2
  Then beams of the huge night [Valley Candle 51-4
  Like blessed beams from out a blessed bush [NH 477-21
  Arabesques of candle beams, [Phases 4-4 P
  Dazzling by simplest beams and soothly still, [Old Woman 46-4 P
BEAN. Fly low, cock bright, and stop on a bean pole. Let [Cred
    377-6
  And on your bean pole, it may be, you detect [Cred 377-17
BEAR. Was blackamoor to bear your blazing tail. [Bantams 75-17
  Bear other perfumes. On your pale head wear [Fictive 88-15
  And yet it brings the storm to bear. [MBG 169-11
  Young ox, bow-legged bear, [Destructive 192-16
  The winter is made and you have to bear it, [Dwarf 208-3
  The sunlight. They bear brightly the little beyond [Extracts
    254-22

May truly bear its heroic fortunes [Hero 281-4
In which to bear with the exactest force [Repet 310-7
Until its wings bear off night's middle witch; [Pure 333-1
Tall and unfretted, a figure meant to bear [Pastor 379-19
Must bear no name, gold flourisher, but be [NSF 381-14
Shattering velvetest far-away. The bear, [NSF 384-14
The wild orange trees continued to bloom and to bear, [NSF 393-2
Beyond the burning body that I bear. [NSF 395-24
They bud and bloom and bear their fruit without change. [Rock
    527-5
They bear their fruit so that the year is known, [Rock 527-12
What mattered was that they should bear [Planet 532-17
And your braids bear brightening of crimson bands. [Burnshaw
    51-29 P
Which, by its repetition, comes to bear [Duck 65-15 P
The future must bear within it every past, [Sombre 70-5 P
To bear virile grace before their fellows, [Stan Hero 83-20 P
Did not the age that bore him bear him among [Someone 85-1 A
See ice-bear.
BEARD. What was the ointment sprinkled on my beard? [Hoon 65-10
His beard moves in the wind. [Six Sig 73-12
Salt masks of beard and mouths of bellowing, [Sea Surf 101-17
Blessed, whose beard is cloak against the snows. [NE Verses 105-6
His beard is of fire and his staff is a leaping flame. [Nigger
    150-14
"The Well Dressed Man with a Beard" [247-title
A great bosom, beard and being, alive with age. [NH 466-3
He from whose beard the future springs, elect. [Duck 64-31 P
The jewels in his beard, the mystic wand, [Bship 79-4 P
BEARDED. And bearded bronze, but not a man, [MBG 165-14
And of a father bearded in his fire. [Celle 438-20
Bearded with chains of blue-green glitterings [Bouquet 449-7
The father, the ancestor, the bearded peer, [Aug 494-22
In that distant chamber, a bearded queen, wicked in her dead
    light. [Madame 507-13
BEARDS. Or in the Yangtse studied out their beards? [Monocle 14-3
My beards, attend [Estracts 253-16
And dewy bearings of their light-locked beards. [Bouquet 449-24
Of the Balkan shoes, the bonnets from Moldau, beards [Duck 62-14P
One is a child again. The gold beards of waterfalls [Discov
    95-10 P
BEARER. Lantern without a bearer, you drift, [Vari 232-16
BEARER-BEING. The idea and the bearer-being of the idea [NH 466-21
BEARERS. Majestic bearers or solemn haulers trapped [Greenest
    57-14 P
BEARING. They are bearing his body into the sky. [Cortege 80-10
Those bearing balsam, its field fragrance, [Vari 235-11
Tipped out with largeness, bearing the heavy [Gigan 289-16
Flotillas, willed and wanted, bearing in them [New Set 352-11
It might come bearing, out of chaos, kin [Page 422-27
Bearing the odors of the summer fields, [Wom Sun 445-13
And breeding and bearing birth of harmony, [Study II 465-2
Yet it has a bearing; [Three 133-26 P
BEARINGS. And dewy bearings of their light-locked beards. [Bouquet
    449-24
BEARS. It comes, it blooms, it bears its fruit and dies. [Monocle
    16-3
But, after all, I know a tree that bears [Monocle 17-2
And pink, the water bright that dogwood bears. [C 37-31
A hand that bears a thick-leaved fruit, [Venereal 48-16
There are no bears among the roses, [Virgin 71-1
A languid janitor bears [Public Sq 109-6
Bears us toward time, on its [Analysis 349-8
And shapes of fire, and wind that bears them down. [Two V 355-12
The actual form bears outwardly this grace, [Pastor 379-17
Caparison elephants, teach bears to juggle. [NSF 385-3
Are they really mechanical bears, [Drum-Majors 37-4 P
Bears words that are the speech of marble men. [Burnshaw 52-5 P
As if it bears all darkness in its bulk. [Sombre 68-18 P
That of the son who bears upon his back [Recit 87-12 P
The father that he loves, and bears him from [Recit 87-13 P
His own bright red. But he bears him out of love, [Recit 87-18P
And bears its floraisons of imagery. [Ulysses 102-31 P
BEAST. Pardie! Summer is like a fat beast, sleepy in mildew,
    [Banal 62-15
Mystic Garden & Middling Beast [Thought 185-title 2
The middling beast, the garden of paradise [Thought 185-21
In the body of a violent beast. [Destructive 193-2
And yet remains the same, the beast of light, [Pure 333-2
And plays his guitar. Ha-ee-me is a beast. [Jouga 337-3
Or perhaps his guitar is a beast or perhaps they are [Jouga 337-4
Ha-ee-me is the male beast . . . an imbecile, [Jouga 337-6
Who knocks out a noise. The guitar is another beast [Jouga 337-7
And polished beast, this complex falls apart. [Cred 377-16
Seeming, at first, a beast disgorged, unlike, [NSF 404-7
On his gold horse striding, like a conjured beast, [Antag 426-1
BEASTS. From beasts or from the incommunicable mass. [Less 328-6
Two beasts. But of the same kind--two conjugal beasts.[Jouga 337-5
    337-5
Two beasts but two of a kind and then not beasts. [Jouga 337-9

There are many of these beasts that one never sees, [Jouga 337-11
Ah, good God! That all beasts should have [Parasol 20-7 P
BEAT. Meantime, centurions guffaw and beat [Monocle 15-22
The crickets beat their tambours in the wind, [C 42-11
. . . Evening, when the measure skips a beat [Eve Angels 137-26
Could beat, yet not alarm the populace. [Havana 143-7
That do not beat by pain, but calendar, [Phenom 286-5
The wind beat in the roof and half the walls. [Repet 306-2
Words, in a storm, that beat around the shapes. [Sketch 335-22
That beat out slimmest edges in the ear, [Greenest 56-30 P
In the beat of the blood. [Sombre 67-27 P
BEATEN. See wind-beaten.
BEATER. The father, the beater of the rigid drums, [Thought 186-4
BEATING. In east wind beating the shutters at night. [Vase 246-16
Comes from the beating of the locust's wings, [Phenom 286-4
Even breathing is the beating of time, in kind: [Pure 330-4
A beating and a beating in the centre of [Two V 354-11
Beating in the heart, as if blood newly came, [NSF 382-21
He wanted his heart to stop beating and his mind to rest [Cata
    425-6
Its being beating heavily in the veins, [Novel 459-2
On her pillow? The thought kept beating in her like her heart.
    [World 521-11
The two kept beating together. It was only day. [World 521-12
Or Death was a rider beating his horse, [Soldat 16-4 P
BEATITUDE. Of Phoebus Apothicaire the first beatitude: [NE Verses
    105-3
BEATS. A fat thumb beats out ai-yi-yi. [MBG 178-22
One sits and beats an old tin can, lard pail. [Dump 202-26
One beats and beats for that which one believes. [Dump 202-27
It is time that beats in the breast and it is time [Pure 329-13
The human ocean beats against this rock [Two V 354-19
BEAU. In a beau language without a drop of blood. [Repet 310-9
Adam of beau regard, from fat Elysia, [Pure 331-20
Just where it was, oh beau caboose . . . It was part [Liadoff
    347-14
Beau linguist. But the MacCullough is MacCullough. [NSF 387-7
On a hill of stones to make beau mont thereof. [NH 466-24
If the black of night stands glistening on beau mont, [NH 467-2
For the beau of illusions. [Coroner 29-17 P
BEAUTE. Is it, once more, the mysterious beauté, [Soldat 12-1 P
BEAUTIES. You know how Utamaro's beauties sought [Monocle 14-5
BEAUTIFIED. Beautified the simplest men. [Phases 4-16 P
BEAUTIFIES. The white iris beautifies me. [Carolinas 5-5
BEAUTIFUL. Abundantly beautiful, eager, [Homunculus 26-24
And beautiful barenesses as yet unseen, [C 31-26
"Jasmine's Beautiful Thoughts underneath the Willow" [79-title
What a beautiful history, beautiful surprise! [Mice 123-3
What a beautiful tableau tinted and towering, [Mice 123-11
And the beautiful trombones--behold [MBG 170-9
"Anything Is Beautiful if You Say It Is" [211-title
"God Is Good. It Is a Beautiful Night" [God 285-title
There is no beautiful eye [Analysis 348-6
Like a book at evening beautiful but untrue, [AA 418-14
Like a book on rising beautiful and true. [AA 418-15
On This Beautiful World Of Ours composes himself [Ulti 429-10
In This Beautiful World Of Ours and not as now, [Ulti 430-6
Like beautiful and abandoned refugees. [Our Stars 455-16
Of the most beautiful, the most beautiful maid [Golden 461-1
Beauty of each beautiful enigma [NH 472-6
Beautiful alliterations of shadows and of things shadowed.
    [Primordia 8-7 P
Or be beautiful [Parasol 20-9 P
A beautiful thing, milord, is beautiful [Red Kit 31-5 P
Ugly as an idea, not beautiful [Burnshaw 47-7 P
That were the moments of the classic, the beautiful. [Local
    112-10 P
That nothing is beautiful [Three 133-14 P
As beautiful. [Three 136-18 P
She was as beautiful as a porcelain water bottle. [Three 136-19 P
BEAUTY. And the beauty [Peacocks 58-21
In any balm or beauty of the earth, [Sunday 67-17
Death is the mother of beauty; hence from her, [Sunday 68-29
Death is the mother of beauty, mystical, [Sunday 69-25
About the lantern of the beauty [Virgin 71-4
Beauty is momentary in the mind-- [Peter 91-22
The body dies; the body's beauty lives. [Peter 92-1
The beauty of inflections [Thirteen 93-8
Or the beauty of innuendoes, [Thirteen 93-9
For him cold's glacial beauty is his fate. [Bad Time 426-15
Beauty of each beautiful enigma [NH 472-6
The multiform beauty, sinking in night wind, [Soldat 12-4 P
Her beauty in your love. She should reflect [Red Kit 31-12 P
And she have beauty of a kind, but such [Red Kit 31-18 P
And shines, perhaps, for the beauty of shining. [Three 131-11 P
Such seclusion knows beauty [Three 131-15 P
When the court knew beauty only, [Three 132-5 P
Let the candle shine for the beauty of shining. [Three 133-10 P
For the beauty of shining. [Three 139-1 P
BECAME. How explicit the coiffures became, [Ord Women 11-21

Became an introspective voyager. [C 29-23
Lettered herself demurely as became [C 44-31
And the nakedness became the broadest blooms, [Sea Surf 101-20
Whatever self it had, became the self [Key W 129-28
Rose out of promise and became the sooth [Havana 143-2
And their blackness became apparent, that one first [Nigger 151-2
And what we said of it became [Postcard 159-12
Sure enough, moving, the thunder became men, [Thunder 220-1
High blue became particular [Vase 246-18
Became--how the central, essential red [Vase 246-21
Escaped its large abstraction, became, [Vase 246-22
Became the form and the fragrance of things [Vase 247-7
Each man himself became a giant, [Gigan 289-15
His hands became his feelings. His thick shape [Repet 306-12
On his balcony at night. Warblings became [EM 314-18
Like earth and sky. Then he became nothing else [Wild 329-1
Her time becomes again, as it became, [Descrip 339-15
And reaches, beaches, tomorrow's regions became [Descrip 343-13
The reader became the book; and summer night [House Q 358-8
In smoke. The blue petals became [Attempt 370-16
Became to-day, among our children and [Lot 371-6
By her coming became a freedom of the two, [AA 419-17
As if the central poem became the world, [Orb 441-19
To understand, as if to know became [Novel 459-5
Became divided in the leisure of blue day [NH 468-22
It became, the nameless, flitting characters-- [NH 479-22
The commonplace became a rumpling of blazons. [NH 483-22
When was it that the particles became [Aug 494-1
The whole man, that tempers and beliefs became [Aug 494-2
So formed, became himself and he breathed [Two Illus 513-14
Became transformed. But his mastery [Two Illus 515-2
He became an inhabitant, obedient [Quiet 523-5
A broken wall--and it ceased to exist, became [Greenest 53-7 P
BECOME. Until they become thoughtlessly willing [Homunculus 26-11
Monotonous earth I saw become [Vincentine 53-13
One might in turn become less diffident, [Pharynx 96-13
He does not become a three-days personage, [Soldier 97-4
It might become his hole of fate. [Snow Stars 133-6
Makes me conceive how dark I have become, [Sun March 133-14
Becomes the stones. Women become [MBG 170-22
The cities, children become the fields [MBG 171-1
And men in waves become the sea. [MBG 171-2
You become a self that fills the four corners of night. [Rabbit K 209-19
Man must become the hero of his world. [Montra 261-12
The sounds that soon become a voluble speech-- [Liadoff 347-20
Become an over-crystal out of ice, [Pieces 351-16
You must become an ignorant man again [NSF 380-15
Become the soft-footed phantom, the irrational [NSF 406-18
It might become a wheel spoked red and white [Page 422-21
They become our gradual possession. The poet [Papini 447-18
Become a single being, sure and true. [Pecul 454-9
So that they become an impalpable town, full of [NH 466-5
The great structure has become a minor house. [Plain 502-15
Become the figures of heaven, the majestic movement [Rome 508-2
Two parallels become one, a perspective, of which [Rome 508-9
Become accompaniments of fortune, but [Rome 508-13
And there become a spirit's mannerism, [Look 519-11
A mood that had become so fixed it was [Old Woman 45-12 P
Deadly and deep. It would become a yew [Old Woman 45-30 P
The porcelain bell-borrowings become [Burnshaw 52-11 P
Become rude robes among white candle lights, [Greenest 53-4 P
And the serpent might become a god, quick-eyed, [Greenest 54-23 P
To be the musician's own and, thence, become [Sombre 67-23 P
The portent would become man-haggard to [Sombre 70-26 P
The way it came, let be what it may become. [Sombre 71-16 P
When earth has become a paradise, it will be [Bship 77-19 P
The ship would become the center of the world. [Bship 78-5 P
On her lips familiar words become the words [Woman Had 83-9 P
Or clouds that hang lateness on the sea. They become [Role 93-10P
The contents of the mind become solid show [Conversat 108-13 P
And that, in his knowledge, local objects become [Local 111-12 P
BECOMES. Yet leaves us in them, until earth becomes, [Fictive 87-16
Becomes the place of things as they are, [MBG 168-7
Becomes the stones. Women become [MBG 170-22
If neatly glazed, becomes the same as the fruit [Extracts 253-9
The mass of meaning becomes composed again. [Extracts 256-3
Comes close to the prisoner's ear, becomes a throat [Montra 261-2
Inhale the purple fragrance. It becomes [News 265-2
It becomes the scholar again, seeking celestial [God 285-11
Of what is secret becomes, for me, a voice [Choc 298-19
The giants that each one of them becomes [Repet 307-3
The sun, its grossest appetite becomes less gross, [EM 318-14
That has lost the folly of the moon becomes [EM 320-23
Her time becomes again, as it became, [Descrip 339-15
Yet coo becomes rou-coo, rou-coo. How close [Think 356-16
It is a spectacle. Scene 10 becomes 11, [Chaos 357-11
The rest look down. One man becomes a race, [Cred 374-22
As placid air becomes. But it is not [Cred 375-15
Everything becomes morning, summer, the hero, [Past Nun 378-17

The importance of its hat to a form becomes [Pastor 379-4
In the sweeping brim becomes the origin [Pastor 379-13
The truth itself, the first idea becomes [NSF 381-20
How simply the fictive hero becomes the real; [NSF 408-1
What has he that becomes his heart's strong core? [Bad Time 426-20
His poverty becomes his heart's strong core-- [Bad Time 427-2
When Swatara becomes this undulant river [Degen 444-20
And the river becomes the landless, waterless ocean? [Degen 444-21
As that which was incredible becomes, [NH 470-14
Becomes amassed in a total double-thing. [NH 472-7
And Juda becomes New Haven or else must. [NH 473-6
Becomes the rock of autumn, glittering, [NH 476-10
The glass of the air becomes an element-- [NH 488-1
Of autumnal space becomes [Leben 505-5
Becomes another murmuring; the smell [Rome 508-19
That its barrenness becomes a thousand things [Rock 527-18
The stage becomes an atmosphere [Soldat 15-19 P
If properly misunderstood becomes a myth. [Lytton 38-15 P
Becomes the hero without heroics. [Stan Hero 84-14 P
Now, here, the warmth I had forgotten becomes [Warmth 90-2 P
Yet the nothingness of winter becomes a little less. [Course 96-11 P
In which the litter of truths becomes [Ulysses 102-7 P
The mode of the person becomes the mode of the world, [Conversat 108-11 P
Now, here, the snow I had forgotten becomes [As Leave 117-8 P
And in this tangent it becomes a thing [Someone 83-20 A
BECOMING. Emotions becoming one. The actor is [Of Mod 240-13
Becoming emeralds. He might watch the palms [Landsc 243-4
The clouds becoming braided girls. [Vase 246-6
Being, becoming seeing and feeling and self, [Extracts 255-21
Of time and place, becoming certain, [Hero 279-26
Like more and more becoming less and less, [Two V 354-13
And of becoming, for which the chapel spreads out [Armor 530-13
Of other lives becoming a total drone, [Americana 94-4 P
BED. A bed of radishes. [Pourtraicte 21-2
A high bed sheltered by curtains. [Theory 87-3
But leave a bed beneath the myrtles. [Norfolk 111-6
Make a bed and leave the iris in it. [Norfolk 112-3
Fears of my bed, [Brave 138-16
Half-way to bed, when the phrase will be spoken, [Nigger 156-8
And to have found the bed empty? [Chateau 161-8
It is good. The bed is empty, [Chateau 161-17
Our bed and we shall sleep by night. [MBG 184-3
Ah! Yes, desire . . . this leaning on his bed, [Men Fall 187-15
This leaning on his elbows on his bed, [Men Fall 187-16
On the edge of his bed. He said, [Freed 204-15
For a moment on rising, at the edge of the bed, to be, [Freed 205-8
To lie on one's bed in the dark, close to a face [Yellow 237-8
Yet a spider spins in the left shoe under the bed-- [Phenom 286-10
Of time's red soldier deathless on his bed. [EM 319-10
"The Bed of Old John Zeller" [326-title
To sleep in that bed for its disorder, talking of ghostly [Bed 327-3
Who lay in bed on the west wall of the sea, [Pure 331-6
To prepare for bed, in the frame of the house, and move [Lot 372-2
In silence upon your bed. You clutch the corner [NSF 384-19
Descending to the children's bed, on which [NSF 403-6
He would go to bed, cover himself with blankets-- [Novel 457-9
This sat beside his bed, with its guitar, [NH 483-16
The bed, the books, the chair, the moving nuns, [Rome 508-21
In a confusion on bed and books, a portent [Rome 509-3
In the warmth of your bed, at the edge of your chair, alive [Rome 509-19
Its domes are the architecture of your bed. [Rome 510-14
No more than a bed, a chair and moving nuns, [Rome 510-23
Than now. No: nor the ploughman in his bed [Burnshaw 47-32 P
And in a bed in one room, alone, a listener [Sick 90-13 P
The chords above your bed to-night. [Child 106-21 P
See marriage-bed.
BEDAZZLED. From cold, slightly irised, slightly bedazzled, [Bus 116-10 P
BED-CLOTHES. On bed-clothes, in an apple on a plate. [Blue Bldg 217-16
BEDIZENED. Turning, bedizened, [Sugar-Cane 12-14
BEDS. Rising upon the doctors in their beds [Freed 205-3
And on their beds. . . ." [Freed 205-4
Men on green beds and women half of sun [Cuisine 227-19
When cooks wake, clawing at their beds [Adequacy 244-3
Underground, a king as candle by our beds [Owl 435-2
The children heard him in their chilly beds, [Phases 5-9 P
And dancers danced ballets on top of their beds-- [Agenda 42-5 P
Their beds, their faces drawn in distant sleep. [Sombre 68-23 P
See: oyster-beds; salad-beds.
BEE. The bee may have all sweet [Anything B 211-9
The President ordains the bee to be [NSF 390-10

Why should the bee recapture a lost blague, [NSF 390-16
Booming and booming of the new-come bee. [NSF 391-6
A bee for the remembering of happiness. [Owl 434-18
And purpose, to hear the wild bee drone, to feel [Greenest
  56-25 P
BEE-LOUD. In the bee-loud glade. Lights on the steamer moved.
  [Page 422-4
BEEN. Too venerably used. That might have been. [NSF 400-19
It right and night have been. But as it was, [NSF 400-20
As he has been and is and, with the Queen [NH 485-17
BEES. And the bees still sought the chrysanthemums' odor. [Contra
  II 270-18
The bees came booming as if they had never gone, [NSF 389-19
Violets, doves, girls, bees and hyacinths [NSF 389-22
It is a repetition. The bees come booming [NSF 390-5
Small bees of spring, sniffing the coldest buds [Duck 65-7 P
The bees to scorpions blackly-barbed, a shade [Duck 65-9 P
And the bees, the scorpions, the men that think, [Duck 66-3 P
BEETLED. Beetled, in chapels, on the chaste bouquets. [C 29-20
BEETLES. Mechanical beetles never quite warm? [MBG 168-15
BEETLING. And beetling of belts and lights of general stones,
  [NH 477-20
BEFORE. I shall run before him, [Plot Giant 6-13
I shall run before him, [Plot Giant 6-17
I shall run before him, [Plot Giant 7-5
Before one merely reads to pass the time. [Monocle 14-22
Before these visible, voluble delugings, [Geneva 24-9
Before they sleep! [Homunculus 26-16
Here was no help before reality. [C 30-5
Before the winter's vacancy returned. [C 34-12
May, after all, stop short before a plum [C 40-28
Who will embrace her before summer comes. [Lilacs 49-15
"Depression before Spring" [63-title
Before they fly, test the reality [Sunday 68-13
That crew before the clocks. [Watermelon 89-6
Have I stopped and thought of its point before? [Grapes 110-11
To rest before the heroic height. [How Live 125-12
The swans . . . Before the bills of the swans fell flat [Havana
  142-13
Upon the ground, and before the chronicle [Havana 142-14
To that casino. Long before the rain [Havana 142-18
Before the colors deepened and grew small. [Anglais 149-5
Before the lion locked in stone. [MBG 175-16
Like the night before Christmas and all the carols.[Thought 185-3
A fate intoned, a death before they die, [Thought 186-15
From a doctor into an ox, before standing up, [Freed 205-11
Someone before him to see and to know. [Scavoir 232-4
Of the silence before the armies, armies without [Martial 237-21
Before the speaker's youngest breath is taken! [Montra 261-21
Ruled us before, from over Asia, by [Montra 262-14
A soldier walks before my door. [Contra I 266-12
Before, before, before my door. [Contra I 266-14
Before, before, before my door. [Contra I 266-17
Before, before. Blood smears the oaks. [Contra I 267-3
A soldier stalks before my door. [Contra I 267-4
She held her hand before him in the air, [Hand 271-5
Who has gone before us in experience. [EM 315-19
Before we were wholly human and knew ourselves. [EM 317-29
Before it comes, the just anticipation [Descrip 344-12
Lifts up its heavy scowl before them. [Pediment 362-3
Before winter freezes and grows black-- [Burghers 362-14
As if twelve princes sat before a king. [Cred 375-25
There was a muddy centre before we breathed. [NSF 383-19
There was a myth before the myth began, [NSF 383-20
Than nakedness, standing before an inflexible [NSF 396-2
Or before, not the white of an aging afternoon, [AA 412-12
Had ever been before, no longer known, [Page 422-14
It fills the being before the mind can think. [John 436-17
Like the snow before it softened [Celle 438-6
Or Gawks of hay . . . Augusta Moon, before [Golden 460-12
Before the thought of evening had occurred [NH 482-23
Before and after one arrives or, say, [NH 485-24
Go back to a parent before thought, before speech, [Irish 501-11
Like tales that were told the day before yesterday-- [Hermit
  505-13
So that he that stood up in the boat leaning and looking before
  him [Prol 515-11
Than seventy, where one looks, one has been there before. [Slug
  522-2
Before one comes to the first black cataracts [R Conn 533-5
A bird's cry, at daylight or before, [Not Ideas 534-5
The time will come for these children, seated before their long
  black instruments, to strike the themes of love-- [Piano 21-16P
Seated before these shining forms, like the duskiest glass,
  reflecting the piebald of roses or what you will. [Piano 21-18P
Lulu sang of barbarians before the eunuchs [Lulu G 26-9 P
Before the horses, clouds of bronze imposed [Old Woman 43-7 P
Would soon be brilliant, as it was, before [Old Woman 45-24 P
Went crying their desolate syllables, before [Old Woman 45-26 P
Of fear before the disorder of the strange, [Burnshaw 48-14 P

Before the strange, having wept and having thought [Burnshaw
  50-7 P
Basilewsky's bulged before it floated, turned [Duck 63-23 P
And the portent end in night, composed, before [Sombre 71-5 P
A lamp, in a day of the week, the time before spring, [Woman Had
  83-6 P
Before the sun brought them that destruction [Stan Hero 83-18 P
To bear virile grace before their fellows, [Stan Hero 83-20 P
There is this bubbling before the sun, [Dove 98-13 P
As if none of us had ever been here before [Clear Day 113-17 P
Before it shines on any house. [Three 130-6 P
Before it rises, [Three 131-2 P
Before one can tell [Three 131-4 P
Before it shines on any house. [Three 131-13 P
At the window, as before. [Three 134-15 P
BEFRIENDED. By which at least I am befriended. [Idiom 201-10
BEGAN. His western voyage ended and began. [C 37-20
Madame, we are where we began. Allow, [High-Toned 59-13
The square began to clear. [Public Sq 109-10
At which the flight began, [Pascagoula 126-20
Music began to fail him. Brahms, although [Anglais 148-13
And that would be perfection, if each began [Nigger 156-20
Then the tree, at night, began to change, [On Road 203-19
There was a myth before the myth began, [NSF 383-20
Turn back to where we were when we began: [AA 420-13
Began, the return to phantomerei, if not [What We 459-8
BEGAT. Begat the tubas and the fire-wind strings, [NSF 398-14
See John-begat-Jacob.
BEGETS. The essential poem begets the others. The light [Orb
  441-26
BEGETTING. The world was round. But not from my begetting.
  [NE Verses 104-4
War's miracle begetting that of peace. [Cats 368-5
BEGETTINGS. A thousand begettings of the broken bold. [Owl 434-21
BEGGAR. But the beggar gazes on calamity [Bad Time 426-12
Weeps in Segovia. The beggar in Rome [Greenest 59-17 P
Is the beggar in Bogota. The kraal [Greenest 59-18 P
BEGGARS. He sat among beggars wet with dew, [Thought 187-5
And beggars dropping to sleep, [Add 198-9
Three beggars, you see, [Three 139-11 P
BEGGAR-TREE. Bare beggar-tree, hung low for fruited red [NH 483-24
BEGGED. In a black glove, holds a novel by Camus. She begged
  [Novel 457-11
BEGGING. Begging for one another. [Three 139-12 P
BEGIN. Do I begin and end? And where, [MBG 171-18
Begin, ephebe, by perceiving the idea [NSF 380-12
Speak softly, to begin with, in the eaves. [Beginning 428-8
To the end. Alpha continues to begin. [NH 469-20
Its actual appearance, suppose we begin [Recit 86-5 P
BEGINNER. Day's invisible beginner, [Song Fixed 520-7
BEGINNING. In the beginning, four blithe instruments [C 45-3
Philosopher, beginning with green brag, [C 46-1
Not by beginning but at the last man's end. [Nigger 156-21
The evening star, at the beginning of winter, the star [Martial
  237-11
At the beginning of winter, and I walked and talked [Martial
  233-14
Again, in the imagination's new beginning, [EM 320-11
And not to have is the beginning of desire. [NSF 382-4
Belief in an immaculate beginning [NSF 382-15
Their love, this beginning, not resuming, this [NSF 391-5
"The Beginning" [427-title
Nor the beginning nor end of a form: [Wom Sun 445-7
Reality is the beginning not the end, [NH 469-4
And yet this end and this beginning are one, [Hermit 506-1
That which is always beginning because it is part [Armor 530-17
Of that which is always beginning, over and over. [Armor 530-18
Beginning of a green Cockaigne to be, disliked, abandoned,
  [Inelegance 25-14 P
Without beginning or the concept of an end. [Grotesque 76-24 P
The beginning of a final order, [Ulysses 101-12 P
Not the beginning but the end of artifice, [Conversat 109-9 P
BEGINNINGS. Of these beginnings, gay and green, propose [NSF 398-5
The drafts of gay beginnings and bright ends, [Greenest 57-13 P
BEGINS. Except that it begins and ends, [Human 363-3
Begins again and ends again-- [Human 363-4
Be still. the summarium in excelsis begins . . . [Puel 456-16
In a perspective that begins again [Rock 528-12
Its wheel begins to turn. [Sombre 71-6 P
BEGONE. Begone! An inchling bristles in these pines, [Bantams 76-2
BEGONIAS. To sully the begonias, nor vex [Archi 18-14 P
BEGOT. An image that begot its infantines, [NH 479-7
BEGOTTEN. His thoughts begotten at clear sources, [Hero 277-14
BEGUILE. Green bosoms and black legs, beguile [Stan MMO 19-10 P
BEGUILES. Like these, autumn beguiles the fatalist. [Nigger 155-5
BEGUN. Nor half begun, but, when it is, leave room [C 33-19
The return to social nature, once begun, [C 43-20
Yet the house is not built, not even begun. [Ghosts 119-2
The tragedy, however, may have begun, [EM 320-10
The life of the poem in the mind has not yet begun.[Slug 522-16

(Her pale smock sparkles in a light begun [Infernale 25-9 P
BEHELD. And maidenly greenhorns, now beheld himself, [C 28-12
  Crispin beheld and Crispin was made new. [C 30-6
  Who, then, beheld the rising of the clouds [Sea Surf 99-23
  Who then beheld the figures of the clouds [Sea Surf 101-11
  Beheld the sovereign clouds as jugglery [Sea Surf 102-6
  Just to be there, just to be beheld, [Adieu 128-5
  As we beheld her striding there alone, [Key W 129-30
  Our man beheld the naked, nameless dame, [Hand 271-3
  So seeing, I beheld you walking, white, [Phenom 287-12
  How mad would he have to be to say, "He beheld [Bad Time 426-9
  To it"? He beheld the order of the northern sky [Bad Time 426-11
  For simple pleasure, he beheld, [Sat Night 27-17 P
  Acquired transparence and beheld itself [Greenest 54-6 P
  And beheld the source from which transparence came; [Greenest
    54-7 P
  Beheld the truth and knew it to be true. [Greenest 54-18 P
BEHIND. They flung monotony behind, [Ord Women 10-17
  Behind the bougainvilleas, [Venereal 47-20
  As if he that lived there left behind [Postcard 159-17
  And although my mind perceives the force behind the moment,
    [Fish-Scale 161-3
  That was what I painted behind the loaf, [Loaf 199-19
  And left beside and left behind. [Country 207-18
  And light behind the body of night [Adequacy 244-7
  In the greenish greens he flung behind [News 264-17
  Yet there is that idea behind the marbles, [Hero 276-14
  An image that leaves nothing much behind. [Repet 307-18
  A shape left behind, with like wings spreading out, [Myrrh 350-2
  Left thoughtlessly behind, [Prejudice 368-18
  Moving around and behind, a following, [Orb 442-22
  Of the image spreading behind it in idea. [Bouquet 449-21
  Behind all actual seeing, in the actual scene, [NH 467-11
  Behind the outer shields, the sheets of music [NH 488-10
  Behind its melancholy mask, [Secret Man 36-14 P
  We shall have gone behind the symbols [Ulysses 102-13 P
  You have left your lantern behind you. [Three 135-7 P
  Came clapping behind them [Three 139-4 P
BEHOLD. Behold, already on the long parades [Swans 4-9
  To behold the junipers shagged with ice, [Snow Man 10-2
  Like a dull scholar, I behold, in love, [Monocle 16-1
  Just to be there and just to behold. [Adieu 127-16
  To behold the sublime, [Am Sub 130-17
  And the beautiful trombones--behold [MBG 170-9
  Behold the moralist hidalgo [Thought 186-17
  To go to the Louvre to behold himself. [Prelude 194-21
  Behold the men in helmets borne on steel, [Extracts 259-19
  There to behold, there to proclaim, the grace [Montra 263-9
  And you, my semblables, behold in blindness [Dutch 292-22
  As on an elevation, and behold [NSF 386-20
  When in my coppice you behold me be. [NSF 393-24
  Behold them, not choses of Provence, growing [Bouquet 449-12
  The meta-men behold the idea as part [Bouquet 449-22
  Of the image, behold it with exactness through beads [Bouquet
    449-23
  Did they behold themselves in this [Sat Night 28-4 P
  Behold how order is the end [Room Gard 41-1
  The volcano Apostrophe, the sea Behold? [Duck 63-29 P
BEHOLDEN. Saved and beholden, in a robe of rays. [NH 477-24
BEHOLDER. From the beholder, [Nomad 95-12
  That the beholder knew their subtle purpose, [New Set 353-2
  The world images for the beholder. [Aug 492-16
BEHOLDING. Beholding all these green sides [Nomad 95-13
BEHOLDS. And, nothing himself, beholds [Snow Man 10-11
  The audience beholds you, not your gown. [Bad Time 427-9
  Its fire fails to pierce the vision that beholds it, [Questions
    462-7
  Beholds himself in you, and hears his voice [Rome 509-15
  The exhausted realist beholds [Abnormal 24-15 P
  The man below beholds the portent poised, [Sombre 69-25 P
BEING. of my being, shine like fire, that mirrors nothing.
    [Nuances 18-10
  The magnificent cause of being, [Weep Woman 25-7
  From whose being by starlight, on sea-coast, [Homunculus 26-26
  As being, in a world so falsified, [C 36-19
  Seemed to suckle themselves on his arid being, [Frogs 78-13
  I am too dumbly in my being pent. [Pharynx 96-4
  The being that yielded so little, acquired [Adieu 127-18
  These had a being, breathing frost; [Postcard 159-3
  It was being without description, being an ox. [Freed 205-16
  Of being, more than birth or death. [Country 207-22
  Neither as mask nor as garment but as a being, [Dwarf 208-11
  Moving and being, the image at its source, [Candle 223-13
  As one loves one's own being, [Yellow 236-15
  There he touches his being. There as he is [Yellow 237-4
  From any future, the ever-living and being, [Martial 238-8
  A gaiety that is being, not merely knowing, [Gala 248-13
  Whose merely being was his valiance, [Extracts 254-11
  And being would be being himself again, [Extracts 255-20
  Being, becoming seeing and feeling and self, [Extracts 255-21

Out of the hero's being, the deliverer [Montra 261-6
  Whose single being, single form [Jumbo 269-8
  "The Hand as a Being" [271-title
  I am and have a being and play a part. [Phenom 287-21
  The A B C of being, [Motive 288-16
  No self in the mass: the braver being, [Gigan 289-3
  Who died, the being that was an abstraction, [Gigan 289-6
  The glitter of a being, which the eye [Choc 297-14
  Of what men are. The collective being knew [Choc 299-22
  They lived, in which they lacked a pervasive being, [Somnam
    304-15
  This being in a reality beyond [Repet 307-11
  A being of sound, whom one does not approach [Creat 311-5
  The mind, which is our being, wrong and wrong, [EM 317-1
  Of the being's deepest darling, we forego [EM 317-14
  Was a return to birth, a being born [EM 321-18
  Mature: A capable being may replace [Pure 330-11
  A poet's metaphors in which being would [Descrip 341-8
  His being felt the need of soaring, the need [Liadoff 347-12
  The knowledge of being, sense without sense of time. [Myrrh 350-9
  Was like the conscious being of the book. [House Q 358-9
  That is a being, a will, a fate. [Human 363-16
  As of a general being or human universe. [Past Nun 378-22
  For a moment in the central of our being, [NSF 380-10
  Or a leaner being, moving in on him, [NSF 387-14
  In being more than an exception, part, [NSF 388-21
  Again, an inexhaustible being, rise [NSF 390-13
  Here, being visible is being white, [AA 412-16
  Is being of the solid of white, the accomplishment [AA 412-17
  The outlines of being and its expressings, the syllables of its
    law: [Large 424-5
  At the moment's being, without history, [Beginning 427-16
  And because being there in the heavy hills [Countryman 429-3
  Being there is being in a place, [Countryman 429-5
  It fills the being before the mind can think. [John 436-17
  Captives the being, widens--and was there. [Orb 440-16
  And others, make certain how being [Degen 444-8
  It not Swatara. It is being. [Degen 444-16
  And a dissociated abundance of being, [Wom Sun 445-10
  Become a single being, sure and true. [Pecul 454-9
  Its being beating heavily in the veins, [Novel 459-2
  Much rough-end being to smooth Paradise, [Luther 461-11
  Participants of its being. It is, we are. [Study I 463-10
  A great bosom, beard and being, alive with age. [NH 466-3
  A naked being with a naked will [NH 480-6
  Within his being, [Aug 492-6
  But, of my being and its knowing, part. [Angel 496-12
  I am one of you and being one of you [Angel 496-13
  Is being and knowing what I am and know. [Angel 496-14
  In which being there together is enough. [Final 524-18
  Were being alive, an incessant being alive, [Rock 526-8
  A particular of being, that gross universe. [Rock 526-9
  This vif, this dizzle-dazzle of being new [Armor 530-12
  It is as if being was to be observed, [Moonlight 531-5
  In the days when the mood of love will be swarming for solace
    and sink deeply into the thin stuff of being, [Piano 22-8 P
  For the gaudium of being, Jocundus instead [Sombre 71-29 P
  It might be the candle of another being, [Theatre 91-7 P
  The first word would be of the susceptible being arrived, [Discov
    96-1 P
  And being are one: the right to know [Ulysses 101-18 P
  And being are one--the right to know [Presence 106-3 P
  And bodying, and being there, [Presence 106-10 P
  The bouquet of being--enough to realize [Conversat 109-21 P
  That the sense of being changes as we talk, [Conversat 109-22 P
  Astute in being what they are made to be. [Art Pop 112-20 P
  "Of Mere Being" [117-title P
  See bearer-being.
BEINGS. The basses of their beings throb [Peter 90-10
  Even of death, the beings of the mind [Owl 436-5
  Beings of other beings manifold-- [Study II 464-12
BEKNOWN. Sinks into likeness blessedly beknown. [Spaniard 35-20 P
BELEAGUERED. See, now, the ways beleaguered by black, dropsical
  duennas, [Inelegance 26-7 P
BELCHED. But with a speech belched out of hoary darks [C 29-26
  And hears the nigger's prayer in motets, belched [Greenest
  59-12 P
BELFRY. The purple dress in autumn and the belfry breath [NE
  Verses 106-7
BELGIAN. This fat pistache of Belgian grapes exceeds [Nigger 154-17
  Belgian Farm, October, 1914 [Phases 5-title 5
BELIE. That must belie the racking masquerade, [C 39-16
BELIEF. If ever the search for a tranquil belief should end,
  [Nigger 151-9
  This death was his belief though death is a stone. [Men Fall
  188-17
  The will to be and to be total in belief, [Gala 248-44
  Of final belief. So, say that final belief [Oboe 250-7
  Of improvisations and seasons of belief. [Extracts 255-24
  (That being as much belief as we may have,) [Extracts 257-23

Whatever it may be; then one's belief [Extracts 257-26
 Of the weather are the belief in one's element, [Extracts 258-4
 Incapable of belief, in the difference. [Extracts 258-13
 Belief, that what it believes in is not true. [Pure 332-12
 We believe without belief, beyond belief. [Flyer 336-15
 Belief in an immaculate beginning [NSF 382-15
 Temper and belief and that differences lost [Aug 494-3
 A thing not planned for imagery or belief, [Look 518-6
 Babyishness of forsythia, a snatch of belief, [Slug 522-13
BELIEFS. The whole man, that tempers and beliefs became [Aug 494-2
 Your beliefs and disbeliefs, your whole peculiar plot; [Old Man
   501-4
 See rose-beliefs.
BELIEVE. To make believe a starry connaissance. [Monocle 13-22
 Do they believe they range the gusty cold, [Heaven 56-12
 Whom all believe that all believe, [MBG 170-11
 I can believe, in face of the object, [MBG 174-16
 Is it ideas that I believe? [MBG 175-19
 Good air, my only friend, believe, [MBG 175-20
 Believe would be a brother full [MBG 175-21
 Of love, believe would be a friend, [MBG 175-22
 The spirit laughs to see the eye believe [Extracts 253-5
 Than this, in this alone I may believe, [Extracts 257-25
 To believe in the weather and in the things and men [Extracts
   258-8
 Unless we believe in the hero, what is there [Hero 275-19
 To believe? Incisive what, the fellow [Hero 275-20
 Time. What a thing it is to believe that [Lack 303-14
 And the desire to believe in a metaphor. [Pure 332-10
 To believe, more than the casual hero, more [Paisant 335-9
 We believe without belief, beyond belief. [Flyer 336-15
 What am I to believe? If the angel in his cloud, [NSF 404-13
 Mesdames, one might believe that Shelley lies [Burnshaw 48-9 P
 The incredible gave him a purpose to believe. [Someone 85-18 A
 See make-believe.
BELIEVED. Out of a thing believed, a thing affirmed: [Beard 247-22
 From the water in which he believed and out of desire [New Set
   352-13
 Were not and are not. It is not to be believed. [Rock 525-11
 And one of us spoke and all of us believed [Letters 107-14 P
BELIEVER. The lover, the believer and the poet. [Orb 441-6
 That's it. The lover writes, the believer hears, [Orb 443-15
BELIEVES. The approach of him whom none believes, [MBG 170-10
 One beats and beats for that which one believes. [Dump 202-27
 The eye believes and its communion takes. [Extracts 253-4
 One believes is what matters. Ecstatic identities [Extracts 258-2
 Belief, that what it believes in is not true. [Pure 332-12
 An age is green or red. An age believes [Descrip 340-6
BELIEVING. No, not believing, but to make the cell [Montra 261-10
BELITTLES. Belittles those carefully chosen daubs. [Grapes 110-16
BELL. Forgather and bell boldly Crispin's last [C 43-13
 Raise reddest columns. Toll a bell [MBG 170-5
 Round and round goes the bell of the water [Vari 235-6
 The bell of its dome, the patron of sound. [Vari 235-9
 To hold by the ear, even though it wished for a bell, [Uruguay
   249-10
 Wished faithfully for a falsifying bell. [Uruguay 249-11
 Of people, as big bell-billows from its bell [EM 322-13
 The choir that choirs the first fatigue in deep bell of canzoni?
   [Inelegance 25-20 P
 As a church is a bell and people are an eye, [Sombre 67-19 P
 "Dinner Bell in the Woods" [109 title P
 He was facing phantasma when the bell rang. [Dinner 109-24
BELLA. He is, we are, Ah, bella! He is, we are, [Study I 463-11
BELL-BELLOW. Bell-bellow in the village steeple. Violets, [EM 322-14
BELL-BILLOWS. Of people, as big bell-billows from its bell [EM
   322-13
BELL-BORROWINGS. The porcelain bell-borrowings become [Burnshaw
   52-11 P
BELLE. "Homunculus et La Belle Étoile" [25-title
 When its black branches came to bud, belle day, [C 39-3
 "The spring is like a belle undressing." [Of Surface 57-5
 I come as belle design [W Burgher 61-12
 "Bouquet of Belle Scavoir" [231-title
 Ceylon, wants nothing from the sea, la belle [Extracts 257-28
 At home; or: In the woods, belle Belle alone [Golden 460-14
 See tea-belle.
BELLED. Where the fattest women belled the glass. [Dinner 110-4 P
BELLES. "Les Plus Belles Pages" [244-title
BELLICOSE. Another, still more bellicose, came on [C 37-22
BELLIES. Within our bellies, we her chariot. [Worms 49-17
 Smacking their muzzy bellies in parade, [High-Toned 59-16
 There is the same color in the bellies of frogs, in clays,
   withered reeds, skins, wood, sunlight. [Primordia 8-2 P
 Of buzzards and eat the bellies of the rich, [Burnshaw 49-8 P
BELLISHINGS. Like daylight, with time's bellishings, [Two Illus
   54-18
BELLISSIMO. Bellissimo, pomposo, [Orangeade 103-3
BELLOW. See bell-bellow.
BELLOWING. Eager for the brine and bellowing [Paltry 5-14

The ribboned stick, the bellowing breeches, cloak [C 28-8
 Salt masks of beard and mouths of bellowing, [Sea Surf 101-17
 The bells are the bellowing of bulls. [MBG 181-12
 In mid-Atlantic, bellowing, to command, [Bship 78-13 P
BELLS. Descensions of their tinkling bells arrive. [Monocle 15-20
 "Winter Bells" [141-title
 That church without bells. [Winter B 141-4
 He preferred the brightness of bells, [Winter B 141-5
 The heavy bells are tolling rowdy-dow. [Nigger 155-9
 The bells are the bellowing of bulls. [MBG 181-12
 The bells grow longer. This is not sleep. This is desire. [Men
   Fall 187-14
 The bells of the chapel pullulate sounds at [Peaches 224-9
 The church bells clap one night in the week. [Cuisine 227-16
 Impatient of the bells and midnight forms, [Uruguay 250-1
 So many clappers going without bells, [NSF 394-5
 Inwoven by a weaver to twelve bells . . . . [Beginning 428-5
 An attic glass, hums of the old Lutheran bells [Golden 460-13
 "The Old Lutheran Bells at Home" [461-title
 Each sexton has his sect. The bells have none. [Luther 461-15
 Each truth is a sect though no bells ring for it. [Luther 462-1
 And the bells belong to the sextons, after all, [Luther 462-2
 Impalpable bells, transparencies of sound, [NH 466-6
 The far-fire flowing and the dim-coned bells [NH 466-10
 Or mind, uncertain in the clearest bells, [NH 466-17
 There was a clearing, a readiness for first bells, [NH 483-1
 The bells keep on repeating solemn names [Rome 510-15
 Bells of the dogs chinked. [Cab 21-1 P
BELLY. Boomed from his very belly odious chords. [Monocle 17-17
 Deeper within the belly's dark [MBG 171-9
 Then the bird from his ruddy belly blew [Horn 230-5
 Feel everything starving except the belly [Hero 278-3
 The flowering Judas grows from the belly or not at all. [Holiday
   312-12
 "The Dove in the Belly" [366-title
 The dove in the belly builds his nest and coos, [Belly 366-17
 Like a belly puckered by a spear. [Lulu M 27-4 P
 And the mighty, musty belly of tears. [Sat Night 28-3 P
 See water-belly.
BELLY-SOUNDS. Bland belly-sounds in somnolent troughs, [Frogs 78-3
BELONG. And the bells belong to the sextons, after all, [Luther
   462-2
BELONGED. The very Place Du Puy, in fact, belonged [NSF 391-24
 An order and thereafter he belonged [Bad Time 426-10
 He belonged to the far-foreign departure of his vessel and was
   part of it, [Prol 516-1
BELONGS. And, otherwise, the rainy rose belongs [Extracts 252-13
 And thereafter he belongs to it, to bread [Bad Time 426-13
 Without understanding, he belongs to it [Bad Time 426-16
 The statue belongs to the cavernous past, belongs [Greenest 58-28P
BELOW. To the dusk of a whistling south below the south, [C 38-13
 Below Key West. [Two Figures 86-12
 The sea-clouds whitened far below the calm [Sea Surf 99-10
 What's down below is in the past [Botanist 2 135-18
 Like last night's crickets, far below. [Botanist 2 135-19
 From below and walks without meditation, [Brave 138-20
 Below me, on the asphalt, under the trees. [Loaf 200-12
 Containing the mind, below which it cannot descend, [Of Mod
   240-17
 Brought down to one below the eaves, [Silent 359-14
 Of flame on the line, with a second wheel below, [Page 422-23
 To most incredible depths. I speak below [John 437-9
 Prostrate below the singleness of its will. [NH 478-24
 Of summer and that unused hearth below, [Phases 5-7 P
 The silent watcher, far below her, hears:) [Infernale 25-11 P
 Of the dank imagination, much below [Burnshaw 47-5 P
 The man below the man below the man, [Sombre 66-16 P
 He thinks and it is not true. The man below [Sombre 66-19 P
 He dwells below, the man below, in less [Sombre 67-13 P
 The man, but not the man below, for whom [Sombre 68-2 P
 The man and the man below were reconciled, [Sombre 68-14 P
 The man below beholds the portent poised, [Sombre 69-25 P
 Leaves of the autumns in which the man below [Sombre 69-32 P
 The year's dim elongations stretch below [Sombre 70-2 P
 Not the space in camera of the man below, [Sombre 70-31 P
 Even the man below, the subverter, stops [Sombre 71-17 P
 Below the prerogative jumble. The fruit so seen [Someone 84-16 A
BELSHAZZAR. In a canton of Belshazzar [Country 207-3
 To Belshazzar, putrid rock, [Country 207-4
 Belshazzar's brow, O, ruler, rude [Country 207-14
 It wants Belshazzar reading right [Country 207-20
BELT. The spouse. She opened her stone-studded belt. [NSF 395-21
 And her belt, the final fortune of their desire. [World 521-9
BELTED. Prime paramour and belted paragon, [Lilacs 49-12
 Of blue and yellow, sky and sun, belted [Cred 378-4
 See dark-belted.
BELTS. The stars are putting on their glittering belts. [AA 419-22
 And beetling of belts and lights of general stones, [NH 477-20
 Angels returning after war with belts [Greenest 56-10 P
BE-MISTED. To that be-misted one and apart from her. [Wild 328-14

BENCH. Lenin on a bench beside a lake disturbed [Descrip 342-21
  A bench was his catalepsy, Theatre [NSF 397-10
  Or the bench with the pot of geraniums, the stained mattress
    and the washed overalls drying in the sun? [Indigo 22-12 P
BEND. He will bend his ear then. [Plot Giant 7-7
  She sees a barer sky that does not bend. [Anatomy 108-7
  He could not bend against its propelling force. [R Conn 533-12
  Oh, bend against the invisible; and lean [Blanche 10-6 P
  Of everything. The roses bend [Room Gard 41-2 P
BENDING. Bending over and pulling themselves erect on the wooden
    handles, [Prol 515-8
  Where the bending iris grew; [Phases 4-8 P
  Only the surfaces--the bending arm, [Blanche 10-3 P
  Bending in blue dresses to touch something, [Clear Day 113-12 P
BENDS. Which pierces clouds and bends on half the world. [NSF
    393-15
  Too long, is like a bayonet that bends. [Soldat 13-7 P
  That bends the particulars to the abstract, [Ulysses 103-23 P
BENEATH. Obliquities of those who pass beneath, [C 41-4
  Of bliss submerged beneath appearance, [Jasmine 79-10
  But leave a bed beneath the myrtles. [Norfolk 111-6
  Beneath the arches and their spangled air, [Eve Angels 138-2
  Beneath the rhapsodies of fire and fire, [Eve Angels 138-3
  I have never--shall never hear. And yet beneath [Autumn 160-7
  Where do you lie, beneath snow, [Bagatelles 213-2
  It glares beneath the webs [Common 221-17
  Beneath summer and the sky [Scavoir 231-10
  We sat beneath it and sang our songs. [Vari 233-7
  Of air, who looked for the world beneath the blue, [Landsc 241-17
  Seized her and wondered: why beneath the tree [Hand 271-4
  And the soldier of time lies calm beneath that stroke. [EM 319-18
  And beneath that handkerchief drapeau, severe, [Pure 331-3
  Beneath his tip-tap-tap. It is she that responds. [Jouga 337-8
  Beneath, far underneath, the surface of [NSF 403-1
  Cinderella fulfilling herself beneath the roof? [NSF 405-9
  His head is air. Beneath his tip at night [AA 411-2
  Under the buttonwoods, beneath a moon nailed fast. [Cata 425-5
  Feeling the fear that creeps beneath the wool, [Novel 458-23
  Beneath the innocence [Inhab 504-14
  His crisp knowledge is devoured by her, beneath a dew. [Madame
    507-4
  And these beneath the shadow of a shape [Rome 509-2
  It is not to be seen beneath the appearances [R Conn 533-13
  The space beneath it still, a smooth domain, [Old Woman 46-5 P
  In a heaven of death. Beneath the heavy foils, [Greenest 54-21 P
  Beneath the spangling greens, fear might placate [Greenest
    54-22 P
  The father. He hides his ancient blue beneath [Recit 87-17 P
  Brooder, brooder, deep beneath its walls-- [Dove 97-16 P
  Beneath the middle stars and said: [Presence 105-18 P
  1. The hut stands by itself beneath the palms. [Someone 86-4 A
BENEDICTION. This may be benediction, sepulcher, [Havana 145-3
BENEFICENCE. The actual is a deft beneficence. [Nigger 155-16
  Beneficence, a repose, utmost repose, [Orb 442-14
  Reveals her, rounded in beneficence, [Spaniard 34-4 P
BENEVOLENCES. Than clouds, benevolences, distant heads. [EM 317-21
BENEVOLENT. As grim as it is benevolent, the just [AA 417-5
BENIGN. Can I take fire from so benign an ash? [Stan MMO 19-7 P
BENIGNLY. The relation comes, benignly, to its end? [C 46-12
BENITIA. Benitia, lapis Ville des Pins must soothe [Greenest
    58-22 P
BENJAMIN. The père Benjamin, the mère Blandenah, [Grotesque 77-11P
BENT. The man bent over his guitar, [MBG 165-1
  The night wind blows upon the dreamer, bent [Men Fall 188-19
  Bent and broken them down, [Weak Mind 212-19
  Shadows of scholars bent upon their books, [Montra 262-17
  Bent over work, anxious, content, alone, [NSF 406-16
  And the coroner bent [Coroner 30-9 P
  The body bent, like Hercules, to build. [Sombre 69-10 P
BEQUEATHING. Bequeathing your white feathers to the moon [Swans 4-7
BERCEUSE. Berceuse, transatlantic. The children are men, old men,
    [Woman Had 82-10 P
BERGAMO. Bergamo on a postcard, Rome after dark, [NH 486-1
BERRIES. Berries of villages, a barber's eye, [C 27-15
  Sweet berries ripen in the wilderness; [Sunday 70-24
BERRY. A white, pink, purple berry tree, [Banjo 114-3 P
  A very dark-leaved berry tree. [Banjo 114-4 P
BERSERK. I met Berserk, [Peacocks 57-10
BESEECH. Beseech them for an overpowering gloom. [Red Kit 32-4 P
BESIDE. Last night, we sat beside a pool of pink, [Monocle 17-14
  That lay beside him, the quotidian [C 43-4
  What were the hymns that buzzed beside my ears? [Hoon 65-11
  And left beside and left behind. [Country 207-18
  Sitting beside your lamp, there citron to nibble [Dwarf 208-13
  A black line beside a white line; [Common 221-3
  Into place beside her, where she was, [Vase 247-2
  And lay beside her underneath the tree. [Hand 271-21
  And darkly beside the vulcanic [Hero 274-28
  From beside us, from where we have yet to live. [Sketch 336-9
  Lenin on a bench beside a lake disturbed [Descrip 342-21

And the pines above and along and beside the sea. [AA 411-9
To keep on flowing. He wanted to walk beside it, [Cata 425-4
A countryman walks beside you. [Countryman 428-16
The name. He does not speak beside you. [Countryman 429-1
Beyond the object. He sits in his room, beside [NH 475-7
This sat beside his bed, with its guitar, [NH 483-16
Of Fact, lies at his ease beside the sea." [NH 485-18
Beside the statue, while you sang. Your eyes [Burnshaw 50-28 P
In the Duft of towns, beside a window, beside [Woman Had 83-5 P
BESIDES. Besides the people, his knowledge of them. In [EM 323-8
  Besides, when the sky is so blue, things sing themselves,
    [Debris 338-10
  There are things in a man besides his reason. [Pieces 351-10
  Like men besides, like men in light secluded, [NSF 405-12
  Besides, the world is a tower. [Secret Man 36-5 P
BESIEGING. The voice of this besieging pain. [Mozart 132-12
BESPOKEN. See bad-bespoken.
BESPRENT. Rose up besprent and sought the flaming red [Hibiscus
    22-20
BESPRINKLED. Arching cloths besprinkled with colors [Plot Giant
    6-18
BEST. And the best cock of red feather [Watermelon 89-5
  Bare night is best. Bare earth is best. Bare, bare, [Eve Angels
    137-29
  Black man, bright nouveautés leave one, at best, pseudonymous.
    [Nudity Col 145-12
  And in perceiving this I best perceive myself [Re-state 146-3
  And the dew and the ploughman still will best be one. [Burnshaw
    48-2 P
BETA. At beta b and gamma g, [Ord Women 11-10
BETHOU. Bethou me, said sparrow, to the crackled blade, [NSF 393-22
  And you, and you, bethou me as you blow, [NSF 393-23
  Bethou, bethou, bethou me in my glade. [NSF 394-3
  Of stone, that never changes. Bethou him, you [NSF 394-16
  And you, bethou him and bethou. It is [NSF 394-17
BETHOUS. That these bethous compose a heavenly gong. [NSF 394-6
BETRAYED. And Lazarus betrayed him to the rest, [Good Man 364-8
BETROTHAL. Of things were waiting in a betrothal known [Study II
    464-17
BETTER. It is better that, as scholars, [Homunculus 26-17
  That's better. That's worth crossing seas to find. [C 36-25
  The oncoming fantasies of better birth. [C 39-28
  Or better not of myself at all, [MBG 175-13
  It would have been better, the time conceived, [Thunder 220-13
  It would have been better for his hands [Thunder 220-21
  Had he been better able to suppose: [Landsc 243-1
  Of things no better than paper things, of days [Extracts 253-2
  Better without an author, without a poet, [Creat 310-18
  Stronger and freer, a little better off. [Good Man 364-4
  It is better for me [Secret Man 36-1 P
  Memory without passion would be better lost. [Lytton 38-18 P
BETWEEN. Between himself and his environment, [C 34-27
  An up and down between two elements, [C 35-7
  A fluctuating between sun and moon, [C 35-8
  Between a Carolina of old time, [C 35-22
  Killing the time between corpses [Venereal 47-15
  I figured you as nude between [Vincentine 52-11
  The lines are straight and swift between the stars. [Tallap 71-10
  I found between moon-rising and moon-setting [NE Verses 104-3
  The mountains between our lands and the sea-- [Grapes 110-9
  But in between lies the sphere of my fortune [Nigger 151-4
  Between farewell and the absence of farewell, [Nigger 152-5
  To this returns. Between the two, [MBG 176-1
  Between issue and return, there is [MBG 176-18
  Between you and the shapes you take [MBG 183-11
  One of many, between two poles. So, [Glass 197-10
  Between that disgust and this, between the things [Dump 202-14
  The distance between the dark steeple [Jersey 210-9
  Spurted from between the fingers [Weak Mind 212-3
  Until the difference between air [Vari 235-3
  The hand between the candle and the wall [Rhythms 245-9
  The mind between this light or that and space, [Rhythms 245-11
  With the ferocious chu-chot-chu between, the sobs [Extracts
    253-18
  There was that difference between the and an, [Extracts 255-7
  The difference between himself and no man, [Extracts 255-8
  A good agreement between himself and night, [Extracts 256-5
  A chord between the mass of men and himself, [Extracts 256-6
  Between one's self and the weather and the things [Extracts
    258-3
  One of the sacraments between two breaths, [Montra 262-8
  Between two neatly measured stations, [Hero 275-17
  Between the thing as idea and [Couch 295-19
  Between cities is a gesticulation of forms, [Choc 296-14
  The soldier seeking his point between the two, [Repet 309-9
  And, between his letters, reading paragraphs [EM 313-12
  Between us and the place in which we stood. [Wild 329-12
  There was no difference between the town [Liadoff 347-17
  "Thinking of a Relation between the Images of Metaphors" [356-
    title

Between the two we live and die-- [Silent 359-6
Than creatures, of the sky between the banks, [Lot 371-14
To an irmaculate end. We move between these points: [NSF 382-17
Between a great captain and the maiden Bawda. [NSF 401-6
Between excluding things. It was not a choice [NSF 403-12
Between, but of. He chose to include the things [NSF 403-13
Soldier, there is a war between the mind [NSF 407-4,
And sky, between thought and day and night. It is [NSF 407-5
Between loud water and loud wind, between that [Page 421-7
Und so lau, between sound without meaning and speech, [Page
    421-10
And she that in the syllable between life [Owl 432-12
Between us and the object, external cause, [John 437-15
Not wholly spoken in a conversation between [NH 471-7
In the area between is and was are leaves, [NH 474-2
Only a little way, and not beyond, unless between himself [Prol
    516-12
An invention, an embrace between one desperate clod [Rock 525-13
A theorem proposed between the two-- [Rock 525-16
Between the slouchings of a gunman and a lover, [Moonlight
    531-15
There is a connection between the colors, [Primordia 9-17 P
Between the matin air and color, goldenest generating,
    [Inelegance 25-16 P
And away, dialogues between incognitos. [Sombre 67-12 P
Between chimeras and garlanded the way, [Sombre 67-29 P
"The war between classes is [Bship 77-16 P
Of the war between individuals. In time, [Bship 77-18 P
Distance between me and the five-times-sensed, [Souls 94-19 P
BEWARE. (He shouts.) Hola! Of that strange light, beware!
    [Infernale 25-3 P
BEWITCH. Health-o, when ginger and fromage bewitch [NE Verses 104-5
BEYOND. The soul, O ganders, flies beyond the parks [Swans 4-1
    And far beyond the discords of the wind. [Swans 4-2
    Beyond your chilly chariots, to the skies. [Swans 4-12
    The blazing passes, from beyond the sun. [Monocle 15-19
    Among the blooms beyond the open sand; [Hibiscus 22-11
    Blotched out beyond unblotching. Crispin, [C 28-6
    Polyphony beyond his baton's thrust. [C 28-21
    From which he sailed. Beyond him, westward, lay [C 33-13
    It irked beyond his patience. Hence it was, [C 39-21
    Beyond Bordeaux, beyond Havana, far [C 40-9
    Beyond carked Yucatan, he might have come [C 40-10
    Beyond these changes, good, fat, guzzly fruit. [C 41-7
    In my room, the world is beyond my understanding; [Of Surface
    57-1
    Beyond the planets. Thus, our bawdiness, [High-Toned 59-9
    Is beyond us, as the firmament, [Curtains 62-8
    Of bliss beyond the mutes of plaster, [Jasmine 79-8
    Beyond revelries of sleep, [Watermelon 89-9
    A blue beyond the rainy hyacinth, [Sea Surf 101-1
    Requiring order beyond their speech. [Sad Gay 122-9
    That passed beyond us through the narrow sky. [Medit 124-6
    Beyond all trees, the ridges thrown [How Live 125-19
    She sang beyond the genius of the sea. [Key W 128-11
    So far beyond the casual solitudes, [Re-state 146-9
    Yet radiantly beyond much lustier blurs. [Nigger 155-19
    Beyond our gate and the windy sky [Postcard 159-9
    A tune beyond us, yet ourselves, [MBG 165-8
    A tune beyond us as we are, [MBG 167-15
    Placed, so, beyond the compass of change, [MBG 168-1
    What is beyond the cathedral, outside, [MBG 181-3
    In the catastrophic room . . . beyond despair, [Men Fall 187-18
    Wax wasted, monarchies beyond [Prelude 195-6
    And of him that sees, beyond the astronomers, [Candle 223-9
    With his men, beyond the barbican. [Vari 234-12
    Beyond which it has no will to rise. [Of Mod 240-18
    A truth beyond all truths. [Landsc 242-19
    Beyond the keenest diamond day [Adequacy 244-1
    Beyond the knowledge of nakedness, as part [Extracts 252-18
    Of reality, beyond the knowledge of what [Extracts 252-19
    Is real, part of a land beyond the mind? [Extracts 252-20
    The sunlight. They bear brightly the little beyond [Extracts
    254-22
    Far, far beyond the putative canzones [Extracts 256-7
    Of anywhere beyond, to a different element, [Extracts 258-11
    Beyond a second death, as evil's end? [Extracts 258-28
    Again and fated to endure beyond [Extracts 259-5
    Beyond, futura's fuddle-fiddling lumps, [Montra 260-15
    Sings of an heroic world beyond the cell, [Montra 261-9
    Beyond the oyster-beds, indigo [Hero 274-26
    Beyond his circumstance, projected [Hero 277-21
    Beyond the sleep of those that did not know, [Choc 299-10
    But not the thinker, large in their largeness, beyond [Choc
    299-16
    Their form, beyond their life, yet of themselves, [Choc 299-17
    And the associations beyond death, even if only [Lack 303-13
    This being in a reality beyond [Repet 307-11
    And beyond the days, beyond the slow-foot litters [Repet 309-1
    Beyond intelligence, an artificial man [Creat 311-3

Beyond invention. Within what we permit, [EM 317-6
Was it that--a sense and beyond intelligence? [Pure 331-10
Could the future rest on a sense and be beyond [Pure 331-11
That is different. They are characters beyond [Paisant 335-4
We believe without belief, beyond belief. [Flyer 336-15
A palm that rises up beyond the sea, [Descrip 344-2
Pure coruscations, that lie beyond [Analysis 349-1
There is a sense in sounds beyond their meaning. [Pieces 352-1
Beyond relation to the parent trunk: [Red Fern 365-10
Beyond which there is nothing left of time. [Cred 372-12
But a tower more precious than the view beyond, [Cred 373-18
His slouching pantaloons, beyond the town, [NSF 389-6
There was an island beyond him on which rested, [NSF 393-10
The spouse beyond emerald or amethyst, [NSF 395-23
Beyond the burning body that I bear. [NSF 395-24
Beyond which fact could not progress as fact. [NSF 402-22
Beyond which thought could not progress as thought. [NSF 403-10
Beyond the habit of sense, anarchic shape [Page 422-18
So far beyond the rhetorician's touch. [Roses 431-12
A diamond jubilance beyond the fire, [Owl 433-21
With a sad splendor, beyond artifice, [Owl 435-16
The effect of the object is beyond the mind's [John 436-18
Is more difficult to find than the way beyond it. [Papini 446-6
The sky was blue beyond the vaultiest phrase. [What We 459-12
Nothing beyond reality. Within it, [NH 471-21
Beyond the object. He sits in his room, beside [NH 475-7
Beyond the horizon with its masculine [NH 476-24
It buzzes beyond the horizon or in the ground: [NH 487-14
Beyond, the two alike in the make of the mind. [Rome 508-7
Of the fortune of the spirit, beyond the eye, [Rome 508-14
Not of its sphere, and yet not far beyond, [Rome 508-15
Outside of and beyond the dirty light, [Two Illus 513-17
Did not pass like someone voyaging out of and beyond the
    familiar. [Prol 515-13
Was beyond his recognizing. By this he knew that likeness of him
    extended [Prol 516-11
Only a little way, and not beyond, unless between himself [Prol
    516-12
And things beyond resemblance there was this and that intended
    to be recognized, [Prol 516-13
No doubt we live beyond ourselves in air, [Look 518-3
We hear, what we are, beyond mystic disputation, [Look 518-11
Of the ground, a cure beyond forgetfulness. [Rock 526-13
Beyond any order, [Polo 38-1 P
Beyond any rebellion, [Polo 38-2 P
Grown great and grave beyond imagined trees, [Old Woman 45-31 P
And there are the white-maned horses' heads, beyond [Burnshaw
    49-19 P
Itself, beyond the utmost increase come [Greenest 53-30 P
Beyond thought's regulation. There each man, [Greenest 54-2 P
In one, except a throne raised up beyond [Greenest 55-10 P
Men's bones, beyond their breaths, the black sublime, [Greenest
    55-11 P
For races, not for men, powerful beyond [Greenest 59-29 P
To the camellia-chateaux and an inch beyond, [Duck 60-14 P
By harmonies beyond known harmony. [Duck 62-8 P
Than the color white and high beyond any height [Duck 64-6 P
An image of his making, beyond the eye, [Sombre 69-26 P
A life beyond this present knowing, [Ulysses 101-22 P
As toward an absolute foyer beyond romance. [Local 112-12 P
An understanding beyond journalism, [Bus 116-12 P
Beyond the last thought, rises [Of Mere 117-16 P
BEZELED. To which we come as into bezeled plain, [Montra 262-3
BIBBLING. Sepulchral señors, bibbling pale mescal, [C 38-21
BID. The muscular one, and bid him whip [Emperor 64-2
BIDDEN. It is easy to say to those bidden--But where, [Ghosts 119-4
BIDDERS. Bidders and biders for its ecstasies, [C 44-1
BIDDING. That would be bidding farewell, be bidding farewell.
    [Adieu 128-6
BIDERS. Bidders and biders for its ecstasies, [C 44-1
BIG. Call the roller of big cigars, [Emperor 64-1
    It was everything bulging and blazing and big in itself,
    [Freed 205-22
    Working, with big hands, on the town, [Hartford 227-2
    Of the armies, the solid men, make big the fable. [Choc 301-15
    Rejected years. A big bird pecks at him [EM 318-8
    For food. The big bird's bony appetite [EM 322-13
    Of people, as big bell-billows from its bell [EM 322-13
    It is that and a very big hat. [Prejudice 368-13
    It does no good to speak of the big, blue bush [Study I 463-4
    Within the big, blue bush and its vast shade [Study I 463-12
    In the big X of the returning primitive. [NH 474-18
    Lighted by space, big over those that sleep, [NH 482-5
    Looked on big women, whose ruddy-ripe images [NH 486-17
    In the land of big mariners, the words they spoke [NH 486-20
    So well, that which we do for ourselves, too big, [Look 518-5
    Last Friday, in the big light of last Friday night, [Real 110-7 P
BIG-BAGGED. Flat-ribbed and big-bagged. [Orangeade 102-19
BIG-BRUSHED. That big-brushed green. Or in a tragic mode, [John
    437-3

BIG-FINNED. The big-finned palm [Nomad 95-8
BIGGEST. People that live in the biggest houses [Grotesque 74-17 P
BIG-SHADOWED. Against gold whipped reddened in big-shadowed black,
    [Repet 309-19
BIJOU. C'était mon enfant, mon bijou, mon âme. [Sea Surf 99-9
    The bijou of Atlas, the moon, [Public Sq 109-11
BILLOWING. There was an insolid billowing of the solid. [Real
    111-1 P
BILLOWS. Of billows, downward, toward the drift-fire shore. [Page
    422-26
    See bell-billows.
BILLS. The bills of the swans are flat upon the ground. [Havana
    142-10
    The swans . . . Before the bills of the swans fell flat [Havana
    142-13
BIND. That is their mind, these men, and that will bind [Farewell
    118-18
BINDERS. The binders did it with armorial books. [Greenest 53-16 P
BING. And make much bing, high bing. [Snow Stars 133-9
BIRCH. The birch trees draw up whiteness from the ground.
    [Primordia 8-21 P
BIRD. A red bird flies across the golden floor. [Monocle 13-12
    It is a red bird that seeks out his choir [Monocle 13-13
    Like a widow's bird [Nuances 18-16
    It did not give of bird or bush, [Jar 76-15
    "The Bird with the Coppery, Keen Claws" [82-title
    For all his purple, the purple bird must have [Nigger 155-20
    In measureless measures, not a bird for me [Autumn 160-5
    But the name of a bird and the name of a nameless air [Autumn
    160-6
    Though I have never--shall never hear that bird. [Autumn 160-12
    It is the leaf the bird brings back to the boat. [Blue Bldg
    217-18
    The bird kept saying that birds had once been men, [Horn 230-1
    Then the bird from his ruddy belly blew [Horn 230-5
    Of the iris bore white blooms. The bird then boomed. [Horn 230-10
    The red bird most and the strongest sky-- [Adequacy 244-14
    Plato, the reddened flower, the erotic bird. [Extracts 253-29
    Look round, brown moon, brown bird, as you rise to fly, [God
    285-1
    The single bird, the obscure moon-- [Motive 288-8
    Noiselessly, noiselessly, resembling a thin bird, [Somnam 304-2
    The generations of the bird are all [Somnam 304-7
    Without this bird that never settles, without [Somnam 304-10
    Rejected years. A big bird pecks at him [EM 318-8
    For food. The big bird's bony appetite [EM 318-9
    Is as insatiable as the sun's. The bird [EM 318-10
    The sun is the country wherever he is. The bird [EM 318-18
    Already the green bird of summer has flown [Myrrh 349-15
    Selah, tempestuous bird. How is it that [Belly 366-18
    In an abandoned spot. Soft, civil bird, [Cred 377-12
    Of leaves, in which the sparrow is a bird [NSF 394-15
    A bird's cry, at daylight or before, [Not Ideas 534-5
    The humming-bird is the national bird [Grotesque 75-1 P
    Or almost solid seem show--the way a fly bird [Conversat 108-14P
    A gold-feathered bird [Of Mere 117-18 P
    The bird sings. Its feathers shine. [Of Mere 118-3 P
    The bird's fire-fangled feathers dangle down. [Of Mere 118-6 P
    See: blue-bird; cock-bird; humming-bird; mi-bird; night-bird;
    red-bird.
BIRD-NEST. Of bird-nest arches and of rain-stained vaults. [Rome
    510-10
BIRDS. That are like birds, [Sugar-Cane 12-13
    To which all birds come sometime in their time. [Monocle 17-5
    She says, "I am content when wakened birds, [Sunday 68-12
    But when the birds are gone, and their warm fields [Sunday 68-15
    Like her remembrance of awakened birds, [Sunday 68-24
    The clambering wings of birds of black revolved, [Babies 77-14
    Why do you imagine golden birds? [Thirteen 93-20
    The grass is in seed. The young birds are flying. [Ghosts 119-1
    It goes and the birds go, [Gray 140-15
    Birds that never fly [Gray 140-17
    The birds are singing in the yellow patios, [Nigger 152-15
    Brown as the bread, thinking of birds [Loaf 200-1
    Birds that came like dirty water in waves [Loaf 200-3
    And still the birds came, came in watery flocks, [Loaf 200-14
    Because it was spring and the birds had to come.[Loaf 200-15
    Solace itself in peevish birds? Is it peace, [Dump 203-4
    On human heads. True, birds rebuild [Cuisine 227-14
    The bird kept saying that birds had once been men, [Horn 230-1
    The wind dissolving into birds, [Vase 246-13
    "Of Bright & Blue Birds & the Gala Sun" [248-title
    Item: The cocks crow and the birds cry and [Montra 263-13
    Birds and people of this too voluminous [Hero 278-1
    Dry Birds Are Fluttering in Blue Leaves [Pure 332-title 4
    Not speaking worms, nor birds [Analysis 348-18
    First fruits, without the virginal of birds, [NSF 385-10
    The theatre is filled with flying birds, [AA 416-16
    Birds twitter pandemoniums around [Antag 426-3
    Under the birds, among the perilous owls, [NH 474-17

Dangling and spangling, the mic-mac of mocking birds. [NH 486-15
    Of birds called up by more than the sun, [Hermit 505-17
    Birds of more wit, that substitute-- [Hermit 505-18
    "Looking across the Fields and Watching the Birds Fly" [517-title
    Birds of intermitted bliss, [Phases 4-9 P
    The birds that wait out rain in willow leaves. [Soldat 13-13 P
    And not all birds sing cuck [Lulu M 27-7 P
    No doubt, the well-tuned birds are singing, [Agenda 42-11 P
    For a little time, again, rose-breasted birds [Burnshaw 49-30 P
    Leaves are not always falling and the birds [Burnshaw 50-24 P
    Is all the birds he ever heard and that, [Duck 62-3 P
    As of insects or cloud-stricken birds, away [Sombre 67-11 P
    This rock and the dry birds [Including 88-3 P
    See cock-birds.
BIRTH. The oncoming fantasies of better birth. [C 39-28
    Jove in the clouds had his inhuman birth. [Sunday 67-27
    Now, of the music summoned by the birth [Fictive 87-14
    Of the bride, love being a birth, have need to see [Ghosts 119-13
    Of being, more than birth or death. [Country 207-22
    Should be illusion, that the mobs of birth [Dutch 292-25
    In what new spirit had his body birth? [Choc 299-8
    Was a return to birth, a being born [EM 321-18
    Are of our earthy birth and here and now [NSF 395-8
    And breeding and bearing birth of harmony, [Study II 465-2
    In a birth of sight. The blooming and the musk [Rock 526-7
    And chant the rose-points of their birth, and when [Burnshaw
    49-29 P
    Of a ruddier summer, a birth that fetched along [Nuns 92-13 P
    But an antipodal, far-fetched creature, worthy of birth, [Discov
    96-5 P
    And thirty years, in the galaxies of birth, [Ideal 88-9 A
BIRTHS. Virgin of boorish births, [Venereal 47-17
BISCAYNE. In the sea, Biscayne, there prinks [Homunculus 25-13
BISCUIT. And a biscuit cheek. [Coroner 30-8 P
BISHOP. The bishop rests. [Gray 140-8
    Except when the bishop passes by, [Gray 140-18
BISHOPS. I have been pupil under bishops' rods [Soldat 11-4 P
    A board for bishops' grapes, the happy form [Sombre 70-8 P
    At least that was the theory, when bishops' books [Connois 215-15
BISQUED. An Alp, a purple Southern mountain bisqued [Someone 87-3A
BIT. At home, a bit like the slenderest courtesan. [NE Verses 106-6
    That it made the General a bit absurd, [NSF 391-18
    Out of a violet sea. They rise a bit [Duck 60-10 P
    The ship, make it my own and, bit by bit, [Bship 77-21 P
BITCH. Keep quiet in the heart, O wild bitch. O mind [Puel 456-13
    It is an old bitch, an old drunk, [Grotesque 77-3 P
BITE. That grips the centre, the actual bite, that life [Choc
    298-22
    And makes flame flame and makes it bite the wood [Novel 458-7
    And bite the hard-bite, barking as it bites. [Novel 458-8
    See hard-bite.
BITES. And bite the hard-bite, barking as it bites. [Novel 458-8
BITS. There are bits of blue. [Pears 196-14
    And pallid bits, that tend to comply with blue, [Bouquet 452-2
BITTER. From your too bitter heart, [Weep Woman 25-2
    Bitter eyes, hands hostile and cold. [Chateau 161-10
    You lovers that are bitter at heart. [MBG 174-4
    The almond and deep fruit. This bitter meat [Cuisine 228-13
    Life is a bitter aspic. We are not [EM 322-9
    A man of bitter appetite despises [EM 322-20
    A bitter utterance from your writhing, dumb, [NSF 384-21
    But her he had not foreseen: the bitter mind [Old Woman 44-1 P
    The blood of his bitter brain; and there the sun [Burnshaw 49-11P
BITTERNESS. Note that, in this bitterness, delight, [Poems Clim
    194-8
BITTEREST. But not of romance, the bitterest vulgar do [Bouquet
    450-4
BLACK. "Domination of Black" [8-title
    Fill your black hull [Fabliau 23-12
    Its black blooms rise. [Weep Woman 25-6
    When its black branches came to bud, belle day, [C 39-3
    The black man said, [Jack Rabbit 50-8
    The black man said, [Jack-Rabbit 50-14
    Should have a black barouche. [W Burgher 61-6
    The sky is a blue gum streaked with rose. The trees are black.
    [Banal 62-12
    But an eye that studies its black lid. [Tallap 71-17
    This old, black dress, [Explan 72-14
    The clambering wings of birds of black revolved, [Babies 77-14
    A black vestibule; [Theory 87-2
    The shrouding shadows, made the petals black [Sea Surf 100-23
    And you, black Sly, [Pascagoula 126-10
    And, dressed in black, he walks [Gray 140-3
    Black man, bright nouveautes leave one, at best, pseudonymous.
    [Nudity Col 145-12
    Do the drummers in black hoods [Circulat 150-3
    A little later when the sky is black. [Nigger 156-14
    Staring, at midnight, at the pillow that is black [Men Fall 187-17
    The rugged black, the image. Design [Prelude 195-18
    You are humped higher and higher, black as stone-- [Rabbit K 210-1

The black wind of the sea [Weak Mind 212-11
Rose up, tallest, in the black sun, [Thunder 220-6
A black line beside a white line; [Common 221-3
A black line drawn on flat air. [Common 221-5
For these black lines. [Common 221-16
And as the black Spaniard plays his guitar. [Peaches 224-6
Whether the water was black and lashed about [Extracts 255-13
Black water breaking into reality. [Extracts 255-22
Blue's last transparence as it turned to black, [Choc 297-13
Against gold whipped reddened in big-shadowed black, [Repet
    309-19
On a black piano practiced epi-tones. [Liadoff 346-16
Before winter freezes and grows black-- [Burghers 362-14
White houses in villages, black communicants-- [Cats 367-19
The waitress heaped up black Hermosas [Attempt 370-2
Among fomentations of black bloom and of white bloom. [Attempt
    370-18
Black beaded on the rock, the flecked animal, [AA 412-2
And proclaim it, the white creator of black, jetted [AA 417-11
Swatara, Swatara, black river, [Countryman 428-9
Say that it is a crude effect, black reds, [Roses 430-10
So there is a man in black space [Degen 444-4
The man in the black wood descends unchanged. [Degen 444-11
Here the black violets grow down to its banks [Degen 445-1
In a black glove, holds a novel by Camus. She begged [Novel
    457-11
A second that grows first, a black unreal [Novel 458-14
If the black of night stands glistening on beau mont, [NH 467-2
Romanza out of the black shepherd's isle, [NH 480-13
In the hearing of the shepherd and his black forms [NH 480-15
Effete green, the woman in black cassimere. [NH 482-2
The black fugatos are strumming the blackness of black . . .
    [Madame 507-9
Before one comes to the first black cataracts [R Conn 533-5
A black figure dances in a black field. [Plough-Boy 6-4 P
It wraps the sheet around its body, until the black figure is
    silver. [Plough-Boy 6-6 P
How soon the silver fades in the dust! How soon the black figure
    slips from the wrinkled sheet! [Plough-Boy 6-8 P
In the flowing of black water. [Primordia 7-22 P
The child's hair is of the color of the hay in the haystack,
    around which the four black horses stand. [Primordia 8-1 P
The black mother of eleven children [Primordia 9-15 P
Green bosoms and black legs, beguile [Stan MMO 19-10 P
Black fact emerges from her swishing dreams. [Stan MMO 19-22
The time will come for these children, seated before their
    long black instruments, to strike the themes of love-- [Piano
    21-16 P
And these long, black instruments will be so little to them
    that will be needing so much, seeking so much in their music.
    [Piano 22-9 P
Fly from the black toward the purple air. [Infernale 25-2 P
See, now, the ways beleaguered by black, dropsical duennas,
    [Inelegance 26-7 P
Cover the golden altar deepest black, [Red Kit 31-21 P
And you, good galliard, to enchant black thoughts [Red Kit 32-3P
The whole of them burning black; [Agenda 42-9 P
Of the park with chalky brow scratched over black [Old Woman
    44-3 P
And black by thought that could not understand [Old Woman 44-4 P
Lay black and full of black misshapen? Wings [Old Woman 44-21 P
Stood stiffly, as if the black of what she thought [Old Woman
    44-24 P
Men's bones, beyond their breaths, the black sublime, [Greenest
    55-11 P
The black and ruin his sepulchral throne. [Greenest 55-29 P
Loosing black slaves to make black infantry, [Greenest 56-9 P
Of purple flowers, to see? The black will still [Greenest 58-32P
Except that this is an image of black spring [Sombre 69-30 P
Bands of black men seem to be drifting in the air, [Sick 90-7 P
In the South, bands of thousands of black men, [Sick 90-8 P
Such black constructions, such public shapes [Ulysses 100-28 P
Here comes our black man. [Three 135-6 P
Without which it would all be black. [Three 143-9 P
See: blue-black; sun-black.
BLACKAMOOR. Was blackamoor to bear your blazing tail. [Bantams
    75-17
BLACKBIRD. Yes, and the blackbird spread its tail, [Watermelon 89-10
    "Thirteen Ways of Looking at a Blackbird" [92-title
    Was the eye of the blackbird. [Thirteen 92-16
    The blackbird whirled in the autumn winds. [Thirteen 93-5
    A man and a woman and a blackbird [Thirteen 93-5
    The blackbird whistling [Thirteen 93-10
    The shadow of the blackbird [Thirteen 93-14
    Do you not see how the blackbird [Thirteen 93-21
    That the blackbird is involved [Thirteen 94-4
    When the blackbird flew out of sight, [Thirteen 94-6
    The blackbird must be flying. [Thirteen 94-20
    The blackbird sat [Thirteen 95-4
BLACKBIRDS. In which there are three blackbirds. [Thirteen 92-19

At the sight of blackbirds [Thirteen 94-9
    For blackbirds. [Thirteen 94-18
BLACK-BLOODED. Of the black-blooded scholar, the man of the cloud,
    to be [Sombre 71-30 P
BLACKEN. And blacken into indigo. [Stan MBG 73-14 P
BLACKEST. Blackest of pickanines, [Mud 148-4
    A mass overtaken by the blackest sky, [Sombre 69-4 P
BLACKLY. Move blackly and without crystal. [Countryman 428-15
BLACKLY-BARBED. The bees to scorpions blackly-barbed, a shade
    [Duck 65-9 P
BLACKNESS. And their blackness became apparent, that one first
    [Nigger 151-2
BLACKNESSES. The black fugatos are strumming the blacknesses of
    black . . . [Madame 507-9
BLACKS. A slash of angular blacks [Public Sq 108-19
    Colossal blacks that leaped across the points [Greenest 53-13 P
BLACK-SLATTED. On the still, black-slatted eastward shutters
    [Aug 492-23
BLADE. Bethou me, said sparrow, to the crackled blade, [NSF 393-22
    And Crispine, the blade, reddened by some touch, demanding the
    most from the phrases [Piano 22-6 P
BLADED. See long-bladed.
BLADES. It dances down a furrow, in the early light, back of a
    crazy plough, the green blades following. [Plough-Boy 6-7 P
BLAGUE. Why should the bee recapture a lost blague. [NSF 390-16
BLAMED. "The Woman Who Blamed Life on a Spaniard" [34-title P
BLANCA. Saying: Olalla blanca en el blanco, [Novel 457-18
BLANCHE. The sun is a corbeil of flowers the moon Blanche [Dump
    201-12
    Blanche, the blonde, whose eyes are not wholly straight, in a
    room of lustres, shed by turquoise falling, [Piano 22-1 P
BLANCHE McCARTHY. "Blanche McCarthy" [10-title
BLANCO. Saying: Olalla blanca en el blanco, [Novel 457-18
BLAND. And giving your bland motions to the air. [Swans 4-8
    With bland complaisance on pale parasols, [C 29-19
    These bland excursions into time to come, [C 39-9
    Bland belly-sounds in somnolent troughs, [Frogs 78-3
BLANDENAH. The père Benjamin, the mère Blandenah, [Grotesque 77-11P
BLANDINA. How happy I was the day I told the young Blandina of
    three-legged giraffes . . . [Analysis 348-1
BLANK. And each blank window of the building balked [Babies 77-8
    Blinking and blank? [Am Sub 131-3
    They warded the blank waters of the lakes [Havana 142-16
    A spirit storming in blank walls, [Postcard 159-18
    Look down now, Cotton Mather, from the blank. [Blue Bldg 217-13
    With the blank skies over England, over France [Martial 238-4
    The page is blank or a frame without a glass [Phosphor 267-7
    In a feeling mass, a blank emotion, [Hero 276-27
    It is a kind of blank in which one sees. [Phenom 287-11
    With the blank uneasiness which one might feel [EM 324-25
    Gives one a blank uneasiness, as if [EM 325-9
    In the much-mottled motion of blank time. [Descrip 342-10
    Propounds blank final music. [Burghers 362-18
    A will to make iris frettings on the blank. [NSF 397-18
    A blank underlies the trials of device, [NH 477-15
    The dominant blank, the unapproachable. [NH 477-16
    He is born the blank mechanic of the mountains, [Aug 492-17
    The blank frere of fields, their matin laborer. [Aug 492-18
    For this blank cold, this sadness without cause. [Plain 502-14
    A civilization formed from the outward blank, [Armor 529-22
    That we desired, a day of blank, blue wheels, [Ideal 88-3 A
    See: Mr. Blank; point-blank.
BLANKEST. This vast inelegance may seem the blankest desolation,
    [Inelegance 25-13 P
BLANKETS. He would go to bed, cover himself with blankets-- [Novel
    457-9
BLANKLY. The man who is walking turns blankly on the sand. [AA
    412-23
BLANKS. A dewy flashing blanks away from fire, [Burnshaw 51-23 P
BLARE. This barbarous chanting of what is strong, this blare.
    [Parochial 191-16
    This future, although the elephants pass and the blare, [Duck
    63-31 P
BLARES. Blares oftener and soon, will soon be constant. [Sad Gay
    122-14
    Breaches the darkness of Ceylon with blares, [NSF 384-12
BLARING. The elephant on the roof and its elephantine blaring,
    [Fuel 456-5
BLASPHEMOUSLY. All din and gobble, blasphemously pink. [C 44-23
BLATHER. Shut to the blather that the water made, [Hibiscus 22-19
BLATTER. Is it to hear the blatter of grackles and say [Dump 203-8
BLAU. Which cries so blau and cries again so lind [Page 421-9
    So blau, so blau . . . Hans listened by the fire. [Page 421-14
BLAZE. Like a blaze of summer straw, in winter's nick. [AA 421-3
    This one star's blaze. [Inhab 504-11
    So radiance of dead blaze, but something seen [Armor 529-13
BLAZED. So lind. The wind blazed as they sang. [Page 421-17
    But his actual candle blazed with artifice. [Quiet 523-15
BLAZING. The blazing passes, from beyond the sun. [Monocle 15-19
    Was blackamoor to bear your blazing tail. [Bantams 75-17

Dew-dapper clapper-traps, blazing [MBG 182-3
  It was everything bulging and blazing and big in itself, [Freed
    205-22
BLAZONED. And hard it is in spite of blazoned days. [NSF 383-24
BLAZONS. Without diamond--blazons or flashing or [Pediment 361-11
  The commonplace became a rumpling of blazons. [NH 483-22
BLEACHED. See sun-bleached.
BLEACHING. And to feel sure and to forget the bleaching sand . . .
    [Farewell 117-20
BLEAK. In this bleak air the broken stalks [Possum 293-17
  And wear humanity's bleak crown; [Crude 305-8
  In space, wherever he sits, of bleak regard, [AA 414-6
  Morbid and bleak? [Drum-Majors 37-6 P
  Categories of bleak necessity, [Ulysses 104-26 P
BLEAKER. The step to the bleaker depths of his descents . . .
    [Rock 528-3
BLEAKEST. To find of sound the bleakest ancestor, [NSF 398-17
BLEAKLY. Persisting bleakly in an icy haze, [Pharynx 96-12
BLEATING. So heaven collects its bleating lambs. [Thought 184-10
BLEATS. Playing a crackled reed, wind-stopped, in bleats. [Sombre
    67-2 P
BLEED. The wound kills that does not bleed. [Woman Song 360-4
BLEMISHES. Unhappy love reveals vast blemishes. [Red Kit 31-19 P
BLENDED. The red and the blue house blended, [Idiom 200-21
  The great men will not be blended   ... [Idiom 201-6
  To momentary ones, are blended, [Hero 279-21
BLENDINGS. To blot this with its dove-winged blendings. [Ghosts
    119-10
BLESSED. To blessed syllable affined, and sound [C 43-9
  And blessed mornings, [Nomad 95-15
  Blessed, who is his nation's multitude. [NE Verses 105-4
  Blessed, whose beard is cloak against the snows. [NE Verses 105-6
  Oh! Blessed rage for order, pale Ramon, [Key W 130-11
  The blessed regal dropped in daggers' dew, [Montra 260-18
  Like blessed beams from out a blessed bush [NH 477-21
BLESSEDLY. Sinks into likeness blessedly beknown. [Spaniard 35-20P
BLESSEDNESS. Having attained a present blessedness, [Past Nun
    378-12
  Of the poem, the figuration of blessedness, [Rock 526-19
BLEW. Until the wind blew. [Valley Candle 51-3
  Until the wind blew. [Valley Candle 51-6
  Then the bird from his ruddy belly blew [Horn 230-5
  And dirt. The wind blew in the empty place. [Extracts 255-5
  The winter wind blew in an empty place-- [Extracts 255-6
  In the genius of summer that they blew up [NH 482-18
  Winds that blew [Phases 4-7 P
  Blew against them or bowed from the hips, when I turned [Bship
    78-17 P
BLIGHTS. Is difficult. It blights in the studios. [Greenest 58-2 P
BLIND. Afraid, the blind man as astronomer, [C 37-18
  Might help the blind, not him, serenely sly. [C 39-20
  His lids are white because his eyes are blind. [Bird Claws 82-6
  Hi! The creator too is blind, [Negation 97-13
  As it descended, blind to her velvet and [Uruguay 249-19
  The lesser seeming original in the blind [Descrip 340-2
  Of blind men tapping their way [Soldat 12-11 P
  (The blind men strike him down with their sticks.) [Soldat 13-5P
  Is a blind thing fumbling for its form, [Ulysses 104-16 P
BLINDNESS. And you, my semblables, behold in blindness [Dutch
    292-22
  That the lilacs came and bloomed, like a blindness cleaned,
    [Rock 526-5
  Sight least, but metaphysical blindness gained, [Souls 94-21 P
  The blindness in which seeing would be false, [Souls 95-1 P
BLINKING. Blinking and blank? [Am Sub 131-3
BLISS. Yet you persist with anecdotal bliss [Monocle 13-21
  "That bliss of starts, that princox of evening heaven!" remind-
    ing of seasons, [Banal 63-1
  The need of some imperishable bliss." [Sunday 68-28
  Of bliss beyond the mutes of plaster, [Jasmine 79-8
  Of bliss submerged beneath appearance, [Jasmine 79-10
  So great a unity, that it is bliss, [EM 317-8
  The lover sighs as for accessible bliss, [NSF 395-4
  The book, hot for another accessible bliss: [NSF 395-13
  Filled with expressible bliss, in which I have [NSF 404-24
  Birds of intermitted bliss, [Phases 4-9 P
  In which the bliss of clouds is mark of an intended meeting
    [Inelegance 25-15 P
  Perhaps at so much mastery, the bliss [Spaniard 35-2 P
  The understanding of heaven, would be bliss, [Lytton 38-20 P
  If anything would be bliss. [Lytton 38-21 P
BLISSFUL. The liaison, the blissful liaison, [C 34-26
  The peaceful, blissful words, well-tuned, well-sung, well-spoken.
    [Sick 90-21 P
BLISSFULLER. Creates, in the blissfuller perceptions, [Hero 280-3
BLITHE. In the beginning, four blithe instruments [C 45-3
BLOATED. Our old bane, green and bloated, serene, who cries,
    [Banal 62-16
  Sleeps by his basket. He snores. His bloated breath [Feo 333-19
BLOBS. Are blobs on the green cloth. [Pears 197-4

In opal blobs along the walls and floor. [Blue Bldg 217-12
BLOCK. Time in its final block, not time [MBG 183-18
  Her self in her manner not the solid block, [Pure 332-15
BLOCKING. And blocking steel. [Peacocks 58-18
BLOCKS. Was full of blocks [Peacocks 58-17
  Scenes of the theatre, vistas and blocks of woods [AA 415-14
  Split it and make blocks, [Archi 17-23 P
  See apple-blocks.
BLOND. At last, in that blond atmosphere, bronzed hard, [NH 487-2
  Blond weather. One is born a saint, [Stan MBG 73-9 P
  Blond weather. Give the mule his hay. [Stan MBG 73-17
BLONDE. Her prismy blonde and clapped her in his hands, [C 42-3
  A blonde to tip the silver and to taste [C 42-19
  The hair of my blonde [Depression 63-9
  Blanche, the blonde, whose eyes are not wholly straight, in a
    room of lustres, shed by turquoise falling, [Piano 22-1
BLOOD. Dominion of the blood and sepulchre. [Sunday 67-11
  Until our blood, commingling, virginal, [Sunday 68-2
  Shall our blood fail? Or shall it come to be [Sunday 68-5
  The blood of paradise? And shall the earth [Sunday 68-6
  Out of their blood, returning to the sky; [Sunday 70-5
  In witching chords, and their thin blood [Peter 90-11
  Is the spot on the floor, there, wine or blood [MBG 173-11
  Or else whose hell, foamed with their blood [Thought 186-13
  Taste of the blood upon his martyred lips, [Men Fall 188-15
  He tastes its blood, not spit. [Destructive 192-17
  He squeezed it and the blood [Weak Mind 212-2
  The blood of the mind fell [Weak Mind 212-14
  Him chanting for those buried in their blood, [Oboe 251-19
  The poison in the blood will have been purged, [Montra 262-4
  Before, before. Blood smears the oaks. [Contra I 267-3
  Grows sharp in blood. The armies kill themselves, [Dutch 292-19
  And in their blood an ancient evil dies-- [Dutch 292-20
  In a beau language without a drop of blood. [Repet 310-9
  The soldiers that have fallen, red in blood, [EM 319-1
  One feels its action moving in the blood. [EM 324-23
  The more than human commonplace of blood, [Descrip 341-3
  The fantastic fortune of fantastic blood, [Liadoff 347-10
  These earlier dissipations of the blood [Extraord 369-12
  Beating in the heart, as if blood newly came, [NSF 382-21
  Inevitably modulating, in the blood. [NSF 407-20
  Peace stood with our last blood adorned, last mind, [Owl 434-19
  The blood refreshes with its stale demands. [Study I 464-3
  In denial that cannot contain its blood, [NH 467-14
  Suppose it was a drop of blood . . . [Inhab 504-12
  As in the last drop of the deepest blood, [Rome 509-26
  Even as the blood of an empire, it might be, [Rome 510-1
  The final pulse of blood from this good heart [Soldat 11-11 P
  The blood of his bitter brain; and there the sun [Burnshaw 49-11P
  With interruptions by vast hymns, blood odes, [Duck 66-1 P
  In the beat of the blood. [Sombre 67-27 P
  A duckling of the wildest blood [Grotesque 75-12 P
  As hangman, a little sick of blood, of [Stan Hero 84-17 P
  You said the dew falls in the blood. [Memo 89-5 P
  Of the color of blood. [Three 137-4 P
  Of the color of blood . . . [Three 142-1 P
  The color of blood, [Three 142-13 P
BLOODED. An abstraction blooded, as a man by thought. [NSF 385-24
  See: black-blooded; briny-blooded; dark-blooded.
BLOODLESS. Glass-blower's destiny, bloodless episcopus, [NSF 394-11
BLOODMAN. Where, butcher, seducer, bloodman, reveller, [Ghosts
    119-5
BLOOD-RED. The blood-red redness of the sun, [Adequacy 243-18
BLOOD-ROSE. And rain, the blood-rose living in its smell,
    [Extracts 252-5
BLOOD-WORLD. This warmth of the blood-world for the pure idea,
    [Extracts 256-12
BLOODY. And the jasmine islands were bloody martyrdoms. [Oboe 251-9
  Ah, ké! the bloody wren, the felon jay, [NSF 394-1
  The bloody lion in the yard at night or ready to spring [Puel
    456-6
  Would shudder on a bloody salver. [Three 132-14 P
BLOOM. A damsel heightened by eternal bloom. [Monocle 15-28
  Our bloom is gone. We are the fruit thereof. [Monocle 16-5
  Of moonlight on the thick, cadaverous bloom [C 31-28
  In bloom. Yet it survives in its own form, [C 41-6
  In the door-yard by his own capacious bloom. [C 44-5
  But that this bloom grown riper, showing nibs [C 44-6
  A pungent bloom against your shade. [Venereal 48-17
  That this bloom is the bloom of soap [Lilacs 48-21
  Moisture and heat have swollen the garden into a slum of bloom.
    [Banal 62-14
  Most near, most clear, and of the clearest bloom, [Fictive 87-7
  The near, the clear, and vaunts the clearest bloom, [Fictive 88-3
  To touch again the hottest bloom, to strike [Havana 143-15
  Though the blue bushes bloomed--and bloom, [Arcades 225-14
  Still bloom in the agate eyes, red blue, [Arcades 225-15
  Bloomed in sheets, as they bloom, and the girl, [Forces 229-1
  To feed on the yellow bloom of the yellow fruit [EM 318-12
  And Bloom would see what Puvis did, protest [Anach 366-6

And flare and Bloom with his vast accumulation [Anach 366-14
Among fomentations of black bloom and of white bloom. [Attempt
   37C-18
A mountain luminous half way in bloom [Cred 375-22
The wild orange trees continued to bloom and to bear, [NSF 393-2
The purple odor, the abundant bloom. [NSF 395-3
If they broke into bloom, if they bore fruit, [Rock 526-15
They bud and bloom and bear their fruit without change. [Rock
   527-5
They bloom as a man loves, as he lives in love. [Rock 527-11
Maidens in bloom, bulls under sea, the lark [Sombre 67-33 P
BLOOMED. The myrtle, if the myrtle ever bloomed, [C 34-13
   Though the blue bushes bloomed--and bloom, [Arcades 225-14
   Bloomed in sheets, as they bloom, and the girl, [Forces 229-1
   That the lilacs came and bloomed, like a blindness cleaned,
      [Rock 526-5
   Speaking and strutting broadly, fair and bloomed, [Burnshaw
   52-17 P
BLOOMING. Blooming and beaming and voluming colors out. [NH 484-6
   In a birth of sight. The blooming and the musk [Rock 526-7
   Of magenta blooming in the Judas-tree [Primordia 9-11 P
   And of purple blooming in the eucalyptus-- [Primordia 9-12 P
BLOOMS. It comes, it blooms, it bears its fruit and dies.
      [Monocle 16-3
   Among the blooms beyond the open sand; [Hibiscus 22-11
   Its black blooms rise. [Weep Woman 25-6
   Elations when the forest blooms; gusty [Sunday 67-22
   Out of the light evolved the moving blooms, [Sea Surf 99-6
   And moved, as blooms move, in the swimming green [Sea Surf 99-11
   Who saw the mortal massives of the blooms [Sea Surf 100-1
   Who, seeing silver petals of white blooms [Sea Surf 100-17
   Like blooms secluded in the thick marine? [Sea Surf 101-12
   Like blooms? Like damasks that were shaken off [Sea Surf 101-13
   And the nakedness became the broadest blooms, [Sea Surf 101-20
   Of green blooms turning crisped the motley hue [Sea Surf 102-12
   Of waving weeds. I hated the vivid blooms [Farewell 118-3
   Blue buds or pitchy blooms. Be content-- [MBG 172-3
   Of the iris bore white blooms. The bird then boomed. [Horn
      230-10
   Are nothing but frothy clouds; the frothy blooms [NSF 399-16
   And savage blooms; [Cab 21-9 P
   Bring down from nowhere nothing's wax-like blooms, [Burnshaw
      47-20 P
   See: ocean-blooms; sea-blooms.
BLOOMY-LEAFED. On dung." Come now, pearled and pasted, bloomy-
      leafed, [Ghosts 119-17
BLOSSOMED. See evil-blossomed.
BLOSSOMS. Nor that the sexual blossoms should repose [NSF 399-8
   And saw the blossoms, snow-bred pink and white, [Good Bad 33-17P
BLOT. To blot this with its dove-winged blendings. [Ghosts 119-10
BLOTCHED. Blotched out beyond unblotching. Crispin, [C 28-6
BLOTCHES. To blotches, angular anonymids [Lot 371-11
   And his orange blotches, these were his zero green, [NSF 393-6
   How facilely the purple blotches fell [NH 484-4
   See moon-blotches.
BLOW. Remus, blow your horn! [Ploughing 20-9
   Blow your horn! [Ploughing 20-12
   And his nostrils blow out salt around each man. [Grapes 111-3
   At what we saw. The spring clouds blow [Postcard 159-7
   The wind in which the dead leaves blow. [MBG 180-14
   And you, and you, bethou me as you blow, [NSF 393-23
   The four winds blow through the rustic arbor, [Vacancy 511-12
   Must blow. [Room Gard 40-18 P
   At the unbeliever's touch. Cloud-cloisters blow [Greenest 58-10P
BLOWER. Are sounds blown by a blower into shapes, [Parochial 191-5
   The blower squeezed to the thinnest mi of falsetto. [Parochial
      191-6
   See glass-blower.
BLOWING. Blowing upon her hands [Paltry 5-17
   That is blowing in the same bare place [Snow Man 10-9
   And my ears made the blowing hymns they heard. [Hoon 65-14
   Freshness is more than the east wind blowing round one. [Nigger
      157-11
   The freshness of morning, the blowing of day, one says [Dump
      202-2
   Is blowing after days of constant rain. [Connois 216-5
   Blowing itself upon the tedious ear. [NSF 400-17
   The wind is blowing the sand across the floor. [AA 412-15
   Of baker and butcher blowing, as if to hear, [NH 475-2
   As rain and booming, gleaming, blowing, swept [NH 484-10
   Blowing among the trees its meaningless sound. [Old Woman 44-28P
BLOWN. Of dampened lumber, emanations blown [C 36-8
   If thinking could be blown away [Nigger 153-5
   Are sounds blown by a blower into shapes, [Parochial 191-5
   The pines along the river and the dry men blown [Loaf 199-21
   The blown sheen--or is it air? [Degen 444-18
   Are like newspapers blown by the wind. He speaks [NH 473-21
   The wind has blown the silence of summer away. [NH 487-13
   How easily the blown banners change to wings . . . [Rome 508-11
   Hallooing haggler; for the wax is blown, [Infernale 25-6 P

Were solemn and your gowns were blown and grief [Burnshaw 50-29P
   In a storm blown into glittering shapes, and flames [Burnshaw
      52-21 P
   It was not a night blown at a glassworks in Vienna [Real 110-9 P
   See dark-blown; full-blown.
BLOWS. Blows on the shutters of the metropoles, [Pharynx 96-6
   Well, after all, the north wind blows [MBG 174-12
   He lies down and the night wind blows upon him here. [Men Fall
      187-13
   The night wind blows upon the dreamer, bent [Men Fall 188-19
   The wind blows. In the wind, the voices [Parochial 191-3
   The trumpet of morning blows in the clouds and through [Cred
      376-16
   Nor brilliant blows thereof, ti-rill-a-roo, [John 437-12
   The wind blows quaintly [Our Stars 454-15
   It blows a glassy brightness on the fire [Novel 458-6
   That blows about in such a hopeless way, [Phases 5-13 P
   And blows, with heaped-up shoulders loudly blows [Greenest
      58-12 P
   Of other images blows, images of time [Sombre 69-28 P
   The blows and buffets of fresh senses [Fare Guit 99-5 P
   See wind-blows.
BLUBBER. With a blubber of tom-toms harrowing the sky? [C 41-13
BLUSTER. And bluster in the wind. [Ploughing 20-8
BLUE. A blue pigeon it is, that circles the blue sky, [Monocle
      17-18
   Blue, gold, pink, and green. [Pourtraicte 21-6
   Which had lain folded against the blue [Hibiscus 22-16
   Of blue and green? A wordy, watery age [C 28-25
   So streaked with yellow, blue and green and red [C 32-6
   When the sky is blue. The blue infected will. [C 40-18
   As buffo, yet divers, four mirrors blue [C 45-6
   Of red and blue and red, [Venereal 48-8
   Monotonous earth and dark blue sky. [Vincentine 52-12
   The gold tree is blue. [Of Surface 57-6
   In this milky blue?" [Peacocks 58-4
   That the blue ground [Peacocks 58-16
   Two wooden tubs of blue hydrangeas stand at the foot of the
      stone steps. [Banal 62-11
   The sky is a blue gum streaked with rose. The trees are black.
      [Banal 62-12
   Or yellow with blue rings. [Ten O'C 66-6
   Not this dividing and indifferent blue. [Sunday 68-11
   Blue and white, [Six Sig 73-9
   With certain blue crystallizations [Six Sig 74-20
   Say that the palms are clear in a total blue, [Two Figures 86-13
   Poured brilliant iris on the glistening blue. [Sea Surf 99-15
   The gongs grew still. And then blue heaven spread [Sea Surf
      100-6
   Until the rolling heaven made them blue, [Sea Surf 100-24
   A blue beyond the rainy hyacinth, [Sea Surf 101-1
   Deluged the ocean with a sapphire blue. [Sea Surf 101-3
   Came fresh transfigurings of freshest blue. [Sea Surf 102-15
   O ashen admiral of the hale, hard blue . . . . [NE Verses 105-8
   That was buttressed by blue slants [Public Sq 108-21
   But this gross blue under rolling bronzes [Grapes 110-15
   Through the mustiest blue of the lake [Sailing 120-18
   It might become his hole of blue. [Snow Stars 133-6
   To gold in broadest blue, and be a part [Sun March 133-16
   Which changed light green to olive then to blue. [Nigger 152-10
   A bridge above the bright and blue of water [Nigger 154-11
   The sun rises green and blue in the fields and in the heavens.
      [Fish-Scale 161-5
   "The Man with the Blue Guitar" [165-title
   They said, "You have a blue guitar, [MBG 165-3
   Are changed upon the blue guitar." [MBG 165-6
   A tune upon the blue guitar [MBG 165-9
   Of a man that plays a blue guitar. [MBG 166-2
   To bang it from a savage blue, [MBG 166-11
   It picks its way on the blue guitar. [MBG 166-14
   This buzzing of the blue guitar. [MBG 167-2
   Yet nothing changed by the blue guitar; [MBG 167-16
   As you play them, on the blue guitar, [MBG 167-20
   The tune is space. The blue guitar [MBG 168-6
   The strings are cold on the blue guitar. [MBG 168-22
   And the color, the overcast blue [MBG 169-13
   Of the air, in which the blue guitar [MBG 169-14
   Roll a drum upon the blue guitar. [MBG 170-13
   Tom-tom, c'est moi. The blue guitar [MBG 171-11
   The pale intrusions into blue [MBG 172-1
   Blue buds or pitchy blooms. Be content-- [MBG 172-3
   Of blue, blue sleek with a hundred chins, [MBG 172-7
   One sits and plays the blue guitar. [MBG 172-22
   An animal. The blue guitar-- [MBG 174-8
   The blue guitar a mould? That shell? [MBG 174-11
   Of things as they are, as the blue guitar [MBG 174-18
   And say they are on the blue guitar. [MBG 180-18
   The nuances of the blue guitar. [MBG 182-22
   The blue guitar surprises you. [MBG 183-14
   There are bits of blue. [Pears 196-14

The red and the blue house blended, [Idiom 200-21
Myrtle, viburnums, daffodils, blue phlox), [Dump 202-13
Smoking through green and smoking blue. [On Road 203-20
The blue of the rug, the portrait of Vidal, [Freed 205-23
If all the green of spring was blue, and it is; [Connois 215-4
"The Blue Buildings in the Summer Air" [216-title
A fruit for pewter, thorned and palmed and blue, [Poem Morn
    219-6
Though the blue bushes bloomed--and bloom, [Arcades 225-14
Still bloom in the agate eyes, red blue, [Arcades 225-15
Old nests and there is blue in the woods. [Cuisine 227-15
The sky is too blue, the earth too wide. [Scavoir 231-13
In light blue air over dark blue sea. [Vari 232-6
As a boat feels when it cuts blue water. [Vari 234-5
The sky was blue. He wanted imperceptible air. [Landsc 241-13
And not be touched by blue. He wanted to know, [Landsc 241-15
Of air, who looked for the world beneath the blue, [Landsc
    241-17
Without blue, without any turquoise tint or phase, [Landsc
    241-18
And the irregular turquoise, part, and perceptible blue [Landsc
    242-23
High blue became particular [Vase 246-18
"Of Bright & Blue Birds & the Gala Sun" [248-title
Is blue, clear, cloudy, high, dark, wide and round; [Extracts
    252-11
Hoy, hoy, the blue bulls kneeling down to rest. [Montra 260-6
The blue sun in his red cockade [News 264-7
Cloud-clown, blue painter, sun as horn, [Jumbo 269-13
Turns blue and on its empty table [Hero 280-20
Of red and blue, the hard sound-- [Motive 288-18
Swarm from the little blue of the horizon [Dutch 290-2
To the great blue of the middle height. [Dutch 290-3
Eyes dripping blue, so much to learn. [Couch 295-9
He was a shell of dark blue glass, or ice, [Choc 297-9
Blue's last transparence as it turned to black, [Choc 297-13
A fusion of night, its blue of the pole of blue [Choc 297-16
Blue friends in shadows, rich conspirators, [Choc 300-9
It was a blue scene washing white in the rain, [Repet 306-19
Blue and its deep inversions in the moon [Repet 309-18
And, with him, many blue phenomena. [EM 319-22
The visible, a zone of blue and orange [EM 324-13
Dry Birds Are Fluttering in Blue Leaves [Pure 332-title 4
Besides, when the sky is so blue, things sing themselves,
    [Debris 338-10
The red, the blue, the argent queen. If not, [Descrip 340-13
Ovation on ovation of large blue men [Liadoff 346-8
That breathed on ground, more blue than red, more red [Pieces
    352-3
Like space dividing its blue and by division [Two V 354-14
The old brown hen and the old blue sky, [Silent 359-5
Of the place, blue and green, both streaked. [Attempt 370-5
In smoke. The blue petals became [Attempt 370-16
We bathed in yellow green and yellow blue [Lot 371-8
Not fustian. The more than casual blue [Cred 375-5
With the gold bugs, in blue meadows, late at night. [Cred 377-23
Of blue and yellow, sky and sun, belted [Cred 378-1
It observes the effortless weather turning blue [NSF 382-7
Wetted by blue, colder for white. Not to [NSF 385-8
And yellow, yellow thins the Northern blue. [NSF 385-13
On a blue island in a sky-wide water [NSF 393-1
The blue woman, linked and lacquered, at her window [NSF 399-4
The blue woman looked and from her window named [NSF 399-21
Gothic blue, speed home its portents to their ends. [Page 422-20
As he sat there reading, aloud, the great blue tabulae. [Large
    423-12
Is changed. It is not so blue as we thought. To be blue, [Ulti
    429-18
Blue for all that and white and hard, [Celle 438-13
A space grown wide, the inevitably blue [Orb 440-2
The composition of blue sea and of green, [Orb 442-3
Of blue light and of green, as lesser poems, [Orb 442-4
For whom no blue in the sky prevents them, as [Bouquet 449-4
The rose, the delphinium, the red, the blue, [Bouquet 451-1
And pallid bits, that tend to comply with blue, [Bouquet 452-2
The sky was blue beyond the vaultiest phrase. [What We 459-12
It does no good to speak of the big, blue bush [Study I 463-4
Within the big, blue bush and its vast shade [Study I 463-12
Became divided in the leisure of blue day [NH 468-22
To the lover, and blue, as of a secret place [NH 470-21
The Oklahoman--the Italian blue [NH 476-23
Blue verdured into a damask's lofty symbol, [NH 477-18
Yet the transcripts of it when it was blue remain; [NH 479-20
On the walk, purple and blue, and red and gold, [NH 484-5
Which, being green and blue, appease him, [Aug 491-4
And blue broke on him from the sun, [Two Illus 514-16
A bullioned blue, a blue abulge, [Two Illus 514-17
Blue and vermilion, purple and white, [Mandolin 28-20 P
In the morning in the blue snow [An Gaiety 32-15 P
Its winds are blue. [Secret Man 36-6 P

Washed over by their green, their flowing blue. [Old Woman 45-11P
An abysmal migration into a possible blue? [Burnshaw 51-9 P
Seized by that possible blue. Be maidens formed [Burnshaw 51-18 P
Of the most evasive hue of a lesser blue, [Burnshaw 51-19 P
The triumph of the arcs of heaven's blue [Duck 60-16 P
The darkest blue of the dome and the wings around [Duck 65-22 P
The green, white, blue of the ballad-eye, by night [Sombre 71-9 P
I play them on a blue guitar [Stan MBG 72-15 P
Quiver upon the blue guitar. [Stan MBG 73-6 P
One could watch the blue sea's blueness flow [Stan MBG 73-13 P
On such a peak, the blue guitar-- [Stan MBG 73-16 P
Covered one morning with blue, one morning with white, [Bship
    80-10 P
The father. He hides his ancient blue beneath [Recit 87-17 P
Fluttering in blue leaves, [Including 88-4 P
The plums are blue on the trees. The katy-dids [Memo 89-14 P
Green, more or less, in green and blue in blue, [Theatre 91-2 P
Are dissolved as in an infancy of blue snow. [Discov 95-11 P
Held in the hands of blue men that are lead within, [Discov
    95-16
The green-edged yellow and yellow and blue and blue-edged green--
    [How Now 97-8 P
Bending in blue dresses to touch something, [Clear Day 113-12 P
That we desired, a day of blank, blue wheels, [Ideal 88-3 A
See: bright-blue-resembling; dark-blue; eye-blue; gray-blue;
    green-blue; mountain-blue; night-blue; red-blue; red-slitted-
    blue; sky-blue; yellow-blue.
BLUE-BIRD. And of the blue-bird [Primordia 7-18 P
BLUE-BLACK. Clipped frigidly blue-black meridians, [C 34-16
BLUE-BOLD. Blue-bold on its pedestal--that seems to say, [Role
    93-13 P
BLUED. The bays of heaven, brighted, blued? [Botanist 2 136-4
BLUE DANUBE. Whipped creams and the Blue Danube, [Agenda 41-16 P
BLUE-EDGED. The green edged yellow and yellow and blue and blue-
    edged green-- [How Now 97-8 P
BLUE-GREEN. The nocturnal, the antique, the blue-green pines
    [Parochial 191-9
Bearded with chains of blue-green glitterings [Bouquet 449-7
Abhorring green-blue north and blue-green south. [Archi 18-1 P
BLUEJAY. Could you have said the bluejay suddenly [Sleight 222-9
BLUE-JAY. He does not lie there remembering the blue-jay, say the
    jay. [Madame 507-11
BLUELY. Instant of millefiori bluely magnified-- [Pieces 351-13
BLUENESS. In an air of freshness, clearness, greenness, blueness,
    [Armor 530-16
The blueness of the half-night, fill the air [Red Kit 31-23 P
One could watch the blue sea's blueness flow [Stan MBG 73-13 P
BLUE-RED. With its frigid brilliances, its blue-red sweeps [AA
    413-1
BLUES. The ephemeral blues must merge for them in one, [Monocle
    15-8
And night blues. [Fabliau 23-8
The two alike, distinguish blues, [Vari 235-2
And, in the brown blues of evening, the lady said, [Uruguay
    248-17
BLUE-SHADOWED. Thinking of your blue-shadowed silk, [Peter 90-4
BLUEST. Its bluest sea-clouds in the thinking green, [Sea Surf
    101-19
We hardened ourselves to live by bluest reason [Medit 124-2
BLUE-STRUTTED. Blue-strutted curule, true-unreal, [Human 363-12
BLUET-EYED. The chits came for his jigging, bluet-eyed, [C 43-16
BLUISH. Occur as they occur. So bluish clouds [Sleight 222-3
BLUNT. Blunt yellow in such a room! [Bananas 54-3
And the booming is blunt, not broken in subtleties. [NSF 390-9
Whose blunt laws made an affectation of mind, [Look 519-9
The blunt ice flows down the Mississippi, [Primordia 8-3 P
No memorable muffing, bare and blunt. [Burnshaw 48-8 P
Of the shape of eyes, like blunt intaglios, [Greenest 59-5 P
BLUNTED. As if a blunted player clutched [MBG 182-21
Of one wilder than the rest (like music blunted, [Thunder 220-23
Clumped carvings, circular, like blunted fans, [Old Woman 43-16 P
BLUNTEST. The spokesman at our bluntest barriers, [NSF 397-2
BLUNTLY. Game bluntly thundering, more terrible [C 32-24
BLURRING. Whose head lies blurring here, for this he died. [Men
    Fall 188-14
BLURS. Yet radiantly beyond much lustier blurs. [Nigger 155-19
BLUSHED. So delicately blushed, so humbly eyed, [C 44-13
BLUSTERINESS. Mere blusteriness that gewgaws jollified, [C 44-22
BOARD. To lay his brain upon the board [MBG 166-5
The air is not a mirror but bare board, [NSF 384-2
A board for bishops' grapes, the happy form [Sombre 70-8 P
Returned on board The Masculine. That night, [Bship 77-14 P
BOARDED. The hotel is boarded and bare. [Botanist 1 135-12
Swept through its boarded windows and the leaves [Havana 142-19
BOARDS. On the boards of the bridge. [Magnifico 19-17
As they tread the boards [Cortege 80-18
Sordid Melpomene, why strut bare boards, [Bad Time 427-4
See table-boards.
BOAT. My old boat goes round on a crutch [Sailing 120-2
In a really vertiginous boat [Sailing 120-19

It is the leaf the bird brings back to the boat. [Blue Bldg
  217-18
As a boat feels when it cuts blue water [Vari 234-5
"Landscape with Boat" [241-title
It is like a boat that has pulled away [Vacancy 511-6
There was an ease of mind that was like being alone in a boat at
  sea, [Prol 515-5
A boat carried forward by waves resembling the bright backs of
  rowers, [Prol 515-6
The boat was built of stones that had lost their weight and
  being no longer heavy [Prol 515-10
So that he that stood up in the boat leaning and looking before
  him [Prol 515-12
A meaning which, as he entered it, would shatter the boat and
  leave the oarsmen quiet [Prol 516-7
The right to be." Guiding his boat [Ulysses 99-14 P
The right to be." He guided his boat [Presence 105-17 P
See glade-boat; man-boat.
BOATMAN. Of the boatman. [Sugar-Cane 12-19
  O, boatman, [Primordia 9-1 P
  O, boatman, [Primordia 9-3 P
  The boatman goes humming. He smokes a cigar [Stan MBG 72-11 P
BOATMEN. Are you two boatmen [Primordia 9-5 P
BOATS. The lights in the fishing boats at anchor there, [Key W
  130-6
  Dutch ice on English boats? The memory [Recit 86-25 P
BODIES. And shave their heads and bodies. [Homunculus 26-20
  Gives comfort, so that other bodies come, [Anatomy 108-10
  The sky would be full of bodies like wood. [Thunder 220-17
  To shaking out heavy bodies in the glares [Cuisine 228-7
  Two bodies disembodied in their talk, [NH 471-8
  The earth as the bodies rose on feathery wings, [Old Woman
    43-15 P
  Would flash in air, and the muscular bodies thrust [Old Woman
    46-9 P
  When younger bodies, because they are younger, rise [Burnshaw
    49-28 P
  Pitched into swelling bodies, upward, drift [Burnshaw 52-20 P
  The leaping bodies, come from the truculent hand, [Duck 64-15 P
  The leaping bodies to his strength, convulsed [Duck 64-18 P
BODILESS. Of absolutes, bodiless, a head [Men Fall 188-7
  This is where the serpent lives, the bodiless. [AA 411-1
  Another bodiless for the body's slough? [AA 411-6
  The bodiless half. There is always this bodiless half, [NH 481-23
BODY. The pine-tree sweetens my body [Carolinas 5-4
  And my body, the old animal, [Joost 46-15
  Her body quivering in the Floréal [Lilacs 49-10
  The bundle of the body and the feet. [Worms 50-2
  The body is no body to be seen [Tallap 71-16
  They are bearing his body into the sky. [Cortege 80-10
  Body and soul, [Cortege 81-5
  The body dies; the body's beauty lives. [Peter 92-1
  When the body of Jesus hangs in a pallor, [Lunar 107-5
  The body walks forth naked in the sun [Anatomy 108-8
  To make the body covetous in desire [Anatomy 108-13
  In which the body walks and is deceived, [Anatomy 108-16
  Like a body wholly body, fluttering [Key W 128-13
  A body in rags. [Mozart 132-1
  Lord of the body, looking down, [MBG 176-6
  In the body of a violent beast. [Destructive 193-2
  Of music--Her body lies [Add 199-2
  And then the body fell. [Weak Mind 212-5
  With my whole body I taste these peaches, [Peaches 224-1
  To escape from the body, so to feel [Vari 234-2
  Those feelings that the body balks, [Vari 234-3
  And light behind the body of night [Adequacy 244-7
  Green in the body, out of a petty phrase, [Beard 247-21
  Then bathed its body in the leaping lake. [Hand 271-12
  Eyes and bruted ears: the man-like body [Hero 277-9
  The body that could never be wounded, [Gigan 289-4
  To think of him destroyed the body's form. [Choc 297-8
  The night. The substance of his body seemed [Choc 297-20
  In what new spirit had his body birth? [Choc 299-8
  A giant without a body. If, as giant, [Repet 308-10
  As the body trembles at the end of life. [EM 314-7
  The genius of the body, which is our world, [EM 317-2
  In his body, fiercer in his mind, merciless [EM 321-21
  The slouch of his body and his look were not [Descrip 343-1
  Until his body smothered him, until [Liadoff 347-11
  Lascar, is there a body, turbulent [Two V 354-1
  Without his envious pain in body, in mind, [Past Nun 378-20
  A composing as the body tires, a stop [NSF 386-4
  An erotic perfume, half of the body, half [NSF 390-7
  The body lift its heavy wing, take up, [NSF 390-12
  That walk away as one in the greenest body. [NSF 392-15
  The body, it touches. The captain and his men [NSF 392-21
  Beyond the burning body that I bear. [NSF 395-24
  Another bodiless for the body's slough? [AA 411-6
  And the serpent body flashing without the skin. [AA 411-12
  Of body and air and forms and images, [AA 411-17

The giant body the meanings of its folds, [Owl 433-16
A massive body and long legs, stretched out, [Orb 443-9
The pulse of the object, the heat of the body grown cold [Study
  I 463-16
A reader without a body, [Inhab 503-19
The spirit comes from the body of the world, [Look 519-7
Or so Mr. Homburg thought; the body of a world [Look 519-8
The body quickened and the mind in root. [Rock 527-10
It wraps the sheet around its body, until the black figure is
  silver. [Plough-Boy 6-6 P
Than body and in less than mind, ogre, [Sombre 67-14 P
The body bent, like Hercules, to build. [Sombre 69-10 P
Of the very body instinctively crying [Stan Hero 84-27 P
Is its body visible to the important eye. [Recit 86-14 P
BODYING. And bodying, and being there, [Presence 106-10 P
BOGOTA. Is the beggar in Bogota. The kraal [Greenest 59-18 P
BOISTEROUS. Their boisterous devotion to the sun, [Sunday 70-1
  The double fruit of boisterous epicures, [Someone 85-20 A
BOISTEROUSLY. Celestial sneering boisterously. Crispin [C 29-22
BOLD. The last largeness, bold to see. [Curtains 62-10
  A thousand begettings of the broken bold. [Owl 434-21
  O bold, that rode your horses straight away. [Duck 61-31 P
  The bold, obedience to Ananke. [Stan Hero 83-24 P
  See blue-bold.
BOLDLY. Forgather and bell boldly Crispin's last [C 43-13
  We must enter boldly that interior world [Feo 333-16
BOMBASTIC. From the bombastic intimations of winter [Contra II
  270-8
BOMBAY. We drank Meursault, ate lobster Bombay with mango [NSF
  401-22
BOND. Found inklings of your bond to all that dust. [Monocle 15-6
BONDAGE. The bondage of the Stygian concubine, [Infernale 25-5 P
BONE. The grackles crack their throats of bone in the smooth air.
  [Banal 62-13
  The flesh, the bone, the dirt, the stone. [MBG 176-14
  Heard the dogs howl at barren bone, [Thought 187-6
  The gate is not jasper. It is not bone. [Stan MBG 72-5 P
  Of her airs, as surely cologne as that she was bone [Grotesque
  74-6 P
BONES. To the flesh and bones of you [Tattoo 81-17
  Curled over the shadowless hut, the rust and bones, [Farewell
  118-4
  The trees like bones and the leaves half sand, half sun.
    [Farewell 118-5
  The spittling tissues tight across the bones. [Nigger 155-8
  Children picking up our bones [Postcard 158-14
  And least will guess that with our bones [Postcard 159-4
  Of bones, he rejected, he denied, to arrive [Landsc 241-20
  Lost in an integration of the martyrs' bones, [Uruguay 249-23
  Eventual victor, out of the martyrs' bones, [Uruguay 250-4
  Summer is in bones. [Metamorph 265-17
  Flesh on the bones. The skeleton throwing [Hero 278-15
  I grieve the pinch of her long-stiffening bones. [Stan MMO 19-19P
  O spirit of bones, O mountain of graves? [Sat Night 28-6 P
  There buzzards pile their sticks among the bones [Burnshaw 49-7 P
  Men's bones, beyond their breaths, the black sublime, [Greenest
  55-11 P
  A countryman of all the bones of the world? [Warmth 90-1 P
  A countryman of all the bones in the world? [As Leave 117-7 P
  Under the bones of time's philosophers? [Ideal 89-9 A
BONHEUR. Encore un instant de bonheur. The words [Nigger 157-14
BONNETS. Of the Balkan shoes, the bonnets from Moldau, beards
  [Duck 62-14 P
BONNIE. Bonnie and Josie, [Motion 83-2
BONY. And which had drowsed along the bony shores, [Hibiscus 22-18
  The bony buttresses, the bony spires [Gray 140-5
  For food. The big bird's bony appetite [EM 318-9
BOO-HA. Are a single voice in the boo-ha of the wind. [NH 481-3
BOOK. To be the book in which to read a round, [Monocle 14-17
  Of love, it is a book too mad to read [Monocle 14-21
  In any book. [Pourtraicte 22-8
  The book of moonlight is not written yet [C 33-18
  Leave room, therefore, in that unwritten book [C 33-26
  If joy shall be without a book [Fading 139-11
  All night I sat reading a book, [Reader 146-13
  Sat reading as if in a book [Reader 146-14
  There might have been a light on a book [Chateau 161-11
  The book and bread, things as they are, [MBG 172-20
  That scholar hungriest for that book, [MBG 178-1
  The very book, or, less, a page [MBG 178-2
  The voice, the book, the hidden well, [Thought 186-2
  In how severe a book he read, [Thought 186-21
  At the book and shoe, the rotted rose [God 285-5
  In your light, the head is speaking. It reads the book. [God
  285-10
  Holds in his hand a book you have never written [Lack 303-2
  Andrew Jackson Something. But this book [Lack 303-7
  And not yet to have written a book in which [Lack 303-17
  There were roses in the cool café. His book [EM 314-9
  The reader by the window has finished his book [Pure 330-2

Of access like the page of a wiggy book, [Pure 333-6
And moon, the book of reconciliation, [Descrip 345-1
Book of a concept only possible [Descrip 345-2
The reader became the book; and summer night [House Q 358-8
Was like the conscious being of the book. [House Q 358-9
The words were spoken as if there was no book, [House Q 358-11
The scholar to whom his book is true, to whom [House Q 358-14
Sour wine to warm him, an empty book to read; [Good Man 364-11
Who reads no book. His ruddy ancientness [Cred 374-2
Do I press the extremest book of the wisest man [NSF 380-5
Who chants by book, in the heat of the scholar, who writes
   [NSF 395-12
The book, hot for another accessible bliss: [NSF 395-13
In a book in a barrack, a letter from Malay. [NSF 407-14
Like a book at evening beautiful but untrue, [AA 418-14
Like a book on rising beautiful and true. [AA 418-15
The fire falls a little and the book is done. [Novel 458-17
The total excellence of its total book." [NH 485-9
The book and candle in your ambered room, [Rome 510-25
Even when the book lay turned in the dust of his table. [Poem
   Mt 512-4
No book of the past in which time's senators [Recit 86-10 P
See note-book.
BOOKED. That the guerilla I should be booked [Prelude 195-10
BOOKS. Holding their books toward the nearer stars, [Polish Aunt
   84-4
Of affected homage foxed so many books, [Havana 142-15
At least that was the theory, when bishops' books [Connois
   215-15
Cotton Mather died when I was a boy. The books [Blue Bldg 216-15
Shadows of scholars bent upon their books, [Montra 262-17
In brown books. The marbles of what he was stand [Hero 276-25
The house will crumble and the books will burn. [AA 413-17
The bed, the books, the chair, the moving nuns, [Rome 508-21
In a confusion on bed and books, a portent [Rome 509-3
A Schloss, and empty Schlossbibliothek, the books [Greenest 53-8P
The binders did it with armorial books. [Greenest 53-16 P
BOOMED. Boomed from his very belly odious chords. [Monocle 17-17
Of the iris bore white blooms. The bird then boomed. [Horn
   230-10
BOOMER. "Banjo Boomer" [114-title P
BOOMING. There has been a booming all the spring, [Nightgown 214-3
And that booming wintry and dull, [Nightgown 214-8
The bees came booming as if they had never gone, [NSF 389-19
It is a repetition. The bees come booming [NSF 390-5
And the booming is blunt, not broken in subtleties. [NSF 390-9
Booming and booming of the new-come bee. [NSF 391-6
As rain and booming, gleaming, blowing, swept [NH 484-10
BOOMINGS. With its organic boomings, to be changed [Freed 205-10
BOOMS. The gongs rang loudly as the windy booms [Sea Surf 100-4
BOOMY. The statue of Jove among the boomy clouds. [NH 482-19
BOOR. [A boor of night in middle earth cries out.) [Infernale
   24-19 P
BOORISH. Virgin of boorish births, [Venereal 47-17
Or by whatever boorish name a man [Choc 300-22
BOOTED. See well-booted.
BOOTS. The boots of the men clump [Magnifico 19-16
Drunk and asleep in his boots, [Ten O'C 66-13
And boots of fur [Cortege 80-17
Sing in clownish boots [Orangeade 103-7
BORDEAUX. Bordeaux to Yucatan, Havana next, [C 29-9
Beyond Bordeaux, beyond Havana, far [C 40-9
BORDER. An acrobat on the border of the sea [Woman Had 81-12 P
BORDERED. That bordered Hell. [Phases 4-14 P
BORDERING. In the swags of pine-trees bordering the lake. [NSF 386-8
BORE. Bore up, in time, the somnolent, deep songs. [C 33-25
A sinewy nakedness. A river bore [C 36-5
That bore us as a part of all the things [Anatomy 107-14
Regretful that she bore her; [Sonatina 109-18
The sombre pages bore no print [Reader 147-10
As if the sky was a current that bore them along, [Loaf 200-5
Of the iris bore white blooms. The bird then boomed. [Horn 230-10
Bore off the residents of its noble Place. [NSF 391-9
The trees have a look as if they bore sad names [Slug 522-5
If they broke into bloom, if they bore fruit, [Rock 526-15
Were wings that bore [Phases 4-2 P
Did not the age that bore him bear him among [Someone 85-1 A
BOREAL. And cold in a boreal mistiness of the moon. [C 34-8
Together, all together. Boreal night [AA 413-20
BORN. Come now. Those to be born have need [Ghosts 119-12
The starry voluptuary will be born. [Nigger 156-9
Born, as she was, at twenty-one, [Couch 295-6
Born old, familiar with the depths of the heart, [Repet 306-17
Was a return to birth, a being born [EM 321-18
Man, that is not born of woman but of air, [Pure 331-16
A text we should be born that we might read, [Descrip 344-21
Of the land's children, easily born, its flesh, [Cred 375-4
He is born the blank mechanic of the mountains, [Aug 492-17
You were not born yet when the trees were crystal [Slug 522-17
It is not that he was born in another land, [Sombre 66-23 P

He was born within us as a second self, [Sombre 67-3 P
Blond weather. One is born a saint, [Stan MBG 73-9 P
That is its life preserved, the effort to be born [Discov 96-8 P
Surviving being born, the event of life. [Discov 96-9 P
See new-born.
BORNE. With lanterns borne aloft to light the way, [Heaven 56-13
Behold the men in helmets borne on steel, [Extracts 259-19
Could be borne, as if we were sure to find our way. [EM 316-6
The uptopping top and tip of things, borne up [Two V 355-6
Could not have borne his labor nor have died [NSF 393-20
To speak of joy and to sing of it, borne on [NSF 398-10
Which counts for most, the anger borne [Sombre 69-21 P
See half-borne.
BORROWINGS. See bell-borrowings.
BOSH. Concentric bosh. To their tabernacles, then, [Greenest 56-21P
For poverty are gaudy bosh to these. [Duck 61-20 P
BOSKAGE. Yet there is no spring in Florida, neither in boskage
   perdu, nor on the nunnery beaches. [Indian 112-7
BOSOM. Within whose burning bosom we devise [Sunday 69-26
A great bosom, beard and being, alive with age. [NH 466-3
From the sleepy bosom of the real, re-creates, [NH 481-20
BOSOMS. Green bosoms and black legs, beguile [Stan MMO 19-10 P
BOSSUET. Unless Racine or Bossuet held the like. [Geneva 24-6
BOSTON. Boston with a Note-book [NE Verses 104-title 5
   Boston without a Note-book [NE Verses 105-title 6
Over wooden Boston, the sparkling Byzantine [Blue Bldg 217-1
Boston should be in the keys [Agenda 41-19 P
BOTANIST. Of hum, inquisitorial botanist, [C 28-10
"Botanist on Alp (No. 1)" [134-title
"Botanist on Alp (No. 2)" [135-title
BOTCHES. Out of her botches, hot embosomer. [C 44-29
BOTH. But that of earth both comes and goes at once. [Monocle
   15-26
A sunken voice, both of remembering [C 29-5
True daughters both of Crispin and his clay. [C 44-2
Are both alike in the routine I know. [Pharynx 96-3
Both of men and clouds, a slime of men in crowds. [Farewell
   118-12
Each is both star and orb; and day [MBG 172-11
And so the moon, both come, and the janitor's poems [Dump 201-16
Out of the changes of both light and dew [Scavoir 231-8
Both substance and non-substance, luminous flesh [Choc 297-21
Or what hell was, since now both heaven and hell [EM 315-12
Weaken our fate, relieve us of woe both great [EM 315-21
The peopled and the unpeopled. In both, he is [EM 323-6
Of them and of himself destroys both worlds, [EM 323-16
And him. Both wanted the same thing. Both sought [Liadoff 347-18
Of the place, blue and green, both streaked. [Attempt 370-5
Invisible or visible or both: [NSF 385-20
Does it move to and fro or is it of both [NSF 396-15
Is the poem both peculiar and general? [NSF 396-20
That speaks, denouncing separate selves, both one. [Orb 441-25
Both size and solitude or thinks it does, [Orb 443-1
Since both alike appoint themselves the choice [NH 469-16
In space and the self, that touched them both at once [NH 483-7
Men are part both in the inch and in the mile. [Rome 508-10
Both late and alone, above the crickets' chords, [Quiet 523-12
His words are both the icon and the man. [Rock 527-21
In whose hard service both of us endure [Soldat 14-7 P
The fowl of Venus may consist of both [Spaniard 35-7 P
On the sea, is both law and evidence in one, [Bship 78-29
And at what time both of the year and day; [Ideal 89-3 A
BOTHER. Of things, why bother about the back of stars? [Greenest
   58-27 P
BOTTLE. "Man and Bottle" [238-title
This bottle of indigo glass in the grass, [Indigo 22-11 P
Your porcelain water bottle. [Three 129-1 P
This bottle is earth: [Three 130-9 P
What the bottle is going to be-- [Three 131-5 P
That we are painted on this very bottle, [Three 132-20 P
As there are sides to a round bottle. [Three 136-16 P
She was as beautiful as a porcelain water bottle. [Three 136-19P
2. Out of their bottle the green genii come. [Someone 86-5 A
BOTTLES. Nudes or bottles. [Pears 196-3
Bottles, pots, shoes and grass and murmur aptest eve: [Dump 203-7
BOTTOM. And so it is one damns that green shade at the bottom of
   the land. [Banal 63-3
If that remains concealed, what does the bottom matter? [Nudity
   Cap 145-11
That he was at the bottom of things [Yellow 236-5
The brown at the bottom of red [Plant 506-10
Is at the bottom of her as pique-pain [Spaniard 34-22 P
At the bottom of imagined artifice, [Someone 83-9 A
BOTTOMLESS. The bottomless trophy, new hornsman after old? [NSF
   390-18
It is not an empty clearness, a bottomless sight. [NH 488-4
BOTTOMNESS. Upon the rumpling bottomness, and nights [C 42-31
BOUCHER. An empty land; the gods that Boucher killed; [Oboe 250-10
Of Boucher pink, the sheens of Venetian gray. [Greenest 53-14 P
BOUGAINVILLEAS. Behind the bougainvilleas, [Venereal 47-20

BOUGH. The bough of summer and the winter branch. [Sunday 67-25
   O bough and bush and scented vine, in whom [Fictive 88-8
   As pleasant as the brush-strokes of a bough, [Connois 215-11
   An upper, particular bough in, say, Marchand. [Connois 215-12
   It is a bough in the electric light [NH 477-7
BOUGHS. Just as they flew from the boughs of the hemlocks
      [Domination 8-22
   To regard the frost and the boughs [Snow Man 9-22
   I know no magic trees, no balmy boughs, [Monocle 16-27
   Does ripe fruit never fall? Or do the boughs [Sunday 69-14
   Comes through boughs that lie in wait, [Brave 138-8
   The parrot in its palmy boughs [Grotesque 75-10 P
BOULEVARDS. A refrain from the end of the boulevards. [Nightgown
      214-4
   The boulevards of the generals. Why should [Feo 334-5
BOUND. Her mind had bound me round. The palms were hot [Farewell
      117-11
   And bound. Its nigger mystics should change [Prelude 195-11
   And bound by a sound which does not change, [Human 363-2
   See: light-bound; place-bound; time-bound.
BOUNDARY. It was like passing a boundary to dive [Lot 371-1
   It was passing a boundary, floating without a head [Lot 371-16
   Within its vital boundary, in the mind. [Final 524-13
BOUNTY. Why should she give her bounty to the dead? [Sunday 67-12
BOUQUET. Places there, a bouquet. Ho-ho . . . The dump is full
      [Dump 201-13
   On the irised hunks, the stone bouquet. [Hartford 227-12
   "Bouquet of Belle Scavoir" [231-title
   Each false thing ends. The bouquet of summer [Hero 280-19
   "Bouquet of Roses in Sunlight" [430-title
   "The Bouquet" [448-title
   The bouquet stands in a jar, as metaphor, [Bouquet 448-8
   The green bouquet comes from the place of the duck. [Bouquet
      450-1
   And the eccentric twistings of the rapt bouquet [Bouquet 450-20
   Are questions of the looks they get. The bouquet, [Bouquet 451-2
   They are. The bouquet is a part of a dithering: [Bouquet 452-17
   He bumps the table. The bouquet falls on its side. [Bouquet
      453-1
   The bouquet has slopped over the edge and lies on the floor.
      [Bouquet 453-3
   The bouquet of being--enough to realize [Conversat 109-21 P
BOUQUETS. Beetled, in chapels, on the chaste bouquets. [C 29-20
   The bouquets come here in the papers. So the sun, [Dump 201-15
BOURGEOIS. And the bourgeois, are different, much. [Hero 276-9
   And there are many bourgeois heroes. [Hero 276-11
BOURGEOISE. "Cuisine Bourgeoise" [227-title
BOURGEOISIE. The rape of the bourgeoisie accomplished, the men
      [Bship 77-13 P
BOW. See hail-bow.
BOWED. Who bowed and, bowing, brought, in her mantilla, [Attempt
      370-7
   Blew against them or bowed from the hips, when I turned [Bship
      78-17 P
BOWING. Came, bowing and voluble, upon the deck, [Sea Surf 101-24
   Who bowed and, bowing, brought, in her mantilla, [Attempt 370-9
BOWL. Clear water in a brilliant bowl, [Poems Clim 193-7
   Is simplified: a bowl of white, [Poems Clim 193-14
   "Bowl" [6-title P
   Was this bowl of Earth designed? [Bowl 6-11 P
   Than on any bowl of the Sungs, [Bowl 6-13 P
BOW-LEGGED. Young ox, bow-legged bear, [Destructive 192-16
BOWMEN. The milkiest bowmen. This makes a new design, [Greenest
      56-6 P
   The heavenly cocks, the bowmen, and the gourds, [Greenest 56-18P
BOX. The cat in the paper-bag, the corset, the box [Dump 201-18
BOXES. On tins and boxes? What about horses eaten by wind?
      [Parochial 191-18
BOY. When the music of the boy fell like a fountain, [Norfolk
      111-14
   Cotton Mather died when I was a boy. The books [Blue Bldg 216-15
   One boy swims under a tub, one sits [Vari 235-16
   He walked with his year-old boy on his shoulder. [Contra II
      270-4
   An abstract, of which the sun, the dog, the boy [Contra II 270-10
   Tom McGreevy, in America, Thinks of Himself as a Boy [Our Stars
      454-title 1
   See plough-boy.
BOYS. It is for fiery boys that star was set [Monocle 14-24
   As they are used to wear, and let the boys [Emperor 64-5
   She causes boys to pile new plums and pears [Sunday 69-10
   Piece the world together, boys, but not with your hands.
      [Parochial 192-8
   Young boys resembling pastry, hip-hip, [Hero 278-11
BRACELET. Like a bracelet [Six Sig 74-2
BRACELETS. Her useless bracelets fondly fluttered, [Thought 184-11
BRAG. Philosopher, beginning with green brag, [C 46-1
BRAHMS. Music began to fail him. Brahms, although [Anglais 148-13
   Turning in time to Brahms as alternate [Anglais 149-6
BRAIDED. The clouds becoming braided girls. [Vase 246-14

BRAIDS. The end of love in their all-speaking braids. [Monocle 14-6
   And your braids bear brightening of crimson bands. Burnshaw 51-29P
BRAIN. To lay his brain upon the board [MBG 166-5
   Fire-monsters in the Milky Brain [Pure 331-title 3
   And brain, as the extraordinary references [Extraord 369-13
   The blood of his bitter brain; and there the sun [Burnshaw 49-11P
BRANCH. The bough of summer and the winter branch. [Sunday 67-25
BRANCHES. When its black branches came to bud, belle day, [C 39-3
   Her old light moves along the branches, [Lunar 107-3
   The grunting, shuffling branches, the robust, [Parochial 191-8
   These trees and their argentines, their dark-spiced branches,
      [Holiday 313-3
   If only in the branches sweeping in the rain: [NH 481-1
   Today the leaves cry, hanging on branches swept by wind, [Course
      96-10 P
   The wind moves slowly in the branches. [Of Mere 118-5 P
   See tree-branches.
BRANCHING. Branching through heavens heavy with the sheen [Old
      Woman 46-1 P
BRANCHINGS. And more, in branchings after day. One part [NH 468-23
BRASS. Was he to bray this in profoundest brass [C 41-10
   You could almost see the brass on her gleaming, [Vari 235-19
   And the brass was played. [Coroner 29-13 P
   And the brass grew cold [Coroner 29-23 P
   Making your heart of brass to intercept [Good Bad 33-18 P
   Why was it that you cast the brass away [Good Bad 33-20 P
   Keep whanging their brass wings . . . [Memo 89-8 P
BRASSY. Where triumph rang its brassy phrase, or love [Sunday 69-5
BRAVE. For somehow the brave dicta of its kings [Surprises 98-10
   "The Brave Man" [138-title
   The sun, that brave man, [Brave 138-7
   That brave man. [Brave 138-9
   That brave man comes up [Brave 138-19
   That brave man. [Brave 138-21
   Of his brave quickenings, the human [Hero 279-3
   What are the major men? All men are brave. [Paisant 334-13
   To be admired by nations. The race is brave. [Paisant 334-20
   Within them right for terraces--oh, brave salut! [Belly 367-11
   As the fox and snake do. It is a brave affair. [NSF 403-17
BRAVER. No self in the mass: the braver being, [Gigan 289-3
BRAVEST. That is the common, the bravest fundament, [NSF 398-12
   But bravest at midnight and in lonely spaces, [Page 421-22
BRAVURA. Bravura adequate to this great hymn? [Monocle 16-22
   From a bravura of the mind, [Aug 494-26
BRAY. Was he to bray this in profoundest brass [C 41-10
BRAZEN. Like brazen shells. [Cab 21-3 P
BRAZIL. Then came Brazil to nourish the emaciated [Pure 330-16
BRAZILIANS. And dark Brazilians in their cafés, [C 38-24
BREACHES. Breaches the darkness of Ceylon with blares, [NSF 384-12
   Breaches of that which held them fast. It is [Orb 441-18
BREAD. What bread does one eat? [Am Sub 131-13
   The tea is bad, bread sad. [Fading 139-8
   The wine is good. The bread, [Fading 139-18
   Has no more meaning than tomorrow's bread. [Havana 144-29
   The book and bread, things as they are, [MBG 172-20
   Here is the bread of time to come, [MBG 183-20
   Here is its actual stone. The bread [MBG 184-1
   Will be our bread, the stone will be [MBG 184-2
   Brown as the bread, thinking of birds [Loaf 200-1
   One man, their bread and their remembered wine? [Extracts 254-17
   The bread and wine of the mind, permitted [Hero 275-27
   Lenin took bread from his pocket, scattered it-- [Descrip 343-6
   If he must, or lives on the bread of faithful speech. [NSF 408-3
   And thereafter he belongs to it, to bread [Bad Time 426-13
   What wheaten bread and oaten cake and kind, [Orb 440-18
   In the mind: the tin plate, the loaf of bread on it, [NH 485-20
BREADTH. The breadth of an accelerando moves, [Orb 440-15
BREAK. Broke dialect in a break of memory. [Page 422-10
   Spread outward. Crack the round dome. Break through. [Aug 490-11
   Hola! Hola! What steps are those that break [Infernale 24-20 P
   See day-break.
BREAKFAST. Of breakfast ribands, fruits laid in their leaves,
      [C 42-26
   At breakfast jelly yellow streaked the deck [Sea Surf 99-18
   Theology after breakfast sticks to the eye. [Les Plus 245-8
   Breakfast in Paris, music and madness and mud, [Bship 80-3 P
BREAKING. Black water breaking into reality. [Extracts 255-22
   Abba, dark death is the breaking of a glass. [Golden 460-16
BREAST. He for her burning breast and she for his arms. [Norfolk
      111-19
   For whom the towers are built. The burgher's breast, [Havana
      143-27
   Winter devising summer in its breast, [Thought 186-8
   A lion, an ox in his breast, [Destructive 192-13
   And weeps on his breast, though he never comes. [Rhythms 245-17
   And his breast is greatness. All his speeches [Hero 277-12
   The breast is covered with violets. It is a green leaf.
      [Holiday 312-16
   It is time that beats in the breast and it is time [Pure 329-13
   In whose breast, the dove, alighting, would grow still. [Think

357-6
Your brown breast redden, while you wait for warmth. [Cred 377-7
On a breast forever precious for that touch, [NSF 388-6
But what his mother was returns and cries on his breast. [Pecul 453-9
And the poverty of dirt, the thing upon his breast, [Pecul 454-7
Lies on the breast and pierces into the heart, [Novel 458-24
BREASTED. See rose-breasted.
BREASTING. It is the same jingle of the red-bird breasting the
    orange-trees out of the cedars. [Indian 112-6
BREATH. He felt the Andean breath. His mind was free [C 33-9
    That the air was heavy with the breath of these swine, [Frogs
    78-4
    The breath of turgid summer, and [Frogs 78-5
    A breath upon her hand [Peter 91-7
    So gardens die, their meek breath scenting [Peter 92-4
    The purple dress in autumn and the belfry breath [NE Verses
    106-7
    To his breath that lies awake at night. [MBG 171-16
    The grunted breath serene and final, [MBG 177-15
    It wants words virile with his breath. [Country 207-23
    A music more than a breath, but less [Vari 232-7
    Among men, in a woman--she caught his breath-- [Yellow 237-6
    For breath to laugh the louder, the deeper gasps [Extracts
    253-19
    Before the speaker's youngest breath is taken! [Montra 261-21
    The breath life's latest, thousand senses. [Montra 264-2
    When the deep breath fetches another year of life. [News 265-12
    Sleeps by his basket. He snores. His bloated breath [Feo 333-19
    The breath that gushes upward and is gone, [Descrip 341-4
    And another breath emerging out of death, [Descrip 341-5
    And breathes again for us a fragile breath. [Extraord 369-18
    Which he can take within him on his breath, [NSF 395-5
    Of breath, obedient to his trumpet's touch. [AA 415-19
    Breathing his bronzen breath at the azury centre of time.
    [Cata 425-12
    The ocean breathed out morning in one breath. [Our Stars 455-24
    And catches from nowhere brightly-burning breath. [Novel 458-5
    Our breath is like a desperate element [NH 470-23
    The breath of another nature as his own, [Two Illus 513-15
    But only its momentary breath, [Two Illus 513-16
    His own: a chapel of breath, an appearance made [Armor 529-11
    This crust of air? . . (He pauses.) Can breath shake [Infernale
    24-21 P
    As I wished, once they fell backward when my breath [Bship 78-16P
    A longer, deeper breath sustains [Ulysses 101-16 P
    The right to use. Need names on its breath [Ulysses 104-25 P
    A longer, deeper breath sustains [Presence 106-1 P
    A refreshment of cold air, cold breath, [Bus 116-6 P
    A perception of cold breath, more revealing than [Bus 116-7 P
    See land-breath.
BREATHE. Breathe in a crevice of earth? [Bagatelles 213-4
    Item: Breathe, breathe upon the centre of [Montra 264-1
    He is, the air changes and grows fresh to breathe. [Choc 301-8
    And to breathe is a fulfilling of desire, [Choc 301-10
    In which we sit and breathe [Crude 305-12
    It was impossible to breathe at Durand-Ruel's. [Holiday 312-14
    Of the lover that lies within us and we breathe [NSF 394-24
    Breathe slightly, slightly move or seem to move [Bouquet 450-8
    Or down a well. Breathe freedom, oh, my native, [Aug 490-13
    In the excellences of the air we breathe, [Conversat 109-20 P
BREATHED. Again, and lived and was again, and breathed again
    [Martial 238-15
    And then returning from the moon, if one breathed [Extracts
    258-14
    One breathed the cold evening, the deepest inhalation [Extracts
    258-20
    Illumination of movement as he breathed. [Choc 297-18
    Upon my top he breathed the pointed dark. [Choc 298-1
    He breathed in crystal-pointed change the whole [Choc 298-6
    Experience of night, as if he breathed [Choc 298-7
    That breathed on ground, more blue than red, more red [Pieces
    352-3
    Breathing as if they breathed themselves, [Pediment 361-18
    There was a muddy centre before we breathed. [NSF 383-19
    Created the time and place in which we breathed . . . [AA 419-3
    Then he breathed deeply the deep atmosphere [Owl 433-23
    The ocean breathed out morning in one breath. [Our Stars 455-24
    He breathed its oxygen, [Poem Mt. 512-3
    So formed, became himself and he breathed [Two Illus 513-14
    Are old men breathed on by a maternal voice, [Woman Had 82-14 P
BREATHES. In the high night, the summer breathes for them [EM
    319-12
    For the soldier of time, it breathes a summer sleep, [EM 319-14
    In which your father died, still breathes for him [Extraord
    369-17
    And breathes again for us a fragile breath. [Extraord 369-18
BREATHING. These had a being, breathing frost; [Postcard 159-3
    I know that timid breathing. Where [MBG 171-17
    To feel it breathing there. [Destructive 192-14

Even breathing is the beating of time, in kind: [Pure 330-4
Breathing as if they breathed themselves, [Pediment 361-18
To be a bronze man breathing under archaic lapis, [Cata 425-10
Breathing his bronzen breath at the azury centre of time. [Cata
    425-12
Of which Swatara is the breathing, [Countryman 428-20
And what we think, a breathing like the wind, [Look 518-13
No longer of air but of the breathing earth, [Burnshaw 52-18 P
And the shoulders turn, breathing immense intent. [Sombre 68-27P
See ever-breathing.
BREATHINGS. In which, for all the breathings [Aug 495-1
    In the breathings of this soliloquy, [Ulysses 105-8 P
    In the breathings of that soliloquy, [Presence 106-8 P
BREATHLESS. Is breathless to attend each quirky turn. [Monocle
    15-13
    Among the breathless spices and, sometimes, [Pecul 454-5
    Interior: breathless things broodingly abreath [NH 481-9
BREATHS. Men fat as feathers, misers counting breaths, [Horn 230-3
    One of the sacraments between two breaths, [Montra 262-8
    And breaths as true [Lulu G 26-21 P
    Men's bones, beyond their breaths, the black sublime, [Greenest
    55-11 P
    Often have the worst breaths. [Grotesque 74-18 P
BRED. The powerful seasons bred and killed, [Joost 46-17
    This was no worm bred in the moon, [Cuban 65-1
    Are the cities to breed as mountains bred, the streets [Duck
    61-3 P
    See snow-bred.
BREECH-CLOTH. And a breech-cloth might wear, [Cab 21-7 P
    What breech-cloth might you wear-- [Cab 21-13 P
BREECHES. The ribboned stick, the bellowing breeches, cloak [C 28-8
    Wear the breeches of a mask, [Orangeade 103-9
BREED. That yuccas breed, and of the panther's tread. [C 31-29
    Are the cities to breed as mountains bred, the streets [Duck
    61-3 P
BREEDING. Of sun and slaves, breeding and death, [Joost 46-21
    And breeding and bearing birth of harmony, [Study II 465-2
BREEDS. It breeds and that was lewder than it is. [Anatomy 107-15
    These are the heroic children whom time breeds [NSF 385-1
BREEZE. Now, soldiers, hear me: mark this very breeze, [Phases
    5-12 P
BRICK. The fields entrap the children, brick [MBG 171-5
BRICKS. Without scenery or lights, in the theatre's bricks, [Bad
    Time 427-5
    The bricks grown brittle in time's poverty, [NH 480-23
BRIDE. Like jades affecting the sequestered bride; [C 34-23
    The vetch has turned purple. But where is the bride? [Ghosts
    119-3
    Of the bride, love being a birth, have need to see [Ghosts
    119-13
    The bride come jingling, kissed and cupped, or else [Repet 308-17
    Then Ozymandias said the spouse, the bride [NSF 396-10
BRIDGE. Twenty men crossing a bridge, [Magnifico 19-1
    Crossing a single bridge into a village. [Magnifico 19-6
    Twenty men crossing a bridge, [Magnifico 19-9
    Twenty men crossing a bridge, [Magnifico 19-12
    On the boards of the bridge. [Magnifico 19-17
    A bridge above the bright and blue of water [Nigger 154-11
    And the same bridge when the river is frozen. [Nigger 154-12
BRIDGES. Are twenty men crossing twenty bridges, [Magnifico 19-3
BRIEF. For this, then, we endure brief lives, [Negation 98-3
BRIGHT. Late, the firecat closed his bright eyes [Earthy 3-19
    Clippered with lilies scudding the bright chromes, [Monocle 17-15
    And pink, the water bright that dogwood bears. [C 37-31
    The pungent oranges and bright, green wings [Sunday 67-5
    In pungent fruit and bright, green wings, or else [Sunday 67-16
    Strapped and buckled bright. [Orangeade 103-8
    Black man, bright nouveautés leave one, at best, pseudonymous.
    [Nudity Col 145-12
    A bridge above the bright and blue of water [Nigger 154-11
    The sun is seeking something bright to shine on. [Nigger 157-20
    The clouds tumultuously bright [MBG 169-4
    It wants the diamond pivot bright. [Country 207-19
    If the flowers of South Africa were bright [Connois 215-5
    To avoid the bright, discursive wings, [Adequacy 243-14
    "Of Bright & Blue Birds & the Gala Sun" [248-title
    There was a bright scienza outside of ourselves, [Gala 248-12
    And if there be nothing more, O bright, O bright, [Montra 260-2
    Bright is the malice in his eye . . . [Possum 294-16
    Of Gothic prong and practick bright, [Couch 295-12
    That a bright red woman will be rising [Debris 338-6
    Sprinklings of bright particulars from the sky. [Descrip 344-6
    The bright obvious stands motionless in cold. [Man Car 351-8
    At last the good life came, good sleep, bright fruit, [Good Man
    364-7
    It was his clarity that made the vista bright. [Anach 366-3
    These mountains being high be, also, bright, [Belly 367-5
    Fly low, cock bright, and stop on a bean pole. Let [Cred 377-6
    This foundling of the infected past, so bright, [NSF 388-11
    I am the spouse, divested of bright gold, [NSF 395-22

And in bright excellence adorned, crested [Orb 442-17
Not the predicate of bright origin. [NH 481-13
The cold and earliness and bright origin [NH 481-16
Or of a new aspect, bright in discovery-- [Aug 489-7
The total of human shadows bright as glass. [Aug 494-23
A boat carried forward by waves resembling the bright backs of
    rowers, [Prol 515-6
Exclaiming bright sight, as it was satisfied, [Rock 526-6
Turquoise the rock, at odious evening bright [Rock 528-7
That, from her helmet, terrible and bright, [Soldat 14-10 P
Is evil, crisply bright, disclosing you [Spaniard 34-13 P
Raced with the horses in bright hurricanes. [Old Woman 43-4 P
The space above the trees might still be bright [Old Woman
    44-29 P
Yet were not bright, came shining as things come [Burnshaw
    51-25 P
The drafts of gay beginnings and bright ends, [Greenest 57-13 P
Created, like a bubble, of bright sheens, [Duck 63-21 P
With senses chiseled on bright stone. They see [Duck 64-10 P
To rumbled rock, its bright projections lie [Sombre 70-3 P
Previous from the region of the hand, still bright [Bship 81-1 P
His own bright red. But he bears him out of love, [Recit 87-18 P
Spring's bright paradise has come to this. [Fare Guit 98-16 P
On the dark side of the heavens or the bright, [Local 112-2 P
And bright, or like a venerable urn, [Someone 83-16 A
See hollow-bright.
BRIGHT-BLUE-RESEMBLING. Not as in air, bright-blue-resembling air,
    [Rhythms 246-7
BRIGHT-DARK. Coulisse bright-dark, tragic chiaroscuro [NSF 384-3
BRIGHTED. The bays of heaven, brighted, blued? [Botanist 2 136-4
BRIGHT-EDGED. Their pleasure that is all bright-edged and cold;
    [Tallap 72-9
BRIGHTEN. The banners should brighten the sun. [Drum-Majors 37-10P
BRIGHTENED. The air attends the brightened guns, [Dutch 290-16
BRIGHTENER. "How, Now, O, Brightener . . ." [97-title P
BRIGHTENING. And your braids bear brightening of crimson bands.
    [Burnshaw 51-29 P
  Color and color brightening into one, [Greenest 58-5 P
  See ever-brightening.
BRIGHTER. The slightly brighter sky, the melting clouds, [Motive
    288-7
  Is brighter than the sun itself. [Poesie 302-16
  Brighter, perfected and distant away, [Ulysses 101-24 P
BRIGHTEST. In the brightest landscape downwardly revolves [EM
    318-19
  The dazzling, bulging, brightest core, [Red Fern 365-11
  Wind-beaten into freshest, brightest fire. [Burnshaw 52-22 P
  Of azure round an upper dome, brightest [Greenest 54-13 P
BRIGHT-ETHERED. The knowledge of bright-ethered things [Analysis
    349-7
BRIGHTLY. And then rush brightly through the summer air. [Sailing
    121-7
  The sunlight. They bear brightly the little beyond [Extracts
    254-22
  Like seeing fallen brightly away. [Possum 294-5
  To hear more brightly the contriving chords. [Descrip 340-22
  Brightly empowered with like colors, swarmingly, [Myrrh 350-3
  Into the sun-filled water, brightly leafed [Lot 371-2
BRIGHTLY-BURNING. And catches from nowhere brightly-burning
    breath. [Novel 458-5
BRIGHTLY-CROWNED. Unless in the darkness, brightly-crowned,
    [Vari 233-1
BRIGHTNESS. The exceeding brightness of this early sun [Sun March
    133-13
  He preferred the brightness of bells, [Winter B 141-5
  The brightness of arms, said Roma wasted [Hero 273-8
  Was always the other mind. The brightness [Hero 273-11
  These hymns are like a stubborn brightness [Hero 279-24
  In the hard brightness of that winter day [Page 421-4
  Its brightness burned the way good solace seethes. [Owl 434-6
  It blows a glassy brightness on the fire [Novel 458-6
BRILLIANCE. Their brilliance through the lattices, crippled
    [Blue Bldg 217-10
  And hollow of him by its brilliance calmed, [Owl 434-5
  Always, in brilliance, fatal, final, formed [Owl 434-23
  Had left in them only a brilliance, of unaccustomed origin,
    [Prol 515-11
BRILLIANCES. With its frigid brilliances, its blue-red sweeps
    [AA 413-1
BRILLIANCIES. These nebulous brilliancies in the smallest look
    [EM 317-13
  Of ten brilliancies of battered gold [Imago 439-6
BRILLIANCY. Faces to people night's brilliancy, [Dezem 218-14
  The brilliancy at the central of the earth. [NH 473-15
BRILLIANT. A sheaf of brilliant arrows flying straight, [Tallap
    72-7
  Poured brilliant iris on the glistening blue. [Sea Surf 99-15
  Clear water in a brilliant bowl, [Poems Clim 193-7
  A crinkled paper makes a brilliant sound. [Extracts 252-1
  And saints are brilliant in fresh cloaks. [Contra I 266-16

A woman brilliant and pallid-skinned, [Attempt 370-10
The brilliant mercy of a sure repose, [Cred 375-18
Or spill night out in brilliant vanishings, [Page 423-4
Stood flourishing the world. The brilliant height [Owl 434-4
Nor brilliant blows thereof, ti-rill-a-roo, [John 437-12
A brilliant air [Polo 38-3 P
Would soon be brilliant, as it was, before [Old Woman 45-24 P
As brilliant as mystic, as mystic as single, all [Greenest 55-9P
BRILLIANT-EDGED. A world of clear water, brilliant-edged, [Poems
    Clim 194-1
BRILLIANTER. The statue is white and high, white brillianter
    [Duck 64-5 P
BRILLIANTEST. In the brilliantest descriptions of new day,
    [Descrip 344-11
BRILLIANTLY. That is an instant nature, brilliantly. [Choc 301-13
  A mask up-gathered brilliantly from the dirt, [Sombre 70-13 P
BRIM. More definite. The sweeping brim of the hat [Pastor 379-5
  In the sweeping brim becomes the origin [Pastor 379-13
  These two go well together, the sinuous brim [Pastor 380-2
BRIMMED. See broad-brimmed.
BRIMMING. Stands brimming white, chiaroscuro scaled [Sombre 70-20P
BRINE. Eager for the brine and bellowing [Paltry 5-14
  The dead brine melted in him like a dew [C 29-14
BRING. Knowing that they can bring back thought [Homunculus 26-13
  Out of the tomb, we bring Badroulbadour, [Worms 49-16
  Out of the tomb we bring Badroulbadour. [Worms 50-3
  Bring flowers in last month's newspapers. [Emperors 64-6
  I cannot bring a world quite round, [MBG 165-11
  With white wine, sugar and lime juice. Then bring it, [Phenom
    286-15
  The vivid transparence that you bring is peace. [NSF 380-11
  She wanted nothing he could not bring her by coming alone.
    [World 521-7
  Sorrow bring-- [Phases 5-2 P
  To bring destruction, often seems high-pitched. [Spaniard 34-17P
  Bring down from nowhere nothing's wax-like blooms, [Burnshaw
    47-20 P
  Bring us fresh water [Three 141-1 P
BRINGING. Bringing the lights of Norway and all that. [Hartford
    226-6
  Pine-figures bringing sleep to sleep. [Vari 235-12
  Shadows of friends, of those he knew, each bringing [New Set
    352-12
BRINGS. Brings no rou-cou, [Depression 63-15
  The difference that heavenly pity brings. [Fictive 88-13
  Brings forth [Nomad 95-7
  Brings forth hymn and hymn [Nomad 95-11
  Brings back an earlier season of quiet [Lunar 107-10
  Brings voices as of lions coming down. [Sun March 134-6
  And yet it brings the storm to bear. [MBG 169-11
  It is the leaf the bird brings back to the boat. [Blue Bldg
    217-18
  That the buxom eye brings merely its element [Poem Morn 219-14
  It is safe to sleep to a sound that time brings back. [Phenom
    286-12
  Brings the day to perfection and then fails. He dwells [EM 318-2
  The poem, through candor, brings back a power again [NSF 382-23
  No more that which most of all brings back the known, [Page
    422-15
  Now, he brings all that he saw into the earth, to the waiting
    parent. [Madame 507-3
BRINY-BLOODED. And picador? Be briny-blooded bull. [Spaniard
    34-23 P
BRISTLED. A firecat bristled in the way. [Earthy 3-3
  Bristled in the way. [Earthy 3-18
BRISTLES. Begone! An inchling bristles in these pines, [Bantams
    76-2
  Bristles, and points their Appalachian tangs, [Bantams 76-3
BRISTLING. And bristling thorn-trees spinning on the bank [Nigger
    155-15
  The brooks are bristling in the field, [Poesie 302-6
  Now, brooks are bristling in the fields [Poesie 302-7
  The bristling soldier, weather-foxed, who looms [Cred 375-2
BRITAIN. Who can pick up the weight of Britain, [Imago 439-1
BRITTLE. The bricks grown brittle in time's poverty, [NH 480-23
BROACHINGS. And you forgive dark broachings growing great
    [Spaniard 34-7 P
BROAD-BRIMMED. His broad-brimmed hat came close upon his eyes.
    [Babies 77-18
BROADENED. The rumbling broadened as it fell. The wind, [C 32-22
BROADENING. Is not too lusty for your broadening. [Monocle 16-18
BROADEST. These are the broadest instances. Crispin, [C 38-28
  And the nakedness became the broadest blooms, [Sea Surf 101-20
  To gold in broadest blue, and be a part [Sun March 133-16
BROADLY. Speaking and strutting broadly, fair and bloomed,
    [Burnshaw 52-17 P
BROCADE. She dressed in red and gold brocade [Pourtraicte 21-7
BROKE. And the wheel that broke as the cart went by. [Silent 359-17
  Broke dialect in a break of memory. [Page 422-10
  And blue broke on him from the sun, [Two Illus 514-16

And yet the leaves, if they broke into bud, [Rock 526-14
If they broke into bloom, if they bore fruit, [Rock 526-15
BROKEN. Bent and broken them down, [Weak Mind 212-19
  Be broken and winter would be broken and done, [Extracts 255-19
  In this bleak air the broken stalks [Possum 293-17
  Lay a passion for yes that had never been broken. [EM 320-14
  The broken cartwheel on the hill. [Silent 359-7
  The rock cannot be broken. It is the truth. [Cred 375-11
  As if the waves at last were never broken, [NSF 387-16
  And the booming is blunt, not broken in subtleties. [NSF 390-9
  A thousand begettings of the broken bold. [Owl 434-21
  But the images, disembodied, are not broken. [Golden 460-19
  With the broken statues standing on the shore. [Aug 491-8
  A broken wall--and it ceased to exist, became [Greenest 53-7 P
  The circle would no longer be broken but closed. [Letters 108-8P
BRONZE. A bronze rain from the sun descending marks [Swans 4-3
  Shine alone, shine nakedly, shine like bronze, [Nuances 18-8
  The arm of bronze outstretched against all evil! [Mice 123-12
  Theatrical distances, bronze shadows heaped [Key W 129-20
  And bearded bronze, but not a man, [MBG 165-14
  That is fluent in even the wintriest bronze. [Sleight 222-19
  The hand can touch, neither green bronze nor marble, [Montra
    261-3
  Changed his true flesh to an inhuman bronze. [NSF 391-19
  To be a bronze man breathing under archaic lapis, [Cata 425-10
  Of bronze whose mind was made up and who, therefore, died.
    [NH 472-10
  We are not men of bronze and we are not dead. [NH 472-11
  Before the horses, clouds of bronze imposed [Old Woman 43-7 P
  On clouds of gold, and green engulfing bronze, [Old Woman 43-8 P
  The golden clouds that turned to bronze, the sounds [Old Woman
    44-7 P
  Now felt, now known as this. The clouds of bronze [Old Woman
    45-4 P
  Complete in bronze on enormous pedestals. [Duck 64-4 P
  The bronze of the wise man seated in repose [Recit 86-15 P
  In the bronze distance, [Of Mere 117-17 P
BRONZED. And, arbored and bronzed, in autumn. [Yellow 236-12
  At last, in that blond atmosphere, bronzed hard, [NH 487-2
  See sun-bronzed.
BRONZE-FILLED. The bronze-filled plazas [Archi 18-19 P
BRONZEN. Breathing his bronzen breath at the azury centre of time.
  [Cata 425-12
BRONZES. But this gross blue under rolling bronzes [Grapes 110-15
  The bronzes liquid through gay light. [Thought 187-3
BROOD. A majestic mother's flocking brood, [Ulysses 103-25 P
BROODER. Of the brooder seeking the acutest end [Extracts 259-14
  Brooder, brooder, deep beneath its walls-- [Dove 97-16 P
BROODING. Brooding on centuries like shells. [Oak 272-12
  And of the brooding mind, fixed but for a slight [Choc 297-17
  Brooding sounds of the images of death, [Degen 444-3
  Brooding sounds of river noises; [Degen 444-6
BROODINGLY. Interior: breathless things broodingly abreath
  [NH 481-9
BROODING-SIGHT. To know; a missal for brooding-sight. [MBG 178-5
BROODS. Except because he broods there and is still. [Bird Claws
  82-9
  As the acorn broods on former oaks [Oak 272-13
  To the first autumnal inhalations, young broods [Cred 372-6
  He broods of neither cap nor cape, [Countryman 428-17
  Broods in tense meditation, constantly, [Sombre 68-20 P
  There is one, unnamed, that broods [Child 106-14 P
BROOK. If any duck in any brook, [Sonatina 109-13
BROOKS. The brooks are bristling in the field, [Poesie 302-6
  Now, brooks are bristling in the fields [Poesie 302-7
BROTHER. Believe would be a brother full [MBG 175-21
  Not father, but bare brother, megafrere, [Choc 300-21
  This brother even in the father's eye, [EM 317-10
  This brother half-spoken in the mother's throat [EM 317-11
  Sister and solace, brother and delight. [NSF 392-24
  There sleep the brother is the father, too, [Owl 432-10
  This was peace after death, the brother of sleep, [Owl 434-7
  The inhuman brother so much like, so near, [Owl 434-8
BROTHERS. And that made brothers of us in a home [AA 419-11
  In which we fed on being brothers, fed [AA 419-12
  Two brothers. And a third form, she that says [Owl 431-16
BROUGHT. Suppose these couriers brought amid their train [Monocle
  15-27
  His trees were planted, his duenna brought [C 42-2
  With heaven, brought such requital to desire [Sunday 68-3
  We feast on human heads, brought in on leaves, [Cuisine 228-10
  The snow hangs heavily on the rocks, brought [Hero 273-5
  Brought down to one below the eaves, [Silent 359-14
  Who bowed and, bowing, brought, in her mantilla, [Attempt 370-9
  A dead shepherd brought tremendous chords from hell [NSF 400-21
  Children in love with them brought early flowers [NSF 400-23
  You brought the incredible calm in ecstasy, [Red Kit 30-17 P
  Before the sun brought them that destruction [Stan Hero 83-18 P
BROW. Though the brow in your palm may grieve [Delight 162-3
  Belshazzar's brow, O, ruler, rude [Country 207-14

Merely by putting hand to brow, [Oak 272-11
  A wider brow, large and less human [Hero 277-8
  The frown like serpents basking on the brow, [NSF 400-11
  Dark Juan looks outward through his mystic brow . . . [Luther
    461-14
  Of the park with chalky brow scratched over black [Old Woman
    44-3 P
BROWN. Brown as the bread, thinking of birds [Loaf 200-1
  Flying from burning countries and brown sand shores, [Loaf 200-2
  And, in the brown blues of evening, the lady said, [Uruguay
    248-17
  Of a still-life, symbols, brown things to think of [Hero 276-24
  In brown books. The marbles of what he was stand [Hero 276-25
  Look round, brown moon, brown bird, as you rise to fly, [God
    285-1
  Look round you as you start to rise, brown moon, [God 285-4
  The deer-grass is thin. The timothy is brown. [Myrrh 350-11
  The old brown hen and the old blue sky, [Silent 359-5
  Your brown breast redden, while you wait for warmth. [Cred 377-7
  They came. But, brown, the ice-bear sleeping in ice-month [Study
    II 464-8
  Were mere brown clods, mere catching weeks of talk. [NH 486-21
  Of its brown wheat rapturous in the wind, [Aug 491-15
  The brown at the bottom of red [Plant 506-10
  As if its understanding was brown skin, [Rock 527-13
  And the awnings are too brown, [Mandolin 28-16 P
  Will laugh in the brown grass, [Secret Man 36-15 P
  And brown, an Italy of the mind, a place [Burnshaw 48-13 P
BROWS. Are shining on all brows of Neversink. [Myrrh 349-14
BRUNE. A brune figure in winter evening resists [Man Car 350-15
BRUNETTE. Brunette, [Vincentine 52-17
  But yet not too brunette, [Vincentine 52-18
BRUNT. Was name for this short-shanks in all that brunt? [C 28-16
BRUSH. A brush of white, the obscure, [Add 199-6
  And, standing in violent golds, will brush her hair. [Debris
    338-7
BRUSHED. He brushed away the thunder, then the clouds, [Landsc
  241-11
  Brushed up by brushy winds in brushy clouds, [NSF 385-7
  And most in what we hear, sound brushed away, [Sombre 67-9 P
  See big-brushed.
BRUSHES. At the finger that brushes this aside [Ulysses 101-1 P
BRUSHINGS. Burns us with brushings of her dress [Wom Sun 445-9
BRUSH-STROKES. As pleasant as the brush-strokes of a bough,
  [Connois 215-11
BRUSHY. Brushed up by brushy winds in brushy clouds, [NSF 385-7
BRUTE. Fear never the brute clouds nor winter-stop [Montra 261-22
BRUTED. Eyes and bruted ears: the man-like body [Hero 277-9
BRUTE-LIKE. These hospitaliers? These brute-like guests? [AA 415-23
BUBBLE. The radiant bubble that she was. And then [Monocle 13-9
  The bubbling sun will bubble up, [MBG 182-12
  Or in a bubble examines the bubble of air. [Phenom 286-8
  Created, like a bubble, of bright sheens. [Duck 63-21 P
  A bubble without a wall on which to hang. [Theatre 91-12 P
BUBBLES. Bubbles up in the night and drowns the crickets' sound.
  [EM 321-9
BUBBLING. Bubbling felicity in cantilene, [C 43-10
  The bubbling sun will bubble up, [MBG 182-12
  To the bubbling of bassoons. That's the time [Dump 202-20
  There is this bubbling before the sun, [Dove 98-13 P
BUCKLED. Strapped and buckled bright. [Orangeade 103-8
BUCKS. Every time the bucks went clattering [Earthy 3-1
  The bucks clattered. [Earthy 3-14
BUCKS COUNTY. "Dutch Graves in Bucks County" [290-title
BUCKSKIN. O buckskin, O crosser of snowy divides, [Duck 61-1 P
  These things he thinks of, as the buckskin hoop-la, [Americana
    94-13 P
BUD. In beak and bud and fruity gobbet-skins, [C 32-7
  When its black branches came to bud, belle day, [C 39-3
  In the leaf and bud and how the red, [Vase 246-19
  The bud of the apple is desire, the down-falling gold, [Holiday
    313-5
  And yet the leaves, if they broke into bud, [Rock 526-14
  They bud and bloom and bear their fruit without change. [Rock
    527-5
  They bud the whitest eye, the pallidest sprout, [Rock 527-7
  See peach-bud.
BUDDED. Still weaving budded aureoles, [Postcard 159-14
BUDDING. Without her, evening like a budding yew [Old Woman 45-23P
BUDGETS. Geranium budgets, pay-roll water-falls, [Duck 62-24 P
BUDS. And pettifogging buds, [Bananas 54-6
  Pushing their buds above the dark green leaves, [Nigger 156-11
  Blue buds or pitchy blooms. Be content-- [MBG 172-3
  As a young lover sees the first buds of spring [Peaches 224-5
  Crowned with the first, cold buds. On these we live, [Cuisine
    228-11
  Small bees of spring, sniffing the coldest buds [Duck 65-7 P
BUFFETS. That buffets the shapes of its possible halcyon [EM 321-7
  The blows and buffets of fresh senses [Fare Guit 99-5 P
BUFFO. As buffo, yet divers, four mirrors blue [C 45-6

Poor buffo! Look at the lavender [Lilacs 49-6
Buffo! A ball, an opera, a bar. [AA 420-12
BUG. And the little green cat is a bug in the grass. [Rabbit K
  210-3
BUGLE. Cock bugler, whistle and bugle and stop just short, [NSF
  405-15
BUGLER. Enjoying angels. Whistle, forced bugler, [NSF 405-13
  Cock bugler, whistle and bugle and stop just short, [NSF 405-15
BUGLES. There is a battering of the drums. The bugles [Dutch 291-8
  That bugles for the mate, nearby the nest, [NSF 405-14
  But the bugles, in the night, [Phases 4-1 P
BUGS. With the gold bugs, in blue meadows, late at night. [Cred
  377-23
BUILD. And from the nave build haunted heaven. Thus, [High-Toned
  59-3
  No more. I can build towers of my own, [Montra 263-8
  And shone. And a small cabin build there. [Page 421-16
  What manner of building shall we build? [Archi 16-13 P
  Let us build the building of light. [Archi 17-14 P
  To build a ruddy palace? [Archi 17-24 P
  The body bent, like Hercules, to build. [Sombre 69-10 P
  Instead of building ships, in numbers, build [Bship 78-1 P
BUILDER. He is the final builder of the total building, [Sketch
  335-17
BUILDING. And each blank window of the building balked [Babies
  77-8
  But the wise man avenges by building his city in snow. [Nigger
  158-13
  Sees a familiar building drenched in cloud [Repet 308-4
  He is the final builder of the total building, [Sketch 335-17
  Or will be. Building and dream are one. [Sketch 335-19
  There is a total building and there is [Sketch 335-20
  There is a building stands in a ruinous storm, [Sketch 336-7
  What manner of building shall we build? [Archi 16-13 P
  Let us build the building of light. [Archi 17-14 P
  Instead of building ships, in numbers, build [Bship 78-1 P
BUILDINGS. The buildings pose in the sky [Add 198-12
  "The Blue Buildings in the Summer Air" [216-title
  The buildings were of marble and stood in marble light. [Anach
  366-2
  The sounds drift in. The buildings are remembered. [Rome 510-11
BUILDS. The dove in the belly builds his nest and coos, [Belly
  366-17
  Next he builds capitols and in their corridors, [NSF 403-18
BUILT. Because he built a cabin who once planned [C 41-19
  Yet the house is not built, not even begun. [Ghosts 119-2
  For whom the towers are built. The burgher's breast, [Havana
  143-27
  The boat was built of stones that had lost their weight and
    being no longer heavy [Prol 515-10
  If her eyes were chinks in which the sparrows built; [Woman Had
  83-1 P
BULGAR. The Bulgar said, "After pineapple with fresh mint [Duck
  60-7 P
  Again the Bulgar said, "There are more things [Duck 62-1 P
BULGE. With a tendency to bulge as it floats away. [Duck 63-22 P
BULGED. Basilewsky's bulged before it floated, turned [Duck 63-23P
BULGES. Whose green mind bulges with complicated hues: [Choc 300-5
BULGING. Of bulging green [Mud 147-18
  Bulging toward the base. [Pears 196-7
  It was everything bulging and blazing and big in itself, [Freed
  205-22
  The dazzling, bulging, brightest core, [Red Fern 365-11
  Last terms, the largest bulging still with more, [Orb 441-11
BULK. In spite of this, the gigantic bulk of him [Choc 299-4
  As if it bears all darkness in its bulk. [Sombre 68-18 P
BULL. Comes up as the sun, bull fire, [Add 198-20
  And picador? Be briny-blooded bull. [Spaniard 34-23 P
BULLIONED. A bullioned blue, a blue abulge, [Two Illus 514-17
BULLS. The bells are the bellowing of bulls. [MBG 181-12
  Hoy, hoy, the blue bulls kneeling down to rest. [Montra 260-6
  Maidens in bloom, bulls under sea, the lark [Sombre 67-33 P
BUM. Meyer is a bum. He eats his pie. [Grotesque 75-18 P
  But Meyer is a bum. [Grotesque 76-3 P
BUMPS. He bumps the table. The bouquet falls on its side. [Bouquet
  453-1
BUNDLE. The bundle of the body and the feet. [Worms 50-2
BURGHER. "The Weeping Burgher" [61-title
  For whom the towers are built. The burgher's breast, [Havana
  143-27
BURGHERS. "Burghers of Petty Death" [362-title
BURIAL. That burial, pillared up each day as porte [Heaven 56-16
  Of chance. Finally, the most solemn burial [Paisant 334-15
BURIED. Of dreamers buried in our sleep, and not [C 39-27
  We buried the fallen without jasmine crowns. [Oboe 251-13
  Him chanting for those buried in their blood, [Oboe 251-19
  The wounds. Yet to lie buried in evil earth, [Extracts 259-2
  Lie harshly buried there? [Extracts 259-10
  To be buried in desert and deserted earth. [Dutch 290-21
  Great tufts, spring up from buried houses [EM 322-15

Moved on the buried water where they lay. [Descrip 343-5
These figures verdant with time's buried verdure [New Set 352-16
So much guilt lies buried [Inhab 504-13
BURLY. He inhaled the rancid rosin, burly smells [C 36-7
  Single, of burly ivory, inched of gold, [Greenest 55-6 P
BURN. As if last night's lamps continued to burn, [Cuisine 228-4
  Yet the freshness of the leaves, the burn [Scavoir 231-6
  Burn everything not part of it to ash. [Cred 373-5
  The house will crumble and the books will burn. [AA 413-17
BURNED. For the legendary moonlight that once burned [C 33-27
  My candle burned alone in an immense valley. [Valley Candle 51-1
  Its brightness burned the way good solace seethes. [Owl 434-6
BURNING. Among the people burning in me still, [W Burgher 61-11
  Within whose burning bosom we devise [Sunday 69-26
  To read, in secret, burning secrecies . . . . [Polish Aunt 84-11
  He for her burning breast and she for his arms, [Norfolk 111-19
  No lamp was burning as I read, [Reader 147-4
  Except the trace of burning stars [Reader 147-11
  Flying from burning countries and brown sand shores, [Loaf 200-2
  The furiously burning father-fire . . . [Red Fern 365-12
  Beyond the burning body that I bear. [NSF 395-24
  Of right joining, a music of ideas, the burning [Study II 465-1
  A shape, the vista twisted and burning, a thing [Bship 80-5 P
  See brightly-burning.
BURNISHED. The well-composed in his burnished solitude, [Antag
  426-5
  Leaves burnished in autumnal burnished trees [NH 474-3
BURNS. In the high west there burns a furious star. [Monocle 14-23
  Burns in the mind on lost remembrances. [Men Fall 187-12
  Burns us with brushings of her dress [Wom Sun 445-9
  The fire burns as the novel taught it how. [Novel 458-3
BURNSHAW. See Mr. Burnshaw.
BURST. It is shaken now. It will burst into flames, [Nightgown
  214-19
  And the banners of the nation flutter, burst [NSF 390-22
  At the burst of day, crepuscular images [Burnshaw 46-23 P
  In a burse of shouts, under the trees [Dinner 110-1 P
BURSTING. Came bursting from the clouds. So the wind [Sleight 222-7
  Leader, the creator of bursting color [Hero 274-2
BURSTS. Within me, bursts its watery syllable. [Monocle 13-11
  Bursts back. What not quite realized transit [Feo 333-20
BURY. And they bury him there, [Cortege 81-4
  Everywhere the spruce trees bury soldiers: [Vari 234-10
  Everywhere spruce trees bury spruce trees. [Vari 234-13
BUS. "On the Way to the Bus" [116-title P
BUSH. It did not give of bird or bush, [Jar 76-15
  O bough and bush and scented vine, in whom [Fictive 88-8
  Tristesses, the fund of life and death, suave bush [Cred 377-15
  And sees the myosotis on its bush. [NSF 382-8
  A lasting visage in a lasting bush, [NSF 400-4
  It does no good to speak of the big, blue bush [Study I 463-4
  Within the big, blue bush and its vast shade [Study I 463-12
  Like blessed beams from out a blessed bush [NH 477-21
  It seizes a sheet, from the ground, from a bush, as if spread
    there by some wash-woman for the night. [Plough-Boy 6-5 P
  Do I happen to like red bush, [Table 40-5 P
  Of the great sizes of an outer bush [Dove 98-8 P
  Fixes itself in its inevitable bush . . . [Conversat 108-15 P
  A churchyard kind of bush as well, [Banjo 114-6 P
  A silent sort of bush, as well, [Banjo 114-7 P
BUSHES. The colors of the bushes [Domination 8-8
  Though the blue bushes bloomed--and bloom, [Arcades 225-14
  To the ruddier bushes at the garden's end. [Hand 271-19
  As one that is strong in the bushes of his eyes. [AA 414-7
  In the swamps, bushes draw up dark red, [Primordia 8-22 P
  Take away the bushes. [Three 139-15 P
BUSHMEN. Combatting bushmen for a patch of gourds, [Greenest 56-8P
BUSHY. On the bushy plain. [Peacocks 57-12
  "On the bushy plain, [Peacocks 58-11
  Of the bushy plain, [Peacocks 58-20
BUSINESS. And writhing wheels of this world's business, [Repet
  308-21
BUSKIN. And the north wind's mighty buskin seems to fall [Antag
  426-7
BUSTS. And the general fidget from busts of Constantine [NH 488-14
BUSY. It is a busy cry, concerning someone else. [Course 96-14 P
BUTCHER. Where, butcher, seducer, bloodman, reveller, [Ghosts 119-5
  There was the butcher's hand. [Weak Mind 212-1
  And, according to the composer, this butcher, [Thunder 220-9
  Each night, an incessant butcher, whose knife [Dutch 292-18
  Of baker and butcher blowing, as if to hear, [NH 475-2
  Oh! Sal, the butcher's wife ate clams [Lulu M 27-9 P
BUTT. See rifle-butt.
BUTTER. And father nature, full of butter [Lulu M 27-13 P
BUTTERFLIES. Already the butterflies flutter above the cabins.
  [Carolinas 4-4
  "Frogs Eat Butterflies. Snakes Eat Frogs. Hogs Eat Snakes. Men
    Eat Hogs" [78-title
BUTTERS. Fat with a thousand butters, and the crows [Burnshaw
  49-9 P

BUTTOCKS. O caliper, do you scratch your buttocks [Lilacs 48-19
BUTTONS. Of buttons, measure of his salt. Such trash [C 39-19
  For buttons, how many women have covered themselves [Dump 202-8
BUTTONWOODS. Under the buttonwoods, beneath a moon nailed fast.
    [Cata 425-5
BUTTRESSED. That was buttressed by blue slants [Public Sq 108-21
BUTTRESSES. The bony buttresses, the bony spires [Gray 140-5
  Pierce, too, with buttresses of coral air [Archi 18-5 P
BUXOM. That the buxom eye brings merely its element [Poem Morn
    219-14
BUZZ. Find a deep echo in a horn and buzz [NSF 390-17
BUZZARD. Crochet me this buzzard [Jack-Rabbit 50-10
  The entrails of the buzzard [Jack-Rabbit 50-16
BUZZARDS. Buzzards and live-moss, [Venereal 47-6
  Say, puerile, that the buzzards crouch on the ridge-pole [Two
    Figures 86-10
  There buzzards pile their sticks among the bones [Burnshaw 49-7P
  Of buzzards and eat the bellies of the rich, [Burnshaw 49-8 P
BUZZED. What were the hymns that buzzed beside my ears? [Hoon
    65-11
BUZZES. It buzzes beyond the horizon or in the ground: [NH 487-14
BUZZING. Like a buzzing of flies in autumn air, [MBG 166-20
  This buzzing of the blue guitar. [MBG 167-2
  The buzzing world and lisping firmament. [Descrip 345-8
BYZANTINE. Over wooden Boston, the sparkling Byzantine [Blue Bldg
    217-1
  Is almost Byzantine. [Abnormal 24-7 P
BYZANTINES. Came her attendant Byzantines. [Peter 91-13
  And then, the simpering Byzantines [Peter 91-20
BYZANTIUM. Cleansed clean of lousy Byzantium. [Memo 89-12 P

C. "The Comedian as the Letter C" [27-title
  The A B C of being, [Motive 288-16
  This is the final Projection, C. [Couch 295-21
c. A chorister whose c preceded the choir. [Not Ideas 534-14
CAB. "Exposition of the Contents of a Cab" [20-title P
  To ride in a cab. [Cab 20-17 P
CABALA. In the sky, as crown and diamond cabala? [AA 417-15
  Except for that crown and mystical cabala. [AA 417-21
CABALLERO. "The Pastor Caballero" [379-title
CABBAGES. The florist asking aid from cabbages, [C 37-16
CAB-HORSE. There's a cab-horse at the corner, [Phases 3-5 P
CABILDO. Inspecting the cabildo, the façade [C 32-15
  The white cabildo darkened, the façade, [C 32-19
CABIN. Because he built a cabin who once planned [C 41-19
  And so it came, his cabin shuffled up, [C 42-1
  Annealed them in their cabin rivalries! [C 42-21
  His cabin counted as phylactery, [C 43-23
  Gave to the cabin, lordlier than it was, [C 44-25
  That the man who erected this cabin, planted [Frogs 78-7
  You dweller in the dark cabin, [Watermelon 88-19
  You dweller in the dark cabin, [Watermelon 89-13
  Farewell to an idea . . . A cabin stands, [AA 412-4
  And shone. And a small cabin build there. [Page 421-16
  My cabin as the center of the ship and I [Bship 78-6 P
  As the center of the cabin, the center of [Bship 78-7 P
CABINET. Everything ticks like a clock. The cabinet [Nigger 157-17
  A skeleton out of its cabinet. Nor am I. [As Leave 116-14 P
CABINS. Already the butterflies flutter above the cabins.
  [Carolinas 4-14
CABLES. Supporting heavy cables, slung [MBG 181-22
CABOOSE. Just where it was, oh beau caboose . . . It was part
  [Liadoff 347-14
CACHINNATION. Its envious cachinnation. [Mozart 131-17
CACKLE. As the cackle of toucans [Men 1000 52-1
CADAVER. By the cadaver of these caverns, half-asleep. [Two V
  355-7
CADAVEROUS. Of moonlight on the thick, cadaverous bloom [C 31-28
  Its ruddy pallor had grown cadaverous. [Anglais 149-4
  To touch a woman cadaverous, [Arcades 225-23
  Cadaverous undulations. Rest, old mould . . . [Two V 355-14
  There entered a cadaverous person, [Attempt 370-8
  The cadaverous persons were dispelled. [Attempt 370-19
  In your cadaverous Eden, they desire [Duck 61-13 P
CADENCES. In which his voice would roll its cadences, [Blue Bldg
  216-19
  To his Virgilian cadences, up down, [NSF 407-8
CADENZA "Martial Cadenza" [237-title
CAFE. As the flag above the old café-- [Hibiscus 23-2
  Which one recalls at a concert or in a café. [Nigger 154-3
  One had come early to a crisp café. [Forces 229-18
  There were roses in the cool café. His book [EM 314-9
  A café. There may be a dish of country cheese [Paisant 335-15
  Or Paris in conversation at a café. [NH 486-3
CAFES. And dark Brazilians in their cafés, [C 38-24
  The diplomats of the cafés expound: [Greenest 57-28 P
  In the streets. There will always be cafés and cards [Greenest
  58-15 P
CAFTAN. Chieftain Iffucan of Azcan in caftan [Bantams 75-14
CAJOLED. Mile-mallows that a mallow sun cajoled. [Sea Surf 101-21
CAKE. No longer on the ancient cake of seed, [Cuisine 228-12
  What wheaten bread and oaten cake and kind, [Orb 440-18
CALAMITOUS. Jovial Crispin, in calamitous crape? [C 41-22
CALAMITY. Calamity, proclaimed himself, was proclaimed. [Horn
  230-16
  In the sense against calamity, it is not [AA 418-8
  But the beggar gazes on calamity [Bad Time 426-12
CALCINED. I, weeping in a calcined heart, [W Burgher 61-16
CALCULATED. In a calculated chaos: he that takes form [Repet 307-4
CALENDAR. That do not beat by pain, but calendar, [Phenom 286-5
  Being virile, it hears the calendar hymn. [NSF 382-9
  Cousins of the calendar if not of kin, [Recit 86-3 P
  Like the chromatic calendar of time to come. [Theatre 91-6 P
CALICO. Dressed in calico, [Motion 83-3
  The civil fiction, the calico idea, [Duck 65-12 P
CALIPER. O caliper, do you scratch your buttocks [Lilacs 48-19
CALL. Which, let the tall musicians call and call, [C 41-16
  Should merely call him dead? Pronounce amen [C 41-17
  Call the roller of big cigars, [Emperor 64-1
  The feelings crazily, craftily call, [MBG 166-19
  I stand in the moon, and call it good, [MBG 168-17
  Remote and call it merciful? [MBG 168-21
  A dream (to call it a dream) in which [MBG 174-15
  Thinking the thoughts I call my own, [MBG 180-8
  Climb through the night, because his cuckoos call. [Oboe 251-7
  An anti-pathos, until we call it [Hero 276-28
  Suppose we call it Projection A. [Couch 295-3
  Might call the common self, interior fons. [Choc 301-1
  Ourselves, in the clearest green--well, call it green. [Lot 371-7

I call you by name, my green, my fluent mundo. [NSF 407-2
Call it, once more, a river, an unnamed flowing, [R Conn 533-18
Of each of the senses; call it, again and again, [R Conn 533-20
Is constant. The time you call serene descends [Burnshaw 50-22 P
"What They Call Red Cherry Pie" [75-title 4 P
He says "That's what I call red cherry pie." [Grotesque 76-4 P
CALLED. The western day through what you called [Hoon 65-8
  As now and called most high, [MBG 176-7
  An invisible gesture. Let this be called [Couch 295-15
  Of birds called up by more than the sun, [Hermit 505-17
  He called hydrangeas purple. And they were. [Abnormal 23-16 P
  Of gobs, who called her orchidean, [Lulu G 26-10 P
  Called Mistress and Maid. [Three 133-23 P
CALLING. Calling for pomp. [Soldier 97-6
  Her days, her oceanic nights, calling [Farewell 117-17
  Falls down, the cock-birds calling at the time. [NSF 388-8
  These are the voices of the pastors calling [Luther 461-4
  These are the voices of the pastors calling [Luther 461-10
  These are the voices of the pastors calling [Luther 461-16
  And calling like the long echoes in long sleep, [Luther 461-17
  Calling them what you will but loosely-named [Burnshaw 47-21 P
CALLS. To watch the fire-feinting sea and calls it good,
  [EM 324-15
  He enters the room and calls. No one is there. [Bouquet 452-21
CALM. In an intenser calm, [Paltry 6-7
  As a calm darkens among water-lights. [Sunday 67-4
  Diffusing balm in that Pacific calm? [Sea Surf 99-8
  The sea-clouds whitened far below the calm [Sea Surf 99-10
  A calm November. Sunday in the fields. [Nigger 156-1
  And the soldier of time lies calm beneath that stroke. [EM
  319-18
  "The House Was Quiet and the World Was Calm" [358-title
  The house was quiet and the world was calm. [House Q 358-7
  The house was quiet and the world was calm. [House Q 358-10
  And the world was calm. The truth in a calm world, [House Q 359-1
  Is calm, itself is summer and night, itself [House Q 359-3
  That we must calm, the origin of a mother tongue [NH 470-24
  Too wide, too irised, to be more than calm, [Look 518-19
  You brought the incredible calm in ecstasy, [Red Kit 30-17 P
  Where is that calm and where that ecstasy? [Red Kit 31-2 P
  In lilies' stately-statued calm; [Room Gard 41-11 P
  To momentary calm, spectacular flocks [Burnshaw 51-2 P
CALMED. And hollow of him by its brilliance calmed, [Owl 434-5
CALMEST. In an ever-changing, calmest unity, [Owl 433-13
CALVIN. Things are as they seemed to Calvin or to Anne [Descrip
  341-21
CALYPSO. Gone, as in Calypso's isle or in Citare, [Bship 79-24 P
CAME. Came to be sleights of sails [Infanta 7-18
  Came striding. [Domination 8-15
  I saw how the night came, [Domination 9-17
  Came striding like the color of the heavy hemlocks [Domination
  9-18
  And you? Remember how the crickets came [Monocle 15-3
  That coolness for his heat came suddenly, [C 31-17
  Came like two spirits parleying, adorned [C 31-31
  But they came parleying of such an earth, [C 32-1
  Came bluntly thundering, more terrible [C 32-24
  The spring came there in clinking pannicles [C 34-9
  Of half-dissolving frost, the summer came, [C 34-10
  He came. The poetic hero without palms [C 35-26
  And as he came he saw that it was spring, [C 35-28
  Another, still more bellicose, came on. [C 37-22
  When its black branches came to bud, belle day, [C 39-3
  And so it came, his cabin shuffled up, [C 42-1
  The chits came for his jigging, bluet-eyed, [C 43-16
  Came reproduced in purple, family font, [C 45-16
  Then you came walking, [Vincentine 53-4
  Yes: you came walking, [Vincentine 53-8
  Yes: you came talking. [Vincentine 53-10
  Came then. [Vincentine 53-12
  When radiance came running down, slim through the bareness.
  [Banal 63-2
  Or heard or felt came not but from myself; [Hoon 65-17
  And whence they came and whither they shall go [Sunday 70-12
  If in a shimmering room the babies came, [Babies 77-10
  His broad-brimmed hat came close upon his eyes. [Babies 77-18
  Came her attendant Byzantines. [Peter 91-13
  Came, bowing and voluble, upon the deck, [Sea Surf 101-24
  The sovereign clouds came clustering. The conch [Sea Surf 102-10
  Came fresh transfigurings of freshest blue. [Sea Surf 102-15
  If from the earth we came, it was an earth [Anatomy 107-13
  To Monsieur Dufy's Hamburg whence they came. [Lions 125-7
  Birds that came like dirty water in waves [Loaf 200-3
  And still the birds came, came in watery flocks, [Loaf 200-14
  It was how the sun came shining into his room: [Freed 205-6
  It was how he was free. It was how his freedom came. [Freed
  205-15
  Came bursting from the clouds. So the wind [Sleight 222-7
  In their hands. The lilacs came long after. [Arcades 225-12
  But he came back as one comes back from the sun [Yellow 237-7

Again . . . as if it came back, as if life came back, [Martial 237-13

The people that turned off and came [Adequacy 243-13

The milkman came in the moonlight and the moonlight [Les Plus 244-17

We had always been partly one. It was as we came [Oboe 251-17

This was the place to which you came last night, [God 285-7

Men came as the sun comes, early children [Dutch 291-23

To this prodigious shadow, who then came [Choc 297-2

Of daylight came while he sat thinking. He said, [Choc 298-12

Now, time stands still. He came from out of sleep. [Choc 299-12

So that it came to him of its own, [Creat 310-11

Then came Brazil to nourish the emaciated [Pure 330-16

In the golden vacancy she came, and comes, [Descrip 339-13

The early constellations, from which came the first [Myrrh 350-7

From a Schuylkill in mid-earth there came emerging [New Set 352-10

Came paddling their canoes, a thousand thousand, [New Set 352-17

At last the good life came, good sleep, bright fruit, [Good Man 364-7

Beating in the heart, as if blood newly came, [NSF 382-21

The bees came booming as if they had never gone, [NSF 389-19

He thought often of the land from which he came, [NSF 393-16

When at long midnight the Canon came to sleep [NSF 402-19

The rendezvous, when she came alone, [AA 419-16

New stars that were a foot across came out [Page 421-15

There came a day, there was a day--one day [Owl 432-19

They came. But, brown, the ice-bear sleeping in ice-month [Study II 464-8

As if the crude collops came together as one, [NH 466-1

At another time, the radial aspect came [NH 479-2

When the mariners came to the land of the lemon trees, [NH 487-1

Is still warm with the love with which she came, [Aug 496-1

That the green leaves came and covered the high rock, [Rock 526-4

That the lilacs came and bloomed, like a blindness cleaned, [Rock 526-5

And so hydrangeas came to be. [Abnormal 24-3 P

Then the coroner came [Coroner 29-14 P

Came not from you. Shall the world be spent again, [Red Kit 30-20 P

Deploring sentiment. When May came last [Good Bad 33-14 P

It lost the common shape of night and came [Old Woman 45-16 P

Yet were not bright, came shining as things come [Burnshaw 51-25 P

That enter day from night, came mirror-dark, [Burnshaw 51 26 P

From which they came, make real the attitudes [Burnshaw 52-3 P

The foul immovables, came through the clouds, [Greenest 53-12 P

And beheld the source from which transparence came; [Greenest 54-7 P

Its surfaces came from distant fire; and it [Greenest 57-2 P

And drenching crimsons, or endure? It came [Greenest 57-23 P

Day came upon the spirit as life comes [Duck 61-5 P

The way it came, let be what it may become. [Sombre 71-16 P

He came to this by knowledge or [Ulysses 102-19

The picnic of children came running then, [Dinner 109-25 P

Came tinkling on the grass to the table [Dinner 110-3 P

Of feeling, the things that came of their own accord, [Local 112-8 P

These came through poverty [Three 132-8 P

We came for isolation, [Three 138-15 P

Came clapping behind them [Three 139-4

He came crying, [Three 139-6

CAMELLIA-CHATEAUX. To the camellia-chateaux and an inch beyond, [Duck 60-14 P

CAMERA. In what camera do you taste [Bagatelles 213-5

Not the space in camera of the man below, [Sombre 70-31 P

CAMP. We live in a camp . . . Stanzas of final peace [Extracts 258-22

CAMPAGNA. Enough. Ah! douce campagna of that thing! [Beard 247-19

Ah! douce campagna, honey in the heart, [Beard 247-20

CAMPHOR. He has left his robes folded in camphor [Gray 140-2

It is full of the myrrh and camphor of summer [Aug 490-4

CAMPS. And above the German camps? It looked apart. [Martial 238-5

CAMUS. In a black glove, holds a novel by Camus. She begged [Novel 457-11

CAN. Of every day, the wrapper on the can of pears, [Dump 201-17

Smacks like fresh water in a can, like the sea [Dump 202-6

One sits and beats an old tin can, lard pail. [Dump 202-26

On a fuchsia in a can--and iridescences [NH 478-14

A trash can at the end of the world, the dead [Burnshaw 49-5 P

CANARIES. Canaries in the morning, orchestras [Havana 142-17

CANCELLINGS. Farewell to an idea . . . The cancellings, [AA 414-4

CANDID. That gives a candid kind to everything. [NSF 382-24

CANDIDE. He once thought necessary. Like Candide, [C 42-16

CANDLE. "Valley Candle" [51-title

My candle burned alone in an immense valley. [Valley Candle 51-1

Furtively, by candle and out of need. [Nigger 153-4

A candle is enough to light the world. [MBG 172-16

"The Candle a Saint" [223-title

The hand between the candle and the wall [Rhythms 245-9

On flames. The scholar of one candle sees [AA 417-1

Underground, a king as candle by our beds [Owl 435-2

The candle as it evades the sight, these are [Rome 508-22

A light on the candle tearing against the wick [Rome 509-5

The book and candle in your ambered room, [Rome 510-25

But his actual candle blazed with artifice. [Quiet 523-15

How high that highest candle lights the dark. [Final 524-15

Arabesques of candle beams, [Phases 4-4 P

Become rude robes among white candle lights, [Greenest 53-4 P

It might be the candle of another being, [Theatre 91-7 P

It would have been like lighting a candle, [Letters 107-10 P

This candle is the sun; [Three 130-8 P

When the candle, sputtering up, [Three 131-9 P

The light of the most tranquil candle [Three 132-13 P

Holding this candle to us, [Three 132-22 P

The candle would tremble in his hands; [Three 132-26 P

Held the candle. [Three 133-7 P

Let the candle shine for the beauty of shining. [Three 133-10 P

By the hermit and his candle [Three 137-11 P

The hermit's candle would have thrown [Three 138-3 P

In the meantime, the candle shines, [Three 138-22 P

Needs no candle [Three 140-2 P

One candle replaces [Three 141-4 P

The candle of the sun, [Three 142-4 P

CANDLES. In the strokes of thunder, dead candles at the window [NH 488-11

CANDOR. From that ever-early candor to its late plural [NSF 382-18

And the candor of them is the strong exhilaration [NSF 382-19

The poem, through candor, brings back a power again [NSF 382-23

CANE. See sugar-cane.

CANNA. "Anecdote of Canna" [55-title

Huge are the canna in the dreams of [Canna 55-1

Observes the canna with a clinging eye, [Canna 55-8

CANOES. Came paddling their canoes, a thousand thousand, [New Set 352-17

CANON. In description, canon central in itself, [Descrip 345-3

When at long midnight the Canon came to sleep [NSF 402-19

CANON ASPIRIN. Chutney. Then the Canon Aspirin declaimed [NSF 401-23

The Canon Aspirin, having said these things, [NSF 402-13

CANONS. Himself. The author of man's canons is man, [Conversat 109-14 P

CANOPIES. And island canopies which were entailed [Havana 142-17

CANTANKEROUS. Oozing cantankerous gum [Bananas 54-20

CANTICLE. In the first canto of the final canticle, [Hand 271-1

In the first canto of the final canticle, [Hand 271-8

In the first canto of the final canticle. [Hand 271-16

CANTILENE. Bubbling felicity in cantilene, [C 43-10

And cantilene? [Archi 17-1 P

CANTINA. Close the cantina. Hood the chandelier. [Havana 144-23

CANTING. The canting curlicues [Ord Women 11-12

CANTO. I sang a canto in a canton, [Country 207-1

In the first canto of the final canticle, [Hand 271-1

In the first canto of the final canticle, [Hand 271-8

In the first canto of the final canticle. [Hand 271-16

CANTON. I sang a canto in a canton, [Country 207-1

In a canton of Belshazzar [Country 207-3

Ontario, Canton. It was the way [Greenest 53-10 P

CANZONES. Far, far beyond the putative canzones [Extracts 256-7

CANZONI. The choir that choirs the first fatigue in deep bell of canzoni? [Inelegance 25-20 P

CAP. Of China, cap of Spain, imperative haw [C 28-9

Without cap or strap, you are the cynic still. [NE Verses 106-4

Once more the longest resonance, to cap [Havana 143-16

Descending, out of the cap of midnight, [Countryman 428-10

He broods of neither cap nor cape, [Countryman 428-17

A visible clear cap, a visible wreath [Greenest 57-7 P

See cloud-cap.

CAPABLE. Crispin as hermit, pure and capable, [C 40-4

What figure of capable imagination? [Uruguay 249-17

Rushing from what was real; and capable? [Uruguay 249-24

The villages slept as the capable man went down, [Uruguay 249-25

And, capable, created in his mind, [Uruguay 250-3

We have and are the man, capable [Hero 279-2

Mature: a capable being may replace [Pure 330-11

By a feeling capable of nothing more. [Cred 374-5

And capable of incapably evil thought? [Page 423-1

It is the question of what he is capable. [Questions 462-13

With which to speak to her, the capable [NH 471-1

CAPACIOUS. In the door-yard by his own capacious bloom. [C 44-5

CAPARISON. It was caparison of wind and cloud [C 30-13

Caparison elephants, teach bears to juggle. [NSF 385-3

CAPE. Toward the cape at which [Countryman 428-11

He broods of neither cap nor cape, [Countryman 428-17

CAPES. Away from them, capes, along the afternoon Sound, [NH 484-7

CAPITAL. "Nudity at the Capital" [145-title

For the imagination. A capital [EM 319-20

And you, you say that the capital things of the mind [Conversat 109-3 P

Without the furious roar in his capital. [Someone 85-6 A

CAPITAN. Capitan profundo, capitan geloso, [Orangeade 102-16
  Makes of the form Most Merciful Capitan, [Pastor 379-6
CAPITOL. They fill the terrace of his capitol. [Canna 55-3
  Or massive portico. A capitol, [AA 416-19
CAPITOLS. Next he builds capitols and in their corridors, [NSF
  403-18
CAPON. To be followed by a platter of capon! [Winter B 141-14
CAPPED. Capped summer-seeming on the tense machine [Sea Surf 99-21
CAPRICE. And, being full of the caprice, inscribed [C 37-15
  It must change from destiny to slight caprice. [AA 417-23
CAPRICIOUS. Of long, capricious fugues and chorals. [Jasmine 79-12
CAPRICORN. In Capricorn. The statue has a form [Greenest 58-17 P
  Of Capricorn or as the sign demands, [Someone 86-18 A
CAPTAIN. The outer captain, the inner saint, [Thought 185-26
  Captain, the man of skill, the expert [Hero 27-1
  The captain squalid on his pillow, the great [Choc 300-1
  This is their captain and philosopher, [Choc 301-16
  "Repetitions of a Young Captain" [306-title
  All men endure. The great captain is the choice [Paisant 334-14
  The body, it touches. The captain and his men [NSF 392-21
  Between a great captain and the maiden Bawda. [NSF 401-6
  The great captain loved the ever-hill Catawba [NSF 401-16
  And Bawda loved the captain as she loved the sun. [NSF 401-18
  The captain said, [Bship 77-15 P
  Of which I am the captain. Given what I intend, [Bship 78-4 P
  So posed, the captain drafted rules of the world, [Bship 78-20 P
  Of this the captain said, [Bship 78-25 P
  The captain said, [Bship 79-19 P
  Captain, high captain, how is it, now, [Bship 80-18 P
  A hand that fails to seize it. High captain, the grand [Bship
  80-25 P
CAPTAINS. Crude captains, the naked majesty, if you like, [Rome
  510-9
CAPTIOUS. It is not a question of captious repartee. [Bad Time
  426-19
  In our captious hymns, erect and sinuous, [John 437-20
  The scholar, captious, told him what he could [Someone 85-10 A
CAPTIVE. They have heads in which a captive cry [Possum 294-2
  Once to make captive, once to subjugate [Cred 376-12
CAPTIVES. Captives the being, widens--and was there. [Orb 440-16
CAPTIVITY. What milk there is in such captivity, [Orb 440-17
CAPTURE. The meaning of the capture, this hard prize, [Cred 376-14
CAPTURED. This time, like damsels captured by the sky, [Burnshaw
  51-17 P
CAPUCHIN. A few years more and the vermeil capuchin [C 44-24
CAPUCHINS. She seemed, of a country of the capuchins, [C 44-12
CAR. A pagan in a varnished car. [MBG 170-12
  A car drives up. A soldier, an officer, [Bouquet 452-19
  The first car out of a tunnel en voyage [Armor 530-2
CARACAS. Cock-robin's at Caracas. [Metamorph 265-18
CARACOLES. He carolled in caracoles [Jack-Rabbit 50-6
CARAMEL. Caramel and would not, could not float. And yet [Duck
  63-24 P
CARCASS. See water-carcass.
CARDINAL. Cardinal, saying the prayers of earliest day; [Choc
  300-2
CARDS. Playing cards. In a village of the indigenes, [Glass 198-3
  A pack of cards is falling toward the floor. [Bouquet 450-22
  In the streets. There will always be cafés and cards [Greenest
  58-15 P
  In the oblivion of cards [Sol Oaks 111-3 P
  Neither the cards nor the trees nor the air [Sol Oaks 111-5 P
CARE. For who can care at the wigs despoiling the Satan ear?
  [Banal 63-4
  Who does not care. [Shifts 84-3
  So little, too little to care, to turn [Adieu 128-1
  Nor kin to care. [Woman Song 360-6
  Themselves with care, sought out the nerveless frame [NSF 391-16
  And didn't care a fig, [Drum-Majors 36-18 P
  I care for neither fugues nor feathers. [Lytton 38-7 P
  Knows, knowing that he does not care, and knows, [Greenest 59-9P
  Knowing and meaning that he cannot care. [Greenest 59-10 P
CAREFULEST. Her dress, the carefulest, commodious weave [Beginning
  428-4
CAREFULLY. Belittles those carefully chosen daubs. [Grapes 110-16
CARES. Do you suppose that she cares a tick, [Lilacs 49-1
CARESSED. Kicked through the roof, caressed by the river-side.
  [Bship 80-6 P
CARESSES. The tongue caresses these exacerbations. [EM 323-1
CARIB. Plucked from the Carib trees, [Bananas 54-18
CARIBBEAN. Of the Caribbean amphitheatre, [C 30-17
CARICATURE. And its tawny caricature and tawny life, [What We 460-4
  If you caricature the way they rise, yet they rise. [Duck 60-18 P
CARICATURES. Of golden quirks and Paphian caricatures, [Swans 4-6
CARING. Forgetting work, not caring for angels, hunting a lift,
  [Duck 60-15 P
CARKED. Beyond carked Yucatan, he might have come [C 40-10
CARLOTTA. Are full of the songs of Jamanda and Carlotta; [Norfolk
  111-17
CARNATIONS. Pink and white carnations. The light [Poems Clim 193-8

  Pink and white carnations--one desires [Poems Clim 193-12
  With nothing more than the carnations there. [Poems Clim 193-16
CAROLINA. And then to Carolina. Simple jaunt. [C 29-10
  Approaching Carolina [C 33-title 3
  Between a Carolina of old time, [C 35-22
CAROLINAS. "In the Carolinas" [4-title
  The lilacs wither in the Carolinas. [Carolinas 4-13
CAROLLED. He carolled in caracoles [Jack-Rabbit 50-6
CAROLLER. "Look out, O caroller, [Jack-Rabbit 50-15
CAROLS. Like the night before Christmas and all the carols.
  [Thought 185-3
CAROUSE. Abashed him by carouse to humble yet [C 40-24
  And bade the sheep carouse. Or so they said. [NSF 400-22
CARPENTER. The life and death of this carpenter depend [NH 478-13
  Or thinks he does, a carpenter's iridescences, [NH 478-18
CARPET. In the street, in a room, on a carpet or a wall, [NH 467-12
CARRIAGE. A hundred yards from a carriage. [Theory 86-19
CARRIED. Sacked up and carried overseas, daubed out [C 45-13
  With nothing else compounded, carried full, [Cred 374-11
  A boat carried forward by waves resembling the bright backs of
  rowers, [Prol 515-6
CARRIERS. And his finical carriers tread, [Cortege 79-14
  The tread of the carriers does not halt [Cortege 80-7
  The spirit's natural images, carriers, [Greenest 57-12 P
CARRIES. Identity. The thing he carries resists [Man Car 350-16
CARROUSEL. The clank of the carrousel and, under the trees, [Duck
  62-25 P
CARRY. They carry the wizened one [Cortege 80-1
  Me round, carry me, misty deck, carry me [Farewell 118-19
  It is because they carry down the stairs [Mozart 131-20
  They could not carry much, as soldiers. [Gigan 289-1
CARRYING. "The Virgin Carrying a Lantern" [71-title
  "Man Carrying Thing" [350-title
  Carrying such shapes, of such alleviation, [New Set 353-1
CART. And the wheel that broke as the cart went by. [Silent 359-17
  It is Marianna's Swedish cart. [Prejudice 368-12
  Aquiline pedants treat the cart, [Prejudice 368-15
  The Swedish cart to be part of the heart. [Prejudice 369-6
CARTWHEEL. The broken cartwheel on the hill. [Silent 359-7
CARVE. Can carve [Six Sig 75-1
  What one star can carve, [Sig Sig 75-2
  How carve the violet moon [Archi 17-25 P
CARVED. That will replace it shall be carved, "The Mass [Burnshaw
  48-5 P
  In this he carved himself, he carved his age, [Duck 64-21 P
  He carved the feathery walkers standing by, [Duck 64-22 P
  So that a carved king found in a jungle, huge [Conversat 109-5 P
CARVING. You sit with your head like a carving in space [Rabbit K
  210-2
  The necklace is a carving not a kiss. [AA 413-15
CARVINGS. Clumped carvings, circular, like blunted fans, [Old
  Woman 43-16 P
  Long after the worms and the curious carvings of [Burnshaw 47-12P
CASE. But I am, in any case, [Sailing 120-8
  And in any case never grim, the human grim [NH 475-17
CASINO. Life is an old casino in a park. [Havana 142-18
  To that casino. Long before the rain [Havana 142-18
  Life is an old casino in a wood. [Havana 144-11
  And the old casino likewise may define [Havana 145-7
CASQUE. In casque and scaffold orator, fortified [Stan Hero 84-21P
CASSIA. The tomtit and the cassia and the rose, [C 42-27
CASSIMERE. Effete green, the woman in black cassimere. [NH 482-2
CAST. Cast corners in the glass. He could describe [EM 314-1
  Still promises perfections cast away. [EM 318-25
  Of the past is description without place, a cast [Descrip 345-20
  But if they do, they cast it widely round. [Bouquet 451-24
  They cast deeply round a crystal crystal-white [Bouquet 452-1
  They cast closely round the facture of the thing [Bouquet 452-6
  Why was it that you cast the brass away [Good Bad 33-20 P
  Is cast in pandemonium, flittered, howled [Duck 62-7 P
CAST-IRON. Have gorging the cast-iron of our lives with good [Orb
  440-3
  And the cast-iron of our works. But it is, dear sirs, [Orb 440-4
CASTLE-FORTRESS-HOME. Can we compose a castle-fortress-home, [NSF
  386-22
CAST-OFF. The dress is lying, cast-off, on the floor. [Beginning
  428-6
CASTRATOS. Castratos of moon-mash--Life consists [Men Made 355-17
CASTS. Across the unscrawled fores the future casts [NSF 383-4
CASUAL. In the casual evocations of your tread [On Manner 56-2
  At evening, casual flocks of pigeons make [Sunday 70-26
  They nourish Jupiters. Their casual pap [Havana 144-7
  So far beyond the casual solitudes, [Re-state 146-9
  The casual reunions, the long-pondered [Extracts 258-5
  Casual poet, that to add your own disorder to disaster [Bed
  326-15
  To believe, more than the casual hero, more [Paisant 335-9
  Not fustian. The more than casual blue [Cred 375-5
  That catches our own. The casual is not [NSF 397-23
  The town, the weather, in a casual litter, [NH 474-8

These casual exfoliations are [Someone 86-16 A
See cloud-casual.
CAT. The cat in the paper-bag, the corset, the box [Dump 201-18
  There was the cat slopping its milk all day, [Rabbit K 209-4
  Fat cat, red tongue, green mind, white milk [Rabbit K 209-5
  Without that monument of cat, [Rabbit K 209-8
  The cat forgotten in the moon; [Rabbit K 209-9
  The red cat hides away in the fur-light [Rabbit K 209-20
  And the little green cat is a bug in the grass. [Rabbit K 210-3
  She strides above the rabbit and the cat, [Candle 223-3
  The topaz rabbit and the emerald cat, [Candle 223-10
  I affirm and then at midnight the great cat [Montra 264-5
  Of a cat, twelve dollars for the devil, [Hero 275-9
  Cat's milk is dry in the saucer. Sunday song [Phenom 286-3
  The gardener's cat is dead, the gardener gone [Cred 377-9
  It is a cat of a sleek transparency [NH 473-1
  The great cat must stand potent in the sun. [NH 473-3
  And Adirondack glittering. The cat hawks it [Aug 490-5
  La-la! The cat is in the violets [Mandolin 28-13 P
  The cat should not be where she is [Mandolin 28-15 P
  Cat's taste possible or possibly Danish lore, [Someone 87-5 A
CATAFALQUES. Rest immobile, though neighboring catafalques [NSF
  391-8
CATALEPSY. A bench was his catalepsy, Theatre [NSF 397-10
CATALOGUE. The catalogue is too commodious. [Cats 367-20
CATARACT. Slid over the western cataract, yet one, [Beard 247-13
CATARACTS. By such long-rolling opulent cataracts [Geneva 24-5
  Is an absolute. Item: The cataracts [Montra 263-21
  "This Solitude of Cataracts" [424-title
  Before one comes to the first black cataracts [R Conn 533-5
CATARRHAL. But a ghost for Andrew, not lean, catarrhal [Lack
  303-10
CATARRHS. From dry catarrhs, and to guitars [Ord Women 10-14
  From dry guitars, and to catarrhs [Ord Women 12-4
CATA-SISTERS. A fantastic irruption. Salute you, cata-sisters,
  [Souls 95-2 P
CATASTROPHE. Encroachment of that old catastrophe, [Sunday 67-3
  That evil made magic, as in catastrophe, [Extracts 253-8
  The maker of catastrophe invents the eye [Extracts 253-12
  Made sure of the most correct catastrophe. [EM 314-10
  So epical a twist, catastrophe [Duck 65-25 P
CATASTROPHIC. In the catastrophic room . . . beyond despair,
  [Men Fall 187-18
CATAWBA. There was a mystic marriage in Catawba, [NSF 401-4
  The great captain loved the ever-hill Catawba [NSF 401-16
CATBIRD. The catbird's gobble in the morning half-awake-- [Holiday
  313-6
CATCH. On the image of what we see, to catch from that [NSF 398-21
  One thinks, when the houses of New England catch the first sun,
  [Discov 95-21 P
CATCHES. Catches tigers [Ten O'C 66-14
  That catches our own. The casual is not [NSF 397-23
  And catches from nowhere brightly-burning breath. [Novel 458-5
CATCHING. Catching at Good-bye, harvest moon, [MBG 173-5
  Catching the lesser dithyrambs. [Thought 184-9
  Were mere brown clods, mere catching weeds of talk. [NH 486-21
CATECHIZE. For Crispin and his quill to catechize. [C 31-33
CATECHUMEN. Young catechumen answering the worms? [Sombre 69-24 P
CATEGORICAL. But on the banjo's categorical gut, [C 38-19
  The stone, the categorical effigy; [Choc 300-3
  The categorical predicate, the arc, [Descrip 344-8
CATEGORIES. He disposes the world in categories, thus: [EM 323-5
  Of the categories. So said, this placid space [Ulti 429-17
  Categories of bleak necessity, [Ulysses 104-26 P
CATERPILLAR. By one caterpillar is great Africa devoured [Puel
  456-2
CAT-EYED. Were the fluid, the cat-eyed atmosphere, in which [Sombre
  68-13 P
CATHEDRAL. Of the cathedral, making notes, he heard [C 32-16
  He knelt in the cathedral with the rest, [C 32-29
  In the cathedral, I sat there, and read, [MBG 180-19
  What is beyond the cathedral, outside, [MBG 181-3
  See the river, the railroad, the cathedral . . . [Hartford 227-6
CATHEDRAL-SHANTY. In the cathedral-shanty. [Grotesque 77-8 P
CATHOLIC. The catholic sun, its majesty, [An Gaiety 32-16 P
  Of evil, evil springs; or catholic hope, [Sombre 69-23 P
CATS. Sombre as fir-trees, liquid cats [MBG 178-15
  The cats had cats and the grass turned gray [MBG 178-16
  Kiss, cats: for the deer and the dachshund [Jersey 210-13
  The lean cats of the arches of the churches, [Extracts 254-1
  The lean cats of the arches of the churches [Extracts 254-18
  "Mountains Covered with Cats" [367-title
  And the hawk cats it and we say spread sail, [Aug 490-6
CATTLE. The cattle skulls in the woods? [Circulat 150-2
CAUGHT. Is a weed and all the flies are caught, [MBG 171-6
  Among men, in a woman--she caught his breath-- [Yellow 237-6
  He caught the flags and the picket-lines [News 264-11
  There were looks that caught him out of empty air. [NH 483-13
  The mannerism of nature caught in a glass [Look 519-10
  Wood-smoke rises through trees, is caught in an upper flow

[Slug 522-3
CAUSE. The magnificent cause of being, [Weep Woman 25-7
  An indecipherable cause. [Thirteen 93-18
  To be an intellectual structure. The cause [EM 324-30
  Are inconstant objects of inconstant cause [NSF 389-23
  Between us and the object, external cause, [John 437-15
  For this blank cold, this sadness without cause, [Plain 502-14
  Of which he is the cause, have never changed [Sombre 66-13 P
CAUSED. Made constant cry, caused constantly a cry, [Key W 128-15
  He, only, caused the statue to be made [Greenest 60-1 P
CAUSES. She causes boys to pile new plums and pears [Sunday 69-10
  To stuff the ear? It causes him to make [Havana 144-14
CAVE. Another image at the end of the cave, [AA 411-5
  In his cave, remains dismissed without a dream, [Study II 464-9
CAVERN. Flying like insects of fire in a cavern of night, [Horn
  230-18
  Of what do you lie thinking in your cavern? [Extracts 256-19
  In its cavern, wings subtler than any mercy, [Hero 273-13
CAVERNOUS. A cavernous and a cruel past, tropic [Greenest 58-21 P
  The statue belongs to the cavernous past, belongs [Greenest
  58-28 P
CAVERNS. By the cadaver of these caverns, half-asleep. [Two V
  355-7
  And crisply musical, or holy caverns temple-toned, [Burnshaw
  47-16 P
CAVES. See tree-caves.
CEASE. Never cease to deploy the structure. [Archi 16-16 P
CEASED. This pundit of the weather, who never ceased [Nigger 156-5
  As if the paradise of meaning ceased [EM 320-28
  In the way what was has ceased to be what is. [Owl 435-12
  A broken wall--and it ceased to exist, became [Greenest 53-7 P
CEASELESSLY. Across the spick torrent, ceaselessly, [Paltry 6-9
CEASES. His will, yet never ceases, perfect cock, [Bird Claws 82-17
CEDAR-LIMBS. In the cedar-limbs. [Thirteen 95-5
CEDARS. It is the same jingle of the red-bird breasting the orange-
  trees out of the cedars. [Indian 112-6
CEILING. Looking at the ceiling. [Six Sig 75-7
  Or in the ceiling, in sounds not chosen, [Creat 310-13
  In the ceiling of the distant room, in which he lies, [Sick
  90-17 P
CEINTURE. The dark-blown ceinture loosened, not relinquished.
  [NSF 385-11
CEINTURES. And beaded ceintures. [Ten O'C 66-9
CELEBRANTS. Of his first central hymns, the celebrants [C 37-12
CELEBRATE. Their curious fates in war, come, celebrate [Monocle
  16-15
  With these they celebrate the central poem, [Orb 441-9
CELEBRATING. Celebrating the marriage [Motion 83-8
CELEBRATION. And celebration. Shrewd novitiates [C 39-7
  Celebration of a maiden's choral. [Peter 92-7
  Which choir makes the most faultless medley in its celebration?
  [Inelegance 25-19 P
  Shall be the celebration in the words [Ideal 89-5 A
CELEBRATIONS. The ghostly celebrations of the picnic, [Aug 492-14
CELESTE. If awnings were celeste and gay, [Mandolin 28-18 P
CELESTIAL. Celestial sneering boisterously. Crispin [C 29-22
  "Meditation Celestial & Terrestrial" [123-title
  The poem of long celestial death; [Botanist 2 136-6
  The rhythm of this celestial pantomine." [Landsc 243-8
  It becomes the scholar again, seeking celestial [God 285-11
  Indulgence out of all celestial sight. [EM 318-17
  It is the celestial ennui of apartments [NSF 381-16
  The desire for its celestial ease in the heart, [NH 467-6
  With lanterns, like a celestial ancientness. [NH 476-21
  The clear. A celestial mode is paramount, [NH 480-24
  Fire is the symbol: the celestial possible. [Rome 509-8
  Arpeggi of celestial souvenirs, [Spaniard 35-16 P
  Come, all celestial paramours, [Burnshaw 47-14 P
CELESTIN. To say what Celestin should say for himself? [Papini
  446-2
  Is Celestin dislodged? The way through the world [Papini 446-5
  Celestin, the generous, the civilized, [Papini 447-7
CELL. Salt-flicker, amen to our accustomed cell, [Montra 260-20
  The moonlight in the cell, words on the wall. [Montra 260-21
  Sings of an heroic world beyond the cell, [Montra 261-9
  No, not believing, but to make the cell [Montra 261-10
CELLS. With squalid cells, unless New York is Cocos [Duck 63-13 P
CEMETERY. Mow the grass in the cemetery, darkies, [Norfolk 111-4
  "Like Decorations in a Nigger Cemetery" [150-title
CENTAVOS. Two coins were lying--dos centavos. [Attempt 370-21
CENTER. The heraldic center of the world [MBG 172-6
  "The Hermitage at the Center" [505-title
  At the center of the mass, the haunches low, [Old Woman 43-13 P
  The ship would become the center of the world. [Bship 78-5 P
  My cabin as the center of the ship and I [Bship 78-6 P
  As the center of the cabin, the center of [Bship 78-7 P
  Merely the center of a circle, spread [Bship 81-10 P
  The center of the self, the self [Ulysses 101-8 P
  The center that he sought was a state of mind, [Art Pop 112-13 P
  The angel at the center of this rind, [Someone 83-6 A

At last, the center of resemblance, found [Ideal 89-8 A
Stand at the center of ideal time, [Ideal 89-11 A
CENTI-COLORED. It is centi-colored and mille-flored and ripe,
   [Bouquet 450-2
CENTRAL. Of his first central hymns, the celebrants [C 37-12
   To the central composition, [Botanist 1 135-4
   The central flaw in the solar morn. [Thought 187-8
   Our faces circling round a central face [Dames 206-12
   Of central things, [Adequacy 243-16
   Became--how the central, essential red [Vase 246-21
   The central man, the human globe, responsive [Oboe 250-20
   How was it then with the central man? Did we [Oboe 251-10
   If we found the central evil, the central good. [Oboe 251-12
   Panjandrum and central heart and mind of minds-- [Extracts
      254-12
   Iciest core, a north star, central [Hero 275-24
   Are the meditations of a central mind. [Choc 298-17
   Central responses to a central fear, [Repet 308-1
   Of central sense, these minutiae mean more [EM 317-20
   Was central in distances the wild ducks could [Wild 329-6
   In description, canon central in itself, [Descrip 345-3
   Of sapphires flashing from the central sky, [Cred 375-24
   For a moment in the central of our being, [NSF 380-10
   And night, colored from distances, central [Owl 433-11
   With these they celebrate the central poem, [Orb 441-9
   As if the central poem became the world, [Orb 441-10
   And the world the central poem, each one the mate [Orb 441-20
   The central poem is the poem of the whole, [Orb 442-1
   The recognizable, medium, central whole-- [Bouquet 450-12
   And one from central earth to central sky [NH 469-1
   The brilliancy at the central of the earth. [NH 473-15
   As at a point of central arrival, an instant moment, much or
      little, [Prol 516-8
   Out of this same light, out of the central mind, [Final 521-16
   Disposed upon the central of what we see, [Greenest 55-7 P
   The central of the composition, in which [Duck 64-12 P
   In a clamor thudding up from central earth. [Sombre 70-30 P
   Who, when they think and speak of the central man, [Woman Had
      82-11 P
   Of the humming of the central man, the whole sound [Woman Had
      82-12 P
   Of the sea, the central humming of the sea, [Woman Had 82-13 P
   At the exactest central of the earth [Ulysses 104-14 P
   That in that ever-dark central, wherever it is, [Conversat
      108-18 P
   In the central of earth or sky or air or thought, [Conversat
      108-19 P
CENTRE. Will go, like the centre of sea-green pomp, [Paltry 6-6
   Farewell in the eyes and farewell at the centre, [Adieu 127-11
   Here in the centre stands the glass. Light [Glass 197-13
   About what stands here in the centre, not the glass, [Glass
      197-21
   But in the centre of our lives, this time, this day, [Glass
      198-1
   At the centre of reality, seeing it. [Freed 205-21
   A light at the centre of many lights, [Bottle 239-3
   A man at the centre of men. [Bottle 239-4
   At the neutral centre, the ominous element, [Landsc 242-1
   Would come from that return to the subtle centre. [Extracts
      258-21
   Item: Breathe, breathe upon the centre of [Montra 264-1
   Even now, the centre of something else, [Oak 272-10
   What any fury to its noble centre. [Hero 274-18
   The organic centre of responses, [Hero 279-27
   March toward a generation's centre. [Dutch 293-10
   That grips the centre, the actual bite, that life [Choc 298-22
   At the centre of a diamond. At dawn, [EM 322-10
   However known, at the centre of the heart? [EM 323-25
   A beating and a beating in the centre of [Two V 354-11
   The centre of transformations that [Human 363-13
   In the punctual centre of all circles white [Anach 366-8
   In the centre of its cones, the resplendent flights [Cats 367-17
   And say this, this is the centre that I seek. [Cred 373-9
   There was a muddy centre before we breathed. [NSF 383-19
   And in your centre mark them and are cowed . . . [NSF 384-24
   Forgets the gold centre, the golden destiny, [NSF 404-18
   Breathing his bronzen breath at the azury centre of time. [Cata
      425-12
   The essential poem at the centre of things, [Orb 440-1
   At the centre on the horizon, concentrum, grave [Orb 443-13
   And final. This is the centre. The poet is [Papini 448-1
   As if the centre of images had its [Study II 464-10
   It fails. The strength at the centre is serious. [NH 477-12
   At the centre, the object of the will, this place, [NH 480-20
   At the centre of the unintelligible, [Aug 495-14
CENTURIES. The voice of centuries [Winter B 141-7
   The centuries of excellence to be [Havana 143-1
   His strutting studied through centuries. [MBG 181-19
   Brooding on centuries like shells. [Oak 272-12
   Through centuries he lived in poverty. [Good Man 364-1

The early centuries were full [Agenda 42-7 P
   And fill the earth with young men centuries old [Ideal 88-11 A
CENTURIONS. Meantime, centurions guffaw and beat [Monocle 15-22
CENTURY. That century of wind in a single puff. [C 28-4
   A century in which everything was part [NH 479-4
   Of that century and of its aspect, a personage, [NH 479-5
   For a moment, once each century or two. [Duck 65-20 P
   Once each century or two. But then so great, [Duck 65-24 P
   An eighteenth century fern or two [Stan MBG 72-7 P
   See eighteenth-century.
CEREMONIAL. This was their ceremonial hymn: Anon [NSF 401-7
CERISE. Cerise sopranos, [Primordia 7-11 P
CERTAIN. It stand gigantic, with a certain tip [Monocle 17-4
   Yet is certain as meaning . . . [Magnifico 19-15
   With certain blue crystallizations [Six Sig 74-20
   Certain of its uncertainty, in which [Anglais 148-16
   After long strumming on certain nights [MBG 174-19
   Of time and place, becoming certain, [Hero 279-26
   "Certain Phenomena of Sound" [Phenom 286-title
   Of the certain solid, the primary free from doubt, [Man Car
      351-2
   This is the last day of a certain year [Cred 372-11
   Things certain sustaining us in certainty. [Cred 375-20
   In the uncertain light of single, certain truth, [NSF 380-7
   A definition growing certain and [NSF 386-6
   And others, make certain how being [Degen 444-8
   It is certain that the river [Degen 444-12
   A view of New Haven, say, through the certain eye, [NH 471-18
   A knowing that something certain had been proposed, [NH 483-4
   He would be certain to see [Aug 493-16
   Come back to see a certain house. [Vacancy 511-11
   Certain and ever more fresh. Ah! Certain, for sure . . .
      [Moonlight 532-6
   To hear the stroke of one's certain solitude, [Old Woman 44-15 P
   He seeks an image certain as meaning is [Someone 84-12 A
CERTAINLY. As certainly as night is the color [Prelude 194-15
CERTAINTY. Things certain sustaining us in certainty. [Cred 375-20
   A wait within that certainty, a rest [NSF 386-7
   The fluctuations of certainty, the change [NSF 395-14
   Uncertain certainty, Apollo [Ulysses 101-5 P
CERTITUDE. And by a hand of certitude to cut [Greenest 56-17 P
CERTITUDES. With a logic of transforming certitudes. [Sombre 66-22P
CESSATION. There must be no cessation [Solitaires 60-6
CETERA. In Series X, Act IV, et cetera. [Chaos 357-12
CEYLON. The wind of Ceylon, [Weak Mind 212-8
   If Englishmen lived without tea in Ceylon, and they do; [Connois
      215-7
   Ceylon, wants nothing from the sea, la belle [Extracts 257-28
   Of England, to Pablo Neruda in Ceylon, [Descrip 341-22
   Breaches the darkness of Ceylon with blares, [NSF 384-12
CHAFFERER. No chafferer, may come [Archi 18-13 P
CHAFFERS. And one that chaffers the time away? [NSF 396-19
CHAIN. The chain of the turquoise hen and sky [Silent 359-16
CHAINS. With dew, dew dresses, stones and chains of dew, heads
      [Dump 202-9
   Chains of circumstance, [Pediment 361-12
   Bearded with chains of blue-green glitterings [Bouquet 449-7
   See watch-chains.
CHAIR. Coffee and oranges in a sunny chair, [Sunday 66-17
   In the sky, an imagined, wooden chair [Human 363-9
   Forced up from nothing, evening's chair, [Human 363-11
   This is the chair from which she gathered up [Beginning 428-3
   And, seated in the nature of his chair, [Aug 493-22
   The bed, the books, the chair, the moving nuns, [Rome 508-21
   On the chair, a moving transparence on the nuns, [Rome 509-4
   In the warmth of your bed, at the edge of your chair, alive
      [Rome 509-19
   No more than a bed, a chair and moving nuns, [Rome 510-23
   In his chair, the most tranquil thought grew peaked [Quiet 523-9
CHAIRS. Qui fait fi des joliesses banales, the chairs. [Freed
      205-24
   The arrangement of the chairs is so and so, [Novel 458-9
CHALK. In his chalk and violet robes. [Nigger 151-14
CHALKED. For a vista in the Louvre. They are things chalked
      [Connois 216-11
CHALKY. Of the park with chalky brow scratched over black [Old
      Woman 44-3 P
CHALLENGE. A challenge to a final solution. [Stan Hero 84-28 P
CHALLENGER. Most supple challenger. The elephant [NSF 384-11
CHALLENGES. He mocks the guinea, challenges [Vari 233-14
CHAMBER. In this chamber the pure sphere escapes the impure [NH
      480-3
   In that distant chamber, a bearded queen, wicked in her dead
      light. [Madame 507-13
CHAMBERMAIDS. The palais de justice of chambermaids [Surprises 98-6
CHAMBERS. In diverse chambers. [Archi 18-4 P
CHAMPAGNE. Of April here and May to come. Champagne [Greenest 58-24P
CHANCE. Grotesque apprenticeship to chance event, [C 39-23
   That's not by chance. It comes to this: [Prelude 195-9
   Has any chance to mate his life with life [Sleight 222-17

Unwished for, chance, the merest riding [Hero 275-12
Itself non-physical, may, by chance, observe [EM 325-22
Of chance. Finally, the most solemn burial [Paisant 334-15
One person should come by chance, [Woman Song 360-17
But it dare not leap by chance in its own dark. [AA 417-22
By chance, or happy chance, or happiness, [Aug 491-5
By print or paper, the trivial chance foregone, [Duck 61-23 P
The ephemeras of the tangent swarm, the chance [Someone 84-1 A
CHANCED. They chanced to think. Suppose the future fails. [Duck
    63-2 P
CHANDELIER. Close the cantina. Hood the chandelier. [Havana 144-23
One says a German chandelier-- [MBG 172-15
CHANDELIERS. And the chandeliers are neat . . . [Anything B 211-12
The chandeliers, their morning glazes spread [Blue Bldg 217-11
CHANGE. Is there no change of death in paradise? [Sunday 69-13
Placed, so, beyond the compass of change, [MBG 168-1
And bound. Its nigger mystics should change [Prelude 195-11
One feels the purifying change. One rejects [Dump 202-17
Then the tree, at night, began to change, [On Road 203-19
To know that the change and that the ox-like struggle [Freed
    205-12
To change nature, not merely to change ideas, [Vari 234-1
Though the air change. Only this evening I saw it again,
    [Martial 238-13
Neither the moonlight could change it. And for her, [Uruguay
    249-12
And the most distant, single color, about to change, [Extracts
    258-17
Magical only for the change they make. [Montra 262-9
He breathed in crystal-pointed change the whole [Choc 298-6
Nothing of place. There is no change of place [Repet 308-6
Of this precarious music, the change of key [Pure 332-3
Not quite detected at the moment of change [Pure 332-4
By her own seeming made the summer change. [Descrip 339-12
There might be, too, a change immenser than [Descrip 341-7
The instant of the change that was the poem, [Liadoff 347-5
And bound by a sound which does not change, [Human 363-3
Rain without change within or from [Human 363-5
And in this sound, which do not change, [Human 363-7
Round the rooms, which do not ever seem to change . . .[Lot 372-3
Of change still possible. Exile desire [Cred 373-13
It Must Change [NSF 389-title 2
On the real. This is the origin of change. [NSF 392-7
The fluctuations of certainty, the change [NSF 395-14
To which the swans curveted, a will to change, [NSF 397-17
There was a will to change, a necessitous [NSF 397-19
In a moving contour, a change not quite completed? [NSF 406-9
He measures the velocities of change. [AA 414-10
He observes how the north is always enlarging the change, [AA
    412-24
Except the lavishing of itself in change, [AA 416-10
It must change from destiny to slight caprice. [AA 417-23
Our sense of these things changes and they change, [Roses 431-4
Invisible change discovers what is changed, [Owl 435-11
And the giant ever changing, living in change. [Orb 443-22
Made suddenly luminous, themselves a change, [Our Stars 455-19
There was an end at which in a final change, [Our Stars 455-22
His spirit is imprisoned in constant change. [NH 472-12
The sea shivered in transcendent change, rose up [NH 484-9
Of words that was a change of nature, more [NH 487-6
He does not change the sea from crumpled tinfoil [Aug 492-20
How easily the blown banners change to wings . . . [Rome 508-11
When the summer was over, when the change [Two Illus 514-7
Part of a discovery, a change part of a change, [Look 518-15
Not subject to change . . . [Song Fixed 520-6
They bud and bloom and bear their fruit without change. [Rock
    527-5
A new-colored sun, say, that will soon change forms [Armor
    529-19
A change of color in the plain poet's mind, [Moonlight 532-1
Whose heart will murmur with the music that will be a voice for
    her, speaking the dreaded change of speech; [Piano 22-2 P
Free from images and change. [Demoiselle 23-11 P
A change so felt, a fear in her so known, [Old Woman 45-3 P
And change. If ploughmen, peacocks, doves alike [Burnshaw 48-26P
To live incessantly in change. See how [Burnshaw 50-17 P
Is no longer a sound of summer. So great a change [Burnshaw
    50-21 P
But change composes, too, and chaos comes [Burnshaw 51-1 P
Are chaos and of archaic change. Shall you, [Burnshaw 51-5 P
A change, until the waterish ditherings turn [Burnshaw 52-14 P
There is a man whom rhapsodies of change, [Sombre 66-12 P
For a change, the englistered woman, seated [Ulysses 104-2 P
It follows that to change modes is to change the world.
    [Conversat 108-16 P
Either in distance, change or nothingness, [Real 110-15 P
CHANGEABLE. It was a purple changeable to see. [Abnormal 24-2 P
CHANGED. Which changed light green to olive then to blue. [Nigger
    152-10
Are changed upon the blue guitar." [MBG 165-6

Yet nothing changed by the blue guitar; [MBG 167-16
Yet nothing changed, except the place [MBG 167-18
To have the ant of the self changed to an ox [Freed 205-9
With its organic boomings, to be changed [Freed 205-10
Then the theatre was changed [Of Mod 239-21
Kept speaking, of God. I changed the word to man. [Les Plus
    245-4
The classic changed. There have been many. [Hero 276-10
The precisions of fate, nothing fobbed off, nor changed [Repet
    310-8
The feeling of Liadoff was changed. It is [Liadoff 347-4
A little changed by tips of artifice, changed [Myrrh 350-5
Being changed from space to the sailor's metier, [Two V 354-15
Summer is changed to winter, the young grow old, [Chaos 357-14
My house has changed a little in the sun. [NSF 385-16
Is that it has not changed enough. It remains, [NSF 390-4
Changed his true flesh to an inhuman bronze. [NSF 391-19
Nothing had happened because nothing had changed. [NSF 392-2
Is changed. It is not so blue as we thought. To be blue, [Ulti
    429-18
Too much as they are to be changed by metaphor, [Roses 430-13
Invisible change discovers what is changed, [Owl 435-11
The whole habit of the mind is changed by them, [Our Stars 455-17
When the whole habit of the mind was changed, [Our Stars 455-23
The countrymen were changed and each constant thing. [NH 487-8
To chromatic crawler. But it is changed. [Aug 492-21
Changed them, at last, to its triumphant hue, [Old Woman 44-26 P
And are your feelings changed to sound, without [Burnshaw 52-13P
As death itself, and never can be changed [Duck 61-22 P
Of which he is the cause, have never changed [Sombre 66-13 P
Until they changed to eagle in white air, [Sombre 68-4 P
And must be, when the portent, changed, takes on [Sombre 70-12 P
That changed in sleep. It is, it is, let be [Sombre 71-15 P
Its land-breath to be stifled, its color changed, [Sombre 71-33P
Were mechanical, muscular. They never changed, [Woman Had 81-20P
The rioter that appears when things are changed, [Pagoda 91-20 P
And yet nothing has been changed except what is [As Leave 117-13P
Unreal, as if nothing had been changed at all. [As Leave 117-14 P
CHANGELESS. A grace to nature, a changeless element. [Greenest
    59-30 P
CHANGES. Through sweating changes, never could forget [C 33-22
Beyond these changes, good, fat, guzzly fruit. [C 41-7
Of the colors, are tinsel changes, [Scavoir 231-7
Out of the changes of both light and dew [Scavoir 231-8
The vivid thing in the air that never changes, [Martial 238-12
In glittering seven-colored changes, [Oak 272-20
In hymns, through iridescent changes, [Hero 279-22
Desiring the exhilarations of changes: [Motive 288-13
To confront with plainest eye the changes, [Gigan 289-11
He is, the air changes and grows fresh to breathe. [Choc 301-8
The air changes, creates and re-creates, like strength, [Choc
    301-9
With the metaphysical changes that occur, [EM 326-11
This changes and that changes. Thus the constant [NSF 389-21
The partaker partakes of that which changes him. [NSF 392-19
Of stone, that never changes. Bethou him, you [NSF 394-16
The season changes. A cold wind chills the beach. [AA 412-19
A season changes color to no end, [AA 416-9
As light changes yellow into gold and gold [AA 416-11
Our sense of these things changes and they change, [Roses 431-4
It exceeds the heavy changes of the light. [Roses 431-7
Of fear changes the scorpions to skins [Duck 65-10 P
That the sense of being changes as we talk, [Conversat 109-22 P
Is fertile with more than changes of the light [Someone 84-18 A
CHANGING. Or the changing of light, the dropping [Curtains 62-5
Were seraphs, were saints, were changing essences. [NSF 397-15
And the giant ever changing, living in change. [Orb 443-22
Of colonies, a sense in the changing sense [NH 479-12
The flights through space, changing habitudes. [Ulysses 103-6 P
See: ever-changing; ever-never-changing.
CHANGINGNESS. Equal in living changingness to the light [NSF 380-8
CHANNEL. The channel slots of rain, the red-rose-red [NSF 400-8
CHANT. Shall chant in orgy on a summer morn [Sunday 69-29
Their chant shall be a chant of paradise, [Sunday 70-4
And in their chant shall enter, voice by voice, [Sunday 70-6
While the domes resound with chant involving chant. [Ghosts
    119-18
Chant, O ye faithful, in your paths [Botanist 2 136-5
Chorals for mountain voices and the moral chant, [Though 185-16
We chant if we live in evil and afterward [Extracts 259-9
From which the chant comes close upon the ear, [Montra 261-5
Here in the west indifferent crickets chant [EM 321-3
Another chant, an incantation, as in [EM 321-5
The wood-dove used to chant his hoobla-hoo [NSF 383-6
And chant the January fire [An Gaiety 33-6 P
Chant sibilant requiems for this effigy. [Burnshaw 47-19 P
And chant the rose-points of their birth, and when [Burnshaw
    49-29 P
Each other moving in a chant and danced [Burnshaw 50-27 P
The father does not come to adorn the chant. [Role 93-6 P

The chant and discourse there, more than wild weather [Role
 93-9 P
CHANTE. In Paris, celui qui chante et pleure, [Thought 186-7
CHANTERING. Like chantering from an abundant [Hero 277-16
CHANTERS. Fresh from the sacred clarities, chanters [Greenest
 56-4 P
CHANTICLEER. Nature as Pinakothek. Whist! Chanticleer . . . [NE
 Verses 106-10
CHANTING. He is singing and chanting the things that are part of
 him, [Nigger 150-11
 This barbarous chanting of what is strong, this blare.
 [Parochial 191-16
 Those that lie chanting green is the night. [Candle 223-6
 Him chanting for those buried in their blood, [Oboe 251-19
CHANTS. The night know nothing of the chants of night. [Re-state
 146-1
 Nothing is final, he chants. No man shall see the end. [Nigger
 150-13
 Any moral end. The chants of final peace [Extracts 259-6
 We live. Thence come the final chants, the chants [Extracts
 259-13
 Who chants by book, in the heat of the scholar, who writes
 [NSF 395-12
 Rugged and luminous, chants in the dark [NH 479-14
 Chants a death that is a medieval death . . . [Greenest 59-19 P
CHAOS. We live in an old chaos of the sun, [Sunday 70-18
 For his rage against chaos [Winter B 141-10
 I heard two workers say, "This chaos [Idiom 200-18
 This chaos will not be ended, [Idiom 200-20
 "Connoisseur of Chaos" [215-title
 The law of chaos is the law of ideas, [Extracts 255-23
 The mass of men are one. Chaos is not [Extracts 255-26
 In chaos and his song is a consolation. [Extracts 256-9
 Of a chaos composed in more than order, [Dutch 293-9
 In a calculated chaos: he that takes form [Repet 307-4
 "Chaos in Motion and Not in Motion" [357-title
 It might come bearing, out of chaos, kin [Page 422-27
 Streamed over chaos their civilities. [NH 479-9
 No introspective chaos . . . I accept: [Soldat 11-1 P
 Through a moving chaos that never ends. Mesdames, [Burnshaw
 50-23 P
 Of chaos are not always sad nor lost [Burnshaw 50-25 P
 But change composes, too, and chaos comes [Burnshaw 51-1 P
 Are chaos and of archaic change. Shall you, [Burnshaw 51-5 P
 Wrenched out of chaos . . . The quiet lamp [Ulysses 100-23 P
CHAPEAUX. Inside our queer chapeaux, we seem, on this bank, [Nuns
 92-15 P
CHAPEL. The bells of the chapel pullulate sounds at [Peaches 224-9
 Its chapel rises from Terre Ensevelie, [Armor 529-9
 His own: a chapel of breath, an appearance made [Armor 529-11
 The chapel rises, his own, his period, [Armor 529-21
 And of becoming, for which the chapel spreads out [Armor 530-13
 The chapel underneath St. Armorer's walls, [Armor 530-19
CHAPELS. Beetled, in chapels, on the chaste bouquets. [C 29-20
 In the presence of such chapels and such schools, [NH 469-22
CHAPLET. And the icon is the man. The pearled chaplet of spring,
 [Rock 526-20
CHARACTER. Any character. It is more than any scene: [Parochial
 192-6
 Too vaguely that it be written in character. [Extracts 257-21
 Signal, a character out of solitude, [Pure 331-4
 Lives in the mountainous character of his speech; [Descrip
 345-12
 The child that touches takes character from the thing, [NSF
 392-20
 As of a character everywhere, [Countryman 429-6
 Some lineament or character, [Planet 532-18
 By giving it a form. But the character [Recit 86-6 P
 You speak. You say: Today's character is not [As Leave 116-15 P
CHARACTERS. But that concerns the secondary characters. [EM 324-1
 That is different. They are characters beyond [Paisant 335-4
 Like their particular characters, addicts [Lot 371-10
 The personae of summer play the characters [Cred 377-21
 He does not hear his characters talk. He sees [Cred 377-24
 In which the characters speak because they want [Cred 378-6
 To speak, the fat, the roseate characters, [Cred 378-4
 They were love's characters come face to face. [NSF 401-21
 Poesis, poesis, the literal characters, the vatic lines,
 [Large 424-6
 These characters are around us in the scene. [NH 469-13
 It became, the nameless, flitting characters-- [NH 479-22
 All your characters [Demoiselle 23-5 P
 Are we characters in an arithmetic [Recit 87-7 P
CHARIOT. Within our bellies, we her chariot. [Worms 49-17
 That comes here in the solar chariot, [Pure 331-17
 To say the solar chariot is junk [Pure 332-6
CHARIOTS. Beyond your chilly chariots, to the skies. [Swans 4-12
 In which he sat. All chariots were drowned. The swans [Descrip
 343-4
 His mind raised up, down-drowned, the chariots. [Descrip 343-12

CHARITABLE. The charitable majesty of her whole kin? [Cred 375-1
CHARLESTON. Charleston should be New York. [Agenda 41-21 P
CHARMS. That this emerald charms philosophers, [Homunculus 26-10
CHARTS. The charts destroyed, even disorder may, [Burnshaw 48-28 P
 Barbers with charts of the only possible modes, [Sombre 68-8 P
CHASTE. Beetled, in chapels, on the chaste bouquets. [C 29-20
CHASTEL. Let us design a chastel de chasteté. [Archi 16-14 P
CHASTETE. Let us design a chastel de chasteté. [Archi 16-14 P
CHASTITY. So lewd spring comes from winter's chastity. [NH 468-4
CHATEAU. "Gallant Château" [161-title
 For example: Au Château. Un Salon. A glass [Golden 460-10
CHATEAUX. Bastard chateaux and smoky demoiselles, [Montra 263-7
 See camellia-chateaux.
CHATILLON. This then is Chatillon or as you please. [AA 415-20
CHATTER. To the chatter that is then the true legend, [Ulysses
 102-16 P
CHATTERING. Even in the chattering of your guitar. [MBG 167-14
CHEAP. And that confident one, Marie, the wearer of cheap stones,
 who will have grown still and restless; [Piano 22-5 P
CHECK. It will check him. [Plot Giant 6-16
 Check your evasions, hold you to yourself. [NSF 406-14
CHECKERED. Of the land, on a checkered cover, red and white.
 [Bouquet 450-6
 The checkered squares, the skeleton of repose, [Bouquet 450-7
CHEEK. Here is the cheek on which that lid declined, [Worms 49-20
 The genius of that cheek. Here are the lips, [Worms 50-1
 And a biscuit cheek. [Coroner 30-8 P
CHEEKS. And the cheeks like flower-pots under her hair. [Grotesque
 74-16 P
CHEERFUL. Of familiar things in a cheerful voice, [Thought 185-2
CHEESE. Of the pears and of the cheese [Anything B 211-19
 A café. There may be a dish of country cheese [Paisant 335-15
 Of yesterday's cheese, [Soldat 12-14 P
CHEF. Eternal chef d'orchestre? [Eve Angels 136-15
CHEMICAL. One chemical afternoon in mid-autumn, [Contra II 270-1
CHEMISTRY. Us. Good chemistry, good common man, what [Hero 273-16
CHERE. O chère maman, another, who, in turn, [Soldat 14-5 P
CHERISHED. Things to be cherished like the thought of heaven?
 [Sunday 67-18
CHERRIES. Cherries are ri . . . He would never say that. [Grotesque
 76-1 P
 When cherries are in season, or, at least [Grotesque 76-8 P
CHERRY. "What They Call Red Cherry Pie" [75-title 4 P
 He eats red cherry pie and never says-- [Grotesque 75-19 P
 He says "That's what I call red cherry pie." [Grotesque 76-4 P
 What is it that we share? Red cherry pie [Grotesque 76-7 P
 And that's red cherry pie. [Grotesque 76-12 P
CHEST. From Esthonia: the tiger chest, for tea. [Dump 201-19
 On more than muscular shoulders, arms and chest, [Choc 297-12
 A city slapped up like a chest of tools, [NH 478-24
CHESTNUT. The redness of your reddish chestnut trees, [Old Man
 501-5
CHEVALERE. As the rider, no chevalere and poorly dressed, [Uruguay
 249-28
CHEVALIER. The idea of the chevalier of chevaliers, [Antag 426-4
CHEVALIERS. The idea of the chevalier of chevaliers, [Antag 426-4
CHEVAUX. Et sabots durs aux chevaux . . . [Parasol 20-2 P
CHEWER. See pebble-chewer.
CHIAROSCURO. Morose chiaroscuro, gauntly drawn. [C 34-17
 In a chiaroscuro where [MBG 172-21
 Coulisse bright-dark, tragic chiaroscuro [NSF 384-3
 Stands brimming white, chiaroscuro scaled [Sombre 70-20 P
CHICAGO. Or Chicago a Kaffir kraal. It means this mob. [Duck 63-14 P
CHICK. The chick, the chidder-barn and grassy chives [Montra 260-3
CHIDDER-BARN. The chick, the chidder-barn and grassy chives
 [Montra 260-3
CHIEF. Which was, and is, chief motive, first delight, [C 34-28
 Because, in chief, it, only, can defend [John 436-11
 In the much-horned night, as its chief personage. [Souls 94-17 P
CHIEFEST. Our chiefest dome a demoiselle of gold. [Archi 18-2 P
 Whose chiefest embracing of all wealth [Ulysses 104-12 P
CHIEFTAIN. Chieftain Iffucan of Azcan in caftan [Bantams 75-14
 What chieftain, walking by himself, crying [NSF 389-2
CHILD. Desiring fiercely, the child of a mother fierce [EM 321-20
 The mother ties the hair-ribbons of the child [Extraord 369-7
 The child's three ribbons are in her plaited hair. [Extraord
 369-21
 The child that touches takes character from the thing, [NSF
 392-20
 It is a child that sings itself to sleep, [Owl 436-7
 Mistress of an idea, child [Celle 438-18
 The child's hair is of the color of the hay in the haystack,
 around which the four black horses stand. [Primordia 8-1 P
 As for a child in an oblivion: [Soldat 13-16 P
 One is a child again. The gold beards of waterfalls [Discov
 95-10 P
 A child asleep in its own life. [Ulysses 104-22 P
 "A Child Asleep in Its Own Life" [106-title P
 And who shall speak it, what child or wanderer [Ideal 88-19 A
CHILDISH. The childish onslaughts of such innocence, [Good Bad

33-19 P
CHILDREN. Already the new-born children interpret love [Carolinas
  4-15
  Of children nibbling at the sugared void, [C 43-25
  The children will be crying on the stair, [Nigger 156-7
  Children picking up our bones [Postcard 158-14
  A part of what it is . . . Children, [Postcard 159-13
  The cities, children become the fields [MBG 171-1
  The fields entrap the children, brick [MBG 171-5
  In trombones roaring for the children, [Hero 278-10
  Men came as the sun comes, early children [Dutch 291-23
  And you, my semblables, know that your children [Dutch 292-8
  Are not your children, not your selves. [Dutch 292-9
  Natives of poverty, children of malheur, [EM 322-18
  It is as if we were never children. [Debris 338-2
  Do you remember the children there like wicks, [Liadoff 346-11
  The air is full of children, statues, roofs [Chaos 357-15
  Day is the children's friend. [Prejudice 368-11
  Of day, then, children make [Prejudice 368-20
  Became to-day, among our children and [Lot 371-6
  Of the land's children, easily born, its flesh, [Cred 375-4
  These are the heroic children whom time breeds [NSF 385-1
  Children in love with them brought early flowers [NSF 400-23
  Yet when her children slept, his sister herself [NSF 402-16
  Descending to the children's bed, on which [NSF 403-6
  Among the children, like curious ripenesses [AA 415-8
  The children laugh and jangle a tinny time. [AA 415-12
  Lie down like children in this holiness, [AA 418-23
  The children of a desire that is the will, [Owl 436-4
  And scintillant sizzlings such as children like, [Orb 442-20
  So that this cold, a children's tale of ice, [NH 468-8
  At lucent children round her in a ring. [Hermit 506-3
  The children heard him in their chilly beds, [Phases 5-9 P
  The black mother of eleven children [Primordia 9-15 P
  And the eleven children . . . [Primordia 9-19 P
  The time will come for these children, seated before their long
    black instruments, to strike the themes of love-- [Piano
    21-16 P
  Contains for its children not a gill of sweet. [Greenest 55-26 P
  To trundle children like the sea? For you, [Duck 61-4 P
  There is a mother whose children need more than that. [Woman Had
    82-1 P
  Berceuse, transatlantic. The children are men, old men, [Woman
    Had 82-10 P
  Children and old men and philosophers, [Woman Had 82-15 P
  The picnic of children came running then, [Dinner 109-25 P
CHILLED. And thereby polar, polar-purple, chilled [C 34-4
  A most desolate wind has chilled Rouge-Fatima [Havana 142-11
  A shivering residue, chilled and foregone, [AA 417-20
CHILLING. Were contours. Cold was chilling the wide-moving swans.
    [Contra II 270-11
CHILLS. The season changes. A cold wind chills the beach. [AA
    412-19
CHILLY. Beyond your chilly chariots, to the skies. [Swans 4-12
  The children heard him in their chilly beds, [Phases 5-9 P
CHIME. And triple chime . . . The self-same rhythm [Stan Hero
    83-22 P
CHIMERA. Be not chimera of morning, [Nuances 18-13
  Nor any old chimera of the grave, [Sunday 68-18
CHIMERAS. Between chimeras and garlanded the way, [Sombre 67-29 P
CHIMERES. So that the stars, my semblables, chimeres, [Dutch 293-4
CHIMERICAL. This hallowed visitant, chimerical, [Spaniard 35-19 P
CHIMING. A thousand crystals' chiming voices, [Hero 279-19
CHIMNEY. The chimney is fifty years old and slants to one side.
    [Plain 502-18
  As if some Old Man of the Chimney, sick [Phases 5-6 P
CHIMNEY-TOPS. When it sings. The gull sits on chimney-tops. [Vari
    233-13
CHINA. Of China, cap of Spain, imperative haw [C 28-9
  In China. [Six Sig 73-7
CHINESE. Is it for nothing, then, that old Chinese [Monocle 14-1
  Good clown. . . .One thought of Chinese chocolate [Sea Surf 102-1
CHINKED. Bells of the dogs chinked. [Cab 21-1 P
CHINKS. If her eyes were chinks in which the sparrows built;
    [Woman Had 83-1 P
CHINS. Of blue, blue sleek with a hundred chins, [MBG 172-7
CHIROPODIST. "Saturday Night at the Chiropodist's" [27-title P
CHIRR. To a chirr of gongs [Cortege 80-21
CHISELED. With sense chiseled on bright stone. They see [Duck
    64-10 P
CHISELS. Nor the chisels of the long streets, [Six Sig 74-24
  Chisels of the stone-cutters cutting the stones. [Archi 16-19 P
CHITS. And jig his chits upon a cloudy knee. [C 40-12
  The chits came for his jigging, bluet-eyed, [C 43-16
CHITTER. And a chitter of cries [Cortege 80-22
CHIVES. The chick, the chidder-barn and grassy chives [Montra 260-3
CHOCOLATE. And made one think of rosy chocolate [Sea Surf 99-1
  And made one think of chop-house chocolate [Sea Surf 99-19
  And made one think of porcelain chocolate [Sea Surf 100-13
  And made one think of musky chocolate [Sea Surf 101-7

  Good clown. . . . One thought of Chinese chocolate [Sea Surf
    102-1
CHOCORUA. The shadow of Chocorua [MBG 176-8
  "Chocorua to Its Neighbor" [296-title
  Now, I, Chocorua, speak of this shadow as [Choc 300-16
CHOICE. The choice is made. Green is the orator [Repet 309-22
  All men endure. The great captain is the choice [Paisant 334-14
  He had to choose. But it was not a choice [NSF 403-11
  Between excluding things. It was not a choice [NSF 403-12
  Inescapable romance, inescapable choice [NH 468-10
  Since both alike appoint themselves the choice [NH 469-16
  God in the object itself, without much choice. [NH 475-10
  It is a choice of the commodious adjective [NH 475-21
  The choice twixt dove and goose is over-close. [Spaniard 35-6 P
  In heaven. But I have no choice. [Lytton 39-15 P
  He makes no choice of words-- [Grotesque 75-20 P
  That the choice should come on them so early. [Stan Hero 83-16 P
  "Of Ideal Time and Choice" [88-title A
  Because what they have chosen is their choice [Ideal 88-13 A
  Much choosing is the final choice made up [Ideal 88-18 A
  The inhuman making choice of a human self. [Ideal 89-12 A
CHOIR. It is a red bird that seeks out his choir [Monocle 13-13
  These choirs of welcome choir for me farewell. [Monocle 13-19
  That choir among themselves long afterward. [Sunday 70-9
  In masks, can choir it with the naked wind? [AA 415-3
  A chorister whose c preceded the choir. [Not Ideas 534-14
  Which choir makes the most faultless medley in its celebration?
    [Inelegance 25-19 P
  The choir that choirs the first fatigue in deep bell of canzoni?
    [Inelegance 25-20 P
  Is any choir the whole voice of this fretful habitation,
    [Inelegance 26-5 P
CHOIRS. Among the choirs of wind and wet and wing. [Monocle 13-14
  These choirs of welcome choir for me farewell. [Monocle 13-19
  Through choirs infolded to the outmost clouds? [C 41-18
  Struggling toward impassioned choirs, [MBG 169-6
  But would it be amen, in choirs, if once [Extracts 258-24
  Swarm, not with secondary sounds, but choirs, [Cred 374-12
  Not evocations but last choirs, last sounds [Cred 374-13
  Of praise, a conjugation done by choirs. [NSF 402-15
  In choruses and choirs of choruses, [Rome 510-16
  The choir that choirs the first fatigue in deep bell of canzoni?
    [Inelegance 25-20 P
  Drifting choirs, long movements and turnings of sounds. [Sick
    90-12 P
CHOKE. Choke every ghost with acted violence, [Nigger 155-6
CHOME. Chome! clicks the clock, if there be nothing more. [Montra
    260-7
CHOOSE. What lover, what dreamer, would choose [Watermelon 89-2
  The moments when we choose to play [MBG 184-9
  Must be in a fiction. It is time to choose. [Oboe 250-8
  He had to choose. But it was not a choice [NSF 403-11
  It is difficult even to choose the adjective [Plain 502-13
CHOOSING. Choosing his element from droll confect [C 40-7
  Choosing out of himself, out of everything within him, [Sick
    90-19 P
  Much choosing is the final choice made up, [Ideal 88-18 A
CHOP. To chop the sullen psaltery, [MBG 173-20
CHOP-HOUSE. And made one think of chop-house chocolate [Sea Surf
    99-19
CHOPINIANA. The mountain collapses. Chopiniana. [Hero 275-4
CHORAL. Celebration of a maiden's choral. [Peter 92-7
  Surrounded by its choral rings, [Not Ideas 534-16
CHORALE. The reverberating psalm, the right chorale. [EM 326-2
CHORALS. Of long, capricious fugues and chorals. [Jasmine 79-12
  Chorals for mountain voices and the moral chant, [Thought 185-16
  When shall lush chorals spiral through our fire [Duck 66-10 P
  And the dissolving chorals, waits for it and imagines [Sick
    90-15 P
CHORD. Strike the piercing chord. [Mozart 132-8
  It is the chord that falsifies. [MBG 171-3
  A chord between the mass of men and himself, [Extracts 256-6
CHORDS. Boomed from his very belly odious chords. [Monocle 17-17
  In witching chords, and their thin blood [Peter 90-11
  Of the still finer, more implacable chords. [Anatomy 108-14
  And the feeling heavy in cold chords [MBG 169-5
  And chords, the morning exercises, [Hero 274-6
  To hear more brightly the contriving chords. [Descrip 340-22
  A dead shepherd brought tremendous chords from hell [NSF 400-21
  Should give you more than their peculiar chords [Rome 510-19
  Both late and alone, above the crickets' chords, [Quiet 523-12
  The chords above your bed to-night. [Child 106-21 P
CHORISTER. No chorister, nor priest. There was [How Live 126-2
  One voice repeating, one tireless chorister, [NSF 394-11
  A chorister whose c preceded the choir. [Not Ideas 534-14
CHORISTERS. Great choristers, propounders of hymns, trumpeters,
    [Luther 461-7
CHORUS. This chorus as of those that wanted to live. [Aug 491-18
  Voices in chorus, singing without words, remote and deep, [Sick
    90-11 P

CHORUSES. In choruses and choirs of choruses, [Rome 510-16
CHOSE. The figures of speech, as why she chose [Scavoir 231-3
  Between, but of. He chose to include the things [NSF 403-13
CHOSEN. Belittles those carefully chosen daubs. [Grapes 110-16
  Or in the ceiling, in sounds not chosen, [Creat 310-13
  Or chosen quickly, in a freedom [Creat 310-14
  Their words are chosen out of their desire, [Orb 441-7
  The woman is chosen but not by him, [Aug 493-1
  Chosen by an inquisitor of structures [Rome 510-27
  And gazed on chosen mornings, [Three 131-19 P
  On chosen porcelain. [Three 131-21 P
  And old men, who have chosen, and are cold [Ideal 88-12 A
  Because what they have chosen is their choice [Ideal 88-13 A
CHOSES. Behold them, not choses of Provence, growing [Bouquet
  449-12
CHRISTIAN. "A High-Toned Old Christian Woman" [59-title
  See Hans Christian.
CHRISTMAS. Like the night before Christmas and all the carols.
  [Thought 185-3
  Policed by the hope of Christmas. Summer night, [Sombre 68-11 P
CHROMATIC. By Howzen, the chromatic Lowzen. [Oak 272-21
  To chromatic crawler. But it is changed. [Aug 492-21
  Like the chromatic calendar of time to come. [Theatre 91-6 P
CHROMATICS. That spread chromatics in hilarious dark, [C 45-9
CHROMES. Clippered with lilies scudding the bright chromes,
  [Monocle 17-15
CHRONICLE. Upon the ground, and before the chronicle [Havana 142-14
  "Paisant Chronicle" [title-334
  Is a paisant chronicle. [Paisant 334-16
  And the chronicle of humanity is the sum [Paisant 335-1
CHRONICLES. Of paisant chronicles. [Paisant 335-2
CHRONOLOGIES. Rose up like phantoms from chronologies. [NSF 389-15
CHRYSALIS. No man. The self, the chrysalis of all men [NH 468-21
CHRYSANTHEMUM. And the bees still sought the chrysanthemums' odor.
  [Contra II 270-18
CHRYSANTHEMUMS. The chrysanthemums' astringent fragrance comes
  [Nigger 157-1
CHU-CHOT-CHU. With the ferocious chu-chot-chu between, the sobs
  [Extracts 253-18
CHUCKLED. They pied and chuckled like a flock, [Sat Night 28-10 P
CHUCKLING. Stepped in and dropped the chuckling down his craw,
  [C 45-18
CHURCH. The archbishop is away. The church is gray. [Gray 140-1
  He is away. The church is gray. [Gray 140-9
  That church without bells. [Winter B 141-4
  To abate on the way to church, [Winter B 141-11
  That made him preach the louder, long for a church [Blue Bldg
  216-18
  The grinding in the arches of the church, [Blue Bldg 217-4
  Principally the church steeple, [Common 221-2
  The church bells clap one night in the week. [Cuisine 227-16
  "St. Armorer's Church from the Outside" [529-title
  As a church is a bell and people are an eye, [Sombre 67-19 P
CHURCHES. The lean cats of the arches of the churches, [Extracts
  254-1
  The lean cats of the arches of the churches [Extracts 254-18
  Colliding with deaf-mute churches and optical trains. [Chaos
  357-17
  The churches and their long parades, Seville [Greenest 53-18 P
  The churches, like dalmatics stooped in prayer, [Sombre 69-1 P
CHURCH-WALL. Like a figure on the church-wall. [Explan 73-4
CHURCH-YARD. In its church-yard, in the province of St. Armorer's,
  [Armor 529-3
CHURCHYARD. A churchyard kind of bush as well, [Banjo 114-6 P
CHUTE. Anabasis or slump, ascent or chute, [C 43-21
CHUTNEY. Chutney. Then the Canon Aspirin declaimed [NSF 401-23
CICADA. Syringa, cicada, his flea. [Thought 186-20
CIEL. C'était mon frère du ciel, ma vie, mon or [Sea Surf 100-3
CIGAR. The poet striding among the cigar stores, [Thought 185-5
  On a hot night and a long cigar and talk [Greenest 58-25 P
  The boatman goes humming. He smokes a cigar [Stan MBG 72-11 P
CIGARS. Call the roller of big cigars, [Emperor 64-1
CINDERELLA. Cinderella fulfilling herself beneath the roof? [NSF
  405-9
CINDERY. An ember yes among its cindery noes, [Armor 529-10
CINERARIAS. Cinerarias have a speaking sheen. [Poesie 302-17
CINNAMON. Than wettest cinnamon. It was cribled pears [Poem Morn
  219-10
  The ponderous cinnamon, snarls in his mountain [NSF 384-15
CIRCLE. In the circle of her traverse of the sea. [Paltry 5-20
  But in a circle, not in the arc [Celle 438-2
  Of winter, in the unbroken circle [Celle 438-10
  In the midst of a circle of trees, from which the leaves [Old
  Woman 43-3 P
  To touch the grass and, as you circle, turn [Burnshaw 51-12 P
  The circle of the sceptre growing large [Bship 80-23 P
  Merely the center of a circle, spread [Bship 81-10 P
  The circle would no longer be broken but closed. [Letters 108-8 P
CIRCLES. A blue pigeon it is, that circles the blue sky, [Monocle
  17-18

  Of one of many circles. [Thirteen 94-8
  There are circles of weapons in the sun. [Dutch 290-15
  Concentric circles of shadows, motionless [EM 319-7
  In the punctual centre of all circles white [Anach 366-8
  Stands truly. The circles nearest to it share [Anach 366-9
  And the circles quicken and crystal colors come [Anach 366-13
  A shape within the ancient circles of shapes, [Rome 509-1
CIRCLET. Opaque, in orange circlet, nearer than it [Page 422-13
CIRCLING. Our faces circling round a central face [Dames 206-12
CIRCULAR. In a swift, circular line [Earthy 3-7
  In a swift, circular line [Earthy 3-11
  Clumped carvings, circular, like blunted fans, [Old Woman 43-16 P
  A leaden ticking circular in width. [Duck 66-5 P
CIRCULATE. Yet invisible currents clearly circulate. [Nigger 156-3
CIRCULATING. "The Pleasures of Merely Circulating" [149-title
CIRCUMSPECT. And the visible, circumspect presentment drawn [C
  35-24
CIRCUMSTANCE. Beyond his circumstance, projected [Hero 277-21
  Chains of circumstance, [Pediment 361-12
  The state of circumstance. [Aug 492-3
CIRCUS. Passed like a circus. [Havana 143-20
CITARE. Gone, as in Calypso's isle or in Citare, [Bship 79-24 P
CITHERN. His hymn, his psalm, his cithern song of praise [Greenest
  59-21 P
CITHERNS. Like windy citherns hankering for hymns. [High-Toned 59-5
CITIES. The cities, children become the fields [MBG 171-1
  The armies are forms in number, as cities are. [Choc 296-12
  The armies are cities in movement. But a war [Choc 296-13
  Between cities is a gesticulation of forms, [Choc 296-14
  The silks they wear in all the cities [Melancholy 32-13 P
  Are the cities to breed as mountains bred, the streets [Duck
  61-3 P
  Cities that would not wash away in the mist, [Sombre 68-9 P
CITIZEN. For a citizen of heaven though still of Rome. [Rome 510-2
CITIZENS. Like molten citizens of the vacuum? [Liadoff 346-10
CITRON. Sitting beside your lamp, there citron to nibble [Dwarf
  208-13
CITRONS. Citrons, oranges and greens [Pears 197-1
  They rolled their r's, there, in the land of the citrons.
  [NH 486-19
  Their dark-colored words had redescribed the citrons. [NH 487-9
CITRON-SAP. Yellow-blue, yellow-green, pungent with citron-sap,
  [NH 486-14
CITRON-SKIN. They might be sugar or paste or citron-skin [Burnshaw
  46-19 P
CITY. Until the steeples of his city clanked and sprang [Geneva
  24-13
  But the wise man avenges by building his city in snow. [Nigger
  158-13
  A city slapped up like a chest of tools, [NH 478-20
  Lucidity of his city, joy of his nation, [Aug 492-2
  The life of the city never lets go, nor do you [Rome 510-12
  On the city, on which it leans, the people there, [Sombre 68-21 P
  If the fane were clear, if the city shone in mind, [Sombre
  69-11 P
CIVIL. Of the civil fans! [Ord Women 11-24
  A civil nakedness in which to be, [Repet 310-6
  In an abandoned spot. Soft, civil bird, [Cred 377-12
  So soft, so civil, and you make a sound, [Cred 377-19
  Civil, madam, I am, but underneath [NSF 406-11
  The civil fiction, the calico idea, [Duck 65-12 P
  See over-civil.
CIVILER. For every day. In a civiler manner, [Hero 275-22
CIVILEST. Diffusing the civilest odors [Plot Giant 6-14
CIVILITIES. Streamed over chaos their civilities. [NH 479-9
CIVILIZATION. Civilization must be destroyed. The hairy saints
  [NE Verses 106-1
  A civilization formed from the outward blank, [Armor 529-22
CIVILIZED. Celestin, the generous, the civilized, [Papini 447-7
CLACK. See click-clack.
CLAIRVOYANCE. Without clairvoyance, close to her. [Vase 247-8
  The romantic intoning, the declaimed clairvoyance [NSF 387-19
CLAIRVOYANT. There the distant fails the clairvoyant eye [Cred
  374-10
  For the clairvoyant men that need no proof: [Orb 441-5
CLAMBERING. The clambering wings of birds of black revolved,
  [Babies 77-14
CLAMOR. In a clamor thudding up from central earth. [Sombre 70-30P
  An immense drum rolls through a clamor of people. [Stan Hero
  83-11 P
CLAMORINGS. As the sea has in its coastal clamorings. [Red Kit
  31-9 P
CLAMS. Oh! Sal, the butcher's wife ate clams [Lulu M 27-9 P
CLAN. Fit for a kinky clan. [Pascagoula 126-18
CLANDESTINE. Clandestine steps upon imagined stairs [Oboe 251-6
CLANGING. The angry day-son clanging as its make: [Papini 448-2
CLANK. The alto clank of the long recitation, in these [Burnshaw
  52-7 P
  The clank of the carrousel and, under the trees, [Duck 62-25 P
CLANKED. Until the steeples of his city clanked and sprang

[Geneva 24-13

CLANKING. Each year to disguise the clanking mechanism [Nigger
  157-2
CLAP. In which the thunder, lapsing in its clap, [C 33-15
  And clap the hollows full of tin. [MBG 170-6
  The church bells clap one night in the week. [Cuisine 227-16
CLAPPED. Her prismy blonde and clapped her in his hands, [C 42-3
CLAPPERS. So many clappers going without bells, [NSF 394-5
CLAPPER-TRAPS. Dew-dapper clapper-traps, blazing [MBG 182-3
CLAPPING. Cane clapping behind them [Three 139-4 P
CLARIFIED. Clarified. It is silence made still dirtier. [Creat
  311-8
CLARION. Tempestuous clarion, with heavy cry, [C 32-23
  Of its cry as clarion, its diction's way [Cred 377-3
  Racking the world with clarion puffs. This must [Greenest 56-12P
CLARITIES. Implicit clarities in the way you cry [Burnshaw 52-12 P
  Fresh from the sacred clarities, chanters [Greenest 56-4 P
CLARITY. Dazzle yields to a clarity and we observe, [Descrip 341-10
  It was his clarity that made the vista bright. [Anach 366-3
CLASHED. Like the clashed edges of two words that kill." [Monocle
  13-4
CLASHES. Loudened by cries, by clashes, quick and sure [Monocle
  16-13
CLASHING. Mobs of ten thousand, clashing together, [Thunder 220-3
CLASP. Clasp me, [Demoiselle 23-14 P
CLASPED. Morning and afternoon are clasped together [NSF 392-12
CLASSES. "The war between classes is [Bship 77-16 P
CLASSIC. Of L'Observateur, the classic hero [Hero 276-8
  The classic changed. There have been many. [Hero 276-10
  A steeple that tip-tops the classic sun's [EM 322-25
  Is part of the classic imagination, posed [Recit 87-1 P
  That were the moments of the classic, the beautiful. [Local
  112-10 P
CLASSICAL. Has rather a classical sound. [Circulat 150-8
CLATTER. As if--The pigeons clatter in the air. [NSF 390-6
CLATTERED. The bucks clattered. [Earthy 3-14
  Whose horse clattered on the road on which she rose, [Uruguay
  249-18
CLATTERING. Every time the bucks went clattering [Earthy 3-1
  They went clattering.[Earthy 3-5
  Of autumn, these horses should go clattering [Burnshaw 47-9 P
CLAUDE. Claude has been dead a long time [Botanist 1 134-10
  But in Claude how near one was [Botanist 1 135-1
CLAVIER. "Peter Quince at the Clavier" [89-title
CLAW. Will claw sleep. Morning is not sun, [MBG 102-19
CLAWED. Clawed on the ear these consonants? [Jumbo 269-6
  So clawed, so sopped with sun, that in these things [Greenest
  57-20 P
CLAWING. When cocks wake, clawing at their beds [Adequacy 244-3
  And wildly free, whose clawing thumb [Jumbo 269-5
  Clawing the sing-song of their instruments. [AA 415-11
CLAWS. "The Bird with the Coppery, Keen Claws" [82-title
  He moves not on his coppery, keen claws. [Bird Claws 82-15
  On that its claws propound, its fangs [MBG 174-9
  Ruddy are his eyes and ruddy are his claws [Glass 197-15
  The claws keep scratching on the shale, the shallow shale,
  [Somnam 304-5
  And memory and claws: a paragon [Spaniard 35-14 P
CLAY. True daughters both of Crispin and his clay. [C 44-2
  Of clay and wattles made as it ascends [Page 421-11
CLAYS. There is the same color in the bellies of frogs, in clays,
  withered reeds, skins, wood, sunlight. [Primordia 8-2 P
CLEAN. As warm, as clean. [Vincentine 52-19
  Among the lascivious poisons, clean of them, [Extracts 252-16
  How clean the sun when seen in its idea, [NSF 381-4
  Cleansed clean of lousy Byzantium. [Memo 89-12 P
CLEANED. That the lilacs came and bloomed, like a blindness
  cleaned, [Rock 526-5
CLEANLINESS. In these, I wear a vital cleanliness, [Rhythms 246-6
  Washed in the remotest cleanliness of a heaven [NSF 381-5
CLEANSED. Cleansed clean of lousy Byzantium. [Memo 89-12 P
CLEAR. Was clear. The last distortion of romance [C 30-2
  Much trumpeted, made desperately clear, [C 30-26
  Wearing a clear tiara [Venereal 48-7
  We agree in principle. That's clear. But take [High-Toned 59-6
  Say that the palms are clear in a total blue, [Two Figures 86-13
  Are clear and are obscure; that it is night; [Two Figures 86-14
  Most near, most clear, and of the clearest bloom, [Fictive 87-7
  The near, the clear, and vaunts the clearest bloom, [Fictive
  88-3
  Too near, too clear, saving a little to endow [Fictive 88-11
  Of a green evening, clear and warm, [Peter 90-7
  In the green water, clear and warm, [Peter 90-13
  On the clear viol of her memory, [Peter 92-12
  Statue against a Clear Sky [NE Verses 105-title 9
  The square began to clear. [Public Sq 109-10
  "In the Clear Season of Grapes" [110-title
  Rides clear of her mind and the waves make a refrain [Farewell
  117-8
  However clear, it would have been deep air, [Key W 129-14

Let this be clear that we are men of sun [Eve Angels 137-13
By mere example opulently clear. [Havana 145-6
It makes it clear. Even at noon [MBG 172-17
Clear water in a brilliant bowl, [Poems Clim 193-7
A world of clear water, brilliant-edged, [Poems Clim 194-1
The mountains are scratched and used, clear fakes. [Arcades
  226-3
Of the town, the river, the railroad were clear. [Hartford 227-8
Is blue, clear, cloudy, high, dark, wide and round; [Extracts
  252-11
His thoughts begotten at clear sources, [Hero 277-14
Of the clear sovereign that is reality, [Repet 307-21
The spirits of all the impotent dead, seen clear, [Cats 368-8
The corals of the dogwood, cold and clear, [NSF 400-1
Clear and, except for the eye, without intrusion. [NSF 400-3
From cloud to cloudless, cloudless to keen clear [AA 414-15
Invisibly clear, the only love. [Wom Sun 445-15
By growing clear, transparent magistrates, [Bouquet 449-6
The eye made clear of uncertainty, with the sight [NH 471-19
To the nations of the clear invisible, [NH 474-24
The clear. A celestial mode is paramount, [NH 480-24
In the morning, the clear river [Primordia 8-5 P
On the clear grass, [Polo 38-5 P
A visible clear cap, a visible wreath [Greenest 57-7 P
If the fane were clear, if the city shone in mind, [Sombre 69-11P
A wandering orb upon a path grown clear. [Sombre 70-17 P
It is clear that it is not a moral law. [Bship 78-31 P
It has a clear, a single, a solid form, [Recit 87-11 P
Tradition wears, the clear, the single form [Recit 87-21 P
Say that in the clear Atlantic night [Memo 89-13 P
"A Clear Day and No Memories" [113-title P
Today the air is clear of everything. [Clear Day 113-14 P
And seen in a clear light. [Three 131-24 P
There, of clear, revolving crystalline; [Ideal 88-7 A
CLEARED. Cleared from the north and in that height [Country 207-12
  Cleared of its stiff and stubborn, man-locked set, [Angel 497-1
  Nothing more, like weather after it has cleared-- [Art Pop
  112-14 P
  Well, more than that, like weather when it has cleared [Art Pop
  112-15 P
CLEAREST. Most near, most clear, and of the clearest bloom,
  [Fictive 87-7
  The near, the clear, and vaunts the clearest bloom, [Fictive
  88-3
  The clearest woman with apt weed, to mount [Havana 143-17
  Of the clearest reality that is sovereign, [Repet 307-22
  Ourselves, in the clearest green--well, call it green. [Lot 371-7
  Or mind, uncertain in the clearest bells, [NH 466-17
CLEARING. To clearing opalescence. Then the sea [Sea Surf 102-13
  A clearing, a detecting, a completing, [Choc 301-11
  There was a clearing, a readiness for first bells, [NH 483-1
CLEARLY. Yet invisible currents clearly circulate. [Nigger 156-3
  There the man sees the image clearly at last. [Rhythms 245-15
  And see it clearly in the idea of it. [NSF 380-17
  And we make of what we see, what we see clearly [NSF 401-2
  Of night. How clearly that would be defined! [Old Woman 46-12 P
CLEARNESS. A clearness has returned. It stands restored. [NH 488-3
  It is not an empty clearness, a bottomless sight. [NH 488-4
  In an air of freshness, clearness, greenness, blueness, [Armor
  530-16
  To search for clearness all an afternoon [Old Woman 44-13 P
  To be a part of a tissue, a clearness of the air, [Nuns 92-16 P
  That matches, today, a clearness of the mind. [Nuns 92-17 P
  Than a power of sleep, a clearness emerging [Bus 116-9 P
CLEAR-POINT. Is the clear-point of an edifice, [Human 363-10
CLEARS. An edge of song that never clears; [Country 207-9
  Clears deeply, when the moon hangs on the wall [NSF 398-24
  But clears and clears until an open night [Spaniard 34-3 P
  If she is like the moon, she never clears [Spaniard 34-11 P
CLEMENTINA. See Victoria Clementina.
CLERESTORY. From pipes that swarm clerestory walls. The voice
  [Greenest 59-13
CLERKS. Should be the clerks of our experience. [C 39-8
CLICK. Click, click, the Got whom we serve is able, [Hero 273-20
CLICK-CLACK. They differ from reason's click-clack, its applied
  [NSF 387-22
CLICKERING. What word split up in clickering syllables [C 28-14
CLICKS. Chome! clicks the clock, if there be nothing more. [Montra
  260-7
CLIFF. Ashen man on ashen cliff above the salt halloo, [NE Verses
  105-7
CLIFFS. Like light in a mirroring of cliffs, [MBG 175-3
  The rocks of the cliffs are the heads of dogs [Vari 232-12
  "The Irish Cliffs of Moher" [501-title
  They go to the cliffs of Moher rising out of the mist, [Irish
  501-13
  The cliffs are rough. [Lulu M 27-5 P
CLIMATE. "The Poems of our Climate" [193-title
  Like things produced by a climate, the world [Ulysses 102-29 P
  In a season, a climate of morning, of elucidation, [Bus 116-5 P

CLIMATES. Goes round in the climates of the mind [Ulysses 102-30 P
CLIMB. Climb through the night, because his cuckoos call. [Oboe
      251-7
   Of the mind--They would soon climb down the side of the ship.
      [Page 123-8
   As they climb the stairs [Archi 17-9 P
   As they climb the flights [Archi 17-11 P
   Toward which, in the nights, the glittering serpents climb,
      [Greenest 55-12 P
   Here, if there was a peak to climb, [Stan MBG 73-12 P
   The way, when we climb a mountain, [July 115-4 P
   To climb the hill [Three 136-7 P
   The momentary footings of a climb [Someone 87-1 A
CLIMBED. Must struggle like the rest." She climbed until [Uruguay
      249-1
   Come home, wind, he said as he climbed the stair-- [Pieces
      351-14
   3. A vine has climbed the other side of the wall. [Someone 86-6 A
CLING. A vibrancy of petals, fallen, that still cling [Bouquet
      450-10
CLINGING. Observes the canna with a clinging eye, [Canna 55-8
   That keep clinging to a tree, [Burghers 362-13
   And reverberations clinging to whisper still. [Rome 510-20
   She was represented as clinging [Three 138-7 P
CLINGS. That clings to the mind like that right sound, that song
      [Extracts 256-14
CLINK. Pass the whole of life earing the clink of the [Archi 16-18P
CLINKING. The spring came there in clinking pannicles [C 34-9
CLINKINGS. Except for delicate clinkings not explained. [Descrip
      340-16
CLIPPED. Clipped frigidly blue-black meridians, [C 34-16
   So may the relation of each man be clipped. [C 46-13
   The cloak to be clipped, the night to be re-designed, [Sombre
      71-32 P
CLIPPERED. Clippered with lilies scudding the bright chromes,
      [Moncole 17-15
CLOAK. The ribboned stick, the bellowing breeches, cloak [C 28-8
   The singer has pulled his cloak over his head. [Of Surface 57-7
   The moon is in the folds of the cloak, [Of Surface 57-8
   Blessed, whose beard is cloak against the snows. [NE Verses 105-6
   The era of the idea of man, the cloak [Thought 185-13
   In a flapping cloak. She walked along the paths [Old Woman 44-2P
   Thoughts by descent. To flourish the great cloak we wear [Sombre
      71-19 P
   That we conceal? A passion to fling the cloak, [Sombre 71-26 P
   The cloak to be clipped, the night to be re-designed, [Sombre
      71-32 P
CLOAKED. The figures of the past go cloaked. [Poesie 302-12
CLOAKS. Of voluminous cloaks, [Homunculus 26-19
   And saints are brilliant in fresh cloaks. [Contra I 266-16
   They throw around their shoulders cloaks that flash [AA 419-23
CLOCK. Everything ticks like a clock. The cabinet [Nigger 157-17
   Chome! clicks the clock, if there be nothing more. [Montra 260-7
   Is largely another winding of the clock. [Duck 65-30 P
CLOCKS. That crew before the clocks. [Watermelon 89-6
   Of the cuckoos, a man with a mania for clocks. [Nigger 157-19
   Time swished on the village clocks and dreams were alive, [Uru-
      guay 249-26
   The eccentric exterior of which the clocks talk. [NH 478-21
   A zone of time without the ticking of clocks, [Aug 494-7
CLOCK-SHOP. In a clock-shop. . . . Soldier, think, in the darkness,
      [Hero 275-15
CLOD. An invention, an embrace between one desperate clod [Rock
      525-13
CLODS. Of letters, prophecies, perceptions, clods [Orb 443-20
   Were mere brown clods, mere catching weeks of talk. [NH 486-21
CLOG. Clog, therefore, purple Jack and crimson Jill. [Nigger 154-6
CLOISTER. That in his Mediterranean cloister a man, [EM 324-11
   The self is a cloister full of remembered sounds [Woman Had 82-17P
   See cloud-cloister-porches.
CLOISTERS. See cloud-cloisters.
CLOPPING. And on the clopping foot-ways of the moon [C 28-28
CLOSE. And for sweet-smelling virgins close to them. [Monocle 14-25
   Drawn close by dreams of fledgling wing, [Babies 77-11
   His broad-brimmed hat came close upon his eyes. [Babies 77-18
   Close the cantina. Hood the chandelier. [Havana 144-23
   To lie on one's bed in the dark, close to a face [Yellow 237-8
   The present close, the present realized, [Martial 238-10
   Without clairvoyance, close to her. [Vase 247-8
   Comes close to the prisoner's ear, becomes a throat [Montra 261-2
   From which the chant comes close upon the ear, [Montra 261-5
   Flew close to, flew to without rising away. [God 285-8
   There is so little that is close and warm. [Debris 338-1
   Yet coo becomes rou-coo, rou-coo. How close [Think 356-16
   Close to me, hidden in me day and night? [NSF 380-6
   The fragrance of the magnolias comes close, [NSF 385-17
   False flick, false form, but falseness close to kin. [NSF 385-18
   Of it, a close, parental magnitude, [Orb 443-12
   The window, close to the ramshackle spout in which [NH 475-8
   Close to the senses there lies another isle [NH 480-17

Shrunk in the poverty of being close, [NH 484-18
   The deep sigh with which the hanging ends, close [Stan Hero
      84-18 P
   Distant, yet close enough to wake [Child 106-20 P
   See over-close.
CLOSED. Later, the firecat closed his bright eyes [Earthy 3-19
   The curtains flittered and the door was closed. [C 42-4
   And with eyes closed [Bagatelles 213-3
   He must be incapable of speaking, closed, [Less 327-15
   Their eyes closed, in a young palaver of lips. [NH 477-1
   The circle would no longer be broken but closed. [Letters 108-8 P
CLOSED-IN. The closed-in smell of hay. A sumac grows [Armor 529-6
CLOSELIER. Them closelier to her by rejecting dreams. [NSF 402-9
CLOSELY. He gripped more closely the essential prose [C 36-18
   And touch each other, even touching closely, [Norfolk 112-1
   Of autumn's halloo in its hair. So that closely, then, [Parochial
      192-2
   The gray grass like a pallet, closely pressed; [Extracts 255-4
   Now, closely the ear attends the varying [Pure 332-2
   Yet not too closely the double of our lives, [Descrip 344-19
   She held men closely with discovery, [Owl 435-9
   They cast closely round the facture of the thing [Bouquet 452-6
CLOSER. Be near me, come closer, touch my hand, phrases [EM 317-17
CLOSES. As the eye closes . . . How cold the vacancy [EM 320-6
   To the closes [Archi 17-12 P
CLOSEST. Closest and strongest. [On Road 204-12
   As color, even the closest to us, is; [Less 328-1
   With meanings, doubled by the closest sound, [Sombre 67-25 P
CLOTH. Are blobs on the green cloth. [Pears 197-4
   With the whole spirit sparkling in its cloth, [Owl 434-12
   See: breech-cloth; table-cloth.
CLOTHE. Clothe me entire in the final filament, [NSF 396-7
CLOTHES. In suavest keeping. The shoes, the clothes, the hat
      [Descrip 343-2
   And walked in fine clothes, [Parasol 20-13 P
   See bed-clothes.
CLOTHS. Arching cloths besprinkled with colors [Plot Giant 6-18
CLOU. Of majesty, of an invincible clou, [NH 473-11
CLOUD. Foam and cloud are one. [Fabliau 23-9
   It was caparison of wind and cloud [C 30-13
   But when I walk I see that it consists of three or four hills and
      a cloud. [Of Surface 57-2
   Out of his cloud and from his sky. [Cuban 64-19
   A mountain-blue cloud arose [Public Sq 109-3
   And cloud, of the sunken coral water-walled, [Key W 129-13
   The cloud rose upward like a heavy stone [Nigger 152-8
   (Omitting reefs of cloud): [Delight 162-5
   Cloud's red, earth feeling, sky that thinks? [MBG 177-4
   But if it did . . . If the cloud that hangs [Country 207-10
   Of a cloud on sand, a shape on the side of a hill. [Connois 215-20
   Seeming to be liquid as leaves made of cloud, [Forces 229-14
   Is a cloud in which a voice mumbles. [Lack 303-8
   It is a ghost that inhabits a cloud, [Lack 303-9
   Sees a familiar building drenched in cloud [Repet 308-4
   At a piano in a cloud sat practicing, [Liadoff 346-15
   As they fell down, as they heard Liadoff's cloud [Liadoff 346-18
   When the cloud pressed suddenly the whole return [Liadoff 347-6
   From thought, like a violent pulse in the cloud itself, [Liadoff
      347-7
   Of air . . . But then that cloud, that piano placed [Liadoff
      347-13
   That the rocket was only an inferior cloud. [Liadoff 347-16
   Lie lengthwise like the cloud of sleep, not quite [Two V 354-4
   Be silent in your luminous cloud and hear [NSF 404-11
   What am I to believe? If the angel in his cloud [NSF 404-13
   Whether fresher or duller, whether of winter cloud [AA 412-13
   From cloud to cloudless, cloudless to keen clear [AA 414-15
   Itself a cloud, although of misted rock [AA 416-5
   Through waves of light. It is of cloud transformed [AA 416-7
   To cloud transformed again, idly, the way [AA 416-16
   The cloud drifts idly through half-thought-of forms. [AA 416-15
   A saying out of a cloud, but innocence. [AA 418-20
   And cloud, the used-to tree and used-to cloud, [Orb 441-13
   Cloud's gold, of a whole appearance that stands and is. [Bouquet
      452-18
   A thing on the side of a house, not deep in a cloud, [NH 474-21
   The dry eucalyptus seeks god in the rainy cloud. [NH 475-4
   Of a woman with a cloud on her shoulder rose [Aug 494-11
   Of wind and light and cloud [Inhab 503-16
   It was not the shadow of cloud and cold, [Two Illus 513-4
   Of the black-blooded scholar, the man of the cloud, to be
      [Sombre 71-30 P
   A single ship, a cloud on the sea, the largest [Bship 78-2 P
   The Masculine, much magnified, that cloud [Bship 78-28 P
   As if in a golden cloud. The son restores [Recit 87-16 P
   See: thunder cloud; top-cloud.
CLOUD-CAP. Like a cloud-cap in the corner of the looking-glass,
      [Moonlight 531-22
CLOUD-CASUAL. Cloud-casual, metaphysical metaphor, [Choc 301-4
CLOUD-CLOISTER-PORCHES. Through long cloud-cloister-porches, walked

alone, [Greenest 54-3 P
CLOUD-CLOISTERS. At the unbeliever's touch. Cloud-cloisters blow
  [Greenest 58-10 P
CLOUD-CLOWN. Cloud-clown, blue painter, sun as horn, [Jumbo
  269-13
CLOUDLESS. Cloudless the morning. It is he. The man [NSF 389-8
  From cloud to cloudless, cloudless to keen clear [AA 414-15
CLOUD-MAN. What avuncular cloud-man beamier than spears? [Greenest
  52-25 P
CLOUD-POLE. Everywhere in space at once, cloud-pole [Ulti 430-3
CLOUDS. She touches the clouds, where she goes [Paltry 5-19
  "Mother of heaven, regina of the clouds, [Monocle 13-1
  Through choirs infolded to the utmost clouds? [C 41-18
  "On the Manner of Addressing Clouds" [55-title
  Their evocations are the speech of clouds. [On Manner 55-16
  Deflations of distance; or as clouds [Curtains 62-3
  Jove in the clouds had his inhuman birth. [Sunday 67-27
  The clouds go, nevertheless, [Soldier 97-11
  "Sea Surface Full of Clouds" [98-title
  Who, then, evolved the sea-blooms from the clouds [Sea Surf 99-7
  Who, then, beheld the rising of the clouds [Sea Surf 99-23
  The sea unfolding in the sunken clouds? [Sea Surf 100-20
  Who then beheld the figures of the clouds [Sea Surf 101-11
  Beheld the sovereign clouds as jugglery [Sea Surf 102-6
  The sovereign clouds came clustering. The conch [Sea Surf 102-10
  Scaffolds and derricks rise from the reeds to the clouds [NE
    Verses 105-9
  Key West sank downward under massive clouds [Farewell 117-3
  Both of men and clouds, a slime of men in crowds. [Farewell
    118-12
  These sudden clouds of faces and arms, [Sad Gay 122-4
  Like giant arms among the clouds. [How Live 125-20
  So that corridors of clouds, [Botanist 1 134-15
  Why should the future leap the clouds [Botanist 2 136-3
  Who can think of the sun costuming clouds [Fading 139-1
  Arranged under the stony clouds [Gray 140-6
  The angel flew round the clouds, [Circulat 149-17
  And the clouds flew round and the clouds flew round [Circulat
    149-18
  And the clouds flew round with the clouds. [Circulat 149-19
  Under the mat of frost and over the mat of clouds. [Nigger 151-4
  And the fortunes of frost and of clouds, [Nigger 151-6
  Happy men, distinguishing frost and clouds. [Nigger 151-8
  At what we saw. The spring clouds blow [Postcard 159-7
  The clouds foretell a swampy rain. [Fish-Scale 161-6
  The clouds tumultuously bright [MBG 169-4
  Crying among the clouds, enraged [MBG 169-7
  With the undertaker: a voice in the clouds, [MBG 177-8
  In the clouds serene and final, next [MBG 177-14
  Sand heaped in the clouds, giant that fought [MBG 179-7
  And, as you paint, the clouds, [Add 198-13
  Out of the clouds, pomp of the air, [Idiom 201-9
  Could have risen to the clouds, [Weak Mind 212-17
  Occur as they occur. So bluish clouds [Sleight 222-3
  Came bursting from the clouds. So the wind [Sleight 222-7
  The fire eye in the clouds survives the gods. [Sleight 222-12
  With a single sense, though he smells clouds [Arcades 225-21
  More nights, more days, more clouds, more worlds. [Vari 233-22
  He brushed away the thunder, then the clouds, [Landsc 241-11
  Upon by clouds, the ear so magnified [Landsc 242-25
  The clouds becoming braided girls. [Vase 246-14
  Fear never the brute clouds nor winter-stop [Montra 261-22
  Taken with withered weather, crumpled clouds, [News 265-6
  Jumps from the clouds or, from his window, [Hero 280-10
  The slightly brighter sky, the melting clouds, [Motive 288-7
  Men scatter throughout clouds. [Dutch 290-4
  Then clouds, benevolences, distant heads. [EM 317-21
  By a lake, with clouds like lights among great tombs, [EM 325-8
  In a world of ideas. He would not be aware of the clouds, [EM
    325-12
  In a conscious world, the great clouds [Analysis 348-2
  Crystal on crystal until crystal clouds [Pieces 351-4
  Under the white clouds piled and piled [Woman Song 360-10
  The clouds are over the village, the town, [Woman Song 360-13
  There are doubles of this fern in clouds, [Red Fern 365-5
  The trumpet of morning blows in the clouds and through [Cred
    376-10
  But the first idea was not to shape the clouds [NSF 383-17
  In imitation. The clouds preceded us [NSF 383-18
  We are the mimics. Clouds are pedagogues [NSF 384-1
  Brushed up by brushy winds in brushy clouds, [NSF 385-7
  Which pierces clouds and bends on half the world. [NSF 393-15
  Should be cold silver, neither that frothy clouds [NSF 399-6
  To cool their ruddy pulses; the frothy clouds [NSF 399-15
  Are nothing but frothy clouds; the frothy blooms [NSF 399-16
  It is a theatre floating through the clouds, [AA 416-7
  From the clouds in the midst of trembling trees [Puel 456-7
  The imaginative transcripts were like clouds, [NH 479-16
  It may be that they mingle, clouds and men, in the air [NH 479-24
  To have evaded clouds and men leaves him [NH 480-5

The statue of Jove among the boomy clouds. [NH 482-19
Than that of their clouds. These lineaments were the earth, [NH
  484-13
Than the difference that clouds make over a town. [NH 487-7
Shifted the rocks and picked his way among clouds, [PoemMt 512-8
To think away the grass, the trees, the clouds, [Look 517-14
Or melancholy crows as shadowing clouds? [Stan MMO 19-18 P
In which the bliss of clouds is mark of an intended meeting
  [Inelegance 25-15 P
The high clouds will move, [Secret Man 36-11 P
Before the horses, clouds of bronze imposed [Old Woman 43-7 P
On clouds of gold, and green engulfing bronze, [Old Woman 43-8 P
The golden clouds that turned to bronze, the sounds [Old Woman
  44-7 P
Now felt, now known as this. The clouds of bronze [Old Woman
  45-4 P
Whether in-dwelling haughty clouds, frigid [Burnshaw 47-15 P
The foul immovables, came through the clouds, [Greenest 53-12 P
The heart in slattern pinnacles, the clouds, [Duck 61-10 P
His roles, would leave to the clouds the righting, [Stan Hero
  84-25 P
Of clouds that hang lateness on the sea. They become [Role
  93-10 P
See sea-clouds.
CLOUD-STRICKEN. As of insects or cloud-stricken birds, away
  [Sombre 67-11 P
CLOUD-TIP. On every cloud-tip over the heavens, [Letters 107-2 P
CLOUD-TOP. Like evening Venus in a cloud-top. [Three 135-9
CLOUDY! His cloudy drift and planned a colony. [C 36-27
  Their azure has a cloudy edge, their white [C 37-30
  And jig his chits upon a cloudy knee. [C 40-12
  Leaving no room upon his cloudy knee, [C 43-18
  And cloudy constellations, [Venereal 48-13
  Nor visionary south, nor cloudy palm [Sunday 68-21
  Of cloudy silver sprinkles in your gown [Fictive 87-11
  "Statue against a Cloudy Sky" [NE Verses 105-title 10
  Corridors of cloudy thoughts, [Botanist 1 134-16
  This cloudy world, by aid of land and sea, [Vari 233-20
  Is blue, clear, cloudy, high, dark, wide and round; [Extracts
    252-11
  Or the concentration of a cloudy day? [NSF 396-17
CLOUDY-CONJURING. At tossing saucers--cloudy-conjuring sea? [Sea
  Surf 102-8
CLOVEN. This darkened water cloven by sullen swells [Farewell
  118-14
CLOWN. A clown, perhaps, but an aspiring clown. [C 39-24
  Good clown. . . . One thought of Chinese Chocolate [Sea Surf 102-1
  The sun, in clownish yellow, but not a clown, [EM 318-1
  See cloud-clown.
CLOWNISH. Sing in clownish boots [Orangeade 103-7
  The sun, in clownish yellow, but not a clown, [EM 318-1
CLOWNS. This parlor of farcical dames, this clowns' colonnade, this
  kites' pavilion? [Inelegance 26-6 P
CLUMP. The boots of the men clump [Magnifico 19-16
CLUMPED. Clumped carvings, circular, like blunted fans, [Old Woman
  43-16 P
  And clumped stars dangled all the way. [Ulysses 105-12 P
  Through clumped stars dangling all the way. [Presence 106-12 P
CLUSTER. And seraphs cluster on the domes, [Contra I 266-15
CLUSTERED. See pink-clustered.
CLUSTERING. The sovereign clouds came clustering. The conch [Sea
  Surf 102-10
CLUTCH. The clutch of the others. [Thunder 220-8
  In silence upon your bed. You clutch the corner [NSF 384-19
CLUTCHED. As if a blunted player clutched [MBG 182-21
COACH. In a glass coach. [Thirteen 94-14
COAST. See sea-coast.
COASTAL. As the sea has in its coastal clamorings. [Red Kit 31-9 P
COAT. His passion's permit, hang of coat, degree [C 39-18
  Coat half-flare and half galloon; [Orangeade 103-14
  And yet see only one, in his old coat, [NSF 389-5
  In that old coat, those sagging pantaloons, [NSF 389-9
COAXING. A kind of cozening and coaxing sound, [NH 482-8
COAXINGS. We obey the coaxings of our end. [Ulysses 103-30 P
COBBLE. And cobble ten thousand and three [Jersey 210-10
COCHON. Cochon! Master, the grapes are here and now. [Nigger 154-19
COCK. The white cock's tail [Ploughing 20-1
  The white cock's tail [Ploughing 20-17
  But let the rabbit run, the cock declaim. [C 39-32
  The cock crows [Depression 63-7
  Damned universal cock, as if the sun [Bantams 75-16
  His will, yet never ceases, perfect cock, [Bird Claws 82-17
  And the best cock of red feather [Watermelon 89-5
  In the museum of the sky. The cock [MBG 182-18
  Cunning-coo, O, cuckoo cock, [Country 207-2
  Fly low, cock bright, and stop on a bean pole. Let [Cred 377-6
  As when the cock crows on the left and all [NSF 386-10
  Cock bugler, whistle and bugle and stop just short, [NSF 405-15
  They cock small ears, more glistening and pale [Soldat 14-2 P
  See: a-cock; hen-cock; turkey-cock.

COCKADE. Without panache, without cockade, [Thought 185-24
  The blue sun in his red cockade [News 264-7
  His red cockade topped off a parade. [News 264-15
COCKAIGNE. Beginning of a green Cockaigne to be, disliked,
  abandoned, [Inelegance 25-14 P
CUCKATOO. And the green freedom of a cuckatoo [Sunday 66-18
COCK-BIRD. Spring sparkle and the cock-bird shriek. [MBG 182-13
COCK-BIRDS. Falls down, the cock-birds calling at the time. [NSF
  388-8
COCK-CRY. The tips of cock-cry pinked out pastily, [NH 470-13
COCKEREL. The cock-hen crows all day. But cockerel shrieks,
  [Nigger 155-11
  9. The coconut and cockerel in one. [Someone 86-12 A
COCK-HEN. The cock-hen crows all day. But cockerel shrieks, [Nig-
  ger 155-11
COCKLE-SHELL. A cockle-shell, a trivial emblem great [Bship 79-10P
COCK-ROBIN. Cock-robin's at Caracas. [Metamorph 265-18
COCKS. The cocks are crowing and crowing loud, [Fish-Scale 161-2
  When cocks wake, clawing at their beds [Adequacy 244-3
  And who, for that, turn toward the cocks [Adequacy 244-5
  Item: The cocks crow and the birds cry and [Montra 263-13
  No pain (ignoring the cocks that crow us up [EM 314-13
  The heavenly cocks, the bowmen, and the gourds, [Greenest 56-18P
COCK-TOPS. To the cock-tops. [Archi 17-16 P
COCOANUT. On a cocoanut--how many men have copied dew [Dump 202-7
COCONUT. 9. The coconut and cockerel in one. [Someone 86-12 A
COCOONS. "Ghosts as Cocoons" [119-title
COCOS. With squalid cells, unless New York is Cocos [Duck 63-13 P
CODDLING. To the group of Flora Coddling Hecuba? [Archi 17-10 P
CODES. Have inscribed life's do and don't. The commanding codes
  [Recit 86-11 P
COFFEE. Coffee and oranges in a sunny chair, [Sunday 66-17
  And coffee dribble . . . Frost is in the stubble. [Dwarf 208-14
  Fromage and coffee and cognac and no gods. [Greenest 57-29 P
COGNAC. Fromage and coffee and cognac and no gods. [Greenest
  57-29 P
COHANSEY. Under Tinicum or small Cohansey, [New Set 353-5
COHEN. A tiara from Cohen's, this summer sea. [Stan MBG 72-14 P
COHERENCES. (In the pale coherences of moon and mood [Anglais 149-1
COIFFEUR. Coiffeur of haloes, fecund jeweller-- [Eve Angels 137-8
COIFFURES. How explicit the coiffures became, [Ord Women 11-21
  You know the mountainous coiffures of Bath. [Monocle 14-7
COIGN. In radiance from the Atlantic coign, [C 31-32
COIL. There lies the misery, the coldest coil [Choc 298-21
COILED. And against the most coiled thorn, have seized on what
  was ugly [Large 424-3
COILS. Rising from indolent coils. If the statue rose, [Greenest
  54-24 P
COINS. Two coins were lying--dos centavos. [Attempt 370-21
COLD. And have been cold a long time [Snow Man 10-1
  And the cold dresses that they wore, [Ord Women 11-5
  From hearing signboards whimper in cold nights [C 33-2
  And cold in a boreal mistiness of the moon. [C 34-8
  Indifferent to the tepid summer cold, [C 43-2
  Do they believe they range the gusty cold, [Heaven 56-12
  To show how cold she is, and dumb. [Emperor 64-14
  Their pleasure that is all bright-edged and cold; [Tallap 72-9
  And in his heart his disbelief lay cold. [Babies 77-17
  And spouting new orations of the cold. [Pharynx 96-15
  It turned cold and silent. Then [Public Sq 109-9
  From my North of cold whistled in a sepulchral South, [Farewell
  117-14
  To the cold, go on, high ship, go on, plunge on. [Farewell
  118-20
  There was the cold wind and the sound [How Live 126-5
  Cold is our element and winter's air [Sun March 134-5
  Everyone, grows suddenly cold. [Fading 139-7
  And a grand decadence settles down like cold. [Havana 142-12
  It is too cold for work, now, in the fields. [Nigger 151-18
  Bitter eyes, hands hostile and cold. [Chateau 161-10
  The strings are cold on the blue guitar. [MBG 168-22
  And the feeling heavy in cold chords [MBG 169-5
  At a table on which the food is cold? [MBG 173-9
  Cold, a cold porcelain, low and round, [Poems Clim 193-15
  That the water would freeze in cold, [Glass 197-8
  Torn from insipid summer, for the mirror of cold, [Dwarf 208-12
  We are cold, the parrots cried, [Anything B 211-14
  Forehead's cold, spite of the eye [Bagatelles 213-14
  Crowned with the first, cold buds. On these we live, [Cuisine
  228-11
  It is cold to be forever young, [Vari 233-8
  And cold. The moon follows the sun like a French [Vari 234-8
  The glass man, cold and numbered, dewily cries, [Oboe 251-4
  It had been cold since December. Snow fell, first, [Extracts
  255-1
  The cold evening, without any scent or the shade [Extracts
  258-15
  One breathed the cold evening, the deepest inhalation [Extracts
  258-20
  Were contours. Cold was chilling the wide-moving swans. [Contra

II 270-11
  And cold, my element. Death is my [Hero 273-3
  Of arms, the will opposed to cold, fate [Hero 273-12
  In an elemental freedom, sharp and cold. [Choc 297-3
  Fell on him, high and cold, searching for what [Choc 301-21
  The pleasure of his spirit in the cold. [Choc 301-23
  A sun in an almost colorless, cold heaven. [Holiday 312-6
  As the eye closes . . . How cold the vacancy [EM 320-6
  The wild ducks were enveloped. The weather was cold. [Wild 329-3
  The bright obvious stands motionless in cold. [Man Car 351-8
  Winter and spring, cold copulars, embrace [NSF 392-8
  Should be cold silver, neither that frothy clouds [NSF 399-6
  The corals of the dogwood, cold and clear, [NSF 400-1
  Cold, coldly delineating, being real; [NSF 400-2
  The season changes. A cold wind chills the beach. [AA 412-19
  The wet weed sputtered, the fire died down, the cold [Page 422-1
  For him cold's glacial beauty is his fate. [Bad Time 426-15
  She found a helping from the cold, [Celle 438-4
  Cold with an under impotency that they know, [Bouquet 449-9
  But she that he loved turns cold at his light touch. [Pecul
  453-12
  The late, least foyer in a qualm of cold. [Novel 457-15
  Its knowledge cold within one as one's own; [Novel 459-3
  The pulse of the object, the heat of the body grown cold [Study
  I 463-15
  Comes the cold volume of forgotten ghosts, [NH 468-6
  So that this cold, a children's tale of ice, [NH 468-8
  With the inhalations of original cold [NH 481-10
  Of cold and earliness is a daily sense, [NH 481-12
  The cold and earliness and bright origin [NH 481-16
  For this blank cold, this sadness without cause. [Plain 502-14
  It was not the shadow of cloud and cold, [Two Illus 513-4
  To gallant notions on the part of cold. [Quiet 523-6
  In its permanent cold, an illusion so desired [Rock 526-3
  And the brass grew cold [Coroner 29-23 P
  Crying against a need that pressed like cold, [Old Woman 45-29 P
  The marble was imagined in the cold. [Greenest 56-28 P
  Stood on a plain of marble; high and cold; [Woman Had 82-29 P
  The iron settee is cold. [Including 88-15 P
  A refreshment of cold air, cold breath, [Bus 116-6 P
  A perception of cold breath, more revealing than [Bus 116-7 P
  From cold, slightly irised, slightly bedazzled, [Bus 116-10 P
  And old men, who have chosen, and are cold [Ideal 88-12 A
COLDER. Cries up for us and colder than the frost [Anatomy 108-4
  Wetted by blue, colder for white. Not to [NSF 385-8
COLDEST. There lies the misery, the coldest coil [Choc 298-21
  Less real. For the oldest and coldest philosopher, [AA 418-9
  Small bees of spring, sniffing the coldest buds [Duck 65-7 P
COLDLY. Coldly the wind fell upon them [How Live 125-13
  Cold, coldly delineating, being real, [NSF 400-2
COLDNESS. Falls back to coldness, [Reader 147-6
  A coldness in a long, too-constant warmth, [NH 474-20
COLLAPSED. Collapsed. The denouement has to be postponed . . .
  [AA 416-21
  The mass of stone collapsed to marble hulk, [Old Woman 44-23 P
COLLAPSES. The mountain collapses. Chopiniana. [Hero 275-4
COLLATION. He made a singular collation. Thus: [C 37-26
COLLECT. Collect their thoughts together into one, [Extracts 254-7
  Through any exaggeration. From him, we collect. [Great 311-6
  It is in that thought that we collect ourselves, [Final 524-5
COLLECTED. Or air collected in a deep essay, [Choc 297-10
  An age is a manner collected from a queen. [Descrip 340-5
COLLECTING. Like excellence collecting excellence? [Belly 367-1
  As of sections collecting toward the greenest cone. [Someone
  87-21 A
COLLECTIVE. Of what men are. The collective being knew [Choc
  299-22
COLLECTS. So heaven collects its bleating lambs. [Thought 184-10
  While the shaggy top collects itself to do [Sombre 68-26 P
COLLEGE OF HERALDS. Yet in trees round the College of Heralds,
  [Agenda 42-10 P
COLLIDING. A revolution of things colliding. [Nightgown 214-13
  Colliding with deaf-mute churches and optical trains. [Chaos
  357-17
COLLOPS. As if the crude collops came together as one, [NH 466-1
COLLOQUY. "Colloquy with a Polish Aunt" [84-title
COLOGNE. Of her airs, as surely cologne as that she was bone
  [Grotesque 74-6 P
COLONIES. "Nudity in the Colonies" [145-title
  Of colonies, a sense in the changing sense [NH 479-12
COLONISTS. No place in the sense of colonists, no place [Greenest
  58-8 P
COLONIZE. To colonize his polar planterdom [C 40-11
COLONIZER. Effective colonizer sharply stopped [C 44-4
COLONNADE. This parlor of farcical dames, this clowns' colonnade,
  this kites' pavilion? [Inelegance 26-6 P
COLONNADES. Tops the horizon with its colonnades. [Surprises 98-7
  His lantern through colonnades [Public Sq 109-7
COLONY. The Idea of a Colony [C 36-title 4
  His cloudy drift and planned a colony. [C 36-27

Projected a colony that should extend [C 38-12
This present colony of a colony [NH 479-11
COLOR. Yes: but the color of the heavy hemlocks [Domination 8-14
  Came striding like the color of the heavy hemlocks [Domination
    9-18
  Into a savage color he went on. [C 30-29
  The night is of the color [Six Sig 73-16
  Of the color of horn [Cortege 80-2
  And the color, the overcast blue [MBG 169-13
  The color like a thought that grows [MBG 169-19
  Stormer, is the color of a self [Prelude 194-14
  As certainly as night is the color [Prelude 194-15
  Escaped from the truth, the morning is color and mist, [Freed
    204-18
  Women invisible in music and motion and color," [Waldorf 241-8
  And the most distant, single color, about to change, [Extracts
    258-17
  Leader, the creator of bursting color [Hero 274-2
  As color, even the closest to us, is; [Less 328-1
  The day in its color not perpending time, [Pure 332-16
  And feel that her color is a meditation, [Debris 338-12
  Its color, but less as they recede, impinged [Anach 366-10
  And comic color of the rose, in which [NSF 384-4
  Like a momentary color, in which swans [NSF 397-14
  The way a painter of pauvred color paints. [NSF 402-3
  The color of ice and fire and solitude. [AA 413-3
  A season changes color to no end, [AA 416-9
  Took on color, took on shape and the size of things as they are
    [Large 424-8
  Of yellow as first color and of white, [Roses 431-1
  A sudden color on the sea. But it is not [John 437-2
  Of color, the giant of nothingness, each one [Orb 443-21
  In the anonymous color of the universe. [NH 470-22
  The color is almost the color of comedy, [NH 477-10
  A color that moved us with forgetfulness. [Aug 494-8
  The forgetful color of the autumn day [Aug 494-16
  By an access of color, a new and unobserved, slight dithering,
    [Prol 517-2
  A sharing of color and being part of it. [Look 518-16
  A change of color in the plain poet's mind, [Moonlight 532-1
  The child's hair is of the color of the hay in the haystack,
    around which the four black horses stand. [Primordia 8-1 P
  There is the same color in the bellies of frogs, in clays,
    withered reeds, skins, wood, sunlight. [Primordia 8-2 P
  Between the matin air and color, goldenest generating, [Inele-
    gance 25-16 P
  Color and color brightening into one, [Greenest 58-5 P
  Than the color white and high beyond any height [Duck 64-6 P
  Give only their color to the leaves. The trees [Sombre 71-3 P
  Its land-breath to be stifled, its color changed, [Sombre 71-33P
  The earth remains of one color-- [Three 130-15 P
  What the court saw was always of the same color, [Three 131-22 P
  Of the color of blood. [Three 137-4 P
  Of the color of blood . . . [Three 142-1 P
  The color of blood, [Three 142-13 P
  See after-color.
COLORED. And the colored purple of the lazy sea, [Hibiscus 22-17
  In the sunshine placidly, colored by ground [C 41-3
  That rose, or even colored by many waves; [Key W 129-11
  Dressed in his colored robes. [Gray 140-20
  Of the fishes of the sea, the colored [Hero 277-28
  The very pool, his thoughts the colored forms, [Descrip 342-12
  Yet look not at his colored eyes. Give him [NSF 388-13
  And night, colored from distances, central [Owl 433-11
  See centi-colored; dark-colored; geranium-colored; new-colored;
    red-colored; seven-colored; sharply-colored; simple-colored;
    single-colored; sun-colored.
COLOR-FRETS. And more. It may have feathery color-frets, [Spaniard
  35-8 P
COLORINGS. And if we ate the incipient colorings [Rock 526-16
  In colorings harmonious, dewed and dashed [Ulysses 104-3 P
  See elephant-colorings.
COLORLESS. The single-colored, colorless, primitive. [Landsc 242-2
  A sun in an almost colorless, cold heaven. [Holiday 312-6
  The colorless light in which this wreckage lies [Burnshaw 49-25P
COLORS. Arching cloths besprinkled with colors [Plot Giant 6-18
  The colors of the bushes [Domination 8-8
  The colors of their tails [Domination 8-17
  Alas, that they should wear our colors there, [Sunday 69-22
  And lightning colors [Nomad 95-17
  Before the colors deepened and grew small. [Anglais 149-15
  It must create its colors out of itself. [Nigger 158-2
  And pick the acrid colors out, [MBG 166-6
  They are full of the colors of my village [Peaches 224-13
  To spread colors. There was not an idea [Forces 229-6
  Could one say that he sang the colors in the stones, [Horn 230-11
  Of the colors, are tinsel changes, [Scavoir 231-7
  Hoot how the inhuman colors fell [Vase 247-1
  With the half colors of quarter-things, [Motive 288-6
  And the words for them and the colors that they possessed.

[Holiday 312-13
  Of the country colors crowding against it, since [EM 318-23
  All final, colors subjected in revery [Descrip 342-16
  Of incredible colors ex, ex and ex and out? [Liadoff 347-3
  His epi-tones, the colors of the ear, [Liadoff 347-19
  Brightly empowered with like colors, swarmingly, [Myrrh 350-3
  And the circles quicken and crystal colors come [Anach 366-13
  And in these comic colors dangled down, [Lot 371-9
  And mingling of colors at a festival. [Cred 374-20
  Its colors make, the migratory daze, [Bouquet 451-17
  Perhaps, these colors, seen in insight, assume [Bouquet 451-22
  In the movement of the colors of the mind, [NH 466-9
  Obscure, in colors whether of the sun [NH 466-16
  Or, say, the late going colors of that past, [NH 482-1
  Blooming and beaming and voluming colors out. [NH 484-6
  He discovered the colors of the moon [Two Illus 514-13
  There is a connection between the colors, [Primordia 9-17 P
  Because new colors make new things [Abnormal 24-11 P
  Conflicting with the moving colors there [Old Woman 44-25 P
  A winter's noon, in which the colors sprang [Greenest 57-25 P
  And felt and known in the colors in which we live, [Conversat
    109-19 P
  The weak colors, [Three 132-1 P
  On the table or in the colors of the room. [Someone 84-19 A
COLOR-SCARRED. Wildly curvetted, color-scarred, so beaked,
  [Greenest 57-18 P
COLOSSAL. Then the colossal illusion of heaven. Yet still [Landsc
  241-12
  It was part of the colossal sun, [Not Ideas 534-15
  Colossal blacks that leaped across the points [Greenest 53-13 P
COLUMN. Incognito, the column in the desert, [Descrip 343-20
COLUMNS. Loquacious columns by the ructive sea? [C 41-20
  Raise reddest columns. Toll a bell [MBG 170-5
  Shines without fire on columns intercrossed, [Burnshaw 49-12 P
  Because time moves on columns intercrossed [Burnshaw 50-13 P
  That a figure reclining among columns toppled down, [Conversat
    109-7 P
COMA. In a coma of the moon. [Public Sq 108-22
COMB. To comb her dewy hair, a touchless light, [Beginning 427-13
  See honey-comb.
COMBAT. I have finished my combat with the sun; [Joost 46-14
  Combat, compose their droll affair. [MBG 182-11
  Are to combat what his exaltations [Hero 274-16
COMBATTING. Combatting bushmen for a patch of gourds, [Greenest
  56-8 P
COMBED. She would talk a little to herself as she combed her hair,
  [World 521-16
COMBINED. Which is like zithers and tambourines combined: [Mice
  123-8
  The mirror of other nights combined in one. [Sombre 71-10 P
COMBING. Combing. The poem of the act of the mind. [Of Mod 240-22
COMBS. The hives are heavy with the combs. [Contra I 266-13
  Might be enough, as if the golden combs [EM 316-2
COME. For it has come that thus I greet the spring. [Monocle 13-18
  Do you come dripping in your hair from sleep? [Monocle 14-11
  The mules that angels ride come slowly down [Monocle 15-18
  The honey of heaven may or may not come, [Monocle 15-25
  Their curious fates in war, come, celebrate [Monocle 16-15
  To which all birds come sometime in their time. [Monocle 17-5
  Might come in the simplest of speech. [Homunculus 27-2
  A man come out of luminous traversing, [C 30-25
  These bland excursions into time to come, [C 39-9
  Beyond carked Yucatan, he might have come [C 40-10
  You come tormenting, [Venereal 48-2
  Permit that if as ghost I come [W Burgher 61-10
  I come as belle Burgher 61-12
  If her horny feet protrude, they come [Emperor 64-13
  What is divinity if it can come [Sunday 67-13
  Shall our blood fail? Or shall it come to be [Sunday 68-5
  Alone, shall come fulfilment to our dreams [Sunday 69-1
  A feme may come, leaf-green, [Watermelon 89-7
  So, in me, come flinging [Nomad 95-18
  Perhaps our wretched state would soon come right. [Surprises 98-9
  Gives comfort, so that other bodies come, [Anatomy 108-10
  The son and the daughter, who come to the darkness, [Norfolk
    111-18
  She must come now. The grass is in seed and high. [Ghosts 119-11
  Come now. Those to be born have need [Ghosts 119-12
  On dung." Come now, pearled and pasted, bloomy-leafed, [Ghosts
    119-17
  Like an hallucination come to daze [Sun March 134-3
  Made earth come right; a peanut parody [Havana 143-9
  A pear should come to the table popped with juice, [Nigger 155-3
  Is it bad to have come here [Chateau 161-7
  When shall I come to say of the sun, [MBG 168-11
  To come, a wrangling of two dreams. [MBG 183-19
  Here is the bread of time to come, [MBG 183-20
  That's where his hymns come crowding, hero-hymns, [Thought 185-15
  So that one would want to escape, come back [Poems Clim 194-5
  Because it was spring and the birds had to come. [Loaf 200-15

The bouquets come here in the papers. So the sun, [Dump 201-15
And so the moon, both come, and the janitor's poem [Dump 201-16
Come from the strength that is the strength of the sun, [Freed
  205-13
All this, of course, will come to summer soon. [Connois 216-6
But suppose the disorder of truths should ever come [Connois
  216-7
A long time the ocean has come with you, [Hartford 226-7
One had come early to a crisp café. [Forces 229-19
To come to tragic shores and flow, [Vari 233-9
Of these. In these, I come forth outwardly. [Rhythms 246-5
Would come from that return to the subtle centre. [Extracts
  258-21
We live. Thence come the final chants, the chants [Extracts
  259-13
Approaching the feelings or come down from them, [Montra 260-12
To which we come as into bezeled plain, [Montra 262-3
How did we come to think that autumn [Hero 280-26
An end must come in a merciless triumph, [Dutch 291-15
And from what thinking did his radiance come? [Choc 299-7
The bride come jingling, kissed and cupped, or else [Repet
  308-17
And come to nothing. Let the rainy arcs [Repet 310-3
Softly let all true sympathizers come, [EM 317-4
Be near me, come closer, touch my hand, phrases [EM 317-17
Whines in its hole for puppies to come see, [Pure 332-21
Words that come out of us like words within, [Sketch 336-2
Come true, a point in the fire of music where [Descrip 341-9
Were one and swans far off were swans to come. [Descrip 343-10
Come home, wind, he kept crying and crying, [Pieces 351-11
Come home, wind, he said as he climbed the stair-- [Pieces
  351-14
"A Woman Sings a Song for a Soldier Come Home" [360-title
One person should come by chance, [Woman Song 360-17
And the circles quicken and crystal colors come [Anach 366-13
Now in midsummer come and all fools slaughtered [Cred 372-4
The fidgets of remembrance come to this. [Cred 372-10
It is a repetition. The bees come booming [NSF 390-5
And forth the particulars of rapture come. [NSF 392-9
Of spring come to their places in the grape leaves [NSF 399-14
They were love's characters come face to face. [NSF 401-21
Out of nothing to have come on major weather, [NSF 404-3
The real will from its crude compoundings come, [NSF 404-6
It may come tomorrow in the simplest word, [AA 420-1
It might come bearing, out of chaos, kin [Page 422-27
Where luminous agitations come to rest, [Owl 433-12
Presence is not the woman, come upon, [John 437-7
"Our Stars Come from Ireland" [454-title
Of his self, come at upon wide delvings of wings. [NH 475-24
Being part of everything come together as one. [NH 482-11
Will come stamping here, the ruler of less than men, [Aug 495-22
We had come to an end of the imagination, [Plain 502-11
Of a sort, silence of a rat come out to see, [Plain 503-5
Come back to see a certain house. [Vacancy 511-11
And old voice cried out, "Come!" [Phases 6-2 P
Come swelling, when, regardless of my end, [Soldat 14-15 P
And how shall those come vested that come there? [Archi 17-6 P
No chafferer, may come [Archi 18-13 P
The time will come for these children, seated before their long
  black instruments, to strike the themes of love-- [Piano 21-16P
She needs will come consolingly. Alas, [Spaniard 35-3 P
And yet the damned thing doesn't come right. [Agenda 41-18 P
Come, all celestial paramours, [Burnshaw 47-14 P
Into a hopeful waste to come. There even [Burnshaw 49-24 P
Yet were not bright, came shining as things come [Burnshaw 51-25P
Itself, beyond the utmost increase come [Greenest 53-30 P
The angels come, armed, gloriously to slay [Greenest 55-28 P
Of April here and May to come. Champagne [Greenest 58-24 P
To April here and May to come. Why think, [Greenest 58-29 P
The leaping bodies, come from the truculent hand, [Duck 64-15 P
Of a time to come--A shade of horror turns [Duck 65-8 P
Come, baffling discontent. These, too, must be [Sombre 69-19 P
And memory may itself be time to come [Sombre 70-11 P
The ideas that come to it with a sense of speech. [Woman Had
  82-22 P
That the choice should come on them so early. [Stan Hero 83-16 P
Come to us every day. And yet they are [Recit 87-28 P
The words of winter in which these two will come together, [Sick
  90-16 P
Like the chromatic calendar of time to come. [Theatre 91-6 P
That could come in a slight lurching of the scene, [Nuns 92-10 P
The father does not come to adorn the chant. [Role 93-6 P
Spring's bright paradise has come to this. [Fare Guit 98-16 P
That place, and it seems to come to that; [Ulysses 99-19 P
And the right to be are one. We come [Ulysses 101-19 P
To knowledge when we come to life. [Ulysses 101-20 P
Will come. His mind presents the world [Ulysses 102-20 P
The worse end they come to; [Three 137-17 P
2. Out of their bottle the green genii come. [Someone 86-5 A
See new-come.

COMEDIAN. "The Comedian as the Letter C" [27-title
  Of a comedian, this critique; [Crude 305-11
COMEDIANS. Make hue among the dark comedians, [Heaven 56-21
COMEDIES. Light's comedies, dark's tragedies, [Ulysses 102-28 P
COMEDY. The darkened ghosts of our old comedy? [Heaven 56-11
  The comedy of hollow sounds derives [Nigger 154-4
  Men turning into things, as comedy, [NH 470-5
  The color is almost the color of comedy, [NH 477-10
  With tragedy or comedy? [Demoiselle 23-13 P
COMES. When this yokel comes maundering, [Plot Giant 6-11
  Of what, like skulls, comes rotting back to ground. [Monocle
    14-19
  But that of earth both comes and goes at once. [Monocle 15-26
  It comes, it blooms, it bears its fruit and dies. [Monocle 16-3
  Of music, as it comes to unison, [C 43-12
  The relation comes, benignly, to its end? [C 46-12
  And say how it comes that you see [Lilacs 49-8
  Who will embrace her before summer comes. [Lilacs 49-15
  Or thing. . . . Now day-break comes . . . [Canna 55-6
  It comes about that the drifting of these curtains [Curtains 62-1
  But no queen comes [Depression 63-17
  Our nature is her nature. Hence it comes, [Anatomy 107-16
  The truth is that there comes a time [Sad Gay 121-8
  There comes a time when the waltz [Sad Gay 121-11
  Have I except it comes from the sun? [Adieu 128-10
  And the sublime comes down [Am Sub 131-7
  Gleam sharply as the sun comes up. [Botanist 2 135-17
  Comes through boughs that lie in wait. [Brave 138-8
  That brave man comes up [Brave 138-19
  The chrysanthemums' astringent fragrance comes [Nigger 157-1
  The wind-gloss. Or as daylight comes, [MBG 175-2
  When spring comes and the skeletons of the hunters [Parochial
    191-19
  That's not by chance. It comes to this: [Prelude 195-9
  Is the lion that comes down to drink. There [Glass 197-13
  When light comes down to wet his frothy jaws [Glass 197-16
  Comes up as the sun, bull fire, [Add 198-20
  Everything is shed; and the moon comes up as the moon [Dump
    202-22
  Whether it comes directly or from the sun. [Freed 205-14
  Then there is nothing to think of. It comes of itself; [Rabbit K
    209-13
  Should play in the trees when morning comes. [Nightgown 214-16
  On top. Hurroo, the man-boat comes, [Vari 235-17
  Everything comes to him [Yellow 237-1
  But he came back as one comes back from the sun [Yellow 237-7
  And weeps on his breast, though he never comes. [Rhythms 245-17
  After the final no there comes a yes [Beard 247-9
  Comes close to the prisoner's ear, becomes a throat [Montra 261-2
  From which the chant comes close upon the ear, [Montra 261-5
  Comes from the beating of the locust's wings, [Phenom 286-4
  Men came as the sun comes, early children [Dutch 291-23
  To anyone that comes--panic, because [EM 320-19
  That comes here in the solar chariot, [Pure 331-17
  The sun comes up like news from Africa. [Feo 334-12
  In the golden vacancy she came, and comes, [Descrip 339-13
  Before it comes, the just anticipation [Descrip 344-12
  The shadow of an external world comes near. [Myrrh 350-12
  To the unstated theme each variation comes . . . [Think 357-1
  It comes to this and the imagination's life. [Cred 372-13
  Who comes and goes and comes and goes all day. [NSF 381-22
  The fragrance of the magnolias comes close, [NSF 385-17
  At which a kind of Swiss perfection comes [NSF 386-12
  The origin of the major man. He comes, [NSF 387-24
  As when the sun comes rising, when the sea [NSF 398-23
  The way wine comes at a table in a wood. [NSF 405-24
  So summer comes in the end to these few stains [Beginning 427-10
  Now that they know, because they know. One comes [Bouquet 449-10
  The green bouquet comes from the place of the duck. [Bouquet
    450-1
  Comes from a great distance and is heard. [Our Stars 455-12
  In the weed of summer comes this green sprout why. [Questions
    462-4
  So lewd spring comes from winter's chastity. [NH 468-4
  Comes the cold volume of forgotten ghosts, [NH 468-6
  For what he sees, it comes in the end to that: [NH 475-12
  Not quite. It comes to the point and at the point, [NH 477-11
  When day comes, fire-foams in the motions of the sea, [NH 488-12
  That comes from ourselves, neither from knowing [Aug 495-9
  A welcome at the door to which no one comes? [Angel 496-6
  That comes and goes in silences of its own. [Look 518-22
  The spirit comes from the body of the world, [Look 519-7
  Of what one sees, the purpose that comes first, [Moonlight 531-7
  Before one comes to the first black cataracts [R Conn 533-5
  It is enough she comes upon the eye. [Stan MMO 19-8 P
  When morning comes [Secret Man 36-10 P
  But change composes, too, and chaos comes [Burnshaw 51-1 P
  Day came upon the spirit as life comes [Duck 61-5 P
  And deep winds flooded you; for these, day comes, [Duck 61-6 P
  Suppose, instead of failing, it never comes, [Duck 63-30 P

Which, by its repetition, comes to bear [Duck 65-15 P
Say that the American moon comes up [Memo 89-11 P
Comes to this thunder of light [Fare Guit 98-20 P
Here comes our black man. [Three 135-6 P
COMETS. Enjoys his comets. [Analysis 349-12
COMFORT. Gives comfort, so that other bodies come, [Anatomy 108-10
Notes for his comfort that he may repeat [Nigger 155-21
And this must comfort the heart's core against [Cred 372-15
To where our comfort was; [Phases 4-3 P
What sound could comfort away the sudden sense? [Old Woman
    44-16 P
The deep comfort of the world and fate. [Ulysses 100-4 P
COMFORTABLE. And on a comfortable sofa dreamed. [Cuban 65-3
COMFORTED. Themselves transposed, muted and comforted [NH 467-24
COMFORTERS. Confiders and comforters and lofty kin [Choc 300-10
COMFORTS. Shall she not find in comforts of the sun, [Sunday 67-15
COMIC. To think of man the abstraction, the comic sum. [Nigger
    156-6
Are comic trash, the ears are dirt, [Arcades 225-18
And nothing is left but comic ugliness [EM 320-21
And in these comic colors dangled down, [Lot 371-9
And comic color of the rose, in which [NSF 384-4
Neither of comic nor tragic but of commonplace. [NH 478-3
A comic infanta among the tragic drapings, [Slug 522-12
COMING. And sounds of music coming to accord [C 45-26
Whose coming may give revel [Watermelon 89-8
Brings voices as of lions coming down. [Sun March 134-6
By her coming became a freedom of the two, [AA 419-17
Coming together in a sense in which we are poised, [NH 466-11
We keep coming back and coming back [NH 471-10
The coming on of feasts and the habits of saints, [NH 472-2
It is a coming on and a coming forth. [NH 487-19
The way some first thing coming into Northern trees [Prol 517-6
She wanted nothing he could not bring her by coming alone.
    [World 521-7
Never forgetting him that kept coming constantly so near.
    [World 521-18
The sun was coming from outside. [Not Ideas 534-12
Coming from the East, forcing itself to the West, [Bship 80-11 P
Without the forfeit scholar coming in, [Someone 85-4 A
COMMAND. The wind will command them with invincible sound. [AA
    414-3
In mid-Atlantic, bellowing, to command, [Bship 78-13 P
COMMANDERS. Either trumpets or drums, the commanders mute, the
    arms [Martial 238-1
COMMANDING. Have inscribed life's do and don't. The commanding
    codes [Recit 86-11 P
COMMANDS. Commands the armies; the relentless arm, [Soldat 14-11 P
COMME. Comme Dieu Dispense de Graces [Soldat 13-title 5 P
COMMENCING. Of sneers, the fugues commencing at the toes [Extracts
    253-21
COMMEND. Do I commend myself to leafy things [Stan MMO 19-17 P
COMMINGLE. Commingle, not like the commingling of sun and moon
    [Burnshaw 50-2 P
COMMINGLED. Commingled souvenirs and prophecies. [C 37-25
COMMINGLING. Until our blood, commingling, virginal, [Sunday 68-2
Commingle, not like the commingling of sun and moon [Burnshaw
    50-2 P
COMMISERABLE. In yours, master and commiserable man, [Rome 509-16
COMMODIOUS. The catalogue is too commodious. [Cats 367-20
Her dress, the carefulest, commodious weave [Beginning 428-4
It is a choice of the commodious adjective [NH 475-11
COMMON. By apparition, plain and common things, [C 46-7
Thus, on the basis of the common drudge, [Polish Aunt 84-8
Disclosed in common forms. Set up [Prelude 195-17
"The Common Life" [221-title
Us. Good chemistry, good common man, what [Hero 273-16
The common man is the common hero. [Hero 275-5
The common hero is the hero. [Hero 275-6
Imprimatur. But then there's common fortune, [Hero 275-7
And common fortune, induced by nothing, [Hero 275-11
In the will of what is common to all men, [Dutch 291-18
Might call the common self, interior fons. [Choc 301-12
They had known that there was not even a common speech, [Holiday
    312-7
Palabra of a common man who did not exist. [Holiday 312-8
It seems as if the honey of common summer [EM 316-1
Running in the rises of common speech, [Sketch 336-5
They sang of summer in the common fields. [Cred 376-5
That is the common, the bravest fundament, [NSF 398-12
Ruffling its common reflections, thought-like Monadnocks. [Cata
    424-14
Held fast tenaciously in common earth [NH 468-24
Common Soldier [Soldat 11-title 1 P
The common grass is green. [Abnormal 24-4 P
And there the common grass is never seen. [Abnormal 24-8 P
It lost the common shape of night and came [Old Woman 45-16 P
There it would be of the mode of common dreams, [Greenest 57-9 P
Fatal Ananke is the common god. [Greenest 59-1 P
It is the common man against evil, [Stan Hero 84-15 P

The one thing common to all life, the human [Conversat 109-1 P
COMMONAL. Though an heroic part, of the commonal, [NSF 388-22
The major abstraction is the commonal, [NSF 388-23
COMMONNESS. It is the third commonness with light and air, [R Conn
    533-16
COMMONPLACE. In any commonplace the sought-for aid. [C 30-23
The more than human commonplace of blood, [Descrip 341-3
As well, not merely as to the commonplace [NH 470-10
Neither of comic nor tragic but of commonplace. [NH 478-3
The commonplace became a rumpling of blazons. [NH 483-22
A name and privilege over the ordinary of his commonplace--
    [Prol 517-4
Shall tuft the commonplace. [Archi 17-19 P
COMMON-PLACE. I mark the virtue of the common-place. [Soldat 11-6P
COMMON-PLACES. Of less neatly measured common-places. [Hero 275-18
The common-places of which it formed a part [Greenest 57-5 P
COMMUNAL. A mot into a dictum, communal, [Spaniard 34-19 P
COMMUNE. The thinker knows. The gunman of the commune [Bship
    80-16 P
Kills the commune. [Bship 80-17 P
COMMUNICANTS. White houses in villages, black communicants--
    [Cats 367-19
COMMUNICATE. That would form themselves, in time, and communicate
    [EM 314-21
COMMUNICATION. Say, a flippant communication under the moon.
    [AA 418-3
Of communication. It would be enough [Ulti 430-4
COMMUNICATIONS. Words, lines, not meanings, not communications,
    [NH 465-12
"Communications of Meaning" [75-title 3 P
COMMUNION. The eye believes and its communion takes. [Extracts
    253-4
And its communion take. And now of that. [Extracts 253-6
Of this tabernacle, this communion, [Hero 278-17
COMMUNITY. Then, fear a drastic community evolved [Burnshaw 51-6 P
COMPACT. Compact in invincible foils, from reason, [NSF 388-1
The whole, the essential compact of the parts, [Orb 442-7
COMPANIES. For companies of voices moving there, [NSF 398-16
COMPANION. And tell the divine ingénue, your companion, [Lilacs
    48-20
The man and his companion stopped [How Live 125-11
That dark companion left him unconsoled [Anglais 148-17
The companion in nothingness, [Jumbo 269-10
Ours, like a familiar companion. [Hero 276-4
In my presence, the companion of presences [Choc 302-3
Follow after, O my companion, my fellow, my self, [NSF 392-23
Companion to his self for her, which she imagined, [World 521-2
The luminous companion, the hand, [Ulysses 100-9 P
COMPANIONS. However tarnished, companions out of the past,
    [Burnshaw 50-10 P
COMPANY. Was he to company vastest things defunct [C 41-12
One joins him there for company, [Possum 294-17
Of nakedness, in the company of the sun, [Lot 371-19
Its actors approaching, in company, in their masks. [AA 414-21
Look at this present throne. What company, [AA 415-2
Of larger company than one. Therefore, [Good Bad 33-11 P
COMPARATIVE. Comparative. The assassin discloses himself, [EM
    324-19
COMPARE. The false roses--Compare the silent rose of the sun
    [Extracts 252-4
COMPARED. The two things compared their tight resemblances: [Past
    Nun 379-2
The metaphor stirred his fear. The object with which he was
    compared [Prol 516-10
COMPASS. Into the compass and curriculum [Monocle 15-15
I was myself the compass of that sea: [Hoon 65-15
Placed, so, beyond the compass of change, [MBG 168-1
COMPASSION. That whispered to the sun's compassion, made [C 28-26
COMPELLED. Compelled thereto by an innate music. [Hero 277-18
COMPELLING. An east in their compelling westwardness, [Our Stars
    155-20
COMPENDIA. Must be the crux for our compendia. [Havana 143-24
COMPENDIUM. Autumn's compendium, strident in itself [C 45-23
COMPETENT. This urgent, competent, serener myth [Havana 143-19
COMPILATION. Compilation of the effects [Primordia 9-10 P
COMPLACENCIES. Complacencies of the peignoir, and late [Sunday
    66-16
COMPLACENT. But to strip off the complacent trifles, [Gigan 289-8
COMPLAIN. This man to complain to the grocer [Soldat 12-13 P
Complain and prophesy, in their complaints, [Burnshaw 48-18 P
COMPLAINTS. Of the North have earned this crumb by their com-
    plaints. [NE Verses 106-2
Complain and prophesy, in their complaints, [Burnshaw 48-18 P
COMPLAISANCE. With bland complaisance on pale parasols, [C 29-19
COMPLETE. Say even that this complete simplicity [Poems Clim
    193-17
A sunny day's complete Poussiniana [Poem Morn 219-1
The organic consolation, the complete [Repet 309-10
That we do not need to understand, complete [Descrip 341-13
Complete in a completed scene, speaking [Cred 378-9

Venerable and articulate and complete. [NSF 383-21
Complete, because at the middle, if only in sense, [Ulti 430-8
That it is complete, that it is an end, [Pecul 453-14
But not for him. His question is complete. [Questions 462-12
His question is complete because it contains [Questions 462-16
Where he would be complete in an unexplained completion: [Poem
    Mt 512-10
Complete in bronze on enormous pedestals. [Duck 64-4 P
Complete in wind-sucked poverty. [Stan MBG 73-10 P
COMPLETED. Complete in a completed scene, speaking [Cred 378-9
In a moving contour, a change not quite completed? [NSF 406-9
COMPLETELY. All approaches gone, being completely there, [Waldorf
    240-25
The eye, completely anonymous, [Couch 295-5
Completely physical in a physical world. [EM 325-26
"A Completely New Set of Objects" [352-title
But that which destroys it completely by this light [Page 422-16
Each person completely touches us [Leben 505-7
That is completely waste, that moves from waste [Burnshaw 49-22P
Response, the completely answering voice, [Ulysses 100-11 P
Under the oak trees, completely released. [Sol Oaks 111-10 P
COMPLETEST. Uplifting the completest rhetoric [Extracts
COMPLETING. A clearing, a detecting, a completing, [Choc 301-11
And observing is completing and we are content, [Descrip 341-11
Enormous, in a completing of his truth. [Roses 431-3
COMPLETION. Where he would be complete in an unexplained comple-
    tion: [Poem Mt 512-10
COMPLEX. Of spiced and weathery rouges, should complex [C 14-8
A complex of emotions falls apart, [Cred 377-11
And polished beast, this complex falls apart. [Cred 377-16
Another complex of other emotions, not [Cred 377-18
COMPLEXITIES. The complexities of the world, when apprehended,
    [Papini 447-16
COMPLICATE. The complicate, the amassing harmony. [NSF 403-15
COMPLICATED. Whose green mind bulges with complicated hues:
    [Choc 300-5
The tempo, in short, of this complicated shift, [Duck 65-31 P
COMPLICATION. To the complication, is good, is a good. [Lack
    303-20
He lacks this venerable complication. [Great 311-10
COMPLICATIONS. An object the sum of its complications, seen
    [Someone 87-10 A
COMPLY. And pallid bits, that tend to comply with blue, [Bouquet
    452-2
COMPOSE. Combat, compose their droll affair. [MBG 182-11
"This image, this love, I compose myself [Rhythms 246-4
We compose these propositions, torn by dreams, [Men Made 356-2
A subject for Puvis. He would compose [Anach 366-4
Compose us in a kind of eulogy. [Extraord 369-15
Of this idea nor for that mind compose [NSF 381-2
Can we compose a castle-fortress-home, [NSF 386-22
That these bethous compose a heavenly gong. [NSF 394-6
COMPOSED. And is as excellent, in that it is composed [Monocle
    14-18
But the quotidian composed as his, [C 42-25
Composed of evenings like cracked shutters flung [C 42-30
The soul, he said, is composed [Men 1000 51-7
To what had been so long composed. [Poems Clim 194-6
Composed of curves [Pears 196-6
The mass of meaning becomes composed again. [Extracts 256-3
Her hand composed him and composed the tree. [Hand 271-9
Her hand composed him like a hand appeared, [Hand 271-13
Of a chaos composed in more than order, [Dutch 293-9
Composed, appropriate to the incomplete, [Repet 309-13
Reality, composed thereof. They are [Paisant 335-5
Composed of a sight indifferent to the eye, [Descrip 343-22
Which is not of our lives composed . . . [Imago 439-18
Flame, sound, fury composed . . . Hear what he says, [Puel
    456-17
The shadowless moon wholly composed of shade, [Study II 464-13
Of what is this house composed if not of the sun, [NH 465-9
Suppose these houses are composed of ourselves, [NH 466-4
In a permanence composed of impermanence, [NH 472-14
The serious reflection is composed [NH 478-2
There was a willingness not yet composed, [NH 483-3
She has composed, so long, a self with which to welcome him,
    [World 521-1
In venting lacerations. So composed, [Spaniard 35-18 P
And because the temple is never quite composed, [Burnshaw 50-14P
And the portent end in night, composed, before [Sombre 71-5 P
And the painted hairs that composed her hair. [Grotesque 74-4 P
See well-composed.
COMPOSER. And, according, to the composer, this butcher, [Thunder
    220-9
COMPOSES. On This Beautiful World Of Ours composes himself [Ulti
    429-10
But change composes, too, and chaos comes [Burnshaw 51-1 P
COMPOSING. A composing of senses of the guitar. [MBG 168-8
Is a worm composing on a straw. [MBG 174-14
A composing as the body tires, a stop [NSF 386-4

COMPOSITE. Which in a composite season, now unknown, [John 437-18
COMPOSITES. A right red with its composites glutted full, [Bouquet
    452-3
COMPOSITION. To the central composition, [Botanist 1 135-4
What composition is there in all this: [Botanist 1 135-6
The poem of the composition of the whole, [Orb 442-2
The composition of blue sea and of green, [Orb 442-3
The central of the composition, in which [Duck 64-12 P
The Johnsonian composition, abstract man, [Duck 65-13 P
Undescribed composition of the sugar-cane, [Someone 86-20 A
COMPOSURE. The unique composure, harshest streakings joined [Owl
    433-14
COMPOUND. To compound the imagination's Latin with [NSF 397-8
COMPOUNDED. The evilly compounded, vital I [Poems Clim 193-19
With an understanding compounded by death [Lack 303-12
Compounded of dear relation, spoken twice, [EM 317-18
With nothing else compounded, carried full, [Cred 374-11
Compounded and compounded, life by life, [Owl 436-1
COMPOUNDER. Ethereal compounder, pater patriae, [Duck 64-28 P
COMPOUNDINGS. The real will from its crude compoundings come,
    [NSF 404-6
COMPREHENSIVE. A comprehensive island hemisphere. [C 38-14
COMPRESSED. It appears to be what there is of life compressed
    [Bship 79-1 P
COMPRISE. So that one lives all the lives that comprise it [Yellow
    236-20
Mere repetitions. These things at least comprise [NSF 405-17
COMPROMISE. A world agrees, thought's compromise, resolved [Ideal
    89-7 A
COMRADE. To walk another room . . . Monsieur and comrade, [NSF
    407-17
CONCEAL. Conceal yourself or disclose [Venereal 48-14
Possess in his heart, conceal and nothing known, [NSF 395-6
That power to conceal they had as men, [NH 470-8
That we conceal? A passion to fling the cloak, [Sombre 71-26 P
CONCEALED. It was as if the solitude concealed [C 42-7
Concealed imaginings. [Peter 90-18
If that remains concealed, what does the bottom matter? [Nudity
    Cap 145-11
Stripped one of all one's torments, concealed [Poems Clim 193-18
Concealed creator. One walks easily [Ccuch 296-3
Concealed in glittering grass, dank reptile skins. [Duck 65-11 P
CONCEALS. Conceals herself. [Six Sig 73-21
Is like your port which conceals [Demoiselle 23-4 P
CONCEDE. As every man in Sweden will concede, [Lions 125-3
CONCEIT. Most venerable heart, the lustiest conceit [Monocle 16-17
CONCEITS. We are conceived in your conceits. [Prelude 195-21
CONCEIVE. Makes me conceive how dark I have become, [Sun March
    133-14
From the sea, conceive for the courts [Prelude 195-15
Can we conceive of him as rescuing less, [EM 316-20
Conceive that while you dance the statue falls, [Burnshaw 51-30P
In the soil and rest. Conceive that marble men [Burnshaw 52-1 P
At least, conceive what these hands from Sweden mean, [Duck
    60-21 P
CONCEIVED. Thus he conceived his voyaging to be [C 35-6
We are conceived in your conceits. [Prelude 195-21
It would have been better, the time conceived, [Thunder 220-13
That he be not conceived, being real. [Hero 279-14
A largeness lived and not conceived, a space [Choc 301-12
In humanity has not conceived of a race [EM 325-25
Or say from that which was conceived to that [Two V 354-16
Thereon the learning of the man conceived [NSF 402-23
And Eden conceived on Morningside, [Ulysses 101-7 A
CONCEIVES. As the night conceives the sea-sounds in silence,
    [Two Figures 86-7
Each matters only in that which it conceives. [Past Nun 379-3
CONCEIVING. Conceiving words, [Two Figures 86-6
Conceiving from its perfect plenitude, [Havana 143-12
A while, conceiving his passage as into a time [Owl 432-23
CONCENTRATION. Or the concentration of a cloudy day? [NSF 396-17
CONCENTRED. Three times the concentred self takes hold, three
    times [Cred 376-9
The thrice concentred self, having possessed [Cred 376-10
CONCENTRIC. Concentric circles of shadows, motionless [EM 319-7
Concentric bosh. To their tabernacles, then, [Greenest 56-21 P
In an age of concentric mobs would any sphere [Duck 63-25 P
CONCENTRUM. At the centre on the horizon, concentrum, grave
    [Orb 443-13
CONCEPT. Book of a concept only possible [Descrip 345-2
Without beginning or the concept of an end. [Grotesque 76-24 P
CONCEPTION. It is a part of his conception, [Hero 279-13
The conception sparkling in still obstinate thought. [Papini
    448-4
CONCEPTIONS. We were the appropriate conceptions, less [Lot 371-13
Conceptions of new mornings of new worlds, [NH 470-12
CONCERN. Sealed pensive purple under its concern. [C 40-20
CONCERNED. Men and the affairs of men seldom concerned [Nigger
    156-4
CONCERNING. "Concerning the Thunderstorms of Yucatan" [C 30-title 2

Concerning the nature of things as they are. [MBG 177-20
It has to content the reason concerning war, [Bottle 239-5
Concerning an immaculate imagery. [Oboe 250-14
It is a busy cry, concerning someone else. [Course 96-14 P
CONCERNS. But nakedness, woolen massa, concerns an innermost atom.
     [Nudity Cap 145-10
But that concerns the secondary characters. [EM 324-1
Itself, until, at last, the cry concerns no one at all. [Course
     97-3 P
CONCERT. Which one recalls at a concert or in a café. [Nigger
     154-3
In concert with the eagle's valiance. [Spaniard 35-12 P
CONCERTINA. Must be played on the concertina. [Grotesque 76-16 P
To the sound of the concertina, [Grotesque 77-9 P
CONCERTINAS. And play concertinas all night. [Jersey 210-19
CONCERTO. The unclouded concerto . . . [Mozart 132-6
"Concerto for Airplane and Pianoforte," [Duck 62-29 P
CONCH. The sovereign clouds came clustering. The conch [Sea Surf
     102-10
CONCILIATIONS. Like human conciliations, more like [Vase 247-3
CONCLUDING. Concluding fadedly, if as a man [C 46-2
CONCLUSIONS. The premiss from which all things were conclusions,
     [Contra II 270-16
CONCOCT. Was the sun concoct for angels or for men? [Eve Angels 137-9
CONCOCTED. Crispin concocted doctrine from the rout. [C 45-11
CONCORD. To Concord, at the edge of things, was this: [Look 517-13
CONCOURSE. Concourse of planetary originals, [Someone 84-2 A
CONCUBINE. The fretful concubine [Anything B 211-2
The bondage of the Stygian concubine, [Infernale 25-5 P
CONCUPISCENT. In kitchen cups concupiscent curds. [Emperor 64-3
CONCUSSION. Ubiquitous concussion, slap and sigh, [C 28-20
CONDIGN. Less prickly and much more condign than that [C 42-15
CONDONED. Confined him, while it cosseted, condoned, [C 40-22
CONDUCTS. This light conducts [Homunculus 26-5
CONE. As of sections collecting toward the greenest cone. [Someone
     87-21 A
CONE. See sugar-cone.
CONED. See dim-coned.
CONES. Cones, waving lines, ellipses-- [Six Sig 75-11
In the centre of its cones, the resplendent flights [Cats 367-17
Angels tiptoe upon the snowy cones [Greenest 56-1 P
CONFECT. Choosing his element from droll confect [C 40-7
It is of him, ephebe, to make, to confect [NSF 389-10
That vast confect of telegrams, [Mandolin 29-7 P
Or a confect of leafy faces in a tree-- [Art Pop 113-2 P
CONFECTED. A ship that rolls on a confected ocean, [EM 322-23
CONFESSING. Confessing the taciturn and yet indifferent, [Wom Sun
     145-14
CONFIDENT. And that confident one, Marie, the wearer of cheap
     stones, who will have grown still and restless; [Piano 22-5 P
CONFIDERS. Confiders and comforters and lofty kin. [Choc 300-10
CONFIDES. The artist. But one confides in what has no [Couch 296-2
CONFINE. They confine themselves [Six Sig 75-8
The little confine soon unconfined [Ulysses 103-20 P
CONFINED. Confined him, while it cosseted, condoned, [C 40-22
Confined by what they see, [Prejudice 368-14
CONFLICT. There is a conflict, there is a resistance involved;
     [Course 96-16 P
CONFLICTING. Conflicting with the moving colors there [Old Woman
     44-25 P
CONFORMER. The stubborn eye, of the conformer who conforms [Duck
     64-16 P
CONFORMS. The stubborn eye, of the conformer who conforms [Duck
     64-16 P
CONFOUNDS. Confounds all opposites and spins a sphere [Duck 63-20P
CONFRONT. To confront the mockers, [Am Sub 130-18
Confront you, hoo-ing the slick trombones, [MBG 170-16
To confront with plainest eye the changes, [Gigan 289-11
CONFRONTED. Confronted Ozymandias. She went [NSF 395-17
CONFRONTING. Crispin confronting it, a vocable thing, [C 29-25
CONFRONTS. Gloomily, the journalist confronts [Bus 116-2 P
CONFUSE. The words of things entangle and confuse. [C 41-1
CONFUSED. Confused illuminations and sonorities, [NH 466-19
CONFUSION. The torments of confusion. [Homunculus 27-6
Confusion solved, as in a refrain [MBG 177-18
In a confusion on bed and books, a portent [Rome 509-3
The confusion of men's voices, intricate [Greenest 54-9 P
CONFUSIONS. He shares the confusions of intelligence.[Papini 446-12
CONGENIAL. And covered him and his congenial sleep. [C 42-8
And lit the snow to a light congenial [Choc 297-1
Congenial mannequins, alert to please, [Study II 464-11
CONGREGATION. Read to the congregation, for today [AA 420-16
CONJUGAL. Two beasts. But of the same kind--two conjugal beasts.
     [Jouga 337-5
CONJUGATION. Of praise, a conjugation done by choirs. [NSF 402-15
CONJUNCTION. This conjunction of mountains and sea and our lands--
     [Grapes 110-10
CONJURATION. Of loyal conjuration trumped. The wind [Sea Surf
     102-11
CONJURED. On his gold horse striding, like a conjured beast,

[Antag 426-1
CONJURING. See cloudy-conjuring.
CONNAISSANCE. To make believe a starry connaissance. [Monocle 13-22
CONNECTICUT. He rode over Connecticut [Thirteen 94-13
On the tables of Connecticut, and they are; [Connois 215-6
"The River of Rivers in Connecticut" [533-title
In Connecticut, we never lived in a time [Myth 118-8 P
CONNECTION. There is a connection between the colors, [Primordia
     9-17 P
CONNOISSEUR. This connoisseur of elemental fate, [C 32-30
The taste of even a country connoisseur. [Nigger 157-16
"Connoisseur of Chaos" [215-title
CONNOISSEURS. That revolution takes for connoisseurs: [Sombre 70-9P
CONSCIENCE. The conscience is converted into palms, [High-Toned
     59-4
You rest intact in conscience and intact [Good Bad 33-9 P
CONSCIENTIOUS. The sensitive and conscientious schemes [Soldat
     13-9 P
CONSCIOUS. Too conscious of too many things at one, [Hand 271-2
Too conscious of too many things at once, [Hand 271-7
He was too conscious of too many things [Hand 271-15
In the conscious world, the great clouds [Analysis 348-2
Was like the conscious being of the book. [House Q 358-9
CONSCIOUSNESS. A consciousness from solitude, inhaled [Choc 298-8
Pretend they are shapes of another consciousness? [Feo 334-8
Toward a consciousness of red and white as one, [Bouquet 450-9
And another in a fantastic consciousness, [Rock 525-14
And thinks about it without consciousness, [Sol Oaks 111-9 P
CONSEQUENCE. An ancestral theme or as a consequence [AA 412-7
And yet this effect is a consequence of the way [Roses 430-16
CONSIDER. Consider the odd morphology of regret. [Nigger 154-10
Consider how the speechless, invisible gods [Montra 262-13
By the lake at Geneva and consider logic: [EM 325-3
Consider that I had asked [Desire 85-14 P
CONSIDERED. "Of Heaven Considered as a Tomb" [56-title
Contrasting our two names, considered speech. [Phenom 287-16
CONSIDERS. Now the mind lays by its trouble and considers. [Cred
     372-9
CONSIST. The fowl of Venus may consist of both [Spaniard 35-7 P
CONSISTS. But when I walk I see that it consists of three or four
     hills and a cloud. [Of Surface 57-2
Castratos of moon-mash--Life consists [Men Made 355-17
CONSOLATION. In chaos and his song is a consolation. [Extracts
     256-9
The organic consolation, the complete [Repet 309-10
CONSOLATIONS. Nor stand there making orotund consolations.
     [Papini 446-11
The consolations of space are nameless things. [NH 482-16
CONSOLE. The final elegance, not to console [NSF 389-11
CONSOLINGLY. She needs will come consolingly. Alas, [Spaniard 35-3P
CONSONANTS. Clawed on the ear these consonants? [Jumbo 269-6
CONSORT. "He is the consort of the Queen of Fact. [NH 485-6
CONSPIRATORS. Blue friends in shadows, rich conspirators, [Choc
     300-9
CONSTABLE. From constable to god, from earth to air, [Bship 80-22 P
See John Constable.
CONSTANT. And makes a constant sacrament of praise. [Peter 92-13
Blares oftener and soon, will soon be constant. [Sad Gay 122-14
Made constant cry, caused constantly a cry, [Key W 128-15
Is blowing after days of constant rain. [Connois 216-5
The ever-breathing and moving, the constant fire, [Martial 238-9
Mouthing its constant smatter throughout space. [Montra 263-19
And small, a constant fellow of destiny, [EM 315-22
Ill of a constant question in his thought, [Pure 331-8
Which was realized, like reason's constant ruin. [Two V 354-17
This changes and that changes. Thus the constant [NSF 389-21
Of volatile world, too constant to be denied, [NSF 397-21
Above the table spins its constant spin, [NSF 406-2
His spirit is imprisoned in constant change. [NH 472-12
Like the constant sound of the water of the sea [NH 480-14
The countrymen were changed and each constant thing. [NH 487-8
In a constant secondariness, [Plant 506-14
The Constant Disquisition of the Wind [Two Illus 513-title 1
The constant cry against an old order, [Polo 37-13 P
Is constant. The time you call serene descends [Burnshaw 50-22 P
The need for a thesis, a music constant to move. [Woman Had 82-9P
See too-constant.
CONSTANTINE. And the general fidget from busts of Constantine
     [NH 488-14
CONSTANTLY. Made constant cry, caused constantly a cry, [Key W
     128-15
The adobe of the angels? Constantly, [Repet 308-2
That constantly sparkled their small gold? The town [Liadoff
     346-12
We flint ourselves, constantly longing, on this form. [NH 470-16
Never forgetting him that kept coming constantly so near. [World
     521-18
Piercing the tide by which it moves, is constantly within us?
     [Inelegance 26-2 P
And order constantly old, [Polo 37-14 P

Broods in tense meditation, constantly, [Sombre 68-20 P
CONSTELLATED. Day hymns instead of constellated rhymes, [Thought
  185-18
CONSTELLATION. In day's constellation, and yet remain, yet be,
  [Choc 300-20
  We live in a constellation [July 114-14 P
CONSTELLATIONS. And cloudy constellations, [Venereal 48-13
  The early constellations, from which came the first [Myrrh 350-7
  She will leap back from the swift constellations, [Soldat 12-7 P
  Of constellations on the beachy air [Greenest 58-1 P
CONSTRUCT. To construct a new stage. It has to be on that stage
  [Of Mod 240-5
CONSTRUCTED. In anything that he constructed, so frail, [Quiet 523-2
CONSTRUCTION. Are a final construction, [Fare Guit 99-7 P
CONSTRUCTIONS. Such black constructions, such public shapes
  [Ulysses 100-28 P
CONSUME. Except for us, Vesuvius might consume [EM 314-11
CONSUMMATE. In a consummate prime, yet still desires [EM 318-3
CONSUMMATION. By the consummation of the swallow's wings. [Sunday
  68-26
  A further consummation. For the lunar month [EM 318-4
CONTACT. Then the relentless contact be desired; [C 34-20
CONTAIN. In denial that cannot contain its blood, [NH 467-14
  What self, for example, did he contain that had not yet been
    loosed, [Prol 516-16
  The streets contain a crowd [Soldat 12-10 P
CONTAINED. Contained in their afflatus the reproach [C 39-12
  Has lost the whole in which he was contained, [Chaos 358-2
  This is nothing until in a single man contained, [AA 416-22
  That it contained the meaning into which he wanted to enter,
    [Prol 516-6
  As if nothingness contained a métier, [Rock 526-1
  That in which space itself is contained, the gate [Rock 528-17
  See self-contained.
CONTAINING. Containing the mind, below which it cannot descend,
  [Of Mod 240-17
CONTAINS. The arrangement contains the desire of [Couch 296-1
  Contains the year and other years and hymns [Cred 375-6
  His question is complete because it contains [Questions 462-16
  The cry that contains its converse in itself, [NH 471-4
  Which of these truly contains the world? [Indigo 22-13 P
  Contains for its children not a gill of sweet. [Greenest 55-26 P
CONTEMPLATE. To contemplate time's golden paladin [Greenest 56-24 P
CONTEMPLATED. Order, saying I am the contemplated spouse. [NSF 396-3
CONTEMPLATES. O juventes, O filii, he contemplates [Someone 83-1 A
  As a part of the nature that he contemplates [Someone 84-17 A
CONTEND. The employer and employee contend, [MBG 182-10
  One would continue to contend with one's ideas. [Glass 198-5
CONTENDING. Although contending featly in its veils, [C 36-2
  Less than contending with fictitious doom. [Spaniard 35-5 P
CONTENT. He could not be content with counterfeit, [C 39-14
  And be content and still be realist. [C 40-29
  She says, "I am content when wakened birds, [Sunday 68-12
  How content I shall be in the North to which I sail [Farewell
    117-19
  Blue buds or pitchy blooms. Be content-- [MBG 172-3
  Expansions, diffusions--content to be [MBG 172-4
  It has to content the reason concerning war, [Bottle 239-5
  Of the least, minor, vital metaphor content, [Crude 305-19
  Evading the point of redness, not content [EM 318-21
  And observing is completing and we are content, [Descrip 341-11
  Bent over work, anxious, content, alone, [NSF 406-16
  To make its factories content, must have [Greenest 58-20 P
  Yet I am content [Three 128-6
CONTENTION. Idea. She floats in the contention, the flux [Couch
  295-18
CONTENTMENT. She says, "But in contentment I still feel [Sunday
  68-27
CONTENTS. Is still to stick to the contents of the mind [Pure 332-9
  "Exposition of the Contents of a Cab" [20-title P
  The contents of the mind become solid show [Conversat 108-13 P
CONTINENT. In Crispin's mind above a continent. [C 34-1
  A still new continent in which to dwell. [C 37-4
  Slid from his continent by slow recess [C 40-15
  Whoever hunts a matinal continent [C 40-27
  "The Greenest Continent" [52-title P
CONTINUAL. Yet in excess, continual, [W Burgher 61-8
  "Continual Conversation with a Silent Man" [359-title
  With continual ululation. [Lulu G 26-18 P
CONTINUALLY. Continually. And old John Zeller stands [Two V 354-21
  Continually--There is a woman has had [Woman Had 81-22 P
CONTINUATION. And manifold continuation; [Solitaires 60-9
CONTINUE. And continue their affair. The shriek [MBG 182-15
  One would continue to contend with one's ideas. [Glass 198-5
  And the two poles continue to maintain it [Art Pop 112-16 P
CONTINUED. As if last night's lamps continued to burn, [Cuisine
  228-4
  As if yesterday's people continued to watch [Cuisine 228-5
  The wild orange trees continued to bloom and to bear, [NSF 393-2
CONTINUES. Observes and then continues to observe. [Canna 55-9

To the end. Alpha continues to begin. [NH 469-20
CONTORTED. Threw its contorted strength around the sky. [Sleight
  222-8
  Contorted, staggering from the thrust against [Old Woman 43-14 P
  The contorted glass. [Three 132-2 P
  Contorted glass . . . [Three 138-21 P
CONTOUR. In a moving contour, a change not quite completed? [NSF
  406-9
CONTOURS. Were contours. Cold was chilling the wide-moving swans.
  [Contra II 270-11
  In misted contours, credible day again. [NH 470-15
CONTRACTED. Contracted like a withered stick. [Two Illus 513-3
CONTRACTS. Life contracts and death is expected, [Soldier 97-1
CONTRADICTION. In a kind of uproar, because an opposite, a contra-
  diction, [Slug 522-7
CONTRARY. "Contrary Theses (I)" [266-title
  "Contrary Theses (II)" [270-title
CONTRAST. After all the pretty contrast of life and death [Connois
  215-13
CONTRASTING. Contrasting our two names, considered speech.
  [Phenom 287-16
CONTRIVANCE. This contrivance of the spectre of the spheres,
  [AA 420-18
CONTRIVE. Contriving balance to contrive a whole, [AA 420-19
CONTRIVED. It is most happily contrived. Here, then, [Antag 425-14
  Apocalypse was not contrived for parks, [Duck 62-23 P
CONTRIVES. Of the phrase. It contrives the self-same evocations
  [NH 473-5
CONTRIVING. To hear more brightly the contriving chords. [Descrip
  340-22
  Contriving balance to contrive a whole, [AA 420-19
CONVENT. The crosses on the convent roofs [Botanist 2 135-16
CONVERGED. Beams of the huge night converged upon it, [Valley
  Candle 51-2
  Converged upon its image, [Valley Candle 51-5
CONVERGING. In alternate stripes converging at a point [Page 422-22
  Converging on the statue, white and high." [Duck 62-27 P
CONVERSATION. "Continual Conversation with a Silent Man" [359-title
  In this conversation, but the sound [Silent 360-1
  Not wholly spoken in a conversation between [NH 471-7
  Or Paris in conversation at a café. [NH 486-3
  "Conversation with Three Women of New England" [108-title P
CONVERSE. The cry that contains its converse in itself, [NH 471-4
CONVERTED. The conscience is converted into palms, [High-Toned 59-4
  Is equally converted into palms, [High-Toned 59-11
CONVEY. A meaning within the meaning they convey, [Duck 65-17 P
CONVINCES. Convinces Athens with its quack. [Grotesque 75-13 P
CONVOCATION. A convocation, nightly, of the sea-stars, [C 28-27
CONVOLUTIONS. Form mystical convolutions in the sleep [EM 319-9
CONVOLVULUS. Convolvulus and coral, [Venereal 47-5
CONVULSED. To be convulsed, to have remained the hands [Thunder
  220-22
  The leaping bodies to his strength, convulsed [Duck 64-18 P
CONVULSIVE. Ten times ten times dynamite, convulsive [Hero 273-18
  Angel, convulsive shatterer, gun, [Hero 273-19
  Impelled by a convulsive harmony. [Red Kit 31-15 P
COO. Yet coo becomes rou-coo, rou-coo. How close [Think 356-16
  Sing coo, sing cuck, cuckoo. [Lulu M 27-8 P
  See: cunning-coo; rou-coo.
COOK. Made by a cook that never rode the back [Burnshaw 46-20 P
COOKS. And the cooks, the cooks, the bar-men and the maids,
  [Greenest 53-17 P
COOL. Toward the cool night and its fantastic star, [Lilacs 49-11
  In the cool [Peter 90-22
  Ballatta dozed in the cool on a straw divan [NE Verses 106-5
  There were roses in the cool café. His book [EM 314-9
  The cool sun of the Tulpehocken refers [Extraord 369-10
  And là-bas, là-bas, the cool bananas grew, [NSF 393-13
  To cool their ruddy pulses; the frothy clouds [NSF 399-15
COOLING. Or cooling in late leaves, not false except [Study I
  463-17
  Cooling the sugary air. [Agenda 42-3 P
COOLNESS. That coolness for his heat came suddenly, [C 31-17
  That will not hear us when we speak: a coolness, [Less 328-8
COOS. The dove in the belly builds his nest and coos, [Belly 366-17
COPERNICUS. At the elbow of Copernicus, a sphere, [Theatre 91-15 P
COPIED. On a cocoanut--how many men have copied dew [Dump 202-7
COPIOUS. Hen shudders: the copious egg is made and laid. [Nigger
  155-12
COPPER. There must be a planet that is copper [Mandolin 29-2 P
COPPERY. "The Bird with the Coppery, Keen Claws" [82-title
  He moves not on his coppery, keen claws. [Bird Claws 82-15
COPPICE. When in my coppice you behold me be. [NSF 393-24
COPULARS. Winter and spring, cold copulars, [NSF 392-8
COPY. Its copy of the sun, these cover the rock. [Rock 527-1
COQUELICOT. The marguerite and coquelicot, [Pourtraicte 21-13
CORAL. Convolvulus and coral, [Venereal 47-5
  Her South of pine and coral and coraline sea, [Farewell 117-15
  And cloud, of the sunken coral water-walled, [Key W 129-13
  Pierce, too, with buttresses of coral air [Archi 18-5 P

CORALINE. Her South of pine and coral and coraline sea, [Farewell
   117-15
CORALS. The corals of the dogwood, cold and clear, [NSF 400-1
CORAZON. Corazon, stout dog, [Destructive 192-15
CORBEIL. The sun is a corbeil of flowers the moon Blanche [Dump
   201-12
CORE. Iciest core, a north star, central [Hero 275-24
   The dazzling, bulging, brightest core, [Red Fern 365-11
   And this must comfort the heart's core against [Cred 372-15
   And hear it as it falls in the deep heart's core. [Page 421-12
   What has he that becomes his heart's strong core? [Bad Time
   426-20
   His poverty becomes his heart's strong core-- [Bad Time 427-2
   It is more than the odor of this core of earth [Someone 87-16 A
CORES. Planting his pristine cores in Florida, [C 38-17
CORN. The green corn gleaming and experience [EM 325-23
   The green corn gleams and the metaphysicals [EM 325-27
   And this great esplanade of corn, miles wide, [Belly 367-7
CORNELIAN. An effulgence faded, dull cornelian [NSF 400-18
CORNELIUS NEPOS. That it puffs as Cornelius Nepos reads, it puffs
   [Dump 202-3
CORNER. The corner of the eye. Our element, [Sun March 134-4
   In silence upon your bed. You clutch the corner [NSF 384-19
   Like a cloud-cap in the corner of a looking-glass, [Moonlight
   531-22
   There's a cab-horse at the corner, [Phases 3-5 P
CORNERED. So near detachment, the cover's cornered squares,
   [Bouquet 450-13
   Is soft in three-four cornered fragrances [NH 470-19
   From five-six cornered leaves, and green, the signal [NH 470-20
CORNERS. You become a self that fills the four corners of night.
   [Rabbit K 209-19
   Cast corners in the glass. He could describe [EM 314-1
   Or street or about the corners of a man, [NH 480-1
   Who sits thinking in the corners of a room. [NH 480-2
   Involving the four corners of the sky, [Ideal 88-4 A
CORNES. Aux taureaux Dieu cornes donne [Parasol 20-1 P
CORNETS. And pines that are cornets, so it occurs, [Sleight 222-14
CORNS. Stabbing at his teat-like corns [Lulu M 27-15 P
CORNWALL. We drove home from Cornwall to Hartford, late [Real
   110-8 P
CORONAL. Attentive to a coronal of things [C 44-14
   The crown and week-day coronal of her fame. [Descrip 339-16
   Set on me the spirit's diamond coronal. [NSF 396-6
CORONER. "The Shape of the Coroner" [29-title P
   Then the coroner came [Coroner 29-14 P
   And the coroner's hand [Coroner 30-1 P
   It was the coroner [Coroner 30-3 P
   And the coroner bent [Coroner 30-9 P
COROT. The album of Corot is premature. [Nigger 156-13
CORPSES. Killing the time between corpses [Venereal 47-15
CORRECT. Made sure of the most correct catastrophe. [EM 314-10
CORRECTED. Yet, when corrected, has its curious lapses, [EM 318-15
CORRIDOR. And vanishing, a web in a corridor [AA 416-18
   In an excessive corridor, alas! [Antag 426-8
CORRIDORS. So that corridors of clouds, [Botanist 1 134-15
   Corridors of cloudy thoughts, [Botanist 1 134-16
   Next he builds capitols and in their corridors, [NSF 403-18
   Rage in the ring and shake the corridors. [Spaniard 35-1 P
CORRODE. She can corrode your world, if never you. [Good Bad
   33-22 P
CORRUPTING. Are corrupting pallors . . . ay di mi, [MBG 172-2
CORSET. The cat in the paper-bag, the corset, the box [Dump 201-18
CORTEGE. "Cortege for Rosenbloom" [79-title
CORUSCATIONS. Pure coruscations, that lie beyond [Analysis 349-1
COSMOS. In an always incipient cosmos, [July 115-3 P
COSSETED. Confined him, while it cosseted, condoned, [C 40-22
COSTUMES. And something more. And the people in costumes, [Belly
   367-9
   Them mottled, in the moodiest costumes, [Cred 377-25
   Full of Raphael's costumes; [Phases 5-17 P
   Maligning his costumes and disputing [Stan Hero 84-24 P
COSTUMING. Who can think of the sun costuming clouds [Fading 139-1
COTTON. Tell me more of the eagle, Cotton, [Pascagoula 126-9
COTTON MATHER. Cotton Mather died when I was a boy. The books
   [Blue Bldg 216-15
   Was everything that Cotton Mather was [Blue Bldg 217-2
   Look down now, Cotton Mather, from the blank. [Blue Bldg 217-13
COUCH. In couch, four more personae, intimate [C 45-5
   "So-and-So Reclining on her Couch" [295-title
COULISSE. Coulisse bright-dark, tragic chiaroscuro [NSF 384-3
COUNSEL. Take counsel, all hierophants [Sat Night 28-7 P
COUNTED. What counted was mythology of self, [C 28-5
   His cabin counted as phylactery, [C 43-23
   Has been counted, the genealogy [Ulysses 102-9 P
COUNTERFEIT. He could not be content with counterfeit, [C 39-14
COUNTER-IDEAS. And counter-ideas. There was nothing one had.
   [Forces 229-8
COUNTERPART. A second similar counterpart, a maid [C 44-16
   The instinct for heaven had its counterpart: [NH 476-1

For its counterpart a kind of counterpoint [NH 476-5
COUNTERPOINT. For its counterpart a kind of counterpoint [NH 476-5
COUNTING. Men fat as feathers, misers counting breaths, [Horn 230-3
   Are time for counting and remembering, [Ideal 88-10 A
COUNTRIES. Flying from burning countries and brown sand shores,
   [Loaf 200-2
   "He will be thinking in strange countries [Three 134-6 P
   "He will be thinking in strange countries [Three 134-12 P
   "He will be thinking in strange countries [Three 134-16 P
COUNTRY. She seemed, of a country of the capuchins, [C 44-12
   The taste of even a country connoisseur. [Nigger 157-16
   "Country Words" [207-title
   This arrival in the wild country of the soul, [Waldorf 240-24
   The sun is the country wherever he is. The bird [EM 318-18
   Of the country colors crowding against it, since [EM 318-23
   A café. There may be a dish of country cheese [Paisant 335-15
   How that whole country was a melon, pink [NSF 393-17
   Afraid of the country angels of those skies, [Page 422-7
   And feel its country gayety and smile [Beginning 428-1
   It cannot mean a sea-wide country strewn [Duck 63-12 P
   A jar of the shoots of an infant country, green [Someone 83-15 A
COUNTRYMAN. "The Countryman" [428-title
   A countryman walks beside you. [Countryman 428-16
   A countryman of all the bones of the world? [Warmth 90-1 P
   A countryman of all the bones in the world? [As Leave 117-7 P
COUNTRYMEN. The countrymen were changed and each constant thing.
   [NH 487-8
COUNTS. Which counts for most, the anger borne [Sombre 69-21 P
   That counts. [Three 132-12 P
   That counts. [Three 132-16 P
COUPLE. And North and South are an intrinsic couple [NSF 392-13
COUPLET. That wrote his couplet yearly to the spring, [C 31-5
COUPLETS. Patron and patriarch of couplets, walk [NE Verses 105-11
COURAGE. It's a strange courage [Nuances 18-4
   A giant's heart in the veins, all courage. [Gigan 289-7
   As in the courage of the ignorant man, [NSF 395-11
   A courage of the eye, [Aug 494-27
COURIERS. Suppose these couriers brought amid their train [Monocle
   15-27
   The one-foot stars were couriers of its death [Page 421-19
COURSE. And still pursue, the origin and course [Monocle 18-1
   All this, of course, will come to summer soon. [Connois 216-6
   You, too, are drifting, in spite of your course; [Vari 232-17
   Of an infinite course. The flowers against the wall [AA 412-8
   "The Course of a Particular" [96-title P
   Objects not present as a matter of course [Local 112-1 P
COURT. "The court had known poverty and wretchedness; hu- [Three
   129-9 P
   As the court knew it. [Three 131-16 P
   The court woke [Three 131-17 P
   What the court saw was always of the same color, [Three 131-22 P
   When the court knew beauty only, [Three 132-5
COURTESAN. At home, a bit like the slenderest courtesan. [NE
   Verses 106-6
COURTS. From the sea, conceive for the courts [Prelude 195-15
COUSIN. The human that has no cousin in the moon. [Less 328-4
   An ethereal cousin, another milleman. [Pieces 352-9
   And peace is cousin by a hundred names [Owl 432-11
COUSINS. Cousins of the calendar if not of kin, [Recit 86-3 P
COVER. And spread it so as to cover her face. [Emperor 64-23
   There are not leaves enough to cover the face [Dames 206-1
   To cover, to crown, to cover--let it go-- [Dames 206-19
   Cover the sea with the sand rose. Fill [Vari 234-14
   Of the land, on a checkered cover, red and white. [Bouquet 450-6
   So near detachment, the cover's cornered squares, [Bouquet 450-13
   He would go to bed, cover himself with blankets-- [Novel 457-9
   It is not enough to cover the rock with leaves. [Rock 526-10
   Its copy of the sun, these cover the rock. [Rock 527-1
   They are more than leaves that cover the barren rock [Rock 527-6
   Cover the golden altar deepest black, [Red Kit 31-21 P
COVERED. Made on the sea-weeds and the covered stones [Hibiscus
   22-13
   And covered him and his congenial sleep. [C 42-8
   Monsieur is on horseback. The horse is covered with mice. [Mice
   123-4
   Covered the shrivelled forms [Reader 147-2
   For buttons, how many women have covered themselves [Dump 202-8
   Or whether the ice still covered the lake. There was still
   [Extracts 255-14
   The breast is covered with violets. It is a green leaf. [Holiday
   312-16
   "Mountains Covered with Cats" [Cats 367-title
   That the green leaves came and covered the high rock, [Rock 526-4
   Covered one morning with blue, one morning with white, [Bship
   80-10 P
COVERING. And depth, covering all surfaces, [Burghers 362-9
   Is never naked. A fictive covering [NSF 396-11
COVERS. When the shapeless shadow covers the sun [Rabbit K 209-2
   It rises from land and sea and covers them. [Cred 375-12
COVERT. And in what covert, may we, naked, be [Extracts 252-17

COVERTS. Upward, from unimagined coverts, fly. [Blanche 10-12 P
COVETOUS. To make the body covetous in desire [Anatomy 108-13
COW. Shot lightning at the kind cow's milk. [Lulu M 27-12 P
COWED. And in your centre mark them and are cowed . . . [NSF
   384-24
COWL. The cowl of winter, done repenting. [Peter 92-5
COWRY-KIN. And Rosa, the muslin dreamer of satin and cowry-kin,
   disdaining the empty keys; and the young infanta, [Piano 22-3P
COWS. As the spittle of cows [Depression 63-11
COZENER. With Crispin as the tiptoe cozener? [C 40-2
COZENING. A king of cozening and coaxing sound, [NH 482-8
CRACK. The grackles crack their throats of bone in the smooth air.
   [Banal 62-13
   The crack across the pane, [Anything B 211-22
   Spread outward. Crack the round dome. Break through. [Aug 490-11
CRACKED. Composed of evenings like cracked shutters flung [C 42-30
   A tempest cracked on the theatre. Quickly, [Repet 306-1
CRACKING. The drivers in the wind-blows cracking whips, [Repet
   308-22
CRACKLED. Bethou me, said sparrow, to the crackled blade, [NSF
   393-22
   Playing a crackled reed, wind-stopped, in bleats. [Sombre 67-2 P
CRACKLING. What is this crackling of voices in the mind, [Dutch
   292-12
   They find her in the crackling summer night, [Woman Had 83-4 P
CRADLE. The night is not the cradle that they cry, [Tallap 71-11
CRAFTILY. The feelings crazily, craftily call, [MBG 166-19
CRAMMERS. Green crammers of the green fruits of the world, [C 43-28
CRAPE. Jovial Crispin, in calamitous crape? [C 41-22
CRASH. Crash in the mind--But, fat Jocundus, worrying [Glass
   197-20
CRASHED. A cymbal crashed, [Peter 91-10
CRASHING. In flowery nations, crashing and alert. [Greenest 55-4 P
CRAVE. The imagination that we spurned and crave. [Fictive 88-18
CRAVES. Suckled on ponds, the spirit craves a watery mountain.
   [NE Verses 105-2
CRAW. Stepped in and dropped the chuckling down his craw, [C 45-18
CRAWL. The way the ants crawl [Six Sig 74-12
CRAWLER. To chromatic crawler. But it is changed. [Aug 492-21
CRAWLING. The crawling railroad spur, the rotten fence, [C 36-14
CRAWLS. It crawls over the water. [Tattoo 81-10
   It crawls over the edges of the snow. [Tattoo 81-11
   It crawls under your eyelids [Tattoo 81-12
   And crawls on them, as if feathers of the duck [Bouquet 450-17
   A fly crawls on the balustrades. [Including 88-16 P
CRAWS. Darting out of their purple craws [Bananas 54-22
CRAYFISH. Fishing for crayfish . . . [Venereal 47-16
CRAZILY. The feelings crazily, craftily call, [MBG 166-19
CRAZY. It dances down a furrow, in the early light, back of a
   crazy plough, the green blades following. [Plough-Boy 6-7 P
CREAK. The oldest-newest night does not creak by, [NH 476-20
CREAKING. Creaking in the night wind. [Three 137-6 P
   There would be no creaking [Three 137-7 P
CREAKS. While it creaks hail. [Watermelon 89-12
CREAM. And cream for the fig and silver for the cream, [C 42-18
   And remains inarticulate, horses with cream. [Burnshaw 47-3 P
   See ice-cream.
CREAMS. Whipped creams and the Blue Danube, [Agenda 41-16 P
CREATE. It must create its colors out of itself. [Nigger 158-2
   What unisons create in music. [Hero 280-4
   Desire prolongs its adventure to create [NH 482-14
   Which, just to name, is to create [Ulysses 104-27 P
   See re-create.
CREATED. Created, in his day, a touch of doubt. [C 27-13
   And he that created the garden and peopled it. [Thought 185-22
   And, capable, created in his mind, [Uruguay 250-3
   So she in Hydaspia created [Oak 272-16
   You were created of your name, the word [Phenom 287-17
   That his revenge created filial [EM 319-24
   The fictive man created out of men. [Paisant 335-6
   Created the time and place in which we breathed . . . [AA 419-3
   In things seen and unseen, created from nothingness, [NH 486-11
   A nature that is created in what it says, [Aug 490-21
   In that which is created as its symbol. [Armor 529-16
   Created, like a bubble, of bright sheens, [Duck 63-21 P
   Was it desire that created Raël [Desire 85-15 P
   Or was it Jaffa that created desire? [Desire 85-16 P
CREATES. The sense creates the pose. [Add 199-9
   Creates, in the blissfuller perceptions, [Hero 280-3
   The air changes, creates and re-creates, like strength, [Choc
   301-9
   This creates a third world without knowledge, [EM 323-19
   Creates a logic not to be distinguished [EM 325-1
   Vertumnus creates an equilibrium. [Extraord 369-20
   This is the refuge that the end creates. [Cred 373-25
   That, nameless, it creates an affectionate name, [Pastor 379-15
   Creates a fresh universe out of nothingness by adding itself,
   [Prol 517-9
CREATING. Of darkness, creating from nothingness [Ulysses 100-27 P
CREATION. Creation is not renewed by images [NH 481-14

Are the fulfilling rhapsodies that hymn it to creation?
   [Inelegance 26-4 P
CREATIONS. "The Creations of Sound" [310-title
   Exhaling these creations of itself. [Pieces 351-17
CREATOR. Hi! The creator too is blind, [Negation 97-13
   Leader, the creator of bursting color [Hero 274-2
   Concealed creator. One walks easily [Couch 296-3
   And proclaim it, the white creator of black, jetted [AA 417-11
   This is the true creator, the waver [Ulysses 100-18 P
   For this creator is a lamp [Ulysses 100-24 P
   The unnamed creator of an unknown sphere, [Ulysses 101-3 P
   The image must be of the nature of its creator. [Myth 118-11 P
   It is the nature of its creator increased, [Myth 118-12
CREATURE. Of this creature of the evening [Infanta 7-17
   To the auroral creature musing in the mind. [Montra 263-24
   Speaks as you speak, a creature that [Search 268-14
   Of that angelic sword? Creature of [Hero 273-17
   He sought the most grossly maternal, the creature [EM 321-13
   But an antipodal, far-fetched creature, worthy of birth, [Discov
   96-5 P
CREATURES. Weather of night creatures, whistling all day, too,
   [Montra 261-17
   Of the appropriate creatures, jubilant, [Descrip 344-13
   Of what are these the creatures, what element [Two V 355-1
   If they were creatures of the sea alone, [Two V 355-4
   Than creatures, of the sky between the banks, [Lot 371-14
   The mind, among the creatures that it makes, [Owl 436-8
CREDENCES. "Credences of Summer" [372-title
CREDIBLE. In misted contours, credible day again. [NH 470-15
   Repose, always, the credible thought [Ulysses 103-7 P
   The one about the credible hero, the one [As Leave 117-3 P
CREEP. Of the steadfast lanterns creep across the dark? [Heaven
   56-20
CREEPER. A creeper under jaunty leaves. And fourth, [C 44-21
CREEPING. And the earth is alive with creeping men, [MBG 168-14
   Day creeps down. The moon is creeping up. [Dump 201-11
   And late wanderers creeping under the barb of night, [Dutch
   291-24
CREEPS. The sun of Asia creeps above the horizon [Nigger 153-8
   Day creeps down. The moon is creeping up. [Dump 201-11
   That's the moment when the moon creeps up [Dump 202-19
   Feeling the fear that creeps beneath the wool, [Novel 458-23
CREPUSCULAR. The green palmettoes in crepuscular ice [C 34-15
   At the burst of day, crepuscular images [Burnshaw 46-23 P
CRESCENT. Even if there had been a crescent moon [Letters 107-1 P
CRESS. These streaked the mother-of-pearl, the lunar cress.
   [Greenest 53-24 P
CRESTED. There was neither voice nor crested image, [How Live 126-1
   To be crested and wear the mane of a multitude [NSF 398-8
   And in bright excellence adorned, crested [Orb 442-17
CRESTS. In aureoles that are over-dazzling crests . . . [Nuns
   92-20 P
CRETONNES. A form of fire approaches the cretonnes of Penelope,
   [World 520-15
CREVASSES. And smiting the crevasses of the leaves [Sea Surf 101-2
CREVICE. Breathe in a crevice of earth? [Bagatelles 213-4
   In what crevice do you find [Bagatelles 213-13
CREW. That crew before the clocks. [Watermelon 89-6
CRIBLED. Than wettest cinnamon. It was cribled pears [Poem Morn
   219-10
CRICKET. No greater than a cricket's horn, no more [Beard 247-15
   The cricket in the telephone is still. [Phenom 286-1
   The cricket of summer forming itself out of ice. [Discov 95-14 P
CRICKET-IMPRESARIO. And great moon, cricket-impresario, [Montra
   260-4
CRICKETS. And you? Remember how the crickets came [Monocle 15-3
   The crickets beat their tambours in the wind, [C 42-15
   Like last night's crickets, far below. [Botanist 2 135-19
   And crickets are loud again in the grass. The moon [Men Fall
   187-14
   Here in the west indifferent crickets chant [EM 321-3
   Bubbles up in the night and drowns the crickets' sound. [EM 321-9
   These locuts by day, these crickets by night [Aug 489-4
   Both late and alone, above the crickets' chords, [Quiet 523-12
   Through these crickets?-- [Soldat 12-18 P
CRIED. Cried quittance [Ord Women 12-1
   Against his pipping sounds a trumpet cried [C 29-21
   They cried, [Motion 83-5
   They wondered why Susanna cried [Peter 91-14
   It was hunger, it was the hungry that cried [Loaf 200-9
   We are cold, the parrots cried, [Anything B 211-14
   And cried out to feel it again, have run fingers over leaves
   [Large 424-2
   An old voice cried out, "Come!" [Phases 6-2 P
   "Olu" the eunuchs cried. "Ululalu." [Lulu G 26-23 P
   And possibly the emperor would have cried, [Three 137-13 P
CRIERS. The criers, undulating the deep-oceaned phrase. [Tallap
   71-12
CRIES. Loudened by cries, by clashes, quick and sure [Monocle 16-13
   Our old bane, green and bloated, serene, who cries, [Banal 62-16

A voice that cries, "The tomb in Palestine [Sunday 70-15
Whistle about us their spontaneous cries; [Sunday 70-23
And a chitter of cries [Cortege 80-22
Cries up for us and colder than the frost [Anatomy 108-4
And the welter of frost and the fox cries do. [Grapes 110-20
For which more than any words cries deeplier? [Ghosts 119-7
And the streets are full of cries. [Mozart 132-21
Cries out a literate despair. [Postcard 159-10
Thick-lipped from riot and rebellious cries, [Men Fall 188-8
This halloo, halloo, halloo heard over the cries [Parochial
    191-12
There would have been the cries of the dead [Thunder 220-18
He sets this peddler's pie and cries in summer, [Oboe 251-3
The glass man, cold and numbered, dewily cries, [Oboe 251-4
Than sharp, illustrious scene. The trumpet cries [Cred 376-19
Which cries so blau and cries again so lind [Page 421-9
And death cries quickly, in a flash of voice, [Owl 432-13
But what his mother was returns and cries on his breast. [Pecul
    453-9
They only know a savage assuagement cries [NH 467-22
(A boor of night in middle earth cries out.) [Infernale 24-19 P
In the glassy sound of your voices, the porcelain cries,
    [Burnshaw 52-6 P
CRIMSON. A sally into gold and crimson forms, [C 35-9
Clog, therefore, purple Jack and crimson Jill. [Nigger 154-6
Iris and orange, crimson and green, [Mandolin 28-9 P
Of crimson and hoods of Venezuelan green [Burnshaw 51-3 P
And your braids bear brightening of crimson bands. [Burnshaw
    51-29 P
CRIMSONS. Dressed in its azure-doubled crimsons, [Hero 281-3
And drenching crimsons, or endure? It came [Greenest 57-23 P
CRINKLED. A crinkled paper makes a brilliant sound. [Extracts
    252-1
CRINKLING. The weaving and the crinkling and the vex. [Owl 433-17
CRINOLINE. Of crinoline spread, but of a pining sweet, [C 42-29
CRINOLINES. Aux crinolines, smears out mad mountains. [Extracts
    257-29
CRIPPLE. The wind moves like a cripple among the leaves [Motive
    288-3
CRIPPLED. Their brilliance through the lattices, crippled [Blue
    Bldg 217-10
CRISES. Through our indifferent crises. Yet we require [EM 321-4
CRISP. One had come early to a crisp café. [Forces 229-19
His crisp knowledge is devoured by her, beneath a dew. [Madame
    507-4
CRISPED. Of green blooms turning crisped the motley hue [Sea Surf
    102-12
CRISPEST. A crown within him of crispest diamonds, [Aug 492-7
CRISPIN. Preceptor to the sea? Crispin at sea [C 27-12
Of honest quilts, the eye of Crispin, hung [C 27-17
Blotched out beyond unblotching. Crispin, [C 28-6
Crispin was washed away by magnitude. [C 28-17
Could Crispin stem verboseness in the sea, [C 28-22
Just so an ancient Crispin was dissolved. [C 29-7
Crispin, merest minuscule in the gales, [C 29-11
Celestial sneering boisterously. Crispin [C 29-22
Crispin confronting it, a vocable thing, [C 29-25
Crispin beheld and Crispin was made new. [C 30-6
But Crispin was too destitute to find [C 30-22
Crispin foresaw a curious promenade [C 31-23
For Crispin and his quill to catechize. [C 31-33
Made pallid flitter. Crispin, here, took flight. [C 32-27
For Crispin to vociferate again. [C 33-17
For Crispin, fagot in the lunar fire, [C 33-20
In Crispin's mind above a continent. [C 34-1
Grind their seductions on him, Crispin knew [C 35-15
Crispin in one laconic phrase laid bare [C 36-26
Whatever shape it took in Crispin's mind, [C 37-6
Be plain. For application Crispin strove, [C 38-8
These are the broadest instances. Crispin, [C 38-28
That first drove Crispin to his wandering. [C 39-13
With Crispin as the tiptoe cozener? [C 40-2
Crispin as hermit, pure and capable, [C 40-4
Crispin dwelt in the land and dwelling there [C 40-14
So Crispin hasped on the surviving form, [C 41-8
Jovial Crispin, in calamitous crape? [C 41-22
Crispin, magister of a single room, [C 42-5
In the presto of the morning, Crispin trod, [C 42-13
And men like Crispin like them in intent, [C 42-23
Forgather and bell boldly Crispin's last [C 43-13
True daughters both of Crispin and his clay. [C 44-2
Was unforeseen. First Crispin smiled upon [C 44-10
Crispin concocted doctrine from the rout. [C 45-11
In form though in design, as Crispin willed, [C 45-21
Is false, if Crispin is a profitless [C 45-31
CRISPINE. And Crispine, the blade, reddened by some touch, demand-
    ing the most from the phrases [Piano 22-6 P
CRISPING. Of crisping light along the statue's rim. [Old Woman
    43-18 P
CRISPIN-SAINT. Crispin-valet, Crispin-saint! [Abnormal 24-14 P

CRISPIN-VALET. Crispin-valet, Crispin-saint! [Abnormal 24-14 P
CRISPLY. Is evil, crisply bright, disclosing you [Spaniard 34-13 P
And crisply musical, or holy caverns temple-toned, [Burnshaw
    47-16 P
CRITIC. It is like a critic of God, the world [Region 115-13 P
CRITIQUE. In which we read the critique of paradise [Crude 305-9
Of a comedian, this critique; [Crude 305-11
CROCHET. Crochet me this buzzard [Jack-Rabbit 50-10
CRONIES. Who are the mossy cronies muttering, [Dutch 292-10
CROOKED. Among the bare and crooked trees, [Celle 438-3
CROONERS. The sort of thing that August crooners sing, [Aug 489-9
CROSS. Just rising, accompanying, arranged to cross, [Page 422-24
CROSSED. Crossed it, to and fro. [Thirteen 93-15
I crossed in '38 in the Western Head. [NE Verses 104-7
It depends which way you crossed, the tea-belle said. [NE Verses
    104-8
CROSSER. O buckskin, O crosser of snowy divides, [Duck 61-1 P
CROSSES. The crosses on the convent roofs [Botanist 2 135-16
As of those crosses, glittering, [Botanist 2 136-10
CROSSING. Twenty men crossing a bridge, [Magnifico 19-1
Are twenty men crossing twenty bridges, [Magnifico 19-3
Crossing a single bridge into a village. [Magnifico 19-6
Twenty men crossing a bridge, [Magnifico 19-9
Twenty men crossing a bridge [Magnifico 19-12
That's better. That's worth crossing seas to find. [C 36-25
Symbol of the seeker, crossing by night [Ulysses 99-11 P
Symbol of the seeker, crossing by night [Presence 105-14 P
CROSS-PIECE. A-cock at the cross-piece on a pole [MBG 181-21
CROUCH. Say, puerile, that the buzzards crouch on the ridge-pole
    [Two Figures 86-10
CROUCHED. Crouched in the moonlight. [Reader 147-3
CROW. From oriole to crow, note the decline [Nigger 154-14
In music. Crow is realist. But, then, [Nigger 154-15
To a crow's voice? Did the nightingale torture the ear, [Dump
    203-2
The crow, inciting various modes. [Vari 233-15
Item: The cocks crow and the birds cry and [Montra 263-13
The crow looks rusty as he rises up. [Possum 294-15
No pain (ignoring the cocks that crow us up [EM 314-13
The statue in a crow's perspective of trees [Sombre 70-19 P
CROWD. Tonight the stars are like a crowd of faces [Dezem 218-9
And laughing, a crowd of men, [Dezem 218-11
Wrapped in their seemings, crowd on curious crowd, [Descrip
    342-14
A little string speaks for a crowd of voices. [NSF 392-18
The streets contain a crowd [Soldat 12-10 P
CROWDED. They crowded [Ord Women 10-19
Had crowded into the rocket and touched the fuse. [Liadoff 346-13
Crowded with apparitions suddenly gone [Bouquet 448-10
CROWDING. That's where his hymns come crowding, hero-hymns,
    [Thought 185-15
Of the country colors crowding against it, since [EM 318-23
CROWDS. Meditating the will of men in formless crowds. [NE Verses
    105-10
Both of men and clouds, a slime of men in crowds. [Farewell
    118-12
CROWING. The cocks are crowing and crowing loud, [Fish-Scale 161-2
CROWN. O sceptre of the sun, crown of the moon, [Monocle 13-2
No crown is simpler than the simple hair. [Fictive 87-13
By the wise. There are not leaves enough to crown, [Dames 206-18
To cover, to crown, to cover--let it go-- [Dames 206-19
That in spring will crown every western horizon, [Martial 237-12
Suspended in air, the slightest crown [Couch 295-11
And wear humanity's bleak crown; [Crude 305-8
The crown and week-day coronal of her fame. [Descrip 339-16
A little roughened and ruder, a crown [NSF 400-15
Straight to the utmost crown of night he flew. [NSF 403-8
Profound, and yet the king and yet the crown, [AA 415-1
In the sky, as crown and diamond cabala? [AA 417-15
Except for that crown and mystical cabala. [AA 417-21
They have, or they may have, their glittering crown, [Golden
    460-20
A crown within him of crispest diamonds, [Aug 492-7
Sultan of African sultans, starless crown. [Greenest 60-6 P
Progenitor wearing the diamond crown of crowns, [Duck 64-30 P
Like any other, rex by right of the crown, [Bship 79-3 P
And their directing sceptre, the crown [Ulysses 104-8 P
CROWNED. Crowned with the first, cold buds. On these we live,
    [Cuisine 228-11
See brightly-crowned.
CROWNS. Among the purple tufts, the scarlet crowns, [C 32-4
We buried the fallen without jasmine crowns. [Oboe 251-13
Progenitor wearing the diamond crown of crowns, [Duck 64-30 P
CROWS. The crows anoint the statues with their dirt. [Swans 4-10
The cock crows [Depression 63-7
The hen-cock crows at midnight and lays no egg, [Nigger 155-10
The cock-hen crows all day. But cockerel shrieks, [Nigger 155-11
As when the cock crows on the left and all [NSF 386-10
The crows are flying above the foyer of summer. [Novel 457-1
The syllables of the gulls and of the crows [Primordia 7-17 P

Or melancholy crows as shadowing clouds? [Stan MMO 19-18 P
Rest, crows upon the edges of the moon, [Red Kit 31-20 P
Fat with a thousand butters, and the crows [Burnshaw 49-9 P
The statue stands in true perspective. Crows [Sombre 71-2 P
CRUDE. The piano, that time: the time when the crude [Vase 246-10
  The crude and jealous formlessness [Vase 247-6
  "Crude Foyer" [305-title
  The real will from its crude compoundings come, [NSF 404-6
  Say that it is a crude effect, black reds, [Roses 430-10
  As if the crude collops came together as one, [NH 466-1
  Crude captains, the naked majesty, if you like, [Rome 510-9
  Twitching a little with crude souvenirs [Duck 64-23 P
CRUEL. A cavernous and a cruel past, tropic [Greenest 58-21 P
CRUMB. Of the North have earned this crumb by their complaints.
    [NE Verses 106-2
  For your crumb, [Sonatina 109-15
CRUMBLE. The house will crumble and the books will burn. [AA 413-17
CRUMBLED. The moonlight crumbled to degenerate forms, [Uruguay
    249-7
CRUMBLING. Day's arches are crumbling into the autumn night.
    [Novel 458-16
CRUMBS. And nourish ourselves on crumbs of whimsy? [Hero 278-4
CRUMPLED. Taken with withered weather, crumpled clouds, [News
    265-6
  He does not change the sea from crumpled tinfoil [Aug 492-20
  See much-crumpled.
CRUSH. Still questioning if to crush the soaring stacks, [Sombre
    68-31 P
  There was a crush of strength in a grinding going round, [Real
    110-11 P
CRUST. When the crust of shape has been destroyed. [MBG 183-12
  His crust away eats of this meat, drinks [Hero 278-16
  This crust of air? . . (He pauses.) Can breath shake [Infernale
    24-21 P
CRUSTED. Of the pine-trees crusted with snow; [Snow Man 9-23
  Our crusted outlines hot and huge with fact, [Burnshaw 47-6 P
CRUSTS. And you, my semblables, are crusts that lie [Dutch 291-6
CRUSTY. That was not in him in the crusty town [C 33-12
  From crusty stacks above machines. [MBG 182-4
CRUTCH. My old boat goes round on a crutch [Sailing 120-2
CRUX. Must be the crux for our compendia. [Havana 143-24
CRY. And I remembered the cry of the peacocks. [Domination 8-16
  I heard them cry--the peacocks. [Domination 9-2
  Was it a cry against the twilight [Domination 9-3
  Full of the cry of the peacocks? [Domination 9-11
  Or was it a cry against the hemlocks? [Domination 9-12
  And I remembered the cry of the peacocks.[Domination 9-20
  Tempestuous clarion, with heavy cry, [C 32-23
  The night is not the cradle that they cry, [Tallap 71-11
  And hail, cry hail, cry hail. [Watermelon 89-15
  Would cry out sharply. [Thirteen 94-12
  For which the voices cry, these, too, may be [Sad Gay 122-11
  Made constant cry, caused constantly a cry, [Key W 128-15
  And cry and cry for help? [Fading 139-5
  And cry and cry for help? [Fading 139-15
  Lean from the steeple. Cry aloud, [MBG 170-14
  And the long echo of their dying cry, [Thought 186-14
  The day to pieces and cry stanza my stone? [Dump 203-10
  Item: The cocks crow and the birds cry and [Montra 263-13
  Cry loudly, cry out in the powerful heart. [Dutch 291-9
  A force gathers that will cry loudlier [Dutch 291-10
  They have heads in which a captive cry [Possum 294-2
  The enlarging of the simplest soldier's cry [Choc 298-14
  The cry is part. My solitaria [Choc 298-16
  And is not to be distinguished, when we cry [EM 315-16
  The cry of an embryo? The spirit tires, [Feo 334-1
  Replaces what is not. The resounding cry [Cred 376-24
  Of its cry as clarion, its diction's way [Cred 377-3
  Free, for a moment, from malice and sudden cry, [Cred 378-8
  Cry out, "I am the purple muse." Make sure [Bad Time 427-8
  With a savage voice; and in that cry they hear [NH 467-23
  Of recognition, avowal, impassioned cry, [NH 471-3
  The cry that contains its converse in itself, [NH 471-4
  The poem is the cry of its occasion, [NH 473-18
  In March, a scrawny cry from outside [Not Ideas 534-2
  A bird's cry, at daylight or before, [Not Ideas 534-5
  The scrawny cry--it was [Not Ideas 534-13
  The mightier mother raises up her cry; [Soldat 14-16 P
  The constant cry against an old order, [Polo 37-13
  Dance, now, and with sharp voices cry, but cry [Burnshaw 51-10 P
  Your hands held high and cry again, but cry, [Burnshaw 51-16 P
  Implicit clarities in the way you cry [Burnshaw 52-12 P
  To whom the jaguars cry and lions roar [Greenest 55-19
  Each look and each necessitous, as a god [Greenest 59-8 P
  A cry, the pallor of a dress, a touch. [Sombre 67-20 P
  Today the leaves cry, hanging on branches swept by wind, [Course
    96-10 P
  The leaves cry . . . One holds off and merely hears the cry.
    [Course 96-13 P
  It is a busy cry, concerning someone else. [Course 96-14 P

The leaves cry. It is not a cry of divine attention, [Course
    96-19 P
  Nor the smoke-drift of puffed-out heroes, nor human cry. [Course
    96-20 P
  It is the cry of leaves that do not transcend themselves,
    [Course 96-21 P
  Itself, until, at last, the cry concerns no one at all. [Course
    97-3 P
  See cock-cry.
CRYING. These voices crying without knowing for what, [Sad Gay
    122-6
  That would be waving and that would be crying, [Adieu 127-9
  Crying and shouting and meaning farewell, [Adieu 127-10
  The children will be crying on the stair, [Nigger 156-7
  Crying among the clouds, enraged [MBG 169-7
  And with mouths crying and crying day by day. [Dames 206-10
  There is a storm much like the crying of the wind, [Sketch 336-1
  Crying as that speech falls as if to fail. [Sketch 336-6
  Come home, wind, he kept crying and crying. [Pieces 351-11
  The savage transparence. They go crying [Pediment 361-16
  What chieftain, walking by himself, crying [NSF 389-2
  Went crying their desolate syllables, before [Old Woman 45-26 P
  Crying against a need that pressed like cold, [Old Woman 45-29 P
  Of the very body instinctively crying [Stan Hero 84-27 P
  He came crying, [Three 139-6 P
CRYPT. A fringed eye in a crypt. [Add 199-8
CRYPTIC. Adorned with cryptic stones and sliding shines, [Owl
    434-10
CRYSTAL. At the end of night last night a crystal star, [Choc
    296-17
  Crystal on crystal until crystal clouds [Pieces 351-15
  And the circles quicken and crystal colors come [Anach 366-13
  Logos and logic, crystal hypothesis, [NSF 387-4
  You will have stopped revolving except in crystal. [NSF 407-3
  Move blackly and without crystal. [Countryman 428-15
  They cast deeply round a crystal crystal-white [Bouquet 452-1
  You were not born yet when the trees were crystal [Slug 522-17
  The light wings lifted through the crystal space [Old Woman
    46-11 P
  In the crystal atmospheres of the mind, [Ulysses 102-27 P
  Shiftings of an inchoate crystal tableau, [Someone 86-21 A
  See over-crystal.
CRYSTALLED. Goat-leaper, crystalled and luminous, sitting [AA 417-9
CRYSTALLINE. Its crystalline pendentives on the sea [Sea Surf 100-7
  There, of clear, revolving crystalline; [Ideal 88-7 A
CRYSTALLIZATIONS. With certain blue crystallizations [Six Sig 74-20
CRYSTAL-POINTED. The crystal-pointed star of morning, rose [Choc
    296-18
  He breathed in crystal-pointed change the whole [Choc 298-6
CRYSTALS. A thousand crystals' chiming voices, [Hero 279-19
  Naked of hindrance, a thousand crystals. [Hero 279-28
  Drenching the evening with crystals' light, [Letters 107-3 P
CRYSTAL-WHITE. They cast deeply round a crystal crystal-white
    [Bouquet 452-1
CUBA. To Cuba. Jot these milky matters down. [Havana 144-6
  Is lunar Habana the Cuba of the self? [Feo 333-15
  This husk of Cuba, tufted emerald, [Someone 83-7 A
CUBAN. The Cuban, Polodowsky, [Venereal 47-12
  "The Cuban Doctor" [64-title
  A mountain, a pineapple pungent as Cuban summer. [NSF 393-12
CUCK. And not all birds sing cuck [Lulu M 27-7 P
  Sing coo, sing cuck, cuckoo. [Lulu M 27-8 P
CUCKOO. Cunning-coo, O, cuckoo cock, [Country 207-2
  Sing coo, sing cuck, cuckoo. [Lulu M 27-8 P
  The cuckoo trees and the widow of Madrid [Greenest 59-16 P
CUCKOOS. Of the cuckoos, a man with a mania for clocks. [Nigger
    157-19
  Climb through the night, because his cuckoos call. [Oboe 251-7
  The improvisations of the cuckoos [Hero 275-14
CUFFS. They should think hard in the dark cuffs [Homunculus 26-18
CUIRASSIERS. Of the pith of mind, cuirassiers against [Greenest
    56-5 P
CUISINE. "Cuisine Bourgeoise" [227-title
CULLS. Of their fresh culls might be a cure of the ground. [Rock
    526-17
CUNNING-COO. Cunning-coo, O, cuckoo cock, [Country 207-2
CUP. One's cup and never to say a word, [Adieu 128-3
  Regard. But for that salty cup, [MBG 179-19
CUPIDO. The faith of forty, ward of Cupido. [Monocle 16-16
CUPPED. The bride came jingling, kissed and cupped, or else [Repet
    308-17
CUPS. In kitchen cups concupiscent curds. [Emperor 64-3
CURDS. In kitchen cups concupiscent curds. [Emperor 64-3
CURE. There is cure of sorrow. [W Burgher 61-9
  We must be cured of it by a cure of the ground [Rock 526-11
  Or a cure of ourselves, that is equal to a cure [Rock 526-12
  Of the ground, a cure beyond forgetfulness. [Rock 526-13
  Of their fresh culls might be a cure of the ground. [Rock 526-17
  These are a cure of the ground and of ourselves, [Rock 527-3
  And so exists no more. This is the cure [Rock 527-19

CURED. We must be cured of it by a cure of the ground [Rock 526-11
CURIOS. It will be fecund in rapt curios. [Red Kit 32-5 P
CURIOUS. With a curious puffing. [Plot Giant 7-6
  Their curious fates in war, come, celebrate [Monocle 16-15
  Crispin foresaw a curious promenade [C 31-23
  Each day, still curious, but in a round [C 42-14
  The fourth, pent now, a digit curious. [C 45-1
  It is curious that the density of life [Nigger 157-7
  He felt curious about the winter hills [Extracts 254-26
  Within the difference. He felt curious [Extracts 255-12
  Yet, when corrected, has its curious lapses, [EM 318-15
  Wrapped in their seemings, crowd on curious crowd, [Descrip
    342-14
  Among the children, like curious ripenesses [AA 415-8
  It was curious to have to descend [Aug 493-21
  Long after the worms and the curious carvings of [Burnshaw
    47-12 P
  It is curious that I should have spoken of Raël, [Desire 85-1 P
  Curious that I should have spoken of Jaffa [Desire 85-4 P
  Or letters of a curious alphabet; [Recit 87-8 P
CURL. That not one curl in nature has survived? [Monocle 14-9
  Each one in her decent curl. [Bananas 54-8
CURLED. Curled over the shadowless hut, the rust and bones,
    [Farewell 118-4
CURLICUES. The canting curlicues [Ord Women 11-12
CURLING. Curling round the steeple and the people, [Hero 278-8
CURLING-OUT. There might be in the curling-out of spring [Descrip
    341-15
CURLS. "And Daughters with Curls" [C 43-title 6
  At the roots of her indifferent curls. [Thought 184-14
  Green were the curls upon that head. [Poem Morn 219-17
  The winds batter it. The water curls. The leaves [Novel 457-2
CURRENT. As if the sky was a current that bore them along,
    [Loaf 200-5
CURRENTS. Yet invisible currents clearly circulate. [Nigger 156-3
CURRICULUM. Into the compass and curriculum [Monocle 15-15
  Curriculum for the marvelous sophomore. [C 36-15
  A curriculum, a vigor, a local abstraction . . . [R Conn 533-17
CURTAINS. The curtains flittered and the door was closed. [C 42-4
  "The Curtains in the House of the Metaphysician" [62-title
  It comes about that the drifting of these curtains [Curtains
    62-1
  A high bed sheltered by curtains. [Theory 87-3
  Of the wind upon the curtains. [Chateau 161-14
  The curtains are stiff and prim and still. [Chateau 161-18
  The curtains. Even the drifting of the curtains, [Peaches 224-17
  The curtains to a metaphysical t [NSF 390-21
  And curtains like a naive pretence of sleep. [AA 415-15
  The curtains, when pulled, might show another whole, [Theatre
    91-13 P
CURULE. Blue-strutted curule, true--unreal, [Human 363-12
CURVED. Having curved outlines. [Pears 196-10
CURVES. Composed of curves [Pears 196-6
CURVETED. To which the swans curveted, a will to change, [NSF
    397-17
CURVETTED. Wildly curvetted, color-scarred, so beaked, [Greenest
    57-18 P
CURVING. The curving of her hip, as motionless gesture, [Couch
    295-8
  Not fixed and deadly (like a curving line [Abnormal 23-17 P
CUSTODIANS. Marching a motionless march, custodians. [C 42-12
  In which those frail custodians watched, [C 43-1
  Custodians of the glory of the scene, [NH 469-17
CUSTOM. It was the custom [Winter B 141-9
  As by a custom or according to [AA 412-6
CUT. Cut summer down to find the honey-comb. [Blue Bldg 217-21
  Like a spectral cut in its perception, a tilt [What We 460-3
  And the oldest and the warmest heart was cut [Quiet 523-10
  And by a hand of certitude to cut [Greenest 56-17 P
CUTS. As a boat feels when it cuts blue water. [Vari 234-5
  To be in scale, unless virtue cuts him, snips [Orb 442-26
  Still on the horizon elongates his cuts, [Orb 443-4
CUTTERS. See stone-cutters.
CUTTING. Chisels of the stone-cutters cutting the stones. [Archi
    16-19 P
CYCLE. To have what is not is its ancient cycle. [NSF 382-5
  The cycle of the solid having turned. [Sombre 68-16 P
  That talk shifts the cycle of the scenes of kings? [Conversat
    109-23 P
CYCLOPS. To watch us in the summer of Cyclops [Owl 435-1
CYMBAL. A cymbal crashed, [Peter 91-10
CYMBALS. The shoo-shoo-shoo of secret cymbals round. [NSF 401-13
  Bang cymbals as they used to do. [Memo 89-15 P
CYNIC. Dark cynic, strip and bathe and bask at will. [NE Verses
    106-3
  Without cap or strap, you are the cynic still. [NE Verses 106-4
CYTHERE. The opposite of Cythère, an isolation [NH 480-19

DA. Damariscotta da da doo. [Vari 235-15
  Dee, dum, diddle, dee, dee, diddle, dee, da. [Primordia 8-20 P
DAB. To dab things even nicely pink [Melancholy 32-9 P
DABBLED. Dabbled with yellow pollen--red as red [Hibiscus 23-1
DACHSHUND. The deer and the dachshund are one. [Jersey 210-4
  Kiss, cats: for the deer and the dachshund [Jersey 210-13
  Since the deer and the dachshund are one. [Jersey 210-21
DAFFODILS. Myrtle, viburnums, daffodils, blue phlox), [Dump 202-13
DAGGER. To drive the dagger in his heart, [MBG 166-4
  An arrogant dagger darting its arrogance, [Aug 491-24
DAGGERS. The blessed regal dropped in daggers' dew, [Montra 260-18
DAGOES. And make the Dagoes squeal. [Drum-Majors 36-22 P
DAILY. Of cold and earliness is a daily sense, [NH 481-12
  A daily majesty of meditation, [Look 518-21
DAIMLERS. The flute on the gramophone, the Daimlers that [Greenest
  53-21 P
DAINTY. These muleteers are dainty of their way. [Monocle 15-21
DALLY. The imaginative, ghosts that dally [Hero 279-6
DALLYING. The second sister dallying was shy [C 44-27
DALMATICS. The churches, like dalmatics stooped in prayer, [Sombre
  69-1 P
DAMARISCOTTA. Damariscotta da da doo. [Vari 235-15
DAMASK. Blue verdured into a damask's lofty symbol, [NH 477-18
  Is, after all, draped damask pampaluned, [Greenest 58-4 P
DAMASKED. And the damasked memory of the golden forms [EM 317-26
  Of the damasked memory of the golden forms, [EM 317-28
  Damasked in the originals of green, [Owl 434-20
DAMASKS. Like blooms? Like damasks that were shaken off [Sea Surf
  101-13
DAME. Our man beheld the naked, nameless dame, [Hand 271-3
  My dame, sing for this person accurate songs. [NSF 388-9
  See diva-dame.
DAMES. "United Dames of America" [206-title
  This parlor of farcical dames, this clowns' colonnade, this
  kites' pavilion? [Inelegance 26-6 P
DAMNED. Damned universal cock, as if the sun [Bantams 75-16
  With his damned hoobla-hoobla-hoobla-how, [NSF 383-2
  And yet the damned thing doesn't come right. [Agenda 41-18 P
  Say this to Pravda, tell the damned rag [Memo 89-9 P
DAMNS. And so it is one damns that green shade at the bottom of
  the land. [Banal 63-3
  And died amid uproarious damns. [Lulu M 27-10 P
DAMOZELS. "One of Those Hibiscuses of Damozels" [74-title 1 P
DAMPENED. Of dampened lumber, emanations blown [C 36-8
DAMSEL. A damsel heightened by eternal bloom. [Monocle 15-28
DAMSELS. Like damsels daubed and let your feet be bare [Burnshaw
  51-11 P
  This time, like damsels captured by the sky, [Burnshaw 51-17 P
DANCE. Shaken in a dance. [Six Sig 74-3
  "Dance of the Macabre Mice" [123-title
  This dance has no name. It is a hungry dance. [Mice 123-5
  We dance it out to the tip of Monsieur's sword, [Mice 123-6
  The salty skeleton must dance because [Montra 261-13
  Of each old revolving dance, the music [Hero 274-7
  The father fetches negresses to dance, [AA 415-7
  Of pattern in the dance's ripening. [AA 415-9
  Or dance the death of doves, most sallowly, [Burnshaw 48-22 P
  Dance, now, and with sharp voices cry, but cry [Burnshaw 51-10 P
  Conceive that while you dance the statue falls, [Burnshaw 51-30P
DANCED. Danced around a stump. [Motion 83-4
  And dancers danced ballets on top of their beds-- [Agenda 42-5 P
  Each other moving in a chant and danced [Burnshaw 50-27 P
DANCER. Like a dancer's skirt, flung round and settling down.
  [Woman Had 81-18 P
DANCERS. And dancers danced ballets on top of their beds--
  [Agenda 42-5 P
DANCES. A black figure dances in a black field. [Plough-Boy 6-4 P
  It dances down a furrow, in the early light, back of a crazy
  plough, the green blades following. [Plough-Boy 6-7 P
DANCING. Today is today and the dancing is done. [Fish-Scale
  160-16
  Be of a man skating, a woman dancing, a woman [Of Mod 240-21
DANES. We were as Danes in Denmark all day long [AA 419-7
DANGLE. As they jangle and dangle and kick their feet. [Luther
  462-3
  The bird's fire-fangled feathers dangle down. [Of Mere 118-6 P
DANGLED. And in these comic colors dangled down, [Lot 371-9
  And clumped stars dangled all the way. [Ulysses 105-12 P
DANGLING. Fibrous and dangling down, [Bananas 54-19
  Dangling in an illogical [Metamorph 266-8
  And mist-mites, dangling seconds, grown [Red Fern 365-9
  Dangling and spangling, the mic-mac of mocking birds. [NH 486-15
  Through clumped stars dangling all the way. [Presence 106-12 P
DANISH. Cat's taste possibly or possibly Danish lore, [Someone
  87-5 A
DANK. Of ocean, pondering dank stratagem. [Sea Surf 101-10
  Of the dank imagination, much below [Burnshaw 47-5 P
  Concealed in glittering grass, dank reptile skins. [Duck 65-11 P

DANUBE. See Blue Danube.
DAPPER. See dew-dapper.
DARE. But it dare not leap by chance in its own dark. [AA 417-22
DARK. Grown tired of flight. Like a dark rabbi, I [Monocle 17-21
  Poison grows in this dark. [Week Woman 25-4
  They should think hard in the dark cuffs [Homunculus 26-18
  And dark Brazilians in their cafés, [C 38-24
  That spread chromatics in hilarious dark, [C 45-9
  Donna, donna, dark, [Venereal 48-11
  Monotonous earth and dark blue sky. [Vincentine 52-12
  Of the steadfast lanterns creep across the dark? [Heaven 56-20
  Make hue among the dark comedians, [Heaven 56-21
  On the dark, green water-wheel, [Solitaires 60-4
  She dreams a little, and she feels the dark [Sunday 67-2
  The lines are much too dark and much too sharp. [Tallap 71-13
  Night nursed not him in whose dark mind [Babies 77-13
  You dweller in the dark cabin, [Watermelon 88-19
  You dweller in the dark cabin, [Watermelon 89-13
  Dark cynic, strip and bathe and bask at will. [NE Verses 106-3
  The dark shadows of the funereal magnolias [Norfolk 111-16
  To stand here on the deck in the dark and say [Farewell 118-6
  If it was only the dark voice of the sea [Key W 129-10
  Makes me conceive how dark I have become, [Sun March 133-11
  And true savant of this dark nature be. [Sun March 134-8
  Of dark, which in its very darkening [Eve Angels 137-24
  In dark forms of the grass [Brave 138-11
  True reconcilings, dark, pacific words, [Havana 144-21
  His dark familiar, often walked apart. [Anglais 148-14
  That dark companion left him unconsoled [Anglais 148-17
  Pushing their buds above the dark green leaves, [Nigger 156-11
  Deeper within the belly's dark [MBG 171-9
  It glistens in essential dark. [MBG 172-18
  And say of what you see in the dark [MBG 183-4
  At a head upon the pillow in the dark, [Men Fall 188-5
  The distance between the dark steeple [Jersey 210-9
  This dark, particular rose. [Scavoir 231-4
  In light blue air over dark blue sea. [Vari 232-6
  To lie on one's bed in the dark, close to a face [Yellow 237-8
  A metaphysician in the dark, twanging [Of Mod 240-14
  He had only not to live, to walk in the dark, [Landsc 242-12
  Is blue, clear, cloudy, high, dark, wide and round; [Extracts
  252-11
  It is difficult to read. The page is dark. [Phosphor 267-5
  Approaching in the dark approaches [Hero 279-25
  He was a shell of dark blue glass, or ice, [Choc 297-9
  Upon my top he breathed the pointed dark. [Choc 298-1
  Too dark, too far, too much the accents of [EM 314-19
  Is ease, stands in the dark, a shadows' hill, [EM 319-5
  But the dark italics it could not propound. [EM 326-6
  Dark horse and walker walking rapidly. [Pure 330-12
  Or in the dark musician, listening [Descrip 340-21
  Of degrees of perception in the scholar's dark. [NSF 395-15
  But it dare not leap by chance in its own dark. [AA 417-22
  As if the innocent mother sang in the dark [AA 419-1
  The dead. Only the thought of those dark three [Owl 432-17
  Is dark, thought of the forms of dark desire. [Owl 432-18
  Slowly the room grows dark. It is odd about [Novel 458-19
  Abba, dark death is the breaking of a glass. [Golden 460-16
  Dark Juan looks outward through his mystic brow . . . [Luther
  461-14
  Dark things without a double, after all, [NH 465-13
  And on the ground. The hibernal dark that hung [NH 476-8
  Rugged and luminous, chants in the dark [NH 479-14
  At evening, after dark, is the other half, [NH 482-4
  Shook off their dark marine in lapis light. [NH 484-8
  Bergamo on a postcard, Rome after dark, [NH 486-1
  Things dark on the horizons of perception, [Rome 508-12
  How high that highest candle lights the dark. [Final 524-15
  A gesture in the dark, a fear one feels [Moonlight 531-16
  In the swamps, bushes draw up dark red, [Primordia 8-22 P
  Of your dark self, and how the wings of stars, [Blanche 10-11 P
  I peopled the dark park with gowns [Stan MMO 19-1 P
  And you forgive dark broachings growing great [Spaniard 34-7 P
  Whitened, again, forms formless in the dark, [Old Woman 45-8 P
  Be marble after the drenching reds, the dark [Greenest 57-22 P
  That has been yelling in the dark. [Grotesque 77-4 P
  At the antipodes of poetry, dark winter, [Discov 95-7 P
  The little and the dark, and that [Dove 98-1 P
  Light's comedies, dark's tragedies, [Ulysses 102-28 P
  On the dark side of the heavens or the bright, [Local 112-2 P
  Like precious scholia jotted down in the dark. [Someone 84-21 A
  See: bright-dark; ever-dark; mirror-dark.
DARK-BELTED. Of a lunar light, dark-belted sorcerers [Old Woman
  46-3 P
DARK-BLOODED. Hot-hooded and dark-blooded, rescued the rose [EM
  316-17
DARK-BLOWN. The dark-blown ceinture loosened, not relinquished.
  [NSF 385-11
DARK-BLUE. Or into a dark-blue king, un roi tonnerre, [Extracts
  254-10

The golden fingers picking dark-blue air: [NSF 398-15
DARK-COLORED. Their dark-colored words had redescribed the citrons.
  [NH 487-9
DARKEN. Darken your speech. [Two Figures 86-3
  And darken it, make an unbroken mat [Red Kit 31-24 P
DARKENED. The white cabildo darkened, the façade, [C 32-19
  The darkened ghosts of our old comedy? [Heaven 56-11
  Hoo-hooed it in the darkened ocean-blooms. [Sea Surf 100-5
  This darkened water cloven by sullen swells [Farewell 118-14
  All of them, darkened by time, moved by they know not what,
    amending the airs they play to fulfill themselves; [Piano
    21-17 P
DARKENING. Of dark, which in its very darkening [Eve Angels 137-24
DARKENS. As a calm darkens among water-lights. [Sunday 67-4
DARKER. Perplexed by its darker iridescences. [Beginning 427-14
DARKEST. The darkest blue of the dome and the wings around [Duck
  65-22 P
DARKIES. Mow the grass in the cemetery, darkies, [Norfolk 111-4
DARK-LEAVED. A very dark-leaved berry tree. [Banjo 114-4 P
DARKLY. And darkly beside the vulcanic [Hero 274-28
DARKNESS. A scholar of darkness, [Venereal 48-5
  Downward to darkness, on extended wings. [Sunday 70-28
  And quieting dreams in the sleepers in darkness-- [Lunar 107-11
  The son and the daughter, who come to the darkness, [Norfolk
    111-18
  The floor. Go on through the darkness. The waves fly back.
    [Farewell 117-10
  The darkness shattered, turbulent with foam. [Farewell 118-16
  This gloom is the darkness of the sea. [MBG 179-17
  Poison, in what darkness set [Bagatelles 213-4
  Unless in the darkness, brightly-crowned, [Vari 233-1
  With lofty darkness. The donkey was there to ride, [Uruguay 249-9
  In a clock-shop. . . . Soldier, think, in the darkness, [Hero
    275-15
  Flutters in tiny darkness. [Dutch 290-14
  Like the head of fate, looked out in darkness, part [Choc 299-20
  Darkness, nothingness of human after-death, [Flyer 336-12
  Breaches the darkness of Ceylon with blares. [NSF 384-12
  A darkness gathers though it does not fall [AA 412-21
  Whirlpools of darkness in whirlwinds of light . . . [Page 423-5
  Good-by in the darkness, speaking quietly there, [Owl 431-17
  As if it bears all darkness in its bulk. [Sombre 68-18 P
  Farewells and, in the darkness, to feel again [Sombre 71-21 P
  Of darkness, creating from nothingness [Ulysses 100-27 P
  A home against one's self, a darkness, [Letters 107-6 P
DARKNESSES. These Gaeled and fitful-fangled darknesses [Our Stars
  455-18
DARKS. But with a speech belched out of hoary darks [C 29-26
DARK-SKINNED. Dark-skinned and sinuous, winding upwardly,
  [Greenest 55-13 P
DARK-SPICED. These trees and their argentines, their dark-spiced
  branches, [Holiday 313-3
DARK-SYLLABLED. Then I, Semiramide, dark-syllabled, [Phenom 287-15
DARLING. Of the being's deepest darling, we forego [EM 317-14
DARTING. Darting out of their purple craws [Bananas 54-22
  An arrogant dagger darting its arrogance, [Aug 491-24
  Darting envenomed eyes about, like fangs, [Greenest 55-15 P
DASHED. In colorings harmonious, dewed and dashed [Ulysses 104-3 P
DAUBED. Sacked up and carried overseas, daubed out [C 45-13
  Like damsels daubed and let your feet be bare [Burnshaw 51-11 P
DAUBS. Belittles those carefully chosen daubs. [Grapes 110-16
DAUGHTER. Seemed the helpless daughter [Sonatina 109-16
  This skeleton had a daughter and that, a son. [Norfolk 111-7
  And his daughter was a foreign thing. [Norfolk 111-11
  The son and the daughter, who come to the darkness, [Norfolk
    111-18
  Not in a later son, a different daughter, another place, [Martial
    237-14
  He disappeared with his neighbor's daughter. [Three 135-15 P
DAUGHTERS. And Daughters with Curls [C 43-title 6
  True daughters both of Crispin and his clay. [C 44-2
  Four daughters in a world too intricate [C 45-2
  Her daughters to the peached and ivory wench [Havana 143-26
  Of her sons and of her daughters. They found themselves [NSF
    383-13
  She lived in her house. She had two daughters, one [NSF 402-1
DAUNT. And daunt that old assassin, heart's desire? [Duck 66-11 P
DAUNTLESS. The dauntless master, as he starts the human tale.
  [Fuel 456-18
DAUNTLESSLY. It was not yet the hour to be dauntlessly leaping.
  [Vari 236-3
DAWDLE. Let the wenches dawdle in such dress [Emperor 64-4
DAWN. At the centre of a diamond. At dawn, [EM 322-10
  Men would be starting at dawn to walk ashore. [Page 422-5
  At dawn, nor of summer-light and winter-light [Burnshaw 50-3 P
  Seraphim of Europe? Pouring out of dawn, [Greenest 56-3 P
DAY. Of a later day [Paltry 6-5
  In lordly study. Every day, I found [Monocle 17-23
  I say now, Fernando, that on that day [Hibiscus 22-9
  Created, in his day, a touch of doubt. [C 27-13

When its black branches came to bud, belle day, [C 39-3
But day by day, now this thing and now that [C 40-21
Each day, still curious, but in a round [C 42-14
That burial, pillared up each day as porte [Heaven 56-16
The western day through what you called [Hoon 65-8
The day is like wide water, without sound, [Sunday 67-8
Or old dependency of day and night, [Sunday 70-19
And queen, and of diviner love the day [Fictive 87-9
Of the two dreams, night and day, [Watermelon 89-1
Night stilled the slopping of the sea. The day [Sea Surf 101-23
And the time of the day. [Sailing 120-5
Day after day, throughout the winter, [Medit 124-1
And men of day and never of pointed night, [Eve Angels 137-14
To moodiest nothings, as, desire for day [Eve Angels 137-21
The worlds that were and will be, death and day. [Nigger 150-12
The cock-hen crows all day. But cockerel shrieks, [Nigger 155-11
A shearsman of sorts. The day was green. [MBG 165-2
Day is desire and night is sleep. [MBG 167-7
Each is both star and orb; and day [MBG 172-11
We shall forget by day, except [MBG 184-4
Day hymns instead of constellated rhymes, [Thought 185-18
So much more than that. The day itself [Poems Clim 193-13
But in the centre of our lives, this time, this day, [Glass
  198-1
Day creeps down. The moon is creeping up. [Dump 201-11
Of every day, the wrapper on the can of pears, [Dump 201-17
The freshness of morning, the blowing of day, one says [Dump
  202-2
The day to pieces and cry stanza my stone? [Dump 203-10
And with mouths crying and crying day by day. [Dames 206-10
The difficulty to think at the end of day, [Rabbit K 209-1
There was the cat slopping its milk all day, [Rabbit K 209-4
Either now or tomorrow or the day after that. [Nightgown 214-20
He read, all day, all night and all the nights, [Blue Bldg
  216-16
Searching all day, all night, for the honey-comb. [Blue Bldg
  217-24
A sunny day's complete Poussiniana [Poem Morn 219-1
And it is not, it is day and it not, [Cuisine 228-3
"Variations on a Summer Day" [232-title
Night and day, wind and quiet, produces [Vari 233-21
Beyond the keenest diamond day [Adequacy 244-1
And toward the start of day and trees [Adequacy 244-6
Than a thought to be rehearsed all day, a speech [Beard 247-16
On an early Sunday in April, a feeble day, [Extracts 254-25
Weather of night creatures, whistling all day, too, [Montra
  261-17
For every day. In a civiler manner, [Hero 275-22
This is his day. With nothing lost, he [Hero 280-16
The feeling of him was the feel of day, [Choc 297-4
And of a day as yet unseen, in which [Choc 297-5
Against the whole experience of day. [Choc 298-10
They wanted him by day to be, image, [Choc 299-4
Cardinal, saying the prayers of earliest day; [Choc 300-2
In day's constellation, and yet remain, yet be, [Choc 300-20
Brings the day to perfection and then fails. He dwells [EM 318-2
The day in its color not perpending time, [Pure 332-16
Things look each day, each morning, or the style [Descrip
  339-18
The spirit's universe, then a summer's day, [Descrip 343-16
Even the seeming of a summer's day, [Descrip 343-17
In the brilliantest descriptions of new day, [Descrip 344-11
How happy I was the day I told the young Blandina of three-
  legged giraffes . . . [Analysis 348-1
The large-leaved day grows rapidly, [Red Fern 365-1
And hold them round the sultry day? Why should [Belly 367-4
Day is the children's friend. [Prejudice 368-11
Of day, then, children make [Prejudice 368-20
No, not of day, but of themselves, [Prejudice 369-2
That's how the stars shine during the day. There, then, [Lot
  371-4
This is the last day of a certain year [Cred 372-11
One day enriches a year. One woman makes [Cred 374-21
And people, without souvenir. The day [Cred 375-7
To share the day. The trumpet supposes that [Cred 377-1
Close to me, hidden in me day and night? [NSF 380-6
Who comes and goes and comes and goes all day. [NSF 381-22
And throws his stars around the floor. By day [NSF 383-5
On a woman, day on night, the imagined [NSF 392-6
Or the concentration of a cloudy day? [NSF 396-17
And if there is an hour there is a day, [NSF 405-3
They will get it straight one day at the Sorbonne. [NSF 406-22
And sky, between thought and day and night. It is [NSF 407-5
We were as Danes in Denmark all day long [AA 419-6
For whom the outlandish was another day [AA 419-9
In the hard brightness of that winter day [Page 421-4
This day writhes with what? The lecturer [Ulti 429-4
If the day writhes, it is not with revelations. [Ulti 429-15
There came a day, there was a day--one day [Owl 432-19
As a moving mountain is, moving through day [Owl 433-10

We shall be heavy with the knowledge of that day. [John 437-23
The day is great and strong-- [Pecul 453-4
She is the day, the walk of the moon [Pecul 454-4
Day's arches are crumbling into the autumn night. [Novel 458-16
Of day. If the study of his images [Study I 463-5
Became divided in the leisure of blue day [NH 468-22
And more, in branchings after day. One part [NH 468-23
In misted contours, credible day again. [NH 470-15
The oldest-newest day is the newest alone. [NH 476-19
Unfretted by day's separate, several selves, [NH 482-10
It took all day to quieten the sky [NH 482-20
When day comes, fire-foams in the motions of the sea, [NH 488-12
These locusts by day, these crickets by night [Aug 489-4
The forgetful color of the autumn day [Aug 494-16
Like tales that were told the day before yesterday-- [Hermit
  505-13
The sky seemed so small that winter day, [Two Illus 513-1
A knowledge that the actual day [Two Illus 513-7
Is only what the sun does every day, [Look 517-16
Day's invisible beginner, [Song Fixed 520-7
The two kept beating together. It was only day. [World 521-12
The difficult rightness of half-risen day. [Rock 528-9
To the enclosure, day, the things illumined [Rock 528-18
By day, night and that which night illumines, [Rock 528-19
Fixed one for good in geranium-colored day. [Armor 529-1
Stands in a light, its natural light and day, [Armor 530-20
And little will or wish, that day, for tears. [Soldat 14-17 P
In a parlor of day. [Coroner 30-12 P
"The Drum-Majors in the Labor Day Parade" [36-title P
At the burst of day, crepuscular images [Burnshaw 46-23 P
Astral and Shelleyan, diffuse new day; [Burnshaw 47-26 P
On a day still full of summer, when the leaves [Burnshaw 50-18 P
And the sound of z in the grass all day, though these [Burnshaw
  51-4 P
That enter day from night, came mirror-dark, [Burnshaw 51-26 P
From youngest day or oldest night and far [Greenest 54-1 P
By waverings of stars, the joy of day [Greenest 54-15 P
Day came upon the spirit as life comes [Duck 61-5 P
And deep winds flooded you; for these, day comes, [Duck 61-6 P
Steeped in night's opium, evading day. [Sombre 66-17 P
In hum-drum space, farewell, farewell, by day [Sombre 71-8 P
The day is green and the wind is young. [Stan MBG 72-1 P
The greenish quaverings of day [Stan MBG 73-5 P
This was repeated day by day. The waves [Woman Had 81-19 P
A lamp, in a day of the week, the time before spring, [Woman Had
  83-6 P
When I was sleeping, nor by day, [Desire 85-8 P
Come to us every day. And yet they are [Recit 87-28 P
A few more hours of day, the unravelling [Nuns 92-12 P
It is a special day. We mumble the words [Nuns 92-18 P
Therein, day settles and thickens round a form-- [Role 93-12 P
The only sun of the only day, [Ulysses 100-2 P
A whole, the day on which the last star [Ulysses 102-8 P
The revolutions through day and night, [Ulysses 102-22 P
A land would hold her in its arms that day [Letters 108-6 P
"A Clear Day and No Memories" [113-title P
Since the day we left Pekin. [Three 128-9 P
Day, night and man and his endless effigies. [Someone 83-13 A
A day of which we say, this is the day [Ideal 88-2 A
That we desired, a day of blank, blue wheels, [Ideal 88-3 A
And at what time both of the year and day; [Ideal 89-3 A
See: a-day; green-a-day; mid-day; to-day; week-day.
DAY-BREAK. Or thing. . . . Now day-break comes. . . [Canna 55-6
DAYLIGHT. The wind-gloss. Or as daylight comes, [MBG 175-2
Of daylight came while he sat thinking. He said, [Choc 298-12
Like daylight, with time's bellishings, [Two Illus 514-18
A bird's cry, at daylight or before, [Not Ideas 534-5
Daylight evaporates, like a sound one hears in sickness. [Discov
  95-9 P
For daylight and too near for sleep. [Dove 98-15 P
DAYS. That the hours of his indolent, arid days, [Frogs 78-10
Her days, her oceanic nights, calling [Farewell 117-17
To go to Florida one of these days, [Winter B 141-16
Articulate its desert days. [MBG 174-10
Of images. Days pass like papers from a press. [Dump 201-14
Of days that will be wasted, [Bagatelles 213-18
Is blowing after days of constant rain. [Connois 216-5
These days of disinheritance, we feast [Cuisine 227-13
More nights, more days, more clouds, more worlds. [Vari 233-22
Of things no better than paper things, of days [Extracts 253-2
That are paper days. The false and true are one. [Extracts
  253-3
Elysia, these days, half earth, half mind; [Extracts 257-1
And beyond the days, beyond the slow-foot litters [Repet 309-1
Baked through long days, is piled in mows. It is [Cred 374-8
Or do the other days enrich the one? [Cred 374-24
And hard it is in spite of blazoned days. [NSF 383-24
Fertile of its own leaves and days and wars, [Aug 491-14
Of autumn days." [Inhab 504-15
In the days when the mood of love will be swarming for solace

and sink deeply into the thin stuff of being, [Piano 22-8 P
Of his orange days [Coroner 29-19 P
In self, a man of longer time than days, [Good Bad 33-10 P
As summer would return to weazened days. [Greenest 57-27 P
Farewell, my days. [Fare Guit 98-18 P
Green had, those days, its own implacable sting. [Someone 85-7 A
See: mid-days; three-days.
DAY-SON. The angry day-son clanging at its make: [Papini 448-2
DAZE. Like an hallucination come to daze [Sun March 134-3
Its colors make, the migratory daze, [Bouquet 451-17
DAZZLE. Words add to the senses. The words for the dazzle [Vari
  234-17
Dazzle yields to a clarity and we observe, [Descrip 341-10
On the flag-poles in a red-blue dazzle, whack [NSF 390-23
A dazzle of remembrance and of sight. [Owl 433-6
See dizzle-dazzle.
DAZZLED. The dazzled flakes and splinters disappear. [Golden
  460-17
DAZZLING. Is dazzling, [Depression 63-10
Speak of the dazzling wings. [Pascagoula 127-8
The dazzling, bulging, brightest core, [Red Fern 365-11
The tree stood dazzling in the air [Two Illus 514-15
Dazzling by simplest beams and soothly still, [Old Woman 46-4 P
Resolved in dazzling discovery. [Ulysses 102-1 P
See over-dazzling.
DAZZLINGLY. From loftiness, misgivings dazzlingly [Ulysses 101-29 P
DEAD. The dead brine melted in him like a dew [C 29-14
Should merely call him dead? Pronounce amen [C 41-17
Seem things in some procession of the dead, [Sunday 67-6
Why should she give her bounty to the dead? [Sunday 67-12
Now, the wry Rosenbloom is dead [Cortege 79-13
Of the dead. [Cortege 79-16
Rosenbloom is dead. [Cortege 79-17
In unison for the dead. [Cortege 80-5
Rosenbloom is dead. [Cortege 80-6
Of the ascending of the dead. [Cortege 80-15
Rosenbloom is dead. [Cortege 81-8
And of the sisterhood of the living dead [Fictive 87-6
Is at the mast-head and the past is dead. [Farewell 117-5
A state that was free, in the dead of winter, from mice? [Mice
  123-10
Claude has been dead a long time [Botanist 1 134-10
Of the dead, majestic in their seals. [MBG 170-8
Have I? Am I a man that is dead [MBG 173-8
The wind in which the dead leaves blow. [MBG 180-14
On the dump? Is it to sit among mattresses of the dead, [Dump
  203-6
Of this dead mass and that. The wind might fill [Dames 206-8
Never angels, nothing of the dead, [Dezem 218-13
There would have been the cries of the dead [Thunder 220-18
This outpost, this douce, this dumb, this dead, in which
  [Cuisine 228-9
The Arachne integument of dead trees, [Vari 234-19
The dead rocks not the green rocks, the live rocks. If,
  [Extracts 255-16
Because everything is half dead. [Motive 288-2
Would be a geography of the dead: not of that land [Somnam
  304-13
The spirits of all the impotent dead, seen clear, [Cats 368-8
The gardener's cat is dead, the gardener gone [Cred 377-9
Phoebus is dead, ephebe. But Phoebus was [NSF 381-10
We encounter in the dead middle of the night [NSF 395-2
A dead shepherd brought tremendous chords from hell [NSF 400-21
To imagine winter? When the leaves are dead, [AA 417-7
Two forms move among the dead, high sleep [Owl 431-13
The dead. Only the thought of those dark three [Owl 432-17
We are not men of bronze and we are not dead. [NH 472-11
In the strokes of thunder, dead candles at the window [NH 488-11
In that distant chamber, a bearded queen, wicked in her dead
  light. [Madame 507-13
Profound poetry of the poor and of the dead, [Rome 509-25
No radiance of dead blaze, but something seen [Armor 529-13
A dead hand tapped the drum, [Phases 6-1 P
And not in this dead glass, which can reflect [Blanche 10-2 P
The thing is dead . . . Everything is dead [Burnshaw 46-13 P
That is is dead except what ought to be. [Burnshaw 46-15 P
A trash can at the end of the world, the dead [Burnshaw 49-5 P
Give up dead things and the living turn away. [Burnshaw 49-6 P
As against each other, the dead, the phantomesque. [Duck 65-5 P
No thoughts of people now dead, [Clear Day 113-8 P
That we are painted as three dead men, [Three 133-2 P
He is dead. [Three 140-8 P
Even dead eyes, [Three 143-13 P
DEADLIEST. Out of the deadliest heat. [Attempt 370-7
DEADLY. As the deadly thought of men accomplishing [Monocle 16-14
From the spun sky and the high and deadly view, [Aug 493-10
Not fixed and deadly (lie a curving line [Abnormal 23-17 P
Observe her shining in the deadly trees. [Spaniard 34-15 P
Deadly and deep. It would become a yew [Old Woman 45-30 P
(Remote from the deadly general of men, [Americana 94-1 P

DEAF. If she was deaf with falling grass in her ears-- [Woman Had
  83-2 P
DEAF-MUTE. Colliding with deaf-mute churches and optical trains.
  [Chaos 357-17
DEAL. Take from the dresser of deal, [Emperor 64-9
  Matisse at Vence and a great deal more than that, [Armor 529-18
DEAR. She said, "My dear, [Pourtraicte 21-10
  And of the fragrant mothers the most dear [Fictive 87-8
  Compounded of dear relation, spoken twice, [EM 317-18
  Distortion, however fragrant, however dear. [NSF 406-19
  And the cast-iron of our works. But it is, dear sirs, [Orb 440-4
  Two in a deep-founded sheltering, friend and dear friend. [World
    521-3
  Friend and dear friend and a planet's encouragement. [World
    521-14
DEATH. The death of summer, which that time endures [Swans 4-4
  And you are pierced by a death. [Weep Woman 25-12
  Of sun and slaves, breeding and death, [Joost 46-21
  Freemen of death, about and still about [Heaven 56-14
  Death is the mother of beauty; hence from her, [Sunday 68-29
  Is there no change of death in paradise? [Sunday 69-13
  Death is the mother of beauty, mystical, [Sunday 69-25
  Left only Death's ironic scraping. [Peter 92-10
  "The Death of a Soldier" [97-title
  Life contracts and death is expected, [Soldier 97-1
  Death is absolute and without memorial, [Soldier 97-7
  Hinted autumnal farewells of academic death. [NE Verses 106-8
  The same. We parallel the mother's death. [Anatomy 108-2
  The poem of long celestial death; [Botanist 2 136-6
  Which led them back to angels, after death. [Eve Angels 137-12
  Fears of life and fears of death, [Brave 138-17
  The worlds that were and will be, death and day. [Nigger 150-12
  We should die except for Death [Nigger 151-13
  Not to die a parish death. [Nigger 151-15
  An oppressor that grudges them their death, [MBG 173-17
  A fate intoned, a death before they die, [Thought 186-15
  This death was his belief though death is a stone. [Men Fall
    188-17
  If he will be heaven after death, [Prelude 194-11
  Of being, more than birth or death. [Country 207-22
  After all the pretty contrast of life and death [Connois 215-13
  One year, death and war prevented the jasmine scent [Oboe 251-8
  And ending at the finger-tips. . . . It is death [Extracts
    253-22
  That is ten thousand deaths and evil death. [Extracts 253-23
  Be tranquil in your wounds. It is good death [Extracts 253-24
  That puts an end to evil death and dies. [Extracts 253-25
  Shall be the gentler for the death you die [Extracts 253-27
  To think it is to think the way of death . . . [Extracts 256-20
  In total war we died and after death [Extracts 258-25
  Beyond a second death, as evil's end? [Extracts 258-28
  To evil after death, unable to die [Extracts 259-4
  Its evil after death, it dissolves it while [Extracts 259-12
  In vain, life's season or death's element. [Montra 263-6
  And cold, my element. Death is my [Hero 273-3
  With an understanding compounded by death [Lack 303-12
  And the associations beyond death, even if only [Lack 303-13
  Unless indifference to deeper death [EM 319-4
  No part of him was ever part of death. [EM 319-16
  The death of Satan was a tragedy [EM 319-19
  After death, the non-physical people, in paradise, [EM 325-21
  In the death of a soldier, like the utmost will, [Descrip 341-2
  And another breath emerging out of death, [Descrip 341-5
  That speaks for him such seemings as death gives. [Descrip 341-6
  That night, Liadoff, a long time after his death, [Liadoff 346-14
  The human revery or poem of death? [Men Made 355-16
  "Burghers of Petty Death" [362-title
  Are a slight part of death. [Burghers 362-5
  But there is a total death. [Burghers 362-7
  A devastation, a death of great height [Burghers 362-8
  These are the small townsmen of death, [Burghers 362-11
  Epitaphium to his death, which read, [Good Man 364-13
  Tristesses, the fund of life and death, suave bush [Cred 377-15
  The death of one god is the death of all. [NSF 381-7
  Of death in memory's dream? Is spring a sleep? [NSF 391-3
  Long after the planter's death. A few limes remained, [NSF 393-3
  Except reflections, the escapades of death, [NSF 405-8
  The one-foot stars were couriers of its death [Page 421-19
  And death cries quickly, in a flash of voice, [Owl 434-7
  This was peace after death, the brother of sleep, [Owl 434-7
  Out of our lives to keep us in our death, [Owl 434-24
  This is the mythology of modern death [Owl 435-22
  These are death's own supremest images, [Owl 436-2
  Even of death, the beings of the mind [Owl 436-5
  Brooding sounds of the images of death, [Degen 444-3
  Includes death and the imagination. [Degen 444-9
  This pastoral of endurance and of death [Papini 447-3
  Abba, dark death is the breaking of a glass. [Golden 460-16
  And something of death's poverty is heard. [NH 477-5
  As if life and death were ever physical. [NH 478-12

The life and death of this carpenter depend [NH 478-13
  He is the theorist of life, not death, [NH 485-8
  Death's nobility again [Phases 4-15 P
  Death was a reaper with sickle and stone, [Soldat 16-1 P
  Or Death was a rider beating his horse, [Soldat 16-4 P
  Of the truth of Death-- [Soldat 16-9 P
  Death, that will never be satisfied, [Soldat 16-10 P
  Death ought to spare their passions. [Lytton 38-17 P
  Or dance the death of doves, most sallowly, [Burnshaw 48-22 P
  No heaven, had death without a heaven, death [Greenest 54-20 P
  In a heaven of death. Beneath the heavy foils, [Greenest 54-21 P
  Death, only, sits upon the serpent throne: [Greenest 55-17 P
  Death, the herdsman of elephants, [Greenest 55-18 P
  Chants a death that is a medieval death . . . [Greenest 59-19 P
  As death itself, and never can be changed [Duck 61-22 P
  In anger; or the fear that from the death [Sombre 69-22 P
  And imperator because of death to oppose [Bship 79-5 P
  The strength of death or triumph. Oheu! [Stan Hero 83-15 P
  Forgetful of death in war, there rises [Stan Hero 84-2 P
  Death, the hermit, [Three 140-1 P
  See after-death.
DEATHLESS. The soldier of time grown deathless in great size.
  [EM 319-2
  And there the soldier of time has deathless rest. [EM 319-6
  Of time's red soldier deathless on his bed. [EM 319-10
DEATHS. And through the eye equates ten thousand deaths [Extracts
    253-13
  That is ten thousand deaths and evil death. [Extracts 253-23
DEBONAIR. In a place so debonair. [Anything B 211-15
DEBRIS. "Debris of Life and Mind" [338-title
  So severed and so much forlorn debris. [Bouquet 450-15
DECADENCE. And a grand decadence settles down like cold. [Havana
    142-12
  In the grand decadence of the perished swans. [Havana 145-9
  Suited the decadence of those silences, [Descrip 343-3
DECAY. The decay that you regard: of the arranged [Cred 377-13
DECAYS. Decays of sacks, and all the arrant stinks [C 36-10
DECEIVED. In which the body walks and is deceived, [Anatomy 108-16
DECEMBER. It had been cold since December. Snow fell, first,
  [Extracts 255-1
DECENT. Each one in her decent curl. [Bananas 54-8
DECK. And deck the bananas in leaves [Bananas 54-17
  And in the morning summer hued the deck [Sea Surf 98-14
  At breakfast jelly yellow streaked the deck [Sea Surf 99-18
  And a pale silver patterned on the deck [Sea Surf 100-12
  A mallow morning dozed upon the deck [Sea Surf 101-6
  Came, bowing and voluble, upon the deck, [Sea Surf 101-24
  To stand here on the deck in the dark and say [Farewell 118-6
  Me round, carry me, misty deck, carry me [Farewell 118-19
DECLAIM. But let the rabbit run, the cock declaim. [C 39-32
  The actor that will at last declaim our end. [Dames 206-20
DECLAIMED. The romantic intoning, the declaimed clairvoyance
  [NSF 387-19
  Chutney. Then the Canon Aspirin declaimed [NSF 401-23
DECLAIMING. Subtler than look's declaiming, although she moved
  [Owl 435-15
  Of a vacant sea declaiming with wide throat, [Puel 456-9
DECLARATION. It is a declaration, a primitive ecstasy, [EM 321-10
DECLARE. That will not declare itself . . . [Magnifico 19-8
  That will not declare itself [Magnifico 19-14
DECLARES. That which momentously declares [MBG 171-20
  Turns to its own figurations and declares, [Rhythms 246-3
DECLINE. From oriole to crow, note the decline [Nigger 154-14
DECLINED. Here is the cheek on which that lid declined, [Worms
    49-20
DECLINES. And being part is an exertion that declines: [Course
    96-17 P
DECORATIONS. "Floral Decorations for Bananas" [53-title
  "Like Decorations in a Nigger Cemetery" [150-title
DECOROUS. By way of decorous melancholy; he [C 31-4
  And fattened as on a decorous honeycomb. [AA 419-13
DECORUM. The huge decorum, the manner of the time, [Cred 378-4
DECOYING. Well-wetted; a decoying voice that sings [Spaniard 35-15P
DEDUCTION. Deduction. Thrum with a proud douceur [C 43-14
DEE. Dee, dum, diddle, dee, dee, diddle, dee, da. [Primordia 8-20 P
DEEP. A deep up-pouring from some saltier well [Monocle 13-10
  Bore up, in time, the somnolent, deep songs. [C 33-25
  Latched up the night. So deep a sound fell down [C 42-6
  So deep a sound fell down it grew to be [C 42-9
  However clear, it would have been deep air, [Key W 129-14
  The almond and deep fruit. This bitter meat [Cuisine 228-13
  When the deep breath fetches another year of life. [News 265-12
  It is deep January. The sky is hard. [Possum 294-7
  Of air collected in a deep essay, [Choc 297-10
  Blue and its deep inversions in the moon [Repet 309-18
  Nietzsche in Basel studied the deep pool [Descrip 342-7
  Yet in time's middle deep, [Analysis 348-12
  Sleep deep, good eel, in your perverse marine. [Two V 354-18
  The bass lie deep, still afraid of the Indians. [Think 356-8
  Deep dove, placate you in your hiddenness. [Belly 367-12

Or else avert the object. Deep in the woods [Cred 376-4
Find a deep echo in a horn and buzz [NSF 390-17
On his spredden wings, needs nothing but deep space, [NSF 404-17
And the lowest ear, the deep ear that discerns, [AA 414-17
And hear it as it falls in the deep heart's core. [Page 421-12
Then he breathed deeply the deep atmosphere [Owl 433-23
Presence lies far too deep, for me to know [John 437-25
Deep in their sound the stentor Martin sings. [Luther 461-13
Possess. It is desire, set deep in the eye, [NH 467-10
A thing on the side of a house, not deep in a cloud, [NH 474-21
And the egg of the earth lies deep within an egg. [Aug 490-10
The choir that choirs the first fatigue in deep bell of canzoni?
    [Inelegance 25-20 P
Deadly and deep. It would become a yew [Old Woman 45-30 P
Even in sleep, deep in the grass of sleep, [Greenest 51-31 P
Deep grass that totters under the weight of light. [Greenest
    55-1 P
And deep winds flooded you; for these, day comes, [Duck 61-6 P
The deep sigh with which the hanging ends, close [Stan Hero
    81-18 P
The dew falls deep in the mind [Memo 89-6 P
Voices in chorus, singing without words, remote and deep, [Sick
    90-11 P
Brooder, brooder, deep beneath its walls-- [Dove 97-16 P
The deep comfort of the world and fate. [Ulysses 100-4 P
DEEPEN. Deepen the feelings to inhuman depths. [Parochial 191-10
DEEPENED. Describe with deepened voice [Pascagoula 126-13
    Before the colors deepened and grew small. [Anglais 149-15
    Or power of the wave, or deepened speech, [NSF 387-13
DEEPENING. Mildew of summer and the deepening snow [Pharynx 96-2
    Arranging, deepening, enchanting night. [Key W 130-10
DEEPENS. Of the wind, of the wind as it deepens, and late sleep,
    [Art Pop 113-5 P
DEEPER. Deeper than a truer ditty [Orangeade 103-18
    Deeper within the belly's dark [MBG 171-9
    For breath to laugh the louder, the deeper gasps [Extracts 253-19
    Unless indifference to deeper death [EM 319-4
    Something returning from a deeper quarter, [Imago 439-15
    And light lay deeper for her than her sight. [Old Woman 44-22 P
    A longer, deeper breath sustains [Ulysses 101-16 P
    A longer, deeper breath sustains [Presence 106-1 P
DEEPEST. One breathed the cold evening, the deepest inhalation
    [Extracts 258-20
    Of the being's deepest darling, we forego [EM 317-14
    Derived from adjectives of deepest mine. [Pastor 379-16
    As in the last drop of the deepest blood, [Rome 509-26
    Cover the golden altar deepest black, [Red Kit 31-21 P
    The future for them is always the deepest dome, [Duck 65-21 P
DEEP-FOUNDED. Two in a deep-founded sheltering, friend and dear
    friend. [World 521-3
DEEPLIER. For which more than any words cries deeplier? [Ghosts
    119-7
    Deeplier, deeplier, loudlier, loudlier, [Region 115-16 P
DEEPLY. So deeply sunken were they that the shrouds, [Sea Surf
    100-22
    So much alone, so deeply by ourselves, [Re-state 146-8
    Of earth penetrates more deeply than any word. [Yellow 237-3
    Down deeply in the empty glass . . . [Phosphor 267-10
    Clears deeply, when the moon hangs on the wall [NSF 398-24
    Then he breathed deeply the deep atmosphere [Owl 433-23
    They cast deeply round a crystal crystal-white [Bouquet 452-1
    In the days when the mood of love will be swarming for solace
        and sink deeply into the thin stuff of being, [Piano 22-8 P
    They sway, deeply and loudly, in an effort, [Region 115-8 P
DEEPNESS. His revery was the deepness of the pool, [Descrip 342-11
DEEPNESSES. Receive and keep him in the deepnesses of space--
    [Flyer 336-13
DEEP-OCEANED. The criers, undulating the deep-oceaned phrase.
    [Tallap 71-24
DEER. Deer walk upon our mountains, and the quail [Sunday 70-22
    In the taste for iron dogs and iron deer. [Nigger 155-2
    The deer and the dachshund are one. [Jersey 210-12
    Kiss, cats: for the deer and the dachshund [Jersey 210-13
    Since the deer and the dachshund are one. [Jersey 210-21
DEER-GRASS. The deer-grass is thin. The timothy is brown. [Myrrh
    350-11
DEFAULTS. Excluding by his largeness their defaults. [Choc 299-18
DEFEAT. On the ground, fixed fast in a profound defeat. [Martial
    238-2
    Discolored, how they are going to defeat. [Extracts 259-20
    It implies a flaw in the battleship, a defeat [Bship 79-15 P
DEFEATED. Year, year and year, defeated at last and lost [Dutch
    291-25
DEFEATS. By the terrible incantations of defeats [Men Made 356-3
    And by the fear that defeats and dreams are one. [Men Made 356-4
DEFEND. I nourish myself. I defend myself against [Repet 308-14
    Because, in chief, it, only, can defend [John 436-11
DEFIES. Defies red emptiness to evolve his match [NSF 384-9
DEFINE. And the old casino likewise may define [Havana 145-7
    Is to define its form, to say: this image [Recit 86-13 P

DEFINED. Of night. How clearly that would be defined! [Old Woman
    46-12 P
DEFINES. An incantation that the moon defines [Havana 145-5
    As a tone defines itself and separates [Anach 366-12
    At the moment when the angelic eye defines [AA 414-20
    It is a fresh spiritual that he defines, [NH 474-19
DEFINITE. More definite. The sweeping brim of the hat [Pastor
    379-5
    More definite for what she is-- [Wom Sun 445-11
DEFINITION. There is a feeling as definition. [Hero 278-21
    By difference and then by definition [Anach 366-11
    A definition growing certain and [NSF 386-6
    A definition with an illustration, not [Orb 443-10
DEFINITIONS. Throw away the lights, the definitions, [MBG 183-3
    That only in man's definitions of himself, [Conversat 109-12 P
DEFLATIONS. Deflations of distance; or as clouds [Curtains 62-3
DEFORMATION. Escape all deformation, much less this, [Duck 63-26 P
DEFORMED. Do I sit, deformed, a naked egg, [MBG 173-4
DEFT. The actual is a deft beneficence. [Nigger 155-16
DEFTER. Of a primitive. He walks with a defter [Hero 277-10
DEFUNCT. Was he to company vastest things defunct [C 41-12
DEFY. Not true, nor think it, less. He must defy [Someone 84-5 A
DEGENERATE. The moonlight crumbled to degenerate forms, [Uruguay
    249-7
DEGENERATION. "Metaphor as Degeneration" [444-title
    How, then, is metaphor degeneration, [Degen 444-19
DEGREE. His passion's permit, hang of coat, degree [C 39-18
    Of less degree than flame and lesser shine. [Choc 297-23
DEGREES. Of degrees of perception in the scholar's dark. [NSF
    395-15
DEGUSTATE. In the alien freedom that such selves degustate:
    [Pagoda 92-2 P
DEGUSTATIONS. "These degustations in the vaults [MBG 181-1
DEJECTED. Dejected his manner to the turbulence. [C 29-12
DELAYS. Could ever make them fat, these are delays [Sombre 69-15 P
DELICATE. A minor meeting, facile, delicate. [C 35-5
    And not a delicate ether star-impaled, [Havana 144-1
    Except for delicate clinkings not explained. [Descrip 340-16
DELICATELY. So delicately blushed, so humbly eyed, [C 44-13
DELICATEST. In the delicatest ear of the mind, repeat, [Of Mod
    240-8
    Delicatest machine. [Demoiselle 23-15 P
DELIGHT. From madness or delight, without regard [Monocle 17-12
    As dissertation of profound delight, [C 31-6
    Which was, and is, chief motive, first delight, [C 34-28
    Let these be your delight, secretive hunter, [Tallap 72-1
    A mirror of a mere delight? [Botanist 2 136-12
    His spirit grew uncertain of delight, [Anglais 148-15
    When to be and delight to be seemed to be one, [Anglais 149-14
    Note that, in this bitterness, delight, [Poems Clim 194-8
    This is the thesis scrivened in delight, [EM 326-1
    Sister and solace, brother and delight. [NSF 392-24
    To its opal elements and fire's delight, [AA 416-12
DELIGHTFUL. "Delightful Evening" [162-title
DELIGHTS. The windy lake wherein their lord delights, [Sunday 70-7
DELINEATING. Cold, coldly delineating, being real, [NSF 400-2
DELIRIUM. A glacier running through delirium, [Imago 439-16
DELIVER. The Got whome we serve is able to deliver [Hero 273-15
    Still, still to deliver us, still magic, [Hero 273-21
DELIVERED. Delivered with a deluging onwardness. [C 45-29
DELIVERER. Out of the hero's being, the deliverer [Montra 261-6
DELIVERING. Delivering the prisoner by his words, [Montra 261-7
DELPHINIUM. The rose, the delphinium, the red, the blue, [Bouquet
    451-1
DELUGED. Deluged the ocean with a sapphire blue. [Sea Surf 101-3
    The morning deluged still by night, [MBG 169-3
DELUGING. Delivered with a deluging onwardness. [C 45-29
DELUGINGS. Before these visible, voluble delugings, [Geneva 24-9
DELUSION. From an old delusion, an old affair with the sun, [Bottle
    239-10
DELUSIONS. Universal delusions of universal grandeurs, [Someone
    87-7 A
DELVING. And final effulgence and delving show. [Ulysses 104-9 P
DELVINGS. Of his self, come at upon wide delvings of wings. [NH
    475-24
DEMAGOGUES. O pensioners, O demagogues and pay-men! [Men Fall
    188-16
DEMANDED. Demanded of sleep, in the excitements of silence [NSF
    402-17
    A hatching that stared and demanded an answering look. [NH 484-3
DEMANDING. Greater than mine, of his demanding, head [Choc 302-4
    And Crispine, the blade, reddened by some touch, demanding the
    most from the phrases [Piano 22-6 P
DEMANDS. The will demands that what he thinks be true? [EM 323-11
    Demands. It accepts whatever is as true, [EM 323-21
    It is the human that demands his speech [Less 328-5
    The blood refreshes with its stale demands. [Study I 464-3
    Of Capricorn or as the sign demands, [Someone 86-18 A
DEMARCATIONS. In ghostlier demarcations, keener sounds. [Key W
    130-15

DEMESNE. How greatly had he grown in his demesne, [C 31-1
DEMI-MONDE. The demi-monde [Anything B 211-5
DEMOISELLE. His goldenest demoiselle, inhabitant, [C 44-11
  Our chiefest dome a demoiselle of gold. [Archi 18-2 P
  "Romance for a Demoiselle Lying in the Grass" [23-title P
DEMOISELLES. Bastard chateaux and smoky demoiselles, [Montra 263-7
DEMON. The demon that cannot be himself, [MBG 180-3
DEMONSTRATION. A demonstration, and a woman, [Common 221-11
DEMURELY. Lettered herself demurely as became [C 44-31
DENIAL. Another denial. If she is everywhere, [Scavoir 231-19
  Made single, made one. This was not denial. [Gigan 289-14
  In denial that cannot contain its blood, [NH 467-14
DENIED. How many poems he denied himself [C 34-18
  Of bones, he rejected, he denied, to arrive [Landsc 242-20
  Accepting. He received what he denied. [Landsc 242-17
  If the rejected things, the things denied, [Beard 247-12
  The assassin flash and rumble . . . He was denied. [EM 320-1
  Of volatile world, too constant to be denied, [NSF 397-21
  Denied, dismissed, may hold a serpent, loud [John 437-19
  In which knowledge cannot be denied, [Ulysses 100-7 P
DENIES. Denies that abstraction is a vice except [Thought 185-7
  Or it denies. An age is solitude [Descrip 340-7
DENMARK. We were as Danes in Denmark all day long [AA 419-7
DENOUEMENT. Attach. It seemed haphazard denouement. [C 40-25
  Collapsed. The denouement has to be postponed . . . [AA 416-21
DENOUNCING. That speaks, denouncing separate selves, both one.
  [Orb 441-25
DENSE. Prickly and obdurate, dense, harmonious, [C 35-18
  Involved him in midwifery so dense [C 43-22
  "Two Figures in Dense Violet Night" [85-title
  And plated up, dense silver shine, in a land [Bouquet 449-15
  Of dense investiture, with luminous vassals, [NH 469-6
  By dense unreason, irreproachable force, [Duck 62-6 P
DENSENESS. Out of the whirl and denseness of your wings, [Red Kit
  31-25 P
DENSER. Grown denser, part, the eye so touched, so played [Landsc
  242-24
DENSITY. It is curious that the density of life [Nigger 157-7
DENYING. And denying what he heard. He would arrive. [Landsc
  242-11
  And suddenly denying itself away. [Real 110-18 P
DEPARTED. Have departed. [Leben 504-18
DEPARTING. Nor of time. The departing soldier is as he is, [Repet
  308-7
DEPARTS. The sun stands like a Spaniard as he departs, [Novel
  457-4
DEPARTURE. He belonged to the far-foreign departure of his vessel
  and was part of it, [Prol 516-1
DEPEND. Two things of opposite natures seem to depend [NSF 392-4
  Against itself. At its mercy we depend [John 436-12
  The life and death of this carpenter depend [NH 478-13
  The inner direction on which we depend, [Ulysses 100-15 P
  As these depend, so must they use. [Ulysses 104-23 P
  Like a direction on which I depend . . . [Presence 105-24 P
DEPENDENCY. Or old dependency of day and night, [Sunday 70-19
DEPENDENT. That makes them our dependent heirs, the heirs [C 39-26
  Evade, this hot, dependent orator, [NSF 397-1
  And have seen, a place dependent on ourselves. [NSF 401-3
DEPENDING. Feebly, slowly, depending upon them; [Lunar 107-4
DEPENDS. It depends which way you crossed, the tea-belle said.
  [NE Verses 104-8
  And on that yes the future world depends. [Beard 247-10
  The life of the world depends on that he is [Wild 328-11
  The truth depends on a walk around a lake, [NSF 386-3
  On one another, as a man depends [NSF 392-5
  Yet it depends on yours. The two are one. [NSF 407-10
  It may be the future depends on an orator, [Duck 63-16 P
DEPLORED. The queen of ignorance, you have deplored [Feo 333-11
DEPLORING. Deploring sentiment. When May came last [Good Bad 33-14 P
DEPLOY. Panache upon panache, his tails deploy [Bird Claws 82-10
  Never cease to deploy the structure. [Archi 16-16 P
DEPRESSION. "Depression before Spring" [63-title
DEPRIVATION. A deprivation muffled in eclipse, [Red Kit 30-22 P
DEPRIVED. He is not himself. He is vitally deprived . . .) [Ameri-
  cana 94-12 P
DEPTH. To speak humanly from the height or from the depth [Choc
  300-14
  And depth, covering all surfaces, [Burghers 362-9
  Of great height and depth [Burghers 362-15
  Not merely as to depth but as to height [NH 470-9
  The dove's adagio may lose its depth [Burnshaw 48-25 P
DEPTHS. Deepen the feelings to inhuman depths. [Parochial 191-10
  Like insects in the depths of the mind, that kill [Extracts
  254-14
  Born old, familiar with the depths of the heart, [Repet 306-17
  To most incredible depths. I speak below [John 437-9
  The world is still profound and in its depths [Papini 447-9
  Your dozing in the depths of wakefulness, [Rome 509-18
  The step to the bleaker depths of his descents . . . [Rock 528-3
DERISIVE. Where shall we find more than derisive words? [Duck 66-9 P

DERIVED. Derived from adjectives of deepest mine. [Pastor 379-16
DERIVES. The comedy of hollow sounds derives [Nigger 154-4
DERRICKS. Scaffolds and derricks rise from the reeds to the clouds
  [NE Verses 105-9
DESCANT. This health is holy, this descant of a self, [Parochial
  191-15
DESCANTS. And what descants, he sent to banishment! [C 34-24
DESCARTES. In Eden was the father of Descartes [NSF 383-11
  Descartes: [Bship 78-22 P
DESCEND. Containing the mind, below which it cannot descend,
  [Of Mod 240-17
  We descend to the street and inhale a health of air [NH 470-17
  It was curious to have to descend [Aug 493-21
DESCENDED. Not less because in purple I descended [Hoon 65-7
  Tell me how he descended [Pascagoula 126-11
  As the night descended, tilting in the air, [Key W 130-7
  As it descended, blind to her velvet and [Uruguay 249-19
DESCENDING. A bronze rain from the sun descending marks [Swans 4-3
  Desire for rest, in that descending sea [Eve Angels 137-23
  Descending to the children's bed, on which [NSF 403-6
  Descending, out of the cap of midnight, [Countryman 428-10
  To symbols of descending night; and search [Blanche 10-7 P
  Descending, did not touch her eye and left [Old Woman 44-8 P
DESCENDS. The man in the black wood descends unchanged. [Degen
  444-11
  Is constant. The time you call serene descends [Burnshaw 50-22 P
  The great Omnium descends on us [Ulysses 102-3 P
  The great Omnium descends on me, [Presence 106-5 P
DESCENSIONS. Descensions of their tinkling bells arrive. [Monocle
  15-20
DESCENT. Thoughts by descent. To flourish the great cloak we wear
  [Sombre 71-19 P
  See down-descent.
DESCENTS. The step to the bleaker depths of his descents . . .
  [Rock 528-3
DESCRIBE. Imposing forms they cannot describe, [Sad Gay 122-8
  Describe with deepened voice [Pascagoula 126-13
  Cast corners in the glass. He could describe [EM 314-1
DESCRIBED. Is a form, described but difficult, [MBG 169-15
  To be described. They are preaching in a time [Extracts 254-4
  To be described. Evangelists of what? [Extracts 254-5
  The thing described, nor false facsimile. [Descrip 344-16
  Sweden described, Salzburg with shaded eyes [NH 486-2
  She described for them [Lulu G 26-14 P
  She described how the barbarians kissed her [Lulu G 26-19
  It is a shape of life described [Banjo 114-9 P
DESCRIBES. He will never ride the red horse she describes. [Ques-
  tions 462-15
DESCRIPTION. To be without a description of to be, [Freed 205-7
  It was being without description, being an ox. [Freed 205-16
  Description of a Platonic Person [Pure 330-title 2
  "Description without Place" [339-title
  If seeming is description without place, [Descrip 343-15
  Is description without place. It is a sense [Descrip 343-18
  On which the dove alights. Description is [Descrip 343-21
  The future is description without place, [Descrip 344-7
  Description is revelation. It is not [Descrip 344-15
  In description, canon central in itself, [Descrip 345-3
  Thus the theory of description matters most. [Descrip 345-5
  In a description hollowed out of hollow-bright, [Descrip 345-17
  Of the past is description without place, a cast [Descrip 345-20
  The description that makes it divinity, still speech [NH 475-13
DESCRIPTIONS. Tired of the old descriptions of the world, [Freed
  204-13
  Air-earth--Can we live on dry descriptions, [Hero 278-2
  In the brilliantest descriptions of new day, [Descrip 344-11
DESERT. Articulate its desert days. [MBG 174-10
  To be buried in desert and deserted earth. [Dutch 290-21
  Incognito, the column in the desert, [Descrip 343-20
  The lion roars at the enraging desert, [NSF 384-7
  Basking in desert Florida? [An Gaiety 33-4 P
DESERTED. To be buried in desert and deserted earth. [Dutch 290-21
  Deserted, on a beach. It is white, [AA 412-5
DESIGN. In form though in design, as Crispin willed, [C 45-21
  I come as belle design [W Burgher 61-12
  Knew the eccentric to be the base of design. [Nigger 151-3
  The rugged black, the image. Design [Prelude 195-18
  They have a sense of their design and savor [Extracts 254-21
  A design, a marble soiled by pigeons? [Hero 278-23
  As if the design of all his words takes form [Rome 511-2
  In the sun's design of its own happiness, [Rock 525-18
  Let us design a chastel de chasteté. [Archi 16-14 P
  The milkiest bowmen. This makes a new design, [Greenest 56-6 P
  Midmost in its design, the arms grown swift, [Sombre 69-9 P
  The joy of meaning in design [Ulysses 100-22 P
DESIGNED. As if designed by X, the per-noble master. [Extracts
  254-20
  Was this bowl of Earth designed? [Bowl 6-11 P
  See re-designed.
DESIGNS. Of wire, the designs of ink, [Common 221-18

DESIRE. Insinuations of desire, [Ord Women 11-25
  With heaven, brought such requital to desire [Sunday 68-3
  Of her desire for June and evening, tipped [Sunday 68-25
  To make the body covetous in desire [Anatomy 108-13
  Is no longer a mode of desire, a mode [Sad Gay 121-12
  Of revealing desire and is empty of shadows. [Sad Gay 121-13
  For whom desire was never that of the waltz, [Sad Gay 121-16
  Modes of desire, modes of revealing desire, [Sad Gay 122-12
  To moodiest nothings, as, desire for day [Eve Angels 137-21
  Desire for rest, in that descending sea [Eve Angels 137-23
  Day is desire and night is sleep. [MBG 167-7
  The bells grow longer. This is not sleep. This is desire. [Men
    Fall 187-14
  Ah! Yes, desire . . . this leaning on his bed, [Men Fall 187-15
  Yet life itself, the fulfilment of desire [Men Fall 188-3
  God and all angels, this was his desire, [Men Fall 188-13
  Like the response to desire. [Dezem 218-20
  Half desire for indifference about the sky. [Extracts 257-3
  The arrangement contains the desire of [Couch 296-1
  Of what was this the force? From what desire [Choc 299-6
  Thereof and part desire and part the sense [Choc 299-21
  And to breathe is a fulfilling of desire, [Choc 301-10
  The bud of the apple is desire, the down-falling gold, [Holiday
    313-5
  Reclining, eased of desire, establishes [EM 324-12
  In a physical world, to feel that one's desire [EM 325-19
  And the desire to believe in a metaphor. [Pure 332-10
  It is an expectation, a desire, [Descrip 344-1
  From the water in which he believed and out of desire [New Set
    352-13
  Knows desire without an object of desire, [Chaos 358-3
  Of change still possible. Exile desire [Cred 373-13
  In face of which desire no longer moved, [Cred 376-7
  And not to have is the beginning of desire. [NSF 382-4
  It is desire at the end of winter, when [NSF 382-6
  Did not desire that feathery argentines [NSF 399-5
  Is dark, thought of the forms of dark desire. [Owl 432-18
  The children of a desire that is the will, [Owl 436-4
  Their words are chosen out of their desire, [Orb 441-7
  When the image itself is false, a mere desire, [Study I 463-18
  The point of vision and desire are the same. [NH 466-22
  And next to love is the desire for love, [NH 467-5
  The desire for its celestial ease in the heart, [NH 467-6
  Possess. It is desire, set deep in the eye, [NH 467-10
  By the hand of desire, faint, sensitive, the soft [NH 476-14
  Desire prolongs its adventure to create [NH 482-14
  Or the same thing without desire, [Aug 491-1
  And her belt, the final fortune of their desire. [World 521-9
  The desire to be at the end of distances, [Rock 527-9
  Or rising in the appointments of desire, [Greenest 57-11 P
  The memory moves on leopards' feet, desire [Greenest 57-16 P
  In your cadaverous Eden, they desire [Duck 61-13 P
  And daunt that old assassin, heart's desire? [Duck 66-11 P
  In the images of desire, the forms that speak, [Woman Had 82-21P
  The desire, for the fiery lullaby. [Woman Had 82-27 P
  "Desire & the Object" [85-title
  Was it desire that created Raël [Desire 85-15 P
  Or was it Jaffa that created desire? [Desire 85-16 P·
  Because I desire it to shine or else [Desire 85-20 P
  That I desire it to shine because it shines. [Desire 85-21 P
  "The Desire to Make Love in a Pagoda" [91-title
  The desire for speech and meaning gallantly fulfilled, [Discov
    95-18 P
  And of that other and her desire. [Fare Guit 99-9 P
DESIRED. Than the relentless contact he desired; [C 34-20
  The more invidious, the more desired: [C 37-15
  Without a name and nothing to be desired, [NSF 385-14
  How soft the grass on which the desired [Hermit 505-11
  In its permanent cold, an illusion so desired [Rock 526-3
  Not merely desired, for sale, and market things [Armor 530-4
  That I desired. It could be-- [Desire 85-3 P
  Because he desired without knowing quite what, [Local 112-9 P
  That we desired, a day of blank, blue wheels, [Ideal 88-3 A
DESIRES. In all desires, his destitution's mark. [C 31-11
  And our desires. Although she strews the leaves [Sunday 69-2
  Like an intenser instinct. What is it he desires? [Men Fall 188-1
  Pink and white carnations--one desires [Poems Clim 193-12
  So that he that suffers most desires [Adequacy 244-13
  In a consummate prime, yet still desires [EM 318-3
  But the priest desires. The philosopher desires. [NSF 382-3
  And their desires. [Demoiselle 23-6 P
DESIRING. Here in this room, desiring you, [Peter 90-3
  Desiring the exhilarations of changes: [Motive 288-13
  Desiring fiercely, the child of a mother fierce [EM 321-20
  They sang desiring an object that was near, [Cred 376-6
DESOLATE. A most desolate wind has chilled Rouge-Fatima [Havana
    142-11
  The stillness is all in the key of that desolate sound. [Autumn
    160-14
  Went crying their desolate syllables, before [Old Woman 45-26 P

DESOLATION. This vast inelegance may seem the blankest desolation,
    [Inelegance 25-13 P
DESPAIR. Yet the panorama of despair [Botanist 1 135-13
  Cries out a literate despair. [Postcard 159-10
  In the catastrophic room . . . beyond despair, [Men Fall 187-18
  The intelligence of his despair, express [EM 314-22
  Is too difficult to tell from despair. Perhaps, [EM 325-20
  If more than pity and despair were sure, [Sombre 69-13 P
DESPAIRINGLY. And despairingly. [Shifts 83-13
DESPERADO. Fate is the present desperado. [Dutch 291-5
DESPERATE. As if they were desperate with a know-and-know, [Repet
    307-24
  In desperate hallow, rugged gesture, fault [EM 316-26
  Which is more desperate in the moments when [EM 323-10
  Warmed by a desperate milk. To find the real, [NSF 404-8
  Our breath is like a desperate element [NH 470-23
  An invention, an embrace between one desperate clod [Rock 525-13
DESPERATELY. Much trumpeted, made desperately clear, [C 30-26
DESPICABLE. And despicable shades of red, just seen, [Burnshaw
    51-21 P
DESPISE. To be one's singular self, to despise [Adieu 127-17
DESPISES. A man of bitter appetite despises [EM 322-20
  Select adieux; and he despises this: [EM 322-22
DESPISING. The very man despising honest quilts [C 41-29
DESPITE. Lies quilted to his poll in his despite. [C 41-30
DESPOILING. For who can care at the wigs despoiling the Satan ear?
    [Banal 63-4
DESPOILS. When the trees glitter with that which despoils them,
    [Discov 95-8 P
DESTINATION. Gripping their oars, as if they were sure of the way
    to their destination, [Prol 515-7
DESTINED. These are the measures destined for her soul. [Sunday
    67-26
DESTINY. And small, a constant fellow of destiny, [EM 315-22
  Tragedy. This is destiny unperplexed, [EM 324-9
  Glass-blower's destiny, bloodless episcopus, [NSF 394-11
  Forgets the gold centre, the golden destiny, [NSF 404-18
  It must change from destiny to slight caprice. [AA 417-23
  Their destiny is just as much machine [Duck 61-21 P
  Is not our grandiose destiny. [Grotesque 77-2 P
  With our affair, our destiny, our hash? [Bship 80-19 P
DESTITUTE. But Crispin was too destitute to find [C 30-22
  To be paradise, it is this to be destitute. [EM 321-1
  So destitute that nothing but herself [Old Woman 44-10 P
  A dream too poor, too destitute [Ulysses 104-18 P
DESTITUTION. In all desires, his destitution's mark. [C 31-11
DESTROY. Destroy all references. This actor [Hero 279-17
  Fails to destroy the antique acceptances, [Questions 462-8
  All things destroy themselves or are destroyed. [Burnshaw 46-16 P
DESTROYED. Civilization must be destroyed. The hairy saints [NE
    Verses 106-1
  Things as they are have been destroyed. [MBG 173-7
  When the crust of shape has been destroyed. [MBG 183-12
  To think of him destroyed the body's form. [Choc 297-8
  The total past felt nothing when destroyed. [EM 314-16
  Negation destroyed him in his tenement [EM 319-21
  The mind that knows it is destroyed by time. [Pure 329-15
  And yet she too is dissolved, she is destroyed. [AA 413-13
  And is destroyed. He opens the door of his house [AA 416-24
  All things destroy themselves or are destroyed. [Burnshaw 46-16 P
  The charts destroyed, even disorder may, [Burnshaw 48-28 P
  The east wind in the west, order destroyed, [Sombre 68-15 P
  Destroyed by a vengeful movement of the arms, [Sombre 69-3 P
  Not least the pasts destroyed. magniloquent [Sombre 70-6 P
  Of gods and men destroyed, the right [Ulysses 102-10 P
DESTROYERS. Shall I grapple with my destroyers [Nigger 153-11
  But my destroyers avoid the museums. [Nigger 153-13
  Surly masks and destroyers? [Bagatelles 213-20
DESTROYING. Of destroying, as the mind destroys, [Bottle 239-8
  Of a destroying spiritual that digs-a-dog, [Pure 332-20
DESTROYS. Destroys romantic tenements [Bottle 238-19
  Of destroying, as the mind destroys, [Bottle 239-8
  As the mind, to find what will suffice, destroys [Bottle 239-15
  Of them and of himself destroys both worlds, [EM 323-16
  The force that destroys us is disclosed, within [EM 324-20
  But that which destroys it completely by this light [Page 422-16
  These he destroys with wafts of wakening, [NH 473-9
DESTRUCTION. Out of what swift destruction did it spring? [C 30-12
  Just to know how it would feel, released from destruction, [Cata
    425-9
  To bring destruction, often seems high-pitched. [Spaniard 34-17P
  Before the sun brought them that destruction [Stan Hero 83-18 P
DESTRUCTIONS. Of destructions," a picture of ourselves, [MBG 173-2
DESTRUCTIVE. "Poetry Is a Destructive Force" [192-title
DETACHED. Detached from us, from things as they are? [MBG 168-19
  And, when detached, so unimportantly gone, [Bouquet 450-14
DETACHMENT. So near detachment, the cover's cornered squares,
    [Bouquet 450-13
DETAIL. Was not indifferent to smart detail. [C 38-30
DETECT. And on your bean pole, it may be, you detect [Cred 377-17

DETECTED. Not quite detected at the moment of change [Pure 332-4
DETECTING. A clearing, a detecting, a completing, [Choc 301-11
DETECTS. Detects the sound of a voice that doubles its own,
    [Woman Had 82-20 P
DETERMINED. Determined thereto, perhaps by his father's ghost,
    [Role 93-4 P
DETESTABLE. And slightly detestable operandum, free [Look 517-19
DETRITUS. Parts of the immense detritus of a world [Burnshaw 49-21P
DEVASTATION. A devastation, a death of great height [Burghers
    362-8
DEVASTATIONS. These devastations are the divertissements [Pure
    332-19
DEVELOPS. Union of the weakest develops strength [Nigger 158-10
DEVIATION. By trope or deviation, straight to the word, [NH 471-14
    Lord without any deviation, lord [Greenest 60-4 P
    The accent of deviation in the living thing [Discov 96-7 P
DEVIATIONS. The faculty of ellipses and deviations, [Aug 493-7
DEVICE. Twinning our phantasy and our device, [Anatomy 108-11
    A blank underlies the trials of device, [NH 477-15
DEVIL. The devil take it, wear it, too. [Snow Stars 133-5
    Of a cat, twelve dollars for the devil, [Hero 275-9
DEVISE. His grand pronunciamento and devise. [C 43-15
    Within whose burning bosom we devise [Sunday 69-26
    Of what good. Devise. Make him of mud, [Hero 275-21
    Devise, devise, and make him of winter's [Hero 275-23
DEVISED. So much he had devised: white forelegs taut [Old Woman
    43-10 P
DEVISING. Winter devising summer in its breast, [Thought 186-8
    Devising proud, majestic issuance. [Soldat 14-12 P
DEVOTION. Their boisterous devotion to the sun, [Sunday 70-1
DEVOTIONS. Of old devotions. [Peter 90-26
    And yet what good were yesterday's devotions? [Montra 264-4
DEVOURED. By one caterpillar is great Africa devoured [Puel 456-2
    His crisp knowledge is devoured by her, beneath a dew. [Madame
    507-4
DEW. The dead brine melted in him like a dew [C 29-14
    With his own quill, in its indigenous dew, [C 31-19
    Irised in dew and early fragrancies, [C 36-3
    The dew upon their feet shall manifest. [Sunday 70-13
    The melon-flower nor dew nor web of either [Tallap 72-5
    The dew [Peter 90-25
    As the immense dew of Florida [Nomad 95-6
    As the immense dew of Florida [Nomad 95-10
    Dew lies on the instruments of straw that you were playing,
    [Fish-Scale 160-17
    The thinking of god is smoky dew. [MBG 168-5
    He sat among beggars wet with dew, [Thought 187-5
    The green smacks in the eye, the dew in the green [Dump 202-5
    On a cocoanut--how many men have copied dew [Dump 202-7
    With dew, dew dresses, stones and chains of dew, heads [Dump
    202-9
    Of the floweriest flowers dewed with the dewiest dew. [Dump
    202-10
    And of fair weather, summer, dew, peace. [Peaches 224-14
    Out of the changes of both light and dew [Scavoir 231-8
    The philosophers' man alone still walks in dew, [Oboe 250-12
    The blessed regal dropped in daggers' dew, [Montra 260-18
    His crisp knowledge is devoured by her, beneath a dew. [Madame
    507-4
    And the dew and the ploughman still will best be one. [Burnshaw
    48-2 P
    Motionless, knowing neither dew nor frost. [Burnshaw 49-15 P
    Each fretful fern drops down a fear like dew [Greenest 55-24 P
    You said the dew falls in the blood. [Memo 89-5 P
    The dew falls deep in the mind [Memo 89-6 P
    Than the dew on the barns. [Three 128-2 P
    Dew is water to see, [Three 128-3
DEW-DAPPER. Dew-dapper clapper-traps, blazing [MBG 182-3
DEWED. Harlequined and mazily dewed and mauved [C 41-5
    Of the floweriest flowers dewed with the dewiest dew. [Dump
    202-10
    In colorings harmonious, dewed and dashed [Ulysses 104-3 P
DEWIEST. Of the floweriest flowers dewed with the dewiest dew.
    [Dump 202-10
    And the dewiest beads of insipid fruit [Stan MBG 72-8 P
DEWILY. The glass man, cold and numbered, dewily cries, [Oboe 251-4
DEWY. X promenades the dewy stones, [Canna 55-7
    To comb her dewy hair, a touchless light, [Beginning 427-13
    And dewy bearings of their light-locked beards. [Bouquet 449-24
    A dewy flashing blanks away from fire, [Burnshaw 51-23 P
    The impoverished waste with dewy vibrancies [Greenest 58-23 P
    In which the spectra have dewy favor and live [How Now 97-13 P
DEZEMBRUM. "Dezembrum" [218-title
DIABETES. A lady dying of diabetes [Thought 184-7
DIALECT. Broke dialect in a break of memory. [Page 422-10
DIALOGUES. And away, dialogues between incognitos. [Sombre 67-12 P
DIAMOND. The diamond point, the sapphire point, [Ord Women 11-22
    It wants the diamond pivot bright. [Country 207-19
    Beyond the keenest diamond day [Adequacy 244-1
    But we and the diamond globe at last were one. [Oboe 251-16

At the centre of a diamond. At dawn, [EM 322-10
    Without diamond--blazons or flashing or [Pediment 361-11
    Set on me the spirit's diamond coronal. [NSF 396-6
    In the sky, as crown and diamond cabala? [AA 417-15
    A diamond jubilance beyond the fire, [Owl 433-21
    Progenitor wearing the diamond crown of crowns, [Duck 64-30 P
    The self as sibyl, whose diamond, [Ulysses 104-11 P
    See: egg-diamond; omni-diamond.
DIAMONDS. Who in a million diamonds sums us up. [Oboe 250-22
    Summer, jangling the savagest diamonds and [Hero 281-2
    Take the diamonds from your hair and lay them down. [Myrrh 350-10
    A crown within him of crispest diamonds, [Aug 492-7
DIAPHANES. Triton, dissolved in shifting diaphanes [C 28-24
DIBBLED. Dibbled in waves that were mustachios, [C 27-20
DICHTUNG. And the truth, Dichtung und Wahrheit, all [MBG 177-17
DICTA. For somehow the brave dicta of its kings [Surprises 98-10
DICTATE. What super-animal dictate our fates? [Duck 63-8 P
DICTION. Of its cry as clarion, its diction's way [Cred 377-3
DICTUM. A not into a dictum, communal, [Spaniard 34-19 P
DID. That he spoke only by doing what he did. [Men Fall 188-12
    And Bloom would see what Puvis did, protest [Anach 366-6
    What they did with their thumbs. [Lulu G 26-16 P
    That's what did it. Everything did it at last. [Greenest 53-15 P
    The binders did it with armorial books. [Greenest 53-16 P
    One the assassins wore stone masks and did [Bship 78-15 P
DIDDLE. Dee, dum, diddle, dee, dee, diddle, dee, da. [Primordia
    8-20 P
DIE. So evenings die, in their green going, [Peter 92-2
    So gardens die, their meek breath scenting [Peter 92-4
    So maidens die, to the auroral [Peter 92-6
    That the people die? [Fading 139-10
    And they will not die. [Fading 139-20
    We should die except for Death [Nigger 151-13
    Not to die a parish death. [Nigger 151-15
    Place honey on the altars and die, [MBG 174-3
    Not yet, however, a thing to die in. [Thought 184-16
    It seemed serener just to die, [Thought 184-17
    A fate intoned, a death before they die, [Thought 186-15
    This man loved earth, not heaven, enough to die. [Men Fall 188-18
    Shall be the gentler for the death you die [Extracts 253-27
    Returned, unable to die again, fated [Extracts 258-26
    It is only that we are able to die, to escape [Extracts 259-1
    To evil after death, unable to die [Extracts 259-4
    To die). This is a part of the sublime [EM 314-14
    He might die was the innocence of living, if life [EM 322-6
    Live, work, suffer and die in that idea [EM 325-14
    Between the two we live and die-- [Silent 359-6
    Let Phoebus slumber and die in autumn umber, [NSF 381-9
    And die. It stands on a table at a window [Bouquet 450-5
    Granted, we die for good. [Table 40-1 P
DIED. Whose head lies blurring here, for this he died. [Men Fall
    188-14
    Cotton Mather died when I was a boy. The books [Blue Bldg 216-15
    In total war we died and after death [Extracts 258-25
    Who died, the being that was an abstraction, [Gigan 289-6
    Knowing that he died nobly, as he died. [Flyer 336-11
    In which your father died, still breathes for him [Extraord
    369-17
    Could not have borne his labor nor have died [NSF 393-20
    The wet weed sputtered, the fire died down, the cold [Page 422-1
    He stayed in Kerry, died there. [Our Stars 455-3
    Of bronze whose mind was made up and who, therefore, died. [NH
    472-10
    When he died. [Phases 4-19 P
    And died amid uproarious damns. [Lulu M 27-10 P
    A self of parents who have never died, [Sombre 67-4 P
DIES. It comes, it blooms, it bears its fruit and dies. [Monocle
    16-3
    The body dies; the body's beauty lives. [Peter 92-1
    That puts an end to evil death and dies. [Extracts 253-25
    And in their blood an ancient evil dies-- [Dutch 292-20
    And the man dies that does not fall. [Woman Song 360-7
    He walks and dies. Nothing survives [Woman Song 360-8
    How gladly with proper words the soldier dies, [NSF 408-2
    The people, those by which it lives and dies. [Owl 436-9
    The solid wax from which the warmth dies out? . . [Infernale
    24-22 P
DIEU. Mon Dieu, hear the poet's prayer. [Sailing 120-11
    Mon Dieu, and must never again return. [Sailing 120-16
    Comme Dieu Dispense de Graces [Soldat 13-title 5 P
    Aux taureaux Dieu cornes donne [Parasol 20-1
DIEUX. Encore, encore, encore les dieux . . . [Jersey 210-8
DIFFER. They differ from reason's click-clack, its applied [NSF
    387-22
DIFFERENCE. The difference that heavenly pity brings. [Fictive
    88-13
    A difference, at least, from nightingales, [Havana 142-3
    Until the difference between air [Vari 235-3
    There was that difference between the and an, [Extracts 255-7
    The difference between himself and no man, [Extracts 255-8

Within the difference. He felt curious [Extracts 255-12
One would be drowned in the air of difference, [Extracts 258-12
Incapable of belief, in the difference. [Extracts 258-13
But in that dream a heavy difference [Montra 263-4
And, now, it attends the difficult difference. [Pure 332-5
The difference that we make in what we see [Descrip 344-4
And our memorials of that difference, [Descrip 344-5
There was no difference between the town [Liadoff 347-17
By difference and then by definition [Anach 366-11
How is it I find you in difference, see you there [NSF 406-8
Read, rabbi, the phases of this difference. [AA 420-1
By his drift-fire, on the shore, the difference [Page 421-6
He, too, is human and difference disappears [Pecul 454-6
But that's the difference: in the end and the way [NH 469-19
Than the difference that clouds make over a town. [NH 487-7
Difference and were one? It had to be [Aug 494-4
It makes so little difference, at so much more [Slug 522-1
Make little difference, for being wrong [Red Kit 30-14 P
Philosophers' end . . . What difference would it make, [Theatre
  91-17 P
The point of difference from reality [Three 130-12 P
DIFFERENCES. Temper and belief and that differences lost [Aug 494-3
  And felt and known the differences we have seen [Conversat
  109-18 P
DIFFERENT. It would have been different, [Explan 72-21
  Not in a later son, a different daughter, another place, [Mar-
  tial 237-14
  Or anywhere beyond, to a different element, [Extracts 258-11
  And the bourgeois, are different, much. [Hero 276-9
  Or having a separate author, a different poet, [Creat 311-1
  It was something to see that their white was different,
  [Holiday 312-1
  That is different. They are characters beyond [Paisant 335-4
  A little different from reality: [Descrip 344-3
  That was different, something else, last year [AA 412-11
  From a different source. But there was always one: [NH 479-3
  Different from each other? [Primordia 9-6 P
  Things would be different. [Mandolin 28-22 P
  Are two quite different things, in particular [Lytton 39-8 P
DIFFERENTLY. Than to be, she could never differently be, [Uruguay
  249-14
DIFFERING. Of differing struts, four voices several [C 45-4
DIFFICULT. In moody rucks, and difficult and strange [C 31-10
  Is a form, described but difficult, [MBG 169-15
  It is difficult to read. The page is dark. [Phosphor 267-5
  Is too difficult to tell from despair. Perhaps, [EM 325-20
  He might slowly forget. It is more difficult to evade [Bed 327-5
  And, now, it attends the difficult difference. [Pure 332-5
  The difficult images of possible shapes, [Two V 354-9
  Its unfamiliar, difficult fern, [Red Fern 365-3
  Secure. It was difficult to sing in face [Cred 376-2
  The inanimate, difficult visage. Who is it? [NSF 388-24
  A difficult apperception, this gorging good, [Orb 440-5
  Is more difficult to find than the way beyond it. [Papini 446-6
  Made difficult by salt fragrance, intricate. [Bouquet 452-15
  These houses, these difficult objects, dilapidate [NH 465-10
  It is the window that makes it difficult [NH 478-4
  It is difficult even to choose the adjective [Plain 503-13
  The difficult rightness of half-risen day. [Rock 528-9
  Is difficult. It blights in the studios. [Greenest 58-2 P
  Always and always, the difficult inch, [Ulysses 103-16
DIFFICULTEST. But the difficultest rigor is forthwith, [NSF 398-20
DIFFICULTY. To the difficulty of rebellious thought [C 40-17
  The difficulty to think at the end of day, [Rabbit K 209-1
  In the difficulty of what it is to be. [NSF 381-15
  A difficulty that we predicate: [NH 474-22
  The difficulty of the visible [NH 474-23
DIFFIDENT. One might in turn become less diffident, [Pharynx 96-13
DIFFUSE. Astral and Shelleyan, diffuse new day; [Burnshaw 47-26 P
DIFFUSED. To be diffused, and, as she disappears, [Infernale
  25-10 P
DIFFUSING. Diffusing the civilest odors [Plot Giant 6-14
  Diffusing balm in that Pacific calm? [Sea Surf 99-8
DIFFUSIONS. Expansions, diffusions--content to be [MBG 172-4
DIGIT. The fourth, pent now, a digit curious. [C 45-1
DIGNITY. It is as if in a human dignity [Rome 508-8
DIGS. Digs up the earth when want returns . . . [Soldat 16-11 P
DIGS-A-DOG. Of a destroying spiritual that digs-a-dog, [Pure
  332-19
DILAPIDATE. These houses, these difficult objects, dilapidate
  [NH 465-10
DILAPIDATION. The dilapidation of dilapidations. [NH 476-18
DILAPIDATIONS. The dilapidation of dilapidations. [NH 476-18
DIM. And our streams rejected the dim Academy. [Nigger 154-21
  As if nothing had happened. The dim actor spoke. [Repet 306-11
  The year's dim elongations stretch below [Sombre 70-2 P
DIM-CONED. The far-fire flowing and the dim-coned bells [NH 466-10
DIMENSION. Profundum, physical thunder, dimension in which [Flyer
  336-14
DIMINISHED. True genii for the diminished, spheres, [Choc 300-7

DIMLY-STARRED. Words of the fragrant portals, dimly-starred,
  [Key W 130-13
DIMS. That lights and dims the stars? [Sonatina 110-6
DIN. In verses wild with motion, full of din, [Monocle 16-12
  All din and gobble, blasphemously pink. [C 44-23
DING. Here was the veritable ding an sich, at last, [C 29-24
  Of ding, ding, dong. [Snow Stars 133-12
DINNER. "A Duck for Dinner" [60-title P
  "Recitation after Dinner" [86-title P
  "Dinner Bell in the Woods" [109-title P
DIP. Or of a town poised at the horizon's dip. [NH 483-9
DIPLOMATS. The diplomats of the cafes expound: [Greenest 57-28 P
DIRECTING. And their directing sceptre, the crown [Ulysses 104-8 P
DIRECTION. In their direction. [Soldier 97-12
  Direction, shrinking from the spit and splash [Think 356-12
  Things stop in that direction and since they stop [Cred 374-16
  The direction stops and we accept what is [Cred 374-17
  A place to go to in his own direction, [Poem Mt 512-6
  The inner direction on which we depend, [Ulysses 100-15 P
  Like a direction on which I depend . . . [Presence 105-24 P
DIRECTIONS. Going in many directions [Homunculus 26-3
DIRECTLY. Whether it comes directly or from the sun. [Freed 205-11
  It is she that he wants, to look at directly, [Scavoir 232-3
  Of statement, directly and indirectly getting at, [NH 488-18
DIRGE. His active force in an inactive dirge, [C 41-15
DIRGES. Their petty dirges of fallen forest-men, [Greenest 55-20 P
DIRT. The crows anoint the statues with their dirt. [Swans 4-10
  Incredible to prudes, the mint of dirt, [C 31-21
  Of dirt . . . It is not possible for the moon [Ghosts 119-9
  The flesh, the bone, the dirt, the stone. [MBG 176-14
  The dirt along the sill. [Anything B 211-23
  Are comic trash, the ears are dirt, [Arcades 225-18
  And dirt. The wind blew in the empty place. [Extracts 255-5
  In its own dirt, said Avignon was [Hero 273-9
  In the poverty of dirt. [Pecul 453-6
  And the poverty of dirt, the thing upon his breast, [Pecul 454-7
  The seal is as relaxed as dirt, perdu. [Golden 460-18
  A mask up-gathered brilliantly from the dirt, [Sombre 70-13 P
DIRTIER. Clarified. It is silence made still dirtier. [Creat 311-8
DIRTY. That slight transcendence to the dirty sail, [Sailing 121-5
  A dirty house in a gutted world, [Postcard 159-19
  In the mud, in Monday's dirty light, [MBG 183-16
  Birds that came like dirty water in waves [Loaf 200-3
  Tell X that speech is not dirty silence [Creat 311-7
  This man escaped the dirty fates, [Flyer 336-10
  Mud, water like dirty glass, expressing silence [Plain 503-4
  A dirty light on a lifeless world, [Two Illus 513-2
  Outside of and beyond the dirty light, [Two Illus 513-17
DISAFFECTED. Your disaffected flagellants, well-stuffed, [High-
  Toned 59-15
DISAPPEAR. But of nothing, trash of sleep that will disappear
  [Choc 300-18
  The dazzled flakes and splinters disappear. [Golden 460-17
DISAPPEARANCES. Skin flashing to wished-for disappearances
  [AA 411-11
DISAPPEARED. The moonlight fiction disappeared. The spring, [C 36-1
  The Indian struck and disappeared. [Cuban 65-4
  As if hell, so modified, had disappeared, [EM 316-4
  From a shore at night and disappeared. [Vacancy 511-7
  Slowly submerging in flatness disappeared. [Old Woman 45-5 P
  He disappeared with his neighbor's daughter. [Three 135-15 P
DISAPPEARS. He, too, is human and difference disappears [Pecul
  454-6
  To be diffused, and, as she disappears, [Infernale 25-10 P
DISASTER. Of the mind, result only in disaster. It follows, [Bed
  326-14
  Casual poet, that to add your own disorder to disaster [Bed
  326-15
  Of what disaster is this the imminence: [AA 419-20
DISASTERS. Its false disasters--these fathers standing round,
  [Cred 372-16
DISBAND. If the stars that move together as one, disband, [Horn
  230-17
DISBELIEF. And in his heart his disbelief lay cold. [Babies 77-17
  Too many waltzes--The epic of disbelief [Sad Gay 122-13
DISBELIEFS. Your beliefs and disbeliefs, your whole peculiar plot;
  [Old Man 501-4
DISBELIEVE. This is his poison: that we should disbelieve [AA
  411-19
DISBELIEVED. A man. The lawyers disbelieved, the doctors [NSF
  391-21
DISBELIEVER. As a disbeliever in reality, [As Leave 117-6 P
  The disbeliever walked the moonlit place, [Babies 77-1
DISCERN. But in our amours amorists discern [Monocle 15-11
DISCERNED. The very hinds discerned it, in a star. [Sunday 68-4
  Mimics that play on instruments discerned [Sombre 67-26 P
DISCERNS. And the lowest ear, the deep ear that discerns, [AA
  414-17
DISCIPLINE. As he is, the discipline of his scope [Ulysses 101-14 P
DISCLOSE. Disclose to the lover. [Venereal 47-10

Conceal yourself or disclose [Venereal 48-14
It is to disclose the essential presence, say, [Moonlight 531-10
To disclose in the figure waiting on the road [Moonlight 531-13
Disclose the rude and ruddy at their jobs [Burnshaw 48-20 P
DISCLOSED. Disclosed the sea floor and the wilderness [Farewell
   118-2
Thus one is most disclosed when one is most anonymous. [Nudity
   Col 145-13
Disclosed in common forms. Set up [Prelude 195-17
And these regalia, these things disclosed, [EM 317-12
The force that destroys us is disclosed, within [EM 324-20
Of a human avocation, so disclosed [Pastor 379-14
Disclosed in everything, transcended, poised [Duck 62-21 P
See well-disclosed.
DISCLOSES. Comparative. The assassin discloses himself, [EM 324-19
Discloses [Primordia 9-22 P
DISCLOSING. A note or two disclosing who it was. [NH 483-18
Is evil, crisply bright, disclosing you [Spaniard 34-13 P
DISCLOSURE. State the disclosure. In that one eye the dove [Think
   357-3
The violent disclosure trimly leafed, [Bouquet 452-9
The immaculate disclosure of the secret no more obscured. [Dis-
   cov 96-2 P
DISCLOSURES. One understands, in the intense disclosures [Lack
   303-15
Since the radiant disclosures that you make [Burnshaw 48-11 P
DISCOLORATIONS. Of these discolorations, mastering [Descrip 342-8
DISCOLORED. Discolored, how they are going to defeat. [Extracts
   259-20
It is stale and the water is discolored. [Hero 280-21
DISCOMPOSED. And fire and air and things not discomposed [Two V
   355-9
DISCONTENT. She too is discontent [Paltry 5-11
Dwelt in the land. Perhaps if discontent [C 40-5
Come, baffling discontent. These, too, must be [Sombre 69-19 P
DISCORD. The discord merely magnifies. [MBG 171-8
DISCORDS. And far beyond the discords of the wind. [Swans 4-2
DISCOURSE. "Academic Discourse at Havana" [142-title
The chant and discourse there, more than wild weather [Role
   93-9 P
DISCOVER. One would have still to discover. Among the dogs and
   dung, [Glass 198-4
Secrete us in reality. Discover [Repet 310-5
"Attempt to Discover Life" [370-title
To discover. To discover an order as of [NSF 403-23
A season, to discover summer and know it, [NSF 403-24
To discover winter and know it well, to find, [NSF 404-1
Would discover, at last, the view toward which they had edged,
   [Poem Mt 512-12
DISCOVERED. This platonic person discovered a soul in the world
   [Pure 331-13
He discovered the colors of the moon [Two Illus 514-13
DISCOVERER. Discoverer walked through the harbor streets [C 32-14
DISCOVERIES. Fresh from discoveries of tidal skies, [C 30-27
DISCOVERS. Almost as speed discovers, in the way [Owl 435-10
Invisible change discovers what is changed, [Owl 435-11
DISCOVERY. Discovery still possible to make, [C 36-21
She held men closely with discovery, [Owl 435-9
Or of a new aspect, bright in discovery-- [Aug 489-7
Snarling in him for discovery as his attentions spread, [Prol
   516-17
A moving part of a motion, a discovery [Look 518-14
Part of a discovery, a change part of a change, [Look 518-15
"A Discovery of Thought" [95-title P
Resolved in dazzling discovery. [Ulysses 102-1 P
DISCURSIVE. To avoid the bright, discursive wings, [Adequacy 243-14
DISDAIN. The appointed power unwielded from disdain. [C 37-19
As a seraglio-parrot; feel disdain [Spaniard 35-11 P
DISDAINING. Disdaining each astringent ripening, [EM 318-20
And Rosa, the muslin dreamer of satin and cowry-kin, disdaining
   the empty keys; and the young infanta, [Piano 22-3 P
DISEMBODIED. Because she is disembodied, [Wom Sun 445-12
But the images, disembodied, are not broken. [Golden 460-19
Two bodies disembodied in their talk, [NH 471-8
DISEMBODIMENTS. In this identity, disembodiments [NH 482-12
DISENTANGLED. Disentangled him from sleek ensolacings. [EM 322-8
DISGORGED. Seeming, at first, a beast disgorged, unlike, [NSF
   404-7
DISGUISE. Each year to disguise the clanking mechanism [Nigger
   157-2
DISGUISED. Disguised pronunciamento, summary, [C 45-22
DISGUST. Between that disgust and this, between the things [Dump
   202-14
DISH. In an eighteenth-century dish, [Bananas 54-5
"A Dish of Peaches in Russia" [224-title
Or the majolica dish heaped up with phosphored fruit [EM 320-17
A café. There may be a dish of country cheese [Paisant 335-15
DISHONEST. Of poor, dishonest people, for whom the steeple, [EM
   322-16
DISILLUSION. Of dreams, disillusion as the last illusion, [NH

468-11
DISILLUSIONMENT. "Disillusionment of Ten O'Clock" [66-title
DISINHERITANCE. These days of disinheritance, we feast [Cuisine
   227-13
DISINHERITED. The much too many disinherited [Dutch 292-6
Is the exile of the disinherited, [Greenest 59-22 P
DISINTEGRATION. At twelve, the disintegration of afternoon [What
   We 459-7
DISLIKE. Nevertheless, I dislike [Six Sig 74-11
I dislike the invasion [Three 133-11 P
DISLIKED. Beginning of a green Cockaigne to be, disliked, aban-
   doned, [Inelegance 25-14 P
DISLODGED. Is Celestin dislodged? The way through the world
   [Papini 446-5
DISMISS. No names. Dismiss him from your images. [NSF 388-14
DISMISSED. Dismissed, absolved [Mozart 132-16
Denied, dismissed, may hold a serpent, loud [John 437-19
In his cave, remains dismissed without a dream, [Study II 464-9
Dismissed the band. [Coroner 30-2 P
DISORDER. A. A violent order is disorder; and [Connois 215-1
B. A great disorder is an order. These [Connois 215-2
Element in the immense disorder of truths. [Connois 216-3
But suppose the disorder of truths should ever come [Connois
   216-7
A great disorder is an order. Now, A [Connois 216-9
Casual poet, that to add your own disorder to disaster [Bed
   326-15
To sleep in that bed for its disorder, talking of ghostly [Bed
   327-3
Of fear before the disorder of the strange, [Burnshaw 48-14 P
In vast disorder live in the ruins, free, [Burnshaw 48-27 P
The charts destroyed, even disorder may, [Burnshaw 48-28 P
DISORDERED. What festival? This loud, disordered mooch? [AA 415-22
DISPARATE. As if, as if, as if the disparate halves [Study II
   464-16
DISPELLED. The cadaverous persons were dispelled. [Attempt 370-19
DISPENSE. Comme Dieu Dispense de Graces [Soldat 13-title 5
DISPLAY. His own pageant and procession and display, [Questions
   462-18
Stood, dressed in antic symbols, to display [NH 470-6
DISPLAYS. Stripped of remembrance, it displays its strength--
   [Cred 375-9
Displays the theory of poetry, [NH 486-5
DISPOSED. This fortune's finding, disposed and re-disposed [Orb
   440-7
Disposed upon the central of what we see, [Greenest 55-7 P
See re-disposed.
DISPOSES. He disposes the world in categories, thus: [EM 323-5
DISPUTATION. We hear, what we are, beyond mystic disputation,
   [Look 518-11
DISPUTING. Maligning his costumes and disputing [Stan Hero 84-24 P
DISQUISITION. The Constant Disquisition of the Wind [Two Illus 513-
   title 1
DISREGARDED. On disregarded plate. The maidens taste [Sunday 69-11
DISSEMBLED. That are dissembled in vague memory [Sombre 67-16 P
DISSERTATION. As dissertation of profound delight, [C 31-6
Upon whose lips the dissertation sounds, [Ideal 89-1 A
DISSIPATE. Upon a rug mingle to dissipate [Sunday 66-19
DISSIPATIONS. These earlier dissipations of the blood [Extraord
   369-12
DISSOCIATED. And a dissociated abundance of being, [Wom Sun 445-10
DISSOLVED. Triton, dissolved in shifting diaphanes [C 28-24
Just so an ancient Crispin was dissolved. [C 29-7
Dissolved. The distances of space and time [Descrip 343-9
It is evening. The house is evening, half dissolved. [AA 413-8
And yet she too is dissolved, she is destroyed. [AA 413-13
And Gibraltar is dissolved like spit in the wind. [Fuel 456-3
Which suddenly is all dissolved and gone-- [Hermit 505-19
Dissolved the woods, war and the fatal farce [Greenest 53-22 P
Are dissolved as in an infancy of blue snow. [Discov 95-11 P
As things emerged and moved and were dissolved, [Real 110-14 P
DISSOLVES. If earth dissolves [Extracts 259-11
Its evil after death, it dissolves it while [Extracts 259-12
DISSOLVING. Are dissolving. [Fabliau 23-11
The wind dissolving into birds, [Vase 246-13
And the dissolving chorals, waits for it and imagines [Sick
   90-15 P
See half-dissolving.
DISTANCE. Deflations of distance; or as clouds [Curtains 62-3
The distance between the dark steeple [Jersey 210-9
High, low, far, wide, against the distance, [Hero 277-22
But at a distance, in another tree. [Possum 294-18
To speak quietly at such a distance, to speak [Choc 296-7
At a distance, a secondary expositor, [Great 311-4
Comes from a great distance and is heard. [Our Stars 455-12
But, here, the inamorata, without distance [NH 484-16
But a sense of the distance of the sun-- [Two Illus 513-5
Yourselves away and at a distance join [Burnshaw 51-15 P
Around him and in that distance meditates [Recit 86-19 P
Distance between me and the five-times-sensed, [Souls 94-19 P

The miles of distance away [Letters 108-9 P
Either in distance, change of nothingness, [Real 110-15 P
In the bronze distance, [Of Merc 117-17 P
DISTANCES. Halloo them in the topmost distances [Heaven 56-22
In the distances of sleep? [Roaring 113-6
Theatrical distances, bronze shadows heaped [Key W 129-20
"Wild Ducks, People and Distances" [328-title
Was central in distances the wild ducks could [Wild 329-6
That held the distances off: the villages [Wild 329-10
Held off the final, fatal distances, [Wild 329-11
Dissolved. The distances of space and time [Descrip 343-9
These fields, these hills, these tinted distances, [AA 411-8
Writhings in wrong obliques and distances, [Ulti 430-1
And night, colored from distances, central [Owl 433-11
In the pallid perceptions of its distances. [NH 469-10
On his balcony, outsensing distances, [NH 483-12
Of men growing small in the distances of space, [Rome 508-3
The desire to be at the end of distances, [Rock 527-9
In melancholy distances. You held [Burnshaw 50-26 P
The sheep-like falling-in of distances, [Duck 62-26 P
DISTANT. The spruces rough in the distant glitter [Snow Man 10-3
And the most distant, single color, about to change, [Extracts
    258-17
Than clouds, benevolences, distant heads. [EM 317-21
As if they knew of distant beaches; and were [Descrip 343-8
There the distant fails the clairvoyant eye [Cred 374-10
To seize, the obscurest as, the distant was . . . [Orb 441-3
The two romanzas, the distant and the near, [NH 481-2
In that distant chamber, a bearded queen, wicked in her dead
    light. [Madame 507-13
Frail princes of distant Monaco, [Primordia 9-20 P
Its surfaces came from distant fire; and it [Greenest 57-2 P
Their beds, their faces drawn in distant sleep, [Sombre 68-23 P
The scholar is always distant in the space [Recit 86-18 P
Things still more distant. And tradition is near. [Recit 86-20 P
In the ceiling of the distant room, in which he lies, [Sick
    90-17 P
Brighter, perfected and distant away, [Ulysses 101-24 P
Distant, yet close enough to wake [Child 106-20 P
6. White sky, pink sun, trees on a distant peak. [Someone 86-9 A
DISTANTLY. Of which we are too distantly a part. [Less 328-10
DISTASTE. It means the distaste we feel for this withered scene
    [NSF 390-3
DISTASTING. Like taste distasting the first fruit of a vine,
    [Theatre 91-3 P
DISTEMPER. Prone to distemper he abates in taste, [C 46-3
DISTENDED. Two golden gourds distended on our vines, [Monocle 16-6
DISTILLED. What pulpy dram distilled of innocence, [C 38-3
And water. It is that which is distilled [Someone 87-17 A
DISTINCT. That fluttering things have so distinct a shade. [Monocle
    18-3
DISTINGUISH. The two alike, distinguish blues, [Vari 235-2
To distinguish. The town was a residuum, [NH 479-18
DISTINGUISHED. And is not to be distinguished, when we cry [EM
    315-16
Creates a logic not to be distinguished [EM 325-1
DISTINGUISHING. Happy men, distinguishing frost and clouds.
    [Nigger 151-8
They press it as epicure, distinguishing [EM 323-2
DISTORT. That I distort the world. [W Burgher 61-2
Distort the shape of what I meant, [Stan MBG 72-18 P
DISTORTED. Distorted by hale fatness, turned grotesque. [Monocle
    16-8
DISTORTING. And so distorting, proving what he proves [C 46-10
DISTORTION. Was clear. The last distortion of romance [C 30-2
Distortion, however fragrant, however dear. [NSF 406-19
That's it: the more than rational distortion, [NSF 406-20
DISTORTIONS. Without the distortions of the theatre, [Lytton 39-3P
DISTURBED. Disturbed not even the most idle ear. [Hibiscus 22-14
Lenin on a bench beside a lake disturbed [Descrip 342-21
Night and silence disturbed by an interior sound, [Moonlight
    532-2
DISTURBS. Slight as it is, disturbs me. I did not know [Peaches
    224-18
DISUSED. Of an old and disused ambit of the soul [Aug 489-6
A disused ambit of the spirit's way, [Aug 489-8
DITHERING. Of mica, the dithering of grass, [Vari 234-18
They are. The bouquet is a part of a dithering: [Bouquet 452-17
By an access of color, a new and unobserved, slight dithering,
    [Prol 517-2
DITHERINGS. A change, until the waterish ditherings turn [Burnshaw
    52-14 P
DITHERY. A dithery gold falls everywhere. [Gray 140-13
DITHYRAMB. What heavenly dithyramb [Archi 16-21 P
DITHYRAMBS. Catching the lesser dithyrambs. [Thought 184-9
DITS. Musing immaculate, pampean dits, [C 38-25
DITTY. Half prayer and half ditty, [Pourtraicte 22-3
Deeper than a truer ditty [Orangeade 103-18
DIVA-DAME. An appearance of Again, the diva-dame. [Adult 353-10
DIVAGATION. Wrong as a divagation to Peking, [C 34-31

DIVAN. Ballatta dozed in the cool on a straw divan [NE Verses
    106-5
DIVE. It was like passing a boundary to dive [Lot 371-1
DIVERGENCE. No: nor divergence made too steep to follow down.
    [Dutch 293-12
DIVERGING. These lines are swift and fall without diverging.
    [Tallap 72-4
DIVERS. As buffo, yet divers, four mirrors blue [C 45-6
DIVERSE. Of an aesthetic tough, diverse, untamed, [C 31-20
In diverse chambers. [Archi 18-4 P
DIVERTIMENTO. The divertimento; [Mozart 132-4
DIVERTING. For Isaac Watts: the diverting of the dream [Duck
    65-26 P
DIVERTISSEMENTS. These devastations are the divertissements [Pure
    332-19
DIVEST. A single self. Divest reality [Someone 86-1 A
DIVESTED. This is the sky divested of its fountains. [EM 321-2
I am the spouse, divested of bright gold, [NSF 395-22
As a man among other men, divested [Stan Hero 84-10 P
DIVIDE. Divide it from itself. It is this or that [Poem Morn 219-2
DIVIDED. Actor and act but not divided. [Hero 279-12
Who has divided the world, what entrepreneur? [NH 468-20
Became divided in the leisure of blue day [NH 468-22
DIVIDES. This great world, it divides itself in two, [Dezem 218-6
O buckskin, O crosser of snowy divides, [Duck 61-1 P
DIVIDING. Not this dividing and indifferent blue. [Sunday 68-11
By dividing the number of legs one sees by two. [Nigger 157-9
Like space dividing its blue and by division [Two V 354-14
DIVINATION. Some merciful divination, you forgive. [Spaniard 34-6P
A divination, a letting down [Ulysses 101-28 P
DIVINATIONS. Its glitters, its divinations of serene [EM 318-16
Our divinations, [Inhab 503-9
DIVINE. And tell the divine ingénue, your companion, [Lilacs 48-20
C'était ma foi, la nonchalance divine. [Sea Surf 101-15
Parts, and more things, parts. He never supposed divine [Landsc
    242-27
Things might not look divine, nor that if nothing [Landsc 242-28
Was divine then all things were, the world itself, [Landsc 242-29
There must be mercy in Asia and divine [Montra 262-16
Divine orations from lean sacristans [Montra 262-18
We knew one parent must have been divine, [Pure 331-19
The leaves cry. It is not a cry of divine attention, [Course
    96-19 P
DIVINER. Prophetic joint, for its diviner young. [C 43-19
Sister and mother and diviner love, [Fictive 87-5
And queen, and of diviner love the day [Fictive 87-9
Of these academies, the diviner health [Prelude 195-16
A responding to a diviner opposite. [NH 468-3
DIVINITY. What is divinity if it can come [Sunday 67-13
Divinity must live within herself: [Sunday 67-19
The description that makes it divinity, still speech [NH 475-13
Don Juan turned furious divinity, [Duck 64-27 P
Possible machine, a divinity of steel, [Bship 78-3 P
The divinity, the divinity's mind, the mind [Bship 78-8 P
Into its own illustration, a divinity [Bship 79-2 P
DIVISION. Like space dividing its blue and by division [Two V
    354-14
A mind exists, aware of division, aware [Cred 377-2
DIXHUITIÈME. Dixhuitième and Georgian and serene. [Lytton 39-25 P
DIZZLE-DAZZLE. This vif, this dizzle-dazzle of being new [Armor
    530-12
DO. Well, nuncle, this plainly won't do. [Bananas 53-20
Won't do with your eglantine. [Bananas 54-1
"How to Live. What to Do" [125-title
What had this star to do with the world it lit, [Martial 238-3
Do all that angels can. I enjoy like them, [NSF 405-9
But not of romance, the bitterest vulgar do [Bouquet 450-4
In an element that does not do for us, [Look 518-4
So well, that which we do for ourselves, too big, [Look 518-5
While the shaggy top collects itself to do [Sombre 68-26 P
Have inscribed life's do and don't. The commanding codes [Recit
    86-11 P
Not having to do with love. [Letters 108-5 P
See nether-do.
DOCK. He marked the marshy ground around the dock, [C 36-13
DOCKS. The trade-wind jingles the rings in the nets around the
    racks by the docks on Indian River. [Indian 112-4
Seize yards and docks, machinery and men, [Bship 77-22 P
DOCTOR. "The Doctor of Geneva" [24-title
The doctor of Geneva stamped the sand [Geneva 24-1
The doctor used his handkerchief and sighed. [Geneva 24-15
"The Cuban Doctor" [64-title
From a doctor into an ox, before standing up, [Freed 205-11
DOCTORS. Rising upon the doctors in their beds [Freed 205-3
To study the past, and doctors, having bathed [NSF 391-15
A man. The lawyers disbelieved, the doctors [NSF 391-21
DOCTRINAL. Invented for its pith, not doctrinal [C 45-20
DOCTRINE. Crispin concocted doctrine from the rout. [C 45-11
A doctrine to this landscape. Yet, having just [Freed 204-17
Overtaking the doctrine of this landscape. Of him [Freed 204-21

Like a man without a doctrine. The light he gives-- [Freed 205-1
Perennial doctrine and most florid truth; [Duck 63-10 P
DODGES. Of windings round and dodges to and fro, [Ulti 429-20
DOES. To what he does. He is the heroic [Hero 279-11
It does no good to speak of the big, blue bush [Study I 463-4
At evening and at night. It does no good. [Study I 463-13
Is only what the sun does every day, [Look 517-16
And there he walks and does as he lives and likes. [Armor 530-22
DOG. Corazon, stout dog, [Destructive 192-15
A pink girl took a white dog walking. [Forces 229-2
The dog had to walk. He had to be taken. [Forces 229-3
No large white horses. But there was the fluffy dog. [Forces
229-12
The sun shone and the dog barked and the baby slept. [Contra II
270-5
An abstract, of which the sun, the dog, the boy [Contra II 270-10
The wind is like a dog that runs away. [Pieces 352-5
See digs-a-dog.
DOG-EARED. On the pedestal, an ambitious page dog-eared [What We
460-1
DOGS. In the taste for iron dogs and iron deer. [Nigger 155-2
Heard the dogs howl at barren bone, [Thought 187-6
One would have still to discover. Among the dogs and dung,
[Glass 198-4
The rocks of the cliffs are the heads of dogs [Vari 232-12
No winds like dogs watched over her at night. [World 521-6
Took seven white dogs [Cab 20-16 P
Bells of the dogs chinked. [Cab 21-1 P
White dogs at bay. [Cab 21-12 P
DOGWOOD. And pink, the water bright that dogwood bears. [C 37-31
The corals of the dogwood, cold and clear, [NSF 400-1
DOGWOODS. There the dogwoods, the white ones and the pink ones,
[Forces 228-22
At the time of the dogwoods, handfuls thrown up [Forces 229-5
In the woods of the dogwoods, [Forces 229-11
DOING. That he spoke only by doing what he did. [Men Fall 188-12
DOKTOR. See Herr Doktor.
DOLEFUL. Doleful heroics, pinching gestures forth [Monocle 17-11
It is a doleful ballad, [Three 138-11 P
DOLEFULLY. In swift, successive shadows, dolefully. [C 32-21
DOLLARS. Of a cat, twelve dollars for the devil, [Hero 275-9
DOLLS. Could make us squeak, like dolls, the wished-for words.
[Monocle 17-8
DOMAIN. The space beneath it still, a smooth domain, [Old Woman
46-5 P
DOME. Infants yet eminently old, then dome [C 43-26
The bell of its dome, the patron of sound. [Vari 235-9
Spread outward. Crack the round dome. Break through. [Aug 490-11
Our chiefest dome a demoiselle of gold. [Archi 18-2 P
Of azure round an upper dome, brightest [Greenest 54-13 P
And its immaculate fire, the middle dome, [Greenest 54-16 P
The future for them is always the deepest dome, [Duck 65-21 P
The darkest blue of the dome and the wings around [Duck 65-22 P
DOMES. Nor the mallets of the domes [Six Sig 74-25
While the domes resound with chant involving chant. [Ghosts
119-18
And seraphs cluster on the domes, [Contra I 266-15
Its domes are the architecture of your bed. [Rome 510-14
There, too, he saw, since he must see, the domes [Greenest
54-12 P
From the rumors of the speech-full domes, [Ulysses 102-15 P
DOMINANCE. One of the songs of that dominance.) [Bagatelles 213-24
DOMINANT. The vital, arrogant, fatal, dominant X. [Motive 288-20
The dominant blank, the unapproachable. [NH 477-16
DOMINATION. "Domination of Black" [8-title
DOMINION. Dominion of the blood and sepulchre. [Sunday 67-11
It took dominion everywhere. [Jar 76-13
DON. Yet Franciscan don was never more [MBG 181-13
DON DON. Why nag at the ideas of Hercules, Don Don? [NE Verses
104-1
DONE. The cowl of winter, done repenting. [Peter 92-5
Today is today and the dancing is done. [Fish-Scale 160-16
But that's all done. It is what used to be, [Cuisine 227-17
Be broken and winter would be broken and done, [Extracts 255-19
Of praise, a conjugation done by choirs. [NSF 402-15
The fire falls a little and the book is done. [Novel 458-17
It would be done. If, only to please myself, [Bship 78-10 P
It would be done. And once the thing was done, [Bship 78-14 P
DONG. Of ding, ding, dong. [Snow Stars 133-12
DON JOHN. Patron and imager of the gold Don John, [Lilacs 49-14
DON JOOST. "From the Misery of Don Joost" [46-title
DON JUAN. Don Juan turned furious divinity, [Duck 64-27 P
DONKEY. In the donkey's ear, "I fear that elegance [Uruguay 248-18
With lofty darkness. The donkey was there to ride, [Uruguay
249-9
DONNA. Donna, donna, dark, [Venereal 48-11
DONNE. Aux taureaux Dieu cornes donne [Parasol 20-1 P
DON'T. Have inscribed life's do and don't. The commanding codes
[Recit 86-11 P
DOO. Damariscotta da da doo. [Vari 235-15

DOOLEY. Nor of a widow Dooley, [Aug 491-11
See Mrs. Dooley.
DOOM. To a jangle of doom [Cortege 80-26
By which to spell out holy doom and end, [Owl 434-17
Less than contending with fictitious doom. [Spaniard 35-5 P
DOOR. The curtains flittered and the door was closed. [C 42-4
Here is the plantain by your door [Watermelon 89-4
To nail his thought across the door, [MBG 166-7
Pass through the door and through the walls, [Vari 235-10
A soldier walks before my door. [Contra I 266-12
Before, before, before my door. [Contra I 266-14
Before, before, before my door. [Contra I 266-17
A soldier stalks before my door. [Contra I 267-4
At the door. [God 285-6
And knock like a rifle-butt against the door. [AA 414-2
And is destroyed. He opens the door of his house [AA 416-24
And the rust and rot of the door through which she went.
[Beginning 427-11
Through the door one sees on the lake that the white duck swims
[Bouquet 449-19
Steps out. He rings and knocks. The door is not locked. [Bouquet
452-20
A glassy ocean lying at the door, [NH 468-15
A welcome at the door to which no one comes? [Angel 496-6
Seen for a moment standing in the door. [Angel 496-8
The old woman that knocks at the door [Grotesque 77-1 P
In the green, outside the door of phantasma. [Dinner 110-6 P
Of the white stones near my door, [Three 134-7 P
Of the white stones near her door; [Three 134-13 P
DOORS. From warehouse doors, the gustiness of ropes, [C 36-9
DOORWAY. True autumn stands then in the doorway. [Hero 280-22
It filled my doorway, [Three 128-10 P
DOOR-YARD. In the door-yard by his own capacious bloom. [C 44-5
DOS. Two coins were lying--dos centavos. [Attempt 370-21
DOT. The dot, the pale pole of resemblances [Ideal 88-16 A
DOTE. On what strange froth does the gross Indian dote, [C 38-1
DOUBLE. Yet not too closely the double of our lives, [Descrip
344-19
And every latent double in the word, [NSF 387-6
Dark things without a double, after all, [NH 465-13
His life made double by his father's life, [Recit 87-19 P
The mulberry is a double tree. [Banjo 114-1 P
The double fruit of boisterous epicures, [Someone 85-20 A
DOUBLED. With meanings, doubled by the closest sound, [Sombre
67-25 P
See azure-doubled.
DOUBLES. There are doubles of this fern in clouds, [Red Fern 365-5
Detects the sound of a voice that doubles its own, [Woman Had
82-20 P
DOUBLE-THING. Becomes amassed in a total double-thing. [NH 472-7
DOUBLING. The doubling second things, not mystical, [Bouquet 451-18
DOUBLY. And you, my semblables, are double killed [Dutch 290-20
DOUBT. Created, in his day, a touch of doubt. [C 27-13
No doubt that soldiers had to be marching [Loaf 200-16
Had got him nowhere. There was always the doubt, [Blue Bldg
216-17
An affirmation free from doubt. [Vase 247-5
Grew strong, as if doubt never touched his heart. [Choc 299-5
Of the certain solid, the primary free from doubt, [Man Car 351-2
Gulping for shape among the reeds. No doubt, [Lot 371-12
No doubt we live beyond ourselves in air, [Look 518-3
As for myself, I feel a doubt: [Lytton 39-10 P
I'd rather not. No doubt there's a quarter here, [Lytton 39-24 P
No doubt, the well-tuned birds are singing, [Agenda 42-11 P
And the great misery of the doubt of it, [Dove 98-9 P
DOUCE. This outpost, this douce, this dumb, this dead, in which
[Cuisine 228-9
Enough. Ah! douce campagna of that thing! [Beard 247-19
Ah! douce campagna, honey in the heart, [Beard 247-20
DOUCEUR. Deduction. Thrum with a proud douceur [C 43-14
DOUCEURS. And of the spirit of the arranged, douceurs, [Cred 377-14
DOVE. What of the dove, [Sonatina 110-1
To think of a dove with an eye of grenadine [Sleight 222-13
On which the dove alights. Description is [Descrip 343-21
One eye, in which the dove resembles the dove. [Think 356-14
There is one dove, one bass, one fisherman. [Think 356-15
State the disclosure. In that one eye the dove [Think 357-3
Might spring to sight and yet remain a dove. [Think 357-4
In whose breast, the dove, alighting, would grow still. [Think
357-6
"The Dove in the Belly" [366-title
The dove in the belly builds his nest and coos, [Belly 366-17
Deep dove, placate you in your hiddenness. [Belly 367-12
Rou-cou spoke the dove, [Song Fixed 519-13
The choice twixt dove and goose is over-close. [Spaniard 35-6 P
The dove's adagio may lose its depth [Burnshaw 48-25 P
"The Dove in Spring" [97-title P
A small howling of the dove [Dove 97-17 P
It is established. There the dove [Dove 98-3 P
See wood-dove.

DOVES. Inhaled the appointed odor, while the doves [NSF 389-14
  Violets, doves, girls, bees and hyacinths [NSF 389-22
  Are like the sound of doves. [Secret Man 35-22 P
  It is long since there have been doves [Secret Man 35-23 P
  The doves will fly round. [Secret Man 36-9 P
  Or dance the death of doves, most sallowly, [Burnshaw 48-22 P
  And change. If ploughmen, peacocks, doves alike [Burnshaw 48-26P
  That the vista retain ploughmen, peacocks, doves, [Burnshaw
    50-9 P
  See wood-doves.
DOVE-WINGED. To blot this with its dove-winged blendings. [Ghosts
  119-10
DOWN. Down to the ground. [Domination 9-1
  The mules that angels ride come slowly down [Monocle 15-18
  The wind pours down. [Ploughing 20-6
  The wind pours down. [Ploughing 20-20
  Up and down. [Homunculus 26-4
  The drenching of stale lives no more fell down. [C 30-10
  Let down gigantic quavers of its voice, [C 33-16
  And up and down between two elements, [C 35-7
  And sinking down to the indulgences [C 35-12
  Latched up the night. So deep a sound fell down [C 42-6
  So deep a sound fell down it grew to be [C 42-9
  A long soothsaying silence down and down. [C 42-10
  Stepped in and dropped the chuckling down his craw, [C 45-18
  Fibrous and dangling down, [Bananas 54-19
  When radiance came running down, slim through the bareness.
    [Banal 63-2
  Wriggling far down the phantom air, [Cuban 65-2
  Pylon and pier fell down. [Public Sq 109-2
  Down to the fishy sea. [Pascagoula 126-16
  Down to the sand, the glare [Pascagoula 127-4
  And the sublime comes down [Am Sub 131-7
  It is because they carry down the stairs [Mozart 131-20
  Brings voices as of lions coming down. [Sun March 134-6
  What's down below is in the past [Botanist 2 135-18
  And a great decadence settles down like cold. [Havana 142-12
  To Cuba. Jot these milky matters down. [Havana 144-6
  Stamp down the phosphorescent toes, tear off [Nigger 155-7
  Lord of the body, looking down, [MBG 176-6
  He lies down and the night wind blows upon him here. [Men Fall
    187-13
  Of those whom the statues torture and keep down. [Parochial
    191-14
  Is the lion that comes down to drink. There [Glass 197-13
  When light comes down to wet his frothy jaws [Glass 197-16
  Worn out, her arm falls down, [Add 199-3
  Day creeps down. The moon is creeping up. [Dump 201-11
  And east rushes west and west rushes down, [Rabbit K 209-14
  Bent and broken them down, [Weak Mind 212-19
  The plaster dropping, even dripping down, [Blue Bldg 217-5
  Look down now, Cotton Mather, from the blank. [Blue Bldg 217-13
  Cut summer down to find the honey-comb. [Blue Bldg 217-21
  So what said the others and the sun went down [Uruguay 248-16
  The villages slept as the capable man went down, [Uruguay 249-25
  Rode over the picket rocks, rode down the road, [Uruguay 250-2
  Hoy, hoy, the blue bulls kneeling down to rest. [Montra 260-6
  Approaching the feelings or come down from them, [Montra 260-12
  Fall down through nakedness to nakedness, [Montra 263-23
  Down deeply in the empty glass . . . [Phosphor 267-10
  No: nor divergence made too steep to follow down. [Dutch 293-12
  Like a machine left running, and running down. [Repet 306-18
  Makes him rise above the houses, looking down. [Repet 307-14
  My orator. Let this giantness fall down [Repet 310-2
  When B. sat down at the piano and made [EM 316-9
  Dropped down from turquoise leaves. In the landscape of [EM
    318-13
  As they fell down, as they heard Liadoff's cloud [Liadoff 346-18
  Take the diamonds from your hair and lay them down. [Myrrh 350-10
  And shapes of fire, and wind that bears them down. [Two V 355-12
  The whole race is a poet that writes down [Men Made 356-5
  The rain is pouring down. It is July. [Chaos 357-9
  People fall out of windows, trees tumble down. [Chaos 357-13
  Brought down to one below the eaves, [Silent 359-14
  And in these comic colors dangled down, [Lot 371-9
  The rest look down. One man becomes a race, [Cred 374-22
  Is like ten thousand tumblers tumbling down [Cred 376-25
  Falls down, the cock-birds calling at the time. [NSF 388-8
  The suitable amours. Time will write them down. [NSF 398-6
  To his Virgilian cadences, up down, [NSF 407-8
  Up down. It is a war that never ends. [NSF 407-9
  Lie down like children in this holiness, [AA 418-23
  The wet weed sputtered, the fire died down, the cold [Page 422-1
  Of the mind—They would soon climb down the side of the ship.
    [Page 423-8
  Here the black violets grow down to its banks [Degen 445-1
  Or down a well. Breathe freedom, oh, my native, [Aug 490-13
  The orange far down in yellow, [Plant 506-11
  A turning down toward finality-- [Plant 506-15
  Weight him down, O side-stars, with the great weightings of the

    end. [Madame 507-1
  Where he could lie and, gazing down at the sea, [Poem Mt 512-13
  Has enraged them and made them want to talk it down. [Slug 522-8
  It dances down a furrow, in the early light, back of a crazy
    plough, the green blades following. [Plough-Boy 6-7 P
  The blunt ice flows down the Mississippi, [Primordia 8-3 P
  (The blind men strike him down with their sticks.) [Soldat 13-5P
  And the awnings are let down. [Mandolin 28-14 P
  Bring down from nowhere nothing's wax-like blooms, [Burnshaw
    47-20 P
  Each fretful fern drops down a fear like dew [Greenest 55-24 P
  Like a dancer's skirt, flung round and settling down. [Woman Had
    81-18 P
  Head down. The reflections and repetitions, [Fare Guit 99-4 P
  A divination, a letting down [Ulysses 101-28 P
  A woman looking down the road, [Ulysses 104-21 P
  That a figure reclining among columns toppled down, [Conversat
    109-7 P
  The bird's fire-fangled feathers dangle down. [Of Mere 118-6 P
  Like precious scholia jotted down in the dark. [Someone 84-21 A
  See jotting-down.
DOWN-DESCENT. The down-descent into November's void. [Sombre 67-30P
DOWN-DROPPING. The same down-dropping fruit in yellow leaves,
  [Duck 61-14 P
DOWN-DROWNED. His mind raised up, down-drowned, the chariots.
  [Descrip 343-12
DOWN-FALLING. Up-rising and down-falling, bares [Curtains 62-9
  The bud of the apple is desire, the down-falling gold, [Holiday
    313-5
DOWN-POURING. Down-pouring, up-springing and inevitable, [NH
  465-17
DOWN-TOWN. That's the down-town frieze, [Common 221-1
DOWNWARD. Downward to darkness, on extended wings. [Sunday 70-28
  Key West sank downward under massive clouds [Farewell 117-3
  Shadow, up the great sea and downward [Hero 274-27
  Leaps downward through evening's revelations, [NSF 404-16
  Of billows, downward, toward the drift-fire shore. [Page 422-26
  And downward, from this purple region, thrown; [Infernale 25-7 P
  Look suddenly downward with their shining eyes [Red Kit 31-29 P
DOWNWARDLY. In the brightest landscape downwardly revolves [EM
  318-19
DOZED. A mallow morning dozed upon the deck [Sea Surf 101-6
  Ballatta dozed in the cool on a straw divan [NE Verses 106-5
DOZEN. The whole. The sound of a dozen orchestras [Bship 79-26 P
  A vacuum for the dozen orchestras [Bship 80-1 P
DOZES. And old John Rocket dozes on his pillow. [Phenom 286-11
DOZING. Your dozing in the depths of wakefulness, [Rome 509-18
DRAFTED. So posed, the captain drafted rules of the world, [Bship
  78-20 P
DRAFTINGS. In addition, there were draftings of him, thus: [NH
  485-5
DRAFTS. The drafts of gay beginnings and bright ends [Greenest
  57-13 P
DRAM. What pulpy dram distilled of innocence, [C 38-3
DRAMA. This drama that we live--We lay sticky with sleep. [AA
  419-14
DRANK. We drank Meursault, ate lobster Bombay with mango [NSF 401-22
DRAPEAU. And beneath the handkerchief drapeau, severe, [Pure 331-3
DRAPED. Is, after all, draped damask pampaluned, [Greenest 58-4 P
DRAPERY. Hangs heaven with flash drapery. Sight [Hero 274-12
DRAPINGS. A comic infanta among the tragic drapings, [Slug 522-12
DRASTIC. Then, fear a drastic community evolved [Burnshaw 51-6 P
DRAW. The birch trees draw up whiteness from the ground. [Primordia
  8-21 P
  In the swamps, bushes draw up dark red, [Primordia 8-22 P
  Sleekly the serpent would draw himself across. [Greenest 54-27 P
DRAWING. Themselves, the slightly unjust drawing that is [Extracts
  254-23
  What are you drawing from the rain-pointed water? [Primordia
    9-2 P
  What are you drawing from the rain-pointed water? [Primordia
    9-4 P
DRAWN. Morose chiaroscuro, gauntly drawn. [C 34-17
  And the visible, circumspect presentment drawn [C 35-24
  Drawn close by dreams of fledgling wing, [Babies 77-11
  A black line drawn on flat air. [Common 221-5
  Their beds, their faces drawn in distant sleep. [Sombre 68-23 P
DREAD. I knew the dread [Peacocks 58-19
DREADED. Whose heart will murmur with the music that will be a
  a voice for her, speaking the dreaded change of speech;
  [Piano 22-2 P
DREADFUL. The dreadful sundry of this world, [Venereal 47-11
DREAM. To dream of baboons and periwinkles. [Ten O'C 66-11
  When my dream was near the moon, [Six Sig 74-14
  You dream of women, swathed in indigo, [Polish Aunt 84-9
  That airy dream of the future, [Mozart 132-5
  A dream (to call it a dream) in which [MBG 174-15
  A dream no longer a dream, a thing, [MBG 174-17
  That generation's dream, aviled [MBG 183-15
  That's it, the only dream they knew, [MBG 183-17

But in that dream a heavy difference [Montra 263-4
The final dreamer of the total dream, [Sketch 335-18
Or will be. Building and dream are one. [Sketch 335-19
A total dream. There are words of this, [Sketch 335-21
A dream interrupted out of the past, [Sketch 336-8
Of death in memory's dream? Is spring a sleep? [NSF 391-3
Eye without lid, mind without any dream-- [NSF 394-12
Not of the enigma of the guilty dream. [AA 419-6
In his cave, remains dismissed without a dream, [Study II 464-9
The weight we lift with the finger of a dream, [NH 476-12
Without any pity in a somnolent dream. [Old Woman 44-6 P
Made to affect a dream they never had, [Burnshaw 47-1 P
For Isaac Watts: the diverting of the dream [Duck 65-26 P
A dream too poor, too destitute [Ulysses 104-18 P
DREAMED. The apprentice knew these dreamers. If he dreamed [C 39-29
And on a comfortable sofa dreamed. [Cuban 65-3
I dreamed, of autumn rivers, silvas green, [Montra 263-2
Was like a sleep. The sea was a sea he dreamed. [Page 422-2
DREAMER. What lover, what dreamer, would choose [Watermelon 89-2
The night wind blows upon the dreamer, bent [Men Fall 188-19
The final dreamer of the total dream, [Sketch 355-18
And Rosa, the muslin dreamer of satin and cowry-kin, disdaining
 the empty keys; and the young infanta, [Piano 22-3 P
Not the agony of a single dreamer, but [Duck 61-25 P
DREAMERS. Of dreamers buried in our sleep, and not [C 39-27
The apprentice knew these dreamers. If he dreamed [C 39-29
DREAMING. Stilled for the passing of her dreaming feet [Sunday
 67-9
DREAMS. There is a monotonous babbling in our dreams [C 39-25
Their dreams, he did it in a gingerly way. [C 39-30
All dreams are vexing. Let them be expunged. [C 39-31
Arointing his dreams with fugal requiems? [C 41-11
Huge are the canna in the dreams of [Canna 55-1
In the midst of dreams." [Peacocks 58-14
She dreams a little, and she feels the dark [Sunday 67-2
Only in silent shadows and in dreams? [Sunday 67-14
Alone, shall come fulfilment to our dreams [Sunday 69-1
Drawn close by dreams of fledgling wing, [Babies 77-11
Of the two dreams, night and day, [Watermelon 89-1
And quieting dreams in the sleepers in darkness-- [Lunar 107-11
The swarm of thoughts, the swarm of dreams [MBG 179-9
To come, a wrangling of two dreams. [MBG 183-19
Time swished on the village clocks and dreams were alive, [Uru-
 guay 249-26
Romantic with dreams of her avoirdupois, green glade [Pure 330-17
We compose these propositions, torn by dreams, [Men Made 356-2
And by the fear that defeats and dreams are one. [Men Made 356-4
Should strengthen her abortive dreams and take [NSF 399-11
Them closelier to her by rejecting dreams. [NSF 402-9
With none of the prescience of oncoming dreams, [AA 413-7
Of dreams, disillusion as the last illusion, [NH 468-11
With redness that sticks fast to evil dreams; [Rock 528-8
Through our heavy dreams; [Phases 4-6 P
Black fact emerges from her swishing dreams. [Stan MMO 19-22 P
There it would be of the mode of common dreams, [Greenest 57-9 P
And only an agony of dreams can help, [Duck 61-24 P
DRENCHED. Sees a familiar building drenched in cloud [Repet 308-4
Yet drenched with its identity, [Red Fern 365-7
DRENCHING. The drenching of stale lives no more fell down. [C 30-10
It needed the heavy nights of drenching weather [Nigger 158-6
The drenching thunder rolling by, [MBG 169-2
Be marble after the drenching reds, the dark [Greenest 57-22 P
And drenching crimsons, or endure? It came [Greenest 57-23 P
Drenching the evening with crystals' light, [Letters 107-3 P
DRESS. The dress of a woman of Lhassa, [Men 1000 52-7
Your dress was green, [Vincentine 53-1
Let the wenches dawdle in such dress [Emperor 64-4
This old, black dress, [Explan 72-14
The purple dress in autumn and the belfry breath [NE Verses
 106-7
His speech, the dress of his meaning, silk [MBG 170-2
And her dress were one and she said, "I have said no [Uruguay
 249-3
To feast . . . Slice the mango, Naaman, and dress it [Phenom
 286-14
Her dress, the carefulest, commodious weave [Beginning 428-4
The dress is lying, cast-off, on the floor. [Beginning 428-6
Burns us with brushings of her dress [Wom Sun 445-9
One remembers a woman standing in such a dress. [Bouquet 450-24
I said, "She thumbs the memories of dress." [Stan MMO 19-6 P
A cry, the pallor of a dress, a touch. [Sombre 67-20 P
DRESSED. She dressed in red and gold brocade [Pourtraicte 21-7
Dressed in calico, [Motion 83-3
And, dressed in black, he walks [Gray 140-3
Dressed in his colored robes. [Gray 140-20
Dressed in metal, silk and stone, [Thought 186-19
"The Well Dressed Man with a Beard" [247-title
Dressed poorly, arrogant of his streaming forces, [Uruguay 249-22
As the rider, no chevalere and poorly dressed, [Uruguay 249-28
Dressed in its azure-doubled crimsons, [Hero 281-3

Of four, and one of seven, whom she dressed [NSF 402-2
Dressed high in heliotrope's inconstant hue, [Bad Time 427-6
Stood, dressed in antic symbols, to display [NH 470-6
DRESSER. Take from the dresser of deal, [Emperor 64-9
DRESSES. And the cold dresses that they wore, [Ord Women 11-5
With dew, dew dresses, stones and chains of dew, heads [Dump
 202-9
The dresses of women, [Bowl 7-6 P
Bending in blue dresses to touch something, [Clear Day 113-12 P
DREW. Her hand took his and drew him near to her. [Hand 271-17
DRIBBLE. And coffee dribble . . . Frost is in the stubble. [Dwarf
 208-14
DRIED. We dried our nets and mended sail [Silent 359-9
Are white, a little dried, a kind of mark [AA 412-9
DRIFT. His cloudy drift and planned a colony. [C 36-27
Followed the drift of the obese machine [Sea Surf 102-3
Lantern without a bearer, you drift, [Vari 232-16
The sounds drift in. The buildings are remembered. [Rome 510-11
Pitched into swelling bodies, upward, drift [Burnshaw 52-20 P
See smoke-drift.
DRIFTED. The green roses drifted up from the table [Attempt 370-15
DRIFT-FIRE. By his drift-fire, on the shore, the difference [Page
 421-6
Of billows, downward, toward the drift-fire shore. [Page 422-26
DRIFTING. To magnify, if in that drifting waste [On Manner 56-6
It comes about that the drifting of these curtains [Curtains
 62-1
Drifting through space, [Explan 73-3
The curtains. Even the drifting of the curtains, [Peaches 224-17
You, too, are drifting, in spite of your course; [Vari 232-17
Bands of black men seem to be drifting in the air, [Sick 90-7 P
Drifting choirs, long movements and turnings of sounds. [Sick
 90-12 P
Waits for the unison of the music of the drifting bands [Sick
 90-14 P
DRIFTS. The sea drifts through the winter air. [MBG 179-14
The cloud drifts idly through half-thought-of forms. [AA 416-15
DRILL. The drill of a submarine. The voyage [Hero 274-25
DRILLED. A running forward, arms stretched out as drilled. [Nigger
 153-15
In the rowdy serpentines. He drilled. [News 264-14
DRINK. What wine does one drink? [Am Sub 131-12
Of ether, the other smelling of drink, [MBG 177-10
Is the lion that comes down to drink. There [Glass 197-13
The long-bladed knife, the little to drink and her [NH 485-21
The trees drink. [Primordia 8-17 P
Not water to drink: [Three 128-4 P
We have forgotten water to drink. [Three 128-5 P
I drink from it, dry as it is, [Three 129-3 P
Drink from wise men? From jade? [Three 129-16 P
DRINKS. His crust away eats of this meat, drinks [Hero 278-16
DRIPPING. Do you come dripping in your hair from sleep? [Monocle
 14-11
The plaster dropping, even dripping, down, [Blue Bldg 217-5
Dripping a morning sap. [Poem Morn 219-11
Eyes dripping blue, so much to learn. [Couch 295-9
DRIVE. If not, when all is said, to drive away [C 37-7
To drive the dagger in his heart, [MBG 166-4
DRIVERS. The drivers in the wind-blows cracking whips, [Repet
 308-22
DRIVES. A car drives up. A soldier, an officer, [Bouquet 452-19
DRIVING. The driving rain, the willows in the rain, [Soldat 13-12P
DROLL. Choosing his element from droll confect [C 40-7
What pistache one, ingenious and droll, [Sea Surf 102-5
Combat, compose their droll affair. [MBG 182-11
DRONE. To drone the green phrases of its juvenal? [NSF 390-15
And, in my hearing, you hear its tragic drone [Angel 497-2
And purpose, to hear the wild bee drone, to feel [Greenest
 56-25 P
Hard to be told from thoughts, the repeated drone [Americana
 94-3 P
Of other lives becoming a total drone, [Americana 94-4 P
DRONED. And while the torrent on the roof still droned [C 33-8
DRONING. To this droning of the surf. [Fabliau 23-15
And out of their droning sibilants makes [Two Figures 86-8
DROP. His tip a drop of water full of storms. [Bird Claws 82-12
Will drop like sweetness in the empty nights [Havana 144-8
Each drop a petty tricolor. For this, [Hartford 226-10
In a beau language without a drop of blood. [Repet 310-9
Is a drop of lightning in an inner world, [Bouquet 448-6
Is more or less. The pearly women that drop [Study II 464-5
Suppose it was a drop of blood . . . [Inhab 504-12
As in the last drop of the deepest blood, [Rome 509-26
The skeletons sit on the wall. They drop [Stan MBG 72-3 P
There is a drop that is life's element, [Conversat 108-20 P
DROPPED. Stepped in and dropped the chuckling down his craw,
 [C 45-18
Dropped out of this amber-ember pod, [MBG 182-6
And speech of Virgil dropped, that's where he walks, [Thought
 185-14

And knowledge dropped upon his heart [Thought 186-23
The blessed regal dropped in daggers' dew, [Montra 260-18
Dropped down from turquoise leaves. In the landscape of [EM
   318-13
DROPPING. Or the changing of light, the dropping [Curtains 62-5
Dropping in sovereign rings [Pascagoula 127-6
And beggars dropping to sleep, [Add 198-9
The plaster dropping, even dripping, down, [Blue Bldg 217-5
Or melt Arcturus to ingots dropping drops, [Page 423-3
See down-dropping.
DROPS. Making gulped potions from obstreperous drops, [C 46-9
That splatters incessant thousands of drops, [Hartford 226-9
Or melt Arcturus to ingots dropping drops, [Page 423-3
Each fretful fern drops down a fear like dew [Greenest 55-24 P
The maid drops her eyes and says to her mistress, [Three 135-1 P
DROPSICAL. See, now, the ways beleaguered by black, dropsical
   duennas, [Inelegance 26-7 P
DROVE. That first drove Crispin to his wandering. [C 39-13
We drove home from Cornwall to Hartford, late. [Real 110-8 P
DROWNED. One would be drowned in the air of difference, [Extracts
   258-12
In which he sat. All chariots were drowned. The swans [Descrip
   343-4
Drowned in its washes, reading in the sound, [NSF 387-10
See down-drowned.
DROWNS. Bubbles up in the night and drowns the crickets' sound.
   [EM 321-9
DROWSED. And which had drowsed along the bony shores, [Hibiscus
   22-18
DROWSES. Enters the room, it drowses and is the night. [NSF 399-19
DROWSING. Drowsing in summer's sleepiest horn. [Cuban 65-6
DROWSY. The way the drowsy, infant, old men do. [Questions 463-3
The river motion, the drowsy motion of the river R. [Old Man
   501-6
DRUDGE. Thus, on the basis of the common drudge, [Polish Aunt 84-8
DRUM. Roll a drum upon the blue guitar. [MBG 170-13
In the heavy drum of speech, the inner men [NH 488-9
A dead hand tapped the drum, [Phases 6-1 P
An immense drum rolls through a clamor of people. [Stan Hero
   83-11 P
And the drum [Three 136-3 P
DRUM-MAJORS. "The Drum-Majors in the Labor Day Parade" [36-title P
DRUMMERS. Do the drummers in black hoods [Circulat 150-3
DRUMS. Approaching like a gasconade of drums. [C 32-18
The eye and tinkling to the ear. Gruff drums [Havana 143-6
Rumble anything out of their drums? [Circulat 150-4
The father, the beater of the rigid drums, [Thought 186-4
It was the battering of drums I heard [Loaf 200-8
And that drums had to be rolling, rolling, rolling. [Loaf 200-17
Massive drums and leaden trumpets, [Nightgown 214-11
Either trumpets or drums, the commanders mute, the arms [Martial
   238-1
Tap skeleton drums inaudibly. [Dutch 290-7
There is a battering of the drums. The bugles [Dutch 291-8
Hear the loud drums roll-- [Phases 3-11 P
DRUNK. Drunk and asleep in his boots, [Ten O'C 66-13
After we've drunk the Moselle, to the thickest shade [Phenom
   286-16
It is an old bitch, an old drunk, [Grotesque 77-3 P
DRUNKARDS. Good light for drunkards, poets, widows, [Homunculus
   25-15
The thoughts of drunkards, the feelings [Homunculus 26-6
DRUNKEN. Of summer, the drunken mother? [Medit 124-9
Smeared, smoked, and drunken of thin potencies, [Page 422-28
DRY. From dry catarrhs, and to guitars [Ord Women 10-14
From dry guitars, and to catarrhs [Ord Women 12-4
He munches a dry shell while he exerts [Bird Claws 82-16
Suggested malice in the dry machine [Sea Surf 101-9
Turn dry, [Gray 140-16
A hard dry leaf hangs [Pears 196-15
"Dry Loaf" [199-title
The pines along the river and the dry men blown [Loaf 199-21
Dry seconds and insipid thirds, [Arcades 225-25
Of the wind, rain in a dry September, [Hero 275-13
Air-earth--Can we live on dry descriptions, [Hero 278-2
Cat's milk is dry in the saucer. Sunday song [Phenom 286-3
The field is frozen. The leaves are dry. [Possum 293-15
And pathetic magnificences dry in the sky. [Repet 310-4
Dry Birds Are Fluttering in Blue Leaves [Pure 332-title 4
These lovers waiting in the soft dry grass. [Cred 372-18
The dry eucalyptus seeks god in the rainy cloud. [NH 475-4
The male voice of the wind in the dry leaves [Primordia 7-14 P
Returns and returns, along the dry, salt shore. [Woman Had 81-24P
This rock and the dry birds [Including 88-3 P
I drink from it, dry as it is, [Three 129-3 P
DRYING. Or the bench with the pot of geraniums, the stained mat-
   tress and the washed overalls drying in the sun? [Indigo
   22-12 P
DUBBING. These musicians dubbing at a tragedy, [AA 415-24
DUCHESS. One is not duchess [Theory 86-18

DUCK. If any duck in any brook, [Sonatina 109-13
Through the door one sees on the lake that the white duck swims
   [Bouquet 449-19
The green bouquet comes from the place of the duck. [Bouquet
   450-1
And crawls on them, as if feathers of the duck [Bouquet 450-17
In other shapes, as if duck and tablecloth [Bouquet 450-19
"A Duck for Dinner" [60-title P
On summer Sundays in the park, a duck [Duck 60-11 P
To a million, a duck with apples and without wine. [Duck 60-12 P
For themselves, and space and time and ease for the duck. [Duck
   60-17 P
But of what are they thinking, of what, in spite of the duck,
   [Duck 62-12 P
But man means more, means the million and the duck. [Duck 63-11 P
DUCKLING. A duckling of the wildest blood [Grotesque 75-12 P
DUCKS. "Wild Ducks, People and Distances" [328-title
The wild ducks were enveloped. The weather was cold. [Wild 329-3
Was central in distances the wild ducks could [Wild 329-6
Fixed like a lake on which the wild ducks fluttered, [Cata 424-13
In a permanent realization, without any wild ducks [Cata 425-7
And one last look at the ducks is a look [Hermit 506-2
For the million, perhaps, two ducks instead of one; [Duck 65-2 P
DUENNA. His trees were planted, his duenna brought [C 42-2
Old pantaloons, duenna of the spring! [Polish Aunt 84-6
DUENNAS. See, now, the ways beleaguered by black, dropsical
   duennas, [Inelegance 26-7 P
DUET. A few final solutions, like a duet [MBG 177-7
DUFT. In the Duft of towns, beside a window, beside [Woman Had
   83-5 P
DUFY. See Monsieur Dufy.
DULCE. Of dulce atmosphere, the fore of lofty scenes [Bouquet 450-3
DULCET. The dulcet omen fit for such a house. [C 44-26
DULCIED. With someone to speak her dulcied native tongue, [Letters
   107-17 P
DULL. Like a dull scholar, I behold, in love, [Monocle 16-1
And that booming wintry and dull, [Nightgown 214-8
An effulgence faded, dull cornelian [NSF 400-18
DULLER. Whether fresher or duller, whether of winter cloud [AA
   412-13
DUM. Dee, dum, diddle, dee, dee, diddle, dee, da. [Primordia 8-20 P
DUMB. To show how cold she is, and dumb. [Emperor 64-14
This outpost, this douce, this dumb, this dead, in which
   [Cuisine 228-9
A bitter utterance from your writhing, dumb, [NSF 384-21
Yet voluble dumb violence. You look [NSF 384-22
A dumb sense possesses them in a kind of solemnity. [Old Man
   501-2
We were obedient and dumb. [Phases 6-3 P
DUMBFOUNDERING. They help us face the dumbfoundering abyss [John
   437-14
DUMBLY. I am too dumbly in my being pent. [Pharynx 96-4
DUMP. "The Man on the Dump" [201-title
Places there, a bouquet. Ho-ho . . . The dump is full [Dump
   201-13
One grows to hate these things except on the dump. [Dump 202-11
That are on the dump (azaleas and so on) [Dump 202-15
(All its images are in the dump) and you see [Dump 202-23
On the dump? Is it to sit among mattresses of the dead, [Dump
   203-6
DUNG. On dung." Come now, pearled and pasted, bloomy-leafed,
   [Ghosts 119-17
One would have still to discover. Among the dogs and dung,
   [Glass 198-4
DU PUY. See: General Du Puy; Place Du Puy.
DURAND-RUEL. It was impossible to breathe at Durand-Ruel's.
   [Holiday 312-14
DURING. That's how the stars shine during the day. There, then,
   [Lot 371-4
Of Mr. Homburg during his visits home [Look 517-12
A light snow, like frost, has fallen during the night. [Bus
   116-14
DURS. Et sabots durs aux chevaux . . . [Parasol 20-2 P
DUSK. To the dusk of a whistling south below the south, [C 38-13
DUSKIEST. Seated before these shining forms, like the duskiest
   glass, reflecting the piebald of roses or what you will.[Piano
   21-18 P
DUSKY. Use dusky words and dusky images. [Two Figures 86-2
Then the sides of peaches, of dusky pears. [Vase 246-24
DUST. Found inklings of your bond to all that dust. [Monocle 15-6
Feel the wind of it, smell the dust of it? [Arcades 225-9
With this paper, this dust. That states the point. [Extracts
   252-6
Grow out of the spirit or they are fantastic dust. [Holiday
   313-4
Springs outward, being large, and, in the dust, [Pure 332-22
A dust, a force that traverses a shade. [NH 489-3
Even when the book lay turned in the dust of his table. [Poem Mt
   512-4
How soon the silver fades in the dust! How soon the black figure

slips from the wrinkled sheet! [Plough-Boy 6-8 P
  Flutter her lance with your tempestuous dust, [Spaniard 34-24 P
  And that, heavily, you move with them in the dust. [Burnshaw
    50-11 P
  In Africa. The serpent's throne is dust [Greenest 58-9 P
  Or Venice, motionless, gathering time and dust. [Real 110-10 P
DUTCH. "Dutch Graves in Bucks County" [290-title
  Dutch ice on English boats? The memory [Recit 86-25 P
DUTY. Who walks there, as a farewell duty, [Virgin 71-5
  The making of his son was one more duty. [Norfolk 111-13
DWARF. "The Dwarf" [208-title
  It is all that you are, the final dwarf of you, [Dwarf 208-9
DWARFS. A race of dwarfs, the meditative arms [Sombre 70-27 P
DWELL. A still new continent in which to dwell. [C 37-4
  Master and, without light, I dwell. There [Hero 273-4
  His stars on the wall. He must dwell quietly. [Less 327-14
DWELLER. You dweller in the dark cabin, [Watermelon 88-19
  You dweller in the dark cabin, [Watermelon 89-13
DWELLING. Crispin dwelt in the land and dwelling there [C 40-14
  In which no scholar, separately dwelling, [Somnam 304-16
  The spirit of one dwelling in a seed, [Descrip 341-19
  We make a dwelling in the evening air, [Final 524-17
  See in-dwelling.
DWELLING-PLACE. Yet this remain the dwelling-place [Nigger 153-6
DWELLINGS. Sounding in transparent dwellings of the self, [NH
    466-7
DWELLS. Brings the day to perfection and then fails. He dwells
    [EM 318-2
  Whose mere savage presence awakens the world in which she
    dwells. [World 520-16
  He dwells below, the man below, in less [Sombre 67-13 P
  It is the fate that dwells in truth. [Ulysses 103-29 P
DWELT. Dwelt in the land. Perhaps if discontent [C 40-5
  Crispin dwelt in the land and dwelling there [C 40-14
DWINDLED. Dwindled to one sound strumming in his ear, [C 28-19
  And dwindled into patches, [Celle 438-7
  Natives of a dwindled sphere. [Leben 504-21
DWINDLES. Of a multitude dwindles, all said, [MBG 171-15
DYING. A lady dying of diabetes [Thought 184-7
  Dying lady, rejoice, rejoice! [Thought 185-4
  And the long echo of their dying cry, [Thought 186-14
  Spelled from spent living and spent dying. [Dutch 291-19
DYNAMITE. Ten times ten times dynamite, convulsive [Hero 273-18

EAGER. Eager for the brine and bellowing [Paltry 5-14
  Abundantly beautiful, eager, [Homunculus 26-24
  He well might find that eager balm [Room Gard 41-10 P
EAGERLY. Who still thinks eagerly [Shifts 83-12
EAGLE. Tell me more of the eagle, Cotton, [Pascagoula 126-9
  The pensive man . . . He sees that eagle float [Connois 216-13
  In concert with the eagle's valiance. [Spaniard 35-12 P
  Until they changed to eagle in white air, [Sombre 68-4 P
EAR. He will bend his ear then. [Plot Giant 7-7
  Disturbed not even the most idle ear. [Hibiscus 22-14
  Dwindled to one sound strumming in his ear, [C 28-19
  He shut out from his tempering ear; what thoughts, [C 34-22
  For who can care at the wigs despoiling the Satan ear? [Banal
    63-4
  With my ear. [Six Sig 74-10
  Be the voice of night and Florida in my ear. [Two Figures 86-1
  The eye and tinkling to the ear. Gruff drums [Havana 143-6
  To stuff the ear? It causes him to make [Havana 144-14
  The agate in the eye, the tufted ear, [Nigger 153-19
  Be merely oneself, as superior as the ear [Dump 203-1
  To a crow's voice? Did the nightingale torture the ear [Dump
    203-2
  Pack the heart and scratch the mind? And does the ear [Dump
    203-3
  With meditation, speak words that in the ear, [Of Mod 240-7
  In the delicatest ear of the mind, repeat, [Of Mod 240-8
  Upon by clouds, the ear so magnified [Landsc 242-25
  In the donkey's ear, "I fear that elegance [Uruguay 248-18
  I have wiped away moonlight like mud. Your innocent ear [Uruguay
    249-5
  To hold by the ear, even though it wished for a bell, [Uruguay
    249-10
  And the ear is glass, in which the noises pelt, [Extracts 252-3
  Comes close to the prisoner's ear, becomes a throat [Montra
    261-2
  From which the chant comes close upon the ear, [Montra 261-5
  Clawed on the ear these consonants? [Jumbo 269-6
  That is my own voice speaking in my ear. [Choc 298-20
  It is more than an imitation for the ear. [Creat 311-9
  Speech found the ear, for all the evil sound, [EM 326-5
  Now, closely the ear attends the varying [Pure 332-2
  His epi-tones, the colors of the ear, [Liadoff 347-19
  In the one ear of the fisherman, who is all [Think 356-9
  One ear, the wood-doves are singing a single song. [Think 356-10
  In that one ear it might strike perfectly: [Think 357-2
  And the secondary senses of the ear [Cred 374-11
  Blowing itself upon the tedious ear. [NSF 400-11
  His ear, the very material of his mind. [NSF 403-3
  In flights of eye and ear, the highest eye [AA 414-16
  And the lowest ear, the deep ear that discerns, [AA 414-17
  The third form speaks, because the ear repeats, [Owl 432-3
  A source of pleasant outbursts on the ear. [Orb 442-24
  Gritting the ear, whispers humane repose. [NH 484-21
  These sounds are long in the living of the ear. [Aug 489-17
  Her ear unmoved. She was that tortured one, [Old Woman 44-9 P
  That beat out slimmest edges in the ear, [Greenest 56-30 P
  This howling at one's ear, too far [Dove 98-14 P
  See elephant's ear.
EARED. See: dog-eared; tuft-eared.
EARING. Pass the whole of life earing the clink of the [Archi
    16-18 P
EARLIER. Brings back an earlier season of quiet [Lunar 107-10
  Of a turning spirit in an earlier self. [Sun March 134-1
  These earlier dissipations of the blood [Extraord 369-12
EARLIEST. He hears the earliest poems of the world [Montra 261-19
  Cardinal, saying the prayers of earliest day; [Choc 300-2
  The way the earliest single light in the evening sky, in spring,
    [Prol 517-8
  At the earliest ending of winter, [Not Ideas 534-1
  The giant Phosphor of their earliest prayers. [Duck 65-23 P
EARLINESS. And of original earliness. Yet the sense [NH 481-11
  Of cold and earliness is a daily sense, [NH 481-12
  The cold and earliness and bright origin [NH 481-16
EARLY. Irised in dew and early fragrancies, [C 36-3
  To warblings early in the hilarious trees [Medit 124-8
  The exceeding brightness of this early sun [Sun March 133-13
  Serve the rouged fruits in early snow. [Nigger 153-1
  The gold façade round early squares, [Thought 187-2
  One had come early to a crisp café. [Forces 229-19
  On an early Sunday in April, a feeble day, [Extracts 254-25
  Men came as the sun comes, early children [Dutch 291-23
  Is not an early time that has grown late. [Dutch 292-2
  The early constellations, from which came the first [Myrrh 350-7
  Children in love with them brought early flowers [NSF 400-23
  In the early March wind. [Not Ideas 534-6
  It dances down a furrow, in the early light, back of a crazy
    plough, the green blades following. [Plough-Boy 6-7 P
  The early centuries were full [Agenda 42-7 P

That the choice should come on them so early. [Stan Hero 83-16 P
  See ever-early.
EARNED. Of the North have earned this crumb by their complaints.
    [NE Verses 106-2
EAR-RINGS. I wore gold ear-rings. [Three 141-10 P
EARS. What were the hymns that buzzed beside my ears? [Hoon 65-11
  And my ears made the blowing hymns they heard. [Hoon 65-14
  Queer, in this Vallombrosa of ears, [Arcades 225-5
  Are comic trash, the ears are dirt, [Arcades 225-18
  Flap green ears in the heat. He might observe [Landsc 243-5
  Eyes and bruted ears: the man-like body [Hero 277-9
  Which in those ears and in those thin, those spended hearts,
    [Large 421-7
  As if the ears heard any shocking sound, [NH 478-11
  Why do the horses have eyes and ears? [Primordia 8-11 P
  They cock small ears, more glistening and pale [Soldat 14-2 P
  Ears, eyes, souls, skins, hair? [Parasol 20-6 P
  Filleted angels over flapping ears, [Greenest 56-7 P
  She was all of her airs and ears and hairs, [Grotesque 74-2 P
  Her pearly ears, her jeweler's ears [Grotesque 74-3 P
  You saw the eye-blue, sky-blue, eye-blue, and the powdered ears
    [Grotesque 74-15 P
  Bald heads with their mother's voice still in their ears.
    [Woman Had 82-16 P
  If she was deaf with falling grass in her ears-- [Woman Had
    83-2 P
EARTH. Falls, it appears, of its own weight to earth. [Monocle
    14-13
  Is measure, also, of the verve of earth. [Monocle 14-27
  But that of earth both comes and goes at once. [Monocle 15-26
  But they came parleying of such an earth, [C 32-1
  That earth was like a jostling festival [C 32-8
  Monotonous earth and dark blue sky. [Vincentine 52-12
  Monotonous earth I saw become [Vincentine 53-13
  In any balm or beauty of the earth, [Sunday 67-17
  The blood of paradise? And shall the earth [Sunday 68-6
  Unchanging, yet so like our perishing earth, [Sunday 69-16
  Yet leaves us in them, until earth becomes, [Fictive 87-16
  If from the earth we came, it was an earth [Anatomy 107-13
  Since by our nature we grow old, earth grows [Anatomy 108-1
  For who could tolerate the earth [Botanist 2 136-7
  Bare night is best. Bare earth is best. Bare, bare, [Eve Angels
    137-29
  Is not so elemental nor the earth [Havana 142-5
  Made earth come right; a peanut parody [Havana 143-9
  The earth, for us, is flat and bare. [MBG 167-9
  And the earth is alive with creeping men, [MBG 168-14
  The earth is not earth but a stone, [MBG 173-13
  Cloud's red, earth feeling, sky that thinks? [MBG 177-4
  Another on earth, the one a voice [MBG 177-9
  This man loved earth, not heaven, enough to die. [Men Fall 188-18
  Breathe in a crevice of earth? [Bagatelles 213-4
  Would swoop to earth? It is a wheel, the rays [Sleight 222-10
  Of poorness as an earth, to taste [Arcades 225-24
  The sky is too blue, the earth too wide. [Scavoir 231-13
  It was in the earth only [Yellow 236-4
  Of earth penetrates more deeply than any word. [Yellow 237-3
  Elysia, these days, half earth, half mind; [Extracts 257-1
  It cannot be half earth, half mind; half sun, [Extracts 257-16
  The wounds. Yet to lie buried in evil earth, [Extracts 259-2
  If earth dissolves [Extracts 259-11
  When the grand mechanics of earth and sky were near, [Contra II
    270-2
  To be buried in desert and deserted earth. [Dutch 290-21
  Snow sparkles like eyesight falling to earth, [Possum 294-4
  Of sky, of sea, large earth, large air. It is [Choc 296-10
  To find for himself his earth, his sky, his sea. [Holiday 312-12
  In solid fire the utmost earth and know [EM 314-12
  In form, lovers of heaven and earth, she-wolves [EM 321-24
  We grew used so soon, too soon, to earth itself, [Wild 328-16
  Like earth and sky. Then he became nothing else [Wild 329-1
  Of earth, rises against it, tide by tide, [Two V 354-20
  But if they are of sea, earth, sky--water [Two V 355-8
  Fetched up with snow that never falls to earth? [Belly 367-6
  In heaven as in a glass; a second earth; [NSF 383-14
  And in the earth itself they found a green-- [NSF 383-15
  Of an earth in which the first leaf is the tale [NSF 394-14
  Even of earth, even of sight, in snow, [AA 417-13
  An innocence of the earth and no false sign [AA 418-21
  Of the work, in the idiom of an innocent earth, [AA 419-5
  There were ghosts that returned to earth to hear his phrases,
    [Large 423-11
  And, if of substance, a likeness of the earth, [Owl 433-2
  Until the used-to earth and sky, and the tree [Orb 441-12
  And they: these men, and earth and sky, inform [Orb 441-15
  That flows round the earth and through the skies, [Degen 444-14
  What good is it that the earth is justified, [Pecul 453-13
  It is the earth itself that is humanity . . . [Pecul 454-1
  Held fast tenaciously in common earth [NH 468-24
  And one from central earth to central sky [NH 469-1

The brilliancy at the central of the earth. [NH 473-15
The instinct for earth, for New Haven, for his room, [NH 476-2
And alike, a point of the sky or of the earth [NH 483-8
Than that of their clouds. These lineaments were the earth,
  [NH 484-13
And the egg of the earth lies deep within an egg. [Aug 490-10
But as of an exhumation returned to earth, [Aug 491-12
The rich earth, of its own self made rich, [Aug 491-13
Yet I am the necessary angel of earth, [Angel 496-15
Since, in my sight, you see the earth again, [Angel 496-16
The self and the earth--your thoughts, your feelings, [Old Man
  501-3
A likeness, one of the race of fathers: earth [Irish 502-7
Seal him there. He looked in a glass of the earth and thought
  he lived in it. [Madame 507-2
Now, he brings all that he saw into the earth, to the waiting
  parent. [Madame 507-3
And earth, [Phases 5-18 P
Was this bowl of Earth designed? [Bowl 6-11 P
Map of yesterday's earth [Primordia 9-13 P
Of men and earth: I quote the line and page, [Soldat 11-8 P
Digs up the earth when want returns . . . [Soldat 16-11 P
(A boor of night in middle earth cries out.) [Infernale 24-19 P
Naked and stamping the earth, [Drum-Majors 37-8 P
Applied on earth to those that were myths [Lytton 39-12 P
The gardener searches earth and sky [Room Gard 41-7 P
The earth as the bodies rose on feathery wings, [Old Woman 43-15P
Thinking of heaven and earth and of herself [Old Woman 45-19 P
Hoofs grinding against the stubborn earth, until [Old Woman
  46-10 P
No longer of air but of the breathing earth, [Burnshaw 52-18 P
And bares an earth that has no gods, and bares [Greenest 58-13 P
In a clamor thudding up from central earth. [Sombre 70-30 P
When earth has become a paradise, it will be [Bship 77-19 P
From constable to god, from earth to air, [Bship 80-22 P
If the sceptre returns to earth, still moving, still [Bship
  80-31 P
At the exactest central of the earth [Ulysses 104-14 P
In the central of earth or sky or air or thought, [Conversat
  108-19 P
This bottle is earth: [Three 130-9 P
The earth remains of one color-- [Three 130-15 P
But when the sun shines on the earth, [Three 130-18 P
On whatever the earth happens to be. [Three 130-23 P
On this hermit earth. [Three 142-6 P
Like the earth on which it shines, [Three 143-11 P
It is more than the odor of this core of earth [Someone 87-16 A
And fill the earth with young men centuries old [Ideal 88-11 A
See: air-earth; man-earth; mid-earth.
EARTHIER. An earthier one, tum, tum-ti-tum, [Botanist 2 136-9
EARTH-LINES. Mounting the earth-lines, long and lax, lethargic.
  [Tallap 72-3
EARTHLY. Our earthly mothers waiting, sleeplessly. [Sunday 69-27
  He sought an earthly leader who could stand [Thought 185-23
  The earthly mother and the mother of [Owl 432-16
EARTHY. "Earthy Anecdote" [3-title
  Are of our earthy birth and here and now [NSF 395-8
  Less in the stars than in their earthy wake, [Burnshaw 48-10 P
EASE. A mountain in which no ease is ever found, [EM 319-3
  Is ease, stands in the dark, a shadows' hill, [EM 319-5
  The man that suffered, lying there at ease, [Past Nun 378-19
  As if the language suddenly, with ease, [NSF 387-17
  They are at ease in a shelter of the mind [AA 413-18
  The desire for its celestial ease in the heart, [NH 467-6
  Of Fact, lies at his ease beside the sea." [NH 485-18
  There was an ease of mind that was like being alone in a boat at
    sea, [Prol 515-5
  For themselves, and space and time and ease for the duck. [Duck
    60-17 P
  The only access to true ease, [Ulysses 100-3 P
  This is not poet's ease of mind. [Ulysses 103-28 P
  An ease in which to live a moment's life, [Letters 107-7 P
EASED. Reclining, eased of desire, establishes [EM 324-12
EASIER. It was easier to think it lay there. If [Landsc 242-5
EASILY. How easily the feelings flow this afternoon [Nigger 151-16
  Concealed creator. One walks easily [Couch 296-3
  Of the land's children, easily born, its flesh, [Cred 375-4
  Extremest pinch and, easily, as in [Page 437-1
  How easily the blown banners change to wings . . . [Rome 508-11
  A poem about tradition could easily be [Recit 86-1 P
  Of tradition does not easily take form. [Recit 86-7 P
EASINGS. Gold easings and ouncings and fluctuations of thread
  [NH 477-19
EAST. There are men of the East, he said, [Men 1000 51-9
  Who are the East. [Men 1000 51-10
  Accomplished in the immensely flashing East, [Eve Angels 137-22
  Freshness is more than the east wind blowing round one. [Nigger
    157-11
  And east rushes west and west rushes down, [Rabbit K 209-14
  In east wind beating the shutters at night. [Vase 246-16

On the east, sister and nun, and opened wide [Phenom 287-8
  An east in their compelling westwardness, [Our Stars 455-20
  Is it Ulysses that approaches from the east, [World 520-11
  Let us fix portals, east and west, [Archi 17-27 P
  The east wind in the west, order destroyed, [Sombre 68-15 P
  Coming from the East, forcing itself to the West, [Bship 80-11 P
EASTER. At Easter on a London screen, the seeds [Greenest 53-19 P
EAST HARTFORD. Whimpers when the moon above East Hartford [Gro-
  tesque 76-18 P
EASTWARD. On the still, black-slatted eastward shutters. [Aug
  492-23
EAST-WIND. O stagnant east-wind, palsied mare, [Room Gard 40-16 P
EASY. It is easy to say to those bidden--But where, [Ghosts 119-4
  She made it. It is easy to say [Scavoir 231-2
  Makes more of it. It is easy to wish for another structure [Bed
    326-16
  The easy projection long prohibited. [Paisant 335-11
  The easy passion, the ever-ready love [NSF 394-23
  For easy passion and ever-ready love [NSF 395-7
EAT. "Frogs Eat Butterflies. Snakes Eat Frogs. Hogs Eat Snakes.
  Men Eat Hogs" [78-title
  What bread does one eat? [Am Sub 131-13
  Of buzzards and eat the bellies of the rich, [Burnshaw 49-8 P
EATEN. On tins and boxes? What about horses eaten by wind?
  [Parochial 191-18
EATING. Are they men eating reflections of themselves? [Cuisine
  228-16
EATS. One eats one paté, even of salt, quotha. [C 28-1
  His crust away eats of this meat, drinks [Hero 278-16
  Meyer is a bum. He eats his pie. [Grotesque 75-18 P
  He eats red cherry pie and never says-- [Grotesque 75-19 P
EAVES. But for the icicles on the eaves-- [MBG 179-20
  Brought down to one below the eaves, [Silent 359-14
  It is not a voice that is under the eaves. [Silent 359-18
  Speak softly, to begin with, in the eaves. [Beginning 428-8
  And exhalations in the eaves, so little [NH 477-8
EBBING. Of mountain pallors ebbing into air; [Soldat 13-10 P
EBON. Of pick of ebon, pick of halcyon. [Havana 144-16
EBONY. Syllables, pewter on ebony, yet still [Sombre 70-7 P
ECCE. Ecce, Oxidia is the seed [MBG 182-5
ECCENTRIC. Of thought evoked a peace eccentric to [Havana 143-5
  Knew the eccentric to be the base of design. [Nigger 151-3
  To grasp the hero, the eccentric [Hero 274-3
  Revenges. And negation was eccentric. [EM 319-25
  The eccentric souvenirs of human shapes, [Descrip 342-13
  The eccentric propositions of its fate. [Men Made 356-6
  At it spinning its eccentric measure. Perhaps, [NSF 406-4
  And the eccentric twistings of the rapt bouquet [Bouquet 450-20
  The eccentric exterior of the clocks talk. [NH 478-21
ECCENTRICITY. But muses on its eccentricity, [Jasmine 79-6
  Each one, his fated eccentricity, [Orb 443-17
ECCLESIAST. Of things? A figure like Ecclesiast, [NH 479-13
ECHO. And the long echo of their dying cry, [Thought 186-14
  Find a deep echo in a horn and buzz [NSF 390-17
ECHOES. And calling like the long echoes in long sleep, [Luther
  461-17
ECHOING. The trees, like serafin, and echoing hills, [Sunday 70-8
  And echoing rhetorics more than our own. [Montra 261-18
ECHOINGS. Rock, of valedictory echoings, [MBG 179-4
ECLIPSE. A deprivation muffled in eclipse, [Red Kit 30-22 P
ECSTASIES. Bidders and biders for its ecstasies, [C 44-1
ECSTASY. And you, my semblables, whose ecstasy [Dutch 292-15
  In an ecstasy of its associates, [EM 316-13
  It is a declaration, a primitive ecstasy, [EM 321-10
  Of his sister, in what a sensible ecstasy [NSF 401-24
  You brought the incredible calm in ecstasy, [Red Kit 30-17 P
  Where is that calm and where that ecstasy? [Red Kit 31-2 P
  The ecstasy of sense in a sensuous air. [Greenest 56-26 P
ECSTATIC. Of this ecstatic air. [Botanist 1 135-15
  One believes is what matters. Ecstatic identities [Extracts
  258-2
EDEN. What Eden sapling gum, what honeyed gore, [C 38-2
  In Eden was the father of Descartes [NSF 383-11
  In your cadaverous Eden, they desire [Duck 61-13 P
  And Eden conceived on Morningside, [Ulysses 101-7 P
EDGE. Their azure has a cloudy edge, their white [C 37-30
  At the edge of the shadow, [Six Sig 73-10
  It marked the edge [Thirteen 94-7
  On the edge of his bed. He said, [Freed 204-15
  For a moment on rising, at the edge of the bed, to be, [Freed
    205-8
  An edge of song that never clears; [Country 207-9
  Against the edge of the ice, the abstraction would [Extracts
    255-18
  Just out of the village, at its edge, [Woman Song 361-5
  We more than awaken, sit on the edge of sleep, [NSF 386-19
  Helplessly at the edge, enough to be [Ulti 430-7
  Of summer, at the windy edge, [Celle 438-11
  The bouquet has slopped over the edge and lies on the floor.
    [Bouquet 453-3

He that kneels always on the edge of space [NH 469-9
So that at the edge of afternoon, not over, [NH 482-22
From the edge of night, [Aug 495-2
In the warmth of your bed, at the edge of your chair, alive
   [Rome 509-19
To Concord, at the edge of things, was this: [Look 517-13
The meeting at noon at the edge of the field seems like [Rock
   525-12
Is there a sharp edge? [Lulu M 27-1 P
Is there a sharp edge? [Lulu M 27-2 P
Arranged for phantasy to form an edge [Old Woman 43-17 P
How shall we face the edge of time? We walk [Duck 66-6 P
In glimpses, on the edge or at the tip. [Sombre 67-1 P
Permitting nothing to the evening's edge. [Role 93-5 P
The palm stands on the edge of space. [Of Mere 118-4
Apposites, to the slightest edge, of the whole [Someone 86-19 A
EDGED. Would discover, at last, the view toward which they had
   edged, [Poem Mt 512-12
Those English noses and edged, Italian eyes, [Duck 60-22 P
See: blue-edged; bright-edged; brilliant-edged; green-edged.
EDGES. Like the clashed edges of two words that kill." [Monocle
   13-4
It crawls over the edges of the snow. [Tattoo 81-11
And in the edges of the snow. [Tattoo 81-21
A self that touches all edges, [Rabbit K 209-18
The enormous gongs gave edges to their sounds, [Uruguay 249-27
There on the edges of oblivion. [Owl 435-18
Rest, crows, upon the edges of the moon, [Red Kit 31-20 P
Along the edges of your eye [An Gaiety 33-3 P
Its edges were taken from tumultous wind [Greenest 56-29 P
That beat out slimmest edges in the ear, [Greenest 56-30 P
EDGING. Of the pine trees edging the sand, [Pascagoula 127-5
EDGINGS. These are the edgings and inchings of final form, [NH
   488-16
EDIFICE. Like a fractured edifice [Public Sq 108-20
A slash and the edifice fell, [Public Sq 109-1
Is the clear-point of an edifice, [Human 363-10
Total grandeur of a total edifice, [Rome 510-26
These are the pointings of our edifice, [Archi 17-17 P
EEL. Sleep deep, good eel, in your perverse marine. [Two V 354-18
EFFECT. Say that it is a crude effect, black reds, [Roses 430-10
And yet this effect is a consequence of the way [Roses 430-16
The effect of the object is beyond the mind's [John 436-18
The frame of a repeated effect, is it that? [Recit 87-6 P
EFFECTIVE. Effective colonizer sharply stopped [C 44-4
EFFECTS. Compilation of the effects [Primordia 9-10 P
EFFECTUAL. Is something wished for made effectual [Belly 367-8
EFFENDI. Panic in the face of the moon--round effendi [EM 320-15
Or a lustred nothingness. Effendi, he [EM 320-22
EFFETE. Effete green, the woman in black cassimere. [NH 482-2
The effete vocabulary of summer [Plant 506-8
EFFIGIES. Day, night and man and his endless effigies. [Someone
   83-13 A
EFFIGY. Gross effigy and simulacrum, none [Fictive 87-18
Ah, but the meaningless, natural effigy! [Nigger 153-17
The stone, the categorical effigy; [Choc 300-3
Approached this strongly-heightened effigy [NSF 391-14
Chant sibilant requiems for this effigy. [Burnshaw 47-19 P
EFFLORISANT. Of sounds resembling sounds, efflorisant, [Montra
   260-11
EFFORT. Of the world, the heroic effort to live expressed [Papini
   446-9
A fantastic effort has failed, a repetition [Plain 502-19
That is its life preserved, the effort to be born [Discov 96-8 P
They sway, deeply and loudly, in an effort, [Region 115-8 P
EFFORTLESS. It observes the effortless weather turning blue [NSF
   382-7
EFFULGENCE. The yellowing fomentations of effulgence, [Attempt
   370-17
An effulgence faded, dull cornelian [NSF 400-18
An Arctic effulgence flaring on the frame [AA 417-2
And final effulgence and delving show. [Ulysses 104-9 P
EFFULGENT. Although they paint effulgent, azure lakes, [C 37-28
Remoter than Athos, the effulgent hordes [Greenest 56-22 P
EGG. The hen-cock crows at midnight and lays no egg, [Nigger 155-10
Hen shudders: the copious egg is made and laid. [Nigger 155-12
Do I sit, deformed, a naked egg, [MBG 173-4
Or is this another wriggling out of the egg, [AA 411-4
We make, although inside an egg, [Aug 490-1
The morning-glories grow in the egg. [Aug 490-3
The shell is a shore. The egg of the sea [Aug 490-8
And the egg of the sky are in shells, in walls, in skins [Aug
   490-9
And the egg of the earth lies deep within an egg. [Aug 490-10
EGG-DIAMOND. Held in his hand the suave egg-diamond [Thunder 220-10
EGG-PLANT. Of an emperor, the egg-plant of a prince. [Extracts
   253-10
An egg-plant of good air. [Extracts 253-15
EGGS. See fish-eggs.
EGLANTINE. Won't do with your eglantine. [Bananas 54-1

Under the eglantine [Anything B 211-1
EGLANTINE-O. From the eglantine-o. [Anything B 211-11
EGOIST. Is only another egoist wearing a mask, [Duck 63-5 P
EGOTIST. Forsook the insatiable egotist. The sea [C 30-3
EGRESS. The pity that her pious egress [Virgin 71-7
EGYPT. I went to Egypt to escape [Cuban 64-17
EGYPTIAN. Egyptian . . . [Three 131-7 P
Egyptian, [Three 138-20 P
EHEU. Eheu! Eheu! With what a weedy face [Stan MMO 19-21 P
EIGHTEENTH. An eighteenth century fern or two [Stan MBG 72-7 P
EIGHTEENTH-CENTURY. In an eighteenth-century dish, [Bananas 54-5
EJECT. Invisible priest; is it to eject, to pull [Dump 203-9
EKE. To see nor, reverberating, eke out the mind [Creat 311-13
EKED. On peculiar horns, themselves eked out [Creat 311-14
Still eked out luminous wrinklings on the leaves, [Old Woman
   45-7 P
ELABORATING. This endlessly elaborating poem [NH 486-4
ELAN. Straight up, an élan without harrowing, [What We 459-14
ELATE. And more than free, elate, intent, profound [C 33-10
ELATIONS. Elations when the forest blooms; gusty [Sunday 67-22
ELBOW. On her side, reclining on her elbow. [Couch 295-1
A mumbling at the elbow, turgid tunes, [Sombre 67-10 P
At the elbow of Copernicus, a sphere, [Theatre 91-15 P
ELBOWS. This leaning on his elbows on his bed, [Men Fall 187-16
ELDERLY. By elderly women? [Cab 21-15 P
ELDERS. Waked in the elders by Susanna. [Peter 90-6
The red-eyed elders watching, felt [Peter 90-9
Against the elders by her side; [Peter 91-15
Of those white elders; but, escaping, [Peter 92-9
ELECT. He from whose beard the future springs, elect. [Duck 64-31 P
Its inhabitant and elect expositor. [Someone 83-10 A
ELECTRIC. For me, the firefly's quick, electric stroke [Monocle
   15-1
And the stack of the electric plant, [Common 221-4
Like an electric lamp [Common 221-8
They would march single file, with electric lamps, alert [Page
   423-9
It is a bough in the electric light [NH 477-7
ELECTRIFY. To electrify the nimbuses-- [MBG 174-2
ELEGANCE. The sweep of an impossible elegance, [Prelude 195-4
In the donkey's ear, "I fear that elegance [Uruguay 248-18
The ultimate elegance: the imagined land. [Uruguay 250-5
God only was his only elegance. [Good Man 364-2
The final elegance, not to console [NSF 389-11
ELEGIES. In endless elegies. But in Africa [Greenest 57-15 P
ELEGY. A kind of elegy he found in space: [EM 315-3
And these, in their mufflings, monsters of elegy, [Owl 435-23
ELEMENT. Choosing his element from droll confect [C 40-7
Is an invisible element of that place [Men 1000 52-9
The corner of the eye. Our element, [Sun March 134-4
Cold is our element and winter's air [Sun March 134-5
Element in the immense disorder of truths. [Connois 216-3
That the buxom eye brings merely its element [Poem Morn 219-14
At the neutral centre, the ominous element, [Landsc 242-1
Of an element, the exactest element for us, [Gala 248-7
Without the labor of thought, in that element, [Gala 248-10
Of the weather are the belief in one's element, [Extracts 258-4
Or anywhere beyond, to a different element, [Extracts 258-11
In vain, life's season or death's element. [Montra 263-6
And cold, my element. Death is my [Hero 273-3
Of this element, this force. Transfer it [Hero 277-3
That was their element, we should not know [Creat 310-15
As an element; to the sky, as an element. [Wild 328-17
People might share but were never an element, [Wild 328-18
The need of its element, the final need [Pure 333-4
Of final access to its element-- [Pure 333-5
A purple-leaping element that forth [Descrip 341-16
Of what are these the creatures, what element [Two V 355-1
Evade us, as in a senseless element? [NSF 396-24
"In the Element of Antagonisms" [425-title
In an element not the heaviness of time, [Owl 432-8
Our breath is like a desperate element [NH 470-23
The glass of the air becomes an element-- [NH 488-1
Of filial love. Or is it the element, [Aug 491-20
An approximation of- an element, [Aug 491-21
In an element that does not do for us, [Look 518-4
Its arches in its vivid element, [Armor 530-14
In the air of newness of that element, [Armor 530-15
A grace to nature, a changeless element. [Greenest 59-30 P
Asserting itself in an element that is free, [Pagoda 92-1 P
A time, an apparition and nourishing element [How Now 97-11 P
There is a drop that is life's element, [Conversat 108-20 P
ELEMENTAL. Or, nobler, sensed an elemental fate, [C 31-24
And elemental potencies and pangs, [C 31-25
This connoisseur of elemental fate, [C 32-30
Is not so elemental nor the earth [Havana 142-5
That elemental parent, the green night, [Phosphor 267-15
In an elemental freedom, sharp and cold. [Choc 297-3
ELEMENTS. An up and down between two elements, [C 35-7
Of the visible elements and of ours [Vari 232-11

Or--yes: what elements, unreconciled [Two V 355-2
To stop the whirlwind, balk the elements. [NSF 401-15
To its opal elements and fire's delight [AA 416-12
ELEPHANT. Most supple challenger. The elephant [NSF 384-11
  The elephant on the roof and its elephantine blaring, [Puel 456-5
  The tusks of the elephant, [Parasol 20-8 P
ELEPHANT-COLORINGS. One looks at the elephant-colorings of tires.
  [Dump 202-21
ELEPHANTINE. The elephant on the roof and its elephantine blaring,
  [Puel 456-5
  Thinly, among the elephantine palms, [Greenest 54-26 P
ELEPHANTS. The elephants of sound, the tigers [Hero 278-9
  Caparison elephants, teach bears to juggle. [NSF 385-3
  Of elephants. But to impose is not [NSF 403-22
  Death, the herdsman of elephants, [Greenest 55-18 P
  Hé quoi! Angels go pricking elephants? [Greenest 55-30 P
  This future, although the elephants pass and the blare, [Duck
  63-31 P
ELEPHANT'S-EAR. When the elephant's-ear in the park [Tea 112-8
ELEVATED. Of a mountain, expanded and elevated almost [Moonlight
  531-11
ELEVATION. As from an inhuman elevation [Gigan 289-18
  This elevation, in which he seems to be tall, [Repet 307-13
  As on an elevation, and behold [NSF 386-20
  This illumination, this elevation, this future [NH 481-24
  Of an elevation, an elixir of the whole. [Woman Had 83-10 P
  And thus an elevation, as if I lived [Warmth 90-5 P
  And thus an elevation, as if I left [As Leave 117-11 P
ELEVEN. The black mother of eleven children [Primordia 9-15 P
  And the eleven children . . . [Primordia 9-19 P
ELICITING. Eliciting the still sustaining pomps [On Manner 55-12
ELISION. The romance of the precise is not the elision [Adult 353-7
ELIXIR. An elixir, an excitation, a pure power. [NSF 382-22
  Poured this elixir [Coroner 30-4 P
  Of an elevation, an elixir of the whole. [Woman Had 83-10 P
ELLIPSE. As, for example, the ellipse of the half-moon-- [Six Sig
  75-12
ELLIPSES. Cones, waving lines, ellipses-- [Six Sig 75-11
  The faculty of ellipses and deviations, [Aug 493-7
  In the prolific ellipses that we know, [Someone 87-18 A
ELM. In the land of the elm trees, wandering mariners [NH 486-16
  They said, "We are back once more in the land of the elm trees,
  [NH 487-3
ELMS. They rise to the muddy, metropolitan elms, [Duck 60-13 P
ELONCATES. Still on the horizon elongates his cuts, [Orb 443-4
ELONGATIONS. The year's dim elongations stretch below [Sombre 70-2P
ELOPEMENT. It was not an elopement. [Three 136-5 P
  It does not sound like an elopement. [Three 138-10 P
ELOPING. The first eloping footfall [Three 136-2 P
ELOQUENCE. Mountains appeared with greater eloquence [NH 484-12
  And without eloquence, O, half-asleep, [Rome 509-11
  The eloquence of right, since knowing [Ulysses 101-17 P
  This eloquence of right, since knowing [Presence 106-2 P
  Like an absolute out of this eloquence." [Presence 106-6 P
ELOQUENCES. The eloquences of light's faculties. [Pure 333-9
ELSE. In pungent fruit and bright, green wings, or else [Sunday
  67-16
  Like nothing else in Tennessee. [Jar 76-16
  Or else sat spinning on the pinnacles, [Babies 77-5
  Must be. It could be nothing else. [MBG 171-22
  Or else whose hell, foamed with their blood [Thought 186-13
  They resemble nothing else. [Pears 196-4
  The form of her in something else [Scavoir 231-15
  To something else. Its past was a souvenir. [Of Mod 239-22
  It was nowhere else, it was there and because [Landsc 242-6
  It was nowhere else, its place had to be supposed, [Landsc 242-7
  Even now, the centre of something else, [Oak 272-10
  Is that which produces everything else, in which [Phenom 287-3
  He was not man yet he was nothing else. [Choc 298-2
  The bride come jingling, kissed and cupped, or else [Repet 308-17
  Spring is umbilical or else it is not spring. [Holiday 313-1
  Like earth and sky. Then he became nothing else [Wild 329-1
  And they were nothing else. It was late in the year. [Wild 329-2
  Let's see the very thing and nothing else. [Cred 373-3
  With nothing else compounded, carried full, [Cred 374-14
  Or else avert the object. Deep in the woods [Cred 376-4
  What else, prodigious scholar, should there be? [NSF 381-24
  With six meats and twelve wines or else without [NSF 407-16
  That was different, something else, last year [AA 412-11
  To be anything else in the sunlight of the room, [Roses 430-12
  Or else an inherent order active to be [Orb 442-12
  Poor procurator, why do you ask someone else, [Papini 446-1
  Alpha fears men or else Omega's men [NH 469-11
  Or else his prolongations of the human. [NH 469-12
  And Juda becomes New Haven or else must. [NH 473-6
  Or else a new aspect, say the spirit's sex, [Aug 489-12
  The power to transform itself, or else, [Two Illus 514-11
  In the predicate that there is nothing else. [Rock 527-4
  Into a sense, an object the less; or else [Moonlight 531-12
  What else remains? But red, [Table 40-7 P

Be merely a masquerade or else a rare [Greenest 56-13 P
Because I desire it to shine or else [Desire 85-20 P
It is a busy cry, concerning someone else. [Course 96-14 P
That which is more than anything else [Ulysses 100-12 P
Free from everything else, free above all from thought. [Letters
  107-9 P
At last, is the pineapple on the table or else [Someone 87-9 A
ELSEWHERE. That lay elsewhere around him. Severance [C 30-1
ELUCIDATION. In a season, a climate of morning, of elucidation,
  [Bus 116-5 P
ELYSEE. For answer from their icy Élysée. [Heaven 56-23
ELYSIA. Elysia, these days, half earth, half mind; [Extracts 257-1
  In these Elysia, these origins, [Extracts 257-9
  Adam of beau regard, from fat Elysia, [Pure 331-20
ELYSIUM. The elysium lay [Coroner 30-11 P
EMACIATED. Then came Brazil to nourish the emaciated [Pure 330-16
EMANATIONS. Of dampened lumber, emanations blown [C 36-8
EMBELLISHED. Embellished by the quicknesses of sight, [Bouquet
  451-10
EMBELLISHMENT. Enriches the year, not as embellishment. [Cred 375-8
  Like a great shadow's last embellishment. [AA 419-24
EMBER. An ember yes among its cindery noes, [Armor 529-10
  See amber-ember.
EMBLAZONED. Fixing emblazoned zones and fiery poles, [Key W 130-9
EMBLEM. If the hero is not a person, the emblem [Hero 277-5
  A cockle-shell, a trivial emblem great [Bship 79-10 P
  And men look inwardly, for the emblem: [Stan Hero 83-13 P
EMBLEMATA. The flight of emblemata through his mind, [Sombre 71-18P
EMBODIED. Or light embodied, or almost, a flash [Choc 297-11
EMBOSOMER. Out of her botches, hot embosomer. [C 44-29
EMBOSSINGS. Embossings of the sky. [Archi 18-8 P
EMBRACE. Who will embrace her before summer comes. [Lilacs 49-15
  Winter and spring, cold copulars, embrace [NSF 392-8
  An invention, an embrace between one desperate clod [Rock 525-13
  To embrace autumn, without turning [Secret Man 36-3 P
  And the Orient and the Occident embrace [Art Pop 112-17 P
EMBRACED. I had as lief be embraced by the porter at the hotel
  [Two Figures 85-14
  Walked toward him on the stage and they embraced. [Repet 306-15
EMBRACES. Than himself, his self, the self that embraces [Hero
  280-6
EMBRACING. Whose chiefest embracing of all wealth [Ulysses 104-12 P
EMBRACINGS. They polished the embracings of a pair [Repet 306-16
EMBROIDERED. On which she embroidered fantails once [Emperor 64-11
  In their embroidered slippers, touch your spleen? [Polish Aunt 84-5
  Except linen, embroidered [Cab 21-14 P
EMBROIDERING. I have been embroidering [Explan 72-15
EMBRYO. The cry of an embryo? The spirit tires, [Feo 334-1
EMBRYOS. Gigantic embryos of populations, [Choc 300-8
EMERALD. The young emerald, evening star, [Homunculus 25-14
  That this emerald charms philosophers, [Homunculus 26-10
  The topaz rabbit and the emerald cat, [Candle 223-10
  Above the Mediterranean, emerald [Landsc 243-3
  And white roses shaded emerald on petals [Attempt 370-6
  The spouse beyond emerald or amethyst, [NSF 395-23
  This husk of Cuba, tufted emerald, [Someone 83-7 A
  Its tuft of emerald that is real, for all [Someone 85-16 A
  See red-emerald.
EMERALDINE. Lapised and lacqued and freely emeraldine [Ideal 88-5 A
EMERALDS. Becoming emeralds. He might watch the palms [Landsc 243-4
EMERGE. The pines that were fans and fragrances emerge, [NH 487-20
EMERGED. As things emerged and moved and were dissolved, [Real
  110-14 P
EMERGES. Black fact emerges from her swishing dreams. [Stan MMO
  19-22 P
EMERGING. The future might stop emerging out of the past, [Nigger
  151-10
  And the future emerging out of us seem to be one. [Nigger 151-12
  And another breath emerging out of death, [Descrip 341-5
  From a Schuylkill in mid-earth there came emerging [New Set
  352-10
  This is the height emerging and its base [AA 411-13
  It may be, is emerging or has just [AA 416-20
  A meeting, an emerging in the light, [Owl 433-5
  Among the endlessly emerging accords. [Aug 493-2
  Than a power of sleep, a clearness emerging [Bus 116-9 P
  But a perfection emerging from a new known, [Bus 116-11 P
EMIGRANT. So much for that. The affectionate emigrant found [C 32-11
EMINENCE. A human thing. It is an eminence, [Choc 300-17
EMINENT. And more. Yet the eminent thunder from the mouse, [Blue
  Bldg 217-3
  Made eminent in a reflected seeming-so. [Recit 88-2 P
EMINENTLY. Infants yet eminently old, then dome [C 43-26
EMOTION. In an emotion as of two people, as of two [Of Mod 240-12
  In a feeling mass, a blank emotion, [Hero 276-27
  As if the eye was an emotion, [Hero 278-25
  The politics of emotion must appear [EM 324-29
  And movement of emotion through the air, [Bouquet 449-17
  Wakes us to the emotion, grand fortissimo, [Grotesque 76-19 P
EMOTIONAL. Mature emotional gesture, that-- [Stan MBG 73-8 P

EMOTIONS. Emotions on wet roads on autumn nights; [Sunday 67-23
  Of spent emotions. [Peter 90-23
  Emotions becoming one. The actor is [Of Mod 240-13
  The rotund emotions, paradise unknown [EM 325-29
  A complex of emotions falls apart, [Cred 377-11
  Another complex of other emotions, not [Cred 377-18
EMPEROR. "The Emperor of Ice-Cream" [64-title
  The only emperor is the emperor of ice-cream. [Emperor 64-8
  The only emperor is the emperor of ice-cream. [Emperor 64-16
  Of an emperor, the egg-plant of a prince. [Extracts 253-10
  Led the emperor astray, the torn trumpets [Hero 278-7
  For what emperor [Bowl 6-10 P
  The sole emperor of what they are, [Child 106-19 P
  If the emperor himself [Three 133-6 P
  And possibly the emperor would have cried, [Three 137-13 P
  And the emperor would have held [Three 138-5 P
EMPERORS. Or emperors, [Three 133-25 P
EMPHATICALLY. Emphatically so. [Mandolin 28-17 P
EMPIRE. False empire . . . These are the works and pastimes [Hero
  280-13
  Even as the blood of an empire, it might be, [Rome 510-1
EMPLOYEE. The employer and employee contend, [MBG 182-10
  The employer and employee will hear [MBG 182-14
EMPLOYER. The employer and employee contend, [MBG 182-10
  The employer and employee will hear [MBG 182-14
EMPOWERED. Brightly empowered with like colors, swarmingly,
  [Myrrh 350-3
EMPRIZE. But his emprize to that idea soon sped. [C 10-13
EMPTIER. The room is emptier than nothingness. [Phenom 286-9
  The long lines of it grow longer, emptier, [AA 412-20
EMPTIEST. The shallowest iris on the emptiest eye. [Sombre 70-4 P
EMPTINESS. Intones its single emptiness, [Possum 294-11
  Has its emptiness and tragic expirations. [EM 320-9
  Defies red emptiness to evolve his match,[NSF 384-9
  Of the past, the rodomontadean emptiness. [Novel 457-6
  Always in emptiness that would be filled, [NH 467-13
  And then to refill its emptiness again, [NH 482-21
  Though they are rigid in rigid emptiness. [Rock 525-6
EMPTY. Of revealing desire and is empty of shadows. [Sad Gay 121-13
  Its empty sleeves; and yet its mimic motion [Key W 128-14
  The empty spirit [Am Sub 131-10
  Will drop like sweetness in the empty nights [Havana 144-8
  Empty and grandiose, let us make hymns [Nigger 151-20
  The ruts in your empty road are red. [Fish-Scale 160-18
  And to have found the bed empty? [Chateau 161-8
  It is good. The bed is empty, [Chateau 161-17
  Of empty heaven and its hymns, [MBG 167-12
  You see the moon rise in the empty sky. [Dump 202-25
  The steeples are empty and so are the people, [Jersey 210-16
  Occurred above the empty house and the leaves [Sleight 222-4
  Nor in their empty hearts to feel [Adequacy 243-17
  An empty land; the gods that Boucher killed; [Oboe 250-10
  And dirt. The wind blew in the empty place. [Extracts 255-5
  The winter wind blew in an empty place-- [Extracts 255-6
  No man that heard a wind in an empty place. [Extracts 255-9
  Or a glass that is empty when he looks. [Phosphor 267-8
  Down deeply in the empty glass . . . [Phosphor 267-10
  Turns blue and on its empty table [Hero 280-20
  Sour wine to warm him, an empty book to read; [Good Man 364-11
  The house is empty. But here is where she sat [Beginning 427-12
  It is empty. But a woman in threadless gold [Wom Sun 445-8
  It is fatal in the moon and empty there. [NH 472-4
  There were looks that caught him out of empty air. [NH 483-13
  It is not an empty clearness, a bottomless sight. [NH 488-4
  So much just to be seen--a purpose, empty [Moonlight 532-4
  And Rosa, the muslin dreamer of satin and cowry-kin, disdaining
    the empty keys; and the young infanta, [Piano 22-3 P
  But they are empty as balloons [Drum-Majors 37-1 P
  The heaven of Europe is empty, like a Schloss [Greenest 53-1 P
  A Schloss, and empty Schlossbibliothek, the books [Greenest
    53-8 P
EMPURPLED. Empurpled garden grass; [Delight 162-6
ENCHANT. And you, good galliard, to enchant black thoughts [Red
  Kit 32-3 P
ENCHANTED. In which the enchanted preludes have their place. [Pure
  330-15
ENCHANTERED. The inimical music, the enchantered space [Pure 330-14
ENCHANTING. Arranging, deepening, enchanting night. [Key W 130-10
  Abortion, fit for the enchanting of basilisks. [Duck 63-1 P
ENCHANTMENT. As in an enchantment, analyzed and fixed [Papini
  447-20
ENCIRCLING. Encircling us, speaks always with our speech. [Eve
  Angels 137-18
ENCLOSURE. To the enclosure, day, the things illumined [Rock 528-18
ENCLOSURES. The this and that in the enclosures of hypotheses
  [Prol 516-14
ENCOILED. So intertwined with serpent-kin encoiled [C 32-3
ENCOMPASSED. Only encompassed in humanity, is he [Conversat 109-13P
ENCORE. Encore un instant de bonheur. The words [Nigger 157-14
  Encore, encore, encore les dieux . . . [Jersey 210-8

ENCOUNTER. We encounter in the dead middle of the night [NSF 395-2
ENCOURAGEMENT. Friend and dear friend and a planet's encourage-
  ment. [World 521-14
ENCROACHMENT. Encroachment of that old catastrophe, [Sunday 67-3
ENCRUSTED. Filled its encrusted fountains, they arrayed [Havana
  142-20
  Then faintly encrusted, a tissue of the moon [Repet 306-14
  See gold-encrusted.
ENCRUSTS. Light, too, encrusts us making visible [Eve Angels 137-19
ENCYCLOPAEDISTS. Lean encyclopaedists, inscribe an Iliad. [NE
  Verses 104-9
END. The end of love in their all-speaking braids. [Monocle 14-6
  There will never be an end [Fabliau 23-14
  The relation comes, benignly, to its end? [C 16-12
  When, at the wearier end of November, [Lunar 107-7
  Pricks in our spirits at the summer's end, [Anatomy 108-5
  Repeated in a summer without end [Key W 129-16
  Nothing is final, he chants. No man shall see the end. [Nigger
    150-13
  If ever the search for a tranquil belief should end, [Nigger
    151-9
  Not by beginning but at the last man's end. [Nigger 156-21
  Ever the prelude to your end, [MBG 170-19
  Do I begin and end? And where, [MBG 171-18
  At the end of winter when afternoons return. [Poems Clim 193-11
  The actor that will at last declaim our end. [Dames 206-20
  The difficulty to think at the end of day, [Rabbit K 209-1
  A refrain from the end of the boulevards. [Nightgown 214-4
  Like a tottering, a falling and an end, [Nightgown 214-9
  As one loves that which is the end [Yellow 236-16
  In the end, however naked, tall, there is still [Oboe 250-17
  That puts an end to evil death and dies. [Extracts 253-25
  In the end, these philosophic assassins pull [Extracts 256-1
  That the mind is the end and must be satisfied. [Extracts 257-15
  Beyond a second death, as evil's end? [Extracts 258-28
  Any mortal end. The chants of final peace [Extracts 259-6
  Of the brooder seeking the acutest end [Extracts 259-14
  I am a poison at the winter's end, [News 265-5
  To the ruddier bushes at the garden's end. [Hand 271-19
  The life that never would end, no matter [Gigan 289-5
  An end must come in a merciless triumph, [Dutch 291-15
  An end of evil in a profounder logic, [Dutch 291-16
  This is the pit of torment that placid end [Dutch 292-24
  At the end of night last night a crystal star, [Choc 296-17
  Last night at the end of night his starry head, [Choc 299-19
  Last night at the end of night and in the sky, [Choc 301-19
  A few sounds of meaning, a momentary end [Lack 303-19
  That there lies at the end of thought [Crude 305-5
  As the body trembles at the end of life. [EM 314-7
  How that which rejects it saves it in the end. [EM 315-10
  It was not the end he had foreseen. He knew [EM 319-23
  Is not a variation but an end. [Pure 332-7
  It is a world of words to the end of it, [Descrip 345-9
  This is the refuge that the end creates. [Cred 373-25
  It is desire at the end of winter, when [NSF 382-6
  To an immaculate end. We move between these points: [NSF 382-17
  Yet the General was rubbish in the end. [NSF 392-3
  A sound like any other. It will end. [NSF 394-18
  Another image at the end of the cave, [AA 411-5
  A season changes color to no end, [AA 416-9
  As pure principle. Its nature is its end, [AA 418-11
  Gothic blue, speed home its portents to their ends. [Page 422-20
  So summer comes in the end to these few stains [Beginning 427-10
  By which to spell out holy doom and end, [Owl 434-17
  This is that figure stationed at our end, [Owl 434-22
  Nor the beginning nor end of a form: [Wom Sun 445-7
  That it is complete, that it is an end, [Pecul 453-14
  Themselves an issue as at an end, as if [Our Stars 455-21
  There was an end at which in a final change, [Our Stars 455-22
  Twelve meant as much as: the end of normal time, [What We 459-13
  Reality is the beginning not the end, [NH 469-4
  But that's the difference: in the end and the way [NH 469-19
  To the end. Alpha continues to begin. [NH 469-20
  Omega is refreshed at every end. [NH 469-21
  In the end, in the whole psychology, the self, [NH 474-7
  For what he sees, it comes in the end to that: [NH 475-12
  We had come to an end of the imagination, [Plain 502-11
  And yet this end and this beginning are one, [Hermit 506-1
  Weight him down, O side-stars, with the great weightings of the
    end. [Madame 507-1
  Unintelligible absolution and an end-- [Rome 508-5
  The human end in the spirit's greatest reach, [Rome 508-16
  It is a kind of total grandeur at the end, [Rome 510-21
  The lives these lived in the mind are at an end. [Rock 525-8
  The desire to be at the end of distances, [Rock 527-9
  The starting point of the human and the end, [Rock 528-16
  Come swelling, when, regardless of my end, [Soldat 14-15 P
  Behold how order is the end [Room Gard 41-1 P
  A trash can at the end of the world, the dead [Burnshaw 49-5 P
  And origin and resplendent end of law, [Greenest 60-5 P

The rest, to whom in the end the rest return, [Sombre 66-15 P
And the portent end in night, composed, before [Sombre 71-5 P
Even imagination has an end, [Sombre 71-13 P
Without beginning or the concept of an end. [Grotesque 76-24 P
As man is natural, would be at an end." [Bship 78-19 P
To the final full, an end without rhetoric. [Bship 81-11 P
Philosophers' end . . . What difference would it make, [Theatre
    91-17 P
We obey the coaxings of our end. [Ulysses 103-30 P
From everything would end. It would all meet. [Letters 108-10 P
Not the beginning but the end of artifice, [Conversat 109-9 P
The palm at the end of the mind, [Of Mere 117-15 P
The worse end they come to; [Three 137-17 P
And can you tell how it will end?-- [Three 138-18 P
Oh! it will end badly. [Three 139-2 P
And the end of the ballad. [Three 139-14 P
See: rough-end; week-end.
ENDAZZLED. Or of night endazzled, proud, [Fading 139-3
ENDED. His western voyage ended and began. [C 37-20
    Too many waltzes have ended. And then [Sad Gay 121-14
    Too many waltzes have ended. Yet the shapes [Sad Gay 122-10
    Why, when the singing ended and we turned [Key W 130-4
    Will soon be ended." [Idiom 200-19
    This chaos will not be ended, [Idiom 200-20
    Not ended, never and never ended, [Idiom 201-1
ENDING. And ending at the finger-tips. . . . It is death [Extracts
    253-22
    At the earliest ending of winter, [Not Ideas 534-1
    See never-ending.
ENDINGS. Would be endings, more poignant than partings, profounder,
    [Adieu 127-14
ENDLESS. In endless ledges, glittering, submerged [C 34-7
    Of the endless tread [Cortege 80-24
    Endless pursuit or endlessly pursued, [Greenest 55-22 P
    In endless elegies. But in Africa [Greenest 57-15 P
    Day, night and man and his endless effigies. [Someone 83-13 A
ENDLESSLY. This endlessly elaborating poem [NH 486-4
    Among the endlessly emerging accords. [Aug 493-2
    Endless pursuit or endlessly pursued, [Greenest 55-22 P
ENDLESSNESS. Lol-lolling the endlessness of poetry. [Novel 458-1
ENDOW. Too near, too clear, saving a little to endow [Fictive 88-11
ENDS. Of their own ends. [Joost 46-19
    An opening of portals when night ends, [Nigger 153-14
    That had flashed (like vicious music that ends [Thunder 220-11
    If evil never ends, is to return [Extracts 259-3
    Each false thing ends. The bouquet of summer [Hero 280-19
    Except that it begins and ends, [Human 363-3
    Begins again and ends again-- [Human 363-4
    Up down. It is a war that never ends. [NSF 407-9
    But your war ends. And after it you return [NSF 407-15
    Like the last muting of winter as it ends. [Look 519-3
    Through a moving chaos that never ends. Mesdames, [Burnshaw
    50-23 P
    The drafts of gay beginnings and bright ends, [Greenest 57-13 P
    For whom men were to be ends in themselves, [Duck 61-2 P
    The deep sigh with which the hanging ends, close [Stan Hero
    84-18 P
ENDURANCE. This pastoral of endurance and of death [Papini 447-3
ENDURE. As April's green endures; or will endure [Sunday 68-23
    For this, then, we endure brief lives, [Negation 98-3
    To endure thereafter every mortal wound, [Extracts 258-27
    Again and fated to endure beyond [Extracts 259-5
    All men endure. The great captain is the choice [Paisant 334-14
    Out of a storm we must endure all night, [Man Car 351-4
    We must endure our thoughts all night, until [Man Car 351-7
    In whose hard service both of us endure [Soldat 14-7 P
    And drenching crimsons, or endure? It came [Greenest 57-23 P
ENDURED. Remote on heaven's hill, that has endured [Sunday 68-22
    This maximum, an adventure to be endured [EM 324-21
ENDURES. The death of summer, which that time endures [Swans 4-4
    As April's green endures; or will endure [Sunday 68-23
    The race endures. The funeral pomps of the race [Paisant 334-21
ENDURING. And next in glory to enduring love, [Sunday 68-10
    Of the enduring, visionary love, [NH 466-15
ENEMIES. Against enemies, against the prester, [Hero 274-4
ENEMY. I knew my enemy was near--I, [Cuban 65-5
    The happiest enemy. And it may be [EM 324-10
    Felicity, ah! Time is the hooded enemy, [Pure 330-13
ENFANT. C'etait mon enfant, mon bijou, mon âme. [Sea Surf 99-9
ENFANTILLAGES. Upon the horizon amid adult enfantillages. [Ques-
    tions 462-6
ENFLASHINGS. Enflashings. But apotheosis is not [NSF 387-23
ENFOLD. Does it take its place in the north and enfold itself,
    [AA 417-8
ENFOLDS. It enfolds the head in a vital ambiance, [Pastor 379-11
ENGAGED. Engaged in the most prolific narrative, [Phenom 287-5
ENGAGEMENTS. Spent in the false engagements of the mind. [EM 317-3
ENGENDERINGS. New senses in the engenderings of sense, [Rock 527-8
ENGINED. Streamed white and stoked and engined wrick-a-wrack.
    [Duck 61-12 P

ENGLAND. With the blank skies over England, over France [Martial
    238-4
    Of England, to Pablo Neruda in Ceylon, [Descrip 341-22
ENGLISH. These English noses and edged, Italian eyes, [Duck 60-22 P
    With appropriate, largely English, furniture, [Sombre 68-7 P
    Dutch ice on English boats? The memory [Recit 86-25 P
ENGLISHMEN. If Englishmen lived without tea in Ceylon, and they do;
    [Connois 215-7
ENGLISTERED. For a change, the englistered woman, seated [Ulysses
    104-2 P
    The englistered woman is now seen [Ulysses 104-31 P
ENGLUTTED. Like things submerged with their englutted sounds,
    [EM 321-27
ENGULFING. On clouds of gold, and green engulfing bronze, [Old
    Woman 43-8 P
ENIGMA. Not of the enigma of the guilty dream. [AA 419-6
    Beauty of each beautiful enigma [NH 472-6
    Alive with an enigma's flittering . . . [Ulysses 105-9 P
    Alive with an enigma's flittering, [Presence 106-9 P
ENIGMAS. A land too ripe for enigmas, too serene. [Cred 374-9
ENIGMATICAL. But, here, allons. The enigmatical [NH 472-5
ENJOY. We enjoy the ithy oonts and long-haired [Analysis 349-10
    Do all that angels can. I enjoy like them, [NSF 405-11
    And we enjoy like men, the way a leaf [NSF 406-1
    And in that enormous sense, merely enjoy. [Ulti 430-9
ENJOYING. Enjoying angels. Whistle, forced bugler, [NSF 405-13
ENJOYS. Enjoys his comets. [Analysis 349-12
    The perquisites of sanctity, enjoys [NH 474-12
ENKINDLING. So that, where he was, there is an enkindling, where
    [Choc 301-7
ENKINDLINGS. And gusts of great enkindlings, its polar green,
    [AA 413-2
ENLARGED. Found his vicissitudes had much enlarged [C 31-8
    It was increased, enlarged, made simple, [Gigan 289-13
    With every visible thing enlarged and yet [Rome 510-22
ENLARGEMENT. "The moments of enlargement overlook [Choc 298-13
ENLARGING. The enlarging of the simplest soldier's cry [Choc 298-14
    He observes how the north is always enlarging the change, [AA
    412-24
    Enlarging like a nocturnal ray [Ulysses 100-25 P
ENLARGINGS. Without his enlargings and pale arrondissements,
    [Someone 85-5 A
ENNOBLED. Ennobled as in a mirror to sanctity. [Nigger 157-6
ENNUI. It is the celestial ennui of apartments [NSF 381-16
    May there be an ennui of the first idea? [NSF 381-23
    So sullen with sighing and surrender to marauding ennui.
    [Inelegance 25-18 P
ENORMOUS. In an enormous undulation fled. [Sea Surf 100-9
    The enormous gongs gave edges to their sounds, [Uruguay 249-27
    Of the giant sense, the enormous harnesses [Repet 308-20
    And in that enormous sense, merely enjoy. [Ulti 430-9
    Enormous, in a completing of his truth. [Roses 431-3
    An enormous nation happy in a style, [NH 468-17
    Complete in bronze on enormous pedestals. [Duck 64-4 P
ENOUGH. Enough, for heaven. Ever-jubilant, [Adieu 128-8
    That's world enough, and more, if one includes [Havana 143-25
    Herr Doktor, and that's enough, [Delight 162-2
    A candle is enough to light the world. [MBG 172-16
    This man loved earth, not heaven, enough to die. [Men Fall 188-18
    Which is enough: the moment's rain and sea, [Freed Man 204-19
    There are not leaves enough to cover the face [Dames 206-1
    Enough to hide away the face of the man [Dames 206-7
    By the wise. There are not leaves enough to crown, [Dames 206-18
    Sure enough, moving, the thunder became men, [Thunder 220-1
    Is not enough. [Scavoir 231-16
    Enough. Ah! douce campagna of that thing! [Beard 247-19
    If you say on the hautboy man is not enough, [Oboe 250-15
    The man who has had the time to think enough, [Oboe 250-19
    Where is that summer warm enough to walk [Extracts 252-15
    There is nothing more and that it is enough [Extracts 258-7
    Physical if the eye is quick enough, [Choc 301-6
    As if the health of the world might be enough. [EM 315-25
    Might be enough, as if the golden combs [EM 316-2
    Were part of a sustenance itself enough, [EM 316-3
    What place in which to be is not enough [EM 320-3
    Infant, it is enough in life [Red Fern 365-13
    Is that it has not changed enough. It remains, [NSF 390-4
    Enough. The freshness of transformation is [NSF 397-24
    In sleep its natural form. It was enough [NSF 399-12
    It was enough for her that she remembered. [NSF 399-20
    Of communication. It would be enough [Ulti 430-4
    Helplessly at the edge, enough to be [Ulti 430-7
    That in itself it is enough? [Pecul 453-15
    For one it is enough; for one it is not; [NH 469-14
    And willed. She has given too much, but not enough. [Aug 496-3
    In which being there together is enough. [Final 524-18
    It is not enough to cover the rock with leaves. [Rock 526-10
    It is enough she comes upon the eye. [Stan MMO 19-8 P
    Mesdames, it is not enough to be reconciled [Burnshaw 50-6 P
    And having said farewell. It is not enough [Burnshaw 50-8 P

It is not enough that you are indifferent, [Burnshaw 50-12 P
Visible over the sea. It is only enough [Burnshaw 50-16 P
Abandoned because of taxes . . . It was enough: [Greenest 53-2 P
Was what she was and flesh, sure enough, but airs; [Grotesque
  74-7 P
Distant, yet close enough to wake [Child 106-20 P
What we heard and the light, though little, was enough. [Letters
  107-15 P
The most at home? Or is it enough to have seen [Conversat 109-17P
The bouquet of being--enough to realize [Conversat 109-21 P
When a pineapple on the table was enough, [Someone 85-3 A
ENRAGED. Crying among the clouds, enraged [MBG 169-7
  Has enraged them and made them want to talk it down. [Slug 522-8
ENRAGING. The lion roars at the enraging desert, [NSF 384-7
ENRAPTURED. The enraptured woman, the sequestered night, [Past Nun
  378-18
ENRICH. Or do the other days enrich the one? [Cred 374-24
ENRICHES. One day enriches a year. One woman makes [Cred 374-21
  Enriches the year, not as embellishment. [Cred 375-8
ENSAMPLE. Of pomp, in love and good ensample, see [Stan MMO 19-13P
ENSEVELIE. Its chapel rises from Terre Ensevelie, [Armor 529-9
ENSIGNS. The spirit and all ensigns of the self? [Repet 308-18
ENSOLACINGS. Disentangled him from sleek ensolacings. [EM 322-8
ENTAILED. And island canopies which were entailed [Havana 142-17
ENTANGLE. The words of things entangle and confuse. [C 41-1
ENTER. And in their chant shall enter, voice by voice, [Sunday 70-6
  We must enter boldly that interior world [Feo 333-16
  You enter the swarthy sea, [Countryman 428-12
  That it contained the meaning into which he wanted to enter,
    [Prol 516-6
  As they enter the place of their western [Soldat 12-8 P
  That enter day from night, came mirror-dark, [Burnshaw 51-26 P
ENTERED. There entered a cadaverous person, [Attempt 370-8
  A meaning which, as he entered it, would shatter the boat and
    leave the oarsmen quiet [Prol 516-7
ENTERING. Of the other eye. One enters, entering home, [Bouquet
  448-15
ENTERS. Enters the room, it drowses and is the night. [NSF 399-19
  Of the other eye. One enters, entering home, [Bouquet 448-15
  He enters the room and calls. No one is there. [Bouquet 452-21
  "Lytton Strachey, Also, Enters into Heaven" [38-title P
ENTHRONED. Even enthroned on rainbows in the sight [Hero 277-27
  Is there an imagination that sits enthroned [AA 417-4
ENTINSELLED. Entinselled and gilderlinged and gone, [Celle 438-15
ENTIRE. Clothe me entire in the final filament, [NSF 396-7
ENTIRELY. A race that is a hero, entirely [Stan Hero 84-4 P
ENTRAILS. The entrails of the buzzard [Jack-Rabbit 50-16
  Induced by what you will: the entrails [Hero 275-8
ENTRANCE. The leaden pigeon on the entrance gate [Nigger 152-18
ENTRAP. The fields entrap the children, brick [MBG 171-5
ENTREPRENEUR. Who has divided the world, what entrepreneur? [NH
  468-20
ENTWINE. Entwine your arms and moving to and fro, [Burnshaw 47-17 P
ENTWINING. A band entwining, set with fatal stones. [Fictive 88-16
ENUNCIATION. Portentous enunciation, syllable [C 43-8
ENVELOPED. The wild ducks were enveloped. The weather was cold.
  [Wild 329-3
ENVENOMED. Darting envenomed eyes about, like fangs, [Greenest 55-15P
ENVIOUS. The thing that makes him envious in phrase. [C 33-7
  Its envious cachinnation. [Mozart 131-17
  Without his envious pain in body, in mind, [Past Nun 378-20
ENVIRONMENT. Between himself and his environment, [C 34-27
ENVOI. And practical. The envoi to the past [Duck 65-29 P
EPHEBE. Begin, ephebe, by perceiving the idea [NSF 380-12
  Phoebus is dead, ephebe. But Phoebus was [NSF 381-10
  But you, ephebe, look from your attic window, [NSF 384-17
  It is of him, ephebe, to make, to confect [NSF 389-10
  The ephebe is solitary in his walk. [NH 474-10
EPHEBI. "The ephebi say that there is only the whole, [Bship 79-20P
EPHEMERAL. The ephemeral blues must merge for them in one, [Monocle
  15-8
EPHEMERAS. The ephemeras of the tangent swarm, the chance [Someone
  84-1 A
EPHRATA. The katy-dids at Ephrata return [Memo 89-1 P
  But it is not Ephrata. [Memo 89-4 P
EPIC. Too many waltzes--The epic of disbelief [Sad Gay 122-13
EPICAL. So epical a twist, catastrophe [Duck 65-25 P
EPICURE. They press it as epicure, distinguishing [EM 323-2
EPICURES. The double fruit of boisterous epicures, [Someone 85-20 A
EPIGRAM. "Adult Epigram" [353-title
EPISCOPATE. The spirit's episcopate, hallowed and high, [Greenest
  53-28 P
EPISCOPUS. Glass-blower's destiny, bloodless episcopus, [NSF 394-11
EPITAPH. Unpurged by epitaph, indulged at last, [High-Toned 59-10
  And epitaph. It may, however, be [Havana 145-4
EPITAPHIUM. Epitaphium to his death, which read, [Good Man 364-13
EPITAPHS. Of Xenophon, his epitaphs, should [Hero 276-20
EPITOME. The last man given for epitome, [Ideal 88-21 A
EPI-TONES. On a black piano practiced epi-tones. [Liadoff 346-16
  His epi-tones, the colors of the ear, [Liadoff 347-19

EQUAL. It is equal to living in a tragic land [Loaf 199-14
  Equal to memory, one line in which [Extracts 259-17
  Equal in living changingness to the light [NSF 380-8
  Or a cure of ourselves, that is equal to a cure [Rock 526-12
  Is the equal of the whole. [Bship 79-18 P
  Where I or one or the part is the equal of [Bship 79-25 P
  Strike fire, but the part is the equal of the whole, [Bship
    79-29 P
  Is equal to the right to be. [Presence 106-4 P
EQUALLY. Is equally converted into palms, [High-Toned 59-11
  And the father alike and equally are spent, [EM 324-4
  And equally as scientist you walked [Good Bad 33-15 P
EQUATE. To equate the root-man and the super-man, [Montra 262-22
EQUATES. And through the eye equates ten thousand deaths [Extracts
  253-13
EQUILIBRIUM. Vertumnus creates an equilibrium. [Extraord 369-20
EQUIPAGE. The shadow of his equipage [Thirteen 94-17
EQUIPAGES. In parades like several equipages, [Hero 277-23
ERA. The era of the idea of man, the cloak [Thought 185-13
  To repose in an hour or season or long era [EM 318-22
ERCOLE. Of systematic thinking . . . Ercole, [Extracts 256-17
  O, skin and spine and hair of you, Ercole, [Extracts 256-18
ERECT. Let us erect in the Basin a lofty fountain. [NE Verses 105-1
  In our captious hymns, erect and sinuous, [John 437-20
  Bending over and pulling themselves erect on the wooden handles,
    [Prol 515-8
  The sprawling of winter might suddenly stand erect, [Discov
    96-3 P
ERECTED. That the man who erected this cabin, planted [Frogs 78-7
EROTIC. Plato, the reddened flower, the erotic bird. [Extracts
  253-29
  An erotic perfume, half of the body, half [NSF 390-7
ERRORS. Their genius: the exquisite errors of time. [Extracts
  254-24
ERUDITE. And erudite in happiness, with nothing learned, [Gala
  248-8
  Who surpassed the most literate owl, the most erudite [NSF 403-21
  Its propagations are more erudite, [Someone 84-20 A
ESCAPADES. Except reflections, the escapades of death, [NSF 405-8
  And unfamiliar escapades: whirroos [Orb 442-19
ESCAPE. I went to Egypt to escape [Cuban 64-17
  Without an escape in the lapses of their kisses. [Norfolk 112-2
  So that one would want to escape, come back [Poems Clim 194-5
  To escape from the body, so to feel [Vari 234-2
  It is only that we are able to die, to escape [Extracts 259-1
  Perhaps these forms are seeking to escape [Two V 355-13
  The eye could not escape, a red renown [NSF 400-6
  An escape from repetition, a happening [NH 483-6
  To join a hovering excellence, to escape [Rome 509-6
  Escape all deformation, much less this, [Duck 63-26 P
  Persist as facts. This is an escape [Sol Oaks 111-6 P
ESCAPED. Escaped from the truth, the morning is color and mist,
    [Freed 204-18
  Escaped its large abstraction, became, [Vase 246-22
  The moon rose up as if it had escaped [EM 314-24
  This man escaped the dirty fates, [Flyer 336-10
ESCAPES. So the meaning escapes. [Magnifico 19-21
  Except when he escapes from it. To be [EM 323-17
  In this chamber the pure sphere escapes the impure [NH 480-3
  Because the thinker himself escapes. And yet [NH 480-4
ESCAPING. Of those white elders; but, escaping, [Peter 92-9
  And am escaping from you. [Soldat 13-3 P
ESCENT. Or these--escent--issant pre-personae: first fly, [Slug
  522-11
ESPECIAL. As he saw it, exist in his own especial eye. [EM 316-19
ESPLANADE. And this great esplanade of corn, miles wide, [Belly
  367-7
ESPLANADES. And the nut-shell esplanades. [Archi 18-20 P
ESPOUSAL. To none, awaiting espousal to the sound [Study II 464-18
ESPOUSED. Espoused each morning, each long afternoon, [Orb 441-22
ESPRIT. C'était mon esprit bâtard, l'ignominie. [Sea Surf 102-9
ESPY. The truth in nature to espy [Room Gard 41-8 P
ESQUIMAU. Abhorring Turk as Esquimau, the lute [C 38-9
ESSAY. Or air collected in a deep essay, [Choc 297-10
ESSENCE. This is his essence: the old fantoche [MBG 181-16
  It is of the essence not yet well perceived. [NH 475-21
ESSENCES. Were seraphs, were saints, were changing essences. [NSF
  397-15
ESSENTIAL. He gripped more closely the essential prose [C 36-18
  The essential theme. [Botanist 1 135-5
  It glistens in essential dark. [MBG 172-18
  Of essential unity, is as pleasant as port, [Connois 215-10
  The noble figure, the essential shadow, [Candle 223-12
  Became--how the central, essential red [Vase 246-21
  Themselves from its essential savor, [EM 323-3
  Of this essential ornament [Pediment 361-21
  Look at it in its essential barrenness [Cred 373-8
  The essential poem at the centre of things, [Orb 440-1
  Fetched by such slick-eyed nymphs, this essential gold, [Orb
    440-6

The essential poem begets the others. The light [Orb 441-26
The whole, the essential compact of the parts, [Orb 442-7
Hear hard, gets at an essential integrity. [NH 475-3
The trees had been mended, as an essential exercise [World 521-4
It is to disclose the essential presence, say, [Moonlight 531-10
ESTABLISHED. It is established. There the dove [Dove 98-3 P
   In that which is and is established . . . It howls [Dove 98-7 P
   To know established as the right to be. [Ulysses 102-11 P
ESTABLISHES. Reclining, eased of desire, establishes [EM 324-12
   Versicolorings, establishes a time [EM 324-14
   He establishes statues of reasonable men, [NSF 403-20
ESTABLISHMENTS. When the establishments [Inhab 503-15
ESTATE. His only testament and estate. [Ulysses 103-9 P
ESTHETIQUE. "Esthétique du Mal" [313-title
ESTHONIA. From Esthonia: the tiger chest, for tea. [Dump 201-19
ESTRANGED. There peace, the godolphin and fellow, estranged,
   estranged, [Owl 434-1
ETERNAL. A damsel heightened by eternal bloom. [Monocle 15-28
   Eternal chef d'orchestre? [Eve Angels 136-15
   And the nose is eternal, that-a-way. [MBG 178-19
   Hip, hip, hurrah. Eternal morning . . . [Hero 278-14
   Fix it in an eternal foliage [Cred 373-10
   Are of an eternal vista, manqué and gold [Burnshaw 48-12 P
   Stiff in eternal lethargy, should be, [Conversat 109-8 P
ETHER. Of his gold ether, golden alguazil, [Bird Claws 82-8
   And not a delicate ether star-impaled, [Havana 144-1
   Of ether, the other smelling of drink, [MBG 177-10
   The voice of ether prevailing, the swell [MBG 177-11
   The volcano trembled in another ether, [EM 314-6
   It is like a thing of ether that exists [AA 418-16
   Of the skeleton of the ether, the total [Orb 443-19
   Of ether, exceed the excelling witches, whence [Study II 464-7
   His place is large and high, an ether flamed [Greenest 59-31 P
ETHEREAL. An ethereal cousin, another milleman. [Pieces 352-9
   Ethereal compounder, pater patriae, [Duck 64-28 P
ETHERED. See bright-ethered.
ETOILE. "Homunculus et La Belle Étoile" [25-title
EUCALYPTUS. The dry eucalyptus seeks god in the rainy cloud. [NH
   475-4
   And of purple blooming in the eucalyptus-- [Primordia 9-12 P
   See Professor Eucalyptus.
EUCLID. On a page of Euclid. [Common 221-9
   The shadows that are absent from Euclid, [Common 221-13
EULALIA. Eulalia, I lounged on the hospital porch, [Phenom 287-7
   That of that light Eulalia was the name. [Phenom 287-14
   You are that white Eulalia of the name. [Phenom 287-22
EULOGY. Compose us in a kind of eulogy. [Extraord 369-15
EUNUCHS. Lulu sang of barbarians before the eunuchs [Lulu G 26-9 P
   She made the eunuchs ululate. [Lulu G 26-13 P
   The eunuchs heard her [Lulu G 26-17 P
   "Olu" the eunuchs cried. "Ululalu." [Lulu G 26-23 P
EUPHONIES. Of euphonies, a skin from Nubia, [Hero 274-9
EUPHONIOUS. I am Solange, euphonious bane, she said. [News 265-4
EUPHONY. Even the bawds of euphony [Thirteen 94-11
   Like a euphony in a museum [Hero 274-8
EUROPE. He was a Jew from Europe or might have been. [Pure 331-15
   On Europe, to the last Alp, [Inhab 504-4
   The heaven of Europe is empty, like a Schloss [Greenest 53-1 P
   Seraphim of Europe? Pouring out of dawn, [Greenest 56-3 P
EVADE. The imagination, here, could not evade, [C 30-7
   He might slowly forget. It is more difficult to evade [Bed 327-5
   Evade us, as in a senseless element? [NSF 396-24
   Evade, this hot, dependent orator, [NSF 397-1
   And everything to make. He may evade [NH 480-7
   But he may not. He may not evade his will, [NH 480-10
   Nor the wills of other men; and he cannot evade [NH 480-11
EVADED. His meditation. It evaded his mind. [EM 314-25
   The hum of thoughts evaded in the mind, [NSF 388-4
   To have evaded clouds and men leaves him [NH 480-5
EVADES. The candle as it evades the sight, these are [Rome 508-22
EVADING. An evading metaphor. [Add 199-12
   Evading the point of redness, not content [EM 318-21
   Steeped in night's opium, evading day. [Sombre 66-17 P
EVANESCENT. The evanescent symmetries [Negation 98-4
EVANGELISTS. To be described. Evangelists of what? [Extracts 254-5
EVAPORATES. Daylight evaporates, like a sound one hears in sick-
   ness. [Discovery 95-9 P
EVASION. Moonlight was an evasion, or, if not, [C 35-4
   Is another shadow, another evasion, [Scavoir 231-18
   Without evasion by a single metaphor. [Cred 373-7
   To be an evasion, a thing not apprehended or [NSF 396-22
EVASIONS. And grates these evasions of the nightingale [Autumn
   160-11
   Check your evasions, hold you to yourself. [NSF 406-14
   As it is, in the intricate evasions of as, [NH 486-10
   All are evasions like a repeated phrase, [Duck 65-14 P
EVASIVE. Evasive and metamorphorid. [Oak 272-6
   Of the most evasive hue of a lesser blue, [Burnshaw 51-19 P
EVE. When you were Eve, its acrid juice was sweet, [Monocle 14-14
   A very felicitous eve, [Delight 162-1

Bottles, pots, shoes and grass and murmur aptest eve: [Dump 203-7
And Eve made air the mirror of herself, [NSF 383-12
He is neither priest nor proctor at low eve, [NH 474-16
EVEN. Disturbed not even the most idle ear. [Hibiscus 22-14
   One eats one paté, even of salt, quotha. [C 28-1
   Speak, even, as if I did not hear you speaking, [Two Figures
      86-4
   Even the bawds of euphony [Thirteen 94-11
   And touch each other, even touching closely, [Norfolk 112-1
   Yet the house is not built, not even begun. [Ghosts 119-2
   Even if what she sang was what she heard, [Key W 128-20
   That rose, or even colored by many waves; [Key W 129-11
   More even than her voice, and ours, among [Key W 129-18
   Even the musky muscadines, [Reader 147-7
   The taste of even a country connoisseur. [Nigger 157-16
   Even in the chattering of your guitar. [MBG 167-14
   It makes it clear. Even at noon [MBG 172-17
   Say even that this complete simplicity [Poems Clim 193-17
   The rocks not even touched by snow, [Loaf 199-20
   The plaster dropping, even dripping, down, [Blue Bldg 217-5
   Even though he shouted. [Thunder 220-16
   That is fluent in even the wintriest bronze. [Sleight 222-19
   The curtains. Even the drifting of the curtains, [Peaches 224-17
   One only, one thing that was firm, even [Beard 247-14
   To hold by the ear, even though it wished for a bell, [Uruguay
      249-10
   Falls on and makes and gives, even a speech. [Phosphor 267-13
   Even the leaves of the locust were yellow then, [Contra II 270-3
   The leaves, even of the locust, the green locust. [Contra II
      270-6
   Even now, the centre of something else, [Oak 272-10
   Of him, even if Xenophon, seems [Hero 277-6
   Even enthroned on rainbows in the sight [Hero 277-27
   And the associations beyond death, even if only [Lack 303-13
   They had known that there was not even a common speech, [Holiday
      312-7
   This brother even in the father's eye, [EM 317-10
   As color, even the closest to us, is; [Less 328-1
   Even breathing is the beating of time, in kind: [Pure 330-4
   Even for her, already for her. She will listen [Debris 338-11
   Even the seeming of a summer's day, [Descrip 343-17
   Even in Paris, in the Gardens [Analysis 349-4
   Even with the help of Viollet-le-Duc, [NSF 386-23
   Even so when I think of you as strong or tired, [NSF 406-15
   Even that. His meditations in the ferns, [AA 411-20
   By extinguishings, even of planets as may be, [AA 417-12
   Even of earth, even of sight, in snow, [AA 417-13
   Upon whose shoulders even the heavens rest, [Owl 431-15
   Even of death, the beings of the mind [Owl 436-5
   Even his own will and in his nakedness [NH 480-8
   It is difficult even to choose the adjective [Plain 502-13
   Even as the blood of an empire, it might be, [Rome 510-1
   Even when the book lay turned in the dust of his table. [Poem Mt
      512-4
   Even our shadows, their shadows, no longer remain. [Rock 525-7
   Even the rarest-- [Bowl 6-14 P
   Even by mice--these scamper and are still; [Soldat 14-1 P
   To dab things even nicely pink [Melancholy 32-9 P
   These are not even Russian animals. [Burnshaw 46-17 P
   The charts destroyed, even disorder may, [Burnshaw 48-28 P
   Into a hopeful waste to come. There even [Burnshaw 49-24 P
   Even in sleep, deep in the grass of sleep, [Greenest 54-31 P
   Even imagination has an end, [Sombre 71-13 P
   Even the man below, the subverter, stops [Sombre 71-17 P
   Even if there had been a crescent moon [Letters 107-1 P
   No: not even sunrise. [Three 133-19 P
   Even dead eyes, [Three 143-13 P
   One says even of the odor of this fruit, [Someone 87-14 A
EVENING. Of this creature of the evening [Infanta 7-17
   And of the evening, [Infanta 8-4
   The young emerald, evening star, [Homunculus 25-14
   "That bliss of stars, that princox of evening heaven!" reminding
      of seasons, [Banal 63-3
   Or her desire for June and evening, tipped [Sunday 68-25
   At evening, casual flocks of pigeons make [Sunday 70-26
   Of a green evening, clear and warm, [Peter 90-7
   It was evening all afternoon. [Thirteen 95-1
   Last evening the moon rose above this rock [How Live 125-9
   "Evening without Angels" [136-title
   . . . Evening, when the measure skips a beat [Eve Angels 137-26
   The skreak and skritter of evening gone [Autumn 160-1
   "Delightful Evening" [162-title
   Sighed in the evening that he lived [Forces 228-18
   Only this evening I saw again low in the sky [Martial 237-10
   The evening star, at the beginning of winter, the star [Martial
      237-11
   But as if evening found us young, still young, [Martial 237-15
   Though the air change. Only this evening I saw it again, [Martial
      238-13
   And, in the brown blues of evening, the lady said, [Uruguay 248-17

The cold evening, without any scent or the shade [Extracts 258-15
One breathed the cold evening, the deepest inhalation [Extracts
  258-20
A brune figure in winter evening resists [Man Car 350-15
Place-bound and time-bound in evening rain [Human 363-1
Forced up from nothing, evening's chair, [Human 363-11
Leaps downward through evening's revelations, and [NSF 404-16
It is evening. The house is evening, half dissolved. [AA 413-8
At evening, things that attend it until it hears [AA 414-18
Like a book at evening beautiful but untrue, [AA 418-14
At evening and at night. It does no good. [Study I 463-13
"An Ordinary Evening in New Haven" [465-title
So that morning and evening are like promises kept, [NH 472-16
Its evening feast and the following festival, [NH 472-18
Is to search. Likewise to say of the evening star, [NH 481-17
At evening, after dark, is the other half, [NH 482-4
Before the thought of evening had occurred [NH 482-23
Like an evening evoking the spectrum of violet, [NH 488-19
At evening's one star [Inhab 503-13
I am the archangel of evening and praise [Inhab 504-10
The way the earliest single light in the evening sky, in spring,
  [Prol 517-8
Light the first light of evening, as in a room [Final 524-1
We make a dwelling in the evening air, [Final 524-17
Turquoise the rock, at odious evening bright [Rock 528-7
Wavered in evening air, above the roof, [Phases 5-5 P
Another evening in another park, [Old Woman 43-1 P
Without her, evening like a budding yew [Old Woman 45-23 P
The same return at heavy evening, love [Duck 61-15 P
Permitting nothing to the evening's edge. [Role 93-5 P
Drenching the evening with crystals' light, [Letters 107-3 P
Under the front of the westward evening star, [Real 110-12 P
Like evening Venus in a cloud-top. [Three 135-9 P
Such things happen in the evening. [Three 136-10 P
Last evening I met him on the road. [Three 141-11 P
See night-evening.
EVENINGS. Composed of evenings like cracked shutters flung [C 42-30
  So evenings die, in their green going, [Peter 92-2
EVENT. Grotesque apprenticeship to chance event, [C 39-23
  Surviving being born, the event of life. [Discov 96-9 P
EVENTUAL. Of its eventual roundness, puerile tints [C 44-7
  Eventual victor, out of the martyrs' bones, [Uruguay 250-4
EVER-BREATHING. The ever-breathing and moving, the constant fire,
  [Martial 238-9
EVER-BRIGHTENING. Of motion the ever-brightening origin, [AA 414-24
EVER-CHANGING. In an ever-changing, calmest unity, [Owl 433-13
EVER-DARK. That in that ever-dark central, wherever it is, [Con-
  versat 108-18 P
EVER-EARLY. From that ever-early candor to its late plural [NSF
  382-18
EVER-FAITHFUL. That silences the ever-faithful town. [Havana 144-25
EVER-FRESHENED. Her home, not mine, in the ever-freshened Keys,
  [Farewell 117-16
EVER-FRESHENING. Of the ocean, ever-freshening, [Hartford 227-11
EVER-HILL. The great captain loved the ever-hill Catawba [NSF 401-16
EVER-HOODED. The ever-hooded, tragic-gestured sea [Key W 129-5
EVER-JUBILANT. To the ever-jubilant weather, to sip [Adieu 128-2
  Enough, for heaven. Ever-jubilant, [Adieu 128-8
EVER-LIVING. From any future, the ever-living and being, [Martial
  238-8
  He has an ever-living subject. The poet [Papini 446-3
EVER-MALADIVE. The harridan self and ever-maladive fate [Old 45-25P
EVER-MINGLING. Wading the sea-lines, moist and ever-mingling,
  [Tallap 72-2
EVER-JUBILANT. To the ever-jubilant weather, to sip [Adieu 128-2
  Enough, for heaven. Ever-jubilant, [Adieu 128-8
EVER-NEVER-CHANGING. It is the ever-never-changing same, [Adult
  353-9
EVER-PRESENT. To expel the ever-present seductions, [Gigan 289-9
EVER-READY. The easy passion, the ever-ready love [NSF 394-23
  For easy passion and ever-ready love [NSF 395-7
EVERY. Every time the bucks went clattering [Earthy 3-1
  If sex were all, then every trembling hand [Monocle 17-7
  In lordly study. Every day, I found [Monocle 17-23
  As every man in Sweden will concede, [Lions 125-3
  Choke every ghost with acted violence, [Nigger 155-6
  Of every day, the wrapper on the can of pears, [Dump 201-17
  Now, every muscle slops away. [Hartford 227-9
  That in spring will crown every western horizon, [Martial 237-12
  To endure thereafter every mortal wound, [Extracts 258-27
  For every day. In a civiler manner, [Hero 275-22
  Say yes, spoken because under every no [EM 320-13
  And every latent double in the word, [NSF 387-6
  To be stripped of every fiction except one, [NSF 404-9
  With every prodigal, familiar fire, [Orb 442-18
  Every thread of summer is at last unwoven, [Puel 456-1
  Omega is refreshed at every end. [NH 469-21
  With every visible thing enlarged and yet [Rome 510-22
  Is only what the sun does every day, [Look 517-16
  And spread hallucinations on every leaf. [Armor 529-20

In every various sense, ought not to be preferred [Lytton 39-13 P
Was under every temple-tone. You sang [Burnshaw 50-30 P
Of the park. They obey the rules of every skeleton. [Duck 62-11 P
This base of every future, vibrant spring, [Duck 63-28 P
The future must bear within it every past, [Sombre 70-5 P
With something I could touch, touch every way. [As Leave 117-12 P
EVERYBODY. And unseen. This is everybody's world. [Someone 87-11 A
EVERYMAN. The admiral of his race and everyman, [Duck 62-4 P
EVERYONE. Everyone, grows suddenly cold. [Fading 139-7
  It was to be as mad as everyone was, [Desire 85-10 P
EVERYTHING. I quiz all sounds, all thoughts, all everything [Mono-
  cle 16-19
A voice was mumbling, "Everything [Reader 147-5
Everything ticks like a clock. The cabinet [Nigger 157-17
The stillness of everything gone, and being still, [Autumn 160-8
Everything is shed; and the moon comes up as the moon [Dump
  202-22
It was everything being more real, himself [Freed 205-20
It was everything bulging and glazing and big in itself, [Freed
  205-22
In which everything is meant for you [Rabbit K 209-11
Was everything that Cotton Mather was [Blue Bldg 217-2
Everything in it is herself. [Scavoir 231-5
Everything comes to him [Yellow 237-1
To everything, in order to get at myself. [Uruguay 249-4
On everything. Now it had melted, leaving [Extracts 255-3
Feel everything starving except the belly [Hero 278-3
Which, as a man feeling everything, were his. [Somnam 304-18
Why should they not know they had everything of their own
  [Holiday 312-9
Falls out on everything: the genius of [EM 316-27
Is that which produces everything else, in which [Phenom 287-3
Because everything is half dead. [Motive 288-2
From everything, flying the flag of the nude, [Pure 330-21
Makes everything grotesque. Is it because [Feo 333-13
It matters, because everything we say [Descrip 345-19
Like the wind that lashes everything at once. [Chaos 358-6
Burn everything not part of it to ash. [Cred 373-5
Axis of everything, green's apogee [Cred 373-20
Everything becomes morning, summer, the hero, [Past Nun 378-17
That gives a candid kind to everything. [NSF 382-24
Of everything he is. And he feels afraid. [AA 417-3
The little ignorance that is everything, [John 437-16
Like a monster that has everything and rests, [Bouquet 452-4
The Westwardness of Everything [Our Stars 455-title 2
Suppose this was the root of everything. [Golden 460-7
Everything as unreal as real can be, [NH 468-18
Everything, the spirit's alchemicana [NH 471-22
A century in which everything was part [NH 479-4
And everything to make. He may evade [NH 480-7
The sun is half the world, half everything, [NH 481-22
Being part of everything come together as one. [NH 482-11
He had said that everything possessed [Two Illus 514-21
It is like a new account of everything old, [Armor 529-17
Of everything. The roses bend [Room Gard 41-2 P
The thing is dead . . . Everything is dead [Burnshaw 46-13 P
Except the future. Always everything [Burnshaw 46-14 P
It made up for everything, it was all selves [Greenest 53-3 P
That's what did it. Everything did it at last. [Greenest 53-15 P
Everything did. [Greenest 53-25 P
Disclosed in everything, transcended, poised [Duck 62-21 P
Choosing out of himself, out of everything within him, [Sick
  90-19 P
And though one says that one is part of everything, [Course
  96-15 P
Gigantic in everything but size. [Ulysses 101-2 P
Free from everything else, free above all from thought. [Letters
  107-9 P
From everything would end. It would all meet. [Letters 108-10 P
Today the air is clear of everything. [Clear Day 113-14 P
EVERYWHERE. It took dominion everywhere. [Jar 76-13
  It ought to be everywhere. [Sailing 120-14
  Its vacancy glitters round us everywhere. [Eve Angels 137-2
  A dithery gold falls everywhere. [Gray 140-13
  Another denial. If she is everywhere, [Scavoir 231-19
  Everywhere the spruce trees bury soldiers: [Vari 234-10
  Everywhere spruce trees bury spruce trees. [Vari 234-13
  Without existence, existing everywhere. [Choc 298-5
  The sea, a strength that tumbles everywhere, [Two V 354-12
  And where we live and everywhere we live, [NSF 395-9
  As of a character everywhere, [Countryman 429-6
  Everywhere in space at once, cloud-pole [Ulti 430-3
  That will always be and will be everywhere. [Greenest 58-18 P
EVES. The long recessional at parish eves wails round [Greenest
  59-15 P
EVIDENCE. On the sea, is both law and evidence in one, [Bship
  78-29 P
EVIL. The arm of bronze outstretched against all evil! [Mice 123-12
  If we found the central evil, the central good. [Oboe 251-12
  That evil made magic, as in catastrophe, [Extracts 253-8

The good is evil's last invention. Thus [Extracts 253-11
To the laughter of evil: the fierce ricanery [Extracts 253-17
That is ten thousand deaths and evil death. [Extracts 253-23
That puts an end to evil death and dies. [Extracts 253-25
Beyond a second death, as evil's end? [Extracts 258-28
The wounds. Yet to lie buried in evil earth, [Extracts 259-2
If evil never ends, is to return [Extracts 259-3
To evil after death, unable to die [Extracts 259-4
We chant if we live in evil and afterward [Extracts 259-9
Its evil after death, it dissolves it while [Extracts 259-12
An end of evil in a profounder logic, [Dutch 291-16
And in their blood an ancient evil dies-- [Dutch 292-20
That evil, that evil in the self, from which [EM 316-25
The assassin's scene. Evil in evil is [EM 324-18
Speech found the ear, for all the evil sound, [EM 326-5
And capable of incapably evil thought: [Page 423-1
With redness that sticks fast to evil dreams; [Rock 528-8
You do not understand her evil mood. [Spaniard 34-1 P
But spreads an evil lustre whose increase [Spaniard 34-12 P
Is evil, crisply bright, disclosing you [Spaniard 34-13 P
And the people suddenly evil, waked, accused, [Sombre 69-2 P
Of evil, evil springs; or catholic hope, [Sombre 69-23 P
Of our sense of evil, [Grotesque 76-20 P
It is the common man against evil, [Stan Hero 84-15 P
I felt the evil, [Three 141-14 P
EVIL-BLOSSOMED. Until each tree, each evil-blossomed vine,
    [Greenest 55-23 P
EVILLY. The evilly compounded, vital I [Poems Clim 193-19
EVILS. As evils, and if reason, fatuous fire, [Duck 63-4 P
EVOCATION. Of a human evocation, so disclosed [Pastor 379-14
EVOCATIONS. Their evocations are the speech of clouds. [On Manner
    55-16
    In the casual evocations of your tread [On Manner 56-2
    Not evocations but last choirs, last sounds [Cred 374-13
    Of the phrase. It contrives the self-same evocations [NH 473-5
EVOKED. Of thought evoked a peace eccentric to [Havana 143-5
EVOKES. The property of the moon, what it evokes. [Moonlight 531-9
EVOKING. An odor evoking nothing, absolute. [NSF 395-1
    Like an evening evoking the spectrum of violet, [NH 488-19
    Of sense, evoking one thing in many men. [Aug 494-18
    Evoking an archaic space, vanishing [Aug 494-19
EVOLVE. From this I shall evolve a man. [MBG 181-15
    Defies red emptiness to evolve his match. [NSF 384-9
EVOLVED. Out of the light evolved the moving blooms, [Sea Surf 99-6
    Who, then evolved the sea-blooms from the clouds [Sea Surf 99-7
    It is a giant, always, that is evolved, [Orb 442-25
    Then, fear a drastic community evolved [Burnshaw 51-6 P
EX. Rising upward from a sea of ex. [MBG 175-4
    Of incredible colors ex, ex and ex and out? [Liadoff 347-3
EXACERBATIONS. The tongue caresses these exacerbations. [EM 323-1
EXACT. No, no: veracious page on page, exact. [C 40-3
    To sing jubilas at exact, accustomed times, [NSF 398-7
    The exact rock where his inexactnesses [Poem Mt 512-11
EXACTED. Exacted attention with attentive force. [Bouquet 450-21
EXACTEST. Of an element, the exactest element for us, [Gala 248-5
    In the exactest poverty, if then [Extracts 258-19
    In which to bear with the exactest force [Repet 310-7
    Knew well the shapes were the exactest shaping [New Set 353-3
    At the exactest point at which it is itself, [NH 471-16
    At the exactest central of the earth [Ulysses 104-14 P
EXACTING. To this accurate, exacting eye. Sight [Hero 274-11
EXACTLY. Of things exactly as they are." [MBG 165-10
    Exactly, that which it wants to hear, at the sound [Of Mod 240-9
    Too exactly himself, and that there are words [Creat 310-17
    Too exactly labelled, a large among the smalls [Orb 443-11
EXACTNESS. Of the image, behold it with exactness through beads
    [Bouquet 449-23
EXAGGERATION. Through any exaggeration. From him, we collect.
    [Creat 311-6
EXALTATION. They seem an exaltation without sound. [On Manner 55-14
EXALTATIONS. Are to combat what his exaltations [Hero 274-16
EXAMINATION. "Examination of the Hero in a Time of War" [273-title
EXAMINES. Or in a bubble examines the bubble of air. [Phenom 286-8
EXAMPLE. As, for example, the ellipse of the half-moon-- [Six Sig
    75-12
    By mere example opulently clear. [Havana 145-6
    For example, this old man selling oranges [Feo 333-18
    The sun is an example. What it seems [Descrip 339-3
    The queen is an example . . . This green queen [Descrip 339-10
    For example: Au Château. Un Salon. A glass [Golden 460-10
    What self, for example, did he contain that had not yet been
    loosed, [Prol 516-16
    As, for example, a world in which, like snow, [Quiet 523-4
    Or if it be supposed, for example, [Three 133-1 P
EX-BAR. Of ex-bar, in-bar retaining attributes [EM 317-24
    And ex-bar's flower and fire of the festivals [EM 317-27
EXCEED. The squirming facts exceed the squamous mind, [Connois
    215-17
    Of ether, exceed the excelling witches, whence [Study II 464-7
EXCEEDING. The exceeding brightness of this early sun [Sun March

133-13
    Exceeding music must take the place [MBG 167-11
    Exceeding sex, he touched another race, [Duck 64-25 P
EXCEEDS. This fat pistache of Belgian grapes exceeds [Nigger 154-17
    Of them. So sense exceeds all metaphor. [Roses 431-6
    It exceeds the heavy changes of the light. [Roses 431-7
EXCELLENCE. The centuries of excellence to be [Havana 143-1
    Like excellence collecting excellence? [Belly 367-1
    Perhaps there are times of inherent excellence, [NSF 386-9
    And in bright excellence adorned, crested [Orb 442-17
    The total excellence of its total book." [NH 485-9
    To join a hovering excellence, to escape [Rome 509-6
EXCELLENCES. In the excellences of the air we breathe, [Conversat
    109-20 P
EXCELLENT. And is as excellent, in that it is composed [Monocle
    14-18
EXCELLING. Excelling summer, ghost of fragrance falling [Ghosts
    119-16
    Of ether, exceed the excelling witches, whence [Study II 464-7
EXCELS. But it excels in this, that as the fruit [Monocle 14-20
EXCELSIS. Be still. The summarium in excelsis begins . . . [Puel
    456-16
EXCEPT. Except in faint, memorial gesturings, [C 29-1
    Remained, except some starker, barer self [C 29-16
    Except because he broods there and is still. [Bird Claws 82-9
    Except in something false. [Orangeade 103-2
    Or look, nor ever again in thought, except [Farewell 118-9
    Except to be happy, without knowing how, [Sad Gay 122-7
    Have I except it comes from the sun? [Adieu 128-10
    Except the one she sang and, singing, made. [Key W 130-2
    Except for our own houses, huddled low [Eve Angels 138-1
    Except when the bishop passes by, [Gray 140-18
    Except the trace of burning stars [Reader 147-11
    All alike, except for the rules of the rabbis, [Nigger 151-7
    We should die except for Death [Nigger 151-13
    Yet nothing changed, except the place [MBG 167-18
    What is there in life except one's ideas, [MBG 175-17
    We shall forget by day, except [MBG 184-4
    Denies that abstraction is a vice except [Thought 185-7
    One grows to hate these things except on the dump. [Dump 202-11
    And nothing is left except light on your fur-- [Rabbit K 209-3
    Except Polacks that pass in their motors [Jersey 210-18
    Except for the images we make of it, [Extracts 257-11
    Feel everything starving except the belly [Hero 278-3
    There is no life except in the word of it. [Phenom 287-19
    Of the thousands of freedoms except our own? [Dutch 292-14
    Except for us, Vesuvius might consume [EM 314-11
    From which we shrink. And yet, except for us, [EM 314-15
    Except when he escapes from it. To be [EM 323-17
    Not span, without any weather at all, except [Wild 329-7
    Except for delicate clinkings not explained. [Descrip 340-16
    Except that the reader leaned above the page, [House Q 358-12
    Except what was, [Woman Song 360-9
    Except that it begins and ends, [Human 363-3
    And for what, except for you, do I feel love? [NSF 380-4
    Clear and, except for the eye, without intrusion. [NSF 400-3
    To be stripped of every fiction except one, [NSF 404-9
    Except reflections, the escapades of death, [NSF 405-8
    You will have stopped revolving except in crystal. [NSF 407-3
    Except the lavishing of itself in change, [AA 416-10
    Except as needed by way of majesty, [AA 417-14
    Except for that crown and mystical cabala. [AA 417-21
    We feel and, therefore, is not real, except [Roses 430-17
    Are flatly there, unversed except to be, [Bouquet 452-14
    Except that the grandson sees it as it is, [Questions 462-9
    Or cooling in late leaves, not false except [Study I 463-17
    Except this hidalgo and his eye and tune, [NH 483-20
    Except for the adjectives, an alteration [NH 487-5
    Except that a green plant glares, as you look [Plant 506-16
    Except his own--perhaps, his own [Two Illus 514-2
    Except linen, embroidered [Cab 21-14 P
    Remained and nothing of herself except [Old Woman 44-11 P
    Except the thing she felt but did not know. [Old Woman 45-22 P
    Except the future. Always everything [Burnshaw 46-14 P
    That is is dead except what ought to be. [Burnshaw 46-15 P
    In one, except a throne raised up beyond [Greenest 55-10 P
    Except that this is an image of black spring [Sombre 69-30 P
    My head, the sorrow of the world, except [Bship 78-18 P
    They are nothing, except in the universe [Child 106-16 P
    It has no knowledge except of nothingness [Clear Day 113-15 P
    And yet nothing has been changed except what is [As Leave 117-13P
    Except with reference to ourselves, [Three 133-15 P
EXCEPTING. And excepting negligible Triton, free [C 29-28
    Excepting to the motherly footstep, but [C 44-18
EXCEPTION. In being more than an exception, part, [NSF 388-21
EXCEPTIONAL. The man-hero is not the exceptional monster, [NSF
    406-5
    By its faculty of the exceptional, [Aug 493-6
EXCESS. Yet in excess, continual, [W Burgher 61-8
EXCESSIVE. In an excessive corridor, alas! [Antag 426-8

EXCHANGE. That they exchange, [Adequacy 244-12
EXCHEQUERING. Exchequering from Piebald fiscs unkeyed. [C 43-7
EXCITATION. An elixir, an excitation, a pure power. [NSF 382-22
EXCITEMENTS. Demanded of sleep, in the excitements of silence
  [NSF 402-17
EXCLAIMING. Exclaiming bright sight, as it was satisfied, [Rock
  526-6
EXCLUDING. The Whole World Excluding the Speaker [NE Verses 104-
  title 2
  Excluding by his largeness their defaults. [Choc 299-18
  Between excluding things. It was not a choice [NSF 403-12
EXCURSIONS. These bland excursions into time to come, [C 39-9
EXECUTANT. To sound, sound's substance and executant, [Someone
  84-13 A
EXEGESIS. Accompanied by the exegesis [Thought 185-1
EXERCISE. An exercise in viewing the world. [Vari 233-17
  This is a facile exercise. Jerome [NSF 398-13
  An occupation, an exercise, a work, [NSF 405-18
  Of an extremist in an exercise . . . [AA 412-18
  The trees had been mended, as an essential exercise [World 521-4
EXERCISED. He used his reason, exercised his will, [Anglais 149-5
EXERCISES. And chords, the morning exercises, [Hero 274-22
EXERTION. And being part is an exertion that declines: [Course
  96-17 P
EXERTS. He munches a dry shell while he exerts [Bird Claws 82-16
EXEUNT. Shebang. Exeunt omnes. Here was prose [C 37-2
EXFOLIATIONS. These casual exfoliations are [Someone 86-16 A
EXHALATION. O exhalation, O flint without a sleeve [Owl 435-19
  Soother and lustier than this vexed, autumnal exhalation,
  [Inelegance 25-17 P
EXHALATIONS. How full of exhalations of the sea . . . [Havana
  144-27
  And exhalations in the eaves, so little [NH 477-8
EXHALING. Exhaling these creations of itself. [Pieces 351-17
EXHAUSTED. She is exhausted and a little old. [Aug 496-4
  The exhausted realist beholds [Abnormal 24-15 P
EXHIBIT. Exhibit Xenophon, what he was, since [Hero 276-21
EXHIBITED. Truth's favors sonorously exhibited. [EM 321-11
EXHILARATION. And the candor of them is the strong exhilaration
  [NSF 382-19
EXHILARATIONS. Desiring the exhilarations of changes: [Motive
  288-13
EXHORT. How I exhort her, huckstering my woe. [Stan MMO 19-14 P
EXHUMATION. But as of an exhumation returned to earth, [Aug 491-12
EXHUMO. Arrangements; and the violets' exhumo. [EM 322-26
EXILE. That animal, that Russian, that exile, for whom [Peaches
  224-8
  Of change still possible. Exile desire [Cred 373-13
  Is the exile of the disinherited, [Greenest 59-22 P
EXILES. Of introspective exiles, lecturing. [Monocle 15-16
EXIST. Palabra of a common man who did not exist. [Holiday 312-8
  As he saw it, exist in his own especial eye. [EM 316-19
  A broken wall--and it ceased to exist, became [Greenest 53-7 P
  In a Third: The whole cannot exist without [Bship 80-14 P
  Without them it could not exist. That's our affair, [Bship
  80-28 P
EXISTED. Existed by itself. Or did the saint survive? [Les Plus
  245-6
  When it never existed, the order [Desire 85-2 P
  Little existed for him but the few things [Local 112-4 P
EXISTENCE. How pleasant an existence it is [Homunculus 26-9
  Without existence, existing everywhere. [Choc 298-5
  We do not prove the existence of the poem. [Orb 440-9
EXISTING. Without existence, existing everywhere. [Choc 298-5
  Existing in the idea of it, alone, [AA 418-7
  A time existing after much time has passed. [Role 93-11 P
EXISTS. And sea exists by grace alone, [Vari 235-4
  Was less than moonlight. Nothing exists by itself. [Les Plus
  244-18
  It is an artificial thing that exists, [Descrip 344-17
  A mind exists, aware of division, aware [Cred 377-2
  It is like a thing of ether that exists [AA 418-16
  Almost as predicate. But it exists, [AA 418-18
  It exists, it is visible, it is, it is. [AA 418-18
  If it should be true that reality exists [NH 485-19
  In which he exists but never as himself. [Aug 493-9
  And so exists no more. This is the cure [Rock 527-19
  One exists among pure principles. [Sol Oaks 111-4 P
EXIT. Exit the mental moonlight, exit lex, [C 36-28
  Rex and principium, exit the whole [C 37-1
EXPANDED. Of a mountain, expanded and elevated almost [Moonlight
  531-11
EXPANDING. Expanding in the gold's maternal warmth. [C 32-10
  A small relation expanding like the shade [Connois 215-19
  Flies like a bat expanding as it flies, [Pure 332-24
EXPANDS. The sun expands, like a repetition on [Montra 263-14
EXPANSE. An expanse and the abstraction of an expanse, [Aug 494-6
  Around it. Thus it has a large expanse, [Red Kit 31-7 P
EXPANSES. Of the expanses that are mountainous rock and sea; [Repet
  308-24

From that strength, whose armies set their own expanses. [Repet
  309-5
EXPANSIONS. Expansions, diffusions--content to be [MBG 172-4
EXPECT. Look, realist, not knowing what you expect. [Phosphor
  267-11
  And you think that that is what you expect, [Phosphor 267-14
  Did we expect to live in other lives? [Wild 328-15
EXPECTATION. It is an expectation, a desire, [Descrip 344-1
EXPECTED. Life contracts and death is expected, [Soldier 97-1
  They were those from the wilderness of stars that had expected
  more. [Large 423-13
EXPECTING. Ababba, expecting this king's queen to appear? [Golden
  461-3
EXPECTS. Yet he knows what it is that he expects. [Phosphor 267-6
EXPEDIENT. May be the MacCullough, an expedient, [NSF 387-3
EXPEL. To expel the ever-present seductions, [Gigan 289-9
EXPELLED. That has expelled us and our images . . . [NSF 381-6
EXPERIENCE. Should be the clerks of our experience. [C 39-8
  That you do not see, you experience, you feel, [Poem Morn 219-13
  Experience of night, as if he breathed [Choc 298-7
  Against the whole experience of day. [Choc 298-10
  Who has gone before us in experience. [EM 315-19
  The green corn gleaming and experience [EM 325-23
  To which we refer experience, a knowledge [Descrip 343-19
  More explicit than the experience of sun [Descrip 344-22
  Is it he or is it I that experience this? [NSF 404-22
  Increases the aspects of experience, [Papini 447-19
  The vulgate of experience. Of this, [NH 465-5
  Experience in perihelion [Aug 490-16
  At this indifferent experience, [Good Bad 33-13 P
  Is it experience, say, the final form [Recit 87-4 P
EXPERIENCED. Experienced yet not well seen; of how [Ideal 88-17 A
EXPERT. Captain, the man of skill, the expert [Hero 274-1
  It is the extreme, the expert aetat. 2. [Questions 462-14
EXPIRATIONS. Has its emptiness and tragic expirations. [EM 320-9
EXPLAINED. And nothing need be explained; [Rabbit K 209-12
  Of impersonal pain. Reality explained. [EM 322-3
  Except for delicate clinkings not explained. [Descrip 340-16
EXPLAINING. Men of memories explaining what they meant. [Lytton
  38-13 P
EXPLANATION. "Explanation" [72-title
  Maternal voice, the explanation at night. [Woman Had 82-24 P
EXPLICATE. These accents explicate [Inhab 504-2
EXPLICIT. How explicit the coiffures became, [Ord Women 11-21
  More explicit than the experience of sun [Descrip 344-22
EXPLODING. And on, at night, exploding finally [Liadoff 346-6
EXPLOITED. See half-exploited.
EXPONENT. And major man is its exponent, abler [NSF 388-17
  Exponent by a form of speech, the speaker [NSF 397-3
EXPOSING. The barrenness that appears is an exposing. [NH 487-16
EXPOSITION. "Exposition of the Contents of a Cab" [20-title P
EXPOSITOR. At a distance, a secondary expositor, [Creat 311-4
  Its inhabitant and elect expositor. [Someone 83-10 A
EXPOUND. The diplomats of the cafés expound: [Greenest 57-28 P
EXPRESS. The intelligence of his despair, express [EM 314-22
  She walks, triumphing humbly, should express [Red Kit 31-11 P
EXPRESSED. Not to the play, but to itself, expressed [Of Mod 240-11
  Of things that would never be quite expressed, [Motive 288-10
  Of the world, the heroic effort to live expressed [Papini 446-9
  Magnificence most shiningly expressed [Greenest 58-3 P
EXPRESSIBLE. Filled with expressible bliss, in which I have [NSF
  404-24
EXPRESSING. Mud, water like dirty glass, expressing silence [Plain
  503-4
EXPRESSINGS. The outlines of being and its expressings, the sylla-
  bles of its law: [Large 424-5
EXPRESSIVE. An expressive on-dit, a profession. [Dutch 290-19
  On the expressive tongue, the finding fang. [AA 420-10
EXPUNGE. To expunge all people and be a pupil [Sailing 121-3
EXPUNGED. All dreams are vexing. Let them be expunged. [C 39-31
EXQUISITE. Aware of exquisite thought. The storm was one [C 32-31
  More exquisite than any tumbling verse: [C 37-3
  "Nomad Exquisite" [95-title
  Their genius: the exquisite errors of time. [Extracts 254-24
  Exquisite in poverty against the suns [EM 317-23
EXTASE. Oh! C'était mon extase et mon amour. [Sea Surf 100-21
EXTEMPORIZE. More harassing master would extemporize [NH 486-7
EXTEND. Projected a colony that should extend [C 38-12
EXTENDED. Downward to darkness, on extended wings. [Sunday 70-28
  Was beyond his recognizing. By this he knew that likeness of him
  extended [Prol 516-11
EXTENSIONS. And in moonlit extensions of them in the mind [NH 469-2
EXTENSIVE. Progenitor of such extensive scope, [C 38-29
EXTENT. The extent of what they are, the strength [Adequacy 244-11
EXTENUATIONS. And there, by feat extenuations, to make [Greenest
  57-6 P
EXTERIOR. The eccentric exterior of which the clocks talk. [NH
  478-21
  For an interior made exterior [NH 481-7
  And the poet's search for the same exterior made [NH 481-8

EXTERIORIZED. With lesser things, with things exteriorized [NH 470-3
EXTERNAL. Of the external world. [Men 1000 51-8
  The glass man, without external reference. [Oboe 251-21
  He was more than an external majesty, [Choc 299-9
  The ruin stood still in an external world. [Repet 306-3
  Overseas, that stood in an external world. [Repet 306-6
  And goes to an external world, having [Repet 308-5
  The shadow of an external world comes near. [Myrrh 350-12
  These external regions, what do we fill them with [NSF 405-7
  Between us and the object, external cause, [John 437-15
  "Presence of an External Master of Knowledge" [105-title P
EXTINGUISH. May rush to extinguish the theme, the basses thump
  [Bship 79-27 P
EXTINGUISHING. Extinguishing our planets, one by one, [AA 417-17
EXTINGUISHINGS. By extinguishings, even of planets as may be,
  [AA 417-12
EXTRACTS. "Extracts from Addresses to the Academy of Fine Ideas"
  [252-title
EXTRAORDINARY. "Extraordinary References" [369-title
  And brain, as the extraordinary references [Extraord 369-13
EXTRAVAGANZAS. If the flashy extravaganzas of the lean [Sombre
  69-14 P
EXTREME. His extreme of logic would be illogical. [EM 325-17
  It is the rock of summer, the extreme, [Cred 375-21
  Extreme, fortuitous, personal, in which [NSF 386-18
  Of medium nature, this farouche extreme [Bouquet 448-5
  When in a way of seeing seen, an extreme, [Bouquet 451-11
  It is the extreme, the expert aetat. 2. [Questions 462-14
  The extreme of the known in the presence of the extreme [Rome
  508-17
EXTREMEST. West Indian, the extremest power [Hero 276-2
  And then half way in the extremest light [Cred 375-23
  Do I press the extremest book of the wisest man [NSF 380-5
  Extremest pinch and, easily, as in [John 437-1
EXTREMIST. Of an extremist in an exercise . . . [AA 412-18
EXTREMITY. And for tomorrow, this extremity, [AA 420-17
EXTRICATE. Made extricate by meanings, meanings made [Greenest
  54-10 P
EXULT. And so, as part, to exult with its great throat, [NSF 398-9
EXULTANT. And in what place, what exultant terminal, [Ideal 89-2 A
EYE. An eye most apt in gelatines and jupes, [C 27-14
  Berries of villages, a barber's eye, [C 27-15
  And eye of land, of simple salad-beds, [C 27-16
  Of honest quilts, the eye of Crispin, hung [C 27-17
  To things within his actual eye, alert [C 40-16
  Here is an eye. And here are, one by one, [Worms 49-18
  The lashes of that eye and its white lid. [Worms 49-19
  His eye on an outdoor gloom [Bananas 54-12
  Observes the canna with a clinging eye, [Canna 55-8
  But is an eye that studies its black lid. [Tallap 71-17
  With my eye; [Six Sig 74-8
  That animal eye, [Gubbinal 85-7
  And sleep with one eye watching the stars fall [Two Figures
  86-11
  Was the eye of the blackbird. [Thirteen 92-16
  Meet for the eye of the young alligator, [Nomad 95-16
  Hang a feather by your eye, [Orangeade 103-15
  The corner of the eye. Our element, [Sun March 134-4
  The eye and tinkling to the ear. Gruff drums [Havana 143-6
  The agate in the eye, the tufted ear, [Nigger 153-14
  The mind is smaller than the eye. [Fish-Scale 161-4
  I sing a hero's head, large eye [MBG 165-13
  To meet that hawk's eye and to flinch [MBG 178-6
  Not at the eye but at the joy of it. [MBG 178-7
  At last, in spite of his manner, his eye [MBG 181-20
  A fringed eye in a crypt. [Add 199-8
  The green smacks in the eye, the dew in the green [Dump 202-5
  The world must be measured by eye"; [On Road 204-4
  Forehead's cold, spite of the eye [Bagatelles 213-14
  That the buxom eye brings merely its element [Poem Morn 219-14
  The fire eye in the clouds survives the gods. [Sleight 222-12
  To think of a dove with an eye of grenadine [Sleight 222-13
  Are the eye grown larger, more intense. [Vari 234-20
  He wanted to see. He wanted the eye to see [Landsc 241-14
  Grown denser, part, the eye so touched, so played [Landsc 242-24
  Theology after breakfast sticks to the eye. [Les Plus 245-8
  A monster-maker, an eye, only an eye, [Extracts 252-22
  A shapener of shapes for only the eye, [Extracts 253-1
  The eye believes and its communion takes. [Extracts 253-4
  The spirit laughs to see the eye believe [Extracts 253-5
  The maker of catastrophe invents the eye [Extracts 253-12
  And through the eye equates ten thousand deaths [Extracts 253-13
  Taller than any eye could see, [News 264-9
  To this accurate, exacting eye. Sight [Hero 274-11
  As if the eye was an emotion, [Hero 278-25
  Pure eye. Instead of allegory. [Hero 279-1
  To confront with plainest eye the changes, [Gigan 289-11
  Bright is the malice in his eye . . . [Possum 294-16
  The eye, completely anonymous, [Couch 295-5
  The glitter of a being, which the eye [Choc 297-14

Physical if the eye is quick enough, [Choc 301-6
Only the eye as faculty, that the mind [Crude 305-15
Is the eye, and that this landscape of the mind [Crude 305-16
Is a landscape only of the eye; and that [Crude 305-17
As he saw it, exist in his own especial eye. [EM 316-19
This brother even in the father's eye, [EM 317-10
As the eye closes . . . How cold the vacancy [EM 320-6
Like rhetoric in a narration of the eye-- [Pure 331-18
Forward of the eye that, in its backward, sees [Descrip 340-3
In the seeming of an original in the eye, [Descrip 340-11
The eye of Lenin kept the far-off shapes. [Descrip 343-11
Composed of a sight indifferent to the eye. [Descrip 343-22
There is no beautiful eye [Analysis 348-6
One eye, in which the dove resembles the dove. [Think 356-14
State the disclosure. In that one eye the dove [Think 357-3
Until sight wakens the sleepy eye [Red Fern 365-15
Freud's eye was the microscope of potency. [Cats 368-6
There the distant fails the clairvoyant eye [Cred 374-10
With one eye watch the willow, motionless. [Cred 377-8
And see the sun again with an ignorant eye [NSF 380-16
A seeing and unseeing in the eye. [NSF 385-21
Lighted at midnight by the studious eye, [NSF 388-2
Eye without lid, mind without any dream-- [NSF 394-12
The eye of a vagabond in metaphor [NSF 397-22
Clear and, except for the eye, without intrusion. [NSF 400-3
The eye could not escape, a red renown [NSF 400-16
His eye and audible in the mountain of [NSF 403-2
In flights of eye and ear, the highest eye [AA 414-16
At the moment when the angelic eye defines [AA 414-20
These forms are visible to the eye that needs, [Owl 432-1
That gives its power to the wild-ringed eye. [Owl 433-22
A source of trumpeting seraphs in the eye, [Orb 442-23
Of the reality of the eye, an artifice, [Bouquet 448-12
Of the other eye. One enters, entering home, [Bouquet 448-15
Here the eye fastens intently to these lines [Bouquet 450-16
In the eye a special hue of origin [Bouquet 451-23
The eye's plain version is a thing apart, [NH 465-4
Possess. It is desire, set deep in the eye, [NH 467-10
In the inexquisite eye. Why, then, inquire [NH 468-19
A view of New Haven, say, through the certain eye, [NH 471-18
The eye made clear of uncertainty, with the sight [NH 471-19
In New Haven with an eye that does not look [NH 475-6
That is part of the indifference of the eye [NH 475-18
Except this hidalgo and his eye and tune, [NH 483-20
A finger with a ring to guide his eye [Aug 492-10
A courage of the eye, [Aug 494-27
Of the fortune of the spirit, beyond the eye, [Rome 508-14
They bud the whitest eye, the pallidest sprout, [Rock 527-7
But through man's eye, their silent rhapsodist, [Rock 528-6
In a mystic eye, no sign of life but life, [Armor 529-14
The leaning shoulder and the searching eye. [Blanche 10-4 P
Not France! France, also, serves the invincible eye, [Soldat
  14-9 P
("The Naked Eye of the Aunt") [Stan MMO 19-Subtitle P
It is enough she comes upon the eye. [Stan MMO 19-8 P
An eye too sleek, [Coroner 30-7 P
Along the edges of your eye [An Gaiety 33-3 P
A skillful apprehension and eye proud [Spaniard 35-17 P
Descending, did not touch her eye and left [Old Woman 44-8 P
Of lizards, in its eye, is more acute [Burnshaw 49-17 P
Made of the eye an insatiable intellect. [Greenest 57-1 P
Out of the eye when the loud wind gathers up [Greenest 58-11 P
The stubborn eye, of the conformer who conforms [Duck 64-16 P
As a church is a bell and people are an eye, [Sombre 67-19 P
An image of his making, beyond the eye, [Sombre 69-26 P
The shallowest iris on the emptiest eye. [Sombre 70-4 P
From size, backs larger than the eye, not flesh [Sombre 70-23 P
Is its body visible to the important eye. [Recit 86-14 P
Like an eye too young to grapple its primitive, [Theatre 91-4 P
The eye, a geometric glitter, tiltings [Someone 87-20 A
See ballad-eye.
EYEBALL. Only, an eyeball in the mud, [Phases 3-16 P
EYE-BLUE. You saw the eye-blue, sky-blue, eye-blue, and the pow-
  dered ears [Grotesque 74-15 P
EYED. So delicately blushed, so humbly eyed, [C 44-13
  See: bluet-eyed; cat-eyed; fuzz-eyed; palm-eyed; quick-eyed;
  red-eyed; slick-eyed; trenchant-eyed.
EYELIDS. It crawls under your eyelids [Tattoo 81-12
EYES. Later, the firecat closed his bright eyes [Earthy 3-19
  And bangles and slatted eyes. [Bananas 54-4
  His broad-brimmed hat came close upon his eyes. [Babies 77-18
  The webs of your eyes [Tattoo 81-15
  There are filaments of your eyes [Tattoo 81-19
  His lids are white because his eyes are blind. [Bird Claws 82-6
  All eyes and size, and galled Justitia, [Lions 124-13
  Farewell in the eyes and farewell at the centre, [Adieu 127-11
  Green and gloomy eyes [Brave 138-10
  Bitter eyes, hands hostile and cold. [Chateau 161-10
  Ruddy are his eyes and ruddy are his claws [Glass 197-15
  And with eyes closed [Bagatelles 213-3

There they sit, holding their eyes in their hands. [Arcades
  225-4
Out of what they see. They polish their eyes [Arcades 225-11
Still bloom in the agate eyes, red blue, [Arcades 225-15
But the eyes are men in the palm of the hand. [Arcades 225-19
Or were to be, animals with men's eyes, [Horn 230-2
Without eyes or mouth, that looks at one and speaks. [Yellow
  237-9
Eyes and bruted ears: the man-like body [Hero 277-9
Eyes dripping blue, so much to learn. [Couch 295-9
Of fiery eyes and long thin arms. [Attempt 370-11
Yet look not at his colored eyes. Give him [NSF 388-13
Eyes open and fix on us in every sky. [AA 411-3
As one that is strong in the bushes of his eyes. [AA 414-7
Ringed round and barred, with eyes held in their hands, [Page
  422-30
Their eyes closed, in a young palaver of lips. [NH 477-1
As if the eyes were the present or part of it, [NH 478-10
With its attentive eyes. And, as he stood, [NH 483-11
Sweden described, Salzburg with shaded eyes [NH 486-2
In which hundreds of eyes, in one mind, see at once. [NH 488-6
Why do the horses have eyes and ears? [Primordia 8-11 P
Ears, eyes, souls, skins, hair? [Parasol 20-6 P
Blanche, the blonde, whose eyes are not wholly straight, in a
  room of lustres, shed by turquoise falling, [Piano 22-1 P
Then turn your heads and let your spiral eyes [Red Kit 31-27 P
Look suddenly downward with their shining eyes [Red Kit 31-29 P
Beside the statue, while you sang. Your eyes [Burnshaw 50-28 P
Darting envenomed eyes about, like fangs, [Greenest 55-15 P
The jostled ferns, where it might be, having eyes [Greenest
  59-4 P
Of the shape of eyes, like blunt intaglios, [Greenest 59-5 P
These English noses and edged, Italian eyes, [Duck 60-22 P
See more than marble in their eyes, see more [Duck 64-8 P
If her eyes were chinks in which the sparrows built; [Woman Had
  83-1 P
The Women with eyes like opals vanish [Stan Hero 83-12 P
Like leaning on the table, shading one's eyes, [Letters 107-11 P
The maid drops her eyes and says to her mistress, [Three 135-1 P
Of a man's eyes, [Three 143-1 P
By the eyes that open on it, [Three 143-12 P
Even dead eyes, [Three 143-13 P
  8. The owl sits humped. It has a hundred eyes. [Someone 86-11 A
EYESIGHT. Snow sparkles like eyesight falling to earth, [Possum
  294-4

FA. Makes poems on the syllable fa or [Hero 280-9
FABLE. Of the armies, the solid men, make big the fable. [Choc
 301-15
FABLES. And only, in the fables that he scrawled [C 31-18
FABLIAU. "Fabliau of Florida" [23-title
FABULOUS. The fabulous and its intrinsic verse [C 31-30
FAÇADE. Inspecting the cabildo, the façade [C 32-15
 The white cabildo darkened, the façade, [C 32-19
 The gold façade round early squares, [Thought 187-2
FAÇADES. The yellow rocked across the still façades, [Babies 77-4
FACE. that reflects neither my face nor any inner part [Nuances
 18-9
 And spread it so as to cover her face. [Emperor 64-12
 That glistens on your face and hair. [Nigger 152-14
 I can believe, in face of the object, [MBG 174-16
 In face of the monster, be more than part [MBG 175-7
 There are not leaves enough to cover the face [Dames 206-1
 Enough to hide away the face of the man [Dames 206-7
 Our faces circling round a central face [Dames 206-12
 Yet one face keeps returning (never the one), [Dames 206-14
 The face of the man of the mass, never the face [Dames 206-15
 Imagined man, the monkish mask, the face. [Dezem 218-8
 To lie on one's bed in the dark, close to a face [Yellow 237-8
 It has to face the men of the time and to meet [Of Mod 240-2
 To face the weather and be unable to tell [Extracts 257-7
 Panic in the face of the moon--round effendi [EM 320-15
 Secure. It was difficult to sing in face [Cred 376-2
 In face of which desire no longer moved, [Cred 376-7
 One sole face, like a photograph of fate, [NSF 394-10
 A face of stone in an unending red, [NSF 394-10
 Red-emerald, red-slitted-blue, a face of slate, [NSF 400-6
 They were love's characters come face to face. [NSF 401-21
 Farewell to an idea . . . The mother's face, [AA 413-4
 They help us face the dumbfoundering abyss [John 437-14
 This should be tragedy's most moving face. [NH 477-6
 Eheu! Eheu! With what a weedy face [Stan MMO 19-21 P
 How shall we face the edge of time? We walk [Duck 66-6 P
FACES. These sudden clouds of faces and arms, [Sad Gay 122-4
 With faces as with leaves, be gusty with mouths, [Dames 206-9
 Our faces circling round a central face [Dames 206-12
 Tonight the stars are like a crowd of faces [Dezem 218-9
 Faces to people night's brilliancy, [Dezem 218-14
 They looked back at Hans' look with savage faces. [Page 421-23
 Their beds, their faces drawn in distant sleep. [Sombre 68-23 P
 Or a confect of leafy faces in a tree-- [Art Pop 113-2 P
 A health--and the faces in a summer night. [Art Pop 113-3 P
FACILE. A minor meeting, facile, delicate. [C 35-5
 This is a facile exercise. Jerome [NSF 398-13
FACILELY. How facilely the purple blotches fell [NH 484-4
FACING. He was facing phantasma when the bell rang. [Dinner 109-24P
FACSIMILE. The thing described, nor false facsimile. [Descrip
 344-16
FACSIMILES. Of red facsimiles through related trees, [Cats 367-18
FACT. Of force, the quintessential fact, the note [C 33-5
 And free requiting of responsive fact, [Montra 263-10
 To project the naked man in a state of fact, [Montra 263-11
 The very Place Du Puy, in fact, belonged [NSF 391-24
 Beyond which fact could not progress as fact. [NSF 402-22
 The phrase grows weak. The fact takes up the strength [NH 473-4
 "He is the consort of the Queen of Fact. [NH 485-6
 Of Fact, lies at his ease beside the sea." [NH 485-18
 Black fact emerges from her swishing dreams. [Stan MMO 19-22 P
 Our crusted outlines hot and huge with fact, [Burnshaw 47-6 P
FACTORIES. To make its factories content, must have [Greenest
 58-20 P
FACTS. The squirming facts exceed the squamous mind, [Connois
 215-17
 As facts fall like rejuvenating rain, [Montra 263-22
 Persist as facts. This is an escape [Sol Oaks 111-6 P
FACTURE. They cast closely round the facture of the thing [Bouquet
 452-6
FACULTIES. The eloquences of light's faculties. [Pure 333-9
FACULTY. Only the eye as faculty, that the mind [Crude 305-15
 By its faculty of the exceptional, [Aug 493-6
 The faculty of ellipses and deviations, [Aug 493-7
FADED. An effulgence faded, dull cornelian [NSF 400-18
 False, faded and yet inextricably there, [Study I 463-15
 Not faded, if images are all we have. [Study I 464-1
 They can be no more faded than ourselves. [Study I 464-2
 Of sleep's faded papier-mâché . . . [Not Ideas 534-11
FADEDLY. Concluding fadedly, if as a man [C 46-2
FADES. How soon the silver fades in the dust! How soon the black
 figure slips from the wrinkled sheet! [Plough-Boy 6-8 P
FADING. "A Fading of the Sun" [139-title
FAGOT. For Crispin, fagot in the lunar fire, [C 33-20
FAIL. Shall our blood fail? Or shall it come to be [Sunday 68-5
 Music began to fail him. Brahms, although [Anglais 148-13
 Crying as that speech falls as if to fail. [Sketch 336-6

The barbarous strength within her would never fail. [World 521-15
 Why should it fail to stand? Victoria Platz, [Greenest 58-19 P
FAILED. A fantastic effort has failed, a repetition [Plain 502-19
FAILING. Perhaps instead of failing it rejects [NH 477-13
 Suppose, instead of failing, it never comes, [Duck 63-30 P
 See never-failing.
FAILS. Brings the day to perfection and then fails. He dwells
 [EM 318-2
 There the distant fails the clairvoyant eye [Cred 374-10
 Its fire fails to pierce the vision that beholds it, [Questions
 462-7
 Fails to destroy the antique acceptances, [Questions 462-8
 It fails. The strength at the centre is serious. [NH 477-12
 Nothing is lost, loud locusts. No note fails. [Aug 489-16
 They chanced to think. Suppose the future fails. [Duck 63-2 P
 A hand that fails to seize it. High captain, the grand [Bship
 80-25 P
 In which nothing of knowledge fails, [Ulysses 100-8 P
FAINT. Except in faint, memorial gesturings, [C 29-1
 Illusive, faint, more mist than moon, perverse, [C 34-30
 By the hand of desire, faint, sensitive, the soft [NH 476-14
 Has faint, portentous lustres, shades and shapes [Burnshaw
 49-26 P
FAINTLY. Then faintly encrusted, a tissue of the moon [Repet
 306-14
FAIR. And of fair weather, summer, dew, peace. [Peaches 224-14
 Why are not women fair, [Parasol 20-3 P
 I wish they were all fair [Parasol 20-12 P
 Speaking and strutting broadly, fair and bloomed, [Burnshaw
 52-17 P
FAIT. Qui fait fi des joliesses banales, the chairs. [Freed 205-24
FAITH. The faith of forty, ward of Cupido. [Monocle 16-16
 Giovanni Papini, by your faith, know how [Papini 447-1
FAITHFUL. Chant, O ye faithful, in your paths [Botanist 2 136-5
 If he must, or lives on the bread of faithful speech. [NSF 408-3
 See ever-faithful.
FAITHFULLY. Wished faithfully for a falsifying bell. [Uruguay
 249-11
FAITHFULNESS. In a faithfulness as against the lunar light, [NH
 472-15
 This faithfulness of reality, this mode, [NH 472-19
FAKE. Is wholly the vapidest fake. . . . [Sailing 120-10
 One wild rhapsody a fake for another. [Waldorf 241-3
 Spring is the truth of spring or nothing, a waste, a fake.
 [Holiday 313-2
FAKES. The mountains are scratched and used, clear fakes. [Arcades
 226-3
FALCON. In spite of hawk and falcon, green toucan [C 30-18
FALL. A torrent will fall from him when he finds. [Monocle 13-15
 Here, something in the rise and fall of wind [C 29-3
 Does ripe fruit never fall? Or do the boughs [Sunday 69-14
 These lines are swift and fall without diverging. [Tallap 72-4
 And sleep with one eye watching the stars fall [Two Figures 86-11
 And the adroiter harmonies of their fall. [Havana 144-22
 One of the major miracles, that fall [Montra 262-6
 As apples fall, without astronomy, [Montra 262-7
 As facts fall like rejuvenating rain, [Montra 263-22
 Fall down through nakedness to nakedness, [Montra 263-23
 And the rude leaves fall. [Metamorph 266-3
 Apparently in air, fall from him [Hero 277-15
 My orator. Let this giantness fall down [Repet 310-2
 The paratroopers fall and as they fall [EM 322-11
 "Flyer's Fall" [336-title
 People fall out of windows, trees tumble down, [Chaos 357-13
 And the man dies that does not fall. [Woman Song 360-7
 A darkness gathers though it does not fall [AA 412-21
 And the north wind's mighty buskin seems to fall [Antag 426-7
 When the leaves fall like things mournful of the past, [Puel
 456-2
 That fall upon it out of the wind. We seek [NH 471-12
 The last leaf that is going to fall has fallen. [NH 487-10
 The sparkling fall of night [Inhab 504-3
 If I should fall, as soldier, I know well [Soldat 11-10 P
 Of the ways things happen to fall. [Table 40-15 P
 They suddenly fall and the leafless sound of the wind [Burnshaw
 50-20 P
 That hears a pin fall in New Amsterdam [Recit 86-23 P
FALLEN. And of the fallen leaves, [Domination 8-9
 Made by the leaves, that have rotted and fallen; [Lunar 107-8
 One of the leaves that have fallen in autumn? [Nigger 158-12
 We buried the fallen without jasmine crowns. [Oboe 251-13
 Like seeing fallen brightly away. [Possum 294-5
 The soldiers that have fallen, red in blood, [EM 319-1
 Where his house had fallen, three scraggy trees weighted [NSF
 393-4
 A vibrancy of petals, fallen, that still cling [Bouquet 450-10
 The last leaf that is going to fall has fallen. [NH 487-10
 After the leaves have fallen, we return [Plain 502-9
 Fallen Winkle felt the pride [Phases 4-17 P
 Their petty dirges of fallen forest-men, [Greenest 55-20 P

The gods like marble figures fallen, left [Greenest 58-14 P
A light snow, like frost, has fallen during the night. [Bus
    116-1 P
See newly-fallen.
FALLING. Falling there, [Peacocks 58-23
    Falling [Peacocks 58-24
    Passions of rain, or moods in falling snow; [Sunday 67-20
    Flying and falling straightway for their pleasure, [Tallap 72-8
    Excelling summer, ghost of fragrance falling [Ghosts 119-16
    The snow is falling. [Mozart 132-7
    The snow is falling [Mozart 132-20
    It was autumn and falling stars [Reader 147-1
    Falling, far off, from sky to land, [Mud 148-7
    The wind and the sudden falling of the wind. [Nigger 152-7
    To be falling and to be passing away. [MBG 179-12
    The sea is in the falling snow. [MBG 179-16
    "The Men That are Falling" [187-title
    The head of one of the men that are falling, placed [Men Fall
        188-9
    Stones pose in the falling night; [Add 198-8
    Like a tottering, a falling and an end, [Nightgown 214-9
    The leaves were falling like notes from a piano. [Contra II
        270-12
    Snow sparkles like eyesight falling to earth, [Possum 294-4
    The ocean, falling and falling on the hollow shore, [Somnam
        304-12
    The tinsel of August falling was like a flame [Pieces 352-2
    On his hill, watching the rising and falling, and says: [Two V
        354-22
    A pack of cards is falling toward the floor. [Bouquet 450-22
    The rain kept falling loudly in the trees [NH 476-7
    A reddened garment falling to his feet, [Aug 492-8
    Blanche, the blonde, whose eyes are not wholly straight, in a
        room of lustres, shed by turquoise falling, [Piano 22-1 P
    Leaves are not always falling and the birds [Burnshaw 50-24 P
    If she was deaf with falling grass in her ears-- [Woman Had 83-2P
    See: down-falling; slowly-falling.
FALLING-IN. The sheep-like falling-in of distances, [Duck 62-26 P
FALLS. Falls, it appears, of its own weight to earth. [Monocle
        14-13
    As sleep falls [Peacocks 58-25
    The soldier falls. [Soldier 97-3
    Falls from that fatal and that barer sky, [Anatomy 108-17
    A dithery gold falls everywhere. [Gray 140-13
    Falls back to coldness, [Reader 147-6
    The hunger shouts as the pheasant falls. [Nigger 154-9
    Shucks . . . lavender moonlight falls. [Add 198-11
    Worn out, her arm falls down, [Add 199-3
    The rain falls. The sky [Metamorph 266-4
    Falls and lies with the worms. [Metamorph 266-5
    The green falls on you as you look, [Phosphor 267-12
    Falls on and makes and gives, even a speech. [Phosphor 267-13
    The venerable song falls from your fiery wings. [God 285-16
    In what I am, as he falls. Of what I am, [Choc 298-15
    Falls out on everything: the genius of [EM 316-27
    Crying as that speech falls as if to fail. [Sketch 336-6
    Fetched up with snow that never falls to earth? [Belly 367-6
    A complex of emotions falls apart, [Cred 377-11
    And polished beast, this complex falls apart. [Cred 377-16
    Howls hoo and rises and howls hoo and falls. [NSF 383-8
    For whom the good of April falls tenderly, [NSF 388-7
    Falls down, the cock-birds calling at the time. [NSF 388-8
    Music falls on the silence like a sense, [NSF 392-10
    Whereon it falls in more than sensual mode. [NSF 398-19
    And to the mother as she falls asleep [AA 413-22
    And hear it as it falls in the deep heart's core. [Page 421-12
    He bumps the table. The bouquet falls on its side. [Bouquet 453-1
    The fire falls a little and the book is done. [Novel 458-17
    Of growling teeth, and falls at night, snuffed out [NH 467-19
    The rain falls with a ramshackle sound. He seeks [NH 475-9
    Weaker and weaker, the sunlight falls [Leben 504-16
    As it falls from the heart and lies there to be seen, [Rome
        509-27
    How softly the sheet falls to the ground! [Plough-Boy 6-9 P
    The rain falls at its base, [Secret Man 36-7 P
    Conceive that while you dance the statue falls, [Burnshaw 51-30 P
    You said the dew falls in the blood. [Memo 89-5 P
    The dew falls deep in the mind [Memo 89-6 P
    Now the thousand-leaved green falls to the ground. [Fare Guit
        98-17 P
    See: foot-falls; water-falls.
FALSE. Is false, if Crispin is a profitless [C 45-31
    Things false and wrong [Virgin 71-3
    Except in something false. [Orangeade 103-2
    The shapes are wrong and the sounds are false. [MBG 181-11
    False as the mind, instead of the fragrance, warm [Horn 230-12
    The false roses--Compare the silent rose of the sun [Extracts
        252-4
    That are paper days. The false and true are one. [Extracts 253-3
    False empire . . . These are the works and pastimes [Hero 280-13

Each false thing ends. The bouquet of summer [Hero 280-19
    But was the summer false? The hero? [Hero 280-25
    Thought is false happiness: the idea [Crude 305-1
    False happiness, since we know that we use [Crude 305-14
    Spent in the false engagements of the mind. [EM 317-3
    Including pain, which, otherwise is false. [EM 323-22
    The thing described, nor false facsimile. [Descrip 344-16
    Its false disasters--these fathers standing round, [Cred 372-16
    False flick, false form, but falseness close to kin. [NSF 385-18
    An innocence of the earth and no false sign [AA 418-21
    False, faded and yet inextricably there, [Study I 463-15
    Or cooling in late leaves, not false except [Study I 463-17
    When the image itself is false, a mere desire, [Study I 463-18
    Were false. The hidalgo was permanent, abstract, [NH 484-2
    Within us. False hybrids and false heroes, [Stan Hero 84-7 P
    The blindness in which seeing would be false, [Souls 95-1 P
    Its invitation to false metaphor. [Someone 85-17 A
FALSELY. Yet the light fell falsely on the marble skulls, [Old
    Woman 44-30 P
    Fell falsely on the matchless skeletons, [Old Woman 45-2 P
FALSENESS. False flick, false form, but falseness close to kin.
    [NSF 385-18
FALSETTO. The blower squeezed to the thinnest mi of falsetto.
    [Parochial 191-6
FALSIFICATIONS. Are falsifications from a sun [Plant 506-12
FALSIFIED. As being, in a world so falsified, [C 36-19
FALSIFIES. It is the chord that falsifies. [MBG 171-3
FALSIFYING. Wished faithfully for a falsifying bell. [Uruguay
    249-11
FALSITIES. Horrors and falsities and wrongs; [Negation 97-16
FAME. The crown and week-day coronal of her fame. [Descrip 339-16
    Whiter than wax, sonorous, fame as it is, [NSF 403-19
    Seen as inamorata, of loving fame [NH 484-14
FAME-FULL. Added and added out of a fame-full heart . . . [NH
    484-15
FAMILIAR. His dark familiar, often walked apart. [Anglais 148-14
    Of familiar things in a cheerful voice, [Thought 185-2
    Amen to the feelings about familiar things, [Montra 260-17
    Ours, like a familiar companion. [Hero 276-4
    After the hero, the familiar [Hero 280-23
    Was the veritable season, that familiar [Hero 280-27
    Born old, familiar with the depths of the heart, [Repet 306-17
    Sees a familiar building drenched in cloud [Repet 308-4
    Ties us to those we love. For this familiar, [EM 317-9
    Stay here. Speak of familiar things a while. [Debris 338-14
    And opens in this familiar spot [Red Fern 365-2
    And a familiar music of the machine [NSF 386-13
    You are familiar yet an aberration. [NSF 406-10
    With every prodigal, familiar fire, [Orb 442-18
    Of an unfamiliar in the familiar room, [Novel 458-12
    Did not pass like someone voyaging out of and beyond the
        familiar. [Prol 515-13
    On her lips familiar words become the words [Woman Had 83-9 P
FAMILY. Came reproduced in purple, family font, [C 45-16
    A member of the family, a tie, [Pieces 352-8
FAMOUS. Fell, famous and flat, [Coroner 29-20 P
FAN. In the roamings of her fan, [Infanta 8-2
FANCY. The fops of fancy in their poems leave [Monocle 16-23
    Illuminating, from a fancy gorged [C 46-6
FANE. Out of their wilderness, a special fane, [Sombre 69-8 P
    If the fane were clear, if the city shone in mind, [Sombre 69-11P
FANFARES. Are full of fanfares of farewell, as night [Sombre 71-4 P
FANG. On the expressive tongue, the finding fang. [AA 420-10
FANGLED. See: fire-fangled; fitful-fangled.
FANGS. On that its claws propound, its fangs [MBG 174-9
    Darting envenomed eyes about, like fangs, [Greenest 55-15 P
FANS. Of the civil fans! [Ord Women 11-24
    Must see her fans of silver undulate. [Nigger 152-20
    The pines that were fans and fragrances emerge, [NH 487-20
    The termagant fans [Coroner 29-18 P
    Clumped carvings, circular, like blunted fans, [Old Woman 43-16 P
FANTAILS. On which she embroidered fantails once [Emperor 64-11
FANTASIA. A moment on this fantasia. He seeks [Look 519-5
    In the absence of fantasia, without meaning more [Course 97-1 P
FANTASIES. The oncoming fantasies of better birth. [C 39-28
FANTASTIC. Toward the cool night and its fantastic star, [Lilacs
    49-11
    Grow out of the spirit or they are fantastic dust. [Holiday
        313-4 P
    With the sea. These were fantastic. There were homes [EM 321-26
    The fantastic fortune of fantastic blood, [Liadoff 347-10
    A fantastic effort has failed, a repetition [Plain 502-19
    And another in a fantastic consciousness, [Rock 525-14
    A fantastic irruption. Salute you, cata-sisters, [Souls 95-2 P
FANTOCHE. This is his essence: the old fantoche [MBG 181-16
FAR. And far beyond the discords of the wind. [Swans 4-2
    Beyond Bordeaux, beyond Havana, far [C 40-9
    Wriggling far down the phantom air, [Cuban 65-2
    Not far off. [Six Sig 74-22
    The sea-clouds whitened far below the calm [Sea Surf 99-10

Like last night's crickets, far below. [Botanist 2 135-19
So far beyond the casual solitudes, [Re-state 146-9
Falling, far off, from sky to land, [Mud 148-7
In the far South the sun of autumn is passing [Nigger 150-9
Far, far beyond the putative canzones [Extracts 256-7
High, low, far, wide, against the distance, [Hero 277-22
Too dark, too far, too much the accents of [EM 314-19
Were one and swans far off were swans to come. [Descrip 343-10
Far in the woods they sang their unreal songs, [Cred 376-1
Beneath, far underneath, the surface of [NSF 403-1
So far beyond the rhetorician's touch. [Roses 431-12
Presence lies far too deep, for me to know [John 437-25
As far as nothingness permits . . . Hear him. [Questions 463-1
The orange far down in yellow, [Plant 506-11
Not of its sphere, and yet not far beyond, [Rome 508-25
A glass aswarm with things going as far as they can. [Look 519-12
In that river, far this side of Stygia, [R Conn 533-7
Still far away. It was like [Not Ideas 534-17
The silent watcher, far below her, hears:) [Infernale 25-11 P
They would throw their batons far up [Drum-Majors 36-20 P
From youngest day or oldest night and far [Greenest 54-1 P
And of sounds so far forgotten, like her voice, [Woman Had 82-18P
This howling at one's ear, too far [Dove 98-14 P
So far the lady of the present ballad [Three 137-9 P
FAR-AWAY. Shattering velvetest far-away. The bear, [NSF 384-14
FARCE. Dissolved the woods, war and the fatal farce [Greenest
   53-22 P
FARCED. The rudiments in the jar, farced, finikin, [Bouquet 452-13
FARCICAL. This parlor of farcical dames, this clowns' colonnade,
   this kites' pavilion? [Inelegance 26-6 P
FAREWELL. These choirs of welcome choir for me farewell. [Monocle
   13-19
Who walks there, as a farewell duty, [Virgin 71-5
"Farewell to Florida" [117-title
Farewell and to know that that land is forever gone [Farewell
   118-7
That I loved her once . . . Farewell. Go on, high ship. [Fare-
   well 118-10
Crying and shouting and meaning farewell, [Adieu 127-10
Farewell in the eyes and farewell at the centre, [Adieu 127-11
And that would be saying farewell, repeating farewell, [Adieu
   127-15
That would be bidding farewell, be bidding farewell. [Adieu 128-6
Between farewell and the absence of farewell, [Nigger 152-5
A kneeling woman, a moon's farewell; [Hero 275 10
Long since, rang out farewell, farewell, farewell. [EM 322-17
Farewell to an idea . . . A cabin stands, [AA 412-4
Farewell to an idea . . . The mother's face, [AA 413-4
Farewell to an idea . . . The cancellings, [AA 414-4
To no; and in saying yes he says farewell. [AA 414-9
Without a voice, inventions of farewell. [Owl 432-4
Forms of farewell, furtive among green ferns. [NH 482-15
And having said farewell. It is not enough [Burnshaw 50-8 P
Are full of fanfares of farewell, as night [Sombre 71-4 P
In hum-drum space, farewell, farewell, by day [Sombre 71-8 P
"Farewell without a Guitar" [98-title P
Farewell, my days. [Fare Guit 98-18 P
FAREWELLS. Hinted autumnal farewells of academic death. [NE Verses
   106-8
Or light, the relic of farewells, [MBG 179-3
For farewells, a sad hanging on for remembrances. [NH 487-18
Farewells and, in the darkness, to feel again [Sombre 71-21 P
FAR-FETCHED. But an antipodal, far-fetched creature, worthy of
   birth, [Discov 96-5 P
FAR-FIRE. The far-fire flowing and the dim-coned bells [NH 466-10
FAR-FOREIGN. He belonged to the far-foreign departure of his vessel
   and was part of it, [Prol 516-1
FARM. Link, of that tempest, to the farm, [Silent 359-15
"The farm was fat and the land in which it lay [Anach 365-18
He had written them near Athens. The farm was white. [Anach 366-1
Belgian Farm, October, 1914 [Phases 5-title 5 P
Mumbling and musing of the silent farm. [Phases 5-10 P
FARMER. Repeats the farmer's almanac. [Grotesque 75-11 P
FARMINGTON. That tell of it. The steeple at Farmington [R Conn
   533-14
FAR-OFF. The eye of Lenin kept the far-off shapes. [Descrip 343-11
As if, alone on a mountain, it saw far-off [Pagoda 92-5 P
FAROUCHE. Of medium nature, this farouche extreme [Bouquet 448-5
FAST. On the ground, fixed fast in a profound defeat. [Martial
   238-2
Under the buttonwoods, beneath a moon nailed fast. [Cata 425-5
Breaches of that which held them fast. It is [Orb 441-18
Held fast tenaciously in common earth [NH 468-24
With redness that sticks fast to evil dreams; [Rock 528-8
FASTENED. Are fastened [Tattoo 81-16
FASTENS. Here the eye fastens intently to these lines [Bouquet
   450-16
FASTER. The faster's feast and heavy-fruited star, [Thought 186-3
It is faster than the weather, faster than [Parochial 192-5
FASTIDIOUS. The torment of fastidious thought grew slack, [C 37-21

FASTLY. Let your golden hands wave fastly and be gay [Burnshaw
   51-28 P
FAT. Of seeds grown fat, too juicily opulent, [C 32-9
Beyond these changes, good, fat, guzzly fruit. [C 41-7
Pardie! Summer is like a fat beast, sleepy in mildew, [Banal
   62-15
Fat! Fat! Fat! Fat! I am the personal. [Bantams 75-18
You ten-foot poet among inchlings. Fat! [Bantams 76-1
The philosophers alone will be fat [Nigger 152-2
The rabbit fat, at last, in glassy grass. [Nigger 153-20
This fat pistache of Belgian grapes exceeds [Nigger 154-17
A fat thumb beats out ai-yi-yi. [MBG 178-22
Crash in the mind--But, fat Jocundus, worrying [Glass 197-20
Men fat as feathers, misers counting breaths, [Horn 230-3
Loud, general, large, fat, soft [Jumbo 269-15
Adam of beau regard, from fat Elysia, [Pure 331-20
"The farm was fat and the land in which it lay [Anach 365-18
To speak, the fat, the roseate characters, [Cred 378-7
Fat girl, terrestrial, my summer, my night, [NSF 406-7
Fat with a thousand butters, and the crows [Burnshaw 49-9 P
Could ever make them fat, these are delays [Sombre 69-15 P
FATAL. A band entwining, set with fatal stones. [Fictive 88-16
Falls from that fatal and that barer sky, [Anatomy 108-17
As the life of the fatal unity of war. [Yellow 236-21
The vital, arrogant, fatal, dominant X. [Motive 288-20
Held off the final, fatal distances, [Wild 329-11
Are the ravishments of truth, so fatal to [NSF 381-19
Always, in brilliance, fatal, final, formed [Owl 434-23
It is fatal in the moon and empty there. [NH 472-4
The sentiment of the fatal is a part [Aug 491-19
Dissolved the woods, war and the fatal farce [Greenest 53-22 P
Fatal Ananke is the common god. [Greenest 59-1 P
Moves in lamenting and the fatal, [Stan Hero 83-23 P
FATALIST. The stopper to indulgent fatalist [C 44-9
The same insoluble lump. The fatalist [C 45-17
Like these, autumn beguiles the fatalist. [Nigger 155-5
FATALITY. The fatality of seeing things too well. [Novel 459-6
FATE. Scullion of fate, [Paltry 6-8
But note the unconscionable treachery of fate, [Monocle 17-9
Or, nobler, sensed an elemental fate, [C 31-24
This connoisseur of elemental fate, [C 32-30
Of his own fate an instance of all fate? [C 41-24
A fate intoned, a death before they die, [Thought 186-15
Fat cat, red tongue, green mind, white milk [Rabbit K 209-5
Phrases! But of fear and of fate. [Nightgown 214-14
Of arms, the will opposed to cold, fate [Hero 273-12
Fate is the present desperado. [Dutch 291-5
Like the head of fate, looked out in darkness, part [Choc 299-20
The precisions of fate, nothing fobbed off, nor changed [Repet
   310-8
Weaken our fate, relieve us of woe both great [EM 315-21
The eccentric propositions of its fate. [Men Made 356-6
That is a being, a will, a fate. [Human 363-16
One sole face, like a photograph of fate, [NSF 394-10
This sense of the activity of fate-- [AA 419-15
The full of fortune and the full of fate, [AA 420-23
For him cold's glacial beauty is his fate. [Bad Time 426-15
She had heard of the fate of an Argentine writer. At night,
   [Novel 457-8
A scribble of fret and fear and fate, [Aug 494-25
Of inescapable force, itself a fate. [Spaniard 34-20 P
The harridan self and ever-maladive fate [Old Woman 45-25 P
Untroubled by suffering, which fate assigns [Old Woman 46-6 P
It will be all we have. Our fate is our own: [Bship 81-4 P
Grow large and larger. Our fate is our own. The hand, [Bship
   81-7 P
The deep comfort of the world and fate. [Ulysses 100-4 P
It is the fate that dwells in truth. [Ulysses 103-29 P
Which knowledge is: the world and fate. [Presence 105-21 P
FATED. Returned, unable to die again, fated [Extracts 258-26
Again and fated to endure beyond [Extracts 259-5
Each one, his fated eccentricity, [Orb 443-2
FATEFUL. Imagination as the fateful sin. [Havana 143-22
She is the fateful mother, whom he does not know. [Pecul 454-3
No shadow walks. The river is fateful, [R Conn 533-10
Fateful Ananke is the final god. [Greenest 59-20 P
FATES. Their curious fates in war, come, celebrate [Monocle 16-15
This man escaped the dirty fates, [Flyer 336-10
That tragic prattle of the fates, astute [Spaniard 34-16 P
What super-animal dictate our fates? [Duck 63-8 P
FATHER. The father, the beater of the rigid drums, [Thought 186-4
There was a tree that was a father, [Vari 233-6
Not father, but bare brother, megalfrere, [Choc 300-21
This brother even in the father's eye, [EM 317-10
For another, as the son's life for the father's. [EM 323-27
And the father alike and equally are spent, [EM 324-4
In which your father died, still breathes for him [Extraord
   369-17
In Eden was the father of Descartes [NSF 383-11
The negations are never final. The father sits [AA 414-5

And table. The father fetches tellers of tales [AA 415-5
The father fetches negresses to dance, [AA 415-7
The father fetches pageants out of air, [AA 415-13
The father fetches his unherded herds, [AA 415-17
There sleep the brother is the father, too, [Owl 432-10
The mind is the terriblest force in the world, father, [John
   436-10
And of a father bearded in his fire. [Celle 438-20
But his father was strong, that lies now [Pecul 453-5
The father, the ancestor, the bearded peer, [Aug 494-22
Who is my father in this world, in this house, [Irish 501-7
My father's father, his father's father, his-- [Irish 501-9
And the sea. This is my father or, maybe, [Irish 502-5
And father nature, full of butter [Lulu M 27-13 P
The father that he loves, and bears him from [Recit 87-13 P
The father. He hides his ancient blue beneath [Recit 87-17 P
His life made double by his father's life, [Recit 87-19 P
The father keeps on living in the son, the world [Recit 87-25 P
Of the father keeps on living in the world [Recit 87-26 P
Determined thereto, perhaps by his father's ghost, [Role 93-4 P
The father does not come to adorn the chant. [Role 93-6 P
One father proclaims another, the patriarchs [Role 93-7 P
The lady's father [Three 139-3 P
Tell my father: [Three 140-7 P
FATHER-FIRE. The furiously burning father-fire . . . [Red Fern
   365-12
FATHERS. The fathers of the makers may lie and weather. [New Set
   353-6
   Its false disasters--these fathers standing round, [Cred 372-16
   A likeness, one of the race of fathers: earth [Irish 502-7
FATIGUE. The choir that choirs the first fatigue in deep bell of
   canzoni? [Inelegance 25-20 P
FATLY. Who was the musician, fatly soft [Jumbo 269-4
FATNESS. Distorted by hale fatness, turned grotesque. [Monocle
   16-8
FATTENED. And fattened as on a decorous honeycomb. [AA 419-13
FATTER. That the grapes seemed fatter. [On Road 203-14
FATTEST. Where the fattest women belled the glass. [Dinner 110-4 P
FATUOUS. To the fatuous. These are his infernal walls, [Thought
   185-8
   As evils, and if reason, fatuous fire, [Duck 63-4 P
FAULT. If the fault is with the soul, the sovereigns [Lions 124-19
   Of the soul must likewise be at fault, and first. [Lions 124-20
   If the fault is with the souvenirs, yet these [Lions 125-1
   If the fault is with the lions, send them back [Lions 125-6
   The fault lies with an over-human god, [EM 315-14
   In desperate hallow, rugged gesture, fault [EM 316-26
FAULTLESS. Which choir makes the most faultless medley in its
   celebration? [Inelegance 25-19 P
FAULTY. Make more awry our faulty human things. [Surprises 98-11
FAVOR. In which the spectra have dewy favor and live [How Now
   97-13 P
FAVORABLE. The favorable transformations of the wind [Past Nun
   378-21
FAVORS. Truth's favors sonorously exhibited. [EM 321-11
FEAR. For fear the Lord would not accept. [Pourtraicte 21-21
   Once, a fear pierced him, [Thirteen 94-15
   The voice of angry fear, [Mozart 132-11
   Phrases! But of fear and of fate. [Nightgown 214-14
   In the donkey's ear, "I fear that elegance [Uruguay 248-18
   Fear never the brute clouds nor winter-stop [Montra 261-22
   Central responses to a central fear, [Repet 308-1
   And by the fear that defeats and dreams are one. [Men Made 356-4
   Feeling the fear that creeps beneath the wool, [Novel 458-23
   Rattles with fear in unreflecting leaves. [Golden 460-15
   A scribble of fret and fear and fate, [Aug 494-25
   The metaphor stirred his fear. The object with which he was com-
   pared [Prol 516-10
   A gesture in the dark, a fear one feels [Moonlight 531-16
   I fear the understanding, [Lytton 38-16 P
   A fear too naked for her shadow's shape. [Old Woman 44-12 P
   A change so felt, a fear in her so known, [Old Woman 45-3 P
   Of fear before the disorder of the strange, [Burnshaw 48-14 P
   Then, fear a drastic community evolved [Burnshaw 51-6 P
   From the whirling, slowly and by trial; or fear [Burnshaw 51-7 P
   Beneath the spangling greens, fear might placate [Greenest 54-22P
   Each fretful fern drops down a fear like dew [Greenest 55-24 P
   Of fear changes the scorpions to skins [Duck 65-10 P
   In anger; or the fear that from the death [Sombre 69-22 P
FEARS. And fears not portly Azcan nor his hoos. [Bantams 76-4
   Fears of my bed, [Brave 138-16
   Fears of life and fears of death, [Brave 138-17
   Alpha fears men or else Omega's men [NH 469-11
FEAST. The faster's feast and heavy-fruited star, [Thought 186-3
   These days of disinheritance, we feast [Cuisine 227-13
   We feast on human heads, brought in on leaves, [Cuisine 228-10
   To feast . . . Slice the mango, Naaman, and dress it [Phenom
   286-14
   Its evening feast and the following festival, [NH 472-18
FEASTS. The coming on of feasts and the habits of saints, [NH 472-2

5. A symbol of feasts and of oblivion . . . [Someone 86-8 A
FEAT. On the feat sandbars. [Jack-Rabbit 50-7
   And there, by feat extenuations, to make [Greenest 57-6 P
FEATHER. And the best cock of red feather [Watermelon 89-5
   Hang a feather by your eye, [Orangeade 103-15
   And headsman and trumpeteer and feather [Stan Hero 84-20 P
FEATHERED. See gold-feathered.
FEATHERS. Bequeathing your white feathers to the moon [Swans 4-7
   The feathers flare [Ploughing 20-7
   That tuft of jungle feathers, [Gubbinal 85-6
   Men fat as feathers, misers counting breaths, [Horn 230-3
   Who killed him, sticking feathers in his flesh [Good Man 364-9
   And crawls on them, as if feathers of the duck [Bouquet 450-17
   I care for neither fugues nor feathers. [Lytton 38-7 P
   The bird sings. Its feathers shine. [Of Mere 118-3 P
   The bird's fire-fangled feathers dangle down. [Of Mere 118-6 P
FEATHERY. Did not desire that feathery argentines [NSF 399-5
   A maid of forty is no feathery girl. [Stan MMO 19-9 P
   And more. It may have feathery color-frets, [Spaniard 35-8 P
   The earth as the bodies rose on feathery wings, [Old Woman
   43-15 P
   He carved the feathery walkers standing by, [Duck 64-22 P
FEATLY. Although contending featly in its veils, [C 36-2
FEATURES. An inhuman of our features, known [Ulysses 105-4 P
FEBRUAR. And ice is still in Februar. [Poesie 302-10
   It still is ice in Februar. [Poesie 302-11
FEBRUARY. Sees the petty gildings on February . . . [Hero 280-11
   Tinsel in February, tinsel in August. [Pieces 351-9
   In February hears the imagination's hymns [Imago 439-10
   . . . Wanderer, this is the pre-history of February. [Slug 522-15
   White February wind, [Grotesque 77-6 P
FECUND. Fecund, [Homunculus 26-25
   Or searcher for the fecund minimum. [C 35-30
   Coiffeur of haloes, fecund jeweller-- [Eve Angels 137-8
   The gross, the fecund, proved him against the touch [EM 322-2
   More fecund as principle than particle, [NSF 388-19
   Much richer, more fecund, sportive and alive. [NH 469-24
   It will be fecund in rapt curios. [Red Kit 32-5 P
FECUNDITY. Happy fecundity, flor-abundant force, [NSF 388-20
FECUNDLY. Who most fecundly assuaged him, the softest [EM 321-14
FED. In which we fed on being brothers, fed [AA 419-12
FEEBLE. On an early Sunday in April, a feeble day, [Extracts
   254-25
FEEBLY. Feebly, slowly, depending upon them; [Lunar 107-4
FEED. To feed on the yellow bloom of the yellow fruit [EM 318-12
   His grief is that his mother should feed on him, himself and
   what he saw, [Madame 507-12
FEEDS. Like hunger that feeds on its own hungriness. [EM 323-4
   In which he feeds on a new known, [Bus 116-4 P
FEEL. Nothing but trash and that you no longer feel [Lilacs 49-9
   She says, "But in contentment I still feel [Sunday 68-27
   And thus it is that what I feel, [Peter 90-2
   And to feel sure and to forget the bleaching sand . . . [Farewell
   117-20
   But how does one feel? [Am Sub 131-4
   Was not the moon he used to see, to feel [Anglais 148-20
   To feel it breathing there. [Destructive 192-14
   And to feel that the light is a rabbit-light, [Rabbit K 209-10
   That you do not see, you experience, you feel, [Poem Morn 219-13
   Feel the wind of it, smell the dust of it? [Arcades 225-9
   To escape from the body, so to feel [Vari 234-2
   Nor in their empty hearts to feel [Adequacy 243-17
   And we feel, in a way apart, for a moment, as if [Gala 248-11
   Bask in the sun in which they feel transparent, [Extracts 254-19
   Nor feel the x malisons of other men, [Montra 261-24
   Feel everything starving except the belly [Hero 278-3
   The feeling of him was the feel of day, [Choc 297-4
   Something to feel that they needed another yellow, [Holiday 312-3
   With the blank uneasiness which one might feel [EM 324-25
   In a physical world, to feel that one's desire [EM 325-19
   The minor of what we feel. The adventurer [EM 325-24
   And feel that her color is a meditation, [Debris 338-12
   Hear, feel and know. We feel and know them so. [Descrip 340-18
   And for what, except for you, do I feel love? [NSF 380-4
   Or what we feel from what we think, of thought [NSF 382-20
   It means the distaste we feel for this withered scene [NSF 390-3
   A passion that we feel, not understand. [NSF 392-11
   The shoulders of joyous men, to feel the heart [NSF 398-11
   And cried out to feel it again, have run fingers over leaves
   [Large 424-2
   He wanted to feel the same way over and over. [Cata 425-2
   Just to know how it would feel, released from destruction, [Cata
   425-9
   And feel its country gayety and smile [Beginning 428-1
   We feel and, therefore, is not real, except [Roses 430-17
   To feel the satisfactions [Aug 493-23
   So that we feel, in this illumined large, [Rome 509-13
   What we know in what we see, what we feel in what [Look 518-10
   We feel the obscurity of an order, a whole, [Final 524-11
   Stretched out a shadowy arm to feel the night. [Phases 5-8 P

As a seraglio-parrot; feel disdain [Spaniard 35-11 P
As for myself, I feel a doubt: [Lytton 39-10 P
And purpose, to hear the wild bee drone, to feel [Greenest
  56-25 P
Why feel the sun or, feeling, why feel more [Greenest 58-30 P
The metropolitan of mind, they feel [Duck 64-11 P
They live. They see and feel themselves, seeing [Duck 64-13 P
Farewells and, in the darkness, to feel again [Sombre 71-21 P
"Here I feel the human loneliness [Presence 105-19 P
FEELING. The senses and feeling, the very sound [Joost 47-1
Music is feeling, then, not sound; [Peter 90-1
Unfolding in the water, feeling sure [Sea Surf 100-18
And the feeling heavy in cold chords [MBG 169-5
Cloud's red, earth feeling, sky that thinks? [MBG 177-4
One is always seeing and feeling oneself, [Prelude 195-8
What is it that my feeling seeks? [Country 207-16
Perceived by feeling instead of sense, [Nightgown 214-12
Being, becoming seeing and feeling and self, [Extracts 255-21
Like a white abstraction only, a feeling [Hero 276-26
In a feeling mass, a blank emotion, [Hero 276-27
It is not an image. It is a feeling. [Hero 278-19
There is a feeling as definition. [Hero 278-21
The hero is a feeling, a man seen [Hero 278-24
As if in seeing we saw our feeling [Hero 278-26
The feeling of him was the feel of day, [Choc 297-4
Which, as a man feeling everything, were his. [Somnam 304-18
The feeling of Liadoff was changed. It is [Liadoff 347-4
Without any feeling, an imperium of quiet, [Burghers 362-16
By a feeling capable of nothing more. [Cred 374-5
The spent feeling leaving nothing of itself, [NSF 400-12
The fiction that results from feeling. Yes, that. [NSF 406-21
Until flicked by feeling, in a gildered street, [NSF 407-1
And spoke the feeling for them, which was what they had lacked.
  [Large 424-9
Feeling the fear that creeps beneath the wool, [Novel 458-23
Today; and the transcripts of feeling, impossible [NH 479-17
And the shapes that it took in feeling, the persons that [NH
  479-21
Feels not, resembling thought, resembling feeling? [Aug 493-4
It is like the feeling of a man [Vacancy 511-10
Of the well-thumbed, infinite pages of her masters, who will
  seem old to her, requiting less and less her feeling: [Piano
  22-7 P
Why feel the sun or, feeling, why feel more [Greenest 58-30 P
From the steppes, are they being part, feeling the strength,
  [Duck 62-15 P
And feeling the world in which they live. The manes, [Duck 64-14 P
By feeling the like of thought in sleep, [Desire 85-12 P
So that feeling was a madness, and is. [Desire 85-13 P
Of feeling, the things that came of their own accord, [Local
  112-8 P
So much less than feeling, so much less than speech, [Region
  115-9
Without human feeling, a foreign song. [Of Mere 117-20 P
FEELINGS. The thoughts of drunkards, the feelings [Homunculus 26-6
How easily the feelings flow this afternoon [Nigger 151-16
The feelings crazily, craftily call, [MBG 166-19
Deepen the feelings to inhuman depths. [Parochial 191-10
Those feelings that the body balks, [Vari 234-3
The feelings of the natures round us here: [Vari 234-4
Approaching the feelings or come down from them, [Montra 260-12
Amen to the feelings about familiar things, [Montra 260-17
His hands became his feelings. His thick shape [Repet 306-12
In which looks and feelings mingle and are part [NH 471-5
The self and the earth--your thoughts, your feelings, [Old Man
  501-3
And are your feelings changed to sound, without [Burnshaw 52-13 P
FEELS. One has a malady, here, a malady. One feels a malady.
  [Banal 63-6
She dreams a little, and she feels the dark [Sunday 67-2
Who still feels irrational things within her. [Shifts 83-16
It is only the way one feels, to say [Sailing 120-22
By light, the way one feels, sharp white, [Sailing 121-6
He knew how one feels. [Am Sub 131-1
Without pathos, he feels what he hears [Prelude 194-18
One feels the purifying change. One rejects [Dump 202-17
As a boat feels when it cuts blue water. [Vari 234-5
One feels its action moving in the blood. [EM 324-23
Of what one feels, who could have thought to make [EM 326-8
It feels good as it is without the giant, [NSF 386-1
Of everything he is. And he feels afraid. [AA 417-3
And feels the imagination's mercies, [Imago 439-13
Feels not, resembling thought, resembling feeling? [Aug 493-4
A gesture in the dark, a fear one feels [Moonlight 531-16
And so France feels. A menace that impends, [Soldat 13-6 P
And in those regions one still feels the rose [Abnormal 24-9 P
And feels the grass [Abnormal 24-10 P
One feels the life of that which gives life as it is. [Course
  96-18 P
FEEN. A bachelor of feen masquerie, [Oak 272-5

FEET. The bundle of the body and the feet. [Worms 50-2
If her horny feet protrude, they come [Emperor 64-13
Stilled for the passing of her dreaming feet [Sunday 67-9
Upon the grass, relinquished to their feet. [Sunday 69-9
The dew upon their feet shall manifest. [Sunday 70-13
The soles of its feet [Six Sig 74-17
On timid feet, [Peter 91-4
Walks around the feet [Thirteen 93-22
For soldiers, the new moon stretches twenty feet. [Gigan 289-21
As they jangle and dangle and kick their feet. [Luther 462-3
A reddened garment falling to his feet, [Aug 492-8
Like damsels daubed and let your feet be bare [Burnshaw 51-11 P
The memory moves on leopards' feet, desire [Greenest 57-16 P
Of pursuing feet. [Three 136-4 P
FEIGNING. Our feigning with the strange unlike, whence springs
  [Fictive 88-12
FEINTING. See fire-feinting.
FELICITOUS. A very felicitous eve, [Delight 162-1
FELICITY. Bubbling felicity in cantilene, [C 43-10
"All the Preludes to Felicity" [Pure 329-title 1
Felicity, ah! Time is the hooded enemy, [Pure 330-13
FELL. The drenching of stale lives no more fell down. [C 30-10
The rumbling broadened as it fell. The wind, [C 32-22
Latched up the night. So deep a sound fell down [C 42-6
So deep a sound fell down it grew to be [C 42-9
A slash and the edifice fell, [Public Sq 109-1
Pylon and pier fell down. [Public Sq 109-2
Like a thing in which they fell, [Public Sq 109-4
Fell slowly as when at night [Public Sq 109-5
When the music of the boy fell like a fountain, [Norfolk 111-14
Your lamp-light fell [Tea 112-12
Coldly the wind fell upon them [How Live 125-13
The swans . . . Before the bills of the swans fell flat [Havana
  142-13
Not the mother that held men as they fell [MBG 173-14
And fell to the floor. [Weak Mind 212-4
And then the body fell. [Weak Mind 212-5
The blood of the mind fell [Weak Mind 212-14
When male light fell on the naked back [Hartford 227-7
Hoot how the inhuman colors fell [Vase 247-6
It had been cold since December. Snow fell, first, [Extracts
  255-1
Her hair fell on him and the mi-bird flew [Hand 271-18
Fell on him, high and cold, searching for what [Choc 301-21
As they fell down, as they heard Liadoff's cloud [Liadoff 346-18
And is it true that what they said, as they fell, [Liadoff 347-1
Fell openly from the air to reappear [Bouquet 450-18
How facilely the purple blotches fell [NH 484-4
That fell [Phases 4-12 P
Stood by him when the tumbler fell, [Sat Night 28-2 P
Fell, famous and flat, [Coroner 29-20 P
Folded and fell [Coroner 29-22 P
Yet the light fell falsely on the marble skulls, [Old Woman
  44-30 P
Fell falsely on the matchless skeletons, [Old Woman 45-2 P
As I wished, once they fell backward when my breath [Bship
  78-16 P
FELLOW. To believe? Incisive what, the fellow [Hero 275-20
And small, a constant fellow of destiny, [EM 315-22
Follow after, O my companion, my fellow, my self, [NSF 392-23
There peace, the godolphin and fellow, estranged, estranged,
  [Owl 434-1
FELLOWS. I am a yeoman, as such fellows go. [Monocle 16-26
The shadow of his fellows from the skies, [C 37-8
The shadows of his fellows ring him round [EM 319-11
To bear virile grace before their fellows, [Stan Hero 83-20 P
FELLOWSHIP. They shall know well the heavenly fellowship [Sunday
  70-10
FELON. Ah, ké! the bloody wren, the felon jay, [NSF 394-1
FELT. I felt afraid. [Domination 9-19
And He felt a subtle quiver, [Pourtraicte 22-4
The multifarious heavens felt no awe [Geneva 24-8
He felt the Andean breath. His mind was free [C 33-9
And what I knew you felt [Vincentine 53-11
Or heard or felt came not but from myself; [Hoon 65-17
The red-eyed elders watching, felt [Peter 90-9
She felt, among the leaves, [Peter 90-24
The look of things, left what we felt [Postcard 159-6
He felt curious about the winter hills [Extracts 254-26
Within the difference. He felt curious [Extracts 255-12
The total past felt nothing when destroyed. [EM 314-16
His being felt the need of soaring, the need [Liadoff 347-12
All mind and violence and nothing felt. [Chaos 358-4
There is nothing more inscribed nor thought nor felt [Cred 372-14
And what she felt fought off the barest phrase. [NSF 402-12
He never felt twice the same about the flecked river, [Cata
  424-10
And potent, an influence felt instead of seen. [Owl 435-7
The muscles of a magnet aptly felt, [Orb 442-15
A syllable of which he felt, with an appointed sureness,

[Prol 516-5
Fallen Winkle felt the pride [Phases 4-17 P
A change so felt, a fear in her so known, [Old Woman 45-3 P
Now felt, now known as this. The clouds of bronze [Old Woman 45-4 P
Except the thing she felt but did not know. [Old Woman 45-22 P
Joined, the triumphant vigor, felt, [Ulysses 100-14 P
And felt and known the differences we have seen [Conversat 109-18 P
And felt and known in the colors in which we live, [Conversat 109-19 P
I felt the evil, [Three 141-14 P
FEMALE. Night, the female, [Six Sig 73-18
    The Female Nude [NE Verses 106-title 14
FEME. A feme may come, leaf-green, [Watermelon 89-7
FEMES. And halidom for the unbraided femes, [C 43-27
FEMININE. Lights masculine and lights feminine. [Hartford 226-14
FENCE. The crawling railroad spur, the rotten fence, [C 36-14
FEND. Oh! Rabbi, rabbi, fend my soul for me [Sun March 134-7
FERN. "The Red Fern" [365-title
    Its unfamiliar, difficult fern, [Red Fern 365-3
    There are doubles of this fern in clouds, [Red Fern 365-5
    Lean larkspur and jagged fern and rusting rue [Bouquet 452-10
    Each fretful fern drops down a fear like dew [Greenest 55-24 P
    An eighteenth century fern or two [Stan MBG 72-7 P
FERNANDEZ. See Ramon Fernandez.
FERNANDO. I say now, Fernando, that on that day [Hibiscus 22-9
FERNS. Of men suited to public ferns . . . The hero [Hero 276-16
    Even that. His meditations in the ferns, [AA 411-20
    Forms of farewell, furtive among green ferns. [NH 482-15
    The jostled ferns, where it might be, having eyes [Greenest 59-4 P
FEROCIOUS. With the ferocious chu-chot-chu between, the sobs [Extracts 253-18
    Being small, inscribes ferocious alphabets, [Pure 332-23
    As large ferocious tigers are. [Parasol 20-10 P
FEROCITIES. That such ferocities could tear [Peaches 224-19
FERRYMAN. Like the last one. But there is no ferryman. [R Conn 533-11
FERTILE. Of its ancient purple, pruned to the fertile main, [C 45-14
    Himself than in this fertile glass. [MBG 181-14
    Of the fertile thing that can attain no more. [Cred 373-15
    Fertile of its own leaves and days and wars, [Aug 491-14
    Is fertile with more than changes of the light [Someone 84-18 A
FERTILEST. In our sense of it, our sense of the fertilest red, [Roses 430-18
FESTIVAL. That earth was like a jostling festival [C 32-8
    Oppose the past and the festival, [MBG 181-2
    And mingling of colors at a festival. [Cred 374-20
    We stand in the tumult of a festival. [AA 415-21
    What festival? This loud, disordered mooch? [AA 415-22
    A mythological form, a festival sphere, [NH 466-2
    Its evening feast and the following festival, [NH 472-18
FESTIVALS. And ex-bar's flower and fire of the festivals [EM 317-27
FETCH. To fetch the one full-pinioned one himself [C 44-28
FETCHED. True transfigurers fetched out of the human mountain, [Choc 300-6
    Fetched up with snow that never falls to earth? [Belly 367-6
    Fetched by such slick-eyed nymphs, this essential gold, [Orb 440-6
    Of a ruddier summer, a birth that fetched along [Nuns 92-13 P
    See far-fetched.
FETCHES. When the deep breath fetches another year of life. [News 265-14
    And table. The father fetches tellers of tales [AA 415-5
    The father fetches negresses to dance, [AA 415-7
    The father fetches pageants out of air, [AA 415-13
    The father fetches his unherded herds, [AA 415-17
    This fetches its own water. [Three 129-2 P
FETCHING. Fetching her woven scarves, [Peter 91-5
FETCHINGS. She wanted no fetchings. His arms would be her necklace [World 521-8
FEW. In the sound of a few leaves, [Snow Man 10-6
    A few years more and the vermeil capuchin [C 44-24
    A few things for themselves, [Venereal 47-4
    A few things for themselves, [Venereal 47-8
    Pitiless verse? a few words tuned [Chateau 161-15
    A few final solutions, like a duet [MBG 177-7
    Out of the movement of few words, [Oak 272-17
    A few sounds of meaning, a momentary end [Lack 303-19
    On a few words of what is real in the world [Repet 308-13
    A few words, a memorandum voluble [Repet 308-19
    A few words of what is real or may be [Repet 309-6
    Long after the planter's death. A few limes remained, [NSF 393-3
    So summer comes in the end to these few stains [Beginning 427-10
    A few words, an and yet, and yet, and yet-- [NH 465-6
    A look, a few words spoken. [Leben 505-6
    A few more hours of day, the unravelling [Nuns 92-12 P
    In a health of weather, knowing a few, old things, [Americana 93-17 P
    In that sphere with so few objects of its own. [Local 112-3 P
    Little existed for him but the few things [Local 112-4 P
    The few things, the objects of insight, the integrations [Local 112-7 P
FEWEST. Fewest things to the lover-- [Venereal 48-15
FI. Qui fait fi des joliesses banales, the chairs. [Freed 205-24
FIBROUS. Fibrous and dangling down, [Bananas 54-19
FICKLE. Fickle and fumbling, variable, obscure, [C 46-4
FICKLE-FINE. Miraculously preserved, full fickle-fine, [Greenest 56-15 P
FICTION. The moonlight fiction disappeared. The spring, [C 36-1
    Poetry is the supreme fiction, madame. [High-Toned 59-1
    Must be in a fiction. It is time to choose. [Oboe 250-8
    That obsolete fiction of the wide river in [Oboe 250-9
    "Notes toward a Supreme Fiction" [380-title
    To be stripped of every fiction except one, [NSF 404-9
    The fiction of an absolute--Angel, [NSF 404-10
    The fiction that results from feeling. Yes, that. [NSF 406-21
    The fiction of the leaves is the icon [Rock 526-18
    The civil fiction, the calico idea, [Duck 65-12 P
    Merely parts of the general fiction of the mind: [Recit 87-29 P
    Or accessible only in the most furtive fiction. [Nuns 93-2 P
FICTITIOUS. Less than contending with fictitious doom. [Spaniard 35-5 P
FICTIVE. With fictive flourishes that preordained [C 39-17
    This will make widows wince. But fictive things [High-Toned 59-21
    "To the One of Fictive Music" [87-title
    The fictive man created out of men. [Paisant 335-6
    The fictive man. He may be seated in [Paisant 335-14
    Is never naked. A fictive covering [NSF 396-11
    How simply the fictive hero becomes the real; [NSF 408-1
FIDDLES. And the fiddles smack, the horns yahoo, the flutes [Bship 79-28 P
FIDDLING. See fuddle-fiddling.
FIDDLINGS. The arias that spiritual fiddlings make, [Orb 440-2
FIDES. And savings banks, Fides, the sculptor's prize, [Lions 124-12
FIDGET. And the general fidget from busts of Constantine [NH 488-14
FIDGETS. Than green, fidgets of all-related fire. [Pieces 352-4
    The fidgets of remembrance come to this. [Cred 372-10
    He is sitting by the fidgets of a fire, [Novel 457-13
FIELD. This field, and tended it awhile, [Frogs 78-8
    Those bearing balsam, its field fragrance, [Vari 235-11
    From the middle of his field. The odor [Yellow 237-2
    The field is frozen. The leaves are dry. [Possum 293-15
    The brooks are bristling in the field, [Poesie 302-6
    We think as wind skitters on a pond in a field [Look 518-24
    The meeting at noon at the edge of the field seems like [Rock 525-12
    A black figure dances in a black field. [Plough-Boy 6-4 P
    Remembrances, a place of a field of lights, [Sombre 67-18 P
    The pheasant in a field was pheasant, field, [Sombre 68-3 P
    In a field, the man on the side of a hill, all men [Americana 93-16 P
FIELDS. Water in the fields. [Ploughing 20-5
    Water in the fields. [Ploughing 20-19
    It may be that the yarrow in his fields [C 40-19
    Of misty fields, by their sweet questionings; [Sunday 68-14
    But when the birds are gone, and their warm fields [Sunday 68-15
    It is too cold for work, now in the fields. [Nigger 151-18
    A calm November. Sunday in the fields. [Nigger 156-1
    The sun rises green and blue in the fields and in the heavens. [Fish-Scale 161-5
    The cities, children become the fields [MBG 171-1
    The fields entrap the children, brick [MBG 171-5
    Home and the fields give praise, hurrah, hip, [Hero 278-13
    Now, brooks are bristling in the herds, [Poesie 302-7
    They sang of summer in the common fields. [Cred 376-5
    These fields, these hills, these tinted distances, [AA 411-8
    Bearing the odors of the summer fields, [Wom Sun 445-13
    The blank frere of fields, their matin laborer. [Aug 492-18
    "Looking across the Fields and Watching the Birds Fly" [517-title
    Wood of his forests and stone out of his fields [Myth 118-15 P
    When he was in his fields, [Three 141-6 P
FIERCE. To the laughter of evil: the fierce ricanery [Extracts 253-17
    Desiring fiercely, the child of a mother fierce [EM 321-20
    Without their fierce addictions, nor that the heat [NSF 399-9
FIERCELY. The poem lashes more fiercely than the wind, [Bottle 239-14
    Desiring fiercely, the child of a mother fierce [EM 321-20
FIERCER. In his body, fiercer in his mind, merciless [EM 321-21
FIERY. It is for fiery boys that star was set [Monocle 14-24
    Out of his fiery lair. [Pascagoula 127-7
    Fixing emblazoned zones and fiery poles, [Key W 130-9
    The venerable song falls from your fiery wings. [God 285-16
    Of fiery eyes and long thin arms. [Attempt 370-11
    These are the ashes of fiery weather, [Our Stars 455-13

The desire, for the fiery lullaby. [Woman Had 82-27 P
FIFTY. The chimney is fifty years old and slants to one side.
  [Plain 502-18
  As they were fifty years ago, [Clear Day 113-9 P
FIG. Yeoman and grub, but with a fig in sight, [C 42-17
  And cream for the fig and silver for the cream, [C 42-18
  And didn't care a fig, [Drum-Majors 36-18 P
FIGHTER. Your great-grandfather was an Indian fighter. [Extraord
  369-9
FIGURATION. Of the poem, the figuration of blessedness, [Rock
  526-19
  "Sombre Figuration" [66-title P
FIGURATIONS. Turns to its own figurations and declares, [Rhythms
  246-3
  Or the wasted figurations of the wastes [NH 477-22
FIGURE. Like a figure on the church-wall. [Explan 73-4
  Humanly near, and the figure of Mary, [Lunar 107-6
  This is the figure and not [Add 199-11
  Like a noble figure, out of the sky, [Candle 223-4
  The noble figure, the essential shadow, [Candle 223-12
  What figure of capable imagination? [Uruguay 249-17
  For the large, the solitary figure. [Hero 281-5
  To see was to be. He was the figure in [Choc 297-6
  A brune figure in winter evening resists [Man Car 350-15
  In which a wasted figure, with an instrument, [Burghers 362-17
  Tall and unfretted, a figure meant to bear [Pastor 379-19
  You remain the more than natural figure. You [NSF 406-17
  This is that figure stationed at our end, [Owl 434-22
  Of things? A figure like Ecclesiast, [NH 479-13
  Myself, only half of a figure of a sort, [Angel 497-6
  A figure half seen, or seen for a moment, a man [Angel 497-7
  To disclose in the figure waiting on the road [Moonlight 531-13
  A black figure dances in a black field. [Plough-Boy 6-4 P
  It wraps the sheet around its body, until the black figure is
    silver. [Plough-Boy 6-6 P
  How soon the silver fades in the dust! How soon the black figure
    slips from the wrinkled sheet! [Plough-Boy 6-8 P
  The figure of the wise man fixed in sense. [Recit 86-17 P
  A tall figure upright in a giant's air. [Recit 87-24 P
  That a figure reclining among columns toppled down, [Conversat
    109-7 P
FIGURED. I figured you as nude between [Vincentine 52-11
FIGURES. "Two Figures in Dense Violet Night" [85-title
  Who then beheld the figures of the clouds [Sea Surf 101-11
  For whom the shapes were never the figures of men. [Sad Gay
    121-18
  Will unite these figures of men and their shapes [Sad Gay 122-16
  We were two figures in a wood. [On Road 203-21
  The figures of speech, as why she chose [Scavoir 231-3
  The figures of the past go cloaked. [Poesie 302-12
  These figures verdant with time's buried verdure [New Set 352-16
  Does not see these separate figures one by one, [NSF 389-4
  These forms are not abortive figures, rocks, [Owl 432-5
  "Horrid figures of Medusa, [Inhab 504-1
  On the threshold of heaven, the figures in the street [Rome
    508-1
  Become the figures of heaven, the majestic movement [Rome 508-2
  Two figures in a nature of the sun, [Rock 525-17
  The gods like marble figures fallen, left [Greenest 58-14 P
  If it be supposed that we are three figures [Three 132-17 P
  For the figures pointed on it. [Three 133-9 P
  See pine-figures.
FILAMENT. Clothe me entire in the final filament, [NSF 396-7
FILAMENTS. There are filaments of your eyes [Tattoo 81-19
  By trivial filaments to the thing intact: [Bouquet 450-11
FILE. They would march single file, with electric lamps, alert
  [Page 423-9
FILIAL. That his revenge created filial [EM 319-24
  In the sunshine is a filial form and one [Cred 375-3
  Of filial love. Or is it the element, [Aug 491-20
FILII. O juventes, O filii, he contemplates [Someone 83-1 A
FILL. Fill your black hull [Fabliau 23-12
  They fill the terrace of his capitol. [Canna 55-3
  Should fill the vigil of a negress [Virgin 71-8
  And fill the hill and fill it full [Snow Stars 133-11
  Of this dead mass and that. The wind might fill [Dames 206-8
  Cover the sea with the sand rose. Fill [Vari 234-14
  And fill the foliage with arrested peace, [Cred 373-11
  These external regions, what do we fill them with [NSF 405-7
  The blueness of the half-night, fill the air [Red Kit 31-23 P
  There sleep and waking fill with jaguar-men [Greenest 55-2 P
  To fill, the grindstone of antiquest time, [Bship 80-2 P
  Fill it and return. [Three 130-1 P
  And fill the earth with young men centuries old [Ideal 88-11 A
FILLED. Filled with yellow light. [Six Sig 74-16
  Its hair filled [Six Sig 74-19
  Icicles filled the long window [Thirteen 93-12
  Filled its encrusted fountains, they arrayed [Havana 142-20
  I stood and sang and filled the air. [Country 207-7
  To be askew. And space is filled with his [EM 318-7

Filled with expressible bliss, in which I have [NSF 404-24
  The theatre is filled with flying birds, [AA 416-16
  Always in emptiness that would be filled, [NH 467-13
  It filled my doorway, [Three 128-10 P
  See: bronze-filled; space-filled; sun-filled.
FILLETED. Filleted angels over flapping ears, [Greenest 56-7 P
FILLING. Filling the imagination's need. [Dezem 218-16
  Filling the mind. [Burghers 362-10
FILLS. Fills the high hall with shuffling men [MBG 171-13
  You become a self that fills the four corners of night. [Rabbit
    K 209-19
  The windows are open. The sunlight fills [Peaches 224-16
  An acid sunlight fills the halls. [Contra I 267-2
  The purpose of the poem, fills the room. [AA 413-5
  It fills the being before the mind can think. [John 436-17
  In the space it fills, the silent motioner [Ideal 88-6 A
FINAL. Of one vast, subjugating, final tone. [C 30-9
  Through all its purples to the final slate, [Pharynx 96-11
  Nothing is final, he chants. No man shall see the end. [Nigger
    150-13
  The final mercy and the final loss, [Nigger 152-6
  Perceived in a final atmosphere; [MBG 168-2
  For a moment final, in the way [MBG 168-3
  The thinking of art seems final when [MBG 168-4
  A few final solutions, like a duet [MBG 177-7
  In the clouds serene and final, next [MBG 177-14
  The grunted breath serene and final, [MBG 177-15
  Time in its final block, not time [MBG 183-18
  It is all that you are, the final dwarf of you, [Dwarf 208-9
  This is the mute, the final sculpture [Yellow 236-9
  After the final no there comes a yes [Beard 247-9
  Of final belief. So, say that final belief [Oboe 250-7
  We live in a camp . . . Stanzas of final peace [Extracts 258-22
  Any mortal end. The chants of final peace [Extracts 259-6
  We live. Thence come the final chants, the chants [Extracts
    259-13
  He wanted and looked for a final refuge, [Contra II 270-7
  In the first canto of the final canticle, [Hand 271-1
  In the first canto of the final canticle, [Hand 271-8
  In the first canto of the final canticle. [Hand 271-16
  Bad is final in this light. [Possum 293-16
  This is the final Projection, C. [Couch 295-21
  Held off the final, fatal distances, [Wild 329-11
  The need of its element, the final need [Pure 333-4
  Of final access to its element-- [Pure 333-5
  He is the final builder of the total building, [Sketch 335-17
  The final dreamer of the total dream, [Sketch 335-18
  All final, colors subjected in revery [Descrip 342-16
  Propounds blank final music. [Burghers 362-18
  It is the final mountain. Here the sun, [Cred 373-23
  The final elegance, not to console [NSF 389-11
  Suggested that, at the final funeral, [NSF 391-11
  Clothe me entire in the final filament, [NSF 396-7
  A thing final in itself and, therefore, good: [NSF 405-19
  One of the vast repetitions final in [NSF 405-20
  Until merely going round is a final good, [NSF 405-23
  The negations are never final. The father sits [AA 414-5
  Always, in brilliance, fatal, final, formed [Owl 434-23
  The roundness that pulls tight the final ring [Orb 442-8
  And final. This is the centre. The poet is [Papini 448-1
  There was an end at which in a final change, [Our Stars 455-22
  The final relation, the marriage of the rest. [Study II 465-3
  These are the edgings and inchings of final form, [NH 488-16
  And her belt, the final fortune of their desire. [World 521-9
  "Final Soliloquy of the Interior Paramour" [524-title
  The honey in its pulp, the final found, [Rock 527-14
  Their purports to a final seriousness-- [Armor 530-6
  Final for him, the acceptance of such prose, [Armor 530-7
  And that, then, is my final aphorism. [Soldat 11-3 P
  The final pulse of blood from this good heart [Soldat 11-11 P
  The final theft? That you are innocent [Red Kit 30-23 P
  And still the final quarter, still the rim, [Spaniard 34-9 P
  Fateful Ananke is the final god. [Greenest 59-20 P
  As the final simplification is meant to be. [Bship 78-30 P
  With its final force, a thing invincible [Bship 79-11 P
  To the final full, an end without rhetoric. [Bship 81-11 P
  A challenge to a final solution. [Stan Hero 84-28 P
  Is it experience, say, the final form [Recit 87-4 P
  That which is human and yet final, like [Americana 94-6 P
  Than they are in the final finding of the air, in the thing
    [Course 97-2 P
  Are a final construction, [Fare Guit 99-7 P
  The beginning of a final order, [Ulysses 101-12 P
  And final effulgence and delving show. [Ulysses 104-9 P
  Thinkers without final thoughts [July 115-2 P
  Much choosing is the final choice made up, [Ideal 88-18 A
FINALE. Let be be finale of seem. [Emperor 64-7
FINALITY. A turning down toward finality-- [Plant 506-15
FINALLY. Of chance. Finally, the most solemn burial [Paisant 334-15
  And on, at night, exploding finally [Liadoff 346-6

Finally, in the last year of her age, [Past Nun 378-11
These lights may finally attain a pole [AA 411-14
The finally human, [Leben 504-20
From his project, as finally magnified. [Two Illus 515-4
And, finally, set guardians in the grounds, [Archi 18-9 P
And then, finally, it is you that say [Conversat 109-11 P
FIND. To make oblation fit. Where shall I find [Monocle 16-21
But Crispin was too destitute to find [C 30-22
That's better. That's worth crossing seas to find. [C 36-25
To find whatever it is they seek? Or does [Heaven 56-15
Shall she not find in comforts of the sun, [Sunday 67-15
They never find, the same receding shores [Sunday 69-18
I find that I am much taller, [Six Sig 74-6
To make him return to people, to find among them [Nigger 158-7
In what crevice do you find [Bagatelles 213-13
Cut summer down to find the honey-comb. [Blue Bldg 217-21
Who, to find what will suffice, [Bottle 238-18
As the mind, to find what will suffice, destroys [Bottle 239-15
To find: the scene was set; it repeated what [Of Mod 239-19
And it has to find what will suffice. It has [Of Mod 240-4
He is and in his poems we find peace. [Oboe 251-2
Find peace? We found the sum of men. We found, [Oboe 251-11
This inability to find a sound, [Extracts 256-13
And there to find music for a single line, [Extracts 259-16
His manner took what it could find, [News 264-16
It is the route that milky millions find, [Repet 307-17
He find another? The giant of sense remains [Repet 308-9
To find for himself his earth, his sky, his sea. [Holiday 312-12
Could be borne, as if we were sure to find our way. [EM 316-6
And, therefore, aquiline pedants find [Prejudice 369-4
Nor made of itself that which it could not find . . . [Cred 376-8
Find a deep echo in a horn and buzz [NSF 390-17
To find of sound the bleakest ancestor, [NSF 398-17
To find of light a music issuing [NSF 398-18
To discover winter and know it well, to find, [NSF 404-1
Warmed by a desperate milk. To find the real, [NSF 404-8
How is it I find you in difference, see you there [NSF 406-8
In the midmost midnight and find the serpent there, [AA 411-15
And shape and mournful making move to find [AA 418-1
Is more difficult to find than the way beyond it. [Papini 446-6
Searched out such majesty as it could find. [NH 469-3
And to find how much that really matters [Mandolin 29-8 P
He well might find that eager balm [Room Gard 41-10 P
He well might find it in this fret [Room Gard 41-13 P
Where shall we find more than derisive words? [Duck 66-9 P
They find her in the crackling summer night, [Woman Had 83-4 P
To find poetry, [Three 127-2 P
I could find it without, [Three 127-4 P
Do find a melon for me [Three 128-14 P
And find a new thing [Three 142-9 P
FINDING. The poem of the mind in the act of finding [Of Mod 239-17
Be the finding of a satisfaction, and may [Of Mod 240-20
Finding its way from the house, makes music seem [Phenom 287-1
On the expressive tongue, the finding fang. [AA 420-10
This fortune's finding, disposed and re-disposed [Orb 440-7
In so much misery; and yet finding it [Rome 509-23
Than they are in the final finding of the air, in the thing
  [Course 97-2 P
FINDS. A torrent will fall from him when he finds. [Monocle 13-15
Is it a philosopher's honeymoon, one finds [Dump 203-5
The sun steps into, regards and finds itself; [Golden 460-11
A man that looks at himself in a glass and finds [Americana 94-7P
Finds itself in seclusion, [Three 131-10 P
FINE. "Extracts from Addresses to the Academy of Fine Ideas" [252-
  title
Poured forth the fine fins, the gawky beaks, the personalia,
  [Somnam 304-17
Flickings from finikin to fine finikin [NH 488-13
And walked in fine clothes, [Parasol 20-13 P
See fickle-fine.
FINED. Nor fined for the inhibited instruments [C 35-20
FINER. Of the still finer, more implacable chords. [Anatomy 108-14
FINGER. And, finger after finger, here, the hand, [Worms 49-21
The weight we lift with the finger of a dream, [NH 476-12
A finger with a ring to guide his eye [Aug 492-10
At the finger that brushes this aside [Ulysses 101-1 P
FINGERS. Just as my fingers on these keys [Peter 89-16
Her fingers touch the ground. [Add 199-4
Spurted from between the fingers [Weak Mind 212-3
The tongue, the fingers, and the nose [Arcades 225-17
The golden fingers picking dark-blue air: [NSF 398-15
And cried out to feel it again, have run fingers over leaves
  [Large 424-2
Rather rings than fingers, rather fingers than hands. [Grotesque
  74-8 P
FINGER-TIPS. And ending at the finger-tips. . . . It is death
  [Extracts 253-22
FINIAL. The thick strings stutter the finial gutterals. [Madame
  507-10
FINICAL. And his finical carriers tread, [Cortege 79-14

FINIKIN. Poetry is a finikin thing of air [Nigger 155-17
The finikin spectres in the memory, [Repet 307-12
The rudiments in the jar, farced, finikin, [Bouquet 452-13
Flickings from finikin to fine finikin [NH 488-13
FINISHED. I have finished my combat with the sun; [Joost 46-14
The reader by the window has finished his book [Pure 330-2
FINNED. The finned flutterings and gaspings of the ice, [Page
  422-8
See big-finned.
FINS. Poured forth the fine fins, the gawky beaks, the personalia,
  [Somnam 304-17
FIORI. The mille fiori of vestments, [Winter B 141-6
FIRE. At night, by the fire, [Domination 8-7
Turned in the fire, [Domination 9-7
Turned in the loud fire, [Domination 9-9
of my being, shine like fire, that mirrors nothing. [Nuances
  18-10
For Crispin, fagot in the lunar fire, [C 33-20
That savage of fire, [Gubbinal 85-9
And flame and summer and sweet fire, no thread [Fictive 87-10
To seek a sun of fuller fire. [How Live 125-16
Beneath the rhapsodies of fire and fire, [Eve Angels 138-3
His beard is of fire and his staff is a leaping flame. [Nigger
  150-14
Oxidia is the soot of fire, [MBG 182-7
Of those for whom a square room is a fire, [Parochial 191-13
Comes up as the sun, bull fire, [Add 198-20
The fire eye in the clouds survives the gods. [Sleight 222-12
Flying like insects of fire in a cavern of night, [Horn 230-18
Is to fire. And her mainmast tapered to nothing, [Vari 235-21
The ever-breathing and moving, the constant fire, [Martial 238-9
Or shapely fire: fire from an underworld, [Choc 297-22
In solid fire the utmost earth and know [EM 314-12
And ex-bar's flower and fire of the festivals [EM 317-27
Lighting the martyrs of logic with white fire. [EM 325-16
There remained the smoke of the villages. Their fire [Wild 329-5
Come true, a point in the fire of music where [Descrip 341-9
In pantaloons of fire and of women hatched, [Liadoff 346-9
Than green, fidgets of all-related fire. [Pieces 352-4
And fire and air and things not discomposed [Two V 355-9
And shapes of fire, and wind that bears them down. [Two V 355-12
Let's see it with the hottest fire of sight. [Cred 373-4
A voluminous master folded in his fire. [NSF 381-3
The color of ice and fire and solitude. [AA 413-3
Master O master seated by the fire [AA 414-12
To its opal elements and fire's delight, [AA 416-12
So blau, so blau . . . Hans listened by the fire. [Page 421-14
The wet weed sputtered, the fire died down, the cold [Page 422-1
A diamond jubilance beyond the fire, [Owl 433-21
And of a father bearded in his fire. [Celle 438-20
With every prodigal, familiar fire, [Orb 442-18
He is sitting by the fidgets of a fire, [Novel 457-13
The fire burns as the novel taught it how. [Novel 458-3
It blows a glassy brightness on the fire [Novel 458-6
The fire falls a little and the book is done. [Novel 458-17
Its fire fails to pierce the vision that beholds it, [Questions
  462-7
From fire and be part only of that of which [Rome 509-7
Fire is the symbol: the celestial possible. [Rome 509-8
Part of the speculum of fire on its prow, its symbol, whatever
  it was, [Prol 516-2
A form of fire approaches the cretonnes of Penelope, [World
  520-15
Can I take fire from so benign an ash? [Stan MMO 19-7 P
And chant the January fire [An Gaiety 33-6 P
Shines without fire on columns intercrossed, [Burnshaw 49-12 P
A dewy flashing blanks away from fire, [Burnshaw 51-23 P
Wind-beaten into freshest, brightest fire. [Burnshaw 52-22 P
And its immaculate fire, the middle dome, [Greenest 54-16 P
Its surfaces came from distant fire; and it [Greenest 57-2 P
As evils, and if reason, fatuous fire, [Duck 63-4 P
When shall lush chorals spiral through our fire [Duck 66-10 P
Strike fire, but the part is the equal of the whole, [Bship
  79-29 P
Like glitter ascended into fire. [Ulysses 102-17 P
See: drift-fire; far-fire; father-fire.
FIRE-BALLS. Full of javelins and old fire-balls, [Dezem 218-3
FIRECAT. A firecat bristled in the way. [Earthy 3-3
Because of the firecat. [Earthy 3-9
Because of the firecat. [Earthy 3-13
The firecat went leaping, [Earthy 3-15
Later, the firecat closed his bright eyes [Earthy 3-19
FIRED. The word respected, fired ten thousand guns [Bship 78-12 P
FIRE-FANGLED. The bird's fire-fangled feathers dangle down. [Of
  Mere 118-6 P
FIRE-FEINTING. To watch the fire-feinting sea and calls it good,
  [EM 324-15
FIREFLIES. Among fireflies. [Gray 140-4
FIREFLY. For me, the firefly's quick, electric stroke [Monocle 15-1
FIRE-FOAMS. When day comes, fire-foams in the motions of the sea,

[NH 488-12
FIRE-MONSTERS. Fire-monsters in the Milky Brain [Pure 331-title 3
FIRES. On The Masculine one asserts and fires the guns. [Bship
      80-7 P
FIRESIDE. Leaps quickly from the fireside and is gone. [Montra
      264-6
FIRE-WIND. Begat the tubas and the fire-wind strings, [NSF 398-14
FIRM. One only, one thing that was firm, even [Beard 247-14
      His firm stanzas hang like hives in hell [EM 315-11
      Less firm than the paternal flame, [Red Fern 365-6
FIRMAMENT. Is beyond us, as the firmament, [Curtains 62-8
      The buzzing world and lisping firmament. [Descrip 345-8
FIRMLY. The stalks are firmly rooted in ice. [Possum 294-8
FIRST. In the pale nights, when your first imagery [Monocle 15-5
      To that first, foremost law. Anguishing hour! [Monocle 17-13
      The first white wall of the village [Magnifico 19-18
      The first white wall of the village . . . [Magnifico 19-22
      Which was, and is, chief motive, first delight, [C 34-28
      Of his first central hymns, the celebrants [C 37-12
      That first drove Crispin to his wandering. [C 39-13
      He first, as realist, admitted that [C 40-26
      Was unforeseen. First Crispin smiled upon [C 44-10
      Most sisterly to the first, not yet awake [C 44-17
      Of Phoebus Apothicaire the first beatitude: [NE Verses 105-3
      Of the soul must likewise be at fault, and first. [Lions 124-20
      It was when the trees were leafless first in November [Nigger
      151-1
      And their blackness became apparent, that one first [Nigger 151-2
      First one beam, then another, then [MBG 172-9
      Stretch themselves to rest in their first summer's sun,
      [Parochial 191-20
      Where was it one first heard of the truth? The the. [Dump 203-11
      As a young lover sees the first buds of spring [Peaches 224-5
      Crowned with the first, cold buds. On these we live, [Cuisine
      228-11
      First, summer, then a lesser time, [Vase 246-23
      It had been cold since December. Snow fell, first, [Extracts
      255-1
      In the first canto of the final canticle, [Hand 271-1
      In the first canto of the final canticle, [Hand 271-8
      In the first canto of the final canticle. [Hand 271-16
      First sees reality. The mortal no [EM 320-8
      In a kind of total affluence, all first, [Descrip 342-15
      The early constellations, from which came the first [Myrrh 350-7
      Things floating like the first hundred flakes of snow [Men Car
      351-3
      My Jacomyntje! This first spring after the war, [Extraord 369-16
      To the first autumnal inhalations, young broods [Cred 372-6
      That sends us back to the first idea, the quick [NSF 381-17
      The truth itself, the first idea becomes [NSF 381-20
      May there be an ennui of the first idea? [NSF 381-23
      For a moment, the first idea . . . It satisfies [NSF 382-14
      The first idea was not our own. Adam [NSF 383-10
      But the first idea was not to shape the clouds [NSF 383-17
      Against the first idea--to lash the lion, [NSF 385-2
      First fruits, without the virginal of birds, [NSF 385-10
      A thinker of the first idea. Perhaps [NSF 386-2
      The first idea is an imagined thing. [NSF 387-1
      About the thinker of the first idea, [NSF 387-11
      Of an earth in which the first leaf is the tale [NSF 394-14
      Seeming, at first, a beast disgorged, unlike, [NSF 404-7
      Now, the first tutoyers of tragedy [Beginning 428-7
      Of yellow as first color and of white, [Roses 431-1
      And the first flowers upon it, an alphabet [Owl 434-16
      Out of the first warmth of spring, [Celle 438-1
      The first red of red winter, winter-red, [Novel 457-14
      A second that grows first, a black unreal [Novel 458-14
      Twelve and the first gray second after, a kind [What We 459-16
      Unless a second giant kills the first-- [NH 465-14
      There was a clearing, a readiness for first bells, [NH 483-1
      The way some first thing coming into Northern trees [Prol 517-6
      Or these--escent--issant pre-personae: first fly, [Slug 522-11
      Light the first light of evening, as in a room [Final 524-1
      The first car out of a tunnel en voyage [Armor 530-2
      Of what one sees, the purpose that comes first, [Moonlight 531-7
      Before one comes to the first black cataracts [R Conn 533-5
      The choir that choirs the first fatigue in deep bell of canzoni?
      [Inelegance 25-20 P
      The rotting man was first to sing. [Sat Night 28-12 P
      First. The grand simplifications reduce [Bship 78-23 P
      The first and second rules are reconciled [Bship 80-13 P
      And the first line spreading up the beach; again, [Woman Had
      81-14 P
      And the first line foaming over the sand; again, [Woman Had
      81-16 P
      The rising and the swell, the first line's glitter, [Woman Had
      81-17 P
      "First Warmth" [89-title P
      Like taste distasting the first fruit of a vine, [Theatre 91-3 P
      In the first inch of night, the stellar summering [Pagoda 92-3 P

The first soothsayers of the land, the man [Americana 93-15 P
      Flaunts that first fortune, which he wanted so much. [Americana
      94-15 P
      One thinks that it could be that the first word spoken, [Discov
      95-17 P
      One thinks, when the houses of New England catch the first sun,
      [Discov 95-21 P
      The first word would be of the susceptible being arrived,
      [Discov 96-1 P
      Trouble in the spillage and first sparkle of the sun, [How Now
      97-7 P
      The first eloping footfall [Three 136-2 P
FIRST-FOUND. But on the first-found weed [Paltry 5-8
FIR-TREES. Sombre as fir-trees, liquid cats [MBG 178-13
FISCS. Exchequering from piebald fiscs unkeyed. [C 43-7
FISH. The fish are in the fishman's window, [Nigger 154-7
      Item: The green fish pensive in green reeds [Montra 263-20
FISH-EGGS. As small as fish-eggs. [Plot Giant 7-1
FISHERMAN. In the one ear of the fisherman, who is all [Think
      356-9
      Of waterish spears. The fisherman is all [Think 356-13
      There is one dove, one bass, one fisherman. [Think 356-15
      The fisherman might be the single man [Think 357-5
FISHES. By this light the salty fishes [Homunculus 26-1
      The movements of fishes. [Homunculus 26-8
      That turn into fishes and leap [Vari 232-13
      Of the fishes of the sea, the colored [Hero 277-28
      The sea full of fishes in shoals, the woods that let [Cats 367-13
      See half-fishes.
FISHING. Fishing for crayfish . . . [Venereal 47-16
      The lights in the fishing boats at anchor there, [Key W 130-6
FISHMAN. The fish are in the fishman's window, [Nigger 154-7
FISH-SCALE. "A Fish-Scale Sunrise" [160-title
FISHY. Down to the fishy sea. [Pascagoula 126-16
FIT. To make oblation fit. Where shall I find [Monocle 16-21
      The dulcet omen fit for such a house. [C 44-26
      Fit for a kinky clan. [Pascagoula 126-18
      His rarities are ours: may they be fit [Havana 144-19
      Abortion, fit for the enchanting of basilisks. [Duck 63-1 P
      Fit for keyholes. [Three 138-12 P
FITFUL. The fitful tracing of a portal; [Peter 91-23
      These fitful sayings are, also, of tragedy: [NH 478-1
      Where Time, in fitful turns, [Phases 5-21 P
FITFUL-FANGLED. These Gaeled and fitful-fangled darknesses [Our
      Stars 455-18
FITTED. Fitted by men and horses [Polo 37-17 P
FIVE. Ideas or, say, five men or, possibly, six. [Extracts 255-28
      The sum of five, the sum of six, [Song Fixed 520-1
      "Five Grotesque Pieces [74-title P
      Meyer has my five senses. I have his. [Grotesque 76-10 P
      Not one of the five, and keep a rendezvous, [Souls 95-5 P
FIVE-SIX. From five-six cornered leaves, and green, the signal
      [NH 470-20
FIVE-TIMES-SENSED. Distance between me and the five-times-sensed,
      [Souls 94-19 P
FIX. The touch. Fix quiet. Take the place [Prelude 195-19
      And pierces the physical fix of things. [Red Fern 365-16
      Fix it in an eternal foliage [Cred 373-10
      Eyes open and fix on us in every sky. [AA 411-3
      Let us fix portals, east and west, [Archi 17-27 P
      And he shall fix the place where it will stand. [Greenest 60-2 P
FIXED. For this, musician, in your girdle fixed [Fictive 88-14
      Stand in a fixed light. [Gray 140-7
      At least the number of people may thus be fixed. [Nigger 157-10
      And yet are fixed as a photograph, [MBG 180-13
      Here, for the lark fixed in the mind, [MBG 182-17
      To an order, most Plantagenet, most fixed . . . [Connois 216-8
      On the ground, fixed fast in a profound defeat. [Martial 238-2
      And of the brooding mind, fixed by for a slight [Choc 297-17
      That Which Cannot Be Fixed [Two V 353-title 1
      Once more he turned to that which could not be fixed. [Two V
      353-11
      That cannot now be fixed. Only there is [Two V 354-10
      Fixed like a lake on which the wilk ducks fluttered, [Cata 424-13
      If we were ever, just once, at the middle, fixed [Ulti 430-5
      As in an enchantment, analyzed and fixed [Papini 447-20
      Life fixed him, wandering on the stair of glass, [NH 483-10
      "Song of Fixed Accord" [519-title
      Like a fixed heaven, [Song Fixed 520-5
      Fixed one for good in geranium-colored day. [Armor 529-4
      Not fixed and deadly (like a curving line [Abnormal 23-17 P
      A mood that had become so fixed it was [Old Woman 45-12 P
      The figure of the wise man fixed in sense. [Recit 86-17 P
      With nothing fixed by a single word. [Banjo 114-12 P
FIXES. Fixes itself in its inevitable bush . . . [Conversat 108-15 P
FIXING. Fixing emblazoned zones and fiery poles, [Key W 130-9
FLAG. As the flag above the old café-- [Hibiscus 23-2
      And you, my semblables--the old flag of Holland [Dutch 290-13
      From everything, flying the flag of the nude, [Pure 330-21
      The flag of the nude above the holiday hotel. [Pure 331-1

FLAGELLANTS. Your disaffected flagellants, well-stuffed, [High-
Toned 59-15
FLAG-POLES. On the flag-poles in a red-blue dazzle, whack [NSF
390-23
FLAGS. He caught the flags and the picket-lines [News 264-11
The flags are natures newly found. [Dutch 291-1
FLAIL. Or swipling flail, sun-black in the sun, [Soldat 16-2 P
FLAKES. Forms, flames, and the flakes of flames. [Nomad 95-19
Things floating like the first hundred flakes of snow [Man Car
351-3
The dazzled flakes and splinters disappear. [Golden 460-17
FLAMBEAUED. In an old, frizzled, flambeaued manner, [Jasmine 79-5
FLAME. And flame and summer and sweet fire, no thread [Fictive
87-10
Anon, their lamps' uplifted flame [Peter 91-18
His beard is of fire and his staff is a leaping flame. [Nigger
150-14
Of less degree than flame and lesser shine. [Choc 297-23
The tinsel of August falling was like a flame [Pieces 352-2
Less firm than the paternal flame, [Red Fern 365-6
Of flame on the line, with a second wheel below, [Page 422-23
Flame, sound, fury composed . . . Hear what he says, [Puel
456-17
And makes flame flame and makes it bite the wood [Novel 458-7
Yet lord, a mask of flame, the sprawling form [Sombre 70-16 P
FLAMED. His place is large and high, an ether flamed [Greenest
59-31 P
FLAME-FREAKED. They that had left the flame-freaked sun [How
Live 125-15
FLAMES. Turning as the flames [Domination 9-6
Forms, flames, and the flakes of flames. [Nomad 95-19
It is shaken now. It will burst into flames, [Nightgown 214-19
Than bad angels leap from heaven to hell in flames. [AA 414-12
On flames. The scholar of one candle sees [AA 417-1
In a storm blown into glittering shapes, and flames [Burnshaw
52-21 P
FLAMING. Rose up besprent and sought the flaming red [Hibiscus
22-20
FLAMINGOES. Tuck, tuck, while the flamingoes flapped his bays.
[C 38-20
FLANKS. On the flanks of horses, [Polo 38-4 P
FLAP. Flap green ears in the heat. He might observe [Landsc 243-5
FLAPPED. Tuck, tuck, while the flamingoes flapped his bays. [C 38-20
FLAPPING. So that the flapping of wind around me here [Choc 299-2
In a flapping cloak. She walked along the paths [Old Woman 44-2 P
Filleted angels over flapping ears, [Greenest 56-7 P
FLARE. The feathers flare [Ploughing 20-7
To flare, in the sun-pallor of his rock. [Bird Claws 82-18
Touched suddenly by the universal flare [Pure 333-7
And flare and Bloom with his vast accumulation [Anach 366-14
A vital, linear ambiance. The flare [Pastor 379-12
In the light-bound space of the mind, the floreate flare . . .
[Owl 436-6
See half-flare.
FLARING. An arctic effulgence flaring on the frame [AA 417-2
FLASH. Hangs heaven with flash drapery. Sight [Hero 274-12
Steel against intimation--the sharp flash, [Motive 288-19
Or light embodied, or almost, a flash [Choc 297-11
The assassin flash and rumble . . . He was denied. [EM 320-1
They throw around their shoulders cloaks that flash [AA 419-23
And death cries quickly, in a flash of voice, [Owl 432-13
Would flash in air, and the muscular bodies thrust [Old Woman
46-9 P
FLASHED. That had flashed (like vicious music that ends [Thunder
220-11
And moved again and flashed again, time flashed again. [Martial
238-16
Of an imagination flashed with irony [Greenest 56-16 P
Than the horses quivering to be gone, flashed through [Duck 64-9P
FLASHIER. Flashier fruits! A flip for the sun and moon, [Grapes
110-17
FLASHING. Accomplished in the immensely flashing East, [Eve Angels
137-22
Without diamond--blazons or flashing or [Pediment 361-11
Of sapphires flashing from the central sky, [Cred 375-24
Skin flashing to wished-for disappearances [AA 411-11
And the serpent body flashing without the skin. [AA 411-12
Flashing and flashing in the sun. On its banks, [R Conn 533-9
A dewy flashing blanks away from fire, [Burnshaw 51-23 P
FLASHY. If the flashy extravaganzas of the lean [Sombre 69-14 P
FLAT. I shall not play the flat historic scale. [Monocle 14-4
The bills of the swans are flat upon the ground. [Havana 142-10
The swans . . . Before the bills of the swans fell flat [Havana
142-13
The earth, for us, is flat and bare. [MBG 167-9
They are not flat surfaces [Pears 196-9
Spreading them as waves spread flat on the shore, [Loaf 200-6
A black line drawn on flat air. [Common 221-5
Low tide, flat water, sultry sun. [Vari 235-13
In flat appearance we should be and be, [Descrip 340-15

Flat and pale and gory! [Phases 3-18 P
Fell, famous and flat, [Coroner 29-20 P
FLATLY. Of hardy foam, receding flatly, spread [C 34-6
That I should name you flatly, waste no words, [NSF 406-13
Are flatly there, unversed except to be, [Bouquet 452-14
FLATNESS. Of ocean, which in sinister flatness lay. [Sea Surf 99-22
Slowly submerging in flatness disappeared. [Old Woman 45-5 P
FLAT-RIBBED. Flat-ribbed and big-bagged. [Orangeade 102-19
FLAUNTING. Trinket pasticcio, flaunting skyey sheets, [C 40-1
FLAUNTINGS. And the green flauntings of the hours of peace
[Pastor 380-3
FLAUNTS. Flaunts that first fortune, which he wanted so much.
[Americana 94-15 P
FLAW. The central flaw in the solar morn. [Thought 187-8
It implies a flaw in the battleship, a defeat [Bship 79-15 P
FLAWED. Lies in flawed words and stubborn sounds. [Poems Clim
194-10
The flawed jars, [Three 131-27 P
FLAXEN. Then third, a thing still flaxen in the light, [C 44-20
FLEA. Syringa, cicada, his flea. [Thought 186-20
FLEAS. The lutanist of fleas, the knave, the thane, [C 28-7
FLECK. And wearing hats of angular flick and fleck, [Bouquet 449-8
FLECKED. Black beaded on the rock, the flecked animal, [AA 412-2
He never felt twice the same about the flecked river, [Cata
424-10
See flock-flecked.
FLED. Fled, with a noise like tambourines. [Peter 91-21
In an enormous undulation fled. [Sea Surf 100-9
The swans fled outward to remoter reaches, [Descrip 343-7
Left here by moonlit muckers when they fled [Burnshaw 46-22 P
FLEDGLING. Drawn close by dreams of fledgling wing, [Babies 77-11
FLEET. Not an intellect in which we are fleet: present [Ulti 430-2
FLESH. I saw you then, as warm as flesh, [Vincentine 52-16
To the flesh and bones of you [Tattoo 81-17
Of flesh and air. [Motion 83-9
But in the flesh it is immortal. [Peter 91-24
The flesh, the bone, the dirt, the stone. [MBG 176-14
Flesh on the bones. The skeleton throwing [Hero 278-15
Both substance and non-substance, luminous flesh [Choc 297-21
Who killed him, sticking feathers in his flesh [Good Man 364-9
And quickly understand, without their flesh, [Cats 368-9
Of the land's children, easily born, its flesh, [Cred 375-4
Changed his true flesh to an inhuman bronze. [NSF 391-19
She too is flesh, [Cab 21-6 P
From size, backs larger than the eye, not flesh [Sombre 70-23 P
Was what she was and flesh, sure enough, but airs; [Grotesque
74-7 P
FLETRIE. Scène Flétrie [NE Verses 106-title 15
FLEURETTES. The youngest, the still fuzz-eyed, odd fleurettes,
[Nuns 92-9 P
FLEURIE. Scène Fleurie [NE Verses 106-title 16
FLEURS. Livre de Toutes Sortes de Fleurs d'après Nature. [EM 316-7
FLEW. Just as they flew from the boughs of the hemlocks [Domination
8-22
When the blackbird flew out of sight, [Thirteen 94-6
The garden flew round with the angel, [Circulat 149-16
The angel flew round with the clouds, [Circulat 149-17
And the clouds flew round and the clouds flew round [Circulat
149-18
And the clouds flew round with the clouds. [Circulat 149-19
The little owl flew through the night, [Adequacy 243-9
Her hair fell on him and the mi-bird flew [Hand 271-18
Flew close to, flew to without rising away. [God 285-8
Straight to the utmost crown of night he flew. [NSF 403-8
FLICK. Hi! Whisk it, poodle, flick the spray [Hartford 227-10
False flick, false form, but falseness close to kin. [NSF 385-18
And wearing hats of angular flick and fleck, [Bouquet 449-8
The smallest lamp, which added its puissant flick, to which he
gave [Prol 517-3
A flick which added to what was real and its vocabulary, [Prol
517-5
FLICKED. Flicked into pieces, points of air, [Vase 246-20
Until flicked by feeling, in a gildered street, [NSF 407-1
FLICKER. See salt-flicker.
FLICKERING. While the sultriest fulgurations, flickering,
[EM 313-15
The mobile and the immobile flickering [NH 474-1
FLICKING. And lion-men and the flicking serpent-kin [Greenest 55-3P
FLICKINGS. Flickings from finikin to fine finikin [NH 488-13
FLICKS. Glozing his life with after-shining flicks, [C 46-5
FLIES. The soul, O ganders, flies beyond the parks [Swans 4-1
And the soul, O ganders, being lonely, flies [Swans 4-11
A red bird flies across the golden floor. [Monocle 13-12
Like a buzzing of flies in autumn air, [MBG 166-20
Is a weed and all the flies are caught, [MBG 171-6
The noble, Alexandrine verve. The flies [Contra II 270-17
Flies like a bat expanding as it flies, [Pure 332-21
In a repetitiousness of men and flies. [Plain 502-20
See night-flies.
FLIGHT. Grown tired of flight. Like a dark rabbi, I [Monocle 17-21

Made pallid flitter. Crispin, here, took flight. [C 32-27
The vulgar, as his theme and hymn and flight, [C 35-2
At which the flight began, [Pascagoula 126-20
Grows warm in the motionless motion of his flight, [NSF 404-19
Men gathering for a mighty flight of men, [Burnshaw 51-8 P
The flight of emblemata through his mind, [Sombre 71-18 P
FLIGHTS. Related in romance to backward flights, [C 39-10
One's grand flights, one's Sunday baths, [Sleight 222-1
In the centre of its cones, the resplendent flights [Cats 367-17
In flights of eye and ear, the highest eye [AA 414-16
As they climb the flights [Archi 17-11 P
The flights through space, changing habitudes. [Ulysses 103-6 P
FLINCH. To meet that hawk's eye and to flinch [MBG 178-6
FLING. And this-a-way he gave a fling. [MBG 178-10
O exhalation, O fling without a sleeve [Owl 435-19
We fling ourselves, constantly longing, on this form. [NH 470-16
Weaving ring in radiant ring and quickly, fling [Burnshaw 51-14P
That we conceal? A passion to fling the cloak, [Sombre 71-26 P
FLINGING. So, in me, come flinging [Nomad 95-18
FLIP. Flashier fruits! A flip for the sun and moon, [Grapes 110-17
FLIPPANT. Say, a flippant communication under the moon. [AA 418-3
FLITTED. They flitted [Ord Women 10-15
They flitted [Ord Women 12-5
FLITTER. Made pallid flitter. Crispin, here, took flight. [C 32-27
Nothing much, a flitter that reflects itself. [Bouquet 448-13
FLITTERED. The curtains flittered and the door was closed. [C 42-4
Is cast in pandemonium, flittered, howled [Duck 62-7 P
FLITTERING. At once? Is it a luminous flittering [NSF 396-16
Alive with an enigma's flittering . . . [Ulysses 105-9 P
Alive with an enigma's flittering, [Presence 106-9 P
FLITTERINGS. Out of these gawky flitterings, [Possum 294-10
FLITTING. It became, the nameless, flitting characters-- [NH 479-22
FLOAT. To float off in the floweriest barge, [Thought 184-18
The pensive man . . . He sees that eagle float [Connois 216-13
From heaven and float in air, like animals [Study II 464-6
Caramel and would not, could not float. And yet [Duck 63-24 P
FLOATED. Basilewsky's bulged before it floated, turned [Duck 63-23P
FLOATING. Of trombones floating in the trees. [Havana 143-3
Things floating like the first hundred flakes of snow [Man Car
  351-3
It was passing a boundary, floating without a head [Lot 371-16
It is a theatre floating through the clouds, [AA 416-4
FLOATS. She floats in air at the level of [Couch 295-4
Idea. She floats in the contention, the flux [Couch 295-18
With a tendency to bulge as it floats away. [Duck 63-22 P
FLOCK. They pied and chuckled like a flock, [Sat Night 28-10 P
FLOCK-FLECKED. That is the flock-flecked river, the water, [Degen
  444-17
FLOCKING. A majestic mother's flocking brood, [Ulysses 103-25 P
FLOCKS. At evening, casual flocks of pigeons make [Sunday 70-26
And still the birds came, came in watery flocks, [Loaf 200-14
Look backward. Let your swiftly-flying flocks [Red Kit 31-28 P
To momentary calm, spectacular flocks [Burnshaw 51-2 P
FLOGGED. To be flogged. [Winter B 141-2
FLOOD. Flood on flood, of our returning sun. [Medit 123-15
FLOODED. And deep winds flooded you; for these, day comes, [Duck
  61-6 P
FLOODS. As if some one lived there. Such floods of white [Sleight
  222-6
FLOOR. A red bird flies across the golden floor. [Monocle 13-12
Looking at the floor, [Six Sig 75-6
The snake has left its skin upon the floor. [Farewell 117-2
The floor. Go on through the darkness. The waves fly back.
  [Farewell 117-10
Disclosed the sea floor and the wilderness [Farewell 118-2
Is the spot on the floor, there, wine or blood [MBG 173-11
And fell to the floor. [Weak Mind 212-4
To the floor. I slept. [Weak Mind 212-15
In opal blobs along the walls and floor. [Blue Bldg 217-12
From the floor, rising in speech we do not speak. [Creat 311-18
Let him move as the sunlight moves on the floor, [Less 327-11
And throws his stars around the floor. By day [NSF 383-5
The wind is blowing the sand across the floor. [AA 412-15
The dress is lying, cast-off, on the floor. [Beginning 428-6
A pack of cards is falling toward the floor. [Bouquet 450-22
The bouquet has slopped over the edge and lies on the floor.
  [Bouquet 453-3
See water-floor.
FLOORS. Rose on the beachy floors. [Ord Women 11-20
Waken, and watch the moonlight on their floors. [Havana 145-2
No turban walks across the lessened floors. [Plain 502-16
FLORA. Flora she was once. She was florid [Oak 272-4
To the group of Flora Coddling Hecuba? [Archi 17-10 P
FLOR-ABUNDANT. Happy fecundity, flor-abundant force, [NSF 388-20
FLORAISONS. And bears its floraisons of imagery. [Ulysses 102-31 P
FLORAL. "Floral Decorations for Bananas" [53-title
FLORA LOWZEN. Flora Lowzen invigorated [Oak 272-18
FLOREAL. Her body quivering in the Floréal [Lilacs 49-10
FLOREATE. In the light-bound space of the mind, the floreate
  flare . . . [Owl 436-6

FLORED. See mille-flored.
FLORENCE. "Anglais Mort À Florence" [148-title
FLORIBUND. An anti-master-man, floribund ascetic. [Landsc 241-10
FLORID. And by will, unshaken and florid [Medit 124-4
The vivid, florid, turgid sky, [MBG 169-1
Flora she was once. She was florid [Oak 272-4
Appoints its florid messengers with wings [Greenest 57-17 P
Perennial doctrine and most florid truth; [Duck 63-10 P
FLORIDA. "Fabliau of Florida" [23-title
Planting his pristine cores in Florida, [C 38-17
"O Florida, Venereal Soil" [47-title
Florida, venereal soil, [Venereal 47-9
Be the voice of night and Florida in my ear. [Two Figures 86-1
As the immense dew of Florida [Nomad 95-6
As the immense dew of Florida [Nomad 95-10
Yet there is no spring in Florida, neither in boskage perdu, nor
  on the nunnery beaches. [Indian 112-7
"Farewell to Florida" [117-title
To go to Florida one of these days, [Winter B 141-16
Basking in desert Florida? [An Gaiety 33-4 P
FLORIDEST. And speak of the floridest reality . . . [Anach 366-7
FLORIST. The florist asking aid from cabbages, [C 37-16
FLOTILLAS. Round those flotillas. And sometimes the sea [Sea Surf
  99-14
Flotillas, willed and wanted, bearing in them [New Set 352-11
FLOURISH. Thoughts by descent. To flourish the great cloak we
  wear [Sombre 71-19 P
FLOURISHER. A shadow in the mind, a flourisher [Montra 260-10
Must bear no name, gold flourisher, but be [NSF 381-14
FLOURISHES. With fictive flourishes that preordained [C 39-17
The stalk, the weed, the grassy flourishes, [Bouquet 452-8
FLOURISHING. It was a flourishing tropic he required [C 35-16
Stood flourishing the world. The brilliant height [Owl 434-4
FLOW. How easily the feelings flow this afternoon [Nigger 151-16
In which the watery grasses flow and flow, [MBG 180-12
To come to tragic shores and flow, [Vari 233-9
The water flowing in the flow of space. [Lot 371-15
It is like a flow of meanings with no speech [Roses 431-8
Wood-smoke rises through threes, is caught in an upper flow
  [Slug 522-3
One could watch the blue sea's blueness flow [Stan MBG 73-13 P
Our good, from this the rhapsodic strophes flow, [Bship 81-5 P
FLOWED. As they flowed around [Infanta 8-5
FLOWER. That strange flower, the sun, [Gubbinal 85-1
Plato, the reddened flower, the erotic bird. [Extracts 253-29
And ex-bar's flower and fire of the festivals [EM 317-27
See melon-flower.
FLOWERIEST. To float off in the floweriest barge, [Thought 184-18
Of the floweriest flowers dewed with the dewiest dew. [Dump
  202-10
FLOWERING. Flowering over the skin. [Pears 197-2
The flowering Judas grows from the belly or not at all. [Holiday
  312-15
FLOWER-POTS. And the cheeks like flower-pots under her hair.
  [Grotesque 74-16 P
FLOWERS. Out of geraniums and unsmelled flowers. [Plot Giant 6-15
With flowers around, [Pourtraicte 21-5
Of radishes and flowers. [Pourtraicte 21-9
Of radishes and flowers." [Pourtraicte 21-19
Bring flowers in last month's newspapers. [Emperor 64-6
French flowers on it. [Explan 72-16
The sun is a corbeil of flowers the moon Blanche [Dump 201-12
Of the floweriest flowers dewed with the dewiest dew. [Dump
  202-10
If the flowers of South Africa were bright [Connois 215-5
"Woman Looking at a Vase of Flowers" [246-title
All sorts of flowers. That's the sentimentalist. [EM 316-8
Children in love with them brought early flowers [NSF 400-23
Of an infinite course. The flowers against the wall [AA 412-8
And the first flowers upon it, an alphabet [Owl 434-16
Of purple flowers, to see? The black will still [Greenest 58-32P
FLOWERY. In flowery nations, crashing and alert. [Greenest 55-4 P
FLOWING. Is like water flowing; [Sugar-Cane 12-8
Like water flowing [Sugar-Cane 12-9
A wave, interminably flowing. [Peter 92-3
Flowing above the rocks, flowing over the sky, [Loaf 200-4
The water flowing in the flow of space. [Lot 371-15
Which kept flowing and never the same way twice, flowing [Cata
  424-11
He wanted the river to go on flowing the same way, [Cata 425-3
To keep on flowing. He wanted to walk beside it, [Cata 425-4
The far-fire flowing and the dim-coned bells [NH 466-10
The mere flowing of the water is a gayety, [R Conn 533-8
Call it, once more, a river, an unnamed flowing, [R Conn 533-18
In the flowing of black water. [Primordia 7-22 P
Washed over by their green, their flowing blue. [Old Woman 45-11P
FLOWN. Already the green bird of summer has flown [Myrrh 349-15
FLOWS. Thus water flows [Six Sig 73-14
That flows round the earth and through the skies, [Degen 444-14
Upon it, as it flows ahead. [Degen 445-3

The river that flows nowhere, like a sea. [R Conn 533-21
The blunt ice flows down the Mississippi, [Primordia 8-3 P
And it flows over us without meanings, [Clear Day 113-16 P
FLUCTUATING. A fluctuating between sun and moon, [C 35-8
FLUCTUATIONS. Such fluctuations that their scrivening [Monocle
  15-12
The fluctuations of certainty, the change [NSF 395-14
Gold easings and ouncings and fluctuations of thread [NH 477-19
FLUENT. That is fluent in even the wintriest bronze. [Sleight
  222-19
I call you by name, my green, my fluent mundo. [NSF 407-2
See too-fluent.
FLUFFY. No large white horses. But there was the fluffy dog.
  [Forces 229-12
FLUID. But not quite molten, not quite the fluid thing, [Myrrh
  350-4
Lives in a fluid, not on solid rock. [Sombre 68-5 P
Were the fluid, the cat-eyed atmosphere, in which [Sombre 68-13P
FLUNG. They flung monotony behind, [Ord Women 10-17
Composed of evenings like cracked shutters flung [C 42-30
In the greenish greens he flung behind [News 264-17
Like a dancer's skirt, flung round and settling down. [Woman
  Had 81-18 P
FLUSTER. Sequestering the fluster from the year, [C 46-8
FLUTE. The flute on the gramophone, the Daimlers that [Greenest
  53-21 P
FLUTERS. The night should be warm and fluter's fortune [Nightgown
  214-15
FLUTES. And the fiddles smack, the horns yahoo, the flutes
  [Bship 79-28 P
FLUTTER. Already the butterflies flutter above the cabins.
  [Carolinas 4-14
And the banners of the nation flutter, burst [NSF 390-22
Flutter her lance with your tempestuous dust, [Spaniard 34-24 P
FLUTTERED. Her useless bracelets fondly fluttered, [Thought 184-11
Fixed like a lake on which the wild ducks fluttered, [Cata 424-13
FLUTTERING. That fluttering things have so distinct a shade.
  [Monocle 18-3
Fluttering the water [Sonatina 109-14
Like a body wholly body, fluttering [Key W 128-13
Dry Birds Are Fluttering in Blue Leaves [Pure 332-title 4
Fluttering in blue leaves, [Including 88-4 P
FLUTTERINGS. The finned flutterings and gaspings of the ice,
  [Page 422-8
FLUTTERS. A white pigeon it is, that flutters to the ground,
  [Monocle 17-20
Flutters in tiny darkness. [Dutch 290-14
He assumes the great speeds of space and flutters them [AA 414-14
FLUX. Idea. She floats in the contention, the flux [Couch 295-18
FLY. Before they fly, test the reality [Sunday 68-13
The floor. Go on through the darkness. The waves fly back.
  [Farewell 117-10
"The fly on the rose prevents us, O season [Ghosts 119-15
Birds that never fly [Gray 140-17
The little owl fly. [Adequacy 244-16
Look round, brown moon, brown bird, as you rise to fly, [God
  285-1
Fly low, cock bright, and stop on a bean pole. Let [Cred 377-6
"Looking across the Fields and Watching the Birds Fly" [517-title
Or these--escent--issant pre-personae; first fly, [Slug 522-11
Upward, from unimagined coverts, fly. [Blanche 10-12 P
Fly from the black toward the purple air. [Infernale 25-2 P
And I fly forth, the naked Proserpine. [Infernale 25-8 P
Fly upward thick in numbers, fly across [Red Kit 31-22 P
Make a sidereal splendor as you fly. [Red Kit 32-2 P
The doves will fly round. [Secret Man 36-9 P
A fly crawls on the balustrades. [Including 88-16 P
Or almost solid seem show--the way a fly bird [Conversat 108-14P
FLYER. "Flyer's Fall" [336-title
FLYING. A sheaf of brilliant arrows flying straight, [Tallap 72-7
Flying and falling straightway for their pleasure, [Tallap 72-8
Flying in a green light, [Thirteen 94-10
The blackbird must be flying. [Thirteen 94-20
The grass is in seed. The young birds are flying. [Ghosts 119-1
Flying from burning countries and brown sand shores, [Loaf 200-2
Flying like insects of fire in a cavern of night, [Horn 230-18
Say of the gulls that they are flying [Vari 232-5
From everything, flying the flag of the nude, [Pure 330-21
The theatre is filled with flying birds, [AA 416-16
The crows are flying above the foyer of summer. [Novel 457-1
The manes to his image of the flying wind, [Duck 64-17 P
The petals flying through the air. [Grotesque 75-17 P
See swiftly-flying.
FOAM. As her heels foam-- [Paltry 6-3
Foam and cloud are one. [Fabliau 23-9
Of hardy foam, receding flatly, spread [C 34-6
The darkness shattered, turbulent with foam. [Farewell 118-16
Should foam, be foamy waves, should move like them, [NSF 399-7
FOAMED. Or else whose hell, foamed with their blood [Thought 186-13
Poet, patting more nonsense foamed [Prelude 195-14

FOAMING. And the first line foaming over the sand; again, [Woman
  Had 81-16 P
FOAMS. See fire-foams.
FOAMY. Should foam, be foamy waves, should move like them, [NSF 399-7
FOBBED. The precisions of fate, nothing fobbed off, nor changed
  [Repet 310-8
FOI. C'était ma foi, la nonchalance divine. [Sea Surf 101-15
FOILS. Compact in invincible foils, from reason, [NSF 388-1
In a heaven of death. Beneath the heavy foils, [Greenest 54-21 P
FOISTS. The sea of spuming thought foists up again [Monocle 13-8
FOLD. It was because night nursed them in its fold. [Babies 77-12
With each fold sweeping in a sweeping play. [Burnshaw 51-27 P
See seventy-fold.
FOLDED. Which had lain folded against the blue [Hibiscus 22-16
He had left his robes folded in camphor [Gray 140-2
A voluminous master folded in his fire. [NSF 381-3
Of sleep, the whiteness folded into less, [Owl 433-8
But folded over, turned round." It was the same, [NH 487-4
And folded him round, [Coroner 29-21 P
Folded and fell [Coroner 29-22 P
FOLDINGS. There he saw well the foldings in the height [Owl 433-7
FOLDS. The moon is in the folds of the cloak. [Of Surface 57-8
The white folds of its gown [Six Sig 74-15
The giant body the meanings of its folds, [Owl 433-16
Vested in the serious folds of majesty, [Orb 422-21
FOLIAGE. Fix it in an eternal foliage [Cred 373-10
And fill the foliage with arrested peace, [Cred 373-11
FOLK-LAND. And happiest folk-land, mostly marriage-hymns. [Cred
  373-21
FOLK-LORE. Space-filled, reflecting the seasons, the folk-lore
  [R Conn 533-19
What man of folk-lore shall rebuild the world, [Duck 63-6 P
FOLLOW. No spring can follow past meridian. [Monocle 13-20
And that she will not follow in any word [Farewell 118-8
In a world without heaven to follow, the stops [Adieu 127-13
A yellow wine and follow a steamer's track [Landsc 243-6
No: nor divergence made too steep to follow down. [Dutch 293-12
By water washed away. They follow after. [Somnam 304-8
They follow, follow, follow, in water washed away. [Somnam 304-9
Its generations that follow in their universe, [Somnam 304-11
Speaking the phrases that follow the sight [Pediment 361-20
It does not follow that major man is man. [NSF 387-8
Follow after, O my companion, my fellow, my self, [NSF 392-23
Or stars that follow men, not to attend, [Angel 496-11
FOLLOWED. Followed the drift of the obese machine [Sea Surf 102-3
To be followed by a platter of capon! [Winter B 141-14
Victor Serge said, "I followed his argument [EM 324-24
If the sky that followed, smaller than the night, [Old Woman 45-6P
FOLLOWING. Moving around and behind, a following, [Orb 442-22
Its evening feast and the following festival, [NH 472-18
It dances down a furrow, in the early light, back of a crazy
  plough, the green blades following. [Plough-Boy 6-7 P
FOLLOWS. Health follows after health. Salvation there: [Parochial
  192-3
And cold. The moon follows the sun like a French [Vari 234-8
Of the mind, result only in disaster. It follows, [Bed 326-14
From sight, in the silence that follows her last word-- [Owl 435-21
As follows, "The Ruler of Reality, [NH 485-2
Misericordia, it follows that [NH 485-22
It follows that to change modes is to change the world [Conversat
  108-16 P
FOLLY. That has lost the folly of the moon becomes [EM 320-23
FOMENTATIONS. The yellowing fomentations of effulgence, [Attempt
  370-17
Among fomentations of black bloom and of white bloom. [Attempt
  370-18
And fragrant fomentations of the spring [Sombre 69-18 P
FOND. And fond, the total man of glubbal glub, [Choc 301-2
FONDLY. Her useless bracelets fondly fluttered, [Thought 184-11
FONS. Might call the common self, interior fons. [Choc 301-1
FONT. Came reproduced in purple, family font, [C 45-16
FONTAINEBLEAU. In the jungle is a voice in Fontainebleau. [Greenest
  59-14 P
FOOD. At a table on which the food is cold? [MBG 173-9
For food. The big bird's bony appetite [EM 318-9
FOOLS. Now in midsummer come and all fools slaughtered [Cred 372-4
FOOLSCAP. Foolscap for wigs. Academies [Prelude 195-12
FOOT. Two wooden tubs of blue hydrangeas stand at the foot of the
  stone steps. [Banal 62-11
There are men shuffling on foot in air. [Dutch 290-9
One foot approaching, one uplifted arm. [Choc 296-16
Master by foot and jaws and by the mane, [NSF 384-10
New stars that were a foot across came out [Page 421-15
To the foot of the hill. [Three 139-5 P
See: one-foot; seven-foot; slow-foot; ten-foot.
FOOTBALL. The negroes were playing football in the park. [Contra II
  270-14
FOOTED. See: many-footed; soft-footed.
FOOTFALL. The first eloping footfall [Three 136-2 P
FOOT-FALLS. Moving so that the foot-falls are slight and almost

nothing. [Jouga 337-12
FOOTING. To be the footing of noon, [Aug 495-7
FOOTINGS. The momentary footings of a climb [Someone 87-1 A
FOOTNOTES. Notations and footnotes. [Common 221-22
FOOT-NOTES. My titillations have no foot-notes [Jasmine 79-1
FOOTSTEP. Excepting to the motherly footstep, but [C 44-18
FOOT-WAYS. And on the clopping foot-ways of the moon [C 28-28
FOPPISH. Of foppish line. [W Burgher 61-13
FOPPISHNESS. Than this jotting-down of the sculptor's foppishness
    [Burnshaw 47-11 P
FOPS. The fops of fancy in their poems leave [Monocle 16-23
FORBIDDEN. And apostrophes are forbidden on the funicular.
    [Botanist 1 134-11
FORCE. Of force, the quintessential fact, the note [C 33-5
  By force of rudeness, let the principle [C 38-7
  His active force in an inactive dirge, [C 41-15
  Incapable master of all force, [Negation 97-17
  And although my mind perceives the force behind the moment,
    [Fish-Scale 161-3
  "Poetry Is a Destructive Force" [192-title
  Force is my lot and not pink-clustered [Hero 273-1
  Of this element, this force. Transfer it [Hero 277-3
  A force gathers that will cry loudlier [Dutch 291-10
  Of what was this the force? From what desire [Choc 299-6
  In which to bear with the exactest force [Repet 310-7
  This force of nature in action is the major [EM 324-8
  The force that destroys us is disclosed, within [EM 324-20
  Happy fecundity, flor-abundant force, [NSF 388-20
  The west wind was the music, the motion, the force [NSF 397-16
  They lay. Forth then with huge pathetic force [NSF 403-7
  The mind is the terriblest force in the world, father, [John
    436-10
  The world is presence and not force. [John 436-14
  Exacted attention with attentive force. [Bouquet 450-21
  A dust, a force that traverses a shade. [NH 489-3
  He could not bend against its propelling force. [R Conn 533-12
  Of inescapable force, itself a fate. [Spaniard 34-20 P
  By dense unreason, irreproachable force, [Duck 62-6 P
  With its final force, a thing invincible [Bship 79-11 P
  The aid of greatness to be and the force. [Ulysses 100-17 P
FORCED. To the total thing, a shapeless giant forced [Poem Morn
    219-15
  Forced up from nothing, evening's chair, [Human 363-11
  Enjoying angels. Whistle, forced bugler, [NSF 405-13
FORCES. "Forces, the Will & the Weather" [228-title
  Dressed poorly, arrogant of his streaming forces, [Uruguay 249-22
FORCING. Coming from the East, forcing itself to the West, [Bship
    80-11 P
FORE. Of dulce atmosphere, the fore of lofty scenes [Bouquet 450-3
FOREGO. Of the being's deepest darling, we forego [EM 317-14
FOREGOING. As foregoing the nakedest passion for barefoot [EM
    316-22
FOREGONE. A shivering residue, chilled and foregone, [AA 417-20
  By print or paper, the trivial chance foregone, [Duck 61-23 P
FOREHEAD. Forehead's cold, spite of the eye [Bagatelles 213-14
  A woman smoothes her forehead with her hand [NSF 319-17
  An ancient forehead hung with heavy hair, [NSF 400-7
FOREIGN. And his daughter was a foreign thing. [Norfolk 111-11
  Yet vested in a foreign absolute, [Owl 434-9
  What is left has the foreign smell of plaster, [Armor 529-5
  Without human feeling, a foreign song. [Of Mere 117-20 P
  See far-foreign.
FOREIGNER. A funny foreigner of meek address. [Lot 371-21
FOREIGNERS. Life's foreigners, pale aliens of the mud, [Greenest
    59-23 P
FOREIGNNESS. In the midst of foreignness, the syllable [NH 471-2
FORELEG. The right, uplifted foreleg of the horse [NSF 391-10
FORELEGS. So much he had devised: white forelegs taut [Old Woman
    43-10 P
FORE-MEANING. As the fore-meaning in music is." Again, [NH 485-12
FOREMOST. To that first, foremost law. Anguishing hour! [Monocle
    17-13
FORES. Across the unscrawled fores the future casts [NSF 383-4
FORESAW. Crispin foresaw a curious promenade [C 31-23
FORESEEN. It was not the end he had foreseen. He knew [EM 319-23
  So much the sculptor had foreseen: autumn, [Old Woman 43-5 P
  But her he had not foreseen: the bitter mind [Old Woman 44-1 P
FOREST. Elations when the forest blooms; gusty [Sunday 67-22
  Above the forest of the parakeets, [Bird Claws 82-1
  These are the forest. This health is holy, [Parochial 191-11
  And forest tigresses and women mixed [EM 321-25
  At the legend of the maroon and olive forest, [Plant 506-17
FOREST-MEN. Their petty dirges of fallen forest-men, [Greenest
    55-20 P
FORESTS. In the jasmine haunted forests, that we knew [Oboe 251-20
  Wood of his forests and stone out of his fields [Myth 118-15 P
FORESWORE. Foreswore the sipping of the marriage wine. [NSF 401-10
FORETELL. Foretell each night the one abysmal night, [Heaven 56-18
  The clouds foretell a swampy rain. [Fish-Scale 161-6
FOREVER. Farewell and to know that the land is forever gone
    [Farewell 118-7
  Patientia, forever soothing wounds, [Lions 124-15
  It is cold to be forever young, [Vari 233-8
  On a breast forever precious for that touch, [NSF 388-6
  Forever hunting or hunted, rushing through [Greenest 55-21 P
  In a world forever without a plan [Grotesque 76-14 P
FORFEIT. Lament, willingly forfeit the ai-ai [EM 317-15
  Without the forfeit scholar coming in, [Someone 85-4 A
FORGATHER. Forgather and bell boldly Crispin's last [C 43-13
FORGET. Through sweating changes, never could forget [C 33-22
  And do not forget his wry neck [Jack-Rabbit 50-12
  Forget so soon. [Peacocks 58-12
  And to feel sure and to forget the bleaching sand . . . [Farewell
    117-20
  We shall forget by day, except [MBG 184-4
  He might slowly forget. It is more difficult to evade [Bed 327-5
  No need, am happy, forget need's golden hand, [NSF 405-1
  Here, now, we forget each other and ourselves. [Final 524-10
  He would forget the procelain [Three 133-8 P
FORGETFUL. The forgetful color of the autumn day [Aug 494-16
  Forgetful of death in war, there rises [Stan Hero 84-2 P
FORGETFULNESS. And of forgetfulness, in alternate strain. [C 29-6
  Like gathered-up forgetfulness, [Woman Song 360-11
  A forgetfulness of summer at the pole. [Bad Time 427-3
  A color that moved us with forgetfulness. [Aug 494-8
  Of the ground, a cure beyond forgetfulness. [Rock 526-13
FORGETS. Forgets the gold centre, the golden destiny, [NSF 404-18
FORGETTING. There was no past in their forgetting, [Gigan 289-2
  To keep him from forgetting, without a word, [NH 483-17
  Never forgetting him that kept coming constantly so near. [World
    521-18
  Forgetting work, not caring for angels, hunting a lift, [Duck
    60-15 P
FORGIVE. Some merciful divination, you forgive. [Spaniard 34-6 P
  And you forgive dark broachings growing great [Spaniard 34-7 P
FORGOT. Saying we have forgot them, they never lived. [Grotesque
    77-12 P
FORGOTTEN. The cat forgotten in the moon; [Rabbit K 209-9
  Neither remembered nor forgotten, nor old, [Bouquet 451-6
  Comes the cold volume of forgotten ghosts, [NH 468-6
  By a woman, who has forgotten it. [Vacancy 511-9
  And of sounds so far forgotten, like her voice, [Woman Had 82-18P
  Now, here, the warmth I had forgotten becomes [Warmth 90-2 P
  Now, here, the snow I had forgotten becomes [As Leave 117-8 P
  We have forgotten water to drink. [Three 128-5 P
FORLORN. So severed and so much forlorn debris. [Bouquet 450-15
  Mumbling and musing like the most forlorn. [Phases 5-14 P
FORM. In bloom. Yet it survives in its own form, [C 41-6
  So Crispin hasped on the surviving form, [C 41-8
  In form though in design, as Crispin willed, [C 45-21
  Who found all form and order in solitude, [Sad Gay 121-17
  The motions of the mind and giving form [Eve Angels 137-20
  Is a form, described but difficult, [MBG 169-15
  The world was a shore, whether sound or form [MBG 179-2
  The sea is a form of ridicule. [MBG 180-1
  The form of her in something else [Scavoir 231-15
  It was as if thunder took form upon [Vase 246-9
  Became the form and the fragrance of things [Vase 247-7
  The form on the pillow humming while one sleeps, [Beard 247-23
  Whose single being, single form [Jumbo 269-8
  To perceive men without reference to their form. [Choc 296-11
  To think of him destroyed the body's form. [Choc 297-8
  Their form, beyond their life, yet of themselves, [Choc 299-17
  In a calculated chaos: he that takes form [Repet 307-4
  Yet in that form will not return. But does [Repet 308-8
  That would form themselves, in time, and communicate [EM 314-21
  Form mystical convolutions in the sleep [EM 319-9
  In form, lovers of heaven and earth, she-wolves [EM 321-24
  A form, then, protected from the battering, may [Pure 330-10
  They hunt for a form which by its form alone, [Pediment 361-10
  By its form alone, by being right, [Pediment 361-13
  In the sunshine is a filial form and one [Cred 375-3
  The importance of its hat to a form becomes [Pastor 379-4
  Makes of the form Most Merciful Capitan, [Pastor 379-6
  The actual form bears outwardly this grace, [Pastor 379-17
  False flick, false form, but falseness close to kin. [NSF 385-18
  Incipit and a form to speak the word [NSF 387-5
  Exponent by a form of speech, the speaker [NSF 397-3
  In sleep its natural form. It was enough [NSF 399-12
  This is form gulping after formlessness, [AA 411-10
  Two brothers. And a third form, she that says [Owl 431-16
  The third form speaks, because the ear repeats, [Owl 432-3
  Imposes power by the power of his form. [Orb 443-6
  Nor the beginning nor end of a form: [Wom Sun 445-7
  A mythological form, a festival sphere, [NH 466-2
  We fling ourselves, constantly longing, on this form. [NH 470-16
  Or as a voice that, speaking without form, [NH 484-20
  These are the edgings and inchings of final form, [NH 488-16
  Was it as we sat in the park and the archaic form [Aug 494-10
  As if the design of all his words takes form [Rome 511-2

Without any form or any sense of form, [Look 518-9
A form of fire approaches the cretonnes of Penelope, [World
  520-15
An object the more, an undetermined form [Moonlight 531-14
In the great vistas of night air, that takes this form,
  [Moonlight 531-17
Arranged for phantasy to form an edge [Old Woman 43-17 P
In Capricorn. The statue has a form [Greenest 58-17 P
It is the form [Sombre 68-29 P
A board for bishops' grapes, the happy form [Sombre 70-8 P
Yet lord, a mask of flame, the sprawling form [Sombre 70-16 P
By giving it a form. But the character [Recit 86-6 P
Of tradition does not easily take form. [Recit 86-7 P
It is not a set of laws. Therefore, its form [Recit 86-8 P
Is to define its form, to say: this image [Recit 86-13 P
Is not its form. Tradition is wise but not [Recit 86-16 P
Is its true form? Is it the memory [Recit 86-22 P
Is it experience, say, the final form [Recit 87-4 P
It has a clear, a single, a solid form, [Recit 87-11 P
Ascending the humane. This is the form [Recit 87-20 P
Tradition wears, the clear, the single form [Recit 87-21 P
Therein, day settles and thickens round a form-- [Role 93-12 P
Is a blind thing fumbling for its form, [Ulysses 104-16 P
A form that is lame, a hand, a back, [Ulysses 104-17 P
An argentine abstraction approaching form [Real 110-17 P
To form that weather's appropriate people, [Art Pop 112-18 P
The root of a form, as of this fruit, a fund, [Someone 83-5 A
The slight incipiencies, of which the form, [Someone 87-8 A
FORMED. The water never formed to mind or voice, [Key W 128-12
  Always, in brilliance, fatal, final, formed [Owl 434-23
So formed, became himself and he breathed [Two Illus 513-14
A civilization formed from the outward blank, [Armor 529-22
Seized by that possible blue. Be maidens formed [Burnshaw 51-18P
The common-places of which if formed a part [Greenest 57-5 P
But now a habit of the truth had formed [Someone 85-8 A
FORMER. As the acorn broods on former oaks [Oak 272-13
FORMIDABLE. The formidable helmet is nothing now. [Pastor 380-1
FORMING. As if sounds were forming [Dutch 290-17
  The cricket of summer forming itself out of ice. [Discov 95-14 P
FORMLESS. Meditating the will of men in formless crowds. [NE
  Verses 105-10
Whitened, again, forms formless in the dark, [Old Woman 45-8 P
FORMLESSNESS. The crude and jealous formlessness [Vase 247-6
  This is form gulping after formlessness, [AA 411-10
FORMS. A sally into gold and crimson forms, [C 35-9
  Upward and outward, in green-vented forms, [Bird Claws 82-11
Forms, flames, and the flakes of flames, [Nomad 95-19
Now, for him, his forms have vanished. [Sad Gay 121-19
Imposing forms they cannot describe, [Sad Gay 122-8
The vegetation still abounds with forms. [Lions 125-8
In dark forms of the grass [Brave 138-11
Covered the shrivelled forms [Reader 147-2
Disclosed in common forms. Set up [Prelude 195-17
They are yellow forms [Pears 196-5
"Words are not forms of a single word. [On Road 204-2
Of the mind that forms itself [Bagatelles 213-22
The moonlight crumbled to degenerate forms, [Uruguay 249-7
Impatient of the bells and midnight forms, [Uruguay 250-1
Legend were part of what he was, forms [Hero 276-23
The armies are forms in number, as cities are. [Choc 296-12
Between cities is a gesticulation of forms, [Choc 296-14
With which we vested, once, the golden forms [EM 317-25
And the damasked memory of the golden forms [EM 317-26
Of the damasked memory of the golden forms [EM 317-28
The moving and the moving of their forms [Descrip 342-9
The very pool, his thoughts the colored forms, [Descrip 342-12
The forms that are attentive in thin air. [Descrip 344-14
In an ovation of resplendent forms-- [Liadoff 346-7
Perhaps these forms are seeking to escape [Two V 355-13
Of body and air and forms and images, [AA 411-17
The cloud drifts idly through half-thought-of forms. [AA 416-15
Two forms move among the dead, high sleep [Owl 431-13
These forms are visible to the eye that needs, [Owl 432-1
These forms are not abortive figures, rocks, [Owl 432-5
Is dark, thought of the forms of dark desire. [Owl 432-18
A man walked living among the forms of thought [Owl 432-20
In the metaphysical streets, the profoundest forms [NH 473-7
In the hearing of the shepherd and his black forms, [NH 480-15
Forms of farewell, furtive among green ferns. [NH 482-15
Was full of these archaic forms, giants [Aug 494-17
There was no fury in transcendent forms. [Quiet 523-14
Forms of the Rock in a Night-Hymn [Rock 528-title 3
A new-colored sun, say, that will soon change forms [Armor
  529-19
What niggling forms of gargoyle patter? [Archi 17-2 P
Seated before these shining forms, like the duskiest glass,
  reflecting the piebald of roses or what you will. [Piano 21-18P
Whitened, again, forms formless in the dark, [Old Woman 45-8 P
In the images of desire, the forms that speak, [Woman Had 82-21P
To which all other forms, at last, return, [Recit 87-5 P

FORMULAE. The swarming activities of the formulae [NH 488-17
FORMULATES. The vital music formulates the words. [Extracts 259-18
FORMULATIONS. Has only the formulations of midnight [Papini 446-4
FORSOOK. Forsook the insatiable egotist. The sea [C 30-3
FORSYTHIA. Gay is, gay was, the gay forsythia [NSF 385-12
  Babyishness of forsythia, a snatch of belief, [Slug 522-13
FORTE. The poor piano forte [Grotesque 76-17 P
FORTELLEZE. He that is fortelleze, though he be [Choc 301-17
FORTH. Doleful heroics, pinching gestures forth [Monocle 17-11
  Brings forth [Nomad 95-7
  Brings forth hymn and hymn [Nomad 95-11
  The body walks forth naked in the sun [Anatomy 108-8
  Of these. In these, I come forth outwardly. [Rhythms 246-5
  Poured forth the fine fins, the gawky beaks, the personalia,
    [Somnam 304-17
  A purple-leaping element that forth [Descrip 341-16
  And forth the particulars of rapture come. [NSF 392-9
  They lay. Forth then with huge pathetic force [NSF 403-7
  It is a coming on and a coming forth. [NH 487-19
  And I fly forth, the naked Proserpine. [Infernale 25-8 P
  Forth from their tabernacles once again [Greenest 55-27 P
  And steps forth, priestly in severity, [Sombre 70-15 P
FORTHWITH. As a man and woman meet and love forthwith. [NSF 386-16
  But the difficultest rigor is forthwith, [NSF 398-20
FORTIFIED. In casque and scaffold orator, fortified [Stan Hero
  84-21 P
FORTIFIES. Which, from the ash within it, fortifies [Someone 83-17A
FORTIFYING. The fortifying arm, the profound [Ulysses 100-10 P
FORTISSIMO. Wakes us to the emotion, grand fortissimo, [Grotesque
  76-19 P
FORTITUDE. A gorgeous fortitude. Medium man [Imago 439-9
FORTITUDO. And mighty Fortitudo, frantic bass. [Lions 124-16
FORTRESS. Spreading out fortress walls like fortress wings.
  [Luther 461-12
  See castle-fortress-home.
FORTUITOUS. Extreme, fortuitous, personal, in which [NSF 386-18
FORTUNATE. And fortunate stone. It moves its parade [Imago 439-7
FORTUNE. I am a man of fortune greeting heirs; [Monocle 13-17
  But in between lies the sphere of my fortune [Nigger 151-5
  The night should be warm and fluters' fortune [Nightgown 214-15
  Imprimatur. But then there's common fortune, [Hero 275-7
  And common fortune, induced by nothing, [Hero 275-11
  The fantastic fortune of fantastic blood, [Liadoff 347-10
  By fortune, his gray ghost may mediate [Cats 368-7
  And is our fortune and honey hived in the trees [Cred 374-19
  The full of fortune and the full of fate, [AA 420-23
  This fortune's finding, disposed and re-disposed [Orb 440-7
  Become accompaniments of fortune, but [Rome 508-13
  Of the fortune of the spirit, beyond the eye, [Rome 508-14
  And her belt, the final fortune of their desire. [World 521-9
  Time's fortune near, the sleepless sleepers moved [Duck 61-27 P
  Flaunts that first fortune, which he wanted so much. [Americana
    94-15 P
  The moment of life's love and fortune, [Letters 107-8 P
FORTUNER. Like this, saps like the sun, true fortuner. [C 43-5
  See good-fortuner.
FORTUNES. And the fortunes of frost and of clouds, [Nigger 151-6
  May truly bear its heroic fortunes [Hero 281-4
FORTY. If men at forty will be painting lakes [Monocle 15-7
  The faith of forty, ward of Cupido. [Monocle 16-16
  A maid of forty is no feathery girl. [Stan MMO 19-9 P
FORWARD. A running forward, arms stretched out as drilled. [Nigger
  153-15
  Forward of the eye that, in its backward, sees [Descrip 340-3
  A boat carried forward by waves resembling the bright backs of
    rowers, [Prol 515-6
  I had looked forward to understanding. Yet [Lytton 39-22 P
FORWARDLY. Straight forwardly through another night [Ulysses 105-11P
FOSTERS. That fosters seraphim and is to them [Eve Angels 137-7
FOUGHT. Sand heaped in the clouds, giant that fought [MBG 179-7
  And what she felt fought off the barest phrase. [NSF 402-12
  As: the last plainness of a man who has fought [NH 467-17
FOUL. The foul immovables, came through the clouds, [Greenest
  53-12 P
FOUND. Found inklings of your bond to all that dust. [Monocle 15-6
  In lordly study. Every day, I found [Monocle 17-23
  Ursula, in a garden, found [Pourtraicte 21-1
  Which yet found means to set his simmering mind [Geneva 24-10
  Found his vicissitudes had much enlarged [C 31-8
  So much for that. The affectionate emigrant found [C 32-11
  And there I found myself more truly and more strange. [Hoon 65-18
  And found [Peter 90-17
  I found between moon-rising and moon-setting [NE Verses 104-3
  Who found all form and order in solitude, [Sad Gay 121-17
  Whatever it was that he found in their absence, [Nigger 158-8
  And to have found the bed empty? [Chateau 161-8
  One might have found tragic hair, [Chateau 161-9
  A poem like a missal found [MBG 177-21
  Or less, he found a man, or more, against [Horn 230-15
  He is. The thought that he had found all this [Yellow 237-5

But as if evening found us young, still young, [Martial 237-15
Find peace? We found the sum of men. We found, [Oboe 251-11
If we found the central evil, the central good. [Oboe 251-12
A parasol, which I had found, against [Phenom 287-9
The flags are natures newly found. [Dutch 291-1
A kind of elegy he found in space: [EM 315-3
A mountain in which no ease is ever found, [EM 319-3
Speech found the ear, for all the evil sound, [EM 326-5
In his packet Anacharsis found the lines: [Anach 365-17
Fully made, fully apparent, fully found. [Cred 376-15
Of her sons and of her daughters. They found themselves [NSF 383-13
And in earth itself they found a green-- [NSF 383-15
And therefore married Bawda, whom he found there, [NSF 401-17
Shall we be found hanging in the trees next spring? [AA 419-19
Hard found, and water tasting of misery. [Bad Time 426-14
She found a helping from the cold, [Celle 438-4
It was a page he had found in the handbook of heartbreak. [Madame 507-8
Left only the fragments found in the grass, [Two Illus 515-3
The honey in its pulp, the final found, [Rock 527-14
Is poverty, whose jewel found [Ulysses 104-13 P
So that a carved king found in a jungle, huge [Conversat 109-5 P
At last, the center of resemblance, found [Ideal 89-8 A
   See: first-found; new-found.
FOUNDED. The Founder of the State. Whoever founded [Mice 123-9
   See deep-founded.
FOUNDER. The Founder of the State. Whoever founded [Mice 123-9
FOUNDERED. A steamer lay near him, foundered in the ice. [Page 421-13
FOUNDLING. This foundling of the infected past, so bright,[NSF 388-11
FOUNTAIN. Let us erect in the Basin a lofty fountain. [NE Verses 105-1
   When the music of the boy fell like a fountain, [Norfolk 111-14
By a pure fountain, that was a ghost, and is, [Aug 489-10
FOUNTAINS. Filled its encrusted fountains, they arrayed [Havana 142-20
This is the sky divested of its fountains. [EM 321-2
FOUR. Four daughters in a world too intricate [C 45-2
   In the beginning, four blithe instruments [C 45-3
   Of differing struts, four voices several [C 45-4
   In couch, four more personae, intimate [C 45-5
   As buffo, yet divers, four mirrors blue [C 45-6
   That should be silver, four accustomed seeds [C 45-7
   Hinting incredible hues, four selfsame lights [C 45-8
   Four questioners and four sure answerers. [C 45-10
But when I walk I see that it consists of three or four hills
   and a cloud. [Of Surface 57-2
You become a self that fills the four corners of night. [Rabbit K 209-19
The mass of meaning. It is three or four [Extracts 255-27
Of four, and one of seven, whom she dressed [NSF 402-2
The propounding of four seasons and twelve months. [NH 473-14
The four winds blow through the rustic arbor, [Vacancy 511-12
The child's hair is of the color of the hay in the haystack,
   around which the four black horses stand. [Primordia 8-1 P
In which one of these three worlds are the four of us [Conversat 109-16 P
Involving the four corners of the sky, [Ideal 88-4 A
   See three-four.
FOURTH. A creeper under jaunty leaves. And fourth, [C 44-21
   The fourth, pent now, a digit curious. [C 45-1
FOWL. The fowl of Venus may consist of both [Spaniard 35-7 P
FOX. And the welter of frost and the fox cries do. [Grapes 110-20
The fox ran out of his hole. [On Road 203-15
As the fox and snake do. It is a brave affair. [NSF 403-17
FOXED. Of affected homage foxed so many books, [Havana 142-15
   See weather-foxed.
FOXES. As quick as foxes on the hill; [Postcard 158-16
FOYER. "Crude Foyer" [305-title
   A foyer of the spirit in a landscape [Crude 305-6
The crows are flying above the foyer of summer. [Novel 457-1
Stepping from the foyer of summer into that [Novel 457-5
The late, least foyer in a qualm of cold. [Novel 457-15
He knew that he was a spirit without a foyer [Local 111-11 P
The local objects of a world without a foyer, [Local 111-14 P
As toward an absolute foyer beyond romance. [Local 112-12 P
FRACTURED. Like a fractured edifice [Public Sq 108-20
FRAGILE. And breathes again for us a fragile breath. [Extraord 369-18
   Too fragile, too immediate for any speech. [NH 471-9
Than fragile volutes in a rose sea-shell. [Soldat 14-3 P
FRAGMENT. Almost a nigger fragment, a mystique [News 265-9
FRAGMENTARY. It is a fragmentary tragedy [EM 324-2
FRAGMENTS. Left only the fragments found in the grass, [Two Illus 515-3
FRAGRANCE. And this fragrance the fragrance of vegetal? [Lilacs 48-22
   Excelling summer, ghost of fragrance falling [Ghosts 119-16

The chrysanthemums' astringent fragrance comes [Nigger 157-1
The fragrance of the autumn warmest, [On Road 204-11
But the town and the fragrance were never one, [Arcades 225-13
False as the mind, instead of the fragrance, warm [Horn 230-12
Those bearing balsam, its field fragrance, [Vari 235-11
Became the form and the fragrance of things [Vase 247-7
Inhale the purple fragrance. It becomes [News 265-8
Squeezing the reddest fragrance from the stump [God 285-14
Its fragrance, a heavy somnolence, and for him, [EM 319-13
The fragrance of the woman not her self, [Pure 332-14
Of fragrance and the mind lays by its trouble. [Cred 372-8
The fragrance of the magnolias comes close, [NSF 385-17
Made difficult by salt fragrance, intricate. [Bouquet 452-15
Not as the frangrance of Persephone, [Aug 491-10
FRAGRANCES. Is soft in three-four cornered fragrances [NH 470-19
   The pines that were fans and fragrances emerge, [NH 487-20
Night and its midnight-minting fragrances, [Rock 528-20
FRAGRANCIES. Irised in dew and early fragrancies, [C 36-3
FRAGRANT. Fragrant and supple, [Six Sig 73-20
And of the fragrant mothers the most dear [Fictive 87-8
   In fragrant leaves heat-heavy yet nimble in talk. [NE Verses 105-12
Words of the fragrant portals, dimly-starred, [Key W 130-13
Of summer, growing fragrant in the night, [NSF 399-10
Distortion, however fragrant, however dear. [NSF 406-19
Oh-hé-hé! Fragrant puppets [Cab 21-4 P
And fragrant fomentations of the spring [Sombre 69-18 P
FRAGRANTER. By metaphor. The juice was fragranter [Poem Morn 219-9
FRAGRANTNESS. Of medicine, a fragrantness not to be spoiled . . . [Rome 508-20
FRAICHEUR. We are part of a fraicheur, inaccessible [Nuns 93-1 P
FRAIL. Frail as April snow; [Pourtraicte 21-15
   In which those frail custodians watched, [C 43-1
And frail umbrellas. A too-fluent green [Sea Surf 101-8
In anything that he constructed, so frail, [Quiet 523-2
Frail princes of distant Monaco, [Primordia 9-20 P
FRAME. The page is blank or a frame without a glass [Phosphor 267-7
   To prepare for bed, in the frame of the house, and move [Lot 372-2
Themselves with care, sought out the nerveless frame [NSF 391-16
An Arctic effulgence flaring on the frame [AA 417-2
And frame from thinking and is realized. [Rome 511-3
The frame of the hero. Yet, willingly, he [Stan Hero 84-13 P
The frame of a repeated effect, is it that? [Recit 87-6 P
FRANCA. The lingua franca et jocundissima. [NSF 397-9
FRANCE. Or say to the French here is France again? [Imago 439-3
And so France feels. A menace that impends, [Soldat 13-6 P
Not France! France, also, serves the invincible eye, [Soldat 14-9P
With the blank skies over England, over France [Martial 238-4
FRANCIS. Jerome and the scrupulous Francis and Sunday women, [Luther 461-8
FRANCISCAN. Yet Franciscan don was never more [MBG 181-13
FRANTIC. And mighty Fortitudo, frantic bass. [Lions 124-16
FRANZ HALS. Not to be realized. Weather by Franz Hals, [NSF 385-6
FREAKED. See flame-freaked.
FREE. And excepting negligible Triton, free [C 29-28
He felt the Andean breath. His mind was free [C 33-9
And more than free, elate, intent, profound [C 33-10
Or island solitude, unsponsored, free, [Sunday 70-29
I am free. High above the mast the moon [Farewell 117-7
To be free again, to return to the violent mind [Farewell 118-17
A state that was free, in the dead of winter, from mice? [Mice 123-10
It was how he was free. It was how his freedom came. [Freed 205-15
An affirmation free from doubt. [Vase 247-5
And free requiting of responsive fact, [Montra 263-10
"The Search for Sound Free from Motion" [268-title
Singsonged and singsonged, wildly free. [Jumbo 269-3
And wildly free, whose clawing thumb [Jumbo 269-5
And wild and free, the secondary man, [Jumbo 269-12
Above him. The moon was always free from him, [EM 314-27
As night was free from him. The shadow touched [EM 315-4
A large-sculptured, platonic person, free from time, [Pure 330-8
Of the certain solid, the primary free from doubt, [Man Car 351-2
Free, for a moment, from malice and sudden cry, [Cred 378-8
Free knowledges, secreted until then, [Orb 441-17
The imprescriptible zenith, free of harangue, [What We 459-15
Free from their majesty and yet in need [NH 473-10
Nor not knowing, yet free from question, [Aug 495-10
And slightly detestable operandum, free [Look 517-19
Free from images and change. [Demoiselle 23-11 P
Be free to sleep there sounder, for the plough [Burnshaw 48-1 P
In vast disorder live in the ruins, free, [Burnshaw 48-27 P
Be free to sing, if only a sorrowful song. [Greenest 58-33 P
And sighing. These lives are not your lives, O free, [Duck 61-30P
Asserting itself in an element that is free, [Pagoda 92-1 P
As a free race. We know it, one [Ulysses 102-4 P
How then shall the mind be less than free [Ulysses 103-11 P

Since only to know is to be free? [Ulysses 103-12 P
Free from everything else, free above all from thought. [Letters
    107-9 P
FREED. An immense suppression, freed, [Sad Gay 122-5
"The Latest Freed Man" [204-title
The latest freed man rose at six and sat [Freed 204-14
And so the freed man said. [Freed 205-5
FREEDOM. And the green freedom of a cockatoo [Sunday 66-18
It was how he was free. It was how his freedom came. [Freed
    205-15
This pitter-patter of archaic freedom, [Dutch 292-13
Freedom is like a man who kills himself [Dutch 292-17
In an elemental freedom, sharp and cold. [Choc 297-3
A freedom out of silver-shaping size, [Choc 298-9
Or chosen quickly, in a freedom [Creat 310-14
This freedom, this supremacy, and in [EM 315-8
By her coming became a freedom of the two, [AA 419-17
A freedom revealed, a realization touched, [Bouquet 451-20
Or down a well. Breathe freedom, oh, my native, [Aug 490-13
By our own motions in a freedom of air. [Rock 525-3
Regard the freedom of seventy years ago. [Rock 525-4
In the alien freedom that such selves degustate: [Pagoda 92-2 P
A freedom at last from the mystical, [Ulysses 101-11 P
FREEDOMS. Of the thousands of freedoms except our own? [Dutch
    292-14
FREELY. Lapised and lacqued and freely emeraldine [Ideal 88-5 A
FREEMEN. He was in this as other freemen are, [C 31-12
Freemen of death, about and still about [Heaven 56-14
FREER. Stronger and freer, a little better off. [Good Man 364-4
FREEZE. That the water would freeze in cold, [Glass 197-13
Mother was afraid I should freeze in the Parisian hotels.
    [Novel 457-7
FREEZES. Before winter freezes and grows black-- [Burghers 362-14
FRENCH. French flowers on it. [Explan 72-16
And cold. The moon follows the sun like a French [Vari 234-8
Of a parent in the French sense. [Lack 303-16
Or say to the French here is France again? [Imago 439-3
FREQUENCY. The frequency of images of the moon [Study II 464-4
FRERE. C'était mon frère du ciel, ma vie, mon or. [Sea Surf 100-3
The blank frere of fields, their matin laborer. [Aug 492-18
FRESH. Fresh from discoveries of tidal skies, [C 30-27
In which old stars are planets of morning, fresh [Descrip 344-10
Came fresh transfigurings of freshest blue. [Sea Surf 102-15
And made it fresh in a world of white, [Poems Clim 193-20
The freshness of night has been fresh a long time. [Dump 202-1
Smacks like fresh water in a can, like the sea [Dump 202-6
And saints are brilliant in fresh cloaks. [Contra I 266-16
The fresh night. [God 285-18
He is, the air changes and grows fresh to breathe. [Choc 301-8
It is a fresh spiritual that he defines, [NH 474-19
He does not raise the rousing of fresh light [Aug 492-22
Creates a fresh universe out of nothingness by adding itself,
    [Prol 517-9
Of their fresh culls might be a cure of the ground. [Rock 526-17
Certain and ever more fresh. Ah! Certain, for sure . . .
    [Moonlight 532-6
Fresh from the sacred clarities, chanters [Greenest 56-4 P
The Bulgar said, "After pineapple with fresh mint [Duck 60-7 P
The blows and buffets of fresh senses [Fare Guit 99-5 P
For which a fresh name always occurred, as if [Local 112-5 P
Bring us fresh water [Three 141-1 P
FRESHENED. Heightened. It is he, anew, in a freshened youth
    [Myth 118-13 P
See ever-freshened.
FRESHENING. See ever-freshening.
FRESHER. Whether fresher or duller, whether of winter cloud [AA
    412-13
FRESHEST. Came fresh transfigurings of freshest blue. [Sea Surf
    102-15
Wind-beaten into freshest, brightest fire. [Burnshaw 52-22 P
FRESHNESS. Freshness is more than the east wind blowing round one.
    [Nigger 157-11
The freshness of night has been fresh a long time. [Dump 202-1
The freshness of morning, the blowing of day, one says [Dump
    202-2
The freshness of the oak-leaves, not so much [Freed 205-18
Yet the freshness of the leaves, the burn [Scavoir 231-6
Enough. The freshness of transformation is [NSF 397-24
The freshness of a world. It is our own, [NSF 398-1
It is ourselves, the freshness of ourselves, [NSF 398-2
In an air of freshness, clearness, greenness, blueness, [Armor
    530-16
In a freshness of poetry by the sea, [Polo 37-19 P
FRET. A scribble of fret and fear and fate, [Aug 494-25
He well might find it in this fret [Room Gard 41-13 P
FRETFUL. The fretful concubine [Anything B 211-2
Is any choir the whole voice of this fretful habitation,
    [Inelegance 26-5 P
Each fretful fern drops down a fear like dew [Greenest 55-24 P
FRETS. See color-frets.

FRETTINGS. A will to make iris frettings on the blank. [NSF 397-18
FREUD. Freud's eye was the microscope of potency. [Cats 368-6
FRIDAY. Last Friday, in the big light of last Friday night, [Real
    110-7 P
FRIEND. Good air, good friend, what is there in life? [MBG 175-18
Good air, my only friend, believe, [MBG 175-20
Of love, believe would be a friend, [MBG 175-22
Friendlier than my only friend, [MBG 176-1
Day is the children's friend. [Prejudice 368-11
Two in a deep-founded sheltering, friend and dear friend. [World
    521-3
Friend and dear friend and a planet's encouragement. [World 521-14
FRIENDLIER. The sky will be much friendlier then than now, [Sunday
    68-8
Friendlier than my only friend, [MBG 176-1
FRIENDS. "Some Friends from Pascagoula" [126-title
Blue friends in shadows, rich conspirators, [Choc 300-9
Shadows of friends, of those he knew, each bringing [New Set
    352-12
FRIEZE. That's the down-town frieze, [Common 221-1
FRIGHTENED. Were frightened and he frightened them, [Adequacy 243-11
FRIGID. With its frigid brilliances, its blue-red sweeps [AA 413-1
Whether in-dwelling haughty clouds, frigid [Burnshaw 47-15 P
FRIGIDLY. Clipped frigidly blue-black meridians, [C 34-16
FRINGED. A fringed eye in a crypt. [Add 199-8
FRISEURED. The super-man friseured, possessing and possessed.
    [Montra 262-24
FRISSON. Sways slightly and the pinnacles frisson. [Hero 275-3
FRIZZLED. In an old, frizzled, flambeaued manner, [Jasmine 79-5
FRO. Crossed it, to and fro. [Thirteen 93-15
The hunters run to and fro. The heavy trees, [Parochial 191-7
To and to and fro [Metamorph 266-9
Fro Niz - nil - imbo. [Metamorph 266-10
Does it move to and fro or is it of both [NSF 396-15
Of windings round and dodges to and fro, [Ulti 429-20
Entwine your arms and moving to and fro, [Burnshaw 47-17 P
FROG. Keen to the point of starlight, while a frog [Monocle 17-16
FROGS. "Frogs Eat Butterflies. Snakes Eat Frogs. Hogs Eat Snakes.
    Men Eat Hogs." [78-title
There is the same color in the bellies of frogs, in clays,
    withered reeds, skins, wood, sunlight. [Primordia 8-2 P
FROMAGE. Health-o, when ginger and fromage bewitch [NE Verses 104-5
Fromage and coffee and cognac and no gods. [Greenest 57-29 P
FRONT. His puissant front nor for her subtle sound, [NSF 401-12
Under the front of the westward evening star, [Real 110-12 P
He hanged himself in front of me. [Three 141-16 P
FROST. To regard the frost and the boughs [Snow Man 9-22
Into the autumn weather, splashed with frost, [Monocle 16-7
The salt hung on his spirit like a frost, [C 29-13
Of half-dissolving frost, the summer came, [C 34-10
In a region of frost, [Cortege 80-19
Viewing the frost; [Cortege 80-20
Cries up for us and colder than the frost [Anatomy 108-4
And the welter of frost and the fox cries do. [Grapes 110-20
Shrivelled in frost, [Tea 112-9
In a world of wind and frost, [Medit 124-3
Under the mat of frost and over the mat of clouds. [Nigger 151-4
And the fortunes of frost and of clouds, [Nigger 151-6
Happy men, distinguishing frost and clouds. [Nigger 151-8
Add nothing to the horror of the frost [Nigger 152-13
A tiger lamed by nothingness and frost. [Nigger 153-10
These had a being, breathing frost; [Postcard 159-3
And coffee dribble . . . Frost is in the stubble. [Dwarf 208-14
Will look like frost as it approaches them [AA 413-21
That would have wept and been happy, have shivered in the frost
    [Large 424-1
Motionless, knowing neither dew nor frost. [Burnshaw 49-15 P
A light snow, like frost, has fallen during the night. [Bus 116-1P
See: Glasgow-frost; hoar-frost.
FROSTY. In the frosty heaven. [Reader 147-12
FROTH. On what strange froth does the gross Indian dote, [C 38-1
Would froth the whole heaven with its seeming-so, [Descrip 341-17
FROTHY. When light comes down to wet his frothy jaws [Glass 197-16
Should be cold silver, neither that frothy clouds [NSF 399-6
To cool their ruddy pulses; the frothy clouds [NSF 399-15
Are nothing but frothy clouds; the frothy blooms [NSF 399-16
FROWN. The frown like serpents basking on the brow, [NSF 400-11
FROZEN. And the same bridge when the river is frozen. [Nigger 154-12
The field is frozen. The leaves are dry. [Possum 293-15
The sea was frozen solid and Hans heard, [Page 421-18
The great ship, Balayne, lay frozen in the sea. [Page 421-18
FRUIT. This luscious and impeccable fruit of life [Monocle 14-12
But it excels in this, that as the fruit [Monocle 14-20
It comes, it blooms, it bears its fruit and dies. [Monocle 16-3
Our bloom is gone. We are the fruit thereof. [Monocle 16-5
Beyond these changes, good, fat, guzzly fruit. [C 41-7
A hand that bears a thick-leaved fruit, [Venereal 48-16
In pungent fruit and bright, green wings, or else [Sunday 67-16
Does ripe fruit never fall? Or do the boughs [Sunday 69-14
Tongues around the fruit. [Orangeade 103-6

A perfect fruit in perfect atmosphere. [NE Verses 106-9
At night, it lights the fruit and wine, [MBG 172-19
A thing. Thus, the pineapple was a leather fruit, [Poem Morn
  219-5
A fruit for pewter, thorned and palmed and blue, [Poem Morn
  219-6
The almond and deep fruit. This bitter meat [Cuisine 228-13
If neatly glazed, becomes the same as the fruit [Extracts 253-9
To feed on the yellow bloom of the yellow fruit [EM 318-12
Or the majolica dish heaped up with phosphored fruit [EM 320-17
Itself that seed's ripe, unpredictable fruit. [Descrip 341-20
At last the good life came, good sleep, bright fruit, [Good Man
  361-7
If they broke into bloom, if they bore fruit, [Rock 526-15
They bud and bloom and bear their fruit without change. [Rock
  527-5
They bear their fruit so that the year is known, [Rock 527-12
Vines with yellow fruit, [Phases 4-11 P
Than purple paste of fruit, to taste, or leaves [Greenest 58-31P
The same down-dropping fruit in yellow leaves, [Duck 61-14 P
And the dewiest beads of insipid fruit [Stan MBG 72-8 P
A manner of walking, yellow fruit, a house, [Woman Had 83-7 P
Like taste distasting the first fruit of a vine, [Theatre 91-3 P
The root of a form, as of this fruit, a fund, [Someone 83-5 A
He must say nothing of the fruit that is [Someone 84-4 A
Below the prerogative jumble. The fruit so seen [Someone 84-16 A
The double fruit of boisterous epicures, [Someone 85-20 A
One says even of the odor of this fruit, [Someone 87-14 A
FRUITED. Bare beggar-tree, hung low for fruited red [NH 483-24
  See: heavy-fruited.
FRUITFUL. Lusty as June, more fruitful than the weeks [Havana 143-13
FRUITS. No silver-ruddy, gold-vermilion fruits. [Monocle 17-1
  Of breakfast ribands, fruits laid in their leaves, [C 42-26
  Green crammers of the green fruits of the world, [C 43-28
  Flashier fruits! A flip for the sun and moon, [Grapes 110-17
  Serve the rouged fruits in early snow. [Nigger 153-1
  First fruits, without the virginal of birds, [NSF 385-10
  Into lands of ruddy-ruby fruits, achieved [Armor 530-3
FRUIT-TREES. Rises through fruit-trees. [Magnifico 19-19
  The fruit-trees . . . [Magnifico 19-23
FRUITY. In beak and bud and fruity gobbet-skins, [C 32-7
FRUSTRATE. Which nothing can frustrate, that most secure, [NH 467-7
FT. Of the world would have only to ring and ft! [Bship 78-9 P
FUBBED. Fubbed the girandoles. [Ord Women 11-4
FUCHSIA. On a fuchsia in a can—and iridescences [NH 478-14
FUDDLE-FIDDLING. Beyond, futura's fuddle-fiddling lumps, [Montra
  260-15
FUGAL. Arointing his dreams with fugal requiems? [C 41-11
FUGATOS. The black fugatos are strumming the blacknesses of
  black . . . [Madame 507-9
FUGITIVE. Is no gaunt fugitive phantom. [Homunculus 26-22
FUGUE. Reflected, humming an outline of a fugue [NSF 402-14
FUGUES. Of long, capricious fugues and chorals. [Jasmine 79-12
  Of sneers, the fugues commencing at the toes [Extracts 253-21
  I care for neither fugues nor feathers. [Lytton 38-7 P
FULFILL. All of them, darkened by time, moved by they know not
  what, amending the airs they play to fulfill themselves;
  [Piano 21-17 P
FULFILLED. So long as the mind, for once, fulfilled itself?
  [Theatre 91-18 P
  The desire for speech and meaning gallantly fulfilled, [Discov
  95-18 P
FULFILLING. And to breathe is a fulfilling of desire.[Choc 301-10
  Cinderella fulfilling herself beneath the roof? [NSF 405-9
  Fulfilling his meditations, great and small. [AA 420-21
  Of sleep, the accomplished, the fulfilling air. [Owl 433-24
  Are the fulfilling rhapsodies that hymn it to creation?
  [Inelegance 26-4 P
FULFILLMENT. The fulfillment of fulfillments, in opulent, [Orb
  441-10
FULFILMENTS. The fulfillment of fulfillments, in opulent, [Orb
  441-10
FULFILMENT. Alone, shall come fulfilment to our dreams [Sunday
  69-1
  Yet life itself, the fulfilment of desire [Men Fall 188-3
FULFILS. By an understanding that fulfils his age, [Cred 374-4
FULGENT. Seeing the fulgent shadows upward heaped, [Duck 62-16 P
FULGOR. Here the adult one is still banded with fulgor, [Aug
  495-24
FULGURATIONS. While the sultriest fulgurations, flickering, [EM
  313-15
FULL. Full of the cry of the peacocks? [Domination 9-11
  Full of the same wind [Snow Man 10-8
  In verses wild with motion, full of din, [Monocle 16-12
  And, being full of the caprice, inscribed [C 37-24
  Was full of blocks [Peacocks 58-17
  Is full of long motions; as the ponderous [Curtains 62-2
  His tip a drop of water full of storms. [Bird Claws 82-12
  "Sea Surface Full of Clouds" [98-title
  Are full of the songs of Jananda and Carlotta; [Norfolk 111-17

And these two never meet in the air so full of summer [Norfolk
  111-20
Will be motion and full of shadows. [Sad Gay 122-18
And the streets are full of cries. [Mozart 132-21
And fill the hill and fill it full [Snow Stars 133-11
How full of exhalations of the sea . . . [Havana 144-27
Out of what is full of us; yet the search [Nigger 151-11
And clap the hollows full of tin. [MBG 170-6
Believe would be a brother full [MBG 175-21
Places there, a bouquet. Ho-ho . . . The dump is full [Dump
  201-13
No matter. The grass is full [Rabbit K 209-15
And full of yourself. The trees around are for you, [Rabbit K
  209-16
Full of stars and the images of stars— [Nightgown 214-7
Full of javelins and old fire-balls, [Dezem 218-3
The sky would be full of bodies like wood. [Thunder 220-17
And a little island full of geese and stars: [Sleight 222-15
They are full of juice and the skin is soft. [Peaches 224-12
They are full of the colors of my village [Peaches 224-13
It is like a region full of intonings. [Hartford 226-17
Is not, or is of what there was, is full [Martial 237-20
The air is full of children, statues, roofs [Chaos 357-15
Full of their ugly lord, [Pediment 361-19
The sea full of fishes in shoals, the woods that let [Cats 367-13
With nothing else compounded, carried full, [Cred 374-14
The lake was full of artificial things, [NSF 397-12
The full of fortune and the full of fate, [AA 420-23
A right red with its composites glutted full, [Bouquet 452-3
Of nights full of the green stars from Ireland, [Our Stars
  455-14
So that they become an impalpable town, full of [NH 466-5
It is full of the myrrh and camphor of summer [Aug 490-4
Was full of these archaic forms, giants [Aug 494-17
This is not landscape, full of the somnambulations [Irish 502-3
Full of Raphael's costumes; [Phases 5-17 P
Is full of reflections, [Primordia 8-6 P
Like a heart full of pins, [Soldat 12-24 P
In a theatre, full of tragedy, [Soldat 15-18 P
And father nature, full of butter [Lulu M 27-13 P
The early centuries were full [Agenda 42-7 P
Lay black and full of black misshapen? Wings [Old Woman 44-21 P
On a day still full of summer, when the leaves [Burnshaw 50-18 P
Miraculously preserved, full fickle-fine, [Greenest 56-15 P
Are full of fanfares of farewell, as night [Sombre 71-4 P
A paradise full of assassins. Suppose I seize [Bship 77-20 P
To the final full, an end without rhetoric. [Bship 81-11 P
The self is a cloister full of remembered sounds [Woman Had 82-17
It is still full of icy shades and shapen snow. [Course 96-12 P
  See: fame-full; speech-full.
FULL-BLOWN. In the woods, in this full-blown May, [Pediment 362-1
FULLER. To seek a sun of fuller fire. [How Live 125-16
FULL-HEIGHT. And sensuous summer stood full-height. [Two Illus
  514-19
FULL-PINIONED. To fetch the one full-pinioned one himself [C 44-28
FULLY. Have shapes that are not yet fully themselves, [Parochial
  191-4
  Fully made, fully apparent, fully found. [Cred 376-15
FUMBLING. Fickle and fumbling, variable, obscure, [C 46-4
  Is a blind thing fumbling for its form, [Ulysses 104-16 P
FUNCTION. Is the function of the poet here mere sound, [Havana
  144-12
FUND. Tristesses, the fund of life and death, suave bush [Cred
  377-15
  The root of a form, as of this fruit, a fund, [Someone 83-5 A
FUNDAMENT. That is the common, the bravest fundament, [NSF 398-12
FUNERAL. The race endures. The funeral pomps of the race [Paisant
  334-21
  Suggested that, at the final funeral, [NSF 391-11
FUNEREAL. The dark shadows of the funereal magnolias [Norfolk 111-16
FUNEST. Funest philosophers and ponderers, [On Manner 55-15
FUNICULAR. And apostrophes are forbidden on the funicular.
  [Botanist 1 134-11
FUNNY. A funny foreigner of meek address. [Lot 371-21
FUR. And boots of fur [Cortege 80-17
  And nothing is left except light on your fur— [Rabbit K 209-3
FURIOUS. In the high west there burns a furious star. [Monocle
  14-23
  More sharply in more furious selves. [Eve Angels 137-5
  A teeming millpond or a furious mind. [Nigger 155-13
  Angry men and furious machines [Dutch 290-1
  What rabbi, grown furious with human wish, [NSF 389-1
  Don Juan turned furious divinity, [Duck 64-27 P
  In slaughter; or if to match its furious wit [Sombre 69-6 P
  Without the furious roar in his capital. [Someone 85-6 A
FURIOUSLY. The furiously burning father-fire . . . [Red Fern 365-12
FUR-LIGHT. The red cat hides away in the fur-light [Rabbit K 209-20
FURNITURE. With appropriate, largely English, furniture, [Sombre
  68-7 P
FURRED. See star-furred.

FURROW. It dances down a furrow, in the early light, back of a
    crazy plough, the green blades following. [Plough-Boy 6-7 P
FURROWS. Unctuous furrows, [Primordia 9-7 P
FURTHER. To give this further thought. [Winter B 141-19
  Further magnified, sua voluntate, [Hero 277-20
  A further consummation. For the lunar month [EM 318-4
FURTIVE. Forms of farewell, furtive among green ferns. [NH 482-15
  Or accessible only in the most furtive fiction. [Nuns 93-2 P
FURTIVELY. Furtively, by candle and out of need. [Nigger 153-4
FURY. A man with the fury of a race of men, [Bottle 239-2
  What any fury to its noble centre. [Hero 274-18
  At the halyards. Why, then, when in golden fury [NSF 390-24
  Flame, sound, fury composed . . . Hear what he says, [Puel
    456-17
  There was no fury in transcendent forms. [Quiet 523-14
FUSE. Had crowded into the rocket and touched the fuse. [Liadoff
    346-13
FUSION. A fusion of night, its blue of the pole of blue [Choc
    297-16
FUSKY. Teaching a fusky alphabet. [Phosphor 267-16
FUSTIAN. Not fustian. The more than casual blue [Cred 375-5
FUT. "Celle Qui Fût Héaulmiette" [438-title
FUTURA. Beyond, futura's fuddle-fiddling lumps, [Montra 260-15
FUTURE. That airy dream of the future, [Mozart 132-5
  Why should the future leap the clouds [Botanist 2 136-3
  The future might stop emerging out of the past, [Nigger 151-10
  And the future emerging out of us seem to be one. [Nigger 151-12
  From any future, the ever-living and being, [Martial 238-8
  And on that yes the future world depends. [Beard 247-10
  Archaic and future happenings, [Oak 272-19
  Of the future, in which the memory had gone [Pure 330-20
  Could the future rest on a sense and be beyond [Pure 331-11
  The future is description without place, [Descrip 344-7
  And because what we say of the future must portend, [Descrip
    346-2
  Across the unscrawled fores the future casts [NSF 383-4
  This illumination, this elevation, this future [NH 481-24
  Of the single future of night, the single sleep, [NH 482-6
  Except the future. Always everything [Burnshaw 46-14 P
  They chanced to think. Suppose the future fails. [Duck 63-2 P
  It may be the future depends on an orator, [Duck 63-16 P
  This base of every future, vibrant spring, [Duck 63-28 P
  This future, although the elephants pass and the blare, [Duck
    63-31 P
  Yet to think of the future is a genius, [Duck 64-1 P
  To think of the future is a thing and he [Duck 64-2 P
  He from whose beard the future springs, elect. [Duck 64-31 P
  The future for them is always the deepest dome, [Duck 65-21 P
  Of heaven from heaven to the future, as a god, [Duck 65-27 P
  The future must bear within it every past, [Sombre 70-5 P
  And without future, a present time, is that [Sombre 71-24 P
  Of the future, of future man [Ulysses 101-9 P
  And future place, when these are known, [Ulysses 101-10 P
  Or a present future, hoped for in present hope, [Local 111-16 P
FUZZ. Ah! and red; and they have peach fuzz, ah! [Peaches 224-11
FUZZ-EYED. The youngest, the still fuzz-eyed, odd fleurettes,
    [Nuns 92-9 P

G. At beta b and gamma g, [Ord Women 11-10
GAELED. These Gaeled and fitful-fangled darknesses[Our Stars 455-18
GAFFER-GREEN. And you, my semblables, in gaffer-green, [Dutch
  291-20
GAIETY. A gaiety that is being, not merely knowing, [Gala 248-13
  The gaiety of language is our seigneur. [EM 322-19
  "Annual Gaiety" [32-title P
GAINED. Sight least, but metaphysical blindness gained, [Souls
  94-21 P
GALA. The total gala of auburn aureoles. [Nigger 151-18
  "Of Bright & Blue Birds & the Gala Sun" [248-title
GALAXIES. And thirty years, in the galaxies of birth, [Ideal
  88-9 A
GALAXY. And not this tinsmith's galaxy, [Mandolin 28-21 P
GALES. Crispin, merest miniscule in the gales, [C 29-11
GALLANT. "Gallant Château" [161-title
  And war for war, each has its gallant kind. [NSF 407-21
  To gallant notions on the part of cold. [Quiet 523-6
  By gallant notions on the part of night-- [Quiet 523-11
GALLANTLY. The desire for speech and meaning gallantly fulfilled,
  [Discov 95-18 P
GALLED. All eyes and size, and galled Justitia, [Lions 124-13
GALLIARD. And you, good galliard, to enchant black thoughts
  [Red Kit 32-3 P
GALLOON. Coat half-flare and half galloon; [Orangeade 103-10
GALLOPING. In galloping hedges, [Polo 37-20 P
GAMMA. At beta b and gamma g, [Ord Women 11-10
GANDERS. The soul, O ganders, flies beyond the parks [Swans 4-1
  And the soul, O ganders, being lonely, flies [Swans 4-11
GANG. The young man is well-disclosed, one of the gang, [Lack 303-6
GAPERING. Issued thin seconds glibly gapering. [Repet 306-13
GAPING. The third one gaping at the orioles [C 44-30
GARBLED. With garbled green. These were the planter's turquoise
  [NSF 393-5
GARDEN. Ursula, in a garden, found [Pourtraicte 21-1
  The good Lord in His garden sought [Pourtraicte 21-22
  Moisture and heat have swollen the garden into a slum of bloom.
    [Banal 62-14
  Whose garden is wind and moon, [Watermelon 88-21
  She bathed in her still garden, while [Peter 90-8
  Of the leafless garden." [Reader 147-9
  The garden flew round with the angel, [Circulat 149-16
  Empurpled garden grass; [Delight 162-6
  Mystic Garden & Middling Beast [Thought 185-title 2
  And the idea of man, the mystic garden and [Thought 185-20
  The middling beast, the garden of paradise [Thought 185-21
  And he that created the garden and peopled it. [Thought 185-22
  Scattered themselves in the garden, like [Vase 246-12
  To the ruddier bushes at the garden's end. [Hand 271-19
  Of the garden. We must prepare to hear the Roamer's [Phenom
    286-17
  In the inherited garden, a second-hand [Extraord 369-19
  And last year's garden grows salacious weeds. [Cred 377-10
  "A Room on a Garden" [40-title P
  And when I was in his garden [Three 141-9 P
GARDENER. The gardener's cat is dead, the gardener gone [Cred 377-9
  The gardener searches earth and sky [Room Gard 41-7 P
GARDENS. So gardens die, their meek breath scenting [Peter 92-4
  The idea of things for public gardens, [Hero 276-15
  Even in Paris, in the Gardens [Analysis 349-4
GARGOYLE. What niggling forms of gargoyle patter? [Archi 17-2 P
GARLANDED. Between chimeras and garlanded the way, [Sombre 67-29 P
GARMENT. Neither as mask nor as garment but as a being, [Dwarf
  208-11
  Sunrise is his garment's hem, sunset is hers. [NH 485-7
  A reddened garment falling to his feet, [Aug 492-8
GASCONADE. Approaching like a gasconade of drums. [C 32-18
GASPING. The grinding water and the gasping wind; [Key W 129-2
GASPINGS. The finned flutterings and gaspings of the ice, [Page
  422-8
GASPS. For breath to laugh the louder, the deeper gasps [Extracts
  253-19
GAT. Melodious, where spirits gat them home, [Sunday 68-20
GATE. "The Worms at Heaven's Gate" [49-title
  The leaden pigeon on the entrance gate [Nigger 152-18
  Beyond our gate and the windy sky [Postcard 159-9
  That in which space itself is contained, the gate [Rock 528-17
  The gate is not jasper. It is not bone. [Stan MBG 72-5 P
GATES. Outside of gates of hammered serafin, [Babies 77-2
GATHER. If they could gather their theses into one, [Extracts 254-6
GATHERED. I saw how the planets gathered [Domination 9-14
  And gathered them, [Pourtraicte 21-4
  This is the chair from which she gathered up [Beginning 428-3
  The heads held high and gathered in a ring [Old Woman 43-12 P
  See up-gathered.
GATHERED-UP. Like gathered-up forgetfulness, [Woman Song 360-11
GATHERING. Men gathering for a mighty flight of men, [Burnshaw
  51-8 P

The gathering of the imbecile against his motes [Discov 95-14 P
  Or Venice, motionless, gathering time and dust. [Real 110-10 P
GATHERS. A force gathers that will cry loudlier [Dutch 291-10
  A darkness gathers though it does not fall [AA 412-21
  Out of the eye when the loud wind gathers up [Greenest 58-11 P
GAUDIEST. And tallest hero and plus gaudiest vir. [Montra 262-12
GAUDIUM. For the gaudium of being, Jocundus instead [Sombre 71-29P
GAUDY. What was this gaudy, gusty panoply? [C 30-11
  Or gaudy as tulips? [Archi 17-8 P
  For poverty are gaudy bosh to these. [Duck 61-20 P
GAUNT. The gaunt guitarists on the strings [Ord Women 11-17
  Is no gaunt fugitive phantom. [Homunculus 26-22
GAUNTLY. Morose chiaroscuro, gauntly drawn. [C 34-17
GAVE. To whom oracular rockings gave no rest. [C 30-28
  Perhaps the Arctic moonlight really gave [C 34-25
  Gave to the cabin, lordlier than it was [C 44-25
  No mother suckled him, no sweet land gave [Sunday 67-28
  Unreal, give back to us what once you gave: [Fictive 88-17
  Gave suavity to the perplexed machine [Sea Surf 99-3
  And this-a-way he gave a fling. [MBG 178-10
  The enormous gongs gave edges to their sounds, [Uruguay 249-27
  The smallest lamp, which added its puissant flick, to which he
    gave [Prol 517-3
  The incredible gave him a purpose to believe. [Someone 85-18 A
GAWKS. Or: Gawks of hay . . . Augusta Moon, before [Golden 460-12
GAWKY. Out of these gawky flitterings, [Possum 294-10
  Poured forth the fine fins, the gawky beaks, the personalia,
    [Somnam 304-17
  But this gawky plaster will not be here. [Burnshaw 48-3 P
GAY. "Sad Strains of a Gay Waltz" [121-title
  The bronzes liquid through gay light. [Thought 187-3
  That instantly and in themselves they are gay [Gala 248-2
  For a moment they are gay and are a part [Gala 248-4
  The most gay and yet not so gay as it was. [Debris 338-13
  Gay is, gay was, the gay forsythia [NSF 385-12
  Of these beginnings, gay and green, propose [NSF 398-5
  Make gay the hallucinations in surfaces. [NH 472-21
  The gay tournamonde as of a single world [NH 476-3
  "Lulu Gay" [26-title P
  If awnings were celeste and gay, [Mandolin 28-18 P
  Let your golden hands wave fastly and be gay [Burnshaw 51-28 P
  The drafts of gay beginnings and bright ends, [Greenest 57-13 P
GAYETY. With Sunday pearls, her widow's gayety. [NSF 402-7
  And feel its country gayety and smile [Beginning 428-1
  The mere flowing of the water is a gayety, [R Conn 533-8
GAZE. For maidens who were wont to sit and gaze [Sunday 69-8
GAZED. And gazed on chosen mornings, [Three 131-19 P
  As it gazed [Three 131-20 P
GAZES. But the beggar gazes on calamity [Bad Time 426-12
GAZETTE. Gazette Guerrière. A man might happen [Hero 276-5
  The hero of the Gazette and the hero [Hero 276-7
GAZING. As we stand gazing at the rounded moon. [Eve Angels 138-6
  Serenely gazing at the violent abyss, [NSF 404-2
  Where he could lie and, gazing down at the sea, [Poem Mt 512-13
GEESE. And a little island full of geese and stars: [Sleight
  222-15
GELATINES. An eye most apt in gelatines and jupes, [C 27-14
GELID. And gelid Januar has gone to hell. [Poesie 302-8
GELOSO. Capitán profundo, capitán geloso, [Orangeade 102-16
GEMMY. Was gemmy marionette to him that sought [C 36-4
GEMUTLICHKEIT. From sheer Gemütlichkeit. [Nigger 152-17
GENEALOGY. Has been counted, the genealogy [Ulysses 102-9 P
GENERAL. And general lexicographer of mute [C 28-11
  Loud, general, large, fat, soft [Jumbo 269-11
  As of a general being or human universe. [Past Nun 378-22
  That it made the General a bit absurd, [NSF 391-18
  As a setting for geraniums, the General, [NSF 391-23
  Yet the General was rubbish in the end. [NSF 392-3
  Is the poem both peculiar and general? [NSF 396-20
  The peculiar potency of the general, [NSF 397-7
  And beetling of belts and lights of general stones, [NH 477-20
  And the general fidget from busts of Constantine [NH 488-14
  Merely parts of the general fiction of the mind: [Recit 87-29 P
  (Remote from the deadly general of men, [Americana 94-1 P
GENERAL DU PUY. The great statue of the General Du Puy [NSF 391-7
GENERAL JACKSON. When General Jackson [Am Sub 130-21
GENERAL-LARGE. And jumbo, the loud general-large [Jumbo 269-2
GENERALS. The boulevards of the generals. Why should [Feo 334-5
GENERATING. Between the matin air and color, goldenest generating,
  [Inelegance 25-16 P
GENERATION. That generation's dream, aviled [MBG 183-15
  A generation sealed, men remoter than mountains, [Waldorf 241-7
  March toward a generation's centre. [Dutch 293-10
  Then generation by generation he grew [Good Man 364-3
  Than the need of each generation to be itself, [Armor 530-9
  Of a generation that does not know itself, [Sombre 68-30 P
GENERATIONS. The generations of the bird are all [Somnam 304-7
  Its generations that follow in their universe, [Somnam 304-11
  Generations of the imagination piled [Owl 434-13
  Generations of shepherds to generations of sheep. [Luther 461-18

The babble of generations magnifies [Spaniard 34-18 P
In the generations of thought, man's sons [Ulysses 103-7 P
Used by generations of hermits. [Three 130-11 P
GENEROUS. Celestin, the generous, the civilized, [Papini 447-7
GENESIS. And uncourageous genesis . . . It seems [EM 315-24
Another and later genesis, music [EM 321-6
GENEVA. "The Doctor of Geneva" [24-title
The doctor of Geneva stamped the sand [Geneva 24-1
By the lake at Geneva and consider logic: [EM 325-3
GENII. And were themselves the genii [Joost 46-18
True genii for the diminished, spheres, [Choc 300-7
We ask which means most, for us, all the genii [Antag 425-15
By such slight genii in such pale air. [Orb 440-8
2. Out of their bottle the green genii come. [Someone 86-5 A
GENIUS. The genius of that cheek. Here are the lips, [Worms 50-1
She sang beyond the genius of the sea. [Key W 128-11
The planes that ought to have genius, [Common 221-19
Their genius: the exquisite errors of time. [Extracts 254-24
Philandering? . . . The genius of misfortune [EM 316-23
Falls out on everything: the genius of [EM 316-27
The genius of the body, which is our world, [EM 317-2
Its line moves quickly with the genius [Pastor 379-9
The vital, the never-failing genius, [AA 420-20
If it is a world without a genius, [Antag 425-13
In the genius of summer that they blew up [NH 482-18
Yet to think of the future is a genius, [Duck 64-1 P
GENTLE. She makes that gentler that can gentle be. [AA 413-12
GENTLEMAN. The young gentleman was seen [Three 136-6 P
Just as the young gentleman [Three 139-9 P
The young gentleman of the ballad. [Three 139-13 P
GENTLEMEN. Permit me, gentlemen, [Soldat 13-1 P
GENTLER. Shall be the gentler for the death you die [Extracts
253-27
She makes that gentler that can gentle be. [AA 413-12
GEOGRAPHERS. Geographers and philosophers, [MBG 179-18
GEOGRAPHY. Would be a geography of the dead: not of that land
[Somnam 304-13
Of that simplified geography, in which [Feo 334-11
GEOMETRIC. The eye, a geometric glitter, tiltings [Someone 87-20 A
GEORGIA. The man in Georgia waking among pines [C 38-15
GEORGIAN. Dixhuitième and Georgian and serene. [Lytton 39-25 P
GERANIUM. A geranium withers on the window-sill. [Phenom 286-2
Geranium budgets, pay-roll water-falls, [Duck 62-24 P
GERANIUM-COLORED. Fixed one for good in geranium-colored day.
[Armor 529-4
GERANIUMS. Out of geraniums and unsmelled flowers. [Plot Giant
6-15
As a setting for geraniums, the General, [NSF 391-23
The geraniums on the sill. [Aug 493-12
Or the bench with the pot of geraniums, the stained mattress
and the washed overalls drying in the sun! [Indigo 22-12 P
GERMAN. Might well have been German or Spanish, [Circulat 150-6
Act I, Scene 1, at a German Staats-Oper. [Nigger 153-16
One says a German chandelier-- [MBG 172-15
And above the German camps? It looked apart. [Martial 238-5
Who can move the German load [Imago 439-2
GESTICULATING. Gesticulating lightning, mystical, [C 32-26
GESTICULATION. Between cities is a gesticulation of forms, [Choc
296-14
GESTURE. Of the actor, half his gesture, half [MBG 170-1
Of an impersonal gesture, a stranger's hand. [Hand 271-14
The curving of her hip, as motionless gesture, [Couch 295-8
An invisible gesture. Let this be called [Couch 295-15
In desperate hallow, rugged gesture, fault [EM 316-26
A gesture in the dark, a fear one feels [Moonlight 531-16
Adorned for a multitude, in a gesture spent [Sombre 71-27 P
In the gesture's whim, a passion merely to be [Sombre 71-28 P
Mature emotional gesture, that-- [Stan MBG 73-8 P
GESTURED. See tragic-gestured.
GESTURES. The grandiose gestures [Infanta 7-14
Doleful heroics, pinching gestures forth [Monocle 17-11
Vengeful, shadowed by gestures [Bagatelles 213-16
Without gestures is to get at it as [Couch 295-17
Slight gestures that could rend the palpable ice, [Page 423-2
She spoke with backward gestures of her hand. [Owl 435-8
By gestures of a mortal perfection. [Stan Hero 84-22 P
GESTURING. Gesturing grandiose things in the air, [Soldat 16-5 P
GESTURINGS. Except in faint, memorial gesturings, [C 29-1
GESU. Gesu, not native of a mind [MBG 180-7
GET. As to get no more from the moonlight [Two Figures 85-15
And doesn't get under way. [Sailing 120-3
That's what one wants to get near. Could it after all [Dump
202-28
To everything, in order to get at myself. [Uruguay 249-4
Projection B. To get at the thing [Couch 295-16
Without gestures is to get at it as [Couch 295-17
They will get it straight one day at the Sorbonne. [NSF 406-22
Are questions of the looks they get. The bouquet, [Bouquet 451-2
Get out of the way! [Soldat 13-4 P
GETS. Hear hard, gets at an essential integrity. [NH 475-3

GETTING. Of statement, directly and indirectly getting at [NH
488-18
GEWGAWS. Mere blusteriness that gewgaws jollified, [C 44-22
GHOST. The sovereign ghost. As such, the Socrates [C 27-8
Permit that if as ghost I come [W Burgher 61-10
Excelling summer, ghost of fragrance falling [Ghosts 119-16
Choke every ghost with acted violence, [Nigger 155-6
It is a ghost that inhabits a cloud, [Lack 303-9
But a ghost for Andrew, not lean, catarrhal [Lack 303-10
Or moonlight, silently, as Plato's ghost [Less 327-12
As if Liadoff no longer remained a ghost [Liadoff 347-8
By fortune, his gray ghost may meditate [Cats 368-7
By a pure fountain, that was a ghost, and is, [Aug 489-10
From man's ghost, larger and yet a little like, [Look 518-1
Determined thereto, perhaps by his father's ghost, [Role 93-4 P
GHOSTLIER. In ghostlier demarcations, keener sounds. [Key W 130-15
GHOSTLY. This structure of ideas, these ghostly sequences [Bed
326-13
Other ghostly sequences and, it would be, luminous [Bed 326-18
To sleep in that bed for its disorder, talking of ghostly [Bed
327-3
The ghostly celebrations of the picnic, [Aug 492-14
GHOSTS. Why, without pity on these studious ghosts, [Monocle 14-10
The darkened ghosts of our old comedy? [Heaven 56-11
"Ghosts as Cocoons" [119-title
The moon they made their own attendant ghosts, [Eve Angels 137-11
"A Rabbit as King of the Ghosts" [209-title
The imaginative, ghosts that dally [Hero 279-6
There were ghosts that returned to earth to hear his phrases,
[Large 423-11
Comes the cold volume of forgotten ghosts, [NH 468-6
In the presence of the barefoot ghosts! [Lytton 39-5 P
GIANT. "The Plot against the Giant" [6-title
Like giant arms among the clouds. [How Live 125-20
Sand heaped in the clouds, giant that fought [MBG 179-7
To the total thing, a shapeless giant forced [Poem Morn 219-15
A giant's heart in the veins, all courage. [Gigan 289-7
Each man himself became a giant, [Gigan 289-15
To giant red, sweats up a giant sense [Repet 307-8
He find another? The giant of sense remains [Repet 308-9
A giant without a body. If, as a giant, [Repet 308-10
Of the giant sense, the enormous harnesses [Repet 308-20
The weather and the giant of the weather, [NSF 385-22
It feels good as it is without the giant, [NSF 386-1
The pensive giant prone in violet space [NSF 387-2
The giant body the meanings of its folds, [Owl 433-16
A giant, on the horizon, glistening, [Orb 442-16
It is a giant, always, that is evolved, [Orb 442-25
A giant on the horizon, given arms, [Orb 443-8
Of color, the giant of nothingness, each one [Orb 443-21
And the giant ever changing, living in change. [Orb 443-22
Part of the question that is a giant himself: [NH 465-8
Unless a second giant kills the first-- [NH 465-11
The giant Phosphor of their earliest prayers. [Duck 65-23 P
A tall figure upright in a giant's air. [Recit 87-24 P
The giant sea, read his own mind. [Ulysses 99-12 P
Makes them a pack on a giant's back, [Ulysses 103-24 P
The giant sea, read his own mind. [Presence 105-15 P
GIANTNESS. My orator. Let this giantness fall down [Repet 310-2
GIANTS. The giants that each one of them becomes [Repet 307-3
The powdered personals against the giants' rage, [Repet 309-17
Was full of these archaic forms, giants [Aug 491-17
GIBBERISH. The poem goes from the poet's gibberish to [NSF 396-13
The gibberish of the vulgate and back again. [NSF 396-24
It is the gibberish of the vulgate that he seeks. [NSF 397-5
GIBRALTAR. And Gibraltar is dissolved like spit in the wind. [Puel
456-3
GIDDAP. Giddap! The ruby roses' hair [Room Gard 40-17 P
GIFT. In this spent world, she must possess. The gift [Red Kit
30-19 P
GIGANTIC. It stands gigantic, with a certain tip [Monocle 17-4
Let down gigantic quavers of its voice, [C 33-16
In spite of this, the gigantic bulk of him [Choc 299-4
Gigantic embryos of populations, [Choc 300-8
He shares a gigantic life, it is because [Repet 308-11
The gigantic has a reality of its own. [Repet 308-12
At some gigantic, solitary urn, [Burnshaw 49-4 P
Gigantic in everything but size. [Ulysses 101-2 P
12. An uncivil shape like a gigantic haw. [Someone 86-15 A
GIGANTOMACHIA. "Gigantomachia" [289-title
GILDED. See parcel-gilded.
GILDERED. Until flicked by feeling, in a gildered street, [NSF 407-1
GILDERING. The sun of Nietzsche gildering the pool, [Descrip 342-18
Yes: gildering the swarm-like manias [Descrip 342-19
GILDERLINGED. Entinselled and gilderlinged and gone, [Celle 438-15
GILDING. Walking the paths, watching the gilding sun, [Duck 65-18 P
GILDINGS. Sees the petty gildings on February . . . [Hero 280-11
GILL. Contains for its children not a gill of sweet. [Greenest
55-26 P
GILT. And gilt umbrellas. Paradisal green [Sea Surf 99-2

GINGER. Health-o, when ginger and fromage bewitch [NE Verses
    104-5
GINGERLY. Their dreams, he did it in a gingerly way. [C 39-30
GIOVANNI PAPINI. Giovanni Papini, by your faith, know how [Papini
    447-1
GIRAFFES. How happy I was the day I told the young Blandina of
    three-legged giraffes . . . [Analysis 348-1
GIRANDOLES. Fubbed the girandoles. [Ord Women 11-4
GIRDLE. For this, musician, in your girdle fixed, [Fictive 88-14
GIRDLES. From the loosed girdles in the spangling must. [Sea Surf
    101-14
GIRL. "Girl in a Nightgown" [214-title
    Bloomed in sheets, as they bloom, and the girl, [Forces 229-1
    A pink girl took a white dog walking. [Forces 229-2
    The girl had to hold back and lean back to hold him, [Forces 229-4
    Fat girl, terrestrial, my summer, my night, [NSF 406-7
    A maid of forty is no feathery girl. [Stan MMO 19-9 P
    Of a girl's. [Three 143-3 P
GIRLS. Should mask as white girls. [W Burgher 61-4
    Triangles and the names of girls. [Dezem 218-4
    The clouds becoming braided girls. [Vase 246-14
    The Italian girls wore jonquils in their hair [NSF 389-16
    Violets, doves, girls, bees and hyacinths [NSF 389-22
GIVE. you give me, ancient star: [Nuances 18-5
    Why should she give her bounty to the dead? [Sunday 67-12
    It did not give of bird or bush, [Jar 76-15
    We give ourselves our likest issuance. [Fictive 88-9
    Unreal, give back to us what once you gave: [Fictive 88-17
    Whose coming may give revel [Watermelon 89-8
    Of the gorgeous wheel and so to give [Sailing 121-4
    To give this further thought. [Winter B 141-19
    Each in the other what each has to give. [Re-state 146-5
    The reason can give nothing at all [Dezem 218-19
    Home and the fields give praise, hurrah, hip, [Hero 278-13
    Yet look not at his colored eyes. Give him [NSF 388-13
    It Must Give Pleasure [NSF 398-title 3
    And not imagined. The removes must give [Papini 447-5
    And there the senses give and nothing take, [NH 480-18
    We'll give the week-end to wisdom, to Weisheit, the rabbi, [Aug
    492-1
    Should give you more than their peculiar chords [Rome 510-19
    Give him-- [Phases 4-22 P
    Give up dead things and the living turn away. [Burnshaw 49-6 P
    Give only their color to the leaves. The trees [Sombre 71-3 P
    Blond weather. Give the mule his hay. [Stan MBG 73 17 P
GIVEN. And something given to make whole among [C 30-14
    On a given plane is ascertainable [Nigger 157-8
    Here, then, is an abstraction given head, [Orb 443-7
    A giant on the horizon, given arms, [Orb 443-8
    And willed. She has given too much, but not enough. [Aug 496-3
    Time's given perfections made to seem like less [Armor 530-8
    Of which I am the captain. Given what I intend, [Eship 78-4 P
    The last man given for epitome, [Ideal 88-21 A
GIVES. For all it takes it gives a humped return [C 43-6
    Gives motion to perfection more serene [Fictive 87-19
    Gives comfort, so that other bodies come, [Anatomy 108-10
    Gives the touch of the senses, not of the hand, [MBG 174-20
    From these it takes. Perhaps it gives, [MBG 177-5
    Like a man without a doctrine. The light he gives-- [Freed 205-1
    It is how he gives his light. It is how he shines, [Freed 205-2
    An instrument, twanging a wiry string that gives [Of Mod 240-15
    Falls on and makes and gives, even a speech. [Phosphor 267-13
    Gives one a blank uneasiness, as if [EM 325-9
    That speaks for him such seemings as death gives. [Descrip 341-6
    That gives a candid kind to everything. [NSF 382-24
    Who gives transparence to their present peace. [AA 413-11
    She gives transparence. But she has grown old. [AA 413-14
    That gives its power to the wild-ringed eye. [Owl 433-22
    One feels the life of that which gives life as it is. [Course
    96-18 P
GIVING. And giving your bland motions to the air. [Swans 4-8
    The motions of the mind and giving form [Eve Angels 137-20
    By giving it a form. But the character [Recit 86-6 P
GLACIAL. Was like a glacial pink upon the air. [C 34-14
    For him cold's glacial beauty is his fate. [Bad Time 426-15
GLACIER. A glacier running through delirium, [Imago 439-16
GLAD. Ariel was glad he had written his poems. [Planet 532-7
    They were so glad to see the spring. [Sat Night 28-11 P
GLADE. Romantic with dreams of her avoirdupois, green glade [Pure
    330-17
    Green glade and holiday hotel and world [Pure 330-19
    But there was one invalid in that green glade [Pure 331-2
    Bethou, bethou, bethou me in my glade. [NSF 394-3
    The moving grass, the Indian in his glade. [AA 412-3
    In the bee-loud glade. Lights on the steamer moved. [Page 422-4
    See how the absent moon waits in a glade [Blanche 10-10 P
GLADE-BOAT. The going of the glade-boat [Sugar-Cane 12-7
GLADLY. Poet, as if he thought gladly, being [Hero 277-17
    How gladly with proper words the soldier dies, [NSF 408-2
GLAMOROUS. Of the guillotine or of any glamorous hanging.

[Parochial 192-7
GLARE. Down to the sand, the glare [Pascagoula 127-4
    But their mignon, marblish glare! [Anything B 211-13
    And their ordinary glare, [Song Fixed 519-22
    The glare of revelations going by! [Blanche 10-8 P
GLARES. It glares beneath the webs [Common 221-17
    To shaking out heavy bodies in the glares [Cuisine 228-7
    Except that a green plant glares, as you look [Plant 506-16
    Glares, outside of the legend, with the barbarous green [Plant
    506-18
GLASGOW-FROST. Those whose Jerusalem is Glasgow-frost [Greenest
    59-24 P
GLASS. Lacking the three glass knobs, that sheet [Emperor 64-10
    With barbaric glass. [Thirteen 93-13
    In a glass coach. [Thirteen 94-14
    Himself than in this fertile glass. [MBG 181-14
    Granted each picture is a glass, [Prelude 195-1
    "The Glass of Water" [197-title
    That the glass would melt in heat, [Glass 197-7
    Here in the centre stands the glass. Light [Glass 197-12
    And in that state, the glass is a pool. [Glass 197-14
    About what stands here in the centre, not the glass, [Glass
    197-21
    A naked man who regarded himself in the glass [Landsc 241-16
    As a mirror with a voice, the man of glass, [Oboe 250-21
    The glass man, cold and numbered, dewily cries, [Oboe 251-4
    The glass man, without external reference-- [Oboe 251-21
    And the ear is glass, in which the noises pelt, [Extracts 252-3
    The page is blank or a frame without a glass [Phosphor 267-7
    Or a glass that is empty when he looks. [Phosphor 267-8
    Down deeply in the empty glass . . . [Phosphor 267-10
    He was a shell of dark blue glass, or ice, [Choc 297-9
    Cast corners in the glass. He could describe [EM 314-1
    In heaven as in a glass; a second earth; [NSF 383-14
    Are rubbings of a glass in which we peer. [NSF 398-4
    This was the glass in which she used to look [Beginning 427-15
    The world has turned to the several speeds of glass, [Bouquet
    449-3
    For example: Au Château. Un Salon. A glass [Golden 460-10
    An attic glass, hums of the old Lutheran bells [Golden 460-13
    Abba, dark death is the breaking of a glass. [Golden 460-16
    Life fixed him, wandering on the stair of glass, [NH 483-10
    The glass of the air becomes an element-- [NH 488-1
    The total of human shadows bright as glass. [Aug 494-23
    Mud, water like dirty glass, expressing silence [Plain 503-4
    Seal him there. He looked in a glass of the earth and thought
    he lived in it. [Madame 507-2
    It was only a glass because he looked in it. It was nothing he
    could be told. [Madame 507-6
    The mannerism of nature caught in a glass [Look 519-10
    A glass aswarm with things going as far as they can. [Look 519-12
    They sip the glass. [Phases 3-4 P
    And not in this dead glass, which can reflect [Blanche 10-2 P
    Seated before these shining forms, like the duskiest glass,
    reflecting the piebald of roses or what you will. [Piano 21-18P
    "The Indigo Glass in the Grass" [22-title P
    This bottle of indigo glass in the grass, [Indigo 22-11 P
    Until the sharply-colored glass transforms [Burnshaw 52-9 P
    A man that looks at himself in a glass and finds [Americana 94-7P
    It is the man in the glass that lives, not he. [Americana 94-8 P
    Like glass and sun, of male reality [Fare Guit 99-8 P
    Where the fattest women belled the glass. [Dinner 110-4 P
    Porcelain, Venetian glass, [Three 131-6 P
    The contorted glass. [Three 132-2 P
    Contorted glass . . . [Three 138-21 P
    See looking-glass; sea-glass.
GLASS-BLOWER. Glass-blower's destiny, bloodless episcopus, [NSF
    394-11
GLASSILY-SPARKLING. Of the wind, the glassily-sparkling particles
    [Page 423-7
GLASS-LIKE. Part of the glass-like sides on which it glided over
    the salt-stained water, [Prol 516-3
GLASSWORKS. It was not a night blown at a glassworks in Vienna
    [Real 110-9 P
GLASSY. Toward the town, tell why the glassy lights, [Key W 130-5
    The rabbit fat, at last, in glassy grass. [Nigger 153-20
    It blows a glassy brightness on the fire [Novel 458-6
    A glassy ocean lying at the door, [NH 468-15
    In the glassy sound of your voices, the porcelain cries,
    [Burnshaw 52-6 P
GLAZED. If neatly glazed, becomes the same as the fruit [Extracts
    253-9
GLAZES. The chandeliers, their morning glazes spread [Blue Bldg
    217-11
GLEAM. Gleam sharply as the sun comes up. [Botanist 2 135-17
GLEAMING. You could almost see the brass on her gleaming, [Vari
    235-19
    The green corn gleaming and experience [EM 325-23
    As rain and booming, gleaming, blowing, swept [NH 484-10
GLEAMS. The green corn gleams and the metaphysicals [EM 325-27

GLIBLY. Issued thin seconds glibly gapering. [Repet 306-13
GLIDED. Part of the glass-like sides on which it glided over the
  salt-stained water, [Prol 515-3
GLIDES. Glides to his meeting like a lover [Hero 276-17
GLIMPSES. In glimpses, on the edge or at the tip, [Sombre 67-1 P
GLINTS. By the glints of sound from the grass. These are not
  [Myrrh 350-6
GLISTEN. Will glisten again with motion, the music [Sad Gay 122-17
GLISTENING. Poured brilliant iris on the glistening blue. [Sea
  Surf 99-15
  The shapes have lost their glistening. [Sad Gay 122-2
  Or of glistening reference to what is real, [Repet 309-7
  Weaves always glistening from the heart and mind. [NSF 396-12
  A giant, on the horizon, glistening, [Orb 442-16
  If the black of night stands glistening on beau mont, [NH 467-2
  Stands glistening and Haddam shines and sways. [R Conn 533-15
  They cock small ears, more glistening and pale [Soldat 14-2 P
  The rainbow in its glistening serpentines [Burnshaw 47-28 P
  An audience to mimics glistening [Sombre 67-24 P
GLISTENS. That glistens on your face and hair. [Nigger 152-14
  It glistens in essential dark. [MBG 172-18
  The yellow glistens. [Pears 196-17
  It glistens with various yellows, [Pears 196-18
  Snow glistens in its instant in the air, [Pieces 351-12
GLITTER. The spruces rough in the distant glitter [Snow Man 10-3
  The glitter of a being, which the eye [Choc 297-14
  In a glitter that is a life, a gold [Human 363-15
  The oranges glitter as part of the sky, [Stan MBG 72-13 P
  The rising and the swell, the first line's glitter, [Woman Had
  81-17 P
  When the trees glitter with that which despoils them, [Discov
  95-8 P
  Like glitter ascended into fire. [Ulysses 102-17 P
  The eye, a geometric glitter, tiltings [Someone 87-20 A
GLITTER-GOES. The glitter-goes on surfaces of tanks, [NSF 384-13
GLITTERING. In endless ledges, glittering, submerged [C 34-7
  As of those crosses, glittering, [Botanist 2 136-10
  And merely of their glittering, [Botanist 2 136-11
  Glittering scales and point [Bagatelles 213-7
  For him to see, wove round her glittering hair. [Hand 271-6
  In glittering seven-colored changes, [Oak 272-20
  Of the wind and the glittering were real now, [Repet 306-8
  The stars are putting on their glittering belts. [AA 419-22
  They have, or they may have, their glittering crown, [Golden
  460-20
  Becomes the rock of autumn, glittering, [NH 476-10
  And Adirondack glittering. The cat hawks it [Aug 490-5
  To return in a glittering wheel [Drum-Majors 36-21 P
  In a storm blown into glittering shapes, and flames [Burnshaw
  52-21 P
  Toward which, in the nights, the glittering serpents climb,
  [Greenest 55-12 P
  Concealed in glittering grass, dank reptile skins. [Duck 65-11 P
  The vigor of glory, a glittering in the veins, [Real 110-13 P
GLITTERINGS. Bearded with chains of blue-green glitterings
  [Bouquet 449-7
GLITTERS. She scuds the glitters, [Paltry 5-9
  Glitters in the sun. [Ploughing 20-4
  Its vacancy glitters round us everywhere. [Eve Angels 137-2
  Its glitters, its divinations of serene [EM 318-16
  Soaring Olympus glitters in the sun. [Infernale 25-12 P
GLOBE. The central man, the human globe, responsive [Oboe 250-20
  But we and the diamond globe at last were one. [Oboe 251-16
GLOBED. Globed in today and tomorrow, [Gray 140-19
GLOOM. His eye on an outdoor gloom [Bananas 54-12
  This gloom is the darkness of the sea. [MBG 179-17
  Beseech them for an overpowering gloom. [Red Kit 32-4 P
GLOOMILY. Gloomily, the journalist confronts [Bus 116-2 P
GLOOMS. See water-glooms.
GLOOMY. Gloomy grammarians in golden gowns, [On Manner 55-10
  Green and gloomy eyes [Brave 138-10
GLORIAS. Or this, whose jingling glorias, importunate of perfec-
  tion, [Inelegance 26-3 P
GLORIES. See morning-glories.
GLORIOUSLY. The angels come, armed, gloriously to slay [Greenest
  55-28 P
GLORY. And next in glory to enduring love, [Sunday 68-10
  And peculiar and appropriate glory, [Hero 277-26
  Was the glory of heaven in the wilderness-- [Dutch 292-16
  That a new glory of new men assembles. [Dutch 292-23
  Plucks on his strings to pluck abysmal glory, [NSF 404-15
  In a robe that is our glory as he guards. [Owl 435-3
  Custodians of the glory of the scene, [NH 469-17
  This was the salty taste of glory, [Phases 3-13 P
  Her glory in your passion and be proud. [Red Kit 31-13 P
  Be glory to this unmerciful pontifex, [Greenest 60-3 P
  The vigor of glory, a glittering in the veins, [Real 110-13 P
GLOSS. Preferring text to gloss, he humbly served [C 39-22
  See wind-gloss.
GLOVE. In a black glove, holds a novel by Camus. She begged

[Novel 457-11
GLOZING. Glozing his life with after-shining flicks, [C 46-5
GLUB. And fond, the total man of glubbal glub, [Choc 301-2
GLUBBAL. And fond, the total man of glubbal glub, [Choc 301-2
GLUE. In glue, but things transfixed, transpierced and well
  [Bouquet 449-13
GLUEY. That the marbles are gluey pastiches, the stairs [Prelude
  195-3
GLUTTED. A right red with its composites glutted full, [Bouquet
  452-3
GNASHING. Making a great gnashing, over the water wallows [Puel
  456-8
GNAW. The horses gnaw the bark from the trees. [Primordia 8-8 P
GO. Will go, like the centre of sea-green pomp, [Paltry 6-6
  I am a yeoman, as such fellows go. [Monocle 16-26
  But when they go that tip still tips the tree. [Monocle 17-6
  And whence they came and whither they shall go [Sunday 70-12
  The clouds go, nevertheless, [Soldier 97-11
  Go on, high ship, since now, upon the shore, [Farewell 117-1
  The floor. Go on through the darkness. The waves fly back.
  [Farewell 117-10
  That I loved her once . . . Farewell. Go on, high ship.[Farewell
  118-10
  To the cold, go on, high ship, go on, plunge on. [Farewell 118-20
  At the base of the statue, we go round and round. [Mice 123-2
  Shall a man go barefoot [Am Sub 131-2
  It goes and the birds go, [Gray 140-15
  The Jew did not go to his synagogue [Winter B 141-1
  To go to Florida one of these days, [Winter B 141-16
  Yet that things go round and again go round [Circulat 150-7
  Long-tailed ponies go nosing the pine-lands, [Parochial 191-1
  To go to the Louvre to behold himself. [Prelude 195-7
  To cover, to crown, to cover--let it go-- [Dames 206-19
  For all the thoughts of summer that go with it [Dwarf 208-5
  Resolved the world. We cannot go back to that. [Connois 215-16
  Go, mouse, go nibble at Lenin in his tomb. [Blue Bldg 217-19
  You are one . . . Go hunt for honey in his hair. [Blue Bldg
  217-22
  Since in the hero-land to which we go, [Montra 262-1
  Their own, waiting until we go [Dutch 293-2
  The figures of the past go cloaked. [Poesie 302-12
  And go, go slowly, but they go. [Poesie 302-14
  To be? You go, poor phantoms, without place [EM 320-4
  And let it go, with nothing lost, [Woman Song 361-4
  Young men go walking in the woods, [Pediment 361-7
  The savage transparence. They go crying [Pediment 361-16
  These two go well together, the sinuous brim [Pastor 380-2
  He wanted the river to go on flowing the same way, [Cata 425-3
  He would go to bed, cover himself with blankets-- [Novel 457-9
  Go with the walker subtly walking there. [NH 473-8
  Go back to a parent before thought, before speech, [Irish 501-11
  They go to the cliffs of Moher rising out of the mist, [Irish
  501-13
  The life of the city never lets go, nor do you [Rome 510-12
  A place to go to in his own direction, [Poem Mt 512-6
  Let's go home. [Drum-Majors 37-12 P
  Of autumn, these horses should go clattering [Burnshaw 47-9 P
  Hé quoi! Angels go pricking elephants? [Greenest 55-30 P
  Therefore my song should go [Three 137-3 P
  Go. [Three 140-6 P
GOAT-LEAPER. Goat-leaper, crystalled and luminous, sitting [AA
  417-9
GOBBET. Man proved a gobbet in my mincing world. [Monocle 17-24
  How thick this gobbet is with overlays, [Someone 85-19 A
GOBBET-SKINS. In beak and bud and fruity gobbet-skins, [C 32-7
GOBBLE. All din and gobble, blasphemously pink. [C 44-23
  The catbird's gobble in the morning half-awake-- [Holiday 313-6
GOBLIN. Although life seems a goblin mummery, [Soldat 13-14 P
GOBLINRY. As on this voyage, out of goblinry, [C 35-10
GOBS. Of gobs, who called her orchidean, [Lulu G 26-10 P
GOD. Good God! What a precious light! [Bananas 54-9
  Not as a god, but as a god might be, [Sunday 70-2
  He stood at last by God's help and the police; [Anglais 149-10
  God of the sausage-makers, sacred guild, [Nigger 157-4
  The thinking of god is smoky dew. [MBG 168-5
  The idea of god no longer sputtered [Thought 184-13
  Hymns of the struggle of the idea of god [Thought 185-19
  With all his attributes no god but man [Thought 186-11
  God and all angels sing the world to sleep, [Men Fall 187-9
  God and all angels, this was his desire, [Men Fall 188-13
  One part is man, the other god: [Dezem 218-7
  Kept speaking, of God. I changed the word to man. [Les Plus 245-4
  Can never stand as god, is ever wrong [Oboe 250-16
  "God Is Good. It Is a Beautiful Night" [285-title
  The fault lies with an over-human god, [EM 315-14
  A too, too human god, self-pity's kin [EM 315-23
  If there must be a god in the house, must be, [Less 327-9
  If there must be a god in the house, let him be one [Less 328-7
  God only was his only elegance. [Good Man 364-2
  The death of one god is the death of all. [NSF 381-7

Without a god, O silver sheen and shape, [Bouquet 449-16
The dry eucalyptus seeks god in the rainy cloud. [NH 475-4
God in the object itself, without much choice. [NH 475-10
The search for god." It is the philosopher's search [NH 481-6
We say God and the imagination are one . . . [Final 524-14
Ah, good God! That all beasts should have [Parasol 20-7 P
What god rules over Africa, what shape, [Greenest 54-23P
And the serpent might become a god, quick-eyed, [Greenest 54-23P
No god rules over Africa, no throne, [Greenest 55-5 P
Fatal Ananke is the common god. [Greenest 59-1 P
Each look and each necessitous cry, as a god [Greenest 59-8 P
Fateful Ananke is the final god. [Greenest 59-20 P
Of heaven from heaven to the future, as a god, [Duck 65-27 P
From constable to god, from earth to air, [Bship 80-22 P
It is like a critic of God, the world [Region 115-13 P
GODOLPHIN. There peace, the godolphin and fellow, estranged,
    estranged, [Owl 434-1
GODS. A substitute for all the gods: [MBG 176-3
Well, the gods grow out of the weather. [Jersey 210-5
The gods grow out of the people. [Jersey 210-7
The fire eye in the clouds survives the gods. [Sleight 222-12
An empty land; the gods that Boucher killed; [Oboe 250-10
Consider how the speechless, invisible gods [Montra 262-13
All men can speak of it in the voice of his gods . . . [Look 518-2
Without his literature and without his gods . . . [Look 518-2
Fromage and coffee and cognac and no gods. [Greenest 57-29 P
It was a mistake to paint the gods. The gold [Greenest 57-30 P
And bares an earth that has no gods, and bares [Greenest 58-13 P
The gods like marble figures fallen, left [Greenest 58-14 P
Of the gods and, for him, a thousand litanies [Greenest 59-26 P
Regardless of gods that were praised in goldness [Stan Hero
    83-21 P
Of gods and men destroyed, the right [Ulysses 102-10 P
GOES. She touches the clouds, where she goes [Paltry 5-19
But that of earth both comes and goes at once. [Monocle 15-26
And of Phoebus the Tailor the second saying goes: [NE Verses 105-5
My old boat goes round on a crutch [Sailing 120-2
It goes and the birds go, [Gray 140-15
Round and round goes the bell of the water [Vari 235-6
And round and round goes the water itself [Vari 235-7
The greenness of night lies on the page and goes[Phosphor 267-9
Nor meditate the world as it goes round. [Phenom 286-6
And goes to an external world, having [Repet 308-5
Who comes and goes and comes and goes all day. [NSF 381-22
The poem goes from the poet's gibberish to [NSF 396-13
One goes on asking questions. That, then, is one [Ulti 429-16
Included, the spirit that goes roundabout [NH 471-23
That comes and goes in silences of its own. [Look 518-22
Goes off a little on the side and stops. [Duck 63-33 P
The boatman goes humming. He smokes a cigar [Stan MBG 72-11 P
In which the world goes round and round [Ulysses 102-26 P
Goes round in the climates of the mind [Ulysses 102-30 P
See glitter-goes.
GOING. The going of the glade-boat [Sugar-Cane 12-7
Going in many directions [Homunculus 26-3
The rich man going bare, the paladin [C 37-17
People are not going [Ten O'C 66-10
So evenings die, in their green going, [Peter 92-2
And it was going to snow. [Thirteen 95-3
Discolored, how they are going to defeat. [Extracts 259-20
So many clappers going without bells, [NSF 394-5
Red-in-red repetitions never going [NSF 400-13
Themselves and, therefore, good, the going round [NSF 405-21
And round and round, the merely going round, [NSF 405-22
Until merely going round is a final good, [NSF 405-23
Or, say, the late going colors of that past, [NH 482-1
The last leaf that is going to fall has fallen. [NH 487-10
A glass aswarm with things going as far as they can. [Look 519-12
The glare of revelations going by! [Blanche 10-8 P
Quite going? [Soldat 12-6 P
There was a crush of strength in a grinding going round, [Real
    110-11 P
What the bottle is going to be-- [Three 131-5 P
GOLD. Blue, gold, pink, and green. [Pourtraicte 21-6
She dressed in red and gold brocade [Pourtraicte 21-7
Expanding in the gold's maternal warmth. [C 32-10
A sally into gold and crimson forms, [C 35-9
That streaking gold should speak in him [C 38-4
Patron and imager of the gold Don John, [Lilacs 49-14
The gold tree is blue. [Of Surface 57-6
Of his gold ether, golden alguazil, [Bird Claws 82-8
And gold sides of green sides, [Nomad 95-14
To gold in broadest blue, and be a part [Sun March 133-16
A dithery gold falls everywhere. [Gray 140-13
Sky-sides of gold [Mud 148-1
Smeared with the gold of the opulent sun. [Postcard 159-21
By gold antagonists in air-- [MBG 169-8
This self, not that gold self aloft, [MBG 176-4
The gold façade round early squares, [Thought 187-2
Snakes and gold and lice, [On Road 204-7

Of the rhododendrons rattled their gold, [Sleight 222-5
Against the fold whipped reddened in big-shadowed black, [Repet
    309-19
The bud of the apple is desire, the down-falling gold, [Holiday
    313-5
While all the leaves leaked gold. His mind made morning, [Pure
    331-22
That constantly sparkled their small gold? The town [Liadoff
    346-12
In a glitter that is a life, a gold [Human 363-15
Trace the gold sun about the whitened sky [Cred 373-6
With the gold bugs, in blue meadows, late at night. [Cred 377-23
Must bear no name, gold flourisher, but be [NSF 381-14
I am the spouse, divested of bright gold, [NSF 395-22
Once more night's pale illuminations, gold [NSF 402-24
Forgets the gold centre, the golden destiny, [NSF 404-18
As light changes yellow into gold and gold [AA 416-11
On his gold horse striding, like a conjured beast, [Antag 426-1
Of ten brilliancies of battered gold [Imago 439-6
Fetched by such slick-eyed nymphs, this essential gold, [Orb
    440-6
It is empty. But a woman in threadless gold [Wom Sun 445-8
Cloud's gold, of a whole appearance that stands and is.[Bouquet
    452-18
Gold easings and ouncings and fluctuations of thread [NH 477-19
On the walk, purple and blue, and red and gold, [NH 481-5
Our chiefest dome a demoiselle of gold. [Archi 18-2 P
The sun is gold, the moon is silver. [Mandolin 29-1 P
On clouds of gold, and green engulfing bronze, [Old Woman 43-8 P
Are of an eternal vista, manqué and gold [Burnshaw 48-12 P
Single, of burly ivory, inched of gold, [Greenest 55-6 P
And beads and bangles of gold and trumpets raised, [Greenest
    56-11 P
It was a mistake to paint the gods. The gold [Greenest 57-30 P
Night gold, and winter night, night silver, these [Sombre 68-12P
One is a child again. The gold beards of waterfalls [Discov
    95-10 P
Thinking gold thoughts in a golden mind, [Ulysses 100-20 P
I wore gold ear-rings. [Three 141-10 P
A matin gold from gold of Hesperus [Ideal 88-15 A
GOLDEN. Of golden quirks and Paphian caricatures, [Swans 4-6
A red bird flies across the golden floor. [Monocle 13-12
Two golden gourds distended on our vines, [Monocle 16-6
Gloomy grammarians in golden gowns, [On Manner 55-10
Out of my mind the golden ointment rained, [Hoon 65-13
Neither the golden underground, nor isle [Sunday 68-19
Of his gold ether, golden alguazil, [Bird Claws 82-8
Why do you imagine golden birds? [Thirteen 93-20
When over the houses, a golden illusion [Lunar 107-9
Mist that is golden is not wholly mist. [Nigger 156-15
Imagination, the golden rescue: [Hero 275-26
Might be enough, as if the golden combs [EM 316-2
With which we vested, once, the golden forms [EM 317-25
And the damasked memory of the golden forms [EM 317-26
Of the damasked memory of the golden forms, [EM 317-28
In the golden vacancy she came, and comes, [Descrip 339-13
Because there is no golden solvent here? [Two V 355-3
At the halyards. Why, then, when in golden fury [NSF 390-24
The golden fingers picking dark-blue air: [NSF 398-15
Forgets the gold centre, the golden destiny, [NSF 404-18
No need, am happy, forget need's golden hand, [NSF 405-1
"A Golden Woman in a Silver Mirror" [460-title
In a golden sedan, [Cab 21-11 P
Cover the golden altar deepest black, [Red Kit 31-21 P
The golden clouds that turned to bronze, the sounds [Old Woman
    44-7 P
Let your golden hands wave fastly and be gay [Burnshaw 51-28 P
To contemplate time's golden paladin [Greenest 56-24 P
As if in a golden cloud. The son restores [Recit 87-16 P
Thinking gold thoughts in a golden mind, [Ulysses 100-20 P
GOLD-ENCRUSTED. The silver-shapeless, gold-encrusted size [Choc
    298-11
GOLDENER. Not as when the goldener nude [Paltry 6-4
GOLDENEST. His goldenest demoiselle, inhabitant, [C 44-11
Between the matin air and color, goldenest generating,
    [Inelegance 25-16 P
GOLD-FEATHERED. A gold-feathered bird [Of Mere 117-18 P
GOLDNESS. Regardless of gods that were praised in goldness [Stan
    Hero 83-21 P
GOLDS. And, standing in violent golds, will brush her hair.
    [Debris 338-7
GOLD-SHINED. Gold-shined by sun, perceiving as I saw [Phenom
    287-13
GOLD-VERMILION. No silver-ruddy, gold-vermilion fruits. [Monocle
    17-1
GONE. Our bloom is gone. We are the fruit thereof. [Monocle 16-5
But when the birds are gone, and their warm fields [Sunday 68-15
Farewell and to know that that land is forever gone [Farewell
    118-7
Of a man gone mad, after all, for time, in spite [Nigger 157-18

The skreak and skritter of evening gone [Autumn 160-1
And grackles gone and sorrows of the sun, [Autumn 160-2
The sorrows of the sun, too, gone . . . the moon and moon,
  [Autumn 160-3
The stillness of everything gone, and being still, [Autumn 160-8
Of spray. Let all the salt be gone. [Vari 234-16
All approaches gone, being completely there, [Waldorf 240-25
Leaps quickly from the fireside and is gone. [Montra 261-6
The abstract was suddenly there and gone again. [Contra II
  270-13
And gelid Januar has gone to hell. [Poesie 302-8
To which they may have gone, but of the place in which [Somnam
  304-14
Who has gone before us in experience. [EM 315-19
When the phantoms are gone and the shaken realist [EM 320-7
Of the future, in which the memory had gone [Pure 330-20
And after a while, when Ha-ee-me has gone to sleep, [Jouga
  337-14
The breath that gushes upward and is gone, [Descrip 341-4
The gardener's cat is dead, the gardener gone [Cred 377-9
The bees came booming as if they had never gone, [NSF 389-19
As if hyacinths had never gone. We say [NSF 389-20
Keep you, keep you, I am gone, oh keep you as [Owl 432-14
Entinselled and gilderlinged and gone, [Celle 438-15
Crowded with apparitions suddenly gone [Bouquet 448-10
And, when detached, so unimportantly gone, [Bouquet 450-14
Gone wild, be what he tells you to be: Puella. [Puel 456-14
The statues will have gone back to be things about. [NH 473-24
Of my shoulder and quickly, too quickly, I am gone? [Angel 497-10
Which suddenly is all dissolved and gone-- [Hermit 505-19
Of summer and of the sun, were gone. [Two Illus 514-9
Quick to be gone, yet never [Soldat 12-5 P
And if you weep for peacocks that are gone [Burnshaw 48-21 P
Than the horses quivering to be gone, flashed through [Duck
  64-9 P
Gone, as in Calypso's isle or in Citare, [Bship 79-24 P
At three-quarters gone, the morning's prescience, [Pagoda 92-4 P
We shall have gone behind the symbols [Ulysses 102-13 P
GONG. That these bethous compose a heavenly gong. [NSF 394-6
GONGS. To a chirr of gongs [Cortege 80-21
  The gongs rang loudly as the windy booms [Sea Surf 100-4
  The gongs grew still. And then blue heaven spread [Sea Surf
  100-6
  The enormous gongs gave edges to their sounds, [Uruguay 249-27
GOOBER. The twilights of the mythy goober khan. [Havana 142-21
GOOD. The good Lord in His garden sought [Pourtraicte 21-22
  Good light for drunkards, poets, widows, [Homunculus 25-15
  The innermost good of their seeking [Homunculus 27-1
  It is a good light, then, for those [Homunculus 27-3
  Beyond these changes, good, fat, guzzly fruit [C 41-7
  The rapey gouts. Good star, how that to be [C 42-20
  To what good, in the alleys of the lilacs, [Lilacs 48-18
  Good God! What a precious light! [Bananas 54-9
  Good clown. . . . One thought of Chinese chocolate [Sea Surf
  102-17
  The good stars, [Brave 138-13
  The wine is good. The bread, [Fading 139-18
  How good life is, on the basis of propriety, [Winter B 141-13
  It is good. The bed is empty, [Chateau 161-17
  I stand in the moon, and call it good, [MBG 168-17
  The immaculate, the merciful good, [MBG 168-18
  Good air, good friend, what is there in life? [MBG 175-18
  Good air, my only friend, believe, [MBG 175-20
  Good air. Poor pale, poor pale guitar . . . [MBG 176-2
  If we found the central evil, the central good. [Oboe 251-12
  The good is evil's last invention. Thus [Extracts 253-11
  An egg-plant of good air. [Extracts 253-15
  Be tranquil in your wounds. It is good death [Extracts 253-24
  A good agreement between himself and night, [Extracts 256-5
  Of the good, speaking of good in the voice of men. [Montra
  262-19
  But to speak simply of good is like to love, [Montra 262-21
  And yet what good were yesterday's devotions? [Montra 264-4
  Us. Good chemistry, good common man, what [Hero 273-16
  Of what good. Devise. Make him of mud, [Hero 275-21
  "God Is Good. It Is a Beautiful Night" [285-title
  The last purity of the knowledge of good. [Possum 294-14
  To the complication, is good, is a good. [Lack 303-20
  In which his wound is good because life was. [EM 319-15
  To watch the fire-feinting sea and calls it good, [EM 324-15
  The ultimate good, sure of a reality [EM 324-16
  "The Pure Good of Theory" [329-title
  Sleep deep, good eel, in your perverse marine. [Two V 354-18
  "The Good Man Has No Shape" [364-title
  He said a good life would be possible. [Good Man 364-6
  At last the good life came, good sleep, bright fruit, [Good Man
  364-7
  The Good Man Has No Shape, as if they knew. [Good Man 364-14
  How good it was at home again at night [Lot 372-1
  As good. The utmost must be good and is [Cred 374-18

  It feels good as it is without the giant, [NSF 386-1
  For whom the good of April falls tenderly, [NSF 388-7
  A thing final in itself and, therefore, good: [NSF 405-19
  Themselves and, therefore, good, the going round [NSF 405-21
  Until merely going round is a final good, [NSF 405-23
  Its brightness burned the way good solace seethes. [Owl 434-6
  Have gorged the cast-iron of our lives with good [Orb 440-3
  A difficult apperception, this gorging good, [Orb 440-5
  What good is it that the earth is justified, [Pecul 453-13
  It does no good to speak of the big, blue bush [Study I 463-4
  At evening and at night. It does no good. [Study I 463-13
  The world imagined is the ultimate good. [Final 524-3
  Fixed one for good in geranium-colored day. [Armor 529-4
  The final pulse of blood from this good heart [Soldat 11-11 P
  Of pomp, in love and good ensample, see [Stan MMO 19-13 P
  Ah, good God! That all beasts should have [Parasol 20-7 P
  And you, good galliard, to enchant black thoughts [Red Kit 32-3P
  "Good Man, Bad Woman" [33-title P
  The parade's no good. [Drum-Majors 37-3 P
  Granted, we die for good. [Table 40-1 P
  And what a good thing it would be [Agenda 42-1 P
  And true. The good, the strength, the sceptre moves [Bship 80-21P
  Our good, from this the rhapsodic strophes flow, [Bship 81-5 P
  Survivals of a good that we have loved, [Recit 88-1 P
  Speech for the quiet, good hail of himself, good hail, good
  hail, [Sick 90-20 P
GOOD-BY. Good-by in the darkness, speaking quietly there, [Owl
  431-17
  To those that cannot say good-by themselves. [Owl 431-18
  But she that says good-by losing in self [Owl 435-4
  To say good-by to the past and to live and to be [NH 478-5
  He was saying good-by to her." [Three 134-18 P
GOOD-BYE. Catching at Good-bye, harvest moon, [MBG 173-5
  As anything but sculpture. Good-bye, [Couch 296-5
GOOD-FORTUNER. Good-fortuner of the grotesque, patroon, [Lot
  371-20
GOODNESS. That he sends ahead, out of the goodness of his heart,
  [EM 320-18
  And the goodness of lying in a maternal sound, [NH 482-9
GOOD-NIGHT. And as they say good-night, good-night. Upstairs [AA
  413-23
GOOSE. The choice twixt dove and goose is over-close. [Spaniard
  35-6 P
GORE. What Eden sapling gum, what honeyed gore, [C 38-2
GORGE. To his gorge, hangman, once helmet-maker [Stan Hero 84-19 P
GORGED. Illuminating, from a fancy gorged [C 46-6
  Have gorged the cast-iron of our lives with good [Orb 440-3
GORGEOUS. Of the gorgeous wheel and so to give [Sailing 121-4
  A gorgeous fortitude. Medium man [Imago 439-9
  Which, like a gorgeous palm, [Archi 17-18 P
  By them: gorgeous symbol seated [Ulysses 104-4 P
GORGING. A difficult apperception, this gorging good, [Orb 440-5
GORY. Flat and pale and gory! [Phases 3-18 P
GOT. Had got him nowhere. There was always the doubt, [Blue Bldg
  216-17
  The Got whom we serve is able to deliver [Hero 273-15
  Click, click, the Got whom we serve is able, [Hero 273-20
  And got my learning from the orthodox. [Soldat 11-5 P
GOTHIC. Of Gothic prong and practick bright, [Couch 295-12
  Gothic blue, speed home its portents to their ends. [Page 422-20
GOTT. See Herr Gott.
GOURDS. Two golden gourds distended on our vines, [Monocle 16-6
  Combatting bushmen for a patch of gourds, [Greenest 56-8 P
  The heavenly cocks, the bowmen, and the gourds, [Greenest 56-18P
GOUTS. The rapey gouts. Good star, how that to be [C 42-20
GOWN. Stooping in indigo gown [Venereal 48-12
  In an orange gown, [Explan 73-2
  The white folds of its gown [Six Sig 74-15
  Of cloudy silver sprinkles in your gown [Fictive 87-11
  The audience beholds you, not your gown. [Bad Time 427-9
  Of the green gown I wore. [Three 134-17 P
  And it affects the green gown. [Three 135-5 P
GOWNS. Gloomy grammarians in golden gowns, [On Manner 55-10
  I peopled the dark park with gowns [Stan MMO 19-1 P
  Were solemn and your gowns were blown and grief [Burnshaw 50-29P
  As if your gowns were woven of the light [Burnshaw 51-24 P
  See night-gowns.
GRACE. Without grace or grumble. Score this anecdote [C 45-19
  And sea exists by grace alone, [Vari 235-4
  There to behold, there to proclaim, the grace [Montra 263-9
  The actual form bears outwardly this grace, [Pastor 379-17
  And perception as an act of grace [Lytton 39-7 P
  A grace to nature, a changeless element. [Greenest 59-30 P
  To bear virile grace before their fellows, [Stan Hero 83-20 P
GRACES. Comme Dieu Dispense de Graces [Soldat 13-title 5
GRACKLES. The grackles crack their throats of bone in the smooth
  air. [Banal 62-13
  The grackles sing avant the spring [Snow Stars 133-1
  And grackles gone and sorrows of the sun, [Autumn 160-2
  Is it to hear the blatter of grackles and say [Dump 203-8

GRADUAL. They become our gradual possession. The poet [Papini
  147-18
GRAIN. The grain is in the baker's shop, [Nigger 154-8
GRAMAPHOON. All afternoon the gramaphoon, [Search 268-9
  All afternoon the gramaphoon, [Search 268-10
GRAMMARIANS. Gloomy grammarians in golden gowns, [On Manner 55-10
GRAMOPHONE. All afternoon the gramophone [Search 268-1
  The flute on the gramophone, the Daimlers that [Greenest 53-21 P
  We must have the throstle on the gramophone. [Duck 66-8 P
GRAMOPHONES. On the priestly gramophones. [Winter B 141-8
GRAND. His grand pronunciamento and devise. [C 43-15
  The grand ideas of the villages. [Pharynx 96-8
  And a grand decadence settles down like cold. [Havana 142-12
  In the grand decadence of the perished swans. [Havana 145-9
  One's grand flights, one's Sunday baths, [Sleight 222-1
  When the grand mechanics of earth and sky were near, [Contra II
    270-2
  Wakes us to the emotion, grand fortissimo, [Grotesque 76-19 P
  First. The grand simplifications reduce [Bship 78-23 P
  A hand that fails to seize it. High captain, the grand [Bship
    80-25 P
GRANDEUR. In the stale grandeur of annihilation. [Leben 505-9
  Impatient for the grandeur that you need [Rome 509-22
  It is a kind of total grandeur at the end, [Rome 510-21
  Total grandeur of a total edifice, [Rome 510-26
GRANDEURS. And jealous grandeurs of sun and sky [Vase 246-11
  A promenade amid the grandeurs of the mind, [EM 325-7
  A wind will spread its windy grandeurs round [AA 414-1
  Universal delusions of universal grandeurs, [Someone 87-7 A
GRANDFATHER. And pallid. It is the grandfather he liked, [Lack
    303-11
  One is already a grandfather and to have put there [Lack 303-18
  This is the habit of wishing, as if one's grandfather lay [Bed
    327-1
  See great-grandfather.
GRANDILOQUENT. If the observer says so: grandiloquent [Pastor 379-7
GRANDIOSE. The grandiose gestures [Infanta 7-14
  Empty and grandiose, let us make hymns [Nigger 151-20
  To an innate grandiose, an innate light, [Descrip 342-17
  Gesturing grandiose things in the air, [Soldat 16-5 P
  Intensified and grandiose, but among [Greenest 57-4 P
  Is not out grandiose destiny. [Grotesque 77-2 P
  This immemorial grandiose, why not [Bship 79-9 P
  That's this grandiose battleship of yours and your [Bship 80-29 P
GRANDMOTHER. "Now, grandmother, [Jack-Rabbit 50-9
  Grandmother and her basketful of pears [Havana 143-23
GRANDSON. Except that the grandson sees it as it is, [Questions
    462-9
GRANITE. A single text, granite monotony, [NSF 394-9
GRANTED. Granted the Picts impressed us otherwise [Nigger 155-1
  Granted each picture is a glass, [Prelude 195-1
  The S.S. Normandie, granted [Prelude 195-7
  A vibrancy not to be taken for granted, from [Holiday 312-5
  Granted, we die for good. [Table 40-1 P
  And that, too, granted, why [Table 40-4 P
GRANULATES. And the metal heroes that time granulates--[Oboe 250-11
GRAPE. Of spring come to their places in the grape leaves [NSF
    399-14
GRAPE-LEAVES. Shining through the grape-leaves. [Six Sig 75-3
GRAPES. "In the Clear Season of Grapes" [110-title
  This fat pistache of Belgian grapes exceeds [Nigger 154-17
  Cochon! Master, the grapes are here and now. [Nigger 154-19
  And that in autumn, when the grapes [Postcard 159-1
  That the grapes seemed fatter. [On Road 203-14
  I love the metal grapes, [Anything B 211-17
  Now grapes are plush upon the vines. [Contra I 266-11
  A board for bishops' grapes, the happy form [Sombre 70-8 P
GRAPPLE. Shall I grapple with my destroyers [Nigger 153-11
  Like an eye too young to grapple its primitive, [Theatre 91-4 P
GRAPPLED. Gripped it and grappled my thoughts. [Weak Mind 212-10
GRAPPLING. Staked solidly in a gusty grappling with rocks. [NH
    487-21
GRASP. The beads on her rails seemed to grasp at transparence.
    [Vari 236-2
  To grasp the hero, the eccentric [Hero 274-19
GRASS. Out of their mother grass, like little kin, [Monocle 15-4
  And in the grass an offering made [Pourtraicte 21-8
  I make an offering, in the grass [Pourtraicte 21-18
  Upon the grass, relinquished to their feet. [Sunday 69-9
  As to rafters or grass. [Tattoo 81-18
  She walked upon the grass, [Peter 91-1
  Mow the grass in the cemetery, darkies, [Norfolk 111-4
  The grass is in seed. The young birds are flying. [Ghosts 119-1
  She must come now. The grass is in seed and high. [Ghosts 119-11
  In dark forms of the grass [Brave 138-11
  The rabbit fat, at last, in glassy grass. [Nigger 153-20
  The trees are wooden, the grass is yellow and thin. [Nigger
    157-21
  Empurpled garden grass; [Delight 162-6
  Moved in the grass without a sound. [MBG 178-14

They did not know the grass went round. [MBG 178-15
The cats had cats and the grass turned gray [MBG 178-16
The grass turned green and the grass turned gray. [MBG 178-18
And crickets are loud again in the grass. The moon [Men Fall
  187-11
Bottles, pots, shoes and grass and murmur aptest eve: [Dump 203-7
To be, in the grass, in the peacefullest time, [Rabbit K 209-7
No matter. The grass is full [Rabbit K 209-15
And the little green cat is a bug in the grass. [Rabbit K 210-3
As they used to lie in the grass, in the heat, [Cuisine 227-18
Were violet, yellow, purple, pink. The grass [Horn 230-9
Of mica, the dithering of grass, [Vari 234-18
The gray grass like a pallet, closely pressed; [Extracts 255-4
By the glints of sound from the grass. These are not [Myrrh
  350-6
The grass is still green. [Burghers 362-6
Are in the grass, the roses are heavy with a weight [Cred 372-7
These lovers waiting in the soft dry grass. [Cred 372-18
The moving grass, the Indian in his glade. [AA 412-3
From line to line, as we lie on the grass and listen [Aug 492-11
The wet, green grass. [Irish 502-2
How soft the grass on which the desired [Hermit 505-11
These marbles lay weathering in the grass [Two Illus 514-6
Left only the fragments found in the grass, [Two Illus 515-3
To think away the grass, the trees, the clouds, [Look 517-14
The horses weary themselves hunting for green grass. [Primordia
  8-15 P
"The Indigo Glass in the Grass" [22-title P
This bottle of indigo glass in the grass, [Indigo 22-11 P
"Romance for a Demoiselle Lying in the Grass" [23-title P
It is grass. [Demoiselle 23-1 P
The common grass is green. [Abnormal 24-4 P
But there are regions where the grass [Abnormal 24-5 P
And there the common grass is never seen. [Abnormal 24-8 P
And feels the grass [Abnormal 24-10 P
Will laugh in the brown grass, [Secret Man 36-15 P
On the clear grass, [Polo 38-5 P
Gray grass and green-gray sky? [Table 40-6 P
Severed and tumbled into seedless grass, [Burnshaw 49-14 P
And the sound of z in the grass all day, though these [Burnshaw
  51-4 P
To touch the grass and, as you circle, turn [Burnshaw 51-12 P
Even in sleep, deep in the grass of sleep, [Greenest 54-31 P
Deep grass that totters under the weight of light. [Greenest
  55-7 P
That rises in the air. The sprawlers on the grass [Duck 64-7 P
Concealed in glittering grass, dank reptile skins. [Duck 65-11 P
If she was deaf with falling grass in her ears-- [Woman Had
  83-2 P
Other men, and not this grass, this valid air. [Americana 94-11P
Came tinkling on the grass to the table [Dinner 110-3 P
See deer-grass; saw-grass.
GRASSES. Gray grasses rolling windily away [Nigger 155-14
  In which the watery grasses flow [MBG 180-12
  The honky-tonk out of the somnolent grasses [Aug 489-18
GRASSMAN. The yellow grassman's mind is still immense, [EM 318-24
GRASSY. The chick, the chidder-barn and grassy chives [Montra
    260-3
  The stalk, the weed, the grassy flourishes, [Bouquet 452-8
GRATES. And grates these evasions of the nightingale [Autumn
    160-11
GRAVE. Nor any old chimera of the grave, [Sunday 68-18
  It is the grave of Jesus, where he lay." [Sunday 70-17
  To mock him. They placed with him in his grave [Good Man 364-10
  At the centre on the horizon, concentrum, grave [Orb 443-13
  Have liberty not as the air within a grave [Aug 490-12
  Grown great and grave beyond imagined trees, [Old Woman 45-31 P
  Of Vilmorin, Verhaeren in his grave, [Greenest 53-20 P
GRAVES. "Dutch Graves in Bucks County" [290-title
  To think of the logicians in their graves [EM 325-4
  O spirit of bones, O mountain of graves? [Sat Night 28-6 P
GRAY. The jar was gray and bare. [Jar 76-14
  "Gray Stones and Gray Pigeons" [140-title
  The archbishop is away. The church is gray. [Gray 140-1
  He is away. The church is gray. [Gray 140-9
  Gray grasses rolling windily away [Nigger 155-14
  The cats had cats and the grass turned gray [MBG 178-16
  The grass turned green and the grass turned gray. [MBG 178-18
  The gray grass like a pallet, closely pressed; [Extracts 255-4
  By fortune, his gray ghost may meditate [Cats 368-7
  Twelve and the first gray second after, a kind [What We 459-16
  Of violet gray, a green violet, a thread [What We 459-17
  That which was public green turned private gray. [NH 479-1
  The rock is the gray particular of man's life, [Rock 528-1
  Gray, gruesome grumblers. [Archi 18-10 P
  Gray grass and green-gray sky? [Table 40-6 P
  Gray, green, why those of all? [Table 40-8 P
  Of Boucher pink, the sheens of Venetian gray. [Greenest 53-14 P
  See green-gray.
GRAY-BLUE. Their poverty, a gray-blue yellowed out [NSF 402-5

GRAY-ROSE. The scene in his gray-rose with violet rocks.
  [Anach 366-5
GREAT. Pravura adequate to this great hymn? [Monocle 16-22
  Only the great height of the rock [How Live 126-3
  As of the great wind howling, [Mozart 132-14
  Where the voice that is great within us rises up,
    [Eve Angels 138-5
  Jehovah and the great sea-worm. The air [Havana 142-4
  When too great rhapsody is left annulled [Havana 144-9
  Sat alone, his great toe like a horn, [Thought 187-7
  The great men will not be blended . . . [Idiom 201-6
  The sun appeared and reddened great [Country 207-13
  B. A great disorder is an order. These [Connois 215-2
  A great disorder is an order. Now, A [Connois 216-9
  This great world, it divides itself in two, [Dezem 218-6
  The mind is the great poem of winter, the man, [Bottle 238-17
  And great moon, cricket-impresario, [Montra 260-4
  I affirm and then at midnight the great cat [Montra 264-5
  Shadow, up the great sea and downward [Hero 274-27
  The song of the great space of your age pierces [God 285-17
  To the great blue of the middle height. [Dutch 290-3
  The captain squalid on his pillow, the great [Choc 300-1
  Integration for integration, the great arms [Choc 301-14
  Weaken our fate, relieve us of woe both great [EM 315-21
  So great a unity, that it is bliss, [EM 317-8
  The soldier of time grown deathless in great size. [EM 319-2
  Great tufts, spring up from buried houses [EM 322-15
  And of the worlds of logic in their great tombs. [EM 325-5
  By a lake, with clouds like lights among great tombs, [EM 325-8
  All men endure. The great captain is the choice [Paisant 334-14
  A great jaguar running will make a little sound. [Jouga 337-15
  In the conscious world, the great clouds [Analysis 348-2
  Hunting for the great ornament, [Pediment 361-8
  A devestation, a death of great height [Burghers 362-8
  Of great height and depth [Burghers 362-15
  And this great esplanade of corn, miles wide, [Belly 367-7
  The great statue of the General Du Puy [NSF 391-7
  Hung heavily on the great banana tree, [NSF 393-14
  And so, as part, to exult with its great throat, [NSF 398-9
  Between a great captain and the maiden Bawda. [NSF 401-6
  The great captain loved the ever-hill Catawba [NSF 401-16
  And gusts of great enkindlings, its polar green, [AA 413-2
  He assumes the great speeds of space and flutters them [AA 414-14
  Like a great shadow's last embellishment. [AA 419-24
  Fulfilling his meditations, great and small. [AA 420-21
  The great ship, Balayne, lay frozen in the sea. [Page 421-18
  As he sat there reading, aloud, the great blue tabulae.
    [Large 423-12
  It is nothing, no great thing, nor man [Imago 439-5
  The day is great and strong-- [Pecul 453-4
  Comes from a great distance and is heard. [Our Stars 455-12
  By one caterpillar is great Africa devoured [Puel 456-2
  Making a great gnashing, over the water wallows [Puel 456-8
  Great choristers, propounders of hymns, trumpeters, [Luther 461-7
  A great bosom, beard and being, alive with age. [NH 466-3
  Against illusion and was, in a great grinding [NH 467-18
  A great town hanging pendent in a shade, [NH 468-16
  The great cat must stand potent in the sun. [NH 473-3 .
  The great structure has become a minor house. [Plain 502-15
  Itself to be imagined. The great pond, [Plain 503-2
  The great pond and its waste of the lilies, all this [Plain 503-6
  And the wind sways like a great thing tottering-- [Hermit 505-16
  Weight him down, O side-stars, with the great weightings of the
    end. [Madame 507-1
  Matisse at Vence and a great deal more than that, [Armor 529-18
  In the great vistas of night air, that takes this form,
    [Moonlight 531-17
  There is a great river this side of Stygia, [R Conn 533-4
  And you forgive dark broachings growing great [Spaniard 34-7 P
  Grown great and grave beyond imagined trees, [Old Woman 45-31 P
  Is no longer a sound of summer. So great a change [Burnshaw 50-21P
  Great mud-ancestor, oozer and Abraham, [Duck 64-29 P
  Once each century or two. But then so great, [Duck 65-24 P
  Thoughts by descent. To flourish the great cloak we wear
    [Sombre 71-19 P
  A cockle-shell, a trivial emblem great [Bship 79-10 P
  Of the great sizes of an outer bush [Dove 98-8 P
  And the great misery of the doubt of it, [Dove 98-9 P
  The great Omnium descends on us [Ulysses 102-3 P
  The great sail of Ulysses seemed, [Ulysses 105-7 P
  The great Omnium descends on me, [Presence 106-5 P
GREATER. Of men is nothing. The mass is no greater than
    [Dames 206-4
  No greater than a cricket's horn, no more [Beard 247-15
  Greater than mine, of his demanding, head [Choc 302-4
  The greater seeming of the major mind. [Descrip 340-4
  Of greater aptitude and apprehension, [NSF 387-15
  Or one man who, for us, is greater than they, [Antag 425-16
  Mountains appeared with greater eloquence [NH 484-12
GREATEST. The greatest poverty is not to live [EM 325-18

The human end in the spirit's greatest reach, [Rome 508-16
GREAT-GRANDFATHER. Your great-grandfather was an Indian fighter.
    [Extraord 369-9
GREATLY. How greatly had he grown in his demesne, [C 31-1
GREATNESS. Do not speak to us of the greatness of poetry,
    [MBG 167-3
  And his breast is greatness. All his speeches [Hero 277-12
  "I am the greatness of the new-found night." [Role 93-14 P
  The aid of greatness to be and the force. [Ulysses 100-17 P
GREEN. Through the green saw-grass, [Sugar-Cane 12-10
  Blue, gold, pink, and green. [Pourtraicte 21-6
  Of blue and green? A wordy, watery age [C 28-25
  In spite of hawk and falcon, green toucan [C 30-18
  Green barbarism turning paradigm. [C 31-22
  So thick with sides and jagged lops of green, [C 32-2
  So streaked with yellow, blue and green and red [C 32-6
  The green palmettoes in crepuscular ice [C 34-15
  Green crammers of the green fruits of the world, [C 43-28
  Philosopher, beginning with green brag, [C 46-1
  Your dress was green, [Vincentine 53-1
  Was whited green, [Vincentine 53-2
  Green Vincentine. [Vincentine 53-3
  On the dark, green water-wheel, [Solitaires 60-4
  Our old bane, green and bloated, serene, who cries, [Banal 62-16
  And so it is one damns that green shade at the bottom of the
    land. [Banal 63-3
  In slipper green. [Depression 63-18
  None are green, [Ten O'C 66-3
  Or purple with green rings, [Ten O'C 66-4
  Or green with yellow rings, [Ten O'C 66-5
  And the green freedom of a cockatoo [Sunday 66-18
  The pungent oranges and bright, green wings [Sunday 67-5
  In pungent fruit and bright, green wings, or else [Sunday 67-16
  As April's green endures; or will endure [Sunday 68-23
  Of a green evening, clear and warm, [Peter 90-7
  In the green water, clear and warm, [Peter 90-13
  So evenings die, in their green going, [Peter 92-2
  Flying in a green light, [Thirteen 94-10
  And green vine angering for life, [Nomad 95-9
  Beholding all these green sides [Nomad 95-13
  And gold sides of green sides, [Nomad 95-14
  And gilt umbrellas. Paradisal green [Sea Surf 99-2
  And moved, as blooms move, in the swimming green [Sea Surf 99-11
  And sham umbrellas. And a sham-like green [Sea Surf 99-20
  And pied umbrellas. An uncertain green, [Sea Surf 100-14
  And frail umbrellas. A too-fluent green [Sea Surf 101-8
  Its bluest sea-clouds in the thinking green, [Sea Surf 101-19
  And large umbrellas. And a motley green [Sea Surf 102-2
  Of green blooms turning crisped the motley hue [Sea Surf 102-12
  Vermilion smeared over green, arranged for show. [Grapes 110-14
  Green and gloomy eyes [Brave 138-10
  Of bulging green [Mud 147-18
  Which changed light green to olive then to blue. [Nigger 152-10
  Pushing their buds above the dark green leaves, [Nigger 156-11
  The sun rises green and blue in the fields and in the heavens.
    [Fish-Scale 161-5
  A shearsman of sorts. The day was green. [MBG 165-2
  Its true appearances there, sun's green, [MBG 177-3
  The grass turned green and the grass turned gray. [MBG 178-18
  Citrons, oranges and greens [Pears 197-1
  Are blobs on the green cloth. [Pears 197-4
  The green smacks in the eye, the dew in the green [Dump 202-5
  Smoking through green and smoking blue. [On Road 203-20
  Fat cat, red tongue, green mind, white milk [Rabbit K 209-5
  And the little green cat is a bug in the grass. [Rabbit K 210-3
  And the green wind [Weak Mind 212-12
  If all the green of spring was blue, and it is; [Connois 215-4
  Green were the curls upon that head. [Poem Morn 219-17
  Green is the night, green kindled and apparelled. [Candle 223-1
  Those that lie chanting green is the night. [Candle 223-6
  Green is the night and out of madness woven, [Candle 223-7
  The abstract, the archaic queen. Green is the night.[Candle 223-14
  Men on green beds and women half of sun. [Cuisine 227-19
  After that alien, point-blank, green and actual Guatemala.
    [Waldorf 241-9
  Flap green ears in the heat. He might observe [Landsc 243-5
  Green in the body, out of a petty phrase, [Beard 247-21
  The dead rocks not the green rocks, the live rocks. If, [Extracts
    255-16
  The hand can touch, neither green bronze nor marble, [Montra 261-3
  I dreamed, of autumn rivers, silvas green, [Montra 263-2
  Item: The green fish pensive in green reeds [Montra 263-20
  The green falls on you as you look, [Phosphor 267-12
  That elemental parent, the green night, [Phosphor 267-15
  The leaves, even of the locust, the green locust. [Contra II 270-6
  Whose green mind bulges with complicated hues: [Choc 300-5
  The greenhouse on the village green [Poesie 302-2
  The choice is made. Green is the orator [Repet 309-22
  Of our passionate height. He wears a tufted green, [Repet 309-23
  And tosses green for those for whom green speaks. [Repet 309-24

The breast is covered with violets. It is a green leaf.
  [Holiday 312-16
For me, grow green for me and, as you whistle and grow green,
  [Holiday 313-8
The green corn gleaming and experience [EM 325-23
The green corn gleams and the metaphysicals [EM 325-27
Romantic with dreams of her avoirdupois, green glade [Pure 330-17
Green glade and holiday hotel and world [Pure 330-19
But there was one invalid in that green glade [Pure 331-2
Her green mind made the world around her green. [Descrip 339-9
The queen is an example . . . This green queen [Descrip 339-10
An age is green or red. And age believes [Descrip 340-6
In the major manner of a queen, the green [Descrip 340-12
And, being straw, turned green, lived backward, shared [Liadoff
  347-9
Already the green bird of summer has flown [Myrrh 349-15
Than green, fidgets of all-related fire. [Pieces 352-4
The grass is still green. [Burghers 362-6
And live and heap their panniers of green [Belly 367-3
Of the place, blue and green, both streaked. [Attempt 370-5
The green roses drifted up from the table [Attempt 370-15
Ourselves, in the clearest green--well, call it green. [Lot 371-7
We bathed in yellow green and yellow blue [Lot 371-8
The point of survey, green's green apogee, [Cred 373-17
Axis of everything, green's apogee [Cred 373-20
It is a mountain half way green and then, [Cred 375-13
Half pales of green, appropriate habit for [Cred 378-3
And the green flauntings of the hours of peace. [Pastor 380-3
And in earth itself they found a green-- [NSF 383-15
The inhabitants of a very varnished green. [NSF 383-16
To drone the green phrases of its juvenal? [NSF 390-15
With garbled green. These were the planter's turquoise [NSF 393-5
And his orange blotches, these were his zero green, [NSF 393-6
A green baked greener in the greenest sun. [NSF 393-7
Of these beginnings, gay and green, propose [NSF 398-5
I call you by name, my green, my fluent mundo. [NSF 407-2
And gusts of great enkindlings, its polar green, [AA 413-2
Damasked in the originals of green, [Owl 434-20
That big-brushed green. Or in a tragic mode, [John 437-3
Green guests and table in the woods and songs [Orb 440-19
The composition of blue sea and of green, [Orb 442-3
Of blue light and of green, as lesser poems, [Orb 442-4
And the memorial mosses hang their green [Degen 445-2
The green bouquet comes from the place of the duck. [Bouquet
  450-4
Of nights full of the green stars from Ireland, [Our Stars 455-14
One imagined the violet trees but the trees stood green, [What We
  459-10
At twelve, as green as ever they would be. [What We 459-11
Of violet gray, a green violet, a thread [What We 459-17
In the weed of summer comes this green sprout why. [Questions
  462-4
From five-six cornered leaves, and green, the signal [NH 470-20
That which was public green turned private gray. [NH 479-1
Effete green, the woman in black cassimere. [NH 482-2
Forms of farewell, furtive among green ferns. [NH 482-15
The wateriness of green wet in the sky. [NH 484-11
Which, being green and blue, appease him, [Aug 491-4
The wet, green grass. [Irish 502-2
"The Green Plant" [506-title
Except that a green plant glares, as you look [Plant 506-16
Glares, outside of the legend, with the barbarous green
  [Plant 506-18
That the green leaves came and covered the high rock, [Rock 526-4
And green with leaves. [Phases 3-8 P
It dances down a furrow, in the early light, back of a crazy
  plough, the green blades following. [Plough-Boy 6-7 P
The horses weary themselves hunting for green grass. [Primordia
  8-15 P
Green bosoms and black legs, beguile [Stan MMO 19-10 P
By the green lake-pallors, [Cab 21-5 P
The common grass is green. [Abnormal 24-4 P
Beginning of a green Cockaigne to be, disliked, abandoned,
  [Inelegance 25-14 P
Iris and orange, crimson and green, [Mandolin 28-19 P
Gray, green, why those of all? [Table 40-8 P
On clouds of gold, and green engulfing bronze, [Old Woman 43-8 P
Washed over by their green, their flowing blue. [Old Woman 45-11P
Of crimson and hoods of Venezuelan green [Burnshaw 51-3 P
Of the least appreciable shade of green [Burnshaw 51-20 P
Was meant to stand, not in a tumbling green, [Greenest 57-3 P
Green is the path we take [Sombre 67-28 P
The green, white, blue of the ballad-eye, by night [Sombre 71-9 P
The day is green and the wind is young. [Stan MBG 72-1 P
Green more or less, in green and blue in blue, [Theatre 91-2 P
The green-edged yellow and yellow and blue and blue-edged green--
  [How Now 97-8 P
Now the thousand-leaved green falls to the ground. [Fare Guit
  98-17 P
In the green, outside the door of phantasma. [Dinner 110-6 P

Of the green gown I wore. [Three 134-17 P
And if affects the green gown. [Three 135-5 P
So it is the green of one tree [Three 143-7
And the green of another, [Three 143-8
A jar of the shoots of an infant country, green [Someone 83-15 A
A green that is the ash of what green is, [Someone 83-18 A
Green had, those days, its own implacable sting. [Someone 85-7 A
2. Out of their bottle the green genii come. [Someone 86-5 A
See: blue-green; gaffer-green; leaf-green; sea-green; yellow-
  green.
GREEN-A-DAY. But now he sits in quiet and green-a-day. [AA 414-13
GREEN-BLUE. Abhorring green-blue north and blue-green south.
  [Archi 18-1 P
GREEN-EDGED. The green-edged yellow and yellow and blue and
  blue-edged green-- [How Now 97-8 P
GREENER. A green baked greener in the greenest sun. [NSF 393-7
GREENEST. That walk away as one in the greenest body. [NSF 392-15
  A green baked greener in the greenest sun. [NSF 393-7
  Sits in a wood, in the greenest part, [Degen 444-2
  "The Greenest Continent" [52-title P
  As of sections collecting toward the greenest cone. [Someone
  87-21 A
GREEN-GRAY. Gray grass and green-gray sky? [Table 40-6 P
GREENHORNS. And maidenly greenhorns, now beheld himself, [C 28-12
GREENHOUSE. The greenhouse on the village green [Poesie 302-15
  The greenhouse never so badly needed paint. [Plain 502-17
GREENISH. In the greenish greens he flung behind [News 264-17
  The greenish quaverings of day [Stan MBG 73-5 P
GREENNESS. The greenness of night lies on the page and goes
  [Phosphor 267-9
  In an air of freshness, clearness, greenness, blueness, [Armor
  530-16
GREENS. And silvers and greens spread over the sea. The moon
  [Farewell 117-4
  Citrons, oranges and greens [Pears 197-1
  In the greenish greens he flung behind [News 264-17
  Beneath the spangling greens, fear might placate [Greenest 54-22P
GREEN-VENTED. Upward and outward, in green-vented forms, [Bird
  Claws 82-11
GREET. For it has come that thus I greet the spring. [Monocle 13-18
GREETING. I am a man of fortune greeting heirs; [Monocle 13-17
GREETS. In Russia at which the same statue of Stalin greets [Cats
  367-15
GRENADINE. To think of a dove with an eye of grenadine [Sleight
  222-13
GREW. The torment of fastidious thought grew slack, [C 37-21
  So deep a sound fell down it grew to be [C 42-9
  Grew red. [Six Sig 74-18
  The slopping of the sea grew still one night [Sea Surf 98-13
  The slopping of the sea grew still one night. [Sea Surf 99-17
  The gongs grew still. And then blue heaven spread [Sea Surf 100-6
  The slopping of the sea grew still one night [Sea Surf 100-11
  The night-long slopping of the sea grew still. [Sea Surf 101-5
  His spirit grew uncertain of delight, [Anglais 148-15
  Before the colors deepened and grew small. [Anglais 149-15
  The idea of the Alps grew large, [Thought 184-15
  Until his nose grew thin and taut [Thought 186-22
  When he looked, the water ran up the air or grew white
  [Extracts 255-17
  Grew strong, as if doubt never touched his heart. [Choc 299-5
  At a town in which acacias grew, he lay [EM 314-17
  We grew used so soon, too soon, to earth itself, [Wild 328-16
  Then generation by generation he grew [Good Man 364-3
  And là-bas, là-bas, the cool bananas grew, [NSF 393-13
  In his chair, the most tranquil thought grew peaked [Quiet 523-9
  Where the bending iris grew; [Phases 4-8 P
  And the brass grew cold [Coroner 29-23 P
GRIEF. And, out of tenderness or grief, the sun [Anatomy 108-9
  His grief is that his mother should feed on him, himself and
  what he saw, [Madame 507-12
  Were solemn and your gowns were blown and grief [Burnshaw 50-29P
GRIEVE. Thought the brow in your palm may grieve [Delight 162-3
  I grieve the pinch of her long-stiffening bones. [Stan MMO 19-19 P
GRIEVES. There's rain. The season grieves. [Phases 3-6 P
GRIEVING. Which grieving will not sweeten. [Weep Woman 25-3
GRIEVINGS. Grievings in loneliness, or unsubdued [Sunday 67-21
GRIM. As grim as it is benevolent, the just [AA 417-5
  As it touches the point of reverberation--not grim [NH 475-14
  And in any case never grim, the human grim [NH 475-17
GRIMLY. Reality but reality grimly seen [NH 475-15
GRIND. Grind their seductions on him, Crispin knew [C 35-15
GRINDING. Rougher than a grinding shale. [Orangeade 103-14
  The grinding water and the gasping wind; [Key W 129-2
  In the grinding ric-rac, staring steadily [Men Fall 188-4
  The grinding in the arches of the church, [Blue Bldg 217-4
  Against illusion and was, in a great grinding [NH 467-18
  Hoofs grinding against the stubborn earth, until [Old Woman 46-10P
  There was a crush of strength in a grinding going round,
  [Real 110-11 P
GRINDSTONE. To fill, the grindstone of antiquest time, [Bship 80-2P

GRIPPED. He gripped more closely the essential prose [C 36-18
   Meeting, gripped my mind, [Weak Mind 212-9
   Gripped it and grappled my thoughts. [Weak Mind 212-10
GRIPPING. Gripping their oars, as if they were sure of the way to
   their destination, [Prol 515-7
GRIPS. That grips the centre, the actual bite, that life [Choc
   298-22
   The object, grips it in savage scrutiny, [Cred 376-11
GRISAILLE. Grisaille, impearled, profound, [Add 198-14
GRITTING. Gritting the ear, whispers humane repose. [NH 484-21
GRITTY. Spontaneously watering their gritty soils. [Monocle 16-25
GRIZZLED. From which their grizzled voice will speak and be heard."
   [Duck 60-24 P
GROAN. That makes us weep, laugh, grunt and groan, and shout
   [Monocle 17-10
GROANED. On the sublime. Vesuvius had groaned [EM 313-13
GROANING. Groaning in half-exploited gutturals [Pure 333-3
GROANS. Make melic groans and tooter at her strokes, [Spaniard
   34-25 P
GROCER. This man to complain to the grocer [Soldat 12-13 P
GROSS. On what strange froth does the gross Indian dote, [C 38-1
   Gross effigy and simulacrum, none [Fictive 87-18
   But this gross blue under rolling bronzes [Grapes 110-15
   Through the gross tedium of being rare. [Nigger 155-22
   The sun, its grossest appetite becomes less gross, [EM 318-14
   The gross, the fecund, proved him against the touch [EM 322-2
   A particular of being, that gross universe. [Rock 526-9
GROSSEST. The sun, its grossest appetite becomes less gross,
   [EM 318-14
   And still the grossest iridescence of ocean [NSF 383-7
GROSSLY. He sought the most grossly maternal, the creature
   [EM 321-13
GROSSNESS. A grossness of peace. [Bottle 239-12
GROTESQUE. Distorted by hale fatness, turned grotesque. [Monocle
   16-8
   Grotesque apprenticeship to chance event, [C 39-23
   Grotesque with this nosing in banks, [Frogs 78-11
   Makes everything grotesque. Is it because [Feo 333-13
   It says there is an absolute grotesque [Feo 334-3
   There is a nature that is grotesque within [Feo 334-4
   The grotesque is not a visitation. It is [Feo 334-9
   And naked, or almost so, into the grotesque [Lot 371-17
   Good-fortuner of the grotesque, patroon, [Lot 371-20
   "Five Grotesque Pieces " [74-title P
GROTESQUELY. A horse grotesquely taut, a walker like [Pure 330-6
GROUND. Down to the ground. [Domination 9-1
   Of what, like skulls, comes rotting back to ground. [Monocle
   14-19
   A white pigeon it is, that flutters to the ground, [Monocle 17-20
   She kneeled upon the ground [Pourtraicte 21-3
   He marked the marshy ground around the dock, [C 36-13
   In the sunshine placidly, colored by ground [C 41-3
   That the blue ground [Peacocks 58-16
   The jar was round upon the ground [Jar 76-11
   As if I lived in ashen ground, as if [Farewell 117-12
   The bills of the swans are flat upon the ground. [Havana 142-10
   Upon the ground, and before the chronicle [Havana 142-14
   Her fingers touch the ground. [Add 199-4
   On the ground, fixed fast in a profound defeat. [Martial 238-2
   On the ground. [God 285-3
   The leaves hop, scraping on the ground. [Possum 294-6
   That breathed on ground, more blue than red, more red [Pieces
   352-3
   On this present ground, the vividest repose, [Cred 375-19
   And on the ground. The hibernal dark that hung [NH 476-8
   It buzzes beyond the horizon or in the ground; [NH 487-14
   We must be cured of it by a cure of the ground [Rock 526-11
   Of the ground, a cure beyond forgetfulness. [Rock 526-13
   Of their fresh culls might be a cure of the ground. [Rock 526-17
   These are a cure of the ground and of ourselves, [Rock 527-3
   Of leaves and of the ground and of ourselves. [Rock 527-20
   It seizes a sheet, from the ground, from a bush, as if spread
      there by some wash-woman for the night. [Plough-Boy 6-5 P
   How softly the sheet falls to the ground! [Plough-Boy 6-9 P
   Why can the horses move about on the ground? [Primordia 8-13 P
   The birch trees draw up whiteness from the ground.[Primordia 8-21P
   Into the ground, [Coroner 30-5 P
   Now the thousand-leaved green falls to the ground. [Fare Guit
   98-17 P
GROUNDS. And, finally, set guardians in the grounds, [Archi 18-9 P
GROUP. In a group [Vincentine 53-5
   To the group of Flora Coddling Hecuba? [Archi 17-10 P
   A group of marble horses rose on wings [Old Woman 43-2 P
GROVELLING. Lay grovelling. Triton incomplicate with that [C 28-29
GROW. When amorists grow bald, then amours shrink [Monocle 15-14
   Since by our nature we grow old, earth grows [Anatomy 108-1
   The bells grow longer. This is not sleep. This is desire.
      [Men Fall 187-14
   Well, the gods grow out of the weather. [Jersey 210-5
   The people grow out of the weather; [Jersey 210-6

The gods grow out of the people. [Jersey 210-7
   Has a will to grow larger on the wall, [Rhythms 215-19
   To grow larger and heavier and stronger than [Rhythms 216-1
   Rifles grow sharper on the sight. [Dutch 291-2
   Grow out of the spirit or they are fantastic dust. [Holiday 313-4
   For me, grow green for me and, as you whistle and grow green,
      [Holiday 313-8
   In whose breast, the dove, alighting, would grow still. [Think
   357-6
   Summer is changed to winter, the young grow old, [Chaos 357-14
   One seed alone grow wild, the railway-stops [Cats 367-14
   The long lines of it grow longer, emptier, [AA 412-20
   Then the stale turtle will grow limp from age. [John 437-22
   Here the black violets grow down to its banks [Degen 445-1
   The morning-glories grow in the egg. [Aug 490-3
   The mornings grow silent, the never-tiring wonder. [Aug 495-17
   Grow large and larger. Our fate is our own. The hand,[Bship 81-7P
GROWING. It is a wizened starlight growing young, [Descrip 344-9
   A definition growing certain and [NSF 386-6
   Of summer, growing fragrant in the night, [NSF 399-10
   By growing clear, transparent magistrates, [Bouquet 449-6
   Behold them, not choses of Provence, growing [Bouquet 449-12
   Of men growing small in the distances of space, [Rome 508-3
   On the altar, growing toward the lights, inside. [Armor 529-7
   And you forgive dark broachings growing great [Spaniard 34-7 P
   But one lives to think of this growing, this pushing life,
      [Bship 80-8 P
   The circle of the sceptre growing large [Bship 80-23 P
GROWL. No thought at all: a guttural growl, [Grotesque 75-15 P
GROWLING. Of growling teeth, and falls at night, snuffed out
   [NH 467-19
GROWN. Grown tired of flight. Like a dark rabbi, I [Monocle 17-21
   How greatly had he grown in his demesne, [C 31-1
   Of seeds grown fat, too juicily opulent, [C 32-9
   But that this bloom grown riper, showing nibs [C 44-6
   The time of year has grown indifferent. [Pharynx 96-1
   Its ruddy pallor had grown cadaverous. [Anglais 149-4
   Are the eye grown larger, more intense. [Vari 234-20
   Grown denser, part, the eye so touched, so played [Landsc 242-24
   Is not an early time that has grown late. [Dutch 292-2
   The soldier of time grown deathless in great size. [EM 319-2
   It has, long since, grown tired, of such ideas. [Feo 334-2
   And mist-mites, dangling seconds, grown [Red Fern 365-9
   Man's mind grown venerable in the unreal. [Cred 377-5
   What rabbi, grown furious with human wish, [NSF 389-1
   She gives transparence. But she has grown old. [AA 413-14
   A space grown wide, the inevitable blue [Orb 440-21
   The pulse of the object, the heat of the body grown cold
      [Study I 463-16
   The bricks grown brittle in time's poverty, [NH 480-23
   And that confident one, Marie, the wearer of cheap stones, who
      will have grown still and restless; [Piano 22-5 P
   Grown great and grave beyond imagined trees, [Old Woman 45-31 P
   We have grown weary of the man that thinks. [Sombre 66-18 P
   Midmost in its design, the arms grown swift, [Sombre 69-9 P
   A wandering orb upon a path grown clear. [Sombre 70-17 P
   And I play my guitar. The vines have grown wild. [Stan MBG 72-12P
   They had hardly grown to know the sunshine, [Stan Hero 83-17 P
GROWS. Poison grows in this dark. [Weep Woman 25-4
   Since by our nature we grow old, earth grows [Anatomy 108-1
   One grows used to the weather, [Am Sub 131-5
   Everyone, grows suddenly cold. [Fading 139-7
   The color like a thought that grows [MBG 169-19
   Of time, time grows upon the rock. [MBG 171-10
   But in nature it merely grows. [Add 198-7
   What in nature merely grows. [Add 198-17
   One grows to hate these things except on the dump. [Dump 202-11
   Grows large on the wall. [Rhythms 215-10
   Grows large against space: [Rhythms 215-14
   Grows sharp in blood. The armies kill themselves, [Dutch 292-19
   He is, the air changes and grows fresh to breathe. [Choc 301-8
   The flowering Judas grows from the belly or not at all.
      [Holiday 312-15
   Before winter freezes and grows black-- [Burghers 362-14
   The large-leaved day grows rapidly, [Red Fern 365-1
   And last year's garden grows salacious weeds. [Cred 377-10
   Grows warm in the motionless motion of his flight, [NSF 404-19
   And the whiteness grows less vivid on the wall. [AA 412-22
   A second that grows first, a black unreal [Novel 458-14
   Slowly the room grows dark. It is odd about [Novel 458-19
   The phrase grows weak. The fact takes up the strength [NH 473-4
   The closed-in smell of hay. A sumac grows [Armor 529-6
   One likes the way red grows. [Table 40-12 P
GROWTH. The poet but the poem, the growth of the mind [Papini 446-8
   And no less suddenly here again, a growth [Bouquet 448-11
   These pods are part of the growth of life within life:[Nuns 92-7P
GRUB. Yeoman and grub, but with a fig in sight, [C 42-17
GRUDGES. An oppressor that grudges them their death, [MBG 173-17
   As it grudges the living that they live. [MBG 173-18
GRUESOME. Gray, gruesome grumblers. [Archi 18-10 P

GRUFF. The eye and tinkling to the ear. Gruff drums [Havana 143-6
GRUMBLE. Without grace or grumble. Score this anecdote [C 45-19
GRUMBLERS. Gray, gruesome grumblers. [Archi 18-10 P
GRUNT. That makes us weep, laugh, grunt and groan, and shout
    [Monocle 17-10
GRUNTED. The grunted breath serene and final, [MBG 177-15
GRUNTING. The grunting, shuffling branches, the robust, [Parochial
    191-8
GUARDIANS. And, finally, set guardians in the grounds, [Archi 18-9P
GUARDS. In a robe that is our glory as he guards. [Owl 435-3
GUATEMALA. Home from Guatemala, back at the Waldorf. [Waldorf
    240-23
    After that alien, point-blank, green and actual Guatemala.
    [Waldorf 241-9
GUBBINAL. "Gubbinal" [85-title
GUERILLA. That the guerilla I should be booked [Prelude 195-10
GUERRIERE. Gazette Guerrière. A man might happen [Hero 276-5
GUESS. And least will guess that with our bones [Postcard 159-4
GUESTS. These hospitaliers? These brute-like guests? [AA 415-23
    Green guests and table in the woods and songs [Orb 440-19
GUFFAW. Meantime, centurions guffaw and beat [Monocle 15-22
GUIDE. A finger with a ring to guide his eye [Aug 492-10
GUIDED. The right to be." He guided his boat [Presence 105-17 P
GUIDING. The right to be." Guiding his boat [Ulysses 99-14 P
GUILD. God of the sausage-makers, sacred guild, [Nigger 157-4
GUILLOTINE. Of the guillotine or of any glamorous hanging.
    [Parochial 192-7
GUILT. So much guilt lies buried [Inhab 504-13
GUILTY. Not of the enigma of the guilty dream. [AA 419-6
GUINEA. He mocks the guinea, challenges [Vari 233-14
GUISE. That prose should wear a poem's guise at last. [C 36-23
GUITAR. After the guitar is asleep, [Venereal 47-21
    "The Man with the Blue Guitar" [165-title
    The man bent over his guitar, [MBG 165-1
    They said, "You have a blue guitar, [MBG 165-3
    Are changed upon the blue guitar." [MBG 165-6
    A tune upon the blue guitar [MBG 165-9
    Of a man that plays a blue guitar. [MBG 166-2
    It picks its way on the blue guitar. [MBG 166-14
    This buzzing of the blue guitar. [MBG 167-2
    Even in the clattering of your guitar. [MBG 167-14
    Yet nothing changed by the blue guitar; [MBG 167-16
    As you play them, on the blue guitar, [MBG 167-20
    The tune is space. The blue guitar [MBG 168-6
    A composing of senses of the guitar. [MBG 168-8
    The strings are cold on the blue guitar. [MBG 168-22
    Of the air, in which the blue guitar [MBG 169-14
    Roll a drum upon the blue guitar. [MBG 170-13
    Tom-tom, c'est moi. The blue guitar [MBG 171-11
    One sits and plays the blue guitar. [MBG 172-22
    An animal. The blue guitar-- [MBG 174-8
    The blue guitar a mould? That shell? [MBG 174-11
    Of things as they are, as the blue guitar [MBG 174-18
    Good air. Poor pale, poor pale guitar . . . [MBG 176-2
    And say they are on the blue guitar. [MBG 180-18
    The nuances of the blue guitar. [MBG 182-22
    The blue guitar surprises you. [MBG 183-14
    He that at midnight touches the guitar, [Thought 186-5
    And as the black Spaniard plays his guitar. [Peaches 224-6
    And plays his guitar. Ha-ee-me is a beast. [Jouga 337-3
    Or perhaps his guitar is a beast or perhaps they are [Jouga 337-4
    Who knocks out a noise. The guitar is another beast [Jouga 337-7
    This sat beside his bed, with its guitar, [NH 483-16
    It is like a guitar left on a table [Vacancy 511-8
    They never were . . . The sounds of the guitar [Rock 525-9
    The world is young and I play my guitar. [Stan MBG 72-2 P
    Red mango peels and I play my guitar. [Stan MBG 72-4 P
    And honey from thorns and I play my guitar. [Stan MBG 72-9 P
    And I play my guitar. The vines have grown wild. [Stan MBG 72-12P
    I play them on a blue guitar [Stan MBG 72-15 P
    Quiver upon the blue guitar. [Stan MBG 73-6 P
    On such a peak, the blue guitar-- [Stan MBG 73-16 P
    "Farewell without a Guitar" [98-title P
GUITARISTS. The gaunt guitarists on the strings [Ord Women 11-17
GUITARS. From dry catarrhs and to guitars [Ord Women 10-14
    From dry guitars, and to catarrhs [Ord Women 12-4
    Playing mouth-organs in the night or, now, guitars. [Sick 90-9 P
GULL. When it sings. The gull sits on chimney-tops. [Vari 233-13
GULLS. Say of the gulls that they are flying [Vari 232-5
    One sparrow is worth a thousand gulls, [Vari 233-12
    The syllables of the gulls and of the crows [Primordia 7-17 P
GULPED. Making gulped potions from obstreperous drops, [C 46-9
GULPING. Gulping for shape among the reeds. No doubt, [Lot 371-12
    This is form gulping after formlessness, [AA 411-10
GUM. What Eden sapling gum, what honeyed gore, [C 38-2
    Oozing cantankerous gum [Bananas 54-20
    The sky is a blue gum streaked with rose. The trees are black.
    [Banal 62-12
    As the gum of the gum-tree. [Lulu G 26-22 P
GUM-TREE. As the gum of the gum-tree. [Lulu G 26-22 P

GUN. Angel, convulsive shatterer, gun, [Hero 273-19
GUNMAN. Between the slouchings of a gunman and a lover, [Moonlight
    531-15
    The thinker knows. The gunman of the commune [Bship 80-16 P
GUNS. The air attends the brightened guns, [Dutch 290-16
    The word respected, fired ten thousand guns [Bship 78-12 P
    On The Masculine one asserts and fires the guns. [Bship 80-7 P
    Your guns are not rhapsodic strophes, red [Bship 80-20 P
    See machine-guns.
GURRITUCK. The softest word went gurrituck in his skull. [Norfolk
    [111-9
GUSHES. The breath that gushes upward and is gone, [Descrip 341-4
GUSTINESS. From warehouse doors, the gustiness of ropes, [C 36-9
GUSTS. And gusts of great enkindlings, its polar green, [AA 413-2
GUSTY. What was this gaudy, gusty panoply? [C 30-11
    Do they believe they range the gusty cold, [Heaven 56-12
    Elations when the forest blooms; gusty [Sunday 67-22
    With faces as with leaves, be gusty with mouths, [Dames 206-9
    Staked solidly in a gusty grappling with rocks. [NH 487-21
GUT. But on the banjo's categorical gut, [C 38-19
GUTTED. A dirty house in a gutted world, [Postcard 159-19
GUTTER. Like water running in a gutter [Grotesque 76-22 P
GUTTERS. And leaves in whirlings in the gutters, whirlings [NH 471-4
GUTTURAL. No thought at all: a guttural growl, [Grotesque 75-15 P
GUTTURALS. Heavenly labials in a world of gutturals. [Plot Giant
    7-9
    Groaning in half-exploited gutturals [Pure 333-3
    The thick strings stutter the finial gutturals. [Madame 507-10
GUZZ. See Père Guzz.
GUZZLY. Beyond these changes, good, fat, guzzly fruit. [C 41-7

HA. The wind had seized the tree and ha, and ha, [Hand 271-10
  Said ha. [Melancholy 32-8 P
  Oh ha, Oh ha. [Melancholy 32-12 P
HABANA. Is lunar Habana the Cuba of the self? [Feo 333-15
HABIT. This is the habit of wishing, as if one's grandfather lay
    [Bed 327-1
  That habit of wishing and to accept the structure [Bed 327-6
  Half pales of green, appropriate habit for [Cred 378-3
  He might take habit, whether from wave or phrase, [NSF 387-12
  Beyond the habit of sense, anarchic shape [Page 422-18
  The whole habit of the mind is changed by them. [Our Stars
    455-17
  When the whole habit of the mind was changed, [Our Stars 455-23
  But now a habit of the truth had formed [Someone 85-8 A
HABITATION. To the wild limits of its habitation. [Page 421-20
  The rock is the habitation of the whole, [Rock 528-10
  Is any choir the whole voice of this fretful habitation,
    [Inelegance 26-5 P
HABITATIONS. Impalpable habitations that seem to move [NH 466-8
HABITS. The coming on of feasts and the habits of saints, [NH 472-2
HABITUATES. It habituates him to the invisible, [Aug 493-5
HABITUDE. That in the moonlight have their habitude. [C 35-13
HABITUDES. The flights through space, changing habitudes. [Ulysses
    103-6 P
HAC. Said hic, said hac, [Melancholy 32-7 P
HACKED. But bananas hacked and hunched . . . [Bananas 54-10
  This mangled, smutted semi-world hacked out [Ghosts 119-8
HACKED-UP. To see, once more, this hacked-up world of tools,
    [Duck 61-9 P
HACKER. Whetting his hacker, [Plot Giant 6-12
HACKLES. Of tan with henna hackles, halt! [Bantams 75-15
HAD. You should have had plums tonight, [Bananas 54-4
  Jove in the clouds had his inhuman birth. [Sunday 67-27
  I had as lief be embraced by the porter at the hotel [Two Fig
    85-14
  This skeleton had a daughter and that, a son. [Norfolk 111-7
  In his time, this one had little to speak of, [Norfolk 111-8
  Perhaps it's the lunch that we had [Sailing 120-6
  Or the lunch that we should have had. [Sailing 120-7
  Whatever self it had, became the self [Key W 129-28
  These had a being, breathing frost; [Postcard 159-3
  Because it was spring and the birds had to come. [Loaf 200-15
  No doubt that soldiers had to be marching [Loaf 200-16
  And that drums had to be rolling, rolling, rolling. [Loaf 200-17
  To have had him holding--what? [Thunder 220-14
  The dog had to walk. He had to be taken. [Forces 229-3
  The girl had to hold back and lean back to hold him, [Forces
    229-4
  And counter-ideas. There was nothing one had. [Forces 229-8
  It had to be right: nougats. It was a shift [Forces 229-16
  He said I had this that I could love, [Yellow 236-13
  What will suffice. It has not always had [Of Mod 239-18
  It was nowhere else, its place had to be supposed, [Landsc 242-7
  Itself had to be supposed, a thing supposed [Landsc 242-8
  He had only not to live, to walk in the dark, [Landsc 242-12
  The man who has had the time to think enough, [Oboe 250-19
  They had to think it to be. He wanted that, [Extracts 257-6
  In what new spirit had his body birth? [Choc 299-8
  Why should they not know they had everything of their own
    [Holiday 312-9
  As each had a particular woman and her touch? [Holiday 312-10
  After all, they knew that to be real each had [Holiday 312-11
  It had nothing of the Julian thunder-cloud: [EM 319-26
  As if sight had not its own miraculous thrift, [EM 320-26
  The house was quiet because it had to be. [House Q 358-16
  She lived in her house. She had two daughters, one [NSF 402-1
  He had to choose. But it was not a choice [NSF 403-11
  It was not her look but a knowledge that she had. [Owl 435-13
  Impassioned by the knowledge that she had [Owl 435-17
  As if the centre of images had its [Study II 464-10
  That power to conceal they had as men, [NH 470-8
  The instinct for heaven had its counterpart: [NH 476-1
  Difference and were one? It had to be [Aug 494-4
  And it had to be, [Aug 495-12
  Yet the absence of the imagination had [Plain 503-1
  Had to be imagined as an inevitable knowledge, [Plain 503-7
  Made to affect a dream they never had, [Burnshaw 47-1 P
  That was never the heaven of Africa, which had [Greenest 54-19 P
  No heaven, had death without a heaven, death [Greenest 54-20 P
  The scholar's outline that you had, the print [Duck 61-17 P
  "The Woman That Had More Babies than That" [81-title P
  Continually--There is a woman has had [Woman Had 81-22 P
  It had neither love nor wisdom. [Three 132-7 P
  Green had, those days, its own implacable sting. [Someone 85-7 A
HADDAM. O thin men of Haddam, [Thirteen 93-19
  Stands glistening and Haddam shines and sways. [R Conn 533-15
HA-EE-ME. And there is no other. There is Ha-eé-me, who sits
    [Jouga 337-2

And plays his guitar. Ha-eé-me is a beast. [Jouga 337-3
  Ha-eé-me is the male beast . . . an imbecile, [Jouga 337-6
  And after a while, when Ha-eé-me has gone to sleep, [Jouga 337-14
HAGGARD. The pillars are prostrate, the arches are haggard,
    [Botanist 1 135-11
  Into this haggard and tenuous air, [Nigger 153-9
  Monsters antique and haggard with past thought? [Dutch 292-11
  Of place: time's haggard mongrels. [Analysis 348-11
  Spelling out pandects and haggard institutes? [Duck 62-17 P
  See man-haggard.
HAGGARDIE. Against the haggardie . . . A loud, large water [EM 321-8
HAGGLER. Hallooing haggler; for the wax is blown, [Infernale 25-6P
HAGGLING. To a haggling of wind and weather, by these lights [AA
    421-2
HAIL. While it creaks hail. [Watermelon 89-12
  And hail, cry hail, cry hail. [Watermelon 89-15
  Speech for the quiet, good hail of himself, good hail, good
    hail, [Sick 90-20 P
HAIL-BOW. And a hail-bow, hail-bow, [Song Fixed 519-16
HAIR. Do you come dripping in your hair from sleep? [Monocle 14-11
  Inscrutable hair in an inscrutable world. [C 27-21
  The hair of my blonde [Depression 63-9
  Its hair filled [Six Sig 74-19
  No crown is simpler than the simple hair. [Fictive 87-13
  That glistens on your face and hair. [Nigger 152-14
  One might have found tragic hair, [Chateau 161-9
  Of autumn's halloo in its hair. So that closely, then, [Parochial
    192-2
  You are one . . . Go hunt for honey in his hair. [Blue Bldg
    217-22
  A youth, a lover with phosphorescent hair, [Uruguay 249-21
  O, skin and spine and hair of you, Ercole, [Extracts 256-18
  For him to see, wove round her glittering hair. [Hand 271-6
  Her hair fell on him and the mi-bird flew [Hand 271-18
  And, standing in violent golds, will brush her hair. [Debris
    338-7
  Take the diamonds from your hair and lay them down. [Myrrh 350-10
  The child's three ribbons are in her plaited hair. [Extraord
    369-21
  The Italian girls wore jonquils in their hair [NSF 389-16
  An ancient forehead hung with heavy hair, [NSF 400-7
  To comb her dewy hair, a touchless light, [Beginning 427-13
  Women with other lives in their live hair, [Study II 464-14
  She would talk a little to herself as she combed her hair,
    [World 521-16
  The child's hair is of the color of the hay in the haystack,
    around which the four black horses stand. [Primordia 8-1 P
  Ears, eyes, souls, skins, hair? [Parasol 20-6 P
  Giddap! The ruby roses' hair [Room Gard 40-17 P
  And the painted hairs that composed her hair. [Grotesque 74-4 P
  And the cheeks like flower-pots under her hair. [Grotesque 74-16P
HAIRED. See long-haired.
HAIR-RIBBONS. The mother ties the hair-ribbons of the child
    [Extraord 369-7
HAIRS. She was all of her airs and ears and hairs, [Grotesque 74-2P
  And the painted hairs that composed her hair. [Grotesque 74-4 P
HAIRY. Civilization must be destroyed. The hairy saints [NE Verses
    106-1
HAIRY-BACKED. Hairy-backed and hump-armed, [Orangeade 102-18
HALCYON. Of pick of ebon, pick of halcyon. [Havana 144-16
  That buffets the shapes of its possible halcyon [EM 321-7
HALE. Distorted by hale fatness, turned grotesque, [Monocle 16-8
  O ashen admiral of the hale, hard blue . . . [NE Verses 105-8
HALE-HEARTED. And knew each other well, hale-hearted landsmen,
    [AA 419-8
HALF. Half prayer and half ditty, [Pourtraicte 22-3
  Nor half begun, but, when it is, leave room [C 33-19
  Coat half-flare and half galloon; [Orangeade 103-10
  The trees like bones and the leaves half sand, half sun. [Farewell
    118-5
  Of the actor, half his gesture, half [MBG 170-1
  Its pitting poison, half the night. [Thought 186-24
  Men on green beds and women half of sun. [Cuisine 227-19
  The sky, half porcelain, preferring that [Cuisine 228-6
  Elysia, these days, half earth, half mind; [Extracts 257-1
  Half sun, half thinking of the sun; half sky, [Extracts 257-2
  Half desire for indifference about the sky. [Extracts 257-3
  It cannot be half earth, half mind; half sun, [Extracts 257-16
  Half thinking; until the mind has been satisfied, [Extracts
    257-17
  Because everything is half dead. [Motive 288-2
  With the half colors of quarter-things, [Motive 288-6
  The idea is thing. She is half who made her. [Couch 295-20
  The wind beat in the roof and half the walls. [Repet 306-2
  The artificer of subjects still half night. [Descrip 345-18
  It is a mountain half way green and then, [Cred 375-13
  The other immeasurable half, such rock [Cred 375-14
  A mountain luminous half way in bloom [Cred 375-22
  And then half way in the extremest light [Cred 375-23
  And knotted, sashed and seamed, half pales of red, [Cred 378-2

Half pales of green, appropriate habit for [Cred 378-3
An erotic perfume, half of the body, half [NSF 390-7
Which pierces clouds and bends on half the world. [NSF 393-15
It is evening. The house is evening, half dissolved. [AA 413-8
Only the half they can never possess remains, [AA 413-9
The sun is half the world, half everything, [NH 481-22
The bodiless half. There is always this bodiless half, [NH
    481-23
If, then, New Haven is half sun, what remains, [NH 482-3
At evening, after dark, is the other half, [NH 482-4
Myself, only half of a figure of a sort, [Angel 497-6
A figure half seen, or seen for a moment, a man [Angel 497-7
He left half a shoulder and half a head [Two Illus 514-4
On which men speculated in summer when they were half asleep.
    [Prol 516-15
Half men and half new, modern monsters . . . [Stan Hero 84-8 P
See one-half.
HALF-ARC. Alone, the half-arc hanging in mid-air [Repet 309-12
    Supported by a half-arc in mid-earth. [Repet 309-14
HALF-ASLEEP By the cadaver of these caverns, half-asleep. [Two V
    355-7
    And without eloquence, O, half-asleep, [Rome 509-11
HALF-AWAKE. The catbird's gobble in the morning half-awake--
    [Holiday 313-6
HALF-BORNE. The message is half-borne. Could marble still [Greenest
    57-21 P
HALF-DISSOLVING. Of half-dissolving frost, the summer came, [C 34-10
HALF-EXPLOITED. Groaning in half-exploited gutturals [Pure 333-3
HALF-FISHES. Rose--women as half-fishes of salt shine, [Study II
    464-15
HALF-FLARE. Coat half-flare and half galloon; [Orangeade 103-10
HALF-HEARD. Of the room and on an accordion, half-heard, [AA 419-2
HALF-MAN. Half-man, half-star. [Nuances 18-14
HALF-MEANINGS. By repetitions of half-meanings. Am I not, [Angel
    497-5
HALF-MOON. As, for example, the ellipse of the half-moon-- [Six Sig
    75-12
HALF-NAKED. Autumn howls upon half-naked summer. But [John 437-5
HALF-NIGHT. The blueness of the half-night, fill the air [Red Kit
    31-23 P
HALF-PERCEIVED. Some affluence, if only half-perceived, [Planet
    533-1
HALF-RISEN. The difficult rightness of half-risen day. [Rock 528-9
HALF-SPOKEN. This brother half-spoken in the mother's throat
    [EM 317-11
HALF-STAR. Half-man, half-star. [Nuances 18-14
HALF-THOUGHT-OF. The cloud drifts idly through half-thought-of
    forms. [AA 416-15
HALFWAY. For sleepers halfway waking. He perceived [C 31-16
HALF-WAY. Half-way to bed, when the phrase will be spoken, [Nigger
    156-8
HALIDOM. And halidom for the unbraided femes, [C 43-27
    On the seat of halidom, rainbowed, [Ulysses 104-5 P
HALL. Fills the high hall with shuffling men [MBG 171-13
    High as the hall. The whirling noise [MBG 171-14
    In hall harridan, not hushful paradise, [AA 421-1
HALLOO. Halloo them in the topmost distances [Heaven 56-22
    Ashen man on ashen cliff above the salt halloo, [NE Verses 105-7
    This halloo, halloo, halloo heard over the cries [Parochial 191-12
    Of autumn's halloo in its hair. So that closely, then, [Parochial
    192-2
    The sun aches and ails and then returns halloo [Questions 462-5
HALLOOING. Hallooing haggler; for the wax is blown, [Infernale 25-6 P
HALLOW. In desperate hallow, rugged gesture, fault [EM 316-26
    See hap-hallow.
HALLOWED. This hallowed visitant, chimerical, [Spaniard 35-19 P
    The spirit's episcopate, hallowed and high, [Greenest 53-28 P
HALLOW-HO. To avoid the hap-hallow hallow-ho [Adequacy 243-15
HALLS. The nocturnal halls. [Ord Women 10-20
    To the wickless halls. [Ord Women 12-2
    An acid sunlight fills the halls. [Contra I 267-2
HALLUCINATING. That seemed hallucinating horn, and here, [C 29-4
HALLUCINATION. Like an hallucination come to daze [Sun March 134-3
    Its own hallucination never sees [EM 315-9
HALLUCINATIONS. Make gay the hallucinations in surfaces. [NH 472-21
    And spread hallucinations on every leaf. [Armor 529-20
HALOES. Coiffeur of haloes, fecund jeweller-- [Eve Angels 137-8
HALO-JOHN. In the names of St. Paul and of the halo-John [Luther
    461-5
HALS. See Franz Hals.
HALT. Of tan with henna hackles, halt! [Bantams 75-15
    The tread of the carriers does not halt [Cortege 80-7
    It is not part of what is absent, a halt [NH 487-17
HALTED. The music halted and the horse stood still. [NSF 391-12
HALVES. Of barbarous tongue, slavered and panting halves [AA 415-18
    As if, as if, as if the disparate halves [Study II 464-16
HALYARDS. At the halyards. Why, then, when in golden fury [NSF
    390-24
HAMBURG. To Monsieur Dufy's Hamburg when they came. [Lions 125-7
HAMMER. The ruddy temper, the hammer [Motive 288-17

HAMMERED. Outside of gates of hammered serafin, [Babies 77-2
HAND. If sex were all, then every trembling hand [Monocle 17-7
    A hand that bears a thick-leaved fruit, [Venereal 48-16
    And, finger after finger, here, the hand, [Worms 49-21
    Than your moist hand. [Two Figures 85-16
    A breath upon her hand [Peter 91-7
    Just to stand still without moving a hand. [Adieu 127-12
    Gives the touch of the senses, not of the hand, [MBG 174-20
    There was the butcher's hand. [Weak Mind 212-1
    Held in his hand the suave egg-diamond [Thunder 220-10
    But the eyes are men in the palm of the hand. [Arcades 225-19
    The hand between the candle and the wall [Rhythms 245-9
    It must be that the hand [Rhythms 245-18
    The hand can touch, neither green bronze nor marble, [Montra
    261-3
    "The Hand as a Being" [271-title
    She held her hand before him in the air, [Hand 271-5
    Her hand composed him and composed the tree. [Hand 271-9
    Her hand composed him like a hand appeared, [Hand 271-13
    Of an impersonal gesture, a stranger's hand. [Hand 271-14
    Her hand took his and drew him to her. [Hand 271-17
    Merely by putting hand to brow, [Oak 272-1
    The suspending hand withdrawn, would be [Couch 295-14
    Holds in his hand a book you have never written [Lack 303-2
    Be near me, come closer, touch my hand, phrases [EM 317-17
    A woman smoothes her forehead with her hand [EM 319-17
    Locution of a hand in a rhapsody. [Pastor 379-8
    Of the pillow in your hand. You writhe and press [NSF 384-20
    So moving in the manner of his hand. [NSF 388-12
    No need, am happy, forget need's golden hand, [NSF 405-1
    And be surprised and tremble, hand and lip. [Beginning 428-2
    She spoke with backward gestures of her hand. [Owl 435-8
    Protruding from the pile of wool, a hand, [Novel 457-10
    By the hand of desire, faint, sensitive, the soft [NH 476-14
    Touch and trouble of the touch of the actual hand. [NH 476-15
    An opening for outpouring, the hand was raised: [NH 483-2
    Touches, as one hand touches another hand, [NH 484-19
    In the parent's hand, perhaps parental love? [Aug 491-25
    A hand of light to turn the page, [Aug 492-9
    A dead hand tapped the drum, [Phases 6-1 P
    And the coroner's hand [Coroner 30-1 P
    More than his muddy hand was in the manes, [Old Woman 43-19 P
    And by a hand of certitude to cut [Greenest 56-17 P
    The leaping bodies, come from the truculent hand, [Duck 64-15 P
    A hand that fails to seize it. High captain, the grand [Bship
    80-25 P
    Precious from the region of the hand, still bright [Bship 81-1 P
    Grow large and larger. Our fate is our own. The hand, [Bship 81-7P
    It must be the hand of one, it must be the hand [Bship 81-8 P
    The luminous companion, the hand, [Ulysses 100-9 P
    A form that is lame, a hand, a back, [Ulysses 104-17 P
    The porcelain in one hand . . . [Three 138-6 P
    See: second-hand; sleight-of-hand.
HANDBOOK. It was a page he had found in the handbook of heartbreak.
    [Madame 507-8
HANDFULS. At the time of the dogwoods, handfuls thrown up [Forces
    229-5
HANDKERCHIEF. The doctor used his handkerchief and sighed. [Geneva
    24-15
    And beneath that handkerchief drapeau, severe, [Pure 331-3
HANDLES. Bending over and pulling themselves erect on the wooden
    handles, [Prol 515-8
HANDS. Blowing upon her hands [Paltry 5-17
    Her prismy blonde and clapped her in his hands, [C 42-3
    Hands without touch yet touching poignantly, [C 43-17
    My hands such sharp, imagined things. [W Burgher 61-17
    Bitter eyes, hands hostile and cold. [Chateau 161-10
    The spruces' outstretched hands; [Delight 162-7
    Piece the world together, boys, but not with your hands.
    [Parochial 192-8
    It would have been better for his hands [Thunder 220-21
    To be convulsed, to have remained the hands [Thunder 220-22
    There they sit, holding their eyes in their hands. [Arcades 225-4
    In their hands. The lilacs came long after. [Arcades 225-12
    Working, with big hands, on the town, [Hartford 227-2
    "Oak Leaves Are Hands" [272-title
    Have arms without hands. They have trunks [Possum 293-18
    His hands became his feelings. His thick shape [Repet 306-12
    The soft hands are a motion not a touch. [AA 413-16
    Ringed round and barred, with eyes held in their hands, [Page
    422-30
    Sniffed her and slapped heavy hands [Lulu G 26-11 P
    Your hands held high and cry again, but cry, [Burnshaw 51-16 P
    Let your golden hands wave fastly and be gay [Burnshaw 51-28 P
    At least, conceive what these hands from Sweden mean, [Duck 60-21P
    Rather rings than fingers, rather fingers than hands. [Grotesque
    74-8 P
    Held in the hands of blue men that are lead within, [Discov 95-16P
    The candle would tremble in his hands; [Three 132-26 P
HANG. We hang like warty squashes, streaked and rayed, [Monocle 16-9

His passion's permit, hang of coat, degree [C 39-18
The plum survives its poems. It may hang [C 41-2
Hang always heavy in that perfect sky, [Sunday 69-15
Hang a feather by your eye, [Orangeade 103-15
His firm stanzas hang like hives in hell [EM 315-11
Or Aristotle's skeleton. Let him hang out [Less 327-13
And the memorial mosses hang their green [Degen 445-2
A bubble without a wall on which to hang. [Theatre 91-12 P
Or clouds that hang lateness on the sea. They become [Role 93-10P
HANGED. Are those that have been hanged, [Metamorph 266-7
He hanged himself in front of me. [Three 141-16 P
HANGING. Hanging his shawl upon the wind, [MBG 181-17
Of the guillotine or of any glamorous hanging. [Parochial 192-7
Of them in the air still hanging heavily [EM 315-6
Alone, the half-arc hanging in mid-air [Repet 309-12
Shall we be found hanging in the trees next spring? [AA 419-19
Are, hanging above you, as you move, [Countryman 428-14
A great town hanging pendent in a shade, [NH 468-16
For farewells, a sad hanging on for remembrances. [NH 487-18
And shadowy hanging of it, thick with stars [Old Woman 46-2 P
The deep sigh with which the hanging ends, close [Stan Hero
  84-18 P
Today the leaves cry, hanging on branches swept by wind, [Course
  96-10 P
See hoary-hanging.
HANGMAN. As hangman, a little sick of blood, of [Stan Hero 84-17 P
To his gorge, hangman, once helmet-maker [Stan Hero 84-19 P
HANGS. When the body of Jesus hangs in a pallor, [Lunar 107-5
A hard dry leaf hangs [Pears 196-15
But if it did . . . If the cloud that hangs [Country 207-10
The snow hangs heavily on the rocks, brought [Hero 273-5
Hangs heaven with flash drapery. Sight [Hero 274-12
Clears deeply, when the moon hangs on the wall [NSF 398-24
A stellar pallor that hangs on the threads. [Leben 505-3
Hangs her quilt under the pine-trees. [Primordia 9-16 P
HANKERING. Like windy citherns hankering for hymns. [High-Toned
  59-5
HANKERS. Still hankers after lions, or, to shift, [Lions 125-4
Still hankers after sovereign images. [Lions 125-5
HANS. The Johannisberger, Hans. [Anything B 211-16
The sea was frozen solid and Hans heard, [Page 421-5
So blau, so blau . . . Hans listened by the fire. [Page 421-14
They looked back at Hans' look with savage faces. [Page 421-23
Yet Hans lay wide awake. And live alone [Page 422-3
HANS CHRISTIAN. "Sonatina To Hans Christian" [109-title
Do you know, Hans Christian [Sonatina 110-7
HAP-HALLOW. To avoid the hap-hallow hallow-ho [Adequacy 243-15
HAPHAZARD. Attach. It seemed haphazard denouement. [C 40-25
Of very haphazard people and things, [Agenda 42-8 P
HAPLESS. With masquerade of thought, with hapless words [C 39-15
HAPPEN. Gazette Guerrière. A man might happen [Hero 276-5
That we achieve but balances that happen, [NSF 386-15
Do I happen to like red bush, [Table 40-5 P
Of the ways things happen to fall. [Table 40-15 P
And was to be? Could it happen to be this, [Old Woman 44-18 P
Such things happen in the evening. [Three 136-10 P
HAPPENED. As if nothing had happened. The dim actor spoke. [Repet
  306-11
Nothing had happened because nothing had changed. [NSF 392-2
HAPPENING. An escape from repetition, a happening [NH 483-6
HAPPENINGS. Archaic and future happenings, [Oak 272-19
HAPPENS. Of happens to like, not should. [Table 40-3 P
One likes what one happens to like. [Table 40-11 P
Happens to like is one [Table 40-14 P
On whatever the earth happens to be. [Three 130-23 P
HAPPIEST. The happiest enemy. And it may be [EM 324-10
And happiest folk-land, mostly marriage-hymns. [Cred 373-21
Of that oration, the happiest sense in which [Ideal 89-6 A
HAPPILY. It is most happily contrived. Here, then, [Antag 425-14
HAPPINESS. And erudite in happiness, with nothing learned, [Gala
  248-8
And, being unhappy, talk of happiness [Extracts 257-13
And, talking of happiness, know that it means [Extracts 257-14
Thought is false happiness: the idea [Crude 305-1
False happiness, since we know that we use [Crude 305-14
Unhappy about the sense of happiness. [Pure 331-9
Their parts as in a youthful happiness. [Cred 378-10
Relentlessly in possession of happiness. [AA 411-18
A bee for the remembering of happiness. [Owl 434-18
By chance, or happy chance, or happiness, [Aug 491-5
The sources of happiness in the shape of Rome, [Rome 508-23
In the sun's design of its own happiness, [Rock 525-18
And take from this restlessly unhappy happiness [How Now 97-14 P
HAPPY. Except to be happy, without knowing how, [Sad Gay 122-7
Happy men, distinguishing frost and clouds. [Nigger 151-8
Happy rather than holy but happy-high, [Thought 185-17
Laughing and singing and being happy, [Dezem 218-15
To be happy because people were thinking to be. [Extracts 257-5
In the same way, you were happy in spring, [Motive 288-5
How happy I was the day I told the young Blandina of three-

legged giraffes . . . [Analysis 348-1
Happy fecundity, flor-abundant force, [NSF 388-20
No need, am happy, forget need's golden hand, [NSF 405-1
An unhappy people in a happy world-- [AA 420-4
A happy people in an unhappy world-- [AA 420-8
A happy people in a happy world-- [AA 420-11
An unhappy people in a happy world. [AA 420-14
That would have wept and been happy, have shivered in the frost
  [Large 424-1
An enormous nation happy in a style, [NH 468-17
By chance, or happy chance, or happiness, [Aug 491-5
A board for bishops' grapes, the happy form [Sombre 70-8 P
That makes us happy or unhappy. [Of Mere 118-2 P
HAPPY-HIGH. Happy rather than holy but happy-high, [Thought 185-17
HARANGUE. The imprescriptible zenith, free of harangue, [What We
  459-15
HARASSING. More harassing master would extemporize [NH 486-7
HARBOR. Discoverer walked through the harbor streets [C 32-14
HARBORS. Tired of the salty harbors, [Paltry 5-13
HARD. They should think hard in the dark cuffs [Homunculus 26-18
O ashen admiral of the hale, hard blue . . . [NE Verses 105-8
A hard dry leaf hangs [Pears 196-15
Of red and blue, the hard sound-- [Motive 288-18
It is deep January. The sky is hard. [Possum 294-7
Hard to perceive and harder still to touch. [Choc 301-18
They do not make the visible a little hard [Creat 311-12
As, men make themselves their speech: the hard hidalgo [Descrip
  345-11
Voluble but archaic and hard to hear. [Liadoff 347-21
The meaning of the capture, this hard prize, [Cred 376-14
And hard it is in spite of blazoned days. [NSF 383-24
In the hard brightness of that winter day [Page 421-4
Hard found, and water tasting of misery. [Bad Time 426-14
Blue for all that and white and hard, [Celle 438-13
He wishes that all hard poetry were true. [Papini 447-2
Hear hard, gets at an essential integrity. [NH 475-3
At last, in that blond atmosphere, bronzed hard, [NH 487-2
In whose hard service both of us endure [Soldat 14-7 P
And the way was more than the walk and was hard to see. [Gro-
  tesque 74-14 P
The strong music of hard times, [Grotesque 76-13 P
Hard to be told from thoughts, the repeated drone [Americana 94-3P
It is hard to hear the north wind again, [Region 115-6 P
In the planes that tilt hard revelations on [Someone 87-19 A
See ice-hard.
HARD-BITE. And bite the hard-bite, barking as it bites. [Novel 458-8
HARDENED. We hardened ourselves to live by bluest reason [Medit
  124-2
HARDER. Hard to perceive and harder still to touch. [Choc 301-18
HARDLY. Less Aix than Stockholm, hardly a yellow at all, [Holiday
  312-4
Yet hardly to be seen and again the legs [Old Woman 46-8 P
They had hardly grown to know the sunshine, [Stan Hero 83-17 P
HARDY. Of hardy foam, receding flatly, spread [C 34-6
HARLEQUINED. Harlequined and mazily dewed and mauved [C 41-5
HARMONIES. And the adroiter harmonies of their fall. [Havana 144-22
By harmonies beyond known harmony. [Duck 62-8 P
HARMONIOUS. Prickly and obdurate, dense, harmonious, [C 35-18
Struggling toward his harmonious whole, [Negation 97-14
Some harmonious skeptic soon in a skeptical music [Sad Gay 122-15
When the harmonious heat of August pines [NSF 399-18
And in harmonious prodigy to be, [Owl 432-22
In colorings harmonious, dewed and dashed [Ulysses 104-3 P
HARMONY. Yet with a harmony not rarefied [C 35-19
The complicate, the amassing harmony. [NSF 403-15
It is the huge, high harmony that sounds [Orb 440-11
And breeding and bearing birth of harmony, [Study II 465-2
In a savage and subtle and simple harmony, [NH 468-4
Impelled by a convulsive harmony. [Red Kit 31-15 P
By harmonies beyond known harmony. [Duck 62-8 P
HARNESS. Harness of the horses shuffled [Cab 21-2 P
HARNESSES. Of the giant sense, the enormous harnesses [Repet 308-20
HARRIDAN. In hall harridan, not hushful paradise, [AA 421-1
The harridan self and ever-maladive fate [Old Woman 45-25 P
HARROWING. With a blubber of tom-toms harrowing the sky? [C 41-13
Straight up, an élan without harrowing, [What We 459-14
HARSH. Making harsh torment of the solitude. [Babies 77-15
Of the harsh reality of which it is part. [Plant 506-19
The mistress says, in a harsh voice, [Three 134-5 P
HARSHER. Proclaiming something harsher than he learned [C 33-1
HARSHEST. The unique composure, harshest streakings joined [Owl
  433-14
HARSHLY. Lie harshly buried there? [Extracts 259-10
HARTFORD. "Of Hartford in a Purple Light" [226-title
From Havre to Hartford, Master Soleil, [Hartford 226-5
It is Hartford seen in a purple light. [Hartford 226-18
We drove home from Cornwall to Hartford, late. [Real 110-8 P
See East Hartford.
HARVEST. Catching at Good-bye, harvest moon, [MBG 173-5
Without seeing the harvest or the moon? [MBG 173-6

Let purple Phoebus lie in umber harvest, [NSF 381-8
HAS. An annotator has his scruples, too. [C 32-28
  Their azure has a cloudy edge, their white [C 37-30
  One has a malady, here, a malady. One feels a malady. [Banal 63-6
  This dance has no name. It is a hungry dance. [Mice 123-5
  Each in the other what each has to give. [Re-state 146-5
  In speech. He has that music and himself. [Anglais 149-7
  The person has a mould. But not [MBG 174-5
  Having nothing otherwise, he has not [Prelude 194-20
  Has any chance to mate his life with life [Sleight 222-17
  Without time: as that which is not has no time, [Martial 237-19
  It has to content the reason concerning war, [Bottle 239-5
  It has to persuade that war is part of itself, [Bottle 239-6
  It has to be living, to learn the speech of the place. [Of Mod
    240-1
  It has to face the men of the time and to meet [Of Mod 240-2
  The women of the time. It has to think about war [Of Mod 240-3
  And it has to find what will suffice. It has [Of Mod 240-4
  To construct a new stage. It has to be on that stage [Of Mod
    240-5
  Beyond which it has no will to rise. [Of Mod 240-18
  Has a will to grow larger on the wall, [Rhythms 245-19
  To stand taller than a person stands, has [Hero 277-7
  The gigantic has a reality of its own. [Repet 308-12
  Yet, when corrected, has its curious lapses. [EM 318-15
  And there the soldier of time has deathless rest. [EM 319-6
  Has its emptiness and tragic expirations [EM 320-9
  He has no secret from them. This knowledge [EM 323-15
  What lover has one in such rocks, what woman. [EM 323-24
  The human that has no cousin in the moon. [Less 328-4
  He knows he has nothing more to think about. [Chaos 358-5
  It has no nurse nor kin to know [Woman Song 360-5
  "The Good Man Has No Shape" [364-title
  The Good Man Has No Shape, as if they knew. [Good Man 364-14
  And she has peace. My Jacomyntje! [Extraord 369-8
  To its barbed, barbarous rising and has peace. [Extraord 369-11
  It knows that what it has is what is not [NSF 382-10
  The President has apples on the table [NSF 390-19
  And war for war, each has its gallant kind. [NSF 407-21
  Collapsed. The denouement has to be postponed . . . [AA 416-21
  Which has no accurate syllables and that [Page 421-8
  What has he? What he has he has. But what? [Bad Time 426-18
  What has he that becomes his heart's strong core? [Bad Time 426-20
  He has his poverty and nothing more. [Bad Time 427-1
  He has an ever-living subject. The poet [Papini 446-3
  Has only the formulations of midnight. [Papini 446-4
  Like a monster that has everything and rests, [Bouquet 452-4
  Each sexton has his sect. The bells have none. [Luther 461-15
  To that which has no speech, [Aug 492-12
  What is left has the foreign smell of plaster, [Armor 529-5
  St. Armorer's has nothing of this present, [Armor 530-11
  Around it. Thus it has a large expanse, [Red Kit 31-7 P
  As the moon has in its moonlight, worlds away, [Red Kit 31-8 P
  As the sea has in its coastal clamorings. [Red Kit 31-9 P
  Has faint, portentous lustres, shades and shapes [Burnshaw 49-26P
  And bares an earth that has no gods, and bares [Greenest 58-13 P
  And the obese proprietor, who has a son [Greenest 58-16 P
  In Capricorn. The statue has a form [Greenest 58-17 P
  Even imagination has an end, [Sombre 71-13 P
  Meyer has my five senses. I have his. [Grotesque 76-10 P
  A street. She has a supernatural head. [Woman Had 83-8 P
  It has a clear, a single, a solid form, [Recit 87-11 P
  He has nothing but the truth to leave. [Ulysses 103-10 P
  It has no knowledge except of nothingness [Clear Day 113-15 P
  Yet it has a bearing; [Three 133-26 P
  Because the incredible, also, has its truth, [Someone 85-15 A
  8. The owl sits humped. It has a hundred eyes. [Someone 86-11 A
HASH. With our affair, our destiny, our hash? [Bship 80-19 P
HASPED. So Crispin hasped on the surviving form, [C 41-8
HAT. Patted his stove-pipe hat and tugged his shawl. [Geneva 24-3
  His broad-brimmed hat came close upon his eyes. [Babies 77-18
  In suavest keeping. The shoes, the clothes, the hat [Descrip
    343-2
  The knowledge of Spain and of the hidalgo's hat-- [Descrip 345-14
  It is that and a very big hat. [Prejudice 368-15
  They treat the philosopher's hat, [Prejudice 368-17
  The philosopher's hat to be part of the mind, [Prejudice 369-5
  The importance of its hat to a form becomes [Pastor 379-4
  More definite. The sweeping brim of the hat [Pastor 379-5
  The shawl across one shoulder and the hat. [NH 483-21
HATCHED. In pantaloons of fire and of women hatched, [Liadoff 346-9
HATCHING. A hatching that stared and demanded an answering look.
    [NH 484-3
HATE. One grows to hate these things except on the dump. [Dump
    202-11
  In the space of horizons that neither love nor hate. [Aug 490-14
HATED. I hated the weathery yawl from which the pools [Farewell
    118-1
  Of waving weeds. I hated the vivid blooms [Farewell 118-3
  Be seen, not to be loved nor hated because [NSF 385-5

Lived as the man lives now, and hated, loved, [Sombre 69-33 P
  As the man hates now, loves now, the self-same things. [Sombre
    70-1 P
HATING. The hating woman, the meaningless place, [Pecul 454-8
HATS. Rationalists, wearing square hats, [Six Sig 75-4
  And wearing hats of angular flick and fleck, [Bouquet 449-8
HATTERS. Ryan's lunch, hatters, insurance and medicines, [Thought
    185-6
HAUGHTY. Whether in-dwelling haughty clouds, frigid [Burnshaw
    47-15 P
HAULERS. Majestic bearers or solemn haulers trapped [Greenest
    57-14 P
HAUNCHES. At the center of the mass, the haunches low, [Old Woman
    43-13 P
  Would be a ring of heads and haunches, torn [Sombre 70-22 P
HAUNT. Then place of vexing palankeens, then haunt [C 43-24
  There is not any haunt of prophecy, [Sunday 68-17
HAUNTED. And from the nave build haunted heaven. Thus, [High-Toned
    59-3
  The houses are haunted [Ten O'C 66-1
  In the jasmine haunted forests, that we knew [Oboe 251-20
  And its tragical, its haunted arpeggios? [Liadoff 346-19
  We say of the moon, it is haunted by the man [NH 472-9
  The old men, the philosophers, are haunted by that [Woman Had
    82-23 P
  See lapis-haunted.
HAUTBOY. If you say on the hautboy man is not enough, [Oboe 250-15
HAVANA. Bordeaux to Yucatan, Havana next, [C 29-9
  Beyond Bordeaux, beyond Havana, far [C 40-9
  "Academic Discourse At Havana" [142-title
HAVE. And would have purple stuff upon her arms, [Paltry 5-12
  One must have a mind of winter [Snow Man 9-21
  A semblance to the thing I have in mind. [Monocle 17-3
  That fluttering things have so distinct a shade. [Monocle 18-3
  That in the moonlight have their habitude. [C 35-13
  The melon should have apposite ritual, [C 39-4
  Should have an incantation. And again, [C 39-4
  The summer, it should have a sacrament [C 39-6
  What word have you, interpreters, of men [Heaven 56-9
  Should have a black barouche. [W Burgher 61-6
  My titillations have no foot-notes [Jasmine 79-1
  Have it your way. [Gubbinal 85-3
  Have it your way. [Gubbinal 85-11
  Come now. Those to be born have need [Ghosts 119-12
  Of the bride, love being a birth, have need to see [Ghosts 119-13
  And to touch her, have need to say to her, [Ghosts 119-14
  Have I except it comes from the sun? [Adieu 128-10
  For all his purple, the purple bird must have [Nigger 155-20
  They said, "You have a blue guitar, [MBG 165-3
  Have shapes that are not yet fully themselves, [Parochial 191-4
  The spring will have a health of its own, with none [Parochial
    192-1
  Nothing to have at heart. [Destructive 192-10
  It is to have or nothing. [Destructive 192-11
  It is a thing to have, [Destructive 192-12
  To have the ant of the self changed to an ox [Freed 205-9
  The web is woven and you have to wear it. [Dwarf 208-2
  The winter is made and you have to bear it, [Dwarf 208-3
  The bee may have all sweet [Anything B 211-9
  The planes that ought to have genius, [Common 221-19
  The men have no shadows [Common 221-24
  And the women have only one side. [Common 221-25
  Ah! and red; and they have peach fuzz, ah! [Peaches 224-11
  They have a sense of their design and savor [Extracts 254-21
  (That being as much belief as we may have,) [Extracts 257-23
  We have and are the man, capable [Hero 279-2
  I am and have a being and play a part. [Phenom 287-21
  And did not want nor have to be, [Motive 288-12
  The hullaballoo of health and have, [Dutch 292-5
  Have arms without hands. They have trunks [Possum 293-18
  They have heads in which a captive cry [Possum 294-2
  Cinerarias have a speaking sheen. [Poesie 302-17
  In him? If it is himself in them, they have [EM 323-13
  In a world of ideas, who would have all the people [EM 325-13
  In which the enchanted preludes have their place. [Pure 330-15
  What subtlety would apparition have? [Descrip 340-14
  Reposed? And does it have a puissant heart [Two V 354-5
  Though poor, though raggeder than ruin, have that [Belly 367-10
  And not to have is the beginning of desire. [NSF 382-4
  To have what is not is its ancient cycle. [NSF 382-5
  We have not the need of any paradise, [NSF 394-20
  We have not the need of any seducing hymn. [NSF 394-21
  Filled with expressible bliss, in which I have [NSF 404-24
  I have not but I am and as I am, I am. [NSF 405-6
  How mad would he have to be to say, "He beheld [Bad Time 426-9
  They have, or they may have, their glittering crown, [Golden
    460-20
  Each sexton has his sect. The bells have none. [Luther 461-15
  Not faded, if images are all we have. [Study I 464-1
  Have liberty not as the air within a grave [Aug 490-12

It was curious to have to descend [Aug 493-21
I have neither ashen wing nor wear of ore [Angel 496-9
The trees have a look as if they bore sad names [Slug 522-5
Why do the horses have eyes and ears? [Primordia 8-11 P
Wait now; have no rememberings of hope, [Soldat 14-13 P
I, that have a head [Soldat 12-19 P
I have secrets [Soldat 12-22 P
Ah, good God! That all beasts should have [Parasol 20-7 P
Would have a most singular appearance, [Mandolin 29-4 P
And she have beauty of a kind, but such [Red Kit 31-18 P
And more. It may have feathery color-frets, [Spaniard 35-8 P
A paragon of lustre; may have voice [Spaniard 35-9 P
Let this be as it may. It must have tears [Spaniard 35-13 P
In heaven. But I have no choice. [Lytton 39-15 P
So seen, neither have an order of its own, a peace [Burnshaw 49-1 P
It was a mistake to think of them. They have [Greenest 58-7 P
To make its factories content, must have [Greenest 58-20 P
A meaning without a meaning. These people have [Duck 65-16 P
In the park. We regret we have no nightingale. [Duck 66-7 P
We must have the throstle on the gramophone. [Duck 66-8 P
Often have the worst breaths. [Grotesque 74-18 P
Meyer has my five senses. I have his. [Grotesque 76-10 P
Of the world would have only to ring and ft! [Bship 78-9 P
It will be all we have. Our fate is our own: [Bship 81-4 P
The origin could have its origin. [Desire 85-17 P
In which the spectra have dewy favor and live [How Now 97-13 P
He said, "As I know, I am and have [Ulysses 99-13 P
He said, "As I know, I am and have [Presence 105-16 P
If we have no water, [Three 128-13 P
I have a song [Three 133-22 P
HAVEN. See heaven-haven.
HAVING. Having nothing otherwise, he has not [Prelude 194-20
  Having curved outlines. [Pears 196-10
  Outlined and having alphabetical [Common 221-21
  And goes to an external world, having [Repet 308-5
  Or having a separate author, a different poet, [Creat 311-1
  Having, each one, most praisable [Parasol 20-5 P
  The jostled ferns, where it might be, having eyes [Greenest 59-4P
  Not having to do with love. [Letters 108-5 P
HAVRE. From Havre to Hartford, Master Soleil, [Hartford 226-5
HAW. Of China, cap of Spain, imperative haw [C 28-9
  12. An uncivil shape like a gigantic haw. [Someone 86-15 A
HAWK. In spite of hawk and falcon, green toucan [C 30-18
  A hawk of life, that latined phrase: [MBG 178-4
  To meet that hawk's eye and to flinch [MBG 178-6
  And the hawk cats it and we say spread sail, [Aug 490-6
HAWKS. And Adirondack glittering. The cat hawks it [Aug 490-5
HAWS. And hems the planet rose and haws it ripe, [Ulti 429-11
HAY. Presents itself in Oley when the hay, [Cred 374-7
  Or: Gawks of hay . . . Augusta Moon, before [Golden 460-12
  The closed-in smell of hay. A sumac grows [Armor 529-6
  The child's hair is of the color of the hay in the haystack,
    around which the four black horses stand. [Primordia 8-1 P
  Blond weather. Give the mule his hay. [Stan MBG 73-17 P
HAYSTACK. The child's hair is of the color of the hay in the
  haystack, around which the four black horses stand. [Primordia
  8-1 P
HAZE. In the vapid haze of the window-bays, [Ord Women 11-6
  Persisting bleakly in an icy haze, [Pharynx 96-12
HÉ. Hé quoi! Angels go pricking elephants? [Greenest 55-30 P
HEAD. The singer has pulled his cloak over his head. [Of Surface
  57-7
  Its venom of renown, and on your head [Fictive 87-12
  Bear other perfumes. On your pale head wear [Fictive 88-15
  I sing a hero's head, large eye [MBG 165-13
  At a head upon the pillow in the dark, [Men Fall 188-5
  Of absolutes, bodiless, a head [Men Fall 188-7
  The head of one of the men that are falling, placed [Men Fall
  188-9
  Whose head lies blurring here, for this he died. [Men Fall 188-14
  You sit with your head like a carving in space [Rabbit K 210-2
  Green were the curls upon that head. [Poem Morn 219-17
  That kill the single man, starvation's head, [Extracts 254-16
  Neither his head nor horse nor knife nor [Hero 276-22
  Look round at the head and zither [God 285-2
  In your light, the head is speaking. It reads the book. [God
  285-10
  If just above her head there hung, [Couch 295-10
  Last night at the end of night his starry head, [Choc 299-19
  Like the head of fate, looked out in darkness, part [Choc 299-20
  Greater than mine, of his demanding, head [Choc 302-4
  It was passing a boundary, floating without a head [Lot 371-16
  It enfolds the head in a vital ambiance, [Pastor 379-11
  His head is air. Beneath his tip at night [AA 411-2
  Made us no less as sure. We saw in his head, [AA 412-1
  Here, then, is an abstraction given head, [Orb 443-7
  At the head of the past. [Irish 501-12
  He left half a shoulder and half a head [Two Illus 514-4
  I, that have a head [Soldat 12-19 P
  There lies the head of the sculptor in which the thought

[Burnshaw 49-16 P
Massed for a head they mean to make for themselves, [Duck 60-23P
And head a shadow trampled under hoofs, [Sombre 70-28 P
My head, the sorrow of the world, except [Bship 78-18 P
If her head [Woman Had 82-28 P
But there is more than a marble, massive head. [Woman Had 83-3 P
A street. She has a supernatural head. [Woman Had 83-8 P
Head down. The reflections and repetitions, [Fare Guit 99-4 P
See mast-head.
HEADS. And shave their heads and bodies. [Homunculus 26-20
  With dew, dew dresses, stones and chains of dew, heads [Dump 202-9
  On human heads. True, birds rebuild [Cuisine 227-14
  We feast on human heads, brought in on leaves, [Cuisine 228-10
  The rocks of the cliffs are the heads of dogs [Vari 232-12
  Without legs, or, for that, without heads. [Possum 294-1
  They have heads in which a captive cry [Possum 294-2
  Than clouds, benevolences, distant heads. [EM 317-21
  Then turn your heads and let your spiral eyes [Red Kit 31-27 P
  Perhaps if the orchestras stood on their heads [Agenda 42-4 P
  The heads held high and gathered in a ring [Old Woman 43-12 P
  White slapped on white, majestic, marble heads, [Burnshaw 49-13P
  And there are the white-maned horses' heads, beyond [Burnshaw
  49-19 P
  The heads are severed, topple, tumble, tip [Burnshaw 51-31 P
  Would be a ring of heads and haunches, torn [Sombre 70-22 P
  Bald heads with their mother's voice still in their ears.
  [Woman Had 82-16 P
HEADSMAN. And headsman and trumpeteer and feather [Stan Hero 84-20P
HEALING-POINT. A healing-point in the sickness of the mind: [Art
  Pop 112-22 P
HEALTH. These are the forest. This health is holy, [Parochial
  191-11
  This health is holy, this descant of a self, [Parochial 191-15
  The spring will have a health of its own, with none [Parochial
  192-1
  Health follows after health. Salvation there: [Parochial 192-3
  Of these academies, the diviner health [Prelude 195-16
  The hullaballoo of health and have, [Dutch 292-5
  As if the health of the world might be enough. [EM 315-25
  We descend to the street and inhale a health of air [NH 470-17
  The origin and keep of its health and his own. [Armor 530-21
  In a health of weather, knowing a few, old things, [Americana
  93-17 P
  A health--and the faces in a summer night. [Art Pop 113-3 P
HEALTH-O. Health-o, when ginger and fromage bewitch [NE Verses
  104-5
HEAP. And live and heap their panniers of green [Belly 367-3
HEAPED. Theatrical distances, bronze shadows heaped [Key W 129-20
  Sand heaped in the clouds, giant that fought [MBG 179-7
  Or the majolica dish heaped up with phosphored fruit [EM 320-17
  The waitress heaped up black Hermosas [Attempt 370-2
  Seeing the fulgent shadows upward heaped, [Duck 62-16 P
HEAPED-UP. And blows, with heaped-up shoulders loudly blows
  [Greenest 58-12 P
HEAPING. Or sees the new North River heaping up [Recit 86-24 P
HEAR. Speak, even, as if I did not hear you speaking, [Two Figures
  86-4
  Mon Dieu, hear the poet's prayer. [Sailing 120-11
  I have never--shall never hear. And yet beneath [Autumn 160-7
  Though I have never--shall never hear that bird. [Autumn 160-12
  The employer and employee will hear [MBG 182-14
  Is it to hear the blatter of grackles and say [Dump 203-8
  That they never hear the past. To see, [Arcades 225-6
  To hear, to touch, to taste, to smell, that's now, [Arcades
  225-7
  To hear himself and not to speak. [Arcades 225-26
  Exactly, that which it wants to hear, at the sound [Of Mod 240-9
  Not the people in the air that hear [Adequacy 244-15
  Of the garden. We must prepare to hear the Roamer's [Phenom
  286-17
  I hear the motions of the spirit and the sound [Choc 298-18
  To hear only what one hears, one meaning alone, [EM 320-27
  That will not hear us when we speak: a coolness, [Less 328-8
  He can hear them, like people on the walls, [Sketch 336-4
  Hear, feel and know. We feel and know them so. [Descrip 340-18
  To hear more brightly the contriving chords. [Descrip 340-22
  Voluble but archaic and hard to hear. [Liadoff 347-21
  It is not speech, the sound we hear [Silent 359-19
  He does not hear his characters talk. He sees [Cred 377-24
  Be silent in your luminous cloud and hear [NSF 404-11
  And hear it as it falls in the deep heart's core. [Page 421-12
  There were ghosts that returned to earth to hear his phrases,
  [Large 423-11
  There were those that returned to hear him read from the poem
  of life, [Large 423-14
  Flame, sound, fury composed . . . Hear what he says, [Puel 456-17
  As far as nothingness permits . . . Hear him. [Questions 463-1
  With a savage voice; and in that cry they hear [NH 467-23
  Of baker and butcher blowing, as if to hear, [NH 475-2
  Hear hard, gets it an essential integrity. [NH 475-3

And, in my hearing, you hear its tragic drone [Angel 497-2
We hear, what we are, beyond mystic disputation, [Look 518-11
Hear the loud drums roll-- [Phases 3-11 P
Now, soldiers, hear me: mark this very breeze, [Phases 5-12 P
To hear the stroke of one's certain solitude, [Old Woman 44-15P
And purpose, to hear the wild bee drone, to feel [Greenest 56-25P
He does not hear by sound. His spirit knows [Greenest 59-7 P
And most in what we hear, sound brushed away, [Sombre 67-9 P
Or hear her step in the way she walked? [Grotesque 74-12 P
And hearing a tale one wanted intensely to hear, [Letters 107-12P
It is hard to hear the north wind again [Region 115-6 P
Shall we hear more? [Three 138-13 P
HEARD. I heard them cry--the peacocks. [Domination 9-2
He heard her low accord, [Pourtraicte 22-2
Of the cathedral, making notes, he heard [C 32-16
And my ears made the blowing hymns they heard. [Hoon 65-14
Or heard or felt came not but from myself; [Hoon 65-17
Of the milk within the saltiest spurge, heard, then, [Sea Surf
    100-19
Even if what she sang was what she heard, [Key W 128-20
But it was she and not the sea we heard. [Key W 129-3
Heard the dogs howl at barren bone, [Thought 187-6
This halloo, halloo, halloo heard over the cries [Parochial 191-12
It was the battering of drums I heard [Loaf 200-8
I heard two workers say, "This chaos [Idiom 200-18
Where was it one first heard of the truth? The the. [Dump 203-11
And denying what he heard. He would arrive. [Landsc 242-11
To see him, that we were wholly one, as we heard [Oboe 251-18
No man that heard a wind in an empty place. [Extracts 255-9
And to be heard is to be large in space, [Choc 296-8
A transparence in which we heard music, made music, [EM 316-10
In which we heard transparent sounds, did he play [EM 316-11
As they fell down, as they heard Liadoff's cloud [Liadoff 346-18
The words they spoke were voices that she heard. [NSF 402-10
The sea was frozen solid and Hans heard [Page 421-5
As he heard it in Tarbert. [Our Stars 454-17
Comes from a great distance and is heard. [Our Stars 455-12
She had heard of the fate of an Argentine writer. At night,
    [Novel 457-8
And something of death's poverty is heard. [NH 477-5
As if the ears heard any shocking sound, [NH 478-11
When was it that we heard the voice of union? [Aug 494-9
He knew that he heard it, [Not Ideas 534-4
The children heard him in their chilly beds, [Phases 5-9 P
They heard his mumble in the morning light. [Phases 5-11 P
(A woman's voice is heard replying.) Mock [Infernale 25-4 P
The eunuchs heard her [Lulu G 26-17 P
And there he heard the voices that were once [Greenest 54-8 P
From which their grizzled voice will speak and be heard."
    [Duck 60-24 P
Is all the birds he ever heard and that, [Duck 62-3 P
Of saints not heard of until now, unnamed, [Nuns 92-19 P
What we heard and the light, though little, was enough. [Letters
    107-15 P
The point of it was the way he heard it, [Dinner 110-5 P
I heard tonight [Three 135-12 P
I am sure you heard [Three 136-1 P
See half-heard.
HEARING. From hearing signboards whimper in cold nights [C 33-2
In the hearing of the shepherd and his black forms [NH 480-15
And, in my hearing, you hear its tragic drone [Angel 497-2
And hearing a tale one wanted intensely to hear, [Letters 107-12P
HEARS. She hears, upon that water without sound, [Sunday 70-14
If, while he lives, he hears himself [Prelude 194-12
He is what he hears and sees and if, [Prelude 194-14
Without pathos, he feels what he hears [Prelude 194-18
He hears the earliest poems of the world [Montra 261-19
In which man is the hero. He hears the words, [Montra 261-20
To hear only what one hears, one meaning alone, [EM 320-27
And out of what one sees and hears and out [EM 326-7
The mind sits listening and hears it pass. [Pure 329-18
Being virile, it hears the calendar hymn. [NSF 382-9
At evening, things that attend it until it hears [AA 414-18
In February hears the imagination's hymns [Imago 439-10
That's it. The lover writes, the believer hears, [Orb 443-15
Beholds himself in you, and hears his voice [Rome 509-15
The silent watcher, far below her, hears:) [Infernal 25-11 P
And hears the nigger's prayer in motets, belched [Greenest 59-12P
That hears a pin fall in New Amsterdam [Recit 86-23 P
Daylight evaporates, like a sound one hears in sickness. [Discov
    95-9 P
The leaves cry . . . One holds off and merely hears the cry.
    [Course 96-13 P
HEART. Most venerable heart, the lustiest conceit [Monocle 16-17
From your too bitter heart, [Weep Woman 25-2
I, weeping in a calcined heart, [W Burgher 61-16
And in his heart his disbelief lay cold. [Babies 77-17
And that one was never a man of heart. [Norfolk 111-12
To drive the dagger in his heart, [MBG 166-4
At heart, a petty misery, [MBG 170-18

You lovers that are bitter at heart. [MBG 174-4
And knowledge dropped upon his heart [Thought 186-23
Nothing to have at heart. [Destructive 192-10
Pack the heart and scratch the mind? And does the ear [Dump 203-3
Upon the heart and round the mind [Country 207-11
Heart. The peaches are large and round, [Peaches 224-10
There the woman receives her lover into her heart [Rhythms 245-15
Ah! douce campagna, honey in the heart, [Beard 247-20
Panjandrum and central heart and mind of minds-- [Extracts 254-12
Lie in the heart's residuum . . . Amen. [Extracts 258-23
Lie in the heart's residuum. [Extracts 259-7
Of speech: to pierce the heart's residuum [Extracts 259-15
A giant's heart in the veins, all courage. [Gigan 289-7
Cry loudly, cry out in the powerful heart. [Dutch 291-9
Grew strong, as if doubt never touched his heart. [Choc 299-5
Born old, familiar with the depths of the heart, [Repet 306-17
Of the populace of the heart, the reddest lord, [EM 315-18
That he sends ahead, out of the goodness of his heart, [EM 320-18
However known, at the centre of the heart? [EM 323-25
In one's heart and wished as he had always wished, unable [Bed
    327-2
Time is a horse that runs in the heart, a horse [Pure 329-16
Reposed? And does it have a puissant heart [Two V 354-5
As one of the relics of the heart. [Prejudice 368-16
The Swedish cart to be part of the heart. [Prejudice 369-6
And this must comfort the heart's core against [Cred 372-15
Beating in the heart, as if blood newly came, [NSF 382-21
The hot of him is purest in the heart. [NSF 388-15
Possess in his heart, conceal and nothing known. [NSF 395-6
Weaves always glistening from the heart and mind. [NSF 396-12
The shoulders of joyous men, to feel the heart [NSF 398-11
And hear it as it falls in the deep heart's core. [Page 421-12
He wanted his heart to stop beating and his mind to rest [Cata
    425-6
What has he that becomes his heart's strong core? [Bad Time
    426-20
His poverty becomes his heart's strong core-- [Bad Time 427-2
Of motions in the mind and heart, [Imago 439-8
At heart, within an instant's motion, within [Orb 440-20
Keep quiet in the heart. O wild bitch. O mind [Puel 456-13
Lies on the breast and pierces into the heart, [Novel 458-24
The desire for its celestial ease in the heart, [NH 467-6
Added and added out of a fame-full heart . . . [NH 481-15
As it falls from the heart and lies there to be seen, [Rome
    509 27
On her pillow? The thought kept beating in her like her heart.
    [World 521-11
And the oldest and the warmest heart was cut [Quiet 523-10
The final pulse of blood from this good heart [Soldat 11-11 P
Like a heart full of pins. [Soldat 12-24 P
Whose heart will murmur with the music that will be a voice for
    her, speaking the dreaded change of speech; [Piano 22-2 P
The wry of neck and the wry of heart [Sat Night 28-1 P
Making your heart of brass to intercept [Good Bad 33-18 P
The heart in slattern pinnacles, the clouds, [Duck 61-10 P .
And daunt that old assassin, heart's desire? [Duck 66-11 P
The spirit's ring and seal, the naked heart. [Bship 79-13 P
HEARTBREAK. It was a page he had found in the handbook of heart-
    break. [Madame 507-8
HEARTED. See hale-hearted.
HEARTH. Of summer and that unused hearth below, [Phases 5-7 P
HEARTS. To bathe their hearts in later moonlight, [Homunculus 26-12
Nor in their empty hearts to feel [Adequacy 243-17
Which in those ears, and in those thin, those spended hearts,
    [Large 424-7
HEAT. That coolness for his heat came suddenly, [C 31-17
Of heat upon his pane. This was the span [C 33-4
Moisture and heat have swollen the garden into a slum of bloom.
    [Banal 62-14
With heat so strong! [Virgin 71-9
Now that the moon is rising in the heat [Men Fall 187-10
That the glass would melt in heat, [Glass 197-7
As they used to lie in the grass, in the heat, [Cuisine 227-18
That rolled in heat is silver-tipped [Vari 234-7
Flap green ears in the heat. He might observe [Landsc 243-5
Lie sprawling in majors of the August heat, [EM 325-28
Out of the deadliest heat. [Attempt 370-7
Who chants by book, in the heat of the scholar, who writes [NSF
    395-12
Without their fierce addictions, nor that the heat [NSF 399-9
When the harmonious heat of August pines [NSF 399-18
The pulse of the object, the heat of the body grown cold [Study I
    463-16
Seems like a sheen of heat romanticized. [NH 468-9
In a mirror, without heat, [Plant 506-13
HEAT-HEAVY. In fragrant leaves heat-heavy yet nimble in talk.
    [NE Verses 105-12
HEAULMIETTE. "Celle Qui Fût Héaulmiette" [438-title
HEAVED-UP. One with us, in the heaved-up noise, still [Hero 273-23
HEAVEN. Of heaven and of the heavenly script. [Ord Women 11-13

"Mother of heaven, regina of the clouds, [Monocle 13-1
The honey of heaven may or may not come, [Monocle 15-25
Move outward into heaven, [Fabliau 23-6
"The Worms at Heaven's Gate" [49-title
"Of Heaven Considered as a Tomb" [56-title
Who in the tomb of heaven walk by night, [Heaven 56-10
And from the nave build haunted heaven. Thus, [High-Tones 59-3
"That bliss of stars, that princox of evening heaven!" reminding
    of seasons, [Banal 63-1
Things to be cherished like the thought of heaven? [Sunday 67-18
With heaven, brought such requital to desire [Sunday 68-3
Remote on heaven's hill, that has endured [Sunday 68-22
Of heaven in an antique reflection rolled [Sea Surf 99-13
The gongs grew still. And then blue heaven spread [Sea Surf 100-6
Until the rolling heaven made them blue, [Sea Surf 100-24
Would--But more suddenly the heaven rolled [Sea Surf 101-18
And heaven rolled as one and from the two [Sea Surf 102-14
Where is sun and music and highest heaven's lust, [Ghosts 119-6
In a world without heaven to follow, the stops [Adieu 127-13
Enough, for heaven. Ever-jubilant, [Adieu 128-8
The bays of heaven, brighted, blued? [Botanist 2 136-4
In the frosty heaven. [Reader 147-12
I am tired. Sleep for me, heaven over the hill. [Nigger 150-16
Of empty heaven and its hymns, [MBG 167-12
In an immenser heaven, aloft, [MBG 176-9
So heaven collects its bleating lambs. [Thought 184-10
Of men whose heaven is in themselves, [Thought 186-12
This man loved earth, not heaven, enough to die. [Men Fall 188-18
If he will be heaven after death, [Prelude 194-11
Was heaven where you thought? It must be there. [Blue Bldg 217-14
Then the colossal illusion of heaven. Yet still [Landsc 241-12
Hangs heaven with flash drapery. Sight [Hero 274-12
Was the glory of heaven in the wilderness- [Dutch 292-16
A sun in an almost colorless, cold heaven. [Holiday 312-6
Or what hell was, since now both heaven and hell [EM 315-12
In form, lovers of heaven and earth, she-wolves [EM 321-24
Would froth the whole heaven with its seeming-so, [Descrip 341-17
Washed in the remotest cleanliness of a heaven [NSF 381-5
In heaven as in a glass; a second earth; [NSF 383-14
Was what they loved. It was neither heaven nor hell. [NSF 401-20
He leaps from heaven to heaven more rapidly [AA 414-11
Than bad angels leap from heaven to hell in flames. [AA 414-12
From heaven and float in air, like animals [Study II 464-6
The instinct for heaven had its counterpart: [NH 476-1
Reclines in the temperature of heaven-- [Hermit 505-12
On the threshold of heaven, the figures in the street [Rome
    508-1
Become the figures of heaven, the majestic movement [Rome 508-2
For a citizen of heaven though still of Rome. [Rome 510-2
Like a fixed heaven, [Song Fixed 520-5
There was heaven, [Phases 5-16 P
And of tomorrow's heaven. [Primordia 9-14 P
Spread over heaven shutting out the light. [Red Kit 31-26 P
Père Guzz, in heaven thumb your lyre [An Gaiety 33-5 P
"Lytton Strachey, Also, Enters into Heaven" [38-title P
The understanding of heaven, would be bliss, [Lytton 38-20 P
In heaven. But I have no choice. [Lytton 39-15 P
Thinking of heaven and earth and of herself [Old Woman 45-19 P
The heaven of Europe is empty, like a Schloss [Greenest 53-1 P
There was a heaven once, [Greenest 53-26 P
That was never the heaven of Africa, which had [Greenest 54-19 P
No heaven, had death without a heaven, death [Greenest 54-20 P
In a heaven of death. Beneath the heavy foils, [Greenest 54-21 P
The triumph of the arcs of heaven's blue [Duck 60-16 P
Of heaven from heaven to the future, as a god, [Duck 65-27 P
High up in heaven a sprawling portent moves, [Sombre 68-17 P
High up in heaven the sprawling portent moves. [Sombre 70-18 P
HEAVEN-HAVEN. Of heaven-haven. These are not things transformed,
    [NSF 399-1
HEAVENLY. Heavenly labials in a world of gutturals. [Plot Giant 7-9
Of heaven and of the heavenly script. [Ord Women 11-13
Untasted, in its heavenly, orchard air. [Monocle 14-15
That was not heavenly love, [Pourtraicte 22-5
Heavenly Vincentine. [Vincentine 52-15
Turned heavenly Vincentine, [Vincentine 53-17
Turned heavenly, heavenly Vincentine. [Vincentine 53-19
They shall know well the heavenly fellowship [Sunday 70-10
The difference that heavenly pity brings. [Fictive 88-13
That these bethous compose a heavenly gong. [NSF 394-6
What heavenly dithyramb [Archi 16-21 P
The heavenly cocks, the bowmen, and the gourds, [Greenest 56-18P
HEAVENS. The multifarious heavens felt no awe [Geneva 24-8
When the wind stops and, over the heavens, [Soldier 97-10
The sun rises green and blue in the fields and in the heavens.
    [Fish-Scale 161-5
In highest night? And do these heavens adorn [AA 417-10
It leaps through us, through all our heavens leaps, [AA 417-16
Upon whose shoulders even the heavens rest, [Owl 431-15
The pattern of the heavens and high, night air. [NH 472-3
The heavens, the hells, the worlds, the longed-for lands.

    [NH 486-12
Branching through heavens heavy with the sheen [Old Woman 46-1 P
On every cloud-tip over the heavens, [Letters 107-2 P
On the dark side of the heavens or the bright, [Local 112-2 P
HEAVES. Silently it heaves its youthful sleep from the sea--
    [NH 476-22
HEAVIER. To grow larger and heavier and stronger than [Rhythms
    246-1
HEAVILY. The snow hangs heavily on the rocks, brought [Hero 273-5
Of them in the air still hanging heavily [EM 315-6
Hung heavily on the great banana tree, [NSF 393-14
Its being beating heavily in the veins, [Novel 459-2
And that, heavily, you move with them in the dust. [Burnshaw
    50-11 P
HEAVINESS. That lost its heaviness through that same will, [Nigger
    152-9
In an element not the heaviness of time, [Owl 432-8
The heaviness we lighten by light will, [NH 476-13
HEAVING. The heaving speech of air, a summer sound [Key W 129-15
HEAVY. Yes: but the color of the heavy hemlocks [Domination 8-14
Came striding like the color of the heavy hemlocks [Domination
    9-18
Tempestuous clarion, with heavy cry, [C 32-23
Hang always heavy in that perfect sky, [Sunday 69-15
That the air was heavy with the breath of these swine, [Frogs 78-4
Heavy with thunder's rattapallax, [Frogs 78-6
And the heavy thrum [Cortege 80-23
Like a human, heavy and heavy, [Shifts 84-2
This heavy historical sail [Sailing 120-17
Say how his heavy wings, [Pascagoula 127-1
The cloud rose upward like a heavy stone [Nigger 152-8
The heavy bells are tolling rowdy-dow. [Nigger 155-9
It needed the heavy nights of drenching weather [Nigger 158-6
And the feeling heavy in cold chords [MBG 169-5
Supporting heavy cables, slung [MBG 181-22
The hunters run to and fro. The heavy trees, [Parochial 191-7
To shaking out heavy bodies in the glares [Cuisine 228-7
But in that dream a heavy difference [Montra 263-4
The hives are heavy with the combs. [Contra I 266-13
And lither stride. His arms are heavy [Hero 277-11
Tipped out with largeness, bearing the heavy [Gigan 289-16
And shuffling lightly, with the heavy lightness [Dutch 290-11
Its fragrance, a heavy somnolence, and for him, [EM 319-13
Lifts up its heavy scowl before them. [Pediment 362-3
In the heavy air. [Attempt 370-14
Are in the grass, the roses are heavy with a weight [Cred 372-7
The body lift its heavy wing, take up, [NSF 390-12
An ancient forehead hung with heavy hair, [NSF 400-7
Swatara, Swatara, heavy the hills [Countryman 428-13
And because being there in the heavy hills [Countryman 429-3
It exceeds the heavy changes of the light. [Roses 431-7
We shall be heavy with the knowledge of that day. [John 437-23
Making this heavy rock a place, [Imago 439-17
Oh as, always too heavy for the sense [Orb 441-2
In the heavy drum of speech, the inner men [NH 488-9
The boat was built of stones that had lost their weight and
    being no longer heavy [Prol 515-10
Through our heavy dreams; [Phases 4-6 P
Sniffed her and slapped heavy hands [Lulu G 26-11 P
Branching through heavens heavy with the sheen [Old Woman 46-1 P
In a heaven of death. Beneath the heavy foils, [Greenest 54-21 P
The same return at heavy evening, love [Duck 61-15 P
On all the rest, in heavy thought. [Child 106-15 P
See heat-heavy.
HEAVY-FRUITED. The faster's feast and heavy-fruited star, [Thought
    186-3
HECUBA. To the group of Flora Coddling Hecuba? [Archi 17-10 P
HEDGES. In galloping hedges, [Polo 37-20 P
HEELS. As her heels foam-- [Paltry 6-3
HEIGHT. To rest before the heroic height. [How Live 125-12
Only the great height of the rock [How Live 126-3
Cleared from the north and in that height [Country 207-12
To the great blue of the middle height. [Dutch 290-3
To speak humanly from the height or from the depth [Choc 300-14
Was native to him in that height, searching [Choc 301-22
Of our passionate height. He wears a tufted green, [Repet 309-23
A devastation, a death of great height [Burghers 362-8
Of great height and depth [Burghers 362-15
High in the height that is our total height. [Pastor 379-21
This is the height emerging and its base [AA 411-13
There he saw well the foldings in the height [Owl 433-7
Stood flourishing the world. The brilliant height [Owl 434-4
Not merely as to depth but as to height [NH 470-9
The height was not quite proper; [Aug 493-19
Than the color white and high beyond any height [Duck 64-6 P
See full-height.
HEIGHTENED. A damsel heightened by eternal bloom. [Monocle 15-28
Heightened. It is he, anew, in a freshened youth [Myth 118-13 P
See strongly-heightened.
HEIRS. I am a man of fortune greeting heirs; [Monocle 13-17

That makes them our dependent heirs, the heirs [C 39-26
And heirs are powers of the mind, [Ulysses 103-8 P
HELD. Unless Racine or Bossuet held the like. [Geneva 24-6
Piano-polished, held the tranced machine [Sea Surf 100-15
Not the mother that held men as they fell [MBG 173-14
He held the world upon his nose [MBG 178-9
Held in his hand the suave egg-diamond [Thunder 220-10
She held her hand before him in the air, [Hand 271-5
It held the shivering, the shaken limbs, [Hand 271-11
That held the distances off: the villages [Wild 329-10
Held off the final, fatal distances, [Wild 329-11
She hid them under simple names. She held [NSF 402-8
Ringed round and barred, with eyes held in their hands, [Page
422-30
She held men closely with discovery, [Owl 435-9
Breaches of that which held them fast. It is [Orb 441-18
Held fast tenaciously in common earth [NH 468-24
The heads held high and gathered in a ring [Old Woman 43-12 P
In melancholy distances. You held [Burnshaw 50-26 P
Your hands held high and cry again, but cry, [Burnshaw 51-16 P
Held in the hands of blue men that are lead within, [Discov
95-16 P
Held the candle. [Three 133-7 P
And the emperor would have held [Three 138-5 P
HELIO-HORN. A helio-horn. How strange the hero [Hero 274-10
HELIOTROPE. Dressed high in heliotrope's inconstant hue, [Bad Time
427-6
HELL. Or else whose hell, foamed with their blood [Thought 186-13
And gelid Januar has gone to hell. [Poesie 302-8
His firm stanzas hang like hives in hell [EM 315-11
Or what hell was, since now both heaven and hell [EM 315-12
As if hell, so modified, had disappeared, [EM 316-4
A dead shepherd brought tremendous chords from hell [NSF 400-21
Was what they loved. It was neither heaven nor hell. [NSF 401-20
Than bad angels leap from heaven to hell in flames. [AA 414-12
That bordered Hell. [Phases 4-14 P
HELLS. Twelve-legged in her ancestral hells, [Oak 272-8
The heavens, the hells, the worlds, the longed-for lands. [NH
486-12
HELMET. Wear a helmet without reason, [Orangeade 103-11
The formidable helmet is nothing now. [Pastor 380-1
That, from her helmet, terrible and bright, [Soldat 14-10 P
HELMET-HO. The attributions, the plume and helmet-ho" [NH 485-15
HELMET-MAKER. To his gorge, hangman, once helmet-maker [Stan Hero
84-19 P
HELMETS. Behold the men in helmets borne on steel, [Extracts 259-19
HELMS. Pale helms and spiky spurs, [Brave 138-14
HELP. Here was no help before reality. [C 30-5
Might help the blind, not him, serenely sly. [C 39-20
And cry and cry for help? [Fading 139-5
And cry and cry for help? [Fading 139-15
He stood at last by God's help and the police; [Anglais 149-10
Is anonymous and cannot help it. [Hero 279-18
Even with the help of Viollet-le-Duc, [NSF 386-23
They help us face the dumbfoundering abyss [John 437-14
The help of any wind or any sky: [Burnshaw 49-20 P
And only an agony of dreams can help, [Duck 61-24 P
For ponderous revolving, without help. [Sombre 69-16 P
A help, a right to help, a right [Ulysses 104-28 P
HELPED. That helped him round his rude aesthetic out. [C 36-11
And being up high had helped him when up high, [Aug 493-14
And the helpless philosophers say still helpful things. [Extracts
253-28
HELPING. She found a helping from the cold, [Celle 438-4
HELPLESS. Seemed the helpless daughter [Sonatina 109-16
And the helpless philosophers say still helpful things. [Extracts
253-28
For the spirit left helpless by the intelligence. [News 265-10
Without any horror of the helpless loss. [Duck 61-16 P
HELPLESSLY. Helplessly at the edge, enough to be [Ulti 430-7
HELPLESSNESS. With the politest helplessness. Ay-mi! [EM 324-22
HELPS. To know what helps and to attain, [Ulysses 104-29 P
HEM. Sunrise is his garment's hem, sunset is hers. [NH 485-7
HEMISPHERE. A comprehensive island hemisphere. [C 38-14
Night after night because the hemisphere [Spaniard 34-8 P
HEMLOCKS. Yes: but the color of the heavy hemlocks [Domination 8-14
Just as they flew from the boughs of the hemlocks [Domination 8-22
Loud as the hemlocks [Domination 9-10
Or was it a cry against the hemlocks? [Domination 9-12
Came striding like the color of the heavy hemlocks [Domination
9-18
And out of the shine of the hemlocks, [Celle 438-2
HEMS. And hems the planet rose and haws it ripe, [Ulti 429-11
HEN. Hen shudders: the copious egg is made and laid. [Nigger 155-12
The old brown hen and the old blue sky, [Silent 359-5
The chain of the turquoise hen and sky [Silent 359-16
See cock-hen.
HENCE. Hence the reverberations in the words [C 37-11
It irked beyond his patience. Hence it was, [C 39-21
Death is the mother of beauty; hence from her, [Sunday 68-29

Our nature is her nature. Hence it comes, [Anatomy 107-16
That, like your own, is large, hence, to be part [Choc 296-9
Lakes are more reasonable than oceans. Hence, [EM 325-6
By the incalculably plural. Hence [Descrip 340-9
HEN-COCK. The hen-cock crows at midnight and lays no egg, [Nigger
155-10
HENNA. Of tan with henna hackles, halt! [Bantams 75-15
HEPATICA. To see hepatica, a stop to watch [NSF 386-5
HERALDIC. The heraldic center of the world [MBG 172-6
Political tramp with an heraldic air, [Choc 301-3
HERALDIC-HO. Indifferent sounds and not the heraldic-ho [Repet
307-20
HERALDS. See College of Heralds.
HERCULES. Why nag at the ideas of Hercules, Don Don? [NE Verses
104-1
The body bent, like Hercules, to build. [Sombre 69-10 P
HERDS. The father fetches his unherded herds, [AA 415-17
HERDSMAN. Death, the herdsman of elephants, [Greenest 55-18 P
HEREDITARY. As if all his hereditary lights were suddenly increased
[Prol 517-1
HEREIN. The mind herein attains simplicity. [Tallap 71-14
HERMIT. Crispin as hermit, pure and capable, [C 40-4
That hermit on reef sable would have seen, [Dames 206-16
A hermit's truth nor symbol in hermitage. [Cred 375-16
The hermit in a poet's metaphors, [NSF 381-21
The hermit of the place, [Three 132-21 P
By the hermit and his candle [Three 137-11 P
The hermit's candle would have thrown [Three 138-3 P
Death, the hermit, [Three 140-1 P
On this hermit earth. [Three 142-6 P
HERMITAGE. A hermit's truth nor symbol in hermitage. [Cred 375-16
As in a hermitage, for us to think, [Aug 495-15
"The Hermitage at the Center" [505-title
In his hermitage. [Three 140-3 P
HERMITS. Used by generations of hermits. [Three 130-11 P
It is of no interest to hermits [Three 133-24 P
HERMOSAS. The waitress heaped up black Hermosas [Attempt 370-2
HERO. He came. The poetic hero without palms [C 35-26
I sing a hero's head, large eye [MBG 165-13
"Idiom of the Hero [200-title
The hero's throat in which the words are spoken, [Montra 261-4
Out of the hero's being, the deliverer [Montra 261-6
A hero's world in which he is the hero. [Montra 261-11
Man must become the hero of his world. [Montra 261-12
In which man is the hero. He hears the words, [Montra 261-20
And tallest hero and plus gaudiest vir. [Montra 262-12
"Examination of the Hero in a Time of War" [273-title
A helio-horn. How strange the hero [Hero 274-10
To grasp the hero, the eccentric [Hero 274-19
The common man is the common hero. [Hero 275-5
The common hero is the hero. [Hero 275-6
Unless we believe in the hero, what is there [Hero 275-19
The hero of the Gazette and the hero [Hero 276-7
Of L'Observateur, the classic hero [Hero 276-8
Of men suited to public ferns . . . The hero [Hero 276-16
The hero is not a person. The marbles [Hero 276-19
If the hero is not a person, the emblem [Hero 277-5
There is no image of the hero. [Hero 278-20
The hero is a feeling, a man seen [Hero 278-24
Too many references. The hero [Hero 279-9
Say that the hero is his nation, [Hero 279-15
Of the apprehending of the hero. [Hero 279-23
The self of the hero, the solar single, [Hero 280-7
The man-sun being hero rejects that [Hero 280-12
After the hero, the familiar [Hero 280-23
Man makes the hero artificial. [Hero 280-24
But was the summer false? The hero? [Hero 280-25
To believe, more than the casual hero, more [Paisant 335-9
Everything becomes morning, summer, the hero, [Past Nun 378-17
How simply the fictive hero becomes the real; [NSF 408-1
It is to the hero of midnight that we pray [NH 466-23
A race that is a hero, entirely [Stan Hero 84-4 P
The hero is the man who is himself, who [Stan Hero 84-9
The frame of the hero. Yet, willingly, he [Stan Hero 84-13 P
Becomes the hero without heroics. [Stan Hero 84-14 P
Now. War as a punishment. The hero [Stan Hero 84-16 P
The one about the credible hero, the one [As Leave 117-3 P
See man-hero.
HEROES. And the metal heroes that time granulates-- [Oboe 250-11
And there are many bourgeois heroes. [Hero 276-11
There are more heroes than marbles of them. [Hero 276-12
Within us. False hybrids and false heroes, [Stan Hero 84-7 P
Nor the smoke-drift of puffed-out heroes, nor human cry. [Course
96-20 P
HERO-HYMNS. That's where his hymns come crowding, hero-hymns,
[Thought 185-15
HEROIC. To rest before the heroic height. [How Live 125-12
That they had left, heroic sound [How Live 126-7
Arranged its heroic attitudes. [Hartford 227-3
Sings of an heroic world beyond the cell, [Montra 261-9

To what he does. He is the heroic [Hero 279-11
May truly bear its heroic fortunes [Hero 281-4
The youth, the vital son, the heroic power. [Cred 375-10
These are the heroic children whom time breeds [NSF 385-1
Though an heroic part, of the commonal. [NSF 388-22
Of the world, the heroic effort to live expressed [Papini 446-9
Without heroic words, heroic [Stan Hero 84-5 P
And what heroic nature of what text [Ideal 89-4 A
HEROICA. What misanthrope, impugning heroica, [Stan Hero 84-23 P
HEROICS. Doleful heroics, pinching gestures forth [Monocle 17-11
  Becomes the hero without heroics. [Stan Hero 84-14 P
HERO-LAND. Since in the hero-land to which we go, [Montra 262-1
HERR DOKTOR. Herr Doktor, and that's enough, [Delight 162-2
HERR GOTT. Plomets, as the Herr Gott [Analysis 349-11
HERSELF. Lettered herself demurely as became [C 44-31
  Divinity must live within herself: [Sunday 67-19
  Conceals herself. [Six Sig 73-21
  Everything in it is herself . [Scavoir 231-5
  And Eve made air the mirror of herself, [NSF 383-12
  Yet when her children slept, his sister herself [NSF 402-16
  Cinderella fulfilling herself beneath the roof? [NSF 405-9   '
  She would talk a little to herself as she combed her hair,
    [World 521-16
  So destitute that nothing but herself [Old Woman 44-10 P
  Remained and nothing of herself except [Old Woman 43-12 P
  Thinking of heaven and earth and of herself [Old Woman 45-19 P
  Then the maid says, to herself, [Three 134-11 P
HESPERUS. A matin gold from gold of Hesperus [Ideal 88-15 A
HEW. How shall we hew the sun, [Archi 17-22 P
HEWN. Ten thousand, men hewn and tumbling, [Thunder 220-2
  Hewn in their middle as the beam of leaves, [Owl 434-2
HEY-DE-I-DO. And a "Hey-de-i-do!" [Anything B 211-8
HEY-DI-HO. Hey-di-ho. [Grotesque 74-19 P
  Hey-di-ho. [Grotesque 75-3 P
  Hey-di-ho. [Grotesque 75-6 P
  Hey-di-ho. [Grotesque 75-9 P
HI. Hi! The creator too is blind, [Negation 97-13
  To strike his living hi and ho, [MBG 166-9
  Hi! Whisk it, poodle, flick the spray [Hartford 227-10
HIBERNAL. The snug hibernal from that sea and salt, [C 28-3
  And on the ground. The hibernal dark that hung [NH 476-8
HIBISCUS. "Hibiscus on the Sleeping Shores" [22-title
HIBISCUSES. One of Those Hibiscuses of Damozels [74-title 1 P
HIC. Said hic, said hac, [Melancholy 32-7 P
HID. She hid them under simple names. She held [NSF 402-8
HIDALGO. Behold the moralist hidalgo [Thought 186-17
  As, men make themselves their speech: the hard hidalgo [Descrip
    345-11
  The knowledge of Spain and of the hidalgo's hat-- [Descrip 345-14
  Except this hidalgo and his eye and tune, [NH 483-20
  Were false. The hidalgo was permanent, abstract, [NH 484-2
HIDDEN. The voice, the book, the hidden well, [Thought 186-2
  Close to me, hidden in me day and night? [NSF 380-6
  Hidden from other thoughts, he that reposes [NSF 388-5
  In which a real lies hidden and alive. [Novel 458-15
  Unreal today, be hidden and alive. [Novel 458-21
  All this is hidden from sight. [Sombre 68-28 P
HIDDENNESS. Deep dove, placate you in your hiddenness. [Belly 367-12
HIDE. Enough to hide away the face of the man [Dames 206-7
  In which he and the lion and the serpent hide [Greenest 54-30 P
HIDEOUS. "Oh, hideous, horrible, horrendous hocks!" [Stan MMO 19-15 P
HIDES. The red cat hides away in the fur-light [Rabbit K 209-20
  What is it that hides in the night wind, [Soldat 11-14 P
  The father. He hides his ancient blue beneath [Recit 87-17 P
HIEROGLYPHICA. Hieroglyphica [74-title 2 P
HIEROPHANT. Naked Alpha, not the hierophant Omega, [NH 469-5
HIEROPHANTS. Take counsel, all hierophants [Sat Night 28-7 P
HIGH. Of the high interiors of the sea. [Paltry 5-15
  In the high west there burns a furious star. [Monocle 14-23
  High up in orange air, were barbarous. [C 30-21
  In the high sea-shadow. [Venereal 48-10
  And high towers, [Six Sig 74-26
  A high bed sheltered by curtains. [Theory 87-3
  Go on, high ship, since now, upon the shore, [Farewell 117-1
  I am free. High above the mast the moon [Farewell 117-7
  That I loved her once . . . Farewell. Go on, high ship. [Farewell
    118-10
  To the cold, go on, high ship, go on, plunge on. [Farewell 118-20
  She must come now. The grass is in seed and high. [Ghosts 119-11
  Massively rising high and bare [How Live 125-18
  On high horizons, mountainous atmospheres [Key W 129-21
  And make much bing, high bing. [Snow Stars 133-9
  Fills the high hall with shuffling men [MBG 171-13
  High as the hall. The whirling noise [MBG 171-14
  As now and called most high, [MBG 176-7
  Of the men that live in the land, high lord. [MBG 176-11
  And there you are humped high, humped up, [Rabbit K 209-21
  There were the sheets high up on older trees, [Forces 229-13
  High blue became particular [Vase 246-18
  Is blue, clear, cloudy, high, dark, wide and round; [Extracts

252-11
  In the high imagination, triumphantly. [Extracts 256-16
  Of sanctimonious mountains high in snow, [Montra 263-3
  High, low, far, wide, against the distance, [Hero 277-22
  And the high, receiving out of others, [Gigan 289-17
  Fell on him, high and cold, searching for what [Choc 301-21
  In the high night, the summer breathes for them [EM 319-12
  By being high, is the stone [Pediment 361-14
  These mountains being high be, also, bright, [Belly 367-5
  High in the height that is our total height. [Pastor 379-21
  Each must the other take not for his high, [NSF 401-11
  Dressed high in heliotrope's inconstant hue, [Bad Time 427-6
  Two forms move among the dead, high sleep [Owl 431-13
  Who by his highness quiets them, high peace [Owl 431-14
  It is the huge, high harmony that sounds [Orb 440-17
  The pattern of the heavens and high, night air. [NH 472-3
  This is the mirror of the high serious: [NH 477-17
  High poetry and low: [Aug 490-15
  From the spun sky and the high and deadly view, [Aug 493-10
  And being up high had helped him when up high, [Aug 493-14
  Seemed large and loud and high and strong. [Two Illus 513-9
  How high that highest candle lights the dark. [Final 524-15
  That the green leaves came and covered the high rock, [Rock 526-4
  The high clouds will move, [Secret Man 36-11 P
  The heads held high and gathered in a ring [Old Woman 43-12 P
  Your hands held high and cry again, but cry, [Burnshaw 51-16 P
  The spirit's episcopate, hallowed and high, [Greenest 53-28 P
  His place is large and high, an ether flamed [Greenest 59-31 P
  Converging on the statue, white and high." [Duck 62-27 P
  The statue is white and high, white brillianter [Duck 64-5 P
  Than the color white and high beyond any height [Duck 64-6 P
  High up in heaven a sprawling portent moves, [Sombre 68-17 P
  High up in heaven the sprawling portent moves. [Sombre 70-18 P
  Captain, high captain, how is it, now, [Bship 80-18 P
  A hand that fails to seize it. High captain, the grand [Bship
    80-25 P
  Stood on a plain of marble, high and cold; [Woman Had 82-29 P
  By her sexual name, saying that that high marriage [Desire 85-5 P
  Nor high, [Three 133-17 P
  See happy-high.
HIGHER. You are humped higher and higher, black as stone-- [Rabbit
  K 210-1
  The highest man with nothing higher [Hero 280-5
HIGHEST. Where is sun and music and highest heaven's lust, [Ghosts
  119-6
  To meditate the highest man, not [Hero 280-1
  The highest supposed in him and over, [Hero 280-2
  The highest man with nothing higher [Hero 280-5
  Of the highest self: he studies the paper [Hero 280-14
  In flights of eye and ear, the highest eye [AA 414-16
  In highest night? And do these heavens adorn [AA 417-10
  How high that highest candle lights the dark. [Final 524-15
HIGHNESS. Who by his highness quiets them, high peace [Owl 431-14
HIGH-PITCHED. To bring destruction, often seems high-pitched.
  [Spaniard 34-17 P
HIGH-TONED. "A High-Toned Old Christian Woman" [59-title
HILARIOUS. That spread chromatics in hilarious dark, [C 45-9
  To warblings early in the hilarious trees [Medit 124-8
HILL. Remote on heaven's hill, that has endured [Sunday 68-22
  And round it was, upon a hill. [Jar 76-6
  Surround that hill. [Jar 76-8
  To the sullen hill, [Cortege 80-3
  On the hill, but turns [Cortege 80-8
  And fill the hill and fill it full [Snow Stars 133-11
  I am tired. Sleep for me, heaven over the hill. [Nigger 150-16
  As quick as foxes on the hill; [Postcard 158-16
  Ponies of Parisians shooting on the hill. [Parochial 191-2
  Of a cloud on sand, a shape on the side of a hill. [Connois 215-20
  Is ease, stands in the dark, a shadows' hill, [EM 319-5
  On his hill, watching the rising and falling, and says: [Two V
    354-22
  The broken cartwheel on the hill. [Silent 359-7
  On a hill of stones to make beau mont thereof. [NH 466-24
  In a field, the man on the side of a hill, all men [Americana
    93-16 P
  That they are searching the hill [Three 135-13 P
  To climb the hill [Three 136-7 P
  And weeping up the hill. [Three 138-9 P
  To the foot of the hill. [Three 139-5 P
  To the top of the hill. [Three 141-13 P
  See: ever-hill; up-hill.
HILLS. But when I walk I see that it consists of three or four
  hills and a cloud. [Of Surface 57-2
  The trees, like serafin, and echoing hills, [Sunday 70-8
  He felt curious about the winter hills [Extracts 254-26
  These fields, these hills, these tinted distances, [AA 411-8
  Swatara, Swatara, heavy the hills [Countryman 428-13
  And because being there in the heavy hills [Countryman 429-3
HILL-SCHOLAR. Hill-scholar, man that never is, [Jumbo 269-14
HILLSIDES. And April hillsides wooded white and pink, [C 37-29

HIMSELF. And, nothing himself, beholds [Snow Man 10-11
 And maidenly greenhorns, now beheld himself, [C 28-12
 Of winter, until nothing of himself [C 29-15
 From the unavoidable shadow of himself [C 29-29
 How may poems he denied himself [C 34-18
 Between himself and his environment, [C 34-27
 To fetch the one full-pinioned one himself [C 44-28
 Yet he kept promising himself [Winter B 141-15
 In speech. He has that music and himself. [Anglais 149-7
 He yielded himself to that single majesty; [Anglais 149-12
 The weather of his stage, himself. [MBG 170-4
 The demon that cannot be himself, [MBG 180-3
 Himself than in this fertile glass. [MBG 181-14
 He hummed to himself at such a plan. [Thought 187-4
 If, while he lives, he hears himself [Prelude 194-12
 To go to the Louvre to behold himself. [Prelude 194-21
 It was everything being more real, himself [Freed 205-20
 To hear himself and not to speak. [Arcades 225-26
 Calamity, proclaimed himself, was proclaimed. [Horn 230-16
 And of himself. There he could say [Yellow 236-6
 A naked man who regarded himself in the glass [Landsc 241-16
 That he might be truth, himself, or part of it, [Landsc 242-21
 The difference between himself and no man, [Extracts 255-8
 It was time to be himself again, to see [Extracts 255-10
 And being would be being himself again, [Extracts 255-20
 A good agreement between himself and night, [Extracts 256-5
 A chord between the mass of men and himself, [Extracts 256-6
 Who the transformer, himself transformed, [Jumbo 269-7
 Than himself, his self, the self that embraces [Hero 280-6
 Each man himself became a giant, [Gigan 289-15
 Freedom is like a man who kills himself [Dutch 292-17
 Too exactly himself, and that there are words [Creat 310-17
 To find for himself his earth, his sky, his sea. [Holiday 312-12
 Who by sympathy has made himself a man [EM 315-15
 The unpeopled, there is his knowledge of himself. [EM 323-9
 Is it himself in them that he knows or they [EM 323-12
 In him? If it is himself in them, they have [EM 323-13
 Of them and of himself destroys both worlds. [EM 323-16
 Alone is not to know them or himself. [EM 323-18
 Himself, the unalterable necessity [EM 324-6
 Comparative. The assassin discloses himself, [EM 324-19
 If MacCullough himself lay lounging by the sea, [NSF 387-9
 What chieftain, walking by himself, crying [NSF 389-2
 On This Beautiful World Of Ours composes himself [Ulti 429-10
 The marble man remains himself in space. [Degen 444-10
 To say what Celestin should say for himself? [Papini 446-2
 Man sits and studies silence and himself, [Papini 447-10
 Now, once, he accumulates himself and time [Papini 447-12
 Tom McGreevy, in America, Thinks of Himself as a Boy [Our Stars
  454-title 1
 He would go to bed, cover himself with blankets-- [Novel 457-9
 Part of the question that is a giant himself [NH 465-8
 He preserves himself against the repugnant rain [NH 475-22
 Because the thinker himself escapes. And yet [NH 480-4
 "This man abolishes by being himself [NH 485-13
 In which he exists but never as himself. [Aug 493-8
 His grief is that his mother should feed on him, himself and what
  he saw. [Madame 507-12
 Beholds himself in you, and hears his voice [Rome 509-15
 For himself. He stops upon this threshold, [Rome 511-1
 The appropriate image of himself, [Two Illus 513-13
 So formed, became himself and he breathed [Two Illus 513-14
 The master of the spruce, himself, [Two Illus 515-4
 Only a little way, and not beyond, unless between himself [Prol
  516-12
 On the horizon and lifting himself up above it. [World 520-14
 Sleekly the serpent would draw himself across. [Greenest 54-27 P
 In this he carved himself, he carved his age, [Duck 64-21 P
 The hero is the man who is himself, who [Stan Hero 84-9 P
 Choosing out of himself, out of everything within him, [Sick
  90-19 P
 Speech for the quiet, good hail of himself, good hail, good hail,
  [Sick 90-20 P
 A man that looks at himself in a glass and finds [Americana
  94-7 P
 He is not himself. He is vitally deprived . . . [Americana 94-12P
 Observed as an absolute, himself. [Ulysses 101-15 P
 Master of the world and of himself, [Ulysses 102-18 P
 That only in man's definitions of himself, [Conversat 109-12 P
 Himself. The author of man's canons is man, [Conversat 109-14 P
 If the emperor himself [Three 133-6 P
 He hanged himself in front of me. [Three 141-16 P
 Himself, may be, the irreducible X [Someone 83-8 A
 He sees it in this tangent of himself. [Someone 83-19 A
HINDRANCE. Naked of hindrance, a thousand crystals. [Hero 279-28
HINDS. Magnificent, would move among his hinds, [Sunday 68-1
 The very hinds discerned it, in a star. [Sunday 68-4
HINTED. Hinted autumnal farewells of academic death. [NE Verses
  106-8
HINTING. Hinting incredible hues, four selfsame lights [C 45-8

HIP. Home and the fields give praise, hurrah, hip, [Hero 278-13
 Hip, hip, hurrah. Eternal morning . . . [Hero 278-14
 The curving of her hip, as motionless gesture, [Couch 295-8
HIP-HIP. Young boys resembling pastry, hip-hip, [Hero 278-11
 Young men as vegetables, hip-hip, [Hero 278-12
HIPS. Blew against them or bowed from the hips, when I turned
  [Bship 78-17 P
HISSING. Spinning and hissing with oracular [Geneva 24-11
 Hissing, across the silence, puissant sounds. [Greenest 55-16 P
HISTOIRE. Histoire [Sat Night 27-subtitle P
HISTORIC. I shall not play the flat historic scale. [Monocle 14-4
HISTORICAL. This heavy historical sail [Sailing 120-17
HISTORY. What a beautiful history, beautiful surprise! [Mice 123-3
 At the moment's being, without history, [Beginning 427-16
 See pre-history.
HITHERTO. Within us hitherto unknown, he that [Duck 63-19 P
HIVE. See honey-hive-o.
HIVED. And is our fortune and honey hived in the trees [Cred 374-19
HIVES. The hives are heavy with the combs. [Contra I 266-13
 His firm stanzas hang like hives in hell [EM 315-11
HO. Ho! Ho! [Depression 63-13
 To strike his living hi and ho, [MBG 166-9
 The stone from which he rises, up--and--ho, [Rock 528-2
 See: hallow-ho; helmit-ho; heraldic-ho.
HOARD. Is this picture of Picasso's, this "hoard [MBG 173-1
HOAR-FROST. Touched on by hoar-frost, shrinks in a shelter [Lunar
  107-7
HOARY. But with a speech belched out of hoary darks [C 29-26
HOARY-HANGING. In the hoary-hanging night. It does not regard [EM
  315-7
HOCKS. "Oh, hideous, horrible, horrendous hocks!" [Stan MMO 19-15 P
HOES. Order, the law of hoes and rakes, [Room Gard 41-4 P
HOGS. "Frogs Eat Butterflies. Snakes Eat Frogs. Hogs Eat Snakes.
  Men Eat Hogs" [78-title
HO-HO. Places there, a bouquet. Ho-ho . . . The dump is full [Dump
  201-13
HOLA. Hola! Hola! What steps are those that break [Infernale 24-20P
 (He shouts.) Hola! Of that strange light, beware! [Infernale
  25-3 P
HOLD. And the lost vehemence the midnights hold. [Tallap 72-12
 The girl had to hold back and lean back to hold him, [Forces
  229-4
 To hold by the ear, even though it wished for a bell, [Uruguay
  249-10
 Is something in tatters that I cannot hold." [Choc 299-3
 The rivers shine and hold their mirrors up, [Belly 366-19
 And hold them round the sultry day? Why should [Belly 367-4
 Three times the concentred self takes hold, three times [Cred
  376-9
 Check your evasions, hold you to yourself. [NSF 406-14
 Denied, dismissed, may hold a serpent, loud [John 437-19
 Millions hold millions in their arms. [Memo 89-16 P
 A land would hold her in its arms that day [Letters 108-6 P
HOLDING. Holding their books toward the nearer stars, [Polish Aunt
  84-10
 To have had him holding--what? [Thunder 220-14
 There they sit, holding their eyes in their hands. [Arcades 225-4
 Holding this candle to us, [Three 132-22 P
HOLDING-IN. This tendance and venerable holding-in [NH 472-20
HOLDS. Of ocean, as a prelude holds and holds. [Sea Surf 100-16
 And the table that holds a platter of pears, [Grapes 110-13
 Holds in his hand a book you have never written [Lack 303-2
 In a black glove, holds a novel by Camus. She begged [Novel
  457-11
 A sense separate that receives and holds the rest, [Americana
  94-5 P
 The leaves cry . . . One holds off and merely hears the cry.
  [Course 96-13 P
HOLE. It might become his hole of blue. [Snow Stars 133-6
 The fox ran out of his hole. [On Road 203-15
 Whines in its hole for puppies to come see, [Pure 332-21
HOLES. Reverberations leak and lack among holes . . . [Armor 529-8
HOLIDAY. This is his holiday. [Gray 140-10
 "Holiday in Reality" [312-title
 Green glade and holiday hotel and world [Pure 330-19
 The flag of the nude above the holiday hotel. [Pure 331-1
 And studied it in his holiday hotel. [Pure 331-14
 On a holiday. [Analysis 349-6
 Seemed in the morning like a holiday." [Anach 365-19
 She wanted a holiday [Letters 107-16 P
HOLINESS. Lie down like children in this holiness, [AA 418-23
 Say next to holiness is the will thereto, [NH 467-4
HOLLAND. And you, my semblables--the old flag of Holland [Dutch
  290-13
HOLLOW. The comedy of hollow sounds derives [Nigger 154-4
 The savagest hollow of winter-sound. [Possum 294-12
 The ocean, falling and falling on the hollow shore, [Somnam
  304-12
 And hollow of him by its brilliance calmed, [Owl 434-5
 The horses are hollow, [Primordia 8-9 P

The trunks of the trees are hollow. [Primordia 8-10 P
HOLLOW-BRIGHT. In a description hollowed out of hollow-bright,
  [Descrip 345-17
HOLLOWED. In a description hollowed out of hollow-bright, [Descrip
  345-17
HOLLOWS. And clap the hollows full of tin. [MBG 170-6
  To our sepulchral hollows. Love of the real [NH 470-18
  See lake-hollows.
HOLY. The holy hush of ancient sacrifice. [Sunday 67-1
  Out of the spirit of the holy temples, [Nigger 151-19
  Happy rather than holy but happy-high, [Thought 185-17
  These are the forest. This health is holy, [Parochial 191-11
  This health is holy, this descant of a self,[Parochial 191-15
  By which to spell out holy doom and end, [Owl 434-17
  And of other holy and learned men, among them [Luther 461-6
  With holy or sublime ado [Archi 18-15 P
  "Piano Practice at the Academy of the Holy Angels" [21-title P
  And crisply musical, or holy caverns temple-toned, [Burnshaw
  47-16 P
  Or poets with holy magic. [Grotesque 75-8 P
HOMAGE. Of affected homage foxed so many books, [Havana 142-15
HOMBURG. See Mr. Homburg.
HOME. A Nice Shady Home [C 40-title 5
  Melodious, where spirits gat them home, [Sunday 68-20
  At home, a bit like the slenderest courtesan. [NE Verses 106-6
  Her home, not mine, in the ever-freshened Keys, [Farewell 117-16
  "On the Road Home" [203-title
  Home from Guatemala, back at the Waldorf. [Waldorf 240-23
  Home and the fields give praise, hurrah, hip, [Hero 278-13
  So you're home again, Redwood Roamer, and ready [Phenom 286-13
  He was at Naples writing letters home [EM 313-11
  And liked it unsubjugated, so that home [EM 321-17
  Come home, wind, he kept crying and crying. [Pieces 351-11
  Come home, wind, he said as he climbed the stair-- [Pieces 351-14
  "A Woman Sings a Song for a Soldier Come Home" [360-title
  How good it was at home again that night [Lot 372-1
  And that made brothers of us in a home [AA 419-11
  Gothic blue, speed home its portents to their ends. [Page 422-20
  Of the other eye. One enters, entering home, [Bouquet 448-15
  At home; or: In the woods, belle Belle alone [Golden 460-14
  "The Old Lutheran Bells at Home" [461-title
  He could understand the things at home. [Aug 493-13
  Recognize his unique and solitary home. [Poem Mt 512-14
  Of Mr. Homburg during his visits home [Look 517-12
  Let's go home. [Drum-Majors 37-12 P
  In which the horse walks home without a rider, [Fare Guit 99-3 P
  A home against one's self, a darkness, [Letters 107-6 P
  The most at home? Or is it enough to have seen [Conversat 109-17P
  We drove home from Cornwall to Hartford, late. [Real 110-8 P
  More precious than the most precious objects of home: [Local
  111-13 P
  See castle-fortress-home.
HOMES. With the sea. These were fantastic. There were homes [EM
  321-26
HOMUNCULUS. "Homunculus et La Belle Etoile" [25-title
HONEST. Of honest quilts, the eye of Crispin, hung [C 27-17
  The very man despising honest quilts [C 41-29
HONEY. For once vent honey? [Carolinas 5-3
  The honey of heaven may or may not come, [Monocle 15-25
  Place honey on the altars and die, [MBG 174-3
  You are one . . . Go hunt for honey in his hair. [Blue Bldg
  217-22
  Ah! douce campagna, honey in the heart, [Beard 247-20
  It seems as if the honey of common summer [EM 316-1
  And is our fortune and honey hived in the trees [Cred 374-19
  The honey in its pulp, the final found, [Rock 527-14
  Sip the wild honey of the poor man's life, [Burnshaw 49-10 P
  And honey from thorns and I play my guitar. [Stan MBG 72-9 P
HONEYCOMB. And fattened as on a decorous honeycomb. [AA 419-13
HONEY-COMB. It is the honey-comb of the seeing man. [Blue Bldg
  217-17
  Cut summer down to find the honey-comb. [Blue Bldg 217-21
  Searching all day, all night, for the honey-comb. [Blue Bldg
  217-24
HONEYED. What Eden sapling gum, what honeyed gore, [C 38-2
HONEY-HIVE-O. For his honey-hive-o, [Anything B 211-10
HONEYMOON. Is it a philosopher's honeymoon, one finds [Dump 203-5
HONKY-TONK. The honky-tonk of the somnolent grasses [Aug 489-18
HONOR. Your self its honor. [Search 268-8
  Made noble by the honor he receives, [Recit 87-15 P
HOO. Howls hoo and rises and howls hoo and falls. [NSF 383-8
HOOBLA-HOO. The wood-dove used to chant his hoobla-hoo [NSF 383-6
HOOBLA-HOOBLA-HOOBLA-HOW. With his damned hoobla-hoobla-hoobla-how,
  [NSF 383-2
HOOD. Close the cantina. Hood the chandelier. [Havana 144-23
HOODED. Felicity, ah! Time is the hooded enemy, [Pure 330-13
  See ever-hooded; hot-hooded.
HOODS. Do the drummers in black hoods [Circulat 150-3
  Of crimson and hoods of Venezuelan green [Burnshaw 51-3 P
HOOFS. Hoofs grinding against the stubborn earth, until [Old Woman

  46-10 P
  And head a shadow trampled under hoofs, [Sombre 70-28 P
HOO-HOOED. Hoo-hooed it in the darkened ocean-blooms. [Sea Surf
  100-5
HOO-HOO-HOO. Play the present, its hoo-hoo-hoo, [Mozart 131-15
HOO-ING. Confront you, hoo-ing the slick trombones, [MBG 170-16
HOON. "Tea at the Palaz of Hoon" [65-title
  There's that mountain-minded Hoon, [Sad Gay 121-15
HOOPED. The oracular trumpets round and roundly hooped, [Greenest
  56-19 P
HOOP-LA. These things he thinks of, as the buckskin hoop-la, [Am-
  ericana 94-13 P
HOOS. And fears not portly Azcan nor his hoos. [Bantams 76-4
HOOT. Hoot, little owl within her, how [Vase 246-17
  Hoot how the inhuman colors fell [Vase 247-6
HOP. The leaves hop, scraping on the ground. [Possum 294-6
HOPE. Wait now; have no rememberings of hope, [Soldat 14-13 P
  Let's hope for Mademoiselle de Lespinasse, [Lytton 39-19 P
  Policed by the hope of Christmas. Summer night, [Sombre 68-11 P
  Of evil, evil springs; or catholic hope, [Sombre 69-23 P
  Or a present future, hoped for in present hope, [Local 111-16 P
HOPED. Or a present future, hoped for in present hope, [Local
  111-16 P
HOPEFUL. Into a hopeful waste to come. There even [Burnshaw 49-24 P
HOPELESS. That blows about in such a hopeless way, [Phases 5-13 P
  To waste, out of the hopeless waste of the past [Burnshaw
  49-23 P
HOPKINS. And Hopkins, [Phases 3-17 P
HORACE WALPOLE. Instead, or Horace Walpole or Mrs. Thrale. [Lytton
  39-20 P
HORDES. Remoter than Athos, the effulgent hordes [Greenest 56-22 P
HORIZON. Tops the horizon with its colonnades. [Surprises 98-7
  The sun of Asia creeps above the horizon [Nigger 153-8
  That in spring will crown every western horizon, [Martial 237-12
  Swarm from the little blue of the horizon [Dutch 290-2
  Rumbling along the autumnal horizon, [Dutch 293-7
  Or of winter sky, from horizon to horizon. [AA 412-14
  A giant, on the horizon, glistening,[Orb 442-16
  Still on the horizon elongates his cuts, [Orb 443-4
  A giant on the horizon, given arms, [Orb 443-8
  At the centre on the horizon, concentrum, grave [Orb 443-13
  Upon the horizon amid adult enfantillages. [Questions 462-6
  Beyond the horizon with its masculine, [NH 476-24
  Or of a town poised at the horizon's dip [NH 483-9
  It buzzes beyond the horizon or in the ground: [NH 487-14
  On the horizon and lifting himself up above it. [World 520-14
HORIZONS. On high horizons, mountainous atmospheres [Key W 129-21
  In the space of horizons that neither love nor hate. [Aug
  490-14
  Things dark on the horizons of perception, [Rome 508-12
  Young weasels racing steep horizons in pursuit of planets . . .
  [Inelegance 26-8 P
  Along the thin horizons, nobly more [Burnshaw 47-10 P
  Reach from the horizons, rim to rim, [Sombre 68-25 P
HORN. Remus, blow your horn! [Ploughing 20-9
  Blow your horn! [Ploughing 20-12
  That seemed hallucinating horn, and here, [C 29-4
  Drowsing in summer's sleepiest horn. [Cuban 65-6
  Of the color of horn [Cortege 80-2
  A horn, on which its victory [MBG 174-13
  Sat alone, his great toe like a horn, [Thought 187-7
  "On an Old Horn" [230-title
  No greater than a cricket's horn, no more [Beard 247-15
  Cloud-clown, blue painter, sun as horn, [Jumbo 269-13
  Find a deep echo in a horn and buzz [NSF 390-17
  See helio-horn.
HORNED. See much-horned.
HORNS. And roaring horns. [Peter 91-11
  On peculiar horns, themselves eked out [Great 311-14
  The actual landscape with its actual horns [NH 475-1
  The illustrious arms, the symbolic horns, the red [Bship 79-6 P
  And the fiddles smack, the horns yahoo, the flutes [Bship 79-28 P
HORNSMAN. The bottomless trophy, new hornsman after old? [NSF
  390-18
HORNY. If her horny feet protrude, they come [Emperor 64-13
HORRENDOUS. "Oh, hideous, horrible, horrendous hocks!" [Stan MMO
  19-15 P
HORRIBLE. "Oh, hideous, horrible, horrendous hocks!" [Stan MMO
  19-15 P
HORRID. "Horrid figures of Medusa, [Inhab 504-1
HORROR. Add nothing to the horror of the frost [Nigger 152-13
  A horror of thoughts that suddenly are real. [Man Car 351-6
  Without any horror of the helpless loss. [Duck 61-16 P
  Of a time to come--A shade of horror turns [Duck 65-8 P
HORRORS. Horrors and falsities and wrongs; [Negation 97-16
HORSE. Or an old horse. [Nuances 18-17
  Monsieur is on horseback. The horse is covered with mice. [Mice
  123-4
  Who was it passed her there on a horse all will, [Uruguay 249-16
  Whose horse clattered on the road on which she rose, [Uruguay

249-18
On a horse, in a plane, at the piano-- [Hero 274-20
Neither his head nor horse nor knife nor [Hero 276-22
Time is a horse that runs in the heart, a horse [Pure 329-16
A horse grotesquely taut, a walker like [Pure 330-6
Dark horse and walker walking rapidly. [Pure 330-12
But it is like a horse. It is like motion [Pieces 352-6
The right, uplifted foreleg of the horse [NSF 391-10
The music halted and the horse stood still. [NSF 391-12
On his gold horse striding, like a conjured beast, [Antag 426-1
He will never ride the red horse she describes. [Questions
    462-15
Or Death was a rider beating his horse, [Soldat 16-4 P
In which the horse walks home without a rider, [Fare Guit 99-3 P
See cab-horse.
HORSEBACK. Monsieur is on horseback. The horse is covered with
    mice. [Mice 123-4
HORSES. On tins and boxes? What about horses eaten by wind?
    [Parochial 191-18
Abhor the plaster of the western horses, [Hartford 226-12
No horses to ride and no one to ride them [Forces 229-10
No large white horses. But there was the fluffy dog. [Forces
    229-12
Two people, three horses, an ox [Les Plus 245-1
The child's hair is of the color of the hay in the haystack,
    around which the four black horses stand. [Primordia 8-1 P
The horses gnaw the bark from the trees. [Primordia 8-8 P
The horses are hollow, [Primordia 8-9 P
Why do the horses have eyes and ears? [Primordia 8-11 P
Why can the horses move about on the ground? [Primordia 8-13 P
The horses weary themselves hunting for green grass. [Primordia
    8-15 P
The water runs away from the horses. [Primordia 8-18 P
Harness of the horses shuffled [Cab 21-2 P
Fitted by men and horses [Polo 37-17 P
On the flanks of horses, [Polo 38-4 P
A group of marble horses rose on wings [Old Woman 43-2 P
Raced with the horses in bright hurricanes. [Old Woman 43-4 P
Before the horses, clouds of bronze imposed [Old Woman 43-7 P
This atmosphere in which the horses rose, [Old Woman 44-19 P
To the moment. There the horses would rise again, [Old Woman
    46-7 P
They are horses as they were in the sculptor's mind. [Burnshaw
    46-18 P
And remains inarticulate, horses with croam. [Burnshaw 47-3 P
Of autumn, these horses should go clattering [Burnshaw 47-9 P
And on this ring of marble horses shed [Burnshaw 47-27 P
And there are the white-maned horses' heads, beyond [Burnshaw
    49-19 P
The horses are a part of a northern sky [Greenest 54-28 P
A ring of horses rising from memory [Greenest 57-10 P
O bold, that rode your horses straight away. [Duck 61-31 P
Than the horses quivering to be gone, flashed through [Duck 64-9P
HOSANNA. Pulse pizzicati of Hosanna. [Peter 90-12
HOSPITAL. Eulalia, I lounged on the hospital porch, [Phenom 287-7
HOSPITALIERS. These hospitaliers? These brute-like guests? [AA
    415-23
HOST. When the host shall no more wander, nor the light [Heaven
    56-19
HOSTILE. Bitter eyes, hands hostile and cold. [Chateau 161-10
HOT. Out of her botches, hot embosomer. [C 44-29
Her mind had bound me round. The palms were hot [Farewell 117-11
Since the imperfect is so hot in us, [Poems Clim 194-9
The hot of him is purest in the heart. [NSF 388-15
The book, hot for another accessible bliss: [NSF 395-13
Evade, this hot, dependent orator, [NSF 397-1
Our crusted outlines hot and huge with face, [Burnshaw 47-6 P
On a hot night and a long cigar and talk [Greenest 58-25 P
HOTEL. I had as lief be embraced by the porter at the hotel [Two
    Figures 85-14
The hotel is boarded and bare. [Botanist 1 135-12
You touch the hotel the way to touch moonlight [Waldorf 241-4
Green glade and holiday hotel and world [Pure 330-19
The flag of the nude above the holiday hotel. [Pure 331-1
And studied it in his holiday hotel. [Pure 331-14
To the real: to the hotel instead of the hymns [NH 471-11
HOTELS. Mother was afraid I should freeze in the Parisian hotels.
    [Novel 457-7
HOT-HOODED. Hot-hooded and dark-blooded, rescued the rose [EM
    316-17
HOTTEST. To touch again the hottest bloom, to strike [Havana 143-15
Let's see it with the hottest fire of sight. [Cred 373-4
HOUR. To that first, foremost law. Angusishing hour! [Monocle 17-13
She measured to the hour its solitude. [Key W 129-25
It was not yet the hour to be dauntlessly leaping. [Vari 236-3
To repose in an hour or season or long era [EM 318-22
And tells the hour by the lateness of the sounds. [Pure 330-3
Is it I then that keep saying there is an hour [NSF 404-23
And if there is an hour there is a day, [NSF 405-3
HOURS. That the hours of his indolent, arid days, [Frogs 78-10

And the green flauntings of the hours of peace. [Pastor 380-3
A few more hours of day, the unravelling [Nuns 92-12 P
HOUSE. The dulcet omen fit for such a house. [C 44-26
"The Curtains in the House of the Metaphysician" [62-title
When I think of our lands I think of the house [Grapes 110-12
Yet the house is not built, not even begun. [Ghosts 119-2
A dirty house in a gutted world, [Postcard 159-19
The red and the blue house blended, [Idiom 200-21
Occurred above the empty house and the leaves [Sleight 222-4
The aureole above the humming house . . . [Beard 247-24
The bareness of the house returns. [Contra I 267-1
Finding its way from the house, makes music seem [Phenom 287-1
If there must be a god in the house, must be, [Less 327-9
If there must be a god in the house, let him be one [Less 328-7
"The House Was Quiet and the World Was Calm" [358-title
The house was quiet and the world was calm. [House Q 358-7
The house was quiet and the world was calm. [House Q 358-10
The house was quiet because it had to be. [House Q 358-16
To prepare for bed, in the frame of the house, and move [Lot
    372-2
My house has changed a little in the sun. [NSF 385-16
Where his house had fallen, three scraggy trees weighted [NSF
    393-4
She lived in her house. She had two daughters, one [NSF 402-1
It is evening. The house is evening, half dissolved. [AA 413-8
The house will crumble and the books will burn. [AA 413-17
And the house is of the mind and they and time, [AA 413-19
The mother invites humanity to her house [AA 415-4
And is destroyed. He opens the door of his house [AA 416-24
The house is empty. But here is where she sat [Beginning 427-12
He walks through the house, looks round him and then leaves.
    [Bouquet 453-2
Of what is this house composed if not of the sun, [NH 465-9
A thing on the side of a house, not deep in a cloud, [NH 474-21
He turned from the tower to the house, [Aug 493-9
Who is my father in this world, in this house, [Irish 501-7
The great structure has become a minor house. [Plain 502-15
Come back to see a certain house. [Vacancy 511-11
Of a house, that makes one think the house is laughing, [Slug
    522-10
Of year. Here in his house and in his room, [Quiet 523-8
In this house, what manner of utterance shall there be? [Archi
    16-20 P
On any house of mine. [Secret Man 35-24 P
A manner of walking, yellow fruit, a house, [Woman Had 83-7 P
Before it shines on any house. [Three 130-6 P
Before it shines on any house. [Three 131-13 P
See: chop-house; mansion-house.
HOUSES. The houses are haunted [Ten O'C 66-1
When over the houses, a golden illusion [Lunar 107-9
Except for our own houses, huddled low [Eve Angels 138-1
Makes him rise above the houses, looking down. [Repet 307-14
Great tufts, spring up from buried houses [EM 322-15
White houses in villages, black communicants-- [Cats 367-19
These houses, these difficult objects, dilapidate [NH 465-10
Suppose these houses are composed of ourselves, [NH 466-4
Lived in the houses of mothers, arranged ourselves [Rock 525-2
It is no longer air. The houses still stand, [Rock 525-5
To men, to houses, streets and the squalid whole. [Greenest 57-8P
Its shadow on their houses, on their walls, [Sombre 68-22 P
People that live in the biggest houses [Grotesque 74-17 P
One thinks, when the houses of New England catch the first sun,
    [Discov 95-21 P
HOVELS. Regard the hovels of those that live in this land. [Loaf
    199-18
HOVERING. To join a hovering excellence, to escape [Rome 509-6
HOWL. Heard the dogs howl at barren bone, [Thought 187-6
HOWLED. Is cast in pandemonium, flittered, howled [Duck 62-7 P
HOWLING. As of the great wind howling, [Mozart 132-14
A small howling of the dove [Dove 97-17 P
Makes this small howling, like a thought [Dove 98-4 P
This howling at one's ear, too far [Dove 98-14 P
HOWLS. Howls hoo and rises and howls hoo and falls. [NSF 383-8
Autumn howls upon half-naked summer. But [John 437-5
That howls in the mind or like a man [Dove 98-5 P
In that which is and is established . . . It howls [Dove 98-7 P
HOWZEN. In Hydaspia, by Howzen, [Oak 272-1
By Howzen, the chromatic Lowzen. [Oak 272-21
HOY. And, hoy, the impopulous purple-plated past, [Montra 260-5
Hoy, hoy, the blue bulls kneeling down to rest. [Montra 260-6
HUBBUB. Who, in the hubbub of his pilgrimage [C 33-21
HUCKSTERING. How I exhort her, huckstering my woe. [Stan MMO 19-14P
HUDDLE. Huddle together in the knowledge of squirrels. [NH 487-12
HUDDLED. The lacquered loges huddled there [Ord Women 11-1
Except for our own houses, huddled low [Eve Angels 138-1
HUE. The basic slate, the universal hue. [Monocle 15-9
Make hue among the dark comedians, [Heaven 56-21
And in its watery radiance, while the hue [Sea Surf 99-12
Of green blooms turning crisped the motley hue [Sea Surf 102-12
Dressed high in heliotrope's inconstant hue, [Bad Time 427-6

In the eye a special hue of origin. [Bouquet 451-23
Changed them, at last, to its triumphant hue, [Old Woman 44-26 P
Of the most evasive hue of a lesser blue, [Burnshaw 51-19 P
HUED. And in the morning summer hued the deck [Sea Surf 98-14
HUES. Hinting incredible hues, four selfsame lights [C 45-8
The sea appends its tattery hues. [MBG 172-13
Whose green mind bulges with complicated hues: [Choc 300-5
Their words and ours; in what we see, their hues [Sombre 67-6 P
HUGE. Beams of the huge night converged upon it, [Valley Candle
    51-2
Then beams of the huge night [Valley Candle 51-4
Huge are the canna in the dreams of [Canna 55-1
The huge decorum, the manner of the time, [Cred 378-4
They lay. Forth then with huge pathetic force [NSF 403-7
It is the huge, high harmony that sounds [Orb 440-11
Our crusted outlines hot and huge with fact, [Burnshaw 47-6 P
So that a carved king found in a jungle, huge [Conversat 109-5 P
HUGH MARCH. Hugh March, a sergeant, a redcoat, killed, [Vari 234-11
HULK. The mass of stone collapsed to marble hulk, [Old Woman 44-23P
HULL. Fill your black hull [Fabliau 23-12
HULLABALOO. A jovial hullabaloo among the spheres [High-Toned
    59-20
HULLABAILLOO. The hullaballoo of health and have, [Dutch 292-5
HUM. Of hum, inquisitorial botanist, [C 28-10
Or sunlight and you hum and the orchestra [Waldorf 241-5
And say, "The thing I hum appears to be [Landsc 243-7
The hum of thoughts evaded in the mind, [NSF 388-4
The passion, indifferent to the poet's hum, [Sombre 71-25 P
HUMAN. Of human others, [Vincentine 53-6
Like the thoughts of an old human, [Shifts 83-11
Like a human without illusions, [Shifts 83-15
Like a human, heavy and heavy, [Shifts 84-2
Make more awry our faulty human things. [Surprises 98-11
On human heads. True, birds rebuild [Cuisine 227-14
We feast on human heads, brought in on leaves, [Cuisine 228-10
Like human conciliations, more like [Vase 247-3
The central man, the human globe, responsive [Oboe 250-20
A wider brow, large and less human [Hero 277-8
Of his brave quickenings, the human [Hero 279-3
True transfigurers fetched out of the human mountain, [Choc 300-6
To say more than human things with human voice, [Choc 300-11
That cannot be; to say human things with more [Choc 300-12
Than human voice, that, also, cannot be; [Choc 300-13
Of human things, that is acutest speech. [Choc 300-15
A human thing. It is an eminence, [Choc 300-17
And, of human realizings, rugged roy . . . [Choc 302-5
It was almost time for lunch. Pain is human. [EM 314-8
A too, too human god, self-pity's kin [EM 315-23
Before we were wholly human and knew ourselves. [EM 317-29
"Less and Less Human, O Savage Spirit" [327-title
It is the human that is the alien, [Less 328-3
The human that has no cousin in the moon. [Less 328-4
It is the human that demands his speech [Less 328-5
Darkness, nothingness of human after-death, [Flyer 336-12
The more than human commonplace of blood, [Descrip 341-3
The eccentric souvenirs of human shapes, [Descrip 342-13
The human ocean beats against this rock [Two V 354-19
The human revery or poem of death? [Men Made 355-16
Of propositions about life. The human [Men Made 355-18
"Human Arrangement" [363-title
As of a general being or human universe. [Past Nun 378-22
Of a human evocation, so disclosed [Pastor 379-14
What rabbi, grown furious with human wish, [NSF 389-1
He, too, is human and difference disappears [Pecul 454-6
The dauntless master, as he starts the human tale. [Puel 456-18
Or else his prolongations of the human. [NH 469-12
And in any case never grim, the human grim [NH 475-17
The world? The inhuman as human? That which thinks not, [Aug
    493-3
The total of human shadows bright as glass. [Aug 494-23
The finally human, [Leben 504-20
It is as if in a human dignity [Rome 508-8
The human end in the spirit's greatest reach, [Rome 508-16
For a human that can be accounted for. [Look 519-6
The starting point of the human and the end, [Rock 528-16
That which is human and yet final, like [Americana 94-6 P
Of the loftiest amour, in a human midnight? [Souls 95-6 P
Nor the smoke-drift of puffed-out heroes, nor human cry. [Course
    96-20 P
There is a human loneliness, [Ulysses 100-5 P
From the human in humanity, [Ulysses 105-1 P
"Here I feel the human loneliness [Presence 105-19 P
The one thing common to all life, the [Conversat 109-1 P
And weathered, should be part of a human landscape, [Conversat
    109-6 P
And human nature, pensively seated [Region 115-14 P
Sings in the palm, without human meaning, [Of Mere 117-19 P
Without human feeling a foreign song. [Of Mere 117-20 P
Yet, as it seems, of human residence. [Someone 84-3 A
The inhuman making choice of a human self. [Ideal 89-12 A

See: mid-human; over-human.
HUMANE. Not yet accustomed, yet, at sight, humane [John 437-8
For humane triumphals. But a politics [Papini 147-13
Gritting the ear, whispers humane repose. [NH 484-21
Ascending the humane. This is the form [Recit 87-20 P
HUMANITY. Lend no part to any humanity that suffuses [Nuances 18-11
And wear humanity's bleak crown; [Crude 305-8
In humanity has not conceived of a race [EM 325-25
And the chronicle of humanity is the sum [Paisant 335-1
The mother invites humanity to her house [AA 415-4
It is the earth itself that is humanity . . . [Pecul 454-1
In a queer assertion of humanity: [Rock 525-15
From the human in humanity, [Ulysses 105-1 P
Only encompassed in humanity, is he [Conversat 109-13 P
"The court had known poverty and wretchedness; humanity [Three
    129-9-10 P
That humanity never invades. [Three 130-3 P
It is the invasion of humanity [Three 132-11 P
HUMANLY. Humanly near, and the figure of Mary, [Lunar 107-6
To speak humanly from the height or from the depth [Choc 300-14
HUMANS. Like humans approaching proudly, [Shifts 83-18
Like humans approaching angrily. [Shifts 83-19
HUMBLE. Abashed him by carouse to humble yet [C 40-24
And is the queen humble as she seems to be, [Cred 374-25
HUMBLY. Preferring text to gloss, he humbly served [C 39-22
So delicately blushed, so humbly eyed, [C 44-13
She walks, triumphing humbly, should express [Red Kit 31-11 P
HUM-DRUM. In hum-drum space, farewell, farewell, by day [Sombre
    71-8 P
The spring is hum-drum like an instrument, [Sombre 71-11 P
HUMMED. He hummed to himself at such a plan. [Thought 187-4
HUMMING. While he imagined humming sounds and sleep. [Babies 77-6
The form on the pillow humming while one sleeps, [Beard 247-23
The aureole above the humming house . . . [Beard 247-24
Reflected, humming an outline of a fugue [NSF 402-14
Answer, humming, [Primordia 7-13 P
The boatman goes humming. He smokes a cigar [Stan MBG 72-11 P
Of the humming of the central man, the whole sound [Woman Had
    82-12 P
Of the sea, the central humming of the sea, [Woman Had 82-13 P
HUMMING-BIRD. The humming-bird is the national bird [Grotesque
    75-1 P
Of the humming-bird. [Grotesque 75-2 P
HUMORS. Ah! that ill humors [W Burgher 61-3
HUMP-ARMED. Hairy-backed and hump-armed, [Orangeade 102-18
HUMPED. For all it takes it gives a humped return [C 43-6
And there you are humped high, humped up, [Rabbit K 209-21
You are humped higher and higher, black as stone-- [Rabbit K 210-1
    8. The owl sits humped. It has a hundred eyes. [Someone 86-11 A
See star-humped.
HUMPS. Through weltering illuminations, humps [Page 422-25
HUMS. Hums and you say "The world in a verse, [Waldorf 241-6
An attic glass, hums of the old Lutheran bells [Golden 460-13
HUNCHED. But bananas hacked and hunched . . . [Bananas 54-10
And I am merely a shadow hunched [MBG 169-16
HUNDRED. On a hundred legs, the tread [Cortege 79-15
A hundred yards from a carriage. [Theory 86-19
Of blue, blue sleek with a hundred chins, [MBG 172-7
Things floating like the first hundred flakes of snow [Man Car
    351-3
And peace is cousin by a hundred names [Owl 432-11
    8. The owl sits humped. It has a hundred eyes. [Someone 86-11 A
HUNDREDS. In which hundreds of eyes, in one mind, see at once.
    [NH 488-6
HUNG. Of honest quilts, the eye of Crispin, hung [C 27-17
The salt hung on his spirit like a frost, [C 29-13
If just above her head there hung, [Couch 295-10
Hung heavily on the great banana tree, [NSF 393-14
An ancient forehead hung with heavy hair, [NSF 400-7
And on the ground. The hibernal dark that hung [NH 476-8
Bare beggar-tree, hung low for fruited red [NH 483-24
HUNGER. It was hunger, it was the hungry that cried [Loaf 200-9
Like hunger that feeds on its own hungriness. [EM 323-4
HUNGRIEST. That scholar hungriest for that book, [MBG 178-1
HUNGRINESS. Like hunger that feeds on its own hungriness. [EM
    323-4
HUNGRY. This dance has no name. It is a hungry dance. [Mice 123-5
It was hunger, it was the hungry that cried [Loaf 200-9
HUNKS. On the irised hunks, the stone bouquet. [Hartford 227-12
HUNT. You are one . . . Go hunt for honey in his hair. [Blue Bldg
    217-22
They hunt for a form which by its form alone, [Pediment 361-10
HUNTED. Forever hunting or hunted, rushing through [Greenest 55-21P
HUNTER. Let these be your delight, secretive hunter, [Tallap 72-1
A hunter of those sovereigns of the soul [Lions 124-11
The hunter shouts as the pheasant falls. [Nigger 154-9
HUNTERS. The hunters run to and fro. The heavy trees, [Parochial
    191-7
When spring comes and the skeletons of the hunters [Parochial
    191-19

HUNTING. Hunting for the great ornament, [Pediment 361-8
  The horses weary themselves hunting for green grass. [Primordia
    8-15 P
  Forever hunting or hunted, rushing through [Greenest 55-21 P
  Forgetting work, not caring for angels, hunting a lift, [Duck
    60-15 P
HUNTS. Whoever hunts a matinal continent [C 40-27
HURRAH. Home and the fields give praise, hurrah, hip, [Hero 278-13
  Hip, hip, hurrah. Eternal morning . . . [Hero 278-14
HURRICANE. And sullen, hurricane shapes [Bananas 53-22
  Parl-parled the West-Indian hurricane. [Search 268-12
HURRICANES. Raced with the horses in bright hurricanes. [Old Woman
    43-4 P
HURROO. On top. Hurroo, the man-boat comes, [Vari 235-17
HURTS. It is the word pejorative that hurts. [Sailing 120-1
HUSH. The holy hush of ancient sacrifice. [Sunday 67-1
HUSHED. Nothing could be more hushed than the way [Pecul 453-7
HUSHFUL. In hall harridan, not hushful paradise, [AA 421-1
HUSK. This husk of Cuba, tufted emerald, [Someone 83-7 A
HUT. Curled over the shadowless hut, the rust and bones, [Farewell
    118-4
  1. The hut stands by itself beneath the palms. [Someone 86-4 A
HYACINTH. It is a theme for Hyacinth alone. [Monocle 15-17
  A blue beyond the rainy hyacinth, [Sea Surf 101-1
HYACINTHS. As if hyacinths had never gone. We say [NSF 389-20
  Violets, doves, girls, bees and hyacinths [NSF 389-22
  And, while revolving, ancient hyacinths [Sombre 69-17 P
HYBRIDS. Hybrids impossible to the wardens [Stan Hero 84-6 P
  Within us. False hybrids and false heroes, [Stan Hero 84-7 P
HYDASPIA. In Hydaspia, by Howzen, [Oak 272-1
  So she in Hydaspia created [Oak 272-16
HYDRANGEAS. Two wooden tubs of blue hydrangeas stand at the foot
    of the stone steps. [Banal 62-11
  He called hydrangeas purple. And they were. [Abnormal 23-16 P
  And so hydrangeas came to be. [Abnormal 24-3 P
HYMENEAL. In this hymeneal air, what it is [Lilacs 49-2
HYMN. Bravura adequate to this great hymn? [Monocle 16-22
  The vulgar, as his theme and hymn and flight, [C 35-2
  "Hymn from a Watermelon Pavilion" [88-title
  Brings forth hymn and hymn [Nomad 95-11
  All this is older than its oldest hymn, [Havana 144-28
  "Late Hymn from the Myrrh-Mountain" [349-title
  Being virile, it hears the calendar hymn. [NSF 382-9
  We have not the need of any seducing hymn. [NSF 394-21
  This was their ceremonial hymn: Anon [NSF 401-7
  Night's hymn of the rock, as in a vivid sleep. [Rock 528-21
  Are the fulfilling rhapsodies that hymn it to creation?
    [Inelegance 26-4 P
  His hymn, his psalm, his cithern song of praise [Greenest 59-21P
  See night-hymn.
HYMNS. Of his first central hymns, the celebrants [C 37-12
  Like windy citherns hankering for hymns. [High-Toned 59-5
  What were the hymns that buzzed beside my ears? [Hoon 65-11
  And my ears made the blowing hymns they heard. [Hoon 65-14
  Empty and grandiose, let us make hymns [Nigger 151-20
  Of empty heaven and its hymns, [MBG 167-12
  That's where his hymns come crowding, hero-hymns, [Thought
    185-15
  Day hymns instead of constellated rhymes, [Thought 185-18
  Hymns of the struggle of the idea of god [Thought 185-19
  In hymns, through iridescent changes, [Hero 279-22
  These hymns are like a stubborn brightness [Hero 279-24
  Contains the year and other years and hymns [Cred 375-6
  In our captious hymns, erect and sinuous, [John 437-20
  In February hears the imagination's hymns [Imago 439-10
  For triumphals. These are hymns appropriate to [Papini 447-15
  Great choristers, propounders of hymns, trumpeters, [Luther
    461-7
  To the real: to the hotel instead of the hymns [NH 471-11
  Poor penury. There will be voluble hymns [Soldat 14-14 P
  For hymns, [Polo 37-18 P
  With interruptions by vast hymns, blood odes, [Duck 66-1 P
  See: hero-hymns; marriage-hymns.
HYPNOSIS. Inhabit the hypnosis of that sphere. [NH 480-9
HYPOTHESIS. Logos and logic, crystal hypothesis, [NSF 387-4
HYPOTHESES. The this and that in the enclosures of hypotheses
    [Prol 516-14

ICE. To behold the junipers shagged with ice, [Snow Man 10-2
  The green palmettoes in crepuscular ice [C 34-15
  In mornings of angular ice, [Medit 124-5
  To be served by men of ice. [Poem Morn 219-7
  Of rose and ice [Bottle 238-20
  Romantic tenements of rose and ice. [Bottle 239-16
  Or whether the ice still covered the lake. There was still
    [Extracts 255-14
  Against the edge of the ice, the abstraction would [Extracts
    255-18
  The stalks are firmly rooted in ice. [Possum 294-8
  He was a shell of dark blue glass, or ice, [Choc 297-9
  And ice is still in Februar. [Poesie 302-10
  It still is ice in Februar. [Poesie 302-12
  Become an over-crystal out of ice, [Pieces 351-16
  The color of ice and fire and solitude. [AA 413-3
  A steamer lay near him, foundered in the ice. [Page 421-13
  The finned flutterings and gaspings of the ice, [Page 422-8
  Slight gestures that could rend the palpable ice, [Page 423-2
  Sharp in the ice shadow of the sky, [Celle 438-12
  So that this cold, a children's tale of ice, [NH 468-8
  The blunt ice flows down the Mississippi, [Primordia 8-3 P
  Dutch ice on English boats? The memory [Recit 86-25 P
  The cricket of summer forming itself out of ice. [Discov 95-14 P
ICE-BEAR. They came. But, brown, the ice-bear sleeping in ice-
    month [Study II 464-8
ICEBERG. The iceberg settings satirize [MBG 180-2
ICE-CREAM. [The Emperor of Ice-Cream" [64-title
  The only emperor is the emperor of ice-cream. [Emperor 64-8
  The only emperor is the emperor of ice-cream. [Emperor 64-16
ICE-HARD. Pinks and pinks the ice-hard melanchole. [An Gaiety
    32-17 P
ICELAND. The wind of Iceland and [Weak Mind 212-7
ICE-MONTH. They came. But, brown, the ice-bear sleeping in ice-
    month [Study II 464-8
ICICLES. Icicles filled the long window [Thirteen 93-12
  But for the icicles on the eaves-- [MBG 179-20
ICIEST. Iciest core, a north star, central [Hero 275-24
ICON. The Poem as Icon [Rock 526-title 2
  The fiction of the leaves is the icon [Rock 526-18
  And the icon is the man. The pearled chaplet of spring, [Rock
    526-20
  These leaves are the poem, the icon and the man. [Rock 527-2
  His words are both the icon and the man. [Rock 527-21
ICY. For answer from their icy Elysée. [Heaven 56-23
  Persisting bleakly in an icy haze, [Pharynx 96-12
  It is still full of icy shades and shapen snow. [Course 96-12 P
IDEA. The Idea of a Colony [C 36-title 4
  But his emprize to that idea soon sped. [C 40-13
  "The Idea of Order at Key West" [128-title
  The idea of god no longer sputtered [Thought 184-13
  The idea of the Alps grew large, [Thought 184-15
  One man, the idea of man, that is the space, [Thought 185-11
  The era of the idea of man, the cloak [Thought 185-13
  Hymns of the struggle of the idea of god [Thought 185-19
  And the idea of man, the mystic garden and [Thought 185-20
  To spread colors. There was not an idea [Forces 229-4
  This warmth in the blood-world for the pure idea, [Extracts
    256-12
  The marbles are pinchings of an idea, [Hero 276-13
  Yet there is that idea behind the marbles, [Hero 276-14
  The idea of things for public gardens, [Hero 276-15
  Idea. She floats in the contention, the flux [Couch 295-18
  Between the thing as idea and [Couch 295-19
  The idea as thing. She is half who made her. [Couch 295-20
  Thought is false happiness: the idea [Crude 305-1
  He would be the lunatic of one idea [EM 325-12
  Live, work, suffer and die in that idea [EM 325-14
  Begin, ephebe, by perceiving the idea [NSF 380-12
  The inconceivable idea of the sun. [NSF 380-14
  And see it clearly in the idea of it. [NSF 380-17
  Of this idea nor for that mind compose [NSF 381-2
  How clean the sun when seen in its idea, [NSF 381-4
  That sends us back to the first idea, the quick [NSF 381-17
  The truth itself, the first idea becomes [NSF 381-20
  May there be an ennui of the first idea? [NSF 381-23
  For a moment, the first idea . . . It satisfies [NSF 382-14
  The first idea was not our own. Adam [NSF 383-10
  But the first idea was not to shape the clouds [NSF 383-17
  Against the first idea--to lash the lion, [NSF 385-2
  A thinker of the first idea. Perhaps [NSF 386-2
  The first idea is an imagined thing. [NSF 387-1
  About the thinker of the first idea, [NSF 387-11
  The major abstraction is the idea of man [NSF 388-16
  Farewell to an idea . . . A cabin stands, [AA 412-4
  Farewell to an idea . . . The mother's face, [AA 413-4
  Farewell to an idea . . . The cancellings, [AA 414-4
  Existing in the idea of it, alone, [AA 418-7

The idea of the chevalier of chevaliers, [Antag 426-4
  Mistress of an idea, child [Celle 438-18
  Of the image spreading behind it in idea. [Bouquet 449-21
  The meta-men behold the idea as part [Bouquet 449-22
  The idea and the bearer-being of the idea. [NH 466-21
  Ugly as an idea, not beautiful [Burnshaw 47-7 P
  The civil fiction, the calico idea, [Duck 65-12 P
  "The Role of the Idea in Poetry" [93-title P
  The over-populace of the idea, the voices [Americana 94-2 P
IDEAL. Here is nothing of the ideal, [Explan 72-18
  "Of Ideal Time and Choice" [88-title A
  Stand at the center of ideal time, [Ideal 89-11 A
IDEALIST. Too vague idealist, overwhelmed [Negation 98-1
IDEAS. The grand ideas of the villages. [Pharynx 96-8
  Why nag at the idea of Hercules, Don Don? [NE Verses 104-1
  What is there in life except one's ideas, [MBG 175-17
  Is it ideas that I believe? [MBG 175-19
  One would continue to contend with one's ideas. [Glass Water
    198-5
  Without ideas in a land without ideas, [Forces 228-19
  To change nature, not merely to change ideas, [Vari 234-1
  "Extracts from Addresses to the Academy of Fine Ideas" [252-title
  The law of chaos is the law of ideas, [Extracts 255-23
  Ideas are men. The mass of meaning and [Extracts 255-25
  Ideas or, say, five men or, possibly, six. [Extracts 255-28
  In a world of ideas, who would have all the people [EM 325-13
  In a world of ideas. He would not be aware of the clouds,
    [EM 325-15
  This structure of ideas, these ghostly sequences [Bed 326-13
  Of ideas and to say as usual that there must be [Bed 326-17
  Of things as the structure of ideas. It was the structure [Bed
    327-7
  Of ideas moves wrinkled in a motion like [Feo 333-21
  It has, long since, grown tired, of such ideas. [Feo 334-2
  Of right joining, a music of ideas, the burning [Study II 465-1
  Among the more irritating minor ideas [Look 517-11
  "Not Ideas about the Thing but the Thing Itself" [534-title
  The ideas that come to it with a sense of speech. [Woman Had
    82-22 P
  See: anti-ideas; counter-ideas.
IDEE. But twiddling mon idée, as old men will, [Stan MMO 19-4 P
IDENTIFY. To be a part of tradition, to identify [Recit 86-4 P
  Are not tradition. To identify it. [Recit 86-12 P
IDENTITIES. One believes is what matters. Ecstatic identities
    [Extracts 258-2
  Of young identities, Aprilian stubs. [Duck 64-24 P
IDENTITY. Its identity is merely a thing that seems, [Descrip 340-10
  Identity. The thing he carries resists [Man Car 350-16
  Yet drenched with its identity, [Red Fern 365-7
  In this identity, disembodiments [NH 482-12
  Who keeps seeking out his identity [Dove 98-6 P
IDIOM. "Idiom of the Hero" [200-title
  And of its nature, the idiom thereof. [NSF 387-21
  And of each other thought--in the idiom [AA 419-4
  Of the work, in the idiom of an innocent earth, [AA 419-5
IDIOSYNCRATIC. Of idiosyncratic music. [Jasmine 79-3
IDIOT. There was such idiot minstrelsy in rain, [NSF 394-4
IDLE. Disturbed not even the most idle ear. [Hibiscus 22-14
IDLENESS. In a Sunday's violent idleness. [Two Illus 514-3
  See pin-idleness.
IDLY. To cloud transformed again, idly, the way [AA 416-8
  The cloud drifts idly through half-thought-of forms. [AA 416-15
  They sit idly there, [Phases 3-3 P
IDOLS. "The idols have seen lots of poverty, [On Road 204-6
IFFUCAN. Chieftain Iffucan of Azcan in caftan [Bantams 75-14
IGNOMINIE. C'était mon esprit bâtard, l'ignominie. [Sea Surf 102-9
IGNORANCE. In an ignorance of sleep with nothing won. [Dutch
    291-26
  The queen of ignorance, you have deplored [Feo 333-11
  From ignorance, not an undivided whole, [Two V 355-10
  Joy of such permanence, right ignorance [Cred 373-12
  The little ignorance that is everything, [John 437-16
IGNORANT. It may be that the ignorant man, alone, [Sleight 222-16
  We are ignorant men incapable [Crude 305-18
  You must become an ignorant man again [NSF 380-15
  And see the sun again with an ignorant eye [NSF 380-16
  As in the courage of the ignorant man, [NSF 395-11
IGNORED. How many sea-masks he ignored; what sounds [C 34-21
IGNORING. No pain (ignoring the cocks that crow us up [EM 314-13
ILIAD. Lean encyclopaedists, inscribe an Iliad. [NE Verses 104-9
ILL. Ah! that ill humors [W Burgher 61-3
  Of what it sees, for all the ill it sees? [EM 326-4
  Ill of a question like a malady, [Pure 331-7
  Ill of a constant question in his thought, [Pure 331-8
ILLIMITABLE. Illimitable spheres of you, [Vincentine 53-14
ILLOGICAL. Dangling in an illogical [Metamorph 266-8
  His extreme of logic would be illogical. [EM 325-17
ILLOGICALLY. But something illogically received, [Ulysses 101-27 P
ILLUMED. Summer assaulted, thundering, illumed, [Thought 186-9
ILLUMINATING. Illuminating, from a fancy gorged [C 46-6

ILLUMINATION. Illumination of movement as he breathed. [Choc 297-18
  This illumination, this elevation, this future [NH 481-24
ILLUMINATIONS. Once more night's pale illuminations, gold [NSF
  402-24
  Through weltering illuminations, humps [Page 422-25
  Confused illuminations and sonorities, [NH 466-19
ILLUMINED. So that we feel, in this illumined large, [Rome 509-13
  To the enclosure, day, the things illumined [Rock 528-18
ILLUMINES. By day, night and that which night illumines, [Rock
  528-19
  See re-illumines.
ILLUSION. When over the houses, a golden illusion [Lunar 107-9
  Then the colossal illusion of heaven. Yet still [Landsc 241-12
  And naked of any illusion, in poverty, [Extracts 258-18
  Should be illusion, that the mobs of birth [Dutch 292-25
  Of secluded thunder, an illusion, as it was, [Orb 441-1
  Return to their original illusion. [Novel 457-3
  Against illusion and was, in a great grinding [NH 467-18
  Of dreams, disillusion as the last illusion, [NH 468-11
  It is an illusion that we were ever alive, [Rock 525-1
  In its permanent cold, an illusion so desired [Rock 526-3
ILLUSIONS. Like a human without illusions, [Shifts 83-15
  For the beau of illusions. [Coroner 29-17 P
ILLUSIVE. Illusive, faint, more mist than moon, perverse [C 34-30
ILLUSTRATION. Almost successfully. Illustration: [Man Car 350-14
  This is the illustration that she used: [Past Nun 378-14
  There was another illustration, in which [Past Nun 379-1
  A definition with an illustration, not [Orb 443-10
  Into its own illustration, a divinity [Bship 79-2 P
  It is an illustration [Three 130-10 P
  That, in this illustration, [Three 130-14 P
ILLUSTRATIONS. Two things are one. (Pages of illustrations.)
  [Connois 215-3
  These illustrations are neither angels, no, [John 437-11
  "Two Illustrations That the World Is What You Make of It" [513-
  title
ILLUSTRIOUS. By the illustrious nothing of her name. [Descrip
  339-8
  Illustrious intimations--uncertain love, [Myrrh 350-4
  Than sharp, illustrious scene. The trumpet cries [Cred 376-19
  Said that as keen, illustrious ornament, [NSF 391-22
  The illustrious arms, the symbolic horns, the red [Bship 79-6 P
IMAGE. Converged upon its image, [Valley Candle 51-5
  As in your name, an image that is sure, [Fictive 88-6
  There was neither voice nor crested image, [How Live 126-1
  Now, an image of our society? [MBG 173-3
  The rugged black, the image. Design [Prelude 195-18
  As a man (not like an image of a man), [Dump 202-24
  Moving and being, the image at its source, [Candle 223-13
  Another image, it is one she has made. [Scavoir 232-2
  (This man in a room with an image of the world, [Rhythms 245-12
  There the man sees the image clearly at last. [Rhythms 245-15
  "This image, this love, I compose myself [Rhythms 246-4
  Into a barbarism as its image. [Hero 277-4
  It is not an image. It is a feeling. [Hero 278-19
  There is no image of the hero. [Hero 278-20
  How could there be an image, an outline, [Hero 278-22
  They wanted him by day to be, image, [Choc 299-14
  His route lies through an image in his mind: [Repet 307-15
  My route lies through an image in my mind, [Repet 307-16
  An image that leaves nothing much behind. [Repet 307-18
  An image of the mind, an inward mate, [Pastor 379-18
  On the imagination of what we see, to catch from that [NSF 398-21
  Another image at the end of the cave, [AA 411-5
  It is not that there is any image in the air [Wom Sun 445-6
  Of the image spreading behind it in idea. [Bouquet 449-21
  Of the image, behold it with exactness through beads [Bouquet
  449-23
  An image that was mistress of the world. [Golden 460-9
  Is the study of man, this image of Saturday, [Study I 463-6
  When the image itself is false, a mere desire, [Study I 463-18 ,
  An image that begot its infantines, [NH 479-7
  The appropriate image of himself, [Two Illus 513-13
  Pellucid love; and for that image, like [Spaniard 34-5 P
  The manes to his image of the flying wind, [Duck 64-17 P
  An image of his making, beyond the eye, [Sombre 69-26 P
  Except that this is an image of black spring [Sombre 69-30 P
  Is to define its form, to say: this image [Recit 86-13 P
  And meditates an image of itself, [Theatre 91-9 P
  Studies and shapes a tallowy image, swarmed [Theatre 91-10 P
  He is the image, the second, the unreal, [Americana 94-9 P
  That raises the question of the image's truth. [Myth 118-10 P
  The image must be of the nature of its creator. [Myth 118-11 P
  He seeks as image a second of the self, [Someone 84-7 A
  He seeks an image certain as meaning is [Someone 84-12 A
IMAGELESS. And, imageless, it is itself the most, [Montra 263-18
IMAGER. Patron and imager of the gold Don John, [Lilacs 49-14
  And stones, only this imager. [Jumbo 269-18
IMAGERY. In the pale nights, when your first imagery [Monocle
  15-5

Knew not the quirks of imagery, [Frogs 78-9
And noble imagery [Pascagoula 126-14
Concerning an immaculate imagery. [Oboe 250-14
A thing not planned for imagery or belief, [Look 518-6
Of such mixed motion and such imagery [Rock 527-17
And bears its floraisons of imagery. [Ulysses 102-31 P
IMAGES. Or bask within his images and words? [C 38-5
  Use dusky words and dusky images. [Two Figures 86-2
  These lions, these majestic images. [Lions 124-18
  Still hankers after sovereign images. [Lions 125-5
  For all your images, [Add 198-19
  Your images will have left [Add 198-21
  Of images. Days pass like papers from a press. [Dump 201-14
  (All its images are in the dump) and you see [Dump 202-23
  Full of stars and the images of stars-- [Nightgown 214-7
  Except for the images we make of it, [Extracts 257-11
  The difficult images of possible shapes, [Two V 354-9
  It is an ocean of watery images [Two V 355-11
  "Thinking of a Relation between the Images of Metaphors" [356-
  title
  Adieux, shapes, images-- [Prejudice 369-1
  That has expelled us and our images . . . [NSF 381-6
  No names. Dismiss him from your images. [NSF 388-14
  Of body and air and forms and images, [AA 411-17
  Lashing at images in the atmosphere, [Page 422-29
  These are death's own supremest images, [Owl 436-2
  And sees its images, its motions [Imago 439-11
  Brooding sounds of the images of death, [Degen 444-3
  And these images, these reverberations, [Degen 444-7
  But the images, disembodied, are not broken. [Golden 460-19
  "Study of Images I" [463-title
  Of day. If the study of his images [Study I 463-5
  A waking, as in images we awake, [Study I 463-7
  Not faded, if images are all we have. [Study I 464-1
  "Study of Images II" [464-title
  The frequency of images of the moon [Study II 464-4
  As if the centre of images had its [Study II 464-10
  Among time's images, there is not one [NH 476-16
  Creation is not renewed by images [NH 481-18
  Looked on big women, whose ruddy-ripe images [NH 486-17
  The world images for the beholder. [Aug 492-16
  These images return and are increased, [Soldat 13-15 P
  I might make many images of this [Demoiselle 23-7 P
  Free from images and change. [Demoiselle 23-11 P
  At the burst of day, crepuscular images [Burnshaw 46-23 P
  The spirit's natural images, carriers, [Greenest 57-12 P
  Of other images blows, images of time [Sombre 69-28 P
  Like the time of the portent, images like leaves, [Sombre 69-29P
  In the images of desire, the forms that speak, [Woman Had 82-21P
IMAGINARY. Imaginary poles whose intelligence [NH 479-8
IMAGINATION. The imagination, the one reality [Weep Woman 25-8
  The World without Imagination [C 27-title 1
  The imagination, here, could not evade, [C 30-7
  Imagination is the will of things. . . . [Polish Aunt 84-7
  The imagination that we spurned and crave. [Fictive 88-18
  Imagination as the fateful sin. [Havana 143-22
  The world washed in his imagination, [MBG 179-1
  To which his imagination returned, [MBG 179-5
  Filling the imagination's need. [Dezem 218-24
  What figure of capable imagination? [Uruguay 249-17
  In the high imagination, triumphantly. [Extracts 256-16
  Imagination, the golden rescue: [Hero 275-26
  For the imagination. A capital [EM 319-20
  Again, in the imagination's new beginning, [EM 320-11
  Of the imagination, made in sound; [Descrip 346-1
  The imagination, intact [Analysis 349-2
  And impotent, like the imagination seeking [Cats 368-3
  To propagate the imagination or like [Cats 368-4
  It comes to this and the imagination's life. [Cred 372-13
  To compound the imagination's Latin with [NSF 397-8
  Is there an imagination that sits enthroned [AA 417-4
  Generations of the imagination piled [Owl 434-13
  In February hears the imagination's hymns [Imago 439-10
  And feels the imagination's mercies, [Imago 439-13
  Includes death and the imagination. [Degen 444-9
  Over all these the mighty imagination triumphs [Puel 456-10
  Straight from the Arcadian imagination, [Novel 459-1
  Of night, time and the imagination, [NH 477-23
  We had come to an end of the imagination, [Plain 502-11
  Yet the absence of the imagination had [Plain 503-1
  We say God and the imagination are one . . . [Final 524-14
  Of the dank imagination, much below [Burnshaw 47-5 P
  Of an imagination flashed with irony [Greenest 56-16 P
  Even imagination has an end, [Sombre 71-13 P
  Without imagination, without past [Sombre 71-23 P
  Night and the imagination being one. [Sombre 71-34 P
  With saintly imagination and the stains [Bship 81-2 P
  Is part of the classic imagination, posed [Recit 87-1 P
  "Reality Is an Activity of the Most August Imagination"[110-titleP
  The moon and the imagination, or, say, [Someone 83-12 A

IMAGINATIVE. The imaginative, ghosts that dally [Hero 279-6
  The imaginative transcripts were like clouds, [NH 479-16
IMAGINE. Why do you imagine golden birds? [Thirteen 93-20
  And imagine for him the speech he cannot speak, [Pure 330-9
  Am I that imagine this angel less satisfied? [NSF 404-20
  To imagine winter? When the leaves are dead, [AA 417-7
IMAGINED. In this imagined world [Weep Woman 25-9
  My hands such sharp, imagined things. [W Burgher 61-17
  If I had imagined myself, [Explan 73-1
  While he imagined humming sounds and sleep. [Babies 77-6
  The imagined and the real, thought [MBG 177-16
  The imagined pine, the imagined jay. [MBG 184-6
  Imagined man, the monkish mask, the face. [Dezem 218-8
  The ultimate elegance: the imagined land. [Uruguay 250-5
  Clandestine steps upon imagined stairs [Oboe 251-6
  In the sky, an imagined, wooden chair [Human 363-9
  If only imagined but imagined well. [NSF 385-15
  The first idea is an imagined thing. [NSF 387-1
  On a woman, day on night, the imagined [NSF 392-6
  And not imagined. The removes must give, [Papini 447-5
  One imagined the violet trees but the trees stood green, [What
    We 459-10
  It was something imagined that has been washed away. [NH 488-2
  Itself to be imagined. The great pond, [Plain 503-2
  Had to be imagined as in inevitable knowledge, [Plain 503-7
  Companion to his self for her, which she imagined, [World 521-2
  The world imagined is the ultimate good. [Final 524-3
  Grown great and grave beyond imagined trees, [Old Woman 45-31 P
  The marble was imagined in the cold. [Greenest 56-28 P
  When the statue is not a thing imagined, a stone [Sombre 71-14 P
  Imagined among the indigenes [Ulysses 101-6 P
  At the bottom of imagined artifice, [Someone 83-9 A
IMAGINER. Not some outer patron and imaginer. [Conversat 109-15 P
IMAGINES. Imagines and it is true, as if he thought [Sombre 66-20P
  And the dissolving chorals, waits for it and imagines [Sick
    90-15 P
IMAGINING. A recent imagining of reality, [NH 465-15
  By imagining, anti-logician, quick [Sombre 66-21 P
IMAGININGS. Concealed imaginings. [Peter 90-18
  Make any imaginings of them lesser things. [Roses 430-15
IMAGO. "Imago" [439-title
  Imago. Imago. Imago. [Imago 439-4
IMBECILE. The unspotted imbecile revery, [MBG 172-5
  Ha-eé-me is the male beast . . . an imbecile, [Jouga 337-6
  The gathering of the imbecile against his motes [Discov 95-19 P
IMBECILES. How she presides over imbeciles. The night [Feo 333-12
IMITATION. It is more than an imitation for the ear. [Creat 311-9
  In imitation. The clouds preceded us [NSF 383-18
IMMACULATE. Musing immaculate, pampean dits, [C 38-25
  The immaculate, the merciful good, [MBG 168-18
  Speak and say the immaculate syllables [Men Fall 188-11
  Concerning an immaculate imagery. [Oboe 250-14
  Belief in an immaculate beginning [NSF 382-15
  To an immaculate end. We move between these points: [NSF 382-17
  An immaculate personage in nothingness, [Owl 434-11
  The immaculate interpreters of life. [NH 469-18
  And its immaculate fire, the middle dome, [Greenest 54-16 P
  The immaculate disclosure of the secret no more obscured.
    [Discov 96-2 P
IMMATERIAL. Its immaterial monsters move, [Analysis 348-14
IMMEASURABLE. The other immeasurable half, such rock [Cred 375-14
  Immeasurable, the space in which he knows [Sombre 70-32 P
IMMEDIATE. In a world that shrinks to an immediate whole, [Descrip
    341-12
  Too fragile, too immediate for any speech. [NH 471-9
  The immediate and intolerable need [Stan Hero 84-26 P
IMMEMORIAL. This immemorial grandiose, why not [Bship 79-9 P
IMMENSE. My candle burned alone in an immense valley. [Valley
    Candle 51-1
  As the immense dew of Florida [Nomad 95-6
  As the immense dew of Florida [Nomad 95-10
  An immense suppression, freed, [Sad Gay 122-5
  There might have been the immense solitude [Chateau 161-13
  Element in the immense disorder of truths. [Connois 216-3
  The yellow grassman's mind is still immense, [EM 318-24
  In an immense activity, in which [Past Nun 378-16
  St. Armorer's was once an immense success. [Armor 529-1
  Swirled round them in immense autumnal sounds. [Old Woman 43-21 P
  Parts of the immense detritus of a world [Burnshaw 49-21 P
  In an autumn afternoon, but two immense [Burnshaw 50-4 P
  And the shoulders turn, breathing immense intent. [Sombre 68-27 P
  An immense drum rolls through a clamor of people. [Stan Hero
    83-11 P
IMMENSELY. Accomplished in the immensely flashing East, [Eve Angels
    137-22
IMMENSER. In an immenser heaven, aloft, [MBG 176-9
  There might be, too, a change immenser than [Descrip 341-7
IMMENSEST. The immensest theatre, the pillared porch, [Rome 510-24
IMMINENCE. Of what disaster is this the imminence: [AA 419-20
IMMOBILE. Rested immobile, though neighboring catafalques [NSF 391-8

The mobile and the immobile flickering [NH 474-1
IMMORTAL. But in the flesh it is immortal. [Peter 91-24
  Immortal. The president ordains. But does [NSF 390-11
IMMORTALITY. Now, in its immortality, it plays [Peter 92-11
IMMOVABLES. The foul immovables, came through the clouds, [Greenest
    53-12 P
IMPALED. See star-impaled.
IMPALPABLE. So that they become an impalpable town, full of
    [NH 466-5
  Impalpable bells, transparencies of sound, [NH 466-6
  Impalpable habitations that seem to move [NH 466-8
IMPASSIONED. And stray impassioned in the littering leaves. [Sunday
    69-12
  Struggling toward impassioned choirs, [MBG 169-6
  Impassioned by the knowledge that she had, [Owl 435-17
  Of recognition, avowal, impassioned cry, [NH 471-3
  And still the impassioned place of it remain. [Spaniard 34-10 P
  Impassioned seducers and seduced, the pale [Burnshaw 52-19 P
IMPATIENT. Impatient of the bells and midnight forms, [Uruguay
    250-1
  Impatient for the grandeur that you need [Rome 509-22
IMPEACH. If these rude instances impeach themselves [C 38-6
IMPEARLED. Grisaille, impearled, profound, [Add 198-14
IMPECCABLE. This luscious and impeccable fruit of life [Monocle
    14-12
IMPELLED. Impelled by a convulsive harmony. [Red Kit 31-15 P
IMPENDS. And so France feels. A menace that impends, [Soldat 13-6P
IMPENETRABLE. Impenetrable symbols, motionless. They move [Owl
    432-6
IMPENITENT. Yet living in two worlds, impenitent [Rome 509-20
IMPERATIVE. Of China, cap of Spain, imperative haw [C 28-9
IMPERATOR. And imperator because of death to oppose [Bship 79-5 P
IMPERCEPTIBLE. The sky was blue. He wanted imperceptible air.
    [Landsc 241-13
IMPERFECT. The imperfect is our paradise. [Poems Clim 194-7
  Since the imperfect is so hot in us, [Poems Clim 194-9
  It is there, being imperfect, and with these things [Gala 248-7
IMPERFECTION. Rose from an imperfection of its own [EM 318-11
IMPERFECTIONS. Than yours, out of our imperfections wrought,
    [Fictive 87-20
IMPERISHABLE. The need of some imperishable bliss." [Sunday 68-28
IMPERIUM. Without any feeling, an imperium of quiet, [Burghers
    362-16
IMPERMANENCE. In a permanence composed of impermanence, [NH 472-14
  A vital assumption, an impermanence [Rock 526-2
IMPERSONAL. Of an impersonal gesture, a stranger's hand. [Hand
    271-14
  Of impersonal pain. Reality explained. [EM 322-3
  Of the impersonal person, the wanderer, [Aug 494-21
IMPINGED. Its color, but less as they recede, impinged [Anach
    366-10
IMPLACABLE. Of the still finer, more implacable chords. [Anatomy
    108-14
  Green had, those days, its own implacable sting. [Someone 85-7 A
IMPLEMENT. Xenophon, its implement and actor. [Hero 277-1
IMPLICIT. Implicit clarities in the way you cry [Burnshaw 52-12 P
IMPLIES. It implies a flaw in the battleship, a defeat [Bship 79-15P
IMPOLITOR. Waved in pale adieu. The rex Impolitor [Aug 495-21
IMPONDERABLE. Ponderable source of each imponderable, [NH 476-11
IMPOPULOUS. And, hoy, the impopulous purple-plated past, [Montra
    260-5
IMPORT. That should import a universal pith [Havana 144-5
IMPORTANCE. It was the importance of the trees outdoors, [Freed
    205-17
  The importance of its hat to a form becomes [Pastor 379-4
IMPORTANT. It was not important that they survive. [Planet 532-16
  Is its body visible to the important eye. [Recit 86-14 P
IMPORTUNATE. Or this, whose jingling glorias, importunate of
    perfection, [Inelegance 26-3 P
IMPOSE. Of elephants. But to impose is not [NSF 403-22
  Not to impose, not to have reasoned at all, [NSF 404-2
IMPOSED. Before the horses, clouds of bronze imposed [Old Woman
    43-7 P
IMPOSES. He imposes orders as he thinks of them, [NSF 403-16
  Imposes power by the power of his form. [Orb 443-6
IMPOSING. Imposing his separation, [Soldier 97-5
  Imposing forms they cannot describe, [Sad Gay 122-8
IMPOSSIBLE. The sweep of an impossible elegance, [Prelude 195-4
  An impossible aberration with the moon, [Bottle 239-11
  Her no and no made yes impossible. [Uruguay 249-15
  The impossible possible philosophers' man, [Oboe 250-18
  It was impossible to breathe at Durand-Ruel's. [Holiday 312-14
  Today; and the transcripts of feeling, impossible [NH 479-17
  A world impossible for poets, who [Burnshaw 48-17 P
  Hybrids impossible to the wardens [Stan Hero 84-6 P
IMPOTENCY. Cold with an under impotency that they know, [Bouquet
    449-9
IMPOTENT. And impotent, like the imagination seeking [Cats 368-3
  The spirits of all the impotent dead, seen clear, [Cats 368-8
IMPOUNDING. That lay impounding the Pacific swell, [Geneva 24-2

IMPOVERISHED. The impoverished architects appear to be [NH 469-23
  The impoverished waste with dewy vibrancies [Greenest 58-23 P
IMPRECISION. Of the tired romance of imprecision. [Adult 353-8
IMPRESARIO. See cricket-impresario.
IMPRESCRIPTIBLE. The imprescriptible zenith, free of harangue,
  [What We 459-15
IMPRESSED. Granted the Picts impressed us otherwise [Nigger 155-1
IMPRIMATUR. Imprimatur. But then there's common fortune, [Hero
  275-7
IMPRISONED. His spirit is imprisoned in constant change. [NH 472-12
  But ours is not imprisoned. It resides [NH 472-13
IMPROVE. To improve the sewers in Jerusalem, [MBG 174-1
IMPROVISATION. Of its improvisation until, at length, [Pastor
  379-10
IMPROVISATIONS. Of improvisations and seasons of belief. [Extracts
  255-24
  The improvisations of the cuckoos [Hero 275-14
IMPROVISES. As one improvises, on the piano. [Vari 233-19
IMPUGNING. What misanthrope, impugning heroica, [Stan Hero 84-23 P
IMPURE. Impure upon a world unpurged. [How Live 125-10
  In this chamber the pure sphere escapes the impure [NH 480-3
INABILITY. This inability to find a sound, [Extracts 256-13
INACCESSIBLE. Of inaccessible Utopia. [MBG 179-10
  Toward an inaccessible, pure sound. [Montra 263-16
  We are part of a fraicheur, inaccessible [Nuns 93-1 P
INACTIVE. His active force in an inactive dirge, [C 41-15
  Inactive in his singular respect. [NH 474-15
INAMORATA. Seen as inamorata, of loving fame [NH 484-14
  But, here, the inamorata, without distance [NH 484-16
INANIMATE. The inanimate, difficult visage. Who is it? [NSF 388-24
  Inanimate in an inert savoir. [Plain 502-12
INAPPROPRIATE. A most inappropriate man [Sailing 120-9
INARTICULATE. That never touch with inarticulate pang? [Sunday
  69-19
  And remains inarticulate, horses with cream. [Burnshaw 47-3 P
INAUDIBLY. Tap skeleton drums inaudibly. [Dutch 290-7
IN-BAR. These are within what we permit, in-bar [EM 317-22
  Of ex-bar, in-bar retaining attributes [EM 317-24
INCALCULABLE. Is well, incalculable balances, [NSF 386-11
INCALCULABLY. By the incalculably plural. Hence [Descrip 340-9
INCANTATION. Should have an incantation. And again, [C 39-4
  An incantation that the moon defines [Havana 145-5
  An infinite incantation of our selves [Havana 145-8
  Like an instinctive incantation. [Dutch 291-12
  Another chant, an incantation, as in [EM 321-5
INCANTATIONS. By the terrible incantations of defeats [Men Made
  356-3
INCAPABLE. Incapable master of all force, [Negation 97-17
  Incapable of belief, in the difference. [Extracts 258-13
  We are ignorant men incapable [Crude 305-18
  He must be incapable of speaking, closed, [Less 327-15
INCAPABLY. And capable of incapably evil thought: page 423-1
INCESSANT. That splatters incessant thousands of drops, [Hartford
  226-9
  Each night, an incessant butcher, whose knife [Dutch 292-18
  Were being alive, an incessant being alive, [Rock 526-8
INCESSANTLY. To live incessantly in change. See how [Burnshaw
  50-17 P
INCH. Men are part both in the inch and in the mile. [Rome 508-10
  To the camellia-chateaux and an inch beyond, [Duck 60-14 P
  True, only an inch, but an inch at a time, and inch [Duck 60-19P
  By inch, Sunday by Sunday, many men. [Duck 60-20 P
  In the first inch of night, the stellar summering [Pagoda 92-3 P
  Always and always, the difficult inch, [Ulysses 103-16 P
INCHED. Single, of burly ivory, inched of gold, [Greenest 55-6 P
INCHES. By inches-- [Soldat 12-12 P
INCHINGS. These are the edgings and inchings of final form, [NH
  488-16
INCHLING. Begone! An inchling bristles in these pines, [Bantams
  76-2
INCHLINGS. You ten-foot poet among inchlings. Fat! [Bantams 76-2
INCHOATE. Shiftings of an inchoate crystal tableau, [Someone 86-21A
INCHWORM. Is more than a seven-foot inchworm [Jersey 210-11
INCIDENT. To which all poems were incident, unless [C 36-22
INCIPIENCIES. The slight incipiencies, of which the form, [Someone
  87-8 A
INCIPIENT. And if we ate the incipient colorings [Rock 526-16
  In an always incipient cosmos, [July 115-3 P
INCIPIT. Incipit and a form to speak the word [NSF 387-5
INCISIVE. To believe? Incisive what, the fellow [Hero 275-20
INCITING. The crow, inciting various modes. [Vari 233-15
INCLUDE. Between, but of. He chose to include the things [NSF
  403-13
INCLUDED. That in each other are included, the whole, [NSF 403-14
  Included, the spirit that goes roundabout [NH 471-23
  And through included, not merely the visible, [NH 471-24
INCLUDES. That's world enough, and more, if one includes [Havana
  143-25
  Includes death and the imagination. [Degen 444-9
INCLUDING. The Whole World Including the Speaker [NE Verses

  104-title 1
  Including pain, which, otherwise, is false. [EM 323-22
  Including the removes toward poetry. [Papini 447-6
  "This as Including That" [88-title P
INCOGNITO. Incognito, the column in the desert, [Descrip 343-20
INCOGNITOS. And away, dialogues between incognitos. [Sombre 67-12P
INCOMINCIA. Or the sound of Incomincia had been set, [NH 482-24
INCOMMUNICABLE. From beasts or from the incommunicable mass. [Less
  328-6
INCOMPLETE. Composed, appropriate to the incomplete, [Repet 309-13
INCOMPLICATE. Lay grovelling. Triton incomplicate with that [C 28-29
INCONCEIVABLE. The inconceivable idea of the sun. [NSF 380-14
INCONSTANCY. In a universe of inconstancy. This means [NSF 389-24
INCONSTANT. Are inconstant objects of inconstant cause [NSF 389-23
  Night-blue is an inconstant thing. The seraph [NSF 390-1
  Dressed high in heliotrope's inconstant hue, [Bad Time 427-6
INCORRIGIBLE. The action of incorrigible tragedy. [Dutch 292-21
INCREASE. But spreads an evil lustre whose increase [Spaniard
  34-12 P
  To which the spirit ascended, to increase [Greenest 53-29 P
  Itself, beyond the utmost increase come [Greenest 53-30 P
INCREASED. It was increased, enlarged, made simple, [Gigan 289-13
  As if all his hereditary lights were suddenly increased [Prol
  517-1
  These images return and are increased, [Soldat 13-15 P
  It is the nature of its creator increased, [Myth 118-12 P
  The profusion of metaphor has been increased. [Someons 83-3 A
INCREASES. Increases the aspects of experience, [Papini 447-19
INCREDIBLE. Incredible to prudes, the mint of dirt, [C 31-21
  Hinting incredible hues, four selfsame lights [C 45-8
  Of incredible colors ex, ex and ex and out? [Liadoff 347-3
  To most incredible depths. I speak below [John 437-9
  As that which was incredible becomes, [NH 470-14
  You brought the incredible calm in ecstasy, [Red Kit 30-17 P
  From which the incredible systems spring, [Ulysses 103-19 P
  Of the incredible subjects of poetry. [Someone 85-13 A
  He was willing they should remain incredible, [Someone 85-14 A
  Because the incredible, also, has its truth, [Someone 85-15 A
  The incredible gave him a purpose to believe. [Someone 85-18 A
INDECIPHERABLE. An indecipherable cause. [Thirteen 93-18
INDEFINITE. The spirit's speeches, the indefinite, [NH 466-18
INDETERMINATE. And there are indeterminate moments [Three 131-1 P
INDIAN. On what strange froth does the gross Indian dote, [C 38-1
  The Indian, but the Indian struck [Cuban 64-18
  The Indian struck and disappeared. [Cuban 65-4
  West Indian, the extremest power [Hero 276-2
  Your great-grandfather was an Indian fighter. [Extraord 369-9
  The moving grass, the Indian in his glade. [AA 412-3
  See West-Indian.
INDIAN RIVER. "Indian River" [112-title
  The trade-wind jingles the rings in the nets around the racks by
  the docks on Indian River. [Indian 112-4
INDIANS. The bass lie deep, still afraid of the Indians. [Think
  356-8
INDICATE. To indicate the total leaflessness. [NH 477-9
INDIFFERENCE. Half desire for indifference about the sky. [Extracts
  257-3
  Unless indifference to deeper death [EM 319-4
  That is part of the indifference of the eye [NH 475-18
INDIFFERENCES. Out of all the indifferences, into one thing: [Final
  524-6
INDIFFERENT. Was not indifferent to smart detail. [C 38-30
  Indifferent to the tepid summer cold, [C 43-2
  Not this dividing and indifferent blue. [Sunday 68-11
  The time of year has grown indifferent. [Pharynx 96-1
  At the roots of her indifferent curls. [Thought 184-14
  Indifferent sounds and not the heraldic-ho [Repet 307-20
  It is pain that is indifferent to the sky [EM 315-4
  Here in the west indifferent crickets chant [EM 321-3
  Through our indifferent crises. Yet we require [EM 321-4
  Composed of a sight indifferent to the eye. [Descrip 343-22
  Confessing the taciturn and yet indifferent, [Wom Sun 445-14
  Indifferent to what it sees. The tink-tonk [NH 475-19
  At this indifferent experience, [Good Bad 33-13 P
  It is not enough that you are indifferent, [Burnshaw 50-12 P
  The passion, indifferent to the poet's hum, [Sombre 71-25 P
INDIGENCE. Their indigence is an indigence [Leben 505-1
  That is an indigence of the light, [Leben 505-2
INDIGENES. Playing cards. In a village of the indigenes, [Glass
  198-3
  Imagined among the indigenes [Ulysses 101-6 P
INDIGENOUS. With his own quill, in its indigenous dew, [C 31-19
INDIGO. Stooping in indigo gown [Venereal 48-12
  You dream of women, swathed in indigo, [Polish Aunt 84-9
  Beyond the oyster-beds, indigo [Hero 274-26
  "The Indigo Glass in the Grass" [22-title P
  This bottle of indigo glass in the grass, [Indigo 22-11 P
  And blacken into indigo. [Stan MBG 73-14 P
INDIRECTLY. Of statement, directly and indirectly getting at,
  [NH 488-18

INDIVIDUAL. Are a multitude of individual pomps [Paisant 334-22
INDIVIDUALS. Of the war between individuals. In time, [Bship 77-18P
INDOLENCE. Of ocean, perfected in indolence, [Sea Surf 102-4
INDOLENT. That the hours of his indolent, arid days, [Frogs 78-10
  The indolent progressions of the swans [Havana 143-8
  Of indolent summer not quite physical [Bouquet 451-15
  Rising from indolent coils. If the statue rose, [Greenest 54-24P
INDUCED. Induced by what you will: the entrails [Hero 275-8
  And common fortune, induced by nothing, [Hero 275-11
INDULGED. Unpurged by epitaph, indulged at last, [High-Toned 59-10
INDULGENCE. A pleasure, an indulgence, an infatuation. [Nigger
  158-9
  Indulgence out of all celestial sight. [EM 318-17
INDULGENCES. And sinking down to the indulgences [C 35-12
INDULGENT. The stopper to indulgent fatalist [C 44-9
IN-DWELLING. Whether in-dwelling haughty clouds, frigid [Burnshaw
  47-15 P
INDYTERRANEAN. Only Indyterranean [Analysis 348-9
INELEGANCE. This vast inelegance may seem the blankest desolation,
  [Inelegance 25-13 P
  "This Vast Inelegance" [25-title P
INERT. Inanimate in an inert savoir. [Plain 502-12
INESCAPABLE. Of that wide water, inescapable. [Sunday 70-21
  And lucid, inescapable rhythms; [Thirteen 94-2
  Inescapable romance, inescapable choice [NH 468-10
  Of inescapable force, itself a fate. [Spaniard 34-20 P
INEVITABLE. A space grown wide, the inevitable blue [Orb 440-21
  Down-pouring, up-springing and inevitable, [NH 465-17
  As of a long, inevitable sound, [NH 482-7
  Had to be imagined as an inevitable knowledge, [Plain 503-7
  Fixes itself in its inevitable bush . . . [Conversat 108-15 P
INEVITABLY. Inevitably modulating, in the blood. [NSF 407-20
INEXACTNESSES. The exact rock where his inexactnesses [Poem Mt
  512-11
INEXHAUSTIBLE. Again, an inexhaustible being, rise [NSF 390-13
INEXPLICABLE. A space of stone, of inexplicable base [Thought
  185-9
INEXQUISITE. In the inexquisite eye. Why, then, inquire [NH 468-19
INEXTRICABLY. False, faded and yet inextricably there, [Study I
  463-15
INFALLIBLE. One thing remaining, infallible, would be [Beard 247-18
INFANCY. Are dissolved as in an infancy of blue snow. [Discov 95-11P
INFANT. Infant, it is enough in life [Red Fern 365-13
  The way the drowsy, infant, old men do. [Questions 463-3
  It is the infant A standing on infant legs, [NH 469-7
  A jar of the shoots of an infant country, green [Someone 83-15 A
INFANTA. "Infanta Marina" [7-title
  A comic infanta among the tragic drapings, [Slug 522-12
  And Rosa, the muslin dreamer of satin and cowry-kin, disdaining
  the empty keys; and the young infanta, [Piano 22-3 P
INFANTINE. Now like a ballet infantine in awkward steps, [Burnshaw
  47-18 P
INFANTINES. An image that begot its infantines, [NH 479-7
INFANTRY. Loosing black slaves to make black infantry, [Greenest
  56-9 P
INFANTS. Infants yet eminently old, then dome [C 43-26
  It is the infants of misanthropes [Cortege 80-11
  And the infants of nothingness [Cortege 80-12
INFATUATION. A pleasure, an indulgence, an infatuation. [Nigger 158-9
INFECTED. When the sky is blue. The blue infected will. [C 40-18
  This foundling of the infected past, so bright, [NSF 388-11
  Infected by unreality, rapt round [Duck 62-5 P
INFERIOR. That the rocket was only an inferior cloud. [Liadoff
  347-16
INFERNAL. To the fatuous. These are his infernal walls, [Thought
  185-8
INFERNALE. "Infernale" [24-title P
INFIDEL. Are one, and here, O terra infidel. [EM 315-13
INFILTRATIONS. Its infiltrations? There had been an age [Someone
  85-2 A
INFINITE. His infinite repetition and alloys [Havana 144-15
  An infinite incantation of our selves [Havana 145-8
  Of an infinite course. The flowers against the wall [AA 412-8
  The infinite of the actual perceived, [Bouquet 451-19
  Of the well-thumbed, infinite pages of her masters, who will
  seem old to her, requiting less and less her feeling: [Piano
  22-7 P
INFLECTIONS. The beauty of inflections [Thirteen 93-8
INFLEXIBLE. Than nakedness, standing before an inflexible [NSF
  396-2
INFLUENCE. And potent, an influence felt instead of seen. [Owl 435-7
  A light, a power, the miraculous influence. [Final 524-9
INFOLDED. Through choirs infolded to the outmost clouds? [C 41-18
INFORM. And they: these men, and earth and sky, inform [Orb 441-15
INFORMATIONS. Each other by sharp informations, sharp, [Orb 441-16
INFURIATES. If it is misery that infuriates our love, [NH 467-1
INFURIATIONS. And spring's infuriations over and a long way [Cred
  372-5
INGENIOUS. What pistache one, ingenious and droll, [Sea Surf 102-5
INGENUE. And tell the divine ingénue, your companion, [Lilacs 48-20

INGOTS. Or melt Arcturus to ingots dropping drops, [Page 423-3
INHABIT. Inhabit the hypnosis of that sphere. [NH 480-9
INHABITANT. His goldenest demoiselle, inhabitant, [C 44-11
  The last island and its inhabitant, [Vari 235-1
  He became an inhabitant, obedient [Quiet 523-5
  Inhabitant, in less than shape, of shapes [Sombre 67-15 P
  Its inhabitant and elect expositor. [Someone 83-10 A
INHABITANTS. The inhabitants of a very varnished green. [NSF 383-16
  "One of the Inhabitants of the West" [503-title
INHABITS. It is a ghost that inhabits a cloud, [Lack 303-9
  The abstraction. He inhabits another man, [Americana 94-10 P
INHALATION. One breathed the cold evening, the deepest inhalation
  [Extracts 258-20
INHALATIONS. To the first autumnal inhalations, young broods
  [Cred 372-6
  With the inhalations of original cold [NH 481-10
INHALE. Here I inhale profounder strength [MBG 180-15
  Inhale the purple fragrance. It becomes [News 265-8
  We descend to the street and inhale a health of air [NH 470-17
INHALED. He inhaled the rancid rosin, burly smells [C 36-7
  A consciousness from solitude, inhaled [Choc 298-8
  Inhaled the appointed odor, while the doves [NSF 389-14
INHALES. Sleepless, inhales his proper air, and rests. [Cred 373-24
INHERENT. Upon his lap, like their inherent sphere, [C 45-27
  And it does; a law of inherent opposites, [Connois 215-9
  Perhaps there are times of inherent excellence, [NSF 386-9
  Or else an inherent order active to be [Orb 442-12
  Is active with a power, an inherent life, [Moonlight 531-20
INHERITED. In the inherited garden, a second-hand [Extraord 369-19
INHIBITED. Nor fined for the inhibited instruments [C 35-20
INHIBITING. Like a woman inhibiting passion [Soldat 12-2 P
INHUMAN. Jove in the clouds had his inhuman birch. [Sunday 67-27
  Inhuman, of the veritable ocean. [Key W 128-17
  Deepen the feelings to inhuman depths. [Parochial 191-10
  Hoot how the inhuman colors fell [Vase 247-1
  Accelerations that seem inhuman. [Hero 279-4
  As from an inhuman elevation [Gigan 289-18
  And origin, an inhuman person, [Gigan 289-19
  Of an inhuman author, who meditates [Cred 377-22
  Changed his true flesh to an inhuman bronze. [NSF 391-19
  The inhuman brother so much like, so near, [Owl 434-8
  He is the inhuman son and she, [Pecul 454-2
  The world? The inhuman as human? That which thinks not, [Aug 493-3
  In an inhuman meditation, larger than her own. [World 521-5
  A part of the inhuman more, [Ulysses 105-2 P
  The still inhuman more, and yet [Ulysses 105-3 P
  An inhuman of our features, known [Ulysses 105-4 P
  And unknown, inhuman for a little while, [Ulysses 105-5 P
  Inhuman for a little, lesser time." [Ulysses 105-6 P
  And inhuman same, the likeness of things unlike. [Conversat 109-2P
  The inhuman making choice of a human self. [Ideal 89-12 A
INIMICAL. The inimical music, the enchantered space [Pure 330-14
INK. Of wire, the designs of ink, [Common 221-18
INKLINGS. Found inklings of your bond to all that dust. [Monocle
  15-6
INNATE. An intercessor by innate rapport, [Extracts 254-9
  Compelled thereto by an innate music. [Hero 277-18
  To an innate grandiose, an innate light, [Descrip 342-17
INNER. that reflects neither my face nor any inner part [Nuances
  18-9
  The outer captain, the inner saint, [Thought 185-26
  An inner miracle and sun-sacrament, [Montra 262-5
  She was a self that knew, an inner thing, [Owl 435-14
  Is a drop of lightning in an inner world, [Bouquet 448-6
  That it is wholly an inner light, that it shines [NH 481-19
  In the heavy drum of speech, the inner men [NH 488-9
  The inner direction on which we depend, [Ulysses 100-15 P
INNERMOST. The innermost good of their seeking [Homunculus 27-1
  But nakedness, woolen massa, concerns an innermost atom. [Nudity
  Cap 145-10
INNOCENCE. What pulpy dram distilled of innocence, [C 38-3
  That marries her innocence thus, [Lilacs 49-3
  There is no such thing as innocence in autumn, [Nigger 157-12
  Yet, it may be, innocence is never lost. [Nigger 157-13
  An innocence of an absolute, [Crud 305-13
  He might die was the innocence of living, if life [EM 322-6
  There may be always a time of innocence. [AA 418-4
  There is or may be a time of innocence [AA 418-10
  A saying out of a cloud, but innocence. [AA 418-20
  An innocence of the earth and no false sign [AA 418-21
  Almost as part of innocence, almost, [AA 420-2
  The nurses of the spirit's innocence. [Luther 461-9
  Beneath the innocence [Inhab 504-14
  The childish onslaughts of such innocence, [Good Bad 33-19 P
  An innocence approaching toward its peak. [Pagoda 92-6 P
INNOCENT. In the innocent air. [Peacocks 58-26
  I have wiped away moonlight like mud. Your innocent ear [Uruguay
  249-5
  Itself was innocent. To say that it was [EM 322-7
  As if the innocent mother sang in the dark [AA 419-1

Of the work, in the idiom of an innocent earth, [AA 419-5
The final theft? That you are innocent [Red Kit 30-23 P
INNUENDOES. Or the beauty of innuendoes. [Thirteen 93-9
INQUIETUDE. Stooped in a night of vast inquietude. [Spaniard 34-14P
INQUIRE. In the inexquisite eye. Why, then, inquire [NH 468-19
INQUISITOR. Chosen by an inquisitor of structures [Rome 510-27
INQUISITORIAL. Of hum, inquisitorial botanist, [C 28-10
INSATIABLE. Forsook the insatiable egotist. The sea [C 30-3
    Insatiable, [Venereal 48-3
    And, like an insatiable actor, slowly and [Of Mod 240-6
    Is as insatiable as the sun's. The bird [EM 318-10
    Made of the eye an insatiable intellect. [Greenest 57-1 P
INSCRIBE. Lean encyclopaedists, inscribe an Iliad. [NE Verses 104-9
    The mountains inscribe themselves upon the walls. [Extracts
        252-12
INSCRIBED. And, being full of the caprice, inscribed [C 37-24
    There is nothing more inscribed nor thought nor felt [Cred 372-14
    That thinks of it is inscribed on walls and stands [Duck 64-3 P
    Have inscribed life's do and don't. The commanding codes [Recit
        86-11 P
INSCRIBES. Being small, inscribes ferocious alphabets, [Pure 332-23
    Inscribes a primitive astronomy [NSF 383-3
INSCRIPTION. Reading the lordly language of the inscription, [Mice
    123-7
    Writing and reading the rigid inscription. [Aug 495-16
INSCRUTABLE. Inscrutable hair in an inscrutable world. [C 27-21
INSECTS. This auditor of insects! He that saw [C 31-2
    Flying like insects of fire in a cavern of night, [Horn 230-18
    Like insects in the depths of the mind, that kill [Extracts 254-14
    As of insects or cloud-stricken birds, away [Sombre 67-11 P
INSENSIBLE. To shrink to an insensible, [Adequacy 243-19
INSEPARABLE. Inseparable from their afternoons; [Curtains 62-4
INSIDE. We make, although inside an egg, [Aug 490-1
    Nor are you now, in this wakefulness inside a sleep. [Slug 522-18
    On the altar, growing toward the lights, inside. [Armor 529-7
    Inside our queer chapeaux, we seem, on this bank, [Nuns 92-15 P
    A way of pronouncing the word inside of one's tongue [Bus 116-13P
INSIDIOUS. For these the musicians make insidious tones, [AA 415-10
INSIGHT. Perhaps, these colors, seen in insight, assume [Bouquet
    451-22
    By sight and insight as they are. There is no [NH 473-22
    The secretions of insight. [Aug 492-15
    And possesses by sincere insight [Ulysses 103-4 P
    The few things, the objects of insight, the integrations [Local
        112-7 P
INSINUATIONS. Insinuations of desire, [Ord Women 11-25
INSIPID. And pick the strings of our insipid lutes! [Sunday 69-24
    Torn from insipid summer, for the mirror of cold, [Dwarf 208-12
    Dry seconds and insipid thirds, [Arcades 225-25
    And the dewiest beads of insipid fruit [Stan MBG 72-8 P
INSOLENT. These insolent, linear peels [Bananas 53-21
INSOLID. By the sea, insolid rock, stentor, and said: [Two V 353-12
    There was an insolid billowing of the solid. [Real 111-1 P
INSOLUBLE. The same insoluble lump. The fatalist [C 45-17
INSPECTING. Inspecting the cabildo, the façade [C 32-15
INSPIRATION. If platitude and inspiration are alike [Duck 63-3 P
INSTALLMENTS. One-half of all its installments paid. [MBG 182-2
INSTANCE. Of his own fate an instance of all fate? [C 41-24
    Now, you, for instance, are of this mode: You say [Conversat
        108-17 P
INSTANCES. If these rude instances impeach themselves [C 38-6
    These are the broadest instances. Crispin, [C 38-28
    These are merely instances. [Theory 87-4
    Millions of instances of which I am one. [Repet 309-15
INSTANT. Encore un instant de bonheur. The words [Nigger 157-14
    That is an instant nature, brilliantly. [Choc 301-13
    The instant of the change that was the poem, [Liadoff 347-5
    Of the instant to perceive, after the shock, [Liadoff 347-15
    Snow glistens in its instant in the air, [Pieces 351-12
    Instant of millefiori bluely magnified-- [Pieces 351-13
    Is not and, therefore, is. In the instant of speech, [Orb 440-14
    At heart, within an instant's motion, within [Orb 440-22
    As at a point of central arrival, an instant moment, much or
        little, [Prol 516-8
INSTANTLY. That instantly and in themselves they are gay [Gala
    248-2
INSTEAD. On porpoises, instead of apricots, [C 27-18
    Instead there was this tufted rock [How Live 125-17
    Day hymns instead of constellated rhymes, [Thought 185-18
    Perceived by feeling instead of sense, [Nightgown 214-12
    False as the mind, instead of the fragrance, warm [Horn 230-12
    Pure eye. Instead of allegory, [Hero 279-1
    Instead, outcast, without the will to power [Cats 368-2
    And potent, an influence felt instead of seen. [Owl 435-7
    To the real: to the hotel instead of the hymns [NH 471-11
    Perhaps instead of failing it rejects [NH 477-13
    Instead, or Horace Walpole or Mrs. Thrale. [Lytton 39-20 P
    Suppose, instead of failing, it never comes, [Duck 63-30 P
    For the million, perhaps, two ducks instead of one; [Duck 65-2 P
    For the gaudium of being, Jocundus instead [Sombre 71-29 P

Instead of building ships, in numbers, build [Bship 78-1 P
INSTINCT. Like an intenser instinct. What is it he desires? [Men
    Fall 188-1
    By an instinct for a rainless land, the self [NH 475-23
    The instinct for heaven had its counterpart: [NH 476-1
    The instinct for earth, for New Haven, for his room [NH 476-2
INSTINCTIVE. Like an instinctive incantation. [Dutch 291-12
    Among these the musicians strike the instinctive poem. [AA 415-16
INSTINCTIVELY. Instinctively, not otherwise. [Grotesque 75-5 P
    Of the very body instinctively crying [Stan Hero 84-27 P
INSTITUTES. Spelling out pandects and haggard institutes? [Duck
    62-17 P
INSTRUMENT. The mandoline is the instrument [Men 1000 52-3
    An instrument, twanging a wiry string that gives [Of Mod 240-15
    He that remains plays on an instrument [Extracts 256-4
    In which a wasted figure, with an instrument, [Burghers 362-17
    The spring is hum-drum like an instrument, [Sombre 71-11 P
    The shapings of the instrument [Stan MBG 72-17 P
INSTRUMENTS. Nor fined for the inhibited instruments [C 35-20
    In the beginning, four blithe instruments [C 45-3
    Dew lies on the instruments of straw that you were playing,
        [Fish-Scale 160-17
    Abysmal instruments make sounds like pips [NSF 384-5
    Clawing the sing-song of their instruments. [AA 415-11
    But soothingly, with pleasant instruments, [NH 468-7
    Are the instruments on which to play [Aug 489-5
    The time will come for these children, seated before their long
        black instruments, to strike the themes of love-- [Piano 21-16P
    And these long, black instruments will be so little to them
        that will be needing so much, seeking so much in their music.
        [Piano 22-9 P
    An apparition, twanging instruments [Duck 63-18 P
    Mimics that play on instruments discerned [Sombre 67-26 P
INSURANCE. Ryan's lunch, hatters, insurance and medicines,
    [Thought 185-6
INTACT. The imagination, intact [Analysis 349-2
    By trivial filaments to the thing intact: [Bouquet 450-11
    You rest intact in conscience and intact [Good Bad 33-9 P
INTAGLIOS. Of the shape of eyes, like blunt intaglios, [Greenest
    59-5 P
INTANGIBLE. Intangible arrows quiver and stick in the skin
    [Holiday 313-9
INTEGRATION. Lost in an integration of the martyrs' bones,
    [Uruguay 249-23
    Integration for integration, the great arms [Choc 301-14
INTEGRATIONS. But the integrations of the past are like [Descrip
    342-2
    In the tumult of integrations out of the sky, [Look 518-12
    The few things, the objects of insight, the integrations [Local
        112-7 P
INTEGRITY. The one integrity for him, the one [C 36-20
    Hear hard, gets at an essential integrity. [NH 475-3
INTEGUMENT. The Arachne integument of dead trees, [Vari 234-19
INTELLECT. As his pure intellect applies its laws, [Bird Claws
    82-14
    There must be no questions. It is an intellect [Ulti 429-19
    Not an intellect in which we are fleet: present [Ulti 430-2
    Was the whiteness that is the ultimate intellect, [Owl 433-20
    Made of the eye an insatiable intellect. [Greenest 57-1 P
INTELLECTUAL. To be an intellectual structure. The cause [EM 324-30
INTELLIGENCE. Be not an intelligence, [Nuances 18-15
    Nota: man is the intelligence of his soil, [C 27-7
    Nota: his soil is man's intelligence. [C 36-24
    And, from their stale intelligence released, [C 37-9
    To make a new intelligence prevail? [C 37-10
    But of that as its intelligence, [MBG 175-14
    For the spirit left helpless by the intelligence. [News 265-10
    Beyond intelligence, an artificial man [Creat 311-3
    The intelligence of his despair, express [EM 314-22
    To accomplish the truth in his intelligence. [EM 321-22
    Was it that--a sense and beyond intelligence? [Pure 331-10
    Intelligence? On what does the present rest? [Pure 331-12
    The poem must resist the intelligence [Man Car 350-13
    He shares the confusions of intelligence. [Papini 446-12
    In a stubborn literacy, an intelligence, [Bouquet 452-11
    Imaginary poles whose intelligence [NH 479-8
    The peace of the last intelligence; [Aug 490-22
    He that in this intelligence [Aug 491-2
    And trees that lack the intelligence of trees. [R Conn 533-6
    Perception as an act of intelligence [Lytton 39-6 P
    Whose shining is the intelligence of our sleep. [Someone 84-11 A
INTELLIGENT. An accretion from ourselves, intelligent [Creat 311-2
    A text of intelligent men [Aug 495-13
    And move the night by their intelligent motes. [Red Kit 32-1 P
INTELLIGIBLE. Their intelligible twittering [Hermit 505-20
    Itself, the presence of the intelligible [Armor 529-15
INTEND. I still intend things as they are. [Stan MBG 73-4 P
    Of which I am the captain. Given what I intend, [Bship 78-4 P
INTENDED. And things beyond resemblance there was this and that
    intended to be recognized, [Prol 516-13

The one moonlight, the various universe, intended [Moonlight
  532-3
In which the bliss of clouds is mark of an intended meeting
  [Inelegance 25-15 P
A revelation not yet intended. [Region 115-12 P
INTENDING. Makers without knowing, or intending, uses. [New Set
  352-15
INTENDS. Of an obvious acid is sure what it intends [NSF 390-8
INTENSE. Of the intense poem [Cortege 81-1
  Are the eye grown larger, more intense. [Vari 234-20
  One understands, in the intense disclosures [Lack 303-15
INTENSELY. And hearing a tale one wanted intensely to hear,
  [Letters 107-12 P
INTENSER. In an intenser calm, [Paltry 6-7
  Like an intenser instinct. What is it he desires? [Men Fall 188-1
  In this rigid room, an intenser love, [Dezem 218-17
  Intenser than any actual life could be, [Descrip 344-20
INTENSEST. That music is intensest which proclaims [Fictive 88-2
  This is, therefore, the intensest rendezvous. [Final 524-4
INTENSIFIED. Intensified and grandiose, but among [Greenest 57-4 P
INTENSITY. The measure of the intensity of love [Monocle 14-26
INTENT. And more than free, elate, intent, profound [C 33-10
  And men like Crispin like them in intent, [C 42-23
  The preparation is long and of long intent [Nigger 158-4
  The sparrow requites one, without intent. [Vari 233-16
  The moonlight? Was it a rider intent on the sun, [Uruguay 249-20
  He makes the tenderest research, intent [EM 318-5
  Intent on your particles of nether-do, [Rome 509-17
  And the shoulders turn, breathing immense intent. [Sombre 68-27P
INTENTIONS. The intentions of a mind as yet unknown, [Descrip
  341-18
  The voluble intentions of the symbols, [Aug 492-13
INTENTLY. Here the eye fastens intently to these lines [Bouquet
  450-16
INTERCEPT. Making your heart of brass to intercept [Good Bad 33-18P
INTERCESSOR. An intercessor by innate rapport, [Extracts 254-9
INTERCHANGE. And you. Only we two may interchange [Re-state 146-4
INTERCOURSE. In the universal intercourse. [MBG 177-6
INTERCROSSED. Shines without fire on columns intercrossed,
  [Burnshaw 49-12 P
  Because time moves on columns intercrossed [Burnshaw 50-13 P
INTEREST. It is of no interest to hermits [Three 133-24 P
INTERESTED. Who have always interested me most, [Lytton 38-9 P
INTERESTS. What interests me most is the people [Lytton 38-8 P
INTERIOR. Is an interior ocean's rocking [Jasmine 79-11
  The sun. The interior of a parasol, [Phenom 287-10
  Might call the common self, interior fons. [Choc 301-1
  Night is the nature of man's interior world? [Feo 333-14
  We must enter boldly that interior world [Feo 333-16
  We say that it is man's interior world [Feo 334-6
  For an interior made exterior [NH 481-7
  Interior: breathless things broodingly abreath [NH 481-9
  Like interior intonations, [Aug 490-19
  "Final Soliloquy of the Interior Paramour" [524-title
  Night and silence disturbed by an interior sound, [Moonlight
  532-2
  Pierce the interior with pouring shafts, [Archi 18-3 P
  Some true interior to which to return, [Letters 107-5 P
INTERIORS. Of the high interiors of the sea. [Paltry 5-15
INTERMEDIATE. Rejecting intermediate parts, [Negation 97-15
INTERMINABLE. The interminable adventurer? The trees are mended.
  [World 520-12
INTERMINABLY. A wave, interminably flowing. [Peter 92-3
INTERMITTED. Birds of intermitted bliss, [Phases 4-9 P
INTERPRET. Already the new-born children interpret love [Carolinas
  4-15
INTERPRETATIONS. In its interpretations voluble, [Bouquet 451-9
INTERPRETERS. What word have you, interpreters, of men [Heaven 56-9
  The immaculate interpreters of life. [NH 469-18
INTERRUPT. One might meet Konstantinov, who would interrupt [EM
  325-10
INTERRUPTED. A dream interrupted out of the past, [Sketch 336-8
INTERRUPTIONS. With interruptions by vast hymns, blood odes,
  [Duck 66-1 P
INTERTWINED. So intertwined with serpent-kin encoiled [C 32-3
INTIMATE. In couch, four more personae, intimate [C 45-5
INTIMATION. Steel against intimation--the sharp flash, [Motive
  288-19
INTIMATIONS. From the bombastic intimations of winter [Contra II
  270-8
  Illustrious intimations--uncertain love, [Myrrh 350-8
INTOLERABLE. The immediate and intolerable need [Stan Hero 84-26 P
INTONATIONS. And intonations of the trees? [Sonatina 110-4
  Like interior intonations, [Aug 490-19
INTONE. And in their music showering sounds intone. [C 37-32
INTONED. A fate intoned, a death before they die, [Thought 186-15
INTONES. Intones its single emptiness, [Possum 294-11
  The priest of nothingness who intones-- [Including 88-6 P
INTONING. The romantic intoning, the declaimed clairvoyance [NSF
  387-19

INTONINGS. It is like a region full of intonings. [Hartford 226-17
INTRICACIES. The intricacies of appearance, when perceived.
  [Papini 447-17
INTRICATE. His apprehension, made him intricate [C 31-9
  Should make the intricate Sierra scan. [C 38-23
  Four daughters in a world too intricate [C 45-2
  For which the intricate Alps are a single nest. [Connois 216-14
  Made difficult by salt fragrance, intricate. [Bouquet 452-15
  As it is, in the intricate evasions of as, [NH 486-10
  The confusion of men's voices, intricate [Greenest 54-9 P
INTRINSIC. The fabulous and its intrinsic verse [C 31-30
  And North and South are an intrinsic couple [NSF 392-13
INTROSPECTIVE. Of introspective exiles, lecturing. [Monocle 15-16
  Became an introspective voyager. [C 29-23
  No introspective chaos . . . I accept: [Soldat 11-1 P
INTRUSION. Clear and, except for the eye, without intrusion. [NSF
  400-3
INTRUSIONS. The pale intrusions into blue [MBG 172-1
INUNDATIONS. Of life and spring and of the lustrous inundations,
  [Medit 123-14
INVADED.-manity had invaded its seclusion, with its suffering and
  its [Three 129-10 P
INVADES. That humanity never invades. [Three 130-3 P
INVALID. But there was one invalid in that green glade [Pure 331-2
  Regard the invalid personality [Cats 368-1
INVASION. It is the invasion of humanity [Three 132-11 P
  It is the invasion [Three 132-15 P
  I dislike the invasion [Three 133-11 P
INVECTIVE. "Invective against Swans" [4-title
INVENTED. Invented for its pith, not doctrinal [C 45-20
  Of this invention, this invented world, [NSF 380-13
  I had not invented my own thoughts, [Desire 85-7 P
INVENTING. Never suppose an inventing mind as source [NSF 381-1
INVENTION. The good is evil's last invention. Thus [Extracts
  253-11
  Beyond invention. Within what we permit, [EM 317-6
  The invention of a nation in a phrase, [Descrip 345-16
  Of this invention, this invented world, [NSF 380-13
  Of this invention; and yet so poisonous [NSF 381-18
  An invention, an embrace between one desperate clod [Rock 525-13
INVENTIONS. Without the inventions of sorrow or the sob [EM 317-5
  Without a voice, inventions of farewell. [Owl 432-4
INVENTS. The maker of catastrophe invents the eye [Extracts 253-12
INVERSIONS. Blue and its deep inversions in the moon [Repet 309-18
INVESTITURE. Of dense investiture, with luminous vassals. [NH 469-6
INVIDIOUS. The more invidious, the more desired: [C 37-15
INVIGORATED. Flora Lowzen invigorated [Oak 272-18
INVINCIBLE. Compact in invincible foils, from reason, [NSF 388-1
  The wind will command them with invincible sound. [AA 414-3
  Of majesty, of an invincible clou, [NH 473-11
  Not France! France, also, serves the invincible eye, [Soldat 14-9P
  With its final force, a thing invincible [Bship 79-11 P
INVISIBLE. Is an invisible element of that place [Men 1000 52-9
  Yet invisible currents clearly circulate. [Nigger 156-3
  Invisible priest; is it to eject, to pull [Dump 203-9
  Of which, an invisible audience listens, [Of Mod 240-10
  Women invisible in music and motion and color," [Waldorf 241-8
  Consider how the speechless, invisible gods [Montra 262-13
  An invisible gesture. Let this be called [Couch 295-15
  Invisible, they move and are, [Analysis 348-17
  This is the successor of the invisible. [Cred 376-20
  It must be visible or invisible, [NSF 385-19
  Invisible or visible or both: [NSF 385-20
  Invisible change discovers what is changed, [Owl 435-11
  The possible nest in the invisible tree, [John 437-17
  To the nations of the clear invisible, [NH 474-24
  It habituates him to the invisible, [Aug 493-5
  Day's invisible beginner, [Song Fixed 520-7
  Oh, bend against the invisible; and lean [Blanche 10-6 P
  This is invisible. The supporting arms [Sombre 68-24 P
  Now, being invisible, I walk without mantilla, [Souls 94-16 P
  This invisible activity, this sense. [Clear Day 113-19 P
INVISIBLY. Invisibly clear, the only love. [Wom Sun 445-15
INVITATION. Its invitation to false metaphor. [Someone 85-17 A
INVITES. The mother invites humanity to her house [AA 415-4
INVOKE. But I invoke the monotony of monotonies [Demoiselle 23-10P
INVOLVED. Involved him in midwifery so dense [C 43-22
  That the blackbird is involved [Thirteen 94-4
  There is a conflict, there is a resistance involved; [Course
  96-16 P
INVOLVING. While the domes resound with chant involving chant.
  [Ghosts 119-18
  Involving the four corners of the sky, [Ideal 88-4 A
INVULNERABLE. The one invulnerable man among [Rome 510-8
INWARD. The vessel inward. Tilting up his nose, [C 36-6
  An image of the mind, an inward mate, [Pastor 379-18
INWARDLY. Sonorous nutshells rattling inwardly. [C 31-13
  And men look inwardly, for the emblem: [Stan Hero 83-13 P
  Outwardly and knows them inwardly, [Child 106-18 P
INWOVEN. Inwoven by a weaver to twelve bells . . . [Beginning 428-5

IRELAND. "Our Stars Come from Ireland" [454-title
    Over the top of the Bank of Ireland, [Our Stars 454-14
    The stars are washing up from Ireland [Our Stars 455-9
    Of nights full of the green stars from Ireland, [Our Stars 455-14
IRIDESCENCE. And still the grossest iridescence of ocean [NSF 383-7
IRIDESCENCES. Perplexed by its darker iridescences. [Beginning
    427-14
    On a fuchsia in a can--and iridescences [NH 478-14
    Or thinks he does, a carpenter's iridescences, [NH 478-18
IRIDESCENT. In hymns, through iridescent changes, [Hero 279-22
IRIS. The white iris beautifies me. [Carolinas 5-5
    Poured brilliant iris on the glistening blue. [Sea Surf 99-15
    Make a bed and leave the iris in it. [Norfolk 112-3
    Of the iris bore white blooms. The bird then boomed. [Horn 230-10
    A will to make iris frettings on the blank. [NSF 397-18
    Where the bending iris grew; [Phases 4-8 P
    Iris and orange, crimson and green [Mandolin 28-19 P
    The shallowest iris on the emptiest eye. [Sombre 70-4 P
IRISED. Irised in dew and early fragrancies, [C 36-3
    On the irised hunks, the stone bouquet.[Hartford 227-12
    Too wide, too irised, to be more than calm, [Look 518-18
    From cold, slightly irised, slightly bedazzled, [Bus 116-10 P
IRISH. "The Irish Cliffs of Moher" [501-title
IRKED. It irked beyond his patience. Hence it was, [C 39-21
    Irked the wet wallows of the water-spout. [NH 476-6
IRON. In the taste for iron dogs and iron deer. [Nigger 155-2
    The trees were plucked like iron bars [Jumbo 269-1
    The iron settee is cold. [Including 88-15 P
    See cast-iron.
IRONIC. Left only Death's ironic scraping. [Peter 92-10
IRONY. Of an imagination flashed with irony [Greenest 56-16 P
IRRADIATION. Or this, whose music, sweeping irradiation of a sea-
    night, [Inelegance 26-1 P
IRRATIONAL. Who still feels irrational things within her. [Shifts
    83-16
    Irrational moment its unreasoning, [NSF 398-22
    Become the soft-footed phantom, the irrational [NSF 406-18
    Pleased that the irrational is rational, [NSF 406-24
    Its irrational reaction, as from pain. [John 437-26
IRREDUCIBLE. Himself, may be, the irreducible X [Someone 83-8 A
IRREGULAR. And the irregular turquoise, part, the perceptible
    blue [Landsc 242-23
IRREPROACHABLE. By dense unreason, irreproachable force, [Duck
    62-6 P
IRRETRIEVABLE. Upon her irretrievable way. [Paltry 6-10
IRRITATING. Among the more irritating minor ideas [Look 517-11
IRRUPTION. A fantastic irruption. Salute you, cata-sisters, [Souls
    95-2 P
IS. Of was and is and shall or ought to be, [C 40-8
    For him, of shall or ought to be in is. [C 41-9
    For realist, what is is what should be. [C 41-31
    It is what it is as I am what I am: [Re-state 146-2
    A part of what it is . . . Children, [Postcard 159-13
    There he touches his being. There as he is [Yellow 237-4
    He is. The thought that he had found all this [Yellow 237-5
    Without time: as that which is not has no time, [Martial 237-19
    Is not, or is of what there was, is full [Martial 237-20
    Nor of time. The departing soldier is as he is, [Repet 308-7
    Because she is as she was, reality, [EM 322-1
    As the sun is something seeming and it is. [Descrip 339-2
    The direction stops and we accept what is [Cred 374-17
    It knows that what it has is what is not [NSF 382-10
    It feels good as it is without the giant, [NSF 386-1
    He is and may be but oh! he is, he is, [NSF 388-10
    Whiter than wax, sonorous, fame as it is, [NSF 403-19
    It exists, it is visible, it is, it is, [AA 418-18
    To see their lustre truly as it is [Owl 432-21
    In the way what was has ceased to be what is. [Owl 435-12
    By means of a separate sense. It is and it [Orb 440-13
    Is not and, therefore, is. In the instant of speech, [Orb 440-14
    Cloud's gold, of a whole appearance that stands and is. [Bouquet
    452-18
    Except that the grandson sees it as it is, [Questions 462-9
    Participants of its being. It is, we are. [Study I 463-10
    He is, we are. Ah, bella! He is, we are, [Study I 463-11
    Not that which is but that which is apprehended, [NH 468-13
    Transfixing by being purely what it is, [NH 471-17
    The poet speaks the poem as it is, [NH 473-18
    Of a windy night as it is, when the marble statues [NH 473-20
    In the area between is and was are leaves, [NH 474-2
    In which he is and as and is are one. [NH 476-4
    As he has been and is and, with the Queen [NH 485-17
    As it is, in the intricate evasions of as, [NH 486-10
    With what he is and as he is, [Leben 505-8
    The need to be actual and as it is. [Armor 530-10
    That is is dead except what ought to be. [Burnshaw 46-15 P
    That changed in sleep. It is, it is, let be [Sombre 71-15 P
    One feels the life of that which gives life as it is. [Course
    96-18 P
    In that which is and is established . . . It howls [Dove 98-7 P

As he is, the discipline of his scope [Ulysses 101-14 P
    As the total reality. Therefore it is [Someone 87-13 A
ISAAC WATTS. For Isaac Watts: the diverting of the dream [Duck
    65-26 P
ISLAND. A comprehensive island hemisphere. [C 38-14
    Or island solitude, unsponsored, free, [Sunday 70-20
    And island canopies which were entailed [Havana 142-17
    And a little island full of geese and stars: [Sleight 222-15
    The last island and its inhabitant, [Vari 235-1
    On a blue island in a sky-wide water [NSF 393-1
    There was an island beyond him on which rested, [NSF 393-10
    An island to the South, on which rested like [NSF 393-11
    11. There is an island Palahude by name-- [Someone 86-14 A
ISLANDS. And the jasmine islands were bloody martyrdoms. [Oboe
    251-9
ISLE. Neither the golden underground, nor isle [Sunday 68-19
    Romanza out of the black shepherd's isle, [NH 480-13
    Out of the isle, but not of any isle. [NH 480-16
    Close to the senses there lies another isle [NH 480-17
    Gone, as in Calypso's isle or in Citare, [Bship 79-24 P
ISOLATED. In isolated moments--isolations [NH 484-1
ISOLATION. And, in the isolation of the sky, [Sunday 70-25
    An isolation which only the two could share. [AA 419-18
    The opposite of Cythere, an isolation [NH 480-19
    In an isolation, separate [Ulysses 104-32 P
    We came for isolation, [Three 138-15 P
ISOLATIONS. In isolated moments--isolations [NH 484-1
ISSANT. Or these--escent--issant pre-personae: first fly, [Slug
    522-11
ISSUANCE. We give ourselves our likest issuance. [Fictive 88-9
    Devising proud, majestic issuance. [Soldat 14-12 P
ISSUE. Between issue and return, there is [MBG 176-18
    Themselves an issue as at an end, as if [Our Stars 455-21
ISSUED. Issued thin seconds glibly gapering. [Repet 306-13
ISSUES. From this the poem issues and [MBG 176-16
ISSUING. To find of light a music issuing [NSF 398-18
ITALIAN. The Italian girls wore jonquils in their hair [NSF 389-16
    This Italian symbol, this Southern landscape, is like [Study I
    463-7
    The Oklahoman--the Italian blue [NH 476-23
    These English noses and edged, Italian eyes, [Duck 60-22 P
    By poets, the Italian lives preserved [Duck 61-19 P
    For an Italian. [Three 135-14 P
ITALIANATE. Assumes a pale, Italianate sheen-- [Abnormal 24-6 P
ITALICS. But the dark italics it could not propound. [FM 326-6
ITALY. And brown, an Italy of the mind, a place [Burnshaw 48-13 P
ITEM. Item: The cocks crow and the birds cry and [Montra 263-13
    Item: The wind is never rounding O [Montra 263-17
    Item: The green fish pensive in green reeds [Montra 263-20
    Is an absolute. Item: The cataracts [Montra 263-21
    Item: Breathe, breathe upon the centre of [Montra 264-1
ITERATION. And its restless iteration, [Solitaires 60-11
ITHY. We enjoy the ithy oonts and long-haired [Analysis 349-10
ITSELF. That will not declare itself . . . [Magnifico 19-8
    That will not declare itself [Magnifico 19-14
    Autumn's compendium, strident in itself [C 45-23
    Are the soul itself. And the whole of the soul, Swenson, [Lions
    125-2
    To the spirit itself, [Am Sub 131-8
    It must create its colors out of itself. [Nigger 158-2
    Itself not to be I and yet [MBG 171-21
    Yet life itself, the fulfilment of desire [Men Fall 188-3
    So much more than that. The day itself [Poems Clim 193-13
    Solace itself in peevish birds? Is it peace, [Dump 203-4
    It was everything bulging and blazing and big in itself, [Freed
    205-22
    Then there is nothing to think of. It comes of itself; [Rabbit K
    209-13
    Of the mind that forms itself [Bagatelles 213-22
    This great world, it divides itself in two, [Dezem 218-6
    Divide it from itself. It is this or that [Poem Morn 219-2
    As a self that lives on itself. [Thunder 220-20
    Red purple, never quite red itself. [Arcades 225-16
    And round and round goes the water itself [Vari 235-7
    Yet it is this that shall maintain--Itself [Martial 238-6
    It has to persuade that war is part of itself, [Bottle 239-6
    Not to the play, but to itself, expressed [Of Mod 240-11
    Itself had to be supposed, a thing supposed [Landsc 242-8
    Was divine then all things were, the world itself, [Landsc 242-29
    Things were the truth, the world itself was the truth. [Landsc
    242-31
    Was less than moonlight. Nothing exists by itself. [Les Plus
    244-18
    Existed by itself. Or did the saint survive? [Les Plus 245-6
    Of the self that must sustain itself on speech, [Beard 247-17
    And, imageless, it is itself the most, [Montra 263-18
    To be a nature, a place in which itself [Phenom 287-2
    Itself is like a poverty in the space of life, [Choc 299-1
    Is brighter than the sun itself. [Poesie 302-16
    His "That reality secrete itself," [Repet 309-21

Audible at noon, pain torturing itself, [EM 314-4
Were part of a sustenance itself enough, [EM 316-3
And then that Spaniard of the rose, itself [EM 316-16
Itself was innocent. To say that it was [EM 322-7
Itself non-physical, may, by chance, observe [EM 325-22
We grew used so soon, too soon, to earth itself, [Wild 328-16
Itself that seed's ripe, unpredictable fruit. [Descrip 341-20
In description, canon central in itself, [Descrip 345-3
From thought, like a violent pulse in the cloud itself, [Liadoff
   347-7
Exhaling these creations of itself. [Pieces 351-17
In which there is no other meaning, itself [House Q 359-2
Is calm, itself is summer and night, itself [House Q 359-3
As a tone defines itself and separates [Anach 366-12
Presents itself in Oley when the hay, [Cred 374-7
Nor made of itself that which it could not find . . . [Cred
   376-8
The truth itself, the first idea becomes [NSF 381-20
And in the earth itself they found a green-- [NSF 383-15
The spent feeling leaving nothing of itself, [NSF 400-12
Blowing itself upon the tedious ear. [NSF 400-17
A thing final in itself, and, therefore, good: [NSF 405-19
Itself a cloud, although of misted rock [AA 416-5
Except the lavishing of itself in change, [AA 416-10
Does it take its place in the north and enfold itself, [AA 417-8
That of itself stood still, perennial, [Owl 432-24
It is a child that sings itself to sleep, [Owl 436-7
Against itself. At its mercy, we depend [John 436-12
Itself, a nature to its natives all [Orb 442-13
As lightning itself is, likewise, metaphor [Bouquet 448-9
Nothing much, a flitter that reflects itself. [Bouquet 448-13
That in itself it is enough? [Pecul 453-15
It is the earth itself that is humanity . . . [Pecul 454-1
The mirror melts and moulds itself and moves [Novel 458-4
The sun steps into, regards and finds itself; [Golden 460-11
When the image itself is false, a mere desire, [Study I 463-18
The cry that contains its converse in itself, [NH 471-4
At the exactest point at which it is itself, [NH 471-16
Part of the res itself and not about it. [NH 473-17
God in the object itself, without much choice. [NH 475-10
Itself to be imagined. The great pond, [Plain 503-2
The power to transform itself, or else, [Two Illus 514-11
Creates a fresh universe out of nothingness by adding itself,
   [Prol 517-9
That in which space itself is contained, the gate [Rock 528-17
Itself, the presence of the intelligible [Armor 529-15
Than the need of each generation to be itself, [Armor 530-9
"Not Ideas about the Thing but the Thing Itself" [534-title
Not only in itself but in the things [Red Kit 31-6 P
Her music should repeat itself in you. [Red Kit 31-14 P
Of inescapable force, itself a fate. [Spaniard 34-20 P
Is itself old and stale. [Polo 37-15 P
Or, if it understood, repressed itself [Old Woman 44-5 P
Appoints These Marbles Of Itself To Be [Burnshaw 48-6 P
Itself." No more than that, no subterfuge, [Burnshaw 48-7 P
Speak, and in these repeat: To Be Itself, [Burnshaw 52-8 P
Itself into the speech of the spirit, until [Burnshaw 52-10 P
Itself, beyond the utmost increase come [Greenest 53-30 P
Acquired transparence and beheld itself [Greenest 54-6 P
As death itself, and never can be changed [Duck 61-22 P
While the shaggy top collects itself to do [Sombre 68-26 P
Of a generation that does not know itself, [Sombre 68-30 P
The portent may itself be memory; [Sombre 70-10 P
And memory may itself be time to come [Sombre 70-11 P
For itself as a world, [Grotesque 76-15 P
"It is a lesser law than the one itself, [Bship 78-26 P
Unless it is the one itself, or unless [Bship 78-27 P
Coming from the East, forcing itself to the West, [Bship 80-11 P
On life itself and there the katy-dids [Memo 89-7 P
And meditates an image of itself, [Theatre 91-9 P
So long as the mind, for once, fulfilled itself? [Theatre 91-18 P
Asserting itself in an element that is free, [Pagoda 92-1 P
The cricket of summer forming itself out of ice. [Discov 95-14 P
Itself, until, at last, the cry concerns no one at all. [Course
   97-3 P
For that person, and, sometimes, for the world itself. [Conversat
   108-12 P
Fixes itself in its inevitable bush . . . [Conversat 108-15 P
And suddenly denying itself away. [Real 110-18 P
Vermont throws itself together. [July 115-5 P
Finds itself in seclusion, [Three 131-10 P
1. The hut stands by itself beneath the palms. [Someone 86-4 A
Here the total artifice reveals itself [Someone 87-12 A
IVORY. Aloe of ivory, pear of rusty rind.) [Bird Claws 82-5
   Her daughters to the peached and ivory wench [Havana 143-26
   Single, of burly ivory, inched of gold, [Greenest 55-6 P
IVY. Slowly the ivy on the stones [MBG 170-21

JACK. Clog, therefore, purple Jack and crimson Jill. [Nigger 154-6
JACK-RABBIT. "The Jack-Rabbit" [50-title
    The jack-rabbit sang to the Arkansaw. [Jack-Rabbit 50-5
JACKSON. See: Andrew Jackson Something; General Jackson.
JACOB. See John-begat-Jacob.
JACOMYNTJE. And she has peace. My Jacomyntje! [Extraord 369-8
    My Jacomyntje! This first spring after the war, [Extraord 369-16
JADE. Or jade. [Three 129-15 P
    Drink from wise men? From jade? [Three 129-16 P
JADES. Like jades affecting the sequestered bride; [C 34-23
JAFFA. Curious that I should have spoken of Jaffa [Desire 85-4 P
    Or was it Jaffa that created desire? [Desire 85-16 P
JAGGED. So thick with sides and jagged lops of green, [C 32-2
    And over it they set a jagged sign, [Good Man 364-12
    Lean larkspur and jagged fern and rusting rue [Bouquet 452-10
    And through the torrents a jutting, jagged tower, [Greenest 53-6P
    Things jutted up, the way the jagged stacks, [Greenest 53-11 P
JAGUAR. A great jaguar running will make a little sound [Jouga
    337-15
    Too starkly pallid for the jaguar's light, [Greenest 54-29 P
JAGUAR-MEN. There sleep and waking fill with jaguar-men [Greenest
    55-2 P
    Wings spread and whirling over jaguar-men? [Greenest 55-31 P
JAGUARS. To whom the jaguars cry and lions roar [Greenest 55-19 P
JAIMAR LILLYGREEN. Of Jalmar Lillygreen. [Primordia 7-20 P
JAMANDA. Are full of the songs of Jamanda and Carlotta; [Norfolk
    111-17
JANGLE. To a jangle of doom [Cortege 80-26
    The children laugh and jangle a tinny time. [AA 415-12
    As they jangle and dangle and kick their feet. [Luther 462-3
JANGLING. Jangling the metal of the strings . . . [MBG 166-12
    Summer, jangling the savagest diamonds and [Hero 281-2
JANITOR. A languid janitor bears [Public Sq 109-6
    And so the moon, both come, and the janitor's poems [Dump 201-16
JANUAR. And gelid Januar has gone to hell. [Poesie 302-8
JANUARY. Of the January sun; and not to think [Snow Man 10-4
    It is deep January. The sky is hard. [Possum 294-7
    Sharp as white paint in the January sun; [Holiday 312-2
    And chant the January fire [An Gaiety 33-6 P
JAPONICA. And I remember sharp Japonica-- [Soldat 13-11 P
JAR. "Anecdote of the Jar" [76-title
    I placed a jar in Tennessee, [Jar 76-5
    The jar was round upon the ground [Jar 76-11
    The jar was gray and bare. [Jar 76-14
    The bouquet stands in a jar, as metaphor, [Bouquet 448-8
    Turned para-thing, the rudiments in the jar, [Bouquet 452-7
    The rudiments in the jar, farced, finikin, [Bouquet 452-13
    A jar of the shoots of an infant country, green [Someone 83-15 A
JARS. The flawed jars, [Three 131-27 P
JASMINE. "Jasmine's Beautiful Thoughts Underneath the Willow"
    [79-title
    One year, death and war prevented the jasmine scent [Oboe 251-8
    And the jasmine islands were bloody martyrdoms. [Oboe 251-9
    We buried the fallen without jasmine crowns. [Oboe 251-13
    It was not as if the jasmine ever returned. [Oboe 251-15
    In the jasmine haunted forests, that we knew [Oboe 251-20
JASPER. It is not jasper. It is not bone. [Stan MBG 72-5 P
JAUNT. And then to Carolina. Simple jaunt. [C 29-10
JAUNTINESS. Suspended in temporary jauntiness. [Bouquet 448-7
JAUNTY. A creeper under jaunty leaves. And fourth, [C 44-21
JAVA. Like umbrellas in Java. [Tea 113-3
JAVELINS. Full of javelins and old fire-balls, [Dezem 218-3
JAWS. When light comes down to wet his frothy jaws [Glass 197-16
    Master by foot and jaws and by the mane, [NSF 384-10
JAY. And jay, still to the night-bird made their plea, [C 30-19
    The imagined pine, the imagined jay. [MBG 184-6
    Ah, ké! the bloody wren, the felon jay, [NSF 394-1
    He does not lie there remembering the blue-jay, say the jay.
    [Madame 507-11
    See blue-jay.
JEALOUS. And jealous grandeurs of sun and sky [Vase 246-11
    The crude and jealous formlessness [Vase 247-6
    Made subtle by truth's most jealous subtlety, [Someone 84-8 A
JEHOVAH. Jehovah and the great sea-worm. The air [Havana 142-4
JELLY. At breakfast jelly yellow streaked the deck [Sea Surf 99-18
JERKED. It is the mind that is woven, the mind that was jerked
    [Dwarf 208-7
JEROME. This is a facile exercise. Jerome [NSF 398-13
    Jerome and the scrupulous Francis and Sunday women, [Luther 461-8
JERSEY CITY. "Loneliness in Jersey City" [210-title
JERUSALEM. To improve the sewers in Jerusalem, [MBG 174-1
    Those whose Jerusalem is Glasgow-frost [Greenest 59-24 P
JESUS. It is the grave of Jesus, where he lay." [Sunday 70-17
    When the body of Jesus hangs in a pallor, [Lunar 107-5
JETTED. And proclaim it, the white creator of black, jetted [AA
    417-11
    And thus its jetted tragedy, its stele [AA 417-24
JEW. The Jew did not go to his synagogue [Winter B 141-1

He was a Jew from Europe or might have been. [Pure 331-15
JEWEL. Tranquillizing with this jewel [Homunculus 27-5
    Is poverty, whose jewel found [Ulysses 104-13 P
JEWELER. Her pearly ears, her jeweler's ears [Grotesque 74-3 P
JEWELLER. Coiffeur of haloes, fecund jeweller-- [Eve Angels 137-8
JEWELS. The jewels in his beard, the mystic wand, [Bship 79-4 P
JIG. And jig his chits upon a cloudy knee. [C 40-12
JIGGING. The chits came for his jigging, bluet-eyed, [C 43-16
JILL. Clog, therefore, purple Jack and crimson Jill. [Nigger 154-6
JIM. You Jim and you Margaret and you singer of La Paloma, [Fish-
    Scale 161-1
JINGLE. It is the same jingle of the water among the roots under
    the banks of the palmettoes, [Indian 112-5
    It is the same jingle of the red-bird breasting the orange-trees
    out of the cedars. [Indian 112-6
JINGLED. Loftily jingled, radiant, [Ulysses 100-21 P
JINGLES. The trade-wind jingles the rings in the nets around the
    racks by the docks on Indian River. [Indian 112-4
JINGLING. The bride come jingling, kissed and cupped, or else
    [Repet 308-17
    Of this, whose jingling glorias, importunate of perfection,
    [Inelegance 26-3 P
JOB. A majestic weavers' job, a summer's sweat. [Greenest 58-6 P
JOBS. Disclose the rude and ruddy at their jobs [Burnshaw 48-20 P
JOCULAR. Nothing of its jocular procreations? [MBG 183-9
JOCUNDA. Jocunda, who will arrange the roses and rearrange, letting
    the leaves lie on the water-like lacquer; [Piano 22-4 P
JOCUNDISSIMA. The lingua franca et jocundissima. [NSF 397-9
JOCUNDUS. Crash in the mind--But, fat Jocundus, worrying [Glass
    197-20
    For the gaudium of being, Jocundus instead [Sombre 71-29 P
JOHANNISBERGER. The Johannisberger, Hans. [Anything B 211-16
JOHANN SEBASTIAN. He praised Johann Sebastian, as he should.
    [Norfolk 111-15
JOHN. The thesis of the plentifullest John. [Descrip 345-4
    And his son's son John, and-a-one [Soldat 14-19 P
    Lean John, and his son, lean John, [Soldat 15-2 P
    And his lean son's John, and-a-one [Soldat 15-3 P
    Rich John, and his son, rich John, [Soldat 15-6 P
    And his rich son's John, and-a-one [Soldat 15-7 P
    Wise John, and his son, wise John, [Soldat 15-10 P
    And his wise son's John, and-a-one [Soldat 15-11 P
    See: Don John; halo-John; Saint John.
JOHN-BEGAT-JACOB. In the John-begat-Jacob of what we know, [Ulysses
    103-5 P
JOHN CONSTABLE. John Constable they could never quite transplant
    [Nigger 154-20
JOHN ROCKET. And old John Rocket dozes on his pillow. [Phenom
    286-11
JOHN SMITH. John Smith and his son, John Smith, [Soldat 14-18 P
JOHNSONIAN. The Johnsonian composition, abstract man, [Duck 65-13P
JOHN ZELLER. "The Bed of Old John Zeller" [326-title
    Continually. And old John Zeller stands [Two V 354-21
JOIN. To join a hovering excellence, to escape [Rome 509-6
    Yourselves away and at a distance join [Burnshaw 51-15 P
JOINED. The unique composure, harshest streakings joined [Owl
    433-14
    Joined, the triumphant vigor, felt, [Ulysses 100-14 P
    Joined in a triumphant vigor, [Presence 105-23 P
JOINING. Of right joining, a music of ideas, the burning [Study II
    465-1
JOINS. One joins him there for company, [Possum 294-17
    It joins and does not separate. What, then, [Recit 86-21 P
JOINT. Prophetic joint, for its diviner young. [C 43-19
JOLIESSES. Qui fait fi des joliesses banales, the chairs. [Freed
    205-24
JOLLIFIED. Mere blusteriness that gewgaws jollified, [C 44-22
JONQUILS. The Italian girls wore jonquils in their hair [NSF 389-16
JOOST. See Don Joost.
JOSE. That I stay away. These are the words of José . . . [Novel
    457-12
JOSE RODRIGUEZ-FEO. "A Word with José Rodrigues-Feo" [333-title
JOSIE. Bonnie and Josie, [Motion 83-2
JOSTLED. The jostled ferns, where it might be, having eyes [Green-
    est 59-4 P
JOSTLING. That earth was like a jostling festival [C 32-8
JOT. To Cuba. Jot these milky matters down. [Havana 144-6
JOTTED. Like precious scholia jotted down in the dark. [Someone
    84-4 A
JOTTING-DOWN. Than this jotting-down of the sculptor's foppishness
    [Burnshaw 47-11 P
JOUGA. "Jouga" [337-title
JOURNALISM. An understanding beyond journalism, [Bus 116-12 P
JOURNALIST. Gloomily, the journalist confronts [Bus 116-2 P
JOVE. Jove in the clouds had his inhuman birth. [Sunday 67-27
    The statue of Jove among the boomy clouds. [NH 482-19
JOVIAL. Jovial Crispin, in calamitous crape? [C 41-22
    A jovial hullabaloo among the spheres. [High-Toned 59-20
JOY. If joy shall be without a book [Fading 139-11
    Not at the eye but at the joy of it. [MBG 178-7

In which we pronounce joy like a word of our own. [Gala 248-6
Joy of such permanence, right ignorance [Cred 373-12
To speak of joy and to sing of it, borne on [NSF 398-10
The joy of language, when it is themselves. [Orb 441-8
Lucidity of his city, joy of his nation, [Aug 492-2
And joy of snow and snow. [An Gaiety 33-7 P
By waverings of stars, the joy of day [Greenest 54-15 P
The joy of meaning in design [Ulysses 100-22 P
JOYFUL. Shout for me, loudly and loudly, joyful sun, when you
   rise. [Nigger 150-17
JOYOUS. Joyous and jubilant and sure. [How Live 126-8
The shoulders of joyous men, to feel the heart [NSF 398-11
JOYOUSLY. That we are joyously ourselves and we think [Gala 248-9
JUAN. Dark Juan looks outward through his mystic brow . . .
   [Luther 461-14
See Don Juan.
JUBILANCE. A diamond jubilance beyond the fire, [Owl 433-21
JUBILANT. Joyous and jubilant and sure. [How Live 126-8
Of the appropriate creatures, jubilant, [Descrip 344-13
See ever-jubilant.
JUBILAS. To sing jubilas at exact, accustomed times, [NSF 398-7
JUDA. We remember the lion of Juda and we save [NH 472-23
And Juda becomes New Haven or else must. [NH 473-6
JUDAS. The flowering Judas grows from the belly or not at all.
   [Holiday 312-15
JUDAS-TREE. Of magenta blooming in the Judas-tree [Primordia 9-11P
JUGGLE. Caparison elephants, teach bears to juggle. [NSF 385-3
JUGGLERY. Or jugglery, without regalia. [C 35-27
Beheld the sovereign clouds as jugglery [Sea Surf 102-6
JUG-THROATED. Ké-ké, the jug-throated robin pouring out, [NSF 394-2
JUICE. When you were Eve, its acrid juice was sweet, [Monocle 14-14
A pear should come to the table popped with juice, [Nigger 155-3
By metaphor. The juice was fragranter [Poem Morn 219-9
They are full of juice and the skin is soft. [Peaches 224-12
With white wine, sugar and lime juice. Then bring it, [Phenom
   286-15
JUICIER. As by a juicier season; and more our own [Duck 65-4 P
JUICILY. Of seeds grown fat, too juicily opulent, [C 32-9
JULIAN. It had nothing of the Julian thunder-cloud: [EM 319-26
JULY. The rain is pouring down. It is July. [Chaos 357-9
"July Mountain" [114-title P
JUMBLE. And a jumble of words [Cortege 80-27
Below the prerogative jumble. The fruit so seen [Someone 84-16 A
JUMBO. "Jumbo" [269-title
And jumbo, the loud general-large [Jumbo 269-2
JUMPS. Jumps from the clouds or, from his window, [Hero 280-10
JUNE. Or her desire for June and evening, tipped [Sunday 68-25
Lusty as June, more fruitful than the weeks [Havana 143-13
Could measure by moonlight in June. [Jersey 210-12
JUNGLE. Scenting the jungle in their refuges, [C 32-5
That tuft of jungle feathers, [Gubbinal 85-6
The wild warblers are warbling in the jungle [Medit 123-13
Thridding the squawkiest jungle [Cab 21-10 P
That purges the wrack or makes the jungle shine, [Greenest 55-8P
In the jungle is a voice in Fontainebleau. [Greenest 59-14 P
The jungle of tropical part and tropical whole." [Bship 80-12 P
So that a carved king found in a jungle, huge [Conversat 109-5 P
JUNIPERS. To behold the junipers shagged with ice, [Snow Man 10-2
JUNK. To say the solar chariot is junk [Pure 332-6
JUNK-SHOP. The sky is no longer a junk-shop, [Dezem 218-2
JUPES. An eye most apt in gelatines and jupes, [C 27-14
JUPITERS. They nourish Jupiters. Their casual pap [Havana 144-7
JUST. Just as they flew from the boughs of the hemlocks [Domination
   8-22
Just so an ancient Crispin was dissolved. [C 29-7
Is just what you say. [Gubbinal 85-2
Is just what you say. [Gubbinal 85-8
Just as my fingers on these keys [Peter 89-16
Or just after. [Thirteen 93-11
Just to stand still without moving a hand. [Adieu 127-12
Just to be there and just to behold. [Adieu 127-16
Or to sleep or just to lie there still, [Adieu 128-4
Just to be there, just to be beheld, [Adieu 128-5
It seemed serener just to die, [Thought 184-17
A doctrine to this landscape. Yet, having just [Freed 204-17
This proves nothing. Just one more truth, one more [Connois
   216-2
If just above her head there hung, [Couch 295-10
Before it comes, the just anticipation [Descrip 344-12
Just out of the village, at its edge, [Woman Song 361-5
Cock bugler, whistle and bugle and stop just short, [NSF 405-15
It may be, is emerging or has just [AA 416-20
As grim as it is benevolent, the just [AA 417-5
Just rising, accompanying, arranged to cross, [Page 422-24
Or mountains that were not mountains, just to know how it would
   be, [Cata 425-8
Just to know how it would feel, released from destruction, [Cata
   425-9
If we were ever, just once, at the middle, fixed [Ulti 430-5
So much just to be seen--a purpose, empty [Moonlight 532-4

And despicable shades of red, just seen, [Burnshaw 51-21 P
Their destiny is just as much machine [Duck 61-21 P
Which, just to name, is to create [Ulysses 104-27 P
Just to see the sunrise again. [Three 128-7 P
Just as it is true of poets, [Three 129-13 P
Just as the young gentleman [Three 139-9 P
JUSTICE. The palais de justice of chambermaids [Surprises 98-6
JUSTIFIED. What good is it that the earth is justified, [Pecul
   453-13
JUSTITIA. All eyes and size, and galled Justitia, [Lions 124-13
JUTTED. Things jutted up, the way the jagged stacks, [Greenest
   53-11 P
Of war, the rust on the steeples, these jutted up, [Greenest
   53-23 P
JUTTING. And through the torrents a jutting, jagged tower, [Green-
   est 53-6 P
JUVENAL. To drone the green phrases of its juvenal? [NSF 390-15
JUVENILE. A little juvenile, an ancient whim, [C 35-23
JUVENTES. O juventes, O filii, he contemplates [Someone 83-1 A

KAFFIR. Or Chicago a Kaffir kraal. It means this mob. [Duck 63-14 P
KATY-DIDS. The katy-dids at Ephrata return [Memo 89-1 P
   On life itself and there the katy-dids [Memo 89-7 P
   The plums are blue on the trees. The katy-dids [Memo 89-14 P
KE. Ah, ké! the bloody wren, the felon jay, [NSF 394-1
KEEN. Keen to the point of starlight, while a frog [Monocle 17-16
   "The Bird with the Coppery, Keen Claws" [82-title
   He moves not on his coppery, keen claws. [Bird Claws 82-15
   Said that as keen, illustrious ornament, [NSF 391-22
   From cloud to cloudless, cloudless to keen clean [AA 414-15
KEENER. In ghostlier demarcations, keener sounds. [Key W 130-15
KEENEST. Beyond the keenest diamond day [Adequacy 244-1
KEEP. Meekly you keep the mortal rendezvous, [On Manner 55-11
   Of those whom the statues torture and keep down. [Parochial
     191-14
   The wings keep spreading and yet are never wings. [Somnam 304-4
   The claws keep scratching on the shale, the shallow shale,
     [Somnam 304-5
   How should I repeat them, keep repeating them, [Repet 307-23
   Receive and keep him in the deepnesses of space-- [Flyer 336-13
   The bass keep looking ahead, upstream, in one [Think 356-11
   That keep clinging to a tree, [Burghers 362-13
   Is it I then that keep saying there is an hour [NSF 404-23
   To keep on flowing. He wanted to walk beside it, [Cata 425-4
   Keep you, keep you, I am gone, oh keep you as [Owl 432-14
   Out of our lives to keep us in our death, [Owl 434-24
   Keep quiet in the heart, O wild bitch. O mind [Puel 456-13
   We keep coming back and coming back [NH 471-10
   Still keep occurring. What is, uncertainly, [NH 482-13
   To keep him from forgetting, without a word, [NH 483-17
   Is a memorizing, a trying out, to keep. [Aug 489-19
   The bells keep on repeating solemn names [Rome 510-15
   The origin and keep of its health and his own. [Armor 530-21
   Here I keep thinking of the Primitives-- [Soldat 13-8 P
   Keep the laborers shouldering plinths. [Archi 16-17 P
   They keep to the paths of the skeleton architect [Duck 62-10 P
   Keep whanging their brass wings . . . [Memo 89-8 P
   Owls warn me and with tuft-eared watches keep [Souls 94-18 P
   Not one of the five, and keep a rendezvous, [Souls 95-5 P
   He wanted to make them, keep them from perishing, [Local 112-6 P
KEEPING. In suavest keeping. The shoes, the clothes, the hat
   [Descrip 343-2
KEEPS. One keeps on playing year by year, [MBG 177-19
   Yet one face keeps returning (never the one), [Dames 206-14
   The father keeps on living in the son, the world [Recit 87-25 P
   Of the father keeps on living in the world [Recit 87-26 P
   Who keeps seeking out his identity [Dove 98-6 P
   That which keeps us the little that we are, [Ulysses 100-16 P
KE-KE. Ke-ke, the jug-throated robin pouring out, [NSF 394-2
   The phrases of a single phrase, ke-ke, [NSF 394-8
KEPT. Had kept him still the prickling realist, [C 40-6
   The leaves in which the wind kept up its sound [Farewell 117-13
   Yet he kept promising himself [Winter B 141-15
   The bird kept saying that birds had once been men, [Horn 230-1
   Kept speaking, of God. I changed the word to man. [Les Plus 245-4
   Kept waking and a mournful sense sought out, [Descrip 343-11
   The eye of Lenin kept the far-off shapes. [Descrip 343-11
   Come home, wind, he kept crying and crying. [Pieces 351-11
   Which kept flowing and never the same way twice, flowing [Cata
     424-11
   While the water kept running through the mouth of the speaker,
     [Novel 457-17
   So that morning and evening are like promises kept, [NH 472-16
   The rain kept falling loudly in the trees [NH 476-7
   On her pillow? The thought kept beating in her like her heart.
     [World 521-11
   The two kept beating together. It was only day. [World 521-12
   Never forgetting him that kept coming constantly so near. [World
     521-18
   And kept saying over and over one same, same thing, [Slug 522-6
KERMESS. The kremlin of kermess. [Archi 18-16 P
KERRY. He stayed in Kerry, died there. [Our Stars 455-3
KEY. And the stillness is in the key, all of it is, [Autumn 160-13
   The stillness is all in the key of that desolate sound. [Autumn
     160-14
   Of this precarious music, the change of key [Pure 332-3
KEYHOLDS. Fit for keyholes. [Three 138-12 P
KEYS. Tiestas from the keys, [Venereal 47-7
   Just as my fingers on these keys [Peter 89-16
   Her home, not mine, in the ever-freshened Keys, [Farewell 117-16
   And Rosa, the muslin dreamer of satin and cowry-kin, disdaining
     the empty keys; and the young infanta, [Piano 22-3 P
   Boston should be in the keys [Agenda 41-19 P
   To ride an old mule round the keys-- [Stan MBG 73-7 P
KEY WEST. In the porches of Key West, [Venereal 47-19
   Below Key West. [Two Figures 86-12
   Key West sank downward under massive clouds [Farewell 117-3
   "The Idea of Order at Key West" [128-title

   The vine, at the roots, this vine of Key West, splurging, [Bship
     80-9 P
KHAN. The twilights of the mythy goober khan. [Havana 142-21
KICK. As they jangle and dangle and kick their feet. [Luther 462-3
KICKED. Kicked through the roof, caressed by the river-side. [Bship
     80-6 P
KI-KI-RI-KI. But ki-ki-ri-ki [Depression 63-14
KILDEER. As kildeer do, [Sugar-Cane 12-16
KILL. Like the clashed edges of two words that kill." [Monocle 13-4
   It can kill a man. [Destructive 193-6
   Like insects in the depths of the mind, that kill [Extracts
     254-14
   That kill the single man, starvation's head, [Extracts 254-16
   Grows sharp in blood. The armies kill themselves, [Dutch 292-19
KILLED. The powerful seasons bred and killed, [Joost 46-17
   Hugh March, a sergeant, a redcoat, killed, [Vari 234-11
   An empty land; the gods that Boucher killed; [Oboe 250-10
   And you, my semblables, are doubly killed [Dutch 290-20
   Who killed him, sticking feathers in his flesh [Good Man 364-9
   I have killed the mayor, [Soldat 13-2 P
KILLING. Killing the time between corpses [Venereal 47-15
   Pain killing pain on the very point of pain. [EM 314-5
KILLS. Freedom is like a man who kills himself [Dutch 292-17
   The wound kills that does not bleed. [Woman Song 360-4
   Unless a second giant kills the first-- [NH 465-14
   Kills the commune. [Bship 80-17 P
KIN. Out of their mother grass, like little kin, [Monocle 15-4
   Confiders and comforters and lofty kin. [Choc 300-10
   A too, too human god, self-pity's kin [EM 315-23
   It has no nurse nor kin to know [Woman Song 360-5
   Nor kin to care. [Woman Song 360-6
   The charitable majesty of her whole kin? [Cred 375-1
   False flick, false form, but falseness close to kin. [NSF 385-18
   It might come bearing, out of chaos, kin [Page 422-27
   Cousins of the calendar if not of kin, [Recit 86-3 P
   See: cowry-kin; serpent-kin.
KIND. Of many proclamations of the kind, [C 32-32
   It is a kind of blank in which one sees. [Phenom 287-11
   A kind of elegy he found in space: [EM 315-3
   Even breathing is the beating of time, in kind: [Pure 330-4
   Two beasts. But of the same kind--two conjugal beasts. [Jouga
     337-5
   Two beasts but two of a kind and then not beasts. [Jouga 337-9
   Yet two not quite of a kind. It is like that here. [Jouga 337-10
   In a kind of total affluence, all first, [Descrip 342-15
   Compose us in a kind of eulogy. [Extraord 369-15
   That gives a candid kind to everything. [NSF 382-24
   At which a kind of Swiss perfection comes [NSF 386-12
   And present way, a presentation, a kind [NSF 397-20
   And war for war, each has its gallant kind. [NSF 407-21
   Are white, a little dried, a kind of mark [AA 412-9
   What wheaten bread and oaten cake and kind, [Orb 440-18
   Twelve and the first gray second after, a kind [What We 459-16
   For its counterpart a kind of counterpoint [NH 476-5
   A kind of cozening and coaxing sound, [NH 482-8
   A dumb sense possesses them in a kind of solemnity. [Old Man 501-2
   It is a kind of total grandeur at the end, [Rome 510-21
   In a kind of uproar, because an opposite, a contradiction, [Slug
     522-7
   Shot lightning at the kind cow's milk, [Lulu M 27-12 P
   And she have beauty of a kind, but such [Red Kit 31-18 P
   A churchyard kind of bush as well, [Banjo 114-6 P
KINDER-SCENEN. Presence is Kinder-Scenen. [John 436-16
KINDLED. Green is the night, green kindled and apparelled. [Candle
     223-1
KINDRED. Most rare, or ever of more kindred air [Fictive 87-21
KING. He moved among us, as a muttering king, [Sunday 67-30
   "A Rabbit as King of the Ghosts" [209-title
   Or into a dark-blue king, un roi tonnerre, [Extracts 254-10
   As if twelve princes sat before a king. [Cred 375-25
   Profound, and yet the king and yet the crown, [AA 415-1
   Underground, a king as candle by our beds [Owl 435-2
   Ababba, expecting this king's queen to appear? [Golden 461-3
   So that a carved king found in a jungle, huge [Conversat 109-5 P
KINGS. For somehow the brave dicta of its kings [Surprises 98-10
   That talk shifts the cycle of the scenes of kings? [Conversat
     109-23 P
KINKY. Fit for a kinky clan. [Pascagoula 126-18
KISS. Kiss, cats: for the deer and the dachshund [Jersey 210-13
   The necklace is a carving not a kiss. [AA 413-15
KISSED. The bride come jungling, kissed and cupped, or else [Repet
     308-1
   She described how the barbarians kissed her [Lulu G 26-19 P
KISSES. Without an escape in the lapses of their kisses. [Norfolk
     112-2
KIT. "Red Loves Kit" [30-title P
KITCHEN. In kitchen cups concupiscent curds. [Emperor 64-3
KITE. This parlor of farcical dames, this clowns' colonnade, this
     kites' pavilion? [Inelegance 26-6 P
KNAVE. The lutanist of fleas, the knave, the thane, [C 28-7

KNAVES. If not in will, to track the knaves of thought. [C 42-24
KNEE. And jig his chits upon a cloudy knee. [C 40-12
  Leaving no room upon his cloudy knee, [C 43-18
  The luminous pages on his knee, [Country 207-21
KNEELED. She kneeled upon the ground [Pourtraicte 21-3
KNEELING. Hoy, hoy, the blue bulls kneeling down to rest. [Montra
  260-6
  A kneeling woman, a moon's farewell; [Hero 275-10
KNEELS. He that kneels always on the edge of space [NH 469-9
KNELT. He knelt in the cathedral with the rest, [C 32-29
KNEW. Of love, but until now I never knew [Monocle 18-2
  Grind their seductions on him, Crispin knew [C 35-15
  The apprentice knew these dreamers. If he dreamed [C 39-29
  And what I knew you felt [Vincentine 53-11
  I knew from this [Peacocks 58-15
  I knew the dread [Peacocks 58-19
  I knew my enemy was near--I, [Cuban 65-5
  Knew not the quirks of imagery, [Frogs 78-9
  Whose spirit is this? we said, because we knew [Key W 129-7
  It was the spirit that we sought and knew [Key W 129-8
  Knew that there never was a world for her [Key W 130-1
  He knew how one feels. [Am Sub 131-1
  Knew the eccentric to be the base of design. [Nigger 151-3
  We knew for long the mansion's look [Postcard 159-11
  That's it, the only dream they knew, [MBG 183-17
  In the jasmine haunted forests, that we knew [Oboe 251-20
  Of her, of her alone, at last he knew [Hand 271-20
  Of what men are. The collective being knew [Choc 299-22
  After all, they knew that to be real each had [Holiday 312-11
  Before we were wholly human and knew ourselves. [EM 317-29
  It was not the end he had foreseen. He knew [EM 319-23
  We knew one parent must have been divine, [Pure 331-19
  As if they knew of distant beaches; and were [Descrip 343-8
  Shadows of friends, of those he knew, each bringing [New Set
  352-12
  That the beholder knew their subtle purpose, [New Set 353-2
  Knew well the shapes were the exactest shaping [New Set 353-3
  The Good Man Has No Shape, as if they knew. [Good Man 364-14
  We knew each other and of each other thought, [AA 417-19
  And knew each other well, hale-hearted landsmen, [AA 419-8
  She was a self that knew, an inner thing, [Owl 435-14
  Was beyond his recognizing. By this he knew that likeness of him
  extended [Prol 516-11
  He knew that he heard it, [Not Ideas 534-4
  Beheld the truth and knew it to be true. [Greenest 54-18 P
  Knew her, how could you see the woman that wore the beads,
  [Grotesque 74-10 P
  He knew that he was a spirit without a foyer [Local 111-11 P
  As the court knew it. [Three 131-16 P
  And never knew, [Three 131-26 P
  It never knew [Three 132-3 P
  When the court knew beauty only, [Three 132-5 P
KNIFE. Neither his head nor horse nor knife nor [Hero 276-22
  Each night, an incessant butcher, whose knife [Dutch 292-18
  The long-bladed knife, the little to drink and her [NH 485-21
KNIVES. Not all the knives of the lamp-posts, [Six Sig 74-23
KNOBS. Lacking the three glass knobs, that sheet [Emperor 64-10
KNOCK. And knock like a rifle-butt against the door. [AA 414-2
KNOCKS. Who knocks out a noise. The guitar is another beast [Jouga
  337-7
  Steps out. He rings and knocks. The door is not locked. [Bouquet
  452-20
  The old woman that knocks at the door [Grotesque 77-1 P
KNOTTED. And knotted, sashed and seamed, half pales of red, [Cred
  378-2
KNOW. You know how Utamaro's beauties sought [Monocle 14-5
  You know the mountainous coiffures of Bath. [Monocle 14-7
  I know no magic trees, no balmy boughs, [Monocle 16-27
  But, after all, I know a tree that bears [Monocle 17-2
  That know the ultimate Plato, [Homunculus 27-4
  Seem all of paradise that we shall know? [Sunday 68-7
  They shall know well the heavenly fellowship [Sunday 70-10
  I do not know which to prefer, [Thirteen 93-7
  I know noble accents [Thirteen 94-1
  But I know, too, [Thirteen 94-3
  In what I know. [Thirteen 94-5
  Are both alike in the routine I know. [Pharynx 96-3
  Do you know, Hans Christian, [Sonatina 110-7
  Farewell and to know that that land is forever gone [Farewell
  118-7
  Ramon Fernandez, tell me, if you know, [Key W 130-3
  I don't know what. [Botanist 1 134-18
  Will never know that these were once [Postcard 158-15
  Will speak our speech and never know, [Postcard 159-15
  I know my lazy, leaden twang [MBG 169-9
  I know that timid breathing. Where [MBG 171-17
  To know; a missal for brooding-sight. [MBG 178-5
  They did not know the grass went round. [MBG 178-15
  To know that the balance does not quite rest, [MBG 181-9
  How should you walk in that space and know [MBG 183-7

But this he cannot know, the man that thinks, [Men Fall 188-2
I know that I cannot be mended, [Idiom 201-8
To know that the change and that the ox-like struggle [Freed
  205-12
I know from all the things it touched [Country 207-17
Slight as it is, disturbs me. I did not know [Peaches 224-18
Someone before him to see and to know. [Scavoir 232-4
And not be touched by blue. He wanted to know, [Landsc 241-15
And, talking of happiness, know that it means [Extracts 257-14
Know that the past is not part of the present. [Dutch 291-21
And you, my semblables, know that this time [Dutch 292-1
And you, my semblables, know that your children [Dutch 292-8
Beyond the sleep of those that did not know, [Choc 299-10
False happiness, since we know that we use [Crude 305-14
That was their element, we should not know [Creat 310-15
Why should they not know they had everything of their own
  [Holiday 312-9
In solid fire the utmost earth and know [EM 314-12
Alone is not to know them or himself. [EM 323-18
Hear, feel and know. We feel and know them so. [Descrip 340-18
It has no nurse nor kin to know [Woman Song 360-5
A season, to discover summer and know it, [NSF 403-24
To discover winter and know it well, to find, [NSF 404-1
As if he lived all lives, that he might know, [AA 420-24
Or mountains that were not mountains, just to know how it would
  be, [Cata 425-8
Just to know how it would feel, released from destruction, [Cata
  425-9
Presence lies far too deep, for me to know [John 437-25
Sits in nothing that we know, [Degen 444-5
You know that the nucleus of a time is not [Papini 446-7
Giovanni Papini, by your faith, know how [Papini 447-1
Cold with an under impotency that they know, [Bouquet 449-9
Now that they know, because they know. One comes [Bouquet
  449-10
She is the fateful mother, whom he does not know. [Pecul 454-3
To understand, as if to know became [Novel 459-5
They only know a savage assuagement cries [NH 467-22
We do not know what is real and what is not. [NH 472-8
Is being and knowing what I am and know. [Angel 496-14
It was a language he spoke, because he must, yet did not know.
  [Madame 507-7
What we know in what we see, what we feel in what [Look 518-10
If I should fall, as soldier, I know well [Soldat 11-10 P
You know the phrase. [Soldat 16-12 P
All of them, darkened by time, moved by they know not what,
  amending the airs they play to fulfill themselves; [Piano 21-17P
He is nothing, I know, to me nor I to him. [Lytton 39-21 P
Except the thing she felt but did not know. [Old Woman 45-22 P
Of a generation that does not know itself, [Sombre 68-30 P
They had hardly grown to know the sunshine, [Stan Hero 83-17 P
Or is it I that, wandering, know, one-sensed, [Souls 95-4 P
He said. "As I know, I am and have [Ulysses 99-13 P
So that to know a man is to be [Ulysses 99-17 P
That man, to know a place is to be [Ulysses 99-18 P
And if to know one man is to know all [Ulysses 99-20 P
And being are one: the right to know [Ulysses 101-18 P
As a free race. We know it, one [Ulysses 102-4 P
To know established as the right to be. [Ulysses 102-11 P
In the John-begat-Jacob of what we know, [Ulysses 103-5 P
Since only to know is to be free? [Ulysses 103-12 P
To know what helps and to attain, [Ulysses 104-29 P
He said, "As I know, I am and have [Presence 105-16 P
And being are one--the right to know [Presence 106-3 P
Among the old men that you know, [Child 106-13 P
You know then that it is not the reason [Of Mere 118-1 P
In the prolific ellipses that we know, [Someone 87-18 A
See know-and-know.
KNOW-AND-KNOW. As if they were desperate with a know-and-know,
  [Repet 307-24
KNOWING. Knowing that they can bring back thought [Homunculus 26-13
  These voices crying without knowing for what, [Sad Gay 122-6
  Except to be happy, without knowing how, [Sad Gay 122-7
  A gaiety that is being, not merely knowing, [Gala 248-13
  Look, realist, not knowing what you expect. [Phosphor 267-11
  Knowing that he died nobly, as he died. [Flyer 336-11
  Makers without knowing, or intending, uses. [New Set 352-15
  A knowing that something certain had been proposed, [NH 483-4
  That comes from ourselves, neither from knowing [Aug 495-9
  Nor not knowing, yet free from question, [Aug 495-10
  But, of my being and its knowing, part. [Angel 496-12
  Is being and knowing what I am and know. [Angel 496-14
  Of the wind, not knowing that that thought [Two Illus 513-11
  And knowing the monotony of thought, [Stan MMO 19-5 P
  And without knowing, and then upon the wind [Old Woman 44-14 P
  Motionless, knowing neither dew nor frost. [Burnshaw 49-15 P
  Knows, knowing that he does not care, and knows, [Greenest 59-9P
  Knowing and meaning that he cannot care. [Greenest 59-10 P
  In a health of weather, knowing a few, old things, [Americana
  93-17 P

Ancient amigas, knowing partisans-- [Souls 95-3 P
The eloquence of right, since knowing [Ulysses 101-17 P
A life beyond this present knowing, [Ulysses 101-22 P
By right of knowing, another plane. [Ulysses 104-30 P
This eloquence of right, since knowing [Presence 106-2 P
Because he desired without knowing quite what, [Local 112-9 P
KNOWLEDGE. And knowledge dropped upon his heart [Thought 186-23
Beyond the knowledge of nakedness, as part [Extracts 252-18
Of reality, beyond the knowledge of what [Extracts 252-19
The last purity of the knowledge of good. [Possum 294-14
Besides the people, his knowledge of them. In [EM 323-8
The unpeopled, there is his knowledge of himself. [EM 323-9
He has no secret from them. This knowledge [EM 323-15
This creates a third world without knowledge, [EM 323-19
It is to stick to the nicer knowledge of [Pure 332-11
To which we refer experience, a knowledge [Descrip 343-19
The knowledge of Spain and of the hidalgo's hat-- [Descrip 345-14
The knowledge of bright-ethered things [Analysis 349-7
The knowledge of being, sense without sense of time. [Myrrh
   350-9
It was not her look but a knowledge that she had. [Owl 435-13
Impassioned by the knowledge that she had, [Owl 435-17
We shall be heavy with the knowledge of that day. [John 437-23
Its knowledge cold within one as one's own; [Novel 459-3
Huddle together in the knowledge of squirrels. [NH 487-12
The knowledge of things lay round but unperceived: [Aug 493-18
Had to be imagined as an inevitable knowledge, [Plain 503-7
His crisp knowledge is devoured by her, beneath a dew. [Madame
   507-4
A knowledge that the actual day [Two Illus 513-7
A knowledge, that which arranged the rendezvous. [Final 524-12
A new knowledge of reality. [Not Ideas 534-18
"If knowledge and the thing known are one [Ulysses 99-16 P
Then knowledge is the only life, [Ulysses 100-1 P
In which knowledge cannot be denied, [Ulysses 100-7 P
In which nothing of knowledge fails, [Ulysses 100-8 P
To knowledge when we come to life. [Ulysses 101-20 P
He came to this by knowledge or [Ulysses 102-19 P
"Presence of an External Master of Knowledge" [105-title P
Which knowledge is: the world and fate, [Presence 105-21 P
And that, in his knowledge, local objects become [Local 111-12 P
It has no knowledge except of nothingness [Clear Day 113-15 P
On the level of that which is not yet knowledge: [Region 115-11P
KNOWLEDGES. Free knowledges, secreted until then, [Orb 441-17
KNOWN. They had known that there was not even a common speech,
   [Holiday 312-7
However known, at the centre of the heart? [EM 323-25
To pick up relaxations of the known. [Feo 333-17
Possess in his heart, conceal and nothing known. [NSF 395-6
So that I tremble with such love so known [NSF 396-8
Had ever been before, no longer known, [Page 422-14
No more than which most of all brings back the known, [Page
   422-15
It is something seen and known in lesser poems. [Orb 440-10
Of things were waiting in a betrothal known [Study II 464-17
The extreme of the known in the presence of the extreme [Rome
   508-17
They bear their fruit so that the year is known, [Rock 527-12
A change so felt, a fear in her so known, [Old Woman 45-3 P
Now felt, now known as this. The clouds of bronze [Old Woman 45-4P
By harmonies beyond known harmony. [Duck 62-8 P
"If knowledge and the thing known are one [Ulysses 99-16 P
And future place, when these are known, [Ulysses 101-10 P
Not to be reached but to be known, [Ulysses 101-25 P
An inhuman of our features, known [Ulysses 105-4 P
And felt and known the differences we have seen [Conversat 109-18P
And felt and known in the colors in which we live, [Conversat
   109-19 P
In which he feeds on a new known, [Bus 116-4 P
But a perfection emerging from a new known, [Bus 116-11 P
"The court had known poverty and wretchedness; hu- [Three 129-9P
KNOWS. Knows nothing more. [Joost 46-16
Knows nothing more. [Joost 47-3
The night knows nothing of the chants of night. [Re-state 146-1
The race that sings and weeps and knows not why. [Thought 186-16
Yet he knows what it is that he expects. [Phosphor 267-6
Is it himself in them that he knows or they [EM 323-12
The mind that knows it is destroyed by time. [Pure 329-15
Knows desire without an object of desire, [Chaos 358-3
He knows he has nothing more to think about. [Chaos 358-5
A person he knows, with whom he might [Woman Song 361-2
It knows that what it has is what is not [NSF 382-10
Someone looking for he knows not what. [Vacancy 511-5
Who knows? The ploughman may not live alone [Burnshaw 48-23 P
He does not hear by sound. His spirit knows [Greenest 59-7 P
Knows, knowing that he does not care, and knows, [Greenest 59-9P
Immeasurable, the space in which he knows [Sombre 70-32 P
The thinker knows. The gunman of the commune [Bship 80-16 P
Not true to this or that, but true, knows [Stan Hero 84-12 P
Is what one knows of the universe, [Ulysses 99-22 P

Outwardly and knows them inwardly, [Child 106-18 P
One knows at last what to think about [Sol Oaks 111-8 P
Such seclusion knows beauty [Three 131-15 P
KONSTANTINOV. He said it of Konstantinov. Revolution [EM 324-27
One might meet Konstantinov, who would interrupt [EM 325-10
KRAAL. Is the beggar in Bogota. The kraal [Greenest 59-18 P
Or Chicago a Kaffir kraal. It means this mob. [Duck 63-14 P
KREMLIN. The kremlin of kermess. [Archi 18-16 P

LA. Oh, la . . . le pauvre! [Plot Giant 7-4
  La,la,la,la,la,la,la,la, [Primordia 8-19 P
LA-BAS. And là-bas, la-bas, the cool bananas grew, [NSF 393-13
  The robins are là-bas, the squirrels, in tree-caves, [NH 487-11
LABELLED. To exactly labelled, a large among the smalls [Orb 443-11
LABIALS. Heavenly labials in a world of gutturals. [Plot Giant 7-9
LABOR. A part of labor and a part of pain, [Sunday 68-9
  Without the labor of thought, in that element, [Gala 248-10
  Could not have borne his labor nor have died [NSF 393-20
  "The Drum-Majors in the Labor Day Parade" [36-title P
LABORER. The blank frere of fields, their matin laborer. [Aug
  492-18
  A laborer. [Soldat 16-3 P
LABORERS. Keep the laborers shouldering plinths. [Archi 16-17 P
LABORIOUS. In the laborious weaving that you wear. [Fictive 87-22
LABORIOUSLY. Said things it had laboriously spoken. [NSF 387-18
LACE. With socks of lace [Ten O'C 66-8
LACERATIONS. In venting lacerations. So composed, [Spaniard 35-18P
LACK. "The Lack of Repose" [303-title
  Reverberations leak and lack among holes . . . [Armor 529-8
  And trees that lack the intelligence of trees. [R Conn 533-6
  A universe without life's limp and lack, [Theatre 91-16 P
  No more and because they lack the will to tell [Ideal 88-14 A
LACKED. They lived, in which they lacked a pervasive being, [Somnam
  304-15
  And spoke the feeling for them, which was what they had lacked.
  [Large 424-9
LACKER. The bad-bespoken lacker, [Jumbo 269-15
LACKING. Lacking the three glass knobs, that sheet [Emperor 64-10
  These are of minstrels lacking minstrelsy, [NSF 394-13
  Lacking men of stone, [Inhab 504-7
LACKS. He lacks this venerable complication. [Creat 311-10
LACK-TRAGIC. To reject the script for its lack-tragic, [Gigan
  289-10
LACONIC. Crispin in one laconic phrase laid bare [C 36-26
LACQUED. Lapised and lacqued and freely emeraldine [Ideal 88-5 A
LACQUER. Jocunda, who will arrange the roses and rearrange, letting
  the leaves lie on the water-like lacquer; [Piano 22-4 P
LACQUERED. The lacquered loges huddled there [Ord Women 11-1
  The blue woman, linked and lacquered, at her window [NSF 399-4
LACUSTRINE. Lacustrine man had never been assailed [Geneva 24-4
LADIES. And ladies soon to be married. [Homunculus 25-16
  Of widows and trembling ladies, [Homunculus 26-7
LADY. A lady dying of diabetes [Thought 184-7
  Dying lady, rejoice, rejoice! [Thought 185-4
  And, in the brown blues of evening, the lady said, [Uruguay 248-17
  Lived a lady, Lady Lowzen, [Oak 272-2
  Reach the lady quickly. [Three 136-13 P
  So far the lady of the present ballad [Three 137-9 P
  That the lady was poor-- [Three 138-2 P
  The lady's father [Three 139-3 P
LADY LOWZEN. Lived a lady, Lady Lowzen, [Oak 272-2
LA FLEURIE. See Madame La Fleurie.
LAGGING. "Oh, lissomeness turned lagging ligaments!" [Stan MMO
  19-20 P
LAID. Crispin in one laconic phrase laid bare [C 36-26
  Of breakfast ribands, fruits laid in their leaves, [C 42-26
  Hen shudders: the copious egg is made and laid. [Nigger 155-12
  And laid it in the sand. As I am, I am [NSF 395-20
LAIN. Which had lain folded against the blue [Hibiscus 22-16
LAIR. Out of his fiery lair. [Pascagoula 127-7
LAKE. The windy lake wherein their lord delights, [Sunday 70-7
  Through the mustiest blue of the lake [Sailing 120-18
  And wondered about the water in the lake. [Extracts 254-27
  Or whether the ice still covered the lake. There was still
  [Extracts 255-14
  Then bathed its body in the leaping lake. [Hand 271-12
  By the lake at Geneva and consider logic: [EM 325-3
  By a lake, with clouds like lights among great tombs, [EM 325-8
  With his lunacy. He would not be aware of the lake. [EM 325-11
  To Nietzsche in Basel, to Lenin by a lake. [Descrip 342-1
  Lenin on a bench beside a lake disturbed [Descrip 342-21
  The truth depends on a walk around a lake, [NSF 386-3
  In the swags of pine-trees bordering the lake. [NSF 386-8
  The lake was full of artificial things, [NSF 397-12
  Fixed like a lake on which the wild ducks fluttered, [Cata 424-13
  Through the door one sees on the lake that the white duck swims
  [Bouquet 449-19
  A mirror, a lake of reflections in a room, [NH 468-14
  Night's moonlight lake was neither water nor air. [Real 111-2 P
LAKE-HOLLOWS. Of the lake-hollows. [Primordia 7-15 P
LAKE-PALLORS. By the green lake-pallors, [Cab 21-5 P
LAKES. If men at forty will be painting lakes [Monocle 15-7
  Although they paint effulgent, azure lakes, [Havana 142-16
  They warded the blank waters of the lakes [Havana 142-16
  Lakes are more reasonable than oceans. Hence, [EM 325-6
LA-LA. La-la! The cat is in the violets [Mandolin 28-13 P
LAMBS. So heaven collects its bleating lambs. [Thought 184-10

LAME. A form that is lame, a hand, a back, [Ulysses 104-17 P
LAMED. A tiger lamed by nothingness and frost. [Nigger 153-10
LAMENT. Lament, willingly forfeit the ai-ai [EM 317-15
LAMENTABLE. The lamentable tread! [Cortege 81-7
LAMENTING. Moves in lamenting and the fatal, [Stan Hero 83-23 P
LAMP. Let the lamp affix its beam. [Emperor 64-15
  No lamp was burning as I read, [Reader 147-4
  Sitting beside your lamp, there citron to nibble [Dwarf 208-13
  Like an electric lamp [Common 221-8
  The smallest lamp, which added its puissant flick, to which he
  gave [Prol 517-3
  A lamp, in a day of the week, the time before spring, [Woman Had
  83-6 P
  Wrenched out of chaos . . . The quiet lamp [Ulysses 100-23 P
  For this creator is a lamp [Ulysses 100-24 P
LAMP-LIGHT. Your lamp-light fell [Tea 112-12
LAMP-POSTS. Not all the knives of the lamp-posts, [Six Sig 74-23
LAMPS. Anon, their lamps' uplifted flame [Peter 91-18
  As if last night's lamps continued to burn, [Cuisine 228-4
  The street lamps [Metamorph 266-6
  They would march single file, with electric lamps, alert [Page
  423-9
LANCE. Flutter her lance with your tempestuous dust, [Spaniard
  34-24 P
LAND. Which is the sound of the land [Snow Man 10-7
  An eye of land, of simple salad-beds, [C 27-16
  Stopping, on voyage, in a land of snakes, [C 31-7
  Dwelt in the land. Perhaps if discontent [C 40-5
  Crispin dwelt in the land and dwelling there [C 40-14
  And so it is one damns that green shade at the bottom of the
  land. [Banal 63-3
  No mother suckled him, no sweet land gave [Sunday 67-28
  Land of Locust [NE Verses 105-title 11
  Land of Pine and Marble [NE Verses 106-title 12
  Farewell and to know that that land is forever gone [Farewell
  118-7
  In the land of turkeys in turkey weather [Mice 123-1
  It made, away from the muck of the land [How Live 126-6
  Falling, far off, from sky to land, [Mud 148-7
  Alone, lord of the land and lord [MBG 176-10
  Of the men that live in the land, high lord, [MBG 176-11
  One's self and the mountains of one's land, [MBG 176-12
  It is equal to living in a tragic land [Loaf 199-14
  Regard the hovels of those that live in this land. [Loaf 199-18
  Without ideas in a land without ideas, [Forces 228-19
  This cloudy world, by aid of land and sea, [Vari 233-20
  In the land of war. More than the man, it is [Bottle 239-1
  The ultimate elegance: the imagined land. [Uruguay 250-5
  An empty land; the gods that Boucher killed; [Oboe 250-10
  Is real, part of a land beyond the mind? [Extracts 252-20
  They preach and they are preaching in a land [Extracts 254-3
  Would be a geography of the dead: not of that land [Somnam 304-13
  "The farm was fat and the land in which it lay [Anach 365-18
  A land too ripe for enigmas, too serene. [Cred 374-9
  Of the land's children, easily born, its flesh, [Cred 375-4
  It rises from land and sea and covers them. [Cred 375-12
  He thought often of the land from which he came, [NSF 393-16
  Lightly and lightly, O my land, [Imago 439-19
  And plated up, dense silver shine, in a land [Bouquet 449-15
  Of the land, on a checkered cover, red and white. [Bouquet 450-6
  By an instinct for a rainless land, the self [NH 475-23
  In the land of the lemon trees, yellow and yellow were [NH 486-13
  In the land of the elm strees, wandering mariners [NH 486-16
  They rolled their r's, there, in the land of the citrons. [NH
  486-19
  In the land of big mariners, the words they spoke [NH 486-20
  When the mariners came to the land of the lemon trees, [NH 487-1
  They said, "We are back once more in the land of the elm trees,
  [NH 487-3
  It is not that he was born in another land, [Sombre 66-23 P
  The first soothsayers of the land, the man [Americana 93-15 P
  Is a residue, a land, a rain, a warmth, [How Now 97-10 P
  A land would hold her in its arms that day [Letters 108-6 P
  Or something much like a land. [Letters 108-7 P
  See: folk-land; hero-land.
LAND-BREATH. Its land-breath to be stifled, its color changed,
  [Sombre 71-33 P
LANDLESS. And the river becomes the landless, waterless ocean?
  [Degen 444-21
LANDS. Severs not only lands but also selves. [C 30-4
  The mountains between our lands and the sea-- [Grapes 110-9
  This conjunction of mountains and sea and our lands-- [Grapes
  110-10
  When I think of our lands I think of the house [Grapes 110-12
  And mountains and the sea do. And our lands. [Grapes 110-19
  The heavens, the hells, the worlds, the longed-for lands. [NH
  486-12
  Into lands of ruddy-ruby fruits, achieved [Armor 530-3
  See pine-lands.
LANDSCAPE. The landscape and that; [Am Sub 131-6

A doctrine to this landscape. Yet, having just [Freed 204-17
Overtaking the doctrine of this landscape. Of him [Freed 204-21
"Landscape with Boat" [241-title
"On the Adequacy of Landscape" [243-title
A foyer of the spirit in a landscape [Crude 305-6
Is the eye, and that this landscape of the mind [Crude 305-16
Is a landscape only of the eye; and that [Crude 305-17
Dropped down from turquoise leaves. In the landscape of [EM
  318-13
In the brightest landscape downwardly revolves [EM 318-19
This Italian symbol, this Southern landscape, is like [Study I
  463-7
The actual landscape with its actual horns [NH 475-1
This is not landscape, full of the somnambulations [Irish 502-3
And weathered, should be part of a human landscape, [Conversat
  109-6 P
LANDSCAPES. "Six Significant Landscapes" [73-title
  She is not the mother of landscapes but of those [Woman Had 82-2P
LANDSMEN. And knew each other well, hale-hearted landsmen, [AA
  419-8
LANGUAGE. Reading the lordly language of the inscription, [Mice
  123-7
  Without lineage or language, only [Couch 295-7
  In a beau language without a drop of blood. [Repet 310-9
  The gaiety of language is our seigneur. [EM 322-19
  Pure rhetoric of a language without words. [Cred 374-15
  As if the language suddenly, with ease, [NSF 387-17
  The joy of language, when it is themselves. [Orb 441-8
  It was a language he spoke, because he must, yet did not know.
    [Madame 507-7
LANGUID. A languid janitor bears [Public Sq 109-6
LANK. And lank, rising and slumping from a sea [C 34-5
LANKIER. More leanly shining from a lankier sky. [Anglais 149-3
LANTERN. "The Virgin Carrying a Lantern" [71-title
  About the lantern of the beauty [Virgin 71-4
  His lantern through colonnades [Public Sq 109-7
  Lantern without a bearer, you drift, [Vari 232-16
  Is to look for it with a lantern. [Three 127-3 P
  You have left your lantern behind you. [Three 135-7 P
LANTERNS. With lanterns borne aloft to light the way, [Heaven 56-13
  Of the steadfast lanterns creep across the dark? [Heaven 56-20
  With lanterns, like a celestial ancientness. [NH 476-21
LAP. Upon his lap, like their inherent sphere, [C 45-27
  The moonlight in her lap, mewing her velvet, [Uruguay 249-2
LAPIS. To be a bronze man breathing under archaic lapis, [Cata
  425-10
  Shook off their dark marine in lapis light. [NH 484-8
  Benitia, lapis Ville des Pins must soothe [Greenest 58-22 P
LAPISED. Lapised and lacqued and freely emeraldine [Ideal 88-5 A
LAPIS-HAUNTED. Are the wings his, the lapis-haunted air? [NSF
  404-21
LAPSES. But let these backward lapses, if they would, [C 35-14
  Without an escape in the lapses of their kisses. [Norfolk 112-2
  Yet, when corrected, has its curious lapses, [EM 318-15
LAPSING. In which the thunder, lapsing in its clap, [C 33-15
LARD. One sits and beats an old tin can, lard pail. [Dump 202-26
LARGE. The ruses that were shattered by the large. [C 30-15
  And large umbrellas. And a motley green [Sea Surf 102-2
  I sing a hero's head, large eye [MBG 165-13
  The idea of the Alps grew large, [Thought 184-15
  Heart. The peaches are large and round, [Peaches 224-10
  No large white horses. But there was the fluffy dog. [Forces
  229-12
  Grows large on the wall. [Rhythms 245-10
  Grows large against space: [Rhythms 245-14
  Escaped its large abstraction, became, [Vase 246-22
  Loud, general, large, fat, soft [Jumbo 269-11
  A wider brow, large and less human [Hero 277-8
  For the large, the solitary figure. [Hero 281-5
  The wheels are too large for any noise. [Dutch 290-5
  And to be heard is to be large in space, [Choc 296-8
  That, like your own, is large, hence, to be part [Choc 296-9
  Of sky, of sea, large earth, large air. It is [Choc 296-10
  But not the thinker, large in their largeness, beyond [Choc
  299-16
  How singular he was as man, how large, [Choc 302-1
  If nothing more than that, for the moment, large [Choc 302-2
  Against the haggardie . . . A loud, large water [EM 321-8
  Springs outward, being large, and, in the dust, [Pure 332-22
  Ovation on ovation of large blue men [Liadoff 346-8
  "Large Red Man Reading" [423-title
  Too exactly labelled, a large among the smalls [Orb 443-11
  So that we feel, in this illumined large, [Rome 509-13
  Seemed large and loud and high and strong. [Two Illus 513-9
  As large ferocious tigers are. [Parasol 20-10 P
  Around it. Thus it has a large expanse, [Red Kit 31-7 P
  His place is large and high, an ether flamed [Greenest 59-31 P
  The circle of the sceptre growing large [Bship 80-23 P
  Grow large and larger. Our fate is our own. The hand, [Bship
  81-7 P

That move in the air as large as air, [Including 88-10 P
And state of being large and light. [Dove 98-12 P
See general-large.
LARGE-LEAVED. The large-leaved day grows rapidly, [Red Fern 365-1
  Large-leaved and many-footed shadowing, [Greenest 52-23 P
LARGELY. Life, then, is largely a thing [Table 40-2 P
  Is largely another winding of the clock. [Duck 65-30 P
  With appropriate, largely English, furniture, [Sombre 68-7 P
LARGE-MANNERED. Large-mannered motions to his mythy mind [Sunday
  67-29
LARGENESS. The last largeness, bold to see. [Curtains 62-10
  Tipped out with largeness, bearing the heavy [Gigan 289-16
  But not the thinker, large in their largeness, beyond [Choc
  299-16
  Excluding by his largeness their defaults. [Choc 299-18
  A largeness lived and not conceived, a space [Choc 301-12
LARGENESSES. In stellar largenesses--these [Ulysses 103-21 P
LARGER. Are the eye grown larger, more intense. [Vari 234-20
  Has a will to grow larger on the wall, [Rhythms 245-19
  To grow larger and heavier and stronger than [Rhythms 246-1
  From the others, being larger than he was, [Repet 307-5
  A larger poem for a larger audience, [NH 465-18
  The World Is Larger in Summer [Two Illus 514-title 2
  From man's ghost, larger and yet a little like, [Look 518-1
  In an inhuman meditation, larger than her own. [World 521-5
  Of larger sentiment. [Demoiselle 23-9 P
  Of larger company than one. Therefore, [Good Bad 33-11 P
  From size, backs larger than the eye, not flesh [Sombre 70-23 P
  And larger as it moves, moving toward [Bship 80-24 P
  Grow large and larger. Our fate is our own. The hand, [Bship
  81-7 P
LARGE-SCULPTURED. A large-sculptured, platonic person, free from
  time, [Pure 330-8
LARGEST. It was at that time, that the silence was largest [On Road
  204-9
  Last terms, the largest, bulging still with more, [Orb 441-11
  A single ship, a cloud on the sea, the largest [Bship 78-2 P
LARK. Here, for the lark fixed in the mind, [MBG 182-17
  Maidens in bloom, bulls under sea, the lark [Sombre 67-33 P
LARKSPUR. He sees larkspur, [Six Sig 73-8
  Lean larkspur and jagged fern and rusting rue [Bouquet 452-10
LASCAR. Lascar, is there a body, turbulent [Two V 354-1
  Lascar, and water-carcass never-named, [Two V 354-7
LASCIVE. Licentious violet and lascive rose, [Montra 261-15
LASCIVIOUS. Pecking at more lascivious rinds than ours, [Nigger
  152-16
  Among the lascivious poisons, clean of them, [Extracts 252-16
LASCIVIOUSLY. Lasciviously as the wind, [Venereal 48-1
LASH. Against the first idea--to lash the lion, [NSF 385-2
LASHED. Whether the water was black and lashed about [Extracts
  255-13
LASHES. The lashes of that eye and its white lid. [Worms 49-19
  The poem lashes more fiercely than the wind, [Bottle 239-14
  Like the wind that lashes everything at once. [Chaos 358-6
LASHING. Oh, that this lashing wind was something more [Chaos 357-7
  Lashing at images in the atmosphere, [Page 422-29
LAST. Last night, we sat beside a pool of pink, [Monocle 17-14
  Here was the veritable ding an sich, at last, [C 29-24
  Was clear. The last distortion of romance [C 30-2
  That prose should wear a poem's guise at last. [C 36-23
  Forgather and bell boldly Crispin's last [C 43-13
  "Last Looks at the Lilacs" [48-title
  And look your last and look still steadily, [Lilacs 49-7
  Unpurged by epitaph, indulged at last, [High-Toned 59-10
  The last largeness, bold to see. [Curtains 62-10
  Bring flowers in last month's newspapers. [Emperor 64-6
  Was last with its porcelain leer. [Public Sq 109-12
  Last evening the moon rose above this rock [How Live 125-9
  Like last night's crickets, far below. [Botanist 2 135-19
  Only last year he said that the naked moon [Anglais 148-19
  He stood at last by God's help and the police; [Anglais 149-10
  The rabbit fat, at last, in glassy grass. [Nigger 153-20
  Not by beginning but at the last man's end. [Nigger 156-21
  Melodious skeletons, for all of last night's music [Fish-Scale
  160-15
  At last, in spite of his manner, his eye [MBG 181-20
  The actor that will at last declaim our end. [Dames 206-20
  As if last night's lamps continued to burn, [Cuisine 228-4
  The last island and its inhabitant, [Vari 235-1
  There the man sees the image clearly at last. [Rhythms 245-15
  But we and the diamond globe at last were one. [Oboe 251-16
  The good is evil's last invention. Thus [Extracts 253-11
  The naked man, the naked man as last [Montra 262-11
  Of her, of her alone, at last he knew [Hand 271-20
  This was the place to which you came last night, [God 285-7
  Year, year and year, defeated at last and lost [Dutch 291-25
  The last purity of the knowledge of good. [Possum 294-14
  At the end of night last night a crystal star, [Choc 296-17
  Blue's last transparence as it turned to black, [Choc 297-13
  Last night at the end of night his starry head, [Choc 299-19

Last night at the end of night and in the sky, [Choc 301-19
At last, there, when it turns out to be here. [Crude 305-20
The last, or sounds so single they seemed one? [EM 316-15
It was the last nostalgia: that he [EM 322-4
At last the good life came, good sleep, bright fruit, [Good Man
  364-7
This is the last day of a certain year [Cred 372-11
Not evocations but last choirs, last sounds [Cred 374-13
And last year's garden grows salacious weeds. [Cred 377-10
Finally, in the last year of her age, [Past Nun 378-11
As if the waves at last were never broken, [NSF 387-16
This warmth is for lovers at last accomplishing [NSF 391-4
That was different, something else, last year [AA 412-11
What must unmake it and, at last, what can, [AA 418-2
Like a great shadow's last embellishment. [AA 419-24
Peace stood with our last blood adorned, last mind, [Owl 434-19
From sight, in the silence that follows her last word-- [Owl
  435-21
Last terms, the largest, bulging still with more, [Orb 441-11
Every thread of summer is at last unwoven. [Puel 456-1
And one trembles to be so understood and, at last, [Novel 459-4
As: the last plainness of a man who has fought [NH 467-17
Of dreams, disillusion as the last illusion, [NH 468-11
At last, in that blond atmosphere, bronzed hard, [NH 487-2
The last leaf that is going to fall has fallen. [NH 487-10
The peace of the last intelligence; [Aug 490-22
On Europe, to the last Alp, [Inhab 504-4
And one last look at the ducks is a look [Hermit 506-2
As in the last drop of the deepest blood, [Rome 509-26
Would discover, at last, the view toward which they had edged,
  [Poem Mt 512-12
Like the last muting of winter as it ends. [Look 519-3
Like the last one. But there is no ferryman. [R Conn 533-11
Deploring sentiment. When May came last [Good Bad 33-14 P
Changed them, at last, to its triumphant hue, [Old Woman 44-26 P
That is yourselves, when, at last, you are yourselves, [Burnshaw
  52-16 P
That's what did it. Everything did it at last. [Greenest 53-15 P
To which all other forms, at last, return, [Recit 87-5 P
Itself, until, at last, the cry concerns no one at all. [Course
  97-3 P
A freedom at last from the mystical, [Ulysses 101-11 P
A whole, the day on which the last star [Ulysses 102-8 P
Last Friday, in the big light of last Friday night, [Real 110-7 P
One knows at last what to think about [Sol Oaks 111-8 P
Beyond the last thought, rises [Of Mere 117-16 P
Last evening I met him on the road. [Three 141-11 P
At last, is the pineapple on the table or else [Someone 87-9 A
The last man given for epitome, [Ideal 88-21 A
At last, the center of resemblance, found [Ideal 89-8 A
LASTING. A lasting visage in a lasting bush, [NSF 400-4
LASTS. And music that lasts long and lives the more. [Art Pop
  113-6 P
LATCHED. Latched up the night. So deep a sound fell down [C 42-6
LATE. Complacencies of the peignoir, and late [Sunday 66-16
  How long and late the pheasant sleeps . . . [MBG 182-9
  And late wanderers creeping under the barb of night, [Dutch
    291-24
  Is not an early time that has grown late. [Dutch 292-2
  And they were nothing else. It was late in the year. [Wild 329-2
  "Late Hymn from the Myrrh-Mountain" [349-title
  Is the reader leaning late and reading there. [House Q 359-4
  With the gold bugs, in blue meadows, late at night. [Cred 377-23
  From that ever-early candor to its late plural [NSF 382-18
  The late, least foyer in a qualm of cold. [Novel 457-15
  Or cooling in late leaves, not false except [Study I 463-17
  Or, say, the late going colors of that past, [NH 488-11
  To photographs of the late president, Mr. Blank, [NH 488-15
  Both late and alone, above the crickets' chords, [Quiet 523-12
  Here in the North, late, late, there are voices of men, [Sick
    90-10 P
  We drove home from Cornwall to Hartford, late. [Real 110-8 P
  Of the wind, of the wind as it deepens, and late sleep, [Art Pop
    113-5 P
LATENESS. And tells the hour by the lateness of the sounds. [Pure
  330-3
  And an air of lateness. The moon is a tricorn [Aug 495-20
  Or clouds that hang lateness on the sea. They become [Role 93-10P
LATENT. And every latent double in the word, [NSF 387-6
LATER. Later, the firecat closed his bright eyes [Earthy 3-19
  Of a later day [Paltry 6-5
  Like a rose rabbi, later, I pursued, [Monocle 17-25
  To bathe their hearts in later moonlight, [Homunculus 26-12
  A little later when the sky is black. [Nigger 156-14
  Not in a later son, a different daughter, another place, [Martial
    237-14
  Another and later genesis, music [EM 321-6
  We reason about them with a later reason. [NSF 399-3
  We reason of these things with later reason [NSF 401-1
  Longer and later, in which the lilacs opened [Aug 491-27

Seventy Years Later [Rock 525-title 1
LATEST. To be their latest, lucent paramour. [C 38-27
  "The Latest Freed Man" [204-title
  The latest freed man rose at six and sat [Freed 204-14
  The breath life's latest, thousand senses. [Montra 264-2
LATIN. To compound the imagination's Latin with [NSF 397-8
LATINED. A hawk of life, that latined phrase: [MBG 178-4
LATITUDE. Who, then, in that ambrosial latitude [Sea Surf 99-5
LATTICES. Their brilliance through the lattices, crippled [Blue
  Bldg 217-10
  7. These lozenges are nailed-up lattices. [Someone 86-10 A
LAU. Und so lau, between sound without meaning and speech, [Page
  421-10
  So lind. The wind blazed as they sang. So lau. [Page 421-17
LAUGH. That makes us weep, laugh, grunt and groan, and shout
  [Monocle 17-10
  For breath to laugh the louder, the deeper gasps [Extracts
    253-19
  The children laugh and jangle a tinny time. [AA 415-12
  Will laugh in the brown grass, [Secret Man 36-15 P
LAUGHED. And laughed, as he sat there reading, from out of the
  purple tabulae, [Large 424-4
LAUGHING. The laughing sky will see the two of us [Monocle 16-10
  And laughing, a crowd of men, [Dezem 218-11
  Laughing and singing and being happy, [Dezem 218-15
  Of a house, that makes one think the house is laughing, [Slug
    522-10
LAUGHS. The spirit laughs to see the eye believe [Extracts 253-5
LAUGHTER. Whose singing is a mode of laughter, [Dezem 218-12
  Provoking a laughter, an agreement, by surprise, [Gala 248-15
  To the laughter of evil: the fierce ricanery [Extracts 253-17
LAUNDRY. The negro with laundry passes me by. [Stan MBG 72-10 P
LAURELS. Its poisoned laurels in this poisoned wood, [Pastor
  379-20
LAVENDER. Poor buffo! Look at the lavender [Lilacs 49-6
  Shucks . . . lavender moonlight falls. [Add 198-11
  A purple woman with a lavender tongue [Melancholy 32-6 P
LAVISHING. Except the lavishing of itself in change, [AA 416-10
LAVISHINGS. And queered by lavishings of their will to see.
  [Bouquet 451-4
LAW. To that first, foremost law. Anguishing hour! [Monocle 17-13
  Take the moral law and make a nave of it [High-Toned 59-2
  The opposing law and make a peristyle, [High-Toned 59-7
  Trained to poise the tables of the law, [Lions 124-14
  And it does; a law of inherent opposites, [Connois 215-9
  The law of chaos is the law of ideas, [Extracts 255-23
  If I live according to this law I live [Past Nun 378-15
  The outlines of being and its expressings, the syllables of its
    law: [Large 424-5
  Order, the law of hoes and rakes, [Room Gard 41-4 P
  And origin and resplendent end of law, [Greenest 60-5 P
  "It is a lesser law than the one itself, [Bship 78-26 P
  On the sea, is both law and evidence in one, [Bship 78-29 P
  It is clear that it is not a moral law. [Bship 78-31 P
  Are the manifestations of a law [Ulysses 103-22 P
LAWN. They mow the lawn. A vessel sinks in waves [EM 322-12
LAWS. As his pure intellect applies its laws, [Bird Claws 82-14
  Whose blunt laws make an affectation of mind, [Look 519-9
  It is not a set of laws. Therefore, its form [Recit 86-8 P
LAWYERS. On Sundays, lawyers in their promenades [NSF 391-13
  A man. The lawyers disbelieved, the doctors [NSF 391-21
LAX. Mounting the earth-lines, long and lax, lethargic. [Tallap
  72-3
LAY. That lay impounding the Pacific swell, [Geneva 24-2
  Lay groveling. Triton incomplicate with that [C 28-29
  That lay elsewhere around him. Severance [C 30-1
  From which he sailed. Beyond him, westward, lay [C 33-13
  Should he lay by the personal and make [C 41-23
  That lay beside him, the quotidian [C 43-4
  It is the grave of Jesus, where he lay." [Sunday 70-17
  And in his heart his disbelief lay cold. [Babies 77-17
  Susanna lay. [Peter 90-14
  Of ocean, which like limpid water lay. [Sea Surf 99-4
  Of ocean, which in sinister flatness lay. [Sea Surf 99-22
  To lay his brain upon the board [MBG 166-5
  It was not as if the truth lay where he thought, [Landsc 242-3
  It was easier to think it lay there. If [Landsc 242-5
  At New Year and, from then until April, lay [Extracts 255-2
  And lay beside her underneath the tree. [Hand 271-21
  At a town in which acacias grew, he lay [EM 314-17
  Lay a passion for yes that had never been broken. [EM 320-14
  This is the habit of wishing, as if one's grandfather lay [Bed
    327-1
  Who lay in bed on the west wall of the sea, [Pure 331-6
  Moved on the buried water where they lay. [Descrip 343-5
  Take the diamonds from your hair and lay them down. [Myrrh 350-10
  "The farm was fat and the land in which it lay [Anach 365-18
  If MacCullough himself lay lounging by the sea, [NSF 387-9
  They lay. Forth then with huge pathetic force [NSF 403-7
  As if, awake, we lay in the quiet of sleep, [AA 418-24

This drama that we live--We lay sticky with sleep. [AA 419-14
A steamer lay near him, foundered in the ice. [Page 421-13
The great ship, Balayne, lay frozen in the sea. [Page 421-18
Yet Hans lay wide awake. And live alone [Page 422-3
The knowledge of things lay round but unperceived: [Aug 493-18
Even when the book lay turned in the dust of his table. [Poem
    Mt 512-4
These marbles lay weathering in the grass [Two Illus 514-6
She lay upon the roof, [Song Fixed 519-18
Lay on the roof [Song Fixed 520-9
The elysium lay [Coroner 30-11 P
Lay black and full of black misshapen? Wings [Old Woman 44-21 P
And light lay deeper for her than her sight. [Old Woman 44-22 P
LAYS. The hen-cock crows at midnight and lays no egg, [Nigger
    155-10
Of fragrance and the mind lays by its trouble. [Cred 372-8
Now the mind lays by its trouble and considers. [Cred 372-9
LAZARUS. And Lazarus betrayed him to the rest, [Good Man 364-8
LAZY. And the colored purple of the lazy sea, [Hibiscus 22-17
I know my lazy, leaden twang [MBG 169-9
LEAD. What path could lead apart from what she was [Old Woman
    44-17 P
Held in the hands of blue men that are lead within, [Discov
    95-16 P
LEADEN. The leaden pigeon on the entrance gate [Nigger 152-18
Must miss the symmetry of a leaden mate, [Nigger 152-19
I know my lazy, leaden twang [MBG 169-9
Massive drums and leaden trumpets, [Nightgown 214-11
A leaden ticking circular in width. [Duck 66-5 P
And always at this antipodes, of leaden loaves [Discov 95-15 P
LEADER. He sought an earthly leader who could stand [Thought 185-23
The Leader [Thought 186-title 4
Leader, the creator of bursting color [Hero 274-2
LEAF. New leaf and shadowy tinct, [Pourtraicte 21-23
There is no moon, on single, silvered leaf. [Tallap 71-15
A hard dry leaf hangs [Pears 196-15
It is the leaf the bird brings back to the boat. [Blue Bldg
    217-18
In the leaf and bud and how the red, [Vase 246-19
The breast is covered with violets. It is a green leaf. [Holiday
    312-16
Of an earth in which the first leaf is the tale [NSF 394-14
And we enjoy like men, the way a leaf [NSF 406-1
The last leaf that is going to fall has fallen. [NH 487-10
And spread hallucinations on every leaf. [Armor 529-20
LEAFED. The violent disclosure trimly leafed, [Bouquet 452-9
Leafed out in adjectives as private [Hero 277-25
Into the sun-filled water, brightly leafed [Lot 371-2
See bloomy-leafed.
LEAF-GREEN. A feme may come, leaf-green, [Watermelon 89-7
LEAFLESS. My North is leafless and lies in a wintry slime [Fare-
    well 118-11
Of the leafless garden." [Reader 147-9
It was when the trees were leafless first in November [Nigger
    151-1
They suddenly fall and the leafless sound of the wind [Burnshaw
    50-20 P
LEAFLESSNESS. To indicate the total leaflessness. [NH 477-9
LEAFY. Do I commend myself to leafy things [Stan MMO 19-17 P
Or a confect of leafy faces in a tree-- [Art Pop 113-2 P
LEAK. Reverberations leak and lack among holes . . . [Armor 529-8
LEAKED. While all the leaves leaked gold. His mind made morning,
    [Pure 331-22
LEAN. It made you seem so small and lean [Vincentine 52-13
And that white animal, so lean, [Vincentine 53-15
And that white animal, so lean, [Vincentine 53-18
Lean encyclopaedists, inscribe an Iliad. [NE Verses 104-9
Lean from the steeple. Cry aloud, [MBG 170-14
Alone, a lean Review and said, [MBG 180-20
The girl had to hold back and lean back to hold him, [Forces
    229-4
The lean cats of the arches of the churches, [Extracts 254-1
The lean cats of the arches of the churches [Extracts 254-18
Divine orations from lean sacristans [Montra 262-18
But a ghost for Andrew, not lean, catarrhal [Lack 303-10
Wanted to lean, wanted much most to be [House Q 358-13
Lean larkspur and jagged fern and rusting rue [Bouquet 452-10
Oh, death against the invisible; and lean [Blanche 10-6 P
Lean John, and his son, lean John, [Soldat 15-2 P
And his lean son's John, and-a-one [Soldat 15-3 P
On which to lean [Lulu M 27-3 P
If the flashy extravaganzas of the lean [Sombre 69-14 P
Is not lean marble, trenchant-eyed. There is [Recit 86-9 P
LEANED. As they leaned and looked [Ord Women 11-8
Except that the reader leaned above the page, [House Q 358-12
LEANER. Or a leaner being, moving in on him, [NSF 387-14
LEANING. Ah! Yes, desire . . . this leaning on his bed, [Men Fall
    187-15
This leaning on his elbows on his bed, [Men Fall 187-16
Is the reader leaning late and reading there. [House Q 359-4

So that he that stood up in the boat leaning and looking before
    him [Prol 515-12
The leaning shoulder and the searching eye. [Blanche 10-4 P
Worn and leaning to nothingness, [Ulysses 104-20 P
Like leaning on the table, shading one's eyes, [Letters 107-11 P
LEANLY. More leanly shining from a lankier sky. [Anglais 149-3
LEANS. On the city, on which it leans, the people there, [Sombre
    68-21 P
LEAP. Why should the future leap the clouds [Botanist 2 136-3
That turn into fishes and leap [Vari 232-13
Than bad angels leap from heaven to hell in flames. [AA 414-12
But it dare not leap by chance in its own dark. [AA 417-22
She will leap back from the swift constellations, [Soldat 12-7 P
LEAPED. Colossal blacks that leaped across the points [Greenest
    53-13 P
LEAPER. See goat-leaper.
LEAPING. The firecat went leaping, [Earthy 3-15
His beard is of fire and his staff is a leaping flame. [Nigger
    150-14
It was not yet the hour to be dauntlessly leaping. [Vari 236-3
Then bathed its body in the leaping lake. [Hand 271-12
The marble leaping in the storms of light. [Old Woman 43-9 P
The leaping bodies, come from the truculent hand, [Duck 64-15 P
The leaping bodies to his strength, convulsed [Duck 64-18 P
See purple-leaping.
LEAPS. Leaps quickly from the fireside and is gone. [Montra 264-6
Leaps downward through evening's revelations, and [NSF 404-16
He leaps from heaven to heaven more rapidly [AA 414-11
It leaps through us, through all our heavens leaps, [AA 417-16
LEARN. It has to be living, to learn the speech of the place. [Of
    Mod 240-1
Eyes dripping blue, so much to learn. [Couch 295-9
LEARNED. Proclaiming something harsher than he learned [C 33-1
And erudite in happiness, with nothing learned, [Gala 248-8
And of other holy and learned men, among them [Luther 461-6
LEARNING. Thereon the learning of the man conceived [NSF 402-23
And got my learning from the orthodox. [Soldat 11-5 P
LEAST. It is least what one ever sees, [Sailing 120-21
A difference, at least, from nightingales, [Havana 142-3
At least the number of people may thus be fixed. [Nigger 157-10
And least will guess that with our bones [Postcard 159-4
Or, at the least, a phrase, that phrase, [MBG 178-3
By which at least I am befriended. [Idiom 201-10
At least that was the theory, when bishops' books [Connois 215-15
Of the least, minor, vital metaphor, content, [Crude 305-19
Of things at least that was thought of in the old peak of night.
    [Bed 327-8
Mere repetitions. These things at least comprise [NSF 405-17
The late, least foyer in a qualm of cold. [Novel 457-15
Perhaps, absurd perhaps, but at least a purpose, [Moonlight 532-5
At least one baby in you. [Primordia 9-23 P
Of the least appreciable shade of green [Burnshaw 51-20 P
At least, conceive what these hands from Sweden mean, [Duck
    60-21 P
Not the least the pasts destroyed, magniloquent [Sombre 70-6 P
We two share that at least. [Grotesque 76-6 P
When cherries are in season, or, at least [Grotesque 76-8 P
This matters most in things that matter least. [Grotesque 76-11 P
Sight least, but metaphysical blindness gained, [Souls 94-21 P
LEATHER. A thing. Thus, the pineapple was a leather fruit, [Poem
    Morn 219-5
LEAVE. The fops of fancy in their poems leave [Monocle 16-23
Nor half begun, but, when it is, leave room [C 33-19
Leave room, therefore, in that unwritten book [C 33-26
But leave a bed beneath the myrtles. [Norfolk 111-6
Make a bed and leave the iris in it. [Norfolk 112-3
Black man, bright nouveautés leave one, at best, pseudonymous.
    [Nudity Col 145-12
I twang it out and leave it there. [MBG 169-12
To picnic in the ruins that we leave. [Dutch 293-3
Sighing that he should leave the banjo's twang. [NSF 393-21
A meaning which, as he entered it, would shatter the boat and
    leave the oarsmen quiet [Prol 516-7
His roles, would leave to the clouds the righting, [Stan Hero
    84-25 P
He has nothing but the truth to leave. [Ulysses 103-10 P
"As You Leave the Room" [116-title P
LEAVED. See: dark-leaved; large-leaved; thick-leaved; thousand-
    leaved.
LEAVES. And of the fallen leaves, [Domination 8-9
Like the leaves themselves [Domination 8-12
Were like the leaves themselves [Domination 8-18
Or against the leaves themselves [Domination 9-4
Like the leaves themselves [Domination 9-15
In the sound of a few leaves, [Snow Man 10-6
Leaves you [Weep Woman 25-10
Of breakfast ribands, fruits laid in their leaves, [C 42-26
A creeper under jaunty leaves. And fourth, [C 44-21
And deck the bananas in leaves [Bananas 54-17
And our desires. Although she strews the leaves [Sunday 69-2

And stray impassioned in the littering leaves. [Sunday 69-12
Yet leaves us in them, until earth becomes, [Fictive 87-16
She felt, among the leaves, [Peter 90-24
And smiting the crevasses of the leaves [Sea Surf 101-2
Necks among the thousand leaves, [Orangeade 103-5
In fragrant leaves heat-heavy yet nimble in talk. [NE Verses
    105-12
Made by the leaves, that have rotted and fallen; [Lunar 107-8
And the leaves on the paths [Tea 112-10
The leaves in which the wind kept up its sound [Farewell 117-13
The trees like bones and the leaves half sand, half sun. [Fare-
    well 118-5
For myself, I live by leaves, [Botanist 1 134-14
Swept through its boarded windows and the leaves [Havana 142-19
Sigh for me, night-wind, in the noisy leaves of the oak. [Nigger
    150-15
Pushing their buds above the dark green leaves, [Nigger 156-11
One of the leaves that have fallen in autumn? [Nigger 158-12
The wind in which the dead leaves blow. [MBG 180-14
There are not leaves enough to cover the face [Dames 206-1
Each one its paradigm." There are not leaves [Dames 206-6
With faces as with leaves, be gusty with mouths, [Dames 206-9
By the wise. There are not leaves enough to crown, [Dames 206-18
Occurred above the empty house and the leaves [Sleight 222-4
We feast on human heads, brought in on leaves, [Cuisine 228-10
Seeming to be liquid as leaves made of cloud, [Forces 229-14
Yet the freshness of the leaves, the burn [Scavoir 231-6
The leaves of the sea are shaken and shaken. [Vari 233-5
And the rude leaves fall. [Metamorph 266-3
The zebra leaves, the sea [Search 268-3
The many-stanzaed sea, the leaves [Search 268-5
Even the leaves of the locust were yellow then, [Contra II 270-3
The leaves, even of the locust, the green locust. [Contra II
    270-6
The leaves were falling like notes from a piano. [Contra II
    270-12
"Oak Leaves Are Hands" [title-272
The wind moves like a cripple among the leaves [Phenom 288-3
The field is frozen. The leaves are dry. [Possum 293-15
The leaves hop, scraping on the ground. [Possum 294-6
An image that leaves nothing much behind. [Repet 307-18
Dropped down from turquoise leaves. In the landscape of [EM
    318-13
While all the leaves leaked gold. His mind made morning, [Pure
    331-22
Dry Birds Are Fluttering in Blue Leaves [Pure 332-title 4
Of many meanings in the leaves, [Silent 359-13
A man and a woman, like two leaves [Burghers 362-12
Of leaves, in which the sparrow is a bird [NSF 394-15
Of spring come to their places in the grape leaves [NSF 399-14
To imagine winter? When the leaves are dead, [AA 417-7
And cried out to feel it again, have run fingers over leaves
    [Large 424-2
Hewn in their middle as the beam of leaves, [Owl 434-2
But the virtuoso never leaves his shape, [Orb 443-4
He walks through the house, looks round him and then leaves.
    [Bouquet 453-2
The red ripeness of round leaves is thick [Pecul 453-10
When the leaves fall like things mournful of the past, [Puel
    456-12
The winds batter it. The water curls. The leaves [Novel 457-2
Rattles with fear in unreflecting leaves. [Golden 460-15
Or cooling in late leaves, not false except [Study I 463-17
From five-six cornered leaves, and green, the signal [NH 470-20
In the area between and was are leaves, [NH 474-2
Leaves burnished in autumnal burnished trees [NH 474-3
And leaves in whirlings in the gutters, whirlings [NH 474-4
To have evaded clouds and men leaves him [NH 480-5
Fertile of its own leaves and days and wars, [Aug 491-14
After the leaves have fallen, we return [Plain 502-9
The plain sense of it, without reflections, leaves, [Plain 503-3
The leaves on the macadam make a noise-- [Hermit 505-10
That the green leaves came and covered the high rock, [Rock 526-4
It is not enough to cover the rock with leaves. [Rock 526-10
And yet the leaves, if they broke into bud, [Rock 526-14
The fiction of the leaves is the icon [Rock 526-18
These leaves are the poem, the icon and the man. [Rock 527-2
They are more than leaves that cover the barren rock [Rock 527-6
Of leaves and of the ground and of ourselves. [Rock 527-20
And green with leaves. [Phases 3-8 P
And leaves that would be loose upon the wind, [Bowl 7-4 P
The male voice of the wind in the dry leaves [Primordia 7-14 P
The birds that wait out rain in willow leaves. [Soldat 13-13 P
Jocunda, who will arrange the roses and rearrange, letting the
    leaves lie on the water-like lacquer; [Piano 22-4 P
And love her still, still leaves you in the wrong. [Red Kit 31-1 P
In the midst of a circle of trees, from which the leaves [Old
    Woman 43-3 P
More than his mind in the wings. The rotten leaves [Old Woman
    43-20 P

Still eked out luminous wrinklings on the leaves, [Old Woman
    45-7 P
A woman walking in the autumn leaves, [Old Woman 45-18 P
On pattering leaves and suddenly with lights, [Burnshaw 47-25 P
On a day still full of summer, when the leaves [Burnshaw 50-18 P
Leaves are not always falling and the birds [Burnshaw 50-24 P
Than purple paste of fruit, to taste, or leaves [Greenest 58-31 P
The same down-dropping fruit in yellow leaves, [Duck 61-14 P
Like the time of the portent, images like leaves, [Sombre 69-29 P
And those the leaves of autumn-afterwards, [Sombre 69-31 P
Leaves of the autumns in which the man below [Sombre 69-32 P
Give only their color to the leaves. The trees [Sombre 71-3 P
Fluttering in blue leaves, [Including 88-4 P
Today the leaves cry, hanging on branches swept by wind, [Course
    96-10 P
The leaves cry . . . One holds off and merely hears the cry.
    [Course 96-13 P
The leaves cry. It is not a cry of divine attention, [Course
    96-19 P
It is the cry of leaves that do not transcend themselves,
    [Course 96-21 P
Among its leaves. [Three 135-11 P
As red is multiplied by the leaves of trees. [Three 143-14 P
See: grape-leaves; locust-leaves; oak-leaves.
LEAVING. Leaving no room upon his cloudy knee, [C 43-18
  On everything. Now it had melted, leaving [Extracts 255-3
  The spent feeling leaving nothing of itself, [NSF 400-12
  Leaving, of where we were and looked, of where [AA 417-18
  In the space, leaving an outline of the size [Aug 494-20
LEBENSWEISHEITSPIELEREI. "Lebensweisheitspielerei" [504-title
LECTURE. We shall return at twilight from the lecture [NSF 406-23
LECTURER. This day writhes with what? The lecturer [Ulti 429-9
LECTURING. Of introspective exiles, lecturing. [Monocle 15-16
LED. Which led them back to angels, after death. [Eve Angels 137-12
  Led the emperor astray, the tom trumpets [Hero 278-7
LEDGES. In endless ledges, glittering, submerged [C 34-7
LEER. Was last with its porcelain leer. [Public Sq 109-12
LEFT. To the left, [Earthy 3-12
  To the right, to the left, [Earthy 3-16
  Which made him Triton, nothing left of him, [C 28-30
  Left only Death's ironic scraping. [Peter 92-10
  The snake has left its skin upon the floor. [Farewell 117-2
  They that had left the flame-freaked sun [How Live 125-15
  That they had left, heroic sound [How Live 126-7
  He has left his robes folded in camphor [Gray 140-2
  When too great rhapsody is left annulled [Havana 144-9
  That dark companion left him unconsoled [Anglais 148-17
  We left much more, left what still is [Postcard 159-5
  The look of things, left what we felt [Postcard 159-6
  As if he that lived there left behind [Postcard 159-17
  Your images will have left [Add 198-21
  Above her, to the left, [Add 199-5
  And left beside and left behind. [Country 207-18
  And nothing is left except light on your fur-- [Rabbit K 209-3
  For the spirit left helpless by the intelligence. [News 265-10
  Someone has left for a ride in a balloon [Phenom 286-7
  Yet a spider spins in the left shoe under the bed-- [Phenom
    286-10
  Like a machine left running, and running down. [Repet 306-18
  Phantoms, what have you left? What underground? [EM 320-2
  And nothing is left but comic ugliness [EM 320-21
  A shape left behind, with like wings spreading out, [Myrrh 350-2
  Left thoughtlessly behind, [Prejudice 368-18
  Beyond which there is nothing left of time. [Cred 372-12
  As when the cock crows on the left and all [NSF 386-10
  They are a plural, a right and left, a pair, [NSF 407-11
  A scholar, in his Segmenta, left a note, [NH 485-1
  Those that are left are the unaccomplished, [Leben 504-19
  It is like a guitar left on a table [Vacancy 511-8
  He left half a shoulder and half a head [Two Illus 514-4
  Left only the fragments found in the grass, [Two Illus 515-3
  Had left in them only a brilliance, of unaccustomed origin,
    [Prol 515-11
  What is left has the foreign smell of plaster, [Armor 529-5
  Descending, did not touch her eye and left [Old Woman 44-8 P
  Left here by moonlit muckers when they fled [Burnshaw 46-22 P
  The gods like marble figures fallen, left [Greenest 58-14 P
  The ruins of the past, out of nothing left, [Recit 87-14 P
  And thus an elevation, as if I left [As Leave 117-11 P
  Since the day we left Pekin. [Three 128-9 P
  You have left your lantern behind you. [Three 135-7 P
LEG. To weave a shadow's leg or sleeve, a scrawl [What We 459-18
LEGEND. Legend were part of what he was, forms [Hero 276-23
  At the legend of the maroon and olive forest, [Plant 506-17
  Glares, outside of the legend, with the barbarous green [Plant
    506-18
  A legend scrawled in script we cannot read? [Recit 87-10 P
  To the chatter that is then the true legend, [Ulysses 102-16 P
LEGENDARY. For the legendary moonlight that once burned [C 33-27
LEGENDS. But over the wind, over the legends of its roaring,

[Puel 456-4

LEGGED. See: bow-legged; three-legged; twelve-legged.
LEGIBLE. The less legible meanings of sounds, the little reds
    [NH 488-7
LEGIONS. White and star-furred for his legions, [Snow Stars
    133-8
    One thinking of apocalyptic legions. [Descrip 343-14
LEGS. On a hundred legs, the tread [Cortege 79-15
    By dividing the number of legs one sees by two. [Nigger 157-9
    Without legs or, for that, without heads. [Possum 294-1
    A massive body and long legs, stretched out, [Orb 443-9
    It is the infant A standing on infant legs, [NH 469-7
    Green bosoms and black legs, beguile [Stanzas MMO 19-10 P
    Yet hardly to be seen and again the legs [Old Woman 46-8 P
LEISURE. Became divided in the leisure of blue day [NH 468-22
LEMON. And the window's lemon light, [Anything B 211-20
    In the land of the lemon trees, yellow and yellow were [NH
    486-13
    When the mariners came to the land of the lemon trees, [NH 487-1
LEMONS. On the wall, the lemons on the table. [Hero 280-15
LEND. toward which you lend no part! [Nuances 18-7
    Lend no part to any humanity that suffuses [Nuances 18-11
LENGTH. Of its improvisation until, at length, [Pastor 379-10
LENGTHENING. A swerving, a tilting, a little lengthening, [Nuns
    92-11 P
LENGTHWISE. Lie lengthwise like the cloud of sleep, not quite
    [Two V 354-4
LENIN. Go, mouse, go nibble at Lenin in his tomb. [Blue Bldg
    217-19
    To Nietzsche in Basel, to Lenin by a lake. [Descrip 342-1
    Lenin on a bench beside a lake disturbed [Descrip 342-21
    Lenin took bread from his pocket, scattered it-- [Descrip 343-6
    The eye of Lenin kept the far-off shapes. [Descrip 343-11
    Might muff the mighty spirit of Lenin. [Lytton 39-17 P
LEONARDO. In Leonardo's way, to magnify [Greenest 56-20 P
LEOPARDS. The memory moves on leopards' feet, desire [Greenest
    57-16 P
LESPINASSE. See Mademoiselle de Lespinasse.
LESS. Less prickly and much more condign than that [C 42-15
    Not less because in purple I descended [Hoon 65-7
    The loneliest air, not less was I myself. [Hoon 65-9
    One might in turn become less diffident, [Pharynx 96-13
    A little less returned for him each spring. [Anglais 148-12
    The very book, or, less, a page [MBG 178-2
    More than, less than or it puffs like this or that. [Dump 202-4
    Or less, he found a man, or more, against [Horn 230-15
    A music more than a breath, but less [Vari 232-7
    Was less than moonlight. Nothing exists by itself. [Les Plus
    244-18
    Of less neatly measured common-places. [Hero 275-18
    A wider brow, large and less human [Hero 277-8
    Of less degree than flame and lesser shine. [Choc 297-23
    The lesser night, the less than morning light, [Choc 301-20
    Less Aix than Stockholm, hardly a yellow at all, [Holiday 312-4
    Can we conceive of him as rescuing less, [EM 316-20
    The sun, its grossest appetite becomes less gross, [EM 318-14
    "Less and Less Human, O Savage Spirit" [327-title
    Like more and more becoming less and less, [Two V 354-13
    Less firm than the paternal flame, [Red Fern 365-6
    Its color, but less as they recede, impinged [Anach 366-10
    We were the appropriate conceptions, less [Lot 371-13
    Am I that imagine this angel less satisfied? [NSF 404-20
    Made us no less as sure. We saw in his head, [AA 412-1
    And the whiteness grows less vivid on the wall. [AA 412-22
    Less real. For the oldest and coldest philosopher, [AA 418-9
    Less time than place, less place than thought of place [Owl 433-1
    Of sleep, the whiteness folded into less, [Owl 433-8
    And no less suddenly here again, a growth [Bouquet 448-11
    Is more or less. The pearly women that drop [Study II 464-5
    The less legible meanings of sounds, the little reds [NH 488-7
    Will come stamping here, the ruler of less than men, [Aug 495-22
    In less than nature. He is not here yet. [Aug 495-23
    Was so much less. Only the wind [Two Illus 513-8
    Too much like thinking to be less than thought, [Look 518-19
    Time's given perfections made to seem like less [Armor 530-8
    Into a sense, an object the less; or else [Moonlight 531-12
    Were no less makings of the sun. [Planet 532-15
    Of the well-thumbed, infinite pages of her masters, who will
    seem old to her, requiting less and less her feeling: [Piano
    22-7 P
    Less than contending with fictitious doom. [Spaniard 35-5 P
    Less in the stars than in their earthy wake, [Burnshaw 48-10 P
    Escape all deformation, much less this, [Duck 63-26 P
    He dwells below, the man below, in less [Sombre 67-13 P
    Than body and in less than mind, ogre, [Sombre 67-14 P
    Inhabitant, in less than shape, of shapes [Sombre 67-15 P
    Of more or less, ascetically sated [Woman Had 82-5 P
    Green, more or less, in green and blue in blue, [Theatre 91-2 P
    Yet the nothingness of winter becomes a little less. [Course
    96-11 P

How then shall the mind be less than free [Ulysses 103-11 P
    So much less than feeling, so much less than speech, [Region
    115-9 P
    Not true, nor think it, less. He must defy [Someone 84-5 A
LESSEN. The shadows lessen on the walls. [Contra I 266-18
LESSENED. No turban walks across the lessened floors. [Plain 502-16
LESSER. In his observant progress, lesser things [C 34-19
    Catching the lesser dithyrambs. [Thought 184-9
    First, summer, then a lesser time, [Vase 246-23
    Of less degree than flame and lesser shine. [Choc 297-23
    The lesser night, the less than morning light, [Choc 301-20
    The lesser seeming original in the blind [Descrip 340-2
    Make any imaginings of them lesser things. [Roses 430-15
    It is something seen and known in lesser poems. [Orb 440-10
    Of blue light and of green, as lesser poems, [Orb 442-4
    And the miraculous multiplex of lesser poems, [Orb 442-5
    With lesser things, with things exteriorized [NH 470-3
    Of the most evasive hue of a lesser blue, [Burnshaw 51-19 P
    What lesser man shall measure sun and moon, [Duck 63-7 P
    "It is a lesser law than the one itself, [Bship 78-26 P
    Inhuman for a little, lesser time." [Ulysses 105-6 P
LET. Yet let that trifle pass. Now, as this odd [C 32-13
    Let down gigantic quavers of its voice, [C 33-16
    But let these backward lapses, if they would, [C 35-14
    By force of rudeness, let the principle [C 38-7
    All dreams are vexing. Let them be expunged. [C 39-31
    But let the rabbit run, the cock declaim. [C 39-32
    Which, let the tall musicians call and call, [C 41-16
    Let the place of the solitaires [Solitaires 60-1
    Let the wenches dawdle in such dress [Emperor 64-4
    As they are used to wear, and let the boys [Emperor 64-5
    Let be be finale of seem. [Emperor 64-7
    Let the lamp affix its beam. [Emperor 64-15
    Let these be your delight, secretive hunter, [Tallap 72-1
    Let us erect in the Basin a lofty fountain. [NE Verses 105-1
    Let him remove it to his regions, [Snow Stars 133-7
    Let this be clear that we are men of sun [Eve Angels 137-13
    But let the poet on his balcony [Havana 144-30
    Empty and grandiose, let us make hymns [Nigger 151-20
    To cover, to crown, to cover--let it go-- [Dames 206-19
    Of spray. Let all the salt be gone. [Vari 234-16
    Let the Secretary for Porcelain observe [Extracts 253-7
    And let the water-belly of ocean roar, [Montra 261-23
    But let this one sense be the single main. [Montra 264-3
    An invisible gesture. Let this be called [Couch 295-15
    My orator. Let this giantness fall down [Repet 310-2
    And come to nothing. Let the rainy arcs [Repet 310-3
    Softly let all true sympathizers come, [EM 317-4
    Let him move as the sunlight moves on the floor, [Less 327-11
    Or Aristotle's skeleton. Let him hang out [Less 327-13
    If there must be a god in the house, let him be one [Less 328-7
    And let it go, with nothing lost, [Woman Song 361-4
    The sea full of fishes in shoals, the woods that let [Cats 367-13
    Let's see the very thing and nothing else. [Cred 373-3
    Let's see it with the hottest fire of sight. [Cred 373-4
    Fly low, cock bright, and stop on a bean pole. Let [Cred 377-6
    Let purple Phoebus lie in umber harvest, [NSF 381-8
    Let Phoebus slumber and die in autumn umber, [NSF 381-9
    Let us design a chastel de chasteté. [Archi 16-14 P
    Let us build the building of light. [Archi 17-14 P
    Let us fix portals, east and west, [Archi 17-27 P
    And the awnings are let down. [Mandolin 28-14 P
    Then turn your heads and let your spiral eyes [Red Kit 31-27 P
    Look backward. Let your swiftly-flying flocks [Red Kit 31-28 P
    Let this be as it may. It must have tears [Spaniard 35-13 P
    Let's go home. [Drum-Majors 37-12 P
    Let's hope for Mademoiselle de Lespinasse, [Lytton 39-19 P
    Like damsels daubed and let your feet be bare [Burnshaw 51-11 P
    Let your golden hands wave fastly and be gay [Burnshaw 51-28 P
    The way it came, let be what it may become. [Sombre 71-16 P
    Let wise men piece the world together with wisdom [Grotesque
    75-7 P
    It was a rabbi's question. Let the rabbis reply. [Bship 79-14 P
    Let the candle shine for the beauty of shining [Three 133-10 P
LETHARGIC. Mounting the earth-lines, long and lax, lethargic.
    [Tallap 72-3
LETHARGY. Stiff in eternal lethargy, should be, [Conversat 109-8 P
LETS. The life of the city never lets go, nor do you [Rome 510-12
LETTER. "The Comedian as the Letter C" [27-title
    In a barrack in a barrack, a letter from Malay. [NSF 407-14
    A Letter From [Letters 107-title 1 P
    A Letter To [Letters 107-title 2 P
LETTERED. Lettered herself demurely as became [C 44-31
LETTERS. Letters of rock and water, words [Vari 232-10
    These letters of him for the little, [Hero 279-5
    He was at Naples writing letters home [EM 313-10
    And, between his letters, reading paragraphs [EM 313-12
    Of letters, prophecies, perceptions, clods [Orb 443-20
    Or letters of a curious alphabet; [Recit 87-8 P
    "Two Letters" [107-title P

LETTING. Jocunda, who will arrange the roses and rearrange, letting
    the leaves lie on the water-like lacquer; [Piano 22-4 P
   A divination, a letting down [Ulysses 101-28 P
LETTRES. "Poems from 'Lettres d'un Soldat'" [10-title P
LEVEL. She floats in air at the level of [Couch 295-4
   On the level of that which is not yet knowledge: [Region 115-11 P
LEWD. So lewd spring comes from winter's chastity. [NH 468-4
LEWDER. It breeds and that was lewder than it is. [Anatomy 107-15
LEWDEST. Of parents, lewdest of ancestors. [Prelude 195-20
   There are the lewdest and the lustiest, [Dutch 292-4
LEX. And lex. Sed quaeritur: is this same wig [C 27-10
   Exit the mental moonlight, exit lex, [C 36-28
LEXICOGRAPHER. And general lexicographer of mute [C 28-11
LEYDEN. Roma ni Avignon ni Leyden, [Hero 273-2
   Peace in a time of peace, said Leyden [Hero 273-10
LHASSA. The dress of a woman of Lhassa, [Men 1000 52-7
LIADOFF. A poem for Liadoff, the self of selves: [Choc 297-7
   "Two Tales of Liadoff" [346-title
   That night, Liadoff, a long time after his death, [Liadoff 346-14
   As they fell down, as they heard Liadoff's cloud [Liadoff 346-18
   Was repeated by Liadoff in a narration [Liadoff 347-2
   The feeling of Liadoff was changed. It is [Liadoff 347-4
   As if Liadoff no longer remained a ghost [Liadoff 347-8
LIAISON. The liaison, the blissful liaison, [C 34-26
LIBERTY. Have liberty not as the air within a grave [Aug 490-12
LICE. Snakes and gold and lice, [On Road 204-7
LICENTIOUS. Licentious violet and lascive rose, [Montra 261-15
LID. The lashes of that eye and its white lid. [Worms 49-19
   Here is the cheek on which that lid declined, [Worms 49-20
   But is an eye that studies its black lid. [Tallap 71-17
   Eye without lid, mind without any dream-- [NSF 394-12
LIDS. His lids are white because his eyes are blind. [Bird Claws
    82-6
LIE. Or to sleep or just to lie there still, [Adieu 128-4
   Comes through boughs that lie in wait, [Brave 138-8
   Where do you lie, beneath snow, [Bagatelles 213-2
   Those that lie chanting green is the night. [Candle 223-6
   As they used to lie in the grass, in the heat, [Cuisine 227-18
   To lie on one's bed in the dark, close to a face [Yellow 237-8
   Of what do you lie thinking in your cavern? [Extracts 256-19
   Lie in the heart's residuum . . . Amen. [Extracts 258-23
   The wounds. Yet to lie buried in evil earth, [Extracts 259-2
   Lie in the heart's residuum. [Extracts 259-7
   Lie harshly buried there? [Extracts 259-10
   And you, my semblables, are crusts that lie [Dutch 291-6
   Lie sprawling in majors of the August heat, [EM 325-28
   Pure coruscations, that lie beyond [Analysis 349-1
   The fathers of the makers may lie and weather. [New Set 353-6
   Lie lengthwise like the cloud of sleep, not quite [Two V 354-4
   The bass lie deep, still afraid of the Indians. [Think 356-8
   Let purple Phoebus lie in umber harvest, [NSF 381-8
   Your mansard with a rented piano. You lie [NSF 384-18
   Lie down like children in this holiness, [AA 418-23
   From line to line, as we lie on the grass and listen [Aug 492-11
   He does not lie there remembering the blue-jay, say the jay.
    [Madame 507-11
   Where he could lie and, gazing down at the sea, [Poem Mt 512-13
   It rose loftily and stood massively; and to lie [Armor 529-2
   Jocunda, who will arrange the roses and rearrange, letting the
    leaves lie on the water-like lacquer; [Piano 22-4 P
   Or is it that alligators lie [An Gaiety 33-2 P
   To rumbled rock, its bright projections lie [Sombre 70-3 P
LIEBCHEN. Liebchen, [Explan 72-22
LIEF. I had as lief be embraced by the porter at the hotel [Two
    Figures 85-14
LIES. Lies quilted to his poll in his despite. [C 41-30
   My North is leafless and lies in a wintry slime [Farewell 118-11
   It lies, themselves within themselves, [Fading 139-12
   But in between lies the sphere of my fortune [Nigger 151-5
   Dew lies on the instruments of straw that you were playing,
    [Fish-Scale 160-17
   To his breath that lies awake at night. [MBG 171-16
   He lies down and the night wind blows upon him here. [Men Fall
    187-13
   Whose head lies blurring here, for this he died. [Men Fall 188-14
   Lies in flawed words and stubborn sounds. [Poems Clim 194-10
   Of music--Her body lies [Add 199-2
   Around which silence lies on silence. [Yellow 236-10
   Falls and lies with the worms. [Metamorph 266-5
   The greenness of night lies on the page and goes [Phosphor 267-9
   There lies the misery, the coldest coil [Choc 298-21
   That there lies at the end of thought [Crude 305-5
   His route lies through an image in his mind: [Repet 307-15
   My route lies through an image in my mind, [Repet 307-16
   The fault lies with an over-human god, [EM 315-14
   And the soldier of time lies calm beneath that stroke. [EM 319-18
   With time, in wavering water lies, swollen [Two V 354-2
   Of the lover that lies within us and we breathe [NSF 394-24
   In which the sense lies still, as a man lies, [Roses 431-2
   Presence lies far too deep, for me to know [John 437-25

The bouquet has slopped over the edge and lies on the floor.
    [Bouquet 453-3
But his father was strong, that lies now [Pecul 453-5
In which a real lies hidden and alive [Novel 458-15
Lies on the breast and pierces into the heart, [Novel 458-24
Close to the senses there lies another isle [NH 480-17
Of Fact, lies at his ease beside the sea." [NH 485-18
And the egg of the earth lies deep within an egg. [Aug 490-10
So much guilt lies buried [Inhab 504-13
As it falls from the heart and lies there to be seen, [Rome
    509-27
On which the quiet moonlight lies. [Archi 17-21 P
Mesdames, one might believe that Shelley lies [Burnshaw 48-9 P
There lies the head of the sculptor in which the thought [Burn-
    shaw 49-16 P
The colorless light in which this wreckage lies [Burnshaw 49-25 P
In the ceiling of the distant room, in which he lies, [Sick
    90-17 P
LIFE. This luscious and impeccable fruit of life [Monocle 14-12
   The whole of life that still remained in him [C 28-18
   Glozing his life with after-shining flicks, [C 46-5
   A pip of life amid a mort of tails. [Bird Claws 82-3
   "Life Is Motion" [83-title
   And green vine angering for life, [Nomad 95-9
   Life contracts and death is expected, [Soldier 97-1
   Of life and spring and of the lustrous inundations, [Medit 123-14
   Fears of life and fears of death, [Brave 138-17
   How good life is, on the basis of propriety, [Winter B 141-13
   Life is an old casino in a park. [Havana 142-9
   Life is an old casino in a wood. [Havana 144-17
   It is curious that the density of life [Nigger 157-7
   So that's life, then: things as they are? [MBG 166-13
   And that's life, then: things as they are, [MBG 167-1
   What is there in life except one's ideas, [MBG 175-17
   Good air, good friend, what is there in life? [MBG 175-18
   A hawk of life, that latined phrase: [MBG 178-4
   Yet life itself, the fulfilment of desire [Men Fall 188-3
   Over words that are life's voluble utterance. [Men Fall 188-20
   There's no such thing as life; or if there is, [Parochial 192-4
   By the trash of life, [Bagatelles 213-11
   Of the life that you will not live, [Bagatelles 213-17
   After all the pretty contrast of life and death [Connois 215-13
   "The Common Life" [221-title
   Has any chance to mate his life with life [Sleight 222-17
   That is the sensual, pearly spouse, the life [Sleight 222-18
   A unity that is the life one loves, [Yellow 236-19
   As the life of the fatal unity of war. [Yellow 236-21
   Again . . . as if it came back, as if life came back, [Martial
    237-13
   That other one wanted to think his way to life, [Extracts 256-21
   He, that one, wanted to think his way to life, [Extracts 257-4
   In vain, life's season or death's element. [Montra 263-6
   The breath life's latest, thousand senses. [Montra 264-2
   When the deep breath fetches another year of life. [News
    265-12
   With life's salt upon their lips and savor [Hero 279-7
   There is no life except in the word of it. [Phenom 287-19
   The life that never would end, no matter [Gigan 289-5
   That grips the centre, the actual bite, that life [Choc 298-22
   Itself is like a poverty in the space of life, [Choc 299-1
   Their form, beyond their life, yet of themselves, [Choc 299-17
   He shares a gigantic life, it is because [Repet 308-11
   His poems are not of the second part of life. [Creat 311-11
   As the body trembles at the end of life. [EM 314-7
   In which his wound is good because life was. [EM 319-15
   He might die was the innocence of living, if life [EM 322-6
   Life is a bitter aspic. We are not [EM 322-9
   It may be that one life is a punishment [EM 323-26
   For another, as the son's life for the father's. [EM 323-27
   The life of the world depends on that he is [Wild 328-11
   "Debris of Life and Mind" [338-title
   Intenser than any actual life could be, [Descrip 344-20
   A seeming of the Spaniard, a style of life, [Descrip 345-15
   Castratos of moon-mash--Life consists [Men Made 355-17
   Of propositions about life. The human [Men Made 355-18
   The world is myself, life is myself, [Pediment 361-17
   In a glitter that is a life, a gold [Human 363-15
   He lived each life because, if it was bad, [Good Man 364-5
   He said a good life would be possible. [Good Man 364-6
   At last the good life came, good sleep, bright fruit, [Good Man
    364-7
   Infant, it is enough in life [Red Fern 365-13
   "Attempt to Discover Life" [370-title
   It comes to this and the imagination's life. [Cred 372-13
   Tristesses, the fund of life and death, suave bush [Cred
    377-15
   The poem refreshes life so that we share, [NSF 382-13
   Life's nonsense pierces us with strange relation. [NSF 383-9
   There were those that returned to hear him read from the poem of
    life, [Large 423-14

And she that in the syllable between life [Owl 432-12
Compounded and compounded, life by life, [Owl 436-1
And its tawny caricature and tawny life, [What We 460-4
The immaculate interpreters of life. [NH 469-18
Together, said words of the world are the life of the world.
    [NH 474-9
As if life and death were ever physical. [NH 478-12
The life and death of this carpenter depend [NH 478-13
Life fixed him, wandering on the stair of glass, [NH 483-10
He is the theorist of life, not death, [NH 485-8
As the life of poetry. A more severe, [NH 486-6
Of poetry is the theory of life, [NH 486-9
The life of the city never lets go, nor do you [Rome 510-12
Ever want it to. It is part of the life in your room. [Rome
    510-13
Of summer and of the sun, the life [Two Illus 514-8
The life of the poem in the mind has not yet begun. [Slug 522-16
"A Quiet Normal Life" [523-title
The rock is the gray particular of man's life, [Rock 528-1
In a mystic eye, no sign of life but life, [Armor 529-14
Is active with a power, an inherent life, [Moonlight 531-20
Although life seems a goblin mummery, [Soldat 13-14 P
Pass the whole of life earing the clink of the [Archi 16-18 P
"The Woman Who Blamed Life on a Spaniard" [34-title P
Life, then, is largely a thing [Table 40-2 P
Made to remember a life they never lived [Burnshaw 46-24 P
Sip the wild honey of the poor man's life, [Burnshaw 49-10 P
Life's foreigners, pale aliens of the mud, [Greenest 59-23 P
Day came upon the spirit as life comes [Duck 61-5 P
More of ourselves, the mood of life made strong [Duck 65-3 P
"Life on a Battleship" [77-title P
It appears to be what there is of life compressed [Bship 79-1 P
But one lives to think of this growing, this pushing life,
    [Bship 80-8 P
From the middens of life, rotten and acrid, [Stan Hero 84-3 P
Have inscribed life's do and don't. The commanding codes [Recit
    86-11 P
His life made double by his father's life, [Recit 87-19 P
On life itself and there the katy-dids [Memo 89-7 P
I wonder, have I lived a skeleton's life, [Warmth 89-17 P
A universe without life's limp and lack, [Theatre 91-16 P
These pods are part of the growth of life within life: [Nuns
    92-7 P
Pronouncing its new life and ours, not autumn's prodigal re-
    turned, [Discov 96-4 P
That is its life preserved, the effort to be born [Discov 96-8 P
Surviving being born, the event of life. [Discov 96-9 P
One feels the life of that which gives life as it is. [Course
    96-18 P
Then knowledge is the only life, [Ulysses 100-1 P
To knowledge when we come to life. [Ulysses 101-20 P
Yet always there is another life. [Ulysses 101-21 P
A life beyond this present knowing, [Ulysses 101-22 P
A life lighter than this present splendor, [Ulysses 101-23 P
A child asleep in its own life. [Ulysses 104-22 P
"A Child Asleep in Its Own Life" [106-title P
An ease in which to live a moment's life, [Letters 107-7 P
The moment of life's love and fortune, [Letters 107-8 P
There is a drop that is life's element, [Conversat 108-20 P
The one thing common to all life, the human [Conversat 109-1 P
It is a shape of life described [Banjo 114-9 P
I wonder, have I lived a skeleton's life, [As Leave 117-5 P
See still-life.
LIFELESS. A dirty light on a lifeless world, [Two Illus 513-2
LIFT. The body lift its heavy wing, take up, [NSF 390-12
The weight we lift with the finger of a dream, [NH 476-12
Forgetting work, nor caring for angels, hunting a lift, [Duck 60-15P
LIFTED. The light wings lifted through the crystal space [Old
    Woman 46-11 P
By tautest pinions lifted through his thought. [Duck 64-19 P
LIFTING. On the horizon and lifting himself up above it. [World
    520-14
LIFTS. Lifts up its heavy scowl before them. [Pediment 362-3
LIGAMENTS. "Oh, lissomeness turned lagging ligaments!" [Stan MMO
    19-20 P
LIGHT. you in its own light. [Nuances 18-12
Good light for drunkards, poets, widows, [Homunculus 25-15
By this light the salty fishes [Homunculus 26-1
This light conducts [Homunculus 26-5
It is a good light, then, for those [Homunculus 27-3
Then third, a thing still flaxen in the light, [C 44-20
Good God! What a precious light! [Bananas 54-9
With lanterns borne aloft to light the way, [Heaven 56-13
When the host shall no more wander, nor the light [Heaven 56-19
Or the changing of light, the dropping [Curtains 62-5
Filled with yellow light. [Six Sig 74-16
The light is like a spider. [Tattoo 81-9
Flying in a green light, [Thirteen 94-10
Out of the light evolved the moving blooms, [Sea Surf 99-6
Her old light moves along the branches, [Lunar 107-3

So be it. Yet the spaciousness and light [Anatomy 108-15
To say the light wind worries the sail, [Sailing 121-1
By light, the way one feels, sharp white, [Sailing 121-6
Stockholm slender in a slender light, [Botanist 1 135-7
And light [Eve Angels 137-6
Light, too, encrusts us making visible [Eve Angels 137-19
Stand in a fixed light. [Gray 140-7
In the pale light that each upon the other throws. [Re-state
    146-12
The shaft of light [Mud 148-6
Which changed light green to olive then to blue. [Nigger 152-10
There might have been a light on a book [Chateau 161-11
At the vernacular of light [Delight 162-4
Of the structure of vaults upon a point of light. [MBG 167-5
A candle is enough to light the world. [MBG 172-16
Like light in a mirroring of cliffs, [MBG 175-3
Or light, the relic of farewells, [MBG 179-3
In the mud, in Monday's dirty light, [MBG 183-16
The bronzes liquid through gay light. [Thought 187-3
Pink and white carnations. The light [Poems Clim 193-8
Here in the centre stands the glass. Light [Glass 197-12
When light comes down to wet his frothy jaws [Glass 197-16
Like a man without a doctrine. The light he gives-- [Freed 205-1
It is how he gives his light. It is how he shines, [Freed 205-2
And nothing is left except light on your fur-- [Rabbit K 209-3
And to feel that the light is a rabbit-light, [Rabbit K 209-10
And the window's lemon light, [Anything B 211-20
Through winter's meditative light? [Bagatelles 213-12
It must be where you think it is, in the light [Blue Bldg 217-15
It is a morbid light [Common 221-6
In this light a man is a result, [Common 221-10
"Of Hartford in a Purple Light" [226-title
It is Hartford seen in a purple light. [Hartford 226-18
A moment ago, light masculine, [Hartford 227-1
When male light fell on the naked back [Hartford 227-7
Out of the changes of both light and dew [Scavoir 231-8
In light blue air over dark blue sea. [Vari 232-6
Not quite. The mist was to light what red [Vari 235-20
A light at the centre of many lights, [Bottle 239-3
And light behind the body of night [Adequacy 244-7
The mind between this light or that and space, [Rhythms 245-11
How much of it was light and how much thought, [Extracts 257-8
Of any woman, watched the thinnest light [Extracts 258-16
"Phosphor Reading by His Own Light" [267-title
Master and, without light, I dwell. There [Hero 273-4
In your light, the head is speaking. It reads the book. [God
    285-10
That of that light Eulalia was the name. [Phenom 287-14
Bad is final in this light. [Possum 293-16
And lit the snow to a light congenial [Choc 297-1
Or light embodied, or almost, a flash [Choc 297-11
The lesser night, the less than morning light, [Choc 301-20
As those are: as light, for all its motion, is; [Less 327-16
And yet remains the same, the beast of light, [Pure 333-2
The eloquences of light's faculties. [Pure 333-9
To an innate grandiose, an innate light, [Descrip 342-17
The buildings were of marble and stood in marble light. [Anach
    366-2
And then half way in the extremest light [Cred 375-23
In the uncertain light of single, certain truth, [NSF 380-7
Equal in living changingness to the light [NSF 380-8
An unaffected man in a negative light [NSF 393-19
To find of light a music issuing [NSF 398-18
Like men besides, like men in light secluded, [NSF 405-12
Through waves of light. It is of cloud transformed [AA 416-7
As light changes yellow into gold and gold [AA 416-11
So, then, these lights are not a spell of light, [AA 418-19
But that which destroys it completely by this light [Page 422-16
Whirlpools of darkness in whirlwinds of light . . . [Page 423-5
To comb her dewy hair, a touchless light, [Beginning 427-13
It exceeds the heavy changes of the light. [Roses 431-7
About the night. They live without our light, [Owl 432-7
A meeting, an emerging in the light, [Owl 433-5
The essential poem begets the others. The light [Orb 441-26
Of it is not a light apart, up-hill. [Orb 441-27
Of blue light and of green, as lesser poems, [Orb 442-4
But she that he loved turns cold at his light touch. [Pecul
    453-12
In a faithfulness as against the lunar light, [NH 472-15
The heaviness we lighten by light will, [NH 476-13
It is a bough in the electric light [NH 477-7
The most ancient light in the most ancient sky, [NH 481-18
That it is wholly an inner light, that it shines [NH 481-19
Shook off their dark marine in lapis light. [NH 484-8
A hand of light to turn the page, [Aug 492-9
He does not raise the rousing of fresh light [Aug 492-22
Of wind and light and cloud [Inhab 503-16
That is an indigence of the light, [Leben 505-2
In that distant chamber, a bearded queen, wicked in her dead
    light. [Madame 507-13

A light on the candle tearing against the wick [Rome 509-5
A dirty light on a lifeless world, [Two Illus 513-2
Outside of and beyond the dirty light, [Two Illus 513-17
The way the earliest single light in the evening sky, in spring,
    [Prol 517-8
Light the first light of evening, as in a room [Final 524-1
A light, a power, the miraculous influence. [Final 524-9
Out of this same light, out of the central mind, [Final 524-16
Stands in a light, its natural light and day, [Armor 530-20
It is the third commonness with light and air, [R Conn 533-16
They heard his mumble in the morning light. [Phases 5-11 P
It dances down a furrow, in the early light, back of a crazy
    plough, the green blades following. [Plough-Boy 6-7 P
Let us build the building of light. [Archi 17-14 P
(He shouts.) Hola! Of that strange light, beware! [Infernale
    25-3 P
(Her pale smock sparkles in a light begun [Infernale 25-9 P
And in whose light the roses [Mandolin 29-3 P
Spread over heaven shutting out the light. [Red Kit 31-26 P
The marble leaping in the storms of light. [Old Woman 43-9 P
Of crisping light along the statue's rim. [Old Woman 43-18 P
And light lay deeper for her than her sight. [Old Woman 44-22 P
Yet the light fell falsely on the marble skulls, [Old Woman
    44-30 P
Manes matted of marble across the air, the light [Old Woman
    45-1 P
Of a lunar light, dark-belted sorcerers [Old Woman 46-3 P
The light wings lifted through the crystal space [Old Woman
    46-11 P
The colorless light in which this wreckage lies [Burnshaw 49-25 P
As if your gowns were woven of the light [Burnshaw 51-24 P
Too starkly pallid for the jaguar's light, [Greenest 54-29 P
Deep grass that totters under the weight of light. [Greenest
    55-1 P
And state of being large and light. [Dove 98-12 P
Comes to this thunder of light [Fare Guit 98-20 P
Light's comedies, dark's tragedies, [Ulysses 102-28 P
Drenching the evening with crystals' light, [Letters 107-3 P
What we heard and the light, though little, was enough. [Letters
    107-15 P
Last Friday, in the big light of last Friday night, [Real 110-7 P
A light snow, like frost, has fallen during the night. [Bus
    116-1 P
And seen in a clear light. [Three 131-24 P
The light of the most tranquil candle [Three 132-13 P
He could not see the steadiest light [Three 133-3 P
"More light!" [Three 137-14 P
Like the true light of the truest sun, the true [Someone 84-9 A
Is fertile with more than changes of the light [Someone 84-18 A
See: fur-light; lamp-light; rabbit-light; stage-light; summer-
    light; two-light; winter-light.
LIGHT-BOUND. In the light-bound space of the mind, the floreate
    flare . . . [Owl 436-6
LIGHTED. And limbed and lighted out from bank to bank. [Lot 371-3
    Lighted at midnight by the studious eye, [NSF 388-2
    The windows will be lighted, not the rooms. [AA 413-24
    Lighted by space, big over those that sleep, [NH 482-5
LIGHTEN. The heaviness we lighten by light will, [NH 476-13
LIGHTER. Not often realized, the lighter words [NH 488-8
    A life lighter than this present splendor, [Ulysses 101-23 P
LIGHTEST. Apparels of such lightest look that a turn [Angel 497-9
LIGHTING. Lighting a pitiless verse or two. [Chateau 161-12
    The obscure moon lighting an obscure world [Motive 288-9
    Lighting the martyrs of logic with white fire. [EM 325-16
    It would have been like lighting a candle, [Letters 107-10 P
LIGHT-LOCKED. And dewy bearings of their light-locked beards.
    [Bouquet 449-24
LIGHTLY. And shuffling lightly, with the heavy lightness [Dutch
    290-11
    Lightly and lightly, O my land, [Imago 439-19
    Move lightly through the air again. [Imago 439-20
LIGHTNESS. And shuffling lightly, with the heavy lightness [Dutch
    290-11
LIGHTNING. Gesticulating lightning, mystical, [C 32-26
    And lightning colors [Nomad 95-17
    There is lightning and the thickest thunder. [Chaos 357-10
    Is a drop of lightning in an inner world, [Bouquet 448-6
    As lightning itself is, likewise, metaphor [Bouquet 448-9
    Shot lightning at the kind cow's milk. [Lulu M 27-12 P
LIGHTS. Hinting incredible hues, four selfsame lights [C 45-8
    That lights and dims the stars? [Sonatina 110-6
    Toward the town, tell why the glassy lights, [Key W 130-5
    The lights in the fishing boats at anchor there, [Key W 130-6
    At night, it lights the fruit and wine, [MBG 172-19
    Throw away the lights, the definitions, [MBG 183-3
    Throw the lights away. Nothing must stand [MBG 183-10
    Lights out. Shades up. [Nightgown 214-1
    Bringing the lights of Norway and all that. [Hartford 226-6
    Lights masculine and lights feminine. [Hartford 226-14
    A light at the centre of many lights, [Bottle 239-3

Like the shiddow-shaddow of lights revolving [Hero 279-20
By a lake, with clouds like lights among great tombs, [EM 325-8
These lights may finally attain a pole [AA 411-14
So, then, these lights are not a spell of light, [AA 418-19
To a haggling of wind and weather, by these lights [AA 421-2
In the bee-loud glade. Lights on the steamer moved. [Page 422-4
Without scenery or lights, in the theatre's bricks, [Bad Time
    427-5
The prince of shither-shade and tinsel lights, [Owl 434-3
And beetling of belts and lights of general stones, [NH 477-20
As if all his hereditary lights were suddenly increased [Prol
    517-1
How high that highest candle lights the dark. [Final 524-15
On the altar, growing toward the lights, inside. [Armor 529-7
On pattering leaves and suddenly with lights, [Burnshaw 47-25 P
Sing rose-beliefs. Above that urn two lights [Burnshaw 50-1 P
Become rude robes among white candle lights, [Greenest 53-4 P
Powdered with primitive lights, and lives with us [Sombre 66-24 P
Remembrances, a place of a field of lights, [Sombre 67-18 P
The poor lights. [Three 132-4 P
See water-lights.
LIKE. Like one who scrawls a listless testament [Swans 4-5
Noiselessly, like one more wave. [Paltry 5-10
Will go, like the centre of sea-green pomp, [Paltry 6-6
Like the leaves themselves [Domination 8-12
Were like the leaves themselves [Domination 8-18
Like the leaves themselves [Domination 9-15
Came striding like the color of the heavy hemlocks [Domination
    9-18
Is like water flowing; [Sugar-Cane 12-8
Like water flowing [Sugar-Cane 12-9
That are like birds, [Sugar-Cane 12-13
Like the clashed edges of two words that kill." [Monocle 13-4
Of what, like skulls, comes rotting back to ground. [Monocle
    14-19
Out of their mother grass, like little kin, [Monocle 15-4
Like a dull scholar, I behold, in love, [Monocle 16-1
We hang like warty squashes, streaked and rayed, [Monocle 16-9
Could make us squeak, like dolls, the wished-for words. [Monocle
    17-8
Grown tired of flight. Like a dark rabbi, I [Monocle 17-21
Like a rose rabbi, later, I pursued, [Monocle 17-25
Shine alone, shine nakedly, shine like bronze, [Nuances 18-8
of my being, shine like fire, that mirrors nothing. [Nuances
    18-10
Like a widow's bird [Nuances 18-16
Unless Racine or Bossuet held the like. [Geneva 24-6
Arch in the sea like tree-branches, [Homunculus 26-2
That were like arms and shoulders in the waves, [C 29-2
The salt hung on his spirit like a frost, [C 29-13
The dead brine melted in him like a dew [C 29-14
Came like two spirits parleying, adorned [C 31-31
That earth was like a jostling festival [C 32-8
Approaching like a gasconade of drums. [C 32-18
Was like a glacial pink upon the air. [C 34-14
Like jades affecting the sequestered bride; [C 34-23
And then retirement like a turning back [C 35-11
He savored rankness like a sensualist. [C 36-12
He once thought necessary. Like Candide, [C 42-15
And men like Crispin like them in intent, [C 42-23
Composed of evenings like cracked shutters flung [C 42-30
Like this, saps like the sun, true fortuner. [C 43-5
Upon his lap, like their inherent sphere, [C 45-27
Of speech which are like music so profound [On Manner 55-13
"The spring is like a belle undressing." [Of Surface 57-5
Like windy citherns hankering for hymns. [High-Toned 59-5
Squiggling like saxaphones. And palm for palm, [High-Toned 59-12
Pardie! Summer is like a fat beast, sleepy in mildew, [Banal
    62-15
The day is like wide water, without sound, [Sunday 67-8
Things to be cherished like the thought of heaven? [Sunday 67-18
Like her remembrance of awakened birds, [Sunday 68-24
Unchanging, yet so like our perishing earth, [Sunday 69-16
With rivers like our own that seek for seas [Sunday 69-17
Naked among them, like a savage source. [Sunday 70-3
The trees, like serafin, and echoing hills, [Sunday 70-8
Is like to these. But in yourself is like: [Tallap 72-6
Like a figure on the church-wall. [Explan 73-4
Like a bracelet [Six Sig 74-2
Like nothing else in Tennessee. [Jar 76-16
It is true that the rivers went nosing like swine, [Frogs 78-1
Is like a vivid apprehension [Jasmine 79-7
The light is like a spider. [Tattoo 81-9
Like the thoughts of an old human, [Shifts 83-11
The wind shifts like this: [Shifts 83-14
Like a human without illusions, [Shifts 83-15
The wind shifts like this: [Shifts 83-17
Like humans approaching proudly, [Shifts 83-18
Like humans approaching angrily. [Shifts 83-19
Like a human, heavy and heavy, [Shifts 84-2

Yet not too like, yet not so like to be [Fictive 88-10
Is music. It is like the strain [Peter 90-5
The winds were like her maids, [Peter 91-3
Soon, with a noise like tambourines, [Peter 91-12
Was like a willow swept by rain. [Peter 91-17
Fled, with a noise like tambourines. [Peter 91-21
Like a tree [Thirteen 92-18
Of ocean, which like limpid water lay. [Sea Surf 99-4
Like blooms secluded in the thick marine? [Sea Surf 101-12
Like blooms? Like damasks that were shaken off [Sea Surf 101-13
At home, a bit like the slenderest courtesan. [NE Verses 106-6
Like a fractured edifice [Public Sq 108-20
Like a thing in which they fell, [Public Sq 109-4
When the music of the boy fell like a fountain, [Norfolk 111-14
Ran like rats, [Tea 112-11
Like umbrellas in Java. [Tea 113-3
The trees like bones and the leaves half sand, half sun. [Farewell 118-5
Which is like zithers and tambourines combined: [Mice 123-8
Like giant arms among the clouds. [How Live 125-20
Like a body wholly body, fluttering [Key W 128-13
Like an hallucination come to daze [Sun March 134-3
Like last night's crickets, far below. [Botanist 2 135-19
Why seraphim like lutanists arranged [Eve Angels 136-13
And a grand decadence settles down like cold. [Havana 142-12
Passed like a circus. [Havana 143-20
Will drop like sweetness in the empty nights [Havana 144-8
"Like Decorations in a Nigger Cemetery" [150-title
Like Walt Whitman walking along a ruddy shore. [Nigger 150-10
The cloud rose upward like a heavy stone [Nigger 152-8
Like these, autumn beguiles the fatalist. [Nigger 155-5
Everything ticks like a clock. The cabinet [Nigger 157-17
Like a buzzing of flies in autumn air, [MBG 166-20
Is like the reason in a storm; [MBG 169-10
The color like a thought that grows [MBG 169-19
But stone, but like a stone, no: not [MBG 173-15
The mother, but an oppressor, but like [MBG 173-16
Like light in a mirroring of cliffs, [MBG 175-3
A few final solutions, like a duet [MBG 177-7
A poem like a missal found [MBG 177-21
And like a native think in it. [MBG 180-10
To say of one mask it is like, [MBG 181-7
To say of another it is like, [MBG 181-8
That the mask is strange, however like." [MBG 181-10
Like something on the stage, puffed out, [MBG 181-18
Like the night before Christmas and all the carols. [Thought 185-3
Sat alone, his great toe like a horn, [Thought 187-7
Like an intenser instinct. What is it he desires? [Men Fall 188-1
He is like a man [Destructive 193-1
In the room more like a snowy air, [Poems Clim 193-9
Birds that came like dirty water in waves [Loaf 200-3
Like the man that is rich and right. [Idiom 201-5
Of images. Days pass like papers from a press. [Dump 201-14
More than, less than or it puffs like this or that. [Dump 202-4
Smacks like fresh water in a can, like the sea [Dump 202-6
As a man (not like an image of a man), [Dump 202-24
Like a man without a doctrine. The light he gives-- [Freed 205-1
You sit with your head like a carving in space [Rabbit K 210-2
Like a tottering, a falling and an end, [Nightgown 214-9
A small relation expanding like the shade [Connois 215-19
And B are not like statuary, posed [Connois 216-10
Tonight the stars are like a crowd of faces [Dezem 218-9
Like the response to desire. [Dezem 218-20
That had flashed (like vicious music that ends [Thunder 220-11
The sky would be full of bodies like wood. [Thunder 220-17
Of one wilder than the rest (like music blunted, [Thunder 220-23
Like an electric lamp [Common 221-8
The volumes like marble ruins [Common 221-20
Like a noble figure, out of the sky, [Candle 223-4
Shaking the water off, like a poodle, [Hartford 226-8
It is like a region full of intonings. [Hartford 226-17
It is like the season when, after summer, [Cuisine 228-1
The weather was like a waiter with a tray. [Forces 229-18
In the little of his voice, or the like, [Horn 230-14
Flying like insects of fire in a cavern of night, [Horn 230-18
Than the wind, sub-music like sub-speech, [Vari 232-8
And cold. The moon follows the sun like a French [Vari 234-8
It was like sudden time in a world without time, [Martial 237-17
And, like an insatiable actor, slowly and [Of Mod 240-6
Like a phantom, in an uncreated night. [Landsc 242-4
Scattered themselves in the garden, like [Vase 246-12
It was like the sea poured out again [Vase 246-15
Like human conciliations, more like [Vase 247-3
Some things, niño, some things are like this, [Gala 248-1
In which we pronounce joy like a word of our own. [Gala 248-6
Must struggle like the rest." She climbed until [Uruguay 249-1
I have wiped away moonlight like mud. Your innocent ear [Uruguay 249-5
Like insects in the depths of the mind, that kill [Extracts 254-14

The gray grass like a pallet, closely pressed; [Extracts 255-4
That clings to the mind like that right sound, that song [Extracts 256-14
But to speak simply of good is like to love, [Montra 262-21
The sun expands, like a repetition on [Montra 263-14
As facts fall like rejuvenating rain, [Montra 263-22
The trees were plucked like iron bars [Jumbo 269-1
The leaves were falling like notes from a piano. [Contra II 270-12
The abstract that he saw, like the locust-leaves, plainly: [Contra II 270-15
Her hand composed him like a hand appeared, [Hand 271-13
Brooding on centuries like shells. [Oak 272-12
Like a euphony in a museum [Hero 274-8
Ours, like a familiar companion. [Hero 276-4
Glides to his meeting like a lover [Hero 276-17
Like a white abstraction only, a feeling [Hero 276-26
Like chantering from an abundant [Hero 277-16
In parades like several equipages, [Hero 277-23
Like the shiddow-shaddow of lights revolving [Hero 279-20
These hymns are like a stubborn brightness [Hero 279-24
You like it under the trees in autumn, [Motive 288-1
The wind moves like a cripple among the leaves [Motive 288-3
Like an instinctive incantation. [Dutch 291-12
Freedom is like a man who kills himself [Dutch 292-17
Snow sparkles like eyesight falling to earth, [Possum 294-4
Like seeing fallen brightly away. [Possum 294-5
That, like your own, is large, hence, to be part [Choc 296-9
The mind's own limits, like a tragic thing [Choc 298-4
Itself is like a poverty in the space of life, [Choc 299-1
Like the head of fate, looked out in darkness, part [Choc 299-20
There were others like him safely under roof: [Choc 299-23
The air changes, creates and re-creates, like strength, [Choc 301-9
Like a machine left running, and running down. [Repet 306-18
Like something I remembered overseas. [Repet 306-20
Millions of major men against their like [Repet 307-1
We do not say ourselves like that in poems. [Great 311-16
His firm stanzas hang like hives in hell [EM 315-11
Like silver in the sheathing of the sight, [EM 320-5
Like things submerged with their englutted sounds, [EM 321-27
Like hunger that feeds on its own hungriness. [EM 323-4
By a lake, with clouds like lights among great tombs, [EM 325-8
Like earth and sky. Then he became nothing else [Wild 329-1
A horse grotesquely taut, a walker like [Pure 330-6
Of serpents like z rivers simmering, [Pure 330-18
Ill of a question like a malady, [Pure 331-7
Like rhetoric in a narration of the eye-- [Pure 331-18
Flies like a bat expanding as it flies, [Pure 331-24
Of access like the page of a wiggy book, [Pure 333-6
Of ideas moves wrinkled in a motion like [Feo 333-21
The sun comes up like news from Africa. [Feo 334-12
There is a storm much like the crying of the wind, [Sketch 336-1
Words that come out of us like words within, [Sketch 336-2
He can hear them, like people on the walls, [Sketch 336-4
Yet not not quite of a kind. It is like that here. [Jouga 337-10
This afternoon the wind and the sea were like that-- [Jouga 337-13
Thus things are like a seeming of the sun [Descrip 339-5
Or like a seeming of the moon or night [Descrip 339-6
In the death of a soldier, like the utmost will, [Descrip 341-2
But the integrations of the past are like [Descrip 342-2
Like rubies reddened by rubies reddening. [Descrip 346-4
Like molten citizens of the vacuum? [Liadoff 346-10
Do you remember the children there like wicks, [Liadoff 346-11
From thought, like a violent pulse in the cloud itself, [Liadoff 347-2
Of summer. Tomorrow will look like today, [Myrrh 349-18
Will appear like it. But it will be an appearance, [Myrrh 350-1
A shape left behind, with like wings spreading out, [Myrrh 350-2
Brightly empowered with like colors, swarmingly, [Myrrh 350-3
Things floating like the first hundred flakes of snow [Man Car 351-3
The tinsel of August falling was like a flame [Pieces 352-2
The wind is like a dog that runs away. [Pieces 352-5
But it is like a horse. It is like motion [Pieces 352-6
Lie lengthwise like the cloud of sleep, not quite [Two V 354-4
Like more and more becoming less and less, [Two V 354-13
Like space dividing its blue and by division [Two V 354-14
Which was realized, like reason's constant ruin. [Two V 354-17
But singular, they would, like water, scale [Two V 355-5
Like the wind that lashes everything at once. [Chaos 358-6
Was like the conscious being of the book. [House Q 358-9
The summer night is like a perfection of thought. [House Q 358-15
Like gathered-up forgetfulness, [Woman Song 360-11
A man and a woman, like two leaves [Burghers 362-12
Seemed in the morning like a holiday." [Anach 365-19
Like excellence collecting excellence? [Belly 367-1
And impotent, like the imagination seeking [Cats 368-3
To propagate the imagination or like [Cats 368-4
It was like passing a boundary to dive [Lot 371-1
Like their particular characters, addicts [Lot 371-10

A point of survey squatting like a throne, [Cred 373-19
Lofty like him, like him perpetual. [Cred 374-23
Is like ten thousand tumblers tumbling down [Cred 376-25
And throws it away like a thing of another time, [NSF 382-11
Abysmal instruments make sounds like pips [NSF 384-5
The academies like structures in a mist. [NSF 386-21
Rose up like phantoms from chronologies. [NSF 389-15
Music falls on the silence like a sense, [NSF 392-10
And sun and rain a plural, like two lovers [NSF 392-14
An island to the South, on which rested like [NSF 393-11
One sole face, like a photograph of fate, [NSF 394-10
A sound like any other. It will end. [NSF 394-18
Alone and like a vestal long-prepared. [NSF 395-18
Like a page of music, like an upper air, [NSF 397-13
Like a momentary color, in which swans [NSF 397-14
Should foam, be foamy waves, should move like them, [NSF 399-7
The frown like serpents basking on the brow, [NSF 400-11
Like men besides, like men in light secluded, [NSF 405-12
And we enjoy like men, the way a leaf [NSF 406-2
Will look like frost as it approaches them [AA 413-21
And knock like a rifle-butt against the door. [AA 414-2
Among the children, like curious ripenesses [AA 415-8
And curtains like a naive pretence of sleep. [AA 415-15
And mountains running like water, wave on wave, [AA 416-6
Like a book at evening beautiful but untrue, [AA 418-14
Like a book on rising beautiful and true. [AA 418-15
It is like a thing of ether that exists [AA 418-16
Lie down like children in this holiness, [AA 418-23
Like a great shadow's last embellishment. [AA 419-24
Like a blaze of summer straw, in winter's nick. [AA 421-3
Was like a sleep. The sea was a sea he dreamed. [Page 422-2
Fixed like a lake on which the wild ducks fluttered, [Cata 424-13
On his gold horse striding, like a conjured beast, [Antag 426-1
It is like a flow of meanings with no speech [Roses 431-8
Like many robings, as moving masses are, [Owl 433-9
The inhuman brother so much like, so near, [Owl 434-8
Like a meaning in nothingness, [Celle 438-5
Like the snow before it softened [Celle 438-6
Like a shelter not in an arc [Celle 438-8
"A Primitive Like an Orb" [440-title
And scintillant sizzlings such as children like, [Orb 442-20
It is only that this warmth and movement are like [Wom Sun 445-4
Like a monster that has everything and rests, [Bouquet 452-4
Like beautiful and abandoned refugees. [Our Stars 455-16
And Gibraltar is dissolved like spit in the wind. [Puel 456-3
Like a trumpet and says, in this season of memory, [Puel 456-11
When the leaves fall like things mournful of the past, [Puel 456-12
The sun stands like a Spaniard as he departs, [Novel 457-4
A retrato that is strong because it is like, [Novel 458-13
Like a spectral cut in its perception, a tilt [What We 460-3
Spreading out fortress walls like fortress wings. [Luther 461-12
And calling like the long echoes in long sleep, [Luther 461-17
This Italian symbol, this Southern landscape, is like [Study I 463-7
From heaven and float in air, like animals [Study II 464-6
Much like a new resemblance of the sun, [NH 465-16
Seems like a sheen of heat romanticized. [NH 468-9
Our breath is like a desperate element [NH 470-23
So that morning and evening are like promises kept, [NH 472-16
Are like newspapers blown by the wind. He speaks [NH 473-21
With lanterns, like a celestial ancientness. [NH 476-21
Like blessed beams from out a blessed bush [NH 477-21
A city slapped up like a chest of tools, [NH 478-20
Of things? A figure like Ecclesiast, [NH 479-13
The imaginative transcripts were like clouds, [NH 479-16
Like the constant sound of the water of the sea [NH 480-14
Like an evening evoking the spectrum of violet, [NH 488-19
Like interior intonations, [Aug 490-19
Like watery words awash; like meanings said [Angel 497-4
Shadows like winds [Irish 501-10
Mud, water like dirty glass, expressing silence [Plain 503-4
Like tales that were told the day before yesterday-- [Hermit 505-13
And the wind sways like a great thing tottering-- [Hermit 505-16
Are like wrecked umbrellas. [Plant 506-7
Crude captains, the naked majesty, if you like, [Rome 510-9
It is like a boat that has pulled away [Vacancy 511-6
It is like a guitar left on a table [Vacancy 511-8
It is like the feeling of a man [Vacancy 511-10
Contracted like a withered stick. [Two Illus 513-3
Like daylight, with time's bellishings, [Two Illus 514-18
There was an ease of mind that was like being alone in a boat at
    sea, [Prol 515-5
Did not pass like someone voyaging out of and beyond the familiar.
    [Prol 515-13
As he traveled alone, like a man lured on by a syllable without
    any meaning, [Prol 516-4
From man's ghost, larger and yet a little like, [Look 518-1
And what we think, a breathing like the wind, [Look 518-13

Too much like thinking to be less than thought, [Look 518-19
Like the last muting of winter as it ends. [Look 519-3
Like the sooth lord of sorrow, [Song Fixed 519-14
Like a fixed heaven, [Song Fixed 520-5
No winds like dogs watched over her at night. [World 521-6
On her pillow? The thought kept beating in her like her heart.
    [World 521-11
As, for example, a world in which, like snow, [Quiet 523-4
The meeting at noon at the edge of the field seems like [Rock 525-12
That the lilacs came and bloomed, like a blindness cleaned,
    [Rock 526-5
It is like a new account of everything old, [Armor 529-17
Time's given perfections made to seem like less [Armor 530-8
Like a plain poet revolving in his mind [Moonlight 531-2
Like a cloud-cap in the corner of a looking-glass, [Moonlight 531-22
Like the last one. But there is no ferryman. [R Conn 533-11
The river that flows nowhere, like a sea. [R Conn 533-21
Seemed like a sound in his mind. [Not Ideas 534-3
Still far away. It was like [Not Ideas 534-17
Like Agamemnon's story. [Phases 3-15 P
Mumbling and musing like the most forlorn. [Phases 5-14 P
Like a woman inhibiting passion [Soldat 12-2 P
Like a heart full of pins. [Soldat 12-24 P
Too long, is like a bayonet that bends. [Soldat 13-7 P
Which, like a gorgeous palm, [Archi 17-18 P
Like brazen shells. [Cab 21-3 P
Seated before these shining forms, like the duskiest glass,
    reflecting the piebald of roses or what you will. [Piano 21-18P
Is like your port which conceals [Demoiselle 23-4 P
Not fixed and deadly (like a curving line [Abnormal 23-17 P
Like a belly puckered by a spear. [Lulu M 27-4 P
They pied and chuckled like a flock, [Sat Night 28-10 P
Which, like a virgin visionary spent [Red Kit 30-18 P
You think that like the moon she is obscured [Spaniard 34-2 P
Pellucid love; and for that image, like [Spaniard 34-5 P
If she is like the moon, she never clears [Spaniard 34-11 P
Like the mother of all nightingales; be wise [Spaniard 35-10 P
Are like the sound of doves. [Secret Man 35-22 P
The trombones are like baboons, [Drum-Majors 37-2 P
Of happens to like, not should. [Table 40-3 P
Do I happen to like red bush, [Table 40-5 P
One likes what one happens to like. [Table 40-11 P
Happens to like is one [Table 40-14 P
Clumped carvings, circular, like blunted fans, [Old Woman 43-16 P
The statue stood in stars like water-spheres, [Old Woman 45-10 P
Without her, evening like a budding yew [Old Woman 45-23 P
Crying against a need that pressed like cold, [Old Woman 45-29 P
Like a word in the mind that sticks at artichoke [Burnshaw 47-2 P
Now like a ballet infantine in awkward steps, [Burnshaw 47-18 P
In a mortal lullaby, like porcelain. [Burnshaw 47-22 P
Long autumn sheens and pittering sounds like sounds [Burnshaw
    47-24 P
Commingle, not like the commingling of sun and moon [Burnshaw
    50-2 P
A tragic lullaby, like porcelain. [Burnshaw 50-31 P
Like damsels daubed and let your feet be bare [Burnshaw 51-11 P
This time, like damsels captured by the sky, [Burnshaw 51-17 P
The heaven of Europe is empty, like a Schloss [Greenest 53-1 P
Like a solitude of the sun, in which the mind [Greenest 54-5 P
Darting envenomed eyes about, like fangs, [Greenest 55-15 P
Each fretful fern drops down a fear like dew [Greenest 55-24 P
If not from winter, from a summer like [Greenest 57-24 P
The gods like marble figures fallen, left [Greenest 58-14 P
Of the shape of eyes, like blunt intaglios, [Greenest 59-5 P
Are like the perpetual verses in a poet's mind. [Greenest 59-27 P
To trundle children like the sea? For you, [Duck 61-4 P
Created, like a bubble, of bright sheens, [Duck 63-21 P
If these were theoretical people, like [Duck 65-6 P
All are evasions like a repeated phrase, [Duck 65-14 P
The churches, like dalmatics stooped in prayer, [Sombre 69-1 P
The body bent, like Hercules, to build. [Sombre 69-10 P
Like the time of the portent, images like leaves, [Sombre 69-29 P
The spring is hum-drum like an instrument, [Sombre 71-11 P
And the cheeks like flower-pots under her hair. [Grotesque 74-16P
Like water running in a gutter [Grotesque 76-22 P
Like the voice of all our ancestors, [Grotesque 77-10 P
Like any other, rex by right of the crown, [Bship 79-3 P
Like a dancer's skirt, flung round and settling down. [Woman Had
    81-18 P
And of sounds so far forgotten, like her voice, [Woman Had 82-18P
The women with eyes like opals vanish [Stan Hero 83-12 P
By feeling the like of thought in sleep, [Desire 85-12 P
In an association like yours [Including 88-13 P
Like taste distasting the first fruit of a vine, [Theatre 91-3 P
Like an eye too young to grapple its primitive, [Theatre 91-4 P
Like the artifice of a new reality, [Theatre 91-5 P
Like the chromatic calendar of time to come. [Theatre 91-6 P
That which is human and yet final, like [Americana 94-6 P

Daylight evaporates, like a sound one hears in sickness. [Discov
    95-9 P
Makes this small howling, like a thought [Dove 98-4 P
That howls in the mind or like a man [Dove 98-5 P
Like slits across a space, a place [Dove 98-11 P
Like glass and sun, of male reality [Fare Guit 99-8 P
Enlarging like a nocturnal ray [Ulysses 100-25 P
Like glitter ascended into fire. [Ulysses 102-17 P
Like things produced by a climate, the world [Ulysses 102-29 P
Like a direction on which I depend . . . [Presence 105-24 P
Like an absolute out of this eloquence." [Presence 106-6 P
It would have been like lighting a candle, [Letters 107-10 P
Like leaning on the table, shading one's eyes, [Letters 107-11 P
Or something much like a land. [Letters 108-7 P
Nothing more, like weather after it has cleared-- [Art Pop
    112-14 P
Well, more than that, like weather when it has cleared [Art Pop
    112-15 P
This artificial population is like [Art Pop 112-21 P
Like angels resting on a rustic steeple [Art Pop 113-1 P
It is like a critic of God, the world [Region 115-13 P
A light snow, like frost, has fallen during the night. [Bus
    116-1 P
Like whispering women. [Three 128-11 P
It is like the seclusion of sunrise, [Three 130-5 P
Like this, [Three 131-3 P
Like evening Venus in a cloud-top. [Three 135-9 P
Or like a ripe strawberry [Three 135-10 P
It does not sound like an elopement. [Three 138-10 P
Like the earth on which it shines, [Three 143-11 P
If he sees an object on a table, much like [Someone 83-14 A
And bright, or like a venerable urn, [Someone 83-16 A
Like the true light of the truest sun, the true [Someone 84-9 A
Like precious scholia jotted down in the dark. [Someone 84-21 A
Like the same orange repeating on one tree [Someone 85-21 A
12. An uncivil shape like a gigantic haw. [Someone 86-15 A
See: ball-like; brute-like; glass-like; man-like; ox-like; sham-
    like; sheep-like; swarm-like; swine-like; teat-like; thought-
    like; water-like; wax-like.
LIKED. He liked the nobler works of man, [Thought 187-1
And pallid. It is the grandfather he liked, [Lack 303-11
Maman. His anima liked its animal [EM 321-16
And liked it unsubjugated, so that home [EM 321-17
Or of something seen that he liked. [Planet 532-9
LIKENESS. And, if of substance, a likeness of the earth, [Owl 433 2
A likeness, one of the race of fathers: earth [Irish 502-7
Was beyond his recognizing. By this he knew that likeness of him
    extended [Prol 516-11
Sinks into likeness blessedly beknown. [Spaniard 35-20 P
And inhuman same, the likeness of things unlike. [Conversat
    109-2 P
LIKES. One likes to practice the thing. They practice, [Adieu 128-7
Splashed wide-wise because it likes magnificence [AA 416-13
And there he walks and does as he lives and likes. [Armor 530-22
One likes what one happens to like. [Table 40-11 P
One likes the way red grows. [Table 40-12 P
LIKEST. We give ourselves our likest issuance. [Fictive 88-9
LIKEWISE. Of the soul must likewise be at fault, and first. [Lions
    124-20
And the old casino likewise may define [Havana 145-7
As lightning itself is, likewise, metaphor [Bouquet 448-9
Is to search. Likewise to say of the evening star, [NH 481-17
LILACS. The lilacs wither in the Carolinas. [Carolinas 4-13
"Last Looks at the Lilacs" [48-title
To what good, in the alleys of the lilacs, [Lilacs 48-18
In their hands. The lilacs came long after. [Arcades 225-12
It is true. Tonight the lilacs magnify [NSF 394-22
The sad smell of the lilacs--one remembered it, [Aug 491-9
Longer and later, in which the lilacs opened [Aug 491-27
That the lilacs came and bloomed, like a blindness cleaned,
    [Rock 526-5
LILIES. Clippered with lilies scudding the bright chromes, [Monocle
    17-15
The great pond and its waste of the lilies, all this [Plain 503-6
In lilies' stately-statued calm; [Room Gard 41-11 P
Of lilies rusted, rutting, wet [Room Gard 41-14 P
See water-lilies.
LILLYGREEN. Of Jalmar Lillygreen. [Primordia 7-20 P
LIMBED. And limbed and lighted out from bank to bank. [Lot 371-3
LIMBS. Bare limbs, bare trees and a wind as sharp as salt? [AA
    419-21
It held the shivering, the shaken limbs, [Hand 271-11
See cedar-limbs.
LIME. With white wine, sugar and lime juice. Then bring it,
    [Phenom 286-15
LIMES. Long after the planter's death. A few limes remained, [NSF
    393-24
LIMITS. The mind's own limits, like a tragic thing [Choc 298-4
One of the limits of reality [Cred 374-6
To the wild limits of its habitation. [Page 421-20

LIMP. Then the stale turtle will grow limp from age. [John 437-22
A universe without life's limp and lack, [Theatre 91-16 P
LIMPID. Of ocean, which like limpid water lay. [Sea Surf 99-4
In his limpid shoes. [Coroner 29-15 P
LIND. Which cries so blau and cries again so lind [Page 421-9
So lind. The wind blazed as they sang. So lau. [Page 421-17
LINE. In a swift, circular line [Earthy 3-7
In a swift, circular line [Earthy 3-11
Of foppish line. [W Burgher 61-13
Always the standard repertoire in line [Nigger 156-19
A black line beside a white line; [Common 221-3
A black line drawn on flat air. [Common 221-5
And there to find music for a single line, [Extracts 259-16
Equal to memory, one line in which [Extracts 259-17
She will speak thoughtfully the words of a line. [Debris 338-8
Its line moves quickly with the genius [Pastor 379-9
Of flame on the line, with a second wheel below, [Page 422-23
From line to line, as we lie on the grass and listen [Aug 492-11
The vaguest line of smoke (a year ago) [Phases 5-4 P
Of men and earth: I quote the line and page, [Soldat 11-8 P
Men of the line, take this new phrase [Soldat 16-8 P
Not fixed and deadly (like a curving line [Abnormal 23-17 P
And the first line spreading up the beach; again, [Woman Had
    81-14 P
And the first line foaming over the sand; again, [Woman Had
    81-16 P
The rising and the swell, the first line's glitter, [Woman Had
    81-17 P
LINEAGE. Without lineage or language, only [Couch 295-7
LINEAMENT. Some lineament or character, [Planet 532-18
LINEAMENTS. Than that of their clouds. These lineaments were the
    earth, [NH 484-13
LINEAR. These insolent, linear peels [Bananas 53-21
A vital, linear ambiance. The flare [Pastor 379-12
LINEN. Except linen, embroidered [Cab 21-14 P
LINES. The lines are straight and swift between the stars. [Tallap
    71-10
The lines are much too dark and much too sharp. [Tallap 71-13
These lines are swift and fall without diverging. [Tallap 72-4
Cones, waving lines, ellipses-- [Six Sig 75-11
For these black lines. [Common 221-16
Still by the sea-side mutters milky lines [Oboe 250-13
In his packet Anacharsis found the lines: [Anach 365-17
Stands and regards and repeats the primitive lines. [Anach 366-15
The soldier is poor without the poet's lines, [NSF 407-18
The long lines of it grow longer, emptier, [AA 412-20
That there are no lines to speak? There is no play. [AA 416-2
Poesis, poesis, the literal characters, the vatic lines, [Large
    424-6
The muse of misery? Speak loftier lines. [Bad Time 427-7
Here the eye fastens intently to these lines [Bouquet 450-16
Words, lines, not meanings, not communications, [NH 465-12
These actors still walk in a twilight muttering lines. [NH 479-23
"Long and Sluggish Lines" [522-title
See: earth-lines; picket-lines; sea-lines.
LINGERING. Is not the porch of spirits lingering. [Sunday 70-16
Of ripest summer, always lingering [Havana 143-14
LINGERINGS. Rise liquidly in liquid lingerings, [Angel 497-3
LINGUA. The lingua franca et jocundissima. [Pastor 379-9
LINGUIST. Beau linguist. But the MacCullough is MacCullough. [NSF
    387-7
LINK. Link, of that tempest, to the farm, [Silent 359-15
LINKED. The blue woman, linked and lacquered, at her window [NSF
    399-4
LIN-LAN-LONE. The lin-lan-lone of Babson, [Agenda 41-17 P
LION. Being the lion in the lute [MBG 175-15
Before the lion locked in stone. [MBG 175-16
A lion, an ox in his breast, [Destructive 192-13
The lion sleeps in the sun. [Destructive 193-14
Is the lion that comes down to drink. There [Glass 197-13
The lion roars at the enraging desert, [NSF 384-7
Against the first idea--to lash the lion, [NSF 385-2
The bloody lion in the yard at night or ready to spring [Puel
    456-6
We remember the lion of Juda and we save [NH 472-23
The phrase . . . Say of each lion of the spirit [NH 472-24
In which he and the lion and the serpent hide [Greenest 54-30 P
LION-MEN. And lion-men and the flicking serpent-kin [Greenest 55-3P
LION-ROSES. Otu-bre's lion-roses have turned to paper [Plant 506-5
LIONS. "Lions in Sweden" [124-title
These lions, these majestic images. [Lions 124-18
Still hankers after lions, or, to shift, [Lions 125-4
If the fault is with the lions, send them back [Lions 125-6
Brings voices as of lions coming down. [Sun March 134-6
To whom the jaguars cry and lions roar [Greenest 55-19 P
LIP. And be surprised and tremble, hand and lip. [Beginning 428-2
LIPPED. See thick-lipped.
LIPS. While he poured out upon the lips of her [C 43-3
The genius of that cheek. Here are the lips, [Worms 50-1
Taste of the blood upon his martyred lips, [Men Fall 188-15

With life's salt upon their lips and savor [Hero 279-7
Once by the lips, once by the services [EM 317-19
Smiling and wetting her lips [Attempt 370-13
The vines around the throat, the shapeless lips, [NSF 400-10
Their eyes closed, in a young palaver of lips. [NH 477-1
Whose lives return, simply, upon our lips, [Sombre 67-5 P
On her lips familiar words become the words [Woman Had 83-9 P
Upon whose lips the dissertation sounds, [Ideal 89-1 A
LIQUEURS. "Mandolin and Liqueurs" [28-title P
LIQUID. Sombre as fir-trees, liquid cats [MBG 178-13
  The bronzes liquid through gay light. [Thought 187-3
  Seeming to be liquid as leaves made of cloud, [Forces 229-14
  Rise liquidly in liquid lingerings, [Angel 497-3
LIQUIDLY. Rise liquidly in liquid lingerings, [Angel 497-3
LIQUORISH. And liquorish prayer provokes new sweats: so, so:
  [Havana 144-10
LISPING. The buzzing world and lisping firmament. [Descrip 345-8
LISSOMENESS. "Oh, lissomeness turned lagging ligaments!" [Stan MMO
  19-20 P
LISTEN. Even for her, already for her. She will listen [Debris
  338-11
  From line to line, as we lie on the grass and listen [Aug 492-11
LISTENED. Listened to the radio, [Thought 184-8
  So blau, so blau . . . Hans listened by the fire. [Page 421-14
LISTENER. For the listener, who listens in the snow, [Snow Man
  10-10
  Which is not part of the listener's own sense. [Cred 377-20
  And in a bed in one room, alone, a listener [Sick 90-13 P
  The listener, listening to the shadows, seeing them, [Sick
  90-18 P
LISTENING. The mind sits listening and hears it pass. [Pure 329-18
  Or in the dark musician, listening [Descrip 340-21
  Listening to the whole sea for a sound [Woman Had 82-4 P
  The listener, listening to the shadows, seeing them, [Sick 90-18P
LISTENS. For the listener, who listens in the snow, [Snow Man 10-10
  Of which, an invisible audience listens, [Of Mod 240-10
LISTLESS. Like one who scrawls a listless testament [Swans 4-5
LIT. What had this star to do with the world it lit, [Martial
  238-3
  And lit the snow to a light congenial [Choc 297-1
  So barely lit, so shadowed over and naught, [Quiet 523-3
LITANIES. Of the gods and, for him, a thousand litanies [Greenest
  59-26 P
LITERACY. In a stubborn literacy, an intelligence, [Bouquet 452-11
LITERAL. Poesis, poesis, the literal characters, the vatic lines,
  [Large 424-6
LITERATE. Cries out a literate despair. [Postcard 159-10
  Who surpassed the most literate owl, the most erudite [NSF 403-21
LITERATURE. Without his literature and without his gods . . .
  [Look 518-2
LITHER. And lither stride. His arms are heavy [Hero 277-11
LITTER. The town, the weather, in a casual litter, [NH 474-8
  In which the litter of truths becomes [Ulysses 102-7 P
LITTERING. And stray impassioned in the littering leaves. [Sunday
  69-12
LITTERS. And beyond the days, beyond the slow-foot litters [Repet
  309-1
LITTLE. Out of their mother grass, like little kin, [Monocle 15-4
  A little juvenile, an ancient whim, [C 35-23
  Little by little, as if the suzerain soil [C 40-23
  She dreams a little, and she feels the dark [Sunday 67-2
  Whispered a little out of tenderness, [Sunday 69-6
  Too near, too clear, saving a little to endow [Fictive 88-11
  Nod and look a little sly. [Orangeade 103-16
  In his time, this one had little to speak of, [Norfolk 111-8
  The being that yielded so little, acquired [Adieu 127-18
  So little, too little to care, to turn [Adieu 128-4
  And in one of the little arrondissements [Winter B 141-17
  A little less returned for him each spring. [Anglais 148-12
  A little later when the sky is black. [Nigger 156-14
  And the little green cat is a bug in the grass. [Rabbit K 210-3
  And a little island full of geese and stars: [Sleight 222-15
  They seem a little painted, now. [Arcades 226-2
  In the little of his voice, or the like, [Horn 230-14
  The little owl flew through the night, [Adequacy 243-9
  The little owl fly. [Adequacy 244-16
  Hoot, little owl within her, how [Vase 246-17
  The sunlight. They bear brightly the little beyond [Extracts
  254-22
  A little nearer by each multitude, [Montra 262-2
  A little while of Terra Paradise [Montra 263-1
  These letters of him for the little, [Hero 279-5
  Swarm from the little blue of the horizon [Dutch 290-2
  With the special things of night, little by little, [Choc 300-19
  Accoutred in a little of the strength [Repet 307-6
  They do not make the visible a little hard [Creat 311-12
  A great jaguar running will make a little sound. [Jouga 337-15
  There is so little that is close and warm. [Debris 338-1
  So little, our affair, which is the affair [Descrip 342-4
  A little different from reality: [Descrip 344-3

A little changed by tips of artifice, changed [Myrrh 350-5
So much a part of the place, so little [Woman Song 361-1
Stronger and freer, a little better off. [Good Man 364-4
My house has changed a little in the sun. [NSF 385-16
A little string speaks for a crowd of voices. [NSF 392-18
Of a speech only a little of the tongue? [NSF 397-4
Away, a little rusty, a little rouged, [NSF 400-14
A little roughened and ruder, a crown [NSF 400-15
Are white, a little dried, a kind of mark [AA 412-9
The little ignorance that is everything, [John 437-16
A little and a little, suddenly, [Orb 440-12
The fire falls a little and the book is done. [Novel 458-17
And exhalations in the eaves, so little [NH 477-8
The long-bladed knife, the little to drink and her [NH 485-21
The less legible meanings of sounds, the little reds [NH 488-7
A little thing to think of on Sunday walks, [Aug 491-22
She is exhausted and a little old. [Aug 496-14
Little by little, the poverty [Leben 505-4
As at a point of central arrival, an instant moment, much or
  little, [Prol 516-8
Only a little way, and not beyond, unless between himself [Prol
  516-12
From man's ghost, larger and yet a little like, [Look 518-1
A little wet of wing and woe, [Song Fixed 519-19
She would talk a little to herself as she combed her hair,
  [World 521-16
It makes so little difference, at so much more [Slug 522-1
There's a little square in Paris, [Phases 3-1 P
And little will or wish, that day, for tears. [Soldat 14-17 P
And these long, black instruments will be so little to them that
  will be needing so much, seeking so much in their music.
  [Piano 22-9 P
Make little difference, for being wrong [Red Kit 30-14 P
Adds very little, [Melancholy 32-10 P
For a little time, again, rose-breasted birds [Burnshaw 49-30 P
Goes off a little on the side and stops. [Duck 63-33 P
Twitching a little with crude souvenirs [Duck 64-23 P
Much too much thought, too little thought, [Grotesque 75-14 P
As hangman, a little sick of blood, of [Stan Hero 84-17 P
A swerving, a tilting, a little lengthening, [Nuns 92-11 P
Yet the nothingness of winter becomes a little less. [Course
  96-11 P
Makes something of the little there, [Dove 97-18 P
The little and the dark, and that [Dove 98-1 P
That which keeps us the little that we are, [Ulysses 100-16 P
The little confine soon unconfined [Ulysses 103-20 P
And unknown, inhuman for a little while, [Ulysses 105-5 P
Inhuman for a little, lesser time." [Ulysses 105-6 P
What we heard and the light, though little, was enough. [Letters
  107-15 P
Little existed for him but the few things [Local 112-4 P
That makes it say the little thing it says, [Someone 84-15 A
LIVE. Divinity must live within herself: [Sunday 67-19
We live in an old chaos of the sun, [Sunday 70-18
We hardened ourselves to live by bluest reason [Medit 124-2
"How to Live. What to Do" [125-title
For myself, I live by leaves, [Botanist 1 134-14
As it grudges the living that they live. [MBG 173-18
To live in war, to live at war, [MBG 173-19
Of the men that live in the land, high lord. [MBG 176-11
To live in a tragic time. [Loaf 199-15
Regard the hovels of those that live in this land. [Loaf 199-18
Of the life that you will not live, [Bagatelles 199-4
Crowned with the first, cold buds. On these we live, [Cuisine
  228-11
He had only not to live, to walk in the dark, [Landsc 242-12
The dead rocks not the green rocks, the live rocks. If, [Extracts
  255-16
We live in a camp . . . Stanzas of final peace [Extracts 258-22
We chant if we live in evil and afterward [Extracts 259-9
We live. Thence come the final chants, the chants [Extracts 259-13
The world lives as you live, [Search 268-13
Air--earth--Can we live on dry descriptions, [Hero 278-2
Live, work, suffer and die in that idea [EM 325-14
The greatest poverty is not to live [EM 325-18
Merely in living as and where we live. [EM 326-12
Did we expect to live in other lives? [Wild 328-15
Men live to be [Paisant 334-17
Admired by men and all men, therefore, live [Paisant 334-18
To be admired by all men. Nations live [Paisant 334-19
From beside us, from where we have yet to live. [Sketch 336-9
Between the two we live and die-- [Silent 359-6
And live and heap their panniers of green [Belly 367-3
If I live according to this law I live [Past Nun 378-15
From this the poem springs: that we live in a place [NSF 383-22
And where we live and everywhere we live, [NSF 395-9
This drama that we live--We lay sticky with sleep. [AA 419-14
Yet Hans lay wide awake. And live alone [Page 422-3
About the night. They live without our light, [Owl 432-7
Of the world, the heroic effort to live expressed [Papini 446-9

I live in Pennsylvania. [Our Stars 455-4
Women with other lives in their live hair, [Study II 464-14
To say good-by to the past and to live and to be [NH 478-5
This chorus as of those that wanted to live. [Aug 491-18
And live without a tepid aureole, [Angel 496-10
No doubt we live beyond ourselves in air, [Look 518-3
And are never of the world in which they live. [Burnshaw 48-19 P
Who knows? The ploughman may not live alone [Burnshaw 48-23 P
In vast disorder live in the ruins, free, [Burnshaw 48-27 P
To live incessantly in change. See how [Burnshaw 50-17 P
They live. They see and feel themselves, seeing [Duck 64-13 P
And feeling the world in which they live. The manes, [Duck
    64-14 P
People that live in the biggest houses [Grotesque 74-17 P
It is true that you live on this rock [Including 88-7 P
In which the spectra have dewy favor and live [How Now 97-13 P
An ease in which to live a moment's life, [Letters 107-7 P
And felt and known in the colors in which we live, [Conversat
    109-19 P
Young and living in a live air, [Clear Day 113-10 P
We live in a constellation [July 114-14 P
LIVED. Alas! Have all the barbers lived in vain [Monocle 14-8
As if I lived in ashen ground, as if [Farewell 117-12
As if he that lived there left behind [Postcard 159-17
If Englishmen lived without tea in Ceylon, and they do; [Connois
    215-7
As if someone lived there. Such floods of white [Sleight 222-6
Sighed in the evening that he lived [Forces 228-18
Again, and lived and was again, and breathed again [Martial
    238-15
Lived a lady, Lady Lowzen, [Oak 272-2
A largeness lived and not conceived, a space [Choc 301-12
They lived, in which they lacked a pervasive being, [Somnam
    304-15
And, being straw, turned green, lived backward, shared [Liadoff
    347-9
Through centuries he lived in poverty. [Good Man 364-1
He lived each life because, if it was bad, [Good Man 364-5
She lived in her house. She had two daughters, one [NSF 402-1
As if he lived all lives, that he might know, [AA 420-24
And mother. How long have you lived and looked, [Golden 461-2
Seal him there. He looked in a glass of the earth and thought he
    lived in it. [Madame 507-2
Lived in the houses of mothers, arranged ourselves [Rock 525-2
The lives these lived in the mind are at an end. [Rock 525-8
Made to remember a life they never lived [Burnshaw 46-24 P
Lived as the man lives now, and hated, loved, [Sombre 69-33 P
Saying we have forgot them, they never lived. [Grotesque 77-12 P
I wonder, have I lived a skeleton's life, [Warmth 89-17 P
And thus an elevation, as if I lived [Warmth 90-5 P
I wonder, have I lived a skeleton's life, [As Leave 117-5 P
In Connecticut, we never lived in a time [Myth 118-8 P
LIVE-MOSS. Buzzards and live-moss, [Venereal 47-6
LIVERY. Without a season, unstinted in livery, [Sombre 67-7 P
LIVES. The drenching of stale lives no more fell down. [C 30-10
The body dies; the body's beauty lives. [Peter 92-1
For this, then, we endure brief lives, [Negation 98-3
From truth and not from satire on our lives. [Nigger 154-5
That lives uncertainly and not for long [Nigger 155-18
If, while he lives, he hears himself [Prelude 194-12
But in the centre of our lives, this time, this day, [Glass 198-1
As a self that lives on itself. [Thunder 220-20
So that one lives all the lives that comprise it [Yellow 236-20
The world lives as you live, [Search 268-13
Did we expect to live in other lives? [Wild 328-15
The weather of other lives, from which there could [Wild 329-8
That have rankled for many lives and made no sound. [Sketch 336-3
Yet not too closely the double of our lives, [Descrip 344-19
Lives in the mountainous character of his speech; [Descrip 345-12
That lives in space. It is a person at night, [Piece 352-7
If he must, or lives on the bread of faithful speech. [NSF 408-3
This is where the serpent lives, the bodiless. [AA 411-1
This is where the serpent lives. This is his nest, [AA 411-7
As if he lived all lives, that he might know, [AA 420-24
Out of our lives to keep us in our death, [Owl 434-24
The people, those by which it lives and dies. [Owl 436-9
Which is not of our lives composed . . . [Imago 439-18
Have gorged the cast-iron of our lives with good [Orb 440-3
Women with other lives in their live hair, [Study II 464-14
The lives these lived in the mind are at an end. [Rock 525-8
They bloom as a man loves, as he lives in love. [Rock 527-11
And there he walks and does as he lives and likes. [Armor 530-22
Or Paris-rain. He thinks of the noble lives [Greenest 59-25 P
By poets, the Italian lives preserved [Duck 61-19 P
And sighing. These lives are not your lives, O free, [Duck 61-30P
Powdered with primitive lights, and lives with us [Sombre 66-24 P
Whose lives return, simply, upon our lips, [Sombre 67-5 P
Lives in a fluid, not on solid rock. [Sombre 68-5 P
Lived as the man lives now, and hated, loved, [Sombre 69-33 P
But one lives to think of this growing, this pushing life,

[Bship 80-8 P
Of other lives becoming a total drone, [Americana 94-4 P
It is the man in the glass that lives, not he. [Americana 94-8 P
A summing up of the loftiest lives [Ulysses 104-7 P
And music that lasts long and lives the more. [Art Pop 113-6 P
LIVING. And of the sisterhood of the living dead [Fictive 87-6
To strike his living hi and ho, [MBG 166-9
Wingless and withered, but living alive. [MBG 171-7
As it grudges the living that they live. [MBG 173-18
It is equal to living in a tragic land [Loaf 199-14
And the living would be speaking, [Thunder 220-19
It has to be living, to learn the speech of the place. [Of Mod
    240-1
And rain, the blood-rose living in its smell, [Extracts 252-5
Living and being about us and being [Hero 276-3
Spelled from spent living and spent dying. [Dutch 291-19
Shine on the very living of those alive. [Dutch 293-5
He might die was the innocence of living, if life [EM 322-6
Merely in living as and where we live. [EM 326-12
Equal in living changingness to the light [NSF 380-8
A man walked living among the forms of thought [Owl 432-20
And the giant ever changing, living in change. [Orb 443-22
These sounds are long in the living of the ear. [Aug 489-17
Yet living in two worlds, impenitent [Rome 509-20
Give up dead things and the living turn away. [Burnshaw 49-6 P
The father keeps on living in the son, the world [Recit 87-25 P
Of the father keeps on living in the world [Recit 87-26 P
The accent of deviation in the living thing [Discov 96-7 P
The living man in the present place, [Ulysses 103-13 P
Young and living in a live air, [Clear Day 113-10 P
See ever-living.
LIVRE. Livre de Toutes Sortes de Fleurs d'après Nature. [EM 316-7
LIZARDS. Of lizards, in its eye, is more acute [Burnshaw 49-17 P
LOAD. "The Load of Sugar-Cane" [12-title
Who can move the German load [Imago 439-2
LOAF. "Dry Loaf" [199-title
That was what I painted behind the loaf, [Loaf 199-19
In the mind: the tin plate, the loaf of bread on it, [NH 485-20
LOAVES. And always at this antipodes, of leaden loaves [Discov
    95-15 P
LOBSTER. We drank Meursault, ate lobster Bombay with mango [NSF
    401-22
LOCAL. A curriculum, a vigor, a local abstraction . . . [R Conn
    533-17
    "Local Objects" [111-title P
And that, in his knowledge, local objects become [Local 111-12 P
The local objects of a world without a foyer, [Local 111-14 P
LOCKED. Before the lion locked in stone. [MBG 175-16
Steps out. He rings and knocks. The door is not locked. [Bouquet
    452-20
    See: light-locked; man-locked.
LOCUST. Land of Locust [NE Verses 105-title 11
Even the leaves of the locust were yellow then, [Contra II 270-3
The leaves, even of the locust, the green locust. [Contra II
    270-6
Comes from the beating of the locust's wings, [Phenom 286-4
The locust's titter and the turtle's sob. [Sombre 71-1 P
LOCUST-LEAVES. The abstract that he saw, like the locust-leaves,
    plainly: [Contra II 270-15
LOCUSTS. These locusts by day, these crickets by night [Aug 489-4
Nothing is lost, loud locusts. No note fails. [Aug 489-16
LOCUTION. Locution of a hand in a rhapsody. [Pastor 379-8
LOFTIER. The muse of misery? Speak loftier lines. [Bad Time 427-7
LOFTIEST. Over the loftiest antagonist [NSF 390-14
The loftiest syllables among loftiest things, [Rome 510-7
Of the loftiest amour, in a human midnight? [Souls 95-6 P
A summing up of the loftiest lives [Ulysses 104-7 P
LOFTILY. It rose loftily and stood massively; and to lie [Armor
    529-2
Loftily jingled, radiant, [Ulysses 100-21 P
LOFTINESS. From loftiness, misgivings dazzlingly [Ulysses 101-29 P
LOFTY. Let us erect in the Basin a lofty fountain. [NE Verses 105-1
With lofty darkness. The donkey was there to ride, [Uruguay 249-9
Confiders and comforters and lofty kin.[Choc 300-10
Lofty like him, like him perpetual. [Cred 374-23
Of dulce atmosphere, the fore of lofty scenes [Bouquet 450-3
Blue verdured into a damask's lofty symbol, [NH 477-18
LOGES. The lacquered loges huddled there [Ord Women 11-1
LOGIC. It weights him with nice logic for the prim. [Havana 144-17
The automaton, in logic self-contained, [Les Plus 245-5
An end of evil in a profounder logic, [Dutch 291-16
Creates a logic not to be distinguished [EM 325-1
By the lake at Geneva and consider logic: [EM 325-3
And of the worlds of logic in their great tombs. [EM 325-5
Lighting the martyrs of logic with white fire. [EM 325-16
His extreme of logic would be illogical. [EM 325-17
Logos and logic, crystal hypothesis, [NSF 387-4
With a logic of transforming certitudes. [Sombre 66-22 P
LOGICAL. In the presence of a logical lunatic." [EM 324-26
Is the affair of logical lunatics. [EM 324-28

LOGICIAN. See anti-logician.
LOGICIANS. To think of the logicians in their graves [EM 325-4
LOGOS. Logos and logic, crystal hypothesis, [NSF 387-4
LOLLING. See lol-lolling.
LOL-LOLLING. Lol-lolling the endlessness of poetry. [Novel 458-1
LONDON. What could London's [Phases 4-20 P
  What could London's [Phases 5-1 P
  At Easter on a London screen, the seeds [Greenest 53-19 P
  Of London, the paper of Paris magnified [Duck 61-18 P
LONE. Of lone wanderers. To re-create, to use [NH 481-15
LONELIEST. The loneliest air, not less was I myself. [Hoon 65-9
LONELINESS. Grievings in loneliness, or unsubdued [Sunday 67-21
  His loneliness and what was in his mind: [Babies 77-9
  "Loneliness in Jersey City" [210-title
  There is a human loneliness, [Ulysses 100-5 P
  "Here I feel the human loneliness [Presence 105-19 P
LONELY. And the soul, O ganders, being lonely, flies [Swans 4-11
  But bravest at midnight and in lonely spaces, [Page 421-22
LONG. Behold, already on the long parades [Swans 4-9
  And have been cold a long time [Snow Man 10-1
  And they read right long. [Ord Women 11-16
  Can one man think one thing and think it long? [C 41-27
  Can one man be one thing and be it long? [C 41-28
  A long soothsaying silence down and down. [C 42-10
  Is full of long motions; as the ponderous [Curtains 62-2
  That choir among themselves long afterward. [Sunday 70-9
  Walks long and long. [Virgin 71-6
  Mounting the earth-lines, long and lax, lethargic. [Tallap 72-3
  Nor the chisels of the long streets, [Six Sig 74-24
  Of long, capricious fugues and chorals. [Jasmine 79-12
  Icicles filled the long window [Thirteen 93-12
  Claude has been dead a long time [Botanist 1 134-10
  The poem of long celestial death; [Botanist 2 136-6
  To that casino. Long before the rain [Havana 142-18
  That lives uncertainly and not for long [Nigger 155-18
  The preparation is long and of long intent [Nigger 158-4
  We knew for long the mansion's look [Postcard 159-11
  After long strumming on certain nights [MBG 174-19
  How long and late the pheasant sleeps . . . [MBG 182-9
  And the long echo of their dying cry, [Thought 186-14
  To what had been so long composed. [Poems Clim 194-6
  The freshness of night has been fresh a long time. [Dump 202-1
  That made him preach the louder, long for a church [Blue Bldg
    216-18
  In their hands. The lilacs came long after. [Arcades 225-12
  A long time you have been making the trip [Hartford 226-1
  A long time the ocean has come with you, [Hartford 226-7
  To repose in an hour or season or long era [EM 318-22
  Long since, rang out farewell, farewell, farewell. [EM 322-17
  It has, long since, grown tired, of such ideas. [Feo 334-2
  The easy projection long prohibited. [Paisant 335-11
  That night, Liadoff, a long time after his death, [Liadoff 346-14
  Of fiery eyes and long thin arms. [Attempt 370-11
  And spring's infuriations over and a long way [Cred 372-5
  Baked through long days, is piled in mows. It is [Cred 374-8
  And these the seraph saw, had seen long since, [NSF 389-17
  Long after the planter's death. A few limes remained, [NSF 393-3
  White sand, his patter of the long sea-slushes. [NSF 393-9
  When at long midnight the Canon came to sleep [NSF 402-19
  The long lines of it grow longer, emptier, [AA 412-20
  We were as Danes in Denmark all day long [AA 419-7
  Espoused each morning, each long afternoon, [Orb 441-22
  A massive body and long legs, stretched out, [Orb 443-9
  And mother. How long have you lived and looked, [Golden 461-2
  And calling like the long echoes in long sleep, [Luther 461-17
  A coldness in a long, too-constant warmth, [NH 474-20
  As of a long, inevitable sound, [NH 482-7
  These sounds are long in the living of the ear. [Aug 489-17
  She has composed, so long, a self with which to welcome him,
    [World 521-1
  "Long and Sluggish Lines" [522-title
  Too long, is like a bayonet that bends. [Soldat 13-7 P
  The time will come for these children, seated before their long
    black instruments, to strike the themes of love-- [Piano 21-16P
  And these long, black instruments will be so little to them that
    will be needing so much, seeking so much in their music. [Piano
    22-9 P
  It is long since there have been doves [Secret Man 35-23 P
  Long after the worms and the curious carvings of [Burnshaw 47-12P
  Long autumn sheens and pittering sounds like sounds [Burnshaw
    47-24 P
  The alto clank of the long recitation, in these [Burnshaw 52-7 P
  The churches and their long parades, Seville [Greenest 53-18 P
  Through long cloud-cloister-porches, walked alone, [Greenest
    54-3 P
  On a hot night and a long cigar and talk [Greenest 58-25 P
  The long recessional at parish eves wails round [Greenest 59-15 P
  It is mud and mud long baked in the sun, [Stan MBG 72-6 P
  Drifting choirs, long movements and turnings of sounds. [Sick
    90-12 P

  So long as the mind, for once, fulfilled itself? [Theatre 91-18 P
  And music that lasts long and lives the more. [Art Pop 113-6 P
  And long for the windless pavilions. [Three 133-12 P
  See night-long.
LONG-BLADED. The long-bladed knife, the little to drink and her
    [NH 485-21
LONGED-FOR. The heavens, the hells, the world, the longed-for lands.
    [NH 486-12
LONGER. Nothing but trash and that you no longer feel [Lilacs 49-9
  And sprawled around, no longer wild. [Jar 76-10
  Is no longer a mode of desire, a mode [Sad Gay 121-12
  The sun no longer shares our works [MBG 168-13
  A dream no longer a dream, a thing, [MBG 174-17
  The idea of god no longer sputtered [Thought 184-13
  The bells grow longer. This is not sleep. This is desire. [Men
    Fall 187-14
  The sky is no longer a junk-shop, [Dezem 218-2
  No longer on the ancient cake of seed, [Cuisine 228-12
  Are prodigies in longer phrases. [Hero 277-13
  As if pain, no longer satanic mimicry, [EM 316-5
  The moon is no longer these nor anything [EM 320-20
  As if Liadoff no longer remained a ghost [Liadoff 347-8
  In face of which desire no longer moved, [Cred 376-7
  The long lines of it grow longer, emptier, [AA 412-20
  Had ever been before, no longer known, [Page 422-14
  Longer and later, in which the lilacs opened [Aug 491-27
  No longer says anything. [Plant 506-9
  The boat was built of stones that had lost their weight and
    being no longer heavy [Prol 515-10
  It is no longer air. The houses still stand, [Rock 525-5
  Even our shadows, their shadows, no longer remain. [Rock 525-7
  No longer a battered panache above snow . . . [Not Ideas 534-8
  In self, a man of longer time than days, [Good Bad 33-10 P
  Is no longer a sound of summer. So great a change [Burnshaw
    50-21 P
  No longer of air but of the breathing earth, [Burnshaw 52-18 P
  A longer, deeper breath sustains [Ulysses 101-16 P
  A longer, deeper breath sustains [Presence 106-1 P
  The circle would no longer be broken but closed. [Letters 108-8 P
LONGEST. Once more the longest resonance, to cap [Havana 143-16
  And longest, the night was roundest, [On Road 204-10
  Of the longest meditation, the maximum, [EM 324-17
LONG-HAIRED. We enjoyed the ithy oonts and long-haired [Analysis
    349-10
LONGING. Barren, and longing for her; [Sonatina 109-20
  We fling ourselves, constantly longing, on this form. [NH 470-16
LONG-PONDERED. The casual reunions, the long-pondered [Extracts
    258-5
LONG-PREPARED. Alone and like a vestal long-prepared. [NSF 395-18
LONG-ROLLING. By such long-rolling opulent cataracts, [Geneva 24-5
LONG-STIFFENING. I grieve the pinch of her long-stiffening bones.
    [Stan MMO 19-19 P
LONG-TAILED. Long-tailed ponies go nosing the pine-lands,
    [Parochial 191-1
LOOK. Poor buffo! Look at the lavender [Lilacs 49-6
  And look your last and look still steadily, [Lilacs 49-7
  "Look out, O caroller, [Jack-Rabbit 50-15
  Nod and look a little sly. [Orangeade 103-16
  Or look, nor ever again in thought, except [Farewell 118-9
  If they will look [Fading 139-13
  The look of things, left what we felt [Postcard 159-6
  We knew for long the mansion's look [Postcard 159-11
  A look at the weather. [Nightgown 214-2
  Look down now, Cotton Mather, from the blank. [Blue Bldg 217-13
  Purple sets purple round. Look, Master, [Hartford 227-5
  Is the table a mirror in which they sit and look? [Cuisine 228-15
  It is she that he wants, to look at directly, [Scavoir 232-3
  Things might not look divine, nor that if nothing [Landsc 242-28
  And turn to look and say there is no more [Extracts 257-14
  Look, realist, not knowing what you expect. [Phosphor 267-11
  The green falls on you as you look, [Phosphor 267-12
  Look round, brown moon, brown bird, as you rise to fly, [God
    285-1
  Look round at the head and zither [God 285-2
  Look round you as you start to rise, brown moon, [God 285-4
  That was to look on what war magnified. [Gigan 289-12
  These nebulous brilliancies in the smallest look [EM 317-13
  Things look each day, each morning, or the style [Descrip 339-18
  The slouch of his body and his look were not [Descrip 343-1
  Of summer. Tomorrow will look like today, [Myrrh 349-18
  Look at it in its essential barrenness [Cred 373-8
  The rest look down. One man becomes a race, [Cred 374-22
  But you, ephebe, look from your attic window, [NSF 384-17
  Yet voluble dumb violence. You look [NSF 384-22
  Yet look not at his colored eyes. Give him [NSF 388-13
  So that we look at it with pleasure, look [NSF 406-3
  Will look like frost as it approaches them [AA 413-21
  Look at this present throne. What company, [AA 415-2
  They looked back at Hans' look with savage faces. [Page 421-23
  This was the glass in which she used to look [Beginning 427-15

Slowly, to the look of a swarthy name. [Countryman 429-8
It was not her look but a knowledge that she had. [Owl 435-13
Subtler than look's declaiming, although she moved [Owl 435-15
And the mate of summer: her mirror and her look, [Orb 441-23
In New Haven with an eye that does not look [NH 475-6
A hatching that stared and demanded an answering look. [NH 484-3
He wears the words he reads to look upon [Aug 492-5
Apparels of such lightest look that a turn [Angel 497-9
A look, a few words spoken. [Leben 505-6
And one last look at the ducks is a look [Hermit 506-2
Except that a green plant glares, as you look [Plant 506-16
The way a look or a touch reveals its unexpected magnitudes.
      [Prol 517-10
The trees have a look as if they bore sad names [Slug 522-5
Look in the terrible mirror of the sky [Blanche 10-1 P
Look in the terrible mirror of the sky. [Blanche 10-5 P
Look in the terrible mirror of the sky. [Blanche 10-9 P
Look backward. Let your swiftly-flying flocks [Red Kit 31-28 P
Look suddenly downward with their shining eyes [Red Kit 31-29 P
Pure scientist, you look with nice aplomb [Good Bad 33-12 P
Each look and each necessitous cry, as a god [Greenest 59-8 P
And men look inwardly, for the emblem: [Stan Hero 83-13 P
Is to look for it with a lantern. [Three 127-3 P
LOOKED. As they leaned and looked [Ord Women 11-8
   That they were oak-leaves, as the way they looked. [Freed 205-19
   And above the German camps? It looked apart. [Martial 238-5
   Of air, who looked for the world beneath the blue, [Landsc 241-17
   When he looked, the water ran up the air or grew white [Extracts
      255-17
   He wanted and looked for a final refuge, [Contra II 270-7
   Like the head of fate, looked out in darkness, part [Choc 299-20
   The blue woman looked and from her window named [NSF 399-21
   She looked at them and saw them as they were [NSF 402-11
   Leaving, of where we were and looked, of where [AA 417-18
   They looked back at Hans' look with savage faces. [Page 421-23
   And mother. How long have you lived and looked, [Golden 461-2
   Looked on big women, whose ruddy-ripe images [NH 486-17
   Seal him there. He looked in a glass of the earth and thought he
      lived in it. [Madame 507-2
   It was only a glass because he looked in it. It was nothing he
      could be told. [Madame 507-6
   I had looked forward to understanding. Yet [Lytton 39-22 P
LOOKING. Looking at the floor, [Six Sig 75-6
   Looking at the ceiling. [Six Sig 75-7
   "Thirteen Ways of Looking at a Blackbird" [92-title
   Lord of the body, looking down, [MBG 176-6
   "Woman Looking at a Vase of Flowers" [246-title
   Makes him rise above the houses, looking down. [Repet 307-14
   The bass keep looking ahead, upstream, in one [Think 356-11
   For which they are looking: [Pediment 361-15
   Looking for what was, where it used to be? [NSF 389-7
   Of thirty years ago. It is looking out [NH 478-8
   Someone looking for he knows not what. [Vacancy 511-5
   So that he that stood up in the boat leaning and looking before
      him [Prol 515-12
   "Looking across the Fields and Watching the Birds Fly" [517-title
   And looking at the place in which she walked, [Old Woman 45-20 P
   A woman looking down the road, [Ulysses 104-21 P
LOOKING-GLASS. Like a cloud-cap in the corner of a looking-glass,
      [Moonlight 531-22
LOOKS. "Last Looks at the Lilacs" [48-title
   One looks at the elephant-colorings of tires. [Dump 202-21
   On the motive! But one looks at the sea [Vari 233-18
   Without eyes or mouth, that looks at one and speaks. [Yellow
      237-9
   Or a glass that is empty when he looks. [Phosphor 267-8
   The crow looks rusty as he rises up. [Possum 294-15
   Are questions of the looks they get. The bouquet, [Bouquet 451-2
   He walks through the house, looks round him and then leaves.
      [Bouquet 453-2
   Dark Juan looks outward through his mystic brow . . . [Luther
      461-14
   In which looks and feelings mingle and are part [NH 471-5
   There were looks that caught him out of empty air. [NH 483-13
   Than seventy, where one looks, one has been there before. [Slug
      522-2
   He looks upon the statue, where it is, [Greenest 59-2 P
   A man that looks at himself in a glass and finds [Americana
      94-7 P
   Their stunted looks. [How Now 97-15 P
   10. This is how yesterday's volcano looks. [Someone 86-13 A
LOOMS. The bristling soldier, weather-foxed, who looms [Cred 375-2
LOOSE. And leaves that would be loose upon the wind, [Bowl 7-4 P
LOOSED. From the loosed girdles in the spangling must. [Sea Surf
      101-14
   What self, for example, did he contain that had not yet been
      loosed, [Prol 516-16
LOOSELY-NAMED. Calling them what you will but loosely-named
      [Burnshaw 47-21 P
LOOSENED. The dark-blown ceinture loosened, not relinquished.

[NSF 385-11
LOOSING. Loosing black slaves to make black infantry, [Greenest
      56-9 P
LOPS. So thick with sides and jagged lops of green, [C 32-2
LOQUACIOUS. Loquacious columns by the ructive sea? [C 41-20
LORD. For fear the Lord would not accept. [Pourtraicte 21-21
   The good Lord in His garden sought [Pourtraicte 21-22
   The windy lake wherein their lord delights, [Sunday 70-7
   Lord of the body, looking down, [MBG 176-6
   Alone, lord of the land and lord [MBG 176-10
   Of the men that live in the land, high lord. [MBG 176-11
   Of the populace of the heart, the reddest lord, [EM 315-18
   Time in its weather, our most sovereign lord, [Pure 332-17
   Full of their ugly lord, [Pediment 361-19
   Like the sooth lord of sorrow, [Song Fixed 519-14
   The lord of love and of sooth sorrow, [Song Fixed 520-8
   Lord without any deviation, lord [Greenest 60-4 P
   And memory's lord is the lord of prophecy [Sombre 70-14 P
   Yet lord, a mask of flame, the sprawling form [Sombre 70-16 P
LORDLIER. Gave to the cabin, lordlier than it was, [C 44-25
LORDLY. In lordly study. Every day, I found [Monocle 17-23
   Reading the lordly language of the inscription, [Mice 123-7
LORE. Cat's taste possibly or possibly Danish lore, [Someone 87-5 A
   See folk-lore.
LOSE. To lose sensibility, to see what one sees, [EM 320-25
   Lose the old uses that they made of them, [Orb 441-14
   The dove's adagio may lose its depth [Burnshaw 48-25 P
LOSING. But she that says good-by losing in self [Owl 435-4
LOSS. The final mercy and the final loss, [Nigger 152-6
   Without any horror of the helpless loss. [Duck 61-16 P
LOST. It was not so much the lost terrestrial, [C 28-2
   And the lost vehemence the midnights hold. [Tallap 72-12
   If it were lost in Übermenschlichkeit, [Surprises 98-8
   The shapes have lost their glistening. [Sad Gay 122-2
   That lost its heaviness through that same will, [Nigger 152-9
   Yet, it may be, innocence is never lost. [Nigger 157-13
   Burns in the mind on lost remembrances. [Men Fall 187-12
   Lost in an integration of the martyrs' bones, [Uruguay 249-23
   This is his day. With nothing lost, he [Hero 280-16
   Year, year and year, defeated at last and lost [Dutch 291-25
   That has lost the folly of the moon becomes [EM 320-23
   Has lost the whole in which he was contained, [Chaos 358-2
   And let it go, with nothing lost, [Woman Song 361-4
   For souvenirs of time, lost time, [Prejudice 368-22
   Why should the bee recapture a lost blague, [NSF 390-16
   The truth about themselves, having lost, as things, [NH 470-7
   And thereby lost, and naked or in rags, [NH 484-17
   Nothing is lost, loud locusts. No note fails. [Aug 489-16
   Temper and belief and that differences lost [Aug 494-3
   The boat was built of stones that had lost their weight and being
      no longer heavy [Prol 515-10
   It is that Old Man, lost among the trees. [Phases 5-15 P
   Memory without passion would be better lost, [Lytton 38-18 P
   It lost the common shape of night and came [Old Woman 45-16 P
   Of chaos are not always sad nor lost [Burnshaw 50-25 P
   In these stations, in which nothing has been lost, [Souls 94-20 P
LOT. Force is my lot and not pink-clustered [Hero 273-1
   "A Lot of People Bathing in a Stream" [371-title
LOTS. "The idols have seen lots of poverty, [On Road 204-6
LOUD. Turned in the loud fire, [Domination 9-9
   Loud as the hemlocks [Domination 9-10
   The cocks are crowing and crowing loud, [Fish-Scale 161-2
   And crickets are loud again in the grass. The moon [Men Fall
      187-11
   And jumbo, the loud general-large [Jumbo 269-2
   Loud, general, large, fat, soft [Jumbo 269-11
   Against the haggardie . . . A loud, large water [EM 321-8
   What festival? This loud, disordered mooch? [AA 415-22
   Between loud water and loud wind, between that [Page 421-7
   Denied, dismissed, may hold a serpent, loud [John 437-19
   Nothing is lost, loud locusts. No note fails. [Aug 489-16
   Seemed large and loud and high and strong. [Two Illus 513-9
   Hear the loud drums roll-- [Phases 3-11 P
   Out of the eye when the loud wind gathers up [Greenest 58-11 P
   See bee-loud.
LOUDENED. Loudened by cries, by clashes, quick and sure [Monocle
      16-13
LOUDER. That made him preach the louder, long for a church [Blue
      Bldg 216-18
   For breath to laugh the louder, the deeper gasps [Extracts 253-19
LOUDLIER. A force gathers that will cry loudlier [Dutch 291-10
   Than the most metal music, loudlier, [Dutch 291-11
   Deeplier, deeplier, loudlier, loudlier, [Region 115-16 P
LOUDLY. The gongs rang loudly as the windy booms [Sea Surf 100-4
   Shout for me, loudly and loudly, joyful sun, when you rise.
      [Nigger 150-17
   Cry loudly, cry out in the powerful heart. [Dutch 291-9
   The rain kept falling loudly in the trees [NH 476-7
   And blows, with heaped-up shoulders loudly blows [Greenest 58-12P
   They sway, deeply and loudly, in an effort, [Region 115-8 P

LOUNGED. Eulalia, I lounged on the hospital porch, [Phenom 287-7
LOUNGING. If MacCullough himself lay lounging by the sea, [NSF
  387-9
LOUSY. Cleansed clean of lousy Byzantium. [Memo 89-12 P
LOUVRE. To go to the Louvre to behold himself. [Prelude 194-21
  For a vista in the Louvre. They are things chalked [Connois
  216-11
LOVE. Already the new-born children interpret love [Carolinas 4-15
  The end of love in their all-speaking braids. [Monocle 14-6
  Of love, it is a book too mad to read [Monocle 14-21
  The measure of the intensity of love [Monocle 14-26
  Like a dull scholar, I behold, in love, [Monocle 16-1
  Of love, but until now I never knew [Monocle 18-2
  That was not heavenly love, [Pourtraicte 22-5
  And next in glory to enduring love, [Sunday 68-10
  Where triumph rang its brassy phrase, or love [Sunday 69-5
  The love that will not be transported [Jasmine 79-4
  Sister and mother and diviner love, [Fictive 87-5
  And queen, and of diviner love the day [Fictive 87-9
  Of the bride, love being a birth, have need to see [Ghosts 119-13
  Of love, believe would be a friend, [MBG 175-22
  I love the metal grapes, [Anything B 211-17
  In this rigid room, an intenser love, [Dezem 218-17
  He said I had this that I could love, [Yellow 236-13
  For the woman one loves or ought to love, [Waldorf 241-2
  "This image, this love, I compose myself [Rhythms 246-4
  Of love and summer. The assassin sings [Extracts 256-8
  What more is there to love than I have loved? [Montra 260-1
  But if, but if there be something more to love, [Montra 260-8
  But if there be something more to love, amen, [Montra 260-16
  Midsummer love and softest silences, [Montra 261-16
  But to speak simply of good is like to love, [Montra 262-21
  Ties us to those we love. For this familiar, [EM 317-9
  Illustrious intimations--uncertain love, [Myrrh 350-8
  And for what, except for you, do I feel love? [NSF 380-4
  As a man and woman meet and love forthwith. [NSF 386-16
  Their love, this beginning, not resuming, this [NSF 391-5
  The easy passion, the ever-ready love [NSF 394-23
  For easy passion and ever-ready love [NSF 395-7
  So that I tremble with such love so known [NSF 396-8
  Children in love with them brought early flowers [NSF 400-23
  They were love's characters come face to face. [NSF 401-21
  Invisibly clear, the only love. [Wom Sun 445-15
  Of the enduring, visionary love, [NH 466-15
  If it is misery that infuriates our love, [NH 467-1
  And next to love is the desire for love, [NH 467-5
  Unlike love in possession of that which was [NH 467-8
  To our sepulchral hollows. Love of the real [NH 470-18
  In the space of horizons that neither love nor hate. [Aug 490-14
  Of filial love. Or is it the element, [Aug 491-20
  In the parent's hand, perhaps parental love? [Aug 491-25
  Is still warm with the love with which she came, [Aug 496-1
  Of sooth love and sorrow, [Song Fixed 519-15
  The lord of love and of sooth sorrow, [Song Fixed 520-8
  They bloom as a man loves, as he lives in love. [Rock 527-11
  There is another mother whom I love, [Soldat 14-4 P
  Of pomp, in love and good ensample, see [Stan MMO 19-13 P
  The time will come for these children, seated before their long
    black instruments, to strike the themes of love-- [Piano 21-16P
  In the days when the mood of love will be swarming for solace and
    sink deeply into the thin stuff of being, [Piano 22-8 P
  Why should I savor love [Demoiselle 23-12 P
  I love to sit and read the Telegraph, [Mandolin 29-6 P
  And love her still, still leaves you in the wrong. [Red Kit 31-1P
  Her beauty in your love. She should reflect [Red Kit 31-12 P
  Does she will to be proud? True, you may love [Red Kit 31-17 P
  Unhappy love reveals vast blemishes. [Red Kit 31-19 P
  Pellucid love; and for that image, like [Spaniard 34-5 P
  The same return at heavy evening, love [Duck 61-15 P
  His own bright red. But he bears him out of love, [Recit 87-18 P
  "The Desire to Make Love in a Pagoda" [91-title P
  And simple love. [How Now 97-12 P
  The moment of life's love and fortune, [Letters 107-8 P
  Not having to do with love. [Letters 108-5 P
  It had neither love nor wisdom. [Three 132-7 P
LOVED. That I loved her once . . . Farewell. Go on, high ship.
  [Farewell 118-10
  This man loved earth, not heaven, enough to die. [Men Fall 188-18
  And must be loved, as one loves that [Yellow 236-17
  What more is there to love than I have loved? [Montra 260-1
  Be seen, not to be loved nor hated because [NSF 385-5
  We loved but would no marriage make. Anon [NSF 401-8
  The great captain loved the ever-hill Catawba [NSF 401-16
  And Bawda loved the captain as she loved the sun. [NSF 401-18
  Was what they loved. It was neither heaven nor hell. [NSF 401-20
  But she that he loved turns cold at his light touch. [Pecul 453-12
  Out of him that I loved, [Our Stars 454-10
  Lived as the man lives now, and hated, loved, [Sombre 69-33 P
  Survivals of a good that we have loved, [Recit 88-1 P
LOVER. Disclose to the lover. [Venereal 47-10

Fewest things to the lover-- [Venereal 48-15
What lover, what dreamer, would choose [Watermelon 89-2
Absorbs Anjou. I see them as a lover sees, [Peaches 224-4
As a young lover sees the first buds of spring [Peaches 224-5
There the woman receives her lover into her heart [Rhythms 245-16
A youth, a lover with phosphorescent hair, [Uruguay 249-21
Glides to his meeting like a lover [Hero 276-17
What lover has one in such rocks, what woman, [EM 323-24
Of the lover that lies within us and we breathe [NSF 394-24
The lover sighs as for accessible bliss, [NSF 395-4
The lover, the believer and the poet. [Orb 441-6
That's it. The lover writes, the believer hears, [Orb 443-15
To the lover, and blue, as of a secret place [NH 470-21
Between the slouchings of a gunman and a lover, [Moonlight 531-15
LOVERS. And sing them in secrecy as lovers do. [Nigger 151-21
You lovers that are bitter at heart. [MBG 174-4
In form, lovers of heaven and earth, she-wolves [EM 321-24
These lovers waiting in the soft dry grass. [Cred 372-18
This warmth is for lovers at last accomplishing [NSF 391-4
And sun and rain a plural, like two lovers [NSF 392-14
LOVES. As one loves visible and responsive peace, [Yellow 236-14
As one loves one's own being, [Yellow 236-15
As one loves that which is the end [Yellow 236-16
And must be loved, as one loves that [Yellow 236-17
A unity that is the life one loves, [Yellow 236-19
For the woman one loves or ought to love, [Waldorf 241-2
That woman waiting for the man she loves,) [Rhythms 245-13
They bloom as a man loves, as he lives in love. [Rock 527-11
"Red Loves Kit" [30-title P
As the man hates now, loves now, the self-same things. [Sombre
  70-1 P
The father that he loves, and bears him from [Recit 87-13 P
LOVING. Seen as inamorata, of loving fame [NH 484-14
LOW. He heard her low accord, [Pourtraicte 22-2
  Except for our own houses, huddled low [Eve Angels 138-1
  Cold, a cold porcelain, low and round, [Poems Clim 193-15
  Low tide, flat water, sultry sun. [Vari 235-13
  Only this evening I saw again low in the sky [Martial 237-10
  High, low, far, wide, against the distance, [Hero 277-22
  Fly low, cock bright, and stop on a bean pole. Let [Cred 377-6
  He is neither priest nor proctor at low eve, [NH 474-16
  Bare beggar-tree, hung low for fruited red [NH 483-24
  High poetry and low: [Aug 490-15
  At the center of the mass, the haunches low, [Old Woman 43-13 P
  Nor low. [Three 133-18 P
LOWEST. And the lowest ear, the deep ear that discerns, [AA 414-17
LOWZEN. By Howzen, the chromatic Lowzen. [Oak 272-21
  See: Flora Lowzen; Lady Lowzen.
LOYAL. Of loyal conjuration trumped. The wind [Sea Surf 102-11
LOZENGES. 7. These lozenges are nailed-up lattices. [Someone 86-10A
LUCENT. To be their latest, lucent paramour. [C 38-27
  At lucent children round her in a ring. [Hermit 506-3
LUCID. And lucid, inescapable rhythms; [Thirteen 94-2
  That lucid souvenir of the past, [Mozart 132-3
LUCIDITY. Lucidity of his city, joy of his nation, [Aug 492-2
LUCK. Nor all one's luck at once in a play of strings. [John 437-13
LUDWIG RICHTER. Than the spirit of Ludwig Richter . . . [Chaos
  357-9
  And Ludwig Richter, turbulent Schlemihl, [Chaos 358-1
LULLABY. In a mortal lullaby, like porcelain. [Burnshaw 47-22 P
  A tragic lullaby, like porcelain. [Burnshaw 50-31 P
  The desire, for the fiery lullaby. [Woman Had 82-27 P
LULU. "Lulu Gay" [26-title P
  Lulu sang of barbarians before the eunuchs [Lulu G 26-9 P
  "Lulu Morose" [27-title P
LUMBER. Of dampened lumber, emanations blown [C 36-8
LUMINOUS. A man come out of luminous traversing, [C 30-25
  The luminous pages on his knee, [Country 207-21
  Both substance and non-substance, luminous flesh [Choc 297-21
  Other ghostly sequences and, it would be, luminous [Bed 326-18
  A mountain luminous half way in bloom [Cred 375-22
  At once? Is it a luminous flittering [NSF 396-16
  Be silent in your luminous cloud and hear [NSF 404-11
  The luminous melody of proper sound. [NSF 404-12
  Goat-leaper, crystalled and luminous, sitting [AA 417-9
  Where luminous agitations come to rest, [Owl 433-12
  Made suddenly luminous, themselves a change, [Our Stars 455-19
  Of dense investiture, with luminous vassals. [NH 469-6
  Rugged and luminous, chants in the dark [NH 479-14
  Still eked out luminous wrinklings on the leaves, [Old Woman
  45-7 P
  The luminous companion, the hand, [Ulysses 100-9 P
LUMINOUSLY. Wet out of the sea, and luminously wet, [Our Stars
  455-15
LUMP. The same insoluble lump. The fatalist [C 45-17
LUMPS. Beyond, futura's fuddle-fiddling lumps, [Montra 260-15
LUNACY. From lunacy . . . One wants to be able to walk [EM 325-2
  With his lunacy. He would not be aware of the lake. [EM 325-11
LUNAR. For Crispin, fagot in the lunar fire, [C 33-20
  "Lunar Paraphrase" [107-title

A further consummation. For the lunar month [EM 318-4
Is lunar Habana the Cuba of the self? [Feo 333-15
In a faithfulness as against the lunar light, [NH 472-15
Of a lunar light, dark-belted sorcerers [Old Woman 46-3 P
These streaked the mother-of-pearl, the lunar cress. [Greenest
   53-24 P
LUNATIC. In the presence of a logical lunatic." [EM 324-26
  He would be the lunatic of one idea [EM 325-12
LUNATICS. Is the affair of logical lunatics. [EM 324-28
LUNCH. "Sailing after Lunch" [120-title
  Perhaps it's the lunch that we had [Sailing 120-6
  Or the lunch that we should have had. [Sailing 120-7
  Ryan's lunch, hatters, insurance and medicines, [Thought 185-6
  It was almost time for lunch. Pain is human. [EM 314-8
LURCHING. That could come in a slight lurching of the scene,
   [Nuns 92-10 P
LURED. As he traveled alone, like a man lured on by a syllable
   without any meaning, [Prol 516-4
LUSCIOUS. This luscious and impeccable fruit of life [Monocle
   14-12
LUSH. When shall lush chorals spiral through our fire [Duck 66-10 P
LUST. Where is sun and music and highest heaven's lust, [Ghosts
   119-6
LUSTIER. Yet radiantly beyond much lustier blurs. [Nigger 155-19
  Soother and lustier than this vexed, autumnal exhalation,
   [Inelegance 25-17 P
LUSTIEST. Most venerable heart, the lustiest conceit [Monocle
   16-17
  There are the lewdest and the lustiest, [Dutch 292-4
LUSTRE. After a lustre of the moon, we say [NSF 394-19
  To see their lustre truly as it is [Owl 432-21
  But spreads an evil lustre whose increase [Spaniard 34-12 P
  A paragon of lustre; may have voice [Spaniard 35-9 P
LUSTRED. Or a lustred nothingness. Effendi, he [EM 320-22
LUSTRES. These ample lustres from the new-come moon. [Stan MMO
   19-11 P
  Blanche, the blonde, whose eyes are not wholly straight, in a
   room of lustres, shed by turquoise falling, [Piano 22-1 P
  Has faint, portentous lustres, shades and shapes [Burnshaw 49-26P
LUSTROUS. Of life and spring and of the lustrous inundations,
   [Medit 123-14
LUSTY. Is not too lusty for your broadening. [Monocle 16-18
  Lusty as June, more fruitful than the weeks [Havana 143-13
  Only the lusty and the plenteous [Archi 18-17 P
LUTANIST. Tho lutanist of fleas, the knave, the thane, [C 28-7
LUTANISTS. Why seraphim like lutanists arranged [Eve Angels 136-13
LUTE. Abhorring Turk as Esquimau, the lute [C 38-9
  Being the lion in the lute [MBG 175-15
LUTES. And pick the strings of our insipid lutes! [Sunday 69-24
  One of its monstrous lutes, not be [MBG 175-9
LUTHERAN. An attic glass, hums of the old Lutheran bells [Golden
   460-13
  "The Old Lutheran Bells at Home" [461-title
LUXURIATIONS. The small luxuriations that portend [Someone 87-6 A
LYING. Two coins were lying--dos centavos. [Attempt 370-21
  The man that suffered, lying there at ease, [Past Nun 378-19
  The dress is lying, cast-off, on the floor. [Beginning.428-6
  A glassy ocean lying at the door, [NH 468-15
  And the goodness of lying in a maternal sound, [NH 482-9
  "Romance for a Demoiselle Lying in the Grass" [23-title P
LYRE. The tension of the lyre. My point is that [John 437-10
  Père Guzz, in heaven thumb your lyre [An Gaiety 33-5 P
LYTTON STRACHEY. "Lytton Strachey, Also, Enters into Heaven"
   [38-title P

MACABRE. And the macabre of the water-glooms [Sea Surf 100-8
  "Dance of the Macabre Mice" [123-title
MACADAM. The leaves on the macadam make a noise-- [Hermit 505-10
MacCULLOUGH. And set the MacCullough there as major man? [NSF
  386-24
  May be the MacCullough, an expedient, [NSF 387-3
  Beau linguist. But the MacCullough is MacCullough [NSF 387-7
  If MacCullough himself lay lounging by the sea, [NSF 387-9
MACHE. See papier-mache.
MACHINE. Gave suavity to the perplexed machine [Sea Surf 99-3
  Capped summer-seeming on the tense machine [Sea Surf 99-21
  Piano-polished, held the tranced machine [Sea Surf 100-15
  Suggested malice in the dry machine [Sea Surf 101-9
  Followed the drift of the obese machine [Sea Surf 102-3
  Of machine within machine within machine. [Nigger 157-3
  Like a machine left running, and running down. [Repet 306-18
  And a familiar music of the machine [NSF 386-13
  Of seeping rose--banal machine [Soldat 15-20 P
  Delicatest machine. [Demoiselle 23-15 P
  Their destiny is just as much machine [Duck 61-21 P
  Possible machine, a divinity of steel, [Bship 78-3 P
  The universal machine. There he perceived [Woman Had 82-8 P
  They are more than parts of the universal machine. [Woman Had
    82-25 P
MACHINE-GUNS. Of palmy peaks sighting machine-guns? These,
  [Greenest 56-2 P
MACHINERY. Seize yards and docks, machinery and men, [Bship 77-22P
MACHINES. From crusty stacks above machines. [MBG 182-4
  Angry men and furious machines [Dutch 290-1
MAC MORT. Mac Mort she had been, ago, [Oak 272-7
MAD. Of love, it is a book too mad to read [Monocle 14-21
  How can the world so old be so mad [Fading 139-9
  Of a man gone mad, after all, for time, in spite [Nigger 157-18
  Aux crinolines, smears out mad mountains. [Extracts 257-29
  How mad would he have to be to say, "He beheld [Bad Time 426-9
  It was to be as mad as everyone was, [Desire 85-10 P
MADAM. Civil madam, I am, but underneath [NSF 406-11
MADAME. "Cy Est Pourtraicte, Madame Ste Ursule, et les Unze Mille
    Vierges" [21-title
  Poetry is the supreme fiction, madame. [High-Toned 59-1
  Madame, we are where we began. Allow, [High-Toned 59-13
  May, merely may, madame, whip from themselves [High-Toned 59-19
MADAME LA FLEURIE. "Madame La Fleurie" [507-title
MADANNA. Unsnack your snood, madanna, for the stars [Myrrh 349-13
MADE. She made of the motions of her wrist [Infanta 7-13
  And in the grass an offering made [Pourtraicte 21-8
  Made on the sea-weeds and the covered stones [Hibiscus 22-13
  Shut to the blather that the water made, [Hibiscus 22-19
  That whispered to the sun's compassion, made [C 28-26
  Which made him Triton, nothing left of him, [C 28-30
  Crispin beheld and Crispin was made new. [C 30-6
  And jay, still to the night-bird made their plea, [C 30-19
  He was a man made vivid by the sea, [C 30-24
  Much trumpeted, made desperately clear, [C 30-26
  His apprehension, made him intricate [C 31-9
  Made pallid flitter. Crispin, here, took flight. [C 32-27
  It purified. It made him see how much [C 36-16
  He made a singular collation. Thus: [C 37-26
  Made visible. [Men 1000 52-10
  It made you seem so small and lean [Vincentine 52-13
  And my ears made the blowing hymns they heard. [Hoon 65-14
  It made the slovenly wilderness [Jar 76-7
  And made one think of rosy chocolate [Sea Surf 99-1
  And made one think of chop-house chocolate [Sea Surf 99-19
  And made one think of porcelain chocolate [Sea Surf 100-13
  The shrouding shadows, made the petals black [Sea Surf 100-23
  Until the rolling heaven made them blue, [Sea Surf 100-24
  And made one think of musky chocolate [Sea Surf 101-7
  Made by the leaves, that have rotted and fallen; [Lunar 107-8
  It made, away from the muck of the land [How Live 126-6
  Made constant cry, caused constantly a cry, [Key W 128-15
  It was her voice that made [Key W 129-23
  Except the one she sang and, singing, made [Key W 130-2
  Sad men made angels of the sun, and of [Eve Angels 137-10
  The moon they made their own attendant ghosts, [Eve Angels 137-11
  Made earth come right, a peanut parody [Havana 143-9
  Hen shudders: the copious egg is made and laid. [Nigger 155-12
  Made sharp air sharper by their smell [Postcard 159-2
  The maker of a thing yet to be made; [MBG 169-18
  And made it fresh in a world of white, [Poems Clim 193-20
  The winter is made and you have to bear it, [Dwarf 208-3
  That made him preach the louder, long for a church [Blue Bldg
    216-18
  Seeming to be liquid as leaves made of cloud, [Forces 229-14
  She made it. It is easy to say [Scavoir 231-2
  But this she has made. If it is [Scavoir 232-1
  Another image, it is one she has made. [Scavoir 232-2
  Her no and no made yes impossible. [Uruguay 249-15

That evil made magic, as in catastrophe, [Extracts 253-8
In him made one, and in that saying [Hero 279-16
It was increased, enlarged, made simple, [Gigan 289-13
Made single, made one. This was not denial. [Gigan 289-14
No: Nor divergence made too steep to follow down. [Dutch 293-12
The idea as thing. She is half who made her. [Couch 295-20
The choice is made. Green is the orator [Repet 309-22
Clarified. It is silence made still dirtier. [Creat 311-8
Made sure of the most correct catastrophe. [EM 314-10
Who by sympathy has made himself a man [EM 315-15
When B. sat down at the piano and made [EM 316-9
A transparence in which we heard music, made music, [EM 316-10
While all the leaves leaked gold. His mind made morning, [Pure
  331-22
That have rankled for many lives and made no sound. [Sketch 336-3
Or sleep. It was a queen that made it seem [Descrip 339-7
Her green mind made the world around her green. [Descrip 339-9
By her own seeming made the summer change. [Descrip 339-12
Of the imagination, made in sound; [Descrip 346-1
Things made by mid-terrestrial, mid-human [New Set 352-14
"Men Made out of Words" [355-title
It was his clarity that made the vista bright. [Anach 366-3
Is something wished for made effectual [Belly 367-8
Nor made of itself that which it could not find . . . [Cred
  376-8
Fully made, fully apparent, fully found. [Cred 376-15
And Eve made air the mirror of herself, [NSF 383-12
That it made the General a bit absurd, [NSF 391-18
Made us no less as sure. We saw in his head, [AA 412-1
A-dub, a-dub, which is made up of this: [AA 416-1
And that made brothers of us in a home [AA 419-11
Of clay and wattles made as it ascends [Page 421-11
Of their own marvel made, of pity made, [Owl 435-24
Lose the old uses that they made of them, [Orb 441-14
The real made more acute by an unreal. [Bouquet 451-21
Made difficult by salt fragrance, intricate. [Bouquet 452-15
Mal Bay I made, [Our Stars 454-11
I made Mal Bay [Our Stars 454-12
These things were made of him [Our Stars 455-1
Out of him I made Mal Bay [Our Stars 455-5
Made suddenly luminous, themselves a change, [Our Stars 455-19
The eye made clear of uncertainty, with the sight [NH 471-19
Of bronze whose mind was made up and who, therefore, died. [NH
  472-10
For an interior made exterior [NH 481-7
And the poet's search for the same exterior made [NH 481-8
The rich earth, of its own self made rich, [Aug 491-13
And made much within her. [Song Fized 520-10
Has enraged them and made them want to talk it down. [Slug 522-8
His own: a chapel of breath, an appearance made [Armor 529-11
Time's given perfections made to seem like less [Armor 530-8
She made the eunuchs ululate. [Lulu G 26-13 P
Made the maelstrom oceans mutter. [Lulu M 27-14 P
Made by a cook that never rode the back [Burnshaw 46-20 P
Made to remember a life they never lived [Burnshaw 46-24 P
Made to affect a dream they never had, [Burnshaw 47-1 P
Made by the sun ascending seventy seas. [Burnshaw 47-29 P
It made up for everything, it was all selves [Greenest 53-3 P
Made extricate by meanings, meanings made [Greenest 54-10 P
Made of the eye an insatiable intellect. [Greenest 57-1 P
He, only, caused the statue to be made [Greenest 60-1 P
More of ourselves, the mood of life made strong [Duck 65-3 P
Made noble by the honor he receives, [Recit 87-15 P
His life made double by his father's life, [Recit 87-19 P
Made eminent in a reflected seeming-so. [Recit 88-2 P
Astute in being what they are made to be. [Art Pop 112-20 P
Made subtle by truth's most jealous subtlety, [Someone 84-8 A
Much choosing is the final choice made up, [Ideal 88-18 A
See well-made.
MADEMOISELLE DE LESPINASSE. Let's hope for Mademoiselle de
  Lespinasse, [Lytton 39-19 P
MAD-MEN. Painted by mad-men, seen as magic, [Hero 277-24
MADNESS. From madness or delight, without regard [Monocle 17-12
  Nothing of the madness of space, [MBG 183-8
  Green is the night and out of madness woven, [Candle 223-7
  The self-same madness of the astronomers [Candle 223-8
  Breakfast in Paris, music and madness and mud, [Bship 80-3 P
  So that thinking was a madness, and is: [Desire 85-9 P
  So that feeling was a madness, and is. [Desire 85-13 P
MADRID. The cuckoo trees and the widow of Madrid [Greenest 59-16 P
MADRIGALS. "The Bagatelles the Madrigals" [213-title
MAELSTROM. Made the Maelstrom oceans mutter. [Lulu M 27-14 P
MAGENTA. Of magenta blooming in the Judas-tree [Primordia 9-11 P
MAGIC. I know no magic trees, no balmy boughs, [Monocle 16-27
  That evil made magic, as in catastrophe, [Extracts 253-8
  Still, still to deliver us, still magic, [Hero 273-21
  Painted by mad-men, seen as magic, [Hero 277-24
  Or poets with holy magic. [Grotesque 75-8 P
MAGICAL. Magical only for the change they make. [Montra 262-9
MAGISTER. Crispin, magister of a single room, [C 42-5

MAGISTRATES. By growing clear, transparent magistrates, [Bouquet 449-6
MAGNET. The muscles of a magnet aptly felt, [Orb 442-15
MAGNIFICENCE. Without shadows, without magnificence, [MBG 176-13
  In the magnificence of a volcano. [Attempt 370-3
  Splashed wide-wise because it likes magnificence [AA 416-13
  Magnificence most shiningly expressed [Greenest 58-3 P
MAGNIFICENCES. And pathetic magnificences dry in the sky. [Repet 310-4
MAGNIFICENT. And so I mocked her in magnificent measure. [Monocle 13-5
  The magnificent cause of being, [Weep Woman 25-7
  Magnificent, would move among his hinds, [Sunday 68-1
  And the solemn pleasures of magnificent space. [AA 416-14
MAGNIFICO. "Metaphors of a Magnifico" [19-title
MAGNIFIED. Alone, one's shadow magnified, [MBG 176-5
  Upon by clouds, the ear so magnified [Landsc 242-25
  And if the phenomenon, magnified, is [Hero 277-19
  Further magnified, sua voluntate, [Hero 277-20
  That was to look on what war magnified. [Gigan 289-12
  Instant of millefiori bluely magnified-- [Pieces 351-13
  From his project, as finally magnified. [Two Illus 515-4
  A night that was that mind so magnified [Old Woman 45-15 P
  Of London, the paper of Paris magnified [Duck 61-18 P
  The Masculine, much magnified, that cloud [Bship 78-28 P
MAGNIFIES. The discord merely magnifies. [MBG 171-8
  The babbly of generations magnifies [Spaniard 34-18 P
MAGNIFY. To magnify, if in that drifting waste [On Manner 56-6
  It is true. Tonight the lilacs magnify [NSF 394-22
  In Leonardo's way, to magnify [Greenest 56-20 P
MAGNILOQUENT. Not least the pasts destroyed, magniloquent [Sombre 70-6 P
MAGNITUDE. Crispin was washed away by magnitude. [C 28-17
  Of it, a close, parental magnitude, [Orb 443-12
MAGNITUDES. The way a look or a touch reveals its unexpected magnitudes. [Prol 517-10
MAGNOLIA. As the marimba, the magnolia as rose. [C 38-10
  Solange, the magnolia to whom I spoke, [News 265-1
  The spook and makings of the nude magnolia? [Slug 522-14
MAGNOLIAS. The dark shadows of the funereal magnolias [Norfolk 111-16
  The fragrance of the magnolias comes close, [NSF 385-17
MAGNUM. The magnum wreath of summer, time's autumn snood, [Rock 526-21
MAID. A second similar counterpart, a maid [C 44-16
  Of the most beautiful, the most beautiful maid [Golden 461-1
  A maid of forty is no feathery girl. [Stan MMO 19-9 P
  Called Mistress and Maid. [Three 133-23 P
  She says sharply, to her maid, [Three 134-9 P
  Then the maid says, to herself, [Three 134-11 P
  The maid drops her eyes and says to her mistress, [Three 135-1
MAIDEN. Celebration of a maiden's choral. [Peter 92-7
  Between a great captain and the maiden Bawda. [NSF 401-6
MAIDENLY. And maidenly greenhorns, now beheld himself, [C 28-12
MAIDENS. For maidens who were wont to sit and gaze [Sunday 69-8
  On disregarded plate. The maidens taste [Sunday 69-11
  So maidens die, to the auroral [Peter 92-6
  Seized by that possible blue. Be maidens formed [Burnshaw 51-18P
  Maidens in bloom, bulls under sea, the lark [Sombre 67-33 P
MAIDS. The winds were like her maids, [Peter 91-3
  As muffing the mistress for her several maids, [EM 316-21
  And the cooks, the cooks, the bar-men and the maids, [Greenest 53-17 P
MAIN. Of its ancient purple, pruned to the fertile main, [C 45-14
  But let this one sense be the single main. [Montra 264-3
  Its tranquil self, the main of things, the mind, [Rock 528-15
MAINE. For sale in Vienna and Zurich to people in Maine, [Greenest 53-9 P
MAINMAST. Is to fire. And her mainmast tapered to nothing, [Vari 235-21
MAINTAIN. Yet it is this that shall maintain--Itself [Martial 238-6
  And the two poles continue to maintain it [Art Pop 112-16 P
MAJESTIC. These lions, these majestic images. [Lions 124-18
  Of the dead, majestic in their seals. [MBG 170-8
  Become the figures of heaven, the majestic movement [Rome 508-2
  Devising proud, majestic issuance. [Soldat 14-12 P
  White slapped on white, majestic, marble heads, [Burnshaw 49-13F
  Majestic bearers or solemn haulers trapped [Greenest 57-14 P
  A majestic weavers' job, a summer's sweat. [Greenest 58-6 P
  A majestic mother's flocking brood, [Ulysses 103-25 P
MAJESTIES. In many majesties of sound: [How Live 125-14
MAJESTY. They were particles of order, a single majesty: [Anglais 149-8
  He yielded himself to that single majesty; [Anglais 149-12
  He was more than an external majesty, [Cred 375-1
  The charitable majesty of her whole kin? [Cred 375-1
  Am satisfied without solacing majesty, [NSF 405-2
  In which majesty is a mirror of the self: [NSF 405-5
  Except as needed by way of majesty, [AA 417-14
  Vested in the serious folds of majesty, [Orb 442-21

Searched out such majesty as it could find. [NH 469-3
Free from their majesty and yet in need [NH 473-10
Of majesty, of an invincible clou, [NH 473-11
Crude captains, the naked majesty, if you like, [Rome 510-9
A daily majesty of meditation, [Look 518-21
The catholic sun, its majesty, [An Gaiety 32-16 P
MAJOLICA. Or the majolica dish heaped up with phosphored fruit [EM 320-17
MAJOR. One of the major miracles, that fall [Montra 262-6
  Millions of major men against their like [Repet 307-1
  This force of nature in action is the major [EM 324-8
  What are the major men? All men are brave. [Paisant 334-13
  The major men-- [Paisant 335-3
  The greater seeming of the major mind. [Descrip 340-4
  In this major manner of a queen, the green [Descrip 340-12
  And set the MacCullough there as major man? [NSF 386-4
  It does not follow that major man is man. [NSF 387-8
  The origin of the major man. He comes, [NSF 387-24
  The major abstraction is the idea of man [NSF 388-16
  And major man is its exponent, abler [NSF 388-17
  The major abstraction is the commonal, [NSF 388-23
  Out of nothing to have come on major weather, [NSF 404-3
  Part of the major reality, part of [Warmth 90-3 P
  Part of a major reality, part of [As Leave 117-9 P
MAJORS. Lie sprawling in majors of the August heat, [EM 325-28
  See drum-majors.
MAKE. To make believe a starry connaissance. [Monocle 13-22
  To make oblation fit. Where shall I find [Monocle 16-21
  Could make us squeak, like dolls, the wished-for words. [Monocle 17-8
  I make an offering, in the grass, [Pourtraicte 21-18
  And something given to make whole among [C 30-4
  Discovery still possible to make, [C 36-21
  To make a new intelligence prevail? [C 37-10
  Should make the intricate Sierra scan. [C 38-23
  Should he lay by the personal and make [C 41-23
  Make hue among the dark comedians, [Heaven 56-21
  Take the moral law and make a nave of it [High-Toned 59-2
  The opposing law and make a peristyle, [High-Toned 59-7
  This will make widows wince. But fictive things [High-Toned 59-21
  At evening, casual flocks of pigeons make [Sunday 70-26
  Make music, so the selfsame sounds [Peter 89-17
  On my spirit make a music, too. [Peter 89-18
  Make more awry our faulty human things. [Surprises 98-11
  To make the body covetous in desire [Anatomy 108-13
  Make a bed and leave the iris in it. [Norfolk 112-3
  Rides clear of her mind and the waves make a refrain. [Farewell 117-7
  And make much bing, high bing. [Snow Stars 133-9
  To stuff the ear? It causes him to make [Havana 144-14
  Empty and grandiose, let us make hymns [Nigger 151-20
  To make him return to people, to find among them [Nigger 158-7
  "Thou art not August unless I make thee so." [Oboe 251-5
  Except for the images we make of it, [Extracts 257-11
  No, not believing, but to make the cell [Montra 261-10
  Magical only for the change they make. [Montra 262-9
  Make o, make o, make o, [Metamorph 266-1
  Of what good. Devise. Make him of mud, [Hero 275-21
  Devise, devise, and make him of winter's [Hero 275-23
  Obscure Satanas, make a model [Hero 277-2
  Of the armies, the solid men, make big the fable. [Choc 301-15
  Make more than thunder's rural rumbling. They make [Repet 307-2
  They do not make the visible a little hard [Creat 311-12
  These are real only if I make them so. Whistle [Holiday 313-7
  Of what one feels, who could have thought to make [EM 326-8
  A great jaguar running will make a little sound. [Jouga 337-15
  The difference that we make in what we see [Descrip 344-4
  As, men make themselves their speech: the hard hidalgo [Descrip 345-11
  These vigors make, thrice-triple-syllabled, [Two V 354-8
  Of day, then, children make [Prejudice 368-20
  Once to make captive, once to subjugate [Cred 376-12
  So soft, so civil, and you make a sound, [Cred 377-19
  Abysmal instruments make sounds like pips [NSF 384-5
  It is of him, ephebe, to make, to confect [NSF 389-10
  A will to make iris frettings on the blank. [NSF 397-18
  And we make of what we see, what we see clearly [NSF 401-2
  We loved but would no marriage make. Anon [NSF 401-8
  When he moved so slightly to make sure of sun, [NSF 411-21
  For these the musicians make insidious tones, [AA 415-10
  Cry out, "I am the purple muse." Make sure [Bad Time 427-8
  Make any imaginings of them lesser things. [Roses 430-15
  The arias that spiritual fiddlings make, [Orb 440-2
  And others, make certain how being [Degen 444-8
  The angry day-son clanging at its make: [Papini 448-7
  Its colors make, the migratory daze, [Bouquet 451-17
  On a hill of stones to make beau mont thereof. [NH 466-24
  Make gay the hallucinations in surfaces. [NH 472-21
  And everything to make. He may evade [NH 480-7
  Than the difference that clouds make over a town. [NH 487-7

We make, although inside an egg, [Aug 490-1
The leaves on the macadam make a noise-- [Hermit 505-10
Beyond, the two alike in the make of the mind. [Rome 508-7
"Two Illustrations that the World is What You Make of It"
    [513-title
Not one of the masculine myths we used to make, [Look 518-7
Whose blunt laws make an affectation of mind, [Look 519-9
We make a dwelling in the evening air, [Final 524-17
Split it and make blocks, [Archi 17-23 P
I might make many images of this [Demoiselle 23-7 P
Because new colors make new things [Abnormal 24-11 P
And new things make old things again . . . [Abnormal 24-12 P
Make little difference, for being wrong [Red Kit 30-14 P
And darken it, make an unbroken mat [Red Kit 31-24 P
Make a sidereal splendor as you fly. [Red Kit 32-2 P
Make melic groans and tooter at her strokes, [Spaniard 34-25 P
And make the Dagoes squeal. [Drum-Majors 36-22 P
That was whatever the mind might make of it, [Old Woman 45-14 P
Then, while the music makes you, make, yourselves, [Burnshaw
    47-23 P
Since the radiant disclosures that you make [Burnshaw 48-11 P
From which they came, make real the attitudes [Burnshaw 52-3 P
Loosing black slaves to make black infantry, [Greenest 56-9 P
And there, by feat extenuations, to make [Greenest 57-6 P
To make its factories content, must have [Greenest 58-20 P
Massed for a head they mean to make for themselves, [Duck 60-23P
Could ever make them fat, these are delays [Sombre 69-15 P
The ship, make it my own and, bit by bit, [Bship 77-21 P
I said that man should wear stone masks and, to make [Bship
    78-11 P
Another sunlight might make another world, [Theatre 91-1 P
Philosophers' end . . . What difference would it make, [Theatre
    91-17 P
"The Desire to Make Love in a Pagoda" [91-title P
He wanted to make them, keep them from perishing, [Local 112-6 P
Since thirty mornings are required to make [Ideal 88-1 A
MAKE-BELIEVE. As of a make-believe. [Bship 79-16 P
MAKE-MATTER. To the make-matter, matter-nothing mind, [Repet 307-9
MAKENESSE. See Man-makenesse.
MAKER. For she was the maker of the song she sang. [Key W 129-4
    That was her song, for she was the maker. Then we, [Key W 129-29
    The maker's rage to order words of the sea, [Key W 130-12
    The peach-bud maker, [Mud 148-9
    The maker of a thing yet to be made; [MBG 169-18
    The maker of catastrophe invents the eye [Extracts 253-12
    See: helmet-maker; monster-maker.
MAKERS. Makers without knowing, or intending, uses. [New Set
    352-15
    The fathers of the makers may lie and weather. [New Set 353-6
    See sausage-makers.
MAKES. That makes us weep, laugh, grunt and groan, and shout
    [Monocle 17-10
    And not for stupor, such as music makes [C 31-15
    The thing that makes him envious in phrase. [C 33-7
    That makes them our dependent heirs, the heirs [C 39-26
    She makes the willow shiver in the sun [Sunday 69-7
    And out of their droning sibilants makes [Two Figures 86-8
    And makes a constant sacrament of praise. [Peter 92-13
    Makes me conceive how dark I have become, [Sun March 133-14
    Where the voice that is in us makes a true response, [Eve Angels
    138-4
    It makes it clear. Even at noon [MBG 172-17
    It is the sea that the north wind makes. [MBG 179-15
    A crinkled paper makes a brilliant sound. [Extracts 252-1
    Falls on and makes and gives, even a speech, [Phosphor 267-13
    Makes poems on the syllable fa or [Hero 280-9
    Man makes the hero artificial. [Hero 280-24
    Finding its way from the house, makes music seem [Phenom 287-1
    Makes him rise above the houses, looking down. [Repet 307-14
    He makes the tenderest research, intent [EM 318-5
    In which no one peers, in which the will makes no [EM 323-20
    Makes more of it. It is easy to wish for another structure [Bed
    326-16
    Makes everything grotesque. Is it because [Feo 333-13
    One day enriches a year. One woman makes [Cred 374-21
    Makes of the form Most Merciful Capitan, [Pastor 379-6
    She makes that gentler that can gentle be. [AA 413-12
    In seeing them. This is what makes them seem [Roses 431-11
    The mind, among the creatures that it makes, [Owl 436-8
    Without that that he makes of it? [Our Stars 455-8
    And makes flame flame and makes it bite the wood [Novel 458-7
    The description that makes it divinity, still speech [NH 475-13
    It is the window that makes it difficult [NH 478-4
    The same wind, rising and rising, makes a sound [Look 519-2
    It makes so little difference, at so much more [Slug 522-1
    Of a house, that makes one think the house is laughing; [Slug
    522-10
    In this plenty, the poem makes meanings of the rock, [Rock
    527-16
    That merely makes a ring). [Abnormal 24-1 P

Which choir makes the most faultless medley in its celebration?
    [Inelegance 25-19 P
Then, while the music makes you, make, yourselves, [Burnshaw
    47-23 P
That purges the wrack or makes the jungle shine, [Greenest 55-8P
The milkiest bowmen. This makes a new design, [Greenest 56-6 P
He makes no choice of words-- [Grotesque 75-20 P
Makes something of the little there, [Dove 97-18 P
Makes this small howling, like a thought [Dove 98-4 P
Makes them a pack on a giant's back, [Ulysses 103-24 P
They measure the right to use. Need makes [Ulysses 104-24 P
That makes us happy or unhappy. [Of Mere 118-2 P
That makes it say the little thing it says, [Someone 84-15 A
See matter-makes.
MAKING. Making the most of savagery of palms, [C 31-27
    Of the cathedral, making notes, he heard [C 32-16
    Making gulped potions from obstreperous drops, [C 46-9
    Making recoveries of young nakedness [Tallap 72-11
    Making harsh torment of the solitude. [Babies 77-15
    The making of his son was one more duty. [Norfolk 111-13
    Light, too, encrusts us making visible [Eve Angels 137-19
    A long time you have been making the trip [Hartford 226-4
    From nature, each time he saw it, making it, [EM 316-18
    For whom the word is the making of the world, [Descrip 345-7
    And shape and mournful making move to find [AA 418-1
    Making this heavy rock a place, [Imago 439-17
    Nor stand there making orotund consolations. [Papini 446-11
    Making a great gnashing, over the water wallows [Puel 456-8
    A minimum of making in the mind, [NH 473-12
    Making your heart of brass to intercept [Good Bad 33-18 P
    An image of his making, beyond the eye, [Sombre 69-26 P
    The inhuman making choice of a human self. [Ideal 89-12 A
MAKINGS. The spook and makings of the nude magnolia? [Slug 522-14
    Other makings of the sun [Planet 532-10
    And his poems, although makings of his self, [Planet 532-14
    Were no less makings of the sun. [Planet 532-15
MAL. "Esthétique du Mal" [313-title
MALADIVE. See ever-maladive.
MALADY. One has a malady, here, a malady. One feels a malady.
    [Banal 63-6
    The malady of the quotidian . . . [Pharynx 96-9
    Ill of a question like a malady, [Pure 331-7
MALAY. In a book in a barrack, a letter from Malay. [NSF 407-14
MAL BAY. Mal Bay I made, [Our Stars 454-11
    I made Mal Bay [Our Stars 454-12
    Out of him I made Mal Bay [Our Stars 455-5
MALE. Well-booted, rugged, arrogantly male, [Lilacs 49-13
    The Male Nude [NE Verses 106-title 13
    When male light fell on the naked back [Hartford 227-7
    Ha-ee-me is the male beast . . . an imbecile, [Jouga 337-6
    The male voice of the wind in the dry leaves [Primordia 7-14 P
    Like glass and sun, of male reality [Fare Guit 99-8 P
MALEVOLENT. That strode submerged in that malevolent sheen, [Sea
    Surf 99-24
MALFORMED. Whose mind malformed this morning metaphor, [Pure 331-21
    Malformed, the world was paradise malformed . . . [Pure 332-1
MALHEUR. Natives of poverty, children of malheur, [EM 322-18
MALICE. It is with a strange malice [W Burgher 61-1
    Suggested malice in the dry machine [Sea Surf 101-9
    Bright is the malice in his eye . . . [Possum 294-16
    Free, for a moment, from malice and sudden cry, [Cred 378-8
    Or symbol of malice. That we partake thereof, [AA 418-22
MALIGNING. Maligning his costumes and disputing [Stan Hero 84-24 P
MALISONS. Nor feel the x malisons of other men, [Montra 261-24
MALLETS. Nor the mallets of the domes [Six Sig 74-25
MALLOW. A mallow morning dozed upon the deck [Sea Surf 101-6
    Mile-mallows that a mallow sun cajoled. [Sea Surf 101-21
MALLOWS. See mile-mallows.
MAMAN. Maman. His anima liked its animal [EM 321-16
    O chère maman, another, who, in turn, [Soldat 14-5 P
MAN. "The Snow Man" [9-title
    I am a man of fortune greeting heirs; [Monocle 13-17
    Man proved a gobbet in my mincing world. [Monocle 17-24
    Or one man [Magnifico 19-5
    Lacustrine man had never been assailed [Geneva 24-4
    He did not quail. A man so used to plumb [Geneva 24-7
    Nota: man is the intelligence of his soil, [C 27-7
    He was a man made vivid by the sea, [C 30-24
    A man come out of luminous traversing, [C 30-25
    Nota: his soil is man's intelligence. [C 36-24
    The rich man going bare, the paladin [C 37-17
    Afraid, the blind man as astronomer, [C 37-18
    The man in Georgia waking among pines [C 38-15
    Should be pine-spokesman. The responsive man, [C 38-16
    What is one man among so many men? [C 41-25
    Can one man think one thing and think it long? [C 41-27
    Can one man be one thing and be it long? [C 41-28
    The very man despising honest quilts [C 41-29
    All this with many multcings of the man, [C 44-3
    Concluding fadedly, if as a man [C 46-2

So may the relation of each man be clipped. [C 46-13
The black man said, [Jack-Rabbit 50-8
The black man said, [Jack-Rabbit 50-14
X, the mighty thought, the mighty man. [Canna 55-2
An old man sits [Six Sig 73-5
That the man who erected this cabin, planted [Frogs 78-7
A man and a woman [Thirteen 93-3
A man and a woman and a blackbird [Thirteen 93-5
"The Man Whose Pharynx Was Bad" [96-title
Ashen man on ashen cliff above the salt halloo, [NE Verses 105-7
And his nostrils blow out salt around each man. [Grapes 111-3
And that one was never a man of heart. [Norfolk 111-12
A most inappropriate man [Sailing 120-9
As every man in Sweden will concede, [Lions 125-3
The man and his companion stopped [How Live 125-11
Shall a man go barefoot [Am Sub 131-2
"The Brave Man" [138-title
The sun, that brave man, [Brave 138-7
That brave man. [Brave 138-9
That brave man comes up [Brave 138-19
That brave man. [Brave 138-21
The thickest man on the thickest stallion-back, [Havana 143-18
Politic man ordained [Havana 143-21
Black man, bright nouveautes leave one, at best, pseudonymous.
   [Nudity Col 145-12
Nothing is final, he chants. No man shall see the end. [Nigger
   150-13
To think of man the abstraction, the comic sum. [Nigger 156-6
Not by beginning but at the last man's end. [Nigger 156-21
Of a man gone mad, after all, for time, in spite [Nigger 157-18
Of the cuckoos, a man with a mania for clocks. [Nigger 157-19
But the wise man avenges by building his city in snow. [Nigger
   158-13
"The Man with the Blue Guitar" [165-title
The man bent over his guitar, [MBG 165-1
The man replied, "Things as they are [MBG 165-5
And bearded bronze, but not a man, [MBG 165-14
And reach through him almost to man. [MBG 165-16
If to serenade almost to man [MBG 165-17
Of a man that plays a blue guitar. [MBG 166-2
Ah, but to play man number one, [MBG 166-3
Have I? Am I a man that is dead [MBG 173-8
In the mud, a missal for that young man, [MBG 177-22
From this I shall evolve a man. [MBG 181-15
One man, the idea of man, that is the space, [Thought 185-11
The era of the idea of man, the cloak [Thought 185-13
And the idea of man, the mystic garden and [Thought 185-20
Son only of man and sun of men, [Thought 185-25
With all his attributes no god but man [Thought 186-11
He liked the nobler works of man, [Thought 187-1
But this he cannot know, the man that thinks, [Men Fall 188-2
This man loved earth, not heaven, enough to die. [Men Fall 188-18
He is like a man [Destructive 193-1
It can kill a man. [Destructive 193-6
The weak man mended, [Idiom 201-2
The man that is poor at night [Idiom 201-3
Like the man that is rich and right. [Idiom 201-5
"The Man on the Dump" [201-title
As a man (not like an image of a man), [Dump 202-24
"The Latest Freed Man" [204-title
The latest freed man rose at six and sat [Freed 204-14
The moment's sun (the strong man vaguely seen), [Freed 204-20
Like a man without a doctrine. The light he gives-- [Freed 205-1
And so the freed man said. [Freed 205-5
The singular man of the mass. Masses produce [Dames 206-5
Enough to hide away the face of the man [Dames 206-7
The face of the man of the mass, never the face [Dames 206-15
Yet there was a man within me [Weak Mind 212-16
On the sidewalk so that the pensive man may see. [Connois 216-12
The pensive man . . . He sees that eagle float [Connois 216-13
It is the honey-comb of the seeing man. [Blue Bldg 217-17
One part is man, the other god: [Dezem 218-2
Imagined man, the monkish mask, the face. [Dezem 218-8
Slowly, one man, savager than the rest, [Thunder 220-5
In this light a man is a result, [Common 221-10
Is not a woman for a man. [Common 221-14
"The Sense of the Sleight-of-Hand Man" [222-title
It may be that the ignorant man, alone, [Sleight 222-16
This? A man must be very poor [Arcades 225-20
Or less, he found a man, or more, against [Horn 230-15
"Man and Bottle" [238-title
The mind is the great poem of winter, the man, [Bottle 238-17
In the land of war. More than the man, it is [Bottle 239-1
A man with the fury of a race of men, [Bottle 239-2
A man at the centre of men. [Bottle 239-4
Be of a man skating, a woman dancing, a woman [Of Mod 240-21
A naked man who regarded himself in the glass [Landsc 241-16
Kept speaking, of God. I changed the word to man. [Les Plus
   245-4
(This man in a room with an image of the world, [Rhythms 245-12

That woman waiting for the man she loves,) [Rhythms 245-13
There the man sees the image clearly at last. [Rhythms 245-15
"The Well Dressed Man with a Beard" [247-title
The villages slept as the capable man went down, [Uruguay 249-25
The philosophers' man alone still walks in dew, [Oboe 250-12
If you say on the hautboy man is not enough, [Oboe 250-15
The impossible possible philosophers' man, [Oboe 250-18
The man who has had the time to think enough, [Oboe 250-19
The central man, the human globe, responsive [Oboe 250-20
As a mirror with a voice, the man of glass, [Oboe 250-21
The glass man, cold and numbered, dewily cries, [Oboe 251-4
How was it then with the central man? Did we [Oboe 251-10
The glass man, without external reference. [Oboe 251-21
That kill the single man, starvation's head, [Extracts 254-16
One man, their bread and their remembered wine? [Extracts 254-17
The difference between himself and no man, [Extracts 255-8
No man that heard a wind in an empty place. [Extracts 255-9
Man must become the hero of his world. [Montra 261-12
In which man is the hero. He hears the words, [Montra 261-20
The naked man, the naked man as last [Montra 262-11
To project the naked man in a state of fact, [Montra 263-11
Older than any man could be. [News 264-10
And wild and free, the secondary man, [Jumbo 269-12
Hill-scholar, man that never is, [Jumbo 269-14
Our man beheld the naked, nameless dame, [Hand 271-3
Each man spoke in winter. Yet each man spoke of [Hero 273-7
Us. Good chemistry, good common man, what [Hero 273-16
Captain, the man of skill, the expert [Hero 274-1
In war, observes each man profoundly. [Hero 274-14
The common man is the common hero. [Hero 275-5
Gazette Guerrière. A man might happen [Hero 276-5
The hero is a feeling, a man seen [Hero 278-24
We have and are the man, capable [Hero 279-2
To meditate the highest man, not [Hero 280-1
The highest man with nothing higher [Hero 280-5
Man makes the hero artificial. [Hero 280-24
Man was the veritable man? So [Hero 281-1
Each man himself became a giant, [Gigan 289-15
Freedom is like a man who kills himself [Dutch 292-17
He was not man yet he was nothing else. [Choc 298-2
Or by whatever boorish name a man [Choc 300-22
And fond, the total man of glubbal glub, [Choc 301-2
How singular he was as man, how large, [Choc 302-1
A young man seated at his table [Lack 303-1
The young man is well-disclosed, one of the gang, [Lack 303-6
Which, as a man feeling everything, were his. [Somnam 304-18
That X is an obstruction, a man [Creat 310-16
Beyond intelligence, an artificial man [Creat 311-3
Palabra of a common man who did not exist. [Holiday 312-8
Who by sympathy has made himself a man [EM 315-15
A man of bitter appetite despises [EM 322-20
That in his Mediterranean cloister a man, [EM 324-11
Man, that is not born of woman but of air, [Pure 331-16
Night is the nature of man's interior world? [Feo 333-14
For example, this old man selling oranges [Feo 333-18
We say that it is man's interior world [Feo 334-6
The fictive man created out of men. [Paisant 335-6
The baroque poet may see him as still a man [Paisant 335-12
The fictive man. He may be seated in [Paisant 335-14
This man escaped the dirty fates, [Flyer 336-10
Or a barricade against the singular man [Descrip 340-8
The swans. He was not the man for swans. [Descrip 342-22
"Man Carrying Thing" [350-title
There are things in a man besides his reason. [Pieces 351-10
The fisherman might be the single man [Think 357-5
"Continual Conversation with a Silent Man" [359-title
Of things and their motion: the other man, [Silent 360-2
And the man dies that does not fall. [Woman Song 360-7
This man or that, [Woman Song 360-18
A man and a woman, like two leaves [Burghers 362-12
"The Good Man Has No Shape" [364-title
The Good Man Has No Shape, as if they knew. [Good Man 364-14
It is the old man standing on the tower, [Cred 374-1
The rest look down. One man becomes a race, [Cred 374-22
Man's mind grown venerable in the unreal. [Cred 377-5
The man that suffered, lying there at ease, [Past Nun 378-19
Do I press the extremest book of the wisest man [NSF 380-5
You must become an ignorant man again [NSF 380-15
The monastic man is an artist. The philosopher [NSF 382-1
Appoints man's place in music, say, today. [NSF 382-2
An abstraction blooded, as a man by thought. [NSF 385-24
As a man and woman meet and love forthwith. [NSF 386-16
And set the MacCullough there as major man? [NSF 386-24
It does not follow that major man is man. [NSF 387-8
The origin of the major man. He comes, [NSF 388-16
The major abstraction is the idea of man [NSF 388-16
And major man is its exponent, abler [NSF 388-17
Cloudless the morning. It is he. The man [NSF 389-8
A man. The lawyers disbelieved, the doctors [NSF 391-21
On one another, as a man depends [NSF 392-5

An unaffected man in a negative light [NSF 393-19
As in the courage of the ignorant man, [NSF 395-11
Thereon the learning of the man conceived [NSF 402-23
The man who is walking turns blankly on the sand. [AA 412-23
This is nothing until in a single man contained, [AA 416-22
That pinches the pity of the pitiful man, [AA 418-13
"Large Red Man Reading" [423-title
To be a bronze man breathing under archaic lapis, [Cata 425-10
Or one man who, for us, is greater than they, [Antag 425-16
In which the sense lies still, as a man lies, [Roses 431-2
A man walked living among the forms of thought [Owl 432-20
It is nothing, no great thing, nor man [Imago 439-5
A gorgeous fortitude. Medium man [Imago 439-9
If there is a man white as marble [Degen 444-1
So there is a man in black space [Degen 444-4
The marble man remains himself in space. [Degen 444-10
The man in the black wood descends unchanged. [Degen 444-11
Man sits and studies silence and himself, [Papini 447-10
Is the study of man, this image of Saturday, [Study I 463-6
As: the last plainness of a man who has fought [NH 467-17
No man. The self, the chrysalis of all men [NH 468-21
We say of the moon, it is haunted by the man [NH 472-9
A serious man without the serious, [NH 474-14
A man who was the axis of his time, [NH 479-6
Or street or about the corners of a man, [NH 480-1
"This man abolishes by being himself [NH 485-13
The whole man, that tempers and beliefs became [Aug 494-2
A figure half seen, or seen for a moment, a man [Angel 497-7
"An Old Man Asleep" [501-title
In yours, master and commiserable man, [Rome 509-16
The one invulnerable man among [Rome 510-8
It is like the feeling of a man [Vacancy 511-10
As he traveled alone, like a man lured on by a syllable without
   any meaning, [Prol 516-4
Removed from any shore, from any man or woman, and needing none.
   [Prol 516-9
From man's ghost, larger and yet a little like, [Look 518-1
And the icon is the man. The pearled chaplet of spring, [Rock
   526-20
These leaves are the poem, the icon and the man. [Rock 527-2
They bloom as a man loves, as he lives in love. [Rock 527-11
His words are both the icon and the man. [Rock 527-21
The rock is the gray particular of man's life, [Rock 528-1
But through man's eye, their silent rhapsodist, [Rock 528-6
As if some Old Man of the Chimney, sick [Phases 5-6 P
It is that Old Man, lost among the trees. [Phases 5-15 P
This man to complain to the grocer [Soldat 12-13 P
This man to visit a woman, [Soldat 12-15 P
This man to take the air. [Soldat 12-16 P
The rotting man for pleasure saw, [Sat Night 27-18 P
The rotting man was first to sing. [Sat Night 28-12 P
And a shabby man, [Coroner 30-6 P
You never can be right. You are the man. [Red Kit 30-16 P
"Good Man, Bad Woman" [33-title P
In self, a man of longer time than days, [Good Bad 33-10 P
"Secret Man" [35-title P
The man of autumn, [Secret Man 36-13 P
One man opposing a society [Lytton 38-14 P
Sip the wild honey of the poor man's life, [Burnshaw 49-10 P
Beyond thought's regulation. There each man, [Greenest 54-2 P
The temple of the altar where each man [Greenest 54-17 P
Than poodles in Pomerania. This man [Duck 62-2 P
Is each man thinking his separate thoughts or, for once, [Duck
   62-18 P
What man of folk-lore shall rebuild the world, [Duck 63-6 P
What lesser man shall measure sun and moon, [Duck 63-7 P
As the man the state, not as the state the man, [Duck 63-9 P
But man means more, means the million and the duck. [Duck 63-11P
The man in the band-stand could be orator. [Duck 63-15 P
The Johnsonian composition, abstract man, [Duck 65-13 P
There is a man whom rhapsodies of change, [Sombre 66-12 P
The man below the man below the man, [Sombre 66-16 P
We have grown weary of the man that thinks. [Sombre 66-18 P
He thinks and it is not true. The man below [Sombre 66-19 P
He dwells below, the man below, in less [Sombre 67-13 P
The man, but not the man below, for whom [Sombre 68-2 P
Each man in his asylum maundering, [Sombre 68-10 P
The man and the man below were reconciled, [Sombre 68-14 P
The man below beholds the portent poised, [Sombre 69-25 P
Leaves of the autumns in which the man below [Sombre 69-32 P
Lived as the man lives now, and hated, loved, [Sombre 69-33 P
As the man hates now, loves now, the self-same things. [Sombre
   70-1 P
Not the space in camera of the man below, [Sombre 70-31 P
That a man without passion plays in an aimless way. [Sombre 71-12P
Even the man below, the subverter, stops [Sombre 71-17 P
Of the black-blooded scholar, the man of the cloud, to be [Sombre
   71-30 P
The medium man among other medium men, [Sombre 71-31 P
As man is natural, would be at an end." [Bship 78-19 P

Of a man, that seizes our strength, will seize it to be [Bship
   81-9 P
Who, when they think and speak of the central man, [Woman Had
   82-11 P
Of the humming of the central man, the whole sound [Woman Had
   82-12 P
The hero is the man who is himself, who [Stan Hero 84-9 P
As a man among other men, divested [Stan Hero 84-10 P
It is the common man against evil, [Stan Hero 84-15 P
The bronze of the wise man seated in repose [Recit 86-15 P
The figure of the wise man fixed in sense. [Recit 86-17 P
"The Sick Man" [90-title P
The first soothsayers of the land, the man [Americana 93-15 P
In a field, the man on the side of a hill, all men [Americana
   93-16 P
A man that looks at himself in a glass and finds [Americana
   94-7 P
It is the man in the glass that lives, not he. [Americana 94-8 P
The abstraction. He inhabits another man, [Americana 94-10 P
That howls in the mind or like a man [Dove 98-5 P
So that to know a man is to be [Ulysses 99-17 P
That man, to know a place is to be [Ulysses 99-18 P
And if to know one man is to know all [Ulysses 99-20 P
Of the future, of future man [Ulysses 101-9 P
The order of man's right to be [Ulysses 101-13 P
By one, in the right of all. Each man [Ulysses 102-5 P
In the generations of thought, man's sons [Ulysses 103-7 P
The living man in the present place, [Ulysses 103-13 P
That only in man's definitions of himself, [Conversat 109-12 P
Himself. The author of man's canons is man, [Conversat 109-14 P
Transparent man in a translated world, [Bus 116-3 P
Here comes our black man. [Three 135-6 P
Of a man's eyes, [Three 143-1 P
Day, night and man and his endless effigies. [Someone 83-13 A
Or woman weeping in a room or man, [Ideal 88-20 A
The last man given for epitome, [Ideal 88-21 A
See: anti-master-man; cloud-man; half-man; man-man; root-man;
   super-man.
MAN-BOAT. On top. Hurroo, the man-boat comes, [Vari 235-17
MANDOLIN. "Mandolin and Liqueurs" [28-title P
MANDOLINE. The mandoline is the instrument [Men 1000 52-3
MANDOLINS. Are there mandolines of western mountains? [Men 1000
   52-5
   Are there mandolines of northern moonlight? [Men 1000 52-6
MANDOLINS. Stop at the terraces of mandolins, [Study I 463-14
MANE. Master by foot and jaws and by the mane, [NSF 384-10
   To be crested and wear the mane of a multitude [NSF 398-8
MAN-EARTH. Man-sun, man-moon, man-earth, man-ocean, [Hero 280-8
MANED. See white-maned.
MANES. More than his muddy hand was in the manes, [Old Woman 43-19P
   Manes matted of marble across the air, the light [Old Woman 45-1P
   And feeling the world in which they live. The manes, [Duck 64-14P
   The manes to his image of the flying wind, [Duck 64-17 P
MANGLED. This mangled, smutted semi-world hacked out [Ghosts 119-8
MANGO. To feast . . . Slice the mango, Naaman, and dress it
   [Phenom 286-14
   We drank Meursault, ate lobster Bombay with mango [NSF 401-22
   At B: the origin of the mango's rind. [Rock 528-13
   Red mango peels and I play my guitar. [Stan MBG 72-4 P
MAN-HAGGARD. The portent would become man-haggard to [Sombre 70-26P
MAN-HERO. The man-hero is not the exceptional monster, [NSF 406-5
MANIA. Of the cuckoos, a man with a mania for clocks. [Nigger
   157-19
MANIAS. Yes: gildering the swarm-like manias [Descrip 342-19
MANIFEST. The dew upon their feet shall manifest. [Sunday 70-13
MANIFESTATIONS. Are the manifestations of a law [Ulysses 103-22 P
MANIFOLD. And manifold continuation; [Solitaires 60-9
   Beings of other beings manifold-- [Study II 464-12
MANIKIN. His tattered manikin arise, [Abnormal 24-16 P
MANKIND. Observed, when young, the nature of mankind, [Monocle
   17-22
MAN-LIKE. Eyes and bruted ears: the man-like body [Hero 277-9
MAN-LOCKED. Cleared of its stiff and stubborn, man-locked set,
   [Angel 497-1
MAN-MAKENESSE. In a man-makenesse, neater than Naples. [Vari 235-18
MAN-MAN. Arrives at the man-man as he wanted. [Hero 280-17
MAN-MISTY. Man-misty to a race star-humped, astride [Sombre 70-29 P
MAN-MOON. Man-sun, man-moon, man-earth, man-ocean, [Hero 280-8
MANNEQUINS. Congenial mannequins, alert to please, [Study II
   464-11
MANNER. For the music and manner of the paladins [Monocle 16-20
   Dejected his manner to the turbulence. [C 29-12
   "On the Manner of Addressing Clouds" [55-title
   In an old, frizzled, flambeaued manner, [Jasmine 79-5
   And all their manner in the thing, [MBG 166-16
   And all their manner, right and wrong, [MBG 166-17
   And all their manner, weak and strong? [MBG 166-18
   At last, in spite of his manner, his eye [MBG 181-20
   A manner of thinking, a mode [Bottle 239-7
   His manner slickened them. He milled [News 264-13

His manner took what it could find, [News 264-16
For every day. In a civiler manner, [Hero 275-22
Her self in her manner not the solid block, [Pure 332-15
An age is a manner collected from a queen. [Descrip 340-5
In the major manner of a queen, the green [Descrip 340-12
The huge decorum, the manner of the time, [Cred 378-4
So moving in the manner of his hand. [NSF 388-12
In the manner of its stitchings, of its thread, [Owl 434-14
In an Ancient, Solemn Manner [Soldat 11-title 2 P
What manner of building shall we build? [Archi 16-13 P
In this house, what manner of utterance shall there be? [Archi
    16-20 P
A manner of the mind, a mind in a night [Old Woman 45-13 P
A manner of walking, yellow fruit, a house, [Woman Had 83-7 P
In the manner of a tragedian [Three 136-8 P
MANNERED. See large-mannered.
MANNERISM. The mannerism of nature caught in a glass [Look 519-10
    And there become a spirit's mannerism, [Look 519-11
MANNERS. The manners of the barbarians, [Lulu G 26-15 P
MAN-OCEAN. Man-sun, man-moon, man-earth, man-ocean, [Hero 280-8
MANQUE. The universe that supplements the manqué, [Repet 309-8
    Are of an eternal vista, manqué and gold [Burnshaw 48-12 P
MANSARD. Your mansard with a rented piano. You lie [NSF 384-18
MANSION. We knew for long the mansion's look [Postcard 159-11
    Will say of the mansion that it seems [Postcard 159-16
MANSION-HOUSE. Above the shuttered mansion-house, [Postcard 159-8
MAN-SUN. Man-sun, man-moon, man-earth, man-ocean, [Hero 280-8
    The man-sun being hero rejects that [Hero 280-12
MANTELPIECE. As in a signed photograph on a mantelpiece. [Orb 443-2
MANTILLA. Who bowed and, bowing, brought, in her mantilla, [Attempt
    370-9
    Now, being invisible, I walk without mantilla, [Souls 94-16 P
MANTLES. Or we put mantles on our words because [Look 519-1
MANY. Going in many directions [Homunculus 26-3
    Of many proclamations of the kind, [C 32-32
    How many poems he denied himself [C 34-18
    How many sea-masks he ignored; what sounds [C 34-21
    What is one man among so many men? [C 41-25
    What are so many men in such a world? [C 41-26
    All this with many mulctings of the man, [C 44-3
    The path sick sorrow took, the many paths [Sunday 69-4
    Of one of many circles. [Thirteen 94-8
    Too many waltzes have ended. And then [Sad Gay 121-14
    Too many waltzes have ended. Yet the shapes [Sad Gay 122-10
    Too many waltzes--The epic of disbelief [Sad Gay 122-13
    In many majesties of sound: [How Live 125-14
    That rose, or even colored by many waves; [Key W 129-11
    Of affected homage foxed so many books, [Havana 142-15
    One of many, between two poles. So, [Glass 197-10
    On a cocoanut--how many men have copied dew [Dump 202-7
    For buttons, how many women have covered themselves [Dump 202-8
    "There are many truths, [On Road 203-17
    A light at the centre of many lights, [Bottle 239-3
    The sea is so many written words; the sky [Extracts 252-10
    Too conscious of too many things at once, [Hand 271-2
    Too conscious of too many things at once, [Hand 271-7
    He was too conscious of too many things [Hand 271-15
    Weaving and weaving many arms. [Oak 272-9
    The classic changed. There have been many. [Hero 276-10
    And there are many bourgeois heroes. [Hero 276-11
    Too many references. The hero [Hero 279-9
    Of those that are marching, many together. [Dutch 290-12
    The much too many disinherited [Dutch 292-6
    The wounds of many soldiers, the wounds of all [EM 318-27
    And, with him, many blue phenomena. [EM 319-22
    So many selves, so many sensuous worlds, [EM 326-9
    That have rankled for many lives and made no sound. [Sketch
    336-3
    There are many of these beasts that one never sees, [Jouga 337-11
    One will and many wills, and the wind, [Silent 359-12
    Of many meanings in the leaves, [Silent 359-13
    So many clappers going without bells, [NSF 394-5
    Here are too many mirrors for misery. [AA 420-7
    Through many places, as if it stood still in one, [Cata 424-12
    And of as many meanings as of men. [Roses 431-9
    Like many robings, as moving masses are, [Owl 433-9
    Of sense, evoking one thing in many men, [Aug 494-18
    I might make many images of this [Demoiselle 23-7 P
    By inch, Sunday by Sunday, many men. [Duck 60-20 P
    There are as many points of view [Three 136-14 P
    But always so many things. He had not to be told [Someone 85-12 A
MANY-FOOTED. Large-leaved and many-footed shadowing, [Greenest
    52-23 P
MANY-STANZAED. The many-stanzaed sea, the leaves [Search 268-5
MAP. Map of yesterday's earth [Primordia 9-13 P
    There is no map of paradise. [Ulysses 102-2 P
MARAUDING. So sullen with sighing and surrender to marauding
    ennui. [Inelegance 25-18 P
MARBLE. Land of Pine and Marble [NE Verses 106-title 12
    The volumes like marble ruins [Common 221-20

The hand can touch, neither green bronze nor marble, [Montra
    261-3
A design, a marble soiled by pigeons? [Hero 278-23
The buildings were of marble and stood in marble light. [Anach
    366-2
If there is a man white as marble [Degen 444-1
The marble man remains himself in space. [Degen 444-10
Of a windy night as it is, when the marble statues [NH 473-20
In that splay of marble [Archi 17-4 P
A group of marble horses rose on wings [Old Woman 43-2 P
The marble leaping in the storms of light. [Old Woman 43-9 P
The mass of stone collapsed to marble hulk, [Old Woman 44-23 P
Yet the light fell falsely on the marble skulls, [Old Woman
    44-30 P
Manes matted of marble across the air, the light [Old Woman
    45-1 P
And on this ring of marble horses shed [Burnshaw 47-27 P
White slapped on white, majestic, marble heads, [Burnshaw 49-13P
In the soil and rest. Conceive that marble men [Burnshaw 52-1 P
Bears words that are the speech of marble men. [Burnshaw 52-5 P
The marble was imagined in the cold. [Greenest 56-28 P
The message is half-borne. Could marble still [Greenest 57-21 P
Be marble after the drenching reds, the dark [Greenest 57-22 P
The gods like marble figures fallen, left [Greenest 58-14 P
See more than marble in their eyes, see more [Duck 64-8 P
In marble, but marble massive as the thrust [Sombre 70-24 P
Stood on a plain of marble, high and cold; [Woman Had 82-29 P
But there is more than a marble, massive head. [Woman Had 83-3 P
Is not lean marble, trenchant-eyed. There is [Recit 86-9 P
A nature of marble in a marble world. [Conversat 109-10 P
MARBLES. That the marbles are gluey pastiches, the stairs [Prelude
    195-3
    There are more heroes than marbles of them. [Hero 276-12
    The marbles are pinchings of an idea, [Hero 276-13
    Yet there is that idea behind the marbles, [Hero 276-14
    The hero is not a person. The marbles [Hero 276-19
    In brown books. The marbles of what he was stand [Hero 276-25
    These marbles lay weathering in the grass [Two Illus 514-6
    Appoints These Marbles Of Itself To Be [Burnshaw 48-6 P
MARBLISH. But their mignon, marblish glare! [Anything B 211-13
MARCH. Marching a motionless march, custodians. [C 42-12
    "The Sun This March" [133-title
    March toward a generation's centre. [Dutch 293-10
    They would march single file, with electric lamps, alert [Page
    423-9
    March . . . Someone has walked across the snow, [Vacancy 511-4
    In March, a scrawny cry from outside [Not Ideas 534-2
    In the early March wind. [Not Ideas 534-6
    The women should sing as they march. [Drum-Majors 37-11 P
    See Hugh March.
MARCHAND. An upper, particular bough in, say, Marchand. [Connois
    215-12
MARCHERS. These violent marchers of the present, [Dutch 293-6
MARCHING. Marching a motionless march, custodians. [C 42-12
    Marching and marching in a tragic time [Loaf 200-11
    It was soldiers went marching over the rocks [Loaf 200-13
    No doubt that soldiers had to be marching [Loaf 200-16
    Men are moving and marching [Dutch 290-10
    Of those that are marching, many together. [Dutch 290-12
    There is a rumble of autumnal marching, [Dutch 291-3
MARE. O stagnant east-wind, palsied mare, [Room Gard 40-16 P
MARGARET. You Jim and you Margaret and you singer of La Paloma,
    [Fish-Scale 161-1
MARGUERITE. The marguerite and coquelicot, [Pourtraicte 21-13
MARIANNA. It is Marianna's Swedish cart. [Prejudice 368-12
MARIE. And that confident one, Marie, the wearer of cheap stones,
    who will have grown still and restless; [Piano 22-5 P
MARIMBA. As the marimba, the magnolia as rose. [C 38-10
MARINA. "Infanta Marina" [7-title
MARINE. Like blooms secluded in the thick marine? [Sea Surf 101-12
    Sleep deep, good eel, in your perverse marine. [Two V 354-18
    Shook off their dark marine in lapis light. [NH 484-8
MARINERS. In the land of the elm trees, wandering mariners [NH
    486-16
    In the land of big mariners, the words they spoke [NH 486-20
    When the mariners came to the land of the lemon trees, [NH 487-1
MARIONETTE. Was gemmy marionette to him that sought [C 36-4
MARK. In all desires, his destitution's mark. [C 31-11
    And in your centre mark them and are cowed . . . [NSF 384-24
    Are white, a little dried, a kind of mark [AA 412-9
    Now, soldiers, hear me: mark this very breeze, [Phases 5-12 P
    I mark the virtue of the common-place. [Soldat 11-6 P
    In which the bliss of clouds is mark of an intended meeting
    [Inelegance 25-15 P
MARKED. He marked the marshy ground around the dock, [C 36-13
    It marked the edge [Thirteen 94-7
MARKET. Not merely desired, for sale, and market things [Armor
    530-4
MARKS. A bronze rain from the sun descending marks [Swans 4-3
MAROON. At the legend of the maroon and olive forest, [Plant 506-17

MARRIAGE. Celebrating the marriage [Motion 83-8
  There was a mystic marriage in Catawba, [NSF 401-4
  We loved but would no marriage make. Anon [NSF 401-8
  Foreswore the sipping of the marriage wine. [NSF 401-10
  The final relation, the marriage of the rest. [Study II 465-3
  By her sexual name, saying that that high marriage [Desire 85-5 P
MARRIAGE-BED. And there they read of marriage-bed. [Ord Women
  11-14
MARRIAGE-HYMNS. And happiest folk-land, mostly marriage-hymns.
  [Cred 373-21
MARRIAGE-PLACE. They married well because the marriage-place [NSF
  401-19
MARRIED. And ladies soon to be married. [Homunculus 25-16
  And therefore married Dawda, whom he found there, [NSF 401-17
  They married well because the marriage-place [NSF 401-19
MARRIES. That marries her innocence thus, [Lilacs 49-3
MARSHY. He marked the marshy ground around the dock, [C 36-13
MARTIAL. "Martial Cadenza" [237-title
MARTIN. Deep in their sound the stentor Martin sings. [Luther
  461-13
MARTYRDOMS. And the jasmine islands were bloody martyrdoms. [Oboe
  251-9
MARTYRED. Taste of the blood upon his martyred lips, [Men Fall
  188-15
MARTYRS. Lost in an integration of the martyrs' bones, [Uruguay
  249-23
  Eventual victor, out of the martyrs's bones, [Uruguay 250-4
  And the martyrs à la mode. He walked toward [Contra II 270-9
  Lighting the martyrs of logic with white fire. [EM 325-16
  Of martyrs, to be arrogant in our need, [Bship 81-3 P
MARVEL. Of their own marvel made, of pity made, [Owl 435-24
MARVELLING. Marvelling sometimes at the shaken sleep. [C 44-19
MARVELOUS. Curriculum for the marvelous sophomore. [C 36-15
MARX. Marx has ruined Nature, [Botanist 1 134-12
MARY. Humanly near, and the figure of Mary, [Lunar 107-6
MASCULINE. Lights masculine and lights feminine. [Hartford 226-14
  A moment ago, light masculine, [Hartford 227-1
  Beyond the horizon with its masculine, [NH 476-24
  Not one of the masculine myths we used to make, [Look 518-7
  Returned on board The Masculine. That night, [Bship 77-14 P
  The Masculine, much magnified, that cloud [Bship 78-28 P
  In more than phrase? There's the true masculine, [Bship 79-12 P
  On The Masculine one asserts and fires the guns. [Bship 80-7 P
MASH. See moon-mash.
MASK. Should mask as white girls. [W Burgher 61-4
  Wear the breeches of a mask, [Orangeade 103-9
  The sea was not a mask. No more was she. [Key W 128-18
  But the ugly alien, the mask that speaks [Nigger 156-17
  To say of one mask it is like, [MBG 181-7
  That the mask is strange, however like." [MBG 181-10
  Neither as mask nor as garment but as a being, [Dwarf 208-11
  Imagined man, the monkish mask, the face. [Dezem 218-8
  A mask, a spirit, an accoutrement. [Gigan 289-20
  Of this present, the venerable mask above [NH 476-17
  In the western night. The venerable mask, [NH 477-3
  Behind its melancholy mask, [Secret Man 36-14 P
  Is only another egoist, wearing a mask, [Duck 63-5 P
  The masks of music. We perceive each mask [Sombre 67-22 P
  A mask up-gathered brilliantly from the dirt, [Sombre 70-13 P
  Yet lord, a mask of flame, the sprawling form [Sombre 70-16 P
MASKS. Salt masks of beard and mouths of bellowing, [Sea Surf 101-17
  Surly masks and destroyers? [Bagatelles 213-20
  Its actors approaching, in company, in their masks. [AA 414-21
  In masks, can choir it with the naked wind? [AA 415-3
  The masks of music. We perceive each mask [Sombre 67-22 P
  I said that men should wear stone masks and, to make [Bship
  78-11 P
  Once the assassins wore stone masks and did [Bship 78-15 P
  See sea-masks.
MASONRY. And murky masonry, one wonders [Ulysses 100-29 P
MASQUE. And from the peristyle project a masque [High-Toned 59-8
MASQUERADE. With masquerade of thought, with hapless words [C 39-15
  That must belie the racking masquerade, [C 39-16
  Be merely a masquerade or else a rare [Greenest 56-13 P
MASQUERIE. A bachelor of feen masquerie, [Oak 272-5
MASS. "The mass is nothing. The number of men in a mass [Dames
  206-3
  Of men is nothing. The mass is no greater than [Dames 206-4
  The singular man of the mass. Masses produce [Dames 206-5
  Of this dead mass and that. The wind might fill [Dames 206-8
  The face of the man of the mass, never the face [Dames 206-15
  Ideas are men. The mass of meaning and [Extracts 255-25
  The mass of men are one. Chaos is not [Extracts 255-26
  The mass of meaning. It is three or four [Extracts 255-27
  The mass of meaning becomes composed again. [Extracts 256-3
  A chord between the mass of men and himself, [Extracts 256-6
  It is the music of the mass of meaning. [Extracts 256-10
  The root-man swarming, tortured by his mass, [Montra 262-23
  In a feeling mass, a blank emotion, [Hero 276-27
  No self in the mass: the braver being, [Gigan 289-3

From beasts or from the incommunicable mass. [Less 328-6
A vermilioned nothingness, any stick of the mass [Less 328-9
At the center of the mass, the haunches low, [Old Woman 43-13 P
The mass of stone collapsed to marble hulk, [Old Woman 44-23 P
That will replace it shall be carved, "The Mass [Burnshaw 48-5 P
A mass overtaken by the blackest sky, [Sombre 69-4 P
Unless society is a mystical mass. [Bship 79-30 P
MASSA. But nakedness, woolen massa, concerns an innermost atom.
  [Nudity Cap 145-10
MASSED. Massed for a head they mean to make for themselves, [Duck
  60-23 P
MASSES. The singular man of the mass. Masses produce [Dames 206-5
  Like many robings, as moving masses are, [Owl 433-9
MASSIVE. Key West sank downward under massive clouds [Farewell
  117-3
  Massive drums and leaden trumpets, [Nightgown 214-11
  The most massive sopranos are singing songs of scales. [Chaos
  357-18
  Or massive portico. A capitol, [AA 416-19
  A massive body and long legs, stretched out, [Orb 443-9
  In marble, but marble massive as the thrust [Sombre 70-24 P
  But there is more than a marble, massive head. [Woman Had 83-3 P
MASSIVELY. Massively rising high and bare [How Live 125-18
  It rose loftily and stood massively; and to lie [Armor 529-2
MASSIVES. Who saw the mortal massives of the blooms [Sea Surf 100-1
MAST. I am free. High above the mast the moon [Farewell 117-7
MASTER. Incapable master of all force, [Negation 97-17
  "Mud Master" [147-title
  There is a master of mud. [Mud 148-5
  The mud master, [Mud 148-10
  The master of the mind. [Mud 148-11
  Cochon! Master, the grapes are here and now. [Nigger 154-19
  From Havre to Hartford, Master Soleil, [Hartford 226-5
  Souvenirs of museums. But, Master, there are [Hartford 226-13
  Purple sets purple round. Look, Master, [Hartford 227-5
  As if designed by X, the per-noble master. [Extracts 254-20
  Master and, without light, I dwell. There [Hero 273-4
  A voluminous master folded in his fire. [NSF 381-3
  Master by foot and jaws and by the mane, [NSF 384-10
  But he that of repetition is most master. [NSF 406-6
  In another nest, the master of the maze [AA 411-16
  Master O master seated by the fire [AA 414-22
  The dauntless master, as he starts the human tale. [Puel 456-18
  More harassing master would extemporize [NH 486-7
  In yours, master and commiserable man, [Rome 509-16
  The master of the spruce, himself, [Two Illus 515-1
  Master of the world and of himself, [Ulysses 102-18 P
  "Presence of an External Master of Knowledge" [105-title P
  See anti-master-man.
MASTERED. Mastered the night and portioned out the sea, [Key W
  130-8
MASTERING. Of these discolorations, mastering [Descrip 342-8
MASTERS. I quote the very phrase my masters used. [Soldat 11-9 P
  Of the well-thumbed, infinite pages of her masters, who will
    seem old to her, requiting less and less her feeling: [Piano
    22-7 P
  Of truth. They stride across and are masters of [Role 93-8 P
MASTERY. Became transformed. But his mastery [Two Illus 515-2
  Perhaps at so much mastery, the bliss [Spaniard 35-2 P
MAST-HEAD. Is at the mast-head and the past is dead. [Farewell
  117-5
MAT. Under the mat of frost and over the mat of clouds. [Nigger
  151-4
  And darken it, make an unbroken mat [Red Kit 31-24 P
MATCH. Defies red emptiness to evolve his match, [NSF 384-9
  In slaughter; or if to match its furious wit [Sombre 69-6 P
MATCHED. Are matched by other revolutions [Ulysses 102-25 P
MATCHES. That matches, today, a clearness of the mind. [Nuns 92-17P
MATCHING. A matching and mating of surprised accords, [NH 468-2
MATCHLESS. Fell falsely on the matchless skeletons, [Old Woman
  45-2 P
MATE. Must miss the symmetry of a leaden mate, [Nigger 152-19
  Has any chance to mate his life with life [Sleight 222-17
  An image of the mind, an inward mate, [Pastor 379-18
  That bugles for the mate, nearby the nest, [NSF 405-14
  And the world the central poem, each one the mate [Orb 441-20
  And the mate of summer: her mirror and her look, [Orb 441-23
MATERIAL. His ear, the very material of his mind. [NSF 403-3
MATERNAL. Expanding in the gold's maternal warmth. [C 32-10
  He sought the most grossly maternal, the creature [EM 321-13
  And the goodness of lying in a maternal sound, [NH 482-9
  Are old men breathed on by a maternal voice, [Woman Had 82-14 P
  Maternal voice, the explanation at night. [Woman Had 82-24 P
MATHER. See Cotton Mather.
MATIN. The blank frere of fields, their matin laborer. [Aug 492-18
  Between the matin air and color, goldenest generating, [Inele-
    gance 25-16 P
  A matin gold from gold of Hesperus [Ideal 88-15 A
MATINAL. Whoever hunts a matinal continent [C 40-27
  And vaguely to be seen, a matinal red, [Burnshaw 51-22 P

MATING. A matching and mating of surprised accords, [NH 468-2
MATISSE. Matisse at Vence and a great deal more than that, [Armor 529-18
MATTED. Manes matted of marble across the air, the light [Old Woman 45-1 P
MATTER. Is nothing, what can all this matter since [C 46-11
   If that remains concealed, what does the bottom matter? [Nudity Cap 145-11
   No matter. The grass is full [Rabbit K 209-15
   The life that never would end, no matter [Gigan 289-5
   Does not really matter [Mandolin 29-9 P
   It cannot matter at all. [Table 40-13 P
   This matters most in things that matter least. [Grotesque 76-11 P
   Objects not present as a matter of course [Local 112-1 P
   See make-matter.
MATTERED. What mattered was that they should bear [Planet 532-17
MATTER-MAKES. Until this matter-makes in years of war. [Repet 307-10
MATTER-NOTHING. To the make-matter, matter-nothing mind, [Repet 307-9
MATTERS. To Cuba. Jot these milky matters down. [Havana 144-6
   It is she alone that matters. [Scavoir 231-1
   One believes is what matters. Ecstatic identities [Extracts 258-2
   Thus the theory of description matters most. [Descrip 345-5
   It matters, because everything we say [Descrip 345-19
   Each matters only in that which it conceives. [Past Nun 379-3
   And to find how much that really matters [Mandolin 29-8 P
   This matters most in things that matter least. [Grotesque 76-11 P
MATTRESS. Or the bench with the pot of geraniums, the stained mattress and the washed overalls drying in the sun? [Indigo 22-12 P
MATTRESSES. On the dump? Is it to sit among mattresses of the dead, [Dump 203-6
   Under its mattresses of vines. [Vacancy 511-13
MATURE. Mature: A capable being may replace [Pure 330-11
   Mature emotional gesture, that-- [Stan MBG 73-8 P
MAUDLIN. To the tense, the maudlin, true meridian [Burnshaw 52-15P
MAUNDERING. When this yokel comes maundering, [Plot Giant 6-11
   Each man in his asylum maundering, [Sombre 68-10 P
MAUVE. Woman with a vague moustache and not the mauve [EM 321-15
MAUVED. Harlequined and mazily dewed and mauved [C 41-5
MAWS. Out of their purple maws, [Bananas 54-21
MAXIMS. As you from maxims, [Three 129-4 P
   Well, it is true of maxims. [Three 129-8 P
   Yes: it is true of maxims, [Three 129-12 P
MAXIMUM. Of the longest meditation, the maximum, [EM 324-17
   This maximum, an adventure to be endured [EM 324-21
MAY. In the woods, in this full-blown May, [Pediment 362-1
   As in the top-cloud of a May night-evening, [NSF 395-10
   Deploring sentiment. When May came last [Good Bad 33-14 P
   Of April here and May to come. Champagne [Greenest 58-24 P
   To April here and May to come. Why think, [Greenest 58-29 P
MAYA. In Yucatan, the Maya sonneteers [C 30-16
MAYBE. And the sea. This is my father or, maybe, [Irish 502-5
MAYOR. I have killed the mayor, [Soldat 13-2 P
MAZE. In another nest, the master of the maze [AA 411-16
MAZILY. Harlequined and mazily dewed and mauved [C 41-5
McCARTHY. See Blance McCarthy.
McGREEVY. See Tom McGreevy.
MEADOWS. With the gold bugs, in blue meadows, late at night. [Cred 377-23
MEAGRE. Yet this is meagre play [Paltry 6-1
MEAN. If they mean no more than that. But they do. [Grapes 110-18
   Of central sense, these minutiae mean more [EM 317-20
   At least, conceive what these hands from Sweden mean, [Duck 60-21 P
   Massed for a head they mean to make for themselves, [Duck 60-23 P
   It cannot mean a sea-wide country strewn [Duck 63-12 P
   Yet what I mean I always say. [Stan MBG 73-2 P
MEANING. Yet is certain as meaning . . . [Magnifico 19-15
   So the meaning escapes. [Magnifico 19-21
   Crying and shouting and meaning farewell, [Adieu 127-10
   Has no more meaning than tomorrow's bread. [Havana 144-29
   His speech, the dress of his meaning, silk [MBG 170-2
   Ideas are men. The mass of meaning and [Extracts 255-25
   The mass of meaning. It is three or four [Extracts 255-27
   The mass of meaning becomes composed again. [Extracts 256-3
   It is the music of the mass of meaning. [Extracts 256-10
   And repeats words without meaning. [Motive 288-4
   A few sounds of meaning, a momentary end [Lack 303-19
   To hear only what one hears, one meaning alone, [EM 320-27
   As if the paradise of meaning ceased [EM 320-28
   There is a sense in sounds beyond their meaning. [Pieces 352-1
   The quiet was part of the meaning, part of the mind: [House Q 358-17
   In which there is no other meaning, itself [House Q 359-2
   The meaning of the capture, this hard prize, [Cred 376-14
   Und so lau, between sound without meaning and speech, [Page 421-10
   Like a meaning in nothingness, [Celle 438-5

As he traveled alone, like a man lured on by a syllable without any meaning, [Prol 516-4
That it contained the meaning into which he wanted to enter, [Prol 516-6
A meaning which, as he entered it, would shatter the boat and leave the oarsmen quiet [Prol 516-7
For a sign of meaning in the meaningless, [Armor 529-12
Knowing and meaning that he cannot care. [Greenest 59-10 P
A meaning without a meaning. These people have [Duck 65-16 P
A meaning within the meaning they convey, [Duck 65-17 P
Communications of Meaning [75-title 3 P
The desire for speech and meaning gallantly fulfilled, [Discov 95-18 P
   In the absence of fantasia, without meaning more [Course 97-1 P
   The joy of meaning in design [Ulysses 100-22 P
   Sings in the palm, without human meaning, [Of Mere 117-19 P
   He seeks an image certain as meaning is [Someone 84-12 A
   See fore-meaning.
MEANINGLESS. The meaningless plungings of water and the wind, [Key W 129-19
   Ah, but the meaningless, natural effigy! [Nigger 153-17
   The physical world is meaningless tonight [Jouga 337-1
   The hating woman, the meaningless place, [Pecul 454-8
   For a sign of meaning in the meaningless, [Armor 529-12
   Blowing among the trees its meaningless sound. [Old Woman 44-28P
MEANINGS. Of many meanings in the leaves, [Silent 359-13
   Of the sweeping meanings that we add to them. [NSF 384-6
   It is like a flow of meanings with no speech [Roses 431-8
   And of as many meanings as of men. [Roses 431-9
   The giant body the meanings of its folds, [Owl 433-16
   Words, lines, not meanings, not communications, [NH 465-12
   The less legible meanings of sounds, the little reds [NH 488-7
   The meanings are our own-- [Aug 495-5
   Like watery words awash; like meanings said [Angel 497-4
   In this plenty, the poem makes meanings of the rock, [Rock 527-16
   Made extricate by meanings, meanings made [Greenest 54-10 P
   With meanings, doubled by the closest sound, [Sombre 67-25 P
   And it flows over us without meanings, [Clear Day 113-16 P
   See half-meanings.
MEANS. Which yet found means to set his simmering mind [Geneva 24-10
   And, talking of happiness, know that it means [Extracts 257-14
   In a universe of inconstancy. This means [NSF 389-24
   It means the distaste we feel for this withered scene [NSF 390-3
   We ask which means most, for us, all the genii [Antag 425-15
   By means of a separate sense. It is and it [Orb 440-13
   The means of prophecy, [Inhab 503-11
   But man means more, means the million and the duck. [Duck 63-11P
   Or Chicago a Kaffir kraal. It means this mob. [Duck 63-14 P
MEANT. In which everything is meant for you [Rabbit K 209-11
   Tall and unfretted, a figure meant to bear [Pastor 379-11
   Twelve meant as much as: the end of normal time, [What We 459-13
   And what meant more, to be transformed. [Two Illus 514-12
   Men of memories explaining what they meant. [Lytton 38-13 P
   Was meant to stand, not in a tumbling green, [Greenest 57-3 P
   Distort the shape of what I meant, [Stan MBG 72-18 P
   As the final simplification is meant to be. [Bship 78-30 P
MEANTIME. Meantime, centurions guffaw and beat [Monocle 15-22
   In the meantime, the candle shines, [Three 138-22 P
MEASURE. And so I mocked her in magnificent measure. [Monocle 13-5
   The measure of the intensity of love [Monocle 14-26
   Is measure, also, of the verve of earth. [Monocle 14-27
   Of buttons, measure of his salt. Such trash [C 39-19
   I measure myself [Six Sig 74-4
   . . . Evening, when the measure skips a beat [Eve Angels 137-26
   Could measure by moonlight in June. [Jersey 210-12
   Without teetering a millimeter's measure. [Vari 236-1
   At it spinning its eccentric measure. Perhaps, [NSF 406-4
   Its strength and measure, that which is near, point A [Rock 528-11
   What lesser man shall measure sun and moon, [Duck 63-7 P
   And ours, of rigid measure, a miser's paint; [Sombre 67-8 P
   They measure the right to use. Need makes [Ulysses 104-24 P
MEASURED. She measured to the hour its solitude. [Key W 129-25
   The world must be measured by eye"; [On Road 204-4
   Between two neatly measured stations, [Hero 275-17
   Of less neatly measured common-places. [Hero 275-18
MEASURELESS. In measureless measures, not a bird for me [Autumn 160-5
MEASURES. These are the measures destined for her soul. [Sunday 67-26
   In measureless measures, not a bird for me [Autumn 160-5
   He measures the velocities of change. [AA 414-10
MEAT. The meat is sweet. [Fading 139-19
   The almond and deep fruit. This bitter meat [Cuisine 228-13
   His crust away eats of this meat, drinks [Hero 278-16
MEATS. With six meats and twelve wines or else without [NSF 407-16
MECHANIC. He is born the blank mechanic of the mountains, [Aug 492-17

MECHANICAL. Mechanical beetles never quite warm? [MBG 168-15
  The Mechanical Optimist [Thought 184-title 1
  A pensive nature, a mechanical [Look 517-18
  Are they really mechanical bears, [Drum-Majors 37-4 P
  Were mechanical, muscular. They never changed, [Woman Had 81-20P
MECHANICS. When the grand mechanics of earth and sky were near,
  [Contra II 270-2
MECHANISM. Each year to disguise the clanking mechanism [Nigger
  157-2
  This mechanism, this apparition, [Couch 295-2
MECHANISMS. Mechanisms of angelic thought, [Inhab 503-10
MEDICINE. Of medicine, a fragrantness not to be spoiled . . .
  [Rome 508-20
MEDICINES. Ryan's lunch, hatters, insurance and medicines,
  [Thought 185-6
MEDIEVAL. Chants a death that is a medieval death . . . [Greenest
  59-19 P
MEDITATE. To meditate the highest man, not [Hero 280-1
  Nor meditate the world as it goes round. [Phenom 286-6
  By fortune, his gray ghost may meditate [Cats 368-7
MEDITATES. Of an inhuman author, who meditates [Cred 377-22
  In these unhappy he meditates a whole, [AA 420-22
  Around him and in that distance meditates [Recit 86-19 P
  And meditates an image of itself, [Theatre 91-9 P
MEDITATING. That wakefulness or meditating sleep, [C 33-23
  Meditating the will of men in formless crowds. [NE Verses 105-10
MEDITATION. "Meditation Celestrial & Terrestrial" [123-title
  From below and walks without meditation, [Brave 138-20
  With meditation, speak words that in the ear, [Of Mod 240-7
  This is his night and meditation. [Hero 280-18
  What meditation never quite achieved. [EM 314-23
  His meditation. It evaded his mind. [EM 314-24
  Of the longest meditation, the maximum, [EM 324-17
  And feel that her color is a meditation, [Debris 338-12
  Of a vast people old in meditation . . . [New Set 353-4
  There's a meditation there, in which there seems [NSF 396-21
  The meditation of a principle, [Orb 442-11
  As part of the never-ending meditation, [NH 465-7
  Of the perpetual meditation, point [NH 466-14
  A daily majesty of meditation. [Look 518-21
  "The World as Meditation" [520-title
  In an inhuman meditation, larger than her own. [World 521-5
  Broods in tense meditation, constantly, [Sombre 68-20 P
  To principium, to meditation. [Sol Oaks 111-7 P
MEDITATIONS. Are the meditations of a central mind. [Choc 298-17
  Even that. His meditations in the ferns, [AA 411-20
  Fulfilling his meditations, great and small. [AA 420-21
MEDITATIVE. Through winter's meditative light? [Bagatelles 213-12
  A race of dwarfs, the meditative arms [Sombre 70-27 P
MEDITERRANEAN. Above the Mediterranean, emerald [Landsc 243-3
  That in his Mediterranean cloister a man, [EM 324-11
  According to his thought, in the Mediterranean [Aug 491-6
MEDIUM. A gorgeous fortitude. Medium man [Imago 439-9
  Of medium nature, this farouche extreme [Bouquet 448-5
  To the things of medium nature, as meta-men [Bouquet 449-11
  The recognizable, medium, central whole-- [Bouquet 450-12
  The medium man among other medium men. [Sombre 71-31 P
MEDLEY. Which choir makes the most faultless medley in its
  celebration? [Inelegance 25-19 P
MEDLEYED. The song and water were not medleyed sound [Key W 128-19
MEDUSA. "Horrid figures of Medusa, [Inhab 504-1
MEEK. So gardens die, their meek breath scenting [Peter 92-4
  A funny foreigner of meek address. [Lot 371-21
MEEKLY. Meekly you keep the mortal rendezvous, [On Manner 55-11
MEET. In sleep may never meet another thought [Canna 55-5
  Are the music of meet resignation; these [On Manner 56-4
  Meet for the eye of the young alligator, [Nomad 95-16
  And these two never meet in the air so full of summer [Norfolk
  111-20
  To meet that hawk's eye and to flinch [MBG 178-6
  It has to face the men of the time and to meet [Of Mod 240-2
  One might meet Konstantinov, who would interrupt [EM 325-10
  In which I meet you, in which we sit at rest, [NSF 380-9
  As a man and woman meet and love forthwith. [NSF 386-16
  Two parallels that meet if only in [NSF 407-12
  The meeting of their shadows or that meet [NSF 407-13
  Meet in the name [Primordia 7-19 P
  From everything would end. It would all meet. [Letters 108-10 P
MEETING. A minor meeting, facile, delicate. [C 35-5
  Meeting, gripped my mind, [Weak Mind 212-9
  Glides to his meeting like a lover [Hero 276-17
  The meeting of their shadows or that meet [NSF 407-13
  A meeting, an emerging in the light, [Owl 433-5
  The meeting at noon at the edge of the field seems like [Rock
  525-12
  In which the bliss of clouds is mark of an intended meeting
  [Inelegance 25-15 P
MEETS. Meets nakedly another's naked voice. [Aug 489-15
MEGALFRERE. Not father, but bare brother, megalfrere, [Choc 300-21
MELANCHOLE. Pinks and pinks the ice-hard melanchole. [An Gaiety

32-17 P
MELANCHOLY. By way of decorous melancholy; he [C 31-4
  Sodden with his melancholy words, [MBG 170-3
  Women of a melancholy one could sing. [Horn 230-4
  Or melancholy crows as shadowing clouds? [Stan MMO 19-18 P
  "Metropolitan Melancholy" [32-title P
  Behind its melancholy mask, [Secret Man 36-14 P
  In melancholy distances. You held [Burnshaw 50-26 P
MELIC. Make melic groans and tooter at her strokes, [Spaniard
  34-25 P
MELODIC. Paddling the melodic swirls, [Thought 184-12
MELODIOUS. Melodious, where spirits gat them home, [Sunday 68-20
  Melodious skeletons, for all of last night's music [Fish-Scale
  160-15
  Takes time and tinkering, melodious [Duck 65-28 P
MELODY. For so much melody. [Peter 90-20
  The luminous melody of proper sound. [NSF 404-12
  Releasing an abysmal melody, [Owl 433-4
MELON. The melon should have apposite ritual, [C 39-1
  How that whole country was a melon, pink [NSF 393-17
  Do find a melon for me [Three 128-14 P
MELON-FLOWER. The melon-flower nor dew nor web of either [Tallap
  72-4
MELONS. The melons, the vermilion pears [Reader 147-8
  Or you from melons. [Three 129-5 P
  Not as I, from melons. [Three 129-6 P
MELPOMENE. Sordid Melpomene, why strut bare boards, [Bad Time
  427-4
MELT. That the glass would melt in heat, [Glass 197-7
  Or melt Arcturus to ingots dropping drops, [Page 423-3
MELTED. The dead brine melted in him like a dew [C 29-14
  On everything. Now it had melted, leaving [Extracts 255-3
MELTING. The slightly brighter sky, the melting clouds, [Motive
  288-7
MELTS. The mirror melts and moulds itself and moves [Novel 458-4
MEMBER. A member of the family, a tie, [Pieces 352-8
MEMORABILIA. Memorabilia of the mystic spouts, [Monocle 16-24
MEMORABLE. No memorable muffing, bare and blunt. [Burnshaw 48-8 P
MEMORANDUM. A few words, a memorandum voluble [Repet 308-19
  A memorandum of the people sprung [Repet 309-4
  "Memorandum" [89-title P
MEMORIAL. Except in faint, memorial gesturings, [C 29-1
  Death is absolute and without memorial, [Soldier 97-7
  And the memorial mosses hang their green [Degen 445-2
  Of the pity that is the memorial of this room, [Rome 509-12
MEMORIALS. And their memorials are the phrases [Jasmine 79-2
  In memorials of Northern sound, [Oak 272-14
  And our memorials of that difference, [Descrip 344-5
MEMORIES. I said, "She thumbs the memories of dress." [Stan MMO
  19-6 P
  Men of memories explaining what they meant. [Lytton 38-13 P
  "A Clear Day and No Memories" [113-title P
MEMORIZING. Is a memorizing, a trying out, to keep. [Aug 489-19
MEMORY. On the clear viol of her memory, [Peter 92-12
  For a self returning mostly memory. [Anglais 148-18
  She was a shadow as thin in memory [Nigger 154-1
  Is my thought a memory, not alive? [MBG 173-10
  Equal to memory, one line in which [Extracts 259-17
  The finikin spectres in the memory, [Repet 307-12
  And the damasked memory of the golden forms, [EM 317-26
  Of the damasked memory of the golden forms, [EM 317-28
  Of the future, in which the memory had gone [Pure 330-20
  Of the spirit. This, in sight and memory, [Cred 376-22
  Of death in memory's dream? Is spring a sleep? [NSF 391-3
  Broke dialect in a break of memory. [Page 422-10
  My memory, is the mother of us all, [Owl 432-15
  Nor new, nor in the sense of memory. [Bouquet 451-7
  Like a trumpet and says, in this season of memory, [Puel 456-11
  And memory and claws: a paragon [Spaniard 35-14 P
  Memory without passion would be better lost. [Lytton 38-18 P
  But memory and passion, and with these [Lytton 38-19 P
  A ring of horses rising from memory, [Greenest 57-10 P
  The memory moves on leopards' feet, desire [Greenest 57-16 P
  That are dissembled in vague memory [Sombre 67-16 P
  The portent may itself be memory; [Sombre 70-10 P
  And memory may itself be time to come [Sombre 70-11 P
  And memory's lord is the lord of prophecy [Sombre 70-14 P
  Is its true form? Is it the memory [Recit 86-22 P
  Dutch ice on English boats? The memory [Recit 86-25 P
  Tradition is much more than the memory. [Recit 87-3 P
MEN. If men at forty will be painting lakes [Monocle 15-7
  As the deadly thought of men accomplishing [Monocle 16-14
  Twenty men crossing a bridge, [Magnifico 19-1
  Are twenty men crossing twenty bridges, [Magnifico 19-3
  Twenty men crossing a bridge, [Magnifico 19-9
  Twenty men crossing a bridge [Magnifico 19-12
  The boots of the men clump [Magnifico 19-16
  The natives of the rain are rainy men. [C 37-27
  What is one man among so many men? [C 41-25
  What are so many men in such a world? [C 41-26

And men like Crispin like them in intent, [C 42-23
"Anecdote of Men by the Thousand" [51-title
There are men of the East, he said, [Men 1000 51-9
There are men of a province [Men 1000 51-11
There are men of a valley [Men 1000 51-13
There are men whose words [Men 1000 51-15
What word have you, interpreters, of men [Heaven 56-9
Supple and turbulent, a ring of men [Sunday 69-28
Of men that perish and of summer morn. [Sunday 70-11
"Frogs Eat Butterflies. Snakes Eat Frogs. Hogs Eat Snakes. Men
  Eat Hogs" [78-title
For so retentive of themselves are men [Fictive 88-1
O thin men of Haddam, [Thirteen 93-19
Meditating the will of men in formless crowds. [NE Verses 105-10
Both of men and clouds, a slime of men in crowds. [Farewell
  118-12
The men are moving as the water moves, [Farewell 118-13
That is their mind, these men, and that will bind [Farewell
  118-18
For whom the shapes were never the figures of men. [Sad Gay
  121-18
There are these sudden mobs of men, [Sad Gay 122-3
Will unite these figures of men and their shapes [Sad Gay 122-16
Was the sun concoct for angels or for men? [Eve Angels 137-9
Sad men made angels of the sun, and of [Eve Angels 137-10
Let this be clear that we are men of sun [Eve Angels 137-13
And men of day and never of pointed night, [Eve Angels 137-14
Men that repeat antiquest sounds of air [Eve Angels 137-15
Happy men, distinguishing frost and clouds. [Nigger 151-8
Men and the affairs of men seldom concerned [Nigger 156-4
Not wisdom. Can all men, together, avenge [Nigger 158-11
And the earth is alive with creeping men, [MBG 168-14
The touch that topples men and rock." [MBG 170-20
And men in waves become the sea. [MBG 171-2
The sea returns upon the men, [MBG 171-4
Fills the high hall with shuffling men [MBG 171-13
Not the mother that held men as they fell [MBG 173-14
Of the men that live in the land, high lord. [MBG 176-11
Son only of man and sun of men, [Thought 185-25
Of men whose heaven is in themselves, [Thought 186-12
"The Men That Are Falling" [187-title
The head of one of the men that are falling, placed [Men Fall
  188-9
The pines along the river and the dry men blown [Loaf 199-21
The great men will not be blended . . . [Idiom 201-6
On a cocoanut--how many men have copied dew [Dump 202-7
"The mass is nothing. The number of men in a mass [Dames 206-3
Of men is nothing. The mass is no greater than [Dames 206-4
And laughing, a crowd of men, [Dezem 218-11
To be served by men of ice. [Poem Morn 219-7
Sure enough, moving, the thunder became men, [Thunder 220-1
Ten thousand, men hewn and tumbling, [Thunder 220-2
The men have no shadows [Common 221-24
Moving among the sleepers, the men, [Candle 223-5
But the eyes are men in the palm of the hand. [Arcades 225-19
Men on green beds and women half of sun. [Cuisine 227-19
Are they men eating reflections of themselves? [Cuisine 228-16
The bird kept saying that birds had once been men, [Horn 230-1
Or were to be, animals with men's eyes, [Horn 230-2
Men fat as feathers, misers counting breaths, [Horn 230-3
Being, for old men, time of their time. [Vari 233-11
With his men, beyond the barbican. [Vari 234-12
Among men, in a woman--she caught his breath-- [Yellow 237-6
A man with the fury of a race of men, [Bottle 239-2
A man at the centre of men. [Bottle 239-4
It has to face the men of the time and to meet [Of Mod 240-2
A generation sealed, men remoter than mountains, [Waldorf 241-7
Find peace? We found the sum of men. We found, [Oboe 251-11
To naked men, to women naked as rain. [Extracts 252-14
That's the old world. In the new, all men are priests. [Extracts
  254-2
The single thought? The multitudes of men [Extracts 254-15
Ideas are men. The mass of meaning and [Extracts 255-25
The mass of men are one. Chaos is not [Extracts 255-26
Ideas or, say, five men or, possibly, six. [Extracts 255-28
A chord between the mass of men and himself, [Extracts 256-6
To believe in the weather and in the things and men [Extracts
  258-8
Behold the men in helmets borne on steel, [Extracts 259-19
Nor feel the x malisons of other men, [Montra 261-24
Of the good, speaking of good in the voice of men. [Montra
  262-19
All men can speak of it in the voice of gods. [Montra 262-20
Of the secondary men. There are no rocks [Jumbo 269-17
Of men suited to public ferns . . . The hero [Hero 276-16
Young men as vegetables, hip-hip, [Hero 278-12
Angry men and furious machines [Dutch 290-1
Men scatter throughout clouds. [Dutch 290-4
There are men shuffling on foot in air. [Dutch 290-9
Men are moving and marching [Dutch 290-10

In the will of what is common to all men, [Dutch 291-18
Men came as the sun comes, early children [Dutch 291-23
That a new glory of new men assembles. [Dutch 292-23
To perceive men without reference to their form. [Choc 296-11
He rose because men wanted him to be. [Choc 299-13
Of what men are. The collective being knew [Choc 299-22
Of the armies, the solid men, make big the fable. [Choc 301-15
We are ignorant men incapable [Crude 305-18
Millions of major men against their like [Repet 307-1
What are the major men? All men are brave. [Paisant 334-13
All men endure. The great captain is the choice [Paisant 334-14
Men live to be [Paisant 334-17
Admired by men and all men, therefore, live [Paisant 334-18
To be admired by all men. Nations live [Paisant 334-19
The major men-- [Paisant 335-3
The fictive man created out of men. [Paisant 335-6
They are men but artificial men. They are [Paisant 335-7
As, men make themselves their speech: the hard hidalgo [Descrip
  345-11
Ovation on ovation of large blue men [Liadoff 346-8
"Men Made out of Words" [355-title
Young men go walking in the woods, [Pediment 361-7
The body, it touches. The captain and his men [NSF 392-21
The shoulders of joyous men, to feel the heart [NSF 398-11
He establishes statues of reasonable men, [NSF 403-20
Like men besides, like men in light secluded, [NSF 405-12
And we enjoy like men, the way a leaf [NSF 406-1
Men would be starting at dawn to walk ashore. [Page 422-5
And of as many meanings as of men. [Roses 431-9
She held men closely with discovery, [Owl 435-9
For the clairvoyant men that need no proof, [Orb 441-5
And they: these men, and earth and sky, inform [Orb 441-15
And yet still men though meta-men, still things [Bouquet 449-1
And of other holy and learned men, among them [Luther 461-6
The way the drowsy, infant, old men do. [Questions 463-3
By the obese opiates of sleep. Plain men in plain towns [NH
  467-20
No man. The self, the chrysalis of all men [NH 468-21
Alpha fears men or else Omega's men [NH 469-11
Men turning into things, as comedy, [NH 470-5
That power to conceal they had as men, [NH 470-8
We are not men of bronze and we are not dead. [NH 472-11
A verity of the most veracious men, [NH 473-13
It may be that they mingle, clouds and men, in the air [NH 479-24
To have evaded clouds and men leaves him [NH 480-5
Nor the wills of other men; and he cannot evade [NH 480-11
In the heavy drum of speech, the inner men [NH 488-9
The stern voices of its necessitous men, [Aug 491-17
Of sense, evoking one thing in many men, [Aug 494-18
A text of intelligent men [Aug 495-13
Will come stamping here, the ruler of less than men, [Aug
  495-22
In a repetitiousness of men and flies. [Plain 502-20
Lacking men of stone, [Inhab 504-7
Of men growing small in the distances of space, [Rome 508-3
Men are part both in the inch and in the mile. [Rome 508-10
On which men speculated in summer when they were half asleep.
  [Prol 516-15
Beautified the simplest men. [Phases 4-16 P
Of men and earth: I quote the line and page, [Soldat 11-8 P
Of blind men tapping their way [Soldat 12-11 P
(The blind men strike him down with their sticks.) [Soldat 13-5 P
Men of the line, take this new phrase [Soldat 16-8 P
But twiddling mon idée, as old men will, [Stan MMO 19-4 P
And so with men. [Abnormal 24-13 P
They ought to be muscular men, [Drum-Majors 37-7 P
Fitted by men and horses [Polo 37-17 P
Men of memories explaining what they meant. [Lytton 38-13 P
Men gathering for a mighty flight of men, [Burnshaw 51-8 P
In the soil and rest. Conceive that marble men [Burnshaw 52-1 P
Bears words that are the speech of marble men. [Burnshaw 52-5 P
The confusion of men's voices, intricate [Greenest 54-9 P
Men's bones, beyond their breaths, the black sublime, [Greenest
  55-11 P
To men, to houses, streets and the squalid whole. [Greenest 57-8P
For races, not for men, powerful beyond [Greenest 59-29 P
By inch, Sunday by Sunday, many men. [Duck 60-20 P
For whom men were to be ends in themselves, [Duck 61-2 P
Are all men thinking together as one, thinking [Duck 62-19 P
And the bees, the scorpions, the men that think, [Duck 66-3 P
The medium man among other medium men, [Sombre 71-31 P
Let wise men piece the world together with wisdom [Grotesque
  75-7 P
The rape of the bourgeoisie accomplished, the men [Bship 77-13 P
Seize yards and docks, machinery and men, [Bship 77-22 P
I said that men should wear stone masks and, to make [Bship 78-11P
Berceuse, transatlantic. The children are men, old men, [Woman
  Had 82-10 P
Are old men breathed on by a maternal voice, [Woman Had 82-14 P
Children and old men and philosophers, [Woman Had 82-15 P

The old men, the philosophers, are haunted by that [Woman Had
  82-23 P
And men look inwardly, for the emblem: [Stan Hero 83-13 P
Half men and half new, modern monsters . . . [Stan Hero 84-8 P
As a man among other men, divested [Stan Hero 84-10 P
Bands of black men seem to be drifting in the air, [Sick 90-7 P
In the South, bands of thousands of black men, [Sick 90-8 P
Here in the North, late, late, there are voices of men, [Sick
  90-10 P
In a field, the man on the side of a hill, all men [Americana
  93-16 P
(Remote from the deadly general of men, [Americana 94-1 P
Other men, and not this grass, this valid air. [Americana 94-11 P
Held in the hands of blue men that are lead within, [Discov
  95-16 P
Of gods and men destroyed, the right [Ulysses 102-10 P
Among the old men that you know, [Child 106-13 P
The rosy men and the women of the rose, [Art Pop 112-19 P
Or wise men, or nobles, [Three 129-14 P
Drink from wise men? From jade? [Three 129-16 P
That we are painted as three dead men, [Three 133-2 P
And fill the earth with young men centuries old [Ideal 88-11 A
And old men, who have chosen, and are cold [Ideal 88-12 A
See: bar-men; forest-men; jaguar-men; lion-men; mad-men; meta-
  men; pay-men.
MENACE. And so France feels. A menace that impends, [Soldat 13-6 P
MENDED. The weak man mended, [Idiom 201-2
  I know that I cannot be mended, [Idiom 201-8
  We dried our nets and mended sail [Silent 359-9
  The interminable adventurer? The trees are mended. [World 520-12
  The trees had been mended, as an essential exercise [World 521-4
MENTAL. Exit the mental moonlight, exit lex, [C 36-28
MENTIONED. Something not to be mentioned to Mrs. Dooley, [Aug 491-23
MERCIES. And feels the imagination's mercies, [Imago 439-13
MERCIFUL. The immaculate, the merciful good, [MBG 168-18
  Remote and call it merciful? [MBG 168-21
  Makes of the form Most Merciful Capitan, [Pastor 379-6
  The threshold, Rome, and that more merciful Rome [Rome 508-6
  Some merciful divination, you forgive. [Spaniard 34-6 P
MERCILESS. An end must come in a merciless triumph, [Dutch 291-15
  In his body, fiercer in his mind, merciless [EM 321-21
MERCY. The final mercy and the final loss, [Nigger 152-6
  There must be mercy in Asia and divine [Montra 262-16
  In its cavern, wings subtler than any mercy, [Hero 273-13
  The brilliant mercy of a sure repose, [Cred 375-18
  Against itself. At its mercy, we depend [John 436-12
  Unwilling that mercy should be a mystery [Rome 510-17
MERE. Mere blusteriness that gewgaws jollified, [C 44-22
  A mirror of a mere delight? [Botanist 2 136-12
  Is the function of the poet here mere sound, [Havana 144-12
  By mere example opulently clear. [Havana 145-6
  Say the weather, the mere weather, the mere air: [NSF 385-23
  Mere repetitions. These things at least comprise [NSF 405-17
  When the image itself is false, a mere desire, [Study I 463-18
  Were mere brown clods, mere catching weeds of talk. [NH 486-21
  Whose mere savage presence awakens the world in which she dwells.
    [World 520-16
  Shines on the mere objectiveness of things. [Moonlight 531-4
  In spite of the mere objectiveness of things, [Moonlight 531-21
  The ever flowing of the water is a gayety, [R Conn 533-8
  "Of Mere Being" [117-title P
MÈRE. The père Benjamin, the mère Blandenah, [Grotesque 77-11 P
MERELY. Before one merely reads to pass the time. [Monocle 14-22
  Should merely call him dead? Pronounce amen [C 41-17
  May, merely may, madame, whip from themselves [High-Toned 59-19
  These are merely instances. [Theory 87-4
  Was merely a place by which she walked to sing. [Key W 129-6
  And merely of their glittering, [Botanist 2 136-11
  "The Pleasures of Merely Circulating" [149-title.
  And I am merely a shadow hunched [MBG 169-16
  The discord merely magnifies. [MBG 171-8
  Shows that this object is merely a state, [Class 197-9
  But in nature it merely grows. [Add 198-7
  What in nature merely grows. [Add 198-17
  Be merely oneself, as superior as the ear [Dump 203-1
  That the buxom eye brings merely its element [Poem Morn 219-14
  To change nature, not merely to change ideas, [Vari 234-1
  A gaiety that is being, not merely knowing, [Gala 248-13
  Whose merely being was his valiance, [Extracts 254-11
  Merely by putting hand to brow, [Oak 272-11
  Is merely the moving of a tongue. [Possum 294-3
  That merely by thinking one can, [Crude 305-3
  Or merely seemed to touch him as he spoke [EM 315-2
  Merely in living as and where we live. [EM 326-12
  Its identity is merely a thing that seems, [Descrip 340-10
  And round and round, the merely going round, [NSF 405-22
  Until merely going round is a final good, [NSF 405-23
  Or, the persons act one merely by being here. [AA 416-3
  And in that enormous sense, merely enjoy. [Ulti 430-9
  Not merely into a whole, but a poem of [Orb 442-6

Not merely as to depth but as to height [NH 470-9
As well, not merely as to the commplace [NH 470-10
And through included, not merely the visible, [NH 471-24
Not merely desired, for sale, and market things [Armor 530-4
That merely makes a ring). [Abnormal 24-1 P
Be merely a masquerade or else a rare [Greenest 56-13 P
In the gesture's whim, a passion merely to be [Sombre 71-28 P
Merely the center of a circle, spread [Bship 81-10 P
More babies than that. The merely revolving wheel [Woman Had
  81-23 P
Merely parts of the general fiction of the mind: [Recit 87-29 P
The leaves cry . . . One holds off and merely hears the cry.
  [Course 96-13 P
MEREST. Crispin, merest minuscule in the gales, [C 29-11
  Or possibly, the merest patron saint [Nigger 157-5
  Our merest apprehension of their will. [Montra 262-15
  Unwished for, chance, the merest riding [Hero 275-12
MERGE. The ephemeral blues must merge for them in one, [Monocle
  15-8
MERIDIAN. No spring can follow past meridian. [Monocle 13-20
  To the tense, the maudlin, true meridian [Burnshaw 52-15 P
MERIDIANS. Clipped frigidly blue-black meridians, [C 34-16
MESCAL. Sepulchral señors, bibbling pale mescal, [C 38-21
MESDAMES. Mesdames, one might believe that Shelley lies [Burnshaw
  48-9 P
  Mesdames, it is not enough to be reconciled [Burnshaw 50-6 P
  Through a moving chaos that never ends. Mesdames, [Burnshaw
    50-23 P
MESSAGE. Mumbling a secret, passionate message. [Hero 276-18
  The message is half-borne. Could marble still [Greenest 57-21 P
MESSENGERS. Appoints its florid messengers with wings [Greenest
  57-17 P
MESSIEURS. Messieurs, [Extracts 252-7
MET. I met Berserk, [Peacocks 57-10
  It was Ulysses and it was not. Yet they had met, [World 521-13
  Last evening I met him on the road. [Three 141-11 P
METAL. Jangling the metal of the strings . . . [MBG 166-12
  Dressed in metal, silk and stone, [Thought 186-19
  I love the metal grapes, [Anything B 211-17
  And the metal heroes that time granulates-- [Oboe 250-11
  Than the most metal music, loudlier, [Dutch 291-11
  The true tone of the metal of winter in what it says: [Discov
    96-6 P
META-MEN. The place of meta-men and para-things, [Bouquet 448-16
  And yet still men though meta-men, still things [Bouquet 449-1
  Though para-things; the meta-men for whom [Bouquet 449-2
  To the things of medium nature, as meta-men [Bouquet 449-11
  The meta-men behold the idea as part [Bouquet 449-22
  Regarded by the meta-men, is quirked [Bouquet 451-3
METAMORPHORID. Evasive and metamorphorid. [Oak 272-6
METAMORPHOSIS. "Metamorphosis" [265-title
  A metamorphosis of paradise, [Pure 331-24
METAPHOR. An evading metaphor. [Add 199-12
  By metaphor you paint [Poem Morn 219-4
  By metaphor. The juice was fragranter [Poem Morn 219-9
  "The Motive for Metaphor" [288-title
  The motive for metaphor, shrinking from [Motive 288-14
  Cloud-casual, metaphysical metaphor, [Choc 301-4
  Of the least, minor, vital metaphor, content, [Crude 305-19
  Whose mind malformed this morning metaphor, [Pure 331-21
  As he slept. He woke in a metaphor: this was [Pure 331-23
  Yet to speak of the whole world as metaphor [Pure 332-8
  And the desire to believe in a metaphor. [Pure 332-10
  Without evasion by a single metaphor. [Cred 373-7
  The eye of a vagabond in metaphor [NSF 397-22
  Too much as they are to be changed by metaphor, [Roses 430-13
  Not as in metaphor, but in our sense [Roses 431-5
  Of them. So sense exceeds all metaphor. [Roses 431-6
  "Metaphor as Degeneration" [444-title
  How, then, is metaphor degeneration, [Degen 444-19
  The bouquet stands in a jar, as metaphor, [Bouquet 448-8
  As lightning itself is, likewise, metaphor [Bouquet 448-9
  The metaphor stirred his fear. The object with which he was com-
    pared [Prol 516-10
  The profusion of metaphor has been increased. [Someone 83-3 A
  The metaphor that murders metaphor. [Someone 84-6 A
  Its invitation to false metaphor. [Someone 85-17 A
METAPHORS. "Metaphors of a Magnifico" [19-title
  Of wormy metaphors. [Delight 162-9
  A poet's metaphors in which being would [Descrip 341-8
  "Thinking of a Relation between the Images of Metaphors" [356-
    title
  The hermit in a poet's metaphors, [NSF 381-21
METAPHYSICA. The metaphysica, the plastic parts of poems [Glass
  197-19
METAPHYSICAL. In the metaphysical, there are these poles. [Glass
  197-11
  Cloud-casual, metaphysical metaphor, [Choc 301-4
  With the metaphysical changes that occur, [EM 326-11
  The physical pine, the metaphysical pine. [Cred 373-2

The curtains to a metaphysical t [NSF 390-21
In the metaphysical streets of the physical town [NH 472-22
In the metaphysical streets, the profoundest forms [NH 473-7
That sack the sun, though metaphysical. [Red Kit 31-4 P
Sight least, but metaphysical blindness gained, [Souls 94-21 P
METAPHYSICALS. The green corn gleams and the metaphysicals [EM
  325-27
METAPHYSICIAN. "The Curtains in the House of the Metaphysician"
  [62-title
  A metaphysician in the dark, twanging [Of Mod 240-14
METICULOUS. From that meticulous potter's thumb. [Negation 98-5
METIER. Being changed from space to the sailor's metier, [Two V
  354-15
  As if nothingness contained a métier, [Rock 526-1
METROPOLES. Blows on the shutters of the metropoles, [Pharynx 96-6
  Does not sustain us in the metropoles. [Havana 142-8
METROPOLITAN. "Metropolitan Melancholy" [32-title P
  They rise to the muddy, metropolitan elms, [Duck 60-13 P
  The metropolitan of mind, they feel [Duck 64-11 P
MEURSAULT. We drank Meursault, ate lobster Bombay with mango
  [NSF 401-22
MEWING. The moonlight in her lap, mewing her velvet, [Uruguay
  249-2
MEXICAN. The Mexican women, [Venereal 47-13
MEXICO. A rumbling, west of Mexico, it seemed, [C 32-17
MEZZANINE. On the mezzanine [Anything B 211-6
MEYER. Meyer is a bum. He eats his pie. [Grotesque 75-18 P
  But Meyer is a bum. [Grotesque 76-3 P
  Meyer has my five senses. I have his. [Grotesque 76-10 P
MI. The blower squeezed to the thinnest mi of falsetto. [Parochial
  191-6
MI-BIRD. Her hair fell on him and the mi-bird flew [Hand 271-18
MICA. Of mica, the dithering of grass, [Vari 234-18
MICE. "Dance of the Macabre Mice" [123-title
  Monsieur is on horseback. The horse is covered with mice. [Mice
  123-4
  A state that was free, in the dead of winter, from mice? [Mice
  123-10
  You are one of the not-numberable mice [Blue Bldg 217-23
  Even by mice--these scamper and are still; [Soldat 14-1 P
MICKEY. The mickey mockers [Am Sub 130-19
MIC-MAC. Dangling and spangling, the mic-mac of mocking birds.
  [NH 486-15
MICROSCOPE. Freud's eye was the microscope of potency. [Cats 368-6
MID-AIR. Alone, the half-arc hanging in mid-air [Repet 309-12
MID-ATLANTIC. In mid-Atlantic, bellowing, to command, [Bship 78-13P
MID-AUTUMN. One chemical afternoon in mid-autumn, [Contra II 270-1
MID-DAY. It is not midnight. It is mid-day, [Lack 303-5
  As if the air, the mid-day air, was swarming [EM 326-10
  At noon it was on the mid-day of the year [NSF 401-5
MID-DAYS. Sometimes at sleepy mid-days it succeeds, [Extracts
  257-20
MIDDENS. From the middens of life, rotten and acrid, [Stan Hero
  84-3 P
MIDDLE. From the middle of his field. The odor [Yellow 237-2
  To the great blue of the middle height. [Dutch 290-3
  He was as tall as a tree in the middle of [Choc 297-19
  Until its wings bear off night's middle witch; [Pure 333-1
  Yet in time's middle deep, [Analysis 348-12
  We encounter in the dead middle of the night [NSF 395-2
  If we were ever, just once, at the middle, fixed [Ulti 430-5
  Complete, because at the middle, if only in sense, [Ulti 430-8
  Hewn in their middle as the beam of leaves, [Owl 434-2
  Of the quiet of the middle of the night, [Aug 491-7
  (A boor of night in middle earth cries out.) [Infernale 24-19 P
  And its immaculate fire, the middle dome, [Greenest 54-16 P
  Under the middle stars, he said: [Ulysses 99-15 P
  Beneath the middle stars [Presence 105-18 P
MIDDLING. Mystic Garden & Middling Beast [Thought 185-title 2
  The middling beast, the garden of paradise [Thought 185-21
MID-EARTH. Supported by a half-arc in mid-earth. [Repet 309-14
  A shadow in mid-earth . . . If we propose [Pure 330-7
  From a Schuylkill in mid-earth there came emerging [New Set
  352-10
MID-HUMAN. Things made by mid-terrestrial, mid-human [New Set
  352-14
MIDMOST. In the midmost midnight and find the serpent there, [AA
  411-15
  Midmost in its design, the arms grown swift, [Sombre 69-9 P
MIDNIGHT. The hen-cock crows at midnight and lays no egg, [Nigger
  155-10
  He that at midnight touches the guitar, [Thought 186-5
  Staring, at midnight, at the pillow that is black [Men Fall
  187-17
  Impatient of the bells and midnight forms, [Uruguay 250-1
  I affirm and then at midnight the great cat [Montra 264-5
  It is not midnight. It is mid-day, [Lack 303-5
  Lighted at midnight by the studious eye, [NSF 388-2
  When at long midnight the Canon came to sleep [NSF 402-19
  In the midmost midnight and find the serpent there, [AA 411-15

But bravest at midnight and in lonely spaces, [Page 421-22
And the night, and midnight, and after, where it is. [Bad Time
  426-17
Descending, out of the cap of midnight, [Countryman 428-10
Has only the formulations of midnight. [Papini 446-6
It is to the hero of midnight that we pray [NH 466-23
The pillar of midnight, [Aug 495-8
Of the loftiest amour, in a human midnight? [Souls 95-6 P
MIDNIGHT-MINTING. Night and its midnight-minting fragrances,
  [Rock 528-20
MIDNIGHTS. And the lost vehemence the midnights hold. [Tallap 72-12
MID-SEA. Whether it be in mid-sea [Solitaires 60-3
MIDST. In the midst of sleep?" [Peacocks 58-8
  In the midst of dreams." [Peacocks 58-14
  And the unjust, which in the midst of summer stops [AA 417-6
  From the clouds in the midst of trembling trees [Puel 456-7
  In the midst of foreignness, the syllable [NH 471-2
  In the midst of a circle of trees, from which the leaves [Old
  Woman 43-3 P
MIDSUMMER. Or seeing the midsummer artifice [C 33-3
  Midsummer love and softest silences, [Montra 261-16
  Now in midsummer come and all fools slaughtered [Cred 372-4
MID-TERRESTRIAL. Things made by mid-terrestrial, mid-human [New
  Set 352-14
MIDWIFERY. Involved him in midwifery so dense [C 43-22
MIFF-MAFF-MUFF. The miff-maff-muff of water, the vocables [Page
  423-6
MIGHTIER. The mightier mother raises up her cry; [Soldat 14-16 P
MIGHTY. X, the mighty thought, the mighty man. [Canna 55-2
  And mighty Fortitudo, frantic bass. [Lions 124-16
  And the north wind's mighty buskin seems to fall [Antag 426-7
  Over all these the mighty imagination triumphs [Puel 456-10
  And the mighty, musty belly of tears. [Sat Night 28-3 P
  Might muff the mighty spirit of Lenin. [Lytton 39-17 P
  Men gathering for a mighty flight of men, [Burnshaw 51-8 P
MIGNON. But their mignon, marblish glare! [Anything B 211-13
MIGRATING. Be no migrating. It was that they were there [Wild
  329-9
MIGRATION. An abysmal migration into a possible blue? [Burnshaw
  51-9 P
MIGRATIONS. Yet, under the migrations to solitude, [Wild 329-4
MIGRATORY. Its colors make, the migratory daze, [Bouquet 451-17
MILDEW. Pardie! Summer is like a fat beast, sleepy in mildew,
  [Banal 62-15
  Mildew of summer and the deepening snow [Pharynx 96-2
  Out of such mildew plucking neater mould [Pharynx 96-14
MILE. Men are part both in the inch and in the mile. [Rome 508-10
MILE-MALLOWS. Mile-mallows that a mallow sun cajoled. [Sea Surf
  101-21
MILES. And this great esplanade of corn, miles wide, [Belly 367-7
  The miles of distance away [Letters 108-9 P
MILITARY. Tractatus, of military things, with plates, [Greenest
  56-14 P
MILK. Of the milk within the saltiest spurge, heard, then, [Sea
  Surf 100-19
  There was the cat slopping its milk all day, [Rabbit K 209-4
  Fat cat, red tongue, green mind, white milk [Rabbit K 209-5
  Cat's milk is dry in the saucer. Sunday song [Phenom 286-3
  Warmed by a desperate milk. To find the real, [NSF 404-8
  What milk there is in such captivity, [Orb 440-17
  Shot lightning at the kind cow's milk. [Lulu M 27-12 P
MILKIEST. The milkiest bowmen. This makes a new design, [Greenest
  56-6 P
MILKMAN. The milkman came in the moonlight and the moonlight [Les
  Plus 244-17
MILKY. In this milky blue?" [Peacocks 58-4
  To Cuba. Jot these milky matters down. [Havana 144-6
  Still by the sea-side mutters milky lines [Oboe 250-13
  It is the route that milky millions find, [Repet 307-17
  Fire-monsters in the Milky Brain [Pure 331-title 3
MILLE. "Cy Est Pourtraicte, Madame Ste Ursule, et Les Unze Mille
  Vierges" [21-title
  The mille fiori of vestments, [Winter B 141-6
MILLED. His manner slickened them. He milled [News 264-13
MILLEFIORI. Instant of millefiori bluely magnified-- [Pieces 351-13
MILLE-FLORED. It is centi-colored and mille-flored and ripe,
  [Bouquet 450-2
MILLEMAN. An ethereal cousin, another milleman. [Pieces 352-9
MILLIMETER. Without teetering a millimeter's measure. [Vari 236-1
MILLION. A million people on one string? [MBG 166-15
  Who in a million diamonds sums us up. [Oboe 250-22
  Are really much a million pities. [Melancholy 32-14 P
  To a million, a duck with apples and without wine. [Duck 60-12 P
  But man means more, means the million and the duck. [Duck 63-11 P
  For the million, perhaps, two ducks instead of one; [Duck 65-2 P
MILLIONAIRES. Toys of the millionaires, [Drum-Majors 37-5 P
MILLIONS. Millions of major men against their like [Repet 307-1
  It is the route that milky millions find, [Repet 307-17
  Millions of instances of which I am one. [Repet 309-15
  Millions hold millions in their arms. [Memo 89-16 P

MILLPOND. A teeming millpond or a furious mind. [Nigger 155-13
MILORD. A beautiful thing, milord, is beautiful [Red Kit 31-5 P
  Milord, I ask you, though you will to sing, [Red Kit 31-16 P
MIMIC. Its empty sleeves; and yet its mimic motion [Key W 128-14
MIMIC-MOTES. Reflections and off-shoots, mimic-motes [Red Fern
  365-8
MIMICRY. As if pain, no longer satanic mimicry, [EM 316-5
MIMICS. We are the mimics. Clouds are pedagogues [NSF 384-1
  An audience to mimics glistening [Sombre 67-24 P
  Mimics that play on instruments discerned [Sombre 67-26 P
MINCING. Man proved a gobbet in my mincing world. [Monocle 17-24
MIND. One must have a mind of winter [Snow Man 9-21
  An ancient aspect touching a new mind. [Monocle 16-2
  A semblance to the thing I have in mind. [Monocle 17-3
  The mind roamed as a moth roams, [Hibiscus 22-10
  Which yet found means to set his simmering mind [Geneva 24-10
  He felt the Andean breath. His mind was free [C 33-9
  In Crispin's mind above a continent. [C 34-1
  Whatever shape it took in Crispin's mind, [C 37-6
  Out of my mind the golden ointment rained, [Hoon 65-13
  Large-mannered motions to his mythy mind [Sunday 67-29
  The mind herein attains simplicity. [Tallap 71-4
  His loneliness and what was in his mind: [Babies 77-9
  Night nursed not him in whose dark mind [Babies 77-13
  Beauty is momentary in the mind-- [Peter 91-22
  Her mind will never speak to me again. [Farewell 117-6
  Rides clear of her mind and the waves make a refrain [Farewell
    117-8
  Her mind had bound me round. The palms were hot [Farewell 117-11
  To be free again, to return to the violent mind [Farewell 118-17
  That is their mind, these men, and that will bind [Farewell
    118-18
  The water never formed to mind or voice, [Key W 128-12
  The motions of the mind and giving form [Eve Angels 137-20
  The mind is muddy. [Mud 147-16
  As yet, for the mind, new banks [Mud 147-17
  The mind snarls. [Mud 148-3
  The master of the mind. [Mud 148-11
  A teeming millpond or a furious mind. [Nigger 155-13
  And although my mind perceives the force behind the moment,
    [Fish-Scale 161-3
  The mind is smaller than the eye. [Fish-Scale 161-4
  Speak of the soul, the mind. It is [MBG 174-7
  Gesu, not native of a mind [MBG 180-7
  It could not be a mind, the wave [MBG 180-11
  Here, for the lark fixed in the mind, [MBG 182-17
  Burns in the mind on lost remembrances. [Men Fall 187-12
  There would still remain the never-resting mind, [Poems Clim
    194-4
  Crash in the mind--But, fat Jocundus, worrying [Glass 197-20
  Pack the heart and scratch the mind? And does the ear [Dump
    203-3
  Upon the heart and round the mind [Country 207-11
  In the mind, pupa of straw, moppet of rags. [Dwarf 208-6
  It is the mind that is woven, the mind that was jerked [Dwarf
    208-7
  Fat cat, red tongue, green mind, white milk [Rabbit K 209-5
  "A Weak Mind in the Mountains" [212-title
  Meeting, gripped my mind, [Weak Mind 212-9
  The blood of the mind fell [Weak Mind 212-14
  Of the mind that forms itself [Bagatelles 213-22
  The squirming facts exceed the squamous mind, [Connois 215-17
  False as the mind, instead of the fragrance, warm [Horn 230-12
  To receive her shadow into his mind . . . [Scavoir 231-11
  The mind is the great poem of winter, the man, [Bottle 238-17
  Of destroying, as the mind destroys, [Bottle 239-8
  As the mind, to find what will suffice, destroys [Bottle 239-15
  The poem of the mind in the act of finding [Of Mod 239-17
  In the delicatest ear of the mind, repeat, [Of Mod 240-17
  Containing the mind, below which it cannot descend, [Of Mod
    240-17
  Combing. The poem of the act of the mind. [Of Mod 240-22
  The mind between this light or that and space, [Rhythms 245-11
  The wall; and that the mind [Rhythms 246-2
  It can never be satisfied, the mind, never. [Beard 247-25
  And, capable, created in his mind, [Uruguay 250-3
  Is real, part of a land beyond the mind? [Extracts 252-20
  Panjandrum and central heart and mind of minds-- [Extracts 254-12
  Like insects in the depths of the mind, that kill [Extracts
    254-14
  That clings to the mind like that right sound, that song [Ex-
    tracts 256-14
  Sure that the ultimate poem was the mind, [Extracts 256-22
  Or of the mind, or of the mind in these [Extracts 256-23
  Elysia, these days, half earth, half mind; [Extracts 257-1
  That the mind is the end and must be satisfied. [Extracts 257-15
  It cannot be half earth, half mind; half sun, [Extracts 257-16
  Half thinking; until the mind has been satisfied, [Extracts
    257-17
  Until, for him, his mind is satisfied. [Extracts 257-18

  To have satisfied the mind and turn to see, [Extracts 257-22
  A shadow in the mind, a flourisher [Montra 260-10
  These other shadows, not in the mind, players [Montra 260-13
  To the auroral creature musing in the mind. [Montra 263-24
  And the sound of pianos in his mind. [News 264-18
  Was always the other mind. The brightness [Hero 273-11
  The bread and wine of the mind, permitted [Hero 275-27
  What is this crackling of voices in the mind, [Dutch 292-12
  And of the brooding mind, fixed but for a slight [Choc 297-17
  If in the mind, he vanished, taking there [Choc 298-3
  The mind's own limits, like a tragic thing [Choc 298-4
  Are the meditations of a central mind. [Choc 298-17
  Whose green mind bulges with complicated hues: [Choc 300-5
  Of the mind, in which we sit [Crude 305-7
  Only the eye as faculty, that the mind [Crude 305-15
  Is the eye, and that this landscape of the mind [Crude 305-16
  To the make-matter, matter-nothing mind, [Repet 307-9
  His route lies through an image in his mind. [Repet 307-15
  My route lies through an image in my mind, [Repet 307-16
  To see nor, reverberating, eke out the mind [Creat 311-13
  His meditation. It evaded his mind. [EM 314-25
  The mind, which is our being, wrong and wrong, [EM 317-1
  Spent in the false engagements of the mind. [EM 317-3
  The yellow grassman's mind is still immense, [EM 318-24
  In his body, fiercer in his mind, merciless [EM 321-21
  A promenade amid the grandeurs of the mind, [EM 325-7
  Of the mind, result only in disaster. It follows, [Bed 326-14
  That batters against the mind, silent and proud, [Pure 329-14
  The mind that knows it is destroyed by time. [Pure 329-15
  The mind sits listening and hears it pass. [Pure 329-18
  Whose mind malformed this morning metaphor, [Pure 331-21
  While all the leaves leaked gold. His mind made morning, [Pure
    331-22
  Is still to stick to the contents of the mind [Pure 332-9
  "Debris of Life and Mind" [title 338
  Her green mind made the world around her green. [Descrip 339-9
  The greater seeming of the major mind. [Descrip 340-4
  Without secret arrangements of it in the mind. [Descrip 341-14
  The intentions of a mind as yet unknown, [Descrip 341-14
  His mind raised up, down-drowned, the chariots. [Descrip 343-12
  All mind and violence and nothing felt. [Chaos 358-4
  The quiet was part of the meaning, part of the mind: [House Q
    358-17
  Filling the mind. [Burghers 362-10
  As one of the relics of the mind . . . [Prejudice 368-19
  The philosopher's hat to be part of the mind, [Prejudice 369-5
  Now the mind lays by its trouble and considers. [Cred 372-9
  Of fragrance and the mind lays by its trouble. [Cred 372-8
  A mind exists, aware of division, aware [Cred 377-2
  Man's mind grown venerable in the unreal. [Cred 377-5
  Without his envious pain in body, in mind, [Past Nun 378-20
  An image of the mind, an inward mate, [Pastor 379-18
  Never suppose an inventing mind as source [NSF 381-1
  Of this idea nor for that mind compose [NSF 381-2
  The hum of thoughts evaded in the mind, [NSF 388-4
  Among our more vestigial states of mind. [NSF 392-1
  Eye without lid, mind without any dream-- [NSF 394-12
  Weaves always glistening from the heart and mind. [NSF 396-12
  His ear, the very material of his mind. [NSF 403-3
  Soldier, there is a war between the mind [NSF 407-4
  They are at ease in a shelter of the mind [AA 413-18
  And the house is of the mind and they and time, [AA 413-19
  Of the mind--They would soon climb down the side of the ship.
    [Page 423-8
  He wanted his heart to stop beating and his mind to rest [Cata
    425-6
  Peace stood with our last blood adorned, last mind, [Owl 434-19
  Even of death, the beings of the mind [Owl 436-5
  In the light-bound space of the mind, the floreate flare . . .
    [Owl 436-6
  The mind, among the creatures that it makes, [Owl 436-8
  The mind is the terriblest force in the world, father, [John
    436-10
  Presence is not mind. [John 436-15
  It fills the being before the mind can think. [John 436-17
  The effect of the object is beyond the mind's [John 436-18
  Of motions in the mind and heart, [Imago 439-8
  The poet but the poem, the growth of the mind [Papini 446-8
  The whole habit of the mind is changed by them, [Our Stars 455-17
  When the whole habit of the mind was changed, [Our Stars 455-23
  Keep quiet in the heart, O wild bitch. O mind [Puel 456-13
  The stillness is the stillness of the mind. [Novel 458-18
  In the movement of the colors of the mind, [NH 466-9
  Or mind, uncertain in the clearest bells, [NH 466-17
  Reality as a thing seen by the mind, [NH 468-12
  And in moonlit extensions of them in the mind [NH 469-2
  Of bronze whose mind was made up and who, therefore, died. [NH
    472-10
  A minimum of making in the mind, [NH 473-12
  A strong mind in a weak neighborhood and is [NH 474-13

The moon rose in the mind and each thing there [NH 478-22
In the mind: the tin plate, the loaf of bread on it, [NH 485-20
In which hundreds of eyes, in one mind, see at once. [NH 488-6
From a bravura of the mind, [Aug 494-26
Of the mind, an apparition apparelled in [Angel 497-8
Beyond, the two alike in the make of the mind. [Rome 508-7
There was an ease of mind that was like being alone in a boat at
  sea, [Prol 515-5
Whose blunt laws make an affectation of mind, [Look 519-9
The life of the poem in the mind has not yet begun. [Slug 522-16
Within its vital boundary, in the mind. [Final 524-13
Out of this same light, out of the central mind, [Final 524-16
The lives these lived in the mind are at an end. [Rock 525-8
The body quickened and the mind in root. [Rock 527-10
Its tranquil self, the main of things, the mind, [Rock 528-15
Like a plain poet revolving in his mind [Moonlight 531-2
A change of color in the plain poet's mind, [Moonlight 532-1
Seemed like a sound in his mind. [Not Ideas 534-3
On the shapes of the mind. [Polo 38-6 P
More than his mind in the wings. The rotten leaves [Old Woman
  43-20 P
But her he had not foreseen: the bitter mind [Old Woman 44-1 P
This atmosphere in which her musty mind [Old Woman 44-20 P
It was as if transparence touched her mind. [Old Woman 45-9 P
A manner of the mind, a mind in a night [Old Woman 45-13 P
That was whatever the mind might make of it, [Old Woman 45-14 P
A night that was that mind so magnified [Old Woman 45-15 P
They are horses as they were in the sculptor's mind. [Burnshaw
  46-18 P
Like a word in the mind that sticks at artichoke [Burnshaw 47-2 P
And brown, an Italy of the mind, a place [Burnshaw 48-13 P
Like a solitude of the sun, in which the mind [Greenest 54-5 P
Of the pith of mind, cuirassiers against [Greenest 56-5 P
He sees the angel in the nigger's mind [Greenest 59-11 P
Are like the perpetual verses in a poet's mind. [Greenest 59-27 P
The metropolitan of mind, they feel [Duck 64-11 P
Than body and in less than mind, ogre, [Sombre 67-14 P
If the fane were clear, if the city shone in mind, [Sombre 69-11P
Poised, but poised as the mind through which a storm [Sombre
  69-27 P
The flight of emblemata through his mind, [Sombre 71-18 P
The divinity, the divinity's mind, the mind [Bship 78-8 P
Merely parts of the general fiction of the mind: [Recit 87-29 P
The dew falls deep in the mind [Memo 89-6
So long as the mind, for once, fulfilled itself? [Theatre 91-18 P
That matches, today, a clearness of the mind. [Nuns 92-17 P
Something of the trouble of the mind [How Now 97-4 P
The trouble of the mind [How Now 97-9 P
That howls in the mind or like a man [Dove 98-5 P
The giant sea, read his own mind. [Ulysses 99-12 P
Thinking gold thoughts in a golden mind, [Ulysses 100-20 P
Will come. His mind presents the world [Ulysses 102-20 P
And in his mind the world revolves. [Ulysses 102-21 P
In the crystal atmospheres of the mind, [Ulysses 102-27 P
Goes round in the climates of the mind [Ulysses 102-30 P
The mind renews the world in a verse, [Ulysses 103-1 P
And heirs are powers of the mind, [Ulysses 103-8 P
How then shall the mind be less than free [Ulysses 103-11 P
This is not poet's ease of mind. [Ulysses 103-28 P
The giant sea, read his own mind. [Presence 105-15 P
Of that single mind. He regards them [Child 106-17 P
The contents of the mind become solid show [Conversat 108-13 P
And you, you say that the capital things of the mind [Conversat
  109-3 P
The center that he sought was a state of mind, [Art Pop 112-13 P
A healing-point in the sickness of the mind: [Art Pop 112-22 P
Today the mind is not part of the weather. [Clear Day 113-13 P
About the mind as never satisfied, [As Leave 117-2 P
The palm at the end of the mind, [Of Mere 117-15 P
MINDED. See mountain-minded.
MINDS. I was of three minds, [Thirteen 92-17
  Out of all the minds, [Bagatelles 213-23
  Panjandrum and central heart and mind of minds-- [Extracts
  254-12
MINE. Derived from adjectives of deepest mine. [Pastor 379-16
MINGLE. Upon a rug mingle to dissipate [Sunday 66-19
  In which looks and feelings mingle and are part [NH 471-5
  It may be that they mingle, clouds and men, in the air [NH 479-24
MINGLING. And mingling of colors at a festival. [Cred 374-20
  See ever-mingling.
MINIMUM. Or searcher for the fecund minimum. [C 35-30
  A minimum of making in the mind, [NH 473-12
  Sole, single source and minimum patriarch, [Conversat 108-21 P
MINNESOTA. All over Minnesota, [Primordia 7-10 P
MINOR. A minor meeting, facile, delicate. [C 35-5
  To a seething minor swiftly modulate. [Eve Angels 137-28
  Of the least, minor, vital metaphor, content, [Crude 305-19
  The minor of what we feel. The adventurer [EM 325-24
  The great structure has become a minor house. [Plain 502-15
  Among the more irritating minor ideas [Look 517-11

MINSTRELS. These are of minstrels lacking minstrelsy, [NSF 394-13
MINSTRELSY. There was such idiot minstrelsy in rain, [NSF 394-4
  These are of minstrels lacking minstrelsy, [NSF 394-13
MINT. Incredible to prudes, the mint of dirt, [C 31-21
  The Bulgar said, "After pineapple with fresh mint [Duck 60-7 P
MINTING. See midnight-minting.
MINUSCULE. Crispin, merest minuscule in the gales, [C 29-11
MINUTIAE. Of central sense, these minutiae mean more [EM 317-20
MIRACLE. An inner miracle and sun-sacrament, [Montra 262-5
  War's miracle begetting that of peace. [Cats 368-5
MIRACLES. One of the major miracles, that fall [Montra 262-6
MIRACULOUS. As if sight had not its own miraculous thrift, [EM
  320-26
  Miraculous in its panache and swish? [Antag 426-2
  And the miraculous multiplex of lesser poems, [Orb 442-5
  But, also, as to their miraculous, [NH 470-11
  A light, a power, the miraculous influence. [Final 524-9
MIRACULOUSLY. Miraculously preserved, full fickle-fine, [Greenest
  56-15 P
MIRROR. A mirror of a mere delight? [Botanist 2 136-12
  Ennobled as in a mirror to sanctity. [Nigger 157-6
  Torn from insipid summer, for the mirror of cold, [Dwarf 208-12
  Is the table a mirror in which they sit and look? [Cuisine 228-15
  But as in the powerful mirror of my wish and will." [Rhythms
  246-8
  As a mirror with a voice, the man of glass, [Oboe 250-21
  And in that mountainous mirror Spain acquires [Descrip 345-13
  And Eve made air the mirror of herself, [NSF 383-12
  The air is not a mirror but bare board, [NSF 384-2
  In which majesty is a mirror of the self: [NSF 405-5
  And the mate of summer: her mirror and her look, [Orb 441-23
  The mirror melts and moulds itself and moves [Novel 458-4
  "A Golden Woman in a Silver Mirror" [460-title
  A mirror, a lake of reflections in a room, [NH 468-14
  This is the mirror of the high serious: [NH 477-17
  In a mirror, without heat, [Plant 506-13
  The mirror of the planets, one by one, [Rock 528-5
  Look in the terrible mirror of the sky [Blanche 10-1 P
  Look in the terrible mirror of the sky. [Blanche 10-5 P
  Look in the terrible mirror of the sky. [Blanche 10-9 P
  The mirror of other nights combined in one. [Sombre 71-10 P
MIRROR-DARK. That enter day from night, came mirror-dark, [Burnshaw
  51-26 P
MIRRORING. Like light in a mirroring of cliffs, [MBG 175-3
MIRRORS. of my being, shine like fire, that mirrors nothing.
  [Nuances 18-10
  As buffo, yet divers, four mirrors blue [C 45-6
  That the walls are mirrors multiplied, [Prelude 195-2
  The rivers shine and hold their mirrors up, [Belly 366-19
  Here are too many mirrors for misery. [AA 420-7
MISANTHROPE. What misanthrope, impugning heroica, [Stan Hero 84-23P
MISANTHROPES. It is the infants of misanthropes [Cortege 80-11
MISER. And ours, of rigid measure, a miser's paint; [Sombre 67-8 P
MISERABLE. Miserable that it was not she. [Scavoir 231-12
  And you and I are such things, O most miserable . . . [Gala 248-3
  Most miserable, most victorious, [NSF 389-3
  Un miserable. [Three 136-12 P
MISERICORDIA. Misericordia, it follows that [NH 485-22
MISERS. Men fat as feathers, misers counting breaths, [Horn 230-3
MISERY. Of any misery in the sound of the wind, [Snow Man 10-5
  "From the Misery of Don Joost" [46-title
  Yet with a petty misery [MBG 170-17
  At heart, a petty misery, [MBG 170-18
  That's what misery is, [Destructive 192-9
  To smother the wry spirit's misery. [News 265-7
  There lies the misery, the coldest coil [Choc 298-21
  Here are too many mirrors for misery. [AA 420-7
  Hard found, and water tasting of misery. [Bad Time 426-14
  The muse of misery? Speak loftier lines. [Bad Time 427-7
  If it is misery that infuriates our love, [NH 467-1
  In so much misery; and yet finding it [Rome 509-23
  Only in misery, the afflatus of ruin, [Rome 509-24
  And the great misery of the doubt of it, [Dove 98-9 P
MISFORTUNE. Philandering? . . . The genius of misfortune [EM 316-23
MISGIVINGS. From loftiness, misgivings dazzlingly [Ulysses 101-29 P
MISS. Must miss the symmetry of a leaden mate, [Nigger 152-19
  Is to miss, by that, things as they are, [MBG 165-18
MISSAL. A poem like a missal found [MBG 177-21
  In the mud, a missal for that young man, [MBG 177-22
  To know; a missal for brooding-sight. [MBG 178-5
MISSHAPEN. Lay black and full of black misshapen? Wings [Old
  Woman 44-21 P
MISSISSIPPI. The blunt ice flows down the Mississippi, [Primordia
  8-3 P
MIST. Illusive, faint, more mist than moon, perverse, [C 34-30
  Mist that is golden is not wholly mist. [Nigger 156-15
  The shores are banks of muffling mist. [MBG 172-14
  Escaped from the truth, the morning is color and mist, [Freed
  204-18
  And of his works, I am sure. He bathes in the mist [Freed 204-22

Not quite. The mist was to light what red [Vari 235-20
The walk in mist and rain and snow [Poesie 302-13
The academies like structures in a mist. [NSF 386-21
They go to the cliffs of Moher rising out of the mist, [Irish 501-13
Cities that would not wash away in the mist, [Sombre 68-9 P
It is an arbor against the wind, a pit in the mist, [Discov 95-12 P
MISTAKE. It was a mistake to paint the gods. The gold [Greenest 57-30 P
It was a mistake to think of them. They have [Greenest 58-7 P
MISTAKES. Mistakes it for a world of objects, [Aug 491-3
MISTED. Itself a cloud, although of misted rock [AA 416-5
In misted contours, credible day again. [NH 470-15
See be-misted.
MISTINESS. And cold in a boreal mistiness of the moon. [C 34-8
MIST-MITES. And mist-mites, dangling seconds, grown [Red Fern 365-9
MISTOOK. In that he mistook [Thirteen 94-16
MISTRESS. It might well be that their mistress [Homunculus 26-21
As muffing the mistress for her several maids, [EM 316-21
Mistress of an idea, child [Celle 438-18
An image that was mistress of the world. [Golden 460-9
Called Mistress and Maid. [Three 133-23 P
The mistress says, in a harsh voice, [Three 134-5 P
The maid drops her eyes and says to her mistress, [Three 135-1 P
MISTY. Of misty fields, by their sweet questionings; [Sunday 68-14
Me round, carry me, misty deck, carry me [Farewell 118-19
See man-misty.
MISUNDERSTOOD. If properly misunderstood becomes a myth. [Lytton 38-15 P
MITES. See mist-mites.
MIXED. And forest tigresses and women mixed [EM 321-25
Of such mixed motion and such imagery [Rock 527-17
MIXINGS. With the molten mixings of related things, [Someone 87-4 A
MOB. Or Chicago a Kaffir kraal. It means this mob. [Duck 63-14 P
MOBILE. The mobile and the immobile flickering [NH 474-1
MOBS. There are these sudden mobs of men, [Sad Gay 122-4
Mobs of ten thousand, clashing together, [Thunder 220-3
Should be illusion, that the mobs of birth [Dutch 292-25
In an age of concentric mobs would any sphere [Duck 63-25 P
MOCK. To mock him. They placed with him in his grave [Good Man 364-10
(A woman's voice is heard, replying.) Mock [Infernale 25-4 P
MOCKED. And so I mocked her in magnificent measure. [Monocle 13-5
Or was it that I mocked myself alone? [Monocle 13-6
MOCKERS. To confront the mockers, [Am Sub 130-18
The mickey mockers [Am Sub 130-19
MOCKING. Dangling and spangling, the mic-mac of mocking birds. [NH 486-15
MOCKS. He mocks the guinea, challenges [Vari 233-14
MODE. Is no longer a mode of desire, a mode [Sad Gay 121-12
Whose singing is a mode of laughter, [Dezem 218-12
A manner of thinking, a mode [Bottle 239-7
And the martyrs à la mode. He walked toward [Contra II 270-9
Whereon it falls in more than sensual mode. [NSF 398-19
That big-brushed green. Or in a tragic mode, [John 437-3
This faithfulness of reality, this mode, [NH 472-19
The clear. A celestial mode is paramount, [NH 480-24
There it would be of the mode of common dreams, [Greenest 57-9 P
The mode of the person becomes the mode of the world, [Conversat 108-11 P
Now, you, for instance, are of this mode: You say [Conversat 108-17P
MODEL. Obscure Satanas, make a model [Hero 277-2
Wooden, the model for astral apprentices, [NH 478-19
MODELLED. In the way they are modelled [Pears 196-13
MODERN. "Of Modern Poetry" [239-title
This is the mythology of modern death [Owl 435-22
Half men and half new, modern monsters . . . [Stan Hero 84-8 P
MODES. It follows that to change modes is to change the world [Conversat 108-16 P
Modes of desire, modes of revealing desire. [Sad Gay 122-12
The crow, inciting various modes. [Vari 233-15
Barbers with charts of the only possible modes, [Sombre 68-8 P
MODIFIED. As if hell, so modified, had disappeared, [EM 316-4
MODIFIES. As a quick answer modifies a question, [NH 471-6
MODULATE. To a seething minor swiftly modulate. [Eve Angels 137-28
MODULATING. Inevitably modulating, in the blood. [NSF 407-20
MOHER. "The Irish Cliffs of Moher" [501-title
They go to the cliffs of Moher rising out of the mist, [Irish 501-13
MOIST. Wading the sea-lines, moist and ever-mingling, [Tallap 72-2
Than your moist hand. [Two Figures 85-16
MOISTURE. Moisture and heat have swollen the garden into a slum of bloom. [Banal 62-14
MOLDAU. Of the Balkan shoes, the bonnets from Moldau, beards [Duck 62-14 P
MOLIERE. Than Tartuffe as myth, the most Molière, [Paisant 335-10
MOLTEN. Like molten citizens of the vacuum? [Liadoff 346-10
But not quite molten, not quite the fluid thing, [Myrrh 350-4
With the molten mixings of related things, [Someone 87-4 A

MOMENT. For the moment. [Botanist 1 134-13
And although my mind perceives the force behind the moment, [Fish-Scale 161-3
For a moment final, in the way [MBG 168-3
That's the moment when the moon creeps up [Dump 202-19
Which is enough: the moment's rain and sea, [Freed 204-19
The moment's sun (the strong man vaguely seen), [Freed 204-20
For a moment on rising, at the edge of the bed, to be, [Freed 205-8
A moment ago, light masculine, [Hartford 227-1
For a moment they are gay and are a part [Gala 248-4
And we feel, in a way apart, for a moment, as if [Gala 248-11
There's a moment in the year, Solange, [News 265-11
If nothing more than that, for the moment, large [Choc 302-2
Not quite detected at the moment of change [Pure 332-4
For a moment, a moment in which we read and repeat [Pure 333-8
Free, for a moment, from malice and sudden cry, [Cred 378-8
For a moment in the central of our being, [NSF 380-10
For a moment, the first idea . . . It satisfies [NSF 382-14
Irrational moment its unreasoning, [NSF 398-22
At the moment when the angelic eye defines [AA 414-20
At the moment's being, without history, [Beginning 427-16
As at the moment of the year when, tick, [John 437-4
The solid, but the movable, the moment, [NH 472-1
Seen for a moment standing in the door. [Angel 496-8
A figure half seen, or seen for a moment, a man [Angel 497-7
As at a point of central arrival, an instant moment, much or little, [Prol 516-8
A moment on this fantasia. He seeks [Look 519-5
Here is the world of a moment, [Polo 37-16 P
To the moment. There the horses would rise again, [Old Woman 46-7 P
For a moment, once each century or two. [Duck 65-20 P
An ease in which to live a moment's life, [Letters 107-7 P
The moment of life's love and fortune, [Letters 107-8 P
MOMENTARY. Beauty is momentary in the mind-- [Peter 91-22
To momentary ones, are blended, [Hero 279-21
A few sounds of meaning, a momentary end [Lack 303-19
Like a momentary color, in which swans [NSF 397-14
But only its momentary breath, [Two Illus 513-16
To momentary calm, spectacular flocks [Burnshaw 51-2 P
The momentary footings of a climb [Someone 87-1 A
MOMENTOUS. For reality is as momentous as [NH 481-5
MOMENTOUSLY. That which momentously declares [MBG 171-20
MOMENTS. The moments when we choose to play [MBG 184-5
"The moments of enlargement overlook [Choc 298-13
Which is more desperate in the moments when [EM 323-10
Perhaps there are moments of awakening, [NSF 386-17
In isolated moments--isolations [NH 484-1
That were the moments of the classic, the beautiful. [Local 112-10 P
And there are indeterminate moments [Three 131-1 P
Well, there are moments [Three 131-8 P
MONACO. Frail princes of distant Monaco, [Primordia 9-20 P
MONADNOCKS. Ruffling its common reflections, thought-like Monadnocks. [Cata 424-14
MONARCHIES. Wax wasted, monarchies beyond [Prelude 195-6
MONASTIC. The monastic man is an artist. The philosopher [NSF 382-1
MONDAY. In the mud, in Monday's dirty light, [MBG 183-16
MONDE. See demi-monde.
MONGRELS. Of place: time's haggard mongrels. [Analysis 348-11
MONHEGAN. Star over Monhegan, Atlantic star, [Vari 232-15
MONKISH. Imagined man, the monkish mask, the face. [Dezem 218-8
MONOCLE. "Le Monocle de Mon Oncle" [13-title
MONOTONIES. But I invoke the monotony of monotonies [Demoiselle 23-10 P
MONOTONOUS. There is a monotonous babbling in our dreams [C 39-25
Monotonous earth and dark blue sky. [Vincentine 52-12
Monotonous earth I saw become [Vincentine 53-13
It is monotonous. [Demoiselle 23-2 P
MONOTONY. They flung monotony behind, [Ord Women 10-17
"Anatomy of Monotony" [107-title
A single text, granite monotony, [NSF 394-9
And knowing the monotony of thought, [Stan MMO 19-5 P
The monotony [Demoiselle 23-3 P
But I invoke the monotony of monotonies [Demoiselle 23-10 P
MONSIEUR. Monsieur is on horseback. The horse is covered with mice. [Mice 123-4
We dance it out to the tip of Monsieur's sword, [Mice 123-6
To walk another room . . . Monsieur and comrade, [NSF 407-17
MONSIEUR DUFY. To Monsieur Dufy's Hamburg whence they came. [Lions 125-7
MONSTER. That I may reduce the monster to [MBG 175-5
In face of the monster, be more than part [MBG 175-7
Alone, but reduce the monster and be, [MBG 175-10
And play of the monster and of myself, [MBG 175-12
A turquoise monster moving round. [Silent 360-3
The man-hero is not the exceptional monster, [NSF 406-5
Like a monster that has everything and rests, [Bouquet 452-4
MONSTERED. Then it was that that monstered moth [Hibiscus 22-15

MONSTER-MAKER. A monster-maker, an eye, only an eye, [Extracts
    252-22
MONSTERS. Monsters antique and haggard with past thought? [Dutch
    292-11
  Its immaterial monsters move, [Analysis 348-14
  And these, in their mufflings, monsters of elegy, [Owl 435-23
  Half men and half new, modern monsters . . . [Stan Hero 84-8 P
  See: fire-monsters; moon-monsters.
MONSTROUS. Of it, more than the monstrous player of [MBG 175-8
  One of its monstrous lutes, not be [MBG 175-9
MONT. On a hill of stones to make beau mont thereof. [NH 466-24
  If the black of night stands glistening on beau mont, [NH 467-2
MONTH. Bring flowers in last month's newspapers. [Emperor 64-6
  And August the most peaceful month. [Rabbit K 209-6
  For a month. It was pleasant to be sitting there, [EM 313-14
  A further consummation. For the lunar month. [EM 318-4
  There is a month, a year, there is a time [NSF 405-4
  See ice-month.
MONTHS. The months of understanding. The pediment [Pediment 362-2
  The propounding of four seasons and twelve months. [NH 473-14
MONTRACHET-LE-JARDIN. "Montrachet-le-Jardin" [260-title
MONUMENT. Without that monument of cat, [Rabbit K 209-8
MOOCH. What festival? This loud, disordered mooch? [AA 415-22
MOOD. The mood [Thirteen 93-16
  (In the pale coherences of moon and mood [Anglais 149-1
  Out of a mood, the tragic robe [MBG 169-20
  Part of the mottled mood of summer's whole, [Cred 378-5
  In the days when the mood of love will be swarming for solace
    and sink deeply into the thin stuff of being, [Piano 22-8 P
  You do not understand her evil mood. [Spaniard 34-1 P
  A mood that had become so fixed it was [Old Woman 45-12 P
  More of ourselves, the mood of life made strong [Duck 65-3 P
MOODIEST. To moodiest nothings, as, desire for day [Eve Angels
    137-21
  Them mottled, in the moodiest costumes, [Cred 377-25
MOODS. Passions of rain, or moods in falling snow; [Sunday 67-20
MOODY. In moody rucks, and difficult and strange [C 31-10
MOON. Bequeathing your white feathers to the moon [Swans 4-7
  O sceptre of the sun, crown of the moon, [Monocle 13-2
  Streams to the moon. [Ploughing 20-18
  And on the clopping foot-ways of the moon [C 28-28
  And cold in a boreal mistiness of the moon. [C 34-8
  Illusive, faint, more mist than moon, perverse, [C 34-30
  A fluctuating between sun and moon, [C 35-8
  Than mute bare splendors of the sun and moon. [On Manner 56 8
  The moon is in the folds of the cloak. [Of Surface 57-8
  This was no worm bred in the moon, [Cuban 65-1
  There is no moon, on single, silvered leaf. [Tallap 71-15
  When my dream was near the moon, [Six Sig 74-14
  That the moon shines. [Two Figures 86-15
  Whose garden is wind and moon, [Watermelon 88-21
  The moon is the mother of pathos and pity. [Lunar 107-1
  The moon is the mother of pathos and pity. [Lunar 107-12
  In a coma of the moon. [Public Sq 108-22
  The bijou of Atlas, the moon, [Public Sq 109-11
  Flashier fruits! A flip for the sun and moon, [Grapes 110-17
  For him the moon was always in Scandinavia [Norfolk 111-10
  And silvers and greens spread over the sea. The moon [Farewell
    117-4
  I am free. High above the mast the moon [Farewell 117-7
  Of dirt . . . It is not possible for the moon [Ghosts 119-9
  Last evening the moon rose above this rock [How Live 125-9
  The moon they made their own attendant ghosts, [Eve Angels 137-11
  As we stand gazing at the rounded moon. [Eve Angels 138-6
  An incantation that the moon defines [Havana 145-5
  Only last year he said that the naked moon [Anglais 148-19
  Was not the moon he used to see, to feel [Anglais 148-20
  (In the pale coherences of moon and mood [Anglais 149-1
  The sorrows of the sun, too, gone . . . the moon and moon,
    [Autumn 160-3
  The yellow moon of words about the nightingale [Autumn 160-4
  The moon shares nothing. It is a sea. [MBG 168-10
  I stand in the moon, and call it good, [MBG 168-17
  Catching at Good-bye, harvest moon, [MBG 173-5
  Without seeing the harvest or the moon? [MBG 173-6
  Now that the moon is rising in the heat [Men Fall 187-10
  And crickets are loud again in the grass. The moon [Men Fall
    187-11
  The moon without a shape, [Add 199-7
  Day creeps down. The moon is creeping up. [Dump 201-11
  The sun is a corbeil of flowers the moon Blanche [Dump 201-12
  And so the moon, both come, and the janitor's poems [Dump 201-16
  That's the moment when the moon creeps up [Dump 202-19
  Everything is shed; and the moon comes up as the moon [Dump
    202-22
  You see the moon rise in the empty sky. [Dump 202-25
  The cat forgotten in the moon; [Rabbit K 209-9
  And cold. The moon follows the sun like a French [Vari 234-8
  An impossible aberration with the moon, [Bottle 239-11
  And nothing more. So that if one went to the moon, [Extracts

    258-10
  And then returning from the moon, if one breathed [Extracts
    258-14
  And great moon, cricket-impresario, [Montra 260-4
  A kneeling woman, a moon's farewell; [Hero 275-10
  Look round, brown moon, brown bird, as you rise to fly, [God
    285-1
  Look round you as you start to rise, brown moon, [God 285-4
  The single bird, the obscure moon-- [Motive 288-8
  The obscure moon lighting an obscure world [Motive 288-9
  For soldiers, the new moon stretches twenty feet. [Gigan 289-21
  The faintly encrusted, a tissue of the moon [Repet 306-14
  Blue and its deep inversions in the moon [Repet 309-18
  The moon rose up as if it had escaped [EM 314-24
  Above him. The moon was always free from him, [EM 314-27
  Panic in the face of the moon--round effendi [EM 320-15
  The moon is no longer these nor anything [EM 320-20
  That has lost the folly of the moon becomes [EM 320-23
  The human that has no cousin in the moon. [Less 328-4
  As one of the secretaries of the moon, [Feo 333-10
  Or like a seeming of the moon or night [Descrip 339-6
  And moon, the book of reconciliation, [Descrip 345-1
  After a lustre of the moon, we say [NSF 394-19
  Clears deeply, when the moon hangs on the wall [NSF 398-24
  Patches the moon together in his room [NSF 407-7
  Say, a flippant communication under the moon. [AA 418-3
  Under the buttonwoods, beneath a moon nailed fast. [Cata 425-5
  The moon moves toward the night. [Pecul 453-8
  She is the day, the walk of the moon [Pecul 454-4
  Or: Gawks of hay . . . Augusta Moon, before [Golden 460-12
  The frequency of images of the moon [Study II 464-4
  The shadowless moon wholly composed of shade, [Study II 464-13
  It is fatal in the moon and empty there. [NH 472-4
  We say of the moon, it is haunted by the man [NH 472-9
  The moon rose in the mind and each thing there [NH 478-22
  And on air of lateness. The moon is a tricorn [Aug 495-20
  Weight him, weight, weight him with the sleepiness of the moon.
    [Madame 507-5
  He discovered the colors of the moon [Two Illus 514-13
  The property of the moon, what it evokes. [Moonlight 531-9
  The various obscurities of the moon, [Bowl 7-2 P
  See how the absent moon waits in a glade [Blanche 10-10 P
  How carve the violet moon [Archi 17-25 P
  These ample lustres from the new-come moon. [Stan MMO 19-11 P
  Tho sun is gold, the moon is silver. [Mandolin 29-1 P
  As the moon has in its moonlight, worlds away, [Red Kit 31-8 P
  Rest, crows, upon the edges of the moon, [Red Kit 31-20 P
  Wherefore those prayers to the moon? [An Gaiety 33-1 P
  You think that like the moon she is obscured [Spaniard 34-2 P
  If she is like the moon, she never clears [Spaniard 34-11 P
  Commingle, not like the commingling of sun and moon [Burnshaw
    50-2 P
  What lesser man shall measure sun and moon, [Duck 63-7 P
  Whimpers when the moon above East Hartford [Grotesque 76-18 P
  Say that the American moon comes up [Memo 89-11 P
  Even if there had been a crescent moon [Letters 107-1 P
  The moon and the imagination, or, say, [Somone 83-12 A
  Power in the waving of the wand of the moon, [Someone 84-10 A
  See: half-moon; man-moon.
MOON-BLOTCHES. Observing the moon-blotches on the walls. [Babies
    77-3
MOONLIGHT. The moonlight [Ord Women 11-3
  The moonlight [Ord Women 11-19
  With white moonlight. [Fabliau 23-13
  To bathe their hearts in later moonlight, [Homunculus 26-12
  Of moonlight on the thick, cadaverous bloom [C 31-28
  The book of moonlight is not written yet [C 33-18
  For the legendary moonlight that once burned [C 33-27
  Perhaps the Arctic moonlight really gave [C 34-25
  Moonlight was an evasion, or, if not, [C 35-4
  That in the moonlight have their habitude. [C 35-13
  The moonlight fiction disappeared. The spring, [C 36-1
  Exit lex mental moonlight, exit lex, [C 36-28
  Are there mandolines of northern moonlight? [Men 1000 52-6
  In the moonlight [Peacocks 57-9
  In the moonlight [Peacocks 57-11
  Of the moonlight [Peacocks 58-22
  The walker in the moonlight walked alone, [Babies 77-7
  The walker in the moonlight walked alone, [Babies 77-16
  As to get no more from the moonlight [Two Figures 85-15
  The moonlight is not yellow but a white [Havana 144-24
  Waken, and watch the moonlight on their floors. [Havana 145-2
  Crouched in the moonlight. [Reader 147-3
  Shucks . . . lavender moonlight falls. [Add 198-11
  Could measure by moonlight in June. [Jersey 210-12
  You touch the hotel the way you touch moonlight [Waldorf 241-4
  The milkman came in the moonlight and the moonlight [Les Plus
    244-17
  Was less than moonlight. Nothing exists by itself. [Les Plus
    244-18

The moonlight seemed to. [Les Plus 244-19
The moonlight and Aquinas seemed to. He spoke, [Les Plus 245-3
The moonlight in her lap, mewing her velvet, [Uruguay 249-2
I have wiped away moonlight like mud. Your innocent ear [Uruguay 249-5
The moonlight crumbled to degenerate forms, [Uruguay 249-7
Neither the moonlight could change it. And for her, [Uruguay 249-12
The moonlight? Was it a rider intent on the sun, [Uruguay 249-20
The moonlight in the cell, words on the wall. [Montra 260-21
So that the skeleton in the moonlight sings, [Montra 261-8
Or moonlight, silently, as Plato's ghost [Less 327-12
Sit in the room. It is true in the moonlight [Debris 338-3
As morning throws off stale moonlight and shabby sleep.[NSF 382-12
"Note on Moonlight" [531-title
The one moonlight, in the simple-colored night, [Moonlight 531-1
The one moonlight, the various universe, intended [Moonlight 532-3
On which the quiet moonlight lies. [Archi 17-21 P
As the moon has in its moonlight, worlds away, [Red Kit 31-8 P
Night's moonlight lake was neither water nor air. [Real 111-2 P
MOONLIT. The disbeliever walked the moonlit place, [Babies 77-1
And in moonlit extensions of them in the mind [NH 469-2
Left here by moonlit muckers when they fled [Burnshaw 46-22 P
MOON-MASH. Castratos of moon-mash--Life consists [Men Made 355-17
MOON-MONSTERS. Sultry moon-monsters [Fabliau 23-10
MOON-RISING. I found between moon-rising and moon-setting [NE Verses 104-3
MOONS. Through wild spaces of other suns and moons, [Ulysses 102-23 P
MOON-SETTING. I found between moon-rising and moon-setting [NE Verses 104-3
MOPPET. In the mind, pupa of straw, moppet of rags. [Dwarf 208-6
MORAL. Take the moral law and make a nave of it [High-Toned 59-2
Chorals for mountain voices and the moral chant, [Thought 185-16
It is clear that it is not a moral law. [Bship 78-31 P
MORALE. Morale [Soldat 13-title 4 P
MORALIST. Behold the moralist hidalgo [Thought 186-17
MORBID. It is a morbid light [Common 221-6
Morbid and bleak? [Drum-Majors 37-6 P
MORN. Shall chant in orgy on a summer morn [Sunday 69-29
Of men that perish and of summer morn. [Sunday 70-11
The central flaw in the solar morn. [Thought 187-8
It was the morn [Coroner 29-11 P
MORNING. Be not chimera of morning, [Nuances 18-13
In the presto of the morning, Crispin trod, [C 42-13
In the morning, [Jack-Rabbit 50-4
"Sunday Morning" [66-title
And in the morning summer hued the deck [Sea Surf 98-14
A mallow morning dozed upon the deck [Sea Surf 101-6
Out of the morning sky. [Pascagoula 126-12
Canaries in the morning, orchestras [Havana 142-1
The morning deluged still by night, [MBG 169-3
Will claw sleep. Morning is not sun, [MBG 182-19
Whose whore is Morning Star [Thought 186-18
The freshness of morning, the blowing of day, one says [Dump 202-2
Escaped from the truth, the morning is color and mist, [Freed 204-18
Should play in the trees when morning comes. [Nightgown 214-16
The chandeliers, their morning glazes spread [Blue Bldg 217-11
"Poem Written at Morning" [219-title
Dripping a morning sap. [Poem Morn 219-11
And chords, the morning exercises, [Hero 274-22
Hip, hip, hurrah. Eternal morning . . . [Hero 278-14
The crystal-pointed star of morning, rose [Choc 296-18
The lesser night, the less than morning light, [Choc 301-20
That sweats the sun up on its morning way [Repet 307-7
The catbird's gobble in the morning half-awake-- [Holiday 313-6
Whose mind malformed this morning metaphor, [Pure 331-21
While all the leaves leaked gold. His mind made morning, [Pure 331-22
Things look each day, each morning, or the style [Descrip 339-18
In which old stars are planets of morning, fresh [Descrip 344-10
Seemed in the morning like a holiday." [Anach 365-19
The trumpet of morning blows in the clouds and through [Cred 376-16
Everything becomes morning, summer, the hero, [Past Nun 378-17
As morning throws off stale moonlight and shabby sleep. [NSF 382-12
Cloudless the morning. It is he. The man [NSF 389-8
Morning and afternoon are clasped together [NSF 392-12
Espoused each morning, each long afternoon, [Orb 441-22
Of today, of this morning, of this afternoon, [Bouquet 451-13
The ocean breathed out morning in one breath. [Our Stars 455-24
So that morning and evening are like promises kept, [NH 472-16
They heard his mumble in the morning light. [Phases 5-11 P
In the morning, the clear river [Primordia 8-5 P
In the morning in the blue snow [An Gaiety 32-15 P

When morning comes [Secret Man 36-10 P
Covered one morning with blue, one morning with white, [Bship 80-10 P
At three-quarters gone, the morning's prescience, [Pagoda 92-4 P
In a season, a climate of morning, of elucidation, [Bus 116-5 P
MORNING-GLORIES. The morning-glories grow in the egg. [Aug 490-3
MORNINGS. And blessed mornings, [Nomad 95-15
In mornings of angular ice, [Medit 124-5
Conceptions of new mornings of new worlds, [NH 470-12
The mornings grow silent, the never-tiring wonder. [Aug 495-17
And gazed on chosen mornings, [Three 131-19 P
Since thirty mornings are required to make [Ideal 88-1 A
MORNINGSIDE. And Eden conceived on Morningside, [Ulysses 101-7 P
MOROSE. Morose chiaroscuro, gauntly drawn. [C 34-17
"Lulu Morose" [27-title P
MORPHOLOGY. Consider the odd morphology of regret. [Nigger 154-10
MORROW. To this morrow. [Song Fixed 519-17
MORT. A pip of life amid a mort of tails. [Bird Claws 82-3
"Anglais Mort à Florence" [148-title
See Mac Mort.
MORTAL. Meekly you keep the mortal rendezvous, [On Manner 55-11
Who saw the mortal massives of the blooms [Sea Surf 100-1
To endure thereafter every mortal wound, [Extracts 258-27
Any mortal end. The chants of final peace [Extracts 259-6
First sees reality. The mortal no [EM 320-8
In a mortal lullaby, like porcelain. [Burnshaw 47-22 P
By gestures of a mortal perfection. [Stan Hero 84-22 P
MOSCOW. This side of Moscow. There were anti-ideas [Forces 229-7
MOSELLE. After we've drunk the Moselle, to the thickest shade [Phenom 286-16
MOSS. The mouse, the moss, the woman on the shore . . . [Blue Bldg 217-6
See live-moss.
MOSSES. And the memorial mosses hang their green [Degen 445-2
MOSSY. Who are the mossy cronies muttering, [Dutch 292-10
MOST. Most venerable heart, the lustiest conceit [Monocle 16-17
Disturbed not even the most idle ear. [Hibiscus 22-14
An eye most apt in gelatines and jupes, [C 27-14
Making the most of savagery of palms, [C 31-27
Most sisterly to the first, not yet awake [C 44-17
Wink as they will. Wink most when widows wince. [High-Toned 59-22
And, most, of the motion of thought [Solitaires 60-10
Most near, most clear, and of the clearest bloom, [Fictive 87-7
And of the fragrant mothers the most dear [Fictive 87-8
Most rare, or ever of more kindred air [Fictive 87-21
That apprehends the most which sees and names, [Fictive 88-5
A most inappropriate man [Sailing 120-9
In a most unpropitious place. [Sailing 120-10
Most spiss--oh! Yes, most spissantly. [Snow Stars 133-2
A most desolate wind has chilled Rouge-Fatima [Havana 142-11
Thus one is most disclosed when one is most anonymous. [Nudity Col 145-13
As now and called most high, [MBG 176-7
And August the most peaceful month. [Rabbit K 209-6
To an order, most Plantagenet, most fixed . . . [Connois 216-8
So that he that suffers most desires [Adequacy 244-13
The red bird most and the strongest sky-- [Adequacy 244-14
And you and I are such things, O most miserable . . . [Gala 248-3
And the most distant, single color, about to change, [Extracts 258-17
And, imageless, it is itself the most, [Montra 263-18
Engaged in the most prolific narrative, [Phenom 287-5
Than the most metal music, loudlier, [Dutch 291-11
Made sure of the most correct catastrophe. [EM 314-10
He sought the most grossly maternal, the creature [EM 321-13
Who most fecundly assuaged him, the softest [EM 321-14
Time in its weather, our most sovereign lord, [Pure 332-17
Of chance. Finally, the most solemn burial [Paisant 334-15
Than Tartuffe as myth, the most Molière, [Paisant 335-10
The most gay and yet not so gay as it was. [Debris 338-13
Thus the theory of description matters most. [Descrip 345-5
The most necessitous sense. Accept them, then, [Man Car 350-17
The most massive sopranos are singing songs of scales. [Chaos 357-18
Wanted to lean, wanted much most to be [House Q 358-13
Makes of the form Most Merciful Capitan, [Pastor 379-6
Most supple challenger. The elephant [NSF 384-11
Most miserable, most victorious, [NSF 389-3
Who surpassed the most literate owl, the most erudite [NSF 403-21
But he that of repetition is most master. [NSF 406-6
No more that which most of all brings back the known, [Page 422-15
And against the most coiled thorn, have seized on what was ugly [Large 424-3
It is most happily contrived. Here, then, [Antag 425-14
We ask which means most, for us, all the genii [Antag 425-15
To most incredible depths. I speak below [John 437-9
Of the most beautiful, the most beautiful maid [Golden 461-1
Which nothing can frustrate, that most secure, [NH 467-7
A verity of the most veracious men, [NH 473-13
This should be tragedy's most moving face. [NH 477-6

The most ancient light in the most ancient sky, [NH 481-18
What was real turned into something most unreal, [NH 483-23
Alert us most [Inhab 503-12
As to one, and, as to one, most penitent, [Rome 509-21
It is poverty's speech that seeks us out the most. [Rome 510-3
In his chair, the most tranquil thought grew peaked [Quiet 523-9
Mumbling and musing like the most forlorn. [Phases 5-14 P
Having, each one, most praisable [Parasol 20-5 P
And Crispin, the blade, reddened by some touch, demanding the
     most from the phrases [Piano 22-6 P
Which choir makes the most faultless medley in its celebration?
     [Inelegance 25-19 P
Would have a most singular appearance, [Mandolin 29-4 P
It is a most spectacular role, and yet [Spaniard 35-4 P
What interests me most is the people [Lytton 38-8 P
Who have always interested me most, [Lytton 38-9 P
Or dance the death of doves, most sallowly, [Burnshaw 48-22 P
Of the most evasive hue of a lesser blue, [Burnshaw 51-19 P
Magnificence most shiningly expressed [Greenest 58-3 P
Perennial doctrine and most florid truth; [Duck 63-10 P
And most in what we hear, sound brushed away, [Sombre 67-9 P
Which counts for most, the anger borne [Sombre 69-21 P
This matters most in things that matter least. [Grotesque 76-11 P
Or accessible only in the most furtive fiction. [Nuns 93-2 P
The most at home? Or is it enough to have seen [Conversat 109-17P
"Reality Is an Activity of the Most August Imagination" [110-
     title P
More precious than the most precious objects of home: [Local
     111-13 P
The light of the most tranquil candle [Three 132-13 P
Made subtle by truth's most jealous subtlety, [Someone 84-8 A
MOSTLY. For a self returning mostly memory. [Anglais 148-18
And happiest folk-land, mostly marriage-hymns. [Cred 373-21
MOT. A mot into a dictum, communal, [Spaniard 34-19 P
MOTES. And move the night by their intelligent motes. [Red Kit
     32-1 P
     The gathering of the imbecile against his motes [Discov 95-19 P
     See mimic-motes.
MOTETS. And hears the nigger's prayer in motets, belched [Greenest
     59-12 P
MOTH. The mind roamed as a moth roams, [Hibiscus 22-10
     Then it was that that monstered moth [Hibiscus 22-15
MOTHER. Timeless mother, [Carolinas 5-1
     "Mother of heaven, regina of the clouds, [Monocle 13-1
     Out of their mother grass, like little kin, [Monocle 15-4
     No mother suckled him, no sweet land gave [Sunday 67-13
     Death is the mother of beauty; hence from her, [Sunday 68-29
     Death is the mother of beauty, mystical, [Sunday 69-25
     Sister and mother and diviner love, [Fictive 87-5
     The moon is the mother of pathos and pity. [Lunar 107-1
     The moon is the mother of pathos and pity. [Lunar 107-12
     The same. We parallel the mother's death. [Anatomy 108-2
     Of a mother [Sonatina 109-17
     Of summer, the drunken mother? [Medit 124-9
     Not the mother that held men as they fell [MBG 173-14
     The mother, but an oppressor, but like [MBG 173-16
     And the mother, the music, the name; the scholar, [Choc 300-4
     This brother half-spoken in the mother's throat [EM 317-11
     Desiring fiercely, the child of a mother fierce [EM 321-20
     The mother ties the hair-ribbons of the child [Extraord 369-7
     Farewell to an idea . . . The mother's face, [AA 413-4
     Still-starred. It is the mother they possess, [AA 413-10
     And to the mother as she falls asleep [AA 413-22
     The mother invites humanity to her house [AA 415-4
     As if the innocent mother sang in the dark [AA 419-1
     My memory, is the mother of us all, [Owl 432-15
     The earthly mother and the mother of [Owl 432-16
     Of a mother with vague severed arms [Celle 438-19
     But what his mother was returns and cries on his breast. [Pecul
     453-9
     She is the fateful mother, whom he does not know. [Pecul 454-3
     Mother was afraid I should freeze in the Parisian hotels. [Novel
     457-7
     And mother. How long have you lived and looked, [Golden 461-2
     Peter the voyant, who says "Mother, what is that"-- [Questions
     462-10
     He does not say, "Mother, my mother, who are you," [Questions
     463-2
     That we must calm, the origin of a mother tongue [NH 470-24
     His grief is that his mother should feed on him, himself and
     what he saw, [Madame 507-12
     The black mother of eleven children [Primordia 9-15 P
     There is another whom I love, [Soldat 14-4 P
     Is mother to the two of us, and more, [Soldat 14-6 P
     And mother nature sick of silk [Lulu M 27-11 P
     Like the mother of all nightingales; be wise [Spaniard 35-10 P
     There is a mother whose children need more than that. [Woman Had
     82-1 P
     She is not the mother of landscapes but of those [Woman Had 82-2P

Bald heads with their mother's voice still in their ears.
     [Woman Had 82-16 P
     A majestic mother's flocking brood, [Ulysses 103-25 P
MOTHERLY. Excepting to the motherly footstep, but [C 44-18
MOTHER-OF-PEARL. These streaked the mother-of-pearl, the lunar
     cress. [Greenest 53-24 P
MOTHERS. In the voices of mothers. [Carolinas 4-16
     Our earthly mothers waiting, sleeplessly. [Sunday 69-27
     And of the fragrant mothers the most dear [Fictive 87-8
     It is true there were other mothers, singular [EM 321-23
     These mothers touching, speaking, being near, [Cred 372-17
     In the bandeaux of the mothers, would see again. [NSF 389-18
     Lived in the houses of mothers, arranged ourselves [Rock 525-2
MOTION. In verses wild with motion, full of din, [Monocle 16-12
     And that whatever noise the motion of the waves [Hibiscus 22-12
     Of motion, or of the noise of motion, [Solitaires 60-7
     And, most, of the motion of thought [Solitaires 60-10
     Of night, in which all motion [Curtains 62-7
     "Life Is Motion" [83-title
     Gives motion to perfection more serene [Fictive 87-19
     And apt in versatile motion, touch and sound [Anatomy 108-12
     Will glisten again with motion, the music [Sad Gay 122-17
     Will be motion and full of shadows. [Sad Gay 122-18
     Its empty sleeves; and yet its mimic motion [Key W 128-14
     And that which is the pitch of its motion, [Vari 235-8
     Women invisible in music and motion and color," [Waldorf 241-8
     "The Search for Sound Free from Motion" [268-title
     The weather pink, the wind in motion; and this: [EM 322-24
     As those are: as light, for all its motion, is; [Less 327-16
     Of ideas moves wrinkled in a motion like [Feo 333-21
     In the much-mottled motion of blank time. [Descrip 342-10
     In its abstract motion, [Analysis 348-13
     But it is like a horse. It is like motion [Pieces 352-6
     "Chaos in Motion and Not in Motion" [357-title
     Of things and their motion: the other man, [Silent 360-2
     The west wind was the music, the motion, the force [NSF 397-16
     Grows warm in the motionless motion of his flight, [NSF 404-19
     The soft hands are a motion not a touch. [AA 413-16
     Of motion the ever-brightening origin, [AA 414-24
     For that, or a motion not in the astronomies, [Page 422-17
     But only of your swarthy motion, [Countryman 428-18
     And motion outward, reddened and resolved [Owl 435-20
     At heart, within an instant's motion, within [Orb 440-20
     The river motion, the drowsy motion of the river R. [Old Man
     501-6
     Wet with water and sparkling in the one-ness of their motion.
     [Prol 515-9
     A moving part of a motion, a discovery [Look 518-14
     Of such mixed motion and such imagery [Rock 527-17
     There is his motion [Primordia 7-21 P
MOTIONER. In the space it fills, the silent motioner [Ideal 88-6 A
MOTIONLESS. Marching a motionless march, custodians. [C 42-12
     That is so much motionless sound. [Sad Gay 121-10
     Still moving yet motionless in smoke, still [Hero 273-22
     The curving of her hip, as motionless gesture, [Couch 295-8
     Concentric circles of shadows, motionless [EM 319-7
     The bright obvious stands motionless in cold. [Man Car 351-8
     With one eye watch the willow, motionless. [Cred 377-8
     Grows warm in the motionless motion of his flight, [NSF 404-19
     And yet in space and motionless and yet [AA 414-23
     Impenetrable symbols, motionless. They move [Owl 432-6
     As a place in which each thing was motionless [Old Woman 45-21 P
     Motionless, knowing neither dew nor frost. [Burnshaw 49-15 P
     Of Venice, motionless, gathering time and dust. [Real 110-10 P
MOTIONS. And giving your bland motions to the air. [Swans 4-8
     She made of the motions of her wrist [Infanta 7-13
     Is full of long motions; as the ponderous [Curtains 62-2
     Large-mannered motions to his mythy mind [Sunday 67-29
     Or, if not arrows, then the nimblest motions, [Tallap 72-10
     The motions of the mind and giving form [Eve Angels 137-20
     I hear the motions of the spirit and the sound [Choc 298-18
     Of motions in the mind and heart, [Imago 439-8
     And sees its images, its motions [Imago 439-11
     And multitude of motions [Imago 439-12
     When day comes, fire-foams in the motions of the sea, [NH 488-12
     By our own motions in a freedom of air. [Rock 525-3
     Motions of air, robes moving in torrents of air, [Greenest 53-5 P
     These bands, these swarms, these motions, what of them? [Duck
     62-9 P
MOTIVE. Which was, and is, chief motive, first delight [C 34-28
     On the motive! But one looks at the sea [Vari 233-18
     "The Motive for Metaphor" [288-title
     The motive for metaphor, shrinking from [Motive 288-14
MOTLEY. And large umbrellas. And a motley green [Sea Surf 102-2
     Of green blooms turning crisped the motley hue [Sea Surf 102-12
MOTORS. Except Polacks that pass in their motors [Jersey 210-18
MOTTLED. Them mottled, in the moodiest costumes, [Cred 377-25
     Part of the mottled mood of summer's whole, [Cred 378-5
     See much-mottled.
MOULD. Out of such mildew plucking neater mould [Pharynx 96-14

The person has a mould. But not [MBG 174-5
The blue guitar a mould? That shell? [MBG 174-11
Cadaverous undulations. Rest, old mould . . . [Two V 355-14
MOULDS. The mirror melts and moulds itself and moves [Novel 458-4
MOUNT. The clearest woman with apt weed, to mount [Havana 143-17
MOUNTAIN. Sat tittivating by their mountain pools [Monocle 14-2
  Suckled on ponds, the spirit craves a watery mountain. [NE Verses
   105-2
  Chorals for mountain voices and the moral chant, [Thought 185-16
  While she approached the real, upon her mountain, [Uruguay 249-8
  The mountain collapses. Chopiniana. [Hero 275-4
  True transfigurers fetched out of the human mountain, [Choc
   300-6
  A mountain in which no ease is ever found, [EM 319-3
  It is the mountain on which the tower stands, [Cred 373-22
  It is the final mountain. Here the sun, [Cred 373-23
  It is a mountain half way green and then, [Cred 375-13
  A mountain luminous half way in bloom [Cred 375-22
  The ponderous cinnamon, snarls in his mountain [NSF 384-15
  A mountain, a pineapple pungent as Cuban summer. [NSF 393-12
  His eye and audible in the mountain of [NSF 403-2
  As a moving mountain is, moving through day [Owl 433-10
  Under the sun-slides of a sloping mountain; [Aug 489-11
  "The Poem that Took the Place of a Mountain" [512-title
  The poem that took the place of a mountain. [Poem Mt 512-2
  Of a mountain, expanded and elevated almost [Moonlight 531-11
  Of mountain pallors ebbing into air; [Soldat 13-10 P
  O spirit of bones, O mountain of graves? [Sat Night 28-6 P
  As if, alone on a mountain, it saw far-off [Pagoda 92-5 P
  "July Mountain" [114-title P
  The way, when we climb a mountain, [July 115-4 P
  An Alp, a purple Southern mountain bisqued [Someone 87-3 A
  See: myrrh-mountain; sea-mountain.
MOUNTAIN-BLUE. A mountain-blue cloud arose [Public Sq 109-3
MOUNTAIN-MINDED. There's that mountain-minded Hoon, [Sad Gay 121-15
MOUNTAINOUS. You know the mountainous coiffures of Bath. [Monocle
  14-7
  The mountainous ridges, purple balustrades, [C 33-14
  On high horizons, mountainous atmospheres [Key W 129-21
  A mountainous music always seemed [MBG 179-11
  Regard now the sloping, mountainous rocks [Loaf 199-16
  Of the expanses that are mountainous rock and sea; [Repet 308-24
  Lives in the mountainous character of his speech; [Descrip
   345-12
  And in that mountainous mirror Spain acquires [Descrip 345-13
MOUNTAINS. Are there mandolines of western mountains? [Men 1000
  52-5
  Deer walk upon our mountains, and the quail [Sunday 70-22
  Among twenty snowy mountains, [Thirteen 92-14
  The mountains between our lands and the sea-- [Grapes 110-9
  This conjunction of mountains and sea and our lands-- [Grapes
   110-10
  And mountains and the sea do. And our lands. [Grapes 110-19
  One's self and the mountains of one's land, [MBG 176-12
  One after another washing the mountains bare. [Loaf 200-7
  "A Weak Mind in the Mountains" [212-title
  The mountains are scratched and used, clear fakes. [Arcades
   226-3
  A generation sealed, men remoter than mountains, [Waldorf 241-7
  The mountains inscribe themselves upon the walls. [Extracts
   252-12
  Aux crinolines, smears out mad mountains. [Extracts 257-29
  Of sanctimonious mountains high in snow, [Montra 263-3
  These mountains being high be, also, bright, [Belly 367-5
  "Mountains Covered with Cats" [367-title
  And mountains running like water, wave on wave, [AA 416-6
  Or mountains that were not mountains, just to know how it would
   be, [Cata 425-8
  Mountains appeared with greater eloquence [NH 484-12
  He is born the blank mechanic of the mountains, [Aug 492-17
  Are the cities to breed as mountains bred, the streets [Duck
   61-3 P
  Or from under his mountains. [Myth 118-16 P
MOUNTING. Mounting the earth-lines, long and lax, lethargic.
  [Tallap 72-3
MOURN. When we can mourn no more over music [Sad Gay 121-9
MOURNFUL. Kept waking and a mournful sense sought out, [Montra
  263-5
  And shape and mournful making move to find [AA 418-1
  When the leaves fall like things mournful of the past, [Puel
   456-12
MOUSE. After the sermon, to quiet that mouse in the wall. [Blue
  Bldg 216-20
  And more. Yet the eminent thunder from the mouse, [Blue Bldg
   217-3
  The mouse, the moss, the woman on the shore . . . [Blue Bldg
   217-6
  If the mouse should swallow the steeple, in its time . . . [Blue
   Bldg 217-7
  Go, mouse, go nibble at Lenin in his tomb. [Blue Bldg 217-19

MOUSTACHE. Woman with a vague moustache and not the mauve [EM
  321-15
MOUTH. Without eyes or mouth, that looks at one and speaks. [Yellow
  237-9
  While the water kept running through the mouth of the speaker,
   [Novel 457-17
MOUTHING. Mouthing its constant smatter throughout space. [Montra
  263-19
MOUTH-ORGANS. Playing mouth-organs in the night or, now, guitars.
  [Sick 90-9 P
MOUTHS. Salt masks of beard and mouths of bellowing, [Sea Surf
  101-17
  With faces as with leaves, be gusty with mouths, [Dames 206-9
  And with mouths crying and crying day by day. [Dames 206-10
  With their wide mouths [Lulu G 26-20 P
  See sea-mouths.
MOVABLE. The solid, but the movable, the moment, [NH 472-1
MOVE. Move outward into heaven, [Fabliau 23-6
  Magnificent, would move among his hinds, [Sunday 68-1
  Move in the wind. [Six Sig 73-11
  And moved, as blooms move, in the swimming green [Sea Surf 99-11
  Speak and the sleepers in their sleep shall move, [Havana 145-1
  And as I am, I speak and move [MBG 180-16
  And in the water winding weeds move round. [Glass 197-17
  If the stars that move together as one, disband, [Horn 230-17
  Let him move as the sunlight moves on the floor, [Less 327-11
  Its immaterial monsters move, [Analysis 348-14
  Invisible, they move and are, [Analysis 348-17
  To prepare for bed, in the frame of the house, and move [Lot
   372-2
  To an immaculate end. We move between these points: [NSF 382-17
  Does it move to and fro or is it of both [NSF 396-15
  Should foam, be foamy waves, should move like them, [NSF 399-7
  And shape and mournful making move to find [AA 418-1
  Are, hanging above you, as you move, [Countryman 428-14
  Move blackly and without crystal. [Countryman 428-15
  Two forms move among the dead, high sleep [Owl 431-13
  Impenetrable symbols, motionless. They move [Owl 432-6
  Who can move the German load [Imago 439-2
  Move lightly through the air again. [Imago 439-20
  Breathe slightly, slightly move or seem to move [Bouquet 450-8
  Impalpable habitations that seem to move [NH 466-8
  Why can the horses move about on the ground? [Primordia 8-13 P
  And move the night by their intelligent motes. [Red Kit 32-1 P
  The high clouds will move, [Secret Man 36-11 P
  And that, heavily, you move with them in the dust. [Burnshaw
   50-11 P
  The need for a thesis, a music constant to move. [Woman Had 82-9P
  That move in the air as large as air, [Including 88-10 P
MOVED. He moved among us, as a muttering king, [Sunday 67-30
  And moved, as blooms move, in the swimming green [Sea Surf 99-11
  Moved in the grass without a sound. [MBG 178-14
  And moved again and flashed again, time flashed again. [Martial
   238-16
  Moved on the buried water where they lay. [Descrip 343-5
  In face of which desire no longer moved, [Cred 376-7
  And moved on them in orbits' outer stars [NSF 403-5
  When he moved so slightly to make sure of sun, [AA 411-21
  In the bee-loud glade. Lights on the steamer moved. [Page 422-4
  Subtler than look's declaiming, although she moved [Owl 435-15
  A color that moved us with forgetfulness. [Aug 494-6
  All of them, darkened by time, moved by they know not what,
   amending the airs they play to fulfill themselves; [Piano 21-17P
  Time's fortune near, the sleepless sleepers moved [Duck 61-27 P
  And is. Perhaps I had been moved [Desire 85-11 P
  As he moved, straightly, on and on, [Presence 106-11 P
  As things emerged and moved and were dissolved, [Real 110-14 P
MOVEMENT. Out of the movement of few words, [Oak 272-17
  The armies are cities in movement. But a war [Choc 296-13
  Illumination of movement as he breathed. [Choc 297-18
  It is only that this warmth and movement are like [Wom Sun 445-4
  The warmth and movement of a woman. [Wom Sun 445-5
  And movement of emotion through the air, [Bouquet 449-17
  In the movement of the colors of the mind, [NH 466-9
  In a movement of the outlines of similarity? [Aug 494-14
  Become the figures of heaven, the majestic movement [Rome 508-2
  Destroyed by a vengeful movement of the arms, [Sombre 69-3 P
MOVEMENTS. The movements of fishes. [Homunculus 26-8
  Drifting choirs, long movements and turnings of sounds. [Sick
   90-12 P
MOVES. With him for whom no phantasy moves, [Weep Woman 25-11
  His beard moves in the wind. [Six Sig 73-12
  The pine tree moves in the wind. [Six Sig 73-13
  He moves not on his coppery, keen claws. [Bird Claws 82-15
  Her old light moves along the branches, [Lunar 107-3
  The men are moving as the water moves, [Farewell 118-13
  The sexton moves with a sexton's stare [Gray 140-11
  In this it moves and speaks. [Add 199-10
  The wind moves like a cripple among the leaves [Motive 288-3
  Let him move as the sunlight moves on the floor, [Less 327-11

Of ideas moves wrinkled in a motion like [Feo 333-21
Its line moves quickly with the genius [Pastor 379-9
And fortunate stone. It moves its parade [Imago 439-7
The breadth of an accelerando moves, [Orb 440-15
The moon moves toward the night. [Pecul 453-8
The mirror melts and moulds itself and moves [Novel 458-4
The objects tingle and the spectator moves [NH 470-1
With the objects. But the spectator also moves [NH 470-2
Piercing the tide by which it moves, is constantly within us?
    [Inelegance 26-2 P
Nobly as autumn moves. [Secret-Man 36-12 P
That is completely waste, that moves from waste [Burnshaw 49-22 P
Because time moves on columns intercrossed [Burnshaw 50-13 P
The memory moves on leopards' feet, desire [Greenest 57-16 P
High up in heaven a sprawling portent moves, [Sombre 68-17 P
High up in heaven the sprawling portent moves. [Sombre 70-18 P
And true. The good, the strength, the sceptre moves [Bship
    80-21 P
And larger as it moves, moving toward [Bship 80-24 P
Moves in lamenting and the fatal, [Stan Hero 83-23 P
The wind moves slowly in the branches. [Of Mere 118-5 P
MOVING. The only moving thing [Thirteen 92-15
    The river is moving. [Thirteen 94-19
    Out of the light evolved the moving blooms, [Sea Surf 99-6
    Of water moving on the water-floor? [Sea Surf 100-2
    The men are moving as the water moves, [Farewell 118-13
    Just to stand still without moving a hand. [Adieu 127-12
    And the waves, the waves were soldiers moving, [Loaf 200-10
    Moving round the sky and singing [Dezem 218-10
    Sure enough, moving, the thunder became men, [Thunder 220-1
    Moving among the sleepers, the men, [Candle 223-5
    Moving and being, the image at its source, [Candle 223-13
    The ever-breathing and moving, the constant fire, [Martial 238-9
    Still moving yet motionless in smoke, still [Hero 273-22
    Men are moving and marching [Dutch 290-10
    Is merely the moving of a tongue. [Possum 294-3
    Of their own part, yet moving on the wind, [EM 319-8
    One feels its action moving in the blood. [EM 324-23
    Moving so that the foot-falls are slight and almost nothing.
        [Jouga 337-12
    The moving and the moving of their forms [Descrip 342-9
    A turquoise monster moving round. [Silent 360-3
    Or a leaner being, moving in on him, [NSF 387-14
    So moving in the manner of his hand. [NSF 388-12
    For companies of voices moving there, [NSF 398-16
    In a moving contour, a change not quite completed? [NSF 406-9
    The moving grass, the Indian in his glade. [AA 412-3
    And along the moving of the water-- [Countryman 429-5
    The place of a swarthy presence moving, [Countryman 429-7
    Like many robings, as moving masses are, [Owl 433-9
    As a moving mountain is, moving through day [Owl 433-10
    Moving around and behind, a following, [NH 477-6
    This should be tragedy's most moving face. [NH 477-6
    The bed, the books, the chair, the moving nuns, [Rome 508-21
    On the chair, a moving transparence on the nuns, [Rome 509-4
    No more than a bed, a chair and moving nuns, [Rome 510-4
    A moving part of a motion, a discovery [Look 518-14
    That winter is washed away. Someone is moving [World 520-13
    Conflicting with the moving colors there [Old Woman 44-25 P
    Entwine your arms and moving to and fro, [Burnshaw 47-17 P
    Through a moving chaos that never ends. Mesdames, [Burnshaw 50-23P
    Each other moving in a chant and danced [Burnshaw 50-27 P
    Motions of air, robes moving in torrents of air, [Greenest 53-5 P
    And larger as it moves, moving toward [Bship 80-24 P
    If the sceptre returns to earth, still moving, still [Bship 80-31P
    See wide-moving.
MOW. Mow the grass in the cemetery, darkies, [Norfolk 111-4
    They mow the lawn. A vessel sinks in waves [EM 322-12
MOWS. Baked through long days, is piled in mows. It is [Cred 374-8
MOZART. "Mozart, 1935" [131-title
    We may return to Mozart. [Mozart 132-18
MR. BLANK. To photographs of the late president, Mr. Blank, [NH
    488-15
MR. BURNSHAW. "Mr. Burnshaw and the Statue" [46-title P
    A solemn voice, not Mr. Burnshaw's says: [Burnshaw 49-3 P
MR. HOMBURG. Of Mr. Homburg during his visits home [Look 517-12
    Or so Mr. Homburg thought: the body of a world [Look 519-8
MRS. ALFRED URUGUAY. "Mrs. Alfred Uruguay" [248-title
MRS. ANDERSON. Mrs. Anderson's Swedish baby [Circulat 150-5
MRS. DOOLEY. Something not to be mentioned to Mrs. Dooley, [Aug
    491-23
MRS. PAPPADOPOULOS. Mrs. Pappadopoulos, and thanks. [Couch 296-6
MRS. THRALE. Instead, or Horace Walpole or Mrs. Thrale. [Lytton
    39-20 P
MUCH-CRUMPLED. Shall I uncrumple this much-crumpled thing? [Monocle
    13-16
MUCH-HORNED. In the much-horned night, as its chief personage.
    [Souls 94-17 P
MUCH-MOTTLED. In the much-mottled motion of blank time. [Descrip
    342-10

MUCK. It made, away from the muck of the land [How Live 126-6
MUCKERS. Left here by moonlit muckers when they fled [Burnshaw
    46-22 P
MUD. "Mud Master" [147-title
    There is a master of mud. [Mud 148-5
    The mud master, [Mud 148-10
    In the mud, a missal for that young man, [MBG 177-22
    In the mud, in Monday's dirty light, [MBG 183-16
    I have wiped away moonlight like mud. Your innocent ear [Uruguay
        249-5
    Of what good. Devise. Make him of mud, [Hero 275-21
    In mud under ponds, where the sky used to be reflected. [NH
        487-15
    Mud, water like dirty glass, expressing silence [Plain 503-4
    Only, an eyeball in the mud, [Phases 3-16 P
    Of his angel through the skies. They might be mud [Burnshaw
        46-21 P
    Life's foreigners, pale aliens of the mud, [Greenest 59-23 P
    It is mud and mud long baked in the sun, [Stan MBG 72-6 P
    Breakfast in Paris, music and madness and mud, [Bship 80-3 P
MUD-ANCESTOR. Great mud-ancestor, oozer and Abraham, [Duck 64-29 P
MUDDY. The muddy rivers of spring [Mud 147-13
    Under muddy skies. [Mud 147-15
    The mind is muddy. [Mud 147-17
    There was a muddy centre before we breathed. [NSF 383-19
    More than his muddy hand was in the manes, [Old Woman 43-19 P
    They rise to the muddy, metropolitan elms, [Duck 60-13 P
MUFF. Might muff the mighty spirit of Lenin. [Lytton 39-17 P
MUFFING. As muffing the mistress for her several maids, [EM 316-21
    No memorable muffing, bare and blunt. [Burnshaw 48-8 P
MUFFLED. A deprivation muffled in eclipse, [Red Kit 30-22 P
MUFFLING. The shores are banks of muffling mist. [MBG 172-14
MUFFLINGS. And these, in their mufflings, monsters of elegy, [Owl
    435-23
MULBERRY. The mulberry is a double tree. [Banjo 114-1 P
    Mulberry, shade me, shade me awhile. [Banjo 114-2 P
    Mulberry, shade me, shade me awhile. [Banjo 114-5 P
    Mulberry, shade me, shade me awhile. [Banjo 114-8 P
    Mulberry, shade me, shade me awhile-- [Banjo 114-11 P
    Mulberry, shade me, shade me awhile. [Banjo 114-13 P
MULCTINGS. All this with many mulctings of the man, [C 44-3
MULE. To ride an old mule round the keys-- [Stan MBG 73-7 P
    In such an air, poor as one's mule. [Stan MBG 73-11 P
    Blond weather. Give the mule his hay. [Stan MBG 73-17 P
MULES. The mules that angels ride come slowly down [Monocle 15-18
MULETEERS. These muleteers are dainty of their way. [Monocle 15-21
MULTIFARIOUS. The multifarious heavens felt no awe [Geneva 24-8
MULTIFORM. The multiform beauty, sinking in night wind, [Soldat
    12-4 P
MULTIPLEX. And the miraculous multiplex of lesser poems, [Orb 442-5
MULTIPLIED. That the walls are mirrors multiplied, [Prelude 195-2
    Sunrise is multiplied, [Three 143-10 P
    As red is multiplied by the leaves of trees. [Three 143-14 P
MULTITUDE. Blessed, who is his nation's multitude. [NE Verses 105-4
    Of a multitude dwindles, all said, [MBG 171-15
    If they could! Or is it the multitude of thoughts, [Extracts
        254-13
    A little nearer by each multitude, [Montra 262-2
    Are a multitude of individual pomps [Paisant 334-22
    As that of a personage in a multitude: [Cred 377-4
    To be crested and wear the mane of a multitude [NSF 398-8
    And multitude of motions [Imago 439-12
    Adorned for a multitude, in a gesture spent [Sombre 71-27 P
MULTITUDES. The single thought? The multitudes of men [Extracts
    254-15
MULTITUDINOUS. And storming under multitudinous tones [C 28-15
MUMBLE. They heard his mumble in the morning light. [Phases 5-11 P
    It is a special day. We mumble the words [Nuns 92-18 P
MUMBLED. Mumbled zay-zay and a-zay, a-zay. [Ord Women 11-2
MUMBLES. Is a cloud in which a voice mumbles. [Lack 303-8
    The poet mumbles and the painter sees, [Orb 443-16
MUMBLING. A voice was mumbling, "Everything [Reader 147-5
    Mumbling a secret, passionate message. [Hero 276-18
    Mumbling and musing of the silent farm. [Phases 5-10 P
    Mumbling and musing like the most forlorn. [Phases 5-14 P
    A mumbling at the elbow, turgid tunes, [Sombre 67-10 P
MUMMERY. Although life seems a goblin mummery, [Soldat 13-14 P
MUNCHES. He munches a dry shell while he exerts [Bird Claws 82-16
MUNDI. Regulae mundi, as apprentice of [Bship 78-21 P
    Regulae mundi . . . . That much is out of the way. [Bship 80-30 P
MUNDO. I call you by name, my green, my fluent mundo. [NSF 407-2
MURDEROUS. Against the murderous alphabet: [MBG 179-8
MURDERS. The metaphor that murders metaphor. [Someone 84-6 A
MURKY. And murky masonry, one wonders [Ulysses 100-29 P
MURMUR. Bottles, pots, shoes and grass and murmur aptest eve:
    [Dump 203-7
    Whose heart will murmur with the music that will be a voice for
        her, speaking the dreaded change of speech; [Piano 22-2 P
MURMURING. To-night, night's undeciphered murmuring [Montra 261-1
    Becomes another murmuring; the smell [Rome 508-19

MUSCADINES. Even the musky muscadines, [Reader 147-7
MUSCLE. Now, every muscle slops away. [Hartford 227-9
MUSCLES. Its muscles are his own . . . [Destructive 193-3
   The muscles of a magnet aptly felt, [Orb 442-15
   To the muscles' very tip for the vivid plunge, [Old Woman 43-11 P
MUSCULAR. The muscular one, and bid him whip [Emperor 64-2
   In the muscular poses of the museums? [Nigger 153-12
   On more than muscular shoulders, arms and chest, [Choc 297-12
   They ought to be muscular men, [Drum-Majors 37-7 P
   Would flash in air, and the muscular bodies thrust [Old Woman
     46-9 P
   Were mechanical, muscular. They never changed, [Woman Had 81-20 P
MUSE. And musicians who mute much, muse much, on the tales. [AA
     415-6
   The muse of misery? Speak loftier lines. [Bad Time 427-7
   Cry out, "I am the purple muse." Make sure [Bad Time 427-8
   Seen by a muse. . . . [Soldat 16-6 P
MUSED. But muted, mused, and perfectly revolved [C 45-24
   The wide night mused by tell-tale muttering, [Duck 61-26 P
MUSEO. A Museo Olimpico, so much [Descrip 342-3
MUSES. But muses on its eccentricity, [Jasmine 79-6
MUSEUM. In the museum of the sky. The cock [MBG 182-18
   Like a euphony in a museum [Hero 274-8
   Is a museum of things seen. Sight, [Hero 274-13
MUSEUMS. In the muscular poses of the museums? [Nigger 153-12
   But my destroyers avoid the museums. [Nigger 153-13
   Souvenirs of museums. But, Master, there are [Hartford 226-13
MUSIC. For the music and manner of the paladins [Monocle 16-20
   And not for stupor, such as music makes [C 31-15
   Than the revenge of music on bassoons. [C 32-25
   And in their music showering sounds intone. [C 37-32
   Of music, as it comes to unison, [C 43-12
   And sounds of music coming to accord [C 45-26
   Or if the music sticks, if the anecdote [C 45-30
   Of speech which are like music so profound [On Manner 55-13
   Are the music of meet resignation; these [On Manner 56-4
   Of idiosyncratic music. [Jasmine 79-3
   "To the One of Fictive Music" [87-title
   Now, of the music summoned by the birth [Fictive 87-14
   That music is intensest which proclaims [Fictive 88-2
   Make music, so the selfsame sounds [Peter 89-17
   On my spirit make a music, too. [Peter 89-18
   Music is feeling, then, not sound; [Peter 90-1
   Is music. It is like the strain [Peter 90-5
   Susanna's music touched the bawdy strings [Peter 92-8
   There is no pith in music [Orangeade 103-1
   When the music of the boy fell like a fountain, [Norfolk 111-14
   For music, for whisperings from the reefs. [Farewell 117-18
   Where is sun and music and highest heaven's lust, [Ghosts 119-6
   When we can mourn no more over music [Sad Gay 121-9
   Some harmonious skeptic soon in a skeptical music [Sad Gay 122-15
   Will glisten again with motion, the music [Sad Gay 122-17
   Music began to fail him. Brahms, although [Anglais 148-13
   In speech. He has that music and himself. [Anglais 149-7
   In music. Crow is realist. But, then, [Nigger 154-15
   Music is not yet written but is to be. [Nigger 158-3
   Melodious skeletons, for all of last night's music [Fish-Scale
     160-15
   Exceeding music must take the place [MBG 167-11
   A mountainous music always seemed [MBG 179-11
   Sounded in music, if the sun, [Prelude 194-13
   Of music--Her body lies [Add 199-2
   That had flashed (like vicious music that ends [Thunder 220-11
   Of one wilder than the rest (like music blunted, [Thunder 220-23
   A music more than a breath, but less [Vari 232-7
   Women invisible in music and motion and color," [Waldorf 241-8
   It is the music of the mass of meaning. [Extracts 256-10
   And there to find music for a single line, [Extracts 259-16
   The vital music formulates the words. [Extracts 259-18
   Of each old revolving dance, the music [Hero 274-7
   Compelled thereto by an innate music. [Hero 277-18
   What unisons create in music. [Hero 280-4
   Picking thin music on the rustiest string, [God 285-13
   Finding its way from the house, makes music seem [Phenom 287-1
   Than the most metal music, loudlier, [Dutch 291-11
   And the mother, the name, the name; the scholar, [Choc 300-4
   If the poetry of X was music, [Creat 310-10
   A transparence in which we heard music, made music, [EM 316-10
   Another and later genesis, music [EM 321-6
   The inimical music, the enchantered space [Pure 330-14
   Of this precarious music, the change of key [Pure 332-3
   Come true, a point in the fire of music where [Descrip 341-9
   Propounds blank final music. [Burghers 362-18
   Appoints man's place in music, say, today. [NSF 382-2
   And a familiar music of the machine [NSF 386-13
   The music halted and the horse stood still. [NSF 391-12
   Music falls on the silence like a sense, [NSF 392-10
   Like a page of music, like an upper air, [NSF 397-13
   The west wind was the music, the motion, the force [NSF 397-16
   To find of light a music issuing [NSF 398-18

Its thin-stringed music, [Our Stars 454-16
   Of right joining, a music of ideas, the burning [Study II 465-1
   As the fore-meaning in music is." Again, [NH 485-12
   Behind the outer shields, the sheets of music [NH 488-10
   Whose heart will murmur with the music that will be a voice for
     her, speaking the dreaded change of speech; [Piano 22-2 P
   And these long, black instruments will be so little to them that
     will be needing so much, seeking so much in their music.
     [Piano 22-9 P
   Or this, whose music, sweeping irradiation of a sea-night,
     [Inelegance 26-1 P
   Her music should repeat itself in you, [Red Kit 31-14 P
   Then, while the music makes you, make, yourselves, [Burnshaw
     47-23 P
   Into a music never touched to sound. [Greenest 54-11 P
   The masks of music. We perceive each mask [Sombre 67-22 P
   The strong music of hard times, [Grotesque 76-13 P
   Breakfast in Paris, music and madness and mud, [Bship 80-3 P
   The need for a thesis, a music constant to move, [Woman Had 82-9P
   Waits for the unison of the music of the drifting bands [Sick
     90-14 P
   A passage of music, a paragraph [Ulysses 103-2 P
   And music that lasts long and lives the more. [Art Pop 113-6 P
   In things said well in music, [July 114-17 P
   See sub-music.
MUSICAL. And crisply musical, or holy caverns temple-toned, [Burn-
    shaw 47-16 P
MUSICIAN. Of snails, musician of pears, principium [C 27-9
   For this, musician, in your girdle fixed [Fictive 88-14
   "Thunder by the Musician" [220-title
   Who was the musician, fatly soft [Jumbo 269-4
   Or in the dark musician, listening [Descrip 340-21
   To be the musician's own and, thence, become [Sombre 67-23 P
MUSICIANS. Which, let the tall musicians call and call, [C 41-16
   For these the musicians make insidious tones, [AA 415-10
   And musicians who mute much, muse much, on the tales. [AA 415-6
   Among these the musicians strike the instinctive poem. [AA
     415-16
   These musicians dubbing at a tragedy, [AA 415-24
MUSING. Musing immaculate, pampean dits, [C 38-25
   And of all vigils musing the obscure, [Fictive 88-4
   To the auroral creature musing in the mind. [Montra 263-24
   Mumbling and musing of the silent farm. [Phases 5-10 P
   Mumbling and musing like the most forlorn. [Phases 5-14 P
MUSK. In a birth of sight. The blooming and the musk [Rock 526-7
MUSKY. Their musky and tingling tongues. [Bananas 54-23
   And made one think of musky chocolate [Sea Surf 101-7
   Even the musky muscadines, [Reader 147-7
MUSLIN. And Rosa, the muslin dreamer of satin and cowry-kin, dis-
    daining the empty keys; and the young infanta, [Piano 22-3 P
MUST. One must have a mind of winter [Snow Man 9-21
   The ephemeral blues must merge for them in one, [Monocle 15-8
   That must belie the racking masquerade, [C 39-16
   There must be no cessation [Solitaires 60-6
   Divinity must live within herself: [Sunday 67-19
   The blackbird must be flying. [Thirteen 94-20
   From the loosed girdles in the spangling must. [Sea Surf 101-14
   This must be the vent of pity, [Orangeade 103-17
   Civilization must be destroyed. The hairy saints [NE Verses 106-1
   She must come now. The grass is in seed and high. [Ghosts 119-11
   But the romantic must never remain, [Sailing 120-15
   Mon Dieu, and must never again return. [Sailing 120-16
   Of the soul must likewise be at fault, and first. [Lions 124-20
   Must be the crux for our compendia. [Havana 143-24
   Must be the place for prodigy, unless [Havana 144-2
   Must miss the symmetry of a leaden mate, [Nigger 152-19
   Must see her fans of silver undulate. [Nigger 152-20
   For all his purple, the purple bird must have [Nigger 155-20
   It must create its colors out of itself. [Nigger 158-2
   And they said then, "But play, you must, [MBG 165-7
   Exceeding music must take the place [MBG 167-11
   Ourselves in poetry must take their place, [MBG 167-13
   Must be. It could be nothing else. [MBG 171-22
   It must be this rhapsody or none, [MBG 183-1
   Throw the lights away. Nothing must stand [MBG 183-10
   The world must be measured by eye"; [On Road 204-4
   Was heaven where you thought? It must be there. [Blue Bldg 217-14
   It must be where you think it is, in the light [Blue Bldg 217-15
   The truth must live within herself. [Poem Morn 219-12
   Who speaks? But it must be that I, [Peaches 224-7
   This? A man must be very poor [Arcades 225-20
   And must be loved, as one loves that [Yellow 236-17
   It must [Of Mod 240-19
   It must be that the hand [Rhythms 245-18
   Of the self that must sustain itself on speech, [Beard 247-17
   Must struggle like the rest." She climbed until [Uruguay 249-1
   Must be in a fiction. It is time to choose. [Oboe 250-8
   That the mind is the end and must be satisfied. [Extracts 257-15
   Man must become the hero of his world. [Montra 261-12
   The salty skeleton must dance because [Montra 261-13

He must, in the aroma of summer nights, [Montra 261-14
There must be mercy in Asia and divine [Montra 262-16
Of the garden. We must prepare to hear the Roamer's [Phenom
  286-17
An end must come in a merciless triumph, [Dutch 291-15
In the yes of the realist spoken because he must [EM 320-12
The politics of emotion must appear [EM 324-29
Of ideas and to say as usual that there must be [Bed 326-17
If there must be a god in the house, must be, [Less 327-9
His stars on the wall. He must dwell quietly. [Less 327-14
He must be incapable of speaking, closed, [Less 327-15
If there must be a god in the house, let him be one [Less 328-7
We knew one parent must have been divine, [Pure 331-19
We must enter boldly that interior world [Feo 333-16
And a pineapple on the table. It must be so. [Paisant 335-16
And because what we say of the future must portend, [Descrip
  346-2
The poem must resist the intelligence [Man Car 350-13
Out of a storm we must endure all night, [Man Car 351-4
We must endure our thoughts all night, until [Man Car 351-7
And this must comfort the heart's core against [Cred 372-15
As good. The utmost must be good and is [Cred 374-18
Must take its place, as what is possible [Cred 376-23
It Must Be Abstract [NSF 380-title 1
You must become an ignorant man again [NSF 380-15
Must bear no name, gold flourisher, but be [NSF 381-14
It must be visible or invisible, [NSF 385-19
It Must Change [NSF 389-title 2
It Must Give Pleasure [NSF 398-title 3
Each must the other take not for his high, [NSF 401-11
Each must the other take as sign, short sign [NSF 401-14
It is possible, possible, possible. It must [NSF 404-4
Be possible. It must be that in time [NSF 404-5
If he must, or lives on the bread of faithful speech. [NSF 408-3
It must change from destiny to slight caprice. [AA 417-23
What must unmake it and, at last, what can, [AA 418-2
There must be no questions. It is an intellect [Ulti 429-19
Is of a nature that must be perceived [Papini 447-4
And not imagined. The removes must give, [Papini 447-5
That we must calm, the origin of a mother tongue [NH 470-24
The great cat must stand potent in the sun. [NH 473-3
And Juda becomes New Haven or else must. [NH 473-15
It was a language he spoke, because he must, yet did not know.
  [Madame 507-7
We must be cured of it by a cure of the ground [Rock 526-11
It is the rock where tranquil must adduce [Rock 528-14
There must be a planet that is copper [Mandolin 29-2 P
In this spent world, she must possess. The gift [Red Kit 30-19 P
Let this be as it may. It must have tears [Spaniard 35-13 P
Must blow. [Room Gard 40-18 P
There, too, he saw, since he must see, the domes [Greenest
  54-12 P
Racking the world with clarion puffs. This must [Greenest 56-12 P
To make its factories content, must have [Greenest 58-20 P
Benitia, lapis Ville des Pins must soothe [Greenest 58-22 P
The summer Sundays in the park, must be [Duck 66-4 P
We must have the throstle on the gramophone. [Duck 66-8 P
Come, baffling discontent. These too, must be [Sombre 69-19 P
The future must bear within it every past, [Sombre 70-5 P
And must be, when the portent, changed, takes on [Sombre 70-12 P
Must be played on the concertina. [Grotesque 76-16 P
It is the absolute why must it be [Bship 79-8 P
It must be the hand of one, it must be the hand [Bship 81-8 P
As these depend, so must they use. [Ulysses 104-23 P
The image must be of the nature of its creator. [Myth 118-11 P
He must say nothing of the fruit that is [Someone 84-4 A
Not true, nor think it, less. He must defy [Someone 84-5 A
MUSTACHIOS. Dibbled in waves that were mustachios, [C 27-20
MUSTIEST. Through the mustiest blue of the lake [Sailing 120-18
MUSTY. And the mighty, musty belly of tears. [Sat Night 28-3 P
  This atmosphere in which her musty mind [Old Woman 44-20 P
MUTABLE. Of mutable plume, [Analysis 348-19
MUTE. And general lexicographer of mute [C 28-11
  Than mute bare splendors of the sun and moon. [On Manner 56-8
  This is the mute, the final sculpture [Yellow 236-9
  Either trumpets or drums, the commanders mute, the arms [Martial
  238-1
And musicians who mute much, muse much, on the tales. [AA 415-6
  See deaf-mute.
MUTED. But muted, mused, and perfectly revolved [C 45-24
  Muted the night. [Peter 91-8
  Themselves transposed, muted and comforted [NH 467-24
MUTES. Of bliss beyond the mutes of plaster, [Jasmine 79-8
MUTING. Like the last muting of winter as it ends. [Look 519-3
MUTTER. Ach, Mutter, [Explan 72-13
  Made the maelstrom oceans mutter. [Lulu M 27-14 P
MUTTERING. He moved among us, as a muttering king, [Sunday 67-30
  Who are the mossy cronies muttering, [Dutch 292-10
  These actors still walk in a twilight muttering lines. [NH
  479-23

Of the unknown. The newsboys' muttering [Rome 508-18
  The wide night mused by tell-tale muttering, [Duck 61-26 P
MUTTERS. Still by the sea-side mutters milky lines [Oboe 250-13
MUZZY. Smacking their muzzy bellies in parade, [High-Toned 59-16
MYOSOTIS. And sees the myosotis on its bush. [NSF 382-8
MYRRH. It is full of the myrrh and camphor of summer [Aug 490-4
MYRRH-MOUNTAIN. "Late Hymn from the Myrrh-Mountain" [349-title
MYRTLE. The myrtle, if the myrtle ever bloomed, [C 34-13
  Myrtle, viburnums, daffodils, blue phlox), [Dump 202-13
MYRTLES. But leave a bed beneath the myrtles. [Norfolk 111-6
  See sea-myrtles.
MYSELF. Or was it that I mocked myself alone? [Monocle 13-6
  The loneliest air, not less was I myself. [Hoon 65-9
  I was myself the compass of that sea: [Hoon 65-15
  Or heard or felt came not but from myself; [Hoon 65-17
  And there I found myself more truly and more strange. [Hoon
  65-18
  If I had imagined myself, [Explan 73-1
  I measure myself [Six Sig 74-4
  For myself, I live by leaves, [Botanist 1 134-14
  And in perceiving this I best perceive myself [Re-state 146-3
  Myself, and then may be myself [MBG 175-6
  And play of the monster and of myself, [MBG 175-12
  Or better not of myself at all, [MBG 175-13
  "This image, this love, I compose myself [Rhythms 246-4
  To everything, in order to get at myself. [Uruguay 249-4
  I nourish myself. I defend myself against [Repet 308-14
  The world is myself, life is myself, [Pediment 361-17
  And myself am precious for your perfecting. [NSF 396-9
  And out of myself. [Our Stars 455-2
  Myself, only half of a figure of a sort, [Angel 497-6
  Do I commend myself to leafy things [Stan MMO 19-17 P
  As for myself, I feel a doubt: [Lytton 39-10 P
  It would be done. If, only to please myself, [Bship 78-10 P
  "I shall sing to myself no more." [Three 135-2 P
MYSTERIES. Or thrush, or any singing mysteries? [Sonatina 110-2
MYSTERIOUS. Across the stale, mysterious seasons. These [On Manner
  56-3
  Is it, once more, the mysterious beauté, [Soldat 12-1 P
MYSTERY. Unwilling that mercy should be a mystery [Rome 510-17
MYSTIC. Memorabilia of the mystic spouts, [Monocle 16-24
  Mystic Garden & Middling Beast [Thought 185-title 2
  And the idea of man, the mystic garden and [Thought 185-20
  In the object seen and saved that mystic [Hero 278-27
  There was a mystic marriage in Catawba, [NSF 401-4
  Dark Juan looks outward through his mystic brow . . . [Luther
  461-14
  We hear, what we are, beyond mystic disputation, [Look 518-11
  In a mystic eye, no sign of life but life, [Armor 529-14
  So she, when in her mystic aureole [Red Kit 31-10 P
  As brilliant as mystic, as mystic as single, all [Greenest 55-9 P
  The jewels in his beard, the mystic wand, [Bship 79-4 P
MYSTICAL. Gesticulating lightning, mystical, [C 32-26
  Death is the mother of beauty, mystical, [Sunday 69-25
  Form mystical convolutions in the sleep [EM 319-9
  Except for that crown and mystical cabala. [AA 417-21
  The doubling second things, not mystical, [Bouquet 451-18
  Unless society is a mystical mass. [Bship 79-30 P
  A freedom at last from the mystical, [Ulysses 101-11 P
MYSTICS. And bound. Its nigger mystics should change [Prelude
  195-11
MYSTIQUE. Almost a nigger fragment, a mystique [News 265-9
MYTH. And serener myth [Havana 143-11
  This urgent, competent, serener myth [Havana 143-19
  Than Tartuffe as myth, the most Molière, [Paisant 335-10
  What should we be without the sexual myth, [Men Made 355-15
  There was a myth before the myth began, [NSF 383-20
  If properly misunderstood becomes a myth. [Lytton 38-15 P
  Of attributes, naked of myth, true, [Stan Hero 84-11 P
MYTHICAL. When applied to the mythical. [Lytton 39-9 P
MYTHOLOGICAL. A mythological form, a festival sphere, [NH 466-2
MYTHOLOGY. What counted was mythology of self, [C 28-5
  This is the mythology of modern death [Owl 435-22
  "A Mythology Reflects Its Region" [118-title P
  A mythology reflects its region. Here [Myth 118-7 P
  When mythology was possible --But if we had-- [Myth 118-9 P
MYTHS. Around the sun. The wheel survives the myths. [Sleight
  222-11
  Not one of the masculine myths we used to make, [Look 518-7
  Applied on earth to those that were myths [Lytton 39-12 P
MYTHY. Large-mannered motions to his mythy mind [Sunday 67-29
  The twilights of the mythy goober khan. [Havana 142-21

NAAMAN. To feast . . . Slice the mango, Naaman, and dress it
    [Phenom 286-14
NABOB. Any azure under-side of after-color. Nabob [Landsc 241-19
NAG. Why nag at the ideas of Hercules, Don Don? [NE Verses 104-1
NAIL. To nail his thought across the door, [MBG 166-7
NAILED. Under the buttonwoods, beneath a moon nailed fast. [Cata
    425-5
NAILED-UP. 7. These lozenges are nailed-up lattices. [Someone
    86-10 A
NAIVE. And curtains like a naive pretence of sleep. [AA 415-15
NAKED. Naked among them, like a savage source. [Sunday 70-3
    The body walks forth naked in the sun [Anatomy 108-8
    Only last year he said that the naked moon [Anglais 148-19
    When he was young), naked and alien, [Anglais 149-2
    Do I sit, deformed, a naked egg, [MBG 173-4
    Never the naked politician taught [Dames 206-17
    When male light fell on the naked back [Hartford 227-7
    A naked man who regarded himself in the glass [Landsc 241-16
    And I, if I rode naked, are what remain." [Uruguay 249-6
    In the end, however naked, tall, there is still [Oboe 250-17
    To naked men, to women naked as rain. [Extracts 252-14
    And in what covert, may we, naked, be [Extracts 252-17
    And naked of any illusion, in poverty, [Extracts 258-18
    The naked man, the naked man as last [Montra 262-11
    To project the naked man in a state of fact, [Montra 263-11
    Our man beheld the naked, nameless dame, [Hand 271-3
    Naked of hindrance, a thousand crystals. [Hero 279-28
    And naked, or almost so, into the grotesque [Lot 371-17
    Of being naked, or almost so, in a world [Lot 371-18
    Is never naked. A fictive covering [NSF 396-11
    In masks, can choir it with the naked wind? [AA 415-3
    Naked Alpha, not the hierophant Omega, [NH 469-5
    A naked being with a naked will [NH 480-6
    And thereby lost, and naked or in rags, [NH 484-17
    Meets nakedly another's naked voice. [Aug 489-15
    Crude captains, the naked majesty, if you like, [Rome 510-9
    The spirit wakes in the night wind--is naked. [Soldat 11-13 P
    ("The Naked Eye of the Aunt") [Stan MMO 19-Subtitle P
    And I fly forth, the naked Proserpine.[Infernale 25-8 P
    Naked and stamping the earth, [Drum-Majors 37-8 P
    A fear too naked for her shadow's shape. [Old Woman 44-12 P
    The spirit's ring and seal, the naked heart. [Bship 79-13 P
    Of attributes, naked of myth, true, [Stan Hero 84-11 P
    See half-naked.
NAKEDEST. As foregoing the nakedest passion for barefoot [EM 316-22
NAKEDLY. Shine alone, shine nakedly, shine like bronze, [Nuances
    18-8
    I am the woman stripped more nakedly [NSF 396-1
    Meets nakedly another's naked voice. [Aug 489-15
NAKEDNESS. A sinewy nakedness. A river bore [C 36-5
    So that her nakedness is near, [Lilacs 49-4
    Making recoveries of young nakedness [Tallap 72-11
    The nakedness would rise and suddenly turn [Sea Surf 101-16
    And the nakedness became the broadest blooms, [Sea Surf 101-20
    But nakedness, woolen massa, concerns an innermost atom. [Nudity
    Cap 145-10
    Beyond the knowledge of nakedness, as part [Extracts 252-18
    Fall down through nakedness to nakedness, [Montra 263-23
    A civil nakedness in which to be, [Repet 310-6
    Of nakedness, in the company of the sun, [Lot 371-19
    Than nakedness, standing before an inflexible [NSF 396-2
    The nothingness was a nakedness, a point, [NSF 402-21
    The nothingness was a nakedness, a point [NSF 403-9
    Even his own will and in his nakedness [NH 480-8
    Sleek in a natural nakedness, [Hermit 505-14
NAME. Was name for this short-shanks in all that brunt? [C 28-16
    As in your name, an image that is sure, [Fictive 88-6
    This dance has no name. It is a hungry dance. [Mice 123-5
    But the name of a bird and the name of a nameless air [Autumn
    160-6
    A nigger tree and with a nigger name, [News 265-2
    That of that light Eulalia was the name. [Phenom 287-14
    You were created of your name, the word [Phenom 287-17
    You are that white Eulalia of the name. [Phenom 287-22
    And the mother, the music, the name; the scholar, [Choc 300-4
    Or by whatever boorish name a man [Choc 300-22
    By the illustrious nothing of her name. [Descrip 339-8
    And seems to be on the saying of her name. [Descrip 339-14
    Or any name. [Analysis 348-16
    That, nameless, it creates an affectionate name, [Pastor 379-15
    A name for something that never could be named. [NSF 381-11
    Must bear no name, gold flourisher, but be [NSF 381-14
    Without a name and nothing to be desired, [NSF 385-14
    That I should name you flatly, waste no words, [NSF 406-13
    I call you by name, my green, my fluent mundo. [NSF 407-2
    The name. He does not speak beside you. [Countryman 429-1
    Slowly, to the look of a swarthy name. [Countryman 429-8
    A name and privilege over the ordinary of his commonplace--

    [Prol 517-4
    Repeating his name with its patient syllables, [World 521-17
    Meet in the name [Primordia 7-19 P
    By her sexual name, saying that that high marriage [Desire 85-5 P
    Which, just to name, is to create [Ulysses 104-27 P
    For which a fresh name always occurred, as if [Local 112-5 P
    11. There is an island Palahude by name-- [Someone 86-14 A
NAMED. A name for something that never could be named. [NSF 381-11
    The blue woman looked and from her window named [NSF 399-21
    Nothing until this named thing nameless is [AA 416-23
    See: loosely-named; never-named.
NAMELESS. And nameless, [Vincentine 52-14
    But the name of a bird and the name of a nameless air [Autumn
    160-6
    Our man beheld the naked, nameless dame, [Hand 271-3
    That, nameless, it creates an affectionate name, [Pastor 379-15
    Nothing until this named thing nameless is [AA 416-23
    It became, the nameless, flitting characters-- [NH 479-22
    The consolations of space are nameless things. [NH 482 16
NAMES. That apprehends the most which sees and names, [Fictive 88-5
    But do not use the rotted names. [MBG 183-6
    Triangles and the names of girls. [Dezem 218-4
    Contrasting our two names, considered speech. [Phenom 287-16
    No names. Dismiss him from your images. [NSF 388-14
    She hid them under simple names. She held [NSF 402-8
    And peace is cousin by a hundred names [Owl 432-11
    In the names of St. Paul and of the halo-John [Luther 461-5
    The bells keep on repeating solemn names [Rome 510-15
    The trees have a look as if they bore sad names [Slug 522-5
    The right to use. Need names on its breath [Ulysses 104-25 P
NANZIA NUNZIO. On her trip around the world, Nanzia Nunzio [NSF
    395-16
NAPLES. In a man-makenesse, neater than Naples. [Vari 235-18
    He was at Naples writing letters home [EM 313-11
NARCISSUS. Ancestor of Narcissus, prince [Jumbo 269-16
NARRATION. Like rhetoric in a narration of the eye-- [Pure 331-18
    Was repeated by Liadoff in a narration [Liadoff 347-2
NARRATIVE. Engaged in the most prolific narrative, [Phenom 287-5
NARROW. That passed beyond us through the narrow sky. [Medit 124-6
NASSAU. If Shasta roared up in Nassau, [Agenda 42-2 P
NATION. Blessed, who is his nation's multitude. [NE Verses 105-4
    Say that the hero is his nation, [Hero 279-15
    The invention of a nation in a phrase, [Descrip 345-16
    And the banners of the nation flutter, burst [NSF 390-22
    An enormous nation happy in a style, [NH 468-17
    Lucidity of his city, joy of his nation, [Aug 492-2
    The race, the nation, the state. But society [Bship 79-21 P
NATIONAL. The humming-bird is the national bird [Grotesque 75-1 P
NATIONS. To be admired by all men. Nations live [Paisant 334-19
    To be admired by nations. The race is brave. [Paisant 334-20
    To the nations of the clear invisible, [NH 474-24
    In flowery nations, crashing and alert. [Greenest 55-4 P
NATIVE. I am a native in this world [MBG 180-5
    And think in it as a native thinks, [MBG 180-6
    Gesu, not native of a mind [MBG 180-7
    Native, a native in the world [MBG 180-9
    And like a native think in it. [MBG 180-10
    Was native to him in that height, searching [Choc 301-22
    Into that native shield she slid, [Celle 438-17
    Or down a well. Breathe freedom, oh, my native, [Aug 490-13
    Than the thought that once was native to the skull; [Burnshaw
    49-18 P
    With someone to speak her dulcied native tongue, [Letters 107-17P
NATIVES. The natives of the rain are rainy men. [C 37-27
    Natives of poverty, children of malheur, [EM 322-18
    Itself, a nature to its natives all [Orb 442-13
    Natives of a dwindled sphere. [Leben 504-21
NATURAL. Are as natural sounds [Men 1000 51-16
    Ah, but the meaningless, natural effigy! [Nigger 153-17
    It is the natural tower of all the world, [Cred 373-16
    In sleep its natural form. It was enough [NSF 399-12
    You remain the more than natural figure. You [NSF 406-17
    Sleek in a natural nakedness, [Hermit 505-14
    Stands in a light, its natural light and day, [Armor 530-20
    The spirit's natural images, carriers, [Greenest 57-12 P
    As man is natural, would be at an end." [Bship 78-19 P
    Should be as natural as natural objects, [Conversat 109-4 P
NATURE. That not one curl in nature has survived? [Monocle 14-9
    Observed, when young, the nature of mankind, [Monocle 17-22
    The return to social nature, once begun, [C 43-20
    Nature as Pinakothek. Whist! Chanticleer. . . . [NE Verses 106-10
    Our nature is her nature. Hence it comes, [Anatomy 107-16
    Since by our nature we grow old, earth grows [Anatomy 108-1
    And true savant of this dark nature be. [Sun March 134-8
    Marx has ruined Nature, [Botanist 1 134-12
    As part of nature he is part of us. [Havana 144-18
    Concerning the nature of things as they are. [MBG 177-20
    But in nature it merely grows. [Add 198-7
    What in nature merely grows. [Add 198-17
    To change nature, not merely to change ideas, [Vari 234-1

It was his nature to suppose, [Landsc 242-15
Of paper is of the nature of its world. [Extracts 252-9
To be a nature, a place in which itself [Phenom 287-2
That is an instant nature, brilliantly. [Choc 301-13
Livre de Toutes Sortes de Fleurs d'après Nature. [EM 316-7
From nature, each time he saw it, making it, [EM 316-18
This force of nature in action is the major [EM 324-8
Night is the nature of man's interior world? [Feo 333-14
There is a nature that is grotesque within [Feo 334-4
And of its nature, the idiom thereof. [NSF 387-21
As pure principle. Its nature is its end, [AA 418-11
Itself, a nature to its natives all [Orb 442-13
Is of a nature that must be perceived [Papini 447-4
Of medium nature, this farouche extreme [Bouquet 448-5
To the things of medium nature, as meta-men [Bouquet 449-11
Of words that was a change of nature, more [NH 487-6
A nature that is created in what it says, [Aug 490-21
The nature of its women in the air, [Aug 491-16
And, seated in the nature of his chair, [Aug 493-22
In less than nature. He is not here yet. [Aug 495-23
The breath of another nature as his own, [Two Illus 513-15
A nature still without a shape, [Two Illus 514-1
A pensive nature, a mechanical [Look 517-18
The mannerism of nature caught in a glass [Look 519-10
Two figures in a nature of the sun, [Rock 525-17
And mother nature sick of silk [Lulu M 27-11 P
And father nature, full of butter [Lulu M 27-13 P
The truth in nature to espy [Room Gard 41-8 P
A grace to nature, a changeless element. [Greenest 59-30 P
A nature of marble in a marble world. [Conversat 109-10 P
And human nature, pensively seated [Region 115-14 P
The image must be of the nature of its creator. [Myth 118-11 P
It is the nature of its creator increased, [Myth 118-12 P
A wholly artificial nature, in which [Someone 83-2 A
As a part of the nature that he contemplates [Someone 84-17 A
And what heroic nature of what text [Ideal 89-4 A
NATURES. The feelings of the natures round us here: [Vari 234-4
The flags are natures newly found. [Dutch 291-1
Two things of opposite natures seem to depend [NSF 392-4
NAUGHT. So barely lit, so shadowed over and naught, [Quiet 523-3
NAVE. Take the moral law and make a nave of it [High-Toned 59-2
And from the nave build haunted heaven. [High-Toned 59-3
NEAR. So that her nakedness is near, [Lilacs 49-4
I knew my enemy was near--I, [Cuban 65-5
When my dream was near the moon, [Six Sig 74-14
Most near, most clear, and of the clearest bloom, [Fictive 87-7
The near, the clear, and vaunts the clearest bloom, [Fictive 88-3
Too near, too clear, saving a little to endow [Fictive 88-11
Humanly near, and the figure of Mary, [Lunar 107-6
But in Claude how near one was [Botanist 1 135-1
So near. [Havana 142-6
That's what one wants to get near. Could it after all [Dump 202-28
To which I spoke, near which I stood and spoke, [News 265-3
When the grand mechanics of earth and sky were near, [Contra II 270-2
Her hand took his and drew him near to her. [Hand 271-17
Within the actual, the warm, the near, [EM 317-6
Be near me, come closer, touch my hand, phrases [EM 317-17
The shadow of an external world comes near. [Myrrh 350-12
He had written them near Athens. The farm was white. [Anach 366-1
On the table near which they stood [Attempt 370-20
These mothers touching, speaking, being near, [Cred 372-17
They sang desiring an object that weas near, [Cred 376-6
A steamer lay near him, foundered in the ice. [Page 421-13
The inhuman brother so much like, so near, [Owl 434-8
So near detachment, the cover's cornered squares, [Bouquet 450-13
The two romanzas, the distant and the near, [NH 481-2
Never forgetting him that kept coming constantly so near. [World 521-18
Its strength and measure, that which is near, point A [Rock 528-11
Near by it? [Soldat 11-15 P
Time's fortune near, the sleepless sleepers moved [Duck 61-27 P
Things still more distant. And tradition is near. [Recit 86-20 P
For daylight and too near for sleep. [Dove 98-15 P
Of the white stones near my door, [Three 134-7 P
Of the white stones near her door; [Three 134-13 P
NEARBY. That bugles for the mate, nearby the nest, [NSF 405-14
NEARER. Holding their books toward the nearer stars, [Polish Aunt 84-10
A little nearer by each multitude, [Montra 262-2
Opaque, in orange circlet, nearer than it [Page 422-13
NEAREST. Stands truly. The circles nearest to it share [Anach 366-9
NEARLY. Or nearly so. [Mandolin 29-5 P
NEAT. And the sea as turquoise-turbaned Sambo, neat [Sea Surf 102-7
And the chandeliers are neat . . . [Anything B 211-12
NEATER. Out of such mildew plucking neater mould [Pharynx 96-14
In a man-makenesse, neater than Naples. [Vari 235-18
NEATLY. If neatly glazed, becomes the same as the fruit [Extracts

253-9
Between two neatly measured stations, [Hero 275-17
Of less neatly measured common-places. [Hero 275-18
NEBULOUS. These nebulous brilliancies in the smallest look [EM 317-13
NECESSARY. He once thought necessary. Like Candide, [C 42-16
Yet I am the necessary angel of earth, [Angel 496-15
NECESSITOUS. The most necessitous sense. Accept them, then, [Man Car 350-17
There is a will to change, a necessitous [NSF 397-19
The stern voices of its necessitous men, [Aug 491-17
Each look and each necessitous cry, as a god [Greenest 59-8 P
NECESSITY. Each one, by the necessity of being [EM 324-5
Himself, the unalterable necessity [EM 324-6
And that necessity and that presentation [NSF 398-3
Needs out of the whole necessity of sight. [Owl 432-2
The will of necessity, the will of wills-- [NH 480-12
Required, as a necessity requires. [Plain 503-8
Categories of bleak necessity, [Ulysses 104-26 P
NECK. And do not forget his wry neck [Jack-Rabbit 50-12
The wry of neck and the wry of heart [Sat Night 28-1 P
NECKLACE. I am the spouse. She took her necklace off [NSF 395-19
The necklace is a carving not a kiss. [AA 413-15
She wanted no fetchings. His arms would be her necklace [World 521-8
NECKS. Necks among the thousand leaves, [Orangeade 103-5
NEED. The need of some imperishable bliss." [Sunday 68-28
Come now. Those to be born have need [Ghosts 119-12
Of the bride, love being a birth, have need to see [Ghosts 119-13
And to touch her, have need to say to her, [Ghosts 119-14
Furtively, by candle and out of need. [Nigger 153-4
Still one would want more, one would need more, [Poems Clim 194-2
And nothing need be explained; [Rabbit K 209-12
Filling the imagination's need. [Dezem 218-16
The need of its element, the final need [Pure 333-4
That we do not need to understand, complete [Descrip 341-13
His being felt the need of soaring, the need [Liadoff 347-12
We have not the need of any paradise, [NSF 394-20
We have not the need of any seducing hymn. [NSF 394-21
No need, am happy, forget need's golden hand, [NSF 405-2
In the weaving round the wonder of its need, [Owl 434-15
For the clairvoyant men that need no proof: [Orb 441-5
Are not precise about the appeasement they need. [NH 467-21
Free from their majesty and yet in need [NH 473-10
Impatient for the grandeur that you need [Rome 509-22
Than the need of each generation to be itself, [Armor 530-9
The need to be actual and as it is. [Armor 530-10
Crying against a need that pressed like cold, [Old Woman 45-29 P
Of martyrs, to be arrogant in our need, [Bship 81-3 P
There is a mother whose children need more than that. [Woman Had 82-1 P
The need for a thesis, a music constant to move. [Woman Had 82-9P
Their need in solitude: that is the need, [Woman Had 82-26 P
The immediate and intolerable need [Stan Hero 84-26 P
Is need. For this, the sibyl's shape [Ulysses 104-15 P
They measure the right to use. Need makes [Ulysses 104-24 P
The right to use. Need names on its breath [Ulysses 104-25 P
All you need, [Three 127-1 P
NEEDED. It needed the heavy nights of drenching weather [Nigger 158-6
Something to feel that they needed another yellow, [Holiday 312-3
Except as needed by way of majesty, [AA 417-14
The greenhouse never so badly needed paint. [Plain 502-17
It reminded him how he had needed [Poem Mt 512-5
Since thirty summers are needed for a year [Ideal 88-8 A
NEEDING. It is a text that we shall be needing, [Aug 495-6
Removed from any shore, from any man or woman, and needing none. [Prol 516-9
And these long, black instruments will be so little to them that will be needing so much, seeking so much in their music. [Piano 22-9 P
NEEDLE. It was a theologian's needle, much [Blue Bldg 217-8
NEEDS. On his spredden wings, needs nothing but deep space, [NSF 404-17
These forms are visible to the eye that needs, [Owl 432-1
Needs out of the whole necessity of sight. [Owl 432-2
She needs will come consolingly. Alas, [Spaniard 35-3 P
Needs no candle [Three 140-2 P
NEGATION. "Negation" [97-title
Negation destroyed him in his tenement [EM 319-21
Revenges. And negation was eccentric. [EM 319-25
NEGATIONS. The negations are never final. The father sits [AA 414-5
NEGATIVE. An unaffected man in a negative light [NSF 393-19
NEGLIGIBLE. And excepting negligible Triton, free [C 29-28
NEGRESS. Only a negress who supposes [Virgin 71-2
Should fill the vigil of a negress [Virgin 71-8
Victoria Clementina, negress, [Cab 20-15 P
NEGRESSES. The father fetches negresses to dance, [AA 415-7
NEGRO. The negro undertaker [Venereal 47-14
The negro with laundry passes me by. [Stan MBG 72-10 P

NEGROES. The negroes were playing football in the park. [Contra II
    270-14
NEIGHBOR. "Chocorua to its Neighbor" [296-title
    He disappeared with his neighbor's daughter. [Three 135-15 P
NEIGHBORHOOD. A strong mind in a weak neighborhood and is [NH
    474-13
NEIGHBORING. Rested immobile, though neighboring catafalques [NSF
    391-8
NEIN. Nein, [Explan 72-19
    Nein. [Explan 72-20
NEPOS. See Cornelius Nepos.
NERUDA. See Pablo Neruda.
NERVELESS. Themselves with care, sought out the nerveless frame
    [NSF 391-16
NERVES. It is this posture of the nerves, [MBG 182-20
    The very will of the nerves, [Anything B 211-21
NEST. For which the intricate Alps are a single nest. [Connois
    216-14
    That thinks of settling, yet never settles, on a nest. [Somnam
    304-3
    The dove in the belly builds his nest and coos, [Belly 366-17
    That bugles for the mate, nearby the nest, [NSF 405-14
    This is where the serpent lives. This is his nest, [AA 411-7
    In another nest, the master of the maze [AA 411-16
    The possible nest in the invisible tree, [John 437-17
    See bird-nest.
NESTS. Old nests and there is blue in the woods. [Cuisine 227-15
NETHER-DO. Intent on your particles of nether-do, [Rome 509-17
NETS. The trade-wind jingles the rings in the nets around the
    racks by the docks on Indian River. [Indian 112-4
    We dried our nets and mended sail [Silent 359-9
NETTED. Netted of topaz and ruby [Cab 21-8 P
NEUROSIS. It was after the neurosis of winter. It was [NH 482-17
NEUTER. A neuter shedding shapes in an absolute. [NH 479-19
NEUTRAL. At the neutral centre, the ominous element, [Landsc 242-1
NEVER. There is not nothing, no, no, never nothing, [Monocle 13-3
    Of love, but until now I never knew [Monocle 18-2
    There will never be an end [Fabliau 23-14
    Lacustrine man had never been assailed [Geneva 24-4
    Was not the sun because it never shone [C 29-18
    Through sweating changes, never could forget [C 33-22
    Of what he saw he never saw at all. [C 36-17
    In sleep may never meet another thought [Canna 55-5
    Does ripe fruit never fall? Or do the boughs [Sunday 69-14
    They never find, the same receding shores [Sunday 69-18
    That never touch with inarticulate pang? [Sunday 69-19
    His will, yet never ceases, perfect cock, [Bird Claws 82-17
    And that one was never a man of heart. [Norfolk 111-12
    And these two never meet in the air so full of summer [Norfolk
    111-20
    Her mind will never speak to me again. [Farewell 117-6
    But the romantic must never remain, [Sailing 120-15
    Mon Dieu, and must never again return. [Sailing 120-16
    For whom desire was never that of the waltz, [Sad Gay 121-16
    For whom the shapes were never the figures of men. [Sad Gay
    121-18
    One's cup and never to say a word, [Adieu 128-3
    The water never formed to mind or voice, [Key W 128-12
    Knew that there never was a world for her [Key W 130-1
    And men of day and never of pointed night, [Eve Angels 137-14
    Birds that never fly [Gray 140-17
    John Constable they could never quite transplant [Nigger 154-20
    This pundit of the weather, who never ceased [Nigger 156-5
    Yet, it may be, innocence is never lost, [Nigger 157-13
    Will never know that these were once [Postcard 158-15
    Will speak our speech and never know, [Postcard 159-15
    I have never--shall never hear. And yet beneath [Autumn 160-7
    Though I have never--shall never hear that bird. [Autumn 160-12
    Mechanical beetles never quite warm? [MBG 168-15
    Yet Franciscan don was never more [MBG 181-13
    Not ended, never and never ended, [Idiom 201-1
    Yet one face keeps returning (never the one), [Dames 206-14
    The face of the man of the mass, never the face [Dames 206-15
    Never the naked politician taught [Dames 206-17
    An edge of song that never clears; [Country 207-9
    Never angels, nothing of the dead, [Dezem 218-13
    That they never hear the past. To see, [Arcades 225-6
    They do not touch it. Sounds never rise [Arcades 225-10
    But the town and the fragrance were never one, [Arcades 225-13
    Red purple, never quite red itself. [Arcades 225-16
    The vivid thing in the air that never changes, [Martial 238-12
    He never supposed [Landsc 242-20
    Parts, and more things, parts. He never supposed divine [Landsc
    242-27
    And weeps on his breast, though he never comes. [Rhythms 245-17
    It can never be satisfied, the mind, never. [Beard 247-25
    To be, regardless of velvet, could never be more [Uruguay 249-13
    Than to be, she could never differently be, [Uruguay 249-14
    Can never stand as god, is ever wrong [Oboe 250-16
    If evil never ends, is to return [Extracts 259-3

Fear never the brute clouds nor winter-stop [Montra 261-22
Item: The wind is never rounding O [Montra 263-17
Hill-scholar, man that never is, [Jumbo 269-14
Of things that would never be quite expressed, [Motive 288-10
Where you yourself were never quite yourself [Motive 288-11
The body that could never be wounded, [Gigan 289-4
The life that never would end, no matter [Gigan 289-5
Grew strong, as if doubt never touched his heart. [Choc 299-5
Holds in his hand a book you have never written [Lack 303-2
That thinks of settling, yet never settles, on a nest. [Somnam
    304-3
The wings keep spreading and yet are never wings. [Somnam 304-4
Without this bird that never settles, without [Somnam 304-10
What meditation never quite achieved. [EM 314-23
Its own hallucination never sees [EM 315-9
Lay a passion for yes that had never been broken. [EM 320-14
That were never wholly still. The softest woman, [EM 321-28
People might share but were never an element, [Wild 328-18
It is never the thing but the version of the thing: [Pure 332-13
There are many of these beasts that one never sees, [Jouga 337-11
It is as if we were never children. [Debris 338-2
That it is as if we had never been young. [Debris 338-4
Fetched up with snow that never falls to earth? [Belly 367-6
Never suppose an inventing mind as source [NSF 381-1
A name for something that never could be named. [NSF 381-11
As if the waves at last were never broken, [NSF 387-16
The bees came booming as if they had never gone, [NSF 389-19
As if hyacinths had never gone. We say [NSF 389-20
There never had been, never could be, such [NSF 391-20
Of stone, that never changes. Bethou him, you [NSF 394-16
Is never naked. A fictive covering [NSF 396-11
Is there a poem that never reaches words [NSF 396-18
Red-in-red repetitions never going [NSF 400-13
Up down. It is a war that never ends. [NSF 407-9
Only the half they can never possess remains, [AA 413-9
The negations are never final. The father sits [AA 414-5
There is never a place. Or if there is no time, [AA 418-5
We never felt twice the same about the flecked river, [Cata
    424-10
Which kept flowing and never the same way twice, flowing [Cata
    424-11
But the virtuoso never leaves his shape, [Orb 443-3
Since what we think is never what we see. [What We 460-6
He will never ride the red horse she describes. [Questions 462-15
And in any case never grim, the human grim [NH 475-17
Of petals that will never be realized, [NH 478-15
In which he exists but never as himself. [Aug 493-8
The greenhouse never so badly needed paint. [Plain 502-17
The life of the city never lets go, nor do you [Rome 510-12
That never could be animal, [Two Illus 513-18
The barbarous strength within her would never fail. [World 521-15
Never forgetting him that kept coming constantly so near. [World
    521-18
They never were . . . The sounds of the guitar [Rock 525-9
I never tire [Bowl 7-8 P
Quick to be gone, yet never [Soldat 12-5 P
Death, that will never be satisfied, [Soldat 16-10 P
Never cease to deploy the structure. [Archi 16-16 P
And there the common grass is never seen. [Abnormal 24-8 P
You never can be right. You are the man. [Red Kit 30-16 P
She can corrode your world, if never you. [Good Bad 33-22 P
If she is like the moon, she never clears [Spaniard 34-11 P
Made by a cook that never rode the back [Burnshaw 46-20 P
Made to remember a life they never lived [Burnshaw 46-24 P
Made to affect a dream they never had, [Burnshaw 47-1 P
And are never of the world in which they live. [Burnshaw 48-19 P
And because the temple is never quite composed, [Burnshaw 50-14 P
Through a moving chaos that never ends. Mesdames, [Burnshaw
    50-23 P
Into a music never touched to sound. [Greenest 54-11 P
That was never the heaven of Africa, which had [Greenest 54-19 P
As death itself, and never can be changed [Duck 61-22 P
Suppose, instead of failing, it never comes, [Duck 63-30 P
Of which he is the cause, have never changed [Sombre 66-13 P
And never will, a subman under all [Sombre 66-14 P
A self of parents who have never died, [Sombre 67-4 P
He eats red cherry pie and never says-- [Grotesque 75-19 P
Cherries are ri . . . He would never say that. [Grotesque 76-1 P
Saying we have forgot them, they never lived. [Grotesque 77-12 P
Were mechanical, muscular. They never changed, [Woman Had 81-20 P
They never stopped, a repetition repeated [Woman Had 81-21 P
When it never existed, the order [Desire 85-2 P
About the mind as never satisfied, [As Leave 117-2 P
In Connecticut, we never lived in a time [Myth 118-8 P
And I have never seen it. [Three 128-12 P
That humanity never invades. [Three 130-3 P
It never woke to see, [Three 131-25 P
And never knew, [Three 131-26 P
It never knew [Three 132-3 P
See ever-never-changing.

NEVER-ENDING. And talked of never-ending things, [Silent 359-10
  Of the never-ending storm of will, [Silent 359-11
  As part of the never-ending meditation. [NH 465-7
NEVER-FAILING. The vital, the never-failing genius, [AA 420-20
NEVER-NAMED. Lascar, and water-carcass never-named, [Two V 354-7
NEVER-RESTING. There would still remain the never-resting mind,
  [Poems Clim 194-4
NEVERSINK. Are shining on all brows of Neversink. [Myrrh 349-14
NEVER-TIRING. The mornings grow silent, the never-tiring wonder.
  [Aug 495-17
NEW. An ancient aspect touching a new mind. [Monocle 16-2
  New leaf and shadowy tinct, [Pourtraicte 21-23
  Crispin beheld and Crispin was made new. [C 30-6
  A new reality in parrot-squawks. [C 32-12
  A still new continent in which to dwell. [C 37-4
  To make a new intelligence prevail? [C 37-10
  She causes boys to pile new plums and pears [Sunday 69-10
  And spouting new orations of the cold. [Pharynx 96-15
  And liquorish prayer provokes new sweats: so, so: [Havana 144-10
  As yet, for the mind, new banks [Mud 147-17
  Read in the ruins of a new society, [Nigger 153-3
  To construct a new stage. It has to be on that stage [Of Mod
  240-5
  That's the old world. In the new, all men are priests. [Extracts
  254-2
  At New Year and, from then until April, lay [Extracts 255-2
  For soldiers, the new moon stretches twenty feet. [Gigan 289-21
  That a new glory of new men assembles. [Dutch 292-23
  In what new spirit had his body birth? [Choc 299-8
  In the spectacle of a new reality. [Repet 306-9
  Again, in the imagination's new beginning, [EM 320-11
  In the brilliantest descriptions of new day, [Descrip 344-11
  "A Completely New Set of Objects" [352-title
  The bottomless trophy, new hornsman after old? [NSF 390-18
  New stars that were a foot across came out [Page 421-15
  Nor new, nor in the sense of memory. [Bouquet 451-7
  Much like a new resemblance of the sun, [NH 465-16
  Conceptions of new mornings of new worlds, [NH 470-12
  And spoken in paradisal parlance new [NH 475-16
  Which, without the statue, would be new, [NH 483-5
  Or of a new aspect, bright in discovery-- [Aug 489-7
  Or else a new aspect, say the spirit's sex, [Aug 489-12
  A new text of the world, [Aug 494-24
  By an access of color, a new and unobserved, slight dithering,
  [Prol 517-2
  A new scholar replacing an older one reflects [Look 519-4
  New senses in the engenderings of sense, [Rock 527-8
  It is like a new account of everything old, [Armor 529-17
  This vif, this dizzle-dazzle of being new [Armor 530-12
  A new knowledge of reality. [Not Ideas 534-18
  Men of the line, take this new phrase, [Soldat 16-8 P
  Because new colors make new things [Abnormal 24-11 P
  And new things make old things again . . . [Abnormal 24-12 P
  The new spring tumble in the sky. [Sat Night 27-19 P
  Astral and Shellyan, diffuse new day; [Burnshaw 47-26 P
  The milkiest bowmen. This makes a new design, [Greenest 56-6 P
  Half men and half new, modern monsters . . . [Stan Hero 84-8 P
  Or sees the new North River heaping up [Recit 86-24 P
  Like the artifice of a new reality, [Theatre 91-5 P
  Pronouncing its new life and ours, not autumn's prodigal re-
  turned, [Discov 96-4 P
  In which he feeds on a new known, [Bus 116-4 P
  But a perfection emerging from a new known, [Bus 116-11 P
  And find a new thing [Three 142-9 P
NEW AMSTERDAM. That hears a pin fall in New Amsterdam [Recit 86-23P
NEW-BORN. Already the new-born children interpret love [Carolinas
  4-15
NEW-COLORED. A new-colored sun, say, that will soon change forms
  [Armor 529-19
NEW-COME. Booming and booming of the new-come bee. [NSF 391-6
  These ample lustres from the new-come moon. [Stan MMO 19-11 P
NEW ENGLAND. "New England Verses" [104-title
  One thinks, when the houses of New England catch the first sun,
  [Discov 95-21 P
  "Conversation with Three Women of New England" [108-title P
NEWEST. The oldest-newest day is the newest alone. [NH 476-19
  The newest Soviet réclame. Profound [Duck 62-30 P
  See oldest-newest.
NEW-FOUND. "I am the greatness of the new-found night." [Role
  93-14 P
NEW HAVEN. "An Ordinary Evening in New Haven" [465-title
  A view of New Haven, say, through the certain eye, [NH 471-18
  And Juda becomes New Haven or else must. [NH 473-6
  Professor Eucalyptus of New Haven seeks him [NH 475-5
  In New Haven with an eye that does not look [NH 475-6
  The instinct for earth, for New Haven, for his room, [NH 476-2
  If, then, New Haven is half sun, what remains, [NH 482-3
  If more unreal than New Haven, is not [NH 485-3
  Real and unreal are two in one: New Haven [NH 485-23
NEWLY. The flags are natures newly found. [Dutch 291-1

Beating in the heart, as if blood newly came, [NSF 382-21
NEWLY-FALLEN. Reflecting snow. A newly-fallen snow [Poems Clim
  193-10
NEWNESS. In the air of newness of that element, [Armor 530-15
NEWS. "The News and the Weather" [264-title
  The sun comes up like news from Africa. [Feo 334-12
NEWSBOYS. Of the unknown. The newsboys' muttering [Rome 508-18
NEWSPAPERS. Bring flowers in last month's newspapers. [Emperor
  64-6
  Are like newspapers blown by the wind. He speaks [NH 473-21
NEW YORK. Charleston should be New York. [Agenda 41-21 P
  With squalid cells, unless New York is Cocos [Duck 63-13 P
NEXT. Bordeaux to Yucatan, Havana next, [C 29-9
  And next in glory to enduring love, [Sunday 68-10
  In the clouds serene and final, next [MBG 177-14
  Next he builds capitols and in their corridors, [NSF 403-18
  Shall we be found hanging in the trees next spring? [AA 419-19
  Say next to holiness is the will thereto, [NH 467-4
  And next to love is the desire for love, [NH 467-5
NIBBLE. Sitting beside your lamp, there citron to nibble [Dwarf
  208-13
  Go, mouse, go nibble at Lenin in his tomb. [Blue Bldg 217-19
NIBBLING. Of children nibbling at the sugared void, [C 43-25
NIBS. But that this bloom grown riper, showing nibs [C 44-6
NICE. A Nice Shady Home [C 40-title 5
  It weights him with nice logic for the prim. [Havana 144-17
  Pure scientist, you look with nice aplomb [Good Bad 33-12 P
NICELY. To dab things even nicely pink [Melancholy 32-9 P
NICER. It is to stick to the nicer knowledge of [Pure 332-11
NICHOLAS POUSSIN. By Nicholas Poussin, yet nevertheless [Recit
  87-23 P
NICKS. To set in nicks? [Archi 17-26 P
NIETZSCHE. To Nietzsche in Basel, to Lenin by a lake. [Descrip
  342-1
  Nietzsche in Basel studied the deep pool [Descrip 342-7
  The sun of Nietzsche gildering the pool, [Descrip 342-18
NIGGER. "Like Decorations in a Nigger Cemetery" [150-title
  And bound. Its nigger mystics should change [Prelude 195-11
  A nigger tree and with a nigger name, [News 265-2
  Almost a nigger fragment, a mystique [News 265-9
  He sees the angel in the nigger's mind [Greenest 59-11 P
  And hears the nigger's prayer in motets, belched [Greenest 59-12P
NIGGLING. A passionately niggling nightingale. [C 35-3
  What niggling forms of gargoyle patter? [Archi 17-2 P
NICK. Like a blaze of summer straw, in winter's nick. [AA 421-3
NIGHT. At night, by the fire, [Domination 8-7
  I saw how the night came, [Domination 9-17
  Last night, we sat beside a pool of pink, [Monocle 17-14
  And night blues. [Fabliau 23-8
  In the night that is still to be silent, [Homunculus 26-14
  Latched up the night. So deep a sound fell down [C 42-6
  Toward the cool night and its fantastic star, [Lilacs 49-11
  Beams of the huge night converged upon it, [Valley Candle 51-2
  Then beams of the huge night [Valley Candle 51-4
  Who in the tomb of heaven walk by night, [Heaven 56-10
  Foretell each night the one abysmal night, [Heaven 56-18
  Of night, in which all motion [Curtains 62-7
  Or old dependency of day and night, [Sunday 70-19
  The night is not the cradle that they cry, [Tallap 71-11
  The night is of the color [Six Sig 73-16
  Night, the female, [Six Sig 73-18
  It was because night nursed them in its fold. [Babies 77-12
  Night nursed not him in whose dark mind [Babies 77-13
  "Two Figures in Dense Violet Night" [85-title
  Be the voice of night and Florida in my ear. [Two Figures 86-1
  As the night conceives the sea-sounds in silence, [Two Figures
  86-7
  Are clear and are obscure; that it is night; [Two Figures 86-14
  Of the two dreams, night and day, [Watermelon 89-1
  Muted the night. [Peter 91-8
  The slopping of the sea grew still one night [Sea Surf 98-13
  The slopping of the sea grew still one night. [Sea Surf 99-17
  The slopping of the sea grew still one night [Sea Surf 100-11
  Night stilled the slopping of the sea. The day [Sea Surf 101-23
  Fell slowly as when at night [Public Sq 109-5
  What of the night [Sonatina 110-5
  Now that you see the night? [Sonatina 110-8
  As the night descended, tilting in the air, [Key W 130-7
  Mastered the night and portioned out the sea, [Key W 130-8
  Arranging, deepening, enchanting night. [Key W 130-10
  Like last night's crickets, far below. [Botanist 2 135-19
  And men of day and never of pointed night, [Eve Angels 137-14
  Bare night is best. Bare earth is best. Bare, bare, [Eve Angels
  137-29
  Or of night endazzled, proud, [Fading 139-3
  Supports of night. The tea, [Fading 139-17
  In the afternoon, balloons at night. That is [Havana 142-2
  How pale and how possessed a night it is, [Havana 144-26
  The night knows nothing of the chants of night. [Re-state 146-1
  Only we two are one, not you and night, [Re-state 146-6

Nor night and I, but you and I, alone, [Re-state 146-7
That night is only the background of our selves, [Re-state 146-10
All night I sat reading a book, [Reader 146-13
An opening of portals when night ends, [Nigger 153-14
Melodious skeletons, for all of last night's music [Fish-Scale
  160-15
Day is desire and night is sleep. [MBG 167-7
The morning deluged still by night, [MBG 169-3
To his breath that lies awake at night. [MBG 171-16
At night, it lights the fruit and wine, [MBG 172-19
Our bed and we shall sleep by night. [MBG 184-3
Like the night before Christmas and all the carols. [Thought
  185-3
Its pitting poison, half the night. [Thought 186-24
He lies down and the night wind blows upon him here. [Men Fall
  187-13
The night wind blows upon the dreamer, bent [Men Fall 188-19
As certainly as night is the color [Prelude 194-15
Stones pose in the falling night; [Add 198-8
The man that is poor at night [Idiom 201-3
The freshness of night has been fresh a long time. [Dump 202-1
Then the tree, at night, began to change, [On Road 203-19
And longest, the night was roundest, [On Road 204-10
The whole of the wideness of night is for you, [Rabbit K 209-17
You become a self that fills the four corners of night. [Rabbit
  K 209-19
And play concertinas all night. [Jersey 210-19
So afterward, at night, [Weak Mind 212-6
This is the silence of night, [Nightgown 214-5
The night should be warm and fluter's fortune [Nightgown 214-15
Once it was, the repose of night, [Nightgown 214-17
He read, all day, all night and all the nights, [Blue Bldg 216-16
Searching all day, all night, for the honey-comb. [Blue Bldg
  217-24
Faces to people night's brilliancy, [Dezem 218-14
Green is the night, green kindled and apparalled. [Candle 223-1
Those that lie chanting green is the night. [Candle 223-6
Green is the night and out of madness woven, [Candle 223-7
The abstract, the archaic queen. Green is the night. [Candle
  223-14
The church bells clap one night in the week. [Cuisine 227-16
As if last night's lamps continued to burn, [Cuisine 228-4
Flying like insects of fire in a cavern of night, [Horn 230-18
Night and day, wind and quiet, produces [Vari 233-21
Like a phantom, in an uncreated night. [Landsc 242-4
The little owl flew through the night, [Adequacy 243-9
And light behind the body of night [Adequacy 244-7
In east wind beating the shutters at night. [Vase 246-16
No was the night. Yes is this present sun. [Beard 247-11
Climb through the night, because his cuckoos call. [Oboe 251-7
A good agreement between himself and night, [Extracts 256-5
To-night, night's undeciphered murmuring [Montra 261-1
Weather of night creatures, whistling all day, too, [Montra
  261-17
The greenness of night lies on the page and goes [Phosphor 267-9
That elemental parent, the green night, [Phosphor 267-15
The afternoon's reading, the night's reflection, [Hero 274-23
This is his night and meditation. [Hero 280-18
"God is Good. It is a Beautiful Night" [285-title
This was the place to which you came last night, [God 285-7
The fresh night. [God 285-18
And late wanderers creeping under the barb of night, [Dutch 291-24
Each night, an incessant butcher, whose knife [Dutch 292-18
At the end of night last night a crystal star, [Choc 296-17
A fusion of night, its blue of the pole of blue [Choc 297-16
The night. The substance of his body seemed [Choc 297-20
Experience of night, as if he breathed [Choc 298-7
More than a spokesman of the night to say [Choc 299-11
Last night at the end of night his starry head, [Choc 299-19
With the special things of night, little by little, [Choc 300-19
Last night at the end of night and in the sky, [Choc 301-19
The lesser night, the less than morning light, [Choc 301-20
On his balcony at night. Warblings became [EM 314-18
As night was free from him. The shadow touched [EM 315-1
In the hoary-hanging night. It does not regard [EM 315-7
In the high night, the summer breathes for them [EM 319-12
Bubbles up in the night and drowns the crickets' sound. [EM 321-9
Sequences, thought of among spheres in the old peak of night:
  [Bed 326-19
Of things at least that was thought of in the old peak of night.
  [Bed 327-8
Without a rider on a road at night. [Pure 329-17
Until its wings bear off night's middle witch; [Pure 333-1
How she presides over imbeciles. The night [Feo 333-12
Night is the nature of man's interior world? [Feo 333-14
Or seeing the spent, unconscious shapes of night, [Feo 334-7
Or like a seeming of the moon or night [Descrip 339-6
The artificer of subjects still half night. [Descrip 345-18
And on, at night, exploding finally [Liadoff 346-6
That night, Liadoff, a long time after his death, [Liadoff 346-14

Predestined to this night, this noise and the place [Myrrh 349-17
Out of a storm we must endure all night, [Man Car 351-4
We must endure our thoughts all night, until [Man Car 351-7
That lives in space. It is a person at night, [Pieces 352-7
The reader became the book; and summer night [House Q 358-8
The summer night is like a perfection of thought. [House Q 358-15
Is calm, itself is summer and night, itself [House Q 359-3
How good it was at home again at night [Lot 372-1
With the gold bugs, in blue meadows, late at night. [Cred 377-23
The enraptured woman, the sequestered night, [Past Nun 378-18
Close to me, hidden in me day and night? [NSF 380-6
We say: At night an Arabian in my room, [NSF 383-1
On a woman, day on night, the imagined [NSF 392-6
We encounter in the dead middle of the night [NSF 395-2
Of summer, growing fragrant in the night, [NSF 399-10
Enters the room, it drowses and is the night. [NSF 399-19
Once more night's pale illuminations, gold [NSF 402-24
Straight to the utmost crown of night he flew. [NSF 403-8
Fat girl, terrestrial, my summer, my night, [NSF 406-7
And sky, between thought and day and night. It is [NSF 407-5
His head is air. Beneath his tip at night [AA 411-2
Together, all together. Boreal night [AA 413-20
In highest night? And do these heavens adorn [AA 417-10
Or spill night out in brilliant vanishings, [Page 423-4
And the night, and midnight, and after, where it is. [Bad Time
  426-17
About the night. They live without our light, [Owl 432-7
And night, colored from distances, central [Owl 433-11
The moon moves toward the night. [Pecul 453-8
The bloody lion in the yard at night or ready to spring [Puel
  456-6
She had heard of the fate of an Argentine writer. At night,
  [Novel 457-8
Day's arches are crumbling into the autumn night. [Novel 458-16
At evening and at night. It does no good. [Study I 463-13
If the black of night stands glistening on beau mont, [NH 467-2
Of growling teeth, and falls at night, snuffed out [NH 467-19
The pattern of the heavens and high, night air. [NH 472-3
Of a windy night as it is, when the marble statues [NH 473-20
The oldest-newest night does not creak by, [NH 476-20
In the western night. The venerable mask, [NH 477-3
Of night, time and the imagination, [NH 477-23
Picked up its radial aspect in the night, [NH 478-23
Of the single future of night, the single sleep, [NH 482-6
These locusts by day, these crickets by night [Aug 489-4
Or in the penumbra of summer night-- [Aug 490-17
Of the quiet of the middle of the night, [Aug 491-7
From the edge of night, [Aug 495-2
The sparkling fall of night [Inhab 504-3
From a shore at night and disappeared. [Vacancy 511-7
No winds like dogs watched over her at night. [World 521-6
By gallant notions on the part of night-- [Quiet 523-11
By day, night and that which night illumines, [Rock 528-19
Night and its midnight-minting fragrances, [Rock 528-20
Night's hymn of the rock, as in a vivid sleep. [Rock 528-21
The one moonlight, in the simple-colored night, [Moonlight 531-1
In the great vistas of night air, that takes this form, [Moon-
  light 531-17
Night and silence disturbed by an interior sound, [Moonlight
  532-2
But the bugles, in the night, [Phases 4-1 P
Singing in the night's abyss; [Phases 4-10 P
Stretched out a shadowy arm to feel the night. [Phases 5-8 P
It seizes a sheet, from the ground, from a bush, as if spread
  there by some wash-woman for the night. [Plough-Boy 6-5 P
At night. [Primordia 8-4 P
To symbols of descending night; and search [Blanche 10-7 P
The spirit wakes in the night wind--is naked. [Soldat 11-13 P
What is it that hides in the night wind [Soldat 11-14 P
The multiform beauty, sinking in night wind, [Soldat 12-4 P
(A boor of night in middle earth cries out.) [Infernale 24-19 P
"Saturday Night at the Chiropodist's" [27-title P
And move the night by their intelligent motes. [Red Kit 32-1 P
But clears and clears until an open night [Spaniard 34-3 P
Night after night because the hemisphere [Spaniard 34-8 P
Stooped in a night of vast inquietude. [Spaniard 34-14 P
If the sky that followed, smaller than the night, [Old Woman
  45-6 P
A manner of the mind, a mind in a night [Old Woman 45-13 P
A night that was that mind so magnified [Old Woman 45-15 P
It lost the common shape of night and came [Old Woman 45-16 P
Of night. How clearly that would be defined! [Old Woman 46-12 P
In the witching wilderness, night's witchingness, [Burnshaw
  46-25 P
That enter day from night, came mirror-dark, [Burnshaw 51-26 P
From youngest day or oldest night and far [Greenest 54-1 P
On a hot night and a long cigar and talk [Greenest 58-25 P
The wide night mused by tell-tale muttering, [Duck 61-26 P
Steeped in night's opium, evading day. [Sombre 66-17 P
Policed by the hope of Christmas. Summer night, [Sombre 68-11 P

Night gold, and winter night, night silver, these [Sombre 68-12 P
If more than the wished-for ruin racked the night, [Sombre
    69-12 P
Are full of fanfares of farewell, as night [Sombre 71-4 P
And the portent end in night, composed, before [Sombre 71-5 P
The green, white, blue of the ballad-eye, by night [Sombre
    71-9 P
At night, to turn away from the abominable [Sombre 71-20 P
The cloak to be clipped, the night to be re-designed, [Sombre
    71-32 P
Night and the imagination being one. [Sombre 71-34 P
Returned on board The Masculine. That night, [Bship 77-14 P
Maternal voice, the explanation at night. [Woman Had 82-24 P
They find her in the crackling summer night, [Woman Had 83-4 P
Say that in the clear Atlantic night [Memo 89-13 P
Playing mouth-organs in the night or, now, guitars. [Sick 90-9 P
In the first inch of night, the stellar summering [Pagoda 92-3 P
"I am the greatness of the new-found night." [Role 93-14 P
"The Souls of Women at Night" [94-title P
In the much-horned night, as its chief personage. [Souls 94-17 P
Symbol of the seeker, crossing by night [Ulysses 99-11 P
The revolutions through day and night, [Ulysses 102-22 P
Straight forwardly through another night [Ulysses 105-11 P
Symbol of the seeker, crossing by night [Presence 105-14 P
Last Friday, in the big light of last Friday night, [Real 110-7 P
It was not a night blown at a glassworks in Vienna [Real 110-9 P
The visible transformations of summer night, [Real 110-16 P
Night's moonlight lake was neither water nor air. [Real 111-2 P
A health--and the faces in a summer night. [Art Pop 113-3 P
A light snow, like frost, has fallen during the night. [Bus
    116-1 P
On an August night, [Three 127-5 P
Creaking in the night wind. [Three 137-6 P
Day, night and man and his endless effigies. [Someone 83-13 A
See: good-night; half-night; sea-night; to-night.
NIGHT-BIRD. And jay, still to the night-bird made their plea,
    [C 30-19
NIGHT-BLUE. Night-blue is an inconstant thing. The seraph [NSF
    390-1
NIGHT-EVENING. As in the top-cloud of a May night-evening, [NSF
    395-10
NIGHT-FLIES. Away. The night-flies acknowledge these planets,
    [Myrrh 349-16
NIGHTGOWN. "Girl in a Nightgown" [214-title
NIGHT-GOWNS. By white night-gowns. [Ten O'C 66-2
NIGHT-HYMN. Forms of the Rock in a Night-Hymn [Rock 528-title 3
NIGHTINGALE. A passionately niggling nightingale. [C 35-3
    The yellow moon of words about the nightingale [Autumn 160-4
    And grates these evasions of the nightingale [Autumn 160-11
    To a crow's voice? Did the nightingale torture the ear, [Dump
        203-2
    In the park. We regret we have no nightingale. [Duck 66-7 P
NIGHTINGALES. A difference, at least, from nightingales, [Havana
    142-3
    Like the mother of all nightingales; be wise [Spaniard 35-10 P
NIGHT-LONG. The night-long slopping of the sea grew still. [Sea
    Surf 101-5
NIGHTLY. A convocation, nightly, of the sea-stars, [C 28-27
NIGHTS. In the pale nights, when your first imagery [Monocle 15-5
    From hearing signboards whimper in cold nights [C 33-2
    Upon the rumpling bottomness, and nights [C 42-31
    Swiftly in the nights, [Venereal 47-18
    Emotions on wet roads on autumn nights; [Sunday 67-23
    Her days, her oceanic nights, calling [Farewell 117-17
    Will drop like sweetness in the empty nights [Havana 144-8
    It needed the heavy nights of drenching weather [Nigger 158-6
    After long strumming on certain nights [MBG 174-19
    Of nights that will not be more than [Bagatelles 213-19
    He read, all day, all night and all the nights, [Blue Bldg 216-16
    More nights, more days, more clouds, more worlds. [Vari 233-22
    He must, in the aroma of summer nights, [Montra 261-14
    Of the nights, the actual, universal strength, [Repet 309-2
    Of nights full of the green stars from Ireland, [Our Stars
        455-14
    Toward which, in the nights, the glittering serpents climb,
        [Greenest 55-12 P
    The mirror of other nights combined in one. [Sombre 71-10 P
NIGHT-WIND. Sigh for me, night-wind, in the noisy leaves of the
    oak. [Nigger 150-15
NIHILIST. A time abhorrent to the nihilist [C 35-29
NIMBLE. In fragrant leaves heat-heavy yet nimble in talk. [NE
    Verses 105-12
NIMBLEST. Or, if not arrows, then the nimblest motions, [Tallap
    72-10
NIMBUSES. To electrify the nimbuses-- [MBG 174-2
NINCOMPATED. Of things, this nincompated pedagogue, [C 27-11
NINO. Some things, niño, some things are like this, [Gala 248-1
NIPPLES. How is it that your aspic nipples [Carolinas 5-2
NIZ - NIL - IMBO. Fro Niz - nil - imbo. [Metamorph 266-10
NO. There is not nothing, no, no, never nothing, [Monocle 13-3

No, no: veracious page on page, exact. [C 40-3
But stone, but like a stone, no: not [MBG 173-15
After the final no there comes a yes [Beard 247-9
No was the night. Yes is this present sun. [Beard 247-11
And her dress were one and she said, "I have said no [Uruguay
    249-3
Her no and no made yes impossible. [Uruguay 249-15
There was nothing he did not suffer, no; nor we. [Oboe 251-14
No, not believing, but to make the cell [Montra 261-10
No: nor divergence made too steep to follow down. [Dutch 293-12
First sees reality. The mortal no [EM 320-8
Say yes, spoken because under every no [EM 320-13
No, not of day, but of themselves, [Prejudice 369-2
He says no to no and yes to yes. He says yes [AA 414-8
To no; and in saying yes he says farewell. [AA 414-9
These illustrations are neither angels, no, [John 437-11
Your yes her no, your no her yes. The words [Red Kit 30-13 P
Than now. No: nor the ploughman in his bed [Burnshaw 47-32 P
No: not even sunrise. [Three 133-19 P
NOBILITY. Death's nobility again [Phases 4-15 P
NOBLE. Although the rose was not the noble thorn [C 42-28
    I know noble accents [Thirteen 94-1
    And noble imagery [Pascagoula 126-14
    Noble in autumn, yet nobler than autumn. [Nigger 156-12
    Like a noble figure, out of the sky, [Candle 223-4
    The noble figure, the essential shadow, [Candle 223-12
    The noble, Alexandrine verve. The flies [Contra II 270-17
    What any fury to its noble centre. [Hero 274-18
    Bore off the residents of its noble Place. [NSF 391-9
    Noble within perfecting solitude, [Greenest 54-4 P
    Or Paris-rain. He thinks of the noble lives [Greenest 59-25 P
    Made noble by the honor he receives, [Recit 87-15 P
    See per-noble.
NOBLER. Or, nobler, sensed an elemental fate, [C 31-24
    Noble in autumn, yet nobler than autumn. [Nigger 156-12
    He liked the nobler works of man, [Thought 187-1
    And twang nobler notes [Demoiselle 23-8 P
NOBLES. Or wise men, or nobles, [Three 129-14 P
NOBLY. Knowing that he died nobly, as he died. [Flyer 336-11
    Nobly as autumn moves. [Secret Man 36-12 P
    Along the thin horizons, nobly more [Burnshaw 47-10 P
NOCTURNAL. The nocturnal halls. [Ord Women 10-20
    The nocturnal, the antique, the blue-green pines [Parochial 191-9
    That shines with a nocturnal shine alone. [NH 473-2
    Enlarging like a nocturnal ray [Ulysses 100-25 P
NOD. Nod and look a little sly. [Orangeade 103-16
NOES. An ember yes among its cindery noes, [Armor 529-10
NOISE. And that whatever noise the motion of the waves [Hibiscus
    22-12
    Of motion, or of the noise of motion, [Solitaires 60-7
    The renewal of noise [Solitaires 60-8
    Soon, with a noise like tambourines, [Peter 91-12
    Fled, with a noise like tambourines. [Peter 91-21
    High as the hall. The whirling noise [MBG 171-14
    One with us, in the heaved-up noise, still [Hero 273-23
    The wheels are too large for any noise. [Dutch 290-5
    Who knocks out a noise. The guitar is another beast [Jouga 337-7
    Predestined to this night, this noise and the place [Myrrh 349-17
    Reddens the sand with his red-colored noise, [NSF 384-8
    The leaves on the macadam make a noise-- [Hermit 505-10
NOISELESSLY. Noiselessly, like one more wave. [Paltry 5-10
    Noiselessly, noiselessly, resembling a thin bird, [Somnam 304-2
NOISES. And the ear is glass, in which the noises pelt, [Extracts
    252-3
    Brooding sounds of river noises; [Degen 444-6
NOISY. Sigh for me, night-wind, in the noisy leaves of the oak.
    [Nigger 150-15
NOMAD. "Nomad Exquisite" [95-title
NONCHALANCE. C'était ma foi, la nonchalance divine. [Sea Surf
    101-15
NONCHALANT. Turned from their want, and, nonchalant, [Ord Women
    10-18
NONE. "Where none can see, [Pourtraicte 21-17
    None are green, [Ten O'C 66-3
    None of them are strange, [Ten O'C 66-7
    Gross effigy and simulacrum, none [Fictive 87-18
    The approach of him whom none believes, [MBG 170-10
    It must be this rhapsody or none, [MBG 183-1
    The spring will have a health of its own, with none [Parochial
        192-1
    With none of the prescience of oncoming dreams, [AA 413-7
    Each sexton has his sect. The bells have none. [Luther 461-15
    To none, awaiting espousal to the sound [Study II 464-18
    Removed from any shore, from any man or woman, and needing none.
        [Prol 516-9
    As if none of us had ever been here before [Clear Day 113-17 P
NON-PHYSICAL. After death, the non-physical people, in paradise,
    [EM 325-21
    Itself non-physical, may, by chance, observe [EM 325-22
NONSENSE. Poet, patting more nonsense foamed [Prelude 195-14

Life's nonsense pierces us with strange relation. [NSF 383-9
NON-SUBSTANCE. Both substance and non-substance, luminous flesh
   [Choc 297-21
NOON. It makes it clear. Even at noon [MBG 172-17
   The weight of primary noon, [Motive 288-15
   Audible at noon, pain torturing itself, [EM 314-4
   At noon it was on the mid-day of the year [NSF 401-5
   To be the footing of noon, [Aug 495-7
   The meeting at noon at the edge of the field seems like [Rock
     525-12
   A winter's noon, in which the colors sprang [Greenest 57-25 P
NORFOLK. "Two at Norfolk" [111-title
NORMAL. And normal things had yawned themselves away, [NSF 402-20
   Twelve meant as much as: the end of normal time, [What We 459-13
   "A Quiet Normal Life" [523-title
NORMANDIE. See S.S. Normandie.
NORTH. America was always north to him, [C 34-2
   A northern west or western north, but north, [C 34-3
   Of the North have earned this crumb by their complaints. [NE
     Verses 106-2
   From my North of cold whistled in a sepulchral South, [Farewell
     117-14
   How content I shall be in the North to which I sail [Farewell
     117-19
   My North is leafless and lies in a wintry slime [Farewell 118-11
   Well, after all, the north wind blows [MBG 174-12
   It is the sea that the north wind makes. [MBG 179-15
   Cleared from the north and in that height [Country 207-12
   Iciest core, a north star, central [Hero 275-24
   And North and South are an intrinsic couple [NSF 392-13
   He observes how the north is always enlarging the change, [AA
     412-24
   Does it take its place in the north and enfold itself, [AA 417-8
   And the north wind's mighty buskin seems to fall [Antag 426-7
   Abhorring green-blue north and blue-green south. [Archi 18-1 P
   Here in the North, late, late, there are voices or men, [Sick
     90-10 P
   A trinkling in the parentage of the north, [Discov 95-13 P
   It is hard to hear the north wind again, [Region 115-6 P
NORTH AMERICA. Ploughing North America. [Ploughing 20-11
NORTHERN. A northern west or western north, but north, [C 34-3
   Are there mandolines of northern moonlight? [Men 1000 52-6
   Snow under the trees and on the northern rocks, [Extracts 255-15
   In memorials of Northern sound, [Oak 272-14
   And yellow, yellow twins the Northern blue. [NSF 385-13
   To it"? He beheld the order of the northern sky. [Bad Time 426-11
   The way some first thing coming into Northern trees [Prol 517-6
   The horses are a part of a northern sky [Greenest 54-28 P
NORTH RIVER. Or sees the new North River heaping up [Recit 86-24 P
NORTHWEST. In the Northwest [Primordia 7-title 1 P
NORWAY. Bringing the lights of Norway and all that. [Hartford
   226-6
NOSE. The vessel inward. Tilting up his nose, [C 36-6
   He held the world upon his nose [MBG 178-9
   And the nose is eternal, that-a-way. [MBG 178-19
   Until his nose grew thin and taut [Thought 186-22
   Its nose is on its paws. [Destructive 193-5
   The tongue, the fingers, and the nose [Arcades 225-17
NOSES. These English noses and edged, Italian eyes [Duck 60-22 P
NOSING. It is true that the rivers went nosing like swine, [Frogs
   78-1
   Grotesque with this nosing in banks, [Frogs 78-11
   Long-tailed ponies go nosing the pine-lands, [Parochial 191-1
NOSTALGIA. It was the last nostalgia: that he [EM 322-4
NOSTALGIAS. He had studied the nostalgias. In these [EM 321-12
NOSTRILS. And his nostrils blow out salt around each man. [Grapes
   111-3
NOTA. Nota: man is the intelligence of his soil, [C 27-7
   Nota: his soil is man's intelligence. [C 36-24
NOTATIONS. Notations of the wild, the ruinous waste, [Geneva 24-12
   Notations and footnotes. [Common 221-22
NOTE. But note the unconscionable treachery of fate, [Monocle 17-9
   Of force, the quintessential fact, the note [C 33-5
   From oriole to crow, note the decline [Nigger 154-14
   Note that, in this bitterness, delight, [Poems Clim 194-8
   A note or two disclosing who it was. [NH 483-18
   A scholar, in his Segmenta, left a note, [NH 485-1
   A woman writing a note and tearing it up. [NH 488-21
   Nothing is lost, loud locusts. No note fails. [Aug 489-16
   "Note on Moonlight" [531-title
NOTE-BOOK. Boston with a Note-book [NE Verses 104-title 5
   Boston without a Note-book [NE Verses 105-title 6
NOTES. Of the cathedral, making notes, he heard [C 32-16
   Notes for his comfort that he may repeat [Nigger 155-21
   The leaves were falling like notes from a piano. [Contra II
     270-12
   All sorts of notes? Or did he play only one [EM 316-12
   "Notes toward a Supreme Fiction" [380-title
   And twang nobler notes [Demoiselle 23-8 P
   See foot-notes.

NOTHING. And, nothing himself, beholds [Snow Man 10-11
   Nothing that is not there and the nothing that is. [Snow Man
     10-12
   There is not nothing, no, no, never nothing, [Monocle 13-3
   Is it for nothing, then, that old Chinese [Monocle 14-1
   Of my being, shine like fire, that mirrors nothing. [Nuances
     18-10
   Which made him Triton, nothing left of him, [C 28-30
   Of winter, until nothing of himself [C 29-15
   Is nothing, what can all this matter since [C 46-11
   Knows nothing more. [Joost 46-16
   Knows nothing more. [Joost 47-3
   Nothing but trash and that you no longer feel [Lilacs 49-9
   Here is nothing of the ideal, [Explan 72-18
   Like nothing else in Tennessee. [Jar 76-16
   The night knows nothing of the chants of night. [Re-state 146-1
   Nothing is final, he chants. No man shall see the end. [Nigger
     150-13
   Add nothing to the horror of the frost [Nigger 152-13
   Yet nothing changed by the blue guitar; [MBG 167-16
   Yet nothing changed, except the place [MBG 167-18
   The moon shares nothing. It is a sea. [MBG 168-10
   It is a sea; it shares nothing; [MBG 168-12
   Must be. It could be nothing else. [MBG 171-22
   Nothing of the madness of space, [MBG 183-8
   Nothing of its jocular procreations? [MBG 183-9
   Throw the lights away. Nothing must stand [MBG 183-10
   Nothing to have at heart. [Destructive 192-10
   It is to have or nothing. [Destructive 192-11
   With nothing more than the carnations there. [Poems Clim 193-16
   And sees, being nothing otherwise, [Prelude 194-19
   Having nothing otherwise, he has not [Prelude 194-20
   They resemble nothing else. [Pears 196-4
   "The mass is nothing. The number of men in a mass [Dames 206-3
   Of men is nothing. The mass is no greater than [Dames 206-4
   And nothing is left except light on your fur-- [Rabbit K 209-3
   And nothing need be explained; [Rabbit K 209-12
   Then there is nothing to think of. It comes of itself; [Rabbit K
     209-13
   There's nothing whatever to see [Jersey 210-17
   This proves nothing. Just one more truth, one more [Connois 216-2
   Never angels, nothing of the dead, [Dezem 218-13
   The reason can give nothing at all [Dezem 218-19
   And counter-ideas. There was nothing one had. [Forces 229-8
   Is to fire. And her mainmast tapered to nothing. [Vari 235-21
   Things might not look divine, nor that if nothing [Landsc 242-28
   And that if nothing was the truth, then all [Landsc 242-30
   Was less than moonlight. Nothing exists by itself. [Les Plus
     244-18
   And erudite in happiness, with nothing learned, [Gala 248-8
   There was nothing he did not suffer, no; nor we. [Oboe 251-14
   Ceylon, wants nothing from the sea, la belle [Extracts 257-28
   There is nothing more and that it is enough [Extracts 258-7
   And nothing more. So that if one went to the moon, [Extracts
     258-10
   And if there be nothing more, O bright, O bright, [Montra 260-2
   Chome! clicks the clock, if there be nothing more. [Montra 260-7
   And common fortune, induced by nothing, [Hero 275-11
   Acts in reality, adds nothing [Hero 279-10
   The highest man with nothing higher [Hero 280-5
   This is his day. With nothing lost, he [Hero 280-16
   Of remembrance share nothing of ourselves. [Dutch 291-14
   In an ignorance of sleep with nothing won. [Dutch 291-26
   Accepted yet which nothing understood, [Choc 297-15
   He was not man yet he was nothing else. [Choc 298-2
   But of nothing, trash of sleep that will disappear [Choc 300-18
   If nothing more than that, for the moment, large [Choc 302-2
   As if nothing had happened. The dim actor spoke. [Repet 306-11
   An image that leaves nothing much behind. [Repet 307-18
   Nothing of place. There is no change of place [Repet 308-6
   And come to nothing. Let the rainy arcs [Repet 310-3
   The precisions of fate, nothing fobbed off, nor changed [Repet
     310-8
   Spring is the truth of spring or nothing, a waste, a fake.
     [Holiday 313-2
   The total past felt nothing when destroyed. [EM 314-16
   It had nothing of the Julian thunder-cloud: [EM 319-26
   And nothing is left but comic ugliness [EM 320-21
   Like earth and sky. Then he became nothing else [Wild 329-1
   And they were nothing else. It was late in the year. [Wild 329-2
   Nothing in which it is not possible [Paisant 335-8
   Moving so that the foot-falls are slight and almost nothing.
     [Jouga 337-12
   By the illustrious nothing of her name. [Descrip 339-8
   In which nothing solid is its solid self. [Descrip 345-10
   All mind and violence and nothing felt. [Chaos 358-4
   He knows he has nothing more to think about. [Chaos 358-5
   He walks and dies. Nothing survives [Woman Song 360-8
   And let it go, with nothing lost, [Woman Song 361-4
   Forced up from nothing, evening's chair, [Human 363-11

Beyond which there is nothing left of time. [Cred 372-12
There is nothing more inscribed nor thought nor felt [Cred 372-14
Let's see the very thing and nothing else. [Cred 373-3
By a feeling capable of nothing more. [Cred 374-5
With nothing else compounded, carried full, [Cred 374-14
The formidable helmet is nothing now. [Pastor 380-1
Without a name and nothing to be desired, [NSF 385-14
Nothing had happened because nothing had changed. [NSF 392-2
An odor evoking nothing, absolute. [NSF 395-1
Possess in his heart, conceal and nothing known, [NSF 395-6
Are nothing but frothy clouds; the frothy blooms [NSF 399-16
The spent feeling leaving nothing of itself, [NSF 400-12
Out of nothing to have come on major weather, [NSF 404-3
On this spredden wings, needs nothing but deep space, [NSF
   404-17
This is nothing until in a single man contained, [AA 416-22
Nothing until this named thing nameless is [AA 416-23
It cannot be. There's nothing there to roll [AA 420-9
He has his poverty and nothing more. [Bad Time 427-1
It is nothing, no great thing, nor man [Imago 439-5
Sits in nothing that we know, [Degen 444-5
Nothing much, a flitter that reflects itself. [Bouquet 448-13
True nothing, yet accosted self to self. [Bouquet 449-18
Nothing could be more hushed than the way [Pecul 453-7
Which nothing can frustrate, that most secure, [NH 467-7
Nothing beyond reality. Within it, [NH 471-21
And there the senses give and nothing take, [NH 480-18
Nothing about him every stayed the same, [NH 483-19
Nothing is lost, loud locusts. No note fails. [Aug 489-16
It was only a glass because he looked in it. It was nothing he
   could be told. [Madame 507-6
She wanted nothing he could not bring her by coming alone.
   [World 521-7
In the predicate that there is nothing else. [Rock 527-4
St. Armorer's has nothing of this present, [Armor 530-11
You say that spite avails her nothing, that [Good Bad 33-8 P
Now, then, if nothing more than vanity [Spaniard 34-21 P
He is nothing, I know, to me nor I to him. [Lytton 39-21 P
So destitute that nothing but herself [Old Woman 44-10 P
Remained and nothing of herself except [Old Woman 44-11 P
Bring down from nowhere nothing's wax-like blooms, [Burnshaw
   47-20 P
And nothing more. He sees but not by sight. [Greenest 59-6 P
The ruins of the past, out of nothing left, [Recit 87-14 P
Permitting nothing to the evening's edge. [Role 93-5 P
In these stations, in which nothing has been lost, [Souls 94-20 P
In which nothing of knowledge fails, [Ulysses 100-8 P
The ancient symbols will be nothing then. [Ulysses 102-12 P
He has nothing but the truth to leave. [Ulysses 103-10 P
They are nothing, except in the universe [Child 106-16 P
Nothing more, like weather after it has cleared-- [Art Pop
   112-14 P
With nothing, fixed by a single word.[Banjo 114-12 P
And yet nothing has been changed except what is [As Leave 117-13P
Unreal, as if nothing had been changed at all. [As Leave 117-14 P
That nothing is beautiful [Three 133-14 P
But he wanted nothing. [Three 141-15 P
He must say nothing of the fruit that is [Someone 84-4 A
See matter-nothing.
NOTHINGNESS. And spiritous passage into nothingness, [Heaven 56-17
   And the infants of nothingness [Cortege 80-12
   A tiger lamed by nothingness and frost. [Nigger 153-10
   The companion in nothingness, [Jumbo 269-10
   The room is emptier than nothingness. [Phenom 286-9
   Or a lustred nothingness. Effendi, he [EM 320-22
   A vermilioned nothingness, any stick of the mass [Less 328-9
   Darkness, nothingness of human after-death, [Flyer 336-12
   The nothingness was a nakedness, a point, [NSF 402-21
   The nothingness was a nakedness, a point [NSF 403-9
   An immaculate personage in nothingness, [Owl 434-11
   Like a meaning in nothingness, [Celle 438-5
   Of color, the giant of nothingness, each one [Orb 443-21
   As far as nothingness permits . . . Hear him. [Questions 463-1
   In things seen and unseen, created from nothingness, [NH 486-11
   Creates a fresh universe out of nothingness by adding itself,
      [Prol 517-9
   As if nothingness contained a métier, [Rock 526-1
   The priest of nothingness who intones-- [Including 88-6 P
   Yet the nothingness of winter becomes a little less. [Course
      96-11 P
   Of darkness, creating from nothingness [Ulysses 100-27 P
   Worn and leaning to nothingness, [Ulysses 104-20 P
   Either in distance, change or nothingness, [Real 110-15 P
   It has no knowledge except of nothingness [Clear Day 113-15 P
NOTHINGS. To moodiest nothings, as, desire for day [Eve Angels
   137-21
NOTIONS. To gallant notions on the part of cold. [Quiet 523-6
   By gallant notions on the part of night-- [Quiet 523-11
NOT-NUMBERABLE. You are one of the not-numberable mice [Blue Bldg
   217-23

NOTORIOUS. And the notorious views from the windows [Prelude 195-5
NOUGATS. At the time of nougats, the peer yellow [Forces 228-17
   It was at the time, the place, of nougats. [Forces 228-21
   Shells under water. These were nougats. [Forces 229-15
   It had to be right: nougats. It was a shift [Forces 229-16
NOURISH. They nourish Jupiters. Their casual pap [Havana 144-7
   And nourish ourselves on crumbs of whimsy? [Hero 278-4
   I nourish myself. I defend myself against [Repet 308-14
   Then came Brazil to nourish the emaciated [Pure 330-16
NOURISHING. A time, an apparition and nourishing element [How Now
   97-11 P
NOUVEAUTES. Black man, bright nouveautés leave one, at best,
   pseudonymous. [Nudity Col 145-12
NOVEL. "The Novel" [457-title
   In a black glove, holds a novel by Camus. She begged [Novel 457-11
   The fire burns as the novel taught it how [Novel 458-3
   But in the style of the novel, its tracing [Novel 458-11
NOVELS. To the novels on the table, [Aug 493-11
NOVELTIES. Proud of such novelties of the sublime, [High-Toned 59-17
NOVEMBER. In that November off Tehuantepec, [Sea Surf 98-12
   In that November off Tehuantepec [Sea Surf 99-16
   In that November off Tehuantepec [Sea Surf 100-10
   In that November off Tehuantepec [Sea Surf 101-4
   In that November off Tehuantepec [Sea Surf 101-22
   When, at the wearier end of November, [Lunar 107-2
   It was when the trees were leafless first in November [Nigger
      151-3
   A calm November. Sunday in the fields. [Nigger 156-1
   The down-descent into November's void. [Sombre 67-30 P
   "The Region November" [115-title P
NOVITIATES. And celebration. Shrewd novitiates [C 39-7
NOWAY. Noway resembling his, a visible thing, [C 29-27
NOWHERE. And then nowhere again, away and away? [Dames 206-13
   Had got him nowhere. There was always the doubt, [Blue Bldg 216-17
   She is nowhere, to him. [Scavoir 231-20
   It was nowhere else, it was there and because [Landsc 242-6
   It was nowhere else, its place had to be supposed, [Landsc 242-7
   And catches from nowhere brightly-burning breath. [Novel 458-5
   The river that flows nowhere, like a sea. [R Conn 533-24
   Bring down from nowhere nothing's wax-like blooms, [Burnshaw
      47-20 P
   Through an alley to nowhere, [Grotesque 76-23 P
NOXIOUS. And a stiff and noxious place. [Bananas 54-13
NUANCES. "Nuances of a Theme by Williams" [18-title
   The nuances of the blue guitar. [MBG 182-22
NUBIA. Of euphonies, a skin from Nubia, [Hero 274-9
NUCLEUS. You know that the nucleus of a time is not [Papini 446-7
NUDE. "The Paltry Nude Starts on a Spring Voyage" [5-title
   Not as when the goldener nude [Paltry 6-4
   I figured you as nude between [Vincentine 52-11
   The Male Nude [NE Verses 106-title 13
   The Female Nude [NE Verses 106-title 14
   From everything, flying the flag of the nude, [Pure 330-21
   The flag of the nude above the holiday hotel. [Pure 331-1
   The spook and makings of the nude magnolia? [Slug 522-14
NUDES. Nudes or bottles. [Pears 196-3
NUDITY. "Nudity at the Capital" [145-title
   "Nudity in the Colonies" [145-title
NUMBER. By dividing the number of legs one sees by two. [Nigger
   157-9
   At least the number of people may thus be fixed. [Nigger 157-10
   Ah, but to play man number one, [MBG 166-3
   "The mass is nothing. The number of men in a mass [Dames 206-3
   The armies are forms in number, as cities are. [Choc 296-12
   A swarming of number over number, not [Choc 296-15
   The parts. Thus: Out of the number of his thoughts [Bship 80-15 P
NUMBERABLE. See not-numberable.
NUMBERED. The glass man, cold and numbered, dewily cries, [Oboe
   251-4
NUMBERS. Fly upward thick in numbers, fly across [Red Kit 31-22 P
   Instead of building ships, in numbers, build [Bship 78-1 P
NUN. On the east, sister and nun, and opened wide [Phenom 287-8
   "A Pastoral Nun" [378-title
NUNCLE. Well, nuncle, this plainly won't do. [Bananas 53-20
NUNNERY. Yet there is no spring in Florida, neither in boskage
   perdu, nor on the nunnery beaches. [Indian 112-7
NUNS. The bed, the books, the chair, the moving nuns, [Rome 508-21
   On the chair, a moving transparence on the nuns, [Rome 509-4
   No more than a bed, a chair and moving nuns, [Rome 510-23
   "Nuns Painting Water-Lilies" [92-title P
NUNZIO. See Nanzia Nunzio.
NUPTIAL. Balances with nuptial song. [MBG 181-4
NURSE. It has no nurse nor kin to know [Woman Song 360-5
NURSED. It was because night nursed them in its fold. [Babies 77-12
   Night nursed not him in whose dark mind [Babies 77-13
NURSES. The nurses of the spirit's innocence. [Luther 461-9
NUT-SHELL. And the nut-shell esplanades. [Archi 18-20 P
NUTSHELLS. Sonorous nutshells rattling inwardly. [C 31-13
NYMPHS. Fetched by such slick-eyed nymphs, this essential gold,
   [Orb 440-6

O. The soul, O ganders, flies beyond the parks [Swans 4-1
  And the soul, O ganders, being lonely, flies [Swans 4-11
  O sceptre of the sun, crown of the moon, [Monocle 13-2
  "O Florida, Venereal Soil" [47-title
  O caliper, do you scratch your buttocks [Lilacs 48-19
  "Look out, O caroller, [Jack-Rabbit 50-15
  O bough and bush and scented vine, in whom [Fictive 88-8
  O thin men of Haddam, [Thirteen 93-19
  O ashen admiral of the hale, hard blue. . . . [NE Verses 105-8
  "The fly on the rose prevents us, O season [Ghosts 119-15
  Chant, O ye faithful, in your paths [Botanist 2 136-5
  O pensioners, O demagogues and pay-men! [Men Fall 188-16
  Cunning-coo, O, cuckoo cock, [Country 207-2
  Belshazzar's brow, O, ruler, rude [Country 207-14
  And you and I are such things, O most miserable . . . [Gala
    248-3
  O, skin and spine and hair of you, Ercole, [Extracts 256-18
  And if there be nothing more, O bright, O bright, [Montra 260-2
  Item: The wind is never rounding O [Montra 263-17
  Make o, make o, make o, [Metamorph 266-1
  Are one, and here, O terra infidel. [EM 315-13
  "Less and Less Human, O Savage Spirit" [327-title
  Fellow after, O my companion, my fellow, my self, [NSF 392-23
  Master O master seated by the fire [AA 414-22
  O exhalation, O fling without a sleeve [Owl 435-19
  Lightly and lightly, O my land, [Imago 439-19
  Without a god, O silver sheen and shape, [Bouquet 449-16
  Keep quiet in the heart, O wild bitch. O mind [Puel 456-13
  Weight him down, O side-stars, with the great weightings of the
    end. [Madame 507-1
  And without eloquence, O, half-asleep, [Rome 509-11
  O, boatman, [Primordia 9-1 P
  O, boatman, [Primordia 9-3 P
  O chère maman, another, who, in turn, [Soldat 14-5 P
  O spirit of bones, O mountain of graves? [Sat Night 28-6 P
  O stagnant east-wind, palsied mare, [Room Gard 40-16 P
  O buckskin, O crosser of snowy divides, [Duck 61-1 P
  And sighing. These lives are not your lives, O free, [Duck 61-30P
  O bold, that rode your horses straight away. [Duck 61-31 P
  "How, Now, O, Brightener . . ." [97-title P
  O juventes, O filii, he contemplates [Someone 83-1 A
OAK. Sigh for me, night-wind, in the noisy leaves of the oak.
    [Nigger 150-15
  "Oak Leaves Are Hands" [title-272
  Under the oak trees, completely released. [Sol Oak 111-10 P
OAK-LEAVES. The freshness of the oak-leaves, not so much [Freed
    205-18
  That they were oak-leaves, as the way they looked. [Freed 205-19
  On urns and oak-leaves twisted into rhyme. [Sombre 68-1 P
OAKS. Before, before. Blood smears the oaks. [Contra I 267-3
  As the acorn broods on former oaks [Oak 272-13
  "Solitaire under the Oaks" [111-title P
OARS. Gripping their oars, as if they were sure of the way to
    their destination, [Prol 515-7
OARSMEN. A meaning which, as he entered it, would shatter the
    boat and leave the oarsmen quiet [Prol 516-7
OATEN. What wheaten bread and oaten cake and kind, [Orb 440-18
OBDURATE. Prickly and obdurate, dense, harmonious, [C 35-18
  He is that obdurate ruler who ordains [Greenest 59-28 P
OBEDIENCE. The bold, obedience to Ananke. [Stan Hero 83-24 P
OBEDIENT. Of breath, obedient to his trumpet's touch. [AA 415-19
  He became an inhabitant, obedient [Quiet 523-5
  We were obedient and dumb. [Phases 6-3 P
  And of obedient pillars? [Archi 17-5 P
OBESE. Followed the drift of the obese machine [Sea Surf 102-3
  By the obese opiates of sleep. Plain men in plain towns [NH
    467-20
  And the obese proprietor, who has a son [Greenest 58-16 P
OBEY. Of the park. They obey the rules of every skeleton. [Duck
    62-11 P
  We obey the coaxings of our end. [Ulysses 103-30 P
OBJECT. I can believe, in face of the object, [MBG 174-16
  Shows that this object is merely a state, [Glass 197-9
  In the object seen and saved that mystic [Hero 278-27
  Knows desire without an object of desire, [Chaos 358-3
  Of the object. The singers had to avert themselves [Cred 376-3
  Or else avert the object. Deep in the woods [Cred 376-4
  They sang desiring an object that was near, [Cred 376-6
  The object, grips it in savage scrutiny, [Cred 376-11
  Swaddled in revery, the object of [NSF 388-3
  The effect of the object is beyond the mind's [John 436-18
  Between us and the object, external cause, [John 437-15
  The object that rises with so much rhetoric, [Questions 462-11
  Within the very object that we seek, [Study I 463-9
  The pulse of the object, the heat of the body grown cold [Study I
    463-16
  In the perpetual reference, object [NH 466-13
  Straight to the transfixing object, to the object [NH 471-15

Beyond the object. He sits in his room, beside [NH 475-7
  God in the object itself, without much choice. [NH 475-10
  At the centre, the object of the will, this place, [NH 480-20
  The metaphor stirred his fear. The object with which he was com-
    pared [Prol 516-10
  Into a sense, an object the less; or else [Moonlight 531-12
  An object the more, an undetermined form [Moonlight 531-14
  "Desire & the Object" [85-title P
  If he sees an object on a table, much like [Someone 83-11 A
  An object the sum of its complications, seen [Someone 87-10 A
OBJECTIVENESS. In spite of the mere objectiveness of things,
    [Moonlight 531-21
  Shines on the mere objectiveness of things. [Moonlight 531-4
OBJECTS. "Prelude to Objects" [194-title
  In objects, as white this, white that. [Vari 235-5
  "A Completely New Set of Objects" [352-title
  Are inconstant objects of inconstant cause [NSF 389-23
  These houses, these difficult objects, dilapidate [NH 465-10
  The objects tingle and the spectator moves [NH 470-1
  With the objects. But the spectator also moves [NH 470-2
  Mistakes it for a world of objects, [Aug 491-3
  Should be as natural as natural objects, [Conversat 109-4 P
  "Local Objects" [111-title P
  And that, in his knowledge, local objects become [Local 111-12 P
  More precious than the most precious objects of home: [Local
    111-13 P
  The local objects of a world without a foyer, [Local 111-14 P
  Objects not present as a matter of course [Local 112-1 P
  In that sphere with so few objects of its own. [Local 112-3 P
  The few things, the objects of insight, the integrations [Local
    112-7 P
OBLATION. To make oblation fit. Where shall I find [Monocle 16-21
OBLIQUES. Writhings in wrong obliques and distances, [Ulti 430-1
OBLIQUITIES. Obliquities of those who pass beneath, [C 41-4
OBLITERATION. Of such obliteration on our paths, [Sunday 69-3
OBLIVION. Small oblivion, [Adequacy 243-20
  In our oblivion, of summer's [Hero 275-25
  There on the edges of oblivion. [Owl 435-18
  As for a child in an oblivion: [Soldat 13-16 P
  In the oblivion of cards [Sol Oaks 111-3 P
  5. The symbol of feasts and of oblivion . . . [Someone 86-8 A
OBLIVIOUS. Oblivious to the Aztec almanacs, [C 38-22
OBOE. "Asides on the Oboe" [250-title
OBSCURE. Fickle and fumbling, variable, obscure, [C 46-4
  Obscure, [Six Sig 73-19
  Are clear and are obscure; that it is night; [Two Figures 86-14
  And of all vigils musing the obscure, [Fictive 88-4
  A brush of white, the obscure, [Add 199-6
  Obscure Satanas, make a model [Hero 277-2
  The single bird, the obscure moon-- [Motive 288-8
  The obscure moon lighting an obscure world [Motive 288-9
  Obscure, in colors whether of the sun [NH 466-16
  A text that is an answer, although obscure. [NH 479-15
  Each one as part of the total wrath, obscure [Sombre 69-5 P
OBSCURED. The one obscured by sleep? [Watermelon 89-3
  You think that like the moon she is obscured [Spaniard 34-2 P
  The immaculate disclosure of the secret no more obscured,
    [Discov 96-2 P
OBSCURER. Of parades in the obscurer selvages. [EM 317-16
OBSCUREST. To seize, the obscurest as, the distant was . . . [Orb
    441-3
  Obscurest parent, obscurest patriarch, [Look 518-20
OBSCURITIES. The various obscurities of the moon, [Bowl 7-2 P
OBSCURITY. We feel the obscurity of an order, a whole, [Final
    524-11
OBSERVANT. In his observant progress, lesser things [C 34-19
OBSERVATEUR. To prefer L'Observateur de la Paix, since [Hero 276-6
  Of L'Observateur, the classic hero [Hero 276-8
OBSERVE. Observes and then continues to observe. [Canna 55-9
  Flap green ears in the heat. He might observe [Landsc 243-5
  Let the Secretary for Porcelain observe [Extracts 253-7
  Itself non-physical, may, by chance, observe [EM 325-22
  Dazzle yields to a clarity and we observe, [Descrip 341-10
  Observe her shining in the deadly trees. [Spaniard 34-15 P
  Among the second selves, sailor, observe [Pagoda 91-19 P
OBSERVED. Observed, when young, the nature of mankind, [Monocle
    17-22
  It is as if being was to be observed, [Moonlight 531-5
  Observed the waves, the rising and the swell [Woman Had 81-13 P
  The acrobat observed [Woman Had 82-7 P
  Observed as an absolute, himself. [Ulysses 101-15 P
OBSERVER. As the observer wills. [Pears 197-6
  If the observer says so: grandiloquent [Pastor 379-7
OBSERVES. Observes the canna with a clinging eye, [Canna 55-8
  Observes and then continues to observe. [Canna 55-9
  One observes profoundest shadows rolling. [Vari 235-14
  In war, observes each man profoundly. [Hero 274-14
  It observes the effortless weather turning blue [NSF 382-7
  He observes how the north is always enlarging the change, [AA
    412-24

OBSERVING. Observing the moon-blotches on the walls. [Babies 77-3
   And observing is completing and we are content, [Descrip 341-11
OBSOLETE. That obsolete fiction of the wide river in [Oboe 250-9
OBSTINATE. The conception sparkling in still obstinate thought.
   [Papini 448-4
OBSTREPEROUS. Making gulped potions from obstreperous drops,
   [C 46-9
OBSTRUCTION. That X is an obstruction, a man [Creat 310-16
OBVIOUS. Of the obvious whole, uncertain particles [Man Car 351-1
   The bright obvious stands motionless in cold. [Man Car 351-8
   Of an obvious acid is sure what it intends [NSF 390-8
OCCASION. The poem is the cry of its occasion, [NH 473-16
OCCASIONALLY. In this perfection, occasionally speaks [NH 477-4
OCCIDENT. And the Orient and the Occident embrace [Art Pop 112-17 P
OCCUPATION. An occupation, an exercise, a work, [NSF 405-18
OCCUR. Occur as they occur. So bluish clouds [Sleight 222-3
   With the metaphysical changes that occur, [EM 326-11
OCCURRED. Occurred above the empty house and the leaves [Sleight
   222-4
   Before the thought of evening had occurred [NH 482-23
   For which a fresh name always occurred, as if [Local 112-5 P
OCCURRING. Still keep occuring. What is, uncertainly, [NH 482-13
OCCURS. And pines that are cornets, so it occurs, [Sleight 222-14
OCEAN. In an interior ocean's rocking [Jasmine 79-11
   Of ocean, which like limpid water lay. [Sea Surf 99-4
   Of ocean, which in sinister flatness lay. [Sea Surf 99-22
   Of ocean, as a prelude holds and holds. [Sea Surf 100-16
   Deluged the ocean with a sapphire blue. [Sea Surf 101-3
   Of ocean, pondering dank stratagem. [Sea Surf 101-10
   Of ocean, perfected in indolence. [Sea Surf 102-4
   Inhuman, of the veritable ocean. [Key W 128-17
   Not the ocean of the virtuosi [Nigger 156-16
   A long time the ocean has come with you, [Hartford 226-7
   Of the ocean, ever-freshening, [Hartford 227-14
   And let the water-belly of ocean roar, [Montra 261-23
   On an old shore, the vulgar ocean rolls [Somnam 304-1
   The ocean, falling and falling on the hollow shore, [Somnam
   304-12
   A ship that rolls on a confected ocean, [EM 322-23
   The human ocean beats against this rock [Two V 354-19
   It is an ocean of watery images [Two V 355-11
   And still the grossest iridescence of ocean [NSF 383-7
   And the river becomes the landless, waterless ocean? [Degen
   444-21
   The ocean breathed out morning in one breath. [Our Stars 455-24
   A glassy ocean lying at the door, [NH 468-15
   See man-ocean.
OCEAN-BLOOMS. Hoo-hooed it in the darkened ocean-blooms. [Sea Surf
   100-5
OCEANED. See deep-oceaned.
OCEANIC. Her days, her oceanic nights, calling [Farewell 117-17
OCEANS. Lakes are more reasonable than oceans. Hence, [EM 325-6
   Made the maelstrom oceans mutter. [Lulu M 27-14 P
O'CLOCK. "Disillusionment of Ten O'Clock" [66-title
OCTOBER. Belgian Farm, October, 1914 [Phases 5-title 5
ODD. Yet let that trifle pass. Now, as this odd [C 32-13
   Consider the odd morphology of regret. [Nigger 154-10
   Slowly the room grows dark. It is odd about [Novel 458-19
   It is odd, too, how that Argentine is oneself, [Novel 458-22
   The youngest, the still fuzz-eyed, odd fleurettes, [Nuns 92-9 P
ODES. With interruptions by vast hymns, blood odes, [Duck 66-1 P
ODIOUS. Boomed from his very belly odious chords. [Monocle 17-17
   Turquoise the rock, at odious evening bright [Rock 528-7
ODOR. From the middle of his field. The odor [Yellow 237-2
   And the bees still sought the chrysanthemums' odor. [Contra II
   270-18
   Inhaled the appointed odor, while the doves [NSF 389-14
   An odor evoking nothing, absolute. [NSF 395-1
   The purple odor, the abundant bloom. [NSF 395-3
   And spread about them a warmer, rosier odor. [Aug 491-28
   One says even of the odor of this fruit, [Someone 87-14 A
   It is more than the odor of this core of earth [Someone 87-16 A
ODORS. Diffusing the civilest odors [Plot Giant 6-14
   Or spice the shores with odors of the plum? [Sunday 69-21
   Bearing the odors of the summer fields, [Wom Sun 445-13
OFF. Not far off. [Six Sig 74-22
   In that November off Tehuantepec, [Sea Surf 98-12
   In that November off Tehuantepec, [Sea Surf 99-16
   In that November off Tehuantepec [Sea Surf 100-10
   In that November off Tehuantepec [Sea Surf 101-4
   Like blooms? Like damasks that were shaken off [Sea Surf 101-13
   In that November off Tehuantepec [Sea Surf 101-22
   Falling, far off, from sky to land, [Mud 148-7
   Stamp down the phosphorescent toes, tear off [Nigger 155-7
   To float off in the floweriest barge, [Thought 184-18
   Stood up straight in the air, struck off [Thunder 220-7
   Shaking the water off, like a poodle, [Hartford 226-8
   The people that turned off and came [Adequacy 243-13
   His red cockade topped off a parade. [News 264-15
   But to strip off the complacent trifles, [Gigan 289-8

The precisions of fate, nothing fobbed off, nor changed [Repet
   310-8
That held the distances off: the villages [Wild 329-10
Held off the final, fatal distances, [Wild 329-11
Until its wings bear off night's middle witch; [Pure 333-1
Were one and swans far off were swans to come. [Descrip 343-10
Stronger and freer, a little better off. [Good Man 364-4
As morning throws off stale moonlight and shabby sleep. [NSF
   382-12
Bore off the residents of its noble Place. [NSF 391-9
I am the spouse. She took her necklace off [NSF 395-19
And what she felt fought off the barest phrase. [NSF 402-12
Shook off their dark marine in lapis light. [NH 484-8
Goes off a little on the side and stops. [Duck 63-33 P
The leaves cry . . . One holds off and merely hears the cry.
   [Course 96-13 P
See: cast-off; far-off.
OFFERING. And in the grass an offering made [Pourtraicte 21-8
   I make an offering, in the grass, [Pourtraicte 21-18
OFFICER. A car drives up. A soldier, an officer, [Bouquet 452-19
OFF-SHOOTS. Reflections and off-shoots, mimic-motes [Red Fern
   365-8
OFTEN. That we should ask this often as she sang. [Key W 129-9
   His dark familiar, often walked apart. [Anglais 148-14
   How often had he walked [Scavoir 231-9
   He thought often of the land from which he came, [NSF 393-16
   Not often realized, the lighter words [NH 488-8
   Of air and whirled away. But it has been often so. [Slug 522-4
   To bring destruction, often seems high-pitched. [Spaniard 34-17 P
   Often have the worst breaths. [Grotesque 74-18 P
   Too often to be more than secondhand. [Recit 87-2 P
OFTENER. Blares oftener and soon, will soon be constant. [Sad Gay
   122-14
OGRE. The table was set by an ogre, [Bananas 54-11
   Than body and in less than mind, ogre, [Sombre 67-14 P
OH. Oh, la . . . le pauvre! [Plot Giant 7-4
   Oh, but the very self of the storm [Joost 46-20
   Oh, sharp he was [Peacocks 58-1
   Oh! C'était mon extase et mon amour. [Sea Surf 100-21
   Oh! Blessed rage for order, pale Ramon, [Key W 130-11
   Most spiss--oh! Yes, most spissantly. [Snow Stars 133-2
   Oh! Rabbi, rabbi, fend my soul for me [Sun March 134-7
   Just where it was, oh beau caboose . . . It was part [Liadoff
   347-14
   Oh, that this lashing wind was something more [Chaos 357-7
   Within them right for terraces--oh, brave salut! [Belly 367-11
   He is and may be but oh! he is, he is, [NSF 388-10
   Keep you, keep you, I am gone, oh keep you as [Owl 432-14
   Oh as, always too heavy for the sense [Orb 441-2
   Or down a well. Breathe freedom, oh, my native, [Aug 490-13
   Oh, bend against the invisible; and lean [Blanche 10-6 P
   Oh! How suave a purple passed me by! [Stan MMO 19-3 P
   "Oh, hideous, horrible, horrendous hocks!" [Stan MMO 19-15 P
   "Oh, lissomeness turned lagging ligaments!" [Stan MMO 19-20 P
   Oh! Sal, the butcher's wife ate clams [Lulu M 27-9 P
   Oh ha, Oh ha. [Melancholy 32-12 P
   Oh! it will end badly. [Three 139-2 P
OHEU. The strength of death or triumph. Oheu! [Stan Hero 83-15 P
OH-HE-HE. Oh-hé-hé! Fragrant puppets [Cab 21-4 P
OHOO. Ohoo". . . [Motion 83-7
OHOYAHO. "Ohoyaho, [Motion 83-6
OINTMENT. What was the ointment sprinkled on my beard? [Hoon 65-10
   Out of my mind the golden ointment rained, [Hoon 65-13
OKLAHOMA. Over Oklahoma [Earthy 3-2
   In Oklahoma, [Motion 83-1
OKLAHOMAN. The Oklahoman--the Italian blue [NH 476-23
OLALLA. Saying: Olalla blanca en el blanco, [Novel 457-18
OLD. Is it for nothing, then, that old Chinese [Monocle 14-1
   Or an old horse. [Nuances 18-17
   This is old song [Magnifico 19-7
   As the flag above the old café-- [Hibiscus 23-2
   The old age of a watery realist, [C 28-23
   Between a Carolina of old time, [C 35-22
   Infants yet eminently old, then dome [C 43-26
   And my body, the old animal, [Joost 46-15
   The old animal, [Joost 46-22
   The darkened ghosts of our old comedy? [Heaven 56-11
   "A High-Toned Old Christian Woman" [59-title
   And I, then, tortured for old speech, [W Burgher 61-14
   Our old bane, green and bloated, serene, who cries, [Banal 62-16
   Only, here and there, an old sailor, [Ten O'C 66-12
   Encroachment of that old catastrophe, [Sunday 67-3
   Nor any old chimera of the grave, [Sunday 68-18
   We live in an old chaos of the sun, [Sunday 70-18
   Or old dependency of day and night, [Sunday 70-19
   This old, black dress, [Explan 72-14
   An old man sits [Six Sig 73-5
   In an old, frizzled, flambeaued manner, [Jasmine 79-5
   Like the thoughts of an old human, [Shifts 83-11
   Old pantaloons, duenna of the spring! [Polish Aunt 84-6

Of old devotions. [Peter 90-26
Her old light moves along the branches, [Lunar 107-3
Since by our nature we grow old, earth grows [Anatomy 108-1
My old boat goes round on a crutch [Sailing 120-2
He was young, and we, we are old. [Mozart 132-19
How can the world so old be so mad [Fading 139-9
Life is an old casino in a park. [Havana 142-9
Life is an old casino in a wood. [Havana 144-11
And the old casino likewise may define [Havana 145-7
This is his essence: the old fantoche [MBG 181-16
One sits and beats an old tin can, lard pail. [Dump 202-26
Tired of the old descriptions of the world, [Freed 204-13
It was an old rebellious song, [Country 207-8
A. Well, an old order is a violent one. [Connois 216-1
Full of javelins and old fire-balls, [Dezem 218-3
Old nests and there is blue in the woods. [Cuisine 227-15
"On an Old Horn" [230-title
Being, for old men, time of their time. [Vari 233-11
From an old delusion, an old affair with the sun, [Bottle 239-10
That's the old world. In the new, all men are priests. [Extracts
   254-2
Old worm, my pretty quirk, [Metamorph 265-14
They are sick of each old romance, returning. [Hero 274-6
Of each old revolving dance, the music [Hero 274-7
And old John Rocket dozes on his pillow. [Phenom 286-11
And you, my semblables--the old flag of Holland [Dutch 290-13
He is not here, the old sun, [Possum 293-13
On an old shore, the vulgar ocean rolls [Somnam 304-1
Born old, familiar with the depths of the heart, [Repet 306-17
Is it the old, the roseate parent or [Repet 308-16
"The Bed of Old John Zeller" [326-title
Sequences, thought of among spheres in the old peak of night:
   [Bed 326-19
Of things at least that was thought of in the old peak of night.
   [Bed 327-8
For example, this old man selling oranges [Feo 333-18
In which old stars are planets of morning, fresh [Descrip 344-10
Of a vast people old in meditation . . . [New Set 353-4
Continually. And old John Zeller stands [Two V 354-21
Cadaverous undulations. Rest, old mould . . . [Two V 355-14
Summer is changed to winter, the young grow old, [Chaos 357-14
The old brown hen and the old blue sky, [Silent 359-5
It is the old man standing on the tower, [Cred 374-1
And yet see only one, in his old coat, [NSF 389-5
In that old coat, those sagging pantaloons, [NSF 389-9
The old seraph, parcel-gilded, among violets [NSF 389-13
The bottomless trophy, new hornsman after old? [NSF 390-18
She gives transparence. But she has grown old, [AA 413-14
Lose the old uses that they made of them, [Orb 441-14
Neither remembered nor forgotten, nor old, [Bouquet 451-6
An attic glass, hums of the old Lutheran bells [Golden 460-13
"The Old Lutheran Bells at Home" [461-title
The way the drowsy, infant, old men do. [Questions 463-3
And yet the wind whimpers oldly of old age [NH 477-2
Of an old and disused ambit of the soul [Aug 489-6
She is exhausted and a little old. [Aug 496-4
"An Old Man Asleep" [501-title
The chimney is fifty years old and slants to one side. [Plain
   502-18
"To an Old Philosopher in Rome" [508-title
It is like a new account of everything old, [Armor 529-17
As if some Old Man of the Chimney, sick [Phases 5-6 P
It is that Old Man, lost among the trees. [Phases 5-15 P
And old voice cried out, "Come!" [Phases 6-2 P
But twiddling mon idée, as old men will, [Stan MMO 19-4 P
Of the well-thumbed, infinite pages of her masters, who will
   seem old to her, requiting less and less her feeling: [Piano
   22-7 P
And new things make old things again . . . [Abnormal 24-12 P
The constant cry against an old order, [Polo 37-13 P
An order constantly old, [Polo 37-14 P
Is itself old and stale. [Polo 37-15 P
"The Old Woman and the Statue" [43-title P
And daunt that old assassin, heart's desire? [Duck 66-11 P
To ride an old mule round the keys-- [Stan MBG 73-7 P
The old woman that knocks at the door [Grotesque 77-1 P
It is an old bitch, an old drunk, [Grotesque 77-3 P
Berceuse, transatlantic. The children are men, old men, [Woman
   Had 82-10 P
Are old men breathed on by a maternal voice, [Woman Had 82-14 P
Children and old men and philosophers, [Woman Had 82-15 P
The old men, the philosophers, are haunted by that [Woman Had
   82-23 P
In a health of weather, knowing a few, old things, [Americana
   93-17 P
To be remembered, the old shape [Ulysses 104-19 P
Among the old men that you know, [Child 106-13 P
And fill the earth with young men centuries old [Ideal 88-11 A
And old men, who have chosen, and are cold [Ideal 88-12 A
See year-old.

OLDER. All this is older than its oldest hymn, [Havana 144-28
   There were the sheets high up on older trees, [Forces 229-13
   Older than any man could be. [News 264-10
   It is older than the oldest speech of Rome. [Rome 510-4
   A new scholar replacing an older one reflects [Look 519-4
OLDEST. All this is older than its oldest hymn, [Havana 144-28
   Because we suffer, our oldest parent, peer [EM 315-17
   Less real. For the oldest and coldest philosopher, [AA 418-9
   It is older than the oldest speech of Rome. [Rome 510-4
   And the oldest and the warmest heart was cut [Quiet 523-10
   From youngest day or oldest night and far [Greenest 54-1 P
OLDEST-NEWEST. The oldest-newest day is the newest alone. [NH
   476-19
   The oldest-newest night does not creak by, [NH 476-20
OLDLY. And yet the wind whimpers oldly of old age [NH 477-2
OLEY. Presents itself in Oley when the hay, [Cred 374-7
OLIMPICO. A Museo Olimpico, so much [Descrip 342-3
OLIVE. Which changed light green to olive then to blue. [Nigger
   152-10
   At the legend of the maroon and olive forest, [Plant 506-17
OLU. "Olu" the eunuchs cried. "Ululalu." [Lulu G 26-23 P
OLYMPIA. Oxidia is Olympia. [MBG 182-8
OLYMPUS. Soaring Olympus glitters in the sun. [Infernale 25-12 P
OMEGA. Naked Alpha, not the hierophant Omega, [NH 469-5
   Alpha fears men or else Omega's men [NH 469-11
   Omega is refreshed at every end. [NH 469-21
OMEN. The dulcet omen fit for such a house. [C 44-26
OMINOUS. At the neutral centre, the ominous element, [Landsc 242-1
OMITTING. (Omitting reefs of cloud): [Delight 162-5
OMNES. Shebang. Exeunt omnes. Here was prose [C 37-2
OMNI-DIAMOND. Sound-soothing pearl and omni-diamond, [Golden 460-21
OMNIUM. The great Omnium descends on us [Ulysses 102-3 P
   The great Omnium descends on me, [Presence 106-5 P
ONCE. For once vent honey? [Carolinas 5-3
   But that of earth both comes and goes at once. [Monocle 15-26
   For the legendary moonlight that once burned [C 33-27
   Because he built a cabin who once planned [C 41-19
   He once thought necessary. Like Candide, [C 42-16
   The return to social nature, once begun, [C 43-20
   The world, a turnip once so readily plucked, [C 45-12
   On which she embroidered fantails once [Emperor 64-11
   Unreal, give back to us what once you gave: [Fictive 88-17
   Once, a fear pierced him, [Thirteen 94-15
   Perhaps, if winter once could penetrate [Pharynx 96-10
   That I loved her once . . . Farewell. Go on, high ship. [Farewell
      118-10
   No more phrases, Swenson: I was once [Lions 124-10
   Once more the longest resonance, to cap [Havana 143-16
   Will never know that these were once [Postcard 158-15
   Once it was, the repose of night, [Nightgown 214-17
   The strawberries once in the Apennines, [Arcades 225-2
   The strawberries once in the Apennines . . . [Arcades 226-1
   The bird kept saying that birds had once been men, [Horn 230-1
   But would it be amen, in choirs, if once [Extracts 258-24
   Too conscious of too many things at once, [Hand 271-2
   Too conscious of too many things at once, [Hand 271-7
   Flora she was once. She was florid [Oak 272-4
   Once by the lips, once by the services [EM 317-19
   With which we vested, once, the golden forms [EM 317-25
   Once more he turned to that which could not be fixed. [Two V
      353-11
   Like the wind that lashes everything at once. [Chaos 358-6
   Once to make captive, once to subjugate [Cred 376-12
   Or yield to subjugation, once to proclaim [Cred 376-13
   At once? Is it a luminous flittering [NSF 396-16
   Once more night's pale illuminations, gold [NSF 402-24
   Everywhere in space at once, cloud-pole [Ulti 430-3
   If we were ever, just once, at the middle, fixed [Ulti 430-5
   Nor all one's luck at once in a play of strings. [John 437-13
   Now, once, he accumulates himself and time [Papini 447-12
   In space and the self, that touched them both at once [NH 483-7
   They said, "We are back once more in the land of the elm trees,
      [NH 487-3
   In which hundreds of eyes, in one mind, see at once. [NH 488-6
   And the sense of the archaic touched us at once [Aug 494-13
   That were rosen once, [Aug 495-4
   St. Armorer's was once an immense success. [Armor 529-1
   Call it, once more, a river, an unnamed flowing, [R Conn 533-18
   It was silver once, [Phases 3-7 P
   Is it, once more, the mysterious beauté, [Soldat 12-1 P
   And see themselves as once they were, [Sat Night 28-5 P
   Than the thought that once was native to the skull; [Burnshaw
      49-18 P
   Of rose, or what will once more rise to rose, [Burnshaw 49-27 P
   There was a heaven once, [Greenest 53-26 P
   And there he heard the voices that were once [Greenest 54-8 P
   If once the statue were to rise, if it stood, [Greenest 54-25 P
   Forth from their tabernacles once again [Greenest 55-27 P
   To see, once more, this hacked-up world of tools, [Duck 61-9 P
   Is each man thinking his separate thoughts or, for once, [Duck

62-18 P
Prolonged, repeated and once more prolonged, [Duck 63-32 P
For a moment, once each century or two. [Duck 65-20 P
Once each century or two. But then so great, [Duck 65-24 P
It would be done. And once the thing was done, [Bship 78-14 P
Once the assassins wore stone masks and did [Bship 78-15 P
As I wished, once they fell backward when my breath [Bship
  78-16 P
To his gorge, hangman, once helmet-maker [Stan Hero 84-19 P
So long as the mind, for once, fulfilled itself? [Theatre 91-18 P
ONCLE. "Le Monocle de Mon Oncle" [13-title
ONCOMING. The oncoming fantasies of better birth. [C 39-28
  With none of the prescience of oncoming dreams, [AA 413-7
ON-DIT. An expressive on-dit, a profession. [Dutch 290-19
ONE. Like one who scrawls a listless testament [Swans 4-5
  Noiselessly, like one more wave. [Paltry 5-10
  That not one curl in nature has survived? [Monocle 14-9
  Ticks tediously the time of one more year. [Monocle 15-2
  The ephemeral blues must merge for them in one, [Monocle 15-8
  Or one man [Magnifico 19-5
  Foam and cloud are one. [Fabliau 23-9
  The imagination, the one reality [Weep Woman 25-8
  One eats one paté, even of salt, quotha. [C 28-1
  Dwindled to one sound strumming in his ear, [C 28-19
  Of one vast, subjugating, final tone. [C 30-9
  Aware of exquisite thought. The storm was one [C 32-31
  The one integrity for him, the one [C 36-20
  Crispin in one laconic phrase laid bare [C 36-26
  What is one man among so many men? [C 41-25
  Can one man think one thing and think it long? [C 41-27
  Can one man be one thing and be it long? [C 41-28
  To fetch the one full-pinioned one himself [C 44-28
  The third one gaping at the orioles [C 44-30
  Here is an eye. And here are, one by one, [Worms 49-18
  Each one in her decent curl. [Bananas 54-8
  Foretell each night the one abysmal night, [Heaven 56-18
  The muscular one, and bid him whip [Emperor 64-2
  What one star can carve, [Six Sig 75-2
  They carry the wizened one [Cortege 80-1
  And sleep with one eye watching the stars fall [Two Figures
    86-11
  "To the One of Fictive Music" [87-title
  The one obscured by sleep? [Watermelon 89-3
  Are one. [Thirteen 93-4
  Are one. [Thirteen 93-6
  Of one of many circles. [Thirteen 94-8
  The slopping of the sea grew still one night [Sea Surf 98-13
  The slopping of the sea grew still one night. [Sea Surf 99-17
  The slopping of the sea grew still one night [Sea Surf 100-11
  What pistache one, ingenious and droll, [Sea Surf 102-5
  And heaven rolled as one and from the two [Sea Surf 102-14
  In his time, this one had little to speak of, [Norfolk 111-8
  And that one was never a man of heart. [Norfolk 111-12
  The making of his son was one more duty. [Norfolk 111-13
  Except the one she sang and, singing, made. [Key W 130-2
  See pretty much one: [Botanist 1 134-17
  An earthier one, tum, tum-ti-tum, [Botanist 2 136-9
  And then another, one by one, and all [Eve Angels 137-27
  To go to Florida one of these days, [Winter B 141-16
  And in one of the little arrondissements [Winter B 141-17
  Only we two are one, not you and night, [Re-state 146-6
  When to be and delight to be seemed to be one, [Anglais 149-14
  And their blackness became apparent, that one first [Nigger 151-2
  And the future emerging out of us seem to be one. [Nigger 151-12
  By dividing the number of legs one sees by two. [Nigger 157-9
  One of the leaves that have fallen in autumn? [Nigger 158-12
  Ah, but to play man number one, [MBG 166-3
  A million people on one string? [MBG 166-15
  And I are one. The orchestra [MBG 171-12
  First one beam, then another, then [MBG 172-9
  One of its monstrous lutes, not be [MBG 175-9
  Two things, the two together as one, [MBG 175-11
  Another on earth, the one a voice [MBG 177-9
  To say of one mask it is like, [MBG 181-7
  One man, the idea of man, that is the space, [Thought 185-11
  The head of one of the men that are falling, placed [Men Fall
    188-9
  One of many, between two poles. So, [Glass 197-10
  One after another washing the mountains bare. [Loaf 200-7
  Each one its paradigm." There are not leaves [Dames 206-6
  Yet one face keeps returning (never the one), [Dames 206-14
  The deer and the dachshund are one. [Jersey 210-4
  Are one. My window is twenty-nine three [Jersey 210-14
  Since the deer and the dachshund are one. [Jersey 210-21
  (This is one of the thoughts [Bagatelles 213-21
  One of the songs of that dominance.) [Bagatelles 213-24
  Two things are one. (Pages of illustrations.) [Connois 215-3
  Proves that these opposite things partake of one, [Connois 215-14
  A. Well, an old order is a violent one. [Connois 216-1
  This proves nothing. Just one more truth, one more [Connois 216-2

Are you not le plus pur, you ancient one? [Blue Bldg 217-20
You are one . . . Go hunt for honey in his hair. [Blue Bldg
  217-22
You are one of the not-numberable mice [Blue Bldg 217-23
One part is man, the other god: [Dezem 218-7
Slowly, one man, savager than the rest, [Thunder 220-5
Of one wilder than the rest (like music blunted, [Thunder 220-23
And the women have only one side. [Common 221-25
One self from another, as these peaches do. [Peaches 224-20
But the town and the fragrance were never one, [Arcades 225-13
The church bells clap one night in the week. [Cuisine 227-16
No horses to ride and no one to ride them [Forces 229-10
If the stars that move together as one, disband, [Horn 230-17
Another image, it is one she has made. [Scavoir 232-2
One of the portents of the will that was. [Vari 233-4
One sparrow is worth a thousand gulls, [Vari 233-12
One boy swims under a tub, one sits [Vari 235-16
Of which one is a part as in a unity, [Yellow 236-18
Emotions becoming one. The actor is [Of Mod 240-13
One wild rhapsody a fake for another. [Waldorf 241-3
To be projected by one void into [Landsc 242-13
Slid over the western cataract, yet one, [Beard 247-13
One only, one thing that was firm, even [Beard 247-14
One thing remaining, infallible, would be [Beard 247-18
And her dress were one and she said, "I have said no [Uruguay
  249-3
One year, death and war prevented the jasmine scent [Oboe 251-8
But we and the diamond globe at last were one. [Oboe 251-16
We had always been partly one. It was as we came [Oboe 251-17
To see him, that we were wholly one, as we heard [Oboe 251-18
That are paper days. The false and true are one. [Extracts 253-3
If they could gather their theses into one, [Extracts 254-6
Collect their thoughts together into one, [Extracts 254-7
One man, their bread and their remembered wine? [Extracts 254-17
The mass of men are one. Chaos is not [Extracts 255-26
Revolvers and shoot each other. One remains. [Extracts 256-2
That other one wanted to think his way to life, [Extracts 256-21
He, that one, wanted to think his way to life, [Extracts 257-4
Equal to memory, one line in which [Extracts 259-17
One of the major miracles, that fall [Montra 262-6
One of the sacraments between two breaths, [Montra 262-8
One string, an absolute, not varying [Montra 263-15
But let this one sense be the single main. [Montra 264-3
One chemical afternoon in mid-autumn, [Contra II 270-1
One with us, in the heaved-up noise, still [Hero 273-23
In him made one, and in that saying [Hero 279-16
Made single, made one. This was not denial. [Gigan 289-14
One foot approaching, one uplifted arm. [Choc 296-16
The young man is well-disclosed, one of the gang, [Lack 303-6
The giants that each one of them becomes [Repet 307-3
Millions of instances of which I am one. [Repet 309-15
Are one, and here, O terra infidel. [EM 315-13
All sorts of notes? Or did he play only one [EM 316-12
The last, or sounds so single they seemed one? [EM 316-15
To hear only what one hears, one meaning alone, [EM 320-27
What lover has one in such rocks, what woman, [EM 323-24
It may be that one life is a punishment [EM 323-26
Each one, by the necessity of being [EM 324-5
He would be the lunatic of one idea [EM 325-12
If there must be a god in the house, let him be one [Less 328-7
To that be-misted one and apart from her. [Wild 328-14
But there was one invalid in that green glade [Pure 331-2
We knew one parent must have been divine, [Pure 331-19
As one of the secretaries of the moon, [Feo 333-10
Or will be. Building and dream are one. [Sketch 335-19
The spirit of one dwelling in a seed, [Descrip 341-19
Were one and swans far off were swans to come. [Descrip 343-10
One thinking of apocalyptic legions. [Descrip 343-14
And by the fear that defeats and dreams are one. [Men Made 356-4
In the one ear of the fisherman, who is all [Think 356-9
One ear, the wood-doves are singing a single song. [Think 356-10
The bass keep looking ahead, upstream, in one [Think 356-11
One eye, in which the dove resembles the dove. [Think 356-14
There is one dove, one bass, one fisherman. [Think 356-15
In that one ear it might strike perfectly: [Think 357-2
State the disclosure. In that one eye the dove [Think 357-3
One will and many wills, and the wind, [Silent 359-12
Brought down to one below the eaves, [Silent 359-14
One person should come by chance, [Woman Song 360-17
In which the rain is all one thing, [Human 363-8
One seed alone grow wild, the railway-stops [Cats 367-14
As one of the relics of the heart. [Prejudice 368-16
As one of the relics of the mind . . . [Prejudice 368-19
One of the limits of reality [Cred 374-6
One day enriches a year. One woman makes [Cred 374-21
The rest look down. One man becomes a race, [Cred 374-22
Or do the other days enrich the one? [Cred 374-24
In the sunshine is a filial form and one [Cred 375-3
With one eye watch the willow, motionless. [Cred 377-8
She said poetry and apotheosis are one. [Past Nun 378-13

The death of one god is the death of all. [NSF 381-7
Does not see these separate figures one by one [NSF 389-4
And yet see only one, in his old coat, [NSF 389-5
On one another, as a man depends [NSF 392-5
That walk away as one in the greenest body. [NSF 392-15
Are one and the sailor and the sea are one. [NSF 392-22
One voice repeating, one tireless chorister, [NSF 394-7
One sole face, like a photograph of fate, [NSF 394-10
And one that chaffers the time away? [NSF 396-19
The one refused the other one to take, [NSF 401-9
She lived in her house. She had two daughters, one [NSF 402-1
Of four, and one of seven, whom she dressed [NSF 402-2
To be stripped of every fiction except one, [NSF 404-9
One of the vast repetitions final in [NSF 405-20
They will get it straight one day at the Sorbonne. [NSF 406-22
Yet it depends on yours. The two are one. [NSF 407-10
As one that is strong in the bushes of his eyes. [AA 414-7
Or, the persons act one merely by being here. [AA 416-3
On flames. The scholar of one candle sees [AA 417-1
Extinguishing our planets, one by one, [AA 417-17
Through many places, as if it stood still in one, [Cata 424-12
Or one man who, for us, is greater than they, [Antag 425-16
One goes on asking questions. That, then, is one [Ulti 429-16
There came a day, there was a day--one day [Owl 432-19
Whose venom and whose wisdom will be one. [John 437-21
One poem proves another and the whole, [Orb 441-4
And the world the central poem, each one the mate [Orb 441-20
That speaks, denouncing separate selves, both one. [Orb 441-25
Each one, his fated eccentricity, [Orb 443-17
Of color, the giant of nothingness, each one [Orb 443-21
Toward a consciousness of red and white as one, [Bouquet 450-9
He enters the room and calls. No one is there. [Bouquet 452-21
The ocean breathed our morning in one breath. [Our Stars 455-24
By one caterpillar is great Africa devoured [Puel 456-2
At the upper right, a pyramid with one side [What We 460-2
As if the crude collops came together as one, [NH 461-1
And more, in branchings after day. One part [NH 468-23
And one from central earth to central sky [NH 469-1
For one it is enough; for one it is not; [NH 469-14
In which he is and as and is are one. [NH 476-4
Among time's images there is not one [NH 476-16
From a different source. But there was always one: [NH 479-3
Being part of everything come together as one. [NH 482-11
The shawl across one shoulder and the hat. [NH 483-21
Touches, as one hand touches another hand, [NH 484-19
Real and unreal are two in one: New Haven [NH 485-23
In which hundreds of eyes, in one mind, see at once. [NH 488-6
And the sex of its voices, as the voice of one [Aug 489-14
Difference and were one? It had to be [Aug 494-4
We resembled one another at the sight. [Aug 494-15
Of sense, evoking one thing in many men, [Aug 494-18
Here the adult one is still banded with fulgor, [Aug 495-24
A welcome at the door to which no one comes? [Angel 496-6
I am one of you and being one of you [Angel 496-13
A likeness, one of the race of fathers: earth [Irish 502-7
The chimney is fifty years old and slants to one side. [Plain
  502-18
"One of the Inhabitants of the West" [503-title
At evening's one star [Inhab 503-13
This one star's blaze. [Inhab 504-11
And yet this end and this beginning are one, [Hermit 506-1
And one last look at the ducks is a look [Hermit 506-2
Two parallels become one, a perspective, of which [Rome 508-9
As to one, and, as to one, most penitent, [Rome 509-21
The one invulnerable man among [Rome 510-8
Not one of the masculine myths we used to make, [Look 518-7
A new scholar replacing an older one reflects [Look 519-4
And kept saying over and over one same, same thing, [Slug 522-6
Babbling, each one, the uniqueness of its sound. [Quiet 523-13
Out of all the indifferences, into one thing: [Final 524-6
We say God and the imagination are one . . . [Final 524-14
An invention, an embrace between one desperate clod [Rock 525-13
The mirror of the planets, one by one, [Rock 528-5
Fixed one for good in geranium-colored day. [Armor 529-4
The one moonlight, in the simple-colored night, [Moonlight 531-1
The one moonlight, the various universe, intended [Moonlight
  532-3
His self and the sun were one [Planet 532-13
Like the last one. But there is no ferryman. [R Conn 533-11
For one, [Primordia 7-16 P
At least one baby in you. [Primordia 9-23 P
For no one proud, nor stiff, [Archi 18-11 P
No solemn one, nor pale, [Archi 18-12 P
Is there one word of sunshine in this plaint? [Stan MMO 19-16 P
Having, each one, most praisable [Parasol 20-5 P
And that confident one, Marie, the wearer of cheap stones,
  who will have grown still and restless; [Piano 22-5 P
Neither one, nor the two together. [Indigo 22-14 P
Of larger company than one. Therefore, [Good Bad 33-11 P
One man opposing a society [Lytton 38-14 P

Happens to like is one [Table 40-14 P
As one. [Room Gard 41-3 P
Her ear unmoved. She was that tortured one, [Old Woman 44-9 P
Their voice and the voice of the tortured wind were one, [Old
  Woman 45-27 P
Each voice within the other, seeming one, [Old Woman 45-28 P
And the dew and the ploughman still will best be one. [Burnshaw
  48-2 P
In one, except a throne raised up beyond [Greenest 55-10 P
Color and color brightening into one, [Greenest 58-5 P
Are all men thinking together as one, thinking [Duck 62-19 P
For the million, perhaps, two ducks instead of one; [Duck
  65-2 P
Each one as part of the total wrath, obscure [Sombre 69-5 P
The mirror of other nights combined in one. [Sombre 71-10 P
Night and the imagination being one. [Sombre 71-34 P
One of Those Hibiscuses of Damozels [Grotesque 74-title 1
Themselves to one. [Bship 78-24 P
"It is a lesser law than the one itself, [Bship 78-26 P
Unless it is the one itself, or unless [Bship 78-27 P
On the sea, is both law and evidence in one, [Bship 78-29 P
Where I or one or the part is the equal of [Bship 79-25 P
Where I or one or the part is the equal of [Bship 79-25 P
Covered one morning with blue, one morning with white, [Bship
  80-10 P
The ultimate one, though they are parts of it. [Bship 80-27 P
It must be the hand of one, it must be the hand [Bship 81-8 P
And in a bed in one room, alone, a listener [Sick 90-13 P
One father proclaims another, the patriarchs [Role 93-7 P
Not one of the five, and keep a rendezvous, [Souls 95-5 P
Itself, until, at last, the cry concerns no one at all. [Course
  97-3 P
"If knowledge and the thing known are one [Ulysses 99-16 P
And if to know one man is to know all [Ulysses 99-20 P
And being are one: the right to know [Ulysses 101-18 P
And the right to be are one. We come [Ulysses 101-19 P
As a free race. We know it, one [Ulysses 102-4 P
By one, in the right of all. Each man [Ulysses 102-5 P
And being are one--the right to know [Presence 106-3 P
There is one, unnamed, that broods [Child 106-14 P
And one of us spoke and all of us believed [Letters 107-14 P
The one thing common to all life, the human [Conversat 109-1 P
In which one of these three worlds are the four of us [Conversat
  109-16 P
That poem about the pineapple, the one [As Leave 117-1 P
The one about the credible hero, the one [As Leave 117-3 P
The earth remains of one color-- [Three 130-15 P
The porcelain in one hand . . . [Three 138-6 P
Begging for one another. [Three 139-12 P
One candle replaces [Three 141-4 P
Is one thing to me [Three 143-5 P
And one thing to another, [Three 143-6 P
So it is the green of one tree [Three 143-7 P
Of there, where the truth was not the respect of one, [Someone
  85-11 A
Like the same orange repeating on one tree [Someone 85-21 A
9. The coconut and cokerel in one. [Someone 86-12 A
See and-a-one.
ONE-FOOT. The one-foot stars were couriers of its death [Page
  421-19
ONE-HALF. One-half of all its installments paid. [MBG 182-2
ONE-NESS. Wet with water and sparkling in the one-ness of their
  motion. [Prol 515-9
ONES. Its animal. The angelic ones [MBG 174-6
  There the dogwoods, the white ones and the pink ones, [Forces
  228-22
  The wrinkled roses tinkle, the paper ones, [Extracts 252-2
  To momentary ones, are blended, [Hero 279-21
  Such seemings are the actual ones: the way [Descrip 339-17
  And through the air. The smaller ones [Dinner 110-2 P
ONESELF. One is always seeing and feeling oneself, [Prelude 195-8
  Be merely oneself, as superior as the ear [Dump 203-1
  Not as one would have arranged them for oneself, [Novel 458-10
  It is odd, too, how that Argentine is oneself, [Novel 458-22
ONE-SENSED. Or is it I that, wandering, know, one-sensed, [Souls
  95-4 P
ONLY. Severs not only lands but also selves. [C 30-4
  And only, in the fables that he scrawled [C 31-18
  The only emperor is the emperor of ice-cream [Emperor 64-8
  The only emperor is the emperor of ice cream. [Emperor 64-16
  Only, here and there, an old sailor, [Ten O'C 66-12
  Only in silent shadows and in dreams? [Sunday 67-14
  Only a negress who supposes [Virgin 71-2
  Left only Death's ironic scraping. [Peter 92-10
  The only moving thing [Thirteen 92-15
  It is only the way one feels, to say [Sailing 120-22
  Only the great height of the rock [How Live 126-3
  If it was only the dark voice of the sea [Key W 129-10
  If it was only the outer voice of sky [Key W 129-12
  And you. Only we two may interchange [Re-state 146-4

Only we two are one, not you and night, [Re-state 146-6
That night is only the background of our selves, [Re-state
  146-10
Only last year he said that the naked moon [Anglais 148-19
Of things as they are and only the place [MBG 167-19
Good air, my only friend, believe, [MBG 175-20
Friendlier than my only friend, [MBG 176-1
That's it, the only dream they knew, [MBG 183-17
Son only of man and sun of men, [Thought 185-25
That he spoke only by doing what he did. [Men Fall 188-12
In the sum of the parts, there are only the parts. [On Road
  204-3
Tonight there are only the winter stars. [Dezem 218-1
And the women have only one side. [Common 221-25
Only the rich remember the past, [Arcades 225-1
It was in the earth only [Yellow 236-4
Only this evening I saw again low in the sky [Martial 237-10
Though the air change. Only this evening I saw it again, [Martial
  238-13
He had only not to live, to walk in the dark, [Landsc 242-12
One only, one thing that was firm, even [Beard 247-14
A monster-maker, an eye, only an eye, [Extracts 252-22
A shapener of shapes for only the eye, [Extracts 253-1
It is only that we are able to die, to escape [Extracts 259-1
Magical only for the change they make. [Montra 262-9
And stones, only this imager. [Jumbo 269-18
Like a white abstraction only, a feeling [Hero 276-26
Without lineage or language, only [Couch 295-7
And the associations beyond death, even if only [Lack 303-13
Only the eye as faculty, that the mind [Crude 305-15
Is a landscape only of the eye; and that [Crude 305-17
If these were only words that I am speaking [Repet 307-19
These are real only if I make them so. Whistle [Holiday 313-7
If only he would not pity us so much, [EM 315-20
All sorts of notes? Or did he play only one [EM 316-12
To hear only what one hears, one meaning alone, [EM 320-27
Of the mind, result only in disaster. It follows, [Bed 326-14
Book of a concept only possible [Descrip 345-2
That the rocket was only an inferior cloud. [Liadoff 347-16
Only Indyterranean [Analysis 348-9
That cannot now be fixed. Only there is [Two V 354-10
God only was his only elegance. [Good Man 364-2
Each matters only in that which it conceives. [Past Nun 379-3
If only imagined but imagined well. [NSF 385-15
And yet see only one, in his old coat, [NSF 389-5
In its own only precious ornament. [NSF 396-5
Of a speech only a little of the tongue? [NSF 397-4
Only the unmuddled self of sleep, for them. [NSF 402-18
Two parallels that meet if only in [NSF 407-12
Only the half they can never possess remains, [AA 413-9
An isolation which only the two could share. [AA 419-18
But only of your swarthy motion, [Countryman 428-18
Complete, because at the middle, if only in sense, [Ulti 430-8
The dead. Only the thought of those dark three [Owl 432-17
Because, in chief, it, only, can defend [John 436-11
Her only place and person, a self of her [Orb 441-24
It is only that this warmth and movement are like [Wom Sun 445-4
Invisibly clear, the only love. [Wom Sun 445-15
Has only the formulations of midnight. [Papini 446-4
That Argentine. Only the real can be [Novel 458-20
They only know a savage assuagement cries [NH 467-22
If only in the branches sweeping in the rain: [NH 481-1
Myself, only half of a figure of a sort, [Angel 497-6
It was only a glass because he looked in it. It was nothing he
  could be told. [Madame 507-6
From fire and be part only of that of which [Rome 509-7
Only in misery, the afflatus of ruin, [Rome 509-24
Was so much less. Only the wind [Two Illus 513-8
But only its momentary breath, [Two Illus 513-16
Left only the fragments found in the grass, [Two Illus 515-3
Had left in them only a brilliance, of unaccustomed origin,
  [Prol 515-11
Only a little way, and not beyond, unless between himself
  [Prol 516-12
Is only what the sun does every day, [Look 517-16
But was it Ulysses? Or was it only the warmth of the sun [World
  521-10
The two kept beating together. It was only day. [World 521-12
Some affluence, if only half-perceived, [Planet 533-1
Only, an eyeball in the mud, [Phases 3-16 P
Only the surfaces--the bending arm, [Blanche 10-3 P
Only the lusty and the plenteous [Archi 18-17 P
And wronging her, if only as she thinks, [Red Kit 30-15 P
Not only in itself but in the things [Red Kit 31-6 P
Visible over the sea. It is only enough [Burnshaw 50-16 P
Death, only, sits upon the serpent throne: [Greenest 55-17 P
Be free to sing, if only a sorrowful song. [Greenest 58-33 P
He, only, caused the statue to be made [Greenest 60-1 P
True, only an inch, but an inch at a time, and inch [Duck 60-19 P
And only an agony of dreams can help, [Duck 61-24 P

Is only another egoist wearing a mask, [Duck 63-5 P
Barbers with charts of the only possible modes, [Sombre 68-8 P
Give only their color to the leaves. The trees [Sombre 71-3 P
Of the world would have only to ring and ft! [Bship 78-9 P
It would be done. If, only to please myself, [Bship 78-10 P
"The ephebi say that there is only the whole, [Bship 79-20 P
Or accessible only in the most furtive fiction. [Nuns 93-2 P
Then knowledge is the only life, [Ulysses 100-1 P
The only sun of the only day, [Ulysses 100-2 P
The only access to true ease, [Ulysses 100-3 P
His only testament and estate. [Ulysses 103-9 P
Since only to know is to be free? [Ulysses 103-12 P
That only in man's definitions of himself, [Conversat 109-12 P
Only encompassed in humanity, is he [Conversat 109-13 P
When the court knew beauty only, [Three 132-5 P
It is only a tree [Three 137-5 P
Red is not only [Three 142-12 P
ONSLAUGHTS. The childish onslaughts of such innocence, [Good Bad
  33-19 P
ONTARIO. Ontario, Canton. It was the way [Greenest 53-10 P
ONWARDNESS. Delivered with a deluging onwardness. [C 45-29
OONTS. We enjoy the ithy oonts and long-haired [Analysis 349-10
OOZER. Great mud-ancestor, oozer and Abraham, [Duck 64-29 P
OOZING. Oozing cantankerous gum [Bananas 54-20
OPAL. In opal blobs along the walls and floor. [Blue Bldg 217-12
  To its opal elements and fire's delight, [AA 416-12
OPALESCENCE. To clearing opalescence. Then the sea [Sea Surf 102-13
OPALS. The women with eyes like opals vanish [Stan Hero 83-12 P
OPAQUE. Opaque, in orange circlet, nearer than it [Page 422-13
OPEN. Among the blooms beyond the open sand; [Hibiscus 22-11
  The windows are open. The sunlight fills [Peaches 224-16
  Eyes open and fix on us in every sky. [AA 411-3
  But clears and clears until an open night [Spaniard 34-3 P
  By the eyes that open on it, [Three 143-12 P
OPENED. On the east, sister and nun, and opened wide [Phenom
  287-8
  The spouse. She opened her stone-studded belt. [NSF 395-21
  Longer and later, in which the lilacs opened [Aug 491-27
  Opened out within a secrecy of place, [Letters 108-4 P
OPENING. An opening of portals when night ends, [Nigger 153-14
  An opening for outpouring, the hand was raised: [NH 483-2
OPENLY. Fell openly from the air to reappear [Bouquet 450-18
OPENS. And opens in this familiar spot [Red Fern 365-2
  And is destroyed. He opens the door of his house [AA 416-24
OPER. See Staats-Oper.
OPERA. This stage-light of the Opera? [Hartford 226-16
  Buffo! A ball, an opera, a bar. [AA 420-12
OPERANDUM. And slightly detestable operandum, free [Look 517-19
OPIATES. By the obese opiates of sleep. Plain men in plain towns
  [NH 467-20
OPIUM. Steeped in night's opium, evading day. [Sombre 66-17 P
OPPOSE. Oppose the past and the festival, [MBG 181-2
  And imperator because of death to oppose [Bship 79-5 P
OPPOSED. Of arms, the will opposed to cold, fate [Hero 273-12
OPPOSING. The opposing law and make a peristyle, [High-Toned 59-7
  One man opposing a society [Lytton 38-14 P
OPPOSITE. Proves that these opposite things partake of one,
  [Connois 215-14
  Two things of opposite natures seem to depend [NSF 392-4
  A responding to a diviner opposite. [NH 468-3
  The opposite of Cythère, an isolation [NH 480-19
  In a kind of uproar, because an opposite, a contradiction, [Slug
  522-7
  What opposite? Could it be that yellow patch, the side [Slug
  522-9
OPPOSITES. And it does; a law of inherent opposites, [Connois
  215-9
  Confounds all opposites and spins a sphere [Duck 63-20 P
OPPRESSOR. The mother, but an oppressor, but like [MBG 173-16
  An oppressor that grudges them their death, [MBG 173-17
OPTICAL. Colliding with deaf-mute churches and optical trains.
  [Chaos 357-17
OPTIMIST. The Mechanical Optimist [Thought 184-title 1
OPULENT. By such long-rolling opulent cataracts, [Geneva 24-5
  Of seeds grown fat, too juicily opulent, [C 32-9
  Smeared with the gold of the opulent sun. [Postcard 159-21
  The fulfillment of fulfillments, in opulent, [Orb 441-10
OPULENTLY. By mere example opulently clear. [Havana 145-6
OPUSCULUM. Opusculum paedagogum. [Pears 196-1
OR. C'était mon frère du ciel, ma vie, mon or. [Sea Surf 100-3
ORACULAR. Spinning and hissing with oracular [Geneva 24-11
  To whom oracular rockings gave no rest. [C 30-28 P
  The oracular trumpets round and roundly hooped, [Greenest 56-19 P
ORANGE. High up in orange air, were barbarous. [C 30-21
  In an orange gown, [Explan 73-2
  The visible, a zone of blue and orange [EM 324-13
  The wild orange trees continued to bloom and to bear, [NSF 393-2
  And his orange blotches, these were his zero green, [NSF 393-6
  Opaque, in orange circlet, nearer than it [Page 422-13
  Pink yellows, orange whites, too much as they are [Roses 430-11

The orange far down in yellow, [Plant 506-11
Iris and orange, crimson and green, [Mandolin 28-19 P
Of his orange days [Coroner 29-19 P
Like the same orange repeating on one tree [Someone 85-21 A
ORANGEADE. "The Revolutionists Stop for Orangeade" [102-title
ORANGED. An azure outre-terre, oranged and rosed, [Theatre 91-14 P
ORANGES. Coffee and oranges in a sunny chair, [Sunday 66-17
The pungent oranges and bright, green wings [Sunday 67-5
Citrons, oranges and greens [Pears 197-1
For example, this old man selling oranges [Feo 333-18
The oranges glitter as part of the sky, [Stan MBG 72-13 P
ORANGE-TREES. It is the same jingle of the red-bird breasting the
orange-trees out of the cedars. [Indian 112-6
ORATION. Of that oration, the happiest sense in which [Ideal 89-6 A
ORATIONS. And spouting new orations of the cold. [Pharynx 96-15
Divine orations from lean sacristans [Montra 262-18
ORATOR. It wears. This is the way the orator spoke: [Dames 206-2
The choice is made. Green is the orator [Repet 309-22
My orator. Let this giantness fall down [Repet 310-2
Evade, this hot, dependent orator, [NSF 397-1
Be orator but with an accurate tongue [Rome 509-10
The man in the band-stand could be orator. [Duck 63-15 P
It may be the future depends on an orator, [Duck 63-16 P
In casque and scaffold orator, fortified [Stan Hero 84-21 P
The orator will say that we ourselves [Ideal 89-10 A
ORB. Each is both star and orb; and day [MBG 172-11
"A Primitive Like an Orb" [440-title
A wandering orb upon a path grown clear. [Sombre 70-17 P
ORBITS. And moved on them in orbits' outer stars [NSF 403-5
ORCHARD. Untasted, in its heavenly, orchard air. [Monocle 14-15
Agree: the apple in the orchard, round [Burnshaw 47-30 P
ORCHARDS. Among the orchards in the apple-blocks [Good Bad 33-16 P
ORCHESTRA. And I are one. The orchestra [MBG 171-12
Or sunlight and you hum and the orchestra [Waldorf 241-5
ORCHESTRAS. Canaries in the morning, orchestras [Havana 142-1
Perhaps if the orchestras stood on their heads [Agenda 42-4 P
The whole. The sound of a dozen orchestras [Bship 79-26 P
A vacuum for the dozen orchestras [Bship 80-1 P
ORCHESTRE. Eternal chef d'orchestre? [Eve Angels 136-15
ORCHIDEAN. Of gobs, who called her orchidean, [Lulu G 26-10 P
ORDAINED. Politic man ordained [Havana 143-21
ORDAINS. The President ordains the bee to be [NSF 390-10
Immortal. The President ordains. But does [NSF 390-11
He is that obdurate ruler who ordains [Greenest 59-28 P
ORDER. Who found all form and order in solitude, [Sad Gay 121-17
There is order in neither sea nor sun. [Sad Gay 122-1
Requiring order beyond their speech. [Sad Gay 122-9
"The Idea of Order at Key West" [128-title
Oh! Blessed rage for order, pale Ramon, [Key W 130-11
The maker's rage to order words of the sea, [Key W 130-12
They were particles of order, a single majesty: [Anglais 149-8
A. A violent order is disorder; and [Connois 215-1
B. A great disorder is an order. These [Connois 215-2
A. Well, an old order is a violet one. [Connois 216-1
To an order, most Plantagenet, most fixed . . . [Connois 216-8
A great disorder is an order. Now, A [Connois 216-9
To everything, in order to get at myself. [Uruguay 249-4
Of a chaos composed in more than order, [Dutch 293-9
Order, saying I am the contemplated spouse. [NSF 396-3
To discover. To discover an order as of [NSF 403-23
An order and thereafter he belonged [Bad Time 426-10
To it"? He beheld the order of the northern sky. [Bad Time
426-11
Or else an inherent order active to be [Orb 442-12
We feel the obscurity of an order, a whole, [Final 524-11
The constant cry against an old order, [Polo 37-13 P
An order constantly old, [Polo 37-14 P
Beyond any order, [Polo 38-1 P
Behold how order is the end [Room Gard 41-1 P
Order, the law of hoes and rakes, [Room Gard 41-4 P
So seen, have an order of its own, a peace [Burnshaw 49-1 P
Not now to be perceived yet order's own. [Burnshaw 49-2 P
The east wind in the west, order destroyed, [Sombre 68-15 P
When it never existed, the order [Desire 85-2 P
The beginning of a final order, [Ulysses 101-12 P
The order of man's right to be [Ulysses 101-13 P
ORDERLY. And if it all went on in an orderly way, [Connois 215-8
ORDERS. He imposes orders as he thinks of them, [NSF 403-16
ORDINARINESS. Their ordinariness, [Song Fixed 520-2
And the ordinariness of seven, [Song Fixed 520-3
ORDINARY. "The Ordinary Women" [10-title
Or ordinary people, places, things, [Extraord 369-14
"An Ordinary Evening in New Haven" [465-title
A name and privilege over the ordinary of his commonplace--
[Prol 517-4
And their ordinary glare, [Song Fixed 519-22
ORE. I have neither ashen wing nor wear of ore [Angel 496-9
ORGANIC. With its organic boomings, to be changed [Freed 205-10
The organic centre of responses, [Hero 279-27
The organic consolation, the complete [Repet 309-10

ORGANS. See mouth-organs.
ORGY. Shall chant in orgy on a summer morn [Sunday 69-29
ORIENT. And the Orient and the Occident embrace [Art Pop 112-17 P
ORIGIN. And still pursue, the origin and course [Monocle 18-1
And origin, an inhuman person, [Gigan 289-19
In the sweeping brim becomes the origin [Pastor 379-13
The origin of the major man. He comes, [NSF 387-24
On the real. This is the origin of change. [NSF 392-7
Of motion the ever-brightening origin, [AA 414-24
In the eye a special hue of origin. [Bouquet 451-23
That we must calm, the origin of a mother tongue [NH 470-24
Not the predicate of bright origin. [NH 481-13
The cold and earliness and bright origin [NH 481-16
Had left in them only a brilliance, of unaccustomed origin,
[Prol 515-11
At B: the origin of the mango's rind. [Rock 528-13
The origin and keep of its health and his own. [Armor 530-21
And origin and resplendent end of law, [Greenest 60-5 P
The origin could have its origin. [Desire 85-17 P
The supernatural of its origin. [Nuns 92-14 P
ORIGINAL. The lesser seeming original in the blind [Descrip 340-2
In the seeming of an original in the eye, [Descrip 340-11
Return to their original illusion. [Novel 457-3
With the inhalations of original cold [NH 481-10
And of original earliness. Yet the sense [NH 481-11
ORIGINALS. Damasked in the originals of green, [Owl 434-20
Concourse of planetary originals, [Someone 84-2 A
ORIGINS. And of ourselves and of our origins, [Key W 130-14
In these Elysia, these origins, [Extracts 257-9
And prodigious person, patron of origins. [Orb 443-14
ORIOLE. From oriole to crow, note the decline [Nigger 154-14
Oriole, also, may be realist. [Nigger 154-16
ORIOLES. The third one gaping at the orioles [C 44-30
ORNAMENT. Hunting for the great ornament, [Pediment 361-8
Of this essential ornament [Pediment 361-21
Said that as keen, illustrious ornament, [NSF 391-22
In its own only precious ornament. [NSF 396-5
ORNATEST. Subtler than the ornatest prophecy, [Havana 144-13
OROTUND. Nor stand there making orotund consolations. [Papini
446-11
ORTHODOX. And got my learning from the orthodox. [Soldat 11-5 P
OSCILLATIONS. Without the oscillations of planetary pass-pass,
[Cata 425-11
OTHERWISE. Granted the Picts impressed us otherwise [Nigger
155-1
And sees, being nothing otherwise, [Prelude 194-19
Having nothing otherwise, he has not [Prelude 194-20
And, otherwise, the rainy rose belongs [Extracts 252-13
Including pain, which, otherwise, is false. [EM 323-22
Instinctively, not otherwise. [Grotesque 75-5 P
OTO - OTU - BRE. Oto - otu - bre. [Metamorph 266-2
OTTOMAN. From an ottoman of thorns. [Lulu M 27-16 P
OTU-BRE. Otu-bre's lion-roses have turned to paper [Plant 506-5
OUGHT. Of was and is and shall or ought to be, [C 40-8
For him, of shall or ought to be in is. [C 41-9
It ought to be everywhere. [Sailing 120-14
The planes that ought to have genius, [Common 221-19
For the woman one loves or ought to love, [Waldorf 241-2
We ought not to be awake. It is from this [Debris 338-5
They ought to be muscular men, [Drum-Majors 37-7 P
Death ought to spare their passions. [Lytton 38-17 P
And how strange it ought to be again, this time [Lytton 39-2 P
In every various sense, ought not to be preferred [Lytton 39-13 P
That is is dead except what ought to be.[Burnshaw 46-15 P
OUNCINGS. Gold easings and ouncings and fluctuations of thread
[NH 477-19
OURSELVES. We give ourselves our likest issuance. [Fictive 88-9
We hardened ourselves to live by bluest reason [Medit 124-2
And of ourselves and of our origins, [Key W 130-14
So much alone, so deeply by ourselves, [Re-state 146-8
For the time when sound shall be subtler than we ourselves.
[Nigger 158-5
A tune beyond us, yet ourselves, [MBG 165-8
Ourselves in poetry must take their place, [MBG 167-13
Ourselves in the tune as if in space, [MBG 167-17
Of destructions," a picture of ourselves, [MBG 173-2
Could all these be ourselves, sounding ourselves, [Dames 206-11
That we are joyously ourselves and we think [Gala 248-9
There was a bright scienza outside of ourselves, [Gala 248-12
And nourish ourselves on crumbs of whimsy? [Hero 278-4
Of remembrance share nothing of ourselves. [Dutch 291-14
An accretion from ourselves, intelligent [Creat 311-2
We do not say ourselves like that in poems. [Creat 311-16
We say ourselves in syllables that rise [Creat 311-17
Before we were wholly human and knew ourselves. [EM 317-29
Ourselves, in the clearest green--well, call it green. [Lot 371-7
That is not our own and, much more, not ourselves [NSF 383-23
It is ourselves, the freshness of ourselves, [NSF 398-2
And have seen, a place dependent on ourselves. [NSF 401-3
They can be no more faded than ourselves. [Study I 464-2

Suppose these houses are composed of ourselves, [NH 466-4
So much ourselves, we cannot tell apart [NH 466-20
We fling ourselves, constantly longing, on this form. [NH 470-16
That which is not ourselves: the regalia, [NH 485-14
That comes from ourselves, neither from knowing [Aug 495-9
Until we say to ourselves that there may be [Look 517-17
No doubt we live beyond ourselves in air, [Look 518-3
So well, that which we do for ourselves, too big, [Look 518-5
It is in that thought that we collect ourselves, [Final 524-5
Here, now, we forget each other and ourselves. [Final 524-10
Lived in the houses of mothers, arranged ourselves [Rock 525-2
Or a cure of ourselves, that is equal to a cure [Rock 526-12
These are a cure of the ground and of ourselves, [Rock 527-3
Of leaves and of the ground and of ourselves. [Rock 527-20
Above our race, yet of ourselves transformed, [Duck 64-26 P
More of ourselves in a world that is more our own, [Duck 65-1 P
More of ourselves, the mood of life made strong [Duck 65-3 P
Except with reference to ourselves, [Three 133-15 P
The orator will say that we ourselves [Ideal 89-10 A
OUT. Out of geraniums and unsmelled flowers. [Plot Giant 6-15
Out of their mother grass, like little kin, [Monocle 15-4
But with a speech belched out of hoary darks [C 29-26
Out of what swift destruction did it spring? [C 30-12
A man come out of luminous traversing, [C 30-25
As on this voyage, out of goblinry, [C 35-10
Out of her botches, hot embosomer. [C 44-29
Sacked up and carried overseas, daubed out [C 45-13
Out of the tomb, we bring Badroulbadour, [Worms 49-16
Out of the tomb we bring Badroulbadour. [Worms 50-3
Out of their purple maws, [Bananas 54-21
Darting out of their purple craws [Bananas 54-22
Out of his cloud and from his sky. [Cuban 64-19
Out of my mind the golden ointment rained, [Hoon 65-13
Whispered a little out of tenderness, [Sunday 69-6
Out of their blood, returning to the sky; [Sunday 70-5
In and out of my shadow. [Six Sig 74-13
And out of their droning sibilants makes [Two Figures 86-8
Than yours, out of our imperfections wrought, [Fictive 87-20
When the blackbird flew out of sight, [Thirteen 94-6
Out of such mildew plucking neater mould [Pharynx 96-14
Out of the light evolved the moving blooms, [Sea Surf 99-6
And, out of tenderness or grief, the sun [Anatomy 108-9
It is the same jingle of the red-bird breasting the orange-trees
    out of the cedars. [Indian 112-6
This mangled, smutted semi-world hacked out [Ghosts 119-8
Out of the morning sky. [Pascagoula 126-12
Out of his fiery lair. [Pascagoula 127-7
That, too, returns from out the winter's air, [Sun March 134-2
Rose out of promise and became the sooth [Havana 143-2
Rumble anything out of their drums? [Circulat 150-4
The future might stop emerging out of the past, [Nigger 151-10
Out of what is full of us; yet the search [Nigger 151-11
And the future emerging out of us seem to be one. [Nigger 151-12
Out of the spirit of the holy temples, [Nigger 151-19
Furtively, by candle and out of need. [Nigger 153-4
It must create its colors out of itself. [Nigger 158-2
Out of a mood, the tragic robe [MBG 169-20
Dropped out of this amber-ember pod, [MBG 182-6
Out of the clouds, pomp of the air, [Idiom 201-9
The fox ran out of his hole. [On Road 203-15
Well, the gods grow out of the weather. [Jersey 210-5
The people grow out of the weather; [Jersey 210-6
The gods grow out of the people. [Jersey 210-7
Out of all the minds, [Bagatelles 213-23
Like a noble figure, out of the sky, [Candle 223-4
Green is the night and out of madness woven, [Candle 223-7
Out of what they see. They polish their eyes [Arcades 225-11
Out of the changes of both light and dew [Scavoir 231-8
Green in the body, out of a petty phrase, [Beard 247-21
Out of a thing believed, a thing affirmed: [Beard 247-22
Eventual victor, out of the martyrs' bones, [Uruguay 250-4
Out of the hero's being, the deliverer [Montra 261-6
Out of the movement of few words, [Oak 272-17
And the high, receiving out of others, [Gigan 289-17
Out of themselves, a saying, [Dutch 290-18
Out of these gawky flitterings, [Possum 294-10
A freedom out of silver-shaping size, [Choc 298-9
Now, time stands still. He came from out of sleep. [Choc 299-12
True transfigurers fetched out of the human mountain, [Choc 300-6
Without understanding, out of the wall [Creat 310-12
Grow out of the spirit or they are fantastic dust. [Holiday 313-4
Indulgence out of all celestial sight. [EM 318-17
That he sends ahead, out of the goodness of his heart, [EM 320-18
And out of what one sees and hears and out [EM 326-7
Signal, a character out of solitude, [Pure 331-4
The fictive man created out of men. [Paisant 335-6
Words that come out of us like words within, [Sketch 336-2
A dream interrupted out of the past, [Sketch 336-8
And another breath emerging out of death, [Descrip 341-5
In a description hollowed out of hollow-bright, [Descrip 345-17

Of incredible colors ex, ex and ex and out? [Liadoff 347-3
Out of a storm we must endure all night, [Man Car 351-4
Out of a storm of secondary things), [Man Car 351-5
Become an over-crystal out of ice, [Pieces 351-16
From the water in which he believed and out of desire [New Set
    352-13
"Men Made out of Words" [355-title
People fall out of windows, trees tumble down, [Chaos 357-13
Just out of the village, at its edge, [Woman Song 361-5
Out of the deadliest heat. [Attempt 370-7
Out of nothing to have come on major weather, [NSF 404-3
Or is this another wriggling out of the egg, [AA 411-4
The father fetches pageants out of air, [AA 415-13
A saying out of a cloud, but innocence. [AA 418-20
It might come bearing, out of chaos, kin [Page 422-27
And laughed, as he sat there reading, from out of the purple
    tabulae, [Large 424-4
Descending, out of the cap of midnight, [Countryman 428-10
Needs out of the whole necessity of sight. [Owl 432-2
Out of our lives to keep us in our death, [Owl 434-24
The sense of self, rosed out of prestiges [Owl 435-5
Out of the first warmth of spring, [Celle 438-1
And out of the shine of the hemlocks, [Celle 438-2
Their words are chosen out of their desire, [Orb 441-7
Out of him that I loved, [Our Stars 454-10
And out of myself. [Our Stars 455-2
Out of him I made Mal Bay [Our Stars 455-5
Wet out of the sea, and luminously wet, [Our Stars 455-15
Out of rigid realists. It is as if [NH 470-4
That fall upon it out of the wind. We seek [NH 471-12
Like blessed beams from out a blessed bush [NH 477-21
Romanza out of the black shepherd's isle, [NH 480-13
Out of the isle, but not of any isle. [NH 480-16
Out of the surfaces, the windows, the walls, [NH 480-22
There were looks that caught him out of empty air. [NH 483-13
Added and added out of a fame-full heart . . . [NH 484-15
The honky-tonk out of the somnolent grasses [Aug 489-18
They go to the cliffs of Moher rising out of the mist, [Irish
    501-13
Rising out of present time and place, above [Irish 502-1
Did not pass like someone voyaging out of and beyond the familiar.
    [Prol 515-13
Creates a fresh universe out of nothingness by adding itself,
    [Prol 517-9
In the tumult of integrations out of the sky, [Look 518-12
Out of all the indifferences, into one thing: [Final 524-6
Out of this same light, out of the central mind, [Final 524-16
The first car out of a tunnel en voyage [Armor 530-2
Out of the whirl and denseness of your wings, [Red Kit 31-25 P
To waste, out of the hopeless waste of the past [Burnshaw 49-23 P
However tarnished, companions out of the past, [Burnshaw 50-10 P
Seraphim of Europe? Pouring out of dawn, [Greenest 56-3 P
Out of the eye when the loud wind gathers up [Greenest 58-11 P
Out of a violet sea. They rise a bit [Duck 60-10 P
Out of their wilderness, a special fane, [Sombre 69-8 P
The parts. Thus: Out of the number of his thoughts [Bship 80-15 P
The ruins of the past, out of nothing left, [Recit 87-14 P
His own bright red. But he bears him out of love, [Recit 87-18 P
Of the son. These survivals out of time and space [Recit 87-27 P
Choosing out of himself, out of everything within him, [Sick
    90-19 P
The cricket of summer forming itself out of ice. [Discov 95-14 P
Wrenched out of chaos . . . the quiet lamp [Ulysses 100-23 P
Like an absolute out of this eloquence." [Presence 106-6 P
A skeleton out of its cabinet. Nor am I. [As Leave 116-16 P
Wood of his forests and stone out of his fields [Myth 118-15 P
2. Out of their bottle the green genii come. [Someone 86-5 A
4. The sea is spouting upward out of rocks. [Someone 86-7 A
OUTBURSTS. A source of pleasant outbursts on the ear. [Orb 442-24
OUTCAST. Instead, outcast, without the will to power [Cats 368-2
OUTDOOR. His eye on an outdoor gloom [Bananas 54-12
OUTDOORS. It was the importance of the trees outdoors, [Freed
    205-17
OUTER. If it was only the outer voice of sky [Key W 129-12
    The outer captain, the inner saint, [Thought 185-26
    And moved on them in orbits' outer stars [NSF 403-5
    Behind the outer shields, the sheets of music [NH 488-10
    Of the great sizes of an outer bush [Dove 98-8 P
    Not some outer patron and imaginer. [Conversat 109-15 P
OUTLANDISH. For whom the outlandish was another day [AA 419-9
OUTLINE. How could there be an image, an outline, [Hero 278-22
    Reflected, humming an outline of a fugue [NSF 402-14
    In the space, leaving an outline of the size [Aug 494-20
    The scholar's outline that you had, the print [Duck 61-17 P
OUTLINED. Outlined and having alphabetical [Common 221-21
OUTLINES. Having curved outlines. [Pears 196-10
    The outlines of being and its expressings, the syllables of its
        law: [Large 424-5
    In a movement of the outlines of similarity? [Aug 494-14
    Our crusted outlines hot and huge with fact, [Burnshaw 47-6 P

OUTLOOK. For the outlook that would be right, [Poem Mt 512-9
OUTMOST. Through choirs infolded to the outmost clouds? [C 41-18
OUTPOST. This outpost, this douce, this dumb, this dead, in which
    [Cuisine 228-9
OUTPOURING. An opening for outpouring, the hand was raised: [NH
    483-2
OUTRE-TERRE. An azure outre-terre, oranged and rosed, [Theatre
    91-14 P
OUTSENSING. On his balcony, outsensing distances, [NH 483-12
OUTSIDE. Outside of gates of hammered serafin, [Babies 77-2
  What is beyond the cathedral, outside, [MBG 181-3
  There was a bright scienza outside of ourselves, [Gala 248-12
  Glares, outside of the legend, with the barbarous green [Plant
    506-18
  Outside of and beyond the dirty light, [Two Illus 513-17
  "St. Armorer's Church from the Outside" [529-title
  In March, a scrawny cry from outside [Not Ideas 534-2
  It would have been outside. [Not Ideas 534-9
  The sun was coming from outside. [Not Ideas 534-12
  Outside of Wedlock [Grotesque 76-title 5 P
  In the green, outside the door of phantasma. [Dinner 110-6 P
OUTSOARING. And peaks outsoaring possible adjectives. [Thought
    185-10
OUTSTRETCHED. The arm of bronze outstretched against all evil!
    [Mice 123-12
  The spruces' outstretched hands; [Delight 162-7
OUTWARD. Move outward into heaven, [Fabliau 23-6
  Upward and outward, in green-vented forms, [Bird Claws 82-11
  Springs outward, being large, and, in the dust, [Pure 332-22
  The swans fled outward to remoter reaches, [Descrip 343-7
  And motion outward, reddened and resolved [Owl 435-20
  Dark Juan looks outward through his mystic brow . . . [Luther
    461-14
  Spread outward. Crack the round dome. Break through. [Aug 490-11
  A civilization formed from the outward blank, [Armor 529-22
OUTWARDLY. Of these. In these, I come forth outwardly. [Rhythms
    246-5
  The actual form bears outwardly this grace, [Pastor 379-17
  Outwardly and knows them inwardly, [Child 106-18 P
OVATION. In an ovation of resplendent forms-- [Liadoff 346-7
  Ovation on ovation of large blue men [Liadoff 346-8
OVER. Over Oklahoma [Earthy 3-2
  Over the sea. [Infanta 7-19
  They swept over the room, [Domination 8-21
  Sequestered over the sea, [Venereal 48-6
  The singer has pulled his cloak over his head. [Of Surface 57-7
  Over the seas, to silent Palestine, [Sunday 67-10
  Over weeds. [Six Sig 73-15
  It crawls over the water. [Tattoo 81-10
  It crawls over the edges of the snow. [Tattoo 81-11
  He rode over Connecticut [Thirteen 94-13
  When the wind stops and, over the heavens, [Soldier 97-10
  When over the houses, a golden illusion [Lunar 107-9
  And over the bare spaces of our skies [Anatomy 108-6
  Vermilion smeared over green, arranged for show. [Grapes 110-14
  And silvers and greens spread over the sea. The moon [Farewell
    117-4
  Curled over the shadowless hut, the rust and bones, [Farewell
    118-4
  When we can mourn no more over music [Sad Gay 121-9
  I am tired. Sleep for me, heaven over the hill. [Nigger 150-16
  Under the mat of frost and over the mat of clouds. [Nigger 151-4
  Over the simplest words: [Nigger 151-17
  The man bent over his guitar, [MBG 165-1
  Over words that are life's voluble utterance. [Men Fall 188-20
  This halloo, halloo, halloo heard over the cries [Parochial
    191-12
  Flowering over the skin. [Pears 197-2
  And the river that batters its way over stones, [Loaf 199-17
  Flowing above the rocks, flowing over the sky, [Loaf 200-4
  It was soldiers went marching over the rocks [Loaf 200-13
  Over wooden Boston, the sparkling Byzantine [Blue Bldg 217-1
  Over and over again you have said, [Dezem 218-5
  In light blue air over dark blue sea. [Vari 232-6
  Star over Monhegan, Atlantic star, [Vari 232-15
  With the blank skies over England, over France [Martial 238-4
  Slid over the western cataract, yet one, [Beard 247-5
  Rode over the picket rocks, rode down the road, [Uruguay 250-2
  The prologues are over. It is a question, now, [Oboe 250-6
  Ruled us before, from over Asia, by [Montra 262-14
  The highest supposed in him and over, [Hero 280-2
  Under the arches, over the arches, in arcs [Dutch 293-8
  A swarming of number over number, not [Choc 296-15
  How she presides over imbeciles. The night [Feo 333-12
  The clouds are over the village, the town, [Woman Song 360-13
  And over it they set a jagged sign, [Good Man 364-12
  And spring's infuriations over and a long way [Cred 372-5
  Over the loftiest antagonist [NSF 390-14
  Bent over work, anxious, content, alone, [NSF 406-16
  And cried out to feel it again, have run fingers over leaves

  [Large 424-2
  He wanted to feel the same way over and over. [Cata 425-2
  The bouquet has slopped over the edge and lies on the floor.
    [Bouquet 453-3
  Over the top of the Bank of Ireland, [Our Stars 454-14
  And through and over the puddles of Swatara [Our Stars 455-10
  But over the wind, over the legends of its roaring, [Puel 456-4
  Making a great gnashing, over the water wallows [Puel 456-8
  Over all these the mighty imagination triumphs [Puel 456-10
  Streamed over chaos their civilities. [NH 479-9
  Lighted by space, big over those that sleep, [NH 482-5
  So that at the edge of afternoon, not over, [NH 482-22
  But folded over, turned round." It was the same, [NH 487-4
  Than the difference that clouds make over a town. [NH 487-7
  When the summer was over, when the change [Two Illus 514-7
  Bending over and pulling themselves erect on the wooden handles,
    [Prol 515-8
  Part of the glass-like sides on which it glided over the salt-
    stained water, [Prol 516-3
  A name and privilege over the ordinary of his commonplace--
    [Prol 517-4
  No winds like dogs watched over her at night. [World 521-6
  And kept saying over and over one same, same thing, [Slug 522-6
  So barely lit, so shadowed over and naught, [Quiet 523-3
  Of that which is always beginning, over and over. [Armor 530-18
  All over Minnesota, [Primordia 7-10 P
  Slung over my shoulder? [Soldat 12-21 P
  Over the palms. [Coroner 30-10 P
  Spread over heaven shutting out the light. [Red Kit 31-26 P
  Of the park with chalky brow scratched over black [Old Woman
    44-3 P
  Washed over by their green, their flowing blue. [Old Woman
    45-10 P
  Visible over the sea. It is only enough [Burnshaw 50-16 P
  What god rules over Africa, what shape, [Greenest 52-24 P
  No god rules over Africa, no throne, [Greenest 55-5 P
  Wings spread and whirling over jaguar-men? [Greenest 55-31 P
  Filleted angels over flapping ears, [Greenest 56-7 P
  And the first line foaming over the sand; again, [Woman Had
    81-16 P
  On every cloud-tip over the heavens, [Letters 107-2 P
  And it flows over us without meanings, [Clear Day 113-16 P
OVERALLS. Or the bench with the pot of geraniums, the stained
    mattress and the washed overalls drying in the sun? [Indigo
    22-12 P
OVERCAST. And the color, the overcast blue [MBG 169-13
OVER-CIVIL. Of over-civil stops. And thus he tossed [C 35-21
OVER-CLOSE. The choice twixt dove and goose is over-close.
    [Spaniard 35-6 P
OVER-CRYSTAL. Become an over-crystal out of ice, [Pieces 351-16
OVER-DAZZLING. In aureoles that are over-dazzling crests . . .
    [Nuns 92-20 P
OVERFULL. The twilight overfull [Delight 162-8
OVER-HUMAN. The fault lies with an over-human god, [EM 315-14
OVERHUNG. Are overhung by the shadows of the rocks [Grapes 111-2
OVERLAYS. How thick this gobbet is with overlays, [Someone 85-19 A
OVERLOOK. "The moments of enlargement overlook [Choc 298-13
OVERLOOKING. Overlooking whole seasons? [Archi 17-13 P
OVER-POPULACE. The over-populace of the idea, the voices [Americana
    94-2 P
OVERPOWERING. Beseech them for an overpowering gloom. [Red Kit 32-4P
OVERSEAS. Sacked up and carried overseas, daubed out [C 45-13
  It had been real. It was something overseas [Repet 306-4
  Like something I remembered overseas. [Repet 306-20
  It was something overseas that I remembered. [Repet 306-21
OVERTAKEN. A mass overtaken by the blackest sky, [Sombre 69-4 P
OVERTAKING. Overtaking the doctrine of this landscape. Of him
    [Freed 204-21
OVERWHELMED. Too vague idealist, overwhelmed [Negation 98-1
OWL. The little owl flew through the night, [Adequacy 243-9
  The little owl fly. [Adequacy 244-16
  Hoot, little owl within her, how [Vase 246-17
  Who surpassed the most literate owl, the most erudite [NSF 403-21
  "The Owl in the Sarcophagus" [431-title
  8. The owl sits humped. It has a hundred eyes. [Someone 86-11 A
OWLS. Owls warn me and with tuft-eared watches keep [Souls 94-18 P
  Under the birds, among the perilous owls, [NH 474-17
OWN. Falls, it appears, of its own weight to earth. [Monocle 14-13
  you in its own light. [Nuances 18-12
  With his own quill, in its indigenous dew, [C 31-19
  Of Vulcan, that a valet seeks to own, [C 33-6
  In bloom. Yet it survives in its own form, [C 41-6
  Of his own fate an instance of all fate? [C 41-24
  In the door-yard by his own capacious bloom. [C 44-5
  Of their own ends. [Joost 46-19
  With rivers like our own that seek for seas [Sunday 69-17
  The moon they made their own attendant ghosts, [Eve Angels 137-11
  Except for our own houses, huddled low [Eve Angels 138-1
  Thinking the thoughts I call my own, [MBG 180-8
  The spring will have a health of its own, with none [Parochial

192-1
Its muscles are his own . . . [Destructive 193-3
As one loves one's own being, [Yellow 236-15
Still walking in a present of our own. [Martial 237-16
Turns to its own figurations and declares, [Rhythms 246-3
In which we pronounce joy like a word of our own. [Gala 248-6
And echoing rhetorics more than our own. [Montra 261-18
No more. I can build towers of my own, [Montra 263-8
"Phosphor Reading by His Own Light" [267-title
In its own dirt, said Avignon [Hero 273-9
Of the thousands of freedoms except our own? [Dutch 292-14
Their own, waiting until we go [Dutch 293-2
That, like your own, is large, hence, to be part [Choc 296-9
The mind's own limits, like a tragic thing [Choc 298-4
That is my own voice speaking in my ear. [Choc 298-20
The gigantic has a reality of its own. [Repet 308-12
From that strength, whose armies set their own expanses. [Repet
  309-5
So that it came to him of its own, [Creat 310-11
Why should they not know they had everything of their own
  [Holiday 312-9
Its own hallucination never sees [EM 315-9
As he saw it, exist in his own especial eye. [EM 316-19
Rose from an imperfection of its own [EM 318-11
Of their own part, yet moving on the wind, [EM 319-8
As if sight had not its own miraculous thrift, [EM 320-26
Like hunger that feeds on its own hungriness. [EM 323-4
Casual poet, that to add your own disorder to disaster [Bed
  326-15
By her own seeming made the summer change. [Descrip 339-12
In its own seeming, plainly visible, [Descrip 344-18
Be alive with its own seemings, seeming to be [Descrip 346-3
Which is not part of the listener's own sense. [Cred 377-20
The first idea was not our own. Adam [NSF 383-10
That is not our own and, much more, not ourselves [NSF 383-23
In its own only precious ornament. [NSF 396-5
That catches our own. The casual is not [NSF 397-23
The freshness of a world. It is our own, [NSF 398-1
The supernatural preludes of its own, [AA 414-19
But it dare not leap by chance in its own dark. [AA 417-22
Of their own marvel made, of pity made, [Owl 435-24
These are death's own supremest images, [Owl 436-2
Its knowledge cold within one as one's own; [Novel 459-3
His utmost statement. It is his own array, [Questions 462-17
His own pageant and procession and display, [Questions 462-18
Even his own will and in his nakedness [NH 480-8
The rich earth, of its own self made rich, [Aug 491-13
Fertile of its own leaves and days and wars, [Aug 491-14
The meanings are our own-- [Aug 495-5
Of their own. [Inhab 504-9
A place to go to in his own direction, [Poem Mt 512-6
The shadow of a sense of his own, [Two Illus 513-6
The breath of another nature as his own, [Two Illus 513-15
Except his own--perhaps, his own [Two Illus 514-2
That comes and goes in silences of its own. [Look 518-22
In an inhuman meditation, larger than her own. [World 521-5
By our own motions in a freedom of air. [Rock 525-3
In the sun's design of its own happiness, [Rock 525-18
His own: a chapel of breath, an appearance made [Armor 529-11
The chapel rises, his own, his period, [Armor 529-21
The origin and keep of its health and his own. [Armor 530-21
His own . . . [Phases 5-23 P
So seen, have an order of its own, a peace [Burnshaw 49-1 P
Not now to be perceived yet order's own. [Burnshaw 49-2 P
More of ourselves in a world that is more our own, [Duck 65-1 P
As by a juicier season; and more our own [Duck 65-4 P
To be the musician's own and, thence, become [Sombre 67-23 P
The ship, make it my own and, bit by bit, [Bship 77-21 P
Into its own illustration, a divinity [Bship 79-2 P
It will be all we have. Our fate is our own: [Bship 81-4 P
Grow large and larger. Our fate is our own. The hand, [Bship
  81-7 P
Detects the sound of a voice that doubles its own, [Woman Had
  82-20 P
I had not invented my own thoughts, [Desire 85-7 P
His own bright red. But he bears him out of love, [Recit 87-18 P
That are almost not our own, but thoughts [Including 88-11 P
The giant sea, read his own mind. [Ulysses 99-12 P
A child asleep in its own life. [Ulysses 104-22 P
The giant sea, read his own mind. [Presence 105-15 P
"A Child Asleep in Its Own Life" [106-title P
In that sphere with so few objects of its own. [Local 112-3 P
Of feeling, the things that came of their own accord, [Local
  112-8 P
On the waste throne of his own wilderness. [Region 115-15 P
This fetches its own water. [Three 129-2 P
Green had, those days, its own implacable sting. [Someone 85-7 A
OX. A lion, an ox in his breast, [Destructive 192-13
  Young ox, bow-legged bear, [Destructive 192-16
  To have the ant of the self changed to an ox [Freed 205-9

From a doctor into an ox, before standing up, [Freed 205-11
  It was being without description, being an ox. [Freed 205-16
  Two people, three horses, an ox [Les Plus 245-1
OXEN. Oxen . . . [Bowl 7-7 P
OXIDIA. Through Oxidia, banal suburb, [MBG 182-1
  Ecce, Oxidia is the seed [MBG 182-5
  Oxidia is the soot of fire, [MBG 182-7
  Oxidia is Olympia. [MBG 182-8
OX-LIKE. To know that the change and that the ox-like struggle
  [Freed 205-12
OXYGEN. He breathed its oxygen, [Poem Mt 512-3
OYSTER-BEDS. Beyond the oyster-beds, indigo. [Hero 274-26
OZYMANDIAS. Confronted Ozymandias. She went [NSF 395-17
  Then Ozymandias said the spouse, the bride [NSF 396-10

PABLO NERUDA. Of England, to Pablo Neruda in Ceylon, [Descrip
    341-22
PACES. Repeating your appointed paces [Hero 275-16
PACIFIC. That lay impounding the Pacific swell, [Geneva 24-2
    Diffusing balm in that Pacific calm? [Sea Surf 99-8
    True reconcilings, dark, pacific words, [Havana 144-21
PACK. Pack the heart and scratch the mind? And does the ear [Dump
    203-3
    A pack of cards is falling toward the floor. [Bouquet 450-22
    Makes them a pack on a giant's back, [Ulysses 103-24 P
PACKET. "From the Packet of Anacharsis" [365-title
    In his packet Anacharsis found the lines: [Anach 365-17
PAD. There's a weltanschauung of the penny pad. [NE Verses 104-10
PADDLING. Paddling the melodic swirls, [Thought 184-12
    Came paddling their canoes, a thousand thousand, [New Set 352-17
PAEDAGOGUM. Opusculum paedagogum. [Pears 196-1
PAGAN. A pagan in a varnished car. [MBG 170-12
PAGE. No, no: veracious page on page, exact. [C 40-3
    They resemble a page of Toulet [Nigger 153-4
    The very book, or, less, a page [MBG 178-2
    On a page of Euclid. [Common 221-9
    It is not the snow that is the quill, the page. [Bottle 239-13
    It is difficult to read. The page is dark. [Phosphor 267-5
    The page is blank or a frame without a glass [Phosphor 267-7
    The greenness of night lies on the page and goes [Phosphor 267-9
    Of access like the page of a wiggy book, [Pure 333-6
    To be, as on the youngest poet's page, [Descrip 340-20
    Except that the reader leaned above the page, [House Q 358-12
    The access of perfection to the page. [House Q 358-18
    Like a page of music, like an upper air, [NSF 397-13
    "Page from a Tale" [421-title
    On the pedestal, an ambitious page dog-eared [What We 460-1
    A hand of light to turn the page, [Aug 492-9
    It was a page he had found in the handbook of heartbreak.
        [Madame 507-8
    Of men and earth: I quote the line and page, [Soldat 11-8 P
    As in a page of poetry-- [July 115-1 P
PAGEANT. His own pageant and procession and display, [Questions
    462-18
PAGEANTS. The father fetches pageants out of air, [AA 415-13
PAGES. Of sombre pages. [Reader 146-15
    The sombre pages bore no print [Reader 147-10
    The luminous pages on his knee, [Country 207-21
    Two things are one. (Pages of illustrations.) [Connois 215-3
    "Les Plus Belles Pages" [244-title
    Of the well-thumbed, infinite pages of her masters, who will
        seem old to her, requiting less and less her feeling: [Piano
        22-7 P
PAGODA. "The Desire to Make Love in a Pagoda" [91-title P
PAID. One-half of all its installments paid. [MBG 182-2
PAIL. One sits and beats an old tin can, lard pail. [Dump 202-26
PAIN. A part of labor and a part of pain, [Sunday 68-9
    The voice of this besieging pain. [Mozart 132-12
    Of people sensible to pain, [Adequacy 244-2
    That do not beat by pain, but calendar, [Phenom 286-5
    Was ancient. He tried to remember the phrases: pain [EM 314-3
    Audible at noon, pain torturing itself, [EM 314-4
    Pain killing pain on the very point of pain. [EM 314-5
    It was almost time for lunch. Pain is human. [EM 314-8
    No pain (ignoring the cocks that crow us up [EM 314-13
    It is pain that is indifferent to the sky [EM 315-4
    As if pain, no longer satanic mimicry, [EM 316-5
    Of impersonal pain. Reality explained. [EM 322-3
    Including pain, which, otherwise, is false. [EM 323-22
    In the third world, then, there is no pain. Yes, but [EM 323-23
    Without his envious pain in body, in mind, [Past Nun 378-20
    Its irrational reaction, as from pain. [John 437-26
    See pique-pain.
PAINS. All pleasures and all pains, remembering [Sunday 67-24
PAINT. Although they paint effulgent, azure lakes, [C 37-28
    And, as you paint, the clouds, [Add 198-13
    The poses of speech, of paint, [Add 199-1
    By metaphor you paint [Poem Morn 219-4
    The senses paint [Poem Morn 219-8
    Sharp as white paint in the January sun; [Holiday 312-2
    In the present state of things as, say, to paint [NH 478-6
    The greenhouse never so badly needed paint. [Plain 502-17
    It was a mistake to paint the gods. [Greenest 57-30 P
    And ours, of rigid measure, a miser's paint; [Sombre 67-8 P
PAINTED. That was what I painted behind the loaf, [Loaf 199-19
    They seem a little painted, now. [Arcades 226-2
    Painted by mad-men, seen as magic, [Hero 277-24
    But still she painted them, appropriate to [NSF 402-4
    And the painted hairs that composed her hair. [Grotesque 74-4 P
    Painted on porcelain [Three 132-18 P
    That we are painted on this very bottle, [Three 132-20 P
    That we are painted as warriors, [Three 132-25 P
    That we are painted as three dead men, [Three 133-2 P

For the figures painted on it. [Three 133-9 P
    Painted on this porcelain, [Three 142-10 P
PAINTER. Cloud-clown, blue painter, sun as horn, [Jumbo 269-13
    The way a painter of pauvred color paints. [NSF 402-3
    The poet mumbles and the painter sees, [Orb 443-16
PAINTING. If men at forty will be painting lakes [Monocle 15-7
    In the present state of painting and not the state [NH 478-7
    Painting the saints among palms. [Agenda 41-20 P
    "Nuns Painting Water-Lilies" [92-title P
PAINTS. The way a painter of pauvred color paints. [NSF 402-3
PAIR. The pair yellow, the peer. [Forces 228-20
    They polished the embracings of a pair [Repet 306-16
    They are a plural, a right and left, a pair, [NSF 407-11
PAIRS. And plated pairs? [Am Sub 130-20
PAISANT. "Paisant Chronicle" [title-334
    Is a paisant chronicle. [Paisant 334-16
    Of paisant chronicles. [Paisant 335-2
PAIX. To prefer L'Observateur de la Paix, since [Hero 276-6
PALABRA. Palabra of a common man who did not exist. [Holiday 312-8
PALACE. Through the palace walls. [Ord Women 10-16
    Through the palace walls. [Ord Women 12-6
    "Palace of the Babies" [77-title
    To build a ruddy palace? [Archi 17-24 P
PALADIN. The rich man going bare, the paladin [C 37-17
    To contemplate time's golden paladin [Greenest 56-24 P
PALADINS. For the music and manner of the paladins [Monocle 16-20
PALAHUDE. ll. There is an island Palahude by name-- [Someone
    86-14 P
PALAIS. The palais de justice of chambermaids [Surprises 98-6
PALANKEENS. Then place of vexing palankeens, then haunt [C 43-24
PALAVER. Their eyes closed, in a young palaver of lips. [NH 477-1
PALAZ. "Tea at the Palaz of Hoon" [65-title
PALE. In the pale nights, when your first imagery [Monocle 15-5
    With bland complaisance on pale parasols, [C 29-19
    Sepulchral señors, bibbling pale mescal, [C 38-21
    Bear other perfumes. On your pale head wear [Fictive 88-15
    And a pale silver patterned on the deck [Sea Surf 100-12
    Oh! Blessed rage for order, pale Ramon, [Key W 130-11
    Pale helms and spiky spurs, [Brave 138-14
    How pale and how possessed a night it is, [Havana 144-26
    In the pale light that each upon the other throws. [Re-state
        146-12
    (In the pale coherences of moon and mood [Anglais 149-1
    The pale intrusions into blue [MBG 172-1
    Good air. Poor pale, poor pale guitar . . . [MBG 176-2
    Once more night's pale illuminations, gold [NSF 402-24
    By such slight genii in such pale air. [Orb 440-8
    Waved in pale adieu. The rex Impolitor [Aug 495-21
    Flat and pale and gory! [Phases 3-18 P
    They cock small ears, more glistening and pale [Soldat 14-2 P
    No solemn one, nor pale, [Archi 18-12 P
    Assumes a pale, Italianate sheen-- [Abnormal 24-6 P
    (Her pale smock sparkles in a light begun [Infernale 25-9 P
    Impassioned seducers and seduced, the pale [Burnshaw 52-19 P
    Life's foreigners, pale aliens of the mud, [Greenest 59-23 P
    Without his enlargings and pale arrondissements, [Someone 85-5 A
    The dot, the pale pole of resemblances [Ideal 88-16 A
PALES. And knotted, sashed and seamed, half pales of red, [Cred
    378-2
    Half pales of green, appropriate habit for [Cred 378-3
PALESTINE. Over the seas, to silent Palestine, [Sunday 67-10
    A voice that cries, "The tomb in Palestine [Sunday 70-15
PALLET. The gray grass like a pallet, closely pressed; [Extracts
    255-4
PALLID. Made pallid flitter. Crispin, here, took flight. [C 32-27
    And pallid. It is the grandfather he liked, [Lack 303-11
    And pallid bits, that tend to comply with blue, [Bouquet 452-2
    In the pallid perceptions of its distances. [NH 469-10
    Too starkly pallid for the jaguar's light, [Greenest 54-29 P
PALLIDEST. They bud the whitest eye, the pallidest sprout, [Rock
    527-7
PALLID-SKINNED. A woman brilliant and pallid-skinned, [Attempt
    370-10
PALLOR. When the body of Jesus hangs in a pallor, [Lunar 107-5
    Its ruddy pallor had grown cadaverous. [Anglais 149-4
    A stellar pallor that hangs on the threads. [Leben 505-3
    A cry, the pallor of a dress, a touch. [Sombre 67-20 P
    See sun-pallor.
PALLORS. Are corrupting pallors . . . ay di mi, [MBG 172-2
    Of mountain pallors ebbing into air; [Soldat 13-10 P
    See lake-pallors.
PALM. Squiggling like saxaphones. And palm for palm, [High-Toned
    59-12
    Nor visionary south, nor cloudy palm [Sunday 68-21
    The big-finned palm [Nomad 95-8
    Though the brow in your palm may grieve [Delight 162-3
    But the eyes are men in the palm of the hand. [Arcades 225-19
    A palm that rises up beyond the sea, [Descrip 344-2
    Which, like a gorgeous palm, [Archi 17-18 P
    The palm at the end of the mind, [Of Mere 117-15 P

Sings in the palm, without human meaning, [Of Mere 117-19 P
The palm stands on the edge of space. [Of Mere 118-4 P
PALMED. A fruit for pewter, thorned and palmed and blue, [Poem
    Morn 219-6
PALMETTOES. The green palmettoes in crepuscular ice [C 34-15
    It is the same jingle of the water among the roots under the
        banks of the palmettoes, [Indian 112-5
PALM-EYED. Wild wedges, as of a volcano's smoke, palm-eyed [AA
    416-17
PALMS. And the palms and the twilight. [Infanta 7-12
    As if raspberry tanagers in palms, [C 30-20
    Making the most of savagery of palms, [C 31-27
    He came. The poetic hero without palms. [C 35-26
    The conscience is converted into palms, [High-Toned 59-4
    Is equally converted into palms, [High-Toned 59-11
    Say that the palms are clear in a total blue, [Two Figures 86-13
    Her mind had bound me round. The palms were hot [Farewell 117-11
    Becoming emeralds. He might watch the palms [Landsc 243-4
    And the palms were waved [Coroner 29-12 P
    The palms were waved [Coroner 29-16 P
    Over the palms. [Coroner 30-10 P
    Painting the saints among palms. [Agenda 41-20 P
    Thinly, among the elephantine palms, [Greenest 54-26 P
    1. The hut stands by itself beneath the palms. [Someone 86-4 A
PALMY. On the palmy beach, [Fabliau 23-5
    Of palmy peaks sighting machine-guns? These, [Greenest 56-2 P
    The parrot in its palmy boughs [Grotesque 75-10 P
PALOMA. You Jim and you Margaret and you singer of La Paloma, [Fish-
    Scale 161-1
PALPABLE. Slight gestures that could rend the palpable ice, [Page
    423-2
PALSIED. O stagnant east-wind, palsied mare, [Room Gard 40-16 P
PALTRY. "The Paltry Nude Starts on a Spring Voyage" [5-title
PAMPALUNED. Is, after all, draped damask pampaluned, [Greenest
    58-4 P
PAMPEAN. Musing immaculate, pampean dits, [C 38-25
PANACHE. Panache upon panache, his tails deploy [Bird Claws 82-10
    Without panache, without cockade, [Thought 185-24
    Miraculous in its panache and swish? [Antag 426-2
    No longer a battered panache above snow . . . [Not Ideas 534-8
PANDECTS. Spelling out pandects and haggard institutes? [Duck
    62-17 P
PANDEMONIUM. Is cast in pandemonium, flittered, howled [Duck 62-7 P
PANDEMONIUMS. Birds twitter pandemoniums around [Antag 426-3
PANE. Of heat upon his pane. This was the span [C 33-4
    The crack across the pane, [Anything B 211-22
    Write pax across the window pane. And then [Puel 456-15
PANG. That never touch with inarticulate pang? [Sunday 69-19
PANGS. And elemental potencies and pangs, [C 31-25
PANIC. Panic in the face of the moon--round effendi [EM 320-15
    To anyone that comes--panic, because [EM 320-19
PANJANDRUM. Panjandrum and central heart and mind of minds--
    [Extracts 254-12
PANNICLES. The spring came there in clinking pannicles [C 34-9
PANNIERS. And live and heap their panniers of green [Belly 367-3
PANOPLY. What was this gaudy, gusty panoply? [C 30-11
PANORAMA. Yet the panorama of despair [Botanist 1 135-13
PANORAMAS. Panoramas are not what they used to be. [Botanist 1
    134-9
PANS. Of the pans above the stove, the pots on the table, the
    tulips among them. [Large 423-15
PANTALOONS. Old pantaloons, duenna of the spring! [Polish Aunt
    84-6
    In pantaloons of fire and of women hatched, [Liadoff 346-9
    His slouching pantaloons, beyond the town, [NSF 389-6
    In that old coat, those sagging pantaloons, [NSF 389-9
PANTHER. That yuccas breed, and of the panther's tread. [C 31-29
PANTING. Of barbarous tongue, slavered and panting halves [AA
    415-18
PANTOMIME. It was a small part of the pantomime. [Thirteen 93-2
    The rhythm of this celestial pantomime." [Landsc 243-8
PAP. They nourish Jupiters. Their casual pap [Havana 144-7
PAPER. Or paper souvenirs of rapture, [Jasmine 79-9
    The paper is whiter [Common 221-15
    The paper is whiter. [Common 221-23
    A crinkled paper makes a brilliant sound. [Extracts 252-1
    The wrinkled roses tinkle, the paper ones, [Extracts 252-2
    With this paper, this dust. That states the point. [Extracts
        252-6
    Of paper is of the nature of its world. [Extracts 252-9
    Of things no better than paper things, of days [Extracts 253-2
    That are paper days. The false and true are one. [Extracts 253-3
    Of the highest self: he studies the paper [Hero 280-14
    Otu-bre's lion-roses have turned to paper [Plant 506-5
    Of London, the paper of Paris magnified [Duck 61-18 P
    By print or paper, the trivial chance foregone, [Duck 61-23 P
PAPER-BAG. The cat in the paper-bag, the corset, the box [Dump
    201-18
PAPERS. Throw papers in the streets, the wills [MBG 170-7
    Of images. Days pass like papers from a press. [Dump 201-14

The bouquets come here in the papers. So the sun, [Dump 201-15
PAPHIAN. Of golden quirks and Paphian caricatures, [Swans 4-6
PAPIER-MACHE. Of sleep's faded papier-mâché . . . [Not Ideas 534-11
PAPINI. "Reply to Papini" [446-title
    See Giovanni Papini.
PAPPADOPOULOS. See Mrs. Pappadopoulos.
PARABLE. This parable, in sense, amounts to this: [Monocle 15-24
PARADE. Smacking their muzzy bellies in parade, [High-Toned 59-16
    His red cockade topped off a parade. [News 264-15
    But a profane parade, the basso [Hero 278-5
    And fortunate stone. It moves its parade [Imago 439-7
    Will see us on parade, [Phases 3-10 P
    "The Drum-Majors in the Labor Day Parade" [36-title P
    The parade's no good. [Drum-Majors 37-3 P
PARADES. Behold, already on the long parades [Swans 4-9
    In parades like several equipages, [Hero 277-23
    Of parades in the obscurer selvages. [EM 317-16
    The churches and their long parades, Seville [Greenest 53-18 P
    Parades of whole races with attendant bands, [Duck 66-2 P
PARADIGM. Green barbarism turning paradigm. [C 31-22
    Each one its paradigm." There are not leaves [Dames 206-6
PARADISAL. And gilt umbrellas. Paradisal green [Sea Surf 99-2
    And spoken in paradisal parlance new [NH 475-26
PARADISE. The blood of paradise? And shall the earth [Sunday 68-6
    Seem all of paradise that we shall know? [Sunday 68-7
    Return no more, where, then, is paradise?" [Sunday 68-16
    Is there no change of death in paradise? [Sunday 69-13
    Their chant shall be a chant of paradise, [Sunday 70-4
    He is not paradise of parakeets, [Bird Claws 82-7
    The middling beast, the garden of paradise [Thought 185-21
    The imperfect is our paradise. [Poems Clim 194-7
    A little while of Terra Paradise [Montra 263-1
    In which we read the critique of paradise [Crude 305-9
    As if the paradise of meaning ceased [EM 320-28
    To be paradise, it is this to be destitute. [EM 321-1
    After death, the non-physical people, in paradise, [EM 325-21
    The rotund emotions, paradise unknown. [EM 325-29
    A metamorphosis of paradise, [Pure 331-24
    Malformed, the world was paradise malformed . . . [Pure 332-1
    We have not the need of any paradise, [NSF 394-20
    In hall harridan, not hushful paradise, [AA 421-1
    Much rough-end being to smooth Paradise, [Luther 461-11
    When earth has become a paradise, it will be [Bship 77-19 P
    A paradise full of assassins. Suppose I seize [Bship 77-20 P
    Spring's bright paradise has come to this. [Fare Guit 98-16 P
    There is no map of paradise. [Ulysses 102-2 P
PARAGON. Prime paramour and belted paragon, [Lilacs 49-12
    That paragon of a parasol [Primordia 9-21 P
    A paragon of lustre; may have voice [Spaniard 35-9 P
    And memory and claws: a paragon [Spaniard 35-14 P
PARAGRAPH. A passage of music, a paragraph [Ulysses 103-2 P
PARAGRAPHS. And, between his letters, reading paragraphs [EM 313-12
PARAKEET. A parakeet of parakeets prevails, [Bird Claws 82-2
PARAKEETS. Above the forest of the parakeets, [Bird Claws 82-1
    A parakeet of parakeets prevails, [Bird Claws 82-2
    He is not paradise of parakeets, [Bird Claws 82-7
PARALLEL. The same. We parallel the mother's death. [Anatomy 108-2
    Two parallels that meet if only in [NSF 407-12
PARALLELS. Two parallels become one, a perspective, of which [Rome
    508-9
PARAMOUNT. Another thought, the paramount ado . . . [What We 460-5
    The clear. A celestial mode is paramount, [NH 480-24
PARAMOUR. To be their latest, lucent paramour. [C 38-27
    Prime paramour and belted paragon, [Lilacs 49-12
    "Final Soliloquy of the Interior Paramour" [524-title
PARAMOURS. Come, all celestial paramours, [Burnshaw 47-14 P
PARAPHRASE. "Lunar Paraphrase" [107-title
PARASOL. What is this purple, this parasol, [Hartford 226-15
    A parasol, which I had found, against [Phenom 287-9
    The sun. The interior of a parasol, [Phenom 287-10
    That paragon of a parasol [Primordia 9-21 P
    "Peter Parasol" [20-title P
PARASOLS. With bland complaisance on pale parasols, [C 29-19
    With parasols, in the afternoon air. [Parasol 20-14 P
PARA-THING. Turned para-thing, the rudiments in the jar, [Bouquet
    452-7
PARA-THINGS. The place of meta-men and para-things, [Bouquet 448-16
    Though para-things; the meta-men for whom [Bouquet 449-2
PARATROOPERS. The paratroopers fall and as they fall [EM 322-11
    A well-made scene in which paratroopers [EM 322-21
PARCEL-GILDED. The old seraph, parcel-gilded, among violets [NSF
    389-13
PARDIE. Pardie! Summer is like a fat beast, sleepy in mildew,
    [Banal 62-15
PARENT. That elemental parent, the green night, [Phosphor 267-15
    Of a parent in the French sense. [Lack 303-16
    Is it the old, the roseate parent or [Repet 308-16
    Because we suffer, our oldest parent, peer [EM 315-17
    We knew one parent must have been divine, [Pure 331-19
    Beyond relation to the parent trunk: [Red Fern 365-10

In the parent's hand, perhaps parental love? [Aug 491-25
Go back to a parent before thought, before speech, [Irish 501-11
Now, he brings all that he saw into the earth, to the waiting
  parent. [Madame 507-3
Obscurest parent, obscurest patriarch, [Look 518-20
PARENTAGE. A trinkling in the parentage of the north, [Discov
  95-13 P
PARENTAL. The pure perfections of parental space,[Owl 436-3
Of it, a close, parental magnitude, [Orb 443-12
In the parent's hand, perhaps parental love? [Aug 491-25
PARENTS. Of parents, lewdest of ancestors. [Prelude 195-20
A self of parents who have never died, [Sombre 67-4 P
PARIS. In Paris, celui qui chante et pleure, [Thought 186-7
Even in Paris, in the Gardens [Analysis 349-4
Or Paris in conversation at a café. [NH 486-3
There's a little square in Paris, [Phases 3-1 P
Of London, the paper of Paris magnified [Duck 61-18 P
Breakfast in Paris, music and madness and mud, [Bship 80-3 P
PARISH. Not to die a parish death. [Nigger 151-15
The long recessional at parish eves wails round [Greenest 59-15 P
PARISIAN. Mother was afraid I should freeze in the Parisian hotels.
  [Novel 457-7
PARISIANS. Ponies of Parisians shooting on the hill. [Parochial
  191-2
PARIS-RAIN. Or Paris-rain. He thinks of the noble lives [Greenest
  59-25 P
PARK. The stride of vanishing autumn in a park [C 31-3
When the elephant's-ear in the park [Tea 112-8
Life is an old casino in a park. [Havana 142-9
The negroes were playing football in the park. [Contra II 270-14
Of Trope. He sat in the park. The water of [NSF 397-11
Was it as we sat in the park and the archaic form [Aug 494-10
"Vacancy in the Park" [511-title
I peopled the dark park with gowns [Stan MMO 19-1 P
Another evening in another park, [Old Woman 43-1 P
Of the park with chalky brow scratched over black [Old Woman
  44-3 P
We went to walk in the park; for, after all, [Duck 60-8 P
On summer Sundays in the park, a duck [Duck 60-11 P
Of the park. They obey the rules of every skeleton. [Duck 62-11 P
The summer Sundays in the park, must be [Duck 66-4 P
In the park. We regret we have no nightingale. [Duck 66-7 P
PARKS. The soul, O ganders, flies beyond the parks [Swans 4-1
Apocalypse was not contrived for parks, [Duck 62-9 P
PARLANCE. And spoken in paradisal parlance new [NH 475-16
PARLED. See parl-parled.
PARLEYING. Came like two spirits parleying, adorned [C 31-31
But they came parleying of such an earth, [C 32-1
PARLOR. This parlor of farcical dames, this clowns' colonnade,
  this kites' pavilion? [Inelegance 26-6 P
In a parlor of day. [Coroner 30-12 P
PARL-PARLED. Parl-parled the West-Indian weather. [Search 268-2
Parl-parled the West-Indian hurricane. [Search 268-12
PAROCHIAL. "Parochial Theme" [191-title
PARODY. Made earth come right; a peanut parody [Havana 143-9
PARROT. There's a parrot in a window, [Phases 3-9 P
The parrot in its palmy boughs [Grotesque 75-10 P
See seraglio-parrot.
PARROTS. We are cold, the parrots cried, [Anything B 211-14
PARROT-SQUAWKS. A new reality in parrot-squawks. [C 32-12
PART. toward which you lend no part! [Nuances 18-7
that reflects neither my face nor any inner part [Nuances 18-9
Lend no part to any humanity that suffuses [Nuances 18-11
A part of labor and a part of pain, [Sunday 68-9
It was a small part of the pantomime. [Thirteen 93-2
That bore us as a part of all the things [Anatomy 107-14
To gold in broadest blue, and be a part [Sun March 133-16
As part of nature he is part of us. [Havana 144-18
He is singing and chanting the things that are part of him,
  [Nigger 150-11
A part of what it is . . . Children, [Postcard 159-13
Not to be part of the sun? To stand [MBG 168-20
In face of the monster, be more than part [MBG 175-7
One part is man, the other god: [Dezem 218-7
Of which one is a part as in a unity, [Yellow 236-18
It has to persuade that war is part of itself, [Bottle 239-6
That he might be truth, himself, or part of it, [Landsc 242-21
That the things that he rejected might be part [Landsc 242-22
And the irregular turquoise, part, the perceptible blue [Landsc
  242-23
Grown denser, part, the eye so touched, so played [Landsc 242-24
For a moment they are gay and are a part [Gala 248-4
Beyond the knowledge of nakedness, as part [Extracts 252-18
Is real, part of a land beyond the mind? [Extracts 252-20
Of the weather and in one's self, as part of that [Extracts 258-9
Legend were part of what he was, forms [Hero 276-23
It is a part of his conception, [Hero 279-13
I am and have a being and play a part. [Phenom 287-21
Know that the past is not part of the present. [Dutch 291-21
That, like your own, is large, hence, to be part [Choc 296-9

The cry is part. My solitaria [Choc 298-16
Like the head of fate, looked out in darkness, part [Choc 299-20
Thereof and part desire and part the sense [Choc 299-21
His poems are not of the second part of life. [Creat 311-11
To die). This is a part of the sublime [EM 314-14
It was part of a supremacy always [EM 314-26
Were part of a sustenance itself enough, [EM 316-3
Of their own part, yet moving on the wind, [EM 319-8
No part of him was ever part of death. [EM 319-16
Of which we are too distantly a part. [Less 328-10
Not apparition but appearance, part [Feo 334-10
Just where it was, oh beau caboose . . . It was part [Liadoff
  347-14
The quiet was part of the meaning, part of the mind: [House Q
  358-17
So much a part of the place, so little [Woman Song 361-1
Are a slight part of death. [Burghers 362-5
The philosopher's hat to be part of the mind, [Prejudice 369-5
The Swedish cart to be part of the heart. [Prejudice 369-6
Burn everything not part of it to ash. [Cred 373-5
Which is not part of the listener's own sense. [Cred 377-20
Part of the mottled mood of summer's whole, [Cred 378-5
In being more than an exception, part, [NSF 388-21
Though an heroic part, of the commonal. [NSF 388-22
And so, as part, to exult with its great throat, [NSF 398-9
Almost as part of innocence, almost, [AA 420-2
Almost as the tenderest and the truest part. [AA 420-3
As a part, but part, but tenacious particle, [Orb 443-18
Sits in a wood, in the greenest part, [Degen 444-2
The meta-men behold the idea as part [Bouquet 449-22
They are. The bouquet is a part of a dithering: [Bouquet 452-17
As part of the never-ending meditation, [NH 465-7
Part of the question that is a giant himself: [NH 465-8
And more, in branchings after day. One part [NH 468-23
In which looks and feelings mingle and are part [NH 471-5
Part of the res itself and not about it. [NH 473-17
Not as it was: part of the reverberation [NH 473-19
That is part of the indifference of the eye [NH 475-18
As if the eyes were the present or part of it, [NH 478-10
A century in which everything was part [NH 479-4
Being part of everything come together as one. [NH 482-11
It is not part of what is absent, a halt [NH 487-17
The sentiment of the fatal is a part [Aug 491-19
But, of my being and its knowing, part. [Angel 496-12
Of the harsh reality of which it is part. [Plant 506-19
Men are part both in the inch and in the mile. [Rome 508-10
From fire and be part only of that of which [Rome 509-7
Ever want it to. It is part of the life in your room. [Rome
  510-13
He belonged to the far-foreign departure of his vessel and was
  part of it, [Prol 516-1
Part of the speculum of fire on its prow, its symbol, whatever
  it was, [Prol 516-2
Part of the glass-like sides on which it glided over the salt-
  stained water, [Prol 516-3
A moving part of a motion, a discovery [Look 518-14
Part of a discovery, a change part of a change, [Look 518-15
A sharing of color and being part of it. [Look 518-16
To gallant notions on the part of cold. [Quiet 523-6
By gallant notions on the part of night-- [Quiet 523-11
That which is always beginning because it is part [Armor 530-17
Of the planet of which they were part. [Planet 533-3
It was part of the colossal sun, [Not Ideas 534-15
The horses are a part of a northern sky [Greenest 54-28 P
The common-places of which if formed a part [Greenest 57-5 P
From the steppes, are they being part, feeling the strength,
  [Duck 62-15 P
Each one as part of the total wrath, obscure [Sombre 69-5 P
The oranges glitter as part of the sky, [Stan MBG 72-13 P
Second. The part [Bship 79-17 P
Where I or one or the part is the equal of [Bship 79-25 P
Strike fire, but the part is the equal of the whole, [Bship
  79-29 P
The jungle of tropical part and tropical whole." [Bship 80-12 P
To be a part of tradition, to identify [Recit 86-4 P
Is part of the classic imagination, posed [Recit 87-1 P
Part of the major reality, part of [Warmth 90-3 P
These pods are part of the growth of life within life: [Nuns
  92-7 P
Part of the unpredictable sproutings, as of [Nuns 92-8 P
To be part of a tissue, a clearness of the air, [Nuns 92-16 P
We are part of a fraicheur, inaccessible [Nuns 93-1 P
And though one says that one is part of everything, [Course
  96-5 P
And being part is an exertion that declines: [Course 96-17 P
A part of space and solitude, [Ulysses 100-6 P
A part of the inhuman more, [Ulysses 105-2 P
And weathered, should be part of a human landscape, [Conversat
  109-6 P
But this will be a part of sunrise, [Three 138-17 P

Today the mind is not part of the weather. [Clear Day 113-13 P
Part of a major reality, part of [As Leave 117-9 P
As a part of the nature that he contemplates [Someone 84-17 A
PARTAKE. Proves that these opposite things partake of one, [Connois 215-14
Or symbol of malice. That we partake thereof, [AA 418-22
PARTAKER. The partaker partakes of that which changes him. [NSF 392-19
PARTAKES. The partaker partakes of that which changes him. [NSF 392-19
PARTAKING. Partaking of the sea, [Infanta 8-3
PARTICIPANTS. Participants of its being. It is, we are. [Study I 463-10
PARTICLE. More fecund as principle than particle, [NSF 388-19
As a part, but part, but tenacious particle, [Orb 443-18
PARTICLES. They were particles of order, a single majesty: [Anglais 149-8
Of the obvious whole, uncertain particles [Man Car 351-1
Of the wind, the glassily-sparkling particles [Page 423-7
When was it that the particles became [Aug 494-1
Intent on your particles of nether-do, [Rome 509-17
PARTICULAR. An upper, particular bough in, say, Marchand. [Connois 215-12
This dark, particular rose. [Scavoir 231-4
High blue became particular [Vase 246-18
As each had a particular woman and her touch? [Holiday 312-10
Like their particular characters, addicts [Lot 371-10
And red, and right. The particular question--here [Ulti 429-12
The particular answer to the particular question [Ulti 429-13
A particular of being, the gross universe. [Rock 526-9
The rock is the gray particular of man's life, [Rock 528-1
The rock is the stern particular of the air, [Rock 528-4
Are two quite different things, in particular [Lytton 39-8 P
"The Course of a Particular" [96-title P
Always, the particular thought [Ulysses 103-14 P
The particular tingle in a proclamation [Someone 84-14 A
PARTICULARS. By the spontaneous particulars of sound. [Creat 311-15
Sprinklings of bright particulars from the sky. [Descrip 344-6
And forth the particulars of rapture come. [NSF 392-9
That bends the particulars to the abstract, [Ulysses 103-23 P
Particulars of a relative sublime. [Ulysses 103-27 P
PARTINGS. Would be endings, more poignant than partings, profounder, [Adieu 127-14
PARTISANS. Ancient amigas, knowing partisans-- [Souls 95-3 P
PARTLY. We had always been partly one. It was as we came [Oboe 251-17
Of partly his. His voice is audible, [NH 485-11
PARTS. Rejecting intermediate parts, [Negation 97-15
The metaphysica, the plastic parts of poems [Glass 197-19
But they are not parts of a truth." [On Road 203-18
In the sum of the parts, there are only the parts. [On Road 204-3
By thunder, parts, and all these things together, [Landsc 242-26
Parts, and more things, parts. He never supposed divine [Landsc 242-27
As secondary (parts not quite perceived [Man Car 350-18
Their parts as in a youthful happiness. [Cred 378-10
Are parts of apotheosis, appropriate [NSF 387-20
The whole, the essential compact of the parts, [Orb 442-7
Parts of the immense detritus of a world [Burnshaw 49-21 P
The parts. Thus: Out of the number of his thoughts [Bship 80-15 P
The ultimate one, though they are parts of it. [Bship 80-27 P
They are more than parts of the universal machine. [Woman Had 82-25 P
Merely parts of the general fiction of the mind: [Recit 87-29 P
PARVULA. "Puella Parvula" [456-title
PASADENA. The aunts in Pasadena, remembering, [Hartford 226-11
PASCAGOULA. "Some Friends from Pascagoula" [126-title
PASS. Before one merely reads to pass the time. [Monocle 14-22
Yet let that trifle pass. Now, as this odd [C 32-13
Obliquities of those who pass beneath, [C 41-4
Of images. Days pass like papers from a press. [Dump 201-14
Except Polacks that pass in their motors [Jersey 210-18
Pass through the door and through the walls, [Vari 235-10
The mind sits listening and hears it pass. [Pure 329-18
Did not pass like someone voyaging out of and beyond the familiar. [Prol 515-13
Waiting until we pass. [Phases 3-2 P
Pass the whole of life earing the clink of the [Archi 16-18 P
This future, although the elephants pass and the blare, [Duck 63-31 P
See pass-pass.
PASSAGE. And spiritous passage into nothingness, [Heaven 56-17
A while, conceiving his passage as into a time [Owl 432-23
A passage of music, a paragraph [Ulysses 103-2 P
PASSAGES. Much more than that. Autumnal passages [Grapes 111-1
PASSED. That passed beyond us through the narrow sky. [Medit 124-6
Passed like a circus. [Havana 143-20
Who was it passed her there on a horse all will, [Uruguay 249-16
After the wind has passed. Sleep realized [Owl 433-19

Tomorrow for him. The wind will have passed by, [NH 473-23
Silence is a shape that has passed. [Plant 506-4
Oh! How suave a purple passed me by! [Stan MMO 19-3 P
A time existing after much time has passed. [Role 93-11 P
PASSENGER. The same railway passenger, the ancient tree [Cats 367-16
PASSES. The blazing passes, from beyond the sun. [Monocle 15-19
Except when the bishop passes by, [Gray 140-18
The negro with laundry passes me by. [Stan MBG 72-10 P
PASSING. Stilled for the passing of her dreaming feet [Sunday 67-9
In the far South the sun of autumn is passing [Nigger 150-9
To be falling and to be passing away. [MBG 179-12
Sounds passing through sudden rightnesses, wholly [Of Mod 240-16
It was like passing a boundary to dive [Lot 371-1
It was passing a boundary, floating without a head [Lot 371-16
PASSION. His passion's permit, hang of coat, degree [C 39-18
As foregoing the nakedest passion for barefoot [EM 316-22
Lay a passion for yes that had never been broken. [EM 320-14
A passion that we feel, not understand. [NSF 392-11
The easy passion, the ever-ready love [NSF 394-23
For easy passion and ever-ready love [NSF 395-7
Like a woman inhibiting passion [Soldat 12-2 P
Her glory in your passion and be proud. [Red Kit 31-13 P
Memory without passion would be better lost. [Lytton 38-18 P
But memory and passion, and with these [Lytton 38-19 P
That a man without passion plays in an aimless way. [Sombre 71-12 P
The passion, indifferent to the poet's hum, [Sombre 71-25 P
That we conceal? A passion to fling the cloak, [Sombre 71-26 P
In the gesture's whim, a passion merely to be [Sombre 71-28 P
PASSIONATE. Mumbling a secret, passionate message. [Hero 276-18
Of our passionate height. He wears a tufted green, [Repet 309-23
PASSIONATELY. A passionately niggling nightingale. [C 35-3
PASSIONS. Passions of rain, or moods in falling snow; [Sunday 67-20
To see them without their passions [Lytton 38-10 P
Perhaps, without their passions, they will be [Lytton 38-12 P
Death ought to spare their passions. [Lytton 38-17 P
PASS-PASS. Without the oscillations of planetary pass-pass, [Cata 425-11
PAST. No spring can follow past meridian.'[Monocle 13-20
Is at the mast-head and the past is dead. [Farewell 117-5
That lucid souvenir of the past, [Mozart 132-3
What's down below is in the past [Botanist 2 135-18
And what's above is in the past [Botanist 2 136-1
The future might stop emerging out of the past, [Nigger 151-10
Oppose the past and the festival, [MBG 181-2
"Arcades of Philadelphia the Past" [225-title
Only the rich remember the past, [Arcades 225-1
That they never hear the past. To see, [Arcades 225-6
Is time, apart from any past, apart [Martial 238-7
To something else. Its past was a souvenir. [Of Mod 239-22
Resists each past apocalypse, rejects [Extracts 257-27
And, hoy, the impopulous purple-plated past, [Montra 260-5
There was no past in their forgetting, [Gigan 289-2
Know that the past is not part of the present. [Dutch 291-21
Monsters antique and haggard with past thought? [Dutch 292-11
The figures of the past go cloaked. [Poesie 302-12
The total past felt nothing when destroyed. [EM 314-16
A dream interrupted out of the past, [Sketch 336-8
But the integrations of the past are like [Descrip 342-2
Of the past is description without place, a cast [Descrip 345-20
"The Prejudice against the Past" [368-title
This foundling of the infected past, so bright, [NSF 388-11
To study the past, and doctors, having bathed [NSF 391-15
When the leaves fall like things mournful of the past, [Puel 456-12
Of the past, the rodomontadean emptiness. [Novel 457-6
To say good-by to the past and to live and to be [NH 478-5
Or, say, the late going colors of that past, [NH 482-1
At the head of the past. [Irish 501-12
To waste, out of the hopeless waste of the past [Burnshaw 49-23 P
However tarnished, companions out of the past, [Burnshaw 50-10 P
A cavernous and a cruel past, tropic [Greenest 58-21 P
The statue belongs to the cavernous past, belongs [Greenest 58-28 P
And practical. The envoi to the past [Duck 65-29 P
The future must bear within it every past, [Sombre 70-5 P
Without imagination, without past [Sombre 71-23 P
No book of the past in which time's senators [Recit 86-10 P
The ruins of the past, out of nothing left, [Recit 87-14 P
Without a remembered past, a present past, [Local 111-15 P
PASTE. They might be sugar or paste or citron-skin [Burnshaw 46-19P
Than purple paste of fruit, to taste, or leaves [Greenest 58-31 P
PASTED. On dung." Come now, pearled and pasted, bloomy-leafed, [Ghosts 119-17
PASTICCIO. Trinket pasticcio, flaunting skyey sheets, [C 40-1
PASTICHES. That the marbles are gluey pastiches, the stairs, [Prelude 195-3
PASTILY. The tips of cock-cry pinked out pastily, [NH 470-13
PASTIMES. False empire . . . These are the works and pastimes

Hero 280-13
PASTOR. "The Pastor Caballero" [379-title
PASTORAL. "A Pastoral Nun" [378-title
  This pastoral of endurance and of death [Papini 447-3
  And its pastoral text, [Inhab 503-14
PASTORS. These are the voices of the pastors calling [Luther 461-4
  These are the voices of the pastors calling [Luther 461-10
  These are the voices of the pastors calling [Luther 461-16
PASTRY. Young boys resembling pastry, hip-hip, [Hero 278-11
PASTS. Not least the pasts destroyed, magniloquent [Sombre 70-6 P
PATCH. Although I patch it as I can. [MBG 165-12
  Although I patch him as I can [MBG 165-15
  What opposite? Could it be that yellow patch, the side [Slug
    522-9
  Combatting bushmen for a patch of gourds, [Greenest 56-8 P
PATCHES. Patches the moon together in his room [NSF 407-7
  And dwindled into patches, [Celle 438-7
  The shapes of the patches, [Primordia 9-18 P
  Of patches and of pitches, [July 114-15 P
PATE. One eats one paté, even of salt, quotha. [C 28-1
PATER. Ethereal compounder, pater patriae, [Duck 64-28 P
PATERNAL. Less firm than the paternal flame, [Red Fern 365-6
PATH. The path sick sorrow took, the many paths [Sunday 69-4
  What path could lead apart from what she was [Old Woman 44-17 P
  Green is the path we take [Sombre 67-28 P
  A wandering orb upon a path grown clear. [Sombre 70-17 P
PATHETIC. And pathetic magnificences dry in the sky. [Repet 310-4
  They lay. Forth then with huge pathetic force [NSF 403-7
PATHOS. The moon is the mother of pathos and pity. [Lunar 107-1
  The moon is the mother of pathos and pity. [Lunar 107-12
  Without pathos, he feels what he hears [Prelude 194-18
  See anti-pathos.
PATHS. Of sure obliteration on our paths, [Sunday 69-3
  The path sick sorrow took, the many paths [Sunday 69-4
  And the leaves on the paths [Tea 112-10
  Chant, O ye faithful, in your paths [Botanist 2 136-5
  In a flapping cloak. She walked along the paths [Old Woman 44-2 P
  They keep to the paths of the skeleton architect [Duck 62-10 P
  Walking the paths, watching the gilding sun, [Duck 65-18 P
PATIENCE. It irked beyond his patience. Hence it was, [C 39-21
PATIENT. Repeating his name with its patient syllables, [World 521-17
PATIENTIA. Patientia, forever soothing wounds, [Lions 124-15
PATIOS. The birds are singing in the yellow patios, [Nigger 152-15
PATRIAE. Ethereal compounder, pater patriae, [Duck 64-28 P
PATRIARCH. Patron and patriarch of couplets, walk [NE Verses 105-11
  Of this I am, this is the patriarch, [Yellow 236-7
  Obscurest parent, obscurest patriarch, [Look 518-20
  This source and patriarch of other spheres, [Duck 63-27 P
  Sole, single source and minimum patriarch, [Conversat 108-21 P
PATRIARCHS. One father proclaims another, the patriarchs [Role
    93-7 P
PATRON. Patron and imager of the gold Don John, [Lilacs 49-14
  Patron and patriarch of couplets, walk [NE Verses 105-11
  Or possibly, the merest patron saint [Nigger 157-5
  The bell of its dome, the patron of sound. [Vari 235-9
  And prodigious person, patron of origins. [Orb 443-14
  Not some outer patron and imaginer. [Conversat 109-15 P
PATROON. Good-fortuner of the grotesque, patroon, [Lot 371-20
PATTED. Patted his stove-pipe hat and tugged his shawl. [Geneva
    24-3
PATTER. White sand, his patter of the long sea-slushes. [NSF 393-9
  What niggling forms of gargoyle patter? [Archi 17-2 P
  See pitter-patter.
PATTERING. On pattering leaves and suddenly with lights, [Burnshaw
    47-25 P
PATTERN. Of pattern in the dance's ripening. [AA 415-9
  The pattern of the heavens and high, night air. [NH 472-3
PATTERNED. And a pale silver patterned on the deck [Sea Surf 100-12
PATTING. Poet, patting more nonsense foamed [Prelude 195-14
PAUL. See St. Paul.
PAUSE. Or that she will pause at scurrilous words? [Lilacs 49-5
PAUSES. This crust of air? . . . (He pauses.) Can breath shake
    [Infernale 24-21 P
PAUVRE. Oh, la . . . le pauvre! [Plot Giant 7-4
PAUVRED. The way a painter of pauvred color paints. [NSF 402-3
PAVILION. "Hymn for a Watermelon Pavilion" [88-title
  This parlor of farcical dames, this clowns' colonnade, this
    kites' pavilion? [Inelegance 26-6 P
PAVILIONS. In its windless pavilions, [Three 131-18 P
  And long for the windless pavilions. [Three 133-12 P
  In the windless pavilions. [Three 137-8 P
PAWS. Its nose on its paws. [Destructive 193-5
PAX. Write pax across the window pane. And then [Puel 456-15
PAY-MEN. O pensioners, O demagogues and pay-men! [Men Fall 188-16
PAY-ROLL. Geranium budgets, pay-roll water-falls, [Duck 62-24 P
PAYSANS. "Angel Surrounded by Paysans" [496-title
PEACE. Of thought evoked a peace eccentric to [Havana 143-5
  Solace itself in peevish birds? Is it peace, [Dump 203-4
  And of fair weather, summer, dew, peace. [Peaches 224-14
  As one loves visible and responsive peace, [Yellow 236-14

A grossness of peace. [Bottle 239-12
He is and in his poems we find peace. [Oboe 251-2
Find peace? We found the sum of men. We found, [Oboe 251-11
We live in a camp . . . Stanzas of final peace [Extracts 258-22
Any mortal end. The chants of final peace [Extracts 259-6
Peace in a time of peace, said Leyden [Hero 273-10
In a peace that is more than a refuge, [Dutch 291-17
War's miracle begetting that of peace. [Cats 368-5
And she has peace. My Jacomyntje! [Extraord 369-8
To its barbed, barbarous rising and has peace. [Extraord 369-11
And fill the foliage with arrested peace, [Cred 373-11
And the green flauntings of the hours of peace. [Pastor 380-3
The vivid transparence that you bring is peace. [NSF 380-11
Who gives transparence to their present peace. [AA 413-11
Who by his highness quiets them, high peace [Owl 431-14
And peace is cousin by a hundred names [Owl 432-11
There peace, the godolphin and fellow, estranged, estranged,
    [Owl 434-1
This was peace after death, the brother of sleep, [Owl 434-7
Peace stood with our last blood adorned, last mind, [Owl 434-19
The peace of the last intelligence; [Aug 490-22
So seen, have an order of its own, a peace [Burnshaw 49-1 P
PEACEFUL. And August the most peaceful month. [Rabbit K 209-6
  The peaceful, blissful words, well-tuned, well-sung, well-
    spoken. [Sick 90-21 P
PEACEFULLEST. To be, in the grass, in the peacefullest time,
    [Rabbit K 209-7
PEACH. Performed in verd apparel, and the peach, [C 39-2
  Ah! and red; and they have peach fuzz, ah! [Peaches 224-11
PEACH-BUD. The peach-bud maker, [Mud 148-9
PEACHED. Her daughters to the peached and ivory wench [Havana
    143-26
PEACHES. "A Dish of Peaches in Russia" [224-title
  With my whole body I taste these peaches, [Peaches 224-1
  Heart. The peaches are large and round, [Peaches 224-10
  One self from another, as these peaches do. [Peaches 224-20
  Then the sides of peaches, of dusky pears. [Vase 246-24
  That the peaches are slowly ripening. [Memo 89-10 P
PEACOCK. With his plough, the peacock may abandon pride, [Burnshaw
    48-24 P
PEACOCKS. And I remembered the cry of the peacocks. [Domination
    8-16
  I heard them cry--the peacocks. [Domination 9-2
  Turning as the tails of the peacocks [Domination 9-8
  Full of the cry of the peacocks? [Domination 9-11
  And I remembered the cry of the peacocks. [Domination 9-20
  "Anecdote of the Prince of Peacocks" [57-title
  And if you weep for peacocks that are gone [Burnshaw 48-21 P
  And change. If ploughmen, peacocks, doves alike [Burnshaw 48-26 P
  That the vista retain ploughmen, peacocks, doves [Burnshaw 50-9 P
PEAK. Sequences, thought of among spheres in the old peak of night:
    [Bed 326-19
  Of things at least that was thought of in the old peak of night.
    [Bed 327-8
  Here, if there was a peak to climb, [Stan MBG 73-12 P
  On such a peak, the blue guitar-- [Stan MBG 73-16 P
  An innocence approaching toward its peak. [Pagoda 92-6 P
  6. White sky, pink sun, trees on a distant peak. [Someone 86-9 A
PEAKED. A pearly poetess, peaked for rhapsody. [C 44-32
  A tatter of shadows peaked to white, [Postcard 159-20
  In his chair, the most tranquil thought grew peaked [Quiet 523-9
  And the sun and the sun-reek piled and peaked above [Greenest
    59-3 P
PEAKS. And peaks outsoaring possible adjectives. [Thought 185-10
  Of palmy peaks sighting machine-guns? These, [Greenest 56-2 P
PEANUT. Made earth come right; a peanut parody [Havana 143-9
  For peanut people. [Havana 143-10
PEAR. Why set the pear upon those river-banks [Sunday 69-20
  Aloe of ivory, pear of rusty rind.) [Bird Claws 82-5
  A pear should come to the table popped with juice, [Nigger 155-3
PEARL. See mother-of-pearl.
PEARLED. On dung." Come now, pearled and pasted, bloomy-leafed,
    [Ghosts 119-17
  And the icon is the man. The pearled chaplet of spring, [Rock
    526-20
PEARLS. With Sunday pearls, her widow's gayety. [NSF 402-7
PEARLY. A pearly poetess, peaked for rhapsody. [C 44-32
  That is the sensual, pearly spouse, the life [Sleight 222-18
  Is more or less. The pearly women that drop [Study II 464-5
  Her pearly ears, her jeweler's ears [Grotesque 74-3 P
PEARS. Of snails, musician of pears, principium [C 27-9
  She causes boys to pile new plums and pears [Sunday 69-10
  And the table that holds a platter of pears, [Grapes 110-13
  Grandmother and her basketful of pears [Havana 143-23
  The melons, the vermilion pears [Reader 147-8
  "Study of Two Pears" [196-title
  The pears are not viols, [Pears 196-2
  The shadows of the pears [Pears 197-3
  The pears are not seen [Pears 197-5
  Of every day, the wrapper on the can of pears, [Dump 201-17

Of the pears and of the cheese [Anything B 211-19
Than wettest cinnamon. It was cribled pears [Poem Morn 219-10
Then the sides of peaches, of dusky pears. [Vase 246-24
Pears on pointed trees, [Bowl 7-5 P
PEASANT. That press, strong peasants in a peasant world, [Armor
   530-5
PEASANTS. That press, strong peasants in a peasant world, [Armor
   530-5
PEBBLE-CHEWER. Some pebble-chewer practiced in Tyrian speech,
   [Duck 63-17 P
PECKING. Pecking at more lascivious rinds than ours, [Nigger
   152-16
PECKS. Rejected years. A big bird pecks at him [EM 318-8
PECULIAR. And peculiar and appropriate glory, [Hero 277-26
   On peculiar horns, themselves eked out [Creat 311-14
   Peculiar to the queen, this queen or that, [Descrip 340-1
   Is the poem both peculiar and general? [NSF 396-20
   He tries by a peculiar speech to speak [NSF 397-6
   The peculiar potency of the general, [NSF 397-7
   Your beliefs and disbeliefs, your whole peculiar plot; [Old Man
   501-4
   Should give you more than their peculiar chords [Rome 510-19
PECULIARITY. "World without Peculiarity" [453-title
PEDAGOGUE. Of things, this nincompated pedagogue, [C 27-11
PEDAGOGUES. We are the mimics. Clouds are pedagogues [NSF 384-1
PEDANTRY. Without physical pedantry [Analysis 348-15
PEDANTS. Aquiline pedants treat the cart, [Prejudice 368-15
   What aquiline pedants take [Prejudice 368-21
   And, therefore, aquiline pedants find [Prejudice 369-4
PEDDLER. He sets this peddler's pie and cries in summer, [Oboe
   251-3
PEDESTAL. On the pedestal, an ambitious page dog-eared [What We
   460-1
   Blue-bold on its pedestal--that seems to say, [Role 93-13 P
PEDESTALS. Complete in bronze on enormous pedestals. [Duck 64-4 P
PEDIMENT. "The Pediment of Appearance" [361-title
   The pediment of appearance. [Pediment 361-9
   The months of understanding. The pediment [Pediment 362-2
   Appointed for them and that the pediment [Burnshaw 52-4 P
PEELS. These insolent, linear peels [Bananas 53-21
   Red mango peels and I play my guitar. [Stan MBG 72-4 P
PEER. At the time of nougats, the peer yellow [Forces 228-17
   The pair yellow, the peer. [Forces 228-20
   Because we suffer, our oldest parent, peer [EM 315-17
   Are rubbings of a glass in which we peer. [NSF 398-4
   The father, the ancestor, the bearded peer, [Aug 494-22
PEERING. A skinny sailor peering in the sea-glass. [C 28-13
PEERS. In which no one peers, in which the will makes no [EM 323-20
PEEVISH. Solace itself in peevish birds? Is it peace, [Dump 203-4
PEIGNOIR. Complacencies of the peignoir, and late [Sunday 66-16
PEJORATIVE. It is the word pejorative that hurts. [Sailing 120-1
PEKIN. Since the day we left Pekin. [Three 128-9 P
PEKING. Wrong as a divagation to Peking, [C 34-31
PELLUCID. Pellucid love; and for that image, like [Spaniard 34-5 P
PELT. And the ear is glass, in which the noises pelt, [Extracts
   252-3
PEMAQUID. Now, the timothy at Pemaquid [Vari 234-6
PENDENT. A great town hanging pendent in a shade, [NH 468-16
PENDENTIVES. Its crystalline pendentives on the sea [Sea Surf 100-7
PENELOPE. A form of fire approaches the cretonnes of Penelope,
   [World 520-15
PENETRATE. Perhaps, if winter once could penetrate [Pharynx 96-10
   Or may, penetrate, not may, [Crude 305-3
PENETRATES. Of earth penetrates more deeply than any word. [Yellow
   237-3
PENETRATING. Against the sight, the penetrating, [Hero 278-28
PENITENT. As to one, and, as to one, most penitent, [Rome 509-21
PENNSYLVANIA. I live in Pennsylvania. [Our Stars 455-5
PENNY. There's a weltanschauung of the penny pad. [NE Verses 104-10
   A penny sun in a tinsel sky, unrhymed, [Duck 61-7 P
PENSEE. De pensée . . . [Archi 16-15 P
PENSIONERS. O pensioners, O demagogues and pay-men! [Men Fall
   188-16
PENSIVE. Sealed pensive purple under its concern. [C 40-20
   On the sidewalk so that the pensive man may see. [Connois 216-12
   The pensive man . . . He sees that eagle float [Connois 216-13
   Item: The green fish pensive in green reeds [Montra 263-20
   The pensive giant prone in violet space [NSF 387-2
   A pensive nature, a mechanical [Look 517-18
PENSIVELY. And human nature, pensively seated [Region 115-14 P
PENT. The fourth, pent now, a digit curious. [C 45-1
   I am too dumbly in my being pent. [Pharynx 96-4
PENUMBRA. They are not splashings in a penumbra. They stand.
   [Bouquet 452-16
   Or in the penumbra of summer night-- [Aug 490-17
PENURY. Poor penury. There will be voluble hymns [Soldat 14-14 P
PEOPLE. Among the people burning in me still, [W Burgher 61-11
   People are not going [Ten O'C 66-10
   And the people are sad. [Gubbinal 85-5
   And the people are sad. [Gubbinal 85-13

To expunge all people and be a pupil [Sailing 121-3
When all people are shaken [Fading 139-2
When people awaken [Fading 139-4
That the people die? [Fading 139-10
For peanut people. [Havana 143-10
At least the number of people may thus be fixed. [Nigger 157-10
To make him return to people, to find among them [Nigger 158-7
A million people on one string? [MBG 166-15
Pillar of a putrid people, [Country 207-5
The people grow out of the weather; [Jersey 210-6
The gods grow out of the people. [Jersey 210-7
The steeples are empty and so are the people, [Jersey 210-16
And where is it, you, people, [Bagatelles 213-9
Faces to people night's brilliancy, [Dezem 218-14
As if yesterday's people continued to watch [Cuisine 228-5
In an emotion as of two people, as of two [Of Mod 240-12
As if the people in the air [Adequacy 243-10
The people that turned off and came [Adequacy 243-13
Of people sensible to pain, [Adequacy 244-2
Not the people in the air that hear [Adequacy 244-15
Two people, three horses, an ox [Les Plus 245-1
To be happy because people were thinking to be. [Extracts 257-5
Of people, round the auto-works: [News 264-12
Birds and people of this too voluminous [Hero 278-1
Curling round the steeple and the people, [Hero 278-8
There were other soldiers, other people, [Dutch 291-22
The people sat in the theatre, in the ruin, [Repet 306-10
A memorandum of the people sprung [Repet 309-4
Of people, as big bell-billows from its bell [EM 322-13
Of poor, dishonest people, for whom the steeple, [EM 322-16
Besides the people, his knowledge of them. In [EM 323-8
In a world of ideas, who would have all the people [EM 325-13
After death, the non-physical people, in paradise, [EM 325-21
"Wild Ducks, People and Distances" [328-title
Alive, on that people are alive, on that [Wild 328-12
People might share but were never an element, [Wild 328-18
Who was what people had been and still were, [Pure 331-5
He can hear them, like people on the walls, [Sketch 336-4
Of a vast people old in meditation . . . [New Set 353-4
People fall out of windows, trees tumble down, [Chaos 357-13
Without a word to the people, unless [Woman Song 360-16
And something more. And the people in costumes, [Belly 367-9
Of ordinary people, places, things, [Extraord 369-14
"A Lot of People Bathing in a Stream" [371-title
And people, without souvenir. The day [Cred 375-7
An unhappy people in a happy world-- [AA 420-4
An unhappy people in an unhappy world-- [AA 420-6
A happy people in an unhappy world-- [AA 420-8
A happy people in a happy world-- [AA 420-11
An unhappy people in a happy world. [AA 420-14
The people, those by which it lives and dies. [Owl 436-9
What interests me most is the people [Lytton 38-8 P
Of very haphazard people and things, [Agenda 42-8 P
For sale in Vienna and Zurich to people in Maine, [Greenest
   53-9 P
If these were theoretical people, like [Duck 65-6 P
A meaning without a meaning. These people have [Duck 65-16 P
As a church is a bell and people are an eye, [Sombre 67-19 P
On the city, on which it leans, the people there, [Sombre 68-21 P
And the people suddenly evil, waked, accused, [Sombre 69-2 P
But squint and squeak, where no people are: [Stan MBG 73-15 P
True, things are people as they are. [Stan MBG 73-18 P
People that live in the biggest houses [Grotesque 74-17 P
An immense drum rolls through a clamor of people. [Stan Hero
   83-11 P
To form that weather's appropriate people, [Art Pop 112-18 P
So, too, of the races of appropriate people [Art Pop 113-4 P
No thoughts of people now dead, [Clear Day 113-8 P
PEOPLED. And he that created the garden and peopled it. [Thought
   185-22
The peopled and the unpeopled. In both, he is [EM 323-6
Alone. But in the peopled world, there is, [EM 323-7
I peopled the dark park with gowns [Stan MMO 19-1 P
PERCEIVE. And in perceiving this I best perceive myself [Re-state
   146-3
To perceive men without reference to their form. [Choc 296-11
Hard to perceive and harder still to touch. [Choc 301-18
Of the instant to perceive, after the shock, [Liadoff 347-15
The masks of music. We perceive each mask [Sombre 67-22 P
PERCEIVED. For sleepers halfway waking. He perceived [C 31-16
Perceived in a final atmosphere; [MBG 168-2
Perceived by feeling instead of sense, [Nightgown 214-12
As secondary (parts not quite perceived [Man Car 350-18
The self of summer perfectly perceived, [Beginning 427-17
Is of a nature that must be perceived [Papini 447-4
The intricacies of appearance, when perceived. [Papini 447-17
Perceived: the white seen smoothly argentine [Bouquet 449-14
The infinite of the actual perceived, [Bouquet 451-19
It is of the essence not yet well perceived. [NH 475-21
May be perceived in windy quakes [Room Gard 41-5 P

Not now to be perceived yet order's own. [Burnshaw 49-2 P
The universal machine. There he perceived [Woman Had 82-8 P
See half-perceived.
PERCEIVES. And although my mind perceives the force behind the
    moment, [Fish-Scale 161-3
PERCEIVING. And in perceiving this I best perceive myself [Re-state
    146-3
Gold-shined by sun, perceiving as I saw [Phenom 287-13
Begin, ephebe, by perceiving the idea [NSF 380-12
PERCEIVES. Things not yet true which he perceives through truth,
    [NH 478-16
Or thinks he does, as he perceives the present, [NH 478-17
PERCEPTIBLE. And the irregular turquoise, part, the perceptible
    blue [Landsc 242-23
PERCEPTION. Of degrees of perception in the scholar's dark. [NSF
    395-15
Like a spectral cut in its perception, a tilt [What We 460-3
Things dark on the horizons of perception, [Rome 508-12
Perception as an act of intelligence [Lytton 39-6 P
And perception as an act of grace [Lytton 39-7 P
I am uncertain whether the perception [Lytton 39-11 P
To an untried perception applied [Lytton 39-14 P
A perception of cold breath, more revealing than [Bus 116-7 P
A perception of sleep, more powerful [Bus 116-8 P
PERCEPTIONS. Creates, in the blissfuller perceptions, [Hero 280-3
Of letters, prophecies, perceptions, clods [Orb 443-20
In the pallid perceptions of its distances. [NH 469-10
Ragged in unkempt perceptions, that stands [Theatre 91-8 P
PERDU. Yet there is no spring in Florida, neither in boskage
    perdu, nor on the nunnery beaches. [Indian 112-7
The seal is as relaxed as dirt, perdu. [Golden 460-18
PERE. The père Benjamin, the mère Blandenah [Grotesque 77-11 P
PERE GUZZ. Père Guzz, in heaven thumb your lyre [An Gaiety 33-5 P
PERENNIAL. That of itself stood still, perennial, [Owl 432-24
Perennial doctrine and most florid truth; [Duck 63-10 P
PERFECT. Hang always heavy in that perfect sky, [Sunday 69-15
His will, yet never ceased, perfect cock, [Bird Claws 82-17
A perfect fruit in perfect atmosphere. [NE Verses 106-9
Conceiving from its perfect plenitude, [Havana 143-12
PERFECTED. Of ocean, perfected in indolence, [Sea Surf 102-4
Brighter, perfected and distant away, [Ulysses 101-24 P
PERFECTING. And myself am precious for your perfecting. [NSF 396-9
Noble within perfecting solitude, [Greenest 54-4 P
PERFECTION. Gives motion to perfection more serene [Fictive 87-19
And that would be perfection, if each began [Nigger 156-20
Brings the day to perfection and then fails. He dwells [EM 318-2
The summer night is like a perfection of thought. [House Q 358-15
The access of perfection to the page. [House Q 358-18
At which a kind of Swiss perfection comes [NSF 386-12
In this perfection, occasionally speaks [NH 477-4
Or this, whose jingling glorias, importunate of perfection,
    [Inelegance 26-3 P
By gestures of a mortal perfection. [Stan Hero 84-22 P
But a perfection emerging from a new known, [Bus 116-11 P
PERFECTIONS. Avoid our stale perfections, seeking out [Dutch 293-1
Still promises perfections cast away. [EM 318-25
The pure perfections of parental space, [Owl 436-3
Time's given perfections made to seem like less [Armor 530-8
PERFECTIVE. Perfective wings. [Analysis 349-9
PERFECTLY. But muted, mused, and perfectly revolved [C 45-24
But spoke for you perfectly in my thoughts, [Two Figures 86-5
In that one ear it might strike perfectly: [Think 357-2
The self of summer perfectly perceived, [Beginning 427-17
PERFORMED. Performed in verd apparel, and the peach, [C 39-2
PERFUME. An erotic perfume, half of the body, half [NSF 390-7
PERFUMES. Bear other perfumes. On your pale head wear [Fictive
    88-15
PERHAPS. Perhaps the Arctic moonlight really gave [C 34-25
A clown, perhaps, but an aspiring clown. [C 39-24
Dwelt in the land. Perhaps if discontent [C 40-5
Perhaps, if winter once could penetrate [Pharynx 96-10
Perhaps our wretched state would soon come right. [Surprises
    98-9
Perhaps it's the lunch that we had [Sailing 120-6
From these it takes. Perhaps it gives, [MBG 177-5
Is too difficult to tell from despair. Perhaps, [EM 325-20
Or perhaps his guitar is a beast or perhaps they are [Jouga 337-4
Perhaps these forms are seeking to escape [Two V 355-13
A thinker of the first idea. Perhaps [NSF 386-2
Perhaps there are times of inherent excellence, [NSF 386-9
Perhaps there are moments of awakening, [NSF 386-17
At it spinning its eccentric measure. Perhaps, [NSF 406-4
Perhaps, these colors, seen in insight, assume [Bouquet 451-22
Perhaps instead of failing it rejects [NH 477-13
In the parent's hand, perhaps parental love? [Aug 491-25
Except his own--perhaps, his own [Two Illus 514-2
Perhaps, absurd perhaps, but at least a purpose, [Moonlight 532-5
Perhaps at so much mastery, the bliss [Spaniard 35-2 P
Perhaps, without their passions, they will be [Lytton 38-12 P
Perhaps if the orchestras stood on their heads [Agenda 42-4 P

For the million, perhaps, two ducks instead of one; [Duck 65-2 P
And is. Perhaps I had been moved [Desire 85-11 P
The solid shape, Aeneas seen, perhaps, [Recit 87-22 P
Determined thereto, perhaps by his father's ghost, [Role 93-4 P
And shines, perhaps, for the beauty of shining. [Three 131-11 P
PERIHELION. Experience in perihelion [Aug 490-16
PERILOUS. Under the birds, among the perilous owls, [NH 474-17
PERIOD. The chapel rises, his own, his period, [Armor 529-21
The solid was an age, a period [Sombre 68-6 P
PERISH. Of men that perish and of summer morn. [Sunday 70-11
PERISHED. In the grand decadence of the perished swans. [Havana
    145-9
PERISHING. Unchanging, yet so like our perishing earth, [Sunday
    69-16
He wanted to make them, keep them from perishing, [Local 112-6 P
PERISTYLE. The opposing law and make a peristyle, [High-Toned 59-7
And from the peristyle project a masque [High-Toned 59-8
PERIWINKLES. To dream of baboons and periwinkles. [Ten O'C 66-11
PERKIOMEN. The wood-doves are singing along the Perkiomen. [Think
    356-7
PERLES. Soupe Aux Perles [NE Verses 104-title 3
    Soupe Sans Perles [NE Verses 104-title 4
PERMANENCE. Joy of such permanence, right ignorance [Cred 373-12
Of a suspension, a permanence, so rigid [NSF 391-17
In a permanence composed of impermanence, [NH 472-14
PERMANENT. In a permanent realization, without any wild ducks [Cata
    425-7
Were false. The hidalgo was permanent, abstract, [NH 484-2
In its permanent cold, an illusion so desired [Rock 526-3
PERMIT. His passion's permit, hang of coat, degree [C 39-18
Permit that if as ghost I come [W Burgher 61-10
Beyond invention. Within what we permit, [EM 317-6
These are within what we permit, in-bar [EM 317-22
Permit me, gentlemen, [Soldat 13-1 P
PERMITS. As far as nothingness permits . . . Hear him. [Questions
    463-1
PERMITTED. The bread and wine of the mind, permitted [Hero 275-27
PERMITTING. Permitting nothing to the evening's edge. [Role 93-5 P
PER-NOBLE. As if designed by X, the per-noble master. [Extracts
    254-20
PERPENDING. The day in its color not perpending time, [Pure 332-16
PERPETUAL. Be a place of perpetual undulation. [Solitaires 60-2
Which is to be a place of perpetual undulation. [Solitaires 60-13
In an autumn that will be perpetual. [Nigger 152-4
In perpetual revolution, round and round . . . [Descrip 342-20
Not of perpetual time. [Prejudice 369-3
Lofty like him, like him perpetual. [Cred 374-23
In the perpetual reference, object [NH 466-13
Of the perpetual meditation, point [NH 466-14
Silent and turquoised and perpetual, [Burnshaw 50-15 P
Are like the perpetual verses in a poet's mind. [Greenest 59-27 P
PERPLEXED. Gave suavity to the perplexed machine [Sea Surf 99-3
Perplexed by its darker iridescences. [Beginning 427-14
PERQUISITES. The perquisites of sanctity, enjoys [NH 474-12
PERSEPHONE. Not as the fragrance of Persephone, [Aug 491-10
PERSIST. Yet you persist with anecdotal bliss [Monocle 13-21
Persist as facts. This is an escape [Sol Oaks 111-6 P
PERSISTING. Persisting bleakly in an icy haze, [Pharynx 96-12
PERSISTS. By an afflatus that persists. [Negation 98-2
PERSON. The person has a mould. But not [MBG 174-5
The hero is not a person. The marbles [Hero 276-19
If the hero is not a person, the emblem [Hero 277-5
To stand taller than a person stands, has [Hero 277-7
And origin, an inhuman person, [Gigan 289-19
But not the person, of their power, thought, [Choc 299-15
Description of a Platonic Person [Pure 330-title 2
A large-sculptured, platonic person, free from time, [Pure 330-8
This platonic person discovered a soul in space [Pure 331-13
That lives in space. It is a person at night, [Pieces 352-7
One person should come by chance, [Woman Song 360-17
A person he knows, with whom he might [Woman Song 361-2
There entered a cadaverous person, [Attempt 370-8
My dame, sing for this person accurate songs. [NSF 388-9
Her only place and person, a self of her [Orb 441-24
And prodigious person, patron of origins, [Aug 443-14
Of the impersonal person, the wanderer, [Aug 494-21
Each person completely touches us [Leben 505-7
The mode of the person becomes the mode of the world, [Conversat
    108-11 P
For that person, and, sometimes, for the world itself. [Conversat
    108-12 P
PERSONAE. In couch, four more personae, intimate [C 45-5
The personae of summer play the characters [Cred 377-21
See pre-personae.
PERSONAGE. He does not become a three-days personage, [Soldier 97-4
Is that of which you were the personage. [Phenom 287-18
As that of a personage in a multitude: [Cred 377-4
An immaculate personage in nothingness, [Owl 434-11
Of that century and of its aspect, a personage, [NH 479-5
In the much-horned night, as its chief personage. [Souls 94-17 P

PERSONAL. Should he lay by the personal and make [C 41-23
 Fat! Fat! Fat! Fat! I am the personal. [Bantams 75-18
 Extreme, fortuitous, personal, in which [NSF 386-18
PERSONALIA. Poured forth the fine fins, the gawky beaks, the
 personalia, [Somnam 304-17
PERSONALITY. Regard the invalid personality [Cats 368-1
PERSONALS. The powdered personals against the giants' rage, [Repet
 309-17
PERSONS. The cadaverous persons were dispelled. [Attempt 370-19
 Or, the persons act one merely by being here. [AA 416-3
 And the shapes that it took in feeling, the persons that [NH
 479-21
PERSPECTIVE. Two parallels become one, a perspective, of which
 [Rome 508-9
 In a perspective that begins again [Rock 528-12
 The statue in a crow's perspective of trees [Sombre 70-19 P
 The statue stands in true perspective. Crows [Sombre 71-2 P
 The perspective squirming as it tries to take [Bship 80-4 P
PERSUADE. It has to persuade that war is part of itself, [Bottle
 239-6
PERVASIVE. They lived, in which they lacked a pervasive being,
 [Somnam 304-15
PERVERSE. Illusive, faint, more mist than moon, perverse, [C 34-30
 Sleep deep, good eel, in your perverse marine. [Two V 354-18
PETALS. Who, seeing silver petals of white blooms [Sea Surf 100-17
 The shrouding shadows, made the petals black [Sea Surf 100-23
 And white roses shaded emerald on petals [Attempt 370-6
 In smoke. The blue petals became [Attempt 370-16
 A vibrancy of petals, fallen, that still cling [Bouquet 450-10
 Of petals that will never be realized, [NH 478-15
 The petals flying through the air. [Grotesque 75-17 P
PETER. Peter the voyant, who says "Mother, what is that"-- [Ques-
 tions 462-10
 "Peter Parasol" [20-title P
PETER QUINCE. "Peter Quince at the Clavier" [89-title
PETTIFOGGING. And pettifogging buds, [Bananas 54-6
PETTY. Yet with a petty misery [MBG 170-17
 At heart, a petty misery, [MBG 170-18
 Each drop a petty tricolor. For this, [Hartford 226-10
 Green in the body, out of a petty phrase, [Beard 247-21
 Sees the petty gildings on February . . . [Hero 280-11
 "Burghers of Petty Death" [362-title
 His petty syllabi, the sounds that stick, [NSF 407-19
 And yet of summer, the petty tones [Bouquet 451-16
 Our petty portion in the sacrifice. [Soldat 14-8 P
 Their petty dirges of fallen forest-men, [Greenest 55-20 P
PEWTER. A fruit for pewter, thorned and palmed and blue, [Poem
 Morn 219-6
 Syllables, pewter on ebony, yet still [Sombre 70-7 P
PFTT. Pftt. . . . In the way you speak [Add 198-15
PFUI. She whispered, "Pfui!" [Anything B 211-4
PHANTASMA. He was facing phantasma when the bell rang. [Dinner
 109-24 P
 In the green, outside the door of phantasma. [Dinner 110-6 P
PHANTASY. With him for whom no phantasy moves, [Weep Woman 25-11
 Twinning our phantasy and our device, [Anatomy 108-11
 Arranged for phantasy to form an edge [Old Woman 43-17 P
PHANTOM. Is no gaunt fugitive phantom. [Homunculus 26-22
 Wriggling far down the phantom air, [Cuban 65-2
 Like a phantom, in an uncreated night. [Landsc 242-4
 Become the soft-footed phantom, the irrational [NSF 406-18
PHANTOMEREI. Began, the return to phantomerei, if not [What We
 459-8
PHANTOMESQUE. As against each other, the dead, the phantomesque.
 [Duck 65-5 P
PHANTOMS. Phantoms, what have you left? What underground? [EM 320-2
 To be? You go, poor phantoms, without place [EM 320-4
 When the phantoms are gone and the shaken realist [EM 320-7
 Rose up like phantoms from chronologies. [NSF 389-15
 To phantoms. Till then, it had been the other way: [What We
 459-9
PHARYNX. "The Man Whose Pharynx Was Bad" [96-title
PHASE. Without blue, without any turquoise tint or phase, [Landsc
 241-18
 A preliminary, provincial phase, [Bship 77-17 P
 Is a phase. We approach a society [Bship 79-22 P
PHASES. Read, rabbi, the phases of this difference. [AA 420-5
 "Poems from 'Phases'" [3-title P
PHEASANT. The hunter shouts as the pheasant falls. [Nigger 154-9
 How long and late the pheasant sleeps . . . [MBG 182-9
 The pheasant in a field was pheasant, field, [Sombre 68-3 P
PHENOMENA. "Certain Phenomena of Sound" [286-title
 And, with him, many blue phenomena. [EM 319-22
PHENOMENON. And if the phenomenon, magnified, is [Hero 277-19
PHILADELPHIA. "Arcades of Philadelphia the Past" [225-title
 Philadelphia that the spiders ate. [Arcades 225-3
PHILANDERING. Philandering? . . . The genius of misfortune [EM
 316-23
PHILOSOPHER. Philosopher, beginning with green brag, [C 46-1
 Is it a philosopher's honeymoon, one finds [Dump 203-5

This is their captain and philosopher, [Choc 301-16
They treat the philosopher's hat, [Prejudice 368-17
The philosopher's hat to be part of the mind, [Prejudice 369-5
The monastic man is an artist. The philosopher [NSF 382-1
But the priest desires. The philosopher desires. [NSF 382-3
Less real. For the oldest and coldest philosopher, [AA 418-9
The search for god." It is the philosopher's search [NH 481-6
A philosopher practicing scales on his piano, [NH 488-20
"To an Old Philosopher in Rome" [508-title
This is a thing to twang a philosopher's sleep, [Bship 79-31 P
Ask of the philosopher why he philosophizes, [Role 93-3 P
By a right philosopher: renews [Ulysses 103-3 P
PHILOSOPHERS. That this emerald charms philosophers, [Homunculus
 26-10
 Yet the quotidian saps philosophers [C 42-22
 Funest philosophers and ponderers, [On Manner 55-15
 The philosophers alone will be fat [Nigger 152-2
 Geographers and philosophers, [MBG 179-18
 The philosophers' man alone still walks in dew, [Oboe 250-12
 The impossible possible philosophers' man, [Oboe 250-18
 And the helpless philosophers say still helpful things. [Extracts
 253-28
 Children and old men and philosophers, [Woman Had 82-15 P
 The old men, the philosophers, are haunted by that [Woman Had
 82-23 P
 Philosophers' end . . . What difference would it make, [Theatre
 91-17 P
 Under the bones of time's philosophers? [Ideal 89-9 A
PHILOSOPHIC. In the end, these philosophic assassins pull [Extracts
 256-1
PHILOSOPHIZES. Ask of the philosopher why he philosophizes, [Role
 93-3 P
PHILOSOPHY. Of his aesthetic, his philosophy, [C 37-14
 With much philosophy; [Three 137-12 P
PHLOX. Myrtle, viburnums, daffodils, blue phlox), [Dump 202-13
PHOEBUS. Of Phoebus Apothicaire the first beatitude: [NE Verses
 105-3
 And of Phoebus the Tailor the second saying goes: [NE Verses
 105-5
 Let purple Phoebus lie in umber harvest, [NSF 381-8
 Let Phoebus slumber and die in autumn umber, [NSF 381-9
 Phoebus is dead, ephebe. But Phoebus was [NSF 381-10
PHOO. Said, "Phooey! Phoo!" [Anything B 211-3
PHOOEY. Said, "Phooey! Phoo!" [Anything B 211-3
 Said, "Phooey!" too, [Anything B 211-7
PHOSPHOR. Barque of phosphor [Fabliau 23-4
 "Phosphor Reading by His Own Light" [267-title
 The giant Phosphor of their earliest prayers. [Duck 65-23 P
PHOSPHORED. Or the phosphored sleep in which he walks abroad [EM
 320-16
 Or the majolica dish heaped up with phosphored fruit [EM 320-17
PHOSPHORESCENT. Stamp down the phosphorescent toes, tear off
 [Nigger 155-7
 A youth, a lover with phosphorescent hair, [Uruguay 249-21
PHOTOGRAPH. And yet are fixed as a photograph, [MBG 180-13
 One sole face, like a photograph of fate, [NSF 394-10
 As in a signed photograph on a mantelpiece. [Orb 443-2
PHOTOGRAPHS. To photographs of the late president, Mr. Blank, [NH
 488-15
PHRASE. The thing that makes him envious in phrase. [C 33-7
 Crispin in one laconic phrase laid bare [C 36-26
 Where triumph rang its brassy phrase, or love [Sunday 69-5
 The criers, undulating the deep-oceaned phrase. [Tallap 71-12
 Half-way to bed, when the phrase will be spoken, [Nigger 156-8
 Or, at the least, a phrase, that phrase, [MBG 178-3
 A hawk of life, that latined phrase: [MBG 178-4
 Green in the body, out of a petty phrase, [Beard 247-21
 The invention of a nation in a phrase, [Descrip 345-16
 He might take habit, whether from wave or phrase, [NSF 387-12
 The phrases of a single phrase, ké-ké, [NSF 394-8
 And what she felt fought off the barest phrase. [NSF 402-12
 The sky was blue beyond the vaultiest phrase. [What We 459-12
 The phrase . . . Say of each lion of the spirit [NH 472-24
 The phrase grows weak. The fact takes up the strength [NH 473-4
 Of the phrase. It contrives the self-same evocations [NH 473-5
 I quote the very phrase my masters used. [Soldat 11-9 P
 Symbols of sentiment . . . Take this phrase, [Soldat 16-7 P
 Men of the line, take this new phrase [Soldat 16-8 P
 You know the phrase. [Soldat 16-12 P
 All are evasions like a repeated phrase, [Duck 65-14 P
 In more than phrase? There's the true masculine, [Bship 79-12 P
PHRASES. And their memorials are the phrases [Jasmine 79-2
 No more phrases, Swenson: I was once [Lions 124-10
 It may be that in all her phrases stirred [Key W 129-1
 Phrases! But of fear and of fate. [Nightgown 214-14
 Are prodigies in longer phrases. [Hero 277-13
 Was ancient. He tried to remember the phrases: pain [EM 314-3
 Be near me, come closer, touch my hand, phrases [EM 317-17
 Speaking the phrases that follow the sight [Pediment 361-20
 To drone the green phrases of its juvenal? [NSF 390-15

The phrases of a single phrase, ke-ke [NSF 394-8
There were ghosts that returned to earth to hear his phrases,
   [Large 423-11
Again, "The sibilance of phrases is his [NH 485-10
And Crispine, the blade, reddened by some touch, demanding the
   most from the phrases [Piano 22-6 P
PHYLACTERY. His cabin counted as phylactery, [C 43-23
PHYSICAL. Physical if the eye is quick enough, [Choc 301-6
In a physical world, to feel that one's desire [EM 325-19
Completely physical in a physical world. [EM 325-26
Profundum, physical thunder, dimension in which [Flyer 336-14
The physical world is meaningless tonight [Jouga 337-1
Without physical pedantry [Analysis 348-15
And pierces the physical fix of things. [Red Fern 365-16
The physical pine, the metaphysical pine. [Cred 373-2
Of indolent summer not quite physical [Bouquet 451-15
In the metaphysical streets of the physical town [NH 472-22
As if life and death were ever physical. [NH 478-12
See non-physical.
PIANO. Poet, be seated at the piano. [Mozart 131-14
Be seated at the piano. [Mozart 132-2
As one improvises, on the piano. [Vari 233-19
The piano, that time: the time when the crude [Vase 246-10
The leaves were falling like notes from a piano. [Contra II
   270-12
On a horse, in a plane, at the piano-- [Hero 274-20
At the piano, scales, arpeggios [Hero 274-21
When B. sat down at the piano and made [EM 316-9
At a piano in a cloud sat practicing, [Liadoff 346-15
On a black piano practiced epi-tones. [Liadoff 346-16
Of air . . . But then that cloud, that piano placed [Liadoff
   347-13
Your mansard with a rented piano. You lie [NSF 384-18
A philosopher practicing scales on his piano, [NH 488-20
"Piano Practice at the Academy of the Holy Angels" [21-title P
The poor piano forte [Grotesque 76-17 P
On the piano, and in speech, [July 114-18 P
PIANOFORTE. "Concerto for Airplane and Pianoforte," [Duck 62-29 P
PIANO-POLISHED. Piano-polished, held the tranced machine [Sea Surf
   100-15
PIANOS. And the sound of pianos in his mind. [News 264-18
PICADOR. And picador? Be briny-blooded bull. [Spaniard 34-23 P
PICASSO. Is this picture of Picasso's, this "hoard [MBG 173-1
PICK. And pick the strings of our insipid lutes! [Sunday 69-24
Of pick of ebon, pick of halcyon. [Havana 144-16
And pick the acrid colors out, [MBG 166-6
As I strum the thing, do I pick up [MBG 171-19
To pick up relaxations of the known. [Feo 333-17
Who can pick up the weight of Britain, [Imago 439-1
Am I to pick my way [Soldat 12-17 P
PICKANINES. Blackest of pickanines, [Mud 148-4
PICKED. Picked up its radial aspect in the night, [NH 478-23
Shifted the rocks and picked his way among clouds, [Poem Mt 512-8
PICKET. Rode over the picket rocks, rode down the road, [Uruguay
   250-2
PICKET-LINES. He caught the flags and the picket-lines [News 264-11
PICKING. Children picking up our bones [Postcard 158-14
Picking thin music on the rustiest string, [God 285-13
The golden fingers picking dark-blue air: [NSF 398-15
PICKS. It picks its way on the blue guitar. [MBG 166-14
PICNIC. To picnic in the ruins that we leave. [Dutch 293-3
The ghostly celebrations of the picnic, [Aug 492-14
The picnic of children came running then, [Dinner 109-25 P
PICTS. Granted the Picts impressed us otherwise [Nigger 155-1
PICTURE. Is this picture of Picasso's, this "hoard [MBG 173-1
Of destructions," a picture of ourselves, [MBG 173-2
Granted each picture is a glass, [Prelude 195-1
PIE. He sets this peddler's pie and cries in summer, [Oboe 251-3
What They Call Red Cherry Pie [Grotesque 75-title 4 P
Meyer is a bum. He eats his pie. [Grotesque 75-18 P
He eats red cherry pie and never says-- [Grotesque 75-19 P
He says "That's what I call red cherry pie." [Grotesque 76-4 P
What is it that we share? Red cherry pie [Grotesque 76-7 P
And that's red cherry pie. [Grotesque 76-12 P
PIEBALD. Exchequering from piebald fiscs unkeyed. [C 43-7
Seated before these shining forms, like the duskiest glass,
   reflecting the piebald of roses or what you will. [Piano 21-18 P
PIECE. Piece the world together, boys, but not with your hands.
   [Parochial 192-8
Let wise men piece the world together with wisdom [Grotesque
   75-7 P
See cross-piece.
PIECES. The day to pieces and cry stanza my stone? [Dump 203-10
Flicked into pieces, points of air, [Vase 246-20
"Pieces" [351-title
"Five Grotesque Pieces" [74-title P
PIED. And pied umbrellas. An uncertain green, [Sea Surf 100-14
They pied and chuckled like a flock, [Sat Night 28-10 P
PIER. Pylon and pier fell down. [Public Sq 109-2
PIERCE. Of speech: to pierce the heart's residuum [Extracts 259-15

Its fire fails to pierce the vision that beholds it, [Questions
   462-7
Pierce the interior with pouring shafts, [Archi 18-3 P
Pierce, too, with buttresses of coral air [Archi 18-5 P
PIERCED. And you are pierced by a death. [Weep Woman 25-12
Once, a fear pierced him, [Thirteen 94-15
PIERCES. The song of the great space of your age pierces [God
   285-17
And pierces the physical fix of things. [Red Fern 365-16
Life's nonsense pierces us with strange relation. [NSF 383-9
Which pierces clouds and bends on half the world. [NSF 393-15
Lies on the breast and pierces into the heart, [Novel 458-24
PIERCING. Strike the piercing chord. [Mozart 132-8
Piercing the tide by which it moves, is constantly within us?
   [Inelegance 26-2 P
Piercing the spirit by appearance, [Ulysses 104-6 P
PIGEON. A blue pigeon it is, that circles the blue sky, [Monocle
   17-18
A white pigeon it is, that flutters to the ground, [Monocle 17-20
The leaden pigeon on the entrance gate [Nigger 152-18
PIGEONS. At evening, casual flocks of pigeons make [Sunday 70-26
"Gray Stones and Gray Pigeons" [140-title
It wets the pigeons, [Gray 140-14
A design, a marble soiled by pigeons? [Hero 278-23
As if--The pigeons clatter in the air. [NSF 390-6
PILE. Pile the bananas on planks. [Bananas 54-14
She causes boys to pile new plums and pears [Sunday 69-10
Protruding from the pile of wool, a hand, [Novel 457-10
There buzzards pile their sticks among the bones [Burnshaw 49-7 P
PILED. When piled on salvers its aroma steeped [C 39-5
Under the white clouds piled and piled [Woman Song 360-10
Baked through long days, is piled in mows. It is [Cred 374-8
Generations of the imagination piled [Owl 434-13
And the sun and the sun-reek piled and peaked above [Greenest
   59-3 P
PILGRIMAGE. Who, in the hubbub of his pilgrimage [C 33-21
What was the purpose of his pilgrimage, [C 37-5
PILLAR. The pine, the pillar and the priest, [Thought 186-1
Pillar of a putrid people, [Country 207-5
The pillar of midnight, [Aug 495-8
PILLARED. That burial, pillared up each day as porte [Heaven 56-16
The immensest theatre, the pillared porch, [Rome 510-24
PILLARS. (In a world that was resting on pillars, [Botanist 1 135-2
The pillars are prostrate, the arches are haggard, [Botanist 1
   135-11
Within as pillars of the sun, [Fading 139-16
And of obedient pillars? [Archi 17-5 P
PILLOW. Staring, at midnight, at the pillow that is black [Men Fall
   187-17
At a head upon the pillow in the dark, [Men Fall 188-5
Upon the pillow to repose and speak, [Men Fall 188-10
The form on the pillow humming while one sleeps, [Beard 247-23
And old John Rocket dozes on his pillow. [Phenom 286-11
The captain squalid on his pillow, the great [Choc 300-1
Of the pillow in your hand. You writhe and press [NSF 384-20
Speak to your pillow as if it was yourself. [Rome 509-9
On her pillow? The thought kept beating in her like her heart.
   [World 521-11
PILLOWS. On shining pillows, [Tea 113-1
PIMPERNEL. Poets of pimpernel, unlucky pimps [Stan MMO 19-12 P
PIMPS. Poets of pimpernel, unlucky pimps [Stan MMO 19-12 P
PIN. That hears a pin fall in New Amsterdam [Recit 86-23 P
PINAKOTHEK. Nature as Pinakothek. Whist! Chanticleer. . . . [NE
   Verses 106-10
PINCH. Extremest pinch and, easily, as in [John 437-1
I grieve the pinch of her long-stiffening bones. [Stan MMO 19-19P
PINCHES. That pinches the pity of the pitiful man, [AA 418-13
PINCHING. Doleful heroics, pinching gestures forth [Monocle 17-11
PINCHINGS. The marbles are pinchings of an idea, [Hero 276-13
PINE. In the shadow of a pine tree [Six Sig 73-6
The pine tree moves in the wind. [Six Six 73-13
Land of Pine and Marble [NE Verses 106-title 12
Her South of pine and coral and coraline sea, [Farewell 117-15
Of the pine trees edging the sand, [Pascagoula 127-5
The imagined pine, the imagined jay. [MBG 184-6
The pine, the pillar and the priest, [Thought 186-1
The physical pine, the metaphysical pine. [Cred 373-2
PINEAPPLE. A thing. Thus, the pineapple was a leather fruit, [Poem
   Morn 219-5
And a pineapple on the table. It must be so. [Paisant 335-16
A mountain, a pineapple pungent as Cuban summer. [NSF 393-12
The Bulgar said, "After pineapple with fresh mint [Duck 60-7 P
That poem about the pineapple, the one [As Leave 117-1 P
"Someone Puts a Pineapple Together" [83-title A
When a pineapple on the table was enough, [Someone 85-3 A
Up the pineapple, a table Alp and yet [Someone 87-2 A
At last, is the pineapple on the table or else [Someone 87-9 A
PINE-FIGURES. Pine-figures bringing sleep to sleep. [Vari 235-12
PINE-LANDS. Long-tailed ponies go nosing the pine-lands, [Parochial
   191-1

PINES. The man in Georgia waking among pines [C 38-15
  Begone! An inchling bristles in these pines, [Bantams 76-2
  The nocturnal, the antique, the blue-green pines [Parochial
    191-9
  The pines along the river and the dry men blown [Loaf 199-21
  And pines that are cornets, so it occurs, [Sleight 222-14
  When the harmonious heat of August pines [NSF 399-18
  And the pines above and along and beside the sea. [AA 411-9
  The pines that were fans and fragrances emerge, [NH 487-20
  How he had recomposed the pines, [Poem Mt 512-7
PINE-SPOKESMAN. Should be pine-spokesman. The responsive man,
  [C 38-16
PINE-TREE. The pine-tree sweetens my body [Carolinas 5-4
PINE-TREES. Of the pine-trees crusted with snow; [Snow Man 9-23
  In the swags of pine-trees bordering the lake. [NSF 386-8
  Hangs her quilt under the pine-trees. [Primordia 9-16 P
PINE-WOODS. "Bantams in Pine-Woods" [75-title
PIN-IDLENESS. As a serious strength rejects pin-idleness. [NH
  477-14
PINING. Of crinoline spread, but of a pining sweet, [C 42-29
PINIONED. See full-pinioned.
PINIONS. By tautest pinions lifted through his thought. [Duck
  64-19 P
PINK. Last night, we sat beside a pool of pink, [Monocle 17-14
  Blue, gold, pink, and green. [Pourtraicte 21-6
  Was like a glacial pink upon the air. [C 34-14
  And April hillsides wooded white and pink, [C 37-29
  And pink, the water bright that dogwood bears. [C 37-31
  All din and gobble, blasphemously pink. [C 44-23
  Pink and white carnations. The light [Poems Clim 193-8
  Pink and white carnations--one desires [Poems Clim 193-12
  There the dogwoods, the white ones and the pink ones, [Forces
    228-22
  A pink girl took a white dog walking. [Forces 229-2
  Were violet, yellow, purple, pink. The grass [Horn 230-9
  The weather pink, the wind in motion; and this: [EM 322-24
  How that whole country was a melon, pink [NSF 393-17
  Pink yellows, orange whites, too much as they are [Roses 430-11
  To dab things even nicely pink [Melancholy 32-9 P
  And saw the blossoms, snow-bred pink and white, [Good Bad 33-17 P
  Of Boucher pink, the sheens of Venetian gray. [Greenest 53-14 P
  A white, pink, purple berry tree, [Banjo 114-3 P
  6. White sky, pink sun, trees on a distant peak. [Someone 86-9 A
PINK-CLUSTERED. Force is my lot and not pink-clustered [Hero 273-1
PINKED. The tips of cock-cry pinked out pastily, [NH 470-13
PINKS. Pinks and pinks the ice-hard melanchole. [An Gaiety 32-17 P
PINNACLES. Or else sat spinning on the pinnacles, [Babies 77-5
  Sways slightly and the pinnacles frisson. [Hero 275-3
  The heart in slattern pinnacles, the clouds, [Duck 61-10 P
  See sea-pinnacles.
PINS. Like a heart full of pins. [Soldat 12-24 P
PIOUS. The pity that her pious egress [Virgin 71-7
PIP. A pip of life amid a mort of tails. [Bird Claws 82-3
PIPE. See stove-pipe.
PIPED. Softly she piped among the suns [Song Fixed 519-21
PIPES. From pipes that swarm clerestory walls. The voice [Greenest
  59-13 P
PIPPERA. Pipperoo, pippera, pipperum . . . The rest is rot. [Horn
  230-19
PIPPEROO. Pipperoo, pippera, pipperum . . . The rest is rot. [Horn
  230-19
PIPPERUM. Pipperoo, pippera, pipperum . . . The rest is rot. [Horn
  230-19
PIPPING. Against his pipping sounds a trumpet cried [C 29-21
PIPS. Abysmal instruments make sounds like pips [NSF 384-5
PIQUE-PAIN. Is at the bottom of her as pique-pain [Spaniard 34-22 P
PISTACHE. What pistache one, ingenious and droll, [Sea Surf 102-5
  This fat pistache of Belgian grapes exceeds [Nigger 154-17
PIT. This is the pit of torment that placid end [Dutch 292-24
  It is an arbor against the wind, a pit in the mist, [Discov
    95-12
PITCH. And that which is the pitch of its motion, [Vari 235-8
PITCHED. Pitched into swelling bodies, upward, drift [Burnshaw
  52-20 P
  See high-pitched.
PITCHES. Of patches and of pitches, [July 114-15 P
PITCHY. Blue buds or pitchy blooms. Be content-- [MBG 172-3
PITH. Invented for its pith, not doctrinal [C 45-20
  There is no pith in music [Orangeade 103-1
  That should import a universal pith [Havana 144-5
  Of the pith of mind, cuirassiers against [Greenest 56-5 P
PITIES. Are really much a million pities. [Melancholy 32-14 P
PITIFUL. That pinches the pity of the pitiful man, [AA 418-13
PITILESS. Lighting a pitiless verse or two. [Chateau 161-12
  Pitiless verse? a few words tuned [Chateau 161-15
PITTERING. Long autumn sheens and pittering sounds like sounds
  [Burnshaw 47-24 P
PITTER-PATTER. This pitter-patter of archaic freedom, [Dutch 292-13
PITTING. Its pitting poison, half the night. [Thought 186-24
PITY. Why, without pity on these studious ghosts, [Monocle 14-10

Or pity. [Pourtraicte 22-6
The pity that her pious egress [Virgin 71-7
The difference that heavenly pity brings. [Fictive 88-13
This must be the vent of pity, [Orangeade 103-17
The moon is the mother of pathos and pity. [Lunar 107-1
The moon is the mother of pathos and pity. [Lunar 107-12
If only he would not pity us so much, [EM 315-20
That pinches the pity of the pitiful man, [AA 418-13
Of their own marvel made, of pity made, [Owl 435-24
Of the pity that is the memorial of this room, [Rome 509-12
Without any pity in a somnolent dream. [Old Woman 44-6 P
If more than pity and despair were sure, [Sombre 69-13 P
pity." [Three 129-11 P
Through suffering and pity. [Three 132-10 P
It is a pity it is of women. [Three 134-3 P
See self-pity.
PIVOT. It wants the diamond pivot bright. [Country 207-19
PIZZICATI. Pulse pizzicati of Hosanna. [Peter 90-12
PLACATE. Deep dove, placate you in your hiddenness. [Belly 367-12
  Beneath the spangling greens, fear might placate [Greenest 54-22P
PLACATING. In a starry placating. [Mozart 132-17
  Be tranquil in your wounds. The placating star [Extracts 253-26
PLACE. That is blowing in the same bare place [Snow Man 10-9
  Then place of vexing palankeens, then haunt [C 43-24
  In the place of toucans. [Men 1000 52-2
  Of a place. [Men 1000 52-4
  In its place, [Men 1000 52-8
  Is an invisible element of that place [Men 1000 52-9
  And a stiff and noxious place. [Bananas 54-13
  "The Place of the Solitaires" [60-title
  Let the place of the solitaires--the [Solitaires 60-1
  Be a place of perpetual undulation. [Solitaires 60-2
  In the place of the solitaires, [Solitaires 60-12
  Which is to be a place of perpetual undulation. [Solitaires 60-13
  The disbeliever walked the moonlit place, [Babies 77-1
  In a place in the sky. [Cortege 81-6
  In a most unpropitious place. [Sailing 120-10
  Was merely a place by which she walked to sing. [Key W 129-6
  Must be the place for prodigy, unless [Havana 144-2
  Exceeding music must take the place [MBG 167-11
  Ourselves in poetry must take their place, [MBG 167-13
  Yet nothing changed, except the place [MBG 167-18
  Of things as they are and only the place [MBG 167-19
  Becomes the place of things as they are, [MBG 168-7
  Place honey on the altars and die, [MBG 174-3
  Will rack the thickets. There is no place, [MBG 182 16
  The touch. Fix quiet. Take the place [Prelude 195-19
  In a place so debonair. [Anything B 211-15
  Was a place, strong place, in which to sleep. [Nightgown 214-18
  It was at the time, the place, of nougats. [Forces 228-21
  Not in a later son, a different daughter, another place, [Martial
    237-14
  This world, this place, the street in which I was, [Martial 237-18
  It has to be living, to learn the speech of the place. [Of Mod
    240-1
  It was nowhere else, its place had to be supposed, [Landsc 242-7
  In a place supposed, a thing that he reached [Landsc 242-9
  In a place that he reached, by rejecting what he saw [Landsc
    242-10
  Into place beside her, where she was, [Vase 247-2
  He is the transparence of the place in which [Oboe 251-1
  And dirt. The wind blew in the empty place. [Extracts 255-5
  The winter wind blew in an empty place-- [Extracts 255-6
  No man that heard a wind in an empty place. [Extracts 255-9
  If the place, in spite of its witheredness, was still [Extracts
    255-11
  This single place in which we are and stay, [Extracts 257-10
  Of time and place, becoming certain, [Hero 279-26
  This was the place to which you came last night, [God 285-7
  To be a nature, a place in which itself [Phenom 287-2
  In the shrivellings of your time and place. [Dutch 291-7
  To which they may have gone, but of the place in which [Somnam
    304-14
  Nothing of place. There is no change of place [Repet 308-6
  What place in which to be is not enough [EM 320-3
  To be? You go, poor phantoms, without place [EM 320-4
  Between us and the place in which we stood. [Wild 329-12
  In which the enchanted preludes have their place. [Pure 330-15
  "Description without Place"[339-title
  If seeming is description without place, [Descrip 343-15
  Is description without place. It is a sense [Descrip 343-18
  The future is description without place, [Descrip 344-7
  Of the past is description without place, a cast [Descrip 345-20
  There being no subconscious place, [Analysis 348-8
  Of place: time's haggard mongrels. [Analysis 348-11
  Predestined to this night, this noise and the place [Myrrh 349-17
  So much a part of the place, so little [Woman Song 361-1
  Without. In this place and in this time [Human 363-6
  Of the place, blue and green, both streaked. [Attempt 370-5
  Must take its place, as what is possible [Cred 376-23

Appoints man's place in music, say, today. [NSF 382-2
From this the poem springs: that we live in a place [NSF 383-22
Bore off the residents of its noble Place. [NSF 391-9
And have seen, a place dependent on ourselves. [NSF 401-3
Does it take its place in the north and enfold itself, [AA 417-8
There is never a place. Or if there is no time, [AA 418-5
If it is not a thing of time, nor of place, [AA 418-6
Created the time and place in which we breathed . . . [AA 419-3
Being there is being in a place, [Countryman 429-5
The place of a swarthy presence moving, [Countryman 429-7
Less time than place, less place than thought of place [Owl 433-1
Making this heavy rock a place, [Imago 439-17
Her only place and person, a self of her [Orb 441-24
The place of meta-men and para-things, [Bouquet 448-16
The green bouquet comes from the place of the duck. [Bouquet
    450-1
The hating woman, the meaningless place, [Pecul 454-8
To the lover, and blue, as of a secret place [NH 470-21
What is the radial aspect of this place, [NH 479-10
At the centre, the object of the will, this place, [NH 480-20
Rising out of present time and place, above [Irish 502-1
"The Poem that Took the Place of a Mountain" [512-title
The poem that took the place of a mountain. [Poem Mt 512-2
A place to go to in his own direction, [Poem Mt 512-6
His place, as he sat and as he thought, was not [Quiet 523-1
As they enter the place of their western [Soldat 12-8 P
And still the impassioned place of it remain. [Spaniard 34-10 P
And looking at the place in which she walked, [Old Woman 45-20 P
As a place in which each thing was motionless [Old Woman 45-21 P
And brown, an Italy of the mind, a place [Burnshaw 48-13 P
No place in the sense of colonists, no place [Greenest 58-8 P
His place is large and high, an ether flamed [Greenest 59-31 P
And he shall fix the place where it will stand. [Greenest 60-2 P
Remembrances, a place of a field of lights, [Sombre 67-18 P
But this time at another place. [Memo 89-2 P
Like slits across a space, a place [Dove 98-11 P
That man, to know a place is to be [Ulysses 99-18 P
That place, and it seems to come to that; [Ulysses 99-19 P
And future place, when these are known, [Ulysses 101-10 P
The living man in the present place, [Ulysses 103-13 P
Opened out within a secrecy of place, [Letters 108-4 P
The hermit of the place, [Three 132-21 P
And in what place, what exultant terminal, [Ideal 89-2 A
See: common-place; dwelling-place; marriage-place.
PLACE-BOUND. Place-bound and time-bound in evening rain [Human
    363-1
PLACED. I have placed [Pourtraicte 21-12
    I placed a jar in Tennessee, [Jar 76-5
    Placed, so, beyond the compass of change, [MBG 168-1
    The head of one of the men that are falling, placed [Men Fall
    188-9
    Of air . . . But then that cloud, that piano placed [Liadoff
    347-13
    To mock him. They placed with him in his grave [Good Man 364-10
PLACE DU PUY. The very Place Du Puy, in fact, belonged [NSF 391-24
PLACES. Of their places [Men 1000 51-17
    Places there, a bouquet. Ho-ho . . . The dump is full [Dump
    201-13
    Or ordinary people, places, things, [Extraord 369-14
    Of spring come to their places in the grape leaves [NSF 399-14
    These were not tepid stars of torpid places [Page 421-21
    Through many places, as if it stood still in one, [Cata 424-12
    See common-places.
PLACID. This is the pit of torment that placid end [Dutch 292-24
    As placid air becomes. But it is not [Cred 375-15
    Of the categories. So said, this placid space [Ulti 429-17
PLACIDLY. In the sunshine placidly, colored by ground [C 41-3
PLAIN. Be plain. For application Crispin strove, [C 38-8
    By apparition, plain and common things, [C 46-7
    On the bushy plain. [Peacocks 57-12
    "On the bushy plain, [Peacocks 58-11
    Of the bushy plain, [Peacocks 58-20
    To which we come as into bezeled plain, [Montra 262-3
    The eye's plain version is a thing apart, [NH 465-4
    The plainness of plain things is savagery, [NH 467-16
    By the obese opiates of sleep. Plain men in plain towns [NH
    467-20
    "The Plain Sense of Things" [502-title
    To a plain sense of things. It is as if [Plain 502-10
    The plain sense of it, without reflections, leaves, [Plain 503-3
    Like a plain poet revolving in his mind [Moonlight 531-2
    A change of color in the plain poet's mind, [Moonlight 532-1
    Stood on a plain of marble, high and cold; [Woman Had 82-29 P
PLAINEST. To confront with plainest eye the changes, [Gigan 289-11
PLAINLY. Well, nuncle, this plainly won't do. [Bananas 53-20
    The abstract that he saw, like the locust-leaves, plainly:
    [Contra II 270-15
    In its own seeming, plainly visible, [Descrip 344-18
    Nor sanctify, but plainly to propound. [NSF 389-12
PLAINNESS. The plainness of plain things is savagery, [NH 467-16

As: the last plainness of a man who has fought [NH 467-17
PLAINT. Is there one word of sunshine in this plaint? [Stan MMO
    19-16 P
PLAITED. The child's three ribbons are in her plaited hair. [Extra-
    ord 369-21
PLAN. He hummed to himself at such a plan. [Thought 187-4
    In a world forever without a plan [Grotesque 76-14 P
PLANE. On a given plane is ascertainable [Nigger 157-8
    On a horse, in a plane, at the piano-- [Hero 274-20
    By right of knowing, another plane. [Ulysses 104-30 P
PLANES. The planes that ought to have genius, [Common 221-19
    In the planes that tilt hard revelations on [Someone 87-19 A
PLANET. And hems the planet rose and haws it ripe, [Ulti 429-11
    Friend and dear friend and a planet's encouragement. [World
    521-14
    "The Planet on the Table" [532-title
    Of the planet of which they were part. [Planet 533-3
    There must be a planet that is copper [Mandolin 29-2 P
    Of that third planet to the table and then: [Someone 86-3 A
PLANETARY. Therefore, that in the planetary scene [High-Toned 59-14
    Without the oscillations of planetary pass-pass, [Cata 425-11
    Concourse of planetary originals, [Someone 84-2 A
PLANETS. I saw how the planets gathered [Domination 9-14
    Beyond the planets. Thus, our bawdiness, [High-Toned 59-9
    In which old stars are planets of morning, fresh [Descrip 344-10
    Away. The night-flies acknowledge these planets, [Myrrh 349-16
    By extinguishings, even of planets as may be, [AA 417-12
    Extinguishing our planets, one by one, [AA 417-17
    The mirror of the planets, one by one, [Rock 528-5
    Young weasels racing steep horizons in pursuit of planets . . .
    [Inelegance 26-8 P
    It is as if there were three planets: the sun, [Someone 83-11 A
PLANKS. Pile the bananas on planks. [Bananas 54-14
PLANNED. His cloudy drift and planned a colony. [C 36-27
    Because he built a cabin who once planned [C 41-19
    A thing not planned for imagery or belief, [Look 518-6
PLANT. And the stack of the electric plant, [Common 221-4
    "The Green Plant" [506-title
    Except that a green plant glares, as you look [Plant 506-16
    See egg-plant.
PLANTAGENET. To an order, most Plantagenet, most fixed . . .
    [Connois 216-8
    Among Plantagenet abstractions, [Ulysses 103-15 P
PLANTAIN. Here is the plantain by your door [Watermelon 89-4
PLANTED. His trees were planted, his duenna brought [C 42-2
    That the man who erected this cabin, planted [Frogs 78-7
PLANTER. Long after the planter's death. A few limes remained,
    [NSF 393-3
    With garbled green. These were the planter's turquoise [NSF 393-5
PLANTERDOM. To colonize his polar planterdom [C 40-11
PLANTING. Planting his pristine cores in Florida, [C 38-17
PLASTER. Of bliss beyond the mutes of plaster, [Jasmine 79-8
    The plaster dropping, even dripping, down, [Blue Bldg 217-5
    Abhor the plaster of the western horses, [Hartford 226-12
    What is left has the foreign smell of plaster, [Armor 529-5
    But this gawky plaster will not be here. [Burnshaw 48-3 P
PLASTIC. The metaphysica, the plastic parts of poems [Glass 197-19
PLATE. On disregarded plate. The maidens taste [Sunday 69-11
    On bed-clothes, in an apple on a plate. [Blue Bldg 217-16
    In the mind: the tin plate, the loaf of bread on it, [NH 485-20
PLATED. And plated pairs? [Am Sub 130-20
    And plated up, dense silver shine, in a land [Bouquet 449-15
    See purple-plated.
PLATES. Tractatus, of military things, with plates, [Greenest
    56-14 P
PLATITUDE. If platitude and inspiration are alike [Duck 63-3 P
PLATO. That know the ultimate Plato, [Homunculus 27-4
    Plato, the reddened flower, the erotic bird. [Extracts 253-29
    Or moonlight, silently, as Plato's ghost [Less 327-12
PLATONIC. A large-sculptured, platonic person, free from time,
    [Pure 330-8
    Description of a Platonic Person [Pure 330-title 2
    This platonic person discovered a soul in the world [Pure 331-13
PLATTER. And the table that holds a platter of pears, [Grapes 110-13
    To be followed by a platter of capon! [Winter B 141-14
PLAY. Yet this is meagre play [Paltry 6-1
    I shall not play the flat historic scale. [Monocle 14-4
    Play the present, its hoo-hoo-hoo, [Mozart 131-15
    You do not play things as they are." [MBG 165-4
    And they said then, "But play, you must, [MBG 165-7
    Ah, but to play man number one, [MBG 166-3
    As you play them, on the blue guitar, [MBG 167-20
    And play of the monster and of myself, [MBG 175-12
    I play. But this is what I think. [MBG 178-8
    The moments when we choose to play [MBG 184-5
    And play concertinas all night. [Jersey 210-19
    Should play in the trees when morning comes. [Nightgown 214-16
    Not to the play, but to itself, expressed [Of Mod 240-11
    I am and have a being and play a part. [Phenom 287-21
    In which we heard transparent sounds, did he play [EM 316-11

All sorts of notes? Or did he play only one [EM 316-12
The personae of summer play the characters [Cred 377-21
That there are no lines to speak? There is no play. [AA 416-2
Nor all one's luck at once in a play of strings. [John 437-13
Are the instruments on which to play [Aug 489-5
All of them, darkened by time, moved by they know not what,
 amending the airs they play to fulfill themselves; [Piano
 21-17 P
With each fold sweeping in a sweeping play. [Burnshaw 51-27 P
Mimics that play on instruments discerned [Sombre 67-26 P
The world is young and I play my guitar. [Stan MBG 72-2 P
Red mango peels and I play my guitar. [Stan MBG 72-4 P
And honey from thorns and I play my guitar. [Stan MBG 72-9 P
And I play my guitar. The vines have grown wild. [Stan MBG
 72-12 P
I play them on a glue guitar [Stan MBG 72-15 P
The accident is how I play. [Stan MBG 73-3 P
Can you play of this [Three 133-20 P
PLAYED. Grown denser, part, the eye so touched, so played [Landsc
 242-24
And the brass was played. [Coroner 29-13 P
Then Basilewsky in the band-stand played [Duck 62-28 P
Must be played on the concertina. [Grotesque 76-16 P
PLAYER. Of it, more than the monstrous player of [MBG 175-8
As if a blunted player clutched [MBG 182-21
PLAYERS. These other shadows, not in the mind, players [Montra
 260-13
PLAYING. Dew lies on the instruments of straw that you were play-
 ing, [Fish-Scale 160-17
One keeps on playing year by year, [MBG 177-19
Playing cards. In a village of the indigenes, [Glass 198-3
The negroes were playing football in the park. [Contra II 270-14
Playing a crackled reed, wind-stopped, in bleats. [Sombre 67-2 P
Playing mouth-organs in the night or, now, guitars. [Sick 90-9 P
PLAYS. Now, in its immortality, it plays [Peter 92-11
Of a man that plays a blue guitar. [MBG 166-2
One sits and plays the blue guitar. [MBG 172-22
And as the black Spaniard plays his guitar. [Peaches 224-6
He that remains plays on an instrument [Extracts 256-4
And plays his guitar. Ha-ee-me is a beast. [Jouga 337-3
That a man without passion plays in an aimless way. [Sombre
 71-12 P
PLAZA. The sky above the plaza widening [Old Woman 43-6 P
PLAZAS. The bronze-filled plazas [Archi 18-19 P
PLEA. And jay, still to the night-bird made their plea, [C 30-19
PLEASANT. How pleasant an existence it is [Homunculus 26-9
Of essential unity, is as pleasant as port, [Connois 215-10
As pleasant as the brush-strokes of a bough, [Connois 215-11
For a month. It was pleasant to be sitting there, [EM 313-14
A source of pleasant outbursts on the ear. [Orb 442-24
But soothingly, with pleasant instruments, [NH 468-7
PLEASE. This then is Chatillon or as you please. [AA 415-20
Congenial mannequins, alert to please, [Study II 464-11
It would be done. If, only to please myself, [Bship 78-10 P
PLEASED. Pleased that the irrational is rational, [NSF 406-24
PLEASING. That the more pleasing they are [Three 137-16 P
PLEASURE. Flying and falling straightway for their pleasure,
 [Tallap 72-8
Their pleasure that is all bright-edged and cold; [Tallap 72-9
A pleasure, an indulgence, an infatuation. [Nigger 158-9
The pleasure of his spirit in the [Choc 301-23
It Must Give Pleasure [NSF 398-title 3
So that we look at it with pleasure, look [NSF 406-3
For simple pleasure, he beheld, [Sat Night 27-17 P
The rotting man for pleasure saw, [Sat Night 27-18 P
PLEASURES. All pleasures and all pains, remembering [Sunday 67-24
"The Pleasures of Merely Circulating" [149-title
And the solemn pleasures of magnificent space. [AA 416-14
PLENITUDE. Conceiving from its perfect plenitude, [Havana 143-12
PLENTEOUS. And still angelic and still plenteous, [Orb 443-5
Only the lusty and the plenteous [Archi 18-17 P
PLENTIFULLEST. The thesis of the plentifullest John. [Descrip 345-4
PLENTY. And plenty of window for me. [Jersey 210-15
The plenty of the year and of the world. [Rock 527-15
In this plenty, the poem makes meanings of the rock, [Rock 527-16
PLEURE. In Paris, celui qui chante et pleure, [Thought 186-7
PLINTHS. Keep the laborers shouldering plinths. [Archi 16-17 P
PLOMETS. Plomets, as the Herr Gott [Analysis 349-11
PLOT. "The Plot against the Giant" [6-title
Your beliefs and disbeliefs, your whole peculiar plot; [Old Man
 501-4
PLOUGH. It dances down a furrow, in the early light, back of a
 crazy plough, the green blades following. [Plough-Boy 6-7 P
Be free to sleep there sounder, for the plough [Burnshaw 48-1 P
With his plough, the peacock may abandon pride, [Burnshaw 48-24 P
PLOUGH-BOY. "The Silver Plough-Boy" [6-title P
PLOUGHING. "Ploughing on Sunday" [20-title
I'm ploughing on Sunday, [Ploughing 20-10
Ploughing North America. [Ploughing 20-11
PLOUGHMAN. The ploughman portrays in you [Primordia 9-8 P

Than now. No: nor the ploughman in his bed [Burnshaw 47-32 P
And the dew and the ploughman still will best be one. [Burnshaw
 48-2 P
Who knows? The ploughman may not live alone [Burnshaw 48-23 P
PLOUGHMEN. And change. If ploughmen, peacocks, doves alike [Burn-
 shaw 48-26 P
That the vista retain ploughmen, peacocks, doves, [Burnshaw 50-9P
PLUCK. Plucks on his strings to pluck abysmal glory, [NSF 404-15
PLUCKED. The world, a turnip once so readily plucked, [C 45-12
Plucked from the Carib trees, [Bananas 54-18
The trees were plucked like iron bars [Jumbo 269-1
PLUCKING. Out of such mildew plucking neater mould [Pharynx 96-14
PLUCKS. Plucks on his strings to pluck abysmal glory, [NSF 404-15
PLUM. May, after all, stop short before a plum [C 40-28
The plum survives its poems. It may hang [C 41-2
Or spice the shores with odors of the plum? [Sunday 69-21
PLUMB. He did not quail. A man so used to plumb [Geneva 24-7
PLUME. Of mutable plume, [Analysis 348-19
The attributions, the plume and helmet-ho." [NH 485-15
PLUMES. The rumpling of the plumes [Infanta 7-16
PLUMS. In poems of plums, the strict austerity [C 30-8
You should have had plums tonight, [Bananas 54-4
She causes boys to pile new plums and pears [Sunday 69-10
The plums are blue on the trees. The katy-dids [Memo 89-14 P
PLUNGE. To the cold, go on, high ship, go on, plunge on. [Farewell
 118-20
To the muscles' very tip for the vivid plunge, [Old Woman 43-11 P
PLUNGINGS. The meaningless plungings of water and the wind, [Key W
 129-19
PLURAL. By the incalculably plural. Hence [Descrip 340-9
From that ever-early candor to its late plural [NSF 382-18
And sun and rain a plural, like two lovers [NSF 392-14
They are a plural, a right and left, a pair, [NSF 407-11
PLUS. Are you not le plus pur, you ancient one? [Blue Bldg 217-20
"Les Plus Belles Pages" [244-title
And tallest hero and plus gaudiest vir. [Montra 262-12
PLUSH. Now grapes are plush upon the vines. [Contra I 266-11
POCKET. Lenin took bread from his pocket, scattered it-- [Descrip
 343-6
POD. Dropped out of this amber-ember pod, [MBG 182-6
PODS. These pods are part of the growth of life within life: [Nuns
 92-7 P
POEM. That prose should wear a poem's guise at last. [C 36-23
Of the intense poem [Cortege 81-1
The poem of long celestial death; [Botanist 2 136-6
Without that poem, or without [Botanist 2 136-8
Poetry is the subject of the poem, [MBG 176-15
From this the poem issues and [MBG 176-16
An absence for the poem, which acquires [MBG 177-2
A poem like a missal found [MBG 177-21
"Poem Written at Morning" [219-title
The mind is the great poem of winter, the man, [Bottle 238-17
The poem lashes more fiercely than the wind, [Bottle 239-14
The poem of the mind in the act of finding [Of Mod 239-17
Combing. The poem of the act of the mind. [Of Mod 240-22
Where the wild poem is a substitute [Waldorf 241-1
"Poem with Rhythms" [245-title
Sure that the ultimate poem was the mind, [Extracts 256-22
A poem for Liadoff, the self of selves: [Choc 297-7
The instant of the change that was the poem, [Liadoff 347-5
The poem must resist the intelligence [Man Car 350-13
"Two Versions of the Same Poem" [353-title
The human revery or poem of death? [Men Made 355-16
The poem refreshes life so that we share, [NSF 382-13
The poem, through candor, brings back a power again [NSF 382-23
From this the poem springs: that we live in a place [NSF 383-22
The poem goes from the poet's gibberish to [NSF 396-13
Is there a poem that never reaches words [NSF 396-18
Is the poem both peculiar and general? [NSF 396-20
The purpose of the poem, fills the room. [AA 413-5
Among these the musicians strike the instinctive poem. [AA 415-16
There were those that returned to hear him read from the poem of
 life, [Large 423-14
"The Ultimate Poem Is Abstract" [429-title
The essential poem at the centre of things, [Orb 440-1
We do not prove the existence of the poem. [Orb 440-9
One poem proves another and the whole, [Orb 441-4
With these they celebrate the central poem, [Orb 441-9
As if the central poem became the world, [Orb 441-19
And the world the central poem, each one the mate [Orb 441-20
The essential poem begets the others. The light [Orb 441-26
The central poem is the poem of the whole, [Orb 442-1
The poem of the composition of the whole, [Orb 442-2
Not merely into a whole, but a poem of [Orb 442-6
The poet but the poem, the growth of the mind [Papini 446-8
A larger poem for a larger audience, [NH 465-18
The poem of pure reality, untouched [NH 471-13
The poem is the cry of its occasion, [NH 473-16
The poet speaks the poem as it is, [NH 473-18
This endlessly elaborating poem [NH 486-4

"The Poem that Took the Place of a Mountain" [512-title
The poem that took the place of a mountain. [Poem Mt 512-2
The life of the poem in the mind has not yet begun. [Slug 522-16
The Poem as Icon [Rock 526-title 2
Of the poem, the figuration of blessedness, [Rock 526-19
These leaves are the poem, the icon and the man. [Rock 527-2
In this plenty, the poem makes meanings of the rock, [Rock 527-16
A poem about tradition could easily be [Recit 86-1 P
That poem about the pineapple, the one [As Leave 117-1 P
POEMS. The fops of fancy in their poems leave [Monocle 16-23
In poems of plums, the strict austerity [C 30-8
How many poems he denied himself [C 34-18
To which all poems were incident, unless [C 36-22
The plum survives its poems. It may hang [C 41-2
"The Poems of Our Climate" [193-title
The metaphysica, the plastic parts of poems [Glass 197-19
And so the moon, both come, and the janitor's poems [Dump 201-16
He is and in his poems we find peace. [Oboe 251-2
He hears the earliest poems of the world [Montra 261-19
Makes poems on the syllable fa or [Hero 280-9
His poems are not of the second part of life. [Creat 311-11
We do not say ourselves like that in poems. [Creat 311-18
It is something seen and known in lesser poems. [Orb 440-10
Of blue light and of green, as lesser poems, [Orb 442-4
And the miraculous multiplex of lesser poems, [Orb 442-5
Ariel was glad he had written his poems. [Planet 532-7
And his poems, although makings of his self, [Planet 532-14
POESIE. "Poesie Abrutie" [302-title
POESIS. Poesis, poesis, the literal characters, the vatic lines,
    [Large 424-6
POET. You ten-foot poet among inchlings. Fat! [Bantams 76-1
Stirring no poet in his sleep, and tolls [Pharynx 96-7
Mon Dieu, heat the poet's prayer. [Sailing 120-11
Poet, be seated at the piano. [Mozart 131-14
Above the trees? And why the poet as [Eve Angels 136-14
Is the function of the poet here mere sound, [Havana 144-12
But let the poet on his balcony [Havana 144-30
The poet striding among the cigar stores, [Thought 185-5
Poet, patting more nonsense foamed [Prelude 195-14
Translation of a Russian poet. [Vari 234-9
Poet, as if he thought gladly, being [Hero 277-17
Better without an author, without a poet, [Creat 310-18
Or having a separate author, a different poet, [Creat 311-1
Casual poet, that to add your own disorder to disaster [Bed 326-15
The baroque poet may see him as still a man [Paisant 335-12
To be, as on the youngest poet's page, [Descrip 340-20
A poet's metaphors in which being would [Descrip 341-8
The whole race is a poet that writes down [Men Made 356-5
The hermit in a poet's metaphors, [NSF 381-21
The poem goes from the poet's gibberish to [NSF 396-13
Not apprehended well. Does the poet [NSF 396-23
For that the poet is always in the sun, [NSF 407-6
The soldier is poor without the poet's lines, [NSF 407-18
The lover, the believer and the poet. [Orb 441-6
The poet mumbles and the painter sees, [Orb 443-16
He has an ever-living subject. The poet [Papini 446-3
The poet but the poem, the growth of the mind [Papini 446-8
As victory. The poet does not speak in ruins [Papini 446-10
They become our gradual possession. The poet [Papini 447-18
And final. This is the centre. The poet is [Papini 448-1
The poet speaks the poem as it is, [NH 473-18
And the poet's search for the same exterior made [NH 481-8
Like a plain poet revolving in his mind [Moonlight 531-2
A change of color in the plain poet's mind, [Moonlight 532-1
Are like the perpetual verses in a poet's mind. [Greenest 59-27 P
The passion, indifferent to the poet's hum, [Sombre 71-25 P
This is not poet's ease of mind. [Ulysses 103-28 P
POETESS. A pearly poetess, peaked for rhapsody. [C 44-32
POETIC. He came. The poetic hero without palms [C 35-26
POETRY. Poetry is the supreme fiction, madame. [High-Toned 59-1
Poetry is a finikin thing of air [Nigger 155-17
Do not speak to us of the greatness of poetry, [MBG 167-3
There are no shadows. Poetry [MBG 167-10
Ourselves in poetry must take their place, [MBG 167-13
Poetry is the subject of the poem, [MBG 176-15
"Poetry Is a Destructive Force" [192-title
"Of Modern Poetry" [239-title
If the poetry of X was music, [Creat 310-10
She said poetry and apotheosis are one. [Past Nun 378-13
He wishes that all hard poetry were true. [Papini 447-2
Including the removes toward poetry. [Papini 447-6
Lol-lolling the endlessness of poetry. [Novel 458-1
Displays the theory of poetry, [NH 486-5
As the life of poetry. A more severe, [NH 486-6
Of poetry is the theory of life, [NH 486-9
High poetry and low: [Aug 490-15
Of poetry [Irish 502-4
Profound poetry of the poor and of the dead, [Rome 509-25
In a freshness of poetry by the sea, [Polo 37-19 P
"The Role of the Idea in Poetry" [93-title P

At the antipodes of poetry, dark winter, [Discov 95-7 P
As in a page of poetry-- [July 115-1 P
To find poetry, [Three 127-2 P
Of the incredible subjects of poetry. [Someone 85-13 A
POETS. Good light for drunkards, poets, widows, [Homunculus 25-15
Poets of pimpernel, unlucky pimps [Stan MMO 19-12 P
A time in which the poets' politics [Burnshaw 48-15 P
Will rule in a poets' world. Yet that will be [Burnshaw 48-16 P
A world impossible for poets, who [Burnshaw 48-17 P
By poets, the Italian lives preserved [Duck 61-19 P
Or poets with holy magic. [Grotesque 75-8 P
Just as it is true of poets, [Three 129-13 P
POIGNANT. Would be endings, more poignant than partings, profounder,
    [Adieu 127-14
POIGNANTLY. Hands without touch yet touching poignantly, [C 43-17
POINT. The diamond point, the sapphire point, [Ord Women 11-22
Keen to the point of starlight, while a frog [Monocle 17-16
Have I stopped and thought of its point before? [Grapes 110-11
Tell me again of the point [Pascagoula 126-19
Of the structure of vaults upon a point of light. [MBG 167-5
To and to and to the point of still, [MBG 181-6
Glittering scales and point [Bagatelles 213-7
With this paper, this dust. That states the point. [Extracts
    252-6
The soldier seeking his point between the two, [Repet 309-9
Pain killing pain on the very point of pain. [EM 314-5
Evading the point of redness, not content [EM 318-21
Come true, a point in the fire of music where [Descrip 341-9
The point of survey, green's green apogee, [Cred 373-17
A point of survey squatting like a throne, [Cred 373-19
The nothingness was a nakedness, a point, [NSF 402-21
The nothingness was a nakedness, a point [NSF 403-9
In alternate stripes converging at a point [Page 422-22
Is not in point--the question is in point. [Ulti 429-14
The tension of the lyre. My point is that [John 437-10
Of the perpetual meditation, point [NH 466-14
The point of vision and desire are the same. [NH 466-22
At the exactest point at which it is itself, [NH 471-16
As it touches the point of reverberation--not grim [NH 475-14
Not quite. It comes to the point and at the point, [NH 477-11
And alike, a point of the sky or of the earth [NH 483-8
As at a point of central arrival, an instant moment, much or
    little, [Prol 516-8
Its strength and measure, that which is near, point A [Rock
    528-11
The starting point of the human and the end, [Rock 528-16
The point of it was the way he heard it, [Dinner 110-5 P
The point of difference from reality [Three 130-12 P
See: clear-point; healing-point.
POINT-BLANK. After that alien, point-blank, green and actual
    Guatemala. [Waldorf 241-9
POINTED. And men of day and never of pointed night, [Eve Angels
    137-14
Upon my top he breathed the pointed dark. [Choc 298-1
Pears on pointed trees, [Bowl 7-5 P
See: crystal-pointed; rain-pointed.
POINTINGS. These are the pointings of our edifice, [Archi 17-17 P
POINTS. Bristles, and points their Appalachian tangs, [Bantams 76-3
Flicked into pieces, points of air, [Vase 246-20
To an immaculate end. We move between these points: [NSF 382-17
Colossal blacks that leaped across the points [Greenest 53-13 P
There are as many points of view [Three 136-14 P
See rose-points.
POISE. Trained to poise the tables of the law, [Lions 124-14
POISED. Coming together in a sense in which we are poised, [NH
    466-11
Or of a town poised at the horizon's dip. [NH 483-9
Disclosed in everything, transcended, poised [Duck 62-21 P
For the syllable, poised for the touch? But that [Duck 62-22 P
The man below beholds the portent poised, [Sombre 69-25 P
Poised, but poised as the mind through which a storm [Sombre
    69-27 P
POISON. Poison grows in this dark. [Weep Woman 25-4
Its pitting poison, half the night. [Thought 186-24
Poison, in what darkness set [Bagatelles 213-6
The poison in the blood will have been purged, [Montra 262-4
I am a poison at the winter's end, [News 265-5
This is his poison: that we should disbelieve [AA 411-19
POISONED. Its poisoned laurels in this poisoned wood, [Pastor
    379-20
POISONOUS. Of this invention; and yet so poisonous [NSF 381-18
POISONS. Among the lascivious poisons, clean of them, [Extracts
    252-16
POLACKS. Except Polacks that pass in their motors [Jersey 210-18
POLAR. And thereby polar, polar-purple, chilled [C 34-4
To colonize his polar planterdom [C 40-11
And gusts of great enkindlings, its polar green, [AA 413-2
POLAR-PURPLE. And thereby polar, polar-purple, chilled [C 34-4
POLE. A-cock at the cross-piece on a pole [MBG 181-21
The solitude, the barrier, the Pole [Thought 186-6

A fusion of night, its blue of the pole of blue [Choc 297-16
Fly low, cock bright, and stop on a bean pole. Let [Cred 377-6
And on your bean pole, it may be, you detect [Cred 377-17
These lights may finally attain a pole [AA 411-14
A forgetfulness of summer at the pole. [Bad Time 427-3
The dot, the pale pole of resemblances [Ideal 88-16 A
See: cloud-pole; ridge-pole.
POLES. Fixing emblazoned zones and fiery poles, [Key W 130-9
One of many, between two poles. So, [Glass 197-10
In the metaphysical, there are these poles. [Glass 197-11
Imaginary poles whose intelligence [NH 479-8
And the two poles continue to maintain it [Art Pop 112-16 P
See flag-poles.
POLICE. He stood at last by God's help and the police; [Anglais
   149-10
POLICED. Policed by the hope of Christmas. Summer night, [Sombre
   68-11 P
POLISH. "Colloquy with a Polish Aunt" [84-title
Out of what they see. They polish their eyes [Arcades 225-11
POLISHED. They polished the embracings of a pair [Repet 306-16
And polished beast, this complex falls apart. [Cred 377-16
See piano-polished.
POLITEST. With the politest helplessness. Ay-mi! [EM 324-22
POLITIC. Politic man ordained [Havana 143-21
POLITICAL. Political tramp with an heraldic air, [Choc 301-3
POLITICIAN. Never the naked politician taught [Dames 206-17
"Sketch of the Ultimate Politician" [title-335
POLITICIANS. It is a state, this spring among the politicians
   [Glass 198-2
Without a society, the politicians [Bship 79-23 P
POLITICS. The politics of emotion must appear [EM 324-29
For humane triumphals. But a politics [Papini 447-13
A time in which the poets' politics [Burnshaw 48-15 P
POLL. Lies quilted to his poll in his despite. [C 41-30
POLLEN. Dabbled with yellow pollen--red as red [Hibiscus 23-1
POLO. "Polo Ponies Practicing" [37-title P
POLODOWSKY. The Cuban, Polodowsky, [Venereal 47-12
POLYMATHIC. Not twisted, stooping, polymathic Z, [NH 469-8
POLYPHONY. Polyphony beyond his baton's thrust. [C 28-21
POMERANIA. Than poodles in Pomerania. This man [Duck 62-2 P
POMP. Will go, like the centre of sea-green pomp, [Paltry 6-6
Calling for pomp. [Soldier 97-6
Out of the clouds, pomp of the air, [Idiom 201-9
Of pomp, in love and good ensample, see [Stan MMO 19-13 P
POMPOSO. Bellissimo, pomposo, [Orangeade 103-3
POMPS. Eliciting the still sustaining pomps [On Manner 55-12
The responsive, still sustaining pomps for you [On Manner 56-5
The race endures. The funeral pomps of the race [Paisant 334-21
Are a multitude of individual pomps [Paisant 334-22
POND. Itself to be imagined. The great pond, [Plain 503-2
The great pond and its waste of the lilies, all this [Plain 503-6
We think as wind skitters on a pond in a field [Look 518-24
PONDERABLE. Ponderable source of each imponderable, [NH 476-11
PONDERED. See long-pondered.
PONDERERS. Funest philosophers and ponderers, [On Manner 55-15
PONDERING. Of ocean, pondering dank stratagem. [Sea Surf 101-10
PONDEROUS. Is full of long motions; as the ponderous [Curtains
   62-2
The ponderous cinnamon, snarls in his mountain [NSF 384-15
For ponderous revolving, without help. [Sombre 69-16 P
PONDS. Suckled on ponds, the spirit craves a watery mountain.
   [NE Verses 105-2
The ponds are not the surfaces it seeks. [Nigger 158-1
In mud under ponds, where the sky used to be reflected. [NH
   487-15
PONIES. Long-tailed ponies go nosing the pine-lands, [Parochial
   191-1
Ponies of Parisians shooting on the hill. [Parochial 191-2
"Polo Ponies Practicing" [37-title P
PONTIFEX. Be glory to this unmerciful pontifex, [Greenest 60-3 P
POODLE. Shaking the water off, like a poodle, [Hartford 226-8
Hi! Whisk it, poodle, flick the spray [Hartford 227-10
POODLES. Than poodles in Pomerania. This man [Duck 62-2 P
POOH. Pooh! [Three 130-7 P
POOL. Last night, we sat beside a pool of pink, [Monocle 17-14
A pool shines [Six Sig 74-1
And in that state, the glass is a pool. [Glass 197-14
Nietzsche in Basel studied the deep pool [Descrip 342-7
His revery was the deepness of the pool, [Descrip 342-11
The very pool, his thoughts the colored forms, [Descrip 342-12
The sun of Nietzsche gildering the pool, [Descrip 342-18
POOLS. Sat tittivating by their mountain pools [Monocle 14-2
I hated the weathery yawl from which the pools [Farewell 118-1
POOR. Poor buffo! Look at the lavender [Lilacs 49-6
The vile antithesis of poor and rich. [NE Verses 104-6
Rich Tweedle-dum, poor Tweedle-dee. [Nigger 154-13
Good air. Poor pale, poor pale guitar . . . [MBG 176-2
The man that is poor at night [Idiom 201-3
This? A man must be very poor [Arcades 225-20
To be? You go, poor phantoms, without place [EM 320-4

Of poor, dishonest people, for whom the steeple, [EM 322-16
Though poor, though raggeder than ruin, have that [Belly 367-10
The soldier is poor without the poet's lines, [NSF 407-12
Poor procurator, why do you ask someone else [Papini 446-1
Profound poetry of the poor and of the dead, [Rome 509-25
Wrapped tightly round us, since we are poor, a warmth, [Final
   524-8
Poor penury. There will be voluble hymns [Soldat 14-14 P
Sip the wild honey of the poor man's life, [Burnshaw 49-10 P
In such an air, poor as one's mule. [Stan MBG 73-11 P
The poor piano forte [Grotesque 76-17 P
A dream too poor, too destitute [Ulysses 104-18 P
The poor lights. [Three 132-4 P
That the lady was poor-- [Three 138-2 P
POOREST. I am the poorest of all. [Idiom 201-7
POORLY. Dressed poorly, arrogant of his streaming forces, [Uruguay
   249-22
As the rider, no chevalere and poorly dressed, [Uruguay 249-28
POORNESS. Of poorness as an earth, to taste [Arcades 225-24
POPPED. A pear should come to the table popped with juice, [Nigger
   155-3
POPULACE. Could beat, yet not alarm the populace. [Havana 143-7
Of the populace of the heart, the reddest lord, [EM 315-18
See over-populace.
POPULATION. This artificial population is like [Art Pop 112-21 P
POPULATIONS. Gigantic embryos of populations, [Choc 300-8
"Artificial Populations" [112-title P
PORCELAIN. And made one think of porcelain chocolate [Sea Surf
   100-13
Was last with its porcelain leer. [Public Sq 109-12
Cold, a cold porcelain, low and round, [Poems Clim 193-15
The sky, half porcelain, preferring that [Cuisine 228-6
Let the Secretary for Porcelain observe [Extracts 253-7
A porcelain, as yet in the bats thereof. [NH 467-15
In a mortal lullaby, like porcelain. [Burnshaw 47-22 P
A tragic lullaby, like porcelain. [Burnshaw 50-31 P
In the glassy sound of your voices, the porcelain cries, [Burn-
   shaw 52-6 P
The porcelain bell-borrowings become [Burnshaw 52-11 P
Your porcelain water bottle. [Three 129-1 P
There is a seclusion of porcelain [Three 130-2 P
Porcelain! [Three 130-4 P
Porcelain, Venetian glass, [Three 131-6 P
As abstract as porcelain. [Three 131-14 P
On chosen porcelain. [Three 131-21 P
Painted on porcelain [Three 132-18 P
He would forget the porcelain [Three 133-8 P
She was as beautiful as a porcelain water bottle. [Three 136-19 P
The porcelain in one hand . . . [Three 138-6 P
Seclusion of porcelain . . . [Three 142-2 P
Painted on this porcelain, [Three 142-10 P
PORCH. Is not the porch of spirits lingering. [Sunday 70-16
Eulalia, I lounged on the hospital porch, [Phenom 287-7
The immensest theatre, the pillared porch, [Rome 510-24
PORCHES. In the porches of Key West, [Venereal 47-19
See cloud-cloister-porches.
PORPOISES. On porpoises, instead of apricots, [C 27-18
And on silentious porpoises, whose snouts [C 27-19
PORT. And tall and of a port in air. [Jar 76-12
Of essential unity, is as pleasant as port, [Connois 215-10
Is like your port which conceals [Demoiselle 23-4 P
PORTAL. The fitful tracing of a portal; [Peter 91-23
PORTALS. Words of the fragrant portals, dimly-starred, [Key W
   130-13
An opening of portals when night ends, [Nigger 153-14
Let us fix portals, east and west, [Archi 17-27 P
PORTE. That burial, pillared up each day as porte [Heaven 56-16
PORTEND. As shapes, though they portend us, are. [Less 328-2
And because what we say of the future must portend, [Descrip
   346-2
The small luxuriations that portend [Someone 87-6 A
PORTENT. Or the portent of a will that was, [Vari 233-3
In a confusion on bed and books, a portent [Rome 509-32
High up in heaven a sprawling portent moves, [Sombre 68-17 P
The man below beholds the portent poised, [Sombre 69-25 P
Like the time of the portent, images like leaves, [Sombre 69-29 P
The portent may itself be memory; [Sombre 70-10 P
And must be, when the portent, changed, takes on [Sombre 70-12 P
High up in heaven the sprawling portent moves. [Sombre 70-18 P
The portent would become man-haggard to [Sombre 70-26 P
And the portent end in night, composed, before [Sombre 71-5 P
PORTENTOUS. Portentous enunciation, syllable [C 43-8
In those portentous accents, syllables, [C 45-25
Has faint, portentous lustres, shades and shapes [Burnshaw 49-26P
PORTENTS. One of the portents of the will that was. [Vari 233-4
Gothic blue, speed home its portents to their ends. [Page 422-20
PORTER. I had as lief be embraced by the porter at the hotel [Two
   Figures 85-14
PORTICO. Or massive portico. A capitol, [AA 416-19
PORTION. Our petty portion in the sacrifice. [Soldat 14-8 P

PORTIONED. Mastered the night and portioned out the sea, [Key W
   130-8
PORTLY. And fears not portly Azcan nor his hoos. [Bantams 76-4
PORTRAIT. The blue of the rug, the portrait of Vidal, [Freed
   205-23
PORTRAITS. These, then are portraits: [Theory 87-1
PORTRAYS. The ploughman portrays in you [Primordia 9-8 P
POSE. Stones pose in the falling night; [Add 198-8
   They pose themselves and their rags. [Add 198-10
   The buildings pose in the sky [Add 198-12
   The sense creates the pose. [Add 199-9
POSED. Posed for his statue [Am Sub 130-22
   It is posed and it is posed. [Add 198-6
   You arrange, the thing is posed, [Add 198-16
   And B are not like statuary, posed [Connois 216-10
   So posed, the captain drafted rules of the world, [Bship 78-20 P
   Is part of the classic imagination, posed [Recit 87-1 P
POSES. In the muscular poses of the museums? [Nigger 153-12
   The poses of speech, of paint, [Add 199-1
POSITION. The position was wrong. [Aug 493-20
POSSESS. Possess in his heart, conceal and nothing known. [NSF
   395-6
   Only the half they can never possess remains, [AA 413-9
   Still-starred. It is the mother they possess, [AA 413-10
   Possess. It is desire, set deep in the eye, [NH 467-10
   In this spent world, we must possess. The gift [Red Kit 30-19 P
POSSESSED. How pale and how possessed a night it is, [Havana 144-26
   The super-man friseured, possessing and possessed. [Montra 262-24
   And the words for them and the colors that they possessed.
      [Holiday 312-13
   The thrice concentred self, having possessed [Cred 376-10
   To be possessed and is. But this cannot [NH 467-9
   He is the possessed of sense not the possessor. [Aug 492-19
   He had said that everything possessed [Two Illus 514-10
POSSESSES. A dumb sense possesses them in a kind of solemnity.
      [Old Man 501-2
   And possesses by sincere insight [Ulysses 103-4 P
POSSESSING. And studious of a self possessing him, [C 33-11
   The super-man friseured, possessing and possessed. [Montra 262-24
POSSESSION. Relentlessly in possession of happiness. [AA 411-18
   They become our gradual possession. The poet [Papini 447-18
   Unlike love in possession of that which was [NH 467-8
POSSESSOR. He is the possessed of sense not the possessor. [Aug
   492-19
POSSIBLE. Discovery still possible to make, [C 36-21
   Cf dirt . . . It is not possible for the moon [Ghosts 119-9
   And peaks outsoaring possible adjectives. [Thought 185-10
   The impossible possible philosophers' man, [Oboe 250-18
   That buffets the shapes of its possible halcyon [EM 321-7
   Nothing in which it is not possible [Paisant 335-8
   It is possible that to seem--it is to be, [Descrip 339-1
   Of the possible: seemings that are to be, [Descrip 342-5
   Seemings that it is possible may be. [Descrip 342-6
   Book of a concept only possible [Descrip 345-2
   The difficult images of possible shapes, [Two V 354-9
   He said a good life would be possible. [Good Man 364-6
   Of change still possible. Exile desire [Cred 373-13
   Must take its place, as what is possible [Cred 376-23
   If seen rightly and yet a possible red. [NSF 393-18
   It is possible, possible, possible. It must [NSF 404-4
   Be possible. It must be that in time [NSF 404-5
   The possible nest in the invisible tree, [John 437-17
   It may be, may be. It is possible. [John 437-24
   Searches a possible for its possibleness. [NH 481-21
   Fire is the symbol: the celestial possible. [Rome 509-8
   "Prologues to What Is Possible" [515-title
   As if, among the possible purposes [Moonlight 531-6
   An abysmal migration into a possible blue? [Burnshaw 51-9 P
   Seized by that possible blue. Be maidens formed [Burnshaw 51-18 P
   Barbers with charts of the only possible modes, [Sombre 68-8 P
   Possible machine, a divinity of steel, [Bship 78-3 P
   When mythology was possible--But if we had-- [Myth 118-9 P
POSSIBLENESS. Searches a possible for its possibleness. [NH 481-21
POSSIBLY. Or possibly, the merest patron saint [Nigger 157-5
   Ideas or, say, five men or, possibly, six. [Extracts 255-28
   And possibly the emperor would have cried, [Three 137-13 P
   Cat's taste possibly or possibly Danish lore, [Someone 87-5 A
POSSUM. "No Possum, No Sop, No Taters" [293-title
POSTCARD. "A Postcard from the Volcano" [158-title
   Bergamo on a postcard, Rome after dark, [NH 486-1
POSTPONE. Postpone the anatomy of summer, as [Cred 373-1
POSTPONED. Collapsed. The denouement has to be postponed . . . [AA
   416-21
POSTS. See lamp-posts.
POSTULATED. To him that postulated as his theme [C 35-1
POSTURE. It is this posture of the nerves, [MBG 182-20
POT. Or the bench with the pot of geraniums, the stained mattress
      and the washed overalls drying in the sun? [Indigo 22-12 P
POTENCIES. And elemental potencies and pangs, [C 31-25
   Smeared, smoked, and drunken of thin potencies, [Page 422-28

POTENCY. Freud's eye was the microscope of potency. [Cats 368-6
   The peculiar potency of the general, [NSF 397-7
   They understand, and take on potency, [Bouquet 449-5
POTENT. And potent, an influence felt instead of seen. [Owl 435-7
   The great cat must stand potent in the sun. [NH 473-3
POTENTIAL. There are potential seemings, arrogant [Descrip 340-19
   There are potential seemings turbulent [Descrip 341-1
POTIONS. Making gulped potions from obstreperous drops, [C 46-9
POTS. Bottles, pots, shoes and grass and murmur aptest eve: [Dump
   203-7
   Of the pans above the stove, the pots on the table, the tulips
      among them. [Large 423-15
   See flower-pots.
POTTER. From that meticulous potter's thumb. [Negation 98-5
   Potter in the summer sky. [Analysis 348-3
POUR. Pour the unhappiness out [Weep Woman 25-1
POURED. While he poured out upon the lips of her [C 43-3
   Poured brilliant iris on the glistening blue. [Sea Surf 99-15
   It was like the sea poured out again [Vase 246-15
   Poured forth the fine fins, the gawky beaks, the personalia,
      [Somnam 304-17
   Poured this elixir [Coroner 30-4 P
POURING. The rain is pouring down. It is July. [Ghaos 357-9
   Ke-ke, the jug-throated robin pouring out, [NSF 394-2
   Pierce the interior with pouring shafts, [Archi 18-3 P
   Seraphim of Europe? Pouring out of dawn, [Greenest 56-3 P
   See: down-pouring; up-pouring.
POURS. The wind pours down. [Ploughing 20-6
   The wind pours down. [Ploughing 20-20
POURTRAICTE. "Cy Est Pourtraicte, Madame Ste Ursule, et Les Unze
   Mille Vierges" [21-title
POUSSIN. See Nicholas Poussin.
POUSSINIANA. A sunny day's complete Poussiniana [Poem Morn 219-1
POVERTY. Then from their poverty they rose. [Ord Women 10-13
   Then from their poverty they rose, [Ord Women 12-3
   In a world of universal poverty [Nigger 152-1
   "The idols have seen lots of poverty, [On Road 204-6
   And naked of any illusion, in poverty, [Extracts 258-18
   In the exactest poverty, if then [Extracts 258-19
   Itself is like a poverty in the space of life, [Choc 299-1
   Exquisite in poverty against the suns [EM 317-23
   The prince of the proverbs of pure poverty. [EM 320-24
   Natives of poverty, children of malheur, [EM 322-18
   The greatest poverty is not to live [EM 325-18
   Through centuries he lived in poverty. [Good Man 364-1
   Their poverty, a gray-blue yellowed out [NSF 402-5
   He has his poverty and nothing more. [Bad Time 427-1
   His poverty becomes his heart's strong core-- [Bad Time 427-2
   In the poverty of dirt. [Pecul 453-6
   And the poverty of dirt, the thing upon his breast, [Pecul 454-7
   And something of death's poverty is heard. [NH 477-5
   The bricks grown brittle in time's poverty, [NH 480-23
   Shrunk in the poverty of being close, [NH 484-18
   The trees are reappearing in poverty. [Aug 495-18
   Little by little, the poverty [Leben 505-4
   It is poverty's speech that seeks us out the most. [Rome 510-3
   In the poverty of their words, [Planet 533-2
   For poverty are gaudy bosh to these. [Duck 61-20 P
   Complete in wind-sucked poverty. [Stan MBG 73-10 P
   Is poverty, whose jewel found [Ulysses 104-13 P
   "The court had known poverty and wretchedness; hu- [Three 129-9 P
   These came through poverty [Three 132-8 P
POWDERED. The powdered personals against the giants' rage, [Repet
   309-17
   Powdered with primitive lights, and lives with us [Sombre 66-24 P
   You saw the eye-blue, sky-blue, eye-blue, and the powdered ears
      [Grotesque 74-15 P
POWER. The appointed power unwielded from disdain. [C 37-19
   West Indian, the extremest power [Hero 276-2
   But not the person, of their power, thought, [Choc 299-15
   Instead, outcast, without the will to power [Cats 368-2
   The youth, the vital son, the heroic power. [Cred 375-10
   An elixir, an excitation, a pure power. [NSF 382-22
   The poem, through candor, brings back a power again [NSF 382-23
   Or power of the wave, or deepened speech, [NSF 387-13
   That gives its power to the wild-ringed eye. [Owl 433-22
   Imposes power by the power of his form. [Orb 443-6
   That power to conceal they had as men, [NH 470-8
   The power to transform itself, or else, [Two Illus 514-11
   A light, a power, the miraculous influence. [Final 524-9
   Is active with a power, an inherent life, [Moonlight 531-20
   Than a power of sleep, a clearness emerging [Bus 116-9 P
   Power in the waving of the wand of the moon, [Someone 84-10 A
POWERFUL. The powerful seasons bred and killed, [Joost 46-17
   But as in the powerful mirror of my wish and will." [Rhythms
      246-8
   Cry loudly, cry out in the powerful heart. [Dutch 291-9
   For races, not for men, powerful beyond [Greenest 59-29 P
   A perception of sleep, more powerful [Bus 116-8 P
POWERS. And heirs are powers of the mind, [Ulysses 103-8 P

PRACTICAL. And practical. The envoi to the past [Duck 65-29 P
PRACTICE. One likes to practice the thing. They practice, [Adieu
  128-7
  While you practice arpeggios, [Mozart 131-19
  "Piano Practice at the Academy of the Holy Angels" [21-title P
PRACTICED. On a black piano practiced epi-tones. [Liadoff 346-16
  Some pebble-chewer practiced in Tyrian speech, [Duck 63-17 P
PRACTICING. At a piano in a cloud sat practicing, [Liadoff 346-15
  Red robin, stop in your preludes, practicing [NSF 405-16
  A philosopher practicing scales on his piano, [NH 488-20
  "Polo Ponies Practicing" [37-title P
PRACTICK. Of Gothic prong and practick bright, [Couch 295-12
PRAISABLE. Having, each one, most praisable [Parasol 20-5 P
PRAISE. And makes a constant sacrament of praise. [Peter 92-13
  Home and the field give praise, hurrah, hip, [Hero 278-13
  Of praise, a conjugation done by choirs. [NSF 402-15
  I am the archangel of evening and praise [Inhab 504-10
  His hymn, his psalm, his cithern song of praise [Greenest 59-21 P
PRAISED. He praised Johann Sebastian, as he should. [Norfolk 111-15
  Regardless of gods that were praised in goldness [Stan Hero
  83-21 P
PRATTLE. That tragic prattle of the fates, astute [Spaniard 34-16 P
PRAVDA. Say this to Pravda, tell the damned rag [Memo 89-9 P
PRAY. It is to the hero of midnight that we pray [NH 466-23
PRAYER. Half prayer and half ditty, [Pourtraicte 22-3
  Mon Dieu, hear the poet's prayer. [Sailing 120-11
  And liquorish prayer provokes new sweats: so, so: [Havana 144-10
  And hears the nigger's prayer in motets, belched [Greenest
  59-12 P
  The churches, like dalmatics stooped in prayer, [Sombre 69-1 P
PRAYERS. Cardinal, saying the prayers of earliest day; [Choc 300-2
  Wherefore those prayers to the moon? [An Gaiety 33-1 P
  The giant Phosphor of their earliest prayers. [Duck 65-23 P
PREACH. That made him preach the louder, long for a church [Blue
  Bldg 216-18
  They preach and they are preaching in a land [Extracts 254-3
PREACHING. They preach and they are preaching in a land [Extracts
  254-3
  To be described. They are preaching in a time [Extracts 254-4
PRECARIOUS. Of this precarious music, the change of key [Pure 332-3
PRECEDED. In imitation. The clouds preceded us [NSF 383-18
  A chorister whose c preceded the choir. [Not Ideas 534-14
PRECEPTOR. Preceptor to the sea? Crispin at sea [C 27-12
PRECIOUS. Good God! What a precious light! [Bananas 54-9
  But a tower more precious than the view beyond, [Cred 373-18
  On a breast forever precious for that touch, [NSF 388-6
  In its own only precious ornament. [NSF 396-5
  And myself am precious for your perfecting. [NSF 396-9
  Precious from the region of the hand, still bright [Bship 81-1 P
  More precious than the most precious objects of home: [Local
  111-13 P
  Like precious scholia jotted down in the dark. [Someone 84-21 A
PRECISE. The romance of the precise is not the elision [Adult 353-7
  Are not precise about the appeasement they need. [NH 467-21
PRECISELY. Would taste, precisely, as they said it would. [Soldat
  11-12 P
PRECISIONS. The precisions of fate, nothing fobbed off, nor changed
  [Repet 310-8
PREDESTINED. Predestined to this night, this noise and the place
  [Myrrh 349-17
PREDICATE. The categorical predicate, the arc. [Descrip 344-8
  Almost as predicate. But it exists, [AA 418-17
  A difficulty that we predicate: [NH 474-22
  Not the predicate of bright origin. [NH 481-13
  In the predicate that there is nothing else. [Rock 527-4
PREFER. I do not know which to prefer, [Thirteen 93-7
  To prefer L'Observateur de la Paix, since [Hero 276-6
PREFERRED. He preferred the brightness of bells, [Winter B 141-5
  In every various sense, ought not to be preferred [Lytton 39-13 P
PREFERRING. Preferring text to gloss, he humbly served [C 39-22
  The sky, half porcelain, preferring that [Cuisine 228-6
PRE-HISTORY. . . . Wanderer, this is the pre-history of February.
  [Slug 522-15
PREJUDICE. "The Prejudice against the Past" [368-title
PRELIMINARY. A preliminary, provincial phase, [Bship 77-17 P
PRELUDE. Of ocean, as a prelude holds and holds. [Sea Surf 100-16
  Ever the prelude to your end, [MBG 170-19
  "Prelude to Objects" [194-title
PRELUDES. Preludes a-rub, a-rub-rub, for him that [Hero 278-6
  All the Preludes to Felicity [Pure 329-title 1
  In which the enchanted preludes have their place. [Pure 330-15
  Red robin, stop in your preludes, practicing [NSF 405-16
  The supernatural preludes of its own, [AA 414-12
PREMATURE. The album of Corot is premature. [Nigger 156-13
PREMISE. It is not in the premise that reality [NH 489-1
PREMISES. Upon these premises propounding, he [C 38-11
PREMISS. The premiss from which all things were conclusions, [Con-
  tra II 270-16
PREORDAINED. With fictive flourishes that preordained [C 39-17
PREPARATION. The preparation is long and of long intent [Nigger

  158-4
  The rising and the swell, the preparation [Woman Had 81-15 P
PREPARE. Of the garden. We must prepare to hear the Roamer's
  [Phenom 286-17
  To prepare for bed, in the frame of the house, and move [Lot
  372-2
PREPARED. See long-prepared.
PRE-PERSONAE. Or these--escent--issant pre-personae: first fly,
  [Slug 522-11
PREROGATIVE. Below the prerogative jumble. The fruit so seen
  [Someone 84-16 A
PRESCIENCE. With none of the prescience of oncoming dreams, [AA
  413-7
  At three-quarters gone, the morning's prescience, [Pagoda 92-4 P
PRESENCE. In my presence, the companion of presences [Choc 302-3
  In the presence of a logical lunatic." [EM 324-26
  As if, in the presence of the sea, [Silent 359-8
  The place of a swarthy presence moving, [Countryman 429-7
  The world is presence and not force. [John 436-14
  Presence is not mind. [John 436-15
  Presence is Kinder-Scenen. [John 436-16
  Presence is not the woman, come upon, [John 437-7
  Presence lies far too deep, for me to know [John 437-25
  And yet is there, a presence in the way. [Bouquet 452-5
  In the presence of such chapels and such schools, [NH 469-22
  Around and away, resembling the presence of thought, [NH 474-5
  In the presence of a solitude of the self, [Aug 494-5
  The extreme of the known in the presence of the extreme [Rome
  508-17
  Whose mere savage presence awakens the world in which she dwells.
  [World 520-16
  Itself, the presence of the intelligible [Armor 529-15
  It is to disclose the essential presence, say, [Moonlight 531-10
  In the presence of the barefoot ghosts! [Lytton 39-5 P
  By his presence, the seat of his ubiquitous will. [Greenest
  59-32 P
  "Presence of an External Master of Knowledge" [105-title P
PRESENCES. In my presence, the companion of presences [Choc 302-3
  Resembling the presences of thoughts, as if, [NH 474-6
PRESENT. Play the present, its hoo-hoo-hoo, [Mozart 131-15
  Of this present, this science, this unrecognized, [Cuisine 228-8
  Still walking in a present of our own. [Martial 237-16
  The present close, the present realized, [Martial 238-10
  No was the night. Yes is this present sun. [Beard 247-11
  Fate is the present desperado. [Dutch 291-5
  Know that the past is not part of the present. [Dutch 291-21
  These violent marchers of the present, [Dutch 293-6
  Intelligence? On what does the present rest? [Pure 331-12
  On this present ground, the vividest repose, [Cred 375-19
  Having attained a present blessedness, [Past Nun 378-12
  And present way, a presentation, a kind [NSF 397-20
  Who gives transparence to their present peace. [AA 413-11
  Look at this present throne. What company, [AA 415-2
  Not an intellect in which we are fleet: present [Ulti 430-2
  Of this present, the venerable mask above [NH 476-17
  In the present state of things as, say, to paint [NH 478-6
  In the present state of painting and not the state [NH 478-7
  As if the eyes were the present or part of it, [NH 478-10
  Or thinks he does, as he perceives the present, [NH 478-17
  This present colony of a colony [NH 479-11
  Rising out of present time and place, above [Irish 502-1
  St. Armorer's has nothing of this present, [Armor 530-11
  And without future, a present time, is that [Sombre 71-24 P
  A life beyond this present knowing, [Ulysses 101-22 P
  A life lighter than this present splendor, [Ulysses 101-23 P
  The living man in the present place, [Ulysses 103-13 P
  Without a remembered past, a present past, [Local 111-15 P
  Or a present future, hoped for in present hope, [Local 111-16 P
  Objects not present as a matter of course [Local 112-1 P
  So far the lady of the present ballad [Three 137-9 P
  See ever-present.
PRESENTATION. And present way, a presentation, a kind [NSF 397-20
  And that necessity and that presentation [NSF 398-3
PRESENTMENT. And the visible, circumspect presentment drawn [C 35-24
PRESENTS. Presents itself in Oley when the hay, [Cred 374-7
  Will come. His mind presents the world [Ulysses 102-20 P
PRESERVED. Miraculously preserved, full fickle-fine, [Greenest
  56-15 P
  By poets, the Italian lives preserved [Duck 61-19 P
  That is its life preserved, the effort to be born [Discov 96-8 P
PRESERVES. He preserves himself against the repugnant rain [NH
  475-22
PRESIDENT. The President ordains the bee to be [NSF 390-10
  Immortal. The President ordains. But does [NSF 390-11
  The President has apples on the table [NSF 390-19
  To photographs of the late president, Mr. Blank, [NH 488-15
PRESIDES. How she presides over imbeciles. The night [Feo 333-12
PRESS. Of images. Days pass like papers from a press. [Dump 201-14
  They press it as epicure, distinguishing [EM 323-2
  Do I press the extremest book of the wisest man [NSF 380-5

Of the pillow in your hand. You writhe and press [NSF 384-20
That press, strong peasants in a peasant world, [Armor 530-5
PRESSED. The gray grass like a pallet, closely pressed; [Extracts
 255-4
When the cloud pressed suddenly the whole return [Liadoff 347-6
 Crying against a need that pressed like cold, [Old Woman 45-29 P
PRESTER. Against enemies, against the prester, [Hero 274-4
PRESTIGES. The sense of self, rosed out of prestiges [Owl 435-5
PRESTO. In the presto of the morning, Crispin trod, [C 42-13
 Presto, whose whispers prickle the spirit. [Hero 274-5
PRETENCE. And curtains like a naive pretence of sleep. [AA 415-15
PRETEND. Pretend they are shapes of another consciousness? [Feo
 334-8
PRETTY. Seem pretty much one: [Botanist 1 134-17
 After all the pretty contrast of life and death [Connois 215-13
 Old worm, my pretty quirk, [Metamorph 265-14
PREVAIL. To make a new intelligence prevail? [C 37-10
PREVAILING. The voice of ether prevailing, the swell [MBG 177-11
PREVAILS. There is a substance in us that prevails. [Monocle 15-10
 A parakeet of parakeets prevails, [Bird Claws 82-2
PREVENTED. One year, death and war prevented the jasmine scent
 [Oboe 251-8
PREVENTS. "The fly on the rose prevents us, O season [Ghosts 119-15
 For whom no blue in the sky prevents them, as [Bouquet 449-4
PRICK. Should prick thereof, not on the psaltery, [C 38-18
 That prick [Soldat 12-23 P
PRICKING. He quoi! Angels go pricking elephants? [Greenest 55-30 P
PRICKLE. Presto, whose whispers prickle the spirit. [Hero 274-5
PRICKLING. Had kept him still the prickling realist, [C 40-6
PRICKLY. Prickly and obdurate, dense, harmonious, [C 35-18
 Less prickly and much more condign than that [C 42-15
PRICKS. Pricks in our spirits at the summer's end, [Anatomy 108-5
PRIDE. Fallen Winkle felt the pride [Phases 4-17 P
 With his plough, the peacock may abandon pride, [Burnshaw 48-24 P
PRIEST. No chorister, nor priest. There was [How Live 126-2
 The pine, the pillar and the priest, [Thought 186-1
 Invisible priest; is it to eject, to pull [Dump 203-9
 But the priest desires. The philosopher desires. [NSF 382-3
 He is neither priest nor proctor at low eve, [NH 474-16
 This rock and the priest, [Including 88-5 P
 The priest of nothingness who intones-- [Including 88-6 P
PRIESTLY. On the priestly gramophones. [Winter B 141-8
 And steps forth, priestly in severity, [Sombre 70-15 P
PRIESTS. That's the old world. In the new, all men are priests.
 [Extracts 254-2
PRIG. If each of them wasn't a prig [Drum-Majors 36-17 P
PRIM. It weights him with nice logic for the prim. [Havana 144-17
 The curtains are stiff and prim and still. [Chateau 161-18
PRIMARY. The weight of primary noon, [Motive 288-15
 Of the certain solid, the primary free from doubt, [Man Car 351-2
PRIMAVERA. In primavera, the shadow of bare rock, [NH 476-9
PRIME. Prime paramour and belted paragon, [Lilacs 49-12
 In a consummate prime, yet still desires [EM 318-3
PRIMITIVE. The single-colored, colorless, primitive. [Landsc 242-2
 Of a primitive. He walks with a defter [Hero 277-10
 It is a declaration, a primitive ecstasy, [EM 321-10
 Stands and regards and repeats the primitive lines. [Anach 366-15
 Inscribes a primitive astronomy [NSF 383-3
 "A Primitive Like an Orb" [440-title
 In the big X of the returning primitive. [NH 474-18
 Powdered with primitive lights, and lives with us [Sombre 66-24 P
 Like an eye too young to grapple its primitive, [Theatre 91-4 P
PRIMITIVES. Here I keep thinking of the Primitives-- [Soldat 13-8 P
PRIMORDIA. "Poems from 'Primordia'" [7-title P
PRIMROSE. For the women of primrose and purl, [Bananas 54-7
PRINCE. "Anecdote of the Prince of Peacocks" [57-title
 Of an emperor, the egg-plant of a prince. [Extracts 253-10
 Ancestor of Narcissus, prince [Jumbo 269-16
 The prince of the proverbs of pure poverty. [EM 320-24
 The prince of shither-shade and tinsel lights, [Owl 434-3
PRINCES. As if twelve princes sat before a king. [Cred 375-25
 Frail princes of distant Monaco, [Primordia 9-20 P
PRINCIPALLY. Principally the church steeple, [Common 221-2
PRINCIPIUM. Of snails, musician of pears, principium [C 27-9
 Rex and principium, exit the whole [C 37-1
 To principium, to meditation. [Sol Oaks 111-7 P
PRINCIPLE. By force of rudeness, let the principle [C 38-7
 We agree in principle. That's clear. But take [High-Toned 59-6
 More fecund as principle than particle, [NSF 388-19
 As pure principle. Its nature is its end, [AA 418-11
 A vis, a principle or, it may be, [Orb 442-10
 The meditation of a principle, [Orb 442-11
PRINCIPLES. One exists among pure principles. [Sol Oaks 111-4 P
PRINCOX. "That bliss of stars, that princox of evening heaven!"
 reminding of seasons, [Banal 63-1
 And who does not seek the sky unfuzzed, soaring to the princox?
 [Banal 63-5
PRINKS. In the sea, Biscayne, there prinks [Homunculus 25-13
PRINT. The sombre pages bore no print [Reader 147-10
 The scholar's outline that you had, the print [Duck 61-17 P

By print or paper, the trivial chance foregone, [Duck 61-23 P
PRISMATIC. The prismatic sombreness of a torrent's wave. [Bouquet
 452-12
 With slight, prismatic reeks not recollected, [Theatre 91-11 P
PRISMY. Her prismy blonde and clapped her in his hands, [C 42-3
PRISONER. Comes close to the prisoner's ear, becomes a throat
 [Montra 261-2
 Delivering the prisoner by his words, [Montra 261-7
PRISTINE. Planting his pristine cores in Florida, [C 38-17
PRIVACY. To protect him in a privacy, in which [Someone 85-9 A
PRIVATE. Leafed out in adjectives as private [Hero 277-25
 That which was public green turned private gray. [NH 479-1
PRIVILEGE. A name and privilege over the ordinary of his common-
 place-- [Prol 517-4
PRIZE. And savings banks, Fides, the sculptor's prize, [Lions
 124-12
 The meaning of the capture, this hard prize, [Cred 376-14
PROCESSION. Seem things in some procession of the dead, [Sunday
 67-6
 His own pageant and procession and display, [Questions 462-18
PROCESSIONALS. So speech of your processionals returns [On Manner
 56-1
PROCLAIM. There to behold, there to proclaim, the grace [Montra
 263-9
 Or yield to subjugation, once to proclaim [Cred 376-13
 And proclaim it, the white creator of black, jetted [AA 417-11
PROCLAIMED. Calamity, proclaimed himself, was proclaimed. [Horn
 230-16
PROCLAIMING. Proclaiming something harsher than he learned [C 33-1
PROCLAIMS. That music is intensest which proclaims [Fictive 88-2
 One father proclaims another, the patriarchs [Role 93-7 P
PROCLAMATION. The particular tingle in a proclamation [Someone
 84-14 A
PROCLAMATIONS. Of many proclamations of the kind, [C 32-32
 Seraphic proclamations of the pure [C 45-28
PROCREATIONS. Nothing of its jocular procreations? [MBG 183-9
PROCTOR. He is neither priest nor proctor at low eve, [NH 474-16
PROCURATOR. Poor procurator, why do you ask someone else [Papini
 446-1
PRODIGAL. However, prodigal, however proud, [C 39-11
 With every prodigal, familiar fire, [Orb 442-18
 Pronouncing its new life and ours, not autumn's prodigal returned,
 [Discov 96-4 P
PRODIGIES. Are prodigies in longer phrases. [Hero 277-13
PRODIGIOUS. Prodigious things are tricks. The world is not [Havana
 144-3
 To this prodigious shadow, who then came [Choc 297-2
 What else, prodigious scholar, should there be? [NSF 381-24
 And prodigious person, patron of origins. [Orb 443-14
PRODIGY. Must be the place for prodigy, unless [Havana 144-2
 In which reality is prodigy. [Owl 432-9
 And in harmonious prodigy to be, [Owl 432-22
PRODUCE. The singular man of the mass. Masses produce [Dames 206-5
 Time troubles to produce the redeeming thought. [Extracts 257-19
 That's how to produce a virtuoso. [Hero 274-24
PRODUCED. Like things produced by a climate, the world [Ulysses
 102-29 P
PRODUCES. Night and day, wind and quiet, produces [Vari 233-21
 Is that which produces everything else, in which [Phenom 287-3
PRODUCING. A sound producing the things that are spoken. [Phenom
 287-6
PROFANE. But a profane parade, the basso [Hero 278-5
PROFESSION. An expressive on-dit, a profession. [Dutch 290-19
PROFESSOR EUCALYPTUS. Professor Eucalyptus of New Haven seeks him
 [NH 475-5
 Professor Eucalyptus said, "The search [NH 481-4
PROFITLESS. Is false, if Crispin is a profitless [C 45-31
PROFOUND. As dissertation of profound delight, [C 31-6
 And more than free, elate, intent, profound [C 33-10
 Of speech which are like music so profound [On Manner 55-13
 Grisaille, impearled, profound, [Add 198-14
 On the ground, fixed fast in a profound defeat. [Martial 238-2
 Profound, and yet the king and yet the crown, [AA 415-1
 The world is still profound and in its depths [Papini 447-9
 For neither is it profound absentia, [NH 469-15
 Profound poetry of the poor and of the dead, [Rome 509-25
 The newest Soviet réclame. Profound [Duck 62-30 P
 The fortifying arm, the profound [Ulysses 100-10 P
PROFOUNDER. Would be endings, more poignant than partings, pro-
 founder, [Adieu 127-14
 Here I inhale profounder strength [MBG 180-15
 A profounder reconciling, an act, [Vase 247-4
 An end of evil in a profounder logic, [Dutch 291-16
PROFOUNDEST. Was he to bray this in profoundest brass [C 41-10
 One observes profoundest shadows rolling. [Vari 235-14
 In the metaphysical streets, the profoundest forms [NH 473-7
PROFOUNDLY. In war, observes each man profoundly. [Hero 274-14
PROFUNDO. Capitán profundo, capitán geloso, [Orangeade 102-16
PROFUNDUM. Profundum, physical thunder, dimension in which [Flyer
 336-14

PROFUSION. The profusion of metaphor has been increased. [Someone
  83-3 A
PROGENITOR. Progenitor of such extensive scope, [C 38-29
  Progenitor wearing the diamond crown of crowns, [Duck 64-30 P
PROGRESS. In his observant progress, lesser things [C 34-19
  Beyond which fact could not progress as fact. [NSF 402-22
  Beyond which thought could not progress as thought. [NSF 403-10
PROGRESSIONS. The indolent progressions of the swans [Havana 143-8
PROHIBITED. The easy projection long prohibited. [Paisant 335-11
PROJECT. And from the peristyle project a masque [High-Toned 59-8
  To project the naked man in a state of fact, [Montra 263-11
  There was a project for the sun and is. [NSF 381-12
  There is a project for the sun. The sun [NSF 381-13
  From his project, as finally magnified. [Two Illus 515-4
PROJECTED. Projected a colony that should extend [C 38-12
  To be projected by one void into [Landsc 242-13
  Beyond his circumstance, projected [Hero 277-21
PROJECTION. Suppose we call it Projection A. [Couch 295-3
  Projection B. To get at the thing [Couch 295-16
  This is the final Projection, C. [Couch 295-21
  The easy projection long prohibited. [Paisant 335-11
PROJECTIONS. To rumbled rock, its bright projections lie [Sombre
  70-3 P
PROLEGOMENA. He, therefore, wrote his prolegomena, [C 37-23
PROLIFIC. Prolific and tormenting tenderness [C 43-11
  Engaged in the most prolific narrative, [Phenom 287-5
  In the prolific ellipses that we know, [Someone 87-18 A
PROLOGUES. The prologues are over. It is a question, now, [Oboe
  250-6
  "Prologues to What Is Possible" [515-title
PROLONG. Scrawl a tragedian's testament? Prolong [C 41-14
PROLONGATIONS. Or else his prolongations of the human. [NH 469-12
PROLONGED. Prolonged, repeated and once more prolonged, [Duck
  63-32 P
PROLONGS. Desire prolongs its adventure to create [NH 482-14
PROMENADE. Crispin foresaw a curious promenade [C 31-23
  A promenade amid the grandeurs of the mind, [EM 325-7
PROMENADES. X promenades the dewy stones, [Canna 55-7
  The true abstract in which he promenades. [Thought 185-12
  On Sundays, lawyers in their promenades [NSF 391-13
PROMISE. Rose out of promise and became the sooth [Havana 143-2
PROMISES. Still promises perfections cast away. [EM 318-25
  So that morning and evening are like promises kept, [NH 472-16
PROMISING. Yet he kept promising himself [Winter B 141-15
PRONE. Prone to distemper he abates in taste, [C 46 3
  The pensive giant prone in violet space [NSF 387-2
PRONG. Of Gothic prong and practick bright, [Couch 295-12
PRONOUNCE. Should merely call him dead? Pronounce amen [C 41-17
  In which we pronounce joy like a word of our own. [Gala 248-6
PRONOUNCING. Pronouncing its new life and ours, not autumn's
  prodigal returned, [Discov 96-4 P
  A way of pronouncing the word inside of one's tongue [Bus 116-13P
PRONUNCIAMENTO. His grand pronunciamento and devise. [C 43-15
  Disguised pronunciamento, summary, [C 45-22
PROOF. For the clairvoyant men that need no proof: [Orb 441-5
  Subtler, more urgent proof that the theory [NH 486-8
PROPAGATE. To propagate the imagination or like [Cats 368-4
PROPAGATIONS. Its propagations are more erudite, [Someone 84-20 A
PROPELLING. He could not bend against its propelling force. [R
  Conn 533-12
PROPER. Sleepless, inhales his proper air, and rests. [Cred 373-24
  The luminous melody of proper sound. [NSF 404-12
  How gladly with proper words the soldier dies, [NSF 408-2
  The height was not quite proper; [Aug 493-19
PROPERLY. If properly misunderstood becomes a myth. [Lytton 38-15 P
PROPERTY. Of property is not an area [Papini 47-14
  The property of the moon, what it evokes. [Moonlight 531-9
PROPHECIES. Commingled souvenirs and prophecies. [C 37-25
  Of letters, prophecies, perceptions, clods [Orb 443-20
  Through prophets and succeeding prophets, whose prophecies [Bship
  81-6 P
PROPHECY. There is not any haunt of prophecy, [Sunday 68-17
  Subtler than the ornatest prophecy, [Havana 144-13
  The means of prophecy, [Inhab 503-11
  And memory's lord is the lord of prophecy [Sombre 70-14 P
PROPHESY. Complain and prophesy, in their complaints, [Burnshaw
  48-18 P
PROPHET. Are to the unaccountable prophet or [Hero 274-17
PROPHETIC. Prophetic joint, for its diviner young. [C 43-19
PROPHETS. Through prophets and succeeding prophets, whose pro-
  phecies [Bship 81-6 P
PROPOSE. A shadow in mid-earth . . . If we propose [Pure 330-7
  Of these beginnings, gay and green, propose [NSF 398-5
PROPOSED. A knowing that something certain had been proposed,
  [NH 483-4
  A theorem proposed between the two-- [Rock 525-16
PROPOSITIONS. Of propositions about life. The human [Men Made
  355-18
  We compose these propositions, torn by dreams, [Men Made 356-2
  The eccentric propositions of its fate. [Men Made 356-6

PROPOUND. On that its claws propound, its fangs [MBG 174-9
  But the dark italics it could not propound. [EM 326-6
  Nor sanctify, but plainly to propound. [NSF 389-12
PROPOUNDERS. Great choristers, propounders of hymns, trumpeters,
  [Luther 461-7
PROPOUNDING. Upon these premises propounding, he [C 38-11
  The propounding of four seasons and twelve months. [NH 473-14
PROPOUNDS. Propounds blank final music. [Burghers 362-18
PROPRIETOR. And the obese proprietor, who has a son [Greenest
  58-16 P
PROPRIETY. How good life is, on the basis of propriety, [Winter B
  141-13
  Of its propriety. Admit the shaft [Someone 86-2 A
PROSE. He gripped more closely the essential prose [C 36-18
  That prose should wear a poem's guise at last. [C 36-23
  Shebang. Exeunt omnes. Here was prose [C 37-2
  Of the strictest prose [Cortege 81-2
  Final for him, the acceptance of such prose, [Armor 530-7
PROSERPINE. And I fly forth, the naked Proserpine. [Infernale 25-8P
PROSTRATE. The pillars are prostrate, the arches are haggard,
  [Botanist 1 135-11
  Prostrate below the singleness of its will. [NH 478-24
PROTECT. To protect him in a privacy, in which [Someone 85-9 A
PROTECTED. A form, then, protected from the battering, may [Pure
  330-10
PROTEST. And Bloom would see what Puvis did, protest [Anach 366-6
PROTRUDE. If her horny feet protrude, they come [Emperor 64-13
PROTRUDING. Protruding from the pile of wool, a hand, [Novel 457-10
PROUD. However prodigal, however proud, [C 39-11
  Deduction. Thrum with a proud douceur [C 43-14
  Proud of such novelties of the sublime, [High-Toned 59-17
  Or of night endazzled, proud, [Fading 139-3
  That batters against the mind, silent and proud, [Pure 329-14
  In the afternoon. The proud and the strong [Leben 504-17
  Devising proud, majestic issuance. [Soldat 14-12 P
  For no one proud, nor stiff, [Archi 18-11 P
  Her glory in your passion and be proud. [Red Kit 31-13 P
  Does she will to be proud? True, you may love [Red Kit 31-17 P
  A skillful apprehension and eye proud [Spaniard 35-17 P
PROUDLY. Like humans approaching proudly, [Shifts 83-18
PROVE. We do not prove the existence of the poem. [Orb 440-9
PROVED. Man proved a gobbet in my mincing world. [Monocle 17-24
  The gross, the fecund, proved him against the touch [EM 322-4
PROVENCE. Behold them, not choses of Provence, growing [Bouquet
  449-12
PROVERBS. The prince of the proverbs of pure poverty. [EM 320-24
PROVES. And so distorting, proving what he proves [C 46-10
  Proves that these opposite things partake of one, [Connois 215-14
  This proves nothing. Just one more truth, one more [Connois 216-2
  One poem proves another and the whole, [Orb 441-4
PROVINCE. There are men of a province [Men 1000 51-11
  Who are that province. [Men 1000 51-12
  It is a province-- [Analysis 348-4
  In its church-yard, in the province of St. Armorer's, [Armor 529-3
PROVINCIAL. A preliminary, provincial phase, [Bship 77-17 P
PROVING. And so distorting, proving what he proves [C 46-10
PROVOKES. And liquorish prayer provokes new sweats: so, so: [Havana
  144-10
PROVOKING. Provoking a laughter, an agreement, by surprise. [Gala
  248-15
PROW. From what he saw across his vessel's prow. [C 35-25
  Part of the speculum of fire on its prow, its symbol, whatever
  it was, [Prol 516-2
PRUDES. Incredible to prudes, the mint of dirt, [C 31-21
PRUNED. Of its ancient purple, pruned to the fertile main, [C 45-14
PSALM. The reverberating psalm, the right chorale. [EM 326-2
  His hymn, his psalm, his cithern song of praise [Greenest 59-21P
PSALTER. These were the psalter of their sybils. [Hero 273-14
PSALTERY. Should prick thereof, not on the psaltery, [C 38-18
  To chop the sullen psaltery, [MBG 173-20
PSEUDONYMOUS. Black man, bright nouveautés leave one, at best,
  pseudonymous. [Nudity Col 145-12
PSYCHOLOGY. In the end, in the whole psychology, the self, [NH 474-7
PUBERTY. Waste without puberty; and afterward, [NSF 399-17
PUBLIC. "The Public Square" [108-title
  The idea of things for public gardens, [Hero 276-15
  Of men suited to public ferns . . . The hero [Hero 276-16
  That which was public green turned private gray. [NH 479-1
  Such black constructions, such public shapes [Ulysses 100-28 P
PUCKERED. Like a belly puckered by a spear. [Lulu M 27-4 P
PUDDLES. The water puddles puddles are [Poesie 302-9
  And through and over the puddles of Swatara [Our Stars 455-10
PUELLA. "Puella Parvula" [456-title
  Gone wild, be what he tells you to be: Puella. [Puel 456-14
PUERILE. Of its eventual roundness, puerile tints [C 44-7
  Say, puerile, that the buzzards crouch on the ridge-pole [Two
  Figures 86-10
PUFF. That century of wind in a single puff. [C 28-4
PUFFED. Like something on the stage, puffed out, [MBG 181-18
PUFFED-OUT. Nor the smoke-drift of puffed-out heroes, nor human

cry. [Course 96-20 P
PUFFING. With a curious puffing. [Plot Giant 7-6
PUFFS. That it puffs as Cornelius Nepos reads, it puffs [Dump
    202-3
    More than, less than or it puffs like this or that. [Dump 202-4
    Racking the world with clarion puffs. This must [Greenest 56-12 P
PUISSANT. Puissant speech, alike in each, [Ord Women 11-26
    Reposed? And does it have a puissant heart [Two V 354-5
    His puissant front nor for her subtle sound, [NSF 401-12
    The smallest lamp, which added its puissant flick, to which he
    gave [Prol 517-3
    Hissing, across the silence, puissant sounds. [Greenest 55-16 P
PUISSANTLY. They sing right puissantly. [Snow Stars 133-3
PULL. Invisible priest; is it to eject, to pull [Dump 203-9
    In the end, these philosophic assassins pull [Extracts 256-1
PULLED. The singer has pulled his cloak over his head. [Of Surface
    57-7
    It is like a boat that has pulled away [Vacancy 511-6
    The curtains, when pulled, might show another whole, [Theatre
    91-13 P
PULLING. The pulling into the sky and the setting there [Repet
    308-23
    Bending over and pulling themselves erect on the wooden handles,
    [Prol 515-8
PULLS. The roundness that pulls tight the final ring [Orb 442-8
PULLULATE. The bells of the chapel pullulate sounds at [Peaches
    224-9
PULP. The honey in its pulp, the final found, [Rock 527-14
PULPY. What pulpy dram distilled of innocence, [C 38-3
PULSE. Pulse pizzicati of Hosanna. [Peter 90-12
    From thought, like a violent pulse in the cloud itself, [Liadoff
    347-7
    The pulse of the object, the heat of the body grown cold [Study I
    463-16
    The final pulse of blood from this good heart [Soldat 11-11 P
PULSES. To toll its pulses, vigors of its self? [Two V 354-6
    To cool their ruddy pulses; the frothy clouds [NSF 399-15
PUNCTUAL. In the punctual centre of all circles white [Anach 366-8
PUNDIT. This pundit of the weather, who never ceased [Nigger 156-5
PUNGENT. A pungent bloom against your shade. [Venereal 48-17
    The pungent oranges and bright, green wings [Sunday 67-5
    In pungent fruit and bright, green wings, or else [Sunday 67-16
    A mountain, a pineapple pungent as Cuban summer. [NSF 393-12
    Yellow-blue, yellow-green, pungent with citron-sap, [NH 486-14
PUNISHMENT. It may be that one life is a punishment [EM 323-26
    Now. War as a punishment. The hero [Stan Hero 84-16 P
PUPA. In the mind, pupa of straw, moppet of rags. [Dwarf 208-6
PUPIL. To expunge all people and be a pupil [Sailing 121-3
    I have been pupil under bishops' rods [Soldat 11-4 P
PUPPETS. Oh-hé-hé! Fragrant puppets [Cab 21-4 P
PUPPIES. Whines in its hole for puppies to come see, [Pure 332-21
PUR. Are you not le plus pur, you ancient one? [Blue Bldg 217-20
PURE. Crispin as hermit, pure and capable, [C 40-4
    Seraphic proclamations of the pure [C 45-28
    As his pure intellect applies its laws, [Bird Claws 82-14
    This warmth in the blood-world for the pure idea, [Extracts
    256-12
    Toward an inaccessible, pure sound. [Montra 263-16
    Pure eye. Instead of allegory, [Hero 279-1
    The prince of the proverbs of pure poverty. [EM 320-24
    "The Pure Good of Theory" [329-title
    Pure coruscations, that lie beyond [Analysis 349-1
    Pure rhetoric of a language without words. [Cred 374-15
    An elixir, an excitation, a pure power. [NSF 382-22
    As pure principle. Its nature is its end, [AA 418-11
    The pure perfections of parental space, [Owl 436-3
    The poem of pure reality, untouched [NH 471-13
    In this chamber of the pure sphere escapes the impure [NH 480-3
    By a pure fountain, that was a ghost, and is, [Aug 489-10
    Pure scientist, you look with nice aplomb [Good Bad 33-12 P
    One exists among pure principles. [Sol Oaks 111-4 P
PURELY. Transfixing by being purely what it is, [NH 471-17
PUREST. The hot of him is purest in the heart. [NSF 388-15
PURGED. The poison in the blood will have been purged, [Montra
    262-4
PURGES. That purges the wrack or makes the jungle shine, [Greenest
    55-8 P
PURIFIED. It purified. It made him see how much [C 36-16
PURIFYING. One feels the purifying change. One rejects [Dump 202-17
PURITY. The last purity of the knowledge of good. [Possum 294-14
PURL. For the women of primrose and purl, [Bananas 54-7
PURPLE. And would have purple stuff upon her arms, [Paltry 5-12
    And the colored purple of the lazy sea, [Hibiscus 22-17
    Among the purple tufts, the scarlet crowns, [C 32-4
    The mountainous ridges, purple balustrades, [C 33-14
    Sealed pensive purple under its concern. [C 40-20
    Of its ancient purple, pruned to the fertile main, [C 45-14
    Came reproduced in purple, family font, [C 45-16
    Out of their purple maws, [Bananas 54-21
    Darting out of their purple craws [Bananas 54-22

Not less because in purple I descended [Hoon 65-7
Or purple with green rings, [Ten O'C 66-4
To whom the watermelon is always purple, [Watermelon 88-20
The purple dress in autumn and the belfry breath [NE Verses 106-7
The vetch has turned purple. But where is the bride? [Ghosts
    119-3
Clog, therefore, purple Jack and crimson Jill. [Nigger 154-6
For all his purple, the purple bird must have [Nigger 155-20
Red purple, never quite red itself. [Arcades 225-16
"Of Hartford in a Purple Light" [226-title
What is this purple, this parasol, [Hartford 226-15
It is Hartford seen in a purple light. [Hartford 226-18
Purple sets purple round. Look, Master, [Hartford 227-5
Were violet, yellow, purple, pink. The grass [Horn 230-9
Inhale the purple fragrance. It becomes [News 265-8
Let purple Phoebus lie in umber harvest, [NSF 381-8
The purple odor, the abundant bloom. [NSF 395-3
And laughed, as he sat there reading, from out of the purple
    tabulae, [Large 424-4
Cry out, "I am the purple muse." Make sure [Bad Time 427-8
How facilely the purple blotches fell [NH 484-4
On the walk, purple and blue, and red and gold, [NH 484-5
And of purple blooming in the eucalyptus-- [Primordia 9-12 P
And purple timbers, [Archi 18-6 P
Oh! How suave a purple passed me by! [Stan MMO 19-3 P
He called hydrangeas purple. And they were. [Abnormal 23-16
It was a purple changeable to see. [Abnormal 24-2 P
Fly from the black toward the purple air. [Infernale 25-2 P
And downward, from this purple region, thrown; [Infernale 25-7 P
Blue and vermilion, purple and white, [Mandolin 28-20 P
A purple woman with a lavender tongue [Melancholy 32-6 P
Than purple paste of fruit, to taste, or leaves [Greenest 58-31 P
Of purple flowers, to see? The black will still [Greenest 58-32 P
For battle, the purple for victory. But if [Bship 79-7 P
A white, pink, purple berry tree, [Banjo 114-3 P
More purple to see; [Three 141-8 P
An Alp, a purple Southern mountain bisqued [Someone 87-3 A
See polar-purple.
PURPLING. Waving purpling wands, the thinker [Ulysses 100-19 P
PURPLE-LEAPING. A purple-leaping element that forth [Descrip
    341-16
PURPLE-PLATED. And, hoy, the impopulous purple-plated past, [Montra
    260-5
PURPLES. Through all its purples to the final slate, [Pharynx 96-11
PURPORTS. Their purports to a final seriousness-- [Armor 530-6
PURPOSE. What was the purpose of his pilgrimage, [C 37-5
    That the beholder knew their subtle purpose, [New Set 353-2
    The purpose of the poem, fills the room. [AA 413-9
    Of what one sees, the purpose that comes first, [Moonlight 531-7
    The surface, is the purpose to be seen, [Moonlight 531-8
    So much just to be seen--a purpose, empty [Moonlight 532-4
    Perhaps, absurd perhaps, but at least a purpose, [Moonlight 532-5
    And purpose, to hear the wild bee drone, to feel [Greenest 56-25 P
    The incredible gave him a purpose to believe. [Someone 85-18 A
PURPOSES. As if, among the possible purposes [Moonlight 531-6
PURSUE. And still pursue, the origin and course [Monocle 18-1
PURSUED. Like a rose rabbi, later, I pursued, [Monocle 17-25
    Endless pursuit or endlessly pursued, [Greenest 55-22 P
PURSUING. Of pursuing feet. [Three 136-4 P
PURSUIT. Young weasels racing steep horizons in pursuit of planets
    . . . [Inelegance 26-8 P
    Endless pursuit or endlessly pursued, [Greenest 55-22 P
PUSH. Push up the towers [Archi 17-15 P
PUSHING. Pushing their buds above the dark green leaves, [Nigger
    156-11
    Pushing and pushing red after red. [Red Fern 365-4
    But one lives to think of this growing, this pushing life, [Bship
    80-8 P
PUT. One is already a grandfather and to have put there [Lack 303-18
    Or we put mantles on our words because [Look 519-1
PUTATIVE. Far, far beyond the putative canzones [Extracts 256-7
PUTRID. To Belshazzar, putrid rock, [Country 207-4
    Pillar of a putrid people, [Country 207-5
PUTS. That puts an end to evil death and dies. [Extracts 253-25
    "Someone Puts a Pineapple Together" [83-title A
PUTTING. Merely by putting hand to brow, [Oak 272-11
    The stars are putting on their glittering belts. [AA 419-22
PUVIS. A subject for Puvis. He would compose [Anach 366-4
    And Bloom would see what Puvis did, protest [Anach 366-6
PYLON. Pylon and pier fell down. [Public Sq 109-2
PYRAMID. At the upper right, a pyramid with one side [What We 460-2

QUACK. Convinces Athens with its quack. [Grotesque 75-13 P
QUAERITUR. And lex. Sed quaeritur: is this same wig [C 27-10
QUAIL. He did not quail. A man so used to plumb [Geneva 24-7
  Deer walk upon our mountains, and the quail [Sunday 70-22
QUAINTLY. The wind blows quaintly [Our Stars 454-15
QUAKES. May be perceived in windy quakes [Room Gard 41-5 P
QUALM. The late, least foyer in a qualm of cold. [Novel 457-15
QUARTER. Something returning from a deeper quarter, [Imago 439-15
  And still the final quarter, still the rim, [Spaniard 34-9 P
  I'd rather not. No doubt there's a quarter here, [Lytton 39-24 P
QUARTERS. See three-quarters.
QUARTER-THINGS. With the half colors of quarter-things, [Motive 288-6
QUAVERING. Still quavering. [Peter 91-2
QUAVERINGS. The greenish quaverings of day [Stan MBG 73-5 P
QUAVERS. Let down gigantic quavers of its voice, [C 33-16
QUEEN. But no queen rises. [Depression 63-8
  But no queen comes [Depression 63-17
  And queen, and of diviner love the day [Fictive 87-9
  The abstract, the archaic queen. Green is the night. [Candle 223-14
  Into a single thought, thus: into a queen, [Extracts 254-8
  The queen of ignorance, you have deplored [Feo 333-11
  Or sleep. It was a queen that made it seem [Descrip 339-7
  The queen is an example . . . This green queen [Descrip 339-10
  Peculiar to the queen, this queen or that, [Descrip 340-1
  An age is a manner collected from a queen. [Descrip 340-5
  In the major manner of a queen, the green [Descrip 340-12
  The red, the blue, the argent queen. If not, [Descrip 340-13
  And is the queen humble as she seems to be, [Cred 374-25
  Ababba, expecting this king's queen to appear? [Golden 461-3
  "He is the consort of the Queen of Fact. [NH 485-6
  As he has been and is and, with the Queen [NH 485-17
  In that distant chamber, a bearded queen, wicked in her dead light. [Madame 507-13
QUEER. Queer, in this Vallombrosa of ears, [Arcades 225-5
  In a queer assertion of humanity: [Rock 525-15
  Inside our queer chapeaux, we seem, on this bank, [Nuns 92-15 P
QUEERED. And queered by lavishings of their will to see. [Bouquet 451-4
QUEERER. Of the week, queerer than Sunday. We thought alike [AA 419-10
QUESTION. The prologues are over. It is a question, now, [Oboe 250-6
  The skeleton said it is a question of [Montra 262-10
  Ill of a question like a malady, [Pure 331-7
  Ill of a constant question in his thought, [Pure 331-8
  Should there be a question of returning or [NSF 391-2
  It is not a question of captious repartee. [Bad Time 426-19
  And red, and right. The particular question--here [Ulti 429-12
  The particular answer to the particular question [Ulti 429-13
  Is not in point--the question is in point. [Ulti 429-14
  But not for him. His question is complete. [Questions 462-12
  It is the question of what he is capable. [Questions 462-13
  His question is complete because it contains [Questions 462-16
  Part of the question that is a giant himself: [NH 465-8
  As a quick answer modifies a question, [NH 471-6
  Nor not knowing, yet free from question, [Aug 495-10
  It was a rabbi's question. Let the rabbis reply. [Bship 79-14 P
  That question the repetition on the shore, [Woman Had 82-3 P
  That raises the question of the image's truth. [Myth 118-10 P
QUESTIONER. As a questioner about reality, [Warmth 89-18 P
QUESTIONERS. Four questioners and four sure answerers. [C 45-10
QUESTIONING. Still questioning if to crush the soaring stacks, [Sombre 68-31 P
QUESTIONINGS. Of misty fields, by their sweet questionings; [Sunday 68-14
QUESTIONS. One goes on asking questions. That, then, is one [Ulti 429-16
  There must be no questions. It is an intellect [Ulti 429-19
  Are questions of the looks they get. The bouquet, [Bouquet 451-2
  "Questions Are Remarks" [462-title
QUICK. For me, the firefly's quick, electric stroke [Monocle 15-1
  Loudened by cries, by clashes, quick and sure [Monocle 16-13
  Of the quick that's wry. [Orangeade 103-20
  As quick as foxes on the hill; [Postcard 158-16
  Physical if the eye is quick enough, [Choc 301-6
  That sends us back to the first idea, the quick [NSF 381-17
  Of rose, stood tall in self not symbol, quick [Owl 435-6
  As a quick answer modifies a question, [NH 471-6
  Quick to be gone, yet never [Soldat 12-5 P
  By imagining, anti-logician, quick [Sombre 66-21 P
QUICKEN. And the circles quicken and crystal colors come [Anach 366-13
QUICKENED. The body quickened and the mind in root. [Rock 527-10
QUICKENINGS. Of his brave quickenings, the human [Hero 279-3
QUICK-EYED. And the serpent might become a god, quick-eyed, [Greenest 54-23 P

QUICKLY. Leaps quickly from the fireside and is gone. [Montra 264-6
  A tempest cracked on the theatre. Quickly, [Repet 306-1
  Or chosen quickly, in a freedom [Creat 310-14
  And quickly understand, without their flesh, [Cats 368-9
  Its line moves quickly with the genius [Pastor 379-9
  And death cries quickly, in a flash of voice, [Owl 432-13
  Of my shoulder and quickly, too quickly, I am gone? [Angel 497-10
  Weaving ring in radiant ring and quickly, fling [Burnshaw 51-14 P
  Reach the lady quickly. [Three 136-13 P
  That steeps the room, quickly, then not at all, [Someone 87-15 A
QUICKNESSES. Embellished by the quicknesses of sight, [Bouquet 451-10
QUIET. Brings back an earlier season of quiet [Lunar 107-10
  The touch. Fix quiet. Take the place [Prelude 195-19
  After the sermon, to quiet that mouse in the wall. [Blue Bldg 216-20
  The room is quiet where they are. [Peaches 224-15
  Night and day, wind and quiet, produces [Vari 233-21
  "The House Was Quiet and the World Was Calm" [358-title
  The house was quiet and the world was calm. [House Q 358-7
  The house was quiet and the world was calm. [House Q 358-10
  The house was quiet because it had to be. [House Q 358-16
  The quiet was part of the meaning, part of the mind: [House Q 358-17
  In the quiet there. [Woman Song 361-6
  Without any feeling, an imperium of quiet, [Burghers 362-16
  But now he sits in quiet and green-a-day. [AA 414-13
  As if, awake, we lay in the quiet of sleep, [AA 418-24
  Keep quiet in the heart, O wild bitch. O mind [Puel 456-13
  Of the quiet of the middle of the night, [Aug 491-7
  A meaning which, as he entered it, would shatter the boat and leave the oarsmen quiet [Prol 516-7
  "A Quiet Normal Life" [523-title
  On which the quiet moonlight lies. [Archi 17-21 P
  Speech for the quiet, good hail of himself, good hail, good hail, [Sick 90-20 P
  Wrenched out of chaos . . . The quiet lamp [Ulysses 100-23 P
QUIETEN. It took all day to quieten the sky [NH 482-20
QUIETING. And quieting dreams in the sleepers in darkness-- [Lunar 107-11
QUIETLY. To speak quietly at such a distance, to speak [Choc 296-7
  His stars on the wall. He must dwell quietly. [Less 327-14
  Good-by in the darkness, speaking quietly there, [Owl 431-17
  Who reads quietly: [Inhab 503-20
QUIETS. Who by his highness quiets them, high peace [Owl 431-14
QUIETUDE. So, then, this warm, wide, weatherless quietude [Moon-light 531-19
QUILL. With his own quill, in its indigenous dew, [C 31-19
  For Crispin and his quill to catechize. [C 31-33
  It is not the snow that is the quill, the page. [Bottle 239-13
QUILT. Hangs her quilt under the pine-trees. [Primordia 9-16 P
QUILTED. Lies quilted to his poll in his despite. [C 41-30
QUILTS. Of honest quilts, the eye of Crispin, hung [C 27-17
  The very man despising honest quilts [C 41-29
QUINCE. See Peter Quince.
QUINTESSENTIAL. Of force, the quintessential fact, the note [C 33-5
QUIRK. Old worm, my pretty quirk, [Metamorph 265-14
QUIRKED. Regarded by the meta-men, is quirked [Bouquet 451-3
QUIRKS. Of golden quirks and Paphian caricatures, [Swans 4-6
  Knew not the quirks of imagery, [Frogs 78-9
QUIRKY. Is breathless to attend each quirky turn. [Monocle 15-13
QUITE. John Constable they could never quite transplant [Nigger 154-2
  I cannot bring a world quite round, [MBG 165-11
  Mechanical beetles never quite warm? [MBG 168-15
  To know that the balance does not quite rest, [MBG 181-9
  Red purple, never quite red itself. [Arcades 225-16
  Not quite. The mist was to light what red [Vari 235-20
  Of things that would never be quite expressed, [Motive 288-10
  Where you yourself were never quite yourself [Motive 288-11
  What meditation never quite achieved. [EM 314-23
  Not quite detected at the moment of change [Pure 332-4
  Burst back. What not quite realized transit [Feo 333-20
  Yet two not quite of a kind. It is like that here. [Jouga 337-10
  She will think about them not quite able to sing. [Debris 338-9
  But not quite molten, not quite the fluid thing, [Myrrh 350-4
  As secondary (parts not quite perceived [Man Car 350-18
  Lie lengthwise like the cloud of sleep, not quite [Two V 354-4
  In a moving contour, a change not quite completed? [NSF 406-9
  Of indolent summer not quite physical [Bouquet 451-15
  Not quite. It comes to the point and at the point, [NH 477-11
  The height was not quite proper; [Aug 493-19
  Quite going? [Soldat 12-6
  Are two quite different things, in particular [Lytton 39-8 P
  And because the temple is never quite composed, [Burnshaw 50-14 P
  Because he desired without knowing quite what, [Local 112-9 P
QUITTANCE. Cried quittance [Ord Women 12-1
QUIVER. And He felt a subtle quiver, [Pourtraicte 22-4
  Intangible arrows quiver and stick in the skin [Holiday 313-9

Quiver upon the blue guitar. [Stan MBG 73-6 P
QUIVERING. Her body quivering in the Floréal [Lilacs 49-10
  Than the horses quivering to be gone, flashed through [Duck
    64-9 P
QUIZ. I quiz all sounds, all thought, all everything [Monocle
    16-19
QUOI. He quoi! Angels go pricking elephants? [Greenest 55-30 P
QUOTE. Of men and earth: I quote the line and page, [Soldat 11-8 P
  I quote the very phrase my masters used. [Soldat 11-9 P
QUOTHA. One eats one paté, even of salt, quotha. [C 28-1
QUOTIDIAN. Yet the quotidian saps philosophers [C 42-22
  But the quotidian composed as his, [C 42-25
  That lay beside him, the quotidian [C 43-4
  The malady of the quotidian . . . [Pharynx 96-9

R. The river motion, the drowsy motion of the river R. [Old Man
  501-6
RABBI. Grown tired of flight. Like a dark rabbi, I [Monocle 17-21
  Like a rose rabbi, later, I pursued, [Monocle 17-25
  Oh! Rabbi, rabbi, .fend my soul for me [Sun March 134-7
  What rabbi, grown furious with human wish, [NSF 389-1
  Read, rabbi, the phases of this difference. [AA 420-5
  We'll give the week-end to wisdom to Weisheit, the rabbi, [Aug
  492-1
    It was a rabbi's question. Let the rabbis reply. [Bship 79-14 P
RABBIS. All alike, except for the rules of the rabbis, [Nigger
  151-7
    It was a rabbi's question. Let the rabbis reply. [Bship 79-14 P
RABBIT. But let the rabbit run, the cock declaim. [C 39-32
  The rabbit fat, at last, in glassy grass. [Nigger 153-20
  "A Rabbit as King of the Ghosts" [209-title
  She strides above the rabbit and the cat, [Candle 223-3
  The topaz rabbit and the emerald cat, [Candle 223-10
  See jack-rabbit.
RABBIT-LIGHT. And to feel that the light is a rabbit-light,
  [Rabbit K 209-10
RACE. The race that sings and weeps and knows not why. [Thought
  186-16
  A man with the fury of a race of men, [Bottle 239-2
  In humanity has not conceived of a race [EM 325-25
  To be admired by nations. The race is brave. [Paisant 334-20
  The race endures. The funeral pomps of the race [Paisant 334-21
  The whole race is a poet that writes down [Men Made 356-5
  The rest look down. One man becomes a race, [Cred 374-22
  A likeness, one of the race of fathers: earth [Irish 502-7
  The admiral of his race and everyman, [Duck 62-4 P
  Exceeding sex, he touched another race, [Duck 64-25 P
  Above our race, yet of ourselves transformed, [Duck 64-26 P
  A race of dwarfs, the meditative arms [Sombre 70-27 P
  Man-misty to a race star-humped, astride [Sombre 70-29 P
  The race, the nation, the state. But society [Bship 79-21 P
  A race that is a hero, entirely [Stan Hero 84-4 P
  As a free race. We know it, one [Ulysses 102-4 P
RACED. Raced with the horses in bright hurricanes. [Old Woman
  43-4 P
RACES. For races, not for men, powerful beyond [Greenest 59-29 P
  Parades of whole races with attendant bands, [Duck 66-2 P
  So, too, of the races of appropriate people [Art Pop 113-4 P
RACINE. Unless Racine or Bossuet held the like. [Geneva 24-6
RACING. Young weasels racing steep horizons in pursuit of planets
  ... [Inelegance 26-8 P
RACK. Will rack the thickets. There is no place, [MBG 182-16
RACKED. If more than the wished-for ruin racked the night, [Sombre
  69-12 P
RACKING. That must belie the racking masquerade, [C 39-16
  Racking the world with clarion puffs. This must [Greenest 56-12 P
RACKS. The trade-wind jingles the rings in the nets around the
  racks by the docks on Indian River. [Indian 112-4
RADIAL. Picked up its radial aspect in the night, [NH 478-23
  At another time, the radial aspect came [NH 479-2
  What is the radial aspect of this place, [NH 479-10
RADIANCE. In radiance from the Atlantic coign, [C 31-32
  When radiance came running down, slim through the bareness.
  [Banal 63-2
  And in its watery radiance, while the hue [Sea Surf 99-12
  And from what thinking did his radiance come? [Choc 299-7
  No radiance of dead blaze, but something seen [Armor 529-13
RADIANT. The radiant bubble that she was. And then [Monocle 13-9
  But what are radiant reason and radiant will [Medit 124-7
  A thousand are radiant in the sky. [MBG 172-10
  Since the radiant disclosures that you make [Burnshaw 48-11 P
  Weaving ring in radiant ring and quickly, fling [Burnshaw 51-14 P
  Loftily jingled, radiant, [Ulysses 100-21 P
RADIANTIANA. The sky with the radiantiana [Vari 234-15
RADIANTLY. Yet radiantly beyond must lustier blurs. [Nigger 155-19
RADIO. Listened to the radio, [Thought 184-8
RADISHES. A bed of radishes. [Pourtraicte 21-2
  Of radishes and flowers. [Pourtraicte 21-9
  Of radishes and flowers." [Pourtraicte 21-19
RAEL. It is curious that I should have spoken of Raël, [Desire
  85-1 P
  Was it desire that created Raël [Desire 85-15 P
RAFTERS. As to rafters or grass. [Tattoo 81-18
RAG. Say this to Pravda, tell the damned rag [Memo 89-9 P
RAGE. Oh! Blessed rage for order, pale Ramon, [Key W 130-11
  The maker's rage to order words of the sea, [Key W 130-12
  For his rage against chaos [Winter B 141-10
  The powdered personals against the giant's rage, [Repet 309-17
  Rage in the ring and shake the corridors. [Spaniard 35-1 P
RAGGED. Ragged in unkempt perceptions, that stands [Theatre 91-8 P
RAGGEDER. Though poor, though raggeder than ruin, have that [Belly
  367-10
RAGS. A body in rags. [Mozart 132-1

They pose themselves and their rags. [Add 198-10
  In the mind, pupa of straw, moppet of rags. [Dwarf 208-6
  And thereby lost, and naked or in rags, [NH 484-17
RAILROAD. The crawling railroad spur, the rotten fence, [C 36-14
  See the river, the railroad, the cathedral . . . [Hartford 227-6
  Of the town, the river, the railroad were clear. [Hartford 227-8
RAILS. The beads on her rails seemed to grasp at transparence.
  [Vari 236-2
RAILWAY. At the railway station, a soldier steps away, [Repet 308-3
  The same railway passenger, the ancient tree [Cats 367-16
RAILWAY-STOPS. One seed alone grow wild, the railway-stops [Cats
  367-14
RAIN. A bronze rain from the sun descending marks [Swans 4-3
  The natives of the rain are rainy men. [C 37-27
  Passions of rain, or moods in falling snow; [Sunday 67-20
  Was like a willow swept by rain. [Peter 91-17
  To that casino. Long before the rain [Havana 142-18
  The clouds foretell a swampy rain. [Fish-Scale 161-6
  Its wings spread wide to rain and snow, [MBG 166-8
  Which is enough: the moment's rain and sea, [Freed 204-19
  Is blowing after days of constant rain. [Connois 216-5
  And rain, the blood-rose living in its smell, [Extracts 252-5
  To naked men, to women naked as rain. [Extracts 252-14
  Rain is an unbearable tyranny. Sun is [Extracts 252-21
  As facts fall like rejuvenating rain, [Montra 263-22
  The rain falls. The sky [Metamorph 266-4
  Of the wind, rain in a dry September, [Hero 275-13
  They walk in mist and rain and snow [Poesie 302-13
  It was a blue scene washing white in the rain, [Repet 306-19
  The rain is pouring down. It is July. [Chaos 357-9
  Place-bound and time-bound in evening rain [Human 363-1
  Rain without change within or from [Human 363-5
  In which the rain is all one thing, [Human 363-8
  And sun and rain a plural, like two lovers [NSF 392-14
  There was such idiot minstrelsy in rain, [NSF 394-4
  The channel slots in rain, the red-rose-red [NSF 400-8
  The rain falls with a ramshackle sound. He seeks [NH 475-9
  Of the rain in the spout is not a substitute. [NH 475-20
  He preserves himself against the repugnant rain [NH 475-22
  The rain kept falling loudly in the trees [NH 476-7
  If only in the branches sweeping in the rain: [NH 481-1
  As rain and booming, gleaming, blowing, swept [NH 484-10
  Without rain, there is the sadness of rain [Aug 495-19
  There's rain. The season grieves. [Phases 3-6 P
  Approaching rain [Bowl 7-3 P
  Tho driving rain, the willows in the rain, [Soldat 13-12 P
  The birds that wait out rain in willow leaves. [Soldat 13-13 P
  The sounds of rain on the roof [Secret Man 35-21 P
  The rain falls at its base, [Secret Man 36-7 P
  With rain. [Room Gard 41-15 P
  The spontaneities of rain or snow [Sombre 67-31 P
  Is a residue, a land, a rain, a warmth, [How Now 97-10 P
  See Paris-rain.
RAINBOW. And rainbow sortilege, the savage weapon [Hero 274-3
  The rainbow in its glistening serpentines [Burnshaw 47-28 P
RAINBOWED. On the seat of halidom, rainbowed, [Ulysses 104-5 P
RAINBOWS. Under the rainbows; [Sugar-Cane 12-11
  Under the rainbows [Sugar-Cane 12-12
  Even enthroned on rainbows in the sight [Hero 277-27
RAINED. Out of my mind the golden ointment rained, [Hoon 65-13
RAINLESS. By an instinct for a rainless land, the self [NH 475-23
RAIN-POINTED. What are you drawing from the rain-pointed water?
  [Primordia 9-2 P
  What are you drawing from the rain-pointed water? [Primordia
  9-4 P
RAINS. Washed into rinds by rotting winter rains. [Monocle 16-11
RAIN-STAINED-VAULTS. Of bird-nest arches and of rain-stained-
  vaults. [Rome 510-10
RAINY. The natives of the rain are rainy men. [C 37-27
  A blue beyond the rainy hyacinth, [Sea Surf 101-1
  And, otherwise, the rainy rose belongs [Extracts 252-13
  And come to nothing. Let the rainy arcs [Repet 310-3
  The dry eucalyptus seeks god in the rainy cloud. [NH 475-4
RAISE. Raise reddest columns. Toll a bell [MBG 170-5
  He does not raise the rousing of fresh light [Aug 492-22
RAISED. His mind raised up, down-drowned, the chariots. [Descrip
  343-12
  An opening for outpouring, the hand was raised: [NH 483-2
  In one, except a throne raised up beyond [Greenest 55-10 P
  And beads and bangles of gold and trumpets raised, [Greenest
  56-11 P
RAISES. The mightier mother raises up her cry; [Soldat 14-16 P
  That raises the question of the image's truth. [Myth 118-10 P
RAKES. Order, the law of hoes and rakes, [Room Gard 41-4 P
RAMON. Oh! Blessed rage for order, pale Ramon, [Key W 130-11
RAMON FERNANDEZ. Ramon Fernandez, tell me, if you know, [Key W
  130-3
RAMSHACKLE. The window, close to the ramshackle spout in which
  [NH 475-8
  The rain falls with a ramshackle sound. He seeks [NH 475-9

RAN. Ran like rats, [Tea 112-11
  The fox ran out of his hole. [On Road 203-15
  When he looked, the water ran up the air or grew white [Extracts
    255-17
RANCID. He inhaled the rancid rosin, burly smells [C 36-7
  In which were yellow, rancid skeletons. [Stan MMO 19-2 P
RANG. Where triumph rang its brassy phrase, or love [Sunday 69-5
  The gongs rang loudly as the windy booms [Sea Surf 100-4
  Long since, rang out farewell, farewell, farewell. [EM 322-17
  He was facing phantasma when the bell rang. [Dinner 109-24 P
RANGE. Do they believe they range the gusty cold, [Heaven 56-12
  The sharpest self, the sensible range, [Adequacy 244-10
RANKEST. Of rankest trivia, tests of the strength [C 37-13
RANKLED. That have rankled for many lives and made no sound.
  [Sketch 336-3
RANKNESS. He savored rankness like a sensualist. [C 36-12
RANSOM. It would be ransom for the willow [Snow Stars 133-10
RAPE. The rape of the bourgeoisie accomplished, the men [Bship
  77-13 P
RAPEY. The rapey gouts. Good star, how that to be [C 42-20
RAPHAEL. Full of Raphael's costumes; [Phases 5-17 P
RAPIDLY. It is someone walking rapidly in the street. [Pure 330-1
  Dark horse and walker walking rapidly. [Pure 330-12
  The large-leaved day grows rapidly, [Red Fern 365-1
  He leaps from heaven to heaven more rapidly [AA 414-11
RAPPORT. An intercessor by innate rapport, [Extracts 254-9
RAPT. And the eccentric twistings of the rapt bouquet [Bouquet
  450-20
  It will be fecund in rapt curios. [Red Kit 32-5 P
  Infected by unreality, rapt round [Duck 62-5 P
RAPTURE. Or paper souvenirs of rapture, [Jasmine 79-9
  And forth the particulars of rapture come. [NSF 392-9
  The reconciliation, the rapture of a time [Sombre 71-22 P
RAPTUROUS. Of its brown wheat rapturous in the wind, [Aug 491-15
RARE. Most rare, or ever of more kindred air [Fictive 87-21
  Through the gross tedium of being rare. [Nigger 155-22
  Be merely a masquerade or else a rare [Greenest 56-13 P
RAREFIED. Yet with a harmony not rarefied [C 35-19
RAREST. Even the rarest-- [Bowl 6-14 P
RARITIES. His rarities are ours: may they be fit [Havana 144-19
RASPBERRY. As if raspberry tanagers in palms, [C 30-20
RAT. A baby with the tail of a rat? [Horn 230-7
  Of a sort, silence of a rat come out to see, [Plain 503-5
RATHER. Has rather a classical sound. [Circulat 150-8
  Happy rather than holy but happy-high, [Thought 185-17
  That sort of thing was always rather stiff. [Lytton 39-18 P
  I'd rather not. No doubt there's a quarter here, [Lytton 39-24 P
  Rather rings than fingers, rather fingers than hands. [Grotesque
    74-8 P
RATIONAL. That's it: the more than rational distortion, [NSF 406-20
  Pleased that the irrational is rational, [NSF 406-24
RATIONALIST. Surprise the sterile rationalist who sees [Sombre
  67-32 P
RATIONALISTS. Rationalists, wearing square hats, [Six Sig 75-4
  Rationalists would wear sombreros. [Six Sig 75-13
RATS. Ran like rats, [Tea 112-11
RATTAPALLAX. Heavy with thunder's rattapallax, [Frogs 78-6
  This somnolence and rattapallax, [Frogs 78-12
RATTLE. But salvation here? What about the rattle of sticks
  [Parochial 191-17
RATTLED. Of the rhododendrons rattled their gold, [Sleight 222-5
RATTLES. Rattles with fear in unreflecting leaves. [Golden 460-15
RATTLING. Sonorous nutshells rattling inwardly. [C 31-13
  Are rattling." [Jack-Rabbit 50-17
RAVISHMENTS. Are the ravishments of truth, so fatal to [NSF 381-19
RAY. Enlarging like a nocturnal ray [Ulysses 100-25 P
RAYED. We hang like warty squashes, streaked and rayed, [Monocle
  16-9
RAYS. Would swoop to earth? It is a wheel, the rays [Sleight 222-10
  Saved and beholden, in a robe of rays. [NH 477-24
REACH. For I reach right up to the sun, [Six Sig 74-7
  And I reach to the shore of the sea [Six Sig 74-9
  And reach through him almost to man. [MBG 165-16
  It is here, in this bad, that we reach [Possum 294-13
  The human end in the spirit's greatest reach, [Rome 508-16
  Reach from the horizons, rim to rim, [Sombre 68-25 P
  Reach the lady quickly. [Three 136-13 P
REACHED. In a place supposed, a thing that he reached [Landsc 242-9
  In a place that he reached, by rejecting what he saw [Landsc
    242-10
  Not to be reached but to be known, [Ulysses 101-25 P
REACHES. The swans fled outward to remoter reaches, [Descrip 343-7
  And reaches, beaches, tomorrow's regions became [Descrip 343-13
  Is there a poem that never reaches words [NSF 396-18
REACTION. Its irrational reaction, as from pain. [John 437-26
READ. And there they read of marriage-bed. [Ord Women 11-14
  And they read right long. [Ord Women 11-16
  To be the book in which to read a round, [Monocle 14-17
  Of love, it is a book too mad to read [Monocle 14-21
  To read, in secret, burning secrecies. . . . [Polish Aunt 84-11

No lamp was burning as I read, [Reader 147-4
Read in the ruins of a new society, [Nigger 153-3
In the cathedral, I sat there, and read, [MBG 180-19
In how severe a book he read, [Thought 186-21
He read, all day, all night and all the nights, [Blue Bldg 216-16
It is difficult to read. The page is dark. [Phosphor 267-5
In which we read the critique of paradise [Crude 305-9
For a moment, a moment in which we read and repeat [Pure 333-8
A text we should be born that we might read and repeat [Des 344-21
Sour wine to warm him, an empty book to read; [Good Man 364-11
Epitaphium to his death, which read, [Good Man 364-13
Read, rabbi, the phases of this difference. [AA 420-5
Read to the congregation, for today [AA 420-16
There were those that returned to hear him read from the poem of
  life, [Large 423-14
I love to sit and read the Telegraph, [Mandolin 29-6 P
A legend scrawled in script we cannot read? [Recit 87-10 P
The giant sea, read his own mind. [Ulysses 99-12 P
The giant sea, read his own mind. [Presence 105-15 P
READER. "The Reader" [146-title
  The reader by the window has finished his book [Pure 330-2
  The reader became the book; and summer night [House Q 358-8
  Except that the reader leaned above the page, [House Q 358-12
  Is the reader leaning late and reading there. [House Q 359-4
  The thinker as reader reads what has been written. [Aug 492-4
  A reader of the text, [Inhab 503-18
  A reader without a body, [Inhab 503-19
READILY. The world, a turnip once so readily plucked, [C 45-12
READINESS. There was a clearing, a readiness for first bells, [NH
  483-1
READING. Reading where I have written, [Of Surface 57-4
  Reading the lordly language of the inscription, [Mice 123-7
  All night I sat reading a book, [Reader 146-13
  Sat reading as if in a book [Reader 146-14
  It wants Belshazzar reading right [Country 207-20
  "Phosphor Reading by His Own Light" [267-title
  The afternoon's reading, the night's reflection, [Hero 274-23
  And, between his letters, reading paragraphs [EM 313-12
  Is the reader leaning late and reading there. [House Q 359-4
  Drowned in its washes, reading in the sound, [NSF 387-10
  "Large Red Man Reading" [423-title
  As he sat there reading, aloud, the great blue tabulae. [Large
    423-12
  And laughed, as he sat there reading, from out of the purple
    tabulae, [Large 424-4
  Writing and reading the rigid inscription. [Aug 495-16
READS. Before one merely reads to pass the time. [Monocle 14-22
  That it puffs as Cornelius Nepos reads, it puffs [Dump 202-3
  In your light, the head is speaking. It reads the book. [God 285-10
  Who reads no book. His ruddy ancientness [Cred 374-2
  The thinker as reader reads what has been written. [Aug 492-4
  He wears the words he reads to look upon [Aug 492-5
  Who reads quietly: [Inhab 503-20
READY. So you're home again, Redwood Roamer, and ready [Phenom
  286-13
  The bloody lion in the yard at night or ready to spring [Puel
    456-6
  See ever-ready.
REAL. Of the real that wrenches, [Orangeade 103-19
  The imagined and the real, thought [MBG 177-16
  It was everything being more real, himself [Freed 205-20
  While she approached the real, upon her mountain, [Uruguay 249-8
  Rushing from what was real; and capable? [Uruguay 249-24
  Is real, part of a land beyond the mind? [Extracts 252-20
  Skims the real for its unreal, [Oak 272-15
  That he be not conceived, being real. [Hero 279-14
  It had been real. It was something overseas [Repet 306-4
  It had been real. It was not now. The rip [Repet 306-5
  Of the wind and the glittering were real now, [Repet 306-8
  On a few words of what is real in the world [Repet 308-13
  Whatever remains. Of what is real I say, [Repet 308-15
  A few words of what is real or may be [Repet 309-6
  Or of glistening reference to what is real, [Repet 309-7
  After all, they knew that to be real each had [Holiday 312-11
  These are real only if I make them so. Whistle [Holiday 313-7
  And I taste at the root of the tongue the unreal of what is real.
    [Holiday 313-10
  A horror of thoughts that suddenly are real. [Man Car 351-6
  On the real. This is the origin of change. [NSF 392-7
  Cold, coldly delineating, being real, [NSF 400-2
  The real will from its crude compoundings come, [NSF 404-6
  Warmed by a desperate milk. To find the real, [NSF 404-8
  How simply the fictive hero becomes the real; [NSF 408-1
  Less real. For the oldest and coldest philosopher, [AA 418-9
  There was so much that was real that was not real at all. [Cata
    425-1
  Too actual, things that in being real [Roses 430-14
  We feel and, therefore, is not real, except [Roses 430-17
  The real made more acute by an unreal. [Bouquet 451-21
  In which a real lies hidden and alive. [Novel 458-15

That Argentine. Only the real can be [Novel 458-20
Everything as unreal as real can be, [NH 468-18
To our sepulchral hollows. Love of the real [NH 470-18
To the real: to the hotel instead of the hymns [NH 471-11
We do not know what is real and what is not. [NH 472-8
From the sleepy bosom of the real, re-creates, [NH 481-20
What was real turned into something most unreal, [NH 483-23
A real ruler, but rules what is unreal." [NH 485-4
Real and unreal are two in one: New Haven [NH 485-23
Above the real, [Irish 501-14
A flick which added to what was real and its vocabulary, [Prol 517-5
Which is real-- [Indigo 22-10 P
From which they came, make real the attitudes [Burnshaw 52-3 P
Its tuft of emerald that is real, for all [Someone 85-16 A
REALIST. The old age of a watery realist, [C 28-23
Had kept him still the prickling realist, [C 40-6
He first, as realist, admitted that [C 40-26
And be content and still be realist. [C 40-29
For realist, what is is what should be. [C 41-31
And sown again by the stiffest realist, [C 45-15
In music. Crow is realist. But, then, [Nigger 154-15
Oriole, also, may be realist. [Nigger 154-16
Look, realist, not knowing what you expect. [Phosphor 267-11
When the phantoms are gone and the shaken realist [EM 320-7
In the yes of the realist spoken because he must [EM 320-12
The exhausted realist beholds [Abnormal 24-15 P
REALISTS. Out of rigid realists. It is as if [NH 470-4
REALITIES. Of realities, that, in which it could be wrong. [Forces 229-17
REALITY. The imagination, the one reality [Weep Woman 25-8
Here was no help before reality. [C 30-5
A new reality in parrot-squawks. [C 32-12
Before they fly, test the reality [Sunday 68-13
An absence in reality, [MBG 176-19
At the centre of reality, seeing it. [Freed 205-21
Of reality, beyond the knowledge of what [Extracts 252-19
Black water breaking into reality. [Extracts 255-22
Acts in reality, adds nothing [Hero 279-10
In the spectacle of a new reality. [Repet 306-9
This being in a reality beyond [Repet 307-11
Of the clear sovereign that is reality, [Repet 307-21
Of the clearest reality that is sovereign, [Repet 307-22
The gigantic has a reality of its own. [Repet 308-12
Her vague "Secrete me from reality," [Repet 309-20
His "That reality secrete itself," [Repet 309-21
Secrete us in reality. It is there [Repet 310-1
Secrete us in reality. Discover [Repet 310-5
"Holiday in Reality" [312-title
First sees reality. The mortal no [EM 320-8
Because she is as she was, reality, [EM 322-1
Of impersonal pain. Reality explained. [EM 322-3
The ultimate good, sure of a reality [EM 324-16
Reality, composed thereof. They are [Paisant 335-5
A little different from reality: [Descrip 344-3
And speak of the floridest reality . . . [Anach 366-7
One of the limits of reality [Cred 374-6
They were those that would have wept to step barefoot into
  reality, [Large 423-16
In which reality is prodigy. [Owl 432-9
Of the reality of the eye, an artifice, [Bouquet 448-12
One approaches, simply, the reality [Bouquet 448-14
A recent imagining of reality, [NH 465-15
Reality as a thing seen by the mind, [NH 468-12
Reality is the beginning not the end, [NH 469-4
The poem of pure reality, untouched [NH 471-13
Nothing beyond reality. Within it, [NH 471-21
This faithfulness of reality, this mode, [NH 472-19
Reality but reality grimly seen [NH 475-15
For reality is as momentous as [NH 481-5
As follows, "The Ruler of Reality, [NH 485-2
If it should be true that reality exists [NH 485-19
It is not in the premise that reality [NH 489-1
I am the angel of reality, [Angel 496-7
Of the harsh reality of which it is part. [Plant 506-19
A new knowledge of reality. [Not Ideas 534-18
As a questioner about reality, [Warmth 89-18 P
Part of the major reality, part of [Warmth 90-3 P
An appreciation of a reality; [Warmth 90-4 P
Like the artifice of a new reality, [Theatre 91-5 P
Like glass and sun, of male reality [Fare Guit 99-8 P
"Reality Is an Activity of the Most August Imagination" [110-
  title P
As a disbeliever in reality, [As Leave 117-6 P
Part of a major reality, part of [As Leave 117-9 P
An appreciation of a reality [As Leave 117-10 P
The point of difference from reality [Three 130-12 P
In reality [Three 130-19 P
A single self. Divest reality [Someone 86-1 A
As the total reality. Therefore it is [Someone 87-13 A

REALIZATION. In a permanent realization, without any wild ducks
  [Cata 425-7
A freedom revealed, a realization touched, [Bouquet 451-20
REALIZE. The bouquet of being--enough to realize [Conversat 109-21P
REALIZED. But our unfashioned spirits realized [Eve Angels 137-4
The present close, the present realized, [Martial 238-10
Bursts back. What not quite realized transit [Feo 333-20
Which was realized, like reason's constant ruin. [Two V 354-17
Not to be realized because not to [NSF 385-4
Not to be realized. Weather by Franz Hals, [NSF 385-6
After the wind has passed. Sleep realized [Owl 433-19
Of petals that will never be realized, [NH 478-15
Not often realized, the lighter words [NH 488-8
And frame from thinking and is realized. [Rome 511-3
By the torture of things that will be realized, [Duck 61-28 P
REALIZINGS. And, of human realizings, rugged roy . . . [Choc 302-5
REALLY. Perhaps the Arctic moonlight really gave [C 34-25
In a really vertiginous boat [Sailing 120-19
And to find how much that really matters [Mandolin 29-8 P
Does not really matter [Mandolin 29-9 P
Are really much a million pities. [Melancholy 32-14 P
Are they really mechanical bears, [Drum-Majors 37-4 P
REAPER. Death was a reaper with sickle and stone, [Soldat 16-1 P
REAPPEAR. Fell openly from the air to reappear [Bouquet 450-18
REAPPEARING. The trees are reappearing in poverty. [Aug 495-18
REARRANGE. Jocunda, who will arrange the roses and rearrange,
  letting the leaves lie on the water-like lacquer; [Piano 22-4 P
REASON. Wear a helmet without reason, [Orangeade 103-11
We hardened ourselves to live by bluest reason [Medit 124-2
But what are radiant reason and radiant will [Medit 124-7
He used his reason, exercised his will, [Anglais 149-5
Is like the reason in a storm; [MBG 169-10
The reason can give nothing at all [Dezem 218-19
It has to content the reason concerning war, [Bottle 239-5
There are things in a man besides his reason. [Pieces 351-10
Which was realized, like reason's constant ruin. [Two V 354-17
They differ from reason's click-clack, its applied [NSF 387-22
Compact in invincible foils, from reason, [NSF 388-1
We reason about them with a later reason. [NSF 399-3
We reason of these things with later reason [NSF 401-1
In which we rest and, for small reason, think [Final 524-2
As evils, and if reason, fatuous fire, [Duck 63-4 P
You know then that it is not the reason [Of Mere 118-1 P
REASONABLE. Lakes are more reasonable than oceans. Hence, [EM 325-6
He establishes statues of reasonable men, [NSF 403-20
REASONED. Not to impose, not to have reasoned at all, [NSF 404-2
REBELLION. Beyond any rebellion, [Polo 38-2 P
REBELLIOUS. To the difficulty of rebellious thought [C 40-17
Thick-lipped from riot and rebellious cries, [Men Fall 188-8
It was an old rebellious song, [Country 207-8
REBUILD. On human heads. True, birds rebuild [Cuisine 227-14
What man of folk-lore shall rebuild the world, [Duck 63-6 P
RECALLING. Sleeps in the sun no thing recalling. [Hero 278-18
RECALLS. Which one recalls at a concert or in a café. [Nigger 154-3
RECAPTURE. Why should the bee recapture a lost blague, [NSF 390-16
RECEDE. Its color, but less as they recede, impinged [Anach 366-10
RECEDING. Of hardy foam, receding flatly, spread [C 34-6
They never find, the same receding shores [Sunday 69-18
RECEIVE. To receive her shadow into his mind . . . [Scavoir 231-11
To receive what others had supposed, without [Landsc 242-16
Receive and keep him in the deepnesses of space-- [Flyer 336-13
RECEIVED. Accepting. He received what he denied. [Landsc 242-17
But something illogically received, [Ulysses 101-27 P
RECEIVES. There the woman receives her lover into her heart
  [Rhythms 245-16
Made noble by the honor he receives, [Recit 87-15 P
A sense separate that receives and holds the rest, [Americana 94-5 P
RECEIVING. And the high, receiving out of others, [Gigan 289-17
RECENT. A recent imagining of reality, [NH 465-15
RECESS. Slid from his continent by slow recess [C 40-15
RECESSIONAL. The long recessional at parish eves wails round
  [Greenest 59-15 P
RECITATION. The alto clank of the long recitation, in these [Burn-
  shaw 52-7 P
"Recitation after Dinner" [86-title P
RECLAME. The newest Soviet réclame. Profound [Duck 62-30 P
RECLINES. Reclines in the temperature of heaven-- [Hermit 505-12
RECLINING. "So-and-So Reclining on Her Couch" [295-title
On her side, reclining on her elbow. [Couch 295-1
Reclining, eased of desire, establishes [EM 324-12
That a figure reclining among columns toppled down, [Conversat 109-7 P
RECOGNITION. Of recognition, avowal, impassioned cry, [NH 471-3
RECOGNIZABLE. The recognizable, medium, central whole-- [Bouquet 450-12
RECOGNIZE. Recognize his unique and solitary home. [Poem Mt 512-14
To recognize him in after time. [Two Illus 514-5
RECOGNIZED. And things beyond resemblance there was this and that
  intended to be recognized, [Prol 516-13

RECOGNIZING. Was beyond his recognizing. By this he knew that
    likeness of him extended [Prol 516-11
RECOLLECTED. With slight, prismatic reeks not recollected, [Theatre
    91-11 P
RECOMPOSED. How he had recomposed the pines, [Poem Mt 512-7
RECONCILE. And reconcile us to our selves in those [Havana 144-20
RECONCILED. Mesdames, it is not enough to be reconciled [Burnshaw
    50-6 P
    The man and the man below were reconciled, [Sombre 68-14 P
    The first and second rules are reconciled [Bship 80-13 P
RECONCILIATION. And moon, the book of reconciliation, [Descrip
    345-1
    The reconciliation, the rapture of a time [Sombre 71-22 P
RECONCILING. A profounder reconciling, an act, [Vase 247-4
RECONCILINGS. True reconcilings, dark, pacific words, [Havana
    144-21
RECOVERIES. Making recoveries of young nakedness [Tallap 72-11
RE-CREATE. Of lone wanderers. To re-create, to use [NH 481-15
    Against the sleepers to re-create for them, [Sombre 69-7 P
RE-CREATES. The air changes, creates and re-creates, like
    strength, [Choc 301-9
    From the sleepy bosom of the real, re-creates, [NH
    481-20
RED. At the red turban [Sugar-Cane 12-18
    A red bird flies across the golden floor. [Monocle 13-12
    It is a red bird that seeks out his choir [Monocle 13-13
    She dressed in red and gold brocade [Pourtraicte 21-7
    Rose up besprent and sought the flaming red [Hibiscus 22-20
    Dabbled with yellow pollen--red as red [Hibiscus 23-1
    So streaked with yellow, blue and green and red [C 32-6
    Of red and blue and red, [Venereal 48-8
    And, "Why are you red [Peacocks 58-3
    In red weather. [Ten O'C 66-15
    Crew red. [Six Sig 74-18
    And the best cock of red feather [Watermelon 89-5
    The ruts in your empty road are red. [Fish-Scale 160-18
    Cloud's red, earth feeling, sky that thinks? [MBG 177-4
    They are touched red. [Pears 196-8
    The red and the blue house blended, [Idiom 200-21
    Fat cat, red tongue, green mind, white milk [Rabbit K 209-5
    The red cat hides away in the fur-light [Rabbit K 209-20
    Ah! and red; and they have peach fuzz, ah! [Peaches 224-11
    Still bloom in the agate eyes, red blue, [Arcades 225-15
    Red purple, never quite red itself. [Arcades 225-16
    Not quite. The mist was to light what red [Vari 235-20
    The red bird most and the strongest sky-- [Adequacy 244-14
    In the leaf and bud and how the red, [Vase 246-19
    Became--how the central, essential red [Vase 246-21
    The blue sun in his red cockade [News 264-7
    His red cockade topped off a parade. [News 264-15
    Red as a red table-cloth, its windows [Hero 276-1
    Of red and blue, the hard sound-- [Motive 288-18
    To giant red, sweats up a giant sense [Repet 307-8
    How red the rose that is the soldier's wound, [EM 318-26
    The soldiers that have fallen, red in blood, [EM 319-1
    Of time's red soldier deathless on his bed. [EM 319-10
    That a bright red woman will be rising [Debris 338-6
    An age is green or red. An age believes [Descrip 340-6
    The red, the blue, the argent queen. If not, [Descrip 340-13
    That breathed on ground, more blue than red, more red [Pieces
    352-3
    "The Red Fern" [365-title
    Pushing and pushing red after red. [Red Fern 365-4
    Of red facsimiles through related trees, [Cats 367-18
    And knotted, sashed and seamed, half pales of red, [Cred 378-2
    Defies red emptiness to evolve his match.[NSF 384-9
    If seen rightly and yet a possible red. [NSF 393-18
    A face of stone in an unending red, [NSF 400-5
    The eye could not escape, a red renown [NSF 400-16
    Red robin, stop in your preludes, practicing [NSF 405-16
    It rose, ashen and red and yellow, each [Page 422-12
    It might become a wheel spoked red and white [Page 422-21
    "Large Red Man Reading" [423-title
    And red, and right. The particular question--here [Ulti 429-12
    In our sense of it, our sense of the fertilest red, [Roses
    430-18
    Of the land, on a checkered cover, red and white. [Bouquet 450-6
    Toward a consciousness of red and white as one, [Bouquet 450-9
    The rose, the delphinium, the red, the blue, [Bouquet 451-1
    A right red with its composites glutted full, [Bouquet 452-3
    The red ripeness of round leaves is thick [Pecul 453-10
    With the spices of red summer. [Pecul 453-11
    The first red of red winter, winter-red, [Novel 457-14
    He will never ride the red horse she describes. [Questions 462-15
    Bare beggar-tree, hung low for fruited red [NH 483-24
    On the walk, purple and blue, and red and gold, [NH 484-5
    The brown at the bottom of red [Plant 506-10
    In the swamps, bushes draw up dark red, [Primordia 8-22 P
    "Red Loves Kit" [30-title P
    Do I happen to like red bush, [Table 40-5 P

What else remains? But red, [Table 40-7 P
One likes the way red grows. [Table 40-12 P
As sequels without thought. In the rudest red [Burnshaw 47-8 P
And red, will not be redder, rounder then [Burnshaw 47-31 P
And despicable shades of red, just seen, [Burnshaw 51-21 P
And vaguely to be seen, a matinal red, [Burnshaw 51-22 P
Red mango peels and I play my guitar. [Stan MBG 72-4 P
What They Call Red Cherry Pie [Grotesque 75-title 4 P
He eats red cherry pie and never says-- [Grotesque 75-19 P
He says "That's what I call red cherry pie." [Grotesque 76-4 P
What is it that we share? Red cherry pie [Grotesque 76-7 P
And that's red cherry pie. [Grotesque 76-12 P
The illustrious arms, the symbolic horns, the red [Bship 79-6 P
Your guns are not rhapsodic strophes, red [Bship 80-20 P
His own bright red. But he bears him out of love, [Recit 87-18 P
The thousand-leaved red [Fare Guit 98-19 P
It remains red, [Three 130-16 P
Red is not only [Three 142-12 P
And as the red of the sun [Three 143-4 P
As red is multiplied by the leaves of trees. [Three 143-14 P
See: blood-red; blue-red; red-in-red; red-rose-red; winter-red.
RED-BIRD. It is the same jingle of the red-bird breasting the
    orange-trees out of the cedars. [Indian 112-6
RED-BLUE. On the flag-poles in a red-blue dazzle, whack [NSF 390-23
REDCOAT. Hugh March, a sergeant, a redcoat, killed, [Vari 234-11
RED-COLORED. Reddens the sand with his red-colored noise, [NSF
    384-8
REDDEN. Your brown breast redden, while you wait for warmth. [Cred
    377-7
REDDENED. The sun appeared and reddened great [Country 207-13
    Plato, the reddened flower, the erotic bird. [Extracts 253-29
    Against gold whipped reddened in big-shadowed black, [Repet 309-19
    Like rubies reddened by rubies reddening. [Descrip 346-4
    And motion outward, reddened and resolved [Owl 435-20
    A reddened garment falling to his feet, [Aug 492-8
    And Crispine, the blade reddened by some touch, demanding the
    most from the phrases [Piano 22-6 P
REDDENING. Like rubies reddened by rubies reddening. [Descrip 346-4
REDDENS. Reddens the sand with his red-colored noise, [NSF 384-8
REDDER. And red, will not be redder, rounder then [Burnshaw 47-31 P
REDDEST. Raise reddest columns. Toll a bell [MBG 170-5
    Squeezing the reddest fragrance from the stump [God 285-14
    Of the populace of the heart, the reddest lord, [EM 315-18
REDDISH. The redness of your reddish chestnut trees, [Old Man 501-5
REDEEMING. Time troubles to produce the redeeming thought.[Extracts
    257-19
RED-EMERALD. Red-emerald, red-slitted-blue, a face of slate, [NSF
    400-6
REDESCRIBED. Their dark-colored words had redescribed the citrons.
    [NH 487-9
RE-DESIGNED. The cloak to be clipped, the night to be re-designed,
    [Sombre 71-32 P
RED-EYED. The red-eyed elders watching, felt [Peter 90-9
RED-IN-RED. Red-in-red repetitions never going [NSF 400-13
RE-DISPOSED. This fortune's finding, disposed and re-disposed [Orb
    440-7
REDNESS. The blood-red redness of the sun, [Adequacy 243-18
    Evading the point of redness, not content [EM 318-21
    The redness of your reddish chestnut trees, [Old Man 501-5
    With redness that sticks fast to evil dreams; [Rock 528-8
RED-ROSE-RED. The channel slots of rain, the red-rose-red [NSF
    400-8
REDS. Say that it is a crude effect, black reds, [Roses 430-10
    The less legible meanings of sounds, the little reds [NH 488-7
    Be marble after the drenching reds, the dark [Greenest 57-22 P
RED-SLITTED-BLUE. Red-emerald, red-slitted-blue, a face of slate,
    [NSF 400-6
REDUCE. That I may reduce the monster to [MBG 175-5
    Alone, but reduce the monster and be, [MBG 175-10
    First. The grand simplifications reduce [Bship 78-23 P
REDWOOD. So you're home again, Redwood Roamer, and ready [Phenom
    286-13
REDWOODS. The Roamer is a voice taller than the redwoods, [Phenom
    287-4
REED. Playing a crackled reed, wind-stopped, in bleats. [Sombre
    67-2 P
REEDS. Scaffolds and derricks rise from the reeds to the clouds
    [NE Verses 105-9
    Item: The green fish pensive in green reeds [Montra 263-20
    Gulping for shape among the reeds. No doubt, [Lot 371-12
    There is the same color in the bellies of frogs, in clays,
    withered reeds, skins, wood, sunlight. [Primordia 8-2 P
REEF. That hermit on reef sable would have seen, [Dames 206-16
REEFS. For music, for whisperings from the reefs. [Farewell 117-18
    (Omitting reefs of cloud): [Delight 162-5
REEK. See sun-reek.
REEKS. With slight, prismatic reeks not recollected, [Theatre
    91-11 P
REFER. To which we refer experience, a knowledge [Descrip 343-19
REFERENCE. The glass man, without external reference. [Oboe 251-21

To perceive men without reference to their form. [Choc 296-11
Or of glistening reference to what is real, [Repet 309-7
In the perpetual reference, object [NH 466-13
Except with reference to ourselves, [Three 133-15 P
REFERENCES. Too many references. The hero [Hero 279-9
Destroy all references. This actor [Hero 279-17
"Extraordinary References" [369-title
And brain, as the extraordinary references [Extraord 369-13
REFERS. The cool sun of the Tulpehocken refers [Extraord 369-10
REFILL. And then to refill its emptiness again, [NH 482-21
REFLECT. And not in this dead glass, which can reflect [Blanche
10-2 P
Her beauty in your love. She should reflect [Red Kit 31-12 P
REFLECTED. Reflected, humming an outline of a fugue [NSF 402-14
In mud, under ponds, where the sky used to be reflected. [NH
487-15
Made eminent in a reflected seeming-so. [Recit 88-2 P
REFLECTING. Reflecting this thing and that, [Homunculus 26-15
Reflecting snow. A newly-fallen snow [Poems Clim 193-10
Space-filled, reflecting the seasons, the folk-lore [R Conn
533-19
Seated before these shining forms, like the duskiest glass, re-
flecting the piebald of roses or what you will [Piano 21-18 P
REFLECTION. Of heaven in an antique reflection rolled [Sea Surf
99-13
A reflection stagnant in a stagnant stream. [Nigger 156-2
The reflection of her here, and then there, [Scavoir 231-17
The afternoon's reading, the night's reflection, [Hero 274-23
Of simple seeing, without reflection. We seek [NH 471-20
The serious reflection is composed [NH 478-2
REFLECTIONS. Are they men eating reflections of themselves?
[Cuisine 228-16
Reflections and off-shoots, mimic-motes [Red Fern 365-8
Except reflections, the escapades of death, [NSF 405-8
Ruffling its common reflections, thought-like Monadnocks. [Cata
424-14
A mirror, a lake of reflections in a room, [NH 468-14
The plain sense of it, without reflections, leaves, [Plain 503-3
Is full of reflections, [Primordia 8-6 P
Reflections, whirling apart and wide away. [Burnshaw 50-5 P
Head down. The reflections and repetitions, [Fare Guit 99-4 P
REFLECTS. that reflects neither my face nor any inner part [Nuances
18-9
Nothing much, a flitter that reflects itself. [Bouquet 448-13
A new scholar replacing an older one reflects [Look 519-4
"A Mythology Reflects Its Region" [118-title P
A mythology reflects its region. Here [Myth 118-7 P
REFRACTIONS. And there and in another state--the refractions,
[Glass 197-18
REFRAIN. And as they whispered, the refrain [Peter 91-16
Rides clear of her mind and the waves make a refrain [Farewell
117-8
"Autumn Refrain" [160-title
Confusion solved, as in a refrain [MBG 177-18
A refrain from the end of the boulevards. [Nightgown 214-4
REFRESHED. The yellow that was yesterday, refreshed, [Lot 371-5
Omega is refreshed at every end. [NH 469-21
REFRESHES. The poem refreshes life so that we share, [NSF 382-13
The blood refreshes with its stale demands. [Study I 464-3
REFRESHMENT. For his refreshment, an abundant zone, [C 35-17
A refreshment of cold air, cold breath, [Bus 116-6 P
REFUGE. He wanted and looked for a final refuge, [Contra II 270-7
In a peace that is more than a refuge, [Dutch 291-17
This is the refuge that the end creates. [Cred 373-25
REFUGEES. Like beautiful and abandoned refugees. [Our Stars 455-16
REFUGES. Scenting the jungle in their refuges, [C 32-5
REFUSED. Seeing that which is refused, [Bagatelles 213-15
The one refused the other one to take, [NSF 401-20
REGAL. The blessed regal dropped in daggers' dew, [Montra 260-18
REGALIA. Of jugglery, without regalia. [C 35-27
And these regalia, these things disclosed, [EM 317-12
That which is not ourselves: the regalia, [NH 485-14
REGARD. To regard the frost and the boughs [Snow Man 9-22
From madness or delight, without regard [Monocle 17-12
Regard. But for that salty cup, [MBG 179-19
Regard now the sloping, mountainous rocks [Loaf 199-16
Regard the hovels of those that live in this land. [Loaf 199-18
In the hoary-hanging night. It does not regard [EM 315-7
There is village and village of them, without regard [Wild 328-13
Adam of beau regard, from fat Elysia, [Pure 331-20
Regard the invalid personality [Cats 368-1
The decay that you regard: of the arranged [Cred 377-13
In space, wherever he sits, of bleak regard, [AA 414-6
Without regard to time or where we are, [NH 466-12
Regard the freedom of seventy years ago, [Rock 525-4
From which to regard her [Three 136-15 P
REGARDE. C'est toujours la vie qui me regarde . . . This was [NH
483-14
REGARDED. A naked man who regarded himself in the glass [Landsc
241-16

Regarded by the meta-men, is quirked [Bouquet 451-3
REGARDLESS. To be, regardless of velvet, could never be more
[Uruguay 249-13
Come swelling, when, regardless of my end, [Soldat 14-15 P
Regardless of gods that were praised in goldness [Stan Hero 83-21 P
REGARDS. Stands and regards and repeats the primitive lines.
[Anach 366-15
The sun steps into, regards and finds itself; [Golden 460-11
Of that single mind. He regards them [Child 106-17 P
REGINA. "Mother of heaven, regina of the clouds, [Monocle 13-1
REGION. In a region of frost, [Cortege 80-19
It is like a region full of intonings. [Hartford 226-17
And downward, from this purple region, thrown; [Infernale 25-7 P
Precious from the region of the hand, still bright [Bship 81-1 P
"The Region November" [115-title P
"A Mythology Reflects Its Region" [118-title P
A mythology reflects its region. Here [Myth 118-7 P
And it is he in the substance of his region, [Myth 118-14 P
REGIONS. Let him remove it to his regions, [Snow Stars 133-7
And reaches, beaches, tomorrow's regions became [Descrip 343-13
These external regions, what do we fill them with [NSF 405-7
But there are regions where the grass [Abnormal 24-5 P
And in those regions one still feels the rose [Abnormal 24-9 P
REGRET. Consider the odd morphology of regret. [Nigger 154-10
In the park. We regret we have no nightingale. [Duck 66-7 P
REGRETFUL. Regretful that she bore her; [Sonatina 109-18
REGULAE. Regulae mundi, as apprentice of [Bship 78-21 P
Regulae mundi . . . That much is out of the way. [Bship 80-30 P
REGULATION. Beyond thought's regulation. There each man, [Greenest
54-2 P
REGULATIONS. In regulations of his spirit. [Winter B 141-12
REHEARSED. Than a thought to be rehearsed all day, a speech [Beard
247-16
RE-ILLUMINES. And re-illumines things that used to turn [Sun March
133-15
REJECT. To reject the script for its lack-tragic, [Gigan 289-10
REJECTED. And our streams rejected the dim Academy. [Nigger 154-21
Rejected years. A big bird pecks at him [EM 318-8
Of bones, he rejected, he denied, to arrive [Landsc 241-20
That the things that he rejected might be part [Landsc 242-22
If the rejected things, the things denied, [Beard 247-12
REJECTING. Rejecting intermediate parts, [Negation 97-15
In a place that he reached, by rejecting what he saw [Landsc
242-10
Them closelier to her by rejecting dreams. [NSF 402-9
REJECTS. One feels the purifying change. One rejects [Dump 202-17
Resists each past apocalypse, rejects [Extracts 257-27
The man-sun being hero rejects that [Hero 280-12
How that which rejects it saves it in the end. [EM 315-10
Perhaps instead of failing it rejects [NH 477-13
As a serious strength rejects pin-idleness. [NH 477-14
REJOICE. Dying lady, rejoice, rejoice! [Thought 185-4
REJUVENATING. As facts fall like rejuvenating rain, [Montra 263-22
RELATED. Related in romance to backward flights, [C 39-10
Of red facsimiles through related trees, [Cats 367-18
To which we are related, [Including 88-12 P
With the molten mixings of related things, [Someone 87-4 A
See all-related.
RELATION. The relation comes, benignly, to its end? [C 46-12
So may the relation of each man be clipped. [C 46-13
If one may say so. And yet relation appears, [Connois 215-18
A small relation expanding like the shade [Connois 215-19
Compounded of dear relation, spoken twice, [EM 317-18
"Thinking of a Relation between the Images of Metaphors" [356-
title
Beyond relation to the parent trunk: [Red Fern 365-10
Life's nonsense pierces us with strange relation. [NSF 383-9
The final relation, the marriage of the rest. [Study II 465-3
RELATIVE. Particulars of a relative sublime. [Ulysses 103-27 P
RELAXATIONS. To pick up relaxations of the known. [Feo 333-17
RELAXED. The seal is as relaxed as dirt, perdu. [Golden 460-18
RELEASED. And, from their stale intelligence released, [C 37-9
By which sorrow is released, [Mozart 132-15
Just to know how it would feel, released from destruction, [Cata
425-9
Under the oak trees, completely released. [Sol Oaks 111-10 P
RELEASING. Releasing an abysmal melody, [Owl 433-4
RELENT. One might. One might. But time will not relent. [Pharynx
96-16
RELENTLESS. Than the relentless contact he desired; [C 34-20
Commands the armies; the relentless arm, [Soldat 14-11 P
RELENTLESSLY. Relentlessly in possession of happiness. [AA 411-18
RELIC. Or light, the relic of farewells, [MBG 179-3
RELICS. As one of the relics of the heart. [Prejudice 368-16
As one of the relics of the mind . . . [Prejudice 368-19
RELIEVE. Weaken our fate, relieve us of woe both great [EM 315-21
RELIEVES. From which no soft sleeve relieves us. [Dutch 291-4
RELINQUISHED. Upon the grass, relinquished to their feet. [Sunday
69-9
The dark-blown ceinture loosened, not relinquished. [NSF 385-11

REMAIN. But the romantic must never remain, [Sailing 120-15
   Yet this remain the dwelling-place [Nigger 153-6
   There would still remain the never-resting mind, [Poems Clim
      194-4
   And I, if I rode naked, are what remain." [Uruguay 249-6
   In day's constellation, and yet remain, yet be, [Choc 300-20
   Might spring to sight and yet remain a dove. [Think 357-4
   You remain the more than natural figure. You [NSF 406-17
   Yet the transcripts of it when it was blue remain; [NH 479-20
   Even our shadows, their shadows, no longer remain. [Rock 525-7
   And still the impassioned place of it remain. [Spaniard 34-10 P
   Yet still retain resemblances, remain [Sombre 67-17 P
   He was willing they should remain incredible, [Someone 85-14 A
REMAINED. The whole of life that still remained in him [C 28-18
   Remained, except some starker, barer self [C 29-16
   To be convulsed, to have remained the hands [Thunder 220-22
   There remained the smoke of the villages. Their fire [Wild 329-5
   As if Liadoff no longer remained a ghost [Liadoff 347-8
   Long after the planter's death. A few limes remained, [NSF 393-3
   Remained and nothing of herself except [Old Woman 44-11 P
REMAINING. One thing remaining, infallible, would be [Beard 247-18
REMAINS. If that remains concealed, what does the bottom matter?
      [Nudity Cap 145-11
   Revolvers and shoot each other. One remains. [Extracts 256-2
   He that remains plays on an instrument. [Extracts 256-4
   Of the assassin that remains and sings [Extracts 256-15
   He find another? The giant of sense remains [Repet 308-9
   Whatever remains. Of what is real I say, [Repet 308-15
   And yet remains the same, the beast of light, [Pure 333-2
   Is that it has not changed enough. It remains, [NSF 390-4
   Only the half they can never possess remains, [AA 413-9
   The marble man remains himself in space. [Degen 444-10
   In his cave, remains dismissed without a dream, [Study II 464-9
   If, then, New Haven is half sun, what remains, [NH 482-3
   What else remains? But red, [Table 40-7 P
   And remains inarticulate, horses with cream. [Burnshaw 47-3 P
   Remains in the sight, and in sayings of the sight, [How Now
      97-5 P
   The earth remains of one color-- [Three 130-15 P
   It remains red, [Three 130-16 P
   It remains what it is. [Three 130-17 P
   It does not shine on a thing that remains [Three 130-20 P
REMARKS. "Questions Are Remarks" [462-title
REMEMBER. And you? Remember how the crickets came [Monocle 15-3
   Only the rich remember the past, [Arcades 225-1
   Was ancient. He tried to remember the phrases: pain [EM 314-3
   Do you remember how the rocket went on [Liadoff 346-5
   Do you remember the children there like wicks, [Liadoff 346-11
   Do you remember what the townsmen said, [Liadoff 346-17
   We remember the lion of Juda and we save [NH 472-23
   And I remember sharp Japonica-- [Soldat 13-11 P
   To remember summer. [Secret Man 36-4 P
   Made to remember a life they never lived [Burnshaw 46-24 P
REMEMBERED. And I remembered the cry of the peacocks. [Domination
      8-16
   And I remembered the cry of the peacocks. [Domination 9-20
   But he remembered the time when he stood alone. [Anglais 149-9
   But he remembered the time when he stood alone. [Anglais 149-11
   But he remembered the time when he stood alone, [Anglais 149-13
   One man, their bread and their remembered wine? [Extracts 254-17
   That I remembered, something that I remembered [Repet 306-5
   Like something I remembered overseas. [Repet 306-20
   It was something overseas that I remembered. [Repet 306-21
   For her that she remembered: the argentines [NSF 399-13
   It was enough for her that she remembered. [NSF 399-20
   Neither remembered nor forgotten, nor old, [Bouquet 451-6
   The sad smell of the lilacs--one remembered it, [Aug 491-9
   The sounds drift in. The buildings are remembered. [Rome 510-11
   They were of a remembered time [Planet 532-8
   The self is a cloister full of remembered sounds [Woman Had 82-17P
   To be remembered, the old shape [Ulysses 104-19 P
   Without a remembered past, a present past, [Local 111-15 P
REMEMBERING. A sunken voice, both of remembering [C 29-5
   All pleasures and all pains, remembering [Sunday 67-24
   The aunts in Pasadena, remembering, [Hartford 226-11
   A bee for the remembering of happiness. [Owl 434-18
   He does not lie there remembering the blue-jay, say the jay.
      [Madame 507-11
   Are time for counting and remembering, [Ideal 88-10 A
REMEMBERINGS. Wait now; have no rememberings of hope, [Soldat
      14-13 P
REMEMBERS. One remembers a woman standing in such a dress. [Bouquet
      450-24
REMEMBRANCE. Like her remembrance of awakened birds, [Sunday 68-24
   Of remembrance share nothing of ourselves. [Dutch 291-14
   The fidgets of remembrance come to this. [Cred 372-10
   Stripped of remembrance, it displays its strength-- [Cred 375-9
   A dazzle of remembrance and of sight. [Owl 433-6
REMEMBRANCES. Burns in the mind on lost remembrances. [Men Fall
      187-12

For farewells, a sad hanging on for remembrances. [NH 487-18
   Remembrances, a place of a field of lights, [Sombre 67-18 P
REMIND. Reminding, trying to remind, of a white [AA 412-10
REMINDED. It reminded him how he had needed [Poem Mt 512-5
REMINDERS. In their ugly reminders? [Archi 17-7 P
REMINDING. "That bliss of stars, that princox of evening heaven!"
      reminding of seasons, [Banal 63-1
   Reminding, trying to remind, of a white [AA 412-10
REMOTE. Remote on heaven's hill, that has endured [Sunday 68-22
   Remote and call it merciful? [MBG 168-21
   Voices in chorus, singing without words, remote and deep, [Sick
      90-11 P
   (Remote from the deadly general of men, [Americana 94-1 P
REMOTER. A generation sealed, men remoter than mountains, [Waldorf
      241-7
   The swans fled outward to remoter reaches, [Descrip 343-7
   Remoter than Athos, the effulgent hordes [Greenest 56-22 P
REMOTEST. Washed in the remotest cleanliness of a heaven [NSF
      381-5
REMOVE. Let him remove it to his regions, [Snow Stars 133-7
REMOVED. Removed from any shore, from any man or woman, and needing
      none. [Prol 516-9
REMOVES. And not imagined. The removes must give, [Papini 447-5
   Including the removes toward poetry. [Papini 447-6
REMUS. Remus, blow your horn! [Ploughing 20-9
REND. Slight gestures that could rend the palpable ice, [Page 423-2
RENDEZVOUS. Meekly you keep the mortal rendezvous, [On Manner
      55-11
   Rendezvous, [God 285-12
   The rendezvous, when she came alone, [AA 419-16
   This is, therefore, the intensest rendezvous. [Final 524-4
   A knowledge, that which arranged the rendezvous. [Final 524-12
   Not one of the five, and keep a rendezvous, [Souls 95-5 P
RENEWAL. The renewal of noise [Solitaires 60-8
RENEWED. Creation is not renewed by images [NH 481-14
RENEWS. The mind renews the world in a verse, [Ulysses 103-1 P
   By a right philosopher: renews [Ulysses 103-3 P
RENOWN. Its venom of renown, and on your head [Fictive 87-12
   The eye could not escape, a red renown [NSF 400-16
RENTED. Your mansard with a rented piano. You lie [NSF 384-18
REPARTEE. It is not a question of captious repartee. [Bad Time
      426-19
REPEAT. Men that repeat antiquest sounds of air [Eve Angels 137-15
   If we repeat, it is because the wind [Eve Angels 137-17
   Notes for his comfort that he may repeat [Nigger 155-21
   In the delicatest ear of the mind, repeat, [Of Mod 240-8
   How should I repeat them, keep repeating them, [Repet 307-23
   For a moment, a moment in which we read and repeat [Pure 333-8
   Her music should repeat itself in you, [Red Kit 31-14 P
   Speak, and in these repeat: To Be Itself, [Burnshaw 52-8 P
REPEATED. Repeated in a summer without end [Key W 129-16
   To find: the scene was set; it repeated what [Of Mod 239-19
   Surrenders, the repeated sayings that [Extracts 258-6
   Was repeated by Liadoff in a narration [Liadoff 347-2
   Prolonged, repeated and once more prolonged, [Duck 63-32 P
   All are evasions like a repeated phrase, [Duck 65-14 P
   This was repeated day by day. The waves [Woman Had 81-19 P
   They never stopped, a repetition repeated [Woman Had 81-21 P
   The frame of a repeated effect, is it that? [Recit 87-6 P
   Hard to be told from thoughts, the repeated drone [Americana
      94-3 P
REPEATING. Repeating themselves, [Domination 8-10
   And that would be saying farewell, repeating farewell, [Adieu
      127-15
   Repeating your appointed paces [Hero 275-16
   How should I repeat them, keep repeating them, [Repet 307-23
   One voice repeating, one tireless chorister, [NSF 394-7
   The bells keep on repeating solemn names [Rome 510-15
   Repeating his name with its patient syllables, [World 521-17
   Like the same orange repeating on one tree [Someone 85-21 A
REPEATS. Repeats its vital words, yet balances [Search 268-15
   And repeats words without meaning. [Motive 288-4
   Stands and regards and repeats the primitive lines. [Anach 366-15
   The third form speaks, because the ear repeats, [Owl 432-3
   Repeats the farmer's almanac. [Grotesque 75-11 P
REPENTING. The cowl of winter, done repenting. [Peter 92-5
REPERTOIRE. Always the standard repertoire in line [Nigger 156-19
   In an appointed repertoire . . . [Soldat 15-21 P
REPETITION. His infinite repetition and alloys [Havana 144-15
   A repetition of unconscious things, [Vari 232-9
   The sun expands, like a repetition on [Montra 263-14
   It is a repetition. The bees come booming [NSF 390-5
   But he that of repetition is most master. [NSF 406-6
   An escape from repetition, a happening [NH 483-6
   A fantastic effort has failed, a repetition [Plain 502-19
   Which, by its repetition, comes to bear [Duck 65-15 P
   They never stopped, a repetition repeated [Woman Had 81-21 P
   That question the repetition on the shore, [Woman Had 82-3 P
REPETITIONS. In an accord of repetitions. Yet, [Eve Angels 137-16
   "Repetitions of a Young Captain" [306-title

Red-in-red repetitions never going [NSF 400-13
  Mere repetitions. These things at least comprise [NSF 405-17
  One of the vast repetitions final in [NSF 405-20
  By repetitions of half-meanings. Am I not, [Angel 497-5
  Head down. The reflections and repetitions, [Fare Guit 99-4 P
REPETITIOUSNESS. In a repetitiousness of men and flies. [Plain
  502-20
REPLACE. Mature: A capable being may replace [Pure 330-11
  That will replace it shall be carved, "The Mass [Burnshaw 48-5 P
REPLACES. Replaces what is not. The resounding cry [Cred 376-24
  One candle replaces [Three 141-4 P
REPLACING. A new scholar replacing an older one reflects [Look
  519-4
REPLIED. The man replied, "Things as they are [MBG 165-5
REPLY. "Reply to Papini" [446-title
  It was a rabbi's question. Let the rabbis reply. [Bship 79-14 P
REPLYING. (A woman's voice is heard, replying.) Mock [Infernal
  25-4 P
REPOSE. Upon the pillow to repose and speak, [Men Fall 188-10
  Once it was, the repose of night, [Nightgown 214-17
  "The Lack of Repose" [303-title
  To repose in an hour or season or long era [EM 318-22
  The brilliant mercy of a sure repose, [Cred 375-18
  On this present ground, the vividest repose, [Cred 375-19
  Nor that the sexual blossoms should repose [NSF 399-8
  Beneficence, a repose, utmost repose, [Orb 442-14
  The checkered squares, the skeleton of repose, [Bouquet 450-7
  Gritting the ear, whispers humane repose. [NH 484-21
  The bronze of the wise man seated in repose [Recit 86-15 P
  Repose, always, the credible thought [Ulysses 103-18 P
REPOSED. Reposed? And does it have a puissant heart [Two V 354-5
REPOSES. This reposes alike in springtime [Yellow 236-11
  Hidden from other thoughts, he that reposes [NSF 388-5
REPRESENTED. She was represented to me [Three 136-17 P
  She was represented to me [Three 137-1 P
  For here it was also represented [Three 138-1 P
  She was represented as clinging [Three 138-7 P
REPRESSED. Or, if it understood, repressed itself [Old Woman 44-5P
REPROACH. Contained in their afflatus the reproach [C 39-12
REPRODUCED. Came reproduced in purple, family font, [C 45-16
REPTILE. Concealed in glittering grass, dank reptile skins. [Duck
  65-11 P
REPUGNANT. He preserves himself against the repugnant rain [NH
  475-22
REQUIEMS. Arointing his dreams with fugal requiems? [C 41-11
  Chant sibilant requiems for this effigy. [Burnshaw 47-19 P
REQUIESCATS. Study the symbols and the requiescats, [Norfolk 111-5
REQUIRE. They require something serpentine. [Bananas 54-2
  Through our indifferent crises. Yet we require [EM 321-4
REQUIRED. It was a flourishing tropic he required [C 35-16
  Required, as a necessity requires. [Plain 503-8
  Since thirty mornings are required to make [Ideal 88-1 A
REQUIRES. A tree, this unprovoked sensation requires [NSF 406-12
  Required, as a necessity requires. [Plain 503-8
REQUIRING. Requiring order beyond their speech. [Sad Gay 122-9
REQUITAL. With heaven, brought such requital to desire [Sunday 68-3
REQUITES. The sparrow requites one, without intent. [Vari 233-16
REQUITING. And free requiting of responsive fact, [Montra 263-10
  Of the well-thumbed, infinite pages of her masters, who will
    seem old to her, requiting less and less her feeling: [Piano
    22-7 P
RES. Part of the res itself and not about it. [NH 473-17
RESCUE. Imagination, the golden rescue: [Hero 275-26
RESCUED. Hot-hooded and dark-blooded, rescued the rose [EM 316-17
RESCUING. Can we conceive of him as rescuing less, [EM 316-20
RESEARCH. He makes the tenderest research, intent [EM 318-5
RESEMBLANCE. That by resemblance twanged him through and through,
  [Owl 433-3
  Much like a new resemblance of the sun, [NH 465-16
  And things beyond resemblance there was this and that intended
    to be recognized, [Prol 516-13
  Of the tropic of resemblance, sprigs [Someone 86-17 A
  At last, the center of resemblance, found [Ideal 89-8 A
RESEMBLANCES. Were their resemblances to ours? [Jumbo 269-9
  Resemblances [Analysis 348-10
  The two things compared their tight resemblances: [Past Nun 379-2
  Yet still retain resemblances, remain [Sombre 67-17 P
  The dot, the pale pole of resemblances [Ideal 88-16 A
RESEMBLE. They resemble a page of Toulet [Nigger 153-2
  They resemble nothing else. [Pears 196-4
RESEMBLED. We resembled one another at the sight. [Aug 494-15
RESEMBLES. One eye, in which the dove resembles the dove. [Think
  356-14
RESEMBLING. Noway resembling his, a visible thing, [C 29-27
  Of sounds resembling sounds, efflorisant, [Montra 260-11
  Young boys resembling pastry, hip-hip [Hero 278-11
  Noiselessly, noiselessly, resembling a thin bird, [Somnam 304-2
  Around and away, resembling the presence of thought, [NH 474-5
  Resembling the presences of thoughts, as if, [NH 474-6
  Feels not, resembling thought, resembling feeling? [Aug 493-4

A boat carried forward by waves resembling the bright backs of
    rowers, [Prol 515-6
  See bright-blue-resembling.
RESIDENCE. And you, my semblables, in sooty residence [Dutch 290-6
  Yet, as it seems, of human residence. [Someone 84-3 A
RESIDENTS. Bore off the residents of its noble Place. [NSF 391-9
RESIDES. Being and sitting still, something resides, [Autumn 160-9
  But ours is not imprisoned. It resides [NH 472-13
RESIDUE. A shivering residue, chilled and foregone, [AA 417-20
  Is a residue, a land, a rain, a warmth, [How Now 97-10 P
RESIDUUM. Some skreaking and skrittering residuum, [Autumn 160-10
  Lie in the heart's residuum . . . Amen. [Extracts 258-23
  Lie in the heart's residuum. [Extracts 259-7
  Of speech: to pierce the heart's residuum [Extracts 259-15
  To distinguish. The town was a residuum, [NH 479-18
RESIGNATION. Are the music of meet resignation; these [On Manner
  56-4
RESIST. The poem must resist the intelligence [Man Car 350-13
RESISTANCE. There is a conflict, there is a resistance involved;
  [Course 96-16 P
RESISTS. Resists each past apocalypse, rejects [Extracts 257-27
  A brune figure in winter evening resists [Man Car 350-15
  Identity. The thing he carries resists [Man Car 350-16
RESOLVED. Resolved the world. We cannot go back to that. [Connois
  215-16
  And motion outward, reddened and resolved [Owl 435-20
  Resolved in dazzling discovery. [Ulysses 102-1 P
  A world agrees, thought's compromise, resolved [Ideal 89-7 A
RESONANCE. Once more the longest resonance, to cap [Havana 143-16
RESOUND. While the domes resound with chant involving chant.
  [Ghosts 119-18
RESOUNDING. Replaces what is not. The resounding cry [Cred 376-24
  Are not of another solitude resounding; [NSF 392-17
RESPECT. Inactive in his singular respect. [NH 474-15
  Of there, where the truth was not the respect of one, [Someone
  85-11 A
RESPECTED. The word respected, fired ten thousand guns [Bship 78-12P
RESPLENDENT. In an ovation of resplendent forms-- [Liadoff 346-7
  In the centre of its cones, the resplendent flights [Cats 367-17
  And origin and resplendent end of law, [Greenest 60-5 P
RESPONDING. A responding to a diviner opposite. [NH 468-3
RESPONDS. Beneath his tip-tap-tap. It is she that responds. [Jouga
  337-8
RESPONSE. Where the voice that is in us makes a true response,
  [Eve Angels 138-4
  Like the response to desire. [Dezem 218-20
  Response, the completely answering voice, [Ulysses 100-11 P
RESPONSES. The organic centre of responses, [Hero 279-27
  Central responses to a central fear, [Repet 308-1
RESPONSIVE. Should be pine-spokesman. The responsive man, [C 38-16
  The responsive, still sustaining pomps for you [On Manner 56-5
  As one loves visible and responsive peace, [Yellow 236-14
  The central man, the human globe, responsive [Oboe 250-20
  And free requiting of responsive fact, [Montra 263-10
REST. To whom oracular rockings gave no rest. [C 30-28
  He knelt in the cathedral with the rest, [C 32-29
  To rest before the heroic height. [How Live 125-12
  And the two of them standing still to rest. [How Live 126-4
  Desire for rest, in that descending sea [Eve Angels 137-23
  Is rest and silence spreading into sleep. [Eve Angels 137-25
  To know that the balance does not quite rest, [MBG 181-9
  Stretch themselves to rest in their first summer's sun, [Parochial
  191-20
  Slowly, one man, savager than the rest, [Thunder 220-5
  Of one wilder than the rest (like music blunted, [Thunder 220-23
  Pipperoo, pippera, pipperum . . . The rest is rot. [Horn 230-19
  Must struggle like the rest." She climbed until [Uruguay 249-1
  Hoy, hoy, the blue bulls kneeling down to rest. [Montra 260-19
  And there the soldier of time has deathless rest. [EM 319-6
  Could the future rest on a sense and be beyond [Pure 331-11
  Intelligence? On what does the present rest? [Pure 331-12
  Cadaverous undulations. Rest, old mould . . . [Two V 355-14
  And Lazarus betrayed him to the rest, [Good Man 364-8
  The rest look down. One man becomes a race, [Cred 374-22
  In which I meet you, in which we sit at rest, [NSF 380-9
  A wait within that certainty, a rest [NSF 386-7
  He wanted his heart to stop beating and his mind to rest [Cata
  425-6
  Upon whose shoulders even the heavens rest, [Owl 431-15
  Where luminous agitations come to rest, [Owl 433-12
  The final relation, the marriage of the rest. [Study II 465-3
  In which we rest and, for small reason, think [Final 524-2
  Rest, crows, upon the edges of the moon, [Red Kit 31-20 P
  You rest intact in conscience and intact [Good Bad 33-9 P
  In the soil and rest. Conceive that marble men [Burnshaw 52-1 P
  The rest, to whom in the end the rest return, [Sombre 66-15 P
  A sense separate that receives and holds the rest, [Americana 94-5P
  On all the rest, in heavy thought. [Child 106-15 P
  To rest in sunrise. [Three 138-16 P
RE-STATEMENT. "Re-statement of Romance" [146-title

RESTED. Rested immobile, though neighboring catafalques [NSF 391-8
  There was an island beyond him on which rested, [NSF 393-10
  An island to the South, on which rested like [NSF 393-11
RESTING. (In a world that was resting on pillars, [Botanist 1
  135-2
  But resting on me, thinking in my snow, [Choc 301-5
  Like angels resting on a rustic steeple [Art Pop 113-1 P
  See never-resting.
RESTLESS. And its restless iteration, [Solitaires 60-11
  And that confident one, Marie, the wearer of cheap stones, who
    will have grown still and restless; [Piano 22-5 P
RESTLESSLY. And take from this restlessly unhappy happiness [How
  Now 97-14 P
RESTORED. A clearness has returned. It stands restored. [NH 488-3
RESTORES. As if in a golden cloud. The son restores [Recit 87-16 P
RESTS. The bishop rests. [Gray 140-8
  Sleepless, inhales his proper air, and rests. [Cred 373-24
  Like a monster that has everything and rests, [Bouquet 452-4
  Of weight, on which the weightless rests: from which [Someone
    83-21 A
RESULT. In this light a man is a result, [Common 221-10
  Of the mind, result only in disaster. It follows, [Bed 326-14
RESULTS. The fiction that results from feeling. Yes, that. [NSF
  406-21
RESUMES. Resumes [Phases 5-22 P
RESUMING. Their love, this beginning, not resuming, this [NSF 391-5
RETAIN. That the vista retain ploughmen, peacocks, doves, [Burn-
  shaw 50-9 P
  Yet still retain resemblances, remain [Sombre 67-17 P
RETAINING. Of ex-bar, in-bar retaining attributes [EM 317-24
RETARDATION. A retardation of its battering, [Pure 330-5
RETENTIVE. For so retentive of themselves are men [Fictive 88-1
RETIREMENT. And then retirement like a turning back [C 35-11
RETRATO. A retrato that is strong because it is like, [Novel
  458-13
RETURN. For all it takes it gives a humped return [C 43-6
  The return to social nature, once begun, [C 43-20
  Return no more, where, then, is paradise?" [Sunday 68-16
  To be free again, to return to the violent mind [Farewell 118-17
  Mon Dieu, and must never again return. [Sailing 120-16
  We may return to Mozart. [Mozart 132-18
  To make him return to people, to find among them [Nigger 158-7
  Between issue and return, there is [MBG 176-18
  At the end of winter when afternoons return. [Poems Clim 193-11
  Would come from that return to the subtle centre. [Extracts
    258-21
  If evil never ends, is to return [Extracts 259-3
  Yet in that form will not return. But does [Repet 308-8
  Was a return to birth, a being born [EM 321-18
  When the cloud pressed suddenly the whole return [Liadoff 347-6
  We shall return at twilight from the lecture [NSF 406-23
  But your war ends. And after it you return [NSF 407-15
  Return to their original illusion. [Novel 457-3
  Began, the return to phantomerei, if not [What We 459-8
  After the leaves have fallen, we return [Plain 502-9
  These images return and are increased, [Soldat 13-15 P
  To return in a glittering wheel [Drum-Majors 36-21 P
  Return, affecting roseate aureoles, [Greenest 56-23 P
  From snow, and would return again to snow, [Greenest 57-26 P
  As summer would return to weazened days. [Greenest 57-27 P
  The same return at heavy evening, love [Duck 61-15 P
  The rest, to whom in the end the rest return, [Sombre 66-15 P
  Whose lives return, simply, upon our lips, [Sombre 67-5 P
  That they return unrecognized. The self [Woman Had 82-19 P
  To which all other forms, at last, return, [Recit 87-5 P
  The katy-dids at Ephrata return [Memo 89-1 P
  In a returning, a seeming of return, [Americana 94-14 P
  Some true interior to which to return, [Letters 107-5 P
  Fill it and return. [Three 130-1 P
RETURNED. Before the winter's vacancy returned. [C 34-12
  A little less returned for him each spring. [Anglais 148-12
  To which his imagination returned, [MBG 179-5
  It was not as if the jasmine ever returned. [Oboe 251-15
  Returned, unable to die again, fated [Extracts 258-26
  There were ghosts that returned to earth to hear his phrases,
    [Large 423-11
  There were those that returned to hear him read from the poem
    of life, [Large 423-14
  A clearness has returned. It stands restored. [NH 488-3
  But as of an exhumation returned to earth, [Aug 491-12
  Returned on board The Masculine. That night, [Bship 77-14 P
  Pronouncing its new life and ours, not autumn's prodigal
    returned, [Discov 96-4 P
RETURNING. Out of their blood, returning to the sky; [Sunday 70-5
  Flood on flood, of our returning sun. [Medit 123-15
  For a self returning mostly memory. [Anglais 148-18
  Yet one face keeps returning (never the one), [Dames 206-14
  And then returning from the moon, if one breathed [Extracts
    258-14
  They are sick of each old romance, returning, [Hero 274-6

Should there be a question of returning or [NSF 391-2
Something returning from a deeper quarter, [Imago 439-15
In the big X of the returning primitive. [NH 474-18
Angels returning after war with belts [Greenest 56-10 P
In a returning, a seeming of return, [Americana 94-14 P
RETURNS. So speech of your processionals returns [On Manner 56-1
  That, too, returns from out the winter's air, [Sun March 134-2
  But what his mother was returns and cries on his breast. [Pecul
    453-9
  The sea returns upon the men, [MBG 171-4
  To this returns. Between the two, [MBG 176-17
  The bareness of the house returns. [Contra I 267-1
  The sun aches and ails and then returns halloo [Questions 462-5
  Digs up the earth when want returns . . . [Soldat 16-11 P
  If the sceptre returns to earth, still moving, still [Bship
    80-31 P
  Returns and returns, along the dry, salt shore. [Woman Had 81-24P
REUNIONS. The casual reunions, the long-pondered [Extracts 258-5
REVEAL. They reveal themselves. [Lack 303-4
REVEALED. Revealed Susanna and her shame. [Peter 91-19
  A freedom revealed, a realization touched, [Bouquet 451-20
  To be swept across them when they are revealed, [Duck 65-19 P
REVEALING. Of revealing desire and is empty of shadows. [Sad Gay
    121-13
  Modes of desire, modes of revealing desire. [Sad Gay 122-12
  The revealing aberration should appear, [Nigger 153-18
  A perception of cold breath, more revealing than [Bus 116-7 P
REVEALS. This trivial trope reveals a way of truth. [Monocle 16-4
  The way a look or a touch reveals its unexpected magnitudes.
    [Prol 517-10
  Unhappy love reveals vast blemishes. [Red Kit 31-19 P
  Reveals her, rounded in beneficence, [Spaniard 34-4 P
  Here the total artifice reveals itself [Someone 87-12 A
REVEL. Whose coming may give revel [Watermelon 89-8
REVELATION. Description is revelation. It is not [Descrip 344-15
  A revelation not yet intended. [Region 115-12 P
REVELATIONS. Leaps downward through evening's revelations, and
    [NSF 404-16
  If the day writhes, it is not with revelations. [Ulti 429-15
  The glare of revelations going by! [Blanche 10-8 P
  In the planes that tilt hard revelations on [Someone 87-19 A
REVELLER. Where, butcher, seducer, bloodman, reveller, [Ghosts
    119-5
REVELRIES. Beyond revelries of sleep, [Watermelon 89-9
REVENGE. Than the revenge of music on bassoons. [C 32-25
  That his revenge created filial [EM 319-24
REVENGES. Revenges. And negation was eccentric. [EM 319-25
REVERBERATING. To see nor, reverberating, eke out the mind [Creat
    311-13
  The reverberating psalm, the right chorale. [EM 326-2
REVERBERATION. Not as it was: part of the reverberation [NH 473-19
  As it touches the point of reverberation--not grim [NH 475-14
REVERBERATIONS. Hence the reverberations in the words [C 37-11
  And these images, these reverberations, [Degen 444-7
  Abiding the reverberations in the vaults. [Papini 447-11
  And reverberations clinging to whisper still. [Rome 510-20
  Reverberations leak and lack among holes . . . [Armor 529-8
REVERY. The unspotted imbecile revery, [MBG 172-5
  His revery was the deepness of the pool, [Descrip 342-11
  All final, colors subjected in revery [Descrip 342-16
  The human revery or poem of death? [Men Made 355-16
  Revery is a solitude in which [Men Made 356-1
  Swaddled in revery, the object of [NSF 388-3
  Anecdotal Revery [Soldat 12-title 3 P
REVIEW. Alone, a lean Review and said, [MBG 180-20
REVOLUTION. A revolution of things colliding. [Nightgown 214-13
  He said it of Konstantinov. Revolution [EM 324-27
  In perpetual revolution, round and round . . . [Descrip 342-20
  That revolution takes for connoisseurs: [Sombre 70-9 P
REVOLUTIONISTS. "The Revolutionists Stop for Orangeade" [102-
    title
REVOLUTIONS. Without the revolutions' ruin, [Lytton 39-4 P
  The revolutions through day and night, [Ulysses 102-22 P
  Are matched by other revolutions [Ulysses 102-25 P
REVOLVED. But muted, mused, and perfectly revolved [C 45-24
  The clambering wings of birds of black revolved, [Babies 77-14
  "A Thought Revolved" [184-title
  Revolved. [Sombre 69-20 P
REVOLVERS. Revolvers and shoot each other. One remains. [Extracts
    256-2
REVOLVES. In the brightest landscape downwardly revolves [EM 318-19
  And in his mind the world revolves. [Ulysses 102-21 P
REVOLVING. Of each old revolving dance, the music [Hero 274-7
  Like the shiddow-shaddow of lights revolving [Hero 279-20
  You will have stopped revolving except in crystal. [NSF 407-3
  Like a plain poet revolving in his mind [Moonlight 531-2
  For ponderous revolving, without help. [Sombre 69-16 P
  And, while revolving, ancient hyacinths [Sombre 69-17 P
  More babies than that. The merely revolving wheel [Woman Had
    81-23 P

There, of clear, revolving crystalline; [Ideal 88-7 A
REX. Rex and principium, exit the whole [C 37-1
  Waved in pale adieu. The rex Impolitor [Aug 495-21
  Like any other, rex by right of the crown, [Bship 79-3 P
RHAPSODIC. Your guns are not rhapsodic strophes, red [Bship 80-20P
  Our good, from this the rhapsodic strophes flow, [Bship 81-5 P
RHAPSODIES. Beneath the rhapsodies of fire and fire, [Eve Angels
  138-3
  Are the fulfilling rhapsodies that hymn it to creation?
    [Inelegance 26-4 P
  There is a man whom rhapsodies of change, [Sombre 66-12 P
RHAPSODIST. But through man's eye, their silent rhapsodist, [Rock
  528-6
RHAPSODY. A pearly poetess, peaked for rhapsody. [C 44-32
  When too great rhapsody is left annulled [Havana 144-9
  It must be this rhapsody or none, [MBG 183-1
  The rhapsody of things as they are. [MBG 183-2
  One wild rhapsody a fake for another. [Waldorf 241-3
  Locution of a hand in a rhapsody. [Pastor 379-8
RHETORIC. "Add This to Rhetoric" [198-title
  Uplifting the completest rhetoric [Extracts 253-20
  Without a word of rhetoric--there it is. [Repet 309-3
  Like rhetoric in a narration of the eye-- [Pure 331-18
  Pure rhetoric of a language without words. [Cred 374-15
  The object that rises with so much rhetoric, [Questions 462-11
  To the final full, an end without rhetoric. [Bship 81-11 P
RHETORICIAN. So far beyond the rhetorician's touch. [Roses 431-12
RHETORICS. And echoing rhetorics more than our own. [Montra 261-18
RHODODENDRONS. Of the rhododendrons rattled their gold, [Sleight
  222-5
RHOMBOIDS. If they tried rhomboids, [Six Sig 75-10
RHYME. On urns and oak-leaves twisted into rhyme. [Sombre 68-1 P
RHYMES. Day hymns instead of constellated rhymes, [Thought 185-18
RHYTHM. The rhythm of this celestial pantomime." [Landsc 243-8
  And triple chime . . . The self-same rhythm [Stan Hero 83-22 P
RHYTHMS. And lucid, inescapable rhythms; [Thirteen 94-2
  "Poem with Rhythms" [245-title
RI. Cherries are ri . . . He would never say that. [Grotesque
  76-1 P
RIBALDRIES. Annealed them in their cabin ribaldries! [C 42-21
RIBANDS. Of breakfast ribands, fruits laid in their leaves,
  [C 42-26
RIBBED. See flat-ribbed.
RIBBON. With ribbon, a rigid statement of them, white, [NSF 402-6
RIBBONED. The ribboned stick, the bellowing breeches, cloak
  [C 28-8
RIBBONS. The child's three ribbons are in her plaited hair.
    [Extraord 369-21
  See hair-ribbons.
RICANERY. To the laughter of evil: the fierce ricanery [Extracts
  253-17
RIC-A-NIC. Its shoo-shoo-shoo, its ric-a-nic, [Mozart 131-16
RICH. The rich man going bare, the paladin [C 37-17
  The vile antithesis of poor and rich. [NE Verses 104-6
  Rich Tweedle-dum, poor Tweedle-dee. [Nigger 154-13
  Like the man that is rich and right. [Idiom 201-5
  Only the rich remember the past, [Arcades 225-1
  Blue friends in shadows, rich conspirators, [Choc 300-9
  The rich earth, of its own self made rich, [Aug 491-13
  Rich John, and his son, rich John, [Soldat 15-6 P
  And his rich son's John, and-a-one [Soldat 15-7 P
  Of buzzards and eat the bellies of the rich, [Burnshaw 49-8 P
RICHER. Much richer, more fecund, sportive and alive. [NH 469-24
RICHES. Is the riches of their atmosphere. [MBG 172-12
RICHTER. See Ludwig Richter.
RIC-RAC. In the grinding ric-rac, staring steadily [Men Fall 188-4
RIDE. The mules that angels ride come slowly down [Monocle 15-18
  No horses to ride and no one to ride them [Forces 229-10
  With lofty darkness. The donkey was there to ride, [Uruguay
    249-9
  Someone has left for a ride in a balloon [Phenom 286-7
  He will never ride the red horse she describes. [Questions
    462-15
  To ride in a cab. [Cab 20-17 P
  To ride an old mule round the keys-- [Stan MBG 73-7 P
RIDER. The moonlight? Was it a rider intent on the sun, [Uruguay
    249-20
  As the rider, no chevalere and poorly dressed, [Uruguay 249-28
  Without a rider on a road at night. [Pure 329-17
  Or Death was a rider beating his horse, [Soldat 16-4 P
  In which the horse walks home without a rider, [Fare Guit 99-3 P
  Of the rider that was, [Fare Guit 99-6 P
RIDES. Rides clear of her mind and the waves make a refrain
    [Farewell 117-8
RIDGE-POLE. Say, puerile, that the buzzards crouch on the ridge-
    pole [Two Figures 86-10
RIDGES. The mountainous ridges, purple balustrades, [C 33-14
  Beyond all trees, the ridges thrown [How Live 125-19
RIDICULE. The sea is a form of ridicule. [MBG 180-1
RIDING. Unwished for, chance, the merest riding [Hero 275-12

RIFLE-BUTT. And knock like a rifle-butt against the door. [AA
  414-2
RIFLES. Rifles grow sharper on the sight. [Dutch 291-2
RIGHT. To the right, [Earthy 3-8
  To the right, to the left, [Earthy 3-16
  And they read right long. [Ord Women 11-16
  For I reach right up to the sun, [Six Sig 74-7
  Perhaps our wretched state would soon come right. [Surprises
    98-9
  They sing right puissantly. [Snow Stars 133-3
  Made earth come right; a peanut parody [Havana 143-9
  And all their manner, right and wrong, [MBG 166-17
  Like the man that is rich and right. [Idiom 201-5
  It wants Belshazzar reading right [Country 207-20
  They think that things are all right, [Jersey 210-20
  It had to be right: nougats. It was a shift [Forces 229-16
  That clings to the mind like that right sound, that song
    [Extracts 256-14
  The reverberating psalm, the right chorale. [EM 326-2
  By its form alone, by being right, [Pediment 361-13
  Within them right for terraces--oh, brave salut! [Belly 367-11
  Joy of such permanence, right ignorance [Cred 373-12
  The right, uplifted foreleg of the horse [NSF 391-10
  They are a plural, a right and left, a pair, [NSF 407-11
  And red, and right. The particular question--here [Ulti 429-12
  A right red with its composites glutted full, [Bouquet 452-3
  At the upper right, a pyramid with one side [What We 460-2
  Of right joining, a music of ideas, the burning [Study II 465-1
  For the outlook that would be right, [Poem Mt 512-9
  You never can be right. You are the man. [Red Kit 30-16 P
  And yet the damned thing doesn't come right. [Agenda 41-18 P
  Like any other, rex by right of the crown, [Bship 79-3 P
  The right to be." Guiding his boat [Ulysses 99-14 P
  The right within us and about us, [Ulysses 100-13 P
  The order of man's right to be [Ulysses 101-13 P
  The eloquence of right, since knowing [Ulysses 101-17 P
  And being are one: the right to know [Ulysses 101-18 P
  And the right to be are one. We come [Ulysses 101-19 P
  By one, in the right of all. Each man [Ulysses 102-5 P
  Of gods and men destroyed, the right [Ulysses 102-10 P
  To know established as the right to be. [Ulysses 102-11 P
  By a right philosopher: renews [Ulysses 103-3 P
  They measure the right to use. Need makes [Ulysses 104-24 P
  The right to use. Need names on its breath [Ulysses 104-25 P
  A help, a right to help, a right [Ulysses 104-28 P
  By right of knowing, another plane. [Ulysses 104-30 P
  The right to be." He guided his boat [Presence 105-17 P
  The right within me and about me, [Presence 105-22 P
  This eloquence of right, since knowing [Presence 106-2 P
  And being are one--the right to know [Presence 106-3 P
  Is equal to the right to be. [Presence 106-4 P
RIGHT-ANGLED. To right-angled triangles. [Six Sig 75-9
RIGHTING. His roles, would leave to the clouds the righting,
    [Stan Hero 84-25 P
RIGHTLY. If seen rightly and yet a possible red. [NSF 393-18
RIGHTNESS. The difficult rightness of half-risen day. [Rock 528-9
RIGHTNESSES. Sounds passing through sudden rightnesses, wholly
    [Of Mod 240-16
RIGID. The father, the beater of the rigid drums, [Thought 186-4
  In this rigid room, an intenser love, [Dezem 218-17
  Of a suspension, a permanence, so rigid [NSF 391-17
  With ribbon, a rigid statement of them, white, [NSF 402-6
  Out of rigid realists. It is as if [NH 470-4
  Writing and reading the rigid inscription. [Aug 495-16
  Though they are rigid in rigid emptiness. [Rock 525-6
  And ours, of rigid measure, a miser's paint; [Sombre 67-8 P
RIGOR. But the difficultest rigor is forthwith, [NSF 398-20
RIM. And still the final quarter, still the rim, [Spaniard 34-9 P
  Will shout from the tower's rim. [Secret Man 36-16 P
  Of crisping light along the statue's rim. [Old Woman 43-18 P
  Reach from the horizons, rim to rim, [Sombre 68-25 P
RIND. Aloe of ivory, pear of rusty rind.) [Bird Claws 82-5
  At B: the origin of the mango's rind. [Rock 528-13
  The angel at the center of this rind, [Someone 83-6 A
RINDS. Washed into rinds by rotting winter rains. [Monocle 16-11
  Pecking at more lascivious rinds than ours, [Nigger 152-16
RING. Supple and turbulent, a ring of men [Sunday 69-28
  The shadows of his fellows ring him round [EM 319-11
  The roundness that pulls tight the final ring [Orb 442-8
  Each truth is a sect though no bells ring for it. [Luther 462-1
  A finger with a ring to guide his eye [Aug 492-10
  At lucent children round her in a ring. [Hermit 506-3
  That merely makes a ring). [Abnormal 24-1 P
  Rage 'n the ring and shake the corridors. [Spaniard 35-1 P
  The heads held high and gathered in a ring [Old Woman 43-12 P
  And on this ring of marble horses shed [Burnshaw 47-27 P
  Weaving ring in radiant ring and quickly, fling [Burnshaw 51-14P
  A ring of horses rising from memory [Greenest 57-10 P
  Would be a ring of heads and haunches, torn [Sombre 70-22 P
  Of the world would have only to ring and ft! [Bship 78-9 P

The spirit's ring and seal, the naked heart. [Bship 79-13 P
RINGED. Ringed round and barred, with eyes held in their hands,
   [Page 422-30
   See wild-ringed.
RINGS. A white of wildly woven rings; [W Burgher 61-15
   Or purple with green rings, [Ten O'C 66-4
   Or green with yellow rings, [Ten O'C 66-5
   Or yellow with blue rings. [Ten O'C 66-6
   The trade-wind jingles the rings in the nets around the racks
      by the docks on Indian River. [Indian 112-4
   Dropping in sovereign rings [Pascagoula 127-6
   Steps out. He rings and knocks. The door is not locked. [Bouquet
      452-20
   Surrounded by its choral rings, [Not Ideas 534-16
   Rather rings than fingers, rather fingers than hands. [Grotesque
      74-8 P
   See ear-rings.
RIOT. Thick-lipped from riot and rebellious cries, [Men Fall 188-8
RIOTER. The rioter that appears when things are changed, [Pagoda
   91-20 P
RIP. It had been real. It was not now. The rip [Repet 306-7
RIPE. Does ripe fruit never fall? Or do the boughs [Sunday 69-14
   Itself that seed's ripe, unpredictable fruit. [Descrip 341-20
   A land too ripe for enigmas, too serene. [Cred 374-9
   And hems the planet rose and haws it ripe, [Ulti 429-11
   It is centi-colored and mille-flored and ripe [Bouquet 450-2
   And the ripe shrub writhed. [Planet 532-12
   Or like a ripe strawberry [Three 135-10 P
   See ruddy-ripe.
RIPEN. Sweet berries ripen in the wilderness; [Sunday 70-24
RIPENED. Ripened in warmth and served in warmth. On terms [Nigger
   155-4
RIPENESS. The red ripeness of round leaves is thick [Pecul 453-10
RIPENESSES. Among the children, like curious ripenesses [AA 415-8
RIPENING. If ever, whisked and wet, not ripening, [C 34-11
   Disdaining each astringent ripening, [EM 318-20
   Of pattern in the dance's ripening. [AA 415-9
   That the peaches are slowly ripening. [Memo 89-10 P
RIPER. But that this bloom grown riper, showing nibs [C 44-6
RIPEST. Of ripest summer, always lingering [Havana 143-14
RISE. When they rise [Sugar-Cane 12-17
   Its black blooms rise. [Weep Woman 25-6
   Here, something in the rise and fall of wind [C 29-3
   Rise, since rising will not waken, [Watermelon 89-14
   The nakedness would rise and suddenly turn [Sea Surf 101-16
   Scaffolds and derricks rise from the reeds to the clouds [NE
      Verses 105-9
   Shout for me, loudly and loudly, joyful sun, when you rise.
      [Nigger 150-17
   As of a tragic science should rise. [Prelude 195-13
   You see the moon rise in the empty sky. [Dump 202-25
   That sees above them, that sees rise up above them, [Candle
      223-11
   They do not touch it. Sounds never rise [Arcades 225-10
   Beyond which it has no will to rise. [Of Mod 240-18
   Look round, brown moon, brown bird, as you rise to fly, [God
      285-1
   Look round you as you start to rise, brown moon, [God 285-4
   Makes him rise above the houses, looking down. [Repet 307-14
   We say ourselves in syllables that rise [Creat 311-17
   Again, an inexhaustible being, rise [NSF 390-13
   The sun might rise and it might not and if [Page 422-11
   Rise liquidly in liquid lingerings, [Angel 497-3
   To the moment. There the horses would rise again, [Old Woman
      46-7 P
   Of rose, or what will once more rise to rose, [Burnshaw 49-27 P
   When younger bodies, because they are younger, rise [Burnshaw
      49-28 P
   If once the statue were to rise, if it stood, [Greenest 54-25 P
   The workers do not rise, as Venus rose, [Duck 60-9 P
   Out of a violet sea. They rise a bit [Duck 60-10 P
   They rise to the muddy, metropolitan elms, [Duck,60-13 P
   If you caricature the way they rise, yet they rise. [Duck 60-18 P
RISEN. Could have risen to the clouds, [Weak Mind 212-17
   See half-risen.
RISES. Rises through fruit-trees. [Magnifico 19-19
   But no queen rises. [Depression 63-8
   Where the voice that is great within us rises up, [Eve Angels
      138-5
   The sun rises green and blue in the fields and in the heavens.
      [Fish-Scale 161-5
   The crow looks rusty as he rises up. [Possum 294-15
   Running in the rises of common speech, [Sketch 336-5
   A palm that rises up beyond the sea, [Descrip 344-2
   Of earth, rises against it, tide by tide, [Two V 354-20
   It rises from land and sea and covers them. [Cred 375-12
   Howls hoo and rises and howls hoo and falls. [NSF 383-8
   The object that rises with so much rhetoric, [Questions 462-11
   Wood-smoke rises through trees, is caught in an upper flow
      [Slug 522-3

The stone from which he rises, up--and--ho, [Rock 528-2
   Its chapel rises from Terre Ensevelie, [Armor 529-9
   The chapel rises, his own, his period, [Armor 529-21
   That rises in the air. The sprawlers on the grass [Duck 64-7 P
   Forgetful of death in war, there rises [Stan Hero 84-2 P
   Beyond the last thought, rises [Of Mere 117-16 P
   The sun rises [Three 130-22 P
   Before it rises, [Three 131-2 P
RISING. And lank, rising and slumping from a sea [C 34-5
   Rise, since rising will not waken, [Watermelon 89-14
   Who, then, beheld the rising of the clouds [Sea Surf 99-23
   Massively rising high and bare [How Live 125-18
   An Adriatic riva rising, [Botanist 1 135-8
   Yesterday the roses were rising upward, [Nigger 156-10
   Rising upward from a sea of ex. [MBG 175-4
   Now that the moon is rising in the heat [Men Fall 187-10
   Rising upon the doctors in their beds [Freed 205-3
   For a moment on rising, at the edge of the bed, to be, [Freed
      205-8
   Flew close to, flew to without rising away. [God 285-8
   From the floor, rising in speech we do not speak. [Creat 311-18
   That a bright red woman will be rising [Debris 338-6
   On his hill, watching the rising and falling, and says: [Two V
      354-22
   To its barbed, barbarous rising and has peace. [Extraord 369-11
   As when the sun comes rising, when the sea [NSF 398-23
   Like a book on rising beautiful and true. [AA 418-15
   Just rising, accompanying, arranged to cross, [Page 422-24
   They go to the cliffs of Moher rising out of the mist, [Irish
      501-13
   Rising out of present time and place, above [Irish 502-1
   The same wind, rising and rising, makes a sound [Look 519-2
   A sacred syllable rising from sacked speech, [Armor 530-1
   The sun was rising at six, [Not Ideas 534-7
   Rising from indolent coils. If the statue rose, [Greenest 54-24P
   A ring of horses rising from memory [Greenest 57-10 P
   Or rising in the appointments of desire, [Greenest 57-11 P
   Observed the waves, the rising and the swell [Woman Had 81-13 P
   The rising and the swell, the preparation [Woman Had 81-15 P
   The rising and the swell, the first line's glitter, [Woman Had
      81-17 P
   See: moon-rising; up-rising.
RITUAL. The melon should have apposite ritual, [C 39-1
RIVA. An Adriatic riva rising, [Botanist 1 135-8
RIVER. A sinewy nakedness. A river bore [C 36-5
   The river is moving. [Thirteen 94-19
   And the same bridge when the river is frozen. [Nigger 154-12
   And the river that batters its way over stones, [Loaf 199-17
   The pines along the river and the dry men blown [Loaf 199-21
   See the river, the railroad, the cathedral . . . [Hartford 227-6
   Of the town, the river, the railroad were clear. [Hartford 227-8
   That obsolete fiction of the wide river in [Oboe 250-9
   He never felt twice the same about the flecked river, [Cata
      424-10
   He wanted the river to go on flowing the same way, [Cata 425-3
   Swatara, Swatara, black river, [Countryman 428-9
   Brooding sounds of river noises; [Degen 444-6
   It is certain that the river [Degen 444-12
   That is the flock-flecked river, the water, [Degen 444-17
   When Swatara becomes this undulant river [Degen 444-20
   And the river becomes the landless, waterless ocean? [Degen
      444-21
   The river motion, the drowsy motion of the river R. [Old Man
      501-6
   "The River of Rivers in Connecticut" [533-title
   There is a great river this side of Stygia, [R Conn 533-4
   In that river, far this side of Stygia, [R Conn 533-7
   No shadow walks. The river is fateful, [R Conn 533-10
   Call it, once more, a river, an unnamed flowing, [R Conn 533-18
   The river that flows nowhere, like a sea. [R Conn 533-21
   In the morning, the clear river [Primordia 8-5 P
   See: Indian River; North River.
RIVER-BANKS. Why set the pear upon those river-banks [Sunday 69-20
RIVERS. With rivers like our own that seek for seas [Sunday 69-17
   It is true that the rivers went nosing like swine, [Frogs 78-1
   As the swine-like rivers suckled themselves [Frogs 78-14
   The muddy rivers of spring [Mud 147-13
   I dreamed, of autumn rivers, silvas green, [Montra 263-2
   Of serpents like z rivers simmering, [Pure 330-1
   The rivers shine and hold their mirrors up, [Belly 366-19
   "The River of Rivers in Connecticut" [533-title
RIVER-SIDE. Kicked through the roof, caressed by the river-side.
      [Bship 80-6 P
ROAD. The ruts in your empty road are red. [Fish-Scale 160-18
   "On the Road Home" [203-title
   Whose horse clattered on the road on which she rose, [Uruguay
      249-18
   Rode over the picket rocks, rode down the road, [Uruguay 250-2
   Without a rider on a road at night. [Pure 329-17
   To disclose in the figure waiting on the road [Moonlight 531-13

ROAD. A woman looking down the road, [Ulysses 104-21 P
  Last evening I met him on the road. [Three 141-11 P
ROADS. Emotions on wet roads on autumn nights; [Sunday 67-23
ROAMED. And thus she roamed [Infanta 8-1
  The mind roamed as a moth roams, [Hibiscus 22-10
  And roamed there all the stupid afternoon. [Hibiscus 23-3
ROAMER. So you're home again, Redwood Roamer, and ready [Phenom
    286-13
  Of the garden. We must prepare to hear the Roamer's [Phenom
    286-17
  The Roamer is a voice taller than the redwoods, [Phenom 287-4
ROAMINGS. In the roamings of her fan, [Infanta 8-2
ROAMS. The mind roamed as a moth roams, [Hibiscus 22-10
ROAR. And let the water-belly of ocean roar, [Montra 261-23
  To whom the jaguars cry and lions roar [Greenest 55-19 P
  Without the furious roar in his capital. [Someone 85-6 A
ROARED. If Shasta roared up in Nassau, [Agenda 42-2 P
ROARING. And roaring horns. [Peter 91-11
  "To the Roaring Wind" [113-title
  In trombones roaring for the children, [Hero 278-10
  But over the wind, over the legends of its roaring, [Puel 456-4
ROARS. The lion roars at the enraging desert, [NSF 384-7
ROBE. This robe of snow and winter stars, [Snow Stars 133-4
  Out of a mood, the tragic robe [MBG 169-20
  In a robe that is our glory as he guards. [Owl 435-3
  Saved and beholden, in a robe of rays. [NH 477-24
ROBES. He has left his robes folded in camphor [Gray 140-2
  Dressed in his colored robes. [Gray 140-20
  In his chalk and violet robes. [Nigger 151-14
  His robes and symbols, ai-yi-yi-- [MBG 178-11
  Become rude robes among white candle lights, [Greenest 53-4 P
  Motions of air, robes moving in torrents of air, [Greenest
    53-5 P
ROBIN. Ke-ke, the jug-throated robin pouring out, [NSF 394-2
  Red robin, stop in your preludes, practicing [NSF 405-16
  See cock-robin.
ROBINGS. Like many robings, as moving masses are, [Owl 433-9
ROBINS. The robins are là-bas, the squirrels, in tree-caves
    [NH 487-11
ROBUST. The grunting, shuffling branches, the robust, [Parochial
    191-8
ROCK. To flare, in the sun-pallor of his rock. [Bird Claws 82-18
  Last evening the moon rose above this rock [How Live 125-9
  Instead there was this tufted rock [How Live 125-17
  Only the great height of the rock [How Live 126-3
  The touch that topples men and rock." [MBG 170-20
  Of time, time grows upon the rock. [MBG 171-10
  Rock, of valedictory echoings, [MBG 179-4
  To Belshazzar, putrid rock, [Country 207-4
  Letters of rock and water, words [Vari 232-10
  Of the expanses that are mountainous rock and sea; [Repet 308-24
  By the sea, insolid rock, stentor, and said: [Two V 353-12
  The human ocean beats against this rock [Two V 354-19
  The rock cannot be broken. It is the truth. [Cred 375-11
  The other immeasurable half, such rock [Cred 375-14
  It is the visible rock, the audible. [Cred 375-17
  It is the rock of summer, the extreme, [Cred 375-21
  Black beaded on the rock, the flecked animal, [AA 412-2
  Itself a cloud, although of misted rock [AA 416-5
  Making this heavy rock a place, [Imago 439-17
  In primavera, the shadow of bare rock, [NH 476-9
  Becomes the rock of autumn, glittering, [NH 476-10
  The exact rock where his inexactnesses [Poem Mt 512-11
  "The Rock" [525-title
  That the green leaves came and covered the high rock, [Rock
    526-4
  It is not enough to cover the rock with leaves. [Rock 526-10
  Its copy of the sun, these cover the rock. [Rock 527-1
  They are more than leaves that cover the barren rock, [Rock 527-6
  In this plenty, the poem makes meanings of the rock, [Rock 527-16
  Forms of the Rock in a Night-Hymn [Rock 528-title 3
  The rock is the gray particular of man's life, [Rock 528-1
  The rock is the stem particular of the air, [Rock 528-4
  Turquoise the rock, at odious evening bright [Rock 528-7
  The rock is the habitation of the whole, [Rock 528-10
  It is the rock where tranquil must adduce [Rock 528-14
  Night's hymn of the rock, as in a vivid sleep. [Rock 528-21
  Lives in a fluid, not on solid rock. [Sombre 68-5 P
  To rumbled rock, its bright projections lie [Sombre 70-3 P
  This rock and the dry birds [Including 88-3 P
  This rock and the priest, [Including 88-5 P
  It is true that you live on this rock [Including 88-7 P
  With the rock and mine with you. [Including 88-14 P
ROCKED. The yellow rocked across the still façades, [Babies 77-4
ROCKET. Do you remember how the rocket went on [Liadoff 346-5
  Had crowded into the rocket and touched the fuse. [Liadoff
    346-13
  That the rocket was only an inferior cloud. [Liadoff 347-16
  See John Rocket.
ROCKING. In an interior ocean's rocking [Jasmine 79-11

ROCKINGS. To whom oracular rockings gave no rest. [C 30-28
ROCKS. Are overhung by the shadows of the rocks [Grapes 111-2
  Regard now the sloping, mountainous rocks [Loaf 199-16
  The rocks not even touched by snow, [Loaf 199-20
  Flowing above the rocks, flowing over the sky, [Loaf 200-4
  It was soldiers went marching over the rocks [Loaf 200-13
  The rocks of the cliffs are the heads of dogs [Vari 232-12
  Rode over the picket rocks, rode down the road, [Uruguay 250-2
  Snow under the trees and on the northern rocks, [Extracts 255-15
  The dead rocks not the green rocks, the live rocks. If,
    [Extracts 255-16
  Of the secondary men. There are no rocks [Jumbo 269-17
  The snow hangs heavily on the rocks, brought [Hero 273-5
  What lover has one in such rocks, what woman, [EM 323-24
  The scene in his gray-rose with violet rocks. [Anach 366-5
  These forms are not abortive figures, rocks, [Owl 432-5
  Staked solidly in a gusty grappling with rocks. [NH 487-21
  Shifted the rocks and picked his way among clouds, [Poem Mt
    512-8
  4. The sea is spouting upward out of rocks. [Someone 86-7 A
RODE. He rode over Connecticut [Thirteen 94-13
  And I, if I rode naked, are what remain." [Uruguay 249-6
  Rode over the picket rocks, rode down the road, [Uruguay 250-2
  Made by a cook that never rode the back [Burnshaw 46-20 P
  O bold, that rode your horses straight away. [Duck 61-31 P
RODOMONTADEAN. Of the past, the rodomontadean emptiness. [Novel
    457-6
RODRIGUEZ-FEO. See José Rodriguez-Feo.
RODS. I have been pupil under bishops' rods [Soldat 11-4 P
ROI. Or into a dark-blue king, un roi tonnerre, [Extracts 254-10
ROISTERERS. And sentimental roisterers, [Sat Night 28-8 P
ROLE. It is a most spectacular role, and yet [Spaniard 35-4 P
  "The Role of the Idea in Poetry" [93-title P
ROLES. His roles, would leave to the clouds the righting, [Stan
    Hero 84-25 P
ROLL. Roll a drum upon the blue guitar. [MBG 170-13
  In which his voice would roll its cadences, [Blue Bldg 216-19
  It cannot be. There's nothing there to roll [AA 420-9
  Hear the loud drums roll-- [Phases 3-11 P
  See pay-roll.
ROLLED. Of heaven in an antique reflection rolled [Sea Surf 99-13
  Would--But more suddenly the heaven rolled [Sea Surf 101-18
  And heaven rolled as one and from the two [Sea Surf 102-14
  That rolled in heat is silver-tipped [Vari 234-7
  They rolled their r's, there, in the land of the citrons.
    [NH 486-19
ROLLER. Call the roller of big cigars, [Emperor 64-1
ROLLING. Until the rolling heaven made them blue, [Sea Surf 100-24
  But this gross blue under rolling bronzes [Grapes 110-15
  Gray grasses rolling windily away [Nigger 155-14
  The drenching thunder rolling by, [MBG 169-2
  And that drums had to be rolling, rolling, rolling. [Loaf 200-17
  One observes profoundest shadows rolling. [Vari 235-14
  See long-rolling.
ROLLS. On an old shore, the vulgar ocean rolls [Somnam 304-1
  A ship that rolls on a confected ocean, [EM 322-23
  An immense drum rolls through a clamor of people. [Stan Hero
    83-11 P
ROMA. Roma ni Avignon ni Leyden, [Hero 273-2
  The brightness of arms, said Roma wasted [Hero 273-8
ROMANCE. Was clear. The last distortion of romance [C 30-2
  Related in romance to backward flights, [C 39-10
  Not by way of romance, [Explan 72-17
  "Re-statement of Romance" [146-title
  And yet it is a singular romance, [Extracts 256-11
  They are sick of each old romance, returning. [Hero 274-6
  The romance of the precise is not the elision [Adult 353-7
  Of the tired romance of imprecision. [Adult 353-8
  But not of romance, the bitterest vulgar do [Bouquet 450-4
  Inescapable romance, inescapable choice [NH 468-10
  "Romance for a Demoiselle Lying in the Grass" [23-title P
  As toward an absolute foyer beyond romance. [Local 112-12 P
ROMANESQUE. Romanesque Affabulation [Thought 185-title 3
ROMANTIC. The romantic should be here. [Sailing 120-12
  The romantic should be there. [Sailing 120-13
  But the romantic must never remain, [Sailing 120-15
  Destroys romantic tenements [Bottle 238-19
  Romantic tenements of rose and ice. [Bottle 239-16
  Romantic with dreams of her avoirdupois, green glade [Pure 330-17
  The romantic intoning, the declaimed clairvoyance [NSF 387-19
ROMANTICIZED. Seems like a sheen of heat romanticized. [NH 468-9
ROMANZA. Romanza out of the black shepherd's isle, [NH 480-13
  The things around--the alternate romanza [NH 480-21
ROMANZAS. The two romanzas, the distant and the near, [NH 481-2
ROME. Bergamo on a postcard, Rome after dark, [NH 486-1
  "To an Old Philosopher in Rome" [508-title
  The threshold, Rome, and that more merciful Rome [Rome 508-6
  The sources of happiness in the shape of Rome, [Rome 508-23
  For a citizen of heaven though still of Rome. [Rome 510-2
  It is older than the oldest speech of Rome. [Rome 510-4

Weeps in Segovia. The beggar in Rome [Greenest 59-17 P
ROOF. And while the torrent on the roof still droned [C 33-8
   If they throw stones upon the roof [Mozart 131-18
   It is the sea that whitens the roof. [MBG 179-13
   There were others like him safely under roof: [Choc 299-23
   The wind beat in the roof and half the walls. [Repet 306-2
   Be spoken to, without a roof, without [NSF 385-9
   Cinderella fulfilling herself beneath the roof? [NSF 405-9
   The elephant on the roof and its elephantine blaring, [Puel
     456-5
   She lay upon the roof, [Song Fixed 519-18
   Lay on the roof [Song Fixed 520-9
   Wavered in evening air, above the roof, [Phases 5-5 P
   The sounds of rain on the roof [Secret Man 35-21 P
   Kicked through the roof, caressed by the river-side. [Bship 80-6P
ROOFS. The crosses on the convent roofs [Botanist 2 135-16
   The air is full of children, statues, roofs [Chaos 357-15
   Across the roofs as sigil and as ward [NSF 384-23
ROOM. Turned in the room, [Domination 8-11
   They swept over the room, [Domination 8-21
   Nor half begun, but, when it is, leave room [C 33-19
   Leave room, therefore, in that unwritten book [C 33-26
   Crispin magister of a single room, [C 42-5
   Leaving no room upon his cloudy knee, [C 43-18
   Blunt yellow in such a room! [Bananas 54-3
   In my room, the world is beyond my understanding; [Of Surface
     57-1
   If in a shimmering room the babies came, [Babies 77-10
   Here in this room, desiring you, [Peter 90-3
   In the catastrophic room . . . beyond despair, [Men Fall 187-18
   Of those for whom a square room is a fire, [Parochial 191-13
   In the room more like a snowy air, [Poems Clim 193-9
   It was how the sun came shining into his room: [Freed 205-6
   In this rigid room, an intenser love, [Dezem 218-14
   The room is quiet where they are. [Peaches 224-15
   (This man in a room with an image of the world, [Rhythms 245-12
   In an ascetic room, its table [Hero 275-28
   The room is emptier than nothingness. [Phenom 286-9
   Sit in the room. It is true in the moonlight [Debris 338-3
   We say: At night an Arabian in my room, [NSF 383-1
   Enters the room, it drowses and is the night. [NSF 399-19
   Patches the moon together in his room [NSF 407-7
   To walk another room . . . Monsieur and comrade, [NSF 407-17
   The purpose of the poem, fills the room. [AA 413-5
   Of the room and on an accordion, half-heard, [AA 419-2
   To be anything else in the sunlight of the room, [Roses 430-12
   He enters the room and calls. No one is there. [Bouquet 452-21
   Of an unfamiliar in the familiar room, [Novel 458-12
   Slowly the room grows dark. It is odd about [Novel 458-19
   In the street, in a room, on a carpet or a wall, [NH 467-12
   A mirror, a lake of reflections in a room, [NH 468-14
   Beyond the object. He sits in his room, beside [NH 475-7
   The instinct for earth, for New Haven, for his room, [NH 476-2
   Who sits thinking in the corners of a room. [NH 480-2
   Of the pity that is the memorial of this room, [Rome 509-12
   Ever want it to. It is part of the life in your room. [Rome
     510-13
   The book and candle in your ambered room, [Rome 510-25
   Of year. Here in his house and in his room, [Quiet 523-8
   Light the first light of evening, as in a room [Final 524-1
   Blanche, the blonde, whose eyes are not wholly straight, in a
     room of lustres, shed by turquoise falling, [Piano 22-1 P
   "A Room on a Garden" [40-title P
   And in a bed in one room, alone, a listener [Sick 90-13 P
   In the ceiling of the distant room, in which he lies, [Sick
     90-17 P
   "As You Leave the Room" [116-title P
   On the table or in the colors of the room. [Someone 84-19 A
   That steeps the room, quickly, then not at all, [Someone 87-15 A
   Or woman weeping in a room or man, [Ideal 88-20 A
ROOMS. Think, in square rooms, [Six Sig 75-5
   Saying things in the rooms and on the stair, [Less 327-10
   Round the rooms, which do not ever seem to change . . . [Lot
     372-3
   The windows will be lighted, not the rooms. [AA 413-24
ROOT. And I taste at the root of the tongue the unreal of what is
   real. [Holiday 313-10
   Suppose this was the root of everything. [Golden 460-7
   The body quickened and the mind in root. [Rock 527-10
   The root of a form, as of this fruit, a fund, [Someone 83-5 A
ROOTED. The stalks are firmly rooted in ice. [Possum 294-8
ROOT-MAN. To equate the root-man and the super-man, [Montra 262-22
   The root-man swarming, tortured by his mass, [Montra 262-23
ROOTS. It is the same jingle of the water among the roots under
   the banks of the palmettoes, [Indian 112-5
   At the roots of her indifferent curls. [Thought 184-14
   The vine, at the roots, this vine of Key West, splurging, [Bship
     80-9 P
ROPES. From warehouse doors, the gustiness of ropes, [C 36-9
ROSA. And Rosa, the muslin dreamer of satin and cowry-kin,

disdaining the empty keys; and the young infanta, [Piano 22-3 P
ROSE. Then from their poverty they rose, [Ord Women 10-13
   Rose on the beachy floors. [Ord Women 11-20
   Then from their poverty they rose, [Ord Women 12-3
   Like a rose rabbi, later, I pursued, [Monocle 17-25
   Rose up besprent and sought the flaming red [Hibiscus 22-20
   As the marimba, the magnolia as rose. [C 38-10
   The tomtit and the cassia and the rose, [C 42-27
   Although the rose was not the noble thorn [C 42-28
   The sky is a blue gum streaked with rose. The trees are black.
     [Banal 62-12
   The wilderness rose up to it, [Jar 76-9
   "The fly on the rose prevents us, O season [Ghosts 119-15
   Last evening the moon rose above this rock [How Live 125-9
   That rose, or even colored by many waves; [Key W 129-11
   Rose out of promise and became the sooth [Havana 143-2
   The cloud rose upward like a heavy stone [Nigger 152-8
   The latest freed man rose at six and sat [Freed 204-14
   Rose up, tallest, in the black sun, [Thunder 220-6
   Without rose and without violet, [Common 221-12
   This dark, particular rose. [Scavoir 231-4
   Cover the sea with the sand rose. Fill [Vari 234-14
   Of rose and ice [Bottle 238-20
   Romantic tenements of rose and ice. [Bottle 239-16
   Whose horse clattered on the road on which she rose, [Uruguay
     249-18
   The false roses--Compare the silent rose of the sun [Extracts
     252-4
   It is an artificial world. The rose [Extracts 252-8
   And, otherwise, the rainy rose belongs [Extracts 252-13
   Licentious violet and lascive rose, [Montra 261-15
   At the book and shoe, the rotted rose [God 285-5
   The crystal-pointed star of morning, rose [Choc 296-18
   He rose because man wanted him to be. [Choc 299-13
   The moon rose up as if it had escaped [EM 314-24
   And then that Spaniard of the rose, itself [EM 316-16
   Hot-hooded and dark-blooded, rescued the rose [EM 316-17
   Rose from an imperfection of its own [EM 318-11
   How red the rose that is the soldier's wound, [EM 318-26
   And comic color of the rose, in which [NSF 384-4
   Rose up like phantoms from chronologies. [NSF 389-15
   It rose, ashen and red and yellow, each [Page 422-12
   And hems the planet rose and haws it ripe, [Ulti 429-11
   Of rose, stood tall in self not symbol, quick [Owl 435-6
   The rose, the delphinium, the red, the blue, [Bouquet 451-1
   Rose--women as half-fishes of salt shine, [Study II 464-15
   The moon rose in the mind and each thing there [NH 478-22
   The sea shivered in transcendent change, rose up [NH 484-9
   Of a woman with a cloud on her shoulder rose [Aug 494-11
   It rose loftily and stood massively; and to lie [Armor 529-2
   Than fragile volutes in a rose sea-shell. [Soldat 14-3 P
   Of seeping rose--banal machine [Soldat 15-20 P
   And in those regions one still feels the rose [Abnormal 24-9 P
   A group of marble horses rose on wings [Old Woman 43-2 P
   The earth as the bodies rose on feathery wings, [Old Woman
     43-15 P
   This atmosphere in which the horses rose, [Old Woman 44-19 P
   Of rose, or what will once more rise to rose, [Burnshaw 49-27 P
   Because it rose above them all, stippled [Greenest 54-14 P
   Rising from indolent coils. If the statue rose, [Greenest 54-24P
   The workers do not rise, as Venus rose, [Duck 60-9 P
   The rosy men and the women of the rose, [Art Pop 112-19 P
   See: blood-rose; gray-rose; red-rose-red.
ROSEATE. Is it the old, the roseate parent or [Repet 308-16
   To speak, the fat, the roseate characters, [Cred 378-7
   Return, affecting roseate aureoles, [Greenest 56-23 P
ROSE-BELIEFS. Sing rose-beliefs. Above that urn two lights [Burn-
   shaw 50-1 P
ROSE-BREASTED. For a little time, again, rose-breasted birds
   [Burnshaw 49-30 P
ROSED. The sense of self, rosed out of prestiges [Owl 435-5
   An azure outre-terre, oranged and rosed, [Theatre 91-14 P
   See well-rosed.
ROSEN. That were rosen once, [Aug 495-4
ROSENBLOOM. "Cortege for Rosenbloom" [79-title
   Now, the wry Rosenbloom is dead [Cortege 79-13
   Rosenbloom is dead. [Cortege 79-17
   Rosenbloom is dead. [Cortege 80-6
   Of Rosenbloom. [Cortege 81-3
   Rosenbloom is dead. [Cortege 81-8
ROSE-POINTS. And chant the rose-points of their birth, and when
   [Burnshaw 49-29 P
ROSES. And roses [Pourtraicte 21-14
   There are no bears among the roses, [Virgin 71-1
   Yesterday the roses were rising upward, [Nigger 156-10
   The wrinkled roses tinkle, the paper ones, [Extracts 252-2
   The false roses--Compare the silent rose of the sun [Extracts
     252-4
   There were roses in the cool café. His book [EM 314-9
   Round them she spilled the roses [Attempt 370-4

And white roses shaded emerald on petals [Attempt 370-6
The green roses drifted up from the table [Attempt 370-15
Are in the grass, the roses are heavy with a weight [Cred 372-7
"Bouquet of Roses in Sunlight" [430-title
We are two that use these roses as we are, [Roses 431-10
Seated before these shining forms, like the duskiest glass, re-
   flecting the piebald of roses or what you will. [Piano 21-18 P
Jocunda, who will arrange the roses and rearrange, letting the
   leaves lie on the water-like lacquer; [Piano 22-4 P
And in whose light the roses [Mandolin 29-3 P
Giddap! The ruby roses' hair [Room Gard 40-17 P
Of everything. The roses bend [Room Gard 41-2 P
See lion-roses.
ROSIER. And spread about them a warmer, rosier odor. [Aug 491-28
ROSIN. He inhaled the rancid rosin, burly smells [C 36-7
ROSY. And made one think of rosy chocolate [Sea Surf 99-1
   The rosy men and the women of the rose, [Art Pop 112-19 P
ROT. Pipperoo, pippera, pipperum . . . The rest is rot. [Horn
   230-19
   And the rust and rot of the door through which she went.
      [Beginning 427-11
ROTTED. Made by the leaves, that have rotted and fallen; [Lunar
   107-8
   But do not use the rotted names. [MBG 183-6
   At the book and shoe, the rotted rose [God 285-5
ROTTEN. The crawling railroad spur, the rotten fence, [C 36-14
   More than his mind in the wings. The rotten leaves [Old Woman
   43-20 P
   From the middens of life, rotten and acrid, [Stan Hero 84-3 P
ROTTING. Of what, like skulls, comes rotting back to ground.
      [Monocle 14-19
   Washed into rinds by rotting winter rains. [Monocle 16-11
   The rotting man for pleasure saw, [Sat Night 27-18 P
   The rotting man was first to sing. [Sat Night 28-12 P
   Of lilies rusted, rotting, wet [Room Gard 41-14 P
ROTUND. The rotund emotions, paradise unknown. [EM 325-29
ROU-COO. Yet coo becomes rou-coo, rou-coo. How close [Think 356-16
ROU-COU. Brings no rou-cou, [Depression 63-15
   Rou-cou spoke the dove, [Song Fixed 519-13
ROU-COU-COU. No rou-cou-cou. [Depression 63-16
ROU-ED. And she rou-ed there, [Song Fixed 519-20
ROUGED. Serve the rouged fruits in early snow. [Nigger 153-1
   Away, a little rusty, a little rouged, [NSF 400-14
ROUGE-FATIMA. A most desolate wind has chilled Rouge-Fatima
   [Havana 142-11
ROUGES. Of spiced and weathery rouges, should complex [C 44-8
ROUGH. The spruces rough in the distant glitter [Snow Man 10-3
   The cliffs are rough. [Lulu M 27-5 P
   Are rough [Lulu M 27-6 P
ROUGH-END. Much rough-end being to smooth Paradise, [Luther 461-11
ROUGHENED. A little roughened and ruder, a crown [NSF 400-15
ROUGHER. Rougher than a grinding shale. [Orangeade 103-14
ROUND. To be the book in which to read a round, [Monocle 14-17
   On sidelong wing, around and round and round. [Monocle 17-19
   That helped him round his rude aesthetic out. [C 36-11
   Each day, still curious, but in a round [C 42-14
   And round it was, upon a hill. [Jar 76-6
   The jar was round upon the ground [Jar 76-11
   Round those flotillas. And sometimes the sea [Sea Surf 99-14
   The world was round. But not from my begetting. [NE Verses
   104-4
   Her mind had bound me round. The palms were hot [Farewell 117-11
   Me round, carry me, misty deck, carry me [Farewell 118-19
   My old boat goes round on a crutch [Sailing 120-2
   At the base of the statue, we go round and round. [Mice 123-2
   His slowly-falling round [Pascagoula 126-15
   Its vacancy glitters round us everywhere. [Eve Angels 137-2
   The garden flew round with the angel, [Circulat 149-16
   The angel flew round with the clouds, [Circulat 149-17
   And the clouds flew round and the clouds flew round [Circulat
   149-18
   And the clouds flew round with the clouds. [Circulat 149-19
   Yet that things go round and again go round [Circulat 150-7
   Freshness is more than the east wind blowing round one. [Nigger
   157-11
   I cannot bring a world quite round, [MBG 165-11
   They did not know the grass went round. [MBG 178-15
   The gold façade round early squares, [Thought 187-2
   Cold, a cold porcelain, low and round, [Poems Clim 193-15
   They are round [Pears 196-11
   And in the water winding weeds move round. [Glass 197-17
   Our faces circling round a central face [Dames 206-12
   Upon the heart and round the mind [Country 207-11
   Moving round the sky and singing [Dezem 218-10
   Heart. The peaches are large and round, [Peaches 224-10
   Purple sets purple round. Look, Master, [Hartford 227-5
   A trumpet round the trees. Could one say that it was [Horn 230-6
   In sapphire, round the sun-bleached stones, [Vari 233-10
   The feelings of the natures round us here: [Vari 234-4
   Round and round goes the bell of the water [Vari 235-6

And round and round goes the water itself [Vari 235-7
Is blue, clear, cloudy, high, dark, wide and round; [Extracts
   252-11
Of people, round the auto-works: [News 264-12
For him to see, wove round her glittering hair, [Hand 271-6
Curling round the steeple and the people, [Hero 278-8
Look round, brown moon, brown bird, as you rise to fly, [God
   285-1
Look round at the head and zither [God 285-2
Look round you as you start to rise, brown moon, [God 285-4
Nor meditate the world as it goes round. [Phenom 286-6
The shadows of his fellows ring him round [EM 319-11
Panic in the face of the moon--round effendi [EM 320-15
In perpetual revolution, round and round . . . [Descrip 342-20
And snow. The theatre is spinning round, [Chaos 357-16
A turquoise monster moving round. [Silent 360-3
And hold them round the sultry day? Why should [Belly 367-4
Round them she spilled the roses [Attempt 370-4
Round the rooms, which do not ever seem to change . . . [Lot
   372-3
Its false disasters--these fathers standing round, [Cred 372-16
And barefoot servants round him, who adjust [NSF 390-20
The shoo-shoo-shoo of secret cymbals round. [NSF 401-13
Themselves and, therefore, good, the going round [NSF 405-21
And round and round, the merely going round, [NSF 405-22
Until merely going round is a final good, [NSF 405-23
A wind will spread its windy grandeurs round [AA 414-1
Ringed round and barred, with eyes held in their hands, [Page
   422-30
Of windings round and dodges to and fro, [Ulti 429-20
In a vanishing-vanished violet that wraps round [Owl 433-15
In the weaving round the wonder of its need, [Owl 433-15
That flows round the earth and through the skies, [Degen 444-14
But if they do, they cast it widely round. [Bouquet 451-24
They cast deeply round a crystal crystal-white [Bouquet 452-1
They cast closely round the facture of the thing [Bouquet 452-6
He walks through the house, looks round him and then leaves.
   [Bouquet 453-2
The red ripeness of round leaves is thick [Pecul 453-10
Wreathed round and round the round wreath of autumn. [NH 486-18
But folded over, turned round." It was the same, [NH 487-4
Spread outward. Crack the round dome. Break through. [Aug 490-11
The knowledge of things lay round but unperceived: [Aug 493-18
At lucent children round her in a ring. [Hermit 506-3
Wrapped tightly round us, since we are poor, a warmth, [Final
   524-8
And folded him round, [Coroner 29-21 P
The doves will fly round. [Secret Man 36-9 P
Yet in trees round the College of Heralds, [Agenda 42-10 P
Swirled round them in immense autumnal sounds. [Old Woman 43-21P
Agree: the apple in the orchard, round [Burnshaw 47-30 P
Of azure round an upper dome, brightest [Greenest 54-13 P
The oracular trumpets round and roundly hooped, [Greenest 56-19P
The long recessional at parish eves wails round [Greenest 59-15P
Infected by unreality, rapt round [Duck 62-5 P
To ride an old mule round the keys-- [Stan MBG 73-7 P
Like a dancer's skirt, flung round and settling down. [Woman Had
   81-18 P
Therein, day settles and thickens round a form-- [Role 93-12 P
And the wry antipodes whirled round the world away-- [Discov
   95-20 P
Round summer and angular winter and winds, [Ulysses 102-24 P
In which the world goes round and round [Ulysses 102-26 P
Goes round in the climates of the mind [Ulysses 102-30 P
There was a crush of strength in a grinding going round, [Real
   110-11 P
As there are sides to a round bottle. [Three 136-16 P
ROUNDABOUT. Included, the spirit that goes roundabout [NH 471-23
ROUNDED. As we stand gazing at the rounded moon. [Eve Angels 138-6
   Reveals her, rounded in beneficence, [Spaniard 34-4 P
ROUNDER. And red, will not be redder, rounder then [Burnshaw 47-31P
ROUNDEST. And longest, the night was roundest, [On Road 204-10
ROUNDING. Item: The wind is never rounding O [Montra 263-17
ROUNDLY. The oracular trumpets round and roundly hooped, [Greenest
   56-19 P
ROUNDNESS. Of its eventual roundness, puerile tints [C 44-7
   The roundness that pulls tight the final ring [Orb 442-8
ROUSING. He does not raise the rousing of fresh light [Aug 492-22
ROUT. Crispin concocted doctrine from the rout. [C 45-11
ROUTE. His route lies through an image in his mind: [Repet 307-15
   My route lies through an image in my mind, [Repet 307-16
   It is the route that milky millions find, [Repet 307-17
ROUTINE. Are both alike in the routine I know. [Pharynx 96-3
ROWDY. In the rowdy serpentines. He drilled. [News 264-14
ROWDY-DOW. The heavy bells are tolling rowdy-dow. [Nigger 155-9
ROWERS. A boat carried forward by waves resembling the bright
   backs of rowers, [Prol 515-6
ROY. And, of human realizings, rugged roy . . . [Choc 302-5
R'S. They rolled their r's, there, in the land of the citrons.
   [NH 486-20

RUBBINGS. Are rubbings of a glass in which we peer. [NSF 398-4
RUBBISH. Yet the General was rubbish in the end. [NSF 392-3
RUBIES. With rubies then, attend me now. [Country 207-15
  Like rubies reddened by rubies reddening. [Descrip 316-4
RUBY. Netted of topaz and ruby [Cab 21-8 P
  Giddap! The ruby roses' hair [Room Gard 40-17 P
  See ruddy-ruby.
RUBY-WATER-WORN. And weathered and the ruby-water-worn, [NSF 400-9
RUCKS. In moody rucks, and difficult and strange [C 31-10
RUCTIVE. Loquacious columns by the ructive sea? [C 41-20
RUDDIER. To the ruddier bushes at the garden's end. [Hand 271-19
  Of a ruddier summer, a birth that fetched along [Nuns 92-13 P
RUDDY. Its ruddy pallor had grown cadaverous. [Anglais 149-4
  Like Walt Whitman walking along a ruddy shore. [Nigger 150-10
  Ruddy are his eyes and ruddy are his claws [Glass 197-15
  Then the bird from his ruddy belly blew [Horn 230-5
  The ruddy temper, the hammer [Motive 288-17
  Who reads no book. His ruddy ancientness [Cred 374-2
  Absorbs the ruddy summer and is appeased. [Cred 374-3
  To cool their ruddy pulses; the frothy clouds [NSF 399-15
  To build a ruddy palace? [Archi 17-24 P
  Disclose the rude and ruddy at their jobs [Burnshaw 48-20 P
  See silver-ruddy.
RUDDY-RIPE. Looked on big women, whose ruddy-ripe images [NH 486-17
RUDDY-RUBY. Into lands of ruddy-ruby fruits, achieved [Armor 530-3
RUDE. That helped him round his rude aesthetic out. [C 36-11
  If these rude instances impeach themselves [C 38-6
  Belshazzar's brow, O, ruler, rude [Country 207-14
  And the rude leaves fall. [Metamorph 266-3
  Disclose the rude and ruddy at their jobs [Burnshaw 48-20 P
  Become rude robes among white candle lights, [Greenest 53-4 P
RUDENESS. By force of rudeness, let the principle [C 38-7
RUDER. A little roughened and ruder, a crown [NSF 400-15
RUDEST. As sequels without thought. In the rudest red [Burnshaw 47-8 P
RUDIMENTS. (The rudiments of tropics are around, [Bird Claws 82-4
  Turned para-thing, the rudiments in the jar, [Bouquet 452-7
  The rudiments in the jar, farced, finikin, [Bouquet 452-13
RUE. Lean larkspur and jagged fern and rusting rue [Bouquet 452-10
RUFFLING. Ruffling its common reflections, thought-like Monadnocks.
  [Cata 424-14
RUG. Upon a rug mingle to dissipate [Sunday 66-19
  The blue of the rug, the portrait of Vidal, [Freed 205-23
RUGGED. Well-booted, rugged, arrogantly male, [Lilacs 49-13
  The rugged black, the image. Design [Prelude 195-18
  And, of human realizings, rugged roy . . . [Choc 302-5
  In desperate hallow, rugged gesture, fault [EM 316-26
  Rugged and luminous, chants in the dark [NH 479-14
RUIN. The ruin stood still in an external world. [Repet 306-3
  The people sat in the theatre, in the ruin, [Repet 306-10
  Which was realized, like reason's constant ruin. [Two V 354-17
  Though poor, though raggeder than ruin, have that [Belly 367-10
  Only in misery, the afflatus of ruin, [Rome 509-24
  Without the revolutions's ruin, [Lytton 39-4 P
  The black and ruin his sepulchral throne. [Greenest 55-29 P
  If more than the wished-for ruin racked the night, [Sombre 69-12 P
RUINED. Marx has ruined Nature, [Botanist 1 134-12
RUINOUS. Notations of the wild, the ruinous waste, [Geneva 24-12
  There is a building stands in a ruinous storm, [Sketch 336-7
RUINS. Read in the ruins of a new society, [Nigger 153-3
  The volumes like marble ruins [Common 221-20
  To picnic in the ruins that we leave. [Dutch 293-3
  As victory. The poet does not speak in ruins [Papini 446-10
  In vast disorder live in the ruins, free, [Burnshaw 48-27 P
  The ruins of the past, out of nothing left, [Recit 87-14 P
RULE. Will rule in a poets' world. Yet that will be [Burnshaw 48-16 P
RULED. Ruled us before, from over Asia, by [Montra 262-14
RULER. Belshazzar's brow, O, ruler, rude [Country 207-14
  As follows, "The Ruler of Reality, [NH 485-2
  A real ruler, but rules what is unreal." [NH 485-4
  Will come stamping here, the ruler of less than men, [Aug 495-22
  He is that obdurate ruler who ordains [Greenest 59-28 P
RULES. All alike, except for the rules of the rabbis, [Nigger 151-7
  A real ruler, but rules what is unreal." [NH 485-4
  What god rules over Africa, what shape, [Greenest 52-24 P
  No god rules over Africa, no throne, [Greenest 55-5 P
  Of the park. They obey the rules of every skeleton. [Duck 62-11P
  So posed, the captain drafted rules of the world, [Bship 78-20 P
  The first and second rules are reconciled [Bship 80-13 P
RUMBLE. Rumble anything out of their drums? [Circulat 150-4
  There is a rumble of autumnal marching, [Dutch 291-3
  The assassin flash and rumble . . . He was denied. [EM 320-1
RUMBLED. Rumbled a-day and a-day, a-day. [Ord Women 11-18
  To rumbled rock, its bright projections lie [Sombre 70-3 P
RUMBLING. A rumbling, west of Mexico, it seemed, [C 32-17
  The rumbling broadened as it fell. The wind, [C 32-22
  Rumbling along the autumnal horizon, [Dutch 293-7

Make more than thunder's rural rumbling. They make [Repet 307-2
RUMORS. From the rumors of the speech-full domes, [Ulysses 102-15P
RUMPLING. The rumpling of the plumes [Infanta 7-16
  Upon the rumpling bottomness, and nights [C 42-31
  The commonplace became a rumpling of blazons. [NH 483-22
RUN. I shall run before him, [Plot Giant 6-13
  I shall run before him, [Plot Giant 6-17
  I shall run before him, [Plot Giant 7-5
  But let the rabbit run, the cock declaim. [C 39-32
  Run away. [Brave 138-12
  Run away. [Brave 138-15
  Run away. [Brave 138-18
  The hunters run to and fro. The heavy trees, [Parochial 191-7
  And cried out to feel it again, have run fingers over leaves
  [Large 424-2
RUNNING. When radiance came running down, slim through the bare-
    ness. [Banal 63-2
  A running forward, arms stretched out as drilled. [Nigger 153-15
  Like a machine left running, and running down. [Repet 306-18
  Running in the rises of common speech, [Sketch 336-5
  A great jaguar running will make a little sound. [Jouga 337-15
  And mountains running like water, wave on wave, [AA 416-6
  And yet with water running in the sun, [Celle 438-14
  A glacier running through delirium, [Imago 439-16
  While the water kept running through the mouth of the speaker,
    [Novel 457-17
  Like water running in a gutter [Grotesque 76-22 P
  The picnic of children came running then, [Dinner 109-25 P
RUNS. Time is a horse that runs in the heart, a horse [Pure 329-16
  The wind is like a dog that runs away. [Pieces 352-5
  The water runs away from the horses. [Primordia 8-18 P
RURAL. Make more than thunder's rural rumbling. They make [Repet
    307-2
RUSES. The ruses that were shattered by the large. [C 30-15
RUSH. And then rush brightly through the summer air. [Sailing 121-7
  May rush to extinguish the theme, the basses thump [Bship 79-27 P
RUSHES. And east rushes west and west rushes down, [Rabbit K 209-14
  In the rushes of autumn wind [Secret Man 36-2 P
RUSHING. Rushing from what was real; and capable? [Uruguay 249-24
  Forever hunting or hunted, rushing through [Greenest 55-21 P
RUSSIA. "A Dish of Peaches in Russia" [224-title
  In Russia at which the same statue of Stalin greets [Cats
    367-15
RUSSIAN. That animal, that Russian, that exile, for whom [Peaches
    224-8
  Translation of a Russian poet. [Vari 234-9
  These are not even Russian animals. [Burnshaw 46-17 P
RUST. Curled over the shadowless hut, the rust and bones, [Farewell
    118-4
  And the rust and rot of the door through which she went.
    [Beginning 427-11
  Of war, the rust on the steeples, these jutted up, [Greenest
    53-23 P
RUSTED. But these are not those rusted armies. [Dutch 292-3
  Of lilies rusted, rotting, wet [Room Gard 41-14 P
RUSTIC. The four winds blow through the rustic arbor, [Vacancy
    511-12
  Like angels resting on a rustic steeple [Art Pop 113-1 P
RUSTIEST. Picking thin music on the rustiest string, [God 285-13
RUSTING. Lean larkspur and jagged fern and rusting rue [Bouquet
    452-10
RUSTY. Aloe of ivory, pear of rusty rind.) [Bird Claws 82-5
  The rusty, battered shapes [Anything B 211-18
  The crow looks rusty as he rises up. [Possum 294-15
  Away, a little rusty, a little rouged, [NSF 400-14
RUTS. The ruts in your empty road are red. [Fish-Scale 160-18
RYAN. Ryan's lunch, hatters, insurance and medicines, [Thought
    185-6

SABLE. That hermit on reef sable would have seen, [Dames 206-16
SABOTS. Et sabots durs aux chevaux . . . [Parasol 20-2 P
SACK. That sack the sun, though metaphysical. [Red Kit 31-4 P
SACKED. Sacked up and carried overseas, daubed out [C 45-13
  A sacred syllable rising from sacked speech, [Armor 530-1
SACKS. Decays of sacks, and all the arrant stinks [C 36-10
SACRAMENT. The summer, it should have a sacrament [C 39-6
  And makes a constant sacrament of praise. [Peter 92-13
  See sun-sacrament.
SACRAMENTS. One of the sacraments between two breaths, [Montra
  262-8
SACRED. God of the sausage-makers, sacred guild, [Nigger 157-4
  A sacred syllable rising from sacked speech, [Armor 530-1
  Fresh from the sacred clarities, chanters [Greenest 56-4 P
SACRIFICE. The holy hush of ancient sacrifice. [Sunday 67-1
  Our petty portion in the sacrifice. [Soldat 14-8 P
SACRIFICIAL. To that salty, sacrificial taste? [Phases 4-23 P
SACRISTANS. Divine orations from lean sacristans [Montra 262-18
SAD. And the people are sad. [Gubbinal 85-5
  And the people are sad. [Gubbinal 85-13
  "Sad Strains of a Gay Waltz" [121-title
  Sad men made angels of the sun, and of [Eve Angels 137-10
  The tea is bad, bread sad. [Fading 139-8
  With a sad splendor, beyond artifice, [Owl 435-16
  For farewells, a sad hanging on for remembrances. [NH 487-18
  The sad smell of the lilacs--one remembered it, [Aug 491-9
  The trees have a look as if they bore sad names [Slug 522-5
  Of chaos are not always sad nor lost [Burnshaw 50-25 P
SADNESS. Without rain, there is the sadness of rain [Aug 495-19
  For this blank cold, this sadness without cause. [Plain 502-14
SAFE. It is safe to sleep to a sound that time brings back.
  [Phenom 286-12
SAFELY. There were others like him safely under roof: [Choc 299-23
SAGGING. In that old coat, those sagging pantaloons, [NSF 389-9
SAID. She said, "My dear, [Pourtraicte 21-10
  But here," she said, [Pourtraicte 21-16
  If not, when all is said, to drive away [C 37-7
  The black man said, [Jack-Rabbit 50-8
  The black man said, [Jack-Rabbit 50-14
  The soul, he said, is composed [Men 1000 51-7
  There are men of the East, he said, [Men 1000 51-9
  I said. [Peacocks 58-5
  So he said, [Peacocks 58-10
  It depends which way you crossed, the tea-belle said. [NE
  Verses 104-8
  Whose spirit is this? we said, because we knew [Key W 129-7
  Only last year he said that the naked moon [Anglais 148-19
  And what we said of it became [Postcard 159-12
  They said, "You have a blue guitar, [MBG 165-3
  And they said then, "But play, you must, [MBG 165-7
  Of a multitude dwindles, all said, [MBG 171-15
  Alone, a lean Review and said, [MBG 180-20
  It was when I said, [On Road 203-12
  You . . . You said, [On Woad 203-16
  We said we stood alone. [On Road 203-22
  It was when I said, [On Road 204-1
  It was when you said, [On Road 204-5
  On the edge of his bed. He said, [Freed 204-15
  And so the freed man said. [Freed 205-5
  Said, "Phooey! Phoo!" [Anything B 211-3
  Said, "Phooey!" too, [Anything B 211-7
  Over and over again you have said, [Dezem 218-5
  Could you have said the bluejay suddenly [Sleight 222-9
  The words are written, though not yet said. [Cuisine 227-20
  He said I had this that I could love, [Yellow 236-13
  So what said the others and the sun went down [Uruguay 248-16
  And, in the brown blues of evening, the lady said, [Uruguay
  248-17
  And her dress were one and she said, "I have said no [Uruguay
  249-3
  The skeleton said it is a question of [Montra 262-10
  I am Solange, euphonious bane, she said. [News 265-4
  The brightness of arms, said Roma wasted [Hero 273-8
  In its own dirt, said Avignon was [Hero 273-9
  Peace in a time of peace, said Leyden [Hero 273-10
  Of daylight came while he sat thinking. He said, [Choc 298-12
  Victor Serge said, "I followed his argument [EM 324-24
  He said it of Konstantinov. Revolution [EM 324-27
  Do you remember what the townsmen said, [Liadoff 346-17
  And is it true that what they said, as they fell, [Liadoff 347-1
  Come home, wind, he said as he climbed the stair-- [Pieces 351-14
  By the sea, insolid rock, stentor, and said: [Two V 353-12
  He said a good life would be possible. [Good Man 364-6
  She said poetry and apotheosis are one. [Past Nun 378-13
  Said things it had laboriously spoken. [NSF 387-18
  Said that as keen, illustrious ornament. [NSF 391-22
  Bethou me, said sparrow, to the crackled blade, [NSF 393-22
  Then Ozymandias said the spouse, the bride [NSF 396-10

And bade the sheep carouse. Or so they said. [NSF 400-22
The Canon Aspirin, having said these things, [NSF 402-13
Of the categories. So said, this placid space [Ulti 429-17
Together, said words of the world are the life of the world.
  [NH 474-9
Professor Eucalyptus said, "The search [NH 481-4
They said, "We are back once more in the land of the elm trees,
  [NH 487-3
Like watery words awash; like meanings said [Angel 497-4
He had said that everything possessed [Two Illus 514-10
Would taste, precisely, as they said it would. [Soldat 11-12 P
I said, "She thumbs the memories of dress." [Stan MMO 19-6 P
Said hic, said hac, [Melancholy 32-7 P
Said ha. [Melancholy 32-8 P
That is not what I said: [Table 40-9 P
And having said farewell. It is not enough [Burnshaw 50-8 P
The Bulgar said, "After pineapple with fresh mint [Duck 60-7 P
Again the Bulgar said, "There are more things [Duck 62-1 P
The captain said, [Bship 77-15 P
I said that men should wear stone masks and, to make [Bship
  78-11 P
Of this the captain said, [Bship 78-25 P
The captain said, [Bship 79-19 P
He said, "As I know, I am and have [Ulysses 99-13 P
Under the middle stars, he said: [Ulysses 99-15 P
He said, "As I know, I am and have [Presence 105-16 P
Beneath the middle stars and said: [Presence 105-18 P
In things said well in music, [July 114-17 P
SAIL. How content I shall be in the North to which I sail [Fare-
  well 117-19
  This heavy historical sail [Sailing 120-17
  To say the light wind worries the sail, [Sailing 121-1
  That slight transcendence to the dirty sail, [Sailing 121-5
  We dried our nets and mended sail [Silent 359-5
  Variations on the words spread sail. [Aug 490-2
  And the hawk cats it and we say spread sail, [Aug 490-6
  Spread sail, we say spread white, spread way. [Aug 490-7
  "The Sail of Ulysses" [99-title P
  Under the shape of his sail, Ulysses, [Ulysses 99-10 P
  The great sail of Ulysses seemed, [Ulysses 105-7 P
  As if another sail went on [Ulysses 105-10 P
  Under the shape of his sail, Ulysses, [Presence 105-13 P
  The sharp sail of Ulysses seemed, [Presence 106-7 P
SAILED. From which he sailed. Beyond him, westward, lay [C 33-13
SAILING. "Sailing after Lunch" [120-title
SAILOR. A skinny sailor peering in the sea-glass. [C 28-13
  Only, here and there, an old sailor, [Ten O'C 66-12
  Being changed from space to the sailor's metier, [Two V 354-15
  Are one and the sailor and the sea are one. [NSF 392-22
  Among the second selves, sailor, observe [Pagoda 91-19 P
SAILS. Came to be sleights of sails [Infanta 7-18
SAINT. Or possibly, the merest patron saint [Nigger 157-5
  The outer captain, the inner saint, [Thought 185-26
  "The Candle a Saint" [223-title
  Existed by itself. Or did the saint survive? [Les Plus 245-6
  And not a bald and tasselled saint. [Our Stars 455-6
  Then, ancientest saint ablaze with ancientest truth, [NH 467-3
  Blond weather. One is born a saint, [Stan MBG 73-9 P
  See Crispin-saint.
SAINT JOHN. "Saint John and the Back-Ache" [436-title
SAINTLY. With saintly imagination and the stains [Bship 81-2 P
SAINTS. How is it that my saints from Voragine, [Polish Aunt 84-4
  Civilization must be destroyed. The hairy saints [NE Verses
  106-1
  And saints are brilliant in fresh cloaks. [Contra I 266-16
  Were seraphs, were saints, were changing essences. [NSF 397-15
  The coming on of feasts and the habits of saints, [NH 472-2
  Painting the saints among palms. [Agenda 41-20 P
  Of saints not heard of until now, unnamed, [Nuns 92-19 P
SAL. Oh! Sal, the butcher's wife ate clams [Lulu M 27-9 P
SALACIOUS. And last year's garden grows salacious weeds. [Cred
  377-10
SALAD-BEDS. An eye of land, of simple salad-beds, [C 27-16
  Because he turned to salad-beds again? [C 41-21
SALE. Not merely desired, for sale, and market things [Armor 530-4
  For sale in Vienna and Zurich to people in Maine, [Greenest
  53-9 P
SALLOWLY. Or dance the death of doves, most sallowly, [Burnshaw
  48-22 P
SALLY. A sally into gold and crimson forms, [C 35-9
SALON. For example: Au Château. Un Salon. A glass [Golden 460-10
SALT. One eats one paté, even of salt, quotha. [C 28-1
  The snug hibernal from that sea and salt, [C 28-3
  The salt hung on his spirit like a frost, [C 29-13
  Of buttons, measure of his salt. Such trash [C 39-19
  Salt masks of beard and mouths of bellowing, [Sea Surf 101-17
  Ashen man on ashen cliff above the salt halloo, [NE Verses 105-7
  And his nostrils blow out salt around each man. [Grapes 111-3
  Of spray. Let all the salt be gone. [Vari 234-16
  With life's salt upon their lips and savor [Hero 279-7

Bare limbs, bare trees and a wind as sharp as salt? [AA 419-21
Made difficult by salt fragrance, intricate. [Bouquet 452-15
Rose--women as half-fishes of salt shine, [Study II 464-15
Returns and returns, along the dry, salt shore. [Woman Had
   81-24 P
SALT-FLICKER. Salt-flicker, amen to our accustomed cell, [Montra
   260-20
SALTIER. A deep up-pouring from some saltier well [Monocle 13-10
SALTIEST. Of the milk within the saltiest spurge, heard, then,
   [Sea Surf 100-19
SALT-STAINED. Part of the glass-like sides on which it glided
   over the salt-stained water. [Prol 516-3
SALTY. Tired of the salty harbors, [Paltry 51-13
By this light the salty fishes [Homunculus 26-1
Regard. But for that salty cup, [MBG 179-19
The salty skeleton must dance because [Montra 261-13
This was the salty taste of glory, [Phases 3-13 P
To that salty, sacrificial taste? [Phases 4-23 P
SALUT. Within them right for terraces--oh, brave salut! [Belly
   367-11
SALUTE. A fantastic irruption. Salute you, cata-sisters, [Souls
   95-2 P
SALVATION. But salvation here? What about the rattle of sticks
   [Parochial 191-17
Health follows after health. Salvation there: [Parochial 192-3
SALVER. Would shudder on a bloody salver. [Three 132-14 P
SALVERS. When piled on salvers its aroma steeped [C 39-5
SALZBURG. Sweden described, Salzburg with shaded eyes [NH 486-2
But not that Salzburg of the skies. It was [Greenest 53-27 P
SAMBO. And the sea as turquoise-turbaned Sambo, neat [Sea Surf
   102-7
SAME. Full of the same wind [Snow Man 10-8
That is blowing in the same bare place [Snow Man 10-9
And lex. Sed quaeritur: is this same wig [C 27-10
The same insoluble lump. The fatalist [C 45-17
They never find, the same receding shores [Sunday 69-18
The same. We parallel the mother's death. [Anatomy 108-2
It is the same jingle of the water among the roots under the
   banks of the palmettoes, [Indian 112-5
It is the same jingle of the red-bird breasting the orange-trees
   out of the cedars. [Indian 112-6
That lost its heaviness through that same will, [Nigger 152-9
And the same bridge when the river is frozen. [Nigger 154-12
If neatly glazed, becomes the same as the fruit [Extracts 253-9
In the same way, you were happy in spring, [Motive 288-5
And yet remains the same, the beast of light, [Pure 333-2
Two beasts. But of the same kind--two conjugal beasts. [Jouga
   337-5
And him. Both wanted the same thing. Both sought [Liadoff 347-18
"Two Versions of the Same Poem" [353-title
It is the ever-never-changing same, [Adult 353-9
In Russia at which the same statue of Stalin greets [Cats 367-15
The same railway passenger, the ancient tree [Cats 367-16
He never felt twice the same about the flecked river, [Cata
   424-10
Which kept flowing and never the same way twice, flowing [Cata
   424-11
He wanted to feel the same way over and over. [Cata 425-2
He wanted the river to go on flowing the same way, [Cata 425-3
The point of vision and desire are the same. [NH 466-22
And the poet's search for the same exterior made [NH 481-8
Nothing about him ever stayed the same, [NH 483-19
But folded over, turned round." It was the same, [NH 487-4
Of the same thing without desire, [Aug 491-1
The same wind, rising and rising, makes a sound [Look 519-2
And kept saying over and over one same, same thing, [Slug 522-6
Out of this same light, out of the central mind, [Final 524-16
There is the same color in the bellies of frogs, in clays,
   withered reeds, skins, wood, sunlight. [Primordia 8-2 P
The same down-dropping fruit in yellow leaves, [Duck 61-14 P
The same return at heavy evening, love [Duck 61-15 P
It is the same sound, the same season, [Memo 89-3 P
And inhuman same, the likeness of things unlike. [Conversat
   109-2 P
What the court saw was always of the same color, [Three 131-22 P
Like the same orange repeating on one tree [Someone 85-21 A
See self-same.
SAMENESS. The sameness of his various universe, [Moonlight 531-3
SANCTIFY. Nor sanctify, but plainly to propound. [NSF 389-12
SANCTIMONIOUS. Of sanctimonious mountains high in snow, [Montra
   263-3
SANCTION. The star-yplaited, visible sanction, [Stan Hero 83-14 P
SANCTITY. Ennobled as in a mirror to sanctity. [Nigger 157-6
The perquisites of sanctity, enjoys [NH 474-12
SAND. Her terrace was the sand [Infanta 7-11
Among the blooms beyond the open sand; [Hibiscus 22-11
The doctor of Geneva stamped the sand [Geneva 24-1
And to feel sure and to forget the bleaching sand . . . [Fare-
   well 117-20
The trees like bones and the leaves half sand, half sun. [Fare-

well 118-5
Down to the sand, the glare [Pascagoula 127-4
Of the pine trees edging the sand, [Pascagoula 127-5
Sand heaped in the clouds, giant that fought [MBG 179-7
Flying from burning countries and brown sand shores, [Loaf 200-2
Of a cloud on sand, a shape on the side of a hill. [Connois
   215-20
Cover the sea with the sand rose. Fill [Vari 234-14
Reddens the sand with his red-colored noise, [NSF 384-8
White sand, his patter of the long sea-slushes. [NSF 393-9
And laid it in the sand. As I am, I am [NSF 395-20
The wind is blowing the sand across the floor. [AA 412-15
The man who is walking turns blankly on the sand. [AA 412-23
And the first line foaming over the sand; again, [Woman Had
   81-16 P
SANDBARS. On the feat sandbars. [Jack-Rabbit 50-7
SANG. The jack-rabbit sang to the Arkansaw. [Jack-Rabbit 50-5
She sang beyond the genius of the sea. [Key W 128-11
Even if what she sang was what she heard, [Key W 128-20
Since what she sang was uttered word by word. [Key W 128-21
For she was the maker of the song she sang. [Key W 129-4
That we should ask this often as she sang. [Key W 129-9
In which she sang. And when she sang, the sea, [Key W 129-27
Except the one she sang and, singing, made. [Key W 130-2
I sang a canto in a canton, [Country 207-1
I stood and sang and filled the air. [Country 207-7
Could one say that he sang the colors in the stones, [Horn
   230-11
We sat beneath it and sang our songs. [Vari 233-7
Far in the woods they sang their unreal songs, [Cred 376-1
They sang of summer in the common fields. [Cred 376-5
They sang desiring an object that was near, [Cred 376-6
As if the innocent mother sang in the dark [AA 419-1
So lind. The wind blazed as they sang. So lau. [Page 421-17
Lulu sang of barbarians before the eunuchs [Lulu G 26-9 P
Beside the statue, while you sang. Your eyes [Burnshaw 50-28 P
Was under every temple-tone. You sang [Burnshaw 50-30 P
SAN MIGUEL DE LOS BAÑOS. At San Miguel de los Baños, [Attempt
   370-1
SANK. Key West sank downward under massive clouds [Farewell 117-3
SANS. Soupe Sans Perles [NE Verses 104-title 4
SAP. Dripping a morning sap. [Poem Morn 219-11
See citron-sap.
SAPLING. What Eden sapling gum, what honeyed gore, [C 38-2
SAPPHIRE. The diamond point, the sapphire point, [Ord Women 11-22
Deluged the ocean with a sapphire blue. [Sea Surf 101-3
In sapphire, round the sun-bleached stones, [Vari 233-10
SAPPHIRES. Of sapphires flashing from the central sky, [Cred
   375-24
SAPS. Yet the quotidian saps philosophers [C 42-21
Like this, saps like the sun, true fortuner. [C 43-5
SARCOPHAGUS. "The Owl in the Sarcophagus" [431-title
SASHED. And knotted, sashed and seamed, half pales of red, [Cred
   378-2
SAT. Sat tittivating by their mountain pools [Monocle 14-2
Last night, we sat beside a pool of pink, [Monocle 17-14
Or else sat spinning on the pinnacles, [Babies 77-5
The blackbird sat [Thirteen 95-4
All night I sat reading a book, [Reader 146-13
Sat reading as if in a book [Reader 146-14
In the cathedral, I sat there, and read, [MBG 180-19
He sat among beggars wet with dew, [Thought 187-5
Sat alone, his great toe like a horn, [Thought 187-7
The latest freed man rose at six and sat [Freed 204-14
We sat beneath it and sang our songs. [Vari 233-7
Of daylight came while he sat thinking. He said, [Choc 298-12
The people sat in the theatre, in the ruin, [Repet 306-10
When B. sat down at the piano and made [EM 316-9
In which he sat. All chariots were drowned. The swans [Descrip
   343-4
At a piano in a cloud sat practicing, [Liadoff 346-15
As if twelve princes sat before a king. [Cred 375-25
Of Trope. He sat in the park. The water of [NSF 397-11
As he sat there reading, aloud, the great blue tabulae. [Large
   423-12
And laughed, as he sat there reading, from out of the purple
   tabulae, [Large 424-4
The house is empty. But here is where she sat [Beginning 427-12
This sat beside his bed, with its guitar, [NH 483-16
Was it as we sat in the park and the archaic form [Aug 494-10
His place, as he sat and as he thought, was not [Quiet 523-1
SATAN. For who can care at the wigs despoiling the Satan ear?
   [Banal 63-4
The death of Satan was a tragedy [EM 319-19
SATANAS. Obscure Satanas, make a model [Hero 277-2
SATANIC. As if pain, no longer satanic mimicry, [EM 316-5 P
SATED. Of more or less, ascetically sated [Woman Had 82-5 P
SATIN. And Rosa, the muslin dreamer of satin and cowry-kin, dis-
   daining the empty keys; and the young infanta, [Piano 22-3 P
SATIRE. From truth and not from satire on our lives. [Nigger 154-5

SATIRIZE. The iceberg settings satirize [MBG 180-2
SATISFACTION. Be the finding of a satisfaction, and may [Of Mod
    240-20
  The satisfaction underneath the sense, [Papini 448-3
SATISFACTIONS. To feel the satisfactions [Aug 493-23
SATISFIED. It can never be satisfied, the mind, never. [Beard
    247-25
  That the mind is the end and must be satisfied. [Extracts 257-15
  Half thinking; until the mind has been satisfied, [Extracts
    257-17
  Until, for him, his mind is satisfied. [Extracts 257-18
  To have satisfied the mind and turn to see, [Extracts 257-22
  Am I that imagine this angel less satisfied? [NSF 404-20
  Am satisfied without solacing majesty, [NSF 405-2
  Exclaiming bright sight, as it was satisfied, [Rock 526-6
  Death, that will never be satisfied, [Soldat 16-10 P
  About the mind as never satisfied, [As Leave 117-2 P
SATISFIES. For a moment, the first idea . . . It satisfies [NSF
    382-14
SATISFY. Are a woman's words, unlikely to satisfy [Nigger 157-15
SATURDAY. Is the study of man, this image of Saturday, [Study I
    463-6
  "Saturday Night at the Chiropodist's" [27-title P
SATURN. Is satyr in Saturn, according to his thoughts. [NSF 390-2
SATURN-STAR. In the arbors that are as if of Saturn-star. [Moon-
    light 531-18
SATYR. Is satyr in Saturn, according to his thoughts. [NSF 390-2
SAUCER. Cat's milk is dry in the saucer. Sunday song [Phenom 286-3
SAUCERS. At tossing saucers--cloudy-conjuring sea? [Sea Surf 102-8
SAUSAGE-MAKERS. God of the sausage-makers, sacred guild, [Nigger
    157-4
SAVAGE. Into a savage color he went on. [C 30-29
  Naked among them, like a savage source. [Sunday 70-3
  That savage of fire, [Gubbinal 85-9
  To bang it from a savage blue, [MBG 166-11
  And rainbow sortilege, the savage weapon [Hero 274-3
  "Less and Less Human, O Savage Spirit" [327-title
  The savage transparence. They go crying [Pediment 361-16
  The object, grips it in savage scrutiny, [Cred 376-11
  They looked back at Hans' look with savage faces. [Page 421-23
  They only know a savage assuagement cries [NH 467-22
  With a savage voice; and in that cry they hear [NH 467-23
  In a savage and subtle and simple harmony, [NH 468-1
  Whose mere savage presence awakens the world in which she dwells.
    [World 520-16
  And savage blooms; [Cab 21-9 P
SAVAGER. Slowly, one man, savager than the rest, [Thunder 220-5
SAVAGERY. Making the most of savagery of palms, [C 31-27
  The plainness of plain things is savagery, [NH 467-16
SAVAGEST. Summer, jangling the savagest diamonds and [Hero 281-2
  The savagest hollow of winter-sound. [Possum 294-12
  Again in the savagest severity. [EM 321-19
SAVANT. And true savant of this dark nature be. [Sun March 134-8
SAVE. We remember the lion of Juda and we save [NH 472-23
SAVED. In the object seen and saved that mystic [Hero 278-27
  Saved and beholden, in a robe of rays. [NH 477-24
SAVES. How that which rejects it saves it in the end. [EM 315-10
SAVING. Too near, too clear, saving a little to endow [Fictive
    88-11
SAVINGS. And savings banks, Fides, the sculptor's prize, [Lions
    124-12
SAVOIR. Inanimate in an inert savoir. [Plain 502-12
SAVOR. They have a sense of their design and savor [Extracts
    254-21
  With life's salt upon their lips and savor [Hero 279-7
  Themselves from its essential savor, [EM 323-3
  Why should I savor love [Demoiselle 23-12 P
SAVORED. He savored rankness like a sensualist. [C 36-12
SAW. I saw how the planets gathered [Domination 9-14
  I saw how the night came, [Domination 9-17
  This auditor of insects! He that saw [C 31-2
  From what he saw across his vessel's prow. [C 35-25
  And as he came he saw that it was spring, [C 35-28
  Of what he saw he never saw at all. [C 36-17
  I saw you then, as warm as flesh, [Vincentine 52-16
  Monotonous earth I saw become [Vincentine 53-13
  I was the world in which I walked, and what I saw [Hoon 65-16
  Who saw the mortal massives of the blooms [Sea Surf 100-1
  At what we saw. The spring clouds blow [Postcard 159-7
  Only this evening I saw again low in the sky [Martial 237-10
  Though the air change. Only this evening I saw it again, [Martial
    238-13
  In a place that he reached, by rejecting what he saw [Landsc
    242-10
  The abstract that he saw, like the locust-leaves, plainly:
    [Contra II 270-15
  As if in seeing we saw our feeling [Hero 278-26
  Gold-shined by sun, perceiving as I saw [Phenom 287-13
  From nature, each time he saw it, making it, [EM 316-18
  As he saw it, exist in his own especial eye. [EM 316-19

And these the seraph saw, had seen long since, [NSF 389-17
She looked at them and saw them as they were [NSF 402-11
So that he was the ascending wings he saw [NSF 403-4
Made us no less as sure. We saw in his head, [AA 412-1
There he saw well the foldings in the height [Owl 433-7
Now, he brings all that he saw into the earth, to the waiting
    parent. [Madame 507-3
His grief is that his mother should feed on him, himself and
    what he saw. [Madame 507-12
I saw a waxen woman in a smock [Infernale 25-1 P
The rotting man for pleasure saw, [Sat Night 27-18 P
And saw the blossoms, snow-bred pink and white, [Good Bad 33-17P
There, too, he saw, since he must see, the domes [Greenest
    54-12 P
How could you ever, how could think that you saw her, [Grotesque
    74-9 P
You saw the eye-blue, sky-blue, eye-blue, and the powdered ears
    [Grotesque 74-15 P
As if, alone on a mountain, it saw far-off [Pagoda 92-5 P
If I saw no more [Three 128-1 P
What the court saw was always of the same color, [Three 131-22 P
SAW-GRASS. Through the green saw-grass, [Sugar-Cane 12-10
SAXAPHONES. Squiggling like saxaphones. And palm for palm, [High-
    Toned 59-12
SAY. I say now, Fernando, that on that day [Hibiscus 22-9
  And say how it comes that you see [Lilacs 49-8
  Is just what you say. [Gubbinal 85-2
  Is just what you say. [Gubbinal 85-8
  Say, puerile, that the buzzards crouch on the ridge-pole [Two
    Figures 86-10
  Say that the palms are clear in a total blue, [Two Figures 86-13
  To stand here on the deck in the dark and say [Farewell 118-6
  It is easy to say to those bidden--But where, [Ghosts 119-4
  And to touch her, have need to say to her, [Ghosts 119-14
  It is only the way one feels, to say [Sailing 120-22
  To say the light wind worries the sail, [Sailing 121-1
  To say the water is swift today, [Sailing 121-2
  Say how his heavy wings, [Pascagoula 127-1
  One's cup and never to say a word, [Adieu 128-3
  Will say of the mansion that it seems [Postcard 159-16
  Say that it is the serenade [MBG 166-1
  When shall I come to say of the sun, [MBG 168-11
  Things as they are. Or so we say. [MBG 176-20
  And say they are on the blue guitar. [MBG 180-18
  To say of one mask it is like, [MBG 181-7
  To say of another it is like, [MBG 181-8
  And say of what you see in the dark [MBG 183-4
  Speak and say the immaculate syllables [Men Fall 188-11
  Say even that this complete simplicity [Poems Clim 193-17
  I heard two workers say, "This chaos [Idiom 200-18
  Is it to hear the blatter of grackles and say [Dump 203-8
  "Anything is Beautiful if You Say It Is" [211-title
  An upper, particular bough in, say, Marchand. [Connois 215-12
  If one may say so. And yet relation appears, [Connois 215-18
  A trumpet round the trees. Could one say that it was [Horn 230-6
  Could one say that he sang the colors in the stones, [Horn 230-11
  She made it. It is easy to say [Scavoir 231-2
  Say of the gulls that they are flying [Vari 232-5
  And of himself. There he could say [Yellow 236-6
  Hums and you say "The world in a verse, [Waldorf 241-6
  And say, "The thing I hum appears to be [Landsc 243-7
  Of final belief. So, say that final belief [Oboe 250-7
  If you say on the hautboy man is not enough, [Oboe 250-15
  With a single well-tempered apricot, or, say, [Extracts 253-14
  And the helpless philosophers say still helpful things. [Extracts
    253-28
  Ideas or, say, five men or, possibly, six. [Extracts 255-28
  And turn to look and say there is no more [Extracts 257-24
  Say that the hero is his nation, [Hero 279-15
  More than a spokesman of the night to say [Choc 299-11
  To say more than human things with human voice, [Choc 300-11
  That cannot be; to say human things with more [Choc 300-12
  And say it is the work [Crude 305-10
  Whatever remains. Of what is real I say, [Repet 308-15
  We do not say ourselves like that in poems. [Creat 311-16
  We say ourselves in syllables that rise [Creat 311-17
  Say yes, spoken because under every no [EM 320-13
  Itself was innocent. To say that it was [EM 322-7
  Of ideas and to say as usual that there must be [Bed 326-17
  To say the solar chariot is junk [Pure 332-6
  We say that it is man's interior world [Feo 334-6
  It matters, because everything we say [Descrip 345-19
  And because what we say of the future must portend, [Descrip
    346-2
  Or say from that which was conceived to that [Two V 354-16
  And say this, this is the centre that I seek. [Cred 373-9
  Appoints man's place in music, say, today. [NSF 382-2
  We say: At night an Arabian in my room, [NSF 383-1
  Say the weather, the mere weather, the mere air: [NSF 385-23
  As if hyacinths had never gone. We say [NSF 389-20

After a lustre of the moon, we say [NSF 394-19
And as they say good-night, good-night. Upstairs [AA 413-23
Say, a flippant communication under the moon. [AA 418-3
How mad would he have to be to say, "He beheld [Bad Time 426-9
Say that it is a crude effect, black reds, [Roses 430-10
To those that cannot say good-by themselves. [Owl 431-18
Or say to the French here is France again? [Imago 439-3
To say what Celestin should say for himself? [Papini 446-2
He does not say, "Mother, my mother, who are you," [Questions
    463-2
Say next to holiness is the will thereto, [NH 467-4
A view of New Haven, say, through the certain eye, [NH 471-18
We say of the moon, it is haunted by the man [NH 472-9
The phrase . . . Say of each lion of the spirit [NH 472-24
To say good-by to the past and to live and to be [NH 478-5
In the present state of things as, say, to paint [NH 478-6
Is to search. Likewise to say of the evening star, [NH 481-17
Or, say, the late going colors of that past, [NH 482-1
Before and after one arrives or, say, [NH 485-24
Or else a new aspect, say the spirit's sex, [Aug 489-12
And the hawk cats it and we say spread sail, [Aug 490-6
Spread sail, we say spread white, spread way. [Aug 490-7
He does not lie there remembering the blue-jay, say the jay.
    [Madame 507-11
Until we say to ourselves that there may be [Look 517-17
We say God and the imagination are one . . . [Final 524-14
A new-colored sun, say, that will soon change forms [Armor 529-19
It is disclose the essential presence, say, [Moonlight 531-10
You say that spite avails her nothing, that [Good Bad 33-8 P
Yet what I mean I always say. [Stan MBG 73-2 P
Cherries are ri . . . He would never say that. [Grotesque 76-1 P
He could not. Neither of us could ever say that. [Grotesque 76-2P
"The ephebi say that there is only the whole, [Bship 79-20 P
Is to define its form, to say: this image [Recit 86-13 P
Is it experience, say, the final form [Recit 87-4 P
Say this to Pravda, tell the damned rag [Memo 89-9 P
Say that the American moon comes up [Memo 89-11 P
Say that in the clear Atlantic night [Memo 89-13 P
Blue-bold on its pedestal--that seems to say, [Role 93-13 P
Now, you, for instance, are of this mode: You say [Conversat
    108-17 P
And you, you say that the capital things of the mind [Conversat
    109-3 P
And then, finally, it is you that say [Conversat 109-11 P
Saying and saying, the way things say [Region 115-10 P
You speak. You say: Today's character is not [As Leave 116-15 P
As you say, [Three 138-23 P
The moon and the imagination, or, say, [Someone 83-12 A
He must say nothing of the fruit that is [Someone 84-4 A
That makes it say the little thing it says, [Someone 84-15 A
A day of which we say, this is the day [Ideal 88-2 A
The orator will say that we ourselves [Ideal 89-10 A
SAYING. And of Phoebus the Tailor the second saying goes: [NE
    Verses 105-5
And that would be saying farewell, repeating farewell, [Adieu
    127-15
The bird kept saying that birds had once been men, [Horn 230-1
In him made one, and in that saying [Hero 279-16
Out of themselves, a saying, [Dutch 290-18
Cardinal, saying the prayers of earliest day; [Choc 300-2
Saying things in the rooms and on the stair, [Less 327-10
And seems to be on the saying of her name. [Descrip 339-14
Order, saying I am the contemplated spouse. [NSF 396-3
Is it I then that keep saying there is an hour [NSF 404-23
To no; and in saying yes he says farewell. [AA 414-9
A saying out of a cloud, but innocence. [AA 418-20
Saying: Olalla blanca en el blanco, [Novel 457-18
And kept saying over and over one same, same thing, [Slug 522-6
Saying we have forgot them, they never lived. [Grotesque 77-12 P
By her sexual name, saying that that high marriage [Desire 85-5P
Saying and saying, the way things say [Region 115-10 P
He was saying good-by to her." [Three 134-18 P
SAYINGS. Surrenders, the repeated sayings that [Extracts 258-6
These fitful sayings are, also, of tragedy: [NH 478-1
Remains in the sight, and in sayings of the sight, [How Now 97-5P
SAYS. She says, "I am content when wakened birds, [Sunday 68-12
She says, "But in contentment I still feel [Sunday 68-27
One says a German chandelier-- [MBG 172-15
The freshness of morning, the blowing of day, one says [Dump
    202-2
It says there is an absolute grotesque. [Feo 334-3
On his hill, watching the rising and falling, and says: [Two V
    354-22
If the observer says so: grandiloquent [Pastor 379-7
He says no to no and yes to yes. He says yes [AA 414-8
To no; and in saying yes he says farewell. [AA 414-9
Two brothers. And a third form, she that says [Owl 431-16
But she that says good-by losing in self [Owl 435-4
Like a trumpet and says, in this season of memory, [Puel 456-11
Flame, sound, fury composed . . . Hear what he says [Puel 456-17

Peter the voyant, who says "Mother, what is that"-- [Questions
    462-10
A nature that is created in what it says, [Aug 490-21
No longer says anything. [Plant 506-9
A solemn voice, not Mr. Burnshaw's says: [Burnshaw 49-3 P
He eats red cherry pie and never says-- [Grotesque 75-19 P
He says, "That's what I call red cherry pie." [Grotesque 76-4 P
The true tone of the metal of winter in what it says: [Discov
    96-6 P
And though one says that one is part of everything. [Course
    96-15 P
The mistress says, in a harsh voice, [Three 134-5 P
She says sharply, to her maid, [Three 134-9 P
Then the maid says, to herself, [Three 134-11 P
The maid drops her eyes and says to her mistress, [Three 135-1 P
That makes it say the little thing it says, [Someone 84-15 A
One says even of the odor of this fruit, [Someone 87-14 A
SCAFFOLD. In casque and scaffold orator, fortified [Stan Hero
    84-21 P
SCAFFOLDS. Scaffolds and derricks rise from the reeds to the clouds
    [NE Verses 105-9
SCALE. I shall not play the flat historic scale. [Monocle 14-4
But singular, they would, like water, scale [Two V 355-5
To be in scale, unless virtue cuts him, snips [Orb 442-26
See fish-scale.
SCALED. Stands brimming white, chiaroscuro scaled [Sombre 70-20 P
To space. To space? The statue scaled to space [Sombre 70-21 P
SCALES. Glittering scales and point [Bagatelles 213-7
At the piano, scales, arpeggios [Hero 274-21
The most massive sopranos are singing songs of scales. [Chaos
    357-18
A philosopher practicing scales on his piano, [NH 488-20
SCAMPER. Even by mice--these scamper and are still; [Soldat 14-1 P
SCAN. Should make the intricate Sierra scan. [C 38-23
SCANDINAVIA. For him the moon was always in Scandinavia [Norfolk
    111-10
SCARAMOUCHE. And ah! that Scaramouche [W Burgher 61-5
SCARLET. Among the purple tufts, the scarlet crowns, [C 32-4
SCARRED. See color-scarred.
SCARVES. Fetching her woven scarves, [Peter 91-5
SCATTER. Men scatter throughout clouds. [Dutch 290-4
SCATTERED. Scattered themselves in the garden, like [Vase 246-12
Lenin took bread from his pocket, scattered it-- [Descrip 343-6
And scattered them about, no two alike. [NSF 400-24
SCAVOIR. "Bouquet of Belle Scavoir" [231-title
SCENE. Therefore, that in the planetary scene [High-Toned 59-14
Scène Flétrie [NE Verses 106-title 15
Scène Fleurie [NE Verses 106-title 16
Act I, Scene 1, at a German Staats-Oper. [Nigger 153-16
That tours to shift the shifting scene. [MBG 180-4
Any character. It is more than any scene: [Parochial 192-6
To find: the scene was set; it repeated what [Of Mod 239-19
It was a blue scene washing white in the rain, [Repet 306-19
A well-made scene in which paratroopers [EM 322-21
The assassin's scene. Evil in evil is [EM 324-18
It is a spectacle. Scene 10 becomes 11, [Chaos 357-11
The scene in his gray-rose with violet rocks. [Anach 366-5
Than sharp, illustrious scene. The trumpet cries [Cred 376-19
Complete in a completed scene, speaking [Cred 378-9
It means the distaste we feel for this withered scene [NSF 390-3
Behind all actual seeing, in the actual scene, [NH 467-11
These characters are around us in the scene. [NH 469-13
Custodians of the glory of the scene, [NH 469-17
This is the tragic accent of the scene. [Rome 510-5
That could come in a slight lurching of the scene, [Nuns 92-10 P
SCENEN. See Kinder-Scenen.
SCENERY. Without scenery or lights, in the theatre's bricks, [Bad
    Time 427-5
No soldiers in the scenery, [Clear Day 113-7 P
SCENES. Scenes of the theatre, vistas and blocks of woods [AA
    415-14
Of dulce atmosphere, the fore of lofty scenes [Bouquet 450-3
That talk shifts the cycle of the scenes of kings? [Conversat
    109-23 P
SCENT. One year, death and war prevented the jasmine scent [Oboe
    251-8
The cold evening, without any scent or the shade [Extracts
    258-15
In spite of the yellow of the acacias, the scent [EM 315-5
SCENTED. O bough and bush and scented vine, in whom [Fictive 88-8
SCENTING. Scenting the jungle in their refuges, [C 32-5
So gardens die, their meek breath scenting [Peter 92-4
SCENTS. More than a world of white and snowy scents [Poems Clim
    194-3
SCEPTRE. O sceptre of the sun, crown of the moon, [Monocle 13-2
And true. The good, the strength, the sceptre moves [Bship
    80-21 P
The circle of the sceptre growing large [Bship 80-23 P
If the sceptre returns to earth, still moving, still [Bship
    80-31 P

And their directing sceptre, the crown [Ulysses 104-8 P
SCHEMES. The sensitive and conscientious schemes [Soldat 13-9 P
SCHLEMIHL. And Ludwig Richter, turbulent Schlemihl [Chaos 358-1
SCHLOSS. The heaven of Europe is empty, like a Schloss [Greenest
    53-1 P
  A Schloss, and empty Schlossbibliothek, the books [Greenest
    53-8 P
SCHLOSSBIBLIOTHEK. A Schloss, and empty Schlossbibliothek, the
  books [Greenest 53-8 P
SCHOLAR. Like a dull scholar, I behold, in love, [Monocle 16-1
  A scholar of darkness, [Venereal 48-5
  That scholar hungriest for that book, [MBG 178-1
  It becomes the scholar again, seeking celestial [God 285-11
  And the mother, the music, the name; the scholar, [Choc 300-4
  In which no scholar, separately dwelling, [Somnan 304-16
  The scholar to whom his book is true, to whom [House Q 358-14
  What else, prodigious scholar, should there be? [NSF 381-24
  Who chants by book, in the heat of the scholar, who writes [NSF
    395-12
  Of degrees of perception in the scholar's dark. [NSF 395-15
  On flames. The scholar of one candle sees [AA 417-1
  A scholar, in his Segmenta, left a note, [NH 485-1
  A new scholar replacing an older one reflects [Look 519-4
  The scholar's outline that you had, the print [Duck 61-17 P
  Of the black-blooded scholar, the man of the cloud, to be
    [Sombre 71-30 P
  The scholar is always distant in the space [Recit 86-18 P
  Without the forfeit scholar coming in, [Someone 85-4 A
  The scholar, captious, told him what he could [Someone 85-10 A
  See hill-scholar.
SCHOLARS. It is better that, as scholars, [Homunculus 26-17
  Shadows of scholars bent upon their books, [Montra 262-17
  He turns us into scholars, studying [Sombre 67-21 P
SCHOLIA. Like precious scholia jotted down in the dark. [Someone
    84-21 A
SCHOOLS. In the presence of such chapels and such schools, [NH
    469-22
SCHUYLKILL. From a Schuylkill in mid-earth there came emerging
    [New Set 352-10
  And Schuylkill. The sound of him [Our Stars 455-11
SCHWARMEREI. Sets up its Schwärmerei, not balances [NSF 386-14
SCHWARZ. The statue seems a thing from Schwarz's, a thing [Burn-
    shaw 47-4 P
SCIENCE. As of a tragic science should rise. [Prelude 195-13
  Of this present, this science, this unrecognized, [Cuisine 228-8
SCIENTIST. Pure scientist, you look with nice aplomb [Good Bad
    33-12 P
  And equally as scientist you walked [Good Bad 33-15 P
SCIENZA. There was a bright scienza outside of ourselves, [Gala
    248-12
SCINTILLANT. And scintillant sizzlings such as children like, [Orb
    442-20
SCOPE. Progenitor of such extensive scope, [C 38-29
  As he is, the discipline of his scope [Ulysses 101-14 P
SCORE. Without grace or grumble. Score this anecdote [C 45-19
SCORPIONS. The bees to scorpions blackly-barbed, a shade [Duck
    65-9 P
  Of fear changes the scorpions to skins [Duck 65-10 P
  And the bees, the scorpions, the men that think, [Duck 66-3 P
SCOWL. Lifts up its heavy scowl before them. [Pediment 362-3
SCRAGGY. Where his house had fallen, three scraggy trees weighted
    [NSF 393-4
SCRAPING. Left only Death's ironic scraping. [Peter 92-10
  The leaves hop, scraping on the ground. [Possum 294-6
SCRAPS. Spring vanishes the scraps of winter, why [NSF 391-1
SCRATCH. O caliper, do you scratch your buttocks [Lilacs 48-19
  Pack the heart and scratch the mind? And does the ear [Dump
    203-3
SCRATCHED. The mountains are scratched and used, clear fakes.
    [Arcades 226-3
  Of the park with chalky brow scratched over black [Old Woman
    44-3 P
SCRATCHING. The claws keep scratching on the shale, the shallow
    shale, [Somnan 304-5
SCRAWL. Should scrawl a vigilant anthology, [C 38-26
  Scrawl a tragedian's testament? Prolong [C 41-14
  To weave a shadow's leg or sleeve, a scrawl [What We 459-18
SCRAWLED. And only, in the fables that he scrawled [C 31-18
  A legend scrawled in script we cannot read? [Recit 87-10 P
SCRAWLS. Like one who scrawls a listless testament [Swans 4-5
SCRAWNY. In March, a scrawny cry from outside [Not Ideas 534-2
  That scrawny cry--it was [Not Ideas 534-14
SCREEN. At Easter on a London screen, the seeds [Greenest 53-19 P
SCRIBBLE. A scribble of fret and fear and fate, [Aug 494-25
SCRIPT. Of heaven and of the heavenly script. [Ord Women 11-13
  Was in the script. [Of Mod 239-20
  I write Semiramide and in the script [Phenom 287-20
  To reject the script for its lack-tragic, [Gigan 289-10
  A legend scrawled in script we cannot read? [Recit 87-10 P
SCRIVENED. This is the thesis scrivened in delight, [EM 326-1

SCRIVENING. Such fluctuations that their scrivening [Monocle 15-12
SCRUPLES. An annotator has his scruples, too. [C 32-28
SCRUPULOUS. Jerome and the scrupulous Francis and Sunday women,
    [Luther 461-8
SCRURRY. In the scrurry and water-shine, [Paltry 6-2
SCRUTINY. The object, grips it in savage scrutiny, [Cred 376-11
SCUDDING. Clippered with lilies scudding the bright chromes,
    [Monocle 17-15
SCUDS. She scuds the glitters, [Paltry 5-9
SCULLION. Scullion of fate, [Paltry 6-8
SCULPTOR. And savings banks, Fides, the sculptor's prize, [Lions
    124-12
  So much the sculptor had foreseen: autumn, [Old Woman 43-5 P
  They are horses as they were in the sculptor's mind. [Burnshaw
    46-18 P
  Than this jotting-down of the sculptor's foppishness [Burnshaw
    47-11 P
  There lies the head of the sculptor in which the thought [Burn-
    shaw 49-16 P
  The statue is the sculptor not the stone. [Duck 64-20 P
SCULPTURE. This is the mute, the final sculpture [Yellow 236-9
  As anything but sculpture. Good-bye, [Couch 296-5
SCULPTURED. See large-sculptured.
SCURRILOUS. Or that she will pause at scurrilous words? [Lilacs
    49-5
SEA. Archaic, for the sea. [Paltry 5-7
  Of the high interiors of the sea. [Paltry 5-15
  In the circle of her traverse of the sea. [Paltry 5-20
  Over the sea. [Infanta 7-19
  Partaking of the sea, [Infanta 8-3
  The sea of spuming thought foists up again [Monocle 13-8
  And the colored purple of the lazy sea, [Hibiscus 22-17
  In the sea, Biscayne, there prinks [Homunculus 25-13
  Arch in the sea like tree-branches, [Homunculus 26-2
  Preceptor to the sea? Crispin at sea [C 27-12
  The snug hibernal from that sea and salt, [C 28-3
  Could Crispin stem verboseness in the sea, [C 28-22
  Forsook the insatiable egotist. The sea [C 30-3
  He was a man made vivid by the sea, [C 30-24
  And lank, rising and slumping from a sea [C 34-5
  Loquacious columns by the ructive sea? [C 41-20
  Sequestered over the sea, [Venereal 48-6
  What was the sea whose tide swept through me there? [Hoon 65-12
  I was myself the compass of that sea: [Hoon 65-15
  And I reach to the shore of the sea [Six Sig 74-9
  That separates us from the wind and sea, [Fictive 87-15
  "Sea Surface Full of Clouds [98-title
  The slopping of the sea grew still one night [Sea Surf 98-13
  Round those flotillas. And sometimes the sea [Sea Surf 99-14
  The slopping of the sea grew still one night. [Sea Surf 99-17
  Its crystalline pendentives on the sea [Sea Surf 100-7
  The slopping of the sea grew still one night [Sea Surf 100-11
  The sea unfolding in the sunken clouds? [Sea Surf 100-20
  The night-long slopping of the sea grew still. [Sea Surf 101-5
  Night stilled the slopping of the sea. The day [Sea Surf 101-23
  And the sea as turquoise-turbaned Sambo, neat [Sea Surf 102-7
  At tossing saucers--cloudy-conjuring sea? [Sea Surf 102-8
  To clearing opalescence. Then the sea [Sea Surf 102-13
  The mountains between our lands and the sea-- [Grapes 110-9
  This conjunction of mountains and sea and our lands-- [Grapes
    110-10
  And mountains and the sea do. And our lands. [Grapes 110-19
  And silvers and greens spread over the sea. The moon [Farewell
    117-4
  Her South of pine and coral and coraline sea, [Farewell 117-15
  Disclosed the sea floor and the wilderness [Farewell 118-2
  There is order in neither sea nor sun. [Sad Gay 122-1
  Down to the fishy sea. [Pascagoula 126-16
  She sang beyond the genius of the sea. [Key W 128-11
  The sea was not a mask. No more was she. [Key W 128-18
  But it was she and not the sea we heard. [Key W 129-3
  The ever-hooded, tragic-gestured sea [Key W 129-5
  If it was only the dark voice of the sea [Key W 129-10
  Of sky and sea. [Key W 129-22
  In which she sang. And when she sang, the sea, [Key W 129-27
  Mastered the night and portioned out the sea, [Key W 130-8
  The maker's rage to order words of the sea, [Key W 130-12
  Desire for rest, in that descending sea [Eve Angels 137-23
  Of the sea there, [Winter B 141-18
  How full of exhalations of the sea . . . [Havana 144-27
  The moon shares nothing. It is a sea. [MBG 168-10
  It is a sea; it shares nothing; [MBG 168-12
  And men in waves become the sea. [MBG 171-2
  The sea returns upon the men, [MBG 171-4
  The sea appends its tattery hues. [MBG 172-13
  Rising upward from a sea of ex. [MBG 175-4
  It is the sea that whitens the roof. [MBG 179-13
  The sea drifts through the winter air. [MBG 179-14
  It is the sea that the north wind makes. [MBG 179-15
  The sea is in the falling snow. [MBG 179-16

This gloom is the darkness of the sea. [MBG 179-17
The sea is a form of ridicule. [MBG 180-1
From the sea, conceive for the courts [Prelude 195-15
Smacks like fresh water in a can, like the sea [Dump 202-6
Which is enough: the moment's rain and sea, [Freed 204-19
The black wind of the sea [Weak Mind 212-11
Too sharp for that. The shore, the sea, the sun, [Blue Bldg 217-9
Or to see the sea on Sunday, or [Arcades 225-22
In light blue air over dark blue sea. [Vari 232-6
Into the sea. [Vari 232-14
The leaves of the sea are shaken and shaken. [Vari 233-5
On the motive! But one looks at the sea [Vari 233-18
This cloudy world, by aid of land and sea, [Vari 233-20
Cover the sea with the sand rose. Fill [Vari 234-14
And sea exists by grace alone, [Vari 235-4
And the sun, the waves together in the sea. [Les Plus 245-2
It was like the sea poured out again [Vase 246-15
The sea is so many written words; the sky [Extracts 252-10
Ceylon, wants nothing from the sea, la belle [Extracts 257-28
The zebra leaves, the sea [Search 268-3
The many-stanzaed sea, the leaves [Search 268-5
Shadow, up the great sea and downward [Hero 274-27
Of the fishes of the sea, the colored [Hero 277-28
Of sky, of sea, large earth, large air. It is [Choc 296-10
Of the expanses that are mountainous rock and sea; [Repet 308-24
To find for himself his earth, his sky, his sea. [Holiday 312-12
With the sea. These were fantastic. There were homes [EM 321-26
To watch the fire-feinting sea and calls it good, [EM 324-15
Who lay in bed on the west wall of the sea, [Pure 331-6
This afternoon the wind and the sea were like that-- [Jouga 337-13
A palm that rises up beyond the sea, [Descrip 344-2
By the sea, insolid rock, stentor, and said: [Two V 353-12
The sea, a strength that tumbles everywhere, [Two V 354-12
If they were creatures of the sea alone, [Two V 355-4
But if they are of sea, earth, sky--water [Two V 355-8
As if, in the presence of the sea, [Silent 359-8
The sea full of fishes in shoals, the woods that let [Cats 367-13
It rises from land and sea and covers them. [Cred 375-12
If MacCullough himself lay lounging by the sea, [NSF 387-9
Are one and the sailor and the sea are one. [NSF 392-22
As when the sun comes rising, when the sea [NSF 398-23
And the pines above and along and beside the sea. [AA 411-9
The sea was frozen solid and Hans heard, [Page 421-5
The great ship, Balayne, lay frozen in the sea. [Page 421-18
Was like a sleep. The sea was a sea he dreamed. [Page 422-2
You enter the swarthy sea, [Countryman 428-12
A sudden color on the sea. But it is not [John 437-2
The composition of blue sea and of green, [Orb 442-3
Wet out of the sea, and luminously wet, [Our Stars 455-15
Of a vacant sea declaiming with wide throat, [Puel 456-9
Silently it heaves its youthful sleep from the sea-- [NH 476-22
Like the constant sound of the water of the sea [NH 480-14
The sea shivered in transcendent change, rose up [NH 484-9
Of Fact, lies at his ease beside the sea." [NH 485-18
When day comes, fire-foams in the motions of the sea, [NH 488-12
The shell is a shore. The egg of the sea [Aug 490-8
He does not change the sea from crumpled tinfoil [Aug 492-20
And the sea. This is my father or, maybe, [Irish 502-5
And sea and air. [Irish 502-8
Where he could lie and, gazing down at the sea, [Poem Mt 512-13
There was an ease of mind that was like being alone in a boat
    at sea, [Prol 515-5
The river that flows nowhere, like a sea. [R Conn 533-21
As the sea has in its coastal clamorings, [Red Kit 31-9 P
In a freshness of poetry by the sea, [Polo 37-19 P
Visible over the sea. It is only enough [Burnshaw 50-16 P
Out of a violet sea. They rise a bit [Duck 60-10 P
To trundle children like the sea? For you, [Duck 61-4 P
The volcano Apostrophe, the sea Behold? [Duck 63-29 P
Maidens in bloom, bulls under sea, the lark [Sombre 67-33 P
A tiara from Cohen's, this summer sea. [Stan MBG 72-14 P
One could watch the blue sea's blueness flow [Stan MBG 73-13 P
A single ship, a cloud on the sea, the largest [Bship 78-2 P
On the sea, is both law and evidence in one, [Bship 78-29 P
An acrobat on the border of the sea [Woman Had 81-12 P
Listening to the whole sea for a sound [Woman Had 82-4 P
Of the sea, the central humming of the sea, [Woman Had 82-13 P
Or clouds that hang lateness on the sea. They become [Role 93-10 P
The giant sea, read his own mind. [Ulysses 99-12 P
The giant sea, read his own mind. [Presence 105-15 P
4. The sea is spouting upward out of rocks. [Someone 86-7 A
See mid-sea.
SEA-BLOOMS. Who, then, evolved the sea-blooms from the clouds [Sea
    Surf 99-7
SEA-CLOUDS. The sea-clouds whitened far below the calm [Sea Surf
    99-10
    Its bluest sea-clouds in the thinking green, [Sea Surf 101-19

SEA-COAST. From whose being by starlight, on sea-coast, [Homunculus
    26-26
SEA-GLASS. A skinny sailor peering in the sea-glass. [C 28-13
SEA-GREEN. Will go, like the centre of sea-green pomp, [Paltry 6-6
SEAL. The seal is as relaxed as dirt, perdu. [Golden 460-18
    Seal him there. He looked in a glass of the earth and thought he
    lived in it. [Madame 507-2
    The spirit's ring and seal, the naked heart. [Bship 79-13 P
SEALED. Sealed pensive purple under its concern. [C 40-20
    A generation sealed, men remoter than mountains, [Waldorf 241-7
SEA-LINES. Wading the sea-lines, moist and ever-mingling, [Tallap
    72-2
SEALS. Of the dead, majestic in their seals. [MBG 170-8
SEA-MASKS. How many sea-masks he ignored; what sounds [C 34-21
SEAMED. And knotted, sashed and seamed, half pales of red, [Cred
    378-2
SEA-MOUNTAIN. Sea-tower, sea-pinnacles, sea-mountain. [Hero 275-1
SEA-MOUTHS. While they went seaward to the sea-mouths. [Frogs
    78-15
SEA-MYRTLES. These were his beaches, his sea-myrtles in [NSF 393-8
SEA-NIGHT. Or this, whose music, sweeping irradiation of a sea-
    night, [Inelegance 26-1 P
SEA-PINNACLES. Sea-tower, sea-pinnacles, sea-mountain. [Hero 275-1
SEARCH. If ever the search for a tranquil belief should end,
    [Nigger 151-9
    Out of what is full of us; yet the search [Nigger 151-11
    "The Search for Sound Free from Motion" [268-title
    Professor Eucalyptus said, "The search [NH 481-4
    The search for god." It is the philosopher's search [NH 481-6
    And the poet's search for the same exterior made [NH 481-8
    Is to search. Likewise to say of the evening star, [NH 481-17
    To symbols of descending night; and search [Blanche 10-7 P
    To search for clearness all an afternoon [Old Woman 44-13 P
SEARCHED. She searched [Peter 90-15
    Searched out such majesty as it could find. [NH 469-3
SEARCHER. Or searcher for the fecund minimum. [C 35-30
SEARCHES. Searches a possible for its possibleness. [NH 481-21
    The gardener searches earth and sky [Room Gard 41-7 P
SEARCHING. Searching all day, all night, for the honey-comb.
    [Blue Bldg 217-24
    Fell on him, high and cold, searching for what [Choc 301-21
    Was native to him in that height, searching [Choc 301-22
    The leaning shoulder and the searching eye. [Blanche 10-4 P
    That they are searching the hill [Three 135-13 P
SEAS. That's better. That's worth crossing seas to find. [C 36-25
    Over the seas, to silent Palestine, [Sunday 67-10
    With rivers like our own that seek for seas [Sunday 69-17
    Made by the sun ascending seventy seas. [Burnshaw 47-29 P
SEA-SHADES. Of sea-shades and sky-shades, [Tea 113-2
SEA-SHADOW. In the high sea-shadow. [Venereal 48-10
SEA-SHELL. Than fragile volutes in a rose sea-shell. [Soldat 14-3P
SEA-SIDE. Still by the sea-side mutters milky lines [Oboe 250-13
SEA-SLUSHES. White sand, his patter of the long sea-slushes. [NSF
    393-9
SEASON. As in a season of autumn. [Soldier 97-2
    As in a season of autumn, [Soldier 97-8
    Brings back an earlier season of quiet [Lunar 107-10
    "In the Clear Season of Grapes" [110-title
    "The fly on the rose prevents us, O season [Ghosts 119-15
    It is like the season when, after summer, [Cuisine 228-1
    In vain, life's season or death's element. [Montra 263-6
    Was the veritable season, that familiar [Hero 280-27
    To repose in an hour or season or long era [EM 318-22
    A season, to discover summer and know it, [NSF 403-24
    The season changes. A cold wind chills the beach. [AA 412-19
    A season changes color to no end, [AA 416-5
    Which in a composite season, now unknown, [John 437-18
    In a season more than sun and south wind, [Imago 439-14
    Like a trumpet and says, in this season of memory, [Puel 456-11
    One wished that there had been a season, [Aug 491-26
    There's rain. The season grieves. [Phases 3-6 P
    As by a juicier season; and more our own [Duck 65-4 P
    Without a season, unstinted in livery, [Sombre 67-7 P
    When cherries are in season, or, at least [Grotesque 76-8 P
    It is the same sound, the same season, [Memo 89-3 P
    In a season, a climate of morning, of elucidation, [Bus 116-5 P
SEASONS. The powerful seasons bred and killed, [Joost 46-17
    Across the stale, mysterious seasons. These [On Manner 56-3
    "That bliss of stars, that princox of evening heaven!" reminding
    of seasons, [Banal 63-1
    Of improvisations and seasons of belief. [Extracts 255-24
    The propounding of four seasons and twelve months. [NH 473-14
    Space-filled, reflecting the seasons, the folk-lore [R Conn
    533-19
    Overlooking whole seasons? [Archi 17-13 P
SEA-SOUNDS. As the night conceives the sea-sounds in silence, [Two
    Figures 86-7
SEA-STARS. A convocation, nightly, of the sea-stars, [C 28-27
SEAT. By his presence, the seat of his ubiquitous will. [Greenest
    59-32 P

On the seat of halidom, rainbowed, [Ulysses 104-5 P
SEATED. Poet, be seated at the piano. [Mozart 131-14
  Be seated at the piano. [Mozart 132-2
  Be seated, thou. [Mozart 132-22
  Sustains us . . . who, then, are they, seated here? [Cuisine
    228-14
  A young man seated at his table [Lack 303-1
  The fictive man. He may be seated in [Paisant 335-14
  Master O master seated by the fire [AA 414-22
  And, seated in the nature of his chair, [Aug 493-22
  The time will come for these children, seated before their long
    black instruments, to strike the themes of love-- [Piano 21-16P
  Seated before these shining forms, like the duskiest glass, re-
    flecting the piebald of roses or what you will. [Piano 21-18 P
  The bronze of the wise man seated in repose [Recit 86-15 P
  For a change, the englistered woman, seated [Ulysses 104-2 P
  By them: gorgeous symbol seated [Ulysses 104-4 P
  As if we were all seated together again [Letters 107-13 P
  And human nature, pensively seated [Region 115-14 P
SEA-TOWER. Sea-tower, sea-pinnacles, sea-mountain. [Hero 275-1
  The signal . . . The sea-tower, shaken, [Hero 275-2
SEAWARD. While they went seaward to the sea-mouths. [Frogs 78-15
SEA-WEEDS. Made on the sea-weeds and the covered stones [Hibiscus
  22-13
SEA-WIDE. It cannot mean a sea-wide country strewn [Duck 63-12 P
SEA-WORM. Jehovah and the great sea-worm. The air [Havana 142-4
SEBASTIAN. See Johann Sebastian.
SECLUDED. Like blooms secluded in the thick marine? [Sea Surf
  101-12
  Like men besides, like men in light secluded, [NSF 405-12
  Of secluded thunder, an illusion, as it was, [Orb 441-1
SECLUSION. Seclusion. [Soldat 12-9 P
  -manity had invaded its seclusion, with its suffering and its
    [Three 129-10 P
  There is a seclusion of porcelain [Three 130-2 P
  It is like the seclusion of sunrise, [Three 130-5 P
  Finds itself in seclusion, [Three 131-10 P
  That is the seclusion of sunrise [Three 131-12 P
  Such seclusion knows beauty [Three 131-15 P
  And in seclusion, [Three 132-6 P
  Seclusion of porcelain . . . [Three 142-2 P
  Seclusion of sunrise . . . [Three 142-3 P
SECOND. Secret and singular. Second, upon [C 44-15
  A second similar counterpart, a maid [C 44-16
  The second sister dallying was shy [C 44-27
  And of Phoebus the Tailor the second saying goes: [NE Verses
    105-5
  Beyond a second death, as evil's end? [Extracts 258-28
  His poems are not of the second part of life. [Creat 311-11
  In heaven as in a glass; a second earth; [NSF 383-14
  Of flame on the line, with a second wheel below, [Page 422-23
  The doubling second things, not mystical, [Bouquet 451-18
  A second that grows first, a black unreal [Novel 458-14
  Twelve and the first gray second after, a kind [What We 459-16
  Unless a second giant kills the first-- [NH 465-14
  He was born within us as a second self, [Sombre 67-3 P
  Second. The part [Bship 79-17 P
  The first and second rules are reconciled [Bship 80-13 P
  Among the second selves, sailor, observe [Pagoda 91-19 P
  He is the image, the second, the unreal, [Americana 94-9 P
  He seeks as image a second of the self, [Someone 84-7 A
SECONDARINESS. In a constant secondariness, [Plant 506-14
SECONDARY. And wild and free, the secondary man, [Jumbo 269-12
  Of the secondary men. There are no rocks [Jumbo 269-17
  At a distance, a secondary expositor, [Creat 311-4
  But that concerns the secondary characters. [Creat 311-?
  As secondary (parts not quite perceived [Man Car 350-18
  Out of a storm of secondary things), [Man Car 351-5
  And the secondary senses of the ear [Cred 374-7
  Swarm, not with secondary sounds, but choirs, [Cred 374-12
SECONDHAND. Too often to be more than secondhand. [Recit 87-2 P
SECOND-HAND. In the inherited garden, a second-hand [Extraord
  369-19
SECONDS. Dry seconds and insipid thirds, [Arcades 225-25
  Issued thin seconds glibly gapering. [Repet 306-13
  And mist-mites, dangling seconds, grown [Red Fern 365-9
SECRECIES. To read, in secret, burning secrecies . . . [Polish
  Aunt 84-11
SECRECY. And sing them in secrecy as lovers do. [Nigger 151-21
  In a secrecy of words [Letters 108-3 P
  Opened out within a secrecy of place, [Letters 108-4 P
SECRET. Secret and singular. Second, upon [C 44-15
  To read, in secret, burning secrecies . . . [Polish Aunt 84-11
  Is there any secret in skulls, [Circulat 150-1
  Mumbling a secret, passionate message. [Hero 276-18
  Of what is secret becomes, for me, a voice [Choc 298-19
  No secret from him. If it is they in him, [EM 323-14
  He has no secret from them. This knowledge [EM 323-15
  Without secret arrangements of it in the mind. [Descrip 341-14
  The shoo-shoo-shoo of secret cymbals round. [NSF 401-13

To the lover, and blue, as of a secret place [NH 470-21
  "Secret Man" [35-title P
  The immaculate disclosure of the secret no more obscured.
    [Discov 96-2 P
SECRETARIES. As one of the secretaries of the moon, [Feo 333-10
SECRETARY. Let the Secretary for Porcelain observe [Extracts 253-7
SECRETE. The taste of it, secrete within them [Hero 279-8
  Her vague "Secrete me from reality," [Repet 309-20
  His "That reality secrete itself," [Repet 309-21
  Secrete us in reality. It is there [Repet 310-1
  Secrete us in reality. Discover [Repet 310-5
SECRETED. Free knowledges, secreted until then, [Orb 441-17
SECRETIONS. Staring at the secretions of the words as [Lack 303-3
  The secretions of insight. [Aug 492-15
SECRETIVE. Let these be your delight, secretive hunter, [Tallap
  72-1
  Now, solemnize the secretive syllables. [AA 420-15
SECRETLY. The sun is secretly shining on a wall. [Bouquet 450-23
SECRETS. I have secrets [Soldat 12-22 P
SECT. Each sexton has his sect. The bells have none. [Luther 461-15
  Each truth is a sect though no bells ring for it. [Luther 462-1
SECTIONS. As of sections collecting toward the greenest cone.
  [Someone 87-21 A
SECURE. Secure. It was difficult to sing in face [Cred 376-2
  Which nothing can frustrate, that most secure, [NH 467-7
SEDAN. In a golden sedan, [Cab 21-11 P
SEDUCED. Impassioned seducers and seduced, the pale [Burnshaw 52-19P
SEDUCER. Where, butcher, seducer, bloodman, reveller, [Ghosts 119-5
SEDUCERS. Impassioned seducers and seduced, the pale [Burnshaw
  52-19 P
SEDUCING. We have not the need of any seducing hymn. [NSF 394-21
SEDUCTIONS. Grind their seductions on him, Crispin knew [C 35-15
  To expel the ever-present seductions, [Gigan 289-9
SEE. The laughing sky will see the two of us [Monocle 16-10
  "Where none can see, [Pourtraicte 21-17
  It purified. It made him see how much [C 36-16
  And say how it comes that you see [Lilacs 49-8
  But when I walk I see that it consists of three or four hills
    and a cloud. [Of Surface 57-2
  The last largeness, bold to see. [Curtains 62-10
  Do you not see how the blackbird [Thirteen 93-21
  Now that you see the night? [Sonatina 110-8
  Of the bride, love being a birth, have need to see [Ghosts 119-13
  Was not the moon he used to see, to feel [Anglais 148-20
  Nothing is final, he chants. No man shall see the end. [Nigger
    150-13
  Must see her fans of silver undulate. [Nigger 152-20
  And say of what you see in the dark [MBG 183-4
  (All its images are in the dump) and you see [Dump 202-23
  You see the moon rise in the empty sky. [Dump 202-25
  There's nothing whatever to see [Jersey 210-17
  On the sidewalk so that the pensive man may see. [Connois 216-12
  That you do not see, you experience, you feel, [Poem Morn 219-13
  Absorbs Anjou. I see them as a lover sees, [Peaches 224-4
  That they never hear the past. To see, [Arcades 225-6
  That's this. Do they touch the thing they see, [Arcades 225-8
  Out of what they see. They polish their eyes [Arcades 225-11
  Or to see the sea on Sunday, or [Arcades 225-22
  See the river, the railroad, the cathedral . . . [Hartford 227-6
  Someone before him to see and to know. [Scavoir 232-4
  You could almost see the brass on her gleaming, [Vari 235-19
  He wanted to see. He wanted the eye to see [Landsc 241-14
  To see him, that we were wholly one, as we heard [Oboe 251-18
  The spirit laughs to see the eye believe [Extracts 253-5
  It was time to be himself again, to see [Extracts 255-10
  To have satisfied the mind and turn to see, [Extracts 257-22
  Taller than any eye could see, [News 264-9
  For him to see, wove round her glittering hair. [Hand 271-6
  To see was to be. He was the figure in [Choc 297-6
  To see nor, reverberating, eke out the mind [Creat 311-13
  It was something to see that their white was different, [Holiday
    312-1
  To lose sensibility, to see what one sees, [EM 320-25
  Whines in its hole for puppies to come see, [Pure 332-21
  The baroque poet may see him as still a man [Paisant 335-12
  As Virgil, abstract. But see him for yourself, [Paisant 335-13
  These are the actual seemings that we see, [Descrip 340-17
  The difference that we make in what we see [Descrip 344-4
  With thought, through which it cannot see? Does it [Two V 354-3
  To speak of what you see. But wait [Red Fern 365-11
  And Bloom would see what Puvis did, protest [Anach 366-6
  Confined by what they see, [Prejudice 368-14
  Let's see the very thing and nothing else. [Cred 373-3
  Let's see it with the hottest fire of sight. [Cred 373-4
  And see the sun again with an ignorant eye [NSF 380-16
  And see it clearly in the idea of it. [NSF 380-17
  To see hepatica, a stop to watch [NSF 386-5
  Does not see these separate figures one by one, [NSF 389-4
  And yet see only one, in his old coat, [NSF 389-5
  In the bandeaux of the mothers, would see again. [NSF 389-18

On the image of what we see, to catch from that [NSF 398-21
And we make of what we see, what we see clearly [NSF 401-2
How is it I find you in difference, see you there [NSF 406-8
To see their lustre truly as it is [Owl 432-21
And queered by lavishings of their will to see. [Bouquet 451-4
"What We See Is What We Think" [459-title
Since what we think is never what we see. [What We 460-6
In which hundreds of eyes, in one mind, see at once. [NH 488-6
He would be certain to see [Aug 493-16
Since, in my sight, you see the earth again [Angel 496-16
Of a sort, silence of a rat come out to see, [Plain 503-5
Come back to see a certain house. [Vacancy 511-11
What we know in what we see, what we feel in what [Look 518-10
Will see us on parade, [Phases 3-10 P
See how the absent moon waits in a glade [Blanche 10-10 P
Of pomp, in love and good ensample, see [Stan MMO 19-13 P
It was a purple changeable to see. [Abnormal 24-2 P
See, now, the ways beleaguered by black, dropsical duennas,
   [Inelegance 26-7 P
And see themselves as once they were, [Sat Night 28-5 P
They were so glad to see the spring. [Sat Night 28-11 P
To see them without their passions [Lytton 38-10 P
To live incessantly in change. See how [Burnshaw 50-17 P
There, too, he saw, since he must see, the domes [Greenest
   54-12 P
Disposed upon the central of what we see, [Greenest 55-7 P
Of purple flowers, to see? The black will still [Greenest 58-32P
To see, once more, this hacked-up world of tools, [Duck 61-9 P
See more than marble in their eyes, see more [Duck 64-8 P
With senses chiseled on bright stone. They see [Duck 64-10 P
They live. They see and feel themselves, seeing [Duck 64-13 P
Their words and ours; in what we see, their hues [Sombre 67-6 P
But this we cannot see. The shaggy top [Sombre 68-19 P
Knew her, how could you see the woman that wore the beads,
   [Grotesque 74-10 P
And the way was more than the walk and was hard to see.
   [Grotesque 74-14 P
Dew is water to see, [Three 128-3 P
Just to see the sunrise again. [Three 128-7 P
It never woke to see, [Three 131-25 P
He could not see the steadiest light [Three 133-3 P
But it is me he will see [Three 134-14 P
Three beggars, you see, [Three 139-11 P
Wore purple to see; [Three 141-8 P
SEED. That seed, [Gubbinal 85-10
   The grass is in seed. The young birds are flying. [Ghosts 119-1
   She must come now. The grass is in seed and high. [Ghosts 119-11
   Ecce, Oxidia is the seed [MBG 182-5
   No longer on the ancient cake of seed, [Cuisine 228-12
   The spirit of one dwelling in a seed, [Descrip 341-19
   Itself that seed's ripe, unpredictable fruit. [Descrip 341-20
   One seed alone grow wild, the railway-stops [Cats 367-14
SEEDLESS. Severed and tumbled into seedless grass, [Burnshaw 49-14P
SEEDS. Of seeds grown fat, too juicily opulent, [C 32-9
   That should be silver, four accustomed seeds [C 45-7
   At Easter on a London screen, the seeds [Greenest 53-19 P
SEEING. Or seeing the midsummer artifice [C 33-3
   Who, seeing silver petals of white blooms [Sea Surf 100-17
   Without seeing the harvest or the moon? [MBG 173-6
   One is always seeing and feeling onself, [Prelude 195-8
   At the centre of reality, seeing it. [Freed 205-21
   Seeing that which is refused, [Bagatelles 213-15
   It is the honey-comb of the seeing man. [Blue Bldg 217-17
   Being, becoming seeing and feeling and self, [Extracts 255-21
   As if in seeing we saw our feeling [Hero 278-26
   So seeing, I beheld you walking, white, [Phenom 287-12
   Like seeing fallen brightly away. [Possum 294-5
   Or seeing the spent, unconscious shapes of night, [Feo 334-7
   A seeing and unseeing in the eye. [NSF 385-21
   In seeing them. This is what makes them seem [Roses 431-11
   When in a way of seeing seen, an extreme, [Bouquet 451-11
   The fatality of seeing things too well. [Novel 459-6
   Behind all actual seeing, in the actual scene, [NH 467-11
   Of simple seeing, without reflection. We seek [NH 471-20
   Of the window and walking in the street and seeing, [NH 478-9
   Seeing the fulgent shadows upward heaped, [Duck 62-16 P
   They live. They see and feel themselves, seeing [Duck 64-13 P
   The listener, listening to the shadows, seeing them, [Sick 90-18P
   The blindness in which seeing would be false, [Souls 95-1 P
SEEK. To find whatever it is they seek? Or does [Heaven 56-15
   And who does not seek the sky unfuzzed, soaring to the princox?
   [Banal 63-5
   With rivers like our own that seek for seas [Sunday 69-17
   To seek a sun of fuller fire. [How Live 125-16
   And say this, this is the centre that I seek. [Cred 373-9
   Within the very object that we seek, [Study I 463-9
   That fall upon it out of the wind. We seek [NH 471-12
   Of simple seeing, without reflection. We seek [NH 471-20
SEEKER. Symbol of the seeker, crossing by night [Ulysses 99-11 P
   Symbol of the seeker, crossing by night [Presence 105-14 P

SEEKING. The innermost good of their seeking [Homunculus 27-1
   What syllable are you seeking, [Roaring 113-4
   The sun is seeking something bright to shine on. [Nigger 157-20
   Of the brooder seeking the acutest end [Extracts 259-14
   It becomes the scholar again, seeking celestial [God 285-11
   Avoid our stale perfections, seeking out [Dutch 293-1
   The soldier seeking his point between the two, [Repet 309-9
   Perhaps these forms are seeking to escape [Two V 355-13
   And impotent, like the imagination seeking [Cats 368-3
   And these long, black instruments will be so little to them
      that will be needing so much, seeking so much in their music.
      [Piano 22-9 P
   Who keeps seeking out his identity [Dove 98-6 P
SEEKS. It is a red bird that seeks out his choir [Monocle 13-13
   Of Vulcan, that a valet seeks to own, [C 33-6
   The ponds are not the surfaces it seeks. [Nigger 158-1
   What is it that my feeling seeks? [Country 207-16
   By a wind that seeks out shelter from snow. Thus [Hero 273-6
   It is the gibberish of the vulgate that he seeks. [NSF 397-5
   He skips the journalism of subjects, seeks out [NH 474-11
   The dry eucalyptus seeks god in the rainy cloud. [NH 475-4
   Professor Eucalyptus of New Haven seeks him [NH 475-5
   The rain falls with a ramshackle sound. He seeks [NH 475-9
   It is poverty's speech that seeks us out the most, [Rome 510-3
   A moment on this fantasia. He seeks [Look 519-5
   He seeks as image a second of the self, [Someone 84-7 A
   He seeks an image certain as meaning is [Someone 84-12 A
SEEM. It made you seem so small and lean [Vincentine 52-13
   They seem an exaltation without sound. [On Manner 55-14
   Let be be finale of seem. [Emperor 64-7
   Seem things in some procession of the dead, [Sunday 67-6
   Seem all of paradise that we shall know? [Sunday 68-7
   Seem pretty much one: [Botanist 1 134-17
   And the future emerging out of us seem to be one. [Nigger 151-12
   They seem a little painted, now. [Arcades 226-2
   Accelerations that seem inhuman. [Hero 279-4
   Finding its way from the house, makes music seem [Phenom 287-1
   It is possible that to seem--it is to be, [Descrip 339-1
   Or sleep. It was a queen that made it seem [Descrip 339-7
   Round the rooms, which do not ever seem to change . . . [Lot
      372-3
   Two things of opposite natures seem to depend [NSF 392-4
   In seeing them. This is what makes them seem [Roses 431-11
   Breathe slightly, slightly move or seem to move [Bouquet 450-8
   Impalpable habitations that seem to move [NH 466-8
   Time's given perfections made to seem like less [Armor 530-8
   Of the well-thumbed, infinite pages of her masters, who will
      seem old to her, requiting less and less her feeling: [Piano
      22-7 P
   This vast inelegance may seem the blankest desolation, [Inele-
      gance 25-13 P
   Bands of black men seem to be drifting in the air, [Sick 90-7 P
   Inside our queer chapeaux, we seem, on this bank, [Nuns 92-15 P
   Or almost solid seem show--the way a fly bird [Conversat 108-14 P
SEEMED. That seemed hallucinating horn, and here, [C 29-4
   A rumbling, west of Mexico, it seemed, [C 32-17
   For him, and not for him alone. It seemed [C 34-29
   Attach. It seemed haphazard denouement. [C 40-25
   She seemed, of a country of the capuchins, [C 44-12
   Tugging at banks, until they seemed [Frogs 78-2
   Seemed to suckle themselves on his arid being, [Frogs 78-13
   Seemed the helpless daughter [Sonatina 109-16
   When to be and delight to be seemed to be one, [Anglais 149-14
   A mountainous music always seemed [MBG 179-11
   It seemed serener just to die, [Thought 184-17
   That the grapes seemed fatter. [On Road 203-14
   The beads on her rails seemed to grasp at transparence. [Vari
      236-2
   The moonlight seemed to. [Les Plue 244-19
   The moonlight and Aquinas seemed to. He spoke, [Les Plus 245-3
   The night. The substance of his body seemed [Choc 297-20
   Or merely seemed to touch him as he spoke [EM 315-2
   The last, or sounds so single they seemed one? [EM 316-15
   Things are as they seemed to Calvin or to Anne [Descrip 341-21
   Seemed in the morning like a holiday." [Anach 365-19
   There seemed to be an apostrophe that was not spoken. [Cata 424-15
   The sky seemed so small that winter day, [Two Illus 513-4
   Seemed large and loud and high and strong. [Two Illus 513-9
   Seemed like a sound in his mind. [Not Ideas 534-3
   The great sail of Ulysses seemed, [Ulysses 105-7 P
   The sharp sail of Ulysses seemed, [Presence 106-7 P
SEEMING. Seeming to be liquid as leaves made of cloud, [Forces
      229-14
   As the sun is something seeming and it is. [Descrip 339-2
   It is and in such seeming all things are. [Descrip 339-4
   Thus things are like a seeming of the sun [Descrip 339-5
   Or like a seeming of the moon or night [Descrip 339-6
   In the seeming of the summer of her sun [Descrip 339-11
   By her own seeming made the summer change. [Descrip 339-12
   The lesser seeming original in the blind [Descrip 340-2

The greater seeming of the major mind. [Descrip 340-4
In the seeming of an original in the eye, [Descrip 340-11
If seeming is description without place, [Descrip 343-15
Even the seeming of a summer's day, [Descrip 343-17
In its own seeming, plainly visible, [Descrip 344-18
A seeming of the Spaniard, a style of life, [Descrip 345-15
Be alive with its own seemings, seeming to be [Descrip 346-3
Seeming, at first, a beast disgorged, unlike, [NSF 404-7
Each voice within the other, seeming one, [Old Woman 45-28 P
In a returning, a seeming of return, [Americana 94-14 P
See summer-seeming.
SEEMINGS. Such seemings are the actual ones: the way [Descrip
   339-17
These are the actual seemings that we see, [Descrip 340-17
There are potential seemings, arrogant [Descrip 340-19
There are potential seemings turbulent [Descrip 341-1
That speaks for him such seemings as death gives. [Descrip 341-6
Of the possible: seemings that are to be, [Descrip 342-5
Seemings that it is possible may be. [Descrip 342-6
Wrapped in their seemings, crowd on curious crowd, [Descrip
   342-14
Be alive with its own seemings, seeming to be [Descrip 346-3
SEEMING-SO. Would froth the whole heaven with its seeming-so,
   [Descrip 341-17
Made eminent in a reflected seeming-so. [Recit 88-2 P
SEEMS. Will say of the mansion that it seems [Postcard 159-16
The thinking of art seems final when [MBG 168-4
Of him, even if Xenophon, seems [Hero 277-6
This elevation, in which he seems to be tall, [Repet 307-13
And uncourageous genesis . . . It seems [EM 315-24
It seems as if the honey of common summer [EM 316-1
The sun is an example. What it seems [Descrip 339-3
And seems to be on the saying of her name. [Descrip 339-14
Its identity is merely a thing that seems, [Descrip 340-10
And is the queen humble as she seems to be, [Cred 371-25
There's meditation there, in which there seems [NSF 396-21
And the north wind's mighty buskin seems to fall [Antag 426-7
Seems like a sheen of heat romanticized. [NH 468-9
The meeting at noon at the edge of the field seems like [Rock
   525-12
Although life seems a goblin mummery, [Soldat 13-14 P
To bring destruction, often seems high-pitched. [Spaniard 34-17P
The statue seems a thing from Schwarz's, a thing [Burnshaw 47-4P
Blue-bold on its pedestal--that seems to say, [Role 93-13 P
That place, and it seems to come to that; [Ulysses 99-19 P
Yet, as it seems, of human residence. [Someone 84-3 A
SEEN. The body is no body to be seen [Tallap 71-16
That was seen through arches) [Botanist 1 135-3
The pears are not seen [Pears 197-5
"The idols have seen lots of poverty, [On Road 204-6
The moment's sun (the strong man vaguely seen), [Freed 204-20
That hermit on reef sable would have seen, [Dames 206-16
It is Hartford seen in a purple light. [Hartford 226-18
Is a museum of things seen. Sight, [Hero 274-13
Painted by mad-men, seen as magic, [Hero 277-24
The hero is a feeling, a man seen [Hero 278-24
In the object seen and saved that mystic [Hero 278-27
On a transmutation which, when seen, appears [EM 318-6
The spirits of all the impotent dead, seen clear, [Cats 368-8
How clean the sun when seen in its idea, [NSF 381-4
Be seen, not to be loved nor hated because [NSF 385-5
And these the seraph saw, had seen long since, [NSF 389-17
If seen rightly and yet a possible red. [NSF 393-18
And have seen, a place dependent on ourselves. [NSF 401-3
And potent, an influence felt instead of seen. [Owl 435-7
It is something seen and known in lesser poems. [Orb 440-10
Perceived: the white seen smoothly argentine [Bouquet 449-14
When in a way of seeing seen, an extreme, [Bouquet 451-11
Perhaps, these colors, seen in insight, assume [Bouquet 451-22
Reality as a thing seen by the mind, [NH 468-12
Reality but reality grimly seen [NH 475-15
Seen as inamorata, of loving fame [NH 484-14
In things seen and unseen, created from nothingness, [NH 486-11
Seen for a moment standing in the door. [Angel 496-8
A figure half seen, or seen for a moment, a man [Angel 497-7
As it falls from the heart and lies there to be seen, [Rome
   509-27
No radiance of dead blaze, but something seen [Armor 529-13
The surface, is the purpose to be seen, [Moonlight 531-8
So much just to be seen--a purpose, empty [Moonlight 532-4
Or of something seen that he liked. [Planet 532-9
It is not to be seen beneath the appearances [R Conn 533-13
Seen by a muse . . . [Soldat 16-6 P
And there the common grass is never seen. [Abnormal 24-8 P
Yet hardly to be seen and again the legs [Old Woman 46-8 P
So seen, have an order of its own, a peace [Burnshaw 49-1 P
And despicable shades of red, just seen, [Burnshaw 51-21 P
And vaguely to be seen, a matinal red, [Burnshaw 51-22 P
Of that which is not seen and cannot be. [Sombre 70-25 P
The solid shape. Aeneas seen, perhaps, [Recit 87-22 P

The englistered woman is now seen [Ulysses 104-31 P
The most at home? Or is it enough to have seen [Conversat 109-17P
And felt and known the differences we have seen [Conversat 109-18P
I have not seen it [Three 128-8 P
And I have never seen it. [Three 128-12 P
And seen in a clear light. [Three 131-24 P
The young gentlemen was seen [Three 136-6 P
Below the prerogative jumble. The fruit so seen [Someone 84-16 A
An object the sum of its complications, seen [Someone 87-10 A
Experienced yet not well seen; of how [Ideal 88-17 A
SEEPING. Of seeping rose--banal machine [Soldat 15-20 P
SEES. He sees larkspur, [Six Sig 73-8
That apprehends the most which sees and names. [Fictive 88-5
She sees a barer sky that does not bend. [Anatomy 108-7
And this the spirit sees and is aggrieved. [Anatomy 108-18
It is least what one ever sees. [Sailing 120-21
By dividing the number of legs one sees by two. [Nigger 157-9
He is what he hears and sees and if, [Prelude 194-17
And sees, being nothing otherwise, [Prelude 194-19
The pensive man . . . He sees that eagle float [Connois 216-13
And of him that sees, beyond the astronomers, [Candle 223-9
That sees above them, that sees rise up above them, [Candle
   223-11
Absorbs Anjou. I see them as a lover sees, [Peaches 224-4
As a young lover sees the first buds of spring [Peaches 224-5
There the man sees the image clearly at last. [Rhythms 245-15
Sees the petty gildings on February . . . [Hero 280-11
It is a kind of blank in which one sees. [Phenom 287-11
Sees a familiar building drenched in cloud [Repet 308-4
Its own hallucination never sees [EM 315-9
First sees reality. The mortal no [EM 320-8
To lose sensibility, to see what one sees, [EM 320-25
Of what it sees, for all the ill it sees? [EM 326-4
And out of what one sees and hears and out [EM 326-7
There are many of these beasts that one never sees, [Jouga
   337-11
Forward of the eye that, in its backward, sees [Descrip 340-3
He does not hear his characters talk. He sees [Cred 377-24
And sees the myosotis on its bush, [NSF 382-8
On flames. The scholar of one candle sees [AA 417-1
And sees its images, its motions [Imago 439-11
The poet mumbles and the painter sees, [Orb 443-16
Through the door one sees on the lake that the white duck swims
   [Bouquet 449-19
Except that the grandson sees it as it is, [Quotions 462-9
For what he sees, it comes in the end to that: [NH 475-12
Indifferent to what it sees. The tink-tonk [NH 475-19
Of what one sees, the purpose that comes first, [Moonlight 531-7
And nothing more. He sees but not by sight. [Greenest 59-6 P
He sees the angel in the nigger's mind [Greenest 59-11 P
Surprise the sterile rationalist who sees [Sombre 67-32 P
Or sees the new North River heaping up [Recit 86-24 P
It is something on a table that he sees, [Someone 83-4 A
If he sees an object on a table, much like [Someone 83-14 A
He sees it in this tangent of himself. [Someone 83-19 A
SEETHES. Its brightness burned the way good solace seethes. [Owl
   434-6
SEETHING. To a seething minor swiftly modulate. [Eve Angels 137-28
SEGMENTA. A scholar, in his Segmenta, left a note, [NH 485-1
SEGOVIA. Weeps in Segovia. The beggar in Rome [Greenest 59-17 P
SEIGNEUR. The gaiety of language is our seigneur. [EM 322-19
SEIZE. To seize, the obscurest as, the distant was . . . [Orb
   441-3
A paradise full of assassins. Suppose I seize [Bship 77-20 P
Seize yards and docks, machinery and men, [Bship 77-22 P
A hand that fails to seize it. High captain, the grand [Bship
   80-25 P
Of a man, that seizes our strength, will seize it to be [Bship
   81-9 P
SEIZED. Seized her and wondered: why beneath the tree [Hand 271-4
The wind had seized the tree and ha, and ha, [Hand 271-10
And against the most coiled thorn, have seized on what was ugly
   [Large 424-3
Seized by that possible blue. Be maidens formed [Burnshaw 51-18 P
SEIZES. It seizes a sheet, from the ground, from a bush, as if
   spread there by some wash-woman for the night. [Plough-Boy 6-5P
Of a man, that seizes our strength, will seize it to be [Bship
   81-9 P
SELAH. Selah, tempestuous bird. How is it that [Belly 366-18
SELDOM. Men and the affairs of men seldom concerned [Nigger 156-4
SELECT. Select adieux; and he despises this: [EM 322-22
SELF. What counted was mythology of self, [C 28-5
Remained, except some starker, barer self [C 29-16
And studious of a self possessing him, [C 33-11
Oh, but the very self of the storm [Joost 46-20
To one's singular self, to despise [Adieu 127-17
Whatever self it had, became the self [Key W 129-28
Of a turning spirit in an earlier self. [Sun March 134-1
The warm antiquity of self, [Fading 139-6
Supremely true each to its separate self, [Re-state 146-11

For a self returning mostly memory. [Anglais 148-18
This self, not that gold self aloft, [MBG 176-4
One's self and the mountains of one's land, [MBG 176-12
This health is holy, this descant of a self, [Parochial 191-15
Stormer, is the color of a self [Prelude 194-14
Of a self, if, without sentiment, [Prelude 194-16
To have the ant of the self changed to an ox [Freed 205-9
A self that touches all edges, [Rabbit K 209-18
You become a self that fills the four corners of night. [Rabbit
    K 209-19
As a self that lives on itself. [Thunder 220-20
One self from another, as these peaches do. [Peaches 224-20
The sharpest self, the sensible range, [Adequacy 244-10
Of the self that must sustain itself on speech, [Beard 247-17
Being, becoming seeing and feeling and self, [Extracts 255-21
Between one's self and the weather and the things [Extracts 258-3
Of the weather and in one's self, as part of that [Extracts 258-9
Your self its honor. [Search 268-8
Than himself, his self, the self that embraces [Hero 280-6
The self of the hero, the solar single, [Hero 280-7
Of the highest self: he studies the paper [Hero 280-14
No self in the mass: the braver being, [Gigan 289-3
A poem for Liadoff, the self of selves: [Choc 297-7
Might call the common self, interior fons. [Choc 301-1
The spirit and all ensigns of the self? [Repet 308-18
That evil, that evil in the self, from which [EM 316-25
The fragrance of the woman not her self, [Pure 332-14
Her self in her manner not the solid block, [Pure 332-15
Is lunar Habana the Cuba of the self? [Feo 333-15
In which nothing solid is its solid self. [Descrip 345-10
To toll its pulses, vigors of its self? [Two V 354-6
Transform for transformation's self, [Human 363-14
Three times the concentred self takes hold, three times [Cred
    376-9
The thrice concentred self, having possessed [Cred 376-10
Follow after, O my companion, my fellow, my self, [NSF 392-23
Only the unmuddled self of sleep, for them. [NSF 402-18
In which majesty is a mirror of the self: [NSF 405-9
The self of summer perfectly perceived, [Beginning 427-17
But she that says good-by losing in self [Owl 435-4
The sense of self, rosed out of prestiges [Owl 435-5
Of rose, stood tall in self not symbol, quick [Owl 435-6
She was a self that knew, an inner thing, [Owl 435-14
Her only place and person, a self of her [Orb 441-24
True nothing, yet accosted self to self. [Bouquet 449-18
Sounding in transparent dwellings of the self, [NH 466-7
No man. The self, the chrysalis of all men [NH 468-21
In the end, in the whole psychology, the self, [NH 474-7
By an instinct for a rainless land, the self [NH 475-23
Of his self, come at upon wide delvings of wings. [NH 475-24
In space and the self, that touched them both at once [NH 483-7
The rich earth, of its own self made rich, [Aug 491-13
In the presence of a solitude of the self, [Aug 494-5
The self and the earth--your thoughts, your feelings, [Old Man
    501-3
What self, for example, did he contain that had not yet been
    loosed, [Prol 516-16
She has composed, so long, a self with which to welcome him,
    [World 521-1
Companion to his self for her, which she imagined, [World 521-2
Its tranquil self, the main of things, the mind, [Rock 528-15
His self and the sun were one [Planet 532-13
And his poems, although makings of his self, [Planet 532-14
Of your dark self, and how the wings of stars, [Blanche 10-11 P
In self, a man of longer time than days, [Good Bad 33-10 P
The harridan self and ever-maladive fate [Old Woman 45-25 P
He was born within us as a second self, [Sombre 67-3 P
A self of parents who have never died, [Sombre 67-4 P
The self is a cloister full of remembered sounds [Woman Had
    82-17 P
That they return unrecognized. The self [Woman Had 82-19 P
The center of the self, the self [Ulysses 101-8 P
It is the sibyl of the self, [Ulysses 104-10 P
The self as sibyl, whose diamond, [Ulysses 104-11 P
A home against one's self, a darkness, [Letters 107-6 P
He seeks as image a second of the self, [Someone 84-7 A
A single self. Divest reality [Someone 86-1 A
The inhuman making choice of a human self. [Ideal 89-12 A
SELF-CONTAINED. The automaton, in logic self-contained, [Les Plus
    245-5
SELF-PITY. A too, too human god, self-pity's kin [EM 315-23
SELFSAME. Hinting incredible hues, four selfsame lights [C 45-8
Make music, so the selfsame sounds [Peter 89-17
SELF-SAME. The self-same madness of the astronomers [Candle 223-8
Of the phrase. It contrives the self-same evocations [NH 473-5
As the man hates now, loves now, the self-same things. [Sombre
    70-1 P
And triple chime . . . The self-same rhythm [Stan Hero 83-22 P
SELLING. For example, this old man selling oranges [Feo 333-18
SELVAGES. Of parades in the obscurer selvages. [EM 317-16

SELVES. Severs not only lands but also selves. [C 30-4
More sharply in more furious selves. [Eve Angels 137-5
And reconcile us to our selves in those [Havana 144-20
An infinite incantation of our selves [Havana 145-8
That night is only the background of our selves, [Re-state 146-10
Are not your children, not your selves. [Dutch 292-9
A poem for Liadoff, the self of selves: [Choc 297-7
So many selves, so many sensuous worlds, [EM 326-9
That speaks, denouncing separate selves, both one. [Orb 441-25
Unfretted by day's separate, several selves, [NH 482-10
Serenely selves, transfigured by the selves [Burnshaw 52-2 P
It made up for everything, it was all selves [Greenest 53-3 P
Among the second selves, sailor, observe [Pagoda 91-19 P
In the alien freedom that such selves degustate: [Pagoda 92-2 P
SEMBLABLES. And you, my semblables, in sooty residence [Dutch 290-6
And you, my semblables--the old flag of Holland [Dutch 290-13
And you, my semblables, are doubly killed [Dutch 290-20
And you, my semblables, are crusts that lie [Dutch 291-6
And you, my semblables, in the total [Dutch 291-13
And you, my semblables, in gaffer-green, [Dutch 291-20
And you, my semblables, know that this time [Dutch 292-1
And you, my semblables, know that your children [Dutch 292-8
And you, my semblables, whose ecstasy [Dutch 292-15
And you, my semblables, behold in blindness [Dutch 292-22
So that the stars, my semblables, chimeres, [Dutch 292-25
SEMBLANCE. A semblance to the thing I have in mind. [Monocle 17-3
SEMIRAMIDE. Then I, Semiramide, dark-syllabled, [Phenom 287-15
I write Semiramide and in the script [Phenom 287-20
SEMI-WORLD. This mangled, smutted semi-world hacked out [Ghosts
    119-8
SENATORS. No book of the past in which time's senators [Recit
    86-10 P
SEND. If the fault is with the lions, send them back [Lions 125-6
SENDS. That he sends ahead, out of the goodness of his heart, [EM
    320-18
That sends us back to the first idea, the quick [NSF 381-17
And sends us, winged by an unconscious will, [NSF 382-16
SENORS. Sepulchral señors, bibbling pale mescal, [C 38-21
SENSATION. A tree, this unprovoked sensation requires [NSF 406-12
SENSE. This parable, in sense, amounts to this: [Monocle 15-24
Widen your sense. All things in the sun are sun. [NE Verses 104-2
The sense of the serpent in you, Ananke, [Nigger 152-11
Of those with a sense for simple space. [Nigger 153-4
The sense creates the pose. [Add 199-9
Perceived by feeling instead of sense, [Nightgown 214-12
"The Sense of the Sleight-of-Hand Man" [222-title
With a single sense, though he smells clouds, [Arcades 225-21
They have a sense of their design and savor [Extracts 254-21
Kept waking and a mournful sense sought out, [Montra 263-5
But let this one sense be the single main. [Montra 264-3
Thereof and part desire and part the sense [Choc 299-21
Of a parent in the French sense. [Lack 303-15
To giant red, sweats up a giant sense [Repet 307-8
He find another? The giant of sense remains [Repet 308-9
Of the giant sense, the enormous harnesses [Repet 308-20
Of central sense, these minutiae mean more [EM 317-20
Unhappy about the sense of happiness. [Pure 331-9
Was it that--a sense and beyond intelligence? [Pure 331-10
Could the future rest on a sense and be beyond [Pure 331-11
Is description without place. It is a sense [Descrip 343-18
The knowledge of being, sense without sense of time. [Myrrh
    350-9
The most necessitous sense. Accept them, then, [Man Car 350-17
There is a sense in sounds beyond their meaning. [Pieces 352-1
Which is not part of the listener's own sense. [Cred 377-20
Music falls on the silence like a sense, [NSF 392-10
In the sense against calamity, it is not [AA 418-8
This sense of the activity of fate-- [AA 419-15
Beyond the habit of sense, anarchic shape [Page 422-18
Complete, because at the middle, if only in sense, [Ulti 430-8
And in that enormous sense, merely enjoy. [Ulti 430-9
In our sense of it, our sense of the fertilest red, [Roses 430-18
In which the sense lies still, as a man lies, [Roses 431-2
Our sense of these things changes and they change, [Roses 431-4
Not as in metaphor, but in our sense [Roses 431-5
Of them. So sense exceeds all metaphor. [Roses 431-6
The sense of self, rosed out of prestiges [Owl 435-5
By means of a separate sense. It is and it [Orb 440-13
Oh as, always too heavy for the sense [Orb 441-2
The satisfaction underneath the sense, [Papini 448-3
Nor new, nor in the sense of memory. [Bouquet 451-7
Coming together in a sense in which we are poised, [NH 466-11
Of colonies, a sense in the changing sense [NH 479-12
And of original earliness. Yet the sense [NH 481-11
Of cold and earliness is a daily sense, [NH 481-21
He is the possessed of sense not the possessor. [Aug 492-19
And the sense of the archaic touched us at once [Aug 494-13
Of sense, evoking one thing in many men, [Aug 494-18
A dumb sense possesses them in a kind of solemnity. [Old Man
    501-2

"The Plain Sense of Things" [502-title
To a plain sense of things. It is as if [Plain 502-10
The plain sense of it, without reflections, leaves, [Plain 503-3
Of silence, that any solitude of sense [Rome 510-18
But a sense of the distance of the sun-- [Two Illus 513-5
The shadow of a sense of his own, [Two Illus 513-6
Without any form or any sense of form, [Look 518-9
New senses in the engenderings of senses, [Rock 527-8
Into a sense, an object the less; or else [Moonlight 531-12
In every various sense, ought not to be preferred [Lytton 39-13P
What could comfort away the sudden sense? [Old Woman 44-16P
The ecstasy of sense in a sensuous air. [Greenest 56-26 P
No place in the sense of colonists, no place [Greenest 58-8 P
Of our sense of evil, [Grotesque 76-20 P
Of our sense that time has been [Grotesque 76-21 P
The ideas that come to it with a sense of speech. [Woman Had
    82-22 P
The figure of the wise man fixed in sense. [Recit 86-17 P
A sense separate that receives and holds the rest, [Americana
    94-5 P
And if one's sense of a single spot [Ulysses 99-21 P
That the sense of being changes as we talk, [Conversat 109-22 P
This invisible activity, this sense. [Clear Day 113-19 P
Of that oration, the happiest sense in which [Ideal 89-6 A
SENSED. Or, nobler, sensed an elemental fate, [C 31-24
    See: five-times-sensed; one-sensed.
SENSELESS. Something in now a senseless syllable, [Montra 260-9
    Evade us, as in a senseless element? [NSF 396-24
SENSES. The senses and feeling, the very sound [Joost 47-1
    A composing of senses of the guitar. [MBG 168-8
    Gives the touch of the senses, not of the hand, [MBG 174-20
    But the very senses as they touch [MBG 175-1
    The senses paint [Poem Morn 219-8
    Words add to the senses. The words for the dazzle [Vari 234-17
    The breath life's latest, thousand senses. [Montra 264-2
    And the secondary senses of the ear [Cred 374-11
    Close to the senses there lies another isle [NH 480-17
    And there the senses give and nothing take, [NH 480-18
    New senses in the engenderings of sense, [Rock 527-8
    Of each of the senses; call it, again and again, [R Conn 533-20
    With senses chisled on bright stone. They see [Duck 64-10 P
    Meyer has my five senses. I have his. [Grotesque 76-10 P
    The blows and buffets of fresh senses [Fare Guit 99-5 P
SENSIBILITY. To lose sensibility, to see what one sees, [EM 320-25
SENSIBLE. Of people sensible to pain, [Adequacy 244-2
    The sharpest self, the sensible range, [Adequacy 244-10
    Of his sister, in what a sensible ecstasy [NSF 401-24
SENSITIVE. By the hand of desire, faint, sensitive, the soft [NH
    476-14
    The sensitive and conscientious schemes [Soldat 13-9 P
SENSUAL. That is the sensual, pearly spouse, the life [Sleight
    222-18
    Whereon it falls in more than sensual mode. [NSF 398-19
SENSUALIST. He savored rankness like a sensualist. [C 36-12
SENSUOUS. So many selves, so many sensuous worlds, [EM 326-9
    And sensuous summer stood full-height. [Two Illus 514-19
    The ecstasy of sense in a sensuous air. [Greenest 56-26 P
SENT. And what descants, he sent to banishment! [C 34-24
SENTENCES. The solemn sentences, [Aug 490-18
SENTIMENT. Of a self, if, without sentiment, [Prelude 194-16
    The sentiment of the fatal is a part [Aug 491-19
    Symbols of sentiment . . . Take this phrase, [Soldat 16-7 P
    Of larger sentiment. [Demoiselle 23-9 P
SENTIMENTAL. And sentimental roisterers, [Sat Night 28-8 P
    Deploring sentiment. When May came last [Good Bad 33-14 P
SENTIMENTALIST. All sorts of flowers. That's the sentimentalist.
    [EM 316-8
    Is not a sentimentalist. He is [EM 316-24
SEPARATE. Supremely true each to its separate self, [Re-state
    146-11
    But are these separate? Is it [MBG 177-1
    Or having a separate author, a different poet, [Creat 311-1
    Does not see these separate figures one by one, [NSF 389-4
    By means of a separate sense. It is and it [Orb 440-13
    That speaks, denouncing separate selves, both one. [Orb 441-25
    Unfretted by day's separate, several selves, [NH 482-10
    Is each man thinking his separate thoughts or, for once, [Duck
    62-18 P
    It joins and does not separate. What, then, [Recit 86-21 P
    A sense separate that receives and holds the rest, [Americana
    94-5 P
    In an isolation, separate [Ulysses 104-32 P
SEPARATELY. In which no scholar, separately dwelling, [Somnam
    304-16
SEPARATES. That separates us from the wind and sea, [Fictive 87-15
    As a tone defines itself and separates [Anach 366-12
SEPARATION. Imposing his separation, [Soldier 97-5
SEPTEMBER. Now it is September and the web is woven. [Dwarf 208-1
    Of the wind, rain in a dry September, [Hero 275-13
SEP-TEM-BER. Sep - tem - ber . . . [Metamorph 265-16

SEPULCHER. This may be benediction, sepulcher, [Havana 145-3
SEPULCHRAL. Sepulchral señors, bibbling pale mescal, [C 38-21
    From my North of cold whistled in a sepulchral South, [Farewell
    117-14
    To our sepulchral hollows. Love of the real [NH 470-18
    The black and ruin his sepulchral throne. [Greenest 55-29 P
SEPULCHRE. Dominion of the blood and sepulchre. [Sunday 67-11
SEQUELS. As sequels without thought. In the rudest red [Burnshaw
    47-8 P
SEQUENCES. This structure of ideas, these ghostly sequences [Bed
    326-13
    Other ghostly sequences and, it would be, luminous [Bed 326-18
    Sequences, thought of among spheres in the old peak of night:
    [Bed 326-19
    Sequences that would be sleep and ting-tang tossing, so that
    [Bed 327-4
SEQUESTERED. Like jades affecting the sequestered bride; [C 34-23
    Sequestered over the sea, [Venereal 48-6
    The enraptured woman, the sequestered night, [Past Nun 378-18
SEQUESTERING. Sequestering the fluster from the year, [C 46-8
SEQUINS. The sequins [Ord Women 11-23
SERAFIN. The trees, like serafin, and echoing hills, [Sunday 70-8
    Outside of gates of hammered serafin, [Babies 77-2
SERAGLIO-PARROT. As a seraglio-parrot; feel disdain [Spaniard 35-11P
SERAPH. The old seraph, parcel-gilded, among violets [NSF 389-13
    And these the seraph saw, had seen long since, [NSF 389-17
    Night-blue is an inconstant thing. The seraph [NSF 390-1
SERAPHIC. Seraphic proclamations of the pure [C 45-28
SERAPHIM. Why seraphim like lutanists arranged [Eve Angels 136-13
    That fosters seraphim and is to them [Eve Angels 137-7
    Seraphim of Europe? Pouring out of dawn. [Greenest 56-3 P
SERAPHS. And seraphs cluster on the domes, [Contra I 266-15
    Were seraphs, were saints, were changing essences. [NSF 397-15
    A source of trumpeting seraphs in the eye, [Orb 442-23
SERENADE. A serenade. [Two Figures 86-9
    If to serenade almost to man [MBG 165-17
    Say that it is the serenade [MBG 166-1
    And serenade. [Phases 3-12 P
SERENE. Our old bane, green and bloated, serene, who cries, [Banal
    62-16
    Gives motion to perfection more serene [Fictive 87-19
    In the clouds serene and final, next [MBG 177-14
    The grunted breath serene and final, [MBG 177-15
    Its glitters, its divinations of serene [EM 318-16
    A land too ripe for enigmas, too serene. [Cred 374-9
    Dixhuitième and Georgian and serene. [Lytton 39-25 P
    Is constant. The time you call serene descends [Burnshaw 50-22 P
    These were that serene he had always been approaching. [Local
    112-11 P
SERENELY. Might help the blind, not him, serenely sly. [C 39-20
    Serenely gazing at the violent abyss, [NSF 401-14
    Serenely selves, transfigured by the selves [Burnshaw 52-2 P
SERENER. And serener myth [Havana 143-11
    This urgent, competent, serener myth [Havana 143-19
    It seemed serener just to die, [Thought 184-17
SERGE. See Victor Serge.
SERGEANT. Hugh March, a sergeant, a redcoat, killed, [Vari 234-11
SERIES. In Series X, Act IV, et cetera. [Chaos 357-12
SERIOUS. Vested in the serious folds of majesty, [Orb 442-21
    A serious man without the serious, [NH 474-14
    It fails. The strength at the centre is serious. [NH 477-12
    As a serious strength rejects pin-idleness. [NH 477-14
    This is the mirror of the high serious: [NH 477-17
    The serious reflection is composed [NH 478-2
SERIOUSNESS. Their purports to a final seriousness-- [Armor 530-6
SERMON. After the sermon, to quiet that mouse in the wall. [Blue
    Bldg 216-20
SERPENT. The sense of the serpent in you, Ananke, [Nigger 152-11
    Where do you think, serpent, [Bagatelles 213-1
    This is where the serpent lives, the bodiless. [AA 411-1
    This is where the serpent lives. This is his nest, [AA 411-7
    And the serpent body flashing without the skin. [AA 411-12
    In the midmost midnight and find the serpent there, [AA 411-15
    Denied, dismissed, may hold a serpent, loud [John 437-19
    And the serpent might become a god, quick-eyed, [Greenest 54-23P
    Sleekly the serpent would draw himself across. [Greenest 54-27 P
    In which he and the lion and the serpent hide [Greenest 54-30 P
    Death, only, sits upon the serpent throne: [Greenest 55-17 P
    In Africa. The serpent's throne is dust [Greenest 58-9 P
SERPENTINE. They require something serpentine. [Bananas 54-2
SERPENTINES. In the rowdy serpentines. He drilled. [News 264-14
    The rainbow in its glistening serpentines [Burnshaw 47-28 P
SERPENT-KIN. So intertwined with serpent-kin encoiled [C 32-3
    Sing a song of serpent-kin, [Orangeade 103-4
    And lion-men and the flicking serpent-kin [Greenest 55-3 P
SERPENTS. Of serpents like z rivers simmering, [Pure 330-18
    The frown like serpents basking on the brow, [NSF 400-11
    Toward which, in the nights, the glittering serpents climb,
    [Greenest 55-12 P
SERVANTS. And barefoot servants round him, who adjust [NSF 390-20

SERVE. Serve the rouged fruits in early snow. [Nigger 153-1
  The Got whome we serve is able to deliver [Hero 273-15
  Click, click, the Got whom we serve is able, [Hero 273-20
SERVED. Preferring text to gloss, he humbly served [C 39-22
  Ripened in warmth and served in warmth. On terms [Nigger 155-4
  To be served by men of ice. [Poem Morn 219-7
SERVES. An apple serves as well as any skull [Monocle 14-16
  Not France! France, also, serves the invincible eye, [Soldat
    14-9 P
SERVICE. In whose hard service both of us endure [Soldat 14-7 P
SERVICES. Once by the lips, once by the services [EM 317-19
SET. It is for fiery boys that star was set [Monocle 14-24
  Which yet found means to set his simmering mind [Geneva 24-10
  The table was set by an ogre, [Bananas 54-11
  But I set my traps [Peacocks 58-13
  Why set the pear upon those river-banks [Sunday 69-20
  A band entwining, set with fatal stones, [Fictive 88-16
  Disclosed in common forms. Set up [Prelude 195-17
  Poison, in what darkness set [Bagatelles 213-6
  To find: the scene was set; it repeated what [Of Mod 239-19
  From that strength, whose armies set their own expanses. [Repet
    309-5
  "A Completely New Set of Objects" [352-title
  And over it they set a jagged sign, [Good Man 364-12
  And set the MacCullough as major man? [NSF 386-24
  Set on me the spirit's diamond coronal. [NSF 396-6
  Possess. It is desire, set deep in the eye, [NH 467-10
  Or the sound of Incomincia had been set, [NH 482-24
  Cleared of its stiff and stubborn, man-locked set, [Angel 497-1
  To set in nicks? [Archi 17-26 P
  And, finally, set guardians in the grounds, [Archi 18-9 P
  It is not a set of laws. Therefore, its form [Recit 86-8 P
SETS. Purple sets purple round. Look, Master, [Hartford 227-5
  He sets this peddler's pie and cries in summer, [Oboe 251-3
  Sets up its Schwärmerei, not balances [NSF 386-14
SETTEE. The iron settee is cold. [Including 88-15 P
SETTING. The pulling into the sky and the setting there [Repet
    308-23
  As a setting for geraniums, the General, [NSF 391-23
  It was here. This was the setting and the time [Quiet 523-7
  See moon-setting.
SETTINGS. The iceberg settings satirize [MBG 180-2
SETTLES. And a grand decadence settles down like cold. [Havana
    142-12
  That thinks of settling, yet never settles, on a nest. [Somnam
    304-3
  Without this bird that never settles, without [Somnam 304-10
  Therein, day settles and thickens round a form-- [Role 93-12 P
SETTLING. That thinks of settling, yet never settles, on a nest.
    [Somnam 304-3
  Like a dancer's skirt, flung round and settling down. [Woman Had
    81-18 P
SEVEN. Of four, and one of seven, whom she dressed [NSF 402-2
  And the ordinariness of seven, [Song Fixed 520-3
  Took seven white dogs [Cab 20-16 P
SEVEN-COLORED. In glittering seven-colored changes, [Oak 272-20
SEVEN-FOOT. Is more than a seven-foot inchworm [Jersey 210-11
SEVENTY. Than seventy, where one looks, one has been there before.
    [Slug 522-2
  Seventy Years Later [Rock 525-title 1
  Regard the freedom of seventy years ago. [Rock 525-4
  Made by the sun ascending seventy seas. [Rock 47-29 P
SEVENTY-FOLD. Sing for her the seventy-fold Amen, [Grotesque 77-5P
SEVERAL. Of differing struts, four voices several [C 45-4
  Did several spirits assume a single shape? [Les Plus 245-7
  In parades like several equipages, [Hero 277-23
  As muffing the mistress for her several maids, [EM 316-21
  The world has turned to the several speeds of glass, [Bouquet
    449-3
  Unfretted by day's separate, several selves, [NH 482-10
SEVERANCE. That lay elsewhere around him. Severance [C 30-1
SEVERE. In how severe a book he read, [Thought 186-21
  And beneath that handkerchief drapeau, severe, [Pure 331-3
  As the life of poetry. A more severe, [NH 486-6
SEVERED. Of a mother with vague severed arms [Celle 438-19
  So severed and so much forlorn debris. [Bouquet 450-15
  Severed and tumbled into seedless grass, [Burnshaw 49-14 P
  The heads are severed, topple, tumble, tip [Burnshaw 51-31 P
SEVERITY. Again in the savagest severity, [EM 321-19
  And steps forth, priestly in severity, [Sombre 70-15 P
SEVERS. Severs not only lands but also selves. [C 30-4
SEVILLE. The churches and their long parades, Seville [Greenest
    53-18 P
SEWERS. To improve the sewers in Jerusalem, [MBG 174-1
SEX. If sex were all, then every trembling hand [Monocle 17-7
  Or else a new aspect, say the spirit's sex, [Aug 489-12
  And the sex of its voices, as the voice of one [Aug 489-14
  Exceeding sex, he touched another race, [Duck 64-25 P
SEXTON. The sexton moves with a sexton's stare [Gray 140-11
  Each sexton has his sect. The bells have none. [Luther 461-15

SEXTONS. And the bells belong to the sextons, after all, [Luther
    462-2
SEXUAL. What should we be without the sexual myth, [Men Made 355-15
  Nor that the sexual blossoms should repose [NSF 399-8
  By her sexual name, saying that that high marriage [Desire 85-5P
SHABBY. As morning throws off stale moonlight and shabby sleep.
    [NSF 382-12
  And a shabby man, [Coroner 30-6 P
SHADDOW. See shiddow-shaddow.
SHADE. That fluttering things have so distinct a shade. [Monocle
    18-3
  A pungent bloom against your shade. [Venereal 48-17
  And so it is one damns that green shade at the bottom of the
    land. [Banal 63-3
  A small relation expanding like the shade [Connois 215-19
  The cold evening, without any scent or the shade [Extracts 258-15
  After we've drunk the Moselle, to the thickest shade [Phenom
    286-16
  Within the big, blue bush and its vast shade [Study I 463-12
  The shadowless moon wholly composed of shade, [Study II 464-13
  A great town hanging pendent in a shade, [NH 468-16
  Is a solid. It may be a shade that traverses [NH 489-2
  A dust, a force that traverses a shade. [NH 489-3
  Of the least appreciable shade of green [Burnshaw 51-20 P
  Of a time to come--A shade of horror turns [Duck 65-8 P
  The bees to scorpions blackly-barbed, a shade [Duck 65-9 P
  Mulberry, shade me, shade me awhile. [Banjo 114-2 P
  Mulberry, shade me, shade me awhile. [Banjo 114-5 P
  Mulberry, shade me, shade me awhile. [Banjo 114-8 P
  Mulberry, shade me, shade me awhile-- [Banjo 114-11 P
  Mulberry, shade me, shade me awhile. [Banjo 114-13 P
  See shither-shade.
SHADED. And white roses shaded emerald on petals [Attempt 370-6
  Sweden described, Salzburg with shaded eyes [NH 486-2
SHADES. Lights out. Shades up. [Nightgown 214-1
  Has faint, portentous lustres, shades and shapes [Burnshaw 49-26P
  And despicable shades of red, just seen, [Burnshaw 51-21 P
  It is still full of icy shades and shapen snow. [Course 96-12 P
  See: sea-shades; sky-shades.
SHADING. Like leaning on the table, shading one's eyes, [Letters
    107-11 P
SHADOW. From the unavoidable shadow of himself [C 29-29
  The shadow of his fellows from the skies, [C 37-8
  In the shadow of a pine tree [Six Sig 73-6
  At the edge of the shadow, [Six Sig 73-10
  In and out of my shadow, [Six Sig 74-13
  The shadow of the blackbird [Thirteen 93-14
  Traced in the shadow [Thirteen 93-17
  The shadow of his equipage [Thirteen 94-17
  She was a shadow as thin in memory [Nigger 154-1
  And I am merely a shadow hunched [MBG 169-16
  Alone, one's shadow magnified, [MBG 176-5
  The shadow of Chocorua [MBG 176-8
  No shadow of themselves. [Add 198-22
  When the shapeless shadow covers the sun [Rabbit K 209-2
  The noble figure, the essential shadow, [Candle 223-12
  To receive her shadow into his mind . . . [Scavoir 231-11
  Is another shadow, another evasion, [Scavoir 231-18
  A shadow in the mind, a flourisher [Montra 260-10
  Shadow, up the great sea and downward [Hero 274-27
  To this prodigious shadow, who then came [Choc 297-2
  Now, I, Chocorua, speak of this shadow as [Choc 300-16
  As night was free from him. The shadow touched [EM 315-1
  A shadow in mid-earth . . . If we propose [Pure 330-7
  The shadow of an external world comes near. [Myrrh 350-12
  Like a great shadow's last embellishment. [AA 419-24
  Sharp in the ice shadow of the sky, [Celle 438-12
  To weave a shadow's leg or sleeve, a scrawl [What We 459-18
  In primavera, the shadow of bare rock, [NH 476-9
  And these beneath the shadow of a shape [Rome 509-2
  It was not the shadow of cloud and cold, [Two Illus 513-4
  The shadow of a sense of his own, [Two Illus 513-6
  No shadow walks. The river is fateful, [R Conn 533-10
  A fear too naked for her shadow's shape. [Old Woman 44-12 P
  Its shadow on their houses, on their walls, [Sombre 68-22 P
  And head a shadow trampled under hoofs, [Sombre 70-28 P
  See sea-shadow.
SHADOWED. Vengeful, shadowed by gestures [Bagatelles 213-16
  So barely lit, so shadowed over and naught, [Quiet 523-3
  Beautiful alliterations of shadows and of things shadowed.
    [Primordia 8-7 P
  See: big-shadowed; blue-shadowed.
SHADOWING. Or melancholy crows as shadowing clouds? [Stan MMO 19-18P
  Large-leaved and many-footed shadowing, [Greenest 52-23 P
SHADOWLESS. Curled over the shadowless hut, the rust and bones,
    [Farewell 118-4
  The shadowless moon wholly composed of shade, [Study II 464-13
  That, in the shadowless atmosphere, [Aug 493-17
SHADOWS. In swift, successive shadows, dolefully. [C 32-21
  Only in silent shadows and in dreams? [Sunday 67-14

The shrouding shadows, made the petals black [Sea Surf 100-23
Are overhung by the shadows of the rocks [Grapes 111-2
The dark shadows of the funereal magnolias [Norfolk 111-16
Of revealing desire and is empty of shadows. [Sad Gay 121-13
Will be motion and full of shadows. [Sad Gay 122-18
Theatrical distances, bronze shadows heaped [Key W 129-20
A tatter of shadows peaked to white, [Postcard 159-20
There are no shadows in our sun. [MBG 167-6
There are no shadows anywhere. [MBG 167-8
There are no shadows. Poetry [MBG 167-10
Without shadows, without magnificence, [MBG 176-13
The shadows of the pears [Pears 197-3
The shadows that are absent from Euclid, [Common 221-13
The men have no shadows [Common 221-24
One observes profoundest shadows rolling. [Vari 235-14
These other shadows, not in the mind, players [Montra 260-13
Shadows of scholars bent upon their books, [Montra 262-17
The shadows lessen on the walls. [Contra I 266-18
Blue friends in shadows, rich conspirators, [Choc 300-9
Is ease, stands in the dark, a shadows' hill, [EM 319-5
Concentric circles of shadows, motionless [EM 319-7
The shadows of his fellows ring him round [EM 319-11
Shadows of friends, of those he knew, each bringing [New Set
   352-12
The meeting of their shadows or that meet [NSF 407-13
The total of human shadows bright as glass. [Aug 494-23
Shadows like winds [Irish 501-10
And the shadows of the trees [Plant 506-6
Even our shadows, their shadows, no longer remain. [Rock 525-7
A thing of shadows, [Phases 5-19 P
Beautiful alliterations of shadows and of things shadowed.
   [Primordia 8-7 P
Seeing the fulgent shadows upward heaped, [Duck 62-16 P
The listener, listening to the shadows, seeing them, [Sick 90-18P
In the shadows of a wood . . . [Letters 108-1 P
Shadows, woods . . . and the two of them in speech, [Letters
   108-2 P
Alarming shadows, [Three 138-4 P
SHADOWY. New leaf and shadowy tinct, [Pourtraicte 21-23
   Stretched out a shadowy arm to feel the night. [Phases 5-8 P
   And shadowy hanging of it, thick with stars [Old Woman 46-2 P
SHADY. A Nice Shady Home [C 40-title 5
SHAFT. The shaft of light [Mud 148-6
   Of its propriety. Admit the shaft [Someone 86-2 A
SHAFTS. Pierce the interior with pouring shafts, [Archi 18-3 P
SHAGGED. To behold the junipers shagged with ice, [Snow Man 10-2
SHAGGY. But this we cannot see. The shaggy top [Sombre 68-19 P
   While the shaggy top collects itself to do [Sombre 68-26 P
SHAKE. This crust of air? . . (He pauses.) Can breath shake
   [Infernale 24-21 P
   Rage in the ring and shake the corridors. [Spaniard 35-1 P
SHAKEN. Marvelling sometimes at the shaken sleep. [C 44-19
   Shaken in a dance. [Six Sig 74-3
   Like blooms? Like damasks that were shaken off [Sea Surf 101-13
   When all people are shaken [Fading 139-2
   This is what could not be shaken, [Nightgown 214-6
   It is shaken now. It will burst into flames, [Nightgown 214-19
   The leaves of the sea are shaken and shaken. [Vari 233-5
   It held the shivering, the shaken limbs, [Hand 271-11
   The signal . . . The sea-tower, shaken, [Hero 275-2
   When the phantoms are gone and the shaken realist [EM 320-7
   Yet we are shaken by them as if they were. [NSF 399-2
SHAKING. Shaking the water off, like a poodle, [Hartford 226-8
   To shaking out heavy bodies in the glares [Cuisine 228-7
SHALE. Rougher than a grinding shale, [Orangeade 103-14
   The claws keep scratching on the shale, the shallow shale,
   [Somnam 304-5
SHALLOW. The claws keep scratching on the shale, the shallow shale,
   [Somnam 304-5
   The sounding shallow, until by water washed away. [Somnam 304-6
   And are not now: in this shallow spectacle, [Clear Day 113-18 P
SHALLOWEST. The shallowest iris on the emptiest eye. [Sombre 70-4P
SHAM. And sham umbrellas. And a sham-like green [Sea Surf 99-20
SHAME. Revealed Susanna and her shame. [Peter 91-19
SHAM-LIKE. And sham umbrellas. And a sham-like green [Sea Surf
   99-20
SHANKS. The women will be all shanks [Bananas 54-15
   See short-shanks.
SHANTY. See cathedral-shanty.
SHAPE. Whatever shape it took in Crispin's mind, [C 37-6
   When the crust of shape has been destroyed. [MBG 183-12
   The moon without a shape, [Add 199-7
   Of a cloud on sand, a shape on the side of a hill. [Connois
   215-20
   Did several spirits assume a single shape? [Les Plus 245-7
   His hands became his feelings. His thick shape [Repet 306-12
   A shape left behind, with like wings spreading out, [Myrrh 350-2
   "The Good Man Has No Shape" [364-title
   The Good Man Has No Shape, as if they knew. [Good Man 364-14
   Gulping for shape among the reeds. No doubt, [Lot 371-12

But the first idea was not to shape the clouds [NSF 383-17
And shape and mournful making move to find [AA 418-1
Beyond the habit of sense, anarchic shape [Page 422-18
Took on color, took on shape and the size of things as they are
   [Large 424-8
But the virtuoso never leaves his shape, [Orb 443-3
Without a god, O silver sheen and shape, [Bouquet 449-16
Silence is a shape that has passed. [Plant 506-4
The sources of happiness in the shape of Rome, [Rome 508-23
A shape within the ancient circles of shapes, [Rome 509-1
And these beneath the shadow of a shape [Rome 509-2
A nature still without a shape, [Two Illus 514-1
"The Shape of the Coroner" [29-title P
A fear too naked for her shadow's shape. [Old Woman 44-12 P
It lost the common shape of night and came [Old Woman 45-16 P
To be the sovereign shape in a world of shapes. [Old Woman 45-17P
What god rules over Africa, what shape, [Greenest 52-24 P
Of the shape of eyes, like blunt intaglios, [Greenest 59-5 P
Inhabitant, in less than shape, of shapes [Sombre 67-15 P
Distort the shape of what I meant, [Stan MBG 72-18 P
Which takes a shape by accident. [Stan MBG 73-1 P
A shape, the vista twisted and burning, a thing [Bship 80-5 P
The solid shape, Aeneas seen, perhaps, [Recit 87-22 P
Under the shape of his sail, Ulysses, [Ulysses 99-10 P
What is the shape of the sibyl? Not, [Ulysses 104-1 P
Is need. For this, the sibyl's shape [Ulysses 104-15 P
To be remembered, the old shape [Ulysses 104-19 P
Under the shape of his sail, Ulysses, [Presence 105-13 P
It is a shape of life described [Banjo 114-9 P
By another shape without a word. [Banjo 114-10 P
12. An uncivil shape like a gigantic haw. [Someone 86-15 A
SHAPED. And well shaped, [Three 131-23 P
SHAPELESS. When the shapeless shadow covers the sun [Rabbit K 209-2
   To the total thing, a shapeless giant forced [Poem Morn 219-15
   The vines around the throat, the shapeless lips, [NSF 400-10
   See silver-shapeless.
SHAPELY. Or shapely fire: fire from an underworld, [Choc 297-22
SHAPEN. It is still full of icy shades and shapen snow. [Course
   96-12 P
SHAPENER. A shapener of shapes for only the eye, [Extracts 253-1
SHAPES. And sullen, hurricane shapes [Bananas 53-22
   For whom the shapes were never the figures of men. [Sad Gay
   121-18
   The shapes have lost their glistening. [Sad Gay 122-2
   Too many waltzes have ended. Yet the shapes [Sad Gay 122-10
   Will unite these figures of men and their shapes [Sad Gay 122-16
   The shapes are wrong and the sounds are false. [MBG 181-11
   Between you and the shapes you take [MBG 183-11
   Have shapes that are not yet fully themselves, [Parochial 191-4
   Are sounds blown by a blower into shapes, [Parochial 191-5
   The rusty, battered shapes [Anything B 211-18
   A shapener of shapes for only the eye, [Extracts 253-1
   That buffets the shapes of its possible halcyon [EM 321-7
   As shapes, though they portent us, are. [Less 328-2
   Or seeing the spent, unconscious shapes of night, [Feo 334-7
   Pretend they are shapes of another consciousness? [Feo·334-8
   Words, in a storm, that beat around the shapes. [Sketch 335-22
   The eccentric souvenirs of human shapes, [Descrip 342-2
   The eye of Lenin kept the far-off shapes. [Descrip 343-11
   Carrying such shapes, of such alleviation, [New Set 353-1
   Knew well the shapes were the exactest shaping [New Set 353-3
   The difficult images of possible shapes, [Two V 354-9
   And shapes of fire, and wind that bears them down. [Two V 355-12
   Adieux, shapes, images-- [Prejudice 369-1
   In other shapes, as if duck and tablecloth [Bouquet 450-19
   A neuter shedding shapes in an absolute. [NH 479-19
   And the shapes that it took in feeling, the persons that [NH
   479-21
   A shape within the ancient circles of shapes, [Rome 509-1
   The shapes of the patches, [Primordia 9-18 P
   On the shapes of the mind. [Polo 38-6 P
   To be the sovereign shape in a world of shapes. [Old Woman 45-17P
   Has faint, portentous lustres, shades and shapes [Burnshaw 49-26P
   In a storm blown into glittering shapes, and flames [Burnshaw
   52-21 P
   Which were their thoughts, squeezed into shapes, the sun [Duck
   61-11 P
   Inhabitant, in less than shape, of shapes [Sombre 76-15 P
   Studies and shapes a tallow image, swarmed [Theatre 91-10 P
   Such black constructions, such public shapes [Ulysses 100-28 P
SHAPING. Knew well the shapes were the exactest shaping [New Set
   353-3
   See silver-shaping.
SHAPINGS. The shapings of the instrument [Stan MBG 72-17 P
SHARE. Of remembrance share nothing of ourselves. [Dutch 291-14
   People might share but were never an element, [Wild 328-18
   Stands truly. The circles nearest to it share [Anach 366-9
   To share the day. The trumpet supposes that [Cred 377-1
   The poem refreshes life so that we share, [NSF 382-13
   An isolation which only the two could share. [AA 419-18

We two share that at least. [Grotesque 76-6 P
What is it that we share? Red cherry pie [Grotesque 76-7 P
SHARED. And, being straw, turned green, lived backward, shared
    [Liadoff 347-9
SHARES. It is the sun that shares our works. [MBG 168-9
    The moon shares nothing. It is a sea. [MBG 168-10
    It is a sea; it shares nothing; [MBG 168-12
    The sun no longer shares our works [MBG 168-13
    He shares a gigantic life, it is because [Repet 308-11
    He shares the confusions of intelligence. [Papini 446-12
SHARING. A sharing of color and being part of it. [Look 518-16
SHARP. Oh, sharp he was [Peacocks 58-1
    My hands such sharp, imagined things. [W Burgher 61-17
    The lines are much too dark and much too sharp. [Tallap 71-13
    By light, the way one feels, sharp white, [Sailing 121-6
    Made sharp air sharper by their smell [Postcard 159-2
    Too sharp for that. The shore, the sea, the sun, [Blue Bldg
        217-9
    Steel against intimation--the sharp flash, [Motive 288-19
    Grows sharp in blood. The armies kill themselves, [Dutch 292-19
    In an elemental freedom, sharp and cold. [Choc 297-3
    Sharp as white paint in the January sun; [Holiday 312-2
    Than sharp, illustrious scene. The trumpet cries [Cred 376-19
    Bare limbs, bare trees and a wind as sharp as salt? [AA 419-21
    Sharp in the ice shadow of the sky, [Celle 438-12
    Each other by sharp informations, sharp, [Orb 441-16
    And I remember sharp Japonica-- [Soldat 13-11 P
    Is there a sharp edge? [Lulu M 27-1 P
    Is there a sharp edge? [Lulu M 27-2 P
    Dance, now, and with sharp voices cry, but cry [Burnshaw 51-10 P
    The sharp sail of Ulysses seemed, [Presence 106-7 P
SHARPER. Made sharp air sharper by their smell [Postcard 159-2
    Rifles grow sharper on the sight. [Dutch 291-2
SHARPEST. Were what they are, the sharpest sun: [Adequacy 244-9
    The sharpest self, the sensible range, [Adequacy 244-10
SHARPLY. Effective colonizer sharply stopped [C 44-4
    Would cry out sharply. [Thirteen 94-12
    Gleam sharply as the sun comes up. [Botanist 2 135-17
    More sharply in more fruious selves. [Eve Angels 137-5
    Could have stood up sharply in the sky. [Weak Mind 212-20
    She says sharply, to her maid, [Three 134-9 P
SHARPLY-COLORED. Until the sharply-colored glass transforms [Burn-
    shaw 52-9 P
SHASTA. If Shasta roared up in Nassau, [Agenda 42-2 P
SHATTER. A meaning which, as he entered it, would shatter the boat
    and leave the oarsmen quiet [Prol 516-7
SHATTERED. The ruses that were shattered by the large. [C 30-15
    The darkness shattered, turbulent with foam. [Farewell 118-16
    And tufted in straggling thunder and shattered sun. [Dwarf 208-8
SHATTERER. Angel, convulsive shatterer, gun, [Hero 273-19
SHATTERING. Shattering velvetest far-away. The bear, [NSF 384-14
SHAVE. And shave their heads and bodies. [Homunculus 26-20
SHAWL. Patted his stove-pipe hat and tugged his shawl. [Geneva
    24-3
    Hanging his shawl upon the wind, [MBG 181-17
    The shawl across one shoulder and the hat. [NH 483-21
    Within a single thing, a single shawl [Final 524-7
SHEAF. A sheaf of brilliant arrows flying straight, [Tallap 72-7
SHEARSMAN. A shearsman of sorts. The day was green. [MBG 165-2
SHEATHING. Like silver in the sheathing of the sight, [EM 320-5
SHEBANG. Shebang. Exeunt omnes. Here was prose [C 37-2
SHED. Of this: that the snake has shed its skin upon [Farewell
    117-9
    Everything is shed; and the moon comes up as the moon [Dump
        202-22
    Blanche, the blonde, whose eyes are not wholly straight, in a
        room of lustres, shed by turquoise falling, [Piano 22-1 P
    And on this ring of marble horses shed [Burnshaw 47-27 P
SHEDDING. A neuter shedding shapes in an absolute. [NH 479-19
SHEEN. That strode submerged in that malevolent sheen, [Sea Surf
    99-24
    Cinerarias have a speaking sheen. [Poesie 302-17
    The blown sheen--or is it air? [Degen 444-18
    Without a god, O silver sheen and shape, [Bouquet 449-16
    Seems like a sheen of heat romanticized. [NH 468-9
    Assumes a pale, Italianate sheen-- [Abnormal 24-6 P
    Branching through heavens heavy with the sheen [Old Woman 46-1 P
SHEENS. Long autumn sheens and pittering sounds like sounds [Burn-
    shaw 47-24 P
    Of Boucher pink, the sheens of Venetian gray. [Greenest 53-14 P
    Created, like a bubble, of bright sheens, [Duck 63-21 P
SHEEP. And bade the sheep carouse. Or so they said. [NSF 400-22
    Generations of shepherds to generations of sheep. [Luther 461-18
SHEEP-LIKE. The sheep-like falling-in of distances, [Duck 62-26 P
SHEER. From sheer Gemütlichkeit. [Nigger 152-17
SHEET. Lacking the three glass knobs, that sheet [Emperor 64-10
    It seizes a sheet, from the ground, from a bush, as if spread
        there by some wash-woman for the night. [Plough-Boy 6-5 P
    It wraps the sheet around its body, until the black figure is
        silver. [Plough-Boy 6-6 P

How soon the silver fades in the dust! How soon the black figure
    slips from the wrinkled sheet! [Plough-Boy 6-8 P
    How softly the sheet falls to the ground! [Plough-Boy 6-9 P
    See winding-sheet.
SHEETED. And the sheeted Atlantic. [Inhab 504-5
SHEETS. Trinket pasticcio, flaunting skeyey sheets, [C 40-1
    Bloomed in sheets, as they bloom, and the girl, [Forces 229-1
    There were the sheets high up on older trees, [Forces 229-13
    Behind the outer shields, the sheets of music [NH 488-10
SHELL. But not on a shell, she starts, [Paltry 5-6
    He munches a dry shell while he exerts [Bird Claws 82-16
    The blue guitar is a mould? [MBG 174-11
    He was a shell of dark blue glass, or ice, [Choc 297-9
    The shell is a shore. The egg of the sea [Aug 490-8
    See: cockle-shell; nut-shell; sea-shell.
SHELLEY. Mesdames, one might believe that Shelley lies [Burnshaw
    48-9 P
SHELLEYAN. Astral and Shelleyan, diffuse new day; [Burnshaw 47-26 P
SHELLS. Shells under water. These were nougats. [Forces 229-15
    Brooding on centuries like shells. [Oak 272-12
    And the egg of the sky are in shells, in walls, in skins [Aug
        490-9
    Like brazen shells. [Cab 21-3 P
SHELTER. Touched on by hoar-frost, shrinks in a shelter [Lunar
    107-7
    Shelter yet thrower of the summer spear, [Thought 186-10
    By a wind that seeks out shelter from snow. Thus [Hero 273-6
    They are at ease in a shelter of the mind [AA 413-18
    Like a shelter not in an arc [Celle 438-4
SHELTERED. A high bed sheltered by curtains. [Theory 87-3
SHELTERING. Two in a deep-founded sheltering, friend and dear
    friend. [World 521-3
SHEPHERD. A dead shepherd brought tremendous chords from hell
    [NSF 400-21
    Romanza out of the black shepherd's isle, [NH 480-13
    In the hearing of the shepherd and his black forms [NH 480-15
SHEPHERDS. Generations of shepherds to generations of sheep.
    [Luther 461-18
SHE-WOLVES. In form, lovers of heaven and earth, she-wolves [EM
    321-24
SHIDDOW-SHADDOW. Like the shiddow-shaddow of lights revolving
    [Hero 279-20
SHIELD. Into that native shield she slid, [Celle 438-17
SHIELDS. Behind the outer shields, the sheets of music [NH 488-10
SHIFT. Still hankers after lions, or, to shift, [Lions 125-4
    That tours to shift the shifting scene. [MBG 180-4
    It had to be right: nougats. It was a shift [Forces 229-16
    It is not the unravelling of her yellow shift. [John 437-6
    The tempo, in short, of this complicated shift, [Duck 65-31 P
SHIFTED. Shifted the rocks and picked his way among clouds [Poem
    Mt 512-8
SHIFTING. Triton, dissolved in shifting diaphanes [C 28-24
    That tours to shift the shifting scene. [MBG 180-4
SHIFTINGS. Shiftings of an inchoate crystal tableau, [Someone
    86-21 A
SHIFTS. "The Wind Shifts" [83-title
    This is how the wind shifts: [Shifts 83-10
    The wind shifts like this: [Shifts 83-14
    The wind shifts like this: [Shifts 83-17
    This is how the wind shifts: [Shifts 84-1
    That talk shifts the cycle of the scenes of kings? [Conversat
        109-23 P
SHIMMERING. If in a shimmering room the babies came, [Babies 77-10
SHINE. Shine alone in the sunrise [Nuances 18-6
    Shine alone, shine nakedly, shine like bronze, [Nuances 18-8
    of my being, shine like fire, that mirrors nothing. [Nuances
        18-10
    The sun is seeking something bright to shine on. [Nigger 157-20
    Shine on the very living of those alive. [Dutch 293-5
    Of less degree than flame and lesser shine. [Choc 297-23
    The rivers shine and hold their mirrors up, [Belly 366-19
    That's how the stars shine during the day. There, then, [Lot
        371-4
    And out of the shine of the hemlocks, [Celle 438-2
    And plated up, dense silver shine, in a land [Bouquet 449-15
    Rose-women as half-fishes of salt shine, [Study II 464-15
    That shines with a nocturnal shine alone. [NH 473-2
    That purges the wrack or makes the jungle shine, [Greenest 55-8 P
    Because I desire it to shine or else [Desire 85-20 P
    That I desire it to shine because it shines. [Desire 85-21 P
    The space in which it stands, the shine [Ulysses 100-26 P
    The bird sings. Its feathers shine. [Of Mere 118-3 P
    It does not shine on a thing that remains [Three 130-20 P
    Let the candle shine for the beauty of shining. [Three 133-10 P
    Will shine soon [Three 142-5 P
    It will shine soon [Three 142-7 P
    See water-shine.
SHINED. See gold-shined.
SHINES. A pool shines, [Six Sig 74-1
    That the moon shines. [Two Figures 86-15

It is how he gives his light. It is how he shines, [Freed 205-2
Adorned with cryptic stones and sliding shines, [Owl 434-10
That shines with a nocturnal shine alone. [NH 473-2
That it is wholly an inner light, that it shines [NH 481-19
We think, then, as the sun shines or does not. [Look 518-23
Shines on the mere objectiveness of things. [Moonlight 531-4
Stands glistening and Haddam shines and sways. [R Conn 533-15
Shines without fire on columns intercrossed, [Burnshaw 49-12 P
It could be that the sun shines [Desire 85-19 P
That I desire it to shine because it shines. [Desire 85-21 P
Before it shines on any house. [Three 130-6 P
But when the sun shines on the earth, [Three 130-18 P
And shines, perhaps, for the beauty of shining. [Three 131-11 P
Before it shines on any house. [Three 131-13 P
It shines, among the trees, [Three 135-8 P
In the meantime, the candle shines, [Three 138-22 P
Like the earth on which it shines, [Three 143-11 P
SHINING. Shining through the grape-leaves. [Six Sig 75-3
On shining pillows, [Tea 113-1
More leanly shining from a lankier sky. [Anglais 149-3
It was how the sun came shining into his room: [Freed 205-6
Are shining on all brows of Neversink. [Myrrh 349-14
The sun is secretly shining on a wall. [Bouquet 450-23
Seated before these shining forms, like the duskiest glass, re-
     flecting the piebald of roses or what you will. [Piano 21-18 P
Look suddenly downward with their shining eyes. [Red Kit 31-29 P
Observe her shining in the deadly trees. [Spaniard 34-15 P
Yet were not bright, came shining as things come [Burnshaw 51-25P
And shines, perhaps, for the beauty of shining. [Three 131-11 P
Let the candle shine for the beauty of shining. [Three 133-10 P
For the beauty of shining. [Three 139-1 P
Whose shining is the intelligence of our sleep. [Someone 84-11 A
See after-shining.
SHININGLY. Magnificence most shiningly expressed [Greenest 58-3 P
SHIP. Go on, high ship, since now, upon the shore [Farewell 117-1
That I loved her once . . . Farewell. Go on, high ship. [Fare-
     well 118-10
To the cold, go on, high ship, go on, plunge on. [Farewell 118-20
A ship that rolls on a confected ocean. [EM 322-23
The great ship, Balayne, lay frozen in the sea. [Page 421-18
Of the mind--They would soon climb down the side of the ship.
     [Page 423-8
The ship, make it my own and, bit by bit, [Bship 77-21 P
A single ship, a cloud on the sea, the largest [Bship 78-2 P
The ship would become the center of the world. [Bship 78-5 P
My cabin as the center of the ship and I [Bship 78-6 P
SHIPS. Instead of building ships, in numbers, build [Bship 78-1 P
SHITHER-SHADE. The prince of shither-shade and tinsel lights, [Owl
     434-3
SHIVER. She makes the willow shiver in the sun [Sunday 69-7
SHIVERED. That would have wept and been happy, have shivered in
     the frost [Large 424-1
The sea shivered in transcendent change, rose up [NH 484-9
SHIVERING. It held the shivering, the shaken limbs, [Hand 271-11
A shivering residue, chilled and foregone, [AA 417-20
SHOALS. The sea full of fishes in shoals, the woods that let [Cats
     367-13
SHOCK. Of the instant to perceive, after the shock, [Liadoff 347-15
SHOCKING. As if the ears heard any shocking sound, [NH 478-11
SHOE. At the book and shoe, the rotted rose [God 285-5
Yet a spider spins in the left shoe under the bed-- [Phenom
     286-10
SHOES. Bottles, pots, shoes and grass and murmur aptest eve: [Dump
     203-7
In suavest keeping. The shoes, the clothes, the hat [Descrip
     343-2
In his limpid shoes. [Coroner 29-15 P
Of the Balkan shoes, the bonnets from Moldau, beards [Duck 62-14P
SHONE. Was not the sun because it never shone [C 29-18
The sun shone and the dog barked and the baby slept. [Contra II
     270-5
And shone. And a small cabin build there. [Page 421-16
If the fane were clear, if the city shone in mind, [Sombre 69-11P
SHOOK. Shook off their dark marine in lapis light. [NH 484-8
SHOO-SHOO-SHOO. Its shoo-shoo-shoo, its ric-a-nic, [Mozart 131-16
The shoo-shoo-shoo of secret cymbals round. [NSF 401-13
SHOOT. Revolvers and shoot each other. One remains. [Extracts 256-2
SHOOTING. Ponies of Parisians shooting on the hill. [Parochial
     191-2
SHOOTS. A jar of the shoots of an infant country, green [Someone
     83-15 A
See off-shoots.
SHOP. The grain is in the baker's shop, [Nigger 154-8
See: clock-shop; junk-shop.
SHORE. And I reach to the shore of the sea [Six Sig 74-9
Go on, high ship, since now, upon the shore, [Farewell 117-1
Like Walt Whitman walking along a ruddy shore. [Nigger 150-10
The world was a short, whether sound or form [MBG 179-2
Spreading them as waves spread flat on the shore, [Loaf 200-6
The mouse, the moss, the woman on the shore . . . [Blue Bldg
     217-6
Too sharp for that. The shore, the sea, the sun, [Blue Bldg 217-9
The unpainted shore, accepts the world [Couch 296-4
On an old shore, the vulgar ocean rolls [Somnam 304-1
The ocean, falling and falling on the hollow shore, [Somnam
     304-12
By his drift-fire, on the shore, the difference [Page 421-6
Of billows, downward, toward the drift-fire shore. [Page 422-26
The shell is a shore. The egg of the sea [Aug 490-8
With the broken statues standing on the shore. [Aug 491-8
From a shore at night and disappeared. [Vacancy 511-7
Removed from any shore, from any man or woman, and needing none.
     [Prol 516-9
Returns and returns, along the dry, salt shore. [Woman Had 81-24P
That question the repetition on the shore, [Woman Had 82-3 P
SHORES. "Hibiscus on the Sleeping Shores" [22-title
And which had drowsed along the bony shores, [Hibiscus 22-18
They never find, the same receding shores [Sunday 69-18
Or spice the shores with odors of the plum? [Sunday 69-21
The shores are banks of muffling mist. [MBG 172-14
Flying from burning countries and brown sand shores, [Loaf 200-2
To come to tragic shores and flow, [Vari 233-9
SHORT. May, after all, stop short before a plum [C 40-28
Each must the other take as sign, short sign [NSF 401-14
Cock bugler, whistle and bugle and stop just short, [NSF 405-15
To that short, triumphant sting? [Phases 5-3 P
The tempo, in short, of this complicated shift, [Duck 65-31 P
SHORT-SHANKS. Was name for this short-shanks in all that brunt?
     [C 28-16
SHOT. Shot lightning at the kind cow's milk. [Lulu M 27-12 P
SHOULDER. He walked with his year-old boy on his shoulder. [Contra
     II 270-4
The shawl across one shoulder and the hat. [NH 483-21
Of a woman with a cloud on her shoulder rose [Aug 494-11
Of my shoulder and quickly, too quickly, I am gone? [Angel 497-10
He left half a shoulder and half a head [Two Illus 514-4
The leaning shoulder and the searching eye. [Blanche 10-4 P
Slung over my shoulder? [Soldat 12-21 P
SHOULDERING. Keep the laborers shouldering plinths. [Archi 16-17 P
SHOULDERS. That were like arms and shoulders in the waves, [C 29-2
On more than muscular shoulders, arms and chest, [Choc 297-12
The shoulders of joyous men, to feel the heart [NSF 398-11
They throw around their shoulders cloaks that flash [AA 419-23
Upon whose shoulders even the heavens rest, [Owl 431-15
And blows, with heaped-up shoulders loudly blows [Greenest 57-12P
And the shoulders turn, breathing immense intent. [Sombre 68-27P
SHOUT. That makes us weep, laugh, grunt and groan, and shout
     [Monocle 17-10
Shout for me, loudly and loudly, joyful sun, when you rise. [Nig-
     ger 150-17
Will shout from the tower's rim. [Secret Man 36-16 P
SHOUTED. Even though he shouted. [Thunder 220-16
SHOUTING. Crying and shouting and meaning farewell, [Adieu 127-10
SHOUTS. The hunter shouts as the pheasant falls. [Nigger 154-9
There are shouts and voices. [Dutch 290-8
(He shouts.) Hola! Of that strange light, beware! [Infernale
     25-3 P
In a burst of shouts, under the trees [Dinner 110-1 P
SHOVING. Against your sides, then shoving and slithering, [Fare-
     well 118-15
SHOW. To show how cold she is, and dumb. [Emperor 64-14
Vermilion smeared over green, arranged for show. [Grapes 110-14
They would show it. [Drum-Majors 36-19 P
The curtains, when pulled, might show another whole, [Theatre
     91-13 P
And final effulgence and delving show. [Ulysses 104-9 P
The contents of the mind become solid show [Conversat 108-13 P
Or almost solid seem show--the way a fly bird [Conversat 108-14P
SHOWERING. And in their music showering sounds intone. [C 37-32
SHOWING. But that this bloom grown riper, showing nibs [C 44-6
SHOWS. Shows that this object is merely a state, [Glass 197-9
SHREWD. And celebration. Shrewd novitiates [C 39-7
SHRIEK. Spring sparkle and the cock-bird shriek. [MBG 182-13
And continue their affair. The shriek [MBG 182-15
SHRIEKS. The cock-hen crows all day. But cockerel shrieks, [Nigger
     155-11
SHRILLING. Their shrilling tankards on the table-boards. [Monocle
     15-23
SHRINK. When amorists grow bald, then amours shrink [Monocle 15-14
To shrink to an insensible. [Adequacy 243-19
From which we shrink. And yet, except for us, [EM 314-15
SHRINKING. The motive for metaphor, shrinking from [Motive 288-14
Direction, shrinking from the spit and splash [Think 356-12
SHRINKS. Touched on by hoar-frost, shrinks in a shelter [Lunar
     107-7
In a world that shrinks to an immediate whole, [Descrip 341-12
SHRIVELED. Shrivelled in frost, [Tea 112-9
Covered the shrivelled forms [Reader 147-2
SHRIVELLINGS. In the shrivellings of your time and place. [Dutch
     291-7

SHROUDING. The shrouding shadows, made the petals black [Sea Surf
    100-23
SHROUDS. So deeply sunken were they that the shrouds, [Sea Surf
    100-22
SHRUB. And the ripe shrub writhed. [Planet 532-12
SHRUNK. Shrunk in the poverty of being close, [NH 484-18
SHUCKS. Shucks . . . lavender moonlight falls. [Add 198-11
SHUDDER. Would shudder on a bloody salver. [Three 132-14 P
SHUDDERS. Hen shudders: the copious egg is made and laid. [Nigger
    155-12
SHUFFLED. And so it came, his cabin shuffled up, [C 42-1
    Harness of the horses shuffled [Cab 21-2 P
SHUFFLING. Fills the high hall with shuffling men [MBG 171-13
    The grunting, shuffling branches, the robust, [Parochial 191-8
    There are men shuffling on foot in air. [Dutch 290-9
    And shuffling lightly, with the heavy lightness [Dutch 290-11
SHUT. Shut to the blather that the water made, [Hibiscus 22-19
    He shut out from his tempering ear; what thoughts, [C 34-22
SHUTTERED. Above the shuttered mansion-house, [Postcard 159-8
SHUTTERS. Composed of evenings like cracked shutters flung [C 42-30
    Blows on the shutters of the metropoles, [Pharynx 96-6
    In east wind beating the shutters at night. [Vase 246-16
    On the still, black-slatted eastward shutters, [Aug 492-23
SHUTTING. Spread over heaven shutting out the light. [Red Kit
    31-26 P
SHY. The second sister dallying was shy [C 44-27
SIBILANCE. Again, "The sibilance of phrases is his [NH 485-10
SIBILANT. Chant sibilant requiems for this effigy. [Burnshaw
    47-19 P
SIBILANTS. And out of their droning sibilants makes [Two Figures
    86-8
SIBYL. What is the shape of the sibyl? Not, [Ulysses 104-1 P
    It is the sibyl of the self, [Ulysses 104-10 P
    The self as sibyl, whose diamond, [Ulysses 104-11 P
    Is need. For this, the sibyl's shape [Ulysses 104-15 P
SICK. The path sick sorrow took, the many paths [Sunday 69-4
    They are sick of each old romance, returning. [Hero 274-6
    As if some Old Man of the Chimney, sick [Phases 5-6 P
    And mother nature sick of silk [Lulu M 27-11 P
    As hangman, a little sick of blood, of [Stan Hero 84-17 P
    "The Sick Man" [90-title P
SICKLE. Death was a reaper with sickle and stone, [Soldat 16-1 P
SICKNESS. Daylight evaporates, like a sound one hears in sickness.
    [Dixcov 95-9 P
    A healing-point in the sickness of the mind: [Art Pop 112-22 P
SIDE. Against the elders by her side; [Peter 91-15
    Of a cloud on sand, a shape on the side of a hill. [Connois
    215-20
    And the women have only one side. [Common 221-25
    This side of Moscow. There were anti-ideas [Forces 229-7
    On her side, reclining on her elbow. [Couch 295-1
    Of the mind--They would soon climb down the side of the ship.
    [Page 423-8
    He bumps the table. The bouquet falls on its side. [Bouquet 453-1
    At the upper right, a pyramid with one side [What We 460-2
    A thing on the side of a house, not deep in a cloud, [NH 474-21
    The chimney is fifty years old and slants to one side. [Plain
    502-18
    What opposite? Could it be that yellow patch, the side [Slug
    522-9
    There is a great river this side of Stygia, [R Conn 533-4
    In that river, far this side of Stygia, [R Conn 533-7
    Goes off a little on the side and stops. [Duck 63-33 P
    In a field, the man on the side of a hill, all men [Americana
    93-16 P
    On the dark side of the heavens or the bright, [Local 112-2 P
    3. A vine has climbed the other side of the wall. [Someone 86-6A
    See: river-side; sea-side; under-side.
SIDELONG. On sidelong wing, around and round and round. [Monocle
    17-19
SIDEREAL. Make a sidereal splendor as you fly. [Red Kit 32-2 P
SIDES. So thick with sides and jagged lops of green, [C 32-2
    Beholding all these green sides [Nomad 95-13
    And gold sides of green sides, [Nomad 95-14
    Against your sides, then shoving and slithering, [Farewell 118-15
    Then the sides of peaches, of dusky pears. [Vase 246-24
    Part of the glass-like sides on which it glided over the salt-
    stained water, [Prol 516-3
    As there are sides to a round bottle. [Three 136-16 P
    See sky-sides.
SIDE-STARS. Weight him down, O side-stars, with the great weight-
    ings of the end. [Madame 507-1
SIDEWALK. On the sidewalk so that the pensive man may see. [Connois
    216-12
SIERRA. Should make the intricate Sierra scan. [C 38-23
SIGH. Ubiquitous concussion, slap and sigh, [C 28-20
    Sigh for me, night-wind, in the noisy leaves of the oak. [Nigger
    150-15
    The deep sigh with which the hanging ends, close [Stan Hero
    84-18 P

SIGHED. The doctor used his handkerchief and sighed. [Geneva 24-15
    She sighed, [Peter 90-19
    Sighed in the evening that he lived [Forces 228-18
SIGHING. Sighing that he should leave the banjo's twang. [NSF 393-21
    So sullen with sighing and surrender to marauding ennui. [Inele-
    gance 25-18 P
    And sighing. These lives are not your lives, O free, [Duck 61-30P
SIGHS. The lover sighs as for accessible bliss, [NSF 395-4
SIGHT. Yeoman and grub, but with a fig in sight, [C 42-17
    And sight, and all there was of the storm, [Joost 47-2
    When the blackbird flew out of sight, [Thirteen 94-6
    At the sight of blackbirds [Thirteen 94-9
    Here was a sovereign sight, [Pascagoula 126-17
    To this accurate, exacting eye. Sight [Hero 274-11
    Hangs heaven with flash drapery. Sight [Hero 274-12
    Is a museum of things seen. Sight, [Hero 274-13
    Even enthroned on rainbows in the sight [Hero 277-27
    Against the sight, the penetrating, [Hero 278-28
    Rifles grow sharper on the sight. [Dutch 291-2
    Indulgence out of all celestial sight. [EM 318-17
    Like silver in the sheathing of the sight, [EM 320-5
    As if sight had not its own miraculous thrift, [EM 320-26
    One might have thought of sight, but who could think [EM 326-3
    Composed of a sight indifferent to the eye. [Descrip 343-22
    Might spring to sight and yet remain a dove. [Think 357-4
    Speaking the phrases that follow the sight [Pediment 361-20
    Until sight wakens the sleepy eye [Red Fern 365-15
    Let's see it with the hottest fire of sight. [Cred 373-4
    Of the spirit. This, in sight and memory, [Cred 376-22
    Even of earth, even of sight, in snow, [AA 417-13
    Needs out of the whole necessity of sight. [Owl 432-2
    A dazzle of remembrance and of sight. [Owl 433-6
    From sight, in the silence that follows her last word-- [Owl
    435-21
    Not yet accustomed, yet, at sight, humane [John 437-8
    Embellished by the quicknesses of sight, [Bouquet 451-10
    The eye made clear of uncertainty, with the sight [NH 471-19
    By sight and insight as they are. There is no [NH 473-22
    It is not an empty clearness, a bottomless sight. [NH 488-4
    We resembled one another at the sight. [Aug 494-15
    Since, in my sight, you see the earth again, [Angel 496-16
    The candle is it evades the sight, these are [Rome 508-22
    Exclaiming bright sight, as it was satisfied, [Rock 526-6
    In a birth of sight. The blooming and the musk [Rock 526-7
    And light lay deeper for her than her sight. [Old Woman 44-22 P
    And nothing more. He sees but not by sight. [Greenest 59-6 P
    All this is hidden from sight. [Sombre 68-28 P
    Sight least, but metaphysical blindness gained, [Souls 94-21 P
    Remains in the sight, and in sayings of the sight, [How Now 97-5P
    See brooding-sight.
SIGHTING. Of palmy peaks sighting machine-guns? These, [Greenest
    56-2 P
SIGIL. Across the roofs as sigil and as ward [NSF 384-23
SIGN. And over it they set a jagged sign, [Good Man 364-12
    Each must the other take as sign, short sign [NSF 401-14
    An innocence of the earth and no false sign [AA 418-21
    A sovereign, a souvenir, a sign. [Bouquet 451-12
    For a sign of meaning in the meaningless, [Armor 529-12
    In a mystic eye, no sign of life but life, [Armor 529-14
    Of Capricorn or as the sign demands, [Someone 86-18 A
SIGNAL. The signal . . . The sea-tower, shaken, [Hero 275-2
    Signal, a character out of solitude, [Pure 331-4
    From five-six cornered leaves, and green, the signal [NH 470-20
SIGNBOARDS. From hearing signboards whimper in cold nights [C 33-2
SIGNED. As in a signed photograph on a mantelpiece. [Orb 443-2
SIGNIFICANT. "Six Significant Landscapes" [73-title
SILENCE. A long soothsaying silence down and down. [C 42-10
    Of the silence, wide sleep and solitude [Curtains 62-6
    As the night conceives the sea-sounds in silence, [Two Figures
    86-7
    Is rest and silence spreading into sleep. [Eve Angels 137-25
    It was at that time, that the silence was largest [On Road 204-9
    This is the silence of night, [Nightgown 214-5
    Around which silence lies on silence. [Yellow 236-10
    Of the silence before the armies, armies without [Martial 237-21
    Tell X that speech is not dirty silence [Creat 311-7
    Clarified. It is silence made still dirtier. [Creat 311-8
    In silence upon your bed. You clutch the corner [NSF 384-19
    Music falls on the silence like a sense, [NSF 392-10
    Demanded of sleep, in the excitements of silence [NSF 402-17
    From sight, in the silence that follows her last word-- [Owl
    435-21
    Man sits and studies silence and himself, [Papini 447-10
    The wind has blown the silence of summer away. [NH 487-13
    Mud, water like dirty glass, expressing silence [Plain 503-4
    Of a sort, silence of a rat come out to see, [Plain 503-5
    Silence is a shape that has passed. [Planet 506-4
    Of silence, that any solitude of sense [Rome 510-18
    Night and silence disturbed by an interior sound, [Moonlight
    532-2

Hissing, across the silence, puissant sounds. [Greenest 55-16 P
SILENCES. That silences the ever-faithful town. [Havana 144-25
   Midsummer love and softest silences. [Montra 261-16
   Suited the decadence of those silences, [Descrip 343-3
   That comes and goes in silences of its own. [Look 518-22
SILENT. In the night that is still to be silent, [Homunculus 26-14
   Over the seas, to silent Palestine, [Sunday 67-10
   Only in silent shadows and in dreams? [Sunday 67-14
   It turned cold and silent. Then [Public Sq 109-9
   The false roses--Compare the silent rose of the sun [Extracts
      252-4
   That batters against the mind, silent and proud, [Pure 329-14
   "Continual Conversation with a Silent Man" [359-title
   Be silent in your luminous cloud and hear [NSF 404-11
   The mornings grow silent, the never-tiring wonder. [Aug 495-17
   But through man's eye, their silent rhapsodist, [Rock 528-6
   Mumbling and musing of the silent farm. [Phases 5-10 P
   The silent watcher, far below her, hears:) [Infernale 25-11 P
   Silent and turquoised and perpetual, [Burnshaw 50-15 P
   A silent sort of bush, as well. [Banjo 114-7 P
   In the space it fills, the silent motioner [Ideal 88-6 A
SILENTIOUS. And on silentious porpoises, whose snouts [C 27-19
SILENTLY. Or moonlight, silently, as Plato's ghost [Less 327-12
   Silently it heaves its youthful sleep from the sea-- [NH 476-22
SILK. Thinking of your blue-shadowed silk, [Peter 90-4
   His speech, the dress of his meaning, silk [MBG 170-2
   Dressed in metal, silk and stone, [Thought 186-19
   And mother nature sick of silk [Lulu M 27-11 P
SILKEN. The silken weavings of our afternoons, [Sunday 69-23
SILKS. The silks they wear in all the cities [Melancholy 32-13 P
SILL. The dirt along the sill. [Anything B 211-23
   The geraniums on the sill. [Aug 493-12
   See window-sill.
SILLS. See window-sills.
SILVAS. I dreamed, of autumn rivers, silvas green. [Montra 263-2
SILVER. And cream for the fig and silver for the cream, [C 42-18
   A blonde to tip the silver and to taste [C 42-19
   That should be silver, four accustomed seeds [C 45-7
   Of cloudy silver sprinkles in your gown [Fictive 87-11
   And a pale silver patterned on the deck [Sea Surf 100-12
   Who, seeing silver petals of white blooms [Sea Surf 100-17
   Must see her fans of silver undulate. [Nigger 152-20
   Like silver in the sheathing of the sight, [EM 320-5
   Should be cold silver, neither that frothy clouds [NSF 399-6
   And plated up, dense silver shine, in a land [Bouquet 449-15
   Without a god, O silver sheen and shape, [Bouquet 449-16
   "A Golden Woman in a Silver Mirror" [460-title
   It was silver once, [Phases 3-7 P
   "The Silver Plough-Boy" [6-title P
   It wraps the sheet around its body, until the black figure is
      silver. [Plough-Boy 6-6 P
   How soon the silver fades in the dust! How soon the black figure
      slips from the wrinkled sheet! [Plough-Boy 6-8 P
   The sun is gold, the moon is silver. [Mandolin 29-1 P
   Night gold, and winter night, night silver, these [Sombre 68-12P
   Of stripes of silver that are strips [Dove 98-10 P
SILVERED. There is no moon, on single, silvered leaf. [Tallap 71-15
SILVER-RUDDY. No silver-ruddy, gold-vermilion fruits. [Monocle 17-1
SILVERS. And silvers and greens spread over the sea. The moon
      [Farewell 117-4
SILVER-SHAPELESS. The silver-shapeless, gold-encrusted size [Choc
      298-11
SILVER-SHAPING. A freedom out of silver-shaping size, [Choc 298-9
SILVER-TIPPED. That rolled in heat is silver-tipped [Vari 234-7
SILVERWARE. A snort across the silverware. [Grotesque 75-16 P
SIMILAR. A second similar counterpart, a maid [C 44-16
SIMILARITY. In a movement of the outlines of similarity? [Aug 494-14
SIMMERING. Which yet found means to set his simmering mind [Geneva
      24-10
   Of serpents like z rivers simmering, [Pure 330-18
SIMPERING. And then, the simpering Byzantines [Peter 91-20
SIMPLE. An eye of land, of simple salad-beds, [C 27-16
   And then to Carolina. Simple jaunt. [C 29-10
   No crown is simpler than the simple hair. [Fictive 87-13
   Of those with a sense for simple space. [Nigger 153-7
   It was increased, enlarged, made simple, [Gigan 289-13
   She hid them under simple names. She held [NSF 402-8
   In a savage and subtle and simple harmony, [NH 468-1
   Of simple seeing, without reflection. We seek [NH 471-20
   For simple pleasure, he beheld, [Sat Night 27-17 P
   And simple love. [How Now 97-12 P
SIMPLE-COLORED. The one moonlight, in the simple-colored night,
      [Moonlight 531-1
SIMPLER. No crown is simpler than the simple hair. [Fictive 87-13
SIMPLEST. Might come in the simplest of speech. [Homunculus 27-2
   Over the simplest words: [Nigger 151-17
   The enlarging of the simplest soldier's cry [Choc 298-14
   It may come tomorrow in the simplest word, [AA 420-1
   Beautified the simplest men. [Phases 4-16 P
   Dazzling by simplest beams and soothly still, [Old Woman 46-4 P

SIMPLICITY. The mind herein attains simplicity. [Tallap 71-14
   Say even that this complete simplicity [Poems Clim 193-17
SIMPLIFICATION. As the final simplification is meant to be. [Bship
      78-30 P
SIMPLIFICATIONS. First. The grand simplifications reduce [Bship
      78-23 P
   Simplifications approach but do not touch [Bship 80-26 P
SIMPLIFIED. Is simplified: a bowl of white, [Poems Clim 193-14
   Of that simplified geography, in which [Feo 334-11
SIMPLY. But to speak simply of good is like to love, [Montra
      262-21
   How simply the fictive hero becomes the real; [NSF 408-1
   One approaches, simply, the reality [Bouquet 448-14
   Whose lives return, simply, upon our lips, [Sombre 67-5 P
SIMULACRUM. Gross effigy and simulacrum, none [Fictive 87-18
SIN. Imagination as the fateful sin. [Havana 143-22
SINCERE. And possesses by sincere insight [Ulysses 103-4 P
SINEWY. A sinewy nakedness. A river bore [C 36-5
SING. Ask us not to sing standing in the sun, [Orangeade 102-17
   Sing a song of serpent-kin, [Orangeade 103-4
   Sing in clownish boots [Orangeade 103-7
   Was merely a place by which he walked to sing. [Key W 129-6
   The grackles sing avant the spring [Snow Stars 133-1
   They sing right puissantly. [Snow Stars 133-3
   And sing them in secrecy as lovers do. [Nigger 151-21
   I sing a hero's head, large eye [MBG 165-13
   God and all angels sing the world to sleep, [Men Fall 187-9
   Women of a melancholy one could sing. [Horn 230-4
   She will think about them not quite able to sing. [Debris 338-9
   Besides, when the sky is so blue, things sing themselves,
      [Debris 338-10
   Secure. It was difficult to sing in face [Cred 376-2
   My dame, sing for this person accurate songs. [NSF 388-9
   To sing jubilas at exact, accustomed times, [NSF 398-7
   To speak of joy and to sing of it, borne on [NSF 398-10
   The sort of thing that August crooners sing, [Aug 489-9
   And not all birds sing cuck [Lulu M 27-7 P
   Sing coo, sing cuck, cuckoo. [Lulu M 27-8 P
   The rotting man was first to sing. [Sat Night 28-12 P
   Milord, I ask you, though you will to sing, [Red Kit 31-16 P
   The women should sing as they march. [Drum-Majors 37-11 P
   Sing rose-beliefs. Above that urn two lights [Burnshaw 50-1 P
   Be free to sing, if only a sorrowful song. [Greenest 58-33 P
   Sing for her the seventy-fold Amen, [Grotesque 77-5 P
   Sing it. [Three 134-4 P
   "Sing to yourself no more." [Three 134-10 P
   "I shall sing to myself no more." [Three 135-2 P
SINGER. The singer has pulled his cloak over his head. [Of Surface
      57-7
   You Jim and you Margaret and you singer of La Paloma, [Fish-
      Scale 161-1
SINGERS. Of the object. The singers had to avert themselves [Cred
      376-3
SINGING. Start the singing in a voice [Orangeade 103-13
   Or thrush, or any singing mysteries? [Sonatina 110-2
   Except the one she sang and, singing, made. [Key W 130-2
   Why, when the singing ended and we turned [Key W 130-4
   He is singing and chanting the things that are part of him,
      [Nigger 150-11
   The birds are singing in the yellow patios, [Nigger 152-15
   Moving round the sky and singing [Dezem 218-10
   Whose singing is a mode of laughter, [Dezem 218-12
   Laughing and singing and being happy, [Dezem 218-15
   The wood-doves are singing along the Perkiomen. [Think 356-7
   One ear, the wood-doves are singing a single song. [Think
      356-10
   The most massive sopranos are singing songs of scales [Chaos
      357-18
   Singing, with smaller and still smaller sound, [Rome 508-4
   Singing in the night's abyss; [Phases 4-10 P
   No doubt, the well-tuned birds are singing, [Agenda 42-11 P
   Voices in chorus, singing without words, remote and deep, [Sick
      90-11 P
SINGLE. Crossing a single bridge into a village. [Magnifico 19-6
   That century of wind in a single puff. [C 28-4
   Crispin, magister of a single room, [C 42-5
   There is no moon, on single, silvered leaf. [Tallap 71-15
   She was the single artificer of the world [Key W 129-26
   They were particles of order, a single majesty: [Anglais 149-8
   He yielded himself to that single majesty; [Anglais 149-12
   "Words are not forms of a single word. [On Road 204-2
   For which the intricate Alps are a single nest. [Connois 216-14
   With a single sense, though he smells clouds, [Arcades 225-21
   Did several spirits assume a single shape? [Les Plus 245-7
   With a single well-tempered apricot, or, say, [Extracts 253-14
   Into a single thought, thus: into a queen, [Extracts 254-8
   The single thought? The multitudes of men [Extracts 254-15
   That kill the single man, starvation's head, [Extracts 254-16
   This single place in which we are and stay, [Extracts 257-10
   And the most distant, single color, about to change, [Extracts

258-17
  And there to find music for a single line, [Extracts 259-16
  But let this one sense be the single main. [Montra 264-3
  Whose single being, single form [Jumbo 269-8
  The self of the hero, the solar single, [Hero 280-7
  The single bird, the obscure moon-- [Motive 288-8
  Made single, made one. This was not denial. [Gigan 289-14
  Intones its single emptiness, [Possum 294-11
  Variations in the tones of a single sound, [EM 316-14
  The last, or sounds so single they seem one? [EM 316-15
  One ear, the wood-doves are singing a single song. [Think 356-10
  The fisherman might be the single man [Think 357-5
  Without evasion by a single metaphor. [Cred 373-7
  In the uncertain light of single, certain truth, [NSF 380-7
  The phrases of a single phrase, ke-ke, [NSF 394-8
  A single text, granite monotony, [NSF 394-9
  This is nothing until in a single man contained, [AA 416-22
  They would march single file, with electric lamps, alert [Page
      423-9
  Become a single being, sure and true. [Pecul 454-9
  The gay tournamonde as of a single world [NH 476-3
  Are a single voice in the boo-ha of the wind. [NH 481-3
  Of the single future of night, the single sleep, [NH 482-6
  In a single spruce, when, suddenly, [Two Illus 514-14
  The way the earliest single light in the evening sky, in spring,
      [Prol 517-8
  Within a single thing, a single shawl [Final 524-7
  Single, of burly ivory, inched of gold, [Greenest 55-6 P
  As brilliant as mystic, as mystic as single, all [Greenest 55-9P
  Not the agony of a single dreamer, but [Duck 61-25 P
  Each other's thoughts, thinking a single thought, [Duck 62-20 P
  A single ship, a cloud on the sea, the largest [Bship 78-2 P
  It has a clear, a single, a solid form, [Recit 87-11 P
  Tradition wears, the clear, the single form [Recit 87-21 P
  And if one's sense of a single spot [Ulysses 99-21 P
  Of that single mind. He regards them [Child 106-17 P
  Sole, single source and minimum patriarch, [Conversat 108-21 P
  With nothing fixed by a single word. [Banjo 114-12 P
  Not in a single world, [July 114-16 P
  A single self. Divest reality [Someone 86-1 A
SINGLE-COLORED. The single-colored, colorless, primitive. [Landsc
    242-2
SINGLENESS. Prostrate below the singleness of its will. [NH 478-24
SINGS. The race that sings and weeps and knows not why. [Thought
    186-16
  When it sings. The gull sits on chimney-tops. [Vari 233-13
  Of love and summer. The assassin sings [Extracts 256-8
  Of the assassin that remains and sings [Extracts 256-15
  So that the skeleton in the moonlight sings, [Montra 261-8
  Sings of an heroic world beyond the cell, [Montra 261-9
  "A Woman Sings a Song for a Soldier Come Home" [360-title
  It is a child that sings itself to sleep, [Owl 436-7
  Deep in their sound the stentor Martin sings. [Luther 461-13
  Well-wetted; a decoying voice that sings [Spaniard 35-15 P
  Sings in the palm, without human meaning, [Of Mere 117-19 P
  The bird sings. Its feathers shine. [Of Mere 118-3 P
SING-SONG. Clawing the sing-song of their instruments. [AA 415-11
SINGSONGED. Singsonged and singsonged, wildly free. [Jumbo 269-3
SINGULAR. He made a singular collation. Thus: [C 37-26
  Secret and singular. Second, upon [C 44-15
  To be one's singular self, to despise [Adieu 127-17
  The singular man of the mass. Masses produce [Dames 206-5
  And yet it is a singular romance, [Extracts 256-11
  Amen to thought, our singular skeleton, [Montra 260-19
  How singular he was as man, how large, [Choc 302-1
  It is true there were other mothers, [EM 321-23
  Or a barricade against the singular man [Descrip 340-8
  But singular, they would, like water, scale [Two V 355-5
  In the abstract than in his singular, [NSF 388-18
  Inactive in his singular respect. [NH 474-15
  Would have a most singular appearance, [Mandolin 29-4 P
SINISTER. Of ocean, which in sinister flatness lay. [Sea Surf 99-22
SINK. Ambiguous undulations as they sink, [Sunday 70-27
  In the days when the mood of love will be swarming for solace
      and sink deeply into the thin stuff of being, [Piano 22-8 P
  Summers sink from it. [Secret Man 36-8 P
SINKING. And sinking down to the indulgences [C 35-12
  The multiform beauty, sinking in night wind, [Soldat 12-4 P
SINKS. They mow the lawn. A vessel sinks in waves [EM 322-12
  Sinks into likeness blessedly beknown. [Spaniard 35-20 P
SINUOUS. These two go well together, the sinuous brim [Pastor 380-2
  In our captious hymns, erect and sinuous, [John 437-20
  Dark-skinned and sinuous, winding upwardly, [Greenest 55-13 P
SIP. Two the ever-jubilant weather, to sip [Adieu 128-2
  They sip the glass. [Phases 3-4 P
  Sip the wild honey of the poor man's life, [Burnshaw 49-10 P
SIPPING. Foreswore the sipping of the marriage wine. [NSF 401-10
SIRS. And the cast-iron of our works. But it is, dear sirs, [Orb
    440-4
SISTER. The second sister dallying was shy [C 44-27

Sister and mother and diviner love, [Fictive 87-5
  On the east, sister and nun, and opened wide [Phenom 287-8
  Sister and solace, brother and delight.[NSF 392-24
  Of his sister, in what a sensible ecstasy [NSF 401-24
  Yet when her children slept, his sister herself [NSF 402-16
SISTERHOOD. And of the sisterhood of the living dead [Fictive
    87-6
SISTERLY. Most sisterly to the first, not yet awake [C 44-17
SISTERS. See cata-sisters.
SIT. When you might sit, [Venereal 48-4
  For maidens who were wont to sit and gaze [Sunday 69-8
  So I sit, deformed, a naked egg, [MBG 173-4
  So it is to sit and to balance things [MBG 181-5
  On the dump? Is it to sit among mattresses of the dead, [Dump
    203-6
  You sit with your head like a carving in space [Rabbit K 210-2
  There they sit, holding their eyes in their hands. [Arcades
    225-4
  Is the table a mirror in which they sit and look? [Cuisine
    228-15
  He might sit on a sofa on a balcony [Landsc 243-2
  Of the mind, in which we sit [Crude 305-7
  In which we sit and breathe [Crude 305-12
  Sit in the room. It is true in the moonlight [Debris 338-3
  In which I meet you, in which we sit at rest, [NSF 380-9
  We more than awaken, sit on the edge of sleep, [NSF 386-19
  They sit idly there, [Phases 3-3 P
  I love to sit and read the Telegraph, [Mandolin 29-6 P
  The skeletons sit on the wall. They drop [Stan MBG 72-3 P
  As we sit here, [Three 132-19 P
SITS. An old man sits [Six Sig 73-5
  One sits and plays the blue guitar. [MBG 172-22
  One sits and beats an old tin can, lard pail. [Dump 202-26
  When it sings. The gull sits on chimney-tops. [Vari 233-13
  One boy swims under a tub, one sits [Vari 235-16
  The mind sits listening and hears it pass. [Pure 329-18
  And there is no other. There is Ha-ee-me, who sits [Jouga 337-2
  The negations are never final. The father sits [AA 414-5
  In space, wherever he sits, of bleak regard, [AA 414-6
  But now he sits in quiet and green-a-day. [AA 414-13
  Is there an imagination that sits enthroned [AA 417-4
  Sits in a wood, in the greenest part, [Degen 444-2
  Sits in nothing that we know, [Degen 444-4
  Man sits and studies silence and himself, [Papini 447-10
  Beyond the object. He sits in his room, beside [NH 475-7
  Who sits thinking in the corners of a room. [NH 480-2
  Death, only, sits upon the serpent throne: [Greenest 55-17 P
  8. The owl sits humped. It has a hundred eyes. [Someone 86-11 A
SITTING. Being and sitting still, something resides, [Autumn 160-9
  Sitting beside your lamp, there citron to nibble [Dwarf 208-13
  For a month. It was pleasant to be sitting there, [EM 313-14
  Goat-leaper, crystalled and luminous, sitting [AA 417-9
  He is sitting by the fidgets of a fire, [Novel 457-13
SIX. "Six Significant Landscapes" [73-title
  The latest freed man rose at six and sat [Freed 204-14
  Ideas or, say, five men or, possibly, six. [Extracts 255-28
  With six meats and twelve wines or else without [NSF 407-16
  The sun of five, the sun of six, [Song Fixed 520-1
  The sun was rising at six, [Not Ideas 534-7
  See five-six.
SIZE. All eyes and size, and galled Justitia, [Lions 124-13
  A freedom out of silver-shaping size, [Choc 298-9
  The silver-shapeless, gold-encrusted size [Choc 298-11
  The soldier of time grown deathless in great size. [EM 319-2
  Took on color, took on shape and the size of things as they are
      [Large 424-8
  The tower, the ancient accent, the wintry size. [Antag 426-6
  Both size and solitude or thinks it does, [Orb 443-1
  In the space, leaving an outline of the size [Aug 494-20
  From size, backs larger than the eye, not flesh [Sombre 70-23 P
  Gigantic in everything but size. [Ulysses 101-2 P
SIZES. Of the great sizes of an outer bush [Dove 98-8 P
SIZZLINGS. And scintillant sizzlings such as children like, [Orb
    442-20
SKATING. Be of a man skating, a woman dancing, a woman [Of Mod
    240-21
SKELETON. This skeleton had a daughter and that, a son. [Norfolk
    111-7
  Amen to thought, our singular skeleton, [Montra 260-19
  So that the skeleton in the moonlight sings, [Montra 261-8
  The salty skeleton must dance because [Montra 261-13
  The skeleton said it is a question of [Montra 262-10
  Flesh on the bones. The skeleton throwing [Hero 278-15
  Tap skeleton drums inaudibly. [Dutch 290-7
  Or Aristotle's skeleton. Let him hang out [Less 327-13
  Of the skeleton of the ether, the total [Orb 443-19
  The checkered squares, the skeleton of repose, [Bouquet 450-7
  They keep to the paths of the skeleton architect [Duck 62-10 P
  Of the park. They obey the rules of every skeleton. [Duck 62-11 P
  I wonder, have I lived a skeleton's life, [Warmth 89-17 P

A skeleton out of its cabinet. Nor am I. [As Leave 116-16 P
I wonder, have I lived a skeleton's life, [As Leave 117-5 P
SKELETONS. Melodious skeletons, for all of last night's music
    [Fish-Scale 160-15
  When spring comes and the skeletons of the hunters [Parochial
    191-19
  In which were yellow, rancid skeletons. [Stan MMO 19-2 P
  Fell falsely on the matchless skeletons, [Old Woman 45-2 P
  The skeletons sit on the wall. They drop [Stan MBG 72-3 P
  About summer, are not what skeletons think about. [As Leave
    117-4 P
SKEPTIC. Some harmonious skeptic soon in a skeptical music [Sad
    Gay 122-15
SKEPTICAL. Some harmonious skeptic soon in a skeptical music [Sad
    Gay 122-15
SKETCH. "Sketch of the Ultimate Politician" [335-title
SKIES. Beyond your chilly chariots, to the skies. [Swans 4-12
  Fresh from discoveries of tidal skies, [C 30-27
  The shadow of his fellows from the skies, [C 37-8
  And over the bare spaces of our skies [Anatomy 108-6
  Under muddy skies. [Mud 147-15
  With the blank skies over England, over France [Martial 238-4
  Afraid of the country angels of those skies, [Page 422-7
  That flows round the earth and through the skies, [Degen 444-14
  And stalk the skies. [Abnormal 24-18 P
  Of his angel through the skies. They might be mud [Burnshaw
    46-21 P
  But not that Salzburg of the skies. It was [Greenest 53-27 P
SKILL. Captain, the man of skill, the expert [Hero 274-1
SKILLFUL. A skillful apprehension and eye proud [Spaniard 35-17 P
SKIMS. Skims the real for its unreal, [Oak 272-15
SKIN. The snake has left its skin upon the floor. [Farewell 117-2
  Of this: that the snake has shed its skin upon [Farewell 117-9
  Flowering over the skin. [Pears 197-2
  They are full of juice and the skin is soft. [Peaches 224-12
  O, skin and spine and hair of you, Ercole, [Extracts 256-18
  Of euphonies, a skin from Nubia, [Hero 274-9
  Intangible arrows quiver and stick in the skin [Holiday 313-9
  Skin flashing to wished-for disappearances [AA 411-11
  And the serpent body flashing without the skin. [AA 411-12
  As if its understanding was brown skin, [Rock 527-13
  See citron-skin.
SKINNED. See: dark-skinned; pallid-skinned.
SKINNY. A skinny sailor peering in the sea-glass. [C 28-13
SKINS. And the egg of the sky are in shells, in walls, in skins
    [Aug 490-9
  There is the same color in the bellies of frogs, in clays,
    withered reeds, skins, wood, sunlight. [Primordia 8-2 P
  Ears, eyes, souls, skins, hair? [Parasol 20-6 P
  Of fear changes the scorpions to skins [Duck 65-10 P
  Concealed in glittering grass, dank reptile skins. [Duck 65-11 P
  See gobbet-skins.
SKIPS. . . . Evening, when the measure skips a beat [Eve Angels
    137-26
  He skips the journalism of subjects, seeks out [NH 474-11
SKIRT. Like a dancer's skirt, flung round and settling down.
    [Woman Had 81-18 P
SKITTERS. We think as wind skitters on a pond in a field [Look
    518-24
SKREAK. The skreak and skritter of evening gone [Autumn 160-1
SKREAKING. Some skreaking and skrittering residuum, [Autumn 160-10
SKRITTER. The skreak and skritter of evening gone [Autumn 160-1
SKRITTERING. Some skreaking and skrittering residuum, [Autumn
    160-10
SKULL. An apple serves as well as any skull [Monocle 14-16
  The softest word went gurrituck in his skull. [Norfolk 111-9
  Than the thought that once was native to the skull; [Burnshaw
    49-18 P
SKULLS. Of what, like skulls, comes rotting back to ground. [Mono-
    cle 14-19
  Is there any secret in skulls, [Circulat 150-1
  The cattle skulls in the woods? [Circulat 150-2
  Yet the light fell falsely on the marble skulls, [Old Woman
    44-30 P
SKY. The laughing sky will see the two of us [Monocle 16-10
  A blue pigeon it is, that circles the blue sky, [Monocle 17-18
  As sullen as the sky, was swallowed up [C 32-20
  When the sky is blue. The blue infected will. [C 40-18
  With a blubber of tom-toms harrowing the sky? [C 41-13
  Monotonous earth and dark blue sky. [Vincentine 52-12
  The sky is a blue gum streaked with rose. The trees are black.
    [Banal 62-12
  And who does not seek the sky unfuzzed, soaring to the princox?
    [Banal 63-5
  Out of his cloud and from his sky. [Cuban 64-19
  The sky will be much friendlier then than now, [Sunday 68-8
  Hang always heavy in that perfect sky, [Sunday 69-15
  Out of their blood, returning to the sky; [Sunday 70-5
  And, in the isolation of the sky, [Sunday 70-25
  Up the sky. [Cortege 80-9

They are bearing his body into the sky. [Cortege 80-10
In a place in the sky. [Cortege 81-6
Statue against a Clear Sky [NE Verses 105-title 9
Statue against a Cloudy Sky [NE Verses 105-title 10
She sees a barer sky that does not bend. [Anatomy 108-7
Falls from that fatal and that barer sky, [Anatomy 108-17
That passed beyond us through the narrow sky. [Medit 124-6
Out of the morning sky. [Pascagoula 126-12
If it was only the outer voice of sky [Key W 129-12
Of sky and sea. [Key W 129-22
The sky acutest at its vanishing. [Key W 129-24
Falling, far off, from sky to land, [Mud 148-7
More leanly shining from a lankier sky. [Anglais 149-3
A little later when the sky is black. [Nigger 156-14
Beyond our gate and the windy sky [Postcard 159-9
The vivid, florid, turgid sky, [MBG 169-1
A thousand are radiant in the sky. [MBG 172-10
Cloud's red, earth feeling, sky that thinks? [MBG 177-4
In the museum of the sky. The cock [MBG 182-18
The buildings pose in the sky [Add 198-12
Flowing above the rocks, flowing over the sky, [Loaf 200-4
As if the sky was a current that bore them along, [Loaf 200-5
You see the moon rise in the empty sky. [Dump 202-25
Could have stood up sharply in the sky. [Weak Mind 212-20
The sky is no longer a junk-shop, [Dezem 218-2
Moving round the sky and singing [Dezem 218-10
The sky would be full of bodies like wood. [Thunder 220-17
Threw its contorted strength around the sky. [Sleight 222-8
Like a noble figure, out of the sky, [Candle 223-4
The sky, half porcelain, preferring that [Cuisine 228-6
Beneath summer and the sky [Scavoir 231-10
The sky is too blue, the earth too wide. [Scavoir 231-13
The sky with the radiantiana [Vari 234-15
Only this evening I saw again low in the sky [Martial 237-10
The sky was blue. He wanted imperceptible air. [Landsc 241-13
The red bird most and the strongest sky-- [Adequacy 244-14
And jealous grandeurs of sun and sky [Vase 246-11
The sea is so many written words; the sky [Extracts 252-10
Half sun, half thinking of the sun; half sky, [Extracts 257-2
Half desire for indifference about the sky. [Extracts 257-3
The rain falls. The sky [Metamorph 266-4
When the grand mechanics of earth and sky were near, [Contra II
    270-2
The slightly brighter sky, the melting clouds, [Motive 288-7
It is deep January. The sky is hard. [Possum 294-7
Of sky, of sea, large earth, large air. It is [Choc 296-10
Last night at the end of night and in the sky, [Choc 301-19
The pulling into the sky and the setting there [Repet 308-23
And pathetic magnificences dry in the sky. [Repet 310-4
To find for himself his earth, his sky, his sea. [Holiday 312-12
It is pain that is indifferent to the sky [EM 315-4
This is the sky divested of its fountains. [EM 321-2
As an element; to the sky, as an element. [Wild 328-17
Like earth and sky. Then he became nothing else [Wild 329-1
Besides, when the sky is so blue, things sing themselves,
    [Debris 338-10
Sprinklings of bright particulars from the sky. [Descrip 344-6
Potter in the summer sky. [Analysis 348-3
But if they are of sea, earth, sky--water [Two V 355-8
The old brown hen and the old blue sky, [Silent 359-5
The chain of the turquoise hen and sky [Silent 359-16
In the sky, an imagined, wooden chair [Human 363-9
Than creatures, of the sky between the banks, [Lot 371-14
Trace the gold sun about the whitened sky [Cred 373-6
Of sapphires flashing from the central sky, [Cred 375-24
The sky. It is the visible announced, [Cred 376-17
Of blue and yellow, sky and sun, belted [Cred 378-1
And sky, between thought and day and night. It is [NSF 407-5
Eyes open and fix on us in every sky. [AA 411-15
Or of winter sky, from horizon to horizon. [AA 412-14
In the sky, as crown and diamond cabala? [AA 417-15
To it"? He beheld the order of the northern sky. [Bad Time
    426-11
Sharp in the ice shadow of the sky, [Celle 438-12
Until the used-to earth and sky, and the tree [Orb 411-12
And they: these men, and earth and sky, inform [Orb 441-15
For whom no blue in the sky prevents them, as [Bouquet 449-4
The sky was blue beyond the vaultiest phrase. [What We 459-12
And one from central earth to central sky [NH 469-1
The most ancient light in the most ancient sky, [NH 481-18
It took all day to quieten the sky [NH 482-20
And alike, a point of the earth [NH 483-8
The wateriness of green wet in the sky. [NH 484-11
In mud under ponds, where the sky used to be reflected. [NH
    487-15
And the egg of the sky are in shells, in walls, in skins [Aug
    490-9
From the spun sky and the high and deadly view, [Aug 493-10
Against the trees and then against the sky [Aug 494-12
The sky seemed so small that winter day, [Two Illus 513-1

The way the earliest single light in the evening sky, in spring,
  [Prol 517-8
In the tumult of integrations out of the sky, [Look 518-12
Look in the terrible mirror of the sky [Blanche 10-1 P
Look in the terrible mirror of the sky. [Blanche 10-5 P
Look in the terrible mirror of the sky. [Blanche 10-9 P
Embossings of the sky. [Archi 18-8 P
The new spring tumble in the sky. [Sat Night 27-19 P
Gray grass and green-gray sky? [Table 40-6 P
The gardener searches earth and sky [Room Gard 41-7 P
The sky above the plaza widening [Old Woman 43-6 P
If the sky that followed, smaller than the night, [Old Woman
  45-6 P
The help of any wind or any sky: [Burnshaw 49-20 P
This time, like damsels captured by the sky, [Burnshaw 51-17 P
The horses are a part of a northern sky [Greenest 54-28 P
A penny sun in a tinsel sky, unrhymed, [Duck 61-7 P
A mass overtaken by the blackest sky, [Sombre 69-4 P
The oranges glitter as part of the sky, [Stan MBG 72-13 P
In the central of earth or sky or air or thought, [Conversat
  108-19 P
6. White sky, pink sun, trees on a distant peak. [Someone 86-9 A
Involving the four corners of the sky, [Ideal 88-4 A
SKY-BLUE. You saw the eye-blue, sky-blue, eye-blue, and the
  powdered ears [Grotesque 74-15 P
SKYEY. Trinket pasticcio, flaunting skyey sheets, [C 40-1
SKY-SHADES. Of sea-shades and sky-shades, [Tea 113-2
SKY-SIDES. Sky-sides of gold [Mud 148-1
SKY-WIDE. On a blue island in a sky-wide water [NSF 393-1
SLACK. The torment of fastidious thought grew slack, [C 37-21
SLANTS. That was buttressed by blue slants [Public Sq 108-21
  The chimney is fifty years old and slants to one side. [Plain
  502-18
SLAP. Ubiquitous concussion, slap and sigh, [C 28-20
SLAPPED. A city slapped up like a chest of tools, [NH 478-20
  Sniffed her and slapped heavy hands [Lulu G 26-11 P
  White slapped on white, majestic, marble heads, [Burnshaw 49-13 P
SLASH. A slash of angular blacks [Public Sq 108-19
  A slash and the edifice fell, [Public Sq 109-1
SLATE. The basic slate, the universal hue. [Monocle 15-9
  Through all its purples to the final slate, [Pharynx 96-11
  Red-emerald, red-slitted-blue, a face of slate, [NSF 400-6
SLATTED. And bangles and slatted eyes. [Bananas 54-16
  See black-slatted.
SLATTERN. The heart in slattern pinnacles, the clouds, [Duck 61-10P
SLAUGHTER. In slaughter; or if to match its furious wit [Sombre
  69-6 P
SLAUGHTERED. Now in midsummer come and all fools slaughtered [Cred
  372-4
SLAVERED. Of barbarous tongue, slavered and panting halves [AA
  415-18
SLAVES. Of sun and slaves, breeding and death, [Joost 46-21
  Loosing black slaves to make black infantry, [Greenest 56-9 P
SLAY. The angels come, armed, gloriously to slay [Greenest 55-28 P
SLEEK. Of blue, blue sleek with a hundred chins, [MBG 172-7
  Disentangled him from sleek ensolacings. [EM 322-8
  It is a cat of a sleek transparency [NH 473-1
  Sleek in a natural nakedness, [Hermit 505-14
  An eye too sleek, [Coroner 30-7 P
SLEEKLY. Sleekly the serpent would draw himself across. [Greenest
  54-27 P
SLEEP. Do you come dripping in your hair from sleep? [Monocle
  14-11
  Before they sleep! [Homunculus 26-16
  That wakefulness or meditating sleep, [C 33-23
  Of dreamers buried in our sleep, and not [C 39-27
  And covered him and his congenial sleep. [C 42-8
  Marvelling sometimes at the shaken sleep. [C 44-19
  In sleep may never meet another thought [Canna 55-5
  In the midst of sleep?" [Peacocks 58-8
  As sleep falls [Peacocks 58-25
  Of the silence, wide sleep and solitude [Curtains 62-6
  While he imagined humming sounds and sleep. [Babies 77-6
  And sleep with one eye watching the stars fall [Two Figures
  86-11
  The one obscured by sleep? [Watermelon 89-3
  Beyond revelries of sleep, [Watermelon 89-9
  Stirring no poet in his sleep, and tolls [Pharynx 96-7
  In the distances of sleep? [Roaring 113-6
  Or to sleep or just to lie there still, [Adieu 128-4
  Is rest and silence spreading into sleep. [Eve Angels 137-25
  Speak and the sleepers in their sleep shall move, [Havana 145-1
  I am tired. Sleep for me, heaven over the hill. [Nigger 150-16
  Day is desire and night is sleep. [MBG 167-7
  Will claw sleep. Morning is not sun, [MBG 182-19
  Our bed and we shall sleep by night. [MBG 184-3
  God and all angels sing the world to sleep, [Men Fall 187-9
  The bells grow longer. This is not sleep. This is desire. [Men
  Fall 187-14
  And beggars dropping to sleep, [Add 198-9

Was a place, strong place, in which to sleep. [Nightgown 214-18
Pine-figures bringing sleep to sleep. [Vari 235-12
It is safe to sleep to a sound that time brings back. [Phenom
  286-12
In an ignorance of sleep with nothing won. [Dutch 291-26
Beyond the sleep of those that did not know, [Choc 299-10
Now, time stands still. He came from out of sleep. [Choc 299-12
But of nothing, trash of sleep that will disappear [Choc 300-18
Afflicted sleep, too much the syllables [EM 314-20
Form mystical convolutions in the sleep [EM 319-9
For the soldier of time, it breathes a summer sleep, [EM 319-14
Or the phosphored sleep in which he walks abroad [EM 320-16
To sleep in that bed for its disorder, talking of ghostly [Bed
  327-3
Sequences that would be sleep and ting-tang tossing, so that
  [Bed 327-4
And after a while, when Ha-eé-me has gone to sleep. [Jouga
  337-14
Or sleep. It was a queen that made it seem [Descrip 339-7
Lie lengthwise like the cloud of sleep, not quite [Two V 354-4
Sleep deep, good eel, in your perverse marine. [Two V 354-18
At last the good life came, good sleep, bright fruit, [Good
  Man 364-7
As morning throws off stale moonlight and shabby sleep. [NSF
  382-12
We more than awaken, sit on the edge of sleep, [NSF 386-19
Of death in memory's dream? Is spring a sleep? [NSF 391-3
In sleep its natural form. It was enough [NSF 399-12
Demanded of sleep, in the excitements of silence [NSF 402-17
Only the unmuddled self of sleep, for them. [NSF 402-18
When at long midnight the Canon came to sleep [NSF 402-19
And curtains like a naive pretence of sleep. [AA 415-15
As if, awake, we lay in the quiet of sleep, [AA 418-24
This drama that we live--We lay sticky with sleep. [AA 419-14
Was like a sleep. The sea was a sea he dreamed. [Page 422-2
Two forms move among the dead, high sleep [Owl 431-13
There sleep the brother is the father, too, [Owl 432-10
Of sleep, the whiteness folded into less, [Owl 433-8
After the wind has passed. Sleep realized [Owl 433-19
Of sleep, the accomplished, the fulfilling air. [Owl 433-24
This was peace after death, the brother of sleep, [Owl 434-7
It is a child that sings itself to sleep, [Owl 436-7
And calling like the long echoes in long sleep, [Luther 461-17
By the obese opiates of sleep. Plain men in plain towns [NH
  467-20
Silently it heaves its youthful sleep from the sea-- [NH 476-22
Lighted by space, big over those that sleep, [NH 482-5
Of the single future of night, the single sleep, [NH 482-6
Nor are you now, in this wakefulness inside a sleep. [Slug
  522-18
Night's hymn of the rock, as in a vivid sleep. [Rock 528-21
Of sleep's faded papier-mâché . . . [Not Ideas 534-11
Be free to sleep there sounder, for the plough [Burnshaw 48-1 P
Appear to sleep within a sleeping air, [Burnshaw 50-19 P
Even in sleep, deep in the grass of sleep, [Greenest 54-31 P
There sleep and waking fill with jaguar-men [Greenest 55-2 P
Their beds, their faces drawn in distant sleep. [Sombre 68-23 P
That changed in sleep. It is, it is, let be [Sombre 71-15 P
This is a thing to twang a philosopher's sleep, [Bship 79-31 P
By feeling the like of thought in sleep, [Desire 85-12 P
For daylight and too near for sleep. [Dove 98-15 P
Of the wind, of the wind as it deepens, and late sleep, [Art
  Pop 113-5 P
A perception of sleep, more powerful [Bus 116-8 P
Than a power of sleep, a clearness emerging [Bus 116-9 P
Whose shining is the intelligence of our sleep. [Someone 84-11 A
SLEEPERS. For sleepers halfway waking. He perceived [C 31-16
  And quieting dreams in the sleepers in darkness-- [Lunar 107-11
  Speak and the sleepers in their sleep shall move, [Havana 145-1
  Moving among the sleepers, the men, [Candle 223-5
  Time's fortune near, the sleepless sleepers moved [Duck 61-27 P
  Against the sleepers to re-create for them, [Sombre 69-7 P
SLEEPIEST. Drowsing in summer's sleepiest horn. [Cuban 65-6
SLEEPINESS. Weight him, weight, weight him with the sleepiness of
  the moon. [Madame 507-5
SLEEPING. "Hibiscus on the Sleeping Shores" [22-title
  In sleeping air. [Woman Song 360-12
  They came. But, brown, the ice-bear sleeping in ice-month [Study
  II 464-8
  The two worlds are asleep, are sleeping, now. [Old Man 501-1
  Appear to sleep within a sleeping air, [Burnshaw 50-19 P
  When I was sleeping, nor by day, [Desire 85-8 P
SLEEPLESS. As the sleepless! [Peacocks 58-2
  The bauble of the sleepless nor a word [Havana 144-4
  Sleepless, inhales his proper air, and rests. [Cred 373-24
  Time's fortune near, the sleepless sleepers moved [Duck 61-27 P
SLEEPLESSLY. Our earthly mothers waiting, sleeplessly. [Sunday
  69-27
SLEEPS. His thought sleeps not. Yet thought that wakes [Canna 55-4
  How long and late the pheasant sleeps . . . [MBG 182-9

The lion sleeps in the sun. [Destructive 193-4
The form on the pillow humming while one sleeps, [Beard 247-23
Sleeps in the sun no thing recalling. [Hero 278-18
Sleeps by his basket. He snores. His bloated breath [Feo 333-19
At summer thunder and sleeps through winter snow. [NSF 384-16
SLEEPY. Pardie! Summer is like a fat beast, sleepy in mildew,
    [Banal 62-15
Sometimes at sleepy mid-days it succeeds, [Extracts 257-20
Until sight wakens the sleepy eye [Red Fern 365-15
From the sleepy bosom of the real, re-creates, [NH 481-20
SLEEVE. From which no soft sleeve relieves us. [Dutch 291-4
O exhalation, O fling without a sleeve [Owl 435-19
To weave a shadow's leg or sleeve, a scrawl [What We 459-18
SLEEVES. Its empty sleeves; and yet its mimic motion [Key W 128-14
SLEIGHT-OF-HAND. "The Sense of the Sleight-of-Hand Man" [222-title
SLEIGHTS. Came to be sleights of sails [Infanta 7-18
SLENDER. Stockholm slender in a slender light, [Botanist 1 135-7
SLENDEREST. At home, a bit like the slenderest courtesan. [NE
    Verses 106-6
SLEPT. And slept. [Earthy 3-20
To the floor. I slept. [Weak Mind 212-15
The villages slept as the capable man went down, [Uruguay 249-25
The sun shone and the dog barked and the baby slept. [Contra II
    270-5
As he slept. He woke in a metaphor: this was [Pure 331-23
Yet when her children slept, his sister herself [NSF 402-16
SLICE. To feast . . . Slice the mango, Naaman, and dress it
    [Phenom 286-14
SLICK. Confront you, hoo-ing the slick trombones, [MBG 170-16
Story . . . The sound of that slick sonata, [Phenom 286-18
SLICKENED. His manner slickened them. He milled [News 264-13
SLICK-EYED. Fetched by such slick-eyed nymphs, this essential
    gold, [Orb 440-6
SLID. Slid from his continent by slow recess [C 40-15
Slid over the western cataract, yet one, [Beard 247-13
Into that native shield she slid, [Celle 438-17
SLIDES. See sun-slides.
SLIDING. Adorned with cryptic stones and sliding shines, [Owl
    434-10
SLIGHT. That slight transcendence to the dirty sail, [Sailing
    121-5
Slight as it is, disturbs me. I did not know [Peaches 224-18
And of the brooding mind, fixed but for a slight [Choc 297-17
Moving so that the foot-falls are slight and almost nothing.
    [Jouga 337-12
Are a slight part of death. [Burghers 362-5
It must change from destiny to slight caprice. [AA 417-23
Slight gestures that could rend the palpable ice, [Page 423-2
By such slight genii in such pale air. [Orb 440-8
By an access of color, a new and unobserved, slight dithering,
    [Prol 517-2
With slight, prismatic reeks not recollected, [Theatre 91-11 P
That could come in a slight lurching of the scene, [Nuns 92-10 P
The slight incipiencies, of which the form, [Someone 87-8 A
SLIGHTEST. Suspended in air, the slightest crown [Couch 295-11
Apposites, to the slightest edge, of the whole [Someone 86-19 A
SLIGHTLY. Themselves, the slightly unjust drawing that is [Ex-
    tracts 254-23
Sways slightly and the pinnacles frisson. [Hero 275-3
The slightly brighter sky, the melting clouds, [Motive 288-7
When he moved so slightly to make sure of sun, [AA 411-21
Breathe slightly, slightly move or seem to move [Bouquet 450-8
And slightly detestable operandum, free [Look 517-19
From cold, slightly irised, slightly bedazzled, [Bus 116-10 P
SLIM. When radiance came running down, slim through the bareness.
    [Banal 63-2
SLIME. My North is leafless and lies in a wintry slime [Farewell
    118-11
Both of men and clouds, a slime of men in crowds. [Farewell
    118-12
SLIMMEST. That beat out slimmest edges in the ear, [Greenest 56-30P
SLIPPER. In slipper green. [Depression 63-18
SLIPPERS. In their embroidered slippers, touch your spleen? [Polish
    Aunt 84-5
SLIPS. How soon the silver fades in the dust! How soon the black
    figure slips from the wrinkled sheet! [Plough-Boy 6-8 P
SLITHERING. Against your sides, then shoving and slithering,
    [Farewell 118-15
SLITS. Like slits across a space, a place [Dove 98-11 P
SLITTED. See red-slitted-blue.
SLOPING. Regard now the sloping, mountainous rocks [Loaf 199-16
Under the sun-slides of a sloping mountain; [Aug 489-11
SLOPPED. The bouquet has slopped over the edge and lies on the
    floor. [Bouquet 453-3
SLOPPING. The slopping of the sea grew still one night [Sea Surf
    98-13
The slopping of the sea grew still one night. [Sea Surf 99-17
The slopping of the sea grew still one night [Sea Surf 100-11
The night-long slopping of the sea grew still. [Sea Surf 101-5
Night stilled the slopping of the sea. The day [Sea Surf 101-23

There was the cat slopping its milk all day, [Rabbit K 209-4
SLOPS. Now, every muscle slops away. [Hartford 227-9
SLOTS. The channel slots of rain, the red-rose-red [NSF 400-8
SLOUCH. The slouch of his body and his look were not [Descrip
    343-1
SLOUCHING. His slouching pantaloons, beyond the town, [NSF 389-6
SLOUCHINGS. Between the slouchings of a gunman and a lover, [Moon-
    light 531-15
SLOUGH. Another bodiless for the body's slough? [AA 411-6
SLOVENLY. It made the slovenly wilderness [Jar 76-7
SLOW. Slid from his continent by slow recess [C 40-15
SLOW-FOOT. And beyond the days, beyond the slow-foot litters
    [Repet 309-1
SLOWLY. The mules that angels ride come slowly down [Monocle 15-18
Feebly, slowly, depending upon them; [Lunar 107-4
Fell slowly as when at night [Public Sq 109-5
Slowly the ivy on the stones [MBG 170-21
Slowly, one man, savager than the rest, [Thunder 220-5
And, like an insatiable actor, slowly and [Of Mod 240-6
They go, go slowly, but they go. [Poesie 302-14
He might slowly forget. It is more difficult to evade [Bed 327-5
Slowly, to the look of a swarthy name. [Countryman 429-8
Slowly the room grows dark. It is odd about [Novel 458-19
Slowly and sweetly. [Agenda 42-12 P
Slowly submerging in flatness disappeared. [Old Woman 45-5 P
From the whirling, slowly and by trial; or fear [Burnshaw 51-7 P
Winding and waving, slowly, waving in air, [Greenest 55-14 P
That the peaches are slowly ripening. [Memo 89-10 P
The wind moves slowly in the branches. [Of Mere 118-5 P
SLOWLY-FALLING. His slowly-falling round [Pascagoula 126-15
SLUGGISH. "Long and Sluggish Lines" [522-title
SLUM. Moisture and heat have swollen the garden into a slum of
    bloom. [Banal 62-14
SLUMBER. Let Phoebus slumber and die in autumn umber, [NSF 381-9
SLUMP. Anabasis or slump, ascent or chute, [C 43-21
SLUMPING. And lank, rising and slumping from a sea [C 34-5
SLUNG. Supporting heavy cables, slung [MBG 181-22
Slung over my shoulder? [Soldat 12-21 P
SLUSHES. See sea-slushes.
SLY. Might help the blind, not him, serenely sly. [C 39-20
Nod and look a little sly. [Orangeade 103-16
And you, black Sly, [Pascagoula 126-10
SMACK. And the fiddles smack, the horns yahoo, the flutes [Bship
    79-28 P
SMACKING. Smacking their muzzy bellies in parade, [High-Toned
    59-16
SMACKS. The green smacks in the eye, the dew in the green [Dump
    202-5
Smacks like fresh water in a can, like the sea [Dump 202-6
SMALL. As small as fish-eggs. [Plot Giant 7-1
It made you seem so small and lean [Vincentine 52-13
It was a small part of the pantomime. [Thirteen 93-2
Before the colors deepened and grew small. [Anglais 149-15
A small relation expanding like the shade [Connois 215-19
Small oblivion, [Adequacy 243-20
And small, a constant fellow of destiny, [EM 315-22
Being small, inscribes ferocious alphabets, [Pure 332-23
That constantly sparkled their small gold? The town [Liadoff
    346-12
Under Tinicum or small Cohansey, [New Set 353-5
These are the small townsmen of death, [Burghers 362-11
Fulfilling his meditations, great and small. [AA 420-21
And shone. And a small cabin build there. [Page 421-16
Of men growing small in the distances of space, [Rome 508-3
The veritable small, so that each of us [Rome 509-11
The sky seemed so small that winter day, [Two Illus 513-1
In which we rest and, for small reason, think [Final 524-2
They cock small ears, more glistening and pale [Soldat 14-2 P
Small bees of spring, sniffing the coldest buds [Duck 65-7 P
A small howling of the dove [Dove 97-17 P
Makes this small howling, like a thought [Dove 98-4 P
The small luxuriations that portend [Someone 87-6 A
SMALLER. The mind is smaller than the eye. [Fish-Scale 161-4
Singing, with smaller and still smaller sound, [Rome 508-4
If the sky that followed, smaller than the night, [Old Woman
    45-6 P
And through the air. The smaller ones [Dinner 110-2 P
SMALLEST. These nebulous brilliancies in the smallest look [EM
    317-13
The smallest lamp, which added its puissant flick, to which he
    gave [Prol 517-3
SMALLS. Too exactly labelled, a large among the smalls [Orb 443-11
SMART. Was not indifferent to smart detail. [C 38-30
SMATTER. Mouthing its constant smatter throughout space [Montra
    263-19
SMEARED. Vermilion smeared over green, arranged for show. [Grapes
    110-14
Smeared with the gold of the opulent sun. [Postcard 159-21
Smeared, smoked, and drunken of thin potencies, [Page 422-28
SMEARS. Aux Crinolines, smears out mad mountains. [Extracts 257-29

Before, before. Blood smears the oaks. [Contra I 267-3
SMELL. Made sharp air sharper by their smell [Postcard 159-2
  I touch them and smell them. Who speaks? [Peaches 224-2
  To hear, to touch, to taste, to smell, that's now, [Arcades
    225-7
  Feel the wind of it, smell the dust of it? [Arcades 225-9
  And rain, the blood-rose living in its smell, [Extracts 252-5
  The sad smell of the lilacs--one remembered it, [Aug 491-9
  Becomes another murmuring; the smell [Rome 508-19
  What is left has the foreign smell of plaster, [Armor 529-5
  The closed-in smell of hay. A sumac grows [Armor 529-6
SMELLING. Of ether, the other smelling of drink, [MBG 177-10
  See sweet-smelling.
SMELLS. He inhaled the rancid rosin, burly smells [C 36-7
  With a single sense, though he smells clouds, [Arcades 225-21
SMILE. And feel its country gayety and smile [Beginning 428-1
SMILED. Was unforeseen. First Crispin smiled upon [C 44-10
SMILING. Smiling and wetting her lips [Attempt 370-13
SMITH. See John Smith.
SMITING. And smiting the crevasses of the leaves [Sea Surf 101-2
SMOCK. I saw a waxen woman in a smock [Infernale 25-1 P
  (Her pale smock sparkles in a light begun [Infernale 25-9 P
SMOKE. Still moving yet motionless in smoke, still [Hero 273-22
  There remained the smoke of the villages. Their fire [Wild 329-5
  In smoke. The blue petals became [Attempt 370-16
  Wild wedges, as of a volcano's smoke, palm-eyed [AA 416-17
  The vaguest line of smoke (a year ago) [Phases 5-4 P
  See wood-smoke.
SMOKED. Smeared, smoked, and drunken of thin potencies [Page 422-28
SMOKE-DRIFT. Nor the smoke-drift of puffed-out heroes, nor human
    cry. [Course 96-20 P
SMOKES. The boatman goes humming. He smokes a cigar [Stan MBG
    72-11 P
SMOKING. Smoking through green and smoking blue. [On Road 203-20
SMOKY. The thinking of god is smoky dew. [MBG 168-5
  Bastard chateaux and smoky demoiselles. [Montra 263-7
SMOOTH. The grackles crack their throats of bone in the smooth air.
    [Banal 62-13
  Much rough-end being to smooth Paradise, [Luther 461-11
  The space beneath it still, a smooth domain, [Old Woman 46-5 P
SMOOTHES. A woman smoothes her forehead with her hand [EM 319-17
SMOOTHLY. Perceived: the white seen smoothly argentine [Bouquet
    449-14
SMOTHER. To smother the wry spirit's misery. [News 265-7
SMOTHERED. Until his body smothered him, until [Liadoff 347-11
SMUTTED. This mangled, smutted semi-world hacked out [Ghosts 119-8
SNAILS. Of snails, musician of pears, principium [C 27-9
SNAKE. The snake has left its skin upon the floor. [Farewell 117-2
  Of this: that the snake has shed its skin upon [Farewell 117-9
  As the fox and snake do. It is a brave affair. [NSF 403-17
SNAKES. Stopping, on voyage, in a land of snakes, [C 31-7
  "Frogs Eat Butterflies. Snakes Eat Frogs. Hogs Eat Snakes. Men
    Eat Hogs" [78-title
  Snakes and gold and lice, [On Road 204-7
SNARLING. Are snarling [Mud 147-14
  Snarling in him for discovery as his attentions spread, [Prol
    516-17
SNARLS. The mind snarls. [Mud 148-3
  The ponderous cinnamon, snarls in his mountain [NSF 384-15
SNATCH. Babyishness of forsythia, a snatch of belief, [Slug 522-13
SNEERING. Celestial sneering boisterously. Crispin [C 29-22
SNEERS. Of sneers, the fugues commencing at the toes [Extracts
    253-21
SNIFFED. Sniffed her and slapped heavy hands [Lulu G 26-11 P
SNIFFING. Small bees of spring, sniffing the coldest buds [Duck
    65-7 P
SNIPS. To be in scale, unless virtue cuts him, snips [Orb 442-26
SNOOD. Unsnack your snood, madanna, for the stars [Myrrh 349-13
  The magnum wreath of summer, time's autumn snood, [Rock 526-21
SNORES. Sleeps by his basket. He snores. His bloated breath [Feo
    333-19
SNORT. A snort across the silverware, [Grotesque 75-16 P
SNOUTS. And on silentious porpoises, whose snouts [C 27-19
  Their snouts. [Burnshaw 47-13 P
SNOW. "The Snow Man" [9-title
  Of the pine-trees crusted with snow; [Snow Man 9-23
  For the listener, who listens in the snow, [Snow Man 10-10
  Frail as April snow; [Pourtraicte 21-15
  Passions of rain, or moods in falling snow; [Sunday 67-20
  It crawls over the edges of the snow. [Tattoo 81-11
  And in the edges of the snow. [Tattoo 81-21
  And it was going to snow. [Thirteen 95-3
  Mildew of summer and the deepening snow [Pharynx 96-2
  The snow is falling. [Mozart 132-7
  The snow is falling [Mozart 132-20
  "Snow and Stars" [133-title
  This robe of snow and winter stars, [Snow Stars 133-4
  Serve the rouged fruits in early snow. [Nigger 153-1
  As an autumn ancient underneath the snow, [Nigger 154-2
  But the wise man avenges by building his city in snow. [Nigger

158-13
  Its wings spread wide to rain and snow, [MBG 166-8
  Of the undertaker's song in the snow [MBG 177-12
  The sea is in the falling snow. [MBG 179-16
  Reflecting snow. A newly-fallen snow [Poems Clim 193-10
  The rocks not even touched by snow, [Loaf 199-20
  Where do you lie, beneath snow, [Bagatelles 213-2
  It is not the snow that is the quill, the page. [Bottle 239-13
  It had been cold since December. Snow fell, first, [Extracts
    255-1
  Snow under the trees and on the northern rocks, [Extracts 255-15
  Of sanctimonious mountains high in snow, [Montra 263-3
  The snow hangs heavily on the rocks, brought [Hero 273-5
  By a wind that seeks out shelter from snow. Thus [Hero 273-6
  Snow sparkles like eyesight falling to earth, [Possum 294-4
  And lit the snow to a light congenial [Choc 297-1
  But resting on me, thinking in my snow, [Choc 301-5
  They walk in mist and rain and snow [Poesie 302-13
  Things floating like the first hundred flakes of snow [Man Car
    351-3
  Snow glistens in its instant in the air, [Pieces 351-12
  And snow. The theatre is spinning round, [Chaos 357-16
  Fetched up with snow that never falls to earth? [Belly 367-6
  At summer thunder and sleeps through winter snow. [NSF 384-16
  Even of earth, even of sight, in snow, [AA 417-13
  Like the snow before it softened [Celle 438-6
  March . . . Someone has walked across the snow, [Vacancy 511-4
  As, for example, a world in which, like snow, [Quiet 523-4
  No longer a battered panache above snow . . . [Not Ideas 534-8
  Walking in the snow, [Primordia 7-12 P
  In the morning in the blue snow [An Gaiety 32-15 P
  And joy of snow and snow. [An Gaiety 33-7 P
  From snow, and would return again to snow, [Greenest 57-26 P
  The spontaneities of rain or snow [Sombre 67-31 P
  Are dissolved as in an infancy of blue snow. [Discov 95-11 P
  It is still full of icy shades and shapen snow. [Course 96-12 P
  A light snow, like frost, has fallen during the night. [Bus
    116-1 P
  Now, here, the snow I had forgotten becomes [As Leave 117-8 P
SNOW-BRED. And saw the blossoms, snow-bred pink and white, [Good
    Bad 33-17 P
SNOWING. It was snowing [Thirteen 95-2
SNOWS. Blessed, whose beard is cloak against the snows. [NE Verses
    105-6
SNOWY. Among twenty snowy mountains, [Thirteen 92-14
  In the room more like a snowy air, [Poems Clim 193-9
  More than a world of white and snowy scents. [Poems Clim 194-3
  Angels tiptoe upon the snowy cones [Greenest 56-1 P
  O buckskin, O crosser of snowy divides, [Duck 61-1 P
SNUFFED. Of growling teeth, and falls at night, snuffed out [NH
    467-19
SNUG. The snug hibernal from that sea and salt, [C 28-3
SO-AND-SO. "So-and-So Reclining on her Couch" [295-title
SOAP. That this bloom is the bloom of soap [Lilacs 48-21
SOAR. And that which in an altitude would soar, [Orb 442-9
SOARING. And who does not seek the sky unfuzzed, soaring to the
    princox? [Banal 63-5
  His being felt the need of soaring, the need [Liadoff 347-12
  Soaring Olympus glitters in the sun. [Infernale 25-12 P
  Still questioning if to crush the soaring stacks, [Sombre 68-31P
SOB. Without the inventions of sorrow or the sob [EM 317-5
  The locust's titter and the turtle's sob. [Sombre 71-1 P
SOBS. With the ferocious chu-chot-chu between, the sobs [Extracts
    253-18
SOCIAL. The return to social nature, once begun, [C 43-20
SOCIETY? Read in the ruins of a new society, [Nigger 153-3
  Now, an image of our society? [MBG 173-3
  Society of the spirit when it is [Repet 309-11
  One man opposing a society [Lytton 38-14 P
  The race, the nation, the state. But society [Bship 79-21 P
  Is a phase. We approach a society [Bship 79-22 P
  Without a society, the politicians [Bship 79-23 P
  Unless society is a mystical mass. [Bship 79-30 P
SOCKS. With socks of lace [Ten O'C 66-8
SOCRATES. The sovereign ghost. As such, the Socrates [C 27-8
SODDEN. Sodden with his melancholy words, [MBG 170-3
SOFA. And on a comfortable sofa dreamed. [Cuban 65-3
  He might sit on a sofa on a balcony [Landsc 243-2
SOFT. They are full of juice and the skin is soft. [Peaches 224-12
  Who was the musician, fatly soft [Jumbo 269-4
  Loud, general, large, fat, soft [Jumbo 269-11
  From which no soft sleeve relieves us. [Dutch 291-4
  These lovers waiting in the soft dry grass. [Cred 372-18
  In an abandoned spot. Soft, civil bird, [Cred 377-12
  So soft, so civil, and you make a sound, [Cred 377-19
  The soft hands are a motion not a touch. [AA 413-16
  Is soft in three-four cornered fragrances [NH 470-19
  By the hand of desire, faint, sensitive, the soft [NH 476-14
  How soft the grass on which the desired [Hermit 505-11
SOFTENED. Like the snow before it softened [Celle 438-6

SOFTEST. The softest word went gurrituck in his skull. [Norfolk
  111-9
  Midsummer love and softest silences, [Montra 261-16
  Who most fecundly assuaged him, the softest [EM 321-14
  That were never wholly still. The softest woman, [EM 321-28
SOFT-FOOTED. Become the soft-footed phantom, the irrational [NSF
  406-18
SOFTLY. Softly let all true sympathizers come, [EM 317-4
  Speak softly, to begin with, in the eaves. [Beginning 428-8
  Softly she piped among the suns [Song Fixed 519-21
  How softly the sheet falls to the ground! [Plough-Boy 6-9 P
SOIL. Nota: man is the intelligence of his soil, [C 27-7
  Nota: his soil is man's intelligence. [C 36-24
  Little by little, as if the suzerain soil [C 40-23
  "O Florida, Venereal Soil" [47-title
  Florida, venereal soil, [Venereal 47-9
  In the soil and rest. Conceive that marble men [Burnshaw 52-1 P
SOILED. A design, a marble soiled by pigeons? [Hero 278-23
SOILS. Spontaneously watering their gritty soils. [Monocle 16-25
SOJOURN. "Banal Sojourn" [62-title
SOLACE. Solace itself in peevish birds? Is it peace, [Dump 203-4
  Sister and solace, brother and delight. [NSF 392-24
  Its brightness burned the way good solace seethes. [Owl 434-6
  In solace-- [Soldat 12-3 P
  In the days when the mood of love will be swarming for solace
    and sink deeply into the thin stuff of being, [Piano 22-8 P
SOLACING. Am satisfied without solacing majesty, [NSF 405-2
SOLANGE. Solange, the magnolia to whom I spoke, [News 265-1
  I am Solange, euphonious bane, she said. [News 265-4
  There's a moment in the year, Solange, [News 265-11
SOLAR. The central flaw in the solar morn. [Thought 187-8
  The self of the hero, the solar single, [Hero 280-7
  That comes here in the solar chariot, [Pure 331-17
  To say the solar chariot is junk [Pure 332-6
SOLDAT. "Poems from 'Letters d'un Soldat'" [10-title P
SOLDIER. "The Death of a Soldier" [97-title
  The soldier falls. [Soldier 97-3
  A soldier walks before my door. [Contra I 266-12
  A soldier stalks before my door. [Contra I 267-4
  In a clock-shop . . . Soldier, think, in the darkness, [Hero
    275-15
  The enlarging of the simplest soldier's cry [Choc 298-14
  At the railway station, a soldier steps away, [Repet 308-3
  Nor of time. The departing soldier is as he is, [Repet 308-7
  The soldier seeking his point between the two, [Repet 309-9
  How red the rose that is the soldier's wound, [EM 318-26
  The soldier of time grown deathless in great size. [EM 319-2
  And there the soldier of time has deathless rest. [EM 319-6
  Of time's red soldier deathless on his bed. [EM 319-10
  For the soldier of time, it breathes a summer sleep, [EM 319-14
  And the soldier of time lies calm beneath that stroke. [EM
    319-18
  In the death of a soldier, like the utmost will, [Descrip 341-2
  "A Woman Sings a Song for a Soldier Come Home" [360-title
  The bristling soldier, weather-foxed, who looms [Cred 375-2
  Soldier, there is a war between the mind [NSF 407-4
  The soldier is poor without the poet's lines, [NSF 407-18
  How gladly with proper words the soldier dies, [NSF 408-2
  A car drives up. A soldier, an officer, [Bouquet 452-19
  Common Soldier [Soldat 11-title 1
  If I should fall, as soldier, I know well [Soldat 11-10 P
SOLDIERS. And the waves, the waves were soldiers moving, [Loaf
  200-10
  It was soldiers went marching over the rocks [Loaf 200-13
  No doubt that soldiers had to be marching [Loaf 200-16
  Everywhere the spruce trees bury soldiers: [Vari 234-10
  They could not carry much, as soldiers. [Gigan 289-1
  For soldiers, the new moon stretches twenty feet. [Gigan 289-21
  There were other soldiers, other people, [Dutch 291-22
  The wounds of many soldiers, the wounds of all [EM 318-27
  The soldiers that have fallen, red in blood, [EM 319-1
  Now, soldiers, hear me: mark this very breeze, [Phases 5-12 P
  No soldiers in the scenery, [Clear Day 113-7 P
SOLE. One sole face, like a photograph of fate, [NSF 394-10
  The sole emperor of what they are, [Chile 106-19 P
  Sole, single source and minimum patriarch, [Conversat 108-21 P
SOLEIL. From Havre to Hartford, Master Soleil, [Hartford 226-5
SOLEMN. But it was solemn, [Winter B 141-3
  Of chance. Finally, the most solemn burial [Paisant 334-15
  And the solemn pleasures of magnificent space. [AA 416-14
  The solemn sentences, [Aug 490-18
  The bells keep on repeating solemn names [Rome 510-15
  In an Ancient, Solemn Manner [Soldat 11-title 2 P
  No solemn one, nor pale, [Archi 18-12 P
  A solemn voice, not Mr. Burnshaw's says: [Burnshaw 49-3 P
  Were solemn and your gowns were blown and grief [Burnshaw 50-29 P
  Majestic bearers or solemn haulers trapped [Greenest 57-14 P
SOLEMNITY. A dumb sense possesses them in a kind of solemnity. [Old
  Man 501-2
SOLEMNIZE. Now, solemnize the secretive syllables. [AA 420-15

SOLEMNLY. Still touches solemnly with what she was [Aug 496-2
SOLES. The soles of its feet [Six Sig 74-17
SOLID. The suspension, as in solid space, [Couch 295-13
  Of the armies, the solid men, make big the fable. [Choc 301-15
  In solid fire the utmost earth and know [EM 314-12
  Her self in her manner not the solid block, [Pure 332-15
  In which nothing solid is its solid self. [Descrip 345-10
  Of the certain solid, the primary free from doubt, [Man Car 351-2
  Is being of the solid of white, the accomplishment [AA 412-17
  The sea was frozen solid and Hans heard, [Page 421-5
  The solid, but the movable, the moment, [NH 472-1
  Is a solid. It may be a shade that traverses [NH 489-2
  The solid wax from which the warmth dies out? . . [Infernale
    24-22 P
  Lives in a fluid, not on solid rock. [Sombre 68-5 P
  The solid was an age, a period [Sombre 68-6 P
  The cycle of the solid having turned. [Sombre 68-16 P
  It has a clear, a single, a solid form, [Recit 87-11 P
  The solid shape, Aeneas seen, perhaps, [Recit 87-22 P
  The contents of the mind become solid show [Conversat 108-13 P
  Or almost solid seem show--the way a fly bird [Conversat 108-14 P
  There was an insolid billowing of the solid. [Real 111-1 P
SOLIDLY. Staked solidly in a gusty grappling with rocks. [NH 487-21
SOLILOQUY. "Final Soliloquy of the Interior Paramour" [524-title
  In the breathings of this soliloquy, [Ulysses 105-8 P
  In the breathings of that soliloquy, [Presence 106-8 P
SOLITAIRE. "Solitaire under the Oaks" [111-title P
SOLITAIRES. "The Place of the Solitaires" [60-title
  Let the place of the solitaires [Solitaires 60-1
  In the place of the solitaires, [Solitaires 60-12
SOLITARIA. The cry is part. My solitaria [Choc 298-16
SOLITARY. Sparkling, solitary, still, [Venereal 48-9
  For the large, the solitary figure. [Hero 281-5
  The ephebe is solitary in his walk. [NH 474-10
  Recognize his unique and solitary home. [Poem Mt 512-14
  At some gigantic, solitary urn, [Burnshaw 49-4 P
SOLITUDE. It was as if the solitude concealed [C 42-7
  Of the silence, wide sleep and solitude [Curtains 62-6
  Or island solitude, unsponsored, free, [Sunday 70-20
  Making harsh torment of the solitude. [Babies 77-15
  Who found all form and order in solitude, [Sad Gay 121-17
  She measured to the hour its solitude. [Key W 129-25
  There might have been the immense solitude [Chateau 161-13
  The solitude, the barrier, the Pole [Thought 186-6
  It is in this solitude, a syllable, [Possum 294-9
  A consciousness from solitude, inhaled [Choc 298-8
  Yet, under the migrations to solitude, [Wild 329-4
  Signal, a character out of solitude, [Pure 331-4
  Or it denies. An age is solitude [Descrip 340-7
  Revery is a solitude in which [Men Made 356-1
  In solitude the trumpets of solitude [NSF 392-16
  Are not of another solitude resounding; [NSF 392-17
  The color of ice and fire and solitude. [AA 413-3
  "This Solitude of Cataracts" [424-title
  The well-composed in his burnished solitude, [Antag 426-5
  Both size and solitude or thinks it does, [Orb 443-1
  The speech of truth in its true solitude, [Aug 490-20
  In the presence of a solitude of the self, [Aug 494-5
  Of silence, that any solitude of sense [Rome 510-18
  To hear the stroke of one's certain solitude, [Old Woman 44-15 P
  Noble within perfecting solitude, [Greenest 54-4 P
  Like a solitude of the sun, in which the mind [Greenest 54-5 P
  Their need in solitude: that is the need, [Woman Had 82-26 P
  A part of space and solitude, [Ulysses 100-6 P
  And that, in space and solitude, [Presence 105-20 P
SOLITUDES. So far beyond the casual solitudes, [Re-state 146-9
SOLSTICES. The wind attendant on the solstices [Pharynx 96-5
SOLUTION. A challenge to a final solution. [Stan Hero 84-28 P
SOLUTIONS. A few final solutions, like a duet [MBG 177-7
SOLVED. Confusion solved, as in a refrain [MBG 177-18
SOLVENT. Because there is no golden solvent here? [Two V 355-3
SOMBRE. Of sombre pages. [Reader 146-15
  The sombre pages bore no print [Reader 147-10
  Sombre as fir-trees, liquid cats [MBG 178-13
  "Sombre Figuration" [66-title P
SOMBRENESS. The prismatic sombreness of a torrent's wave. [Bouquet
  452-12
SOMBREROS. Rationalists would wear sombreros. [Six Sig 75-13
SOME. A deep up-pouring from some saltier well [Monocle 13-10
  Remained, except some starker, barer self [C 29-16
  Seem things in some procession of the dead, [Sunday 67-6
  The need of some imperishable bliss." [Sunday 68-28
  Some harmonious skeptic soon in a skeptical music [Sad Gay 122-15
  "Some Friends from Pascagoula" [126-title
  Some skreaking and skrittering residuum, [Autumn 160-10
  Some things, niño, some things are like this, [Gala 248-1
  The way some first thing coming into Northern trees [Prol 517-6
  As if some Old Man of the Chimney, sick [Phases 5-6 P
  It seizes a sheet, from the ground, from a bush, as if spread
    there by some wash-woman for the night. [Plough-Boy 6-5 P

And Crispine, the blade reddened by some touch, demanding the
   most from the phrases [Piano 22-6 P
Some merciful divination, you forgive. [Spaniard 34-6 P
At some gigantic, solitary urn, [Burnshaw 49-4 P
Not some outer patron and imaginer. [Conversat 109-15 P
SOMEHOW. For somehow the brave dicta of its kings [Surprises 98-10
SOMEONE. As if someone lived there. Such floods of white [Sleight
   222-6
Someone before him to see and to know. [Scavoir 232-4
Someone has left for a ride in a balloon [Phenom 286-7
It is someone walking rapidly in the street. [Pure 330-1
Poor procurator, why do you ask someone else [Papini 446-1
March . . . Someone has walked across the snow, [Vacancy 511-4
Someone looking for he knows not what. [Vacancy 511-6
Did not pass like someone voyaging out of and beyond the
   familiar. [Prol 515-13
That winter is washed away. Someone is moving [World 520-13
It is a busy cry, concerning someone else. [Course 96-4 P
With someone to speak her dulcied native tongue, [Letters 107-17P
"Someone Puts a Pineapple Together" [83-title A
SOMETHING. Here, something in the rise and fall of wind [C 29-3
And something given to make whole among [C 30-14
Proclaiming something harsher than he learned [C 33-1
They require something serpentine. [Bananas 54-2
Except in something false. [Orangeade 103-2
The sun is seeking something bright to shine on. [Nigger 157-20
Being and sitting still, something resides, [Autumn 160-9
Like something on the stage, puffed out, [MBG 181-18
The form of her in something else [Scavoir 231-15
To something else. Its past was a souvenir. [Of Mod 239-22
But if, but if there be something more to love, [Montra 260-8
Something in now a senseless syllable, [Montra 260-9
But if there be something more to love, amen, [Montra 260-16
Even now, the centre of something else, [Oak 272-10
Is something in tatters that I cannot hold." [Choc 299-3
It had been real. It was something overseas [Repet 306-4
That I remembered, something that I remembered [Repet 306-5
Like something I remembered overseas. [Repet 306-20
It was something overseas that I remembered. [Repet 306-21
It was something to see that their white was different, [Holiday
   312-1
Something to feel that they needed another yellow, [Holiday 312-3
As the sun is something seeming and it is. [Descrip 339-2
Oh, that this lashing wind was something more [Chaos 357-7
Is something wished for made effectual [Belly 367-8
And something more. And the people in costumes, [Belly 367-9
A name for something that never could be named. [NSF 381-11
That was different, something else, last year [AA 412-11
Something returning from a deeper quarter, [Imago 439-15
It is something seen and known in lesser poems. [Orb 440-10
And something of death's poverty is heard. [NH 477-5
A knowing that something certain had been proposed, [NH 483-4
What was real turned into something most unreal, [NH 483-23
It was something imagined that has been washed away. [NH 488-2
Something not to be mentioned to Mrs. Dooley, [Aug 491-23
No radiance of dead blaze, but something seen, [Armor 529-13
Or of something seen that he liked. [Planet 532-9
With something I could touch, touch every way. [Warmth 90-6 P
Something of the trouble of the mind [How Now 97-4 P
Makes something of the little there, [Dove 97-18 P
But something illogically received, [Ulysses 101-27 P
Or something much like a land. [Letters 108-7 P
Bending in blue dresses to touch something, [Clear Day 113-12 P
With something I could touch, touch every way. [As Leave 117-12P
It is something on a table that he sees, [Someone 83-4 A
See Andrew Jackson Something.
SOMETIME. To which all birds come sometime in their time. [Monocle
   17-5
SOMETIMES. Marvelling sometimes at the shaken sleep. [C 44-19
Round those flotillas. And sometimes the sea [Sea Surf 99-14
Sometimes at sleepy mid-days it succeeds, [Extracts 257-20
Among the breathless spices and, sometimes, [Pecul 454-4
For that person, and, sometimes, for the world itself. [Conversat
   108-12 P
SOMNABULATIONS. This is not landscape, full of the somnambulations
   [Irish 502-3
SOMNAMBULISMA. "Somnambulisma" [304-title
SOMNOLENCE. This somnolence and rattapallax, [Frogs 78-12
Its fragrance, a heavy somnolence, and for him, [EM 319-13
SOMNOLENT. Bore up, in time, the somnolent, deep songs. [C 33-25
Bland belly-sounds in somnolent troughs, [Frogs 78-3
The honky-tonk out of the somnolent grasses [Aug 489-18
Without any pity in a somnolent dream. [Old Woman 44-6 P
SON. This skeleton had a daughter and that, a son. [Norfolk 111-7
The making of his son was one more duty. [Norfolk 111-13
The son and the daughter, who come to the darkness, [Norfolk
   111-18
Son only of man and sun of men, [Thought 185-25
Not in a later son, a different daughter, another place, [Martial
   237-14

For another, as the son's life for the father's. [EM 323-27
Within the universal whole. The son [EM 324-3
The youth, the vital son, the heroic power. [Cred 375-10
He is the inhuman son and she, [Pecul 454-2
John Smith and his son, John Smith, [Soldat 14-18 P
And his son's son John, and-a-one [Soldat 14-19 P
Lean John, and his son, lean John, [Soldat 15-2 P
And his lean son's John, and-a-one [Soldat 15-3 P
Rich John, and his son, rich John, [Soldat 15-6 P
And his rich son's John, and-a-one [Soldat 15-7 P
Wise John, and his son, wise John, [Soldat 15-10 P
And his wise son's John, and-a-one [Soldat 15-11 P
And the obese proprietor, who has a son [Greenest 58-16 P
That of the son who bears upon his back [Recit 87-12 P
As if in a golden cloud. The son restores [Recit 87-16 P
The father keeps on living in the son, the world [Recit 87-25 P
Of the son. These survivals out of time and space [Recit 87-27 P
See day-son.
SONATA. Story . . . The sound of that slick sonata, [Phenom 286-18
SONATINA. "Sonatina to Hans Christian" [109-title
SONG. This is old song [Magnifico 19-7
Sing a song of serpent-kin, [Orangeade 103-4
The song and water were not medleyed sound [Key W 128-19
For she was the maker of the song she sang. [Key W 129-4
That was her song, for she was the maker. Then we, [Key W 129-29
Of the undertaker's song in the snow [MBG 177-12
Balances with nuptial song. [MBG 181-4
It was an old rebellious song, [Country 207-8
An edge of song that never clears; [Country 207-9
In chaos and his song is a consolation. [Extracts 256-9
That clings to the mind like that right sound, that song [Ex-
   tracts 256-14
The venerable song falls from your fiery wings. [God 285-16
The song of the great space of your age pierces [God 285-17
Cat's milk is dry in the saucer. Sunday song [Phenom 286-3
One ear, the wood-doves are singing a single song. [Think
   356-10
"A Woman Sings a Song for a Soldier Come Home" [360-title
"Song of Fixed Accord" [519-title
Be free to sing, if only a sorrowful song. [Greenest 58-33 P
His hymn, his psalm, his cithern song of praise [Greenest 59-21 P
Without human feeling, a foreign song. [Of Mere 117-20 P
I have a song [Three 133-22 P
Therefore my song should go [Three 137-3 P
See sing-song.
SONGS. Bore up, in time, the somnolent, deep songs. [C 33-25
Are full of the songs of Jamanda and Carlotta; [Norfolk 111-17
One of the songs of that dominance.) [Bagatelles 213-24
We sat beneath it and sang our songs. [Vari 233-7
The most massive sopranos are singing songs of scales. [Chaos
   357-18
Far in the woods they sang their unreal songs, [Cred 376-1
My dame, sing for this person accurate songs. [NSF 388-9
Green guests and table in the woods and songs [Orb 440-19
SONNETEERS. In Yucatan, the Maya sonneteers [C 30-16
SONORITIES. Confused illuminations and sonorities, [NH 466-19
SONOROUS. Sonorous nutshells rattling inwardly. [C 31-13
Whiter than wax, sonorous, fame as it is, [NSF 403-19
SONOROUSLY. Truth's favors sonorously exhibited. [EM 321-11
SONS. Of her sons and of her daughters. They found themselves [NSF
   383-13
In the generations of thought, man's sons [Ulysses 103-7 P
SOON. And ladies soon to be married. [Homunculus 25-16
But his emprize to that idea soon sped. [C 40-13
Forget so soon. [Peacocks 58-12
Soon, with a noise like tambourines, [Peter 91-12
Perhaps our wretched state would soon come right. [Surprises 98-9
Blares oftener and soon, will soon be constant. [Sad Gay 122-14
Some harmonious skeptic soon in a skeptical music [Sad Gay 122-15
Will soon be ended." [Idiom 200-19
All this, of course, will come to summer soon. [Connois 216-6
We grew used to soon, too soon, to earth itself, [Wild 328-16
The sounds that soon become a voluble speech-- [Liadoff 347-20
Of the mind--They would soon climb down the side of the ship.
   [Page 423-8
A new-colored sun, say, that will soon change forms [Armor 529-19
How soon the silver fades in the dust! How soon the black figure
   slips from the wrinkled sheet! [Plough-Boy 6-8 P
Would soon be brilliant, as it was, before [Old Woman 45-24 P
The little confine soon unconfined [Ulysses 103-20 P
It will soon be sunrise. [Three 141-3 P
Will shine soon [Three 142-5 P
It will shine soon [Three 142-7 P
SOOT. Oxidia is the soot of fire, [MBG 182-7
SOOTH. Rose out of promise and became the sooth [Havana 143-2
Like the sooth lord of sorrow, [Song Fixed 519-14
Of sooth love and sorrow, [Song Fixed 519-15
The lord of love and of sooth sorrow, [Song Fixed 520-8
SOOTHE. Benitia, lapis Ville des Pins must soothe [Greenest 58-22P
SOOTHER. Soother and lustier than this vexed, autumnal exhalation,

[Inelegance 25-17 P
SOOTHING. Patientia, forever soothing wounds, [Lions 124-15
  See sound-soothing.
SOOTHINGLY. But soothingly, with pleasant instruments, [NH 468-7
SOOTHLY. Dazzling by simplest beams and soothly still, [Old Woman
  46-4 P
SOOTHSAYERS. The first soothsayers of the land, the man [Americana
  93-15 P
SOOTHSAYING. A long soothsaying silence down and down. [C 42-10
SOOTY. And you, my semblables, in sooty residence [Dutch 290-6
SOP. "No Possum, No Sop, No Taters" [293-title
SOPHOMORE. Curriculum for the marvelous sophomore. [C 36-15
SOPPED. So clawed, so sopped with sun, that in these things
  [Greenest 57-20 P
SOPRANOS. The most massive sopranos are singing songs of scales.
  [Chaos 357-18
  Cerise sopranos, [Primordia 7-11 P
SORBONNE. They will get it straight one day at the Sorbonne. [NSF
  406-22
SORCERERS. Of a lunar light, dark-belted sorcerers [Old Woman
  46-3 P
SORDID. Sordid Melpomene, why strut bare boards, [Bad Time 427-4
SORROW. There is cure of sorrow. [W Burgher 61-9
  The path sick sorrow took, the many paths [Sunday 69-4
  By which sorrow is released, [Mozart 132-15
  Without the inventions of sorrow or the sob [EM 317-5
  Like the sooth lord of sorrow, [Song Fixed 519-14
  Of sooth love and sorrow, [Song Fixed 519-15
  The lord of love and of sooth sorrow [Song Fixed 520-8
  Sorrow bring-- [Phases 5-2 P
  My head, the sorrow of the world, except [Bship 78-18 P
  For sorrow. [Three 133-4 P
SORROWFUL. Be free to sing, if only a sorrowful song. [Greenest
  58-33 P
SORROWS. And grackles gone and sorrows of the sun, [Autumn 160-2
  The sorrows of sun, too, gone . . . the moon and moon, [Autumn
  160-3
SORRY. The sorry verities! [W Burgher 61-7
SORT. The sort of thing that August crooners sing, [Aug 489-9
  Myself, only half of a figure of a sort, [Angel 497-6
  Of a sort, silence of a rat come out to see, [Plain 503-5
  That sort of thing was always rather stiff. [Lytton 39-18 P
  A silent sort of bush, as well, [Banjo 114-7 P
SORTES. Livre de Toutes Sortes de Fleurs d'apres Nature. [EM
  316-7
SORTILEGE. And rainbow sortilege, the savage weapon [Hero 274-3
SORTS. A shearsman of sorts. The day was green. [MBG 165-2
  All sorts of flowers. That's the sentimentalist. [EM 316-8
  All sorts of notes? Or did he play only one [EM 316-12
SOUGHT. You know how Utamaro's beauties sought [Monocle 14-5
  The good Lord in His garden sought [Pourtraicte 21-22
  Rose up besprent and sought the flaming red [Hibiscus 22-20
  Was gemmy marionette to him that sought [C 36-4
  It was the spirit that we sought and knew [Key W 129-8
  He sought an earthly leader who could stand [Thought 185-23
  Kept waking and a mournful sense sought out, [Montra 263-5
  And the bees still sought the chrysanthemums' odor. [Contra II
  270-18
  He sought the most grossly maternal, the creature [EM·321-13
  And him. Both wanted the same thing. Both sought [Liadoff
  347-18
  Themselves with care, sought out the nerveless frame [NSF 391-16
  The center that he sought was a state of mind, [Art Pop 112-13 P
SOUGHT-FOR. In any commonplace the sought-for aid. [C 30-23
SOUL. The soul, O ganders, flies beyond the parks [Swans 4-1
  And the soul, O ganders, being lonely, flies [Swans 4-11
  The soul, he said, is composed [Men 1000 51-7
  These are the measures destined for her soul. [Sunday 67-26
  Body and soul, [Cortege 81-5
  A hunter of those sovereigns of the soul [Lions 124-11
  If the fault is with the soul, the sovereigns [Lions 124-19
  Of the soul must likewise be at fault, and first. [Lions 124-20
  Are the soul itself. And the whole of the soul, Swenson, [Lions
  125-2
  Oh! Rabbi, rabbi, fend my soul for me [Sun March 134-7
  Speak of the soul, the mind. It is [MBG 174-7
  One's tootings at the weddings of the soul [Sleight 222-2
  This arrival in the wild country of the soul, [Waldorf 240-24
  This platonic persons discovered a soul in the world [Pure 331-13
  Of an old and disused ambit of the soul [Aug 489-6
SOULS. Ears, eyes, souls, skins, hair? [Parasol 20-6 P
  "The Souls of Women at Night" [94-title P
SOUND. And uttered their subsiding sound. [Infanta 8-6
  Of any misery in the sound of the wind, [Snow Man 10-5
  In the sound of a few leaves, [Snow Man 10-7
  Which is the sound of the land [Snow Man 10-7
  Dwindled to one sound strumming in his ear, [C 28-19
  Latched up the night. So deep a sound fell down [C 42-6
  So deep a sound fell down it grew to be [C 42-9
  To blessed syllable affined, and sound [C 43-9

The senses and feeling, the very sound [Joost 47-1
They seem an exaltation without sound. [On Manner 55-14
Winding across wide water, without sound. [Sunday 67-7
The day is like wide water, without sound, [Sunday 67-8
She hears, upon that water without sound, [Sunday 70-14
Music is feeling, then, not sound; [Peter 90-1
And apt in versatile motion, touch and sound [Anatomy 108-12
The leaves in which the wind kept up its sound [Farewell 117-13
That is so much motionless sound. [Sad Gay 121-10
In many majesties of sound: [How Live 125-14
There was the cold wind and the sound [How Live 126-5
That they had left, heroic sound [How Live 126-7
The song and water were not medleyed sound [Key W 128-19
The heaving speech of air, a summer sound [Key W 129-15
And sound alone. But it was more than that, [Key W 129-17
Be thou that wintry sound [Mozart 132-13
Is the function of the poet here mere sound, [Havana 144-12
Has rather a classical sound. [Circulat 150-8
For the time when sound shall be subtler than we ourselves.
  [Nigger 158-5
The stillness is all in the key of that desolate sound. [Autumn
  160-14
Moved in the grass without a sound. [MBG 178-14
The world was a shore, whether sound or form [MBG 179-2
Yet the sound of that). [Thunder 220-24
The bell of its dome, the patron of sound. [Vari 235-9
Exactly, that which it wants to hear, at the sound [Of Mod 240-9
A crinkled paper makes a brilliant sound. [Extracts 252-1
This inability to find a sound, [Extracts 256-13
That clings to the mind like that right sound, that song [Ex-
  tracts 256-14
Toward an inaccessible, pure sound. [Montra 263-16
And the sound of pianos in his mind. [News 264-18
"The Search for Sound Free from Motion" [268-title
In memorials of Northern sound, [Oak 272-14
The elephants of sound, the tigers [Hero 278-9
"Certain Phenomena of Sound" [286-title
It is safe to sleep to a sound that time brings back. [Phenom
  286-12
Story . . . The sound of that slick sonata, [Phenom 286-18
A sound producing the things that are spoken. [Phenom 287-6
Of red and blue, the hard sound-- [Motive 288-18
I hear the motions of the spirit and the sound [Choc 298-18
"The Creations of Sound" [310-title
A being of sound, whom one does not approach [Creat 311-5
By the spontaneous particulars of sound. [Creat 311-15
The terror of the sound because the sound [EM 314-2
Variations in the tones of a single sound, [EM 316-14
Bubbles up in the night and drowns the crickets' sound. [EM
  321-9
Speech found the ear, for all the evil sound, [EM 326-5
The weather in words and words in sounds of sound. [Pure 332-18
That have rankled for many lives and made no sound. [Sketch
  336-3
A great jaguar running will make a little sound. [Jouga 337-15
Of the imagination, made in sound; [Descrip 346-1
By the glints of sound from the grass. These are not [Myrrh
  350-6
It is not speech, the sound we hear [Silent 359-19
In this conversation, but the sound [Silent 360-1
And bound by a sound which does not change, [Human 363-2
And in this sound, which do not change, [Human 363-7
So soft, so civil, and you make a sound, [Cred 377-19
Drowned in its washes, reading in the sound, [NSF 387-10
A sound like any other. It will end. [NSF 394-18
To find of sound the bleakest ancestor, [NSF 398-17
His puissant front nor for her subtle sound, [NSF 401-12
The luminous melody of proper sound. [NSF 404-12
The wind will command them with invincible sound. [AA 414-3
Und so lau, between sound without meaning and speech, [Page
  421-10
And Schuylkill. The sound of him [Our Stars 455-11
Flame, sound, fury composed . . . Hear what he says, [Puel
  456-17
Deep in their sound the stentor Martin sings. [Luther 461-13
To none, awaiting espousal to the sound [Study II 464-18
Impalpable bells, transparencies of sound, [NH 466-6
The rain falls with a ramshackle sound. He cocks [NH 475-9
As if the ears heard any shocking sound, [NH 478-11
Like the constant sound of the water of the sea [NH 480-14
As of a long, inevitable sound, [NH 482-7
A kind of cozening and coaxing sound, [NH 482-8
And the goodness of lying in a maternal sound, [NH 482-9
Or the sound of Incomincia had been set, [NH 482-24
Away from them, capes, along the afternoon Sound, [NH 484-7
Singing, with smaller and still smaller sound, [Rome 508-4
The same wind, rising and rising, makes a sound [Look 519-2
Babbling, each one, the uniqueness of its sound. [Quiet 523-13
Night and silence disturbed by an interior sound, [Moonlight
  532-2

Seemed like a sound in his mind. [Not Ideas 534-3
Are like the sound of doves. [Secret Man 35-22 P
What sound could comfort away the sudden sense? [Old Woman
    44-16 P
Blowing among the trees its meaningless sound. [Old Woman 44-28P
They suddenly fall and the leafless sound of the wind [Burnshaw
    50-20 P
Is no longer a sound of summer. So great a change [Burnshaw
    50-21 P
And the sound of z in the grass all day, though these [Burnshaw
    51-4 P
In the glassy sound of your voices, the porcelain cries, [Burn-
    shaw 52-6 P
And are your feelings changed to sound, without [Burnshaw 52-13P
Into a music never touched to sound. [Greenest 54-11 P
He does not hear by sound. His spirit knows [Greenest 59-7 P
And most in what we hear, sound brushed away, [Sombre 67-9 P
With meanings, doubled by the closest sound, [Sombre 67-25 P
To the sound of the concertina, [Grotesque 77-9 P
The whole. The sound of a dozen orchestras [Bship 79-26 P
Listening to the whole sea for a sound [Woman Had 82-4 P
Of the humming of the central man, the whole sound [Woman Had
    82-12 P
Detects the sound of a voice that doubles its own, [Woman Had
    82-20 P
It is the same sound, the same season, [Memo 89-3 P
Daylight evaporates, like a sound one hears in sickness. [Discov
    95-9 P
It does not sound like an elopement. [Three 138-10 P
To sound, sound's substance and executant, [Someone 84-13 A
See: winter-sound.
SOUNDED. Sounded in music, if the sun, [Prelude 194-13
SOUNDER. Be free to sleep there sounder, for the plough [Burnshaw
    48-1 P
SOUNDING. Could all these be ourselves, sounding ourselves, [Dames
    206-11
    The sounding shallow, until by water washed away. [Somnam 304-6
    Sounding in transparent dwellings of the self, [NH 466-7
SOUNDS. I quiz all sounds, all thoughts, all everything [Monocle
    16-19
    Against his pipping sounds a trumpet cried [C 29-21
    How many sea-masks he ignored; what sounds [C 34-21
    And in their music showering sounds intone. [C 37-32
    And sounds of music coming to accord [C 45-26
    Are as natural sounds [Men 1000 51-16
    While he imagined humming sounds and sleep. [Babies 77-6
    Make music, so the selfsame sounds [Peter 89-17
    In ghostlier demarcations, keener sounds. [Key W 130-15
    Its sounds are not angelic syllables [Eve Angels 137-3
    Men that repeat antiquest sounds of air [Eve Angels 137-15
    The comedy of hollow sounds derives [Nigger 154-4
    The shapes are wrong and the sounds are false. [MBG 181-11
    Are sounds blown by a blower into shapes, [Parochial 191-5
    Lies in flawed words and stubborn sounds. [Poems Clim 194-10
    The bells of the chapel pullulate sounds at [Peaches 224-9
    They do not touch it. Sounds never rise [Arcades 225-10
    Sounds passing through sudden rightnesses, wholly [Of Mod 240-16
    The enormous gongs gave edges to their sounds, [Uruguay 249-27
    Of sounds resembling sounds, efflorisant, [Montra 260-11
    As if sounds were forming [Dutch 290-17
    A few sounds of meaning, a momentary end [Lack 303-19
    Indifferent sounds and not the heraldic-ho [Repet 307-20
    Or in the ceiling, in sounds not chosen, [Creat 310-13
    In which we heard transparent sounds, did he play [EM 316-11
    The last, or sounds so single they seemed one? [EM 316-15
    Like things submerged with their englutted sounds, [EM 321-27
    And tells the hours by the lateness of the sounds. [Pure 330-3
    The weather in words and words in sounds of sound. [Pure 332-18
    The sounds that soon become a voluble speech-- [Liadoff 347-20
    There is a sense in sounds beyond their meaning. [Pieces 352-1
    Swarm, not with secondary sounds, but choirs, [Cred 374-12
    Not evocations but last choirs, last sounds [Cred 374-13
    Abysmal instruments make sounds like pips [NSF 384-5
    His petty syllabi, the sounds that stick, [NSF 407-19
    It is the huge, high harmony that sounds [Orb 440-20
    Brooding sounds of the images of death, [Degen 444-3
    Brooding sounds of river noises; [Degen 444-6
    The less legible meanings of sounds, the little reds [NH 488-7
    These sounds are long in the living of the ear. [Aug 489-17
    The sounds drift in. The buildings are remembered. [Rome 510-11
    They never were . . . The sounds of the guitar [Rock 525-9
    The sounds of rain on the roof [Secret Man 35-21 P
    Swirled round them in immense autumnal sounds. [Old Woman 43-21P
    The golden clouds that turned to bronze, the sounds [Old Woman
    44-7 P
    Long autumn sheens and pittering sounds like sounds [Burnshaw
    47-24 P
    Hissing, across the silence, puissant sounds. [Greenest 55-16 P
    The self is a cloister full of remembered sounds [Woman Had
    82-17 P

And of sounds so far forgotten, like her voice, [Woman Had 82-18P
    Drifting choirs, long movements and turnings of sounds. [Sick
    90-12 P
    Upon whose lips the dissertation sounds, [Ideal 89-1 A
    See: belly-sounds; sea-sounds.
SOUND-SOOTHING. Sound-soothing pearl and omni-diamond, [Golden
    460-21
SOUPE. Soupe aux Perles [NE Verses 104-title 3
    Soupe Sans Perles [NE Verses 104-title 4
SOUR. Sour wine to warm him, an empty book to read; [Good Man
    364-11
SOURCE. Naked among them, like a savage source. [Sunday 70-3
    Moving and being, the image at its source, [Candle 223-13
    Never suppose an inventing mind as source [NSF 381-1
    A source of trumpeting seraphs in the eye, [Orb 442-23
    A source of pleasant outbursts on the ear. [Orb 442-24
    Ponderable source of each imponderable, [NH 476-11
    From a different source. But there was always one: [NH 479-3
    The afternoon is visibly a source, [Look 518-17
    And beheld the source from which transparence came; [Greenest
    54-7 P
    This source and patriarch of other spheres, [Duck 63-27 P
    Sole, single source and minimum patriarch, [Conversat 108-21 P
SOURCES. His thoughts begotten at clear sources, [Hero 277-14
    The sources of happiness in the shape of Rome, [Rome 508-23
SOUTH. To the dusk of a whistling south below the south, [C 38-13
    Nor visionary south, nor cloudy palm [Sunday 68-21
    From my North of cold whistled in a sepulchral South, [Farewell
    117-14
    Her South of pine and coral and coraline sea, [Farewell 117-15
    In the far South the sun of autumn is passing [Nigger 150-9
    And North and South are in intrinsic couple [NSF 392-14
    An island to the South, on which rested like [NSF 393-11
    In a season more than sun and south wind, [Imago 439-14
    Adds to them the whole vocabulary of the South, [Prol 517-7
    In the South [Primordia 9-title 6 P
    Abhorring green-blue north and blue-green south. [Archi 18-1 P
    In the South, bands of thousands of black men, [Sick 90-8 P
SOUTH AFRICA. If the flowers of South Africa were bright [Connois
    215-5
SOUTHERN. This Italian symbol, this Southern landscape, is like
    [Study I 463-7
    An Alp, a purple Southern mountain bisqued [Someone 87-3 A
SOUVENIR. That lucid souvenir of the past, [Mozart 132-3
    To something else. Its past was a souvenir. [Of Mod 239-22
    And people, without souvenir. The day [Cred 375-7
    A sovereign, a souvenir, a sign, [Bouquet 451-12
SOUVENIRS. Commingled souvenirs and prophecies. [C 37-25
    Or paper souvenirs of rapture, [Jasmine 79-9
    But these shall not adorn my souvenirs, [Lions 124-17
    If the fault is with the souvenirs, yet these [Lions 125-1
    Souvenirs of museums. But, Master, there are [Hartford 226-13
    The eccentric souvenirs of human shapes, [Descrip 342-13
    For souvenirs of time, lost time, [Prejudice 368-22
    It stands a sovereign of souvenirs [Bouquet 451-5
    Arpeggi of celestial souvenirs, [Spaniard 35-16 P
    Twitching a little with crude souvenirs [Duck 64-23 P
SOVEREIGN. The sovereign ghost. As such, the Socrates [C 27-8
    Beheld the sovereign clouds as jugglery [Sea Surf 102-6
    The sovereign clouds came clustering. The conch [Sea Surf 102-10
    Still hankers after sovereign images. [Lions 125-5
    Here was a sovereign sight, [Pascagoula 126-17
    Dropping in sovereign rings [Pascagoula 127-6
    Of the clear sovereign that is reality, [Repet 307-21
    Of the clearest reality that is sovereign, [Repet 307-22
    Time in its weather, our most sovereign lord, [Pure 332-17
    It stands a sovereign of souvenirs [Bouquet 451-5
    It is a symbol, a sovereign of symbols [Bouquet 451-8
    A sovereign, a souvenir, a sign. [Bouquet 451-12
    To be the sovereign shape in a world of shapes. [Old Woman 45-17P
SOVEREIGNS. A hunter of those sovereigns of the soul [Lions 124-11
    If the fault is with the soul, the sovereigns [Lions 124-19
SOVIET. The newest Soviet réclame. Profound [Duck 62-30 P
SOWN. And sown again by the stiffest realist, [C 45-15
SPACE. Drifting through space, [Explan 73-3
    The spirit and space, [Am Sub 131-9
    In vacant space. [Am Sub 131-11
    Of those with a sense for simple space. [Nigger 153-7
    Ourselves in the tune as if in space, [MBG 167-17
    The tune is space. The blue guitar [MBG 168-6
    From which it sped, a bar in space, [MBG 179-6
    How should you walk in that space and know [MBG 183-7
    Nothing of the madness of space, [MBG 183-8
    A space of stone, of inexplicable base [Thought 185-9
    One man, the idea of man, that is the space, [Thought 185-11
    You sit with your head like a carving in space [Rabbit K 210-2
    The mind between this light or that and space, [Rhythms 245-11
    Grows large against space: [Rhythms 245-14
    Mouthing its constant smatter throughout space. [Montra 263-19
    The song of the great space of your age pierces [God 285-17

The suspension, as in solid space, [Couch 295-13
And to be heard is to be large in space, [Choc 296-8
Itself is like a poverty in the space of life, [Choc 299-1
A largeness lived and not conceived, a space [Choc 301-12
A kind of elegy he found in space: [EM 315-3
To be askew. And space is filled with his [EM 318-7
The inimical music, the enchantered space [Pure 330-14
Receive and keep him in the deepnesses of space-- [Flyer 336-13
Dissolved. The distances of space and time [Descrip 343-9
That lives in space. It is a person at night, [Pieces 352-7
Like space dividing its blue and by division [Two V 354-14
Being changed from space to the sailor's metier, [Two V 354-15
The water flowing in the flow of space. [Lot 371-15
The pensive giant prone in violet space [NSF 387-2
On his spredden wings, needs nothing but deep space, [NSF
   404-17
In space, wherever he sits, of bleak regard, [AA 414-6
He assumes the great speeds of space and flutters them [AA
   414-14
And yet in space and motionless and yet [AA 414-23
And the solemn pleasures of magnificent space. [AA 416-14
Of the categories. So said, this placid space [Ulti 429-17
Everywhere in space at once, cloud-pole [Ulti 430-3
The pure perfections of parental space, [Owl 436-5
In the light-bound space of the mind, the floreate flare . . .
   [Owl 436-6
A space grown wide, the inevitable blue [Orb 440-21
So there is a man in black space [Degen 444-4
The marble man remains himself in space. [Degen 444-10
He that kneels always on the edge of space [NH 469-9
Lighted by space, big over those that sleep, [NH 482-5
The consolations of space are nameless things. [NH 482-16
In space and the self, that touched them both at once [NH 483-7
In the space of horizons that neither love nor hate. [Aug 490-14
Evoking an archaic space, vanishing [Aug 494-19
In the space, leaving an outline of the size [Aug 494-20
Of autumnal space becomes [Leben 505-5
Of men growing small in the distances of space, [Rome 508-3
That in which space itself is contained, the gate [Rock 528-17
The space above the trees might still be bright [Old Woman
   44-29 P
The space beneath it still, a smooth domain, [Old Woman 46-5 P
The light wings lifted through the crystal space [Old Woman
   46-11 P
For themselves, and space and time and ease for the duck. [Duck
   60-17 P
To space. To space? The statue scaled to space [Sombre 70-21 P
Not the space in camera of the man below, [Sombre 70-31 P
Immeasurable, the space in which he knows [Sombre 70-32 P
In hum-drum space, farewell, farewell, by day [Sombre 71-8 P
The scholar is always distant in the space [Recit 86-18 P
Of the son. These survivals out of time and space [Recit 87-27 P
Like slits across a space, a place [Dove 98-11 P
A part of space and solitude, [Ulysses 100-6 P
The space in which it stands, the shine [Ulysses 100-26 P
The flights through space, changing habitudes. [Ulysses 103-6 P
On which the vast arches of space [Ulysses 103-17 P
And that, in space and solitude, [Presence 105-20 P
The palm stands on the edge of space. [Of Mere 118-4 P
In the space it fills, the silent motioner [Ideal 88-6 A
SPACE-FILLED. Space-filled, reflecting the seasons, the folk-lore
   [R Conn 533-19
SPACES. And over the bare spaces of our skies [Anatomy 108-6
  But bravest at midnight and in lonely spaces, [Page 421-22
  Twisting among the universal spaces, [Degen 444-15
  Through wild spaces of other suns and moons, [Ulysses 102-23 P
SPACIOUSNESS. So be it. Yet the spaciousness and light [Anatomy
   108-15
SPAIN. Of China, cap of Spain, imperative haw [C 28-9
  And in that mountainous mirror Spain acquires [Descrip 345-13
  The knowledge of Spain and of the hidalgo's hat-- [Descrip
   345-14
SPAN. Of heat upon his pane. This was the span [C 33-4
  Not span, without any weather at all, except [Wild 329-7
SPANGLED. Beneath the arches and their spangled air, [Eve Angels
   138-2
SPANGLING. From the loosed girdles in the spangling must. [Sea
   Surf 101-14
  Dangling and spangling, the mic-mac of mocking birds. [NH 486-15
  Beneath the spangling greens, fear might placate [Greenest 54-22P
SPANIARD. And as the black Spaniard plays his guitar. [Peaches
   224-6
  And then that Spaniard of the rose, itself [EM 316-16
  A seeming of the Spaniard, a style of life, [Descrip 345-15
  The sun stands like a Spaniard as he departs, [Novel 457-4
  "The Woman Who Blamed Life on a Spaniard" [34-title P
SPANISH. Might well have been German or Spanish, [Circulat 150-6
  A Spanish storm, [Fare Guit 99-1 P
SPARE. Death ought to spare their passions. [Lytton 38-17 P
SPARKLE. Spring sparkle and the cock-bird shriek. [MBG 182-13

Trouble in the spillage and first sparkle of sun, [How Now 97-7P
SPARKLED. That constantly sparkled their small gold? The town
   [Liadoff 346-12
SPARKLES. Snow sparkles like eyesight falling to earth, [Possum
   294-4
  (Her pale smock sparkles in a light begun [Infernale 25-9 P
SPARKLING. Sparkling, solitary, still, [Venereal 48-9
  Over wooden Boston, the sparkling Byzantine [Blue Bldg 217-1
  With the whole spirit sparkling in its cloth, [Owl 434-12
  The conception sparkling in still obstinate thought. [Papini
   448-4
  The sparkling fall of night [Inhab 504-3
  Wet with water and sparkling in the one-ness of their motion.
   [Prol 515-9
  See glassily-sparkling.
SPARROW. One sparrow is worth a thousand gulls, [Vari 233-12
  The sparrow requites one, without intent. [Vari 233-16
  Bethou me, said sparrow, to the crackled blade, [NSF 393-22
  Of leaves, in which the sparrow is a bird [NSF 394-15
SPARROWS. If her eyes were chinks in which the sparrows built;
   [Woman Had 83-1 P
SPEAK. That streaking gold should speak in him [C 38-4
  Speak, even, as if I did not hear you speaking, [Two Figures
   86-4
  In his time, this one had little to speak of, [Norfolk 111-8
  Speak it. [Roaring 113-7
  Her mind will never speak to me again. [Farewell 117-6
  Speak of the dazzling wings. [Pascagoula 127-8
  Speak and the sleepers in their sleep shall move, [Havana 145-1
  Will speak our speech and never know, [Postcard 159-15
  Do not speak to us of the greatness of poetry, [MBG 167-3
  Speak of the soul, the mind. It is [MBG 174-7
  And as I am, I speak and move [MBG 180-16
  Upon the pillow to repose and speak, [Men Fall 188-10
  Speak and say the immaculate syllables [Men Fall 188-11
  Pftt. . . . In the way you speak [Add 198-15
  To hear himself and not to speak. [Arcades 225-26
  With meditation, speak words that in the ear, [Of Mod 240-7
  All men can speak of it in the voice of gods. [Montra 262-20
  But to speak simply of good is like to love, [Montra 262-21
  Speaks as you speak, a creature that [Search 268-14
  To speak quietly at such a distance, to speak [Choc 296-7
  To speak humanly from the height or from the depth [Choc 300-14
  Now, I, Chocorua, speak of this shadow as [Choc 300-16
  From the floor, rising in speech we do not speak. [Creat 311-18
  That will not hear us when we speak: a coolness, [Less 328-8
  And imagine for him the speech he cannot speak, [Pure 330-9
  Yet to speak of the whole world as metaphor [Pure 332-8
  She will speak thoughtfully the words of a line. [Debris 338-8
  Stay here. Speak of familiar things a while. [Debris 338-14
  To speak of what you see. But wait [Red Fern 365-14
  And speak of the floridest reality . . . [Anach 366-7
  In which the characters speak because they want [Cred 378-6
  To speak, the fat, the roseate characters, [Cred 378-7
  Incipit and a form to speak the word [NSF 387-5
  Speak to me that, which spoken, will array me [NSF 396-4
  He tries by a peculiar speech to speak [NSF 397-6
  To speak of joy and to sing of it, borne on [NSF 398-10
  That there are no lines to speak? There is no play. [AA 416-2
  As if whatever in water strove to speak [Page 422-9
  The muse of misery? Speak loftier lines. [Bad Time 427-7
  Speak softly, to begin with, in the eaves. [Beginning 428-8
  The name. He does not speak beside you. [Countryman 429-1
  To most incredible depths. I speak below [John 437-9
  As victory. The poet does not speak in ruins [Papini 446-10
  It does no good to speak of the big, blue bush [Study I 463-4
  With which to speak to her, the capable [NH 471-1
  Speak to your pillow as if it was yourself. [Rome 509-9
  And you--it is you that speak it, without speech, [Rome 510-6
  Speak, and in these repeat: To Be Itself, [Burnshaw 52-8 P
  From which their grizzled voice will speak and be heard." [Duck
   60-24 P
  The way we speak of it. [Grotesque 76-9 P
  Who, when they think and speak of the central man, [Woman Had
   82-11 P
  In the images of desire, the forms that speak, [Woman Had 82-21P
  With someone to speak her dulcied native tongue, [Letters 107-17P
  You speak. You say: Today's character is not [As Leave 116-15 P
  And who shall speak it, what child or wanderer [Ideal 88-19 A
SPEAKER. The Whole World Including the Speaker [NE Verses
   104-title 1
  The Whole World Excluding the Speaker [NE Verses 104-title 2
  Before the speaker's youngest breath is taken! [Montra 261-21
  Exponent by a form of speech, the speaker [NSF 397-3
  While the water kept running through the mouth of the speaker,
   [Novel 457-17
SPEAKING. Speak, even, as if I did not hear you speaking, [Two
   Figures 86-4
  More than sudarium, speaking the speech [Men Fall 188-6
  And the living would be speaking, [Thunder 220-19

Kept speaking, of God. I changed the word to man. [Les Plus
  245-4
Of the good, speaking of good in the voice of men. [Montra
  262-19
In your light, the head is speaking. It reads the book. [God
  285-10
That is my own voice speaking in my ear. [Choc 298-20
Cinerarias have a speaking sheen. [Poesie 302-17
If these were only words that I am speaking [Repet 307-19
He must be incapable of speaking, closed, [Less 327-15
Not speaking worms, nor birds [Analysis 348-18
Speaking the phrases that follow the sight [Pediment 361-20
These mothers touching, speaking, being near, [Cred 372-17
Complete in a completed scene, speaking [Cred 378-9
Good-by in the darkness, speaking quietly there, [Owl 431-17
Or as a voice that, speaking without form, [NH 484-20
Whose heart will murmur with the music that will be a voice for
  her, speaking the dreaded change of speech; [Piano 22-2 P
Speaking and strutting broadly, fair and bloomed, [Burnshaw
  52-17 P
See all-speaking.
SPEAKS. Encircling us, speaks always with our speech. [Eve Angels
  137-18
But the ugly alien, the mask that speaks [Nigger 156-17
In this it moves and speaks. [Add 199-10
I touch them and smell them. Who speaks? [Peaches 224-2
Who speaks? But it must be that I, [Peaches 224-7
Without eyes or mouth, that looks at one and speaks. [Yellow
  237-9
Speaks as you speak, a creature that [Search 268-14
And tosses green for those for whom green speaks. [Repet 309-24
That speaks for him such seemings as death gives. [Descrip
  341-6
To which the walker speaks [Woman Song 360-14
A little string speaks for a crowd of voices. [NSF 392-18
The third form speaks, because the ear repeats, [Owl 432-3
That speaks, denouncing separate selves, both one. [Orb 441-25
The poet speaks the poem as it is, [NH 473-18
Are like newspapers blown by the wind. He speaks [NH 473-21
In this perfection, occasionally speaks [NH 477-4
SPEAR. Shelter yet thrower of the summer spear, [Thought 186-10
Like a belly puckered by a spear. [Lulu M 27-4 P
SPEARS. Of waterish spears. The fisherman is all [Think 356-13
What avuncular cloud-man beamier than spears? [Greenest 52-25 P
SPECIAL. With the special things of night, little by little,
  [Choc 300-19
In the eye a special hue of origin [Bouquet 451-23
Out of their wilderness, a special fane, [Sombre 69-8 P
It is a special day. We mumble the words [Nuns 92-18 P
SPECIALTY. Cannot be the specialty [Botanist 1 135-14
SPECKLE. So that the sun may speckle, [Watermelon 89-11
SPECTACLE. In the spectacle of a new reality. [Repet 306-9
It is a spectacle. Scene 10 becomes 11, [Chaos 357-11
And are not now: in this shallow spectacle, [Clear Day 113-18 P
SPECTACULAR. It is a most spectacular role, and yet [Spaniard
  35-4 P
To momentary calm, spectacular flocks [Burnshaw 51-2 P
SPECTATOR. The objects tingle and the spectator moves [NH 470-1
With the objects. But the spectator also moves [NH 470-2
SPECTRA. In which the spectra have dewy favor and live [How Now
  97-13 P
SPECTRAL. Like a spectral cut in its perception, a tilt [What We
  460-3
SPECTRE. This contrivance of the spectre of the spheres, [AA
  420-18
SPECTRES. The finikin spectres in the memory, [Repet 307-12
SPECTRUM. Like an evening evoking the spectrum of violet, [NH
  488-19
SPECULATED. On which men speculated in summer when they were half
  asleep. [Prol 516-15
SPECULUM. Part of the speculum of fire on its prow, its symbol,
  whatever it was, [Prol 516-2
SPED. But his emprize to that idea soon sped. [C 40-13
From which it sped, a bar in space, [MBG 179-6
SPEECH. Puissant speech, alike in each. [Ord Women 11-26
Might come in the simplest of speech. [Homunculus 27-2
But with a speech belched out of hoary darks [C 29-26
Of speech which are like music so profound [On Manner 55-13
Their evocations are the speech of clouds. [On Manner 55-16
So speech of your processionals returns [On Manner 56-1
And I, then, tortured for old speech, [W Burgher 61-14
Darken your speech. [Two Figures 86-3
Requiring order beyond their speech. [Sad Gay 122-9
The heaving speech of air, a summer sound [Key W 129-15
Encircling us, speaks always with our speech. [Eve Angels 137-18
In speech. He has that music and himself. [Anglais 149-7
Will speak our speech and never know, [Postcard 159-15
His speech, the dress of his meaning, silk [MBG 170-2
And speech of Virgil dropped, that's where he walks, [Thought
  185-14

More than sudarium, speaking the speech [Men Fall 188-6
The poses of speech, of paint, [Add 199-1
The figures of speech, as why she chose [Scavoir 231-3
It has to be living, to learn the speech of the place. [Of Mod
  240-1
Than a thought to be rehearsed all day, a speech [Beard 247-16
Of the self that must sustain itself on speech, [Beard 247-17
Of speech: to pierce the heart's residuum [Extracts 259-15
Falls on and makes and gives, even a speech. [Phosphor 267-13
Contrasting our two names, considered speech. [Phenom 287-16
Of human things, that is acutest speech. [Choc 300-15
Tell X that speech is not dirty silence [Creat 311-7
From the floor, rising in speech we do not speak. [Creat 311-18
They had known that there was not even a common speech, [Holiday
  312-7
Speech found the ear, for all the evil sound, [EM 326-5
It is the human that demands his speech [Less 328-5
And imagine for him the speech he cannot speak, [Pure 330-9
Running in the rises of common speech, [Sketch 336-5
Crying as that speech falls as if to fail. [Sketch 336-6
As, men make themselves their speech: the hard hidalgo [Descrip
  345-11
Lives in the mountainous character of his speech; [Descrip 345-12
The sounds that soon become a voluble speech-- [Liadoff 347-20
It is not speech, the sound we hear [Silent 359-19
Or power of the wave, or deepened speech, [NSF 387-13
Exponent by a form of speech, the speaker [NSF 397-3
Of a speech only a little of the tongue? [NSF 397-4
He tries by a peculiar speech to speak [NSF 397-6
If he must, or lives on the bread of faithful speech. [NSF 408-3
Und so lau, between sound without meaning and speech, [Page
  421-10
It is like a flow of meanings with no speech [Roses 431-8
Is not and, therefore, is. In the instant of speech, [Orb 440-14
Too fragile, too immediate for any speech. [NH 471-9
The description that makes it divinity, still speech [NH 475-13
In the heavy drum of speech, the inner men [NH 488-9
The speech of truth in its true solitude, [Aug 490-20
To that which has no speech, [Aug 492-12
Go back to a parent before thought, before speech, [Irish 501-11
It is poverty's speech that seeks us out the most, [Rome 510-3
It is older than the oldest speech of Rome. [Rome 510-4
And you--it is you that speak it, without speech, [Rome 510-6
A sacred syllable rising from sacked speech, [Armor 530-1
Of what shall the speech be, [Archi 17-3 P
Whose heart will murmur with the music that will be a voice for
  her, speaking the dreaded change of speech; [Piano 22-2 P
Bears words that are the speech of marble men. [Burnshaw 52-5 P
Itself into the speech of the spirit, until [Burnshaw 52-10 P
Some pebble-chewer practiced in Tyrian speech, [Duck 63-17 P
The ideas that come to it with a sense of speech. [Woman Had
  82-22 P
Speech for the quiet, good hail of himself, good hail, good hail,
  [Sick 90-20 P
The desire for speech and meaning gallantly fulfilled, [Discov
  95-18 P
Shadows, woods . . . and the two of them in speech, [Letters
  108-2 P
On the piano, and in speech, [July 114-18 P
So much less than feeling, so much less than speech, [Region
  115-9 P
See sub-speech.
SPEECHES. And his breast is greatness. All his speeches [Hero
  277-12
The spirit's speeches, the indefinite. [NH 466-18
SPEECH-FULL. From the rumors of the speech-full domes, [Ulysses
  102-15 P
SPEECHLESS. Consider how the speechless, invisible gods [Montra
  262-13
SPEED. Gothic blue, speed home its portents to their ends. [Page
  422-20
Almost as speed discovers in the way [Owl 435-10
SPEEDS. The wind speeds her, [Paltry 5-16
The world has turned to the several speeds of glass, [Bouquet
  449-5
He assumes the great speeds of space and flutters them [AA 414-14
SPELL. So, then, these lights are not a spell of light, [AA 418-19
By which to spell out holy doom and end, [Owl 434-17
SPELLED. Spelled from spent living and spent dying. [Dutch 291-19
SPELLING. Spelling out pandects and haggard institutes? [Duck
  62-17 P
SPELLS. How the wind spells out [Metamorph 265-15
SPENDED. Which in those ears and in those thin, those spended
  hearts, [Large 424-7
SPENT. Of spent emotions. [Peter 90-23
Spelled from spent living and spent dying. [Dutch 291-19
Spent in the false engagements of the mind. [EM 317-3
And the father alike and equally are spent, [EM 324-4
Or seeing the spent, unconscious shapes of night, [Feo 334-7
The spent feeling leaving nothing of itself, [NSF 400-12

Which, like a virgin visionary spent [Red Kit 30-18 P
In this spent world, she must possess. The gift [Red Kit 30-19 P
Came not from you. Shall the world be spent again, [Red Kit 30-20 P
Adorned for a multitude, in a gesture spent [Sombre 71-27 P
SPHERE. Upon his lap, like their inherent sphere, [C 45-27
But in between lies the sphere of my fortune [Nigger 151-5
A mythological form, a festival sphere, [NH 466-2
In this chamber the pure sphere escapes the impure [NH 480-3
Inhabit the hypnosis of that sphere. [NH 480-9
Natives of a dwindled sphere. [Leben 504-21
Not of its sphere, and yet not far beyond, [Rome 508-15
Confounds all opposites and spins a sphere [Duck 63-20 P
In an age of concentric mobs would any sphere [Duck 63-25 P
At the elbow of Copernicus, a sphere, [Theatre 91-15 P
The unnamed creator of an unknown sphere, [Ulysses 101-3 P
In that sphere with so few objects of its own. [Local 112-3 P
SPHERES. Illimitable spheres of you, [Vincentine 53-14
A jovial hullabaloo among the spheres. [High-Toned 59-20
True genii for the diminished, spheres, [Choc 300-7
Sequences, thought of among spheres in the old peak of night: [Bed 326-19
This contrivance of the spectre of the spheres, [AA 420-18
This source and patriarch of other spheres, [Duck 63-27 P
See water-spheres.
SPICE. Or spice the shores with odors of the plum? [Sunday 69-21
SPICED. Of spiced and weathery rouges, should complex [C 44-8
See dark-spiced.
SPICES. Among the arrant spices of the sun, [Fictive 88-7
With the spices of red summer. [Pecul 453-11
Among the breathless spices and, sometimes, [Pecul 454-5
SPICK. Across the spick torrent, ceaselessly, [Paltry 6-9
SPIDER. The light is like a spider. [Tattoo 81-9
Yet a spider spins in the left shoe under the bed-- [Phenom 286-10
SPIDERS. Philadelphia that the spiders ate. [Arcades 225-3
SPIKY. Pale helms and spiky spurs, [Brave 138-14
SPILL. Or spill night out in brilliant vanishings, [Page 423-4
SPILLAGE. Trouble in the spillage and first sparkle of sun, [How Now 97-7 P
SPILLED. Round them she spilled the roses [Attempt 370-4
SPIN. Above the able spins its constant spin, [NSF 406-2
SPINE. O, skin and spine and hair of you, Ercole, [Extracts 256-18
SPINNING. Spinning and hissing with oracular [Geneva 24-11
Or else sat spinning on the pinnacles, [Babies 77-5
And bristling thorn-trees spinning on the bank [Nigger 155-15
And snow. The gheatre is spinning round, [Chaos 357-16
At it spinning its eccentric measure. Perhaps, [NSF 406-4
SPINS. Yet a spider spins in the left shoe under the bed-- [Phenom 286-10
Above the table spins its constant spin, [NSF 406-2
Confounds all opposites and spins a sphere [Duck 63-20 P
SPIRAL. Then turn your heads and let your spiral eyes [Red Kit 31-27 P
When shall lush chorals spiral through our fire [Duck 66-10 P
SPIRES. The bony buttresses, the bony spires [Gray 140-5
SPIRIT. The salt hung on his spirit like a frost, [C 29-13
On my spirit make a music, too. [Peter 89-18
Suckled on ponds, the spirit craves a watery mountain. [NE Verses 105-2
And this the spirit sees and is aggrieved. [Anatomy 108-18
Where my spirit is I am, [Sailing 120-23
What is there here but weather, what spirit [Adieu 128-9
Whose spirit is this? we said, because we knew [Key W 129-7
It was the spirit that we sought and knew [Key W 129-8
To the spirit itself, [Am Sub 131-8
The spirit and space, [Am Sub 131-9
The empty spirit [Am Sub 131-10
Of a turning spirit in an earlier self. [Sun March 134-1
In regulations of his spirit. [Winter B 141-12
His spirit grew uncertain of delight, [Anglais 148-15
Out of the spirit of the holy temples, [Nigger 151-19
A spirit storming in blank walls, [Postcard 159-18
The spirit laughs to see the eye believe [Extracts 253-5
To smother the wry spirit's misery. [News 265-7
For the spirit left helpless by the intelligence. [News 265-10
Presto, whose whispers prickle the spirit. [Hero 274-5
A mask, a spirit, an accoutrement. [Gigan 289-20
I hear the motions of the spirit and the sound [Choc 298-18
In what new spirit had his body birth? [Choc 299-8
The pleasure of his spirit in the cold. [Choc 301-23
A foyer of the spirit in a landscape [Crude 305-6
The spirit and all ensigns of the self? [Repet 308-18
Society of the spirit when it is [Repet 309-11
Grow out of the spirit or they are fantastic dust. [Holiday 313-4
"Less and Less Human, O Savage Spirit" [327-title
The cry of an embryo? The spirit tires, [Feo 334-1
The spirit of one dwelling in a seed, [Descrip 341-19
The spirit's universe, then a summer's day, [Descrip 343-16
Than the spirit of Ludwig Richter . . . [Chaos 357-8

Of the spirit. This, in sight and memory, [Cred 376-22
And of the spirit of the arranged, douceurs, [Cred 377-14
Set on me the spirit's diamond coronal. [NSF 396-6
With the whole spirit sparkling in its cloth, [Owl 434-12
The nurses of the spirit's innocence. [Luther 461-9
The spirit's speeches, the indefinite, [NH 466-18
Everything, the spirit's alchemicana [NH 471-22
Included, the spirit, that goes roundabout [NH 471-23
His spirit is imprisoned in constant change. [NH 472-12
The phrase . . . Say of each lion of the spirit [NH 472-24
A disused ambit of the spirit's way, [Aug 489-8
Or else a new aspect, say the spirit's sex, [Aug 489-12
At the spirit's base? [Irish 501-8
Of the fortune of the spirit, beyond the eye, [Rome 508-14
The human end in the spirit's greatest reach. [Rome 508-16
The spirit comes from the body of the world, [Look 519-7
And there become a spirit's mannerism, [Look 519-11
The spirit wakes in the wind--is naked. [Soldat 11-13 P
O spirit of bones, O mountain of graves? [Sat Night 28-6 P
Might muff the mighty spirit of Lenin. [Lytton 39-17 P
Itself into the speech of the spirit, until [Burnshaw 52-10 P
The spirit's episcopate, hallowed and high, [Greenest 53-28 P
To which the spirit ascended, to increase [Greenest 53-29 P
The spirit's natural images, carriers, [Greenest 57-12 P
He does not hear by sound. His spirit knows [Greenest 59-7 P
Day came upon the spirit as life comes [Duck 61-5 P
And the spirit writhes to be wakened, writhes [Duck 61-8 P
The spirit's ring and seal, the naked heart. [Bship 79-13 P
Piercing the spirit by appearance, [Ulysses 104-6 P
He knew that he was a spirit without a foyer [Local 111-11 P
SPIRITOUS. And spiritous passage into nothingness, [Heaven 56-17
SPIRITS. Came like two spirits parleying, adorned [C 31-31
Melodious, where spirits gat them home, [Sunday 68-20
Is not the porch of spirits lingering. [Sunday 70-16
Pricks in our spirits at the summer's end, [Anatomy 108-5
But our unfashioned spirits realized [Eve Angels 137-4
Did several spirits assume a single shape. [Les Plus 245-7
The spirits of all the impotent dead, seen clear, [Cats 368-8
SPIRITUAL. Of a destroying spiritual that digs-a-dog, [Pure 332-20
The arias that spiritual fiddlings make, [Orb 440-2
It is a fresh spiritual that he defines, [NH 474-19
SPISS. Most spiss--oh! Yes, most spissantly. [Snow Stars 133-2
SPISSANTLY. Most spiss--oh! Yes, most spissantly, [Snow Stars 133-2
SPIT. He tastes its blood, not spit. [Destructive 192-17
Direction, shrinking from the spit and splash [Think 356-12
And Gibraltar is dissolved like spit in the wind. [Puel 456-3
SPITE. In spite of hawk and falcon, green toucan [C 30-18
Of a man gone mad, after all, for time, in spite [Nigger 157-18
At last, in spite of his manner, his eye [MBG 181-20
Forehead's cold, spite of the eye [Bagatelles 213-14
You, too, are drifting, in spite of your course; [Vari 232-17
If the place, in spite of its witheredness, was still [Extracts 255-11
In spite of this, the gigantic bulk of him [Choc 299-4
In spite of the yellow of the acacias, the scent [EM 315-5
And hard it is in spite of blazoned days. [NSF 383-24
In spite of the mere objectiveness of things, [Moonlight 531-21
You say that spite avails her nothing, that [Good Bad 33-8 P
But of what are they thinking, of what, in spite of the duck, [Duck 62-12 P
In spite of the watch-chains aus Wien, in spite [Duck 62-13 P
In spite of her airs, that's what she was. She was all [Grotesque 74-5 P
SPITTLE. As the spittle of cows [Depression 63-11
SPITTLING. The spittling tissues tight across the bones. [Nigger 155-8
SPLASH. Direction, shrinking from the spit and splash [Think 356-12
SPLASHED. Into the autumn weather, splashed with frost, [Monocle 16-7
Splashed wide-wise because it likes magnificence [AA 416-13
SPLASHINGS. They are not splashings in a penumbra. They stand. [Bouquet 452-16
SPLATTERS. That splatters incessant thousands of drops, [Hartford 226-9
SPLAY. In that splay of marble [Archi 17-4 P
SPLEEN. In their embroidered slippers, touch your spleen? [Polish Aunt 84-5
SPLENDOR. With a sad splendor, beyond artifice, [Owl 435-16
Make a sidereal splendor as you fly. [Red Kit 32-2 P
A life lighter than this present splendor, [Ulysses 101-23 P
SPLENDORS. Than mute bare splendors of the sun and moon. [On Manner 56-8
SPLINTERS. The dazzled flakes and splinters disappear. [Golden 460-17
SPLIT. What ward split up in clickering syllables [C 28-14
Split it and make blocks, [Archi 17-23 P
SPLURGING. The vine, at the roots, this vine of Key West, splurging [Bship 80-9 P
SPOILED. Of medicine, a fragrantness not to be spoiled . . . [Rome 508-20

SPOKE. But spoke for you perfectly in my thoughts, [Two Figures
      86-5
    That he spoke only by doing what he did. [Men Fall 188-12
    It wears. This is the way the orator spoke: [Dames 206-2
    The moonlight and Aquinas seemed to. He spoke, [Les Plus 245-3
    Solange, the magnolia to whom I spoke, [News 265-1
    To which I spoke, near which I stood and spoke, [News 265-3
    And it all spoke together. [Search 268-4
    And it spoke all together. [Search 268-6
    Each man spoke in winter. Yet each man spoke of [Hero 273-7
    As if nothing had happened. The dim actor spoke. [Repet 306-11
    Or merely seemed to touch him as he spoke [EM 315-2
    The words they spoke were voices that she heard. [NSF 402-10
    And spoke the feeling for them, which was what they had lacked.
      [Large 424-9
    She spoke with backward gestures of her hand. [Owl 435-8
    In the land of big mariners, the words they spoke [NH 486-20
    It was a language he spoke, because he must, yet did not know.
      [Madame 507-7
    Rou-cou spoke the dove, [Song Fixed 519-13
    And one of us spoke and all of us believed [Letters 107-14 P
SPOKED. It might become a wheel spoked red and white [Page 422-21
SPOKEN. Half-way to bed, when the phrase will be spoken, [Nigger
      156-8
    The hero's throat in which the words are spoken, [Montra 261-4
    A sound producing the things that are spoken. [Phenom 287-6
    Compounded of dear relation, spoken twice, [EM 317-18
    In the yes of the realist spoken because he must [EM 320-12
    Say yes, spoken because under every no [EM 320-13
    The words were spoken as if there was no book, [House Q 358-11
    Be spoken to, without a roof, without [NSF 385-9
    Said things it had laboriously spoken. [NSF 387-18
    Speak to me that, which spoken, will array me [NSF 396-4
    There seemed to be an apostrophe that was not spoken. [Cata
      424-15
    Not wholly spoken in a conversation between [NH 471-7
    And spoken in paradisal parlance new [NH 475-16
    A look, a few words spoken. [Leben 505-6
    Were not and are not. Absurd. The words spoken [Rock 525-10
    It is curious that I should have spoken of Raël, [Desire 85-1 P
    Curious that I should have spoken of Jaffa [Desire 85-4 P
    One thinks that it could be that the first word spoken, [Discov
      95-17 P
    See: half-spoken; well-spoken.
SPOKESMAN. More than a spokesman of the night to say [Choc 299-11
    The spokesman at our bluntest barriers, [NSF 397-2
    See pine-spokesman.
SPONTANEITIES. The spontaneities of rain or snow [Sombre 67-31 P
SPONTANEOUS. Whistle about us their spontaneous cries; [Sunday
      70-23
    By the spontaneous particulars of sound. [Creat 311-15
SPONTANEOUSLY. Spontaneously watering their gritty soils. [Monocle
      16-25
SPOOK. The spook and makings of the nude magnolia? [Slug 522-14
SPORTIVE. Much richer, more fecund, sportive and alive. [NH 469-24
SPOT. Is the spot on the floor, there, wine or blood [MBG 173-11
    And opens in this familiar spot [Red Fern 365-2
    In an abandoned spot. Soft, civil bird, [Cred 377-12
    And if one's sense of a single spot [Ulysses 99-21 P
SPOUSE. That is the sensual, pearly spouse, the life [Sleight
      222-18
    I am the spouse. She took her necklace off [NSF 395-19
    The spouse. She opened her stone-studded belt. [NSF 395-21
    I am the spouse, divested of bright gold, [NSF 395-22
    The spouse beyond emerald or amethyst, [NSF 395-23
    Order, saying I am the contemplated spouse. [NSF 396-3
    Then Ozymandias said the spouse, the bride [NSF 396-10
    Of the other, as if summer was a spouse, [Orb 441-20
SPOUT. The window, close to the ramshackle spout in which [NH 475-8
    Of the rain in the spout is not a substitute. [NH 475-20
    See water-spout.
SPOUTING. And spouting new orations of the cold. [Pharynx 96-15
    4. The sea is spouting upward out of rocks. [Someone 86-7 A
SPOUTS. Memorabilia of the mystic spouts, [Monocle 16-24
SPRANG. Until the steeples of his city clanked and sprang [Geneva
      24-13
    A winter's noon, in which the colors sprang [Greenest 57-25 P
SPRAWLED. And sprawled around, no longer wild. [Jar 76-10
SPRAWLERS. That rises in the air. The sprawlers on the grass [Duck
      64-7 P
SPRAWLING. Lie sprawling in majors of the August heat, [EM 325-28
    High up in heaven a sprawling portent moves, [Sombre 68-17 P
    Yet lord, a mask of flame, the sprawling form [Sombre 70-16 P
    High up in heaven the sprawling portent moves. [Sombre 70-18 P
    The sprawling of winter might suddenly stand erect, [Discov
      96-3 P
SPRAY. Hi! Whisk it, poodle, flick the spray [Hartford 227-10
    Of spray. Let all the salt be gone. [Vari 234-16
SPREAD. Of hardy foam, receding flatly, spread [C 34-6
    Of crinoline spread, but of a pining sweet, [C 42-29

That spread chromatics in hilarious dark, [C 45-9
    And spread it so as to cover her face. [Emperor 64-12
    Yes, and the blackbird spread its tail, [Watermelon 89-10
    The gongs grew still. And then blue heaven spread [Sea Surf 100-6
    And silvers and greens spread over the sea. The moon [Farewell
      117-4
    Spread on the sun-bronzed air, [Pascagoula 127-2
    Its wings spread wide to rain and snow, [MBG 166-8
    Spreading them as waves spread flat on the shore, [Loaf 200-6
    The chandeliers, their morning glazes spread [Blue Bldg 217-11
    To spread colors. There was not an idea [Forces 229-6
    A wind will spread its windy grandeurs round [AA 414-1
    Variations on the words spread sail. [Aug 490-2
    And the hawk cats it and we say spread sail, [Aug 490-6
    Spread sail, we say spread white, spread way. [Aug 490-7
    Spread outward. Crack the round dome. Break through. [Aug 490-11
    And spread about them a warmer, rosier odor. [Aug 491-28
    Snarling in him for discovery as his attentions spread, [Prol
      516-17
    And spread hallucinations on every leaf. [Armor 529-20
    It seizes a sheet, from the ground, from a bush, as if spread
      There by some wash-woman for the night. [Plough-Boy 6-5 P
    Spread over heaven shutting out the light. [Red Kit 31-26 P
    Wings spread and whirling over jaguar-men? [Greenest 55-31 P
    Merely the center of a circle, spread [Bship 81-10 P
SPREADING. Is rest and silence spreading into sleep. [Eve Angels
      137-25
    Spreading them as waves spread flat on the shore, [Loaf 200-6
    The wings keep spreading and yet are never wings. [Somnam 304-4
    A shape left behind, with like wings spreading out, [Myrrh 350-2
    Of the image spreading behind it in idea. [Bouquet 449-20
    Spreading out fortress walls like fortress wings, [Luther 461-12
    And the first line spreading up the beach; again, [Woman Had
      81-14 P
SPREADS. Spreads to the sun. [Ploughing 20-16
    And spreads its webs there-- [Tattoo 81-13
    And of becoming, for which the chapel spreads out [Armor 530-13
    But spreads an evil lustre whose increase [Spaniard 34-12 P
SPREDDEN. On his spredden wings, needs nothing but deep space,
      [NSF 404-17
SPRIGS. Of the tropic of resemblance, sprigs [Someone 86-17 A
SPRING. "The Paltry Nude Starts on a Spring Voyage" [5-title
    For it has come that thus I greet the spring. [Monocle 13-18
    No spring can follow past meridian. [Monocle 13-20
    Out of what swift destruction did it spring? [C 30-12
    That wrote his couplet yearly to the spring, [C 31-5
    The spring came there in clinking pannicles [C 34-9
    And as he came he saw that it was spring, [C 35-28
    The moonlight fiction disappeared. The spring, [C 36-1
    "The spring is like a belle undressing." [Of Surface 57-5
    "Depression before Spring" [63-title
    Old pantaloons, duenna of the spring! [Polish Aunt 84-6
    Yet there is no spring in Florida, neither in boskage perdu,
      nor on the nunnery beaches. [Indian 112-7
    Of life and spring and of the lustrous inundations, [Medit 123-14
    The grackles sing avant the spring [Snow Stars 133-1
    The muddy rivers of spring [Mud 147-13
    A little less returned for him each spring, [Anglais 148-12
    At what we saw. The spring clouds blow [Postcard 159-7
    Spring sparkle and the cock-bird shriek. [MBG 182-13
    When spring comes and the skeletons of the hunters [Parochial
      191-19
    The spring will have a health of its own, with none [Parochial
      192-1
    It is a state, this spring among the politicians [Glass 198-2
    Because it was spring and the birds had to come. [Loaf 200-15
    Now, in the time of spring (azaleas, trilliums, [Dump 202-12
    There has been a booming all the spring, [Nightgown 214-3
    If all the green of spring was blue, and it is; [Connois 215-4
    As a young lover sees the first buds of spring [Peaches 224-5
    That in spring will crown every western horizon, [Martial 237-12
    In the same way, you were happy in spring, [Motive 288-5
    Spring is umbilical or else it is not spring. [Holiday 313-1
    Spring is the truth of spring or nothing, a waste, a fake.
      [Holiday 313-2
    Great tufts, spring up from buried houses [EM 322-15
    There might be in the curling-out of spring [Descrip 341-15
    Might spring to sight and yet remain a dove. [Think 357-4
    My Jacomyntje! This first spring after the war, [Extraord 369-16
    And spring's infuriations over and a long way [Cred 372-5
    Spring vanishes the scraps of winter, why [NSF 391-1
    Of death in memory's dream? Is spring a sleep? [NSF 391-3
    Winter and spring, cold copulars, embrace [NSF 392-8
    Of spring come to their places in the grape leaves [NSF 399-14
    Shall we be found hanging in the trees next spring? [AA 419-19
    Out of the first warmth of spring, [Celle 438-1
    The bloody lion in the yard at night or ready to spring [Puel
      456-6
    So lewd spring comes from winter's chastity. [NH 468-4
    The way the earliest single light in the evening sky, in spring,

[Prol 517-8
And the icon is the man. The pearled chaplet of spring, [Rock
    526-20
The spring about him: [Primordia 9-9 P
The new spring tumble in the sky. [Sat Night 27-19 P
They were so glad to see the spring. [Sat Night 28-11 P
This base of every future, vibrant spring, [Duck 63-28 P
Small bees of spring, sniffing the coldest buds [Duck 65-7 P
And fragrant fomentations of the spring [Sombre 69-18 P
Except that this is an image of black spring [Sombre 69-30 P
The spring is hum-drum like an instrument, [Sombre 71-11 P
A lamp, in a day of the week, the time before spring, [Woman
    Had 83-6 P
Of the spring of the year, [How Now 97-6 P
"The Dove in Spring" [97-title P
Spring's bright paradise has come to this. [Fare Guit 98-16 P
From which the incredible systems spring, [Ulysses 103-19 P
Is there no spring? [Three 128-16 P
Is there no spring? [Three 129-17 P
From the spring. [Three 141-2 P
SPRINGING. See up-springing.
SPRINGS. Our feigning with the strange unlike, whence springs
    [Fictive 88-12
    The touch of springs, [Peter 90-16
    Springs outward, being large, and, in the dust, [Pure 332-22
    From this the poem springs: that we live in a place [NSF 383-22
    He from whose beard the future springs, elect. [Duck 64-31 P
    Of evil, evil springs; or catholic hope, [Sombre 69-23 P
SPRINGTIME. This reposes alike in springtime [Yellow 236-11
SPRINKLED. What was the ointment sprinkled on my beard? [Hoon
    65-10
SPRINKLES. Of cloudy silver sprinkles in your gown [Fictive 87-11
SPRINKLINGS. Sprinklings of bright particulars from the sky. [De-
    scrip 344-6
SPROUT. In the weed of summer comes this green sprout why.
    [Questions 462-4
    They bud the whitest eye, the pallidest sprout, [Rock 527-7
SPROUTINGS. Part of the unpredictable sproutings, as of [Nuns
    92-8 P
SPRUCE. Everywhere the spruce trees bury soldiers: [Vari 234-10
    Everywhere spruce trees bury spruce trees. [Vari 234-13
    In a single spruce, when, suddenly, [Two Illus 514-14
    The master of the spruce, himself, [Two Illus 515-1
SPRUCES. The spruces rough in the distant glitter [Snow Man 10-3
    The spruces' outstretched hands; [Delight 162-7
SPRUNG. A memorandum of the people sprung [Repet 309-4
SPUMING. The sea of spuming thought foists up again [Monocle 13-8
SPUN. From the spun sky and the high and deadly view, [Aug 493-10
SPUR. The crawling railroad spur, the rotten fence, [C 36-14
SPURGE. Of the milk within the saltiest spurge, heard, then,
    [Sea Surf 100-19
SPURNED. The imagination that we spurned and crave. [Fictive 88-18
SPURS. Pale helms and spiky spurs, [Brave 138-14
SPURTED. Spurted from between the fingers [Weak Mind 212-3
SPUTTERED. The idea of god no longer sputtered [Thought 184-13
    The wed weed sputtered, the fire died down, the cold [Page 422-1
SPUTTERING. When the candle, sputtering up, [Three 131-9 P
SQUALID. The captain squalid on his pillow, the great [Choc 300-1
    To men, to houses, streets and the squalid whole. [Greenest
    57-8 P
    With squalid cells, unless New York is Cocos [Duck 63-13 P
SQUALLS. And squalls. [Room Gard 41-6 P
SQUAMOUS. The squirming facts exceed the squamous mind, [Connois
    215-17
SQUARE. Rationalists, wearing square hats, [Six Sig 75-4
    Think, in square rooms, [Six Sig 75-5
    "The Public Square" [108-title
    The square began to clear. [Public Sq 109-10
    Of those for whom a square room is a fire, [Parochial 191-13
    There's a little square in Paris, [Phases 3-1 P
SQUARES. The gold façade round early squares, [Thought 187-2
    The checkered squares, the skeleton of repose, [Bouquet 450-7
    So near detachment, the cover's cornered squares, [Bouquet
    450-13
SQUASHES. We hang like warty squashes, streaked and rayed, [Monocle
    16-9
SQUATTING. A point of survey squatting like a throne, [Cred 373-19
SQUAWKIEST. Thridding the squawkiest jungle [Cab 21-10 P
SQUAWKS. See parrot-squawks.
SQUEAK. Could make us squeak, like dolls, the wished-for words.
    [Monocle 17-8
    But squint and squeak, where no people are: [Stan MBG 73-15 P
SQUEAL. And make the Dagoes squeal. [Drum-Majors 36-22 P
SQUEEZED. The blower squeezed to the thinnest mi of falsetto.
    [Parochial 191-6
    He squeezed it and the blood [Weak Mind 212-2
    Which were their thoughts, squeezed into shapes, the sun [Duck
    61-11 P
SQUEEZING. Squeezing the reddest fragrance from the stump [God
    285-14

SQUIGGLING. Squiggling like saxaphones. And palm for palm, [High-
    Toned 59-12
SQUINT. But squint and squeak, where no people are: [Stan MBG
    73-15 P
SQUIRMING. The squirming facts exceed the squamous mind, [Connois
    215-17
    The perspective squirming as it tries to take [Bship 80-4 P
SQUIRRELS. The robins are là-bas, the squirrels, in tree-caves,
    [NH 487-11
    Huddle together in the knowledge of squirrels. [NH 487-12
S.S. NORMANDIE. The S.S. Normandie, granted [Prelude 195-7
STAATS-OPER. Act I, Scene 1, at a German Staats-Oper. [Nigger
    153-16
STABBING. Stabbing at his teat-like corns [Lulu M 27-15 P
STACK. And the stack of the electric plant, [Common 221-4
STACKS. From crusty stacks above machines. [MBG 182-4
    Things jutted up, the way the jagged stacks, [Greenest 53-11 P
    Still questioning if to crush the soaring stacks, [Sombre
    68-31 P
STAFF. His beard is of fire and his staff is a leaping flame.
    [Nigger 150-14
STAGE. The weather of his stage, himself. [MBG 170-4
    Like something on the stage, puffed out, [MBG 181-18
    To construct a new stage. It has to be on that stage [Of Mod
    240-5
    Walked toward him on the stage and they embraced. [Repet 306-15
    The stage becomes an atmosphere [Soldat 15-19 P
STAGE-LIGHT. This stage-light of the Opera? [Hartford 226-16
STAGGERING. Contorted, staggering from the thrust against [Old
    Woman 43-14 P
STAGNANT. A reflection stagnant in a stagnant stream. [Nigger 156-2
    O stagnant east-wind, palsied mare, [Room Gard 40-16 P
STAINED. Or the bench with the pot of geraniums, the stained
    mattress and the washed overalls drying in the sun? [Indigo
    22-12 P
    See: rain-stained-vaults; salt-stained.
STAINS. So summer comes in the end to these few stains [Beginning
    427-10
    With saintly imagination and the stains [Bship 81-2 P
STAIR. The children will be crying on the stair, [Nigger 156-7
    Saying things in the rooms and on the stair, [Less 327-10
    Come home, wind, he said as he climbed the stair-- [Pieces 351-14
    Life fixed him, wandering on the stair of glass. [NH 483-10
STAIRS. It is because they carry down the stairs [Mozart 131-20
    That the marbles are gluey pastiches, the stairs [Prelude 195-3
    Clandestine steps upon imagined stairs [Oboe 251-6
    As they climb the stairs [Archi 17-9 P
STAKED. Staked solidly in a gusty grappling with rocks. [NH 487-21
STALE. The drenching of stale lives no more fell down. [C 30-10
    And, from their stale intelligence released, [C 37-9
    Across the stale, mysterious seasons. These [On Manner 56-3
    It is stale and the water is discolored. [Hero 280-21
    Avoid our stale perfections, seeking out [Dutch 293-1
    As morning throws off stale moonlight and shabby sleep. [NSF
    382-12
    Then the stale turtle will grow limp from age. [John 437-22
    The blood refreshes with its stale demands. [Study I 464-3
    In the stale grandeur of annihilation. [Leben 505-9
    Is itself old and stale. [Polo 37-15 P
STALIN. In Russia at which the same statue of Stalin greets [Cats
    367-15
STALK. The stalk, the weed, the grassy flourishes, [Bouquet 452-8
    And stalk the skies. [Abnormal 24-18 P
STALKS. A soldier stalks before my door. [Contra I 267-4
    In this bleak air the broken stalks [Possum 293-17
    The stalks are firmly rooted in ice. [Possum 294-8
STALLION-BACK. The thickest man on the thickest stallion-back,
    [Havana 143-18
STAMP. Stamp down the phosphorescent toes, tear off [Nigger 155-7
STAMPED. The doctor of Geneva stamped the sand [Geneva 24-1
STAMPING. Will come stamping here, the ruler of less than men,
    [Aug 495-22
    Naked and stamping the earth, [Drum-Majors 37-8 P
STAND. Two wooden tubs of blue hydrangeas stand at the foot of the
    stone steps. [Banal 62-11
    To stand here on the deck in the dark and say [Farewell 118-6
    Just to stand still without moving a hand. [Adieu 127-12
    How does one stand [Am Sub 130-16
    As we stand gazing at the rounded moon. [Eve Angels 138-6
    Stand in a fixed light. [Gray 140-7
    And shall I then stand in the sun, as now [MBG 168-16
    I stand in the moon, and call it good, [MBG 168-17
    Not to be part of the sun? To stand [MBG 168-20
    Throw the lights away. Nothing must stand [MBG 183-10
    He sought an earthly leader who could stand [Thought 185-23
    In which they stand, [Common 221-7
    Can never stand as god, is ever wrong [Oboe 250-16
    In brown books. The marbles of what he was stand [Hero 276-25
    To stand taller than a person stands, has [Hero 277-7
    How is it that the wooden trees stand up [Belly 367-2

We stand in the tumult of a festival. [AA 415-21
Nor stand there making orotund consolations. [Papini 446-11
They are not splashings in a penumbra. They stand. [Bouquet
    452-16
The great cat must stand potent in the sun. [NH 473-3
It is no longer air. The houses still stand, [Rock 525-5
The child's hair is of the color of the hay in the haystack,
    around which the four black horses stand. [Primordia 8-1 P
The trees stand still, [Primordia 8-16 P
But could the statue stand in Africa? [Greenest 56-27 P
Was meant to stand, not in a tumbling green, [Greenest 57-3 P
Why should it fail to stand? Victoria Platz, [Greenest 58-19 P
And he shall fix the place where it will stand. [Greenst 60-2 P
The sprawling of winter might suddenly stand erect, [Discov 96-3P
Stand at the center of ideal time, [Ideal 89-11 A
    See band-stand.
STANDARD. Always the standard repertoire in line [Nigger 156-19
STANDING. Ask us not to sing standing in the sun, [Orangeade 102-17
And the two of them standing still to rest. [How Live 126-4
From a doctor into an ox, before standing up, [Freed 205-11
And, standing in violent golds, will brush her hair. [Debris
    338-7
Its false disasters--these fathers standing round, [Cred 372-16
It is the old man standing on the tower, [Cred 374-1
Than nakedness, standing before an inflexible [NSF 396-2
One remembers a woman standing in such a dress. [Bouquet 450-24
It is the infant A standing on infant legs, [NH 469-7
With the broken statues standing on the shore. [Aug 491-8
Seen for a moment standing in the door. [Angel 496-8
He carved the feathery walkers standing by, [Duck 64-22 P
STANDS. It stands gigantic, with a certain tip [Monocle 17-4
Here in the centre stands the glass. Light [Glass 197-12
About what stands here in the centre, not the glass, [Glass
    197-12
Not the symbol but that for which the symbol stands, [Martial
    238-11
To stand taller than a person stands, has [Hero 277-7
True autumn stands then in the doorway. [Hero 280-22
Now, time stands still. He came from out of sleep. [Choc 299-12
Is ease, stands in the dark, a shadows' hill, [EM 319-5
There is a building stands in a ruinous storm, [Sketch 336-7
The bright obvious stands motionless in cold. [Man Car 351-8
Continually. And old John Zeller stands [Two V 354-21
Stands truly. The circles nearest to it share [Anach 366-9
Stands and regards and repeats the primitive lines. [Anach
    366-15
It is the mountain on which the tower stands, [Cred 373-22
Farewell to an idea . . . A cabin stands, [AA 412-4
The bouquet stands in a jar, as metaphor, [Bouquet 448-8
And die. It stands on a table at a window [Bouquet 450-5
It stands a sovereign of souvenirs [Bouquet 451-5
Cloud's gold, of a whole appearance that stands and is. [Bouquet
    452-18
The sun stands like a Spaniard as he departs, [Novel 457-4
If the black of night stand glistening on beau mont, [NH 467-2
A clearness has returned. It stands restored. [NH 488-3
Stands in a light, its natural light and day, [Armor 530-20
Stands glistening and Haddam shines and sways. [R Conn 533-15
That thinks of it is incribed on walls and stands [Duck 64-3 P
Stands brimming white, chiaroscuro scaled [Sombre 70-20 P
The state stands in true perspective. Crows [Sombre 71-2 P
The statue stands [Sombre 71-7 P
Ragged in unkempt perceptions, that stands [Theatre 91-8 P
The space in which it stands, the shine [Ulysses 100-26 P
The palm stands on the edge of space. [Of Mere 118-4 P
1. The hut stands by itself beneath the palms. [Someone 86-4 A
STANZA. The day to pieces and cry stanza my stone? [Dump 203-10
STANZAED. See many-stanzaed.
STANZAS. We live in a camp . . . Stanzas of final peace [Extracts
    258-22
His firm stanzas hang like hives in hell [EM 315-11
STAR. In the high west there burns a furious star. [Monocle 14-23
It is for fiery boys that star was set [Monocle 14-24
you give me, ancient star: [Nuances 18-5
The young emerald, evening star, [Homunculus 25-14
The rapey gouts. Good star, how that to be [C 42-20
Toward the cool night and its fantastic star, [Lilacs 49-11
The very hinds discerned it, in a star. [Sunday 68-4
What one star can carve, [Six Sig 75-2
Each is both star and orb; and day [MBG 172-11
The faster's feast and heavy-fruited star, [Thought 186-3
Whose whore is Morning Star [Thought 186-18
Star over Monhegan, Atlantic star, [Vari 232-15
The evening star, at the beginning of winter, the star [Martial
    237-11
What had this star to do with the world it lit, [Martial 238-3
Be tranquil in your wounds. The placating star [Extracts 253-26
Iciest core, a north star, central [Hero 275-24
At the end of night last night a crystal star, [Choc 296-17
The crystal-pointed star of morning, rose [Choc 296-18

Is to search. Likewise to say of the evening star, [NH 481-17
At evening's one star [Inhab 503-13
This one star's blaze. [Inhab 504-11
A whole, the day on which the last star [Ulysses 102-8 P
Under the front of the westward evening star, [Real 110-12 P
    See: half-star; Saturn-star.
STARE. The sexton moves with a sexton's stare [Gray 140-11
STARED. A hatching that stared and demanded an answering look.
    [NH 484-3
STAR-FURRED. White and star-furred for his legions, [Snow Stars
    133-8
STAR-HUMPED. Man-misty to a race star-humped, astride [Sombre
    70-29 P
STAR-IMPALED. And not a delicate ether star-impaled, [Havana 144-1
STARING. Staring, at midnight, at the pillow that is black [Men
    Fall 187-17
In the grinding ric-rac, staring steadily [Men Fall 188-4
Staring at the secretions of the words as [Lack 303-3
STARKER. Remained, except some starker, barer self [C 29-16
In a starker, barer world, in which the sun [C 29-17
STARKLY. Too starkly pallid for the jaguar's light, [Greenest
    54-29 P
STARLESS. Sultan of African sultans, starless crown. [Greenest
    60-6 P
STARLIGHT. Keen to the point of starlight, while a frog [Monocle
    17-16
From whose being by starlight, on sea-coast, [Homunculus 26-26
It is a wizened starlight growing young, [Descrip 344-9
ST. ARMORER. "St. Armorer's Church from the Outside" [529-title
St. Armorer's was once an immense success. [Armor 529-1
In its church-yard, in the province of St. Armorer's, [Armor 529-3
St. Armorer's has nothing of this present, [Armor 530-11
The chapel underneath St. Armorer's walls, [Armor 530-19
STARRED. See: dimly-starred; still-starred.
STARRY. To make believe a starry connaissance. [Monocle 13-22
In a starry placating. [Mozart 132-17
The starry voluptuary will be born. [Nigger 156-9
Last night at the end of night his starry head, [Choc 299-19
STARS. "That bliss of stars, that princox of evening heaven!"
    reminding of seasons, [Banal 63-1
"Stars at Tallapoosa" [71-title
The lines are straight and swift between the stars. [Tallap 71-10
From stars, [Six Sig 74-21
Holding their books toward the nearer stars, [Plish Aunt 84-10
And sleep with one eye watching the stars fall [Two Figures
    86-11
That lights and dims the stars? [Sonatina 110-6
"Snow and Stars" [133-title
This robe of snow and winter stars, [Snow Stars 133-4
Statues and stars, [Botanist 1 135-9
The good stars, [Brave 138-13
It was autumn and falling stars [Reader 147-1
Except the trace of burning stars [Reader 147-11
Full of stars and the images of stars-- [Nightgown 214-7
Tonight there are only the winter stars. [Dezem 218-1
Tonight the stars are like a crowd of faces [Dezem 218-9
And a little island full of geese and stars: [Sleight 222-15
If the stars that move together as one, disband, [Horn 230-17
So that the stars, my semblables, chimeres, [Dutch 293-4
His stars on the wall. He must dwell quietly. [Less 327-14
In which old stars are planets of morning, fresh [Descrip 344-10
Unsnack your snood, madanna, for the stars [Myrrh 349-13
That's how the stars shine during the day. There, then, [Lot
    371-4
And throws his stars around the floor. By day [NSF 383-5
And moved on them in orbits' outer stars [NSF 383-5
The stars are putting on their glittering belts. [AA 419-22
New stars that were a foot across came out [Page 421-15
The one-foot stars were couriers of its death [Page 421-19
These were not tepid stars of torpid places [Page 421-21
They were those from the wilderness of stars that had expected
    more. [Large 423-13
"Our Stars Come from Ireland" [454-title
The stars are washing up from Ireland [Our Stars 455-9
Of nights full of the green stars from Ireland, [Our Stars 455-14
Or stars that follow men, not to attend, [Angel 496-11
Of your dark self, and how the wings of stars, [Blanche 10-11 P
The statue stood in stars like water-spheres, [Old Woman 45-10 P
And shadowy hanging of it, thick with stars [Old Woman 46-2 P
Less in the stars than in their earthy wake, [Burnshaw 48-10 P
By waverings of stars, the joy of day [Greenst 54-15 P
Of things, why bother about the back of stars? [Greenst 58-27 P
Under the middle stars, he said: [Ulysses 99-15 P
And clumped stars dangled all the way. [Ulysses 105-12 P
Beneath the middle stars and said: [Presence 105-18 P
Through clumped stars dangling all the way. [Presence 106-12 P
    See: sea-stars; side-stars.
START. Start the singing in a voice [Orangeade 103-13
And toward the start of day and trees [Adequacy 244-6
Look round you as you start to rise, brown moon, [God 285-4

STARTING. Men would be starting at dawn to walk ashore. [Page
    422-5
    The starting point of the human and the end, [Rock 528-16
STARTS. "The Paltry Nude Starts on a Spring Voyage" [5-title
    But not on a shell, she starts, [Paltry 5-6
    The dauntless master, as he starts the human tale. [Puel 456-18
STARVATION. That kill the single man, starvation's head, [Extracts
    254-16
STARVING. Feel everything starving except the belly [Hero 278-3
STAR-YPLAITED. The star-yplaited, visible sanction, [Stan Hero
    83-14 P
STATE. Perhaps our wretched state would soon come right. [Sur-
    prises 98-9
    The Founder of the State. Whoever founded [Mice 123-9
    A state that was free, in the dead of winter, from mice? [Mice
    123-10
    Shows that this object is merely a state, [Glass 197-9
    And in that state, the glass is a pool. [Glass 197-14
    And there and in another state--the refractions, [Glass 197-18
    It is a state, this spring among the politicians [Glass 198-2
    To project the naked man in a state of fact, [Montra 263-11
    State the disclosure. In that one eye the dove [Think 357-3
    In the present state of things as, say, to paint [NH 478-6
    In the present state of painting and not the state [NH 478-7
    The state of circumstance. [Aug 492-3
    As the man the state, not as the state the man, [Duck 63-9 P
    The race, the nation, the state. But society [Bship 79-21 P
    And state of being large and light. [Dove 98-12 P
    The center that he sought was a state of mind, [Art Pop 112-13 P
STATED. I take all things as stated--so and so [Soldat 11-7 P
STATELY-STATUED. In lilies' stately-statued calm; [Room Gard 41-11P
STATEMENT. With ribbon, a rigid statement of them, white, [NSF
    402-6
    His utmost statement. It is his own array, [Questions 462-17
    Of statement, directly and indirectly getting at, [NH 488-18
    See re-statement.
STATES. With this paper, this dust. That states the point. [Ex-
    tracts 252-6
    Among are more vestigial states of mind. [NSF 392-1
STATION. At the railway station, a soldier steps away, [Repet
    308-3
STATIONED. This is that figure stationed at our end, [Owl 434-22
STATIONS. Between two neatly measured stations, [Hero 275-17
    In these stations, in which nothing has been lost, [Souls 94-20 P
STATUARY. And B are not like statuary, posed [Connois 216-10
STATUE. Statue against a Clear Sky [NE Verses 105-title 9
    Statue against a Cloudy Sky [NE Verses 105-title 10
    At the base of the statue, we go round and round. [Mice 123-2
    Posed for his statue [Am Sub 130-22
    In Russia at which the same statue of Stalin greets [Cats 367-15
    The great statue of the General Du Puy [NSF 391-7
    The statue of Jove among the boomy clouds. [NH 482-19
    Which, without the statue, would be new, [NH 483-5
    "The Old Woman and the Statue" [43-title P
    Of crisping light along the statue's rim. [Old Woman 43-18 P
    The statue stood in stars like water-spheres. [Old Woman 45-10 P
    "Mr. Burnshaw and the Statue" [46-title P
    The statue seems a thing from Schwarz's, a thing [Burnshaw 47-4P
    Beside the statue, while you sang. Your eyes [Burnshaw 50-28 P
    Your backs upon the vivid statue. Then, [Burnshaw 51-13 P
    Conceive that while you dance the statue falls, [Burnshaw 51-30P
    Rising from indolent coils. If the statue rose, [Greenest 54-24P
    If once the statue were to rise, if it stood, [Greenest 54-25 P
    But could the statue stand in Africa? [Greenest 56-27 P
    In Capricorn. The statue has a form [Greenst 58-17 P
    The statue belongs to the cavernous past, belongs [Greenest
    58-28 P
    He looks upon the statue, where it is, [Greenest 59-2 P
    He, only, caused the statue to be made [Greenest 60-1 P
    Converging on the statue, white and high." [Duck 62-27 P
    The statue is white and high, white brillianter [Duck 64-5 P
    The statue is the sculptor not the stone. [Duck 64-20 P
    The statue in a crow's perspective of trees [Sombre 70-19 P
    To space. To space? The statue scaled to space [Sombre 70-21 P
    The statue stands in true perspective. Crows [Sombre 71-2 P
    The statue stands [Sombre 71-7 P
    When the statue is not a thing imagined, a stone [Sombre 71-14 P
STATUED. See stately-statued.
STATUES. The crows anoint the statues with their dirt. [Swans 4-10
    Statues and stars, [Botanist 1 135-9
    Of those whom the statues torture and keep down. [Parochial
    191-14
    The air is full of children, statues, roofs [Chaos 357-15
    He establishes statues of reasonable men, [NSF 403-20
    Of a windy night as it is, when the marble statues [NH 473-20
    The statues will have gone back to be things about. [NH 473-24
    With the broken statues standing on the shore. [Aug 491-8
STAY. This single place in which we are and stay, [Extracts 257-10
    Stay here. Speak of familiar things a while. [Debris 338-14
    That I stay away. These are the words of José . . . [Novel 457-12

STAYED. He stayed in Kerry, died there. [Our Stars 455-3
    Nothing about him ever stayed the same, [NH 483-19
STEADFAST. Of the steadfast lanterns creep across the dark?
    [Heaven 56-20
STEADIEST. He could not see the steadiest light [Three 133-3 P
STEADILY. And look your last and look still steadily, [Lilacs 49-7
    In the grinding ric-rac, staring steadily [Men Fall 188-4
STEAMER. A yellow wine and follow a steamer's track [Landsc 243-6
    A steamer lay near him, foundered in the ice. [Page 421-13
    In the bee-loud glade. Lights on the steamer moved. [Page 422-4
STEEL. And blocking steel. [Peacocks 58-18
    Behold the men in helmets borne on steel, [Extracts 259-19
    Steel against intimation--the sharp flash, [Motive 288-19
    Possible machine, a divinity of steel, [Bship 78-3 P
STEEP. No: nor divergence made too steep to follow down. [Dutch
    293-12
    Young weasels racing steep horizons in pursuit of planets . . .
    [Inelegance 26-8 P
STEEPED. When piled on salvers its aroma steeped [C 39-5
    Steeped in night's opium, evading day. [Sombre 66-17 P
STEEPLE. Lean from the steeple. Cry aloud, [MBG 170-14
    The distance between the dark steeple [Jersey 210-9
    If the mouse should swallow the steeple, in its time . . . [Blue
    Bldg 217-7
    Principally the church steeple, [Common 221-2
    Curling round the steeple and the people, [Hero 278-8
    Bell-bellow in the village steeple. Violets, [EM 322-14
    Of poor, dishonest people, for whom the steeple, [EM 322-16
    A steeple that tip-tops the classic sun's [EM 322-25
    That tell of it. The steeple at Farmington [R Conn 533-14
    Like angels resting on a rustic steeple [Art Pop 113-1 P
STEEPLES. Until the steeples of his city clanked and sprang
    [Geneva 24-13
    The steeples are empty and so are the people, [Jersey 210-16
    Of war, the rust on the steeples, these jutted up, [Greenest
    53-23 P
STEEPS. That steeps the room, quickly, then not at all, [Someone
    87-15 A
STELE. And thus its jetted tragedy, its stele [AA 417-24
STELLAR. A stellar pallor that hangs on the threads. [Leben 505-3
    In the first inch of night, the stellar summering [Pagoda 92-3 P
    In stellar largenesses--these [Ulysses 103-21 P
STEM. Could Crispin stem verboseness in the sea, [C 28-22
    From the stem. [Pears 196-16
STENTOR. By the sea, insolid rook, otontor, and said: [Two V 353-12
    Deep in their sound the stentor Martin sings. [Luther 461-13
STEP. They were those that would have wept to step barefoot into
    reality, [Large 423-16
    The step to the bleaker depths of his descents . . . [Rock 528-3
    Or hear her step in the way she walked? [Grotesque 74-12 P
STEPPED. Stepped in and dropped the chuckling down his craw, [C
    45-18
STEPPES. From the steppes, are they being part, feeling the
    strength, [Duck 62-15 P
STEPPING. Stepping from the foyer of summer into that [Novel 457-5
STEPS. Two wooden tubs of blue hydrangeas stand at the foot of the
    stone steps. [Banal 62-11
    Clandestine steps upon imagined stairs [Oboe 251-6
    At the railway station, a soldier steps away, [Repet 308-3
    Steps out. He rings and knocks. The door is not locked. [Bouquet
    452-20
    The sun steps into, regards and finds itself; [Golden 460-11
    Hola! Hola! What steps are those that break [Infernale 24-20 P
    Now like a ballet infantine in awkward steps, [Burnshaw 47-18 P
    And steps forth, priestly in severity. [Sombre 70-15 P
STERILE. Surprise the sterile rationalist who sees [Sombre 67-32 P
STERN. The stern voices of its necessitous men, [Aug 491-17
    The rock is the stern particular of the air, [Rock 528-4
STE URSULE. "Cy Est Pourtraicte, Madame Ste Ursule, et Les Unze
    Mille Vierges" [21-title
STICK. The ribboned stick, the bellowing breeches, cloak [C 28-8
    Intangible arrows quiver and stick in the skin [Holiday 313-9
    A vermilioned nothingness, any stick of the mass [Less 328-9
    Is still to stick to the contents of the mind [Pure 332-9
    It is to stick to the nicer knowledge of [Pure 332-11
    His petty syllabi, the sounds that stick, [NSF 407-19
    Contracted like a withered stick. [Two Illus 513-3
STICKING. Who killed him, sticking feathers in his flesh [Good
    Man 364-3
STICKS. Or if the music sticks, if the anecdote [C 45-30
    But salvation here? What about the rattle of sticks [Parochial
    191-17
    Theology after breakfast sticks to the eye. [Les Plus 245-8
    With redness that sticks fast to evil dreams; [Rock 528-8
    (The blind men strike him down with their sticks.) [Soldat 13-5P
    Like a word in the mind that sticks at artichoke [Burnshaw 47-2 P
    There buzzards pile their sticks among the bones [Burnshaw 49-7 P
STICKY. This drama that we live--We lay sticky with sleep. [AA
    419-14
STIFF. And a stiff and noxious place. [Bananas 54-13

The curtains are stiff and prim and still. [Chateau 161-18
Cleared of its stiff and stubborn, man-locked set, [Angel 497-1
Stiff as stone, [Phases 5-20 P
For no one proud, nor stiff, [Archi 18-11 P
That sort of thing was always rather stiff. [Lytton 39-18 P
Stiff in eternal lethargy, should be, [Conversat 109-8 P
STIFFENING. See long-stiffening.
STIFFEST. And sown again by the stiffest realist, [C 45-15
STIFFLY. Stood stiffly, as if the black of what she thought [Old
　Woman 44-24 P
STIFLED. Its land-breath to be stifled, its color changed, [Sombre
　71-33 P
STILL. While the wind still whistles [Sugar-Cane 12-15
　But when they go that tip still tips the tree. [Monocle 17-6
　And still pursue, the origin and course [Monocle 18-1
　In the night that is still to be silent, [Homunculus 26-14
　The whole of life that still remained in him [C 28-18
　And jay, still to the night-bird made their plea [C 30-19
　And while the torrent on the roof still droned [C 33-8
　Discovery still possible to make, [C 36-21
　A still new continent in which to dwell. [C 37-4
　Another, still more bellicose, came on. [C 37-22
　Had kept him still the prickling realist, [C 40-6
　And be content and still be realist. [C 40-29
　Each day, still curious, but in a round [C 42-14
　Then third, a thing still flaxen in the light, [C 44-20
　Sparkling, solitary, still, [Venereal 48-9
　And look your last and look still steadily, [Lilacs 49-7
　Eliciting the still sustaining pomps [On Manner 55-12
　The responsive, still sustaining pomps for you [On Manner 56-5
　Freemen of death, about and still about [Heaven 56-14
　Among the people burning in me still, [W Burgher 61-11
　She says, "But in contentment I still feel [Sunday 68-27
　The yellow rocked across the still façades, [Babies 77-4
　Except because he broods there and is still. [Bird Claws 82-9
　Who still thinks eagerly [Shifts 83-12
　Who still feels irrational things within her. [Shifts 83-16
　She bathed in her still garden, while [Peter 90-8
　Still quavering. [Peter 91-2
　The slopping of the sea grew still one night [Sea Surf 98-13
　The slopping of the sea grew still one night. [Sea Surf 99-17
　The gongs grew still. And then blue heaven spread [Sea Surf 100-6
　The slopping of the sea grew still one night [Sea Surf 100-11
　The night-long slopping of the sea grew still. [Sea Surf 101-5
　Without cap or strap, you are the cynic still. [NE Verses 106-4
　Of the still finer, more implacable chords. [Anatomy 108-14
　Still hankers after lions, or, to shift, [Lions 125-4
　Still hankers after sovereign images. [Lions 125-5
　The vegetation still abounds with forms. [Lions 125-8
　And the two of them standing still to rest. [How Live 126-4
　Just to stand still without moving a hand. [Adieu 127-12
　Or to sleep or just to lie there still, [Adieu 128-4
　We left much more, left what still is [Postcard 159-5
　Still weaving budded aureoles, [Postcard 159-14
　The stillness of everything gone, and being still, [Autumn 160-8
　Being and sitting still, something resides, [Autumn 160-9
　The curtains are stiff and prim and still. [Chateau 161-18
　The morning deluged still by night, [MBG 169-3
　Above the arrowy, still strings, [MBG 169-4
　To and to and to the point of still, [MBG 181-6
　Still one would want more, one would need more, [Poems Clim
　194-2
　There would still remain the never-resting mind, [Poems Clim
　194-4
　One would have still to discover. Among the dogs and dung, [Glass
　198-4
　And still the birds came, came in watery flocks, [Loaf 200-14
　Still bloom in the agate eyes, red blue, [Arcades 225-15
　But as if evening found us young, still young, [Martial 237-15
　Still walking in a present of our own. [Martial 237-16
　Then the colossal illusion of heaven. Yet still [Landsc 241-12
　The philosopher's man alone still walks in dew, [Oboe 250-12
　Still by the sea-side mutters milky lines [Oboe 250-13
　In the end, however naked, tall, there is still [Oboe 250-17
　And the helpless philosophers say still helpful things. [Ex-
　tracts 253-28
　If the place, in spite of its witheredness, was still [Extracts
　255-11
　Or whether the ice still covered the lake. There was still [Ex-
　tracts 255-14
　And the bees still sought the chrysanthemums' odor. [Contra II
　270-18
　Still, still to deliver us, still magic, [Hero 273-21
　Still moving yet motionless in smoke, still [Hero 273-22
　One with us, in the heaved-up noise, still [Hero 273-23
　The cricket in the telephone is still. [Phenom 286-1
　Now, time stands still. He came from out of sleep, [Choc 299-12
　Hard to perceive and harder still to touch. [Choc 301-18
　And ice is still in Februar. [Poesie 302-10
　Is still is ice in Februar. [Poesie 302-11

The ruin stood still in an external world. [Repet 306-3
Clarified. It is silence made still dirtier. [Creat 311-8
Of them in the air still hanging heavily [EM 315-6
In a consummate prime, yet still desires [EM 318-3
The yellow grassman's mind is still immense, [EM 318-24
Still promises perfections cast away. [EM 318-25
That were never wholly still. The softest woman, [EM 321-28
Who was what people had been and still were, [Pure 331-5
Is still to stick to the contents of the mind [Pure 332-9
The baroque poet may see him as still a man [Paisant 335-12
The artificer of subjects still half night. [Descrip 345-18
The bass lie deep, still afraid of the Indians. [Think 356-5
In whose breast, the dove, alighting, would grow still. [Think
　357-6
The grass is still green. [Burghers 362-6
In which your father died, still breathes for him [Extraord
　369-17
Of change still possible. Exile desire [Cred 373-13
And still the grossest iridescence of ocean [NSF 383-7
The music halted and the horse stood still. [NSF 391-12
But still she painted them, appropriate to [NSF 402-4
Through many places, as if it stood still in one, [Cata 424-12
In which the sense lies still, as a man lies, [Roses 431-2
That of itself stood still, perennial, [Owl 432-24
Last terms, the largest, bulging still with more, [Orb 441-11
Still on the horizon elongates his cuts, [Orb 443-4
And still angelic and still plenteous, [Orb 443-5
The world is still profound and in its depths [Papini 447-9
The conception sparkling in still obstinate thought. [Papini
　448-4
And yet still men though meta-men, still things [Bouquet 449-1
A vibrancy of petals, fallen, that still cling [Bouquet 450-10
Be still. The summarium in excelsis begins . . . [Puel 456-16
The description that makes it divinity, still speech [NH 475-13
These actors still walk in a twilight muttering lines. [NH
　479-23
Still keep occurring. What is, uncertainly, [NH 482-13
On the still, black-slatted eastward shutters. [Aug 492-23
Here the adult one is still banded with fulgor, [Aug 495-4
Is still warm with the love with which she came, [Aug 496-1
Still touches solemnly with what she was [Aug 496-2
Singing, with smaller and still smaller sound, [Rome 508-4
For a citizen of heaven though still of Rome, [Rome 510-2
And reverberations clinging to whisper still. [Rome 510-20
A nature still without a shape, [Two Illus 514-1
It is no longer air. The houses still stand, [Rock 525-5
Still far away. It was like [Not Ideas 534-17
The trees stand still, [Primordia 8-16 P
Even by mice--these scamper and are still; [Soldat 14-1 P
And that confident one, Marie, the wearer of cheap stones, who
　will have grown still and restless; [Piano 22-5 P
And in those regions one still feels the rose [Abnormal 24-9 P
And love her still, still leaves you in the wrong. [Red Kit 31-1P
And still the final quarter, still the rim, [Spaniard 34-9 P
And still the impassioned place of it remain. [Spaniard 34-10 P
The space above the trees might still be bright [Old Woman
　44-29 P
Still eked out luminous wrinklings on the leaves, [Old Woman 45-7P
Dazzling by simplest beams and soothly still, [Old Woman 46-4 P
The space beneath it still, a smooth domain, [Old Woman 46-5 P
And the dew and the ploughman still will best be one. [Burnshaw
　48-2 P
On a day still full or summer, when the leaves [Burnshaw 50-18 P
The message is half-borne. Could marble still [Greenest 57-21 P
Of purple flowers, to see? The black will still [Greenest 58-32P
Yet still retain resemblances, remain [Sombre 67-19 P
Still questioning if to crush the soaring stacks, [Sombre 68-31 P
Syllables, pewter on ebony, yet still [Sombre 70-7 P
I still intend things as they are. [Stan MBG 73-4 P
If the sceptre returns to earth, still moving, still [Bship 80-31P
Precious from the region of the hand, still bright [Bship 81-1 P
Bald heads with their mother's voice still in their ears.
　[Woman Had 82-16 P
Things still more distant. And tradition is near. [Recit 86-20 P
The youngest, the still fuzz-eyed, odd fleurettes, [Nuns 92-9 P
It is still full of icy shades and shapen snow. [Course 96-12 P
A wide, still Aragonese, [Fare Guit 99-2 P
The still inhuman more, and yet [Ulysses 105-3 P
STILLED. Stilled for the passing of her dreaming feet [Sunday 67-9
　Night stilled the slopping of the sea. The day [Sea Surf 101-23
STILL-LIFE. Of a still-life, symbols, brown things to think of
　[Hero 276-24
STILLNESS. The stillness of everything gone, and being still,
　[Autumn 160-8
　And the stillness is in the key, all of it is, [Autumn 160-13
　The stillness is all in the key of that desolate sound. [Autumn
　160-14
　The stillness is the stillness of the mind. [Novel 458-18
STILL-STARRED. Still-starred. It is the mother they possess, [AA
　413-10

STING. To that short, triumphant sting? [Phases 5-3 P
  Green had, those days, its own implacable sting. [Someone 85-7 A
STINKS. Decays of sacks, and all the arrant stinks [C 36-10
STIPPLED. Because it rose above them all, stippled [Greenest 54-14P
STIRRED. It may be that in all her phrases stirred [Key W 129-1
  The metaphor stirred his fear. The object with which he was com-
    pared [Prol 516-10
STIRRING. Stirring no poet in his sleep, and tolls [Pharynx 96-7
STITCHINGS. In the manner of its stitchings, of its thread, [Owl
  434-14
STOCKHOLM. Stockholm slender in a slender light, [Botanist 1 135-7
  Less Aix than Stockholm, hardly a yellow at all, [Holiday 312-4
STOKED. Streamed white and stoked and engined wrick-a-wrack. [Duck
  61-12 P
STONE. I wish that I might be a thinking stone. [Monocle 13-7
  Two wooden tubs of blue hydrangeas stand at the foot of the
    stone steps. [Banal 62-11
  The cloud rose upward like a heavy stone [Nigger 152-8
  The earth is not earth but a stone, [MBG 173-13
  But stone, but like a stone, no: not [MBG 173-15
  Before the lion locked in stone. [MBG 175-16
  The flesh, the bone, the dirt, the stone. [MBG 176-14
  Here is its actual stone. The bread [MBG 184-1
  Will be our bread, the stone will be [MBG 184-2
  A space of stone, of inexplicable base [Thought 185-9
  Dressed in metal, silk, and stone, [Thought 186-19
  This death was his belief though death is a stone. [Men Fall
    188-17
  The day to pieces and cry stanza my stone? [Dump 203-10
  You are humped higher and higher, black as stone-- [Rabbit K
    210-1
  On the irised hunks, the stone bouquet. [Hartford 227-12
  The stone, the categorical effigy; [Choc 300-3
  By being high, is the stone [Pediment 361-14
  These two by the stone wall [Burghers 362-4
  Of stone, that never changes. Bethou him, you [NSF 394-16
  A face of stone in an unending red, [NSF 400-5
  And fortunate stone. It moves its parade [Imago 439-7
  Lacking men of stone, [Inhab 504-7
  The stone from which he rises, up--and--ho, [Rock 528-2
  Stiff as stone, [Phases 5-20 P
  Death was a reaper with sickle and stone, [Soldat 16-1 P
  The mass of stone collapsed to marble hulk, [Old Woman 44-23 P
  With senses chiseled on bright stone. They see [Duck 64-10 P
  The statue is the sculptor not the stone. [Duck 64-20 P
  When the statue is not a thing imagined, a stone [Sombre 71-14 P
  I said that men should wear stone masks and, to make [Bship
    78-11 P
  Once the assassins wore stone masks and did [Bship 78-15 P
  Wood of his forests and stone out of his fields [Myth 118-15 P
STONE-CUTTERS. Chisels of the stone-cutters cutting the stones.
  [Archi 16-19 P
STONES. Made on the sea-weeds and the covered stones [Hibiscus
  22-13
  X promenades the dewy stones, [Canna 55-7
  A band entwining, set with fatal stones. [Fictive 88-16
  If they throw stones upon the roof [Mozart 131-18
  "Gray Stones and Gray Pigeons" [140-title
  Slowly the ivy on the stones [MBG 170-21
  Becomes the stones. Women become [MBG 170-22
  Stones pose in the falling night; [Add 198-8
  And the river that batters its way over stones, [Loaf 199-17
  With dew, dew dresses, stones and chains of dew, heads [Dump
    202-9
  The stones [Horn 230-8
  Could one say that he sang the colors in the stones, [Horn 230-11
  In sapphire, round the sun-bleached stones, [Vari 233-10
  And stones, only this imager. [Jumbo 269-18
  Adorned with cryptic stones and sliding shines, [Owl 434-10
  On a hill of stones to make beau mont thereof. [NH 466-24
  And beetling of belts and lights of general stones, [NH 477-20
  The boat was built of stones that had lost their weight and
    being no longer heavy [Prol 515-10
  Chisels of the stone-cutters cutting the stones. [Archi 16-19 P
  And that confident one, Marie, the wearer of cheap stones, who
    will have grown still and restless; [Piano 22-5 P
  The stones [Burnshaw 48-4 P
  Of the white stones near my door, [Three 134-7 P
  Of the white stones near her door; [Three 134-13 P
  That affects the white stones, [Three 135-3 P
STONE-STUDDED. The spouse. She opened her stone-studded belt. [NSF
  395-21
STONY. Arranged under the stony clouds [Gray 140-6
STOOD. Upon the bank, she stood [Peter 90-21
  But he remembered the time when he stood alone. [Anglais 149-9
  He stood at last by God's help and the police; [Anglais 149-10
  But he remembered the time when he stood alone. [Anglais 149-11
  But he remembered the time when he stood alone, [Anglais 149-13
  We said we stood alone. [On Road 203-22
  I stood and sang and filled the air. [Country 207-7

Could have stood up sharply in the sky. [Weak Mind 212-20
Stood up straight in the air, struck off [Thunder 220-7
To which I spoke, near which I stood and spoke, [News 265-3
The ruin stood still in an external world. [Repet 306-3
Overseas, that stood in an external world. [Repet 306-6
Between us and the place in which we stood. [Wild 329-12
The buildings were of marble and stood in marble light. [Anach
  366-2
She stood with him at the table, [Attempt 370-12
On the table near which they stood [Attempt 370-20
The music halted and the horse stood still. [NSF 391-12
Through many places, as if it stood still in one, [Cata 424-12
That of itself stood still, perennial, [Owl 432-24
Stood flourishing the world. The brilliant height [Owl 434-4
Peace stood with our last blood adorned, last mind, [Owl 434-19
Of rose, stood tall in self not symbol, quick [Owl 435-6
One imagined the violet trees but the trees stood green, [What
  We 459-10
Stood, dressed in antic symbols, to display [NH 470-6
With its attentive eyes. And, as he stood, [NH 483-11
The tree stood dazzling in the air [Two Illus 514-15
And sensuous summer stood full-height. [Two Illus 514-19
So that he that stood up in the boat leaning and looking before
  him [Prol 515-12
It rose loftily and stood massively; and to lie [Armor 529-2
Stood by him when the tumbler fell, [Sat Night 28-2 P
Perhaps if the orchestras stood on their heads [Agenda 42-4 P
Stood stiffly, as if the black of what she thought [Old Woman
  44-24 P
The statue stood in stars like water-spheres, [Old Woman 45-10 P
If once the statue were to rise, if it stood, [Greenest 54-25 P
Stood on a plain of marble, high and cold; [Woman Had 82-29 P
STOOPED. Stooped in a night of vast inquietude. [Spaniard 34-14 P
  The churches, like dalmatics stooped in prayer, [Sombre 69-1 P
STOOPING. Stooping in indigo gown [Venereal 48-12
  Not twisted, stooping, polymathic Z, [NH 469-8
STOP. May, after all, stop short before a plum [C 40-28
  "The Revolutionists Stop for Orangeade" [102-title
  The future might stop emerging out of the past, [Nigger 151-10
  Things stop in that direction and since they stop [Cred 374-16
  Fly low, cock bright, and stop on a bean pole. Let [Cred 377-6
  A composing as the body tires, a stop [NSF 386-4
  To see hepatica, a stop to watch [NSF 386-5
  To stop the whirlwind, balk the elements. [NSF 401-15
  Cock bugler, whistle and bugle and stop just short, [NSF 405-15
  Red robin, stop in your preludes, practicing [NSF 405-16
  He wanted his heart to stop beating and his mind to rest [Cata
    425-6
  Stop at the terraces of mandolins, [Study I 463-14
  See winter-stop.
STOPPED. Effective colonizer sharply stopped [C 44-4
  Have I stopped and thought of its point before? [Grapes 110-11
  The man and his companion stopped [How Live 125-11
  You will have stopped revolving except in crystal. [NSF 407-3
  They never stopped, a repetition repeated [Woman Had 81-21 P
  See wind-stopped.
STOPPER. The stopper to indulgent fatalist [C 44-9
STOPPING. Stopping, on voyage, in a land of snakes, [C 31-7
STOPS. Of over-civil stops. And thus he tossed [C 35-21
  When the wind stops, [Soldier 97-9
  When the wind stops and, over the heavens, [Soldier 97-10
  In a world without heaven to follow, the stops [Adieu 127-13
  The direction stops and we accept what is [Cred 374-17
  And the unjust, which in the midst of summer stops [AA 417-6
  For himself. He stops upon this threshold, [Rome 511-1
  Goes off a little on the side and stops. [Duck 63-33 P
  Even the man below, the subverter, stops [Sombre 71-17 P
  See railway-stops.
STORES. The poet striding among the cigar stores, [Thought 185-5
STORM. Aware of exquisite thought. The storm was one [C 32-31
  Oh, but the very self of the storm [Joost 46-20
  And sight, and all there was of the storm, [Joost 47-2
  Is like the reason in a storm; [MBG 169-10
  And yet it brings the storm to bear. [MBG 169-11
  In a storm of torn-up testaments. [Dutch 292-7
  Words, in a storm, that beat around the shapes. [Sketch 335-22
  There is a storm much like the crying of the wind, [Sketch 336-1
  There is a building stands in a ruinous storm, [Sketch 336-7
  Out of a storm we must endure all night, [Man Car 351-4
  Out of a storm of secondary things), [Man Car 351-5
  Of the never-ending storm of will, [Silent 359-11
  In a storm blown into glittering shapes, and flames [Burnshaw
    52-21 P
  Poised, but poised as the mind through which a storm [Sombre
    69-27 P
  A Spanish storm, [Fare Guit 99-1 P
STORMER. Stormer, is the color of a self [Prelude 194-14
STORMING. And storming under multitudinous tones [C 28-15
  A spirit storming in blank walls, [Postcard 159-18
STORMS. His tip a drop of water full of storms. [Bird Claws 82-12

The marble leaping in the storms of light. [Old Woman 43-9 P
STORY. Story . . . The sound of that slick sonata, [Phenom 286-18
    Like Agamemnon's story. [Phases 3-15 P
STOUT. Corazon, stout dog, [Destructive 192-15
STOVE. Of the pans above the stove, the pots on the table, the
    tulips among them. [Large 423-15
STOVE-PIPE. Patted his stove-pipe hat and tugged his shawl.
    [Geneva 24-3
ST. PAUL. In the names of St. Paul and of the halo-John [Luther
    461-5
STRACHEY. See Lytton Strachey.
STRAGGLING. And tufted in straggling thunder and shattered sun.
    [Dwarf 208-8
STRAIGHT. The lines are straight and swift between the stars.
    [Tallap 71-10
    A sheaf of brilliant arrows flying straight, [Tallap 72-7
    Stood up straight in the air, struck off [Thunder 220-7
    Straight to the utmost crown of night he flew. [NSF 403-8
    They will get it straight one day at the Sorbonne. [NSF 406-22
    Straight from the Arcadian imagination, [Novel 459-1
    Straight up, an élan without harrowing, [What We 459-14
    By trope or deviation, straight to the word, [NH 471-14
    Straight to the transfixing object, to the object [NH 471-15
    Blanche, the blonde, whose eyes are not wholly straight, in a
        room of lustres, shed by turquoise falling, [Piano 22-1 P
    O bold, that rode your horses straight away. [Duck 61-31 P
    Straight forwardly through another night [Ulysses 105-11 P
STRAIGHTLY. As he moved, straightly, on and on, [Presence 106-11 P
STRAIGHTWAY. Flying and falling straightway for their pleasure,
    [Tallap 72-8
STRAIN. And of forgetfulness, in alternate strain. [C 29-6
    Is music. It is like the strain [Peter 90-5
STRAINS. "Sad Strains of a Gay Waltz" [121-title
STRANGE. It's a strange courage [Nuances 18-4
    In moody rucks, and difficult and strange [C 31-10
    On what strange froth does the gross Indian dote, [C 38-1
    It is with a strange malice [W Burgher 61-1
    And there I found myself more truly and more strange. [Hoon
        65-18
    None of them are strange, [Ten O'C 66-7
    That strange flower, the sun, [Gubbinal 85-1
    Our feigning with the strange unlike, whence springs [Fictive
        88-12
    That the mask is strange, however like." [MBG 181-10
    A helio-horn. How strange the hero [Hero 274-10
    Life's nonsense pierces us with strange relation. [NSF 383-9
    (He shouts.) Hola! Of that strange light, beware! [Infernale
        25-3 P
    How strange a thing it was to understand [Lytton 39-1 P
    And how strange it ought to be again, this time [Lytton 39-2 P
    Of fear before the disorder of the strange, [Burnshaw 48-14 P
    Before the strange, having wept and having thought [Burnshaw
        50-7 P
    "He will be thinking in strange countries [Three 134-6 P
    "He will be thinking in strange countries [Three 134-12 P
    "He will be thinking in strange countries [Three 134-16 P
STRANGER. Of an impersonal gesture, a stranger's hand. [Hand
    271-14
STRAP. Without cap or strap, you are the cynic still. [NE Verses
    106-4
STRAPPED. Strapped and buckled bright. [Orangeade 103-8
STRATAGEM. Of ocean, pondering dank stratagem. [Sea Surf 101-10
STRATAGEMS. This is its substitute in stratagems [Cred 376-21
STRAW. Ballatta dozed in the cool on a straw divan [NE Verses
    106-5
    Dew lies on the instruments of straw that you were playing,
        [Fish-Scale 160-17
    Is a worm composing on a straw. [MBG 174-14
    In the mind, pupa of straw, moppet of rags. [Dwarf 208-6
    And, being straw, turned green, lived backward, shared [Liadoff
        347-9
    Like a blaze of summer straw, in winter's nick. [AA 421-3
    Tuck in the straw, [Abnormal 24-17 P
STRAWBERRIES. The strawberries once in the Apennines, [Arcades
    225-2
    The strawberries once in the Apennines . . . [Arcades 226-1
STRAWBERRY. Or like a ripe strawberry [Three 135-10 P
STRAY. And stray impassioned in the littering leaves. [Sunday
    69-12
STREAKED. We hang like warty squashes, streaked and rayed,
    [Monocle 16-9
    So streaked with yellow, blue and green and red [C 32-6
    The sky is a blue gum streaked with rose. The trees are black.
        [Banal 62-12
    At breakfast jelly yellow streaked the deck [Sea Surf 99-18
    Of the place, blue and green, both streaked. [Attempt 370-5
    These streaked the mother-of-pearl, the lunar cress. [Greenest
        53-24 P
STREAKING. That streaking gold should speak in him [C 38-4
STREAKINGS. The unique composure, harshest streakings·joined [Owl

433-14
STREAM. A reflection stagnant in a stagnant stream. [Nigger 156-2
    "A Lot of People Bathing in a Stream" [371-title
STREAMED. Streamed over chaos their civilities. [NH 479-9
    Streamed white and stoked and engined wrick-a-wrack. [Duck 61-12P
STREAMING. Dressed poorly, arrogant of his streaming forces,
    [Uruguay 249-22
STREAMS. Streams to the moon. [Ploughing 20-18
    And our streams rejected the dim Academy. [Nigger 154-21
STREET. This world, this place, the street in which I was, [Martial
    237-18
    The street lamps [Metamorph 266-6
    It is someone walking rapidly in the street. [Pure 330-1
    Until flicked by feeling, in a gildered street, [NSF 407-1
    In the street, in a room, on a carpet or a wall, [NH 467-12
    We descend to the street and inhale a health of air [NH 470-17
    Of the window and walking in the street and seeing, [NH 478-9
    Or street or about the corners of a man, [NH 480-1
    On the threshold of heaven, the figures in the street [Rome 508-1
    A street. She has a supernatural head. [Woman Had 83-8 P
STREETS. Discoverer walked through the harbor streets [C 32-14
    Nor the chisels of the long streets, [Six Sig 74-24
    And the streets are full of cries. [Mozart 132-21
    Throw papers in the streets, the wills [MBG 170-7
    In the metaphysical streets of the physical town [NH 472-22
    In the metaphysical streets, the profoundest forms [NH 473-7
    The streets contain a crowd [Soldat 12-10 P
    To men, to houses, streets and the squalid whole. [Greenest
        57-8 P
    In the streets. There will always be cafés and cards [Greenest
        58-15 P
    Are the cities to breed as mountains bred, the streets [Duck
        61-3 P
STRENGTH. Of rankest trivia, tests of the strength [C 37-13
    Union of the weakest develops strength [Nigger 158-10
    Here I inhale profounder strength [MBG 180-15
    Come from the strength that is the strength of the sun, [Freed
        205-13
    Threw its contorted strength around the sky. [Sleight 222-8
    The extent of what they are, the strength [Adequacy 244-11
    The air changes, creates and re-creates, like strength [Choc
        301-9
    Accoutred in a little of the strength [Repet 307-6
    Of the nights, the actual, universal strength, [Repet 309-2
    From that strength, whose armies set their own expanses. [Repet
        309-5
    The sea, a strength that tumbles everywhere, [Two V 354-12
    Stripped of remembrance, it displays its strength-- [Cred 375-9
    The phrase grows weak. The fact takes up the strength [NH 473-4
    It fails. The strength at the centre is serious. [NH 477-12
    As a serious strength rejects pin-idleness. [NH 477-14
    The barbarous strength within her would never fail. [World 521-15
    Its strength and measure, that which is near, point A [Rock
        528-11
    From the steppes, are they being part, feeling the strength,
        [Duck 62-15 P
    The leaping bodies to his strength, convulsed [Duck 64-18 P
    And true. The good, the strength, the sceptre moves [Bship 80-21P
    Of a man, that seizes our strength, will seize it to be [Bship
        81-9 P
    The strength of death or triumph. Oheu! [Stan Hero 83-15 P
    There was a crush of strength in a grinding going round, [Real
        110-14 P
STRENGTHEN. Should strengthen her abortive dreams and take [NSF
    399-11
STRETCH. Stretch themselves to rest in their first summer's sun,
    [Parochial 191-20
    The year's dim elongations stretch below [Sombre 70-2 P
STRETCHED. A running forward, arms stretched out as drilled.
    [Nigger 153-15
    A massive body and long legs, stretched out, [Orb 443-9
    Stretched out a shadowy arm to feel the night. [Phases 5-8 P
STRETCHES. For soldiers, the new moon stretches twenty feet.
    [Givan 289-21
STREWN. It cannot mean a sea-wide country strewn [Duck 63-12 P
STREWS. And our desires. Although she strews the leaves [Sunday
    69-2
STRICKEN. See cloud-stricken.
STRICT. In poems of plums, the strict austerity [C 30-8
STRICTEST. Of the strictest prose [Cortege 81-2
STRIDE. The stride of vanishing autumn in a park [C 31-3
    And your averted stride [Nigger 152-12
    And lither stride. His arms are heavy [Hero 277-11
    Of truth. They stride across and are masters of [Role 93-8 P
STRIDENT. Autumn's compendium, strident in itself [C 45-23
STRIDES. She strides above the rabbit and the cat, [Candle 223-3
STRIDING. Came striding. [Domination 8-15
    Came striding like the color of the heavy hemlocks [Domination
        9-18
    As we beheld her striding there alone, [Key W 129-30

The poet striding among the cigar stores, [Thought 185-5
On his gold horse striding, like a conjured beast, [Antag 426-1
STRIKE. Strike the piercing chord. [Mozart 132-8
  To touch again the hottest bloom, to strike [Havana 143-15
  To strike his living hi and ho, [MBG 166-9
  In that one ear it might strike perfectly: [Think 357-2
  Among these the musicians strike the instinctive poem. [AA 415-16
  (The blind men strike him down with their sticks.) [Soldat 13-5P
  The time will come for these children, seated before their long
    black instruments, to strike the themes of love-- [Piano 21-16P
  Strike fire, but the part is the equal of the whole, [Bship
    79-29 P
STRING. A million people on one string? [MBG 166-15
  An instrument, twanging a wiry string that gives [Of Mod 240-15
  One string, an absolute, not varying [Montra 263-15
  Picking thin music on the rustiest string, [God 285-13
  A little string speaks for a crowd of voices. [NSF 392-18
STRINGED. See thin-stringed.
STRINGS. The gaunt guitarists on the strings [Ord Women 11-17
  And pick the strings of our insipid lutes! [Sunday 69-24
  Susanna's music touched the bawdy strings [Peter 92-8
  Jangling the metal of the strings . . . [MBG 166-12
  The strings are cold on the blue guitar. [MBG 168-22
  Above the arrowy, still strings, [MBG 169-17
  Begat the tubas and the fire-wind strings, [NSF 398-14
  Plucks on his strings to pluck abysmal glory, [NSF 404-15
  Nor all one's luck at once in a play of strings. [John 437-13
  The thick strings stutter the finial gutterals. [Madame 507-10
STRIP. Dark cynic, strip and bathe and bask at will. [NE Verses
    106-3
  But to strip off the complacent trifles, [Gigan 289-8
STRIPES. In alternate stripes converging at a point [Page 422-22
  Of stripes of silver that are strips [Dove 98-10 P
STRIPPED. Stripped one of all one's torments, concealed [Poems
    Clim 193-18
  Stripped of remembrance, it displays its strength-- [Cred 375-9
  I am the woman stripped more nakedly [NSF 396-1
  To be stripped of every fiction except one, [NSF 404-9
STRIPS. Of stripes of silver that are strips [Dove 98-10 P
STRODE. That strode submerged in that malevolent sheen, [Sea Surf
    99-24
STROKE. For me, the firefly's quick, electric stroke [Monocle 15-1
  And the soldier of time lies calm beneath that stroke. [EM 319-18
  To hear the stroke of one's certain solitude, [Old Woman 44-15 P
STROKES. In the strokes of thunder, dead candles at the window
    [NH 488-11
  Make melic groans and tooter at her strokes, [Spaniard 34-25 P
  See brush-strokes.
STRONG. With heat so strong! [Virgin 71-9
  And all their manner, weak and strong? [MBG 166-18
  This barbarous chanting of what is strong, this blare. [Parochial
    191-16
  The moment's sun (the strong man vaguely seen), [Freed 204-20
  Was a place, strong place, in which to sleep. [Nightown 214-18
  Grew strong, as if doubt never touched his heart. [Choc 299-5
  And the candor of them is the strong exhilaration [NSF 382-19
  Even so when I think of you as strong or tired, [NSF 406-15
  As one that is strong in the bushes of his eyes. [AA 414-7
  What has he that becomes his heart's strong core? [Bad Time
    426-20
  His poverty becomes his heart's strong core-- [Bad Time 427-2
  The day is great and strong-- [Pecul 453-4
  But his father was strong, that lies now [Pecul 453-5
  A retrato that is strong because it is like, [Novel 458-13
  A strong mind in a weak neighborhood and is [NH 474-13
  In the afternoon. The proud and the strong [Leben 504-17
  Seemed large and loud and high and strong. [Two Illus 513-9
  That press, strong peasants in a peasant world, [Armor 530-5
  More of ourselves, the mood of life made strong [Duck 65-3 P
  The strong music of hard times, [Grotesque 76-13 P
STRONGER. To grow larger and heavier and stronger than [Rhythms
    246-1
  Stronger and freer, a little better off. [Good Man 364-4
STRONGEST. Closest and strongest. [On Road 204-12
  The red bird most and the strongest sky-- [Adequacy 244-14
STRONGLY-HEIGHTENED. Approached this strongly-heightened effigy
    [NSF 391-14
STROPHES. In which the sulky strophes willingly [C 33-24
  Your guns are not rhapsodic strophes, red [Bship 80-20 P
  Our good, from this the rhapsodic strophes flow, [Bship 81-5 P
STROVE. Be plain. For application Crispin strove, [C 38-8
  As if whatever in water strove to speak [Page 422-9
STRUCK. The Indian, but the Indian struck [Cuban 64-18
  The Indian struck and disappeared. [Cuban 65-4
  Stood up straight in the air, struck off [Thunder 220-7
STRUCTURE. Of the structure of vaults upon a point of light. [MBG
    167-5
  To be an intellectual structure. The cause [EM 324-30
  This structure of ideas, these ghostly sequences [Bed 326-13
  Makes more of it. It is easy to wish for another structure [Bed

326-16
  That habit of wishing and to accept the structure [Bed 327-6
  Of things as the structure of ideas. It was the structure [Bed
    327-7
  The great structure has become a minor house. [Plain 502-15
  Never cease to deploy the structure. [Archi 16-16 P
STRUCTURES. The academies like structures in a mist. [NSF 386-21
  Chosen by an inquisitor of structures [Rome 510-27
STRUGGLE. Hymns of the struggle of the idea of god [Thought 185-19
  To know that the change and that the ox-like struggle [Freed
    205-12
  Must struggle like the rest." She climbed until [Uruguay 249-1
STRUGGLING. Struggling toward his harmonious whole, [Negation 97-14
  Struggling toward impassioned choirs, [MBG 169-6
STRUM. As I strum the thing, do I pick up [MBG 171-19
STRUMMING. Dwindled to one sound strumming in his ear, [C 28-19
  After long strumming on certain nights [MBG 174-19
  The black fugatos are strumming the blacknesses of black . . .
    [Madame 507-9
STRUT. Sordid Melpomene, why strut bare boards, [Bad Time 427-4
STRUTS. Of differing struts, four voices several [C 45-4
STRUTTED. See blue-strutted.
STRUTTING. His strutting studied through centuries. [MBG 181-19
  Speaking and strutting broadly, fair and bloomed, [Burnshaw
    52-17 P
STUBBLE. And coffee dribble . . . Frost is in the stubble. [Dwarf
    208-14
STUBBORN. Lies in flawed words and stubborn sounds. [Poems Clim
    194-10
  These hymns are like a stubborn brightness [Hero 279-24
  In a stubborn literacy, an intelligence, [Bouquet 452-11
  Cleared of its stiff and stubborn, man-locked set, [Angel 497-1
  Hoofs grinding against the stubborn earth, until [Old Woman
    46-10 P
  The stubborn eye, of the conformer who conforms [Duck 64-16 P
STUBS. Of young identities, Aprilian stubs. [Duck 64-24 P
STUDDED. See stone-studded.
STUDIED. Or in the Yangtse studied out their beards? [Monocle 14-3
  His strutting studied through centuries. [MBG 181-19
  He had studied the nostalgias. In these [EM 321-12
  And studied it in his holiday hotel. [Pure 331-14
  Nietzsche in Basel studied the deep pool [Descrip 342-7
  Would have been studied [Three 137-10 P
STUDIES. But is an eye that studies its black lid. [Tallap 71-17
  Of the highest self: he studies the paper [Hero 280-14
  Man sits and studies silence and himself, [Papini 447-10
  Studies and shapes a tallow image, swarmed [Theatre 91-10 P
STUDIOS. Is difficult. It blights in the studios. [Greenest 58-2 P
STUDIOUS. Why, without pity on these studious ghosts, [Monocle
    14-10
  And studious of a self possessing him, [C 33-11
  Lighted at midnight by the studious eye, [NSF 388-2
STUDY. To study [Ord Women 11-11
  In lordly study. Every day, I found [Monocle 17-23
  Study the symbols and the requiescats, [Norfolk 111-5
  "Study of Two Pears" [196-title
  To study the past, and doctors, having bathed [NSF 391-15
  "Study of Images I" [463-title
  Of day. If the study of his images [Study I 463-5
  Is the study of man, this image of Saturday, [Study I 463-6
  "Study of Images II" [464-title
STUDYING. He turns us into scholars, studying [Sombre 67-21 P
STUFF. And would have purple stuff upon her arms, [Paltry 5-12
  To stuff the ear? It causes him to make [Havana 144-14
  In the days when the mood of love will be swarming for solace
    and sink deeply into the thin stuff of being, [Piano 22-8 P
STUFFED. With tongues unclipped and throats so stuffed with thorns,
    [Greenest 57-19 P
  See well-stuffed.
STUMP. Danced around a stump. [Motion 83-4
  Squeezing the reddest fragrance from the stump [God 285-14
STUNTED. Their stunted looks. [How Now 97-15 P
STUPID. And roamed there all the stupid afternoon. [Hibiscus 23-3
STUPOR. And not for stupor, such as music makes [C 31-15
STUTTER. The thick strings stutter the finial gutterals. [Madame
    507-10
STYGIA. There is a great river this side of Stygia, [R Conn 533-4
  In that river, far this side of Stygia, [R Conn 533-7
STYGIAN. The bondage of the Stygian concubine, [Infernale 25-5 P
STYLE. Things look each day, each morning, or the style [Descrip
    339-18
  A seeming of the Spaniard, a style of life, [Descrip 345-15
  But in the style of the novel, its tracing [Novel 458-11
  An enormous nation happy in a style, [NH 468-17
SUAVE. Held in his hand the suave egg-diamond [Thunder 220-10
  Tristesses, the fund of life and death, suave bush [Cred 377-15
  Oh! How suave a purple passed me by! [Stan MMO 19-3 P
SUAVEST. In suavest keeping. The shoes, the clothes, the hat [De-
    scrip 343-2
SUAVITY. Gave suavity to the perplexed machine [Sea Surf 99-3

SUBCONSCIOUS. Of ugly, subconscious time, in which [Analysis 348-5
   There being no subconscious place, [Analysis 348-8
SUBJECT. Poetry is the subject of the poem, [MBG 176-15
   A subject for Puvis. He would compose [Anach 366-4
   He has an ever-living subject. The poet [Papini 446-3
   Not subject to change . . . [Song Fixed 520-6
SUBJECTED. All final, colors subjected in revery [Descrip 342-16
SUBJECTS. The artificer of subjects still half night. [Descrip
   345-18
   He skips the journalism of subjects, seeks out [NH 474-11
   Of the incredible subjects of poetry. [Someone 85-13 A
SUBJUGATE. Once to make captive, once to subjugate [Cred 376-12
SUBJUGATING. Of one vast, subjugating, final tone. [C 30-9
SUBJUGATION. Or yield to subjugation, once to proclaim [Cred 376-13
SUBLIMATIONS. Yes. But these sudden sublimations [Hero 274-15
SUBLIME. Proud of such novelties of the sublime, [High-Toned 59-17
   "The American Sublime" [130-title
   To behold the sublime, [Am Sub 130-17
   And the sublime comes down [Am Sub 131-7
   On the sublime. Vesuvius had groaned [EM 313-13
   To die). This is a part of the sublime [EM 314-14
   With holy or sublime ado [Archi 18-15 P
   Men's bones, beyond their breaths, the black sublime, [Greenest
   55-11 P
   Particulars of a relative sublime. [Ulysses 103-27 P
SUBMAN. And never will, a subman under all [Sombre 66-14 P
SUBMARINE. The drill of a submarine. The voyage [Hero 274-25
SUBMERGED. In endless ledges, glittering, submerged [C 34-7
   Of bliss submerged beneath appearance, [Jasmine 79-10
   That strode submerged in that malevolent sheen, [Sea Surf 99-24
   Like things submerged with their englutted sounds, [EM 321-27
SUBMERGING. Slowly submerging in flatness disappeared. [Old Woman
   45-5 P
SUB-MUSIC. Than the wind, sub-music like sub-speech, [Vari 232-8
SUBSIDING. And uttered their subsiding sound. [Infanta 8-6
SUB-SPEECH. Than the wind, sub-music like sub-speech, [Vari 232-8
SUBSTANCE. There is a substance in us that prevails, [Monocle
   15-10
   The night. The substance of his body seemed [Choc 297-20
   Both substance and non-substance, luminous flesh [Choc 297-21
   And, if of substance, a lineness of the earth, [Owl 433-2
   And it is he in the substance of his region, [Myth 118-14 P
   To sound, sound's substance and executant, [Someone 84-13 A
SUBSTITUTE. A substitute for all the gods: [MBG 176-3
   Where the wild poem is a substitute [Waldorf 241-1
   This is its substitute in stratagems [Cred 376-21
   Of the rain in the spout is not a substitute. [NH 475-20
   Birds of more wit, that substitute-- [Hermit 505-18
SUBTERFUGE. Itself." No more than that, no subterfuge, [Burnshaw
   48-7 P
SUBTLE. And He felt a subtle quiver, [Pourtraicte 22-4
   Would come from that return to the subtle centre. [Extracts
   258-21
   Time was not wasted in your subtle temples. [Dutch 293-11
   That the beholder knew their subtle purpose, [New Set 353-2
   His puissant front nor for her subtle sound, [NSF 401-12
   In a savage and subtle and simple harmony, [NH 468-1
   Made subtle by truth's most jealous subtlety, [Someone 84-8 A
SUBTLER. Subtler than the ornatest prophecy, [Havana 144-13
   For the time when sound shall be subtler than we ourselves.
   [Nigger 158-5
   In its cavern, wings subtler than any mercy, [Hero 273-13
   Subtler than look's declaiming, although she moved [Owl 435-15
   Subtler, more urgent proof that the theory [NH 486-8
SUBTLETIES. And the booming is blunt, not broken in subtleties.
   [NSF 390-9
SUBTLETY. What subtlety would apparition have? [Descrip 340-14
   Made subtle by truth's most jealous subtlety, [Someone 84-8 A
SUBTLY. Go with the walker subtly walking there. [NH 473-8
SUBURB. Through Oxidia, banal suburb, [MBG 182-1
SUBVERTER. Even the man below, the subverter, stops [Sombre 71-17P
SUCCEEDING. Through prophets and succeeding prophets, whose
   prophecies [Bship 81-6 P
SUCCEEDS. Sometimes at sleepy mid-days it succeeds, [Extracts
   257-20
SUCCESS. St. Armorer's was once an immense success. [Armor 529-1
SUCCESSFULLY. Almost successfully. Illustration: [Man Car 350-14
SUCCESSIVE. In swift, successive shadows, dolefully. [C 32-21
SUCCESSOR. This is the successor of the invisible. [Cred 376-20
SUCKED. See wind-sucked.
SUCKLE. Seemed to suckle themselves on his arid being, [Frogs
   78-13
SUCKLED. No mother suckled him, no sweet land gave [Sunday 67-28
   As the swine-like rivers suckled themselves [Frogs 78-14
   Suckled on ponds, the spirit craves a watery mountain. [NE
   Verses 105-2
SUDARIUM. More than sudarium, speaking the speech [Men Fall 188-6
SUDDEN. There are these sudden mobs of men, [Sad Gay 122-3
   These sudden clouds of faces and arms, [Sad Gay 122-4
   The wind and the sudden falling of the wind. [Nigger 152-7

It was like sudden time in a world without time, [Martial 237-17
   Sounds passing through sudden rightnesses, wholly [Of Mod 240-16
   Yes. But these sudden sublimations [Hero 274-15
   Free, for a moment, from malice and sudden cry, [Cred 378-8
   A sudden color on the sea. But it is not [John 437-2
   What sound could comfort away the sudden sense? [Old Woman 44-16P
SUDDENLY. That coolness for his heat came suddenly, [C 31-17
   The nakedness would rise and suddenly turn [Sea Surf 101-16
   Would--But more suddenly the heaven rolled [Sea Surf 101-18
   Everyone, grows suddenly cold. [Fading 139-7
   Could you have said the bluejay suddenly [Sleight 222-9
   The abstract was suddenly there and gone again. [Contra II
   270-13
   Touched suddenly by the universal flare [Pure 333-7
   When the cloud pressed suddenly the whole return [Liadoff 347-6
   A horror of thoughts that suddenly are real. [Man Car 351-6
   As if the language suddenly, with ease, [NSF 387-17
   A little and a little, suddenly, [Orb 440-12
   Crowded with apparitions suddenly gone [Bouquet 448-10
   And no less suddenly here again, a growth [Bouquet 448-11
   Made suddenly luminous, themselves a change, [Our Stars 455-19
   Which suddenly is all dissolved and gone-- [Hermit 505-19
   In a single spruce, when, suddenly, [Two Illus 514-14
   As if all his hereditary lights were suddenly increased [Prol
   517-1
   Look suddenly downward with their shining eyes [Red Kit 31-29 P
   On pattering leaves and suddenly with lights, [Burnshaw 47-25 P
   They suddenly fall and the leafless sound of the wind [Burnshaw
   50-20 P
   And the people suddenly evil, waked, accused, [Sombre 69-2 P
   The sprawling of winter might suddenly stand erect, [Discov
   96-3 P
   And suddenly denying itself away. [Real 110-18 P
SUFFER. There was nothing he did not suffer, no; nor we. [Oboe
   251-14
   Because we suffer, our oldest parent, peer [EM 315-17
   Should understand. That he might suffer or that [EM 322-5
   Live, work, suffer and die in that idea [EM 325-14
SUFFERED. The man that suffered, lying there at ease, [Past Nun
   378-19
SUFFERING. Untroubled by suffering, which fate assigns [Old Woman
   46-6 P
   -manity had invaded its seclusion, with its suffering and its
   [Three 129-10 P
   Through suffering and pity. [Three 132-10 P
SUFFERS. So that he that suffers most desires [Adequacy 244-13
SUFFICE. Who, to find what will suffice, [Bottle 238-18
   As the mind, to find what will suffice, destroys [Bottle 239-15
   What will suffice. It has not always had [Of Mod 239-18
   And it has to find what will suffice. It has [Of Mod 240-4
SUFFUSES. Lend no part to any humanity that suffuses [Nuances 18-11
SUGAR. With white wine, sugar and lime juice. Then bring it,
   [Phenom 286-15
   They might be sugar or paste or citron-skin [Burnshaw 46-19 P
SUGAR-CANE. "The Load of Sugar-Cane" [12-title
SUGAR-CONE. Undescribed composition of the sugar-cone, [Someone
   86-20 A
SUGARED. Of children nibbling at the sugared void, [C 43-25
SUGARY. Cooling the sugary air. [Agenda 42-3 P
SUGGESTED. Suggested malice in the dry machine [Sea Surf 101-9
   Suggested that, at the final funeral, [NSF 391-11
SUITABLE. The suitable amours. Time will write them down. [NSF
   398-6
SUITED. Of men suited to public ferns . . . The hero [Hero 276-16
   Suited the decadence of those silences, [Descrip 343-3
SULKY. In which the sulky strophes willingly [C 33-24
SULLEN. As sullen as the sky, was swallowed up [C 32-20
   And sullen, hurricane shapes [Bananas 53-22
   To the sullen hill, [Cortege 80-3
   This darkened water cloven by sullen swells [Farewell 118-14
   To chop the sullen psaltery, [MBG 173-20
   So sullen with sighing and surrender to marauding ennui.
   [Inelegance 25-18 P
SULLY. To sully the begonias, nor vex [Archi 18-14 P
SULTAN. Sultan of African sultans, starless crown. [Greenest 60-6 P
SULTANS. Sultan of African sultans, starless crown. [Greenest
   60-6 P
SULTRIEST. While the sultriest fulgurations, flickering, [EM 313-15
SULTRY. Sultry moon-monsters [Fabliau 23-10
   Low tide, flat water, sultry sun. [Vari 235-13
   And hold them round the sultry day? Why should [Belly 367-4
SUM. To think of man the abstraction, the comic sum. [Nigger 156-6
   In the sum of the parts, there are only the parts. [On Road 204-3
   Find peace? We found the sum of men. We found, [Oboe 251-14
   And the chronicle of humanity is the sum [Paisant 335-1
   And is tradition an unfamiliar sum, [Recit 87-9 P
   An object the sum of its complications, seen [Someone 87-10 A
SUMAC. The closed-in smell of hay. A sumac grows [Armor 529-6
SUMMARIUM. Be still. The summarium in excelsis begins . . . [Puel
   456-16

SUMMARY. Disguised pronunciamento, summary, [C 45-22
SUMMER. The death of summer, which that time endures [Swans 4-4
Of half-dissolving frost, the summer came, [C 34-10
The summer, it should have a sacrament [C 39-6
Indifferent to the tepid summer cold, [C 43-2
Who will embrace her before summer comes. [Lilacs 49-15
Pardie! Summer is like a fat beast, sleepy in mildew, [Banal
    62-15
Drowsing in summer's sleepiest horn. [Cuban 65-5
The bough of summer and the winter branch. [Sunday 67-25
Shall chant in orgy on a summer morn [Sunday 69-29
Of men that perish and of summer morn. [Sunday 70-11
The breath of turgid summer, and, [Frogs 78-5
And flame and summer and sweet fire, no thread [Fictive 87-10
Mildew of summer and the deepening snow [Pharynx 96-2
And in the morning summer hued the deck [Sea Surf 98-14
Pricks in our spirits at the summer's end, [Anatomy 108-5
And these two never meet in the air so full of summer [Norfolk
    111-20
Excelling summer, ghost of fragrance falling [Ghosts 119-16
And then rush brightly through the summer air. [Sailing 121-7
Of summer, the drunken mother? [Medit 124-9
The heaving speech of air, a summer sound [Key W 129-15
Repeated in a summer without end [Key W 129-16
Of ripest summer, always lingering [Havana 143-14
Winter devising summer in its breast, [Thought 186-8
Summer assaulted, thundering, illumed, [Thought 186-9
Shelter yet thrower of the summer spear, [Thought 186-10
Stretch themselves to rest in their first summer's sun,
    [Parochial 191-20
For all the thoughts of summer that go with it [Dwarf 208-5
Torn from insipid summer, for the mirror of cold, [Dwarf 208-12
All this, of course, will come to summer soon. [Connois 216-6
"The Blue Buildings in the Summer Air" [216-title
Cut summer down to find the honey-comb. [Blue Bldg 217-21
And of fair weather, summer, dew, peace. [Peaches 224-11
It is like the season, when, after summer, [Cuisine 228-1
It is summer and it is not, it is autumn [Cuisine 228-2
Beneath summer and the sky [Scavoir 231-10
"Variations on a Summer Day" [232-title
First, summer, then a lesser time, [Vase 246-23
He sets this peddler's pie and cries in summer, [Oboe 251-3
Where is that summer warm enough to walk [Extracts 252-15
Of love and summer. The assassin sings [Extracts 256-8
He must, in the aroma of summer nights, [Montra 261-14
Summer is in bones. [Metamorph 265-17
In our oblivion, of summer's [Hero 275-25
Each false thing ends. The bouquet of summer [Hero 280-19
But was the summer false? The hero? [Hero 280-25
Summer, jangling the savagest diamonds and [Hero 281-2
Of summer. [God 285-15
It seems as if the honey of common summer [EM 316-1
In the high night, the summer breathes for them [EM 319-12
For the soldier of time, it breathes a summer sleep, [EM 319-14
In the seeming of the summer of her sun [Descrip 339-11
By her own seeming made the summer change. [Descrip 339-12
The spirit's universe, then a summer's day, [Descrip 343-16
Even the seeming of a summer's day, [Descrip 343-17
Potter in the summer sky. [Analysis 348-3
Already the green bird of summer has flown [Myrrh 349-15
Of summer. Tomorrow will look like today, [Myrrh 349-18
Summer is changed to winter, the young grow old, [Chaos 357-14
The reader became the book; and summer night [House Q 358-8
The summer night is like a perfection of thought. [House Q
    358-15
Is calm, itself is summer and night, itself [House Q 359-3
"Credences of Summer" [372-title
Postpone the anatomy of summer, as [Cred 373-1
Absorbs the ruddy summer and is appeased, [Cred 374-3
It is the rock of summer, the extreme, [Cred 375-21
They sang of summer in the common fields. [Cred 376-5
The personae of summer play the characters [Cred 377-21
Part of the mottled mood of summer's whole, [Cred 378-5
Everything becomes morning, summer, the hero, [Past Nun 378-17
At summer thunder and sleeps through winter snow. [NSF 384-16
A mountain, a pineapple pungent as Cuban summer. [NSF 393-12
Of summer, growing fragrant in the night, [NSF 399-10
A season, to discover summer and know it, [NSF 403-24
Fat girl, terrestrial, my summer, my night, [NSF 406-7
And the unjust, which in the midst of summer stops [AA 417-6
Like a blaze of summer straw, in winter's nick. [AA 421-3
A forgetfulness of summer at the pole. [Bad Time 427-3
So summer comes in the end to these few stains [Beginning 427-10
The self of summer perfectly perceived, [Beginning 427-17
To watch us in the summer of Cyclops [Owl 435-1
Autumn howls upon half-naked summer. But [John 437-5
Of summer, at the windy edge, [Celle 438-11
Of the other, as if summer was a spouse, [Orb 441-21
And the mate of summer: her mirror and her look, [Orb 441-23
Bearing the odors of the summer fields, [Wom Sun 445-13

Of indolent summer not quite physical [Bouquet 451-15
And yet of summer, the petty tones [Bouquet 451-16
With the spices of red summer. [Pecul 453-11
Every thread of summer is at last unwoven. [Puel 456-1
The crows are flying above the foyer of summer. [Novel 457-1
Stepping from the foyer of summer into that [Novel 457-5
In the weed of summer comes this green sprout why. [Questions
    462-4
So, after summer, in the autumn air, [NH 468-5
In the genius of summer that they blew up [NH 482-18
The wind has blown the silence of summer away. [NH 487-13
It is full of the myrrh and camphor of summer [Aug 490-4
Or in the penumbra of summer night-- [Aug 490-17
The effete vocabulary of summer [Plant 506-8
The World Is Larger in Summer [Two Illus 514-title 2
When the summer was over, when the change [Two Illus 514-7
Of summer and of the sun, the life [Two Illus 514-8
Of summer and of the sun, were gone. [Two Illus 514-9
And sensuous summer stood full-height. [Two Illus 514-19
On which men speculated in summer when they were half asleep.
    [Prol 516-15
The magnum wreath of summer, time's autumn snood, [Rock 526-21
Of summer and that unused hearth below, [Phases 5-7 P
To remember summer. [Secret Man 36-4 P
On a day still full of summer, when the leaves [Burnshaw 50-18 P
Is no longer a sound of summer. So great a change [Burnshaw
    50-21 P
If not from winter, from a summer like [Greenest 57-24 P
As summer would return to weazened days. [Greenest 57-27 P
A majestic weavers' job, a summer's sweat. [Greenest 58-6 P
On summer Sundays in the park, a duck [Duck 60-11 P
The summer Sundays in the park, must be [Duck 66-4
Policed by the hope of Christmas. Summer night, [Sombre 68-11 P
A tiara from Cohen's, this summer sea. [Stan MBG 72-14 P
They find her in the crackling summer night, [Woman Had 83-4 P
Of a ruddier summer, a birth that fetched along [Nuns 92-13 P
The cricket of summer forming itself out of ice. [Discov 95-14 P
Round summer and angular winter and winds, [Ulysses 102-24 P
The visible transformations of summer night, [Real 110-16 P
A health--and the faces in a summer night. [Art Pop 113-3 P
About summer, are not what skeletons think about. [As Leave
    117-4 P
SUMMERING. In the first inch of night, the stellar summering
    [Pagoda 92-3 P
SUMMER-LIGHT. At dawn, nor of summer-light and winter-light
    [Burnshaw 50-3 P
SUMMERS. Summers sink from it. [Secret Man 36-8 P
  Since thirty summers are needed for a year [Ideal 88-8 A
SUMMER-SEEMING. Capped summer-seeming on the tense machine [Sea
    Surf 99-21
SUMMING. A summing up of the loftiest lives [Ulysses 104-7 P
SUMMONED. Now, of the music summoned by the birth [Fictive 87-14
SUMS. Who in a million diamonds sums us up. [Oboe 250-22
SUN. A bronze rain from the sun descending marks [Swans 4-3
  Of the January sun; and not to think [Snow Man 10-4
  O sceptre of the sun, crown of the moon, [Monocle 13-2
  The blazing passes from beyond the sun. [Monocle 15-19
  Glitters in the sun. [Ploughing 20-4
  Spreads to the sun. [Ploughing 20-16
  That whispered to the sun's compassion, made [C 28-26
  In a starker, barer world, in which the sun [C 29-17
  Was not the sun because it never shone [C 29-18
  A fluctuating between sun and moon, [C 35-8
  Like this, saps like the sun, true fortuner. [C 43-5
  I have finished my combat with the sun; [Joost 46-14
  Of sun and slaves, breeding and death, [Joost 46-21
  Than mute bare splendors of the sun and moon. [On Manner 56-8
  Shall she not find in comforts of the sun, [Sunday 67-15
  She makes the willow shiver in the sun [Sunday 69-7
  Their boisterous devotion to the sun, [Sunday 70-1
  We live in an old chaos of the sun, [Sunday 70-18
  For I reach right up to the sun, [Six Sig 74-7
  Damned universal cock, as if the sun [Bantams 75-16
  That strange flower, the sun, [Gubbinal 85-1
  Among the arrant spices of the sun, [Fictive 88-7
  So that the sun may speckle, [Watermelon 89-11
  Mile-mallows that a mallow sun cajoled. [Sea Surf 101-21
  Ask us not to sing standing in the sun, [Orangeade 102-17
  Widen your sense. All things in the sun are sun. [NE Verses 104-2
  The body walks forth naked in the sun [Anatomy 108-8
  And, out of tenderness or grief, the sun [Anatomy 108-9
  Flashier fruits! A slip for the sun and moon, [Grapes 110-17
  The trees like bones and the leaves half sand, half sun. [Fare-
    well 118-5
  Where is sun and music and highest heaven's lust, [Ghosts 119-6
  There is order in neither sea nor sun. [Sad Gay 122-1
  Flood on flood, of our returning sun. [Medit 123-15
  They that had left the flame-freaked sun [How Live 125-15
  To seek a sun of fuller fire. [How Live 125-16
  Have I except it comes from the sun? [Adieu 128-10

"The Sun this March" [133-title
The exceeding brightness of this early sun [Sun March 133-13
Gleam sharply as the sun comes up. [Botanist 2 135-17
Was the sun concoct for angels or for men? [Eve Angels 137-9
Sad men made angels of the sun, and of [Eve Angels 137-10
Let this be clear that we are men of sun [Eve Angels 137-13
The sun, that brave man, [Brave 138-7
"A Fading of the Sun" [139-title
Who can think of the sun costuming clouds [Fading 139-1
Within as pillars of the sun, [Fading 139-16
In the far South the sun of autumn is passing [Nigger 150-9
Shout for me, loudly and loudly, joyful sun, when you rise.
   [Nigger 150-17
The sun of Asia creeps above the horizon [Nigger 153-8
The sun is seeking something bright to shine on. [Nigger 157-20
Smeared with the gold of the opulent sun. [Postcard 159-21
And grackles gone and sorrows of the sun, [Autumn 160-2
The sorrows of the sun, too, gone . . . the moon and moon,
   [Autumn 160-3
The sun rises green and blue in the fields and in the heavens.
   [Fish-Scale 161-5
There are no shadows in our sun, [MBG 167-6
It is the sun that shares our works. [MBG 168-9
When shall I come to say of the sun, [MBG 168-11
The sun no longer shares our works [MBG 168-13
And shall I then stand in the sun, as now [MBG 168-16
Not to be part of the sun? To stand [MBG 168-20
Its true appearances there, sun's green, [MBG 177-3
The bubbling sun will bubble up, [MBG 182-12
Will claw sleep. Morning is not sun, [MBG 182-19
Son only of man and sun of men, [Thought 185-25
Stretch themselves to rest in their first summer's sun, [Paro-
   chial 191-20
The lion sleeps in the sun. [Destructive 193-4
Sounded in music, if the sun, [Prelude 194-13
To-morrow when the sun, [Add 198-18
Comes up as the sun, bull fire, [Add 198-20
The sun is a corbeil of flowers the moon Blanche [Sump 201-12
The bouquets come here in the papers. So the sun, [Dump 201-15
The moment's sun (the strong man vaguely seen), [Freed 204-20
It was how the sun came shining into his room: [Freed 205-6
Come from the strength that is the strength of the sun, [Freed
   205-13
Whether it comes directly or from the sun. [Freed 205-14
The sun appeared and reddened great [Country 207-13
And tufted in straggling thunder and shattered sun. [Dwarf 208-8
When the shapeless shadow covers the sun [Rabbit K 209-2
Too sharp for that. The shore, the sea, the sun, [Blue Bldg 217-9
Rose up, tallest, in the black sun, [Thunder 220-6
Around the sun. The wheel survives the myths. [Sleight 222-11
Men on green beds and women half of sun. [Cuisine 227-19
With sun? [Horn 230-13
And cold. The moon follows the sun like a French [Vari 234-8
Low tide, flat water, sultry sun. [Vari 235-13
But he came back as one comes back from the sun [Yellow 237-7
From an old delusion, an old affair with the sun, [Bottle
   239-10
The blood-red redness of the sun, [Adequacy 243-18
And sun, as if these [Adequacy 244-8
Were what they are, the sharpest sun: [Adequacy 244-9
And the sun, the waves together in the sun, [Les Plus 245-2
And jealous grandeurs of sun and sky [Vase 246-11
No was the night. Yes is this present sun. [Beard 247-11
"Of Bright & Blue Birds & the Gala Sun" [248-title
So what said the others and the sun went down [Uruguay 248-16
The moonlight? Was it a rider intent on the sun, [Uruguay 249-20
The false roses--Compare the silent rose of the sun [Extracts
   252-4
Rain is an unbearable tyranny. Sun is [Extracts 252-21
Bask in the sun in which they feel transparent, [Extracts 254-19
Half sun, half thinking of the sun, half sky, [Extracts 257-2
It cannot be half earth, half mind; half sun, [Extracts 257-16
The sun expands, like a repetition on [Montra 263-14
The blue sun in his red cockade [News 264-7
Cloud-clown, blue painter, sun as horn, [Jumbo 269-13
The sun shone and the dog barked and the baby slept. [Contra II
   270-5
An abstract, of which the sun, the dog, the boy [Contra II 270-10
Sleeps in the sun no thing recalling. [Hero 278-18
The sun. The interior of a parasol, [Phenom 287-10
Gold-shined by sun, perceiving as I saw [Phenom 287-13
There are circles of weapons in the sun. [Dutch 290-15
Men came as the sun comes, early children [Dutch 291-23
He is not here, the old sun, [Possum 293-13
Is brighter than the sun itself. [Poesie 302-16
That sweats the sun up on its morning way [Repet 307-7
Sharp as white paint in the January sun; [Holiday 312-2
A sun in an almost colorless, cold heaven. [Holiday 312-6
The sun, in clownish yellow, but not a clown, [EM 318-1
Is as insatiable as the sun's. The bird [EM 318-10 ·

The sun, its grossest appetite becomes less gross, [EM 318-14
The sun is the country wherever he is. The bird [EM 318-18
A steeple that tip-tops the classic sun's [EM 322-25
The sun comes up like news from Africa. [Feo 334-12
As the sun is something seeming and it is. [Descrip 339-2
The sun is an example. What it seems [Descrip 339-3
Thus things are like a seeming of the sun [Descrip 339-5
In the seeming of the summer of her sun [Descrip 339-11
The sun of Nietzsche gildering the pool, [Descrip 342-18
More explicit than the experience of sun [Descrip 344-22
The cool sun of the Tulpehocken refers [Extraord 369-10
Of nakedness, in the company of the sun, [Lot 371-19
Trace the gold sun about the whitened sky [Cred 373-6
It is the final mountain. Here the sun, [Cred 373-23
Of blue and yellow, sky and sun, belted [Cred 378-1
The inconceivable idea of the sun. [NSF 380-14
And see the sun again with an ignorant eye [NSF 380-16
How clean the sun when seen in its idea, [NSF 381-4
There was a project for the sun and is. [NSF 381-12
There is a project for the sun. The sun [NSF 381-13
My house has changed a little in the sun. [NSF 385-16
And sun and rain a plural, like two lovers [NSF 392-14
A green baked greener in the greenest sun. [NSF 393-7
As when the sun comes rising, when the sea [NSF 398-23
And Bawda loved the captain as she loved the sun. [NSF 401-18
For that the poet is always in the sun, [NSF 407-6
When he moved so slightly to make sure of sun, [AA 411-21
They would be afraid of the sun: what it might be, [Page 422-6
The sun might rise and it might not and if [Page 422-11
And yet with water running in the sun, [Celle 438-14
In a season more than sun and south wind, [Imago 439-14
The sun is secretly shining on a wall. [Bouquet 450-23
The sun stands like a Spaniard as he departs, [Novel 457-4
The sun steps into, regards and finds itself; [Golden 460-11
The sun aches and ails and then returns halloo [Questions 462-5
Of what is this house composed if not of the sun, [NH 465-9
Much like a new resemblance of the sun, [NH 465-16
Obscure, in colors whether of the sun [NH 466-16
So that the approaching sun and its arrival, [NH 472-17
The great cat must stand potent in the sun. [NH 473-3
The sun is half the world, half everything, [NH 481-22
If, then, New Haven is half sun, what remains, [NH 482-3
Of birds called up by more than the sun, [Hermit 505-17
Are falsifications from a sun [Plant 506-12
But a sense of the distance of the sun-- [Two Illus 513-5
Of summer and of the sun, the life [Two Illus 514-8
Of summer and of the sun, were gone. [Two Illus 514-9
And blue broke on him from the sun, [Two Illus 514-16
Is only what the sun does every day, [Look 517-16
We think, then, as the sun shines or does not. [Look 518-23
The sun of five, the sun of six, [Song Fixed 520-1
But was it Ulysses? Or was it only the warmth of the sun [World
   521-10
Two figures in a nature of the sun, [Rock 525-17
In the sun's design of its own happiness, [Rock 525-18
Its copy of the sun, these cover the rock. [Rock 527-1
A new-colored sun, say, that will soon change forms [Armor
   529-19
Other makings of the sun [Planet 532-10
His self and the sun were one [Planet 532-13
Were no less makings of the sun. [Planet 532-15
Flashing and flashing in the sun. On its banks, [R Conn 533-9
The sun was rising at six, [Not Ideas 534-7
The sun was coming from outside. [Not Ideas 534-12
It was part of the colossal sun, [Not Ideas 534-15
Or swipling flail, sun-black in the sun, [Soldat 16-2 P
How shall we hew the sun, [Archi 17-22 P
Or the bench with the pot of geraniums, the stained mattress
   and the washed overalls drying in the sun? [Indigo 22-12 P
Soaring Olympus glitters in the sun. [Infernale 25-12 P
The sun is gold, the moon is silver. [Mandolin 29-1 P
That sack the sun, though metaphysical. [Red Kit 31-4 P
The catholic sun, its majesty, [An Gaiety 32-16 P
The banners should brighten the sun. [Drum-Majors 37-10 P
Made by the sun ascending seventy seas. [Burnshaw 47-29 P
The blood of his bitter brain; and there the sun [Burnshaw
   49-11 P
Commingle, not like the commingling of sun and moon [Burnshaw
   50-2 P
Like a solitude of the sun, in which the mind [Greenest 54-5 P
And Africa, basking in antiquest sun, [Greenest 55-25 P
So clawed, so sopped with sun, that in these things [Greenest
   57-20 P
Why feel the sun or, feeling, why feel more [Greenest 58-30 P
And the sun and the sun-reek piled and peaked above [Greenest
   59-3 P
A penny sun in a tinsel sky, unrhymed, [Duck 61-7 P
Which were their thoughts, squeezed into shapes, the sun [Duck
   61-11 P
What lesser man shall measure sun and moon, [Duck 63-7 P

Walking the paths, watching the gilding sun, [Duck 65-18 P
It is mud and mud long baked in the sun, [Stan MBG 72-6 P
Before the sun brought them that destruction [Stan Hero 83-18 P
It could be that the sun shines [Desire 85-19 P
One thinks, when the houses of New England catch the first sun,
  [Discov 95-21 P
Trouble in the spillage and first sparkle of sun, [How Now 97-7P
There is this bubbling before the sun, [Dove 98-13 P
Like glass and sun, of male reality [Fare Guit 99-8 P
The only sun of the only day, [Ulysses 100-2 P
This candle is the sun; [Three 130-8 P
But when the sun shines on the earth, [Three 130-18 P
The sun rises [Three 130-22 P
The candle of the sun, [Three 142-4 P
And as the red of the sun [Three 143-4 P
It is as if there were three planets: the sun, [Someone 83-11 A
Like the true light of the truest sun, the true [Someone 84-9 A
6. White sky, pink sun, trees on a distant peak. [Someone 86-9A
See man-sun.
SUN-BLACK. Or swipling flail, sun-black in the sun, [Soldat 16-2 P
SUN-BLEACHED. In sapphire, round the sun-bleached stones, [Vari
  233-10
SUN-BRONZED. Spread on the sun-bronzed air, [Pascagoula 127-2
SUN-COLORED. "Why sun-colored, [Peacocks 58-6
SUNDAY. "Ploughing on Sunday" [20-title
  I'm ploughing on Sunday, [Ploughing 20-10
  "Sunday Morning" [66-title
  A calm November. Sunday in the fields. [Nigger 156-1
  One's grand flights, one's Sunday baths, [Sleight 222-1
  Or to see the sea on Sunday, or [Arcades 225-22
  On an early Sunday in April, a feeble day, [Extracts 254-25
  Cat's milk is dry in the saucer. Sunday song [Phenom 286-3
  With Sunday pearls, her widow's gayety. [NSF 402-7
  Of the week, queerer than Sunday. We thought alike [AA 419-10
  Jerome and the scrupulous Francis and Sunday women, [Luther
    461-8
  A little thing to think of on Sunday walks, [Aug 491-22
  In a Sunday's violent idleness. [Two Illus 514-3
  By inch, Sunday by Sunday, many men. [Duck 60-20 P
SUNDAYS. On Sundays, lawyers in their promenades [NSF 391-13
  On summer Sundays in the park, a duck [Duck 60-11 P
  The summer Sundays in the park, must be [Duck 66-4 P
SUNDRY. The dreadful sundry of this world, [Venereal 47-11
SUN-FILLED. Into the sun-filled water, brightly leafed [Lot 371-2
SUNG. See well-sung.
SUNGS. Than on any bowl of the Sungs, [Bowl 6-13 P
SUNKEN. A sunken voice, both of remembering [C 29-5
  The sea unfolding in the sunken clouds? [Sea Surf 100-20
  So deeply sunken were they that the shrouds, [Sea Surf 100-22
  And cloud, of the sunken coral water-walled, [Key W 129-13
SUNLIGHT. The windows are open. The sunlight fills [Peaches 224-16
  Or sunlight and you hum and the orchestra [Waldorf 241-5
  The sunlight. They bear brightly the little beyond [Extracts
    254-22
  An acid sunlight fills the halls. [Contra I 267-2
  Let him move as the sunlight moves on the floor, [Less 327-11
  "Bouquet of Roses in Sunlight" [430-title
  To be anything else in the sunlight of the room, [Roses 430-12
  Weaker and weaker, the sunlight falls [Leben 504-16
  There is the same color in the bellies of frogs, in clays,
    withered reeds, skins, wood, sunlight. [Primordia 8-2 P
  Another sunlight might make another world, [Theatre 91-1 P
SUNNY. Coffee and oranges in a sunny chair, [Sunday 66-17
  A sunny day's complete Poussiniana [Poem Morn 219-1
SUN-PALLOR. To flare, in the sun-pallor of his rock. [Bird Claws
  82-18
SUN-REEK. And the sun and the sun-reek piled and peaked above
  [Greenest 59-3 P
SUNRISE. Shine alone in the sunrise [Nuances 18-6
  "A Fish-Scale Sunrise" [160-title
  Sunrise is his garment's hem, sunset is hers. [NH 485-7
  "Three Travelers Watch a Sunrise" [127-title P
  Just to see the sunrise again. [Three 128-7 P
  It is like the seclusion of sunrise, [Three 130-5 P
  That is the seclusion of sunrise [Three 131-12 P
  No: not even sunrise. [Three 133-19 P
  For if we affect sunrise, [Three 134-1 P
  To rest in sunrise. [Three 138-16 P
  But this will be a part of sunrise, [Three 138-17 P
  It will soon be sunrise. [Three 141-3 P
  Seclusion of sunrise . . . [Three 142-3 P
  Sunrise is multiplied, [Three 143-10 P
SUNS. Exquisite in poverty against the suns [EM 317-23
  Softly she piped among the suns [Song Fixed 519-21
  Through wild spaces of other suns and moons, [Ulysses 102-23 P
SUN-SACRAMENT. An inner miracle and sun-sacrament, [Montra 262-5
SUNSET. Sunrise is his garment's hem, sunset is hers. [NH 485-7
SUNSHINE. In the sunshine placidly, colored by ground [C 41-3
  In the sunshine is a filial form and one [Cred 375-3
  "The Woman in Sunshine" [445-title

Is there one word of sunshine in this plaint? [Stan MMO 19-16 P
  They had hardly grown to know the sunshine, [Stan Hero 83-17 P
  Young and walking in the sunshine, [Clear Day 113-11 P
SUN-SLIDES. Under the sun-slides of a sloping mountain; [Aug 489-11
SUPER-ANIMAL. What super-animal dictate our fates? [Duck 63-8 P
SUPERHUMAN. "The Surprises of the Superhuman" [98-title
SUPERIOR. Be merely oneself, as superior as the ear [Dump 203-1
SUPER-MAN. To equate the root-man and the super-man, [Montra
  262-22
  The super-man friseured, possessing and possessed. [Montra
  262-24
SUPERNATURAL. The supernatural preludes of its own. [AA 414-19
  A street. She has a supernatural head. [Woman Had 83-8 P
  The supernatural of its origin. [Nuns 92-14 P
SUPPLE. Supple and turbulent, a ring of men [Sunday 69-28
  Fragrant and supple, [Six Sig 73-20
  Most supple challenger. The elephant [NSF 384-11
SUPPLEMENTS. The universe that supplements the manqué, [Repet 309-8
SUPPORTED. Supported by a half-arc in mid-earth. [Repet 309-14
SUPPORTING. Supporting heavy cables, slung [MBG 181-22
  This is invisible. The supporting arms [Sombre 68-24 P
SUPPORTS. Supports of night. The tea, [Fading 139-17
SUPPOSE. Suppose these couriers brought amid their train [Monocle
  15-27
  Do you suppose that she cares a tick, [Lilacs 49-1
  "I suppose there is [Freed 204-16
  But suppose the disorder or truths should ever come [Connois
  216-7
  It was his nature to suppose, [Landsc 242-15
  Had he been better able to suppose: [Landsc 243-1
  Suppose we call it Projection A. [Couch 295-3
  Never suppose an inventing mind as source [NSF 381-1
  Suppose this was the root of everything. [Golden 460-7
  Suppose it turned out to be or that it touched [Golden 460-8
  Suppose these houses are composed of ourselves, [NH 466-4
  Suppose it was a drop of blood . . . [Inhab 504-12
  They chanced to think. Suppose the future fails. [Duck 63-2 P
  Suppose, instead of failing, it never comes, [Duck 63-30 P
  A paradise full of assassins. Suppose I seize [Bship 77-20 P
  Its actual appearance, suppose we begin [Recit 86-5 P
SUPPOSED. It was nowhere else, its place had to be supposed,
  [Landsc 242-7
  Itself had to be supposed, a thing supposed [Landsc 242-8
  In a place supposed, a thing that he reached [Landsc 242-9
  To receive what others had supposed, without [Landsc 242-16
  But as truth to be accepted, he supposed [Landsc 242-18
  He never supposed [Landsc 242-20
  Parts, and more things, parts. He never supposed divine [Landsc
  242-27
  The highest supposed in him and over, [Hero 280-2
  If it be supposed that we are three figures [Three 132-17 P
  But if it be supposed [Three 132-24 P
  Or if it be supposed, for example, [Three 133-1 P
SUPPOSES. Only a negress who supposes [Virgin 71-2
  To share the day. The trumpet supposes that [Cred 377-1
SUPPRESSION. An immense suppression, freed, [Sad Gay 122-5
SUPREMACY. It was part of a supremacy always [EM 314-26
  This freedom, this supremacy, and in [EM 315-8
SUPREME. Poetry is the supreme fiction, madame. [High-Toned 59-1
  "Notes toward a Supreme Fiction" [380-title
SUPREMELY. Supremely true each to its separate self, [Re-state
  146-11
SUPREMEST. These are death's own supremest images, [Owl 436-2
SURE. Loudened by cries, by clashes, quick and sure [Monocle 16-13
  Four questioners and four sure answerers. [C 45-10
  Of sure obliteration on our paths, [Sunday 69-3
  As in your name, an image that is sure, [Fictive 88-6
  Unfolding in the water, feeling sure [Sea Surf 100-18
  And to feel sure and to forget the bleaching sand . . . [Farewell
  117-20
  Joyous and jubilant and sure. [How Live 126-8
  As sure as all the angels are. [Botanist 2 136-2
  And of his works, I am sure. He bathes in the mist [Freed 204-22
  Sure enough, moving, the thunder became men, [Thunder 220-1
  Sure that the ultimate poem was the mind, [Extracts 256-22
  But can, that one is sure to be able-- [Crude 305-4
  Made sure of the most correct catastrophe. [EM 314-10
  Could be borne, as if we were sure to find our way. [EM 316-6
  The ultimate good, sure of a reality [EM 324-16
  The brilliant mercy of a sure repose, [Cred 375-18
  Of an obvious acid is sure what it intends [NSF 390-8
  When he moved so slightly to make sure of sun, [AA 411-21
  Made us no less as sure. We saw in his head, [AA 412-1
  Cry out, "I am the purple muse." Make sure [Bad Time 427-8
  Become a single being, sure and true. [Pecul 454-9
  Gripping their oars, as if they were sure of the way to their
    destination, [Prol 515-7
  Certain and ever more fresh. Ah! Certain, for sure . . . [Moon-
  light 532-6
  If more than pity and despair were sure, [Sombre 69-13 P

Was what she was and flesh, sure enough, but airs: [Grotesque
  74-7 P
Be sure of that. [Three 129-7 P
To be sure. [Three 135-4 P
I am sure you heard [Three 136-1 P
SURELY. Of her airs, as surely cologne as that she was bone
  [Grotesque 74-6 P
SURENESS. A syllable of which he felt, with an appointed sureness,
  [Prol 516-5
SURF. To this droning of the surf. [Fabliau 23-15
SURFACE. "Of the Surface of Things" [57-title
  On the surface of the water [Tattoo 81-20
  "Sea Surface Full of Clouds" [98-title
  Beneath, far underneath, the surface of [NSF 403-1
  The surface, is the purpose to be seen, [Moonlight 531-8
SURFACES. The ponds are not the surfaces it seeks. [Nigger 158-1
  They are not flat surfaces [Pears 196-9
  And depth, covering all surfaces, [Burghers 362-9
  The glitter-goes on surfaces of tanks, [NSF 384-13
  Make gay the hallucinations in surfaces. [NH 472-21
  Out of the surfaces, the windows, the walls, [NH 480-22
  Only the surfaces--the bending arm, [Blanche 10-3 P
  Its surfaces came from distant fire; and it [Greenest 57-2 P
SURLY. Surly masks and destroyers? [Bagatelles 213-20
SURPASSED. Who surpassed the most literate owl, the most erudite
  [NSF 403-21
SURPRISE. What a beautiful history, beautiful surprise! [Mice
  123-3
  Provoking a laughter, an agreement, by surprise. [Gala 248-15
  Surprise the sterile rationalist who sees [Sombre 67-32 P
SURPRISED. And be surprised and tremble, hand and lip. [Beginning
  428-2
  A matching and mating of surprised accords, [NH 468-2
SURPRISES. "The Surprises of the Superhuman" [98-title
  The blue guitar surprises you. [MBG 183-14
SURRENDER. So sullen with sighing and surrender to marauding
  ennui. [Inelegance 25-18 P
SURRENDERS. Surrenders, the repeated sayings that [Extracts 258-6
SURROUND. Surround that hill. [Jar 76-8
SURROUNDED. "Angel Surrounded by Paysans" [496-title
  Surrounded by its choral rings, [Not Ideas 534-16
SURVEY. From my balcony, I survey the yellow air, [Of Surface 57-3
  The point of survey, green's green apogee, [Cred 373-17
  A point of survey squatting like a throne, [Cred 373-19
SURVIVALS. Of the son. These survivals out of time and space
  [Recit 87-27 P
  Survivals of a good that we have loved, [Recit 88-1 P
SURVIVE. Existed by itself. Or did the saint survive? [Les Plus
  245-6
  It was not important that they survive. [Planet 532-16
SURVIVED. That not one curl in nature has survived? [Monocle 14-9
SURVIVES. The plum survives its poems. It may hang [C 41-2
  In bloom. Yet it survives in its own form, [C 41-6
  Around the sun. The wheel survives the myths. [Sleight 222-11
  The fire eye in the clouds survives the gods. [Sleight 222-12
  He walks and dies. Nothing survives [Woman Song 360-8
SURVIVING. So Crispin hasped on the surviving form, [C 41-8
  Surviving being born, the event of life. [Discov 96-9 P
SUSANNA. Waked in the elders by Susanna. [Peter 90-6
  Susanna lay. [Peter 90-14
  They wondered why Susanna cried [Peter 91-14
  Revealed Susanna and her shame. [Peter 91-19
  Susanna's music touched the bawdy strings [Peter 92-8
SUSCEPTIBLE. The first word would be of the susceptible being
  arrived, [Discov 96-1 P
SUSPENDED. Suspended in air, the slightest crown [Couch 295-11
  Suspended in temporary jauntiness. [Bouquet 448-7
SUSPENDING. The suspending hand withdrawn, would be [Couch 295-14
SUSPENSION. The suspension, as in solid space, [Couch 295-13
  Of a suspension, a permanence, so rigid [NSF 391-17
SUSTAIN. Does not sustain us in the metropoles. [Havana 142-8
  Of the self that must sustain itself on speech, [Beard 247-17
SUSTAINING. Eliciting the still sustaining pomps [On Manner 55-12
  The responsive, still sustaining pomps for you [On Manner 56-5
  Things certain sustaining us in certainty. [Cred 375-20
SUSTAINS. Sustains us . . . Who, then, are they, seated here?
  [Cuisine 228-14
  A longer, deeper breath sustains [Ulysses 101-16 P
  A longer, deeper breath sustains [Presence 106-1 P
SUSTENANCE. But the sustenance of the wilderness [Havana 142-7
  Were part of a sustenance itself enough, [EM 316-3
SUZERAIN. Little by little, as if the suzerain soil [C 40-23
SWADDLED. Swaddled in revery, the object of [NSF 388-3
SWAGS. In the swags of pine-trees bordering the lake. [NSF 386-8
SWALLOW. By the consummation of the swallow's wings. [Sunday 68-26
  If the mouse should swallow the steeple, in its time . . . [Blue
  Bldg 217-7
  A transparency through which the swallow weaves, [Look 518-8
SWALLOWED. As sullen as the sky, was swallowed up [C 32-20
SWAMPS. In the swamps, bushes draw up dark red, [Primordia 8-22 P

SWAMPY. The clouds foretell a swampy rain. [Fish-Scale 161-6
SWANS. "Invective against Swans" [4-title
  The bills of the swans are flat upon the ground. [Havana 142-10
  The swans . . . Before the bills of the swans fell flat [Havana
  142-13
  The indolent progressions of the swans [Havana 143-8
  In the grand decadence of the perished swans. [Havana 145-9
  Were contours. Cold was chilling the wide-moving swans. [Contra
  II 270-11
  The swans. He was not the man for swans. [Descrip 342-22
  In which he sat. All chariots were drowned. The swans [Descrip
  343-4
  The swans fled outward to remoter reaches, [Descrip 343-7
  Were one and swans far off were swans to come. [Descrip 343-10
  Like a momentary color, in which swans [NSF 397-14
  To which the swans curveted, a will to change, [NSF 397-17
SWARM. The swarm of thoughts, the swarm of dreams [MBG 179-9
  Swarm from the little blue of the horizon [Dutch 290-2
  Swarm, not with secondary sounds, but choirs, [Cred 374-12
  From pipes that swarm clerestory walls. The voice [Greenest
  59-13 P
  The ephemeras of the tangent swarm, the chance [Someone 84-1 A
SWARMED. Studies and shapes a tallowy image, swarmed [Theatre
  91-10 P
SWARMING. The root-man swarming, tortured by his mass, [Montra
  262-23
  A swarming of number over number, not [Choc 296-15
  As if the air, the mid-day air, was swarming [EM 326-10
  The swarming activities of the formulae [NH 488-17
  In the days when the mood of love will be swarming for solace
  and sink deeply into the thin stuff of being, [Piano 22-8 P
SWARMINGLY. Brightly empowered with like colors, swarmingly,
  [Myrrh 350-3
SWARM-LIKE. Yes: gildering the swarm-like manias [Descrip 342-19
SWARMS. These bands, these swarms, these motions, what of them?
  [Duck 62-9 P
SWARTHY. You enter the swarthy sea, [Countryman 428-12
  But only of your swarthy motion, [Countryman 428-18
  But always of the swarthy water, [Countryman 428-19
  The place of a swarthy presence moving, [Countryman 429-7
  Slowly, to the look of a swarthy name. [Countryman 429-8
  Is not Swatara. The swarthy water [Degen 444-13
SWATARA. Swatara, Swatara, black river, [Countryman 428-9
  Swatara, Swatara, heavy the hills [Countryman 428-13
  Of which Swatara is the breathing, [Countryman 428-20
  Is not Swatara. The swarthy water [Degen 444-13
  Is not Swatara. It is being. [Degen 444-16
  When Swatara becomes this undulant river [Degen 444-20
  And through and over the puddles of Swatara [Our Stars 455-10
SWATHED. You dream of women, swathed in indigo, [Polish Aunt 84-9
SWAY. And to watch the treetops, as they sway. [Region 115-7 P
  They sway, deeply and loudly, in an effort, [Region 115-8 P
SWAYING. The trees are swaying, swaying, swaying. [Region 115-17 P
SWAYS. Sways slightly and the pinnacles frisson. [Hero 275-3
  And the wind sways like a great thing tottering-- [Hermit 505-16
  Stands glistening and Haddam shines and sways. [R Conn 533-15
SWEAT. A majestic weavers' job, a summer's sweat. [Greenest 58-6 P
SWEATING. Through sweating changes, never could forget [C 33-22
SWEATS. And liquorish prayer provokes new sweats: so, so, [Havana
  144-10
  That sweats the sun up on its morning way [Repet 307-7
  To giant red, sweats up a giant sense [Repet 307-8
  Who sweats. [Three 136-9 P
SWEATY. To that sweaty tragedian, [Three 138-8 P
SWEDEN. "Lions in Sweden" [124-title
  As every man in Sweden will concede, [Lions 125-3
  Sweden described, Salzburg with shaded eyes [NH 486-2
  At least, conceive what these hands from Sweden mean, [Duck
  60-21 P
SWEDISH. Mrs. Anderson's Swedish baby [Circulat 150-5
  It is Marianna's Swedish cart. [Prejudice 368-12
  The Swedish cart to be part of the heart. [Prejudice 369-6
SWEEP. The sweep of an impossible elegance, [Prelude 195-4
SWEEPING. More definite. The sweeping brim of the hat [Pastor
  379-5
  In the sweeping brim becomes the origin [Pastor 379-13
  Of the sweeping meanings that we add to them. [NSF 384-6
  If only in the branches sweeping in the rain: [NH 481-1
  Or this, whose music, sweeping irradiation of a sea-night,
  [Inelegance 26-1 P
  With each fold sweeping in a sweeping play. [Burnshaw 51-27 P
SWEEPS. With its frigid brilliances, its blue-red sweeps [AA 413-1
SWEET. When you were Eve, its acrid juice was sweet, [Monocle 14-14
  Of crinoline spread, but of a pining sweet, [C 42-29
  No mother suckled him, no sweet land gave [Sunday 67-28
  Of misty fields, by their sweet questionings; [Sunday 68-14
  Sweet berries ripen in the wilderness; [Sunday 70-24
  And flame and summer and sweet fire, no thread [Fictive 87-10
  The meat is sweet. [Fading 139-19
  The bee may have all sweet [Anything B 211-9

Contains for its children not a gill of sweet. [Greenest 55-26 P
SWEETEN. Which grieving will not sweeten. [Weep Woman 25-3
SWEETENS. The pine-tree sweetens my body [Carolinas 5-4
SWEETLY. Slowly and sweetly. [Agenda 42-12 P
SWEETNESS. Will drop like sweetness in the empty nights [Havana
   144-8
SWEET-SMELLING. And for sweet-smelling virgins close to them.
   [Monocle 14-25
SWELL. That lay impounding the Pacific swell, [Geneva 24-2
   The voice of ether prevailing, the swell [MBG 177-11
   Observed the waves, the rising and the swell [Woman Had 81-13 P
   The rising and the swell, the preparation [Woman Had 81-15 P
   The rising and the swell, the first line's glitter, [Woman Had
   81-17 P
SWELLING. Come swelling, when, regardless of my end, [Soldat 14-15P
   Pitched into swelling bodies, upward, drift [Burnshaw 52-20 P
SWELLS. This darkened water cloven by sullen swells [Farewell
   118-14
SWENSON. No more phrases, Swenson: I was once [Lions 124-10
   Are the soul itself. And the whole of the soul, Swenson, [Lions
   125-2
SWEPT. They swept over the room, [Domination 8-21
   What was the sea whose tide swept through me there? [Hoon 65-12
   Was like a willow swept by rain. [Peter 91-11
   Swept through its boarded windows and the leaves [Havana 142-19
   As rain and booming, gleaming, blowing, swept [NH 484-10
   To be swept across them when they are revealed, [Duck 65-19 P
   Today the leaves cry, hanging on branches swept by wind,
   [Course 96-10 P
SWERVED. Until they swerved [Earthy 3-6
   Or until they swerved [Earthy 3-10
SWERVING. A swerving, a tilting, a little lengthening, [Nuns
   92-11 P
SWIFT. In a swift, circular line [Earthy 3-7
   In a swift, circular line [Earthy 3-11
   Out of what swift destruction did it spring? [C 30-12
   In swift, successive shadows, dolefully. [C 32-21
   The lines are straight and swift between the stars. [Tallap
   71-10
   These lines are swift and fall without diverging. [Tallap 72-4
   To say the water is swift today, [Sailing 121-2
   She will leap back from the swift constellations, [Soldat 12-7 P
   Midmost in its design, the arms grown swift, [Sombre 69-9 P
SWIFTLY. Swiftly in the nights, [Venereal 47-18
   To a seething minor swiftly modulate. [Eve Angels 137-28
SWIFTLY FLYING. Look backward. Let your swiftly-flying flocks
   [Red Kit 31-28 P
SWIMMING. And moved, as blooms move, in the swimming green [Sea
   Surf 99-11
SWIMS. One boy swims under a tub, one sits [Vari 235-16
   Through the door one sees on the lake that the white duck swims
   [Bouquet 449-19
SWINE. It is true that the rivers went nosing like swine, [Frogs
   78-1
   That the air was heavy with the breath of these swine, [Frogs
   78-4
SWINE-LIKE. As the swine-like rivers suckled themselves [Frogs
   78-14
SWIPLING. Or swipling flail, sun-black in the sun, [Soldat 16-2 P
SWIRLED. Swirled round them in immense autumnal sounds. [Old
   Woman 43-21 P
SWIRLS. Paddling the melodic swirls, [Thought 184-12
SWISH. Miraculous in its panache and swish? [Antag 426-2
SWISHED. Time swished on the village clocks and dreams were alive,
   [Uruguay 249-26
SWISHING. Black fact emerges from her swishing dreams. [Stan MMO
   19-22 P
SWISS. At which a kind of Swiss perfection comes [NSF 386-12
SWOLLEN. Moisture and heat have swollen the garden into a slum of
   bloom. [Banal 62-14
   With time, in wavering water lies, swollen [Two V 354-2
SWOONS. And the architecture swoons. [Public Sq 109-8
SWOOP. Would swoop to earth? It is a wheel, the rays [Sleight
   222-10
SWORD. We dance it out to the tip of Monsieur's sword, [Mice 123-6
   Of that angelic sword? Creature of [Hero 273-17
SYBILS. These were the psalter of their sybils. [Hero 273-14
SYLLABI. His petty syllabi, the sounds that stick, [NSF 407-19
SYLLABLE. Within me, bursts its watery syllable. [Monocle 13-11
   Portentous enunciation, syllable [C 43-8
   To blessed syllable affined, and sound [C 43-9
   What syllable are you seeking, [Roaring 113-4
   Something in now a senseless syllable, [Montra 260-9
   The syllable of a syllable. [Search 268-16
   Makes poems on the syllable fa or [Hero 280-9
   It is in this solitude, a syllable, [Possum 294-9
   And she that in the syllable between life [Owl 432-12
   In the midst of foreignness, the syllable [NH 471-2
   As he traveled alone, like a man lured on by a syllable without
   any meaning, [Prol 516-4

A syllable of which he felt, with an appointed sureness, [Prol
   516-5
A sacred syllable rising from sacked speech, [Armor 530-1
For the syllable, poised for the touch? But that [Duck 62-22 P
SYLLABLED. See: dark-syllabled; thrice-triple-syllabled.
SYLLABLES. What word split up in clickering syllables [C 28-14
   In those portentous accents, syllables, [C 45-25
   Its sounds are not angelic syllables [Eve Angels 137-3
   Speak and say the immaculate syllables [Men Fall 188-11
   We say ourselves in syllables that rise [Creat 311-17
   Afflicted sleep, too much the syllables [EM 314-20
   Now, solemnize the secretive syllables. [AA 420-15
   Which has no accurate syllables and that [Page 421-8
   The outlines of being and its expressings, the syllables of its
   law: [Large 424-5
   The loftiest syllables among loftiest things, [Rome 510-7
   Repeating his name with its patient syllables, [World 521-17
   The syllables of the gulls and of the crows [Primordia 7-17 P
   Went crying their desolate syllables, before [Old Woman 45-26 P
   Syllables, pewter on ebony, yet still [Sombre 70-7 P
SYMBOL. Not the symbol but that for which the symbol stands,
   [Martial 238-11
   A hermit's truth nor symbol in hermitage. [Cred 375-16
   Or symbol of malice. That we partake thereof, [AA 418-22
   Of rose, stood tall in self not symbol, quick [Owl 435-6
   It is a symbol, a sovereign of symbols [Bouquet 451-8
   This Italian symbol, this Southern landscape, is like [Study I
   463-7
   Blue verdured into a damask's lofty symbol, [NH 477-18
   Fire is the symbol: the celestial possible. [Rome 509-8
   Part of the speculum of fire on its prow, its symbol, whatever
   it was, [Prol 516-2
   In that which is created as its symbol. [Armor 529-16
   Symbol of the seeker, crossing by night [Ulysses 99-11 P
   By them: gorgeous symbol seated [Ulysses 104-4 P
   Symbol of the seeker, crossing by night [Presence 105-14 P
   5. The symbol of feasts and of oblivion . . . [Someone 86-8 A
SYMBOLIC. The illustrious arms, the symbolic horns, the red
   [Bship 79-6 P
SYMBOLIZED. To that which they symbolized, away [Ulysses 102-14 P
SYMBOLS. Study the symbols and the requiescats, [Norfolk 111-5
   His robes and symbols, ai-yi-yi-- [MBG 178-11
   Of a still-life, symbols, brown things to think of [Hero 276-24
   Impenetrable symbols, motionless. They move [Owl 432-6
   It is a symbol, a sovereign of symbols [Bouquet 451-8
   Stood, dressed in antic symbols, to display [NH 470-6
   The voluble intentions of the symbols, [Aug 492-13
   To symbols of descending night; and search [Blanche 10-7 P
   Symbols of sentiment . . . Take this phrase, [Soldat 16-7 P
   The ancient symbols will be nothing then. [Ulysses 102-12 P
   We shall have gone behind the symbols [Ulysses 102-13 P
SYMMETRIES. The evanescent symmetries [Negation 98-4
SYMMETRY. Must miss the symmetry of a leaden mate, [Nigger 152-19
SYMPATHIZERS. Softly let all true sympathizers come, [EM 317-4
SYMPATHY. Who by sympathy has made himself a man [EM 315-15
SYNAGOGUE. The Jew did not go to his synagogue [Winter B 141-1
SYRINGA. Syringa, cicada, his flea. [Thought 186-20
SYSTEMATIC. Of systematic thinking . . . Ercole, [Extracts 256-17
SYSTEMS. From which the incredible systems spring, [Ulysses
   103-19 P

T. The curtains to a metaphysical t [NSF 390-21
TABERNACLE. Of this tabernacle, this communion, [Hero 278-17
TABERNACLES. Forth from their tabernacles once again [Greenest
    55-27 P
  Concentric bosh. To their tabernacles, then, [Greenest 56-21 P
TABLE. The table was set by an ogre, [Bananas 54-11
  And the table that holds a platter of pears, [Grapes 110-13
  A pear should come to the table popped with juice, [Nigger 155-3
  At a table on which the food is cold? [MBG 173-9
  Is the table a mirror in which they sit and look? [Cuisine
    228-15
  In an ascetic room, its table [Hero 275-28
  On the wall, the lemons on the table. [Hero 280-15
  Turns blue and on its empty table [Hero 280-20
  A young man seated at his table [Lack 303-14
  And a pineapple on the table. It must be so. [Paisant 335-16
  She stood with him at the table, [Attempt 370-12
  The green roses drifted up from the table [Attempt 370-15
  On the table near which they stood [Attempt 370-20
  The President has apples on the table [NSF 390-19
  The way wine comes at a table in a wood. [NSF 405-24
  Above the table spins its constant spin, [NSF 406-2
  And table. The father fetches tellers of tales [AA 415-5
  Of the pans above the stove, the pots on the table, the tulips
    among them. [Large 423-15
  Green guests and table in the woods and songs [Orb 440-19
  And die. It stands on a table at a window [Bouquet 450-5
  He bumps the table. The bouquet falls on its side. [Bouquet
    453-1
  To the novels on the table, [Aug 493-11
  It is like a guitar left on a table [Vacancy 511-8
  Even when the book lay turned in the dust of his table. [Poem
    Mt 512-4
  "The Planet on the Table" [532-title
  "Table Talk" [40-title P
  Like leaning on the table, shading one's eyes, [Letters 107-11 P
  Came tinkling on the grass to the table [Dinner 110-3 P
  It is something on a table that he sees, [Someone 83-4 A
  If he sees an object on a table, much like [Someone 83-14 A
  On the table or in the colors of the room. [Someone 84-19 A
  When a pineapple on the table was enough, [Someone 85-3 A
  Of that third planet to the table and then: [Someone 86-3 A
  Up the pineapple, a table Alp and yet [Someone 87-2 A
  At last, is the pineapple on the table or else [Someone 87-9 A
TABLEAU. What a beautiful tableau tinted and towering, [Mice
    123-11
  Shiftings of an inchoate crystal tableau, [Someone 86-21 A
TABLE-BOARDS. Their shrilling tankards on the table-boards.
    [Monocle 15-23
TABLECLOTH. In other shapes, as if duck and tablecloth [Bouquet
    450-19
TABLE-CLOTH. Red as a red table-cloth, its windows [Hero 276-1
TABLES. Trained to poise the tables of the law, [Lions 124-14
  On the tables of Connecticut, and they are; [Connois 215-6
TABULAE. As he sat there reading, aloud, the great blue tabulae.
    [Large 423-12
  And laughed, as he sat there reading, from out of the purple tab-
    ulae, [Large 424-4
TACITURN. Confessing the taciturn and yet indifferent, [Wom Sun
    445-14
TAIL. The white cock's tail [Ploughing 20-1
  The turkey-cock's tail [Ploughing 20-3
  The turkey-cock's tail [Ploughing 20-15
  The white cock's tail [Ploughing 20-17
  Was blackamoor to bear your blazing tail. [Bantams 75-17
  Yes, and the blackbird spread its tail, [Watermelon 89-10
  A baby with the tail of a rat? [Horn 230-7
TAILED. See long-tailed.
TAILOR. And of Phoebus the Tailor the second saying goes: [NE
    Verses 105-5
TAILS. The colors of their tails [Domination 8-17
  Turning as the tails of the peacocks [Domination 9-8
  A pip of life amid a mort of tails. [Bird Claws 82-3
  Panache upon panache, his tails deploy [Bird Claws 82-10
TAKE. Take the moral law and make a nave of it [High-Toned 59-2
  We agree in principle. That's clear. But take [High-Toned 59-6
  Take from the dresser of deal, [Emperor 64-9
  The devil take it, wear it, too. [Snow Stars 133-5
  Exceeding music must take the place [MBG 167-11
  Ourselves in poetry must take their place, [MBG 167-13
  Between you and the shapes you take [MBG 183-11
  The touch. Fix quiet. Take the place [Prelude 195-19
  And its communion take. And now of that. [Extracts 253-6
  Take the diamonds from your hair and lay them down. [Myrrh 350-10
  What aquiline pedants take [Prejudice 368-21
  Must take its place, as what is possible [Cred 376-23
  He might take habit, whether from wave or phrase, [NSF 387-12
  The body lift its heavy wing, take up, [NSF 390-12

Which he can take within him on his breath, [NSF 395-5
  Should strengthen her abortive dreams and take [NSF 399-11
  The one refused the other one to take, [NSF 401-9
  Each must the other take not for his high, [NSF 401-11
  Each must the other take as sign, short sign [NSF 401-14
  Does it take its place in the north and enfold itself, [AA 417-8
  They understand, and take on potency, [Bouquet 449-5
  And there the senses give and nothing take, [NH 480-18
  Vines that take [Bowl 7-1 P
  I take all things as stated--so and so [Soldat 11-7 P
  This man to take the air. [Soldat 12-16 P
  Symbols of sentiment . . . Take this phrase, [Soldat 16-7 P
  Men of the line, take this new phrase [Soldat 16-8 P
  Can I take fire from so benign an ash? [Stan MMO 19-7 P
  Take counsel, all hierophants [Sat Night 28-7 P
  Green is the path we take [Sombre 67-28 P
  The perspective squirming as it tries to take [Bship 80-4 P
  Of tradition does not easily take form. [Recit 86-7 P
  And take from this restlessly unhappy happiness [How Now 97-14 P
  Take away the bushes. [Three 139-15 P
TAKEN. The dog had to walk. He had to be taken. [Forces 229-3
  Before the speaker's youngest breath is taken! [Montra 261-21
  Taken with withered weather, crumpled clouds, [News 265-6
  A vibrancy not to be taken for granted, from [Holiday 312-5
  Its edges were taken from tumultous wind [Greenest 56-29 P
TAKES. For all it takes it gives a humped return [C 43-6
  From these it takes. Perhaps it gives, [MBG 177-5
  The thought of her takes her away. [Scavoir 231-14
  The eye believes and its communion takes. [Extracts 253-4
  In a calculated chaos: he that takes form [Repet 307-4
  Three times the concentred self takes hold, three times [Cred
    376-9
  The child that touches takes character from the thing, [NSF
    392-20
  The phrase grows weak. The fact takes up the strength [NH 473-4
  As if the design of all his words takes form [Rome 511-2
  In the great vistas of night air, that takes this form, [Moon-
    light 531-17
  Takes time and tinkering, melodious [Duck 65-28 P
  That revolution takes for connoisseurs: [Sombre 70-9 P
  And must be, when the portent, changed, takes on [Sombre 70-12 P
  Which takes a shape by accident. [Stan MBG 73-1 P
TAKING. If in the mind, he vanished, taking there [Choc 298-3
TALE. Of an earth in which the first leaf is the tale [NSF 394-14
  "Page from a Tale" [421-title
  The dauntless master, as he starts the human tale. [Puel 456-18
  So that this cold, a children's tale of ice, [NH 468-8
  And hearing a tale one wanted intensely to hear, [Letters 107-12P
  See tell-tale.
TALES. "Two Tales of Liadoff" [346-title
  And table. The father fetches tellers of tales [AA 415-5
  And musicians who mute much, muse much, on the tales. [AA 415-6
  Like tales that were told the day before yesterday-- [Hermit
    505-3
TALK. In fragrant leaves heat-heavy yet nimble in talk. [NE Verses
    105-12
  And, being unhappy, talk of happiness [Extracts 257-13
  Talk of the weather-- [Woman Song 361-3
  He does not hear his characters talk. He sees [Cred 377-24
  Two bodies disembodied in their talk, [NH 471-8
  The eccentric exterior of which the clocks talk. [NH 478-21
  Were mere brown clods, mere catching weeds of talk. [NH 486-21
  She would talk a little to herself as she combed her hair,
    [World 521-16
  Has enraged them and made them want to talk it down. [Slug 522-8
  "Table Talk" [40-title P
  On a hot night and a long cigar and talk [Greenest 58-25 P
  That the sense of being changes as we talk, [Conversat 109-22 P
  That talk shifts the cycle of the scenes of kings? [Conversat
    109-23 P
TALKED. At the beginning of winter, and I walked and talked
    [Martial 238-14
  And talked of never-ending things, [Silent 359-10
TALKING. Yes: you came talking. [Vincentine 53-10
  And, talking of happiness, know that it means [Extracts 257-14
  To sleep in that bed for its disorder, talking of ghostly [Bed
    327-3
TALL. Which, let the tall musicians call and call, [C 41-16
  Against a tall tree. [Six Sig 74-5
  And tall and of a port in air. [Jar 76-12
  In the end, however naked, tall, there is still [Oboe 250-17
  He was as tall as a tree in the middle of [Choc 297-19
  This elevation, in which he seems to be tall, [Repet 307-13
  Tall and\unfretted, a figure meant to bear [Pastor 379-19
  Of rose, stood tall in self not symbol, quick [Owl 435-6
  A tall figure upright in a giant's air. [Recit 87-24 P
TALLAPOOSA. "Stars at Tallapoosa" [71-title
TALLER. I find that I am much taller, [Six Sig 74-6
  Taller than any eye could see, [News 264-9
  To stand taller than a person stands, has [Hero 277-7

The Roamer is a voice taller than the redwoods, [Phenom 287-4
  As if on a taller tower [Aug 493-15
TALLEST. Rose up, tallest, in the black sun, [Thunder 220-6
  And tallest hero and plus gaudiest vir. [Montra 262-12
TALLOWY. Studies and shapes a tallowy image, swarmed [Theatre
  91-10 P
TAMBOURINES. Soon, with a noise like tambourines, [Peter 91-12
  Fled, with a noise like tambourines. [Peter 91-21
  Which is like zithers and tambourines combined: [Mice 123-8
TAMBOURS. The crickets beat their tambours in the wind [C 42-11
TAN. Of tan with henna hackles, halt! [Bantams 75-15
TANAGERS. As if raspberry tanagers in palms, [C 30-20
TANG. See ting-tang.
TANGENT. He sees it in this tangent of himself. [Someone 83-19 A
  And in this tangent it becomes a thing [Someone 83-20 A
  The ephemeras of the tangent swarm, the chance [Someone 84-1 A
TANGS. Bristles, and points their Appalachian tangs, [Bantams 76-3
TANK. Such tink and tank and tunk-a-tunk-tunk, [High-Toned 59-18
TANKARDS. Their shrilling tankards on the table-boards. [Monocle
  15-23
TANKS. The glitter-goes on surfaces of tanks, [NSF 384-13
TAP. Tap skeleton drums inaudibly. [Dutch 290-7
  See tip-tap-tap.
TAPERED. Is to fire. And her mainmast tapered to nothing, [Vari
  235-21
TAPERING. Tapering toward the top. [Pears 196-12
TAPPED. A dead hand tapped the drum, [Phases 6-1 P
TAPPING. Of blind men tapping their way [Soldat 12-11 P
TARBERT. As he heard it in Tarbert. [Our Stars 454-17
TARNISHED. However tarnished, companions out of the past, [Burn-
  shaw 50-10 P
TARTUFFE. Than Tartuffe as myth, the most Molière, [Paisant 335-10
TASSELLED. And not a bald and tasselled saint. [Our Stars 455-6
TASTE. A blonde to tip the silver and to taste [C 42-19
  Prone to distemper he abates in taste, [C 46-3
  On disregarded plate. The maidens taste [Sunday 69-11
  In the taste for iron dogs and iron deer. [Nigger 155-2
  The taste of even a country connoisseur. [Nigger 157-16
  Taste of the blood upon his martyred lips, [Men Fall 188-15
  In what camera do you taste [Bagatelles 213-5
  With my whole body I taste these peaches, [Peaches 224-1
  To hear, to touch, to taste, to smell, that's now, [Arcades
  225-7
  Of poorness as an earth, to taste [Arcades 225-24
  The taste of it, secrete within them [Hero 279-8
  And I taste at the root of the tongue the unreal of what is
  real. [Holiday 313-10
  This was the salty taste of glory, [Phases 3-13 P
  To that salty, sacrificial taste? [Phases 4-23 P
  Would taste, precisely, as they said it would. [Soldat 11-12 P
  Than purple paste of fruit, to taste, or leaves [Greenest 58-31P
  Like taste distasting the first fruit of a vine, [Theatre 91-3 P
  Cat's taste possibly or possibly Danish lore, [Someone 87-5 A
TASTES. He tastes its blood, not spit. [Destructive 192-17
TASTING. Hard found, and water tasting of misery. [Bad Time 426-14
TATERS. "No Possum, No Sop, No Taters" [293-title
TATTER. A tatter of shadows peaked to white, [Postcard 159-20
TATTERED. His tattered manikin arise, [Abnormal 24-16 P
TATTERS. Is something in tatters that I cannot hold." [Choc 299-3
TATTERY. The sea appends its tattery hues. [MBG 172-13
TATTOO. "Tattoo" [81-title
TAUGHT. Never the naked politician taught [Dames 206-17
  The fire burns as the novel taught it how. [Novel 458-3
TAUREAUX. Aux taureaux Dieu cornes donne [Parasol 20-1 P
TAUT. Until his nose grew thin and taut [Thought 186-22
  A horse grotesquely taut, a walker like [Pure 330-6
  So much he had devised: white forelegs taut [Old Woman 43-10 P
TAUTEST. By tautest pinions lifted through his thought. [Duck
  64-19 P
TAWNY. And its tawny caricature and tawny life, [What We 460-4
TAXES. Abandoned because of taxes . . . It was enough [Greenest
  53-2 P
TEA. "Tea at the Palaz of Hoon" [65-title
  "Tea" [112-title
  The tea is bad, bread sad. [Fading 139-8
  Supports of night. The tea, [Fading 139-17
  From Esthonia: the tiger chest, for tea. [Dump 201-19
  If Englishmen lived without tea in Ceylon, and they do; [Connois
  215-7
TEA-BELLE. It depends which way you crossed, the tea-belle said.
  [NE Verses 104-8
TEACH. Caparison elephants, teach bears to juggle. [NSF 385-3
TEACHING. Teaching a fusky alphabet. [Phosphor 267-16
TEAR. Stamp down the phosphorescent toes, tear off [Nigger 155-7
  That such ferocities could tear [Peaches 224-19
TEARING. A woman writing a note and tearing it up. [NH 488-21
  A light on the candle tearing against the wick [Rome 509-5
TEARS. It is in the water of tears [Weep Woman 25-5
  And little will or wish, that day, for tears. [Soldat 14-17 P
  And the mighty, musty belly of tears. [Sat Night 28-3 P

Let this be as it may. It must have tears [Spaniard 35-13 P
TEAT-LIKE. Stabbing at his teat-like corns [Lulu M 27-15 P
TEDIOUS. Blowing itself upon the tedious ear. [NSF 400-17
TEDIOUSLY. Ticks tediously the time of one more year. [Monocle 15-2
TEDIUM. Through the gross tedium of being rare. [Nigger 155-22
TEEMING. A teeming millpond or a furious mind. [Nigger 155-13
TEETERING. Without teetering a millimeter's measure. [Vari 236-1
TEETH. Of growling teeth, and falls at night, snuffed out [NH
  467-19
TEHAUNTEPEC. In that November off Tehuantepec, [Sea Surf 98-12
  In that November off Tehuantepec [Sea Surf 99-16
  In that November off Tehuantepec, [Sea Surf 100-10
  In that November off Tehuantepec [Sea Surf 101-4
  In that November off Tehuantepec [Sea Surf 101-22
TELEGRAMS. That vast confect of telegrams, [Mandolin 29-7 P
TELEGRAPH. I love to sit and read the Telegraph, [Mandolin 29-6 P
TELEPHONE. The cricket in the telephone is still. [Phenom 286-1
TELL. And tell the divine ingénue, your companion, [Lilacs 48-20
  Tell me more of the eagle, Cotton, [Pascagoula 126-9
  Tell me how he descended [Pascagoula 126-11
  Tell me again of the point [Pascagoula 126-19
  Ramon Fernandez, tell me, if you know, [Key W 130-3
  Toward the town, tell why the glassy lights, [Key W 130-5
  To face the weather and be unable to tell [Extracts 257-7
  Tell X that speech is not dirty silence [Creat 311-7
  Is too difficult to tell from despair. Perhaps, [EM 325-20
  So much ourselves, we cannot tell apart [NH 466-20
  That tell of it. The steeple at Farmington [R Conn 533-14
  Say this to Pravda, tell the damned rag [Memo 89-9 P
  Before one can tell [Three 131-4 P
  And can you tell how it will end?-- [Three 138-18 P
  Tell my father: [Three 140-7 P
  No more and because they lack the will to tell [Ideal 88-14 A
TELLERS. And table. The father fetches tellers of tales [AA 415-5
TELLS. And tells the hour by the lateness of the sounds. [Pure
  330-3
  And tells of his wound, [Woman Song 360-15
  Away--and tells and tells the water tells [Bouquet 449-20
  Gone wild, be what he tells you to be: Puella. [Puel 456-14
TELL-TALE. The wide night mused by tell-tale muttering, [Duck
  61-26 P
TEMPER. The ruddy temper, the hammer [Motive 288-17
  Temper and belief and that differences lost [Aug 494-3
TEMPERATURE. Reclines in the temperature of heaven-- [Hermit
  505-12
TEMPERED. See well-tempered.
TEMPERING. He shut out from his tempering ear; what thoughts, [C
  34-22
TEMPERS. The whole man, that tempers and beliefs became [Aug 494-2
TEMPEST. The valet in the tempest was annulled. [C 29-8
  A tempest cracked on the theatre. Quickly, [Repet 306-1
  Link, of that tempest, to the farm, [Silent 359-15
TEMPESTUOUS. Tempestuous clarion, with heavy cry, [C 32-23
  Selah, tempestuous bird. How is it that [Belly 366-18
  Flutter her lance with your tempestuous dust. [Spaniard 34-24 P
TEMPLE. And because the temple is never quite composed, [Burnshaw
  50-14 P
  The temple of the altar where each man [Greenest 54-17 P
TEMPLES. Out of the spirit of the holy temples, [Nigger 151-19
  Time was not wasted in your subtle temples. [Dutch 293-11
TEMPLE-TONE. Was under every temple-tone. You sang [Burnshaw 50-30P
TEMPLE-TONED. And crisply musical, or holy caverns temple-toned,
  [Burnshaw 47-16 P
TEMPO. The tempo, in short, of this complicated shift, [Duck 65-31P
TEMPORARY. Suspended in temporary jauntiness. [Bouquet 448-7
TEN. "Disillusionment of Ten O'Clock" [66-title
  And cobble ten thousand and three [Jersey 210-10
  Ten thousand, men hewn and tumbling, [Thunder 220-2
  Mobs of ten thousand, clashing together, [Thunder 220-3
  And through the eye equates ten thousand deaths [Extracts 253-13
  That is ten thousand deaths and evil death. [Extracts 253-23
  Ten times ten times dynamite, convulsive [Hero 273-18
  Is like ten thousand tumblers tumbling down [Cred 376-25
  Of ten brilliancies of battered gold [Imago 439-6
  The word respected, fired ten thousand guns [Bship 78-12 P
TENACIOUS. As a part, but part, but tenacious particle, [Orb 443-18
TENACIOUSLY. Held fast tenaciously in common earth [NH 468-24
TEND. And pallid bits, that tend to comply with blue, [Bouquet
  452-2
TENDANCE. This tendance and venerable holding-in [NH 472-20
TENDED. This field, and tended it awhile, [Frogs 78-8
TENDENCY. With a tendency to bulge as it floats away. [Duck 63-22 P
TENDEREST. He makes the tenderest research, intent [EM 318-5
  Almost as the tenderest and the truest part. [AA 420-3
TENDERLY. For whom the good of April falls tenderly, [NSF 388-7
TENDERNESS. Prolific and tormenting tenderness [C 43-11
  Whispered a little out of tenderness, [Sunday 69-6
  And, out of tenderness or grief, the sun [Anatomy 108-9
TENEMENT. Negation destroyed him in his tenement [EM 319-21
TENEMENTS. Destroys romantic tenements [Bottle 238-19

Romantic tenements of rose and ice. [Bottle 239-16
TEN-FOOT. You ten-foot poet among inchlings. Fat! [Bantams 76-1
TENNESSEE. I placed a jar in Tennessee, [Jar 76-5
  Like nothing else in Tennessee. [Jar 76-16
TENSE. Capped summer-seeming on the tense machine [Sea Surf 99-21
  To the tense, the maudlin, true meridian [Burnshaw 52-15 P
  Broods in tense meditation, constantly, [Sombre 68-20 P
TENSION. The tension of the lyre. My point is that [John 437-10
TENUOUS. Into this haggard and tenuous air, [Nigger 153-9
TEPID. Indifferent to the tepid summer cold, [C 43-2
  These were not tepid stars of torpid places [Page 421-21
  And live without a tepid aureole, [Angel 496-10
TERMAGANT. The termagant fans [Coroner 29-18 P
TERMINAL. As its autumnal terminal-- [Fare Guit 98-21 P
  And in what place, what exultant terminal, [Ideal 89-2 A
TERMS. Ripened in warmth and served in warmth. On terms [Nigger 155-4
  Last terms, the largest, bulging still with more, [Orb 441-11
TERRA. A little while of Terra Paradise [Montra 263-1
  Are one, and here, O terra infidel. [EM 315-13
TERRACE. Her terrace was the sand [Infanta 7-11
  They fill the terrace of his capitol. [Canna 55-3
  Under the wintry trees of the terrace. [Bus 116-14 P
TERRACES. Within them right for terraces--oh, brave salut! [Belly
    367-11
  Stop at the terraces of mandolins, [Study I 463-14
TERRE. Its chapel rises from Terre Ensevelie, [Armor 529-9
  See outre-terre.
TERRESTRIAL. It was not so much the lost terrestrial, [C 28-2
  "Meditation Celestial & Terrestrial" [123-title
  Fat girl, terrestrial, my summer, my night, [NSF 406-7
  See mid-terrestrial.
TERRIBLE. Came bluntly thundering, more terrible [C 32-24
  By the terrible incantations of defeats [Men Made 356-3
  Look in the terrible mirror of the sky [Blanche 10-1 P
  Look in the terrible mirror of the sky. [Blanche 10-5 P
  Look in the terrible mirror of the sky. [Blanche 10-9 P
  That, from her helmet, terrible and bright, [Soldat 14-10 P
TERRIBLEST. The mind is the terriblest force in the world, father,
    [John 436-10
TERROR. The terror of the sound because the sound [EM 314-2
TEST. Before they fly, test the reality [Sunday 68-13
TESTAMENT. Like one who scrawls a listless testament [Swans 4-5
  Scrawl a tragedian's testament? Prolong [C 11-14
  His only testament and estate. [Ulysses 103-9 P
TESTAMENTS. In a storm of torn-up testaments. [Dutch 292-7
TESTS. Of rankest trivia, tests of the strength [C 37-13
TEXT. Preferring text to gloss, he humbly served [C 39-22
  A text we should be born that we might read, [Descrip 344-21
  A single text, granite monotony, [NSF 394-9
  A text that is an answer, although obscure. [NH 479-15
  A new text of the world, [Aug 494-24
  It is a text that we shall be needing, [Aug 495-6
  A text of intelligent men [Aug 495-13
  And its pastoral text, [Inhab 503-14
  A reader of the text, [Inhab 503-18
  And what heroic nature of what text [Ideal 89-4 A
THAN. Than the revenge of music on bassoons. [C 32-25
  Proclaiming something harsher than he learned [C 33-1
  And more than free, elate, intent, profound [C 33-10
  Than the relentless contact he desired; [C 34-20
  Illusive, faint, more mist than moon, perverse, [C 34-30
  More exquisite than any tumbling verse: [C 37-3
  Less prickly and much more condign than that [C 42-15
  Gave to the cabin, lordlier than it was, [C 44-25
  Than your moist hand. [Two Fig 85-16
  No crown is simpler than the simple hair. [Fictive 87-13
  Rougher than a grinding shale. [Orangeade 103-14
  Deeper than a truer ditty [Orangeade 103-18
  It breeds and that was lewder than it is. [Anatomy 107-15
  She walks an autumn ampler than the wind [Anatomy 108-3
  Cries up for us and colder than the frost [Anatomy 108-4
  If they mean no more than that. But they do. [Grapes 110-18
  Much more than that. Autumnal passages [Grapes 111-1
  For which more than any words cries deeplier? [Ghosts 119-7
  Would be endings, more poignant than partings, profounder,
    [Adieu 127-14
  And sound alone. But it was more than that, [Key W 129-17
  More even than her voice, and ours, among [Key W 129-18
  Lusty as June, more fruitful than the weeks [Havana 143-13
  Subtler than the ornatest prophecy, [Havana 144-13
  All this is older than its oldest hymn, [Havana 144-28
  Has no more meaning than tomorrow's bread. [Havana 144-29
  Noble in autumn, yet nobler than autumn. [Nigger 156-12
  Freshness is more than the east wind blowing round one. [Nigger
    157-11
  For the time when sound shall be subtler than we ourselves.
    [Nigger 158-5
  The mind is smaller than the eye. [Fish-Scale 161-4
  In face of the monster, be more than part [MBG 175-7
  Friendlier than my only friend, [MBG 176-1

Himself than in this fertile glass. [MBG 181-14
Happy rather than holy but happy-high, [Thought 185-17
More than sudarium, speaking the speech [Men Fall 188-6
It is faster than the weather, faster than [Paroch 192-5
Any character. It is more than any scene: [Paroch 192-6
So much more than that. The day itself [Poems Clim 193-13
With nothing more than the carnations there. [Poems Clim 193-16
More than a world of white and snowy scents. [Poems Clim 194-3
More than, less than or it puffs like this or that. [Dump 202-4
Of men is nothing. The mass is no greater than [Dames 206-4
Of being, more than birth or death. [Country 207-22
Is more than a seven-foot inchworm [Jersey 210-11
Of nights that will not be more than [Bagatelles 213-19
Than wettest cinnamon. It was cribled pears [Poem Morn 219-10
Slowly, one man, savager than the rest, [Thunder 220-5
Of one wilder than the rest (like music blunted, [Thunder 220-23
A music more than a breath, but less [Vari 232-7
Than the wind, sub-music like sub-speech, [Vari 232-8
In a man-makeness, neater than Naples. [Vari 235-18
Of earth penetrates more deeply than any word. [Yellow 237-3
In the land of war. More than the man, it is [Bottle 239-1
The poem lashes more fiercely than the wind, [Bottle 239-14
A generation sealed, men remoter than mountains, [Waldorf 241-7
Was less than moonlight. Nothing exists by itself. [Les Plus
  244-18
To grow larger and heavier and stronger than [Rhythms 246-1
No greater than a cricket's horn, no more [Beard 247-15
Than a thought to be rehearsed all day, a speech [Beard 247-16
Of things no better than paper things, of days [Extracts 253-2
What more is there to love than I have loved? [Montra 260-1
And echoing rhetorics more than our own. [Montra 261-18
Taller than any eye could see, [News 264-9
Older than any man could be. [News 264-10
In its cavern, wings subtler than any mercy, [Hero 273-13
There are more heroes than marbles of them. [Hero 276-12
To stand taller than a person stands, has [Hero 277-7
Than himself, his self, the self that embraces [Hero 280-6
The room is emptier than nothingness. [Phenom 286-9
The Roamer is a voice taller than the redwoods, [Phenom 287-4
Than the most metal music, loudlier, [Dutch 291-11
In a peace that is more than a refuge, [Dutch 291-17
Of a chaos composed in more than order, [Dutch 293-9
Of less degree than flame and lesser shine. [Choc 297-23
He was more than an external majesty, [Choc 299-9
More than a spokesman of the night to say [Choc 299-11
To say more than human things with human voice, [Choc 300-11
Than human voice, that, also, cannot be; [Choc 300-13
The lesser night, the less than morning light, [Choc 301-20
If nothing more than that, for the moment, large [Choc 302-2
Greater than mine, of his demanding, head [Choc 302-4
Is brighter than the sun itself. [Poesie 302-16
Make more than thunder's rural rumbling. They make [Repet 307-2
From the others, being larger than he was, [Repet 307-5
It is more than an imitation for the ear. [Creat 311-9
Less Aix than Stockholm, hardly a yellow at all, [Holiday 312-4
Than clouds, benevolences, distant heads. [EM 317-21
Lakes are more reasonable than oceans. Hence, [EM 325-6
To believe, more than the casual hero, more [Paisant 335-9
Than Tartuffe as myth, the most Molière, [Paisant 335-10
The more than human commonplace of blood, [Descrip 341-3
There might be, too, a change immenser than [Descrip 341-7
Intenser than any actual life could be, [Descrip 344-20
More explicit than the experience of sun [Descrip 344-22
That breathed on ground, more blue than red, more red [Pieces
  352-3
Than green, fidgets of all-related fire. [Pieces 352-4
Than the spirit of Ludwig Richter . . . [Chaos 357-8
Less firm than the paternal flame, [Red Fern 365-6
Though poor, though raggeder than ruin, have that [Belly 367-10
Than creatures, of the sky between the banks, [Lot 371-14
But a tower more precious than the view beyond, [Cred 373-18
Not fustian. The more than casual blue [Cred 375-5
It is the more than visible, the more [Cred 376-18
Than sharp, illustrious scene. The trumpet cries [Cred 376-19
We more than awaken, sit on the edge of sleep, [NSF 386-19
In the abstract than in his singular, [NSF 388-18
More fecund as principle than particle, [NSF 388-19
In being more than an exception, part, [NSF 388-21
Than nakedness, standing before an inflexible [NSF 396-2
Whereon it falls in more than sensual mode. [NSF 398-19
Whiter than wax, sonorous, fame as it is, [NSF 403-19
You remain the more than natural figure. You [NSF 406-19
That's it: the more than rational distortion, [NSF 406-20
Than bad angels leap from heaven to hell in flames. [AA 414-12
Of the week, queerer than Sunday. We thought alike [AA 419-10
Or one man who, for us, is greater than they, [Antag 425-16
Less time than place, less place than thought of place [Owl 433-1
Subtler than look's declaiming, although she moved [Owl 435-15
In a season more than sun and south wind, [Imago 439-14
Is more difficult to find than the way beyond it. [Papini 446-6

Nothing could be more hushed than the way [Pecul 453-7
They can be no more faded than ourselves. [Study I 464-2
Than that of their clouds. These lineaments were the earth, [NH
    484-13
If more unreal than New Haven, is not [NH 485-3
Than the difference that clouds make over a town. [NH 487-7
Will come stamping here, the ruler of less than men, [Aug 495-22
In less than nature. He is not here yet. [Aug 495-23
Of birds called up by more than the sun, [Hermit 505-17
It is older than the oldest speech of Rome. [Rome 510-4
Should give you more than their peculiar chords [Rome 510-19
No more than a bed, a chair and moving nuns, [Rome 510-23
Too much like thinking to be less than thought, [Look 518-19
In an inhuman meditation, larger than her own. [World 521-5
Than seventy, where one looks, one has been there before. [Slug
    522-2
They are more than leaves that cover the barren rock [Rock 527-6
Matisse at Vence and a great deal more than that, [Armor 529-18
Than the need of each generation to be itself, [Armor 530-9
Than on any bowl of the Sungs, [Bowl 6-13 P
Than fragile volutes in a rose sea-shell. [Soldat 14-3 P
Soother and lustier than this vexed, autumnal exhalation, [Inele-
    gance 25-17 P
In self, a man of longer time than days, [Good Bad 33-10 P
Of larger company than one. Therefore, [Good Bad 33-11 P
How, then, if nothing more than vanity [Spaniard 34-21 P
Less than contending with fictitious doom. [Spaniard 35-5 P
More than his muddy hand was in the manes, [Old Woman 43-19 P
More than his mind in the wings. The rotten leaves [Old Woman
    43-20 P
And light lay deeper for her than her sight. [Old Woman 44-22 P
If the sky that followed, smaller than the night, [Old Woman
    45-6 P
Than this jotting-down of the sculptor's foppishness [Burnshaw
    47-11 P
Than now. No: nor the ploughman in his bed [Burnshaw 47-32 P
Itself." No more than that, no subterfuge, [Burnshaw 48-7 P
Less in the stars than in their earthy wake, [Burnshaw 48-10 P
Than the thought that once was native to the skull; [Burnshaw
    49-18 P
What avuncular cloud-man beamier than spears? [Greenest 52-25 P
Remoter than Athos, the effulgent hordes [Greenest 56-22 P
Than purple paste of fruit, to taste, or leaves [Greenest 58-31 P
Than poodles in Pomerania. This man [Duck 62-2 P
Than the color white and high beyond any height [Duck 64-6 P
See more than marble in their eyes, see more [Duck 64-8 P
Than the horses quivering to be gone, flashed through [Duck
    64-9 P
Where shall we find more than derisive words? [Duck 66-9 P
Than body and in less than mind, ogre, [Sombre 67-14 P
If more than the wished-for ruin racked the night, [Sombre
    69-12 P
If more than pity and despair were sure, [Sombre 69-13 P
From size, backs larger than the eye, not flesh [Sombre 70-23 P
Rather rings than fingers, rather fingers than hands. [Grotesque
    74-8 P
"It is a lesser law than the one itself, [Bship 78-26 P
In more than phrase? There's the true masculine, [Bship 79-12 P
"The Woman That Had More Babies than That" [81-title P
More babies than that. The merely revolving wheel [Woman Had
    81-23 P
There is a mother whose children need more than that. [Woman Had
    82-1 P
They are more than parts of the universal machine. [Woman Had
    82-25 P
But there is more than a marble, massive head. [Woman Had 83-3 P
Too often to be more than secondhand. [Recit 87-2 P
Tradition is much more than the memory. [Recit 87-3 P
The chant and discourse there, more than wild weather [Role 93-9P
Than they are in the final finding of the air, in the thing
    [Course 97-2 P
That which is more than anything else [Ulysses 100-12 P
A life lighter than this present splendor, [Ulysses 101-23 P
How then shall the mind be less than free [Ulysses 103-11 P
More precious than the most precious objects of home: [Local
    111-13 P
Well, more than that, like weather when it has cleared [Art Pop
    112-15 P
So much less than feeling, so much less than speech, [Region
    115-9 P
A perception of cold breath, more revealing than [Bus 116-7 P
Than a power of sleep, a clearness emerging [Bus 116-9 P
Than the dew on the barns. [Three 128-2 P
Is fertile with more than changes of the light [Someone 84-18 A
It is more than the odor of this core of earth [Someone 87-16 A
THANE. The lutanist of fleas, the knave, the thane, [C 28-7
THANKS. Mrs. Pappadopoulos, and thanks. [Couch 296-6
THAT-A-WAY. And that-a-way he twirled the thing. [MBG 178-12
    And the nose is eternal, that-a-way. [MBG 178-19
THEATRE. Then the theatre was changed [Of Mod 239-21

A tempest cracked on the theatre. Quickly, [Repet 306-1
The people sat in the theatre, in the ruin, [Repet 306-10
And if it be theatre for theatre, [Repet 309-16
And snow. The theatre is spinning round, [Chaos 357-16
A bench was his catalepsy, Theatre [NSF 397-10
Scenes of the theatre, vistas and blocks of woods [AA 415-14
It is a theatre floating through the clouds, [AA 416-4
The theatre is filled with flying birds, [AA 416-16
Without scenery or lights, in the theatre's bricks, [Bad Time
    427-5
The immensest theatre, the pillared porch, [Rome 510-24
In a theatre, full of tragedy, [Soldat 15-18 P
Without the distortions of the theatre, [Lytton 39-3 P
"As at a Theatre" [91-title P
THEATRICAL. Theatrical distances, bronze shadows heaped [Key W
    129-20
THEE. "Thou art not August unless I make thee so." [Oboe 251-5
THEFT. The final theft? That you are innocent [Red Kit 30-23 P
THEME. It is a theme for Hyacinth alone. [Monocle 15-17
    "Nuances of a Theme by Williams" [18-title
    To him that postulated as his theme [C 35-1
    The vulgar, as his theme and hymn and flight, [C 35-2
    The essential theme. [Botanist 1 135-5
    Without a theme? [Botanist 1 135-10
    "Parochial Theme" [191-title
    "Analysis of a Theme" [348-title
    To the unstated theme each variation comes . . . [Think 357-1
    An ancestral theme or as a consequence [AA 412-7
    May rush to extinguish the theme, the basses thump [Bship 79-27 P
THEMES. The time will come for these children, seated before their
    long black instruments, to strike the themes of love-- [Piano
    21-16 P
THEMSELVES. Repeating themselves, [Domination 8-10
    Like the leaves themselves [Domination 8-12
    Were like the leaves themselves [Domination 8-18
    Or against the leaves themselves [Domination 9-4
    Like the leaves themselves [Domination 9-15
    If these rude instances impeach themselves [C 38-6
    And were themselves the genii [Joost 46-18
    A few things for themselves, [Venereal 47-4
    A few things for themselves, [Venereal 47-8
    May, merely may, madame, whip from themselves [High-Toned 59-19
    That choir among themselves long afterward. [Sunday 70-9
    They confine themselves [Six Sig 75-8
    Seemed to sucklo themselves on his arid being, [Frogs 78-13
    As the swine-like rivers suckled themselves [Frogs 78-14
    For so retentive of themselves are men [Fictive 88-1
    It lies, themselves within themselves, [Fading 139-12
    Within themselves [Fading 139-14
    Of men whose heaven is in themselves, [Thought 186-12
    Have shapes that are not yet fully themselves, [Parochial 191-4
    Stretch themselves to rest in their first summer's sun, [Paro-
    chial 191-20
    They pose themselves and their rags. [Add 198-10
    No shadow of themselves. [Add 198-22
    For buttons, how many women have covered themselves [Dump 202-8
    Are the men eating reflections of themselves? [Cuisine 228-16
    Scattered themselves in the garden, like [Vase 246-12
    That instantly and in themselves they are gay [Gala 248-2
    The mountains inscribe themselves upon the walls. [Extracts
    252-12
    Themselves, the slightly unjust drawing that is [Extracts 254-23
    Out of themselves, a saying, [Dutch 290-18
    Grows sharp in blood. The armies kill themselves, [Dutch 292-19
    Their form, beyond their life, yet of themselves, [Choc 299-17
    They reveal themselves. [Lack 303-4
    On peculiar horns, themselves eked out [Creat 311-14
    That would form themselves, in time, and communicate [EM 314-21
    Themselves from its essential savor, [EM 323-3
    Besides, when the sky is so blue, things sing themselves, [Debris
    338-10
    As, men make themselves their speech: the hard hidalgo [Descrip
    345-11
    Breathing as if they breathed themselves, [Pediment 361-18
    No, not of day, but of themselves, [Prejudice 369-2
    Of the object. The singers had to avert themselves [Cred 376-3
    Of her sons and of her daughters. They found themselves [NSF
    383-3
    Themselves with care, sought out the nerveless frame [NSF 391-16
    And normal things had yawned themselves away, [NSF 402-20
    Themselves and, therefore, good, the going round [NSF 405-21
    To those that cannot say good-by themselves, [Owl 431-18
    The joy of language, when it is themselves. [Orb 441-8
    Made suddenly luminous, themselves a change, [Our Stars 455-19
    Themselves an issue as at an end, as if [Our Stars 455-21
    Themselves transposed, muted and comforted [NH 467-24
    Since both alike appoint themselves the choice [NH 469-16
    The truth about themselves, having lost, as things, [NH 470-7
    Bending over and pulling themselves erect on the wooden handles,
    [Prol 515-8

The horses weary themselves hunting for green grass. [Primordia
  8-15 P
All of them, darkened by time, moved by they know not what,
  amending the airs they play to fulfill themselves; [Piano
  21-17 P
Did they behold themselves in this [Sat Night 28-4 P
And see themselves as once they were, [Sat Night 28-5 P
All things destroy themselves or are destroyed. [Burnshaw 46-16P
For themselves, and space and time and ease for the duck. [Duck
  60-17 P
Massed for a head they mean to make for themselves, [Duck 60-23P
For whom men were to be ends in themselves, [Duck 61-2 P
They live. They see and feel themselves, seeing [Duck 64-13 P
Themselves to one. [Bship 78-24 P
It is the cry of leaves that do not transcend themselves,
  [Course 96-21 P
As if abstractions were, themselves [Ulysses 103-26 P
THENCE. We live. Thence come the final chants, the chants [Ex-
  tracts 259-13
To be the musician's own and, thence, become [Sombre 67-23 P
THEOLOGIAN. It was a theologian's needle, much [Blue Bldg 217-8
THEOLOGY. Theology after breakfast sticks to the eye. [Les Plus
  245-8
THEOREM. A theorem proposed between the two-- [Rock 525-16
THEORETICAL. If these were theoretical people, like [Duck 65-6 P
THEORIST. He is the theorist of life, not death, [NH 485-8
THEORY. "Theory" [86-title
  At least that was the theory, when bishops' books [Connois 215-15
  "The Pure Good of Theory" [329-title
  Thus the theory of description matters most. [Descrip 345-5
  It is the theory of the word for those [Descrip 345-6
  Displays the theory of poetry, [NH 486-5
  Subtler, more urgent proof that the theory [NH 486-8
  Of poetry is the theory of life, [NH 486-9
THEREAFTER. To endure thereafter every mortal wound, [Extracts
  258-27
  An order and thereafter he belonged [Bad Time 426-10
  And thereafter he belongs to it, to bread [Bad Time 426-13
THEREBY. And thereby polar, polar-purple, chilled [C 34-4
  And thereby lost, and naked or in rags, [NH 484-17
THEREIN. Therein, day settles and thickens round a form-- [Role
  93-12 P
THEREOF. Our bloom is gone. We are the fruit thereof. [Monocle
  16-5
  Should prick thereof, not on the psaltery, [C 38-18
  Thereof and part desire and part the sense [Choc 299-21
  Reality, composed thereof. They are [Paisant 335-5
  And of its nature, the idiom thereof. [NSF 387-21
  Or symbol of malice. That we partake thereof, [AA 418-22
  Nor brilliant blows thereof, ti-rill-a-roo, [John 437-12
  On a hill of stones to make beau mont thereof. [NH 466-24
  A porcelain, as yet in the bats thereof, [NH 467-15
THEREON. Thereon the learning of the man conceived [NSF 402-23
THERETO. Compelled thereto by an innate music. [Hero 277-18
  Say next to holiness is the will thereto, [NH 467-4
  Determined thereto, perhaps by his father's ghost, [Role 93-4 P
THESES. If they could gather their theses into one, [Extracts
  254-6
  "Contrary Theses (I)" [266-title
  "Contrary Theses (II)" [270-title
THESIS. This is the thesis scrivened in delight, [EM 326-1
  The thesis of the plentifullest John. [Descrip 345-4
  The need for a thesis, a music constant to move. [Woman Had 82-9P
THICK. Of moonlight on the thick, cadaverous bloom [C 31-28
  So thick with sides and jagged lops of green, [C 32-2
  Like blooms secluded in the thick marine? [Sea Surf 101-12
  His hands became his feelings. His thick shape [Repet 306-12
  The red ripeness of round leaves is thick [Pecul 453-10
  The thick strings stutter the finial gutterals. [Madame 507-10
  Fly upward thick in numbers, fly across [Red Kit 31-22 P
  And shadowy hanging of it, thick with stars [Old Woman 46-2 P
  How thick this gobbet is with overlays, [Someone 85-19 A
THICKENS. Therein, day settles and thickens round a form-- [Role
  93-12 P
THICKEST. The thickest man on thickest stallion-back, [Havana
  143-18
  After we've drunk the Moselle, to the thickest shade [Phenom
  286-16
  There is lightning and the thickest thunder. [Chaos 357-10
THICKETS. Will rack the thickets. There is no place, [MBG 182-16
THICK-LEAVED. A hand that bears a thick-leaved fruit, [Venereal
  48-16
THICK-LIPPED. Thick-lipped from riot and rebellious cries, [Men
  Fall 188-8
THIN. In witching chords, and their thin blood [Peter 90-11
  O thin men of Haddam, [Thirteen 93-19
  She was a shadow as thin in memory [Nigger 154-1
  The trees are wooden, the grass is yellow and thin. [Nigger
  157-21
  Until his nose grew thin and taut [Thought 186-22 ,

Picking thin music on the rustiest string, [God 285-13
Noiselessly, noiselessly, resembling a thin bird, [Somnam 304-2
Issued thin seconds glibly gapering. [Repet 306-13
The forms that are attentive in thin air. [Descrip 344-14
The deer-grass is thin. The timothy is brown. [Myrrh 350-11
Of fiery eyes and long thin arms. [Attempt 370-11
Smeared, smoked, and drunken of thin potencies, [Page 422-28
Which in those ears and in those thin, those spended hearts,
  [Large 424-7
In the days when the mood of love will be swarming for solace
  and sink deeply into the thin stuff of being, [Piano 22-8 P
Along the thin horizons, nobly more [Burnshaw 47-10 P
THING. Shall I uncrumple this much-crumpled thing? [Monocle 13-16
A semblance to the thing I have in mind. [Monocle 17-3
Reflecting this thing and that, [Homunculus 26-15
Crispin confronting it, a vocable thing, [C 29-25
Noway resembling his, a visible thing, [C 29-27
The thing that makes him envious in phrase. [C 33-7
But day by day, now this thing and now that [C 40-21
Can one man think one thing and think it long? [C 41-27
Can one man be one thing and be it long? [C 41-28
Then third, a thing still flaxen in the light, [C 44-20
Or thing . . . Now day-break comes . . . [Canna 55-6
The only moving thing [Thirteen 92-15
Like a thing in which they fell, [Public Sq 109-4
And his daughter was a foreign thing. [Norfolk 111-11
One likes to practice the thing. They practice, [Adieu 128-7
Poetry is a finikin thing of air [Nigger 155-17
There is no such thing as innocence in autumn, [Nigger 157-12
And all their manner in the thing, [MBG 166-16
The maker of a thing yet to be made; [MBG 169-18
As I strum the thing, do I pick up [MBG 171-19
A dream no longer a dream, a thing, [MBG 174-17
And that-a-way he twirled the thing. [MBG 178-12
Not yet, however, a thing to die in. [Thought 184-16
There's no such thing as life; or if there is, [Parochial 192-4
It is a thing to have, [Destructive 192-12
You arrange, the thing is posed, [Add 198-16
"There is no such thing as the truth," [On Road 203-13
A thing. Thus, the pineapple was a leather fruit, [Poem Morn
  219-5
To the total thing, a shapeless giant forced [Poem Morn 219-15
That's this. Do they touch the thing they see, [Arcades 225-8
The vivid thing in the air that never changes, [Martial 238-12
Itself had to be supposed, a thing supposed [Landsc 242-8
In a place supposed, a thing that he reached [Landsc 242-9
And say, "The thing I hum appears to be [Landsc 243-7
One only, one thing that was firm, even [Beard 247-14
One thing remaining, infallible, would be [Beard 247-18
Enough. Ah! douce campagna of that thing! [Beard 247-19
Out of a thing believed, a thing affirmed: [Beard 247-22
Sleeps in the sun no thing recalling. [Hero 278-18
Each false thing ends. The bouquet of summer [Hero 280-19
Projection B. To get at the thing [Couch 295-16
Between the thing as idea and [Couch 295-19
The idea as thing. She is half who made her. [Couch 295-20
The mind's own limits, like a tragic thing [Choc 298-4
A human thing. It is an eminence, [Choc 300-17
Time. What a thing it is to believe that [Lack 303-14
It is never the thing but the version of the thing: [Pure 332-13
Its identity is merely a thing that seems, [Descrip 340-10
The thing described, nor false facsimile. [Descrip 344-16
It is an artificial thing that exists, [Descrip 344-17
And him. Both wanted the same thing. Both sought [Liadoff 347-18
But not quite molten, not quite the fluid thing, [Myrrh 350-4
"Man Carrying Thing" [350-title
Identity. The thing he carries resists [Man Car 350-16
In which the rain is all one thing, [Human 363-8
Let's see the very thing and nothing else. [Cred 373-3
Of the fertile thing that can attain no more. [Cred 373-15
And throws it away like a thing of another time, [NSF 382-11
Night-blue is an inconstant thing. The seraph [NSF 390-1
The child that touches takes character from the thing, [NSF
  392-20
To be an evasion, a thing not apprehended or [NSF 396-22
A thing final in itself and, therefore, good: [NSF 405-19
Nothing until this named thing nameless is [AA 416-23
If it is not a thing of time, nor of place, [AA 418-6
That it should be, and yet not be, a thing [AA 418-12
It is like a thing of ether that exists [AA 418-16
She was a self that knew, an inner thing, [Owl 435-14
It is nothing, no great thing, nor man [Imago 439-5
By trivial filaments to the thing intact: [Bouquet 450-11
They cast closely round the facture of the thing [Bouquet 452-6
And the poverty of dirt, the thing upon his breast, [Pecul 454-7
The eye's plain version is a thing apart, [NH 465-4
Reality as a thing seen by the mind, [NH 468-12
A thing on the side of a house, not deep in a cloud, [NH 474-21
The moon rose in the mind and each thing there [NH 478-22
The countrymen were changed and each constant thing. [NH 487-8

The sort of thing that August crooners sing, [Aug 489-9
Or the same thing without desire, [Aug 491-1
A little thing to think of on Sunday walks, [Aug 491-22
Of sense, evoking one thing in many men, [Aug 494-18
And the wind sways like a great thing tottering-- [Hermit 505-16
With every visible thing enlarged and yet [Rome 510-22
The way some first thing coming into Northern trees [Prol 517-6
A thing not planned for imagery or belief, [Look 518-6
And kept saying over and over one same, same thing, [Slug 522-6
Out of all the indifferences, into one thing: [Final 524-6
Within a single thing, a single shawl [Final 524-7
"Not Ideas about the Thing but the Thing Itself" [534-title
A thing of shadows, [Phases 5-19 P
A beautiful thing, milord, is beautiful [Red Kit 31-5 P
How strange a thing it was to understand [Lytton 39-1 P
That sort of thing was always rather stiff. [Lytton 39-18 P
Life, then, is largely a thing [Table 40-2 P
And yet the damned thing doesn't come right. [Agenda 41-18 P
And what a good thing it would be [Agenda 42-1 P
As a place in which each thing was motionless [Old Woman 45-21 P
Except the thing she felt but did not know. [Old Woman 45-22 P
The thing is dead . . . Everything is dead [Burnshaw 46-13 P
The statue seems a thing from Schwarz's, a thing [Burnshaw 47-4 P
To think of the future is a thing and he [Duck 64-2 P
When the statue is not a thing imagined, a stone [Sombre 71-14 P
It would be done. And once the thing was done, [Bship 78-14 P
With its final force, a thing invincible [Bship 79-11 P
This is a thing to twang a philosopher's sleep, [Bship 79-31 P
A shape, the vista twisted and burning, a thing [Bship 80-5 P
A windy thing . . . However, since we are here, [Recit 86-2 P
The accent of deviation in the living thing [Discov 96-7 P
Than they are in the final finding of the air, in the thing
    [Course 97-2 P
"If knowledge and the thing known are one [Ulysses 99-16 P
Is a blind thing fumbling for its form, [Ulysses 104-16 P
The one thing common to all life, the human [Conversat 109-1 P
It does not shine on a thing that remains [Three 130-20 P
And find a new thing [Three 142-9 P
Is one thing to me [Three 143-5 P
And one thing to another, [Three 143-6 P
And in this tangent it becomes a thing [Someone 83-20 A
That makes it say the little thing it says, [Someone 84-15 A
See: double-thing; para-thing.
THING-A-MA-JIGS. Not toys, not thing-a-ma-jigs-- [Dezem 218-18
THINGS. That fluttering things have so distinct a shade. [Monocle
    18-3
Of things, this nincompated pedagogue, [C 27-11
In his observant progress, lesser things [C 34-19
To things within his actual eye, alert [C 40-16
The words of things entangle and confuse. [C 41-1
Was he to company vastest things defunct [C 41-12
Attentive to a coronal of things [C 44-14
By apparition, plain and common things, [C 46-7
A few things for themselves, [Venereal 47-4
A few things for themselves, [Venereal 47-4
Fewest things to the lover-- [Venereal 48-15
"Of the Surface of Things" [57-title
This will make widows wince. But fictive things [High-Toned
    59-21
My hands such sharp, imagined things. [W Burgher 61-17
Seem things in some procession of the dead, [Sunday 67-6
Things to be cherished like the thought of heaven? [Sunday 67-18
Things false and wrong [Virgin 71-3
Who still feels irrational things within her. [Shifts 83-16
Imagination is the will of things . . . [Polish Aunt 84-7
By being so much of the things we are, [Fictive 87-4
Make more awry our faulty human things. [Surprises 98-11
Widen your sense. All things in the sun are sun. [NE Verses
    104-2
That bore us as a part of all the things [Anatomy 107-14
And re-illumines things that used to turn [Sun March 133-15
Prodigious things are tricks. The world is not [Havana 144-3
Yet that things go round and again go round [Circulat 150-7
He is singing and chanting the things that are part of him,
    [Nigger 150-11
Things unintelligible, yet understood. [Nigger 156-18
The look of things, left what we felt [Postcard 159-6
You do not play things as they are." [MBG 165-4
The man replied, "Things as they are [MBG 165-5
Of things exactly as they are." [MBG 165-10
Is to miss, by that, things as they are, [MBG 165-18
So that's life, then: things as they are? [MBG 166-13
And that's life, then: things as they are, [MBG 167-1
Of things as they are and only the place [MBG 167-19
Becomes the place of things as they are, [MBG 168-7
Detached from us, from things as they are? [MBG 168-19
The book and bread, things as they are, [MBG 172-20
Things as they are have been destroyed. [MBG 173-7
Of things as they are, as the blue guitar [MBG 174-18
Two things, the two together as one, [MBG 175-11

Things as they are. Or so we say. [MBG 176-20
Concerning the nature of things as they are. [MBG 177-20
Things as they were, things as they are, [MBG 178-20
Things as they will be by and by . . . [MBG 178-21
And things are as I think they are [MBG 180-17
So it is to sit and to balance things [MBG 181-5
The rhapsody of things as they are. [MBG 183-2
Of familiar things in a cheerful voice, [Thought 185-2
One grows to hate these things except on the dump. [Dump 202-11
Between that disgust and this, between the things [Dump 202-14
I know from all the things it touched [Country 207-17
They think that things are all right, [Jersey 210-20
A revolution of things colliding. [Nightgown 214-13
Two things are one. (Pages of illustrations.) [Connois 215-3
Proves that these opposite things partake of one, [Connois
    215-14
For a vista in the Louvre. They are things chalked [Connois
    216-11
A repetition of unconscious things, [Vari 232-9
That he was at the bottom of things [Yellow 236-5
That the things that he rejected might be part [Landsc 242-22
By thunder, parts, and all these things together, [Landsc 242-26
Parts, and more things, parts. He never supposed divine [Landsc
    242-27
Things might not look divine, nor that if nothing [Landsc 242-28
Was divine then all things were, the world itself, [Landsc 242-29
Things were the truth, the world itself was the truth. [Landsc
    242-31
Of central things, [Adequacy 243-16
Became the form and the fragrance of things [Vase 247-7
If the rejected things, the things denied, [Beard 247-12
Some things, nino, some things are like this, [Gala 248-1
And you and I are such things, O most miserable . . . [Gala 248-3
It is there, being imperfect, and with these things [Gala 248-7
Of things no better than paper things, of days [Extracts 253-2
And the helpless philosophers say still helpful things. [Ex-
    tracts 253-28
Between one's self and the weather and the things [Extracts 258-3
To believe in the weather and in the things and men [Extracts
    258-8
Amen to the feelings about familiar things, [Montra 260-17
The premiss from which all things were conclusions, [Contra II
    270-16
Too conscious of too many things at once, [Hand 271-2
Too conscious of too many things at once, [Hand 271-7
Ho was too conscious of too many things [Hand 271-15
For whom what is was other things. [Oak 272-3
Is a museum of things seen. Sight, [Hero 274-13
The idea of things for public gardens, [Hero 276-15
Of a still-life, symbols, brown things to think of [Hero 276-24
A sound producing the things that are spoken. [Phenom 287-6
Of things that would never be quite expressed, [Motive 288-10
To say more than human things with human voice, [Choc 300-11
That cannot be; to say human things with more [Choc 300-12
Of human things, that is acutest speech. [Choc 300-15
With the special things of night, little by little, [Choc 300-19
And these regalia, these things disclosed, [EM 317-12
Like things submerged with their englutted sounds, [EM 321-27
Of things as the structure of ideas. It was the structure [Bed
    327-7
Of things at least that was thought of in the old peak of night.
    [Bed 327-8
Saying things in the rooms and on the stair, [Less 327-10
Besides when the sky is so blue, things sing themselves, [Debris
    338-10
Stay here. Speak of familiar things a while. [Debris 338-14
It is and in such seeming all things are. [Descrip 339-4
Thus things are like a seeming of the sun [Descrip 339-5
Things look each day, each morning, or the style [Descrip 339-18
Things are as they seemed to Calvin or to Anne [Descrip 341-21
The knowledge of bright-ethered things [Analysis 349-7
Things floating like the first hundred flakes of snow [Man Car
    351-3
Out of a storm of secondary things), [Man Car 351-5
There are things in a man besides his reason. [Pieces 351-10
Things made by mid-terrestrial, mid-human [New Set 352-14
The uptopping top and tip of things, borne up [Two V 355-6
And fire and air and things not discomposed [Two V 355-9
And talked of never-ending things, [Silent 359-10
Of things and their motion: the other man, [Silent 360-2
And pierces the physical fix of things. [Red Fern 365-16
Of ordinary people, places, things, [Extraord 369-14
Things stop in that direction and since they stop [Cred 374-16
Things certain sustaining us in certainty. [Cred 375-20
The two things compared their tight resemblances: [Past Nun
    379-2
Said things it had laboriously spoken. [NSF 387-18
Two things of opposite natures seem to depend [NSF 392-4
The lake was full of artificial things, [NSF 397-12
Of heaven-haven. These are not things transformed. [NSF 399-1

We reason of these things with later reason [NSF 401-1
The Canon Aspirin, having said these things, [NSF 402-13
And normal things had yawned themselves away, [NSF 402-20
Between excluding things. It was not a choice [NSF 403-12
Between, but of. He chose to include the things [NSF 403-13
Mere repetitions. These things at least comprise [NSF 405-17
At evening, things that attend it until it hears [AA 414-18
Took on color, took on shape and the size of things as they are
  [Large 424-8
Too actual, things that in being real [Roses 430-14
Make any imaginings of them lesser things. [Roses 430-15
Our sense of these things changes and they change, [Roses 431-4
The essential poem at the centre of things, [Orb 440-1
And yet still men though meta-men, still things [Bouquet 449-1
To the things of medium nature, as meta-men [Bouquet 449-11
In glue, but things transfixed, transpierced and well [Bouquet
  449-13
The doubling second things, not mystical, [Bouquet 451-18
These things were made of him [Our Stars 455-1
When the leaves fall like things mournful of the past, [Puel
  456-12
The fatality of seeing things too well. [Novel 459-6
Of things were waiting in a betrothal known [Study II 464-17
Dark things without a double, after all, [NH 465-13
The plainness of plain things is savagery, [NH 467-16
With lesser things, with things exteriorized [NH 470-3
Men turning into things, as comedy, [NH 470-5
The truth about themselves, having lost, as things, [NH 470-7
The statues will have gone back to be things about. [NH 473-24
In the present state of things as, say, to paint [NH 478-6
Things not yet true which he perceives through truth [NH 478-16
Of things? A figure like Ecclesiast, [NH 479-13
The things around--the alternate romanza [NH 480-21
Interior: breathless things broodingly abreath [NH 481-9
The consolations of space are nameless things. [NH 482-16
In things seen and unseen, created from nothingness, [NH 486-11
"Things of August" [489-title
He could understand the things at home. [Aug 493-13
The knowledge of things lay round but unperceived: [Aug 493-18
"The Plain Sense of Things" [502-title
To a plain sense of things. It is as if [Plain 502-10
Things dark on the horizons of perception, [Rome 508-12
The loftiest syllables among loftiest things, [Rome 510-7
And things beyond resemblance there was this and that intended
  to be recognized, [Prol 516-13
To Concord, at the edge of things, was this: [Look 517-13
Not to transform them into other things, [Look 517-15
A glass aswarm with things going as far as they can. [Look
  519-12
That its barrenness becomes a thousand things [Rock 527-18
Its tranquil self, the main of things, the mind, [Rock 528-15
To the enclosure, day, the things illumined [Rock 528-18
Not merely desired, for sale, and market things [Armor 530-4
Shines on the mere objectiveness of things. [Moonlight 531-4
In spite of the mere objectiveness of things, [Moonlight 531-21
Here are more things [Bowl 6-12 P
Beautiful alliterations of shadows and of things shadowed.
  [Primordia 8-7 P
I take all things as stated--so and so [Soldat 11-7 P
Gesturing grandiose things in the air, [Soldat 16-5 P
Do I commend myself to leafy things [Stan MMO 19-17 P
Because new colors make new things [Abnormal 24-11 P
And new things make old things again . . . [Abnormal 24-12 P
Things would be different. [Mandolin 28-22 P
Not only in itself but in the things [Red Kit 31-6 P
To dab things even nicely pink [Melancholy 32-9 P
Are two quite different things, in particular [Lytton 39-8 P
Of the ways things happen to fall. [Table 40-15 P
Of very haphazard people and things, [Agenda 42-8 P
All things destroy themselves or are destroyed. [Burnshaw 46-16P
Give up dead things and the living turn away. [Burnshaw 49-6 P
Yet were not bright, came shining as things come [Burnshaw 51-25P
Things jutted up, the way the jagged stacks, [Greenest 53-11 P
Tractatus, of military things, with plates, [Greenest 56-14 P
So clawed, so sopped with sun, that in these things [Greenest
  57-20 P
Of things, why bother about the back of stars? [Greenest 58-27 P
By the torture of things that will be realized, [Duck 61-28 P
Again the Bulgar said, "There are more things [Duck 62-1 P
As the man hates now, loves now, the self-same things. [Sombre
  70-1 P
And then things are not as they are. [Stan MBG 72-16 P
I still intend things as they are. [Stan MBG 73-4 P
True, things are people as they are. [Stan MBG 73-18 P
This matters most in things that matter least. [Grotesque 76-11 P
Things still more distant. And tradition is near. [Recit 86-20 P
The rioter that appears when things are changed, [Pagoda 91-20 P
In a health of weather, knowing a few, old things, [Americana
  93-17 P
These things he thinks of, as the buckskin hoop-la, [Americana

94-13 P
Like things produced by a climate, the world [Ulysses 102-29 P
And inhuman same, the likeness of things unlike. [Conversat
  109-2 P
And you, you say that the capital things of the mind [Conversat
  109-3 P
As things emerged and moved and were dissolved, [Real 110-14 P
Little existed for him but the few things [Local 112-4 P
The few things, the objects of insight, the integrations [Local
  112-7 P
Of feeling, the things that came of their own accord, [Local
  112-8 P
In things said well in music, [July 114-17 P
Saying and saying, the way things say [Region 115-10 P
We affect all things. [Three 134-2 P
Such things happen in the evening. [Three 136-10 P
But always of many things. He had not to be told [Someone 85-12 A
With the molten mixings of related things, [Someone 87-4 A
See: para-things; quarter-things.
THINK. Of the January sun; and not to think [Snow Man 10-4
They should think hard in the dark cuffs [Homunculus 26-18
Can one man think one think and think it long? [C 41-27
Think, in square rooms, [Six Sig 75-5
And made one think of rosy chocolate [Sea Surf 99-1
And made one think of chop-house chocolate [Sea Surf 99-19
And made one think of porcelain chocolate [Sea Surf 100-13
And made one think of musky chocolate [Sea Surf 101-7
When I think of our lands I think of the house [Grapes 110-12
Who can think of the sun costuming clouds [Fading 139-1
To think of man the abstraction, the comic sum. [Nigger 156-6
I play. But this is what I think. [MBG 178-8
And think in it as a native thinks, [MBG 180-6
And like a native think in it. [MBG 180-10
And things are as I think they are [MBG 180-17
The difficulty to think at the end of day, [Rabbit K 209-1
Then there is nothing to think of. It comes of itself; [Rabbit K
  209-13
They think that things are all right, [Jersey 210-20
Where do you think, serpent, [Bagatelles 213-1
Where is it that you think, baffled [Bagatelles 213-10
It must be where you think it is, in the light [Blue Bldg 217-15
To think of a dove with an eye of grenadine [Sleight 222-13
The women of the time. It has to think about war [Of Mod 240-3
It was easier to think it lay there. If [Landsc 242-5
That we are joyously ourselves and we think [Gala 248-9
The man who has had the time to think enough, [Oboe 250-19
To think it is to think the way to death . . . [Extracts 256-20
That other one wanted to think his way to life, [Extracts 256-21
He, that one, wanted to think his way to life, [Extracts 257-4
They had to think it to be. He wanted that, [Extracts 257-6
And for it, and by which we think the way, [Extracts 257-12
And you think that that is what you expect, [Phosphor 267-14
In a clock-shop . . . Soldier, think, in the darkness, [Hero
  275-15
Of a still-life, symbols, brown things to think of [Hero 276-24
How did we come to think that autumn [Hero 280-26
To think of him destroyed the body's form. [Choc 297-8
To think of the logicians in their graves [EM 325-4
One might have thought of sight, but who could think [EM 326-3
She will think about them not quite able to sing. [Debris 338-9
He knows he has nothing more to think about. [Chaos 358-5
Of what we feel from what we think, of thought [NSF 382-20
The first idea is an imagined thing. [NSF 387-1
Even so when I think of you as strong or tired, [NSF 406-15
It fills the being before the mind can think. [John 436-17
"What We See Is What We Think" [459-title
Since what we think is never what we see. [What We 460-6
A little thing to think of on Sunday walks, [Aug 491-22
As in a hermitage, for us to think, [Aug 495-15
To think away the grass, the trees, the clouds, [Look 517-14
And what we think, a breathing like the wind, [Look 518-13
We think, then, as the sun shines or does not. [Look 518-23
We think as wind skitters on a pond in a field [Look 518-24
Of a house, that makes one think the house is laughing, [Slug
  522-10
In which we rest and, for small reason, think [Final 524-2
To think of this. [Bowl 7-9 P
So I think. [Melancholy 32-11 P
You think that like the moon she is obscured [Spaniard 34-2 P
It was a mistake to think of them. They have [Greenest 58-7 P
To April here and May to come. Why think, [Greenest 58-29 P
They chanced to think. Suppose the future fails. [Duck 63-2 P
Yet to think of the future is a genius, [Duck 64-1 P
To think of the future is a thing and he [Duck 64-2 P
And the bees, the scorpions, the men that think, [Duck 66-3 P
How could you ever, how could think that you saw her, [Grotesque
  74-9 P
But one lives to think of this growing, this pushing life, [Bship
  80-8 P
Who, when they think and speak of the central man, [Woman Had

82-11 P
One knows at last what to think about [Sol Oaks 111-8 P
About summer, are not what skeletons think about. [As Leave
    117-4 P
Not true, nor think it, less. He must defy [Someone 84-5 A
THINKER. But not the thinker, large in their largeness, beyond
    [Choc 299-16
A thinker of the first idea. Perhaps [NSF 386-2
About the thinker of the first idea, [NSF 387-11
Because the thinker himself escapes. And yet [NH 480-4
The thinker as reader reads what has been written. [Aug 492-4
The thinker knows. The gunman of the commune [Bship 80-16 P
Waving purpling wands, the thinker [Ulysses 100-19 P
THINKERS. Thinkers without final thoughts [July 115-2 P
THINKING. I wish that I might be a thinking stone. [Monocle 13-7
Of what was it I was thinking? [Magnifico 19-20
Thinking of your blue-shadowed silk, [Peter 90-4
Its bluest sea-clouds in the thinking green, [Sea Surf 101-19
If thinking could be blown away [Nigger 153-5
The thinking of art seems final when [MBG 168-4
The thinking of god is smoky dew. [MBG 168-5
Thinking the thoughts I call my own, [MBG 180-8
Brown as the bread, thinking of birds [Loaf 200-1
A manner of thinking, a mode [Bottle 239-7
Of systematic thinking . . . Ercole, [Extracts 256-17
Of what do you lie thinking in your cavern? [Extracts 256-19
Half sun, half thinking of the sun; half sky, [Extracts 257-2
To be happy because people were thinking to be. [Extracts 257-5
Half thinking; until the mind has been satisfied, [Extracts
    257-17
Of daylight came while he sat thinking. He said, [Choc 298-12
And from what thinking did his radiance come? [Choc 299-7
But resting on me, thinking in my snow, [Choc 301-5
That merely by thinking one can, [Crude 305-2
One thinking of apocalyptic legions. [Descrip 343-14
"Thinking of a Relation between the Images of Metaphors" [356-
    title
Who sits thinking in the corners of a room. [NH 480-2
And frame from thinking and is realized. [Rome 511-3
Too much like thinking to be less than thought, [Look 518-19
Here I keep thinking of the Primitives-- [Soldat 13-8 P
Thinking of heaven and earth and of herself [Old Woman 45-19 P
But of what are they thinking, of what, in spite of the duck,
    [Duck 62-12 P
Is each man thinking his separate thoughts or, for once, [Duck
    62-18 P
Are all men thinking together as one, thinking [Duck 62-19 P
Each other's thoughts, thinking a single thought, [Duck 62-20 P
So that thinking was a madness, and is: [Desire 85-9 P
Thinking gold thoughts in a golden mind, [Ulysses 100-20 P
"He will be thinking in strange countries [Three 134-6 P
"He will be thinking in strange countries [Three 134-12 P
"He will be thinking in strange countries [Three 134-16 P
THINKS. Who still thinks eagerly [Shifts 83-12
Cloud's red, earth feeling, sky that thinks? [MBG 177-4
And think in it as a native thinks, [MBG 180-6
But this he cannot know, the man that thinks, [Men Fall 188-2
That thinks of settling, yet never settles, on a nest. [Somnam
    304-3
The will demands that what he thinks be true? [EM 323-11
He imposes orders as he thinks of them, [NSF 403-16
Both size and solitude or thinks it does, [Orb 443-1
Tom McGreevy, in America, Thinks of Himself as a Boy [Our Stars
    454-title 1
But here tranquillity is what one thinks. [Novel 458-2
Or thinks he does, as he perceives the present, [NH 478-17
Or thinks he does, a carpenter's iridescences, [NH 478-18
Again, "He has thought it out, he thinks it out, [NH 485-16
The world? The inhuman as human? That which thinks not, [Aug
    493-3
And wronging her, if only as she thinks, [Red Kit 30-15 P
Or Paris-rain. He thinks of the noble lives [Greenest 59-25 P
That thinks of it is inscribed on walls and stands [Duck 64-3 P
We have grown weary of the man that thinks. [Sombre 66-18 P
He thinks and it is not true. The man below [Sombre 66-19 P
These things he thinks of, as the buckskin hoop-la [Americana
    94-13 P
One thinks that it could be that the first word spoken, [Discov
    95-17 P
One thinks, when the houses of New England catch the first sun,
    [Discov 95-21 P
And thinks about it without consciousness, [Sol Oaks 111-9 P
THINLY. Thinly, among the elephantine palms, [Greenest 54-26 P
THINNEST. The blower squeezed to the thinnest _mi_ of falsetto.
    [Parochial 191-6
Of any woman, watched the thinnest light [Extracts 258-16
THINS. And yellow, yellow thins the Northern blue. [NSF 385-13
THIN-STRINGED. Its thin-stringed music, [Our Stars 454-16
THIRD. Then third, a thing still flaxen in the light, [C 44-20
The third one gaping at the orioles [C 44-30

This creates a third world without knowledge, [EM 323-19
In the third world, then, there is no pain. Yes, but [EM 323-23
Two brothers. And a third form, she that says [Owl 431-16
The third form speaks, because the ear repeats, [Owl 432-3
It is the third commonness with light and air, [R Conn 533-16
In a Third: The whole cannot exist without [Bship 80-14 P
Of that third planet to the table and then: [Someone 86-3 A
THIRDS. Dry seconds and insipid thirds, [Arcades 225-25
THIRTEEN. "Thirteen Ways of Looking at a Blackbird" [92-title
THIRTY. Of thirty years ago. It is looking out [NH 478-8
Since thirty mornings are required to make [Ideal 88-1 A
Since thirty summers are needed for a year [Ideal 88-8 A
And thirty years, in the galaxies of birth, [Ideal 88-9 A
THIS-A-WAY. And this-a-way he gave a fling. [MBG 178-10
And the world had worlds, ai, this-a-way: [MBG 178-17
THORN. Although the rose was not the noble thorn [C 42-28
And against the most coiled thorn, have seized on what was ugly
    [Large 424-3
THORNED. A fruit for pewter, thorned and palmed and blue, [Poem
    Morn 219-6
THORNS. From an ottoman of thorns. [Lulu M 27-16 P
With tongues unclipped and throats so stuffed with thorns,
    [Greenest 57-19 P
And honey from thorns and I play my guitar. [Stan MBG 72-9 P
THORN-TREES. And bristling thorn-trees spinning on the bank [Nig-
    ger 155-15
THOU. Be thou the voice, [Mozart 132-9
Not you. Be thou, be thou [Mozart 132-10
Be thou that wintry sound [Mozart 132-13
Be seated, thou. [Mozart 132-22
"Thou art not August unless I make thee so." [Oboe 251-5
THOUGHT. Of her thought. [Infanta 7-15
The sea of spuming thought foists up again [Monocle 13-8
As the deadly thought of men accomplishing [Monocle 16-14
And they were all His thought. [Pourtraicte 22-1
Knowing that they can bring back thought [Homunculus 26-13
Aware of exquisite thought. The storm was one [C 32-31
The torment of fastidious thought grew slack, [C 37-21
With masquerade of thought, with hapless words [C 39-15
To the difficulty of rebellious thought [C 40-17
He once thought necessary. Like Candide, [C 42-16
If not in will, to track the knaves of thought. [C 42-24
X, the mighty thought, the mighty man. [Canna 55-2
His thought sleeps not. Yet thought that wakes [Canna 55-4
In sleep may never meet another thought [Canna 55-5
And, most, of the motion of thought [Solitaires 60-10
Things to be cherished like the thought of heaven? [Sunday 67-18
Good clown . . . One thought of Chinese chocolate [Sea Surf 102-1
Have I stopped and thought of its point before? [Grapes 110-11
Or look, nor ever again in thought, except [Farewell 118-9
To give this further thought. [Winter B 141-19
Of thought evoked a peace eccentric to [Havana 143-5
To nail his thought across the door, [MBG 166-7
The color like a thought that grows [MBG 169-19
Is my thought a memory, not alive? [MBG 173-10
The imagined and the real, thought [MBG 177-16
"A Thought Revolved" [184-title
Was heaven where you thought? It must be there. [Blue Bldg 217-14
The thought of her takes her away. [Scavoir 231-14
He is. The thought that he had found all this [Yellow 237-5
It was not as if the truth lay where he thought, [Landsc 242-3
Than a thought to be rehearsed all day, a speech [Beard 247-16
Without the labor of thought, in that element, [Gala 248-10
Into a single thought, thus: into a queen, [Extracts 254-8
The single thought? The multitudes of men [Extracts 254-15
How much of it was light and how much thought, [Extracts 257-8
Time troubles to produce the redeeming thought. [Extracts 257-19
Amen to thought, our singular skeleton, [Montra 260-19
Poet, as if he thought gladly, being [Hero 277-17
Monsters antique and haggard with past thought? [Dutch 292-11
But not the person, of their power, thought, [Choc 299-15
Thought is false happiness: the idea [Crude 305-1
That there lies at the end of thought [Crude 305-5
One might have thought of sight, but who could think [EM 326-3
Of what one feels, who could have thought to make [EM 326-8
Sequences, thought of among spheres in the old peak of night:
    [Bed 326-19
Of things at least that was thought of in the old peak of night.
    [Bed 327-8
Ill of a constant question in his thought, [Pure 331-8
From thought, like a violent pulse in the cloud itself, [Liadoff
    347-7
With thought, through which it cannot see? Does it [Two V 354-3
The summer night is like a perfection of thought. [House Q
    358-15
There is nothing more inscribed nor thought nor felt [Cred
    372-14
Of what we feel from what we think, of thought [NSF 382-20
An abstraction blooded, as a man by thought. [NSF 385-24
He thought often of the land from which he came, [NSF 393-16

Beyond which thought could not progress as thought. [NSF 403-10
And sky, between thought and day and night. It is [NSF 407-5
We knew each other and of each other thought, [AA 417-19
And of each other thought--in the idiom [AA 419-4
Of the week, queerer than Sunday. We thought alike [AA 419-10
And capable of incapably evil thought: [Page 423-1
Is changed. It is not so blue as we thought. To be blue, [Ulti
    429-18
The dead. Only the thought of those dark three [Owl 432-17
Is dark, thought of the forms of dark desire. [Owl 432-18
A man walked living among the forms of thought [Owl 432-20
Less time than place, less place than thought of place [Owl
    433-1
The conception sparkling in still obstinate thought. [Papini
    448-4
Another thought, the paramount ado . . . [What We 460-5
Around and away, resembling the presence of thought, [NH 474-5
Before the thought of evening had occurred [NH 482-23
Who watched him, always, for unfaithful thought. [NH 483-15
Again, "He has thought it out, he thinks it out, [NH 485-16
It is a visibility of thought, [NH 488-5
According to his thought, in the Mediterranean [Aug 491-6
Feels not, resembling thought, resembling feeling? [Aug 493-4
Go back to a parent before thought, before speech, [Irish 501-11
Mechanisms of angelic thought, [Inhab 503-10
For unintelligible thought. [Hermit 505-21
Seal him there. He looked in a glass of the earth and thought he
    lived in it. [Madame 507-2
And as he thought within the thought [Two Illus 513-10
Of the wind, not knowing that that thought [Two Illus 513-11
Was not his thought, nor anyone's, [Two Illus 513-12
Too much like thinking to be less than thought, [Look 518-19
Or so Mr. Homburg thought: the body of a world [Look 519-8
On her pillow? The thought kept beating in her like her heart.
    [World 521-11
His place, as he sat and as he thought, was not [Quiet 523-1
In his chair, the most tranquil thought grew peaked [Quiet
    523-9
It is in that thought that we collect ourselves, [Final 524-5
And knowing the monotony of thought, [Stan MMO 19-5 P
And black by thought that could not understand [Old Woman 44-4 P
Stood stiffly, as if the black of what she thought [Old Woman
    44-24 P
As sequels without thought. In the rudest red [Burnshaw 47-8 P
There lies the head of the sculptor in which the thought [Burn-
    shaw 49-16 P
Than the thought that once was native to the skull; [Burnshaw
    49-18 P
Before the strange, having wept and having thought [Burnshaw
    50-7 P
Beyond thought's regulation. There each man, [Greenest 54-2 P
Each other's thoughts, thinking a single thought, [Duck 62-20 P
By tautest pinions lifted through his thought. [Duck 64-19 P
Imagines and it is true, as if he thought [Sombre 66-20 P
Much too much thought, too little thought, [Grotesque 75-14 P
No thought at all: a gutteral growl, [Grotesque 75-15 P
By feeling the life of thought in sleep, [Desire 85-12 P
"A Discovery of Thought" [95-title P
Makes this small howling, like a thought [Dove 98-4 P
In the generations of thought, man's sons [Ulysses 103-7 P
Always, the particular thought [Ulysses 103-14 P
Repose, always, the credible thought [Ulysses 103-18 P
On all the rest, in heavy thought. [Child 106-15 P
Free from everything else, free above all from thought. [Letters
    107-9 P
In the central of earth or sky or air or thought, [Conversat
    108-19 P
Beyond the last thought, rises [Of Mere 117-16 P
A world agrees, thought's compromise, resolved [Ideal 89-7 A
See half-thought-of.
THOUGHTFULLY. She will speak thoughtfully the words of a line.
    [Debris 338-8
THOUGHTLESSLY. Until they become thoughtlessly willing [Homunculus
    26-11
    Left thoughtlessly behind, [Prejudice 368-18
THOUGHT-LIKE. Ruffling its common reflections, thought-like
    Monadnocks. [Cata 424-14
THOUGHTS. I quiz all sounds, all thoughts, all everything [Monocle
    16-19
    The thoughts of drunkards, the feelings [Homunculus 26-6
    He shut out from his tempering ear; what thoughts, [C 34-22
    "Jasmine's Beautiful Thoughts underneath the Willow" [79-title
    Like the thoughts of an old human, [Shifts 83-11
    But spoke for you perfectly in my thoughts, [Two Figures 86-5
    Corridors of cloudy thoughts, [Botanist 1 134-16
    The swarm of thoughts, the swarm of dreams [MBG 179-9
    Thinking the thoughts I call my own, [MBG 180-8
    For all the thoughts of summer that go with it [Dwarf 208-5
    Gripped it and grappled my thoughts. [Weak Mind 212-10
    (This is one of the thoughts [Bagatelles 213-21

Collect their thoughts together into one, [Extracts 254-7
If they could! Or is it the multitude of thoughts, [Extracts
    254-13
His thoughts begotten at clear sources, [Hero 277-14
The very pool, his thoughts the colored forms, [Descrip 342-12
A horror of thoughts that suddenly are real. [Man Car 351-6
We must endure our thoughts all night, until [Man Car 351-7
The hum of thoughts evaded in the mind, [NSF 388-4
Hidden from other thoughts, he that reposes [NSF 388-5
Is satyr in Saturn, according to his thoughts. [NSF 390-2
Resembling the presences of thoughts, as if, [NH 474-6
The self and the earth--your thoughts, your feelings, [Old Man
    501-3
And you, good galliard, to enchant black thoughts [Red Kit 32-3P
Which were their thoughts, squeezed into shapes, the sun [Duck
    61-11 P
Is each man thinking his separate thoughts or, for once, [Duck
    62-18 P
Each other's thoughts, thinking a single thought, [Duck 62-20 P
Thoughts by descent. To flourish the great cloak we wear [Sombre
    71-19 P
The parts. Thus: Out of the number of his thoughts [Bship 80-15 P
The words are in the way and thoughts are. [Stan Hero 84-1 P
I had not invented my own thoughts, [Desire 85-7 P
It is true that there are thoughts [Including 88-9 P
That are almost not our own, but thoughts [Including 88-11 P
Hard to be told from thoughts, the repeated drone [Americana 94-3P
Thinking gold thoughts in a golden mind, [Ulysses 100-20 P
No thoughts of people now dead, [Clear Day 113-8 P
Thinkers without final thoughts [July 115-2 P
THOUSAND. "Anecdote of Men by the Thousand" [51-title
    Necks among the thousand leaves, [Orangeade 103-5
    A thousand are radiant in the sky. [MBG 172-10
    And cobble ten thousand and three [Jersey 210-10
    Ten thousand, men hewn and tumbling, [Thunder 220-2
    Mobs of ten thousand, clashing together, [Thunder 220-3
    One sparrow is worth a thousand gulls, [Vari 233-12
    And through the eye equates ten thousand deaths [Extracts 253-13
    That is ten thousand deaths and evil death. [Extracts 253-23
    The breath life's latest, thousand senses. [Montra 264-2
    A thousand crystals' chiming voices, [Hero 279-19
    Naked of hindrance, a thousand crystals. [Hero 279-28
    Came paddling their canoes, a thousand thousand, [New Set 352-17
    Is like ten thousand tumblers tumbling down [Cred 376-25
    A thousand begettings of the broken bold. [Owl 434-21
    That its barrenness becomes a thousand things [Rock 527-18
    Fat with a thousand butters, and the crows [Burnshaw 49-9 P
    Of the gods and, for him, a thousand litanies [Greenest 59-26 P
    The word respected, fired ten thousand guns [Bship 78-12 P
THOUSAND-LEAVED. Now the thousand-leaved green falls to the ground.
    [Fare Guit 98-17 P
    The thousand-leaved red [Fare Guit 98-19 P
THOUSANDS. That splatters incessant thousands of drops, [Hartford
    226-9
    Of the thousands of freedoms except our own? [Dutch 292-14
    In the South, bands of thousands of black men, [Sick 90-8 P
THRALE. See Mrs. Thrale.
THREAD. And flame and summer and sweet fire, no thread [Fictive
    87-10
    In the manner of its stitchings, of its thread, [Owl 434-14
    Every thread of summer is at last unwoven. [Puel 456-1
    Of violet gray, a green violet, a thread [What We 459-17
    Gold easings and ouncings and fluctuations of thread [NH 477-19
THREADING. Threading the wind. [Depression 63-12
THREADLESS. It is empty. But a woman in threadless gold [Wom Sun
    445-8
THREADS. The threads [Plot Giant 7-2
    A stellar pallor that hangs on the threads. [Leben 505-3
THREE. But when I walk I see that it consists of three or four
    hills and a cloud. [Of Surface 57-7
    Lacking the three glass knobs, that sheet [Emperor 64-10
    I was of three minds, [Thirteen 92-17
    In which there are three blackbirds. [Thirteen 92-19
    And cobble then thousand and three [Jersey 210-10
    Are one. My window is twenty-nine three [Jersey 210-14
    Two people, three horses, an ox [Les Plus 245-1
    The mass of meaning. It is three or four [Extracts 255-27
    The child's three ribbons are in her plaited hair. [Extraord
    369-21
    Three times the concentred self takes hold, three times [Cred
    376-9
    Where his house had fallen, three scraggy trees weighted [NSF
    393-4
    The dead. Only the thought of those dark three [Owl 432-17
    "Conversation with Three Women of New England" [108-title P
    In which one of these three worlds are the four of us [Conversat
    109-16 P
    "Three Travelers Watch a Sunrise" [127-title P
    If it be supposed that we are three figures [Three 132-17 P
    That we are painted as three dead men, [Three 133-2 P

Three beggars, you see, [Three 139-11 P
It is as if there were three planets: the sun, [Someone 83-11 A
See and-a-three.
THREE-DAYS. He does not become a three-days personage, [Soldier
   97-4
THREE-FOUR. Is soft in three-four cornered fragrances [NH 470-19
THREE-LEGGED. How happy I was the day I told the young Blandina of
   three-legged giraffes . . . [Analysis 348-1
THREE-QUARTERS. At three-quarters gone, the morning's prescience,
   [Pagoda 92-4 P
THRESHOLD. On the threshold of heaven, the figures in the street
   [Rome 508-1
   The threshold, Rome, and that more merciful Rome [Rome 508-6
   For himself. He stops upon this threshold, [Rome 511-1
THREW. Threw its contorted strength around the sky. [Sleight 222-8
THRICE. The thrice concentred self, having possessed [Cred 376-10
THRICE-TRIPLE-SYLLABLED. These vigors make, thrice-triple-syl-
   labled, [Two V 354-8
THRIDDING. Thridding the squawkiest jungle [Cab 21-10 P
THRIFT. As if sight had not its own miraculous thrift, [EM 320-26
THROAT. Comes close to the prisoner's ear, becomes a throat
   [Montra 261-2
   The hero's throat in which the words are spoken, [Montra 261-4
   This brother half-spoken in the mother's throat [EM 317-11
   And so, as part, to exult with its great throat, [NSF 398-9
   The vines around the throat, the shapeless lips, [NSF 400-10
   Of a vacant sea declaiming with wide throat, [Puel 456-9
THROATED. See jug-throated.
THROATS. The grackles crack their throats of bone in the smooth
   air. [Banal 62-13
   They did not so. But in their throats [Sat Night 28-9 P
   With tongues unclipped and throats so stuffed with thorns,
   [Greenest 57-19 P
THROB. The basses of their beings throb [Peter 90-10
THRONE. A point of survey squatting like a throne, [Cred 373-19
   Look at this present throne. What company, [AA 415-2
   No god rules over Africa, no throne, [Greenest 55-5 P
   In one, except a throne raised up beyond [Greenest 55-10 P
   Death, only, sits upon the serpent throne: [Greenest 55-17 P
   The black and ruin his sepulchral throne. [Greenest 55-29 P
   In Africa. The serpent's throne is dust [Greenest 58-9 P
   On the waste throne of his own wilderness. [Region 115-15 P
THROSTLE. We must have the throstle on the gramophone. [Duck 66-8P
THROW. If they throw stones upon the roof [Mozart 131-18
   Throw papers in the streets, the wills [MBG 170-7
   Throw away the lights, the definitions, [MBG 183 3
   Throw the lights away. Nothing must stand [MBG 183-10
   They throw around their shoulders cloaks that flash [AA 419-23
   They would throw their batons far up [Drum-Majors 36-20 P
THROWER. Shelter yet thrower of the summer spear, [Thought 186-10
THROWING. Flesh on the bones. The skeleton throwing [Hero 278-15
THROWN. Beyond all trees, the ridges thrown [How Live 125-19
   At the time of the dogwoods, handfuls thrown up [Forces 229-5
   And downward, from this purple region, thrown; [Infernale 25-7 P
   The hermit's candle would have thrown [Three 138-3 P
THROWS. In the pale light that each upon the other throws. [Re-
   state 146-12
   And throws it away like a thing of another time, [NSF 382-11
   As morning throws off stale moonlight and shabby sleep. [NSF
   382-12
   And throws his stars around the floor. By day [NSF 383-5
   Vermont throws itself together. [July 115-5 P
THRUM. Deduction. Thrum with a proud douceur [C 43-14
   And the heavy thrum [Cortege 80-23
THRUSH. Or thrush, or any singing mysteries? [Sonatina 110-2
THRUST. Polyphony beyond his baton's thrust. [C 28-21
   Contorted, staggering from the thrust against [Old Woman 43-14 P
   Would flash in air, and the muscular bodies thrust [Old Woman
   46-9 P
   In marble, but marble massive as the thrust [Sombre 70-24 P
THUDDING. In thudding air: [Polo 37-21 P
   In a clamor thudding up from central earth, [Sombre 70-30 P
THUMB. From that meticulous potter's thumb. [Negation 98-5
   A fat thumb beats out ai-yi-yi. [MBG 178-22
   And wildly free, whose clawing thumb [Jumbo 269-5
   Père Guzz, in heaven thumb your lyre [An Gaiety 33-5 P
THUMBED. See well-thumbed.
THUMBS. I said, "She thumbs the memories of dress." [Stan MMO 19-6P
   What they did with their thumbs. [Lulu G 26-16 P
THUMP. May rush to extinguish the theme, the basses thump [Bship
   79-27 P
THUNDER. In which the thunder, lapsing in its clap, [C 33-15
   Heavy with thunder's rattapallax, [Frogs 78-6
   The drenching thunder rolling by, [MBG 169-2
   And tufted in straggling thunder and shattered sun. [Dwarf 208-8
   And more. Yet the eminent thunder from the mouse, [Blue Bldg
   217-3
   "Thunder by the Musician" [220-title
   Sure enough, moving, the thunder became men, [Thunder 220-1
   He brushed away the thunder, then the clouds, [Landsc 241-11

By thunder, parts, and all these things together, [Landsc
   242-26
It was as if thunder took form upon [Vase 246-9
Make more than thunder's rural rumbling. They make [Repet 307-2
Profundum, physical thunder, dimension in which [Flyer 336-14
There is lightning and the thickest thunder. [Chaos 357-10
At summer thunder and sleeps through winter snow. [NSF 384-16
Of secluded thunder, an illusion, as it was, [Orb 441-1
In the strokes of thunder, dead candles at the window [NH 488-11
Comes to this thunder of light [Fare Guit 98-20 P
THUNDER-CLOUD. It had nothing of the Julian thunder-cloud: [EM
   319-26
THUNDERING. Came bluntly thundering, more terrible [C 32-24
   Summer assaulted, thundering, illumed, [Thought 186-9
THUNDERSTORMS. Concerning the Thunderstorms of Yucatan [C 30-title 2
TIARA. Wearing a clear tiara [Venereal 48-7
   A tiara from Cohen's, this summer sea. [Stan MBG 72-14 P
TICK. Do you suppose that she cares a tick, [Lilacs 49-1
   To tick it, tock it, turn it true, [MBG 166-10
   As at the moment of the year when, tick, [John 437-4
TICKING. A zone of time without the ticking of clocks, [Aug 494-7
   A leaden ticking circular in width. [Duck 66-5 P
TICKS. Ticks tediously the time of one more year. [Monocle 15-2
   Everything ticks like a clock. The cabinet [Nigger 157-17
TIDAL. Fresh from discoveries of tidal skies, [C 30-27
   For a tidal undulation underneath. [Page 423-10
TIDE. What was the sea whose tide swept through me there? [Hoon
   65-12
   Low tide, flat water, sultry sun. [Vari 235-13
   Of earth, rises against it, tide by tide, [Two V 354-20
   Piercing the tide by which it moves, is constantly within us?
   [Inelegance 26-2 P
TIE. A member of the family, a tie, [Pieces 352-8
TIES. Ties us to those we love. For this familiar, [EM 317-9
   The mother ties the hair-ribbons of the child [Extraord 369-7
TIESTAS. Tiestas from the keys, [Venereal 47-7
TIGER. A tiger lamed by nothingness and frost. [Nigger 153-10
   From Esthonia: the tiger chest, for tea. [Dump 201-19
TIGERS. Catches tigers [Ten O'C 66-14
   The elephants of sound, the tigers [Hero 278-9
   As large ferocious tigers are. [Parasol 20-10 P
TIGHT. The spittling tissues tight across the bones. [Nigger 155-8
   The two things compared their tight resemblances: [Past Nun 379-2
   The roundness that pulls tight the final ring [Orb 442-3
TIGHTLY. Wrapped tightly round us, since we are poor, a warmth,
   [Final 524-8
TIGRESSES. And forest tigresses and women mixed [EM 321-25
TI-LILL-O. Ti-lill-o! [Ord Women 11-15
TILT. Like a spectral cut in its perception, a tilt [What We 460-3
   In the planes that tilt hard revelations on [Someone 87-19 A
TILTED. Tufted, tilted, twirled, and twisted. [Orangeade 103-12
TILTING. The vessel inward. Tilting up his nose, [C 36-6
   As the night descended, tilting in the air, [Key W 130-7
   A swerving, a tilting, a little lengthening, [Nuns 92-11 P
TILTINGS. The eye, a geometric glitter, tiltings [Someone 87-20 A
TIMBERS. And purple timbers, [Archi 18-6 P
TIME. Every time the bucks went clattering [Earthy 3-1
   The death of summer, which that time endures [Swans 4-4
   And have been cold a long time [Snow Man 10-1
   Before one merely reads to pass the time. [Monocle 14-22
   Ticks tediously the time of one more year. [Monocle 15-2
   To which all birds come sometime in their time. [Monocle 17-5
   Bore up, in time, the somnolent, deep songs. [C 33-25
   Between a Carolina of old time, [C 35-22
   A time abhorrent to the nihilist [C 35-29
   These bland excursions into time to come, [C 39-9
   Killing the time between corpses [Venereal 47-15
   The time of year has grown indifferent. [Pharynx 96-1
   One might. One might. But time will not relent. [Pharynx 96-16
   In his time, this one had little to speak of, [Norfolk 111-8
   It's the time of the year [Sailing 120-4
   And the time of the day. [Sailing 120-5
   The truth is that there comes a time [Sad Gay 121-8
   There comes a time when the waltz [Sad Gay 121-11
   Claude has been dead a long time [Botanist 1 134-10
   Turning in time to Brahms as alternate [Anglais 149-6
   But he remembered the time when he stood alone. [Anglais 149-9
   But he remembered the time when he stood alone. [Anglais 149-11
   But he remembered the time when he stood alone, [Anglais 149-13
   Of a man gone mad, after all, for time, in spite [Nigger 157-18
   For the time when sound shall be subtler than we ourselves [Nig-
   ger 158-5
   Of time, time grows upon the rock. [MBG 171-10
   Time in its final block, not time [MBG 183-18
   Here is the bread of time to come, [MBG 183-20
   But in the centre of our lives, this time, this day, [Glass
   198-1
   To live in a tragic time. [Loaf 199-15
   Marching and marching in a tragic time [Loaf 200-11
   The freshness of night has been fresh a long time. [Dump 202-1

Now, in the time of spring (azaleas, trilliums, [Dump 202-12
To the bubbling of bassoons. That's the time [Dump 202-20
It was at that time, that the silence was largest [On Road 204-9
To be, in the grass, in the peacefullest time, [Rabbit K 209-7
If the mouse should swallow the steeple, in its time . . . [Blue
    Bldg 217-7
It would have been better, the time conceived, [Thunder 220-13
A long time you have been making the trip [Hartford 226-4
A long time the ocean has come with you, [Hartford 226-7
At the time of nougats, the peer yellow [Forces 228-17
It was at the time, the place, of nougats. [Forces 228-21
At the time of the dogwoods, handfuls thrown up [Forces 229-5
Being, for old men, time of their time. [Vari 233-11
It was like sudden time in a world without time, [Martial 237-17
Without time: as that which is not has no time, [Martial 237-19
Is time, apart from any past, apart [Martial 238-7
And moved again and flashed again, time flashed again. [Martial
    238-16
It has to face the men of the time and to meet [Of Mod 240-2
The women of the time. It has to think about war [Of Mod 240-3
The piano, that time: the time when the crude [Vase 246-10
First, summer, then a lesser time, [Vase 246-23
Time swished on the village clocks and dreams were alive, [Uru-
    guay 249-26
Must be in a fiction. It is time to choose. [Oboe 250-8
And the metal heroes that time granulates-- [Oboe 250-11
The man who has had the time to think enough, [Oboe 250-19
To be described. They are preaching in a time [Extracts 254-4
Their genius: the exquisite errors of time. [Extracts 254-24
It was time to be himself again, to see [Extracts 255-10
Time troubles to produce the redeeming thought. [Extracts 257-19
"Examination of the Hero in a Time of War" [273-title
Peace in a time of peace, said Leyden [Hero 273-10
Of time and place, becoming certain, [Hero 279-26
It is safe to sleep to a sound that time brings back. [Phenom
    286-12
In the shrivellings of your time and place. [Dutch 291-7
And you, my semblables, know that this time [Dutch 292-1
Is not an early time that has grown late. [Dutch 292-20
Time was not wasted in your subtle temples. [Dutch 293-11
Now, time stands still. He came from out of sleep. [Choc 299-12
Time. What a thing it is to believe that [Lack 303-14
Nor of time. The departing soldier is as he is, [Repet 308-7
It was almost time for lunch. Pain is human. [EM 314-8
That would form themselves, in time, and communicate [EM 314-21
From nature, each time he saw it, making it, [EM 316-18
The soldier of time grown deathless in great size. [EM 319-2
And there the soldier of time has deathless rest. [EM 319-6
Of time's red soldier deathless on his bed. [EM 319-10
For the soldier of time, it breathes a summer sleep, [EM 319-14
And the soldier of time lies calm beneath that stroke. [EM
    319-18
Versicolorings, establishes a time [EM 324-14
It is time that beats in the breast and it is time [Pure 329-13
The mind that knows it is destroyed by time. [Pure 329-15
Time is a horse that runs in the heart, a horse [Pure 329-16
Even breathing is the beating of time, in kind: [Pure 330-4
A large-sculptured, platonic person, free from time, [Pure 330-8
Felicity, ah! Time is the hooded enemy, [Pure 330-13
The day in its color not perpending time, [Pure 332-16
Time in its weather, our most sovereign lord, [Pure 332-17
Her time becomes again, as it became, [Descrip 339-15
In the much-mottled motion of blank time. [Descrip 342-10
Dissolved. The distances of space and time [Descrip 343-9
That night, Liadoff, a long time after his death, [Liadoff
    346-14
Of ugly, subconscious time, in which [Analysis 348-5
Of place: time's haggard mongrels. [Analysis 348-11
Yet in time's middle deep, [Analysis 348-12
Bears us toward time, on its [Analysis 349-8
The knowledge of being, sense without sense of time. [Myrrh 350-9
These figures verdant with time's buried verdure [New Set 352-16
With time, in wavering water lies, swollen [Two V 354-2
Without. In this place and in this time [Human 363-6
For souvenirs of time, lost time, [Prejudice 368-22
Not of perpetual time. [Prejudice 369-3
Beyond which there is nothing left of time. [Cred 372-12
The huge decorum, the manner of the time, [Cred 378-4
And throws it away like a thing of another time, [NSF 382-11
These are the heroic children whom time breeds [NSF 385-1
Falls down, the cock-birds calling at the time. [NSF 388-8
And one that chaffers the time away? [NSF 396-19
The suitable amours. Time will write them down. [NSF 398-6
Be possible. It must be that in time [NSF 404-5
There is a month, a year, there is a time [NSF 405-4
And the house is of the mind and they and time, [AA 413-19
The children laugh and jangle a tinny time. [AA 415-12
There may be always a time of innocence. [AA 418-4
There is never a place. Or if there is no time, [AA 418-5
If it is not a thing of time, nor of place, [AA 418-6

There is or may be a time of innocence [AA 418-10
Created the time and place in which we breathed . . . [AA 419-3
Breathing his bronzen breath at the azury centre of time. [Cata
    425-12
"In a Bad Time" [426-title
In an element not the heaviness of time, [Owl 432-8
A while, conceiving his passage as into a time [Owl 432-23
Less time than place, less place than thought of place [Owl 433-1
You know that the nucleus of a time is not [Papini 446-7
Now, once, he accumulates himself and time [Papini 447-12
Twelve meant as much as the end of normal time, [What We 459-13
Without regard to time or where we are, [NH 466-12
Among time's images, there is not one [NH 476-16
Of night, time and the imagination, [NH 477-23
At another time, the radial aspect came [NH 479-2
A man who was the axis of his time, [NH 479-6
The bricks grown brittle in time's poverty, [NH 480-23
A zone of time without the ticking of clocks, [Aug 494-7
Rising out of present time and place, above [Irish 502-1
To recognize him in after time. [Two Illus 514-5
Like daylight, with time's bellishings, [Two Illus 514-18
It was here. This was the setting and the time [Quiet 523-7
The magnum wreath of summer, time's autumn snood, [Rock 526-21
Time's given perfections made to seem like less [Armor 530-8
They were of a remembered time [Planet 532-8
Where Time, in fitful turns, [Phases 5-21 P
The time will come for these children, seated before their long
    black instruments, to strike the themes of love-- [Piano
    21-16 P
All of them, darkened by time, moved by they know not what,
    amending the airs they play to fulfill themselves; [Piano
    21-17 P
In self, a man of longer time than days, [Good Bad 33-10 P
And how strange it ought to be again, this time [Lytton 39-2 P
A time in which the poets' politics [Burnshaw 48-15 P
For a little time, again, rose-breasted birds [Burnshaw 49-30 P
Because time moves on columns intercrossed [Burnshaw 50-13 P
Is constant. The time you call serene descends [Burnshaw 50-22 P
This time, like damsels captured by the sky, [Burnshaw 51-17 P
To contemplate time's golden paladin [Greenest 56-24 P
For themselves, and space and time and ease for the duck. [Duck
    60-17 P
True, only an inch, but an inch at a time, and inch [Duck 60-19 P
Time's fortune near, the sleepless sleepers moved [Duck 61-27 P
Of a time to come--A shade of horror turns [Duck 65-8 P
Takes time and tinkering, melodious [Duck 65-28 P
How shall we face the edge of time? We walk [Duck 66-6 P
Of other images blows, images of time [Sombre 69-28 P
Like the time of the portent, images like leaves, [Sombre 69-29 P
And memory may itself be time to come [Sombre 70-11 P
The reconciliation, the rapture of a time [Sombre 71-22 P
And without future, a present time, is that [Sombre 71-24 P
Of our sense that time has been [Grotesque 76-21 P
Of the war between individuals. In time, [Bship 77-18 P
To fill, the grindstone of antiquest time, [Bship 80-2 P
A lamp, in a day of the week, the time before spring, [Woman Had
    83-6 P
No book of the past in which time's senators [Recit 86-10 P
Of the son. These survivals out of time and space [Recit 87-27 P
But this time at another place. [Memo 89-2 P
Like the chromatic calendar of time to come. [Theatre 91-6 P
A time existing after much time has passed. [Role 93-11 P
A time, an apparition and nourishing element [How Now 97-11 P
Inhuman for a little, lesser time." [Ulysses 105-6 P
Or Venice, motionless, gathering time and dust. [Real 110-10 P
In Connecticut, we never lived in a time [Myth 118-8 P
"Of Ideal Time and Choice" [88-title A
Are time for counting and remembering, [Ideal 88-10 A
And at what time both of the year and day; [Ideal 89-3 A
Under the bones of time's philosophers? [Ideal 89-9 A
Stand at the center of ideal time, [Ideal 89-11 A
TIME-BOUND. Place-bound and time-bound in evening rain [Human 363-1
TIMELESS. Timeless mother, [Carolinas 5-1
TIMES. Ten times ten times dynamite, convulsive [Hero 273-18
    Three times the concentred self takes hold, three times [Cred
    376-9
    Perhaps there are times of inherent excellence, [NSF 386-9
    To sing jubilas at exact, accustomed times, [NSF 398-7
    The strong music of hard times, [Grotesque 76-13 P
    See five-times-sensed.
TIMID. On timid feet, [Peter 91-4
    I know that timid breathing. Where [MBG 171-17
TIMOTHY. Now, the timothy at Pemaquid [Vari 234-6
    The deer-grass is thin. The timothy is brown. [Myrrh 350-11
TIN. And clap the hollows full of tin. [MBG 170-6
    One sits and beats an old tin can, lard pail. [Dump 202-26
    In the mind: the tin plate, the loaf of bread on it, [NH 485-20
TINCT. New leaf and shadowy tinct, [Pourtraicte 21-23
TINFOIL. He does not change the sea from crumpled tinfoil [Aug
    492-20

TINGES. But though the turbulent tinges undulate [Bird Claws 82-13
TINGLE. The objects tingle and the spectator moves [NH 470-1
    The particular tingle in a proclamation [Someone 84-14 A
TINGLING. Their musky and tingling tongues. [Bananas 54-23
TING-TANG. Sequences that would be sleep and ting-tang tossing, so
    that [Bed 327-4
TINICUM. Under Tinicum or small Cohansey, [New Set 353-5
TINK. Such tink and tank and tunk-a-tunk-tunk, [High-Toned 59-18
TINKERING. Takes time and tinkering, melodious [Duck 65-28 P
TINKLE. The wrinkled roses tinkle, the paper ones, [Extracts 252-2
TINKLING. Descensions of their tinkling bells arrive. [Monocle
    15-20
    The eye and tinkling to the ear. Gruff drums [Havana 143-6
    Came tinkling on the grass to the table [Dinner 110-3 P
TINK-TONK. Indifferent to what it sees. The tink-tonk [NH 475-19
TINNY. The children laugh and jangle a tinny time. [AA 415-12
TINS. On tins and boxes? What about horses eaten by wind? [Paro-
    chial 191-18
TINSEL. Of the colors, are tinsel changes, [Scavoir 231-7
    Tinsel in February, tinsel in August. [Pieces 351-9
    The tinsel of August falling was like a flame [Pieces 352-2
    The prince of shither-shade and tinsel lights, [Owl 434-3
    A penny sun in a tinsel sky, unrhymed, [Duck 61-7 P
TINSMITH. And not this tinsmith's galaxy, [Mandolin 28-21 P
TINT. Without blue, without any turquoise tint or phase, [Landsc
    241-18
TINTED. What a beautiful tableau tinted and towering, [Mice 123-11
    These fields, these hills, these tinted distances, [AA 411-8
TINTINNABULA. She attends the tintinnabula-- [Hermit 505-15
TINTS. Of its eventual roundness, puerile tints [C 44-7
TINY. Flutters in tiny darkness. [Dutch 290-14
TIP. It stands gigantic, with a certain tip [Monocle 17-4
    But when they go that tip still tips the tree. [Monocle 17-6
    A blonde to tip the silver and to taste [C 42-19
    His tip a drop of water full of storms. [Bird Claws 82-12
    We dance it out to the tip of Monsieur's sword, [Mice 123-6
    Turned tip and tip away, [Pascagoula 127-3
    The uptopping top and tip of things, borne up [Two V 355-6
    His head is air. Beneath his tip at night [AA 411-2
    To the muscles' very tip for the vivid plunge, [Old Woman 43-11P
    The heads are severed, topple, tumble, tip [Burnshaw 51-31 P
    In glimpses, on the edge or at the tip, [Sombre 67-1 P
    See cloud-tip.
TIPPED. Or her desire for June and evening, tipped [Sunday 68-25
    Tipped out with largeness, bearing the heavy [Gigan 289-16
    See silver-tipped.
TIPPING. The tipping tongue? [Bagatelles 213-8
TIPS. But when they go that tip still tips the tree. [Monocle 17-6
    A little changed by tips of artifice, changed [Myrrh 350-5
    The tips of cock-cry pinked out pastily, [NH 470-13
    See finger-tips.
TIP-TAP-TAP. Beneath his tip-tap-tap. It is she that responds.
    [Jouga 337-8
TIPTOE. With Crispin as the tiptoe cozener? [C 40-2
    Angels tiptoe upon the snowy cones [Greenest 56-1 P
TIP-TOPS. A steeple that tip-tops the classic sun's [EM 322-25
TIRE. I never tire [Bowl 7-8 P
TIRED. Tired of the salty harbors, [Paltry 5-13
    Grown tired of flight. Like a dark rabbi, I [Monocle 17-21
    I am tired. Sleep for me, heaven over the hill. [Nigger 150-16
    Tired of the old descriptions of the world, [Freed 204-13
    It has, long since, grown tired, of such ideas. [Feo 334-2
    Of the tired romance of imprecision. [Adult 353-8
    Even so when I think of you as strong or tired, [NSF 406-15
    And I--I am tired of him." [Three 134-8 P
TIRELESS. One voice repeating, one tireless chorister, [NSF 394-7
TIRES. One looks at the elephant-colorings of tires. [Dump 202-21
    The cry of an embryo? The spirit tires, [Feo 334-1
    A composing as the body tires, a stop [NSF 386-4
TIRING. See never-tiring.
TISSUE. Then faintly encrusted, a tissue of the moon [Repet 306-14
    To be part of a tissue, a clearness of the air, [Nuns 92-16 P
TISSUES. The spittling tissues tight across the bones. [Nigger
    155-8
TI-TILL-A-ROO. Nor brilliant blows thereof, ti-rill-a-roo, [John
    437-12
TITILLATIONS. My titillations have no foot-notes [Jasmine 79-1
TITTER. The locust's titter and the turtle's sob. [Sombre 71-1 P
TITTIVATING. Sat tittivating by their mountain pools [Monocle 14-2
TI-TUM-TUM-TUM. Ti-tum-tum-tum! [Ploughing 20-14
TOCK. To tick it, tock it, turn it true, [MBG 166-10
TODAY. To say the water is swift today, [Sailing 121-2
    Globed in today and tomorrow, [Gray 140-19
    Today is today and the dancing is done. [Fish-Scale 160-16
    Walked the United States today, [News 264-8
    Of summer. Tomorrow will look like today, [Myrrh 349-18
    Appoints man's place in music, say today. [NSF 382-2
    Read to the congregation, for today [AA 420-16
    Of today, of this morning, of this afternoon, [Bouquet 451-13
    Unreal today, be hidden and alive. [Novel 458-21

Today; and the transcripts of feeling, impossible [NH 479-17
That matches, today, a clearness of the mind. [Nuns 92-17 P
Today the leaves cry, hanging on branches swept by wind, [Course
    96-10 P
Today the mind is not part of the weather. [Clear Day 113-13 P
Today the air is clear of everything. [Clear Day 113-14 P
You speak. You say: Today's character is not [As Leave 116-15 P
TO-DAY. Became to-day, among our children and [Lot 371-6
TOE. Sat alone, his great toe like a horn, [Thought 187-7
TOES. Stamp down the phosphorescent toes, tear off [Nigger 155-7
    Of sneers, the fugues commencing at the toes [Extracts 253-21
TOGETHER. Not wisdom. Can all men, together, avenge [Nigger 158-11
    Two things, the two together as one, [MBG 175-11
    Piece the world together, boys, but not with your hands. [Paro-
    chial 192-8
    Mobs of ten thousand, clashing together, [Thunder 220-3
    If the stars that move together as one, disband, [Horn 230-17
    By thunder, parts, and all these things together, [Landsc 242-26
    And the sun, the waves together in the sea. [Les Plus 245-2
    Collect their thoughts together into one, [Extracts 254-7
    And it all spoke together. [Search 268-4
    And it spoke all together. [Search 268-6
    Of those that are marching, many together. [Dutch 290-12
    These two go well together, the sinuous brim [Pastor 380-2
    Morning and afternoon are clasped together [NSF 392-12
    Patches the moon together in his room [NSF 407-7
    They are together, here, and it is warm, [AA 413-6
    Together, all together. Boreal night [AA 413-20
    As if the crude collops came together as one, [NH 466-1
    Coming together in a sense in which we are poised, [NH 466-11
    Together, said words of the world are the life of the world.
    [NH 474-9
    Being part of everything come together as one. [NH 482-11
    Huddle together in the knowledge of squirrels. [NH 487-12
    The two kept beating together. It was only day. [World 521-12
    In which being there together is enough. [Final 524-18
    Neither one, nor the two together. [Indigo 22-14 P
    Are all men thinking together as one, thinking [Duck 62-19 P
    Let wise men piece the world together with wisdom [Grotesque
    75-7 P
    The words of winter in which these two will come together, [Sick
    90-16 P
    As if we were all seated together again [Letters 107-13 P
    Vermont throws itself together. [July 115-5 P
    "Someone Puts a Pineapple Together" [83-title A
TOIL. The toil [Havana 143 4
TOLD. How happy I was the day I told the young Blandina of three-
    legged giraffes . . . [Analysis 348-1
    Like tales that were told the day before yesterday-- [Hermit
    505-13
    It was only a glass because he looked in it. It was nothing he
    could be told. [Madame 507-6
    Hard to be told from thoughts, the repeated drone [Americana
    [94-3 P
    The scholar, captious, told him what he could [Someone 85-10 A
    But always of many things. He had not to be told [Someone 85-12A
TOLERATE. For who could tolerate the earth [Botanist 2 136-7
TOLL. Raise reddest columns. Toll a bell [MBG 170-5
    To toll its pulses, vigors of its self? [Two V 354-6
TOLLING. The heavy bells are tolling rowdy-dow. [Nigger 155-9
TOLLS. Stirring no poet in his sleep, and tolls [Pharynx 96-7
TOM. Led the emperor astray, the tom trumpets [Hero 278-7
TOMB. Out of the tomb, we bring Badroulbadour, [Worms 49-16
    Out of the tomb we bring Badroulbadour. [Worms 50-3
    "Of Heaven Considered as a Tomb" [56-title
    Who in the tomb of heaven walk by night, [Heaven 56-10
    A voice that cries, "The tomb in Palestine [Sunday 70-15
    Go, mouse, go nibble at Lenin in his tomb. [Blue Bldg 217-19
TOMBS. And of the world of logic in their great tombs. [EM 325-7
    By a lake, with clouds like lights among great tombs. [EM 325-8
TOM McGREEVY. Tom McGreevy, in America, Thinks of Himself as a
    Boy [Our Stars 454-title 1
TOMORROW. Globed in today and tomorrow, [Gray 140-19
    Has no more meaning than tomorrow's bread. [Havana 144-29
    Either now or tomorrow or the day after that. [Nightgown 214-20
    And reaches, beaches, tomorrow's regions became [Descrip 343-13
    Of summer. Tomorrow will look like today, [Myrrh 349-18
    It may come tomorrow in the simplest word, [AA 420-1
    And for tomorrow, this extremity, [AA 420-14
    Not yesterday, not tomorrow, an appanage [Bouquet 451-14
    Tomorrow for him. The wind will have passed by, [NH 473-23
    And of tomorrow's heaven. [Primordia 9-14 P
TO-MORROW. To-morrow when the sun, [Add 198-18
TOMTIT. The tomtit and the cassia and the rose, [C 42-27
TOM-TOM. Tom-tom, c'est moi. The blue guitar [MBG 171-11
TOM-TOMS. With a blubber of tom-toms harrowing the sky? [C 41-13
TONE. Of one, vast, subjugating, final tone. [C 30-9
    As a tone defines itself and separates [Anach 366-12
    The true tone of the metal of winter in what it says: [Discov
    96-6 P

See temple-tone.
TONED. See: high-toned; temple-toned.
TONES. And storming under multitudinous tones [C 28-15
  Variations in the tones of a single sound, [EM 316-14
  For these the musicians make insidious tones, [AA 415-10
  And yet of summer, the petty tones [Bouquet 451-16
  By amical tones. [Woman Had 82-6 P
  See epi-tones.
TONGUE. Fat cat, red tongue, green mind, white milk [Rabbit K 209-5
  The tipping tongue? [Bagatelles 213-8
  The tongue, the fingers, and the nose [Arcades 225-17
  Is merely the moving of a tongue. [Possum 294-3
  And I taste at the root of the tongue the unreal of what is
    real. [Holiday 313-10
  The tongue caresses these exacerbations. [EM 323-1
  Of a speech only a little of the tongue? [NSF 397-4
  Of barbarous tongue, slavered and panting halves [AA 415-18
  On the expressive tongue, the finding fang. [AA 420-10
  That we must calm, the origin of a mother tongue [NH 470-24
  Be orator but with an accurate tongue [Rome 509-10
  A purple woman with a lavender tongue [Melancholy 32-6 P
  With someone to speak her dulcied native tongue, [Letters 107-17P
  A way of pronouncing the word inside of one's tongue [Bus 116-13P
TONGUES. Their musky and tingling tongues. [Bananas 54-23
  Tongues around the fruit. [Orangeade 103-6
  With tongues unclipped and throats so stuffed with thorns,
    [Greenest 57-19 P
TONIGHT. You should have had plums tonight, [Bananas 54-4
  Tonight there are only the winter stars. [Dezem 218-1
  Tonight the stars are like a crowd of faces [Dezem 218-9
  The physical world is meaningless tonight [Jouga 337-1
  It is true. Tonight the lilacs magnify [NSF 394-22
  I heard tonight [Three 135-12 P
TO-NIGHT. To-night, night's undeciphered murmuring [Montra 261-1
  The chords above your bed to-night. [Child 106-21 P
TONNERRE. Or into a dark-blue kind, un roi tonnerre, [Extracts
  254-10
TOO. Of love, it is a book too mad to read [Monocle 14-21
  Is not too lusty for your broadening. [Monocle 16-18
  From your too bitter heart, [Weep Woman 25-2
  But Crispin was too destitute to find [C 30-22
  Of seeds grown fat, too juicily opulent, [C 32-9
  Four daughters in a world too intricate [C 45-2
  But yet not too brunette, [Vincentine 52-18
  The lines are much too dark and much too sharp. [Tallap 71-13
  Yet not too like, yet not so like to be [Fictive 88-10
  Too near, too clear, saving a little to endow [Fictive 88-11
  I am too dumbly in my being pent. [Pharynx 96-4
  Too vague idealist, overwhelmed [Negation 98-1
  Too many waltzes have ended. And then [Sad Gay 121-14
  Too many waltzes have ended. Yet the shapes [Sad Gay 122-10
  Too many waltzes--The epic of disbelief [Sad Gay 122-13
  So little, too little to care, to turn [Adieu 128-1
  When too great rhapsody is left annulled [Havana 144-9
  It is too cold for work, now, in the fields. [Nigger 151-18
  Too sharp for that. The shore, the sea, the sun, [Blue Bldg
  217-9
  The sky is too blue, the earth too wide. [Scavoir 231-13
  Too vaguely that it be written in character. [Extracts 257-21
  Too conscious of too many things at once, [Hand 271-2
  Too conscious of too many things at once, [Hand 271-7
  He was too conscious of too many things [Hand 271-15
  Birds and people of this too voluminous [Hero 278-1
  Too many references. The hero [Hero 279-9
  The wheels are too large for any noise. [Dutch 290-5
  The much too many disinherited [Dutch 292-6
  No: nor divergence made too steep to follow down. [Dutch 293-12
  Too exactly himself, and that there are words [Creat 310-17
  Too dark, too far, too much the accents of [EM 314-19
  Afflicted sleep, too much the syllables [EM 314-20
  A too, too human god, self-pity's kin [EM 315-23
  Is too difficult to tell from despair. Perhaps, [EM 325-20
  Of which we are too distantly a part. [Less 328-10
  We grew used so soon, too soon, to earth itself, [Wild 328-16
  Yet not too closely the double of our lives, [Descrip 344-19
  The catalogue is too commodious. [Cats 367-20
  A land too ripe for enigmas, too serene. [Cred 374-9
  Of volatile world, too constant to be denied, [NSF 397-21
  Too venerably used. That might have been. [NSF 400-19
  Whistle aloud, too weedy wren. I can [NSF 405-9
  Here are too many mirrors for misery. [AA 420-7
  Pink yellows, orange whites, too much as they are [Roses 430-11
  Too much as they are to be changed by metaphor, [Roses 430-13
  Too actual, things that in being real [Roses 430-14
  Presence lies far too deep, for me to know [John 437-25
  Oh as, always too heavy for the sense [Orb 441-2
  Too exactly labelled, a large among the smalls [Orb 443-11
  The fatality of seeing things too well. [Novel 459-6
  Too fragile, too immediate for any speech. [NH 471-9
  And willed. She has given too much, but not enough. [Aug 496-3

Of my shoulder and quickly, too quickly, I am gone? [Angels
  497-10
So well, that which we do for ourselves, too big, [Look 518-5
Too wide, too irised, to be more than calm, [Look 518-18
Too much like thinking to be less than thought, [Look 518-19
Too long, is like a bayonet that bends. [Soldat 13-7 P
And the awnings are too brown, [Mandolin 28-16 P
An eye too sleek, [Coroner 30-7 P
A fear too naked for her shadow's shape. [Old Woman 44-12 P
Too starkly pallid for the jaguar's light, [Greenest 54-29 P
Much too much thought, too little thought, [Grotesque 75-14 P
Too often to be more than secondhand. [Recit 87-2 P
Like an eye too young to grapple its primitive, [Theatre 91-4 P
This howling at one's ear, too far [Dove 98-14 P
For daylight and too near for sleep. [Dove 98-15 P
A dream too poor, too destitute [Ulysses 104-18 P
TOO-CONSTANT. A coldness in a long, too-constant warmth, [NH
  474-20
TOO-FLUENT. And frail umbrellas. A too-fluent green [Sea Surf
  101-8
TOOK. Made pallid flitter. Crispin, here, took flight. [C 32-27
  Whatever shape it took in Crispin's mind, [C 37-6
  The path sick sorrow took, the many paths [Sunday 69-4
  It took dominion everywhere. [Jar 76-13
  A pink girl took a white dog walking. [Forces 229-2
  It was as if thunder took form upon [Vase 246-9
  His manner took what it could find, [News 264-16
  Her hand took his and drew him near to her. [Hand 271-17
  Lenin took bread from his pocket, scattered it-- [Descrip 343-6
  I am the spouse. She took her necklace off [NSF 395-19
  Took on color, took on shape and the size of things as they are
    [Large 424-8
  And the shapes that it took in feeling, the persons that [NH
  479-21
  It took all day to quieten the sky [NH 482-20
  "The Poem That Took the Place of a Mountain" [512-title
  The poem that took the place of a mountain. [Poem Mt 512-2
  Took seven white dogs [Cab 20-16 P
TOOLS. A city slapped up like a chest of tools, [NH 478-20
  To see, once more, this hacked-up world of tools, [Duck 61-9 P
TOOTER. Make melic groans and tooter at her strokes, [Spaniard
  34-25 P
TOOTINGS. One's tootings at the weddings of the soul [Sleight 222-2
TOP. Tapering toward the top. [Pears 196-12
  On top. Hurroo, the man-boat comes, [Vari 235-17
  Upon my top he breathed the pointed dark. [Choc 298-1
  The uptopping top and tip of things, borne up [Two V 355-6
  Over the top of the Bank of Ireland, [Our Stars 454-14
  And dancers danced ballets on top of their beds-- [Agenda 42-5 P
  But this we cannot see. The shaggy top [Sombre 68-19 P
  While the shaggy top collects itself to do [Sombre 68-26 P
  To the top of the hill. [Three 141-13 P
  See cloud-top.
TOPAZ. The topaz rabbit and the emerald cat, [Candle 223-10
  Netted of topaz and ruby [Cab 21-8 P
TOP-CLOUD. As in the top-cloud of a May night-evening, [NSF 395-10
TOPMOST. Halloo them in the topmost distances [Heaven 56-22
TOPPED. His red cockade topped off a parade. [News 264-15
TOPPLE. The heads are severed, topple, tumble, tip [Burnshaw 51-31P
TOPPLED. That a figure reclining among columns toppled down,
  [Conversat 109-7 P
TOPPLES. The touch that topples men and rock." [MBG 170-20
TOPS. Tops the horizon with its colonnades. [Surprises 98-7
  See: chimney-tops; cock-tops; tip-tops.
TORCHES. Of the torches wisping in the underground, [MBG 167-4
TORMENT. The torment of fastidious thought grew slack, [C 37-21
  Making harsh torment of the solitude. [Babies 77-15
  This is the pit of torment that placid end [Dutch 292-24
TORMENTING. Prolific and tormenting tenderness [C 43-11
  You come tormenting, [Venereal 48-2
TORMENTS. The torments of confusion. [Homunculus 27-6
  Stripped one of all one's torments, concealed [Poems Clim 193-18
TORN. Torn from insipid summer, for the mirror of cold, [Dwarf
  208-12
We compose these propositions, torn by dreams, [Men Made 356-2
  Would be a ring of heads and haunches, torn [Sombre 70-22 P
TORN-UP. In a storm of torn-up testaments. [Dutch 292-7
TORPID. These were not tepid stars of torpid places [Page 421-21
TORRENT. Across the spick torrent, ceaselessly, [Paltry 6-9
  A torrent will fall from him when he finds. [Monocle 13-15
  And while the torrent on the roof still droned [C 33-8
  The prismatic sombreness of a torrent's wave. [Bouquet 452-12
TORRENTS. Motions of air, robes moving in torrents of air,
  [Greenest 53-5 P
  And through the torrents a jutting, jagged tower, [Greenest 53-6P
TORTURE. Of those whom the statues torture and keep down. [Paro-
  chial 191-14
  To a crow's voice? Did the nightingale torture the ear, [Dump
  203-2
  By the torture of things that will be realized, [Duck 61-28 P

TORTURED. And I, then, tortured for old speech, [W Burgher 61-14
   The root-man swarming, tortured by his mass, [Montra 262-23
   Her ear unmoved. She was that tortured one, [Old Woman 44-9 P
   Their voice and the voice of the tortured wind were one, [Old
      Woman 45-27 P
TORTURING. Audible at noon, pain torturing itself, [EM 314-4
TOSSED. Of over-civil stops. And thus he tossed [C 35-21
TOSSES. Tosses in the wind. [Ploughing 20-2
   And tosses green for those for whom green speaks. [Repet 309-24
TOSSING. At tossing saucers--cloudy-conjuring sea? [Sea Surf 102-8
   Sequences that would be sleep and ting-tang tossing, so that
      [Bed 327-4
TOTAL. Say that the palms are clear in a total blue, [Two Figures
      86-13
   The total gala of auburn aureoles. [Nigger 154-18
   To the total thing, a shapeless giant forced [Poem Morn 219-15
   The will to be and to be total in belief, [Gala 248-14
   In total war we died and after death [Extracts 258-25
   And you, my semblables, in the total [Dutch 291-13
   And fond, the total man of glubbal glub, [Choc 301-2
   The total past felt nothing when destroyed. [EM 314-16
   He is the final builder of the total building, [Sketch 335-17
   The final dreamer of the total dream, [Sketch 335-18
   There is a total building and there is [Sketch 335-20
   A total dream. There are words of this, [Sketch 335-21
   In a kind of total affluence, all first, [Descrip 342-15
   But there is a total death, [Burghers 362-7
   High in the height that is our total height. [Pastor 379-21
   Of the skeleton of the ether, the total [Orb 443-19
   Becomes amassed in a total double-thing. [NH 472-7
   To indicate the total leaflessness. [NH 477-9
   The total excellence of its total book." [NH 485-9
   The total of human shadows bright as glass. [Aug 494-23
   It is a kind of total grandeur at the end, [Rome 510-21
   Total grandeur of a total edifice, [Rome 510-26
   Each one as part of the total wrath, obscure [Sombre 69-5 P
   Of other lives becoming a total drone, [Americana 94-4 P
   Here the total artifice reveals itself [Someone 87-12 A
   As the total reality. Therefore it is [Someone 87-13 A
TOTTERING. Like a tottering, a falling and an end, [Nightgown
      214-9
   And the wind sways like a great thing tottering-- [Hermit 505-16
TOTTERS. Deep grass that totters under the weight of light.
      [Greenest 55-1 P
TOUCAN. In spite of hawk and falcon green toucan [C 30-18
TOUCANS. As the cackle of toucans [Men 1000 52-1
   In the place of toucans. [Men 1000 52-2
TOUCH. Created, in his day, a touch of doubt. [C 27-13
   Hands without touch yet touching poignantly, [C 43-17
   That never touch with inarticulate pang? [Sunday 69-19
   In their embroidered slippers, touch your spleen? [Polish Aunt
      84-5
   The touch of springs, [Peter 90-16
   And apt in versatile motion, touch and sound [Anatomy 108-12
   And touch each other, even touching closely, [Norfolk 112-1
   And to touch her, have need to say to her, [Ghosts 119-14
   To touch again the hottest bloom, to strike [Havana 143-15
   The touch that topples men and rock." [MBG 170-20
   Gives the touch of the senses, not of the hand, [MBG 174-20
   But the very senses as they touch [MBG 175-1
   The touch. Fix quiet. Take the place [Prelude 195-19
   Her fingers touch the ground. [Add 199-4
   I touch them and smell them. Who speaks? [Peaches 224-2
   To hear, to touch, to taste, to smell, that's now, [Arcades
      225-7
   That's this. Do they touch the thing they see, [Arcades 225-8
   They do not touch it. Sounds never rise [Arcades 225-10
   To touch a woman cadaverous, [Arcades 225-23
   You touch the hotel the way you touch moonlight [Waldorf 241-4
   The hand can touch, neither green bronze nor marble, [Montra
      261-3
   Hard to perceive and harder still to touch. [Choc 301-18
   As each had a particular woman and her touch? [Holiday 312-10
   Or merely seemed to touch him as he spoke [EM 315-2
   Be near me, come closer, touch my hand, phrases [EM 317-17
   The gross, the fecund, proved him against the touch [EM 322-2
   On a breast forever precious for that touch, [NSF 388-6
   The soft hands are a motion not a touch. [AA 413-16
   Of breath, obedient to his trumpet's touch. [AA 415-19
   So far beyond the rhetorician's touch. [Roses 431-12
   But she that he loved turns cold at his light touch. [Pecul
      453-12
   Touch and trouble of the touch of the actual hand. [NH 476-15
   The way a look or a touch reveals its unexpected magnitudes.
      [Prol 517-10
   And Crispine, the blade, reddened by some touch, demanding the
      most from the phrases [Piano 22-6 P
   Descending, did not touch her eye and left [Old Woman 44-8 P
   To touch the grass and, as you circle, turn [Burnshaw 51-12 P
   At the unbeliever's touch. Cloud-cloisters blow [Greenest 58-10P

For the syllable, poised for the touch? But that [Duck 62-22 P
   A cry, the pallor of a dress, a touch. [Sombre 67-20 P
   Simplifications approach but do not touch [Bship 80-26 P
   With something I could touch, touch every way. [Warmth 90-6 P
   Bending in blue dresses to touch something, [Clear Day 113-12 P
   With something I could touch, touch every way. [As Leave 117-12 P
TOUCHED. Susanna's music touched the bawdy strings [Peter 92-8
   Touched on by hoar-frost, shrinks in a shelter [Lunar 107-7
   They are touched red. [Pears 196-8
   The rocks not even touched by snow, [Loaf 199-20
   I know from all the things it touched [Country 207-17
   Could have touched these winds, [Weak Mind 212-18
   And not be touched by blue. He wanted to know, [Landsc 241-15
   Grown denser, part, the eye so touched, so played [Landsc 242-24
   Grew strong, as if doubt never touched his heart. [Choc 299-5
   As night was free from him. The shadow touched [EM 315-1
   Touched suddenly by the universal flare [Pure 333-7
   Had crowded into the rocket and touched the fuse. [Liadoff 346-13
   A freedom revealed, a realization touched, [Bouquet 451-20
   Suppose it turned out to be or that it touched [Golden 460-8
   In space and the self, that touched them both at once [NH 483-7
   And the sense of the archaic touched us at once [Aug 494-13
   It was as if transparence touched her mind. [Old Woman 45-9 P
   Into a music never touched to sound. [Greenest 54-11 P
   Exceeding sex, he touched another race, [Duck 64-25 P
TOUCHES. She touches the clouds, where she goes [Paltry 5-19
   He that at midnight touches the guitar, [Thought 186-5
   A self that touches all edges, [Rabbit K 209-18
   There he touches his being. There as he is [Yellow 237-4
   The child that touches takes character from the thing, [NSF
      392-20
   The body, it touches. The captain and his men [NSF 392-21
   As it touches the point of reverberation--not grim [NH 475-14
   Touches, as one hand touches another hand, [NH 484-19
   Still touches solemnly with what she was [Aug 496-2
   Each person completely touches us [Leben 505-7
TOUCHING. An ancient aspect touching a new mind. [Monocle 16-2
   Hands without touch yet touching poignantly, [C 43-17
   And touch each other, even touching closely, [Norfolk 112-1
   These mothers touching, speaking, being near, [Cred 372-17
TOUCHLESS. To comb her dewy hair, a touchless light, [Beginning
      427-13
TOUGH. Of an aesthetic tough, diverse, untamed, [C 31-20
TOUJOURS. C'est toujours la vie qui me regarde . . . This was [NH
      483-14]
TOULET. They resemble a page of Toulet [Nigger 153-2
TOURNAMONDE. The gay tournamonde as of a single world [NH 476-3
TOURS. That tours to shift the shifting scene. [MBG 180-4
TOUTES. Livre de Toutes Sortes de Fleurs d'après Nature. [EM 316-7
TOWER. It is the natural tower of all the world, [Cred 373-16
   But a tower more precious than the view beyond, [Cred 373-18
   It is the mountain on which the tower stands, [Cred 373-22
   It is the old man standing on the tower, [Cred 374-1
   The tower, the ancient accent, the wintry size. [Antag 426-6
   He turned from the tower to the house, [Aug 493-9
   As if on a taller tower [Aug 493-15
   Besides, the world is a tower. [Secret Man 36-5 P
   Will shout from the tower's rim. [Secret Man 36-16 P
   And through the torrents a jutting, jagged tower, [Greenest
      53-6 P
   See sea-tower.
TOWERING. What a beautiful tableau tinted and towering, [Mice
      123-11
TOWERS. And high towers, [Six Sig 74-26
   For whom the towers are built. The burgher's breast, [Havana
      143-27
   No more. I can build towers of my own, [Montra 263-8
   Push up the towers [Archi 17-15 P
TOWN. That was not in him in the crusty town [C 33-12
   Toward the town, tell why the glassy lights, [Key W 130-5
   That silences the ever-faithful town. [Havana 144-25
   But the town and the fragrance were never one, [Arcades 225-13
   Working, with big hands, on the town, [Hartford 227-2
   Of the town, the river, the railroad were clear. [Hartford 227-8
   At a town in which acacias grew, he lay [EM 314-17
   That constantly sparkled their small gold? The town [Liadoff
      346-12
   There was no difference between the town [Liadoff 347-17
   The clouds are over the village, the town, [Woman Song 360-13
   His slouching pantaloons, beyond the town, [NSF 389-6
   So that they become an impalpable town, full of [NH 466-5
   A great town hanging pendent in a shade, [NH 468-16
   In the metaphysical streets of the physical town [NH 472-22
   The town, the weather, in a casual litter, [NH 474-8
   To distinguish. The town was a residuum, [NH 479-18
   Or of a town poised at the horizon's dip. [NH 483-9
   Than the difference that clouds make over a town. [NH 487-7
   See down-town.
TOWNS. By the obese opiates of sleep. Plain men in plain towns [NH
      467-20

In the Duft of towns, beside a window, beside [Woman Had 83-5 P
TOWNSMEN. Do you remember what the townsmen said, [Liadoff 346-17
  These are the small townsmen of death, [Burghers 362-11
TOY. The whole of appearance is a toy. For this, [Belly 366-16
TOYS. Not toys, not thing-a-ma-jigs-- [Dezem 218-18
  Toys of the millionaires, [Drum-Majors 37-5 P
TRACE. Except the trace of burning stars [Reader 147-11
  Trace the gold sun about the whitened sky [Cred 373-6
TRACED. Traced in the shadow [Thirteen 93-17
TRACING. The fitful tracing of a portal; [Peter 91-23
  But in the style of the novel, its tracing [Novel 458-11
TRACK. If not in will, to track the knaves of thought. [C 42-24
  A yellow wine and follow a steamer's track [Landsc 243-6
TRACTATUS. Tractatus, of military things, with plates, [Greenest
  56-14 P
TRADE-WIND. The trade-wind jingles the rings in the nets around
  the racks by the docks on Indian River. [Indian 112-4
TRADITION. A poem about tradition could easily be [Recit 86-1 P
  To be a part of tradition, to identify [Recit 86-4 P
  Of tradition does not easily take form. [Recit 86-7 P
  Are not tradition. To identify it [Recit 86-12 P
  Is not its form. Tradition is wise but not [Recit 86-16 P
  Things still more distant. And tradition is near. [Recit 86-20 P
  Tradition is much more than the memory. [Recit 87-3 P
  And is tradition an unfamiliar sum, [Recit 87-9 P
  Tradition wears, the clear, the single form [Recit 87-21 P
TRAGEDIAN. Scrawl a tragedian's testament? Prolong [C 41-14
  In the manner of a tragedian [Three 136-8 P
  To that sweaty tragedian, [Three 138-8 P
TRAGEDIES. Light's comedies, dark's tragedies, [Ulysses 102-28 P
TRAGEDY. The action of incorrigible tragedy. [Dutch 292-21
  The death of Satan was a tragedy [EM 319-19
  The tragedy, however, may have begun, [EM 320-10
  It is a fragmentary tragedy [EM 324-2
  Tragedy. This is destiny unperplexed, [EM 324-9
  These musicians dubbing at a tragedy, [AA 415-24
  And thus its jetted tragedy, its stele [AA 417-24
  Now, the first tutoyers of tragedy [Beginning 428-7
  This should be tragedy's most moving face. [NH 477-6
  These fitful sayings are, also, of tragedy: [NH 478-1
  In a theatre, full of tragedy, [Soldat 15-18 P
  With tragedy or comedy? [Demoiselle 23-13 P
TRAGIC. One might have found tragic hair, [Chateau 161-9
  Out of a mood, the tragic robe [MBG 169-20
  As of a tragic science should rise. [Prelude 195-13
  It is equal to living in a tragic land [Loaf 199-14
  To live in a tragic time. [Loaf 199-15
  Marching and marching in a tragic time [Loaf 200-11
  To come to tragic shores and flow, [Vari 233-9
  The mind's own limits, like a tragic thing [Choc 298-4
  Has its emptiness and tragic expirations. [EM 320-9
  Coulisse bright-dark, tragic chiaroscuro [NSF 384-3
  That big-brushed green. Or in a tragic mode, [John 437-3
  Neither of comic nor tragic but of commonplace. [NH 478-3
  And, in my hearing, you hear its tragic drone [Angel 497-2
  This is the tragic accent of the scene. [Rome 510-5
  A comic infanta among the tragic drapings, [Slug 522-12
  That tragic prattle of the fates, astute [Spaniard 34-16 P
  A tragic lullaby, like porcelain. [Burnshaw 50-31 P
  See lack-tragic.
TRAGICAL. And its tragical, its haunted arpeggios? [Liadoff 346-19
TRAGIC-GESTURED. The ever-hooded, tragic-gestured sea [Key W 129-5
TRAIN. Suppose these couriers brought amid their train [Monocle
  15-27
TRAINED. Trained to poise the tables of the law, [Lions 124-14
TRAINS. Colliding with deaf-mute churches and optical trains.
  [Chaos 357-17
TRAMP. Political tramp with an heraldic air, [Choc 301-3
TRAMPLED. And head a shadow trampled under hoofs, [Sombre 70-28 P
TRANCED. Piano-polished, held the tranced machine [Sea Surf 100-15
TRANQUIL. Were tranquil [Ord Women 11-7
  If ever the search for a tranquil belief should end, [Nigger
  151-9
  Be tranquil in your wounds. It is good death [Extracts 253-24
  Be tranquil in your wounds. The placating star [Extracts 253-26
  How tranquil it was at vividest Varadero, [Novel 457-16
  In his chair, the most tranquil thought grew peaked [Quiet 523-9
  If is the rock where tranquil must adduce [Rock 528-14
  Its tranquil self, the main of things, the mind, [Rock 528-15
  The light of the most tranquil candle [Three 132-13 P
TRANQUILLITY. But here tranquillity is what one thinks. [Novel
  458-2
TRANQUILLIZING. Tranquillizing with this jewel [Homunculus 27-5
TRANSATLANTIC. Berceuse, transatlantic. The children are men, old
  men, [Woman Had 82-10 P
TRANSCEND. It is the cry of leaves that do not transcend themselves,
  [Course 96-21 P
TRANSCENDED. Disclosed in everything, transcended, poised [Duck
  62-21 P
TRANSCENDENCE. That slight transcendence to the dirty sail,

[Sailing 121-5
TRANSCENDENT. The sea shivered in transcendent change, rose up
  [NH 484-9
  There was no fury in transcendent forms. [Quiet 523-14
TRANSCRIPTS. The imaginative transcripts were like clouds, [NH
  479-16
  Today; and the transcripts of feeling, impossible [NH 479-17
  Yet the transcripts of it when it was blue remain: [NH 479-20
TRANSFER. Of this element, this force. Transfer it [Hero 277-3
TRANSFIGURED. Serenely selves, transfigured by the selves [Burn-
  shaw 52-2 P
TRANSFIGURERS. True transfigurers fetched out of the human moun-
  tain, [Choc 300-6
TRANSFIGURINGS. Came fresh transfigurings of freshest blue. [Sea
  Surf 102-15
TRANSFIXED. In glue, but things transfixed, transpierced and well
  [Bouquet 449-13
TRANSFIXING. Straight to the transfixing object, to the object [NH
  471-15
  Transfixing by being purely what it is, [NH 471-17
TRANSFORM. Transform for transformation's self, [Human 363-14
  The power to transform itself, or else, [Two Illus 514-11
  Not to transform them into other things, [Look 517-15
TRANSFORMATION. Transform for transformation's self, [Human 363-14
  Enough. The freshness of transformation is [NSF 397-24
TRANSFORMATIONS. The centre of transformations that [Human 363-13
  The favorable transformations of the wind [Past Nun 378-21
  The visible transformations of summer night, [Real 110-16 P
TRANSFORMED. Who the transformer, himself transformed, [Jumbo
  269-7
  Of heaven-haven. These are not things transformed. [NSF 399-1
  Through waves of light. It is of cloud transformed [AA 416-7
  To cloud transformed again, idly, the way [AA 416-8
  And what meant more, to be transformed. [Two Illus 514-12
  Became transformed. But his mastery [Two Illus 515-2
  Above our race, yet of ourselves transformed, [Duck 64-26 P
TRANSFORMER. Who the transformer, himself transformed, [Jumbo
  269-7
TRANSFORMING. With a logic of transforming certitudes. [Sombre
  66-22 P
TRANSFORMS. Until the sharply-colored glass transforms [Burnshaw
  52-9 P
TRANSIT. Bursts back. What not quite realized transit [Feo 333-20
TRANSLATED. Transparent man in a translated world, [Bus 116-3 P
TRANSLATION. Translation of a Russian poet. [Vari 234-9
TRANSMUTATION. On a transmutation which, when seen, appears [EM
  318-6
TRANSPARENCE. The beads on her rails seemed to grasp at trans-
  parence. [Vari 236-2
  He is the transparence of the place in which [Oboe 251-1
  Blue's last transparence as it turned to black, [Choc 297-13
  A transparence in which we heard music, made music, [EM 316-10
  The savage transparence. They go crying [Pediment 361-16
  The vivid transparence that you bring is peace. [NSF 380-11
  Who gives transparence to their present peace. [AA 413-11
  She gives transparence. But she has grown old. [AA 413-14
  On the chair, a moving transparence on the nuns, [Rome 509-4
  It was as if transparence touched her mind. [Old Woman 45-9 P
  Acquired transparence and beheld itself [Greenest 54-6 P
  And beheld the source from which transparence came; [Greenest
  54-7 P
TRANSPARENCIES. Impalpable bells, transparencies of sound, [NH
  466-6
TRANSPARENCY. It is a cat of a sleek transparency [NH 473-1
  A transparency through which the swallow weaves, [Look 518-8
TRANSPARENT. In transparent accords). [Thunder 220-12
  Bask in the sun in which they feel transparent, [Extracts 254-19
  In which we heard transparent sounds, did he play [EM 316-11
  By growing clear, transparent magistrates, [Bouquet 449-6
  Sounding in transparent dwellings of the self, [NH 466-7
  Of that transparent air. [Aug 493-24
  Transparent man in a translated world, [Bus 116-3 P
TRANSPIERCED. In glue, but things transfixed, transpierced and
  well [Bouquet 449-13
TRANSPLANT. John Constable they could never quite transplant [Nig-
  ger 154-20
TRANSPORTED. The love that will not be transported [Jasmine 79-4
TRANSPOSED. Themselves transposed, muted and comforted [NH 467-24
TRAPPED. Majestic bearers or solemn haulers trapped [Greenest
  57-14 P
TRAPS. But I set my traps [Peacocks 58-13
  See clapper-traps.
TRASH. Of buttons, measure of his salt. Such trash [C 39-19
  Nothing but trash and that you no longer feel [Lilacs 49-9
  The trash. [Dump 202-18
  By the trash of life, [Bagatelles 213-11
  Are comic trash, the ears are dirt, [Arcades 225-18
  But of nothing, trash of sleep that will disappear [Choc 300-18
  A trash can at the end of the world, the dead [Burnshaw 49-5 P
TRAVELED. As he traveled alone, like a man lured on by a syllable

without any meaning, [Prol 516-4
TRAVELERS. "Three Travelers Watch a Sunrise" [127-title P
TRAVERSE. In the circle of her traverse of the sea. [Paltry 5-20
TRAVERSES. Is a solid. It may be a shade that traverses [NH 489-2
    A dust, a force that traverses a shade. [NH 489-3
TRAVERSING. A man come out of luminous traversing, [C 30-25
TRAY. The weather was like a waiter with a tray. [Forces 229-18
TREACHERY. But note the unconscionable treachery of fate, [Monocle
    17-9
TREAD. That yuccas breed, and of the panther's tread. [C 31-29
    In the casual evocations of your tread [On Manner 56-2
    And his finical carriers tread, [Cortege 79-14
    On a hundred legs, the tread [Cortege 79-15
    Treading a tread [Cortege 80-4
    The tread of the carriers does not halt [Cortege 80-7
    That tread [Cortege 80-13
    As they tread the boards [Cortege 80-18
    Of the endless tread [Cortege 80-24
    That they tread; [Cortege 80-25
    The lamentable tread! [Cortege 81-7
TREADING. Treading a tread [Cortege 80-4
TREAT. Aquiline pedants treat the cart, [Prejudice 368-15
    They treat the philosopher's hat, [Prejudice 368-17
TREE. But, after all, I know a tree that bears [Monocle 17-2
    But when they go that tip still tips the tree. [Monocle 17-6
    The gold tree is blue. [Of Surface 57-6
    In the shadow of a pine tree [Six Sig 73-6
    The pine tree moves in the wind. [Six Sig 73-13
    Against a tall tree. [Six Sig 74-5
    Like a tree [Thirteen 92-18
    Then the tree, at night, began to change, [On Road 203-19
    There was a tree that was a father, [Vari 233-6
    A nigger tree and with a nigger name, [News 265-2
    Seized her and wondered: why beneath the tree [Hand 271-4
    Her hand composed him and composed the tree. [Hand 271-9
    The wind had seized the tree and ha, and ha, [Hand 271-10
    And lay beside her underneath the tree. [Hand 271-21
    But at a distance, in another tree. [Possum 294-18
    He was as tall as a tree in the middle of [Choc 297-19
    And no true tree, [Analysis 348-7
    That keep clinging to a tree, [Burghers 362-13
    The same railway passenger, the ancient tree [Cats 367-16
    Hung heavily on the great banana tree, [NSF 393-14
    A tree, this unprovoked sensation requires [NSF 406-12
    The possible nest in the invisible tree, [John 437-17
    Until the used-to earth and sky, and the tree [Orb 441-12
    And cloud, the used-to tree and used-to cloud, [Orb 441-13
    The tree stood dazzling in the air [Two Illus 514-15
    Until each tree, each evil-blossomed vine, [Greenest 55-23 P
    Or a confect of leafy faces in a tree-- [Art Pop 113-2 P
    The mulberry tree is a double tree. [Banjo 114-1 P
    A white, pink, purple berry tree, [Banjo 114-3 P
    A very dark-leaved berry tree. [Banjo 114-4 P
    It is only a tree [Three 137-5 P
    So it is the green of one tree [Three 143-7 P
    Like the same orange repeating on one tree [Someone 85-21 A
    See: beggar-tree; gum-tree; Judas-tree; pine-tree.
TREE-BRANCHES. Arch in the sea like tree-branches, [Homunculus 26-2
TREE-CAVES. The robins are là-bas, the squirrels, in tree-caves,
    [NH 487-11
TREES. I know no magic trees, no balmy boughs, [Monocle 16-27
    His trees were planted, his duenna brought [C 42-2
    Plucked from the Carib trees, [Bananas 54-18
    The sky is a blue gum streaked with rose. The trees are black.
    [Banal 62-12
    The trees, like serafin, and echoing hills, [Sunday 70-8
    What of the trees [Sonatina 110-3
    And intonations of the trees? [Sonatina 110-4
    The trees like bones and the leaves half sand, half sun. [Fare-
    well 118-5
    To warblings early in the hilarious trees [Medit 124-8
    Beyond all trees, the ridges thrown [How Live 125-19
    Of the pine trees edging the sand, [Pascagoula 127-5
    Above the trees? And why the poet as [Eve Angels 136-14
    Of trombones floating in the trees. [Havana 143-3
    It was when the trees were leafless first in November [Nigger
    151-1
    The trees are wooden, the grass is yellow and thin. [Nigger
    157-21
    The hunters run to and fro. The heavy trees, [Parochial 191-7
    Below me, on the asphalt, under the trees. [Loaf 200-12
    It was the importance of the trees outdoors, [Freed 205-17
    And full of yourself. The trees around are for you, [Rabbit K
    209-16
    Should play in the trees when morning comes. [Nightgown 214-16
    There were the sheets high up on older trees, [Forces 229-13
    A trumpet round the trees. Could one say that it was [Horn 230-6
    Everywhere the spruce trees bury soldiers: [Vari 234-10
    Everywhere spruce trees bury spruce trees. [Vari 234-13
    The Arachne integument of dead trees, [Vari 234-19

And toward the start of day and trees [Adequacy 244-6
Snow under the trees and on the northern rocks, [Extracts 255-15
The trees were plucked like iron bars [Jumbo 269-1
You like it under the trees in autumn, [Motive 288-1
These trees and their argentines, their dark-spiced branches,
    [Holiday 313-3
People fall out of windows, trees tumble down, [Chaos 357-13
How is it that the wooden trees stand up [Belly 367-2
Of red facsimiles through related trees, [Cats 367-18
And is our fortune and honey hived in the trees [Cred 374-19
The wild orange trees continued to bloom and to bear, [NSF
    393-2
Where his house had fallen, three scraggy trees weighted [NSF
    393-4
Shall we be found hanging in the trees next spring? [AA 419-19
Bare limbs, bare trees and a wind as sharp as salt? [AA 419-21
Among the bare and crooked trees, [Celle 438-3
From the clouds in the midst of trembling trees [Puel 456-7
One imagined the violet trees but the trees stood green, [What
    We 459-10
Leaves burnished in autumnal burnished trees [NH 474-3
The rain kept falling loudly in the trees [NH 476-7
In the land of the lemon trees, yellow and yellow were [NH
    486-13
In the land of the elm trees, wandering mariners [NH 486-16
When the mariners came to the land of the lemon trees, [NH
    487-1
They said, "We are back once more in the land of the elm trees,
    [NH 487-3
Against the trees and then against the sky [Aug 494-12
The trees are reappearing in poverty. [Aug 495-10
The redness of your reddish chestnut trees, [Old Man 501-5
And the shadows of the trees [Plant 506-6
The way some first thing coming into Northern trees [Prol 517-6
To think away the grass, the trees, the clouds, [Look 517-14
The interminable adventurer? The trees are mended. [World 520-12
The trees had been mended, as an essential exercise [World 521-4
Wood-smoke rises through trees, is caught in an upper flow [Slug
    522-3
The trees have a look as if they bore sad names [Slug 522-5
You were not born yet when the trees were crystal [Slug 522-17
And trees that lack the intelligence of trees. [R Conn 533-6
It is that Old Man, lost among the trees. [Phases 5-15 P
Pears on pointed trees, [Bowl 7-5 P
The horses gnaw the bark from the trees. [Primordia 8-8 P
The trunks of the trees are hollow. [Primordia 8-10 P
The trees do not. [Primordia 8-12 P
The trees cannot. [Primordia 8-14 P
The trees stand still, [Primordia 8-16 P
The trees drink. [Primordia 8-17 P
The birch trees draw up whiteness from the ground. [Primordia
    8-21 P
Observe her shining in the deadly trees. [Spaniard 34-15 P
Yet in trees round the College of Heralds, [Agenda 42-10 P
In the midst of a circle of trees, from which the leaves [Old
    Woman 43-3 P
Blowing among the trees its meaningless sound. [Old Woman 44-28P
The space above the trees might still be bright [Old Woman 44-29P
Grown great and grave beyond imagined trees, [Old Woman 45-31 P
The cuckoo trees and the widow of Madrid [Greenest 59-16 P
The clank of the carrousel and, under the trees, [Duck 62-25 P
The statue in a crow's perspective of trees [Sombre 70-19 P
Give only their color to the leaves. The trees [Sombre 71-3 P
The plums are blue on the trees. The katy-dids [Memo 89-14 P
When the trees glitter with that which despoils them, [Discov
    95-8 P
In a burst of shouts, under the trees [Dinner 110-1 P
Neither the cards nor the trees nor the air [Sol Oaks 111-5 P
Under the oak trees, completely released. [Sol Oaks 111-10 P
The trees are swaying, swaying, swaying. [Region 115-17 P
Under the wintry trees of the terrace. [Bus 116-14 P
It shines, among the trees, [Three 135-8 P
Upon the trees, [Three 142-8 P
As red is multiplied by the leaves of trees. [Three 143-14 P
6. White sky, pink sun, trees on a distant peak. [Someone 86-9 A
See: fir-trees; fruit-trees; orange-trees; pine-trees; thorn-
    trees.
TREETOPS. And to watch the treetops, as they sway. [Region 115-7 P
TREMBLE. So that I tremble with such love so known [NSF 396-8
    And be surprised and tremble, hand and lip. [Beginning 428-2
    The candle would tremble in his hands; [Three 132-26 P
TREMBLED. The volcano trembled in another ether, [EM 314-6
TREMBLES. As the body trembles at the end of life. [EM 314-7
    And one trembles to be so understood and, at last, [Novel 459-4
TREMBLING. If sex were all, then every trembling hand [Monocle
    17-7
    Of widows and trembling ladies, [Homunculus 26-7
    His arm would be trembling, he would be weak, [Thunder 220-15
    From the clouds in the midst of trembling trees [Puel 456-7
TREMENDOUS. A dead shepherd brought tremendous chords from hell

[NSF 400-21
TRENCHANT-EYED. Is not lean marble, trenchant-eyed. There is
    [Recit 86-9 P
TRIAL. From the whirling, slowly and by trial; or fear [Burnshaw
    51-7 P
TRIALS. A blank underlies the trials of device, [NH 477-15
TRIANGLES. To right-angled triangles. [Six Sig 75-9
    Triangles and the names of girls. [Dezem 218-4
TRICKS. Prodigious things are tricks. The world is not [Havana
    144-3
TRICOLOR. Each drop a petty tricolor. For this, [Hartford 226-10
TRICORN. And an air of lateness. The moon is a tricorn [Aug 495-20
TRIED. If they tried rhomboids, [Six Sig 75-10
    Was ancient. He tried to remember the phrases: pain [EM 314-3
    We haven't tried that. [Agenda 42-6 P
TRIES. He tries by a peculiar speech to speak [NSF 397-6
    The perspective squirming as it tries to take [Bship 80-4 P
TRIFLE. Yet let that trifle pass. Now, as this odd [C 32-13
TRIFLES. But to strip off the complacent trifles, [Gigan 289-8
TRILLIUMS. Now, in the time of spring (azaleas, trilliums, [Dump
    202-12
TRIMLY. The violent disclosure trimly leafed, [Bouquet 452-9
TRINKET. Trinket pasticcio, flaunting skyey sheets, [C 40-1
TRINKLING. A trinkling in the parentage of the north, [Discov
    95-13 P
TRIP. A long time you have been making the trip [Hartford 226-4
    On her trip around the world, Nanzia Nunzio [NSF 395-16
TRIPLE. And triple chime . . . The self-same rhythm [Stan Hero
    83-22 P
    See thrice-triple-syllabled.
TRISTESSES. Tristesses, the fund of life and death, suave bush
    [Cred 377-15
TRITON. Triton, dissolved in shifting diaphanes [C 28-24
    Lay grovelling. Triton incomplicate with that [C 28-29
    Which made him Triton, nothing left of him, [C 28-30
    And excepting negligible Triton, free [C 29-28
TRIUMPH. Where triumph rang its brassy phrase, or love [Sunday
    69-5
    An end must come in a merciless triumph, [Dutch 291-15
    The triumph of the arcs of heaven's blue [Duck 60-16 P
    The strength of death or triumph. Oheu! [Stan Hero 83-15 P
TRIUMPHALS. For humane triumphals. But a politics [Papini 447-13
    For triumphals. These are hymns appropriate to [Papini 447-15
TRIUMPHANT. To that short, triumphant sting? [Phases 5-3 P
    Changed them, at last, to its triumphant hue, [Old Woman 44-26 P
    Triumphant as that always upward wind [Old Woman 44-27 P
    Joined, the triumphant vigor, felt, [Ulysses 100-14 P
    Joined in a triumphant vigor, [Presence 105-23 P
TRIUMPHANTLY. In the high imagination, triumphantly. [Extracts
    256-16
TRIUMPHING. She walks, triumphing humbly, should express [Red Kit
    31-11 P
TRIUMPHS. Over all these the mighty imagination triumphs [Puel
    456-10
TRIVIA. Of rankest trivia, tests of the strength [C 37-13
TRIVIAL. This trivial trope reveals a way of truth. [Monocle 16-4
    By trivial filaments to the thing intact: [Bouquet 450-11
    By print or paper, the trivial chance foregone, [Duck 61-23 P
    A cockle-shell, a trivial emblem great [Bship 79-10 P
TROD. In the presto of the morning, Crispin trod, [C 42-13
TROMBONES. Of trombones floating in the trees. [Havana 143-3
    And the beautiful trombones--behold [MBG 170-9
    Confront you, hoo-ing the slick trombones, [MBG 170-16
    In trombones roaring for the children, [Hero 278-10
    The trombones are like baboons, [Drum-Majors 37-2 P
TROPE. This trivial trope reveals a way of truth. [Monocle 16-4
    Of Trope. He sat in the park. The water of [NSF 397-11
    By trope or deviation, straight to the word, [NH 471-14
TROPHY. The bottomless trophy, new hornsman after old? [NSF 390-18
TROPIC. It was a flourishing tropic he required [C 35-16
    Artist in Tropic [NE Verses 105-title 7
    A cavernous and a cruel past, tropic [Greenest 58-21 P
    Of the tropic of resemblance, sprigs [Someone 86-17 A
TROPICAL. The jungle of tropical part and tropical whole." [Bship
    80-12 P
TROPICS. (The rudiments of tropics are around, [Bird Claws 82-4
TROUBLE. Of fragrance and the mind lays by its trouble. [Cred
    372-8
    Now the mind lays by its trouble and considers. [Cred 372-9
    Touch and trouble of the touch of the actual hand. [NH 476-15
    Something of the trouble of the mind [How Now 97-4 P
    Trouble in the spillage and first sparkle of sun, [How Now 97-7P
    The trouble of the mind [How Now 97-9 P
TROUBLES. Time troubles to produce the redeeming thought. [Ex-
    tracts 257-19
TROUBLESOME. An understanding may be troublesome. [Lytton 39-23 P
TROUGHS. Bland belly-sounds in somnolent troughs, [Frogs 78-3
TROVE. As acutest virtue and ascetic trove. [Montra 263-12
TRUCULENT. The leaping bodies, come from the truculent hand, [Duck
    64-15 P

TRUE. Like this, saps like the sun, true fortuner. [C 43-5
    True daughters both of Crispin and his clay. [C 44-2
    It is true that the rivers went nosing like swine, [Frogs 78-1
    And true savant of this dark nature be. [Sun March 134-8
    Where the voice that is in us makes a true response, [Eve Angels
    138-4
    True reconcilings, dark, pacific words, [Havana 144-21
    Supremely true each to its separate self, [Re-state 146-11
    To tick it, tock it, turn it true, [MBG 166-10
    Its true appearances there, sun's green, [MBG 177-3
    The true abstract in which he promenades. [Thought 185-12
    On human heads. True, birds rebuild [Cuisine 227-14
    That are paper days. The false and true are one. [Extracts 253-3
    True autumn stands then in the doorway. [Hero 280-22
    True transfigurers fetched out of the human mountain, [Choc 300-6
    True genii for the diminished, spheres, [Choc 300-7
    Softly let all true sympathizers come, [EM 317-4
    It is true there were other mothers, singular [EM 321-23
    The will demands that what he thinks be true? [EM 323-11
    Demands. It accepts whatever is as true, [EM 323-21
    Belief, that what it believes in is not true. [Pure 332-12
    Sit in the room. It is true in the moonlight [Debris 338-3
    Come true, a point in the fire of music where [Descrip 341-9
    And is it true that what they said, as they fell, [Liadoff 347-1
    And no true tree, [Analysis 348-7
    The scholar to whom his book is true, to whom [House Q 358-14
    Blue-strutted curule, true--unreal, [Human 363-14
    Changed his true flesh to an inhuman bronze. [NSF 391-19
    It is true. Tonight the lilacs magnify [NSF 394-22
    Like a book on rising beautiful and true [AA 418-15
    He wishes that all hard poetry were true. [Papini 447-2
    True nothing, yet accosted self to self. [Bouquet 449-18
    Become a single being, sure and true. [Pecul 454-9
    Things not yet true which he perceives through truth, [NH 478-16
    If it should be true that reality exists [NH 485-19
    The speech of truth in its true solitude, [Aug 490-20
    And breaths as true [Lulu G 26-21 P
    Does she will to be proud? True, you may love [Red Kit 31-17 P
    To the tense, the maudlin, true meridian [Burnshaw 52-15 P
    Beheld the truth and knew it to be true. [Greenest 54-18 P
    True, only an inch, but an inch at a time, and inch [Duck 60-19 P
    He thinks and it is not true. The man below [Sombre 66-19 P
    Imagines and it is true, as if he thought [Sombre 66-20 P
    The statue stands in true perspective. Crows [Sombre 71-2 P
    True, things are people as they are. [Stan MBG 73-18 P
    In more than phrase? There's the true masculine, [Bship 79-12 P
    And true. The good, the strength, the sceptre moves [Bship
    80-21 P
    Of attributes, naked of myth, true, [Stan Hero 84-11 P
    Not true to this or that, but true, knows [Stan Hero 84-12 P
    Is its true form? Is it the memory [Recit 86-22 P
    It is true that you live on this rock [Including 88-7 P
    It is true that there are thoughts [Including 88-9 P
    The true tone of the metal of winter in what it says: [Discov
    96-6 P
    The only access to true ease, [Ulysses 100-3 P
    This is the true creator, the waver [Ulysses 100-18 P
    To the chatter that is then the true legend, [Ulysses 102-16 P
    Some true interior to which to return, [Letters 107-5 P
    Well, it is true of maxims. [Three 129-8 P
    Yes: it is true of maxims, [Three 129-12 P
    Just as it is true of poets, [Three 129-13 P
    It would be true [Three 133-5 P
    And yet it may be true [Three 133-13 P
    Not true, nor think it, less. He must defy [Someone 84-5 A
    Like the true light of the truest sun, the true [Someone 84-9 A
TRUER. Deeper than a truer ditty [Orangeade 103-18
TRUEST. Almost as the tenderest and the truest part. [AA 420-3
    Like the true light of the truest sun, the true [Someone 84-9 A
TRULY. And there I found myself more truly and more strange.
    [Hoon 65-18
    May truly bear its heroic fortunes [Hero 281-4
    Stands truly. The circles nearest to it share [Anach 366-9
    How truly they had not been what they were. [Cats 368-10
    To see their lustre truly as it is [Owl 432-21
    Which of these truly contains the world? [Indigo 22-13 P
TRUMPED. Of loyal conjuration trumped. The wind [Sea Surf 102-11
TRUMPET. Against his pipping sounds a trumpet cried [C 29-21
    A trumpet round the trees. Could one say that it was [Horn 230-6
    The trumpet of morning blows in the clouds and through [Cred
    376-16
    Than sharp, illustrious scene. The trumpet cries [Cred 376-19
    To share the day. The trumpet supposes that [Cred 377-1
    Of breath, obedient to his trumpet's touch. [AA 415-19
    Like a trumpet and says, in this season of memory, [Puel 456-11
TRUMPETED. Much trumpeted, made desperately clear, [C 30-26
TRUMPETEER. And headsman and trumpeteer and feather [Stan Hero
    84-20 P
TRUMPETERS. Great choristers, propounders of hymns, trumpeters,
    [Luther 461-7

TRUMPETING. A source of trumpeting seraphs in the eye, [Orb 442-23
TRUMPETS. Massive drums and leaden trumpets. [Nightgown 214-11
  Either trumpets or drums, the commanders mute, the arms [Martial
    238-1
  Led the emperor astray, the tom trumpets [Hero 278-7
  In solitude the trumpets of solitude [NSF 392-16
  And beads and bangles of gold and trumpets raised, [Greenest
    56-11 P
  The oracular trumpets round and roundly hooped, [Greenest 56-19 P
TRUNDLE. To trundle children like the sea? For you, [Duck 61-4 P
TRUNK. Beyond relation to the parent trunk: [Red Fern 365-10
TRUNKS. Have arms without hands. They have trunks [Possum 293-18
  The trunks of the trees are hollow. [Primordia 8-10 P
TRUTH. This trivial trope reveals a way of truth. [Monocle 16-4
  The truth is that there comes a time [Sad Gay 121-8
  From truth and not from satire on our lives. [Nigger 154-5
  And the truth, Dichtung und Wahrheit, all [MBG 177-17
  Where was it one first heard of the truth? The the. [Dump 203-11
  "There is no such thing as the truth," [On Road 203-13
  But they are not parts of a truth." [On Road 203-18
  But not the truth"; [On Road 204-8
  Escaped from the truth, the morning is color and mist, [Freed
    204-18
  This proves nothing. Just one more truth, one more [Connois
    216-2
  The truth must be [Poem Morn 219-12
  It was not as if the truth lay where he thought, [Landsc 242-3
  But as truth to be accepted, he supposed [Landsc 242-18
  A truth beyond all truths. [Landsc 242-19
  That he might be truth, himself, or part of it, [Landsc 242-21
  And that if nothing was the truth, then all [Landsc 242-30
  Things were the truth, the world itself was the truth. [Landsc
    242-31
  Spring is the truth of spring or nothing, a waste, a fake. [Holi-
    day 313-2
  Truth's favors sonorously exhibited. [EM 321-11
  To accomplish the truth in his intelligence. [EM 321-22
  And the world was calm. The truth in a calm world, [House Q
    359-1
  The rock cannot be broken. It is the truth. [Cred 375-11
  A hermit's truth nor symbol in hermitage. [Cred 375-16
  In the uncertain light of single, certain truth, [NSF 380-7
  Are the ravishments of truth, so fatal to [NSF 381-19
  The truth itself, the first idea becomes [NSF 381-20
  The truth depends on a walk around a lake, [NSF 386-3
  Enormous, in a completing of his truth. [Roses 431-3
  Each truth is a sect though no bells ring for it. [Luther 462-1
  Then, ancientest saint ablaze with ancientest truth, [NH 467-3
  The truth about themselves, having lost, as things, [NH 470-7
  Things not yet true which he perceives through truth, [NH 478-16
  The speech of truth in its true solitude, [Aug 490-20
  Of the truth of Death-- [Soldat 16-9 P
  The truth in nature to espy [Room Gard 41-8 P
  Beheld the truth and knew it to be true. [Greenest 54-18 P
  Perennial doctrine and most florid truth; [Duck 63-10 P
  Of truth. They stride across and are masters of [Role 93-8 P
  He has nothing but the truth to leave. [Ulysses 103-10 P
  It is the fate that dwells in truth. [Ulysses 103-29 P
  That raises the question of the image's truth. [Myth 118-10 P
  Made subtle by truth's most jealous subtlety, [Someone 84-8 A
  But now a habit of the truth had formed [Someone 85-8 A
  Of there, where the truth was not the respect of one, [Someone
    85-11 A
  Because the incredible, also, has its truth, [Someone 85-15 A
TRUTHS. "There are many truths, [On Road 203-17
  Element in the immense disorder of truths. [Connois 216-3
  But suppose the disorder of truths should ever come [Connois
    216-7
  A truth beyond all truths. [Landsc 242-19
  In which the litter of truths becomes [Ulysses 102-7 P
TRYING. Reminding, trying to remind, of a white [AA 412-10
  Is a memorizing, a trying out, to keep. [Aug 489-19
TUB. One boy swims under a tub, one sits [Vari 235-16
TUBAS. Begat the tubas and the fire-wind strings, [NSF 398-14
TUBS. Two wooden tubs of blue hydrangeas stand at the foot of the
    stone steps. [Banal 62-11
TUCK. Tuck, tuck, while the flamingoes flapped his bays. [C 38-20
  Tuck in the straw, [Abnormal 24-17 P
TUFT. That tuft of jungle feathers, [Gubbinal 85-6
  Shall tuft the commonplace. [Archi 17-19 P
  Its tuft of emerald that is real, for all [Someone 85-16 A
TUFT-EARED. Owls warn me and with tuft-eared watches keep [Souls
    94-18 P
TUFTED. Tufted, tilted, twirled, and twisted. [Orangeade 103-12
  Instead there was this tufted rock [How Live 125-17
  The agate in the eye, the tufted ear, [Nigger 153-19
  And tufted in straggling thunder and shattered sun. [Dwarf 208-8
  Of our passionate height. He wears a tufted green, [Repet 309-23
  This husk of Cuba, tufted emerald, [Someone 83-7 A
TUFTS. Among the purple tufts, the scarlet crowns, [C 32-4

Great tufts, spring up from buried houses [EM 322-15
TUGGED. Patted his stove-pipe hat and tugged his shawl. [Geneva
    24-3
TUGGING. Tugging at banks, until they seemed [Frogs 78-2
TULIPS. Of the pans above the stove, the pots on the table, the
    tulips among them. [Large 423-15
  Or gaudy as tulips? [Archi 17-8 P
TULPEHOCKEN. The cool sun of the Tulpehocken refers [Extraord
    369-10
TUM. An earthier one, tum, tum-ti-tum, [Botanist 2 136-9
TUMBLE. People fall out of windows, trees tumble down. [Chaos
    357-13
  The new spring tumble in the sky. [Sat Night 27-19 P
  The heads are severed, topple, tumble, tip [Burnshaw 51-31 P
TUMBLED. Severed and tumbled into seedless grass, [Burnshaw 49-14P
TUMBLER. Stood by him when the tumbler fell, [Sat Night 28-2 P
TUMBLERS. Is like ten thousand tumblers tumbling down [Cred 376-25
TUMBLES. The sea, a strength that tumbles everywhere, [Two V 354-12
TUMBLING. More exquisite than any tumbling verse: [C 37-3
  Ten thousand, men hewn and tumbling, [Thunder 220-2
  Is like ten thousand tumblers tumbling down [Cred 376-25
  Was meant to stand, not in a tumbling green, [Greenest 57-3 P
TUM-TI-TUM. Tum-ti-tum [Ploughing 20-13
  An earthier one, tum, tum-ti-tum, [Botanist 2 136-9
TUMULT. We stand in the tumult of a festival. [AA 415-21
  In the tumult of integrations out of the sky, [Look 518-12
TUMULTOUS. Its edges were taken from tumultous wind [Greenest
    56-29 P
TUMULTUOUSLY. The clouds tumultuously bright [MBG 169-4
TUNE. A tune beyond us, yet ourselves, [MBG 165-8
  A tune upon the blue guitar [MBG 165-9
  A tune beyond us as we are, [MBG 167-15
  Ourselves in the tune as if in space, [MBG 167-17
  The tune is space. The blue guitar [MBG 168-6
  Except this hidalgo and his eye and tune, [NH 483-20
TUNED. Pitiless verse? A few words tuned [Chateau 161-15
  And tuned and tuned and tuned. [Chateau 161-16
  Of aphonies, tuned in from zero and [Montra 260-14
  See well-tuned.
TUNES. A mumbling at the elbow, turgid tunes, [Sombre 67-10 P
TUNK-A-TUNK-TUNK. Such tink and tank and tunk-a-tunk-tunk, [High-
    Toned 59-18
TUNNEL. The first car out of a tunnel en voyage [Armor 530-2
TURBAN. At the red turban [Sugar-Cane 12-18
  No turban walks across the lessened floors. [Plain 502-16
TURBANED. See turquoise-turbaned.
TURBANS. It is turbans they wear [Cortege 80-16
TURBULENCE. Dejected his manner to the turbulence. [C 29-12
TURBULENT. Supple and turbulent, a ring of men [Sunday 69-28
  But though the turbulent tinges undulate [Bird Claws 82-13
  The darkness shattered, turbulent with foam. [Farewell 118-16
  There are potential seemings turbulent [Descrip 341-1
  Lascar, is there a body, turbulent [Two V 354-1
  And Ludwig Richter, turbulent Schlemihl, [Chaos 358-1
TURGID. The breath of turgid summer, and [Frogs 78-5
  The vivid, florid, turgid sky, [MBG 169-1
  A mumbling at the elbow, turgid tunes, [Sombre 67-10 P
TURK. Abhorring Turk as Esquimau, the lute [C 38-9
TURKEY. In the land of turkeys in turkey weather [Mice 123-1
TURKEY-COCK. The turkey-cock's tail [Ploughing 20-3
  The turkey-cock's tail [Ploughing 20-15
TURKEYS. In the land of turkeys in turkey weather [Mice 123-1
TURN. Is breathless to attend each quirky turn. [Monocle 15-13
  One might in turn become less diffident, [Pharynx 96-13
  The nakedness would rise and suddenly turn [Sea Surf 101-16
  So little, too little to care, to turn [Adieu 128-1
  And re-illumines things that used to turn [Sun March 133-15
  Turn dry, [Gray 140-16
  To tick it, tock it, turn it true, [MBG 166-10
  That turn into fishes and leap [Vari 232-13
  And who, for that, turn toward the cocks [Adequacy 244-5
  To have satisfied the mind and turn to see, [Extracts 257-22
  And turn to look and say there is no more [Extracts 257-24
  Turn back to where we were when we began: [AA 420-13
  A hand of light to turn the page, [Aug 492-9
  Apparels of such lightest look that a turn [Angel 497-9
  O chère maman, another, who, in turn, [Soldat 14-5 P
  Then turn your heads and let your spiral eyes [Red Kit 31-27 P
  Give up dead things and the living turn away. [Burnshaw 49-6 P
  To touch the grass and, as you circle, turn [Burnshaw 51-12 P
  A change, until the waterish ditherings turn [Burnshaw 52-14 P
  And the shoulders turn, breathing immense intent. [Sombre 68-27 P
  Its wheel begins to turn. [Sombre 71-6 P
  At night, to turn away from the abominable [Sombre 71-20 P
TURNED. Turned in the room, [Domination 8-11
  Turned in the fire, [Domination 9-7
  Turned in the loud fire, [Domination 9-9
  Turned from their want, and, nonchalant, [Ord Women 10-18
  Distorted by hale fatness, turned grotesque. [Monocle 16-8
  Because he turned to salad-beds again? [C 41-21

Turned Vincentine, [Vincentine 53-16
Turned heavenly Vincentine, [Vincentine 53-17
Turned heavenly, heavenly Vincentine. [Vincentine 53-19
She turned-- [Peter 91-9
It turned cold and silent. Then [Public Sq 109-9
The vetch has turned purple. But where is the bride? [Ghosts
  119-3
Turned tip and tip away, [Pascagoula 127-3
Why, when the singing ended and we turned [Key W 130-4
The cats had cats and the grass turned gray [MBG 178-16
The grass turned green and the grass turned gray. [MBG 178-18
The people that turned off and came [Adequacy 243-13
Blue's last transparence as it turned to black, [Choc 297-13
And, being straw, turned green, lived backward, shared [Liadoff
  347-9
Once more he turned to that which could not be fixed. [Two V
  353-11
The world has turned to the several speeds of glass, [Bouquet
  449-5
Turned para-thing, the rudiments in the jar, [Bouquet 452-7
Suppose it turned out to be or that it touched [Golden 460-8
That which was public green turned private gray. [NH 479-1
What was real turned into something most unreal, [NH 483-23
But folded over, turned round." It was the same, [NH 487-4
He turned from the tower to the house, [Aug 493-9
Otu-bre's lion-roses have turned to paper [Plant 506-5
Even when the book lay turned in the dust of his table. [Poem
  Mt 512-4
"Oh, lissomeness turned lagging ligaments!" [Stan MMO 19-20 P
The golden clouds that turned to bronze, the sounds [Old Woman
  44-7 P
Basilewsky's bulged before it floated, turned [Duck 63-23 P
Don Juan turned furious divinity, [Duck 64-27 P
The cycle of the solid having turned. [Sombre 68-16 P
Blew against them or bowed from the hips, when I turned [Bship
  78-17 P
TURNING. Turning in the wind. [Domination 8-13
  Turning in the wind, [Domination 8-19
  Turning in the wind, [Domination 9-5
  Turning as the flames [Domination 9-6
  Turning as the tails of the peacocks [Domination 9-8
  Turning in the wind. [Domination 9-16
  Turning, bedizened, [Sugar-Cane 12-14
  Green barbarism turning paradigm. [C 31-22
  And then retirement like a turning back [C 35-11
  Of green blooms turning crisped the motley hue [Sea Surf 102-12
  Of a turning spirit in an earlier self. [Sun March 134-1
  Turning in time to Brahms as alternate [Anglais 149-6
  It observes the effortless weather turning blue [NSF 382-7
  Men turning into things, as comedy, [NH 470-5
  A turning down toward finality-- [Plant 506-15
  To embrace autumn, without turning [Secret Man 36-3 P
  The whole of them turning black; [Agenda 42-9 P
TURNINGS. Drifting choirs, long movements and turnings of sounds.
  [Sick 90-12 P
TURNIP. The world, a turnip once so readily plucked, [C 45-12
TURNS. On the hill, but turns [Cortege 80-8
  Turns to its own figurations and declares, [Rhythms 246-3
  Turns blue and on its empty table [Hero 280-20
  At last, there, when it turns out to be here. [Crude 305-20
  The man who is walking turns blankly on the sand. [AA 412-23
  But she that he loved turns cold at his light touch. [Pecul
  453-12
  Where Time, in fitful turns, [Phases 5-21 P
  Of a time to come--A shade of horror turns [Duck 65-8 P
  He turns us into scholars, studying [Sombre 67-21 P
TURQUOISE. Without blue, without any turquoise tint or phase,
  [Landsc 241-18
  And the irregular turquoise, part, the perceptible blue [Landsc
  242-23
  Dropped down from turquoise leaves. In the landscape of [EM 318-13
  The chain of the turquoise hen and sky [Silent 359-16
  A turquoise monster moving round. [Silent 360-3
  With garbled green. These were the planter's turquoise [NSF 393-5
  Turquoise the rock, at odious evening bright [Rock 528-7
  Blanche, the blonde, whose eyes are not wholly straight, in a
    room of lustres, shed by turquoise falling, [Piano 22-1 P
TURQUOISED. Silent and turquoised and perpetual, [Burnshaw 50-15 P
TURQUOISE-TURBANED. And the sea as turquoise-turbaned Sambo, neat
  [Sea Surf 102-7
TURTLE. Then the stale turtle will grow limp from age. [John 437-22
  The locust's titter and the turtle's sob. [Sombre 71-1 P
TUSKS. The tusks of the elephant, [Parasol 20-8 P
TUTOYERS. Now, the first tutoyers of tragedy [Beginning 428-7
TWANG. I know my lazy, leaden twang [MBG 169-9
  I twang it out and leave it there. [MBG 169-12
  Sighing that he should leave the banjo's twang. [NSF 393-21
  And twang nobler notes [Demoiselle 23-8 P
  This is a thing to twang a philosopher's sleep, [Bship 79-31 P
TWANGED. That by resemblance twanged him through and through, [Owl

433-3
TWANGING. A metaphysician in the dark, twanging [Of Mod 240-14
  An instrument, twanging a wiry string that gives [Of Mod 240-15
  An apparition, twanging instruments [Duck 63-18 P
TWEEDLE-DEE. Rich Tweedle-dum, poor Tweedle-dee. [Nigger 154-13
TWEEDLE-DUM. Rich Tweedle-dum, poor Tweedle-dee. [Nigger 154-13
TWELVE. Of a cat, twelve dollars for the devil, [Hero 275-9
  As if twelve princes sat before a king. [Cred 375-25
  With six meats and twelve wines or else without [NSF 407-16
  Inwoven by a weaver to twelve bells . . . [Beginning 428-5
  At twelve, the disintegration of afternoon [What We 459-7
  At twelve, as green as ever they would be. [What We 459-11
  Twelve meant as much as: the end of normal time, [What We 459-13
  Twelve and the first gray second after, a kind [What We 459-16
  The propounding of four seasons and twelve months. [NH 473-14
TWELVE-LEGGED. Twelve-legged in her ancestral hells, [Oak 272-8
TWENTY. Twenty men crossing a bridge, [Magnifico 19-1
  Are twenty men crossing twenty bridges, [Magnifico 19-3
  Into twenty villages, [Magnifico 19-4
  Twenty men crossing a bridge, [Magnifico 19-9
  Twenty men crossing a bridge [Magnifico 19-12
  Among twenty snowy mountains, [Thirteen 92-14
  For soldiers, the new moon stretches twenty feet. [Gigan 289-21
TWENTY-NINE. Are one. My window is twenty-nine three [Jersey 210-14
TWENTY-ONE. Born, as she was, at twenty-one, [Couch 295-6
TWICE. Compounded of dear relation, spoken twice, [EM 317-18
  He never felt twice the same about the flecked river, [Cata
  424-10
  Which kept flowing and never the same way twice, flowing [Cata
  424-11
TWIDDLING. But twiddling mon idée, as old men will, [Stan MMO 19-4 P
TWILIGHT. And the palms and the twilight. [Infanta 7-12
  In the twilight wind. [Domination 8-20
  Was it a cry against the twilight [Domination 9-3
  The twilight overfull [Delight 162-8
  We shall return at twilight from the lecture [NSF 406-23
  These actors still walk in a twilight muttering lines. [NH 479-23
TWILIGHTS. The twilights of the mythy goober khan. [Havana 142-21
TWINNING. Twinning our phantasy and our device, [Anatomy 108-11
TWIRLED. Tufted, tilted, twirled, and twisted. [Orangeade 103-12
  And that-a-way he twirled the thing. [MBG 178-12
TWIST. So epical a twist, catastrophe [Duck 65-25 P
TWISTED. Tufted, tilted, twirled, and twisted. [Orangeade 103-12
  Not twisted, stooping polymathic Z, [NH 469-8
  On urns and oak-leaves twisted into rhyme. [Sombre 68-1 P
  A shape, the vista twisted and burning, a thing [Bship 80-5 P
TWISTING. Twisting among the universal spaces, [Degen 444-15
TWISTINGS. And the eccentric twistings of the rapt bouquet [Bou-
  quet 450-20
TWITCHING. Twitching a little with crude souvenirs [Duck 64-23 P
TWITTER. Birds twitter pandemoniums around [Antag 426-3
TWITTERING. Their intelligible twittering [Hermit 505-20
TWIXT. The choice twixt dove and goose is over-close. [Spaniard
  35-6 P
TWO. Like the clashed edges of two words that kill." [Monocle 13-4
  Two golden gourds distended on our vines, [Monocle 16-6
  The laughing sky will see the two of us [Monocle 16-10
  Came like two spirits parleying, adorned [C 31-31
  An up and down between two elements, [C 35-7
  Two wooden tubs of blue hydrangeas stand at the foot of the
    stone steps. [Banal 62-11
  Its two webs. [Tattoo 81-14
  "Two Figures in Dense Violet Night" [85-title
  Of the two dreams, night and day, [Watermelon 89-1
  And heaven rolled as one and from the two [Sea Surf 102-14
  "Two at Norfolk" [111-title
  And these two never meet in the air so full of summer [Norfolk
  111-20
  And the two of them standing still to rest. [How Live 126-4
  And you. Only we two may interchange [Re-state 146-4
  Only we two are one, not you and night, [Re-state 146-6
  By dividing the number of legs one sees by two. [Nigger 157-9
  Lighting a pitiless verse or two. [Chateau 161-12
  Two things, the two together as one, [MBG 175-11
  To this returns. Between the two, [MBG 176-17
  To come, a wrangling of two dreams. [MBG 183-19
  "Study of Two Pears" [196-title
  One of many, between two poles. So, [Glass 197-10
  I heard two workers say, "This chaos [Idiom 200-18
  We were two figures in a wood. [On Road 203-21
  Two things are one. (Pages of illustrations.) [Connois 215-3
  This great world, it divides itself in two, [Dezem 218-6
  The two alike, distinguish blues, [Vari 235-2
  In an emotion as of two people, as of two [Of Mod 240-12
  Two people, three horses, an ox [Les Plus 245-1
  One of the sacraments between two breaths, [Montra 262-8
  Between two neatly measured stations, [Hero 275-17
  Contrasting our two names, considered speech. [Phenom 287-16
  The soldier seeking his point between the two, [Repet 309-9
  Two beasts. But of the same kind--two conjugal beasts. [Jouga

337-5
Two beasts but two of a kind and then not beasts. [Jouga 337-9
Yet two not quite of a kind. It is like that here. [Jouga 337-10
"Two Tales of Liadoff" [346-title
"Two Versions of the Same Poem" [353-title
Between the two we live and die-- [Silent 359-6
These two by the stone wall [Burghers 362-4
A man and a woman, like two leaves [Burghers 362-12
Two coins were lying--dos centavos. [Attempt 370-21
The two things compared their tight resemblances: [Past Nun
   379-2
These two go well together, the sinuous brim [Pastor 380-2
Two things of opposite natures seem to depend [NSF 392-4
And sun and rain a plural, like two lovers [NSF 392-14
And scattered them about, no two alike. [NSF 400-24
She lived in her house. She had two daughters, one [NSF 402-1
Yet it depends on yours. The two are one. [NSF 407-10
Two parallels that meet if only in [NSF 407-12
By her coming became a freedom of the two, [AA 419-17
An isolation which only the two could share. [AA 419-18
We are two that use these roses as we are, [Roses 431-10
Two forms move among the dead, high sleep [Owl 431-13
Two brothers. And a third form, she that says [Owl 431-16
Two bodies disembodied in their talk, [NH 471-8
The two romanzas, the distant and the near, [NH 481-2
A note or two disclosing who it was. [NH 483-18
Real and unreal are two in one: New Haven [NH 485-23
The two worlds are asleep, are sleeping, now. [Old Man 501-1
Beyond, the two alike in the make of the mind. [Rome 508-7
Two parallels become one, a perspective, of which [Rome 508-9
Yet living in two worlds, impenitent [Rome 509-20
"Two Illustrations that the World is What you Make of It" [513-
   title
Two in a deep-founded sheltering, friend and dear friend. [World
   521-3
The two kept beating together. It was only day. [World 521-12
A theorem proposed between the two-- [Rock 525-16
Two figures in a nature of the sun, [Rock 525-17
Are you two boatmen [Primordia 9-5 P
Is mother to the two of us, and more, [Soldat 14-6 P
Neither one, nor the two together. [Indigo 22-14 P
Are two quite different things, in particular [Lytton 39-8 P
Sing rose-beliefs. Above that urn two lights [Burnshaw 50-1 P
In an autumn afternoon, but two immense [Burnshaw 50-4 P
For the million, perhaps, two ducks instead of one; [Duck 65-2 P
For a moment, once each century or two, [Duck 65-20 P
Once each century or two. But then so great, [Duck 65-24 P
An eighteenth century fern or two [Stan MBG 72-7 P
We two share that at least. [Grotesque 76-6 P
The words of winter in which these two will come together, [Sick
   90-16 P
"Two Letters" [107-title P
Shadows, woods . . . and the two of them in speech, [Letters
   108-2 P
And the two poles continue to maintain it [Art Pop 112-16 P
See and-a-two.
TWO-LIGHT. In a well-rosed two-light [Inhab 504-8
TYRANNY. Rain is an unbearable tyranny. Sun is [Extracts 252-21
TYRIAN. Some pebbly-chewer practiced in Tyrian speech, [Duck 63-17P

UBERMENSCHLICHKEIT. If it were lost in Übermenschlichkeit, [Sur-
   prises 98-8
UBIQUITOUS. Ubiquitous concussion, slap and sigh, [C 28-20
  By his presence, the seat of his ubiquitous will. [Greenest
   59-32 P
UGLINESS. And nothing is left but comic ugliness [EM 320-21
UGLY. The world is ugly, [Gubbinal 85-4
  The world is ugly, [Gubbinal 85-12
  But the ugly alien, the mask that speaks [Nigger 156-17
  Of ugly, subconscious time, in which [Analysis 348-5
  Full of their ugly lord, [Pediment 361-19
  And against the most coiled thorn, have seized on what was ugly
   [Large 424-3
  In their ugly reminders? [Archi 17-7 P
  Ugly as an idea, not beautiful [Burnshaw 47-7 P
  Nor ugly, [Three 133-16 P
ULTIMATE. That know the ultimate Plato, [Homunculus 27-4
  The ultimate elegance: the imagined land. [Uruguay 250-5
  Sure that the ultimate poem was the mind, [Extracts 256-22
  The ultimate good, sure of a reality [EM 324-16
  "Sketch of the Ultimate Politician" [335-title
  "The Ultimate Poem Is Abstract" [429-title
  Was the whiteness that is the ultimate intellect, [Owl 433-20
  The world imagined is the ultimate good. [Final 524-3
  Wasted in what would be an ultimate waste, [Red Kit 30-21 P
  The ultimate one, though they are parts of it. [Bship 80-27 P
ULULALU. "Olu" the enunchs cried. "Ululalu." [Lulu G 26-23 P
ULULATE. She made the eunuchs ululate. [Lulu G 26-13 P
ULULATION. With continual ululation. [Lulu G 26-18 P
ULYSSES. Is it Ulysses that approaches from the east, [World 520-11
  But was it Ulysses? Or was it only the warmth of the sun [World
   521-10
  It was Ulysses and it was not. Yet they had met, [World 521-13
  "The Sail of Ulysses" [99-title P
  Under the shape of his sail, Ulysses, [Ulysses 99-10 P
  The great sail of Ulysses seemed, [Ulysses 105-7 P
  Under the shape of his sail, Ulysses, [Presence 105-13 P
  The sharp sail of Ulysses seemed, [Presence 106-7 P
UMBER. Let purple Phoebus lie in umber harvest, [NSF 381-8
  Let Phoebus slumber and die in autumn umber, [NSF 381-9
UMBILICAL. Spring is umbilical or else it is not spring. [Holiday
   313-1
UMBRELLAS. And gilt umbrellas. Paradisal green [Sea Surf 99-2
  And sham umbrellas. And a sham-like green [Sea Surf 99-20
  And pied umbrellas. An uncertain green, [Sea Surf 100-14
  And frail umbrellas. A too-fluent green [Sea Surf 101-8
  And large umbrellas. And a motley green [Sea Surf 102-2
  Like umbrellas in Java. [Tea 113-3
  Are like wrecked umbrellas. [Plant 506-7
UNABLE. To face the weather and be unable to tell [Extracts 257-7
  Returned, unable to die again, fated [Extracts 258-26
  To evil after death, unable to die [Extracts 259-4
  In one's heart and wished as he had always wished, unable [Bed
   327-2
UNACCOMPLISHED. Those that are left are the unaccomplished, [Leben
   504-19
UNACCOUNTABLE. Are to the unaccountable prophet or [Hero 274-17
UNACCUSTOMED. Had left in them only a brilliance, of unaccustomed
   origin, [Prol 515-11
UNAFFECTED. An unaffected man in a negative light [NSF 393-19
UNALTERABLE. Himself, the unalterable necessity [EM 324-6
  Of being this unalterable animal. [EM 324-7
UNAPPROACHABLE. The dominant blank, the unapproachable. [NH 477-16
UNATTAINED. And unattained, [Analysis 349-3
UNAVOIDABLE. From the unavoidable shadow of himself [C 29-29
UNBEARABLE. Rain is an unbearable tyranny. Sun is [Extracts 252-21
UNBELIEVER. At the unbeliever's touch. Cloud-cloisters blow
   [Greenest 58-10 P
UNBLOTCHING. Blotched out beyond unblotching. Crispin, [C 28-6
UNBRAIDED. And halidom for the unbraided femes, [C 43-27
UNBROKEN. Of winter, in the unbroken circle [Celle 438-10
  And darken it, make an unbroken mat [Red Kit 31-24 P
UNBURGHERLY. In an unburgherly apocalypse. [Geneva 24-14
UNCERTAIN. And pied umbrellas. An uncertain green, [Sea Surf 100-14
  His spirit grew uncertain of delight, [Anglais 148-15
  Illustrious intimations--uncertain love, [Myrrh 350-8
  Of the obvious whole, uncertain particles [Man Car 351-1
  In the uncertain light of single, certain truth, [NSF 380-7
  Or mind, uncertain in the clearest bells, [NH 466-17
  I am uncertain whether the perception [Lytton 39-11 P
  Uncertain certainty, Apollo [Ulysses 101-5 P
UNCERTAINLY. That lives uncertainly and not for long [Nigger 155-18
  Still keep occurring. What is, uncertainly, [NH 482-13
UNCERTAINTY. Certain of its uncertainty, in which [Anglais 148-16
  The eye made clear of uncertainty, with the sight [NH 471-19
UNCHANGED. The man in the black wood descends unchanged. [Degen
   444-11
UNCHANGING. Unchanging, yet so like our perishing earth, [Sunday

   69-16
UNCIVIL. 12. An uncivil shape like a gigantic haw. [Someone 86-15A
UNCLIPPED. With tongues unclipped and throats so stuffed with
   thorns, [Greenest 57-19 P
UNCLOUDED. The unclouded concerto . . . [Mozart 132-6
UNCONFINED. The little confine soon unconfined [Ulysses 103-20 P
UNCONSCIONABLE. But note the unconscionable treachery of fate,
   [Monocle 17-9
UNCONSCIOUS. A repetition of unconscious things, [Vari 232-9
  Or seeing the spent, unconscious shapes of night, [Feo 334-7
  And sends us, winged by an unconscious will, [NSF 382-16
UNCONSOLED. That dark companion left him unconsoled [Anglais 148-17
UNCOURAGEOUS. And uncourageous genesis . . . It seems [EM 315-24
UNCREATED. Like a phantom, in an uncreated night. [Landsc 242-4
UNCRUMPLE. Shall I uncrumple this much-crumpled thing? [Monocle
   13-16
UNCTUOUS. Unctuous furrows, [Primordia 9-7 P
UNDECIPHERED. To-night, night's undeciphered murmuring [Montra
   261-1
UNDER. Under the rainbows: [Sugar-Cane 12-11
  Under the rainbows [Sugar-Cane 12-12
  And storming under multitudinous tones [C 28-15
  Sealed pensive purple under its concern. [C 40-20
  A creeper under jaunty leaves. And fourth, [C 44-21
  It crawls under your eyelids [Tattoo 81-12
  But this gross blue under rolling bronzes [Grapes 110-15
  It is the same jingle of the water among the roots under the
   banks of the palmettoes, [Indian 112-5
  Key West sank downward under massive clouds [Farewell 117-3
  And doesn't get under way. [Sailing 120-3
  Arranged under the stony clouds [Gray 140-6
  Under muddy skies. [Mud 147-15
  Under the mat of frost and over the mat of clouds. [Nigger 151-4
  Below me, on the asphalt, under the trees. [Loaf 200-12
  Under the eglantine [Anything B 211-1
  Shells under water. These were nougats. [Forces 229-15
  One boy swims under a tub, one sits [Vari 235-16
  Snow under the trees and on the northern rocks, [Extracts 255-15
  Yet a spider spins in the left shoe under the bed-- [Phenom
   286-10
  You like it under the trees in autumn, [Motive 288-1
  And late wanderers creeping under the barb of night, [Dutch
   291-24
  Under the arches, over the arches, in arcs [Dutch 293-8
  There were others like him safely under roof: [Choc 299-23
  Say yes, spoken because under every no [EM 320-13
  Yet, under the migrations to solitude, [Wild 329-4
  Under Tinicum or small Cohansey, [New Set 353-5
  It is not a voice that is under the eaves. [Silent 359-18
  Under the white clouds piled and piled [Woman Song 360-10
  She hid them under simple names. She held [NSF 402-8
  Say, a flippant communication under the moon. [AA 418-3
  Under the buttonwoods, beneath a moon nailed fast. [Cata 425-5
  To be a bronze man breathing under archaic lapis, [Cata 425-10
  Cold with an under impotency that they know, [Bouquet 449-9
  Under the birds, among the perilous owls, [NH 474-17
  In mud under ponds, where the sky used to be reflected. [NH
   487-15
  Under the sun-slides of a sloping mountain; [Aug 489-11
  Under its mattresses of vines. [Vacancy 511-13
  Hangs her quilt under the pine-trees. [Primordia 9-16 P
  I have been pupil under bishops' rods [Soldat 11-4 P
  Was under every temple-tone. You sang [Burnshaw 50-30 P
  Deep grass that totters under the weight of light. [Greenest
   55-1 P
  The clank of the carrousel and, under the trees, [Duck 62-25 P
  And never will, a subman under all [Sombre 66-14 P
  Maidens in bloom, bulls under sea, the lark [Sombre 67-33 P
  And head a shadow trampled under hoofs, [Sombre 70-28 P
  And the cheeks like flower-pots under her hair. [Grotesque
   74-16 P
  Under the shape of his sail, Ulysses, [Ulysses 99-10 P
  Under the middle stars, he said: [Ulysses 99-15 P
  Under the shape of his sail, Ulysses, [Presence 105-13 P
  In a burst of shouts, under the trees [Dinner 110-1 P
  Under the front of the westward evening star, [Real 110-12 P
  "Solitaire under the Oaks" [111-title P
  Under the oak trees, completely released. [Sol Oaks 111-10 P
  Under the wintry trees of the terrace. [Bus 116-14 P
  Or from under his mountains. [Myth 118-16 P
  Under the bones of time's philosophers? [Ideal 89-9 A
UNDERGROUND. Neither the golden underground, nor isle [Sunday 68-19
  Of the torches wisping in the underground, [MBG 167-4
  Phantoms, what have you left? What underground? [EM 320-2
  Underground, a king as candle by our beds [Owl 435-2
UNDERLIES. A blank underlies the trials of device, [NH 477-15
UNDERNEATH. "Jasmine's Beautiful Thoughts underneath the Willow"
   [79-title
  As an autumn ancient underneath the snow, [Nigger 154-2
  Underneath a willow there [Country 207-6

And lay beside her underneath the tree. [Hand 271-21
Beneath, far underneath, the surface of [NSF 403-1
Civil, madam, I am, but underneath [NSF 406-11
For a tidal undulation underneath. [Page 423-10
The satisfaction underneath the sense, [Papini 448-3
The chapel underneath St. Armorer's walls, [Armor 530-19
UNDER-SIDE. Any azure under-side or after-color. Nabob [Landsc 241-19
UNDERSTAND. Women understand this. [Theory 86-17
    Should understand. That he might suffer or that [EM 322-5
    That we do not need to understand, complete [Descrip 341-13
    And quickly understand, without their flesh, [Cats 368-9
    A passion that we feel, not understand. [NSF 392-11
    Will understand what it is to understand. [Papini 447-8
    They understand, and take on potency, [Bouquet 449-5
    To understand, as if to know became [Novel 459-5
    He could understand the things at home. [Aug 493-13
    War, too, although I do not understand. [Soldat 11-2 P
    You do not understand her evil mood. [Spaniard 34-1 P
    And to understand them. [Lytton 38-11 P
    How strange a thing it was to understand [Lytton 39-1 P
    And black by thought that could not understand [Old Woman 44-4 P
UNDERSTANDING. In my room, the world is beyond my understanding; [Of Surface 57-1
    With an understanding compounded by death [Lack 303-12
    Without understanding, out of the wall [Creat 310-12
    The months of understanding. The pediment [Pediment 362-2
    By an understanding that fulfils his age, [Cred 374-4
    Without understanding, he belongs to it [Bad Time 426-16
    As if its understanding was brown skin, [Rock 527-13
    I fear the understanding. [Lytton 38-16 P
    The understanding of heaven, would be bliss, [Lytton 38-20 P
    I had looked forward to understanding. Yet [Lytton 39-22 P
    An understanding may be troublesome. [Lytton 39-23 P
    An understanding beyond journalism, [Bus 116-12 P
UNDERSTANDS. One understands, in the intense disclosures [Lack 303-15
    X understands Aristotle [Grotesque 75-4 P
UNDERSTOOD. That was not ours although we understood, [Key W 128-16
    Things unintelligible, yet understood. [Nigger 156-18
    Accepted yet which nothing understood, [Choc 297-15
    And one trembles to be so understood and, at last, [Novel 459-4
    Or, if it understood, repressed itself [Old Woman 44-5 P
UNDERTAKER. The negro undertaker [Venereal 47-14
    With the undertaker: a voice in the clouds, [MBG 177-8
    Of the undertaker's song in the snow [MBG 177-12
UNDERWORLD. Or shapely fire: fire from an underworld, [Choc 297-22
UNDESCRIBED. Undescribed composition of the sugar-cone, [Someone 86-20 A
UNDETERMINED. An object the more, an undetermined form [Moonlight 531-14
UNDIVIDED. From ignorance, not an undivided whole, [Two V 355-10
UNDO. It will undo him. [Plot Giant 7-10
UNDRESSING. "The spring is like a belle undressing." [Of Surface 57-5
UNDULANT. When Swatara becomes this undulant river [Degen 444-20
UNDULATE. But though the turbulent tinges undulate [Bird Claws 82-13
    Must see her fans of silver undulate. [Nigger 152-20
UNDULATING. The criers, undulating the deep-oceaned phrase. [Tallap 71-12
UNDULATION. Be a place of perpetual undulation. [Solitaires 60-2
    Which is to be a place of perpetual undulation. [Solitaires 60-13
    In an enormous undulation fled. [Sea Surf 100-18
    For a tidal undulation underneath. [Page 423-10
UNDULATIONS. Ambiguous undulations as they sink, [Sunday 70-27
    Cadaverous undulations. Rest, old mould . . . [Two V 355-14
UNEASINESS. With the blank uneasiness which one might feel [EM 324-25
    Gives one a blank uneasiness, as if [EM 325-9
UNENDING. A face of stone in an unending red, [NSF 400-5
UNEXPECTED. The way a look or a touch reveals its unexpected magnitudes. [Prol 517-10
UNEXPLAINED. Where he would be complete in an unexplained completion: [Poem Mt 512-10
UNFAITHFUL. Who watched him, always, for unfaithful thought. [NH 483-15
UNFAMILIAR. Its unfamiliar, difficult fern, [Red Fern 365-3
    And unfamiliar escapades: whirroos [Orb 442-19
    Of an unfamiliar in the familiar room, [Novel 458-12
    And is tradition an unfamiliar sum, [Recit 87-9 P
UNFASHIONED. But our unfashioned spirits realized [Eve Angels 137-4
UNFOLDING. Unfolding in the water, feeling sure [Sea Surf 100-18
    The sea unfolding in the sunken clouds? [Sea Surf 100-20
UNFORESEEN. Was unforeseen. First Crispin smiled upon [C 44-10
UNFRETTED. Tall and unfretted, a figure meant to bear [Pastor 379-19
    Unfretted by day's separate, several selves, [NH 482-10
UNFUZZED. And who does not seek the sky unfuzzed, soaring to the princox? [Banal 63-5

UNHAPPINESS. Pour the unhappiness out [Weep Woman 25-1
UNHAPPY. And, being unhappy, talk of happiness [Extracts 257-13
    Unhappy about the sense of happiness. [Pure 331-9
    An unhappy people in a happy world-- [AA 420-4
    An unhappy people in an unhappy world-- [AA 420-6
    A happy people in an unhappy world-- [AA 420-8
    An unhappy people in a happy world. [AA 420-14
    In these unhappy he meditates a whole, [AA 420-22
    Unhappy love reveals vast blemishes. [Red Kit 31-19 P
    And take from this restlessly unhappy happiness [How Now 97-14 P
    That makes us happy or unhappy. [Of Mere 118-2 P
UNHERDED. The father fetches his unherded herds, [AA 415-17
UNIMAGINED. Upward, from unimagined coverts, fly. [Blanche 10-12 P
UNIMPORTANTLY. And, when detached, so unimportantly gone, [Bouquet 450-14
UNINTELLIGIBLE. Things unintelligible, yet understood. [Nigger 156-18
    At the centre of the unintelligible, [Aug 495-14
    For unintelligible thought. [Hermit 505-21
    Unintelligible absolution and an end-- [Rome 508-5
UNION. Union of the weakest develops strength [Nigger 158-10
    When was it that we heard the voice of union? [Aug 494-9
UNIQUE. The unique composure, harshest streakings joined [Owl 433-14
    Recognize his unique and solitary home. [Poem Mt 512-14
UNIQUENESS. Babbling, each one, the uniqueness of its sound. [Quiet 523-13
UNISON. Of music, as it comes to unison, [C 43-12
    In unison for the dead. [Cortege 80-5
    Waits for the unison of the music of the drifting bands [Sick 90-14 P
UNISONS. What unisons create in music. [Hero 280-4
UNITE. Will unite these figures of men and their shapes [Sad Gay 122-16
UNITED. "United Dames of America" [206-title
UNITED STATES. Walked the United States today, [News 264-8
UNITY. Of essential unity, is as pleasant as port, [Connois 215-10
    Of which one is a part as in a unity, [Yellow 236-18
    A unity that is the life one loves, [Yellow 236-19
    As the life of the fatal unity of war. [Yellow 236-21
    So great a unity, that it is bliss, [EM 317-8
    In an ever-changing, calmest unity, [Owl 433-13
UNIVERSAL. The basic slate, the universal hue. [Monocle 15-9
    Damned universal cock, as if the sun [Bantams 75-16
    That should import a universal pith [Havana 144-5
    In a world of universal poverty [Nigger 152-1
    In the universal intercourse. [MBG 177-6
    Of the nights, the actual, universal strength, [Repet 309-2
    Within the universal whole. The son [EM 324-3
    Touched suddenly by the universal flare [Pure 333-7
    Twisting among the universal spaces, [Degen 444-15
    The universal machine. There he perceived [Woman Had 82-8 P
    They are more than parts of the universal machine. [Woman Had 82-25 P
    Universal delusions of universal grandeurs, [Someone 87-7 A
UNIVERSE. Its generations that follow in their universe, [Somnam 304-11
    The universe that supplements the manqué, [Repet 309-8
    The spirit's universe, then a summer's day, [Descrip 343-16
    As of a general being or human universe. [Past Nun 378-22
    In a universe of inconstancy. This means [NSF 389-24
    In the anonymous color of the universe. [NH 470-22
    Creates a fresh universe out of nothingness by adding itself, [Prol 517-9
    A particular of being, that gross universe. [Rock 526-9
    The sameness of his various universe, [Moonlight 531-3
    The one moonlight, the various universe, intended [Moonlight 532-3
    A universe without life's limp and lack, [Theatre 91-16 P
    Is what one knows of the universe, [Ulysses 99-22 P
    They are nothing, except in the universe [Child 106-16 P
UNJUST. Themselves, the slightly unjust drawing that is [Extracts 254-23
    And the unjust, which in the midst of summer stops [AA 417-6
UNKEMPT. Ragged in unkempt perceptions, that stands [Theatre 91-8P
UNKEYED. Exchequering from piebald fiscs unkeyed, [C 43-7
UNKNOWABLE. Unknown as yet, unknowable, [Ulysses 101-4 P
UNKNOWN. The rotund emotions, paradise unknown. [EM 325-29
    The intentions of a mind as yet unknown, [Descrip 341-18
    Which in a composite season, now unknown, [John 437-18
    Of the unknown. The newsboys' muttering [Rome 508-18
    Within us hitherto unknown, he that [Duck 63-19 P
    The unnamed creator of an unknown sphere, [Ulysses 101-3 P
    Unknown as yet, unknowable, [Ulysses 101-4 P
    And unknown, inhuman for a little while, [Ulysses 105-5 P
UNLIKE. Our feigning with the strange unlike, whence springs [Fictive 88-12
    Seeming, at first, a beast disgorged, unlike, [NSF 404-7
    Unlike love in possession of that which was [NH 467-8
    As others have, and then, unlike the others, [Bship 77-23 P
    And inhuman same, the likeness of things unlike. [Conversat 109-2P

UNLIKELY. Are a woman's words, unlikely to satisfy [Nigger 157-15
UNLUCKY. Poets of pimpernel, unlucky pimps [Stan MMO 19-12 P
UNMAKE. What must unmake it and, at last, what can, [AA 418-2
UNMERCIFUL. Be glory to this unmerciful pontifex, [Greenest 60-3 P
UNMOVED. Her ear unmoved. She was that tortured one, [Old Woman
    44-9 P
UNMUDDLED. Only the unmuddled self of sleep, for them. [NSF 402-18
UNNAMED. Call it, once more, a river, an unnamed flowing, [R Conn
    533-18
    Of saints not heard of until now, unnamed, [Nuns 92-19 P
    The unnamed creator of an unknown sphere, [Ulysses 101-3 P
    There is one, unnamed, that broods [Child 106-14 P
UNOBSERVED. By an access of color, a new and unobserved, slight
    dithering, [Prol 517-2
UNPAINTED. The unpainted shore, accepts the world [Couch 296-4
UNPEOPLED. The peopled and the unpeopled. In both, he is [EM 323-6
    The unpeopled, there is his knowledge of himself. [EM 323-9
UNPERCEIVED. The knowledge of things lay round but unperceived:
    [Aug 493-18
UNPERPLEXED. Tragedy. This is destiny unperplexed, [EM 324-9
UNPREDICTABLE. Itself that seed's ripe, unpredictable fruit. [De-
    scrip 341-20
    Part of the unpredictable sproutings, as of [Nuns 92-8 P
UNPROPITIOUS. In a most unpropitious place. [Sailing 120-10
UNPROVOKED. A tree, this unprovoked sensation requires [NSF 406-12
UNPURGED. Unpurged by epitaph, indulged at last, [High-Toned 59-10
    Impure upon a world unpurged. [How Live 125-10
UNRAVELLING. It is not the unravelling of her yellow shift. [John
    437-6
    A few more hours of day, the unravelling [Nuns 92-12 P
UNREAL. Unreal, give back to us what once you gave: [Fictive 88-17
    Skims the real for its unreal, [Oak 272-15
    And I taste at the root of the tongue the unreal of what is real.
    [Holiday 313-10
    Blue-strutted curule, true--unreal, [Human 363-12
    Far in the woods they sang their unreal songs, [Cred 376-1
    Man's mind grown venerable in the unreal. [Cred 377-5
    The real made more acute by an unreal. [Bouquet 451-21
    A second that grows first, a black unreal [Novel 458-14
    Unreal today, be hidden and alive. [Novel 458-21
    Everything as unreal as real can be, [NH 468-18
    What was real turned into something most unreal, [NH 483-23
    If more unreal than New Haven, is not [NH 485-3
    A real ruler, but rules what is unreal." [NH 485-4
    Real and unreal are two in one: New Haven [NH 485-23
    He is the image, the second, the unreal, [Americana 94-9 P
    Unreal, as if nothing had been changed at all. [As Leave 117-14P
UNREALITY. Infected by unreality, rapt round [Duck 62-5 P
UNREASON. By dense unreason, irreproachable force, [Duck 62-6 P
UNREASONING. Irrational moment its unreasoning, [NSF 398-22
UNRECOGNIZED. Of this present, this science, this unrecognized
    [Cuisine 228-8
    That they return unrecognized. The self [Woman Had 82-19 P
UNRECONCILED. Or--yes: what elements, unreconciled [Two V 355-2
UNREFLECTING. Rattles with fear in unreflecting leaves. [Golden
    460-15
UNRHYMED. A penny sun in a tinsel sky, unrhymed, [Duck 61-7 P
UNSCRAWLED. Across the unscrawled fores the future casts [NSF
    383-4
UNSEEING. A seeing and unseeing in the eye. [NSF 385-21
UNSEEN. And beautiful barenesses as yet unseen, [C 31-26
    And of a day as yet unseen, in which [Choc 297-5
    In things seen and unseen, created from nothingness, [NH 486-11
    And unseen. This is everybody's world. [Someone 87-11 A
UNSHAKEN. And by will, unshaken and florid [Medit 124-4
UNSMELLED. Out of geraniums and unsmelled flowers. [Plot Giant
    6-15
UNSNACK. Unsnack your snood, madanna, for the stars [Myrrh 349-13
UNSPONSORED. Or island solitude, unsponsored, free, [Sunday 70-20
UNSPOTTED. The unspotted imbecile revery, [MBG 172-5
UNSTATED. To the unstated theme each variation comes . . . [Think
    357-1
UNSTINTED. Without a season, unstinted in livery. [Sombre 67-7 P
UNSUBDUED. Grievings in loneliness, or unsubdued [Sunday 67-21
UNSUBJUGATED. And liked it unsubjugated, so that home [EM 321-17
UNTAMED. Of an aesthetic tough, diverse, untamed, [C 31-20
UNTASTED. Untasted, in its heavenly, orchard air. [Monocle 14-15
UNTOUCHED. The poem of pure reality, untouched [NH 471-13
UNTRIED. To an untried perception applied [Lytton 39-14 P
UNTROUBLED. Untroubled by suffering, which fate assigns [Old
    Woman 46-6 P
UNTRUE. Like a book at evening beautiful but untrue, [AA 418-14
UNUSED. Of summer and that unused hearth below, [Phases 5-7 P
UNVERSED. Are flatly there, unversed except to be, [Bouquet 452-14
UNWIELDED. The appointed power unwielded from disdain. [C 37-19
UNWILLING. Unwilling that mercy should be a mystery [Rome 510-17
UNWISHED. Unwished for, chance, the merest riding [Hero 275-12
UNWOVEN. Every thread of summer is at last unwoven. [Fuel 456-1
UNWRITTEN. Leave room, therefore, in that unwritten book [C 33-26
UNZE. "Cy Est Pourtraicte, Madame Ste Ursule, et Les Unze Mille

Vierges" [21-title
UP. The sea of spuming thought foists up again [Monocle 13-8
    Rose up besprent and sought the flaming red [Hibiscus 22-20
    Up and down. [Homunculus 26-4
    What word split up in clickering syllables [C 28-14
    High up in orange air, were barbarous. [C 30-21
    As sullen as the sky, was swallowed up [C 32-20
    Bore up, in time, the somnolent, deep songs. [C 33-25
    And up and down between two elements, [C 35-7
    The vessel inward. Tilting up his nose, [C 36-6
    And so it came, his cabin shuffled up, [C 42-1
    Latched up the night. So deep a sound fell down [C 42-6
    Sacked up and carried overseas, daubed out [C 45-13
    That burial, pillared up each day as porte [Heaven 56-16
    For I reach right up to the sun, [Six Sig 74-7
    The wilderness rose up to it, [Jar 76-9
    Up the sky. [Cortege 80-9
    Cries up for us and colder than the frost [Anatomy 108-4
    The leaves in which the wind kept up its sound [Farewell 117-13
    Gleam sharply as the sun comes up. [Botanist 2 135-17
    Where the voice that is great within us rises up, [Eve Angels
    138-5
    That brave man comes up [Brave 138-19
    Children picking up our bones [Postcard 158-14
    As I strum the thing, do I pick up [MBG 171-19
    The bubbling sun will bubble up, [MBG 182-12
    Disclosed in common forms. Set up [Prelude 195-17
    Comes up as the sun, bull fire, [Add 198-20
    Day creeps down. The moon is creeping up. [Dump 201-11
    That's the moment when the moon creeps up [Dump 202-19
    Everything is shed; and the moon comes up as the moon [Dump
    202-22
    From a doctor into an ox, before standing up, [Freed 205-11
    And there you are humped high, humped up, [Rabbit K 209-21
    Could have stood up sharply in the sky. [Weak Mind 212-20
    Lights out. Shades up. [Nightgown 214-1
    Rose up, tallest, in the black sun, [Thunder 220-6
    Stood up straight in the air, struck off [Thunder 220-7
    That sees above them, that sees rise up above them, [Candle
    223-11
    At the time of the dogwoods, handfuls thrown up [Forces 229-5
    There were the sheets high up on older trees, [Forces 229-13
    Who in a million diamonds sums us up. [Oboe 250-22
    When he looked, the water ran up the air or grew white [Extracts
    255-17
    Shadow, up the great sea and downward [Hero 274-27
    The crow looks rusty as he rises up. [Possum 294-15
    That sweats the sun up on its morning way [Repet 307-7
    To giant red, sweats up a giant sense [Repet 307-8
    No pain (ignoring the cocks that crow us up [EM 314-13
    The moon rose up as if it had escaped [EM 314-21
    Or the majolica dish heaped up with phosphored fruit [EM 320-17
    Bubbles up in the night and drowns the crickets' sound. [EM
    321-9
    Great tufts, spring up from buried houses [EM 322-15
    To pick up relaxations of the known. [Feo 333-17
    The sun comes up like news from Africa. [Feo 334-12
    His mind raised up, down-drowned, the chariots. [Descrip 343-12
    A palm that rises up beyond the sea, [Descrip 344-2
    The uptopping top and tip of things, borne up [Two V 355-6
    Lifts up its heavy scowl before them. [Pediment 362-3
    Forced up from nothing, evening's chair, [Human 363-11
    The rivers shine and hold their mirrors up, [Belly 366-19
    How is it that the wooden trees stand up [Belly 367-2
    Fetched up with snow that never falls to earth? [Belly 367-6
    The waitress heaped up black Hermosas [Attempt 370-2
    The green roses drifted up from the table [Attempt 370-15
    Brushed up by brushy winds in brushy clouds, [NSF 385-7
    Sets up its Schwärmerei, not balances [NSF 386-14
    Rose up like phantoms from chronologies. [NSF 389-15
    The body lift its heavy wing, take up, [NSF 390-12
    To his Virgilian cadences, up down, [NSF 407-8
    Up down. It is a war that never ends. [NSF 407-9
    A-dub, a-dub, which is made up of this: [AA 416-1
    This is the chair from which she gathered up [Beginning 428-3
    Who can pick up the weight of Britain, [Imago 439-1
    And plated up, dense silver shine, in a land [Bouquet 449-15
    A car drives up. A soldier, an officer, [Bouquet 452-19
    The stars are washing up from Ireland [Our Stars 455-9
    Straight up, an élan without harrowing, [What We 459-14
    Of bronze whose mind was made up and who, therefore, died. [NH
    472-10
    The phrase grows weak. The fact takes up the strength [NH 473-4
    A city slapped up like a chest of tools, [NH 478-20
    Picked up its radial aspect in the night, [NH 478-23
    In the genius of summer that they blew up [NH 482-18
    The sea shivered in transcendent change, rose up [NH 484-9
    A woman writing a note and tearing it up. [NH 488-21
    And being up high had helped him when up high, [Aug 493-14
    Of birds called up by more than the sun, [Hermit 505-17

So that he that stood up in the boat leaning and looking before
  him [Prol 515-12
On the horizon and lifting himself up above it. [World 520-14
The stone from which he rises, up--and--ho, [Rock 528-2
The birch trees draw up whiteness from the ground. [Primordia
  8-21 P
In the swamps, bushes draw up dark red, [Primordia 8-22 P
The mightier mother raises up her cry; [Soldat 14-16 P
Digs up the earth when want returns . . . [Soldat 16-11 P
Push up the towers [Archi 17-15 P
They would throw their batons far up [Drum-Majors 36-20 P
If Shasta roared up in Nassau, [Agenda 42-2 P
Give up dead things and the living turn away. [Burnshaw 49-6 P
It made up for everything, it was all selves [Greenest 53-3 P
Things jutted up, the way the jagged stacks, [Greenest 53-11 P
Of war, the rust on the steeples, these jutted up, [Greenest
  53-23 P
In one, except a throne raised up beyond [Greenest 55-10 P
Out of the eye when the loud wind gathers up [Greenest 58-11 P
High up in heaven a sprawling portent moves, [Sombre 68-17 P
High up in heaven the sprawling portent moves. [Sombre 70-18 P
In a clamor thudding up from central earth. [Sombre 70-30 P
And the first line spreading up the beach; again, [Woman Had
  81-14 P
Or sees the new North River heaping up [Recit 86-24 P
Say that the American moon comes up [Memo 89-11 P
A summing up of the loftiest lives [Ulysses 104-7 P
When the candle, sputtering up, [Three 131-9 P
And weeping up the hill. [Three 138-9 P
Up the pineapple, a table Alp and yet [Someone 87-2 A
Much choosing is the final choice made up, [Ideal 88-18 A
See: gathered-up; hacked-up; heaped-up; heaved-up; nailed-up;
  torn-up.
UP-GATHERED. A mask up-gathered brilliantly from the dirt, [Sombre
  70-13 P
UP-HILL. Of it is not a light apart, up-hill. [Orb 441-27
UPLIFTED. Anon, their lamps' uplifted flame [Peter 91-18
  One foot approaching, one uplifted arm. [Choc 296-16
  The right, uplifted foreleg of the horse [NSF 391-10
UPLIFTING. Uplifting the completest rhetoric [Extracts
  253-20
UPPER. An upper, particular bough in, say, Marchand. [Connois
  215-12
  Like a page of music, like an upper air, [NSF 397-13
  At the upper right, a pyramid with one side [What We 460-2
  Wood-smoke rises through trees, is caught in an upper flow
  [Slug 522-3
  Of azure round an upper dome, brightest [Greenest 54-13 P
UP-POURING. A deep up-pouring from some saltier well [Monocle
  13-10
UPRIGHT. A tall figure upright in a giant's air. [Recit 87-24 P
UP-RISING. Up-rising and down-falling, bares [Curtains 62-9
UPROAR. In a kind of uproar, because an opposite, a contradiction,
  [Slug 522-7
UPROARIOUS. And died amid uproarious damns. [Lulu M 27-10 P
UP-SPRINGING. Down-pouring, up-springing, and inevitable, [NH
  465-17
UPSTAIRS. And as they say good-night, good-night. Upstairs [AA
  413-23
UPSTREAM. The bass keep looking ahead, upstream, in one [Think
  356-11
UPTOPPING. The uptopping top and tip of things, borne up [Two V
  355-6
UPWARD. Upward and outward, in green-vented forms, [Bird Claws
  82-11
  The cloud rose upward like a heavy stone [Nigger 152-8
  Yesterday the roses were rising upward, [Nigger 156-10
  Rising upward from a sea of ex. [MBG 175-4
  Upward. [Poem Morn 219-16
  The breath that gushes upward and is gone, [Descrip 341-4
  Upward, from unimagined coverts, fly. [Blanche 10-12 P
  Fly upward thick in numbers, fly across [Red Kit 31-22 P
  Triumphant as that always upward wind [Old Woman 44-27 P
  Pitched into swelling bodies, upward, drift [Burnshaw 52-20 P
  Seeing the fulgent shadows upward heaped, [Duck 62-16 P
  4. The sea is spouting upward out of rocks. [Someone 86-7 A
UPWARDLY. Dark-skinned and sinuous, winding upwardly, [Greenest
  55-13 P
URGENT. This urgent, competent, serener myth [Havana 143-19
  Subtler, more urgent proof that the theory [NH 486-8
URN. At some gigantic, solitary urn, [Burnshaw 49-4 P
  Sing rose-beliefs. Above that urn two lights [Burnshaw 50-1 P
  And bright, or like a venerable urn, [Someone 83-16 A
URNS. On urns and oak-leaves twisted into rhyme. [Sombre 68-1 P
URSULA. Ursula, in a garden, found [Pourtraicte 21-1
URSULE. See Ste Ursule.
URUGUAY. See Mrs. Alfred Uruguay.
USE. Use dusky words and dusky images. [Two Figures 86-2
  But do not use the rotted names. [MBG 183-6
  False happiness, since we know that we use [Crude 305-14

We are two that use these roses as we are, [Roses 431-10
Of lone wanderers. To re-create, to use [NH 481-15
As these depend, so must they use. [Ulysses 104-23 P
They measure the right to use. Need makes [Ulysses 104-24 P
The right to use. Need names on its breath [Ulysses 104-25 P
USED. He did not quail. A man so used to plumb [Geneva 24-7
  The doctor used his handkerchief and sighed. [Geneva 24-15
  As they are used to wear, and let the boys [Emperor 64-5
  One grows used to the weather, [Am Sub 131-5
  And re-illumines things that used to turn [Sun March 133-15
  Panoramas are not what they used to be. [Botanist 1 134-9
  Was not the moon he used to see, to feel [Anglais 148-20
  He used his reason, exercised his will, [Anglais 149-5
  The mountains are scratched and used, clear fakes. [Arcades
  226-3
  But that's all done. It is what used to be, [Cuisine 227-17
  As they used to lie in the grass, in the heat, [Cuisine 227-18
  But you, you used the word, [Search 268-7
  We grew used so soon, too soon, to earth itself, [Wild 328-16
  This is the illustration that she used: [Past Nun 378-14
  The wood-dove used to chant his hoobla-hoo [NSF 383-6
  Looking for what was, where it used to be? [NSF 389-7
  Too venerably used. That might have been. [NSF 400-19
  This was the glass in which she used to look [Beginning 427-15
  In mud under ponds, where the sky used to be reflected. [NH
  487-15
  Not one of the masculine myths we used to make, [Look 518-7
  I quote the very phrase my masters used. [Soldat 11-9 P
  Bang cymbals as they used to do. [Memo 89-15 P
  Used by generations of hermits. [Three 130-11 P
USED-TO. Until the used-to earth and sky, and the tree [Orb 441-12
  And cloud, the used-to tree and used-to cloud, [Orb 441-13
USELESS. Her useless bracelets fondly fluttered, [Thought 184-11
USES. Makers without knowing, or intending, uses. [New Set 352-15
  Lose the old uses that they made of them, [Orb 441-14
USUAL. Of ideas and to say as usual that there must be [Bed 326-17
UTAMARO. You know how Utamaro's beauties sought [Monocle 14-5
UTMOST. In solid fire the utmost earth and know [EM 314-12
  In the death of a soldier, like the utmost will, [Descrip 341-2
  As good. The utmost must be good and is [Cred 374-18
  Straight to the utmost crown of night he flew. [NSF 403-8
  Beneficence, a repose, utmost repose, [Orb 442-14
  His utmost statement. It is his own array, [Questions 462-17
  Itself, beyond the utmost increase come [Greenest 53-30 P
UTOPIA. Of inaccessible Utopia. [MBG 179-10
UTTERANCE. Over words that are life's voluble utterance. [Men Fall
  188-20
  A bitter utterance from your writhing, dumb, [NSF 384-21
  In this house, what manner of utterance shall there be? [Archi
  16-20 P
UTTERED. And uttered their subsiding sound. [Infanta 8-6
  Since what she sang was uttered word by word. [Key W 128-21

VACANCY. Before the winter's vacancy returned. [C 34-12
 Its vacancy glitters round us everywhere. [Eve Angels 137-2
 As the eye closes . . . How cold the vacancy [EM 320-6
 In the golden vacancy she came, and comes, [Descrip 339-13
 "Vacancy in the Park" [511-title
VACANT. In vacant space. [Am Sub 131-11
 Of a vacant sea declaiming with wide throat, [Puel 456-9
VACUUM. Like molten citizens of the vacuum? [Liadoff 346-10
 A vacuum for the dozen orchestras [Bship 80-1 P
VAGABOND. The eye of a vagabond in metaphor [NSF 397-22
VAGUE. Too vague idealist, overwhelmed [Negation 98-1
 Her vague "Secrete me from reality," [Repet 309-20
 Woman with a vague moustache and not the mauve [EM 321-15
 Of a mother with vague severed arms [Celle 438-19
 That are dissembled in vague memory [Sombre 67-16 P
VAGUELY. The moment's sun (The strong man vaguely seen), [Freed
 204-20
 Too vaguely that it be written in character. [Extracts 257-21
 And vaguely to be seen, a matinal red, [Burnshaw 51-22 P
VAGUEST. The vaguest line of smoke (a year ago) [Phases 5-4 P
VAIN. Alas! Have all the barbers lived in vain [Monocle 14-8
 In vain, life's season or death's element. [Montra 263-6
 And bared yourself, and bared yourself in vain? [Good Bad 33-21 P
 In vain. [Room Gard 41-9 P
VALEDICTORY. Rock, of valedictory echoings, [MBG 179-4
VALET. The valet in the tempest was annulled. [C 29-8
 Of Vulcan, that a valet seeks to own, [C 33-6
 See Crispin-valet.
VALIANCE. Whose merely being was his valiance, [Extracts 254-11
 In concert with the eagle's valiance. [Spaniard 35-12 P
VALID. Other men, and not this grass, this valid air. [Americana
 94-11 P
VALLEY. "Valley Candle" [51-title
 My candle burned alone in an immense valley. [Valley Candle
 51-1
 There are men of a valley [Men 1000 51-13
 Who are that valley. [Men 1000 51-14
VALLOMBROSA. Queer, in this Vallombrosa of ears, [Arcades 225-5
VANISH. The women with eyes like opals vanish [Stan Hero 83-12 P
VANISHED. Now, for him, his forms have vanished. [Sad Gay 121-19
 If in the mind, he vanished, taking there [Choc 298-3
 See vanishing-vanished.
VANISHES. Spring vanishes the scraps of winter, why [NSF 391-1
VANISHING. The stride of vanishing autumn in a park [C 31-3
 The sky acutest at its vanishing. [Key W 129-24
 And vanishing, a web in a corridor [AA 416-18
 Evoking an archaic space, vanishing [Aug 494-19
VANISHINGS. Or spill night out in brilliant vanishings, [Page
 423-4
VANISHING-VANISHED. In a vanishing-vanished violet that wraps round
 [Owl 433-15
VANITY. How, then, if nothing more than vanity [Spaniard 34-21 P
VAPID. In the vapid haze of the window-bays, [Ord Women 11-6
VAPIDEST. Is wholly the vapidest fake . . . [Sailing 120-20
VARADERO. How tranquil it was at vividest Varadero, [Novel 457-16
VARIABLE. Fickle and fumbling, variable, obscure, [C 46-4
VARIATION. Is not a variation but an end. [Pure 332-7
 To the unstated theme each variation comes . . . [Think 357-1
VARIATIONS. "Variations on a Summer Day" [232-title
 Variations in the tones of a single sound, [EM 316-14
 Variations on the words spread sail. [Aug 490-2
VARIOUS. It glistens with various yellows, [Pears 196-18
 The crow, inciting various modes. [Vari 233-15
 The sameness of his various universe, [Moonlight 531-3
 The one moonlight, the various universe, intended [Moonlight
 532-3
 The various obscurities of the moon, [Bowl 7-2 P
 Various argentines, [Archi 18-7 P
 In every various sense, ought not to be preferred [Lytton 39-13P
VARNISHED. A pagan in a varnished car. [MBG 170-12
 The inhabitants of a very varnished green. [NSF 383-16
VARYING. One string, an absolute, not varying [Montra 263-15
 Now, closely the ear attends the varying [Pure 332-2
VASE. "Woman Looking at a Vase of Flowers" [246-title
VASSALS. Of dense investiture, with luminous vassals. [NH 469-6
VAST. Of one vast, subjugating, final tone. [C 30-9
 Of a vast people old in meditation . . . [New Set 353-4
 And flare and Bloom with his vast accumulation [Anach 366-14
 One of the vast repetitions final in [NSF 405-20
 Within the big, blue bush and its vast shade [Study I 463-12
 It was not from the vast ventriloquism [Not Ideas 534-10
 "This Vast Inelegance" [25-title P
 This vast inelegance may seem the blankest desolation, [Inelegance
 25-13 P
 That vast confect of telegrams, [Mandolin 29-7 P
 Unhappy love reveals vast blemishes. [Red Kit 31-19 P
 Stooped in a night of vast inquietude. [Spaniard 34-14 P
 In vast disorder live in the ruins, free, [Burnshaw 48-27 P

With interruptions by vast hymns, blood odes, [Duck 66-1 P
 On which the vast arches of space [Ulysses 103-17 P
VASTEST. Was he to company vastest things defunct [C 41-12
VATIC. Poesis, poesis, the literal characters, the vatic lines,
 [Large 424-6
VAULTIEST. The sky was blue beyond the vaultiest phrase. [What We
 459-12
VAULTS. Of the structure of vaults upon a point of light. [MBG
 167-5
 "These degustations in the vaults [MBG 181-1
 Abiding the reverberations in the vaults. [Papini 447-11
 See rain-stained-vaults.
VAUNTS. The near, the clear, and vaunts the clearest bloom, [Fic-
 tive 88-3
VEGETABLES. Young men as vegetables, hip-hip, [Hero 278-12
VEGETAL. And this fragrance the fragrance of vegetal? [Lilacs
 48-22
VEGETATION. The vegetation still abounds with forms. [Lions 125-8
VEHEMENCE. And the lost vehemence the midnights hold. [Tallap 72-12
VEILS. Although contending featly in its veils, [C 36-2
VEINS. A giant's heart in the veins, all courage. [Gigan 289-7
 Its being beating heavily in the veins, [Novel 459-2
 The vigor of glory, a glittering in the veins, [Real 110-13 P
VELOCITIES. He measures the velocities of change. [AA 414-10
VELVET. The moonlight in her lap, mewing her velvet, [Uruguay
 249-2
 To be, regardless of velvet, could never be more [Uruguay 249-13
 As it descended, blind to her velvet and [Uruguay 249-19
VELVETEST. Shattering velvetest far-away. The bear, [NSF 384-14
VENCE. Matisse at Vence and a great deal more than that, [Armor
 529-18
VENERABLE. Most venerable heart, the lustiest conceit [Monocle
 16-17
 The venerable song falls from your fiery wings. [God 285-16
 He lacks this venerable complication. [Great 311-10
 Man's mind grown venerable in the unreal. [Cred 377-5
 Venerable and articulate and complete. [NSF 383-21
 This tendance and venerable holding-in [NH 472-20
 Of this present, the venerable mask above [NH 476-17
 In the western night. The venerable mask, [NH 477-3
 And bright, or like a venerable urn, [Someone 83-16 A
VENERABLY. Too venerably used. That might have been. [NSF 400-19
VENEREAL. "O Florida, Venereal Soil" [47-title
 Florida, venereal soil, [Venereal 47-9
VENETIAN. Of Boucher pink, the sheens of Venetian gray. [Greenest
 53-14 P
 Porcelain, Venetian glass, [Three 131-6 P
 Venetian, [Three 138-19 P
VENEZUELAN. Of crimson and hoods of Venezuelan green [Burnshaw
 51-3 P
VENGEFUL. Vengeful, shadowed by gestures [Bagatelles 213-16
 Destroyed by a vengeful movement of the arms, [Sombre 69-3 P
VENICE. Or Venice, motionless, gathering time and dust. [Real
 110-10 P
VENOM. Its venom of renown, and on your head [Fictive 87-12
 Whose venom and whose wisdom will be one. [John 437-21
VENT. For once vent honey? [Carolinas 5-3
 This must be the vent of pity, [Orangeade 103-17
VENTED. See green-vented.
VENTING. In venting lacerations. So composed, [Spaniard 35-18 P
VENTRILOQUISM. It was not from the vast ventriloquism [Not Ideas
 534-10
VENUS. The fowl of Venus may consist of both [Spaniard 35-7 P
 The workers do not rise, as Venus rose, [Duck 60-9 P
 Like evening Venus in a cloud-top. [Three 135-9 P
VERACIOUS. No, no: veracious page on page, exact. [C 40-3
 A verity of the most veracious men, [NH 473-13
VERBOSENESS. Could Crispin stem verboseness in the sea, [C 28-22
VERD. Performed in verd apparel, and the peach, [C 39-2
VERDANT. These figures verdant with time's buried verdure [New Set
 352-16
VERDURE. These figures verdant with time's buried verdure [New Set
 352-16
VERDURED. Blue verdured into a damask's lofty symbol, [NH 477-18
VERHAEREN. Of Vilmorin, Verhaeren in his grave, [Greenest 53-20 P
VERITABLE. Here was the veritable ding an sich, at last, [C 29-24
 Inhuman, of the veritable ocean. [Key W 128-17
 Was the veritable season, that familiar [Hero 280-27
 Man was the veritable man? So [Hero 281-1
 The veritable small, so that each of us [Rome 509-14
VERITIES. The sorry verities! [W Burgher 61-7
VERITY. A verity of the most veracious men, [NH 473-13
VERMEIL. A few years more and the vermeil capuchin [C 44-24
VERMILION. Vermilion smeared over green, arranged for show. [Grapes
 110-14
 The melons, the vermilion pears [Reader 147-8
 Blue and vermilion, purple and white, [Mandolin 28-20 P
 See gold-vermilion.
VERMILIONED. A vermilioned nothingness, any stick of the mass [Less
 328-9

VERMONT. Vermont throws itself together. [July 115-5 P
VERNACULAR. At the vernacular of light [Delight 162-4
VERSATILE. And apt in versatile motion, touch and sound [Anatomy
    108-12
VERSE. The fabulous and its intrinsic verse [C 31-30
    More exquisite than any tumbling verse: [C 37-3
    Lighting a pitiless verse or two. [Chateau 161-12
    Pitiless verse? A few words tuned [Chateau 161-15
    Hums and you say "The world in a verse, [Waldorf 241-6
    The mind renews the world in a verse, [Ulysses 103-1 P
VERSES. In verses wild with motion, full of din, [Monocle 16-12
    "New England Verses" [104-title
    Are like the perpetual verses in a poet's mind. [Greenest 59-27P
VERSICOLORINGS. Versicolorings, establishes a time [EM 324-14
VERSION. It is never the thing but the version of the thing: [Pure
    332-13
    The eye's plain version is a thing apart, [NH 465-4
VERSIONS. "Two Versions of the Same Poem" [353-title
VERTIGINOUS. In a really vertiginous boat [Sailing 120-19
VERTUMNUS. Vertumnus creates an equilibrium. [Extraord 369-20
VERVE. Is measure, also, of the verve of earth. [Monocle 14-27
    The noble, Alexandrine verve. The flies [Contra II 270-17
VERY. Boomed from his very belly odious chords. [Monocle 17-17
    The very man despising honest quilts [C 41-29
    Oh, but the very self of the storm [Joost 46-20
    The senses and feeling, the very sound [Joost 47-1
    The very hinds discerned it, in a star. [Sunday 68-4
    Of dark, which in its very darkening [Eve Angels 137-24
    A very felicitous eve, [Delight 162-1
    But the very senses as they touch [MBG 175-1
    The very book, or, less, a page [MBG 178-2
    The very will of the nerves, [Anything B 211-21
    This? A man must be very poor [Arcades 225-20
    Shine on the very living of those alive. [Dutch 293-5
    Pain killing pain on the very point of pain. [EM 314-5
    The very pool, his thoughts the colored forms, [Descrip 342-12
    It is that and a very big hat. [Prejudice 368-13
    Let's see the very thing and nothing else. [Cred 373-3
    The inhabitants of a very varnished green. [NSF 383-16
    The very Place Du Puy, in fact, belonged [NSF 391-24
    His ear, the very material of his mind. [NSF 403-2
    Within the very object that we seek, [Study I 463-9
    Now, soldiers, hear me: mark this very breeze, [Phases 5-12 P
    I quote the very phrase my masters used. [Soldat 11-9 P
    Adds very little, [Melancholy 32-10 P
    Of very haphazard people and things, [Agenda 42-8 P
    To the muscles' very tip for the vivid plunge, [Old Woman 43-11P
    Of the very body instinctively crying [Stan Hero 84-27 P
    A very dark-leaved berry tree. [Banjo 114-4 P
    That we are painted on this very bottle, [Three 132-20 P
VESSEL. From what he saw across his vessel's prow. [C 35-25
    The vessel inward. Tilting up his nose, [C 36-6
    They mow the lawn. A vessel sinks in waves [EM 322-12
    He belonged to the far-foreign departure of his vessel and was
        part of it, [Prol 516-1
VESTAL. Alone and like a vestal long-prepared. [NSF 395-18
VESTED. With which we vested, once, the golden forms [EM 317-25
    Yet vested in a foreign absolute, [Owl 434-9
    Vested in the serious folds of majesty, [Orb 442-21
    And how shall those come vested that come there? [Archi 17-6 P
VESTIBULE. A black vestibule; [Theory 87-2
VESTIGIAL. Among our more vestigial states of mind. [NSF 392-1
VESTMENTS. The mille fiori of vestments, [Winter B 141-6
VESUVIUS. On the sublime. Vesuvius had groaned [EM 313-13
    Except for us, Vesuvius might consume [EM 314-11
VETCH. The vetch has turned purple. But where is the bride? [Ghosts
    119-3
VEX. The weaving and the crinkling and the vex, [Owl 433-17
    To sully the begonias, nor vex [Archi 18-14 P
VEXED. Soother and lustier than this vexed, autumnal exhalation,
    [Inelegance 25-17 P
VEXING. All dreams are vexing. Let them be expunged. [C 39-31
    Then place of vexing palankeens, then haunt [C 43-24
VIBRANCIES. The impoverished waste with dewy vibrancies [Greenest
    58-23 P
VIBRANCY. A vibrancy not to be taken for granted, from [Holiday
    312-5
    A vibrancy of petals, fallen, that still cling [Bouquet 450-10
VIBRANT. This base of every future, vibrant spring, [Duck 63-28 P
VIBURNUMS. Myrtle, viburnums, daffodils, blue phlox), [Dump 202-13
VICE. Denies that abstraction is a vice except [Thought 185-7
VICIOUS. That had flashed (like vicious music that ends [Thunder
    220-11
VICISSITUDES. Found his vicissitudes had much enlarged [C 31-8
VICTOR. Eventual victor, out of the martyrs' bones, [Uruguay 250-4
VICTORIA CLEMENTINA. Victoria Clementina, negress, [Cab 20-15 P
VICTORIA PLATZ. Why should it fail to stand? Victoria Platz,
    [Greenest 58-19 P
VICTORIOUS. Most miserable, most victorious, [NSF 389-3
VICTOR SERGE. Victor Serge said, "I followed his argument [EM 324-24

VICTORY. A horn, on which its victory [MBG 174-13
    As victory. The poet does not speak in ruins [Papini 446-10
    For battle, the purple for victory. But if [Bship 79-7 P
VIDAL. The blue of the rug, the portrait of Vidal, [Freed 205-23
VIE. C'était mon frère du ciel, ma vie, mon or. [Sea Surf 100-3
    C'est toujours la vie qui me regarde . . . This was [NH 483-14
    Voilà la vie, la vie, la vie, [Soldat 15-15 P
VIENNA. For sale in Vienna and Zurich to people in Maine, [Greenest
    53-9 P
    It was not a night blown at a glassworks in Vienna [Real 110-9 P
VIERGES. "Cy Est Pourtraicte, Madame Ste Ursule, et Les Unze Mille
    Vierges" [21-title
VIEW. But a tower more precious than the view beyond, [Cred 373-18
    A view of New Haven, say, through the certain eye, [NH 471-18
    From the spun sky and the high and deadly view, [Aug 493-10
    Would discover, at last, the view toward which they had edged,
        [Poem Mt 512-12
    There are as many points of view [Three 136-14 P
VIEWING. Viewing the frost; [Cortege 80-20
    An exercise in viewing the world. [Vari 233-17
VIEWS. And the notorious views from the windows [Prelude 195-5
VIF. This vif, this dizzle-dazzle of being new [Armor 530-12
VIGIL. Should fill the vigil of a negress [Virgin 71-8
VIGILANCE. Is an approach to the vigilance [Ulysses 102-6 P
VIGILANT. Should scrawl a vigilant anthology, [C 38-26
VIGILS. And of all vigils musing the obscure, [Fictive 88-4
VIGOR. A curriculum, a vigor, a local abstraction . . . [R Conn
    533-17
    Joined, the triumphant vigor, felt, [Ulysses 100-14 P
    Joined in a triumphant vigor, [Presence 105-23 P
    The vigor of glory, a glittering in the veins, [Real 110-13 P
VIGORS. To toll its pulses, vigors of its self? [Two V 354-6
    These vigors make, thrice-triple-syllabled, [Two V 354-8
VILE. The vile antithesis of poor and rich. [NE Verses 104-6
VILLAGE. Into a village, [Magnifico 19-2
    Crossing a single bridge into a village. [Magnifico 19-6
    Into a village, [Magnifico 19-10
    Into a village, [Magnifico 19-13
    The first white wall of the village [Magnifico 19-18
    The first white wall of the village . . . [Magnifico 19-22
    Playing cards. In a village of the indigenes, [Glass 198-3
    They are full of the colors of my village [Peaches 224-13
    Time swished on the village clocks and dreams were alive, [Uru-
        guay 249-26
    The greenhouse on the village green [Poesie 302-15
    Bell-bellow in the village steeple. Violets, [EM 322-14
    There is village and village of them, without regard [Wild 320-13
    The clouds are over the village, the town, [Woman Song 360-13
    Just out of the village, at its edge, [Woman Song 361-5
VILLAGES. Into twenty villages, [Magnifico 19-4
    Berries of villages, a barber's eye, [C 27-15
    The grand ideas of the villages. [Pharynx 96-8
    The villages slept as the capable man went down, [Uruguay 249-25
    There remained the smoke of the villages. Their fire [Wild 329-5
    That held the distances off: the villages [Wild 329-10
    White houses in villages, black communicants-- [Cats 367-19
VILLE DES PINS. Benitia, lapis Ville des Pins must soothe [Greenest
    58-22 P
VILMORIN. Of Vilmorin, Verhaeren in his grave, [Greenest 53-20 P
VINCENTINE. "The Apostrophe to Vincentine" [52-title
    Heavenly Vincentine. [Vincentine 52-15
    Green Vincentine. [Vincentine 53-3
    Vincentine. [Vincentine 53-9
    Turned Vincentine, [Vincentine 53-16
    Turned heavenly Vincentine, [Vincentine 53-17
    Turned heavenly, heavenly Vincentine. [Vincentine 53-19
VINE. O bough and bush and scented vine, in whom [Fictive 88-8
    And green vine angering for life, [Nomad 95-9
    Until each tree, each evil-blossomed vine, [Greenest 55-23 P
    The vine, at the roots, this vine of Key West, splurging,
        [Bship 80-9 P
    Like taste distasting the first fruit of a vine, [Theatre 91-3 P
    3. A vine has climbed the other side of the wall. [Someone
        86-6 A
VINES. Two golden gourds distended on our vines, [Monocle 16-6
    Now grapes are plush upon the vines. [Contra I 266-11
    The vines around the throat, the shapeless lips, [NSF 400-10
    Under its mattresses of vines. [Vacancy 511-13
    Vines with yellow fruit, [Phases 4-11 P
    Vines that take [Bowl 7-1 P
    And I play my guitar. The vines have grown wild. [Stan MBG 72-12P
VIOL. On the clear viol of her memory, [Peter 92-12
VIOLENCE. His violence was for aggrandizement [C 31-14
    Choke every ghost with acted violence, [Nigger 155-6
    All mind and violence and nothing felt. [Chaos 358-4
    Yet voluble dumb violence. You look [NSF 384-22
VIOLENT. To be free again, to return to the violent mind [Farewell
    118-17
    In the body of a violent beast. [Destructive 193-2
    A. A violent order is disorder; and [Connois 215-1

A. Well, an old order is a violent one. [Connois 216-1
These violent marchers of the present, [Dutch 293-6
And, standing in violent golds, will brush her hair. [Debris
    338-7
From thought, like a violent pulse in the cloud itself, [Liadoff
    347-7
Serenely gazing at the violent abyss, [NSF 404-14
The violent disclosure trimly leafed, [Bouquet 452-9
In a Sunday's violent idleness. [Two Illus 514-3
VIOLET. "Two Figures in Dense Violet Night" [85-title
In his chalk and violet robes. [Nigger 151-14
Without rose and without violet, [Common 221-12
Were violet, yellow, purple, pink. The grass [Horn 230-9
Licentious violet and lascive rose, [Montra 261-15
The scene in his gray-rose with violet rocks. [Anach 366-5
The pensive giant prone in violet space [NSF 387-2
In a vanishing-vanished violet that wraps round [Owl 433-15
One imagined the violet trees but the trees stood green, [What
    We 459-10
Of violet gray, a green violet, a thread [What We 459-17
Like an evening evoking the spectrum of violet, [NH 488-19
How carve the violet moon [Archi 17-25 P
Out of a violet sea. They rise a bit [Duck 60-10 P
VIOLETS. The breast is covered with violets. It is a green leaf.
    [Holiday 312-16
Bell-bellow in the village steeple. Violets, [EM 322-14
Arrangements; and the violets' exhumo. [EM 322-26
The old seraph, parcel-gilded, among violets [NSF 389-13
Violets, doves, girls, bees and hyacinths [NSF 389-22
Here the black violets grow down to its banks [Degen 445-1
La-la! The cat is in the violets [Mandolin 28-13 P
VIOLLET-LE-DUC. Even with the help of Viollet-le-Duc, [NSF 386-23
VIOLS. The pears are not viols, [Pears 196-2
VIR. And tallest hero and plus gaudiest vir. [Montra 262-12
VIRGIL. And speech of Virgil dropped, that's where he walks,
    [Thought 185-14
As Virgil, abstract. But see him for yourself, [Paisant 335-13
VIRGILIAN. To his Virgilian cadences, up down, [NSF 407-8
VIRGIN. Virgin of boorish births, [Venereal 47-17
"The Virgin Carrying a Lantern" [71-title
Which, like a virgin visionary spent [Red Kit 30-18 P
VIRGINAL. Until our blood, commingling, virginal, [Sunday 68-2
First fruits, without the virginal of birds, [NSF 385-10
VIRGINS. And for sweet-smelling virgins close to them. [Monocle
    14-25
VIRILE. It wants words virile with his breath. [Country 207-23
Being virile, it hears the calendar hymn. [NSF 382-9
To bear virile grace before their fellows, [Stan Hero 83-20 P
VIRTUE. As acutest virtue and ascetic trove. [Montra 263-12
To be in scale, unless virtue cuts him, snips [Orb 442-26
I mark the virtue of the common-place. [Soldat 11-6 P
VIRTUOSI. Not the ocean of the virtuosi [Nigger 156-16
VIRTUOSO. That's how to produce a virtuoso. [Hero 274-24
But the virtuoso never leaves his shape, [Orb 443-3
VIS. A vis, a principle or, it may be, [Orb 442-10
VISAGE. The inanimate, difficult visage. Who is it? [NSF 388-24
A lasting visage in a lasting bush, [NSF 400-4
VISIBILITY. It is a visibility of thought, [NH 488-5
VISIBLE. Before these visible, voluble delugings, [Geneva 24-9
Noway resembling his, a visible thing, [C 29-27
And the visible, circumspect presentment drawn [C 35-24
Made visible. [Men 1000 52-10
Light, too, encrusts us making visible [Eve Angels 137-19
Of the visible elements and of ours. [Vari 232-11
As one loves visible and responsive peace, [Yellow 236-14
They do not make the visible a little hard [Creat 311-12
The visible, a zone of blue and orange [EM 324-13
In its own seeming, plainly visible, [Descrip 344-18
It is the visible rock, the audible, [Cred 375-17
The sky. It is the visible announced, [Cred 376-17
It is the more than visible, the more [Cred 376-18
It must be visible or invisible, [NSF 385-19
Invisible or visible or both: [NSF 385-20
Here, being visible is being white, [AA 412-16
It exists, it is visible, it is, it is. [AA 418-18
These forms are visible to the eye that needs, [Owl 432-1
And through included, not merely the visible, [NH 471-24
The difficulty of the visible [NH 474-23
With every visible thing enlarged and yet [Rome 510-22
Visible over the sea. It is only enough [Burnshaw 50-16 P
A visible clear cap, a visible wreath [Greenest 57-7 P
The star-yplaited, visible sanction, [Stan Hero 83-14 P
Is its body visible to the important eye. [Recit 86-14 P
The visible transformations of summer night, [Real 110-16 P
VISIBLY. The afternoon is visibly a source, [Look 518-17
VISION. Its fire fails to pierce the vision that beholds it,
    [Questions 462-7
The point of vision and desire are the same. [NH 466-22
VISIONARY. Nor visionary south, nor cloudy palm [Sunday 68-21
Of the enduring, visionary love, [NH 466-15

Which, like a virgin visionary spent [Red Kit 30-18 P
VISIT. This man to visit a woman, [Soldat 12-15 P
VISITANT. This hallowed visitant, chimerical, [Spaniard 35-19 P
VISITATION. The grotesque is not a visitation. It is [Feo 334-9
VISITS. Of Mr. Homburg during his visits home [Look 517-12
VISTA. For a vista in the Louvre. They are things chalked [Connois
    216-11
It was his clarity that made the vista bright. [Anach 366-3
Are of an eternal vista, manqué and gold [Burnshaw 48-12 P
That the vista retain ploughmen, peacocks, doves, [Burnshaw
    50-9 P
A shape, the vista twisted and burning, a thing [Bship 80-5 P
VISTAS. Scenes of the theatre, vistas and blocks of woods [AA
    415-14
In the great vistas of night air, that takes this form, [Moon-
    light 531-17
VITAL. The evilly compounded, vital I [Poems Clim 193-19
In these, I wear a vital cleanliness, [Rhythms 246-6
The vital music formulates the words. [Extracts 259-18
Repeats its vital words, yet balances [Search 268-15
The vital, arrogant, fatal, dominant X. [Motive 288-20
Of the least, minor, vital metaphor, content, [Crude 305-19
The youth, the vital son, the heroic power. [Cred 375-10
It enfolds the head in a vital ambiance, [Pastor 379-11
A vital, linear ambiance. The flare [Pastor 379-12
The vital, the never-failing genius, [AA 420-20
Within its vital boundary, in the mind. [Final 524-13
A vital assumption, an impermanence [Rock 526-2
VITALLY. He is not himself. He is vitally deprived . . .) [Ameri-
    cana 94-12 P
VIVID. He was a man made vivid by the sea, [C 30-24
Is like a vivid apprehension [Jasmine 79-7
Of waving weeds. I hated the vivid blooms [Farewell 118-3
The vivid, florid, turgid sky, [MBG 169-1
The vivid thing in the air that never changes, [Martial 238-12
The vivid transparence that you bring is peace. [NSF 380-11
And the whiteness grows less vivid on the wall. [AA 412-22
Night's hymn of the rock, as in a vivid sleep. [Rock 528-21
Its arches in its vivid element, [Armor 530-14
To the muscles' very tip for the vivid plunge, [Old Woman 43-11P
Your backs upon the vivid statue. Then, [Burnshaw 51-13 P
VIVIDEST. On this present ground, the vividest repose, [Cred 375-19
How tranquil it was at vividest Varadero, [Novel 457-16
VOCABLE. Crispin confronting it, a vocable thing, [C 29-25
VOCABLES. The miff-maff-muff of water, the vocables [Page 423-6
VOCABULARY. The effete vocabulary of summer [Plant 506-8
A flick which added to what was real and its vocabulary, [Prol
    517-5
Adds to them the whole vocabulary of the South, [Prol 517-7
VOCALISSIMUS. Vocalissimus, [Roaring 113-5
VOCIFERATE. For Crispin to vociferate again. [C 33-17
VOICE. A sunken voice, both of remembering [C 29-5
Let down gigantic quavers of its voice, [C 33-16
And in their chant shall enter, voice by voice, [Sunday 70-6
A voice that cries, "The tomb in Palestine [Sunday 70-15
Be the voice of night and Florida in my ear. [Two Figures 86-1
Start the singing in a voice [Orangeade 103-13
There was neither voice nor crested image, [How Live 126-1
Describe with deepened voice [Pascagoula 126-13
The water never formed to mind or voice, [Key W 128-12
If it was only the dark voice of the sea [Key W 129-10
If it was only the outer voice of sky [Key W 129-12
More even than her voice, and ours, among [Key W 129-18
It was her voice that made [Key W 129-23
Be thou the voice, [Mozart 132-9
The voice of angry fear, [Mozart 132-11
The voice of this besieging pain. [Mozart 132-12
Where the voice that is in us makes a true response, [Eve Angels
    138-4
Where the voice that is great within us rises up, [Eve Angels
    138-5
The voice of centuries [Winter B 141-7
A voice was mumbling, "Everything [Reader 147-5
With the undertaker: a voice in the clouds, [MBG 177-8
Another on earth, the one a voice [MBG 177-9
The voice of ether prevailing, the swell [MBG 177-11
Apostrophizing wreaths, the voice [MBG 177-13
Of familiar things in a cheerful voice, [Thought 185-2
The voice, the book, the hidden well, [Thought 186-2
To a crow's voice? Did the nightingale torture the ear, [Dump
    203-2
In which his voice would roll its cadences, [Blue Bldg 216-19
In the little of his voice, or the like, [Horn 230-14
As a mirror with a voice, the man of glass, [Oboe 250-21
Of the good, speaking of good in the voice of men. [Montra 262-19
All men can speak of it in the voice of gods. [Montra 262-20
The Roamer is a voice taller than the redwoods, [Phenom 287-4
Of what is secret becomes, for me, a voice [Choc 298-19
That is my own voice speaking in my ear. [Choc 298-20
To say more than human things with human voice, [Choc 300-11

Than human voice, that, also, cannot be; [Choc 300-13
Is a cloud in which a voice mumbles. [Lack 303-8
It is not a voice that is under the eaves. [Silent 359-18
One voice repeating, one tireless chorister, [NSF 394-7
Without a voice, inventions of farewell. [Owl 432-4
And death cries quickly, in a flash of voice, [Owl 432-13
With a savage voice; and in that cry they hear [NH 467-23
Are a single voice in the boo-ha of the wind. [NH 481-3
Or as a voice that, speaking without form, [NH 484-20
Or partly his. His voice is audible, [NH 485-11
And the sex of its voices, as the voice of one [Aug 489-14
Meets nakedly another's naked voice. [Aug 489-15
When was it that we heard the voice of union? [Aug 494-9
Beholds himself in you, and hears his voice [Rome 509-15
An old voice cried out, "Come!" [Phases 6-2 P
The male voice of the wind in the dry leaves [Primordia 7-14 P
Whose heart will murmur with the music that will be a voice for
  her, speaking the dreaded change of speech; [Piano 22-2 P
(A woman's voice is heard, replying.) Mock [Infernale 25-4 P
Is any choir the whole voice of this fretful habitation, [Inele-
  gance 26-5 P
A paragon of lustre; may have voice [Spaniard 35-9 P
Well-wetted; a decoying voice that sings [Spaniard 35-15 P
Their voice and the voice of the tortured wind were one, [Old
  Woman 45-27 P
Each voice within the other, seeming one, [Old Woman 45-28 P
A solemn voice, not Mr. Burnshaw's says: [Burnshaw 49-3 P
From pipes that swarm clerestory walls. The voice [Greenest
  59-13 P
In the jungle is a voice in Fontainebleau. [Greenest 59-14 P
From which their grizzled voice will speak and be heard." [Duck
  60-24 P
Like the voice of all our ancestors, [Grotesque 77-10 P
Are old men breathed on by a maternal voice, [Woman Had 82-14 P
Bald heads with their mother's voice still in their ears. [Woman
  Had 82-16 P
And of sounds so far forgotten, like her voice, [Woman Had 82-18P
Detects the sound of a voice that doubles its own, [Woman Had
  82-20 P
Maternal voice, the explanation at night. [Woman Had 82-24 P
Response, the completely answering voice, [Ulysses 100-11 P
The mistress says, in a harsh voice, [Three 134-5 P
VOICES. In the voices of mothers. [Carolinas 4-16
Of differing struts, four voices several [C 45-4
These voices crying without knowing for what, [Sad Gay 122-6
For which the voices cry, these, too, may be [Sad Gay 122-11
Brings voices as of lions coming down. [Sun March 134-6
Chorals for mountain voices and the moral chant, [Thought 185-16
The wind blows. In the wind, the voices [Parochial 191-3
A thousand crystals' chiming voices [Hero 279-19
There are shouts and voices. [Dutch 290-8
What is this crackling of voices in the mind, [Dutch 292-12
A little string speaks for a crowd of voices. [NSF 392-18
For companies of voices moving there, [NSF 398-16
The words they spoke were voices that she heard. [NSF 402-10
These are the voices of the pastors calling [Luther 461-4
These are the voices of the pastors calling [Luther 461-10
These are the voices of the pastors calling [Luther 461-16
And the sex of its voices, as the voice of one [Aug 489-14
The stern voices of its necessitous men, [Aug 491-17
And for all the white voices [Aug 495-3
Dance, now, and with sharp voices cry, but cry [Burnshaw 51-10 P
In the glassy sound of your voices, the porcelain cries, [Burn-
  shaw 52-6 P
And there he heard the voices that were once [Greenest 54-8 P
The confusion of men's voices, intricate [Greenest 54-9 P
Through banks and banks of voices, [Grotesque 77-7 P
Here in the North, late, late, there are voices of men, [Sick
  90-10 P
Voices in chorus, singing without words, remote and deep, [Sick
  90-11 P
The over-populace of the idea, the voices [Americana 94-2 P
VOID. Of children nibbling at the sugared void, [C 43-25
To be projected by one void into [Landsc 242-13
The down-descent into November's void. [Sombre 67-30 P
VOILA. Voilà la vie, la vie, la vie, [Soldat 15-15 P
VOLATILE. Of volatile world, too constant to be denied, [NSF
  397-21
VOLCANO. "A Postcard from the Volcano" [158-title
The volcano trembled in another ether, [EM 314-6
In the magnificence of a volcano. [Attempt 370-3
Wild wedges, as of a volcano's smoke, palm-eyed [AA 416-17
The volcano Apostrophe, the sea Behold? [Duck 63-29 P
10. This is how yesterday's volcano looks. [Someone 86-13 A
VOLUBLE. Before these visible, voluble delugings, [Geneva 24-9
Voluble. [Vincentine 53-7
Came, bowing and voluble, upon the deck, [Sea Surf 101-24
Over words that are life's voluble utterance. [Men Fall 188-20
A few words, a memorandum voluble [Repet 308-19
The sounds that soon become a voluble speech-- [Liadoff 347-20

Voluble but archaic and hard to hear. [Liadoff 347-21
Yet voluble dumb violence. You look [NSF 384-22
In its interpretations voluble, [Bouquet 451-9
The voluble intentions of the symbols, [Aug 492-13
Poor penury. There will be voluble hymns [Soldat 14-14 P
VOLUME. Comes the cold volume of forgotten ghosts, [NH 468-6
VOLUMES. The volumes like marble ruins [Common 221-20
VOLUMING. Blooming and beaming and voluming colors out. [NH 484-6
VOLUMINOUS. Of voluminous cloaks, [Homunculus 26-19
Birds and people of this too voluminous [Hero 278-1
A voluminous master folded in his fire. [NSF 381-3
VOLUNTATE. Further magnified, sua voluntate, [Hero 277-20
VOLUPTUARY. The starry voluptuary will be born. [Nigger 156-9
VOLUTES. Than fragile volutes in a rose sea-shell. [Soldat 14-3 P
VORAGINE. How is it that my saints from Voragine, [Polish Aunt
  84-4
VOYAGE. "The Paltry Nude Starts on a Spring Voyage" [5-title
Stopping, on voyage, in a land of snakes, [C 31-7
As on this voyage, out of goblinry, [C 35-10
His western voyage ended and began. [C 37-20
The drill of a submarine. The voyage [Hero 274-25
The first car out of a tunnel en voyage [Armor 530-2
VOYAGER. Became an introspective voyager. [C 29-23
VOYAGING. Thus he conceived his voyaging to be [C 35-6
Did not pass like someone voyaging out of and beyond the familiar.
  [Prol 515-13
VOYANT. Peter the voyant, who says "Mother, what is that"--
  [Questions 462-10
VULCAN. Of Vulcan, that a valet seeks to own, [C 33-6
VULCANIC. And darkly beside the vulcanic [Hero 274-28
VULGAR. The vulgar, as his theme and hymn and flight, [C 35-2
On an old shore, the vulgar ocean rolls [Somnam 304-1
But not of romance, the bitterest vulgar do [Bouquet 450-4
VULGARITY. Another American vulgarity. [Celle 438-16
VULGATE. The gibberish of the vulgate and back again. [NSF 396-14
It is the gibberish of the vulgate that he seeks. [NSF 397-5
The vulgate of experience. Of this, [NH 465-5

WADING. Wading the sea-lines, moist and ever-mingling, [Tallap 72-2
WAFTS. These he destroys with wafts of wakening, [NH 473-9
WAHRHEIT. And the truth, Dichtung und Wahrheit, all [MBG 177-17
WAILS. The long recessional at parish eves wails round [Greenest
   59-15 P
WAIT. Comes through boughs that lie in wait, [Brave 138-8
  To speak of what you see. But wait [Red Fern 365-14
  Your brown breast redden, while you wait for warmth. [Cred 377-7
  A wait within that certainty, a rest [NSF 386-7
  The birds that wait out rain in willow leaves. [Soldat 13-13 P
  Wait now; have no rememberings of hope, [Soldat 14-13 P
WAITER. The weather was like a waiter with a tray. [Forces 229-18
WAITING. Our earthly mothers waiting, sleeplessly. [Sunday 69-27
  That is woven and woven and waiting to be worn, [Dwarf 208-10
  That woman waiting for the man she loves,) [Rhythms 245-13
  Their own, waiting until we go [Dutch 293-2
  These lovers waiting in the soft dry grass. [Cred 372-18
  Of things were waiting in a betrothal known [Study II 464-17
  Now, he brings all that he saw into the earth, to the waiting
   parent. [Madame 507-3
  To disclose in the figure waiting on the road [Moonlight 531-13
  Waiting until we pass. [Phases 3-2 P
WAITRESS. The waitress heaped up black Hermosas [Attempt 370-2
WAITS. See how the absent moon waits in a glade [Blanche 10-10 P
  Waits for the unison of the music of the drifting bands [Sick
   90-14 P
  And the dissolving chorals, waits for it and imagines [Sick 90-15P
WAKE. When cocks wake, clawing at their beds [Adequacy 244-3
  Less in the stars than in their earthy wake, [Burnshaw 48-10 P
  Distant, yet close enough to wake [Child 106-20 P
WAKED. Waked in the elders by Susanna. [Peter 90-6
  And the people suddenly evil, waked, accused, [Sombre 69-2 P
WAKEFULNESS. That wakefulness or meditating sleep, [C 33-23
  Your dozing in the depths of wakefulness, [Rome 509-18
  Nor are you now, in this wakefulness inside a sleep. [Slug 522-18
WAKEN. Rise, since rising will not waken, [Watermelon 89-14
  Waken, and watch the moonlight on their floors. [Havana 145-2
WAKENED. She says, "I am content when wakened birds, [Sunday 68-12
  And the spirit writhes to be wakened, writhes [Duck 61-8 P
WAKENING. These he destroys with wafts of wakening, [NH 473-9
WAKENS. Until sight wakens the sleepy eye [Red Fern 365-15
WAKES. His thought sleeps not. Yet thought that wakes [Canna 55-4
  The spirit wakes in the night wind--is naked. [Soldat 11-13 P
  Wakes us to the emotion, grand fortissimo, [Grotesque 76-19 P
WAKING. For sleepers halfway waking. He perceived [C 31-16
  The man in Georgia waking among pines [C 38-15
  Kept waking and a mournful sense sought out, [Montra 263-5
  A waking, as in images we awake, [Study I 463-8
  There sleep and waking fill with jaguar-men [Greenest 55-2 P
WALDORF. Home from Guatemala, back at the Waldorf. [Waldorf 240-23
WALK. Who in the tomb of heaven walk by night, [Heaven 56-10
  But when I walk I see that it consists of three or four hills
   and a cloud. [Of Surface 57-2
  Deer walk upon our mountains, and the quail [Sunday 70-22
  Patron and patriarch of couplets, walk [NE Verses 105-11
  How should you walk in that space and know [MBG 183-7
  The dog had to walk. He had to be taken. [Forces 229-3
  He had only not to live, to walk in the dark, [Landsc 242-12
  Where is that summer warm enough to walk [Extracts 252-15
  They walk in mist and rain and snow [Poesie 302-13
  From lunacy . . . One wants to be able to walk [EM 325-2
  The truth depends on a walk around a lake, [NSF 386-3
  That walk away as one in the greenest body. [NSF 392-15
  To walk another room . . . Monsieur and comrade, [NSF 407-17
  Men would be starting at dawn to walk ashore. [Page 422-5
  To keep on flowing. He wanted to walk beside it, [Cata 425-4
  She is the day, the walk of the moon. [Pecul 454-4
  The ephebe is solitary in his walk. [NH 474-10
  These actors still walk in a twilight muttering lines. [NH 479-23
  On the walk, purple and blue, and red and gold, [NH 484-5
  Shall walk [Archi 18-18 P
  We went to walk in the park; for, after all, [Duck 60-8 P
  How shall we face the edge of time? We walk [Duck 66-6 P
  And the way was more than the walk and was hard to see. [Gro-
   tesque 74-14 P
  Now, being invisible, I walk without mantilla, [Souls 94-16 P
  He asked me to walk with him [Three 141-12 P
WALKED. Discoverer walked through the harbor streets [C 32-14
  I was the world in which I walked, and what I saw [Hoon 65-16
  The disbeliever walked the moonlit place, [Babies 77-1
  The walker in the moonlight walked alone, [Babies 77-7
  The walker in the moonlight walked alone, [Babies 77-16
  She walked upon the grass, [Peter 91-1
  Was merely a place by which she walked to sing. [Key W 129-6
  His dark familiar, often walked apart. [Anglais 148-14
  How often had he walked [Scavoir 231-9
  At the beginning of winter, and I walked and talked [Martial
   238-14

Walked the United States today, [News 264-8
He walked with his year-old boy on his shoulder. [Contra II 270-4
And the martyrs à la mode. He walked toward [Contra II 270-9
Walked toward him on the stage and they embraced. [Repet 306-15
A man walked living among the forms of thought [Owl 432-20
March . . . Someone has walked across the snow, [Vacancy 511-4
And walked in fine clothes, [Parasol 20-13 P
And equally as scientist you walked [Good Bad 33-15 P
In a flapping cloak. She walked along the paths [Old Woman 44-2 P
And looking at the place in which she walked, [Old Woman 45-20 P
Through long cloud-cloister-porches, walked alone, [Greenest
  54-3 P
Or hear her step in the way she walked? [Grotesque 74-12 P
This was not how she walked for she walked in a way [Grotesque
  74-13 P
WALKER. The walker in the moonlight walked alone, [Babies 77-7
  The walker in the moonlight walked alone, [Babies 77-16
  A horse grotesquely taut, a walker like [Pure 330-6
  Dark horse and walker walking rapidly. [Pure 330-12
  To which the walker speaks [Woman Song 360-14
  Go with the walker subtly walking there. [NH 473-8
WALKERS. He carved the feathery walkers standing by, [Duck
  64-22 P
WALKING. Then you came walking, [Vincentine 53-4
  Yes: you came walking, [Vincentine 53-8
  Like Walt Whitman walking along a ruddy shore. [Nigger 150-10
  A pink girl took a white dog walking. [Forces 229-2
  Still walking in a present of our own. [Martial 237-16
  So seeing, I beheld you walking, white, [Phenom 287-12
  It is someone walking rapidly in the street. [Pure 330-1
  Dark horse and walker walking rapidly. [Pure 330-12
  Young men go walking in the woods, [Pediment 361-7
  What chieftain, walking by himself, crying [NSF 389-2
  The man who is walking turns blankly on the sand. [AA 412-23
  Go with the walker subtly walking there. [NH 473-8
  Of the window and walking in the street and seeing, [NH 478-9
  Walking in the snow, [Primordia 7-12 P
  A woman walking in the autumn leaves, [Old Woman 45-18 P
  Walking the paths, watching the gilding sun, [Duck 65-18 P
  A manner of walking, yellow fruit, a house, [Woman Had 83-7 P
  Young and walking in the sunshine, [Clear Day 113-11 P
WALKS. Who walks there, as a farewell duty, [Virgin 71-5
  Walks long and long. [Virgin 71-6
  Walks around the feet [Thirteen 93-22
  She walks an autumn ampler than the wind [Anatomy 108-3
  The body walks forth naked in the sun [Anatomy 108-8
  In which the body walks and is deceived, [Anatomy 108-16
  From below and walks without meditation, [Brave 138-20
  And, dressed in black, he walks [Gray 140-3
  And speech of Virgil dropped, that's where he walks, [Thought
   185-14
  It is she that walks among astronomers. [Candle 223-2
  The philosophers' man alone still walks in dew, [Oboe 250-12
  A soldier walks before my door. [Contra I 266-12
  Of a primitive. He walks with a defter [Hero 277-10
  Concealed creator. One walks easily [Couch 296-3
  Or the phosphored sleep in which he walks abroad [EM 320-16
  He walks and dies. Nothing survives [Woman Song 360-8
  A countryman walks beside you. [Countryman 428-6
  He walks through the house, looks round him and then leaves.
   [Bouquet 453-2
  A little thing to think of on Sunday walks, [Aug 491-22
  No turban walks across the lessened floors. [Plain 502-16
  And there he walks and does as he lives and likes. [Armor 530-22
  No shadow walks. The river is fateful, [R Conn 533-10
  She walks, triumphing humbly, should express [Red Kit 31-11 P
  In which the horse walks home without a rider, [Fare Guit 99-3 P
WALL. The first white wall of the village [Magnifico 19-18
  The first white wall of the village . . . [Magnifico 19-22
  After the sermon, to quiet that mouse in the wall. [Blue Bldg
   216-20
  The hand between the candle and the wall [Rhythms 245-9
  Grows large on the wall. [Rhythms 245-10
  Has a will to grow larger on the wall, [Rhythms 245-19
  The wall; and that the mind [Rhythms 246-2
  The moonlight in the cell, words on the wall. [Montra 260-21
  On the wall, the lemons on the table. [Hero 280-15
  Without understanding, out of the wall [Creat 310-12
  His stars on the wall. He must dwell quietly. [Less 327-14
  Who lay in bed on the west wall of the sea, [Pure 331-6
  These two by the stone wall [Burghers 362-4
  Clears deeply, when the moon hangs on the wall [NSF 398-24
  Of an infinite course. The flowers against the wall [AA 412-8
  And the whiteness grows less vivid on the wall. [AA 412-22
  The sun is secretly shining on a wall. [Bouquet 450-23
  In the street, in a room, on a carpet or a wall, [NH 467-12
  A broken wall--and it ceased to exist, became [Greenest 53-7 P
  The skeletons sit on the wall. They drop [Stan MBG 72-3 P
  A bubble without a wall on which to hang. [Theatre 91-12 P
  3. A vine has climbed the other side of the wall. [Someone 86-6 A

See church-wall.
WALLED. See water-walled.
WALLOWS. Making a great gnashing, over the water wallows [Puel 456-8
  Irked the wet wallows of the water-spout. [NH 476-6
WALLS. Through the palace walls. [Ord Women 10-16
  Through the palace walls. [Ord Women 12-6
  Observing the moon-blotches on the walls. [Babies 77-3
  A spirit storming in blank walls, [Postcard 159-18
  To the fatuous. These are his infernal walls, [Thought 185-8
  That the walls are mirrors multiplied, [Prelude 195-2
  In opal blobs along the walls and floor. [Blue Bldg 217-12
  Pass through the door and through the walls, [Vari 235-10
  The mountains inscribe themselves upon the walls. [Extracts
    252-8
  The shadows lessen on the walls. [Contra I 266-18
  The wind beat in the roof and half the walls. [Repet 306-2
  He can hear them, like people on the walls, [Sketch 336-4
  Spreading out fortress walls like fortress wings. [Luther 461-12
  Out of the surfaces, the windows, the walls, [NH 480-22
  And the egg of the sky are in shells, in walls, in skins [Aug
    490-9
  The chapel underneath St. Armorer's walls, [Armor 530-19
  Along the walls [Phases 4-13 P
  From pipes that swarm clerestory walls. The voice [Greenest
    59-13 P
  That thinks of it is inscribed on walls and stands [Duck 64-3 P
  Its shadow on their houses, on their walls, [Sombre 68-22 P
  Brooder, brooder, deep beneath its walls-- [Dove 97-16 P
WALPOLE. See Horace Walpole.
WALT WHITMAN. Like Walt Whitman walking along a ruddy shore. [Nig-
  ger 150-10
WALTZ. "Sad Strains of a Gay Waltz" [121-title
  There comes a time when the waltz [Sad Gay 121-11
  For whom desire was never that of the waltz, [Sad Gay 121-16
WALTZES. Too many waltzes have ended. And then [Sad Gay 121-14
  Too many waltzes have ended. Yet the shapes [Sad Gay 122-10
  Too many waltzes--The epic of disbelief [Sad Gay 122-13
WAND. The jewels in his beard, the mystic wand, [Bship 79-4 P
  Power in the waving of the wand of the moon, [Someone 84-10 A
WANDER. When the host shall no more wander, nor the light [Heaven
  56-19
  "You that wander," [Peacocks 58-9
WANDERER. Of the impersonal person, the wanderer, [Aug 494-21
  . . . Wanderer, this is the pre-history of February. [Slug 522-15
  And who shall speak it, what child or wanderer [Ideal 88-19 A
WANDERERS. And late wanderers creeping under the barb of night,
  [Dutch 291-24
  Of lone wanderers. To re-create, to use [NH 481-15
WANDERING. That first drove Crispin to his wandering. [C 39-13
  Life fixed him, wandering on the stair of glass, [NH 483-10
  In the land of the elm trees, wandering mariners [NH 486-16
  A wandering orb upon a path grown clear. [Sombre 70-17 P
  Or is it I that, wandering, know, one-sensed, [Souls 95-4 P
WANDS. Waving purpling wands, the thinker [Ulysses 100-19 P
WANT. Turned from their want, and, nonchalant, [Ord Women 10-18
  Still one would want more, one would need more, [Poems Clim
    194-2
  So that one would want to escape, come back [Poems Clim 194-5
  And did not want nor have to be, [Motive 288-12
  In which the characters speak because they want [Cred 378-6
  Ever want it to. It is part of the life in your room. [Rome
    510-13
  Has enraged them and made them want to talk it down. [Slug 522-8
  Digs up the earth when want returns . . . [Soldat 16-11 P
WANTED. The sky was blue. He wanted imperceptible air. [Landsc
  241-13
  He wanted to see. He wanted the eye to see [Landsc 241-14
  And not be touched by blue. He wanted to know, [Landsc 241-15
  That other one wanted to think his way to life, [Extracts 256-21
  He, that one, wanted to think his way to life, [Extracts 257-4
  They had to think it to be. He wanted that, [Extracts 257-6
  He wanted and looked for a final refuge, [Contra II 270-7
  Arrives at the man-man as he wanted. [Hero 280-17
  He rose because men wanted him to be. [Choc 299-13
  They wanted him by day to be, image, [Choc 299-14
  And him. Both wanted the same thing. Both sought [Liadoff 347-18
  Flotillas, willed and wanted, bearing in them [New Set 352-11
  Wanted to lean, wanted much most to be [House Q 358-13
  He wanted to feel the same way over and over. [Cata 425-2
  He wanted the river to go on flowing the same way, [Cata 425-3
  To keep on flowing. He wanted to walk beside it, [Cata 425-4
  He wanted his heart to stop beating and his mind to rest [Cata
    425-6
  This chorus as of those that wanted to live. [Aug 491-18
  Because we wanted it so [Aug 495-11
  That it contained the meaning into which he wanted to enter,
    [Prol 516-6
  She wanted nothing he could not bring her by coming alone.
    [World 521-7
  She wanted no fetchings. His arms would be her necklace [World

521-8
  Flaunts that first fortune, which he wanted so much. [Americana
    94-15 P
  One would have wanted more--more--more-- [Letters 107-4 P
  And hearing a tale one wanted intensely to hear, [Letters 107-12P
  She wanted a holiday [Letters 107-16 P
  He wanted to make them, keep them from perishing, [Local 112-6 P
  But he wanted nothing. [Three 141-15 P
WANTON. She might, after all, be a wanton, [Homunculus 26-23
WANTS. That's what one wants to get near. Could it after all [Dump
  202-28
  It wants the diamond pivot bright. [Country 207-19
  It wants Belshazzar reading right [Country 207-20
  It wants words virile with his breath. [Country 207-23
  It is she that he wants, to look at directly, [Scavoir 232-3
  Exactly, that which it wants to hear, at the sound [Of Mod 240-9
  Ceylon, wants nothing from the sea, la belle [Extracts 257-28
  From lunacy . . . One wants to be able to walk [EM 325-2
  He is there because he wants to be [Countryman 429-2
WAR. Their curious fates in war, come, celebrate [Monocle 16-15
  To live in war, to live at war, [MBG 173-19
  As the life of the fatal unity of war. [Yellow 236-21
  In the land of war. More than the man, it is [Bottle 239-1
  It has to content the reason concerning war, [Bottle 239-5
  It has to persuade that war is part of itself, [Bottle 239-6
  The women of the time. It has to think about war [Of Mod 240-3
  One year, death and war prevented the jasmine scent [Oboe 251-8
  In total war we died and after death [Extracts 258-25
  "Examination of the Hero in a Time of War" [273-title
  In war, observes each man profoundly. [Hero 274-14
  That was to look on what war magnified. [Gigan 289-14
  The armies are cities in movement. But a war [Choc 296-13
  Until this matter-makes in years of war. [Repet 307-10
  War's miracle begetting that of peace. [Cats 368-5
  My Jacomyntje! This first spring after the war, [Extraord 369-16
  Soldier, there is a war between the mind [NSF 407-4
  Up down. It is a war that never ends. [NSF 407-9
  But your war ends. And after it you return [NSF 407-15
  And war for war, each has its gallant kind. [NSF 407-21
  War, too, although I do not understand. [Soldat 11-2 P
  Dissolved the woods, war and the fatal farce [Greenest 53-22 P
  Of war, the rust on the steeples, these jutted up, [Greenest
    53-23 P
  Angels returning after war with belts [Greenest 56-10 P
  "The war between classes is [Bship 77-16 P
  Of the war between individuals. In time, [Bship 77-18 P
  Forgetful of death in war, there rises [Stan Hero 84-2 P
  Now. War as a punishment. The hero [Stan Hero 84-16 P
WARBLERS. The wild warblers are warbling in the jungle [Medit
  123-13
WARBLING. The wild warblers are warbling in the jungle [Medit
  123-13
WARBLINGS. To warblings early in the hilarious trees [Medit 124-8
  On his balcony at night. Warblings became [EM 314-18
WARD. The faith of forty, ward of Cupido. [Monocle 16-16
  Across the roofs as sigil and as ward [NSF 384-23
WARDED. They warded the blank waters of the lakes [Havana 142-16
WARDENS. Hybrids impossible to the wardens [Stan Hero 84-6 P
WAREHOUSE. From warehouse doors, the gustiness of ropes, [C 36-9
WARM. I saw you then, as warm as flesh, [Vincentine 52-16
  As warm, as clean. [Vincentine 52-19
  But when the birds are gone, and their warm fields [Sunday 68-15
  Of a green evening, clear and warm, [Peter 90-7
  In the green water, clear and warm, [Peter 90-13
  The warm antiquity of self, [Fading 139-6
  Mechanical beetles never quite warm? [MBG 168-15
  The night should be warm and fluters' fortune [Nightgown 214-15
  False as the mind, instead of the fragrance, warm [Horn 230-12
  Where is that summer warm enough to walk [Extracts 252-15
  Within the actual, the warm, the near, [EM 317-7
  There is so little that is close and warm. [Debris 338-1
  Sour wine to warm him, an empty book to read; [Good Man 364-11
  Grows warm in the motionless motion of his flight, [NSF 404-19
  They are together, here, and it is warm, [AA 413-6
  Is still warm with the love with which she came, [Aug 496-1
  So, then, this warm, wide, weatherless quietude [Moonlight 531-19
WARMED. Warmed by a desperate milk. To find the real, [NSF 404-8
WARMER. And spread about them a warmer, rosier odor. [Aug 491-28
WARMEST. The fragrance of the autumn warmest, [On Road 204-11
  And the oldest and the warmest heart was cut [Quiet 523-10
WARMTH. Expanding in the gold's maternal warmth. [C 32-10
  Ripened in warmth and served in warmth. On terms [Nigger 155-4
  This warmth of the blood-world for the pure idea, [Extracts
    256-12
  Your brown breast redden, while you wait for warmth. [Cred 377-7
  This warmth is for lovers at last accomplishing [NSF 391-4
  Out of the first warmth of spring, [Celle 438-1
  It is only that this warmth and movement are like [Wom Sun 445-4
  The warmth and movement of a woman. [Wom Sun 445-5
  A coldness in a long, too-constant warmth, [NH 474-20

Like the constant sound of the water of the sea [NH 480-14
Mud, water like dirty glass, expressing silence [Plain 503-4
Wet with water and sparkling in the one-ness of their motion.
  [Prol 515-9
Part of the glass-like sides on which it glided over the salt-
  stained water, [Prol 516-3
The mere flowing of the water is a gayety, [R Conn 533-8
In the flowing of black water. [Primordia 7-22 P
The water runs away from the horses. [Primordia 8-18 P
What are you drawing from the rain-pointed water? [Primordia 9-2P
What are you drawing from the rain-pointed water? [Primordia 9-4P
Like water running in a gutter [Grotesque 76-22 P
Night's moonlight lake was neither water nor air. [Real 111-2 P
Dew is water to see, [Three 128-3 P
Not water to drink: [Three 128-4 P
We have forgotten water to drink. [Three 128-5 P
If we have no water, [Three 128-13 P
Your porcelain water bottle. [Three 129-1 P
This fetches its own water. [Three 129-2 P
She was as beautiful as a porcelain water bottle. [Three 136-19P
Bring us fresh water [Three 141-1 P
And water. It is that which is distilled [Someone 87-17 A
See ruby-water-worn.
WATER-BELLY. And let the water-belly of ocean roar, [Montra 261-23
WATER-CARCASS. Lascar, and water-carcass never-named, [Two V 354-7
WATERFALLS. One is a child again. The gold beards of waterfalls
  [Discov 95-10 P
WATER-FALLS. Geranium budgets, pay-roll water-falls, [Duck 62-24 P
WATER-FLOOR. Of water moving on the water-floor? [Sea Surf 100-2
WATER-GLOOMS. And the macabre of the water-glooms [Sea Surf 100-8
WATERINESS. The wateriness of green wet in the sky. [NH 484-11
WATERING. Spontaneously watering their gritty soils. [Monocle
  16-25
WATERISH. Of waterish spears. The fisherman is all [Think 356-13
  A change, until the waterish ditherings turn [Burnshaw 52-14 P
WATERLESS. And the river becomes the landless, waterless ocean?
  [Degen 444-21
WATER-LIGHTS. As a calm darkens among water-lights. [Sunday 67-4
WATER-LIKE. Jocunda, who will arrange the roses and rearrange,
  letting the leaves lie on the water-like lacquer; [Piano 22-4P
WATER-LILIES. "Nuns Painting Water-Lilies" [92-title P
WATERMELON. "Hymn from a Watermelon Pavilion" [88-title
  To whom the watermelon is always purple, [Watermelon 88-20
WATERS. They warded the blank waters of the lakes [Havana 142-16
WATER-SHINE. In the scrurry and water-shine, [Paltry 6-2
WATER-SPHERES. The statue stood in stars like water-spheres, [Old
  Woman 45-10 P
WATER-SPOUT. Irked the wet wallows of the water-spout. [NH 476-6
WATER-WALLED. And cloud, of the sunken coral water-walled, [Key W
  129-13
WATER-WHEEL. On the dark, green water-wheel, [Solitaires 60-4
WATERY. And watery back. [Paltry 5-18
  Within me, bursts its watery syllable. [Monocle 13-11
  The old age of a watery realist, [C 28-23
  Of blue and green? A wordy, watery age [C 28-25
  And in its watery radiance, while the hue [Sea Surf 99-12
  Suckled on ponds, the spirit craves a watery mountain. [NE
    Verses 105-2
  In which the watery grasses flow [MBG 180-12
  And still the birds came, came in watery flocks, [Loaf 200-14
  It is an ocean of watery images [Two V 355-11
  Like watery words awash; like meanings said [Angel 497-4
WATTLES. Of clay and wattles made as it ascends [Page 421-11
WATTS. See Isaac Watts.
WAVE. Noiselessly, like one more wave. [Paltry 5-10
  A wave, interminably flowing. [Peter 92-3
  It could not be a mind, the wave [MBG 180-11
  He might take habit, whether from wave or phrase, [NSF 387-12
  Or power of the wave, or deepened speech, [NSF 387-13
  And mountains running like water, wave on wave, [AA 416-6
  The prismatic sombreness of a torrent's wave. [Bouquet 452-12
  Let your golden hands wave fastly and be gay [Burnshaw 51-28 P
WAVED. Waved in pale adieu. The rex Impolitor [Aug 495-21
  And the palms were waved [Coroner 29-12 P
  The palms were waved [Coroner 29-16 P
WAVER. This is the true creator, the waver [Ulysses 100-18 P
WAVERED. Wavered in evening air, above the roof, [Phases 5-5 P
WAVERING. Yet wavering. [Peter 91-6
  With time, in wavering water lies, swollen [Two V 354-2
WAVERINGS. By waverings of stars, the joy of day [Greenest 54-15 P
WAVES. And that whatever noise the motion of the waves [Hibiscus
  22-12
  Dibbled in waves that were mustachios, [C 27-20
  That were like arms and shoulders in the waves, [C 29-2
  Rides clear of her mind and the waves make a refrain. [Farewell
    117-8
  The floor. Go on through the darkness. The waves fly back. [Fare-
    well 117-10
  That rose, or even colored by many waves; [Key W 129-11
  And men in waves become the sea. [MBG 171-2

Birds that came like dirty water in waves [Loaf 200-3
Spreading them as waves spread flat on the shore, [Loaf 200-6
And the waves, the waves were soldiers moving, [Loaf 200-10
And the sun, the waves together in the sea. [Les Plus 245-2
They mow the lawn. A vessel sinks in waves [EM 322-12
As if the waves at last were never broken, [NSF 387-16
Should foam, be foamy waves, should move like them, [NSF 399-7
Through waves of light. It is of cloud transformed [AA 416-7
A boat carried forward by waves resembling the bright backs of
  rowers, [Prol 515-6
Observed the waves, the rising and the swell [Woman Had 81-13 P
This was repeated day by day. The waves [Woman Had 81-19 P
WAVING. Cones, waving lines, ellipses-- [Six Sig 75-11
  Of waving weeds. I hated the vivid blooms [Farewell 118-3
  "Waving Adieu, Adieu, Adieu" [127-title
  That would be waving and that would be crying, [Adieu 127-9
  Winding and waving, slowly, waving in air, [Greenest 55-14 P
  Waving purpling wands, the thinker [Ulysses 100-19 P
  Power in the waving of the wand of the moon, [Someone 84-10 A
WAX. Wax wasted, monarchies beyond [Prelude 195-6
  Whiter than wax, sonorous, fame as it is, [NSF 403-19
  The solid wax from which the warmth dies out? . . [Infernale
    24-22 P
  Hallooing haggler; for the wax is blown, [Infernale 25-6 P
WAXEN. I saw a waxen woman in a smock [Infernale 25-1 P
WAX-LIKE. Bring down from nowhere nothing's wax-like blooms,
  [Burnshaw 47-20 P
WAY. A firecat bristled in the way. [Earthy 3-3
  Bristled in the way. [Earthy 3-18
  Upon her irretrievable way. [Paltry 6-10
  These muleteers are dainty of their way. [Monocle 15-21
  This trivial trope reveals a way of truth. [Monocle 16-4
  By way of decorous melancholy; he [C 31-4
  Their dreams, he did it in a gingerly way. [C 39-30
  With lanterns borne aloft to light the way, [Heaven 56-13
  Not by way of romance, [Explan 72-17
  The way the ants crawl [Six Sig 74-12
  Have it your way. [Gubbinal 85-3
  Have it your way. [Gubbinal 85-11
  It depends which way you crossed, the tea-belle said. [NE Verses
    104-4
  And doesn't get under way. [Sailing 120-3
  It is only the way one feels, to say [Sailing 120-22
  By light, the way one feels, sharp white, [Sailing 121-6
  To abate on the way to church, [Winter B 141-11
  It picks its way on the blue guitar. [MBG 166-14
  For a moment final, in the way [MBG 168-3
  In the way they are modelled [Pears 196-13
  Pftt. . . . In the way you speak [Add 198-15
  And the river that batters its way over stones, [Loaf 199-17
  That they were oak-leaves, as the way they looked. [Freed 205-19
  It wears. This is the way the orator spoke: [Dames 206-2
  And if it all went on in an orderly way, [Connois 215-8
  This way and that. [Thunder 220-4
  You touch the hotel the way you touch moonlight [Waldorf 241-4
  And we feel, in a way apart, for a moment, as if [Gala 248-11
  To think it is to think the way to death . . . [Extracts 256-20
  That other one wanted to think his way to life, [Extracts 256-21
  He, that one, wanted to think his way to life, [Extracts 257-4
  And for it, and by which we think the way, [Extracts 257-12
  Finding its way from the house, makes music seem [Phenom 287-1
  In the same way, you were happy in spring, [Motive 288-5
  That sweats the sun up on its morning way [Repet 307-7
  Could be borne, as if we were sure to find our way. [EM 316-6
  Such seemings are the actual ones: the way [Descrip 339-17
  And spring's infuriations over and a long way [Cred 372-5
  It is a mountain half way green and then, [Cred 375-13
  A mountain luminous half way in bloom [Cred 375-22
  And then half way in the extremest light [Cred 375-23
  Of its cry as clarion, its diction's way [Cred 377-3
  And present way, a presentation, a kind [NSF 397-20
  The way a painter of pauvred color paints. [NSF 402-3
  The way wine comes at a table in a wood. [NSF 405-24
  And we enjoy like men, the way a leaf [NSF 406-1
  To cloud transformed again, idly, the way [AA 416-8
  Except as needed by way of majesty, [AA 417-14
  Which kept flowing and never the same way twice, flowing [Cata
    424-8
  He wanted to feel the same way over and over. [Cata 425-2
  He wanted the river to go on flowing the same way, [Cata 425-3
  And yet this effect is a consequence of the way [Roses 430-16
  Its brightness burned the way good solace seethes. [Owl 434-6
  Almost as speed discovers, in the way [Owl 435-10
  In the way what was has ceased to be what is. [Owl 435-12
  Is Celestin dislodged? The way through the world [Papini 446-5
  Is more difficult to find than the way beyond it. [Papini 446-6
  When in a way of seeing seen, an extreme, [Bouquet 451-11
  And yet is there, a presence in the way. [Bouquet 452-5
  Nothing could be more hushed than the way [Pecul 453-7
  To phantoms. Till then, it had been the other way: [What We 459-9

The way the drowsy, infant, old men do. [Questions 463-3
But that's the difference: in the end and the way [NH 469-19
A disused ambit of the spirit's way, [Aug 489-8
Spread sail, we say spread white, spread way. [Aug 490-7
Shifted the rocks and picked his way among clouds, [Poem Mt 512-8
Gripping their oars, as if they were sure of the way to their
    destination, [Prol 515-7
Only a little way, and not beyond, unless between himself [Prol
    516-12
The way some first thing coming into Northern trees [Prol 517-6
The way the earliest single light in the evening sky, in spring,
    [Prol 517-8
The way a look or a touch reveals its unexpected magnitudes.
    [Prol 517-10
That blows about in such a hopeless way, [Phases 5-13 P
Of blind men tapping their way [Soldat 12-11 P
Am I to pick my way [Soldat 12-17 P
Get out of the way! [Soldat 13-4 P
One likes the way red grows. [Table 40-12 P
Implicit clarities in the way you cry [Burnshaw 52-12 P
Ontario, Canton. It was the way [Greenest 53-10 P
Things jutted up, the way the jagged stacks, [Greenest 53-11 P
In Leonardo's way, to magnify [Greenest 56-20 P
About the weather and women and the way [Greenest 58-26 P
If you caricature the way they rise, yet they rise. [Duck 60-18P
Between chimeras and garlanded the way, [Sombre 67-29 P
That a man without passion plays in an aimless way. [Sombre
    71-12 P
The way it came, let be what it may become. [Sombre 71-16 P
Or hear her step in the way she walked? [Grotesque 74-12 P
This was not how she walked for she walked in a way [Grotesque
    74-13 P
And the way was more than the walk and was hard to see. [Gro-
    tesque 74-14 P
And that's his way. And that's my way as well. [Grotesque 76-5 P
The way we speak of it. [Grotesque 76-9 P
Regulae mundi . . . That much is out of the way. [Bship 80-30 P
The words are in the way and thoughts are. [Stan Hero 84-1 P
With something I could touch, touch every way. [Warmth 90-6 P
And clumped stars dangled all the way. [Ulysses 105-12 P
Through clumped stars dangling all the way. [Presence 106-12 P
Or almost solid seem show--the way a fly bird [Conversat 108-14P
The point of it was the way he heard it, [Dinner 110-5 P
The way, when we climb a mountain, [July 115-4 P
Saying and saying, the way things say [Region 115-10 P
"On the Way to the Bus" [116-title
A way of pronouncing the word inside of one's tongue [Bus 116-13P
With something I could touch, touch every way. [As Leave 117-12P
But it is a way with ballads [Three 137-15 P
See: half-way; that-a-way; this-a-way.
WAYS. "Thirteen Ways of Looking at a Blackbird" [92-title
See, now, the ways beleaguered by black, dropsical duennas,
    [Inelegance 26-7 P
Of the ways things happen to fall. [Table 40-15 P
See foot-ways.
WEAK. And all their manner, weak and strong? [MBG 166-18
The weak man mended, [Idiom 201-2
"A Weak Mind in the Mountains" [212-title
His arm would be trembling, he would be weak, [Thunder 220-15
The phrase grows weak. The fact takes up the strength [NH 473-4
A strong mind in a weak neighborhood and is [NH 474-13
The weak colors, [Three 132-1 P
WEAKEN. Weaken our fate, relieve us of woe both great [EM 315-21
WEAKER. Weaker and weaker, the sunlight falls [Leben 504-16
WEAKEST. Union of the weakest develops strength [Nigger 158-10
WEALTH. Whose chiefest embracing of all wealth [Ulysses 104-12 P
WEAPON. And rainbow sortilege, the savage weapon [Hero 274-3
WEAPONS. There are circles of weapons in the sun. [Dutch 290-15
WEAR. That prose should wear a poem's guise at last. [C 36-23
As they are used to wear, and let the boys [Emperor 64-5
Alas, that they should wear our colors there, [Sunday 69-22
Rationalists would wear sombreros. [Six Sig 75-13
It is turbans they wear [Cortege 80-16
In the laborious weaving that you wear. [Fictive 87-22
Bear other perfumes. On your pale head wear [Fictive 88-15
Wear the breeches of a mask, [Orangeade 103-9
Wear a helmet without reason, [Orangeade 103-11
The devil take it, wear it, too. [Snow Stars 133-5
The web is woven and you have to wear it. [Dwarf 208-2
In these, I wear a vital cleanliness, [Rhythms 246-6
And wear humanity's bleak crown; [Crude 305-8
To be crested and wear the mane of a multitude [NSF 398-8
I have neither ashen wing nor wear of ore [Angel 496-9
And a breech-cloth might wear, [Cab 21-7 P
What breech-cloth might you wear-- [Cab 21-13 P
The silks they wear in all the cities [Melancholy 32-13 P
Thoughts by descent. To flourish the great cloak we wear [Sombre
    71-19 P
I said that men should wear stone masks and, to make [Bship
    78-11 P

WEARER. And that confident one, Marie, the wearer of cheap stones,
    who will have grown still and restless; [Piano 22-5 P
WEARIER. When, at the wearier end of November, [Lunar 107-2
WEARING. Wearing a clear tiara [Venereal 48-7
Rationalists, wearing square hats, [Six Sig 75-4
And wearing hats of angular flick and fleck, [Bouquet 449-8
Is only another egoist, wearing a mask, [Duck 63-5 P
Progenitor wearing the diamond crown of crowns, [Duck 64-30 P
WEARS. It wears. This is the way the orator spoke: [Dames 206-2
Of our passionate height. He wears a tufted green, [Repet 309-23
He wears the words he reads to look upon [Aug 492-5
Tradition wears, the clear, the single form [Recit 87-21 P
WEARY. The horses weary themselves hunting for green grass.
    [Primordia 8-15 P
We have grown weary of the man that thinks. [Sombre 66-18 P
WEASELS. Young weasels racing steep horizons in pursuit of
    planets . . . [Inelegance 26-8 P
WEATHER. Into the autumn weather, splashed with frost, [Monocle
    16-7
In red weather. [Ten O'C 66-15
In the land of turkeys in turkey weather [Mice 123-1
To the ever-jubilant weather, to sip [Adieu 128-2
What is there here but weather, what spirit [Adieu 128-9
One grows used to the weather, [Am Sub 131-5
This pundit of the weather, who never ceased [Nigger 156-5
It needed the heavy nights of drenching weather [Nigger 158-6
The weather of his stage, himself. [MBG 170-4
It is faster than the weather, faster than [Parochial 192-5
Well, the gods grow out of the weather. [Jersey 210-5
The people grow out of the weather; [Jersey 210-6
A look at the weather. [Nightgown 214-2
And of fair weather, summer dew, peace. [Peaches 224-14
"Forces, the Will & the Weather" [228-title
The weather was like a waiter with a tray. [Forces 229-18
To face the weather and be unable to tell [Extracts 257-7
Between one's self and the weather and the things [Extracts
    258-3
Of the weather are the belief in one's element, [Extracts 258-4
To believe in the weather and in the things and men [Extracts
    258-8
Of the weather and in one's self, as part of that [Extracts
    258-9
Weather of night creatures, whistling all day, too, [Montra
    261-17
"The News and the Weather" [264-title
Taken with withered weather, crumpled clouds, [News 265-6
Parl-parled the West-Indian weather. [Search 268-2
The weather pink, the wind in motion; and this: [EM 322-24
The wild ducks were enveloped. The weather was cold. [Wild 329-3
Not span, without any weather at all, except [Wild 329-7
The weather of other lives, from which there could [Wild 329-8
Time in its weather, our most sovereign lord, [Pure 332-17
The weather in words and words in sounds of sound. [Pure 332-18
The fathers of the makers may lie and weather. [New Set 353-6
Talk of the weather-- [Woman Song 361-3
It observes the effortless weather turning blue [NSF 382-7
Not to be realized. Weather by Franz Hals, [NSF 385-6
The weather and the giant of the weather, [NSF 385-22
Say the weather, the mere weather, the mere air: [NSF 385-23
Out of nothing to have come on major weather, [NSF 404-3
To a haggling of wind and weather, by these lights [AA 421-2
These are the ashes of fiery weather, [Our Stars 455-13
The town, the weather, in a casual litter, [NH 474-8
About the weather and women and the way [Greenest 58-26 P
Blond weather. One is born a saint, [Stan MBG 73-9 P
Blond weather. Give the mule his hay. [Stan MBG 73-17 P
The chant and discourse there, more than wild weather [Role 93-9P
In a health of weather, knowing a few, old things, [Americana
    93-17 P
Nothing more, like weather after it has cleared-- [Art Pop
    112-14 P
Well, more than that, like weather when it has cleared [Art Pop
    112-15 P
To form that weather's appropriate people, [Art Pop 112-18 P
Today the mind is not part of the weather. [Clear Day 113-13 P
WEATHERED. And weathered and the ruby-water-worn, [NSF 400-9
And weathered, should be part of a human landscape, [Conversat
    109-6 P
WEATHER-FOXED. The bristling soldier, weather-foxed, who looms
    [Cred 375-2
WEATHERING. These marbles lay weathering in the grass [Two Illus
    514-6
WEATHERLESS. So, then, this warm, wide, weatherless quietude
    [Moonlight 531-19
WEATHERY. Of spiced and weathery rouges, should complex [C 44-8
I hated the weathery yawl from which the pools [Farewell 118-1
WEAVE. Her dress, the carefulest, commodious weave [Beginning
    428-4
To weave a shadow's leg or sleeve, a scrawl [What We 459-18
WEAVER. Inwoven by a weaver to twelve bells . . . [Beginning 428-5

WEAVERS. A majestic weavers' job, a summer's sweat. [Greenest 58-6 P
WEAVES. Weaves always glistening from the heart and mind. [NSF 396-12
A transparency through which the swallow weaves, [Look 518-8
WEAVING. In the laborious weaving that you wear. [Fictive 87-22
Still weaving budded aureoles, [Postcard 159-14
Weaving and weaving many arms. [Oak 272-9
The weaving and the crinkling and the vex, [Owl 433-17
In the weaving round the wonder of its need, [Owl 434-15
Weaving ring in radiant ring and quickly, fling [Burnshaw 51-14P
WEAVINGS. The silken weavings of our afternoons, [Sunday 69-23
WEAZENED. As summer would return to weazened days. [Greenest 57-27 P
WEB. The melon-flower nor dew nor web of either [Tallap 72-5
Now it is September and the web is woven. [Dwarf 208-1
The web is woven and you have to wear it. [Dwarf 208-2
The winter web, the winter woven, wind and wind, [Dwarf 208-4
And vanishing, a web in a corridor [AA 416-18
WEBS. And spreads its webs there-- [Tattoo 81-13
Its two webs. [Tattoo 81-14
The webs of your eyes [Tattoo 81-15
It glares beneath the webs [Common 221-17
WEDDINGS. One's tootings at the weddings of the soul [Sleight 222-2
WEDGES. Wild wedges, as of a volcano's smoke, palm-eyed [AA 416-17
WEDLOCK. Outside of Wedlock [76-title 5 P
WEED. But on the first-found weed [Paltry 5-8
The clearest woman with apt weed, to mount [Havana 143-17
Is a weed and all the flies are caught, [MBG 171-6
The wet weed sputtered, the fire died down, the cold [Page 422-1
The stalk, the weed, the grassy flourishes, [Bouquet 452-8
In the weed of summer comes this green sprout why. [Questions 462-4
WEEDS. Over weeds. [Six Sig 73-15
Of waving weeds. I hated the vivid blooms [Farewell 118-3
And in the water winding weeds move round. [Glass 197-17
And last year's garden grows salacious weeds. [Cred 377-10
Were mere brown clods, mere catching weeds of talk. [NH 486-21
See sea-weeds.
WEEDY. Whistle aloud, too weedy wren. I can [NSF 405-10
Eheu! Eheu! With what a weedy face [Stan MMO 19-21 P
WEEK. The church bells clap one night in the week. [Cuisine 227-16
Of the week, queerer than Sunday. We thought alike [AA 419-10
A lamp, in a day of the week, the time before spring, [Woman Had 83-6 P
WEEK-DAY. The crown and week-day coronal of her fame. [Descrip 339-16
WEEK-END. We'll give the week-end to wisdom, to Weisheit, the rabbi, [Aug 492-1
WEEKS. Lusty as June, more fruitful than the weeks [Havana 143-13
WEEP. That makes us weep, laugh, grunt and groan, and shout [Monocle 17-10
And if you weep for peacocks that are gone [Burnshaw 48-21 P
WEEPING. "Another Weeping Woman" [25-title
"The Weeping Burgher" [61-title
I, weeping in a calcined heart, [W Burgher 61-16
And weeping up the hill. [Three 138-9 P
Or woman weeping in a room or man, [Ideal 88-20 A
WEEPS. The race that sings and weeps and knows not why. [Thought 186-16
And weeps on his breast, though he never comes. [Rhythms 245-17
Weeps in Segovia. The beggar in Rome [Greenest 59-17 P
WEIGHT. Falls, it appears, of its own weight to earth. [Monocle 14-13
The weight of primary noon, [Motive 288-15
Are in the grass, the roses are heavy with a weight [Cred 372-7
Who can pick up the weight of Britain, [Imago 439-1
The weight we lift with the finger of a dream, [NH 476-12
Weight him down, O side-stars, with the great weightings of the end. [Madame 507-1
Weight him, weight, weight him with the sleepiness of the moon. [Madame 507-5
The boat was built of stones that had lost their weight and being no longer heavy [Prol 515-10
Deep grass that totters under the weight of light. [Greenest 55-1 P
Of weight, on which the weightless rests: from which [Someone 83-21 A
WEIGHTED. Where his house had fallen, three scraggy trees weighted [NSF 393-4
WEIGHTINGS. Weight him down, O side-stars, with the great weightings of the end. [Madame 507-1
WEIGHTLESS. Of weight, on which the weightless rests: from which [Someone 83-21 A
WEIGHTS. It weights him with nice logic for the prim. [Havana 144-17
WEISHEIT. We'll give the week-end to wisdom, to Weisheit, the rabbi, [Aug 492-1
WELCOME. These choirs of welcome choir for me farewell. [Monocle 13-19
A welcome at the door to which no one comes? [Angel 496-6

She has composed, so long, a self with which to welcome him, [World 521-1
WELL. A deep up-pouring from some saltier well [Monocle 13-10
An apple serves as well as any skull [Monocle 14-16
It might well be that their mistress [Homunculus 26-21
Well, nuncle, this plainly won't do. [Bananas 53-20
They shall know well the heavenly fellowship [Sunday 70-10
Might well have been German or Spanish, [Circulat 150-6
Well, after all, the north wind blows [MBG 174-12
The voice, the book, the hidden well, [Thought 186-2
Well, the gods grow out of the weather. [Jersey 210-5
A. Well, an old order is a violent one. [Connois 216-1
"The Well Dressed Man with a Beard" [247-title
Knew well the shapes were the exactest shaping [New Set 353-3
Ourselves, in the clearest green--well, call it green. [Lot 371-7
These two go well together, the sinuous brim [Pastor 380-2
If only imagined but imagined well. [NSF 385-15
Is well, incalculable balances, [NSF 386-11
Not apprehended well. Does the poet [NSF 396-23
They married well because the marriage-place [NSF 401-19
To discover winter and know it well, to find, [NSF 404-1
And knew each other well, hale-hearted landsmen, [AA 419-8
There he saw well the foldings in the height [Owl 433-7
In glue, but things transfixed, transpierced and well [Bouquet 449-13
The fatality of seeing things too well. [Novel 459-6
As well, not merely as to the commonplace [NH 470-10
It is of the essence not yet well perceived. [NH 475-21
Or down a well. Breathe freedom, oh, my native, [Aug 490-13
So well, that which we do for ourselves, too big, [Look 518-5
If I should fall, as soldier, I know well [Soldat 11-10 P
In this apologetic air, one well [Lytton 39-16 P
He well might find that eager balm [Room Gard 41-10 P
He well might find it in this fret [Room Gard 41-11 P
And that's his way. And that's my way as well. [Grotesque 76-5 P
Well, more than that, like weather when it has cleared [Art Pop 112-15 P
A churchyard kind of bush as well, [Banjo 114-6 P
A silent sort of bush, as well. [Banjo 114-7 P
In things said well in music, [July 114-17 P
Well, it is true of maxims. [Three 129-8 P
Well, there are moments [Three 131-8 P
And well shaped, [Three 131-23 P
Experienced yet not well seen; of how [Ideal 88-17 A
WELL-BOOTED. Well-booted, rugged, arrogantly male, [Lilacs 49-13
WELL-COMPOSED. The well-composed in his burnished solitude, [Antag 426-5
WELL-DISCLOSED. The young man is well-disclosed, one of the gang, [Lack 303-6
WELL-MADE. A well-made scene in which paratroopers [EM 322-21
WELL-ROSED. In a well-rosed two-light [Inhab 504-8
WELL-SPOKEN. The peaceful, blissful words, well-tuned, well-sung, well-spoken. [Sick 90-21 P
WELL-STUFFED. Your disaffected flagellants, well-stuffed, [High-Toned 59-15
WELL-SUNG. The peaceful, blissful words, well-tuned, well-sung, well-spoken. [Sick 90-21 P
WELL-TEMPERED. With a single well-tempered apricot, or, say, [Extracts 253-14
WELL-THUMBED. Of the well-thumbed, infinite pages of her masters, who will seem old to her, requiting less and less her feeling: [Piano 22-7 P
WELL-TUNED. No doubt, the well-tuned birds are singing, [Agenda 42-11 P
The peaceful, blissful words, well-tuned, well-sung, well-spoken. [Sick 90-21 P
WELL-WETTED. Well-wetted; a decoying voice that sings [Spaniard 35-15 P
WELTANSCHAUUNG. There's a weltanschauung of the penny pad. [NE Verses 104-10
WELTER. And the welter of frost and the fox cries do. [Grapes 110-20
We waste and welter [Planet 532-11
WELTERING. Through weltering illuminations, humps [Page 422-25
WENCH. Her daughters to the peached and ivory wench [Havana 143-26
WENCHES. Let the wenches dawdle in such dress [Emperor 64-4
WENT. Every time the bucks went clattering [Earthy 3-1
Wherever they went, [Earthy 3-4
They went clattering, [Earthy 3-5
The firecat went leaping, [Earthy 3-15
Into a savage color he went on. [C 30-29
I went to Egypt to escape [Cuban 64-17
It is true that the rivers went nosing like swine, [Frogs 78-1
While they went seaward to the sea-mouths. [Frogs 78-15
The softest word went gurrituck in his skull. [Norfolk 111-9
They did not know the grass went round. [MBG 178-15
It was soldiers went marching over the rocks [Loaf 200-13
And if it all went on in an orderly way, [Connois 215-8
So what said the others and the sun went down [Uruguay 248-16
The villages slept as the capable man went down, [Uruguay 249-25
And nothing more. So that if one went to the moon, [Extracts

258-10
Do you remember how the rocket went on [Liadoff 346-5
And the wheel that broke as the cart went by. [Silent 359-17
Confronted Ozymandias. She went [NSF 395-17
And the rust and rot of the door through which she went. [Be-
    ginning 427-11
Went crying their desolate syllables, before [Old Woman 45-26 P
We went to walk in the park; for, after all, [Duck 60-8 P
As if another sail went on [Ulysses 105-10 P
WEPT. And then she wept [Pourtraicte 21-20
They were those that would have wept to step barefoot into
    reality, [Large 423-16
That would have wept and been happy, have shivered in the frost
    [Large 424-1
Before the strange, having wept and having thought [Burnshaw
    50-7 P
WERE. Things as they were, things as they are, [MBG 178-20
She looked at them and saw them as they were [NSF 402-11
They never were . . . The sounds of the guitar [Rock 525-9
Were not and are not. Absurd. The words spoken [Rock 525-10
Were not and are not. It is not to be believed. [Rock 525-11
He called hydrangeas purple. And they were. [Abnormal 23-16 P
WEST. In the high west there burns a furious star. [Monocle 14-23
A rumbling, west of Mexico, it seemed, [C 32-17
A northern west or western north, but north, [C 34-3
And east rushes west and west rushes down, [Rabbit K 209-14
Here in the west indifferent crickets chant [EM 321-3
Who lay in bed on the west wall of the sea, [Pure 331-6
The west wind was the music, the motion, the force [NSF 397-16
"One of the Inhabitants of the West" [503-title
Let us fix portals, east and west, [Archi 17-27 P
The east wind in the west, order destroyed, [Sombre 68-15 P
Coming from the East, forcing itself to the West, [Bship 80-11 P
WESTERN. A northern west or western north, but north, [C 34-3
His western voyage ended and began. [C 37-20
Are there mandolines of western mountains? [Men 1000 52-5
The western day through what you called [Hoon 65-8
Abhor the plaster of the western horses, [Hartford 226-12
That in spring will crown every western horizon, [Martial 237-12
Slid over the western cataract, yet one, [Beard 247-13
In the western night, the venerable mask, [NH 477-3
As they enter the place of their western [Soldat 12-8 P
WESTERN HEAD. I crossed in '38 in the Western Head. [NE Verses
    104-7
WEST-INDIAN. Parl-parled the West-Indian weather. [Search 268-2
Parl-parled the West-Indian hurricane. [Search 268-12
WEST INDIAN. West Indian, the extremest power [Hero 276-2
WESTWARD. From which he sailed. Beyond him, westward, lay [C 33-13
Under the front of the westward evening star, [Real 110-12 P
WESTWARDNESS. The Westwardness of Everything [Our Stars 455-title 2
An east in their compelling westwardness, [Our Stars 455-20
WET. Among the choirs of wind and wet and wing. [Monocle 13-14
If ever, whisked and wet, not ripening; [C 34-11
Emotions on wet roads on autumn nights; [Sunday 67-23
He sat among beggars wet with dew, [Thought 187-5
When light comes down to wet his frothy jaws [Glass 197-16
The wet weed sputtered, the fire died down, the cold [Page 422-1
Wet out of the sea, and luminously wet, [Our Stars 455-15
Irked the wet wallows of the water-spout. [NH 476-6
The wateriness of green wet in the sky. [NH 484-11
The wet, green grass. [Irish 502-2
Wet with water and sparkling in the one-ness of their motion.
    [Prol 515-9
A little wet of wing and woe, [Song Fixed 519-19
Of lilies rusted, rotting, wet [Room Gard 41-14 P
WETS. It wets the pigeons, [Gray 140-14
WETTED. Wetted by blue, colder for white. Not to [NSF 385-8
See well-wetted.
WETTEST. Than wettest cinnamon. It was cribled pears [Poem Morn
    219-14
WETTING. Smiling and wetting her lips [Attempt 370-12
WHACK. On the flag-poles in a red-blue dazzle, whack [NSF 390-23
WHANGING. Keep whanging their brass wings . . . [Memo 89-8 P
WHEAT. Of its brown wheat rapturous in the wind, [Aug 491-15
WHEATEN. What wheaten bread and oaten cake and kind, [Orb 440-18
WHEEL. Of the gorgeous wheel and so to give [Sailing 121-4
Would swoop to earth? It is a wheel, the rays [Sleight 222-10
Around the sun. The wheel survives the myths. [Sleight 222-11
And the wheel that broke as the cart went by. [Silent 359-17
It might become a wheel spoked red and white [Page 422-21
Of flame on the line, with a second wheel below, [Page 422-23
To return in a glittering wheel [Drum-Majors 36-21 P
Its wheel begins to turn. [Sombre 71-6 P
More babies than that. The merely revolving wheel [Woman Had
    81-23 P
See water-wheel.
WHEELS. The wheels are too large for any noise. [Dutch 290-5
And writhing wheels of this world's business, [Repet 308-21
That we desired, a day of blank, blue wheels, [Ideal 88-3 A
WHENCE. And whence they came and whither they shall go [Sunday

70-12
Our feigning with the strange unlike, whence springs [Fictive
    88-12
To Monsieur Dufy's Hamburg whence they came. [Lions 125-7
Of either, exceed the excelling witches, whence [Study II 464-7
WHEREFORE. Wherefore those prayers to the moon? [An Gaiety 33-1 P
WHEREIN. The windy lake wherein their lord delights, [Sunday 70-7
WHEREON. Whereon it falls in more than sensual mode. [NSF 398-19
WHETTING. Whetting his hacker, [Plot Giant 6-12
WHILE. A little while of Terra Paradise [Montra 263-1
And after a while, when Ha-eé-me has gone to sleep, [Jouga 337-14
Say here. Speak of familiar things a while. [Debris 338-14
A while, conceiving his passage as into a time [Owl 432-23
And unknown, inhuman for a little while, [Ulysses 105-5 P
WHIM. A little juvenile, an ancient whim, [C 35-23
In the gesture's whim, a passion merely to be [Sombre 71-28 P
WHIMPER. From hearing signboards whimper in cold nights [C 33-?
WHIMPERS. And yet the wind whimpers oldly of old age [NH 477-2
Whimpers when the moon above East Hartford [Grotesque 76-18 P
WHIMSY. And nourish ourselves on crumbs of whimsey? [Hero 278-4
WHINES. Whines in its hole for puppies to come see, [Pure 332-21
WHIP. May, merely may, madame, whip from themselves [High-Toned
    59-19
The muscular one, and bid him whip [Emperor 64-2
WHIPPED. Against gold whipped reddened in big-shadowed black,
    [Repet 309-19
Whipped creams and the Blue Danube, [Agenda 41-16 P
WHIPPING. Whipping the air. [Drum-Majors 37-9 P
WHIPS. The drivers in the wind-blows cracking whips, [Repet 308-22
WHIRL. Out of the whirl and denseness of your wings, [Red Kit
    31-25 P
WHIRLED. The blackbird whirled in the autumn winds. [Thirteen 93-1
Whirled upon me. [Weak Mind 212-13
Of air and whirled away. But it has been often so. [Slug 522-4
And the wry antipodes whirled round the world away-- [Discov
    95-20 P
WHIRLING. High as the hall. The whirling noise [MBG 171-14
Reflections, whirling apart and wide away. [Burnshaw 50-5 P
From the whirling, slowly and by trial; or fear [Burnshaw 51-7 P
Wings spread and whirling over jaguar-men? [Greenest 55-31 P
WHIRLINGS. And leaves in whirlings in the gutters, whirlings [NH
    474-4
WHIRLPOOLS. Whirlpools of darkness in whirlwinds of light . . .
    [Page 423-5
WHIRLWIND. To stop the whirlwind, balk the elements. [NSF 401-15
WHIRLWINDS. Whirlpools of darkness in whirlwinds of light . . .
    [Page 423-5
WHIRROOS. And unfamiliar escapades: whirroos [Orb 442-19
WHISK. Hi! Whisk it, poodle, flick the spray [Hartford 227-10
WHISKED. If ever, whisked and wet, not ripening, [C 34-11
WHISPER. I shall whisper [Plot Giant 7-8
And reverberations clinging to whisper still. [Rome 510-20
WHISPERED. That whispered to the sun's compassion, made [C 28-26
Whispered a little out of tenderness, [Sunday 69-6
And as they whispered, the refrain [Peter 91-16
She whispered, "Pfui!" [Anything B 211-4
WHISPERING. Like whispering women. [Three 128-11 P
WHISPERINGS. For music, for whisperings from the reefs. [Farewell
    117-18
WHISPERS. Presto, whose whispers prickle the spirit. [Hero 274-5
Gritting the ear, whispers humane repose. [NH 484-21
WHIST. Nature as Pinakothek. Whist! Chanticleer . . . [NE Verses
    106-10
WHISTLE. Whistle about us their spontaneous cries; [Sunday 70-23
These are real only if I make them so. Whistle [Holiday 313-7
For me, grow green for me and, as you whistle and grow green,
    [Holiday 313-8
Whistle aloud, too weedy wren. I can [NSF 405-10
Enjoying angels. Whistle, forced bugler, [NSF 405-13
Cock bugler, whistle and bugle and stop just short, [NSF 405-15
WHISTLED. From my North of cold whistled in a sepulchral South,
    [Farewell 117-14
WHISTLES. While the wind still whistles [Sugar-Cane 12-15
WHISTLING. To the dusk of a whistling south below the south, [C
    38-13
The blackbird whistling [Thirteen 93-10
Weather of night creatures, whistling all day, too, [Montra
    261-17
WHITE. Bequeathing your white feathers to the moon [Swans 4-7
The white iris beautifies me. [Carolinas 5-5
A white pigeon it is, that flutters to the ground, [Monocle
    17-20
The first white wall of the village [Magnifico 19-18
The first white wall of the village . . . [Magnifico 19-22
The white cock's tail [Ploughing 20-1
The white cock's tail [Ploughing 20-17
With white moonlight. [Fabliau 23-13
The white cabildo darkened, the façade, [C 32-19
And April hillsides wooded white and pink, [C 37-29
Their azure has a cloudy edge, their white [C 37-30

The lashes of that eye and its white lid. [Worms 49-19
And that white animal, so lean, [Vincentine 53-15
And that white animal, so lean, [Vincentine 53-18
Should mask as white girls. [W Burgher 61-4
A white of wildly woven rings; [W Burgher 61-15
By white night-gowns. [Ten O'C 66-2
Blue and white, [Six Sig 73-9
The white folds of its gown [Six Sig 74-15
His lids are white because his eyes are blind. [Bird Claws 82-6
Of those white elders; but, escaping, [Peter 92-9
Who, seeing silver petals of white blooms [Sea Surf 100-17
By light, the way one feels, sharp white, [Sailing 121-6
White and star-furred for his legions, [Snow Stars 133-8
The moonlight is not yellow but a white [Havana 144-24
A tatter of shadows peaked to white, [Postcard 159-20
Pink and white carnations. The light [Poems Clim 193-8
Pink and white carnations--one desires [Poems Clim 193-12
Is simplified: a bowl of white, [Poems Clim 193-14
And made it fresh in a world of white, [Poems Clim 193-20
More than a world of white and snowy scents. [Poems Clim 194-3
A brush of white, the obscure, [Add 199-6
Fat cat, red tongue, green mind, white milk [Rabbit K 209-5
A black line beside a white line; [Common 221-3
As if someone lived there. Such floods of white [Sleight 222-6
There the dogwoods, the white ones and the pink ones, [Forces 228-22
A pink girl took a white dog walking. [Forces 229-2
No large white horses. But there was the fluffy dog. [Forces 229-12
Of the iris bore white blooms. The bird then boomed. [Horn 230-10
In objects, as white this, white that. [Vari 235-5
When he looked, the water ran up the air or grew white [Extracts 255-17
Like a white abstraction only, a feeling [Hero 276-26
With white wine, sugar and lime juice. Then bring it, [Phenom 286-15
So seeing, I beheld you walking, white, [Phenom 287-12
You are that white Eulalia of the name. [Phenom 287-22
It was a blue scene washing white in the rain, [Repet 306-19
It was something to see that their white was different, [Holiday 312-1
Sharp as white paint in the January sun; [Holiday 312-2
Lighting the martyrs of logic with white fire. [EM 325-16
Under the white clouds piled and piled [Woman Song 360-10
He had written them near Athens. The farm was white. [Anach 366-1
In the punctual centre of all circles white [Anach 366-8
White houses in villages, black communicants-- [Cats 367-19
And white roses shaded emerald on petals [Attempt 370-6
Among fomentations of black bloom and of white bloom. [Attempt 370-18
Wetted by blue, colder for white. Not to [NSF 385-8
White sand, his patter of the long sea-slushes. [NSF 393-9
With ribbon, a rigid statement of them, white, [NSF 402-6
Deserted, on a beach. It is white, [AA 412-5
Are white, a little dried, a kind of mark [AA 412-9
Reminding, trying to remind, of a white [AA 412-10
Or before, not the white of an aging afternoon, [AA 412-12
Here, being visible is being white, [AA 412-16
Is being of the solid of white, the accomplishment [AA 412-17
And proclaim it, the white creator of black, jetted [AA 417-11
It might become a wheel spoked red and white [Page 422-21
Of yellow as first color and of white, [Roses 431-1
Blue for all that and white and hard, [Celle 438-13
If there is a man white as marble [Degen 444-1
Perceived: the white seen smoothly argentine [Bouquet 449-14
Through the door one sees on the lake that the white duck swims [Bouquet 449-19
Of the land, on a checkered cover, red and white. [Bouquet 450-6
Toward a consciousness of red and white as one, [Bouquet 450-9
Spread sail, we say spread white, spread way. [Aug 490-7
And for all the white voices [Aug 495-3
Took seven white dogs [Cab 20-16 P
White dogs at bay. [Cab 21-12 P
Blue and vermilion, purple and white, [Mandolin 28-20 P
And saw the blossoms, snow-bred pink and white, [Good Bad 33-17P
So much he had devised: white forelegs taut [Old Woman 43-10 P
White slapped on white, majestic, marble heads, [Burnshaw 49-13P
Become rude robes among white candle lights, [Greenest 53-4 P
Streamed white and stoked and engined wrick-a-wrack. [Duck 61-12P
Converging on the statue, white and high." [Duck 62-27 P
The statue is white and high, white brillianter [Duck 64-5 P
Than the color white and high beyond any height [Duck 64-6 P
Until they changed to eagle in white air, [Sombre 68-4 P
Stands brimming white, chiaroscuro scaled [Sombre 70-20 P
The green, white, blue of the ballad-eye, by night [Sombre 71-9P
White February wind, [Grotesque 77-6 P
Covered one morning with blue, one morning with white, [Bship 80-10 P
A white, pink, purple berry tree, [Banjo 114-3 P

Of the white stones near my door, [Three 134-7 P
Of the white stones near her door; [Three 134-13 P
That affects the white stones, [Three 135-3 P
6. White sky, pink sun, trees on a distant peak. [Someone 86-9 A
See crystal-white.
WHITED. Was whited green, [Vincentine 53-2
WHITE-MANED. And there are the white-maned horses' heads, beyond [Burnshaw 49-19 P
WHITENED. The sea-clouds whitened far below the calm [Sea Surf 99-10
Trace the gold sun about the whitened sky [Cred 373-6
Whitened, again, forms formless in the dark, [Old Woman 45-8 P
WHITENESS. And the whiteness grows less vivid on the wall. [AA 412-22
Of sleep, the whiteness folded into less, [Owl 433-8
Was the whiteness that is the ultimate intellect, [Owl 433-20
The birch trees draw up whiteness from the ground. [Primordia 8-21 P
WHITENS. It is the sea that whitens the roof. [MBG 179-13
WHITER. The paper is whiter [Common 221-15
The paper is whiter. [Common 221-23
Whiter than wax, sonorous, fame as it is, [NSF 403-19
WHITES. Pink yellows, orange whites, too much as they are [Roses 430-11
WHITEST. They bud the whitest eye, the pallidest sprout, [Rock 527-7
WHITHER. And whence they came and whither they shall go [Sunday 70-12
WHITMAN. See Walt Whitman.
WHOLE. The whole of life that still remained in him [C 28-18
And something given to make whole among [C 30-14
Rex and principium, exit the whole [C 37-1
Struggling toward his harmonious whole, [Negation 97-14
The Whole World Including the Speaker [NE Verses 104-title 1
The Whole World Excluding the Speaker [NE Verses 104-title 2
Are the soul itself. And the whole of the soul, Swenson, [Lions 125-2
The whole of the wideness of night is for you, [Rabbit K 209-17
With my whole body I taste these peaches, [Peaches 224-1
He breathed in crystal-pointed change the whole [Choc 298-6
Against the whole experience of day. [Choc 298-10
Within the universal whole. The son [EM 324-3
Yet to speak of the whole world as metaphor [Pure 332-8
In a world that shrinks to an immediate whole, [Descrip 341-12
Would froth the whole heaven with its seeming-so, [Descrip 341-17
When the cloud pressed suddenly the whole return [Liadoff 347-6
Of the obvious whole, uncertain particles [Man Car 351-1
From ignorance, not an undivided whole, [Two V 355-10
The whole race is a poet that writes down [Men Made 356-5
Has lost the whole in which he was contained, [Chaos 358-2
The whole of appearance is a toy. For this, [Belly 366-16
The charitable majesty of her whole kin? [Cred 375-1
Part of the mottled mood of summer's whole, [Cred 378-5
How that whole country was a melon, pink [NSF 393-17
That in each other are included, the whole, [NSF 403-14
Contriving balance to contrive a whole, [AA 420-19
In these unhappy he meditates a whole, [AA 420-22
Needs out of the whole necessity of sight. [Owl 432-2
With the whole spirit sparkling in its cloth, [Owl 434-12
One poem proves another and the whole, [Orb 441-4
The central poem is the poem of the whole, [Orb 442-1
The poem of the composition of the whole, [Orb 442-2
Not merely into a whole, but a poem of [Orb 442-6
The whole, the essential compact of the parts, [Orb 442-7
The recognizable, medium, central whole-- [Bouquet 450-12
Cloud's gold, of a whole appearance that stands and is. [Bouquet 452-16
The whole habit of the mind is changed by them, [Our Stars 455-17
When the whole habit of the mind was changed, [Our Stars 455-23
In the end, in the whole psychology, the self, [NH 474-7
The whole man, that tempers and beliefs became [Aug 494-2
Your beliefs and disbeliefs, your whole peculiar plot; [Old Man 501-4
Adds to them the whole vocabulary of the South, [Prol 517-7
We feel the obscurity of an order, a whole, [Final 524-11
The rock is the habitation of the whole, [Rock 528-10
Pass the whole of life earing the clink of the [Archi 16-18 P
Overlooking whole seasons? [Archi 17-13 P
Is any choir the whole voice of this fretful habitation, [Inelegance 26-5 P
The whole of them turning black; [Agenda 42-9 P
To men, to houses, streets and the squalid whole. [Greenest 57-8P
Parades of whole races with attendant bands, [Duck 66-2 P
Is the equal of the whole. [Bship 79-18 P
"The ephebi say that there is only the whole, [Bship 79-20 P
The whole. The sound of a dozen orchestras [Bship 79-26 P
Strike fire, but the part is the equal of the whole, [Bship 79-29 P
The jungle of tropical part and tropical whole." [Bship 80-12 P

In a Third: The whole cannot exist without [Bship 80-14 P
Listening to the whole sea for a sound [Woman Had 82-4 P
Of the humming of the central man, the whole sound [Woman Had 82-12 P
Of an elevation, an elixir of the whole. [Woman Had 83-10 P
The curtains, when pulled, might show another whole, [Theatre 91-13 P
A whole, the day on which the last star [Ulysses 102-8 P
Apposites, to the slightest edge, of the whole [Someone 86-19 A
WHOLLY. Is wholly the vapidest fake . . . [Sailing 120-20
Like a body wholly body, fluttering [Key W 128-13
Mist that is golden is not wholly mist. [Nigger 156-15
Sounds passing through sudden rightnesses, wholly [Of Mod 240-16
To see him, that we were wholly one, as we heard [Oboe 251-18
Before we were wholly human and knew ourselves. [EM 317-29
That were never wholly still. The softest woman, [EM 321-28
The shadowless moon wholly composed of shade, [Study II 464-13
Not wholly spoken in a conversation between [NH 471-7
That it is wholly an inner light, that it shines [NH 481-19
Blanche, the blonde, whose eyes are not wholly straight, in a room of lustres, shed by turquoise falling, [Piano 22-1 P
And in it. It is wholly you. [Including 88-8 P
A wholly artificial nature, in which [Someone 83-2 A
WHORE. Whose whore is Morning Star [Thought 186-18
WICK. A light on the candle tearing against the wick [Rome 509-5
WICKED. In that distant chamber, a bearded queen, wicked in her dead light. [Madame 507-13
WICKLESS. To the wickless halls. [Ord Women 12-2
WICKS. Do you remember the children there like wicks, [Liadoff 346-11
WIDE. Of the silence, wide sleep and solitude [Curtains 62-6
Winding across wide water, without sound. [Sunday 67-7
The day is like wide water, without sound, [Sunday 67-8
Of that wide water, inescapable. [Sunday 70-21
Its wings spread wide to rain and snow, [MBG 166-8
The sky is too blue, the earth too wide. [Scavoir 231-13
That obsolete fiction of the wide river in [Oboe 250-9
Is blue, clear, cloudy, high, dark, wide and round; [Extracts 252-11
High, low, far, wide, against the distance, [Hero 277-22
On the east, sister and nun, and opened wide [Phenom 287-8
And this great esplanade of corn, miles wide, [Belly 367-7
Yet Hans lay wide awake. And live alone [Page 422-3
A space grown wide, the inevitable blue [Orb 440-21
Of a vacant sea declaiming with wide throat, [Puel 456-9
Of his self, come at upon wide delvings of wings. [NH 475-24
Too wide, too irised, to be more than calm, [Look 518-18
So, then, this warm, wide, weatherless quietude [Moonlight 531-19
With their wide mouths [Lulu G 26-20 P
Reflections, whirling apart and wide away. [Burnshaw 50-5 P
The wide night mused by tell-tale muttering, [Duck 61-26 P
A wide, still Aragonese, [Fare Guit 99-2 P
See: sea-wide; sky-wide.
WIDELY. But if they do, they cast it widely round. [Bouquet 451-24
WIDE-MOVING. Were contours. Cold was chilling the wide-moving swans. [Contra II 270-11
WIDEN. Widen your sense. All things in the sun are sun. [NE Verses 104-2
WIDENESS. The whole of the wideness of night is for you, [Rabbit K 209-17
WIDENING. The sky above the plaza widening [Old Woman 43-6 P
WIDENS. Captives the being, widens--and was there. [Orb 440-16
WIDER. A wider brow, large and less human [Hero 277-8
WIDE-WISE. Splashed wide-wise because it likes magnificence [AA 416-13
WIDOW. Like a widow's bird [Nuances 18-16
With Sunday pearls, her widow's gayety. [NSF 402-7
Nor of a widow Dooley, [Aug 491-11
The cuckoo trees and the widow of Madrid [Greenest 59-16 P
WIDOWS. Good light for drunkards, poets, widows, [Homunculus 25-15
Of widows and trembling ladies, [Homunculus 26-7
This will make widows wince. But fictive things [High-Toned 59-21
Wink as they will. Wink most when widows wince. [High-Toned 59-22
WIDTH. A leaden ticking circular in width. [Duck 66-5 P
WIEN. In spite of the watch-chains aus Wien, in spite [Dutch 62-13 P
WIFE. Oh! Sal, the butcher's wife ate clams [Lulu M 27-9 P
WIG. And lex. Sed quaeritur: is this same wig [C 27-10
WIGGY. Of access like the page of a wiggy book, [Pure 333-6
WIGS. For who can care at the wigs despoiling the Satan ear? [Banal 63-4
Foolscap for wigs. Academies [Prelude 195-12
WILD. In verses wild with motion, full of din, [Monocle 16-12
Notations of the wild, the ruinous waste, [Geneva 24-12
And sprawled around, no longer wild. [Jar 76-10
The wild warblers are warbling in the jungle [Medit 123-13
This arrival in the wild country of the soul, [Waldorf 240-24

Where the wild poem is a substitute [Waldorf 241-1
One wild rhapsody a fake for another. [Waldorf 241-3
And wild and free, the secondary man, [Jumbo 269-12
"Wild Ducks, People and Distances" [328-title
The wild ducks were enveloped. The weather was cold. [Wild 329-3
Was central in distances the wild ducks could [Wild 329-6
One seed alone grow wild, the railway-stops [Cats 367-14
The wild orange trees continued to bloom and to bear, [NSF 393-2
Wild wedges, as of a volcano's smoke, palm-eyed [AA 416-17
To the wild limits of its habitation. [Page 421-20
Fixed like a lake on which the wild ducks fluttered, [Cata 424-13
In a permanent realization, without any wild ducks [Cata 425-7
Keep quiet in the heart, O wild bitch. O mind [Puel 456-13
Gone wild, be what he tells you to be: Puella. [Puel 456-14
Sip the wild honey of the poor man's life, [Burnshaw 49-10 P
And purpose, to hear the wild bee drone, to feel [Greenest 56-25 P
And I play my guitar. The vines have grown wild. [Stan MBG 72-12 P
The chant and discourse there, more than wild weather [Role 93-9 P
Through wild spaces of other suns and moons, [Ulysses 102-23 P
WILDER. Of one wilder than the rest (like music blunted, [Thunder 220-23
WILDERNESS. Sweet berries ripen in the wilderness; [Sunday 70-24
It made the slovenly wilderness [Jar 76-7
The wilderness rose up to it, [Jar 76-9
Disclosed the sea floor and the wilderness [Farewell 118-2
But the sustenance of the wilderness [Havana 142-7
Was the glory of heaven in the wilderness-- [Dutch 292-16
They were those from the wilderness of stars that had expected more. [Large 423-13
In the witching wilderness, night's witchingness, [Burnshaw 46-25 P
Out of their wilderness, a special fane, [Sombre 69-8 P
On the waste throne of his own wilderness. [Region 115-15 P
WILDEST. A duckling of the wildest blood [Grotesque 75-12 P
WILDLY. A white of wildly woven rings; [W Burgher 61-15
Singsonged and singsonged, wildly free. [Jumbo 269-3
And wildly free, whose clawing thumb [Jumbo 269-5
Wildly curvetted, color-scarred, so beaked, [Greenest 57-18 P
WILD-RINGED. That gives its power to the wild-ringed eye. [Owl 433-22
WILL. When the sky is blue. The blue infected will. [C 40-18
If not in will, to track the knaves of thought. [C 42-24
Wink as they will. Wink most when widows wince. [High-Toned 59-22
His will, yet never ceases, perfect cock, [Bird Claws 82-17
Imagination is the will of things . . . [Polish Aunt 84-7
Meditating the will of men in formless crowds. [NE Verses 105-10
Dark cynic, strip and bathe and bask at will. [NE Verses 106-3
And by will, unshaken and florid [Medit 124-4
But what are radiant reason and radiant will [Medit 124-7
He used his reason, exercised his will, [Anglais 149-5
That lost its heaviness through that same will, [Nigger 152-9
The very will of the nerves, [Anything B 211-21
"Forces, the Will & the Weather" [228-title
You are the will, if there is a will, [Vari 233-2
Or the portent of a will that was, [Vari 233-3
One of the portents of the will that was. [Vari 233-4
Beyond which it has no will to rise. [Of Mod 240-18
Has a will to grow larger on the wall, [Rhythms 245-19
But as in the powerful mirror of my wish and will." [Rhythms 246-8
The will to be and to be total in belief, [Gala 248-14
Who was it passed her there on a horse all will, [Uruguay 249-16
Our merest apprehension of their will. [Montra 262-15
Of arms, the will opposed to cold, fate [Hero 273-12
Induced by what you will: the entrails [Hero 275-8
In the will of what is common to all men, [Dutch 291-18
The will demands that what he thinks be true? [EM 323-11
In which no one peers, in which the will makes no [EM 323-20
In the death of a soldier, like the utmost will, [Descrip 341-2
Of the never-ending storm of will, [Silent 359-11
One will and many wills, and the wind, [Silent 359-12
That is a being, a will, a fate. [Human 363-16
Instead, outcast, without the will to power [Cats 368-2
And sends us, winged by an unconscious will, [NSF 382-16
To which the swans curveted, a will to change, [NSF 397-17
A will to make iris frettings on the blank. [NSF 397-18
There was a will to change, a necessitous [NSF 397-19
The real will from its crude compoundings come, [NSF 404-6
The children of a desire that is the will, [Owl 436-11
And queered by lavishings of their will to see. [Bouquet 451-4
Say next to holiness is the will thereto, [NH 467-4
The heaviness we lighten by light will, [NH 476-13
Prostrate below the singleness of its will. [NH 478-24
A naked being with a naked will [NH 480-6
Even his own will and in his nakedness [NH 480-8

But he may not. He may not evade his will, [NH 480-10
The will of necessity, the will of wills-- [NH 480-12
At the centre, the object of the will, this place, [NH 480-20
And little will or wish, that day, for tears. [Soldat 14-17 P
Seated before these shining forms, like the duskiest glass, re-
     flecting the piebald of roses or what you will. [Piano 21-18 P
Milord, I ask you, though you will to sing, [Red Kit 31-16 P
Does she will to be proud? True, you may love [Red Kit 31-17 P
Calling them what you will but loosely-named [Burnshaw 47-21 P
By his presence, the seat of his ubiquitous will. [Greenest
     59-32 P
Not an attainment of the will [Ulysses 101-26 P
No more and because they lack the will to tell [Ideal 88-14 A
WILLED. In form though in design, as Crispin willed, [C 45-21
     Flotillas, willed and wanted, bearing in them [New Set 352-11
     And willed. She has given too much, but not enough. [Aug 496-3
WILLIAMS. "Nuances of a Theme by Williams" [18-title
WILLING. Until they become thoughtlessly willing [Homunculus 26-11
     He was willing they should remain incredible, [Someone 85-14 A
WILLINGLY. In which the sulky strophes willingly [C 33-24
     Lament, willingly forfeit the ai-ai [EM 317-15
     The frame of the hero. Yet, willingly, he [Stan Hero 84-13 P
WILLINGNESS. There was a willingness not yet composed, [NH 483-3
WILLOW. She makes the willow shiver in the sun [Sunday 69-7
     "Jasmine's Beautiful Thoughts underneath the Willow" [79-title
     Was like a willow swept by rain. [Peter 91-17
     It would be ransom for the willow [Snow Stars 133-10
     Underneath a willow there [Country 207-6
     With one eye watch the willow, motionless. [Cred 377-8
     The birds that wait out rain in willow leaves. [Soldat 13-13 P
WILLOWS. The driving rain, the willows in the rain, [Soldat 13-12P
WILLS. Throw papers in the streets, the wills [MBG 170-7
     As the observer wills. [Pears 197-6
     One will and many wills, and the wind, [Silent 359-12
     Nor the wills of other men; and he cannot evade [NH 480-11
     The will of necessity, the will of wills-- [NH 480-12
WINCE. This will make widows wince. But fictive things [High-Toned
     59-21
     Wink as they will. Wink most when widows wince. [High-Toned
     59-22
WIND. And far beyond the discords of the wind. [Swans 4-2
     The wind speeds her, [Paltry 5-16
     Turning in the wind. [Domination 8-13
     Turning in the wind, [Domination 8-19
     In the twilight wind. [Domination 8-20
     Turning in the wind, [Domination 9-5
     Turning in the wind. [Domination 9-16
     Of any misery in the sound of the wind, [Snow Man 10-5
     Full of the same wind [Snow Man 10-8
     While the wind still whistles [Sugar-Cane 12-15
     Among the choirs of wind and wet and wing. [Monocle 13-14
     Tosses in the wind. [Ploughing 20-2
     The wind pours down. [Ploughing 20-6
     And bluster in the wind. [Ploughing 20-8
     The wind pours down. [Ploughing 20-20
     That century of wind in a single puff. [C 28-4
     Here, something in the rise and fall of wind [C 29-3
     It was caparison of wind and cloud [C 30-13
     The rumbling broadened as it fell. The wind, [C 32-22
     The crickets beat their tambours in the wind, [C 42-11
     Lasciviously as the wind, [Venereal 48-1
     Until the wind blew. [Valley Candle 51-3
     Until the wind blew. [Valley Candle 51-6
     Threading the wind. [Depression 63-12
     Move in the wind. [Six Sig 73-11
     His beard moves in the wind. [Six Sig 73-12
     The pine tree moves in the wind. [Six Sig 73-13
     "The Wind Shifts" [83-title
     This is how the wind shifts: [Shifts 83-10
     The wind shifts like this: [Shifts 83-14
     The wind shifts like this: [Shifts 83-17
     This is how the wind shifts: [Shifts 84-1
     That separates us from the wind and sea, [Fictive 87-15
     Whose garden is wind and moon, [Watermelon 88-21
     The wind attendant on the solstices [Pharynx 96-5
     When the wind stops, [Soldier 97-9
     When the wind stops and, over the heavens, [Soldier 97-10
     Of loyal conjuration trumped. The wind [Sea Surf 102-11
     She walks an autumn ampler than the wind [Anatomy 108-3
     "To the Roaring Wind" [113-title
     The leaves in which the wind kept up its sound [Farewell 117-13
     To say the light wind worries the sail, [Sailing 121-1
     In a world of wind and frost, [Medit 124-3
     Coldly the wind fell upon them [How Live 125-13
     There was the cold wind and the sound [How Live 126-5
     The grinding water and the gasping wind; [Key W 129-2
     The meaningless plungings of water and the wind, [Key W 129-19
     As of the great wind howling, [Mozart 132-14
     If we repeat, it is because the wind [Eve Angels 137-17
     A most desolate wind has chilled Rouge-Fatima [Havana 142-11

The wind and the sudden falling of the wind. [Nigger 152-7
Freshness is more than the east wind blowing round one. [Nigger
     157-11
Of the wind upon the curtains. [Chateau 161-14
Well, after all, the north wind blows [MBG 174-12
It is the sea that the north wind makes. [MBG 179-15
The wind in which the dead leaves blow. [MBG 180-14
Hanging his shawl upon the wind, [MBG 181-17
He lies down and the night wind blows upon him here. [Men Fall
     187-13
The night wind blows upon the dreamer, bent [Men Fall 188-19
The wind blows. In the wind, the voices [Parochial 191-3
On tins and boxes? What about horses eaten by wind? [Parochial
     191-18
Of this dead mass and that. The wind might fill [Dames 206-8
The winter web, the winter woven, wind and wind, [Dwarf 208-4
The wind of Iceland and [Weak Mind 212-7
The wind of Ceylon, [Weak Mind 212-8
The black wind of the sea [Weak Mind 212-11
And the green wind [Weak Mind 212-12
B. It is April as I write. The wind [Connois 216-4
Came bursting from the clouds. So the wind [Sleight 222-7
Feel the wind of it, smell the dust of it? [Arcades 225-9
Than the wind, sub-music like sub-speech, [Vari 232-8
Night and day, wind and quiet, produces [Vari 233-21
The poem lashes more fiercely than the wind, [Bottle 239-14
The wind dissolving into birds, [Vase 246-13
In east wind beating the shutters at night. [Vase 246-16
And dirt. The wind blew in the empty place. [Extracts 255-5
The winter wind blew in an empty place-- [Extracts 255-6
No man that heard a wind in an empty place. [Extracts 255-9
Item: The wind is never rounding O [Montra 263-17
How the wind spells out [Metamorph 265-15
The wind had seized the tree and ha, and ha, [Hand 271-10
By a wind that seeks out shelter from snow. Thus [Hero 273-6
Of the wind, rain in a dry September, [Hero 275-13
The wind moves like a cripple among the leaves [Motive 288-3
So that the flapping of wind around me here [Choc 299-2
The wind beat in the roof and half the walls. [Repet 306-2
Of the wind and the glittering were real now, [Repet 306-8
Of their own part, yet moving on the wind, [EM 319-8
The weather pink, the wind in motion; and this: [EM 322-24
There is a storm much like the crying of the wind, [Sketch 336-1
This afternoon the wind and the sea were like that-- [Jouga
     337-13
Come home, wind, he kept crying and crying. [Pieces 351-11
Come home, wind, he said as he climbed the stair-- [Pieces
     351-14
The wind is like a dog that runs away. [Pieces 352-5
And shapes of fire, and wind that bears them down. [Two V 355-12
Oh, that this lashing wind was something more [Chaos 357-7
Like the wind that lashes everything at once. [Chaos 358-6
One will and many wills, and the wind, [Silent 359-12
The favorable transformations of the wind [Past Nun 378-21
The west wind was the music, the motion, the force [NSF 397-16
The wind is blowing the sand across the floor. [AA 412-15
The season changes. A cold wind chills the beach. [AA 412-19
A wind will spread its windy grandeurs round [AA 414-1
The wind will command them with invincible sound. [AA 414-3
In masks, can choir it with the naked wind? [AA 415-3
Bare limbs, bare trees and a wind as sharp as salt? [AA 419-21
To a haggling of wind and weather, by these lights [AA 421-2
Between loud water and loud wind, between that [Page 421-7
So lind. The wind blazed as they sang. So lau. [Page 421-17
Of the wind, the glassily-sparkling particles [Page 423-7
And the north wind's mighty buskin seems to fall [Antag 426-7
As on water of an afternoon in the wind [Owl 433-14
After the wind has passed. Sleep realized [Owl 433-19
In a season more than sun and south wind, [Imago 439-14
The wind blows quaintly [Our Stars 454-15
And Gibraltar is dissolved like spit in the wind. [Puel 456-3
But over the wind, over the legends of its roaring, [Puel 456-4
That fall upon it out of the wind. We seek [NH 471-12
Are like newspapers blown by the wind. He speaks [NH 473-21
Tomorrow for him. The wind will have passed by, [NH 473-23
And yet the wind whimpers oldly of old age [NH 477-2
Are a single voice in the boo-ha of the wind. [NH 481-3
The wind has blown the silence of summer away. [NH 487-13
Of its brown wheat rapturous in the wind, [Aug 491-15
Of wind and light and cloud [Inhab 503-16
And the wind sways like a great thing tottering-- [Hermit 505-16
The Constant Disquisition of the Wind [Two Illus 513-title 1
Was so much less. Only the wind [Two Illus 513-8
Of the wind, not knowing that that thought [Two Illus 513-11
And what we think, a breathing like the wind, [Look 518-13
We think as wind skitters on a pond in a field [Look 518-24
The same wind, rising and rising, makes a sound [Look 519-2
In the early March wind. [Not Ideas 534-6
And leaves that would be loose upon the wind, [Bowl 7-4 P
The male voice of the wind in the dry leaves [Primordia 7-14 P

The spirit wakes in the night wind--is naked. [Soldat 11-13 P
What is it that hides in the night wind [Soldat 11-14 P
The multiform beauty, sinking in night wind, [Soldat 12-4 P
In the rushes of autumn wind [Secret Man 36-2 P
And without knowing, and then upon the wind [Old Woman 44-14 P
Triumphant as that always upward wind [Old Woman 44-27 P
Their voice and the voice of the tortured wind were one, [Old
    Woman 45-27 P
The help of any wind of any sky: [Burnshaw 49-20 P
They suddenly fall and the leafless sound of the wind [Burnshaw
    50-20 P
Its edges were taken from tumultous wind [Greenest 56-29 P
Out of the eye when the loud wind gathers up [Greenest 58-11 P
The manes to his image of the flying wind, [Duck 64-17 P
The east wind in the west, order destroyed, [Sombre 68-15 P
The day is green and the wind is young. [Stan MBG 72-1 P
White February wind, [Grotesque 77-6 P
It is an arbor against the wind, a pit in the mist, [Discov
    95-12 P
Today the leaves cry, hanging on branches swept by wind, [Course
    96-10 P
Of the wind, of the wind as it deepens, and late sleep, [Art
    Pop 113-5 P
It is hard to hear the north wind again, [Region 115-6 P
The wind moves slowly in the branches. [Of Mere 118-5 P
Creaking in the night wind. [Three 137-6 P
See: east-wind; fire-wind; night-wind; trade-wind.
WIND-BEATEN. Wind-beaten into freshest, brightest fire. [Burnshaw
    52-22 P
WIND-BLOWS. The drivers in the wind-blows cracking whips, [Repet
    308-22
WIND-GLOSS. The wind-gloss. Or as daylight comes, [MBG 175-2
WINDILY. Gray grasses rolling windily away [Nigger 155-14
WINDING. Winding across wide water, without sound. [Sunday 67-7
    And in the water winding weeds move round. [Glass 197-17
    Winding [Phases 4-5 P
    Dark-skinned and sinuous, winding upwardly, [Greenest 55-13 P
    Winding and waving, slowly, waving in air, [Greenest 55-14 P
    Is largely another winding of the clock. [Duck 65-30 P
WINDINGS. Of windings round and dodges to and fro, [Ulti 429-20
WINDING-SHEET. On your winding-sheet, [Jack-Rabbit 50-11
WINDLESS. In its windless pavilions, [Three 131-18 P
    And long for the windless pavilions. [Three 133-12 P
    In the windless pavilions. [Three 137-8 P
WINDOW. Out of the window, [Domination 9-13
    And each blank window of the building balked [Babies 77-8
    Icicles filled the long window [Thirteen 93-12
    The fish are in the fishman's window, [Nigger 154-7
    Are one. My window is twenty-nine three [Jersey 210-14
    And plenty of window for me. [Jersey 210-15
    And the window's lemon light, [Anything B 211-20
    Jumps from the clouds or, from his window, [Hero 280-10
    The reader by the window has finished his book [Pure 330-2
    But you, ephebe, look from your attic window, [NSF 384-17
    The blue woman, linked and lacquered, at her window [NSF 399-4
    The blue woman looked and from her window named [NSF 399-21
    And die. It stands on a table at a window [Bouquet 450-5
    Write pax across the window pane. And then [Puel 456-15
    The window, close to the ramshackle spout in which [NH 475-8
    It is the window that makes it difficult [NH 478-4
    Of the window and walking in the street and seeing, [NH 478-9
    In the strokes of thunder, dead candles at the window [NH 488-11
    There's a parrot in a window, [Phases 3-9 P
    In the Duft of towns, beside a window, [Woman Had 83-5 P
    At the window, as before. [Three 134-15 P
WINDOW-BAYS. In the vapid haze of the window-bays, [Ord Women 11-6
WINDOWS. Swept through its boarded windows and the leaves [Havana
    142-19
    And the notorious views from the windows [Prelude 195-5
    The windows are open. The sunlight fills [Peaches 224-16
    Red as a red table-cloth, its windows [Hero 276-1
    People fall out of windows, trees tumble down, [Chaos 357-13
    The windows will be lighted, not the rooms. [AA 413-24
    Out of the surfaces, the windows, the walls, [NH 480-22
WINDOW-SILL. A geranium withers on the window-sill. [Phenom 286-2
    These are the window-sill [Archi 17-20 P
WINDOW-SILLS. From the window-sills at the alphabets, [Ord Women
    11-9
WINDS. The winds were like her maids, [Peter 91-3
    The blackbird whirled in the autumn winds. [Thirteen 93-1
    Against the autumn winds [Nigger 152-3
    Could have touched these winds, [Weak Mind 212-18
    Brushed up by brushy winds in brushy clouds, [NSF 385-7
    The winds batter it. The water curls. The leaves [Novel 457-2
    Shadows like winds [Irish 501-10
    The four winds blow through the rustic arbor, [Vacancy 511-12
    No winds like dogs watched over her at night. [World 521-6
    Winds that blew [Phases 4-7 P
    Its winds are blue. [Secret Man 36-6 P
    And deep winds flooded you, for these, day comes, [Duck 61-6 P

Round summer and angular winter and winds, [Ulysses 102-24 P
WIND-STOPPED. Playing a crackled reed, wind-stopped, in bleats.
    [Sombre 67-2 P
WIND-SUCKED. Complete in wind-sucked poverty. [Stan MBG 73-10 P
WINDY. Like windy citherns hankering for hymns. [High-Toned 59-5
    The windy lake wherein their lord delights, [Sunday 70-7
    The gongs rang loudly as the windy booms [Sea Surf 100-4
    Beyond our gate and the windy sky [Postcard 159-9
    A wind will spread its windy grandeurs round [AA 414-1
    Of summer, at the windy edge, [Celle 438-11
    Of a windy night as it is, when the marble statues [NH 473-20
    May be perceived in windy quakes [Room Gard 41-5 P
    A windy thing . . . However, since we are here, [Recit 86-2 P
WINE. What wine does one drink? [Am Sub 131-12
    The wine is good. The bread, [Fading 139-18
    At night, it lights the fruit and wine, [MBG 172-19
    Is the spot on the floor, there, wine or blood [MBG 173-11
    A yellow wine and follow a steamer's track [Landsc 243-6
    One man, their bread and their remembered wine? [Extracts 254-17
    The bread and wine of the mind, permitted [Hero 275-27
    With white wine, sugar and lime juice. Then bring it, [Phenom
    286-15
    Sour wine to warn him, an empty book to read; [Good Man 364-11
    Foreswore the sipping of the marriage wine. [NSF 401-10
    The way wine comes at a table in a wood. [NSF 405-24
    To a million, a duck with apples and without wine. [Duck 60-12 P
WINES. With six meats and twelve wines or else without [NSF 407-16
WING. Among the choirs of wind and wet and wing. [Monocle 13-14
    On sidelong wing, around and round and round. [Monocle 17-19
    Drawn close by dreams of fledgling wing, [Babies 77-11
    The body lift its heavy wing, take up, [NSF 390-12
    I have neither ashen wing nor wear of ore [Angel 496-9
    A little wet of wing and woe, [Song Fixed 519-19
WINGED. And sends us, winged by an unconscious will, [NSF 382-16
    See dove-winged.
WINGLESS. Wingless and withered, but living alive. [MBG 171-7
WINGS. The pungent oranges and bright, green wings [Sunday 67-5
    In pungent fruit and bright, green wings, or else [Sunday 67-16
    By the consummation of the swallow's wings. [Sunday 68-26
    Downward to darkness, on extended wings. [Sunday 70-28
    The clambering wings of birds of black revolved, [Babies 77-14
    Say how his heavy wings, [Pascagoula 127-1
    Speak of the dazzling wings. [Pascagoula 127-8
    Its wings spread wide to rain and snow, [MBG 166-8
    To avoid the bright, discursive wings, [Adequacy 243-14
    In its cavern, wings subtler than any mercy, [Hero 273-13
    The venerable song falls from your fiery wings. [God 285-16
    Comes from the beating of the locust's wings, [Phenom 286-4
    The wings keep spreading and yet are never wings. [Somnam 304-4
    Until its wings bear off night's middle witch; [Pure 333-1
    Perfective wings. [Analysis 349-9
    A shape left behind, with like wings spreading out, [Myrrh 350-2
    So that he was the ascending wings he saw [NSF 403-4
    On his spredden wings, needs nothing but deep space, [NSF 404-17
    Are the wings his, the lapis-haunted air? [NSF 404-21
    Spreading out fortress walls like fortress wings. [Luther 461-12
    Of his self, come at upon wide delvings of wings. [NH 475-24
    How easily the blown banners change to wings . . . [Rome 508-11
    Were wings that bore [Phases 4-2 P
    Of your dark self, and how the wings of stars, [Blanche 10-11 P
    Out of the whirl and denseness of your wings, [Red Kit 31-25 P
    A group of marble horses rose on wings [Old Woman 43-2 P
    The earth as the bodies rose on feathery wings, [Old Woman 43-15P
    More than his mind in the wings. The rotten leaves [Old Woman
    43-20 P
    Lay black and full of black misshapen? Wings [Old Woman 44-21 P
    The light wings lifted through the crystal space [Old Woman
    46-11 P
    Wings spread and whirling over jaguar-men? [Greenest 55-31 P
    Appoints its florid messengers with wings [Greenest 57-17 P
    The darkest blue of the dome and the wings around [Duck 65-22 P
    Keep whanging their brass wings . . . [Memo 89-8 P
WINK. Wink as they will. Wink most when widows wince. [High-Toned
    59-22
WINKLE. Fallen Winkle felt the pride [Phases 4-17 P
WINTER. One must have a mind of winter [Snow Man 9-21
    Washed into rinds by rotting winter rains. [Monocle 16-11
    Of winter, until nothing of himself [C 29-15
    Before the winter's vacancy returned. [C 34-12
    After the winter." [Jack-Rabbit 50-13
    The bough of summer and the winter branch. [Sunday 67-25
    The cowl of winter, done repenting. [Peter 92-5
    Perhaps, if winter once could penetrate [Pharynx 96-10
    A state that was free, in the dead of winter, from mice? [Mice
    123-10
    Day after day, throughout the winter, [Medit 124-1
    This robe of snow and winter stars, [Snow Stars 133-4
    That, too, returns from out the winter's air, [Sun March 134-2
    Cold is our element and winter's air [Sun March 134-5
    "Winter Bells" [141-title

The sea drifts through the winter air. [MBG 179-14
Winter devising summer in its breast, [Thought 186-8
At the end of winter when afternoons return. [Poems Clim 193-11
The winter is made and you have to bear it, [Dwarf 208-3
The winter web, the winter woven, wind and wind, [Dwarf 208-4
Through winter's meditative light? [Bagatelles 213-12
Tonight there are only the winter stars. [Dezem 218-1
The evening star, at the beginning of winter, the star [Martial
    237-11
At the beginning of winter, and I walked and talked [Martial
    238-14
The mind is the great poem of winter, the man, [Bottle 238-17
He felt curious about the winter hills [Extracts 254-26
The winter wind blew in an empty place-- [Extracts 255-6
Be broken and winter would be broken and done, [Extracts 255-19
I am a poison at the winter's end, [News 265-5
From the bombastic intimations of winter [Contra II 270-8
Each man spoke in winter. Yet each man spoke of [Hero 273-7
Devise, devise, and make him of winter's [Hero 275-23
A brune figure in winter evening resists [Man Car 350-15
Summer is changed to winter, the young grow old, [Chaos 357-14
Before winter freezes and grows black-- [Burghers 362-14
It is desire at the end of winter, when [NSF 382-6
At summer thunder and sleeps through winter snow. [NSF 384-16
Spring vanishes the scraps of winter, why [NSF 391-1
Winter and spring, cold copulars, embrace [NSF 392-8
To discover winter and know it well, to find, [NSF 404-1
Whether fresher or duller, whether of winter cloud [AA 412-13
Or of winter sky, from horizon to horizon. [AA 412-14
To imagine winter? When the leaves are dead, [AA 417-7
Like a blaze of summer straw, in winter's nick. [AA 421-3
In the hard brightness of that winter day [Page 421-4
Of winter, in the unbroken circle [Celle 438-10
The first red of red winter, winter-red, [Novel 457-14
So lewd spring comes from winter's chastity. [NH 468-4
It was after the neurosis of winter. It was [NH 482-17
The sky seemed so small that winter day, [Two Illus 513-1
Like the last muting of winter as it ends. [Look 519-3
That winter is washed away. Someone is moving [World 520-13
At the earliest ending of winter, [Not Ideas 534-1
If not from winter, from a summer like [Greenest 57-24 P
A winter's noon, in which the colors sprang [Greenest 57-25 P
Night gold, and winter night, night silver, these [Sombre 68-12P
The words of winter in which these two will come together, [Sick
    90-16 P
At the antipodes of poetry, dark winter, [Discov 95-7 P
The sprawling of winter might suddenly stand erect, [Discov 96-3P
The true tone of the metal of winter in what it says: [Discov
    96-6 P
Yet the nothingness of winter becomes a little less. [Course
    96-11 P
Round summer and angular winter and winds, [Ulysses 102-24 P
WINTER-LIGHT. At dawn, nor of summer-light and winter-light [Burn-
    shaw 50-3 P
WINTER-RED. The first red of red winter, winter-red, [Novel 457-14
WINTER-SOUND. The savagest hollow of winter-sound. [Possum 294-12
WINTER-STOP. Fear never the brute clouds nor winter-stop [Montra
    261-22
WINTRIEST. That is fluent in even the wintriest bronze. [Sleight
    222-19
WINTRY. My North is leafless and lies in a wintry slime [Farewell
    118-11
Be thou that wintry sound [Mozart 132-13
And that booming wintry and dull, [Nightgown 214-8
The tower, the ancient accent, the wintry size. [Antag 426-6
Under the wintry trees of the terrace. [Bus 116-14 P
WIPED. I have wiped away moonlight like mud. Your innocent ear
    [Uruguay 249-5
WIRE. Of wire, the designs of ink, [Common 221-18
WIRY. An instrument, twanging a wiry string that gives [Of Mod
    240-15
WISDOM. Not wisdom. Can all men, together, avenge [Nigger 158-11
Whose venom and whose wisdom will be one. [John 437-21
We'll give the week-end to wisdom, to Weisheit, the rabbi, [Aug
    492-1
Let wise men piece the world together with wisdom [Grotesque
    75-7 P
It had neither love nor wisdom. [Three 132-7 P
WISE. But the wise man avenges by building his city in snow. [Nig-
    ger 158-13
By the wise. There are not leaves enough to crown, [Dames 206-18
Wise John, and his son, wise John, [Soldat 15-10 P
And his wise son's John, and-a-one [Soldat 15-11 P
Like the mother of all nightingales; be wise [Spaniard 35-10 P
Let wise men piece the world together with wisdom [Grotesque
    75-7 P
The bronze of the wise man seated in repose [Recit 86-15 P
Is not its form. Tradition is wise but not [Recit 86-16 P
The figure of the wise man fixed in sense. [Recit 86-17 P
Or wise men, or nobles, [Three 129-14 P

Drink from wise men? From jade? [Three 129-16 P
    See wide-wise.
WISEST. Do I press the extremest book of the wisest man [NSF 380-5
WISH. I wish that I might be a thinking stone. [Monocle 13-7
    But as in the powerful mirror of my wish and will." [Rhythms
    246-8
Makes more of it. It is easy to wish for another structure [Bed
    326-16
What rabbi, grown furious with human wish, [NSF 389-1
And little will or wish, that day, for tears. [Soldat 14-17 P
I wish they were all fair [Parasol 20-12 P
WISHED. To hold by the ear, even though it wished for a bell,
    [Uruguay 249-10
Wished faithfully for a falsifying bell. [Uruguay 249-11
In one's heart and wished as he had always wished, unable [Bed
    327-2
Is something wished for made effectual [Belly 367-8
One wished that there had been a season, [Aug 491-26
As I wished, once they fell backward when my breath [Bship 78-16P
WISHED-FOR. Could make us squeak, like dolls, the wished-for words.
    [Monocle 17-8
Skin flashing to wished-for disappearances [AA 411-11
If more than the wished-for ruin racked the night, [Sombre 69-12P
WISHES. He wishes that all hard poetry were true. [Papini 447-2
WISHING. This is the habit of wishing, as if one's grandfather lay
    [Bed 327-1
That habit of wishing and to accept the structure [Bed 327-6
And with it, the antiquest wishing [Stan Hero 83-19 P
WISPING. Of the torches wisping in the underground, [MBG 167-4
WIT. Birds of more wit, that substitute-- [Hermit 505-18
In slaughter; or if to match its furious wit [Sombre 69-6 P
WITCH. Until its wings bear off night's middle witch; [Pure 333-1
WITCHES. Of ether, exceed the excelling witches, whence [Study II
    464-7
WITCHING. In witching chords, and their thin blood [Peter 90-11
In the witching wilderness, night's witchingness, [Burnshaw
    46-25 P
WITCHINGNESS. In the witching wilderness, night's witchingness,
    [Burnshaw 46-25 P
WITHDRAWN. The suspending hand withdrawn, would be [Couch 295-14
WITHER. The lilacs wither in the Carolinas. [Carolinas 4-11
WITHERED. Wingless and withered, but living alive. [MBG 171-7
Taken with withered weather, crumpled clouds, [News 265-6
It means the distaste we feel for this withered scene [NSF 390-3
Contracted like a withered stick. [Two Illus 513-3
There is the same color in the bellies of frogs, in clays,
    withered reeds, skins, wood, sunlight. [Primordia 8-2 P
WITHEREDNESS. If the place, in spite of its witheredness, was still
    [Extracts 255-11
WITHERS. A geranium withers on the window-sill. [Phenom 286-2
WITHIN. Within me, bursts its watery syllable. [Monocle 13-11
Or bask within his images and words? [C 38-5
To things within his actual eye, alert [C 40-16
Within our bellies, we her chariot. [Worms 49-17
Divinity must live within herself: [Sunday 67-19
Within whose burning bosom we devise [Sunday 69-26
Who still feels irrational things within her. [Shifts 83-16
Of the milk within the saltiest spurge, heard, then, [Sea Surf
    100-19
Where the voice that is great within us rises up, [Eve Angels
    138-5
It lies, themselves within themselves, [Fading 139-12
Within themselves [Fading 139-14
Within as pillars of the sun, [Fading 139-16
Of machine within machine within machine. [Nigger 157-3
Deeper within the belly's dark [MBG 171-9
Yet there was a man within me [Weak Mind 212-16
Hoot, little owl within her, how [Vase 246-2
Within the difference. He felt curious [Extracts 255-12
The taste of it, secrete within them [Hero 279-8
Beyond invention. Within what we permit, [EM 317-6
Within the actual, the warm, the near, [EM 317-7
These are within what we permit, in-bar [EM 317-22
Within the universal whole. The son [EM 324-3
The force that destroys us is disclosed, within [EM 324-20
There is a nature that is grotesque within [Feo 334-4
Words that come out of us like words within, [Sketch 336-2
Rain without change within or from [Human 363-5
Within them right for terraces--oh, brave salut! [Belly 367-11
A wait within that certainty, a rest [NSF 386-7
Of the lover that lies within us and we breathe [NSF 394-24
Which he can take within him on his breath, [NSF 395-5
At heart, within an instant's motion, within [Orb 440-20
Its knowledge cold within one as one's own; [Novel 459-3
Within the very object that we seek, [Study I 463-9
Within the big, blue bush and its vast shade [Study I 463-12
Nothing beyond reality. Within it, [NH 471-21
And the egg of the earth lies deep within an egg. [Aug 490-10
Have liberty not as the air within a grave [Aug 490-12
Within his being, [Aug 492-6

A crown within him of crispest diamonds, [Aug 492-7
A shape within the ancient circles of shapes, [Rome 509-1
And as he thought within the thought [Two Illus 513-10
And made much within her. [Song Fixed 520-10
The barbarous strength within her would never fail. [World 521-15
Within a single thing, a single shawl [Final 524-7
Within its vital boundary, in the mind. [Final 524-13
Piercing the tide by which it moves, is constantly within us?
    [Inelegance 26-2 P
Each voice within the other, seeming one, [Old Woman 45-28 P
Appear to sleep within a sleeping air, [Burnshaw 50-19 P
Noble within perfecting solitude, [Greenest 54-4 P
Within us hitherto unknown, he that [Duck 63-19 P
A meaning within the meaning they convey, [Duck 65-17 P
He was born within us as a second self, [Sombre 67-3 P
The future must bear within it every past, [Sombre 70-5 P
Within us. False hybrids and false heroes, [Stan Hero 84-7 P
Choosing out of himself, out of everything within him, [Sick
    90-19 P
These pods are part of the growth of life within life: [Nuns
    92-7 P
Held in the hands of blue men that are lead within, [Discov
    95-16 P
The right within us and about us, [Ulysses 100-13 P
The right within me and about me, [Presence 105-22 P
Opened out within a secrecy of place, [Letters 108-4 P
Which, from the ash within it, fortifies [Someone 83-17 A
WITHOUT. Why, without pity on these studious ghosts, [Monocle
    14-10
From madness or delight, without regard [Monocle 17-12
The World without Imagination [C 27-title 1
He came. The poetic hero without palms [C 35-26
Or jugglery, without regalia. [C 35-27
Hands without touch yet touching poignantly, [C 43-17
Without grace or grumble. Score this anecdote [C 45-19
They seem an exaltation without sound. [On Manner 55-14
Winding across the wide water, without sound, [Sunday 67-7
The day is like wide water, without sound, [Sunday 67-8
She hears, upon that water without sound, [Sunday 70-14
These lines are swift and fall without diverging. [Tallap 72-4
Like a human without illusions, [Shifts 83-15
Death is absolute and without memorial, [Soldier 97-7
Wear a helmet without reason, [Orangeade 103-11
Boston without a Note-book [NE Verses 105-title 6
Without cap or strap, you are the cynic still. [NE Verses 106-4
Without an escape in the lapses of their kisses. [Norfolk 112-2
These voices crying without knowing for what, [Sad Gay 122-6
Except to be happy, without knowing how, [Sad Gay 122-7
Just to stand still without moving a hand. [Adieu 127-12
In a world without heaven to follow, the stops [Adieu 127-13
Repeated in a summer without end [Key W 129-16
Without a theme? [Bot 1 135-10
Without that poem, or without [Bot 2 136-8
"Evening without Angels" [136-title
From below and walks without meditation, [Brave 138-20
If joy shall be without a book [Fading 139-11
That church without bells. [Winter B 141-4
Without seeing the harvest or the moon? [MBG 173-6
Without shadows, without magnificence, [MBG 176-13
Moved in the grass without a sound. [MBG 178-14
Without panache, without cockade, [Thought 185-24
Of a self, if, without sentiment, [Prelude 194-16
Without pathos, he feels what he hears [Prelude 194-18
The moon without a shape, [Add 199-7
Like a man without a doctrine. The light he gives-- [Freed 205-1
To be without a description of to be, [Freed 205-7
It was being without description, being an ox. [Freed 205-16
Without that monument of cat, [Rabbit K 209-8
If Englishmen lived without tea in Ceylon, and they do; [Connois
    215-7
Without rose and without violet, [Common 221-12
Without ideas in a land without ideas, [Forces 228-19
Lantern without a bearer, you drift, [Vari 232-16
The sparrow requites one, without intent. [Vari 233-16
Without teetering a millimeter's measure. [Vari 236-1
Without eyes or mouth, that looks at one and speaks. [Yellow
    237-9
It was like sudden time in a world without time, [Martial 237-17
Without time: as that which is not has no time, [Martial 237-19
Of the silence before the armies, armies without [Martial 237-21
Without blue, without any turquoise tint or phase, [Landsc 241-18
To receive what others had supposed, without [Landsc 242-16
Without clairvoyance, close to her. [Vase 247-8
Without the labor of thought, in that element, [Gala 248-10
We buried the fallen without jasmine crowns. [Oboe 251-13
The glass man, without external reference. [Oboe 251-21
The cold evening, without any scent or the shade [Extracts 258-15
As apples fall, without astronomy, [Montra 262-7
The page is blank or a frame without a glass [Phosphor 267-7
Master and, without light, I dwell. There [Hero 273-4

Flew close to, flew to without rising away. [God 285-8
And repeats words without meaning. [Motive 288-4
Have arms without hands. They have trunks [Possum 293-18
Without legs, or, for that, without heads. [Possum 294-1
Without lineage or language, only [Couch 295-7
Without gestures is to get at it as [Couch 295-17
To perceive men without reference to their form. [Choc 296-11
Without existence, existing everywhere. [Choc 298-5
Without this bird that never settles, without [Somnam 304-10
A giant without a body. If, as giant, [Repet 308-10
Without a word of rhetoric--there it is. [Repet 309-3
In a beau language without a drop of blood. [Repet 310-9
Without understanding, out of the wall [Creat 310-12
Better without an author, without a poet, [Creat 310-18
Without the inventions of sorrow or the sob [EM 317-5
To be? You go, poor phantoms, without place [EM 320-4
This creates a third world without knowledge, [EM 323-19
There is village and village of them, without regard [Wild 328-13
Not span, without any weather at all, except [Wild 329-7
Without a rider on a road at night. [Pure 329-17
We believe without belief, beyond belief. [Flyer 336-15
"Description without Place" [339-title
Without secret arrangements of it in the mind. [Descrip 341-14
If seeming is description without place, [Descrip 343-15
Is description without place. It is a sense [Descrip 343-18
The future is description without place, [Descrip 344-7
Of the past is description without place, a cast [Descrip 345-20
Without physical pedantry [Analysis 348-15
The knowledge of being, sense without sense of time. [Myrrh 350-9
Makers without knowing, or intending, uses. [New Set 352-15
What should we be without the sexual myth, [Men Made 355-15
Knows desire without an object of desire, [Chaos 358-3
Without a word to the people, unless [Woman Song 360-16
Without diamond--blazons or flashing or [Pediment 361-11
Without any feeling, an imperium of quiet, [Burghers 362-16
Rain without change within or from [Human 363-5
Without. In this place and in this time [Human 363-6
Instead, outcast, without the will to power [Cats 368-2
And quickly understand, without their flesh, [Cats 368-9
It was passing a boundary, floating without a head [Lot 371-16
Without evasion by a single metaphor. [Cred 373-7
Pure rhetoric of a language without words. [Cred 374-15
And people, without souvenir. The day [Cred 375-7
Without his envious pain in body, in mind, [Past Nun 378-20
Be spoken to, without a roof, without [NSF 385-9
First fruits, without the virginal of birds, [NSF 385-10
Without a name and nothing to be desired, [NSF 385-13
It feels good as it is without the giant, [NSF 386-1
So many clappers going without bells, [NSF 394-5
Eye without lid, mind without any dream-- [NSF 394-12
Without their fierce addictions, nor that the heat [NSF 399-9
Waste without puberty; and afterward, [NSF 399-17
Clear and, except for the eye, without intrusion. [NSF 400-3
Am satisfied without solacing majesty, [NSF 405-2
With six meats and twelve wines or else without [NSF 407-16
The soldier is poor without the poet's lines, [NSF 407-18
And the serpent body flashing without the skin. [AA 411-12
Und so lau, between sound without meaning and speech, [Page
    421-10
In a permanent realization, without any wild ducks [Cata 425-7
Without the oscillations of planetary pass-pass, [Cata 425-11
If it is a world without a genius, [Antag 425-13
Without understanding, he belongs to it [Bad Time 426-16
Without scenery or lights, in the theatre's bricks, [Bad Time
    427-5
At the moment's being, without history, [Beginning 427-16
Move blackly and without crystal. [Countryman 428-15
Without a voice, inventions of farewell. [Owl 432-4
About the night. They live without our light, [Owl 432-7
O exhalation, O fling without a sleeve [Owl 435-19
Without a god, O silver sheen and shape, [Bouquet 449-16
"World without Peculiarity" [453-title
Without that that he makes of it? [Our Stars 455-8
Straight up, an élan without harrowing, [What We 459-14
In his cave, remains dismissed without a dream, [Study II 464-9
Dark things without a double, after all, [NH 465-13
Without regard to time or where we are, [NH 466-12
Of simple seeing, without reflection. We seek [NH 471-20
A serious man without the serious, [NH 474-14
God in the object itself, without much choice. [NH 475-10
Which, without the statue, would be new, [NH 483-5
To keep him from forgetting, without a word, [NH 483-17
But, here, the inamorata, without distance [NH 484-16
Or as a voice that, speaking without form, [NH 484-20
Or the same thing without desire, [Aug 491-1
A zone of time without the ticking of clocks, [Aug 494-7
Without rain, there is the sadness of rain [Aug 495-19
And live without a tepid aureole, [Angel 496-10
For this blank cold, this sadness without cause. [Plain 502-14
The plain sense of it, without reflections, leaves, [Plain 503-3

A reader without a body, [Inhab 503-19
In a mirror, without heat, [Plant 506-13
And without eloquence, O. half-asleep, [Rome 509-11
And you--it is you that speak it, without speech, [Rome 510-6
A nature still without a shape, [Two Illus 514-1
As he traveled alone, like a man lured on by a syllable without
   any meaning, [Prol 516-4
Without his literature and without his gods . . . [Look 518-2
Without any form or any sense of form, [Look 518-9
They bud and bloom and bear their fruit without change. [Rock
   527-5
To embrace autumn, without turning [Secret Man 36-3 P
To see them without their passions [Lytton 38-10 P
Perhaps, without their passions, they will be [Lytton 38-12 P
Memory without passion would be better lost. [Lytton 38-18 P
Without the distortions of the theatre, [Lytton 39-3 P
Without the revolutions' ruin, [Lytton 39-4 P
Without any pity in a somnolent dream. [Old Woman 44-6 P
And without knowing, and then upon the wind [Old Woman 44-14 P
Without her, evening like a budding yew [Old Woman 45-23 P
As sequels without thought. In the rudest red [Burnshaw 47-8 P
Shines without fire on columns intercrossed, [Burnshaw 49-12 P
And are your feelings changed to sound, without [Burnshaw 52-13P
No heaven, had death without a heaven, death [Greenest 54-20 P
Lord without any deviation, lord [Greenest 60-4 P
To a million, a duck with apples and without wine. [Duck 60-12 P
Without any horror of the helpless loss. [Duck 61-16 P
A meaning without a meaning. These people have [Duck 65-16 P
Without a season, unstinted in livery, [Sombre 67-7 P
For ponderous revolving, without help. [Sombre 69-16 P
That a man without passion plays in an aimless way. [Sombre
   71-12 P
Without imagination, without past [Sombre 71-23 P
And without future, a present time, is that [Sombre 71-24 P
In a world forever without a plan [Grotesque 76-14 P
Without beginning or the concept of an end. [Grotesque 76-24 P
Without a society, the politicians [Bship 79-23 P
In a Third: The whole cannot exist without [Bship 80-14 P
Without them it could not exist. That's our affair, [Bship 80-28P
To the final full, an end without rhetoric. [Bship 81-11 P
Without heroic words, heroic [Stan Hero 84-5 P
Becomes the hero without heroics. [Stan Hero 84-14 P
Voices in chorus, singing without words, remote and deep, [Sick
   90-11 P
A bubble without a wall on which to hang. [Theatre 91-12 P
A universe without life's limp and lack, [Theatre 91-16 P
Now, being invisible, I walk without mantilla, [Souls 94-16 P
In the absence of fantasia, without meaning more [Course 97-1 P
"Farewell without a Guitar" [98-title P
In which the horse walks home without a rider, [Fare Guit 99-3 P
And thinks about it without consciousness, [Sol Oaks 111-9 P
He knew that he was a spirit without a foyer [Local 111-11 P
The local objects of a world without a foyer, [Local 111-14 P
Without a remembered past, a present past, [Local 111-15 P
Because he desired without knowing quite what, [Local 112-9 P
And it flows over us without meanings, [Clear Day 113-16 P
By another shape without a word. [Banjo 114-10 P
Thinkers without final thoughts [July 115-2 P
Sings in the palm, without human meaning, [Of Mere 117-19 P
Without human feeling, a foreign song. [Of Mere 117-20 P
I could find it without, [Three 127-4 P
He was alone without her, [Three 139-8 P
Was alone without her: [Three 139-10 P
Without which it would all be black. [Three 143-9 P
Without the forfeit scholar coming in, [Someone 85-4 A
Without his enlargings and pale arrondissements, [Someone 85-5 A
Without the furious roar in his capital. [Someone 85-6 A
WIZENED. They carry the wizened one [Cortege 80-1
It is a wizened starlight growing young, [Descrip 344-9
WOE. Weaken our fate, relieve us of woe both great [EM 315-21
A little wet of wing and woe, [Song Fixed 519-19
How I exhort her, huckstering my woe. [Stan MMO 19-14 P
WOKE. As he slept. He woke in a metaphor: this was [Pure 331-23
The court woke [Three 131-17 P
It never woke to see, [Three 131-25 P
WOLVES. See she-wolves.
WOMAN. "Another Weeping Woman" [25-title
The dress of a woman of Lhassa, [Men 1000 52-7
"A High-Toned Old Christian Woman" [59-title
Of a woman's arm: [Six Sig 73-17
A man and a woman [Thirteen 93-3
A man and a woman and a blackbird [Thirteen 93-5
The clearest woman with apt weed, to mount [Havana 143-17
Are a woman's words, unlikely to satisfy [Nigger 157-15
The mouse, the moss, the woman on the shore . . . [Blue Bldg 217-6
A demonstration, and a woman, [Common 221-11
Is not a woman for a man. [Common 221-14
To touch a woman cadaverous, [Arcades 225-23
Among men, in a woman--she caught his breath-- [Yellow 237-6
Be of a man skating, a woman dancing, a woman [Of Mod 240-21

For the woman one loves or ought to love, [Waldorf 241-2
That woman waiting for the man she loves,) [Rhythms 245-13
There the woman receives her lover into her heart [Rhythms 245-16
"Woman Looking at a Vase of Flowers" [246-title
Of any woman, watched the thinnest light [Extracts 258-16
A kneeling woman, a moon's farewell; [Hero 275-10
As each had a particular woman and her touch? [Holiday 312-10
A woman smoothes her forehead with her hand [EM 319-17
Woman with a vague moustache and not the mauve [EM 321-15
That were never wholly still. The softest woman, [EM 321-28
What lover has one in such rocks, what woman, [EM 323-24
Man, that is not born of woman but of air, [Pure 331-16
The fragrance of the woman not her self, [Pure 332-14
That a bright red woman will be rising [Debris 338-6
"A Woman Sings a Song for a Soldier Come Home" [360-title
A man and a woman, like two leaves [Burghers 362-12
A woman brilliant and pallid-skinned, [Attempt 370-10
One day enriches a year. One woman makes [Cred 374-21
The enraptured woman, the sequestered night, [Past Nun 378-18
As a man and woman meet and love forthwith. [NSF 386-16
On a woman, day on night, the imagined [NSF 392-6
I am the woman stripped more nakedly [NSF 396-1
The blue woman, linked and lacquered, at her window [NSF 399-4
The blue woman looked and from her window named [NSF 399-21
Presence is not the woman, come upon, [John 437-7
"The Woman in Sunshine" [445-title
The warmth and movement of a woman. [Wom Sun 445-5
It is empty. But a woman in threadless gold [Wom Sun 445-8
One remembers a woman standing in such a dress. [Bouquet 450-24
The hating woman, the meaningless place, [Pecul 454-8
"A Golden Woman in a Silver Mirror" [460-title
Effete green, the woman in black cassimere. [NH 482-2
A woman writing a note and tearing it up. [NH 488-21
The woman is chosen but not by him, [Aug 493-1
Of a woman with a cloud on her shoulder rose [Aug 494-11
By a woman, who has forgotten it. [Vacancy 511-9
Removed from any shore, from any man or woman and needing none.
   [Prol 516-9
Like a woman inhibiting passion [Soldat 12-2 P
This man to visit a woman, [Soldat 12-15 P
I saw a waxen woman in a smock [Infernale 25-1 P
(A woman's voice is heard, replying.) Mock [Infernale 25-4 P
A purple woman with a lavender tongue [Melancholy 32-6 P
"Good Man, Bad Woman" [33-title P
"The Woman Who Blamed Life on a Spaniard" [34-title P
"The Old Woman and the Statue" [43-title P
A woman walking in the autumn leaves, [Old Woman 45-18 P
Knew her, how could you see the woman that wore the beads,
   [Grotesque 74-10 P
The old woman that knocks at the door [Grotesque 77-1 P
"The Woman That Had More Babies than That" [81-title P
Continually--There is a woman has had [Woman Had 81-22 P
For a change, the englistered woman, seated [Ulysses 104-2 P
A woman looking down the road, [Ulysses 104-21 P
The englistered woman is now seen [Ulysses 104-31
Or woman weeping in a room or man, [Ideal 88-20 A
See wash-woman.
WOMEN. "The Ordinary Women" [10-title
The Mexican women, [Venereal 47-13
For the women of primrose and purl, [Bananas 54-7
The women will be all shanks [Bananas 54-15
You dream of women, swathed in indigo, [Polish Aunt 84-9
Women understand this. [Theory 86-17
Of the women about you? [Thirteen 93-23
Becomes the stones. Women become [MBG 170-22
For buttons, how many women have covered themselves [Dump 202-8
And the women have only one side. [Common 221-25
But now as in an amour of women [Hartford 227-4
Men on green beds and women half of sun. [Cuisine 227-19
Women of a melancholy one could sing. [Horn 230-4
The women of the time. It has to think about war [Of Mod 240-3
Women invisible in music and motion and color," [Waldorf 241-8
To naked men, to women naked as rain. [Extracts 252-14
And forest tigresses and women mixed [EM 321-25
In pantaloons of fire and of women hatched, [Liadoff 346-9
Jerome and the scrupulous Francis and Sunday women, [Luther
   461-8
Is more or less. The pearly women that drop [Study II 464-5
Women with other lives in their live hair, [Study II 464-14
Rose--women as half-fishes of salt shine, [Study II 464-15
Looked on big women, whose ruddy-ripe images [NH 486-17
The nature of its women in the air, [Aug 491-16
The dresses of women, [Bowl 7-6 P
Why are not women fair, [Parasol 20-3 P
It is not so with women. [Parasol 20-11 P
By elderly women? [Cab 21-15 P
The women should sing as they march. [Drum-Majors 37-11 P
About the weather and women and the way [Greenest 58-26 P
The women with eyes like opals vanish [Stan Hero 83-12 P
"The Souls of Women at Night" [94-title P

"Conversation with Three Women of New England" [108-title P
Where the fattest women belled the glass. [Dinner 110-4 P
The rosy men and the women of the rose, [Art Pop 112-19 P
Like whispering women. [Three 128-11 P
It is a pity it is of women. [Three 134-3 P
WON. In an ignorance of sleep with nothing won. [Dutch 291-26
WONDER. In the weaving round the wonder of its need, [Owl 434-15
The mornings grow silent, the never-tiring wonder. [Aug 495-17
I wonder, have I lived a skeleton's life, [Warmth 89-17 P
I wonder, have I lived a skeleton's life, [As Leave 117-5 P
Would wonder; [Three 132-23 P
WONDERED. They wondered why Susanna cried [Peter 91-14
And wondered about the water in the lake. [Extracts 254-27
Seized her and wondered: why beneath the tree [Hand 271-4
WONDERS. And murky masonry, one wonders [Ulysses 100-29 P
WONT. For maidens who were wont to sit and gaze [Sunday 69-8
WOOD. Life is an old casino in a wood. [Havana 144-11
We were two figures in a wood. [On Road 203-21
The sky would be full of bodies like wood. [Thunder 220-17
Its poisoned laurels in this poisoned wood, [Pastor 379-20
The way wine comes at a table in a wood. [NSF 405-24
Sits in a wood, in the greenest part, [Degen 444-2
The man in the black wood descends unchanged. [Degen 444-11
And makes flame flame and makes it bite the wood [Novel 458-7
There is the same color in the bellies of frogs, in clays,
    withered reeds, skins, wood, sunlight. [Primordia 8-2 P
In the shadows of a wood . . . [Letters 108-1 P
Wood of his forests and stone out of his fields [Myth 118-15 P
WOOD-DOVE. The wood-dove used to chant his hoobla-hoo [NSF 383-6
WOOD-DOVES. The wood-doves are singing along the Perkiomen. [Think
    356-7
One ear, the wood-doves are singing a single song. [Think 356-10
WOODED. And April hillsides wooded white and pink, [C 37-29
WOODEN. Two wooden tubs of blue hydrangeas stand at the foot of the
    stone steps. [Banal 62-11
The wooden ascents [Cortege 80-14
The trees are wooden, the grass is yellow and thin. [Nigger
    157-21
Over wooden Boston, the sparkling Byzantine [Blue Bldg 217-1
In the sky, an imagined, wooden chair [Human 363-9
How is it that the wooden trees stand up [Belly 367-2
Wooden, the model for astral apprentices, [NH 478-19
Bending over and pulling themselves erect on the wooden handles,
    [Prol 515-8
WOODS. The cattle skulls in the woods? [Circulat 150-2
Old nests and there is blue in the woods. [Cuisine 227-15
In the woods of the dogwoods, [Forces 229-11
Young men go walking in the woods, [Pediment 361-7
In the woods, in this full-blown May, [Pediment 362-1
The sea full of fishes in shoals, the woods that let [Cats 367-13
Far in the woods they sang their unreal songs, [Cred 376-1
Or else avert the object. Deep in the woods [Cred 376-4
Scenes of the theatre, vistas and blocks of woods [AA 415-14
Green guests and table in the woods and songs [Orb 440-19
At home; or: In the woods, belle Belle alone [Golden 460-14
Dissolved the woods, war and the fatal farce [Greenest 53-22 P
Shadows, woods . . . and the two of them in speech, [Letters
    108-2 P
"Dinner Bell in the Woods" [109-title P
See pine-woods.
WOOD-SMOKE. Wood-smoke rises through trees, is caught in an upper
    flow [Slug 522-3
WOOL. Protruding from the pile of wool, a hand, [Novel 457-10
Feeling the fear that creeps beneath the wool, [Novel 458-23
WOOLEN. But nakedness, woolen massa, concerns an innermost atom.
    [Nudity Cap 145-10
WORD. What word split up in clickering syllables [C 28-14
What word have you, interpreters, of men [Heaven 56-9
The softest word went gurrituck in his skull. [Norfolk 111-9
And that she will not follow in any word [Farewell 118-8
It is the word pejorative that hurts. [Sailing 120-1
One's cup and never to say a word, [Adieu 128-3
Since what she sang was uttered word by word. [Key W 128-21
The bauble of the sleepless nor a word [Havana 144-4
"Words are not forms of a single word. [On Road 204-2
Of earth penetrates more deeply than any word. [Yellow 237-3
Kept speaking, of God. I changed the word to man. [Les Plus
    245-4
In which we pronounce joy like a word of our own. [Gala 248-6
But you, you used the word, [Search 268-7
The world as word, [Search 268-11
You were created of your name, the word [Phenom 287-17
There is no life except in the word of it. [Phenom 287-19
Without a word of rhetoric--there it is. [Repet 309-3
"A Word with José Rodríguez-Feo" [333-title
It is the theory of the word for those [Descrip 345-6
For whom the word is the making of the world, [Descrip 345-7
Without a word to the people, unless [Woman Song 360-16
Incipit and a form to speak the word [NSF 387-5
And every latent double in the word, [NSF 387-6

It may come tomorrow in the simplest word, [AA 420-1
From sight, in the silence that follows her last word-- [Owl
    435-21
By trope or deviation, straight to the word, [NH 471-14
To keep him from forgetting, without a word, [NH 483-17
There it was, word for word, [Poem Mt 512-1
Is there one word of sunshine in this plaint? [Stan MMO 19-16 P
Like a word in the mind that sticks at artichoke [Burnshaw 47-2P
The word respected, fired ten thousand guns [Bship 78-12 P
One thinks that it could be that the first word spoken, [Discov
    95-17 P
The first word would be of the susceptible being arrived, [Discov
    96-1 P
By another shape without a word. [Banjo 114-10 P
With nothing fixed by a single word. [Banjo 114-12 P
A way of pronouncing the word inside of one's tongue [Bus 116-13P
WORDS. Like the clashed edges of two words that kill." [Monocle
    13-4
Could make us squeak, like dolls, the wished-for words. [Monocle
    17-8
Hence the reverberations in the words [C 37-11
Or bask within his images and words? [C 38-5
With masquerade of thought, with hapless words [C 39-15
The words of things entangle and confuse. [C 41-1
Or that she will pause at scurrilous words? [Lilacs 49-5
There are men whose words [Men 1000 51-15
And a jumble of words [Cortege 80-27
Use dusky words and dusky images. [Two Figures 86-2
Conceiving words, [Two Figures 86-6
For which more than any words cries deeplier? [Ghosts 119-7
The maker's rage to order words of the sea, [Key W 130-12
Words of the fragrant portals, dimly-starred, [Key W 130-13
True reconcilings, dark, pacific words, [Havana 144-21
Over the simplest words: [Nigger 151-17
Encore un instant de bonheur. The words [Nigger 157-14
Are a woman's words, unlikely to satisfy [Nigger 157-15
The yellow moon of words about the nightingale [Autumn 160-4
Pitiless verse? A few words tuned [Chateau 161-15
Sodden with his melancholy words, [MBG 170-3
Over words that are life's voluble utterance. [Men Fall 188-20
Lies in flawed words and stubborn sounds. [Poems Clim 194-10
"Words are not forms of a single word. [On Road 204-2
"Country Words" [207-title
It wants words virile with his breath. [Country 207-23
The words are written, though not yet said. [Cuisine 227-20
Letters of rock and water, words [Vari 232-10
Words add to the senses. The words for the dazzle [Vari 234-17
With meditation, speak words that in the ear, [Of Mod 240-7
The sea is so many written words; the sky [Extracts 252-10
The vital music formulates the words. [Extracts 259-18
The moonlight in the cell, words on the wall. [Montra 260-21
The hero's throat in which the words are spoken, [Montra 261-4
Delivering the prisoner by his words, [Montra 261-7
In which man is the hero. He hears the words, [Montra 261-20
Repeats its vital words, yet balances [Search 268-15
Out of the movement of few words, [Oak 272-1
And repeats words without meaning. [Motive 288-4
Staring at the secretions of the words as [Lack 303-3
If these were only words that I am speaking [Repet 307-19
On a few words of what is real in the world [Repet 308-13
A few words, a memorandum voluble [Repet 308-19
A few words of what is real or may be [Repet 309-6
Too exactly himself, and that there are words [Creat 310-17
And the words for them and the colors that they possessed. [Holi-
    day 312-13
The weather in words and words in sounds of sound. [Pure 332-18
A total dream. There are words of this, [Sketch 335-21
Words, in a storm, that beat around the shapes. [Sketch 335-22
Words that come out of us like words within, [Sketch 336-2
She will speak thoughtfully the words of a line. [Debris 338-8
It is a world of words to the end of it, [Descrip 345-9
"Men Made out of Words" [355-title
The words were spoken as if there was no book, [House Q 358-11
Pure rhetoric of a language without words. [Cred 374-15
Is there a poem that never reaches words [NSF 396-18
The words they spoke were voices that she heard. [NSF 402-10
That I should name you flatly, waste no words, [NSF 406-13
How gladly with proper words the soldier dies, [NSF 408-2
Their words are chosen out of their desire, [Orb 441-7
That I stay away. These are the words of José . . . [Novel 457-12
A few words, an and yet, and yet, and yet-- [NH 465-6
Words, lines, not meanings, not communications, [NH 465-12
Together, said words of the world are the life of the world. [NH
    474-9
In the land of big mariners, the words they spoke [NH 486-20
Of words that was a change of nature, more [NH 487-6
Their dark-colored words had redescribed the citrons. [NH 487-9
Not often realized, the lighter words [NH 488-8
Variations on the words spread sail. [Aug 490-2
He wears the words he reads to look upon [Aug 492-5

Like watery words awash; like meanings said [Angel 497-4
A look, a few words spoken. [Leben 505-6
As if the design of all his words takes form [Rome 511-2
Or we put mantles on our words because [Look 519-1
Were not and are not. Absurd. The words spoken [Rock 525-10
His words are both the icon and the man. [Rock 527-21
In the poverty of their words, [Planet 533-2
Your yes her no, your no her yes. The words [Red Kit 30-13 P
Her words accuse you of adulteries [Red Kit 31-3 P
Bears words that are the speech of marble men. [Burnshaw 52-5 P
Where shall we find more than derisive words? [Duck 66-9 P
Their words and ours; in what we see, their hues [Sombre 67-6 P
He makes no choice of words-- [Grotesque 75-20 P
On her lips familiar words become the words [Woman Had 83-9 P
The words are in the way and thoughts are. [Stan Hero 84-1 P
Without heroic words, heroic [Stan Hero 84-5 P
Voices in chorus, singing without words, remote and deep, [Sick
     90-11 P
The words of winter in which these two will come together, [Sick
     90-16 P
The peaceful, blissful words, well-tuned, well-sung, well-spoken.
     [Sick 90-21 P
It is a special day. We mumble the words [Nuns 92-18 P
In a secrecy of words [Letters 108-3 P
Shall be the celebration in the words [Ideal 89-5 A
WORDY. Of blue and green? A wordy, watery age [C 28-25
WORE. And the cold dresses that they wore, [Ord Women 11-5
The Italian girls wore jonquils in their hair [NSF 389-16
Knew her, how could you see the woman that wore the beads,
     [Grotesque 74-10 P
Once the assassins wore stone masks and did [Bship 78-15 P
Of the green gown I wore. [Three 134-17 P
Wore purple to see; [Three 141-8 P
I wore gold ear-rings. [Three 141-10 P
WORK. It is too cold for work, now, in the fields. [Nigger 151-18
And say it is the work [Crude 305-10
Live, work, suffer and die in that idea [EM 325-14
An occupation, an exercise, a work, [NSF 405-18
Bent over work, anxious, content, alone, [NSF 406-16
Of the work, in the idiom of an innocent earth, [AA 419-5
Work and waste [Phases 4-21 P
Forgetting work, not caring for angels, hunting a lift, [Duck
     60-15 P
WORKED. I worked in ours-- [Three 141-7 P
WORKERS. I heard two workers say, "This chaos [Idiom 200-18
The workers do not rise, as Venus rose, [Duck 60-9 P
WORKING. Working, with big hands, on the town, [Hartford 227-2
WORKS. It is the sun that shares our works. [MBG 168-9
The sun no longer shares our works [MBG 168-13
He liked the nobler works of man, [Thought 187-1
And of his works, I am sure. He bathes in the mist [Freed 204-22
False empire . . . These are the works and pastimes [Hero 280-13
And the cast-iron of our works. But it is, dear sirs, [Orb 440-4
See auto-works.
WORLD. Heavenly labials in a world of gutturals. [Plot Giant 7-9
Man proved a gobbet in my mincing world. [Monocle 17-24
In this imagined world [Weep Woman 25-9
The World without Imagination [C 27-title 1
Inscrutable hair in an inscrutable world. [C 27-21
In a starker, barer world, in which the sun [C 29-17
As being, in a world so falsified, [C 36-19
What are so many men in such a world? [C 41-26
Green crammers of the green fruits of the world, [C 43-28
Four daughters in a world too intricate [C 45-2
The world, a turnip once so readily plucked, [C 45-12
The dreadful sundry of this world, [Venereal 47-11
Of the external world. [Men 1000 51-8
In my room, the world is beyond my understanding; [Of Surface
     57-1
That I distort the world. [W Burgher 61-2
I was the world in which I walked, and what I saw [Hoon 65-16
Your world is you. I am my world. [Bantams 75-19
The world is ugly, [Gubbinal 85-4
The world is ugly, [Gubbinal 85-12
The Whole World Including the Speaker [NE Verses 104-title 1
The Whole World Excluding the Speaker [NE Verses 104-title 2
The world was round. But not from my begetting. [NE Verses 104-4
In a world of wind and frost, [Medit 124-3
Impure upon a world unpurged. [How Live 125-10
In a world without heaven to follow, the stops [Adieu 127-13
She was the single artificer of the world [Key W 129-26
Knew that there never was a world for her [Key W 130-1
(In a world that was resting on pillars, [Botanist 1 135-2
How can the world so old be so mad [Fading 139-9
That's world enough, and more, if one includes [Havana 143-25
Prodigious things are tricks. The world is not [Havana 144-3
In a world of universal poverty [Nigger 152-1
A dirty house in a gutted world, [Postcard 159-19
I cannot bring a world quite round, [MBG 165-11
The heraldic center of the world [MBG 172-6

A candle is enough to light the world. [MBG 172-16
He held the world upon his nose [MBG 178-9
And the world had worlds, ai, this-a-way: [MBG 178-17
The world washed in his imagination, [MBG 179-1
The world was a shore, whether sound or form [MBG 179-2
I am a native in this world [MBG 180-5
Native, a native in the world [MBG 180-9
God and all angels sing the world to sleep, [Men Fall 187-9
Piece the world together, boys, but not with your hands. [Paro-
     chial 192-8
And made it fresh in a world of white, [Poems Clim 193-20
A world of clear water, brilliant-edged, [Poems Clim 194-1
More than a world of white and snowy scents. [Poems Clim 194-3
The world must be measured by eye"; [On Road 204-4
Tired of the old descriptions of the world, [Freed 204-13
Resolved the world. We cannot go back to that. [Connois 215-16
This great world, it divides itself in two, [Dezem 218-6
An exercise in viewing the world. [Vari 233-17
This cloudy world, by aid of land and sea, [Vari 233-20
It was like sudden time in a world without time, [Martial 237-17
This world, this place, the street in which I was, [Martial
     237-18
What had this star to do with the world it lit, [Martial 238-3
An aversion, as the world is averted [Bottle 239-9
Hums and you say "The world in a verse, [Waldorf 241-6
Of air, who looked for the world beneath the blue, [Landsc 241-17
Was divine then all things were, the world itself, [Landsc 242-29
Things were the truth, the world itself was the truth. [Landsc
     242-31
(This man in a room with an image of the world, [Rhythms 245-12
And on that yes the future world depends. [Beard 247-10
It is an artificial world. The rose [Extracts 252-8
Of paper is of the nature of its world. [Extracts 252-9
That's the old world. In the new, all men are priests. [Extracts
     254-2
Sings of an heroic world beyond the cell, [Montra 261-9
A hero's world in which he is the hero. [Montra 261-11
Man must become the hero of his world. [Montra 261-12
He hears the earliest poems of the world [Montra 261-19
The world as word, [Search 268-11
The world lives as you live, [Search 268-13
Nor meditate the world as it goes round. [Phenom 286-6
The obscure moon lighting an obscure world [Motive 288-9
The unpainted shore, accepts the world [Couch 296-4
The ruin stood still in an external world. [Repet 306-3
Overseas, that stood in an external world. [Repet 306-6
And goes to an external world, having [Repet 308-5
On a few words of what is real in the world [Repet 308-13
And writhing wheels of this world's business, [Repet 308-21
As if the health of the world might be enough. [EM 315-25
The genius of the body, which is our world, [EM 317-2
He disposes the world in categories, thus: [EM 323-5
Alone. But in the peopled world, there is, [EM 323-7
This creates a third world without knowledge, [EM 323-19
In the third world, then, there is no pain. Yes, but [EM 323-23
In a world of ideas, who would have all the people [EM 325-13
In a world of ideas. He would not be aware of the clouds, [EM
     325-15
In a physical world, to feel that one's desire [EM 325-19
Completely physical in a physical world. [EM 325-26
The life of the world depends on that he is [Wild 328-11
Green glade and holiday hotel and world [Pure 330-19
This platonic person discovered a soul in the world [Pure 331-13
Malformed, the world was paradise malformed . . . [Pure 332-1
Yet to speak of the whole world as metaphor [Pure 332-8
Night is the nature of man's interior world? [Feo 333-14
We must enter boldly that interior world [Feo 333-16
We say that it is man's interior world [Feo 334-6
The physical world is meaningless tonight [Jouga 337-1
Her green mind made the world around her green. [Descrip 339-9
In a world that shrinks to an immediate whole, [Descrip 341-12
For whom the word is the making of the world, [Descrip 345-7
The buzzing world and lisping firmament. [Descrip 345-8
It is a world of words to the end of it, [Descrip 345-9
In the conscious world, the great clouds [Analysis 348-2
The shadow of an external world comes near. [Myrrh 350-12
"The House Was Quiet and the World Was Calm" [358-title
The house was quiet and the world was calm. [House Q 358-7
The house was quiet and the world was calm. [House Q 358-10
And the world was calm. The truth in a calm world, [House Q 359-1
The world is myself, life is myself, [Pediment 361-17
Of being naked, or almost so, in a world [Lot 371-18
It is the natural tower of all the world, [Cred 373-16
Of this invention, this invented world, [NSF 380-13
Which pierces clouds and bends on half the world. [NSF 393-15
On her trip around the world, Nanzia Nunzio [NSF 395-16
Of volatile world, too constant to be denied, [NSF 397-21
The freshness of a world. It is our own, [NSF 398-1
An unhappy people in a happy world-- [AA 420-4
An unhappy people in an unhappy world-- [AA 420-6

A happy people in an unhappy world-- [AA 420-8
A happy people in a happy world-- [AA 420-11
An unhappy people in a happy world. [AA 420-14
If it is a world without a genius, [Antag 425-13
On This Beautiful World Of Ours composes himself [Ulti 429-10
In This Beautiful World Of Ours and not as now, [Ulti 430-6
Stood flourishing the world. The brilliant height [Owl 434-4
The mind is the terriblest force in the world, father, [John
    436-10
The world is presence and not force. [John 436-14
As if the central poem became the world, [Orb 441-19
And the world the central poem, each one the mate [Orb 441-20
Is Celestin dislodged? The way through the world [Papini 446-5
Of the world, the heroic effort to live expressed [Papini 446-9
The world is still profound and in its depths [Papini 447-9
The complexities of the world, when apprehended, [Papini 447-16
Is a drop of lightning in an inner world, [Bouquet 448-6
The world has turned to the several speeds of glass, [Bouquet
    449-3
"World without Peculiarity" [453-title
An image that was mistress of the world. [Golden 460-9
Who has divided the world, what entrepreneur? [NH 468-20
Together, said words of the world are the life of the world. [NH
    474-9
The gay tournamonde as of a single world [NH 476-3
The sun is half the world, half everything, [NH 481-22
Mistakes it for a world of objects, [Aug 491-3
The world images for the beholder. [Aug 492-16
The world? The inhuman as human? That which thinks not, [Aug
    493-2
A new text of the world, [Aug 494-24
Who is my father in this world, in this house, [Irish 501-7
"Two Illustrations that the World Is What You Make of It" [513-
    title
A dirty light on a lifeless world, [Two Illus 513-2
The World Is Larger in Summer [Two Illus 514-title 2
The spirit comes from the body of the world, [Look 519-7
Or so Mr. Homburg thought: the body of a world [Look 519-8
"The World as Meditation" [520-title
Whose mere savage presence awakens the world in which she dwells.
    [World 520-16
As, for example, a world in which, like snow, [Quiet 523-4
The world imagined is the ultimate good. [Final 524-3
The plenty of the year and of the world. [Rock 527-15
That press, strong peasants in a peasant world, [Armor 530-5
Which of these truly contains the world? [Indigo 22-13 P
In this spent world, she must possess. The gift [Red Kit 30-19 P
Came not from you. Shall the world be spent again, [Red Kit
    30-20 P
She can corrode your world, if never you. [Good Bad 33-22 P
Besides, the world is a tower. [Secret Man 36-5 P
Here is the world of a moment, [Polo 37-16 P
To be the sovereign shape in a world of shapes. [Old Woman 45-17P
Will rule in a poets' world. Yet that will be [Burnshaw 48-16 P
A world impossible for poets, who [Burnshaw 48-17 P
And are never of the world in which they live. [Burnshaw 48-19 P
A trash can at the end of the world, the dead [Burnshaw 49-5 P
Parts of the immense detritus of a world [Burnshaw 49-21 P
Racking the world with clarion puffs. This must [Greenest 56-12P
To see, once more, this hacked-up world of tools, [Duck 61-9 P
What man of folk-lore shall rebuild the world, [Duck 63-6 P
And feeling the world in which they live. The manes, [Duck 64-14P
More of ourselves in a world that is more our own, [Duck 65-1 P
The world is young and I play my guitar. [Stan MBG 72-2 P
Let wise men piece the world together with wisdom [Grotesque
    75-7 P
In a world forever without a plan [Grotesque 76-14 P
For itself as a world, [Grotesque 76-15 P
The ship would become the center of the world. [Bship 78-5 P
Of the world would have only to ring and ft! [Bship 78-9 P
My head, the sorrow of the world, except [Bship 78-18 P
So posed, the captain drafted rules of the world, [Bship 78-20 P
The father keeps on living in the son, the world [Recit 87-25 P
Of the father keeps on living in the world [Recit 87-26 P
A countryman of all the bones of the world? [Warmth 90-1 P
Another sunlight might make another world, [Theatre 91-1 P
And the wry antipodes whirled round the world away-- [Discov
    95-20 P
The deep comfort of the world and fate. [Ulysses 100-4 P
Master of the world and of himself, [Ulysses 102-18 P
Will come. His mind presents the world [Ulysses 102-20 P
And in his mind the world revolves. [Ulysses 102-21 P
In which the world goes round and round [Ulysses 102-26 P
Like things produced by a climate, the world [Ulysses 102-29 P
The mind renews the world in a verse, [Ulysses 103-1 P
Which knowledge is: the world and fate, [Presence 105-21 P
The mode of the person becomes the mode of the world, [Conversat
    108-11 P
For that person, and, sometimes, for the world itself. [Conversat
    108-12 P

It follows that to change modes is to change the world. [Conver-
    sat 108-16 P
A nature of marble in a marble world. [Conversat 109-10 P
The local objects of a world without a foyer, [Local 111-14 P
Not in a single world, [July 114-16 P
It is like a critic of God, the world [Region 115-13 P
Transparent man in a translated world, [Bus 116-3 P
A countryman of all the bones in the world? [As Leave 117-7 P
And unseen. This is everybody's world. [Someone 87-11 A
A world agrees, thought's compromise, resolved [Ideal 89-7 A
See: blood-world; semi-world.
WORLDS. The worlds that were and will be, death and day. [Nigger
    150-12
And the world had worlds, ai, this-a-way: [MBG 178-17
More nights, more days, more clouds, more worlds. [Vari 233-22
Of them and of himself destroys both worlds, [EM 323-16
And of the worlds of logic in their great tombs. [EM 325-5
So many selves, so many sensuous worlds, [EM 326-9
Conceptions of new mornings of new worlds, [NH 470-12
The heavens, the hells, the worlds, the longed-for lands. [NH
    486-12
The two worlds are asleep, are sleeping, now. [Old Man 501-1
Yet living in two worlds, impenitent [Rome 509-20
As the moon has in its moonlight, worlds away, [Red Kit 31-8 P
In which one of these three worlds are the four of us [Conversat
    109-16 P
WORM. This was no worm bred in the moon, [Cuban 65-1
Is a worm composing on a straw. [MBG 174-14
Old worm, my pretty quirk, [Metamorph 265-14
See sea-worm.
WORMS. "The Worms at Heaven's Gate" [49-title
Falls and lies with the worms. [Metamorph 266-5
Not speaking worms, nor birds [Analysis 348-18
Long after the worms and the curious carvings of [Burnshaw
    47-12 P
Young catechumen answering the worms? [Sombre 69-24 P
WORMY. Of wormy metaphors. [Delight 162-9
WORN. Worn out, her arm falls down, [Add 199-3
That is woven and woven and waiting to be worn, [Dwarf 208-10
Worn and leaning to nothingness, [Ulysses 104-20 P
See ruby-water-worn.
WORRIES. To say the light wind worries the sail, [Sailing 121-1
WORRYING. Crash in the mind--But, fat Jocundus, worrying [Glass
    197-20
WORSE. The worse end they come to; [Three 137-17 P
WORST. Often have the worst breaths. [Grotesque 74-18 P
WORTH. That's better. That's worth crossing seas to find. [C 36-25
One sparrow is worth a thousand gulls, [Vari 233-12
WORTHY. But an antipodal, far-fetched creature, worthy of birth,
    [Discov 96-5 P
WOUND. To endure thereafter every mortal wound, [Extracts 258-27
How red the rose that is the soldier's wound, [EM 318-26
In which his wound is good because life was. [EM 319-15
The wound kills that does not bleed. [Woman Song 360-4
And tells of his wound, [Woman Song 360-15
WOUNDED. The body that could never be wounded, [Gigan 289-4
WOUNDS. Patientia, forever soothing wounds, [Lions 124-15
Be tranquil in your wounds. It is good death [Extracts 253-24
Be tranquil in your wounds. The placating star [Extracts 253-26
The wounds. Yet to lie buried in evil earth, [Extracts 259-2
The wounds of many soldiers, the wounds of all [EM 318-27
WOVE. For him to see, wove round her glittering hair. [Hand 271-6
WOVEN. A white of wildly woven rings; [W Burgher 61-15
Fetching her woven scarves, [Peter 91-5
Now it is September and the web is woven. [Dwarf 208-1
The web is woven and you have to wear it. [Dwarf 208-2
The winter web, the winter woven, wind and wind, [Dwarf 208-4
It is the mind that is woven, the mind that was jerked [Dwarf
    208-7
That is woven and woven and waiting to be worn, [Dwarf 208-10
Green is the night and out of madness woven, [Candle 223-7
As if your gowns were woven of the light [Burnshaw 51-24 P
WRACK. That purges the wrack or makes the jungle shine, [Greenest
    55-8 P
WRANGLING. To come, a wrangling of two dreams. [MBG 183-19
WRAPPED. Wrapped in their seemings, crowd on curious crowd, [De-
    scrip 342-14
Wrapped tightly round us, since we are poor, a warmth, [Final
    524-8
WRAPPER. Of every day, the wrapper on the can of pears, [Dump
    201-17
WRAPS. In a vanishing-vanished violet that wraps round [Owl 433-15
It wraps the sheet around its body, until the black figure is
    silver. [Plough-Boy 6-6 P
WRATH. Each one as part of the total wrath, obscure [Sombre 69-5 P
WREATH. Wreathed round and round the round wreath of autumn. [NH
    486-18
The magnum wreath of summer, time's autumn snood, [Rock 526-21
A visible clear cap, a visible wreath [Greenest 57-7 P
WREATHED. Wreathed round and round the round wreath of autumn. [NH

486-18
WREATHS. Apostrophizing wreaths, the voice [MBG 177-13
WRECKAGE. The colorless light in which this wreckage lies [Burn-
  shaw 49-25 P
WRECKED. Are like wrecked umbrellas. [Plant 506-7
WREN. Ah, ke! the bloody wren, the felon jay, [NSF 394-1
  Whistle aloud, too weedy wren. I can [NSF 405-10
WRENCHED. Wrenched out of chaos . . . The quiet lamp [Ulysses
  100-23 P
WRENCHES. Of the real that wrenches, [Orangeade 103-19
WRETCHED. Perhaps our wretched state would soon come right. [Sur-
  prises 98-9
WRETCHEDNESS. "The court had known poverty and wretchedness; hu-
  [Three 129-9 P
  And wretchedness, [Three 132-9 P
WRICK-A-WRACK. Streamed white and stoked and engined wrick-a-
  wrack. [Duck 61-12 P
WRIGGLING. Wriggling far down the phantom air, [Cuban 65-2
  Or is this another wriggling out of the egg, [AA 411-4
WRINKLED. The wrinkled roses tinkle, the paper ones, [Extracts
  252-2
  Of ideas moves wrinkled in a motion like [Feo 333-21
  How soon the silver fades in the dust! How soon the black figure
  slips from the wrinkled sheet! [Plough-Boy 6-8 P
WRINKLINGS. Still eked out luminous wrinklings on the leaves, [Old
  Woman 45-7 P
WRIST. She made the motions of her wrist [Infanta 7-13
WRIT. This is not writ [Pourtraicte 22-7
WRITE. B. It is April as I write. The wind [Connois 216-4
  I write Semiramide and in the script [Phenom 287-20
  The suitable amours. Time will write them down. [NSF 398-6
  Write pax across the window pane. And then [Puel 456-15
  She had heard of the fate of an Argentine writer. At night,
  [Novel 457-8
WRITES. The whole race is a poet that writes down [Men Made 356-5
  Who chants by book, in the heat of the scholar, who writes [NSF
  395-12
  That's it. The lover writes, the believer hears, [Orb 443-15
WRITHE. Of the pillow in your hand. You writhe and press [NSF
  384-20
WRITHED. And the ripe shrub writhed. [Planet 532-12
WRITHES. This day writhes with what? The lecturer [Ulti 429-9
  If the day writhes, it is not with revelations. [Ulti 429-15
  And the spirit writhes to be wakened, writhes [Duck 61-8 P
WRITHING. And writhing wheels of this world's business, [Repet
  308-21
  A bitter utterance from your writhing, dumb, [NSF 384-21
WRITHINGS. Writhings in wrong obliques and distances, [Ulti 430-1
WRITING. He was at Naples writing letters home [EM 313-11
  A woman writing a note and tearing it up. [NH 488-21
  Writing and reading the rigid inscription. [Aug 495-16
WRITTEN. The book of moonlight is not written yet [C 33-18
  Reading where I have written, [Of Surface 57-4
  Music is not yet written but is to be. [Nigger 158-3
  "Poem Written at Morning" [219-title
  The words are written, though not yet said. [Cuisine 227-20
  The sea is so many written words; the sky [Extracts 252-10
  Too vaguely that it be written in character. [Extracts 257-21
  Holds in his hand a book you have never written [Lack 303-2
  And not yet to have written a book in which [Lack 303-17
  He had written them near Athens. The farm was white. [Anach
  366-1
  The thinker as reader reads what has been written. [Aug 492-4
  Ariel was glad he had written his poems. [Planet 532-7
WRONG. Wrong as a divagation to Peking, [C 34-31
  Things false and wrong [Virgin 71-3
  And all their manner, right and wrong, [MBG 166-17
  The shapes are wrong and the sounds are false. [MBG 181-11
  Of realities, that, in which it could be wrong. [Forces 229-17
  Can never stand as god, is ever wrong [Oboe 250-16
  The mind, which is our being, wrong and wrong, [EM 317-1
  Writhings in wrong obliques and distances, [Ulti 430-1
  The position was wrong. [Aug 493-20
  Make little difference, for being wrong [Red Kit 30-14 P
  And love her still, still leaves you in the wrong. [Red Kit 31-1P
WRONGING. And wronging her, if only as she thinks, [Red Kit 30-15 P
WRONGS. Horrors and falsities and wrongs; [Negation 97-16
WROTE. That wrote his couplet yearly to the spring, [C 31-5
  He, therefore, wrote his prolegomena, [C 37-23
WROUGHT. Than yours, out of our imperfections wrought, [Fictive
  87-20
WRY. And do not forget his wry neck [Jack-Rabbit 50-12
  Now, the wry Rosenbloom is dead [Cortege 79-13
  Of the quick that's wry. [Orangeade 103-20
  To smother the wry spirit's misery. [News 265-7
  The wry of neck and the wry of heart [Sat Night 28-1 P
  And the wry antipodes whirled round the world away-- [Discov
  95-20 P

X. X, The mighty thought, the mighty man. [Canna 55-2
  X promenades the dewy stones, [Canna 55-7
  As if designed by X, the per-noble master. [Extracts 254-20
  Nor feel the x malisons of other men, [Montra 261-24
  The vital, arrogant, fatal, dominant X. [Motive 288-20
  If the poetry of X was music, [Creat 310-10
  That X is an obstruction, a man [Creat 310-16
  Tell X that speech is not dirty silence [Creat 311-7
  In the big X of the returning primitive. [NH 474-18
  X understands Aristotle [Grotesque 75-4 P
  Himself, may be, the irreducible X [Someone 83-8 A
XENOPHON. Of Xenophon, his epitaphs, should [Hero 276-20
  Exhibit Xenophon, what he was, since [Hero 276-21
  Xenophon, its implement and actor. [Hero 277-1
  Of him, even if Xenophon, seems [Hero 277-6

YAHOO. And the fiddles smack, the horns yahoo, the flutes [Bship
  79-28 P
YANGTSE. Or in the Yangtse studied out their beards? [Monocle 14-3
YARD. The bloody lion in the yard at night or ready to spring [Puel
  456-6
  See: church-yard; door-yard.
YARDS. A hundred yards from a carriage. [Theory 86-19
  Seize yards and docks, machinery and men, [Bship 77-22 P
YARROW. It may be that the yarrow in his fields [C 40-19
YAWL. I hated the weathery yawl from which the pools [Farewell
  118-1
YAWNED. And normal things had yawned themselves away, [NSF 402-20
YE. Chant, O ye faithful, in your paths [Botanist 2 136-5
YEAR. Ticks tediously the time of one more year. [Monocle 15-2
  Sequestering the fluster from the year, [C 46-8
  The time of year has grown indifferent. [Pharynx 96-1
  It's the time of the year [Sailing 120-4
  Only last year he said that the naked moon [Anglais 148-19
  Each year to disguise the clanking mechanism [Nigger 157-2
  One keeps on playing year by year, [MBG 177-19
  One year, death and war prevented the jasmine scent [Oboe 251-8
  At New Year and, from then until April, lay [Extracts 255-2
  There's a moment in the year, Solange, [News 265-11
  When the deep breath fetches another year of life. [News 265-12
  Year, year and year, defeated at last and lost [Dutch 291-25
  And they were nothing else. It was late in the year. [Wild 329-2
  This is the last day of a certain year [Cred 372-11
  One day enriches a year. One woman makes [Cred 374-21
  Contains the year and other years and hymns [Cred 375-6
  Enriches the year, not as embellishment. [Cred 375-8
  And last year's garden grows salacious weeds. [Cred 377-10
  Finally, in the last year of her age, [Past Nun 378-11
  At noon it was on the mid-day of the year [NSF 401-5
  There is a month, a year, there is a time [NSF 405-4
  That was different, something else, last year [AA 412-11
  As at the moment of the year when, tick, [John 437-4
  Of year. Here in his house and in his room, [Quiet 523-8
  They bear their fruit so that the year is known, [Rock 527-12
  The plenty of the year and of the world. [Rock 527-15
  The vaguest line of smoke (a year ago) [Phases 5-4 P
  The year's dim elongations stretch below [Sombre 70-2 P
  Of the spring of the year, [How Now 97-6 P
  Since thirty summers are needed for a year [Ideal 88-8 A
  And at what time both of the year and day; [Ideal 89-3 A
YEARLY. That wrote his couplet yearly to the spring, [C 31-5
YEAR-OLD. He walked with his year-old boy on his shoulder. [Contra
  II 270-4
YEARS. A few years more and the vermeil capuchin [C 44-24
  Until this matter-makes in years of war. [Repet 307-10
  Rejected years. A big bird pecks at him [EM 318-8
  Contains the year and other years and hymns [Cred 375-6
  Of thirty years ago. It is looking out [NH 478-8
  The chimney is fifty years old and slants to one side. [Plain
  502-18
  Seventy Years Later [Rock 525-title 1
  Regard the freedom of seventy years ago. [Rock 525-4
  As they were fifty years ago, [Clear Day 113-9 P
  And thirty years, in the galaxies of birth, [Ideal 88-9 A
YELLING. That has been yelling in the dark. [Grotesque 77-4 P
YELLOW. Dabbled with yellow pollen--red as red [Hibiscus 23-1
  So streaked with yellow, blue and green and red [C 32-6
  Blunt yellow in such a room! [Bananas 54-3
  From my balcony, I survey the yellow air, [Of Surface 57-3
  Or green with yellow rings, [Ten O'C 66-5
  Or yellow with blue rings. [Ten O'C 66-6
  Filled with yellow light. [Six Sig 74-16
  The yellow rocked across the still façades, [Babies 77-4
  At breakfast jelly yellow streaked the deck [Sea Surf 99-18
  The moonlight is not yellow but a white [Havana 144-24
  The birds are singing in the yellow patios, [Nigger 152-15
  The trees are wooden, the grass is yellow and thin. [Nigger 157-21

The yellow moon of words about the nightingale [Autumn 160-4
They are yellow forms [Pears 196-5
The yellow glistens. [Pears 196-17
At the time of nougats, the peer yellow [Forces 228-17
The pair yellow, the peer. [Forces 228-20
Were violet, yellow, purple, pink. The grass [Horn 230-9
A yellow wine and follow a streamer's track [Landsc 243-6
Even the leaves of the locust were yellow then, [Contra II 270-3
Something to feel that they needed another yellow, [Holiday 312-3
Less Aix than Stockholm, hardly a yellow at all, [Holiday 312-4
In spite of the yellow of the acacias, the scent [EM 315-5
The sun, in clownish yellow, but not a clown, [EM 318-1
To feed on the yellow bloom of the yellow fruit [EM 318-12
The yellow grassman's mind is still immense, [EM 318-24
The yellow that was yesterday, refreshed, [Lot 371-5
We bathed in yellow green and yellow blue [Lot 371-8
Of blue and yellow, sky and sun, belted [Cred 378-1
And yellow, yellow thins the Northern blue. [NSF 385-13
As light changes yellow into gold and gold [AA 416-11
It rose, ashen and red and yellow, each [Page 422-12
Of yellow as first color and of white, [Roses 431-1
It is not the unravelling of her yellow shift. [John 437-6
In the land of the lemon trees, yellow and yellow were [NH 486-13
The orange far down in yellow, [Plant 506-11
What opposite? Could it be that yellow patch, the side [Slug
  522-9
Vines with yellow fruit, [Phases 4-11 P
Or yellow. [Primordia 8-23 P
In which were yellow, rancid skeletons. [Stan MMO 19-2 P
The same down-dropping fruit in yellow leaves, [Duck 61-14 P
A manner of walking, yellow fruit, a house, [Woman Had 83-7 P
The green-edged yellow and yellow and blue and blue-edged green--
  [How Now 97-8 P
YELLOW-BLUE. Yellow-blue, yellow-green, pungent with citron-sap,
  [NH 486-14
YELLOWED. Their poverty, a gray-blue yellowed out [NSF 402-5
YELLOW-GREEN. Yellow-blue, yellow-green, pungent with citron-sap,
  [NH 486-14
YELLOWING. The yellowing fomentations of effulgence, [Attempt
  370-17
YELLOWS. It glistens with various yellows, [Pears 196-18
  Pink yellows, orange whites, too much as they are [Roses 430-11
YEOMAN. I am a yeoman, as such fellows go. [Monocle 16-26
  Yeoman and grub, but with a fig in sight, [C 42-17
YES. Yes: but the color of the heavy hemlocks [Domination 8-14
  Yes: you came walking, [Vincentine 53-8
  Yes: you came talking. [Vincentine 53-10
  Yes, and the blackbird spread its tail, [Watermelon 89-10
  Most spiss--oh! Yes, most spissantly. [Snow Stars 133-2
  Ah! Yes, desire . . . this leaning on his bed, [Men Fall 187-15
  After the final no there comes a yes [Beard 247-9
  And on that yes the future world depends. [Beard 247-10
  No was the night. Yes is this present sun. [Beard 247-11
  Her no and no made yes impossible. [Uruguay 249-15
  Yes. But these sudden sublimations [Hero 274-15
  In the yes of the realist spoken because he must [EM 320-12
  Say yes, spoken because under every no [EM 320-13
  Lay a passion for yes that had never been broken. [EM 320-14
  In the third world, then, there is no pain. Yes, but [EM 323-23
  Yes: gildering the swarm-like manias [Descrip 342-19
  Or--yes: what elements, unreconciled [Two V 355-2
  The fiction that results from feeling. Yes, that. [NSF 406-21
  He says no to no and yes to yes. He says yes [AA 414-8
  To no; and in saying yes he says farewell. [AA 414-9
  An ember yes among its cindery noes, [Armor 529-10
  Your yes here no, your no her yes. The words [Red Kit 30-13 P
  Yes; it is true of maxims, [Three 129-12 P
YESTERDAY. Yesterday the roses were rising upward, [Nigger 156-10
  As if yesterday's people continued to watch [Cuisine 228-5
  And yet what good were yesterday's devotions? [Montra 264-4
  The yellow that was yesterday, refreshed, [Lot 371-5
  Not yesterday, not tomorrow, an appanage [Bouquet 451-14
  Like tales that were told the day before yesterday-- [Hermit
  505-13
  10. This is how yesterday's volcano looks. [Someone 86-13 A
  Map of yesterday's earth [Primordia 9-13 P
  Of yesterday's cheese, [Soldat 12-14 P
  What it was yesterday. [Three 130-21 P
YEW. Without her, evening like a budding yew [Old Woman 45-23 P
  Deadly and deep. It would become a yew [Old Woman 45-30 P
YIELD. Or yield to subjugation, once to proclaim [Cred 376-13
YIELDED. The being that yielded so little, acquired [Adieu 127-18
  He yielded himself to that single majesty; [Anglais 149-12
YIELDS. Dazzle yields to a clarity and we observe, [Descrip 341-10
YILLOW. Yillow, yillow, yillow, [Metamorph 265-13
YOKEL. When this yokel comes maundering, [Plot Giant 6-11
YOUNG. Observed, when young, the nature of mankind, [Monocle 17-22
  The young emerald, evening star, [Homunculus 25-14
  Prophetic joint, for its diviner young. [C 43-19
  Making recoveries of young nakedness [Tallap 72-11

Meet for the eye of the young alligator, [Nomad 95-16
The grass is in seed. The young birds are flying. [Ghosts 119-1
He was young, and we, we are old. [Mozart 132-19
When he was young), naked and alien, [Anglais 149-2
In the mud, a missal for that young man, [MBG 177-22
Young ox, bow-legged bear, [Destructive 192-16
As a young lover sees the first buds of spring [Peaches 224-5
It is cold to be forever young, [Vari 233-8
But as if evening found us young, still young, [Martial 237-15
Young boys resembling pastry, hip-hip, [Hero 278-11
Young men as vegetables, hip-hip.[Hero 278-12
A young man seated at his table [Lack 303-1
The young man is well-disclosed, one of the gang, [Lack 303-6
"Repetitions of a Young Captain" [306-title
That it is as if we had never been young. [Debris 338-4
It is a wizened starlight growing young, [Descrip 344-9
How happy I was the day I told the young Blandina of three-
    legged giraffes . . . [Analysis 348-1
Summer is changed to winter, the young grow old, [Chaos 357-14
Young men go walking in the woods, [Pediment 361-7
To the first autumnal inhalations, young broods [Cred 372-6
Their eyes closed, in a young palaver of lips. [NH 477-1
And Rosa, the muslin dreamer of satin and cowry-kin, disdaining
    the empty keys; and the young infanta, [Piano 22-3 P
Young weasels racing steep horizons in pursuit of planets . . .
    [Inelegance 26-8 P
Of young identities, Aprilian stubs. [Duck 64-24 P
Young catachumen answering the worms? [Sombre 69-24 P
The day is green and the wind is young. [Stan MBG 72-1 P
The world is young and I play my guitar. [Stan MBG 72-2 P
Like an eye too young to grapple its primitive, [Theatre 91-4 P
Young and living in a live air, [Clear Day 113-10 P
Young and walking in the sunshine, [Clear Day 113-11 P
The young gentleman was seen [Three 136-6 P
As young. [Three 137-2 P
Just as the young gentleman [Three 139-9 P
The young gentleman of the ballad. [Three 139-13 P
And fill the earth with young men centuries old [Ideal 88-11 A
YOUNGER. When younger bodies, because they are younger, rise [Burn-
    shaw 49-28 P
YOUNGEST. Before the speaker's youngest breath is taken! [Montra
    261-21
To be, as on the youngest poet's page, [Descrip 340-20
From youngest day or oldest night and far [Greenest 54-1 P
The youngest, the still fuzz-eyed, odd fleurettes, [Nuns 92-9 P
YOURSELF. Conceal yourself or disclose [Venereal 48-14
Is like to these. But in yourself is like: [Tallap 72-6
You as you are? You are yourself. [MBG 183-13
And full of yourself. The trees around are for you, [Rabbit K
    209-16
Where you yourself were never quite yourself [Motive 288-11
As Virgil, abstract. But see him for yourself, [Paisant 335-13
Check your evasions, hold you to yourself. [NSF 406-14
Speak to your pillow as if it was yourself. [Rome 509-9
And bared yourself, and bared yourself in vain? [Good Bad 33-21P
"Sing to yourself no more." [Three 134-10 P
YOURSELVES. Then, while the music makes you, make, yourselves,
    [Burnshaw 47-23 P
Yourselves away and at a distance join [Burnshaw 51-15 P
That is yourselves, when, at last, you are yourselves, [Burnshaw
    52-16 P
YOUTH. A youth, a lover with phosphorescent hair, [Uruguay 249-21
The youth, the vital son, the heroic power. [Cred 375-10
Heightened. It is he, anew, in a freshened youth [Myth 118-13 P
YOUTHFUL. Their parts as in a youthful happiness. [Cred 378-10
Silently it heaves its youthful sleep from the sea-- [NH 476-22
YPLAITED. See star-yplaited.
YUCATAN. Bordeaux to Yucatan, Havana next, [C 29-9
    Concerning the Thunderstorms of Yucatan [C 30-title 2
    In Yucatan, the Maya sonneteers [C 30-16
Beyond carked Yucatan, he might have come [C 40-10
YUCCAS. That yuccas breed, and of the panther's tread. [C 31-29

Z. Of serpents like z rivers simmering, [Pure 330-18
Not twisted, stooping, polymathic Z, [NH 469-8
And the sound of z in the grass all day, though these [Burnshaw
    51-4 P
ZAY-ZAY. Mumbled zay-zay and a-zay, a-zay. [Ord Women 11-2
ZEBRA. The zebra leaves, the sea [Search 268-3
ZELLER. See John Zeller.
ZENITH. The imprescriptible zenith, free of harangue, [What We
    459-15
ZERO. Of aphonies, tuned in from zero and [Montra 260-14
And his orange blotches, these were his zero green, [NSF 393-6
ZITHER. Look round at the head and zither [God 285-2
ZITHERS. Which is like zithers and tambourines combined: [Mice
    123-8
ZONE. For his refreshment, an abundant zone, [C 35-17
The visible, a zone of blue and orange [EM 324-13

A zone of time without the ticking of clocks, [Aug 494-7
ZONES. Fixing emblazoned zones and fiery poles, [Key W 130-9
ZURICH. For sale in Vienna and Zurich to people in Maine, [Greenest
    53-9 P

AS. Although I patch it as I can. [MBG 165-12
  There's no such thing as life; or if there is, [Parochial 192-4
  If the stars that move together as one, disband, [Horn 230-17
  But as truth to be accepted, he supposed [Landsc 242-18
  Born, as she was, at twenty-one, [Couch 295-6
  As he saw it, exist in his own especial eye. [EM 316-19
  The most gay and yet not so gay as it was. [Debris 338-13
  Its knowledge cold within one as one's own; [Novel 459-3
  Not as I, from melons. [Three 129-6 P
  Just as the young gentleman [Three 139-9 P
EVERY. Come to us every day. And yet they are [Recit 87-28 P
  With something I could touch, touch every way. [Warmth 90-6 P
  On every cloud-tip over the heavens, [Letters 107-2 P

HAD. And the world had worlds, ai, this-a-way: [MBG 178-17
  What had this star to do with the world it lit, [Martial 238-3
IS. Nothing that is not there and the nothing that is. [Snow Man
   10-12
  For whom what is was other things. [Oak 272-3
THAN. Than mute bare splendors of the sun and moon. [Manner 56-8
  Than yours, out of our imperfections wrought, [Fictive 87-20
  Of it, more than the monstrous player of [MBG 175-8
  Than this, in this alone I may believe, [Extracts 257-25
  On more than muscular shoulders, arms and chest, [Choc 297-12
WAS. Again, and lived and was again, and breathed again [Martial
   238-15
  Except what was, [Woman Song 360-9